COLLINS
PAPERBACK
GERMAN
DICTIONARY

COLLINS
PAPERBACK
GERMAN
DICTIONARY

COLLINS
PAPERBACK
GERMAN
DICTIONARY

GERMAN▶ENGLISH   ENGLISH▶GERMAN

HarperCollins*Publishers*

second edition/zweite Auflage 1995

© **HarperCollins Publishers 1995**
© **William Collins Sons & Co. Ltd. 1988**

ISBN 0 00 470189 5 (Paperback)
ISBN 0 00 470727 3 (College)

---

first edition/erste Auflage
Dagmar Förtsch • Hildegard Pesch
Veronika Schnorr • Gisela Moohan • Ulrike Seeberger
Lorna Sinclair • Elspeth Anderson • Val McNulty

revised by/Bearbeitung
Eva Vennebusch
Horst Kopleck • Robin Sawers

editorial staff/Redaktion
Nicola Cooke • Joyce Littlejohn
Maree Airlie • Carol MacLeod • Anne Lindsay

computing staff/Datenverarbeitung
André Gautier • Raymund Carrick

series editor/Gesamtleitung
Lorna Sinclair Knight
editorial management/Redaktionsleitung
Vivian Marr

Typeset by Morton Word Processing Ltd, Scarborough

*Printed in Great Britain by
HarperCollins Manufacturing, Glasgow*

INHALT

CONTENTS

Warenzeichen

Wörter, die unseres Wissens eingetragene Warenzeichen darstellen, sind als solche gekennzeichnet. Es ist jedoch zu beachten, daß weder das Vorhandensein noch das Fehlen derartiger Kennzeichnungen die Rechtslage hinsichtlich eingetragener Warenzeichen berührt.

Note on trademarks

Words which we have reason to believe constitute trademarks have been designated as such. However, neither the presence nor the absence of such designation should be regarded as affecting the legal status of any trademark.

EINLEITUNG

Sie möchten Englisch lernen oder vielleicht bereits vorhandene Kenntnisse vertiefen. Sie möchten sich auf englisch ausdrücken, englische Texte lesen oder übersetzen, oder Sie möchten sich ganz einfach mit englischsprechenden Menschen unterhalten können. Ganz gleich, ob Sie nun Schülerin, Student, Tourist, Sekretärin oder geschäftlich tätig sind, Sie haben sich den richtigen Begleiter für Ihre Arbeit ausgesucht! Dieses Buch ist der ideale Helfer, wenn Sie sich in englischer Sprache ausdrücken und verständlich machen möchten, sei es schriftlich oder mündlich. Es ist ganz bewußt praktisch und modern, es räumt vor allem der Alltagssprache und der Sprache, wie sie Ihnen in Zeitungen und Nachrichten, im Geschäftsleben, im Büro und im Urlaub begegnet, großen Raum ein. Wie in allen unseren Wörterbüchern haben wir das Hauptgewicht auf aktuellen Sprachgebrauch und idiomatische Redewendungen gelegt.

WIE MAN DIESES BUCH BENUTZT

Wir möchten Ihnen im folgenden einige kurze Erklärungen über die Art und Weise geben, wie wir Ihnen die Informationen in Ihrem Wörterbuch präsentieren. Unser Ziel: wir wollen Ihnen soviel Information wie möglich bieten, ohne dabei an Klarheit und Verständlichkeit einzubüßen.

Die Wörterbucheinträge

Hier also die verschiedenen Grundelemente, aus denen sich ein typischer Eintrag in Ihrem Wörterbuch zusammensetzt:

Lautschrift

Wie die meisten modernen Wörterbücher geben wir die Aussprache mit Zeichen an, die zum "internationalen phonetischen Alphabet" gehören. Weiter unten (auf den Seiten xvi und xvii) finden Sie eine vollständige Liste der Zeichen, die in diesem System benutzt werden. Die Aussprache englischer Wörter geben wir auf der englisch-deutschen Seite unmittelbar hinter dem jeweiligen Wort in eckigen Klammern an. Die deutsche Aussprache erscheint im deutsch-englischen Teil ebenfalls auf diese Weise unmittelbar hinter den Worteinträgen. Allerdings wird sie nicht immer angegeben, zum Beispiel bei zusammengesetzten Wörtern wie etwa **Liebesbrief**, deren Bestandteile schon an anderer Stelle im Wörterbuch zu finden sind.

Grammatik-Information

Alle Wörter gehören zu einer der folgenden grammatischen Klassen: Substantiv, Verb, Adjektiv, Adverb, Pronomen, Artikel, Konjunktion, Präposition, Abkürzung. Substantive können im Deutschen männlich, weiblich oder sächlich sein; sie können im Singular oder Plural stehen. Verben können transitiv, intransitiv, reflexiv oder auch unpersönlich sein. Die grammatische Klasse der Wörter wird jeweils gleich hinter dem Wort in *Kursivschrift* angezeigt.

Es kommt oft vor, daß ein Wort in verschiedene grammatische Klassen unterteilt wird. So kann z.B. das englische Wort **next** ein Adjektiv (deutsch: "nächste") sein oder ein Adverb (deutsch: "dann"); und das deutsche Wort **gut** kann ein Adjektiv (englisch: "good") oder ein Adverb (englisch: "well") sein. Ebenso kann z.B. das Verb **rauchen** manchmal transitiv sein ("eine gute Zigarre rauchen"), manchmal intransitiv ("hier darf man nicht rauchen"). Damit Sie immer genau die Bedeutung finden, die Sie gerade suchen, und damit der Text leichter überschaubar wird, haben wir die verschiedenen grammatischen Kategorien durch eine schwarze Raute ♦ gegeneinander abgegrenzt. Alle Beispielsätze sowie zusammengesetzte Wörter werden gesammelt am Ende des Eintrags gegeben.

Bedeutungsunterschiede

Viele Wörter haben mehr als eine Bedeutung. So kann z.B. **Rad** einen Teil eines Autos oder Fahrrades bezeichnen, aber auch ein Wort für das ganze Fahrrad sein. Oder Wörter müssen je nach dem Zusammenhang, in dem sie gebraucht werden, anders übersetzt werden: so muß z.B. das englische Wort **to go** für Fußgänger mit "gehen", für Autofahrer mit "fahren" übersetzt werden. Damit Sie in jedem Zusammenhang immer die richtige Übersetzung finden, haben wir die Einträge nach Bedeutungen eingeteilt: jede Kategorie wird durch einen "Verwendungshinweis" bestimmt, der *kursiv* gedruckt ist und in Klammern steht. Die beiden Beispiele von oben sehen dann so aus:

Rad *nt* wheel; (*Fahrrad*) bike
go *vi* gehen; (*travel*) fahren

Außerdem haben manche Wörter eine andere Bedeutung und müssen im Englischen anders übersetzt werden, wenn sie in einem bestimmten Bereich verwendet werden. Ein Beispiel dafür wäre **Rezept**, das einmal die Anleitung sein kann, nach der Sie etwa einen Kuchen backen, in medizinischen Zusammenhängen jedoch angibt, welche Tabletten Ihnen ein Arzt verschreibt. Wir zeigen Ihnen, welche Übersetzung Sie auswählen sollten, indem wir wieder in Klammern solche Fachgebiete in kursiven Großbuchstaben angeben, im vorigen Fall *KOCH* als Abkürzung für *KOCHEN* und *MED* als Abkürzung für *MEDIZIN*:

Rezept *nt* (*KOCH*) recipe; (*MED*) prescription

Sie finden eine Liste aller in diesem Wörterbuch benutzten Abkürzungen für solche Gebiete auf den Seiten xii bis xiv.

Übersetzungen

Die meisten deutschen Wörter können mit einem einzigen englischen Wort übersetzt werden und umgekehrt. Aber manchmal gibt es in der Zielsprache kein Wort, das dem Wort der Ausgangssprache genau entspricht. In solchen Fällen haben wir ein ungefähres Äquivalent angegeben, das durch das Zeichen ≈ gekennzeichnet ist. So z.B. beim deutschen Wort **Abitur**, dessen ungefähres englisches Äquivalent "A-levels" ist: hier handelt es sich aber nur um eine ungefähre Entsprechung, nicht um eine "echte" Übersetzung, weil die beiden Schulsysteme sich stark unterscheiden:

Abitur *nt* ≈ A-levels *pl*

Manchmal kann man nicht einmal ein ungefähres Äquivalent finden. Besonders oft ist das der Fall beim Essen, insbesondere bei lokalen Gerichten wie z.B. bei der folgenden schottischen Spezialität:

haggis *n Gericht aus gehackten Schafsinnereien und Haferschrot, im Schafsmagen gekocht*

Hier wird statt einer Übersetzung (die es einfach gar nicht gibt) eine Erklärung gegeben, die in *Kursivschrift* gesetzt ist.

Manchmal ist es auch wichtig, ein Wort nicht nur für sich allein, sondern auch in einem bestimmten Zusammenhang zu übersetzen. So wird z.B. das deutsche Wort **Hand** im Englischen mit "hand" übersetzt, aber **die Hand für jdn ins Feuer legen** nicht mit "to put one's hand in the fire for sb", sondern mit "to vouch for sb". Manchmal haben auch einfache Zusammensetzungen völlig andere Übersetzungen: so wird **Handschuh** eben nicht mit "hand shoe" übersetzt, sondern mit "glove". Gerade in diesen Bereichen werden Sie feststellen, daß Ihr Wörterbuch ganz besonders hilfreich und vollständig ist: wir haben uns nämlich bemüht, so viele zusammengesetzte Wörter, Redewendungen und idiomatische Ausdrücke aufzunehmen wie möglich.

Sprachniveau

Im Deutschen wissen Sie ganz genau, in welcher Situation Sie den Ausdruck **ich habe genug** verwenden, wann Sie **mir langt's** sagen und wann **ich hab' die Nase voll**. Aber wenn Sie versuchen, jemanden zu verstehen, der englisch redet, oder wenn Sie selbst versuchen, sich auf Englisch auszudrücken, dann sollten Sie wirklich gesagt bekommen, welcher Ausdruck höflich ist und welcher weniger höflich. Wir haben also bei Wörtern, die aus der Umgangssprache stammen, die Kennzeichnung (*umg*) oder (*inf*) hinzugefügt, bei ganz besonders groben Ausdrücken zur Warnung auch noch ein zusätzliches Ausrufungszeichen, (*umg!*) oder (*inf!*), und zwar sowohl in der Ausgangs- als auch in der Zielsprache, um Ihnen anzudeuten, daß diese Ausdrücke mit Vorsicht zu verwenden sind. Bitte beachten Sie ansonsten: Wenn das Sprachniveau der Übersetzung dem des übersetzten Ausdrucks entspricht, finden Sie die Kennzeichnungen (*umg*) und (*inf*) nur in der Ausgangssprache.

Schlüsselwörter

Als *SCHLÜSSELWÖRTER* hervorgehobene Einträge, wie z.B. **be** und **do** und ihre deutschen Entsprechungen **sein** und **machen**, werden besonders eingehend behandelt, da sie grundlegende Elemente der Sprache sind. Diese Sonderbehandlung gewährleistet, daß Sie die notwendige Sicherheit für die Benutzung dieser komplexen Wörter erhalten.

Landeskundliche Informationen

Besondere Einträge, vom restlichen Text durch horizontale Linien abgeteilt, erläutern bestimmte kulturelle Aspekte der deutschen und englischen Sprachräume. Themengebiete sind z.B. Politik, Erziehung, Medien und nationale Feiertage.

INTRODUCTION

You may be starting to learn German, or you may wish to extend your knowledge of the language. Perhaps you want to read and study German books, newspapers and magazines, or perhaps simply have a conversation with Geman speakers. Whatever the reason, whether you're a student, a tourist or want to use German for business, this is the ideal book to help you understand and communicate. This modern, user-friendly dictionary gives priority to everyday vocabulary and the language of current affairs, business and tourism. As in all Collins dictionaries, the emphasis is firmly placed on contemporary language and expressions.

HOW TO USE THE DICTIONARY

You will find below an outline of the way in which information is presented in your dictionary. Our aim is to give you the maximum amount of information whilst still providing a text which is clear and user-friendly.

Entries

A typical entry in your dictionary will be made up of the following elements:

Phonetic transcription

Phonetics appear in square brackets immediately after the headword. They are shown using the International Phonetic Alphabet (IPA), and a complete list of the symbols used in this system can be found on pages xvi and xvii.

Grammatical information

All words belong to one of the following parts of speech: noun, verb, adjective, adverb, pronoun, article, conjunction, preposition, abbreviation. Nouns can be singular or plural and, in German, masculine, feminine, or neuter. Verbs can be transitive, intransitive, reflexive or impersonal. Parts of speech appear in *italics* immediately after the phonetic spelling of the headword. The gender of the translation appears in *italics* immediately following the key element of the translation.

Often a word can have more than one part of speech. Just as the English word **next** can be an adjective or an adverb, the German word **gut** can be an adjective ("good") or an adverb ("well"). In the same way the verb **to walk** is sometimes transitive, ie it takes an object ("to walk the dog") and sometimes intransitive, ie it doesn't take an object ("to walk to school"). To help you find the meaning you are looking for quickly and for clarity of presentation, the different part of speech categories are separated by a black lozenge ♦.

Meaning divisions

Most words have more than one meaning. Take, for example, **punch** which can be, amongst other things, a blow with the fist or an object used for making holes. Other words are translated differently depending on the context in which they are used. The intransitive verb **to recede**, for example, can be translated by "zurückgehen" or "verschwinden" depending on *what* is receding. To help you select the most appropriate translation in every context, entries are divided according to meaning. Each different meaning is introduced by an "indicator" in *italics* and in brackets. Thus, the examples given above will be shown as follows:

    punch n (*blow*) Schlag *m*; (*tool*) Locher *m*
    recede vi (*tide*) zurückgehen; (*lights etc*) verschwinden

Likewise, some words can have a different meaning when used to talk about a specific subject area or field. For example, **bishop**, which in a religious context means a high-ranking clergyman, is also the name of a chess piece. To show English speakers which translation to use, we have added "subject field labels" in capitals and in brackets, in this case (*REL*) and (*CHESS*):

> **bishop** n (*REL*) Bischof m; (*CHESS*) Läufer m

Field labels are often shortened to save space. You will find a complete list of abbreviations used in the dictionary on pages xii to xiv.

Translations

Most English words have a direct translation in German and vice versa, as shown in the examples given above. Sometimes, however, no exact equivalent exists in the target language. In such cases we have given an approximate equivalent, indicated by the sign ≈. Such is the case of **high school**, the German equivalent of which is "Oberschule *f*". This is not an exact translation since the systems of the two countries in question are quite different:

> **high school** n ≈ Oberschule f

On occasion it is impossible to find even an approximate equivalent. This may be the case, for example, with the names of culinary specialities like this German cake:

> **Streuselkuchen** m *cake with crumble topping*

Here the translation (which doesn't exist) is replaced by an explanation. For increased clarity the explanation, or "gloss", is shown in *italics*.

It is often the case that a word, or a particular meaning of a word, cannot be translated in isolation. The translation of **Dutch**, for example, is "holländisch, niederländisch". However, the phrase **to go Dutch** is rendered by "getrennte Kasse machen". Even an expression as simple as **cake shop** needs a separate translation since it translates as "Konditorei", not "Kuchengeschäft". This is where your dictionary will prove to be particularly informative and useful since it contains an abundance of compounds, phrases and idiomatic expressions.

Register

In English you instinctively know when to say **I'm broke** or **I'm a bit short of cash** and when to say **I don't have any money**. When you are trying to understand someone who is speaking German, however, or when you yourself try to speak German, it is especially important to know what is polite and what is less so. To help you with this, we have added the register labels (*umg*) and (*inf*) to colloquial or offensive expressions. Those expressions which are particularly vulgar are also given an exclamation mark (*umg!*) or (*inf!*), warning you to use them with extreme care. Please note that the register labels (*umg*) and (*inf*) are not repeated in the target language when the register of the translation matches that of the word or phrase being translated.

Keywords

Words labelled in the text as *KEYWORDS*, such as **be** and **do** or their German equivalents **sein** and **machen**, have been given special treatment because they form the basic elements of the language. This extra help will ensure that you know how to use these complex words with confidence.

Cultural information

Entries which appear separated from the main text by a line above and below them explain aspects of culture in German- and English-speaking countries. Subject areas covered include politics, education, media and national festivals, for example **Bundestag**, **Abitur**, **BBC** and **Hallowe'en**.

ABKÜRZUNGEN

ABBREVIATIONS

Abkürzung	**abk, abbr**	abbreviation
Adjektiv	**adj**	adjective
Verwaltung	**ADMIN**	administration
Adverb	**adv**	adverb
Agrarwirtschaft	**AGR**	agriculture
Akkusativ	**akk, acc**	accusative
Anatomie	**ANAT**	anatomy
Architektur	**ARCHIT**	architecture
Artikel	**art**	article
Kunst	**ART**	
Astrologie	**ASTROL**	astrology
Astronomie	**ASTRON**	astronomy
attributiv	**attrib**	attributive
Kraftfahrzeugwesen	**AUT**	automobiles
Hilfsverb	**aux**	auxiliary
Luftfahrt	**AVIAT**	aviation
Bergbau	**BERGB**	mining
besonders	**bes**	especially
Biologie	**BIOL**	biology
Botanik	**BOT**	botany
britisch	**BRIT**	British
Kartenspiel	**CARDS**	
Chemie	**CHEM**	chemistry
Film	**CINE**	cinema
Handel	**COMM**	commerce
Komparativ	**comp**	comparative
Computerwesen	**COMPUT**	computers
Konjunktion	**conj**	conjunction
Bauwesen	**CONSTR**	building
zusammengesetztes Wort	**cpd**	compound
Kochen und Backen	**CULIN**	cooking
Dativ	**dat**	dative
bestimmt	**def**	definite
diminutiv	**dimin**	diminutive
dekliniert	**dekl**	declined
kirchlich	**ECCL**	ecclesiastical
Volkswirtschaft	**ECON**	economics
Eisenbahnwesen	**EISENB**	railways
Elektrizität	**ELEK, ELEC**	electricity
besonders	**esp**	especially
und so weiter	**etc**	et cetera
etwas	**etw**	something
Euphemismus	**euph**	euphemism
Ausruf	**excl**	exclamation
Femininum	**f**	feminine
übertragen	**fig**	figurative
Film	**FILM**	cinema
Finanzwesen	**FIN**	finance
formell	**form**	formal
'phrasal verb', bei dem Partikel und Verb nicht getrennt werden können	**fus**	fused: phrasal verb where the particle cannot be separated from the verb
gehoben	**geh**	elevated
Genitiv	**gen**	genitive
Geographie	**GEOG**	geography

ABKÜRZUNGEN

ABBREVIATIONS

Geologie	*GEOL*	geology
Geometrie	*GEOM*	geometry
Grammatik	*GRAM*	grammar
Geschichte	*HIST*	history
scherzhaft	*hum*	humorous
Imperfekt	*imperf*	imperfect
unpersönlich	*impers*	impersonal
unbestimmt	*indef*	indefinite
umgangssprachlich	*inf*	informal
untrennbares Verb	*insep*	inseparable
Interjektion	*interj*	interjection
interrogativ	*interrog*	interrogative
unveränderlich	*inv*	invariable
unregelmäßig	*irreg*	irregular
jemand	*jd*	somebody
jemandem	*jdm*	(to) somebody
jemanden	*jdn*	somebody
jemandes	*jds*	somebody's
Rechtswesen	*JUR*	law
Kartenspiel	*KARTEN*	cards
Kochen und Backen	*KOCH*	cooking
Komparativ	*komp*	comparative
Konjunktion	*konj*	conjunction
Rechtswesen	*LAW*	
Sprachwissenschaft	*LING*	linguistics
wörtlich	*lit*	literal
literarisch	*liter*	literary
Literatur	*LITER*	literature
Maskulinum	*m*	masculine
Mathematik	*MATH*	mathematics
Medizin	*MED*	medicine
Meteorologie	*MET*	meteorology
Militärwesen	*MIL*	military
Bergbau	*MIN*	mining
Musik	*MUS*	music
Substantiv	*n*	noun
nautisch	*NAUT*	nautical
Nominativ	*nom*	nominative
Norddeutschland	*NORDD*	North German
Neutrum	*nt*	neuter
Zahlwort	*num*	numeral
Objekt	*obj*	object
oder	*od*	or
veraltet	*old*	
sich	*o.s.*	oneself
Österreich	*ÖSTERR*	Austria
Parlament	*PARL*	parliament
pejorativ	*pej*	pejorative
Person/persönlich	*pers*	person/personal
Pharmazie	*PHARM*	pharmacy
Photographie	*PHOT*	photography
Physik	*PHYS*	physics
Physiologie	*PHYSIOL*	physiology
Plural	*pl*	plural
Politik	*POL*	politics

ABKÜRZUNGEN

ABBREVIATIONS

possessiv	**poss**	possessive
Partizip Perfekt	**pp**	past participle
Präfix	**präf, pref**	prefix
Präposition	**präp, prep**	preposition
Präsens	**präs, pres**	present
Typographie	*PRINT*	printing
Pronomen	**pron**	pronoun
Psychologie	*PSYCH*	psychology
Imperfekt	**pt**	past tense
Radio	*RADIO*	radio
Eisenbahn	*RAIL*	railways
Relativ-	**rel**	relative
Religion	*REL*	religion
Rundfunk	*RUNDF*	broadcasting
jemand (-en, -em)	**sb**	somebody
Schulwesen	*SCH*	school
Naturwissenschaft	*SCI*	science
Schulwesen	*SCOL*	teaching
schottisch	*SCOT*	Scottish
Singular	**sing**	singular
Skisport	*SKI*	skiing
etwas	**sth**	something
Süddeutschland	*SÜDD*	South German
Suffix	**suff**	suffix
Superlativ	**superl**	superlative
Technik	*TECH*	technology
Nachrichtentechnik	*TEL*	telecommunications
Theater	*THEAT*	theatre
Fernsehen	*TV*	television
Typographie	*TYP*	typography
umgangssprachlich	**umg**	colloquial
Universität	*UNIV*	university
unpersönlich	**unpers**	impersonal
unregelmäßig	**unreg**	irregular
untrennbar	**untr**	inseparable
unveränderlich	**unver**	invariable
(nord)amerikanisch	*US*	(North) American
gewöhnlich	**usu**	usually
und so weiter	**usw**	et cetera
Verb	**vb**	verb
intransitives Verb	**vi**	intransitive verb
reflexives Verb	**vr**	reflexive verb
transitives Verb	**vt**	transitive verb
vulgär	**vulg**	vulgar
Wirtschaft	*WIRTS*	economy
Zoologie	*ZOOL*	zoology
zusammengesetztes Wort	**zW**	compound
zwischen zwei Sprechern	-	change of speaker
ungefähre Entsprechung	≈	cultural equivalent
eingetragenes Warenzeichen	®	registered trademark

GERMAN NOUN ENDINGS

After many noun entries on the German-English side of the dictionary, you will find two pieces of grammatical information, separated by commas, to help you with the declension of the noun, e.g. **-, -n** or **-(e)s, -e.**

The first item shows you the genitive singular form, and the second gives the plural form. The hyphen stands for the word itself and the other letters are endings. Sometimes an umlaut is shown over the hyphen, which means an umlaut must be placed on the vowel of the word, e.g.:

dictionary entry	*genitive singular*	*plural*
Mann *m* **(e)s, ¨er**	**Mannes** *or* **Manns**	**Männer**
Jacht *f* **-, -en**	**Jacht**	**Jachten**

This information is not given when the noun has one of the regular German noun endings below, and you should refer to this table in such cases.

Similarly, genitive and plural endings are not shown when the German entry is a compound consisting of two or more words which are to be found elsewhere in the dictionary, since the compound form takes the endings of the LAST word of which it is formed, e.g.:

for **Nebenstraße**	*see* **Straße**
for **Schneeball**	*see* **Ball**

Regular German Noun Endings

nom		gen	pl
-ant	*m*	-anten	-anten
-anz	*f*	-anz	-anzen
-ar	*m*	-ar(e)s	-are
-chen	*nt*	-chens	-chen
-ei	*f*	-ei	-eien
-elle	*f*	-elle	-ellen
-ent	*m*	-enten	-enten
-enz	*f*	-enz	-enzen
-ette	*f*	-ette	-etten
-eur	*m*	-eurs	-eure
-euse	*f*	-euse	-eusen
-heit	*f*	-heit	-heiten
-ie	*f*	-ie	-ien
-ik	*f*	-ik	-iken
-in	*f*	-in	-innen
-ine	*f*	-ine	-inen
-ion	*f*	-ion	-ionen
-ist	*m*	-isten	-isten
-ium	*nt*	-iums	-ien
-ius	*m*	-ius	-iusse
-ive	*f*	-ive	-iven
-keit	*f*	-keit	-keiten
-lein	*nt*	-leins	-lein
-ling	*m*	-lings	-linge
-ment	*nt*	-ments	-mente
-mus	*m*	-mus	-men
-schaft	*f*	-schaft	-schaften
-tät	*f*	-tät	-täten
-tor	*m*	-tors	-toren
-ung	*f*	-ung	-ungen
-ur	*f*	-ur	-uren

PHONETIC SYMBOLS   LAUTSCHRIFT

NB: All vowels sounds are
approximate only.

NB: Manche Laute sind nur
ungefähre Entsprechungen.

Vowels   Vokale

m*a*tt	[a]	
F*ah*ne	[aː]	
Vat*er*	[ər]	
	[ɑː]	c*a*lm, p*ar*t
	[æ]	s*a*t
R*en*dezvous	[ã]	
Ch*an*ce	[aː]	
	[ɑ̃ː]	cli*en*tele
*E*tage	[e]	
S*ee*le, M*eh*l	[eː]	
W*ä*sche, B*e*tt	[ɛ]	*e*gg
z*äh*len	[ɛː]	
T*ein*t	[ɛ̃ː]	
mach*e*	[ə]	*a*bove
	[əː]	b*ur*n, *ea*rn
K*i*ste	[ɪ]	p*i*t, awfull*y*
V*i*tamin	[i]	
Z*ie*l	[iː]	p*ea*t
*O*ase	[o]	
*o*ben	[oː]	
Champign*on*	[õ]	
Sal*on*	[õː]	
M*o*st	[ɔ]	c*o*t
	[ɔː]	b*or*n, j*aw*
*ö*konomisch	[ø]	
bl*ö*d	[øː]	
G*ö*ttin	[œ]	
	[ʌ]	h*u*t
z*u*letzt	[u]	p*u*t
M*u*t	[uː]	p*oo*l
M*u*tter	[ʊ]	
Ph*y*sik	[y]	
K*ü*bel	[yː]	
S*ü*nde	[ʏ]	

NB: Vowels and consonants which are
frequently elided (not spoken) are
given in *italics*:

Vokale und Konsonanten, die
häufig elidiert (nicht
ausgesprochen) werden, sind
kursiv dargestellt:

convention [kən'venʃən]
attempt [ə'tem*p*t]

Diphthongs

Sty_l_ing	[ai]	
w_ei_t	[aɪ]	b_uy_, d_ie_, m_y_
umb_au_en	[au]	h_ou_se, n_ow_
H_au_s	[aʊ]	
	[eɪ]	p_ay_, m_a_te
	[ɛə]	p_air_, m_a_re
	[əu]	n_o_, b_oa_t
	[ɪə]	m_e_re, sh_ear_
H_eu_, H_äu_ser	[ɔɣ]	
	[ɔɪ]	b_oy_, c_oi_n
	[uə]	t_our_, p_oor_

Consonants

_B_all	[b]	_b_all
mi_ch_	[ç]	
	[tʃ]	_ch_ild
_f_ern	[f]	_f_ield
gern	[g]	good
_H_and	[h]	_h_and
_j_a	[j]	_y_et, milli_o_n
	[dʒ]	_j_ust
_K_ind	[k]	_k_ind, _c_atch
_l_inks, Pu_l_t	[l]	_l_eft, litt_l_e
_m_att	[m]	_m_at
_N_est	[n]	_n_est
la_ng_	[ŋ]	lo_ng_
_P_aar	[p]	_p_ut
_r_ennen	[r]	_r_un
fa_s_t, fa_ss_en	[s]	_s_it
_Ch_ef, _S_tein, _Sch_lag	[ʃ]	_sh_all
_T_afel	[t]	_t_ab
	[θ]	_th_ing
	[ð]	_th_is
_w_er	[v]	_v_ery
	[w]	_w_et
Lo_ch_	[x]	lo_ch_
fi_x_	[ks]	bo_x_
_s_ingen	[z]	pod_s_, _z_ip
_Z_ahn	[ts]	
genieren	[ʒ]	mea_s_ure

Other signs

glottal stop	ǀ	Knacklaut
main stress	[']	Hauptton
long vowel	[ː]	Längezeichen

Diphthonge

Konsonanten

Andere Zeichen

xvii

GERMAN IRREGULAR VERBS

* with 'sein'

Infinitive	Present Indicative 2nd pers sing ◆ 3rd pers sing	Imperfect Indicative	Past Participle
aufschrecken*	schrickst auf ◆ schrickt auf	schrak *od* schreckte auf	aufgeschreckt
ausbedingen	bedingst aus ◆ bedingt aus	bedang *od* bedingte aus	ausbedungen
backen	bäckst ◆ bäckt	backte *od* buk	gebacken
befehlen	befiehlst ◆ befiehlt	befahl	befohlen
beginnen	beginnst ◆ beginnt	begann	begonnen
beißen	beißt ◆ beißt	biß	gebissen
bergen*	birgst ◆ birgt	barg	geborgen
bersten*	birst ◆ birst	barst	geborsten
bescheißen*	bescheißt ◆ bescheißt	beschiß	beschissen
bewegen	bewegst ◆ bewegt	bewog	bewogen
biegen	biegst ◆ biegt	bog	gebogen
bieten	bietest ◆ bietet	bot	geboten
binden	bindest ◆ bindet	band	gebunden
bitten	bittest ◆ bittet	bat	gebeten
blasen	bläst ◆ bläst	blies	geblasen
bleiben*	bleibst ◆ bleibt	blieb	geblieben
braten	brätst ◆ brät	briet	gebraten
brechen*	brichst ◆ bricht	brach	gebrochen
brennen	brennst ◆ brennt	brannte	gebrannt
bringen	bringst ◆ bringt	brachte	gebracht
denken	denkst ◆ denkt	dachte	gedacht
dreschen	drisch(e)st ◆ drischt	drasch	gedroschen
dringen*	dringst ◆ dringt	drang	gedrungen
dürfen	darfst ◆ darf	durfte	gedurft
empfangen	empfängst ◆ empfängt	empfing	empfangen
empfehlen	empfiehlst ◆ empfiehlt	empfahl	empfohlen
erbleichen*	erbleichst ◆ erbleicht	erbleichte	erblichen
erlöschen*	erlischst ◆ erlischt	erlosch	erloschen
erschrecken*	erschrickst ◆ erschrickt	erschrak	erschrocken
essen	ißt ◆ ißt	aß	gegessen
fahren*	fährst ◆ fährt	fuhr	gefahren
fallen*	fällst ◆ fällt	fiel	gefallen
fangen	fängst ◆ fängt	fing	gefangen
fechten	fichtst ◆ ficht	focht	gefochten
finden	findest ◆ findet	fand	gefunden
flechten	flichtst ◆ flicht	flocht	geflochten
fliegen*	fliegst ◆ fliegt	flog	geflogen
fliehen*	fliehst ◆ flieht	floh	geflohen
fließen*	fließt ◆ fließt	floß	geflossen
fressen	frißt ◆ frißt	fraß	gefressen
frieren	frierst ◆ friert	fror	gefroren
gären*	gärst ◆ gärt	gor	gegoren
gebären	gebierst ◆ gebiert	gebar	geboren
geben	gibst ◆ gibt	gab	gegeben
gedeihen*	gedeihst ◆ gedeiht	gedieh	gediehen
gehen*	gehst ◆ geht	ging	gegangen

Infinitive	Present Indicative 2nd pers sing ♦ 3rd pers sing	Imperfect Indicative	Past Participle
gelingen*	- ♦ gelingt	gelang	gelungen
gelten	giltst ♦ gilt	galt	gegolten
genesen*	gene(se)st ♦ genest	genas	genesen
genießen	genießt ♦ genießt	genoß	genossen
geraten*	gerätst ♦ gerät	geriet	geraten
geschehen*	- ♦ geschieht	geschah	geschehen
gewinnen	gewinnst ♦ gewinnt	gewann	gewonnen
gießen	gießt ♦ gießt	goß	gegossen
gleichen	gleichst ♦ gleicht	glich	geglichen
gleiten*	gleitest ♦ gleitet	glitt	geglitten
glimmen	glimmst ♦ glimmt	glomm	geglommen
graben	gräbst ♦ gräbt	grub	gegraben
greifen	greifst ♦ greift	griff	gegriffen
haben	hast ♦ hat	hatte	gehabt
halten	hältst ♦ hält	hielt	gehalten
hängen	hängst ♦ hängt	hing	gehangen
hauen	haust ♦ haut	hieb	gehauen
heben	hebst ♦ hebt	hob	gehoben
heißen	heißt ♦ heißt	hieß	geheißen
helfen	hilfst ♦ hilft	half	geholfen
kennen	kennst ♦ kennt	kannte	gekannt
klimmen*	klimmst ♦ klimmt	klomm	geklommen
klingen	klingst ♦ klingt	klang	geklungen
kneifen	kneifst ♦ kneift	kniff	gekniffen
kommen*	kommst ♦ kommt	kam	gekommen
können	kannst ♦ kann	konnte	gekonnt
kriechen*	kriechst ♦ kriecht	kroch	gekrochen
laden	lädst ♦ lädt	lud	geladen
lassen	läßt ♦ läßt	ließ	gelassen
laufen*	läufst ♦ läuft	lief	gelaufen
leiden	leidest ♦ leidet	litt	gelitten
leihen	leihst ♦ leiht	lieh	geliehen
lesen	liest ♦ liest	las	gelesen
liegen*	liegst ♦ liegt	lag	gelegen
lügen	lügst ♦ lügt	log	gelogen
mahlen	mahlst ♦ mahlt	mahlte	gemahlen
meiden	meidest ♦ meidet	mied	gemieden
melken	milkst ♦ milkt	molk	gemolken
messen	mißt ♦ mißt	maß	gemessen
mißlingen*	- ♦ mißlingt	mißlang	mißlungen
mögen	magst ♦ mag	mochte	gemocht
müssen	mußt ♦ muß	mußte	gemußt
nehmen	nimmst ♦ nimmt	nahm	genommen
nennen	nennst ♦ nennt	nannte	genannt
pfeifen	pfeifst ♦ pfeift	pfiff	gepfiffen
preisen	preist ♦ preist	pries	gepriesen
quellen*	quillst ♦ quillt	quoll	gequollen
raten	rätst ♦ rät	riet	geraten
reiben	reibst ♦ reibt	rieb	gerieben
reißen*	reißt ♦ reißt	riß	gerissen
reiten*	reitest ♦ reitet	ritt	geritten
rennen*	rennst ♦ rennt	rannte	gerannt
riechen	riechst ♦ riecht	roch	gerochen
ringen	ringst ♦ ringt	rang	gerungen

xix

Infinitive	Present Indicative 2nd pers sing ♦ 3rd pers sing	Imperfect Indicative	Past Participle
rinnen*	rinnst ♦ rinnt	rann	geronnen
rufen	rufst ♦ ruft	rief	gerufen
salzen	salzt ♦ salzt	salzte	gesalzen
saufen	säufst ♦ säuft	soff	gesoffen
saugen	saugst ♦ saugt	sog	gesogen *od* gesaugt
schaffen	schaffst ♦ schafft	schuf	geschaffen
schallen	schallst ♦ schallt	scholl	geschollen
scheiden*	scheidest ♦ scheidet	schied	geschieden
scheinen	scheinst ♦ scheint	schien	geschienen
scheißen	scheißt ♦ scheißt	schiß	geschissen
schelten	schiltst ♦ schilt	schalt	gescholten
scheren	scherst ♦ schert	schor	geschoren
schieben	schiebst ♦ schiebt	schob	geschoben
schießen	schießt ♦ schießt	schoß	geschossen
schinden	schindest ♦ schindet	schindete	geschunden
schlafen	schläfst ♦ schläft	schlief	geschlafen
schlagen	schlägst ♦ schlägt	schlug	geschlagen
schleichen*	schleichst ♦ schleicht	schlich	geschlichen
schleifen	schleifst ♦ schleift	schliff	geschliffen
schließen	schließt ♦ schließt	schloß	geschlossen
schlingen	schlingst ♦ schlingt	schlang	geschlungen
schmeißen	schmeißt ♦ schmeißt	schmiß	geschmissen
schmelzen*	schmilzt ♦ schmilzt	schmolz	geschmolzen
schneiden	schneidest ♦ schneidet	schnitt	geschnitten
schreiben	schreibst ♦ schreibt	schrieb	geschrieben
schreien	schreist ♦ schreit	schrie	geschrie(e)n
schreiten	schreitest ♦ schreitet	schritt	geschritten
schweigen	schweigst ♦ schweigt	schwieg	geschwiegen
schwellen*	schwillst ♦ schwillt	schwoll	geschwollen
schwimmen*	schwimmst ♦ schwimmt	schwamm	geschwommen
schwinden*	schwindest ♦ schwindet	schwand	geschwunden
schwingen	schwingst ♦ schwingt	schwang	geschwungen
schwören	schwörst ♦ schwört	schwor	geschworen
sehen	siehst ♦ sieht	sah	gesehen
sein*	bist ♦ ist	war	gewesen
senden	sendest ♦ sendet	sandte	gesandt
singen	singst ♦ singt	sang	gesungen
sinken*	sinkst ♦ sinkt	sank	gesunken
sinnen	sinnst ♦ sinnt	sann	gesonnen
sitzen*	sitzt ♦ sitzt	saß	gesessen
sollen	sollst ♦ soll	sollte	gesollt
speien	speist ♦ speit	spie	gespie(e)n
spinnen	spinnst ♦ spinnt	spann	gesponnen
sprechen	sprichst ♦ spricht	sprach	gesprochen
sprießen*	sprießt ♦ sprießt	sproß	gesprossen
springen*	springst ♦ springt	sprang	gesprungen
stechen	stichst ♦ sticht	stach	gestochen
stecken	steckst ♦ steckt	steckte *od* stak	gesteckt
stehen	stehst ♦ steht	stand	gestanden
stehlen	stiehlst ♦ stiehlt	stahl	gestohlen
steigen*	steigst ♦ steigt	stieg	gestiegen
sterben*	stirbst ♦ stirbt	starb	gestorben

Infinitive	Present Indicative 2nd pers sing ♦ 3rd pers sing	Imperfect Indicative	Past Participle
stinken	stinkst ♦ stinkt	stank	gestunken
stoßen	stößt ♦ stößt	stieß	gestoßen
streichen	streichst ♦ streicht	strich	gestrichen
streiten	streitest ♦ streitet	stritt	gestritten
tragen	trägst ♦ trägt	trug	getragen
treffen	triffst ♦ trifft	traf	getroffen
treiben*	treibst ♦ treibt	trieb	getrieben
treten*	trittst ♦ tritt	trat	getreten
trinken	trinkst ♦ trinkt	trank	getrunken
trügen	trügst ♦ trügt	trog	getrogen
tun	tust ♦ tut	tat	getan
verderben	verdirbst ♦ verdirbt	verdarb	verdorben
verdrießen	verdrießt ♦ verdrießt	verdroß	verdrossen
vergessen	vergißt ♦ vergißt	vergaß	vergessen
verlieren	verlierst ♦ verliert	verlor	verloren
verschleißen	verschleißt ♦ verschleißt	verschliß	verschlissen
wachsen*	wächst ♦ wächst	wuchs	gewachsen
wägen	wägst ♦ wägt	wog	gewogen
waschen	wäschst ♦ wäscht	wusch	gewaschen
weben	webst ♦ webt	webte *od* wob	gewoben
weichen*	weichst ♦ weicht	wich	gewichen
weisen	weist ♦ weist	wies	gewiesen
wenden	wendest ♦ wendet	wendete	gewendet
werben	wirbst ♦ wirbt	warb	geworben
werden*	wirst ♦ wird	wurde	geworden
werfen	wirfst ♦ wirft	warf	geworfen
wiegen	wiegst ♦ wiegt	wog	gewogen
winden	windest ♦ windet	wand	gewunden
wissen	weißt ♦ weiß	wußte	gewußt
wollen	willst ♦ will	wollte	gewollt
wringen	wringst ♦ wringt	wrang	gewrungen
zeihen	zeihst ♦ zeiht	zieh	geziehen
ziehen*	ziehst ♦ zieht	zog	gezogen
zwingen	zwingst ♦ zwingt	zwang	gezwungen

UNREGELMÄSSIGE ENGLISCHE VERBEN

present	pt	pp	present	pt	pp
arise	arose	arisen	drive	drove	driven
awake	awoke	awoken	dwell	dwelt	dwelt
be (am, is,	was, were	been	eat	ate	eaten
are;			fall	fell	fallen
being)			feed	fed	fed
bear	bore	born(e)	feel	felt	felt
beat	beat	beaten	fight	fought	fought
become	became	become	find	found	found
befall	befell	befallen	flee	fled	fled
begin	began	begun	fling	flung	flung
behold	beheld	beheld	fly	flew	flown
bend	bent	bent	forbid	forbad(e)	forbidden
beset	beset	beset	forecast	forecast	forecast
bet	bet, betted	bet, betted	forget	forgot	forgotten
bid (at	bid	bid	forgive	forgave	forgiven
auction,			forsake	forsook	forsaken
cards)			freeze	froze	frozen
bid (say)	bade	bidden	get	got	got, (US)
bind	bound	bound			gotten
bite	bit	bitten	give	gave	given
bleed	bled	bled	go (goes)	went	gone
blow	blew	blown	grind	ground	ground
break	broke	broken	grow	grew	grown
breed	bred	bred	hang	hung	hung
bring	brought	brought	hang	hanged	hanged
build	built	built	(execute)		
burn	burnt,	burnt,	have	had	had
	burned	burned	hear	heard	heard
burst	burst	burst	hide	hid	hidden
buy	bought	bought	hit	hit	hit
can	could	(been able)	hold	held	held
cast	cast	cast	hurt	hurt	hurt
catch	caught	caught	keep	kept	kept
choose	chose	chosen	kneel	knelt,	knelt,
cling	clung	clung		kneeled	kneeled
come	came	come	know	knew	known
cost	cost	cost	lay	laid	laid
cost (work	costed	costed	lead	led	led
out price			lean	leant,	leant,
of)				leaned	leaned
creep	crept	crept	leap	leapt,	leapt,
cut	cut	cut		leaped	leaped
deal	dealt	dealt	learn	learnt,	learnt,
dig	dug	dug		learned	learned
do (3rd	did	done	leave	left	left
person:			lend	lent	lent
he/she/it			let	let	let
does)			lie (lying)	lay	lain
draw	drew	drawn	light	lit, lighted	lit, lighted
dream	dreamed,	dreamed,	lose	lost	lost
	dreamt	dreamt	make	made	made
drink	drank	drunk	may	might	—

xxii

present	pt	pp	present	pt	pp
mean	meant	meant	speed	sped,	sped,
meet	met	met		speeded	speeded
mistake	mistook	mistaken	spell	spelt,	spelt,
mow	mowed	mown,		spelled	spelled
		mowed	spend	spent	spent
must	(had to)	(had to)	spill	spilt,	spilt,
pay	paid	paid		spilled	spilled
put	put	put	spin	spun	spun
quit	quit,	quit,	spit	spat	spat
	quitted	quitted	spoil	spoiled,	spoiled,
read	read	read		spoilt	spoilt
rid	rid	rid	spread	spread	spread
ride	rode	ridden	spring	sprang	sprung
ring	rang	rung	stand	stood	stood
rise	rose	risen	steal	stole	stolen
run	ran	run	stick	stuck	stuck
saw	sawed	sawed,	sting	stung	stung
		sawn	stink	stank	stunk
say	said	said	stride	strode	stridden
see	saw	seen	strike	struck	struck
seek	sought	sought	strive	strove	striven
sell	sold	sold	swear	swore	sworn
send	sent	sent	sweep	swept	swept
set	set	set	swell	swelled	swollen,
sew	sewed	sewn			swelled
shake	shook	shaken	swim	swam	swum
shear	sheared	shorn,	swing	swung	swung
		sheared	take	took	taken
shed	shed	shed	teach	taught	taught
shine	shone	shone	tear	tore	torn
shoot	shot	shot	tell	told	told
show	showed	shown	think	thought	thought
shrink	shrank	shrunk	throw	threw	thrown
shut	shut	shut	thrust	thrust	thrust
sing	sang	sung	tread	trod	trodden
sink	sank	sunk	wake	woke,	woken,
sit	sat	sat		waked	waked
slay	slew	slain	wear	wore	worn
sleep	slept	slept	weave	wove	woven
slide	slid	slid	weave	weaved	weaved
sling	slung	slung	(wind)		
slit	slit	slit	wed	wedded,	wedded,
smell	smelt,	smelt,		wed	wed
	smelled	smelled	weep	wept	wept
sow	sowed	sown,	win	won	won
		sowed	wind	wound	wound
speak	spoke	spoken	wring	wrung	wrung
			write	wrote	written

ZAHLEN

NUMBERS

ein(s)	1	one
zwei	2	two
drei	3	three
vier	4	four
fünf	5	five
sechs	6	six
sieben	7	seven
acht	8	eight
neun	9	nine
zehn	10	ten
elf	11	eleven
zwölf	12	twelve
dreizehn	13	thirteen
vierzehn	14	fourteen
fünfzehn	15	fifteen
sechzehn	16	sixteen
siebzehn	17	seventeen
achtzehn	18	eighteen
neunzehn	19	nineteen
zwanzig	20	twenty
einundzwanzig	21	twenty-one
zweiundzwanzig	22	twenty-two
dreißig	30	thirty
vierzig	40	forty
fünfzig	50	fifty
sechzig	60	sixty
siebzig	70	seventy
achtzig	80	eighty
neunzig	90	ninety
hundert	100	a hundred
hunderteins	101	a hundred and one
zweihundert	200	two hundred
zweihunderteins	201	two hundred and one
dreihundert	300	three hundred
dreihunderteins	301	three hundred and one
tausend	1000	a thousand
tausend(und)eins	1001	a thousand and one
fünftausend	5000	five thousand
eine Million	1000000	a million

ZAHLEN

NUMBERS

erste(r, s)	**1. 1st**	first
zweite(r, s)	**2. 2nd**	second
dritte(r, s)	**3. 3rd**	third
vierte(r, s)	**4. 4th**	fourth
fünfte(r, s)	**5. 5th**	fifth
sechste(r, s)	**6. 6th**	sixth
siebte(r, s)	**7. 7th**	seventh
achte(r, s)	**8. 8th**	eighth
neunte(r, s)	**9. 9th**	ninth
zehnte(r, s)	**10. 10th**	tenth
elfte(r, s)	**11. 11th**	eleventh
zwölfte(r, s)	**12. 12th**	twelfth
dreizehnte(r, s)	**13. 13th**	thirteenth
vierzehnte(r, s)	**14. 14th**	fourteenth
fünfzehnte(r, s)	**15. 15th**	fifteenth
sechzehnte(r, s)	**16. 16th**	sixteenth
siebzehnte(r, s)	**17. 17th**	seventeenth
achtzehnte(r, s)	**18. 18th**	eighteenth
neunzehnte(r, s)	**19. 19th**	nineteenth
zwanzigste(r, s)	**20. 20th**	twentieth
einundzwanzigste(r, s)	**21. 21st**	twenty-first
dreißigste(r, s)	**30. 30th**	thirtieth
hundertste(r, s)	**100. 100th**	hundredth
hunderterste(r, s)	**101. 101st**	hundred-and-first
tausendste(r, s)	**1000. 1000th**	thousandth

UHRZEIT

TIME

*wieviel Uhr ist es?, wie spät ist
 es?*
es ist ...

what time is it?

it is or it's ...

Mitternacht, zwölf Uhr nachts	midnight
ein Uhr (morgens *or* früh)	one o'clock (in the morning), 1am
fünf nach eins, ein Uhr fünf	five (minutes) past one
zehn nach eins, ein Uhr zehn	ten (minutes) past one
Viertel nach eins, ein Uhr fünfzehn	quarter past, fifteen minutes past one
fünf vor halb zwei, ein Uhr fünfundzwanzig	twenty-five (minutes) past two
halb zwei, ein Uhr dreißig	half (past) one, one thirty
fünf nach halb zwei, ein Uhr fünfunddreißig	twenty-five (minutes) to two, one thirty-five
zwanzig vor zwei, ein Uhr vierzig	twenty (minutes) to two, one forty
Viertel vor zwei, ein Uhr fünfundvierzig	a quarter to two, one forty-five
zehn vor zwei, ein Uhr fünfzig	ten minutes to two, one fifty
zwölf Uhr (mittags), Mittag	twelve (o'clock) noon, midday
halb eins (mittags *or* nachmittags), zwölf Uhr dreißig	half (past) twelve *or* twelve thirty in (the afternoon), 12.30pm
zwei Uhr (nachmittags)	two o'clock (in the afternoon), 2pm
sieben Uhr (abends)	7 o'clock (in the evening), 7pm

um wieviel Uhr?

at what time?

um Mitternacht	at midnight
um sieben Uhr	at seven (o'clock)
in zwanzig Minuten	in twenty minutes
vor zehn Minuten	ten minutes ago

DATUM

DATES

heute	today
morgen	tomorrow
übermorgen	the day after tomorrow
gestern	yesterday
vorgestern	the day before yesterday
am Vortag	the day before, on the eve of
am nächsten Tag	the day after

morgens	in the morning
abends	in the evening
heute morgen	this morning
heute abend	this evening
heute nachmittag	this afternoon
gestern morgen	yesterday morning
gestern abend	yesterday evening
morgen vormittag	tomorrow morning
morgen abend	tomorrow evening
in der Nacht von Samstag auf Sonntag	Saturday night, Sunday morning
er kommt am Donnerstag	he's coming on Thursday
samstags	on Saturdays
jeden Samstag	every Saturday
letzten Samstag	last Saturday
nächsten Samstag	next Saturday
Samstag in einer Woche	a week on Saturday
Samstag in zwei Wochen	two weeks on Saturday
von Montag bis Samstag	from Monday to Saturday
jeden Tag	every day
einmal in der Woche	once a week
zweimal in der Woche	twice a week
einmal im Monat	once a month
vor einer Woche *or* acht Tagen	a week *or* seven days ago
vor zwei Wochen *or* vierzehn Tagen	two weeks *or* a fortnight ago
letztes Jahr	last year
in zwei Tagen	in two days time
in acht Tagen *or* einer Woche	in seven days *or* one week
in vierzehn Tagen *or* zwei Wochen	in a fortnight *or* two weeks
nächsten Monat	next month
nächstes Jahr	next year
den wievielten haben wir heute?, der wievielte ist heute?	what is today's date?, what date is it today?
der 1./22. Oktober 1995	the first/22nd October 1995
ich bin am 5 Juni 1991 geboren	I was born on the 5th of June 1991
1995	in 1995
neunzehnhundert(und)fünfundneunzig	nineteen (hundred and) ninety-five
44 v. Chr.	44 B.C.
14 n. Chr.	14 A.D.
im 19. Jahrhundert	in the 19th century
in den 30er Jahren	in the thirties
es war einmal	once upon a time

GERMAN HYPHENATION RULES

German hyphenation follows some basic general rules.

The fundamental rule is that a syllable should begin with a consonant,
eg. **Zei-tung, re-no-vieren**

If two or more consonants stand between vowels, usually only the last comes after the hyphen, eg.

Ver-wand-te, Was-ser, Klemp-ner

However, the consonantal groups ch, sch, ph, st and th cannot be split unless the letters belong to different syllables, eg.

Ta-sche, Phi-lo-so-phie, Mor-gen-stern

but **Häus-chen, Pump-hose, Donners-tag**

Compounds

Compounds can be split into their individual elements, eg.

Sonn-tag, Kranken-haus, Hand-schuh-fach

If necessary, the individual elements can be further split into syllables, following the general rules above.

Kran-ken-haus

NOTE: When three identical consonants come together in a compound, only two of them will appear in normal spelling (like in the word **Schiffahrt** which is made up of **Schiff** and **Fahrt**). However, if a compound like this is hyphenated, all three consonants must be shown.

Schiff-fahrt, Bett-tuch, voll-laufen

This is shown in the dictionary as follows:

Schiff- *zW:* **~(f)ahrt**

Words with prefixes

Prefixes can be split from the rest of the word.

be-treuen, auf-machen, pro-duzieren, dar-um

If necessary, the rest of the word can be split further into syllables, following the general rules above.

be-treu-en, auf-ma-chen, pro-du-zie-ren

Words with suffixes

Suffixes can be split from the rest of the word, eg.

Müdig-keit, Dunkel-heit, rund-lich, Zeug-nis, müh-sam

When the suffix starts with a vowel (eg. **-ei, -in, -ung**), the last consonant before the suffix comes after the hyphen.

Meiste-rin, Freun-din, Behand-lung, Bäcke-rei

If necessary, the rest of the word can be split further into syllables, following the basic rules above.

Mü-dig-keit, Dun-kel-heit, Mei-ste-rin, Be-hand-lung

The consonant combination ck may be split, but it is then spelt k-k.

drucken: druk-ken, Glocke: Glok-ke

Note that it is best to avoid splitting ck where correct spelling is important, in names for example.

Vowels

When splitting words into syllables, vowels may be split as follows:

Generally, vowels may be split as long as they are not pronounced as one sound.

zu-erst, An-schau-ung, Mu-se-um, En-zi-an, na-iv

Two vowels which are pronounced as one sound (like **aa, ee, oo, ie**) and diphthongs (like **au, ei, eu**) must <u>never</u> be split.

Haa-re, Boo-te, er-neu-ern, fei-ern, trau-en, Wie-se

If two vowels form a unit (although they are not pronounced as one sound) they should not be split.

Poe-sie, re-gio-nal, asia-tisch

When two i's are side by side, they can be split.

par-tei-isch, va-ri-ie-ren

Cases where hyphenation is not possible

Words of one syllable cannot be split.

hübsch, Freund, sein

Syllables which consist of one vowel only must not be split from the rest of the word.

Atem	not	**A-tem**
oder	not	**o-der**
edel	not	**e-del**

Deutsch–Englisch

German–English

A, a

A¹, a [aː] *nt* A, a; ~ **wie Anton** ≈ A for Andrew, A for Able (*US*); **das ~ und O** the be-all and end-all; (*eines Wissensgebietes*) the basics *pl*; **wer ~ sagt, muß auch B sagen** (*Sprichwort*) in for a penny, in for a pound (*Sprichwort*).

A² *f abk* (= *Autobahn*) ≈ M (*BRIT*).

a. *abk* = **am.**

à [aː] *präp* (*bes COMM*) at.

AA *nt abk* (= *Auswärtiges Amt*) F.O. (*BRIT*).

Aachen ['aːxən] (**-s**) *nt* Aachen.

Aal [aːl] (**-(e)s, -e**) *m* eel.

aalen ['aːlən] (*umg*) *vr:* **sich in der Sonne ~** to bask in the sun.

a.a.O. *abk* (= *am angegebenen od angeführten Ort*) loc. cit.

Aas [aːs] (**-es, -e** *od* **Äser**) *nt* carrion; **~geier** *m* vulture.

═══════════════ *SCHLÜSSELWORT*

ab [ap] *präp +dat* from; ~ **Werk** (*COMM*) ex works; **Kinder ~ 12 Jahren** children from the age of 12; ~ **morgen** from tomorrow; ~ **sofort** as of now

♦ *adv* **1** off; **links ~** to the left; **der Knopf ist ~** the button has come off; ~ **nach Hause!** off home with you!; ~ **durch die Mitte!** (*umg*) beat it!

2 (*zeitlich*): **von da ~** from then on; **von heute ~** from today, as of today

3 (*auf Fahrplänen*): **München ~ 12.20** leaving Munich 12.20

4: ~ **und zu** *od* **an** now and then *od* again.

abändern ['ap|ɛndərn] *vt:* ~ (**in** +*akk*) to alter (to); (*Gesetzentwurf*) to amend (to); (*Strafe, Urteil*) to revise (to).

Abänderung *f* alteration; amendment; revision.

Abänderungsantrag *m* (*PARL*) proposed amendment.

abarbeiten ['ap|arbaɪtən] *vr* to slave away.

Abart ['ap|aːrt] *f* (*BIOL*) variety.

abartig *adj* abnormal.

Abb. *abk* (= *Abbildung*) illus.

Abbau ['apbaʊ] (**-(e)s**) *m* (+*gen*) dismantling; (*Verminderung*) reduction (in); (*Verfall*) decline (in); (*MIN*) mining; (*über Tage*) quarrying; (*CHEM*) decomposition.

abbaubar *adj:* **biologisch ~** biodegradable.

abbauen *vt* to dismantle; (*verringern*) to reduce; (*MIN*) to mine; to quarry; (*CHEM*) to break down; **Arbeitsplätze ~** to make job cuts.

Abbaurechte *pl* mineral rights *pl*.

abbeißen ['apbaɪsən] *unreg vt* to bite off.

abbekommen ['apbəkɔmən] *unreg vt:* **etwas ~** to get some (of it); (*beschädigt werden*) to get damaged; (*verletzt werden*) to get hurt.

abberufen ['apbəruːfən] *unreg vt* to recall.

Abberufung *f* recall.

abbestellen ['apbəʃtɛlən] *vt* to cancel.

abbezahlen ['apbətsaːlən] *vt* to pay off.

abbiegen ['apbiːgən] *unreg vi* to turn off; (*Straße*) to bend ♦ *vt* to bend; (*verhindern*) to ward off.

Abbiegespur *f* turning lane.

Abbild ['apbɪlt] *nt* portrayal; (*einer Person*) image, likeness; **a~en** ['apbɪldən] *vt* to portray; **~ung** *f* illustration; (*Schaubild*) diagram.

abbinden ['apbɪndən] *unreg vt* (*MED: Arm, Bein etc*) to ligature.

Abbitte ['apbɪtə] *f:* ~ **leisten** *od* **tun (bei)** to make one's apologies (to).

abblasen ['apblaːzən] *unreg vt* to blow off; (*fig: umg*) to call off.

abblättern ['apblɛtərn] *vi* (*Putz, Farbe*) to flake (off).

abblenden ['apblɛndən] *vt* (*AUT*) to dip (*BRIT*), dim (*US*) ♦ *vi* to dip (*BRIT*) *od* dim (*US*) one's headlights.

Abblendlicht ['apblɛntlɪçt] *nt* dipped (*BRIT*) *od* dimmed (*US*) headlights *pl*.

abblitzen ['apblɪtsən] (*umg*) *vi:* **jdn ~ lassen** to send sb packing.

abbrechen ['apbrɛçən] *unreg vt* to break off; (*Gebäude*) to pull down; (*Zelt*) to take down; (*aufhören*) to stop; (*COMPUT*) to abort ♦ *vi* to break off; to stop; **sich** *dat* **einen ~** (*umg: sich sehr anstrengen*) to bust a gut.

abbrennen ['apbrɛnən] *unreg vt* to burn off; (*Feuerwerk*) to let off ♦ *vi* (*Hilfsverb sein*) to burn down; **abgebrannt sein** (*umg*) to be broke.

abbringen ['apbrɪŋən] *unreg vt:* **jdn von etw ~** to dissuade sb from sth; **jdn vom Weg ~** to divert sb; **ich bringe den Verschluß nicht ab** (*umg*) I can't get the top off.

abbröckeln ['apbrœkəln] *vi* to crumble off *od* away; (*BÖRSE: Preise*) to ease.

Abbruch ['apbrʊx] *m* (*von Verhandlungen etc*) breaking off; (*von Haus*) demolition; (*COMPUT*) abort; **jdm/etw ~ tun** to harm sb/sth; **~arbeiten** *pl* demolition work *sing*; **a~reif** *adj* only fit for demolition.

abbrühen ['apbry:ən] *vt* to scald.

abbuchen ['apbu:xən] *vt* to debit; (*durch Dauerauftrag*): **~ (von)** to pay by standing order (from).

abbürsten ['apbʏrstən] *vt* to brush off.

abbüßen ['apby:sən] *vt* (*Strafe*) to serve.

ABC-Waffen *pl abk* (= *atomare, biologische und chemische Waffen*) ABC weapons (= *atomic, biological and chemical weapons*).

abdampfen ['apdampfən] *vi* (*fig: umg: losgehen/-fahren*) to hit the road.

abdanken ['apdaŋkən] *vi* to resign; (*König*) to abdicate.

Abdankung *f* resignation; abdication.

abdecken ['apdɛkən] *vt* to uncover; (*Tisch*) to clear; (*Loch*) to cover.

abdichten ['apdɪçtən] *vt* to seal; (*NAUT*) to caulk.

abdrängen ['apdrɛŋən] *vt* to push off.

abdrehen ['apdre:ən] *vt* (*Gas*) to turn off; (*Licht*) to switch off; (*Film*) to shoot ♦ *vi* (*Schiff*) to change course; **jdm den Hals ~ to** wring sb's neck.

abdriften ['apdrɪftən] *vi* to drift (away).

abdrosseln ['apdrɔsəln] *vt* to throttle; (*AUT*) to stall; (*Produktion*) to cut back.

Abdruck ['apdrʊk] *m* (*Nachdrucken*) reprinting; (*Gedrucktes*) reprint; (*Gips~, Wachs~*) impression; (*Finger~*) print; **a~en** *vt* to print.

abdrücken ['apdrʏkən] *vt* to make an impression of; (*Waffe*) to fire; (*umg: Person*) to hug, squeeze ♦ *vi* to leave imprints; (*abstoßen*) to push o.s. away; **jdm die Luft ~** to squeeze all the breath out of sb.

abebben ['ap|ɛbən] *vi* to ebb away.

Abend ['a:bənt] (**-s, -e**) *m* evening; **gegen ~** towards (the) evening; **den ganzen ~ (über)** the whole evening; **zu ~ essen** to have dinner *od* supper; **a~** *adv:* **heute a~** this

evening; **~anzug** *m* dinner jacket (*BRIT*), tuxedo (*US*); **~brot** *nt* supper; **~essen** *nt* supper; **a~füllend** *adj* taking up the whole evening; **~gymnasium** *nt* night school; **~kasse** *f* (*THEAT*) box office; **~kleid** *nt* evening gown; **~kurs** *m* evening classes *pl*; **~land** *nt* West; **a~lich** *adj* evening; **~mahl** *nt* Holy Communion; **~rot** *nt* sunset.

abends *adv* in the evening.

Abend- *zW:* **~vorstellung** *f* evening performance; **~zeitung** *f* evening paper.

Abenteuer ['a:bəntɔyər] (**-s, -**) *nt* adventure; (*Liebes~*) affair; **a~lich** *adj* adventurous; **~spielplatz** *m* adventure playground.

Abenteurer (**-s, -**) *m* adventurer; **~in** *f* adventuress.

aber ['a:bər] *konj* but; (*jedoch*) however ♦ *adv:* **tausend und ~ tausend** thousands upon thousands; **oder ~** or else; **bist du ~ braun!** aren't you brown!; **das ist ~ schön** that's really nice; **nun ist ~ Schluß!** now that's enough!; **A~** *nt* but.

Aberglaube ['a:bərglaubə] *m* superstition.

abergläubisch ['a:bərglɔybɪʃ] *adj* superstitious.

aberkennen ['ap|ɛrkɛnən] *unreg vt:* **jdm etw ~** to deprive sb of sth, take sth (away) from sb.

Aberkennung *f* taking away.

abermalig *adj* repeated.

abermals *adv* once again.

Abf. *abk* (= *Abfahrt*) dep.

abfahren ['apfa:rən] *unreg vi* to leave, depart ♦ *vt* to take *od* cart away; (*Film*) to start; (*FILM, TV: Kamera*) to roll; (*Strecke*) to drive; (*Reifen*) to wear; (*Fahrkarte*) to use; **der Zug ist abgefahren** (*lit*) the train has left; (*fig*) we've/you've *etc* missed the boat; **der Zug fährt um 8.00 von Bremen ab** the train leaves from Bremen at 8 o'clock; **jdn ~ lassen** (*umg: abweisen*) to tell sb to get lost; **auf jdn ~** (*umg*) to really go for sb.

Abfahrt ['apfa:rt] *f* departure; (*Autobahn~*) exit; (*SKI*) descent; (*Piste*) run; **Vorsicht bei der ~ des Zuges!** stand clear, the train is about to leave!

Abfahrts- *zW:* **~lauf** *m* (*SKI*) downhill; **~tag** *m* day of departure; **~zeit** *f* departure time.

Abfall ['apfal] *m* waste; (*von Speisen etc*) rubbish (*BRIT*), garbage (*US*); (*Neigung*) slope; (*Verschlechterung*) decline; **~eimer** *m* rubbish bin (*BRIT*), garbage can (*US*).

abfallen *unreg vi* (*lit, fig*) to fall *od* drop off; (*POL, vom Glauben*) to break away; (*sich neigen*) to fall *od* drop away; **wieviel fällt bei dem Geschäft für mich ab?** (*umg*) how much do I get out of the deal?

abfällig ['apfɛlɪç] *adj* disparaging, deprecatory.

Abfallprodukt *nt* (*lit, fig*) waste product.

abfangen ['apfaŋən] *unreg vt* to intercept; (*Person*) to catch; (*unter Kontrolle bringen*) to check; (*Aufprall*) to absorb; (*Kunden*) to lure away.

Abfangjäger m (*MIL*) interceptor.

abfärben ['apfɛrbən] vi (*lit*) to lose its colour; (*Wäsche*) to run; (*fig*) to rub off.

abfassen ['apfasən] vt to write, draft.

abfeiern ['apfaiɐrn] (*umg*) vt: **Überstunden** ~ to take time off in lieu of overtime pay.

abfertigen ['apfɛrtɪgən] vt to prepare for dispatch, process; (*an der Grenze*) to clear; (*Kundschaft*) to attend to; **jdn kurz** ~ to give sb short shrift.

Abfertigung f preparing for dispatch, processing; clearance; (*Bedienung: von Kunden*) service; (: *von Antragstellern*): ~ **von** dealing with.

abfeuern ['apfɔyɐrn] vt to fire.

abfinden ['apfɪndən] unreg vt to pay off ♦ vr to come to terms; **sich mit jdm** ~/**nicht** ~ to put up with/not to get on with sb; **er konnte sich nie damit** ~, **daß** ... he could never accept the fact that ...

Abfindung f (*von Gläubigern*) payment; (*Geld*) sum in settlement.

abflachen ['apflaxən] vt to level (off), flatten (out) ♦ vi (*fig: sinken*) to decline.

abflauen ['apflauən] vi (*Wind, Erregung*) to die away, subside; (*Nachfrage, Geschäft*) to fall od drop off.

abfliegen ['apfli:gən] unreg vi to take off ♦ vt (*Gebiet*) to fly over.

abfließen ['apfli:sən] unreg vi to drain away; **ins Ausland** ~ (*Geld*) to flow out of the country.

Abflug ['apflu:k] m departure; (*Start*) take-off; ~**zeit** f departure time.

Abfluß ['apflʊs] m draining away; (*Öffnung*) outlet; ~**rohr** nt drainpipe; (*von sanitären Anlagen*) wastepipe.

abfragen ['apfra:gən] vt to test; (*COMPUT*) to call up; **jdn etw** ~ to question sb on sth.

abfrieren ['apfri:rən] unreg vi: **ihm sind die Füße abgefroren** his feet got frostbitten, he got frostbite in his feet.

Abfuhr ['apfu:r] (-, -en) f removal; (*fig*) snub, rebuff; **sich** dat **eine** ~ **holen** to meet with a rebuff.

abführen ['apfy:rən] vt to lead away; (*Gelder, Steuern*) to pay ♦ vi (*MED*) to have a laxative effect.

Abführmittel nt laxative, purgative.

Abfüllanlage f bottling plant.

abfüllen ['apfʏlən] vt to draw off; (*in Flaschen*) to bottle.

Abgabe ['apga:bə] f handing in; (*von Ball*) pass; (*Steuer*) tax; (*einer Erklärung*) giving.

abgabenfrei adj tax-free.

abgabenpflichtig adj liable to tax.

Abgabetermin m closing date; (*für Dissertation etc*) submission date.

Abgang ['apgaŋ] m (*von Schule*) leaving; (*THEAT*) exit; (*MED: Ausscheiden*) passing;

(: *Fehlgeburt*) miscarriage; (*Abfahrt*) departure; (*der Post, von Waren*) dispatch.

Abgangszeugnis nt leaving certificate.

Abgas ['apga:s] nt waste gas; (*AUT*) exhaust.

ABGB nt abk (*ÖSTERR*: = *Allgemeines Bürgerliches Gesetzbuch*) Civil Code in Austria.

abgeben ['apge:bən] unreg vt (*Gegenstand*) to hand od give in; (*Ball*) to pass; (*Wärme*) to give off; (*Amt*) to hand over; (*Schuß*) to fire; (*Erklärung, Urteil*) to give; (*darstellen*) to make ♦ vr: **sich mit jdm/etw** ~ to associate with sb/bother with sth; „**Kinderwagen abzugeben**" "pram for sale"; **jdm etw** ~ (*überlassen*) to let sb have sth.

abgebrannt ['apgəbrant] (*umg*) adj broke.

abgebrüht ['apgəbry:t] (*umg*) adj (*skrupellos*) hard-boiled, hardened.

abgedroschen ['apgədrɔʃən] adj trite; (*Witz*) corny.

abgefahren ['apgəfa:rən] pp von **abfahren**.

abgefeimt ['apgəfaimt] adj cunning.

abgegeben ['apgəge:bən] pp von **abgeben**.

abgegriffen ['apgəgrɪfən] adj (*Buch*) well-thumbed; (*Redensart*) trite.

abgehackt ['apgəhakt] adj clipped.

abgehalftert ['apgəhalftɐrt] adj (*fig: umg*) run-down, dead beat.

abgehangen ['apgəhaŋən] pp von **abhängen** ♦ adj: (**gut**) ~ (*Fleisch*) well-hung.

abgehärtet ['apgəhɛrtət] adj tough, hardy; (*fig*) hardened.

abgehen ['apge:ən] unreg vi to go away, leave; (*THEAT*) to exit; (*POST*) to go; (*MED*) to be passed; (*sterben*) to die; (*Knopf etc*) to come off; (*abgezogen werden*) to be taken off; (*Straße*) to branch off; (*abweichen*): **von einer Forderung** ~ to give up a demand ♦ vt (*Strecke*) to go od walk along; (*MIL: Gelände*) to patrol; **von seiner Meinung** ~ to change one's opinion; **davon gehen 5% ab** 5% is taken off that; **etw geht jdm ab** (*fehlt*) sb lacks sth.

abgekämpft ['apgəkɛmpft] adj exhausted.

abgekartet ['apgəkartət] adj: **ein** ~**es Spiel** a rigged job.

abgeklärt ['apgəklɛ:rt] adj serene, tranquil.

abgelegen ['apgəle:gən] adj remote.

abgelten ['apgɛltən] unreg vt (*Ansprüche*) to satisfy.

abgemacht ['apgəmaxt] adj fixed; ~! done!

abgemagert ['apgəma:gɐrt] adj (*sehr dünn*) thin; (*ausgemergelt*) emaciated.

abgeneigt ['apgənaikt] adj averse.

abgenutzt ['apgənʊtst] adj worn, shabby; (*Reifen*) worn; (*fig: Klischees*) well-worn.

Abgeordnete(r) ['apgəɔrdnətə(r)] f(m) elected representative; (*von Parlament*) member of parliament.

Abgesandte(r) ['apgəzantə(r)] f(m) delegate; (*POL*) envoy.

abgeschieden ['apgəʃi:dən] adj (*einsam*):

~ **leben/wohnen** to live in seclusion.

abgeschlagen ['apgəʃlaːgən] *adj* (*besiegt*) defeated; (*erschöpft*) exhausted, worn-out.

abgeschlossen ['apgəʃlɔsən] *pp von* **abschließen** ♦ *adj attrib* (*Wohnung*) self-contained.

abgeschmackt ['apgəʃmakt] *adj* tasteless; **A~heit** *f* lack of taste; (*Bemerkung*) tasteless remark.

abgesehen ['apgəzeːən] *adj:* **es auf jdn/etw ~ haben** to be after sb/sth; **~ von ...** apart from ...

abgespannt ['apgəʃpant] *adj* tired out.

abgestanden ['apgəʃtandən] *adj* stale; (*Bier*) flat.

abgestorben ['apgəʃtɔrbən] *adj* numb; (*BIOL, MED*) dead.

abgestumpft ['apgəʃtʊmpft] *adj* (*gefühllos: Person*) insensitive; (*Gefühle, Gewissen*) dulled.

abgetakelt ['apgətaːkəlt] *adj* (*fig*) decrepit, past it.

abgetan ['apgətaːn] *adj:* **damit ist die Sache ~** that settles the matter.

abgetragen ['apgətraːgən] *adj* worn.

abgewinnen ['apgəvɪnən] *unreg vt:* **jdm Geld ~** to win money from sb; **einer Sache etw/ Geschmack ~** to get sth/pleasure from sth.

abgewogen ['apgəvoːgən] *adj* (*Urteil, Worte*) balanced.

abgewöhnen ['apgəvøːnən] *vt:* **jdm/sich etw ~** to cure sb of sth/give sth up.

abgießen ['apgiːsən] *unreg vt* (*Flüssigkeit*) to pour off.

Abglanz ['apglants] *m* (*auch fig*) reflection.

abgleiten ['apglaɪtən] *unreg vi* to slip, slide.

Abgott ['apgɔt] *m* idol.

abgöttisch ['apgœtɪʃ] *adj:* ~ **lieben** to idolize.

abgrasen ['apgraːzən] *vt* (*Feld*) to graze; (*umg: Thema*) to do to death.

abgrenzen ['apgrɛntsən] *vt* (*lit, fig*) to mark off; (*Gelände*) to fence off ♦ *vr:* **sich ~ (gegen)** to dis(as)sociate o.s. (from).

Abgrund ['apgrʊnt] *m* (*lit, fig*) abyss.

abgründig ['apgrʏndɪç] *adj* unfathomable; (*Lächeln*) cryptic.

abgrundtief *adj* (*Haß, Verachtung*) profound.

abgucken ['apgʊkən] *vt, vi* to copy.

Abguß ['apgʊs] *m* (*KUNST, METALLURGIE: Vorgang*) casting; (*: Form*) cast.

abhaben ['apha:bən] *unreg* (*umg*) *vt* (*abbekommen*): **willst du ein Stück ~?** do you want a bit?

abhacken ['aphakən] *vt* to chop off.

abhaken ['apha:kən] *vt* to tick off (*BRIT*), check off (*US*).

abhalten ['aphaltən] *unreg vt* (*Versammlung*) to hold; **jdn von etw ~** (*fernhalten*) to keep sb away from sth; (*hindern*) to keep sb from sth.

abhandeln ['aphandəln] *vt* (*Thema*) to deal with; **jdm die Waren/8 Mark ~** to do a deal

with sb for the goods/beat sb down 8 marks.

abhanden [ap'handən] *adj:* ~ **kommen** to get lost.

Abhandlung ['aphandlʊŋ] *f* treatise, discourse.

Abhang ['aphaŋ] *m* slope.

abhängen ['aphɛŋən] *unreg vt* (*Bild*) to take down; (*Anhänger*) to uncouple; (*Verfolger*) to shake off ♦ *vi* (*Fleisch*) to hang; **von jdm/etw ~** to depend on sb/sth; **das hängt ganz davon ab** it all depends; **er hat abgehängt** (*TEL: umg*) he hung up (on me *etc*).

abhängig ['aphɛŋɪç] *adj:* ~ **(von)** dependent (on); **A~keit** *f:* **A~keit (von)** dependence (on).

abhärten ['aphɛrtən] *vt* to toughen up ♦ *vr* to toughen (o.s.) up; **sich gegen etw ~** to harden o.s. to sth.

abhauen ['aphaʊən] *unreg vt* to cut off; (*Baum*) to cut down ♦ *vi* (*umg*) to clear off *od* out; **hau ab!** beat it!

abheben ['aphe:bən] *unreg vt* to lift (up); (*Karten*) to cut; (*Masche*) to slip; (*Geld*) to withdraw, take out ♦ *vi* (*Flugzeug*) to take off; (*Rakete*) to lift off; (*KARTEN*) to cut ♦ *vr:* **sich ~ von** to stand out from, contrast with.

abheften ['aphɛftən] *vt* (*Rechnungen etc*) to file away; (*NÄHEN*) to tack, baste.

abhelfen ['aphɛlfən] *unreg vi +dat* to remedy.

abhetzen ['aphɛtsən] *vr* to wear *od* tire o.s. out.

Abhilfe ['aphɪlfə] *f* remedy; ~ **schaffen** to put things right.

Abholmarkt *m* cash and carry.

abholen ['apho:lən] *vt* (*Gegenstand*) to fetch, collect; (*Person*) to call for; (*am Bahnhof etc*) to pick up, meet.

abholzen ['aphɔltsən] *vt* (*Wald*) to clear, deforest.

abhorchen ['aphɔrçən] *vt* (*MED*) to listen to, sound.

abhören ['aphø:rən] *vt* (*Vokabeln*) to test; (*Telefongespräch*) to tap; (*Tonband etc*) to listen to; **abgehört werden** (*umg*) to be bugged.

Abhörgerät *nt* bug.

abhungern ['aphʊŋərn] *vr:* **sich** *dat* **10 Kilo ~** to lose 10 kilos by going on a starvation diet.

Abi ['abi] (*-s, -s*) *nt* (*SCH: umg*) = **Abitur**.

Abitur [abi'tu:r] (*-s, -e*) *nt German school-leaving examination*, ≈ A-levels *pl* (*BRIT*); **(das) ~ machen** to take one's school-leaving exam *od* A-levels.

---

*The **Abitur** is the German school-leaving examination which is taken at the age of 18 or 19, after 13 years of school, by pupils at a **Gymnasium**. It is taken in four subjects and is necessary for entry to a university education.*

Abiturient(in) [abitu'rɪɛnt(ɪn)] *m(f)* candidate

for school-leaving certificate.

abkämmen ['apkɛmən] vt (Gegend) to comb, scour.

abkanzeln ['apkantsəln] (umg) vt: jdn ~ to give sb a dressing-down.

abkapseln ['apkapsəln] vr to shut od cut o.s. off.

abkarten ['apkartən] (umg) vt: **die Sache war von vornherein abgekartet** the whole thing was a put-up job.

abkaufen ['apkaufən] vt: **jdm etw** ~ to buy sth from sb.

abkehren ['apke:rən] vt (Blick) to avert, turn away ♦ vr to turn away.

abklappern ['apklapərn] (umg) vt (Kunden) to call on; (: Läden, Straße): ~ **(nach)** to scour (for), comb (for).

abklären ['apklɛ:rən] vt (klarstellen) to clear up, clarify ♦ vr (sich setzen) to clarify.

Abklatsch ['apklatʃ] (-es, -e) m (fig) (poor) copy.

abklemmen ['apklɛmən] vt (Leitung) to clamp.

abklingen ['apklɪŋən] unreg vi to die away; (RUNDF) to fade out.

abknallen ['apknalən] (umg) vt to shoot down.

abknöpfen ['apknœpfən] vt to unbutton; **jdm etw** ~ (umg) to get sth off sb.

abkochen ['apkɔxən] vt to boil; (keimfrei machen) to sterilize (by boiling).

abkommandieren ['apkɔmandi:rən] vt (MIL: zu Einheit) to post; (zu bestimmtem Dienst): ~ **zu** to detail for.

abkommen ['apkɔmən] unreg vi to get away; (vom Thema) ~ to get off the subject, digress; **von der Straße/einem Plan** ~ to leave the road/give up a plan.

Abkommen (-s, -) nt agreement.

abkömmlich ['apkœmlɪç] adj available, free.

Abkömmling m (Nachkomme) descendant; (fig) adherent.

abkönnen ['apkœnən] unreg (umg) vt (mögen): **das kann ich nicht ab** I can't stand it.

abkratzen ['apkratsən] vt to scrape off ♦ vi (umg) to kick the bucket.

abkriegen ['apkri:gən] (umg) vt = abbekommen.

abkühlen ['apky:lən] vt to cool down ♦ vr (Mensch) to cool down od off; (Wetter) to get cool; (Zuneigung) to cool.

Abkunft ['apkunft] (-) f origin, birth.

abkürzen ['apkʏrtsən] vt to shorten; (Wort) to abbreviate; **den Weg** ~ to take a short cut.

Abkürzung f abbreviation; short cut.

abladen ['apla:dən] unreg vi to unload ♦ vt to unload; (fig: umg): **seinen Ärger (bei jdm)** ~ to vent one's anger (on sb).

Ablage ['apla:gə] f place to keep/put sth; (Aktenordnung) filing; (für Akten) tray.

ablagern ['apla:gərn] vt to deposit ♦ vr to be deposited ♦ vi to mature.

Ablagerung f (abgelagerter Stoff) deposit.

ablassen ['aplasən] unreg vt (Wasser, Dampf) to let out od off; (vom Preis) to knock off ♦ vi: **von etw** ~ to give sth up, abandon sth.

Ablauf m (Abfluß) drain; (von Ereignissen) course; (einer Frist, Zeit) expiry (BRIT), expiration (US); **nach** ~ **des Jahres/dieser Zeit** at the end of the year/this time.

ablaufen ['aplaufən] unreg vi (abfließen) to drain away; (Ereignisse) to happen; (Frist, Zeit, Paß) to expire ♦ vt (Sohlen) to wear (down od out); ~ **lassen** (abspulen, abspielen: Platte, Tonband) to play; (Film) to run; **sich** dat **die Beine** od **Hacken nach etw** ~ (umg) to walk one's legs off looking for sth; **jdm den Rang** ~ to steal a march on sb.

Ableben ['aple:bən] nt (form) demise (form).

ablegen ['aple:gən] vt to put od lay down; (Kleider) to take off; (Gewohnheit) to get rid of; (Prüfung) to take, sit (BRIT); (Zeugnis) to give; (Schriftwechsel) to file (away); (nicht mehr tragen: Kleidung) to discard, cast off; (Schwur, Eid) to swear ♦ vi (Schiff) to cast off.

Ableger (-s, -) m layer; (fig) branch, offshoot.

ablehnen ['aple:nən] vt to reject; (mißbilligen) to disapprove of; (Einladung) to decline, refuse ♦ vi to decline, refuse.

Ablehnung f rejection; refusal; **auf** ~ **stoßen** to meet with disapproval.

ableisten ['aplaɪstən] vt (form: Zeit) to serve.

ableiten ['aplaɪtən] vt (Wasser) to divert; (deduzieren) to deduce; (Wort) to derive.

Ableitung f diversion; deduction; (Wort) derivative.

ablenken ['aplɛŋkən] vt to turn away, deflect; (zerstreuen) to distract ♦ vi to change the subject; **das lenkt ab** (zerstreut) it takes your mind off things; (stört) it's distracting.

Ablenkung f deflection; distraction.

Ablenkungsmanöver nt diversionary tactic; (um vom Thema abzulenken) red herring.

ablesen ['aple:zən] unreg vt to read; **jdm jeden Wunsch von den Augen** ~ to anticipate sb's every wish.

ableugnen ['aplɔygnən] vt to deny.

ablichten ['aplɪçtən] vt to photocopy; (fotografieren) to photograph.

abliefern ['apli:fərn] vt to deliver; **etw bei jdm/einer Dienststelle** ~ to hand sth over to sb/in at an office.

Ablieferung f delivery.

abliegen ['apli:gən] unreg vi to be some distance away; (fig) to be far removed.

ablisten ['aplɪstən] vt: **jdm etw** ~ to trick od con sb out of sth.

ablösen ['aplø:zən] vt (abtrennen) to take off, remove; (in Amt) to take over from; (FIN: Schuld, Hypothek) to pay off, redeem; (Methode, System) to supersede ♦ vr (auch: **einander** ~) to take turns; (Fahrer, Kollegen, Wachen) to relieve each other.

Ablösung f removal; relieving.

abluchsen ['apluksən] (umg) vt: **jdm etw** ~ to

get *od* wangle sth out of sb.

Abluft *f* (*TECH*) used air.

ABM *pl abk* (= *Arbeitsbeschaffungsmaßnahmen*) *job-creation scheme.*

abmachen ['apmaxən] *vt* to take off; (*vereinbaren*) to agree; **etw mit sich allein** ~ to sort sth out for o.s.

Abmachung *f* agreement.

abmagern ['apma:gərn] *vi* to get thinner, become emaciated.

Abmagerungskur *f* diet; **eine** ~ **machen** to go on a diet.

Abmarsch ['apmarʃ] *m* departure; **a~bereit** *adj* ready to start.

abmarschieren ['apmarʃi:rən] *vi* to march off.

abmelden ['apmɛldən] *vt* (*Auto*) to take off the road; (*Telefon*) to have disconnected; (*COMPUT*) to log off ♦ *vr* to give notice of one's departure; (*im Hotel*) to check out; **ein Kind von einer Schule** ~ to take a child away from a school; **er/sie ist bei mir abgemeldet** (*umg*) I don't want anything to do with him/her; **jdn bei der Polizei** ~ to register sb's departure with the police.

abmessen ['apmɛsən] *unreg vt* to measure.

Abmessung *f* measurement; (*Ausmaß*) dimension.

abmontieren ['apmɔnti:rən] *vt* to take off; (*Maschine*) to dismantle.

ABM-Stelle *f* *temporary post created as part of a job creation scheme.*

abmühen ['apmy:ən] *vr* to wear o.s. out.

abnabeln ['apna:bəln] *vt*: **jdn** ~ (*auch fig*) to cut sb's umbilical cord.

abnagen ['apna:gən] *vt* to gnaw off; (*Knochen*) to gnaw.

Abnäher ['apnɛ:ər] (**-s, -**) *m* dart.

Abnahme ['apna:mə] *f* (*+gen*) removal; (*COMM*) buying; (*Verringerung*) decrease (in).

abnehmen ['apne:mən] *unreg vt* to take off, remove; (*Führerschein*) to take away; (*Prüfung*) to hold; (*Maschen*) to decrease; (*Hörer*) to lift, pick up; (*begutachten: Gebäude, Auto*) to inspect ♦ *vi* to decrease; (*schlanker werden*) to lose weight; **jdm etw** ~ (*Geld*) to get sth out of sb; (*kaufen: auch umg: glauben*) to buy sth from sb; **kann ich dir etwas** ~? (*tragen*) can I take something for you?; **jdm Arbeit** ~ to take work off sb's shoulders; **jdm ein Versprechen** ~ to make sb promise sth.

Abnehmer (**-s, -**) *m* purchaser, customer; **viele/wenige** ~ **finden** (*COMM*) to sell well/badly.

Abneigung ['apnaigʊŋ] *f* aversion, dislike.

abnorm [ap'nɔrm] *adj* abnormal.

abnötigen ['apnø:tigən] *vt*: **jdm etw/Respekt** ~ to force sth from sb/gain sb's respect.

abnutzen ['apnʊtsən] *vt* to wear out.

Abnutzung *f* wear (and tear).

Abo ['abo] (**-s, -s**) (*umg*) *nt* = **Abonnement.**

Abonnement [abɔn(ə)'mã:] (**-s, -s** *od* **-e**) *nt* subscription; (*Theater~*) season ticket.

Abonnent(in) [abɔ'nɛnt(ɪn)] *m(f)* subscriber.

abonnieren [abɔ'ni:rən] *vt* to subscribe to.

abordnen ['ap|ɔrdnən] *vt* to delegate.

Abordnung *f* delegation.

Abort [a'bɔrt] (**-(e)s, -e**) *m* (*veraltet*) lavatory.

abpacken ['appakən] *vt* to pack.

abpassen ['appasən] *vt* (*Person, Gelegenheit*) to wait for; (*warten auf*) to catch; (*jdm auflauern*) to waylay; **etw gut** ~ to time sth well.

abpausen ['appaʊzən] *vt* to make a tracing of.

abpfeifen ['appfaifən] *unreg vt, vi* (*SPORT*): (**das Spiel**) ~ to blow the whistle (for the end of the game).

Abpfiff ['appfɪf] *m* final whistle.

abplagen ['appla:gən] *vr* to struggle (away).

Abprall ['appral] *m* rebound; (*von Kugel*) ricochet.

abprallen ['appralən] *vi* to bounce off; to ricochet; **an jdm** ~ (*fig*) to make no impression on sb.

abputzen ['appʊtsən] *vt* to clean; (*Nase etc*) to wipe.

abquälen ['apkvɛ:lən] *vr* to struggle (away).

abrackern ['aprakərn] (*umg*) *vr* to slave away.

abraten ['apra:tən] *unreg vi*: **jdm von etw** ~ to advise sb against sth, warn sb against sth.

abräumen ['aprɔymən] *vt* to clear up *od* away; (*Tisch*) to clear ♦ *vi* to clear up *od* away.

abreagieren ['apreagi:rən] *vt*: **seinen Zorn (an jdm/etw)** ~ to work one's anger off (on sb/sth) ♦ *vr* to calm down; **seinen Ärger an anderen** ~ to take it out on others.

abrechnen ['apreçnən] *vt* to deduct, take off ♦ *vi* (*lit*) to settle up; (*fig*) to get even; **darf ich** ~? would you like your bill (*BRIT* *od* check (*US*) now?

Abrechnung *f* settlement; (*Rechnung*) bill; (*Aufstellung*) statement; (*Bilanz*) balancing; (*fig: Rache*) revenge; **in** ~ **stellen** (*form: Abzug*) to deduct; ~ **über** *+akk* bill/statement for.

Abrechnungszeitraum *m* accounting period.

Abrede ['apre:də] *f*: **etw in** ~ **stellen** to deny *od* dispute sth.

abregen ['apre:gən] (*umg*) *vr* to calm *od* cool down.

abreiben ['apraibən] *unreg vt* to rub off; (*säubern*) to wipe; **jdn mit einem Handtuch** ~ to towel sb down.

Abreibung (*umg*) *f* (*Prügel*) hiding, thrashing.

Abreise ['apraizə] *f* departure.

abreisen *vi* to leave, set off.

abreißen ['apraisən] *unreg vt* (*Haus*) to tear down; (*Blatt*) to tear off ♦ *vi*: **den Kontakt nicht** ~ **lassen** to stay in touch.

abrichten ['apriçtən] *vt* to train.

abriegeln ['apri:gəln] *vt* (*Tür*) to bolt; (*Straße,*

Gebiet) to seal off.
abringen ['apriŋən] *unreg vt:* **sich** *dat* **ein Lächeln** ~ to force a smile.
Abriß ['apris] (**-sses, -sse**) *m* (*Übersicht*) outline; (*Abbruch*) demolition.
abrollen ['aprɔlən] *vt* (*abwickeln*) to unwind ♦ *vi* (*vonstatten gehen: Programm*) to run; (: *Veranstaltung*) to go off; (: *Ereignisse*) to unfold.
Abruf ['apru:f] *m:* **auf** ~ on call.
abrufen *unreg vt* (*Mensch*) to call away; (*COMM: Ware*) to request delivery of; (*COMPUT*) to recall, retrieve.
abrunden ['aprondən] *vt* to round off.
abrüsten ['aprystən] *vi* to disarm.
Abrüstung *f* disarmament.
abrutschen ['aprotʃən] *vi* to slip; (*AVIAT*) to sideslip.
Abs. *abk* = **Absender**; (= **Absatz**) par., para.
absacken ['apzakən] *vi* (*sinken*) to sink; (*Boden, Gebäude*) to subside.
Absage ['apza:gə] (**-, -n**) *f* refusal; (*auf Einladung*) negative reply.
absagen *vt* to cancel, call off; (*Einladung*) to turn down ♦ *vi* to cry off; (*ablehnen*) to decline; **jdm** ~ to tell sb that one can't come.
absägen ['apzɛ:gən] *vt* to saw off.
absahnen ['apza:nən] *vt* (*lit*) to skim; **das beste für sich** ~ (*fig*) to take the cream.
Absatz ['apzats] *m* (*COMM*) sales *pl*; (*JUR*) section; (*Bodensatz*) deposit; (*neuer Abschnitt*) paragraph; (*Treppen~*) landing; (*Schuh~*) heel; **~flaute** *f* slump in the market; **~förderung** *f* sales promotion; **~gebiet** *nt* (*COMM*) market; sales territory; **~prognose** *f* sales forecast; **~schwierigkeiten** *pl* sales problems *pl*; **~ziffern** *pl* sales figures *pl*.
absaufen ['apzaufən] *unreg vi* (*umg*) *vi* (*ertrinken*) to drown; (: *Motor*) to flood; (: *Schiff etc*) to go down.
absaugen ['apzaugən] *vt* (*Flüssigkeit*) to suck out *od* off; (*Teppich, Sofa*) to hoover ®, vacuum.
abschaben ['apʃa:bən] *vt* to scrape off; (*Möhren*) to scrape.
abschaffen ['apʃafən] *vt* to abolish, do away with.
Abschaffung *f* abolition.
abschalten ['apʃaltən] *vt, vi* (*lit: umg*) to switch off.
abschattieren ['apʃati:rən] *vt* to shade.
abschätzen ['apʃɛtsən] *vt* to estimate; (*Lage*) to assess; (*Person*) to size up.
abschätzig ['apʃɛtsɪç] *adj* disparaging, derogatory.
Abschaum ['apʃaum] (**-(e)s**) *m* scum.
Abscheu ['apʃɔy] (**-(e)s**) *m* loathing, repugnance; **a~erregend** *adj* repulsive, loathsome; **a~lich** *adj* abominable.
abschicken ['apʃɪkən] *vt* to send off.

abschieben ['apʃi:bən] *unreg vt* to push away; (*Person*) to pack off; (*ausweisen: Ausländer*) to deport; (*fig: Verantwortung, Schuld*): ~ **(auf** +*akk*) to shift (onto).
Abschied ['apʃi:t] (**-(e)s, -e**) *m* parting; (*von Armee*) discharge; (**von jdm**) ~ **nehmen** to say goodbye (to sb), take one's leave (of sb); **seinen** ~ **nehmen** (*MIL*) to apply for discharge; **zum** ~ on parting.
Abschiedsbrief *m* farewell letter.
Abschiedsfeier *f* farewell party.
abschießen ['apʃi:sən] *unreg vt* (*Flugzeug*) to shoot down; (*Geschoß*) to fire; (*umg: Minister*) to get rid of.
abschirmen ['apʃɪrmən] *vt* to screen; (*schützen*) to protect ♦ *vr* (*sich isolieren*): **sich** ~ **(gegen)** to cut o.s. off (from).
abschlaffen ['apʃlafən] (*umg*) *vi* to flag.
abschlagen ['apʃla:gən] *unreg vt* (*abhacken, COMM*) to knock off; (*ablehnen*) to refuse; (*MIL*) to repel.
abschlägig ['apʃlɛ:gɪç] *adj* negative; **jdn/etw** ~ **bescheiden** (*form*) to turn sb/sth down.
Abschlagszahlung *f* interim payment.
abschleifen ['apʃlaifən] *unreg vt* to grind down; (*Holzboden*) to sand (down) ♦ *vr* to wear off.
Abschleppdienst *m* (*AUT*) breakdown service (*BRIT*), towing company (*US*).
abschleppen ['apʃlɛpən] *vt* to (take in) tow.
Abschleppseil *nt* towrope.
abschließen ['apʃli:sən] *unreg vt* (*Tür*) to lock; (*beenden*) to conclude, finish; (*Vertrag, Handel*) to conclude; (*Versicherung*) to take out; (*Wette*) to place ♦ *vr* (*sich isolieren*) to cut o.s. off; **mit abgeschlossenem Studium** with a degree; **mit der Vergangenheit** ~ to break with the past.
abschließend *adj* concluding ♦ *adv* in conclusion, finally.
Abschluß ['apʃlus] *m* (*Beendigung*) close, conclusion; (*COMM: Bilanz*) balancing; (*von Vertrag, Handel*) conclusion; **zum** ~ in conclusion; **~feier** *f* (*SCH*) school-leavers' ceremony; **~prüfer** *m* accountant; **~prüfung** *f* (*SCH*) final examination; (*UNIV*) finals *pl*; **~rechnung** *f* final account; **~zeugnis** *nt* (*SCH*) leaving certificate, diploma (*US*).
abschmecken ['apʃmɛkən] *vt* (*kosten*) to taste; (*würzen*) to season.
abschmieren ['apʃmi:rən] *vt* (*AUT*) to grease, lubricate.
abschminken ['apʃmɪŋkən] *vt:* **sich** ~ to remove one's make-up.
abschmirgeln ['apʃmɪrgəln] *vt* to sand down.
abschnallen ['apʃnalən] *vr* to unfasten one's seat belt ♦ *vi* (*umg: nicht mehr folgen können*) to give up; (: *fassungslos sein*) to be staggered.
abschneiden ['apʃnaidən] *unreg vt* to cut off ♦ *vi* to do, come off; **bei etw gut/schlecht** ~ (*umg*) to come off well/badly in sth.
Abschnitt ['apʃnɪt] *m* section; (*MIL*) sector;

(*Kontroll~*) counterfoil (*BRIT*), stub (*US*); (*MATH*) segment; (*Zeit~*) period.

abschnüren ['apʃnyːrən] *vt* to constrict.

abschöpfen ['apʃœpfən] *vt* to skim off.

abschrauben ['apʃraubən] *vt* to unscrew.

abschrecken ['apʃrɛkən] *vt* to deter, put off; (*mit kaltem Wasser*) to plunge into cold water.

abschreckend *adj* deterrent; **~es Beispiel** warning; **eine ~e Wirkung haben, ~ wirken** to act as a deterrent.

abschreiben ['apʃraibən] *unreg vt* to copy; (*verlorengeben*) to write off; (*COMM*) to deduct; **er ist bei mir abgeschrieben** I'm finished with him.

Abschreibung *f* (*COMM*) deduction; (*Wertverminderung*) depreciation.

Abschrift ['apʃrift] *f* copy.

abschuften ['apʃuftən] (*umg*) *vr* to slog one's guts out (*umg*).

abschürfen ['apʃyrfən] *vt* to graze.

Abschuß ['apʃus] *m* (*eines Geschützes*) firing; (*Herunterschießen*) shooting down; (*Tötung*) shooting.

abschüssig ['apʃysiç] *adj* steep.

Abschußliste *f*: **er steht auf der ~** (*umg*) his days are numbered.

Abschußrampe *f* launch(ing) pad.

abschütteln ['apʃytəln] *vt* to shake off.

abschütten ['apʃytən] *vt* (*Flüssigkeit etc*) to pour off.

abschwächen ['apʃvɛçən] *vt* to lessen; (*Behauptung, Kritik*) to tone down ♦ *vr* to lessen.

abschweifen ['apʃvaifən] *vi* to wander; (*Redner*) to digress.

Abschweifung *f* digression.

abschwellen ['apʃvɛlən] *unreg vi* (*Geschwulst*) to go down; (*Lärm*) to die down.

abschwenken ['apʃvɛŋkən] *vi* to turn away.

abschwören ['apʃvøːrən] *unreg vi* +*dat* to renounce.

absehbar ['apzeːbaːr] *adj* foreseeable; **in ~er Zeit** in the foreseeable future; **das Ende ist ~** the end is in sight.

absehen *unreg vt* (*Ende, Folgen*) to foresee ♦ *vi*: **von etw ~** to refrain from sth; (*nicht berücksichtigen*) to leave sth out of consideration; **jdm etw ~** (*erlernen*) to copy sth from sb.

abseilen ['apzailən] *vt* to lower down on a rope ♦ *vr* (*Bergsteiger*) to abseil (down).

Abseits ['apzaits] *nt* (*SPORT*) offside; **im ~ stehen** to be offside; **im ~ leben** (*fig*) to live in the shadows.

abseits *adv* out of the way ♦ *präp* +*gen* away from.

absenden ['apzɛndən] *unreg vt* to send off, dispatch.

Absender *m* sender.

Absendung *f* dispatch.

absetzbar ['apzɛtsbaːr] *adj* (*Beamter*)

dismissible; (*Waren*) saleable; (*von Steuer*) deductible.

absetzen ['apzɛtsən] *vt* (*niederstellen, aussteigen lassen*) to put down; (*abnehmen; auch Theaterstück*) to take off; (*COMM: verkaufen*) to sell; (*FIN: abziehen*) to deduct; (*entlassen*) to dismiss; (*König*) to depose; (*streichen*) to drop; (*Fußballspiel, Termin*) to cancel; (*hervorheben*) to pick out ♦ *vi*: **er trank das Glas aus, ohne abzusetzen** he emptied his glass in one ♦ *vr* (*sich entfernen*) to clear off; (*sich ablagern*) to be deposited; **das kann man ~** that is tax-deductible.

Absetzung *f* (*FIN: Abzug*) deduction; (*Entlassung*) dismissal; (*von König*) deposing; (*Streichung*) dropping.

absichern ['apzɪçərn] *vt* to make safe; (*schützen*) to safeguard ♦ *vr* to protect o.s.

Absicht ['apzɪçt] *f* intention; **mit ~** on purpose; **a~lich** *adj* intentional, deliberate.

absichtslos *adj* unintentional.

absinken ['apzɪŋkən] *unreg vi* to sink; (*Temperatur, Geschwindigkeit*) to decrease.

absitzen ['apzɪtsən] *unreg vi* to dismount ♦ *vt* (*Strafe*) to serve.

absolut [apzo'luːt] *adj* absolute.

Absolutheitsanspruch *m* claim to absolute right.

Absolutismus [apzolu'tɪsmus] *m* absolutism.

Absolvent(in) *m(f)*: **die ~en eines Lehrgangs** the students who have completed a course.

absolvieren [apzɔl'viːrən] *vt* (*SCH*) to complete.

absonderlich [ap'zɔndərlɪç] *adj* odd, strange.

absondern *vt* to separate; (*ausscheiden*) to give off, secrete ♦ *vr* to cut o.s. off.

Absonderung *f* separation; (*MED*) secretion.

absorbieren [apzɔr'biːrən] *vt* (*lit, fig*) to absorb.

abspalten ['apʃpaltən] *vt* to split off.

Abspannung ['apʃpanuŋ] *f* (*Ermüdung*) exhaustion.

absparen ['apʃpaːrən] *vt*: **sich** *dat* **etw ~** to scrimp and save for sth.

abspecken ['apʃpɛkən] (*umg*) *vt* to shed ♦ *vi* to lose weight.

abspeisen ['apʃpaizən] *vt* (*fig*) to fob off.

abspenstig ['apʃpɛnstɪç] *adj*: **(jdm) ~ machen** to lure away (from sb).

absperren ['apʃpɛrən] *vt* to block *od* close off; (*Tür*) to lock.

Absperrung *f* (*Vorgang*) blocking *od* closing off; (*Sperre*) barricade.

abspielen ['apʃpiːlən] *vt* (*Platte, Tonband*) to play; (*SPORT: Ball*) to pass ♦ *vr* to happen; **vom Blatt ~** (*MUS*) to sight-read.

absplittern ['apʃplɪtərn] *vt, vi* to chip off.

Absprache ['apʃpraːxə] *f* arrangement; **ohne vorherige ~** without prior consultation.

absprechen ['apʃprɛçən] *unreg vt* (*vereinbaren*) to arrange ♦ *vr*: **die beiden hatten sich vorher abgesprochen** they had agreed on what to do/say *etc* in advance; **jdm etw** ~ to deny sb sth; (*in Abrede stellen: Begabung*) to dispute sb's sth.

abspringen ['apʃprɪŋən] *unreg vi* to jump down/off; (*Farbe, Lack*) to flake off; (*AVIAT*) to bale out; (*sich distanzieren*) to back out.

Absprung ['apʃprʊŋ] *m* jump; **den** ~ **schaffen** (*fig*) to make the break (*umg*).

abspulen ['apʃpuːlən] *vt* (*Kabel, Garn*) to unwind.

abspülen ['apʃpyːlən] *vt* to rinse; **Geschirr** ~ to wash up (*BRIT*), do the dishes.

abstammen ['apʃtamən] *vi* to be descended; (*Wort*) to be derived.

Abstammung *f* descent; derivation; **französischer** ~ of French extraction *od* descent.

Abstand ['apʃtant] *m* distance; (*zeitlich*) interval; **davon** ~ **nehmen, etw zu tun to** refrain from doing sth; ~ **halten** (*AUT*) to keep one's distance; ~ **von etw gewinnen** (*fig*) to distance o.s. from sth; **mit großem** ~ **führen** to lead by a wide margin; **mit** ~ **der beste** by far the best.

Abstandssumme *f* compensation.

abstatten ['apʃtatən] *vt* (*form: Dank*) to give; (: *Besuch*) to pay.

abstauben ['apʃtaʊbən] *vt, vi* to dust; (*umg: mitgehen lassen*) to help oneself to, pinch; **(den Ball)** ~ (*SPORT*) to tuck the ball away.

Abstauber(in) ['apʃtaʊbər(ɪn)] (**-s, -**) (*umg*) *m(f)* (*Person*) somebody on the make.

abstechen ['apʃtɛçən] *unreg vt* to cut; (*Tier*) to cut the throat of ♦ *vi:* ~ **gegen** *od* **von** to contrast with.

Abstecher (**-s, -**) *m* detour.

abstecken ['apʃtɛkən] *vt* (*Fläche*) to mark out; (*Saum*) to pin.

abstehen ['apʃteːən] *unreg vi* (*Ohren, Haare*) to stick out; (*entfernt sein*) to stand away.

Absteige *f* cheap hotel.

absteigen ['apʃtaɪgən] *unreg vi* (*vom Rad etc*) to get off, dismount; **in einem Gasthof** ~ to put up at an inn; **(in die zweite Liga)** ~ to be relegated (to the second division); **auf dem** ~**den Ast sein** (*umg*) to be going downhill, be on the decline.

abstellen ['apʃtɛlən] *vt* (*niederstellen*) to put down; (*entfernt stellen*) to pull out; (*hinstellen: Auto*) to park; (*ausschalten*) to turn *od* switch off; (*Mißstand, Unsitte*) to stop; (*abkommandieren*) to order off; (*ausrichten*): ~ **auf** +*akk* to gear to; **das läßt sich nicht/läßt sich** ~ nothing/something can be done about that.

Abstellgleis *nt* siding; **jdn aufs** ~ **schieben** (*fig*) to cast sb aside.

Abstellraum *m* storeroom.

abstempeln ['apʃtɛmpəln] *vt* to stamp; (*fig*): ~ **zu** *od* **als** to brand as.

absterben ['apʃtɛrbən] *unreg vi* to die; (*Körperteil*) to go numb.

Abstieg ['apʃtiːk] (**-(e)s, -e**) *m* descent; (*SPORT*) relegation; (*fig*) decline.

abstimmen ['apʃtɪmən] *vi* to vote ♦ *vt:* ~ **(auf** +*akk*) (*Instrument*) to tune (to); (*Interessen*) to match (with); (*Termine, Ziele*) to fit in (with) ♦ *vr* to agree.

Abstimmung *f* vote; (*geheime* ~) ballot.

abstinent [apstiˈnɛnt] *adj* (*von Alkohol*) teetotal.

Abstinenz [apstiˈnɛnts] *f* teetotalism.

Abstinenzler(in) (**-s, -**) *m(f)* teetotaller.

abstoßen ['apʃtoːsən] *unreg vt* to push off *od* away; (*anekeln*) to repel; (*COMM: Ware, Aktien*) to sell off.

abstoßend *adj* repulsive.

abstottern ['apʃtɔtərn] (*umg*) *vt* to pay off in instalments.

abstrahieren [apstraˈhiːrən] *vt, vi* to abstract.

abstrakt [apˈstrakt] *adj* abstract ♦ *adv* abstractly, in the abstract.

Abstraktion [apstraktsiˈoːn] *f* abstraction.

Abstraktum [apˈstraktʊm] (**-s, Abstrakta**) *nt* abstract concept; (*GRAM*) abstract noun.

abstrampeln ['apʃtrampəln] *vr* (*fig: umg*) to sweat (away).

abstreifen ['apʃtraɪfən] *vt* (*abtreten: Schuhe, Füße*) to wipe; (*abziehen: Schmuck*) to take off, slip off.

abstreiten ['apʃtraɪtən] *unreg vt* to deny.

Abstrich ['apʃtrɪç] *m* (*Abzug*) cut; (*MED*) smear; ~**e machen** to lower one's sights.

abstufen ['apʃtuːfən] *vt* (*Hang*) to terrace; (*Farben*) to shade; (*Gehälter*) to grade.

abstumpfen ['apʃtʊmpfən] *vt* (*lit, fig*) to dull, blunt ♦ *vi* to become dulled.

Absturz ['apʃtʊrts] *m* fall; (*AVIAT*) crash.

abstürzen ['apʃtʏrtsən] *vi* to fall; (*AVIAT*) to crash.

absuchen ['apzuːxən] *vt* to scour, search.

absurd [apˈzʊrt] *adj* absurd.

Abszeß [apsˈtsɛs] (**-sses, -sse**) *m* abscess.

Abt [apt] (**-(e)s, ⁻e**) *m* abbot.

Abt. *abk* (= *Abteilung*) dept.

abtasten ['aptastən] *vt* to feel, probe; (*ELEK*) to scan; (*bei Durchsuchung*): ~ **(auf** +*akk*) to frisk (for).

abtauen ['aptaʊən] *vt, vi* to thaw; (*Kühlschrank*) to defrost.

Abtei [apˈtaɪ] (**-, -en**) *f* abbey.

Abteil [apˈtaɪl] (**-(e)s, -e**) *nt* compartment.

abteilen ['aptaɪlən] *vt* to divide up; (*abtrennen*) to divide off.

Abteilung *f* (*in Firma, Kaufhaus*) department; (*MIL*) unit; (*in Krankenhaus, JUR*) section.

Abteilungsleiter(in) *m(f)* head of department; (*in Kaufhaus*) department manager(ess).

abtelefonieren ['aptelefoniːrən] (*umg*) *vi* to telephone to say one can't make it.

Äbtissin [ɛpˈtɪsɪn] *f* abbess.

abtönen ['aptøːnən] *vt* (*PHOT*) to tone down.

abtöten ['aptøːtən] *vt* (*lit, fig*) to destroy, kill

(off); (*Nerv*) to deaden.
abtragen ['aptraːgən] *unreg vt* (*Hügel, Erde*) to
level down; (*Essen*) to clear away; (*Kleider*)
to wear out; (*Schulden*) to pay off.
abträglich ['aptrɛːklɪç] *adj* (*+dat*) harmful (to).
Abtragung *f* (*GEOL*) erosion.
Abtransport (-(e)s, -e) *m* transportation; (*aus
Katastrophengebiet*) evacuation.
abtransportieren ['aptransportiːrən] *vt* to
transport; to evacuate.
abtreiben ['aptraɪbən] *unreg vt* (*Boot, Flugzeug*)
to drive off course; (*Kind*) to abort ♦ *vi* to be
driven off course; (*Frau*) to have an
abortion.
Abtreibung *f* abortion.
Abtreibungsparagraph *m* abortion law.
Abtreibungsversuch *m* attempted abortion.
abtrennen ['aptrɛnən] *vt* (*lostrennen*) to
detach; (*entfernen*) to take off; (*abteilen*) to
separate off.
abtreten ['aptreːtən] *unreg vt* to wear out;
(*überlassen*) to hand over, cede; (*Rechte,
Ansprüche*) to transfer ♦ *vi* to go off;
(*zurücktreten*) to step down; **sich** *dat* **die Füße**
~ to wipe one's feet; ~! (*MIL*) dismiss!
Abtritt ['aptrɪt] *m* (*Rücktritt*) resignation.
abtrocknen ['aptrɔknən] *vt* to dry ♦ *vi* to do
the drying-up.
abtropfen ['aptrɔpfən] *vi:* **etw** ~ **lassen** to let
sth drain.
abtrünnig ['aptrʏnɪç] *adj* renegade.
abtun ['aptuːn] *unreg vt* to take off; (*fig*) to
dismiss; **etw kurz** ~ to brush sth aside.
aburteilen ['ap|ʊrtaɪlən] *vt* to condemn.
abverlangen ['apfɛrlaŋən] *vt:* **jdm etw** ~ to
demand sth from sb.
abwägen ['apvɛːgən] *unreg vt* to weigh up.
abwählen ['apvɛːlən] *vt* to vote out (of office);
(*SCH: Fach*) to give up.
abwälzen ['apvɛltsən] *vt:* ~ **(auf** *+akk*) (*Schuld,
Verantwortung*) to shift (onto); (*Arbeit*) to
unload (onto); (*Kosten*) to pass on (to).
abwandeln ['apvandəln] *vt* to adapt.
abwandern ['apvandərn] *vi* to move away.
Abwärme ['apvɛrmə] *f* waste heat.
abwarten ['apvartən] *vt* to wait for ♦ *vi* to
wait; **das Gewitter** ~ to wait till the storm is
over; ~ **und Tee trinken** (*umg*) to wait and
see; **eine** ~**de Haltung einnehmen** to play a
waiting game.
abwärts ['apvɛrts] *adv* down; ~**gehen** *vi unpers*
(*fig*): **mit ihm/dem Land geht es** ~ he/the
country is going downhill.
Abwasch ['apvaʃ] (-(e)s) *m* washing-up; **du
kannst das auch machen, das ist (dann) ein**
~ (*umg*) you could do that as well and kill
two birds with one stone.
abwaschen *unreg vt* (*Schmutz*) to wash off;
(*Geschirr*) to wash (up).
Abwasser ['apvasər] (-s, -wässer) *nt* sewage;
~**aufbereitung** *f* sewage treatment; ~**kanal**
m sewer.

abwechseln ['apvɛksəln] *vi, vr* to alternate;
(*Personen*) to take turns.
abwechselnd *adj* alternate.
Abwechslung *f* change; (*Zerstreuung*)
diversion; **für** ~ **sorgen** to provide
entertainment.
abwechslungsreich *adj* varied.
Abweg ['apveːk] *m:* **auf** ~**e geraten/führen** to
go/lead astray.
abwegig ['apveːgɪç] *adj* wrong; (*Verdacht*)
groundless.
Abwehr ['apveːr] (-) *f* defence; (*Schutz*)
protection; (~*dienst*) counter-intelligence
(service); **auf** ~ **stoßen** to be repulsed;
a~**en** *vt* to ward off; (*Ball*) to stop; **a**~**ende
Geste** dismissive gesture; ~**reaktion** *f*
(*PSYCH*) defence (*BRIT*) *od* defense (*US*)
reaction; ~**stoff** *m* antibody.
abweichen ['apvaɪçən] *unreg vi* to deviate;
(*Meinung*) to differ; **vom rechten Weg** ~ (*fig*)
to wander off the straight and narrow.
abweichend *adj* deviant; differing.
Abweichler (-s, -) *m* (*POL*) maverick.
Abweichung *f* (*zeitlich, zahlenmäßig*)
allowance; **zulässige** ~ (*TECH*) tolerance.
abweisen ['apvaɪzən] *unreg vt* to turn away;
(*Antrag*) to turn down; **er läßt sich nicht** ~ he
won't take no for an answer.
abweisend *adj* (*Haltung*) cold.
abwenden ['apvɛndən] *unreg vt* to avert ♦ *vr* to
turn away.
abwerben ['apvɛrbən] *unreg vt:* (**jdm**) ~ to woo
away (from sb).
abwerfen ['apvɛrfən] *unreg vt* to throw off;
(*Profit*) to yield; (*aus Flugzeug*) to drop;
(*Spielkarte*) to discard.
abwerten ['apvɛrtən] *vt* (*FIN*) to devalue.
abwertend *adj* pejorative.
Abwertung *f* devaluation.
abwesend ['apveːzənt] *adj* absent; (*zerstreut*)
far away.
Abwesenheit ['apveːzənhaɪt] *f* absence;
durch ~ **glänzen** (*ironisch*) to be conspicuous
by one's absence.
abwickeln ['apvɪkəln] *vt* to unwind; (*Geschäft*)
to transact, conclude; (*fig: erledigen*) to deal
with.
Abwicklungskosten ['apvɪklʊŋskɔstən] *pl*
transaction costs *pl*.
abwiegen ['apviːgən] *unreg vt* to weigh out.
abwimmeln ['apvɪməln] (*umg*) *vt* (*Person*) to
get rid of; (: *Auftrag*) to get out of.
abwinken ['apvɪŋkən] *vi* to wave it/him *etc*
aside; (*fig: ablehnen*) to say no.
abwirtschaften ['apvɪrtʃaftən] *vi* to go
downhill.
abwischen ['apvɪʃən] *vt* to wipe off *od* away;
(*putzen*) to wipe.
abwracken ['apvrakən] *vt* (*Schiff*) to break
(up); **ein abgewrackter Mensch** a wreck (of
a person).
Abwurf ['apvʊrf] *m* throwing off; (*von Bomben*

etc) dropping; (*von Reiter, SPORT*) throw.

abwürgen ['apvʏrgən] (*umg*) *vt* to scotch; (*Motor*) to stall; **etw von vornherein** ~ to nip sth in the bud.

abzahlen ['aptsaːlən] *vt* to pay off.

abzählen ['aptsɛːlən] *vt* to count (up); **abgezähltes Fahrgeld** exact fare.

Abzählreim ['aptsɛːlraɪm] *m* counting rhyme (*e.g.* eeny meeny miney mo).

Abzahlung *f* repayment; **auf** ~ **kaufen** to buy on hire purchase (*BRIT*) *od* the installment plan (*US*).

abzapfen ['aptsapfən] *vt* to draw off; **jdm Blut** ~ to take blood from sb.

abzäunen ['aptsɔʏnən] *vt* to fence off.

Abzeichen ['aptsaɪçən] *nt* badge; (*Orden*) decoration.

abzeichnen ['aptsaɪçnən] *vt* to draw, copy; (*unterschreiben*) to initial ♦ *vr* to stand out; (*fig: bevorstehen*) to loom.

Abziehbild *nt* transfer.

abziehen ['aptsiːən] *unreg vt* to take off; (*Tier*) to skin; (*Bett*) to strip; (*Truppen*) to withdraw; (*subtrahieren*) to take away, subtract; (*kopieren*) to run off; (*Schlüssel*) to take out, remove ♦ *vi* to go away; (*Truppen*) to withdraw; (*abdrücken*) to pull the trigger, fire.

abzielen ['aptsiːlən] *vi:* ~ **auf** +*akk* to be aimed at.

Abzug ['aptsuːk] *m* departure; (*von Truppen*) withdrawal; (*Kopie*) copy; (*Subtraktion*) subtraction; (*Betrag*) deduction; (*Rauch*~) flue; (*von Waffen*) trigger; (*Rabatt*) discount; (*Korrekturfahne*) proof; (*PHOT*) print; **jdm freien** ~ **gewähren** to grant sb safe passage.

abzüglich ['aptsyːklɪç] *präp* +*gen* less.

abzweigen ['aptsvaɪgən] *vi* to branch off ♦ *vt* to set aside.

Abzweigung *f* junction.

Accessoires [aksɛso'aːrs] *pl* accessories *pl*.

ach [ax] *interj* oh; ~ **so!** I see!; **mit A~ und Krach** by the skin of one's teeth; ~ **was** *od* **wo, das ist doch nicht so schlimm!** come on now, it's not that bad!

Achillesferse [a'xɪlɛsfɛrzə] *f* Achilles heel.

Achse ['aksə] (**-, -n**) *f* axis; (*AUT*) axle; **auf** ~ **sein** (*umg*) to be on the move.

Achsel ['aksəl] (**-, -n**) *f* shoulder; ~**höhle** *f* armpit; ~**zucken** *nt* shrug (of one's shoulders).

Achsenbruch *m* (*AUT*) broken axle.

Achsenkreuz *nt* coordinate system.

Acht[1] [axt] (**-, -en**) *f* eight; (*beim Eislaufen etc*) figure (of) eight.

Acht[2] (**-**) *f* attention; **hab a~** (*MIL*) attention!; **sich in a~ nehmen** (**vor** +*dat*) to be careful (of), watch out (for); **etw außer a~ lassen** to disregard sth.

acht *num* eight; ~ **Tage** a week.

achtbar *adj* worthy.

achte(r, s) *adj* eighth.

Achteck *nt* octagon.

Achtel *nt* eighth; ~**note** *f* quaver, eighth note (*US*).

achten *vt* to respect ♦ *vi:* ~ **(auf** +*akk*) to pay attention (to); **darauf** ~, **daß** ... to be careful that ...

ächten ['ɛçtən] *vt* to outlaw, ban.

Achterbahn *f* roller coaster.

Achterdeck *nt* (*NAUT*) afterdeck.

achtfach *adj* eightfold.

achtgeben *unreg vi:* ~ **(auf** +*akk*) to take care (of); (*aufmerksam sein*) to pay attention (to).

achtlos *adj* careless; **viele gehen** ~ **daran vorbei** many people just pass by without noticing.

achtmal *adv* eight times.

achtsam *adj* attentive.

Achtstundentag *m* eight-hour day.

Achtung ['axtʊŋ] *f* attention; (*Ehrfurcht*) respect ♦ *interj* look out!; (*MIL*) attention!; **alle** ~! good for you/him *etc*!; ~, **fertig, los!** ready, steady, go!; „~ **Hochspannung!"** "danger, high voltage"; „~ **Lebensgefahr/ Stufe!"** "danger/mind the step!".

Achtungserfolg *m* reasonable success.

achtzehn *num* eighteen.

achtzig *num* eighty; **A~er(in)** (**-s, -**) *m(f)* octogenarian.

ächzen ['ɛçtsən] *vi:* ~ **(vor** +*dat*) to groan (with).

Acker ['akər] (**-s, ⸚**) *m* field; ~**bau** *m* agriculture; ~**bau und Viehzucht** farming.

ackern *vi* to plough; (*umg*) to slog away.

a conto [a 'kɔnto] *adv* (*COMM*) on account.

A.D. *abk* (= *Anno Domini*) A.D.

a.D. *abk* = **außer Dienst**.

a.d. *abk* = **an der** (*bei Ortsnamen*).

ad absurdum [at ap'zʊrdʊm] *adv:* ~ **führen** (*Argument etc*) to reduce to absurdity.

ADAC (**-**) *m abk* (= *Allgemeiner Deutscher Automobilclub*) *German motoring organization*, ≈ AA (*BRIT*), AAA (*US*).

ad acta [at 'akta] *adv:* **etw** ~ **legen** (*fig*) to consider sth finished; (*Frage, Problem*) to consider sth closed.

Adam ['aːdam] *m:* **bei** ~ **und Eva anfangen** (*umg*) to start right from scratch *od* from square one.

adaptieren [adap'tiːrən] *vt* to adapt.

adäquat [adɛ'kvaːt] *adj* (*Belohnung, Übersetzung*) adequate; (*Stellung, Verhalten*) suitable.

addieren [a'diːrən] *vt* to add (up).

Addis Abeba ['adɪs'aːbeba] (**-, -s**) *nt* Addis Ababa.

Addition [aditsi'oːn] *f* addition.

ade *interj* bye!

Adel ['aːdəl] (**-s**) *m* nobility; ~ **verpflichtet** noblesse oblige.

adelig *adj* noble.

Adelsstand *m* nobility.

Ader ['aːdər] (**-, -n**) *f* vein; (*fig: Veranlagung*)

bent.
Adhäsionsverschluß [athɛzi'oːnsfɛrʃlʊs] *m* adhesive seal.
Adjektiv ['atjɛktiːf] (**-s, -e**) *nt* adjective.
Adler ['aːdlər] (**-s, -**) *m* eagle.
adlig *adj* = **adelig.**
Admiral [atmi'raːl] (**-s, -e**) *m* admiral.
Admiralität *f* admiralty.
adoptieren [adɔp'tiːrən] *vt* to adopt.
Adoption [adɔptsi'oːn] *f* adoption.
Adoptiveltern *pl* adoptive parents *pl.*
Adoptivkind *nt* adopted child.
Adr. *abk* (= *Adresse*) add.
Adressant [adre'sant] *m* sender.
Adressat [adrɛ'saːt] (**-en, -en**) *m* addressee.
Adreßbuch *nt* directory; (*privat*) address book.
Adresse [a'drɛsə] (**-, -n**) *f* (*auch COMPUT*) address; **an der falschen ~ sein** (*umg*) to have gone/come to the wrong person; **absolute ~** absolute address; **relative ~** relative address.
adressieren [adrɛ'siːrən] *vt:* **~ (an** +*akk*) to address (to).
Adria ['aːdria] (**-**) *f* Adriatic Sea.
Adriatisches Meer [adri'aːtɪʃəs meːr] *nt* (*form*) Adriatic Sea.
Advent [at'vɛnt] (**-(e)s, -e**) *m* Advent; **der erste/zweite ~** the first/second Sunday in Advent.
Advents- *zW:* **~kalender** *m* Advent calendar; **~kranz** *m* Advent wreath.
Adverb [at'vɛrp] *nt* adverb.
adverbial [atvɛrbi'aːl] *adj* adverbial.
aero- [aero] *präf* aero-.
Aerobic [ae'roːbik] (**-s**) *nt* aerobics *sing.*
Affäre [a'fɛːrə] (**-, -n**) *f* affair; **sich aus der ~ ziehen** (*umg*) to get (o.s.) out of it.
Affe ['afə] (**-n, -n**) *m* monkey; (*umg: Kerl*) berk (*BRIT*).
Affekt (**-(e)s, -e**) *m:* **im ~ handeln** to act in the heat of the moment.
affektiert [afɛk'tiːrt] *adj* affected.
Affen- *zW:* **a~artig** *adj* like a monkey; **mit a~artiger Geschwindigkeit** (*umg*) like a flash; **a~geil** (*umg*) *adj* magic, fantastic; **~hitze** (*umg*) *f* incredible heat; **~liebe** *f:* **~liebe (zu)** blind adoration (of); **~schande** (*umg*) *f* crying shame; **~tempo** (*umg*) *nt:* **in** *od* **mit einem ~tempo** at breakneck speed; **~theater** (*umg*) *nt:* **ein ~theater aufführen** to make a fuss.
affig ['afɪç] *adj* affected.
Afghane [af'gaːnə] (**-n, -n**) *m* Afghan.
Afghanin [af'gaːnɪn] *f* Afghan.
afghanisch *adj* Afghan.
Afghanistan [af'gaːnɪstaːn] (**-s**) *nt* Afghanistan.
Afrika ['aːfrika] (**-s**) *nt* Africa.
Afrikaans [afri'kaːns] (**-**) *nt* Afrikaans.
Afrikaner(in) [afri'kaːnər(ɪn)] (**-s, -**) *m(f)* African.

afrikanisch *adj* African.
afro-amerikanisch ['aːfro|ameri'kaːnɪʃ] *adj* Afro-American.
After ['aftər] (**-s, -**) *m* anus.
AG (**-**) *f abk* (= *Aktiengesellschaft*) ≈ plc (*BRIT*), corp., inc. (*US*).
Ägäis [ɛ'gɛːɪs] (**-**) *f* Aegean (Sea).
Ägäisches Meer *nt* Aegean Sea.
Agent(in) [a'gɛnt(ɪn)] *m(f)* agent.
Agententätigkeit *f* espionage.
Agentur [agɛn'tuːr] *f* agency; **~bericht** *m* (news) agency report.
Aggregat [agre'gaːt] (**-(e)s, -e**) *nt* aggregate; (*TECH*) unit; **~zustand** *m* (*PHYS*) state.
Aggression [agrɛsi'oːn] *f* aggression.
aggressiv [agrɛ'siːf] *adj* aggressive.
Aggressivität [agrɛsivi'tɛːt] *f* aggressiveness.
Aggressor [a'grɛsoːr] (**-s, -en**) *m* aggressor.
Agitation [agitatsi'oːn] *f* agitation.
Agrarpolitik *f* agricultural policy.
Agrarstaat *m* agrarian state.
AGV *f abk* (= *Arbeitsgemeinschaft der Verbraucherverbände*) *consumer groups' association.*
Ägypten [ɛ'gyptən] (**-s**) *nt* Egypt.
Ägypter(in) (**-s, -**) *m(f)* Egyptian.
ägyptisch *adj* Egyptian.
aha [a'haː] *interj* aha!
Aha-Erlebnis *nt* sudden insight.
ahd. *abk* (= *althochdeutsch*) OHG.
Ahn [aːn] (**-en, -en**) *m* forebear.
ahnden ['aːndən] *vt* (*geh: Freveltat, Verbrechen*) to avenge; (*Übertretung, Verstoß*) to punish.
ähneln ['ɛːnəln] *vi* +*dat* to be like, resemble ♦ *vr* to be alike *od* similar.
ahnen ['aːnən] *vt* to suspect; (*Tod, Gefahr*) to have a presentiment of; **nichts Böses ~** to be unsuspecting; **du ahnst es nicht!** you have no idea!; **davon habe ich nichts geahnt** I didn't have the slightest inkling of it.
Ahnenforschung *f* genealogy.
ähnlich ['ɛːnlɪç] *adj (+dat)* similar (to); **das sieht ihm (ganz) ~!** (*umg*) that's just like him!, that's him all over!; **Ä~keit** *f* similarity.
Ahnung ['aːnʊŋ] *f* idea, suspicion; (*Vorgefühl*) presentiment.
ahnungslos *adj* unsuspecting.
Ahorn ['aːhɔrn] (**-s, -e**) *m* maple.
Ähre ['ɛːrə] (**-, -n**) *f* ear.
Aids [eːdz] (**-**) *nt* Aids.
Akademie [akade'miː] *f* academy.
Akademiker(in) [aka'deːmikər(ɪn)] (**-s, -**) *m(f)* university graduate.
akademisch *adj* academic.
Akazie [a'kaːtsiə] (**-, -n**) *f* acacia.
Akk. *abk* = **Akkusativ.**
akklimatisieren [aklimati'ziːrən] *vr* to become acclimatized.
Akkord [a'kɔrt] (**-(e)s, -e**) *m* (*MUS*) chord; **im ~ arbeiten** to do piecework; **~arbeit** *f* piecework.

Akkordeon [a'kɔrdeɔn] (-s, -s) nt accordion.
Akkordlohn m piece wages pl, piece rate.
Akkreditiv [akredi'tiːf] (-s, -e) nt (COMM) letter of credit.
Akku ['aku] (-s, -s) (umg) m (Akkumulator) battery.
akkurat [aku'raːt] adj precise; (sorgfältig) meticulous.
Akkusativ ['akuzatiːf] (-s, -e) m accusative (case); ~**objekt** nt accusative od direct object.
Akne ['aknə] (-, -n) f acne.
Akribie [akri'biː] f (geh) meticulousness.
Akrobat(in) [akro'baːt(ɪn)] (-en, -en) m(f) acrobat.
Akt [akt] (-(e)s, -e) m act; (KUNST) nude.
Akte ['aktə] (-, -n) f file; etw zu den ~n legen (lit, fig) to file sth away.
Akten- zW: ~**deckel** m folder; ~**koffer** m attaché case; a~**kundig** adj on record; ~**notiz** f memo(randum); ~**ordner** m file; ~**schrank** m filing cabinet; ~**tasche** f briefcase; ~**zeichen** nt reference.
Aktie ['aktsiə] (-, -n) f share; wie stehen die ~n? (hum: umg) how are things?
Aktien- zW: ~**bank** f joint-stock bank; ~**emission** f share issue; ~**gesellschaft** f joint-stock company; ~**index** m share index; ~**kapital** nt share capital; ~**kurs** m share price.
Aktion [aktsi'oːn] f campaign; (Polizei~, Such~) action.
Aktionär(in) [aktsio'nɛːr(ɪn)] (-s, -e) m(f) shareholder.
Aktionismus [aktsio'nɪsmʊs] m (POL) actionism.
Aktionsradius [aktsi'oːnzraːdiʊs] (-, -ien) m (AVIAT, NAUT) range; (fig: Wirkungsbereich) scope.
aktiv [ak'tiːf] adj active; (MIL) regular; **A~** (-s) nt (GRAM) active (voice).
Aktiva [ak'tiːva] pl assets pl.
aktivieren [akti'viːrən] vt to activate; (fig: Arbeit, Kampagne) to step up; (Mitarbeiter) to get moving.
Aktivität [aktivi'tɛːt] f activity.
Aktivposten m (lit, fig) asset.
Aktivsaldo m (COMM) credit balance.
aktualisieren [aktuali'ziːrən] vt (COMPUT) to update.
Aktualität [aktuali'tɛːt] f topicality; (einer Mode) up-to-dateness.
aktuell [aktu'ɛl] adj topical; up-to-date; eine ~e Sendung (RUNDF, TV) a current affairs programme.
Akupunktur [akupʊŋk'tuːər] f acupuncture.
Akustik [a'kʊstɪk] f acoustics pl.
akustisch [a'kʊstɪʃ] adj acoustic; ich habe dich rein ~ nicht verstanden I simply didn't catch what you said (properly).
akut [a'kuːt] adj acute; (Frage) pressing, urgent.

AKW nt abk = **Atomkraftwerk.**
Akzent [ak'tsɛnt] (-(e)s, -e) m accent; (Betonung) stress; ~**e setzen** (fig) to bring out od emphasize the main points; ~**verschiebung** f (fig) shift of emphasis.
Akzept (-(e)s, -e) nt (COMM: Wechsel) acceptance.
akzeptabel [aktsɛp'taːbl] adj acceptable.
akzeptieren [aktsɛp'tiːrən] vt to accept.
AL f abk (= Alternative Liste) siehe **alternativ.**
Alarm [a'larm] (-(e)s, -e) m alarm; (Zustand) alert; ~ **schlagen** to give od raise the alarm; ~**anlage** f alarm system; a~**bereit** adj standing by; ~**bereitschaft** f stand-by.
alarmieren [alar'miːrən] vt to alarm.
Alaska [a'laska] (-s) nt Alaska.
Albaner(in) [al'baːnər(ɪn)] (-s, -) m(f) Albanian.
Albanien [al'baːniən] (-s) nt Albania.
albanisch adj Albanian.
albern ['albərn] adj silly.
Album ['albʊm] (-s, Alben) nt album.
Aleuten [ale'uːtən] pl Aleutian Islands pl.
Alg (umg) abk = **Arbeitslosengeld.**
Alge ['algə] (-, -n) f alga.
Algebra ['algebra] (-) f algebra.
Algerien [al'geːriən] (-s) nt Algeria.
Algerier(in) (-s, -) m(f) Algerian.
algerisch [al'geːrɪʃ] adj Algerian.
Algier ['alʒiːər] (-s) nt Algiers.
ALGOL ['algɔl] (-(s)) nt (COMPUT) ALGOL.
Algorithmus [algo'rɪtmʊs] m (COMPUT) algorithm.
alias ['aːlias] adv alias.
Alibi ['aːlibi] (-s, -s) nt alibi.
Alimente [ali'mɛntə] pl alimony sing.
Alkohol ['alkohɔl] (-s, -e) m alcohol; unter ~ stehen to be under the influence (of alcohol); a~**arm** adj low alcohol; a~**frei** adj non-alcoholic; ~**gehalt** m proof.
Alkoholika [alko'hoːlika] pl alcoholic drinks pl, liquor (US).
Alkoholiker(in) [alko'hoːlikər(ɪn)] (-s, -) m(f) alcoholic.
alkoholisch adj alcoholic.
Alkoholverbot nt ban on alcohol.
All [al] (-s) nt universe; (RAUMFAHRT) space; (außerhalb unseres Sternsystems) outer space.
allabendlich adj every evening.
allbekannt adj universally known.
alle adj siehe **alle(r, s).**
alledem ['alədeːm] pron: bei/trotz etc ~ with/in spite of etc all that; zu ~ moreover.
Allee [a'leː] (-, -n) f avenue.
allein [a'laɪn] adj, adv alone; (ohne Hilfe) on one's own, by oneself ♦ konj (geh) but, only; von ~ by oneself/itself; nicht ~ (nicht nur) not only; ~ schon der Gedanke the very od mere thought ..., the thought alone ...; ~**erziehend** adj single-parent; A~**erziehende(r)** f(m) single parent; A~**gang** m: im A~**gang** on one's own; A~**herrscher(in)** m(f)

autocrat; **A~hersteller(in)** *m(f)* sole manufacturer.
alleinig [a'lainiç] *adj* sole.
allein- *zW:* **A~sein** *nt* being on one's own; (*Einsamkeit*) loneliness; **~stehend** *adj* single; **A~unterhalter(in)** *m(f)* solo entertainer; **A~vertretung** *f* (*COMM*) sole agency; **A~vertretungsvertrag** *m* (*COMM*) exclusive agency agreement.
allemal ['alə'ma:l] *adv* (*jedesmal*) always; (*ohne weiteres*) with no bother; **ein für ~** once and for all.
allenfalls ['alən'fals] *adv* at all events; (*höchstens*) at most.

═════════════ *SCHLÜSSELWORT*

alle(r, s) *adj* **1** (*sämtliche*) all; **wir ~** all of us; **~ Kinder waren da** all the children were there; **~ Kinder mögen ...** all children like ...; **~ beide** both of us/them; **sie kamen ~** they all came; **~s Gute** all the best; **~ in ~m** all in all; **vor ~m** above all; **das ist ~s andere als ...** that's anything but ...; **es hat ~s keinen Sinn mehr** nothing makes sense any more; **was habt ihr ~s gemacht?** what did you get up to?
2 (*mit Zeit- oder Maßangaben*) every; **~ vier Jahre** every four years; **~ fünf Meter** every five metres
♦ *pron* everything; **~s was er sagt** everything he says, all that he says; **trotz ~m** in spite of everything
♦ *adv* (*zu Ende, aufgebraucht*) finished; **die Milch is ~** the milk's all gone, there's no milk left; **etw ~ machen** to finish sth up.

allerbeste(r, s) ['alər'bɛstə(r, s)] *adj* very best.
allerdings ['alər'dɪŋs] *adv* (*zwar*) admittedly; (*gewiß*) certainly.
Allergie [aler'gi:] *f* allergy.
allergisch [a'lɛrgɪʃ] *adj* allergic; **auf etw** *akk* **~ reagieren** to be allergic to sth.
allerhand (*umg*) *adj inv* all sorts of; **das ist doch ~!** that's a bit much!; **~!** (*lobend*) good show!
Allerheiligen *nt* All Saints' Day.

Allerheiligen (*All Saints' Day*) *is a public holiday in Germany and in Austria. It is a day in honour of all the saints.* Allerseelen (*All Souls' Day*) *is celebrated on November 2nd in the Roman Catholic Church. It is customary to visit cemeteries and place lighted candles on the graves of deceased relatives and friends.*

aller- *zW:* **~höchste(r, s)** *adj* very highest; **es wird ~höchste Zeit, daß ...** it's really high time that ...; **~höchstens** *adv* at the very most; **~lei** *adj inv* all sorts of; **~letzte(r, s)** *adj* very last; **der/das ist das ~letzte** (*umg*) he's/it's the absolute end!; **~neu(e)ste(r, s)** *adj* very latest; **~seits** *adv* on all sides; **prost**

~seits! cheers everyone!
Allerseelen (**-s**) *nt* All Soul's Day; *siehe auch* **Allerheiligen.**
Allerwelts- *in zW* (*Durchschnitts-*) common; (*nichtssagend*) commonplace.
allerwenigste(r, s) *adj* very least; **die ~n Menschen wissen das** very few people know that.
Allerwerteste(r) *m* (*hum*) posterior (*hum*).
alles *pron* everything; *siehe* **alle(r, s).**
allesamt *adv* all (of them/us *etc*).
Alleskleber (**-s, -**) *m* all-purpose adhesive.
Allgäu ['algɔy] *nt part of the alpine region of Bavaria.*
allgegenwärtig *adj* omnipresent, ubiquitous.
allgemein ['algəmain] *adj* general ♦ *adv:* **es ist ~ üblich** it's the general rule; **im ~en Interesse** in the common interest; **auf ~en Wunsch** by popular request; **A~bildung** *f* general *od* all-round education; **~gültig** *adj* generally accepted; **A~heit** *f* (*Menschen*) general public; **Allgemeinheiten** *pl* (*Redensarten*) general remarks *pl*; **~verständlich** *adj* generally intelligible; **A~wissen** *nt* general knowledge.
Allheilmittel [al'hailmɪtəl] *nt* cure-all, panacea (*bes fig*).
Alliierte(r) [ali'i:rtə(r)] *f(m)* ally.
all- *zW:* **~jährlich** *adj* annual; **~mächtig** *adj* all-powerful, omnipotent; **~mählich** *adv* gradually; **es wird ~mählich Zeit** (*umg*) it's about time; **A~radantrieb** *m* all-wheel drive; **~seitig** *adj* (*allgemein*) general; (*ausnahmslos*) universal; **A~tag** *m* everyday life; **~täglich** *adj* daily; (*gewöhnlich*) commonplace; **~tags** *adv* on weekdays.
Allüren [a'ly:rən] *pl* odd behaviour (*BRIT*) *od* behavior (*US*) *sing*; (*eines Stars etc*) airs and graces *pl*.
all- *zW:* **~wissend** *adj* omniscient; **~zu** *adv* all too; **~zugern** *adv* (*mögen*) only too much; (*bereitwillig*) only too willingly; **~zuoft** *adv* all too often; **~zuviel** *adv* too much.
Allzweck- ['altsvɛk-] *in zW* all-purpose.
Alm [alm] (**-, -en**) *f* alpine pasture.
Almosen ['almo:zən] (**-s, -**) *nt* alms *pl*.
Alpen ['alpən] *pl* Alps *pl*; **~blume** *f* alpine flower; **~veilchen** *nt* cyclamen; **~vorland** *nt* foothills *pl* of the Alps.
Alphabet [alfa'be:t] (**-(e)s, -e**) *nt* alphabet.
alphabetisch *adj* alphabetical.
alphanumerisch [alfanu'me:rɪʃ] *adj* (*COMPUT*) alphanumeric.
Alptraum ['alptraum] *m* nightmare.

═════════════ *SCHLÜSSELWORT*

als [als] *konj* **1** (*zeitlich*) when; (*gleichzeitig*) as; **damals, ~ ...** (in the days) when ...; **gerade, ~ ...** just as ...
2 (*in der Eigenschaft*) than; **~ Antwort** as an answer; **~ Kind** as a child
3 (*bei Vergleichen*) than; **ich kam später ~ er**

I came later than he (did) *od* later than him;
lieber ... ~ ... rather ... than ...; **alles andere**
~ anything but; **nichts** ~ **Ärger** nothing but
trouble; **soviel/soweit** ~ **möglich** (*bei
Vergleichen*) as much/far as possible
4: ~ **ob/wenn** as if.

alsbaldig [als'baldıç] *konj:* „**zum** ~**en
Verbrauch bestimmt**" "for immediate use
only".

also ['alzo:] *konj* so; (*folglich*) therefore; ~ **wie
ich schon sagte** well (then), as I said before;
ich komme ~ **morgen** so I'll come
tomorrow; ~ **gut** *od* **schön!** okay then; ~, **so
was!** well really!; **na** ~! there you are then!

Alt [alt] (**-s, -e**) *m* (*MUS*) alto.

alt *adj* old; **ich bin nicht mehr der** ~**e** I am not
the man I was; **alles beim** ~**en lassen** to
leave everything as it was; **ich werde heute
nicht** ~ (**werden**) (*umg*) I won't last long
today/tonight *etc*; ~ **aussehen** (*fig: umg*) to
be in a pickle.

Altar [al'ta:r] (**-(e)s, -äre**) *m* altar.

alt- *zW:* **A~bau** *m* old building;
A~bauwohnung *f* flat (*BRIT*) *od* apartment
(*US*) in an old building; ~**bekannt** *adj* well-
known; ~**bewährt** *adj* (*Methode etc*) well-
tried; (*Tradition etc*) long-standing; **A~bier**
nt top-fermented German dark beer;
~**eingesessen** *adj* old-established; **A~eisen**
nt scrap iron.

Altenheim *nt* old people's home.

Altenteil ['altəntail] *nt:* **sich aufs** ~ **setzen** *od*
zurückziehen (*fig*) to retire from public life.

Alter ['altər] (**-s, -**) *nt* age; (*hohes*) old age; **er
ist in deinem** ~ he's your age; **im** ~ **von** at
the age of.

älter ['ɛltər] *adj* (*comp*) older; (*Bruder,
Schwester*) elder; (*nicht mehr jung*) elderly.

altern ['altərn] *vi* to grow old, age.

Alternativ- [altɛrna'ti:f] *in zW* alternative.

alternativ *adj:* **A~e Liste** *electoral pact
between the Greens and alternative
parties*; ~ **leben** to live an alternative way
of life.

Alternative [altɛrna'ti:və] *f* alternative.

Alternativ- *zW:* ~**medizin** *f* alternative
medicine; ~**szene** *f* alternative scene;
~**-Technologie** *f* alternative technology.

alters ['altərs] *adv* (*geh*): **von** *od* **seit** ~ (**her**)
from time immemorial.

Alters- *zW:* **a~bedingt** *adj* related to a
particular age; caused by old age; ~**grenze**
f age limit; **flexible** ~**grenze** flexible
retirement age; ~**heim** *nt* old people's
home; ~**rente** *f* old age pension; ~**ruhegeld**
nt retirement benefit; **a~schwach** *adj*
(*Mensch*) old and infirm; (*Auto, Möbel*)
decrepit; ~**versorgung** *f* provision for old
age.

Altertum ['altərtu:m] *nt* antiquity.

altertümlich *adj* (*aus dem Altertum*) ancient;

(*veraltet*) antiquated.

alt- *zW:* ~**gedient** *adj* long-serving; **A~glas** *nt*
used glass (*for recycling*), scrap glass;
A~glascontainer *m* bottle bank;
~**hergebracht** *adj* traditional;
A~herrenmannschaft *f* (*SPORT*) *team of
players over thirty*; ~**klug** *adj* precocious;
A~lasten *pl* legacy *sing* of dangerous waste;
A~material *nt* scrap; **A~metall** *nt* scrap
metal; ~**modisch** *adj* old-fashioned;
A~papier *nt* waste paper; **A~stadt** *f* old
town.

Altstimme *f* alto.

Altwarenhändler *m* second-hand dealer.

Altweibersommer *m* Indian summer.

Alu ['a:lu] *abk* = **Arbeitslosenunterstützung;
Aluminium.**

Alufolie ['a:lufo:liə] *f* tinfoil.

Aluminium [alu'mi:niom] (**-s**) *nt* aluminium,
aluminum (*US*); ~**folie** *f* tinfoil.

Alzheimer-Krankheit ['altshaımər'kraŋkhaıt]
f Alzheimer's disease.

am [am] = **an dem;** ~ **Sterben** on the point of
dying; ~ **15. März** on March 15th; ~ **letzten
Sonntag** last Sunday; ~ **Morgen/Abend** in
the morning/evening; ~ **besten/schönsten**
best/most beautiful.

Amalgam [amal'ga:m] (**-s, -e**) *nt* amalgam.

Amateur [ama'tø:r] *m* amateur.

Amazonas [ama'tso:nas] (**-**) *m* Amazon
(river).

Ambiente [ambi'ɛntə] (**-**) *nt* ambience.

Ambition [ambitsi'o:n] *f:* ~**en auf etw** *akk*
haben to have ambitions of getting sth.

Amboß ['ambɔs] (**-sses, -sse**) *m* anvil.

ambulant [ambu'lant] *adj* outpatient.

Ameise ['a:maızə] (**-, -n**) *f* ant.

Ameisenhaufen *m* anthill.

Amerika [a'me:rika] (**-s**) *nt* America.

Amerikaner [ameri'ka:nər] (**-s, -**) *m* American;
(*Gebäck*) *flat iced cake*; ~**in** *f* American.

amerikanisch *adj* American.

Ami ['ami] (**-s, -s**) (*umg*) *m* Yank; (*Soldat*) GI.

Amme ['amə] (**-, -n**) *f* (*veraltet*) foster mother;
(*Nährmutter*) wet nurse.

Ammenmärchen ['amənmɛ:rçən] *nt* fairy tale
od story.

Amok ['a:mɔk] *m:* ~ **laufen** to run amok *od*
amuck.

Amortisation [amɔrtizatsi'o:n] *f*
amortization.

amortisieren [amɔrti'zi:rən] *vr* to pay for
itself.

Ampel ['ampəl] (**-, -n**) *f* traffic lights *pl*.

amphibisch [am'fi:bıʃ] *adj* amphibious.

Ampulle [am'pʊlə] (**-, -n**) *f* (*Behälter*)
ampoule.

amputieren [ampu'ti:rən] *vt* to amputate.

Amsel ['amzəl] (**-, -n**) *f* blackbird.

Amsterdam [amstər'dam] *nt* (**-s**) Amsterdam.

Amt [amt] (**-(e)s, ⁻er**) *nt* office; (*Pflicht*) duty;
(*TEL*) exchange; **zum zuständigen** ~ **gehen**

to go to the relevant authority; **von ~s
wegen** (*auf behördliche Anordnung hin*)
officially.
amtieren [am'ti:rən] *vi* to hold office;
(*fungieren*): **als ... ~** to act as ...
amtierend *adj* incumbent.
amtlich *adj* official; **~es Kennzeichen**
registration (number), license number
(*US*).
Amtmann (-(e)s, *pl* **-männer** *od* **-leute)** *m*
(*VERWALTUNG*) senior civil servant.
Amtmännin *f* (*VERWALTUNG*) senior civil
servant.
Amts- *zW:* **~arzt** *m* medical officer;
a~ärztlich *adj:* **a~ärztlich untersucht werden**
to have an official medical examination;
~deutsch(e) *nt* officialese; **~eid** *m:* **den ~eid
ablegen** to be sworn in, take the oath of
office; **~geheimnis** *nt* (*geheime Sache*)
official secret; (*Schweigepflicht*) official
secrecy; **~gericht** *nt* county (*BRIT*) *od*
district (*US*) court; **~mißbrauch** *m* abuse of
one's position; **~periode** *f* term of office;
~person *f* official; **~richter** *m* district
judge; **~schimmel** *m* (*hum*) officialdom;
~sprache *f* official language; **~stunden** *pl*
office hours *pl*; **~träger** *m* office bearer;
~weg *m:* **auf dem ~weg** through official
channels; **~zeit** *f* period of office.
amüsant [amy'zant] *adj* amusing.
Amüsement [amyzə'mã:] *nt* amusement.
amüsieren [amy'zi:rən] *vt* to amuse ♦ *vr* to
enjoy o.s.; **sich über etw** *akk* **~** to find sth
funny; (*unfreundlich*) to make fun of sth.

═══════════════════ *SCHLÜSSELWORT*

an [an] *präp +dat* **1** (*räumlich: wo?*) at; (*auf, bei*)
on; (*nahe bei*) near; **~ diesem Ort** at this
place; **~ der Wand** on the wall; **zu nahe
~ etw** too near to sth; **unten am Fluß** down
by the river; **Köln liegt am Rhein** Cologne is
on the Rhine; **~ der gleichen Stelle** at *od* on
the same spot; **jdn ~ der Hand nehmen** to
take sb by the hand; **sie wohnen Tür ~ Tür**
they live next door to one another; **es ~ der
Leber** *etc* **haben** (*umg*) to have liver *etc* trouble
2 (*zeitlich: wann?*) on; **~ diesem Tag** on this
day; **~ Ostern** at Easter
3: arm ~ Fett low in fat; **jung ~ Jahren sein**
to be young in years; **~ der ganzen Sache
ist nichts** there is nothing in it; **~ etw
sterben** to die of sth; **~** (*und für*) **sich**
actually ♦ *präp +akk* **1** (*räumlich: wohin?*) to; **er
ging ~s Fenster** he went (over) to the
window; **etw ~ die Wand hängen/schreiben**
to hang/write sth on the wall; **~ die Arbeit
gehen** to get down to work
2 (*zeitlich: woran?*): **~ etw denken** to think of
sth
3 (*gerichtet an*) to; **ein Gruß/eine Frage
~ dich** greetings/a question to you
♦ *adv* **1** (*ungefähr*) about; **~ die hundert** about

a hundred; **~ die 5 DM** around 5 marks
2 (*auf Fahrplänen*): **Frankfurt ~ 18.30**
arriving Frankfurt 18.30
3 (*ab*): **von dort/heute ~** from there/today
onwards
4 (*angeschaltet, angezogen*) on; **das Licht is ~**
the light is on; **ohne etwas ~** with nothing
on; *siehe auch* **am**.

analog [ana'lo:k] *adj* analogous.
Analogie [analo'gi:] *f* analogy.
Analogrechner [ana'lo:krɛçnər] *m* analog
computer.
Analphabet(in) [an|alfa'be:t(ɪn)] **(-en, -en)** *m(f)*
illiterate (person).
Analyse [ana'ly:zə] **(-, -n)** *f* analysis.
analysieren [analy'zi:rən] *vt* to analyse (*BRIT*),
analyze (*US*).
Anämie [anɛ'mi:] **(-, -n)** *f* anaemia (*BRIT*),
anemia (*US*).
Ananas ['ananas] **(-, -** *od* **-se)** *f* pineapple.
Anarchie [anar'çi:] *f* anarchy.
anarchisch [a'narçɪʃ] *adj* anarchic.
Anarchist(in) [anar'çɪst(ɪn)] *m(f)* **(-en, -en)**
anarchist.
Anästhesist(in) [an|ɛste'zɪst(ɪn)] **(-en, -en)**
m(f) anaesthetist (*BRIT*), anesthesiologist
(*US*).
Anatomie [anato'mi:] *f* anatomy.
anbahnen ['anba:nən] *vr* to open up; (*sich
andeuten*) to be in the offing;
(*Unangenehmes*) to be looming ♦ *vt* to
initiate.
Anbahnung *f* initiation.
anbändeln ['anbɛndəln] (*umg*) *vi* to flirt.
Anbau ['anbaʊ] *m* (*AGR*) cultivation;
(*Gebäude*) extension.
anbauen *vt* (*AGR*) to cultivate; (*Gebäudeteil*)
to build on.
Anbaugebiet *nt:* **ein gutes ~ für etw** a good
area for growing sth.
Anbaumöbel *pl* unit furniture *sing*.
anbehalten ['anbəhaltən] *unreg vt* to keep on.
anbei [an'baɪ] *adv* enclosed (*form*); **~ schicken
wir Ihnen ...** please find enclosed ...
anbeißen ['anbaɪsən] *unreg vt* to bite into ♦ *vi*
(*lit*) to bite; (*fig*) to swallow the bait; **zum
A~ aussehen** (*umg*) to look good enough to
eat.
anbelangen ['anbəlaŋən] *vt* to concern; **was
mich anbelangt** as far as I am concerned.
anberaumen ['anbəraʊmən] *vt* (*form*) to fix,
arrange.
anbeten ['anbe:tən] *vt* to worship.
Anbetracht ['anbətraxt] *m:* **in ~** *+gen* in view
of.
Anbetung *f* worship.
anbiedern ['anbi:dərn] (*pej*) *vr:* **sich ~** (**bei**) to
curry favour (with).
anbieten ['anbi:tən] *unreg vt* to offer ♦ *vr* to
volunteer; **das bietet sich als Lösung an** that
would provide a solution.

anbinden ['anbɪndən] *unreg vt* to tie up; (*verbinden*) to connect.

Anblick ['anblɪk] *m* sight.

anblicken *vt* to look at.

anbraten ['anbraːtən] *unreg vt* (*Fleisch*) to brown.

anbrechen ['anbrɛçən] *unreg vt* to start; (*Vorräte*) to break into ♦ *vi* to start; (*Tag*) to break; (*Nacht*) to fall.

anbrennen ['anbrɛnən] *unreg vi* to catch fire; (*KOCH*) to burn.

anbringen ['anbrɪŋən] *unreg vt* to bring; (*Ware*) to sell; (*festmachen*) to fasten; (*Telefon etc*) to install.

Anbruch ['anbrʊx] *m* beginning; ~ **des Tages** dawn; ~ **der Nacht** nightfall.

anbrüllen ['anbrʏlən] *vt* to roar at.

Andacht ['andaxt] (-, -en) *f* devotion; (*Versenkung*) rapt interest; (*Gottesdienst*) prayers *pl*; (*Ehrfurcht*) reverence.

andächtig ['andɛçtɪç] *adj* devout.

andauern ['andaʊərn] *vi* to last, go on.

andauernd *adj* continual.

Anden ['andən] *pl*: **die** ~ the Andes *pl*.

Andenken ['andɛŋkən] (-s, -) *nt* memory; (*Reise~*) souvenir; (*Erinnerungsstück*): **ein** ~ (**an** +*akk*) a memento (of), a keepsake (from).

andere(r, s) *adj* other; (*verschieden*) different; **am** ~**n Tage** the next day; **ein** ~**s Mal** another time; **kein** ~**r** nobody else; **alles** ~ **als zufrieden** anything but pleased, far from pleased; **von etwas** ~**m sprechen** to talk about something else; **es blieb mir nichts** ~**s übrig, als selbst hinzugehen** I had no alternative but to go myself; **unter** ~**m** among other things; **von einem Tag zum** ~**n** overnight; **sie hat einen** ~**n** she has someone else.

andererseits *adv* on the other hand.

andermal *adv*: **ein** ~ some other time.

ändern ['ɛndərn] *vt* to alter, change ♦ *vr* to change.

andernfalls *adv* otherwise.

andernorts ['andərn'ɔrts] *adv* elsewhere.

anders *adv*: ~ (**als**) differently (from); **wer** ~? who else?; **niemand** ~ no-one else; **wie nicht** ~ **zu erwarten** as was to be expected; **wie könnte es** ~ **sein?** how could it be otherwise?; **ich kann nicht** ~ (*kann es nicht lassen*) I can't help it; (*muß leider*) I have no choice; ~ **ausgedrückt** to put it another way; **jemand/irgendwo** ~ somebody/somewhere else; ~ **aussehen/klingen** to look/sound different.

andersartig *adj* different.

Andersdenkende(r) *f(m)* dissident, dissenter.

anderseits ['andər'zaɪts] *adv* = **andererseits**.

anders- *zW*: ~**farbig** *adj* of a different colour; ~**gläubig** *adj* of a different faith; ~**herum** *adv* the other way round; ~**lautend** *adj attrib*

(*form*): ~**lautende Berichte** reports to the contrary; ~**wo** *adv* elsewhere; ~**woher** *adv* from elsewhere; ~**wohin** *adv* elsewhere.

anderthalb ['andərt'halp] *adj* one and a half.

Änderung ['ɛndərʊŋ] *f* alteration, change.

Änderungsantrag ['ɛndərʊŋs|antraːk] *m* (*PARL*) amendment.

anderweitig ['andər'vaɪtɪç] *adj* other ♦ *adv* otherwise; (*anderswo*) elsewhere.

andeuten ['andɔʏtən] *vt* to indicate; (*Wink geben*) to hint at.

Andeutung *f* indication; hint.

andeutungsweise *adv* (*als Anspielung, Anzeichen*) by way of a hint; (*als flüchtiger Hinweis*) in passing.

andichten ['andɪçtən] *vt*: **jdm etw** ~ (*umg: Fähigkeiten*) to credit sb with sth.

Andorra [an'dɔra] (-s) *nt* Andorra.

Andorraner(in) [andɔ'raːnər(ɪn)] *m(f)* Andorran.

Andrang ['andraŋ] *m* crush.

andrehen ['andreːən] *vt* to turn *od* switch on; **jdm etw** ~ (*umg*) to unload sth onto sb.

androhen ['androːən] *vt*: **jdm etw** ~ to threaten sb with sth.

Androhung *f*: **unter** ~ **von Gewalt** with the threat of violence.

anecken ['an|ɛkən] (*umg*) *vi*: (**bei jdm/allen**) ~ to rub (sb/everyone) up the wrong way.

aneignen ['an|aɪɡnən] *vt*: **sich** *dat* **etw** ~ to acquire sth; (*widerrechtlich*) to appropriate sth; (*sich mit etw vertraut machen*) to learn sth.

aneinander [an|aɪ'nandər] *adv* at/on/to *etc* one another *od* each other; ~**fügen** *vt* to put together; ~**geraten** *unreg vi* to clash; ~**legen** *vt* to put together.

anekeln ['an|eːkəln] *vt* to disgust.

Anemone [ane'moːnə] (-, -n) *f* anemone.

anerkannt ['an|ɛrkant] *adj* recognized, acknowledged.

anerkennen ['an|ɛrkɛnən] *unreg vt* to recognize, acknowledge; (*würdigen*) to appreciate; **das muß man** ~ (*zugeben*) you can't argue with that; (*würdigen*) one has to appreciate that.

anerkennend *adj* appreciative.

anerkennenswert *adj* praiseworthy.

Anerkennung *f* recognition, acknowledgement; appreciation.

anerzogen ['an|ɛrtsoːɡən] *adj* acquired.

anfachen ['anfaxən] *vt* (*lit*) to fan into flame; (*fig*) to kindle.

anfahren ['anfaːrən] *unreg vt* to deliver; (*fahren gegen*) to hit; (*Hafen*) to put into; (*umg*) to bawl at ♦ *vi* to drive up; (*losfahren*) to drive off.

Anfahrt ['anfaːrt] *f* (*~sweg, ~szeit*) journey; (*Zufahrt*) approach.

Anfall ['anfal] *m* (*MED*) attack; **in einem** ~ **von** (*fig*) in a fit of.

anfallen *unreg vt* to attack ♦ *vi* (*Arbeit*) to come

up; (*Produkt, Nebenprodukte*) to be obtained; (*Zinsen*) to accrue; (*sich anhäufen*) to accumulate; **die ~den Kosten/Reparaturen** the costs/repairs incurred.

anfällig ['anfɛlɪç] *adj* delicate; ~ **für etw** prone to sth.

Anfang ['anfaŋ] (**-(e)s, -fänge**) *m* beginning, start; **von ~ an** right from the beginning; **zu ~** at the beginning; ~ **Fünfzig** in one's early fifties; ~ **Mai/1994** at the beginning of May/1994.

anfangen ['anfaŋən] *unreg vt* to begin, start; (*machen*) to do ◆ *vi* to begin, start; **damit kann ich nichts** ~ (*nützt mir nichts*) that's no good to me; (*verstehe ich nicht*) it doesn't mean a thing to me; **mit dir ist heute (aber) gar nichts anzufangen!** you're no fun at all today!; **bei einer Firma** ~ to start working for a firm.

Anfänger(in) ['anfɛŋər(ɪn)] (**-s, -**) *m(f)* beginner.

anfänglich ['anfɛŋlɪç] *adj* initial.

anfangs *adv* at first; **wie ich schon ~ erwähnte** as I mentioned at the beginning; **A~buchstabe** *m* initial *od* first letter; **A~gehalt** *nt* starting salary; **A~stadium** *nt* initial stages *pl*.

anfassen ['anfasən] *vt* to handle; (*berühren*) to touch ◆ *vi* to lend a hand ◆ *vr* to feel.

anfechtbar ['anfɛçtbaːr] *adj* contestable.

anfechten ['anfɛçtən] *unreg vt* to dispute; (*Meinung, Aussage*) to challenge; (*Urteil*) to appeal against; (*beunruhigen*) to trouble.

anfeinden ['anfaɪndən] *vt* to treat with hostility.

anfertigen ['anfɛrtɪgən] *vt* to make.

anfeuchten ['anfɔʏçtən] *vt* to moisten.

anfeuern ['anfɔʏərn] *vt* (*fig*) to spur on.

anflehen ['anfleːən] *vt* to implore.

anfliegen ['anfliːgən] *unreg vt* to fly to ◆ *vi* to fly up.

Anflug ['anfluːk] *m* (*AVIAT*) approach; (*Spur*) trace.

anfordern ['anfɔrdərn] *vt* to demand; (*COMM*) to requisition.

Anforderung *f* (*+gen*) demand (for); (*COMM*) requisition.

Anfrage ['anfraːgə] *f* inquiry; (*PARL*) question.

anfragen ['anfraːgən] *vi* to inquire.

anfreunden ['anfrɔʏndən] *vr* to make friends; **sich mit etw** ~ (*fig*) to get to like sth.

anfügen ['anfyːgən] *vt* to add; (*beifügen*) to enclose.

anfühlen ['anfyːlən] *vt, vr* to feel.

anführen ['anfyːrən] *vt* to lead; (*zitieren*) to quote; (*umg: betrügen*) to lead up the garden path.

Anführer(in) ['anfyːrər(ɪn)] (**-s, -**) *m(f)* leader.

Anführung *f* leadership; (*Zitat*) quotation.

Anführungszeichen *pl* quotation marks *pl*, inverted commas *pl* (*BRIT*).

Angabe ['angaːbə] *f* statement; (*TECH*) specification; (*umg: Prahlerei*) boasting; (*SPORT*) service; **Angaben** *pl* (*Auskunft*) particulars *pl*; **ohne ~ von Gründen** without giving any reasons; **~n zur Person** (*form*) personal details *od* particulars.

angeben ['angeːbən] *unreg vt* to give; (*anzeigen*) to inform on; (*bestimmen*) to set ◆ *vi* (*umg*) to boast; (*SPORT*) to serve.

Angeber(in) (**-s, -**) (*umg*) *m(f)* show-off.

Angeberei [angeːbəˈraɪ] (*umg*) *f* showing off.

angeblich ['angeːplɪç] *adj* alleged.

angeboren ['angəboːrən] *adj* (*+dat*) inborn, innate (in); (*MED, fig*): ~ **(bei)** congenital (to).

Angebot ['angəboːt] *nt* offer; (*COMM*): ~ **(an** *+dat*) supply (of); **im ~** (*umg*) on special offer.

angeboten ['angəboːtən] *pp von* **anbieten**.

Angebotspreis *m* offer price.

angebracht ['angəbraxt] *adj* appropriate.

angebrannt ['angəbrant] *adj*: **es riecht hier so ~** there's a smell of burning here.

angebrochen ['angəbrɔxən] *adj* (*Packung, Flasche*) open(ed); **was machen wir mit dem ~en Abend?** (*umg*) what shall we do with the rest of the evening?

angebunden ['angəbundən] *adj*: **kurz ~ sein** (*umg*) to be abrupt *od* curt.

angefangen *pp von* **anfangen**.

angegeben *pp von* **angeben**.

angegossen ['angəgɔsən] *adj*: **wie ~ sitzen** to fit like a glove.

angegriffen ['angəgrɪfən] *adj*: **er wirkt ~** he looks as if he's under a lot of strain.

angehalten ['angəhaltən] *pp von* **anhalten** ◆ *adj*: ~ **sein, etw zu tun** to be required *od* obliged to do sth.

angehaucht ['angəhauxt] *adj*: **links/rechts ~ sein** to have left-/right-wing tendencies *od* leanings.

angeheiratet ['angəhaɪratət] *adj* related by marriage.

angeheitert ['angəhaɪtərt] *adj* tipsy.

angehen ['angeːən] *unreg vt* to concern; (*angreifen*) to attack; (*bitten*): **jdn ~ (um)** to approach sb (for) ◆ *vi* (*Feuer*) to light; (*umg: beginnen*) to begin; **das geht ihn gar nichts an** that's none of his business; **gegen jdn ~** (*entgegentreten*) to fight sb; **gegen etw ~** (*entgegentreten*) to fight sth; (*Mißstände, Zustände*) to take measures against sth.

angehend *adj* prospective; (*Musiker, Künstler*) budding.

angehören ['angəhøːrən] *vi +dat* to belong to.

Angehörige(r) *f(m)* relative.

Angeklagte(r) ['angəklaːktə(r)] *f(m)* accused, defendant.

angeknackst ['angəknakst] (*umg*) *adj* (*Mensch*) uptight; (: *Selbstbewußtsein*) weakened.

angekommen ['angəkɔmən] *pp von*

ankommen.

Angel ['aŋəl] (-, -n) f fishing rod; (*Tür~*) hinge; **die Welt aus den ~n heben** (*fig*) to turn the world upside down.

Angelegenheit ['aŋəle:gənhaɪt] f affair, matter.

angelernt ['aŋəlɛrnt] adj (*Arbeiter*) semi-skilled.

Angelhaken m fish hook.

angeln ['aŋəln] vt to catch ♦ vi to fish; **A~** (**-s**) nt angling, fishing.

Angelpunkt m crucial od central point; (*Frage*) key od central issue.

Angelrute f fishing rod.

Angelsachse ['aŋəlzaksə] (**-n, -n**) m Anglo-Saxon.

Angelsächsin ['aŋəlzɛksɪn] f Anglo-Saxon.

angelsächsisch ['aŋəlzɛksɪʃ] adj Anglo-Saxon.

Angelschein m fishing permit.

angemessen ['aŋəmɛsən] adj appropriate, suitable; **eine der Leistung ~e Bezahlung** payment commensurate with the input.

angenehm ['aŋəne:m] adj pleasant; **~!** (*bei Vorstellung*) pleased to meet you; **das A~e mit dem Nützlichen verbinden** to combine business with pleasure.

angenommen ['aŋənɔmən] pp von **annehmen** ♦ adj assumed; (*Kind*) adopted; **~, wir ...** assuming we ...

angepaßt ['aŋəpast] adj conformist.

angerufen ['aŋəru:fən] pp von **anrufen.**

angesäuselt ['aŋəzɔyzəlt] adj tipsy, merry.

angeschlagen ['aŋəʃla:gən] (*umg*) adj (*Mensch, Aussehen, Nerven*) shattered; (: *Gesundheit*) poor.

angeschlossen ['aŋəʃlɔsən] adj (*+dat*) affiliated (to od with), associated (with).

angeschmiert ['aŋəʃmi:rt] (*umg*) adj in trouble; **der/die A~e sein** to have been had.

angeschrieben ['aŋəʃri:bən] (*umg*) adj: **bei jdm gut/schlecht ~ sein** to be in sb's good/bad books.

angesehen ['aŋəze:ən] pp von **ansehen** ♦ adj respected.

Angesicht ['aŋəzɪçt] nt (*geh*) face.

angesichts ['aŋəzɪçts] präp *+gen* in view of, considering.

angespannt ['aŋəʃpant] adj (*Aufmerksamkeit*) close; (*Nerven, Lage*) tense, strained; (*COMM: Markt*) tight, overstretched; (*Arbeit*) hard.

Angest. abk = **Angestellte(r).**

angestammt ['aŋəʃtamt] adj (*überkommen*) traditional; (*ererbt: Rechte*) hereditary; (: *Besitz*) inherited.

Angestellte(r) ['aŋəʃtɛltə(r)] f(m) employee; (*Büro~*) white-collar worker.

angestrengt ['aŋəʃtrɛŋt] adv as hard as one can.

angetan ['aŋəta:n] adj: **von jdm/etw ~ sein** to be taken with sb/sth; **es jdm ~ haben** to appeal to sb.

angetrunken ['aŋətruŋkən] adj inebriated.

angewiesen ['aŋəvi:zən] adj: **auf jdn/etw ~ sein** to be dependent on sb/sth; **auf sich selbst ~ sein** to be left to one's own devices.

angewöhnen ['aŋəvø:nən] vt: **jdm/sich etw ~** to accustom sb/become accustomed to sth.

Angewohnheit ['aŋəvo:nhaɪt] f habit.

angewurzelt ['aŋəvʊrtsəlt] adj: **wie ~ dastehen** to be rooted to the spot.

angiften ['aŋɪftən] (*pej: umg*) vt to snap at.

angleichen ['aŋlaɪçən] unreg vt, vr to adjust.

Angler ['aŋlər] (**-s, -**) m angler.

angliedern ['aŋli:dərn] vt: **~ (an** *+akk*) (*Verein, Partei*) to affiliate (to od with); (*Land*) to annex (to).

Anglist(in) [aŋ'glɪst(ɪn)] (**-en, -en**) m(f) English specialist; (*Student*) English student; (*Professor etc*) English lecturer/professor.

Angola [aŋ'go:la] (**-s**) nt Angola.

angolanisch [aŋgo'la:nɪʃ] adj Angolan.

angreifen ['aŋraɪfən] unreg vt to attack; (*anfassen*) to touch; (*Arbeit*) to tackle; (*beschädigen*) to damage.

Angreifer(in) (**-s, -**) m(f) attacker.

angrenzen ['aŋrɛntsən] vi: **an etw** akk **~** to border on sth, adjoin sth.

Angriff ['aŋrɪf] m attack; **etw in ~ nehmen** to make a start on sth.

Angriffsfläche f: **jdm/etw eine ~ bieten** (*lit, fig*) to provide sb/sth with a target.

angriffslustig adj aggressive.

Angst [aŋst] (-, **-̈e**) f fear; **~ haben (vor** *+dat*) to be afraid od scared (of); **~ um jdn/etw haben** to be worried about sb/sth; **jdm ~ einflößen** od **einjagen** to frighten sb; **nur keine ~!** I don't be scared; **a~** adj: **jdm ist a~** sb is afraid od scared; **jdm a~ machen** to scare sb; **a~frei** adj free of fear; **~hase** (*umg*) m chicken, scaredy-cat.

ängstigen ['ɛŋstɪgən] vt to frighten ♦ vr: **sich ~ (vor** *+dat od* **um)** to worry (o.s.) (about).

ängstlich adj nervous; (*besorgt*) worried; (*schüchtern*) timid; **Ä~keit** f nervousness.

Angstschweiß m: **mir brach der ~ aus** I broke out in a cold sweat.

angurten ['aŋgʊrtən] vt, vr = **anschnallen.**

Anh. abk (= *Anhang*) app.

anhaben ['anha:bən] unreg vt to have on; **er kann mir nichts ~** he can't hurt me.

anhaften ['anhaftən] vi (*lit*) to stick (to); (*fig*): **~ (an** *+dat*) to stick to, stay with.

anhalten ['anhaltən] unreg vt to stop ♦ vi to stop; (*andauern*) to persist; (*werben*): **um die Hand eines Mädchens ~** to ask for a girl's hand in marriage; (*jdm*) **etw ~** to hold sth up (against sb); **jdn zur Arbeit/Höflichkeit ~** to get sb to work/teach sb to be polite.

anhaltend adj persistent.

Anhalter(in) (**-s, -**) m(f) hitch-hiker; **per ~ fahren** to hitch-hike.

Anhaltspunkt m clue.

anhand [an'hant] *präp +gen* with.
Anhang ['anhaŋ] *m* appendix; (*Leute*) family; (*Anhängerschaft*) supporters *pl*.
anhängen ['anhɛŋən] *unreg vt* to hang up; (*Wagen*) to couple up; (*Zusatz*) to add (on); (*COMPUT*) to append; **sich an jdn** ~ to attach o.s. to sb; **jdm etw** ~ (*umg: nachsagen, anlasten*) to blame sb for sth, blame sth on sb; (: *Verdacht, Schuld*) to pin sth on sb.
Anhänger (**-s, -**) *m* supporter; (*AUT*) trailer; (*am Koffer*) tag; (*Schmuck*) pendant; **~schaft** *f* supporters *pl*.
Anhängeschloß *nt* padlock.
anhängig *adj* (*JUR*) sub judice; **etw** ~ **machen** to start legal proceedings over sth.
anhänglich *adj* devoted; **A~keit** *f* devotion.
Anhängsel (**-s, -**) *nt* appendage.
anhauen ['anhauən] (*umg*) *vt* (*ansprechen*): **jdn** ~ (**um**) to accost sb (for).
anhäufen ['anhɔʏfən] *vt* to accumulate, amass ♦ *vr* to accrue.
Anhäufung ['anhɔʏfoŋ] *f* accumulation.
anheben ['anhe:bən] *unreg vt* to lift up; (*Preise*) to raise.
anheimelnd ['anhaiməlnt] *adj* comfortable, cosy.
anheimstellen [an'haimʃtɛlən] *vt:* **jdm etw** ~ to leave sth up to sb.
anheizen ['anhaitsən] *vt* (*Ofen*) to light; (*fig: umg: Wirtschaft*) to stimulate; (*verschlimmern: Krise*) to aggravate.
anheuern ['anhɔʏərn] *vt, vi* (*NAUT, fig*) to sign on *od* up.
Anhieb ['anhi:b] *m:* **auf** ~ straight off, first go; **es klappte auf** ~ it was an immediate success.
anhimmeln ['anhiməln] (*umg*) *vt* to idolize, worship.
Anhöhe ['anhø:ə] *f* hill.
anhören ['anhø:rən] *vt* to listen to; (*anmerken*) to hear ♦ *vr* to sound.
Anhörung *f* hearing.
Animierdame [ani'mi:rda:mə] *f* nightclub/bar hostess.
animieren [ani'mi:rən] *vt* to encourage, urge on.
Anis [a'ni:s] (**-es, -e**) *m* aniseed.
Ank. *abk* (= *Ankunft*) arr.
ankämpfen ['ankɛmpfən] *vi:* **gegen etw** ~ to fight (against) sth; (*gegen Wind, Strömung*) to battle against sth.
Ankara ['aŋkara] (**-s**) *nt* Ankara.
Ankauf ['ankauf] *m:* ~ **und Verkauf von ...** we buy and sell ...; **a~en** *vt* to purchase, buy.
Anker ['aŋkər] (**-s, -**) *m* anchor; **vor** ~ **gehen** to drop anchor.
ankern *vt, vi* to anchor.
Ankerplatz *m* anchorage.
Anklage ['ankla:gə] *f* accusation; (*JUR*) charge; **gegen jdn** ~ **erheben** (*JUR*) to bring *od* prefer charges against sb; **~bank** *f* dock.

anklagen ['ankla:gən] *vt* to accuse; **jdn (eines Verbrechens)** ~ (*JUR*) to charge sb (with a crime).
Anklagepunkt *m* charge.
Ankläger(in) ['anklɛ:gər(in)] (**-s, -**) *m(f)* accuser.
Anklageschrift *f* indictment.
anklammern ['anklamərn] *vt* to clip, staple ♦ *vr:* **sich an etw** *akk od dat* ~ to cling to sth.
Anklang ['anklaŋ] *m:* **bei jdm** ~ **finden** to meet with sb's approval.
ankleben ['ankle:bən] *vt:* „**Plakate** ~ **verboten!**" "stick no bills".
Ankleidekabine *f* changing cubicle.
ankleiden ['anklaidən] *vt, vr* to dress.
anklingen ['ankliŋən] *vi* (*angeschnitten werden*) to be touched (up)on; (*erinnern*): ~ **an** *+akk* to be reminiscent of.
anklopfen ['anklɔpfən] *vi* to knock.
anknipsen ['anknipsən] *vt* to switch on; (*Schalter*) to flick.
anknüpfen ['anknypfən] *vt* to fasten *od* tie on; (*Beziehungen*) to establish; (*Gespräch*) to start up ♦ *vi* (*anschließen*): ~ **an** *+akk* to refer to.
Anknüpfungspunkt *m* link.
ankommen ['ankɔmən] *unreg vi* to arrive; (*näherkommen*) to approach; (*Anklang finden*): **bei jdm (gut)** ~ to go down well with sb ♦ *vi unpers:* **er ließ es auf einen Streit/einen Versuch** ~ he was prepared to argue about it/to give it a try; **es kommt darauf an** it depends; (*wichtig sein*) that is what matters; **es kommt auf ihn an** it depends on him; **es darauf** ~ **lassen** to let things take their course; **gegen jdn/etw** ~ to cope with sb/sth; **damit kommst du bei ihm nicht an!** you won't get anywhere with him like that.
ankreiden ['ankraidən] *vt* (*fig*): **jdm etw (dick** *od* **übel)** ~ to hold sth against sb.
ankreuzen ['ankrɔʏtsən] *vt* to mark with a cross.
ankündigen ['ankyndigən] *vt* to announce.
Ankündigung *f* announcement.
Ankunft ['ankonft] (**-, -künfte**) *f* arrival.
Ankunftszeit *f* time of arrival.
ankurbeln ['ankorbəln] *vt* (*AUT*) to crank; (*fig*) to boost.
Anl. *abk* (= *Anlage*) enc(l).
anlachen ['anlaxən] *vt* to smile at; **sich** *dat* **jdn** ~ (*umg*) to pick sb up.
Anlage ['anla:gə] *f* disposition; (*Begabung*) talent; (*Park*) gardens *pl*; (*Beilage*) enclosure; (*TECH*) plant; (*Einrichtung: MIL, ELEK*) installation(s *pl*); (*Sport*~ *etc*) facilities *pl*; (*umg: Stereo*~) (stereo) system; (*FIN*) investment; (*Entwurf*) layout; **als** ~ *od* **in der** ~ **erhalten Sie ...** please find enclosed ...; **~berater(in)** *m(f)* investment consultant; **~kapital** *nt* fixed capital.
Anlagenabschreibung *f* capital allowance.
Anlagevermögen *nt* capital assets *pl*, fixed

assets *pl*.

anlangen ['anlaŋən] *vi* (*ankommen*) to arrive.

Anlaß ['anlas] (**-sses, -lässe**) *m:* ~ **(zu)** cause (for); (*Ereignis*) occasion; **aus** ~ *+gen* on the occasion of; ~ **zu etw geben** to give rise to sth; **beim geringsten/bei jedem** ~ for the slightest reason/at every opportunity; **etw zum** ~ **nehmen** to take the opportunity of sth.

anlassen *unreg vt* to leave on; (*Motor*) to start ♦ *vr* (*umg*) to start off.

Anlasser (**-s, -**) *m* (*AUT*) starter.

anläßlich ['anlɛslɪç] *präp +gen* on the occasion of.

anlasten ['anlastən] *vt:* **jdm etw** ~ to blame sb for sth.

Anlauf ['anlauf] *m* run-up; (*fig: Versuch*) attempt, try.

anlaufen *unreg vi* to begin; (*Film*) to be showing; (*SPORT*) to run up; (*Fenster*) to mist up; (*Metall*) to tarnish ♦ *vt* to call at; **rot** ~ to turn *od* go red; **gegen etw** ~ to run into *od* up against sth; **angelaufen kommen** to come running up.

Anlauf- *zW:* **~stelle** *f* place to go (with one's problems); **~zeit** *f* (*fig*) time to get going *od* started.

anläuten ['anlɔʏtən] *vi* to ring.

anlegen ['anleːgən] *vt* to put; (*anziehen*) to put on; (*gestalten*) to lay out; (*Kartei, Akte*) to start; (*COMPUT: Datei*) to create; (*Geld*) to invest ♦ *vi* to dock; (*NAUT*) to berth; **etw an etw** *akk* ~ to put sth against *od* on sth; **ein Gewehr** ~ (**auf** *+akk*) to aim a weapon (at); **es auf etw** *akk* ~ to be out for sth/to do sth; **strengere Maßstäbe** ~ (**bei**) to lay down *od* impose stricter standards (in); **sich mit jdm** ~ (*umg*) to quarrel with sb.

Anlegeplatz *m* landing place.

Anleger(in) (**-s, -**) *m(f)* (*FIN*) investor.

Anlegestelle *f* landing place.

anlehnen ['anleːnən] *vt* to lean; (*Tür*) to leave ajar; (**sich**) **an etw** *akk* ~ to lean on *od* against sth.

Anlehnung *f* (*Imitation*): **in** ~ **an jdn/etw** following sb/sth.

Anlehnungsbedürfnis *nt* need of loving care.

anleiern ['anlaɪərn] (*umg*) *vt* to get going.

Anleihe ['anlaɪə] (**-, -n**) *f* (*FIN*) loan; (*Wertpapier*) bond.

anleiten ['anlaɪtən] *vt* to instruct.

Anleitung *f* instructions *pl*.

anlernen ['anlɛrnən] *vt* to teach, instruct.

anlesen ['anleːzən] *unreg vt* (*aneignen*): **sich** *dat* **etw** ~ to learn sth by reading.

Anliegen ['anliːgən] (**-s, -**) *nt* matter; (*Wunsch*) wish.

anliegen *unreg vi* (*Kleidung*) to cling.

anliegend *adj* adjacent; (*beigefügt*) enclosed.

Anlieger (**-s, -**) *m* resident; ~ **frei** no thoroughfare - residents only.

anlocken ['anlɔkən] *vt* to attract; (*Tiere*) to lure.

anlügen ['anlyːgən] *unreg vt* to lie to.

Anm. *abk* (= *Anmerkung*) n.

anmachen ['anmaxən] *vt* to attach; (*Elektrisches*) to put on; (*Salat*) to dress; **jdn** ~ (*umg*) to try and pick sb up.

anmalen ['anmaːlən] *vt* to paint ♦ *vr* (*pej: schminken*) to paint one's face *od* o.s.

Anmarsch ['anmarʃ] *m:* **im** ~ **sein** to be advancing; (*hum*) to be on the way; **im** ~ **sein auf** *+akk* to be advancing on.

anmaßen ['anmaːsən] *vt:* **sich** *dat* **etw** ~ to lay claim to sth.

anmaßend *adj* arrogant.

Anmaßung *f* presumption.

Anmeldeformular ['anmɛldəfɔrmulaːr] *nt* registration form.

anmelden *vt* to announce; (*geltend machen: Recht, Ansprüche, zu Steuerzwecken*) to declare; (*COMPUT*) to log on ♦ *vr* (*sich ankündigen*) to make an appointment; (*polizeilich, für Kurs etc*) to register; **ein Gespräch nach Deutschland** ~ (*TEL*) to book a call to Germany.

Anmeldung *f* announcement; appointment; registration; **nur nach vorheriger** ~ by appointment only.

anmerken ['anmɛrkən] *vt* to observe; (*anstreichen*) to mark; **jdm seine Verlegenheit** *etc* ~ to notice sb's embarrassment *etc*; **sich** *dat* **nichts** ~ **lassen** not to give anything away.

Anmerkung *f* note.

Anmut ['anmuːt] (**-**) *f* grace.

anmuten *vt* (*geh*): **jdn** ~ to appear *od* seem to sb.

anmutig *adj* charming.

annähen ['annɛːən] *vt* to sew on.

annähern ['annɛːərn] *vr* to get closer.

annähernd *adj* approximate; **nicht** ~ **soviel** not nearly as much.

Annäherung *f* approach.

Annäherungsversuch *m* advances *pl*.

Annahme ['annaːmə] (**-, -n**) *f* acceptance; (*Vermutung*) assumption; **~stelle** *f* counter; (*für Reparaturen*) reception; **~verweigerung** *f* refusal.

annehmbar ['anneːmbaːr] *adj* acceptable.

annehmen *unreg vt* to accept; (*Namen*) to take; (*Kind*) to adopt; (*vermuten*) to suppose, assume ♦ *vr* (*+gen*) to take care (of); **jdn an Kindes Statt** ~ to adopt sb; **angenommen, das ist so** assuming that is so.

Annehmlichkeit *f* comfort.

annektieren [anɛk'tiːrən] *vt* to annex.

anno ['ano] *adj:* **von** ~ **dazumal** (*umg*) from the year dot.

Annonce [a'nõːsə] (**-, -n**) *f* advertisement.

annoncieren [anõ'siːrən] *vt, vi* to advertise.

annullieren [anʊ'liːrən] *vt* to annul.

Anode [a'noːdə] (**-, -n**) *f* anode.

anöden ['an|ø:dən] (*umg*) *vt* to bore stiff.
anomal [ano'ma:l] *adj* (*regelwidrig*) unusual, abnormal; (*nicht normal*) strange, odd.
anonym [ano'ny:m] *adj* anonymous.
Anorak ['anorak] (**-s, -s**) *m* anorak.
anordnen ['an|ɔrdnən] *vt* to arrange; (*befehlen*) to order.
Anordnung *f* arrangement; order; **~en treffen** to give orders.
anorganisch ['an|ɔrga:nɪʃ] *adj* (*CHEM*) inorganic.
anpacken ['anpakən] *vt* to grasp; (*fig*) to tackle; **mit ~** to lend a hand.
anpassen ['anpasən] *vt* (*Kleidung*) to fit; (*fig*) to adapt ♦ *vr* to adapt.
Anpassung *f* fitting; adaptation.
Anpassungsdruck *m* pressure to conform (*to society*).
anpassungsfähig *adj* adaptable.
anpeilen ['anpaɪlən] *vt* (*mit Radar, Funk etc*) to take a bearing on; **etw ~** (*fig: umg*) to have one's sights on sth.
Anpfiff ['anpfɪf] *m* (*SPORT*) (starting) whistle; (*Spielbeginn: Fußball etc*) kick-off; **einen ~ bekommen** (*umg*) to get a rocket (*BRIT*).
anpöbeln ['anpø:bəln] *vt* to abuse; (*umg*) to pester.
Anprall ['anpral] *m:* **~ gegen** *od* **an** +*akk* impact on *od* against.
anprangern ['anpraŋərn] *vt* to denounce.
anpreisen ['anpraɪzən] *unreg vt* to extol; **sich ~ (als)** to sell o.s. (as); **etw ~** to extol (the virtues of) sth; **seine Waren ~** to cry one's wares.
Anprobe ['anpro:bə] *f* trying on.
anprobieren ['anprobi:rən] *vt* to try on.
anpumpen ['anpʊmpən] (*umg*) *vt* to borrow from.
anquatschen ['ankvatʃən] (*umg*) *vt* to speak to; (: *Mädchen*) to try to pick up.
Anrainer ['anraɪnər] (**-s, -**) *m* neighbour (*BRIT*), neighbor (*US*).
anranzen ['anrantsən] (*umg*) *vt:* **jdn ~** to tick sb off.
anraten ['anra:tən] *unreg vt* to recommend; **auf A~ des Arztes** *etc* on the doctor's *etc* advice *od* recommendation.
anrechnen ['anrɛçnən] *vt* to charge; (*fig*) to count; **jdm etw hoch ~** to think highly of sb for sth.
Anrecht ['anrɛçt] *nt:* **~ auf** +*akk* right (to); **ein ~ auf etw haben** to be entitled to sth, have a right to sth.
Anrede ['anre:də] *f* form of address.
anreden *vt* to address.
anregen ['anre:gən] *vt* to stimulate; **angeregte Unterhaltung** lively discussion.
anregend *adj* stimulating.
Anregung *f* stimulation; (*Vorschlag*) suggestion.
anreichern ['anraɪçərn] *vt* to enrich.
Anreise ['anraɪzə] *f* journey there/here.

anreisen *vi* to arrive.
anreißen ['anraɪsən] *unreg vt* (*kurz zur Sprache bringen*) to touch on.
Anreiz ['anraɪts] *m* incentive.
anrempeln ['anrɛmpəln] *vt* (*anstoßen*) to bump into; (*absichtlich*) to jostle.
anrennen ['anrɛnən] *unreg vi:* **gegen etw ~** (*gegen Wind etc*) to run against sth; (*MIL*) to storm sth.
Anrichte ['anrɪçtə] (**-, -n**) *f* sideboard.
anrichten *vt* to serve up; **Unheil ~** to make mischief; **da hast du aber etwas angerichtet!** (*umg: verursacht*) you've started something there all right!; (: *angestellt*) you've really made a mess there!
anrüchig ['anrʏçɪç] *adj* dubious.
anrücken ['anrʏkən] *vi* to approach; (*MIL*) to advance.
Anruf ['anru:f] *m* call; **~beantworter** *m* (telephone) answering machine, answerphone.
anrufen *unreg vt* to call out to; (*bitten*) to call on; (*TEL*) to ring up, phone, call.
anrühren ['anry:rən] *vt* to touch; (*mischen*) to mix.
ans [ans] = **an das.**
Ansage ['anza:gə] *f* announcement.
ansagen *vt* to announce ♦ *vr* to say one will come.
Ansager(in) (**-s, -**) *m(f)* announcer.
ansammeln ['anzaməln] *vt* to collect ♦ *vr* to accumulate; (*fig: Wut, Druck*) to build up.
Ansammlung *f* collection; (*Leute*) crowd.
ansässig ['anzɛsɪç] *adj* resident.
Ansatz ['anzats] *m* start; (*Haar~*) hairline; (*Hals~*) base; (*Verlängerungsstück*) extension; (*Veranschlagung*) estimate; **die ersten Ansätze zu etw** the beginnings of sth; **~punkt** *m* starting point; **~stück** *nt* (*TECH*) attachment.
anschaffen ['anʃafən] *vt* to buy, purchase ♦ *vi:* **~ gehen** (*umg: durch Prostitution*) to be on the game; **sich** *dat* **Kinder ~** (*umg*) to have children.
Anschaffung *f* purchase.
anschalten ['anʃaltən] *vt* to switch on.
anschauen ['anʃaʊən] *vt* to look at.
anschaulich *adj* illustrative.
Anschauung *f* (*Meinung*) view; **aus eigener ~** from one's own experience.
Anschauungsmaterial *nt* illustrative material.
Anschein ['anʃaɪn] *m* appearance; **allem ~ nach** to all appearances; **den ~ haben** to seem, appear.
anscheinend *adj* apparent.
anschieben ['anʃi:bən] *unreg vt* (*Fahrzeug*) to push.
Anschiß ['anʃɪs] (*umg*) *m:* **einen ~ bekommen** to get a telling-off *od* ticking-off (*bes BRIT*).
Anschlag ['anʃla:k] *m* notice; (*Attentat*) attack; (*COMM*) estimate; (*auf Klavier*) touch; (*auf*

Schreibmaschine) keystroke; **einem ~ zum Opfer fallen** to be assassinated; **ein Gewehr im ~ haben** (*MIL*) to have a rifle at the ready; **~brett** *nt* notice board (*BRIT*), bulletin board (*US*).

anschlagen ['anʃlaːgən] *unreg vt* to put up; (*beschädigen*) to chip; (*Akkord*) to strike; (*Kosten*) to estimate ♦ *vi* to hit; (*wirken*) to have an effect; (*Glocke*) to ring; (*Hund*) to bark; **einen anderen Ton ~** (*fig*) to change one's tune; **an etw** *akk* **~** to hit against sth.

anschlagfrei *adj*: **~er Drucker** non-impact printer.

Anschlagzettel *m* notice.

anschleppen ['anʃlɛpən] (*umg*) *vt* (*unerwünscht mitbringen*) to bring along.

anschließen ['anʃliːsən] *unreg vt* to connect up; (*Sender*) to link up; (*in Steckdose*) to plug in; (*fig: hinzufügen*) to add ♦ *vi*: **an etw** *akk* **~** (*zeitlich*) to follow sth ♦ *vr*: **sich jdm/etw ~** to join sb/sth; (*beipflichten*) to agree with sb/sth; **sich an etw** *akk* **~** (*angrenzen*) to adjoin sth.

anschließend *adj* adjacent; (*zeitlich*) subsequent ♦ *adv* afterwards; **~ an** +*akk* following.

Anschluß ['anʃlʊs] *m* (*ELEK, EISENB, TEL*) connection; (*weiterer Apparat*) extension; (*von Wasser etc*) supply; (*COMPUT*) port; **im ~ an** +*akk* following; **~ finden** to make friends; **~ bekommen** to get through; **kein ~ unter dieser Nummer** number unobtainable; **den ~ verpassen** (*EISENB etc*) to miss one's connection; (*fig*) to miss the boat.

anschmiegen ['anʃmiːgən] *vr*: **sich an jdn/etw ~** (*Kind, Hund*) to snuggle *od* nestle up to *od* against sb/sth.

anschmiegsam ['anʃmiːkzaːm] *adj* affectionate.

anschmieren ['anʃmiːrən] *vt* to smear; (*umg*) to take in.

anschnallen ['anʃnalən] *vt* to buckle on ♦ *vr* to fasten one's seat belt.

Anschnallpflicht *f*: **für Kinder besteht ~** children must wear seat belts.

anschnauzen ['anʃnaʊtsən] (*umg*) *vt* to yell at.

anschneiden ['anʃnaɪdən] *unreg vt* to cut into; (*Thema*) to introduce.

Anschnitt ['anʃnɪt] *m* first slice.

anschreiben ['anʃraɪbən] *unreg vt* to write (up); (*COMM*) to charge up; (*benachrichtigen*) to write to; **bei jdm gut/schlecht angeschrieben sein** to be well/badly thought of by sb, be in sb's good/bad books.

anschreien ['anʃraɪən] *unreg vt* to shout at.

Anschrift ['anʃrɪft] *f* address.

Anschriftenliste *f* mailing list.

Anschuldigung ['anʃʊldɪgʊŋ] *f* accusation.

anschwärzen ['anʃvɛrtsən] *vt* (*fig: umg*): **jdn ~ (bei)** to blacken sb's name (with).

anschwellen ['anʃvɛlən] *unreg vi* to swell (up).

anschwemmen ['anʃvɛmən] *vt* to wash ashore.

anschwindeln ['anʃvɪndəln] (*umg*) *vt* to lie to.

ansehen ['anzeːən] *unreg vt* to look at; **jdm etw ~** to see sth (from sb's face); **jdn/etw als etw ~** to look on sb/sth as sth; **~ für** to consider; (**sich** *dat*) **etw ~** to (have a) look at sth; (*Fernsehsendung*) to watch sth; (*Film, Stück, Sportveranstaltung*) to see sth; **etw (mit) ~** to watch sth, see sth happening.

Ansehen (**-s**) *nt* respect; (*Ruf*) reputation; **ohne ~ der Person** (*JUR*) without respect of person.

ansehnlich ['anzeːnlɪç] *adj* fine-looking; (*beträchtlich*) considerable.

anseilen ['anzaɪlən] *vt*: **jdn/sich ~** to rope sb/o.s. up.

ansein ['anzaɪn] *unreg* (*umg*) *vi* to be on.

ansetzen ['anzɛtsən] *vt* (*festlegen*) to fix; (*entwickeln*) to develop; (*Fett*) to put on; (*Blätter*) to grow; (*zubereiten*) to prepare ♦ *vi* (*anfangen*) to start, begin; (*Entwicklung*) to set in; (*dick werden*) to put on weight ♦ *vr* (*Rost etc*) to start to develop; **~ an** +*akk* (*anfügen*) to fit on to; (*anlegen, an Mund etc*) to put to; **zu etw ~** to prepare to do sth; **jdn/etw auf jdn/etw ~** to set sb/sth on sb/sth.

Ansicht ['anzɪçt] *f* (*Anblick*) sight; (*Meinung*) view, opinion; **zur ~** on approval; **meiner ~ nach** in my opinion.

Ansichtskarte *f* picture postcard.

Ansichtssache *f* matter of opinion.

ansiedeln ['anziːdəln] *vt* to settle; (*Tierart*) to introduce ♦ *vr* to settle; (*Industrie etc*) to get established.

ansonsten [an'zɔnstən] *adv* otherwise.

anspannen ['anʃpanən] *vt* to harness; (*Muskel*) to strain.

Anspannung *f* strain.

Anspiel ['anʃpiːl] *nt* (*SPORT*) start of play.

anspielen *vt* (*SPORT*) to play the ball *etc* to ♦ *vi*: **auf etw** *akk* **~** to refer *od* allude to sth.

Anspielung *f*: **~ (auf** +*akk*) reference (to), allusion (to).

Ansporn ['anʃpɔrn] (**-(e)s**) *m* incentive.

Ansprache ['anʃpraːxə] *f* (*Rede*) address.

ansprechen ['anʃprɛçən] *unreg vt* to speak to; (*bitten, gefallen*) to appeal to; (*Eindruck machen auf*) to make an impression on ♦ *vi*: **~ (auf** +*akk*) (*Patient*) to respond (to); (*Meßgerät*) to react (to); **jdn auf etw** *akk* (**hin**) **~** to ask sb about sth.

ansprechend *adj* attractive.

Ansprechpartner *m* contact.

anspringen ['anʃprɪŋən] *unreg vi* (*AUT*) to start ♦ *vt* (*anfallen*) to jump; (*Raubtier*) to pounce (up)on; (*Hund: hochspringen*) to jump up at.

Anspruch ['anʃprʊx] (**-s, -sprüche**) *m* (*Recht*): **~ (auf** +*akk*) claim (to); **den Ansprüchen gerecht werden** to meet the requirements; **hohe Ansprüche stellen/haben** to demand/

expect a lot; **jdn/etw in** ~ **nehmen** to occupy sb/take up sth.
anspruchslos *adj* undemanding.
anspruchsvoll *adj* demanding; (*COMM*) upmarket.
anspucken ['anʃpʊkən] *vt* to spit at.
anstacheln ['anʃtaxəln] *vt* to spur on.
Anstalt ['anʃtalt] (-, -en) *f* institution; ~**en machen, etw zu tun** to prepare to do sth.
Anstand ['anʃtant] *m* decency; (*Manieren*) (good) manners *pl.*
anständig ['anʃtɛndɪç] *adj* decent; (*umg*) proper; (*groß*) considerable; **A**~**keit** *f* propriety, decency.
anstandshalber ['anʃtantshalbər] *adv* out of politeness.
anstandslos *adv* without any ado.
anstarren ['anʃtarən] *vt* to stare at.
anstatt [an'ʃtat] *präp +gen* instead of ♦ *konj:* ~ **etw zu tun** instead of doing sth.
anstauen ['anʃtauən] *vr* to accumulate; (*Blut in Adern etc*) to congest; (*fig: Gefühle*) to build up.
anstechen ['anʃtɛçən] *unreg vt* to prick; (*Faß*) to tap.
anstecken ['anʃtɛkən] *vt* to pin on; (*Ring*) to put *od* slip on; (*MED*) to infect; (*Pfeife*) to light; (*Haus*) to set fire to ♦ *vr:* **ich habe mich bei ihm angesteckt** I caught it from him ♦ *vi* (*fig*) to be infectious.
ansteckend *adj* infectious.
Ansteckung *f* infection.
anstehen ['anʃteːən] *unreg vi* to queue (up) (*BRIT*), line up (*US*); (*Verhandlungspunkt*) to be on the agenda.
ansteigen ['anʃtaigən] *unreg vi* to rise; (*Straße*) to climb.
anstelle [an'ʃtɛlə] *präp +gen* in place of.
anstellen ['anʃtɛlən] *vt* (*einschalten*) to turn on; (*Arbeit geben*) to employ; (*umg: Unfug treiben*) to get up to; (: *machen*) to do ♦ *vr* to queue (up) (*BRIT*), line up (*US*); (*umg*) to act; (: *sich zieren*) to make a fuss, act up.
Anstellung *f* employment; (*Posten*) post, position; ~ **auf Lebenszeit** tenure.
ansteuern ['anʃtɔyərn] *vt* to make *od* steer *od* head for.
Anstich ['anʃtɪç] *m* (*von Faß*) tapping, broaching.
Anstieg ['anʃtiːk] (-(e)s, -e) *m* climb; (*fig: von Preisen etc*) increase.
anstiften ['anʃtɪftən] *vt* (*Unglück*) to cause; **jdn zu etw** ~ to put sb up to sth.
Anstifter (-s, -) *m* instigator.
Anstiftung *f* (*von Tat*) instigation; (*von Mensch*): ~ (**zu**) incitement (to).
anstimmen ['anʃtɪmən] *vt* (*Lied*) to strike up (with); (*Geschrei*) to set up ♦ *vi* to strike up.
Anstoß ['anʃtoːs] *m* impetus; (*Ärgernis*) offence (*BRIT*), offense (*US*); (*SPORT*) kick-off; **der erste** ~ the initiative; **ein Stein des** ~**es** (*umstrittene Sache*) a bone of contention;

~ **nehmen an** +*dat* to take offence at.
anstoßen *unreg vt* to push; (*mit Fuß*) to kick ♦ *vi* to knock, bump; (*mit der Zunge*) to lisp; (*mit Gläsern*) to drink a toast; **an etw** *akk* ~ (*angrenzen*) to adjoin sth; ~ **auf** +*akk* to drink (a toast) to.
anstößig ['anʃtøːsɪç] *adj* offensive, indecent; **A**~**keit** *f* indecency, offensiveness.
anstrahlen ['anʃtraːlən] *vt* to floodlight; (*strahlend ansehen*) to beam at.
anstreben ['anʃtreːbən] *vt* to strive for.
anstreichen ['anʃtraiçən] *unreg vt* to paint; (**jdm**) **etw als Fehler** ~ to mark sth wrong.
Anstreicher(in) (-s, -) *m(f)* painter.
anstrengen ['anʃtrɛŋən] *vt* to strain; (*strapazieren: jdn*) to tire out; (: *Patienten*) to fatigue; (*JUR*) to bring ♦ *vr* to make an effort; **eine Klage** ~ **(gegen)** (*JUR*) to initiate *od* institute proceedings (against).
anstrengend *adj* tiring.
Anstrengung *f* effort.
Anstrich ['anʃtrɪç] *m* coat of paint.
Ansturm ['anʃtʊrm] *m* rush; (*MIL*) attack.
Ansuchen ['anzuːxən] (-s, -) *nt* request.
ansuchen ['anzuːxən] *vi:* **um etw** ~ to apply for sth.
Antagonismus [antago'nɪsmʊs] *m* antagonism.
antanzen ['antantsən] (*umg*) *vi* to turn *od* show up.
Antarktis [ant'ʔarktɪs] (-) *f* Antarctic.
antarktisch *adj* Antarctic.
antasten ['antastən] *vt* to touch; (*Recht*) to infringe upon; (*Ehre*) to question.
Anteil ['antail] (-s, -e) *m* share; (*Mitgefühl*) sympathy; ~ **nehmen an** +*dat* to share in; (*sich interessieren*) to take an interest in; ~ **an etw** *dat* **haben** (*beitragen*) to contribute to sth; (*teilnehmen*) to take part in sth.
anteilig *adj* proportionate, proportional.
anteilmäßig *adj* pro rata.
Anteilnahme (-) *f* sympathy.
Antenne [an'tɛnə] (-, -n) *f* aerial; (*ZOOL*) antenna; **eine/keine** ~ **für etw haben** (*fig: umg*) to have a/no feeling for sth.
Anthrazit [antra'tsiːt] (-s, -e) *m* anthracite.
Anthropologie [antropolo'giː] (-) *f* anthropology.
Anti- ['anti] *in zW* anti; ~**alkoholiker** *m* teetotaller; **a**~**autoritär** *adj* anti-authoritarian; ~**babypille** *f* (contraceptive) pill; ~**biotikum** (-s, -ka) *nt* antibiotic; ~**held** *m* antihero.
antik [an'tiːk] *adj* antique.
Antike (-, -n) *f* (*Zeitalter*) ancient world; (*Kunstgegenstand*) antique.
Antikörper *m* antibody.
Antillen [an'tɪlən] *pl* Antilles *pl.*
Antilope [anti'loːpə] (-, -n) *f* antelope.
Antipathie [antipa'tiː] *f* antipathy.
antippen ['antɪpən] *vt* to tap; (*Pedal, Bremse*) to touch; (*fig: Thema*) to touch on.

Antiquariat [antikvari'aːt] (-(e)s, -e) *nt* secondhand bookshop; **modernes** ~ remainder bookshop/department.

antiquiert [anti'kviːrt] (*pej*) *adj* antiquated.

Antiquitäten [antikvi'tɛːtən] *pl* antiques *pl*; ~**handel** *m* antique business; ~**händler(in)** *m(f)* antique dealer.

Antisemitismus [antizemi'tɪsmʊs] *m* antisemitism.

antiseptisch [anti'zɛptɪʃ] *adj* antiseptic.

Antlitz ['antlɪts] (-es, -e) *nt* (*liter*) countenance (*liter*), face.

antörnen ['antœrnən] *vt, vi* = **anturnen.**

Antrag ['antraːk] (-(e)s, -träge) *m* proposal; (*PARL*) motion; (*Gesuch*) application; **einen** ~ **auf etw** *akk* **stellen** to make an application for sth; (*JUR etc*) to file a petition/claim for sth.

Antragsformular *nt* application form.

Antragsgegner(in) *m(f)* (*JUR*) respondent.

Antragsteller(in) (-s, -) *m(f)* claimant; (*für Kredit etc*) applicant.

antreffen ['antrɛfən] *unreg vt* to meet.

antreiben ['antraɪbən] *unreg vt* to drive on; (*Motor*) to drive; (*anschwemmen*) to wash up ♦ *vi* to be washed up; **jdn zur Eile/Arbeit** ~ to urge sb to hurry up/to work.

Antreiber (-s, -) (*pej*) *m* slave-driver (*pej*).

antreten ['antreːtən] *unreg vt* (*Amt*) to take up; (*Erbschaft*) to come into; (*Beweis*) to offer; (*Reise*) to start, begin ♦ *vi* (*MIL*) to fall in; (*SPORT*) to line up; (*zum Dienst*) to report; **gegen jdn** ~ to play/fight against sb.

Antrieb ['antriːp] *m* (*lit, fig*) drive; **aus eigenem** ~ of one's own accord.

Antriebskraft *f* (*TECH*) power.

antrinken ['antrɪŋkən] *unreg vt* (*Flasche, Glas*) to start to drink from; **sich** *dat* **Mut/einen Rausch** ~ to give o.s. Dutch courage/get drunk; **angetrunken sein** to be tipsy.

Antritt ['antrɪt] *m* beginning, commencement; (*eines Amts*) taking up.

antun ['antuːn] *unreg vt*: **jdm etw** ~ to do sth to sb; **sich** *dat* **Zwang** ~ to force o.s.

anturnen ['antœrnən] (*umg*) *vt* (*Drogen, Musik*) to turn on ♦ *vi*: ... **turnt an** ... turns you on.

Antwerpen [ant'vɛrpən] (-s) *nt* Antwerp.

Antwort ['antvɔrt] (-, -en) *f* answer, reply; **um** ~ **wird gebeten** RSVP.

antworten *vi* to answer, reply.

anvertrauen ['anfɛrtrauən] *vt*: **jdm etw** ~ to entrust sb with sth; **sich jdm** ~ to confide in sb.

anvisieren ['anviziːrən] *vt* (*fig*) to set one's sights on.

anwachsen ['anvaksən] *unreg vi* to grow; (*Pflanze*) to take root.

Anwalt ['anvalt] (-(e)s, -wälte) *m* solicitor; lawyer; (*fig: Fürsprecher*) advocate; (: *der Armen etc*) champion.

Anwältin ['anvɛltɪn] *f* siehe **Anwalt.**

Anwalts- *zW*: ~**honorar** *nt* retainer, retaining

fee; ~**kammer** *f* professional association of lawyers, ≈ Law Society (*BRIT*); ~**kosten** *pl* legal expenses *pl*.

Anwandlung ['anvandlʊŋ] *f* caprice; **eine** ~ **von etw** a fit of sth.

anwärmen ['anvɛrmən] *vt* to warm up.

Anwärter(in) ['anvɛrtər(ɪn)] *m(f)* candidate.

anweisen ['anvaɪzən] *unreg vt* to instruct; (*zuteilen*) to assign.

Anweisung *f* instruction; (*COMM*) remittance; (*Post~, Zahlungs~*) money order.

anwendbar ['anvɛntbaːr] *adj* practicable, applicable.

anwenden ['anvɛndən] *unreg vt* to use, employ; (*Gesetz, Regel*) to apply.

Anwenderprogramm *nt* (*COMPUT*) application program.

Anwendersoftware *f* application package.

Anwendung *f* use; application.

anwerfen ['anvɛrfən] *unreg vt* (*TECH*) to start up.

anwesend ['anveːzənt] *adj* present; **die A~en** those present.

Anwesenheit *f* presence.

Anwesenheitsliste *f* attendance register.

anwidern ['anviːdərn] *vt* to disgust.

Anwohner(in) ['anvoːnər(ɪn)] (-s, -) *m(f)* resident.

Anwuchs ['anvuːks] *m* growth.

Anzahl ['antsaːl] *f:* ~ (**an** +*dat*) number (of).

anzahlen *vt* to pay on account.

Anzahlung *f* deposit, payment on account.

anzapfen ['antsapfən] *vt* to tap.

Anzeichen ['antsaɪçən] *nt* sign, indication; **alle** ~ **deuten darauf hin, daß** ... all the signs are that ...

Anzeige ['antsaɪgə] (-, -n) *f* (*Zeitungs~*) announcement; (*Werbung*) advertisement; (*COMPUT*) display; (*bei Polizei*) report; **gegen jdn** ~ **erstatten** to report sb (to the police).

anzeigen *vt* (*zu erkennen geben*) to show; (*bekanntgeben*) to announce; (*bei Polizei*) to report.

Anzeigenteil *m* advertisements *pl*.

anzeigepflichtig *adj* notifiable.

Anzeiger *m* indicator.

anzetteln ['antsɛtəln] (*umg*) *vt* to instigate.

anziehen ['antsiːən] *unreg vt* to attract; (*Kleidung*) to put on; (*Mensch*) to dress; (*Schraube, Seil*) to pull tight; (*Knie*) to draw up; (*Feuchtigkeit*) to absorb ♦ *vr* to get dressed.

anziehend *adj* attractive.

Anziehung *f* (*Reiz*) attraction.

Anziehungskraft *f* power of attraction; (*PHYS*) force of gravitation.

Anzug ['antsuːk] *m* suit; **im** ~ **sein** to be approaching.

anzüglich ['antsyːklɪç] *adj* personal; (*anstößig*) offensive; **A~keit** *f* offensiveness; (*Bemerkung*) personal remark.

anzünden ['antsyndən] *vt* to light.
Anzünder *m* lighter.
anzweifeln ['antsvaifəln] *vt* to doubt.
AOK (-) *f abk* (= *Allgemeine Ortskrankenkasse*)
siehe **Ortskrankenkasse.**

The **AOK** (*Allgemeine Ortskrankenkasse*)
*forms part of a compulsory medical insurance
scheme for people who are not members of a
private scheme. The AOK has an office in every
large town.*

APA *f abk* (= *Austria Presse-Agentur*) *Austrian
news agency.*
apart [a'part] *adj* distinctive.
Apartheid [a'pa:rthait] *f* apartheid.
Apartment [a'partmənt] (-s, -s) *nt* flat (*BRIT*),
apartment (*bes US*).
Apathie [apa'ti:] *f* apathy.
apathisch [a'pa:tiʃ] *adj* apathetic.
Apenninen [ape'ni:nən] *pl* Apennines *pl.*
Apfel ['apfəl] (-s, -̈) *m* apple; **in den sauren
~ beißen** (*fig: umg*) to swallow the bitter
pill; **etw für einen ~ und ein Ei kaufen** (*umg*)
to buy sth dirt cheap *od* for a song; ~**mus** *nt*
apple purée; (*als Beilage*) apple sauce; ~**saft**
m apple juice.
Apfelsine [apfəl'zi:nə] (-, -n) *f* orange.
Apfeltasche *f* apple turnover.
Apfelwein *m* strong cider.
apl. *abk* = **außerplanmäßig.**
APO, Apo ['a:po] (-) *f abk*
(= *außerparlamentarische Opposition*)
extraparliamentary opposition.

The **APO** *was an extraparliamentary
opposition group formed in West Germany in
the late 1960s by those who felt that their
interests were not being sufficiently
represented in parliament. It was disbanded in
the 1970s. Some of its members then formed
the RAF, a terrorist organisation. Some formed
the Green Party* (**die Grünen**).

apolitisch ['apoli:tiʃ] *adj* non-political,
apolitical.
Apostel [a'postəl] (-s, -) *m* apostle.
Apostroph [apo'stro:f] (-s, -e) *m* apostrophe.
Apotheke [apo'te:kə] (-, -n) *f* chemist's
(shop) (*BRIT*), drugstore (*US*).

The **Apotheke** *is a pharmacy selling medicines
only available on prescription. It also sells
toiletries. The pharmacist is qualified to give
advice on medicines and treatment.*

Apotheker(in) (-s, -) *m(f)* pharmacist,
(dispensing) chemist (*BRIT*), druggist (*US*).
Appalachen [apa'laxən] *pl* Appalachian
Mountains *pl.*
Apparat [apa'ra:t] (-(e)s, -e) *m* piece of
apparatus; (*Foto~*) camera; (*Telefon*)

telephone; (*RUNDF, TV*) set; (*Verwaltungs~,
Partei~*) machinery, apparatus; **am ~** on the
phone; (*als Antwort*) speaking; **am ~ bleiben**
to hold the line.
Apparatur [apara'tu:r] *f* apparatus.
Appartement [apart(ə)'mã:] (-s, -s) *nt* flat
(*BRIT*), apartment (*bes US*).
Appell [a'pɛl] (-s, -e) *m* (*MIL*) muster, parade;
(*fig*) appeal; **zum ~ antreten** to line up for
roll call.
appellieren [apɛ'li:rən] *vi:* ~ **(an** +*akk*) to
appeal (to).
Appetit [ape'ti:t] (-(e)s, -e) *m* appetite; **guten
~!** enjoy your meal; **a~lich** *adj* appetizing;
~**losigkeit** *f* lack of appetite.
Applaus [ap'laus] (-es, -e) *m* applause.
Appretur [apre'tu:r] *f* finish;
(*Wasserundurchlässigkeit*) waterproofing.
approbiert [apro'bi:rt] *adj* (*Arzt*) registered,
certified.
Apr. *abk* (= *April*) Apr.
Aprikose [apri'ko:zə] (-, -n) *f* apricot.
April [a'prıl] (-(s), -e) (*pl selten*) *m* April; **jdn in
den ~ schicken** to make an April fool of sb;
siehe auch **September;** ~**wetter** *nt* April
showers *pl.*
apropos [apro'po:] *adv* by the way, that
reminds me.
Aquaplaning [akva'pla:nıŋ] (-(s)) *nt*
aquaplaning.
Aquarell [akva'rɛl] (-s, -e) *nt* watercolour
(*BRIT*), watercolor (*US*).
Aquarium [a'kva:riom] *nt* aquarium.
Äquator [ɛ'kva:tor] (-s) *m* equator.
Äquivalent [ɛkviva'lɛnt] (-(e)s, -e) *nt*
equivalent.
Ar [a:r] (-s, -e) *nt od m* (*Maß*) are (*100 m²*).
Ära ['ɛ:ra] (-, **Ären**) *f* era.
Araber(in) ['a:rabər(ın)] (-s, -) *m(f)* Arab.
Arabien [a'ra:biən] (-s) *nt* Arabia.
arabisch *adj* Arab; (*Arabien betreffend*)
Arabian; (*Sprache*) Arabic; **A~er Golf**
Arabian Gulf; **A~es Meer** Arabian Sea; **A~e
Wüste** Arabian Desert.
Arbeit ['arbait] (-, -en) *f* work *no art*; (*Stelle*)
job; (*Erzeugnis*) piece of work;
(*wissenschaftliche*) dissertation; (*Klassen~*)
test; **Tag der ~** Labour (*BRIT*) *od* Labor (*US*)
Day; **sich an die ~ machen, an die ~ gehen**
to get down to work, start working; **jdm
~ machen** (*Mühe*) to put sb to trouble; **das
war eine ~** that was a hard job.
arbeiten *vi* to work ♦ *vt* to make ♦ *vr:* **sich
nach oben/an die Spitze ~** (*fig*) to work
one's way up/to the top.
Arbeiter(in) (-s, -) *m(f)* worker; (*ungelernt*)
labourer (*BRIT*), laborer (*US*).
Arbeiter- *zW:* ~**familie** *f* working-class
family; ~**kind** *nt* child from a working-class
family; ~**mitbestimmung** *f* employee
participation; ~**schaft** *f* workers *pl*, labour
(*BRIT*) *od* labor (*US*) force; ~**selbstkontrolle**

f workers' control; **~-und-Bauern-Staat** *m* (*DDR*) workers' and peasants' state; **~wohlfahrt** *f* workers' welfare association.
Arbeit- *zW:* **~geber** (**-s, -**) *m* employer; **~nehmer** (**-s, -**) *m* employee; **a~sam** *adj* industrious.
Arbeits- *in zW* labour (*BRIT*), labor (*US*); **~amt** *nt* employment exchange, Job Centre (*BRIT*); **~aufwand** *m* expenditure of energy; (*INDUSTRIE*) use of labour (*BRIT*) *od* labor (*US*); **~bedingungen** *pl* working conditions *pl*; **~beschaffung** *f* (*~platzbeschaffung*) job creation; **~erlaubnis** *f* work permit; **a~fähig** *adj* fit for work, able-bodied; **~gang** *m* operation; **~gemeinschaft** *f* study group; **~gericht** *nt* industrial tribunal; **a~intensiv** *adj* labour-intensive (*BRIT*), labor-intensive (*US*); **~konflikt** *m* industrial dispute; **~kraft** *f* worker; **~kräfte** *pl* workers *pl*, labour (*BRIT*), labor (*US*); **a~los** *adj* unemployed, out-of-work; **~losengeld** *nt* unemployment benefit; **~losenhilfe** *f* supplementary benefit; **~losenunterstützung** *f* unemployment benefit; **~losenversicherung** *f* compulsory insurance against unemployment; **~losigkeit** *f* unemployment; **~markt** *m* job market; **~moral** *f* attitude to work; (*in Betrieb*) work climate; **~niederlegung** *f* walkout; **~platte** *f* (*Küche*) work-top, work surface; **~platz** *m* place of work; (*Stelle*) job; **~platzrechner** *m* (*COMPUT*) work station; **~recht** *nt* industrial law; **a~scheu** *adj* workshy; **~schutz** *m* maintenance of health and safety standards at work; **~tag** *m* work(ing) day; **~teilung** *f* division of labour (*BRIT*) *od* labor (*US*); **~tier** *nt* (*fig: umg*) glutton for work, workaholic; **a~unfähig** *adj* unfit for work; **~unfall** *m* industrial accident; **~verhältnis** *nt* employee-employer relationship; **~vermittlung** *f* (*Amt*) employment exchange; (*privat*) employment agency; **~vertrag** *m* contract of employment; **~zeit** *f* working hours *pl*; **~zeitverkürzung** *f* reduction in working hours; **~zimmer** *nt* study.
Archäologe [arçɛoˈloːgə] (**-n, -n**) *m* arch(a)eologist.
Archäologin [arçɛoˈloːgɪn] *f* arch(a)eologist.
Arche [ˈarçə] (**-, -n**) *f:* **die ~ Noah** Noah's Ark.
Architekt(in) [arçiˈtɛkt(ɪn)] (**-en, -en**) *m(f)* architect.
architektonisch [arçitɛkˈtoːnɪʃ] *adj* architectural.
Architektur [arçitɛkˈtuːr] *f* architecture.
Archiv [arˈçiːf] (**-s, -e**) *nt* archive.

Arena [aˈreːna] (**-, Arenen**) *f* (*lit, fig*) arena; (*Zirkus~, Stierkampf~*) ring.
arg [ark] *adj* bad, awful ♦ *adv* awfully, very; **es zu ~ treiben** to go too far.
Argentinien [argɛnˈtiːniən] (**-s**) *nt* Argentina, the Argentine.
Argentinier(in) (**-s, -**) *m(f)* Argentine, Argentinian (*BRIT*), Argentinean (*US*).
argentinisch [argɛnˈtiːnɪʃ] *adj* Argentine, Argentinian (*BRIT*), Argentinean (*US*).
Ärger [ˈɛrgər] (**-s**) *m* (*Wut*) anger; (*Unannehmlichkeit*) trouble; **jdm ~ machen** *od* **bereiten** to cause sb a lot of trouble *od* bother; **ä~lich** *adj* (*zornig*) angry; (*lästig*) annoying, aggravating.
ärgern *vt* to annoy ♦ *vr* to get annoyed.
Ärgernis (**-ses, -se**) *nt* annoyance; (*Anstoß*) offence (*BRIT*), offense (*US*), outrage; **öffentliches ~ erregen** to be a public nuisance.
arg- *zW:* **~listig** *adj* cunning, insidious; **~listige Täuschung** fraud; **~los** *adj* guileless, innocent; **A~losigkeit** *f* guilelessness, innocence.
Argument [arguˈmɛnt] *nt* argument.
argumentieren [argumɛnˈtiːrən] *vi* to argue.
Argusauge [ˈargʊsˌaʊgə] *nt* (*geh*): **mit ~n** eagle-eyed.
Argwohn *m* suspicion.
argwöhnisch *adj* suspicious.
Arie [ˈaːriə] *f* aria.
Aristokrat(in) [arɪstoˈkraːt(ɪn)] (**-en, -en**) *m(f)* aristocrat.
Aristokratie [arɪstokraˈtiː] *f* aristocracy.
aristokratisch *adj* aristocratic.
arithmetisch [arɪtˈmeːtɪʃ] *adj* arithmetical; **~es Mittel** arithmetic mean.
Arkaden [arˈkaːdən] *pl* (*Bogengang*) arcade *sing*.
Arktis [ˈarktɪs] (**-**) *f* Arctic.
arktisch *adj* Arctic.
arm [arm] *adj* poor; **~ dran sein** (*umg*) to have a hard time of it.
Arm (**-(e)s, -e**) *m* arm; (*Fluß~*) branch; **jdn auf den ~ nehmen** (*fig: umg*) to pull sb's leg; **jdm unter die ~e greifen** (*fig*) to help sb out; **einen langen/den längeren ~ haben** (*fig*) to have a lot of/more pull (*umg*) *od* influence.
Armatur [armaˈtuːr] *f* (*ELEK*) armature.
Armaturenbrett *nt* instrument panel; (*AUT*) dashboard.
Armband *nt* bracelet; **~uhr** *f* (wrist) watch.
Arme(r) *f(m)* poor man/woman; **die ~n** the poor.
Armee [arˈmeː] (**-, -n**) *f* army; **~korps** *nt* army corps.
Ärmel [ˈɛrməl] (**-s, -**) *m* sleeve; **etw aus dem**

~ **schütteln** (*fig*) to produce sth just like that.
Ärmelkanal *m* (English) Channel.
Armenien [ar'me:niən] (**-s**) *nt* Armenia.
Armenier(in) [ar'me:niər(ın)] (**-s, -**) *m(f)* Armenian.
armenisch [ar'me:nıʃ] *adj* Armenian.
Armenrecht *nt* (*JUR*) legal aid.
Armer *m siehe* **Arme(r)**.
Armlehne *f* armrest.
Armleuchter (*pej: umg*) *m* (*Dummkopf*) twit (*BRIT*), fool.
ärmlich ['ɛrmlıç] *adj* poor; **aus ~en Verhältnissen** from a poor family.
armselig *adj* wretched, miserable; (*mitleiderregend*) pathetic, pitiful.
Armut ['armu:t] (**-**) *f* poverty.
Armutsgrenze *f* poverty line.
Armutszeugnis *nt* (*fig*): **jdm/sich ein ~ ausstellen** to show sb's/one's shortcomings.
Aroma [a'ro:ma] (**-s, Aromen**) *nt* aroma; **~therapie** *f* aromatherapy.
aromatisch [aro'ma:tıʃ] *adj* aromatic.
arrangieren [arã:'ʒi:rən] *vt* to arrange ♦ *vr* to come to an arrangement.
Arrest [a'rɛst] (**-(e)s, -e**) *m* detention.
arretieren [are'ti:rən] *vt* (*TECH*) to lock (in place).
arrogant [aro'gant] *adj* arrogant.
Arroganz *f* arrogance.
Arsch [arʃ] (**-es, ˝e**) (*umg!*) *m* arse (*!*); **leck mich am ~!** (*laß mich in Ruhe*) get stuffed! (*!*), fuck off! (*!*); **am ~ der Welt** (*umg*) in the back of beyond; **~kriecher** (*umg!*) *m* arse licker (*!*), crawler; **~loch** (*umg!*) *nt* (*Mensch*) bastard (*!*).
Arsen [ar'ze:n] (**-s**) *nt* arsenic.
Art [a:rt] (**-, -en**) *f* (*Weise*) way; (*Sorte*) kind, sort; (*BIOL*) species; **eine ~ (von) Frucht** a kind of fruit; **Häuser aller ~** houses of all kinds; **einzig in seiner ~ sein** to be the only one of its kind, be unique; **auf diese ~ und Weise** in this way; **das ist doch keine ~!** that's no way to behave!; **es ist nicht seine ~, das zu tun** it's not like him to do that; **ich mache das auf meine ~** I do that my (own) way; **Schnitzel nach ~ des Hauses** chef's special escalope.
arten *vi*: **nach jdm ~** to take after sb; **der Mensch ist so geartet, daß ...** human nature is such that ...
Artenschutz *m* protection of endangered species.
Arterie [ar'te:riə] *f* artery.
Arterienverkalkung *f* arteriosclerosis.
Artgenosse ['a:rtgənɔsə] *m* animal/plant of the same species; (*Mensch*) person of the same type.
Arthritis [ar'tri:tıs] (**-, -ritiden**) *f* arthritis.
artig ['a:rtıç] *adj* good, well-behaved.
Artikel [ar'ti:kəl] (**-s, -**) *m* article.

Artillerie [artılə'ri:] *f* artillery.
Artischocke [arti'ʃɔkə] (**-, -n**) *f* artichoke.
Artistik [ar'tıstık] (**-**) *f* artistry; (*Zirkus-/Varietékunst*) circus/variety performing.
Arznei [a:rts'naı] *f* medicine; **~mittel** *nt* medicine, medicament.
Arzt [a:rtst] (**-es, ˝e**) *m* doctor; **praktischer ~** general practitioner, GP.
Ärztekammer *f* ≈ General Medical Council (*BRIT*), State Medical Board of Registration (*US*).
Arzthelferin *f* doctor's assistant.
Ärztin ['ɛ:rtstın] *f* woman doctor; *siehe auch* **Arzt**.
ärztlich ['ɛ:rtstlıç] *adj* medical.
Arztpraxis *f* doctor's practice; (*Räume*) doctor's surgery (*BRIT*) *od* office (*US*).
As [as] (**-ses, -se**) *nt* ace; (*MUS*) A flat.
Asbest [as'bɛst] (**-(e)s, -e**) *m* asbestos.
Asche ['aʃə] (**-, -n**) *f* ash.
Aschen- *zW*: **~bahn** *f* cinder track; **~becher** *m* ashtray; **~brödel** *nt* (*LITER, fig*) Cinderella; **~puttel** *nt* (*LITER, fig*) Cinderella.
Aschermittwoch *m* Ash Wednesday.
Aserbaidschan [azɛrbaɪ'dʒa:n] (**-s**) *nt* Azerbaijan.
aserbaidschanisch *adj* Azerbaijani.
Asiat(in) [azi'a:t(ın)] (**-en, -en**) *m(f)* Asian.
asiatisch *adj* Asian, Asiatic.
Asien ['a:ziən] (**-s**) *nt* Asia.
asozial ['azotsia:l] *adj* antisocial; (*Familie*) asocial.
Asoziale(r) (*pej*) *f(m)* antisocial person; **Asoziale** *pl* antisocial elements.
Aspekt [as'pɛkt] (**-(e)s, -e**) *m* aspect.
Asphalt [as'falt] (**-(e)s, -e**) *m* asphalt.
asphaltieren [asfal'ti:rən] *vt* to asphalt.
Asphaltstraße *f* asphalt road.
aß *etc* [a:s] *vb siehe* **essen**.
Ass. *abk* = **Assessor**.
Assekurant(in) [aseku'rant(ın)] (**-en, -en**) *m(f)* underwriter.
Assemblersprache [ə'sɛmblərʃpra:xə] *f* (*COMPUT*) assembly language.
Assessor(in) [a'sɛsɔr(ın)] (**-s, -en**) *m(f)* graduate civil servant who has completed his/her traineeship.
Assistent(in) [asıs'tɛnt(ın)] *m(f)* assistant.
Assistenzarzt [asıs'tɛntsa:rtst] *m* houseman (*BRIT*), intern (*US*).
Assoziation [asotsiatsi'o:n] *f* association.
assoziieren [asotsi'i:rən] *vt* (*geh*) to associate.
Ast [ast] (**-(e)s, ˝e**) *m* branch; **sich** *dat* **einen ~ lachen** (*umg*) to double up (with laughter).
AStA ['asta] (**-(s), -(s)**) *m abk* (= *Allgemeiner Studentenausschuß*) students' association.
Aster ['astər] (**-, -n**) *f* aster.
ästhetisch [ɛs'te:tıʃ] *adj* aesthetic (*BRIT*), esthetic (*US*).
Asthma ['astma] (**-s**) *nt* asthma.
Asthmatiker(in) [ast'ma:tikər(ın)] (**-s, -**) *m(f)*

asthmatic.

astrein ['astraɪn] adj (fig: umg: moralisch einwandfrei) straight, on the level; (: echt) genuine; (prima) fantastic.

Astrologe [astro'lo:gə] (-n, -n) m astrologer.

Astrologie [astrolo'gi:] f astrology.

Astrologin f astrologer.

Astronaut(in) [astro'naʊt(ɪn)] (-en, -en) m(f) astronaut.

Astronautik f astronautics.

Astronom(in) [astro'no:m(ɪn)] (-en, -en) m(f) astronomer.

Astronomie [astrono'mi:] f astronomy.

ASU f abk (= Arbeitsgemeinschaft selbständiger Unternehmer) association of private traders; (= Abgassonderuntersuchung) exhaust emission test.

ASW f abk (= außersinnliche Wahrnehmung) ESP.

Asyl [a'zy:l] (-s, -e) nt asylum; (Heim) home; (Obdachlosen~) shelter.

Asylant(in) [azy'lant(ɪn)] (-en, -en) m(f) person seeking (political) asylum.

Asylrecht nt (POL) right of (political) asylum.

A.T. abk (= Altes Testament) O.T.

Atelier [atəli'e:] (-s, -s) nt studio.

Atem ['a:təm] (-s) m breath; **den ~ anhalten** to hold one's breath; **außer ~** out of breath; **jdn in ~ halten** to keep sb in suspense od on tenterhooks; **das verschlug mir den ~** it took my breath away; **einen langen/den längeren ~ haben** to have a lot of staying power; **a~beraubend** adj breathtaking; **a~los** adj breathless; **~pause** f breather; **~wege** pl (ANAT) respiratory tract; **~zug** m breath.

Atheismus [ate'ɪsmʊs] m atheism.

Atheist(in) m(f) atheist; **a~isch** adj atheistic.

Athen [a'te:n] (-s) nt Athens.

Athener(in) (-s, -) m(f) Athenian.

Äther ['ɛːtər] (-s, -) m ether.

Äthiopien [ɛti'o:piən] (-s) nt Ethiopia.

Äthiopier(in) (-s, -) m(f) Ethiopian.

äthiopisch adj Ethiopian.

Athlet(in) [at'le:t(ɪn)] (-en, -en) m(f) athlete.

Athletik f athletics sing.

Atlanten pl von **Atlas.**

Atlantik [at'lantɪk] (-s) m Atlantic.

atlantisch adj Atlantic; **der A~e Ozean** the Atlantic Ocean.

Atlas ['atlas] (- od -ses, -se od **Atlanten**) m atlas; **~gebirge** nt Atlas Mountains pl.

atmen ['a:tmən] vt, vi to breathe.

Atmosphäre [atmo'sfɛːrə] (-, -n) f atmosphere.

atmosphärisch adj atmospheric.

Atmung ['a:tmʊŋ] f respiration.

Ätna ['ɛːtna] (-(s)) m Etna.

Atom [a'to:m] (-s, -e) nt atom.

atomar [ato'ma:r] adj atomic, nuclear; (Drohung) nuclear.

Atom- zW: **~bombe** f atom bomb; **~energie** f nuclear od atomic energy; **~kern** m atomic nucleus; **~kraft** f nuclear power; **~kraftwerk** nt nuclear power station; **~krieg** m nuclear od atomic war; **~lobby** f nuclear lobby; **~macht** f nuclear od atomic power; **~meiler** m nuclear reactor; **~müll** m nuclear waste; **~physik** f nuclear physics sing; **~pilz** m mushroom cloud; **~sperrvertrag** m (POL) nuclear non-proliferation treaty; **~sprengkopf** m nuclear od atomic warhead; **~strom** m electricity generated by nuclear power; **~test** m nuclear test; **~testgelände** nt nuclear testing range; **~waffen** pl nuclear od atomic weapons pl; **a~waffenfrei** adj (Zone) nuclear-free; **~wirtschaft** f nuclear industry; **~zeitalter** nt atomic age.

Attacke [a'takə] (-, -n) f (Angriff) attack.

Attentat [atɛn'ta:t] (-(e)s, -e) nt: **~ (auf +akk)** (attempted) assassination (of).

Attentäter(in) [atɛn'tɛːtər(ɪn)] (-s, -) m(f) (would-be) assassin.

Attest [a'tɛst] (-(e)s, -e) nt certificate.

Attraktion [atraktsi'o:n] f attraction.

attraktiv [atrak'ti:f] adj attractive.

Attrappe [a'trapə] (-, -n) f dummy; **bei ihr ist alles ~** everything about her is false.

Attribut [atri'bu:t] (-(e)s, -e) nt (GRAM) attribute.

ätzen ['ɛtsən] vi to be caustic.

ätzend adj (lit: Säure) corrosive; (Geruch) pungent; (fig: umg: furchtbar) dreadful, horrible; (: toll) magic.

═══════════════════ SCHLÜSSELWORT

auch [aʊx] adv **1** (ebenfalls) also, too, as well; **das ist ~ schön** that's nice too od as well; **er kommt - ich ~** he's coming - so am I, me too; **~ nicht** not ... either; **ich ~ nicht** nor I, me neither; **oder ~** or; **~ das noch!** not that as well!; **nicht nur ..., sondern ~ ...** not only ... but also ...

2 (selbst, sogar) even; **~ wenn das Wetter schlecht ist** even if the weather is bad; **ohne ~ nur zu fragen** without even asking

3 (wirklich) really; **du siehst müde aus - bin ich ~** you look tired - (so) I am; **so sieht es ~ aus** (and) that's what it looks like

4 (~ immer): **wer ~** whoever; **was ~** whatever; **wozu ~?** (emphatisch) whatever for?; **wie dem ~ sei** be that as it may; **wie sehr er sich ~ bemühte** however much he tried.

Audienz [aʊdi'ɛnts] (-, -en) f (bei Papst, König etc) audience.

Audimax [aʊdi'maks] nt (UNIV: umg) main lecture hall.

audiovisuell [aʊdiovizu'ɛl] adj audiovisual.

Auditorium [aʊdi'to:riʊm] nt (Hörsaal) lecture hall; (geh: Zuhörerschaft) audience.

=========== SCHLÜSSELWORT

auf [aʊf] *präp +dat* (*wo?*) on; ~ **dem Tisch** on the table; ~ **der Reise** on the way; ~ **der Post/dem Fest** at the post office/party; ~ **der Straße** on the road; ~ **dem Land/der ganzen Welt** in the country/the whole world; **was hat es damit** ~ **sich?** what does it mean?
♦ *präp +akk* **1** (*wohin?*) on(to); ~ **den Tisch** on(to) the table; ~ **die Post gehen** to go to the post office; ~ **das Land** into the country; **etw** ~ **einen Zettel schreiben** to write sth on a piece of paper; ~ **eine Tasse Kaffee/eine Zigarette(nlänge)** for a cup of coffee/a smoke; **die Nacht (von Montag)** ~ **Dienstag** Monday night; ~ **einen Polizisten kommen 1.000 Bürger** there is one policeman to every 1,000 citizens
2: ~ **deutsch** in German; ~ **Lebenszeit** for my/his lifetime; **bis** ~ **ihn** except for him; ~ **einmal** at once; ~ **seinen Vorschlag (hin)** at his suggestion
♦ *adv* **1** (*offen*) open; **das Fenster ist** ~ the window is open
2 (*hinauf*) up; ~ **und ab** up and down; ~ **und davon** up and away; ~**!** (*los!*) come on!; **von klein** ~ from childhood onwards
3 (*aufgestanden*) up; **ist er schon** ~**?** is he up yet?
♦ *konj:* ~ **daß** (so) that.

aufarbeiten ['aʊf|arbaɪtən] *vt* (*erledigen: Korrespondenz etc*) to catch up with.
aufatmen ['aʊf|aːtmən] *vi* to heave a sigh of relief.
aufbahren ['aʊfbaːrən] *vt* to lay out.
Aufbau ['aʊfbaʊ] *m* (*Bauen*) building, construction; (*Struktur*) structure; (*aufgebautes Teil*) superstructure.
aufbauen ['aʊfbaʊən] *vt* to erect, build (up); (*Existenz*) to make; (*gestalten*) to construct; (*gründen*): ~ **(auf** *+dat*) to found (on), base (on) ♦ *vr:* **sich vor jdm** ~ to draw o.s. up to one's full height in front of sb.
aufbäumen ['aʊfbɔʏmən] *vr* to rear; (*fig*) to revolt, rebel.
aufbauschen ['aʊfbaʊʃən] *vt* to puff out; (*fig*) to exaggerate.
aufbegehren ['aʊfbəgeːrən] *vi* (*geh*) to rebel.
aufbehalten ['aʊfbəhaltən] *unreg vt* to keep on.
aufbekommen ['aʊfbəkɔmən] *unreg* (*umg*) *vt* (*öffnen*) to get open; (: *Hausaufgaben*) to be given.
aufbereiten ['aʊfbəraɪtən] *vt* to process; (*Trinkwasser*) to purify; (*Text etc*) to work up.
Aufbereitungsanlage *f* processing plant.
aufbessern ['aʊfbɛsərn] *vt* (*Gehalt*) to increase.
aufbewahren ['aʊfbəvaːrən] *vt* to keep; (*Gepäck*) to put in the left-luggage office.
Aufbewahrung *f* (safe)keeping; (*Gepäck~*)

left-luggage office (*BRIT*), baggage check (*US*); **jdm etw zur** ~ **geben** to give sb sth for safekeeping.
Aufbewahrungsort *m* storage place.
aufbieten ['aʊfbiːtən] *unreg vt* (*Kraft*) to summon (up); (*Armee, Polizei*) to mobilize.
Aufbietung *f:* **unter** ~ **aller Kräfte ...** summoning (up) all his/her *etc* strength ...
aufbinden ['aʊfbɪndən] *unreg vt:* **laß dir doch so etwas nicht** ~ (*fig*) don't fall for that.
aufblähen ['aʊfblɛːən] *vr* to blow out; (*Segel*) to billow out; (*MED*) to become swollen; (*fig: pej*) to puff o.s. up.
aufblasen ['aʊfblaːzən] *unreg vt* to blow up, inflate ♦ *vr* (*umg*) to become big-headed.
aufbleiben ['aʊfblaɪbən] *unreg vi* (*Laden*) to remain open; (*Person*) to stay up.
aufblenden ['aʊfblɛndən] *vt* (*Scheinwerfer*) to turn on full beam.
aufblicken ['aʊfblɪkən] *vi* to look up; ~ **zu** (*lit*) to look up at; (*fig*) to look up to.
aufblühen ['aʊfblyːən] *vi* to blossom; (*fig*) to blossom, flourish.
aufblühend *adj* (*COMM*) booming.
aufbocken ['aʊfbɔkən] *vt* (*Auto*) to jack up.
aufbrauchen ['aʊfbraʊxən] *vt* to use up.
aufbrausen ['aʊfbraʊzən] *vi* (*fig*) to flare up.
aufbrausend *adj* hot-tempered.
aufbrechen ['aʊfbrɛçən] *unreg vt* to break open, to prise (*BRIT*) *od* pry (*US*) open ♦ *vi* to burst open; (*gehen*) to start, set off.
aufbringen ['aʊfbrɪŋən] *unreg vt* (*öffnen*) to open; (*in Mode*) to bring into fashion; (*beschaffen*) to procure; (*FIN*) to raise; (*ärgern*) to irritate; **Verständnis für etw** ~ to be able to understand sth.
Aufbruch ['aʊfbrʊx] *m* departure.
aufbrühen ['aʊfbryːən] *vt* (*Tee*) to make.
aufbrummen ['aʊfbrʊmən] (*umg*) *vt:* **jdm die Kosten** ~ to land sb with the costs.
aufbürden ['aʊfbyrdən] *vt:* **jdm etw** ~ to burden sb with sth.
aufdecken ['aʊfdɛkən] *vt* to uncover; (*Spielkarten*) to show.
aufdrängen ['aʊfdrɛŋən] *vt:* **jdm etw** ~ to force sth on sb ♦ *vr:* **sich jdm** ~ to intrude on sb.
aufdrehen ['aʊfdreːən] *vt* (*Wasserhahn etc*) to turn on; (*Ventil*) to open; (*Schraubverschluß*) to unscrew; (*Radio etc*) to turn up; (*Haar*) to put in rollers.
aufdringlich ['aʊfdrɪŋlɪç] *adj* pushy; (*Benehmen*) obtrusive; (*Parfüm*) powerful.
aufeinander [aʊf|aɪˈnandər] *adv* on top of one another; (*schießen*) at each other; (*warten*) for one another; (*vertrauen*) each other; **A~folge** *f* succession, series; ~**folgen** *vi* to follow one another; ~**folgend** *adj* consecutive; ~**legen** *vt* to lay on top of one another; ~**prallen** *vi* (*Autos etc*) to collide; (*Truppen, Meinungen*) to clash.
Aufenthalt ['aʊf|ɛnthalt] *m* stay; (*Verzögerung*)

delay; (*EISENB: Halten*) stop; (*Ort*) haunt.
Aufenthalts- *zW:* **~erlaubnis** *f,*
~genehmigung *f* residence permit; **~raum**
m day room; (*in Betrieb*) recreation room.
auferlegen ['auf|ɛrleːgən] *vt:* (jdm) ~ to
impose (upon sb).
auferstehen ['auf|ɛrʃteːən] *unreg vi untr* to rise
from the dead.
Auferstehung *f* resurrection.
aufessen ['auf|ɛsən] *unreg vt* to eat up.
auffahren ['aufaːrən] *unreg vi* (*herankommen*)
to draw up; (*hochfahren*) to jump up; (*wütend
werden*) to flare up; (*in den Himmel*) to
ascend ♦ *vt* (*Kanonen, Geschütz*) to bring up;
~ **auf** +*akk* (*Auto*) to run *od* crash into.
auffahrend *adj* hot-tempered.
Auffahrt *f* (*Haus~*) drive; (*Autobahn~*) slip
road (*BRIT*), entrance ramp (*US*).
Auffahrunfall *m* pile-up.
auffallen ['auffalən] *unreg vi* to be noticeable;
angenehm/unangenehm ~ to make a good/
bad impression; **jdm** ~ (*bemerkt werden*) to
strike sb.
auffallend *adj* striking.
auffällig ['auffɛlıç] *adj* conspicuous, striking.
auffangen ['auffaŋən] *unreg vt* to catch;
(*Funkspruch*) to intercept; (*Preise*) to peg;
(*abfangen: Aufprall etc*) to cushion, absorb.
Auffanglager *nt* reception camp.
auffassen ['auffasən] *vt* to understand,
comprehend; (*auslegen*) to see, view.
Auffassung *f* (*Meinung*) opinion; (*Auslegung*)
view, conception; (*auch:* **~sgabe**) grasp.
auffindbar ['auffɪntbaːr] *adj* to be found.
aufflammen ['aufflamən] *vi* (*lit, fig: Feuer,
Unruhen etc*) to flare up.
auffliegen ['auffliːgən] *unreg vi* to fly up; (*umg:
Rauschgiftring etc*) to be busted.
auffordern ['auffɔrdərn] *vt* to challenge;
(*befehlen*) to call upon, order; (*bitten*) to ask.
Aufforderung *f* (*Befehl*) order; (*Einladung*)
invitation.
aufforsten ['auffɔrstən] *vt* (*Gebiet*) to
reafforest; (*Wald*) to restock.
auffrischen ['auffrɪʃən] *vt* to freshen up;
(*Kenntnisse*) to brush up; (*Erinnerungen*) to
reawaken ♦ *vi* (*Wind*) to freshen.
aufführen ['auffyːrən] *vt* (*THEAT*) to perform;
(*in einem Verzeichnis*) to list, specify ♦ *vr*
(*sich benehmen*) to behave; **einzeln** ~ to
itemize.
Aufführung *f* (*THEAT*) performance; (*Liste*)
specification.
auffüllen ['auffylən] *vt* to fill up; (*Vorräte*) to
replenish; (*Öl*) to top up.
Aufgabe ['aufgaːbə] (*-, -n*) *f* task; (*SCH*)
exercise; (*Haus~*) homework; (*Verzicht*)
giving up; (*von Gepäck*) registration; (*von
Post*) posting; (*von Inserat*) insertion; **sich** *dat*
etw zur ~ **machen** to make sth one's job *od*
business.
aufgabeln ['aufgaːbəln] *vt* (*fig: umg: jdn*) to

pick up; (: *Sache*) to get hold of.
Aufgabenbereich *m* area of responsibility.
Aufgang ['aufgaŋ] *m* ascent; (*Sonnen~*) rise;
(*Treppe*) staircase.
aufgeben ['aufgeːbən] *unreg vt* (*verzichten auf*)
to give up; (*Paket*) to send, post; (*Gepäck*) to
register; (*Bestellung*) to give; (*Inserat*) to
insert; (*Rätsel, Problem*) to set ♦ *vi* to give up.
aufgeblasen ['aufgəblaːzən] *adj* (*fig*) puffed
up, self-important.
Aufgebot ['aufgəboːt] *nt* supply; (*von Kräften*)
utilization; (*Ehe~*) banns *pl.*
aufgedonnert ['aufgədɔnərt] (*pej: umg*) *adj*
tarted up.
aufgedreht ['aufgədreːt] (*umg*) *adj* excited.
aufgedunsen ['aufgedʊnzən] *adj* swollen,
puffed up.
aufgegeben ['aufgəgeːbən] *pp von* **aufgeben.**
aufgehen ['aufgeːən] *unreg vi* (*Sonne, Teig*) to
rise; (*sich öffnen*) to open; (*THEAT: Vorhang*)
to go up; (*Knopf, Knoten etc*) to come undone;
(*klarwerden*) to become clear; (*MATH*) to
come out exactly; ~ (**in** +*dat*) (*sich widmen*)
to be absorbed (in); **in Rauch/Flammen** ~ to
go up in smoke/flames.
aufgeilen ['aufgailən] (*umg*) *vt* to turn on ♦ *vr*
to be turned on.
aufgeklärt ['aufgəklɛːrt] *adj* enlightened;
(*sexuell*) knowing the facts of life.
aufgekratzt ['aufgəkratst] (*umg*) *adj* in high
spirits, full of beans.
aufgelaufen ['aufgəlaufən] *adj:* **~e Zinsen** *pl*
accrued interest *sing.*
Aufgeld *nt* premium.
aufgelegt ['aufgəleːkt] *adj:* **gut/schlecht** ~ **sein**
to be in a good/bad mood; **zu etw** ~ **sein** to
be in the mood for sth.
aufgenommen ['aufgənɔmən] *pp von*
aufnehmen.
aufgeregt ['aufgəreːkt] *adj* excited.
aufgeschlossen ['aufgəʃlɔsən] *adj* open,
open-minded.
aufgeschmissen ['aufgəʃmɪsən] (*umg*) *adj* in a
fix, stuck.
aufgeschrieben ['aufgəʃriːbən] *pp von*
aufschreiben.
aufgestanden ['aufgəʃtandən] *pp von*
aufstehen.
aufgetakelt ['aufgətaːkəlt] *adj* (*fig: umg*)
dressed up to the nines.
aufgeweckt ['aufgəvɛkt] *adj* bright,
intelligent.
aufgießen ['aufgiːsən] *unreg vt* (*Wasser*) to
pour over; (*Tee*) to infuse.
aufgliedern ['aufgliːdərn] *vr:* **sich** ~ (**in** +*akk*) to
(sub)divide (into), break down (into).
aufgreifen ['aufgraifən] *unreg vt* (*Thema*) to
take up; (*Verdächtige*) to pick up, seize.
aufgrund [auf'grʊnt] *präp* +*gen* on the basis of;
(*wegen*) because of.
Aufgußbeutel ['aufgʊsbɔytəl] *m* sachet
(containing coffee/herbs *etc*) for brewing;

(*Teebeutel*) tea bag.

aufhaben ['aʊfhaːbən] *unreg vt* (*Hut etc*) to have on; (*Arbeit*) to have to do.

aufhalsen ['aʊfhalzən] (*umg*) *vt:* **jdm etw** ~ **to** saddle *od* lumber sb with sth.

aufhalten ['aʊfhaltən] *unreg vt* (*Person*) to detain; (*Entwicklung*) to check; (*Tür, Hand*) to hold open; (*Augen*) to keep open ♦ *vr* (*wohnen*) to live; (*bleiben*) to stay; **jdn (bei etw)** ~ (*abhalten, stören*) to hold *od* keep sb back (from sth); **sich über etw/jdn** ~ to go on about sth/sb; **sich mit etw** ~ to waste time over sth; **sich bei etw** ~ (*sich befassen*) to dwell on sth.

aufhängen ['aʊfhɛŋən] *unreg vt* (*Wäsche*) to hang up; (*Menschen*) to hang ♦ *vr* to hang o.s.

Aufhänger (**-s, -**) *m* (*am Mantel*) hook; (*fig*) peg.

Aufhängung *f* (*TECH*) suspension.

aufheben ['aʊfheːbən] *unreg vt* (*hochheben*) to raise, lift; (*Sitzung*) to wind up; (*Urteil*) to annul; (*Gesetz*) to repeal, abolish; (*aufbewahren*) to keep; (*ausgleichen*) to offset, make up for ♦ *vr* to cancel itself out; **viel A~(s) machen (von)** to make a fuss (about); **bei jdm gut aufgehoben sein** to be well looked after at sb's.

aufheitern ['aʊfhaɪtərn] *vt, vr* (*Himmel, Miene*) to brighten; (*Mensch*) to cheer up.

Aufheiterungen *pl* (*MET*) bright periods *pl*.

aufheizen ['aʊfhaɪtsən] *vt:* **die Stimmung** ~ to stir up feelings.

aufhelfen ['aʊfhɛlfən] *unreg vi* (*lit: beim Aufstehen*): **jdm** ~ to help sb up.

aufhellen ['aʊfhɛlən] *vt, vr* to clear up; (*Farbe, Haare*) to lighten.

aufhetzen ['aʊfhɛtsən] *vt* to stir up.

aufheulen ['aʊfhɔʏlən] *vi* to howl; (*Sirene*) to (start to) wail; (*Motor*) to (give a) roar.

aufholen ['aʊfhoːlən] *vt* to make up ♦ *vi* to catch up.

aufhorchen ['aʊfhɔrçən] *vi* to prick up one's ears.

aufhören ['aʊfhøːrən] *vi* to stop; ~, **etw zu tun** to stop doing sth.

aufkaufen ['aʊfkaʊfən] *vt* to buy up.

aufklappen ['aʊfklapən] *vt* to open; (*Verdeck*) to fold back.

aufklären ['aʊfklɛːrən] *vt* (*Geheimnis etc*) to clear up; (*Person*) to enlighten; (*sexuell*) to tell the facts of life to; (*MIL*) to reconnoitre ♦ *vr* to clear up.

Aufklärung *f* (*von Geheimnis*) clearing up; (*Unterrichtung, Zeitalter*) enlightenment; (*sexuell*) sex education; (*MIL, AVIAT*) reconnaissance.

Aufklärungsarbeit *f* educational work.

aufkleben ['aʊfkleːbən] *vt* to stick on.

Aufkleber (**-s, -**) *m* sticker.

aufknöpfen ['aʊfknœpfən] *vt* to unbutton.

aufkochen ['aʊfkɔxən] *vt* to bring to the boil.

aufkommen ['aʊfkɔmən] *unreg vi* (*Wind*) to come up; (*Zweifel, Gefühl*) to arise; (*Mode*) to start; **für jdn/etw** ~ to be liable *od* responsible for sb/sth; **für den Schaden** ~ to pay for the damage; **endlich kam Stimmung auf** at last things livened up.

aufkreuzen ['aʊfkrɔʏtsən] (*umg*) *vi* (*erscheinen*) to turn *od* show up.

aufkündigen ['aʊfkʏndɪgən] *vt* (*Vertrag etc*) to terminate.

aufladen ['aʊflaːdən] *unreg vt* to load ♦ *vr* (*Batterie etc*) to be charged; (*neu* ~) to be recharged; **jdm/sich etw** ~ (*fig*) to saddle sb/o.s. with sth.

Auflage ['aʊflaːgə] *f* edition; (*Zeitung*) circulation; (*Bedingung*) condition; **jdm etw zur** ~ **machen** to make sth a condition for sb.

Auflage(n)höhe *f* (*von Buch*) number of copies published; (*von Zeitung*) circulation.

auflassen ['aʊflasən] *unreg* (*umg*) *vt* (*offen*) to leave open; (: *aufgesetzt*) to leave on; **die Kinder länger** ~ to let the children stay up (longer).

auflauern ['aʊflaʊərn] *vi:* **jdm** ~ to lie in wait for sb.

Auflauf ['aʊflaʊf] *m* (*KOCH*) pudding; (*Menschen~*) crowd.

auflaufen *unreg vi* (*auf Grund laufen: Schiff*) to run aground; **jdn** ~ **lassen** (*umg*) to drop sb in it.

Auflaufform *f* (*KOCH*) ovenproof dish.

aufleben ['aʊfleːbən] *vi* to revive.

auflegen ['aʊfleːgən] *vt* to put on; (*Hörer*) to put down; (*TYP*) to print ♦ *vi* (*TEL*) to hang up.

auflehnen ['aʊfleːnən] *vt* to lean on ♦ *vr* to rebel.

Auflehnung *f* rebellion.

auflesen ['aʊfleːzən] *unreg vt* to pick up.

aufleuchten ['aʊflɔʏçtən] *vi* to light up.

aufliegen ['aʊfliːgən] *unreg vi* to lie on; (*COMM*) to be available.

auflisten ['aʊflɪstən] *vt* (*auch COMPUT*) to list.

auflockern ['aʊflɔkərn] *vt* to loosen; (*fig: Eintönigkeit etc*) to liven up; (*entspannen, zwangloser machen*) to make relaxed; (*Atmosphäre*) to make more relaxed, ease.

auflösen ['aʊfløːzən] *vt* to dissolve; (*Mißverständnis*) to sort out; (*Konto*) to close; (*Firma*) to wind up; (*Haushalt*) to break up; **in Tränen aufgelöst sein** to be in tears.

Auflösung *f* dissolving; (*fig*) solution; (*Bildschirm*) resolution.

aufmachen ['aʊfmaxən] *vt* to open; (*Kleidung*) to undo; (*zurechtmachen*) to do up ♦ *vr* to set out.

Aufmacher *m* (*PRESSE*) lead.

Aufmachung *f* (*Kleidung*) outfit, get-up; (*Gestaltung*) format.

aufmerksam ['aʊfmɛrkzaːm] *adj* attentive; **auf etw** *akk* ~ **werden** to become aware of sth; **jdn auf etw** *akk* ~ **machen** to point sth out to sb; **(das ist) sehr ~ von Ihnen** (*zuvorkommend*) (that's) most kind of you; **A~keit** *f* attention, attentiveness; (*Geschenk*) token (gift).

aufmöbeln ['aʊfmøːbəln] (*umg*) *vt* (*Gegenstand*) to do up; (: *beleben*) to buck up, pep up.

aufmucken ['aʊfmʊkən] (*umg*) *vi:* ~ **gegen** to protest at *od* against.

aufmuntern ['aʊfmʊntərn] *vt* (*ermutigen*) to encourage; (*erheitern*) to cheer up.

aufmüpfig ['aʊfmʏpfɪç] (*umg*) *adj* rebellious.

Aufnahme ['aʊfnaːmə] (-, -n) *f* reception; (*Beginn*) beginning; (*in Verein etc*) admission; (*in Liste etc*) inclusion; (*Notieren*) taking down; (*PHOT*) shot; (*auf Tonband etc*) recording; ~**antrag** *m* application for membership *od* admission; **a~fähig** *adj* receptive; ~**leiter** *m* (*FILM*) production manager; (*RUNDF, TV*) producer; ~**prüfung** *f* entrance test; ~**stopp** *m* (*für Flüchtlinge etc*) freeze on immigration.

aufnehmen ['aʊfneːmən] *unreg vt* to receive; (*hochheben*) to pick up; (*beginnen*) to take up; (*in Verein etc*) to admit; (*in Liste etc*) to include; (*fassen*) to hold; (*begreifen*) to take in, grasp; (*beim Stricken: Maschen*) to increase, make; (*notieren*) to take down; (*fotografieren*) to photograph; (*auf Tonband, Platte*) to record; (*FIN: leihen*) to take out; **es mit jdm ~ können** to be able to compete with sb.

aufnötigen ['aʊfnøːtɪgən] *vt:* **jdm etw ~ to** force sth on sb.

aufoktroyieren ['aʊf|ɔktroajiːrən] *vt:* **jdm etw ~** (*geh*) to impose *od* force sth on sb.

aufopfern ['aʊf|ɔpfərn] *vt* to sacrifice ♦ *vr* to sacrifice o.s.

aufopfernd *adj* selfless.

aufpassen ['aʊfpasən] *vi* (*aufmerksam sein*) to pay attention; **auf jdn/etw ~** to look after *od* watch sb/sth; **aufgepaßt!** look out!

Aufpasser(in) (-s, -) (*pej*) *m(f)* (*Aufseher, Spitzel*) spy, watchdog; (*Beobachter*) supervisor; (*Wächter*) guard.

aufpflanzen ['aʊfpflantsən] *vr:* **sich vor jdm ~** to plant o.s. in front of sb.

aufplatzen ['aʊfplatsən] *vi* to burst open.

aufplustern ['aʊfpluːstərn] *vr* (*Vogel*) to ruffle (up) its feathers; (*Mensch*) to puff o.s. up.

aufprägen ['aʊfprɛːgən] *vt:* **jdm/etw seinen Stempel ~** (*fig*) to leave one's mark on sb/ sth.

Aufprall ['aʊfpral] (-(e)s, -e) *m* impact.

aufprallen *vi* to hit, strike.

Aufpreis ['aʊfpraɪs] *m* extra charge.

aufpumpen ['aʊfpʊmpən] *vt* to pump up.

aufputschen ['aʊfpʊtʃən] *vt* (*aufhetzen*) to inflame; (*erregen*) to stimulate.

Aufputschmittel *nt* stimulant.

aufraffen ['aʊfrafən] *vr* to rouse o.s.

aufräumen ['aʊfrɔʏmən] *vt, vi* (*Dinge*) to clear

away; (*Zimmer*) to tidy up.

Aufräumungsarbeiten *pl* clearing-up operations *pl*.

aufrecht ['aʊfrɛçt] *adj* (*lit, fig*) upright.

aufrechterhalten *unreg vt* to maintain.

aufregen ['aʊfreːgən] *vt* to excite; (*ärgerlich machen*) to irritate, annoy; (*nervös machen*) to make nervous; (*beunruhigen*) to disturb ♦ *vr* to get excited.

aufregend *adj* exciting.

Aufregung *f* excitement.

aufreiben ['aʊfraɪbən] *unreg vt* (*Haut*) to rub raw; (*erschöpfen*) to exhaust; (*MIL: völlig vernichten*) to wipe out, annihilate.

aufreibend *adj* strenuous.

aufreihen ['aʊfraɪən] *vt* (*in Linie*) to line up; (*Perlen*) to string.

aufreißen ['aʊfraɪsən] *unreg vt* (*Umschlag*) to tear open; (*Augen*) to open wide; (*Tür*) to throw open; (*Straße*) to take up; (*umg: Mädchen*) to pick up.

Aufreißer (-s, -) *m* (*Person*) smooth operator.

aufreizen ['aʊfraɪtsən] *vt* to incite, stir up.

aufreizend *adj* exciting, stimulating.

aufrichten ['aʊfrɪçtən] *vt* to put up, erect; (*moralisch*) to console ♦ *vr* to rise; (*moralisch*): **sich ~ (an** +*dat*) to take heart (from); **sich im Bett ~** to sit up in bed.

aufrichtig ['aʊfrɪçtɪç] *adj* sincere; honest; **A~keit** *f* sincerity.

aufrollen ['aʊfrɔlən] *vt* (*zusammenrollen*) to roll up; (*Kabel*) to coil *od* wind up; **einen Fall/Prozeß wieder ~** to reopen a case/trial.

aufrücken ['aʊfrʏkən] *vi* to move up; (*beruflich*) to be promoted.

Aufruf ['aʊfruːf] *m* summons; (*zur Hilfe*) call; (*des Namens*) calling out.

aufrufen *unreg vt* (*Namen*) to call out; (*auffordern*): **jdn ~ (zu)** to call upon sb (for); **einen Schüler ~** to ask a pupil (to answer) a question.

Aufruhr ['aʊfruːr] (-(e)s, -e) *m* uprising, revolt; **in ~ sein** to be in uproar.

Aufrührer(in) (-s, -) *m(f)* rabble-rouser.

aufrührerisch ['aʊfryːrərɪʃ] *adj* rebellious.

aufrunden ['aʊfrʊndən] *vt* (*Summe*) to round up.

aufrüsten ['aʊfrʏstən] *vt, vi* to arm.

Aufrüstung *f* rearmament.

aufrütteln ['aʊfrʏtəln] *vt* (*lit, fig*) to shake up.

aufs [aʊfs] = **auf das**.

aufsagen ['aʊfzaːgən] *vt* (*Gedicht*) to recite; (*geh: Freundschaft*) to put an end to.

aufsammeln ['aʊfzaməln] *vt* to gather up.

aufsässig ['aʊfzɛsɪç] *adj* rebellious.

Aufsatz ['aʊfzats] *m* (*Geschriebenes*) essay, composition; (*auf Schrank etc*) top.

aufsaugen ['aʊfzaʊgən] *unreg vt* to soak up.

aufschauen ['aʊfʃaʊən] *vi* to look up.

aufscheuchen ['aʊfʃɔʏçən] *vt* to scare, startle.

aufschichten ['aʊfʃɪçtən] *vt* to stack, pile up.

aufschieben ['aʊfʃiːbən] *unreg vt* to push open; (*verzögern*) to put off, postpone.

Aufschlag ['aʊfʃlaːk] *m* (*Ärmel~*) cuff; (*Jacken~*) lapel; (*Hosen~*) turn-up (*BRIT*), cuff (*US*); (*Aufprall*) impact; (*Preis~*) surcharge; (*TENNIS*) service.

aufschlagen ['aʊfʃlaːgən] *unreg vt* (*öffnen*) to open; (*verwunden*) to cut; (*hochschlagen*) to turn up; (*aufbauen: Zelt, Lager*) to pitch, erect; (*Wohnsitz*) to take up ♦ *vi* (*aufprallen*) to hit; (*teurer werden*) to go up; (*TENNIS*) to serve; **schlagt Seite 111 auf** open your books at page 111.

aufschließen ['aʊfʃliːsən] *unreg vt* to open up, unlock ♦ *vi* (*aufrücken*) to close up.

Aufschluß ['aʊfʃlʊs] *m* information.

aufschlüsseln ['aʊfʃlʏsəln] *vt*: ~ (**nach**) to break down (into); (*klassifizieren*) to classify (according to).

aufschlußreich *adj* informative, illuminating.

aufschnappen ['aʊfʃnapən] *vt* (*umg*) to pick up ♦ *vi* to fly open.

aufschneiden ['aʊfʃnaɪdən] *unreg vt* to cut open; (*Brot*) to cut up; (*MED: Geschwür*) to lance ♦ *vi* (*umg*) to brag.

Aufschneider (**-s, -**) *m* boaster, braggart.

Aufschnitt ['aʊfʃnɪt] *m* (slices of) cold meat.

aufschnüren ['aʊfʃnyːrən] *vt* to unlace; (*Paket*) to untie.

aufschrauben ['aʊfʃraʊbən] *vt* (*fest~*) to screw on; (*lösen*) to unscrew.

aufschrecken ['aʊfʃrɛkən] *vt* to startle ♦ *vi* (*unreg*) to start up.

Aufschrei ['aʊfʃraɪ] *m* cry.

aufschreiben ['aʊfʃraɪbən] *unreg vt* to write down.

aufschreien *unreg vi* to cry out.

Aufschrift ['aʊfʃrɪft] *f* (*Inschrift*) inscription; (*Etikett*) label.

Aufschub ['aʊfʃuːp] (**-(e)s, -schübe**) *m* delay, postponement; **jdm** ~ **gewähren** to grant sb an extension.

aufschürfen ['aʊfʃʏrfən] *vt*: **sich** *dat* **die Haut/ das Knie** ~ to graze *od* scrape o.s./one's knee.

aufschütten ['aʊfʃʏtən] *vt* (*Flüssigkeit*) to pour on; (*Kohle*) to put on (the fire); (*Damm, Deich*) to throw up; **Kaffee** ~ to make coffee.

aufschwatzen ['aʊfʃvatsən] (*umg*) *vt*: **jdm etw** ~ to talk sb into (getting/having etc) sth.

Aufschwung ['aʊfʃvʊŋ] *m* (*Elan*) boost; (*wirtschaftlich*) upturn, boom; (*SPORT: an Gerät*) mount.

aufsehen ['aʊfzeːən] *unreg vi* to look up; ~ **zu** (*lit*) to look up at; (*fig*) to look up to; **A~** (**-s**) *nt* sensation, stir.

aufsehenerregend *adj* sensational.

Aufseher(in) (**-s, -**) *m(f)* guard; (*im Betrieb*) supervisor; (*Museums~*) attendant; (*Park~*) keeper.

aufsein ['aʊfzaɪn] *unreg* (*umg*) *vi* to be open;

(*Person*) to be up.

aufsetzen ['aʊfzɛtsən] *vt* to put on; (*Flugzeug*) to put down; (*Dokument*) to draw up ♦ *vr* to sit upright ♦ *vi* (*Flugzeug*) to touch down.

Aufsicht ['aʊfzɪçt] *f* supervision; **die** ~ **haben** to be in charge; **bei einer Prüfung** ~ **führen** to invigilate (*BRIT*) *od* supervise an exam.

Aufsichtsrat *m* board (of directors).

aufsitzen ['aʊfzɪtsən] *unreg vi* (*aufgerichtet sitzen*) to sit up; (*aufs Pferd, Motorrad*) to mount, get on; (*Schiff*) to run aground; **jdn** ~ **lassen** (*umg*) to stand sb up; **jdm** ~ (*umg*) to be taken in by sb.

aufspalten ['aʊfʃpaltən] *vt* to split.

aufspannen ['aʊfʃpanən] *vt* (*Netz, Sprungtuch*) to stretch *od* spread out; (*Schirm*) to put up, open.

aufsparen ['aʊfʃpaːrən] *vt* to save (up).

aufsperren ['aʊfʃpɛrən] *vt* to unlock; (*Mund*) to open wide; **die Ohren** ~ (*umg*) to prick up one's ears.

aufspielen ['aʊfʃpiːlən] *vr* to show off; **sich als etw** ~ to try to come on as sth.

aufspießen ['aʊfʃpiːsən] *vt* to spear.

aufspringen ['aʊfʃprɪŋən] *unreg vi* (*hochspringen*) to jump up; (*sich öffnen*) to spring open; (*Hände, Lippen*) to become chapped; ~ **auf** *+akk* to jump onto.

aufspüren ['aʊfʃpyːrən] *vt* to track down, trace.

aufstacheln ['aʊfʃtaxəln] *vt* to incite.

aufstampfen ['aʊfʃtampfən] *vi*: **mit dem Fuß** ~ to stamp one's foot.

Aufstand ['aʊfʃtant] *m* insurrection, rebellion.

aufständisch ['aʊfʃtɛndɪʃ] *adj* rebellious, mutinous.

aufstauen ['aʊfʃtaʊən] *vr* to collect; (*fig: Ärger*) to be bottled up.

aufstechen ['aʊfʃtɛçən] *unreg vt* to prick open, puncture.

aufstecken ['aʊfʃtɛkən] *vt* to stick on; (*mit Nadeln*) to pin up; (*umg*) to give up.

aufstehen ['aʊfʃteːən] *unreg vi* to get up; (*Tür*) to be open; **da mußt du früher** *od* **eher** ~! (*fig: umg*) you'll have to do better than that!

aufsteigen ['aʊfʃtaɪgən] *unreg vi* (*hochsteigen*) to climb; (*Rauch*) to rise; ~ **auf** *+akk* to get onto; **in jdm** ~ (*Haß, Verdacht, Erinnerung etc*) to well up in sb.

Aufsteiger (**-s,**) *m* (*SPORT*) promoted team; (**sozialer**) ~ social climber.

aufstellen ['aʊfʃtɛlən] *vt* (*aufrecht stellen*) to put up; (*Maschine*) to install; (*aufreihen*) to line up; (*Kandidaten*) to nominate; (*Forderung, Behauptung*) to put forward; (*formulieren: Programm etc*) to draw up; (*leisten: Rekord*) to set up.

Aufstellung *f* (*SPORT*) line-up; (*Liste*) list.

Aufstieg ['aʊfʃtiːk] (**-(e)s, -e**) *m* (*auf Berg*) ascent; (*Fortschritt*) rise; (*beruflich, SPORT*) promotion.

Aufstiegschance f prospect of promotion.
aufstöbern ['aufʃtøːbərn] vt (Wild) to start, flush; (umg: entdecken) to run to earth.
aufstocken ['aufʃtɔkən] vt (Vorräte) to build up.
aufstoßen ['aufʃtoːsən] unreg vt to push open ♦ vi to belch.
aufstrebend ['aufʃtreːbənd] adj ambitious; (Land) striving for progress.
Aufstrich ['aufʃtrɪç] m spread.
aufstülpen ['aufʃtʏlpən] vt (Ärmel) to turn up; (Hut) to put on.
aufstützen ['aufʃtʏtsən] vt (Körperteil) to prop, lean; (Person) to prop up ♦ vr: **sich ~ auf** +akk to lean on.
aufsuchen ['aufzuːxən] vt (besuchen) to visit; (konsultieren) to consult.
auftakeln ['auftaːkəln] vt (NAUT) to rig (out) ♦ vr (pej: umg) to deck o.s. out.
Auftakt ['auftakt] m (MUS) upbeat; (fig) prelude.
auftanken ['auftaŋkən] vi to get petrol (BRIT) od gas (US) ♦ vt to refuel.
auftauchen ['auftauxən] vi to appear; (gefunden werden, kommen) to turn up; (aus Wasser etc) to emerge; (U-Boot) to surface; (Zweifel) to arise.
auftauen ['auftauən] vt to thaw ♦ vi to thaw; (fig) to relax.
aufteilen ['auftailən] vt to divide up; (Raum) to partition.
Aufteilung f division; partition.
auftischen ['auftɪʃən] vt to serve (up); (fig) to tell.
Auftr. abk = **Auftrag**.
Auftrag ['auftraːk] (-(e)s, -träge) m order; (Anweisung) commission; (Aufgabe) mission; **etw in ~ geben (bei)** to order/commission sth (from); **im ~ von** on behalf of; **im ~ od i.A. J. Burnett** pp J. Burnett.
auftragen ['auftraːgən] unreg vt (Essen) to serve; (Farbe) to put on; (Kleidung) to wear out ♦ vi (dick machen): **die Jacke trägt auf** the jacket makes one look fat; **jdm etw ~** to tell sb sth; **dick ~** (umg) to exaggerate.
Auftraggeber(in) (-s, -) m(f) client; (COMM) customer.
Auftragsbestätigung f confirmation of order.
auftreiben ['auftraibən] unreg (umg) vt (beschaffen) to raise.
auftrennen ['auftrɛnən] vt to undo.
auftreten ['auftreːtən] unreg vt to kick open ♦ vi to appear; (mit Füßen) to tread; (sich verhalten) to behave; (fig: eintreten) to occur; (Schwierigkeiten etc) to arise; **als Vermittler** etc ~ to act as intermediary etc; **geschlossen ~** to put up a united front.
Auftreten (-s) nt (Vorkommen) appearance; (Benehmen) behaviour (BRIT), behavior (US).
Auftrieb ['auftriːp] m (PHYS) buoyancy, lift; (fig) impetus.

Auftritt ['auftrɪt] m (des Schauspielers) entrance; (lit, fig: Szene) scene.
auftrumpfen ['auftrumpfən] vi to show how good one is; (mit Bemerkung) to crow.
auftun ['auftuːn] unreg vt to open ♦ vr to open up.
auftürmen ['auftʏrmən] vr (Gebirge etc) to tower up; (Schwierigkeiten) to pile od mount up.
aufwachen ['aufvaxən] vi to wake up.
aufwachsen ['aufvaksən] unreg vi to grow up.
Aufwand ['aufvant] (-(e)s) m expenditure; (Kosten) expense; (Luxus) show; **bitte, keinen ~!** please don't go out of your way.
Aufwandsentschädigung f expense allowance.
aufwärmen ['aufvɛrmən] vt to warm up; (alte Geschichten) to rake up.
aufwarten ['aufvartən] vi (zu bieten haben): **mit etw ~** to offer sth.
aufwärts ['aufvɛrts] adv upwards; **A~entwicklung** f upward trend; **~gehen** unreg vi to look up.
aufwecken ['aufvɛkən] vt to wake(n) up.
aufweichen ['aufvaiçən] vt to soften; (Brot) to soak.
aufweisen ['aufvaizən] unreg vt to show.
aufwenden ['aufvɛndən] unreg vt to expend; (Geld) to spend; (Sorgfalt) to devote.
aufwendig adj costly.
aufwerfen ['aufvɛrfən] unreg vt (Fenster etc) to throw open; (Probleme) to throw up, raise ♦ vr: **sich zu etw ~** to make o.s. out to be sth.
aufwerten ['aufvɛrtən] vt (FIN) to revalue; (fig) to raise in value.
Aufwertung f revaluation.
aufwickeln ['aufvɪkəln] vt (aufrollen) to roll up; (umg: Haar) to put in curlers; (lösen) to untie.
aufwiegeln ['aufviːgəln] vt to stir up, incite.
aufwiegen ['aufviːgən] unreg vt to make up for.
Aufwind ['aufvɪnt] m up-current; **neuen ~ bekommen** (fig) to get new impetus.
aufwirbeln ['aufvɪrbəln] vt to whirl up; **Staub ~** (fig) to create a stir.
aufwischen ['aufvɪʃən] vt to wipe up.
aufwühlen ['aufvyːlən] vt (lit: Erde, Meer) to churn (up); (Gefühle) to stir.
aufzählen ['auftsɛːlən] vt to count out.
aufzeichnen ['auftsaiçnən] vt to sketch; (schriftlich) to jot down; (auf Band) to record.
Aufzeichnung f (schriftlich) note; (Tonband~, Film~) recording.
aufzeigen ['auftsaigən] vt to show, demonstrate.
aufziehen ['auftsiːən] unreg vt (hochziehen) to raise, draw up; (öffnen) to pull open; (: Reißverschluß) to undo; (Gardinen) to draw (back); (Uhr) to wind; (großziehen: Kinder) to raise, bring up; (Tiere) to rear; (umg: necken) to tease; (: veranstalten) to set up; (: Fest) to arrange ♦ vi (Gewitter, Wolken) to gather.

Aufzucht ['aʊftsʊxt] *f (das Großziehen)* rearing, raising.

Aufzug ['aʊftsuːk] *m (Fahrstuhl)* lift *(BRIT)*, elevator *(US)*; *(Aufmarsch)* procession, parade; *(Kleidung)* get-up; *(THEAT)* act.

aufzwingen ['aʊftsvɪŋən] *unreg vt:* **jdm etw ~** to force sth upon sb.

Aug. *abk (= August)* Aug.

Augapfel ['aʊk|apfəl] *m* eyeball; *(fig)* apple of one's eye.

Auge ['aʊɡə] **(-s, -n)** *nt* eye; *(Fett~)* globule of fat; **unter vier ~n** in private; **vor aller ~n** in front of everybody, for all to see; **jdn/etw mit anderen ~n (an)sehen** to see sb/sth in a different light; **ich habe kein ~ zugetan** I didn't sleep a wink; **ein ~/beide ~n zudrücken** *(umg)* to turn a blind eye; **jdn/etw aus den ~n verlieren** to lose sight of sb/sth; *(fig)* to lose touch with sb/sth; **etw ins ~ fassen** to contemplate sth; **das kann leicht ins ~ gehen** *(fig: umg)* it might easily go wrong.

Augenarzt *m* eye specialist, ophthalmologist.

Augenblick *m* moment; **im ~** at the moment; **im ersten ~** for a moment; **a~lich** *adj (sofort)* instantaneous; *(gegenwärtig)* present.

Augen- *zW:* **~braue** *f* eyebrow; **~höhe** *f:* **in ~höhe** at eye level; **~merk** *nt (Aufmerksamkeit)* attention; **~schein** *m:* **jdn/etw in ~schein nehmen** to have a close look at sb/sth; **a~scheinlich** *adj* obvious; **~weide** *f* sight for sore eyes; **~wischerei** *f (fig)* eye-wash; **~zeuge** *m* eye witness; **~zeugin** *f* eye witness.

August [aʊ'ɡʊst] **(-(e)s** *od* **-, -e)** *(pl selten) m* August; *siehe auch* **September.**

Auktion [aʊktsi'oːn] *f* auction.

Auktionator [aʊktsio'naːtɔr] *m* auctioneer.

Aula ['aʊla] **(-, Aulen** *od* **-s)** *f* assembly hall.

Aus [aʊs] **(-)** *nt (SPORT)* outfield; **ins ~ gehen** to go out.

════════════ *SCHLÜSSELWORT* ════════════

aus [aʊs] *präp +dat* **1** *(räumlich)* out of; *(von ... her)* from; **er ist ~ Berlin** he's from Berlin; **~ dem Fenster** out of the window

2 *(gemacht/hergestellt ~)* made of; **ein Herz ~ Stein** a heart of stone

3 *(auf Ursache deutend)* out of; **~ Mitleid** out of sympathy; **~ Erfahrung** from experience; **~ Spaß** for fun

4: ~ ihr wird nie etwas she'll never get anywhere

♦ *adv* **1** *(zu Ende)* finished, over; **~ und vorbei** over and done with

2 *(ausgeschaltet, ausgezogen)* off; **Licht ~!** lights out!

3 *(in Verbindung mit von)*: **von Rom ~** from Rome; **vom Fenster ~** out of the window; **von sich ~** *(selbständig)* of one's own accord; **von mir ~** as far as I'm concerned

4 ~ und ein gehen to come and go; *(bei jdm)* to visit frequently; **weder ~ noch ein wissen** to be at one's wits' end; **auf etw** *akk* **~ sein** to be after sth.

ausarbeiten ['aʊs|arbaɪtən] *vt* to work out.

ausarten ['aʊs|artən] *vi* to degenerate; *(Kind)* to become overexcited.

ausatmen ['aʊs|aːtmən] *vi* to breathe out.

ausbaden ['aʊsbaːdən] *(umg) vt:* **etw ~ müssen** to carry the can for sth.

Ausbau ['aʊsbaʊ] *m* extension, expansion; removal.

ausbauen *vt* to extend, expand; *(herausnehmen)* to take out, remove.

ausbaufähig *adj (fig)* worth developing.

ausbedingen ['aʊsbədɪŋən] *unreg vt:* **sich** *dat* **etw ~** to insist on sth.

ausbeißen ['aʊsbaɪsən] *unreg vr:* **sich** *dat* **an etw** *dat* **die Zähne ~** *(fig)* to have a tough time of it with sth.

ausbessern ['aʊsbɛsərn] *vt* to mend, repair.

Ausbesserungsarbeiten *pl* repair work *sing*.

ausbeulen ['aʊsbɔylən] *vt* to beat out.

Ausbeute ['aʊsbɔytə] *f* yield; *(Gewinn)* profit, gain; *(Fische)* catch.

ausbeuten *vt* to exploit; *(MIN)* to work.

ausbezahlen ['aʊsbətsaːlən] *vt (Geld)* to pay out.

ausbilden ['aʊsbɪldən] *vt* to educate; *(Lehrling, Soldat)* to instruct, train; *(Fähigkeiten)* to develop; *(Geschmack)* to cultivate.

Ausbilder(in) **(-s, -)** *m(f)* instructor, instructress.

Ausbildung *f* education; training; instruction; development; cultivation; **er ist noch in der ~** he's still a trainee; he hasn't finished his education.

Ausbildungs- *zW:* **~förderung** *f* (provision of) grants for students and trainees; *(Stipendium)* grant; **~platz** *m (Stelle)* training vacancy.

ausbitten ['aʊsbɪtən] *unreg vt:* **sich** *dat* **etw ~** *(geh: erbitten)* to ask for sth; *(verlangen)* to insist on sth.

ausblasen ['aʊsblaːzən] *unreg vt* to blow out; *(Ei)* to blow.

ausbleiben ['aʊsblaɪbən] *unreg vi (Personen)* to stay away, not come; *(Ereignisse)* to fail to happen, not happen; **es konnte nicht ~, daß** ... it was inevitable that ...

ausblenden ['aʊsblɛndən] *vt, vi (TV etc)* to fade out.

Ausblick ['aʊsblɪk] *m (lit, fig)* prospect, outlook, view.

ausbomben ['aʊsbɔmbən] *vt* to bomb out.

ausbooten ['aʊsboːtən] *(umg) vt (jdn)* to kick *od* boot out.

ausbrechen ['aʊsbrɛçən] *unreg vi* to break out ♦ *vt* to break off; **in Tränen/Gelächter ~** to burst into tears/out laughing.

Ausbrecher(in) **(-s, -)** *(umg) m(f) (Gefangener)*

escaped prisoner, escapee.
ausbreiten ['aʊsbraɪtən] *vt* to spread (out);
(*Arme*) to stretch out ♦ *vr* to spread; **sich
über ein Thema** ~ to expand *od* enlarge on a
topic.
ausbrennen ['aʊsbrɛnən] *unreg vt* to scorch;
(*Wunde*) to cauterize ♦ *vi* to burn out.
ausbringen ['aʊsbrɪŋən] *unreg vt* (*ein Hoch*) to
propose.
Ausbruch ['aʊsbrʊx] *m* outbreak; (*von Vulkan*)
eruption; (*Gefühls~*) outburst; (*von
Gefangenen*) escape.
ausbrüten ['aʊsbryːtən] *vt* (*lit, fig*) to hatch.
Ausbuchtung ['aʊsbʊxtʊŋ] *f* bulge; (*Küste*)
cove.
ausbügeln ['aʊsbyːgəln] *vt* to iron out; (*umg:
Fehler, Verlust*) to make good.
ausbuhen ['aʊsbuːən] *vt* to boo.
Ausbund ['aʊsbʊnt] *m:* **ein** ~ **an** *od* **von
Tugend/Sparsamkeit** a paragon of virtue/a
model of thrift.
ausbürgern ['aʊsbyrgərn] *vt* to expatriate.
ausbürsten ['aʊsbyrstən] *vt* to brush out.
Ausdauer ['aʊsdaʊər] *f* stamina;
(*Beharrlichkeit*) perseverance.
ausdauernd *adj* persevering.
ausdehnen ['aʊsdeːnən] *vt, vr* (*räumlich*) to
expand; (*zeitlich, auch Gummi*) to stretch;
(*Nebel, fig: Macht*) to extend.
ausdenken ['aʊsdɛŋkən] *unreg vt* (*zu Ende
denken*) to think through; **sich** *dat* **etw** ~ to
think sth up; **das ist nicht auszudenken**
(*unvorstellbar*) it's inconceivable.
ausdiskutieren ['aʊsdɪskutiːrən] *vt* to talk out.
ausdrehen ['aʊsdreːən] *vt* to turn *od* switch
off.
Ausdruck ['aʊsdrʊk] (**-s, -drücke**) *m*
expression, phrase; (*Kundgabe, Gesichts~*)
expression; (*Fach~*) term; (*COMPUT*) hard
copy; **mit dem** ~ **des Bedauerns** (*form*)
expressing regret.
ausdrucken *vt* (*Text*) to print out.
ausdrücken ['aʊsdrykən] *vt* (*auch vr:
formulieren, zeigen*) to express; (*Zigarette*) to
put out; (*Zitrone*) to squeeze.
ausdrücklich *adj* express, explicit.
Ausdrucks- *zW:* ~**fähigkeit** *f* expressiveness;
(*Gewandtheit*) articulateness; **a~los** *adj*
expressionless, blank; **a~voll** *adj*
expressive; ~**weise** *f* mode of expression.
Ausdünstung ['aʊsdynstʊŋ] *f* (*Dampf*) vapour
(*BRIT*), vapor (*US*); (*Geruch*) smell.
auseinander [aʊsʔaɪˈnandər] *adv* (*getrennt*)
apart; **weit** ~ far apart; ~ **schreiben** to
write as separate words; ~**bringen** *unreg vt* to
separate; ~**fallen** *unreg vi* to fall apart;
~**gehen** *unreg vi* (*Menschen*) to separate;
(*Meinungen*) to differ; (*Gegenstand*) to fall
apart; (*umg: dick werden*) to put on weight;
~**halten** *unreg vt* to tell apart; ~**klaffen** *vi* to
gape open; (*fig: Meinungen*) to be far apart,
diverge (wildly); ~**laufen** *unreg* (*umg*) *vi* (*sich*

trennen) to break up; (*Menge*) to disperse;
~**leben** *vr* to drift apart; ~**nehmen** *unreg vt* to
take to pieces, dismantle; ~**setzen** *vt*
(*erklären*) to set forth, explain ♦ *vr* (*sich
verständigen*) to come to terms, settle; (*sich
befassen*) to concern o.s.; **sich mit jdm
~setzen** to talk with sb; (*sich streiten*) to
argue with sb; **A~setzung** *f* argument.
auserkoren ['aʊsʔɛrkoːrən] *adj* (*liter*) chosen,
selected.
auserlesen ['aʊsʔɛrleːzən] *adj* select, choice.
ausersehen ['aʊsʔɛrzeːən] *unreg vt* (*geh*): **dazu
~ sein, etw zu tun** to be chosen to do sth.
ausfahrbar *adj* extendable; (*Antenne,
Fahrgestell*) retractable.
ausfahren ['aʊsfaːrən] *unreg vi* to drive out;
(*NAUT*) to put out (to sea) ♦ *vt* to take out;
(*AUT*) to drive flat out; (*ausliefern: Waren*) to
deliver; **ausgefahrene Wege** rutted roads.
Ausfahrt *f* (*des Zuges etc*) leaving,
departure; (*Autobahn~, Garagen~*) exit, way
out; (*Spazierfahrt*) drive, excursion.
Ausfall ['aʊsfal] *m* loss; (*Nichtstattfinden*)
cancellation; (*das Versagen: TECH, MED*)
failure; (*von Motor*) breakdown;
(*Produktionsstörung*) stoppage; (*MIL*) sortie;
(*Fechten*) lunge; (*radioaktiv*) fallout.
ausfallen ['aʊsfalən] *unreg vi* (*Zähne, Haare*) to
fall *od* come out; (*nicht stattfinden*) to be
cancelled; (*wegbleiben*) to be omitted;
(*Person*) to drop out; (*Lohn*) to be stopped;
(*nicht funktionieren*) to break down; (*Resultat
haben*) to turn out; **wie ist das Spiel
ausgefallen?** what was the result of the
game?; **die Schule fällt morgen aus** there's
no school tomorrow.
ausfallend *adj* impertinent.
Ausfallstraße *f* arterial road.
Ausfallzeit *f* (*Maschine*) downtime.
ausfegen ['aʊsfeːgən] *vt* to sweep out.
ausfeilen ['aʊsfaɪlən] *vt* to file out; (*Stil*) to
polish up.
ausfertigen ['aʊsfɛrtɪgən] *vt* (*form*) to draw
up; (*Rechnung*) to make out; **doppelt** ~ to
duplicate.
Ausfertigung *f* (*form*) drawing up; making
out; (*Exemplar*) copy; **in doppelter/dreifacher
~** in duplicate/triplicate.
ausfindig ['aʊsfɪndɪç] *adj:* ~ **machen** to
discover.
ausfliegen ['aʊsfliːgən] *unreg vi* to fly away ♦ *vt*
to fly out; **sie sind ausgeflogen** (*umg*) they're
out.
ausfließen ['aʊsfliːsən] *unreg vi:* ~ (**aus**)
(*herausfließen*) to flow out (of); (*auslaufen: Öl
etc*) to leak (out of); (*Eiter etc*) to be
discharged (from).
ausflippen ['aʊsflɪpən] (*umg*) *vi* to freak out.
Ausflucht ['aʊsflʊxt] (**-, -flüchte**) *f* excuse.
Ausflug ['aʊsfluːk] *m* excursion, outing.
Ausflügler(in) ['aʊsflyːklər(ɪn)] (**-s, -**) *m(f)*
tripper (*BRIT*), excursionist (*US*).

Ausfluß ['aʊsflʊs] *m* outlet; (*MED*) discharge.
ausfragen ['aʊsfraːgən] *vt* to interrogate, question.
ausfransen ['aʊsfranzən] *vi* to fray.
ausfressen ['aʊsfrɛsən] *unreg* (*umg*) *vt* (*anstellen*) to be up to.
Ausfuhr ['aʊsfuːr] (-, -en) *f* export, exportation; (*Ware*) export ♦ *in zW* export.
ausführbar ['aʊsfyːrbaːr] *adj* feasible; (*COMM*) exportable.
ausführen ['aʊsfyːrən] *vt* (*verwirklichen*) to carry out; (*Person*) to take out; (*Hund*) to take for a walk; (*COMM*) to export; (*erklären*) to give details of; **die ~de Gewalt** (*POL*) the executive.
Ausfuhrgenehmigung *f* export licence.
ausführlich *adj* detailed ♦ *adv* in detail; **A~keit** *f* detail.
Ausführung *f* execution, performance; (*von Waren*) design; (*von Thema*) exposition; (*Durchführung*) completion; (*Herstellungsart*) version; (*Erklärung*) explanation.
Ausfuhrzoll *m* export duty.
ausfüllen ['aʊsfylən] *vt* to fill up; (*Fragebogen etc*) to fill in; (*Beruf*) to be fulfilling for; **jdn (ganz) ~** (*Zeit in Anspruch nehmen*) to take (all) sb's time.
Ausg. *abk* (= *Ausgabe*) ed.
Ausgabe ['aʊsgaːbə] *f* (*Geld*) expenditure, outlay; (*Aushändigung*) giving out; (*Schalter*) counter; (*Ausführung*) version; (*Buch*) edition; (*Nummer*) issue.
Ausgang ['aʊsgaŋ] *m* way out, exit; (*Ende*) end; (~*spunkt*) starting point; (*Ergebnis*) result; (*Ausgehtag*) free time, time off; **ein Unfall mit tödlichem ~** a fatal accident; **kein ~** no exit.
Ausgangs- *zW*: **~basis** *f* starting point; **~punkt** *m* starting point; **~sperre** *f* curfew.
ausgeben ['aʊsgeːbən] *unreg vt* (*Geld*) to spend; (*austeilen*) to issue, distribute; (*COMPUT*) to output ♦ *vr*: **sich für etw/jdn ~** to pass o.s. off as sth/sb; **ich gebe heute abend einen aus** (*umg*) it's my treat this evening.
ausgebeult ['aʊsgəbɔylt] *adj* (*Kleidung*) baggy; (*Hut*) battered.
ausgebucht ['aʊsgəbuːxt] *adj* fully booked ♦
Ausgeburt ['aʊsgəbuːrt] (*pej*) *f* (*der Phantasie etc*) monstrous product *od* invention.
ausgedehnt ['aʊsgədeːnt] *adj* (*breit, groß, fig: weitreichend*) extensive; (*Spaziergang*) long; (*zeitlich*) lengthy.
ausgedient ['aʊsgədiːnt] *adj* (*Soldat*) discharged; (*verbraucht*) no longer in use; **~ haben** to have come to the end of its useful life.
ausgefallen ['aʊsgəfalən] *adj* (*ungewöhnlich*) exceptional.
ausgefuchst ['aʊsgəfʊkst] (*umg*) *adj* clever; (: *listig*) crafty.
ausgegangen ['aʊsgəgaŋən] *pp von* **ausgehen.**
ausgeglichen ['aʊsgəglɪçən] *adj* (well-)bal-

anced; **A~heit** *f* balance; (*von Mensch*) even-temperedness.
Ausgehanzug *m* good suit.
ausgehen ['aʊsgeːən] *unreg vi* (*auch Feuer, Ofen, Licht*) to go out; (*zu Ende gehen*) to come to an end; (*Benzin*) to run out; (*Haare, Zähne*) to fall *od* come out; (*Strom*) to go off; (*Resultat haben*) to turn out; (*spazierengehen*) to go (out) for a walk; (*abgeschickt werden: Post*) to be sent off; **mir ging das Benzin aus** I ran out of petrol (*BRIT*) *od* gas (*US*); **auf etw** *akk* **~** to aim at sth; **von etw ~** (*wegführen*) to lead away from sth; (*herrühren*) to come from sth; (*zugrunde legen*) to proceed from sth; **wir können davon ~, daß ...** we can proceed from the assumption that ..., we can take as our starting point that ...; **leer ~** to get nothing; **schlecht ~** to turn out badly.
ausgehungert ['aʊsgəhʊŋərt] *adj* starved; (*abgezehrt: Mensch etc*) emaciated.
Ausgehverbot *nt* curfew.
ausgeklügelt ['aʊsgəklyːgəlt] *adj* ingenious.
ausgekocht ['aʊsgəkɔxt] (*pej: umg*) *adj* (*durchtrieben*) cunning; (*fig*) out-and-out.
ausgelassen ['aʊsgəlasən] *adj* boisterous, high-spirited, exuberant; **A~heit** *f* boisterousness, high spirits *pl*, exuberance.
ausgelastet ['aʊsgəlastət] *adj* fully occupied.
ausgeleiert ['aʊsgəlaɪərt] *adj* worn; (*Gummiband*) stretched.
ausgelernt ['aʊsgəlɛrnt] *adj* trained, qualified.
ausgemacht ['aʊsgəmaxt] *adj* settled; (*umg: Dummkopf etc*) out-and-out, downright; **es gilt als ~, daß ...** it is settled that ...; **es war eine ~e Sache, daß ...** it was a foregone conclusion that ...
ausgemergelt ['aʊsgəmɛrgəlt] *adj* (*Gesicht*) emaciated, gaunt.
ausgenommen ['aʊsgənɔmən] *konj* except; **Anwesende sind ~** present company excepted.
ausgepowert ['aʊsgəpoːvərt] *adj*: **~ sein** (*umg*) to be tired, be exhausted.
ausgeprägt ['aʊsgəprɛːkt] *adj* prominent; (*Eigenschaft*) distinct.
ausgerechnet ['aʊsgərɛçnət] *adv* just, precisely; **~ du** you of all people; **~ heute** today of all days.
ausgeschlossen ['aʊsgəʃlɔsən] *pp von* **ausschließen** ♦ *adj* (*unmöglich*) impossible, out of the question; **es ist nicht ~, daß ...** it cannot be ruled out that ...
ausgeschnitten ['aʊsgəʃnɪtən] *adj* (*Kleid*) low-necked.
ausgesehen ['aʊsgəzeːən] *pp von* **aussehen.**
ausgesprochen ['aʊsgəʃprɔxən] *adj* (*Faulheit, Lüge etc*) out-and-out; (*unverkennbar*) marked ♦ *adv* decidedly.
ausgestorben ['aʊsgəʃtɔrbən] *adj* (*Tierart*) extinct; (*fig*) deserted.
ausgewogen ['aʊsgəvoːgən] *adj* balanced; (*Maß*) equal.

ausgezeichnet ['aʊsgətsaɪçnət] *adj* excellent.
ausgiebig ['aʊsgiːbɪç] *adj (Gebrauch)* full,
good; *(Essen)* generous, lavish; ~ **schlafen** to
have a good sleep.
ausgießen ['aʊsgiːsən] *unreg vt (aus einem
Behälter)* to pour out; *(Behälter)* to empty;
(weggießen) to pour away.
Ausgleich ['aʊsglaɪç] *(-(e)s, -e)* m balance;
(von Fehler, Mangel) compensation; *(SPORT)*:
den ~ erzielen to equalize; **zum ~** +*gen* in
order to offset sth; **das ist ein guter ~**
(entspannend) that's very relaxing.
ausgleichen ['aʊsglaɪçən] *unreg vt* to balance
(out); *(Konflikte)* to reconcile; *(Höhe)* to even
up ♦ *vi (SPORT)* to equalize; ~**de**
Gerechtigkeit poetic justice.
Ausgleichssport m keep-fit activity.
Ausgleichstor nt equalizer.
ausgraben ['aʊsgraːbən] *unreg vt* to dig up;
(Leichen) to exhume; *(fig)* to unearth.
Ausgrabung f excavation.
ausgrenzen ['aʊsgrɛntsən] *vt* to shut out,
separate.
Ausgrenzung f shut-out, separation.
Ausguck ['aʊsgʊk] m look-out.
Ausguß ['aʊsgʊs] m *(Spüle)* sink; *(Abfluß)*
outlet; *(Tülle)* spout.
aushaben ['aʊshaːbən] *unreg (umg) vt*
(Kleidung) to have taken off; *(Buch)* to have
finished.
aushalten ['aʊshaltən] *unreg vt* to bear, stand;
(umg: Geliebte) to keep ♦ *vi* to hold out; **das
ist nicht zum A~** that is unbearable; **sich
von jdm ~ lassen** to be kept by sb.
aushandeln ['aʊshandəln] *vt* to negotiate.
aushändigen ['aʊshɛndɪgən] *vt:* **jdm etw ~** to
hand sth over to sb.
Aushang ['aʊshaŋ] m notice.
aushängen ['aʊshɛŋən] *unreg vt (Meldung)* to
put up; *(Fenster)* to take off its hinges ♦ *vi* to
be displayed ♦ *vr* to hang out.
Aushängeschild nt *(shop)* sign; *(fig)*: **als
~ für etw dienen** to promote sth.
ausharren ['aʊsharən] *vi* to hold out.
aushäusig ['aʊshɔyzɪç] *adj* gallivanting
around, on the tiles.
ausheben ['aʊsheːbən] *unreg vt (Erde)* to lift
out; *(Grube)* to hollow out; *(Tür)* to take off
its hinges; *(Diebesnest)* to clear out; *(MIL)* to
enlist.
aushecken ['aʊshɛkən] *(umg) vt* to concoct,
think up.
aushelfen ['aʊshɛlfən] *unreg vi:* **jdm ~** to help
sb out.
Aushilfe ['aʊshɪlfə] f help, assistance;
(Person) (temporary) worker.
Aushilfs- zW: ~**kraft** f temporary worker;
~**lehrer(in)** m(f) supply teacher; **a~weise** *adv*
temporarily, as a stopgap.
aushöhlen ['aʊshøːlən] *vt* to hollow out; *(fig:
untergraben)* to undermine.
ausholen ['aʊshoːlən] *vi* to swing one's arm

back; *(zur Ohrfeige)* to raise one's hand;
(beim Gehen) to take long strides; **zum
Gegenschlag ~** *(lit, fig)* to prepare for a
counter-attack.
aushorchen ['aʊshɔrçən] *vt* to sound out,
pump.
aushungern ['aʊshʊŋərn] *vt* to starve out.
auskennen ['aʊskɛnən] *unreg vr* to know a lot;
(an einem Ort) to know one's way about; *(in
Fragen etc)* to be knowledgeable; **man kennt
sich bei ihm nie aus** you never know where
you are with him.
auskippen ['aʊskɪpən] *vt* to empty.
ausklammern ['aʊsklamərn] *vt (Thema)* to
exclude, leave out.
Ausklang ['aʊsklaŋ] m *(geh)* end.
ausklappbar ['aʊsklapbaːr] *adj:* **dieser Tisch ist
~** this table can be opened out.
auskleiden ['aʊsklaɪdən] *vr (geh)* to undress
♦ *vt (Wand)* to line.
ausklingen ['aʊsklɪŋən] *unreg vi* to end; *(Ton,
Lied)* to die away; *(Fest)* to come to an end.
ausklinken ['aʊsklɪŋkən] *vt (Bomben)* to
release ♦ *vi (umg)* to flip one's lid.
ausklopfen ['aʊsklɔpfən] *vt (Teppich)* to beat;
(Pfeife) to knock out.
auskochen ['aʊskɔxən] *vt* to boil; *(MED)* to
sterilize.
auskommen ['aʊskɔmən] *unreg vi:* **mit jdm ~**
to get on with sb; **mit etw ~** to get by with
sth; **A~** *(-s) nt:* **sein A~ haben** to get by; **mit
ihr ist kein A~** she's impossible to get on
with.
auskosten ['aʊskɔstən] *vt* to enjoy to the full.
auskramen ['aʊskraːmən] *(umg) vt* to dig out,
unearth; *(fig: alte Geschichten etc)* to bring
up.
auskratzen ['aʊskratsən] *vt (auch MED)* to
scrape out.
auskugeln ['aʊskuːgəln] *vr:* **sich** *dat* **den Arm ~**
to dislocate one's arm.
auskundschaften ['aʊskʊntʃaftən] *vt* to spy
out; *(Gebiet)* to reconnoitre *(BRIT)*,
reconnoiter *(US)*.
Auskunft ['aʊskʊnft] *(-, -künfte)* f
information; *(nähere)* details pl, particulars
pl; *(Stelle)* information office; *(TEL)*
inquiries; **jdm ~ erteilen** to give sb
information.
auskuppeln ['aʊskʊpəln] *vi* to disengage the
clutch.
auskurieren ['aʊskuriːrən] *(umg) vt* to cure.
auslachen ['aʊslaxən] *vt* to laugh at, mock.
ausladen ['aʊslaːdən] *unreg vt* to unload; *(umg:
Gäste)* to cancel an invitation to ♦ *vi (Äste)* to
spread.
ausladend *adj (Gebärden, Bewegung)*
sweeping.
Auslage ['aʊslaːgə] f shop window (display).
Auslagen pl outlay sing, expenditure sing.
Ausland ['aʊslant] nt foreign countries pl; **im
~** abroad; **ins ~** abroad.

Ausländer(in) [ˈaʊslɛndər(ɪn)] **(-s, -)** *m(f)* foreigner.
Ausländerfeindlichkeit *f* hostility to foreigners, xenophobia.
ausländisch *adj* foreign.
Auslands- *zW:* ~**aufenthalt** *m* stay abroad; ~**gespräch** *nt* international call; ~**korrespondent(in)** *m(f)* foreign correspondent; ~**reise** *f* trip abroad; ~**schutzbrief** *m* international travel cover; ~**vertretung** *f* agency abroad; (*von Firma*) foreign branch.
auslassen [ˈaʊslasən] *unreg vt* to leave out; (*Wort etc*) to omit; (*Fett*) to melt; (*Kleidungsstück*) to let out ♦ *vr:* **sich über etw** *akk* ~ to speak one's mind about sth; **seine Wut** *etc* **an jdm** ~ to vent one's rage *etc* on sb.
Auslassung *f* omission.
Auslassungszeichen *nt* apostrophe.
auslasten [ˈaʊslastən] *vt* (*Fahrzeug*) to make full use of; (*Maschine*) to use to capacity; (*jdn*) to occupy fully.
Auslauf [ˈaʊslaʊf] *m* (*für Tiere*) run; (*Ausfluß*) outflow, outlet.
auslaufen *unreg vi* to run out; (*Behälter*) to leak; (*NAUT*) to put out (to sea); (*langsam aufhören*) to run down.
Ausläufer [ˈaʊslɔyfər] *m* (*von Gebirge*) spur; (*Pflanze*) runner; (*MET: von Hoch*) ridge; (*: von Tief*) trough.
ausleeren [ˈaʊsleːrən] *vt* to empty.
auslegen [ˈaʊsleːgən] *vt* (*Waren*) to lay out; (*Köder*) to put down; (*Geld*) to lend; (*bedecken*) to cover; (*Text etc*) to interpret.
Ausleger **(-s, -)** *m* (*von Kran etc*) jib, boom.
Auslegung *f* interpretation.
Ausleihe [ˈaʊslaɪə] **(-, -n)** *f* issuing; (*Stelle*) issue desk.
ausleihen [ˈaʊslaɪən] *unreg vt* (*verleihen*) to lend; **sich** *dat* **etw** ~ to borrow sth.
auslernen [ˈaʊslɛrnən] *vi* (*Lehrling*) to finish one's apprenticeship; **man lernt nie aus** (*Sprichwort*) you live and learn.
Auslese [ˈaʊsleːzə] **(-, -n)** *f* selection; (*Elite*) elite; (*Wein*) choice wine.
auslesen [ˈaʊsleːzən] *unreg vt* to select; (*umg: zu Ende lesen*) to finish.
ausliefern [ˈaʊsliːfərn] *vt* to hand over; (*COMM*) to deliver ♦ *vr:* **sich jdm** ~ to give o.s. up to sb; ~ (**an** +*akk*) to deliver (up) (to), hand over (to); (*an anderen Staat*) to extradite (to); **jdm/etw ausgeliefert sein** to be at the mercy of sb/sth.
Auslieferungsabkommen *nt* extradition treaty.
ausliegen [ˈaʊsliːgən] *unreg vi* (*zur Ansicht*) to be displayed; (*Zeitschriften etc*) to be available (to the public); (*Liste*) to be up.
auslöschen [ˈaʊslœʃən] *vt* to extinguish; (*fig*) to wipe out, obliterate.
auslosen [ˈaʊsloːzən] *vt* to draw lots for.

auslösen [ˈaʊsløːzən] *vt* (*Explosion, Schuß*) to set off; (*hervorrufen*) to cause, produce; (*Gefangene*) to ransom; (*Pfand*) to redeem.
Auslöser **(-s, -)** *m* trigger; (*PHOT*) release; (*Anlaß*) cause.
ausloten [ˈaʊsloːtən] *vt* (*NAUT: Tiefe*) to sound; (*fig geh*) to plumb.
ausmachen [ˈaʊsmaxən] *vt* (*Licht, Radio*) to turn off; (*Feuer*) to put out; (*entdecken*) to make out; (*vereinbaren*) to agree; (*beilegen*) to settle; (*Anteil darstellen, betragen*) to represent; (*bedeuten*) to matter; **das macht ihm nichts aus** it doesn't matter to him; **macht es Ihnen etwas aus, wenn ...?** would you mind if ...?
ausmalen [ˈaʊsmaːlən] *vt* to paint; (*fig*) to describe; **sich** *dat* **etw** ~ to imagine sth.
Ausmaß [ˈaʊsmaːs] *nt* dimension; (*fig*) scale.
ausmerzen [ˈaʊsmɛrtsən] *vt* to eliminate.
ausmessen [ˈaʊsmɛsən] *unreg vt* to measure.
ausmisten [ˈaʊsmɪstən] *vt* (*Stall*) to muck out; (*fig: umg: Schrank etc*) to tidy out; (*: Zimmer*) to clean out.
ausmustern [ˈaʊsmʊstərn] *vt* (*Maschine, Fahrzeug etc*) to take out of service; (*MIL: entlassen*) to invalid out.
Ausnahme [ˈaʊsnaːmə] **(-, -n)** *f* exception; **eine** ~ **machen** to make an exception; ~**erscheinung** *f* exception, one-off example; ~**fall** *m* exceptional case; ~**zustand** *m* state of emergency.
ausnahmslos *adv* without exception.
ausnahmsweise *adv* by way of exception, for once.
ausnehmen [ˈaʊsneːmən] *unreg vt* to take out, remove; (*Tier*) to gut; (*Nest*) to rob; (*umg: Geld abnehmen*) to clean out; (*ausschließen*) to make an exception of ♦ *vr* to look, appear.
ausnehmend *adj* exceptional.
ausnüchtern [ˈaʊsnʏçtərn] *vt, vi* to sober up.
Ausnüchterungszelle *f* drying-out cell.
ausnutzen [ˈaʊsnʊtsən] *vt* (*Zeit, Gelegenheit*) to use, turn to good account; (*Einfluß*) to use; (*Mensch, Gutmütigkeit*) to exploit.
auspacken [ˈaʊspakən] *vt* to unpack ♦ *vi* (*umg: alles sagen*) to talk.
auspfeifen [ˈaʊspfaɪfən] *unreg vt* to hiss/boo at.
ausplaudern [ˈaʊsplaʊdərn] *vt* (*Geheimnis*) to blab.
ausposaunen [ˈaʊspozaʊnən] (*umg*) *vt* to tell the world about.
ausprägen [ˈaʊsprɛːgən] *vr* (*Begabung, Charaktereigenschaft*) to reveal *od* show itself.
auspressen [ˈaʊspresən] *vt* (*Saft, Schwamm etc*) to squeeze out; (*Zitrone etc*) to squeeze.
ausprobieren [ˈaʊsproːbiːrən] *vt* to try (out).
Auspuff [ˈaʊspʊf] **(-(e)s, -e)** *m* (*TECH*) exhaust; ~**rohr** *nt* exhaust (pipe); ~**topf** *m* (*AUT*) silencer (*BRIT*), muffler (*US*).
ausquartieren [ˈaʊskvartiːrən] *vt* to move out.
ausquetschen [ˈaʊskvɛtʃən] *vt* (*Zitrone etc*) to

squeeze; (*umg: ausfragen*) to grill; (: *aus Neugier*) to pump.

ausradieren ['aʊsradiːrən] *vt* to erase, rub out.

ausrangieren ['aʊsrãʒiːrən] (*umg*) *vt* to chuck out; (*Maschine, Auto*) to scrap.

ausrauben ['aʊsraʊbən] *vt* to rob.

ausräumen ['aʊsrɔʏmən] *vt* (*Dinge*) to clear away; (*Schrank, Zimmer*) to empty; (*Bedenken*) to put aside.

ausrechnen ['aʊsrɛçnən] *vt* to calculate, reckon.

Ausrechnung *f* calculation, reckoning.

Ausrede ['aʊsreːdə] *f* excuse.

ausreden ['aʊsreːdən] *vi* to have one's say ♦ *vt:* **jdm etw ~** to talk sb out of sth; **er hat mich nicht mal ~ lassen** he didn't even let me finish (speaking).

ausreichen ['aʊsraɪçən] *vi* to suffice, be enough.

ausreichend *adj* sufficient, adequate; (*SCH*) adequate.

Ausreise ['aʊsraɪzə] *f* departure; **bei der ~** when leaving the country; **~erlaubnis** *f* exit visa.

ausreisen ['aʊsraɪzən] *vi* to leave the country.

ausreißen ['aʊsraɪsən] *unreg vt* to tear *od* pull out ♦ *vi* (*Riß bekommen*) to tear; (*umg*) to make off, scram; **er hat sich** *dat* **kein Bein ausgerissen** (*umg*) he didn't exactly overstrain himself.

ausrenken ['aʊsrɛŋkən] *vt* to dislocate.

ausrichten ['aʊsrɪçtən] *vt* (*Botschaft*) to deliver; (*Gruß*) to pass on; (*Hochzeit etc*) to arrange; (*in gerade Linie bringen*) to get in a straight line; (*angleichen*) to bring into line; (*TYP etc*) to justify; **etwas/nichts bei jdm ~** to get somewhere/nowhere with sb; **jdm etw ~** to take a message for sb; **ich werde es ihm ~** I'll tell him.

ausrotten ['aʊsrɔtən] *vt* to stamp out, exterminate.

ausrücken ['aʊsrʏkən] *vi* (*MIL*) to move off; (*Feuerwehr, Polizei*) to be called out; (*umg: weglaufen*) to run away.

Ausruf ['aʊsruːf] *m* (*Schrei*) cry, exclamation; (*Verkünden*) proclamation.

ausrufen *unreg vt* to cry out, exclaim; to call out; **jdn ~ (lassen)** (*über Lautsprecher etc*) to page sb.

Ausrufezeichen *nt* exclamation mark.

ausruhen ['aʊsruːən] *vt, vi, vr* to rest.

ausrüsten ['aʊsrʏstən] *vt* to equip, fit out.

Ausrüstung *f* equipment.

ausrutschen ['aʊsrʊtʃən] *vi* to slip.

Ausrutscher (**-s, -**) (*umg*) *m* (*lit, fig*) slip.

Aussage ['aʊszaːgə] (**-, -n**) *f* (*JUR*) statement; **der Angeklagte/Zeuge verweigerte die ~** the accused/witness refused to give evidence.

aussagekräftig *adj* expressive, full of expression.

aussagen ['aʊszaːgən] *vt* to say, state ♦ *vi* (*JUR*) to give evidence.

Aussatz ['aʊszats] (**-es**) *m* (*MED*) leprosy.

aussaugen ['aʊszaʊgən] *vt* (*Saft etc*) to suck out; (*Wunde*) to suck the poison out of; (*fig: ausbeuten*) to drain dry.

ausschalten ['aʊsʃaltən] *vt* to switch off; (*fig*) to eliminate.

Ausschank ['aʊsʃaŋk] (**-(e)s, -schänke**) *m* dispensing, giving out; (*COMM*) selling; (*Theke*) bar.

Ausschankerlaubnis *f* licence (*BRIT*), license (*US*).

Ausschau ['aʊsʃaʊ] *f:* **~ halten (nach)** to look out (for), watch (for).

ausschauen *vi:* **~ (nach)** to look out (for), be on the look-out (for).

ausscheiden ['aʊsʃaɪdən] *unreg vt* (*aussondern*) to take out; (*MED*) to excrete ♦ *vi:* **~ (aus)** to leave; (*aus einem Amt*) to retire (from); (*SPORT*) to be eliminated (from), be knocked out (of); **er scheidet für den Posten aus** he can't be considered for the job.

Ausscheidung *f* (*Aussondern*) removal; (*MED*) excretion; (*SPORT*) elimination.

ausschenken ['aʊsʃɛŋkən] *vt* to pour out; (*am Ausschank*) to serve.

ausscheren ['aʊsʃeːrən] *vi* (*Fahrzeug*) to leave the line *od* convoy; (*zum Überholen*) to pull out.

ausschildern ['aʊsʃɪldərn] *vt* to signpost.

ausschimpfen ['aʊsʃɪmpfən] *vt* to scold, tell off.

ausschlachten ['aʊsʃlaxtən] *vt* (*Auto*) to cannibalize; (*fig*) to make a meal of.

ausschlafen ['aʊsʃlaːfən] *unreg vi, vr* to sleep late ♦ *vt* to sleep off; **ich bin nicht ausgeschlafen** I didn't have *od* get enough sleep.

Ausschlag ['aʊsʃlaːk] *m* (*MED*) rash; (*Pendel~*) swing; (*von Nadel*) deflection; **den ~ geben** (*fig*) to tip the balance.

ausschlagen ['aʊsʃlaːgən] *unreg vt* to knock out; (*auskleiden*) to deck out; (*verweigern*) to decline ♦ *vi* (*Pferd*) to kick out; (*BOT*) to sprout; (*Zeiger*) to be deflected.

ausschlaggebend *adj* decisive.

ausschließen ['aʊsʃliːsən] *unreg vt* to shut *od* lock out; (*SPORT*) to disqualify; (*Fehler, Möglichkeit etc*) to rule out; (*fig*) to exclude; **ich will mich nicht ~** myself not excepted.

ausschließlich *adj* exclusive ♦ *adv* exclusively ♦ *präp +gen* excluding, exclusive of.

ausschlüpfen ['aʊsʃlʏpfən] *vi* to slip out; (*aus Ei, Puppe*) to hatch out.

Ausschluß ['aʊsʃlʊs] *m* exclusion; **unter ~ der Öffentlichkeit stattfinden** to be closed to the public; (*JUR*) to be held in camera.

ausschmücken ['aʊsʃmʏkən] *vt* to decorate; (*fig*) to embellish.

ausschneiden ['aʊsʃnaɪdən] *unreg vt* to cut out; (*Büsche*) to trim.

Ausschnitt ['aʊsʃnɪt] *m* (*Teil*) section; (*von Kleid*) neckline; (*Zeitungs~*) cutting (*BRIT*), clipping (*US*); (*aus Film etc*) excerpt.

ausschöpfen ['aʊsʃœpfən] *vt* to ladle out; (*fig*) to exhaust; **Wasser** *etc* **aus etw** ~ to ladle water *etc* out of sth.

ausschreiben ['aʊsʃraɪbən] *unreg vt* (*ganz schreiben*) to write out (in full); (*Scheck, Rechnung etc*) to write out (out); (*Stelle, Wettbewerb etc*) to announce, advertise.

Ausschreibung *f* (*Bekanntmachung: von Wahlen*) calling; (: *von Stelle*) advertising.

Ausschreitung ['aʊsʃraɪtʊŋ] *f* excess.

Ausschuß ['aʊsʃʊs] *m* committee, board; (*Abfall*) waste, scraps *pl*; (*COMM: auch:* ~**ware**) reject.

ausschütten ['aʊsʃʏtən] *vt* to pour out; (*Eimer*) to empty; (*Geld*) to pay ♦ *vr* to shake (with laughter).

Ausschüttung *f* (*FIN*) distribution.

ausschwärmen ['aʊsʃvɛrmən] *vi* (*Bienen, Menschen*) to swarm out; (*MIL*) to fan out.

ausschweifend ['aʊsʃvaɪfənt] *adj* (*Leben*) dissipated, debauched; (*Phantasie*) extravagant.

Ausschweifung *f* excess.

ausschweigen ['aʊsʃvaɪgən] *unreg vr* to keep silent.

ausschwitzen ['aʊsʃvɪtsən] *vt* to sweat out.

aussehen ['aʊszeːən] *unreg vi* to look; **gut** ~ to look good/well; **wie sieht's aus?** (*umg: wie steht's?*) how's things?; **das sieht nach nichts aus** that doesn't look anything special; **es sieht nach Regen aus** it looks like rain; **es sieht schlecht aus** things look bad; **A~ (-s)** *nt* appearance.

aussein ['aʊssaɪn] *unreg* (*umg*) *vi* to be out; (*zu Ende*) to be over ♦ *vi unpers*: **es ist aus mit ihm** he is finished, he has had it.

außen ['aʊsən] *adv* outside; (*nach* ~) outwards; ~ **ist es rot** it's red (on the) outside.

Außen- *zW*: ~**antenne** *f* outside aerial; ~**arbeiten** *pl* work *sing* on the exterior; ~**aufnahme** *f* outdoor shot; ~**bezirk** *m* outlying district; ~**bordmotor** *m* outboard motor.

aussenden ['aʊszɛndən] *unreg vt* to send out, emit.

Außen- *zW*: ~**dienst** *m* outside *od* field service; (*von Diplomat*) foreign service; ~**handel** *m* foreign trade; ~**minister** *m* foreign minister; ~**ministerium** *nt* foreign office; ~**politik** *f* foreign policy; ~**seite** *f* outside; ~**seiter(in)** (**-s, -**) *m(f)* outsider; ~**spiegel** *m* (*AUT*) outside mirror; ~**stände** *pl* (*bes COMM*) outstanding debts *pl*, arrears *pl*; ~**stehende(r)** *f(m)* outsider; ~**stelle** *f* branch; ~**welt** *f* outside world.

außer ['aʊsər] *präp* +*dat* (*räumlich*) out of; (*abgesehen von*) except ♦ *konj* (*ausgenommen*) except; ~ **Gefahr sein** to be out of danger; ~ **Zweifel** beyond any doubt;

~ **Betrieb** out of order; ~ **sich** *dat* **sein/geraten** to be beside o.s.; ~ **Dienst** retired; ~ **Landes** abroad; ~ **wenn** unless; ~ **daß** except; ~**amtlich** *adj* unofficial, private.

außerdem *konj* besides, in addition ♦ *adv* anyway.

außerdienstlich *adj* private.

äußere(r, s) ['ɔʏsərə(r, s)] *adj* outer, external; **Ä~(s)** *nt* exterior; (*fig: Aussehen*) outward appearance.

außer- *zW*: ~**ehelich** *adj* extramarital; ~**gewöhnlich** *adj* unusual; ~**halb** *präp* +*gen* outside ♦ *adv* outside; ~**irdisch** *adj* extraterrestrial; **A~kraftsetzung** *f* repeal.

äußerlich *adj* external; **rein** ~ **betrachtet** on the face of it; **Ä~keit** *f* (*fig*) triviality; (*Oberflächlichkeit*) superficiality; (*Formalität*) formality.

äußern *vt* to utter, express; (*zeigen*) to show ♦ *vr* to give one's opinion; (*sich zeigen*) to show itself.

außer- *zW*: ~**ordentlich** *adj* extraordinary; ~**planmäßig** *adj* unscheduled; ~**sinnlich** *adj*: ~**sinnliche Wahrnehmung** extrasensory perception.

äußerst ['ɔʏsərst] *adv* extremely, most.

außerstande [aʊsər'ʃtandə] *adv* (*nicht in der Lage*) not in a position; (*nicht fähig*) unable.

Äußerste(s) *nt*: **bis zum ~n gehen** to go to extremes.

äußerste(r, s) *adj* utmost; (*räumlich*) farthest; (*Termin*) last possible; (*Preis*) highest; **mein ~s Angebot** my final offer.

äußerstenfalls *adv* if the worst comes to the worst.

Äußerung *f* (*Bemerkung*) remark, comment; (*Behauptung*) statement; (*Zeichen*) expression.

aussetzen ['aʊszɛtsən] *vt* (*Kind, Tier*) to abandon; (*Boote*) to lower; (*Belohnung*) to offer; (*Urteil, Verfahren*) to postpone ♦ *vi* (*aufhören*) to stop; (*Pause machen*) to have a break; **jdn/sich einer Sache** *dat* ~ to lay sb/o.s. open to sth; **jdm/etw ausgesetzt sein** to be exposed to sb/sth; **was haben Sie daran auszusetzen?** what's your objection to it?; **an jdm/etw etwas** ~ to find fault with sb/sth.

Aussicht ['aʊszɪçt] *f* view; (*in Zukunft*) prospect; **in** ~ **sein** to be in view; **etw in** ~ **haben** to have sth in view; **jdm etw in** ~ **stellen** to promise sb sth.

Aussichts- *zW*: **a~los** *adj* hopeless; ~**punkt** *m* viewpoint; **a~reich** *adj* promising; ~**turm** *m* observation tower.

Aussiedler(in) ['aʊsziːdlər(ɪn)] (**-s, -**) *m(f)* (*Auswanderer*) emigrant.

Aussiedler *are people of German origin from East and South-East Europe who have resettled in Germany. Many come from the former Soviet Union. They are given free*

German language tuition for 6 months and receive financial help for 15 months. The number of Aussiedler increased dramatically in the early 1990s.

aussöhnen ['aʊszøːnən] vt to reconcile ♦ vr (einander) to become reconciled; **sich mit jdm/etw** ~ to reconcile o.s. with sb/to sth.

Aussöhnung f reconciliation.

aussondern ['aʊszɔndərn] vt to separate off, select.

aussorgen ['aʊszɔrgən] vi: **ausgesorgt haben** to have no more money worries.

aussortieren ['aʊszɔrtiːrən] vt to sort out.

ausspannen ['aʊsʃpanən] vt to spread od stretch out; (Pferd) to unharness; (umg: Mädchen): **jdm jdn** ~ to steal sb from sb ♦ vi to relax.

aussparen ['aʊsʃpaːrən] vt to leave open.

aussperren ['aʊsʃpɛrən] vt to lock out.

Aussperrung f (INDUSTRIE) lock-out.

ausspielen ['aʊsʃpiːlən] vt (Karte) to lead; (Geldprämie) to offer as a prize ♦ vi (KARTEN) to lead; **ausgespielt haben** to be finished; **jdn gegen jdn** ~ to play sb off against sb.

Ausspielung f (im Lotto) draw.

ausspionieren ['aʊsʃpioniːrən] vt (Pläne etc) to spy out; (Person) to spy on.

Aussprache ['aʊsʃpraːxə] f pronunciation; (Unterredung) (frank) discussion.

aussprechen ['aʊsʃprɛçən] unreg vt to pronounce; (zu Ende sprechen) to speak; (äußern) to say, express ♦ vr (sich äußern): **sich** ~ (über +akk) to speak (about); (sich anvertrauen) to unburden o.s. (about od on); (diskutieren) to discuss ♦ vi (zu Ende sprechen) to finish speaking; **der Regierung das Vertrauen** ~ to pass a vote of confidence in the government.

Ausspruch ['aʊsʃprʊx] m remark; (geflügeltes Wort) saying.

ausspucken ['aʊsʃpʊkən] vt to spit out ♦ vi to spit.

ausspülen ['aʊsʃpyːlən] vt to wash out; (Mund) to rinse.

ausstaffieren ['aʊsʃtafiːrən] vt to equip, kit out; (Zimmer) to furnish.

Ausstand ['aʊsʃtant] m strike; **in den** ~ **treten** to go on strike; **seinen** ~ **geben** to hold a leaving party.

ausstatten ['aʊsʃtatən] vt (Zimmer etc) to furnish; **jdn mit etw** ~ to equip sb od kit sb out with sth.

Ausstattung f (Ausstatten) provision; (Kleidung) outfit; (Aussteuer) dowry; (Aufmachung) make-up; (Einrichtung) furnishing.

ausstechen ['aʊsʃtɛçən] unreg vt (Torf, Kekse) to cut out; (Augen) to gouge out; (übertreffen) to outshine.

ausstehen ['aʊsʃteːən] unreg vt to stand,

endure ♦ vi (noch nicht dasein) to be outstanding.

aussteigen ['aʊsʃtaɪgən] unreg vi to get out, alight; **alles** ~! (von Schaffner) all change!; **aus der Gesellschaft** ~ to drop out (of society).

Aussteiger(in) (umg) m(f) dropout.

ausstellen ['aʊsʃtɛlən] vt to exhibit, display; (umg: ausschalten) to switch off; (Rechnung etc) to make out; (Paß, Zeugnis) to issue.

Aussteller(in) m(f) (auf Messe) exhibitor; (von Scheck) drawer.

Ausstellung f exhibition; (FIN) drawing up; (einer Rechnung) making out; (eines Passes etc) issuing.

Ausstellungsdatum nt date of issue.

Ausstellungsstück nt (in Ausstellung) exhibit; (in Schaufenster etc) display item.

aussterben ['aʊsʃtɛrbən] unreg vi to die out; **A~** nt extinction.

Aussteuer ['aʊsʃtɔyər] f dowry.

aussteuern ['aʊsʃtɔyərn] vt (Verstärker) to adjust.

Ausstieg ['aʊsʃtiːk] (-(e)s, -e) m (Ausgang) exit; ~ **aus der Atomenergie** abandonment of nuclear energy.

ausstopfen ['aʊsʃtɔpfən] vt to stuff.

ausstoßen ['aʊsʃtoːsən] unreg vt (Luft, Rauch) to give off, emit; (aus Verein etc) to expel, exclude; (herstellen: Teile, Stückzahl) to turn out, produce.

ausstrahlen ['aʊsʃtraːlən] vt, vi to radiate; (RUNDF) to broadcast.

Ausstrahlung f radiation; (fig) charisma.

ausstrecken ['aʊsʃtrɛkən] vt, vr to stretch out.

ausstreichen ['aʊsʃtraɪçən] unreg vt to cross out; (glätten) to smooth out.

ausstreuen ['aʊsʃtrɔyən] vt to scatter; (fig: Gerücht) to spread.

ausströmen ['aʊsʃtrøːmən] vi (Gas) to pour out, escape ♦ vt to give off; (fig) to radiate.

aussuchen ['aʊszuːxən] vt to select, pick out.

Austausch ['aʊstaʊʃ] m exchange; **a~bar** adj exchangeable.

austauschen vt to exchange, swop.

Austauschmotor m replacement engine; (gebraucht) factory-reconditioned engine.

Austauschstudent(in) m(f) exchange student.

austeilen ['aʊstaɪlən] vt to distribute, give out.

Auster ['aʊstər] (-, -n) f oyster.

austoben ['aʊstoːbən] vr (Kind) to run wild; (Erwachsene) to let off steam; (sich müde machen) to tire o.s. out.

austragen ['aʊstraːgən] unreg vt (Post) to deliver; (Streit etc) to decide; (Wettkämpfe) to hold; **ein Kind** ~ (nicht abtreiben) to have a child.

Austräger ['aʊstrɛːgər] m delivery boy; (Zeitungs~) newspaper boy.

Austragungsort m (SPORT) venue.

Australien [aʊsˈtraːliən] (-s) _nt_ Australia.
Australier(in) (-s, -) _m(f)_ Australian.
australisch _adj_ Australian.
austreiben [ˈaʊstraɪbən] _unreg vt_ to drive out, expel; (_Teufel etc_) to exorcize; **jdm etw ~ to** cure sb of sth; (_bes durch Schläge_) to knock sth out of sb.
austreten [ˈaʊstreːtən] _unreg vi_ (_zur Toilette_) to be excused ♦ _vt_ (_Feuer_) to tread out, trample; (_Schuhe_) to wear out; (_Treppe_) to wear down; **aus etw ~** to leave sth.
austricksen [ˈaʊstrɪksən] (_umg_) _vt_ (_SPORT, fig_) to trick.
austrinken [ˈaʊstrɪŋkən] _unreg vt_ (_Glas_) to drain; (_Getränk_) to drink up ♦ _vi_ to finish one's drink, drink up.
Austritt [ˈaʊstrɪt] _m_ emission, (_aus Verein, Partei etc_) retirement, withdrawal.
austrocknen [ˈaʊstrɔknən] _vt, vi_ to dry up.
austüfteln [ˈaʊstyftəln] (_umg_) _vt_ to work out; (_ersinnen_) to think up.
ausüben [ˈaʊs|yːbən] _vt_ (_Beruf_) to practise (_BRIT_), practice (_US_), carry out; (_innehaben: Amt_) to hold; (_Funktion_) to perform; (_Einfluß_) to exert; **einen Reiz auf jdn ~** to hold an attraction for sb; **eine Wirkung auf jdn ~** to have an effect on sb.
Ausübung _f_ practice, exercise; **in ~ seines Dienstes/seiner Pflicht** (_form_) in the execution of his duty.
ausufern [ˈaʊs|uːfərn] _vi_ (_fig_) to get out of hand; (_Konflikt etc_): **~ (zu)** to escalate (into).
Ausverkauf [ˈaʊsfɛrkaʊf] _m_ sale; (_fig: Verrat_) sell-out.
ausverkaufen _vt_ to sell out; (_Geschäft_) to sell up.
ausverkauft _adj_ (_Karten, Artikel_) sold out; (_THEAT: Haus_) full.
auswachsen [ˈaʊsvaksən] _unreg vi:_ **das ist (ja) zum A~** (_umg_) it's enough to drive you mad.
Auswahl [ˈaʊsvaːl] _f:_ **eine ~ (an +dat)** a selection (of), a choice (of).
auswählen [ˈaʊsvɛːlən] _vt_ to select, choose.
Auswahlmöglichkeit _f_ choice.
Auswanderer [ˈaʊsvandərər] (-s, -) _m_ emigrant.
Auswanderin [ˈaʊsvandərɪn] _f_ emigrant.
auswandern _vi_ to emigrate.
Auswanderung _f_ emigration.
auswärtig [ˈaʊsvɛrtɪç] _adj_ (_nicht am/vom Ort_) out-of-town; (_ausländisch_) foreign; **das A~e Amt** the Foreign Office (_BRIT_), the State Department (_US_).
auswärts [ˈaʊsvɛrts] _adv_ outside; (_nach außen_) outwards; **~ essen** to eat out; **A~spiel** _nt_ away game.
auswaschen [ˈaʊsvaʃən] _unreg vt_ to wash out; (_spülen_) to rinse (out).
auswechseln [ˈaʊsvɛksəln] _vt_ to change, substitute.
Ausweg [ˈaʊsveːk] _m_ way out; **der letzte ~** the last resort; **a~los** _adj_ hopeless.

ausweichen [ˈaʊsvaɪçən] _unreg vi:_ **jdm/etw ~** (_lit_) to move aside _od_ make way for sb/sth; (_fig_) to sidestep sb/sth; **jdm/einer Begegnung ~** to avoid sb/a meeting.
ausweichend _adj_ evasive.
Ausweichmanöver _nt_ evasive action.
ausweinen [ˈaʊsvaɪnən] _vr_ to have a (good) cry.
Ausweis [ˈaʊsvaɪs] (-es, -e) _m_ identity card; passport; (_Mitglieds~, Bibliotheks~ etc_) card; **~, bitte** your papers, please.
ausweisen [ˈaʊsvaɪzən] _unreg vt_ to expel, banish ♦ _vr_ to prove one's identity.
Ausweis- _zW:_ **~karte** _f_ identity papers _pl_; **~kontrolle** _f_ identity check; **~papiere** _pl_ identity papers _pl_.
Ausweisung _f_ expulsion.
ausweiten [ˈaʊsvaɪtən] _vt_ to stretch.
auswendig [ˈaʊsvɛndɪç] _adv_ by heart; **~ lernen** to learn by heart.
auswerfen [ˈaʊsvɛrfən] _unreg vt_ (_Anker, Netz_) to cast.
auswerten [ˈaʊsvɛrtən] _vt_ to evaluate.
Auswertung _f_ evaluation, analysis; (_Nutzung_) utilization.
auswickeln [ˈaʊsvɪkəln] _vt_ (_Paket, Bonbon etc_) to unwrap.
auswirken [ˈaʊsvɪrkən] _vr_ to have an effect.
Auswirkung _f_ effect.
auswischen [ˈaʊsvɪʃən] _vt_ to wipe out; **jdm eins ~** (_umg_) to one over on sb.
Auswuchs [ˈaʊsvuːks] _m_ (out)growth; (_fig_) product; (_Mißstand, Übersteigerung_) excess.
auswuchten [ˈaʊsvʊxtən] _vt_ (_AUT_) to balance.
auszacken [ˈaʊstsakən] _vt_ (_Stoff etc_) to pink.
auszahlen [ˈaʊstsaːlən] _vt_ (_Lohn, Summe_) to pay out; (_Arbeiter_) to pay off; (_Miterben_) to buy out ♦ _vr_ (_sich lohnen_) to pay.
auszählen [ˈaʊstsɛːlən] _vt_ (_Stimmen_) to count; (_BOXEN_) to count out.
auszeichnen [ˈaʊstsaɪçnən] _vt_ to honour (_BRIT_), honor (_US_); (_MIL_) to decorate; (_COMM_) to price ♦ _vr_ to distinguish o.s.; **der Wagen zeichnet sich durch ... aus** one of the car's main features is ...
Auszeichnung _f_ distinction; (_COMM_) pricing; (_Ehrung_) awarding of decoration; (_Ehre_) honour (_BRIT_), honor (_US_); (_Orden_) decoration; **mit ~** with distinction.
ausziehen [ˈaʊstsiːən] _unreg vt_ (_Kleidung_) to take off; (_Haare, Zähne, Tisch etc_) to pull out ♦ _vr_ to undress ♦ _vi_ (_aufbrechen_) to leave; (_aus Wohnung_) to move out.
Auszubildende(r) [ˈaʊstsʊbɪldəndə(r)] _f(m)_ trainee; (_als Handwerker_) apprentice.
Auszug [ˈaʊstsuːk] _m_ (_aus Wohnung_) removal; (_aus Buch etc_) extract; (_Konto~_) statement; (_Ausmarsch_) departure.
autark [aʊˈtark] _adj_ self-sufficient (_auch fig_); (_COMM_) autarkical.
Auto [ˈaʊto] (-s, -s) _nt_ (motor-)car, automobile (_US_); **mit dem ~ fahren** to go by car;

~ **fahren** to drive.
Autoatlas *m* road atlas.
Autobahn *f* motorway (*BRIT*), expressway (*US*).

> **Autobahn** is the German for a motorway. In the former West Germany there is a widespread network but in the former **DDR** the motorways are somewhat less extensive. There is no overall speed limit but a limit of 130 km per hour is recommended and there are lower mandatory limits on certain stretches of road. As yet there are no tolls payable on German Autobahnen.

Autobahndreieck *nt* motorway (*BRIT*) *od* expressway (*US*) junction.
Autobahnkreuz *nt* motorway (*BRIT*) *od* expressway (*US*) intersection.
Autobahnzubringer *m* motorway feeder *od* access road.
Autobiographie [autobiogra'fiː] *f* autobiography.
Auto- *zW:* ~**bombe** *f* car bomb; ~**bus** *m* bus; (*Reisebus*) coach (*BRIT*), bus (*US*); ~**fähre** *f* car ferry; ~**fahrer(in)** *m(f)* motorist, driver; ~**fahrt** *f* drive; ~**friedhof** (*umg*) *m* car dump.
autogen [auto'geːn] *adj* autogenous; ~**es Training** (*PSYCH*) relaxation through self-hypnosis.
Autogramm [auto'gram] *nt* autograph.
Automat (-en, -en) *m* machine.
Automatik [auto'maːtɪk] *f* automatic mechanism (*auch fig*); (*Gesamtanlage*) automatic system; (*AUT*) automatic transmission.
automatisch *adj* automatic.
Automatisierung [automati'ziːruŋ] *f* automation.
Automobilausstellung [automo'biːlausʃtɛluŋ] *f* motor show.
autonom [auto'noːm] *adj* autonomous.
Autopsie [auto'psiː] *f* post-mortem, autopsy.
Autor ['autɔr] (-s, -en) *m* author.
Auto- *zW:* ~**radio** *nt* car radio; ~**reifen** *m* car tyre (*BRIT*) *od* tire (*US*); ~**reisezug** *m* motorail train; ~**rennen** *nt* motor race; (*Sportart*) motor racing.
Autorin [au'toːrɪn] *f* authoress.
autoritär [autori'tɛːr] *adj* authoritarian.
Autorität *f* authority.
Auto- *zW:* ~**schalter** *m* drive-in bank (counter); ~**telefon** *nt* car phone; ~**unfall** *m* car *od* motor accident; ~**verleih** *m*, ~**vermietung** *f* car hire (*BRIT*) *od* rental (*US*).
AvD (-) *m abk* (= *Automobilclub von Deutschland*) German motoring organization, ≈ AA (*BRIT*), AAA (*US*).
Axt [akst] (-, ⁻e) *f* axe (*BRIT*), ax (*US*).
AZ, Az. *abk* (= *Aktenzeichen*) ref.
Azoren [a'tsoːrən] *pl* (*GEOG*) Azores *pl*.

Azteke [ats'teːkə] (-n, -n) *m* Aztec.
Aztekin *f* Aztec.
Azubi [a'tsuːbi] (-s, -s) (*umg*) *f(m) abk* = **Auszubildende(r)**.

B, b

B¹, b [beː] *nt* (*letter*) B, b; ~ **wie Bertha** ≈ B for Benjamin, B for Baker (*US*); **B-Dur/b-Moll** (the key of) B flat major/minor.
B² [beː] *f abk* = **Bundesstraße**.
Baby ['beːbi] (-s, -s) *nt* baby; ~**ausstattung** *f* layette; ~**raum** *m* (*Flughafen etc*) nursing room; ~**sitter** ['beːbisɪtər] (-s, -) *m* baby-sitter; ~**speck** (*umg*) *m* puppy fat.
Bach [bax] (-(e)s, ⁻e) *m* stream, brook.
Backblech *nt* baking tray.
Backbord (-(e)s, -e) *nt* (*NAUT*) port.
Backe (-, -n) *f* cheek.
backen ['bakən] *unreg vt, vi* to bake; **frisch/knusprig gebackenes Brot** fresh/crusty bread.
Backenbart *m* sideboards *pl*.
Backenzahn *m* molar.
Bäcker(in) ['bɛkər(ɪn)] (-s, -) *m(f)* baker.
Bäckerei [bɛkə'rai] *f* bakery; (*Bäckerladen*) baker's (shop).
Bäckerjunge *m* (*Lehrling*) baker's apprentice.
Back- *zW:* ~**fisch** *m* fried fish; (*veraltet*) teenager; ~**form** *f* baking tin (*BRIT*) *od* pan (*US*); ~**hähnchen** *nt* fried chicken in breadcrumbs; ~**obst** *nt* dried fruit; ~**ofen** *m* oven; ~**pflaume** *f* prune; ~**pulver** *nt* baking powder; ~**stein** *m* brick.
bäckt [bɛkt] *vb siehe* **backen**.
Bad [baːt] (-(e)s, ⁻er) *nt* bath; (*Schwimmen*) bathing; (*Ort*) spa.
Bade- *zW:* ~**anstalt** *f* swimming pool; ~**anzug** *m* bathing suit; ~**hose** *f* bathing *od* swimming trunks *pl*; ~**kappe** *f* bathing cap; ~**mantel** *m* bath(ing) robe; ~**meister** *m* swimming pool attendant.
baden ['baːdən] *vi* to bathe, have a bath ♦ *vt* to bath; ~ **gehen** (*fig: umg*) to come a cropper.
Baden-Württemberg ['baːdən'vyrtəmbɛrk] *nt* Baden-Württemberg.
Bade- *zW:* ~**ort** *m* spa; ~**sachen** *pl* swimming things *pl*; ~**tuch** *nt* bath towel; ~**wanne** *f* bath(tub); ~**zimmer** *nt* bathroom.
baff [baf] *adj:* ~ **sein** (*umg*) to be flabbergasted.
BAföG, Bafög [ ] *nt abk* (= *Bundesausbildungsförderungsgesetz*) German student grants system.

Bafög is the system which awards grants for living expenses to students at universities and certain training colleges. The amount is based on parental income. Part of the grant must be paid back a few years after graduating.

BAG (-) nt abk (= Bundesarbeitsgericht) German industrial tribunal.

Bagatelle [baga'tɛlə] (-, -n) f trifle.

Bagdad ['bakdat] (-s) nt Baghdad.

Bagger ['bagər] (-s, -) m excavator; (NAUT) dredger.

baggern vt, vi to excavate; (NAUT) to dredge.

Baggersee m (flooded) gravel pit.

Bahamas [ba'haːmas] pl: die ~ the Bahamas pl.

Bahn [baːn] (-, -en) f railway (BRIT), railroad (US); (Weg) road, way; (Spur) lane; (Renn~) track; (ASTRON) orbit; (Stoff~) length; **mit der ~** by train od rail/tram; **frei ~** (COMM) carriage free to station of destination; **jdm/etw die ~ frei machen** (fig) to clear the way for sb/sth; **von der rechten ~ abkommen** to stray from the straight and narrow; **jdn aus der ~ werfen** (fig) to shatter sb; **~beamte(r)** m railway (BRIT) od railroad (US) official; **b~brechend** adj pioneering; **~brecher(in)** (-s, -) m(f) pioneer; **~damm** m railway embankment.

bahnen vt: **sich einen Weg ~** to clear a way.

Bahnfahrt f railway (BRIT) od railroad (US) journey.

Bahnhof m station; **auf dem ~** at the station; **ich verstehe nur ~** (hum: umg) it's all Greek to me.

Bahnhofshalle f station concourse.

Bahnhofsmission f charitable organization for helping rail travellers.

The **Bahnhofsmission** is a charitable organization set up by and run jointly by various churches. At railway stations in most big cities they have an office to which people in need of advice and help can go.

Bahnhofswirtschaft f station restaurant.

Bahn- zW: **b~lagernd** adj (COMM) to be collected from the station; **~linie** f (railway (BRIT) od railroad (US)) line; **~schranke** f level (BRIT) od grade (US) crossing barrier; **~steig** m platform; **~steigkarte** f platform ticket; **~strecke** f railway (BRIT) od railroad (US) line; **~übergang** m level (BRIT) od grade (US) crossing; **beschrankter ~übergang** crossing with gates; **unbeschrankter ~übergang** unguarded crossing; **~wärter** m signalman.

Bahrain [ba'raɪn] (-s) nt Bahrain.

Bahre ['baːrə] (-, -n) f stretcher.

Baiser [bɛ'zeː] (-s, -s) nt meringue.

Baisse ['bɛːsə] (-, -n) f (Börse) fall; (plötzlich) slump.

Bajonett [bajo'nɛt] (-(e)s, -e) nt bayonet.

Bakelit ® [bake'liːt] (-s) nt Bakelite ®.

Bakterien [bak'teːriən] pl bacteria pl.

Balance [ba'lãːsə] (-, -n) f balance, equilibrium.

balancieren vt, vi to balance.

bald [balt] adv (zeitlich) soon; (beinahe) almost; ~ ... ~ ... now ... now ...; ~ **darauf** soon afterwards; **bis ~!** see you soon.

baldig ['baldɪç] adj early, speedy.

baldmöglichst adv as soon as possible.

Baldrian ['baldriaːn] (-s, -e) m valerian.

Balearen [bale'aːrən] pl: **die ~** the Balearics pl.

Balg [balk] (-(e)s, ∺er) (pej: umg) m od nt (Kind) brat.

balgen vr: **sich ~ (um)** to scrap (over).

Balkan ['balkaːn] m: **der ~** the Balkans pl.

Balken ['balkən] (-s, -) m beam; (Trag~) girder; (Stütz~) prop.

Balkon [bal'kõː] (-s, -s od -e) m balcony; (THEAT) (dress) circle.

Ball [bal] (-(e)s, ∺e) m ball; (Tanz) dance, ball.

Ballade [ba'laːdə] (-, -n) f ballad.

Ballast ['balast] (-(e)s, -e) m ballast; (fig) weight, burden; **~stoffe** pl (MED) roughage sing.

Ballen ['balən] (-s, -) m bale; (ANAT) ball.

ballen vt (formen) to make into a ball; (Faust) to clench ♦ vr to build up; (Menschen) to gather.

ballern ['balərn] (umg) vi to shoot, fire.

Ballett [ba'lɛt] (-(e)s, -e) nt ballet; **~(t)änzer(in)** m(f) ballet dancer.

Ballistik [ba'lɪstɪk] f ballistics sing.

Balljunge m ball boy.

Ballkleid nt evening dress.

Ballon [ba'lõː] (-s, -s od -e) m balloon.

Ballspiel nt ball game.

Ballung ['baluŋ] f concentration; (von Energie) build-up.

Ballungs- zW: **~gebiet** nt, **~raum** m conurbation; **~zentrum** nt centre (BRIT) od center (US) (of population, industry etc).

Balsam ['balzaːm] (-s, -e) m balsam; (fig) balm.

Balte ['baltə] (-n, -n) m Balt; **er ist ~** he comes from the Baltic.

Baltikum ['baltikum] (-s) nt: **das ~** the Baltic States pl.

Baltin ['baltɪn] f siehe Balte.

baltisch adj Baltic attrib.

Balz [balts] (-, -en) f (Paarungsspiel) courtship display; (Paarungszeit) mating season.

Bambus ['bambus] (-ses, -se) m bamboo; **~rohr** nt bamboo cane.

Bammel ['baməl] (-s) (umg) m: **(einen) ~ vor jdm/etw haben** to be scared of sb/sth.

banal [ba'naːl] adj banal.

Banalität [banali'tɛːt] f banality.

Banane [ba'naːnə] (-, -n) f banana.

Bananenschale f banana skin.
Bananenstecker m jack plug.
Banause [ba'nauzə] (-n, -n) m philistine.
Band¹ [bant] (-(e)s, ⁼e) m (*Buchband*) volume; **das spricht Bände** that speaks volumes.
Band² (-(e)s, ⁼er) nt (*Stoff~*) ribbon, tape; (*Fließ~*) production line; (*Faß~*) hoop; (*Ziel~, Ton~*) tape; (*ANAT*) ligament; **etw auf ~ aufnehmen** to tape sth; **am laufenden ~** (*umg*) non-stop.
Band³ (-(e)s, -e) nt (*Freundschafts~* etc) bond.
Band⁴ [bɛnt] (-, -s) f band, group.
band etc [bant] vb siehe **binden**.
Bandage [banda:ʒə] (-, -n) f bandage.
bandagieren vt to bandage.
Bandbreite f (*von Meinungen* etc) range.
Bande ['bandə] (-, -n) f band; (*Straßen~*) gang.
bändigen ['bɛndɪgən] vt (*Tier*) to tame; (*Trieb, Leidenschaft*) to control, restrain.
Bandit [ban'di:t] (-en, -en) m bandit.
Band- zW: ~**maß** nt tape measure; ~**nudeln** pl tagliatelle pl; ~**säge** f band saw; ~**scheibe** f (*ANAT*) disc; ~**scheibenschaden** m slipped disc; ~**wurm** m tapeworm.
bange ['baŋə] adj scared; (*besorgt*) anxious; **jdm wird es ~** sb is becoming scared; **jdm ~ machen** to scare sb; **B~macher** (-s, -) m scaremonger.
bangen vi: **um jdn/etw ~** to be anxious od worried about sb/sth.
Bangkok ['baŋkɔk] (-s) nt Bangkok.
Bangladesch [baŋgla'dɛʃ] (-s) nt Bangladesh.
Banjo ['banjo, 'bɛndʒo] (-s, -s) nt banjo.
Bank¹ [baŋk] (-, ⁼e) f (*Sitz~*) bench; (*Sand~* etc) (sand)bank, (sand)bar; **etw auf die lange ~ schieben** (*umg*) to put sth off.
Bank² (-, -en) f (*Geld~*) bank; **bei der ~** at the bank; **Geld auf der ~ haben** to have money in the bank; ~**anweisung** f banker's order; ~**automat** m cash dispenser; ~**beamte(r)** m bank clerk; ~**einlage** f (bank) deposit.
Bankett [baŋ'kɛt] (-(e)s, -e) nt (*Essen*) banquet; (*Straßenrand*) verge (*BRIT*), shoulder (*US*).
Bank- zW: ~**fach** nt (*Schließfach*) safe-deposit box; ~**gebühr** f bank charge; ~**geheimnis** nt confidentiality in banking.
Bankier [baŋki'e:] (-s, -s) m banker.
Bank- zW: ~**konto** nt bank account; ~**leitzahl** f bank code number; ~**note** f banknote; ~**raub** m bank robbery.
bankrott [baŋ'krɔt] adj bankrupt; **B~** (-(e)s, -e) m bankruptcy; **B~ machen** to go bankrupt; **den B~ anmelden** od **erklären** to declare o.s. bankrupt; **B~erklärung** f (*lit*) declaration of bankruptcy; (*fig: umg*) declaration of failure.
Banküberfall m bank raid.
Bann [ban] (-(e)s, -e) m (*HIST*) ban; (*Kirchen~*) excommunication; (*fig: Zauber*) spell; **b~en**

vt (*Geister*) to exorcize; (*Gefahr*) to avert; (*bezaubern*) to enchant; (*HIST*) to banish.
Banner (-s, -) nt banner, flag.
Bar [ba:r] (-, -s) f bar.
bar adj (+gen) (*unbedeckt*) bare; (*frei von*) lacking (in); (*offenkundig*) utter, sheer; ~**e(s) Geld** cash; **etw (in) ~ bezahlen** to pay sth (in) cash; **etw für ~e Münze nehmen** (*fig*) to take sth at face value; ~ **aller Hoffnung** (*liter*) devoid of hope, completely without hope.
Bär [bɛ:r] (-en, -en) m bear; **jdm einen ~en aufbinden** (*umg*) to have sb on.
Baracke [ba'rakə] (-, -n) f hut.
barbarisch [bar'ba:rɪʃ] adj barbaric, barbarous.
Barbestand m money in hand.
Bardame f barmaid.
Bärenhunger (*umg*) m: **einen ~ haben** to be famished.
bärenstark (*umg*) adj strapping, strong as an ox; (*fig*) terrific.
barfuß adj barefoot.
barg etc [bark] vb siehe **bergen**.
Bargeld nt cash, ready money.
bargeldlos adj non-cash; ~**er Zahlungsverkehr** non-cash od credit transactions pl.
barhäuptig adj bareheaded.
Barhocker m bar stool.
Bariton ['ba:ritɔn] m baritone.
Barkauf m cash purchase.
Barkeeper ['ba:rki:pər] (-s, -) m barman, bartender.
Barkredit m cash loan.
Barmann (-(e)s, pl -männer) m barman.
barmherzig [barm'hɛrtsɪç] adj merciful, compassionate; **B~keit** f mercy, compassion.
Barock [ba'rɔk] (-s od -) nt od m baroque.
Barometer [baro'me:tər] (-s, -) nt barometer; **das ~ steht auf Sturm** (*fig*) there's a storm brewing.
Baron [ba'ro:n] (-s, -e) m baron.
Baronesse [baro'nɛsə] (-, -n) f baroness.
Baronin f baroness.
Barren ['barən] (-s, -) m parallel bars pl; (*Gold~*) ingot.
Barriere [bari'ɛ:rə] (-, -n) f barrier.
Barrikade [bari'ka:də] (-, -n) f barricade.
Barsch [barʃ] (-(e)s, -e) m perch.
barsch [barʃ] adj brusque, gruff; **jdn ~ anfahren** to snap at sb.
Barschaft f ready money.
Barscheck m open od uncrossed cheque (*BRIT*), open check (*US*).
barst etc [barst] vb siehe **bersten**.
Bart [ba:rt] (-(e)s, ⁼e) m beard; (*Schlüssel~*) bit.
bärtig ['bɛ:rtɪç] adj bearded.
Barvermögen nt liquid assets pl.
Barzahlung f cash payment.

Basar [ba'zaːr] (-s, -e) *m* bazaar.
Base ['baːzə] (-, -n) *f* (*CHEM*) base; (*Kusine*) cousin.
Basel ['baːzəl] (-s) *nt* Basle.
Basen *pl von* **Base, Basis.**
basieren [ba'ziːrən] *vt* to base ♦ *vi* to be based.
Basilikum [ba'ziːlikʊm] (-s) *nt* basil.
Basis ['baːzɪs] (-, *pl* **Basen**) *f* basis; (*ARCHIT, MIL, MATH*) base; ~ **und Überbau** (*POL, SOZIOLOGIE*) foundation and superstructure; **die** ~ (*umg*) the grass roots.
basisch ['baːzɪʃ] *adj* (*CHEM*) alkaline.
Basisgruppe *f* action group.
Baske ['baskə] (-n, -n) *m* Basque.
Baskenland *nt* Basque region.
Baskenmütze *f* beret.
Baskin *f* Basque.
Baß [bas] (**Basses**, *pl* **Bässe**) *m* bass.
Bassin [ba'sɛː] (-s, -s) *nt* pool.
Bassist [ba'sɪst] *m* bass.
Baßschlüssel *m* bass clef.
Baßstimme *f* bass voice.
Bast [bast] (-(e)s, -e) *m* raffia.
basta ['basta] *interj*: **(und damit)** ~! (and) that's that!
basteln ['bastəln] *vt* to make ♦ *vi* to do handicrafts; **an etw** *dat* ~ (*an etw herum~*) to tinker with sth.
Bastler ['bastlər] (-s, -) *m* do-it-yourselfer; (*handwerklich*) handicrafts enthusiast.
BAT *m abk* (= *Bundesangestelltentarif*) German salary scale for employees.
bat *etc* [baːt] *vb siehe* **bitten.**
Bataillon [batal'joːn] (-s, -e) *nt* battalion.
Batist [ba'tɪst] (-(e)s, -e) *m* batiste.
Batterie [batə'riː] *f* battery.
Bau [baʊ] (-(e)s) *m* (~*en*) building, construction; (*Auf~*) structure; (*Körper~*) frame; (~*stelle*) building site; (*pl ~e: Tier~*) hole, burrow; (: *MIN*) working(s); (*pl ~ten: Gebäude*) building; **sich im** ~ **befinden** to be under construction; ~**arbeiten** *pl* (*Straßen~*) roadworks *pl* (*BRIT*), roadwork *sing* (*US*); building *od* construction work *sing*; ~**arbeiter** *m* building worker.
Bauch [baʊx] (-(e)s, **Bäuche**) *m* belly; (*ANAT*) stomach, abdomen; **sich** *dat* **(vor Lachen) den** ~ **halten** (*umg*) to split one's sides (laughing); **mit etw auf den** ~ **fallen** (*umg*) to come a cropper with sth; ~**ansatz** *m* beginning of a paunch; ~**fell** *nt* peritoneum.
bauchig *adj* bulging.
Bauch- *zW*: ~**landung** *f*: **eine** ~**landung machen** (*fig*) to experience a failure, to flop; ~**muskel** *m* abdominal muscle; ~**nabel** *m* navel, belly-button (*umg*); ~**redner** *m* ventriloquist; ~**schmerzen** *pl* stomachache *sing*; ~**speicheldrüse** *f* pancreas; ~**tanz** *m* belly dance; belly dancing; ~**weh** *nt* stomachache.
Baud-Rate [baʊt'raːtə] *f* (*COMPUT*) baud rate.
bauen ['baʊən] *vt* to build; (*TECH*) to construct; (*umg: verursachen: Unfall*) to cause ♦ *vi* to build; **auf jdn/etw** ~ to depend *od* count upon sb/sth; **da hast du Mist gebaut** (*umg*) you really messed that up.
Bauer¹ ['baʊər] (-n *od* -s, -n) *m* farmer; (*SCHACH*) pawn.
Bauer² (-s, -) *nt od m* (*Vogel~*) cage.
Bäuerchen ['bɔyərçən] *nt* (*Kindersprache*) burp.
Bäuerin ['bɔyərɪn] *f* farmer; (*Frau des Bauern*) farmer's wife.
bäuerlich *adj* rustic.
Bauern- *zW*: ~**brot** *nt* black bread; ~**fänge'rei** *f* deception, confidence trick(s); ~**frühstück** *nt* bacon and potato omelette (*BRIT*) *od* omelet (*US*); ~**haus** *nt* farmhouse; ~**hof** *m* farm; ~**schaft** *f* farming community; ~**schläue** *f* native cunning, craftiness, shrewdness.
Bau- *zW*: **b~fällig** *adj* dilapidated; ~**fälligkeit** *f* dilapidation; ~**firma** *f* construction firm; ~**führer** *m* site foreman; ~**gelände** *nt* building site; ~**genehmigung** *f* building permit; ~**gerüst** *nt* scaffolding; ~**herr** *m* client (*of construction firm*); ~**ingenieur** *m* civil engineer.
Bauj. *abk* = **Baujahr.**
Bau- *zW*: ~**jahr** *nt* year of construction; (*von Auto*) year of manufacture; ~**kasten** *m* box of bricks; ~**klötzchen** *nt* (building) block; ~**kosten** *pl* construction costs *pl*; ~**land** *nt* building land; ~**leute** *pl* building workers *pl*; **b~lich** *adj* structural; ~**löwe** *m* building speculator; ~**lücke** *f* undeveloped building plot.
Baum [baʊm] (-(e)s, *pl* **Bäume**) *m* tree; **heute könnte ich Bäume ausreißen** I feel full of energy today.
Baumarkt *m* DIY superstore.
baumeln ['baʊməln] *vi* to dangle.
bäumen ['bɔymən] *vr* to rear (up).
Baum- *zW*: ~**grenze** *f* tree line; ~**schule** *f* nursery; ~**stamm** *m* tree trunk; ~**stumpf** *m* tree stump; ~**wolle** *f* cotton.
Bau- *zW*: ~**plan** *m* architect's plan; ~**platz** *m* building site; ~**sachverständige(r)** *f(m)* quantity surveyor; ~**satz** *m* construction kit.
Bausch [baʊʃ] (-(e)s, *pl* **Bäusche**) *m* (*Watte~*) ball, wad; **in** ~ **und Bogen** (*fig*) lock, stock, and barrel.
bauschen *vt, vi, vr* to puff out.
bauschig *adj* baggy, wide.
Bau- *zW*: **b~sparen** *vi untr* to save with a building society (*BRIT*) *od a* building and loan association (*US*); ~**sparkasse** *f* building society (*BRIT*), building and loan association (*US*); ~**sparvertrag** *m* savings contract with a building society (*BRIT*) *od* building and loan association (*US*); ~**stein** *m* building stone, freestone; ~**stelle** *f* building site; ~**stil** *m* architectural style;

b~technisch adj in accordance with building od construction methods; **~teil** nt prefabricated part (of building); **~ten** pl von **Bau**; **~unternehmer** m contractor, builder; **~weise** f (method of) construction; **~werk** nt building; **~zaun** m hoarding.

b.a.w. abk (= bis auf weiteres) until further notice.

Bayer(in) ['baɪər(ɪn)] (-n, -n) m(f) Bavarian.

bay(e)risch adj Bavarian.

Bayern nt Bavaria.

Bazillus [ba'tsɪlʊs] (-, pl **Bazillen**) m bacillus.

Bd. abk (= Band) vol.

Bde. abk (= Bände) vols.

beabsichtigen [bə'|apzɪçtɪgən] vt to intend.

beachten [bə'|axtən] vt to take note of; (Vorschrift) to obey; (Vorfahrt) to observe.

beachtenswert adj noteworthy.

beachtlich adj considerable.

Beachtung f notice, attention, observation; **jdm keine ~ schenken** to take no notice of sb.

Beamte(r) [bə'|amtə(r)] (-n, -n) m official; (Staats~) civil servant; (Bank~ etc) employee.

Beamtenlaufbahn f: **die ~ einschlagen** to enter the civil service.

Beamtenverhältnis nt: **im ~ stehen** to be a civil servant.

beamtet adj (form) appointed on a permanent basis (by the state).

Beamtin f siehe **Beamte(r)**.

beängstigend [bə'|ɛŋstɪgənt] adj alarming.

beanspruchen [bə'|anʃprʊxən] vt to claim; (Zeit, Platz) to take up, occupy; **jdn ~** to take up sb's time; **etw stark ~** to put sth under a lot of stress.

beanstanden [bə'|anʃtandən] vt to complain about, object to; (Rechnung) to query.

Beanstandung f complaint.

beantragen [bə'|antra:gən] vt to apply for, ask for.

beantworten [bə'|antvɔrtən] vt to answer.

Beantwortung f reply.

bearbeiten [bə'|arbaɪtən] vt to work; (Material) to process; (Thema) to deal with; (Land) to cultivate; (CHEM) to treat; (Buch) to revise; (umg: beeinflussen wollen) to work on.

Bearbeitung f processing; cultivation; treatment; revision; **die ~ meines Antrags hat lange gedauert** it took a long time to deal with my claim.

Bearbeitungsgebühr f handling charge.

beatmen [bə'|a:tmən] vt: **jdn künstlich ~** to give sb artificial respiration.

Beatmung [bə'|a:tmʊŋ] f respiration.

beaufsichtigen [bə'|aʊfzɪçtɪgən] vt to supervise.

Beaufsichtigung f supervision.

beauftragen [bə'|aʊftra:gən] vt to instruct; **jdn mit etw ~** to entrust sb with sth.

Beauftragte(r) f(m) representative.

bebauen [bə'baʊən] vt to build on; (AGR) to cultivate.

beben ['be:bən] vi to tremble, shake; **B~ (-s -)** nt earthquake.

bebildern [bə'bɪldərn] vt to illustrate.

Becher ['bɛçər] (-s, -) m mug; (ohne Henkel) tumbler.

bechern ['bɛçərn] (umg) vi (trinken) to have a few (drinks).

Becken ['bɛkən] (-s, -) nt basin; (MUS) cymbal; (ANAT) pelvis.

Bedacht [bə'daxt] m: **mit ~** (vorsichtig) prudently, carefully; (absichtlich) deliberately.

bedacht adj thoughtful, careful; **auf etw** akk **~ sein** to be concerned about sth.

bedächtig [bə'dɛçtɪç] adj (umsichtig) thoughtful, reflective; (langsam) slow, deliberate.

bedanken [bə'daŋkən] vr: **sich (bei jdm) ~** to say thank you (to sb); **ich bedanke mich herzlich** thank you very much.

Bedarf [bə'darf] (-(e)s -) m need; (~smenge) requirements pl; (COMM) demand; supply; **alles für den häuslichen ~** all household requirements; **je nach ~** according to demand; **bei ~** if necessary; **~ an etw** dat **haben** to be in need of sth.

Bedarfs- zW: **~artikel** m requisite; **~deckung** f satisfaction of sb's needs; **~fall** m case of need; **~haltestelle** f request stop.

bedauerlich [bə'daʊərlɪç] adj regrettable.

bedauern [bə'daʊərn] vt to be sorry for; (bemitleiden) to pity; **wir ~, Ihnen mitteilen zu müssen, ...** we regret to have to inform you ...; **B~ (-s)** nt regret.

bedauernswert adj (Zustände) regrettable; (Mensch) pitiable, unfortunate.

bedecken [bə'dɛkən] vt to cover.

bedeckt adj covered; (Himmel) overcast.

bedenken [bə'dɛŋkən] unreg vt to think over, consider; **ich gebe zu ~, daß ...** (geh) I would ask you to consider that ...; **B~ (-s, -)** nt (Überlegen) consideration; (Zweifel) doubt; (Skrupel) scruple; **mir kommen B~** I am having second thoughts.

bedenklich adj doubtful; (bedrohlich) dangerous, risky.

Bedenkzeit f time to consider; **zwei Tage ~** two days to think about it.

bedeuten [bə'dɔʏtən] vt to mean; to signify; (wichtig sein) to be of importance; **das bedeutet nichts Gutes** that means trouble.

bedeutend adj important; (beträchtlich) considerable.

bedeutsam adj significant; (vielsagend) meaningful.

Bedeutung f meaning; significance; (Wichtigkeit) importance.

bedeutungslos adj insignificant, unimportant.

bedeutungsvoll adj momentous, significant.

bedienen [bə'di:nən] *vt* to serve; (*Maschine*) to work, operate ♦ *vr* (*beim Essen*) to help o.s.; (*gebrauchen*): **sich jds/einer Sache ~** to make use of sb/sth; **werden Sie schon bedient?** are you being served?; **damit sind Sie sehr gut bedient** that should serve you very well; **ich bin bedient!** (*umg*) I've had enough.

Bedienung *f* service; (*Kellner etc*) waiter/waitress; (*Zuschlag*) service (charge); (*von Maschinen*) operation.

Bedienungsanleitung *f* operating instructions *pl.*

bedingen [bə'diŋən] *vt* (*voraussetzen*) to demand, involve; (*verursachen*) to cause, occasion.

bedingt *adj* limited; (*Straferlaß*) conditional; (*Reflex*) conditioned; **(nur) ~ gelten** to be (only) partially valid; **~ geeignet** suitable up to a point.

Bedingung *f* condition; (*Voraussetzung*) stipulation; **mit** *od* **unter der ~, daß ...** on condition that ...; **zu günstigen ~en** (*COMM*) on favourable (*BRIT*) *od* favorable (*US*) terms.

Bedingungsform *f* (*GRAM*) conditional.

bedingungslos *adj* unconditional.

bedrängen [bə'drɛŋən] *vt* to pester, harass.

Bedrängnis [bə'drɛŋnis] *f* (*seelisch*) distress, torment.

Bedrängung *f* trouble.

bedrohen [bə'dro:ən] *vt* to threaten.

bedrohlich *adj* ominous, threatening.

Bedrohung *f* threat, menace.

bedrucken [bə'drukən] *vt* to print on.

bedrücken [bədrykən] *vt* to oppress, trouble.

bedürfen [bə'dyrfən] *unreg vi +gen* (*geh*) to need, require; **ohne daß es eines Hinweises bedurft hätte, ...** without having to be asked ...

Bedürfnis [bə'dyrfnis] (**-ses, -se**) *nt* need; **das ~ nach etw haben** to need sth; **~anstalt** *f* (*form*) public convenience (*BRIT*), comfort station (*US*); **b~los** *adj* frugal, modest.

bedürftig *adj* in need, poor, needy.

Beefsteak ['bi:fste:k] (**-s, -s**) *nt* steak; **deutsches ~** ≈ hamburger.

beehren [bə'e:rən] *vt* (*geh*) to honour (*BRIT*), honor (*US*); **wir ~ uns ...** we have pleasure in ...

beeilen [bə'ailən] *vr* to hurry.

beeindrucken [bə'aindrukən] *vt* to impress, make an impression on.

beeinflussen [bə'ainflusən] *vt* to influence.

Beeinflussung *f* influence.

beeinträchtigen [bə'aintrɛçtigən] *vt* to affect adversely; (*Sehvermögen*) to impair; (*Freiheit*) to infringe upon.

beend(ig)en [bə'ɛnd(ig)ən] *vt* to end, finish, terminate.

Beend(ig)ung *f* end(ing), finish(ing).

beengen [bə'ɛŋən] *vt* to cramp; (*fig*) to

hamper, inhibit; **~de Kleidung** restricting clothing.

beengt *adj* cramped; (*fig*) stifled.

beerben [bə'ɛrbən] *vt* to inherit from.

beerdigen [bə'e:rdigən] *vt* to bury.

Beerdigung *f* funeral, burial.

Beerdigungsunternehmer *m* undertaker.

Beere ['be:rə] (**-, -n**) *f* berry; (*Trauben~*) grape.

Beerenauslese *f* wine made from specially selected grapes.

Beet [be:t] (**-(e)s, -e**) *nt* (*Blumen~*) bed.

befähigen [bə'fɛ:igən] *vt* to enable.

befähigt *adj* (*begabt*) talented; (*fähig*): **~ (für)** capable (of).

Befähigung *f* capability; (*Begabung*) talent, aptitude; **die ~ zum Richteramt** the qualifications to become a judge.

befahl *etc* [bə'fa:l] *vb siehe* **befehlen.**

befahrbar [bə'fa:rba:r] *adj* passable; (*NAUT*) navigable; **nicht ~ sein** (*Straße, Weg*) to be closed (to traffic); (*wegen Schnee etc*) to be impassable.

befahren [bə'fa:rən] *unreg vt* to use, drive over; (*NAUT*) to navigate ♦ *adj* used.

befallen [bə'falən] *unreg vt* to come over.

befangen [bə'faŋən] *adj* (*schüchtern*) shy, self-conscious; (*voreingenommen*) bias(s)ed; **B~heit** *f* shyness; bias.

befassen [bə'fasən] *vr* to concern o.s.

Befehl [bə'fe:l] (**-(e)s, -e**) *m* command, order; (*COMPUT*) command; **auf ~ handeln** to act under orders; **zu ~, Herr Hauptmann!** (*MIL*) yes, sir; **den ~ haben** *od* **führen (über** +*akk*) to be in command (of).

befehlen *unreg vt* to order ♦ *vi* to give orders; **jdm etw ~** to order sb to do sth; **du hast mir gar nichts zu ~** I won't take orders from you.

befehligen *vt* to be in command of.

Befehls- *zW*: **~empfänger** *m* subordinate; **~form** *f* (*GRAM*) imperative; **~haber** (**-s, -**) *m* commanding officer; **~notstand** *m* (*JUR*) obligation to obey orders; **~verweigerung** *f* insubordination.

befestigen [bə'fɛstigən] *vt* to fasten; (*stärken*) to strengthen; (*MIL*) to fortify; **~ an** +*dat* to fasten to.

Befestigung *f* fastening; strengthening; (*MIL*) fortification.

Befestigungsanlage *f* fortification.

befeuchten [bə'fɔyçtən] *vt* to damp(en), moisten.

befinden [bə'findən] *unreg vr* to be; (*sich fühlen*) to feel ♦ *vt*: **jdn/etw für** *od* **als etw ~** to deem sb/sth to be sth ♦ *vi*: **~ (über** +*akk*) to decide (on), adjudicate (on).

Befinden (**-s**) *nt* health, condition; (*Meinung*) view, opinion.

beflecken [bə'flɛkən] *vt* (*lit*) to stain; (*fig geh: Ruf, Ehre*) to besmirch.

befliegen [bə'fli:gən] *unreg vt* (*Strecke*) to fly.

beflügeln [bə'fly:gəln] vt (geh) to inspire.
befohlen [bə'fo:lən] pp von **befehlen**.
befolgen [bə'fɔlgən] vt to comply with, follow.
befördern [bə'fœrdərn] vt (senden) to transport, send; (beruflich) to promote; **etw mit der Post/per Bahn** ~ to send sth by post/by rail.
Beförderung f transport; promotion.
Beförderungskosten pl transport costs pl.
befragen [bə'fra:gən] vt to question; (um Stellungnahme bitten): ~ (**über** +akk) to consult (about).
Befragung f poll.
befreien [bə'fraɪən] vt to set free; (erlassen) to exempt.
Befreier(in) (-s, -) m(f) liberator.
befreit adj (erleichtert) relieved.
Befreiung f liberation, release; (Erlassen) exemption.
Befreiungs- zW: ~**bewegung** f liberation movement; ~**kampf** m struggle for liberation; ~**versuch** m escape attempt.
befremden [bə'frɛmdən] vt to surprise; (unangenehm) to disturb; **B**~ (-s) nt surprise, astonishment.
befreunden [bə'frɔʏndən] vr to make friends; (mit Idee etc) to acquaint o.s.
befreundet adj friendly; **wir sind schon lange (miteinander)** ~ we have been friends for a long time.
befriedigen [bə'fri:dɪgən] vt to satisfy.
befriedigend adj satisfactory.
Befriedigung f satisfaction, gratification.
befristet [bə'frɪstət] adj limited; (Arbeitsverhältnis, Anstellung) temporary.
befruchten [bə'frʊxtən] vt to fertilize; (fig) to stimulate.
Befruchtung f: **künstliche** ~ artificial insemination.
Befugnis [bə'fu:knɪs] (-, -se) f authorization, powers pl.
befugt adj authorized, entitled.
befühlen [bə'fy:lən] vt to feel, touch.
Befund [bə'fʊnt] (-(e)s, -e) m findings pl; (MED) diagnosis; **ohne** ~ (MED) (results) negative.
befürchten [bə'fʏrçtən] vt to fear.
Befürchtung f fear, apprehension.
befürworten [bə'fy:rvɔrtən] vt to support, speak in favour (BRIT) od favor (US) of.
Befürworter(in) (-s, -) m(f) supporter, advocate.
Befürwortung f support(ing), favouring (BRIT), favoring (US).
begabt [bə'ga:pt] adj gifted.
Begabung [bə'ga:bʊŋ] f talent, gift.
begann etc [bə'gan] vb siehe **beginnen**.
begatten [bə'gatən] vr to mate ♦ vt to mate od pair (with).
begeben [bə'ge:bən] unreg vr (gehen) to proceed; (geschehen) to occur; **sich** ~ **nach** od **zu** to proceed to(wards); **sich in ärztliche Behandlung** ~ to undergo medical

treatment; **sich in Gefahr** ~ to expose o.s. to danger; **B**~**heit** f occurrence.
begegnen [bə'ge:gnən] vi: **jdm** ~ to meet sb; (behandeln) to treat; **Blicke** ~ **sich** eyes meet.
Begegnung f meeting; (SPORT) match.
begehen [bə'ge:ən] unreg vt (Straftat) to commit; (Weg etc) to use, negotiate; (geh: feiern) to celebrate.
begehren [bə'ge:rən] vt to desire.
begehrenswert adj desirable.
begehrt adj in demand; (Junggeselle) eligible.
begeistern [bə'gaɪstərn] vt to fill with enthusiasm; (inspirieren) to inspire ♦ vr: **sich für etw** ~ to get enthusiastic about sth; **er ist für nichts zu** ~ he's not interested in doing anything.
begeistert adj enthusiastic.
Begeisterung f enthusiasm.
Begierde [bə'gi:rdə] (-, -n) f desire, passion.
begierig [bə'gi:rɪç] adj eager, keen; (voll Verlangen) hungry, greedy.
begießen [bə'gi:sən] unreg vt to water; (mit Fett: Braten etc) to baste; (mit Alkohol) to drink to.
Beginn [bə'gɪn] (-(e)s) m beginning; **zu** ~ at the beginning.
beginnen unreg vt, vi to start, begin.
beglaubigen [bə'glaʊbɪgən] vt to countersign; (Abschrift) to authenticate; (Echtheit, Übersetzung) to certify.
Beglaubigung f countersignature.
Beglaubigungsschreiben nt credentials pl.
begleichen [bə'glaɪçən] unreg vt to settle, pay; **mit Ihnen habe ich noch eine Rechnung zu** ~ (fig) I've a score to settle with you.
begleiten [bə'glaɪtən] vt to accompany; (MIL) to escort.
Begleiter(in) (-s, -) m(f) companion; (zum Schutz) escort; (MUS) accompanist.
Begleit- zW: ~**erscheinung** f side effect; ~**musik** f accompaniment; ~**papiere** pl (COMM) accompanying documents pl; ~**schiff** nt escort vessel; ~**schreiben** nt covering letter; ~**umstände** pl attendant circumstances.
Begleitung f company; (MIL) escort; (MUS) accompaniment.
beglücken [bə'glʏkən] vt to make happy, delight.
beglückwünschen [bə'glʏkvʏnʃən] vt: ~ (**zu**) to congratulate (on).
begnadet [bə'gna:dət] adj gifted.
begnadigen [bə'gna:dɪgən] vt to pardon.
Begnadigung f pardon.
begnügen [bə'gny:gən] vr: **sich** ~ **mit** to be satisfied with, content o.s. with.
Begonie [bə'go:niə] f begonia.
begonnen [bə'gɔnən] pp von **beginnen**.
begossen [bə'gɔsən] pp von **begießen** ♦ adj: **er stand da wie ein** ~**er Pudel** (umg) he looked so sheepish.

begraben [bə'graːbən] *unreg vt* to bury; (*aufgeben: Hoffnung*) to abandon; (*beenden: Streit etc*) to end; **dort möchte ich nicht ~ sein** (*umg*) I wouldn't like to be stuck in that hole.

Begräbnis [bə'grɛːpnɪs] (**-ses, -se**) *nt* burial, funeral.

begradigen [bə'graːdɪgən] *vt* to straighten (out).

begreifen [bə'graɪfən] *unreg vt* to understand, comprehend.

begreiflich [bə'graɪflɪç] *adj* understandable; **ich kann mich ihm nicht ~ machen** I can't make myself clear to him.

begrenzen [bə'grɛntsən] *vt* (*beschränken*): **~ (auf +akk)** to restrict (to), limit (to).

Begrenztheit [bə'grɛntsthaɪt] *f* limitation, restriction; (*fig*) narrowness.

Begriff [bə'grɪf] (**-(e)s, -e**) *m* concept, idea; **im ~ sein, etw zu tun** to be about to do sth; **sein Name ist mir ein/kein ~** his name means something/doesn't mean anything to me; **du machst dir keinen ~ (davon)** you've no idea; **für meine ~e** in my opinion; **schwer von ~** (*umg*) slow on the uptake.

Begriffsbestimmung *f* definition.

begriffsstutzig *adj* slow-witted, dense.

begrub *etc* [bə'gruːp] *vb siehe* **begraben.**

begründen [bə'gryndən] *vt* (*Gründe geben*) to justify; **etw näher ~** to give specific reasons for sth.

Begründer(in) (**-s, -**) *m(f)* founder.

begründet *adj* well-founded, justified; **sachlich ~** founded on fact.

Begründung *f* justification, reason.

begrünen [bə'gryːnən] *vt* to plant with greenery.

begrüßen [bə'gryːsən] *vt* to greet, welcome.

begrüßenswert *adj* welcome.

Begrüßung *f* greeting, welcome.

begünstigen [bə'gynstɪgən] *vt* (*Person*) to favour (*BRIT*), favor (*US*); (*Sache*) to further, promote.

Begünstigte(r) *f(m)* beneficiary.

begutachten [bə'guːtʔaxtən] *vt* to assess; (*umg: ansehen*) to have a look at.

begütert [bə'gyːtərt] *adj* wealthy, well-to-do.

begütigend *adj* (*Worte etc*) soothing; **~ auf jdn einreden** to calm sb down.

behaart [bə'haːrt] *adj* hairy.

behäbig [bə'hɛːbɪç] *adj* (*dick*) portly, stout; (*geruhsam*) comfortable.

behaftet [bə'haftət] *adj*: **mit etw ~ sein** to be afflicted by sth.

behagen [bə'haːgən] *vi*: **das behagt ihm nicht** he does not like it; **B~ (-s)** *nt* comfort, ease; **mit B~ essen** to eat with relish.

behaglich [bə'haːklɪç] *adj* comfortable, cosy; **B~keit** *f* comfort, cosiness.

behält [bə'hɛlt] *vb siehe* **behalten.**

behalten [bə'haltən] *unreg vt* to keep, retain; (*im Gedächtnis*) to remember; **~ Sie (doch)**

Platz! please don't get up!

Behälter [bə'hɛltər] (**-s, -**) *m* container, receptacle.

behämmert [bə'hɛmərt] (*umg*) *adj* screwy, crazy.

behandeln [bə'handəln] *vt* to treat; (*Thema*) to deal with; (*Maschine*) to handle; **der ~de Arzt** the doctor in attendance.

Behandlung *f* treatment; (*von Maschine*) handling.

behängen [bə'hɛŋən] *vt* to decorate.

beharren [bə'harən] *vi*: **auf etw** *dat* **~** to stick *od* keep to sth.

beharrlich [bə'harlɪç] *adj* (*ausdauernd*) steadfast, unwavering; (*hartnäckig*) tenacious, dogged; **B~keit** *f* steadfastness; tenacity.

behaupten [bə'haʊptən] *vt* to claim, assert, maintain; (*sein Recht*) to defend ♦ *vr* to assert o.s.; **von jdm ~, daß ...** to say (of sb) that ...; **sich auf dem Markt ~** to establish itself on the market.

Behauptung *f* claim, assertion.

Behausung [bə'haʊzʊŋ] *f* dwelling, abode; (*armselig*) hovel.

beheben [bə'heːbən] *unreg vt* (*beseitigen*) to remove; (*Mißstände*) to remedy; (*Schaden*) to repair; (*Störung*) to clear.

beheimatet [bə'haɪmaːtət] *adj*: **~ (in +dat)** domiciled (at/in); (*Tier, Pflanze*) native (to).

beheizen [bə'haɪtsən] *vt* to heat.

Behelf [bə'hɛlf] (**-(e)s, -e**) *m* expedient, makeshift; **b~en** *unreg vr*: **sich mit etw b~en** to make do with sth.

behelfsmäßig *adj* improvised, makeshift; (*vorübergehend*) temporary.

behelligen [bə'hɛlɪgən] *vt* to trouble, bother.

Behendigkeit [bə'hɛndɪçkaɪt] *f* agility, quickness.

beherbergen [bə'hɛrbɛrgən] *vt* (*lit, fig*) to house.

beherrschen [bə'hɛrʃən] *vt* (*Volk*) to rule, govern; (*Situation*) to control; (*Sprache, Gefühle*) to master ♦ *vr* to control o.s.

beherrscht *adj* controlled; **B~heit** *f* self-control.

Beherrschung *f* rule; control; mastery; **die ~ verlieren** to lose one's temper.

beherzigen [bə'hɛrtsɪgən] *vt* to take to heart.

beherzt *adj* spirited, brave.

behielt *etc* [bə'hiːlt] *vb siehe* **behalten.**

behilflich [bə'hɪlflɪç] *adj* helpful; **jdm ~ sein (bei)** to help sb (with).

behindern [bə'hɪndərn] *vt* to hinder, impede.

Behinderte(r) *f(m)* disabled person.

Behinderung *f* hindrance; (*Körperbehinderung*) handicap.

Behörde [bə'høːrdə] (**-, -n**) *f* authorities *pl*; (*Amtsgebäude*) office(s) *pl*.

behördlich [bə'høːrtlɪç] *adj* official.

behüten [bə'hyːtən] *vt* to guard; **jdn vor etw** *dat* **~** to preserve sb from sth.

behütet *adj* (*Jugend etc*) sheltered.

behutsam [bə'huːtzaːm] *adj* cautious, careful; **man muß es ihr ~ beibringen** it will have to be broken to her gently; **B~keit** *f* caution, carefulness.

═══════════════════ *SCHLÜSSELWORT*

bei [baɪ] *präp +dat* **1** (*nähe ~*) near; (*zum Aufenthalt*) at, with; (*unter, zwischen*) among; **~ München** near Munich; **~ uns** at our place; **~m Friseur** at the hairdresser's; **~ seinen Eltern wohnen** to live with one's parents; **~ einer Firma arbeiten** to work for a firm; **etw ~ sich haben** to have sth on one; **jdn ~ sich haben** to have sb with one; **~ Goethe** in Goethe; **~m Militär** in the army **2** (*zeitlich*) at, on; (*während*) during; (*Zustand, Umstand*) in; **~ Nacht** at night; **~ Nebel** in fog; **~ Regen** if it rains; **~ solcher Hitze** in such heat; **~ meiner Ankunft** on my arrival; **~ der Arbeit** when I'm *etc* working; **~m Fahren** while driving; **~ offenem Fenster schlafen** to sleep with the window open; **~ Feuer Scheibe einschlagen** in case of fire break glass; **~ seinem Talent** with his talent.

beibehalten ['baɪbəhaltən] *unreg vt* to keep, retain.

Beibehaltung *f* keeping, retaining.

Beiblatt ['baɪblat] *nt* supplement.

beibringen ['baɪbrɪŋən] *unreg vt* (*Beweis, Zeugen*) to bring forward; (*Gründe*) to adduce; **jdm etw ~** (*zufügen*) to inflict sth on sb; (*zu verstehen geben*) to make sb understand sth; (*lehren*) to teach sb sth.

Beichte ['baɪçtə] *f* confession.

beichten *vt* to confess ♦ *vi* to go to confession.

Beichtgeheimnis *nt* secret of the confessional.

Beichtstuhl *m* confessional.

beide ['baɪdə] *pron, adj* both; **meine ~n Brüder** my two brothers, both my brothers; **die ersten ~n** the first two; **wir ~** we two; **einer von ~n** one of the two; **alles ~s** both (of them); **~mal** *adv* both times.

beider- *zW:* **~lei** *adj inv* of both; **~seitig** *adj* mutual, reciprocal; **~seits** *adv* mutually ♦ *präp +gen* on both sides of.

beidhändig ['baɪthɛndɪç] *adj* ambidextrous.

beidrehen ['baɪdreːən] *vi* to heave to.

beidseitig ['baɪtzaɪtɪç] *adj* (*auf beiden Seiten*) on both sides.

beieinander [baɪʔaɪ'nandər] *adv* together; **~sein** *unreg vi:* **gut ~sein** (*umg: gesundheitlich*) to be in good shape; (*: geistig*) to be all there.

Beifahrer(in) ['baɪfaːrər(ɪn)] (**-s, -**) *m(f)* passenger; **~sitz** *m* passenger seat.

Beifall ['baɪfal] (**-(e)s**) *m* applause; (*Zustimmung*) approval.

beifallheischend ['baɪfalhaɪʃənt] *adj* fishing for applause/approval.

beifällig ['baɪfɛlɪç] *adj* approving; (*Kommentar*) favourable (*BRIT*), favorable (*US*).

Beifilm ['baɪfɪlm] *m* supporting film.

beifügen ['baɪfyːgən] *vt* to enclose.

Beigabe ['baɪgaːbə] *f* addition.

beige ['beːʒ] *adj* beige.

beigeben ['baɪgeːbən] *unreg vt* (*zufügen*) to add; (*mitgeben*) to give ♦ *vi:* **klein ~** (*nachgeben*) to climb down.

Beigeschmack ['baɪgəʃmak] *m* aftertaste.

Beihilfe ['baɪhɪlfə] *f* aid, assistance; (*Studienbeihilfe*) grant; (*JUR*) aiding and abetting; **wegen ~ zum Mord** (*JUR*) because of being an accessory to the murder.

beikommen ['baɪkɔmən] *vi +dat* to get at; (*einem Problem*) to deal with.

Beil [baɪl] (**-(e)s, -e**) *nt* axe (*BRIT*), ax (*US*), hatchet.

Beilage ['baɪlaːgə] *f* (*Buch~ etc*) supplement; (*KOCH*) accompanying vegetables; (*getrennt serviert*) side dish.

beiläufig ['baɪlɔyfɪç] *adj* casual, incidental ♦ *adv* casually, by the way.

beilegen ['baɪleːgən] *vt* (*hinzufügen*) to enclose, add; (*beimessen*) to attribute, ascribe; (*Streit*) to settle.

beileibe [baɪ'laɪbə] *adv:* **~ nicht** by no means.

Beileid ['baɪlaɪt] *nt* condolence, sympathy; **herzliches ~** deepest sympathy.

beiliegend ['baɪliːgənt] *adj* (*COMM*) enclosed.

beim [baɪm] = **bei dem**.

beimessen ['baɪmɛsən] *unreg vt* to attribute, ascribe.

Bein [baɪn] (**-(e)s, -e**) *nt* leg; **jdm ein ~ stellen** (*lit, fig*) to trip sb up; **wir sollten uns auf die ~e machen** (*umg*) we ought to be making tracks; **jdm ~e machen** (*umg: antreiben*) to make sb get a move on; **die ~e in die Hand nehmen** (*umg*) to take to one's heels; **sich** *dat* **die ~e in den Bauch stehen** (*umg*) to stand about until one is fit to drop; **etw auf die ~e stellen** (*fig*) to get sth off the ground.

beinah(e) [baɪ'naː(ə)] *adv* almost, nearly.

Beinbruch *m* fracture of the leg; **das ist kein ~** (*fig: umg*) it could be worse.

beinhalten [bə'ʔɪnhaltən] *vt* to contain.

beipflichten ['baɪpflɪçtən] *vi:* **jdm/etw ~** to agree with sb/sth.

Beiprogramm ['baɪprogram] *nt* supporting programme (*BRIT*) *od* program (*US*).

Beirat ['baɪraːt] *m* advisory council; (*Eltern~*) parents' council.

beirren [bə'ʔɪrən] *vt* to confuse, muddle; **sich nicht ~ lassen** not to let o.s. be confused.

Beirut [baɪ'ruːt] (**-s**) *nt* Beirut.

beisammen [baɪ'zamən] *adv* together; **~haben** *unreg vi:* **er hat (sie) nicht alle ~** (*umg*) he's not all there; **B~sein** (**-s**) *nt* get-together.

Beischlaf ['baɪʃlaːf] *m* (*JUR*) sexual intercourse.

Beisein ['baɪzaɪn] (**-s**) *nt* presence.

beiseite [baɪ'zaɪtə] *adv* to one side, aside; (*stehen*) on one side, aside; **Spaß** ~! joking apart!; **etw** ~ **legen** (*sparen*) to put sth by; **jdn/etw** ~ **schaffen** to get rid of sb/sth.

beisetzen ['baɪzɛtsən] *vt* to bury.

Beisetzung *f* funeral.

Beisitzer(in) ['baɪzɪtsər(ɪn)] (**-s, -**) *m(f)* (*JUR*) assessor; (*bei Prüfung*) observer.

Beispiel ['baɪʃpiːl] (**-(e)s, -e**) *nt* example; **mit gutem** ~ **vorangehen** to set a good example; **sich** *dat* **an jdm ein** ~ **nehmen** to take sb as an example; **zum** ~ for example; **b~haft** *adj* exemplary; **b~los** *adj* unprecedented.

beispielsweise *adv* for instance, for example.

beispringen ['baɪʃprɪŋən] *unreg vi +dat* to come to the aid of.

beißen ['baɪsən] *unreg vt, vi* to bite; (*stechen: Rauch, Säure*) to burn ♦ *vr* (*Farben*) to clash.

beißend *adj* biting, caustic; (*Geruch*) pungent, sharp; (*fig*) sarcastic.

Beißzange ['baɪtsaŋə] *f* pliers *pl.*

Beistand ['baɪʃtant] (**-(e)s, ⁻e**) *m* support, help; (*JUR*) adviser; **jdm** ~ **leisten** to give sb assistance/one's support.

beistehen ['baɪʃteːən] *unreg vi*: **jdm** ~ to stand by sb.

Beistelltisch ['baɪʃtɛltɪʃ] *m* occasional table.

beisteuern ['baɪʃtɔyərn] *vt* to contribute.

beistimmen ['baɪʃtɪmən] *vi +dat* to agree with.

Beistrich ['baɪʃtrɪç] *m* comma.

Beitrag ['baɪtraːk] (**-(e)s, ⁻e**) *m* contribution; (*Zahlung*) fee, subscription; (*Versicherungs~*) premium; **einen** ~ **zu etw leisten** to make a contribution to sth.

beitragen ['baɪtraːgən] *unreg vt, vi*: ~ (**zu**) to contribute (to); (*mithelfen*) to help (with).

Beitrags- *zW*: **b~frei** *adj* non-contributory; **b~pflichtig** *adj* contributory; **b~pflichtig sein** (*Mensch*) to have to pay contributions; ~**zahlende(r)** *f(m)* fee-paying member.

beitreten ['baɪtreːtən] *unreg vi +dat* to join.

Beitritt ['baɪtrɪt] *m* joining; membership.

Beitrittserklärung *f* declaration of membership.

Beiwagen ['baɪvaːgən] *m* (*Motorrad~*) sidecar; (*Straßenbahn~*) extra carriage.

beiwohnen ['baɪvoːnən] *vi* (*geh*): **einer Sache** *dat* ~ to attend *od* be present at sth.

Beiwort ['baɪvɔrt] *nt* adjective.

Beize ['baɪtsə] (**-, -n**) *f* (*Holz~*) stain; (*KOCH*) marinade.

beizeiten [baɪ'tsaɪtən] *adv* in time.

bejahen [bə'jaːən] *vt* (*Frage*) to say yes to, answer in the affirmative; (*gutheißen*) to agree with.

bejahrt [bə'jaːrt] *adj* elderly, advanced in years.

bejammern [bə'jamərn] *vt* to lament, bewail.

bejammernswert *adj* lamentable.

bekakeln [bə'kaːkəln] (*umg*) *vt* to discuss.

bekam *etc* [bə'kam] *vb siehe* **bekommen.**

bekämpfen [bə'kɛmpfən] *vt* (*Gegner*) to fight; (*Seuche*) to combat ♦ *vr* to fight.

Bekämpfung *f*: ~ (**+gen**) fight (against), struggle (against).

bekannt [bə'kant] *adj* (well-)known; (*nicht fremd*) familiar; **mit jdm** ~ **sein** to know sb; **jdn mit jdm** ~ **machen** to introduce sb to sb; **sich mit etw** ~ **machen** to familiarize o.s. with sth; **das ist mir** ~ I know that; **es/sie kommt mir** ~ **vor** it/she seems familiar; **durch etw** ~ **werden** to become famous because of sth.

Bekannte(r) *f(m)* friend, acquaintance.

Bekanntenkreis *m* circle of friends.

bekanntermaßen *adv* as is known.

bekannt- *zW*: **B~gabe** *f* announcement; ~**geben** *unreg vt* to announce publicly; **B~heitsgrad** *m* degree of fame; ~**lich** *adv* as is well known, as you know; ~**machen** *vt* to announce; **B~machung** *f* publication; (*Anschlag etc*) announcement; **B~schaft** *f* acquaintance.

bekehren [bə'keːrən] *vt* to convert ♦ *vr* to be *od* become converted.

Bekehrung *f* conversion.

bekennen [bə'kɛnən] *unreg vt* to confess; (*Glauben*) to profess ♦ *vr*: **sich zu jdm/etw** ~ to declare one's support for sb/sth; **Farbe** ~ (*umg*) to show where one stands.

Bekenntnis [bə'kɛntnɪs] (**-ses, -se**) *nt* admission, confession; (*Religion*) confession, denomination; **ein** ~ **zur Demokratie ablegen** to declare one's belief in democracy; ~**schule** *f* denominational school.

beklagen [bə'klaːgən] *vt* to deplore, lament ♦ *vr* to complain.

beklagenswert *adj* lamentable, pathetic; (*Mensch*) pitiful; (*Zustand*) deplorable; (*Unfall*) terrible.

beklatschen [bə'klatʃən] *vt* to applaud, clap.

bekleben [bə'kleːbən] *vt*: **etw mit Bildern** ~ to stick pictures onto sth.

bekleckern [bə'klɛkərn] (*umg*) *vt* to stain.

bekleiden [bə'klaɪdən] *vt* to clothe; (*Amt*) to occupy, fill.

Bekleidung *f* clothing; (*form: eines Amtes*) tenure.

Bekleidungsindustrie *f* clothing industry, rag trade (*umg*).

beklemmen [bə'klɛmən] *vt* to oppress.

Beklemmung *f* oppressiveness; (*Gefühl der Angst*) feeling of apprehension.

beklommen [bə'kləmən] *adj* anxious, uneasy; **B~heit** *f* anxiety, uneasiness.

bekloppt [bə'kləpt] (*umg*) *adj* (*Mensch*) crazy; (: *Sache*) lousy.

beknackt [bə'knakt] (*umg*) *adj* = **bekloppt.**

beknien [bə'kniːən] (*umg*) *vt* (*jdn*) to beg.

bekommen [bə'kɔmən] *unreg vt* to get, receive; (*Kind*) to have; (*Zug*) to catch, get

♦ *vi:* **jdm** ~ to agree with sb; **es mit jdm zu tun** ~ to get into trouble with sb; **wohl bekomm's!** your health!
bekömmlich [bə'kœmlıç] *adj* easily digestible.
beköstigen [bə'kœstıgən] *vt* to cater for.
bekräftigen [bə'krɛftıgən] *vt* to confirm, corroborate.
Bekräftigung *f* corroboration.
bekreuzigen [bə'krɔytsıgən] *vr* to cross o.s.
bekritteln [bə'krıtəln] *vt* to criticize, pick holes in.
bekümmern [bə'kʏmərn] *vt* to worry, trouble.
bekunden [bə'kʊndən] *vt* (*sagen*) to state; (*zeigen*) to show.
belächeln [bə'lɛçəln] *vt* to laugh at.
beladen [bə'la:dən] *unreg vt* to load.
Belag [bə'la:k] (-(e)s, -̈e) *m* covering, coating; (*Brot*~) spread; (*auf Pizza, Brot*) topping; (*auf Tortenboden, zwischen Brotscheiben*) filling; (*Zahn*~) tartar; (*auf Zunge*) fur; (*Brems*~) lining.
belagern [bə'la:gərn] *vt* to besiege.
Belagerung *f* siege.
Belagerungszustand *m* state of siege.
Belang [bə'laŋ] (-(e)s) *m* importance.
Belange *pl* interests *pl*, concerns *pl*.
belangen *vt* (*JUR*) to take to court.
belanglos *adj* trivial, unimportant.
Belanglosigkeit *f* triviality.
belassen [bə'lasən] *unreg vt* (*in Zustand, Glauben*) to leave; (*in Stellung*) to retain; **es dabei** ~ to leave it at that.
Belastbarkeit *f* (*von Brücke, Aufzug*) load-bearing capacity; (*von Menschen, Nerven*) ability to take stress.
belasten [bə'lastən] *vt* (*lit*) to burden; (*fig: bedrücken*) to trouble, worry; (*COMM: Konto*) to debit; (*JUR*) to incriminate ♦ *vr* to weigh o.s. down; (*JUR*) to incriminate o.s.; **etw (mit einer Hypothek)** ~ to mortgage sth.
belastend *adj* (*JUR*) incriminating.
belästigen [bə'lɛstıgən] *vt* to annoy, pester.
Belästigung *f* annoyance, pestering; (*körperlich*) molesting.
Belastung [bə'lastʊŋ] *f* (*lit*) load; (*fig: Sorge etc*) weight; (*COMM*) charge, debit(ing); (*mit Hypothek*): ~ (+*gen*) mortgage (on); (*JUR*) incriminating evidence.
Belastungs- *zW:* ~**material** *nt* (*JUR*) incriminating evidence; ~**probe** *f* capacity test; (*fig*) test; ~**zeuge** *m* witness for the prosecution.
belaubt [bə'laʊpt] *adj:* **dicht** ~ **sein** to have thick foliage.
belaufen [bə'laʊfən] *unreg vr:* **sich** ~ **auf** +*akk* to amount to.
belauschen [bə'laʊʃən] *vt* to eavesdrop on.
beleben [bə'le:bən] *vt* (*anregen*) to liven up; (*Konjunktur, jds Hoffnungen*) to stimulate.
belebt [bə'le:pt] *adj* (*Straße*) crowded.
Beleg [bə'le:k] (-(e)s, -e) *m* (*COMM*) receipt; (*Beweis*) documentary evidence, proof;

(*Beispiel*) example.
belegen [bə'le:gən] *vt* to cover; (*Kuchen, Brot*) to spread; (*Platz*) to reserve, book; (*Kurs, Vorlesung*) to register for; (*beweisen*) to verify, prove.
Belegschaft *f* personnel, staff.
belegt *adj* (*Zunge*) furred; (*Stimme*) hoarse; (*Zimmer*) occupied; ~**e Brote** open sandwiches.
belehren [bə'le:rən] *vt* to instruct, teach; **jdn eines Besseren** ~ to teach sb better; **er ist nicht zu** ~ he won't be told.
Belehrung *f* instruction.
beleibt [bə'laıpt] *adj* stout, corpulent.
beleidigen [bə'laıdıgən] *vt* to insult; to offend.
beleidigt *adj* insulted; (*gekränkt*) offended; **die** ~**e Leberwurst spielen** (*umg*) to be in a huff.
Beleidigung *f* insult; (*JUR*) slander; (: *schriftlich*) libel.
beleihen [bə'laıən] *unreg vt* (*COMM*) to lend money on.
belemmert [bə'lɛmərt] (*umg*) *adj* sheepish.
belesen [bə'le:zən] *adj* well-read.
beleuchten [bə'lɔyçtən] *vt* to light, illuminate; (*fig*) to throw light on.
Beleuchter(in) (-s, -) *m(f)* lighting technician.
Beleuchtung *f* lighting, illumination.
beleumdet [bə'lɔymdət] *adj:* **gut/schlecht** ~ **sein** to have a good/bad reputation.
beleumundet [bə'lɔymʊndət] *adj* = **beleumdet**.
Belgien ['bɛlgiən] (-s) *nt* Belgium.
Belgier(in) (-s, -) *m(f)* Belgian.
belgisch *adj* Belgian.
Belgrad ['bɛlgra:t] (-s) *nt* Belgrade.
belichten [bə'lıçtən] *vt* to expose.
Belichtung *f* exposure.
Belichtungsmesser *m* exposure meter.
Belieben [bə'li:bən] *nt:* **(ganz) nach** ~ (just) as you wish.
belieben *vi unpers* (*geh*): **wie es Ihnen beliebt** as you wish.
beliebig [bə'li:bıç] *adj* any you like, as you like; ~ **viel** as much as you like; **in** ~**er Reihenfolge** in any order whatever; **ein** ~**es Thema** any subject you like *od* want.
beliebt [bə'li:pt] *adj* popular; **sich bei jdm** ~ **machen** to make o.s. popular with sb; **B**~**heit** *f* popularity.
beliefern [bə'li:fərn] *vt* to supply.
Belize [bɛ'li:z] (-s) *nt* Belize.
bellen ['bɛlən] *vi* to bark.
Belletristik [bɛle'trıstık] *f* fiction and poetry.
belohnen [bə'lo:nən] *vt* to reward.
Belohnung *f* reward.
Belüftung [bə'lʏftʊŋ] *f* ventilation.
belügen [bə'ly:gən] *unreg vt* to lie to, deceive.
belustigen [bə'lustıgən] *vt* to amuse.
Belustigung *f* amusement.
bemächtigen [bə'mɛçtıgən] *vr:* **sich einer Sache** *gen* ~ to take possession of sth, seize sth.
bemalen [bə'ma:lən] *vt* to paint ♦ *vr* (*pej:*

schminken) to put on one's war paint (umg).
bemängeln [bə'mɛŋəln] vt to criticize.
bemannen [bə'manən] vt to man.
Bemannung f manning; (NAUT, AVIAT etc) crew.
bemänteln [bə'mɛntəln] vt to cloak, hide.
bemerkbar adj perceptible, noticeable; **sich ~ machen** (Person) to make od get o.s. noticed; (Unruhe) to become noticeable.
bemerken [bə'mɛrkən] vt (wahrnehmen) to notice, observe; (sagen) to say, mention; **nebenbei bemerkt** by the way.
bemerkenswert adj remarkable, noteworthy.
Bemerkung f remark, comment; (schriftlich) comment, note.
bemitleiden [bə'mɪtlaɪdən] vt to pity.
bemittelt [bə'mɪtəlt] adj well-to-do, well-off.
bemühen [bə'myːən] vr to take trouble od pains; **sich um eine Stelle ~** to try to get a job.
bemüht adj: **(darum) ~ sein, etw zu tun** to endeavour (BRIT) od endeavor (US) od be at pains to do sth.
Bemühung f trouble, pains pl, effort.
bemüßigt [bə'myːsɪçt] adj: **sich ~ fühlen/ sehen** (geh) to feel called upon.
bemuttern [bə'mʊtərn] vt to mother.
benachbart [bə'naxbaːrt] adj neighbouring (BRIT), neighboring (US).
benachrichtigen [bə'naːxrɪçtɪgən] vt to inform.
Benachrichtigung f notification.
benachteiligen [bə'naːxtaɪlɪgən] vt to (put at a) disadvantage, victimize.
benehmen [bə'neːmən] unreg vr to behave; **B~ (-s)** nt behaviour (BRIT), behavior (US); **kein B~ haben** not to know how to behave.
beneiden [bə'naɪdən] vt to envy.
beneidenswert adj enviable.
Beneluxländer ['beːnelʊkslɛndər] pl Benelux (countries pl).
Beneluxstaaten pl Benelux (countries pl).
benennen [bə'nɛnən] unreg vt to name.
Bengel ['bɛŋəl] (-s, -) m (little) rascal od rogue.
Benimm [bə'nɪm] (-s) (umg) m manners pl.
Benin [be'niːn] (-s) nt Benin.
benommen [bə'nɔmən] adj dazed.
benoten [bə'noːtən] vt to mark.
benötigen [bə'nøːtɪgən] vt to need.
benutzen [bə'nʊtsən] vt to use.
benützen [bə'nʏtsən] vt to use.
Benutzer(in) (-s, -) m(f) user; **b~freundlich** adj user-friendly.
Benutzung f utilization, use; **jdm etw zur ~ überlassen** to put sth at sb's disposal.
Benzin [bɛnt'siːn] (-s, -e) nt (AUT) petrol (BRIT), gas(oline) (US); **~einspritzanlage** f (AUT) fuel injection system; **~kanister** m petrol (BRIT) od gas (US) can; **~tank** m petrol (BRIT) od gas (US) tank; **~uhr** f petrol

(BRIT) od gas (US) gauge.
beobachten [bə'|oːbaxtən] vt to observe.
Beobachter(in) (-s, -) m(f) observer; (eines Unfalls) witness; (PRESSE, TV) correspondent.
Beobachtung f observation.
beordern [bə'|ɔrdərn] vt: **jdn zu sich ~** to send for sb.
bepacken [bə'pakən] vt to load, pack.
bepflanzen [bə'pflantsən] vt to plant.
bequatschen [bə'kvatʃən] (umg) vt (überreden) to persuade; **etw ~** to talk sth over.
bequem [bə'kveːm] adj comfortable; (Ausrede) convenient; (Person) lazy, indolent.
bequemen [bə'kveːmən] vr: **sich ~, etw zu tun** to condescend to do sth.
Bequemlichkeit f convenience, comfort; (Faulheit) laziness, indolence.
Ber. abk = **Bericht; Beruf**.
berät [bə'rɛːt] vb siehe **beraten**.
beraten [bə'raːtən] unreg vt to advise; (besprechen) to discuss, debate ♦ vr to consult; **gut/schlecht ~ sein** to be well/ill advised; **sich ~ lassen** to get advice.
beratend adj consultative; **jdm ~ zur Seite stehen** to act in an advisory capacity to sb.
Berater(in) (-s, -) m(f) adviser; **~vertrag** m consultancy contract.
beratschlagen [bə'raːtʃlaːgən] vi to deliberate, confer ♦ vt to deliberate on, confer about.
Beratung f advice; (Besprechung) consultation.
Beratungsstelle f advice centre (BRIT) od center (US).
berauben [bə'raʊbən] vt to rob.
berauschen [bə'raʊʃən] vt (lit, fig) to intoxicate.
berauschend adj: **das war nicht sehr ~** (ironisch) that wasn't very exciting.
berechenbar [bə'rɛçənbaːr] adj calculable; (Verhalten) predictable.
berechnen [bə'rɛçnən] vt to calculate; (COMM: anrechnen) to charge.
berechnend adj (Mensch) calculating, scheming.
Berechnung f calculation; (COMM) charge.
berechtigen [bə'rɛçtɪgən] vt to entitle; (bevollmächtigen) to authorize; (fig) to justify.
berechtigt [bə'rɛçtɪçt] adj justifiable, justified.
Berechtigung f authorization; (fig) justification.
bereden [bə'reːdən] vt (besprechen) to discuss; (überreden) to persuade ♦ vr to discuss.
beredt [bə'reːt] adj eloquent.
Bereich [bə'raɪç] (-(e)s, -e) m (Bezirk) area; (Ressort, Gebiet) sphere; **im ~ des Möglichen liegen** to be within the bounds of possibility.
bereichern [bə'raɪçərn] vt to enrich ♦ vr to get

rich; **sich auf Kosten anderer** ~ to feather one's nest at the expense of other people.
Bereifung [bə'raɪfʊŋ] f (set of) tyres (BRIT) od tires (US) pl; (Vorgang) fitting with tyres (BRIT) od tires (US).
bereinigen [bə'raɪnɪgən] vt to settle.
bereisen [bə'raɪzən] vt to travel through; (COMM: Gebiet) to travel, cover.
bereit [bə'raɪt] adj ready, prepared; **zu etw** ~ **sein** to be ready for sth; **sich** ~ **erklären** to declare o.s. willing.
bereiten vt to prepare, make ready; (Kummer, Freude) to cause; **einer Sache** dat **ein Ende** ~ to put an end to sth.
bereit- zW: ~**halten** unreg vt to keep in readiness; ~**legen** vt to lay out; ~**machen** vt, vr to prepare, get ready.
bereits adv already.
bereit- zW: **B**~**schaft** f readiness; (Polizei) alert; **in B**~**schaft sein** to be on the alert od on stand-by; **B**~**schaftsarzt** m doctor on call; (im Krankenhaus) duty doctor; **B**~**schaftsdienst** m emergency service; ~**stehen** unreg vi (Person) to be ready; (Ding) to be ready; ~**stellen** vt (Kisten, Pakete etc) to put ready; (Geld etc) to make available; (Truppen, Maschinen) to put at the ready.
Bereitung f preparation.
bereitwillig adj willing, ready; **B**~**keit** f willingness, readiness.
bereuen [bə'rɔyən] vt to regret.
Berg [bɛrk] (-(e)s, -e) m mountain; (kleiner) hill; **mit etw hinterm** ~ **halten** (fig) to keep quiet about sth; **über alle** ~**e sein** to be miles away; **da stehen einem ja die Haare zu** ~**e** it's enough to make your hair stand on end; **b**~**ab** adv downhill; **b**~**an** adv uphill; ~**arbeiter** m miner; **b**~**auf** adv uphill; ~**bahn** f mountain railway (BRIT) od railroad (US); ~**bau** m mining.
bergen ['bɛrgən] unreg vt (retten) to rescue; (Ladung) to salvage; (enthalten) to contain.
Bergführer m mountain guide.
Berggipfel m mountain top, peak, summit.
bergig ['bɛrgɪç] adj mountainous, hilly.
Berg- zW: ~**kamm** m crest, ridge; ~**kette** f mountain range; ~**kristall** m rock crystal; ~**mann** (-(e)s, pl ~**leute**) m miner; ~**not** f: **in** ~**not sein/geraten** to be in/get into difficulties while climbing; ~**predigt** f (REL) Sermon on the Mount; ~**rettungsdienst** m mountain rescue service; ~**rutsch** m landslide; ~**schuh** m walking boot; ~**steigen** nt mountaineering; ~**steiger(in)** m(f) mountaineer, climber; ~**und-Tal-Bahn** f big dipper, roller-coaster.
Bergung ['bɛrgʊŋ] f (von Menschen) rescue; (von Material) recovery; (NAUT) salvage.
Bergwacht f mountain rescue service.
Bergwerk nt mine.
Bericht [bə'rɪçt] (-(e)s, -e) m report, account;

b~**en** vt, vi to report; ~**erstatter** (-s, -) m reporter, (newspaper) correspondent; ~**erstattung** f reporting.
berichtigen [bə'rɪçtɪgən] vt to correct.
Berichtigung f correction.
berieseln [bə'riːzəln] vt to spray with water etc.
Berieselung f watering; **die dauernde** ~ **mit Musik** ... (fig) the constant stream of music.
Berieselungsanlage f sprinkler (system).
Beringmeer ['beːrɪŋmeːr] nt Bering Sea.
beritten [bə'rɪtən] adj mounted.
Berlin [bɛr'liːn] (-s) nt Berlin.
Berliner[1] adj attrib Berlin.
Berliner[2] (-s, -) m (Person) Berliner; (KOCH) jam doughnut.
Berlinerin f Berliner.
berlinerisch (umg) adj (Dialekt) Berlin attr.
Bermudas [bɛr'muːdas] pl: **auf den** ~ in Bermuda.
Bern [bɛrn] (-s) nt Berne.
Bernhardiner [bɛrnhar'diːnər] (-s, -) m Saint Bernard (dog).
Bernstein ['bɛrnʃtaɪn] m amber.
bersten ['bɛrstən] unreg vi to burst, split.
berüchtigt [bə'rʏçtɪçt] adj notorious, infamous.
berücksichtigen [bə'rʏkzɪçtɪgən] vt to consider, bear in mind.
Berücksichtigung f consideration; **in** od **unter** ~ **der Tatsache, daß** ... in view of the fact that ...
Beruf [bə'ruːf] (-(e)s, -e) m occupation, profession; (Gewerbe) trade; **was sind Sie von** ~? what is your occupation etc?, what do you do for a living?; **seinen** ~ **verfehlt haben** to have missed one's vocation.
berufen unreg vt (in Amt): **jdn in etw** akk ~ to appoint sb to sth ♦ vr: **sich auf jdn/etw** ~ to refer od appeal to sb/sth ♦ adj competent, qualified; (ausersehen): **zu etw** ~ **sein** to have a vocation for sth.
beruflich adj professional; **er ist** ~ **viel unterwegs** he is away a lot on business.
Berufs- zW: ~**ausbildung** f vocational od professional training; **b**~**bedingt** adj occupational; ~**berater** m careers adviser; ~**beratung** f vocational guidance; ~**bezeichnung** f job description; ~**erfahrung** f (professional) experience; ~**feuerwehr** f fire service; ~**geheimnis** nt professional secret; ~**krankheit** f occupational disease; ~**kriminalität** f professional crime; ~**leben** nt professional life; **im** ~**leben stehen** to be working od in employment; **b**~**mäßig** adj professional; ~**risiko** nt occupational hazard; ~**schule** f vocational od trade school; ~**soldat** m professional soldier, regular; ~**sportler** m professional (sportsman); **b**~**tätig** adj employed; **b**~**unfähig** adj unable to work (at one's profession); ~**unfall** m occupational

accident; ~**verbot** *nt:* **jdm** ~**verbot erteilen** to ban sb from his/her profession; (*einem Arzt, Anwalt*) to strike sb off; ~**verkehr** *m* commuter traffic; ~**wahl** *f* choice of a job.

Berufung *f* vocation, calling; (*Ernennung*) appointment; (*JUR*) appeal; ~ **einlegen** to appeal; **unter** ~ **auf etw** *akk* (*form*) with reference to sth.

Berufungsgericht *nt* appeal court, court of appeal.

beruhen [bə'ruːən] *vi:* **auf etw** *dat* ~ to be based on sth; **etw auf sich** ~ **lassen** to leave sth at that; **das beruht auf Gegenseitigkeit** the feeling is mutual.

beruhigen [bə'ruːɪgən] *vt* to calm, pacify, soothe ♦ *vr* (*Mensch*) to calm (o.s.) down; (*Situation*) to calm down.

beruhigend *adj* (*Gefühl, Wissen*) reassuring; (*Worte*) comforting; (*Mittel*) tranquillizing.

Beruhigung *f* reassurance; (*der Nerven*) calming; **zu jds** ~ to reassure sb.

Beruhigungsmittel *nt* sedative.

Beruhigungspille *f* tranquillizer.

berühmt [bə'ryːmt] *adj* famous; **das war nicht** ~ (*umg*) it was nothing to write home about; ~-**berüchtigt** *adj* infamous, notorious; **B~heit** *f* (*Ruf*) fame; (*Mensch*) celebrity.

berühren [bə'ryːrən] *vt* to touch; (*gefühlsmäßig bewegen*) to affect; (*flüchtig erwähnen*) to mention, touch on ♦ *vr* to meet, touch; **von etw peinlich berührt sein** to be embarrassed by sth.

Berührung *f* contact.

Berührungspunkt *m* point of contact.

bes. *abk* (= *besonders*) esp.

besagen [bə'zaːgən] *vt* to mean.

besagt *adj* (*form: Tag etc*) in question.

besaiten [bə'zaɪtən] *vt:* **neu** ~ (*Instrument*) to restring.

besänftigen [bə'zɛnftɪgən] *vt* to soothe, calm.

besänftigend *adj* soothing.

Besänftigung *f* soothing, calming.

besaß *etc* [bə'zaːs] *vb siehe* **besitzen**.

besät [bə'zɛːt] *adj* covered; (*mit Blättern etc*) strewn.

Besatz [bə'zats] (-**es**, -̈**e**) *m* trimming, edging.

Besatzung *f* garrison; (*NAUT, AVIAT*) crew.

Besatzungsmacht *f* occupying power.

Besatzungszone *f* occupied zone.

besaufen [bə'zaʊfən] *unreg* (*umg*) *vr* to get drunk *od* stoned.

beschädigen [bə'ʃɛːdɪgən] *vt* to damage.

Beschädigung *f* damage; (*Stelle*) damaged spot.

beschaffen [bə'ʃafən] *vt* to get, acquire ♦ *adj* constituted; **so** ~ **sein wie** ... to be the same as ...; **B~heit** *f* constitution, nature; **je nach B~heit der Lage** according to the situation.

Beschaffung *f* acquisition.

beschäftigen [bə'ʃɛftɪgən] *vt* to occupy; (*beruflich*) to employ; (*innerlich*): **jdn** ~ to be on sb's mind ♦ *vr* to occupy *od* concern o.s.

beschäftigt *adj* busy, occupied; (*angestellt*): (**bei einer Firma**) ~ employed (by a firm).

Beschäftigung *f* (*Beruf*) employment; (*Tätigkeit*) occupation; (*geistige* ~) preoccupation; **einer** ~ **nachgehen** (*form*) to be employed.

Beschäftigungsprogramm *nt* employment scheme.

Beschäftigungstherapie *f* occupational therapy.

beschämen [bə'ʃɛːmən] *vt* to put to shame.

beschämend *adj* shameful; (*Hilfsbereitschaft*) shaming.

beschämt *adj* ashamed.

beschatten [bə'ʃatən] *vt* to shade; (*Verdächtige*) to shadow.

beschaulich [bə'ʃaʊlɪç] *adj* contemplative; (*Leben, Abend*) quiet, tranquil.

Bescheid [bə'ʃaɪt] (-**(e)s**, -**e**) *m* information; (*Weisung*) directions *pl*; ~ **wissen (über** +*akk*) to be well-informed (about); **ich weiß** ~ I know; **jdm** ~ **geben** *od* **sagen** to let sb know; **jdm ordentlich** ~ **sagen** (*umg*) to tell sb where to go.

bescheiden [bə'ʃaɪdən] *unreg vr* to content o.s. ♦ *vt:* **etw abschlägig** ~ (*form*) to turn sth down ♦ *adj* modest; **B~heit** *f* modesty.

bescheinen [bə'ʃaɪnən] *unreg vt* to shine on.

bescheinigen [bə'ʃaɪnɪgən] *vt* to certify; (*bestätigen*) to acknowledge; **hiermit wird bescheinigt, daß** ... this is to certify that ...

Bescheinigung *f* certificate; (*Quittung*) receipt.

bescheißen [bə'ʃaɪsən] *unreg* (*umg!*) *vt* to cheat.

beschenken [bə'ʃɛŋkən] *vt* to give presents to.

bescheren [bə'ʃeːrən] *vt:* **jdm etw** ~ to give sb sth as a present; **jdn** ~ to give presents to sb.

Bescherung *f* giving of presents; (*umg*) mess; **da haben wir die** ~! (*umg*) what did I tell you!

bescheuert [bə'ʃɔʏərt] (*umg*) *adj* stupid.

beschichten [bə'ʃɪçtən] *vt* (*TECH*) to coat, cover.

beschießen [bə'ʃiːsən] *unreg vt* to shoot *od* fire at.

beschildern [bə'ʃɪldərn] *vt* to signpost.

beschimpfen [bə'ʃɪmpfən] *vt* to abuse.

Beschimpfung *f* abuse, insult.

beschirmen [bə'ʃɪrmən] *vt* (*geh: beschützen*) to shield.

Beschiß [bə'ʃɪs] (-**sses**) (*umg*) *m:* **das ist** ~ that is a cheat.

beschiß *etc vb siehe* **bescheißen**.

beschissen *pp von* **bescheißen** ♦ *adj* (*umg!*) bloody awful, lousy.

Beschlag [bə'ʃlaːk] (-**(e)s**, -̈**e**) *m* (*Metallband*) fitting; (*auf Fenster*) condensation; (*auf Metall*) tarnish; finish; (*Hufeisen*) horseshoe; **jdn/etw in** ~ **nehmen** *od* **mit** ~ **belegen** to monopolize sb/sth.

beschlagen [bə'ʃlaːgən] *unreg vt* to cover; (*Pferd*) to shoe; (*Fenster, Metall*) to cover ♦ *vi, vr* (*Fenster etc*) to mist over; ~ **sein** (**in** *od* **auf** +*dat*) to be well versed (in).

beschlagnahmen *vt* to seize, confiscate.

Beschlagnahmung *f* confiscation.

beschleunigen [bə'ʃlɔynɪgən] *vt* to accelerate, speed up ♦ *vi* (*AUT*) to accelerate.

Beschleunigung *f* acceleration.

beschließen [bə'ʃliːsən] *unreg vt* to decide on; (*beenden*) to end, close.

beschlossen [bə'ʃlɔsən] *pp von* **beschließen** ♦ *adj* (*entschieden*) decided, agreed; **das ist ~e Sache** that's been settled.

Beschluß [bə'ʃlus] (**-sses, -schlüsse**) *m* decision, conclusion; (*Ende*) close, end; **einen ~ fassen** to pass a resolution.

beschlußfähig *adj:* ~ **sein** to have a quorum.

beschmieren [bə'ʃmiːrən] *vt* (*Wand*) to bedaub.

beschmutzen [bə'ʃmutsən] *vt* to dirty, soil.

beschneiden [bə'ʃnaɪdən] *unreg vt* to cut; (*stutzen*) to trim; (: *Strauch*) to prune; (*REL*) to circumcise.

beschnuppern [bə'ʃnupərn] *vr* (*Hunde*) to sniff each other; (*fig: umg*) to size each other up.

beschönigen [bə'ʃøːnɪgən] *vt* to gloss over; ~**der Ausdruck** euphemism.

beschränken [bə'ʃrɛŋkən] *vt, vr:* (**sich**) ~ (**auf** +*akk*) to limit *od* restrict (o.s.) (to).

beschrankt [bə'ʃraŋkt] *adj* (*Bahnübergang*) with barrier.

beschränkt [bə'ʃrɛŋkt] *adj* confined, narrow; (*Mensch*) limited, narrow-minded; (*pej: geistig*) dim; **Gesellschaft mit ~er Haftung** limited company (*BRIT*), corporation (*US*); **B~heit** *f* narrowness.

Beschränkung *f* limitation.

beschreiben [bə'ʃraɪbən] *unreg vt* to describe; (*Papier*) to write on.

Beschreibung *f* description.

beschrieb *etc* [bə'ʃriːp] *vb siehe* **beschreiben**.

beschrieben [bə'ʃriːbən] *pp von* **beschreiben**.

beschriften [bə'ʃrɪftən] *vt* to mark, label.

Beschriftung *f* lettering.

beschuldigen [bə'ʃuldɪgən] *vt* to accuse.

Beschuldigung *f* accusation.

beschummeln [bə'ʃuməln] (*umg*) *vt, vi* to cheat.

Beschuß [bə'ʃus] *m:* **jdn/etw unter ~ nehmen** (*MIL*) to (start to) bombard *od* shell sb/sth; (*fig*) to attack sb/sth; **unter ~ geraten** (*lit, fig*) to come into the firing line.

beschützen [bə'ʃytsən] *vt:* ~ (**vor** +*dat*) to protect (from).

Beschützer(in) (**-s, -**) *m(f)* protector.

Beschützung *f* protection.

beschwatzen [bə'ʃvatsən] (*umg*) *vt* (*überreden*) to talk over.

Beschwerde [bə'ʃveːrdə] (**-, -n**) *f* complaint; (*Mühe*) hardship; (*INDUSTRIE*) grievance; **Beschwerden** *pl* (*Leiden*) trouble; ~ **einlegen** (*form*) to lodge a complaint; **b~frei** *adj* fit and healthy; ~**frist** *f* (*JUR*) *period of time during which an appeal may be lodged.*

beschweren [bə'ʃveːrən] *vt* to weight down; (*fig*) to burden ♦ *vr* to complain.

beschwerlich *adj* tiring, exhausting.

beschwichtigen [bə'ʃvɪçtɪgən] *vt* to soothe, pacify.

Beschwichtigung *f* soothing, calming.

beschwindeln [bə'ʃvɪndəln] *vt* (*betrügen*) to cheat; (*belügen*) to fib to.

beschwingt [bə'ʃvɪŋt] *adj* cheery, in high spirits.

beschwipst [bə'ʃvɪpst] *adj* tipsy.

beschwören [bə'ʃvøːrən] *unreg vt* (*Aussage*) to swear to; (*anflehen*) to implore; (*Geister*) to conjure up.

beseelen [bə'zeːlən] *vt* to inspire.

besehen [bə'zeːən] *unreg vt* to look at; **genau ~** to examine closely.

beseitigen [bə'zaɪtɪgən] *vt* to remove.

Beseitigung *f* removal.

Besen ['beːzən] (**-s, -**) *m* broom; (*pej: umg: Frau*) old bag; **ich fresse einen ~, wenn das stimmt** (*umg*) if that's right, I'll eat my hat; ~**stiel** *m* broomstick.

besessen [bə'zɛsən] *adj* possessed; (*von einer Idee etc*): ~ (**von**) obsessed (with).

besetzen [bə'zɛtsən] *vt* (*Haus, Land*) to occupy; (*Platz*) to take, fill; (*Posten*) to fill; (*Rolle*) to cast; (*mit Edelsteinen*) to set.

besetzt *adj* full; (*TEL*) engaged, busy; (*Platz*) taken; (*WC*) engaged; **B~zeichen** *nt* engaged tone (*BRIT*), busy signal (*US*).

Besetzung *f* occupation; (*von Stelle*) filling; (*von Rolle*) casting; (*die Schauspieler*) cast; **zweite ~** (*THEAT*) understudy.

besichtigen [bə'zɪçtɪgən] *vt* to visit, look at.

Besichtigung *f* visit.

besiedeln *vt:* **dicht/dünn besiedelt** densely/thinly populated.

Besied(e)lung [bə'ziːd(ə)luŋ] *f* population.

besiegeln [bə'ziːgəln] *vt* to seal.

besiegen [bə'ziːgən] *vt* to defeat, overcome.

Besiegte(r) [bə'ziːktə(r)] *f(m)* loser.

besinnen [bə'zɪnən] *unreg vr* (*nachdenken*) to think, reflect; (*erinnern*) to remember; **sich anders ~** to change one's mind.

besinnlich *adj* contemplative.

Besinnung *f* consciousness; **bei/ohne ~ sein** to be conscious/unconscious; **zur ~ kommen** to recover consciousness; (*fig*) to come to one's senses.

besinnungslos *adj* unconscious; (*fig*) blind.

Besitz [bə'zɪts] (**-es**) *m* possession; (*Eigentum*) property; ~**anspruch** *m* claim of ownership; (*JUR*) title; **b~anzeigend** *adj* (*GRAM*) possessive.

besitzen *unreg vt* to possess, own; (*Eigenschaft*) to have.

Besitzer(in) **(-s, -)** *m(f)* owner, proprietor.
Besitz- *zW:* **~ergreifung** *f* seizure; **~nahme** *f* seizure; **~tum** *nt* (*Grundbesitz*) estate(s *pl*), property; **~urkunde** *f* title deeds *pl*.
besoffen [bə'zɔfən] (*umg*) *adj* sozzled.
besohlen [bə'zo:lən] *vt* to sole.
Besoldung [bə'zɔldʊŋ] *f* salary, pay.
besondere(r, s) [bə'zɔndərə(r, s)] *adj* special; (*eigen*) particular; (*gesondert*) separate; (*eigentümlich*) peculiar.
Besonderheit *f* peculiarity.
besonders *adv* especially, particularly; (*getrennt*) separately; **das Essen/der Film war nicht ~** the food/film was nothing special *od* out of the ordinary; **wie geht's dir? - nicht ~** how are you? - not too hot.
besonnen [bə'zɔnən] *adj* sensible, level-headed; **B~heit** *f* level-headedness.
besorgen [bə'zɔrgən] *vt* (*beschaffen*) to acquire; (*kaufen*) to purchase; (*erledigen*: *Geschäfte*) to deal with; (*sich kümmern um*) to take care of; **es jdm ~** (*umg*) to sort sb out.
Besorgnis **(-, -se)** *f* anxiety, concern; **b~erregend** *adj* alarming, worrying.
besorgt [bə'zɔrkt] *adj* anxious, worried; **B~heit** *f* anxiety, worry.
Besorgung *f* acquisition; (*Kauf*) purchase; (*Einkauf*): **~en machen** to do some shopping.
bespannen [bə'ʃpanən] *vt* (*mit Saiten, Fäden*) to string.
bespielbar *adj* (*Rasen etc*) playable.
bespielen [bə'ʃpi:lən] *vt* (*Tonband, Kassette*) to make a recording on.
bespitzeln [bə'ʃpɪtsəln] *vt* to spy on.
besprechen [bə'ʃprɛçən] *unreg vt* to discuss; (*Tonband etc*) to record, speak onto; (*Buch*) to review ♦ *vr* to discuss, consult.
Besprechung *f* meeting, discussion; (*von Buch*) review.
bespringen [bə'ʃprɪŋən] *unreg vt* (*Tier*) to mount, cover.
bespritzen [bə'ʃprɪtsən] *vt* to spray; (*beschmutzen*) to spatter.
besser ['bɛsər] *adj* better; **nur ein ~er ...** just a glorified ...; **~e Leute** a better class of people; **~gehen** *unreg vi unpers*: **es geht ihm ~** he feels better.
bessern *vt* to make better, improve ♦ *vr* to improve; (*Mensch*) to reform.
besserstehen *unreg* (*umg*) *vr* to be better off.
Besserung *f* improvement; **auf dem Weg(e) der ~ sein** to be getting better, be improving; **gute ~!** get well soon!
Besserwisser(in) **(-s, -)** *m(f)* know-all (*BRIT*), know-it-all (*US*).
Bestand [bə'ʃtant] **(-(e)s, -̈e)** *m* (*Fortbestehen*) duration, continuance; (*Kassenbestand*) amount, balance; (*Vorrat*) stock; **eiserner ~** iron rations *pl*; **~ haben, von ~ sein** to last long, endure.
bestand *etc vb siehe* **bestehen.**
bestanden *pp von* **bestehen** ♦ *adj*: **nach ~er**

Prüfung after passing the exam.
beständig [bə'ʃtɛndɪç] *adj* (*ausdauernd*) constant; (*auch fig*); (*Wetter*) settled; (*Stoffe*) resistant; (*Klagen etc*) continual.
Bestandsaufnahme *f* stocktaking.
Bestandsüberwachung *f* stock control, inventory control.
Bestandteil *m* part, component; (*Zutat*) ingredient; **sich in seine ~e auflösen** to fall to pieces.
bestärken [bə'ʃtɛrkən] *vt*: **jdn in etw** *dat* **~** to strengthen *od* confirm sb in sth.
bestätigen [bə'ʃtɛːtɪgən] *vt* to confirm; (*anerkennen, COMM*) to acknowledge; **jdn (im Amt) ~** to confirm sb's appointment.
Bestätigung *f* confirmation; acknowledgement.
bestatten [bə'ʃtatən] *vt* to bury.
Bestatter **(-s, -)** *m* undertaker.
Bestattung *f* funeral.
Bestattungsinstitut *nt* undertaker's (*BRIT*), mortician's (*US*).
bestäuben [bə'ʃtɔybən] *vt* to powder, dust; (*Pflanze*) to pollinate.
beste(r, s) ['bɛstə(r, s)] *adj* best; **sie singt am ~n** she sings best; **so ist es am ~n** it's best that way; **am ~n gehst du gleich** you'd better go at once; **jdn zum ~n haben** to pull sb's leg; **einen Witz etc zum ~n geben** to tell a joke *etc*; **aufs ~** in the best possible way; **zu jds B~n** for the benefit of sb; **es steht nicht zum ~n** it does not look too promising.
bestechen [bə'ʃtɛçən] *unreg vt* to bribe ♦ *vi* (*Eindruck machen*): **(durch etw) ~** to be impressive (because of sth).
bestechend *adj* (*Schönheit, Eindruck*) captivating; (*Angebot*) tempting.
bestechlich *adj* corruptible; **B~keit** *f* corruptibility.
Bestechung *f* bribery, corruption.
Bestechungsgelder *pl* bribe *sing*.
Bestechungsversuch *m* attempted bribery.
Besteck [bə'ʃtɛk] **(-(e)s, -e)** *nt* knife, fork and spoon, cutlery; (*MED*) set of instruments; **~kasten** *m* cutlery canteen.
bestehen [bə'ʃteːən] *unreg vi* to exist; (*andauern*) to last ♦ *vt* (*Probe, Prüfung*) to pass; (*Kampf*) to win; **die Schwierigkeit/das Problem besteht darin, daß ...** the difficulty/problem lies in the fact that ..., the difficulty/problem is that ...; **~ auf** +*dat* to insist on; **~ aus** to consist of; **B~** *nt*: **seit B~ der Firma** ever since the firm came into existence *od* has existed.
bestehenbleiben *unreg vi* to last, endure; (*Frage, Hoffnung*) to remain.
bestehlen [bə'ʃteːlən] *unreg vt* to rob.
besteigen [bə'ʃtaɪgən] *unreg vt* to climb, ascend; (*Pferd*) to mount; (*Thron*) to ascend.
Bestellbuch *nt* order book.
bestellen [bə'ʃtɛlən] *vt* to order; (*kommen*

lassen) to arrange to see; (*nominieren*) to name; (*Acker*) to cultivate; (*Grüße, Auftrag*) to pass on; **wie bestellt und nicht abgeholt** (*hum: umg*) like orphan Annie; **er hat nicht viel/nichts zu** ~ he doesn't have much/any say here; **ich bin für 10 Uhr bestellt** I have an appointment for *od* at 10 o'clock; **es ist schlecht um ihn bestellt** (*fig*) he is in a bad way.

Bestell- *zW:* **~formular** *nt* purchase order; **~nummer** *f* order number; **~schein** *m* order coupon.

Bestellung *f* (*COMM*) order; (*Bestellen*) ordering; (*Ernennung*) nomination, appointment.

bestenfalls ['bɛstən'fals] *adv* at best.

bestens ['bɛstəns] *adv* very well.

besteuern [bə'ʃtɔyərn] *vt* to tax.

bestialisch [bɛsti'a:lɪʃ] (*umg*) *adj* awful, beastly.

besticken [bə'ʃtɪkən] *vt* to embroider.

Bestie ['bɛstiə] *f* (*lit, fig*) beast.

bestimmen [bə'ʃtɪmən] *vt* (*Regeln*) to lay down; (*Tag, Ort*) to fix; (*prägen*) to characterize; (*ausersehen*) to mean; (*ernennen*) to appoint; (*definieren*) to define; (*veranlassen*) to induce ♦ *vi:* **du hast hier nicht zu** ~ you don't make the decisions here; **er kann über sein Geld allein** ~ it is up to him what he does with his money.

bestimmend *adj* (*Faktor, Einfluß*) determining, decisive.

bestimmt *adj* (*entschlossen*) firm; (*gewiß*) certain, definite; (*Artikel*) definite ♦ *adv* (*gewiß*) definitely, for sure; **suchen Sie etwas B~es?** are you looking for anything in particular?; **B~heit** *f* certainty; **in** *od* **mit aller B~heit** quite categorically.

Bestimmung *f* (*Verordnung*) regulation; (*Festsetzen*) determining; (*Verwendungszweck*) purpose; (*Schicksal*) fate; (*Definition*) definition.

Bestimmungs- *zW:* **~bahnhof** *m* (*EISENB*) destination; **b~gemäß** *adj* as agreed; **~hafen** *m* (port of) destination; **~ort** *m* destination.

Bestleistung *f* best performance.

bestmöglich *adj* best possible.

Best.-Nr. *abk* = **Bestellnummer.**

bestrafen [bə'ʃtra:fən] *vt* to punish.

Bestrafung *f* punishment.

bestrahlen [bə'ʃtra:lən] *vt* to shine on; (*MED*) to treat with X-rays.

Bestrahlung *f* (*MED*) X-ray treatment, radiotherapy.

Bestreben [bə'ʃtre:bən] (*-s*) *nt* endeavour (*BRIT*), endeavor (*US*), effort.

bestrebt [bə'ʃtre:pt] *adj:* ~ **sein, etw zu tun** to endeavour (*BRIT*) *od* endeavor (*US*) to do sth.

Bestrebung [bə'ʃtre:bʊŋ] *f* = **Bestreben.**

bestreichen [bə'ʃtraiçən] *unreg vt* (*Brot*) to

spread.

bestreiken [bə'ʃtraikən] *vt* (*INDUSTRIE*) to black; **die Fabrik wird zur Zeit bestreikt** there's a strike on in the factory at the moment.

bestreiten [bə'ʃtraitən] *unreg vt* (*abstreiten*) to dispute; (*finanzieren*) to pay for, finance; **er hat das ganze Gespräch allein bestritten** he did all the talking.

bestreuen [bə'ʃtrɔyən] *vt* to sprinkle, dust; (*Straße*) to (spread with) grit.

Bestseller [bɛst'sɛlər] (*-s, -*) *m* best-seller.

bestürmen [bə'ʃtyrmən] *vt* (*mit Fragen, Bitten etc*) to overwhelm, swamp.

bestürzen [bə'ʃtyrtsən] *vt* to dismay.

bestürzt *adj* dismayed.

Bestürzung *f* consternation.

Bestzeit *f* (*bes SPORT*) best time.

Besuch [bə'zu:x] (*-(e)s, -e*) *m* visit; (*Person*) visitor; **einen** ~ **bei jdm machen** to pay sb a visit *od* call; ~ **haben** to have visitors; **bei jdm auf** *od* **zu** ~ **sein** to be visiting sb.

besuchen *vt* to visit; (*SCH etc*) to attend; **gut besucht** well-attended.

Besucher(in) (*-s, -*) *m(f)* visitor, guest.

Besuchserlaubnis *f* permission to visit.

Besuchszeit *f* visiting hours *pl.*

besudeln [bə'zu:dəln] *vt* (*Wände*) to smear; (*fig: Namen, Ehre*) to sully.

betagt [bə'ta:kt] *adj* aged.

betasten [bə'tastən] *vt* to touch, feel.

betätigen [bə'tɛ:tɪgən] *vt* (*bedienen*) to work, operate ♦ *vr* to involve o.s.; **sich politisch** ~ to be involved in politics; **sich als etw** ~ to work as sth.

Betätigung *f* activity; (*beruflich*) occupation; (*TECH*) operation.

betäuben [bə'tɔybən] *vt* to stun; (*fig: Gewissen*) to still; (*MED*) to anaesthetize (*BRIT*), anesthetize (*US*); **ein ~der Duft** an overpowering smell.

Betäubung *f* (*Narkose*): **örtliche** ~ local anaesthetic (*BRIT*) *od* anesthetic (*US*).

Betäubungsmittel *nt* anaesthetic (*BRIT*), anesthetic (*US*).

Bete ['be:tə] (*-, -n*) *f:* **rote** ~ beetroot (*BRIT*), beet (*US*).

beteiligen [bə'tailɪgən] *vr:* **sich (an etw** *dat*) ~ to take part (in sth), participate (in sth); (*an Geschäft: finanziell*) to have a share (in sth) ♦ *vt:* **jdn (an etw** *dat*) ~ to give sb a share *od* interest (in sth); **sich an den Unkosten** ~ to contribute to the expenses.

Beteiligung *f* participation; (*Anteil*) share, interest; (*Besucherzahl*) attendance.

Beteiligungsgesellschaft *f* associated company.

beten ['be:tən] *vi* to pray ♦ *vt* (*Rosenkranz*) to say.

beteuern [bə'tɔyərn] *vt* to assert; (*Unschuld*) to protest; **jdm etw** ~ to assure sb of sth.

Beteuerung *f* assertion; protestation;

assurance.

Beton [be'tõ:] (**-s, -s**) *m* concrete.

betonen [bə'to:nən] *vt* to stress.

betonieren [beto'ni:rən] *vt* to concrete.

Betonmischmaschine *f* concrete mixer.

betont [bə'to:nt] *adj* (*Höflichkeit*) emphatic, deliberate; (*Kühle, Sachlichkeit*) pointed.

Betonung *f* stress, emphasis.

betören [bə'tø:rən] *vt* to beguile.

Betr. *abk* = **Betreff**.

betr. *abk* (= *betreffend, betreffs*) re.

Betracht [bə'traxt] *m:* **in ~ kommen** to be concerned *od* relevant; **nicht in ~ kommen** to be out of the question; **etw in ~ ziehen** to consider sth; **außer ~ bleiben** not to be considered.

betrachten *vt* to look at; (*fig*) to consider, look at.

Betrachter(in) (**-s, -**) *m(f)* onlooker.

beträchtlich [bə'trɛçtlɪç] *adj* considerable.

Betrachtung *f* (*Ansehen*) examination; (*Erwägung*) consideration; **über etw** *akk* **~en anstellen** to reflect on *od* contemplate sth.

betraf *etc* [bə'tra:f] *vb siehe* **betreffen**.

Betrag [bə'tra:k] (**-(e)s, -̈e**) *m* amount, sum; **~ erhalten** (*COMM*) sum received.

betragen [bə'tra:gən] *unreg vt* to amount to ♦ *vr* to behave.

Betragen (**-s**) *nt* behaviour (*BRIT*), behavior (*US*); (*bes in Zeugnis*) conduct.

beträgt [bə'trɛ:kt] *vb siehe* **betragen**.

betrat *etc* [bə'tra:t] *vb siehe* **betreten**.

betrauen [bə'trauən] *vt:* **jdn mit etw ~** to entrust sb with sth.

betrauern [bə'trauərn] *vt* to mourn.

beträufeln [bə'trɔyfəln] *vt:* **den Fisch mit Zitrone ~** to sprinkle lemon juice on the fish.

Betreff *m:* **~: Ihr Schreiben vom ...** re *od* reference your letter of ...

betreffen [bə'trɛfən] *unreg vt* to concern, affect; **was mich betrifft** as for me.

betreffend *adj* relevant, in question.

betreffs [bə'trɛfs] *präp +gen* concerning, regarding.

betreiben [bə'traibən] *unreg vt* (*ausüben*) to practise (*BRIT*), practice (*US*); (*Politik*) to follow; (*Studien*) to pursue; (*vorantreiben*) to push ahead; (*TECH: antreiben*) to drive; **auf jds B~** *akk* **hin** (*form*) at sb's instigation.

betreten [bə'tre:tən] *unreg vt* to enter; (*Bühne etc*) to step onto ♦ *adj* embarrassed; **„B~ verboten"** "keep off/out".

betreuen [bə'trɔyən] *vt* to look after.

Betreuer(in) (**-s, -**) *m(f)* carer; (*Kinderbetreuer*) child-minder.

Betreuung *f:* **er wurde mit der ~ der Gruppe beauftragt** he was put in charge of the group.

Betrieb (**-(e)s, -e**) *m* (*Firma*) firm, concern; (*Anlage*) plant; (*Tätigkeit*) operation; (*Treiben*) bustle; (*Verkehr*) traffic; **außer ~ sein** to be

out of order; **in ~ sein** to be in operation; **eine Maschine in/außer ~ setzen** to start a machine up/stop a machine; **eine Maschine/Fabrik in ~ nehmen** to put a machine/factory into operation; **in den Geschäften herrscht großer ~** the shops are very busy; **er hält den ganzen ~ auf** (*umg*) he's holding everything up.

betrieb *etc* [bə'tri:p] *vb siehe* **betreiben**.

betrieben [bə'tri:bən] *pp von* **betreiben**.

betrieblich *adj* company *attr* ♦ *adv* (*regeln*) within the company.

Betriebs- *zW:* **~anleitung** *f* operating instructions *pl*; **~ausflug** *m* firm's outing; **~ausgaben** *pl* revenue expenditure *sing*; **b~eigen** *adj* company *attr*; **~erlaubnis** *f* operating permission/licence (*BRIT*) *od* license (*US*); **b~fähig** *adj* in working order; **~ferien** *pl* company holidays *pl* (*BRIT*) *od* vacation *sing* (*US*); **~führung** *f* management; **~geheimnis** *nt* trade secret; **~kapital** *nt* capital employed; **~klima** *nt* (working) atmosphere; **~kosten** *pl* running costs; **~leitung** *f* management; **~rat** *m* workers' council; **~rente** *f* company pension; **b~sicher** *adj* safe, reliable; **~stoff** *m* fuel; **~störung** *f* breakdown; **~system** *nt* (*COMPUT*) operating system; **~unfall** *m* industrial accident; **~wirt** *m* management expert; **~wirtschaft** *f* business management.

betrifft [bə'trɪft] *vb siehe* **betreffen**.

betrinken [bə'trɪŋkən] *unreg vr* to get drunk.

betritt [bə'trɪt] *vb siehe* **betreten**.

betroffen [bə'trɔfən] *pp von* **betreffen** ♦ *adj* (*bestürzt*) amazed, perplexed; **von etw ~ werden** *od* **sein** to be affected by sth.

betrüben [bə'try:bən] *vt* to grieve.

betrübt [bə'try:pt] *adj* sorrowful, grieved.

Betrug (**-(e)s**) *m* deception; (*JUR*) fraud.

betrug *etc* [bə'tru:k] *vb siehe* **betragen**.

betrügen [bə'try:gən] *unreg vt* to cheat; (*JUR*) to defraud; (*Ehepartner*) to be unfaithful to ♦ *vr* to deceive o.s.

Betrüger(in) (**-s, -**) *m(f)* cheat, deceiver.

betrügerisch *adj* deceitful; (*JUR*) fraudulent; **in ~er Absicht** with intent to defraud.

betrunken [bə'trʊŋkən] *adj* drunk.

Betrunkene(r) *f(m)* drunk.

Bett [bɛt] (**-(e)s, -en**) *nt* bed; **im ~** in bed; **ins** *od* **zu ~ gehen** to go to bed; **~bezug** *m* duvet cover; **~decke** *f* blanket; (*Daunenbettdecke*) quilt; (*Überwurf*) bedspread.

bettelarm ['bɛtəl|arm] *adj* very poor, destitute.

Bettelei [bɛtə'lai] *f* begging.

Bettelmönch *m* mendicant *od* begging monk.

betteln *vi* to beg.

betten *vt* to make a bed for.

Bett- *zW:* **~hupferl** (*SÜDD*) *nt* bedtime sweet; **b~lägerig** *adj* bedridden; **~laken** *nt* sheet;

~**lektüre** f bedtime reading.
Bettler(in) ['bɛtlər(ɪn)] (**-s, -**) m(f) beggar.
Bett- zW: ~**nässer** (**-s, -**) m bedwetter;
~**schwere** (umg) f: **die nötige** ~**schwere haben/bekommen** to be/get tired enough to sleep; ~**(t)uch** nt sheet; ~**vorleger** m bedside rug; ~**wäsche** f bedclothes pl, bedding; ~**zeug** nt = **Bettwäsche.**
betucht [bə'tuːxt] (umg) adj well-to-do.
betulich [bə'tuːlɪç] adj (übertrieben besorgt) fussing attr; (Redeweise) twee.
betupfen [bə'tupfən] vt to dab; (MED) to swab.
Beugehaft ['bɔygəhaft] f (JUR) coercive detention.
beugen ['bɔygən] vt to bend; (GRAM) to inflect ♦ vr (+dat) (sich fügen) to bow (to).
Beule ['bɔylə] (**-, -n**) f bump.
beunruhigen [bə'|ʊnruːɪgən] vt to disturb, alarm ♦ vr to become worried.
Beunruhigung f worry, alarm.
beurkunden [bə'|uːrkʊndən] vt to attest, verify.
beurlauben [bə'|uːrlaʊbən] vt to give leave od holiday to (BRIT), grant vacation to (US); **beurlaubt sein** to have leave of absence; (suspendiert sein) to have been relieved of one's duties.
beurteilen [bə'|ʊrtaɪlən] vt to judge; (Buch etc) to review.
Beurteilung f judgement; (von Buch etc) review; (Note) mark.
Beute ['bɔytə] (**-**) f booty, loot; (von Raubtieren etc) prey.
Beutel (**-s, -**) m bag; (Geld~) purse; (Tabaks~) pouch.
bevölkern [bə'fœlkərn] vt to populate.
Bevölkerung f population.
Bevölkerungs- zW: ~**explosion** f population explosion; ~**schicht** f social stratum; ~**statistik** f vital statistics pl.
bevollmächtigen [bə'fɔlmɛçtɪgən] vt to authorize.
Bevollmächtigte(r) f(m) authorized agent.
Bevollmächtigung f authorization.
bevor [bə'foːr] konj before; ~**munden** vt untr to dominate; ~**stehen** unreg vi: (jdm) ~**stehen** to be in store (for sb); ~**stehend** adj imminent, approaching; ~**zugen** vt untr to prefer; ~**zugt** [bə'foːrtsuːkt] adv: **etw** ~**zugt abfertigen** etc to give sth priority; **B**~**zugung** f preference.
bewachen [bə'vaxən] vt to watch, guard.
bewachsen [bə'vaksən] adj overgrown.
Bewachung f (Bewachen) guarding; (Leute) guard, watch.
bewaffnen [bə'vafnən] vt to arm.
Bewaffnung f (Vorgang) arming; (Ausrüstung) armament, arms pl.
bewahren [bə'vaːrən] vt to keep; **jdn vor jdm/etw** ~ to save sb from sb/sth; (Gott) **bewahre!** (umg) heaven od God forbid!
bewähren [bə'vɛːrən] vr to prove o.s.;

(Maschine) to prove its worth.
bewahrheiten [bə'vaːrhaɪtən] vr to come true.
bewährt adj reliable.
Bewährung f (JUR) probation; **ein Jahr Gefängnis mit** ~ a suspended sentence of one year with probation.
Bewährungs- zW: ~**frist** f (period of) probation; ~**helfer** m probation officer; ~**probe** f: **etw einer** ~**probe** dat **unterziehen** to put sth to the test.
bewaldet [bə'valdət] adj wooded.
bewältigen [bə'vɛltɪgən] vt to overcome; (Arbeit) to finish; (Portion) to manage; (Schwierigkeiten) to cope with.
bewandert [bə'vandərt] adj expert, knowledgeable.
Bewandtnis [bə'vantnɪs] f: **damit hat es folgende** ~ the fact of the matter is this.
bewarb etc [bə'varp] vb siehe **bewerben.**
bewässern [bə'vɛsərn] vt to irrigate.
Bewässerung f irrigation.
bewegen [bə'veːgən] vt, vr to move; **der Preis bewegt sich um die 50 Mark** the price is about 50 marks; **jdn zu etw** ~ to induce sb to do sth.
Beweggrund m motive.
beweglich adj movable, mobile; (flink) quick.
bewegt [bə'veːkt] adj (Leben) eventful; (Meer) rough; (ergriffen) touched.
Bewegung f movement, motion; (innere) emotion; (körperlich) exercise; **sich** dat ~ **machen** to take exercise.
Bewegungsfreiheit f freedom of movement; (fig) freedom of action.
bewegungslos adj motionless.
Beweis [bə'vaɪs] (**-es, -e**) m proof; (Zeichen) sign; ~**aufnahme** f (JUR) taking od hearing of evidence; **b**~**bar** adj provable.
beweisen unreg vt to prove; (zeigen) to show; **was zu** ~ **war** QED.
Beweis- zW: ~**führung** f reasoning; (JUR) presentation of one's case; ~**kraft** f weight, conclusiveness; **b**~**kräftig** adj convincing, conclusive; ~**last** f (JUR) onus, burden of proof; ~**mittel** nt evidence; ~**not** f (JUR) lack of evidence; ~**stück** nt exhibit.
bewenden [bə'vɛndən] vi: **etw dabei** ~ **lassen** to leave sth at that.
bewerben [bə'vɛrbən] unreg vr: **sich** ~ (**um**) to apply (for).
Bewerber(in) (**-s, -**) m(f) applicant.
Bewerbung f application.
Bewerbungsunterlagen pl application documents.
bewerkstelligen [bə'vɛrkʃtɛlɪgən] vt to manage, accomplish.
bewerten [bə'veːrtən] vt to assess.
bewies etc [bə'viːs] vb siehe **beweisen.**
bewiesen [bə'viːzən] pp von **beweisen.**
bewilligen [bə'vɪlɪgən] vt to grant, allow.
Bewilligung f granting.
bewirbt [bə'vɪrpt] vb siehe **bewerben.**

bewirken [bə'vɪrkən] *vt* to cause, bring about.
bewirten [bə'vɪrtən] *vt* to entertain.
bewirtschaften [bə'vɪrtʃaftən] *vt* to manage.
Bewirtung *f* hospitality; **die ~ so vieler Gäste** catering for so many guests.
bewog *etc* [bə'vo:k] *vb siehe* **bewegen**.
bewogen [bə'vo:gən] *pp von* **bewegen**.
bewohnbar *adj* inhabitable.
bewohnen [bə'vo:nən] *vt* to inhabit, live in.
Bewohner(in) (-s, -) *m(f)* inhabitant; (*von Haus*) resident.
bewölkt [bə'vœlkt] *adj* cloudy, overcast.
Bewölkung *f* clouds *pl.*
Bewölkungsauflockerung *f* break-up of the cloud.
beworben [bə'vɔrbən] *pp von* **bewerben**.
Bewunderer(in) (-s, -) *m(f)* admirer.
bewundern [bə'vʊndərn] *vt* to admire.
bewundernswert *adj* admirable, wonderful.
Bewunderung *f* admiration.
bewußt [bə'vʊst] *adj* conscious; (*absichtlich*) deliberate; **sich** *dat* **einer Sache** *gen* ~ **sein** to be aware of sth; ~**los** *adj* unconscious; **B~losigkeit** *f* unconsciousness; **bis zur B~losigkeit** (*umg*) ad nauseam; ~**machen** *vt:* **jdm etw** ~**machen** to make sb conscious of sth; **sich** *dat* **etw** ~**machen** to realize sth; **B~sein** *nt* consciousness; **bei B~sein** conscious; **im B~sein, daß** ... in the knowledge that ...
Bewußtseins- *zW:* ~**bildung** *f* (*POL*) shaping of political ideas; **b~erweiternd** *adj:* **b~erweiternde Drogen** mind-expanding drugs; ~**erweiterung** *f* consciousness raising.
Bez. *abk* = **Bezirk**.
bez. *abk* (= *bezüglich*) re.
bezahlen [bə'tsa:lən] *vt* to pay (for); **es macht sich bezahlt** it will pay.
Bezahlung *f* payment; **ohne/gegen** *od* **für** ~ without/for payment.
bezaubern [bə'tsaʊbərn] *vt* to enchant, charm.
bezeichnen [bə'tsaɪçnən] *vt* (*kennzeichnen*) to mark; (*nennen*) to call; (*beschreiben*) to describe; (*zeigen*) to show, indicate.
bezeichnend *adj:* ~ (**für**) characteristic (of), typical (of).
Bezeichnung *f* (*Zeichen*) mark, sign; (*Beschreibung*) description; (*Ausdruck*) expression, term.
bezeugen [bə'tsɔʏgən] *vt* to testify to.
bezichtigen [bə'tsɪçtɪgən] *vt* (+*gen*) to accuse (of).
Bezichtigung *f* accusation.
beziehen [bə'tsi:ən] *unreg vt* (*mit Überzug*) to cover; (*Haus, Position*) to move into; (*Standpunkt*) to take up; (*erhalten*) to receive; (*Zeitung*) to subscribe to, take ♦ *vr* (*Himmel*) to cloud over; **die Betten frisch** ~ to change the beds; **etw auf jdn/etw** ~ to relate sth to sb/sth; **sich** ~ **auf** +*akk* to refer to.
Beziehung *f* (*Verbindung*) connection;

(*Zusammenhang*) relation; (*Verhältnis*) relationship; (*Hinsicht*) respect; **diplomatische** ~**en** diplomatic relations; **seine** ~**en spielen lassen** to pull strings; **in jeder** ~ in every respect; ~**en haben** (*vorteilhaft*) to have connections *od* contacts.
Beziehungskiste (*umg*) *f* relationship.
beziehungsweise *adv* or; (*genauer gesagt*) that is, or rather; (*im anderen Fall*) and ... respectively.
beziffern [bə'tsɪfərn] *vt* (*angeben*): ~ **auf** +*akk od* **mit** to estimate at.
Bezirk [bə'tsɪrk] (-(e)s, -e) *m* district.
bezirzen [bə'tsɪrtsən] (*umg*) *vt* to bewitch.
bezogen [bə'tso:gən] *pp von* **beziehen**.
Bezogene(r) [bə'tso:gənə(r)] *f(m)* (*von Scheck etc*) drawee.
Bezug [bə'tsu:k] (-(e)s, ̈-e) *m* (*Hülle*) covering; (*COMM*) ordering; (*Gehalt*) income, salary; (*Beziehung*): ~ (**zu**) relationship (to); **in b~ auf** +*akk* with reference to; **mit** *od* **unter** ~ **auf** +*akk* regarding; (*form*) with reference to; ~ **nehmen auf** +*akk* to refer to.
bezüglich [bə'tsy:klɪç] *präp* +*gen* concerning, referring to ♦ *adj* concerning; (*GRAM*) relative.
Bezugnahme *f:* ~ (**auf** +*akk*) reference (to).
Bezugs- *zW:* ~**person** *f:* **die wichtigste** ~**person des Kleinkindes** the person to whom the small child relates most closely; ~**preis** *m* retail price; ~**quelle** *f* source of supply.
bezuschussen [bə'tsu:ʃʊsən] *vt* to subsidize.
bezwecken [bə'tsvɛkən] *vt* to aim at.
bezweifeln [bə'tsvaɪfəln] *vt* to doubt.
bezwingen [bə'tsvɪŋən] *unreg vt* to conquer; (*Feind*) to defeat, overcome.
bezwungen [bə'tsvʊŋən] *pp von* **bezwingen**.
Bf. *abk* = **Bahnhof; Brief**.
BfA (-) *f abk* (= *Bundesversicherungsanstalt für Angestellte*) *Federal insurance company for employees*.
BfV (-) *nt abk* (= *Bundesamt für Verfassungsschutz*) *Federal Office for Protection of the Constitution*.
BG (-) *f abk* (= *Berufsgenossenschaft*) *professional association*.
BGB (-) *nt abk* (= *Bürgerliches Gesetzbuch*) *siehe* **bürgerlich**.
BGH (-) *m abk* (= *Bundesgerichtshof*) *Federal Supreme Court*.
BGS (-) *m abk* = **Bundesgrenzschutz**.
BH (-s, -(s)) *m abk* (= *Büstenhalter*) bra.
Bhf. *abk* = **Bahnhof**.
BI *f abk* = **Bürgerinitiative**.
Biathlon ['bi:atlɔn] (-s, -s) *nt* biathlon.
bibbern ['bɪbərn] (*umg*) *vi* (*vor Kälte*) to shiver.
Bibel ['bi:bəl] (-, -n) *f* Bible.
bibelfest *adj* well versed in the Bible.
Biber ['bi:bər] (-s, -) *m* beaver.
Biberbettuch *nt* flannelette sheet.
Bibliographie [bibliogra'fi:] *f* bibliography.

Bibliothek [biblio'te:k] (-, -en) f (auch COMPUT) library.
Bibliothekar(in) [bibliote'ka:r(ın)] (-s, -e) m(f) librarian.
biblisch ['bi:blıʃ] adj biblical.
bieder ['bi:dər] adj upright, worthy; (pej) conventional; (Kleid etc) plain.
Biedermann (-(e)s, pl -männer) (pej) m (geh) petty bourgeois.
biegbar ['bi:kba:r] adj flexible.
Biege f: die ~ machen (umg) to buzz off, split.
biegen ['bi:gən] unreg vt, vr to bend ♦ vi to turn; sich vor Lachen ~ (fig) to double up with laughter; auf B~ oder Brechen (umg) by hook or by crook.
biegsam ['bi:kza:m] adj supple.
Biegung f bend, curve.
Biene ['bi:nə] (-, -n) f bee; (veraltet: umg: Mädchen) bird (BRIT), chick (bes US).
Bienen- zW: ~**honig** m honey; ~**korb** m beehive; ~**stich** m (KOCH) sugar-and-almond coated cake filled with custard or cream; ~**stock** m beehive; ~**wachs** nt beeswax.
Bier [bi:r] (-(e)s, -e) nt beer; zwei ~, bitte! two beers, please.
Bier- zW: ~**bauch** (umg) m beer belly; ~**brauer** m brewer; ~**deckel** m beer mat; ~**filz** m beer mat; ~**krug** m beer mug; ~**schinken** m ham sausage; ~**seidel** nt beer mug; ~**wurst** f ham sausage.
Biest [bi:st] (-(e)s, -er) (pej: umg) nt (Mensch) (little) wretch; (Frau) bitch (!).
biestig adj beastly.
bieten ['bi:tən] unreg vt to offer; (bei Versteigerung) to bid ♦ vr (Gelegenheit): sich jdm ~ to present itself to sb; sich dat etw ~ lassen to put up with sth.
Bigamie [biga'mi:] f bigamy.
Bikini [bi'ki:ni] (-s, -s) m bikini.
Bilanz [bi'lants] f balance; (fig) outcome; eine ~ aufstellen to draw up a balance sheet; ~ ziehen (aus) to take stock (of); ~**prüfer** m auditor.
bilateral ['bi:latera:l] adj bilateral; ~er Handel bilateral trade; ~es Abkommen bilateral agreement.
Bild [bılt] (-(e)s, -er) nt (lit, fig) picture; photo; (Spiegel~) reflection; (fig: Vorstellung) image, picture; ein ~ machen to take a photo od picture; im ~e sein (über +akk) to be in the picture (about); ~**auflösung** f (TV, COMPUT) resolution; ~**band** m illustrated book; ~**bericht** m pictorial report; ~**beschreibung** f (SCH) description of a picture.
bilden ['bıldən] vt to form; (erziehen) to educate; (ausmachen) to constitute ♦ vr to arise; (durch Lesen etc) to improve one's knowledge; (erziehen) to educate o.s.
bildend adj: die ~e Kunst art.
Bilderbuch nt picture book.
Bilderrahmen m picture frame.

Bild- zW: ~**fläche** f screen; (fig) scene; von der ~**fläche verschwinden** (fig: umg) to disappear (from the scene); b~**haft** adj (Sprache) vivid; ~**hauer** m sculptor; b~**hübsch** adj lovely, pretty as a picture; b~**lich** adj figurative; pictorial; sich dat etw b~**lich vorstellen** to picture sth in one's mind's eye.
Bildnis ['bıltnıs] nt (liter) portrait.
Bild- zW: ~**platte** f videodisc; ~**röhre** f (TV) cathode ray tube; ~**schirm** m (TV, COMPUT) screen; ~**schirmgerät** nt (COMPUT) visual display unit, VDU; ~**schirmtext** m teletext; ≈ Ceefax ®, Oracle ®; b~**schön** adj lovely.
Bildtelefon nt videophone.
Bildung ['bıldʊŋ] f formation; (Wissen, Benehmen) education.
Bildungs- zW: ~**gang** m school (and university/college) career; ~**gut** nt cultural heritage; ~**lücke** f gap in one's education; ~**politik** f educational policy; ~**roman** m (LITER) Bildungsroman, novel relating hero's intellectual/spiritual development; ~**urlaub** m educational holiday; ~**weg** m: auf dem zweiten ~**weg** through night school/the Open University etc; ~**wesen** nt education system.
Bildweite f (PHOT) distance.
Bildzuschrift f reply enclosing photograph.
Billard ['bıljart] (-s, -e) nt billiards; ~**ball** m billiard ball; ~**kugel** f billiard ball.
billig ['bılıç] adj cheap; (gerecht) fair, reasonable; ~e Handelsflagge flag of convenience; ~es Geld cheap/easy money.
billigen ['bılıgən] vt to approve of; etw stillschweigend ~ to condone sth.
billigerweise adv (veraltet) in all fairness, reasonably.
Billigladen m discount store.
Billigpreis m low price.
Billigung f approval.
Billion [bıli'o:n] f billion (BRIT), trillion (US).
bimmeln ['bıməln] vi to tinkle.
Bimsstein ['bımsʃtain] m pumice stone.
bin [bın] vb siehe sein.
binär [bi'nɛ:r] adj binary; B~**zahl** f binary number.
Binde ['bındə] (-, -n) f bandage; (Armbinde) band; (MED) sanitary towel (BRIT) od napkin (US); sich dat einen hinter die ~ gießen od kippen (umg) to put a few drinks away.
Binde- zW: ~**glied** nt connecting link; ~**hautentzündung** f conjunctivitis; ~**mittel** nt binder.
binden unreg vt to bind, tie ♦ vr (sich verpflichten): sich ~ (an +akk) to commit o.s. (to).
bindend adj binding; (Zusage) definite; ~ für binding on.
Bindestrich m hyphen.
Bindewort nt conjunction.
Bindfaden m string; es regnet Bindfäden

(umg) it's sheeting down.

Bindung *f* bond, tie; *(SKI)* binding.

binnen ['bɪnən] *präp (+dat od gen)* within; **B~hafen** *m* inland harbour *(BRIT)* od harbor *(US)*; **B~handel** *m* internal trade; **B~markt** *m* home market; **Europäischer B~markt** single European market.

Binse ['bɪnzə] *(-, -n)f* rush, reed; **in die ~n gehen** *(fig: umg: mißlingen)* to be a wash-out.

Binsenwahrheit *f* truism.

Biographie [biogra'fi:] *f* biography.

Bioladen ['biola:dən] *m* health food shop *(BRIT)* od store *(US)*.

A **Bioladen** *is a shop which specializes in selling environmentally-friendly products such as phosphate-free washing powders, recycled paper and organically-grown vegetables.*

Biologe [bio'lo:gə] *(-n, -n)* m biologist.

Biologie [biolo'gi:] *f* biology.

Biologin *f* biologist.

biologisch [bio'lo:gɪʃ] *adj* biological; **~e Vielfalt** biodiversity; **~e Uhr** biological clock.

Bio- [bio-] *zW:* **~sphäre** *f* biosphere; **~technik** [bio'tɛçnɪk] *f* biotechnology; **~treibstoff** ['bi:otraipʃtɔf] *m* biofuel.

birgt [bɪrkt] *vb siehe* **bergen**.

Birke ['bɪrkə] *(-, -n)f* birch.

Birma ['bɪrma] *(-s)* nt Burma.

Birnbaum *m* pear tree.

Birne ['bɪrnə] *(-, -n)f* pear; *(ELEK)* (light) bulb.

birst [bɪrst] *vb siehe* **bersten**.

===================== *SCHLÜSSELWORT*

bis [bɪs] *präp +akk, adv* **1** *(zeitlich)* till, until; *(~ spätestens)* by; **Sie haben ~ Dienstag Zeit** you have until od till Tuesday; **~ zum Wochenende** up to od until the weekend; *(spätestens)* by the weekend; **~ Dienstag muß es fertig sein** it must be ready by Tuesday; **~ wann ist das fertig?** when will that be finished?; **~ auf weiteres** until further notice; **~ in die Nacht** into the night; **~ bald!/gleich!** see you later/soon

2 *(räumlich)* (up) to; **ich fahre ~ Köln** I'm going as far as Cologne; **~ an unser Grundstück** (right *od* up) to our plot; **~ hierher** this far; **~ zur Straße kommen** to get as far as the road

3 *(bei Zahlen, Angaben)* up to; **~ zu** up to; **Gefängnis ~ zu 8 Jahren** a maximum of 8 years' imprisonment

4 **~ auf etw** *akk (außer)* except sth; *(einschließlich)* including sth

♦ *konj* **1** *(mit Zahlen)* to; **10 ~ 20** 10 to 20

2 *(zeitlich)* till, until; **~ es dunkel wird** till *od* until it gets dark; **von ... ~ ... from ... to ...**

Bisamratte ['bi:zamratə] *f* muskrat (beaver).

Bischof ['bɪʃɔf] *(-s, ̈-e)* m bishop.

bischöflich ['bɪʃøːflɪç] *adj* episcopal.

bisexuell [bizɛksu'ɛl] *adj* bisexual.

bisher [bɪs'heːr] *adv* till now, hitherto.

bisherig [bɪs'heːrɪç] *adj* till now.

Biskaya [bɪs'kaːya] *f:* **Golf von ~** Bay of Biscay.

Biskuit [bɪs'kviːt] *(-(e)s, -s od -e)* m od nt biscuit; **~gebäck** nt sponge cake(s); **~teig** m sponge mixture.

bislang [bɪs'laŋ] *adv* hitherto.

Biß (**-sses, -sse**) *m* bite.

biß *etc* [bɪs] *vb siehe* **beißen**.

bißchen ['bɪsçən] *adj, adv* bit.

Bissen ['bɪsən] *(-s, -)* m bite, morsel; **sich** *dat* **jeden ~ vom od am Munde absparen** to watch every penny one spends.

bissig ['bɪsɪç] *adj (Hund)* snappy; vicious; *(Bemerkung)* cutting, biting; **„Vorsicht, ~er Hund"** "beware of the dog".

bist [bɪst] *vb siehe* **sein**.

Bistum ['bɪstuːm] *nt* bishopric.

bisweilen [bɪs'vaɪlən] *adv* at times, occasionally.

Bit [bɪt] *(-s), (-s))* nt *(COMPUT)* bit.

Bittbrief *m* petition.

Bitte ['bɪtə] *(-, -n)f* request; **auf seine ~ hin** at his request; **b~** *interj* please; *(als Antwort auf Dank)* you're welcome; **wie b~?** (I beg your) pardon?; **b~ schön!** it was a pleasure; **b~ schön?** *(in Geschäft)* can I help you?; **na b~!** there you are!

bitten *unreg vt* to ask ♦ *vi (einladen):* **ich lasse ~** would you ask him/her *etc* to come in now?; **~ um** to ask for; **aber ich bitte dich!** not at all; **ich bitte darum** *(form)* if you wouldn't mind; **ich muß doch (sehr) ~!** well I must say!

bittend *adj* pleading, imploring.

bitter ['bɪtər] *adj* bitter; *(Schokolade)* plain; **etw ~ nötig haben** to be in dire need of sth; **~böse** *adj* very angry; **~ernst** *adj:* **damit ist es mir ~ernst** I am deadly serious *od* in deadly earnest; **B~keit** *f* bitterness; **~lich** *adj* bitter ♦ *adv* bitterly.

Bittsteller(in) **(-s, -)** *m(f)* petitioner.

Biwak ['bi:vak] *(-s, -s od -e)* nt bivouac.

Bj. *abk =* **Baujahr.**

Blabla [bla:'bla:] *(-s)* *(umg)* nt waffle.

blähen ['blɛːən] *vt, vr* to swell, blow out ♦ *vi (Speisen)* to cause flatulence *od* wind.

Blähungen *pl (MED)* wind *sing.*

blamabel [bla'ma:bəl] *adj* disgraceful.

Blamage [bla'ma:ʒə] *(-, -n)f* disgrace.

blamieren [bla'mi:rən] *vr* to make a fool of o.s., disgrace o.s. ♦ *vt* to let down, disgrace.

blank [blaŋk] *adj* bright; *(unbedeckt)* bare; *(sauber)* clean, polished; *(umg: ohne Geld)* broke; *(offensichtlich)* blatant.

blanko ['blaŋko] *adv* blank; **B~scheck** m blank cheque *(BRIT)* od check *(US)*; **B~vollmacht** f carte blanche.

Bläschen ['blɛ:sçən] *nt* bubble; (*MED*) small blister.

Blase ['bla:zə] (-, -n) *f* bubble; (*MED*) blister; (*ANAT*) bladder.

Blasebalg *m* bellows *pl*.

blasen *unreg vt, vi* to blow; **zum Aufbruch** ~ (*fig*) to say it's time to go.

Blasenentzündung *f* cystitis.

Bläser(in) ['blɛ:zər(ɪn)] (-s, -) *m(f)* (*MUS*) wind player; **die** ~ the wind (section).

blasiert [bla'zi:rt] (*pej*) *adj* (*geh*) blasé.

Blas- *zW:* ~**instrument** *nt* wind instrument; ~**kapelle** *f* brass band; ~**musik** *f* brass band music.

blaß [blas] *adj* pale; (*Ausdruck*) weak, insipid; (*fig: Ahnung, Vorstellung*) faint, vague; ~ **vor Neid werden** to go green with envy.

Blässe ['blɛsə] (-) *f* paleness, pallor.

Blatt [blat] (-(e)s, ⁻er) *nt* leaf; (*von Papier*) sheet; (*Zeitung*) newspaper; (*KARTEN*) hand; **vom** ~ **singen/spielen** to sight-read; **kein** ~ **vor den Mund nehmen** not to mince one's words.

blättern ['blɛtərn] *vi:* **in etw** *dat* ~ to leaf through sth.

Blätterteig *m* flaky *od* puff pastry.

Blattlaus *f* greenfly, aphid.

blau [blaʊ] *adj* blue; (*umg*) drunk, stoned; (*KOCH*) boiled; (*Auge*) black; ~**er Fleck** bruise; **mit einem** ~**en Auge davonkommen** (*fig*) to get off lightly; ~**er Brief** (*SCH*) *letter telling parents a child may have to repeat a year*; **er wird sein** ~**es Wunder erleben** (*umg*) he won't know what's hit him; ~**äugig** *adj* blue-eyed; **B**~**beere** *f* bilberry.

Blaue *nt:* **Fahrt ins** ~ mystery tour; **das** ~ **vom Himmel (herunter) lügen** (*umg*) to tell a pack of lies.

blau- *zW:* **B**~**helm** (*umg*) *m* UN Soldier; **B**~**kraut** *nt* red cabbage; **B**~**licht** *nt* flashing blue light; ~**machen** (*umg*) *vi* to skive off work; **B**~**pause** *f* blueprint; **B**~**säure** *f* prussic acid; **B**~**strumpf** *m* (*fig*) bluestocking.

Blech [blɛç] (-(e)s, -e) *nt* tin, sheet metal; (*Back*~) baking tray; ~ **reden** (*umg*) to talk rubbish *od* nonsense; ~**bläser** *pl* the brass (section); ~**büchse** *f* tin, can; ~**dose** *f* tin, can.

blechen (*umg*) *vt, vi* to pay.

Blechschaden *m* (*AUT*) damage to bodywork.

Blechtrommel *f* tin drum.

blecken ['blɛkən] *vt:* **die Zähne** ~ to bare *od* show one's teeth.

Blei [blaɪ] (-(e)s, -e) *nt* lead.

Bleibe (-, -n) *f* roof over one's head.

bleiben *unreg vi* to stay, remain; **bitte,** ~ **Sie doch sitzen** please don't get up; **wo bleibst du so lange?** (*umg*) what's keeping you?; **das bleibt unter uns** (*fig*) that's (just) between ourselves; ~**lassen** *unreg vt*

(*aufgeben*) to give up; **etw** ~**lassen** (*unterlassen*) to give sth a miss.

bleich [blaɪç] *adj* faded, pale; ~**en** *vt* to bleach; **B**~**gesicht** (*umg*) *nt* (*blasser Mensch*) pasty-face.

bleiern *adj* leaden.

Blei- *zW:* **b**~**frei** *adj* lead-free; ~**gießen** *nt New Year's Eve fortune-telling using lead shapes*; **b**~**haltig** *adj:* **b**~**haltig sein** to contain lead; ~**stift** *m* pencil; ~**stiftabsatz** *m* stiletto heel (*BRIT*), spike heel (*US*); ~**stiftspitzer** *m* pencil sharpener; ~**vergiftung** *f* lead poisoning.

Blende ['blɛndə] (-, -n) *f* (*PHOT*) aperture; (: *Einstellungsposition*) f-stop.

blenden *vt* to blind, dazzle; (*fig*) to hoodwink.

blendend (*umg*) *adj* grand; ~ **aussehen** to look smashing.

Blender (-s, -) *m* con-man.

blendfrei ['blɛntfraɪ] *adj* (*Glas*) non-reflective.

Blick [blɪk] (-(e)s, -e) *m* (*kurz*) glance, glimpse; (*Anschauen*) look, gaze; (*Aussicht*) view; **Liebe auf den ersten** ~ love at first sight; **den** ~ **senken** to look down; **den bösen** ~ **haben** to have the evil eye; **einen (guten)** ~ **für etw haben** to have an eye for sth; **mit einem** ~ at a glance.

blicken *vi* to look; **das läßt tief** ~ that's very revealing; **sich** ~ **lassen** to put in an appearance.

Blick- *zW:* ~**fang** *m* eye-catcher; ~**feld** *nt* range of vision (*auch fig*); ~**kontakt** *m* visual contact; ~**punkt** *m:* **im** ~**punkt der Öffentlichkeit stehen** to be in the public eye.

blieb *etc* [bli:p] *vb siehe* **bleiben**.

blies *etc* [bli:s] *vb siehe* **blasen**.

blind [blɪnt] *adj* blind; (*Glas etc*) dull; (*Alarm*) false; ~**er Passagier** stowaway.

Blinddarm *m* appendix; ~**entzündung** *f* appendicitis.

Blindekuh ['blɪndəku:] *f:* ~ **spielen** to play blind man's buff.

Blindenhund *m* guide dog.

Blindenschrift *f* braille.

Blind- *zW:* ~**gänger** *m* (*MIL, fig*) dud; ~**heit** *f* blindness; **mit** ~**heit geschlagen sein** (*fig*) to be blind; **b**~**lings** *adv* blindly; ~**schleiche** *f* slow worm; **b**~**schreiben** *unreg vi* to touch-type.

blinken ['blɪŋkən] *vi* to twinkle, sparkle; (*Licht*) to flash, signal; (*AUT*) to indicate ♦ *vt* to flash, signal.

Blinker (-s, -) *m* (*AUT*) indicator.

Blinklicht *nt* (*AUT*) indicator.

blinzeln ['blɪntsəln] *vi* to blink, wink.

Blitz [blɪts] (-es, -e) *m* (flash of) lightning; **wie ein** ~ **aus heiterem Himmel** (*fig*) like a bolt from the blue; ~**ableiter** *m* lightning conductor; (*fig*) vent *od* safety valve for feelings; **b**~**en** *vi* (*aufleuchten*) to glint, shine; **es b**~**t** (*MET*) there's a flash of lightning; ~**gerät** *nt* (*PHOT*) flash(gun);

~**licht** nt flashlight; **b~sauber** adj spick and span; **b~schnell** adj, adv as quick as a flash; ~**würfel** m (PHOT) flashcube.

Block [blɔk] (-(e)s, ⁀e) m (lit, fig) block; (von Papier) pad; (POL: Staaten~) bloc; (Fraktion) faction.

Blockade [blɔ'kaːdə] (-, -n) f blockade.

Block- zW: ~**buchstabe** m block letter od capital; ~**flöte** f recorder; **b~frei** adj (POL) non-aligned; ~**haus** nt log cabin; ~**hütte** f log cabin.

blockieren [blɔ'kiːrən] vt to block ♦ vi (Räder) to jam.

Block- zW: ~**schokolade** f cooking chocolate; ~**schrift** f block letters pl; ~**stunde** f double period.

blöd [bløːt] adj silly, stupid.

blödeln ['bløːdəln] (umg) vi to fool around.

Blödheit f stupidity.

Blödian ['bløːdian] (-(e)s, -e) (umg) m idiot.

blöd- zW: **B~mann** (-(e)s, pl -männer) (umg) m idiot; **B~sinn** m nonsense; ~**sinnig** adj silly, idiotic.

blöken ['bløːkən] vi (Schaf) to bleat.

blond [blɔnt] adj blond(e), fair-haired.

Blondine [blɔn'diːnə] f blonde.

══════════ *SCHLÜSSELWORT*

bloß [bloːs] adj **1** (unbedeckt) bare; (nackt) naked; **mit der ~en Hand** with one's bare hand; **mit ~em Auge** with the naked eye
2 (alleinig: nur) mere; **der ~e Gedanke** the very thought; ~**er Neid** sheer envy
♦ adv only, merely; **laß das ~!** just don't do that!; **wie ist das ~ passiert?** how on earth did that happen?

Blöße ['bløːsə] (-, -n) f bareness; nakedness; (fig) weakness; **sich** dat **eine ~ geben** (fig) to lay o.s. open to attack.

bloßlegen vt to expose.

bloßstellen vt to show up.

blühen ['blyːən] vi (lit) to bloom, be in bloom; (fig) to flourish; (umg: bevorstehen): **(jdm) ~** to be in store (for sb).

blühend adj: **wie das ~e Leben aussehen** to look the very picture of health.

Blume ['bluːmə] (-, -n) f flower; (von Wein) bouquet; **jdm etw durch die ~ sagen** to say sth in a roundabout way to sb.

Blumen- zW: ~**geschäft** nt flower shop, florist's; ~**kasten** m window box; ~**kohl** m cauliflower; ~**strauß** m bouquet, bunch of flowers; ~**topf** m flowerpot; ~**zwiebel** f bulb.

Bluse ['bluːzə] (-, -n) f blouse.

Blut [bluːt] (-(e)s) nt (lit, fig) blood; **(nur) ruhig ~** keep your shirt on (umg); **jdn/sich bis aufs ~ bekämpfen** to fight sb/fight bitterly; **b~arm** adj anaemic (BRIT), anemic (US); (fig) penniless; ~**bahn** f bloodstream; ~**bank** f blood bank; **b~befleckt** adj bloodstained;

~**bild** nt blood count; ~**buche** f copper beech; ~**druck** m blood pressure.

Blüte ['blyːtə] (-, -n) f blossom; (fig) prime.

Blutegel ['bluːt|eːgəl] m leech.

bluten vi to bleed.

Blütenstaub m pollen.

Bluter (-s, -) m (MED) haemophiliac (BRIT), hemophiliac (US).

Bluterguß m haemorrhage (BRIT), hemorrhage (US); (auf Haut) bruise.

Blütezeit f flowering period; (fig) prime.

Blutgerinnsel nt blood clot.

Blutgruppe f blood group.

blutig adj bloody; (umg: Anfänger) absolute; (: Ernst) deadly.

Blut- zW: **b~jung** adj very young; ~**konserve** f unit od pint of stored blood; ~**körperchen** nt blood corpuscle; ~**probe** f blood test; **b~rünstig** adj bloodthirsty; ~**schande** f incest; ~**senkung** f (MED): **eine ~senkung machen** to test the sedimentation rate of the blood; ~**spender** m blood donor; **b~stillend** adj styptic; ~**sturz** m haemorrhage (BRIT), hemorrhage (US).

blutsverwandt adj related by blood.

Blutübertragung f blood transfusion.

Blutung f bleeding, haemorrhage (BRIT), hemorrhage (US).

Blut- zW: **b~unterlaufen** adj suffused with blood; (Augen) bloodshot; ~**vergießen** nt bloodshed; ~**vergiftung** f blood poisoning; ~**wurst** f black pudding; ~**zuckerspiegel** m blood sugar level.

BLZ abk = **Bankleitzahl**.

BMX-Rad nt BMX.

BND (-s, -) m abk = **Bundesnachrichtendienst**.

Bö (-, -en) f squall.

Boccia ['bɔtʃa] nt od f bowls sing.

Bock [bɔk] (-(e)s, ⁀e) m buck, ram; (Gestell) trestle, support; (SPORT) buck; **alter ~** (umg) old goat; **den ~ zum Gärtner machen** (fig) to choose the worst possible person for the job; **einen ~ schießen** (fig: umg) to (make a) boob; ~ **haben, etw zu tun** (umg: Lust) to fancy doing sth.

Bockbier nt bock (beer) (type of strong beer).

bocken ['bɔkən] (umg) vi (Auto, Mensch) to play up.

Bocksbeutel m wide, rounded (dumpy) bottle containing Franconian wine.

Bockshorn nt: **sich von jdm ins ~ jagen lassen** to let sb upset one.

Bocksprung m leapfrog; (SPORT) vault.

Bockwurst f bockwurst (large frankfurter).

Boden ['boːdən] (-s, ⁀) m ground; (Fuß~) floor; (Meeres~, Faß~) bottom; (Speicher) attic; **den ~ unter den Füßen verlieren** (lit) to lose one's footing; (fig: in Diskussion) to get out of one's depth; **ich hätte (vor Scham) im ~ versinken können** (fig) I was so ashamed, I wished the ground would swallow me up; **am ~ zerstört sein** (umg) to be shattered;

etw aus dem ~ stampfen (*fig*) to conjure sth up out of nothing; (*Häuser*) to build overnight; **auf dem ~ der Tatsachen bleiben** (*fig: Grundlage*) to stick to the facts; **zu ~ fallen** to fall to the ground; **festen ~ unter den Füßen haben** to be on firm ground, be on terra firma; **~kontrolle** *f* (*RAUMFAHRT*) ground control; **b~los** *adj* bottomless; (*umg*) incredible; **~personal** *nt* (*AVIAT*) ground personnel *pl*, ground staff; **~satz** *m* dregs *pl*, sediment; **~schätze** *pl* mineral wealth *sing*.

Bodensee ['boːdənzeː] *m:* **der ~** Lake Constance.

Bodenturnen *nt* floor exercises *pl*.

Böe (-, -n) *f* squall.

bog *etc* [boːk] *vb siehe* **biegen**.

Bogen ['boːɡən] (-s, -) *m* (*Biegung*) curve; (*ARCHIT*) arch; (*Waffe, MUS*) bow; (*Papier*) sheet; **den ~ heraushaben** (*umg*) to have got the hang of it; **einen großen ~ um jdn/etw machen** (*meiden*) to give sb/sth a wide berth; **jdn in hohem ~ hinauswerfen** (*umg*) to fling sb out; **~gang** *m* arcade; **~schütze** *m* archer.

Bohle ['boːlə] (-, -n) *f* plank.

Böhme ['bøːmə] (-n, -n) *m* Bohemian.

Böhmen (-s) *nt* Bohemia.

Böhmin *f* Bohemian woman.

böhmisch ['bøːmɪʃ] *adj* Bohemian; **das sind für mich ~e Dörfer** (*umg*) that's all Greek to me.

Bohne ['boːnə] (-, -n) *f* bean; **blaue ~** (*umg*) bullet; **nicht die ~** not one little bit.

Bohnen- *zW:* **~kaffee** *m* real coffee; **~stange** *f* (*fig: umg*) beanpole; **~stroh** *nt:* **dumm wie ~stroh** (*umg*) (as) thick as two (short) planks.

bohnern *vt* to wax, polish.

Bohnerwachs *nt* floor polish.

bohren ['boːrən] *vt* to bore; (*Loch*) to drill ♦ *vi* to drill; (*fig: drängen*) to keep on; (*peinigen: Schmerz, Zweifel etc*) to gnaw; **nach Öl/ Wasser ~** drill for oil/water; **in der Nase ~** to pick one's nose.

Bohrer (-s, -) *m* drill.

Bohr- *zW:* **~insel** *f* oil rig; **~maschine** *f* drill; **~turm** *m* derrick.

Boiler ['bɔylər] (-s, -) *m* water heater.

Boje ['boːjə] (-, -n) *f* buoy.

Bolivianer(in) [bolivi'aːnər(ɪn)] (-s, -) *m(f)* Bolivian.

Bolivien [bo'liːviən] *nt* Bolivia.

bolivisch [bo'liːvɪʃ] *adj* Bolivian.

Bollwerk ['bɔlvɛrk] *nt* (*lit, fig*) bulwark.

Bolschewismus [bɔlʃe'vɪsmʊs] (-) *m* Bolshevism.

Bolzen ['bɔltsən] (-s, -) *m* bolt.

bombardieren [bɔmbar'diːrən] *vt* to bombard; (*aus der Luft*) to bomb.

Bombe ['bɔmbə] (-, -n) *f* bomb; **wie eine ~ einschlagen** to come as a (real) bombshell.

Bomben- *zW:* **~alarm** *m* bomb scare; **~angriff** *m* bombing raid; **~anschlag** *m* bomb attack; **~erfolg** (*umg*) *m* huge success; **~geschäft** (*umg*) *nt:* **ein ~geschäft machen** to do a roaring trade; **b~sicher** (*umg*) *adj* dead certain.

bombig (*umg*) *adj* great, super.

Bon [bɔŋ] (-s, -s) *m* voucher; (*Kassenzettel*) receipt.

Bonbon [bõ'bõː] (-s, -s) *nt od m* sweet.

Bonn [bɔn] (-s) *nt* Bonn.

Bonze ['bɔntsə] (-n, -n) *m* big shot (*umg*).

Bonzenviertel (*umg*) *nt* posh quarter (*of town*).

Boot [boːt] (-(e)s, -e) *nt* boat.

Bord [bɔrt] (-(e)s, -e) *m* (*AVIAT, NAUT*) board ♦ *nt* (*Brett*) shelf; **über ~ gehen** to go overboard; (*fig*) to go by the board; **an ~ on board**.

Bordell [bɔr'dɛl] (-s, -e) *nt* brothel.

Bordfunkanlage *f* radio.

Bordstein *m* kerb(stone) (*BRIT*), curb(stone) (*US*).

borgen ['bɔrɡən] *vt* to borrow; **jdm etw ~** to lend sb sth.

Borneo ['bɔrneo] (-s) *nt* Borneo.

borniert [bɔr'niːrt] *adj* narrow-minded.

Börse ['bœrzə] (-, -n) *f* stock exchange; (*Geld~*) purse.

Börsen- *zW:* **~makler** *m* stockbroker; **b~notiert** *adj:* **b~notierte Firma** listed company; **~notierung** *f* quotation (on the stock exchange).

Borste ['bɔrstə] (-, -n) *f* bristle.

Borte ['bɔrtə] (-, -n) *f* edging; (*Band*) trimming.

bös [bøːs] *adj* = **böse**; **~artig** *adj* malicious; (*MED*) malignant.

Böschung ['bœʃʊŋ] *f* slope; (*Ufer~ etc*) embankment.

böse ['bøːzə] *adj* bad, evil; (*zornig*) angry; **das war nicht ~ gemeint** I/he *etc* didn't mean it nastily.

Bösewicht (*umg*) *m* baddy.

boshaft ['boːshaft] *adj* malicious, spiteful.

Bosheit *f* malice, spite.

Bosnien ['bɔsniən] (-s) *nt* Bosnia.

Bosnien-Herzegowina ['bɔsniənhɛrtsə'ɡoːviːna] (-s) *nt* Bosnia-Herzegovina.

Bosnier(in) (-s, -) *m(f)* Bosnian.

bosnisch *adj* Bosnian.

Boß [bɔs] (-sses, -sse) (*umg*) *m* boss.

böswillig ['bøːsvɪlɪç] *adj* malicious.

bot *etc* [boːt] *vb siehe* **bieten**.

Botanik [bo'taːnɪk] *f* botany.

botanisch [bo'taːnɪʃ] *adj* botanical.

Bote ['boːtə] (-n, -n) *m* messenger.

Botengang *m* errand.

Botenjunge *m* errand boy.

Botin ['boːtɪn] *f* messenger.

Botschaft *f* message, news; (*POL*) embassy;

die **Frohe** ~ the Gospel; ~**er (-s, -)** *m* ambassador.
Botswana [bɔ'tsvaːna] **(-s)** *nt* Botswana.
Bottich ['bɔtɪç] **(-(e)s, -e)** *m* vat, tub.
Bouillon [bʊ'ljõː] **(-, -s)** *f* consommé.
Boulevard- [bulə'vaːr] *zW:* ~**blatt** (*umg*) *nt* tabloid; ~**presse** *f* tabloid press; ~**stück** *nt* light play/comedy.
Boutique [bu'tiːk] **(-, -n)** *f* boutique.
Bowle ['boːlə] **(-, -n)** *f* punch.
Bowlingbahn ['boːlɪŋbaːn] *f* bowling alley.
Box [bɔks] *f* (*Lautsprecher~*) speaker.
boxen *vi* to box.
Boxer (-s, -) *m* boxer.
Boxhandschuh *m* boxing glove.
Boxkampf *m* boxing match.
Boykott [bɔy'kɔt] **(-(e)s, -s)** *m* boycott.
boykottieren [bɔykɔ'tiːrən] *vt* to boycott.
BR *abk* (= *Bayerischer Rundfunk*) *German radio station.*
brach *etc* [braːx] *vb siehe* **brechen**.
brachial [braxi'aːl] *adj:* **mit ~er Gewalt** by brute force.
brachliegen ['braːxliːgən] *unreg vi* (*lit, fig*) to lie fallow.
brachte *etc* ['braxtə] *vb siehe* **bringen**.
Branche ['brãːʃə] **(-, -n)** *f* line of business.
Branchenverzeichnis *nt* trade directory.
Brand [brant] **(-(e)s, ̈-e)** *m* fire; (*MED*) gangrene.
Brandanschlag *m* arson attack.
branden ['brandən] *vi* to surge; (*Meer*) to break.
Brandenburg ['brandənbʊrk] **(-s)** *nt* Brandenburg.
Brandherd *m* source of the fire.
brandmarken *vt* to brand; (*fig*) to stigmatize.
brandneu (*umg*) *adj* brand-new.
Brand- *zW:* ~**salbe** *f* ointment for burns; ~**satz** *m* incendiary device; ~**stifter** *m* arsonist, fire-raiser; ~**stiftung** *f* arson.
Brandung *f* surf.
Brandwunde *f* burn.
brannte *etc* ['brantə] *vb siehe* **brennen**.
Branntwein ['brantvaɪn] *m* brandy; ~**steuer** *f* tax on spirits.
Brasilianer(in) [brazili'aːnər(ɪn)] **(-s, -)** *m(f)* Brazilian.
brasilianisch *adj* Brazilian.
Brasilien [bra'ziːliən] *nt* Brazil.
brät [brɛt] *vb siehe* **braten**.
Bratapfel *m* baked apple.
braten ['braːtən] *unreg vt* to roast; (*in Pfanne*) to fry; **B~ (-s, -)** *m* roast, joint; **den B~ riechen** (*umg*) to smell a rat, suss something.
Brat- *zW:* ~**hähnchen** *nt* (*SÜDD, ÖSTERR*) roast chicken; ~**hendl** *nt* roast chicken; ~**huhn** *nt* roast chicken; ~**kartoffeln** *pl* fried/roast potatoes *pl*; ~**pfanne** *f* frying pan; ~**rost** *m* grill.
Bratsche ['braːtʃə] **(-, -n)** *f* viola.
Bratspieß *m* spit.

Bratwurst *f* grilled sausage.
Brauch [braux] **(-(e)s, *pl* Bräuche)** *m* custom.
brauchbar *adj* usable, serviceable; (*Person*) capable.
brauchen *vt* (*bedürfen*) to need; (*müssen*) to have to; (*verwenden*) to use; **wie lange braucht man, um ...?** how long does it take to ...?
Brauchtum *nt* customs *pl*, traditions *pl*.
Braue ['brauə] **(-, -n)** *f* brow.
brauen ['brauən] *vt* to brew.
Brauerei [brauə'raɪ] *f* brewery.
braun [braun] *adj* brown; (*von Sonne*) tanned; (*pej*) Nazi.
Bräune ['brɔynə] **(-, -n)** *f* brownness; (*Sonnen~*) tan.
bräunen *vt* to make brown; (*Sonne*) to tan.
braungebrannt *adj* tanned.
Braunkohle *f* brown coal.
Braunschweig ['braunʃvaɪk] **(-s)** *nt* Brunswick.
Brause ['brauzə] **(-, -n)** *f* shower; (*von Gießkanne*) rose; (*Getränk*) lemonade.
brausen *vi* to roar; (*auch vr: duschen*) to take a shower.
Brausepulver *nt* lemonade powder.
Brausetablette *f* lemonade tablet.
Braut [braut] **(-, *pl* Bräute)** *f* bride; (*Verlobte*) fiancée.
Bräutigam ['brɔytɪgam] **(-s, -e)** *m* bridegroom; (*Verlobter*) fiancé.
Braut- *zW:* ~**jungfer** *f* bridesmaid; ~**kleid** *nt* wedding dress; ~**paar** *nt* bride and bridegroom, bridal pair.
brav [braːf] *adj* (*artig*) good; (*ehrenhaft*) worthy, honest; (*bieder: Frisur, Kleid*) plain; **sei schön ~!** be a good boy/girl.
BRD (-) *f abk* (= *Bundesrepublik Deutschland*) FRG; **die alte ~** former West Germany.

The **BRD** *(Bundesrepublik Deutschland) is the official name for the Federal Republic of Germany. It comprises 16* **Länder** *(see* **Land***). It was originally the name given to the former West Germany as opposed to East Germany (the* **DDR***). The two Germanies were reunited on 3rd October 1990.*

Brechbohne *f* French bean.
Brecheisen *nt* crowbar.
brechen *unreg vt, vi* to break; (*Licht*) to refract; (*speien*) to vomit; **die Ehe ~** to commit adultery; **mir bricht das Herz** it breaks my heart; ~**d voll sein** to be full to bursting.
Brechmittel *nt:* **er/das ist das reinste ~** (*umg*) he/it makes me feel ill.
Brechreiz *m* nausea.
Brechung *f* (*des Lichts*) refraction.
Brei [braɪ] **(-(e)s, -e)** *m* (*Masse*) pulp; (*KOCH*) gruel; (*Hafer~*) porridge (*BRIT*), oatmeal (*US*); (*für Kinder, Kranke*) mash; **um den heißen ~ herumreden** (*umg*) to beat about

the bush.

breit [brait] adj broad; (bei Maßangabe) wide; **die ~e Masse** the masses pl; **~beinig** adj with one's legs apart.

Breite (-, -n) f breadth; (bei Maßangabe) width; (GEOG) latitude.

breiten vt: **etw über etw** akk ~ to spread sth over sth.

Breitengrad m degree of latitude.

Breitensport m popular sport.

breit- zW: **~gefächert** adj: **ein ~gefächertes Angebot** a wide range; **~machen** vr to spread o.s. out; **~schlagen** unreg (umg) vt: **sich ~schlagen lassen** to let o.s. be talked round; **~schult(e)rig** adj broad-shouldered; **~treten** unreg (umg) vt to go on about; **B~wandfilm** m wide-screen film.

Bremen ['breːmən] (-s) nt Bremen.

Bremsbelag m brake lining.

Bremse ['brɛmzə] (-, -n) f brake; (ZOOL) horsefly.

bremsen vi to brake, apply the brakes ♦ vt (Auto) to brake; (fig) to slow down ♦ vr: **ich kann mich ~** (umg) not likely!

Brems- zW: **~flüssigkeit** f brake fluid; **~licht** nt brake light; **~pedal** nt brake pedal; **~schuh** m brake shoe; **~spur** f tyre (BRIT) od tire (US) marks pl; **~weg** m braking distance.

brennbar adj inflammable; **leicht ~** highly inflammable.

Brennelement nt fuel element.

brennen ['brɛnən] unreg vi to burn, be on fire; (Licht, Kerze etc) to burn ♦ vt (Holz etc) to burn; (Ziegel, Ton) to fire; (Kaffee) to roast; (Branntwein) to distil; **wo brennt's denn?** (fig: umg) what's the panic?; **darauf ~, etw zu tun** to be dying to do sth.

Brenn- zW: **~material** nt fuel; **~(n)essel** f nettle; **~ofen** m kiln; **~punkt** m (MATH, OPTIK) focus; **~spiritus** m methylated spirits pl; **~stoff** m liquid fuel.

brenzlig ['brɛntslɪç] adj smelling of burning, burnt; (fig) precarious.

Bresche ['brɛʃə] (-, -n) f: **in die ~ springen** (fig) to step into the breach.

Bretagne [bre'tanjə] f: **die ~** Brittany.

Bretone [bre'toːnə] (-n, -n) m Breton.

Bretonin [bre'toːnɪn] f Breton.

Brett [brɛt] (-(e)s, -er) nt board, plank; (Bord) shelf; (Spiel~) board; **Bretter** pl (SKI) skis pl; (THEAT) boards pl; **Schwarzes ~** notice board; **er hat ein ~ vor dem Kopf** (umg) he's really thick.

brettern (umg) vi to speed.

Bretterzaun m wooden fence.

Brezel ['breːtsəl] (-, -n) f pretzel.

bricht [brɪçt] vb siehe **brechen**.

Brief [briːf] (-(e)s, -e) m letter; **~beschwerer** (-s, -) m paperweight; **~drucksache** f circular; **~freund(in)** m(f) pen friend, pen-pal; **~kasten** m letter box; (COMPUT)

mailbox; **~kopf** m letterhead; **b~lich** adj, adv by letter; **~marke** f postage stamp; **~öffner** m letter opener; **~papier** nt notepaper; **~qualität** f (COMPUT) letter quality; **~tasche** f wallet; **~taube** f carrier pigeon; **~träger** m postman; **~umschlag** m envelope; **~wahl** f postal vote; **~wechsel** m correspondence.

briet etc [briːt] vb siehe **braten**.

Brigade [bri'gaːdə] (-, -n) f (MIL) brigade; (DDR) (work) team od group.

Brikett [bri'kɛt] (-s, -s) nt briquette.

brillant [brɪl'jant] adj (fig) sparkling, brilliant; **B~** (-en, -en) m brilliant, diamond.

Brille ['brɪlə] (-, -n) f spectacles pl; (Schutz~) goggles pl; (Toiletten~) (toilet) seat.

Brillenschlange f (hum) four-eyes.

Brillenträger(in) m(f): **er ist ~** he wears glasses.

bringen ['brɪŋən] unreg vt to bring; (mitnehmen, begleiten) to take; (einbringen: Profit) to bring in; (veröffentlichen) to publish; (THEAT, FILM) to show; (RUNDF, TV) to broadcast; (in einen Zustand versetzen) to get; (umg: tun können) to manage; **jdn dazu ~, etw zu tun** to make sb do sth; **jdn zum Lachen/Weinen ~** to make sb laugh/cry; **es weit ~** to do very well, get far; **jdn nach Hause ~** to take sb home; **jdn um etw ~** to make sb lose sth; **jdn auf eine Idee ~** to give sb an idea.

brisant [bri'zant] adj (fig) controversial.

Brisanz [bri'zants] f (fig) controversial nature.

Brise ['briːzə] (-, -n) f breeze.

Brite ['briːtə] (-n, -n) m Briton, Britisher (US); **die ~n** the British.

Britin f Briton, Britisher (US).

britisch ['briːtɪʃ] adj British; **die B~en Inseln** the British Isles.

bröckelig ['brœkəlɪç] adj crumbly.

Brocken ['brɔkən] (-s, -) m piece, bit; (Felsbrocken) lump of rock; **ein paar ~ Spanisch** a smattering of Spanish; **ein harter ~** (umg) a tough nut to crack.

brodeln ['broːdəln] vi to bubble.

Brokat [bro'kaːt] (-(e)s, -e) m brocade.

Brokkoli ['brɔkoli] pl broccoli.

Brombeere ['brɔmbeːrə] f blackberry, bramble (BRIT).

bronchial [brɔnçi'aːl] adj bronchial.

Bronchien ['brɔnçiən] pl bronchial tubes pl.

Bronchitis [brɔn'çiːtɪs] (-, -tiden) f bronchitis.

Bronze ['brõːsə] (-, -n) f bronze.

Brosame ['broːzaːmə] (-, -n) f crumb.

Brosche ['brɔʃə] (-, -n) f brooch.

Broschüre [brɔ'ʃyːrə] (-, -n) f pamphlet.

Brot [broːt] (-(e)s, -e) nt bread; (~laib) loaf; **das ist ein hartes ~** (fig) that's a hard way to earn one's living.

Brötchen ['brøːtçən] nt roll; **kleine ~ backen** (fig) to set one's sights lower; **~geber** m (hum) employer, provider (hum).

brotlos ['broːtloːs] *adj* (*Person*) unemployed; (*Arbeit etc*) unprofitable.

Brotzeit (*SÜDD*) *f* (*Pause*) ≈ tea break.

BRT *abk* (= *Bruttoregistertonne*) GRT.

Bruch [brʊx] (-(e)s, ⁼e) *m* breakage; (*zerbrochene Stelle*) break; (*fig*) split, breach; (*MED: Eingeweide~*) rupture, hernia; (*Bein~ etc*) fracture; (*MATH*) fraction; **zu ~ gehen** to get broken; **sich einen ~ heben** to rupture o.s.; **~bude** (*umg*) *f* shack.

brüchig ['brʏçɪç] *adj* brittle, fragile.

Bruch- *zW:* **~landung** *f* crash landing; **~schaden** *m* breakage; **~stelle** *f* break; (*von Knochen*) fracture; **~strich** *m* (*MATH*) line; **~stück** *nt* fragment; **~teil** *m* fraction.

Brücke ['brʏkə] (-, -n) *f* bridge; (*Teppich*) rug; (*Turnen*) crab.

Bruder ['bruːdər] (-s, ⁼) *m* brother; **unter Brüdern** (*umg*) between friends.

brüderlich *adj* brotherly; **B~keit** *f* fraternity.

Brudermord *m* fratricide.

Brüderschaft *f* brotherhood, fellowship; **~ trinken** to agree to use the familiar "du" (*over a drink*).

Brühe ['bryːə] (-, -n) *f* broth, stock; (*pej*) muck.

brühwarm ['bryː'varm] (*umg*) *adj:* **er hat das sofort ~ weitererzählt** he promptly spread it around.

Brühwürfel *m* stock cube (*BRIT*), bouillon cube (*US*).

brüllen ['brʏlən] *vi* to bellow, roar.

Brummbär *m* grumbler.

brummeln ['brʊməln] *vt, vi* to mumble.

brummen *vi* (*Bär, Mensch etc*) to growl; (*Insekt, Radio*) to buzz; (*Motor*) to roar; (*murren*) to grumble ♦ *vt* to growl; **jdm brummt der Kopf** sb's head is buzzing.

Brummer ['brʊmər] (-s, -) (*umg*) *m* (*Lastwagen*) juggernaut.

Brummi ['brʊmi] (*umg*) *m* lorry, juggernaut.

brummig (*umg*) *adj* grumpy.

Brummschädel (*umg*) *m* thick head.

brünett [brʏˈnɛt] *adj* brunette, brown-haired.

Brunnen ['brʊnən] (-s, -) *m* fountain; (*tief*) well; (*natürlich*) spring; **~kresse** *f* watercress.

Brunst [brʊnst] *f* (*von männlichen Tieren*) rut; (*von weiblichen Tieren*) heat; **~zeit** *f* rutting season.

brüsk [brʏsk] *adj* abrupt, brusque.

brüskieren [brʏsˈkiːrən] *vt* to snub.

Brüssel ['brʏsəl] (-s) *nt* Brussels.

Brust [brʊst] (-, ⁼e) *f* breast; (*Männer~*) chest; **einem Kind die ~ geben** to breast-feed (*BRIT*) *od* nurse (*US*) a baby.

brüsten ['brʏstən] *vr* to boast.

Brust- *zW:* **~fellentzündung** *f* pleurisy; **~kasten** *m* chest; **~korb** *m* (*ANAT*) thorax; **~schwimmen** *nt* breast-stroke; **~ton** *m:* **im ~ton der Überzeugung** in a tone of utter conviction.

Brüstung ['brʏstʊŋ] *f* parapet.

Brustwarze *f* nipple.

Brut [bruːt] (-, -en) *f* brood; (*Brüten*) hatching.

brutal [bruˈtaːl] *adj* brutal; **B~ität** *f* brutality.

Brutapparat *m* incubator.

brüten ['bryːtən] *vi* (*auch fig*) to brood; **~de Hitze** oppressive *od* stifling heat.

Brüter (-s, -) *m* (*TECH*): **schneller ~** fast-breeder (reactor).

Brutkasten *m* incubator.

Brutstätte *f* (+gen) (*lit, fig*) breeding ground (for).

brutto ['brʊto] *adv* gross; **B~einkommen** *nt* gross salary; **B~gehalt** *nt* gross salary; **B~gewicht** *nt* gross weight; **B~gewinn** *m* gross profit; **B~inlandsprodukt** *nt* gross domestic product; **B~lohn** *m* gross wages *pl*; **B~sozialprodukt** *nt* gross national product.

brutzeln ['brʊtsəln] (*umg*) *vi* to sizzle away ♦ *vt* to fry (up).

Btx *abk* = **Bildschirmtext**.

Bub [buːp] (-en, -en) *m* boy, lad.

Bube ['buːbə] (-n, -n) *m* (*Schurke*) rogue; (*KARTEN*) jack.

Bubikopf *m* bobbed hair.

Buch [buːx] (-(e)s, ⁼er) *nt* book; (*COMM*) account book; **er redet wie ein ~** (*umg*) he never stops talking; **ein ~ mit sieben Siegeln** (*fig*) a closed book; **über etw** *akk* **~ führen** to keep a record of sth; **zu ~(e) schlagen** to make a significant difference, tip the balance; **~binder** *m* bookbinder; **~drucker** *m* printer.

Buche (-, -n) *f* beech tree.

buchen *vt* to book; (*Betrag*) to enter; **etw als Erfolg ~** to put sth down as a success.

Bücherbord ['byːçər-] *nt* bookshelf.

Bücherbrett *nt* bookshelf.

Bücherei [byːçəˈraɪ] *f* library.

Bücherregal *nt* bookshelves *pl*, bookcase.

Bücherschrank *m* bookcase.

Bücherwurm (*umg*) *m* bookworm.

Buchfink ['buːxfɪŋk] *m* chaffinch.

Buch- *zW:* **~führung** *f* book-keeping, accounting; **~halter(in)** (-s, -) *m(f)* book-keeper; **~handel** *m* book trade; **im ~handel erhältlich** available in bookshops; **~händler(in)** *m(f)* bookseller; **~handlung** *f* bookshop; **~prüfung** *f* audit; **~rücken** *m* spine.

Büchse ['bʏksə] (-, -n) *f* tin, can; (*Holz~*) box; (*Gewehr*) rifle.

Büchsenfleisch *nt* tinned meat.

Büchsenöffner *m* tin *od* can opener.

Buchstabe (-ns, -n) *m* letter (of the alphabet).

buchstabieren [buːxʃtaˈbiːrən] *vt* to spell.

buchstäblich ['buːxʃtɛːplɪç] *adj* literal.

Buchstütze *f* book end.

Bucht ['bʊxt] (-, -en) *f* bay.

Buchung ['buːxʊŋ] *f* booking; (*COMM*) entry.

Buchweizen m buckwheat.
Buchwert m book value.
Buckel ['bʊkəl] (-s, -) m hump; **er kann mir den** ~ **runterrutschen** (umg) he can (go and) take a running jump.
buckeln (pej) vi to bow and scrape.
bücken ['bʏkən] vr to bend; **sich nach etw** ~ **to** bend down od stoop to pick sth up.
Bückling ['bʏklɪŋ] m (Fisch) kipper; (Verbeugung) bow.
Budapest ['buːdapɛst] (-s) nt Budapest.
buddeln ['bʊdəln] (umg) vi to dig.
Bude ['buːdə] (-, -n) f booth, stall; (umg) digs pl (BRIT) od place (US); **jdm die** ~ **einrennen** (umg) to pester sb.
Budget [bʏ'dʒeː] (-s, -s) nt budget.
Büfett [bʏ'fɛt] (-s, -s) nt (Anrichte) sideboard; (Geschirrschrank) dresser; **kaltes** ~ cold buffet.
Büffel ['bʏfəl] (-s, -) m buffalo.
büffeln ['bʏfəln] (umg) vi to swot, cram ♦ vt (Lernstoff) to swot up.
Bug [buːk] (-(e)s, -e) m (NAUT) bow; (AVIAT) nose.
Bügel ['byːgəl] (-s, -) m (Kleider~) hanger; (Steig~) stirrup; (Brillen~) arm; ~**brett** nt ironing board; ~**eisen** nt iron; ~**falte** f crease; **b**~**frei** adj non-iron; (Hemd) drip-dry.
bügeln vt, vi to iron.
Buhmann ['buːman] (umg) m bogeyman.
Bühne ['byːnə] (-, -n) f stage.
Bühnenbild nt set, scenery.
Buhruf ['buːruːf] m boo.
buk etc [buːk] vb (veraltet) siehe **backen.**
Bukarest ['buːkarɛst] (-s) nt Bucharest.
Bulette [bu'lɛtə] f meatball.
Bulgare [bʊl'gaːrə] (-n, -n) m Bulgarian.
Bulgarien (-s) nt Bulgaria.
Bulgarin f Bulgarian.
bulgarisch adj Bulgarian.
Bulimie [buli'miː] f (MED) bulimia.
Bull- zW: ~**auge** nt (NAUT) porthole; ~**dogge** f bulldog; ~**dozer** ['bʊldoːzər] (-s, -) m bulldozer.
Bulle (-n, -n) m bull; **die** ~**n** (pej: umg) the fuzz sing, the cops.
Bullenhitze (umg) f sweltering heat.
Bummel ['bʊməl] (-s, -) m stroll; (Schaufenster~) window-shopping (expedition).
Bummelant [bʊmə'lant] m slowcoach.
Bummelei [bʊmə'laɪ] f wandering; dawdling; skiving.
bummeln vi to wander, stroll; (trödeln) to dawdle; (faulenzen) to skive (BRIT), loaf around.
Bummelstreik m go-slow (BRIT), slowdown (US).
Bummelzug m slow train.
Bummler(in) ['bʊmlər(ɪn)] (-s, -) m(f) (langsamer Mensch) dawdler (BRIT), slowpoke (US); (Faulenzer) idler, loafer.

bumsen ['bʊmzən] vi (schlagen) to thump; (prallen, stoßen) to bump, bang; (umg: koitieren) to bonk, have it off (BRIT).
Bund¹ [bʊnt] (-(e)s, ⸚e) m (Freundschafts~ etc) bond; (Organisation) union; (POL) confederacy; (Hosen~, Rock~) waistband; **den** ~ **fürs Leben schließen** to take the marriage vows.
Bund² (-(e)s, -e) nt bunch; (Stroh~) bundle.
Bündchen ['bʏntçən] nt ribbing; (Ärmel~) cuff.
Bündel (-s, -) nt bundle, bale.
bündeln vt to bundle.
Bundes- ['bʊndəs] in zW Federal; ~**bahn** f: **die Deutsche** ~**bahn** German Federal Railways pl; ~**bank** f Federal Bank, Bundesbank; ~**bürger** m German citizen; (vor 1990) West German citizen; ~**gerichtshof** m Federal Supreme Court; ~**grenzschutz** m Federal Border Guard; ~**hauptstadt** f Federal capital; ~**haushalt** m (POL) National Budget; ~**kanzler** m Federal Chancellor.

> The **Bundeskanzler**, head of the German government, is elected for 4 years and determines government guidelines. He is formally proposed by the **Bundespräsident** but needs a majority in parliament to be elected to office.

Bundes- zW: ~**land** nt state, Land; ~**liga** f (SPORT) national league; ~**nachrichtendienst** m Federal Intelligence Service; ~**post** f: **die (Deutsche)** ~**post** the (German) Federal Post (Office).

> The **Bundespräsident** is the head of state of the Federal Republic of Germany who is elected every 5 years by the members of the **Bundestag** and by delegates of the Landtage (regional parliaments). His role is that of a figurehead who represents Germany at home and abroad. No one can be elected more than twice.
> The **Bundesrat** is the Upper House of the German Parliament whose 68 members are not elected but nominated by the parliaments of the individual **Länder**. Its most important function is the approval of federal laws which concern jurisdiction of the Länder. It can raise objections to all other laws but can be outvoted by the Bundestag.

Bundes- zW: ~**regierung** f Federal Government; ~**republik** f Federal Republic (of Germany); ~**staat** m Federal state; ~**straße** f Federal Highway, main road.

> The **Bundestag** is the Lower House of the German Parliament, elected by the people. There are 646 MPs, half of them elected directly from the first vote (**Erststimme**), and half from the regional list of parliamentary

candidates resulting from the second vote
(**Zweitstimme**), and giving proportional
representation to the parties. The Bundestag
exercises parliamentary control over the
government.

Bundes- zW: **~tagsabgeordnete(r)** f(m)
member of the German Parliament;
~tagswahl f (Federal) parliamentary
elections pl; **~verfassungsgericht** nt Federal
Constitutional Court; **~wehr** f German od
(vor 1990) West German Armed Forces pl.

The **Bundeswehr** is the name for the German
armed forces. It was established in 1955, first
of all for volunteers, but since 1956 there has
been compulsory military service for all able-
bodied young men of 18 (see **Wehrdienst**). In
peacetime the Defence Minister is the head of
the Bundeswehr, but in wartime, the
Bundeskanzler takes over. The Bundeswehr
comes under the jurisdiction of NATO.

Bundfaltenhose f pleated trousers pl.
Bundhose f knee breeches pl.
bündig ['byndɪç] adj (kurz) concise.
Bündnis ['byntnɪs] (**-ses, -se**) nt alliance.
Bunker ['buŋkər] (**-s, -**) m bunker;
(Luftschutzbunker) air-raid shelter.
bunt [bʊnt] adj coloured (BRIT), colored (US);
(gemischt) mixed; **jdm wird es zu ~** it's
getting too much for sb; **B~stift** m coloured
(BRIT) od colored (US) pencil, crayon.
Bürde ['byrdə] (**-, -n**) f (lit, fig) burden.
Burg [bʊrk] (**-, -en**) f castle, fort.
Bürge ['byrgə] (**-n, -n**) m guarantor.
bürgen vi to vouch; **für jdn ~** (fig) to vouch
for sb; (FIN) to stand surety for sb.
Bürger(in) (**-s, -**) m(f) citizen; member of the
middle class; **~initiative** f citizen's
initiative; **~krieg** m civil war; **b~lich** adj
(Rechte) civil; (Klasse) middle-class; (pej)
bourgeois; **gut b~liche Küche** good home
cooking; **b~liches Gesetzbuch** Civil Code;
~meister m mayor; **~recht** nt civil rights pl;
~rechtler(in) m(f) civil rights campaigner;
~schaft f population, citizens pl; **~schreck** m
bogey of the middle classes; **~steig** m
pavement (BRIT), sidewalk (US); **~tum** nt
citizens pl; **~wehr** f vigilantes pl.
Burgfriede(n) m (fig) truce.
Bürgin f guarantor.
Bürgschaft f surety; **~ leisten** to give
security.
Burgund [bʊr'gʊnt] (**-(s)**) nt Burgundy.
Burgunder (**-s, -**) m (Wein) burgundy.
Büro [by'roː] (**-s, -s**) nt office; **~angestellte(r)**
f(m) office worker; **~klammer** f paper clip;
~kraft f (office) clerk.
Bürokrat [byro'kraːt] (**-en, -en**) m bureaucrat.
Bürokratie [byrokra'tiː] f bureaucracy.
bürokratisch adj bureaucratic.

Bürokratismus m red tape.
Büroschluß m office closing time.
Bursch ['bʊrʃ(ə)] (**-en, -en**) m = **Bursche**.
Bursche (**-n, -n**) m lad, fellow; (Diener)
servant.
Burschenschaft f student fraternity.
burschikos [bʊrʃi'koːs] adj (jungenhaft)
(tom)boyish; (unbekümmert) casual.
Bürste ['byrstə] (**-, -n**) f brush.
bürsten vt to brush.
Bus [bʊs] (**-ses, -se**) m bus.
Busch [bʊʃ] (**-(e)s, ̈-e**) m bush, shrub; **bei jdm
auf den ~ klopfen** (umg) to sound sb out.
Büschel ['byʃəl] (**-s, -**) nt tuft.
buschig adj bushy.
Busen ['buːzən] (**-s, -**) m bosom; (Meer~) inlet,
bay; **~freund(in)** m(f) bosom friend.
Bushaltestelle f bus stop.
Bussard ['bʊsart] (**-s, -e**) m buzzard.
Buße ['buːsə] (**-, -n**) f atonement, penance;
(Geld) fine.
büßen ['byːsən] vi to do penance, atone ♦ vt to
atone for.
Bußgeld nt fine.
Buß- und Bettag m day of prayer and
repentance.
Büste ['bystə] (**-, -n**) f bust.
Büstenhalter m bra.
Butan [bu'taːn] (**-s**) nt butane.
Büttenrede ['bytənreːdə] f carnival speech.
Butter ['bʊtər] (**-**) f butter; **alles (ist) in ~**
(umg) everything is fine od hunky-dory;
~berg (umg) m butter mountain; **~blume** f
buttercup; **~brot** nt (piece of) bread and
butter; **~brotpapier** nt greaseproof paper;
~cremetorte f gateau with buttercream
filling; **~dose** f butter dish; **~keks** m ≈ Rich
Tea ® biscuit; **~milch** f buttermilk;
b~weich adj soft as butter; (fig: umg) soft.
Butzen ['bʊtsən] (**-s, -**) m core.
BVG nt abk (= Betriebsverfassungsgesetz)
≈ Industrial Relations Act;
= **Bundesverfassungsgericht**.
b.w. abk (= bitte wenden) p.t.o.
Byte [baɪt] (**-s, -s**) nt (COMPUT) byte.
Bz. abk = **Bezirk**.
bzgl. abk (= bezüglich) re.
bzw. abk = **beziehungsweise**.

C, c

C¹, c [tseː] nt C, c; ~ **wie Cäsar** ≈ C for Charlie.

C² [tseː] abk (= Celsius) C.

ca. [ka] abk (= circa) approx.

Cabriolet [kabrio'leː] (-s, -s) nt (AUT) convertible.

Café [ka'feː] (-s, -s) nt café.

Cafeteria [kafete'riːa] (-, -s) f cafeteria.

cal abk (= Kalorie) cal.

Calais [ka'leː] (-') nt: **die Straße von** ~ the Straits of Dover.

Camcorder (-s, -) m camcorder.

campen ['kɛmpən] vi to camp.

Camper(in) (-s, -) m(f) camper.

Camping ['kɛmpɪŋ] (-s) nt camping; ~**bus** m camper; ~**platz** m camp(ing) site.

Caravan ['karavan] (-s, -s) m caravan.

Carnet [kar'nɛ] (-s) nt (COMM) international customs pass, carnet.

Cäsium ['tsɛːziʊm] nt caesium (BRIT), cesium (US).

ccm abk (= Kubikzentimeter) cc, cm³.

CD f abk (= Compact Disc) CD; ~-**ROM** (-, -s) f CD-ROM; ~-**Spieler** m CD player.

CDU [tseːdeː'uː] (-) f abk (= Christlich-Demokratische Union (Deutschlands)) Christian Democratic Union.

The **CDU** (Christlich-Demokratische Union) is a Christian and conservative political party founded in 1945. It operates in all the **Länder** apart from Bavaria where its sister party the **CSU** is active. In the **Bundestag** the two parties form a coalition. It is the second largest party in Germany after the **SPD**, the Social Democratic Party.

Celli pl von **Cello.**

Cellist(in) [tʃɛ'lɪst(ɪn)] m(f) cellist.

Cello ['tʃɛlo] (-s, -s od **Celli**) nt cello.

Celsius ['tsɛlziʊs] m Celsius.

Cembalo ['tʃɛmbalo] (-s, -s) nt cembalo, harpsichord.

Ces [tsɛs] (-, -) nt (MUS) C flat.

ces [tsɛs] (-, -) nt (MUS) C flat.

Ceylon ['tsaɪlɔn] (-s) nt Ceylon.

Chamäleon [ka'mɛːleon] (-s, -s) nt chameleon.

Champagner [ʃam'panjər] (-s, -) m champagne.

Champignon ['ʃampinjõ] (-s, -s) m button mushroom.

Chance ['ʃãːs(ə)] (-, -n) f chance, opportunity.

Chancengleichheit f equality of opportunity.

Chaos ['kaːɔs] (-) nt chaos.

Chaot(in) [ka'oːt(ɪn)] (-en, -en) m(f) (POL: pej) anarchist (pej).

chaotisch [ka'oːtɪʃ] adj chaotic.

Charakter [ka'raktər] (-s, -e) m character; c~**fest** adj of firm character.

charakterisieren [karakteri'ziːrən] vt to characterize.

Charakteristik [karakte'rɪstɪk] f characterization.

charakteristisch [karakte'rɪstɪʃ] adj: ~ **(für)** characteristic (of), typical (of).

Charakter- zW: c~**los** adj unprincipled; ~**losigkeit** f lack of principle; ~**schwäche** f weakness of character; ~**stärke** f strength of character; ~**zug** m characteristic, trait.

charmant [ʃar'mant] adj charming.

Charme [ʃarm] (-s) m charm.

Charta ['karta] (-, -s) f charter.

Charterflug ['tʃartərfluːk] m charter flight.

Chartermaschine ['tʃartərmaʃiːnə] f charter plane.

chartern ['tʃartərn] vt to charter.

Chassis [ʃa'siː] (-, -) nt chassis.

Chauffeur [ʃɔ'føːr] m chauffeur.

Chaussee [ʃo'seː] (-, -n) f (veraltet) high road.

Chauvi ['ʃovi] (-s, -s) (umg) m male chauvinist.

Chauvinismus [ʃovi'nɪsmʊs] m chauvinism.

Chauvinist [ʃovi'nɪst] m chauvinist.

checken ['tʃɛkən] vt (überprüfen) to check; (umg: verstehen) to get.

Chef(in) [ʃɛf(ɪn)] (-s, -s) m(f) head; (umg) boss; ~**arzt** m senior consultant; ~**etage** f executive floor; ~**redakteur** m editor-in-chief; ~**sekretärin** f personal assistant/ secretary; ~**visite** f (MED) consultant's round.

Chemie [çe'miː] (-) f chemistry; ~**faser** f man-made fibre (BRIT) od fiber (US).

Chemikalie [çemi'kaːliə] f chemical.

Chemiker(in) ['çeːmikər(ɪn)] (-s, -) m(f) (industrial) chemist.

chemisch ['çeːmɪʃ] adj chemical; ~**e Reinigung** dry cleaning.

Chemotherapie [çemotera'piː] f chemotherapy.

Chicorée [ʃiko'reː] (-s) f od m chicory.

Chiffre ['ʃifrə] (-, -n) f (Geheimzeichen) cipher; (in Zeitung) box number.

Chiffriermaschine [ʃi'friːrmaʃiːnə] f cipher machine.

Chile ['tʃiːle] (-s) nt Chile.

Chilene [tʃi'leːnə] (-n, -n) m Chilean.

Chilenin [tʃi'leːnɪn] f Chilean.

chilenisch adj Chilean.

China ['çiːna] (-s) nt China.

Chinakohl m Chinese leaves pl.

Chinese [çi'neːzə] (-n, -n) m Chinaman, Chinese.

Chinesin *f* Chinese woman.
chinesisch *adj* Chinese.
Chinin [çi'niːn] (**-s**) *nt* quinine.
Chipkarte ['tʃɪpkartə] *f* smart card.
Chips [tʃɪps] *pl* crisps *pl* (*BRIT*), chips *pl* (*US*).
Chirurg(in) [çi'rʊrg(ɪn)] (**-en, -en**) *m(f)* surgeon.
Chirurgie [çirʊr'giː] *f* surgery.
chirurgisch *adj* surgical; **ein ~er Eingriff** surgery.
Chlor [kloːr] (**-s**) *nt* chlorine.
Chloroform [kloro'fɔrm] (**-s**) *nt* chloroform.
chloroformieren [klorofor'miːrən] *vt* to chloroform.
Chlorophyll [kloro'fʏl] (**-s**) *nt* chlorophyll.
Cholera ['koːlera] (-) *f* cholera.
Choleriker(in) [ko'leːrikər(ɪn)] (**-s**, -) *m(f)* hot-tempered person.
cholerisch [ko'leːrɪʃ] *adj* choleric.
Cholesterin [koleste'riːn] (**-s**) *nt* cholesterol; **~spiegel** [koleste'riːnʃpigəl] *m* cholesterol level.
Chor [koːr] (**-(e)s, ̈-e**) *m* choir; (*Musikstück, THEAT*) chorus.
Choral [ko'raːl] (**-s, -äle**) *m* chorale.
Choreograph(in) [koreo'graːf(ɪn)] (**-en, -en**) *m(f)* choreographer.
Choreographie [koreogra'fiː] *f* choreography.
Chorgestühl *nt* choir stalls *pl*.
Chorknabe *m* choirboy.
Chose ['ʃoːzə] (-, **-n**) (*umg*) *f* (*Angelegenheit*) thing.
Chr. *abk* = **Christus; Chronik.**
Christ [krɪst] (**-en, -en**) *m* Christian; **~baum** *m* Christmas tree.
Christenheit *f* Christendom.
Christentum (**-s**) *nt* Christianity.
Christin *f* Christian.
Christkind *nt* ≈ Father Christmas; (*Jesus*) baby Jesus.
christlich *adj* Christian; **C~er Verein Junger Männer** Young Men's Christian Association.
Christus (Christi) *m* Christ; **Christi Himmelfahrt** Ascension Day.
Chrom [kroːm] (**-s**) *nt* (*CHEM*) chromium; chrome.
Chromosom [kromo'zoːm] (**-s, -en**) *nt* (*BIOL*) chromosome.
Chronik ['kroːnɪk] *f* chronicle.
chronisch *adj* chronic.
Chronologie [kronolo'giː] *f* chronology.
chronologisch *adj* chronological.
Chrysantheme [kryzan'teːmə] (-, **-n**) *f* chrysanthemum.
CIA ['siːaɪ'eɪ] (-) *f od m abk* (= *Central Intelligence Agency*) CIA.
circa ['tsɪrka] *adv* (round) about.
Cis [tsɪs] (-, -) *nt* (*MUS*) C sharp.
cis [tsɪs] (-, -) *nt* (*MUS*) C sharp.
City ['sɪti] (-, **-s**) *f* city centre (*BRIT*); **in der ~** in the city centre (*BRIT*), downtown (*US*); **die ~ von Berlin** the (city) centre of Berlin

(*BRIT*), downtown Berlin (*US*).
clean [kliːn] *adj* (*DROGEN: umg*) off drugs.
clever ['klɛvər] *adj* clever; (*gerissen*) crafty.
Clique ['klɪkə] (-, **-n**) *f* set, crowd.
Clou [kluː] (**-s, -s**) *m* (*von Geschichte*) (whole) point; (*von Show*) highlight, high spot.
Clown [klaʊn] (**-s, -s**) *m* clown.
cm *abk* (= *Zentimeter*) cm.
COBOL ['koːbɔl] *nt* COBOL.
Cockpit ['kɔkpɪt] (**-s, -s**) *nt* cockpit.
Cocktail ['kɔkteːl] (**-s, -s**) *m* cocktail.
Cola ['koːla] (**-(s), -s**) *nt od f* Coke ®.
Comicheft ['kɔmɪkhɛft] *nt* comic.
Computer [kɔm'pjuːtər] (**-s, -**) *m* computer; **c~gesteuert** *adj* computer-controlled; **~kriminalität** *f* computer crime; **~spiel** *nt* computer game; **~technik** *f* computer technology.
Conférencier [kõferãsi'eː] (**-s, -s**) *m* compère.
Container [kɔn'teːnər] (**-s, -**) *m* container; **~schiff** *nt* container ship.
Contergankind [kɔntɛr'gankɪnt] (*umg*) *nt* thalidomide child.
cool [kuːl] (*umg*) *adj* (*gefaßt*) cool.
Cord [kɔrt] (**-(e)s, -e** *od* **-s**) *m* corduroy.
Cornichon [kɔrni'ʃõː] (**-s, -s**) *nt* gherkin.
Costa Rica ['kɔsta 'riːka] (**-s**) *nt* Costa Rica.
Couch [kaʊtʃ] (-, **-es** *od* **-en**) *f* couch; **~garnitur** ['kaʊtʃgarni'tuːr] *f* three-piece suite.
Couleur [ku'løːr] (**-s, -s**) *f* (*geh*) kind, sort.
Coupé [ku'peː] (**-s, -s**) *nt* (*AUT*) coupé, sports version.
Coupon [ku'põː] (**-s, -s**) *m* coupon, voucher; (*Stoff~*) length of cloth.
Courage [ku'raːʒə] (-) *f* courage.
Cousin [ku'zɛ̃ː] (**-s, -s**) *m* cousin.
Cousine [ku'ziːnə] (-, **-n**) *f* cousin.
Crack [krɛk] (-) *nt* (*Droge*) crack.
Creme [krɛːm] (-, **-s**) *f* (*lit, fig*) cream; (*Schuh~*) polish; (*KOCH*) mousse; **c~farben** *adj* cream(-coloured (*BRIT*) *od* -colored (*US*)).
cremig ['kreːmɪç] *adj* creamy.
Crux [krʊks] (-) *f* (*Schwierigkeit*) trouble, problem.
CSU [tseːɛs'uː] (-) *f abk* (= *Christlich-Soziale Union*) Christian Social Union.

> *The CSU (Christlich-Soziale Union) is a party founded in 1945 in Bavaria. Like its sister party the CDU it is a Christian, right-wing party.*

CT-Scanner [tseː'teːskɛnər] *m* CT scanner.
Curriculum [ku'riːkulʊm] (**-s, -cula**) *nt* (*geh*) curriculum.
Curry ['kari] (**-s**) *m od nt* curry powder; **~pulver** ['karipʊlfər] *nt* curry powder; **~wurst** *f* curried sausage.
Cursor ['kœrsər] (**-s**) *m* (*COMPUT*) cursor.
Cutter(in) ['katər(ɪn)] (**-s, -**) *m(f)* (*FILM*) editor.
CVJM [tseːfaʊjɔt'ɛm] (-) *m abk* (= *Christlicher*

Verein Junger Männer) YMCA.

D, d

D, d [de:] *nt* D, d; ~ **wie Dora** ≈ D for David, D for Dog (*US*).
D. *abk* = **Doktor** (*der evangelischen Theologie*).

═══════════════════ SCHLÜSSELWORT

da [da:] *adv* **1** (*örtlich*) there; (*hier*) here;
~ **draußen** out there; ~ **bin ich** here I am;
~ **hast du dein Geld** (there you are,) there's
your money; ~, **wo** where; **ist noch Milch**
~? is there any milk left?
2 (*zeitlich*) then; (*folglich*) so; **es war niemand
im Zimmer,** ~ **habe ich ...** there was nobody
in the room, so I ...
3: ~ **haben wir Glück gehabt** we were lucky
there; **was gibt's denn** ~ **zu lachen?** what's
so funny about that?; ~ **kann man nichts
machen** there's nothing one can do (in a
case like that)
♦ *konj* (*weil*) as, since.

d.Ä. *abk* (= *der Ältere*) Sen., sen.
DAAD (-) *m abk* (= *Deutscher Akademischer
Austauschdienst*) German Academic
Exchange Service.
dabehalten *unreg vt* to keep.
dabei [da'baɪ] *adv* (*räumlich*) close to it; (*noch
dazu*) besides; (*zusammen mit*) with them/it
etc; (*zeitlich*) during this; (*obwohl doch*) but,
however; **was ist schon** ~? what of it?; **es ist
doch nichts** ~, **wenn ...** it doesn't matter if
...; **bleiben wir** ~ let's leave it at that; **es soll
nicht** ~ **bleiben** this isn't the end of it; **es
bleibt** ~ that's settled; **das Dumme/
Schwierige** ~ the stupid/difficult part of it;
er war gerade ~, **zu gehen** he was just
leaving; **hast du** ~ **etwas gelernt?** did you
learn anything from it?; ~ **darf man nicht
vergessen, daß ...** it shouldn't be forgotten
that ...; **die** ~ **entstehenden Kosten** the
expenses arising from this; **es kommt doch
nichts** ~ **heraus** nothing will come of it; **ich
finde gar nichts** ~ I don't see any harm in it;
~**sein** *unreg vi* (*anwesend*) to be present;
(*beteiligt*) to be involved; **ich bin** ~! count
me in!; ~**stehen** *unreg vi* to stand around.
Dach [dax] (-(e)s, ⸚er) *nt* roof; **unter** ~ **und
Fach sein** (*abgeschlossen*) to be in the bag
(*umg*); (*Vertrag, Geschäft*) to be signed and
sealed; (*in Sicherheit*) to be safe; **jdm eins
aufs** ~ **geben** (*umg: ausschimpfen*) to give sb
a (good) talking to; ~**boden** *m* attic, loft;

~**decker** (-s, -) *m* slater, tiler; ~**fenster** *nt*
skylight; (*ausgestellt*) dormer window; ~**first**
m ridge of the roof; ~**gepäckträger** *m* (*AUT*)
roof rack; ~**geschoß** *nt* attic storey (*BRIT*)
od story (*US*); (*oberster Stock*) top floor *od*
storey (*BRIT*) *od* story (*US*); ~**luke** *f*
skylight; ~**pappe** *f* roofing felt; ~**rinne** *f*
gutter.
Dachs [daks] (-es, -e) *m* badger.
Dachschaden (*umg*) *m:* **einen** ~ **haben** to
have a screw loose.
dachte *etc* ['daxtə] *vb siehe* **denken.**
Dach- *zW:* ~**terrasse** *f* roof terrace;
~**verband** *m* umbrella organization; ~**ziegel**
m roof tile.
Dackel ['dakəl] (-s, -) *m* dachshund.
dadurch [da'dʊrç] *adv* (*räumlich*) through it;
(*durch diesen Umstand*) thereby, in that way;
(*deshalb*) because of that, for that reason
♦ *konj:* ~, **daß** because.
dafür [da'fy:r] *adv* for it; (*anstatt*) instead; (*zum
Ausgleich*): **in Latein ist er schlecht,** ~ **kann
er gut Fußball spielen** he's bad at Latin but
he makes up for it at football; **er ist bekannt**
~ he is well-known for that; **was bekomme
ich** ~? what will I get for it?; ~ **ist er immer
zu haben** he never says no to that; ~ **bin ich
ja hier** that's what I'm here for; ~**halten**
(-s) *nt* (*geh*): **nach meinem D**~**halten** in my
opinion; ~**können** *unreg vt:* **er kann nichts** ~ (,
daß ...) he can't help it (that ...).
DAG *f abk* (= *Deutsche Angestellten-
Gewerkschaft*) Clerical and Administrative
Workers' Union.
dagegen [da'ge:gən] *adv* against it; (*im
Vergleich damit*) in comparison with it; (*bei
Tausch*) for it ♦ *konj* however; **haben Sie
etwas** ~, **wenn ich rauche?** do you mind if I
smoke?; **ich habe nichts** ~ I don't mind; **ich
war** ~ I was against it; **ich hätte nichts**
~ (**einzuwenden**) that's okay by me; ~ **kann
man nichts tun** one can't do anything about
it; ~**halten** *unreg vt* (*vergleichen*) to compare
with it; (*entgegnen*) to put forward as an
objection.
dagewesen ['da:gəve:zən] *pp von* **dasein.**
daheim [da'haɪm] *adv* at home; **bei uns** ~ back
home; **D**~ (-s) *nt* home.
daher [da'he:r] *adv* (*räumlich*) from there;
(*Ursache*) from that ♦ *konj* (*deshalb*) that's
why; **das kommt** ~, **daß ...** that is because
...; ~ **kommt er auch** that's where he comes
from too; ~ **die Schwierigkeiten** that's what
is causing the difficulties; ~**gelaufen** *adj:*
jeder ~**gelaufene Kerl** any Tom, Dick or
Harry; ~**reden** *vi* to talk away ♦ *vt* to say
without thinking.
dahin [da'hɪn] *adv* (*räumlich*) there; (*zeitlich*)
then; (*vergangen*) gone; **ist es noch weit bis**
~? is there still far to go?; **das tendiert** ~ it
is tending towards that; **er bringt es noch** ~,
daß ich ... he'll make me ...; ~**gegen** *konj* on

the other hand; ~**gehen** *unreg vi* (*Zeit*) to
pass; ~**gehend** *adv* on this matter; ~**gestellt**
adv: ~**gestellt bleiben** to remain to be seen;
etw ~**gestellt sein lassen** to leave sth open
od undecided; ~**schleppen** *vr* (*lit: sich
fortbewegen*) to drag o.s. along; (*fig:
Verhandlungen, Zeit*) to drag on; ~**schmelzen**
vi to be enthralled.

dahinten [da'hɪntən] *adv* over there.

dahinter [da'hɪntər] *adv* behind it; ~**klemmen**
(*umg*) *vr* to put one's back into it; ~**knien**
(*umg*) *vr* to put one's back into it; ~**kommen**
unreg (*umg*) *vi* to find out.

dahinvegetieren [da'hɪnvege'tiːrən] *vi* to
vegetate.

Dahlie ['daːliə] (-, -n) *f* dahlia.

DAK (-) *f abk* (= *Deutsche Angestellten-
Krankenkasse*) *health insurance company for
employees.*

Dakar ['dakar] (-s) *nt* Dakar.

dalassen ['daːlasən] *unreg vt* to leave (behind).

dalli ['dali] (*umg*) *adv:* ~, ~! on (*BRIT*) *od* at
(*US*) the double!

damalig ['daːmaːlɪç] *adj* of that time, then.

damals ['daːmaːls] *adv* at that time, then.

Damaskus [da'maskus] *nt* Damascus.

Damast [da'mast] (-(e)s, -e) *m* damask.

Dame ['daːmə] (-, -n) *f* lady; (*SCHACH,
KARTEN*) queen; (*Spiel*) draughts (*BRIT*),
checkers (*US*).

Damen- *zW:* ~**besuch** *m* lady visitor *od*
visitors; ~**binde** *f* sanitary towel (*BRIT*) *od*
napkin (*US*); **d~haft** *adj* ladylike; ~**sattel** *m:*
im ~**sattel reiten** to ride side-saddle; ~**wahl**
f ladies' excuse-me.

Damespiel *nt* draughts (*BRIT*), checkers (*US*).

damit [da'mɪt] *adv* with it; (*begründend*) by
that ♦ *konj* in order that *od* to; **was meint er**
~? what does he mean by that?; **was soll ich**
~? what am I meant to do with that?; **muß
er denn immer wieder** ~ **ankommen?** must
he keep on about it?; **was ist** ~? what about
it?; **genug** ~! that's enough!; ~ **basta!** and
that's that!; ~ **eilt es nicht** there's no hurry.

dämlich ['dɛːmlɪç] (*umg*) *adj* silly, stupid.

Damm [dam] (-(e)s, ⁻e) *m* dyke (*BRIT*), dike
(*US*); (*Stau~*) dam; (*Hafen~*) mole; (*Bahn~,
Straßen~*) embankment.

dämmen ['dɛmən] *vt* (*Wasser*) to dam up;
(*Schmerzen*) to keep back.

dämmerig *adj* dim, faint.

Dämmerlicht *nt* twilight; (*abends*) dusk;
(*Halbdunkel*) half-light.

dämmern ['dɛmərn] *vi* (*Tag*) to dawn; (*Abend*)
to fall; **es dämmerte ihm, daß** ... (*umg*) it
dawned on him that ...

Dämmerung *f* twilight; (*Morgen~*) dawn;
(*Abend~*) dusk.

Dämmerzustand *m* (*Halbschlaf*) dozy state;
(*Bewußtseinstrübung*) semi-conscious state.

Dämmung *f* insulation.

Dämon ['dɛːmɔn] (-s, -en) *m* demon.

dämonisch [dɛ'moːnɪʃ] *adj* demonic.

Dampf [dampf] (-(e)s, ⁻e) *m* steam; (*Dunst*)
vapour (*BRIT*), vapor (*US*); **jdm** ~ **machen**
(*umg*) to make sb get a move on; ~ **ablassen**
(*lit, fig*) to let off steam; **d~en** *vi* to steam.

dämpfen ['dɛmpfən] *vt* (*KOCH*) to steam;
(*bügeln*) to iron with a damp cloth; (*mit
Dampfbügeleisen*) to steam iron; (*fig*) to
dampen, subdue.

Dampfer ['dampfər] (-s, -) *m* steamer; **auf dem
falschen** ~ **sein** (*fig*) to have got the wrong
idea.

Dämpfer (-s, -) *m* (*MUS: bei Klavier*) damper;
(*bei Geige, Trompete*) mute; **er hat einen**
~ **bekommen** (*fig*) it dampened his spirits.

Dampf- *zW:* ~**kochtopf** *m* pressure cooker;
~**maschine** *f* steam engine; ~**schiff** *nt*
steamship; ~**walze** *f* steamroller.

Damwild ['damvɪlt] *nt* fallow deer.

danach [da'naːx] *adv* after that; (*zeitlich*)
afterwards; (*gemäß*) accordingly; (*laut
diesem*) according to which *od* that; **mir war
nicht** ~ (**zumute**) I didn't feel like it; **er griff
schnell** ~ he grabbed at it; ~ **kann man
nicht gehen** you can't go by that; **er sieht**
~ **aus** he looks it.

Däne ['dɛːnə] (-n, -n) *m* Dane, Danish man/
boy.

daneben [da'neːbən] *adv* beside it; (*im
Vergleich*) in comparison; ~**benehmen** *unreg
vr* to misbehave; ~**gehen** *unreg vi* to miss;
(*Plan*) to fail; ~**greifen** *unreg vi* to miss; (*fig:
mit Schätzung etc*) to be wide of the mark;
~**sein** *unreg* (*umg*) *vi* (*verwirrt sein*) to be
completely confused.

Dänemark ['dɛːnəmark] (-s) *nt* Denmark.

Dänin ['dɛːnɪn] *f* Dane, Danish woman *od*
girl.

dänisch *adj* Danish.

Dank [daŋk] (-(e)s) *m* thanks *pl*; **vielen** *od*
schönen ~ many thanks; **jdm** ~ **sagen** to
thank sb; **mit (bestem)** ~ **zurück!** many
thanks for the loan; **d~** *präp* (+*dat od gen*)
thanks to; **d~bar** *adj* grateful; (*Aufgabe*)
rewarding; (*haltbar*) hard-wearing; ~**barkeit**
f gratitude.

danke *interj* thank you, thanks.

danken *vi* +*dat* to thank; **nichts zu** ~! don't
mention it; ~**d erhalten/ablehnen** to
receive/decline with thanks.

dankenswert *adj* (*Arbeit*) worthwhile;
rewarding; (*Bemühung*) kind.

Dank- *zW:* ~**gottesdienst** *m* service of
thanksgiving; **d~sagen** *vi* to express one's
thanks; ~**schreiben** *nt* letter of thanks.

dann [dan] *adv* then; ~ **und wann** now and
then; ~ **eben nicht** well, in that case (there's
no more to be said); **erst** ~, **wenn** ... only
when ...; ~ **erst recht nicht!** in that case no
way (*umg*).

dannen ['danən] *adv:* **von** ~ (*liter: weg*) away.

daran [da'ran] *adv* on it; (*stoßen*) against it; **es**

liegt ~, daß ... the cause of it is that ...; **gut/ schlecht ~ sein** to be well/badly off; **das Beste/Dümmste ~** the best/stupidest thing about it; **ich war nahe ~, zu** ... I was on the point of ...; **im Anschluß ~** (*zeitlich: danach anschließend*) following that *od* this; **wir können nichts ~ machen** we can't do anything about it; **es ist nichts ~** (*ist nicht fundiert*) there's nothing in it; (*ist nichts Besonderes*) it's nothing special; **er ist ~ gestorben** he died from *od* of it; **~gehen** *unreg vi* to start; **~machen** (*umg*) *vr:* **sich ~machen, etw zu tun** to set about doing sth; **~setzen** *vt* to stake; **er hat alles ~gesetzt, von Glasgow wegzukommen** he has done his utmost to get away from Glasgow.

darauf [da'rauf] *adv* (*räumlich*) on it; (*zielgerichtet*) towards it; (*danach*) afterwards; **es kommt ganz ~ an, ob** ... it depends whether ...; **seine Behauptungen stützen sich ~, daß** ... his claims are based on the supposition that ...; **wie kommst du ~?** what makes you think that?; **die Tage ~** the days following *od* thereafter; **am Tag ~** the next day; **~folgend** *adj* (*Tag, Jahr*) next, following; **~hin** *adv* (*im Hinblick ~*) in this respect; (*aus diesem Grund*) as a result; **wir müssen es ~hin prüfen, ob** ... we must test it to see whether ...; **~legen** *vt* to lay *od* put on top.

daraus [da'raus] *adv* from it; **was ist ~ geworden?** what became of it?; **~ geht hervor, daß** ... this means that ...

darbieten ['da:rbi:tən] *vt* (*vortragen: Lehrstoff*) to present ♦ *vr* to present itself.

Darbietung *f* performance.

Dardanellen [darda'nɛlən] *pl* Dardanelles *pl*.

darein- *präf* = **drein-**.

Daressalam [daresa'la:m] *nt* Dar-es-Salaam.

darf [darf] *vb siehe* **dürfen**.

darin [da'rɪn] *adv* in (there), in it; **der Unterschied liegt ~, daß** ... the difference is that ...

darlegen ['da:rle:gən] *vt* to explain, expound, set forth.

Darlegung *f* explanation.

Darleh(e)n (-s, -) *nt* loan.

Darm [darm] (-(e)s, ̈-e) *m* intestine; (*Wurst~*) skin; **~ausgang** *m* anus; **~grippe** *f* gastric influenza; **~saite** *f* gut string; **~trägheit** *f* under-activity of the intestines.

darstellen ['da:rʃtɛlən] *vt* (*abbilden, bedeuten*) to represent; (*THEAT*) to act; (*beschreiben*) to describe ♦ *vr* to appear to be.

Darsteller(in) (-s, -) *m(f)* actor, actress.

darstellerisch *adj*: **eine ~e Höchstleistung** a magnificent piece of acting.

Darstellung *f* portrayal, depiction.

darüber [da'ry:bər] *adv* (*räumlich*) over/above it; (*fahren*) over it; (*mehr*) more; (*währenddessen*) meanwhile; (*sprechen, streiten*) about it; **~ hinweg sein** (*fig*) to have

got over it; **~ hinaus** over and above that; **~ geht nichts** there's nothing like it; **seine Gedanken ~** his thoughts about *od* on it; **~liegen** *unreg vi* (*fig*) to be higher.

darum [da'rʊm] *adv* (*räumlich*) round it ♦ *konj* that's why; **~ herum** round about (it); **er bittet ~** he is pleading for it; **es geht ~, daß** ... the thing is that ...; **~ geht es mir/geht es mir nicht** that's my point/that's not the point for me; **er würde viel ~ geben, wenn** ... he would give a lot to ...; *siehe auch* **drum**.

darunter [da'rʊntər] *adv* (*räumlich*) under it; (*dazwischen*) among them; (*weniger*) less; **ein Stockwerk ~** one floor below (it); **was verstehen Sie ~?** what do you understand by that?; **~ kann ich mir nichts vorstellen** that doesn't mean anything to me; **~fallen** *unreg vi* to be included; **~mischen** *vt* (*Mehl*) to mix in ♦ *vr* to mingle; **~setzen** *vt* (*Unterschrift*) to put to it.

das [das] *pron* that ♦ *def art* the; *siehe auch* **der**; **~ heißt** that is; **~ und ~** such and such.

Dasein ['da:zaɪn] (-s) *nt* (*Leben*) life; (*Anwesenheit*) presence; (*Bestehen*) existence.

dasein *unreg vi* to be there; **ein Arzt, der immer für seine Patienten da ist** a doctor who always has time for his patients.

Daseinsberechtigung *f* right to exist.

Daseinskampf *m* struggle for survival.

daß [das] *konj* that.

dasselbe [das'zɛlbə] *nt pron* the same.

dastehen ['da:ʃte:ən] *unreg vi* to stand there; (*fig*): **gut/schlecht ~** to be in a good/bad position; **allein ~** to be on one's own.

Dat. *abk* = **Dativ**.

Datei [da'taɪ] *f* (*COMPUT*) file; **~name** *m* file name; **~verwaltung** *f* file management.

Daten ['da:tən] *pl* (*COMPUT*) data; (*Angaben*) data *pl*, particulars; *siehe auch* **Datum**; **~autobahn** *f* information (super)highway; **~bank** *f* data base; **~erfassung** *f* data capture; **~satz** *m* record; **~schutz** *m* data protection; **~sichtgerät** *nt* visual display unit, VDU; **~träger** *m* data carrier; **~typist(in)** *m(f)* keyboard operator, keyboarder; **~übertragung** *f* data transmission; **~verarbeitung** *f* data processing; **~verarbeitungsanlage** *f* data processing equipment, DP equipment.

datieren [da'ti:rən] *vt* to date.

Dativ ['da:ti:f] (-s, -e) *m* dative; **~objekt** *nt* (*GRAM*) indirect object.

dato ['da:to] *adv*: **bis ~** (*COMM: umg*) to date.

Dattel ['datəl] (-, -n) *f* date.

Datum ['da:tʊm] (-s, Daten) *nt* date; **das heutige ~** today's date.

Datumsgrenze *f* (*GEOG*) (international) date line.

Dauer ['dauər] (-, -n) *f* duration; (*gewisse Zeitspanne*) length; (*Bestand, Fortbestehen*) permanence; **es war nur von kurzer ~** it didn't last long; **auf die** ~ in the long run; (*auf längere Zeit*) indefinitely; ~**auftrag** *m* standing order; **d~haft** *adj* lasting, durable; ~**haftigkeit** *f* durability; ~**karte** *f* season ticket; ~**lauf** *m* long-distance run.

dauern *vi* to last; **es hat sehr lang gedauert, bis er** ... it took him a long time to ...

dauernd *adj* constant.

Dauer- *zW:* ~**obst** *nt* fruit suitable for storing; ~**redner** (*pej*) *m* long-winded speaker; ~**regen** *m* continuous rain; ~**schlaf** *m* prolonged sleep; ~**stellung** *f* permanent position; ~**welle** *f* perm, permanent wave; ~**wurst** *f* German salami; ~**zustand** *m* permanent condition.

Daumen ['daʊmən] (**-s, -**) *m* thumb; **jdm die** ~ **drücken** *od* **halten** to keep one's fingers crossed for sb; **über den** ~ **peilen** to guess roughly; ~**lutscher** *m* thumb-sucker.

Daune ['daʊnə] (**-, -n**) *f* down.

Daunendecke *f* down duvet.

davon [da'fɔn] *adv* of it; (*räumlich*) away; (*weg von*) away from it; (*Grund*) because of it; (*mit Passiv*) by it; **das kommt** ~! that's what you get; ~ **abgesehen** apart from that; **wenn wir einmal** ~ **absehen, daß** ... if for once we overlook the fact that ...; ~ **sprechen/wissen** to talk/know of *od* about it; **was habe ich** ~? what's the point?; ~ **betroffen werden** to be affected by it; ~**gehen** *unreg vi* to leave, go away; ~**kommen** *unreg vi* to escape; ~**lassen** *unreg vt:* **die Finger** ~**lassen** (*umg*) to keep one's hands *od* fingers off (it); ~**laufen** *unreg vi* to run away; ~**machen** *vr* to make off; ~**tragen** *unreg vt* to carry off; (*Verletzung*) to receive.

davor [da'foːr] *adv* (*räumlich*) in front of it; (*zeitlich*) before (that); ~ **warnen** to warn about it.

dazu [da'tsuː] *adv* (*legen, stellen*) by it; (*essen*) with it; **und** ~ **noch** and in addition; **ein Beispiel/seine Gedanken** ~ one example for/his thoughts on this; **wie komme ich denn** ~? why should I?; ... **aber ich bin nicht** ~ **gekommen** ... but I didn't get around to it; **das Recht** ~ the right to do it; ~ **bereit sein, etw zu tun** to be prepared to do sth; ~ **fähig sein** to be capable of it; **sich** ~ **äußern** to say something on it; ~**gehören** *vi* to belong to it; **das gehört** ~ (*versteht sich von selbst*) it's all part of it; **es gehört schon einiges** ~, **das zu tun** it takes a lot to do that; ~**gehörig** *adj* appropriate; ~**kommen** *unreg vi* (*Ereignisse*) to happen too; (*an einen Ort*) to come along; **kommt noch etwas** ~? will there be anything else?; ~**lernen** *vt:* **schon wieder was** ~**gelernt!** you learn something (new) every day!; ~**mal** ['da:tsuma:l] *adv* in those days; ~**tun** *unreg vt* to add; **er hat es ohne dein D~tun geschafft** he managed it without your doing *etc* anything.

dazwischen [da'tsvɪʃən] *adv* in between;

(*zusammen mit*) among them; **der Unterschied** ~ the difference between them; ~**fahren** *unreg vi* (*eingreifen*) to intervene; ~**funken** (*umg*) *vi* (*eingreifen*) to put one's oar in; ~**kommen** *unreg vi* (*hineingeraten*) to get caught in it; **es ist etwas** ~**gekommen** something (has) cropped up; ~**reden** *vi* (*unterbrechen*) to interrupt; (*sich einmischen*) to interfere; ~**treten** *unreg vi* to intervene.

DB *f abk* (= *Deutsche Bahn*) German railways.

DBP *f abk* = **Deutsche Bundespost.**

DDR (**-**) *f abk* (*früher:* = *Deutsche Demokratische Republik*) GDR.

The **DDR** (*Deutsche Demokratische Republik*) was the name by which the former Communist German Democratic Republic was known. It was founded in 1949 from the Soviet-occupied zone. After the building of the Berlin Wall in 1961 it was virtually sealed off from the West until mass demonstrations and demands for reform forced the opening of the borders in 1989. It then merged in 1990 with the **BRD**.

DDT ® *nt abk* DDT.

Dealer(in) ['diːlər(ɪn)] (**-s, -**) (*umg*) *m(f)* pusher.

Debatte [de'batə] (**-, -n**) *f* debate; **das steht hier nicht zur** ~ that's not the issue.

debattieren [deba'tiːrən] *vt* to debate.

Debet ['deːbɛt] (**-s, -s**) *nt* (*FIN*) debits *pl*.

Debüt [de'byː] (**-s, -s**) *nt* debut.

dechiffrieren [deʃɪ'friːrən] *vt* to decode; (*Text*) to decipher.

Deck [dɛk] (**-(e)s, -s** *od* **-e**) *nt* deck; **an** ~ **gehen** to go on deck.

Deckbett *nt* feather quilt.

Deckblatt *nt* (*Schutzblatt*) cover.

Decke (**-, -n**) *f* cover; (*Bett~*) blanket; (*Tisch~*) tablecloth; (*Zimmer~*) ceiling; **unter einer** ~ **stecken** to be hand in glove; **an die** ~ **gehen** to hit the roof; **mir fällt die** ~ **auf den Kopf** (*fig*) I feel really claustrophobic.

Deckel (**-s, -**) *m* lid; **du kriegst gleich eins auf den** ~ (*umg*) you're going to catch it.

decken *vt* to cover ♦ *vr* to coincide ♦ *vi* to lay the table; **mein Bedarf ist gedeckt** I have all I need; (*fig*) I've had enough; **sich an einen gedeckten Tisch setzen** (*fig*) to be handed everything on a plate.

Deckmantel *m:* **unter dem** ~ **von** under the guise of.

Deckname *m* assumed name.

Deckung *f* (*das Schützen*) covering; (*Schutz*) cover; (*SPORT*) defence (*BRIT*), defense (*US*); (*Übereinstimmen*) agreement; **zur** ~ **seiner Schulden** to meet his debts.

deckungsgleich *adj* congruent.

Decoder *m* (*TV*) decoder.

de facto [deː 'fakto] *adv* de facto.

Defekt [de'fɛkt] (**-(e)s, -e**) *m* fault, defect; **d~** *adj* faulty.

defensiv [defɛn'siːf] *adj* defensive.
Defensive *f:* **jdn in die ~ drängen** to force sb onto the defensive.
definieren [defi'niːrən] *vt* to define.
Definition [definitsi'oːn] *f* definition.
definitiv [defini'tiːf] *adj* definite.
Defizit ['deːfitsɪt] **(-s, -e)** *nt* deficit.
defizitär [defitsi'tɛːr] *adj:* **eine ~e Haushaltspolitik führen** to follow an economic policy which can only lead to deficit.
Deflation [deflatsi'oːn] *f* (*ECON*) deflation.
deflationär [deflatsio'nɛːr] *adj* deflationary.
deftig ['dɛftɪç] *adj* (*Essen*) large; (*Witz*) coarse.
Degen ['deːgən] **(-s, -)** *m* sword.
degenerieren [degene'riːrən] *vi* to degenerate.
degradieren [degra'diːrən] *vt* to degrade.
dehnbar ['deːnbaːr] *adj* elastic; (*fig: Begriff*) loose; **D~keit** *f* elasticity; looseness.
dehnen *vt, vr* to stretch.
Dehnung *f* stretching.
Deich [daɪç] **(-(e)s, -e)** *m* dyke (*BRIT*), dike (*US*).
Deichsel ['daɪksəl] **(-, -n)** *f* shaft.
deichseln *vt* (*fig: umg*) to wangle.
dein [daɪn] *pron* (*in Briefen: D~*) your; (*adjektivisch*): **herzliche Grüße, D~e Elke** with best wishes, yours *od* (*herzlicher*) love, Elke.
deine(r, s) *poss pron* yours.
deiner *gen von* **du** ♦ *pron* of you.
deinerseits *adv* on your part.
deinesgleichen *pron* people like you.
deinetwegen ['daɪnət've:gən] *adv* (*für dich*) for your sake; (*wegen dir*) on your account.
deinetwillen ['daɪnət'vɪlən] *adv:* **um ~ = deinetwegen.**
deinige *pron:* **der/die/das ~** yours.
dekadent [deka'dɛnt] *adj* decadent.
Dekadenz *f* decadence.
Dekan [de'kaːn] **(-s, -e)** *m* dean.
deklassieren [dekla'siːrən] *vt* (*SOZIOLOGIE: herabsetzen*) to downgrade; (*SPORT: übertreffen*) to outclass.
Deklination [deklinatsi'oːn] *f* declension.
deklinieren [dekli'niːrən] *vt* to decline.
Dekolleté [dekɔl'teː] **(-s, -s)** *nt* low neckline.
Dekor [de'koːr] **(-s, -s** *od* **-e)** *m od nt* decoration.
Dekorateur(in) [dekora'tøːr(ɪn)] *m(f)* window dresser.
Dekoration [dekoratsi'oːn] *f* decoration; (*in Laden*) window dressing.
dekorativ [dekora'tiːf] *adj* decorative.
dekorieren [deko'riːrən] *vt* to decorate; (*Schaufenster*) to dress.
Dekostoff ['deːkoʃtɔf] *m* (*TEXTIL*) furnishing fabric.
Dekret [de'kreːt] **(-(e)s, -e)** *nt* decree.
Delegation [delegatsi'oːn] *f* delegation.
delegieren [dele'giːrən] *vt:* **~ (an** +*akk*) to delegate (to).
Delegierte(r) *f(m)* delegate.

Delhi ['deːlɪ] **(-s)** *nt* Delhi.
delikat [deli'kaːt] *adj* (*zart, heikel*) delicate; (*köstlich*) delicious.
Delikatesse [delika'tɛsə] **(-, -n)** *f* delicacy.
Delikatessengeschäft *nt* delicatessen (shop).
Delikt [de'lɪkt] **(-(e)s, -e)** *nt* (*JUR*) offence (*BRIT*), offense (*US*).
Delinquent [delɪŋ'kvɛnt] *m* (*geh*) offender.
Delirium [de'liːriʊm] *nt:* **im ~ sein** to be delirious; (*umg: betrunken*) to be paralytic.
Delle ['dɛlə] **(-, -n)** (*umg*) *f* dent.
Delphin [dɛl'fiːn] **(-s, -e)** *m* dolphin.
Delphinschwimmen *nt* butterfly (stroke).
Delta ['dɛlta] **(-s, -s)** *nt* delta.
dem [de(ː)m] *art dat von* **der, das; wie ~ auch sei** be that as it may.
Demagoge [dema'goːgə] **(-n, -n)** *m* demagogue.
Demarkationslinie [demarkatsi'oːnzliːniə] *f* demarcation line.
Dementi [de'mɛnti] **(-s, -s)** *nt* denial.
dementieren [demɛn'tiːrən] *vt* to deny.
dem- *zW:* **~entsprechend** *adj* appropriate ♦ *adv* correspondingly; (*demnach*) accordingly; **~gemäß** *adv* accordingly; **~nach** *adv* accordingly; **~nächst** *adv* shortly.
Demo ['deːmo] **(-s, -s)** (*umg*) *f* demo.
Demographie [demogra'fiː] *f* demography.
Demokrat(in) [demo'kraːt(ɪn)] **(-en, -en)** *m(f)* democrat.
Demokratie [demokra'tiː] *f* democracy; **~verständnis** *nt* understanding of (the meaning of) democracy.
demokratisch *adj* democratic.
demokratisieren [demokrati'ziːrən] *vt* to democratize.
demolieren [demo'liːrən] *vt* to demolish.
Demonstrant(in) [demɔn'strant(ɪn)] *m(f)* demonstrator.
Demonstration [demɔnstratsi'oːn] *f* demonstration.
demonstrativ [demɔnstra'tiːf] *adj* demonstrative; (*Protest*) pointed.
demonstrieren [demɔn'striːrən] *vt, vi* to demonstrate.
Demontage [demɔn'taːʒə] **(-, -n)** *f* (*lit, fig*) dismantling.
demontieren [demɔn'tiːrən] *vt* (*lit, fig*) to dismantle; (*Räder*) to take off.
demoralisieren [demorali'ziːrən] *vt* to demoralize.
Demoskopie [demosko'piː] *f* public opinion research.
demselben *dat von* **derselbe, dasselbe.**
Demut ['deːmuːt] **(-)** *f* humility.
demütig ['deːmyːtɪç] *adj* humble.
demütigen ['deːmyːtɪgən] *vt* to humiliate.
Demütigung *f* humiliation.
demzufolge ['deːmtsu'fɔlgə] *adv* accordingly.
den [de(ː)n] *art akk von* **der.**
denen ['deːnən] *pron dat pl von* **der, die, das.**

Denk- *zW:* **~anstoß** *m:* **jdm ~anstöße geben**
to give sb food for thought; **~art** *f*
mentality; **d~bar** *adj* conceivable.
denken ['dɛŋkən] *unreg vi* to think ♦ *vt:* **für jdn/
etw gedacht sein** to be intended *od* meant
for sb/sth ♦ *vr* (*vorstellen*): **das kann ich mir
~** I can imagine; (*beabsichtigen*): **sich** *dat* **etw
bei etw ~** to mean sth by sth; **wo ~ Sie hin!**
what an idea!; **ich denke schon** I think so; **an
jdn/etw ~** to think of sb/sth; **daran ist gar
nicht zu ~** that's (quite) out of the question;
ich denke nicht daran, das zu tun there's no
way I'm going to do that (*umg*).
Denken (**-s**) *nt* thinking.
Denker(in) (**-s, -**) *m(f)* thinker; **das Volk der
Dichter und ~** the nation of poets and
philosophers.
Denk- *zW:* **~fähigkeit** *f* intelligence; **d~faul**
adj mentally lazy; **~fehler** *m* logical error;
~horizont *m* mental horizon.
Denkmal (**-s, ¨-er**) *nt* monument; **~schutz** *m:*
etw unter ~schutz stellen to classify sth as
a historical monument.
Denk- *zW:* **~pause** *f:* **eine ~pause einlegen** to
have a break to think things over; **~schrift**
f memorandum; **~vermögen** *nt* intellectual
capacity; **d~würdig** *adj* memorable;
~zettel *m:* **jdm einen ~zettel verpassen** to
teach sb a lesson.
denn [dɛn] *konj* for; (*konzessiv*): **es sei ~, (daß)**
unless ♦ *adv* then; (*nach Komparativ*) than.
dennoch ['dɛnnɔx] *konj* nevertheless ♦ *adv:*
und ~, ... and yet ...
denselben *akk von* **derselbe** ♦ *dat von* **dieselben**.
Denunziant(in) [denʊntsi'ant(ɪn)] *m(f)*
informer.
denunzieren [denʊn'tsiːrən] *vt* to inform
against.
Deospray ['deːoʃpreɪ] *nt od m* deodorant spray.
Depesche [de'pɛʃə] (**-, -n**) *f* dispatch.
deplaziert [depla'tsiːrt] *adj* out of place.
Deponent(in) [depo'nɛnt(ɪn)] *m(f)* depositor.
Deponie *f* dump, disposal site.
deponieren [depo'niːrən] *vt* (*COMM*) to
deposit.
deportieren [depɔr'tiːrən] *vt* to deport.
Depot [de'poː] (**-s, -s**) *nt* warehouse; (*Bus~,
EISENB*) depot; (*Bank~*) strongroom (*BRIT*),
safe (*US*).
Depp [dɛp] (**-en, -en**) *m* (*Dialekt: pej*) twit.
Depression [deprɛsi'oːn] *f* depression.
depressiv *adj* depressive; (*FIN*) depressed.
deprimieren [depri'miːrən] *vt* to depress.

═══════════════════ *SCHLÜSSELWORT*

der [deː(r)] (*f* **die**, *nt* **das**) (*gen* **des, der, des,** *dat*
dem, der, dem) (*akk* **den**) *def art* the; **~ Rhein**
the Rhine; **~ Klaus** (*umg*) Klaus; **die Frau** (*im
allgemeinen*) women; **~ Tod/das Leben**
death/life; **~ Fuß des Berges** the foot of the
hill; **gib es ~ Frau** give it to the woman; **er
hat sich** *dat* **die Hand verletzt** he has hurt his

hand
♦ *rel pron* (*bei Menschen*) who, that; (*bei
Tieren, Sachen*) which, that; **~ Mann, den ich
gesehen habe** the man who *od* whom *od* that
I saw
♦ *demon pron* he/she/it; (*jener, dieser*) that; (*pl*)
those; **~/die war es** it was him/her; **~ mit
~ Brille** the one with the glasses; **ich will
den (da)** I want that one.

derart ['deːr'aːrt] *adv* (*Art und Weise*) in such a
way; (*Ausmaß: vor adj*) so; (: *vor vb*) so much.
derartig *adj* such, this sort of.
derb [dɛrp] *adj* sturdy; (*Kost*) solid; (*grob*)
coarse; **D~heit** *f* sturdiness; solidity;
coarseness.
deren ['deːrən] *rel pron* (*gen sing von die*)
whose; (*von Sachen*) of which; (*gen pl von
der, die, das*) their; whose; of whom.
derentwillen ['deːrənt'vɪlən] *adv:* **um ~** (*rel*)
for whose sake; (*von Sachen*) for the sake of
which.
dergestalt *adv* (*geh*): **~, daß ...** in such a way
that ...
der- *zW:* **~gleichen** *pron* such; (*substantivisch*):
er tat nichts ~gleichen he did nothing of the
kind; **und ~gleichen (mehr)** and suchlike;
~jenige *pron* he; she; it; (*rel*) the one (who);
that (which); **~maßen** *adv* to such an
extent, so; **~selbe** *m pron* the same;
~weil(en) *adv* in the meantime; **~zeit** *adv*
(*jetzt*) at present, at the moment; **~zeitig** *adj*
present, current; (*damalig*) then.
des [dɛs] *art gen von* **der**.
Des [dɛs] (**-**) *nt* (*MUS: auch:* **d~**) D flat.
Deserteur [dezɛr'tøːr] *m* deserter.
desertieren [dezɛr'tiːrən] *vi* to desert.
desgl. *abk* = **desgleichen**.
desgleichen ['dɛs'glaɪçən] *pron* the same.
deshalb ['dɛs'halp] *adv, konj* therefore, that's
why.
Design [di'zaɪn] (**-s, -s**) *nt* design.
designiert [dezi'gniːrt] *adj attrib:* **der ~e
Vorsitzende/Nachfolger** the chairman
designate/prospective successor.
Desinfektion [dezɪnfɛktsi'oːn] *f* disinfection.
Desinfektionsmittel *nt* disinfectant.
desinfizieren [dezɪnfi'tsiːrən] *vt* to disinfect.
Desinteresse [dɛs|ɪntə'rɛsə] (**-s**) *nt:* **~ (an** +*dat*)
lack of interest (in).
desinteressiert [dɛs|ɪntərɛ'siːrt] *adj*
uninterested.
desselben *gen von* **derselbe, dasselbe**.
dessen ['dɛsən] *pron gen von* **der, das;
~ungeachtet** *adv* nevertheless, regardless.
Dessert [dɛ'seːr] (**-s, -s**) *nt* dessert.
Dessin [dɛ'sɛ̃ː] (**-s, -s**) *nt* (*TEXTIL*) pattern,
design.
Destillation [dɛstɪlatsi'oːn] *f* distillation.
destillieren [dɛstɪ'liːrən] *vt* to distil.
desto ['dɛsto] *adv* all *od* so much the; **~ besser**
all the better.

destruktiv [destrʊk'tiːf] *adj* destructive.
deswegen ['dɛs'veːgən] *konj* therefore, hence.
Detail [de'taɪ] **(-s, -s)** *nt* detail.
detaillieren [deta'jiːrən] *vt* to specify, give details of.
Detektiv [detɛk'tiːf] **(-s, -e)** *m* detective;
~**roman** *m* detective novel.
Detektor [de'tɛktɔr] *m* (*TECH*) detector.
Detonation [detonatsi'oːn] *f* explosion, blast.
Deut *m*: **(um) keinen** ~ not one iota *od* jot.
deuten ['dɔytən] *vt* to interpret; (*Zukunft*) to read ♦ *vi*: ~ **(auf** +*akk*) to point (to *od* at).
deutlich *adj* clear; (*Unterschied*) distinct; **jdm etw** ~ **zu verstehen geben** to make sth perfectly clear *od* plain to sb; **D~keit** *f* clarity; distinctness.
deutsch [dɔytʃ] *adj* German; ~**e Schrift** Gothic script; **auf** ~ in German; **auf gut** ~ **(gesagt)** (*fig: umg*) ≈ in plain English; **D~e Demokratische Republik** (*HIST*) German Democratic Republic.
Deutsche(r) *f(m)*: **er ist** ~**r** he is (a) German.
Deutschland *nt* Germany; ~**lied** *nt* German national anthem; ~**politik** *f* home *od* domestic policy; (*von fremdem Staat*) policy towards Germany.
deutschsprachig *adj* (*Bevölkerung, Gebiete*) German-speaking; (*Zeitung, Ausgabe*) German-language; (*Literatur*) German.
deutschstämmig *adj* of German origin.
Deutung *f* interpretation.
Devise [de'viːzə] **(-, -n)** *f* motto, device; **Devisen** *pl* (*FIN*) foreign currency *od* exchange.
Devisenausgleich *m* foreign exchange offset.
Devisenkontrolle *f* exchange control.
Dez. *abk* (= *Dezember*) Dec.
Dezember [de'tsɛmbər] **(-(s), -)** *m* December; *siehe auch* **September.**
dezent [de'tsɛnt] *adj* discreet.
Dezentralisation [detsɛntralizatsi'oːn] *f* decentralization.
Dezernat [detsɛr'naːt] **(-(e)s, -e)** *nt* (*VERWALTUNG*) department.
Dezibel [detsi'bɛl] **(-s, -)** *nt* decibel.
dezidiert [detsi'diːrt] *adj* firm, determined.
dezimal [detsi'maːl] *adj* decimal; **D~bruch** *m* decimal (fraction); **D~system** *nt* decimal system.
dezimieren [detsi'miːrən] *vt* (*fig*) to decimate ♦ *vr* to be decimated.
DFB *m abk* (= *Deutscher Fußball-Bund*) *German Football Association.*
DFG *f abk* (= *Deutsche Forschungsgemein-schaft*) *German Research Council.*
DGB *m abk* (= *Deutscher Gewerkschaftsbund*) ≈ TUC.
dgl. *abk* = **dergleichen.**
d.h. *abk* (= *das heißt*) i.e.
Dia ['diːa] **(-s, -s)** *nt* = **Diapositiv.**
Diabetes [dia'beːtɛs] **(-, -)** *m* (*MED*) diabetes.

Diabetiker(in) [dia'beːtikər(ɪn)] **(-s, -)** *m(f)* diabetic.
Diagnose [dia'gnoːzə] **(-, -n)** *f* diagnosis.
diagnostizieren [diagnɔsti'tsiːrən] *vt, vi* (*MED, fig*) to diagnose.
diagonal [diago'naːl] *adj* diagonal.
Diagonale (-, -n) *f* diagonal.
Diagramm [dia'gram] *nt* diagram.
Diakonie [diako'niː] *f* (*REL*) social welfare work.
Dialekt [dia'lɛkt] **(-(e)s, -e)** *m* dialect; ~**ausdruck** *m* dialect expression *od* word; **d~frei** *adj* without an accent.
dialektisch *adj* dialectal; (*Logik*) dialectical.
Dialog [dia'loːk] **(-(e)s, -e)** *m* dialogue.
Diamant [dia'mant] *m* diamond.
Diapositiv [diapozi'tiːf] **(-s, -e)** *nt* (*PHOT*) slide, transparency.
Diaprojektor *m* slide projector.
Diät [di'ɛːt] **(-)** *f* **diet; Diäten** *pl* (*POL*) allowance *sing*; **d~** *adv* (*kochen, essen*) according to a diet; (*leben*) on a special diet.
dich [dɪç] *akk von* **du** ♦ *pron* you ♦ *refl pron* yourself.
dicht [dɪçt] *adj* dense; (*Nebel*) thick; (*Gewebe*) close; (*undurchlässig*) (water)tight; (*fig*) concise; (*umg: zu*) shut, closed ♦ *adv*: ~ **an/bei** close to; **er ist nicht ganz** ~ (*umg*) he's crackers; ~ **machen** to make watertight/airtight; (*Person*) to close one's mind; ~ **hintereinander** right behind one another; ~**bevölkert** *adj* densely *od* heavily populated.
Dichte (-, -n) *f* density; thickness; closeness; (water)tightness; (*fig*) conciseness.
dichten *vt* (*dicht machen*) to make watertight; to seal; (*NAUT*) to caulk; (*LITER*) to compose, write ♦ *vi* (*LITER*) to compose, write.
Dichter(in) (-s, -) *m(f)* poet; (*Autor*) writer; **d~isch** *adj* poetical; **d~ische Freiheit** poetic licence (*BRIT*) *od* license (*US*).
dichthalten *unreg* (*umg*) *vi* to keep one's mouth shut.
dichtmachen (*umg*) *vt* (*Geschäft*) to wind up.
Dichtung *f* (*TECH*) washer; (*AUT*) gasket; (*Gedichte*) poetry; (*Prosa*) (piece of) writing; ~ **und Wahrheit** (*fig*) fact and fantasy.
dick [dɪk] *adj* thick; (*fett*) fat; **durch** ~ **und dünn** through thick and thin; **D~darm** *m* (*ANAT*) colon.
Dicke (-, -n) *f* thickness; fatness.
dickfellig *adj* thick-skinned.
dickflüssig *adj* viscous.
Dickicht (-s, -e) *nt* thicket.
dick- *zW*: **D~kopf** *m* mule; **D~milch** *f* soured milk; **D~schädel** *m* = **Dickkopf.**
die [diː] *def art* the; *siehe auch* **der.**
Dieb(in) [diːp, 'diːbɪn] **(-(e)s, -e)** *m(f)* thief; **haltet den** ~! stop thief!; **d~isch** *adj* thieving; (*umg*) immense; ~**stahl** *m* theft; **d~stahlsicher** *adj* theft-proof.
diejenige ['diːjeːnɪgə] *pron siehe* **derjenige.**

Diele ['di:lə] (-, **-n**) *f* (*Brett*) board; (*Flur*) hall, lobby; (*Eis~*) ice-cream parlour (*BRIT*) *od* parlor (*US*).

dienen ['di:nən] *vi:* (**jdm**) ~ to serve (sb); **womit kann ich Ihnen** ~? what can I do for you?; (*in Geschäft*) can I help you?

Diener (**-s**, **-**) *m* servant; (*umg: Verbeugung*) bow; ~**in** *f* (maid)servant.

dienern *vi* (*fig*): ~ (**vor** +*dat*) to bow and scrape (to).

Dienerschaft *f* servants *pl*.

dienlich *adj* useful, helpful.

Dienst [di:nst] (**-(e)s**, **-e**) *m* service; (*Arbeit, Arbeitszeit*) work; ~ **am Kunden** customer service; **jdm zu** ~**en stehen** to be at sb's disposal; **außer** ~ retired; ~ **haben** to be on duty; **der öffentliche** ~ the civil service.

Dienstag *m* Tuesday; **am** ~ on Tuesday; ~ **in acht Tagen** *od* **in einer Woche** a week on Tuesday, Tuesday week; ~ **vor einer Woche** *od* **acht Tagen** a week (ago) last Tuesday.

dienstags *adv* on Tuesdays.

Dienst- *zW:* ~**alter** *nt* length of service; **d~beflissen** *adj* zealous; ~**bote** *m* servant; ~**boteneingang** *m* tradesmen's *od* service entrance; **d~eifrig** *adj* zealous; **d~frei** *adj* off duty; ~**gebrauch** *m* (*MIL, VERWALTUNG*): **nur für den** ~**gebrauch** for official use only; ~**geheimnis** *nt* professional secret; ~**gespräch** *nt* business call; ~**grad** *m* rank; **d~habend** *adj* (*Arzt, Offizier*) on duty; ~**leistung** *f* service; ~**leistungsbetrieb** *m* service industry business; ~**leistungsgewerbe** *nt* service industries *pl*; **d~lich** *adj* official; (*Angelegenheiten*) business *attrib*; ~**mädchen** *nt* domestic servant; ~**plan** *m* duty rota; ~**reise** *f* business trip; ~**stelle** *f* office; **d~tuend** *adj* on duty; ~**vorschrift** *f* service regulations *pl*; ~**wagen** *m* (*von Beamten*) official car; ~**weg** *m* official channels *pl*; ~**zeit** *f* office hours *pl*; (*MIL*) period of service.

diesbezüglich *adj* (*Frage*) on this matter.

diese(r, s) *pron* this (one) ♦ *adj* this; ~ **Nacht** tonight.

Diesel ['di:zəl] (**-s**) *m* (*Kraftstoff*) diesel fuel; ~**öl** ['di:zələ:l] *nt* diesel oil.

dieselbe [di:'zɛlbə] *f pron* the same.

dieselben [di:'zɛlbən] *pl pron* the same.

diesig *adj* drizzly.

dies- *zW:* ~**jährig** *adj* this year's; ~**mal** *adv* this time; **D~seits** (**-**) *nt* this life; ~**seits** *präp* +*gen* on this side.

Dietrich ['di:trɪç] (**-s**, **-e**) *m* picklock.

Diffamierungskampagne [dɪfa'mi:rʊŋskampanjə] *f* smear campaign.

differential [dɪferɛntsi'a:l] *adj* differential; **D~getriebe** *nt* differential gear; **D~rechnung** *f* differential calculus.

Differenzbetrag *m* difference, balance.

differenzieren [dɪferɛn'tsi:rən] *vt* to make distinctions in ♦ *vi:* ~ (**bei**) to make

distinctions (in).

differenziert *adj* complex.

diffus [dɪ'fu:s] *adj* (*Gedanken etc*) confused.

Digital- [digi'ta:l-] *zW:* ~**anzeige** *f* digital display; ~**rechner** *m* digital computer; ~**uhr** *f* digital watch.

Diktaphon [dɪkta'fo:n] *nt* dictaphone ®.

Diktat [dɪk'ta:t] (**-(e)s**, **-e**) *nt* dictation; (*fig: Gebot*) dictate; (*POL*) diktat, dictate.

Diktator [dɪk'ta:tɔr] *m* dictator; **d~isch** [-a'to:rɪʃ] *adj* dictatorial.

Diktatur [dɪkta'tu:r] *f* dictatorship.

diktieren [dɪk'ti:rən] *vt* to dictate.

Diktion [dɪktsi'o:n] *f* style.

Dilemma [di'lɛma] (**-s**, **-s** *od* **-ta**) *nt* dilemma.

Dilettant [dile'tant] *m* dilettante, amateur; **d~isch** *adj* dilettante.

Dimension [dimɛnzi'o:n] *f* dimension.

DIN *f abk* (= *Deutsche Industrie-Norm*) German Industrial Standard; ≈ **A4** A4.

Ding [dɪŋ] (**-(e)s**, **-e**) *nt* thing; object; **das ist ein** ~ **der Unmöglichkeit** that is totally impossible; **guter** ~**e sein** to be in good spirits; **so wie die** ~**e liegen, nach Lage der** ~**e** as things are; **es müßte nicht mit rechten** ~**en zugehen, wenn** ... it would be more than a little strange if ...; **ein krummes** ~ **drehen** to commit a crime; **to do something wrong**; **d~fest** *adj*: **jdn d~fest machen** to arrest sb; **d~lich** *adj* real, concrete.

Dings (**-**) (*umg*) *nt* thingummyjig (*BRIT*).

Dingsbums ['dɪŋsbums] (**-**) (*umg*) *nt* thingummybob (*BRIT*).

Dingsda (**-**) (*umg*) *nt* thingummyjig (*BRIT*).

Dinosaurier [dino'zauriər] *m* dinosaur.

Diözese [diø'tse:zə] (**-**, **-n**) *f* diocese.

Diphtherie [dɪfte'ri:] *f* diphtheria.

Dipl.-Ing. *abk* = **Diplomingenieur.**

Diplom [di'plo:m] (**-(e)s**, **-e**) *nt* diploma; (*Hochschulabschluß*) degree; ~**arbeit** *f* dissertation.

Diplomat [diplo'ma:t] (**-en**, **-en**) *m* diplomat.

Diplomatie [diploma'ti:] *f* diplomacy.

diplomatisch [diplo'ma:tɪʃ] *adj* diplomatic.

Diplomingenieur *m* academically qualified engineer.

dir [di:r] *dat von* **du** ♦ *pron* (to) you.

direkt [di'rɛkt] *adj* direct; ~ **fragen** to ask outright *od* straight out.

Direktion [dirɛktsi'o:n] *f* management; (*Büro*) manager's office.

Direktmandat *nt* (*POL*) direct mandate.

Direktor(in) *m(f)* director; (*von Hochschule*) principal; (*von Schule*) principal, head (teacher) (*BRIT*).

Direktorium [dirɛk'to:riʊm] *nt* board of directors.

Direktübertragung *f* live broadcast.

Direktverkauf *m* direct selling.

Dirigent(in) [diri'gɛnt(ɪn)] *m(f)* conductor.

dirigieren [diri'gi:rən] *vt* to direct; (*MUS*) to

conduct.

Dirne ['dɪrnə] (-, -n) f prostitute.
Dis [dɪs] (-, -) nt (MUS) D sharp.
dis [dɪs] (-, -) nt (MUS) D sharp.
Disco ['dɪsko] (-s, -s) f disco.
Disharmonie [dɪsharmo'niː] f (lit, fig) discord.
Diskette [dɪs'kɛtə] f disk, diskette.
Diskettenlaufwerk nt disk drive.
Diskont [dɪs'kɔnt] (-s, -e) m discount; ~satz m rate of discount.
Diskothek [dɪsko'teːk] (-, -en) f disco(theque).
diskreditieren [dɪskredi'tiːrən] vt (geh) to discredit.
Diskrepanz [dɪskre'pants] f discrepancy.
diskret [dɪs'kreːt] adj discreet.
Diskretion [dɪskretsi'oːn] f discretion; **strengste ~ wahren** to preserve the strictest confidence.
diskriminieren [dɪskrimi'niːrən] vt to discriminate against.
Diskriminierung f: ~ **(von)** discrimination (against).
Diskussion [dɪskʊsi'oːn] f discussion; **zur ~ stehen** to be under discussion.
Diskussionsbeitrag m contribution to the discussion.
Diskuswerfen ['dɪskʊsvɛrfən] nt throwing the discus.
diskutabel [dɪsku'taːbəl] adj debatable.
diskutieren [dɪsku'tiːrən] vt, vi to discuss; **darüber läßt sich ~** that sounds like something we could talk about.
disponieren [dɪspo'niːrən] vi (geh: planen) to make arrangements.
Disposition [dɪspozitsi'oːn] f (geh: Verfügung): **jdm zur** od **zu jds ~ stehen** to be at sb's disposal.
disqualifizieren [dɪskvalifi'tsiːrən] vt to disqualify.
Dissertation [dɪsɛrtatsi'oːn] f dissertation; doctoral thesis.
Dissident(in) [dɪsi'dɛnt(ɪn)] m(f) dissident.
Distanz [dɪs'tants] f distance; (fig: Abstand, Entfernung) detachment; (Zurückhaltung) reserve.
distanzieren [dɪstan'tsiːrən] vr: **sich von jdm/ etw ~** to dissociate o.s. from sb/sth.
distanziert adj (Verhalten) distant.
Distel ['dɪstəl] (-, -n) f thistle.
Disziplin [dɪstsi'pliːn] (-, -en) f discipline.
Disziplinarverfahren [dɪstsipli'narferfaːrən] nt disciplinary proceedings pl.
dito ['diːto] adv (COMM, hum) ditto.
Diva ['diːva] (-, -s) f star; (FILM) screen goddess.
divers [di'vɛrs] adj various.
Diverses pl sundries pl; „~" "miscellaneous".
Dividende [divi'dɛndə] (-, -n) f dividend.
dividieren [divi'diːrən] vt: ~ **(durch)** to divide (by).

d.J. abk (= der Jüngere) jun.
Djakarta [dʒa'karta] nt Jakarta.
DJH nt abk (= Deutsches Jugendherbergswerk) German Youth Hostel Association.
DKP f abk (= Deutsche Kommunistische Partei) German Communist Party.
DLRG f abk (= Deutsche Lebens-Rettungs-Gesellschaft) German lifesaving association.
DLV m abk (= Deutscher Leichtathletik-Verband) German track and field associaton.
DM f abk (= Deutsche Mark) DM.
d.M. abk (= dieses Monats) inst.
D-Mark ['deːmark] (-, -) f deutschmark, German mark.
DNS f abk (= Desoxyribo(se)nukleinsäure) DNA.

══════════════ SCHLÜSSELWORT

doch [dɔx] adv **1** (dennoch) after all; (sowieso) anyway; **er kam ~ noch** he came after all; **du weißt es ja ~ besser** you know more about it (than I do) anyway; **es war ~ ganz interessant** it was actually quite interesting; **und ~, ...** and yet ...
2 (als bejahende Antwort) yes I do/it does etc; **das ist nicht wahr - ~!** that's not true - yes it is!
3 (auffordernd): **komm ~** do come; **laß ihn ~** just leave him; **nicht ~!** oh no!
4: **sie ist ~ noch so jung** but she's still so young; **Sie wissen ~, wie das ist** you know how it is(, don't you?); **wenn ~** if only
♦ konj (aber) but; (trotzdem) all the same; **und ~ hat er es getan** but still he did it.

Docht [dɔxt] (-(e)s, -e) m wick.
Dock [dɔk] (-s, -s od -e) nt dock; ~gebühren pl dock dues pl.
Dogge ['dɔgə] (-, -n) f bulldog; **deutsche ~** Great Dane.
Dogma ['dɔgma] (-s, -men) nt dogma.
dogmatisch [dɔ'gmaːtɪʃ] adj dogmatic.
Dohle ['doːlə] (-, -n) f jackdaw.
Doktor ['dɔktɔr] (-s, -en) m doctor; **den ~ machen** (umg) to do a doctorate od Ph.D.
Doktorand(in) [dɔktɔ'rant (-dɪn)] (-en, -en) m(f) Ph.D. student.
Doktor- zW: ~**arbeit** f doctoral thesis; ~**titel** m doctorate; ~**vater** m supervisor.
doktrinär [dɔktri'nɛːr] adj doctrinal; (stur) doctrinaire.
Dokument [doku'mɛnt] nt document.
Dokumentar- zW: ~**bericht** m documentary; ~**film** m documentary (film); **d~isch** adj documentary; ~**spiel** nt docudrama.
dokumentieren [dokumɛn'tiːrən] vt to document; (fig: zu erkennen geben) to reveal, show.
Dolch [dɔlç] (-(e)s, -e) m dagger; ~**stoß** m (bes fig) stab.
dolmetschen ['dɔlmɛtʃən] vt, vi to interpret.
Dolmetscher(in) (-s, -) m(f) interpreter.
Dolomiten [dolo'miːtən] pl (GEOG): **die ~** the

Dolomites *pl.*
Dom [doːm] (-(e)s, -e) *m* cathedral.
Domäne [doˈmɛːnə] (-, -n) *f* (*fig*) domain, province.
dominieren [domiˈniːrən] *vt* to dominate ♦ *vi* to predominate.
Dominikanische Republik
[domiˈkaːnɪʃərepuˈbliːk] *f* Dominican Republic.
Dompfaff [ˈdoːmpfaf] (-en, -en) *m* bullfinch.
Dompteur [dɔmpˈtøːr] *m* (*Zirkus*) trainer.
Dompteuse [dɔmpˈtøːzə] *f* (*Zirkus*) trainer.
Donau [ˈdoːnau] *f*: **die ~** the Danube.
Donner [ˈdɔnər] (-s, -) *m* thunder; **wie vom ~ gerührt** (*fig*) thunderstruck.
donnern *vi unpers* to thunder ♦ *vt* (*umg*) to slam, crash.
Donnerschlag *m* thunderclap.
Donnerstag *m* Thursday; *siehe auch* **Dienstag**.
Donnerwetter *nt* thunderstorm; (*fig*) dressing-down ♦ *interj* good heavens!; (*anerkennend*) my word!
doof [doːf] (*umg*) *adj* daft, stupid.
Dopingkontrolle [ˈdoːpɪŋkɔntrɔlə] *f* (*SPORT*) dope check.
Doppel [ˈdɔpəl] (-s, -) *nt* duplicate; (*SPORT*) doubles; **~band** *m* (*von doppeltem Umfang*) double-sized volume; (*zwei Bände*) two volumes *pl*; **~bett** *nt* double bed; **d~bödig** *adj* (*fig*) ambiguous; **d~deutig** *adj* ambiguous; **~fenster** *nt* double glazing; **~gänger(in)** (-s, -) *m(f)* double; **~korn** *m* type of schnapps; **~punkt** *m* colon; **d~seitig** *adj* (*auch COMPUT: Diskette*) double-sided; (*Lungenentzündung*) double; **d~seitige Anzeige** double-page advertisement; **d~sinnig** *adj* ambiguous; **~stecker** *m* two-way adaptor; **~stunde** *f* (*SCH*) double period.
doppelt *adj* double; (*COMM: Buchführung*) double-entry; (*Staatsbürgerschaft*) dual ♦ *adv*: **die Karte habe ich ~** I have two of these cards; **~ gemoppelt** (*umg*) saying the same thing twice over; **in ~er Ausführung** in duplicate.
Doppel- *zW*: **~verdiener** *pl* two-income family; **~zentner** *m* 100 kilograms; **~zimmer** *nt* double room.
Dorf [dɔrf] (-(e)s, ⁻er) *nt* village; **~bewohner** *m* villager.
dörflich [ˈdœrflɪç] *adj* village *attrib*.
Dorn¹ [dɔrn] (-(e)s, -en) *m* (*BOT*) thorn; **das ist mir ein ~ im Auge** (*fig*) it's a thorn in my flesh.
Dorn² [dɔrn] (-(e)s, -e) *m* (*Schnallen~*) tongue, pin.
dornig *adj* thorny.
Dornröschen *nt* Sleeping Beauty.
dörren [ˈdœrən] *vt* to dry.
Dörrobst [ˈdœroːpst] *nt* dried fruit.
Dorsch [dɔrʃ] (-(e)s, -e) *m* cod.
dort [dɔrt] *adv* there; **~ drüben** over there; **~her** *adv* from there; **~hin** *adv* (to) there;

~hinaus *adv*: **frech bis ~hinaus** (*umg*) really cheeky.
dortig *adj* of that place; in that town.
Dose [ˈdoːzə] (-, -n) *f* box; (*Blech~*) tin, can; **in ~n** (*Konserven*) canned, tinned (*BRIT*).
Dosen *pl von* **Dose, Dosis**.
dösen [ˈdøːzən] (*umg*) *vi* to doze.
Dosenmilch *f* evaporated milk.
Dosenöffner *m* tin (*BRIT*) *od* can opener.
dosieren [doˈziːrən] *vt* (*lit, fig*) to measure out.
Dosis [ˈdoːzɪs] (-, **Dosen**) *f* dose.
Dotierung [doˈtiːruŋ] *f* endowment; (*von Posten*) remuneration.
Dotter [ˈdɔtər] (-s, -) *m* egg yolk.
Double [ˈduːbəl] (-s, -s) *nt* (*FILM etc*) stand-in.
Down-Syndrom *nt no pl* (*MED*) Down's Syndrome.
Doz. *abk* = **Dozent(in)**.
Dozent(in) [doˈtsɛnt(ɪn)] (-en, -en) *m(f)*: **~ (für)** lecturer (in), professor (of) (*US*).
dpa (-) *f abk* (= *Deutsche Presse-Agentur*) *German Press Agency*.
Dr. *abk* = **Doktor**.
Drache [ˈdraxə] (-n, -n) *m* (*Tier*) dragon.
Drachen (-s, -) *m* kite; **einen ~ steigen lassen** to fly a kite; **d~fliegen** *vi* to hang-glide; **~fliegen** *nt* (*SPORT*) hang-gliding.
Dragée [draˈʒeː] (-s, -s) *nt* (*PHARM*) dragee, sugar-coated pill.
Draht [draːt] (-(e)s, ⁻e) *m* wire; **auf ~ sein** to be on the ball; **~esel** *m* (*hum*) trusty bicycle; **~gitter** *nt* wire grating; **d~los** *adj* cordless; (*Telefon*) mobile; **~seil** *nt* cable; **Nerven wie ~seile** (*umg*) nerves of steel; **~seilbahn** *f* cable railway; **~zange** *f* pliers *pl*; **~zieher(in)** *m(f)* (*fig*) wire-puller.
Drall *m* (*fig: Hang*) tendency; **einen ~ nach links haben** (*AUT*) to pull to the left.
drall [dral] *adj* strapping; (*Frau*) buxom.
Drama [ˈdraːma] (-s, **Dramen**) *nt* drama.
Dramatiker(in) [draˈmaːtikər(ɪn)] (-s, -) *m(f)* dramatist.
dramatisch [draˈmaːtɪʃ] *adj* dramatic.
Dramaturg(in) [dramaˈtʊrk (-ɡɪn)] (-en, -en) *m(f)* artistic director; (*TV*) drama producer.
dran [dran] (*umg*) *adv* (*an der Reihe*): **jetzt bist du ~** it's your turn now; **früh/spät ~ sein** to be early/late; **ich weiß nicht, wie ich (bei ihm) ~ bin** I don't know where I stand (with him); *siehe auch* **daran**; **~bleiben** *unreg* (*umg*) *vi* to stay close; (*am Apparat*) to hang on.
Drang (-(e)s, ⁻e) *m* (*Trieb*) urge, yearning; (*Druck*) pressure; **~ nach** urge *od* yearning for.
drang *etc* [draŋ] *vb siehe* **dringen**.
drängeln [ˈdrɛŋəln] *vt, vi* to push, jostle.
drängen [ˈdrɛŋən] *vt* (*schieben*) to push, press; (*antreiben*) to urge ♦ *vi* (*eilig sein*) to be urgent; (*Zeit*) to press; **auf etw** *akk* **~** to press for sth.
drangsalieren [draŋzaˈliːrən] *vt* to pester, plague.

dranhalten (*umg*) *vr* to get a move on.
drankommen (*umg*) *unreg vi* (*an die Reihe kommen*) to have one's turn; (*SCH: beim Melden*) to be called; (*Frage, Aufgabe etc*) to come up.
drannehmen (*umg*) *unreg vt* (*Schüler*) to ask.
drasch *etc* [draːʃ] *vb siehe* **dreschen**.
drastisch ['drastɪʃ] *adj* drastic.
drauf [drauf] (*umg*) *adv:* ~ **und dran sein, etw zu tun** to be on the point of doing sth; **etw** ~ **haben** (*können*) to be able to do sth just like that; (*Kenntnisse*) to be well up on sth; *siehe auch* **darauf**; **D~gänger** (*-s, -*) *m* daredevil; ~**gehen** *unreg vi* (*verbraucht werden*) to be used up; (*kaputtgehen*) to be smashed up; ~**zahlen** *vi* (*fig: Einbußen erleiden*) to pay the price.
draußen ['drausən] *adv* outside, out-of-doors.
Drechsler(in) ['drɛkslər(ɪn)] (*-s, -*) *m(f)* (wood) turner.
Dreck [drɛk] (*-(e)s*) *m* mud, dirt; ~ **am Stecken haben** (*fig*) to have a skeleton in the cupboard; **das geht ihn einen** ~ **an** (*umg*) that's none of his business.
dreckig *adj* dirty, filthy; **es geht mir** ~ (*umg*) I'm in a bad way.
Dreckskerl (*umg!*) *m* dirty swine (*!*).
Dreh [dreː] *m:* **den** ~ **raushaben** *od* **weghaben** (*umg*) to have got the hang of it.
Dreh- *zW:* ~**achse** *f* axis of rotation; ~**arbeiten** *pl* (*FILM*) shooting *sing*; ~**bank** *f* lathe; **d~bar** *adj* revolving; ~**buch** *nt* (*FILM*) script.
drehen *vt* to turn, rotate; (*Zigaretten*) to roll; (*Film*) to shoot ♦ *vi* to turn, rotate ♦ *vr* to turn; (*handeln von*): **sich um etw** ~ to be about sth; **ein Ding** ~ (*umg*) to play a prank.
Dreher(in) (*-s, -*) *m(f)* lathe operator.
Dreh- *zW:* ~**orgel** *f* barrel organ; ~**ort** *m* (*FILM*) location; ~**scheibe** *f* (*EISENB*) turntable; ~**tür** *f* revolving door.
Drehung *f* (*Rotation*) rotation; (*Um~, Wendung*) turn.
Dreh- *zW:* ~**wurm** (*umg*) *m:* **einen** ~**wurm haben/bekommen** to be/become dizzy; ~**zahl** *f* rate of revolution; ~**zahlmesser** *m* rev(olution) counter.
drei [drai] *num* three; **aller guten Dinge sind** ~! (*Sprichwort*) all good things come in threes!; (*nach zwei mißglückten Versuchen*) third time lucky!; **D~eck** *nt* triangle; ~**eckig** *adj* triangular; **D~ecksverhältnis** *nt* eternal triangle; ~**einhalb** *num* three and a half; **D~einigkeit** [-'|ainɪçkait] *f* Trinity.
dreierlei *adj inv* of three kinds.
drei- *zW:* ~**fach** *adj* triple, treble ♦ *adv* three times; **die** ~**fache Menge** three times the amount; **D~faltigkeit** *f* trinity; **D~fuß** *m* tripod; (*Schemel*) three-legged stool; **D~gangschaltung** *f* three-speed gear; ~**hundert** *num* three hundred; **D~käsehoch** (*umg*) *m* tiny tot; **D~königsfest** *nt* Epiphany;

~**mal** *adv* three times, thrice; ~**malig** *adj* three times.
dreinblicken ['drainblɪkən] *vi:* **traurig** *etc* ~ to look sad *etc*.
dreinreden ['drainreːdən] *vi:* **jdm** ~ (*dazwischenreden*) to interrupt sb; (*sich einmischen*) to interfere with sb.
Dreirad *nt* tricycle.
Dreisprung *m* triple jump.
dreißig ['draisɪç] *num* thirty.
dreist [draist] *adj* bold, audacious.
Dreistigkeit *f* boldness, audacity.
drei- *zW:* ~**viertel** *num* three-quarters; **D~viertelstunde** *f* three-quarters of an hour; **D~vierteltakt** *m:* **im D~vierteltakt** in three-four time; ~**zehn** *num* thirteen; **jetzt schlägt's** ~**zehn!** (*umg*) that's a bit much.
dreschen ['drɛʃən] *unreg vt* to thresh; **Skat** ~ (*umg*) to play skat.
Dresden ['dreːsdən] (*-s*) *nt* Dresden.
dressieren [drɛˈsiːrən] *vt* to train.
Dressur [drɛˈsuːr] *f* training; (*für ~reiten*) dressage.
Dr.h.c. *abk* (= *Doktor honoris causa*) honorary doctor.
driften ['drɪftən] *vi* (*NAUT, fig*) to drift.
Drillbohrer *m* light drill.
drillen ['drɪlən] *vt* (*bohren*) to drill, bore; (*MIL*) to drill; (*fig*) to train; **auf etw** *akk* **gedrillt sein** (*fig: umg*) to be practised (*BRIT*) *od* practiced (*US*) at doing sth.
Drilling *m* triplet.
drin [drɪn] (*umg*) *adv:* **bis jetzt ist noch alles** ~ everything is still quite open; *siehe auch* **darin**.
dringen ['drɪŋən] *unreg vi* (*Wasser, Licht, Kälte*): ~ (**durch/in** +*akk*) to penetrate (through/into); **auf etw** *akk* ~ to insist on sth; **in jdn** ~ (*geh*) to entreat sb.
dringend ['drɪŋənt] *adj* urgent; ~ **empfehlen** to recommend strongly.
dringlich ['drɪŋlɪç] *adj* = **dringend**.
Dringlichkeit *f* urgency.
Dringlichkeitsstufe *f* priority; ~ **1** top priority.
drinnen ['drɪnən] *adv* inside, indoors.
drinstecken ['drɪnʃtɛkən] (*umg*) *vi:* **da steckt eine Menge Arbeit drin** a lot of work has gone into it.
drischt [drɪʃt] *vb siehe* **dreschen**.
dritt *adv:* **wir kommen zu** ~ three of us are coming together.
dritte(r, s) *adj* third; **D~ Welt** Third World; **im Beisein D~r** in the presence of a third party.
Drittel (*-s, -*) *nt* third.
drittens *adv* thirdly.
drittklassig *adj* third-rate, third-class.
Dr.jur. *abk* (= *Doktor der Rechtswissenschaften*) ≈ L.L.D.
DRK (*-*) *nt abk* (= *Deutsches Rotes Kreuz*) ≈ R.C.
Dr.med. *abk* (= *Doktor der Medizin*) ≈ M.D.

droben ['dro:bən] *adv* above, up there.
Droge ['dro:gə] (-, -n) *f* drug.
dröge ['drø:gə] (*NORDD*) *adj* boring.
Drogen- *zW:* **d~abhängig** *adj* addicted to drugs; **~händler(in)** *m(f)* peddler, pusher; **d~süchtig** *adj* addicted to drugs.
Drogerie [drogə'ri:] *f* chemist's shop (*BRIT*), drugstore (*US*).

> The **Drogerie** as opposed to the **Apotheke** sells medicines not requiring a prescription. It tends to be cheaper and also sells cosmetics, perfume and toiletries.

Drogist(in) [dro'gɪst(ɪn)] *m(f)* pharmacist, chemist (*BRIT*).
Drohbrief *m* threatening letter.
drohen ['dro:ən] *vi:* (**jdm**) ~ to threaten (sb).
Drohgebärde *f* (*lit, fig*) threatening gesture.
Drohne ['dro:nə] (-, -n) *f* drone.
dröhnen ['drø:nən] *vi* (*Motor*) to roar; (*Stimme, Musik*) to ring, resound.
Drohung ['dro:ʊŋ] *f* threat.
drollig ['drɔlɪç] *adj* droll.
Drops [drɔps] (-, -) *m od nt* fruit drop.
drosch *etc* [drɔʃ] *vb siehe* **dreschen.**
Droschke ['drɔʃkə] (-, -n) *f* cab.
Droschkenkutscher *m* cabman.
Drossel ['drɔsəl] (-, -n) *f* thrush.
drosseln ['drɔsəln] *vt* (*Motor etc*) to throttle; (*Heizung*) to turn down; (*Strom, Tempo, Produktion etc*) to cut down.
Dr.phil. *abk* (= *Doktor der Geisteswissenschaften*) ≈ Ph.D.
Dr.theol. *abk* (= *Doktor der Theologie*) ≈ D.D.
drüben ['dry:bən] *adv* over there, on the other side.
drüber ['dry:bər] (*umg*) *adv* = **darüber.**
Druck [drʊk] (-(e)s, -e) *m* (*PHYS, Zwang*) pressure; (*TYP: Vorgang*) printing; (: *Produkt*) print; (*fig: Belastung*) burden, weight; ~ **hinter etw** *akk* **machen** to put some pressure on sth; **~buchstabe** *m* block letter; **in ~buchstaben schreiben** to print.
Drückeberger ['drʏkəbergər] (-s, -) *m* shirker, dodger.
drucken ['drʊkən] *vt, vi* (*TYP, COMPUT*) to print.
drücken ['drʏkən] *vt* (*Knopf, Hand*) to press; (*zu eng sein*) to pinch; (*fig: Preise*) to keep down; (: *belasten*) to oppress, weigh down ♦ *vi* to press; to pinch ♦ *vr:* **sich vor etw** *dat* ~ to get out of (doing) sth; **jdm etw in die Hand** ~ to press sth into sb's hand.
drückend *adj* oppressive; (*Last, Steuern*) heavy; (*Armut*) grinding; (*Wetter, Hitze*) oppressive, close.
Drucker (-s, -) *m* printer.
Drücker (-s, -) *m* button; (*Tür~*) handle; (*Gewehr~*) trigger; **am** ~ **sein** *od* **sitzen** (*fig: umg*) to be the key person; **auf den letzten** ~ (*fig: umg*) at the last minute.

Druckerei [drʊkə'raɪ] *f* printing works, press.
Druckerschwärze *f* printer's ink.
Druck- *zW:* **~fahne** *f* galley(-proof); **~fehler** *m* misprint; **~knopf** *m* press stud (*BRIT*), snap fastener; **~kopf** *m* printhead; **~luft** *f* compressed air; **~mittel** *nt* leverage; **d~reif** *adj* ready for printing, passed for press; (*fig*) polished; **~sache** *f* printed matter; **~schrift** *f* printing; (*gedrucktes Werk*) pamphlet; **~taste** *f* push button; **~welle** *f* shock wave.
drum [drʊm] (*umg*) *adv* around; **mit allem D~ und Dran** with all the bits and pieces *pl*; (*Mahlzeit*) with all the trimmings *pl*.
Drumherum *nt* trappings *pl*.
drunten ['drʊntən] *adv* below, down there.
Drüse ['dry:zə] (-, -n) *f* gland.
DSB (-) *m abk* (= *Deutscher Sportbund*) German Sports Association.
Dschungel ['dʒʊŋəl] (-s, -) *m* jungle.
DSD [ ] *nt abk* (= *Duales System Deutschland*) German waste collection and recycling service.

> The **DSD** (*Duales System Deutschland*) is a scheme introduced in Germany for separating domestic refuse into two types so as to reduce environmental damage. Normal refuse is disposed of in the usual way by burning or dumping at land-fill sites; packets and containers with a green spot (**grüner Punkt**) imprinted on them are kept separate and are then collected for recycling.

dt. *abk* = **deutsch.**
DTC (-) *m abk* (= *Deutscher Touring-Automobil-Club*) German motoring organization.
DTP (-) *nt abk* (= *Desktop publishing*) DTP.
Dtzd. *abk* (= *Dutzend*) doz.
du [du:] *pron* (*D~ in Briefen*) you; **mit jdm per** ~ **sein** to be on familiar terms with sb; **D~** *nt*: **jdm das D~ anbieten** to suggest that sb uses "du", suggest that sb uses the familiar form of address.
Dübel ['dy:bəl] (-s, -) *m* plug; (*Holz~*) dowel.
dübeln ['dy:bəln] *vt, vi* to plug.
Dublin ['dablɪn] *nt* Dublin.
ducken ['dʊkən] *vt* (*Kopf*) to duck; (*fig*) to take down a peg or two ♦ *vr* to duck.
Duckmäuser ['dʊkmɔyzər] (-s, -) *m* yes-man.
Dudelsack ['du:dəlzak] *m* bagpipes *pl*.
Duell [du'ɛl] (-s, -e) *nt* duel.
Duett [du'ɛt] (-(e)s, -e) *nt* duet.
Duft [dʊft] (-(e)s, ̈-e) *m* scent, odour (*BRIT*), odor (*US*); **d~en** *vi* to smell, be fragrant.
duftig *adj* (*Stoff, Kleid*) delicate, diaphanous; (*Muster*) fine.
Duftnote *f* (*von Parfüm*) scent.
dulden ['dʊldən] *vt* to suffer; (*zulassen*) to tolerate ♦ *vi* to suffer.
duldsam *adj* tolerant.
dumm [dʊm] *adj* stupid; **das wird mir zu** ~

that's just too much; **der D~e sein** to be the loser; **der ~e August** (*umg*) the clown; **du willst mich wohl für ~ verkaufen** you must think I'm stupid; **sich ~ und dämlich reden** (*umg*) to talk till one is blue in the face; **so etwas D~es** how stupid; what a nuisance; **~dreist** *adj* impudent.

dummerweise *adv* stupidly.

Dummheit *f* stupidity; (*Tat*) blunder, stupid mistake.

Dummkopf *m* blockhead.

dumpf [dʊmpf] *adj* (*Ton*) hollow, dull; (*Luft*) close; (*Erinnerung, Schmerz*) vague; **D~heit** *f* hollowness, dullness; closeness; vagueness.

dumpfig *adj* musty.

Dumpingpreis ['dampɪŋpraɪs] *m* give-away price.

Düne ['dy:nə] (*-, -n*) *f* dune.

Dung [dʊŋ] (*-(e)s*) *m* manure.

düngen ['dyŋən] *vt* to fertilize.

Dünger (*-s, -*) *m* fertilizer; (*Dung*) manure.

dunkel ['dʊŋkəl] *adj* dark; (*Stimme*) deep; (*Ahnung*) vague; (*rätselhaft*) obscure; (*verdächtig*) dubious, shady; **im ~n tappen** (*fig*) to grope in the dark.

Dünkel ['dyŋkəl] (*-s*) *m* self-conceit; **d~haft** *adj* conceited.

Dunkelheit *f* darkness; (*fig*) obscurity; **bei Einbruch der ~** at nightfall.

Dunkelkammer *f* (*PHOT*) dark room.

dunkeln *vi unpers* to grow dark.

Dunkelziffer *f* estimated number of unnotified cases.

dünn [dyn] *adj* thin; **D~darm** *m* small intestine; **~flüssig** *adj* watery, thin; **~gesät** *adj* scarce; **D~heit** *f* thinness; **~machen** (*umg*) *vr* to make o.s. scarce; **D~schiß** (*umg*) *m* the runs.

Dunst [dʊnst] (*-es, ⁻e*) *m* vapour (*BRIT*), vapor (*US*); (*Wetter*) haze; **~abzugshaube** *f* extractor hood.

dünsten ['dynstən] *vt* to steam.

Dunstglocke *f* haze; (*Smog*) pall of smog.

dunstig ['dʊnstɪç] *adj* vaporous; (*Wetter*) hazy, misty.

düpieren [dy'pi:rən] *vt* to dupe.

Duplikat [dupli'ka:t] (*-(e)s, -e*) *nt* duplicate.

Dur [du:r] (*-, -*) *nt* (*MUS*) major.

===================== *SCHLÜSSELWORT*

durch [dʊrç] *präp +akk* **1** (*hindurch*) through; **~ den Urwald** through the jungle; **~ die ganze Welt reisen** to travel all over the world

2 (*mittels*) through, by (means of); (*aufgrund*) due to, owing to; **Tod ~ Herzschlag/den Strang** death from a heart attack/by hanging; **~ die Post** by post; **~ seine Bemühungen** through his efforts

♦ *adj* **1** (*hin~*) through; **die ganze Nacht ~** all through the night; **den Sommer ~** during the summer; **8 Uhr ~** past 8 o'clock; **~ und**

~ completely; **das geht mir ~ und ~** that goes right through me

2 (*KOCH: umg: durchgebraten*) done; **(gut) ~** well-done.

durcharbeiten *vt, vi* to work through ♦ *vr*: **sich durch etw ~** to work one's way through sth.

durchatmen *vi* to breathe deeply.

durchaus [dʊrç'aʊs] *adv* completely; (*unbedingt*) definitely; **~ nicht** (*in verneinten Sätzen: als Verstärkung*) by no means; (: *als Antwort*) not at all; **das läßt sich ~ machen** that sounds feasible; **ich bin ~ Ihrer Meinung** I quite *od* absolutely agree with you.

durchbeißen *unreg vt* to bite through ♦ *vr* (*fig*) to battle on.

durchblättern *vt* to leaf through.

Durchblick ['dʊrçblɪk] *m* view; (*fig*) comprehension; **den ~ haben** (*fig: umg*) to know what's what.

durchblicken *vi* to look through; (*umg: verstehen*): **(bei etw) ~** to understand (sth); **etw ~ lassen** (*fig*) to hint at sth.

Durchblutung [dʊrç'blu:tʊŋ] *f* circulation (of blood).

durchbohren *vt untr* to bore through, pierce.

durchboxen ['dʊrçbɔksən] *vr* (*fig: umg*): **sich (durch etw) ~** to fight one's way through (sth).

durchbrechen¹ ['dʊrçbrɛçən] *unreg vt, vi* to break.

durchbrechen² [dʊrç'brɛçən] *unreg vt untr* (*Schranken*) to break through.

durchbrennen *unreg vi* (*Draht, Sicherung*) to burn through; (*umg*) to run away.

durchbringen *unreg vt* to get through; (*Geld*) to squander ♦ *vr* to make a living.

Durchbruch ['dʊrçbrʊx] *m* (*Öffnung*) opening; (*MIL*) breach; (*von Gefühlen etc*) eruption; (*der Zähne*) cutting; (*fig*) breakthrough; **zum ~ kommen** to break through.

durchdacht [dʊrç'daxt] *adj* well thought-out.

durchdenken *unreg vt untr* to think out.

durch- *zW:* **~diskutieren** *vt* to talk over, discuss; **~drängen** *vr* to force one's way through; **~drehen** *vt* (*Fleisch*) to mince ♦ *vi* (*umg*) to crack up.

durchdringen¹ ['dʊrçdrɪŋən] *unreg vi* to penetrate, get through.

durchdringen² [dʊrç'drɪŋən] *unreg vt untr* to penetrate.

durchdringend *adj* piercing; (*Kälte, Wind*) biting; (*Geruch*) pungent.

durchdrücken ['dʊrçdrʏkən] *vt* (*durch Presse*) to press through; (*Creme, Teig*) to pipe; (*fig: Gesetz, Reformen etc*) to push through; (*seinen Willen*) to get; (*Knie, Kreuz etc*) to straighten.

durcheinander [dʊrçaɪ'nandər] *adv* in a mess, in confusion; (*verwirrt*) confused; **~ trinken** to mix one's drinks; **D~** (*-s*) *nt* (*Verwirrung*) confusion; (*Unordnung*) mess; ~**bringen** *unreg vt* to mess up; (*verwirren*) to confuse; ~**reden** *vi* to talk at the same time; ~**werfen** *unreg vt* to muddle up.

durch- *zW:* ~**fahren** *unreg vi:* **er ist bei Rot** ~**gefahren** he jumped the lights ♦ *vt:* **die Nacht** ~**fahren** to travel through the night; **D~fahrt** *f* transit; (*Verkehr*) thoroughfare; **D~fahrt bitte freihalten!** please keep access free; **D~fahrt verboten!** no through road; **D~fall** *m* (*MED*) diarrhoea (*BRIT*), diarrhea (*US*); ~**fallen** *unreg vi* to fall through; (*in Prüfung*) to fail; ~**finden** *unreg vr* to find one's way through; ~**fliegen** *unreg* (*umg*) *vi* (*in Prüfung*): (**durch etw** *od* **in etw** *dat*) ~**fliegen** to fail (sth); **D~flug** *m:* **Passagiere auf dem D~flug** transit passengers.

durchforschen *vt untr* to explore.

durchforsten [dʊrç'fɔrstən] *vt untr* (*fig: Akten etc*) to go through.

durchfragen *vr* to find one's way by asking.

durchfressen *unreg vr* to eat one's way through.

durchführbar *adj* feasible, practicable.

durchführen ['dʊrçfyːrən] *vt* to carry out; (*Gesetz*) to implement; (*Kursus*) to run.

Durchführung *f* execution, performance.

Durchgang ['dʊrçgaŋ] *m* passage(way); (*bei Produktion, Versuch*) run; (*SPORT*) round; (*bei Wahl*) ballot; ~ **verboten** no thoroughfare.

durchgängig ['dʊrçgɛŋɪç] *adj* universal, general.

Durchgangs- *zW:* ~**handel** *m* transit trade; ~**lager** *nt* transit camp; ~**stadium** *nt* transitory stage; ~**verkehr** *m* through traffic.

durchgeben ['dʊrçgeːbən] *unreg vt* (*RUNDF, TV: Hinweis, Wetter*) to give; (*Lottozahlen*) to announce.

durchgefroren ['dʊrçgəfroːrən] *adj* (*See*) completely frozen; (*Mensch*) frozen stiff.

durchgehen ['dʊrçgeːən] *unreg vt* (*behandeln*) to go over *od* through ♦ *vi* to go through; (*ausreißen: Pferd*) to break loose; (*Mensch*) to run away; **mein Temperament ging mit mir durch** my temper got the better of me; **jdm etw ~ lassen** to let sb get away with sth.

durchgehend *adj* (*Zug*) through; (*Öffnungszeiten*) continuous.

durchgeschwitzt ['dʊrçgəʃvɪtst] *adj* soaked in sweat.

durch- *zW:* ~**greifen** *unreg vi* to take strong action; ~**halten** *unreg vi* to last out ♦ *vt* to keep up; **D~haltevermögen** *nt* staying power; ~**hängen** *unreg vi* (*lit, fig*) to sag; ~**hecheln** (*umg*) *vt* to gossip about; ~**kommen** *unreg vi* to get through; (*überleben*) to pull through.

durchkreuzen *vt untr* to thwart, frustrate.

durchlassen *unreg vt* (*Person*) to let through; (*Wasser*) to let in.

durchlässig *adj* leaky.

Durchlaucht ['dʊrçlaʊxt] (*-, -en*) *f:* (**Euer**) ~ Your Highness.

Durchlauf ['dʊrçlaʊf] *m* (*COMPUT*) run.

durchlaufen *unreg vt untr* (*Schule, Phase*) to go through.

Durchlauferhitzer (*-s, -*) *m* continuous-flow water heater.

Durchlaufzeit *f* (*COMPUT*) length of the run.

durch- *zW:* ~**leben** *vt untr* (*Zeit*) to live *od* go through; (*Jugend, Gefühl*) to experience; ~**lesen** *unreg vt* to read through; ~**leuchten** *vt untr* to X-ray; ~**löchern** *vt untr* to perforate; (*mit Löchern*) to punch holes in; (*mit Kugeln*) to riddle; ~**machen** *vt* to go through; **die Nacht** ~**machen** to make a night of it.

Durchmarsch *m* march through.

Durchmesser (*-s, -*) *m* diameter.

durchnässen *vt untr* to soak (through).

durch- *zW:* ~**nehmen** *unreg vt* to go over; ~**numerieren** *vt* to number consecutively; ~**organisieren** *vt* to organize down to the last detail; ~**pausen** *vt* to trace; ~**peitschen** *vt* (*lit*) to whip soundly; (*fig: Gesetzentwurf, Reform*) to force through.

durchqueren [dʊrç'kveːrən] *vt untr* to cross.

durch- *zW:* ~**rechnen** *vt* to calculate; ~**regnen** *vi unpers:* **es regnet durchs Dach** ~ the rain is coming through the roof; **D~reiche** (*-, -n*) *f* (serving) hatch, pass-through (*US*); **D~reise** *f* transit; **auf der D~reise** passing through; (*Güter*) in transit; **D~reisevisum** *nt* transit visa; ~**ringen** *unreg vr* to make up one's mind finally; ~**rosten** *vi* to rust through; ~**rutschen** *vi:* (**durch etw**) ~**rutschen** (*lit*) to slip through (sth); (*bei Prüfung*) to scrape through (sth).

durchs [dʊrçs] = **durch das.**

Durchsage ['dʊrçzaːgə] *f* intercom *od* radio announcement.

Durchsatz ['dʊrçzats] *m* (*COMPUT, Produktion*) throughput.

durchschauen¹ ['dʊrçʃaʊən] *vt, vi* (*lit*) to look *od* see through.

durchschauen² [dʊrç'ʃaʊən] *vt untr* (*Person, Lüge*) to see through.

durchscheinen ['dʊrçʃaɪnən] *unreg vi* to shine through.

durchscheinend *adj* translucent.

durchschlafen ['dʊrçʃlaːfən] *unreg vi* to sleep through.

Durchschlag ['dʊrçʃlaːk] *m* (*Doppel*) carbon copy; (*Sieb*) strainer.

durchschlagen *unreg vt* (*entzweischlagen*) to split (in two); (*sieben*) to sieve ♦ *vi* (*zum Vorschein kommen*) to emerge, come out ♦ *vr* to get by.

durchschlagend *adj* resounding; (**eine**) ~**e Wirkung haben** to be totally effective.

Durchschlagpapier *nt* flimsy; (*Kohlepapier*) carbon paper.

Durchschlagskraft *f* (*von Geschoß*) penetration; (*fig: von Argument*) decisiveness.

durch- zW: **~schlängeln** vr (durch etw: Mensch) to thread one's way through; **~schlüpfen** vi to slip through; **~schneiden** unreg vt to cut through.

Durchschnitt ['dʊrçʃnɪt] m (Mittelwert) average; **über/unter dem ~** above/below average; **im ~** on average; **d~lich** adj average; **d~lich begabt/groß** etc of average ability/height etc.

Durchschnitts- zW: **~geschwindigkeit** f average speed; **~mensch** m average man, man in the street; **~wert** m average.

durch- zW: **D~schrift** f copy; **D~schuß** m (Loch) bullet hole; **~schwimmen** unreg vt untr to swim across; **~segeln** (umg) vi (nicht bestehen): **durch** od **bei etw ~segeln** to fail od flunk (umg) (sth); **~sehen** unreg vt to look through.

durchsetzen¹ ['dʊrçzɛtsən] vt to enforce ♦ vr (Erfolg haben) to succeed; (sich behaupten) to get one's way; **seinen Kopf ~** to get one's own way.

durchsetzen² [dʊrç'zɛtsən] vt untr to mix.

Durchsicht ['dʊrçzɪçt] f looking through, checking.

durchsichtig adj transparent; **D~keit** f transparency.

durch- zW: **~sickern** vi to seep through; (fig) to leak out; **~sieben** vt to sieve; **~sitzen** unreg vt (Sessel etc) to wear out (the seat of); **~spielen** vt to go od run through; **~sprechen** unreg vt to talk over; **~stehen** unreg vt to live through; **D~stehvermögen** nt endurance, staying power; **~stellen** vt (TEL) to put through; **~stöbern** [-'ʃtøːbərn] vt untr to ransack, search through; **~stoßen** unreg vt, vi to break through (auch MIL); **~streichen** unreg vt to cross out; **~stylen** vt to ponce up (umg); **~suchen** vt untr to search; **D~suchung** f search; **D~suchungsbefehl** m search warrant; **~trainieren** vt (Sportler, Körper): **gut ~trainiert** in superb condition; **~tränken** vt untr to soak; **~treten** unreg vt (Pedal) to step on; (Starter) to kick; **~trieben** adj cunning, wily; **~wachsen** adj (lit: Speck) streaky; (fig: mittelmäßig) so-so.

Durchwahl ['dʊrçvaːl] f (TEL) direct dialling; (bei Firma) extension.

durch- zW: **~weg** adv throughout, completely; **~wursteln** (umg) vr to muddle through; **~zählen** vt to count ♦ vi to count od number off; **~zechen** vt untr: **eine ~zechte Nacht** a night of drinking; **~ziehen** unreg vt (Faden) to draw through ♦ vi to pass through; **eine Sache ~ziehen** to finish off sth; **~zucken** vt untr to shoot od flash through; **D~zug** m (Luft) draught (BRIT), draft (US); (von Truppen, Vögeln) passage; **~zwängen** vt, vr to squeeze od force through.

dürfen ['dʏrfən] unreg vi **1** (Erlaubnis haben) to be allowed to; **ich darf das** I'm allowed to (do that); **darf ich?** may I?; **darf ich ins Kino?** can od may I go to the cinema?; **es darf geraucht werden** you may smoke

2 (in Verneinungen): **er darf das nicht** he's not allowed to (do that); **das darf nicht geschehen** that must not happen; **da darf sie sich nicht wundern** that shouldn't surprise her; **das darf doch nicht wahr sein!** that can't be true!

3 (in Höflichkeitsformeln): **darf ich Sie bitten, das zu tun?** may od could I ask you to do that?; **wir freuen uns, Ihnen mitteilen zu ~** we are pleased to be able to tell you; **was darf es sein?** what can I get for you?

4 (können): **das ~ Sie mir glauben** you can believe me

5 (Möglichkeit): **das dürfte genug sein** that should be enough; **es dürfte Ihnen bekannte sein, daß ...** as you will probably know ...

durfte etc ['dʊrftə] vb siehe **dürfen.**

dürftig ['dʏrftɪç] adj (ärmlich) needy, poor; (unzulänglich) inadequate.

dürr [dʏr] adj dried-up; (Land) arid; (mager) skinny.

Dürre (-, -n) f aridity; (Zeit) drought.

Durst [dʊrst] (-(e)s) m thirst; **~ haben** to be thirsty; **einen über den ~ getrunken haben** (umg) to have had one too many.

durstig adj thirsty.

Durststrecke f hard times pl.

Dusche ['dʊʃə] (-, -n) f shower; **das war eine kalte ~** (fig) that really brought him/her etc down with a bump.

duschen vi, vr to have a shower.

Duschgelegenheit f shower facilities pl.

Düse ['dyːzə] (-, -n) f nozzle; (Flugzeug~) jet.

Dusel ['duːzəl] (umg) m: **da hat er (einen) ~ gehabt** he was lucky.

Düsen- zW: **~antrieb** m jet propulsion; **~flugzeug** nt jet (plane); **~jäger** m jet fighter.

Dussel ['dʊsəl] (-s, -) (umg) m twit, berk.

Düsseldorf ['dʏsəldɔrf] nt Dusseldorf.

dusselig ['dʊsəlɪç] (umg) adj stupid.

dußlig ['dʊslɪç] (umg) adj stupid.

düster ['dyːstər] adj dark; (Gedanken, Zukunft) gloomy; **D~keit** f darkness, gloom; gloominess.

Dutzend ['dʊtsənt] (-s, -e) nt dozen; **d~(e)mal** adv a dozen times; **~ware** (pej) f (cheap) mass-produced item; **d~weise** adv by the dozen.

duzen ['duːtsən] vt to address with the familiar "du" form ♦ vr to address each other with the familiar "du" form; siehe auch **siezen.**

There are two different forms of address in German: du and Sie. **Duzen** means addressing someone as 'du' and **siezen** means addressing someone as 'Sie'. 'Du' is used to address children, family and close friends. Students almost always use 'du' to each other. 'Sie' is used for all grown-ups and older teenagers.

Duzfreund *m* good friend.

Dynamik [dy'na:mɪk] *f* (*PHYS*) dynamics; (*fig: Schwung*) momentum; (*von Mensch*) dynamism.

dynamisch [dy'na:mɪʃ] *adj* (*lit, fig*) dynamic; (*renten~*) index-linked.

Dynamit [dyna'mi:t] (**-s**) *nt* dynamite.

Dynamo [dy'na:mo] (**-s, -s**) *m* dynamo.

dz *abk* = **Doppelzentner**.

D-Zug ['de:tsu:k] *m* through train; **ein alter Mann ist doch kein ~-~** (*umg*) I am going as fast as I can.

===== *E, e* =====

E¹, e [e:] *nt* E, e; **~ wie Emil** ≈ E for Edward, E for Easy (*US*).

E² [e:] *abk* = **Eilzug; Europastraße**.

Ebbe ['ɛbə] (**-, -n**) *f* low tide; **~ und Flut** ebb and flow.

eben ['e:bən] *adj* level; (*glatt*) smooth ♦ *adv* just; (*bestätigend*) exactly; **das ist ~ so** that's just the way it is; **mein Bleistift war doch ~ noch da** my pencil was there (just) a minute ago; **~ deswegen** just because of that.

Ebenbild *nt*: **das genaue ~ seines Vaters** the spitting image of his father.

ebenbürtig *adj*: **jdm ~ sein** to be sb's peer.

Ebene (**-, -n**) *f* plain; (*MATH, PHYS*) plane; (*fig*) level.

eben- *zW*: **~erdig** *adj* at ground level; **~falls** *adv* likewise; **E~heit** *f* levelness; (*Glätte*) smoothness; **E~holz** *nt* ebony; **~so** *adv* just as; **~sogut** *adv* just as well; **~sooft** *adv* just as often; **~soviel** *adv* just as much; **~soweit** *adv* just as far; **~sowenig** *adv* just as little.

Eber ['e:bər] (**-s, -**) *m* boar.

Eberesche *f* mountain ash, rowan.

ebnen ['e:bnən] *vt* to level; **jdm den Weg ~** (*fig*) to smooth the way for sb.

Echo ['ɛço] (**-s, -s**) *nt* echo; (**bei jdm**) **ein lebhaftes ~ finden** (*fig*) to meet with a lively response (from sb).

Echolot ['ɛçolo:t] *nt* (*NAUT*) echo-sounder, sonar.

Echse ['ɛksə] (**-, -n**) *f* (*ZOOL*) lizard.

echt [ɛçt] *adj* genuine; (*typisch*) typical; **ich hab' ~ keine Zeit** (*umg*) I really don't have any time; **E~heit** *f* genuineness.

Eckball ['ɛkbal] *m* corner (kick).

Ecke ['ɛkə] (**-, -n**) *f* corner; (*MATH*) angle; **gleich um die ~** just around the corner; **an allen ~n und Enden sparen** (*umg*) to pinch and scrape; **jdn um die ~ bringen** (*umg*) to bump sb off; **mit jdm um ein paar ~n herum verwandt sein** (*umg*) to be distantly related to sb, be sb's second cousin twice removed (*hum*).

eckig *adj* angular.

Eckzahn *m* eye tooth.

Eckzins *m* (*FIN*) minimum lending rate.

Ecstasy ['ɛkstəsi] *nt* (*Droge*) ecstasy.

ECU [e'ky:] (**-(s), -(s)**) *m* (*FIN*) ecu.

Ecuador [ekua'do:r] (**-s**) *nt* Ecuador.

edel ['e:dəl] *adj* noble; **E~ganove** *m* gentleman criminal; **E~gas** *nt* rare gas; **E~metall** *nt* rare metal; **E~stein** *m* precious stone.

Edinburg(h) ['e:dɪnburk] *nt* Edinburgh.

EDV (**-**) *f abk* (= **elektronische Datenverarbeitung**) EDP.

EEG (**-**) *nt abk* (= **Elektroenzephalogramm**) EEG.

Efeu ['e:fɔy] (**-s**) *m* ivy.

Effeff [ɛf'|ɛf] (**-**) (*umg*) *nt*: **etw aus dem ~ können** to be able to do sth standing on one's head.

Effekt [ɛ'fɛkt] (**-(e)s, -e**) *m* effect.

Effekten [ɛ'fɛktən] *pl* stocks *pl*; **~börse** *f* Stock Exchange.

Effekthascherei [ɛfɛkthaʃə'raɪ] *f* sensationalism.

effektiv [ɛfɛk'ti:f] *adj* effective, actual.

Effet [ɛ'fe:] (**-s**) *m* spin.

EG (**-**) *f abk* (= **Europäische Gemeinschaft**) EC.

egal [e'ga:l] *adj* all the same; **das ist mir ganz ~** it's all the same to me.

egalitär [egali'tɛ:r] *adj* (*geh*) egalitarian.

Egge ['ɛgə] (**-, -n**) *f* (*AGR*) harrow.

Egoismus [ego'ɪsmʊs] *m* selfishness, egoism.

Egoist(in) *m(f)* egoist; **e~isch** *adj* selfish, egoistic.

egozentrisch [ego'tsɛntrɪʃ] *adj* egocentric, self-centred (*BRIT*), self-centered (*US*).

eh [e:] *adv*: **seit ~ und je** for ages, since the year dot (*umg*); **ich komme ~ nicht dazu** I won't get around to it anyway.

e.h. *abk* = **ehrenhalber**.

Ehe ['e:ə] (**-, -n**) *f* marriage; **die ~ eingehen** (*form*) to enter into matrimony; **sie leben in wilder ~** (*veraltet*) they are living in sin.

ehe *konj* before.

Ehe- *zW*: **~brecher** (**-s, -**) *m* adulterer; **~brecherin** *f* adulteress; **~bruch** *m* adultery; **~frau** *f* wife; **~leute** *pl* married couple *pl*; **e~lich** *adj* matrimonial; (*Kind*) legitimate.

ehemalig *adj* former.

ehemals *adv* formerly.

Ehe- *zW:* ~**mann** *m* married man; (*Partner*) husband; ~**paar** *nt* married couple; ~**partner** *m* husband; ~**partnerin** *f* wife.

eher ['eːər] *adv* (*früher*) sooner; (*lieber*) rather, sooner; (*mehr*) more; **nicht** ~ **als** not before; **um so** ~, **als** the more so because.

Ehe- *zW:* ~**ring** *m* wedding ring; ~**scheidung** *f* divorce; ~**schließung** *f* marriage; ~**stand** *m*: **in den** ~**stand treten** (*form*) to enter into matrimony.

eheste(r, s) ['eːəstə(r, s)] *adj* (*früheste*) first, earliest; **am** ~**n** (*am liebsten*) soonest; (*meist*) most; (*am wahrscheinlichsten*) most probably.

Ehevermittlung *f* (*Büro*) marriage bureau.

Eheversprechen *nt* (*JUR*) promise to marry.

ehrbar ['eːrbaːr] *adj* honourable (*BRIT*), honorable (*US*), respectable.

Ehre (-, -n) *f* honour (*BRIT*), honor (*US*); **etw in** ~**n halten** to treasure *od* cherish sth.

ehren *vt* to honour (*BRIT*), honor (*US*).

Ehren- *zW:* **e**~**amtlich** *adj* honorary; ~**bürgerrecht** *nt:* **die Stadt verlieh ihr das** ~**bürgerrecht** she was given the freedom of the city; ~**gast** *m* guest of honour (*BRIT*) *od* honor (*US*); **e**~**haft** *adj* honourable (*BRIT*), honorable (*US*); **e**~**halber** *adv:* **er wurde e**~**halber zum Vorsitzenden auf Lebenszeit ernannt** he was made honorary president for life; ~**mann** *m* man of honour (*BRIT*) *od* honor (*US*); ~**mitglied** *nt* honorary member; ~**platz** *m* place of honour (*BRIT*) *od* honor (*US*); ~**rechte** *pl* civic rights *pl*; **e**~**rührig** *adj* defamatory; ~**runde** *f* lap of honour (*BRIT*) *od* honor (*US*); ~**sache** *f* point of honour (*BRIT*) *od* honor (*US*); ~**sache!** (*umg*) you can count on me; ~**tag** *m* (*Geburtstag*) birthday; (*großer Tag*) big day; **e**~**voll** *adj* honourable (*BRIT*), honorable (*US*); ~**wort** *nt* word of honour (*BRIT*) *od* honor (*US*); **Urlaub auf** ~**wort** parole.

Ehr- *zW:* **e**~**erbietig** *adj* respectful; ~**furcht** *f* awe, deep respect; **e**~**furchtgebietend** *adj* awesome; (*Stimme*) authoritative; ~**gefühl** *nt* sense of honour (*BRIT*) *od* honor (*US*); ~**geiz** *m* ambition; **e**~**geizig** *adj* ambitious; **e**~**lich** *adj* honest; **e**~**lich verdientes Geld** hard-earned money; **e**~**lich gesagt** ... quite frankly *od* honestly ...; ~**lichkeit** *f* honesty; **e**~**los** *adj* dishonourable (*BRIT*), dishonorable (*US*).

Ehrung *f* honour(ing) (*BRIT*), honor(ing) (*US*).

ehrwürdig *adj* venerable.

Ei [aɪ] (-(e)s, -er) *nt* egg; **Eier** *pl* (*umg!: Hoden*) balls *pl* (*!*); **jdn wie ein rohes** ~ **behandeln** (*fig*) to handle sb with kid gloves; **wie aus dem** ~ **gepellt aussehen** (*umg*) to look spruce.

ei *interj* well, well; (*beschwichtigend*) now, now.

Eibe ['aɪbə] (-, -n) *f* (*BOT*) yew.

Eichamt ['aɪç|amt] *nt* Office of Weights and Measures.

Eiche (-, -n) *f* oak (tree).

Eichel (-, -n) *f* acorn; (*KARTEN*) club; (*ANAT*) glans.

eichen *vt* to calibrate.

Eichhörnchen *nt* squirrel.

Eichmaß *nt* standard.

Eichung *f* standardization.

Eid ['aɪt] (-(e)s, -e) *m* oath; **eine Erklärung an** ~**es Statt abgeben** (*JUR*) to make a solemn declaration.

Eidechse ['aɪdɛksə] (-, -n) *f* lizard.

eidesstattlich *adj:* ~**e Erklärung** affidavit.

Eid- *zW:* ~**genosse** *m* Swiss; ~**genossenschaft** *f:* **Schweizerische** ~**genossenschaft** Swiss Confederation; **e**~**lich** *adj* (sworn) upon oath.

Eidotter *nt* egg yolk.

Eier- *zW:* ~**becher** *m* egg cup; ~**kuchen** *m* pancake; (*Omelett*) omelette (*BRIT*), omelet (*US*); ~**likör** *m* advocaat.

eiern ['aɪərn] (*umg*) *vi* to wobble.

Eier- *zW:* ~**schale** *f* eggshell; ~**stock** *m* ovary; ~**uhr** *f* egg timer.

Eifel ['aɪfəl] (-) *f* Eifel (Mountains).

Eifer ['aɪfər] (-s) *m* zeal, enthusiasm; **mit großem** ~ **bei der Sache sein** to put one's heart into it; **im** ~ **des Gefechts** (*fig*) in the heat of the moment; ~**sucht** *f* jealousy; **e**~**süchtig** *adj:* **e**~**süchtig (auf** +*akk*) jealous (of).

eifrig ['aɪfrɪç] *adj* zealous, enthusiastic.

Eigelb ['aɪgɛlp] (-(e)s, -e *od* -) *nt* egg yolk.

eigen ['aɪgən] *adj* own; (~*artig*) peculiar; (*ordentlich*) particular; (*übergenau*) fussy; **ich möchte kurz in** ~**er Sache sprechen** I would like to say something on my own account; **mit dem ihm** ~**en Lächeln** with that smile peculiar to him; **sich** *dat* **etw zu** ~ **machen** to make sth one's own; ~**art** *f* (*Besonderheit*) peculiarity; (*Eigenschaft*) characteristic; ~**artig** *adj* peculiar; **E**~**bau** *m*: **er fährt ein Fahrrad Marke E**~**bau** (*hum: umg*) he rides a home-made bike; **E**~**bedarf** *m* one's own requirements *pl*; **E**~**brötler(in)** (-s, -) *m(f)* loner, lone wolf; (*komischer Kauz*) oddball (*umg*); **E**~**gewicht** *nt* dead weight; ~**händig** *adj* with one's own hand; **E**~**heim** *nt* owner-occupied house; **E**~**heit** *f* peculiarity; **E**~**initiative** *f* initiative of one's own; **E**~**kapital** *nt* personal capital; (*von Firma*) company capital; **E**~**lob** *nt* self-praise; ~**mächtig** *adj* high-handed; (~*verantwortlich*) taken/done *etc* on one's own authority; (*unbefugt*) unauthorized; **E**~**name** *m* proper name; **E**~**nutz** *m* self-interest.

eigens *adv* expressly, on purpose.

eigen- *zW:* **E**~**schaft** *f* quality, property, attribute; **E**~**schaftswort** *nt* adjective; **E**~**sinn** *m* obstinacy; ~**sinnig** *adj* obstinate; ~**ständig** *adj* independent; **E**~**ständigkeit** *f* independence.

eigentlich *adj* actual, real ◆ *adv* actually, really; **was willst du ~ hier?** what do you want here anyway?

eigen- *zW:* **E~tor** *nt* own goal; **E~tum** *nt* property; **E~tümer(in)** **(-s, -)** *m(f)* owner, proprietor; **~tümlich** *adj* peculiar; **E~tümlichkeit** *f* peculiarity.

Eigentumsdelikt *nt* (*JUR: Diebstahl*) theft.

Eigentumswohnung *f* freehold flat.

eigenwillig *adj* with a mind of one's own.

eignen ['aɪgnən] *vr* to be suited.

Eignung *f* suitability.

Eignungsprüfung *f* aptitude test.

Eignungstest **(-(e)s, -s** *od* **-e)** *m* aptitude test.

Eilbote *m* courier; **per** *od* **durch ~n** express.

Eilbrief *m* express letter.

Eile **(-)** *f* haste; **es hat keine ~** there's no hurry.

Eileiter ['aɪlaɪtər] *m* (*ANAT*) Fallopian tube.

eilen *vi* (*Mensch*) to hurry; (*dringend sein*) to be urgent.

eilends *adv* hastily.

Eilgut *nt* express goods *pl*, fast freight (*US*).

eilig *adj* hasty, hurried; (*dringlich*) urgent; **es ~ haben** to be in a hurry.

Eil- *zW:* **~tempo** *nt:* **etw im ~tempo machen** to do sth in a rush; **~zug** *m* fast stopping train; **~zustellung** *f* special delivery.

Eimer ['aɪmər] **(-s, -)** *m* bucket, pail; **im ~ sein** (*umg*) to be up the spout.

ein(e) ['aɪn(ə)] *num* one ◆ *indef art* a, an ◆ *adv:* **nicht ~ noch aus wissen** not to know what to do; **E~/Aus** (*an Geräten*) on/off; **er ist ihr ~ und alles** he means everything to her; **er geht bei uns ~ und aus** he is always round at our place.

einander [aɪ'nandər] *pron* one another, each other.

einarbeiten ['aɪn|arbaɪtən] *vr:* **sich (in etw** *akk*) **~** to familiarize o.s. (with sth).

Einarbeitungszeit *f* training period.

einarmig ['aɪn|armɪç] *adj* one-armed.

einäschern ['aɪn|ɛʃərn] *vt* (*Leichnam*) to cremate; (*Stadt etc*) to reduce to ashes.

einatmen ['aɪn|aːtmən] *vt, vi* to inhale, breathe in.

einäugig ['aɪn|ɔʏgɪç] *adj* one-eyed.

Einbahnstraße ['aɪnbaːnʃtrasə] *f* one-way street.

Einband ['aɪnbant] *m* binding, cover.

einbändig ['aɪnbɛndɪç] *adj* one-volume.

einbauen ['aɪnbauən] *vt* to build in; (*Motor*) to install, fit.

Einbau- *zW:* **~küche** *f* (fully-)fitted kitchen; **~möbel** *pl* built-in furniture *sing*; **~schrank** *m* fitted cupboard.

einbegriffen ['aɪnbəgrɪfən] *adj* included, inclusive.

einbehalten ['aɪnbəhaltən] *unreg vt* to keep back.

einberufen *unreg vt* to convene; (*MIL*) to call up (*BRIT*), draft (*US*).

Einberufung *f* convocation; call-up (*BRIT*), draft (*US*).

Einberufungsbefehl *m*, **Einberufungs- bescheid** *m* (*MIL*) call-up (*BRIT*) *od* draft (*US*) papers *pl*.

einbetten ['aɪnbɛtən] *vt* to embed.

Einbettzimmer *nt* single room.

einbeziehen ['aɪnbətsiːən] *unreg vt* to include.

einbiegen ['aɪnbiːgən] *unreg vi* to turn.

einbilden ['aɪnbɪldən] *vr:* **sich** *dat* **etw ~** to imagine sth; **sich** *dat* **viel auf etw** *akk* **~** (*stolz sein*) to be conceited about sth.

Einbildung *f* imagination; (*Dünkel*) conceit.

Einbildungskraft *f* imagination.

einbinden ['aɪnbɪndən] *unreg vt* to bind (up).

einblenden ['aɪnblɛndən] *vt* to fade in.

einbleuen ['aɪnblɔʏən] (*umg*) *vt:* **jdm etw ~** to hammer sth into sb.

Einblick ['aɪnblɪk] *m* insight; **~ in die Akten nehmen** to examine the files; **jdm ~ in etw** *akk* **gewähren** to allow sb to look at sth.

einbrechen ['aɪnbrɛçən] *unreg vi* (*einstürzen*) to fall in; (*Einbruch verüben*) to break in; **bei ~der Dunkelheit** at nightfall.

Einbrecher **(-s, -)** *m* burglar.

einbringen ['aɪnbrɪŋən] *unreg vt* to bring in; (*Geld, Vorteil*) to yield; (*mitbringen*) to contribute; **das bringt nichts ein** (*fig*) it's not worth it.

einbrocken ['aɪnbrɔkən] (*umg*) *vt:* **jdm/sich etwas ~** to land sb/o.s. in it.

Einbruch ['aɪnbrux] *m* (*Haus~*) break-in, burglary; (*des Winters*) onset; (*Einsturz, FIN*) collapse; (*MIL: in Front*) breakthrough; **bei ~ der Nacht** at nightfall.

einbruchssicher *adj* burglar-proof.

Einbuchtung ['aɪnbuxtuŋ] *f* indentation; (*Bucht*) inlet, bay.

einbürgern ['aɪnbyrgərn] *vt* to naturalize ◆ *vr* to become adopted; **das hat sich so eingebürgert** that's become a custom.

Einbürgerung *f* naturalization.

Einbuße ['aɪnbuːsə] *f* loss, forfeiture.

einbüßen ['aɪnbyːsən] *vt* to lose, forfeit.

einchecken ['aɪntʃɛkən] *vt, vi* to check in.

eincremen ['aɪnkreːmən] *vt* to put cream on.

eindämmen ['aɪndɛmən] *vt* (*Fluß*) to dam; (*fig*) to check, contain.

eindecken ['aɪndɛkən] *vr:* **sich ~ (mit)** to lay in stocks (of) ◆ *vt* (*umg: überhäufen*): **mit Arbeit eingedeckt sein** to be inundated with work.

eindeutig ['aɪndɔʏtɪç] *adj* unequivocal.

eindeutschen ['aɪndɔʏtʃən] *vt* (*Fremdwort*) to Germanize.

eindösen ['aɪndøːzən] (*umg*) *vi* to doze off.

eindringen ['aɪndrɪŋən] *unreg vi:* **~ (in** +*akk*) to force one's way in(to); (*in Haus*) to break in(to); (*in Land*) to invade; (*Gas, Wasser*) to penetrate; **auf jdn ~** (*mit Bitten*) to pester sb.

eindringlich *adj* forcible, urgent; **ich habe ihn ~ gebeten ...** I urged him ...

Eindringling *m* intruder.

Eindruck ['aındruk] *m* impression.
eindrücken ['aındrykən] *vt* to press in.
eindrucksfähig *adj* impressionable.
eindrucksvoll *adj* impressive.
eine(r, s) *pron* one; (*jemand*) someone; **wie kann ~r nur so dumm sein!** how could anybody be so stupid!; **es kam ~s zum anderen** it was (just) one thing after another; **sich** *dat* **~n genehmigen** (*umg*) to have a quick one.
einebnen ['aın|e:bnən] *vt* (*lit*) to level (off); (*fig*) to level out.
Einehe ['aın|e:ə] *f* monogamy.
eineiig ['aın|aıç] *adj* (*Zwillinge*) identical.
eineinhalb ['aın|aın'halp] *num* one and a half.
einengen ['aın|ɛŋən] *vt* to confine, restrict.
Einer ['aınər] (-) *m* (*MATH*) unit; (*Ruderboot*) single scull.
Einerlei ['aınər'laı] (-s) *nt* monotony; **e~** *adj* (*gleichartig*) the same kind of; **es ist mir e~** it is all the same to me.
einerseits *adv* on the one hand.
einfach ['aınfax] *adj* simple; (*nicht mehrfach*) single ♦ *adv* simply; **E~heit** *f* simplicity.
einfädeln ['aınfɛ:dəln] *vt* (*Nadel*) to thread; (*fig*) to contrive.
einfahren ['aınfa:rən] *unreg vt* to bring in; (*Barriere*) to knock down; (*Auto*) to run in ♦ *vi* to drive in; (*Zug*) to pull in; (*MIN*) to go down.
Einfahrt *f* (*Vorgang*) driving in; pulling in; (*MIN*) descent; (*Ort*) entrance; (*von Autobahn*) slip road (*BRIT*), entrance ramp (*US*).
Einfall ['aınfal] *m* (*Idee*) idea, notion; (*Licht~*) incidence; (*MIL*) raid.
einfallen *unreg vi* (*einstürzen*) to fall in, collapse; (*Licht*) to fall; (*MIL*) to raid; (*einstimmen*): **~ (in** +*akk*) to join in (with); **etw fällt jdm ein** sth occurs to sb; **das fällt mir gar nicht ein!** I wouldn't dream of it; **sich** *dat* **etwas ~ lassen** to have a good idea; **dabei fällt mir mein Onkel ein, der ...** that reminds me of my uncle who ...; **es fällt mir jetzt nicht ein** I can't think of it *od* it won't come to me at the moment.
einfallslos *adj* unimaginative.
einfallsreich *adj* imaginative.
einfältig ['aınfɛltıç] *adj* simple(-minded).
Einfaltspinsel ['aınfaltspınzəl] (*umg*) *m* simpleton.
Einfamilienhaus [aınfa'mi:liənhaus] *nt* detached house.
einfangen ['aınfaŋən] *unreg vt* to catch.
einfarbig ['aınfarbıç] *adj* all one colour (*BRIT*) *od* color (*US*); (*Stoff etc*) self-coloured (*BRIT*), self-colored (*US*).
einfassen ['aınfasən] *vt* (*Edelstein*) to set; (*Beet, Stoff*) to edge.
Einfassung *f* setting; border.
einfetten ['aınfɛtən] *vt* to grease.
einfinden ['aınfındən] *unreg vr* to come, turn up.

einfliegen ['aınfli:gən] *unreg vt* to fly in.
einfließen ['aınfli:sən] *unreg vi* to flow in.
einflößen ['aınflø:sən] *vt*: **jdm etw ~** (*lit*) to give sb sth; (*fig*) to instil sth into sb.
Einfluß ['aınflus] *m* influence; **~ nehmen** to bring an influence to bear; **~bereich** *m* sphere of influence; **e~reich** *adj* influential.
einflüstern ['aınflystərn] *vt*: **jdm etw ~** to whisper sth to sb; (*fig*) to insinuate sth to sb.
einförmig ['aınfœrmıç] *adj* uniform; (*eintönig*) monotonous; **E~keit** *f* uniformity; monotony.
einfrieren ['aınfri:rən] *unreg vi* to freeze (in) ♦ *vt* to freeze; (*POL: Beziehungen*) to suspend.
einfügen ['aınfy:gən] *vt* to fit in; (*zusätzlich*) to add; (*COMPUT*) to insert.
einfühlen ['aınfy:lən] *vr*: **sich in jdn ~** to empathize with sb.
einfühlsam ['aınfy:lza:m] *adj* sensitive.
Einfühlungsvermögen *nt* empathy; **mit großem ~** with a great deal of sensitivity.
Einfuhr ['aınfu:r] (-) *f* import; **~artikel** *m* imported article.
einführen ['aınfy:rən] *vt* to bring in; (*Mensch, Sitten*) to introduce; (*Ware*) to import; **jdn in sein Amt ~** to install sb (in office).
Einfuhr- *zW*: **~genehmigung** *f* import permit; **~kontingent** *nt* import quota; **~sperre** *f* ban on imports; **~stopp** *m* ban on imports.
Einführung *f* introduction.
Einführungspreis *m* introductory price.
Einfuhrzoll *m* import duty.
einfüllen ['aınfylən] *vt* to pour in.
Eingabe ['aınga:bə] *f* petition; (*Daten~*) input; **~/Ausgabe** (*COMPUT*) input/output.
Eingang ['aıngaŋ] *m* entrance; (*COMM: Ankunft*) arrival; (*Sendung*) post; **wir bestätigen den ~ Ihres Schreibens vom ...** we acknowledge receipt of your letter of the ...
eingängig ['aıngɛŋıç] *adj* catchy.
eingangs *adv* at the outset ♦ *präp* +*gen* at the outset of.
Eingangs- *zW*: **~bestätigung** *f* acknowledgement of receipt; **~halle** *f* entrance hall; **~stempel** *m* (*COMM*) receipt stamp.
eingeben ['aınge:bən] *unreg vt* (*Arznei*) to give; (*Daten etc*) to enter; (*Gedanken*) to inspire.
eingebettet ['aıngəbɛtət] *adj*: **in** *od* **zwischen Hügeln ~** nestling among the hills.
eingebildet ['aıngəbıldət] *adj* imaginary; (*eitel*) conceited; **~er Kranker** hypochondriac.
Eingeborene(r) ['aıngəbo:rənə(r)] *f(m)* native.
Eingebung *f* inspiration.
eingedenk ['aıngədɛŋk] *präp* +*gen* bearing in mind.
eingefahren ['aıngəfa:rən] *adj* (*Verhaltensweise*) well-worn.

eingefallen ['aɪŋgəfalən] *adj* (*Gesicht*) gaunt.
eingefleischt ['aɪŋgəflaɪʃt] *adj* inveterate; ~**er Junggeselle** confirmed bachelor.
eingefroren ['aɪŋgəfroːrən] *adj* frozen.
eingehen ['aɪŋgeːən] *unreg vi* (*Aufnahme finden*) to come in; (*Sendung, Geld*) to be received; (*Tier, Pflanze*) to die; (*Firma*) to fold; (*schrumpfen*) to shrink ♦ *vt* (*abmachen*) to enter into; (*Wette*) to make; **auf etw** *akk* ~ to go into sth; **auf jdn** ~ to respond to sb; **jdm** ~ (*verständlich sein*) to be comprehensible to sb; **auf einen Vorschlag/Plan** ~ (*zustimmen*) to go along with a suggestion/plan; **bei dieser Hitze/Kälte geht man ja ein!** (*umg*) this heat/cold is just too much.
eingehend *adj* in-depth, thorough.
eingekeilt ['aɪŋgəkaɪlt] *adj* hemmed in; (*fig*) trapped.
eingekesselt ['aɪŋgəkɛsəlt] *adj*: ~ **sein** to be encircled *od* surrounded.
Eingemachte(s) ['aɪŋgəmaːxtə(s)] *nt* preserves *pl*.
eingemeinden ['aɪŋgəmaɪndən] *vt* to incorporate.
eingenommen ['aɪŋgənɔmən] *adj*: ~ (**von**) fond (of), partial (to); ~ (**gegen**) prejudiced (against).
eingeschnappt ['aɪŋgəʃnapt] (*umg*) *adj* cross; ~ **sein** to be in a huff.
eingeschrieben ['aɪŋgəʃriːbən] *adj* registered.
eingeschworen ['aɪŋgəʃvoːrən] *adj* confirmed; (*Gemeinschaft*) close.
eingesessen ['aɪŋgəzɛsən] *adj* old-established.
eingespannt ['aɪŋgəʃpant] *adj* busy.
eingespielt ['aɪŋgəʃpiːlt] *adj*: **aufeinander** ~ **sein** to be in tune with each other.
Eingeständnis ['aɪŋgəʃtɛntnɪs] *nt* admission, confession.
eingestehen ['aɪŋgəʃteːən] *unreg vt* to confess.
eingestellt ['aɪŋgəʃtɛlt] *adj*: **ich bin im Moment nicht auf Besuch** ~ I'm not prepared for visitors.
eingetragen ['aɪŋgətraːgən] *adj* (*COMM*) registered; ~**er Gesellschaftssitz** registered office; ~**es Warenzeichen** registered trademark.
Eingeweide ['aɪŋgəvaɪdə] (-**s**, -) *nt* innards *pl*, intestines *pl*.
Eingeweihte(r) ['aɪŋgəvaɪtə(r)] *f(m)* initiate.
eingewöhnen ['aɪŋgəvøːnən] *vr*: **sich** ~ (**in** +*dat*) to settle down (in).
eingezahlt ['aɪŋgətsaːlt] *adj*: ~**es Kapital** paid-up capital.
eingießen ['aɪŋgiːsən] *unreg vt* to pour (out).
eingleisig ['aɪŋglaɪzɪç] *adj* single-track; **er denkt sehr** ~ (*fig*) he's completely single-minded.
eingliedern ['aɪŋgliːdərn] *vt*: ~ (**in** +*akk*) to integrate (into) ♦ *vr*: **sich** ~ (**in** +*akk*) to integrate o.s. (into).
eingraben ['aɪŋgraːbən] *unreg vt* to dig in ♦ *vr* to dig o.s. in; **dieses Erlebnis hat sich seinem**

Gedächtnis eingegraben this experience has engraved itself on his memory.
eingreifen ['aɪŋgraɪfən] *unreg vi* to intervene, interfere; (*Zahnrad*) to mesh.
eingrenzen ['aɪŋgrɛntsən] *vt* to enclose; (*fig: Problem*) to delimit.
Eingriff ['aɪŋgrɪf] *m* intervention, interference; (*Operation*) operation.
einhaken ['aɪnhaːkən] *vt* to hook in ♦ *vr*: **sich bei jdm** ~ to link arms with sb ♦ *vi* (*sich einmischen*) to intervene.
Einhalt ['aɪnhalt] *m*: ~ **gebieten** +*dat* to put a stop to.
einhalten *unreg vt* (*Regel*) to keep ♦ *vi* to stop.
einhämmern ['aɪnhɛmərn] *vt*: **jdm etw** ~ (*fig*) to hammer sth into sb.
einhandeln ['aɪnhandəln] *vt*: **etw gegen** *od* **für etw** ~ to trade sth for sth.
einhändig ['aɪnhɛndɪç] *adj* one-handed.
einhändigen ['aɪnhɛndɪgən] *vt* to hand in.
einhängen ['aɪnhɛŋən] *vt* to hang; (*Telefon: auch vi*) to hang up; **sich bei jdm** ~ to link arms with sb.
einheimisch ['aɪnhaɪmɪʃ] *adj* native.
Einheimische(r) *f(m)* local.
einheimsen (*umg*) *vt* to bring home.
einheiraten ['aɪnhaɪraːtən] *vi*: **in einen Betrieb** ~ to marry into a business.
Einheit ['aɪnhaɪt] *f* unity; (*Maß, MIL*) unit; **eine geschlossene** ~ **bilden** to form an integrated whole; **e**~**lich** *adj* uniform.
Einheits- *zW*: ~**front** *f* (*POL*) united front; ~**liste** *f* (*POL*) single *od* unified list of candidates; ~**preis** *m* uniform price.
einheizen ['aɪnhaɪtsən] *vi*: **jdm (tüchtig)** ~ (*umg: die Meinung sagen*) to make things hot for sb.
einhellig ['aɪnhɛlɪç] *adj* unanimous ♦ *adv* unanimously.
einholen ['aɪnhoːlən] *vt* (*Tau*) to haul in; (*Fahne, Segel*) to lower; (*Vorsprung aufholen*) to catch up with; (*Verspätung*) to make up; (*Rat, Erlaubnis*) to ask ♦ *vi* (*einkaufen*) to buy, shop.
Einhorn ['aɪnhɔrn] *nt* unicorn.
einhüllen ['aɪnhylən] *vt* to wrap up.
einhundert ['aɪn'hʊndərt] *num* one hundred.
einig ['aɪnɪç] *adj* (*vereint*) united; **sich** *dat* ~ **sein** to be in agreement; ~ **werden** to agree.
einige(r, s) *adj, pron* some ♦ *pl* some; (*mehrere*) several; **mit Ausnahme** ~**r weniger** with a few exceptions; **vor** ~**n Tagen** the other day, a few days ago; **dazu ist noch** ~**s zu sagen** there are still one or two things to say about that.
einigemal *adv* a few times.
einigen *vt* to unite ♦ *vr*: **sich (auf etw** *akk*) ~ to agree (on sth).
einigermaßen *adv* somewhat; (*leidlich*) reasonably.
einiges *pron siehe* **einige(r, s).**

einiggehen *unreg vi* to agree.
Einigkeit *f* unity; (*Übereinstimmung*) agreement.
Einigung *f* agreement; (*Ver~*) unification.
einimpfen ['aɪnˌɪmpfən] *vt:* **jdm etw ~** to inoculate sb with sth; (*fig*) to impress sth upon sb.
einjagen ['aɪnjaːgən] *vt:* **jdm Furcht/einen Schrecken ~** to give sb a fright.
einjährig ['aɪnjɛːrɪç] *adj* of *od* for one year; (*Alter*) one-year-old; (*Pflanze*) annual.
einkalkulieren ['aɪnkalkuliːrən] *vt* to take into account, allow for.
einkassieren ['aɪnkasiːrən] *vt* (*Geld, Schulden*) to collect.
Einkauf ['aɪnkaʊf] *m* purchase; (*COMM: Abteilung*) purchasing (department).
einkaufen *vt* to buy ♦ *vi* to shop; **~ gehen** to go shopping.
Einkäufer(in) ['aɪnkɔyfər(ɪn)] *m(f)* (*COMM*) buyer.
Einkaufs- *zW:* **~bummel** *m:* **einen ~bummel machen** to go on a shopping spree; **~ korb** *m* shopping basket; **~leiter(in)** *m(f)* (*COMM*) chief buyer; **~netz** *nt* string bag; **~preis** *m* cost price, wholesale price; **~wagen** *m* trolley (*BRIT*), cart (*US*); **~zentrum** *nt* shopping centre.
einkehren ['aɪnkeːrən] *vi* (*geh: Ruhe, Frühling*) to come; **in einem Gasthof ~** to (make a) stop at an inn.
einkerben ['aɪnkɛrbən] *vt* to notch.
einklagen ['aɪnklaːgən] *vt* (*Schulden*) to sue for (the recovery of).
einklammern ['aɪnklamərn] *vt* to put in brackets, bracket.
Einklang ['aɪnklaŋ] *m* harmony.
einkleiden ['aɪnklaɪdən] *vt* to clothe; (*fig*) to express.
einklemmen ['aɪnklɛmən] *vt* to jam.
einknicken ['aɪnknɪkən] *vt* to bend in; (*Papier*) to fold ♦ *vi* (*Knie*) to give way.
einkochen ['aɪnkɔxən] *vt* to boil down; (*Obst*) to preserve, bottle.
Einkommen ['aɪnkɔmən] (**-s, -**) *nt* income.
einkommensschwach *adj* low-income *attrib*.
einkommensstark *adj* high-income *attrib*.
Einkommen(s)steuer *f* income tax; **~erklärung** *f* income tax return.
Einkommensverhältnisse *pl* (level of) income *sing*.
einkreisen ['aɪnkraɪzən] *vt* to encircle.
einkriegen ['aɪnkriːgən] (*umg*) *vr:* **sie konnte sich gar nicht mehr darüber ~, daß ...** she couldn't get over the fact that ...
Einkünfte ['aɪnkʏnftə] *pl* income *sing*, revenue *sing*.
einladen ['aɪnlaːdən] *unreg vt* (*Person*) to invite; (*Gegenstände*) to load; **jdn ins Kino ~** to take sb to the cinema.
Einladung *f* invitation.
Einlage ['aɪnlaːgə] *f* (*Programm~*) interlude;

(*Spar~*) deposit; (*FIN: Kapital~*) investment; (*Schuh~*) insole; (*Fußstütze*) support; (*Zahn~*) temporary filling; (*KOCH*) noodles, vegetables etc (in clear soup).
einlagern ['aɪnlaːgərn] *vt* to store.
Einlaß ['aɪnlas] (**-sses, -lässe**) *m* admission; **jdm ~ gewähren** to admit sb.
einlassen *unreg vt* to let in; (*einsetzen*) to set in ♦ *vr:* **sich mit jdm/auf etw** *akk* **~** to get involved with sb/sth; **sich auf einen Kompromiß ~** to agree to a compromise; **ich lasse mich auf keine Diskussion ein** I'm not having any discussion about it.
Einlauf ['aɪnlaʊf] *m* arrival; (*von Pferden*) finish; (*MED*) enema.
einlaufen *unreg vi* to arrive, come in; (*SPORT*) to finish; (*Wasser*) to run in; (*Stoff*) to shrink ♦ *vt* (*Schuhe*) to break in ♦ *vr* (*SPORT*) to warm up; (*Motor, Maschine*) to run in; **jdm das Haus ~** to invade sb's house; **in den Hafen ~** to enter the harbour.
einläuten ['aɪnlɔytən] *vt* (*neues Jahr*) to ring in; (*SPORT: Runde*) to sound the bell for.
einleben ['aɪnleːbən] *vr* to settle down.
Einlegearbeit *f* inlay.
einlegen ['aɪnleːgən] *vt* (*einfügen: Blatt, Sohle*) to insert; (*KOCH*) to pickle; (*in Holz etc*) to inlay; (*Geld*) to deposit; (*Pause*) to have; (*Protest*) to make; (*Veto*) to use; (*Berufung*) to lodge; **ein gutes Wort bei jdm ~** to put in a good word with sb.
Einlegesohle *f* insole.
einleiten ['aɪnlaɪtən] *vt* to introduce, start; (*Geburt*) to induce.
Einleitung *f* introduction; induction.
einlenken ['aɪnlɛŋkən] *vi* (*fig*) to yield, give way.
einlesen ['aɪnleːzən] *unreg vr:* **sich in ein Gebiet ~** to get into a subject ♦ *vt:* **etw in etw** *+akk* **~** (*Daten*) to feed sth into sth.
einleuchten ['aɪnlɔyçtən] *vi:* **(jdm) ~** to be clear *od* evident (to sb).
einleuchtend *adj* clear.
einliefern ['aɪnliːfərn] *vt:* **~ (in** *+akk*) to take (into); **jdn ins Krankenhaus ~** to admit sb to hospital.
Einlieferungsschein *m* certificate of posting.
einlochen ['aɪnlɔxən] (*umg*) *vt* (*einsperren*) to lock up.
einlösen ['aɪnløːzən] *vt* (*Scheck*) to cash; (*Schuldschein, Pfand*) to redeem; (*Versprechen*) to keep.
einmachen ['aɪnmaxən] *vt* to preserve.
Einmachglas *nt* bottling jar.
einmal ['aɪnmaːl] *adv* once; (*erstens*) first of all, firstly; (*später*) one day; **nehmen wir ~ an** just let's suppose; **noch ~** once more; **nicht ~** not even; **auf ~** all at once; **es war ~** once upon a time there was/were; **~ ist keinmal** (*Sprichwort*) once doesn't count; **waren Sie schon ~ in Rom?** have you ever

been to Rome?
Einmaleins *nt* multiplication tables *pl*; (*fig*) ABC, basics *pl*.
einmalig *adj* unique; (*einmal geschehend*) single; (*prima*) fantastic.
Einmannbetrieb *m* one-man business.
Einmannbus *m* one-man-operated bus.
Einmarsch ['aɪnmarʃ] *m* entry; (*MIL*) invasion.
einmarschieren *vi* to march in.
einmengen ['aɪnmɛŋən] *vr:* **sich (in etw** +*akk*) ~ to interfere (with sth).
einmieten ['aɪnmiːtən] *vr:* **sich bei jdm** ~ to take lodgings with sb.
einmischen ['aɪnmɪʃən] *vr:* **sich (in etw** +*akk*) ~ to interfere (with sth).
einmotten ['aɪnmɔtən] *vt* (*Kleider etc*) to put in mothballs.
einmünden ['aɪnmʏndən] *vi:* ~ **in** +*akk* (*subj: Fluß*) to flow *od* run into, join; (: *Straße: in Platz*) to run into; (: : *in andere Straße*) to run into, join.
einmütig ['aɪnmyːtɪç] *adj* unanimous.
einnähen ['aɪnnɛːən] *vt* (*enger machen*) to take in.
Einnahme ['aɪnnaːmə] (-, -n) *f* (*Geld*) takings *pl*, revenue; (*von Medizin*) taking; (*MIL*) capture, taking; ~**n und Ausgaben** income and expenditure; ~**quelle** *f* source of income.
einnehmen ['aɪnneːmən] *unreg vt* to take; (*Stellung, Raum*) to take up; ~ **für/gegen** to persuade in favour of/against.
einnehmend *adj* charming.
einnicken ['aɪnnɪkən] *vi* to nod off.
einnisten ['aɪnnɪstən] *vr* to nest; (*fig*) to settle o.s.
Einöde ['aɪn|øːdə] (-, -n) *f* desert, wilderness.
einordnen ['aɪn|ɔrdnən] *vt* to arrange, fit in ♦ *vr* to adapt; (*AUT*) to get in(to) lane.
einpacken ['aɪnpakən] *vt* to pack (up).
einparken ['aɪnparkən] *vt, vi* to park.
einpauken ['aɪnpaʊkən] (*umg*) *vt:* **jdm etw** ~ to drum sth into sb.
einpendeln ['aɪnpɛndəln] *vr* to even out.
einpennen ['aɪnpɛnən] (*umg*) *vi* to drop off.
einpferchen ['aɪnpfɛrçən] *vt* to pen in; (*fig*) to coop up.
einpflanzen ['aɪnpflantsən] *vt* to plant; (*MED*) to implant.
einplanen ['aɪnplaːnən] *vt* to plan for.
einprägen ['aɪnprɛːgən] *vt* to impress, imprint; (*beibringen*): **jdm etw** ~ to impress sth on sb; **sich** *dat* **etw** ~ to memorize sth.
einprägsam ['aɪnprɛːkzaːm] *adj* easy to remember; (*Melodie*) catchy.
einprogrammieren ['aɪnprogramiːrən] *vt* (*COMPUT*) to feed in.
einprügeln ['aɪnpryːgəln] (*umg*) *vt:* **jdm etw** ~ to din sth into sb.
einquartieren ['aɪnkvartiːrən] *vt* (*MIL*) to billet; **Gäste bei Freunden** ~ to put visitors up with friends.

einrahmen ['aɪnraːmən] *vt* to frame.
einrasten ['aɪnrastən] *vi* to engage.
einräumen ['aɪnrɔymən] *vt* (*ordnend*) to put away; (*überlassen: Platz*) to give up; (*zugestehen*) to admit, concede.
einrechnen ['aɪnrɛçnən] *vt* to include; (*berücksichtigen*) to take into account.
einreden ['aɪnreːdən] *vt:* **jdm/sich etw** ~ to talk sb/o.s. into believing sth ♦ *vi:* **auf jdn** ~ to keep on and on at sb.
Einreibemittel *nt* liniment.
einreiben ['aɪnraɪbən] *unreg vt* to rub in.
einreichen ['aɪnraɪçən] *vt* to hand in; (*Antrag*) to submit.
einreihen ['aɪnraɪən] *vt* (*einordnen, einfügen*) to put in; (*klassifizieren*) to classify ♦ *vr* (*Auto*) to get in lane; **etw in etw** *akk* ~ to put sth into sth.
Einreise ['aɪnraɪzə] *f* entry; ~**bestimmungen** *pl* entry regulations *pl*; ~**erlaubnis** *f* entry permit; ~**genehmigung** *f* entry permit.
einreisen ['aɪnraɪzən] *vi:* **in ein Land** ~ to enter a country.
Einreiseverbot *nt* refusal of entry.
Einreisevisum *nt* entry visa.
einreißen ['aɪnraɪsən] *unreg vt* (*Papier*) to tear; (*Gebäude*) to pull down ♦ *vi* to tear; (*Gewohnheit werden*) to catch on.
einrenken ['aɪnrɛŋkən] *vt* (*Gelenk, Knie*) to put back in place; (*fig: umg*) to sort out ♦ *vr* (*fig: umg*) to sort itself out.
einrichten ['aɪnrɪçtən] *vt* (*Haus*) to furnish; (*schaffen*) to establish, set up; (*arrangieren*) to arrange; (*möglich machen*) to manage ♦ *vr* (*in Haus*) to furnish one's house; **sich** ~ **(auf** +*akk*) (*sich vorbereiten*) to prepare o.s. (for); (*sich anpassen*) to adapt (to).
Einrichtung *f* (*Wohnungs*~) furnishings *pl*; (*öffentliche Anstalt*) organization; (*Dienste*) service; (*Labor*~ *etc*) equipment; (*Gewohnheit*): **zur ständigen** ~ **werden** to become an institution.
Einrichtungsgegenstand *m* item of furniture.
einrosten ['aɪnrɔstən] *vi* to get rusty.
einrücken ['aɪnrʏkən] *vi* (*MIL: Soldat*) to join up; (: *in Land*) to move in ♦ *vt* (*Anzeige*) to insert; (*Zeile, Text*) to indent.
Eins [aɪns] (-, -en) *f* one; **e~** *num* one; **es ist mir alles e~** it's all one to me; **e~ zu e~** (*SPORT*) one all; **e~ a** (*umg*) first-rate.
einsalzen ['aɪnzaltsən] *vt* to salt.
einsam ['aɪnzaːm] *adj* lonely, solitary; ~**e Klasse/Spitze** (*umg: hervorragend*) absolutely fantastic; **E~keit** *f* loneliness, solitude.
einsammeln ['aɪnzaməln] *vt* to collect.
Einsatz ['aɪnzats] *m* (*Teil*) insert; (*an Kleid*) insertion; (*Tisch*~) leaf; (*Verwendung*) use, employment; (*Spiel*~) stake; (*Risiko*) risk; (*MIL*) operation; (*MUS*) entry; **im** ~ in action; **etw unter** ~ **seines Lebens tun** to risk one's life to do sth; ~**befehl** *m* order to

go into action; **e~bereit** adj ready for action; **~kommando** nt (MIL) task force.

einschalten ['aɪnʃaltən] vt (ELEK) to switch on; (einfügen) to insert; (Pause) to make; (AUT: Gang) to engage; (Anwalt) to bring in ♦ vr (dazwischentreten) to intervene.

Einschaltquote f (TV) viewing figures pl.

einschärfen ['aɪnʃɛrfən] vt: **jdm etw** ~ to impress sth on sb.

einschätzen ['aɪnʃɛtsən] vt to estimate, assess ♦ vr to rate o.s.

einschenken ['aɪnʃɛŋkən] vt to pour out.

einscheren ['aɪnʃeːrən] vi to get back (into lane).

einschicken ['aɪnʃɪkən] vt to send in.

einschieben ['aɪnʃiːbən] unreg vt to push in; (zusätzlich) to insert; **eine Pause** ~ to have a break.

einschiffen ['aɪnʃɪfən] vt to ship ♦ vr to embark, go on board.

einschl. abk (= einschließlich) inc.

einschlafen ['aɪnʃlaːfən] unreg vi to fall asleep, go to sleep; (fig: Freundschaft) to peter out.

einschläfern ['aɪnʃlɛːfərn] vt (schläfrig machen) to make sleepy; (Gewissen) to soothe; (narkotisieren) to give a soporific to; (töten: Tier) to put to sleep.

einschläfernd adj (MED) soporific; (langweilig) boring; (Stimme) lulling.

Einschlag ['aɪnʃlaːk] m impact; (AUT) lock; (fig: Beimischung) touch, hint.

einschlagen ['aɪnʃlaːgən] unreg vt to knock in; (Fenster) to smash, break; (Zähne, Schädel) to smash in; (Steuer) to turn; (kürzer machen) to take up; (Ware) to pack, wrap up; (Weg, Richtung) to take ♦ vi to hit; (sich einigen) to agree; (Anklang finden) to work, succeed; **es muß irgendwo eingeschlagen haben** something must have been struck by lightning; **gut** ~ (umg) to go down well, be a big hit; **auf jdn** ~ to hit sb.

einschlägig ['aɪnʃlɛːgɪç] adj relevant; **er ist** ~ **vorbestraft** (JUR) he has a previous conviction for a similar offence.

einschleichen ['aɪnʃlaɪçən] unreg vr (in Haus, fig: Fehler) to creep in, steal in; (in Vertrauen) to worm one's way in.

einschleppen ['aɪnʃlɛpən] vt (fig: Krankheit etc) to bring in.

einschleusen ['aɪnʃlɔʏzən] vt: ~ **(in** +akk) to smuggle in(to).

einschließen ['aɪnʃliːsən] unreg vt (Kind) to lock in; (Häftling) to lock up; (Gegenstand) to lock away; (Bergleute) to cut off; (umgeben) to surround; (MIL) to encircle; (fig) to include, comprise ♦ vr to lock o.s. in.

einschließlich adv inclusive ♦ präp +gen inclusive of, including.

einschmeicheln ['aɪnʃmaɪçəln] vr: **sich (bei jdm)** ~ to ingratiate o.s. (with sb).

einschmuggeln ['aɪnʃmʊgəln] vt: ~ **(in** +akk) to smuggle in(to).

einschnappen ['aɪnʃnapən] vi (Tür) to click to; (fig) to be touchy; **eingeschnappt sein** to be in a huff.

einschneidend ['aɪnʃnaɪdənt] adj incisive.

einschneien ['aɪnʃnaɪən] vi: **eingeschneit sein** to be snowed in.

Einschnitt ['aɪnʃnɪt] m (MED) incision; (im Tal, Gebirge) cleft; (im Leben) decisive point.

einschnüren ['aɪnʃnyːrən] vt (einengen) to cut into; **dieser Kragen schnürt mir den Hals ein** this collar is strangling me.

einschränken ['aɪnʃrɛŋkən] vt to limit, restrict; (Kosten) to cut down, reduce ♦ vr to cut down (on expenditure); **~d möchte ich sagen, daß** ... I'd like to qualify that by saying ...

einschränkend adj restrictive.

Einschränkung f restriction, limitation; reduction; (von Behauptung) qualification.

Einschreib(e)brief m registered (BRIT) od certified (US) letter.

einschreiben ['aɪnʃraɪbən] unreg vt to write in; (POST) to send by registered (BRIT) od certified mail (US) ♦ vr to register; (UNIV) to enrol; **E~** nt registered (BRIT) od certified (US) letter.

einschreiten ['aɪnʃraɪtən] unreg vi to step in, intervene; ~ **gegen** to take action against.

Einschub ['aɪnʃuːp] (-(e)s, ⁻e) m insertion.

einschüchtern ['aɪnʃʏçtərn] vt to intimidate.

Einschüchterung ['aɪnʃʏçtərʊŋ] f intimidation.

einschulen ['aɪnʃuːlən] vt: **eingeschult werden** (Kind) to start school.

einschweißen ['aɪnʃvaɪsən] vt (in Plastik) to shrink-wrap; (TECH): **etw in etw** akk ~ to weld sth into sth.

einschwenken ['aɪnʃvɛŋkən] vi: ~ **(in** +akk) to turn od swing in(to).

einsehen ['aɪnzeːən] unreg vt (prüfen) to inspect; (Fehler etc) to recognize; (verstehen) to see; **das sehe ich nicht ein** I don't see why; **E~** (-s) nt understanding; **ein E~ haben** to show understanding.

einseifen ['aɪnzaɪfən] vt to soap, lather; (fig: umg) to take in, con.

einseitig ['aɪnzaɪtɪç] adj one-sided; (POL) unilateral; (Ernährung) unbalanced; (Diskette) single-sided; **E~keit** f one-sidedness.

einsenden ['aɪnzɛndən] unreg vt to send in.

Einsender(in) (-s, -) m(f) sender, contributor.

Einsendeschluß m closing date (for entries).

Einsendung f sending in.

einsetzen ['aɪnzɛtsən] vt to put (in); (in Amt) to appoint, install; (Geld) to stake; (verwenden) to use; (MIL) to employ ♦ vi (beginnen) to set in; (MUS) to enter, come in ♦ vr to work hard; **sich für jdn/etw** ~ to support sb/sth; **ich werde mich dafür** ~, **daß** ... I will do what I can to see that ...

Einsicht ['aɪnzɪçt] f insight; (in Akten) look, inspection; **zu der** ~ **kommen, daß** ... to

come to the conclusion that ...
einsichtig *adj* (*Mensch*) judicious; **jdm etw ~ machen** to make sb understand *od* see sth.
Einsichtnahme (-, -n) *f* (*form*) perusal; **„zur ~"** "for attention".
einsichtslos *adj* unreasonable.
einsichtsvoll *adj* understanding.
Einsiedler ['aɪnziːdlər] (-s, -) *m* hermit.
einsilbig ['aɪnzɪlbɪç] *adj* (*lit, fig*) monosyllabic; **E~keit** *f* (*fig*) taciturnity.
einsinken ['aɪnzɪŋkən] *unreg vi* to sink in.
Einsitzer ['aɪnzɪtsər] (-s, -) *m* single-seater.
einspannen ['aɪnʃpanən] *vt* (*Werkstück, Papier*) to put (in), insert; (*Pferde*) to harness; (*umg: Person*) to rope in; **jdn für seine Zwecke ~** to use sb for one's own ends.
einsparen ['aɪnʃpaːrən] *vt* to save, economize on; (*Kosten*) to cut down on; (*Posten*) to eliminate.
Einsparung *f* saving.
einspeichern ['aɪnʃpaɪçərn] *vt:* **etw (in etw +akk) ~** (*COMPUT*) to feed sth in(to sth).
einsperren ['aɪnʃpɛrən] *vt* to lock up.
einspielen ['aɪnʃpiːlən] *vr* (*SPORT*) to warm up ♦ *vt* (*Film: Geld*) to bring in; (*Instrument*) to play in; **sich aufeinander ~** to become attuned to each other; **gut eingespielt** running smoothly.
einsprachig ['aɪnʃpraːxɪç] *adj* monolingual.
einspringen ['aɪnʃprɪŋən] *unreg vi* (*aushelfen*) to stand in; (*mit Geld*) to help out.
einspritzen ['aɪnʃprɪtsən] *vt* to inject.
Einspritzmotor *m* (*AUT*) injection engine.
Einspruch ['aɪnʃprux] *m* protest, objection; **~ einlegen** (*JUR*) to file an objection.
Einspruchsfrist *f* (*JUR*) period for filing an objection.
Einspruchsrecht *nt* veto.
einspurig ['aɪnʃpuːrɪç] *adj* single-lane; (*EISENB*) single-track.
einst [aɪnst] *adv* once; (*zukünftig*) one *od* some day.
Einstand ['aɪnʃtant] *m* (*TENNIS*) deuce; (*Antritt*) entrance (to office); **er hat gestern seinen ~ gegeben** yesterday he celebrated starting his new job.
einstechen ['aɪnʃtɛçən] *unreg vt* to pierce.
einstecken ['aɪnʃtɛkən] *vt* to stick in, insert; (*Brief*) to post, mail (*US*); (*ELEK: Stecker*) to plug in; (*Geld*) to pocket; (*mitnehmen*) to take; (*überlegen sein*) to put in the shade; (*hinnehmen*) to swallow.
einstehen ['aɪnʃteːən] *unreg vi:* **für jdn ~** to vouch for sb; **für ~** to guarantee sth, vouch for sth; (*Ersatz leisten*) to make good sth.
einsteigen ['aɪnʃtaɪgən] *unreg vi* to get in *od* on; (*in Schiff*) to go on board; (*sich beteiligen*) to come in; (*hineinklettern*) to climb in; **~!** (*EISENB etc*) all aboard!
Einsteiger (-s, -) (*umg*) *m* beginner.

einstellbar *adj* adjustable.
einstellen ['aɪnʃtɛlən] *vt* (*in Firma*) to employ, take on; (*aufhören*) to stop; (*Geräte*) to adjust; (*Kamera etc*) to focus; (*Sender, Radio*) to tune in to; (*unterstellen*) to put ♦ *vi* to take on staff/workers ♦ *vr* (*anfangen*) to set in; (*kommen*) to arrive; **Zahlungen ~** to suspend payment; **etw auf etw akk ~** to adjust sth to sth; to focus sth on sth; **sich auf jdn/etw ~** to adapt to sb/prepare o.s. for sth.
einstellig *adj* (*Zahl*) single-digit.
Einstellplatz *m* (*auf Hof*) carport; (*in Großgarage*) (covered) parking space.
Einstellung *f* (*Aufhören*) suspension, cessation; (*von Gerät*) adjustment; (*von Kamera etc*) focusing; (*von Arbeiter etc*) appointment; (*Haltung*) attitude.
Einstellungsgespräch *nt* interview.
Einstellungsstopp *m* halt in recruitment.
Einstieg ['aɪnʃtiːk] (-(e)s, -e) *m* entry; (*fig*) approach; (*von Bus, Bahn*) door; **kein ~** exit only.
einstig ['aɪnstɪç] *adj* former.
einstimmen ['aɪnʃtɪmən] *vi* to join in ♦ *vt* (*MUS*) to tune; (*in Stimmung bringen*) to put in the mood.
einstimmig *adj* unanimous; (*MUS*) for one voice; **E~keit** *f* unanimity.
einstmalig *adj* former.
einstmals *adv* once, formerly.
einstöckig ['aɪnʃtœkɪç] *adj* two-storeyed (*BRIT*), two-storied (*US*).
einstöpseln ['aɪnʃtœpsəln] *vt:* **etw (in etw +akk) ~** (*ELEK*) to plug sth in(to sth).
einstudieren ['aɪnʃtudiːrən] *vt* to study, rehearse.
einstufen ['aɪnʃtuːfən] *vt* to classify.
Einstufung *f:* **nach seiner ~ in eine höhere Gehaltsklasse** after he was put on a higher salary grade.
einstündig ['aɪnʃtyndɪç] *adj* one-hour *attrib*.
einstürmen ['aɪnʃtʏrmən] *vi:* **auf jdn ~** to rush at sb; (*Eindrücke*) to overwhelm sb.
Einsturz ['aɪnʃtʊrts] *m* collapse.
einstürzen ['aɪnʃtʏrtsən] *vi* to fall in, collapse; **auf jdn ~** (*fig*) to overwhelm sb.
Einsturzgefahr *f* danger of collapse.
einstweilen *adv* meanwhile; (*vorläufig*) temporarily, for the time being.
einstweilig *adj* temporary; **~e Verfügung** (*JUR*) temporary *od* interim injunction.
eintägig ['aɪntɛːgɪç] *adj* one-day.
Eintagsfliege ['aɪntaːksfliːgə] *f* (*ZOOL*) mayfly; (*fig*) nine-day wonder.
eintauchen ['aɪntauxən] *vt* to immerse, dip in ♦ *vi* to dive.
eintauschen ['aɪntauʃən] *vt* to exchange.
eintausend ['aɪn'tauzənt] *num* one thousand.
einteilen ['aɪntaɪlən] *vt* (*in Teile*) to divide (up); (*Menschen*) to assign.
einteilig *adj* one-piece.
eintönig ['aɪntøːnɪç] *adj* monotonous; **E~keit** *f*

monotony.

Eintopf ['aɪntɔpf] m stew.

Eintopfgericht ['aɪntɔpfgərɪçt] nt stew.

Eintracht ['aɪntraxt] (-) f concord, harmony.

einträchtig ['aɪntrɛçtɪç] adj harmonious.

Eintrag ['aɪntraːk] (-(e)s, ̈e) m entry;
amtlicher ~ entry in the register.

eintragen ['aɪntraːgən] unreg vt (in Buch) to
enter; (Profit) to yield ♦ vr to put one's name
down; **jdm etw** ~ to bring sb sth.

einträglich ['aɪntrɛːklɪç] adj profitable.

Eintragung f: ~ (**in** +akk) entry (in).

eintreffen ['aɪntrɛfən] unreg vi to happen;
(ankommen) to arrive; (fig: wahr werden) to
come true.

eintreiben ['aɪntraɪbən] unreg vt (Geldbeträge)
to collect.

eintreten ['aɪntreːtən] unreg vi (hineingehen) to
enter; (sich ereignen) to occur ♦ vt (Tür) to
kick open; **in etw** akk ~ to enter sth; (in Club,
Partei) to join sth; **für jdn/etw** ~ to stand up
for sb/sth.

eintrichtern ['aɪntrɪçtərn] (umg) vt: **jdm etw** ~
to drum sth into sb.

Eintritt ['aɪntrɪt] m (Betreten) entrance; (in
Club etc) joining; ~ **frei** admission free;
„~ **verboten"** "no admittance"; **bei** ~ **der
Dunkelheit** at nightfall.

Eintritts- zW: ~**geld** nt admission charge;
~**karte** f (admission) ticket; ~**preis** m
admission charge.

eintrocknen ['aɪntrɔknən] vi to dry up.

eintrudeln ['aɪntruːdəln] (umg) vi to drift in.

eintunken ['aɪntʊŋkən] vt (Brot): **etw in etw**
akk ~ to dunk sth in sth.

einüben ['aɪn|yːbən] vt to practise (BRIT),
practice (US), drill.

einverleiben ['aɪnfɛrlaɪbən] vt to incorporate;
(Gebiet) to annex; **sich** dat **etw** ~ (fig: geistig)
to assimilate sth.

Einvernehmen ['aɪnfɛrneːmən] (-s, -) nt
agreement, understanding.

einverstanden ['aɪnfɛrʃtandən] interj agreed
♦ adj: ~ **sein** to agree, be agreed; **sich mit
etw** ~ **erklären** to give one's agreement to
sth.

Einverständnis ['aɪnfɛrʃtɛntnɪs] (-ses) nt
understanding; (gleiche Meinung)
agreement; **im** ~ **mit jdm handeln** to act
with sb's consent.

Einwand ['aɪnvant] (-(e)s, ̈e) m objection;
einen ~ **erheben** to raise an objection.

Einwanderer ['aɪnvandərər] m immigrant.

Einwanderin f immigrant.

einwandern vi to immigrate.

Einwanderung f immigration.

einwandfrei adj perfect; **etw** ~ **beweisen** to
prove sth beyond doubt.

einwärts ['aɪnvɛrts] adv inwards.

einwecken ['aɪnvɛkən] vt to bottle, preserve.

Einwegflasche ['aɪnveːgflaʃə] f nonreturnable bottle.

Einwegspritze f disposable (hypodermic)
syringe.

einweichen ['aɪnvaɪçən] vt to soak.

einweihen ['aɪnvaɪən] vt (Kirche) to
consecrate; (Brücke) to open; (Gebäude) to
inaugurate; (Person): **in etw** akk ~ to initiate
in sth; **er ist eingeweiht** (fig) he knows all
about it.

Einweihung f consecration; opening;
inauguration; initiation.

einweisen ['aɪnvaɪzən] unreg vt (in Amt) to
install; (in Arbeit) to introduce; (in Anstalt) to
send; (in Krankenhaus): ~ (**in** +akk) to admit
(to); (AUT): ~ (**in** +akk) to guide in(to).

Einweisung f installation; introduction;
sending.

einwenden ['aɪnvɛndən] unreg vt: **etwas**
~ **gegen** to object to, oppose.

einwerfen ['aɪnvɛrfən] unreg vt to throw in;
(Brief) to post; (Geld) to put in, insert;
(Fenster) to smash; (äußern) to interpose.

einwickeln ['aɪnvɪkəln] vt to wrap up; (fig:
umg) to outsmart.

einwilligen ['aɪnvɪlɪgən] vi: (**in etw** akk) ~ to
consent (to sth), agree (to sth).

Einwilligung f consent.

einwirken ['aɪnvɪrkən] vi: **auf jdn/etw** ~ to
influence sb/sth.

Einwirkung f influence.

Einwohner(in) ['aɪnvoːnər(ɪn)] (-s, -) m(f)
inhabitant; ~**meldeamt** nt registration
office; **sich beim** ~**meldeamt (an)melden**
≈ to register with the police; ~**schaft** f
population, inhabitants pl.

Einwurf ['aɪnvʊrf] m (Öffnung) slot; (Einwand)
objection; (SPORT) throw-in.

Einzahl ['aɪntsaːl] f singular.

einzahlen vt to pay in.

Einzahlung f payment; (auf Sparkonto)
deposit.

einzäunen ['aɪntsɔynən] vt to fence in.

einzeichnen ['aɪntsaɪçnən] vt to draw in.

Einzel ['aɪntsəl] (-s, -) nt (TENNIS) singles pl.

Einzel- zW: ~**aufstellung** f (COMM) itemized
list; ~**bett** nt single bed; ~**blattzuführung** f
sheet feed; ~**fall** m single instance,
individual case; ~**gänger(in)** m(f) loner;
~**haft** f solitary confinement; ~**handel** m
retail trade; **im** ~**handel erhältlich** available
retail; ~**handelsgeschäft** nt retail outlet;
~**handelspreis** m retail price; ~**händler** m
retailer; ~**heit** f particular, detail; ~**kind** nt
only child.

Einzeller ['aɪntsɛlər] (-s, -) m (BIOL) single-
celled organism.

einzeln adj single; (von Paar) odd ♦ adv singly;
~ **angeben** to specify; ~**e** some (people), a
few (people); **der/die** ~**e** the individual; **das**
~**e** the particular; **ins** ~**e gehen** to go into
detail(s); **etw im** ~**en besprechen** to discuss
sth in detail; ~ **aufführen** to list separately
od individually; **bitte** ~ **eintreten** please

come in one (person) at a time.

Einzelteil *nt* individual part; (*Ersatzteil*) spare part; **etw in seine ~e zerlegen** to take sth to pieces, dismantle sth.

Einzelzimmer *nt* single room.

einziehen ['aɪntsiːən] *unreg vt* to draw in, take in; (*Kopf*) to duck; (*Fühler, Antenne, Fahrgestell*) to retract; (*Steuern, Erkundigungen*) to collect; (*MIL*) to call up, draft (*US*); (*aus dem Verkehr ziehen*) to withdraw; (*konfiszieren*) to confiscate ♦ *vi* to move in; (*Friede, Ruhe*) to come; (*Flüssigkeit*): **~ (in** +*akk*) to soak in(to).

einzig ['aɪntsɪç] *adj* only; (*ohnegleichen*) unique ♦ *adv*: **~ und allein** solely; **das ~e** the only thing; **der/die ~e** the only one; **kein ~es Mal** not once, not one single time; **kein ~er** nobody, not a single person; **~artig** *adj* unique.

Einzug ['aɪntsuːk] *m* entry, moving in.

Einzugsauftrag *m* (*FIN*) direct debit.

Einzugsbereich *m* catchment area.

Einzugsverfahren *nt* (*FIN*) direct debit.

Eis [aɪs] (*-es, -*) *nt* ice; (*Speise~*) ice cream; **~ am Stiel** ice lolly (*BRIT*), popsicle ® (*US*); **~bahn** *f* ice *od* skating rink; **~bär** *m* polar bear; **~becher** *m* sundae; **~bein** *nt* pig's trotters *pl*; **~berg** *m* iceberg; **~beutel** *m* ice pack; **~café** *nt* = **Eisdiele**.

Eischnee ['aɪʃneː] *m* (*KOCH*) beaten white of egg.

Eisdecke *f* sheet of ice.

Eisdiele *f* ice-cream parlour (*BRIT*) *od* parlor (*US*).

Eisen ['aɪzən] (*-s, -*) *nt* iron; **zum alten ~ gehören** (*fig*) to be on the scrap heap.

Eisenbahn *f* railway, railroad (*US*); **es ist (aller)höchste ~** (*umg*) it's high time; **~er** (*-s, -*) *m* railwayman, railway employee, railroader (*US*); **~netz** *nt* rail network; **~schaffner** *m* railway guard, (railroad) conductor (*US*); **~überführung** *f* footbridge; **~übergang** *m* level crossing, grade crossing (*US*); **~wagen** *m* railway *od* railroad (*US*) carriage; **~waggon** *m* (*Güterwagen*) goods wagon.

Eisen- *zW*: **~erz** *nt* iron ore; **e~haltig** *adj* containing iron; **~mangel** *m* iron deficiency; **~warenhandlung** *f* ironmonger's (*BRIT*), hardware store (*US*).

eisern ['aɪzərn] *adj* iron; (*Gesundheit*) robust; (*Energie*) unrelenting; (*Reserve*) emergency; **der E~e Vorhang** the Iron Curtain; **in etw** *dat* **~ sein** to be adamant about sth; **er ist ~ bei seinem Entschluß geblieben** he stuck firmly to his decision.

Eis- *zW*: **~fach** *nt* freezer compartment, icebox; **e~frei** *adj* clear of ice; **e~gekühlt** *adj* chilled; **~hockey** *nt* ice hockey.

eisig ['aɪzɪç] *adj* icy.

Eis- *zW*: **~kaffee** *m* iced coffee; **e~kalt** *adj* icy cold; **~kunstlauf** *m* figure skating; **~laufen**

nt ice-skating; **~läufer** *m* ice-skater; **~meer** *nt*: **Nördliches/Südliches ~meer** Arctic/Antarctic Ocean; **~pickel** *m* ice-axe (*BRIT*), ice-ax (*US*).

Eisprung ['aɪʃprʊŋ] *m* ovulation.

Eis- *zW*: **~schießen** *nt* ≈ curling; **~scholle** *f* ice floe; **~schrank** *m* fridge, icebox (*US*); **~stadion** *nt* ice *od* skating rink; **~würfel** *m* ice cube; **~zapfen** *m* icicle; **~zeit** *f* Ice Age.

eitel ['aɪtəl] *adj* vain; **E~keit** *f* vanity.

Eiter ['aɪtər] (*-s*) *m* pus.

eiterig *adj* suppurating.

eitern *vi* to suppurate.

Ei- *zW*: **~weiß** (*-es, -e*) *nt* white of an egg; (*CHEM*) protein; **~weißgehalt** *m* protein content; **~zelle** *f* ovum.

EKD *f abk* (= *Evangelische Kirche in Deutschland*) *German Protestant Church*.

Ekel¹ ['eːkəl] (*-s*) *m* nausea, disgust; **vor jdm/etw einen ~ haben** to loathe sb/sth.

Ekel² ['eːkəl] (*-s, -*) (*umg*) *nt* (*Mensch*) nauseating person.

ekelerregend *adj* nauseating, disgusting.

ekelhaft *adj*, **ekelig** *adj* = **ekelerregend**.

ekeln *vt* to disgust ♦ *vr*: **sich vor etw** *dat* **~** to loathe *od* be disgusted at sth; **es ekelt ihn** he is disgusted.

EKG (*-*) *nt abk* (= *Elektrokardiogramm*) *ECG*.

Eklat [e'klaː] (*-s*) *m* (*geh: Aufsehen*) sensation.

eklig *adj* nauseating, disgusting.

Ekstase [ɛk'staːzə] (*-, -n*) *f* ecstasy; **jdn in ~ versetzen** to send sb into ecstasies.

Ekzem [ɛk'tseːm] (*-s, -e*) *nt* (*MED*) eczema.

Elan [e'lãː] (*-s*) *m* élan.

elastisch [e'lastɪʃ] *adj* elastic.

Elastizität [elastitsi'tɛːt] *f* elasticity.

Elbe ['ɛlbə] *f* (*Fluß*) Elbe.

Elch [ɛlç] (*-(e)s, -e*) *m* elk.

Elefant [ele'fant] *m* elephant; **wie ein ~ im Porzellanladen** (*umg*) like a bull in a china shop.

elegant [ele'gant] *adj* elegant.

Eleganz [ele'gants] *f* elegance.

Elektrifizierung [elɛktrifi'tsiːrʊŋ] *f* electrification.

Elektriker [e'lɛktrikər] (*-s, -*) *m* electrician.

elektrisch [e'lɛktrɪʃ] *adj* electric.

elektrisieren [elɛktri'ziːrən] *vt* (*lit, fig*) to electrify; (*Mensch*) to give an electric shock to ♦ *vr* to get an electric shock.

Elektrizität [elɛktritsi'tɛːt] *f* electricity.

Elektrizitätswerk *nt* electric power station.

Elektroartikel [e'lɛktroˌartɪkəl] *m* electrical appliance.

Elektrode [elɛk'troːdə] (*-, -n*) *f* electrode.

Elektro- *zW*: **~gerät** *nt* electrical appliance; **~herd** *m* electric cooker; **~kardiogramm** *nt* (*MED*) electrocardiogram.

Elektrolyse [elektro'lyːzə] (*-, -n*) *f* electrolysis.

Elektromotor *m* electric motor.

Elektron [e'lɛktrɔn] (*-s, -en*) *nt* electron.

Elektronen(ge)hirn *nt* electronic brain.
Elektronenrechner *m* computer.
Elektronik [elɛk'troːnɪk] *f* electronics *sing*; (*Teile*) electronics *pl*.
elektronisch *adj* electronic; **~e Post** electronic mail.
Elektro- *zW:* **~rasierer (-s, -)** *m* electric razor; **~schock** *m* (*MED*) electric shock, electroshock; **~techniker** *m* electrician; (*Ingenieur*) electrical engineer.
Element [ele'mɛnt] **(-s, -e)** *nt* element; (*ELEK*) cell, battery.
elementar [elemɛn'taːr] *adj* elementary; (*naturhaft*) elemental; **E~teilchen** *nt* (*PHYS*) elementary particle.
Elend ['eːlɛnt] **(-(e)s)** *nt* misery; **da kann man das heulende ~ kriegen** (*umg*) it's enough to make you scream; **e~** *adj* miserable; **mir ist ganz e~** I feel really awful.
elendiglich ['eːlɛndɪklɪç] *adv* miserably; **~ zugrunde gehen** to come to a wretched end.
Elendsviertel *nt* slum.
elf [ɛlf] *num* eleven; **E~ (-, en)** *f* (*SPORT*) eleven.
Elfe (-, -n) *f* elf.
Elfenbein *nt* ivory; **~küste** *f* Ivory Coast.
Elfmeter *m* (*SPORT*) penalty (kick).
Elfmeterschießen *nt* (*SPORT*) penalty shoot-out.
eliminieren [elimi'niːrən] *vt* to eliminate.
elitär [eli'tɛːr] *adj* elitist ♦ *adv* in an elitist fashion.
Elite [e'liːtə] **(-, -n)** *f* elite.
Elixier [elɪ'ksiːr] **(-s, -e)** *nt* elixir.
Ellbogen *m* = **Ellenbogen**.
Elle ['ɛlə] **(-, -n)** *f* ell; (*Maß*) ≈ yard.
Ellenbogen *m* elbow; **die ~ gebrauchen** (*umg*) to be pushy; **~freiheit** *f* (*fig*) elbow room; **~gesellschaft** *f* dog-eat-dog society.
Ellipse [e'lɪpsə] **(-, -n)** *f* ellipse.
E-Lok ['eːlɔk] **(-)** *f* *abk* (= *elektrische Lokomotive*) electric locomotive *od* engine.
Elsaß ['ɛlzas] *nt:* **das ~** Alsace.
Elsässer ['ɛlzɛsər] *adj* Alsatian.
Elsässer(in) (-s, -) *m(f)* Alsatian, inhabitant of Alsace.
elsässisch *adj* Alsatian.
Elster ['ɛlstər] **(-, -n)** *f* magpie.
elterlich *adj* parental.
Eltern ['ɛltərn] *pl* parents *pl*; **nicht von schlechten ~ sein** (*umg*) to be quite something; **~abend** *m* (*SCH*) parents' evening; **~haus** *nt* home; **e~los** *adj* orphaned; **~sprechtag** *m* open day (for parents); **~teil** *m* parent.
Email [e'maːj] **(-s, -s)** *nt* enamel.
emaillieren [ema'jiːrən] *vt* to enamel.
Emanze (-, -n) (*meist pej*) *f* women's libber (*umg*).
Emanzipation [emantsipatsi'oːn] *f* emancipation.

emanzipieren [emantsi'piːrən] *vt* to emancipate.
Embargo [ɛm'bargo] **(-s, -s)** *nt* embargo.
Embryo ['ɛmbryo] **(-s, -s** *od* **-nen)** *m* embryo.
Emigrant(in) [emi'grant(ɪn)] *m(f)* emigrant.
Emigration [emigratsi'oːn] *f* emigration.
emigrieren [emi'griːrən] *vi* to emigrate.
Emissionen *npl* emissions *pl*.
Emissionskurs [emɪsi'oːnskʊrs] *m* (*Aktien*) issued price.
EMNID *m* *abk* (= *Erforschung, Meinung, Nachrichten, Informationsdienst*) opinion poll organization.
emotional [emotsio'naːl] *adj* emotional; (*Ausdrucksweise*) emotive.
emotionsgeladen [emotsi'oːnsgəlaːdən] *adj* emotionally-charged.
Empf. *abk* = **Empfänger**.
empfahl *etc* [ɛm'pfaːl] *vb siehe* **empfehlen**.
empfand *etc* [ɛm'pfant] *vb siehe* **empfinden**.
Empfang [ɛm'pfaŋ] **(-(e)s, ̈-e)** *m* reception; (*Erhalten*) receipt; **in ~ nehmen** to receive; **(zahlbar) nach** *od* **bei ~ +gen** (payable) on receipt (of).
empfangen *unreg* *vt* to receive ♦ *vi* (*schwanger werden*) to conceive.
Empfänger(in) [ɛm'pfɛŋər(ɪn)] **(-s, -)** *m(f)* receiver; (*COMM*) addressee, consignee; **~ unbekannt** (*auf Briefen*) not known at this address.
empfänglich *adj* receptive, susceptible.
Empfängnis (-, -se) *f* conception; **e~verhütend** *adj:* **e~verhütende Mittel** contraceptives *pl*; **~verhütung** *f* contraception.
Empfangs- *zW:* **~bestätigung** *f* (acknowledgement of) receipt; **~chef** *m* (*von Hotel*) head porter; **~dame** *f* receptionist; **~schein** *m* receipt; **~störung** *f* (*RUNDF, TV*) interference; **~zimmer** *nt* reception room.
empfehlen [ɛm'pfeːlən] *unreg* *vt* to recommend ♦ *vr* to take one's leave.
empfehlenswert *adj* recommendable.
Empfehlung *f* recommendation; **auf ~ von** on the recommendation of.
Empfehlungsschreiben *nt* letter of recommendation.
empfiehlt [ɛm'pfiːlt] *vb siehe* **empfehlen**.
empfinden [ɛm'pfɪndən] *unreg* *vt* to feel; **etw als Beleidigung ~** to find sth insulting; **E~ (-s)** *nt:* **meinem E~ nach** to my mind.
empfindlich *adj* sensitive; (*Stelle*) sore; (*reizbar*) touchy; **deine Kritik hat ihn ~ getroffen** your criticism cut him to the quick; **E~keit** *f* sensitiveness; (*Reizbarkeit*) touchiness.
empfindsam *adj* sentimental; (*Mensch*) sensitive.
Empfindung *f* feeling, sentiment.
empfindungslos *adj* unfeeling, insensitive.
empfing *etc* [ɛm'pfɪŋ] *vb siehe* **empfangen**.

empfohlen [ɛm'pfoːlən] *pp von* **empfehlen**
♦ *adj:* ~**er Einzelhandelspreis** recommended
retail price.
empfunden [ɛm'pfundən] *pp von* **empfinden**.
empor [ɛm'poːr] *adv* up, upwards.
emporarbeiten *vr (geh)* to work one's way
up.
Empore [ɛm'poːrə] (-, -n) *f (ARCHIT)* gallery.
empören [ɛm'pøːrən] *vt* to make indignant; to
shock ♦ *vr* to become indignant.
empörend *adj* outrageous.
emporkommen *unreg vi* to rise;
(*vorankommen*) to succeed.
Emporkömmling *m* upstart, parvenu.
empört *adj:* ~ **(über** +*akk*) indignant (at),
outraged (at).
Empörung *f* indignation.
emsig ['ɛmzɪç] *adj* diligent, busy.
End- ['ɛnt] *in zW* final; ~**auswertung** *f* final
analysis; ~**bahnhof** *m* terminus; ~**betrag** *m*
final amount.
Ende ['ɛndə] (-s, -n) *nt* end; **am** ~ at the end;
(*schließlich*) in the end; **am** ~ **sein** to be at
the end of one's tether; ~ **Dezember** at the
end of December; **zu** ~ **sein** to be finished;
zu ~ **gehen** to come to an end; **zu** ~ **führen**
to finish (off); **letzten** ~**s** in the end, at the
end of the day; **letzten** ~**s** in the end, at the
end of the day; **etw böses** ~ **nehmen** to come
to a bad end; **ich bin mit meiner Weisheit am**
~ I'm at my wits' end; **er wohnt am** ~ **der**
Welt (*umg*) he lives at the back of beyond.
Endeffekt *m:* **im** ~ (*umg*) when it comes down
to it.
enden *vi* to end.
Endergebnis *nt* final result.
endgültig *adj* final, definite.
Endivie [ɛn'diːviə] *f* endive.
End- *zW:* ~**lager** *nt* permanent waste disposal
site; ~**lagerung** *f* permanent disposal;
e~**lich** *adj* final; (*MATH*) finite ♦ *adv* finally;
e~**lich!** at last!; **hör e**~**lich damit auf!** will
you stop that!; **e**~**los** *adj* endless;
~**lospapier** *nt* continuous paper; ~**produkt**
nt end od final product; ~**spiel** *nt* final(s);
~**spurt** *m* (*SPORT*) final spurt; ~**station** *f*
terminus.
Endung *f* ending.
Endverbraucher *m* consumer, end-user.
Energie [enɛr'giː] *f* energy; ~**aufwand** *m*
energy expenditure; ~**bedarf** *m* energy
requirement; ~**einsparung** *f* energy saving;
~**gewinnung** *f* generation of energy; **e**~**los**
adj lacking in energy, weak; ~**quelle** *f*
source of energy; ~**versorgung** *f* supply of
energy; ~**wirtschaft** *f* energy industry.
energisch [e'nɛrgɪʃ] *adj* energetic;
~ **durchgreifen** to take vigorous *od* firm
action.
eng [ɛŋ] *adj* narrow; (*Kleidung*) tight; (*fig:*
Horizont) narrow, limited; (*Freundschaft,*
Verhältnis) close; ~ **an etw** *dat* close to sth; **in**
die ~**ere Wahl kommen** to be short-listed

(*BRIT*).
Engadin ['ɛŋgadiːn] (-s) *nt:* **das** ~ the
Engadine.
Engagement [ãgaʒə'mãː] (-s, -s) *nt*
engagement; (*Verpflichtung*) commitment.
engagieren [ãga'ʒiːrən] *vt* to engage ♦ *vr* to
commit o.s.; **ein engagierter Schriftsteller** a
committed writer.
Enge ['ɛŋə] (-, -n) *f* (*lit, fig*) narrowness;
(*Land*~) defile; (*Meer*~) straits *pl*; **jdn in die**
~ **treiben** to drive sb into a corner.
Engel ['ɛŋəl] (-s, -) *m* angel; **e**~**haft** *adj* angelic;
~**macher(in)** (-s, -) (*umg*) *m(f)* backstreet
abortionist.
Engelsgeduld *f:* **sie hat eine** ~ she has the
patience of a saint.
Engelszungen *pl:* **(wie) mit** ~ **reden** to use all
one's own powers of persuasion.
engherzig *adj* petty.
engl. *abk* = **englisch**.
England ['ɛŋlant] *nt* England.
Engländer ['ɛŋlɛndər] (-s, -) *m* Englishman;
English boy; **die Engländer** *pl* the English,
the Britishers (*US*); ~**in** *f* Englishwoman;
English girl.
englisch ['ɛŋlɪʃ] *adj* English.
engmaschig ['ɛŋmaʃɪç] *adj* close-meshed.
Engpaß *m* defile, pass; (*fig: Verkehr*)
bottleneck.
en gros [ã'gro] *adv* wholesale.
engstirnig ['ɛŋʃtɪrnɪç] *adj* narrow-minded.
Enkel ['ɛŋkəl] (-s, -) *m* grandson; ~**in** *f*
granddaughter; ~**kind** *nt* grandchild.
en masse [ã'mas] *adv* en masse.
enorm [e'nɔrm] *adj* enormous; (*umg: herrlich,*
kolossal) tremendous.
en passant [ãpa'sã] *adv* en passant, in
passing.
Ensemble [ã'sãbəl] (-s, -s) *nt* ensemble.
entarten [ɛnt'ʔaːrtən] *vi* to degenerate.
entbehren [ɛnt'beːrən] *vt* to do without,
dispense with.
entbehrlich *adj* superfluous.
Entbehrung *f* privation; ~**en auf sich** *akk*
nehmen to make sacrifices.
entbinden [ɛnt'bɪndən] *unreg vt* (+*gen*) to
release (from); (*MED*) to deliver ♦ *vi* (*MED*)
to give birth.
Entbindung *f* release; (*MED*) delivery, birth.
Entbindungsheim *nt* maternity hospital.
Entbindungsstation *f* maternity ward.
entblößen [ɛnt'bløːsən] *vt* to denude,
uncover; (*berauben*): **einer Sache** *gen*
entblößt deprived of sth.
entbrennen [ɛnt'brɛnən] *unreg vi* (*liter: Kampf,*
Streit) to flare up; (: *Liebe*) to be aroused.
entdecken [ɛnt'dɛkən] *vt* to discover; **jdm etw**
~ to disclose sth to sb.
Entdecker(in) (-s, -) *m(f)* discoverer.
Entdeckung *f* discovery.
Ente ['ɛntə] (-, -n) *f* duck; (*fig*) canard, false
report; (*AUT*) Citroën 2CV, deux-chevaux.

entehren [ɛnt'|eːrən] vt to dishonour (BRIT), dishonor (US), disgrace.

enteignen [ɛnt'|aɪɡnən] vt to expropriate; (Besitzer) to dispossess.

enteisen [ɛnt'|aɪzən] vt to de-ice; (Kühlschrank) to defrost.

enterben [ɛnt'|ɛrbən] vt to disinherit.

Enterhaken ['ɛntərhaːkən] m grappling iron od hook.

entfachen [ɛnt'faxən] vt to kindle.

entfallen [ɛnt'falən] unreg vi to drop, fall; (wegfallen) to be dropped; **jdm ~** (vergessen) to slip sb's memory; **auf jdn ~** to be allotted to sb.

entfalten [ɛnt'faltən] vt to unfold; (Talente) to develop ♦ vr to open; (Mensch) to develop one's potential.

Entfaltung f unfolding; (von Talenten) development.

entfernen [ɛnt'fɛrnən] vt to remove; (hinauswerfen) to expel ♦ vr to go away, retire, withdraw.

entfernt adj distant ♦ adv: **nicht im ~esten!** not in the slightest!; **weit davon ~ sein, etw zu tun** to be far from doing sth.

Entfernung f distance; (Wegschaffen) removal; **unerlaubte ~ von der Truppe** absence without leave.

Entfernungsmesser m (PHOT) rangefinder.

entfesseln [ɛnt'fɛsəln] vt (fig) to arouse.

entfetten [ɛnt'fɛtən] vt to take the fat from.

entflammen [ɛnt'flamən] vt (fig) to (a)rouse ♦ vi to burst into flames; (fig: Streit) to flare up; (: Leidenschaft) to be (a)roused od inflamed.

entfremden [ɛnt'frɛmdən] vt to estrange, alienate.

Entfremdung f estrangement, alienation.

entfrosten [ɛnt'frɔstən] vt to defrost.

Entfroster (-s, -) m (AUT) defroster.

entführen [ɛnt'fyːrən] vt to abduct, kidnap; (Flugzeug) to hijack.

Entführer (-s, -) m kidnapper (BRIT), kidnaper (US); hijacker.

Entführung f abduction, kidnapping (BRIT), kidnaping (US); hijacking.

entgegen [ɛnt'ɡeːɡən] präp +dat contrary to, against ♦ adv towards; **~bringen** unreg vt to bring; (fig): **jdm etw ~bringen** to show sb sth; **~gehen** unreg vi +dat to go to meet, go towards; **Schwierigkeiten ~gehen** to be heading for difficulties; **~gesetzt** adj opposite; (widersprechend) opposed; **~halten** unreg vt (fig): **einer Sache** dat **~halten, daß ...** to object to sth that ...; **E~kommen** nt obligingness; **~kommen** unreg vi +dat to come towards, approach; (fig): **jdm ~kommen** to accommodate sb; **das kommt unseren Plänen sehr ~** that fits in very well with our plans; **~kommend** adj obliging; **~laufen** unreg vi +dat to run towards od to meet; (fig) to run counter to; **E~nahme** f (form: Empfang)

receipt; (Annahme) acceptance; **~nehmen** unreg vt to receive, accept; **~sehen** unreg vi +dat to await; **~setzen** vt to oppose; **dem habe ich ~zusetzen, daß ...** against that I'd like to say that ...; **jdm/etw Widerstand ~setzen** to put up resistance to sb/sth; **~stehen** unreg vi: **dem steht nichts ~** there's no objection to that; **~treten** unreg vi +dat (lit) to step up to; (fig) to oppose, counter; **~wirken** vi +dat to counteract.

entgegnen [ɛnt'ɡeːɡnən] vt to reply, retort.

Entgegnung f reply, retort.

entgehen [ɛnt'ɡeːən] unreg vi (fig): **jdm ~** to escape sb's notice; **sich** dat **etw ~ lassen** to miss sth.

entgeistert [ɛnt'ɡaɪstərt] adj thunderstruck.

Entgelt [ɛnt'ɡɛlt] (-(e)s, -e) nt remuneration.

entgelten unreg vt: **jdm etw ~** to repay sb for sth.

entgleisen [ɛnt'ɡlaɪzən] vi (EISENB) to be derailed; (fig: Person) to misbehave; **~ lassen** to derail.

Entgleisung f derailment; (fig) faux pas, gaffe.

entgleiten [ɛnt'ɡlaɪtən] unreg vi: **jdm ~** to slip from sb's hand.

entgräten [ɛnt'ɡrɛːtən] vt to fillet, bone.

Enthaarungsmittel [ɛnt'haːrʊŋsmɪtəl] nt depilatory.

enthält [ɛnt'hɛlt] vb siehe enthalten.

enthalten [ɛnt'haltən] unreg vt to contain ♦ vr +gen to abstain from, refrain from; **sich (der Stimme) ~** to abstain.

enthaltsam [ɛnt'haltzaːm] adj abstinent, abstemious; **E~keit** f abstinence.

enthärten [ɛnt'hɛrtən] vt (Wasser) to soften; (Metall) to anneal.

enthaupten [ɛnt'haʊptən] vt to decapitate; (als Hinrichtung) to behead.

enthäuten [ɛnt'hɔytən] vt to skin.

entheben [ɛnt'heːbən] unreg vt: **jdn einer Sache** gen **~** to relieve sb of sth.

enthemmen [ɛnt'hɛmən] vt: **jdn ~** to free sb from his/her inhibitions.

enthielt etc [ɛnt'hiːlt] vb siehe enthalten.

enthüllen [ɛnt'hʏlən] vt to reveal, unveil.

Enthüllung f revelation; (von Skandal) exposure.

Enthusiasmus [ɛntuzi'asmʊs] m enthusiasm.

entjungfern [ɛnt'jʊŋfərn] vt to deflower.

entkalken [ɛnt'kalkən] vt to decalcify.

entkernen [ɛnt'kɛrnən] vt (Kernobst) to core; (Steinobst) to stone.

entkleiden [ɛnt'klaɪdən] vt, vr (geh) to undress.

entkommen [ɛnt'kɔmən] unreg vi to get away, escape; **jdm/etw od aus etw ~** to get away od escape from sb/sth.

entkorken [ɛnt'kɔrkən] vt to uncork.

entkräften [ɛnt'krɛftən] vt to weaken, exhaust; (Argument) to refute.

entkrampfen [ɛnt'krampfən] vt (fig) to relax,

ease.

entladen [ɛnt'laːdən] *unreg vt* to unload; (*ELEK*) to discharge ♦ *vr* (*ELEK, Gewehr*) to discharge; (*Ärger etc*) to vent itself.

entlang [ɛnt'laŋ] *präp* (+*akk od dat*) along ♦ *adv* along; ~ **dem Fluß, den Fluß** ~ along the river; **hier** ~ this way; ~**gehen** *unreg vi* to walk along.

entlarven [ɛnt'larfən] *vt* to unmask, expose.

entlassen [ɛnt'lasən] *unreg vt* to discharge; (*Arbeiter*) to dismiss; (*nach Stellenabbau*) to make redundant.

entläßt [ɛnt'lɛst] *vb siehe* **entlassen**.

Entlassung *f* discharge; dismissal; **es gab 20** ~**en** there were 20 redundancies.

Entlassungszeugnis *nt* (*SCH*) school-leaving certificate.

entlasten [ɛnt'lastən] *vt* to relieve; (*Arbeit abnehmen*) to take some of the load off; (*Angeklagte*) to exonerate; (*Konto*) to clear.

Entlastung *f* relief; (*COMM*) crediting.

Entlastungszeuge *m* defence (*BRIT*) *od* defense (*US*) witness.

Entlastungszug *m* relief train.

entledigen [ɛnt'leːdɪgən] *vr:* **sich jds/einer Sache** ~ to rid o.s. of sb/sth.

entleeren [ɛnt'leːrən] *vt* to empty; (*Darm*) to evacuate.

entlegen [ɛnt'leːgən] *adj* remote.

entließ *etc* [ɛnt'liːs] *vb siehe* **entlassen**.

entlocken [ɛnt'lɔkən] *vt:* **jdm etw** ~ to elicit sth from sb.

entlohnen *vt* to pay; (*fig*) to reward.

entlüften [ɛnt'lʏftən] *vt* to ventilate.

entmachten [ɛnt'maxtən] *vt* to deprive of power.

entmenscht [ɛnt'mɛnʃt] *adj* inhuman, bestial.

entmilitarisiert [ɛntmilitari'ziːrt] *adj* demilitarized.

entmündigen [ɛnt'mʏndɪgən] *vt* to certify; (*JUR*) to (legally) incapacitate, declare incapable of managing one's own affairs.

entmutigen [ɛnt'muːtɪgən] *vt* to discourage.

Entnahme [ɛnt'naːmə] (-, -n) *f* removal, withdrawal.

Entnazifizierung [ɛntnatsifi'tsiːrʊŋ] *f* denazification.

entnehmen [ɛnt'neːmən] *unreg vt* +*dat* to take out of, take from; (*folgern*) to infer from; **wie ich Ihren Worten entnehme, ...** I gather from what you say that ...

entpuppen [ɛnt'pʊpən] *vr* (*fig*) to reveal o.s., turn out; **sich als etw** ~ to turn out to be sth.

entrahmen [ɛnt'raːmən] *vt* to skim.

entreißen [ɛnt'raɪsən] *unreg vt:* **jdm etw** ~ to snatch sth (away) from sb.

entrichten [ɛnt'rɪçtən] *vt* (*form*) to pay.

entrosten [ɛnt'rɔstən] *vt* to derust.

entrüsten [ɛnt'rʏstən] *vt* to incense, outrage ♦ *vr* to be filled with indignation.

entrüstet *adj* indignant, outraged.

Entrüstung *f* indignation.

Entsafter [ɛnt'zaftər] (-s, -) *m* juice extractor.

entsagen [ɛnt'zaːgən] *vi* +*dat* to renounce.

entschädigen [ɛnt'ʃɛːdɪgən] *vt* to compensate.

Entschädigung *f* compensation.

entschärfen [ɛnt'ʃɛrfən] *vt* to defuse; (*Kritik*) to tone down.

Entscheid [ɛnt'ʃaɪt] (-(e)s, -e) *m* (*form*) decision.

entscheiden [ɛnt'ʃaɪdən] *unreg vt, vi, vr* to decide; **darüber habe ich nicht zu** ~ that is not for me to decide; **sich für jdn/etw** ~ to decide in favour of sb/sth; to decide on sb/sth.

entscheidend *adj* decisive; (*Stimme*) casting; **das E~e** the decisive *od* deciding factor.

Entscheidung *f* decision; **wie ist die** ~ **ausgefallen?** which way did the decision go?

Entscheidungs- *zW:* ~**befugnis** *f* decision-making powers *pl*; **e~fähig** *adj* capable of deciding; ~**spiel** *nt* play-off; ~**träger** *m* decision-maker.

entschied *etc* [ɛnt'ʃiːt] *vb siehe* **entscheiden**.

entschieden [ɛnt'ʃiːdən] *pp von* **entscheiden** ♦ *adj* decided; (*entschlossen*) resolute; **das geht** ~ **zu weit** that's definitely going too far; **E~heit** *f* firmness, determination.

entschlacken [ɛnt'ʃlakən] *vt* (*MED: Körper*) to purify.

entschließen [ɛnt'ʃliːsən] *unreg vr* to decide; **sich zu nichts** ~ **können** to be unable to make up one's mind; **kurz entschlossen** straight away.

Entschließungsantrag *m* (*POL*) resolution proposal.

entschloß *etc* [ɛnt'ʃlɔs] *vb siehe* **entschließen**.

entschlossen [ɛnt'ʃlɔsən] *pp von* **entschließen** ♦ *adj* determined, resolute; **E~heit** *f* determination.

entschlüpfen [ɛnt'ʃlʏpfən] *vi* to escape, slip away; (*fig: Wort etc*) to slip out.

Entschluß [ɛnt'ʃlʊs] *m* decision; **aus eigenem** ~ **handeln** to act on one's own initiative; **es ist mein fester** ~ it is my firm intention.

entschlüsseln [ɛnt'ʃlʏsəln] *vt* to decipher; (*Funkspruch*) to decode.

entschlußfreudig *adj* decisive.

Entschlußkraft *f* determination, decisiveness.

entschuldbar [ɛnt'ʃʊltbaːr] *adj* excusable.

entschuldigen [ɛnt'ʃʊldɪgən] *vt* to excuse ♦ *vr* to apologize ♦ *vi:* ~ **Sie (bitte)!** excuse me; (*Verzeihung*) sorry; **jdn bei jdm** ~ to make sb's excuses *od* apologies to sb; **sich** ~ **lassen** to send one's apologies.

entschuldigend *adj* apologetic.

Entschuldigung *f* apology; (*Grund*) excuse; **jdn um** ~ **bitten** to apologize to sb; ~**!** excuse me; (*Verzeihung*) sorry.

entschwefeln [ɛnt'ʃveːfəln] *vt* to desulphurize.

Entschwefelungsanlage *f* desulphurization plant.

entschwinden [ɛnt'ʃvɪndən] *unreg vi* to disappear.

entsetzen [ɛnt'zɛtsən] *vt* to horrify ♦ *vr* to be horrified *od* appalled; **E~** **(-s)** *nt* horror, dismay.

entsetzlich *adj* dreadful, appalling.

entsetzt *adj* horrified.

entsichern [ɛnt'zɪçərn] *vt* to release the safety catch of.

entsinnen [ɛnt'zɪnən] *unreg vr* +*gen* to remember.

entsorgen [ɛnt'zɔrgən] *vt:* **eine Stadt ~** to dispose of a town's refuse and sewage.

Entsorgung *f* waste disposal; (*von Chemikalien*) disposal.

entspannen [ɛnt'ʃpanən] *vt, vr* (*Körper*) to relax; (*POL: Lage*) to ease.

Entspannung *f* relaxation, rest; (*POL*) détente.

Entspannungspolitik *f* policy of détente.

Entspannungsübungen *pl* relaxation exercises *pl*.

entspr. *abk* = **entsprechend.**

entsprach *etc* [ɛnt'ʃprax] *vb siehe* **entsprechen.**

entsprechen [ɛnt'ʃprɛçən] *unreg vi* +*dat* to correspond to; (*Anforderungen, Wünschen*) to meet, comply with.

entsprechend *adj* appropriate ♦ *adv* accordingly ♦ *präp* +*dat:* **er wird seiner Leistung ~ bezahlt** he is paid according to output.

entspricht [ɛnt'ʃprɪçt] *vb siehe* **entsprechen.**

entspringen [ɛnt'ʃprɪŋən] *unreg vi* (+*dat*) to spring (from).

entsprochen [ɛnt'ʃprɔxən] *pp von* **entsprechen.**

entstaatlichen [ɛnt'ʃtaːtlɪçən] *vt* to denationalize.

entstammen [ɛnt'ʃtamən] *vi* +*dat* to stem *od* come from.

entstand *etc* [ɛnt'ʃtant] *vb siehe* **entstehen.**

entstanden [ɛnt'ʃtandən] *pp von* **entstehen.**

entstehen [ɛnt'ʃteːən] *unreg vi:* **~** (**aus** *od* **durch**) to arise (from), result (from); **wir wollen nicht den Eindruck ~ lassen, ...** we don't want to give rise to the impression that ...; **für ~den** *od* **entstandenen Schaden** for damages incurred.

Entstehung *f* genesis, origin.

entstellen [ɛnt'ʃtɛlən] *vt* to disfigure; (*Wahrheit*) to distort.

Entstellung *f* distortion; disfigurement.

entstören [ɛnt'ʃtøːrən] *vt* (*RUNDF*) to eliminate interference from; (*AUT*) to suppress.

enttäuschen [ɛnt'tɔyʃən] *vt* to disappoint.

Enttäuschung *f* disappointment.

entwachsen [ɛnt'vaksən] *unreg vi* +*dat* to outgrow, grow out of; (*geh: herauswachsen aus*) to spring from.

entwaffnen [ɛnt'vafnən] *vt* (*lit, fig*) to disarm.

entwaffnend *adj* disarming.

Entwarnung [ɛnt'varnʊŋ] *f* all clear (signal).

entwässern [ɛnt'vɛsərn] *vt* to drain.

Entwässerung *f* drainage.

entweder [ɛnt'veːdər] *konj* either; **~ ... oder ...** either ... or ...

entweichen [ɛnt'vaɪçən] *unreg vi* to escape.

entweihen [ɛnt'vaɪən] *unreg vt* to desecrate.

entwenden [ɛnt'vɛndən] *unreg vt* to purloin, steal.

entwerfen [ɛnt'vɛrfən] *unreg vt* (*Zeichnung*) to sketch; (*Modell*) to design; (*Vortrag, Gesetz etc*) to draft.

entwerten [ɛnt'veːrtən] *vt* to devalue; (*stempeln*) to cancel.

Entwerter **(-s, -)** *m* (ticket-)cancelling (*BRIT*) *od* canceling (*US*) machine.

entwickeln [ɛnt'vɪkəln] *vt* to develop (*auch PHOT*); (*Mut, Energie*) to show, display ♦ *vr* to develop.

Entwickler **(-s, -)** *m* developer.

Entwicklung [ɛnt'vɪklʊŋ] *f* development; (*PHOT*) developing; **in der ~** at the development stage; (*Jugendliche etc*) still developing.

Entwicklungs- *zW:* **~abschnitt** *m* stage of development; **~helfer(in)** *m(f)* VSO worker (*BRIT*), Peace Corps worker (*US*); **~hilfe** *f* aid for developing countries; **~jahre** *pl* adolescence *sing*; **~land** *nt* developing country; **~zeit** *f* period of development; (*PHOT*) developing time.

entwirren [ɛnt'vɪrən] *vt* to disentangle.

entwischen [ɛnt'vɪʃən] *vi* to escape.

entwöhnen [ɛnt'vøːnən] *vt* to wean; (*Süchtige*): (**einer Sache** *dat od* **von etw**) **~** to cure (of sth).

Entwöhnung *f* weaning; cure, curing.

entwürdigend [ɛnt'vyrdɪgənt] *adj* degrading.

Entwurf [ɛnt'vʊrf] *m* outline, design; (*Vertrags~, Konzept*) draft.

entwurzeln [ɛnt'vʊrtsəln] *vt* to uproot.

entziehen [ɛnt'tsiːən] *unreg vt* (+*dat*) to withdraw (from), take away (from); (*Flüssigkeit*) to draw (from), extract (from) ♦ *vr* (+*dat*) to escape (from); (*jds Kenntnis*) to be outside *od* beyond; (*der Pflicht*) to shirk (from); **sich jds Blicken ~** to be hidden from sight.

Entziehung *f* withdrawal.

Entziehungsanstalt *f* drug addiction/ alcoholism treatment centre (*BRIT*) *od* center (*US*).

Entziehungskur *f* treatment for drug addiction/alcoholism.

entziffern [ɛnt'tsɪfərn] *vt* to decipher; (*Funkspruch*) to decode.

entzücken [ɛnt'tsykən] *vt* to delight; **E~** **(-s)** *nt* delight.

entzückend *adj* delightful, charming.

Entzug [ɛnt'tsuːk] **(-(e)s)** *m* (*einer Lizenz etc, MED*) withdrawal.

Entzugserscheinung *f* withdrawal

symptom.

entzündbar *adj:* **leicht** ~ highly inflammable; (*fig*) easily roused.

entzünden [ɛnt'tsʏndən] *vt* to light, set light to; (*fig, MED*) to inflame; (*Streit*) to spark off ♦ *vr* (*lit, fig*) to catch fire; (*Streit*) to start; (*MED*) to become inflamed.

Entzündung *f* (*MED*) inflammation.

entzwei [ɛnt'tsvaɪ] *adv* in two; broken; ~**brechen** *unreg vt, vi* to break in two.

entzweien *vt* to set at odds ♦ *vr* to fall out.

entzweigehen *unreg vi* to break (in two).

Enzian ['ɛntsiaːn] (**-s, -e**) *m* gentian.

Enzyklika [ɛn'tsyːklika] (**-, -liken**) *f* (*REL*) encyclical.

Enzyklopädie [ɛntsyklopɛ'diː] *f* encyclop(a)edia.

Enzym [ɛn'tsyːm] (**-s, -e**) *nt* enzyme.

Epen *pl von* **Epos.**

Epidemie [epide'miː] *f* epidemic.

Epilepsie [epile'psiː] *f* epilepsy.

episch ['eːpɪʃ] *adj* epic.

Episode [epi'zoːdə] (**-, -n**) *f* episode.

Epoche [e'pɔxə] (**-, -n**) *f* epoch; **e~machend** *adj* epoch-making.

Epos ['eːpɔs] (**-, Epen**) *nt* epic (poem).

Equipe [e'kɪp] (**-, -n**) *f* team.

er [eːr] *pron* he; it.

erachten [ɛr'|axtən] *vt* (*geh*): ~ **für** *od* **als** to consider (to be); **meines E~s** in my opinion.

erarbeiten [ɛr'|arbaɪtən] *vt* to work for, acquire; (*Theorie*) to work out.

Erbanlage ['ɛrp|anlaːgə] *f* hereditary factor(s *pl*).

erbarmen [ɛr'barmən] *vr* (*+gen*) to have pity *od* mercy (on) ♦ *vt:* **er sieht zum E~ aus** he's a pitiful sight; **Herr, erbarme dich (unser)!** Lord, have mercy (upon us)!; **E~** (**-s**) *nt* pity.

erbärmlich [ɛr'bɛrmlɪç] *adj* wretched, pitiful; **E~keit** *f* wretchedness.

Erbarmungs- *zW:* **e~los** *adj* pitiless, merciless; **e~voll** *adj* compassionate; **e~würdig** *adj* pitiable, wretched.

erbauen [ɛr'bauən] *vt* to build, erect; (*fig*) to edify; **er ist von meinem Plan nicht besonders erbaut** (*umg*) he isn't particularly enthusiastic about my plan.

Erbauer (**-s, -**) *m* builder.

erbaulich *adj* edifying.

Erbauung *f* construction; (*fig*) edification.

erbberechtigt *adj* entitled to inherit.

erbbiologisch *adj:* ~**es Gutachten** (*JUR*) blood test (*to establish paternity*).

Erbe¹ ['ɛrbə] (**-n, -n**) *m* heir; **jdn zum** *od* **als** ~**n einsetzen** to make sb one's/sb's heir.

Erbe² ['ɛrbə] (**-s**) *nt* inheritance; (*fig*) heritage.

erben *vt* to inherit; (*umg: geschenkt bekommen*) to get, be given.

erbeuten [ɛr'bɔytən] *vt* to carry off; (*MIL*) to capture.

Erb- *zW:* ~**faktor** *m* gene; ~**fehler** *m*

hereditary defect; ~**feind** *m* traditional *od* arch enemy; ~**folge** *f* (line of) succession.

Erbin *f* heiress.

erbitten [ɛr'bɪtən] *unreg vt* to ask for, request.

erbittern [ɛr'bɪtərn] *vt* to embitter; (*erzürnen*) to incense.

erbittert [ɛr'bɪtərt] *adj* (*Kampf*) fierce, bitter.

erblassen [ɛr'blasən] *vi* to (turn) pale.

Erblasser(in) (**-s, -**) *m(f)* (*JUR*) person who leaves an inheritance.

erbleichen [ɛr'blaɪçən] *unreg vi* to (turn) pale.

erblich ['ɛrplɪç] *adj* hereditary; **er/sie ist** ~ (**vor)belastet** it runs in the family.

erblichen *pp von* **erbleichen.**

erblicken [ɛr'blɪkən] *vt* to see; (*erspähen*) to catch sight of.

erblinden [ɛr'blɪndən] *vi* to go blind.

Erbmasse ['ɛrpmasə] *f* estate; (*BIOL*) genotype.

erbosen [ɛr'boːzən] *vt* (*geh*) to anger ♦ *vr* to grow angry.

erbrechen [ɛr'brɛçən] *unreg vt, vr* to vomit.

Erbrecht *nt* hereditary right; (*Gesetze*) law of inheritance.

Erbschaft *f* inheritance, legacy.

Erbschaftssteuer *f* estate *od* death duties *pl*.

Erbschleicher(in) ['ɛrpʃlaɪçər(ɪn)] (**-s, -**) *m(f)* legacy-hunter.

Erbse ['ɛrpsə] (**-, -n**) *f* pea.

Erb- *zW:* ~**stück** *nt* heirloom; ~**sünde** *f* (*REL*) original sin; ~**teil** *nt* inherited trait; (*JUR*) (portion of) inheritance.

Erd- *zW:* ~**achse** *f* earth's axis; ~**apfel** (*ÖSTERR*) *m* potato; ~**atmosphäre** *f* earth's atmosphere; ~**bahn** *f* orbit of the earth; ~**beben** *nt* earthquake; ~**beere** *f* strawberry; ~**boden** *m* ground; **etw dem** ~**boden gleichmachen** to level sth, raze sth to the ground.

Erde (**-, -n**) *f* earth; **zu ebener** ~ at ground level; **auf der ganzen** ~ all over the world; **du wirst mich noch unter die** ~ **bringen** (*umg*) you'll be the death of me yet.

erden *vt* (*ELEK*) to earth.

erdenkbar [ɛr'dɛŋkbaːr] *adj* conceivable; **sich** *dat* **alle** ~**e Mühe geben** to take the greatest (possible) pains.

erdenklich [ɛr'dɛŋklɪç] *adj* = **erdenkbar.**

Erdg. *abk* = **Erdgeschoß.**

Erd- *zW:* ~**gas** *nt* natural gas; ~**geschoß** *nt* ground floor (*BRIT*), first floor (*US*); ~**kunde** *f* geography; ~**nuß** *f* peanut; ~**oberfläche** *f* surface of the earth; ~**öl** *nt* (mineral) oil; ~**ölfeld** *nt* oilfield; ~**ölindustrie** *f* oil industry; ~**reich** *nt* soil, earth.

erdreisten [ɛr'draɪstən] *vr* to dare, have the audacity (*to do sth*).

erdrosseln [ɛr'drɔsəln] *vt* to strangle, throttle.

erdrücken [ɛr'drʏkən] *vt* to crush; ~**de Übermacht/~des Beweismaterial** overwhelming superiority/evidence.

Erd- *zW:* ~**rutsch** *m* landslide; ~**stoß** *m*

(seismic) shock; **~teil** m continent.
erdulden [ɛr'dʊldən] vt to endure, suffer.
ereifern [ɛr'|aɪfərn] vr to get excited.
ereignen [ɛr'|aɪgnən] vr to happen.
Ereignis [ɛr'|aɪgnɪs] (**-ses, -se**) nt event; **e~los**
adj uneventful; **e~reich** adj eventful.
Eremit [ere'miːt] (**-en, -en**) m hermit.
erfahren [ɛr'faːrən] unreg vt to learn, find out;
(erleben) to experience ♦ adj experienced.
Erfahrung f experience; **~en sammeln** to
gain experience; **etw in ~ bringen** to learn
od find out sth.
Erfahrungsaustausch m exchange of
experiences.
erfahrungsgemäß adv according to
experience.
erfand etc [ɛr'fant] vb siehe **erfinden**.
erfassen [ɛr'fasən] vt to seize; (fig: einbeziehen)
to include, register; (verstehen) to grasp.
erfinden [ɛr'fɪndən] unreg vt to invent; **frei
erfunden** completely fictitious.
Erfinder(in) (**-s, -**) m(f) inventor; **e~isch** adj
inventive.
Erfindung f invention.
Erfindungsgabe f inventiveness.
Erfolg [ɛr'fɔlk] (**-(e)s, -e**) m success; (Folge)
result; **viel ~!** good luck!
erfolgen [ɛr'fɔlgən] vi to follow; (sich ergeben)
to result; (stattfinden) to take place;
(Zahlung) to be effected; **nach erfolgter
Zahlung** when payment has been made.
Erfolg- zW: **e~los** adj unsuccessful;
~losigkeit f lack of success; **e~reich** adj
successful.
Erfolgserlebnis nt feeling of success, sense
of achievement.
erfolgversprechend adj promising.
erforderlich adj requisite, necessary.
erfordern [ɛr'fɔrdərn] vt to require, demand.
Erfordernis (**-ses, -se**) nt requirement,
prerequisite.
erforschen [ɛr'fɔrʃən] vt (Land) to explore;
(Problem) to investigate; (Gewissen) to
search.
Erforscher(in) (**-s, -**) m(f) explorer;
investigator.
Erforschung f exploration; investigation;
searching.
erfragen [ɛr'fraːgən] vt to inquire, ascertain.
erfreuen [ɛr'frɔyən] vr: **sich ~ an** +dat to enjoy
♦ vt to delight; **sich einer Sache gen ~** (geh)
to enjoy sth; **sehr erfreut!** (form: bei
Vorstellung) pleased to meet you!
erfreulich [ɛr'frɔylɪç] adj pleasing, gratifying.
erfreulicherweise adv happily, luckily.
erfrieren [ɛr'friːrən] unreg vi to freeze (to
death); (Glieder) to get frostbitten; (Pflanzen)
to be killed by frost.
erfrischen [ɛr'frɪʃən] vt to refresh.
Erfrischung f refreshment.
Erfrischungsraum m snack bar, cafeteria.
erfüllen [ɛr'fylən] vt (Raum etc) to fill; (fig: Bitte

etc) to fulfil (BRIT), fulfill (US) ♦ vr to come
true; **ein erfülltes Leben** a full life.
Erfüllung f: **in ~ gehen** to be fulfilled.
erfunden [ɛr'fʊndən] pp von **erfinden**.
ergab etc [ɛr'gaːp] vb siehe **ergeben**.
ergänzen [ɛr'gɛntsən] vt to supplement,
complete ♦ vr to complement one another.
Ergänzung f completion; (Zusatz)
supplement.
ergattern [ɛr'gatərn] (umg) vt to get hold of,
hunt up.
ergaunern [ɛr'gaʊnərn] (umg) vt: **sich** dat **etw
~** to get hold of sth by underhand methods.
ergeben [ɛr'geːbən] unreg vt to yield, produce
♦ vr to surrender; (folgen) to result ♦ adj
devoted; (demütig) humble; **sich einer Sache**
dat **~** (sich hingeben) to give o.s. up to sth,
yield to sth; **es ergab sich, daß unsere
Befürchtungen ...** it turned out that our
fears ...; **dem Trunk ~** addicted to drink;
E~heit f devotion; humility.
Ergebnis [ɛr'geːpnɪs] (**-ses, -se**) nt result; **zu
einem ~ kommen** to come to od reach a
conclusion; **e~los** adj without result,
fruitless; **e~los bleiben** od **verlaufen** to
come to nothing.
ergehen [ɛr'geːən] unreg vi (form) to be issued,
go out ♦ vi unpers: **es ergeht ihm gut/schlecht**
he's faring od getting on well/badly ♦ vr:
sich in etw dat **~** to indulge in sth; **etw über
sich** akk **~ lassen** to put up with sth; **sich (in
langen Reden) über ein Thema ~** (fig) to
hold forth at length on sth.
ergiebig [ɛr'giːbɪç] adj productive.
ergo ['ɛrgo] konj therefore, ergo (liter, hum).
Ergonomie [ɛrgono'miː] f ergonomics pl.
ergötzen [ɛr'gœtsən] vt to amuse, delight.
ergrauen [ɛr'graʊən] vi to turn od go grey
(BRIT) od gray (US).
ergreifen [ɛr'graɪfən] unreg vt (lit, fig) to seize;
(Beruf) to take up; (Maßnahmen) to resort to;
(rühren) to move; **er ergriff das Wort** he
began to speak.
ergreifend adj moving, affecting.
ergriff etc [ɛr'grɪf] vb siehe **ergreifen**.
ergriffen pp von **ergreifen** ♦ adj deeply moved.
Ergriffenheit f emotion.
ergründen [ɛr'gryndən] vt (Sinn etc) to
fathom; (Ursache, Motive) to discover.
Erguß [ɛr'gʊs] (**-sses, ̈-sse**) m discharge; (fig)
outpouring, effusion.
erhaben [ɛr'haːbən] adj (lit) raised, embossed;
(fig) exalted, lofty; **über etw** akk **~ sein** to be
above sth.
Erhalt m: **bei** od **nach ~** on receipt.
erhält [ɛr'hɛlt] vb siehe **erhalten**.
erhalten [ɛr'haltən] unreg vt to receive;
(bewahren) to preserve, maintain; **das Wort
~** to receive permission to speak; **jdn am
Leben ~** to keep sb alive; **gut ~** in good
condition.
erhältlich [ɛr'hɛltlɪç] adj obtainable, available.

Erhaltung f maintenance, preservation.
erhängen [ɛr'hɛŋən] vt, vr to hang.
erhärten [ɛr'hɛrtən] vt to harden; (*These*) to substantiate, corroborate.
erhaschen [ɛr'haʃən] vt to catch.
erheben [ɛr'he:bən] unreg vt to raise; (*Protest, Forderungen*) to make; (*Fakten*) to ascertain ♦ vr to rise (up); **sich über etw** akk ~ to rise above sth.
erheblich [ɛr'he:plɪç] adj considerable.
erheitern [ɛr'haɪtərn] vt to amuse, cheer (up).
Erheiterung f exhilaration; **zur allgemeinen** ~ to everybody's amusement.
erhellen [ɛr'hɛlən] vt (*lit, fig*) to illuminate; (*Geheimnis*) to shed light on ♦ vr (*Fenster*) to light up; (*Himmel, Miene*) to brighten (up); (*Gesicht*) to brighten up.
erhielt etc [ɛr'hi:lt] vb siehe **erhalten**.
erhitzen [ɛr'hɪtsən] vt to heat ♦ vr to heat up; (*fig*) to become heated od aroused.
erhoffen [ɛr'hɔfən] vt to hope for; **was erhoffst du dir davon?** what do you hope to gain from it?
erhöhen [ɛr'hø:ən] vt to raise; (*verstärken*) to increase; **erhöhte Temperatur haben** to have a temperature.
Erhöhung f (*Gehalt*) increment.
erholen [ɛr'ho:lən] vr to recover; (*entspannen*) to have a rest; (*fig: Preise, Aktien*) to rally, pick up.
erholsam adj restful.
Erholung f recovery; relaxation, rest.
erholungsbedürftig adj in need of a rest, run-down.
Erholungsgebiet nt holiday (*BRIT*) od vacation (*US*) area.
Erholungsheim nt convalescent home.
erhören [ɛr'hø:rən] vt (*Gebet etc*) to hear; (*Bitte etc*) to yield to.
Erika ['e:rika] (-, **Eriken**) f heather.
erinnern [ɛr'ɪnərn] vt: ~ (an +akk) to remind (of) ♦ vr: **sich (an etw** akk) ~ to remember (sth).
Erinnerung f memory; (*Andenken*) reminder; **Erinnerungen** pl (*Lebens~*) reminiscences pl; (*LITER*) memoirs pl; **jdn/etw in guter** ~ **behalten** to have pleasant memories of sb/sth.
Erinnerungsschreiben nt (*COMM*) reminder.
Erinnerungstafel f commemorative plaque.
Eritrea [eri'tre:a] (-s) nt Eritrea.
erkalten [ɛr'kaltən] vi to go cold, cool (down).
erkälten [ɛr'kɛltən] vr to catch cold; **sich** dat **die Blase** ~ to catch a chill in one's bladder.
erkältet adj with a cold; ~ **sein** to have a cold.
Erkältung f cold.
erkämpfen [ɛr'kɛmpfən] vt to win, secure.
erkannt [ɛr'kant] pp von **erkennen**.
erkannte etc vb siehe **erkennen**.
erkennbar adj recognizable.
erkennen [ɛr'kɛnən] unreg vt to recognize; (*sehen, verstehen*) to see; **jdm zu** ~ **geben,**

daß to give sb to understand that ...
erkenntlich adj: **sich** ~ **zeigen** to show one's appreciation; **E~keit** f gratitude; (*Geschenk*) token of one's gratitude.
Erkenntnis (-, **-se**) f knowledge; (*das Erkennen*) recognition; (*Einsicht*) insight; **zur** ~ **kommen** to realize.
Erkennung f recognition.
Erkennungsdienst m police records department.
Erkennungsmarke f identity disc.
Erker ['ɛrkər] (-s, -) m bay; **~fenster** nt bay window.
erklärbar adj explicable.
erklären [ɛr'klɛ:rən] vt to explain; (*Rücktritt*) to announce; (*Politiker, Pressesprecher etc*) to say; **ich kann mir nicht** ~, **warum** ... I can't understand why ...
erklärlich adj explicable; (*verständlich*) understandable.
erklärt adj attrib (*Gegner etc*) professed, avowed; (*Favorit, Liebling*) acknowledged.
Erklärung f explanation; (*Aussage*) declaration.
erklecklich [ɛr'klɛklɪç] adj considerable.
erklimmen [ɛr'klɪmən] unreg vt to climb to.
erklingen [ɛr'klɪŋən] unreg vi to resound, ring out.
erklomm etc [ɛr'klɔm] vb siehe **erklimmen**.
erklommen pp von **erklimmen**.
erkranken [ɛr'kraŋkən] vi: ~ (**an** +dat) to be taken ill (with); (*Organ, Pflanze, Tier*) to become diseased (with).
Erkrankung f illness.
erkunden [ɛr'kundən] vt to find out, ascertain; (*bes MIL*) to reconnoitre (*BRIT*), reconnoiter (*US*).
erkundigen vr: **sich** ~ (**nach**) to inquire (about); **ich werde mich** ~ I'll find out.
Erkundigung f inquiry; **~en einholen** to make inquiries.
Erkundung f (*MIL*) reconnaissance, scouting.
erlahmen [ɛr'la:mən] vi to tire; (*nachlassen*) to flag, wane.
erlangen [ɛr'laŋən] vt to attain, achieve.
Erlaß [ɛr'las] (**-sses**, **-̈sse**) m decree; (*Aufhebung*) remission.
erlassen unreg vt (*Verfügung*) to issue; (*Gesetz*) to enact; (*Strafe*) to remit; **jdm etw** ~ to release sb from sth.
erlauben [ɛr'laubən] vt to allow, permit ♦ vr: **sich** dat **etw** ~ (*Zigarette, Pause*) to permit o.s. sth; (*Bemerkung, Verschlag*) to venture sth; (*sich leisten*) to afford sth; **jdm etw** ~ to allow od permit sb (to do) sth; ~ **Sie?** may I?; ~ **Sie mal!** do you mind!; **was** ~ **Sie sich (eigentlich)!** how dare you!
Erlaubnis [ɛr'laupnɪs] (-, **-se**) f permission.
erläutern [ɛr'lɔytərn] vt to explain.
Erläuterung f explanation; **zur** ~ in explanation.

Erle ['ɛrlə] (-, -n) *f* alder.

erleben [ɛr'le:bən] *vt* to experience; (*Zeit*) to live through; (*mit~*) to witness; (*noch mit~*) to live to see; **so wütend habe ich ihn noch nie erlebt** I've never seen *od* known him so furious.

Erlebnis [ɛr'le:pnɪs] (-ses, -se) *nt* experience.

erledigen [ɛr'le:dɪgən] *vt* to take care of, deal with; (*Antrag etc*) to process; (*umg: erschöpfen*) to wear out; (*ruinieren*) to finish; (*umbringen*) to do in ♦ *vr:* **das hat sich erledigt** that's all settled; **das ist erledigt** that's taken care of, that's been done; **ich habe noch einiges in der Stadt zu ~** I've still got a few things to do in town.

erledigt (*umg*) *adj* (*erschöpft*) shattered, done in; (: *ruiniert*) finished, ruined.

erlegen [ɛr'le:gən] *vt* to kill.

erleichtern [ɛr'laɪçtərn] *vt* to make easier; (*fig: Last*) to lighten; (*lindern, beruhigen*) to relieve.

erleichtert *adj* relieved; **~ aufatmen** to breathe a sigh of relief.

Erleichterung *f* facilitation; lightening; relief.

erleiden [ɛr'laɪdən] *unreg vt* to suffer, endure.

erlernbar *adj* learnable.

erlernen [ɛr'lɛrnən] *vt* to learn, acquire.

erlesen [ɛr'le:zən] *adj* select, choice.

erleuchten [ɛr'lɔyçtən] *vt* to illuminate; (*fig*) to inspire.

Erleuchtung *f* (*Einfall*) inspiration.

erliegen [ɛr'li:gən] *unreg vi* +dat (*lit, fig*) to succumb to; (*einem Irrtum*) to be the victim of; **zum E~ kommen** to come to a standstill.

erlischt [ɛr'lɪʃt] *vb siehe* **erlöschen**.

erlogen [ɛr'lo:gən] *adj* untrue, made-up.

Erlös [ɛr'lø:s] (-es, -e) *m* proceeds *pl*.

erlosch *etc* [ɛr'lɔʃ] *vb siehe* **erlöschen**.

erlöschen [ɛr'lœʃən] *unreg vi* (*Feuer*) to go out; (*Interesse*) to cease, die; (*Vertrag, Recht*) to expire; **ein erloschener Vulkan** an extinct volcano.

erlösen [ɛr'lø:zən] *vt* to redeem, save.

Erlöser (-s, -) *m* (*REL*) Redeemer; (*Befreier*) saviour (*BRIT*), savior (*US*).

Erlösung *f* release; (*REL*) redemption.

ermächtigen [ɛr'mɛçtɪgən] *vt* to authorize, empower.

Ermächtigung *f* authorization.

ermahnen [ɛr'ma:nən] *vt* to admonish, exhort.

Ermahnung *f* admonition, exhortation.

Ermang(e)lung [ɛr'maŋəluŋ] *f:* **in ~** +gen because of the lack of.

ermäßigen [ɛr'mɛsɪgən] *vt* to reduce.

Ermäßigung *f* reduction.

ermessen [ɛr'mɛsən] *unreg vt* to estimate, gauge; **E~ (-s)** *nt* estimation; discretion; **in jds E~** *dat* **liegen** to lie within sb's discretion; **nach meinem E~** in my judgement.

Ermessensfrage *f* matter of discretion.

ermitteln [ɛr'mɪtəln] *vt* to determine; (*Täter*) to trace ♦ *vi:* **gegen jdn ~** to investigate sb.

Ermittlung [ɛr'mɪtluŋ] *f* determination; (*Polizei~*) investigation; **~en anstellen (über** +akk**)** to make inquiries (about).

Ermittlungsverfahren *nt* (*JUR*) preliminary proceedings *pl*.

ermöglichen [ɛr'mø:klɪçən] *vt* (+dat) to make possible (for).

ermorden [ɛr'mɔrdən] *vt* to murder.

Ermordung *f* murder.

ermüden [ɛr'my:dən] *vt* to tire; (*TECH*) to fatigue ♦ *vi* to tire.

ermüdend *adj* tiring; (*fig*) wearisome.

Ermüdung *f* fatigue.

Ermüdungserscheinung *f* sign of fatigue.

ermuntern [ɛr'muntərn] *vt* to rouse; (*ermutigen*) to encourage; (*beleben*) to liven up; (*aufmuntern*) to cheer up.

ermutigen [ɛr'mu:tɪgən] *vt* to encourage.

ernähren [ɛr'nɛ:rən] *vt* to feed, nourish; (*Familie*) to support ♦ *vr* to support o.s., earn a living; **sich ~ von** to live on.

Ernährer(in) (-s, -) *m(f)* breadwinner.

Ernährung *f* nourishment; (*MED*) nutrition; (*Unterhalt*) maintenance.

ernennen [ɛr'nɛnən] *unreg vt* to appoint.

Ernennung *f* appointment.

erneuern [ɛr'nɔyərn] *vt* to renew; (*restaurieren*) to restore; (*renovieren*) to renovate.

Erneuerung *f* renewal; restoration; renovation.

erneut *adj* renewed, fresh ♦ *adv* once more.

erniedrigen [ɛr'ni:drɪgən] *vt* to humiliate, degrade.

Ernst [ɛrnst] (-es) *m* seriousness; **das ist mein ~** I'm quite serious; **im ~** in earnest; **~ machen mit etw** to put sth into practice; **e~** *adj* serious; **es steht e~ um ihn** things don't look too good for him; **~fall** *m* emergency; **e~gemeint** *adj* meant in earnest, serious; **e~haft** *adj* serious; **~haftigkeit** *f* seriousness; **e~lich** *adj* serious.

Ernte ['ɛrntə] (-, -n) *f* harvest; **~dankfest** *nt* harvest festival.

ernten *vt* to harvest; (*Lob etc*) to earn.

ernüchtern [ɛr'nyçtərn] *vt* to sober up; (*fig*) to bring down to earth.

Ernüchterung *f* sobering up; (*fig*) disillusionment.

Eroberer [ɛr'ʔobərər] (-s, -) *m* conqueror.

erobern *vt* to conquer.

Eroberung *f* conquest.

eröffnen [ɛr'ʔœfnən] *vt* to open ♦ *vr* to present itself; **jdm etw ~** (*geh*) to disclose sth to sb.

Eröffnung *f* opening.

Eröffnungsansprache *f* inaugural *od* opening address.

Eröffnungsfeier *f* opening ceremony.

erogen [ero'ge:n] *adj* erogenous.

erörtern [ɛr'ʔœrtərn] *vt* to discuss (in detail).

Erörterung *f* discussion.

Erotik [e'ro:tɪk] *f* eroticism.
erotisch *adj* erotic.
Erpel ['ɛrpəl] **(-, -)** *m* drake.
erpicht [ɛr'pɪçt] *adj:* ~ **(auf** +*akk*) keen (on).
erpressen [ɛr'prɛsən] *vt* (*Geld etc*) to extort; (*jdn*) to blackmail.
Erpresser (-s, -) *m* blackmailer.
Erpressung *f* blackmail; extortion.
erproben [ɛr'pro:bən] *vt* to test; **erprobt** tried and tested.
erraten [ɛr'ra:tən] *unreg vt* to guess.
errechnen [ɛr'rɛçnən] *vt* to calculate, work out.
erregbar [ɛr're:kba:r] *adj* excitable; (*reizbar*) irritable; **E~keit** *f* excitability; irritability.
erregen [ɛr're:gən] *vt* to excite; (*sexuell*) to arouse; (*ärgern*) to infuriate; (*hervorrufen*) to arouse, provoke ♦ *vr* to get excited *od* worked up.
Erreger (-s, -) *m* causative agent.
Erregtheit *f* excitement; (*Beunruhigung*) agitation.
Erregung *f* excitement; (*sexuell*) arousal.
erreichbar *adj* accessible, within reach.
erreichen [ɛr'raɪçən] *vt* to reach; (*Zweck*) to achieve; (*Zug*) to catch; **wann kann ich Sie morgen ~?** when can I get in touch with you tomorrow?; **vom Bahnhof leicht zu ~** within easy reach of the station.
errichten [ɛr'rɪçtən] *vt* to erect, put up; (*gründen*) to establish, set up.
erringen [ɛr'rɪŋən] *unreg vt* to gain, win.
erröten [ɛr'rø:tən] *vi* to blush, flush.
Errungenschaft [ɛr'rʊŋənʃaft] *f* achievement; (*umg: Anschaffung*) acquisition.
Ersatz [ɛr'zats] **(-es)** *m* substitute; replacement; (*Schaden~*) compensation; (*MIL*) reinforcements *pl*; **als ~ für jdn einspringen** to stand in for sb; **~befriedigung** *f* vicarious satisfaction; **~dienst** *m* (*MIL*) alternative service; **~kasse** *f* private health insurance; **~mann** *m* replacement; (*SPORT*) substitute; **~mutter** *f* substitute mother; **e~pflichtig** *adj* liable to pay compensation; **~reifen** *m* (*AUT*) spare tyre (*BRIT*) *od* tire (*US*); **~teil** *nt* spare (part); **e~weise** *adv* as an alternative.
ersaufen [ɛr'zaʊfən] *unreg* (*umg*) *vi* to drown.
ersäufen [ɛr'zɔyfən] *vt* to drown.
erschaffen [ɛr'ʃafən] *unreg vt* to create.
erscheinen [ɛr'ʃaɪnən] *unreg vi* to appear.
Erscheinung *f* appearance; (*Geist*) apparition; (*Gegebenheit*) phenomenon; (*Gestalt*) figure; **in ~ treten** (*Merkmale*) to appear; (*Gefühle*) to show themselves.
Erscheinungsform *f* manifestation.
Erscheinungsjahr *nt* (*von Buch*) year of publication.
erschien *etc* [ɛr'ʃi:n] *vb siehe* **erscheinen**.
erschienen *pp von* **erscheinen**.
erschießen [ɛr'ʃi:sən] *unreg vt* to shoot (dead).

erschlaffen [ɛr'ʃlafən] *vi* to go limp; (*Mensch*) to become exhausted.
erschlagen [ɛr'ʃla:gən] *unreg vt* to strike dead ♦ *adj* (*umg: todmüde*) worn out, dead beat (*umg*).
erschleichen [ɛr'ʃlaɪçən] *unreg vt* to obtain by stealth *od* dubious methods.
erschließen [ɛr'ʃli:sən] *unreg vt* (*Gebiet, Absatzmarkt*) to develop, open up; (*Bodenschätze*) to tap.
erschlossen [ɛr'ʃlɔsən] *adj* (*Gebiet*) developed.
erschöpfen [ɛr'ʃœpfən] *vt* to exhaust.
erschöpfend *adj* exhaustive, thorough.
erschöpft *adj* exhausted.
Erschöpfung *f* exhaustion.
erschossen [ɛr'ʃɔsən] (*umg*) *adj:* **(völlig)** ~ **sein** to be whacked, be dead (beat).
erschrak *etc* [ɛr'ʃra:k] *vb siehe* **erschrecken**[2].
erschrecken[1] [ɛr'ʃrɛkən] *vt* to startle, frighten.
erschrecken[2] [ɛr'ʃrɛkən] *unreg vi* to be frightened *od* startled.
erschreckend *adj* alarming, frightening.
erschrickt [ɛr'ʃrɪkt] *vb siehe* **erschrecken**[2].
erschrocken [ɛr'ʃrɔkən] *pp von* **erschrecken**[2] ♦ *adj* frightened, startled.
erschüttern [ɛr'ʃytərn] *vt* to shake; (*ergreifen*) to move deeply; **ihn kann nichts ~** he always keeps his cool (*umg*).
erschütternd *adj* shattering.
Erschütterung *f* (*des Bodens*) tremor; (*tiefe Ergriffenheit*) shock.
erschweren [ɛr'ʃve:rən] *vt* to complicate; ~**de Umstände** (*JUR*) aggravating circumstances; **es kommt noch ~d hinzu, daß** ... to compound matters ...
erschwindeln [ɛr'ʃvɪndəln] *vt* to obtain by fraud.
erschwinglich *adj* affordable.
ersehen [ɛr'ze:ən] *unreg vt:* **aus etw ~, daß** ... to gather from sth that ...
ersehnt [ɛr'ze:nt] *adj* longed-for.
ersetzbar *adj* replaceable.
ersetzen [ɛr'zɛtsən] *vt* to replace; **jdm Unkosten** *etc* ~ to pay sb's expenses *etc.*
ersichtlich [ɛr'zɪçtlɪç] *adj* evident, obvious.
ersparen [ɛr'ʃpa:rən] *vt* (*Ärger etc*) to spare; (*Geld*) to save; **ihr blieb auch nichts erspart** she was spared nothing.
Ersparnis (-, -se) *f* saving.
ersprießlich [ɛr'ʃpri:slɪç] *adj* profitable, useful; (*angenehm*) pleasant.

=========== *SCHLÜSSELWORT*

erst [e:rst] *adv* **1** first; **mach ~ (ein)mal die Arbeit fertig** finish your work first; **wenn du das ~ (ein)mal hinter dir hast** once you've got that behind you
2 (*nicht früher als, nur*) only; (*nicht bis*) not till; ~ **gestern** only yesterday; ~ **morgen** not until tomorrow; ~ **als** only when, not until; **wir fahren ~ später** we're not going

until later; **er ist (gerade)** ~ **angekommen** he's only just arrived **3: wäre er doch** ~ **zurück!** if only he were back!; **da fange ich** ~ **gar nicht an** I simply won't bother to begin; **jetzt** ~ **recht!** that just makes me all the more determined; **da ging's** ~ **richtig los** then things really got going.

erstarren [ɛr'ʃtarən] vi to stiffen; (vor Furcht) to grow rigid; (Materie) to solidify.

erstatten [ɛr'ʃtatən] vt (Unkosten) to refund; **Anzeige gegen jdn** ~ to report sb; **Bericht** ~ to make a report.

Erstattung f (von Unkosten) reimbursement.

Erstaufführung ['e:rst|aʊffy:rʊŋ] f first performance.

erstaunen [ɛr'ʃtaʊnən] vt to astonish ♦ vi to be astonished; **E~** (-s) nt astonishment.

erstaunlich adj astonishing.

Erstausgabe f first edition.

erstbeste(r, s) adj first that comes along.

erste(r, s) adj first; **als** ~s first of all; **in** ~r **Linie** first and foremost; **fürs** ~ for the time being; **E~ Hilfe** first aid.

erstechen [ɛr'ʃtɛçən] unreg vt to stab (to death).

erstehen [ɛr'ʃte:ən] unreg vt to buy ♦ vi to (a)rise.

ersteigen [ɛr'ʃtaigən] unreg vt to climb, ascend.

ersteigern [ɛr'ʃtaigərn] vt to buy at an auction.

erstellen [ɛr'ʃtɛlən] vt to erect, build.

erstemal adv: **das** ~ the first time.

erstens adv firstly, in the first place.

erstere(r, s) pron (the) former.

ersticken [ɛr'ʃtikən] vt (lit, fig) to stifle; (Mensch) to suffocate; (Flammen) to smother ♦ vi (Mensch) to suffocate; (Feuer) to be smothered; **mit erstickter Stimme** in a choked voice; **in Arbeit** ~ to be snowed under with work.

Erstickung f suffocation.

erst- zW: ~**klassig** adj first-class; **E~kommunion** f first communion; ~**malig** adj first; ~**mals** adv for the first time; ~**rangig** adj first-rate.

erstrebenswert [ɛr'ʃtre:bənsve:rt] adj desirable, worthwhile.

erstrecken [ɛr'ʃtrɛkən] vr to extend, stretch.

Erststimme f first vote.

The **Erststimme** and **Zweitstimme** (first and second vote) system is used to elect MPs to the **Bundestag**. Each elector is given two votes. The first is to choose a candidate in his constituency; the candidate with the most votes is elected MP. The second is to choose a party. All the second votes in each **Land** are counted and a proportionate number of MPs from each party is sent to the Bundestag.

Ersttagsbrief m first-day cover.

Ersttagsstempel m first-day (date) stamp.

erstunken [ɛr'ʃtʊŋkən] adj: **das ist** ~ **und erlogen** (umg) that's a pack of lies.

Erstwähler (-s, -) m first-time voter.

ersuchen [ɛr'zu:xən] vt to request.

ertappen [ɛr'tapən] vt to catch, detect.

erteilen [ɛr'tailən] vt to give.

ertönen [ɛr'tø:nən] vi to sound, ring out.

Ertrag [ɛr'tra:k] (-(e)s, ̈-e) m yield; (Gewinn) proceeds pl.

ertragen unreg vt to bear, stand.

erträglich [ɛr'trɛ:klɪç] adj tolerable, bearable.

ertragreich adj (Geschäft) profitable, lucrative.

ertrank etc [ɛr'traŋk] vb siehe **ertrinken**.

ertränken [ɛr'trɛŋkən] vt to drown.

erträumen [ɛr'trɔymən] vt: **sich** dat **etw** ~ to dream of sth, imagine sth.

ertrinken [ɛr'trɪŋkən] unreg vi to drown; **E~** (-s) nt drowning.

ertrunken [ɛr'trʊŋkən] pp von **ertrinken**.

erübrigen [ɛr'|y:brɪgən] vt to spare ♦ vr to be unnecessary.

erwachen [ɛr'vaxən] vi to awake; **ein böses E~** (fig) a rude awakening.

erwachsen [ɛr'vaksən] adj grown-up ♦ unreg vi: **daraus erwuchsen ihm Unannehmlichkeiten** that caused him some trouble.

Erwachsene(r) f(m) adult.

Erwachsenenbildung f adult education.

erwägen [ɛr've:gən] unreg vt to consider.

Erwägung f consideration; **etw in** ~ **ziehen** to take sth into consideration.

erwähnen [ɛr've:nən] vt to mention.

erwähnenswert adj worth mentioning.

Erwähnung f mention.

erwarb etc [ɛr'varp] vb siehe **erwerben**.

erwärmen [ɛr'vɛrmən] vt to warm, heat ♦ vr to get warm, warm up; **sich** ~ **für** to warm to.

erwarten [ɛr'vartən] vt to expect; (warten auf) to wait for; **etw kaum** ~ **können** to hardly be able to wait for sth.

Erwartung f expectation; **in** ~ **Ihrer baldigen Antwort** (form) in anticipation of your early reply.

erwartungsgemäß adv as expected.

erwartungsvoll adj expectant.

erwecken [ɛr'vɛkən] vt to rouse, awake; **den Anschein** ~ to give the impression; **etw zu neuem Leben** ~ to resurrect sth.

erwehren [ɛr've:rən] vr +gen (geh) to fend off, ward off; (des Lachens etc) to refrain from.

erweichen [ɛr'vaiçən] vt to soften; **sich nicht** ~ **lassen** to be unmoved.

erweisen [ɛr'vaizən] unreg vt to prove ♦ vr: **sich** ~ **als** to prove to be; **jdm einen Gefallen/ Dienst** ~ to do sb a favour/service; **sich jdm gegenüber dankbar** ~ to show one's gratitude to sb.

erweitern [ɛr'vaitərn] vt, vr to widen, enlarge;

(*Geschäft*) to expand; (*MED*) to dilate; (*fig: Kenntnisse*) to broaden; (*Macht*) to extend.
Erweiterung *f* expansion.
Erwerb [ɛr'vɛrp] (-(e)s, -e) *m* acquisition; (*Beruf*) trade.
erwerben [ɛr'vɛrbən] *unreg vt* to acquire; **er hat sich** *dat* **große Verdienste um die Firma erworben** he has done great service for the firm.
Erwerbs- *zW:* **e~fähig** *adj* (*form*) capable of gainful employment; **~gesellschaft** *f* acquisitive society; **e~los** *adj* unemployed; **~quelle** *f* source of income; **e~tätig** *adj* (gainfully) employed; **e~unfähig** *adj* unable to work.
erwidern [ɛr'viːdərn] *vt* to reply; (*vergelten*) to return.
Erwiderung *f:* **in ~ Ihres Schreibens vom ...** (*form*) in reply to your letter of the ...
erwiesen [ɛr'viːzən] *adj* proven.
erwirbt [ɛr'vɪrpt] *vb siehe* **erwerben.**
erwirtschaften [ɛr'vɪrtʃaftən] *vt* (*Gewinn etc*) to make by good management.
erwischen [ɛr'vɪʃən] (*umg*) *vt* to catch, get; **ihn hat's erwischt!** (*umg: verliebt*) he's got it bad; (: *krank*) he's got it; **kalt ~** (*umg*) to catch off-balance.
erworben [ɛr'vɔrbən] *pp von* **erwerben.**
erwünscht [ɛr'vʏnʃt] *adj* desired.
erwürgen [ɛr'vʏrgən] *vt* to strangle.
Erz [eːrts] (-es, -e) *nt* ore.
erzählen [ɛr'tsɛːlən] *vt, vi* to tell; **dem werd' ich was ~!** (*umg*) I'll have something to say to him; **~de Dichtung** narrative fiction.
Erzähler(in) (-s, -) *m(f)* narrator.
Erzählung *f* story, tale.
Erzbischof *m* archbishop.
Erzengel *m* archangel.
erzeugen [ɛr'tsɔygən] *vt* to produce; (*Strom*) to generate.
Erzeuger (-s, -) *m* producer; **~preis** *m* manufacturer's price.
Erzeugnis (-ses, -se) *nt* product, produce.
Erzeugung *f* production; generation.
Erzfeind *m* arch enemy.
erziehbar *adj:* **ein Heim für schwer ~e Kinder** a home for difficult children.
erziehen [ɛr'tsiːən] *unreg vt* to bring up; (*bilden*) to educate, train.
Erzieher(in) (-s, -) *m(f)* educator; (*in Kindergarten*) nursery school teacher.
Erziehung *f* bringing up; (*Bildung*) education.
Erziehungs- *zW:* **~berechtigte(r)** *f(m)* parent, legal guardian; **~geld** *nt* payment for new parents; **~heim** *nt* community home; **~urlaub** *m* leave for a new parent.
erzielen [ɛr'tsiːlən] *vt* to achieve, obtain; (*Tor*) to score.
erzkonservativ ['ɛrtskɔnzɛrva'tiːf] *adj* ultraconservative.
erzog *etc* [ɛr'tsoːk] *vb siehe* **erziehen.**

erzogen [ɛr'tsoːgən] *pp von* **erziehen.**
erzürnen [ɛr'tsʏrnən] *vt* (*geh*) to anger, incense.
erzwingen [ɛr'tsvɪŋən] *unreg vt* to force, obtain by force.
Es [ɛs] (-) *nt* (*MUS: Dur*) E flat.
es [ɛs] *nom, akk pron* it.
Esche ['ɛʃə] (-, -n) *f* ash.
Esel ['eːzəl] (-s, -) *m* donkey, ass; **ich ~!** (*umg*) silly me!
Eselsbrücke *f* (*Gedächtnishilfe*) mnemonic, aide-mémoire.
Eselsohr *nt* dog-ear.
Eskalation [ɛskalatsi'oːn] *f* escalation.
eskalieren [ɛska'liːrən] *vt, vi* to escalate.
Eskimo ['ɛskimo] (-s, -s) *m* eskimo.
Eskorte [ɛs'kɔrtə] (-, -n) *f* (*MIL*) escort.
eskortieren [ɛskɔr'tiːrən] *vt* (*geh*) to escort.
Espenlaub ['ɛspənlaʊp] *nt:* **zittern wie ~** to shake like a leaf.
eßbar ['ɛsbaːr] *adj* eatable, edible.
Eßecke *f* dining area.
essen ['ɛsən] *unreg vt, vi* to eat; **~ gehen** (*auswärts*) to eat out; **~ Sie gern Äpfel?** do you like apples?; **E~** (-s, -) *nt* (*Mahlzeit*) meal; (*Nahrung*) food; **E~ auf Rädern** meals on wheels.
Essens- *zW:* **~ausgabe** *f* serving of meals; (*Stelle*) serving counter; **~marke** *f* meal voucher; **~zeit** *f* mealtime.
Eßgeschirr *nt* dinner service.
Essig ['ɛsɪç] (-s, -e) *m* vinegar; **damit ist es ~** (*umg*) it's all off; **~gurke** *f* gherkin.
Eßkastanie *f* sweet chestnut.
Eßl. *abk* (= *Eßlöffel*) tbsp.
Eß- *zW:* **~löffel** *m* tablespoon; **~tisch** *m* dining table; **~waren** *pl* foodstuffs *pl*; **~zimmer** *nt* dining room.
Establishment [ɪs'tæblɪʃmənt] (-s, -s) *nt* establishment.
Este ['eːstə] (-n, -n) *m*, **Estin** *f* Estonian.
Estland ['eːstlant] *nt* Estonia.
estnisch ['eːstnɪʃ] *adj* Estonian.
Estragon ['ɛstragɔn] (-s) *m* tarragon.
Estrich ['ɛstrɪç] (-s, -e) *m* stone/clay *etc* floor.
etablieren [eta'bliːrən] *vr* to establish o.s.; (*COMM*) to set up.
Etage [e'taːʒə] (-, -n) *f* floor, storey (*BRIT*), story (*US*).
Etagenbetten *pl* bunk beds *pl*.
Etagenwohnung *f* flat (*BRIT*), apartment (*US*).
Etappe [e'tapə] (-, -n) *f* stage.
etappenweise *adv* step by step, stage by stage.
Etat [e'taː] (-s, -s) *m* budget; **~jahr** *nt* financial year; **~posten** *m* budget item.
etc *abk* (= *et cetera*) etc.
etepetete [eːtəpe'teːtə] (*umg*) *adj* fussy.
Ethik ['eːtɪk] *f* ethics *sing*.
ethisch ['eːtɪʃ] *adj* ethical.
ethnisch ['ɛtnɪʃ] *adj* ethnic; **~e Säuberung**

ethnic cleansing.

Etikett [eti'kɛt] (-(e)s, -e) nt (lit, fig) label.

Etikette f etiquette, manners pl.

Etikettenschwindel m (POL): **es ist reinster ~, wenn ...** it is just playing od juggling with names if ...

etikettieren [etikɛ'tiːrən] vt to label.

etliche(r, s) ['ɛtlıçə(r, s)] adj quite a lot of ♦ pron pl some, quite a few; **~s** quite a lot.

Etüde [e'tyːdə] (-, -n) f (MUS) étude.

Etui [ɛt'viː] (-s, -s) nt case.

etwa ['ɛtva] adv (ungefähr) about; (vielleicht) perhaps; (beispielsweise) for instance; (entrüstet, erstaunt): **hast du ~ schon wieder kein Geld dabei?** don't tell me you haven't got any money again! ♦ adv (zur Bestätigung): **Sie kommen doch, oder ~ nicht?** you are coming, aren't you?; **nicht ~** by no means; **willst du ~ schon gehen?** (surely) you don't want to go already?

etwaig ['ɛtvaıç] adj possible.

etwas pron something; (fragend, verneinend) anything; (ein wenig) a little ♦ adv a little; **er kann ~** he's good; **E~** nt: **das gewisse E~** that certain something.

Etymologie [etymolo'giː] f etymology.

EU (-) f abk (= Europäische Union) EU.

euch [ɔʏç] pron (akk von ihr) you; yourselves; (dat von ihr) (to/for) you ♦ refl pron yourselves.

euer ['ɔʏər] pron gen von **ihr** of you ♦ adj your.

Eule ['ɔʏlə] (-, -n) f owl.

Euphemismus [ɔʏfe'mısmʊs] m euphemism.

Eurasien [ɔʏ'raːziən] nt Eurasia.

Euratom [ɔʏra'toːm] f abk (= Europäische Atomgemeinschaft) Euratom.

eure(r, s) ['ɔʏrə(r, s)] pron yours.

eurerseits adv on your part.

euresgleichen pron people like you.

euretwegen ['ɔʏrət'veːgən] adv (für euch) for your sakes; (wegen euch) on your account.

euretwillen ['ɔʏrət'vılən] adv: **um ~** = euretwegen.

eurige pron: **der/die/das ~** (geh) yours.

Eurokrat [ɔʏro'kraːt] (-en, -en) m eurocrat.

Europa [ɔʏ'roːpa] (-s) nt Europe.

Europäer(in) [ɔʏro'pɛːər(ın)] (-s, -) m(f) European.

europäisch adj European; **das E~e Parlament** the European Parliament; **E~e Union** European Union; **E~e (Wirtschafts)gemeinschaft** European (Economic) Community, Common Market.

Europa- zW: **~meister** m European champion; **~rat** m Council of Europe; **~straße** f Euroroute.

Euroscheck [ɔʏro'ʃɛk] m Eurocheque.

Euter ['ɔʏtər] (-s, -) nt udder.

Euthanasie [ɔʏtana'ziː] f euthanasia.

E.V., e.V. abk (= eingetragener Verein) registered association.

ev. abk = **evangelisch.**

evakuieren [evaku'iːrən] vt to evacuate.

evangelisch [evaŋ'geːlıʃ] adj Protestant.

Evangelium [evaŋ'geːlium] nt Gospel.

Evaskostüm nt: **im ~** in her birthday suit.

eventuell [evɛntu'ɛl] adj possible ♦ adv possibly, perhaps.

Everest ['evərɛst] (-s) m (Mount) Everest.

Evolution [evolutsi'oːn] f evolution.

Evolutionstheorie f theory of evolution.

evtl. abk = **eventuell.**

EWG [eːveː'geː] (-) f abk (= Europäische Wirtschaftsgemeinschaft) EC.

ewig ['eːvıç] adj eternal ♦ adv: **auf ~** forever; **ich habe Sie ~ lange nicht gesehen** (umg) I haven't seen you for ages; **E~keit** f eternity; **bis in alle E~keit** forever.

EWS (-) nt abk (= Europäisches Währungssystem) EMS.

EWU (-) f abk (= Europäische Währungsunion) EMU.

ex [ɛks] (umg) adv: **etw ~ trinken** to drink sth down in one.

exakt [ɛ'ksakt] adj exact.

exaltiert [ɛksal'tiːrt] adj exaggerated, effusive.

Examen [ɛ'ksaːmən] (-s, - od Examina) nt examination.

Examensangst f exam nerves pl.

Examensarbeit f dissertation.

Exekutionskommando [ɛksekutsi'oːnskomando] nt firing squad.

Exekutive [ɛkseku'tiːvə] f executive.

Exempel [ɛ'ksɛmpəl] (-s, -) nt example; **die Probe aufs ~ machen** to put it to the test.

Exemplar [ɛksɛm'plaːr] (-s, -e) nt specimen; (Buch~) copy; **e~isch** adj exemplary.

exerzieren [ɛksɛr'tsiːrən] vi to drill.

Exhibitionist [ɛkshibitsio'nıst] m exhibitionist.

Exil [ɛ'ksiːl] (-s, -e) nt exile.

existentiell [ɛksıstɛntsi'ɛl] adj: **von ~er Bedeutung** of vital significance.

Existenz [ɛksıs'tɛnts] f existence; (Unterhalt) livelihood, living; (pej: Mensch) character; **~berechtigung** f right to exist; **~grundlage** f basis of one's livelihood; **~kampf** m struggle for existence; **~minimum** (-s, -ma) nt subsistence level.

existieren [ɛksıs'tiːrən] vi to exist.

exkl. abk = **exklusive.**

exklusiv [ɛksklu'ziːf] adj exclusive; **E~bericht** m (PRESSE) exclusive report.

exklusive [ɛksklu'ziːvə] präp +gen exclusive of, not including ♦ adv exclusive of, excluding.

Exkursion [ɛkskʊrzi'oːn] f (study) trip.

Exmatrikulation [ɛksmatrikulatsi'oːn] f (UNIV): **bei seiner ~** when he left university.

exorzieren [ɛksɔr'tsiːrən] vt to exorcize.

exotisch [ɛ'ksoːtıʃ] adj exotic.

expandieren [ɛkspan'diːrən] vi (ECON) to expand.

Expansion [ɛkspanzi'oːn] f expansion.

expansiv [ɛkspan'ziːf] _adj_ expansionist;
(_Wirtschaftszweige_) expanding.
Expedition [ɛkspeditsi'oːn] _f_ expedition;
(_COMM_) forwarding department.
Experiment [ɛksperi'mɛnt] _nt_ experiment.
experimentell [ɛksperimɛn'tɛl] _adj_
experimental.
experimentieren [ɛksperimɛn'tiːrən] _vi_ to
experiment.
Experte [ɛks'pɛrtə] (**-n, -n**) _m_ expert,
specialist.
Expertin [ɛks'pɛrtɪn] _f_ expert, specialist.
explodieren [ɛksplo'diːrən] _vi_ to explode.
Explosion [ɛksplozi'oːn] _f_ explosion.
explosiv [ɛksplo'ziːf] _adj_ explosive.
Exponent [ɛkspo'nɛnt] _m_ exponent.
exponieren [ɛkspo'niːrən] _vt:_ **an exponierter
Stelle stehen** to be in an exposed position.
Export [ɛks'pɔrt] (**-(e)s, -e**) _m_ export.
Exportartikel _m_ export.
Exporteur [ɛkspɔr'tøːr] _m_ exporter.
Exporthandel _m_ export trade.
Exporthaus _nt_ export house.
exportieren [ɛkspɔr'tiːrən] _vt_ to export.
Exportkaufmann _m_ exporter.
Exportland _nt_ exporting country.
Exportvertreter _m_ export agent.
Expreßgut [ɛks'prɛsguːt] _nt_ express goods _pl_
_od_ freight.
Expressionismus [ɛkspresio'nɪsmʊs] _m_
expressionism.
Expreßzug _m_ express (train).
extra ['ɛkstra] _adj inv_ (_umg: gesondert_)
separate; (_besondere_) extra ♦ _adv_ (_gesondert_)
separately; (_speziell_) specially; (_absichtlich_)
on purpose; (_vor Adjektiven, zusätzlich_) extra;
E~ (**-s, -s**) _nt_ extra; **E~ausgabe** _f_ special
edition; **E~blatt** _nt_ special edition.
Extrakt [ɛks'trakt] (**-(e)s, -e**) _m_ extract.
Extratour _f_ (_fig: umg_): **sich** _dat_ ~**en leisten** to
do one's own thing.
extravagant [ɛkstrava'gant] _adj_ extravagant;
(_Kleidung_) flamboyant.
Extrawurst (_umg_) _f_ (_Sonderwunsch_): **er will
immer eine** ~ (**gebraten haben**) he always
wants something different.
Extrem [ɛks'treːm] (**-s, -e**) _nt_ extreme; **e~** _adj_
extreme; ~**fall** _m_ extreme (case).
Extremist(in) _m(f)_ extremist.
Extremistenerlaß [ɛkstre'mɪstən|ɛrlas] _m_
law(s) governing extremism.
extremistisch [ɛkstre'mɪstɪʃ] _adj_ (_POL_)
extremist.
Extremitäten [ɛkstremi'tɛːtən] _pl_ extremities
_pl_.
extrovertiert [ɛkstrover'tiːrt] _adj_ extrovert.
Exzellenz [ɛkstsɛ'lɛnts] _f_ excellency.
exzentrisch [ɛks'tsɛntrɪʃ] _adj_ eccentric.
Exzeß [ɛks'tsɛs] (**-sses, -sse**) _m_ excess.

_F, f_

F, f¹ [ɛf] (**-, -**) _nt_ F, f; ~ **wie Friedrich** ≈ F for
Frederick, F for Fox (_US_); **nach Schema F**
(_umg_) in the usual old way.
f² _abk_ (= _feminin_) fem.
Fa _abk_ (= _Firma_) co.
Fabel ['faːbəl] (**-, -n**) _f_ fable; **f~haft** _adj_
fabulous, marvellous (_BRIT_), marvelous
(_US_).
Fabrik [fa'briːk] _f_ factory; ~**anlage** _f_ plant;
(_Gelände_) factory premises _pl_.
Fabrikant [fabri'kant] _m_ (_Hersteller_)
manufacturer; (_Besitzer_) industrialist.
Fabrikarbeiter(in) _m(f)_ factory worker.
Fabrikat [fabri'kaːt] (**-(e)s, -e**) _nt_ product;
(_Marke_) make.
Fabrikation [fabriːkatsi'oːn] _f_ manufacture,
production.
Fabrikbesitzer _m_ factory owner.
Fabrikgelände _nt_ factory site.
fabrizieren [fabri'tsiːrən] _vt_ (_geistiges Produkt_)
to produce; (_Geschichte_) to concoct,
fabricate.
Fach [fax] (**-(e)s, ̈-er**) _nt_ compartment; (_in
Schrank, Regal etc_) shelf; (_Sachgebiet_) an
subject; **ein Mann/eine Frau vom** ~ an
expert; ~**arbeiter** _m_ skilled worker; ~**arzt** _m_
(medical) specialist; ~**ausdruck** _m_ technical
term; ~**bereich** _m_ (special) field; (_UNIV_)
school, faculty; ~**buch** _nt_ reference book.
Fächer ['fɛçər] (**-s, -**) _m_ fan.
Fach- _zW:_ ~**frau** _f_ expert; ~**gebiet** _nt_ (special)
field; ~**geschäft** _nt_ specialist shop (_BRIT_) _od_
store (_US_); ~**händler** _m_ stockist;
~**hochschule** _f_ college; ~**idiot** (_umg_) _m_
narrow-minded specialist; ~**kraft** _f_
qualified employee; ~**kreise** _pl:_ **in** ~**kreisen**
among experts; **f~kundig** _adj_ expert,
specialist; ~**lehrer** _m_ specialist subject
teacher; **f~lich** _adj_ technical; (_beruflich_)
professional; ~**mann** (**-(e)s,** _pl_ ~**leute**) _m_
expert; **f~männisch** _adj_ professional;
~**richtung** _f_ subject area; ~**schule** _f_
technical college; **f~simpeln** _vi_ to talk shop;
f~spezifisch _adj_ technical; ~**verband** _m_
trade association; ~**welt** _f_ profession;
~**werk** _nt_ timber frame; ~**werkhaus** _nt_ half-
timbered house.
Fackel ['fakəl] (**-, -n**) _f_ torch.
fackeln (_umg_) _vi_ to dither.
Fackelzug _m_ torchlight procession.
fad(e) _adj_ insipid; (_langweilig_) dull; (_Essen_)
tasteless.

Faden ['faːdən] (**-s, ⸚**) *m* thread; **der rote ~** (*fig*) the central theme; **alle Fäden laufen hier zusammen** this is the nerve centre (*BRIT*) *od* center (*US*) of the whole thing; **~nudeln** *pl* vermicelli *sing*; **f~scheinig** *adj* (*lit, fig*) threadbare.

Fagott [fa'gɔt] (**-(e)s, -e**) *nt* bassoon.

fähig ['fɛːɪç] *adj*: **~ (zu** *od* **+gen)** capable (of); able (to); **zu allem ~ sein** to be capable of anything; **F~keit** *f* ability.

Fähnchen ['fɛːnçən] *nt* pennon, streamer.

fahnden ['faːndən] *vi*: **~ nach** to search for.

Fahndung *f* search.

Fahndungsliste *f* list of wanted criminals, wanted list.

Fahne ['faːnə] (**-, -n**) *f* flag; standard; **mit fliegenden ~n zu jdm/etw überlaufen** to go over to sb/sth; **eine ~ haben** (*umg*) to smell of drink.

Fahnenflucht *f* desertion.

Fahrausweis *m* (*form*) ticket.

Fahrbahn *f* carriageway (*BRIT*), roadway.

fahrbar *adj*: **~er Untersatz** (*hum*) wheels *pl*.

Fähre ['fɛːrə] (**-, -n**) *f* ferry.

fahren ['faːrən] *unreg vt* to drive; (*Rad*) to ride; (*befördern*) to drive, take; (*Rennen*) to drive in ♦ *vi* (*sich bewegen*) to go; (*Schiff*) to sail; (*ab~*) to leave; **mit dem Auto/Zug ~** to go *od* travel by car/train; **mit dem Aufzug ~** to take the lift, ride the elevator (*US*); **links/rechts ~** to drive on the left/right; **gegen einen Baum ~** to drive *od* go into a tree; **die U-Bahn fährt alle fünf Minuten** the underground goes *od* runs every five minutes; **mit der Hand ~ über** *+akk* to pass one's hand over; **(bei etw) gut/schlecht ~** (*zurechtkommen*) to do well/badly (with sth); **was ist (denn) in dich gefahren?** what's got (*BRIT*) *od* gotten (*US*) into you?; **einen ~ lassen** (*umg*) to fart (*!*).

fahrend *adj*: **~es Volk** travelling people.

Fahrer(in) ['faːrər(ɪn)] (**-s, -**) *m(f)* driver; **~flucht** *f* hit-and-run driving.

Fahr- *zW*: **~gast** *m* passenger; **~geld** *nt* fare; **~gelegenheit** *f* transport; **~gestell** *nt* chassis; (*AVIAT*) undercarriage.

fahrig ['faːrɪç] *adj* nervous; (*unkonzentriert*) distracted.

Fahr- *zW*: **~karte** *f* ticket; **~kartenausgabe** *f* ticket office; **~kartenautomat** *m* ticket machine; **~kartenschalter** *m* ticket office.

fahrlässig *adj* negligent; **~e Tötung** manslaughter; **F~keit** *f* negligence.

Fahr- *zW*: **~lehrer** *m* driving instructor; **~plan** *m* timetable; **f~planmäßig** *adj* (*EISENB*) scheduled; **~praxis** *f* driving experience; **~preis** *m* fare; **~prüfung** *f* driving test; **~rad** *nt* bicycle; **~radweg** *m* cycle path; **~rinne** *f* (*NAUT*) shipping channel, fairway; **~schein** *m* ticket; **~schule** *f* driving school; **~schüler** *m* learner (driver); **~spur** *f* lane; **~stuhl** *m*

lift (*BRIT*), elevator (*US*); **~stunde** *f* driving lesson.

Fahrt [faːrt] (**-, -en**) *f* journey; (*kurz*) trip; (*AUT*) drive; (*Geschwindigkeit*) speed; **gute ~!** safe journey!; **volle ~ voraus!** (*NAUT*) full speed ahead!

fährt [fɛːrt] *vb siehe* **fahren.**

fahrtauglich ['faːrtaʊklɪç] *adj* fit to drive.

Fährte ['fɛːrtə] (**-, -n**) *f* track, trail; **jdn auf eine falsche ~ locken** (*fig*) to put sb off the scent.

Fahrtenschreiber *m* tachograph.

Fahrtkosten *pl* travelling expenses *pl*.

Fahrtrichtung *f* course, direction.

Fahr- *zW*: **f~tüchtig** ['faːrtʏçtɪç] *adj* fit to drive; **~verhalten** *nt* (*von Fahrer*) behaviour (*BRIT*) *od* behavior (*US*) behind the wheel; (*von Wagen*) road performance; **~zeug** *nt* vehicle; **~zeughalter** (**-s, -**) *m* owner of a vehicle; **~zeugpapiere** *pl* vehicle documents *pl*.

Faible ['fɛːbl] (**-s, -s**) *nt* (*geh*) liking; (*Schwäche*) weakness; (*Vorliebe*) penchant.

fair [fɛːr] *adj* fair.

Fäkalien [fɛ'kaːliən] *pl* faeces *pl*.

Faksimile [fak'ziːmile] (**-s, -s**) *nt* facsimile.

faktisch ['faktɪʃ] *adj* actual.

Faktor *m* factor.

Faktum (**-s, -ten**) *nt* fact.

fakturieren [faktu'riːrən] *vt* (*COMM*) to invoice.

Fakultät [fakul'tɛːt] *f* faculty.

Falke ['falkə] (**-n, -n**) *m* falcon.

Falklandinseln ['falklant'ɪnzəln] *pl* Falkland Islands, Falklands.

Fall [fal] (**-(e)s, ⸚e**) *m* (*Sturz*) fall; (*Sachverhalt, JUR, GRAM*) case; **auf jeden ~, auf alle Fälle** in any case; (*bestimmt*) definitely; **gesetzt den ~** assuming (that); **jds ~ sein** (*umg*) to be sb's cup of tea; **klarer ~!** (*umg*) sure thing!, you bet!; **das mache ich auf keinen ~** there's no way I'm going to do that.

Falle (**-, -n**) *f* trap; (*umg*: *Bett*) bed; **jdm eine ~ stellen** to set a trap for sb.

fallen *unreg vi* to fall; (*im Krieg*) to fall, be killed; **etw ~ lassen** to drop sth.

fällen ['fɛlən] *vt* (*Baum*) to fell; (*Urteil*) to pass.

fallenlassen *unreg vt* (*Bemerkung*) to make; (*Plan*) to abandon, drop.

fällig ['fɛlɪç] *adj* due; (*Wechsel*) mature(d); **längst ~** long overdue; **F~keit** *f* (*COMM*) maturity.

Fallobst *nt* fallen fruit, windfall.

falls *adv* in case, if.

Fall- *zW*: **~schirm** *m* parachute; **~schirmjäger** *m* paratrooper; **~schirmspringer(in)** *m(f)* parachutist; **~schirmtruppe** *f* paratroops *pl*; **~strick** *m* (*fig*) trap, snare; **~studie** *f* case study.

fällt [fɛlt] *vb siehe* **fallen.**

Falltür *f* trap door.

fallweise *adj* from case to case.

falsch [falʃ] *adj* false; (*unrichtig*) wrong; ~ **liegen (bei** od **in** +*dat*) (*umg*) to be wrong (about); ~ **liegen mit** to be wrong in; **ein ~es Spiel (mit jdm) treiben** to play (sb) false; **etw ~ verstehen** to misunderstand sth, get sth wrong.
fälschen ['fɛlʃən] *vt* to forge.
Fälscher(in) (**-s, -**) *m(f)* forger.
Falschgeld *nt* counterfeit money.
Falschheit *f* falsity, falseness; (*Unrichtigkeit*) wrongness.
fälschlich *adj* false.
fälschlicherweise *adv* mistakenly.
Falschmeldung *f* (*PRESSE*) false report.
Fälschung *f* forgery.
fälschungssicher *adj* forgery-proof.
Faltblatt *nt* leaflet; (*in Zeitschrift etc*) insert.
Fältchen ['fɛltçən] *nt* crease, wrinkle.
Falte ['faltə] (**-, -n**) *f* (*Knick*) fold, crease; (*Haut~*) wrinkle; (*Rock~*) pleat.
falten *vt* to fold; (*Stirn*) to wrinkle.
faltenlos *adj* without folds; without wrinkles.
Faltenrock *m* pleated skirt.
Falter ['faltər] (**-s, -**) *m* (*Tag~*) butterfly; (*Nacht~*) moth.
faltig ['faltɪç] *adj* (*Haut*) wrinkled; (*Rock usw*) creased.
falzen ['faltsən] *vt* (*Papierbogen*) to fold.
Fam. *abk* = **Familie.**
familiär [famili'ɛːr] *adj* familiar.
Familie [fa'miːliə] *f* family; ~ **Otto Francke** (*als Anschrift*) Mr. & Mrs. Otto Francke and family; **zur ~ gehören** to be one of the family.
Familien- *zW:* ~**ähnlichkeit** *f* family resemblance; ~**anschluß** *m:* **Unterkunft mit ~anschluß** *accommodation where one is treated as one of the family*; ~**kreis** *m* family circle; ~**mitglied** *nt* member of the family; ~**name** *m* surname; ~**packung** *f* family(-size) pack; ~**planung** *f* family planning; ~**stand** *m* marital status; ~**vater** *m* head of the family; ~**verhältnisse** *pl* family circumstances *pl*.
Fanatiker(in) [fa'naːtikər(ɪn)] (**-s, -**) *m(f)* fanatic.
fanatisch *adj* fanatical.
Fanatismus [fana'tɪsmʊs] *m* fanaticism.
fand *etc* [fant] *vb siehe* **finden.**
Fang [faŋ] (**-(e)s, ⁻e**) *m* catch; (*Jagen*) hunting; (*Kralle*) talon, claw.
fangen *unreg vt* to catch ♦ *vr* to get caught; (*Flugzeug*) to level out; (*Mensch: nicht fallen*) to steady o.s.; (*fig*) to compose o.s.; (*in Leistung*) to get back on form.
Fangfrage *f* catch od trick question.
Fanggründe *pl* fishing grounds *pl*.
fängt [fɛŋkt] *vb siehe* **fangen.**
Farb- *zW:* ~**abzug** *m* coloured (*BRIT*) od colored (*US*) print; ~**aufnahme** *f* colour (*BRIT*) od color (*US*) photograph; ~**band** *nt* typewriter ribbon.

Farbe ['farbə] (**-, -n**) *f* colour (*BRIT*), color (*US*); (*zum Malen etc*) paint; (*Stoff~*) dye; (*KARTEN*) suit.
farbecht ['farp|ɛçt] *adj* colourfast (*BRIT*), colorfast (*US*).
färben ['fɛrbən] *vt* to colour (*BRIT*), color (*US*); (*Stoff, Haar*) to dye.
farben- *zW:* ~**blind** *adj* colour-blind (*BRIT*), color-blind (*US*); ~**froh** *adj* colourful (*BRIT*), colorful (*US*); ~**prächtig** *adj* colourful (*BRIT*), colorful (*US*).
Farbfernsehen *nt* colour (*BRIT*) od color (*US*) television.
Farbfilm *m* colour (*BRIT*) od color (*US*) film.
Farbfoto *nt* colour (*BRIT*) od color (*US*) photo.
farbig *adj* coloured (*BRIT*), colored (*US*).
Farbige(r) *f(m)* coloured (*BRIT*) od colored (*US*) person.
Farb- *zW:* ~**kasten** *m* paintbox; **f~los** *adj* colourless (*BRIT*), colorless (*US*); ~**stift** *m* coloured (*BRIT*) od colored (*US*) pencil; ~**stoff** *m* dye; (*Lebensmittel~*) (artificial) colouring (*BRIT*) od coloring (*US*); ~**ton** *m* hue, tone.
Färbung ['fɛrbʊŋ] *f* colouring (*BRIT*), coloring (*US*); (*Tendenz*) bias.
Farn [farn] (**-(e)s, -e**) *m* fern; (*Adler~*) bracken.
Farnkraut [farn] *nt* = **Farn.**
Färöer [fɛ'røːər] *pl* Faeroe Islands *pl*.
Fasan [fa'zaːn] (**-(e)s, -e(n)**) *m* pheasant.
Fasching ['faʃɪŋ] (**-s, -e** od **-s**) *m* carnival.
Faschismus [fa'ʃɪsmʊs] *m* fascism.
Faschist(in) *m(f)* fascist.
faschistisch [fa'ʃɪstɪʃ] *adj* fascist.
faseln ['faːzəln] *vi* to talk nonsense, drivel.
Faser ['faːzər] (**-, -n**) *f* fibre.
fasern *vi* to fray.
Faß [fas] (**-sses, Fässer**) *nt* vat, barrel; (*für Öl*) drum; **Bier vom ~** draught beer; **ein ~ ohne Boden** (*fig*) a bottomless pit.
Fassade [fa'saːdə] *f* (*lit, fig*) façade.
faßbar *adj* comprehensible.
Faßbier *nt* draught beer.
fassen ['fasən] *vt* (*ergreifen*) to grasp, take; (*inhaltlich*) to hold; (*Entschluß etc*) to take; (*verstehen*) to understand; (*Ring etc*) to set; (*formulieren*) to formulate, phrase ♦ *vr* to calm down; **nicht zu ~** unbelievable; **sich kurz ~** to be brief.
faßlich ['faslɪç] *adj* comprehensible.
Fasson [fa'sõː] (**-, -s**) *f* style; (*Art und Weise*) way; **aus der ~ geraten** (*lit*) to lose its shape.
Fassung ['fasʊŋ] *f* (*Umrahmung*) mounting; (*Lampen~*) socket; (*Wortlaut*) version; (*Beherrschung*) composure; **jdn aus der ~ bringen** to upset sb; **völlig außer ~ geraten** to lose all self-control.
fassungslos *adj* speechless.
Fassungsvermögen *nt* capacity; (*Verständnis*) comprehension.
fast [fast] *adv* almost, nearly; ~ **nie** hardly ever.

fasten ['fastən] *vi* to fast; **F~** **(-s)** *nt* fasting; **F~zeit** *f* Lent.

Fastnacht *f* Shrovetide carnival.

faszinieren [fastsi'niːrən] *vt* to fascinate.

fatal [fa'taːl] *adj* fatal; (*peinlich*) embarrassing.

fauchen ['fauxən] *vt*, *vi* to hiss.

faul [faul] *adj* rotten; (*Person*) lazy; (*Ausreden*) lame; **daran ist etwas ~** there's something fishy about it.

faulen *vi* to rot.

faulenzen ['faulɛntsən] *vi* to idle.

Faulenzer(in) **(-s, -)** *m(f)* idler, loafer.

Faulheit *f* laziness.

faulig *adj* putrid.

Fäulnis ['fɔylnɪs] **(-)** *f* decay, putrefaction.

Faulpelz (*umg*) *m* lazybones *sing*.

Faust ['faust] **(-, Fäuste)** *f* fist; **das paßt wie die ~ aufs Auge** (*paßt nicht*) it's all wrong; **auf eigene ~** (*fig*) on one's own initiative.

Fäustchen ['fɔystçən] *nt*: **sich** *dat* **ins ~ lachen** to laugh up one's sleeve.

faustdick (*umg*) *adj*: **er hat es ~ hinter den Ohren** he's a crafty one.

Fausthandschuh *m* mitten.

Faustregel *f* rule of thumb.

Favorit(in) [favo'riːt(ɪn)] **(-en, -en)** *m(f)* favourite (*BRIT*), favorite (*US*).

Fax [faks] **(-, -e)** *nt* fax; **f~en** *vt* to fax.

Faxen ['faksən] *pl*: **~ machen** to fool around.

Fazit ['faːtsɪt] **(-s, -s** *od* **-e)** *nt*: **wenn wir aus diesen vier Jahren das ~ ziehen** if we take stock of these four years.

FCKW **(-s, -s)** *m abk* (= *Fluorchlorkohlenwasserstoff*) CFC.

FdH (*umg*) *abk* (= *Friß die Hälfte*) eat less.

FDP, F.D.P. *f abk* (= *Freie Demokratische Partei*) Free Democratic Party.

> The **FDP** (*Freie Demokratische Partei*) was founded in 1948 and is Germany's centre party. It is a liberal party which has formed governing coalitions with both the **SPD** and the **CDU/CSU** at times, both in the regions and in the **Bundestag**.

Feb. *abk* (= *Februar*) Feb.

Februar ['feːbruaːr] **(-(s), -e)** (*pl selten*) *m* February; *siehe auch* **September**.

fechten ['fɛçtən] *unreg vi* to fence.

Feder ['feːdər] **(-, -n)** *f* feather; (*Schreib~*) pen nib; (*TECH*) spring; **in den ~n liegen** (*umg*) to be/stay in bed; **~ball** *m* shuttlecock; **~ballspiel** *nt* badminton; **~bett** *nt* continental quilt; **f~führend** *adj* (*Behörde*): **f~führend (für)** in overall charge (of); **~halter** *m* pen; **f~leicht** *adj* light as a feather; **~lesen** *nt*: **nicht viel ~lesens mit jdm/etw machen** to make short work of sb/sth.

federn *vi* (*nachgeben*) to be springy; (*sich bewegen*) to bounce ♦ *vt* to spring.

Federung *f* suspension.

Federvieh *nt* poultry.

Federweiße(r) *m* new wine.

Federzeichnung *f* pen-and-ink drawing.

Fee [feː] **(-, -n)** *f* fairy.

feenhaft ['feːənhaft] *adj* (*liter*) fairylike.

Fegefeuer ['feːgəfɔyər] *nt* purgatory.

fegen ['feːgən] *vt* to sweep.

fehl [feːl] *adj*: **~ am Platz** *od* **Ort** out of place; **F~anzeige** (*umg*) *f* dead loss.

fehlen *vi* to be wanting *od* missing; (*abwesend sein*) to be absent ♦ *vi unpers*: **es fehlte nicht viel, und ich hätte ihn verprügelt** I almost hit him; **etw fehlt jdm** sb lacks sth; **du fehlst mir** I miss you; **was fehlt ihm?** what's wrong with him?; **der/das hat mir gerade noch gefehlt!** (*ironisch*) he/that was all I needed; **weit gefehlt!** (*fig*) you're way out! (*umg*); (*ganz im Gegenteil*) far from it!; **mir ~ die Worte** words fail me; **wo fehlt es?** what's the trouble?, what's up? (*umg*).

Fehlentscheidung *f* wrong decision.

Fehler **(-s, -)** *m* mistake, error; (*Mangel, Schwäche*) fault; **ihr ist ein ~ unterlaufen** she's made a mistake; **~beseitigung** *f* (*COMPUT*) debugging; **f~frei** *adj* faultless; without any mistakes; **f~haft** *adj* incorrect; faulty; **f~los** *adj* = **fehlerfrei**; **~meldung** *f* (*COMPUT*) error message; **~suchprogramm** *nt* (*COMPUT*) debugger.

fehl- *zW*: **F~geburt** *f* miscarriage; **~gehen** *unreg vi* to go astray; **~griff** *m* blunder; **F~konstruktion** *f*: **eine F~konstruktion sein** to be badly designed; **F~leistung** *f*: **Freudsche F~leistung** Freudian slip; **F~schlag** *m* failure; **~schlagen** *unreg vi* to fail; **F~schluß** *m* wrong conclusion; **F~start** *m* (*SPORT*) false start; **F~tritt** *m* false move; (*fig*) blunder, slip; (: *Affäre*) indiscretion; **F~urteil** *nt* miscarriage of justice; **F~zündung** *f* (*AUT*) misfire, backfire.

Feier ['faɪər] **(-, -n)** *f* celebration; **~abend** *m* time to stop work; **~abend machen** to stop, knock off; **was machst du am ~abend?** what are you doing after work?; **jetzt ist ~abend!** that's enough!

feierlich *adj* solemn; **das ist ja nicht mehr ~** (*umg*) that's beyond a joke; **F~keit** *f* solemnity; **Feierlichkeiten** *pl* festivities *pl*.

feiern *vt*, *vi* to celebrate.

Feiertag *m* holiday.

feig *adj* cowardly.

Feige ['faɪgə] **(-, -n)** *f* fig.

feige *adj* cowardly.

Feigheit *f* cowardice.

Feigling *m* coward.

Feile ['faɪlə] **(-, -n)** *f* file.

feilen *vt*, *vi* to file.

feilschen ['faɪlʃən] *vi* to haggle.

fein [faɪn] *adj* fine; (*vornehm*) refined; (*Gehör etc*) keen; **~!** great!; **er ist ~ raus** (*umg*) he's sitting pretty; **sich ~ machen** to get all dressed up.

Feind(in) [faɪnt, 'faɪndɪn] (-**(e)s, -e**) *m(f)* enemy; ~**bild** *nt* concept of an/the enemy; **f~lich** *adj* hostile; ~**schaft** *f* enmity; **f~selig** *adj* hostile; ~**seligkeit** *f* hostility.

Fein- *zW:* **f~fühlend** *adj* sensitive; **f~fühlig** *adj* sensitive; ~**gefühl** *nt* delicacy, tact; ~**heit** *f* fineness; refinement; keenness; ~**kostgeschäft** *nt* delicatessen (shop), deli; ~**schmecker** (**-s, -**) *m* gourmet; ~**waschmittel** *nt* mild(-action) detergent.

feist [faɪst] *adj* fat.

feixen ['faɪksən] (*umg*) *vi* to smirk.

Feld [fɛlt] (-**(e)s, -er**) *nt* field; (*SCHACH*) square; (*SPORT*) pitch; **Argumente ins ~ führen** to bring arguments to bear; **das ~ räumen** (*fig*) to bow out; ~**arbeit** *f* (*AGR*) work in the fields; (*GEOG etc*) fieldwork; ~**blume** *f* wild flower; ~**herr** *m* commander; ~**jäger** *pl* (*MIL*) the military police; ~**lazarett** *nt* (*MIL*) field hospital; ~**salat** *m* lamb's lettuce; ~**stecher** *m* (pair of) binoculars *pl od* field glasses *pl*.

Feld-Wald-und-Wiesen- (*umg*) *in zW* common-or-garden.

Feld- *zW:* ~**webel** (**-s, -**) *m* sergeant; ~**weg** *m* path; ~**zug** *m* (*lit, fig*) campaign.

Felge ['fɛlgə] (**-, -n**) *f* (wheel) rim.

Felgenbremse *f* caliper brake.

Fell [fɛl] (-**(e)s, -e**) *nt* fur; coat; (*von Schaf*) fleece; (*von toten Tieren*) skin; **ein dickes ~ haben** to be thick-skinned, have a thick skin; **ihm sind die ~e weggeschwommen** (*fig*) all his hopes were dashed.

Fels [fɛls] (-**en, -en**) *m* = **Felsen**.

Felsen ['fɛlzən] (**-s, -**) *m* rock; (*Klippe*) cliff; **f~fest** *adj* firm.

felsig *adj* rocky.

Felsspalte *f* crevice.

Felsvorsprung *m* ledge.

feminin [femi'niːn] *adj* feminine; (*pej*) effeminate.

Feministin [femi'nɪstɪn] *f* feminist.

Fenchel ['fɛnçəl] (**-s**) *m* fennel.

Fenster ['fɛnstər] (**-s, -**) *nt* window; **weg vom ~** (*umg*) out of the game, finished; ~**brett** *nt* windowsill; ~**laden** *m* shutter; ~**leder** *nt* chamois, shammy (leather); ~**platz** *m* window seat; ~**putzer** (**-s, -**) *m* window cleaner; ~**scheibe** *f* windowpane; ~**sims** *m* windowsill.

Ferien ['feːriən] *pl* holidays *pl*, vacation (*US*); **die großen ~** the summer holidays (*BRIT*), the long vacation (*US UNIV*); **~ haben** to be on holiday; ~**kurs** *m* holiday course; ~**reise** *f* holiday; ~**wohnung** *f* holiday flat (*BRIT*), vacation apartment (*US*); ~**zeit** *f* holiday period.

Ferkel ['fɛrkəl] (**-s, -**) *nt* piglet.

fern [fɛrn] *adj, adv* far-off, distant; **~ von hier** a long way (away) from here; **F~amt** *nt* (*TEL*) exchange; **F~bedienung** *f* remote control; ~**bleiben** *unreg vi:* **~ bleiben** (**von** *od* +*dat*) to stay away (from).

Ferne (**-, -n**) *f* distance.

ferner *adj, adv* further; (*weiterhin*) in future; **unter „~ liefen" rangieren** (*umg*) to be an also-ran.

fern- *zW:* **F~fahrer** *m* long-distance lorry (*BRIT*) *od* truck driver; **F~flug** *m* long-distance flight; **F~gespräch** *nt* long-distance call (*BRIT*), toll call (*US*); ~**gesteuert** *adj* remote-controlled; (*Rakete*) guided; **F~glas** *nt* binoculars *pl*; ~**halten** *unreg vt, vr* to keep away; **F~kopie** *f* fax; **F~kopierer** *m* fax machine; **F~kurs(us)** *m* correspondence course; **F~lenkung** *f* remote control; **F~licht** *nt* (*AUT*): **mit F~licht fahren** to drive on full beam; ~**liegen** *unreg vi:* **jdm ~liegen** to be far from sb's mind.

Fernmelde- *in zW* telecommunications; (*MIL*) signals.

fern- *zW:* **F~ost: aus/in F~ost** from/in the Far East; ~**östlich** *adj* Far Eastern *attrib*; **F~rohr** *nt* telescope; **F~schreiben** *nt* telex; **F~schreiber** *m* teleprinter; ~**schriftlich** *adj* by telex.

Fernsehapparat *m* television (set).

fernsehen ['fɛrnzeːən] *unreg vi* to watch television; **F~** (**-s**) *nt* television; **im F~** on television.

Fernseher (**-s, -**) *m* television (set).

Fernseh- *zW:* ~**gebühr** *f* television licence (*BRIT*) *od* license (*US*) fee; ~**gerät** *nt* television set; ~**programm** *nt* (*Kanal*) channel, station (*US*); (*Sendung*) programme (*BRIT*), program (*US*); (~*zeitschrift*) (television) programme (*BRIT*) *od* program (*US*) guide; ~**sendung** *f* television programme (*BRIT*) *od* program (*US*); ~**überwachungsanlage** *f* closed-circuit television; ~**zuschauer** *m* (television) viewer.

Fern- *zW:* ~**sprecher** *m* telephone; ~**sprechzelle** *f* telephone box (*BRIT*) *od* booth (*US*); ~**steuerung** *f* remote control; ~**studium** *nt* multimedia course, ≈ Open University course (*BRIT*); ~**verkehr** *m* long-distance traffic; ~**weh** *nt* wanderlust.

Fernstudium *is a distance-learning degree course where students do not go to university but receive their tuition by letter, television or radio programmes. There is no personal contact between student and lecturer. The first* **Fernstudium** *was founded in 1974. Students are free to practise their career or to bring up a family at the same time as studying.*

Ferse ['fɛrzə] (**-, -n**) *f* heel.

Fersengeld *nt:* **~ geben** to take to one's heels.

fertig ['fɛrtɪç] *adj* (*bereit*) ready; (*beendet*) finished; (*gebrauchs~*) ready-made; **~ ausgebildet** fully qualified; **mit jdm/etw ~ werden** to cope with sb/sth; **mit den**

Nerven ~ **sein** to be at the end of one's tether; ~ **essen/lesen** to finish eating/reading; **F~bau** m prefab(ricated house); ~**bringen** unreg vt (fähig sein) to manage, be capable of; (beenden) to finish.

fertigen ['fɛrtɪɡən] vt to manufacture.

fertig- zW: **F~gericht** nt ready-to-serve meal; **F~haus** nt prefab(ricated house); **F~keit** f skill; ~**machen** vt (beenden) to finish; (umg: Person) to finish; (: körperlich) to exhaust; (: moralisch) to get down ♦ vr to get ready; ~**stellen** vt to complete.

Fertigung f production.

Fertigungs- in zW production; ~**straße** f production line.

Fertigware f finished product.

fesch [fɛʃ] (umg) adj (modisch) smart; (: hübsch) attractive.

Fessel ['fɛsəl] (-, -n) f fetter.

fesseln vt to bind; (mit F~) to fetter; (fig) to grip; **ans Bett gefesselt** (fig) confined to bed.

fesselnd adj gripping.

Fest [fɛst] (-(e)s, -e) nt (Feier) celebration; (Party) party; **man soll die ~e feiern, wie sie fallen** (Sprichwort) make hay while the sun shines.

fest adj firm; (Nahrung) solid; (Gehalt) regular; (Gewebe, Schuhe) strong, sturdy; (Freund(in)) steady ♦ adv (schlafen) soundly; ~ **entschlossen sein** to be absolutely determined; ~**e Kosten** (COMM) fixed costs pl.

festangestellt adj employed on a permanent basis.

Festbeleuchtung f illumination.

festbinden unreg vt to tie, fasten.

festbleiben unreg vi to stand firm.

Festessen nt banquet.

festfahren unreg vr to get stuck.

festhalten unreg vt to seize, hold fast; (Ereignis) to record ♦ vr: **sich** ~ **(an** +dat) to hold on (to).

festigen vt to strengthen.

Festigkeit f strength.

fest- zW: ~**klammern** vr: **sich** ~**klammern (an** +dat) to cling on (to); ~**klemmen** vt to wedge fast; **F~komma** nt (COMPUT) fixed point; **F~land** nt mainland; ~**legen** vt to fix ♦ vr to commit o.s.; **jdn auf etw** akk ~**legen** (~nageln) to tie sb (down) to sth; (verpflichten) to commit sb to sth.

festlich adj festive.

fest- zW: ~**liegen** unreg vi (FIN: Geld) to be tied up; ~**machen** vt to fasten; (Termin etc) to fix; ~**nageln: jdn** ~**nageln (auf** +akk) (fig: umg) to pin sb down (to); **F~nahme** (-, -n) f capture; ~**nehmen** unreg vt to capture, arrest; **F~platte** f (COMPUT) hard disk; **F~preis** m (COMM) fixed price.

Festrede f speech, address.

festschnallen vt to strap down ♦ vr to fasten one's seat belt.

festsetzen vt to fix, settle.

Festspiel nt festival.

fest- zW: ~**stehen** unreg vi to be certain; ~**stellbar** adj (herauszufinden) ascertainable; ~**stellen** vt to establish; (sagen) to remark; (TECH) to lock (fast); **F~stellung** f: **die F~stellung machen, daß** ... to realize that ...; (bemerken) to remark od observe that ...; **F~tag** m holiday; ~**umrissen** adj attrib clearcut.

Festung f fortress.

festverzinslich adj fixed-interest attrib.

Festwertspeicher m (COMPUT) read-only memory.

Festzelt nt marquee.

Fete ['feːtə] (-, -n) f party.

Fett [fɛt] (-(e)s, -e) nt fat, grease; **f~** adj fat; (Essen etc) greasy; **f~arm** adj low fat; **f~en** vt to grease; ~**fleck** m grease spot od stain; **f~frei** adj fat-free; **f~gedruckt** adj bold-type; ~**gehalt** m fat content; **f~ig** adj greasy, fatty; ~**näpfchen** nt: **ins** ~**näpfchen treten** to put one's foot in it; ~**polster** nt (hum: umg): ~**polster haben** to be well-padded.

Fetzen ['fɛtsən] (-s, -) m scrap; **..., daß die** ~ **fliegen** (umg) ... like mad.

feucht [fɔyçt] adj damp; (Luft) humid; ~**fröhlich** adj (hum) boozy.

Feuchtigkeit f dampness; humidity.

Feuchtigkeitscreme f moisturizer.

feudal [fɔy'daːl] adj (POL, HIST) feudal; (umg) plush.

Feuer ['fɔyər] (-s, -) nt fire; (zum Rauchen) a light; (fig: Schwung) spirit; **für jdn durchs** ~ **gehen** to go through fire and water for sb; ~ **und Flamme (für etw) sein** (umg) to be dead keen (on sth); ~ **für etw/jdn fangen** (fig) to develop a great interest in sth/sb; ~**alarm** m fire alarm; ~**eifer** m zeal; **f~fest** adj fireproof; ~**gefahr** f danger of fire; **bei** ~**gefahr** in the event of fire; **f~gefährlich** adj inflammable; ~**leiter** f fire escape ladder; ~**löscher** (-s, -) m fire extinguisher; ~**melder** (-s, -) m fire alarm.

feuern vt, vi (lit, fig) to fire.

Feuer- zW: **f~polizeilich** adj (Bestimmungen) laid down by the fire authorities; ~**probe** f acid test; **f~rot** adj fiery red.

Feuersbrunst f (geh) conflagration.

Feuer- zW: ~**schlucker** m fire-eater; ~**schutz** m (Vorbeugung) fire prevention; (MIL: Deckung) covering fire; **f~sicher** adj fireproof; ~**stein** m flint; ~**stelle** f fireplace; ~**treppe** f fire escape; ~**versicherung** f fire insurance; ~**waffe** f firearm; ~**wehr** f fire brigade; ~**wehrauto** nt fire engine; ~**werk** nt fireworks pl; ~**werkskörper** m firework; ~**zangenbowle** f red wine punch containing rum which has been flamed od **zeug** nt (cigarette) lighter.

Feuilleton [fœjə'tõː] (-s, -s) nt (PRESSE) feature section; (Artikel) feature (article).

feurig ['fɔyrɪç] *adj* fiery.
Fiche [fiːʃ] **(-s, -s)** *m od nt* (micro)fiche.
ficht [fɪçt] *vb siehe* **fechten.**
Fichte ['fɪçtə] **(-, -n)** *f* spruce.
ficken ['fɪkən] (*umg!*) *vt, vi* to fuck (*!*).
fick(e)rig ['fɪk(ə)rɪç] (*umg*) *adj* fidgety.
fidel [fi'deːl] (*umg*) *adj* jolly.
Fidschiinseln ['fɪdʒi|ɪnzəln] *pl* Fiji Islands.
Fieber ['fiːbər] **(-s, -)** *nt* fever, temperature;
 (*Krankheit*) fever; ~ **haben** to have a
 temperature; **f~haft** *adj* feverish; ~**messer**
 m thermometer; ~**thermometer** *nt*
 thermometer.
fiel *etc* [fiːl] *vb siehe* **fallen.**
fies [fiːs] (*umg*) *adj* nasty.
Figur [fi'guːr] **(-, -en)** *f* figure; (*Schach~*)
 chessman, chess piece; **eine gute/**
 schlechte/traurige ~ **abgeben** to cut a good/
 poor/sorry figure.
fiktiv [fɪk'tiːf] *adj* fictitious.
Filet [fi'leː] **(-s, -s)** *nt* (*KOCH*) fillet; (*Rinder~*)
 fillet steak; (*zum Braten*) piece of sirloin *od*
 tenderloin (*US*).
Filiale [fili'aːlə] **(-, -n)** *f* (*COMM*) branch.
Filipino [fili'piːno] **(-s, -s)** *m* Filipino.
Film [fɪlm] **(-(e)s, -e)** *m* film, movie (*bes US*);
 da ist bei mir der ~ **gerissen** (*umg*) I had a
 mental blackout; ~**aufnahme** *f* shooting.
Filmemacher(in) *m(f)* film-maker.
filmen *vt, vi* to film.
Film- *zW:* ~**festspiele** *pl* film festival *sing;*
 ~**kamera** *f* cine-camera; ~**riß** (*umg*) *m*
 mental blackout; ~**schauspieler(in)** *m(f)* film
 od movie (*bes US*) actor, film *od* movie
 actress; ~**verleih** *m* film distributors *pl;*
 ~**vorführgerät** *nt* cine-projector.
Filter ['fɪltər] **(-s, -)** *m* filter; ~**kaffee** *m* filter *od*
 drip (*US*) coffee; ~**mundstück** *nt* filter tip.
filtern *vt* to filter.
Filterpapier *nt* filter paper.
Filterzigarette *f* tipped cigarette.
Filz [fɪlts] **(-es, -e)** *m* felt.
filzen (*umg*) *vt* to frisk ♦ *vi* (*Wolle*) to mat.
Filzstift *m* felt-tip (pen).
Fimmel ['fɪməl] **(-s, -)** (*umg*) *m:* **du hast wohl**
 einen ~**!** you're crazy!
Finale [fi'naːlə] **(-s, -(s))** *nt* finale; (*SPORT*)
 final(*s pl*).
Finanz [fi'nants] *f* finance; **Finanzen** *pl*
 finances *pl;* **das übersteigt meine** ~**en** that's
 beyond my means; ~**amt** *nt* ≈ Inland
 Revenue Office (*BRIT*), Internal Revenue
 Office (*US*); ~**beamte(r)** *f(m)* revenue officer.
finanziell [finantsi'ɛl] *adj* financial.
finanzieren [finan'tsiːrən] *vt* to finance, to
 fund.
Finanzierung *f* financing, funding.
Finanz- *zW:* ~**minister** *m* ≈ Chancellor of the
 Exchequer (*BRIT*), Minister of Finance;
 f~schwach *adj* financially weak; ~**wesen** *nt*
 financial system; ~**wirtschaft** *f* public
 finances *pl.*

finden ['fɪndən] *unreg vt* to find; (*meinen*) to
 think ♦ *vr* to be (found); (*sich fassen*) to
 compose o.s. ♦ *vi:* **ich finde schon allein**
 hinaus I can see myself out; **ich finde nichts**
 dabei, wenn ... I don't see what's wrong if
 ...; **das wird sich** ~ things will work out.
Finder(in) **(-s, -)** *m(f)* finder; ~**lohn** *m* reward
 (for the finder).
findig *adj* resourceful.
fing *etc* [fɪŋ] *vb siehe* **fangen.**
Finger ['fɪŋər] **(-s, -)** *m* finger; **mit** ~**n auf jdn**
 zeigen (*fig*) to look askance at sb; **das kann**
 sich jeder an den (fünf) ~**n abzählen** (*umg*) it
 sticks out a mile; **sich** *dat* **etw aus den** ~**n**
 saugen to conjure sth up; **lange** ~ **machen**
 (*umg*) to be light-fingered; ~**abdruck** *m*
 fingerprint; ~**handschuh** *m* glove; ~**hut** *m*
 thimble; (*BOT*) foxglove; ~**nagel** *m*
 fingernail; ~**ring** *m* ring; ~**spitze** *f* fingertip;
 ~**spitzengefühl** *nt* sensitivity; ~**zeig**
 (-(e)s, -e) *m* hint, pointer.
fingieren [fɪŋ'giːrən] *vt* to feign.
fingiert *adj* made-up, fictitious.
Fink [fɪŋk] **(-en, -en)** *m* finch.
Finne ['fɪnə] **(-n, -n)** *m* Finn.
Finnin ['fɪnɪn] *f* Finn.
finnisch *adj* Finnish.
Finnland *nt* Finland.
finster ['fɪnstər] *adj* dark, gloomy; (*verdächtig*)
 dubious; (*verdrossen*) grim; (*Gedanke*) dark;
 jdn ~ **ansehen** to give sb a black look; **F~nis**
 (-) *f* darkness, gloom.
Finte ['fɪntə] **(-, -n)** *f* feint, trick.
Firlefanz ['fɪrləfants] (*umg*) *m* (*Kram*)
 frippery; (*Albernheit*): **mach keinen** ~ don't
 clown around.
firm [fɪrm] *adj* well-up.
Firma **(-, -men)** *f* firm; **die** ~ **dankt** (*hum*)
 much obliged (to you).
Firmen- *zW:* ~**inhaber** *m* proprietor (*of firm*);
 ~**register** *nt* register of companies; ~**schild**
 nt (shop) sign; ~**übernahme** *f* takeover;
 ~**wagen** *m* company car; ~**zeichen** *nt*
 trademark.
Firmung *f* (*REL*) confirmation.
Firnis ['fɪrnɪs] **(-ses, -se)** *m* varnish.
Fis [fɪs] **(-, -)** *nt* (*MUS*) F sharp.
Fisch [fɪʃ] **(-(e)s, -e)** *m* fish; **Fische** *pl* (*ASTROL*)
 Pisces *sing;* **das sind kleine** ~**e** (*fig: umg*)
 that's child's play; ~**bestand** *m* fish
 population.
fischen *vt, vi* to fish.
Fischer **(-s, -)** *m* fisherman.
Fischerei [fɪʃə'raɪ] *f* fishing, fishery.
Fisch- *zW:* ~**fang** *m* fishing; ~**geschäft** *nt*
 fishmonger's (shop); ~**gräte** *f* fishbone;
 ~**gründe** *pl* fishing grounds *pl*, fisheries *pl;*
 ~**stäbchen** *nt* fish finger (*BRIT*), fish stick
 (*US*); ~**zucht** *f* fish-farming; ~**zug** *m* catch
 of fish.
Fisimatenten [fizima'tɛntən] (*umg*) *pl*
 (*Ausflüchte*) excuses *pl;* (*Umstände*) fuss *sing.*

Fiskus ['fɪskʊs] m (fig: Staatskasse) Treasury.
fit [fɪt] adj fit.
Fittich ['fɪtɪç] (-(e)s, -e) m (liter): **jdn unter seine ~e nehmen** (hum) to take sb under one's wing.
fix [fɪks] adj (flink) quick; (Person) alert, smart; **~e Idee** obsession, idée fixe; **~ und fertig** finished; (erschöpft) done in; **jdn ~ und fertig machen** (nervös machen) to drive sb mad.
fixen (umg) vi (Drogen spritzen) to fix.
fixieren [fɪ'ksiːrən] vt to fix; (anstarren) to stare at; **er ist zu stark auf seine Mutter fixiert** (PSYCH) he has a mother fixation.
Fixkosten pl (COMM) fixed costs pl.
FKK abk = **Freikörperkultur**.
flach [flax] adj flat; (Gefäß) shallow; **auf dem ~en Land** in the middle of the country.
Fläche ['flɛçə] (-, -n) f area; (Ober~) surface.
Flächeninhalt m surface area.
Flach- zW: **f~fallen** unreg (umg) vi to fall through; **~heit** f flatness; shallowness; **~land** nt lowland; **f~liegen** unreg (umg) vi to be laid up; **~mann** (-(e)s, pl -männer) (umg) m hip flask.
flachsen ['flaksən] (umg) vi to kid around.
flackern ['flakərn] vi to flare, flicker.
Fladen ['flaːdən] (-s, -) m (KOCH) round flat dough-cake; (umg: Kuh~) cowpat.
Flagge ['flaɡə] (-, -n) f flag; **~ zeigen** (fig) to nail one's colours to the mast.
flaggen vi to fly flags od a flag.
flagrant [fla'ɡrant] adj flagrant; **in ~i** red-handed.
Flak [flak] (-s, -) f (= Flug(zeug)abwehrkanone) anti-aircraft gun; (Einheit) anti-aircraft unit.
flambieren [flam'biːrən] vt (KOCH) to flambé.
Flame ['flaːmə] (-n, -n) m Fleming.
Flämin ['flɛːmɪn] f Fleming.
flämisch ['flɛːmɪʃ] adj Flemish.
Flamme ['flamə] (-, -n) f flame; **in ~n stehen/aufgehen** to be in/go up in flames.
Flandern ['flandərn] nt Flanders sing.
Flanell [fla'nɛl] (-s, -e) m flannel.
Flanke ['flaŋkə] (-, -n) f flank; (SPORT: Seite) wing.
Flasche ['flaʃə] (-, -n) f bottle; (umg: Versager) wash-out; **zur ~ greifen** (fig) to hit the bottle.
Flaschen- zW: **~bier** nt bottled beer; **~öffner** m bottle opener; **~wein** m bottled wine; **~zug** m pulley.
flatterhaft adj flighty, fickle.
flattern ['flatərn] vi to flutter.
flau [flaʊ] adj (Brise, COMM) slack; **jdm ist ~ (im Magen)** sb feels queasy.
Flaum [flaʊm] (-(e)s) m (Feder) down.
flauschig ['flaʊʃɪç] adj fluffy.
Flausen ['flaʊzən] pl silly ideas pl; (Ausflüchte) weak excuses pl.
Flaute ['flaʊtə] (-, -n) f calm; (COMM) recession.
Flechte ['flɛçtə] (-, -n) f (MED) dry scab;

(BOT) lichen.
flechten unreg vt to plait; (Kranz) to twine.
Fleck [flɛk] (-(e)s, -e) m (Schmutz~) stain; (Farb~) patch; (Stelle) spot; **nicht vom ~ kommen** (lit, fig) not to get any further; **sich nicht vom ~ rühren** not to budge; **vom ~ weg** straight away.
Fleckchen nt: **ein schönes ~ (Erde)** a lovely little spot.
Flecken (-s, -) m = **Fleck**; **f~los** adj spotless; **~mittel** nt stain remover; **~wasser** nt stain remover.
fleckig adj marked; (schmutzig) stained.
Fledermaus ['fleːdərmaʊs] f bat.
Flegel ['fleːɡəl] (-s, -) m flail; (Person) lout; **f~haft** adj loutish, unmannerly; **~jahre** pl adolescence sing.
flegeln vr to loll, sprawl.
flehen ['fleːən] vi (geh) to implore.
flehentlich adj imploring.
Fleisch [flaɪʃ] (-(e)s) nt flesh; (Essen) meat; **sich** dat od akk **ins eigene ~ schneiden** to cut off one's nose to spite one's face (Sprichwort); **es ist mir in ~ und Blut übergegangen** it has become second nature to me; **~brühe** f meat stock.
Fleischer (-s, -) m butcher.
Fleischerei [flaɪʃə'raɪ] f butcher's (shop).
fleischig adj fleshy.
Fleisch- zW: **~käse** m meat loaf; **f~lich** adj carnal; **~pastete** f meat pie; **~salat** m diced meat salad with mayonnaise; **~vergiftung** f food poisoning (from meat); **~wolf** m mincer; **~wunde** f flesh wound; **~wurst** f pork sausage.
Fleiß ['flaɪs] (-es) m diligence, industry; **ohne ~ kein Preis** (Sprichwort) success never comes easily.
fleißig adj diligent, industrious; **~ studieren/arbeiten** to study/work hard.
flektieren [flɛk'tiːrən] vt to inflect.
flennen ['flɛnən] (umg) vi to cry, blubber.
fletschen ['flɛtʃən] vt (Zähne) to show.
Fleurop® ['flɔɪrɔp] f ≈ Interflora®.
flexibel [flɛ'ksiːbəl] adj flexible.
Flexibilität [flɛksibili'tɛːt] f flexibility.
flicht [flɪçt] vb siehe **flechten**.
Flicken ['flɪkən] (-s, -) m patch.
flicken vt to mend.
Flickschusterei ['flɪkʃuːstəraɪ] f: **das ist ~** that's a patch-up job.
Flieder ['fliːdər] (-s, -) m lilac.
Fliege ['fliːɡə] (-, -n) f fly; (Schlips) bow tie; **zwei ~n mit einer Klappe schlagen** (Sprichwort) to kill two birds with one stone; **ihn stört die ~ an der Wand** every little thing irritates him.
fliegen unreg vt, vi to fly; **auf jdn/etw ~** (umg) to be mad about sb/sth; **aus der Kurve ~** to skid off the bend; **aus der Firma ~** (umg) to get the sack.
fliegend adj attrib flying; **~e Hitze** hot flushes

pl.
Fliegengewicht *nt (SPORT, fig)* flyweight.
Fliegenklatsche ['fliːgənklatʃə] *f* fly-swat.
Fliegenpilz *m* fly agaric.
Flieger (**-s, -**) *m* flier, airman; ~**alarm** *m* air-raid warning.
fliehen ['fliːən] *unreg vi* to flee.
Fliehkraft ['fliːkraft] *f* centrifugal force.
Fliese ['fliːzə] (**-, -n**) *f* tile.
Fließband ['fliːsbant] *nt* assembly *od* production line; **am** ~ **arbeiten** to work on the assembly *od* production line; ~**arbeit** *f* production-line work; ~**produktion** *f* assembly-line production.
fließen *unreg vi* to flow.
fließend *adj* flowing; (*Rede, Deutsch*) fluent; (*Übergang*) smooth.
Fließ- *zW:* ~**heck** *nt* fastback; ~**komma** *nt* (*COMPUT*) ≈ floating point; ~**papier** *nt* blotting paper (*BRIT*), fleece paper (*US*).
Flimmerkasten (*umg*) *m* (*Fernsehen*) box.
Flimmerkiste (*umg*) *f* (*Fernsehen*) box.
flimmern ['flɪmərn] *vi* to glimmer; **es flimmert mir vor den Augen** my head's swimming.
flink [flɪŋk] *adj* nimble, lively; **mit etw** ~ **bei der Hand sein** to be quick (off the mark) with sth; **F~heit** *f* nimbleness, liveliness.
Flinte ['flɪntə] (**-, -n**) *f* shotgun; **die** ~ **ins Korn werfen** to throw in the sponge.
Flirt [flœrt] (**-s, -s**) *m* flirtation; **einen** ~ (**mit jdm**) **haben** flirt (with sb).
flirten ['flɪrtən] *vi* to flirt.
Flittchen (*pej: umg*) *nt* floozy.
Flitter (**-s, -**) *m* (~*schmuck*) sequins *pl.*
Flitterwochen *pl* honeymoon *sing.*
flitzen ['flɪtsən] *vi* to flit.
Flitzer (**-s, -**) (*umg*) *m* (*Auto*) sporty car.
floaten ['floːtən] *vt, vi* (*FIN*) to float.
flocht *etc* [flɔxt] *vb siehe* **flechten**.
Flocke ['flɔkə] (**-, -n**) *f* flake.
flockig *adj* flaky.
flog *etc* [floːk] *vb siehe* **fliegen**.
Floh [floː] (**-(e)s, ⸚e**) *m* flea; **jdm einen** ~ **ins Ohr setzen** (*umg*) to put an idea into sb's head.
floh *etc vb siehe* **fliehen**.
Flohmarkt *m* flea market.
Flora ['floːra] (**-, -ren**) *f* flora.
Florenz [floˈrɛnts] *nt* Florence.
florieren [floˈriːrən] *vi* to flourish.
Florist(in) *m(f)* florist.
Floskel ['flɔskəl] (**-, -n**) *f* set phrase; **f~haft** *adj* cliché-ridden, stereotyped.
Floß [floːs] (**-es, ⸚e**) *nt* raft.
floß *etc* [flɔs] *vb siehe* **fließen**.
Flosse ['flɔsə] (**-, -n**) *f* fin; (*Taucher~*) flipper; (*umg: Hand*) paw.
Flöte ['fløːtə] (**-, -n**) *f* flute; (*Block~*) recorder.
flötengehen ['fløːtəngeːən] (*umg*) *vi* to go for a burton.
Flötist(in) [fløˈtɪst(ɪn)] *m(f)* flautist, flutist (*bes US*).

flott [flɔt] *adj* lively; (*elegant*) smart; (*NAUT*) afloat.
Flotte (**-, -n**) *f* fleet.
Flottenstützpunkt *m* naval base.
flottmachen *vt* (*Schiff*) to float off; (*Auto, Fahrrad etc*) to put back on the road.
Flöz [fløːts] (**-es, -e**) *nt* layer, seam.
Fluch [fluːx] (**-(e)s, ⸚e**) *m* curse; **f~en** *vi* to curse, swear.
Flucht [flʊxt] (**-, -en**) *f* flight; (*Fenster~*) row; (*Reihe*) range; (*Zimmer~*) suite; (*geglückt*) flight, escape; **jdn/etw in die** ~ **schlagen** to put sb/sth to flight.
fluchtartig *adj* hasty.
flüchten ['flʏçtən] *vi* to flee ♦ *vr* to take refuge.
Fluchthilfe *f:* ~ **leisten** to aid an escape.
flüchtig *adj* fugitive; (*CHEM*) volatile; (*oberflächlich*) cursory; (*eilig*) fleeting; ~**er Speicher** (*COMPUT*) volatile memory; **jdn** ~ **kennen** to have met sb briefly; **F~keit** *f* transitoriness; volatility; cursoriness; **F~keitsfehler** *m* careless slip.
Flüchtling *m* refugee.
Flüchtlingslager *nt* refugee camp.
Flucht- *zW:* ~**versuch** *m* escape attempt; ~**weg** *m* escape route.
Flug [fluːk] (**-(e)s, ⸚e**) *m* flight; **im** ~ airborne, in flight; **wie im** ~ (**e**) (*fig*) in a flash; ~**abwehr** *f* anti-aircraft defence; ~**bahn** *f* flight path; (*Kreisbahn*) orbit; ~**begleiter(in)** *m(f)* (*AVIAT*) flight attendant; ~**blatt** *nt* pamphlet.
Flügel ['flyːgəl] (**-s, -**) *m* wing; (*MUS*) grand piano; ~**tür** *f* double door.
flugfähig *adj* able to fly; (*Flugzeug: in Ordnung*) airworthy.
Fluggast *m* airline passenger.
flügge ['flʏgə] *adj* (fully-)fledged; ~ **werden** (*lit*) to be able to fly; (*fig*) to leave the nest.
Flug- *zW:* ~**geschwindigkeit** *f* flying *od* air speed; ~**gesellschaft** *f* airline (company); ~**hafen** *m* airport; ~**höhe** *f* altitude (of flight); ~**lotse** *m* air traffic *od* flight controller; ~**plan** *m* flight schedule; ~**platz** *m* airport; (*klein*) airfield; ~**reise** *f* flight.
flugs [flʊks] *adv* speedily.
Flug- *zW:* ~**sand** *m* drifting sand; ~**schein** *m* pilot's licence (*BRIT*) *od* license (*US*); ~**schreiber** *m* flight recorder; ~**schrift** *f* pamphlet; ~**steig** *m* gate; ~**strecke** *f* air route; ~**verkehr** *m* air traffic; ~**wesen** *nt* aviation.
Flugzeug (**-(e)s, -e**) *nt* plane, aeroplane (*BRIT*), airplane (*US*); ~**entführung** *f* hijacking of a plane; ~**halle** *f* hangar; ~**träger** *m* aircraft carrier.
fluktuieren [flʊktuˈiːrən] *vi* to fluctuate.
Flunder ['flʊndər] (**-, -n**) *f* flounder.
flunkern ['flʊŋkərn] *vi* to fib, tell stories.
Fluor ['fluːɔr] (**-s**) *nt* fluorine.
Flur[1] [fluːr] (**-(e)s, -e**) *m* hall; (*Treppen~*) staircase.

Flur² [fluːr] (-, -en) *f* (*geh*) open fields *pl*;
allein auf weiter ~ stehen (*fig*) to be out on a
limb.

Fluß [flʊs] (-sses, -̈sse) *m* river; (*Fließen*) flow;
im ~ sein (*fig*) to be in a state of flux; **etw in**
~ akk bringen to get sth moving;
f~ab(wärts) *adv* downstream; **f~auf(wärts)**
adv upstream; **~diagramm** *nt* flow chart.

flüssig ['flʏsɪç] *adj* liquid; (*Stil*) flowing; **~es**
Vermögen (*COMM*) liquid assets *pl*; **F~keit** *f*
liquid; (*Zustand*) liquidity; **~machen** *vt*
(*Geld*) to make available.

Flußmündung *f* estuary.

Flußpferd *nt* hippopotamus.

flüstern ['flʏstərn] *vt, vi* to whisper.

Flüsterpropaganda *f* whispering campaign.

Flut [fluːt] (-, -en) *f* (*lit, fig*) flood; (*Gezeiten*)
high tide; **f~en** *vi* to flood; **~licht** *nt*
floodlight.

flutschen ['flʊtʃən] (*umg*) *vi* (*rutschen*) to
slide; (*funktionieren*) to go well.

Flutwelle *f* tidal wave.

fl.W. *abk* (= *fließendes Wasser*) running water.

focht *etc* [fɔxt] *vb siehe* **fechten**.

föderativ [fødera'tiːf] *adj* federal.

Fohlen ['foːlən] (-s, -) *nt* foal.

Föhn [føːn] (-(e)s, -e) *m* foehn, *warm dry*
alpine wind.

Föhre ['føːrə] (-, -n) *f* Scots pine.

Folge ['fɔlgə] (-, -n) *f* series, sequence;
(*Fortsetzung*) instalment (*BRIT*), installment
(*US*); (*TV, RUNDF*) episode; (*Auswirkung*)
result; **in rascher ~** in quick succession; **etw**
zur ~ haben to result in sth; **~n haben** to
have consequences; **einer Sache** *dat*
~ leisten to comply with sth; **~erscheinung**
f result, consequence.

folgen *vi +dat* to follow ♦ *vi* (*gehorchen*) to
obey; **jdm ~ können** (*fig*) to follow *od*
understand sb; **daraus folgt, daß ...** it
follows from this that ...

folgend *adj* following; **im ~en** in the
following; (*schriftlich*) below.

folgendermaßen ['fɔlgəndər'maːsən] *adv* as
follows, in the following way.

folgenreich *adj* momentous.

folgenschwer *adj* momentous.

folgerichtig *adj* logical.

folgern *vt:* **~ (aus)** to conclude (from).

Folgerung *f* conclusion.

folgewidrig *adj* illogical.

folglich ['fɔlklɪç] *adv* consequently.

folgsam ['fɔlkzaːm] *adj* obedient.

Folie ['foːliə] (-, -n) *f* foil.

Folienschweißgerät *nt* shrink-wrap
machine.

Folklore ['fɔlkloːər] (-) *f* folklore.

Folter ['fɔltər] (-, -n) *f* torture; (*Gerät*) rack;
jdn auf die ~ spannen (*fig*) to keep sb on
tenterhooks.

foltern *vt* to torture.

Fön ® [føːn] (-(e)s, -e) *m* hair dryer.

Fonds [fõː] (-, -) *m* (*lit, fig*) fund; (*FIN:*
Schuldverschreibung) government bond.

fönen *vt* to blow-dry.

Fontäne [fɔn'tɛːnə] (-, -n) *f* fountain.

foppen ['fɔpən] *vt* to tease.

forcieren [fɔr'siːrən] *vt* to push; (*Tempo*) to
force; (*Konsum, Produktion*) to push *od* force
up.

Förderband ['fœrdərbant] *nt* conveyor belt.

Förderer (-s, -) *m* patron.

Fördergebiet *nt* development area.

Förderin *f* patroness.

Förderkorb *m* pit cage.

Förderleistung *f* (*MIN*) output.

förderlich *adj* beneficial.

fordern ['fɔrdərn] *vt* to demand; (*fig: kosten:*
Opfer) to claim; (: *heraus~*) to challenge.

fördern ['fœrdərn] *vt* to promote; (*unterstützen*)
to help; (*Kohle*) to extract; (*finanziell: Projekt*)
to sponsor; (*jds Talent, Neigung*) to
encourage, foster.

Förderplattform *f* production platform.

Förderstufe *f* (*SCH*) *first stage of secondary*
school where abilities are judged.

Förderturm *m* (*MIN*) winding tower; (*auf*
Bohrstelle) derrick.

Forderung ['fɔrdəruŋ] *f* demand.

Förderung ['fœrdəruŋ] *f* promotion; help;
extraction.

Forelle [fo'rɛlə] *f* trout.

Form [fɔrm] (-, -en) *f* shape; (*Gestaltung*)
form; (*Guß~*) mould; (*Back~*) baking tin; **in**
~ von in the shape of; **in ~ sein** to be in
good form *od* shape; **die ~ wahren** to
observe the proprieties; **in aller ~** formally.

formal [fɔr'maːl] *adj* formal; (*Besitzer, Grund*)
technical.

formalisieren [fɔrmali'ziːrən] *vt* to formalize.

Formalität [fɔrmalɪ'tɛːt] *f* formality; **alle ~en**
erledigen to go through all the formalities.

Format [fɔr'maːt] (-(e)s, -e) *nt* format; (*fig*)
quality.

formatieren [fɔrma'tiːrən] *vt* (*Text, Diskette*) to
format.

Formation [fɔrmatsi'oːn] *f* formation.

formbar *adj* malleable.

Formblatt *nt* form.

Formel (-, -n) *f* formula; (*von Eid etc*)
wording; (*Floskel*) set phrase; **f~haft** *adj*
(*Sprache, Stil*) stereotyped.

formell [fɔr'mɛl] *adj* formal.

formen *vt* to form, shape.

Formfehler *m* faux pas, gaffe; (*JUR*)
irregularity.

formieren [fɔr'miːrən] *vt* to form ♦ *vr* to form
up.

förmlich ['fœrmlɪç] *adj* formal; (*umg*) real;
F~keit *f* formality.

formlos *adj* shapeless; (*Benehmen etc*)
informal; (*Antrag*) unaccompanied by a
form *od* any forms.

Formsache *f* formality.

Formular [fɔrmuˈlaːr] (**-s, -e**) *nt* form.
formulieren [fɔrmuˈliːrən] *vt* to formulate.
Formulierung *f* wording.
formvollendet *adj* perfect; (*Vase etc*) perfectly formed.
forsch [fɔrʃ] *adj* energetic, vigorous.
forschen [ˈfɔrʃən] *vi* to search; (*wissenschaftlich*) to (do) research; ~ **nach** to search for.
forschend *adj* searching.
Forscher (**-s, -**) *m* research scientist; (*Natur~*) explorer.
Forschung [ˈfɔrʃʊŋ] *f* research; ~ **und Lehre** research and teaching; ~ **und Entwicklung** research and development.
Forschungsreise *f* scientific expedition.
Forst [fɔrst] (**-(e)s, -e**) *m* forest; ~**arbeiter** *m* forestry worker.
Förster [ˈfœrstər] (**-s, -**) *m* forester; (*für Wild*) gamekeeper.
Forstwesen *nt* forestry.
Forstwirtschaft *f* forestry.
fort [fɔrt] *adv* away; (*verschwunden*) gone; (*vorwärts*) on; **und so** ~ and so on; **in einem** ~ incessantly; ~**bestehen** *unreg vi* to continue to exist; ~**bewegen** *vt, vr* to move away; ~**bilden** *vr* to continue one's education; **F~bildung** *f* further education; ~**bleiben** *unreg vi* to stay away; ~**bringen** *unreg vt* to take away; **F~dauer** *f* continuance; ~**dauernd** *adj* continuing; (*in der Vergangenheit*) continued ♦ *adv* constantly, continuously; ~**fahren** *unreg vi* to depart; (*~setzen*) to go on, continue; ~**führen** *vt* to continue, carry on; **F~gang** *m* (*Verlauf*) progress; (*Weggang*): **F~gang (aus)** departure (from); ~**gehen** *unreg vi* to go away; ~**geschritten** *adj* advanced; ~**kommen** *unreg vi* to get on; (*wegkommen*) to get away; ~**können** *unreg vi* to be able to get away; ~**lassen** *vt* (*auslassen*) to leave out, omit; (*weggehen lassen*): **jdn ~lassen** to let sb go; ~**laufend** *adj*: ~**laufend numeriert** consecutively numbered; ~**müssen** *unreg vi* to have to go; ~**pflanzen** *vr* to reproduce; **F~pflanzung** *f* reproduction.
FORTRAN [ˈfɔrtran] *nt* FORTRAN.
Forts. *abk* = **Fortsetzung**.
fortschaffen *vt* to remove.
fortschreiten *unreg vi* to advance.
Fortschritt [ˈfɔrtʃrɪt] *m* advance; ~**e machen** to make progress; **dem ~ dienen** to further progress; **f~lich** *adj* progressive.
fortschrittsgläubig *adj* believing in progress.
fort- *zW:* ~**setzen** *vt* to continue; **F~setzung** *f* continuation; (*folgender Teil*) instalment (*BRIT*), installment (*US*); **F~setzung folgt** to be continued; **F~setzungsroman** *m* serialized novel; ~**während** *adj* incessant, continual; ~**wirken** *vi* to continue to have an effect; ~**ziehen** *unreg vt* to pull away ♦ *vi* to

move on; (*umziehen*) to move away.
Foto [ˈfoːto] (**-s, -s**) *nt* photo(graph); **ein** ~ **machen** to take a photo(graph); ~**album** *nt* photograph album; ~**apparat** *m* camera; ~**graf(in)** (**-en, -en**) *m(f)* photographer; ~**grafie** *f* photography; (*Bild*) photograph; **f~grafieren** *vt* to photograph ♦ *vi* to take photographs; ~**kopie** *f* photocopy; **f~kopieren** *vt* to photocopy; ~**kopierer** *m* photocopier; ~**kopiergerät** *nt* photocopier.
Foul [faʊl] (**-s, -s**) *nt* foul.
Foyer [foaˈjeː] (**-s, -s**) *nt* foyer; (*in Hotel*) lobby, foyer.
FPÖ (**-**) *f abk* (= *Freiheitliche Partei Österreichs*) Austrian Freedom Party.
Fr. *abk* (= *Frau*) Mrs, Ms.
Fracht [fraxt] (**-, -en**) *f* freight; (*NAUT*) cargo; (*Preis*) carriage; ~ **zahlt Empfänger** (*COMM*) carriage forward; ~**brief** *m* consignment note, waybill.
Frachter (**-s, -**) *m* freighter.
Fracht- *zW:* **f~frei** *adj* (*COMM*) carriage paid *od* free; ~**gut** *nt* freight; ~**kosten** *pl* (*COMM*) freight charges *pl*.
Frack [frak] (**-(e)s, -̈e**) *m* tails *pl*, tail coat.
Frage [ˈfraːgə] (**-, -n**) *f* question; **etw in** ~ **stellen** to question sth; **jdm eine ~ stellen** to ask sb a question, put a question to sb; **das ist gar keine ~, das steht außer ~** there's no question about it; **in ~ kommend** possible; (*Bewerber*) worth considering; **nicht in ~ kommen** to be out of the question; ~**bogen** *m* questionnaire.
fragen *vt, vi* to ask ♦ *vr* to wonder; **nach Arbeit/Post ~** to ask whether there is/was any work/mail; **da fragst du mich zuviel** (*umg*) I really couldn't say; **nach** *od* **wegen** (*umg*) **jdm ~** to ask for sb; (*nach jds Befinden*) to ask after sb; **ohne lange zu ~** without asking a lot of questions.
Fragerei [fraːgəˈraɪ] *f* questions *pl*.
Fragestunde *f* (*PARL*) question time.
Fragezeichen *nt* question mark.
fraglich *adj* questionable, doubtful; (*betreffend*) in question.
fraglos *adv* unquestionably.
Fragment [fraˈgmɛnt] *nt* fragment.
fragmentarisch [fragmɛnˈtaːrɪʃ] *adj* fragmentary.
fragwürdig [ˈfraːkvʏrdɪç] *adj* questionable, dubious.
Fraktion [fraktsiˈoːn] *f* parliamentary party.
Fraktionsvorsitzende(r) *f(m)* (*POL*) party whip.
Fraktionszwang *m* requirement to obey the party whip.
frank [fraŋk] *adj* frank, candid.
Franken[1] [ˈfraŋkən] *nt* Franconia.
Franken[2] [ˈfraŋkən] (**-, -**) *m*: (**Schweizer**) ~ (Swiss) Franc.
Frankfurt [ˈfraŋkfʊrt] (**-s**) *nt* Frankfurt.
Frankfurter(in) *m(f)* native of Frankfurt ♦ *adj*

Frankfurt; ~ **Würstchen** pl frankfurters.

frankieren [fraŋˈkiːrən] vt to stamp, frank.

Frankiermaschine f franking machine.

fränkisch [ˈfrɛŋkɪʃ] adj Franconian.

franko adv carriage paid; (POST) post-paid.

Frankreich [ˈfraŋkraɪç] (**-s**) nt France.

Franse [ˈfranzə] (**-**, **-n**) f fringe.

fransen vi to fray.

franz. abk = **französisch**.

Franzbranntwein m alcoholic liniment.

Franzose [franˈtsoːzə] (**-n**, **-n**) m Frenchman; French boy.

Französin [franˈtsøːzɪn] f Frenchwoman; French girl.

französisch adj French; ~**es Bett** double bed.

Fräse [ˈfrɛːzə] (**-**, **-n**) f (Werkzeug) milling cutter; (für Holz) moulding cutter.

Fraß (**-es**, **-e**) (pej: umg) m (Essen) muck.

fraß etc [fraːs] vb siehe **fressen**.

Fratze [ˈfratsə] (**-**, **-n**) f grimace; **eine ~ schneiden** to pull od make a face.

Frau [frau] (**-**, **-en**) f woman; (Ehe~) wife; (Anrede) Mrs, Ms; ~ **Doktor** Doctor.

Frauen- zW: ~**arzt** m gynaecologist (BRIT), gynecologist (US); ~**bewegung** f feminist movement; **f~feindlich** adj anti-women, misogynous; ~**haus** nt women's refuge; ~**quote** f recommended proportion of women (employed); ~**rechtlerin** f feminist; ~**zentrum** nt women's advice centre; ~**zimmer** (pej) nt female, broad (US).

Fräulein [ˈfrɔʏlaɪn] nt young lady; (Anrede) Miss; (Verkäuferin) assistant (BRIT), sales clerk (US); (Kellnerin) waitress.

fraulich [ˈfraulɪç] adj womanly.

frech [frɛç] adj cheeky, impudent; ~ **wie Oskar sein** (umg) to be a little monkey; **F~dachs** m cheeky monkey; **F~heit** f cheek, impudence; **sich** dat **(einige) F~heiten erlauben** to be a bit cheeky (bes BRIT) od fresh (bes US).

Fregatte [freˈgatə] (**-**, **-n**) f frigate.

frei [fraɪ] adj free; (Stelle) vacant; (Mitarbeiter) freelance; (Geld) available; (unbekleidet) bare; **aus ~en Stücken** od ~**em Willen** of one's own free will; ~ **nach ...** based on ...; **für etw ~e Fahrt geben** (fig) to give sth the go-ahead; **der Film ist ~ ab 16 (Jahren)** the film may be seen by people of 16 years (of age) and over; **unter ~em Himmel** in the open (air); **morgen/Mittwoch ist ~** tomorrow/Wednesday is a holiday; „**Zimmer ~**" "vacancies"; **auf ~er Strecke** (EISENB) between stations; (AUT) on the road; **sich ~ machen** (beim Arzt) to take one's clothes off, strip; ~**er Wettbewerb** fair/open competition; ~ **Haus** (COMM) carriage paid; ~ **Schiff** (COMM) free on board; ~**e Marktwirtschaft** free market economy; **sich** dat **einen Tag ~ nehmen** to take a day off; **von etw ~ sein** to be free of sth; **im F~en** in the open air; ~ **sprechen** to talk without

notes; **F~bad** nt open-air swimming pool; ~**bekommen** unreg vt: **jdn/einen Tag ~bekommen** to get sb freed/get a day off; ~**beruflich** adj self-employed; **F~betrag** m tax allowance.

Freier (**-s**, **-**) m suitor.

Frei- zW: ~**exemplar** nt free copy; **f~geben** unreg vt: **etw zum Verkauf f~geben** to allow sth to be sold on the open market; **f~gebig** adj generous; ~**gebigkeit** f generosity; ~**hafen** m free port; **f~halten** unreg vt to keep free; (bezahlen) to pay for; ~**handel** m free trade; ~**handelszone** f free trade area; **f~händig** adv (fahren) with no hands.

Freiheit f freedom; **sich** dat **die ~ nehmen, etw zu tun** to take the liberty of doing sth; **f~lich** adj liberal; (Verfassung) based on the principle of liberty; (Demokratie) free.

Freiheits- zW: ~**beraubung** f (JUR) wrongful deprivation of personal liberty; ~**drang** m urge/desire for freedom; ~**kampf** m fight for freedom; ~**kämpfer(in)** m(f) freedom fighter; ~**rechte** pl civil liberties pl; ~**strafe** f prison sentence.

frei- zW: ~**heraus** adv frankly; **F~karte** f free ticket; ~**kaufen** vt: **jdn/sich ~kaufen** to buy sb's/one's freedom; ~**kommen** unreg vi to get free; **F~körperkultur** f nudism; ~**lassen** unreg vt to (set) free; **F~lauf** m freewheeling; ~**laufend** adj (Hühner) free-range; ~**legen** vt to expose; ~**lich** adv certainly, admittedly; **ja ~lich!** yes of course; **F~lichtbühne** f open-air theatre; ~**machen** vt (POST) to frank ♦ vr to arrange to be free; **Tage ~machen** to take days off; **F~maurer** m Mason, Freemason.

freimütig [ˈfraɪmyːtɪç] adj frank, honest.

Frei- zW: ~**raum** m: ~**raum (zu)** (fig) freedom (for); **f~schaffend** adj attrib freelance; ~**schärler** (**-s**, **-**) m guerrilla; **f~schwimmen** vr (fig) to learn to stand on one's own two feet; **f~setzen** vt (Energien) to release; **f~sinnig** adj liberal; **f~sprechen** unreg vt: **f~sprechen (von)** to acquit (of); ~**spruch** m acquittal; **f~stehen** unreg vi: **es steht dir f~, das zu tun** you are free to do so; **das steht Ihnen völlig f~** that is completely up to you; **f~stellen** vt: **jdm etw f~stellen** to leave sth (up) to sb; ~**stoß** m free kick; ~**stunde** f free hour; (SCH) free period.

Freitag m Friday; siehe auch **Dienstag**.

freitags adv on Fridays.

Frei- zW: ~**tod** m suicide; ~**übungen** pl (physical) exercises pl; ~**umschlag** m reply-paid envelope; ~**wild** nt (fig) fair game; **f~willig** adj voluntary; ~**willige(r)** f(m) volunteer; ~**zeichen** nt (TEL) ringing tone; ~**zeit** f spare od free time; ~**zeitgestaltung** f organization of one's leisure time; **f~zügig** adj liberal, broad-minded; (mit Geld) generous.

fremd [frɛmt] adj (unvertraut) strange;

(*ausländisch*) foreign; (*nicht eigen*) someone else's; **etw ist jdm ~** sth is foreign to sb; **ich bin hier ~** I'm a stranger here; **sich ~ fühlen** to feel like a stranger; **~artig** *adj* strange.

Fremde (-) *f* (*liter*): **die ~** foreign parts *pl*.

Fremde(r) *f(m)* stranger; (*Ausländer*) foreigner.

Fremden- *zW:* **~führer** *m* (tourist) guide; (*Buch*) guide (book); **~legion** *f* foreign legion; **~verkehr** *m* tourism; **~zimmer** *nt* guest room.

fremd- *zW:* **~gehen** *unreg* (*umg*) *vi* to be unfaithful; **F~kapital** *nt* loan capital; **F~körper** *m* foreign body; **~ländisch** *adj* foreign; **F~ling** *m* stranger; **F~sprache** *f* foreign language; **F~sprachenkorrespondentin** *f* bilingual secretary; **~sprachig** *adj attrib* foreign-language; **F~wort** *nt* foreign word.

frenetisch [fre'neːtɪʃ] *adj* frenetic.

Frequenz [fre'kvɛnts] *f* (*RUNDF*) frequency.

Fresse (-, -n) (*umg!*) *f* (*Mund*) gob; (*Gesicht*) mug.

fressen ['frɛsən] *unreg vt, vi* to eat ♦ *vr:* **sich voll** *od* **satt ~** to gorge o.s.; **einen Narren an jdm/etw gefressen haben** to dote on sb/sth.

Freude ['frɔydə] (-, -n) *f* joy, delight; **~ an etw** *dat* **haben** to get *od* derive pleasure from sth; **jdm eine ~ machen** *od* **bereiten** to make sb happy.

Freudenhaus *nt* (*veraltet*) house of ill repute.

Freudentanz *m:* **einen ~ aufführen** to dance with joy.

freudestrahlend *adj* beaming with delight.

freudig *adj* joyful, happy.

freudlos *adj* joyless.

freuen ['frɔyən] *vt unpers* to make happy *od* pleased ♦ *vr* to be glad *od* happy; **sich auf etw** *akk* **~** to look forward to sth; **sich über etw** *akk* **~** to be pleased about sth; **sich zu früh ~** to get one's hopes up too soon.

Freund ['frɔynt] (-(e)s, -e) *m* friend; (*Liebhaber*) boyfriend; **ich bin kein ~ von so etwas** I'm not one for that sort of thing; **~in** *f* friend; (*Liebhaberin*) girlfriend; **f~lich** *adj* kind, friendly; **bitte recht f~lich!** smile please!; **würden Sie bitte so f~lich sein und das tun?** would you be so kind as to do that?; **f~licherweise** *adv* kindly; **~lichkeit** *f* friendliness, kindness; **~schaft** *f* friendship; **f~schaftlich** *adj* friendly.

Frevel ['freːfəl] (-s, -) *m:* **~ (an** +*dat*) crime *od* offence (against); **f~haft** *adj* wicked.

Frhr. *abk* (= *Freiherr*) baron.

Frieden ['friːdən] (-s, -) *m* peace; **im ~** in peacetime; **~ schließen** to make one's peace; (*POL*) to make peace; **um des lieben ~s willen** (*umg*) for the sake of peace and quiet; **ich traue dem ~ nicht** (*umg*) something (fishy) is going on.

Friedens- *zW:* **~bewegung** *f* peace movement; **~richter** *m* justice of the peace;

~schluß *m* peace agreement; **~truppe** *f* peace-keeping force; **~verhandlungen** *pl* peace negotiations *pl*; **~vertrag** *m* peace treaty; **~zeit** *f* peacetime.

fried- *zW:* **~fertig** *adj* peaceable; **F~hof** *m* cemetery; **~lich** *adj* peaceful; **etw auf ~lichem Wege lösen** to solve sth by peaceful means.

frieren ['friːrən] *unreg vi* to freeze ♦ *vt unpers* to freeze ♦ *vi unpers:* **heute nacht hat es gefroren** it was below freezing last night; **ich friere, es friert mich** I am freezing, I'm cold; **wie ein Schneider ~** (*umg*) to be *od* get frozen to the marrow.

Fries [friːs] (-es, -e) *m* (*ARCHIT*) frieze.

Friese ['friːzə] (-n, -n) *m* Fri(e)sian.

Friesin ['friːzə] *f* Fri(e)sian.

frigid(e) *adj* frigid.

Frikadelle [frika'dɛlə] *f* meatball.

frisch [frɪʃ] *adj* fresh; (*lebhaft*) lively; **~ gestrichen!** wet paint!; **sich ~ machen** to freshen (o.s.) up; **jdn auf ~er Tat ertappen** to catch sb red-handed *od* in the act.

Frische (-) *f* freshness; liveliness; **in alter ~** (*umg*) as always.

Frischhaltebeutel *m* airtight bag.

Frischhaltefolie *f* clingfilm.

frischweg *adv* (*munter*) straight out.

Friseur [fri'zøːr] *m* hairdresser.

Friseuse [fri'zøːzə] *f* hairdresser.

frisieren [fri'ziːrən] *vt* (*Haar*) to do; (*fig: Abrechnung*) to fiddle, doctor ♦ *vr* to do one's hair; **jdn ~, jdm das Haar ~** to do sb's hair.

Frisiersalon *m* hairdressing salon.

Frisiertisch *m* dressing table.

Frisör [fri'zøːr] (-s, -e) *m* hairdresser.

frißt [frɪst] *vb siehe* **fressen**.

Frist [frɪst] (-, -en) *f* period; (*Termin*) deadline; **eine ~ einhalten/verstreichen lassen** to meet a deadline/let a deadline pass; (*bei Rechnung*) to pay/not to pay within the period stipulated; **jdm eine ~ von vier Tagen geben** to give sb four days' grace.

fristen *vt* (*Dasein*) to lead; (*kümmerlich*) to eke out.

Fristenlösung *f* abortion law (*permitting abortion in the first three months*).

fristgerecht *adj* within the period stipulated.

fristlos *adj* (*Entlassung*) instant.

Frisur [fri'zuːr] *f* hairdo, hairstyle.

Friteuse [fri'tøːzə] (-, -n) *f* chip pan (*BRIT*), deep fat fryer.

fritieren [fri'tiːrən] *vt* to deep fry.

frivol [fri'voːl] *adj* frivolous.

Frl. *abk* (= *Fräulein*) Miss.

froh [froː] *adj* happy, cheerful; **ich bin ~, daß ...** I'm glad that ...

fröhlich ['frøːlɪç] *adj* merry, happy; **F~keit** *f* merriment, gaiety.

frohlocken *vi* (*geh*) to rejoice; (*pej*) to gloat.

Frohsinn *m* cheerfulness.

fromm [frɔm] *adj* pious, good; (*Wunsch*) idle.

Frömmelei [frœmə'laɪ] f false piety.
Frömmigkeit f piety.
frönen ['frøːnən] vi +dat to indulge in.
Fronleichnam [froːn'laɪçnaːm] (-(e)s) m Corpus Christi.
Front [frɔnt] (-, -en) f front; **klare ~en schaffen** (fig) to clarify the position.
frontal [frɔn'taːl] adj frontal; **F~angriff** m frontal attack.
fror etc [froːr] vb siehe **frieren**.
Frosch [frɔʃ] (-(e)s, ⁻e) m frog; (Feuerwerk) squib; **sei kein ~!** (umg) be a sport!; **~mann** m frogman; **~perspektive** f: **etw aus der ~perspektive sehen** to get a worm's-eye view of sth; **~schenkel** m frog's leg.
Frost [frɔst] (-(e)s, ⁻e) m frost; **f~beständig** adj frost-resistant; **~beule** f chilblain.
frösteln ['frœstəln] vi to shiver.
frostig adj frosty.
Frostschutzmittel nt anti-freeze.
Frottee [frɔ'teː] (-(s), -s) nt od m towelling.
frottieren [frɔ'tiːrən] vt to rub, towel.
Frottierhandtuch nt towel.
Frottiertuch nt towel.
frotzeln ['frɔtsəln] (umg) vt, vi to tease.
Frucht [fruxt] (-, ⁻e) f (lit, fig) fruit; (Getreide) corn; (Embryo) foetus; **f~bar** adj fruitful, fertile; **~barkeit** f fertility; **~becher** m fruit sundae.
Früchtchen ['frʏçtçən] (umg) nt (Tunichtgut) good-for-nothing.
fruchten vi to be of use.
fruchtlos adj fruitless.
Fruchtsaft m fruit juice.
früh [fryː] adj, adv early; **heute ~** this morning; **~auf** adv: **von ~auf** from an early age; **F~aufsteher** (-s, -) m early riser; **F~dienst** m: **F~dienst haben** to be on early shift.
Frühe (-) f early morning; **in aller ~** at the crack of dawn.
früher adj earlier; (ehemalig) former ♦ adv formerly; **~ war das anders** that used to be different; **~ oder später** sooner or later.
frühestens adv at the earliest.
Frühgeburt f premature birth; (Kind) premature baby.
Frühjahr nt spring.
Frühjahrsmüdigkeit f springtime lethargy.
Frühjahrsputz m spring-cleaning.
Frühling m spring; **im ~** in spring.
früh- zW: **~reif** adj precocious; **F~rentner** m person who has retired early; **F~schicht** f early shift; **F~schoppen** m morning/lunchtime drink; **F~sport** m early morning exercise; **F~stück** nt breakfast; **~stücken** vi to (have) breakfast; **F~warnsystem** nt early warning system; **~zeitig** adj early; (vorzeitig) premature.
Frust (-(e)s) (umg) m frustration.
frustrieren [frus'triːrən] vt to frustrate.
frz. abk = **französisch**.
FSV abk (= Fußball-Sportverein) F.C.

FU (-) f abk (= Freie Universität Berlin) Berlin University.
Fuchs [fuks] (-es, ⁻e) m fox.
fuchsen (umg) vt to rile, annoy ♦ vr to be annoyed.
Füchsin ['fʏksɪn] f vixen.
fuchsteufelswild adj hopping mad.
Fuchtel ['fuxtl] (-, -n) f (fig: umg): **unter jds ~** under sb's control od thumb.
fuchteln ['fuxtəln] vi to gesticulate wildly.
Fuge ['fuːgə] (-, -n) f joint; (MUS) fugue.
fügen ['fyːgən] vt to place, join ♦ vr unpers to happen ♦ vr: **sich ~ (in** +akk) to be obedient (to); (anpassen) to adapt o.s. (to).
fügsam ['fyːkzaːm] adj obedient.
fühlbar adj perceptible, noticeable.
fühlen ['fyːlən] vt, vi, vr to feel.
Fühler (-s, -) m feeler.
Fühlung f: **mit jdm in ~ bleiben/stehen** to stay/be in contact od touch with sb.
fuhr etc [fuːr] vb siehe **fahren**.
Fuhre (-, -n) f (Ladung) load.
führen ['fyːrən] vt to lead; (Geschäft) to run; (Name) to bear; (Buch) to keep; (im Angebot haben) to stock ♦ vi to lead ♦ vr to behave; **was führt Sie zu mir?** (form) what brings you to me?; **Geld/seine Papiere bei sich ~** (form) to carry money/one's papers on one's person; **das führt zu nichts** that will come to nothing.
Führer(in) ['fyːrər(ɪn)] (-s, -) m(f) leader; (Fremden~) guide; **~haus** nt cab; **~schein** m driving licence (BRIT), driver's license (US); **den ~schein machen** (AUT) to learn to drive; (die Prüfung ablegen) to take one's (driving) test; **~scheinentzug** m disqualification from driving.
Fuhrmann ['fuːrman] (-(e)s, pl -leute) m carter.
Führung ['fyːrʊŋ] f leadership; (eines Unternehmens) management; (MIL) command; (Benehmen) conduct; (Museums~) conducted tour.
Führungs- zW: **~kraft** f executive; **~stab** m (MIL) command; (COMM) top management; **~stil** m management style; **~zeugnis** nt certificate of good conduct.
Fuhrunternehmen nt haulage business.
Fuhrwerk nt cart.
Fülle ['fʏlə] (-) f wealth, abundance.
Füllen (-s, -) nt foal.
füllen vt to fill; (KOCH) to stuff ♦ vr to fill (up).
Füller (-s, -) m fountain pen.
Füllfederhalter m fountain pen.
Füllgewicht nt (COMM) weight at time of packing; (auf Dosen) net weight.
füllig ['fʏlɪç] adj (Mensch) corpulent, portly; (Figur) ample.
Füllung f filling; (Holz~) panel.
fummeln ['fʊməln] (umg) vi to fumble.
Fund [funt] (-(e)s, -e) m find.
Fundament [funda'mɛnt] nt foundation.

fundamental *adj* fundamental.
Fundamentalismus *m* fundamentalism.
Fundbüro *nt* lost property office, lost and found (*US*).
Fundgrube *f* (*fig*) treasure trove.
fundieren [fʊn'diːrən] *vt* to back up.
fundiert *adj* sound.
fündig ['fʏndɪç] *adj* (*MIN*) rich; ~ **werden** to make a strike; (*fig*) to strike it lucky.
Fundsachen *pl* lost property *sing*.
fünf [fʏnf] *num* five; **seine ~ Sinne beisammen haben** to have all one's wits about one; ~**(e) gerade sein lassen** (*umg*) to turn a blind eye; ~**hundert** *num* five hundred; ~**jährig** *adj* (*Frist, Plan*) five-year; (*Kind*) five-year-old; **F~kampf** *m* pentathlon; **F~prozentklausel** *f* (*PARL*) clause debarring parties *with less than 5% of the vote from Parliament*; **F~tagewoche** *f* five-day week.

> The **Fünfprozentklausel** is a rule in German Federal elections whereby only those parties who collect at least 5% of the second vote (**Zweitstimme**) receive a parliamentary seat. This is to avoid the parliament being made up of a large number of very small parties which, in the Weimar Republic, led to political instability.

fünfte(r, s) *adj* fifth.
Fünftel (**-s, -**) *nt* fifth.
fünfzehn *num* fifteen.
fünfzig *num* fifty.
fungieren [fʊŋ'giːrən] *vi* to function; (*Person*) to act.
Funk [fʊŋk] (**-s**) *m* radio, wireless (*BRIT old*); ~**ausstellung** *f* radio and television exhibition.
Funke (**-ns, -n**) *m* (*lit, fig*) spark.
funkeln *vi* to sparkle.
funkelnagelneu (*umg*) *adj* brand-new.
Funken (**-s, -**) *m* = **Funke**.
funken *vt* to radio.
Funker (**-s, -**) *m* radio operator.
Funk- *zW*: ~**gerät** *nt* radio set; ~**haus** *nt* broadcasting centre; ~**kolleg** *nt* educational radio broadcasts *pl*; ~**rufempfänger** *m* (*TELEC*) pager, paging device; ~**spot** *m* advertisement on the radio; ~**sprechgerät** *nt* radio telephone; ~**spruch** *m* radio signal; ~**station** *f* radio station; ~**stille** *f* (*fig*) ominous silence; ~**streife** *f* police radio patrol; ~**taxi** *nt* radio taxi; ~**telefon** *nt* cell phone.
Funktion [fʊŋktsi'oːn] *f* function; **in ~ treten/sein** to come into/be in operation.
Funktionär(in) [fʊŋktsio'nɛːr(ɪn)] (**-s, -e**) *m(f)* functionary, official.
funktionieren [fʊŋktsio'niːrən] *vi* to work, function.
Funktions- *zW*: **f~fähig** *adj* working; ~**taste** *f* (*COMPUT*) function key; **f~tüchtig** *adj* in working order.
Funzel [funtsəl] (**-, -n**) (*umg*) *f* dim lamp.
für [fyːr] *präp +akk* for; **was ~** what kind *od* sort of; ~**s erste** for the moment; **was Sie da sagen, hat etwas ~ sich** there's something in what you're saying; **Tag ~ Tag** day after day; **Schritt ~ Schritt** step by step; **das F~ und Wider** the pros and cons *pl*; **F~bitte** *f* intercession.
Furche ['fʊrçə] (**-, -n**) *f* furrow.
furchen *vt* to furrow.
Furcht [fʊrçt] (**-**) *f* fear; **f~bar** *adj* terrible, awful.
fürchten ['fʏrçtən] *vt* to be afraid of, fear ♦ *vr*: **sich ~ (vor +dat)** to be afraid (of).
fürchterlich *adj* awful.
furchtlos *adj* fearless.
furchtsam *adj* timorous.
füreinander [fyːrˌaɪ'nandər] *adv* for each other.
Furie ['fuːriə] (**-, -n**) *f* (*MYTHOLOGIE*) fury; (*fig*) hellcat.
Furnier [fʊr'niːr] (**-s, -e**) *nt* veneer.
Furore [fu'roːrə] *f od nt*: ~ **machen** (*umg*) to cause a sensation.
fürs [fyːrs] = **für das**.
Fürsorge ['fyːrzɔrgə] *f* care; (*Sozial~*) welfare; **von der ~ leben** to live on social security (*BRIT*) *od* welfare (*US*); ~**amt** *nt* welfare office.
Fürsorger(in) (**-s, -**) *m(f)* welfare worker.
Fürsorgeunterstützung *f* social security (*BRIT*), welfare benefit (*US*).
fürsorglich *adj* caring.
Fürsprache *f* recommendation; (*um Gnade*) intercession.
Fürsprecher *m* advocate.
Fürst [fʏrst] (**-en, -en**) *m* prince.
Fürstentum *nt* principality.
Fürstin *f* princess.
fürstlich *adj* princely.
Furt [fʊrt] (**-, -en**) *f* ford.
Furunkel [fu'rʊŋkəl] (**-s, -**) *nt od m* boil.
Fürwort ['fyːrvɔrt] *nt* pronoun.
furzen ['fʊrtsən] (*umg!*) *vi* to fart (*!*).
Fusion [fuzi'oːn] *f* amalgamation; (*von Unternehmen*) merger; (*von Atomkernen, Zellen*) fusion.
fusionieren [fuzio'niːrən] *vt* to amalgamate.
Fuß [fuːs] (**-es, -̈e**) *m* foot; (*von Glas, Säule etc*) base; (*von Möbel*) leg; **zu ~** on foot; **bei ~!** heel!; **jdm etw vor die Füße werfen** (*lit*) to throw sth at sb; (*fig*) to tell sb to keep sth; (**festen**) ~ **fassen** (*lit, fig*) to gain a foothold; (*sich niederlassen*) to settle down; **mit jdm auf gutem ~ stehen** to be on good terms with sb; **auf großem ~ leben** to live the high life.
Fußball *m* football; ~**platz** *m* football pitch; ~**spiel** *nt* football match; ~**spieler** *m* footballer (*BRIT*), football player (*US*); ~**toto** *m od nt* football pools *pl*.

Fußboden m floor; ~**heizung** f underfloor heating.
Fußbremse f (AUT) foot brake.
fusselig ['fʊsəlɪç] adj: **sich** dat **den Mund** ~ **reden** (umg) to talk till one is blue in the face.
fusseln ['fʊsəln] vi (Stoff, Kleid etc) to go bobbly (umg).
fußen vi: ~ **auf** +dat to rest on, be based on.
Fuß- zW: ~**ende** nt foot; ~**gänger(in)** (-s, -) m(f) pedestrian; ~**gängerüberführung** f pedestrian bridge; ~**gängerzone** f pedestrian precinct; ~**leiste** f skirting board (BRIT), baseboard (US); ~**nagel** m toenail; ~**note** f footnote; ~**pfleger** m chiropodist; ~**pilz** m (MED) athlete's foot; ~**spur** f footprint; ~**stapfen** (-s, -) m: **in jds** ~**stapfen treten** (fig) to follow in sb's footsteps; ~**tritt** m kick; (Spur) footstep; ~**volk** nt (fig): **das** ~**volk** the rank and file; ~**weg** m footpath.
futsch [fʊtʃ] (umg) adj (weg) gone, vanished.
Futter ['fʊtər] (-s, -) nt fodder, feed; (Stoff) lining.
Futteral [fʊtəˈraːl] (-s, -e) nt case.
futtern ['fʊtərn] vi (hum: umg) to stuff o.s. ♦ vt to scoff.
füttern ['fʏtərn] vt to feed; (Kleidung) to line; „**F~ verboten**" "do not feed the animals".
Futur [fuˈtuːr] (-s, -e) nt future.

G, g

G, g[1] [geː] nt G, g; ~ **wie Gustav** ≈ G for George.
g[2] abk (ÖSTERR) = **Groschen**; (= Gramm) g.
gab etc [gaːp] vb siehe **geben**.
Gabe ['gaːbə] (-, -n) f gift.
Gabel ['gaːbəl] (-, -n) f fork; (TEL) rest, cradle; ~**frühstück** nt mid-morning light lunch; ~**stapler** (-s, -) m fork-lift truck.
gabeln vr to fork.
Gabelung f fork.
Gabentisch ['gaːbəntɪʃ] m table for Christmas or birthday presents.
Gabun [gaˈbuːn] nt Gabon.
gackern ['gakərn] vi to cackle.
gaffen ['gafən] vi to gape.
Gag [gɛk] (-s, -s) m (Film~) gag; (Werbe~) gimmick.
Gage ['gaːʒə] (-, -n) f fee.
gähnen ['gɛːnən] vi to yawn; ~**de Leere** total emptiness.
GAL (-) f abk (= Grün-Alternative Liste) electoral pact of Greens and alternative parties.
Gala ['gala] (-) f formal dress.
galant [gaˈlant] adj gallant, courteous.
Galavorstellung f (THEAT) gala performance.
Galerie [galəˈriː] f gallery.
Galgen ['galgən] (-s, -) m gallows pl; ~**frist** f respite; ~**humor** m macabre humour (BRIT) od humor (US); ~**strick** (umg) m, ~**vogel** (umg) m gallows bird.
Galionsfigur [galiˈoːnsfiguːr] f figurehead.
gälisch ['gɛːlɪʃ] adj Gaelic.
Galle ['galə] (-, -n) f gall; (Organ) gall bladder; **jdm kommt die** ~ **hoch** sb's blood begins to boil.
Galopp [gaˈlɔp] (-s, -s od -e) m gallop; **im** ~ (lit) at a gallop; (fig) at top speed.
galoppieren [galɔˈpiːrən] vi to gallop.
galt etc [galt] vb siehe **gelten**.
galvanisieren [galvaniˈziːrən] vt to galvanize.
Gamasche [gaˈmaʃə] (-, -n) f gaiter; (kurz) spat.
Gameboy ® ['geːmbɔy] m (COMPUT) games console.
Gammastrahlen ['gamaʃtraːlən] pl gamma rays pl.
gamm(e)lig ['gam(ə)lɪç] (umg) adj (Kleidung) tatty.
gammeln ['gaməln] (umg) vi to loaf about.
Gammler(in) ['gamlər(ɪn)] (-s, -) m(f) dropout.
Gang[1] [gaŋ] (-(e)s, ⁻e) m walk; (Boten~) errand; (~art) gait; (Abschnitt eines Vorgangs) operation; (Essens~, Ablauf) course; (Flur etc) corridor; (Durch~) passage; (AUT, TECH) gear; (THEAT, AVIAT, in Kirche) aisle; **den ersten** ~ **einlegen** to engage first (gear); **einen** ~ **machen/tun** to go on an errand/for a walk; **den** ~ **nach Canossa antreten** (fig) to eat humble pie; **seinen gewohnten** ~ **gehen** (fig) to run its usual course; **in** ~ **bringen** to start up; (fig) to get off the ground; **in** ~ **sein** to be in operation; (fig) to be under way.
Gang[2] [gɛŋ] (-, -s) f gang.
gang adj: ~ **und gäbe** usual, normal.
Gangart f way of walking, walk, gait; (von Pferd) gait; **eine härtere** ~ **einschlagen** (fig) to apply harder tactics.
gangbar adj passable; (Methode) practicable.
Gängelband ['gɛŋəlbant] nt: **jdn am** ~ **halten** (fig) to spoon-feed sb.
gängeln vt to spoonfeed; **jdn** ~ to treat sb like a child.
gängig ['gɛŋɪç] adj common, current; (Ware) in demand, selling well.
Gangschaltung f gears pl.
Gangway ['gæŋweɪ] f (NAUT) gangway; (AVIAT) steps pl.
Ganove [gaˈnoːvə] (-n, -n) (umg) m crook.
Gans [gans] (-, ⁻e) f goose.
Gänse- zW: ~**blümchen** nt daisy; ~**braten** m roast goose; ~**füßchen** (umg) pl inverted

commas *pl* (*BRIT*), quotes *pl*; ~**haut** *f* goose pimples *pl*; ~**marsch** *m*: im ~**marsch** in single file.

Gänserich (**-s, -e**) *m* gander.

ganz [gants] *adj* whole; (*vollständig*) complete ♦ *adv* quite; (*völlig*) completely; (*sehr*) really; (*genau*) exactly; ~ **Europa** all Europe; **im (großen und)** ~**en genommen** on the whole, all in all; **etw wieder** ~ **machen** to mend sth; **sein** ~**es Geld** all his money; ~ **gewiß!** absolutely; **ein** ~ **klein wenig** just a tiny bit; **das mag ich** ~ **besonders gern(e)** I'm particularly fond of that; **sie ist** ~ **die Mutter** she's just *od* exactly like her mother; ~ **und gar nicht** not at all.

Ganze(s) *nt*: **es geht ums** ~ everything's at stake; **aufs** ~ **gehen** to go for the lot.

Ganzheitsmethode ['gantshaitsmeto:də] *f* (*SCH*) look-and-say method.

gänzlich ['gɛntslɪç] *adj* complete, entire ♦ *adv* completely, entirely.

ganztägig ['gantstɛ:gɪç] *adj* all-day *attrib*.

ganztags *adv* (*arbeiten*) full time.

gar [ga:r] *adj* cooked, done ♦ *adv* quite; ~ **nicht/nichts/keiner** not/nothing/nobody at all; ~ **nicht schlecht** not bad at all; ~ **kein Grund** no reason whatsoever *od* at all; **er wäre** ~ **zu gern noch länger geblieben** he would really have liked to stay longer.

Garage [ga'ra:ʒə] (**-, -n**) *f* garage.

Garantie [garan'ti:] *f* guarantee; **das fällt noch unter die** ~ that's covered by the guarantee.

garantieren *vt* to guarantee.

garantiert *adv* guaranteed; (*umg*) I bet.

Garantieschein *m* guarantee.

Garaus ['ga:raus] (*umg*) *m*: **jdm den** ~ **machen** to do sb in.

Garbe ['garbə] (**-, -n**) *f* sheaf; (*MIL*) burst of fire.

Garde ['gardə] (**-, -n**) *f* guard(s); **die alte** ~ the old guard.

Garderobe [gardə'ro:bə] (**-, -n**) *f* wardrobe; (*Abgabe*) cloakroom (*BRIT*), checkroom (*US*); (*Kleiderablage*) hall stand; (*THEAT: Umkleideraum*) dressing room.

Garderobenfrau *f* cloakroom attendant.

Garderobenständer *m* hall stand.

Gardine [gar'di:nə] (**-, -n**) *f* curtain.

Gardinenpredigt (*umg*) *f*: **jdm eine** ~ **halten** to give sb a talking-to.

Gardinenstange *f* curtain rail; (*zum Ziehen*) curtain rod.

garen ['ga:rən] *vt, vi* (*KOCH*) to cook.

gären ['gɛ:rən] *unreg vi* to ferment.

Garn [garn] (**-(e)s, -e**) *nt* thread; (*Häkel*~, *fig*) yarn.

Garnele [gar'ne:lə] (**-, -n**) *f* shrimp, prawn.

garnieren [gar'ni:rən] *vt* to decorate; (*Speisen*) to garnish.

Garnison [garni'zo:n] (**-, -en**) *f* garrison.

Garnitur [garni'tu:r] *f* (*Satz*) set;

(*Unterwäsche*) set of (matching) underwear; **erste** ~ (*fig*) top rank; **zweite** ~ second rate.

garstig ['garstɪç] *adj* nasty, horrid.

Garten ['gartən] (**-s, ⸚**) *m* garden; ~**arbeit** *f* gardening; ~**bau** *m* horticulture; ~**fest** *nt* garden party; ~**gerät** *nt* gardening tool; ~**haus** *nt* summerhouse; ~**kresse** *f* cress; ~**laube** *f* (~*häuschen*) summerhouse; ~**lokal** *nt* beer garden; ~**schere** *f* pruning shears *pl*; ~**tür** *f* garden gate; ~**zaun** *m* garden fence; ~**zwerg** *m* garden gnome; (*pej: umg*) squirt.

Gärtner(in) ['gɛrtnər(ɪn)] (**-s, -**) *m(f)* gardener.

Gärtnerei [gɛrtnə'raɪ] *f* nursery; (*Gemüse*~) market garden (*BRIT*), truck farm (*US*).

gärtnern *vi* to garden.

Gärung ['gɛ:rʊŋ] *f* fermentation.

Gas [ga:s] (**-es, -e**) *nt* gas; ~ **geben** (*AUT*) to accelerate, step on the gas.

Gascogne [gas'kɔnjə] *f* Gascony.

Gas- *zW*: ~**flasche** *f* bottle of gas, gas canister; **g**~**förmig** *adj* gaseous; ~**hahn** *m* gas tap; ~**herd** *m* gas cooker; ~**kocher** *m* gas cooker; ~**leitung** *f* gas pipeline; ~**maske** *f* gas mask; ~**pedal** *nt* accelerator, gas pedal (*US*); ~**pistole** *f* gas pistol.

Gasse ['gasə] (**-, -n**) *f* lane, alley.

Gassenhauer (**-s, -**) (*veraltet: umg*) *m* popular melody.

Gassenjunge *m* street urchin.

Gast [gast] (**-es, ⸚e**) *m* guest; **bei jdm zu** ~ **sein** to be sb's guest(s); ~**arbeiter** *m* foreign worker.

Gäste- *zW*: ~**bett** *nt* spare bed; ~**buch** *nt* visitors' book; ~**zimmer** *nt* guest room.

Gast- *zW*: **g**~**freundlich** *adj* hospitable; ~**freundlichkeit** *f* hospitality; ~**freundschaft** *f* hospitality; ~**geber(in)** (**-s, -**) *m(f)* host(ess); ~**haus** *nt* hotel, inn; ~**hof** *m* hotel, inn; ~**hörer(in)** *m(f)* (*UNIV*) observer, auditor (*US*).

gastieren [gas'ti:rən] *vi* (*THEAT*) to (appear as a) guest.

Gast- *zW*: ~**land** *nt* host country; **g**~**lich** *adj* hospitable; ~**lichkeit** *f* hospitality; ~**rolle** *f* (*THEAT*) guest role; **eine** ~**rolle spielen** to make a guest appearance.

Gastronomie [gastrono'mi:] *f* (*form: Gaststättengewerbe*) catering trade.

gastronomisch [gastro'no:mɪʃ] *adj* gastronomic(al).

Gast- *zW*: ~**spiel** *nt* (*SPORT*) away game; **ein** ~**spiel geben** (*THEAT*) to give a guest performance; (*fig*) to put in a brief appearance; ~**stätte** *f* restaurant; (*Trinklokal*) pub; ~**wirt** *m* innkeeper; ~**wirtschaft** *f* hotel, inn; ~**zimmer** *nt* guest room.

Gas- *zW*: ~**vergiftung** *f* gas poisoning; ~**versorgung** *f* (*System*) gas supply; ~**werk** *nt* gasworks *sing od pl*; ~**zähler** *m* gas meter.

Gatte ['gatə] (**-n, -n**) *m* (*form*) husband, spouse; **die** ~**n** husband and wife.

Gatter ['gatər] (-s, -) nt grating; (Tür) gate.
Gattin f (form) wife, spouse.
Gattung ['gatʊŋ] f (BIOL) genus; (Sorte) kind.
GAU [gaʊ] m abk (= größter anzunehmender Unfall) MCA, maximum credible accident.
Gaudi ['gaʊdi] (SÜDD, ÖSTERR: umg) nt od f fun.
Gaukler ['gaʊklər] (-s, -) m (liter) travelling entertainer; (Zauberkünstler) conjurer, magician.
Gaul [gaʊl] (-(e)s, Gäule) (pej) m nag.
Gaumen ['gaʊmən] (-s, -) m palate.
Gauner ['gaʊnər] (-s, -) m rogue.
Gaunerei [gaʊnə'raɪ] f swindle.
Gaunersprache f underworld jargon.
Gaze ['gaːzə] (-, -n) f gauze.
Geäst [gə'ɛst] nt branches pl.
geb. abk = **geboren.**
Gebäck [gə'bɛk] (-(e)s, -e) nt (Kekse) biscuits pl (BRIT), cookies pl (US); (Teilchen) pastries pl.
gebacken [gə'bakən] pp von **backen.**
Gebälk [gə'bɛlk] (-(e)s) nt timberwork.
gebannt [gə'bant] adj spellbound.
gebar etc [gə'baːr] vb siehe **gebären.**
Gebärde [gə'bɛːrdə] (-, -n) f gesture.
gebärden vr to behave.
Gebaren [gə'baːrən] (-s) nt behaviour (BRIT), behavior (US); (Geschäfts~) conduct.
gebären [gə'bɛːrən] unreg vt to give birth to.
Gebärmutter f uterus, womb.
Gebäude [gə'bɔʏdə] (-s, -) nt building; ~komplex m (building) complex; ~reinigung f (das Reinigen) commercial cleaning; (Firma) cleaning contractors pl.
Gebein [gə'baɪn] (-(e)s, -e) nt bones pl.
Gebell [gə'bɛl] (-(e)s) nt barking.
geben ['geːbən] unreg vt, vi to give; (Karten) to deal ♦ vt unpers: **es gibt** there is/are; there will be ♦ vr (sich verhalten) to behave, act; (aufhören) to abate; **jdm etw ~** to give sb sth od sth to sb; **in die Post ~** to post; **das gibt keinen Sinn** that doesn't make sense; **er gibt Englisch** he teaches English; **viel/nicht viel auf etw** akk **~** to set great store/not much store by sth; **etw von sich ~** (Laute etc) to utter; **ein Wort gab das andere** one angry word led to another; **ein gutes Beispiel ~** to set a good example; **~ Sie mir bitte Herrn Braun** (TEL) can I speak to Mr Braun please?; **ein Auto in Reparatur ~** to have a car repaired; **was gibt's?** what's the matter?, what's up?; **was gibt's zum Mittagessen?** what's for lunch?; **das gibt's doch nicht!** that's impossible!; **sich geschlagen ~** to admit defeat; **das wird sich schon ~** that'll soon sort itself out.
Gebet [gə'beːt] (-(e)s, -e) nt prayer; **jdn ins ~ nehmen** (fig) to take sb to task.
gebeten [gə'beːtən] pp von **bitten.**
gebeugt [gə'bɔʏkt] adj (Haltung) stooped; (Kopf) bowed; (Schultern) sloping.

gebiert [gə'biːrt] vb siehe **gebären.**
Gebiet [gə'biːt] (-(e)s, -e) nt area; (Hoheits~) territory; (fig) field.
gebieten unreg vt to command, demand.
Gebieter (-s, -) m master; (Herrscher) ruler; ~in f mistress; g~isch adj imperious.
Gebietshoheit f territorial sovereignty.
Gebilde [gə'bɪldə] (-s, -) nt object, structure.
gebildet adj cultured, educated.
Gebimmel [gə'bɪməl] (-s) nt (continual) ringing.
Gebirge [gə'bɪrgə] (-s, -) nt mountains pl.
gebirgig adj mountainous.
Gebirgs- zW: ~**bahn** f railway crossing a mountain range; ~**kette** f, ~**zug** m mountain range.
Gebiß [gə'bɪs] (-sses, -sse) nt teeth pl; (künstlich) dentures pl.
gebissen pp von **beißen.**
Gebläse [gə'blɛːzə] (-s, -) nt fan, blower.
geblasen [gə'blaːzən] pp von **blasen.**
geblichen [gə'blɪçən] pp von **bleichen.**
geblieben [gə'bliːbən] pp von **bleiben.**
geblümt [gə'blyːmt] adj flowered; (Stil) flowery.
Geblüt [gə'blyːt] (-(e)s) nt blood, race.
gebogen [gə'boːgən] pp von **biegen.**
geboren [gə'boːrən] pp von **gebären** ♦ adj born; (Frau) née; **wo sind Sie ~?** where were you born?
geborgen [gə'bɔrgən] pp von **bergen** ♦ adj secure, safe.
geborsten [gə'bɔrstən] pp von **bersten.**
Gebot (-(e)s, -e) nt (Gesetz) law; (REL) commandment; (bei Auktion) bid; **das ~ der Stunde** the needs of the moment.
gebot etc [gə'boːt] vb siehe **gebieten.**
geboten [gə'boːtən] pp von **bieten, gebieten** ♦ adj (geh: ratsam) advisable; (: notwendig) necessary; (: dringend ~) imperative.
Gebr. abk (= Gebrüder) Bros., bros.
gebracht [gə'braxt] pp von **bringen.**
gebrannt [gə'brant] pp von **brennen** ♦ adj: **ein ~es Kind scheut das Feuer** (Sprichwort) once bitten twice shy (Sprichwort).
gebraten [gə'braːtən] pp von **braten.**
Gebräu [gə'brɔʏ] (-(e)s, -e) nt brew, concoction.
Gebrauch [gə'braʊx] (-(e)s, Gebräuche) m use; (Sitte) custom; **zum äußerlichen/innerlichen ~** for external use/to be taken internally.
gebrauchen vt to use; **er/das ist zu nichts zu ~** that's/that's (of) no use to anybody.
gebräuchlich [gə'brɔʏçlɪç] adj usual, customary.
Gebrauchs- zW: ~**anweisung** f directions pl for use; ~**artikel** m article of everyday use; **g~fertig** adj ready for use; ~**gegenstand** m commodity.
gebraucht [gə'braʊxt] adj used; **G~wagen** m second-hand od used car.
gebrechlich [gə'brɛçlɪç] adj frail; **G~keit** f

frailty.

gebrochen [gə'brɔxən] *pp von* **brechen.**

Gebrüder [gə'bry:dər] *pl* brothers *pl.*

Gebrüll [gə'bryl] **(-(e)s)** *nt* (*von Mensch*) yelling; (*von Löwe*) roar.

gebückt [gə'bʏkt] *adj:* **eine ~e Haltung** a stoop.

Gebühr [gə'by:r] **(-, -en)** *f* charge; (*Post~*) postage *no pl;* (*Honorar*) fee; **zu ermäßigter ~** at a reduced rate; **~ (be)zahlt Empfänger** postage to be paid by addressee; **nach ~** suitably; **über ~** excessively.

gebühren *vi* (*geh*): **jdm ~** to be sb's due *od* due to sb ♦ *vr* to be fitting.

gebührend *adj* (*verdient*) due; (*angemessen*) suitable.

Gebühren- *zW:* **~einheit** *f* (*TEL*) tariff unit; **~erlaß** *m* remission of fees; **~ermäßigung** *f* reduction of fees; **g~frei** *adj* free of charge; **g~pflichtig** *adj* subject to charges; **g~pflichtige Verwarnung** (*JUR*) fine.

gebunden [gə'bʊndən] *pp von* **binden** ♦ *adj:* **vertraglich ~ sein** to be bound by contract.

Geburt [gə'bu:rt] **(-, -en)** *f* birth; **das war eine schwere ~!** (*fig: umg*) that took some doing.

Geburten- *zW:* **~kontrolle** *f* birth control; **~regelung** *f* birth control; **~rückgang** *m* drop in the birth rate; **g~schwach** *adj* (*Jahrgang*) with a low birth rate; **~ziffer** *f* birth rate.

gebürtig [gə'bʏrtɪç] *adj* born in, native of; **~e Schweizerin** native of Switzerland, Swiss-born woman.

Geburts- *zW:* **~anzeige** *f* birth notice; **~datum** *nt* date of birth; **~fehler** *m* congenital defect; **~helfer** *m* (*Arzt*) obstetrician; **~helferin** *f* (*Ärztin*) obstetrician; (*Hebamme*) midwife; **~hilfe** *f* (*als Fach*) obstetrics *sing;* (*von Hebamme*) midwifery; **~jahr** *nt* year of birth; **~ort** *m* birthplace; **~tag** *m* birthday; **herzlichen Glückwunsch zum ~tag!** happy birthday!, many happy returns (of the day)!; **~urkunde** *f* birth certificate.

Gebüsch [gə'bʏʃ] **(-(e)s, -e)** *nt* bushes *pl.*

gedacht [gə'daxt] *pp von* **denken, gedenken.**

gedachte *etc vb siehe* **gedenken.**

Gedächtnis [gə'dɛçtnɪs] **(-ses, -se)** *nt* memory; **wenn mich mein ~ nicht trügt** if my memory serves me right; **~feier** *f* commemoration; **~hilfe** *f* memory aid, mnemonic; **~schwund** *m* loss of memory; **~verlust** *m* amnesia.

gedämpft [gə'dɛmpft] *adj* (*Geräusch*) muffled; (*Farben, Instrument, Stimmung*) muted; (*Licht, Freude*) subdued.

Gedanke [gə'daŋkə] **(-ns, -n)** *m* thought; (*Idee, Plan, Einfall*) idea; (*Konzept*) concept; **sich über etw** *akk* **~n machen** to think about sth; **jdn auf andere ~n bringen** to make sb think about other things; **etw ganz in ~n** *dat* **tun** to do sth without thinking; **auf einen ~n**

kommen to have *od* get an idea.

Gedanken- *zW:* **~austausch** *m* exchange of ideas; **~freiheit** *f* freedom of thought; **g~los** *adj* thoughtless; **~losigkeit** *f* thoughtlessness; **~sprung** *m* mental leap; **~strich** *m* dash; **~übertragung** *f* thought transference, telepathy; **g~verloren** *adj* lost in thought; **g~voll** *adj* thoughtful.

Gedärme [gə'dɛrmə] *pl* intestines *pl.*

Gedeck [gə'dɛk] **(-(e)s, -e)** *nt* cover(ing); (*Menü*) set meal; **ein ~ auflegen** to lay a place.

gedeckt *adj* (*Farbe*) muted.

Gedeih *m:* **auf ~ und Verderb** for better or for worse.

gedeihen [gə'daɪən] *unreg vi* to thrive, prosper; **die Sache ist so weit gediehen, daß ...** the matter has reached the point *od* stage where ...

gedenken [gə'dɛŋkən] *unreg vi +gen* (*geh: denken an*) to remember; (*beabsichtigen*) to intend; **G~** *nt:* **zum G~ an jdn** in memory *od* remembrance of sb.

Gedenk- *zW:* **~feier** *f* commemoration; **~minute** *f* minute's silence; **~stätte** *f* memorial; **~tag** *m* remembrance day.

Gedicht [gə'dɪçt] **(-(e)s, -e)** *nt* poem.

gediegen [gə'di:gən] *adj* (*good*) quality; (*Mensch*) reliable; (*rechtschaffen*) honest; **G~heit** *f* quality; reliability; honesty.

gedieh *etc* [gə'di:] *vb siehe* **gedeihen.**

gediehen *pp von* **gedeihen.**

gedr. *abk* = **gedruckt.**

Gedränge [gə'drɛŋə] **(-s)** *nt* crush, crowd; **ins ~ kommen** (*fig*) to get into difficulties.

gedrängt *adj* compressed; **~ voll** packed.

gedroschen [gə'drɔʃən] *pp von* **dreschen.**

gedruckt [gə'drʊkt] *adj* printed; **lügen wie ~** (*umg*) to lie right, left and centre.

gedrungen [gə'drʊŋən] *pp von* **dringen** ♦ *adj* thickset, stocky.

Geduld [gə'dʊlt] **(-)** *f* patience; **mir reißt die ~, ich verliere die ~** my patience is wearing thin, I'm losing my patience.

gedulden [gə'dʊldən] *vr* to be patient.

geduldig *adj* patient.

Geduldsprobe *f* trial of (one's) patience.

gedungen [gə'dʊŋən] (*pej*) *adj* (*geh: Mörder*) hired.

gedunsen [gə'dʊnzən] *adj* bloated.

gedurft [gə'dʊrft] *pp von* **dürfen.**

geehrt [gə'|e:rt] *adj:* **Sehr ~e Damen und Herren!** Ladies and Gentlemen!; (*in Briefen*) Dear Sir or Madam.

geeignet [gə'|aɪgnət] *adj* suitable; **im ~en Augenblick** at the right moment.

Gefahr [gə'fa:r] **(-, -en)** *f* danger; **~ laufen, etw zu tun** to run the risk of doing sth; **auf eigene ~** at one's own risk; **außer ~** (*nicht gefährdet*) not in danger; (*nicht mehr gefährdet*) out of danger; (*Patienten*) off the danger list.

gefährden [gə'fɛːrdən] vt to endanger.
gefahren [gə'faːrən] pp von **fahren**.
Gefahren- zW: **~quelle** f source of danger;
~schwelle f threshold of danger;
~stelle f danger spot; **~zulage** f danger
money.
gefährlich [gə'fɛːrlɪç] adj dangerous.
Gefährte [gə'fɛːrtə] (-n, -n) m companion.
Gefährtin [gə'fɛːrtɪn] f companion.
Gefälle [gə'fɛlə] (-s, -) nt (von Land, Straße)
slope; (Neigungsgrad) gradient; **starkes ~!**
steep hill.
Gefallen[1] [gə'falən] (-s, -) m favour; **jdm etw**
zu ~ tun to do sth to please sb.
Gefallen[2] [gə'falən] (-s) nt pleasure; **an etw**
dat **~ finden** to derive pleasure from sth; **an**
jdm ~ finden to take to sb.
gefallen pp von **fallen, gefallen** ♦ vi (unreg): **jdm**
~ to please sb; **er/es gefällt mir** I like him/it;
das gefällt mir an ihm that's one thing I like
about him; **sich** dat **etw ~ lassen** to put up
with sth.
Gefallene(r) m soldier killed in action.
gefällig [gə'fɛlɪç] adj (hilfsbereit) obliging;
(erfreulich) pleasant; **sonst noch etwas ~?**
(veraltet, ironisch) will there be anything
else?; **G~keit** f favour (BRIT), favor (US);
helpfulness; **etw aus G~keit tun** to do sth as
a favour (BRIT) od favor (US).
gefälligst (umg) adv kindly; **sei ~ still!** will
you kindly keep your mouth shut!
gefällt [gə'fɛlt] vb siehe **gefallen**.
gefangen [gə'faŋən] pp von **fangen** ♦ adj
captured; (fig) captivated.
Gefangene(r) f(m) prisoner, captive.
Gefangenenlager nt prisoner-of-war camp.
gefangen- zW: **~halten** unreg vt to keep
prisoner; **G~nahme** (-, -n) f capture;
~nehmen unreg vt to capture; **G~schaft** f
captivity.
Gefängnis [gə'fɛŋnɪs] (-ses, -se) nt prison;
zwei Jahre ~ bekommen to get two years'
imprisonment; **~strafe** f prison sentence; **~wärter** m prison warder (BRIT) od
guard.
gefärbt [gə'fɛrpt] adj (fig: Bericht) biased;
(Lebensmittel) coloured (BRIT), colored (US).
Gefasel [gə'faːzəl] (-s) nt twaddle, drivel.
Gefäß [gə'fɛːs] (-es, -e) nt vessel (auch ANAT),
container.
gefaßt [gə'fast] adj composed, calm; **auf etw**
akk **~ sein** to be prepared od ready for sth;
er kann sich auf etwas ~ machen (umg) I'll
give him something to think about.
Gefecht [gə'fɛçt] (-(e)s, -e) nt fight; (MIL)
engagement; **jdn/etw außer ~ setzen** (lit,
fig) to put sb/sth out of action.
gefedert [gə'feːdərt] adj (Matratze) sprung.
gefeiert [gə'faɪərt] adj celebrated.
gefeit [gə'faɪt] adj: **gegen etw ~ sein** to be
immune to sth.
gefestigt [gə'fɛstɪçt] adj (Charakter) steadfast.

Gefieder [gə'fiːdər] (-s, -) nt plumage,
feathers pl.
gefiedert adj feathered.
gefiel etc [gə'fiːl] vb siehe **gefallen**.
Geflecht [gə'flɛçt] (-(e)s, -e) nt (lit, fig)
network.
gefleckt [gə'flɛkt] adj spotted; (Blume, Vogel)
speckled.
Geflimmer [gə'flɪmər] (-s) nt shimmering;
(FILM, TV) flicker(ing).
geflissentlich [gə'flɪsəntlɪç] adj intentional
♦ adv intentionally.
geflochten [gə'flɔxtən] pp von **flechten**.
geflogen [gə'floːgən] pp von **fliegen**.
geflohen [gə'floːən] pp von **fliehen**.
geflossen [gə'flɔsən] pp von **fließen**.
Geflügel [gə'flyːgəl] (-s) nt poultry.
geflügelt adj: **~e Worte** familiar quotations.
Geflüster [gə'flʏstər] (-s) nt whispering.
gefochten [gə'fɔxtən] pp von **fechten**.
Gefolge [gə'fɔlgə] (-s, -) nt retinue.
Gefolgschaft [gə'fɔlkʃaft] f following.
Gefolgsmann (-(e)s, pl -leute) m follower.
gefragt [gə'fraːkt] adj in demand.
gefräßig [gə'frɛːsɪç] adj voracious.
Gefreite(r) [gə'fraɪtə(r)] m (MIL) lance
corporal (BRIT), private first class (US);
(NAUT) able seaman (BRIT), seaman
apprentice (US); (AVIAT) aircraftman (BRIT),
airman first class (US).
gefressen [gə'frɛsən] pp von **fressen** ♦ adj: **den**
hab(e) ich ~ (umg) I'm sick of him.
gefrieren [gə'friːrən] unreg vi to freeze.
Gefrier- zW: **~fach** nt freezer compartment;
~fleisch nt frozen meat; **g~getrocknet** adj
freeze-dried; **~punkt** nt freezing point;
~schutzmittel nt antifreeze; **~truhe** f deepfreeze.
gefror etc [gə'froːr] vb siehe **gefrieren**.
gefroren pp von **frieren, gefrieren**.
Gefüge [gə'fyːgə] (-s, -) nt structure.
gefügig adj submissive; (gehorsam) obedient.
Gefühl [gə'fyːl] (-(e)s, -e) nt feeling; **etw im**
~ haben to have a feel for sth; **g~los** adj
unfeeling; (Glieder) numb.
Gefühls- zW: **g~betont** adj emotional;
~duselei [-duːzə'laɪ] (pej) f mawkishness;
~leben nt emotional life; **g~mäßig** adj
instinctive; **~mensch** m emotional person.
gefühlvoll adj (empfindsam) sensitive;
(ausdrucksvoll) expressive; (liebevoll) loving.
gefüllt [gə'fʏlt] adj (KOCH) stuffed; (Pralinen)
with soft centres.
gefunden [gə'fʊndən] pp von **finden** ♦ adj: **das**
war ein ~es Fressen für ihn that was
handing it to him on a plate.
gegangen [gə'gaŋən] pp von **gehen**.
gegeben [gə'geːbən] pp von **geben** ♦ adj given;
zu ~er Zeit in due course.
gegebenenfalls [gə'geːbənənfals] adv if need
be.

================= *SCHLÜSSELWORT*

gegen ['ge:gən] *präp +akk* **1** against; **nichts
~ jdn haben** to have nothing against sb; **X
~ Y** (*SPORT, JUR*) X versus Y; **ein Mittel
~ Schnupfen** something for colds
2 (*in Richtung auf*) towards; **~ Osten**
to(wards) the east; **~ Abend** towards
evening; **~ einen Baum fahren** to drive into
a tree
3 (*ungefähr*) round about; **~ 3 Uhr** around 3
o'clock
4 (*gegenüber*) towards; (*ungefähr*) around;
gerecht ~ alle fair to all
5 (*im Austausch für*) for; **~ bar** for cash;
~ Quittung against a receipt
6 (*verglichen mit*) compared with.

Gegen- *zW:* **~angriff** *m* counter-attack;
~besuch *m* return visit; **~beweis** *m*
counter-evidence.
Gegend ['ge:gənt] (*-, -en*) *f* area, district.
Gegen- *zW:* **~darstellung** *f* (*PRESSE*) reply;
g~einander *adv* against one another;
~fahrbahn *f* opposite carriageway; **~frage**
f counterquestion; **~gewicht** *nt*
counterbalance; **~gift** *nt* antidote;
~kandidat *m* rival candidate; **g~läufig** *adj*
contrary; **~leistung** *f* service in return;
~lichtaufnahme *f* back lit photograph;
~liebe *f* requited love; (*fig: Zustimmung*)
approval; **~maßnahme** *f* countermeasure;
~mittel *nt:* **~mittel (gegen)** (*MED*) antidote
(to); **~probe** *f* cross-check.
Gegensatz (*-es, ⁻e*) *m* contrast; **Gegensätze
überbrücken** to overcome differences.
gegensätzlich *adj* contrary, opposite;
(*widersprüchlich*) contradictory.
Gegen- *zW:* **~schlag** *m* counter-attack; **~seite**
f opposite side; (*Rückseite*) reverse;
g~seitig *adj* mutual, reciprocal; **sich
g~seitig helfen** to help each other; **in
g~seitigem Einverständnis** by mutual
agreement; **~seitigkeit** *f* reciprocity;
~spieler *m* opponent; **~sprechanlage** *f*
(two-way) intercom; **~stand** *m* object;
g~ständlich *adj* objective, concrete;
(*KUNST*) representational; **g~standslos** *adj*
(*überflüssig*) irrelevant; (*grundlos*)
groundless; **~stimme** *f* vote against;
~stoß *m* counterblow; **~stück** *nt*
counterpart; **~teil** *nt* opposite; **im ~teil** on
the contrary; **das ~teil bewirken** to have the
opposite effect; (*Mensch*) to achieve the
exact opposite; **ganz im ~teil** quite the
reverse; **ins ~teil umschlagen** to swing to
the other extreme; **g~teilig** *adj* opposite,
contrary; **ich habe nichts ~teiliges gehört**
I've heard nothing to the contrary.
gegenüber [ge:gən'y:bər] *präp +dat* opposite;
(*zu*) to(wards); (*in bezug auf*) with regard to;
(*im Vergleich zu*) in comparison with;

(*angesichts*) in the face of ♦ *adv* opposite; **mir
~ hat er das nicht geäußert** he didn't say
that to me; **G~** (*-s, -*) *nt* person opposite; (*bei
Kampf*) opponent; (*bei Diskussion*) opposite
number; **~liegen** *unreg vr* to face each other;
~stehen *unreg vr* to be opposed (to each
other); **~stellen** *vt* to confront; (*fig*) to
contrast; **G~stellung** *f* confrontation; (*fig*)
contrast; (*: Vergleich*) comparison; **~treten**
unreg vi +dat to face.
Gegen- *zW:* **~veranstaltung** *f* counter-
meeting; **~verkehr** *m* oncoming traffic;
~vorschlag *m* counterproposal.
Gegenwart ['ge:gənvart] *f* present; **in ~ von**
in the presence of.
gegenwärtig *adj* present ♦ *adv* at present;
das ist mir nicht mehr ~ that has slipped my
mind.
gegenwartsbezogen *adj* (*Roman etc*)
relevant to present times.
Gegen- *zW:* **~wert** *m* equivalent; **~wind** *m*
headwind; **~wirkung** *f* reaction;
g~zeichnen *vt* to countersign; **~zug** *m*
countermove; (*EISENB*) corresponding train
in the other direction.
gegessen [gə'gɛsən] *pp von* **essen.**
geglichen [gə'glɪçən] *pp von* **gleichen.**
gegliedert [gə'gli:dərt] *adj* jointed; (*fig*)
structured.
geglitten [gə'glɪtən] *pp von* **gleiten.**
geglommen [gə'glɔmən] *pp von* **glimmen.**
geglückt [gə'glʏkt] *adj* (*Feier*) successful;
(*Überraschung*) real.
Gegner(in) ['ge:gnər(ɪn)] (*-s, -*) *m(f)* opponent;
g~isch *adj* opposing; **~schaft** *f* opposition.
gegolten [gə'gɔltən] *pp von* **gelten.**
gegoren [gə'go:rən] *pp von* **gären.**
gegossen [gə'gɔsən] *pp von* **gießen.**
gegr. *abk* (*= gegründet*) estab.
gegraben [gə'gra:bən] *pp von* **graben.**
gegriffen [gə'grɪfən] *pp von* **greifen.**
Gehabe [gə'ha:bə] (*-s*) (*umg*) *nt* affected
behaviour (*BRIT*) *od* behavior (*US*).
gehabt [gə'ha:pt] *pp von* **haben.**
Gehackte(s) [ge'haktə(s)] *nt* mince(d meat)
(*BRIT*), ground meat (*US*).
Gehalt¹ [gə'halt] (*-(e)s, -e*) *m* content.
Gehalt² [gə'halt] (*-(e)s, ⁻er*) *nt* salary.
gehalten [gə'haltən] *pp von* **halten** ♦ *adj:* **~ sein,
etw zu tun** (*form*) to be required to do sth.
Gehalts- *zW:* **~abrechnung** *f* salary
statement; **~empfänger** *m* salary earner;
~erhöhung *f* salary increase; **~klasse** *f*
salary bracket; **~konto** *nt* current account
(*BRIT*), checking account (*US*); **~zulage** *f*
salary increment.
gehaltvoll [gə'haltfɔl] *adj* (*Speise, Buch*)
substantial.
gehandikapt [gə'hɛndikɛpt] *adj* handicapped.
gehangen [gə'haŋən] *pp von* **hängen.**
geharnischt [gə'harnɪʃt] *adj* (*fig*) forceful,
sharp.

gehässig [gə'hɛsɪç] *adj* spiteful, nasty; **G~keit** *f* spite(fulness).
gehäuft [gə'hɔyft] *adj* (*Löffel*) heaped.
Gehäuse [gə'hɔyzə] (**-s, -**) *nt* case; (*Radio~, Uhr~*) casing; (*von Apfel etc*) core.
gehbehindert ['ge:bəhɪndərt] *adj* disabled.
Gehege [gə'he:gə] (**-s, -**) *nt* enclosure, preserve; **jdm ins ~ kommen** (*fig*) to poach on sb's preserve.
geheim [gə'haɪm] *adj* secret; (*Dokumente*) classified; **streng ~** top secret; **G~dienst** *m* secret service, intelligence service; **G~fach** *nt* secret compartment; **~halten** *unreg vt* to keep secret.
Geheimnis (**-ses, -se**) *nt* secret; (*rätselhaftes ~*) mystery; **~krämer** *m* mystery-monger; **g~voll** *adj* mysterious.
Geheim- *zW:* **~nummer** *f* (*TEL*) secret number; **~polizei** *f* secret police; **~rat** *m* privy councillor; **~ratsecken** *pl:* **er hat ~ratsecken** he is going bald at the temples; **~schrift** *f* code, secret writing; **~tip** *m* (personal) tip.
Geheiß [gə'haɪs] (**-es**) *nt* (*geh*) command; **auf jds ~** *akk* at sb's bidding.
geheißen [gə'haɪsən] *pp von* **heißen**.
gehemmt [gə'hɛmt] *adj* inhibited.
gehen ['ge:ən] *unreg vi* (*auch Auto, Uhr*) to go; (*zu Fuß ~*) to walk; (*funktionieren*) to work; (*Teig*) to rise ♦ *vt* to go; to walk ♦ *vi unpers:* **wie geht es dir?** how are you *od* things?; **~ nach** (*Fenster*) to face; **in sich** *akk* **~** to think things over; **nach etw ~** (*urteilen*) to go by sth; **wieviele Leute ~ in deinen Wagen?** how many people can you get in your car?; **nichts geht über** +*akk* ... there's nothing to beat ..., there's nothing better than ...; **schwimmen/schlafen ~** to go swimming/to bed; **in die Tausende ~** to run into (the) thousands; **mir/ihm geht es gut** I'm/he's (doing) fine; **geht das?** is that possible?; **geht's noch?** can you manage?; **es geht** not too bad, O.K.; **das geht nicht** that's not on; **es geht um etw** it concerns sth, it's about sth; **laß es dir gut ~** look after yourself, take care of yourself; **so geht das, das geht so** that/this is how it's done; **darum geht es (mir) nicht** that's not the point; (*spielt keine Rolle*) that's not important to me; **morgen geht es nicht** tomorrow's no good; **wenn es nach mir ginge** ... if it were *od* was up to me ...
gehenlassen *unreg vr* to lose one's self-control; (*nachlässig sein*) to let o.s. go.
gehetzt [gə'hɛtst] *adj* harassed.
geheuer [gə'hɔyər] *adj:* **nicht ~** eerie; (*fragwürdig*) dubious.
Geheul [gə'hɔyl] (**-(e)s**) *nt* howling.
Gehilfe [gə'hɪlfə] (**-n, -n**) *m* assistant.
Gehilfin [gə'hɪlfɪn] *f* assistant.
Gehirn [gə'hɪrn] (**-(e)s, -e**) *nt* brain; **~erschütterung** *f* concussion; **~schlag** *m*

stroke; **~wäsche** *f* brainwashing.
gehoben [gə'ho:bən] *pp von* **heben** ♦ *adj:* **~er Dienst** *professional and executive levels of the civil service.*
geholfen [gə'hɔlfən] *pp von* **helfen**.
Gehör [gə'hø:r] (**-(e)s**) *nt* hearing; **musikalisches ~** ear; **absolutes ~** perfect pitch; **~ finden** to gain a hearing; **jdm ~ schenken** to give sb a hearing.
gehorchen [gə'hɔrçən] *vi* +*dat* to obey.
gehören [gə'hø:rən] *vi* to belong ♦ *vr unpers* to be right *od* proper; **das gehört nicht zur Sache** that's irrelevant; **dazu gehört (schon) einiges** *od* **etwas** that takes some doing (*umg*); **er gehört ins Bett** he should be in bed.
gehörig *adj* proper; **~ zu** *od* +*dat* (*geh*) belonging to.
gehörlos *adj* (*form*) deaf.
gehorsam [gə'ho:rza:m] *adj* obedient; **G~** (**-s**) *m* obedience.
Gehörsinn *m* sense of hearing.
Gehsteig ['ge:ʃtaɪk] *m*, **Gehweg** *m* pavement (*BRIT*), sidewalk (*US*).
Geier ['gaɪər] (**-s, -**) *m* vulture; **weiß der ~!** (*umg*) God knows.
geifern ['gaɪfərn] *vi* to slaver; (*fig*) to be bursting with venom.
Geige ['gaɪgə] (**-, -n**) *f* violin; **die erste/zweite ~ spielen** (*lit*) to play first/second violin; (*fig*) to call the tune/play second fiddle.
Geiger(in) (**-s, -**) *m(f)* violinist.
Geigerzähler *m* geiger counter.
geil [gaɪl] *adj* randy (*BRIT*), horny (*US*); (*pej: lüstern*) lecherous; (*umg: gut*) fantastic.
Geisel ['gaɪzəl] (**-, -n**) *f* hostage; **~nahme** (**-**) *f* taking of hostages.
Geißel ['gaɪsəl] (**-, -n**) *f* scourge, whip.
geißeln *vt* to scourge.
Geist [gaɪst] (**-(e)s, -er**) *m* spirit; (*Gespenst*) ghost; (*Verstand*) mind; **von allen guten ~ern verlassen sein** (*umg*) to have taken leave of one's senses; **hier scheiden sich die ~er** this is the parting of the ways; **den** *od* **seinen ~ aufgeben** to give up the ghost.
Geister- *zW:* **~fahrer** (*umg*) *m* ghost-driver (*US*), person driving in the wrong direction; **g~haft** *adj* ghostly; **~hand** *f:* **wie von ~hand** as if by magic.
Geistes- *zW:* **g~abwesend** *adj* absent-minded; **~akrobat** *m* mental acrobat; **~blitz** *m* brain wave; **~gegenwart** *f* presence of mind; **g~gegenwärtig** *adj* quick-witted; **g~gestört** *adj* mentally disturbed; (*stärker*) (mentally) deranged; **~haltung** *f* mental attitude; **g~krank** *adj* mentally ill; **~kranke(r)** *f(m)* mentally ill person; **~krankheit** *f* mental illness; **~störung** *f* mental disturbance; **~verfassung** *f* frame of mind; **~wissenschaften** *pl* arts (subjects) *pl*; **~zustand** *m* state of mind; **jdn auf seinen ~zustand untersuchen** to give sb a

psychiatric examination.
geistig adj intellectual; (PSYCH) mental; (Getränke) alcoholic; ~ **behindert** mentally handicapped; ~-**seelisch** mental and spiritual.
geistlich adj spiritual; (religiös) religious; G~**e(r)** m clergyman; G~**keit** f clergy.
geist- zW: ~**los** adj uninspired, dull; ~**reich** adj intelligent; (witzig) witty; ~**tötend** adj soul-destroying; ~**voll** adj intellectual; (weise) wise.
Geiz [gaɪts] (-es) m miserliness, meanness; g~**en** vi to be miserly; ~**hals** m miser.
geizig adj miserly, mean.
Geizkragen m miser.
gekannt [gə'kant] pp von **kennen**.
Gekicher [gə'kɪçər] (-s) nt giggling.
Geklapper [gə'klapər] (-s) nt rattling.
Geklimper [gə'klɪmpər] (-s) (umg) nt (Klavier~) tinkling; (: stümperhaft) plonking; (von Geld) jingling.
geklungen [gə'klʊŋən] pp von **klingen**.
geknickt [gə'knɪkt] adj (fig) dejected.
gekniffen [gə'knɪfən] pp von **kneifen**.
gekommen [gə'kɔmən] pp von **kommen**.
gekonnt [gə'kɔnt] pp von **können** ♦ adj skilful (BRIT), skillful (US).
Gekritzel [gə'krɪtsəl] (-s) nt scrawl, scribble.
gekrochen [gə'krɔxən] pp von **kriechen**.
gekünstelt [ge'kynstəlt] adj artificial; (Sprache, Benehmen) affected.
Gel [geːl] (-s, -e) nt gel.
Gelaber(e) [gə'laːbər(ə)] (-s) (umg) nt prattle.
Gelächter [gə'lɛçtər] (-s, -) nt laughter; **in** ~ **ausbrechen** to burst out laughing.
gelackmeiert [gə'lakmaɪərt] (umg) adj conned.
geladen [ge'laːdən] pp von **laden** ♦ adj loaded; (ELEK) live; (fig) furious.
Gelage [gə'laːgə] (-s, -) nt feast, banquet.
gelagert [gə'laːgərt] adj: **in anders/ähnlich ~en Fällen** in different/similar cases.
gelähmt [gə'lɛːmt] adj paralysed.
Gelände [gə'lɛndə] (-s, -) nt land, terrain; (von Fabrik, Sport~) grounds pl; (Bau~) site; ~**fahrzeug** nt cross-country vehicle; g~**gängig** adj able to go cross-country; ~**lauf** m cross-country race.
Geländer [gə'lɛndər] (-s, -) nt railing; (Treppen~) banister(s).
gelang etc vb siehe **gelingen**.
gelangen [gə'laŋən] vi: ~ **an** +akk od **zu** to reach; (erwerben) to attain; **in jds Besitz** akk ~ to come into sb's possession; **in die richtigen/falschen Hände** ~ to fall into the right/wrong hands.
gelangweilt adj bored.
gelassen [gə'lasən] pp von **lassen** ♦ adj calm; (gefaßt) composed; G~**heit** f calmness; composure.
Gelatine [ʒela'tiːnə] f gelatine.
gelaufen [gə'laʊfən] pp von **laufen**.
geläufig [gə'lɔyfɪç] adj (üblich) common; **das**

ist mir nicht ~ I'm not familiar with that; G~**keit** f commonness; familiarity.
gelaunt [gə'laʊnt] adj: **schlecht/gut** ~ in a bad/good mood; **wie ist er** ~? what sort of mood is he in?
Geläut [gə'lɔyt] (-(e)s) nt ringing; (Läutwerk) chime.
Geläute (-s) nt ringing.
gelb [gɛlp] adj yellow; (Ampellicht) amber (BRIT), yellow (US); G~**e Seiten** Yellow Pages; ~**lich** adj yellowish.
Gelbsucht f jaundice.
Geld [gɛlt] (-(e)s, -er) nt money; **etw zu** ~ **machen** to sell sth off; **er hat** ~ **wie Heu** (umg) he's stinking rich; **am** ~ **hängen** od **kleben** to be tight with money; **staatliche/ öffentliche** ~**er** state/public funds pl od money; ~**adel** m: **der** ~**adel** the moneyed aristocracy; (hum: die Reichen) the rich; ~**anlage** f investment; ~**automat** m cash dispenser; ~**automatenkarte** f cash card; ~**beutel** m purse; ~**börse** f purse; ~**einwurf** m slot; ~**geber** (-s, -) m financial backer; g~**gierig** adj avaricious; ~**institut** nt financial institution; ~**mittel** pl capital sing, means pl; ~**quelle** f source of income; ~**schein** m banknote; ~**schrank** m safe, strongbox; ~**strafe** f fine; ~**stück** nt coin; ~**verlegenheit** f: **in** ~**verlegenheit sein/kommen** to be/run short of money; ~**verleiher** m moneylender; ~**wäsche** f money-laundering; ~**wechsel** m exchange (of money); „~**wechsel**" "bureau de change"; ~**wert** m cash value; (FIN: Kaufkraft) currency value.
geleckt [gə'lɛkt] adj: **wie** ~ **aussehen** to be neat and tidy.
Gelee [ʒe'leː] (-s, -s) m or nt jelly.
gelegen [gə'leːgən] pp von **liegen** ♦ adj situated; (passend) convenient, opportune; **etw kommt jdm** ~ sth is convenient for sb; **mir ist viel/nichts daran** ~ (wichtig) it matters a great deal/doesn't matter to me.
Gelegenheit [gə'leːgənhaɪt] f opportunity; (Anlaß) occasion; **bei** ~ some time (or other); **bei jeder** ~ at every opportunity.
Gelegenheits- zW: ~**arbeit** f casual work; ~**arbeiter** m casual worker; ~**kauf** m bargain.
gelegentlich [gə'leːgəntlɪç] adj occasional ♦ adv occasionally; (bei Gelegenheit) some time (or other) ♦ präp +gen on the occasion of.
gelehrig [gə'leːrɪç] adj quick to learn.
gelehrt adj learned; G~**e(r)** f(m) scholar; G~**heit** f scholarliness.
Geleise [gə'laɪzə] (-s, -) nt = **Gleis**.
Geleit [gə'laɪt] (-(e)s, -e) nt escort; **freies** od **sicheres** ~ safe conduct; g~**en** vt to escort; ~**schutz** m escort.
Gelenk [gə'lɛŋk] (-(e)s, -e) nt joint.
gelenkig adj supple.
gelernt [gə'lɛrnt] adj skilled.

gelesen [gə'le:zən] *pp von* **lesen**.
Geliebte *f* sweetheart; (*Liebhaberin*) mistress.
Geliebte(r) *m* sweetheart; (*Liebhaber*) lover.
geliefert [gə'li:fərt] *adj:* **ich bin ~** (*umg*) I've had it.
geliehen [gə'li:ən] *pp von* **leihen**.
gelind [gə'lɪnt] *adj* = **gelinde**.
gelinde [gə'lɪndə] *adj* (*geh*) mild; **~ gesagt** to put it mildly.
gelingen [gə'lɪŋən] *unreg vi* to succeed; **die Arbeit gelingt mir nicht** I'm not doing very well with this work; **es ist mir gelungen, etw zu tun** I succeeded in doing sth; **G~** *nt* (*geh: Glück*) success; (: *erfolgreiches Ergebnis*) successful outcome.
gelitten [gə'lɪtən] *pp von* **leiden**.
gellen ['gɛlən] *vi* to shrill.
gellend *adj* shrill, piercing.
geloben [gə'lo:bən] *vt, vi* to vow, swear; **das Gelobte Land** (*REL*) the Promised Land.
gelogen [gə'lo:gən] *pp von* **lügen**.
gelten ['gɛltən] *unreg vt* (*wert sein*) to be worth ♦ *vi* (*gültig sein*) to be valid; (*erlaubt sein*) to be allowed ♦ *vb unpers* (*geh*): **es gilt, etw zu tun** it is necessary to do sth; **was gilt die Wette?** do you want a bet?; **das gilt nicht!** that doesn't count!; (*nicht erlaubt*) that's not allowed; **etw gilt bei jdm viel/wenig** sb values sth highly/doesn't value sth very highly; **jdm viel/wenig ~** to mean a lot/not mean much to sb; **jdm ~** (*gemünzt sein auf*) to be meant for *od* aimed at sb; **etw ~ lassen** to accept sth; **für diesmal lasse ich's ~** I'll let it go this time; **als** *od* **für etw ~** to be considered to be sth; **jdm** *od* **für jdn ~** (*betreffen*) to apply to sb.
geltend *adj* (*Preise*) current; (*Gesetz*) in force; (*Meinung*) prevailing; **etw ~ machen** to assert sth; **sich ~ machen** to make itself/o.s. felt; **einen Einwand ~ machen** to raise an objection.
Geltung ['gɛltʊŋ] *f:* **~ haben** to have validity; **sich/etw** *dat* **~ verschaffen** to establish o.s./sth; **etw zur ~ bringen** to show sth to its best advantage; **zur ~ kommen** to be seen/heard *etc* to its best advantage.
Geltungsbedürfnis *nt* desire for admiration.
geltungssüchtig *adj* craving admiration.
Gelübde [gə'lʏpdə] (**-s, -**) *nt* vow.
gelungen [gə'lʊŋən] *pp von* **gelingen** ♦ *adj* successful.
Gem. *abk* = **Gemeinde**.
gemächlich [gə'mɛːçlɪç] *adj* leisurely.
gemacht [gə'maxt] *adj* (*gewollt, gekünstelt*) false, contrived; **ein ~er Mann sein** to be made.
Gemahl [gə'ma:l] (**-(e)s, -e**) *m* (*geh, form*) spouse, husband.
gemahlen [gə'ma:lən] *pp von* **mahlen**.
Gemahlin *f* (*geh, form*) spouse, wife.
Gemälde [gə'mɛːldə] (**-s, -**) *nt* picture, painting.

gemasert [gə'ma:zərt] *adj* (*Holz*) grained.
gemäß [gə'mɛːs] *präp +dat* in accordance with ♦ *adj +dat* appropriate to.
gemäßigt *adj* moderate; (*Klima*) temperate.
Gemauschel [gə'mauʃəl] (**-s**) (*umg*) *nt* scheming.
Gemecker [gə'mɛkər] (**-s**) *nt* (*von Ziegen*) bleating; (*umg: Nörgelei*) moaning.
gemein [gə'maɪn] *adj* common; (*niederträchtig*) mean; **etw ~ haben (mit)** to have sth in common (with).
Gemeinde [gə'maɪndə] (**-, -n**) *f* district; (*Bewohner*) community; (*Pfarr~*) parish; (*Kirchen~*) congregation; **~abgaben** *pl* rates and local taxes *pl*; **~ordnung** *f* by(e) laws *pl*, ordinances *pl* (*US*); **~rat** *m* district council; (*Mitglied*) district councillor; **~schwester** *f* district nurse (*BRIT*); **~steuer** *f* local rates *pl*; **~verwaltung** *f* local administration; **~vorstand** *m* local council; **~wahl** *f* local election.
Gemein- *zW:* **~eigentum** *nt* common property; **g~gefährlich** *adj* dangerous to the public; **~gut** *nt* public property; **~heit** *f* (*Niedertracht*) meanness; **das war eine ~heit** that was a mean thing to do/to say; **g~hin** *adv* generally; **~kosten** *pl* overheads *pl*; **~nutz** *m* public good; **g~nützig** *adj* of benefit to the public; (*wohltätig*) charitable; **~platz** *m* commonplace, platitude; **g~sam** *adj* joint, common (*auch MATH*) ♦ *adv* together; **g~same Sache mit jdm machen** to be in cahoots with sb; **der g~same Markt** the Common Market; **g~sames Konto** joint account; **etw g~sam haben** to have sth in common; **~samkeit** *f* common ground; **~schaft** *f* community; **in ~schaft mit** jointly *od* together with; **eheliche ~schaft** (*JUR*) matrimony; **~schaft Unabhängiger Staaten** Commonwealth of Independent States; **g~schaftlich** *adj* = **gemeinsam**; **~schaftsantenne** *f* party aerial (*BRIT*) *od* antenna (*US*); **~schaftsarbeit** *f* teamwork; **~schaftsbesitz** *m* collective ownership; **~schaftserziehung** *f* coeducation; **~schaftskunde** *f* social studies *pl*; **~schaftsraum** *m* common room; **~sinn** *m* public spirit; **g~verständlich** *adj* generally comprehensible; **~wesen** *nt* community; **~wohl** *nt* common good.
Gemenge [gə'mɛŋə] (**-s, -**) *nt* mixture; (*Hand~*) scuffle.
gemessen [gə'mɛsən] *pp von* **messen** ♦ *adj* measured.
Gemetzel [gə'mɛtsəl] (**-s, -**) *nt* slaughter, carnage.
gemieden [gə'mi:dən] *pp von* **meiden**.
Gemisch [gə'mɪʃ] (**-es, -e**) *nt* mixture.
gemischt *adj* mixed.
gemocht [gə'mɔxt] *pp von* **mögen**.
gemolken [gə'mɔlkən] *pp von* **melken**.

Gemse ['gɛmzə] (-, -n) *f* chamois.
Gemunkel [gə'muŋkəl] (-s) *nt* gossip.
Gemurmel [gə'murməl] (-s) *nt* murmur(ing).
Gemüse [gə'my:zə] (-s, -) *nt* vegetables *pl*;
~**garten** *m* vegetable garden; ~**händler** *m*
greengrocer (*BRIT*), vegetable dealer (*US*);
~**platte** *f* (*KOCH*): **eine** ~**platte** assorted
vegetables.
gemußt [gə'must] *pp von* **müssen**.
gemustert [gə'mustərt] *adj* patterned.
Gemüt [gə'my:t] (-(e)s, -er) *nt* disposition,
nature; (*fig: Mensch*) person; **sich** *dat* **etw zu**
~**e führen** (*umg*) to indulge in sth; **die** ~**er**
erregen to arouse strong feelings; **wir**
müssen warten, bis sich die ~**er beruhigt**
haben we must wait until feelings have
cooled down.
gemütlich *adj* comfortable, cosy; (*Person*)
good-natured; **wir verbrachten einen** ~**en**
Abend we spent a very pleasant evening;
G~**keit** *f* comfortableness, cosiness;
amiability.
Gemüts- *zW:* ~**bewegung** *f* emotion;
g~**krank** *adj* emotionally disturbed;
~**mensch** *m* sentimental person; ~**ruhe** *f*
composure; **in aller** ~**ruhe** (*umg*) (as) cool as
a cucumber; (*gemächlich*) at a leisurely
pace; ~**zustand** *m* state of mind.
gemütvoll *adj* warm, tender.
Gen [ge:n] (-s, -e) *nt* gene.
Gen. *abk* = **Genossenschaft**; (= *Genitiv*) gen.
gen. *abk* (= *genannt*) named, called.
genannt [gə'nant] *pp von* **nennen**.
genas *etc* [gə'na:s] *vb siehe* **genesen**.
genau [gə'nau] *adj* exact, precise ♦ *adv*
exactly, precisely; **etw** ~ **nehmen** to take
sth seriously; **G**~**eres** further details *pl*; **etw**
~ **wissen** to know sth for certain; ~ **auf die**
Minute, auf die Minute ~ exactly on time;
~**genommen** *adv* strictly speaking.
Genauigkeit *f* exactness, accuracy.
genauso [gə'nauzo:] *adv* (*vor Adjektiv*) just as;
(*alleinstehend*) just *od* exactly the same.
Gen.-Dir. *abk* = **Generaldirektor**.
genehm [gə'ne:m] *adj* agreeable, acceptable.
genehmigen *vt* to approve, authorize; **sich**
dat **etw** ~ to indulge in sth.
Genehmigung *f* approval, authorization.
geneigt [gə'naikt] *adj* (*geh*) well-disposed,
willing; ~ **sein, etw zu tun** to be inclined to
do sth.
Genera *pl von* **Genus**.
General [gene'ra:l] (-s, -e *od* ̈-e) *m* general;
~**direktor** *m* chairman (*BRIT*), president
(*US*); ~**konsulat** *nt* consulate general;
~**probe** *f* dress rehearsal; ~**sekretär** *m*
secretary-general; ~**stabskarte** *f* ordnance
survey map; ~**streik** *m* general strike;
g~**überholen** *vt* to overhaul thoroughly;
~**vertretung** *f* sole agency.
Generation [generatsi'o:n] *f* generation.
Generationskonflikt *m* generation gap.

Generator [gene'ra:tɔr] *m* generator, dynamo.
generell [genə'rɛl] *adj* general.
genesen [ge'ne:zən] *unreg vi* (*geh*) to
convalesce, recover.
Genesende(r) *f(m)* convalescent.
Genesung *f* recovery, convalescence.
Genetik [ge'ne:tɪk] *f* genetics.
genetisch [ge'ne:tɪʃ] *adj* genetic.
Genf ['gɛnf] (-s) *nt* Geneva.
Genfer *adj attrib:* **der** ~ See Lake Geneva; **die**
~ **Konvention** the Geneva Convention.
genial [geni'a:l] *adj* brilliant.
Genialität [geniali'tɛ:t] *f* brilliance, genius.
Genick [gə'nɪk] (-(e)s, -e) *nt* (back of the)
neck; **jdm/etw das** ~ **brechen** (*fig*) to finish
sb/sth; ~**starre** *f* stiff neck.
Genie [ʒe'ni:] (-s, -s) *nt* genius.
genieren [ʒe'ni:rən] *vr* to be embarrassed ♦ *vt*
to bother; **geniert es Sie, wenn ...?** do you
mind if ...?
genießbar *adj* edible; (*trinkbar*) drinkable.
genießen [gə'ni:sən] *unreg vt* to enjoy; (*essen*)
to eat; (*trinken*) to drink; **er ist heute nicht zu**
~ (*umg*) he is unbearable today.
Genießer(in) (-s, -) *m(f)* connoisseur; (*des*
Lebens) pleasure-lover; **g**~**isch** *adj*
appreciative ♦ *adv* with relish.
Genitalien [geni'ta:liən] *pl* genitals *pl*.
Genitiv ['ge:niti:f] *m* genitive.
genommen [gə'nɔmən] *pp von* **nehmen**.
genoß *etc* [gə'nɔs] *vb siehe* **genießen**.
Genosse [gə'nɔsə] (-n, -n) *m* comrade (*bes*
POL), companion.
genossen *pp von* **genießen**.
Genossenschaft *f* cooperative
(association).
Genossin *f* comrade (*bes POL*), companion.
genötigt [gə'nø:tɪçt] *adj:* **sich** ~ **sehen, etw zu**
tun to feel obliged to do sth.
Genre [ʒã:rə] (-s, -s) *nt* genre.
Gent [gɛnt] (-s) *nt* Ghent.
Gentechnik *f*, **Gentechnologie** *f* gene
technology.
Genua ['ge:nua] (-s) *nt* Genoa.
genug [gə'nu:k] *adv* enough; **jetzt ist('s) aber**
~**!** that's enough!
Genüge [gə'ny:gə] *f:* **jdm/etw** ~ **tun** *od* **leisten**
to satisfy sb/sth; **etw zur** ~ **kennen** to know
sth well enough; (*abwertender*) to know sth
only too well.
genügen *vi* to be enough; (*den Anforderungen*
etc) to satisfy; **jdm** ~ to be enough for sb.
genügend *adj* enough, sufficient;
(*befriedigend*) satisfactory.
genügsam [gə'ny:kza:m] *adj* modest, easily
satisfied; **G**~**keit** *f* moderation.
Genugtuung [gə'nu:ktu:uŋ] *f* satisfaction.
Genus ['ge:nus] (-, **Genera**) *nt* (*GRAM*) gender.
Genuß [gə'nus] (-sses, ̈-sse) *m* pleasure;
(*Zusichnehmen*) consumption; **etw mit**
~ **essen** to eat sth with relish; **in den** ~ **von**
etw kommen to receive the benefit of sth.

genüßlich [gə'nʏslɪç] *adv* with relish.
Genußmittel *pl* (semi-)luxury items *pl*.
geöffnet [gə'œfnət] *adj* open.
Geograph [geo'graːf] (**-en, -en**) *m* geographer.
Geographie [geogra'fiː] *f* geography.
Geographin *f* geographer.
geographisch *adj* geographical.
Geologe [geo'loːgə] (**-n, -n**) *m* geologist.
Geologie [geolo'giː] *f* geology.
Geologin *f* geologist.
Geometrie [geome'triː] *f* geometry.
geordnet [gə'ɔrdnət] *adj*: **in ~en Verhältnissen leben** to live a well-ordered life.
Georgien [ge'ɔrgiən] (**-s**) *nt* Georgia.
Gepäck [gə'pɛk] *nt* luggage, baggage; **mit leichtem ~ reisen** to travel light; **~abfertigung** *f* luggage desk/office; **~annahme** *f* (*Bahnhof*) baggage office; (*Flughafen*) baggage check-in; **~aufbewahrung** *f* left-luggage office (*BRIT*), baggage check (*US*); **~ausgabe** *f* (*Bahnhof*) baggage office; (*Flughafen*) baggage reclaim; **~netz** *nt* luggage rack; **~schein** *m* luggage *od* baggage ticket; **~stück** *nt* piece of baggage; **~träger** *m* porter; (*Fahrrad*) carrier; **~wagen** *m* luggage van (*BRIT*), baggage car (*US*).
Gepard ['geːpart] (**-(e)s, -e**) *m* cheetah.
gepfeffert [gə'pfɛfərt] (*umg*) *adj* (*Preise*) steep; (*Fragen, Prüfung*) tough; (*Kritik*) biting.
gepfiffen [gə'pfɪfən] *pp von* **pfeifen**.
gepflegt [gə'pfleːkt] *adj* well-groomed; (*Park etc*) well looked after; (*Atmosphäre*) sophisticated; (*Ausdrucksweise, Sprache*) cultured.
Gepflogenheit [gə'pfloːgənhaɪt] *f* (*geh*) custom.
Geplapper [gə'plapər] (**-s**) *nt* chatter.
Geplauder [gə'plaʊdər] (**-s**) *nt* chat(ting).
Gepolter [gə'pɔltər] (**-s**) *nt* din.
gepr. *abk* (= *geprüft*) tested.
gepriesen [gə'priːzən] *pp von* **preisen**.
gequält [gə'kvɛːlt] *adj* (*Lächeln*) forced; (*Miene, Ausdruck*) pained; (*Gesang, Stimme*) strained.
Gequatsche [gə'kvatʃə] (**-s**) (*pej: umg*) *nt* gabbing; (*Blödsinn*) twaddle.
gequollen [gə'kvɔlən] *pp von* **quellen**.
Gerade [gə'raːdə] (**-n, -n**) *f* straight line.

=============== *SCHLÜSSELWORT* ===============

gerade [gə'raːdə] *adj* straight; (*aufrecht*) upright; **eine ~ Zahl** an even number
♦ *adv* **1** (*genau*) just, exactly; (*speziell*) especially; **~ deshalb** that's just *od* exactly why; **das ist es ja ~!** that's just it; **~ du** you especially; **warum ~ ich?** why me (of all people)?; **jetzt ~ nicht!** not now!; **~ neben** right next to; **nicht ~ schön** not exactly beautiful
2 (*eben, soeben*) just; **er wollte ~ aufstehen** he was just about to get up; **da wir ~ von**

Geld sprechen ... talking of money ...; ~ erst only just; **~ noch** (only) just.

gerade- *zW*: **~aus** *adv* straight ahead; **~biegen** *unreg vt* (*lit, fig*) to straighten out; **~heraus** *adv* straight out, bluntly.
gerädert [gə'rɛːdərt] *adj*: **wie ~ sein, sich wie ~ fühlen** to be *od* feel (absolutely) whacked (*umg*).
geradeso *adv* just so; **~ dumm** *etc* just as stupid *etc*; **~ wie** just as.
geradestehen *unreg vi* (*aufrecht stehen*) to stand up straight; **für jdn/etw ~** (*fig*) to answer *od* be answerable for sb/sth.
geradezu *adv* (*beinahe*) virtually, almost.
geradlinig *adj* straight.
gerammelt [gə'raməlt] *adv*: **~ voll** (*umg*) (jam-)packed.
Geranie [gɛ'raːniə] *f* geranium.
gerannt [gə'rant] *pp von* **rennen**.
Gerät [gə'rɛːt] (**-(e)s, -e**) *nt* device; (*Apparat*) gadget; (*elektrisches ~*) appliance; (*Werkzeug*) tool; (*SPORT*) apparatus; (*Zubehör*) equipment *no pl*.
gerät [gə'rɛːt] *vb siehe* **geraten**.
geraten [gə'raːtən] *unreg pp von* **raten, geraten**
♦ *vi* (*gedeihen*) to thrive; (*gelingen*): **~** to turn out well (for sb); (*zufällig gelangen*): **~ in** *+akk* to get into; **gut/schlecht ~** to turn out well/badly; **an jdn ~** to come across sb; **an den Richtigen/Falschen ~** to come to the right/wrong person; **in Angst ~** to get frightened; **nach jdm ~** to take after sb.
Geräteturnen *nt* apparatus gymnastics.
Geratewohl [gəraːtə'voːl] *nt*: **aufs ~** on the off chance; (*bei Wahl*) at random.
geraum [gə'raʊm] *adj*: **seit ~er Zeit** for some considerable time.
geräumig [gə'rɔʏmɪç] *adj* roomy.
Geräusch [gə'rɔʏʃ] (**-(e)s, -e**) *nt* sound; (*unangenehm*) noise; **g~arm** *adj* quiet; **~kulisse** *f* background noise; (*FILM, RUNDF, TV*) sound effects *pl*; **g~los** *adj* silent; **~pegel** *m* sound level; **g~voll** *adj* noisy.
gerben ['gɛrbən] *vt* to tan.
Gerber (**-s, -**) *m* tanner.
Gerberei [gɛrbə'raɪ] *f* tannery.
gerecht [gə'rɛçt] *adj* just, fair; **jdm/etw ~ werden** to do justice to sb/sth; **~fertigt** *adj* justified.
Gerechtigkeit *f* justice, fairness.
Gerechtigkeits- *zW*: **~fanatiker** *m* justice fanatic; **~gefühl** *nt* sense of justice; **~sinn** *m* sense of justice.
Gerede [gə'reːdə] (**-s**) *nt* talk; (*Klatsch*) gossip.
geregelt [gə'reːgəlt] *adj* (*Arbeit, Mahlzeiten*) regular; (*Leben*) well-ordered.
gereizt [gə'raɪtst] *adj* irritable; **G~heit** *f* irritation.
Gericht [gə'rɪçt] (**-(e)s, -e**) *nt* court; (*Essen*) dish; **jdn/einen Fall vor ~ bringen** to take sb/a case to court; **mit jdm ins ~ gehen** (*fig*)

to judge sb harshly; **über jdn zu ~ sitzen** to sit in judgement on sb; **das Jüngste ~** the Last Judgement; **g~lich** *adj* judicial, legal ♦ *adv* judicially, legally; **ein g~liches Nachspiel haben** to finish up in court; **g~lich gegen jdn vorgehen** to take legal proceedings against sb.

Gerichts- *zW:* **~akten** *pl* court records *pl*; **~barkeit** *f* jurisdiction; **~hof** *m* court (of law); **~kosten** *pl* (legal) costs *pl*; **g~medizinisch** *adj* forensic medical *attrib*; **~saal** *m* courtroom; **~stand** *m* court of jurisdiction; **~verfahren** *nt* legal proceedings *pl*; **~verhandlung** *f* court proceedings *pl*; **~vollzieher** *m* bailiff.

gerieben [gə'riːbən] *pp von* **reiben** ♦ *adj* grated; (*umg: schlau*) smart, wily.

geriet *etc* [gə'riːt] *vb siehe* **geraten**.

gering [gə'rɪŋ] *adj* slight, small; (*niedrig*) low; (*Zeit*) short; **~achten** *vt* to think little of; **~fügig** *adj* slight, trivial; **~schätzig** *adj* disparaging; **G~schätzung** *f* disdain.

geringste(r, s) *adj* slightest, least; **nicht im ~n** not in the least *od* slightest.

gerinnen [gə'rɪnən] *unreg vi* to congeal; (*Blut*) to clot; (*Milch*) to curdle.

Gerinnsel [gə'rɪnzəl] (**-s, -**) *nt* clot.

Gerippe [gə'rɪpə] (**-s, -**) *nt* skeleton.

gerissen [gə'rɪsən] *pp von* **reißen** ♦ *adj* wily, smart.

geritten [gə'rɪtən] *pp von* **reiten**.

geritzt [gə'rɪtst] (*umg*) *adj:* **die Sache ist ~** everything's fixed up *od* settled.

Germanist(in) [germa'nɪst(ɪn)] *m(f)* Germanist, German specialist; (*Student*) German student.

Germanistik *f* German (studies *pl*).

gern [gɛrn] *adv* willingly, gladly; (*aber*) **~!** of course!; **~ haben, ~ mögen** to like; **etw ~ tun** to like doing sth; **~ geschehen!** you're welcome!, not at all!; **ein ~ gesehener Gast** a welcome visitor; **ich hätte** *od* **möchte ~ ...** I would like ...; **du kannst mich mal ~ haben!** (*umg*) (you can) go to hell!

gerne ['gɛrnə] *adv* = **gern**.

Gernegroß (**-, -e**) *m* show-off.

gerochen [gə'rɔxən] *pp von* **riechen**.

Geröll [gə'rœl] (**-(e)s, -e**) *nt* scree.

geronnen [gə'rɔnən] *pp von* **rinnen, gerinnen**.

Gerste ['gɛrstə] (**-, -n**) *f* barley.

Gerstenkorn *nt* (*im Auge*) stye.

Gerte ['gɛrtə] (**-, -n**) *f* switch, rod.

gertenschlank *adj* willowy.

Geruch [gə'rʊx] (**-(e)s, -̈e**) *m* smell, odour (*BRIT*), odor (*US*); **g~los** *adj* odourless (*BRIT*), odorless (*US*).

Geruchssinn *m* sense of smell.

Gerücht [gə'rʏçt] (**-(e)s, -e**) *nt* rumour (*BRIT*), rumor (*US*).

geruchtilgend *adj* deodorant.

gerufen [gə'ruːfən] *pp von* **rufen**.

geruhen [gə'ruːən] *vi* to deign.

geruhsam [gə'ruːzaːm] *adj* peaceful; (*Spaziergang etc*) leisurely.

Gerümpel [gə'rʏmpəl] (**-s**) *nt* junk.

gerungen [gə'rʊŋən] *pp von* **ringen**.

Gerüst [gə'rʏst] (**-(e)s, -e**) *nt* (*Bau~*) scaffold(ing); (*fig*) framework.

Ges. *abk* (= *Gesellschaft*) Co., co.

gesalzen [gə'zaltsən] *pp von* **salzen** ♦ *adj* (*fig: umg: Preis, Rechnung*) steep, stiff.

gesamt [gə'zamt] *adj* whole, entire; (*Kosten*) total; (*Werke*) complete; **im ~en** all in all; **G~auflage** *f* gross circulation; **G~ausgabe** *f* complete edition; **G~betrag** *m* total (amount); **~deutsch** *adj* all-German; **G~eindruck** *m* general impression; **G~heit** *f* totality, whole.

Gesamthochschule *f* polytechnic (*BRIT*).

A **Gesamthochschule** *is an institution combining several different kinds of higher education organizations eg. a university, teacher training college and institute of applied science. Students can study for various degrees within the same subject area and it is easier to change course than it is in an individual institution.*

Gesamt- *zW:* **~masse** *f* (*COMM*) total assets *pl*; **~nachfrage** *f* (*COMM*) composite demand; **~schaden** *m* total damage.

Gesamtschule *f* ≈ comprehensive school.

The **Gesamtschule** *is a comprehensive school teaching pupils who have different aims. Traditionally pupils would go to one of three different schools, the* **Gymnasium, Realschule** *or* **Hauptschule,** *depending on ability. The Gesamtschule seeks to avoid the elitist element prevalent in many Gymnasien, but in Germany these schools are still very controversial. Many parents still prefer the traditional system.*

Gesamtwertung *f* (*SPORT*) overall placings *pl*.

gesandt *pp von* **senden**.

Gesandte(r) [gə'zantə(r)] *f(m)* envoy.

Gesandtschaft [gə'zantʃaft] *f* legation.

Gesang [gə'zaŋ] (**-(e)s, -̈e**) *m* song; (*Singen*) singing; **~buch** *nt* (*REL*) hymn book; **~verein** *m* choral society.

Gesäß [gə'zɛːs] (**-es, -e**) *nt* seat, bottom.

gesättigt [gə'zɛtɪçt] *adj* (*CHEM*) saturated.

gesch. *abk* (= *geschieden*) div.

Geschädigte(r) [gə'ʃɛːdɪçtə(r)] *f(m)* victim.

geschaffen [gə'ʃafən] *pp von* **schaffen**.

Geschäft [gə'ʃɛft] (**-(e)s, -e**) *nt* business; (*Laden*) shop; (*~sabschluß*) deal; **mit jdm ins ~ kommen** to do business with sb; **dabei hat er ein ~ gemacht** he made a profit by it; **im ~** at work; (*im Laden*) in the shop; **sein**

~ **verrichten** to do one's business (*euph*).
Geschäftemacher *m* wheeler-dealer.
geschäftig *adj* active, busy; (*pej*) officious.
geschäftlich *adj* commercial ♦ *adv* on business; ~ **unterwegs** away on business.
Geschäfts- *zW:* ~**abschluß** *m* business deal *od* transaction; ~**aufgabe** *f* closure of a/the business; ~**auflösung** *f* closure of a/the business; ~**bedingungen** *pl* terms of business; ~**bereich** *m* (*PARL*) responsibilities *pl*; **Minister ohne** ~**bereich** minister without portfolio; ~**bericht** *m* financial report; ~**computer** *m* business computer; ~**essen** *nt* business lunch; ~**führer** *m* manager; (*Klub*) secretary; ~**geheimnis** *nt* trade secret; ~**inhaber** *m* owner; ~**jahr** *nt* financial year; ~**lage** *f* business conditions *pl*; ~**leitung** *f* management; ~**mann** (-(**e**)**s**, *pl* -**leute**) *m* businessman; **g**~**mäßig** *adj* businesslike; ~**ordnung** *f* standing orders *pl*; **eine Frage zur** ~**ordnung** a question on a point of order; ~**partner** *m* partner; ~**reise** *f* business trip; ~**schluß** *m* closing time; ~**sinn** *m* business sense; ~**stelle** *f* office(s *pl*), place of business; **g**~**tüchtig** *adj* business-minded; ~**viertel** *nt* shopping centre (*BRIT*) *od* center (*US*); (*Banken etc*) business quarter, commercial district; ~**wagen** *m* company car; ~**wesen** *nt* business; ~**zeit** *f* business hours *pl*; ~**zweig** *m* branch (of a business).
geschah *etc* [gə'ʃaː] *vb siehe* **geschehen.**
geschehen [gə'ʃeːən] *unreg vi* to happen; **das geschieht ihm (ganz) recht** it serves him (jolly well (*umg*)) right; **was soll mit ihm/ damit** ~**?** what is to be done with him/it?; **es war um ihn** ~ that was the end of him.
gescheit [gə'ʃaɪt] *adj* clever; (*vernünftig*) sensible.
Geschenk [gə'ʃɛŋk] (-(**e**)**s**, -**e**) *nt* present, gift; ~**artikel** *m* gift; ~**gutschein** *m* gift voucher; ~**packung** *f* gift pack; ~**sendung** *f* gift parcel.
Geschichte [gə'ʃɪçtə] (-, -**n**) *f* story; (*Sache*) affair; (*Historie*) history.
Geschichtenerzähler *m* storyteller.
geschichtlich *adj* historical; (*bedeutungsvoll*) historic.
Geschichtsfälschung *f* falsification of history.
Geschichtsschreiber *m* historian.
Geschick [gə'ʃɪk] (-(**e**)**s**, -**e**) *nt* skill; (*geh: Schicksal*) fate.
Geschicklichkeit *f* skill, dexterity.
Geschicklichkeitsspiel *nt* game of skill.
geschickt *adj* skilful (*BRIT*), skillful (*US*); (*taktisch*) clever; (*beweglich*) agile.
geschieden [gə'ʃiːdən] *pp von* **scheiden** ♦ *adj* divorced.
geschieht [gə'ʃiːt] *vb siehe* **geschehen.**
geschienen [gə'ʃiːnən] *pp von* **scheinen.**

Geschirr [gə'ʃɪr] (-(**e**)**s**, -**e**) *nt* crockery; (*Küchen*~) pots and pans *pl*; (*Pferde*~) harness; ~**spülmaschine** *f* dishwasher; ~**tuch** *nt* tea towel (*BRIT*), dishtowel (*US*).
geschissen [gə'ʃɪsən] *pp von* **scheißen.**
geschlafen [gə'ʃlaːfən] *pp von* **schlafen.**
geschlagen [gə'ʃlaːgən] *pp von* **schlagen.**
geschlaucht [gə'ʃlauxt] *adv:* ~ **sein** (*umg*) to be exhausted *od* knackered.
Geschlecht [gə'ʃlɛçt] (-(**e**)**s**, -**er**) *nt* sex; (*GRAM*) gender; (*Gattung*) race; (*Abstammung*) lineage; **g**~**lich** *adj* sexual.
Geschlechts- *zW:* ~**krankheit** *f* sexually-transmitted disease; **g**~**reif** *adj* sexually mature; **g**~**spezifisch** *adj* (*SOZIOLOGIE*) sex-specific; ~**teil** *nt od m* genitals *pl*; ~**verkehr** *m* sexual intercourse; ~**wort** *nt* (*GRAM*) article.
geschlichen [gə'ʃlɪçən] *pp von* **schleichen.**
geschliffen [gə'ʃlɪfən] *pp von* **schleifen.**
geschlossen [gə'ʃlɔsən] *pp von* **schließen** ♦ *adj:* ~**e Gesellschaft** (*Fest*) private party ♦ *adv:* ~ **hinter jdm stehen** to stand solidly behind sb; ~**e Ortschaft** built-up area.
geschlungen [gə'ʃlʊŋən] *pp von* **schlingen.**
Geschmack [gə'ʃmak] (-(**e**)**s**, ⁼**e**) *m* taste; **nach jds** ~ to sb's taste; ~ **an etw** *dat* **finden** to (come to) like sth; **je nach** ~ to one's own taste; **er hat einen guten** ~ (*fig*) he has good taste; **g**~**los** *adj* tasteless; (*fig*) in bad taste.
Geschmacks- *zW:* ~**sache** *f* matter of taste; ~**sinn** *m* sense of taste; ~**verirrung** *f:* **unter** ~**verirrung leiden** (*ironisch*) to have no taste.
geschmackvoll *adj* tasteful.
Geschmeide [gə'ʃmaɪdə] (-**s**, -) *nt* jewellery (*BRIT*), jewelry (*US*).
geschmeidig *adj* supple; (*formbar*) malleable.
Geschmeiß *nt* vermin *pl*.
Geschmiere [gə'ʃmiːrə] (-**s**) *nt* scrawl; (*Bild*) daub.
geschmissen [gə'ʃmɪsən] *pp von* **schmeißen.**
geschmolzen [gə'ʃmɔltsən] *pp von* **schmelzen.**
Geschnetzelte(s) [gə'ʃnɛtsəltə(s)] *nt* (*KOCH*) meat cut into strips and stewed to produce a thick sauce.
geschnitten [gə'ʃnɪtən] *pp von* **schneiden.**
geschoben [gə'ʃoːbən] *pp von* **schieben.**
geschollen [gə'ʃɔlən] *pp von* **schallen.**
gescholten [gə'ʃɔltən] *pp von* **schelten.**
Geschöpf [gə'ʃœpf] (-(**e**)**s**, -**e**) *nt* creature.
geschoren [gə'ʃoːrən] *pp von* **scheren.**
Geschoß [gə'ʃɔs] (-**sses**, -**sse**) *nt* (*MIL*) projectile; (*Rakete*) missile; (*Stockwerk*) floor.
geschossen [gə'ʃɔsən] *pp von* **schießen.**
geschraubt [gə'ʃraupt] *adj* stilted, artificial.
Geschrei [gə'ʃraɪ] (-**s**) *nt* cries *pl*, shouting; (*fig: Aufheben*) noise, fuss.
geschrieben [gə'ʃriːbən] *pp von* **schreiben.**
geschrie(e)n [gə'ʃriː(ə)n] *pp von* **schreien.**
geschritten [gə'ʃrɪtən] *pp von* **schreiten.**
geschunden [gə'ʃʊndən] *pp von* **schinden.**

Geschütz [gə'ʃyts] (**-es, -e**) *nt* gun, piece of artillery; **ein schweres ~ auffahren** (*fig*) to bring out the big guns; **~feuer** *nt* artillery fire, gunfire.

geschützt *adj* protected; (*Winkel, Ecke*) sheltered.

Geschw. *abk* = **Geschwister.**

Geschwader [gə'ʃvaːdər] (**-s, -**) *nt* (*NAUT*) squadron; (*AVIAT*) group.

Geschwafel [gə'ʃvaːfəl] (**-s**) *nt* silly talk.

Geschwätz [gə'ʃvɛts] (**-es**) *nt* chatter; (*Klatsch*) gossip.

geschwätzig *adj* talkative; **G~keit** *f* talkativeness.

geschweige [gə'ʃvaɪɡə] *adv:* ~ (**denn**) let alone, not to mention.

geschwiegen [gə'ʃviːɡən] *pp von* **schweigen.**

geschwind [gə'ʃvɪnt] *adj* quick, swift.

Geschwindigkeit [gə'ʃvɪndɪçkaɪt] *f* speed, velocity.

Geschwindigkeits- *zW:* **~begrenzung** *f*, **~beschränkung** *f* speed limit; **~messer** *m* (*AUT*) speedometer; **~überschreitung** *f* speeding.

Geschwister [gə'ʃvɪstər] *pl* brothers and sisters *pl.*

geschwollen [gə'ʃvɔlən] *pp von* **schwellen** ♦ *adj* pompous.

geschwommen [gə'ʃvɔmən] *pp von* **schwimmen.**

geschworen [gə'ʃvoːrən] *pp von* **schwören.**

Geschworene(r) *f(m)* juror; **die Geschworenen** *pl* the jury.

Geschwulst [gə'ʃvʊlst] (**-, ⁻e**) *f* growth, tumour.

geschwunden [gə'ʃvʊndən] *pp von* **schwinden.**

geschwungen [gə'ʃvʊŋən] *pp von* **schwingen** ♦ *adj* curved.

Geschwür [gə'ʃvyːr] (**-(e)s, -e**) *nt* ulcer; (*Furunkel*) boil.

gesehen [gə'zeːən] *pp von* **sehen.**

Geselle [gə'zɛlə] (**-n, -n**) *m* fellow; (*Handwerks~*) journeyman.

gesellen *vr:* **sich zu jdm** ~ to join sb.

Gesellenbrief *m* articles *pl.*

Gesellenprüfung *f* examination to become a journeyman.

gesellig *adj* sociable; **~es Beisammensein** get-together; **G~keit** *f* sociability.

Gesellschaft *f* society; (*Begleitung, COMM*) company; (*Abend~ etc*) party; (*pej*) crowd (*umg*); (*Kreis von Menschen*) group of people; **in schlechte ~ geraten** to get into bad company; **geschlossene ~** private party; **jdm ~ leisten** to keep sb company.

Gesellschafter(in) (**-s, -**) *m(f)* shareholder; (*Partner*) partner.

gesellschaftlich *adj* social.

Gesellschafts- *zW:* **~anzug** *m* evening dress; **g~fähig** *adj* socially acceptable; **~ordnung** *f* social structure; **~reise** *f* group tour; **~schicht** *f* social stratum; **~system** *nt* social system.

gesessen [gə'zɛsən] *pp von* **sitzen.**

Gesetz [gə'zɛts] (**-es, -e**) *nt* law; (*PARL*) act; (*Satzung, Regel*) rule; **vor dem ~ in** (the eyes of) the law; **nach dem ~ under** the law; **das oberste ~ (der Wirtschaft etc)** the golden rule (of industry *etc*); **~blatt** *nt* law gazette; **~buch** *nt* statute book; **~entwurf** *m* bill.

Gesetzeshüter *m* (*ironisch*) guardian of the law.

Gesetzesvorlage *f* bill.

Gesetz- *zW:* **g~gebend** *adj* legislative; **~geber** (**-s, -**) *m* legislator; **~gebung** *f* legislation; **g~lich** *adj* legal, lawful; **~lichkeit** *f* legality, lawfulness; **g~los** *adj* lawless; **g~mäßig** *adj* lawful.

gesetzt *adj* (*Mensch*) sedate ♦ *konj:* ~ **den Fall** ... assuming (that) ...

gesetzwidrig *adj* illegal; (*unrechtmäßig*) unlawful.

ges. gesch. *abk* (= *gesetzlich geschützt*) reg.

Gesicht [gə'zɪçt] (**-(e)s, -er**) *nt* face; **das Zweite ~** second sight; **das ist mir nie zu ~ gekommen** I've never laid eyes on that; **jdn zu ~ bekommen** to clap eyes on sb; **jdm etw ins ~ sagen** to tell sb sth to his face; **sein wahres ~ zeigen** to show (o.s. in) one's true colours; **jdm wie aus dem ~ geschnitten sein** to be the spitting image of sb.

Gesichts- *zW:* **~ausdruck** *m* (facial) expression; **~farbe** *f* complexion; **~packung** *f* face pack; **~punkt** *m* point of view; **~wasser** *nt* face lotion; **~züge** *pl* features *pl.*

Gesindel [gə'zɪndəl] (**-s**) *nt* rabble.

gesinnt [gə'zɪnt] *adj* disposed, minded.

Gesinnung [gə'zɪnʊŋ] *f* disposition; (*Ansicht*) views *pl.*

Gesinnungs- *zW:* **~genosse** *m* like-minded person; **~losigkeit** *f* lack of conviction; **~schnüffelei** (*pej*) *f:* **~schnüffelei betreiben** to pry into people's political convictions; **~wandel** *m* change of opinion.

gesittet [gə'zɪtət] *adj* well-mannered.

gesoffen [gə'zɔfən] *pp von* **saufen.**

gesogen [gə'zoːɡən] *pp von* **saugen.**

gesollt [gə'zɔlt] *pp von* **sollen.**

gesondert [gə'zɔndərt] *adj* separate.

gesonnen [gə'zɔnən] *pp von* **sinnen.**

gespalten [gə'ʃpaltən] *adj* (*Bewußtsein*) split; (*Lippe*) cleft.

Gespann [gə'ʃpan] (**-(e)s, -e**) *nt* team; (*umg*) couple.

gespannt *adj* tense, strained; (*neugierig*) curious; (*begierig*) eager; **ich bin ~, ob** I wonder if *od* whether; **auf etw/jdn ~ sein** to look forward to sth/to meeting sb; **ich bin ~ wie ein Flitzebogen** (*hum: umg*) I'm on tenterhooks.

Gespenst [gə'ʃpɛnst] (**-(e)s, -er**) *nt* ghost; (*fig: Gefahr*) spectre (*BRIT*), specter (*US*); **~er**

sehen (fig: umg) to imagine things.
gespensterhaft, gespenstisch adj ghostly.
gespie(e)n [gəˈʃpiː(ə)n] pp von **speien.**
gespielt [gəˈʃpiːlt] adj feigned.
gesponnen [gəˈʃpɔnən] pp von **spinnen.**
Gespött [gəˈʃpœt] (-(e)s) nt mockery; **zum ~ werden** to become a laughing stock.
Gespräch [gəˈʃprɛːç] (-(e)s, -e) nt conversation; (Diskussion) discussion; (Anruf) call; **zum ~ werden** to become a topic of conversation; **ein ~ unter vier Augen** a confidential od private talk; **mit jdm ins ~ kommen** to get into conversation with sb; (fig) to establish a dialogue with sb.
gesprächig adj talkative; **G~keit** f talkativeness.
Gesprächs- zW: **~einheit** f (TEL) unit; **~gegenstand** m topic; **~partner** m: **mein ~partner bei den Verhandlungen** my opposite number at the talks; **~stoff** m topics pl; **~thema** nt subject od topic (of conversation).
gesprochen [gəˈʃprɔxən] pp von **sprechen.**
gesprossen [gəˈʃprɔsən] pp von **sprießen.**
gesprungen [gəˈʃprʊŋən] pp von **springen.**
Gespür [gəˈʃpyːr] (-s) nt feeling.
gest. abk (= gestorben) dec.
Gestalt [gəˈʃtalt] (-, -en) f form, shape; (Person) figure; (LITER: pej: Mensch) character; **in ~ von** in the form of; **~ annehmen** to take shape.
gestalten vt (formen) to shape, form; (organisieren) to arrange, organize ♦ vr: **sich ~ (zu)** to turn out (to be); **etw interessanter** etc **~** to make sth more interesting etc.
Gestaltung f formation; organization.
gestanden [gəˈʃtandən] pp von **stehen, gestehen.**
geständig [gəˈʃtɛndɪç] adj: **~ sein** to have confessed.
Geständnis [gəˈʃtɛntnɪs] (-ses, -se) nt confession.
Gestank [gəˈʃtaŋk] (-(e)s) m stench.
gestatten [gəˈʃtatən] vt to permit, allow; **~ Sie?** may I?; **sich** dat **~, etw zu tun** to take the liberty of doing sth.
Geste [ˈɡɛstə] (-, -n) f gesture.
Gesteck [gəˈʃtɛk] (-(e)s, -e) nt flower arrangement.
gestehen [gəˈʃteːən] unreg vt to confess; **offen gestanden** quite frankly.
Gestein [gəˈʃtaɪn] (-(e)s, -e) nt rock.
Gestell [gəˈʃtɛl] (-(e)s, -e) nt stand; (Regal) shelf; (Bett~, Brillen~) frame.
gestellt adj (unecht) posed.
gestern [ˈɡɛstərn] adv yesterday; **~ abend/ morgen** yesterday evening/morning; **er ist nicht von ~** (umg) he wasn't born yesterday.
gestiefelt [gəˈʃtiːfəlt] adj: **der G~e Kater** Puss-in-Boots.
gestiegen [gəˈʃtiːɡən] pp von **steigen.**

Gestik (-) f gestures pl.
gestikulieren [ɡɛstikuˈliːrən] vi to gesticulate.
Gestirn [gəˈʃtɪrn] (-(e)s, -e) nt star.
gestoben [gəˈʃtoːbən] pp von **stieben.**
Gestöber [gəˈʃtøːbər] (-s, -) nt flurry; (länger) blizzard.
gestochen [gəˈʃtɔxən] pp von **stechen** ♦ adj (Handschrift) clear, neat.
gestohlen [gəˈʃtoːlən] pp von **stehlen** ♦ adj: **der/das kann mir ~ bleiben** (umg) he/it can go hang.
gestorben [gəˈʃtɔrbən] pp von **sterben.**
gestört [gəˈʃtøːrt] adj disturbed; (Rundfunkempfang) poor, with a lot of interference.
gestoßen [gəˈʃtoːsən] pp von **stoßen.**
Gestotter [gəˈʃtɔtər] (-s) nt stuttering, stammering.
Gesträuch [gəˈʃtrɔyç] (-(e)s, -e) nt shrubbery, bushes pl.
gestreift [gəˈʃtraɪft] adj striped.
gestrichen [gəˈʃtrɪçən] pp von **streichen** ♦ adj: **~ voll** (genau voll) level; (sehr voll) full to the brim; **ein ~er Teelöffel voll** a level teaspoon(ful).
gestrig [ˈɡɛstrɪç] adj yesterday's.
gestritten [gəˈʃtrɪtən] pp von **streiten.**
Gestrüpp [gəˈʃtryp] (-(e)s, -e) nt undergrowth.
gestunken [gəˈʃtʊŋkən] pp von **stinken.**
Gestüt [gəˈʃtyːt] (-(e)s, -e) nt stud farm.
Gesuch [gəˈzuːx] (-(e)s, -e) nt petition; (Antrag) application.
gesucht adj (begehrt) sought after.
gesund [gəˈzʊnt] adj healthy; **wieder ~ werden** to get better; **~ und munter** hale and hearty; **jdn ~ schreiben** to certify sb (as) fit; **G~heit** f health; (Sportlichkeit, fig) healthiness; **G~heit!** bless you!; **bei guter G~heit** in good health; **~heitlich** adj health attrib, physical ♦ adv physically; **wie geht es Ihnen ~heitlich?** how's your health?
Gesundheits- zW: **~amt** nt public health department; **~apostel** m (ironisch) health freak (umg); **~fürsorge** f health care; **~reform** f health service reforms pl; **~risiko** nt health hazard; **g~schädlich** adj unhealthy; **~wesen** nt health service; **~zeugnis** nt health certificate; **~zustand** m state of health.
gesungen [gəˈzʊŋən] pp von **singen.**
gesunken [gəˈzʊŋkən] pp von **sinken.**
getan [gəˈtaːn] pp von **tun** ♦ adj: **nach ~er Arbeit** when the day's work is done.
Getier [gəˈtiːər] (-(e)s, -e) nt (Tiere, bes Insekten) creatures pl; (einzelnes) creature.
Getöse [gəˈtøːzə] (-s) nt din, racket.
getragen [gəˈtraːɡən] pp von **tragen.**
Getränk [gəˈtrɛŋk] (-(e)s, -e) nt drink.
Getränkeautomat m drinks machine od dispenser.
Getränkekarte f (in Café) list of beverages; (in Restaurant) wine list.

getrauen [gə'trauən] *vr* to dare.
Getreide [gə'traɪdə] (**-s, -**) *nt* cereal, grain;
~**speicher** *m* granary.
getrennt [gə'trɛnt] *adj* separate; ~ **leben** to be
separated, live apart.
getreten [gə'treːtən] *pp von* **treten.**
getreu [gə'trɔy] *adj* faithful.
Getriebe [gə'triːbə] (**-s, -**) *nt* (*Leute*) bustle;
(*AUT*) gearbox.
getrieben *pp von* **treiben.**
Getriebeöl *nt* transmission oil.
getroffen [gə'trɔfən] *pp von* **treffen.**
getrogen [gə'troːgən] *pp von* **trügen.**
getrost [gə'troːst] *adv* confidently; ~ **sterben**
to die in peace; **du kannst dich** ~ **auf ihn
verlassen** you need have no fears about
relying on him.
getrunken [gə'trʊŋkən] *pp von* **trinken.**
Getto ['gɛto] (**-s, -s**) *nt* ghetto.
Getue [gə'tuːə] (**-s**) *nt* fuss.
Getümmel [gə'tʏməl] (**-s**) *nt* turmoil.
geübt [gə'yːpt] *adj* experienced.
GEW (**-**) *f abk* (= *Gewerkschaft Erziehung und
Wissenschaft*) *union of employees in
education and science.*
Gew. *abk* = **Gewerkschaft.**
Gewächs [gə'vɛks] (**-es, -e**) *nt* growth;
(*Pflanze*) plant.
gewachsen [gə'vaksən] *pp von* **wachsen** ♦ *adj:*
jdm/etw ~ **sein** to be sb's equal/equal to
sth.
Gewächshaus *nt* greenhouse.
gewagt [gə'vaːkt] *adj* daring, risky.
gewählt [gə'vɛːlt] *adj* (*Sprache*) refined,
elegant.
gewahr [gə'vaːr] *adj:* **eine** *od* **einer Sache** *gen* ~
werden to become aware of sth.
Gewähr [gə'vɛːr] (**-**) *f* guarantee; **keine**
~ **übernehmen für** to accept no
responsibility for; **die Angabe erfolgt ohne**
~ this information is supplied without
liability.
gewähren *vt* to grant; (*geben*) to provide; **jdn**
~ **lassen** not to stop sb.
gewährleisten *vt* to guarantee.
Gewahrsam [gə'vaːrzaːm] (**-s, -e**) *m*
safekeeping; (*Polizei~*) custody.
Gewährsmann *m* informant, source.
Gewährung *f* granting.
Gewalt [gə'valt] (**-, -en**) *f* power; (*große Kraft*)
force; (~*taten*) violence; **mit aller** ~ with all
one's might; **die ausübende/
gesetzgebende/richterliche** ~ the
executive/legislature/judiciary; **elterliche** ~
parental authority; **höhere** ~ acts/an act of
God; ~**anwendung** *f* use of force.
Gewaltenteilung *f* separation of powers.
Gewaltherrschaft *f* tyranny.
gewaltig *adj* tremendous; (*Irrtum*) huge; **sich**
~ **irren** to be very much mistaken.
Gewalt- *zW:* **g~los** *adj* non-violent ♦ *adv*
without force/violence; ~**marsch** *m* forced

march; ~**monopol** *nt* monopoly on the use
of force; **g~sam** *adj* forcible; **g~tätig** *adj*
violent; ~**verbrechen** *nt* crime of violence;
~**verzicht** *m* non-aggression.
Gewand [gə'vant] (**-(e)s, -̈er**) *nt* garment.
gewandt [gə'vant] *pp von* **wenden** ♦ *adj* deft,
skilful (*BRIT*), skillful (*US*); (*erfahren*)
experienced; **G~heit** *f* dexterity, skill.
gewann *etc* [gə'van] *vb siehe* **gewinnen.**
gewaschen [gə'vaʃən] *pp von* **waschen.**
Gewässer [gə'vɛsər] (**-s, -**) *nt* waters *pl.*
Gewebe [gə'veːbə] (**-s, -**) *nt* (*Stoff*) fabric;
(*BIOL*) tissue.
Gewehr [gə'veːr] (**-(e)s, -e**) *nt* (*Flinte*) rifle;
(*Schrotbüchse*) shotgun; ~**lauf** *m* rifle barrel;
barrel of a shotgun.
Geweih [gə'vaɪ] (**-(e)s, -e**) *nt* antlers *pl.*
Gewerbe [gə'vɛrbə] (**-s, -**) *nt* trade,
occupation; **Handel und** ~ trade and
industry; **fahrendes** ~ mobile trade;
~**aufsichtsamt** *nt* ≈ factory inspectorate;
~**schein** *m* trading licence; ~**schule** *f*
technical school; **g~treibend** *adj* carrying on
a trade.
gewerblich *adj* industrial.
gewerbsmäßig *adj* professional.
Gewerbszweig *m* line of trade.
Gewerkschaft [gə'vɛrkʃaft] *f* trade *od* labor
(*US*) union.
Gewerkschaft(l)er(in) *m(f)* trade *od* labor
(*US*) unionist.
gewerkschaftlich *adj:* **wir haben uns**
~ **organisiert** we organized ourselves into a
union.
Gewerkschaftsbund *m* federation of trade
od labor (*US*) unions, ≈ Trades Union
Congress (*BRIT*), Federation of Labor (*US*).
gewesen [gə'veːzən] *pp von* **sein.**
gewichen [gə'vɪçən] *pp von* **weichen.**
Gewicht [gə'vɪçt] (**-(e)s, -e**) *nt* weight; (*fig*)
importance.
gewichten *vt* to evaluate.
Gewichtheben (**-s**) *nt* (*SPORT*) weight-
lifting.
gewichtig *adj* weighty.
Gewichtsklasse *f* (*SPORT*) weight
(category).
gewieft [gə'viːft] (*umg*) *adj* shrewd, cunning.
gewiesen [gə'viːzən] *pp von* **weisen.**
gewillt [gə'vɪlt] *adj* willing, prepared.
Gewimmel [gə'vɪməl] (**-s**) *nt* swarm; (*Menge*)
crush.
Gewinde [gə'vɪndə] (**-s, -**) *nt* (*Kranz*) wreath;
(*von Schraube*) thread.
Gewinn [gə'vɪn] (**-(e)s, -e**) *m* profit; (*bei Spiel*)
winnings *pl;* **etw mit** ~ **verkaufen** to sell sth
at a profit; **aus etw** ~ **schlagen** (*umg*) to
make a profit out of sth; ~**anteil** *m* (*COMM*)
dividend; ~**ausschüttung** *f* profit draw;
~**beteiligung** *f* profit-sharing; **g~bringend**
adj profitable; ~**chancen** *pl* (*beim Wetten*)
odds *pl.*

gewinnen *unreg vt* to win; (*erwerben*) to gain; (*Kohle, Öl*) to extract ♦ *vi* to win; (*profitieren*) to gain; **jdn (für etw)** ~ to win sb over (to sth); **an etw** *dat* ~ to gain in sth.
gewinnend *adj* winning, attractive.
Gewinner(in) (**-s,** -) *m(f)* winner.
Gewinn- *zW:* **~(n)ummer** *f* winning number; **~spanne** *f* profit margin; **~sucht** *f* love of gain; **~- und Verlustrechnung** *f* profit and loss account.
Gewinnung *f* (*von Kohle etc*) mining; (*von Zucker etc*) extraction.
Gewirr [gə'vɪr] (**-(e)s,** -e) *nt* tangle; (*von Straßen*) maze.
gewiß [gə'vɪs] *adj* certain ♦ *adv* certainly; **in gewissem Maße** to a certain extent.
Gewissen [gə'vɪsən] (**-s,** -) *nt* conscience; **jdm ins** ~ **reden** to have a serious talk with sb; **g~haft** *adj* conscientious; **~haftigkeit** *f* conscientiousness; **g~los** *adj* unscrupulous.
Gewissens- *zW:* **~bisse** *pl* pangs of conscience *pl*, qualms *pl*; **~frage** *f* matter of conscience; **~freiheit** *f* freedom of conscience; **~konflikt** *m* moral conflict.
gewissermaßen [gəvɪsər'maːsən] *adv* more or less, in a way.
Gewißheit *f* certainty; **sich** *dat* ~ **verschaffen** to find out for certain.
gewißlich *adv* surely.
Gewitter [gə'vɪtər] (**-s,** -) *nt* thunderstorm.
gewittern *vi unpers:* **es gewittert** there's a thunderstorm.
gewitterschwül *adj* sultry and thundery.
Gewitterwolke *f* thundercloud; (*fig: umg*) storm cloud.
gewitzt [gə'vɪtst] *adj* shrewd, cunning.
gewoben [gə'voːbən] *pp von* **weben.**
gewogen [gə'voːgən] *pp von* **wiegen** ♦ *adj* (+*dat*) well-disposed (towards).
gewöhnen [gə'vøːnən] *vt:* **jdn an etw** *akk* ~ to accustom sb to sth; (*erziehen zu*) to teach sb sth ♦ *vr:* **sich an etw** *akk* ~ to get used *od* accustomed to sth.
Gewohnheit [gə'voːnhaɪt] *f* habit; (*Brauch*) custom; **aus** ~ from habit; **zur** ~ **werden** to become a habit; **sich** *dat* **etw zur** ~ **machen** to make a habit of sth.
Gewohnheits- *in zW* habitual; **~mensch** *m* creature of habit; **~recht** *nt* common law; **~tier** (*umg*) *nt* creature of habit.
gewöhnlich [gə'vøːnlɪç] *adj* usual; (*durchschnittlich*) ordinary; (*pej*) common; **wie** ~ as usual.
gewohnt [gə'voːnt] *adj* usual; **etw** ~ **sein** to be used to sth.
Gewöhnung *f:* ~ **(an** +*akk*) getting accustomed (to); (*das Angewöhnen*) training (in).
Gewölbe [gə'vœlbə] (**-s,** -) *nt* vault.
gewollt [gə'vɔlt] *pp von* **wollen** ♦ *adj* forced, artificial.
gewonnen [gə'vɔnən] *pp von* **gewinnen.**

geworben [gə'vɔrbən] *pp von* **werben.**
geworden [gə'vɔrdən] *pp von* **werden.**
geworfen [gə'vɔrfən] *pp von* **werfen.**
gewrungen [gə'vrʊŋən] *pp von* **wringen.**
Gewühl [gə'vyːl] (**-(e)s)** *nt* throng.
gewunden [gə'vʊndən] *pp von* **winden.**
gewunken [gə'vʊŋkən] *pp von* **winken.**
Gewürz [gə'vʏrts] (**-es,** -e) *nt* spice; (*Pfeffer, Salz*) seasoning; **~gurke** *f* pickled gherkin; **~nelke** *f* clove.
gewußt [gə'vʊst] *pp von* **wissen.**
gez. *abk* (= *gezeichnet*) signed.
gezackt [gə'tsakt] *adj* (*Fels*) jagged; (*Blatt*) serrated.
gezähnt [gə'tsɛːnt] *adj* serrated, toothed.
gezeichnet [gə'tsaɪçnət] *adj* marked.
Gezeiten [gə'tsaɪtən] *pl* tides *pl*.
Gezeter [gə'tseːtər] (**-s)** *nt* nagging.
gezielt [gə'tsiːlt] *adj* (*Frage, Maßnahme*) specific; (*Hilfe*) well-directed; (*Kritik*) pointed.
geziemen [gə'tsiːmən] *vr unpers* to be fitting.
geziemend *adj* proper.
geziert [gə'tsiːrt] *adj* affected; **G~heit** *f* affectation.
gezogen [gə'tsoːgən] *pp von* **ziehen.**
Gezwitscher [gə'tsvɪtʃər] (**-s)** *nt* twitter(ing), chirping.
gezwungen [gə'tsvʊŋən] *pp von* **zwingen** ♦ *adj* forced; (*Atmosphäre*) strained.
gezwungenermaßen *adv* of necessity; **etw** ~ **tun** to be forced to do sth, do sth of necessity.
GG *abk* = **Grundgesetz.**
ggf. *abk* = **gegebenenfalls.**
Ghana ['gaːna] (**-s)** *nt* Ghana.
Ghettoblaster ['gɛtoblaːstər] (**-s,** -s) *m* ghettoblaster.
Gibraltar [gi'braltar] (**-s)** *nt* Gibraltar.
gibst [giːpst] *vb siehe* **geben.**
gibt *vb siehe* **geben.**
Gicht [gɪçt] (-) *f* gout; **g~isch** *adj* gouty.
Giebel ['giːbəl] (**-s,** -) *m* gable; **~dach** *nt* gable(d) roof; **~fenster** *nt* gable window.
Gier [giːr] (-) *f* greed.
gierig *adj* greedy.
Gießbach *m* torrent.
gießen ['giːsən] *unreg vt* to pour; (*Blumen*) to water; (*Metall*) to cast; (*Wachs*) to mould ♦ *vi unpers:* **es gießt in Strömen** it's pouring down.
Gießerei [giːsə'raɪ] *f* foundry.
Gießkanne *f* watering can.
Gift [gɪft] (**-(e)s,** -e) *nt* poison; **das ist** ~ **für ihn** (*umg*) that is very bad for him; **darauf kannst du** ~ **nehmen** (*umg*) you can bet your life on it; **g~grün** *adj* bilious green.
giftig *adj* poisonous; (*fig: boshaft*) venomous.
Gift- *zW:* **~müll** *m* toxic waste; **~pilz** *m* poisonous toadstool; **~stoff** *m* toxic substance; **~wolke** *f* poisonous cloud; **~zahn** *m* fang; **~zwerg** (*umg*) *m* spiteful

little devil.

Gigabyte ['gɪgabaɪt] *nt* (*COMPUT*) gigabyte.

Gilde ['gɪldə] (**-, -n**) *f* guild.

gilt [gɪlt] *vb siehe* **gelten.**

ging *etc* [gɪŋ] *vb siehe* **gehen.**

Ginseng ['gɪnzɛŋ] (**-s, -s**) *m* ginseng.

Ginster ['gɪnstər] (**-s, -**) *m* broom.

Gipfel ['gɪpfəl] (**-s, -**) *m* summit, peak; (*fig*) height; **das ist der ~!** (*umg*) that's the limit!; **~konferenz** *f* (*POL*) summit conference.

gipfeln *vi* to culminate.

Gipfeltreffen *nt* summit (meeting).

Gips [gɪps] (**-es, ̦e**) *m* plaster; (*MED*) plaster (of Paris); **~abdruck** *m* plaster cast; **~bein** (*umg*) *nt* leg in plaster; **g~en** *vt* to plaster; **~figur** *f* plaster figure; **~verband** *m* plaster (cast).

Giraffe [gi'rafə] (**-, -n**) *f* giraffe.

Girlande [gɪr'landə] (**-, -n**) *f* garland.

Giro ['ʒiːro] (**-s, -s**) *nt* giro; **~konto** *nt* current account (*BRIT*), checking account (*US*).

girren ['gɪrən] *vi* to coo.

Gis [gɪs] (**-, -**) *nt* (*MUS*) G sharp.

Gischt [gɪʃt] (**-(e)s, -e**) *m od f* spray, foam.

Gitarre [gi'tarə] (**-, -n**) *f* guitar.

Gitter ['gɪtər] (**-s, -**) *nt* grating, bars *pl*; (*für Pflanzen*) trellis; (*Zaun*) railing(s); **~bett** *nt* cot (*BRIT*), crib (*US*); **~fenster** *nt* barred window; **~zaun** *m* railing(s).

Glacéhandschuh [gla'seːhantʃuː] *m* kid glove.

Gladiole [gladi'oːlə] (**-, -n**) *f* gladiolus.

Glanz [glants] (**-es**) *m* shine, lustre (*BRIT*), luster (*US*); (*fig*) splendour (*BRIT*), splendor (*US*); **~abzug** *m* (*PHOT*) glossy *od* gloss print.

glänzen ['glɛntsən] *vi* to shine (*also fig*), gleam.

glänzend *adj* shining; (*fig*) brilliant; **wir haben uns ~ amüsiert** we had a marvellous *od* great time.

Glanz- *zW:* **~lack** *m* gloss (paint); **~leistung** *f* brilliant achievement; **g~los** *adj* dull; **~stück** *nt* pièce de résistance; **~zeit** *f* heyday.

Glas [glaːs] (**-es, ̈er**) *nt* glass; (*Brillen~*) lens *sing*; **zwei ~ Wein** two glasses of wine; **~bläser** *m* glass blower; **~er** (**-s, -**) *m* glazier; **~faser** *f* fibreglass (*BRIT*), fiberglass (*US*); **~faserkabel** *nt* optical fibre (*BRIT*) *od* fiber (*US*) cable.

Glasgow ['glaːsgoʊ] *nt* Glasgow.

glasieren [gla'ziːrən] *vt* to glaze.

glasig *adj* glassy; (*Zwiebeln*) transparent.

glasklar *adj* crystal clear.

Glasscheibe *f* pane.

Glasur [gla'zuːr] *f* glaze; (*KOCH*) icing, frosting (*bes US*).

glatt [glat] *adj* smooth; (*rutschig*) slippery; (*Absage*) flat; (*Lüge*) downright; (*Haar*) straight; (*MED: Bruch*) clean; (*pej: allzu gewandt*) smooth, slick.

Glätte ['glɛtə] (**-, -n**) *f* smoothness;

slipperiness.

Glatteis *nt* (black) ice; **„Vorsicht ~!"** "danger, black ice!"; **jdn aufs ~ führen** (*fig*) to take sb for a ride.

glätten *vt* to smooth out.

glatt- *zW:* **~gehen** *unreg vi* to go smoothly; **~rasiert** *adj* (*Mann, Kinn*) clean-shaven; **~streichen** *unreg vt* to smooth out.

Glatze ['glatsə] (**-, -n**) *f* bald head; **eine ~ bekommen** to go bald.

glatzköpfig *adj* bald.

Glaube ['glaubə] (**-ns, -n**) *m:* **~ (an +akk)** faith (in); (*Überzeugung*) belief (in); **den ~n an jdn/etw verlieren** to lose faith in sb/sth.

glauben *vt, vi* to believe; (*meinen*) to think; **jdm ~** to believe sb; **~ an +akk** to believe in; **jdm (etw) aufs Wort ~** to take sb's word (for sth); **wer's glaubt, wird selig** (*ironisch*) a likely story.

Glaubens- *zW:* **~bekenntnis** *nt* creed; **~freiheit** *f* religious freedom; **~gemeinschaft** *f* religious sect; (*christliche*) denomination.

glaubhaft ['glaubhaft] *adj* credible; **jdm etw ~ machen** to satisfy sb of sth.

Glaubhaftigkeit *f* credibility.

gläubig ['glɔybɪç] *adj* (*REL*) devout; (*vertrauensvoll*) trustful; **G~e(r)** *f(m)* believer; **die Gläubigen** *pl* the faithful.

Gläubiger(in) (**-s, -**) *m(f)* creditor.

glaubwürdig ['glaubvyrdɪç] *adj* credible; (*Mensch*) trustworthy; **G~keit** *f* credibility, trustworthiness.

gleich [glaɪç] *adj* equal; (*identisch*) (the) same, identical ♦ *adv* equally; (*sofort*) straight away; (*bald*) in a minute; (*räumlich*): **~ hinter dem Haus** just behind the house; (*zeitlich*): **~ am Anfang** at the very beginning; **es ist mir ~** it's all the same to me; **zu ~en Teilen** in equal parts; **das ~e, aber nicht dasselbe Auto** a similar car, but not the same one; **ganz ~ wer/was** *etc* no matter who/what *etc*; **2 mal 2 ~ 4** 2 times 2 is *od* equals 4; **bis ~!** see you soon!; **wie war doch ~ Ihr Name?** what was your name again?; **es ist ~ drei Uhr** it's very nearly three o'clock; **sie sind ~ groß** they are the same size; **~ nach/an** right after/at; **~altrig** *adj* of the same age; **~artig** *adj* similar; **~bedeutend** *adj* synonymous; **~berechtigt** *adj* with equal rights; **G~berechtigung** *f* equal rights *pl*; **~bleibend** *adj* constant; **bei ~bleibendem Gehalt** when one's salary stays the same.

gleichen *unreg vi:* **jdm/etw ~** to be like sb/sth ♦ *vr* to be alike.

gleichermaßen *adv* equally.

gleich- *zW:* **~falls** *adv* likewise; **danke ~falls!** the same to you; **G~förmigkeit** *f* uniformity; **~gesinnt** *adj* like-minded; **~gestellt** *adj:* **rechtlich ~gestellt** equal in law; **G~gewicht** *nt* equilibrium, balance; **jdm aus dem G~gewicht bringen** to throw sb off balance; ~**gültig** adj indifferent; (unbedeutend) unimportant; **G~gültigkeit** f indifference; **G~heit** f equality; (Identität) identity; (INDUSTRIE) parity; **G~heitsprinzip** nt principle of equality; **G~heitszeichen** nt (MATH) equals sign; ~**kommen** unreg vi +dat to be equal to; ~**lautend** adj identical; **G~macherei** f egalitarianism, levelling down (pej); ~**mäßig** adj even, equal; **G~mut** m equanimity.

Gleichnis (-ses, -se) nt parable.

gleich- zW: ~**rangig** adj (Probleme etc) equally important; ~**rangig (mit)** (Beamte etc) equal in rank (to), at the same level (as); ~**sam** adv as it were; ~**schalten** (pej) vt to bring into line; **G~schritt** m: **im G~schritt, marsch!** forward march!; ~**sehen** unreg vi: **jdm ~sehen** to be od look like sb; ~**stellen** vt (rechtlich etc) to treat as equal; **G~strom** m (ELEK) direct current; ~**tun** unreg vi: **es jdm ~tun** to match sb.

Gleichung f equation.

gleich- zW: ~**viel** adv no matter; ~**wertig** adj of the same value; (Leistung, Qualität) equal; (Gegner) evenly matched; ~**wohl** adv (geh) nevertheless; ~**zeitig** adj simultaneous.

Gleis [glaɪs] (-es, -e) nt track, rails pl; (am Bahnhof) platform (BRIT), track (US).

gleißend ['glaɪsənt] adj glistening, gleaming.

gleiten unreg vi to glide; (rutschen) to slide.

gleitend ['glaɪtənt] adj: ~**e Arbeitszeit** flexible working hours pl, flex(i)time.

Gleit- zW: ~**flug** m glide; ~**klausel** f (COMM) escalator clause; ~**komma** nt floating point; ~**zeit** f flex(i)time.

Gletscher ['glɛtʃər] (-s, -) m glacier; ~**spalte** f crevasse.

glich etc [glɪç] vb siehe **gleichen**.

Glied [gliːt] (-(e)s, -er) nt member; (Arm, Bein) limb; (Penis) penis; (von Kette) link; (MIL) rank(s); **der Schreck steckt ihr noch in den ~ern** she is still shaking with the shock.

gliedern vt to organize, structure.

Gliederreißen nt rheumatic pains pl.

Gliederschmerz m rheumatic pains pl.

Gliederung f structure, organization.

Gliedmaßen pl limbs pl.

glimmen ['glɪmən] unreg vi to glow.

Glimmer (-s, -) m (MINERAL) mica.

Glimmstengel (umg) m fag (BRIT), butt (US).

glimpflich ['glɪmpflɪç] adj mild, lenient; ~ **davonkommen** to get off lightly.

glitschig ['glɪtʃɪç] (umg) adj slippery, slippy.

glitt etc [glɪt] vb siehe **gleiten**.

glitzern ['glɪtsərn] vi to glitter; (Stern) to twinkle.

global [glo'baːl] adj (weltweit) global, worldwide; (ungefähr, pauschal) general.

Globus ['gloːbus] (- od -ses, **Globen** od -se) m globe.

Glöckchen ['glœkçən] nt (little) bell.

Glocke ['glɔkə] (-, -n) f bell; **etw an die große ~ hängen** (fig) to shout sth from the rooftops.

Glocken- zW: ~**geläut** nt peal of bells; ~**schlag** m stroke (of the bell); (von Uhr) chime; ~**spiel** nt chime(s); (MUS) glockenspiel; ~**turm** m belfry, bell-tower.

glomm etc [glɔm] vb siehe **glimmen**.

Glorie ['gloːriə] f glory; (von Heiligen) halo.

glorreich ['gloːrraɪç] adj glorious.

Glossar [glɔ'saːr] (-s, -e) nt glossary.

Glosse ['glɔsə] (-, -n) f comment.

Glotze (-, -n) (umg) f gogglebox (BRIT), TV set.

glotzen ['glɔtsən] (umg) vi to stare.

Glück [glʏk] (-(e)s) nt luck, fortune; (Freude) happiness; ~ **haben** to be lucky; **viel ~** good luck; **zum ~** fortunately; **ein ~!** how lucky!, what a stroke of luck!; **auf gut ~** (aufs Geratewohl) on the off-chance; (unvorbereitet) trusting to luck; (wahllos) at random; **sie weiß noch nichts von ihrem ~** (ironisch) she doesn't know anything about it yet; **er kann von ~ sagen, daß ...** he can count himself lucky that ...; ~**auf** nt: „~**auf"** (Bergleute) (cry of) "good luck".

Glucke (-, -n) f (Bruthenne) broody hen; (mit Jungen) mother hen.

glücken vi to succeed; **es glückte ihm, es zu bekommen** he succeeded in getting it.

gluckern ['glʊkərn] vi to glug.

glücklich adj fortunate; (froh) happy ♦ adv happily; (umg: endlich, zu guter Letzt) finally, eventually.

glücklicherweise adv fortunately.

glücklos adj luckless.

Glücksbringer (-s, -) m lucky charm.

glückselig [glʏk'zeːlɪç] adj blissful.

Glücks- zW: ~**fall** m stroke of luck; ~**kind** nt lucky person; ~**pilz** m lucky beggar (umg); ~**sache** f matter of luck; ~**spiel** nt game of chance; ~**stern** m lucky star; ~**strähne** f lucky streak.

glückstrahlend adj radiant (with happiness).

Glückszahl f lucky number.

Glückwunsch m: ~ **(zu)** congratulations pl (on), best wishes pl (on).

Glühbirne f light bulb.

glühen ['glyːən] vi to glow.

glühend adj glowing; (heiß~: Metall) red-hot; (Hitze) blazing; (fig: leidenschaftlich) ardent; (: Haß) burning; (Wangen) flushed, burning.

Glüh- zW: ~**faden** m (ELEK) filament; ~**wein** m mulled wine; ~**würmchen** nt glow-worm.

Glut [gluːt] (-, -en) f (Röte) glow; (Feuers~) fire; (Hitze) heat; (fig) ardour (BRIT), ardor (US).

GmbH (-, -s) f abk (= Gesellschaft mit beschränkter Haftung) ≈ Ltd. (BRIT), plc (BRIT), Inc. (US).

Gnade ['gnaːdə] (-, -n) f (Gunst) favour (BRIT), favor (US); (Erbarmen) mercy; (Milde) clemency; ~ **vor Recht ergehen lassen** to temper justice with mercy.

gnaden *vi:* **(dann) gnade dir Gott!** (then) God help you *od* heaven have mercy on you!

Gnaden- *zW:* ~**brot** *nt:* **jdm/einem Tier das** ~**brot geben** to keep sb/an animal in his/her/its old age; ~**frist** *f* reprieve; ~**gesuch** *nt* petition for clemency; **g**~**los** *adj* merciless; ~**stoß** *m* coup de grâce.

gnädig ['gnɛːdɪç] *adj* gracious; (*voll Erbarmen*) merciful; ~**e Frau** (*form*) madam, ma'am.

Gockel ['gɔkəl] **(-s, -)** *m* (*bes SÜDD*) cock.

Gold [gɔlt] **(-(e)s)** *nt* gold; **nicht mit** ~ **zu bezahlen** *od* **aufzuwiegen sein** to be worth one's weight in gold; **g**~**en** *adj* golden; **g**~**ene Worte** words of wisdom; **der Tanz ums g**~**ene Kalb** (*fig*) the worship of Mammon; ~**fisch** *m* goldfish; ~**grube** *f* gold mine; ~**hamster** *m* (golden) hamster.

goldig ['gɔldɪç] *adj* (*fig: umg: allerliebst*) sweet, cute.

Gold- *zW:* ~**regen** *m* laburnum; (*fig*) riches *pl*; **g**~**richtig** (*umg*) *adj* dead right; ~**schmied** *m* goldsmith; ~**schnitt** *m* gilt edging; ~**standard** *m* gold standard; ~**stück** *nt* piece of gold; (*fig: umg*) treasure; ~**waage** *f:* **jedes Wort auf die** ~**waage legen** (*fig*) to weigh one's words; ~**währung** *f* gold standard.

Golf¹ [gɔlf] **(-(e)s, -e)** *m* gulf; **der (Persische)** ~ the Gulf.

Golf² [gɔlf] **(-s)** *nt* golf; ~**platz** *m* golf course; ~**schläger** *m* golf club; ~**spieler** *m* golfer.

Golfstaaten *pl:* **die** ~ the Gulf States *pl*.

Golfstrom *m* (*GEOG*) Gulf Stream.

Gondel ['gɔndəl] **(-, -n)** *f* gondola; (*von Seilbahn*) cable car.

gondeln (*umg*) *vi:* **durch die Welt** ~ to go globetrotting.

Gong [gɔŋ] **(-s, -s)** *m* gong; (*bei Boxkampf etc*) bell.

gönnen ['gœnən] *vt:* **jdm etw** ~ not to begrudge sb sth; **sich** *dat* **etw** ~ to allow o.s. sth.

Gönner **(-s, -)** *m* patron; **g**~**haft** *adj* patronizing; ~**in** *f* patroness; ~**miene** *f* patronizing air.

gor *etc* [goːr] *vb siehe* **gären.**

Gorilla [goˈrɪla] **(-s, -s)** *m* gorilla; (*umg: Leibwächter*) heavy.

goß *etc* [gɔs] *vb siehe* **gießen.**

Gosse ['gɔsə] **(-, -n)** *f* gutter.

Gote ['goːtə] **(-n, -n)** *m* Goth.

Gotik ['goːtɪk] *f* (*KUNST*) Gothic (style); (*Epoche*) Gothic period.

Gotin ['goːtɪn] *f* Goth.

Gott [gɔt] **(-es, -̈er)** *m* god; (*als Name*) God; **um** ~**es Willen!** for heaven's sake!; ~ **sei Dank!** thank God!; **grüß** ~! (*bes SÜDD, ÖSTERR*) hello, good morning/afternoon/evening; **den lieben** ~ **einen guten Mann sein lassen** (*umg*) to take things as they come; **ein Bild für die Götter** (*hum: umg*) a sight for sore

eyes; **das wissen die Götter** (*umg*) God (only) knows; **über** ~ **und die Welt reden** (*fig*) to talk about everything under the sun; **wie** ~ **in Frankreich leben** (*umg*) to be in clover.

Götterspeise *f* (*KOCH*) jelly (*BRIT*), jello (*US*).

Gottes- *zW:* ~**dienst** *m* service; **g**~**fürchtig** *adj* god-fearing; ~**haus** *nt* place of worship; ~**lästerung** *f* blasphemy.

Gottheit *f* deity.

Göttin ['gœtɪn] *f* goddess.

göttlich *adj* divine.

Gott- *zW:* **g**~**lob** *interj* thank heavens!; **g**~**los** *adj* godless; **g**~**verdammt** *adj* goddamn(ed); **g**~**verlassen** *adj* godforsaken; ~**vertrauen** *nt* trust in God.

Götze ['gœtsə] **(-n, -n)** *m* idol.

Grab [graːp] **(-(e)s, -̈er)** *nt* grave.

grabbeln ['grabəln] (*NORDD: umg*) *vt* to rummage.

Graben ['graːbən] **(-s, -̈)** *m* ditch; (*MIL*) trench.

graben *unreg vt* to dig.

Grabesstille *f* (*liter*) deathly hush.

Grab- *zW:* ~**mal** *nt* monument; (~*stein*) gravestone; ~**rede** *f* funeral oration; ~**stein** *m* gravestone.

gräbt *vb siehe* **graben.**

Gracht [graxt] **(-, -en)** *f* canal.

Grad [graːt] **(-(e)s, -e)** *m* degree; **im höchsten** ~**(e)** extremely; **Verbrennungen ersten** ~**es** (*MED*) first-degree burns; ~**einteilung** *f* graduation; **g**~**linig** *adj* straight; **g**~**weise** *adv* gradually.

Graf [graːf] **(-en, -en)** *m* count, earl (*BRIT*).

Grafik *f siehe* **Graphik.**

Grafiker(in) *m(f) siehe* **Graphiker(in).**

Gräfin ['grɛːfɪn] *f* countess.

grafisch *adj siehe* **graphisch.**

Grafschaft *f* county.

Grahambrot ['graːhambroːt] *nt* type of wholemeal (*BRIT*) *od* whole-wheat (*US*) bread.

Gralshüter ['graːlzhyːtər] **(-s, -)** *m* (*fig*) guardian.

Gram [graːm] **(-(e)s)** *m* (*geh*) grief, sorrow.

grämen ['grɛːmən] *vr* to grieve; **sich zu Tode** ~ to die of grief *od* sorrow.

Gramm [gram] **(-s, -e)** *nt* gram(me).

Grammatik [graˈmatɪk] *f* grammar.

grammatisch *adj* grammatical.

Grammophon [gramoˈfoːn] **(-s, -e)** *nt* gramophone.

Granat [graˈnaːt] **(-(e)s, -e)** *m* (*Stein*) garnet; ~**apfel** *m* pomegranate.

Granate **(-, -n)** *f* (*MIL*) shell; (*Hand*~) grenade.

grandios [granˈdioːs] *adj* magnificent, superb.

Granit [graˈniːt] **(-s, -e)** *m* granite; **auf** ~ **beißen (bei ...)** to bang one's head against a brick wall (with ...).

grantig ['grantɪç] (*umg*) *adj* grumpy.

Graphik ['gra:fɪk] f (COMPUT, TECH) graphics; (ART) graphic arts pl.
Graphiker(in) ['gra:fɪkər(ɪn)] (-s, -) m(f) graphic artist; (Illustrator) illustrator.
graphisch ['gra:fɪʃ] adj graphic; ~e Darstellung graph.
grapschen ['grapʃən] (umg) vt, vi to grab; (sich dat) etw ~ to grab sth.
Gras [gra:s] (-es, ⁻er) nt (auch umg: Marihuana) grass; über etw akk ~ wachsen lassen (fig) to let the dust settle on sth; g~en vi to graze; ~halm m blade of grass.
grasig adj grassy.
Grasnarbe f turf.
grassieren [gra'si:rən] vi to be rampant, rage.
gräßlich ['grɛslɪç] adj horrible.
Grat [gra:t] (-(e)s, -e) m ridge.
Gräte ['grɛ:tə] (-, -n) f fish-bone.
Gratifikation [gratifikatsi'o:n] f bonus.
gratis ['gra:tɪs] adj, adv free (of charge); G~probe f free sample.
Grätsche ['grɛ:tʃə] (-, -n) f (SPORT) straddle.
Gratulant(in) [gratu'lant(ɪn)] m(f) well-wisher.
Gratulation [gratulatsi'o:n] f congratulation(s).
gratulieren [gratu'li:rən] vi: jdm (zu etw) ~ to congratulate sb (on sth); (ich) gratuliere! congratulations!
Gratwanderung f (fig) tightrope walk.
grau [grau] adj grey (BRIT), gray (US); der ~e Alltag drab reality; G~brot nt = Mischbrot.
Grauen (-s) nt horror.
grauen vi (Tag) to dawn ♦ vi unpers: es graut jdm vor etw sb dreads sth, sb is afraid of sth ♦ vr: sich ~ vor to dread, have a horror of.
grauenhaft, grauenvoll adj horrible.
grauhaarig adj grey-haired (BRIT), gray-haired (US).
graumeliert adj grey-flecked (BRIT), gray-flecked (US).
Graupelregen ['graupəlre:gən] m sleet.
Graupelschauer m sleet.
Graupen ['graupən] pl pearl barley sing.
grausam ['grauza:m] adj cruel; G~keit f cruelty.
Grausen ['grauzən] (-s) nt horror; da kann man das kalte ~ kriegen (umg) it's enough to give you the creeps.
grausen vb = grauen.
Grauzone f (fig) grey (BRIT) od gray (US) area.
gravieren [gra'vi:rən] vt to engrave.
gravierend adj grave.
Grazie ['gra:tsiə] f grace.
graziös [gratsi'ø:s] adj graceful.
greifbar adj tangible, concrete; in ~er Nähe within reach.
greifen ['graifən] unreg vt (nehmen) to grasp; (grapschen) to seize, grab ♦ vi (nicht rutschen, einrasten) to grip; nach etw ~ to reach for sth; um sich ~ (fig) to spread; zu etw ~ (fig)

to turn to sth; diese Zahl ist zu niedrig gegriffen (fig) this figure is too low; aus dem Leben gegriffen taken from life.
Greifer (-s, -) m (TECH) grab.
Greifvogel m bird of prey.
Greis [grais] (-es, -e) m old man.
Greisenalter nt old age.
greisenhaft adj very old.
Greisin ['graizɪn] f old woman.
grell [grɛl] adj harsh.
Gremium ['gre:miʊm] nt body; (Ausschuß) committee.
Grenadier [grena'di:ər] (-s, -e) m (MIL: Infanterist) infantryman.
Grenzbeamte(r) m frontier official.
Grenze (-, -n) f border; (zwischen Grundstücken, fig) boundary; (Staats~) frontier; (Schranke) limit; über die ~ gehen/fahren to cross the border; hart an der ~ des Erlaubten bordering on the limits of what is permitted.
grenzen vi: ~ an +akk to border on.
grenzenlos adj boundless.
Grenz- zW: ~fall m borderline case; ~gänger m (Arbeiter) international commuter (across a local border); ~gebiet nt (lit, fig) border area; ~kosten pl marginal cost sing; ~linie f boundary; ~übergang m frontier crossing; ~wert m limit; ~zwischenfall m border incident.
Gretchenfrage ['gre:tçənfra:gə] f (fig) crunch question, sixty-four-thousand-dollar question (umg).
Greuel ['grɔyəl] (-s, -) m horror; (~tat) atrocity; etw ist jdm ein ~ sb loathes sth; ~propaganda f atrocity propaganda; ~tat f atrocity.
greulich ['grɔylɪç] adj horrible.
Grieche ['gri:çə] (-n, -n) m Greek.
Griechenland nt Greece.
Griechin ['gri:çɪn] f Greek.
griechisch adj Greek.
griesgrämig ['gri:sgrɛ:mɪç] adj grumpy.
Grieß [gri:s] (-es, -e) m (KOCH) semolina; ~brei m cooked semolina.
Griff [grɪf] (-(e)s, -e) m grip; (Vorrichtung) handle; (das Greifen): der ~ nach etw reaching for sth; jdn/etw in den ~ bekommen (fig) to gain control of sb/sth; etw in den ~ bekommen (geistig) to get a grasp of sth.
griff etc vb siehe **greifen**.
griffbereit adj handy.
Griffel ['grɪfəl] (-s, -) m slate pencil; (BOT) style.
griffig ['grɪfɪç] adj (Fahrbahn etc) that has a good grip; (fig: Ausdruck) useful, handy.
Grill [grɪl] (-s, -s) m grill; (AUT) grille.
Grille ['grɪlə] (-, -n) f cricket; (fig) whim.
grillen vt to grill.
Grimasse [gri'masə] (-, -n) f grimace; ~n schneiden to make faces.

grimmig *adj* furious; (*heftig*) fierce, severe.
grinsen ['grɪnzən] *vi* to grin; (*höhnisch*) to smirk.
Grippe ['grɪpə] (-, -n) *f* influenza, flu.
Grips [grɪps] (-es, -e) (*umg*) *m* sense.
grob [groːp] *adj* coarse, gross; (*Fehler, Verstoß*) gross; (*brutal, derb*) rough; (*unhöflich*) ill-mannered; ~ **geschätzt** at a rough estimate; **G~heit** *f* coarseness; (*Beschimpfung*) coarse expression.
Grobian ['groːbiaːn] (-s, -e) *m* ruffian.
grobknochig *adj* large-boned.
groggy ['grɔgi] *adj* (*BOXEN*) groggy; (*umg: erschöpft*) bushed.
grölen ['grøːlən] (*pej*) *vt, vi* to bawl.
Groll [grɔl] (-(e)s) *m* resentment; **g~en** *vi* (*Donner*) to rumble; **g~en (mit** *od* +*dat*) to bear ill will (towards).
Grönland ['grøːnlant] (-s) *nt* Greenland.
Grönländer(in) (-s, -) *m(f)* Greenlander.
Groschen ['grɔʃən] (-s, -) (*umg*) *m* 10-pfennig piece; (*ÖSTERR*) groschen; (*fig*) penny, cent (*US*); ~**roman** (*pej*) *m* cheap *od* dime (*US*) novel.
groß [groːs] *adj* big, large; (*hoch*) tall; (*Freude, Werk*) great ♦ *adv* greatly; **im ~en und ganzen** on the whole; **wie ~ bist du?** how tall are you?; **die G~en** (*Erwachsene*) the grown-ups; **mit etw ~ geworden sein** to have grown up with sth; **die G~en Seen** the Great Lakes *pl*; ~**en Hunger haben** to be very hungry; ~**e Mode sein** to be all the fashion; ~ **und breit** (*fig: umg*) at great *od* enormous length; **ein Wort ~ schreiben** to write a word with a capital; **G~abnehmer** *m* (*COMM*) bulk buyer; **G~alarm** *m* red alert; ~**angelegt** *adj attrib* large-scale, on a large scale; ~**artig** *adj* great, splendid; **G~aufnahme** *f* (*FILM*) close-up; **G~britannien** (-s) *nt* (Great) Britain; **G~buchstabe** *m* capital (letter).
Größe ['grøːsə] (-, -n) *f* size; (*Länge*) height; (*fig*) greatness; **eine unbekannte ~** (*lit, fig*) an unknown quantity.
Groß- *zW:* ~**einkauf** *m* bulk purchase; ~**einsatz** *m:* ~**einsatz der Polizei** *etc* large-scale operation by the police *etc*; ~**eltern** *pl* grandparents *pl*.
Größenordnung *f* scale; (*Größe*) magnitude; (*MATH*) order (of magnitude).
großenteils *adv* for the most part.
Größen- *zW:* ~**unterschied** *m* difference in size; ~**wahn** *m*, ~**wahnsinn** *m* megalomania, delusions *pl* of grandeur.
Groß- *zW:* ~**format** *nt* large size; ~**handel** *m* wholesale trade; ~**handelspreisindex** *m* wholesale-price index; ~**händler** *m* wholesaler; **g~herzig** *adj* generous; ~**hirn** *nt* cerebrum; ~**industrielle(r)** *f(m)* major industrialist; **g~kotzig** (*umg*) *adj* show-offish, bragging; ~**kundgebung** *f* mass rally; ~**macht** *f* great power; ~**maul** *m*

braggart; ~**mut** (-) *f* magnanimity; **g~mütig** *adj* magnanimous; ~**mutter** *f* grandmother; ~**raum** *m:* **der ~raum München** the Munich area *od* conurbation, Greater Munich; ~**raumbüro** *nt* open-plan office; ~**rechner** *m* mainframe; ~**reinemachen** *nt* thorough cleaning, ≈ spring cleaning; **g~schreiben** *unreg vt:* **g~geschrieben werden** (*umg*) to be stressed; ~**schreibung** *f* capitalization; **g~spurig** *adj* pompous; ~**stadt** *f* city.
größte(r, s) [grøːstə(r, s)] *adj superl von* **groß**.
größtenteils *adv* for the most part.
Groß- *zW:* ~**tuer** (-s, -) *m* boaster; **g~tun** *unreg vi* to boast; ~**vater** *m* grandfather; ~**verbraucher** *m* (*COMM*) heavy user; ~**verdiener** *m* big earner; ~**wild** *nt* big game; **g~ziehen** *unreg vt* to raise; **g~zügig** *adj* generous; (*Planung*) on a large scale.
grotesk [gro'tɛsk] *adj* grotesque.
Grotte ['grɔtə] (-, -n) *f* grotto.
grub *etc* [gruːp] *vb siehe* **graben**.
Grübchen ['gryːpçən] *nt* dimple.
Grube ['gruːbə] (-, -n) *f* pit; (*Bergwerk*) mine.
grübeln ['gryːbəln] *vi* to brood.
Grubenarbeiter *m* miner.
Grubengas *nt* firedamp.
Grübler ['gryːblər] (-s, -) *m* brooder; **g~isch** *adj* brooding, pensive.
Gruft [gruft] (-, ⁼e) *f* tomb, vault.
grün [gryːn] *adj* green; (*ökologisch*) green; (*POL*): **die G~en** the Greens; **G~e Minna** (*umg*) Black Maria (*BRIT*), paddy wagon (*US*); ~**e Welle** phased traffic lights; ~**e Versicherungskarte** (*AUT*) green card; **sich ~ und blau** *od* **gelb ärgern** (*umg*) to be furious; **auf keinen ~en Zweig kommen** (*fig: umg*) to get nowhere; **jdm ~es Licht geben** to give sb the green light; **G~anlage** *f* park.
Grund [grunt] (-(e)s, ⁼e) *m* ground; (*von See, Gefäß*) bottom; (*fig*) reason; **von ~ auf** entirely, completely; **auf ~ von** on the basis of; **aus gesundheitlichen** *etc* **Gründen** for health *etc* reasons; **im ~e genommen** basically; **ich habe ~ zu der Annahme, daß ...** I have reason to believe that ...; **einer Sache** *dat* **auf den ~ gehen** (*fig*) to get to the bottom of sth; **in ~ und Boden** (*fig*) utterly, thoroughly; ~**ausbildung** *f* basic training; ~**bedeutung** *f* basic meaning; ~**bedingung** *f* fundamental condition; ~**begriff** *m* basic concept; ~**besitz** *m* land(ed property), real estate; ~**buch** *nt* land register; **g~ehrlich** *adj* thoroughly honest.
gründen ['gryndən] *vt* to found ♦ *vr:* **sich ~ auf** +*akk* to be based on; ~ **auf** +*akk* to base on.
Gründer(in) (-s, -) *m(f)* founder.
Grund- *zW:* **g~falsch** *adj* utterly wrong; ~**gebühr** *f* basic charge; ~**gedanke** *m* basic idea; ~**gesetz** *nt* constitution.
Grundierung [grun'diːruŋ] *f* (*Farbe*) primer.
Grund- *zW:* ~**kapital** *nt* nominal capital;

~**kurs** m basic course; ~**lage** f foundation;
jeder ~**lage** gen **entbehren** to be completely
unfounded; **g~legend** adj
fundamental.
gründlich adj thorough; **jdm** ~ **die Meinung
sagen** to give sb a piece of one's mind.
Grund- zW: **g~los** adj (fig) groundless;
~**mauer** f foundation wall;
~**nahrungsmittel** nt basic food(stuff).
Gründonnerstag m Maundy Thursday.
Grund- zW: ~**ordnung** f: **die freiheitlich-
demokratische** ~**ordnung** (BRD POL) the
German constitution based on democratic
liberty; ~**rechenart** f basic arithmetical
operation; ~**recht** nt basic od constitutional
right; ~**regel** f basic od ground rule; ~**riß**
m plan; (fig) outline; ~**satz** m principle;
g~sätzlich adj fundamental; (Frage) of
principle ♦ adv fundamentally; (prinzipiell)
on principle; **das ist g~sätzlich verboten** it
is absolutely forbidden; ~**satzurteil** nt
judgement that establishes a principle.
Grundschule f primary (BRIT) od
elementary school.

> The **Grundschule** is a primary school which
> children attend for 4 years from the age of 6 to
> 10. There are no formal examinations in the
> Grundschule but parents receive a report on
> their child's progress twice a year. Many
> children attend a **Kindergarten** from 3-6 years
> before going to the Grundschule, but no formal
> instruction takes place in the Kindergarten.

Grund- zW: ~**stein** m foundation stone;
~**steuer** f rates pl; ~**stück** nt plot (of land);
(Anwesen) estate; ~**stücksmakler** m estate
agent (BRIT), realtor (US); ~**stufe** f first
stage; (SCH) ≈ junior (BRIT) od grade (US)
school.
Gründung f foundation.
Gründungsurkunde f (COMM) certificate of
incorporation.
Gründungsversammlung f
(Aktiengesellschaft) statutory meeting.
Grund- zW: **g~verschieden** adj utterly
different; ~**wasser** nt ground water;
~**wasserspiegel** m water table, ground-
water level; ~**zug** m characteristic; **etw in
seinen** ~**zügen darstellen** to outline (the
essentials of) sth.
Grüne (-n) nt: **im** ~**n** in the open air; **ins**
~ **fahren** to go to the country.
Grüne(r) f(m) (POL) Ecologist, Green; **die
Grünen** pl (als Partei) the Greens.

> **Die Grünen** is the name given to the Green or
> ecological party in Germany which was
> founded in 1980. Since 1993 they have been
> allied with the originally East German party,
> Bündnis 90.
> The **grüner Punkt** is the green spot symbol

which appears on packaging that should not be
thrown into the normal household refuse but
kept separate to be recycled through the **DSD**
system. The recycling is financed by licences
bought by the manufacturer from the DSD and
the cost of this is often passed on to the
consumer.

Grün- zW: ~**kohl** m kale; ~**schnabel** m
greenhorn; ~**span** m verdigris; ~**streifen** m
central reservation.
grunzen ['grʊntsən] vi to grunt.
Gruppe ['grʊpə] (-, -n) f group.
Gruppen- zW: ~**arbeit** f teamwork;
~**dynamik** f group dynamics pl; ~**therapie** f
group therapy; **g~weise** adv in groups.
gruppieren [grʊ'piːrən] vt, vr to group.
gruselig adj creepy.
gruseln ['gruːzəln] vi unpers: **es gruselt jdm vor
etw** sth gives sb the creeps ♦ vr to have the
creeps.
Gruß [gruːs] (-es, ⁻e) m greeting; (MIL) salute;
viele Grüße best wishes; **Grüße an** +akk
regards to; **einen (schönen)** ~ **an Ihre Frau!**
my regards to your wife; **mit freundlichen
Grüßen** (als Briefformel) Yours sincerely.
grüßen ['gryːsən] vt to greet; (MIL) to salute;
jdn von jdm ~ to give sb sb's regards; **jdn**
~ **lassen** to send sb one's regards.
Grütze ['grytsə] (-, -n) f (Brei) gruel; **rote** ~
(type of) red fruit jelly.
Guatemala [guate'maːla] (-s) nt Guatemala.
Guayana [gua'jaːna] (-s) nt Guyana.
gucken ['gʊkən] vi to look.
Guckloch nt peephole.
Guinea [gi'neːa] (-s) nt Guinea.
Gulasch ['guːlaʃ] (-(e)s, -e) nt goulash;
~**kanone** f (MIL: umg) field kitchen.
gültig ['gyltɪç] adj valid; ~ **werden** to become
valid; (Gesetz, Vertrag) to come into effect;
(Münze) to become legal tender; **G~keit** f
validity; **G~keitsdauer** f period of validity.
Gummi ['gʊmi] (-s, -s) nt od m rubber; (~harze)
gum; (umg: Kondom) rubber, Durex ®;
(~band) rubber od elastic band; (Hosen~)
elastic; ~**band** nt rubber od elastic band;
~**bärchen** nt jelly baby; ~**geschoß** nt rubber
bullet; ~**knüppel** m rubber truncheon;
~**paragraph** m ambiguous od meaningless
law od statute; ~**stiefel** m rubber boot,
wellington (boot) (BRIT); ~**strumpf** m elastic
stocking; ~**zelle** f padded cell.
Gunst [gʊnst] (-) f favour (BRIT), favor (US).
günstig ['gynstɪç] adj favourable (BRIT),
favorable (US); (Angebot, Preis etc)
reasonable, good; **bei** ~**er Witterung**
weather permitting; **im** ~**sten Fall(e)** with
luck.
Gurgel ['gʊrgəl] (-, -n) f throat.
gurgeln vi to gurgle; (im Rachen) to gargle.
Gurke ['gʊrkə] (-, -n) f cucumber; **saure** ~
pickled cucumber, gherkin.

Gurt [gʊrt] (-(e)s, -e) *m* belt.
Gurtanlegepflicht *f* (form) obligation to wear a safety belt in vehicles.
Gürtel ['gʏrtəl] (-s, -) *m* belt; (GEOG) zone; **~reifen** *m* radial tyre; **~rose** *f* shingles *sing od pl.*
GUS [geː|uːˈ|ɛs] *f abk* (= Gemeinschaft Unabhängiger Staaten) CIS.
Guß [gʊs] (-sses, Güsse) *m* casting; (Regen~) downpour; (KOCH) glazing; **~eisen** *nt* cast iron.
Gut [guːt] (-(e)s, ̈-er) *nt* (Besitz) possession; (Landgut) estate; **Güter** *pl* (Waren) goods *pl.*

================ *SCHLÜSSELWORT*

gut *adj* good; **das ist ~ gegen** *od* **für** (umg) **Husten** it's good for coughs; **sei so ~ (und) gib mir das** would you mind giving me that; **dafür ist er sich zu ~** he wouldn't stoop to that sort of thing; **das ist ja alles ~ und schön, aber ...** that's all very well but ...; **du bist ~!** (umg) you're a fine one!; **alles G~e** all the best; **also ~** all right then ♦ *adv* well; **du hast es ~!** you've got it made!; **~, aber ...** OK, but ...; **(na) ~, ich komme** all right, I'll come; **~ drei Stunden** a good three hours; **das kann ~ sein** that may well be; **~ und gern** easily; **laß es ~ sein** that'll do.

Gut- *zW:* **~achten** (-s, -) *nt* report; **~achter** (-s, -) *m* expert; **~achterkommission** *f* quango; **g~artig** *adj* good-natured; (MED) benign; **g~bürgerlich** *adj* (Küche) (good) plain; **~dünken** *nt:* nach **~dünken** at one's discretion.
Güte ['gʏːtə] (-) *f* goodness, kindness; (Qualität) quality; **ach du liebe** *od* **meine ~!** (umg) goodness me!; **~klasse** *f* (COMM) grade; **~klasseneinteilung** *f* (COMM) grading.
Güter- *zW:* **~abfertigung** *f* (EISENB) goods office; **~bahnhof** *m* goods station; **~trennung** *f* (JUR) separation of property; **~verkehr** *m* freight traffic; **~wagen** *m* goods waggon (BRIT), freight car (US); **~zug** *m* goods train (BRIT), freight train (US).
Gütesiegel *nt* (COMM) stamp of quality.
gut- *zW:* **~gehen** *unreg vi unpers* to work, come off; **es geht jdm ~** sb's doing fine; **das ist noch einmal ~gegangen** it turned out all right; **~gehend** *adj attrib* thriving; **~gelaunt** *adj* cheerful, in a good mood; **~gemeint** *adj* well meant; **~gläubig** *adj* trusting; **G~haben** (-s) *nt* credit; **~haben** *unreg vt:* **20 Mark (bei jdm) ~haben** to be in credit (with sb) to the tune of 20 marks; **~heißen** *unreg vt* to approve (of); **~herzig** *adj* kind(-hearted).
gütig ['gʏːtɪç] *adj* kind.
gütlich ['gʏːtlɪç] *adj* amicable.
gut- *zW:* **~machen** *vt* (in Ordnung bringen: Fehler) to put right, correct; (Schaden) to make good; **~mütig** *adj* good-natured;

G~mütigkeit *f* good nature.
Gutsbesitzer(in) *m(f)* landowner.
Gut- *zW:* **~schein** *m* voucher; **g~schreiben** *unreg vt* to credit; **~schrift** *f* credit.
Gutsherr *m* squire.
Gutshof *m* estate.
gut- *zW:* **~situiert** *adj attrib* well-off; **~tun** *unreg vi:* **jdm ~tun** to do sb good; **~unterrichtet** *adj attrib* well-informed; **~willig** *adj* willing.
Gymnasiallehrer(in) [gʏmnaziˈaːlleːrər(ɪn)] *m(f)* ≈ grammar school teacher (BRIT), high school teacher (US).
Gymnasium [gʏmˈnaːziʊm] *nt* ≈ grammar school (BRIT), high school (US).

---

*The **Gymnasium** is a selective secondary school. There are nine years of study at a Gymnasium leading to the **Abitur** which gives access to higher education. Pupils who successfully complete six years automatically gain the **mittlere Reife**.*

Gymnastik [gʏmˈnastɪk] *f* exercises *pl*, keep-fit; **~ machen** to do keep-fit (exercises)/gymnastics.
Gynäkologe [gʏnɛkoˈloːgə] (-n, -n) *m* gynaecologist (BRIT), gynecologist (US).
Gynäkologin [gʏnɛkoˈloːgɪn] *f* gynaecologist (BRIT), gynecologist (US).

H, h

H, h [haː] *nt* H, h; **~ wie Heinrich** ≈ H for Harry, H for How (US); (MUS) B.
ha *abk* = **Hektar.**
Haag [haːk] (-s) *m:* **Den ~** The Hague.
Haar [haːr] (-(e)s, -e) *nt* hair; **um ein ~** nearly; **~e auf den Zähnen haben** to be a tough customer; **sich die ~e raufen** (umg) to tear one's hair; **sich** *dat* **in die ~e kriegen** (umg) to quarrel; **das ist an den ~en herbeigezogen** that's rather far-fetched; **~ansatz** *m* hairline; **~bürste** *f* hairbrush.
haaren *vi, vr* to lose hair.
Haaresbreite *f:* **um ~** by a hair's-breadth.
Haarfestiger (-s, -) *m* setting lotion.
haargenau *adv* precisely.
haarig *adj* hairy; (fig) nasty.
Haar- *zW:* **~klammer** *f*, **~klemme** *f* hair grip (BRIT), barrette (US); **h~klein** *adv* in minute detail; **h~los** *adj* hairless; **~nadel** *f* hairpin; **h~scharf** *adv* (beobachten) very sharply; (verfehlen) by a hair's breadth; **~schnitt** *m* haircut; **~schopf** *m* head of hair; **~sieb** *nt* fine sieve; **~spalterei** *f* hair-splitting;

~spange f hair slide; **h~sträubend** adj hair-raising; **~teil** nt hairpiece; **~waschmittel** nt shampoo; **~wasser** nt hair lotion.

Hab [haːp] nt: ~ **und Gut** possessions pl, belongings pl, worldly goods pl.

Habe ['haːbə] (-) f property.

haben ['haːbən] unreg vt, Hilfsverb to have ♦ vr unpers: **und damit hat es sich** (umg) and that's that; **Hunger/Angst** ~ to be hungry/afraid; **da hast du 10 Mark** there's 10 Marks; **die ~'s (ja)** (umg) they can afford it; **Ferien** ~ to be on holiday; **es am Herzen** ~ (umg) to have heart trouble; **sie ist noch zu** ~ (umg: nicht verheiratet) she's still single; **für etw zu** ~ **sein** to be keen on sth; **sie werden schon merken, was sie an ihm** ~ they'll see how valuable he is; **haste was, biste was** (Sprichwort) money brings status; **wie gehabt!** some things don't change; **das hast du jetzt davon** now see what's happened; **woher hast du das?** where did you get that from?; **was hast du denn?** what's the matter (with you)?; **ich habe zu tun** I'm busy.

Haben (-s, -) nt (COMM) credit.

Habenseite f (COMM) credit side.

Habgier f avarice.

habgierig adj avaricious.

habhaft adj: **jds/einer Sache** ~ **werden** (geh) to get hold of sb/sth.

Habicht ['haːbɪçt] (-(e)s, -e) m hawk.

Habilitation [habilitatsi'oːn] f (Lehrberechtigung) postdoctoral lecturing qualification.

Habseligkeiten ['haːpzeːlɪçkaɪtən] pl belongings pl.

Habsucht ['haːpzuxt] f greed.

Hachse ['haksə] (-, -n) f (KOCH) knuckle.

Hackbraten m meat loaf.

Hackbrett nt chopping board; (MUS) dulcimer.

Hacke ['hakə] (-, -n) f hoe; (Ferse) heel.

hacken vt to hack, chop; (Erde) to hoe.

Hacker ['hakər] (-s, -) m (COMPUT) hacker.

Hackfleisch nt mince, minced meat, ground meat (US).

Hackordnung f (lit, fig) pecking order.

Häcksel ['hɛksəl] (-s) m od nt chopped straw, chaff.

hadern ['haːdərn] vi (geh): ~ **mit** to quarrel with; (unzufrieden sein) to be at odds with.

Hafen ['haːfən] (-s, ⁻) m harbour, harbor (US), port; (fig) haven; **~anlagen** pl docks pl; **~arbeiter** m docker; **~damm** m jetty, mole; **~gebühren** pl harbo(u)r dues pl; **~stadt** f port.

Hafer ['haːfər] (-s, -) m oats pl; **ihn sticht der** ~ (umg) he is feeling his oats; **~brei** m porridge (BRIT), oatmeal (US); **~flocken** pl rolled oats pl (BRIT), oatmeal (US); **~schleim** m gruel.

Haff [haf] (-s, -s od -e) nt lagoon.

Haft [haft] (-) f custody; **~anstalt** f detention centre (BRIT) od center (US); **h~bar** adj liable, responsible; **~befehl** m warrant (for arrest); **einen ~befehl gegen jdn ausstellen** to issue a warrant for sb's arrest.

haften vi to stick, cling; ~ **für** to be liable od responsible for; **für Garderobe kann nicht gehaftet werden** all articles are left at owner's risk; **~bleiben** unreg vi: **~bleiben (an** +dat) to stick (to).

Häftling ['hɛftlɪŋ] m prisoner.

Haft- zW: **~pflicht** f liability; **~pflichtversicherung** f third party insurance; **~richter** m magistrate.

Haftschalen pl contact lenses pl.

Haftung f liability.

Hagebutte ['haːgəbʊtə] (-, -n) f rose hip.

Hagedorn m hawthorn.

Hagel ['haːgəl] (-s) m hail; **~korn** nt hailstone; (MED) eye cyst.

hageln vi unpers to hail.

Hagelschauer m (short) hailstorm.

hager ['haːgər] adj gaunt.

Häher ['hɛːər] (-s, -) m jay.

Hahn [haːn] (-(e)s, ⁻e) m cock; (Wasser~) tap, faucet (US); (Abzug) trigger; ~ **im Korb sein** (umg) to be cock of the walk; **danach kräht kein** ~ **mehr** (umg) no one cares two hoots about that any more.

Hähnchen ['hɛːnçən] nt cockerel; (KOCH) chicken.

Hai(fisch) ['haɪ(fɪʃ)] (-(e)s, -e) m shark.

Haiti [ha'iːti] (-s) nt Haiti.

Häkchen ['hɛːkçən] nt small hook.

Häkelarbeit f crochet work.

häkeln ['hɛːkəln] vt to crochet.

Häkelnadel f crochet hook.

Haken ['haːkən] (-s, -) m hook; (fig) catch; **einen ~ schlagen** to dart sideways; **~kreuz** nt swastika; **~nase** f hooked nose.

halb [halp] adj half ♦ adv (beinahe) almost; ~ **eins** half past twelve; **ein ~es Dutzend** half a dozen; **nichts H~es und nichts Ganzes** neither one thing nor the other; **(noch) ein ~es Kind sein** to be scarcely more than a child; **das ist ~ so schlimm** it's not as bad as all that; **mit jdm ~e-~e machen** (umg) to go halves with sb.

halb- zW: **H~blut** nt (Tier) crossbreed; **H~bruder** m half-brother; **H~dunkel** nt semi-darkness.

halber ['halbər] präp +gen (wegen) on account of; (für) for the sake of.

Halb- zW: **h~fett** adj medium fat; **~finale** nt semi-final; **~heit** f half-measure; **h~herzig** adj half-hearted.

halbieren [hal'biːrən] vt to halve.

Halb- zW: **~insel** f peninsula; **h~jährlich** adj half-yearly; **~kreis** m semicircle; **~kugel** f hemisphere; **h~lang** adj: **nun mach mal h~lang!** (umg) now wait a minute!; **h~laut** adv in an undertone; **~leiter** m (PHYS) semiconductor; **h~mast** *adv* at half-mast; **~mond** *m* half-moon; (*fig*) crescent; **h~offen** *adj* half-open; **~pension** *f* half-board (*BRIT*), European plan (*US*); **~schuh** *m* shoe; **~schwester** *f* half-sister; **h~seiden** *adj* (*lit*) fifty per cent silk; (*fig: Dame*) fast; (*: homosexuell*) gay; **h~seitig** *adj* (*Anzeige*) half-page; **~starke(r)** *f(m)* hooligan, rowdy; **h~tags** *adv:* **h~tags arbeiten** to work part-time; **~tagsarbeit** *f* part-time work; **~tagskraft** *f* part-time worker; **~ton** *m* half-tone; (*MUS*) semitone; **h~trocken** *adj* medium-dry; **~waise** *f* child/person who has lost one parent; **h~wegs** *adv* half-way; **h~wegs besser** more or less better; **~welt** *f* demimonde; **~wertzeit** *f* half-life; **~wüchsige(r)** *f(m)* adolescent; **~zeit** *f* (*SPORT*) half; (*Pause*) half-time.

Halde ['haldə] *f* tip; (*Schlacken~*) slag heap.

half *etc vb siehe* **helfen.**

Hälfte ['hɛlftə] (-, -n) *f* half; **um die ~ steigen** to increase by half.

Halfter¹ ['halftər] (-s, -) *m od nt* (*für Tiere*) halter.

Halfter² ['halftər] (-, -n *od* -s, -) *f od nt* (*Pistolen~*) holster.

Hall [hal] (-(e)s, -e) *m* sound.

Halle ['halə] (-, -n) *f* hall; (*AVIAT*) hangar.

hallen *vi* to echo, resound.

Hallen- *in zW* indoor; **~bad** *nt* indoor swimming pool.

hallo [ha'loː] *interj* hallo.

Halluzination [halutsinatsi'oːn] *f* hallucination.

Halm ['halm] (-(e)s, -e) *m* blade, stalk.

Hals [hals] (-es, ̈-e) *m* neck; (*Kehle*) throat; **sich** *dat* **nach jdm/etw den ~ verrenken** (*umg*) to crane one's neck to see sb/sth; **jdm um den ~ fallen** to fling one's arms around sb's neck; **aus vollem ~(e)** at the top of one's voice; **~ über Kopf** in a rush; **jdn auf dem** *od* **am ~ haben** (*umg*) to be lumbered *od* saddled with sb; **das hängt mir zum ~ raus** (*umg*) I'm sick and tired of it; **sie hat es in den falschen ~ bekommen** (*falsch verstehen*) she took it wrongly; **~abschneider** (*pej: umg*) *m* shark; **~band** *nt* (*Hundehalsband*) collar; **h~brecherisch** *adj* (*Tempo*) breakneck; (*Fahrt*) hair-raising; **~kette** *f* necklace; **~krause** *f* ruff; **~- Nasen-Ohren-Arzt** *m* ear, nose and throat specialist; **~schlagader** *f* carotid artery; **~schmerzen** *pl* sore throat *sing*; **h~starrig** *adj* stubborn, obstinate; **~tuch** *nt* scarf; **~- und Beinbruch** *interj* good luck; **~weh** *nt* sore throat; **~wirbel** *m* cervical vertebra.

Halt [halt] (-(e)s, -e) *m* stop; (*fester ~*) hold; (*innerer ~*) stability; **h~!** stop!, halt!

hält [hɛlt] *vb siehe* **halten.**

Halt- *zW:* **h~bar** *adj* durable; (*Lebensmittel*) non-perishable; (*MIL, fig*) tenable; **h~bar bis 6.11.** use by 6 Nov.; **~barkeit** *f* durability;

(non-)perishability; tenability; (*von Lebensmitteln*) shelf life; **~barkeitsdatum** *nt* best-before date.

halten ['haltən] *unreg vt* to keep; (*fest~*) to hold ♦ *vi* to hold; (*frisch bleiben*) to keep; (*stoppen*) to stop ♦ *vr* (*frisch bleiben*) to keep; (*sich behaupten*) to hold out; **den Mund ~** (*umg*) to keep one's mouth shut; **~ für** to regard as; **~ von** to think of; **das kannst du ~ wie du willst** that's completely up to you; **der Film hält nicht, was er verspricht** the film doesn't live up to expectations; **davon halt(e) ich nichts** I don't think much of it; **zu jdm ~** to stand *od* stick by sb; **an sich** *akk* **~** to restrain o.s.; **auf sich** *akk* **~** (*auf Äußeres achten*) to take a pride in o.s.; **er hat sich gut gehalten** (*umg*) he's well-preserved; **sich an ein Versprechen ~** to keep a promise; **sich rechts/links ~** to keep to the right/left.

Halter ['haltər] (-s, -) *m* (*Halterung*) holder.

Haltestelle *f* stop.

Halteverbot *nt:* **absolutes ~** no stopping; **eingeschränktes ~** no waiting; **hier ist ~** you cannot stop here.

Halt- *zW:* **h~los** *adj* unstable; **~losigkeit** *f* instability; **h~machen** *vi* to stop.

Haltung *f* posture; (*fig*) attitude; (*Selbstbeherrschung*) composure; **~ bewahren** to keep one's composure.

Halunke [ha'luŋkə] (-n, -n) *m* rascal.

Hamburg ['hamburk] (-s) *nt* Hamburg.

Hamburger (-s, -) *m* (*KOCH*) burger, hamburger.

Hamburger(in) (-s, -) *m(f)* native of Hamburg.

Hameln ['haːməln] *nt* Hamelin.

hämisch ['hɛːmɪʃ] *adj* malicious.

Hammel ['haməl] (-s, ̈ *od* -) *m* wether; **~fleisch** *nt* mutton; **~keule** *f* leg of mutton.

Hammelsprung *m* (*PARL*) division.

Hammer ['hamər] (-s, ̈-) *m* hammer; **das ist ein ~!** (*umg: unerhört*) that's absurd!

hämmern ['hɛmərn] *vt, vi* to hammer.

Hammondorgel ['hæmənd|ɔrgəl] *f* electric organ.

Hämorrhoiden [hɛmɔro'iːdən] *pl* piles *pl*, haemorrhoids *pl* (*BRIT*), hemorrhoids *pl* (*US*).

Hampelmann ['hampəlman] *m* (*lit, fig*) puppet.

Hamster ['hamstər] (-s, -) *m* hamster.

Hamsterei [hamstə'raɪ] *f* hoarding.

Hamsterer (-s, -) *m* hoarder.

hamstern *vi* to hoard.

Hand [hant] (-, ̈-e) *f* hand; **etw zur ~ haben** to have sth to hand; (*Ausrede, Erklärung*) to have sth ready; **jdm zur ~ gehen** to lend sb a helping hand; **zu Händen von jdm** for the attention of sb; **in festen Händen sein** to be spoken for; **die ~ für jdn ins Feuer legen** to vouch for sb; **hinter vorgehaltener ~** on the quiet; **~ aufs Herz** cross your heart; **jdn auf Händen tragen** to cherish sb; **bei etw die** *od* **seine ~ im Spiel haben** to have a hand in sth; **eine ~ wäscht die andere** (*Sprichwort*) if you scratch my back I'll scratch yours; **das hat weder ~ noch Fuß** that doesn't make sense; **das liegt auf der ~** (*umg*) that's obvious; **an ~ eines Beispiels** by means of an example; **~arbeit** *f* manual work; (*Nadelarbeit*) needlework; **~arbeiter** *m* manual worker; **~ball** *m* handball; **~besen** *m* brush; **~betrieb** *m:* **mit ~betrieb** hand-operated; **~bewegung** *f* gesture; **~bibliothek** *f* (*in Bibliothek*) reference section; (*auf Schreibtisch*) reference books *pl*; **~bremse** *f* handbrake; **~buch** *nt* handbook, manual.

Händedruck *m* handshake.

Händeklatschen *nt* clapping, applause.

Handel[1] ['handəl] (**-s**) *m* trade; (*Geschäft*) transaction; **im ~ sein** to be on the market; (**mit jdm**) **~ treiben** to trade (with sb); **etw in den ~ bringen/aus dem ~ ziehen** to put sth on/take sth off the market.

Handel[2] (**-s**, **⸚**) *m* quarrel.

handeln ['handəln] *vi* to trade; (*tätig werden*) to act ♦ *vr unpers:* **sich ~ um** to be a question of, be about; **~ von** to be about; **ich lasse mit mir ~** I'm open to persuasion; (*in bezug auf Preis*) I'm open to offers.

Handeln (**-s**) *nt* action.

handelnd *adj:* **die ~en Personen in einem Drama** the characters in a drama.

Handels- *zW:* **~bank** *f* merchant bank (*BRIT*), commercial bank; **~bilanz** *f* balance of trade; **aktive/passive ~bilanz** balance of trade surplus/deficit; **~delegation** *f* trade mission; **h~einig** *adj:* **mit jdm h~einig werden** to conclude a deal with sb; **~gesellschaft** *f* commercial company; **~kammer** *f* chamber of commerce; **~klasse** *f* grade; **~marine** *f* merchant navy; **~marke** *f* trade name; **~name** *m* trade name; **~recht** *nt* commercial law; **~register** *nt* register of companies; **~reisende(r)** *f(m)* = Handlungsreisende(r) commercial traveller; **~sanktionen** *pl* trade sanctions *pl*; **~schule** *f* business school; **~spanne** *f* gross margin, mark-up; **~sperre** *f* trade embargo; **h~üblich** *adj* customary; **~vertreter** *m* sales representative; **~vertretung** *f* trade mission; **~ware** *f* commodity.

händeringend ['hɛndərɪŋənd] *adv* wringing one's hands; (*fig*) imploringly.

Hand- *zW:* **~feger** (**-s**, **-**) *m* brush; **~fertigkeit** *f* dexterity; **h~fest** *adj* hefty; **~fläche** *f* palm *od* flat (of one's hand); **h~gearbeitet** *adj* handmade; **~gelenk** *nt* wrist; **aus dem ~gelenk** (*umg: ohne Mühe*) effortlessly; (: *improvisiert*) off the cuff; **~gemenge** *nt* scuffle; **~gepäck** *nt* hand baggage *od* luggage; **h~geschrieben** *adj* handwritten; **~granate** *f* hand grenade; **h~greiflich** *adj* palpable; **h~greiflich werden** to become

violent; **~griff** *m* flick of the wrist; **~habe** *f:* **ich habe gegen ihn keine ~habe** (*fig*) I have no hold on him; **h~haben** *unreg vt untr* to handle; **~karren** *m* handcart; **~käse** *m* strong-smelling, round German cheese; **~kuß** *m* kiss on the hand; **~langer** (**-s**, **-**) *m* odd-job man, handyman; (*fig: Untergeordneter*) dogsbody.

Händler ['hɛndlər] (**-s**, **-**) *m* trader, dealer.

handlich ['hantlɪç] *adj* handy.

Handlung ['handlʊŋ] *f* action; (*Tat*) act; (*in Buch*) plot; (*Geschäft*) shop.

Handlungs- *zW:* **~ablauf** *m* plot; **~bevollmächtigte(r)** *f(m)* authorized agent; **h~fähig** *adj* (*Regierung*) able to act; (*JUR*) empowered to act; **~freiheit** *f* freedom of action; **h~orientiert** *adj* action-orientated; **~reisende(r)** *f(m)* commercial traveller (*BRIT*), traveling salesman (*US*); **~vollmacht** *f* proxy; **~weise** *f* manner of dealing.

Hand- *zW:* **~pflege** *f* manicure; **~schelle** *f* handcuff; **~schlag** *m* handshake; **keinen ~schlag tun** not to do a stroke (of work); **~schrift** *f* handwriting; (*Text*) manuscript; **h~schriftlich** *adj* handwritten ♦ *adv* (*korrigieren, einfügen*) by hand; **~schuh** *m* glove; **~schuhfach** *nt* (*AUT*) glove compartment; **~tasche** *f* handbag (*BRIT*), pocket book (*US*), purse (*US*); **~tuch** *nt* towel; **~umdrehen** *nt:* **im ~umdrehen** (*fig*) in the twinkling of an eye.

Handwerk *nt* trade, craft; **jdm das ~ legen** (*fig*) to put a stop to sb's game.

Handwerker (**-s**, **-**) *m* craftsman, artisan; **wir haben seit Wochen die ~ im Haus** we've had workmen in the house for weeks.

Handwerkskammer *f* trade corporation.

Hand- *zW:* **~werkszeug** *nt* tools *pl*; **~wörterbuch** *nt* concise dictionary; **~zeichen** *nt* signal; (*Geste*) sign; (*bei Abstimmung*) show of hands; **~zettel** *m* leaflet, handbill.

Hanf [hanf] (**-(e)s**) *m* hemp.

Hang [haŋ] (**-(e)s**, **⸚e**) *m* inclination; (*Ab~*) slope.

Hänge- ['hɛŋə] *in zW* hanging; **~brücke** *f* suspension bridge; **~matte** *f* hammock.

Hängen ['hɛŋən] *nt:* **mit ~ und Würgen** (*umg*) by the skin of one's teeth.

hängen *unreg vi* to hang ♦ *vt:* **~ (an +akk)** to hang (on(to)); **an jdm ~** (*fig*) to be attached to sb; **den Kopf ~ lassen** (*fig*) to be downcast; **die ganze Sache hängt an ihm** it all depends on him; **sich ~ an +akk** to hang on to, cling to.

hängenbleiben *unreg vi* to be caught; (*fig*) to remain, stick; **~ an +dat** to catch *od* get caught on; **es bleibt ja doch alles an mir hängen** (*fig: umg*) in the end it's all down to me anyhow.

hängend *adj:* **mit ~er Zunge kam er**

angelaufen (*fig*) he came running up panting.

hängenlassen *unreg vt* (*vergessen*) to leave behind ♦ *vr* to let o.s. go.

Hängeschloß *nt* padlock.

Hanglage *f:* **in ~** situated on a slope.

Hannover [ha'noːfər] (**-s**) *nt* Hanover.

Hannoveraner(in) [hanovə'raːnər(ɪn)] (**-s, -**) *m(f)* Hanoverian.

hänseln ['hɛnzəln] *vt* to tease.

Hansestadt ['hanzəʃtat] *f* Hanseatic *od* Hanse town.

Hanswurst [hans'vʊrst] (**-(e)s, -e** *od* **-würste**) *m* clown.

Hantel ['hantəl] (**-, -n**) *f* (*SPORT*) dumb-bell.

hantieren [han'tiːrən] *vi* to work, be busy; **mit etw ~** to handle sth.

hapern ['haːpərn] *vi unpers:* **es hapert an etw** *dat* there is a lack of sth.

Happen ['hapən] (**-s, -**) *m* mouthful.

happig ['hapɪç] (*umg*) *adj* steep.

Hardware ['haːdwɛə] (**-, -s**) *f* hardware.

Harfe ['harfə] (**-, -n**) *f* harp.

Harke ['harkə] (**-, -n**) *f* rake.

harken *vt, vi* to rake.

harmlos ['harmloːs] *adj* harmless.

Harmlosigkeit *f* harmlessness.

Harmonie [harmo'niː] *f* harmony.

harmonieren *vi* to harmonize.

Harmonika [har'moːnika] (**-, -s**) *f* (*Zieh~*) concertina.

harmonisch [har'moːnɪʃ] *adj* harmonious.

Harmonium [har'moːniʊm] (**-s, -nien** *od* **-s**) *nt* harmonium.

Harn ['harn] (**-(e)s, -e**) *m* urine; **~blase** *f* bladder.

Harnisch ['harnɪʃ] (**-(e)s, -e**) *m* armour, armor (*US*); **jdn in ~ bringen** to infuriate sb; **in ~ geraten** to become angry.

Harpune [har'puːnə] (**-, -n**) *f* harpoon.

harren ['harən] *vi:* **~ auf** +*akk* to wait for.

Harsch [harʃ] (**-(e)s**) *m* frozen snow.

harschig *adj* (*Schnee*) frozen.

hart [hart] *adj* hard; (*fig*) harsh ♦ *adv:* **das ist ~ an der Grenze** that's almost going too far; **~e Währung** hard currency; **~ bleiben** to stand firm; **es geht ~ auf ~** it's a tough fight.

Härte ['hɛrtə] (**-, -n**) *f* hardness; (*fig*) harshness; **soziale ~n** social hardships; **~fall** *m* case of hardship; (*umg: Mensch*) hardship case; **~klausel** *f* hardship clause.

härten *vt, vr* to harden.

hart- *zW:* **H~faserplatte** *f* hardboard, fiberboard (*US*); **~gekocht** *adj* hard-boiled; **~gesotten** *adj* tough, hard-boiled; **~herzig** *adj* hard-hearted; **~näckig** *adj* stubborn; **H~näckigkeit** *f* stubbornness.

Harz¹ [haːrts] (**-es, -e**) *nt* resin.

Harz² (**-es**) *m* (*GEOG*) Harz Mountains *pl.*

Haschee [ha'ʃeː] (**-s, -s**) *nt* hash.

haschen ['haʃən] *vt* to catch, snatch ♦ *vi* (*umg*)

to smoke hash.

Haschisch ['haʃɪʃ] (**-**) *nt* hashish.

Hase ['haːzə] (**-n, -n**) *m* hare; **falscher ~** (*KOCH*) meat loaf; **wissen, wie der ~ läuft** (*fig: umg*) to know which way the wind blows; **mein Name ist ~(, ich weiß von nichts)** I don't know anything about anything.

Haselnuß ['haːzəlnʊs] *f* hazelnut.

Hasenfuß *m* coward.

Hasenscharte *f* harelip.

Haspel (**-, -n**) *f* reel, bobbin; (*Winde*) winch.

Haß [has] (**-sses**) *m* hate, hatred; **einen ~ (auf jdn) haben** (*umg: Wut*) to be really mad (with sb).

hassen ['hasən] *vt* to hate; **etw ~ wie die Pest** (*umg*) to detest sth.

hassenswert *adj* hateful.

häßlich ['hɛslɪç] *adj* ugly; (*gemein*) nasty; **H~keit** *f* ugliness; nastiness.

Haßliebe *f* love-hate relationship.

Hast [hast] (**-**) *f* haste.

hast *vb siehe* **haben.**

hasten *vi, vr* to rush.

hastig *adj* hasty.

hat [hat] *vb siehe* **haben.**

hätscheln ['hɛtʃəln] *vt* to pamper; (*zärtlich*) to cuddle.

hatte *etc* ['hatə] *vb siehe* **haben.**

hätte *etc* ['hɛtə] *vb siehe* **haben.**

Haube ['haubə] (**-, -n**) *f* hood; (*Mütze*) cap; (*AUT*) bonnet (*BRIT*), hood (*US*); **unter der ~ sein/unter die ~ kommen** (*hum*) to be/get married.

Hauch [haux] (**-(e)s, -e**) *m* breath; (*Luft~*) breeze; (*fig*) trace; **h~dünn** *adj* extremely thin; (*Scheiben*) wafer-thin; (*fig: Mehrheit*) extremely narrow; **h~en** *vi* to breathe; **h~fein** *adj* very fine.

Haue ['hauə] (**-, -n**) *f* hoe; (*Pickel*) pick; (*umg*) hiding.

hauen *unreg vt* to hew, cut; (*umg*) to thrash.

Hauer ['hauər] (**-s, -**) *m* (*MIN*) face-worker.

Häufchen ['hɔyfçən] *nt:* **ein ~ Unglück** *od* **Elend** a picture of misery.

Haufen ['haufən] (**-s, -**) *m* heap; (*Leute*) crowd; **ein ~ (Bücher)** (*umg*) loads *od* a lot (of books); **auf einem ~** in one heap; **etw über den ~ werfen** (*umg: verwerfen*) to chuck sth out; **jdn über den ~ rennen** *od* **fahren** *etc* (*umg*) to knock sb down.

häufen ['hɔyfən] *vt* to pile up ♦ *vr* to accumulate.

haufenweise *adv* in heaps; in droves; **etw ~ haben** to have piles of sth.

häufig ['hɔyfɪç] *adj* frequent ♦ *adv* frequently; **H~keit** *f* frequency.

Haupt [haupt] (**-(e)s, Häupter**) *nt* head; (*Ober~*) chief ♦ *in zW* main; **~akteur** *m* (*lit, fig*) leading light; (*pej*) main figure; **~aktionär** *m* major shareholder; **~bahnhof** *m* central station; **h~beruflich** *adv* as one's main occupation;

~**buch** nt (COMM) ledger; ~**darsteller(in)** m(f) leading actor, leading actress; ~**eingang** m main entrance; ~**fach** nt (SCH, UNIV) main subject, major (US); **etw im ~fach studieren** to study sth as one's main subject, major in sth (US); ~**film** m main film; ~**gericht** nt main course; ~**geschäftsstelle** f head office; ~**geschäftszeit** f peak (shopping) period; ~**gewinn** m first prize; **einer der ~gewinne** one of the main prizes; ~**leitung** f mains pl.

Häuptling ['hɔʏptlɪŋ] m chief(tain).

Haupt- zW: ~**mahlzeit** f main meal; ~**mann** (-(e)s, pl -leute) m (MIL) captain; ~**nahrungsmittel** nt staple food; ~**person** f (im Roman usw) main character; (fig) central figure; ~**postamt** nt main post office; ~**quartier** nt headquarters pl; ~**rolle** f leading part; ~**sache** f main thing; **in der ~sache** in the main, mainly; **h~sächlich** adj chief ♦ adv chiefly; ~**saison** f peak od high season; ~**satz** m main clause; ~**schlagader** f aorta; ~**schlüssel** m master key.

Hauptschule f ≈ secondary modern (school) (BRIT), junior high (school) (US).

---

*The **Hauptschule** is a non-selective school which pupils attend after the **Grundschule**. They complete five years of study and most go on to do some training in a practical subject or trade.*

Haupt- zW: ~**sendezeit** f (TV) prime time; ~**stadt** f capital; ~**straße** f main street; ~**verkehrsstraße** f (in Stadt) main street; (Durchgangsstraße) main thoroughfare; (zwischen Städten) main highway, trunk road (BRIT); ~**verkehrszeit** f rush hour; ~**versammlung** f general meeting; ~**wohnsitz** m main place of residence; ~**wort** nt noun.

hau ruck ['hau 'rʊk] interj heave-ho.

Haus [haʊs] (-es, Häuser) nt house; **nach ~e** home; **zu ~e** at home; **fühl dich wie zu ~e!** make yourself at home!; **ein Freund des ~es** a friend of the family; **wir liefern frei ~** (COMM) we offer free delivery; **das erste ~ am Platze** (Hotel) the best hotel in town; ~**angestellte** f domestic servant; ~**arbeit** f housework; (SCH) homework; ~**arrest** m (im Internat) detention; (JUR) house arrest; ~**arzt** m family doctor; ~**aufgabe** f (SCH) homework; ~**besetzung** f squat; ~**besitzer** m house-owner; ~**besuch** m home visit; (von Arzt) house call.

Häuschen ['hɔʏsçən] nt: **ganz aus dem ~ sein** (fig: umg) to be out of one's mind (with excitement/fear etc).

Hauseigentümer m house-owner.

hausen ['haʊzən] vi to live (in poverty); (pej) to wreak havoc.

Häuser- zW: ~**block** m block (of houses); ~**makler** m estate agent (BRIT), real estate

agent (US); ~**reihe** f, ~**zeile** f row of houses; (aneinandergebaut) terrace (BRIT).

Haus- zW: ~**frau** f housewife; ~**freund** m family friend; (umg) lover; ~**friedensbruch** m (JUR) trespass (in sb's house); ~**gebrauch** m: **für den ~gebrauch** (Gerät) for domestic od household use; **h~gemacht** adj homemade; ~**gemeinschaft** f household (community); ~**halt** m household; (POL) budget; **h~halten** unreg vi to keep house; (sparen) to economize; ~**hälterin** f housekeeper.

Haushalts- zW: ~**auflösung** f dissolution of the household; ~**buch** nt housekeeping book; ~**debatte** f (PARL) budget debate; ~**geld** nt housekeeping (money); ~**gerät** nt domestic appliance; ~**hilfe** f domestic od home help; ~**jahr** nt (POL, WIRTS) financial od fiscal year; ~**periode** f budget period; ~**plan** m budget.

Haus- zW: ~**haltung** f housekeeping; ~**herr** m host; (Vermieter) landlord; **h~hoch** adv: **h~hoch verlieren** to lose by a mile.

hausieren [hau'ziːrən] vi to peddle.

Hausierer (-s, -) m pedlar (BRIT), peddler (US).

hausintern ['haʊsɪntɛrn] adj internal company attrib.

häuslich ['hɔʏslɪç] adj domestic; **sich irgendwo ~ einrichten** od **niederlassen** to settle in somewhere; **H~keit** f domesticity.

Hausmacherart ['hausmaxərˌaːrt] f: **Wurst etc nach ~** home-made-style sausage etc.

Haus- zW: ~**mann** (-(e)s, pl -männer) m (den Haushalt versorgender Mann) househusband; ~**marke** f (eigene Marke) own brand; (bevorzugte Marke) favourite (BRIT) od favorite (US) brand; ~**meister** m caretaker, janitor; ~**mittel** nt household remedy; ~**nummer** f house number; ~**ordnung** f house rules pl; ~**putz** m house cleaning; ~**ratversicherung** f (household) contents insurance; ~**schlüssel** m front-door key; ~**schuh** m slipper; ~**schwamm** m dry rot.

Hausse ['hoːsə] (-, -n) f (WIRTS) boom; (BÖRSE) bull market; ~ **an** +dat boom in.

Haus- zW: ~**segen** m: **bei ihnen hängt der ~segen schief** (hum) they're a bit short on domestic bliss; ~**stand** m: **einen ~stand gründen** to set up house od home; ~**suchung** f police raid; ~**suchungsbefehl** m search warrant; ~**tier** nt domestic animal; ~**tür** f front door; ~**verbot** nt: **jdm ~verbot erteilen** to ban sb from the house; ~**verwalter** m property manager; ~**verwaltung** f property management; ~**wirt** m landlord; ~**wirtschaft** f domestic science; ~**-zu-~-Verkauf** m door-to-door selling.

Haut [haʊt] (-, Häute) f skin; (Tier~) hide; **mit ~ und Haar(en)** (umg) completely; **aus der ~ fahren** (umg) to go through the roof;

~arzt *m* skin specialist, dermatologist.
häuten ['hɔytən] *vt* to skin ♦ *vr* to shed one's skin.
hauteng *adj* skintight.
Hautfarbe *f* complexion.
Hautkrebs *m* (*MED*) skin cancer.
Havanna [ha'vana] (**-s**) *nt* Havana.
Havel ['ha:fəl] (**-**) *f* (*Fluß*) Havel.
Haxe ['haksə] (**-**, **-n**) *f* = **Hachse**.
Hbf. *abk* = **Hauptbahnhof**.
H-Bombe ['ha:bɔmbə] *f abk* H-bomb.
Hebamme ['he:ᵖ|amə] *f* midwife.
Hebel ['he:bəl] (**-s**, **-**) *m* lever; **alle ~ in Bewegung setzen** (*umg*) to move heaven and earth; **am längeren ~ sitzen** (*umg*) to have the whip hand.
heben ['he:bən] *unreg vt* to raise, lift; (*steigern*) to increase; **einen ~ gehen** (*umg*) to go for a drink.
Hebräer(in) [he'brɛ:ər(ɪn)] (**-s**, **-**) *m(f)* Hebrew.
hebräisch [he'brɛ:ɪʃ] *adj* Hebrew.
Hebriden [he'bri:dən] *pl:* **die ~** the Hebrides *pl*.
hecheln ['hɛçəln] *vi* (*Hund*) to pant.
Hecht [hɛçt] (**-(e)s**, **-e**) *m* pike; ~**sprung** *m* (*beim Schwimmen*) racing dive; (*beim Turnen*) forward dive; (*FUSSBALL: umg*) dive.
Heck [hɛk] (**-(e)s**, **-e**) *nt* stern; (*von Auto*) rear.
Hecke ['hɛkə] (**-**, **-n**) *f* hedge.
Heckenrose *f* dog rose.
Heckenschütze *m* sniper.
Heck- *zW:* ~**fenster** *nt* (*AUT*) rear window; ~**klappe** *f* tailgate; ~**motor** *m* rear engine.
heda ['he:da] *interj* hey there.
Heer [he:r] (**-(e)s**, **-e**) *nt* army.
Hefe ['he:fə] (**-**, **-n**) *f* yeast.
Heft ['hɛft] (**-(e)s**, **-e**) *nt* exercise book; (*Zeitschrift*) number; (*von Messer*) haft; **jdm das ~ aus der Hand nehmen** (*fig*) to seize control *od* power from sb.
Heftchen *nt* (*Fahrkarten~*) book of tickets; (*Briefmarken~*) book of stamps.
heften *vt:* **~ (an** +*akk*) to fasten (to); (*nähen*) to tack (on to)); (*mit Heftmaschine*) to staple *od* fasten (to) ♦ *vr:* **sich an jds Fersen** *od* **Sohlen ~** (*fig*) to dog sb's heels.
Hefter (**-s**, **-**) *m* folder.
heftig *adj* fierce, violent; **H~keit** *f* fierceness, violence.
Heft- *zW:* ~**klammer** *f* staple; ~**maschine** *f* stapling machine; ~**pflaster** *nt* sticking plaster; ~**zwecke** *f* drawing pin (*BRIT*), thumb tack (*US*).
hegen ['he:gən] *vt* to nurse; (*fig*) to harbour (*BRIT*), harbor (*US*), foster.
Hehl [he:l] *m od nt:* **kein(en) ~ aus etw machen** to make no secret of sth.
Hehler (**-s**, **-**) *m* receiver (of stolen goods), fence.
Heide¹ ['haidə] (**-**, **-n**) *f* heath, moor; (*~kraut*) heather.

Heide² ['haidə] (**-n**, **-n**) *m* heathen, pagan.
Heidekraut *nt* heather.
Heidelbeere *f* bilberry.
Heiden- *zW:* ~**angst** (*umg*) *f:* **eine ~angst vor etw/jdm haben** to be scared stiff of sth/sb; ~**arbeit** (*umg*) *f* real slog; **h~mäßig** (*umg*) *adj* terrific; ~**tum** *nt* paganism.
Heidin *f* heathen, pagan.
heidnisch ['haidnɪʃ] *adj* heathen, pagan.
heikel ['haikəl] *adj* awkward, thorny; (*wählerisch*) fussy.
Heil [hail] (**-(e)s**) *nt* well-being; (*Seelen~*) salvation ♦ *interj* hail; **Ski/Petri ~!** good skiing/fishing!
heil *adj* in one piece, intact; **mit ~er Haut davonkommen** to escape unscathed; **die ~e Welt** an ideal world (*without problems etc*).
Heiland (**-(e)s**, **-e**) *m* saviour (*BRIT*), savior (*US*).
Heil- *zW:* ~**anstalt** *f* nursing home; (*für Sucht- oder Geisteskranke*) home; ~**bad** *nt* (*Bad*) medicinal bath; (*Ort*) spa; **h~bar** *adj* curable.
Heilbutt ['hailbut] (**-s**, **-e**) *m* halibut.
heilen *vt* to cure ♦ *vi* to heal; **als geheilt entlassen werden** to be discharged with a clean bill of health.
heilfroh *adj* very relieved.
Heilgymnastin *f* physiotherapist.
heilig ['hailɪç] *adj* holy; **jdm ~ sein** (*lit, fig*) to be sacred to sb; **die H~e Schrift** the Holy Scriptures *pl*; **es ist mein ~er Ernst** I am deadly serious; **H~abend** *m* Christmas Eve.
Heilige(r) *f(m)* saint.
heiligen *vt* to sanctify, hallow; **der Zweck heiligt die Mittel** the end justifies the means.
Heiligenschein *m* halo.
heilig- *zW:* **H~keit** *f* holiness; ~**sprechen** *unreg vt* to canonize; **H~tum** *nt* shrine; (*Gegenstand*) relic.
Heilkunde *f* medicine.
heillos *adj* unholy; (*Schreck*) terrible.
Heil- *zW:* ~**mittel** *nt* remedy; ~**praktiker(in)** (**-s**, **-**) *m(f)* non-medical practitioner; **h~sam** *adj* (*fig*) salutary.
Heilsarmee *f* Salvation Army.
Heilung *f* cure.
heim [haim] *adv* home.
Heim (**-(e)**, **-e**) *nt* home; (*Wohn~*) hostel.
Heimarbeit *f* (*INDUSTRIE*) homework, outwork.
Heimat ['haima:t] (**-**, **-en**) *f* home (town/ country *etc*); ~**film** *m* sentimental film in idealized regional setting; ~**kunde** *f* (*SCH*) local history; ~**land** *nt* homeland; **h~lich** *adj* native, home *attrib*; (*Gefühle*) nostalgic; **h~los** *adj* homeless; ~**museum** *nt* local history museum; ~**ort** *m* home town *od* area; ~**vertriebene(r)** *f(m)* displaced person.
heimbegleiten *vt* to accompany home.
Heimchen *nt:* **~ (am Herd)** (*pej: Frau*)

housewife.
Heimcomputer *m* home computer.
heimelig ['haɪməlɪç] *adj* homely.
Heim- *zW:* **h~fahren** *unreg vi* to drive *od* go home; **~fahrt** *f* journey home; **~gang** *m* return home; (*Tod*) decease; **h~gehen** *unreg vi* to go home; (*sterben*) to pass away; **h~isch** *adj* (*gebürtig*) native; **sich h~isch fühlen** to feel at home; **~kehr** (-, **-en**) *f* homecoming; **h~kehren** *vi* to return home; **~kind** *nt child brought up in a home*; **h~kommen** *unreg vi* to come home; **~leiter** *m* warden of a home/hostel.
heimlich *adj* secret ♦ *adv:* ~, **still und leise** (*umg*) quietly, on the quiet; **H~keit** *f* secrecy; **H~tuerei** *f* secrecy.
Heim- *zW:* **~reise** *f* journey home; **~spiel** *nt* home game; **h~suchen** *vt* to afflict; (*Geist*) to haunt; **h~tückisch** *adj* malicious; **h~wärts** *adv* homewards; **~weg** *m* way home; **~weh** *nt* homesickness; **~weh haben** to be homesick; **~werker** *m* handyman; **h~zahlen** *vt:* **jdm etw h~zahlen** to pay back sb for sth.
Heini ['haɪni] (-s, -s) *m:* **blöder** ~ (*umg*) silly idiot.
Heirat ['haɪraːt] (-, **-en**) *f* marriage; **h~en** *vt, vi* to marry.
Heirats- *zW:* **~antrag** *m* proposal (of marriage); **~anzeige** *f* (*Annonce*) advertisement for a marriage partner; **~schwindler** *m person who makes a marriage proposal under false pretences*; **~urkunde** *f* marriage certificate.
heiser ['haɪzər] *adj* hoarse; **H~keit** *f* hoarseness.
heiß [haɪs] *adj* hot; (*Thema*) hotly disputed; (*Diskussion, Kampf*) heated, fierce; (*Begierde, Liebe, Wunsch*) burning; **es wird nichts so ~ gegessen, wie es gekocht wird** (*Sprichwort*) things are never as bad as they seem; **~er Draht** hot line; **~es Eisen** (*fig: umg*) hot potato; **~es Geld** hot money; **jdn/etw ~ und innig lieben** to love sb/sth madly; **~blütig** *adj* hot-blooded.
heißen ['haɪsən] *unreg vi* to be called; (*bedeuten*) to mean ♦ *vt* to command; (*nennen*) to name ♦ *vi unpers:* **es heißt hier ...** it says here ...; **es heißt, daß ...** they say that ...; **wie ~ Sie?** what's your name?; ... **und wie sie alle ~** ... and the rest of them; **das will schon etwas ~** that's quite something; **jdn willkommen ~** to bid sb welcome; **das heißt** that is; (*mit anderen Worten*) that is to say.
Heiß- *zW:* **h~ersehnt** *adj* longed for; **~hunger** *m* ravenous hunger; **h~laufen** *unreg vi, vr* to overheat; **~luft** *f* hot air; **h~umstritten** *adj attrib* hotly debated; **~wasserbereiter** *m* water heater.
heiter ['haɪtər] *adj* cheerful; (*Wetter*) bright; **aus ~em Himmel** (*fig*) out of the blue;

H~keit *f* cheerfulness; (*Belustigung*) amusement.
heizbar *adj* heated; (*Raum*) with heating; **leicht** ~ easily heated.
Heizdecke *f* electric blanket.
heizen *vt* to heat.
Heizer (-s, -) *m* stoker.
Heiz- *zW:* **~gerät** *nt* heater; **~körper** *m* radiator; **~öl** *nt* fuel oil; **~sonne** *f* electric fire.
Heizung *f* heating.
Heizungsanlage *f* heating system.
Hektar [hɛk'taːr] (-s, -e) *nt od m* hectare.
Hektik ['hɛktɪk] *f* hectic rush; (*von Leben etc*) hectic pace.
hektisch ['hɛktɪʃ] *adj* hectic.
Hektoliter [hɛkto'liːtər] *m od nt* hectolitre (*BRIT*), hectoliter (*US*).
Held [hɛlt] (-en, -en) *m* hero; **h~enhaft** ['hɛldənhaft] *adj* heroic; **~in** *f* heroine.
helfen ['hɛlfən] *unreg vi* to help; (*nützen*) to be of use ♦ *vb unpers:* **es hilft nichts, du mußt ...** it's no use, you'll have to ...; **jdm (bei etw) ~** to help sb (with sth); **sich** *dat* **zu ~ wissen** to be resourceful; **er weiß sich** *dat* **nicht mehr zu ~** he's at his wits' end.
Helfer(in) (-s, -) *m(f)* helper, assistant.
Helfershelfer *m* accomplice.
Helgoland ['hɛlgolant] (-s) *nt* Heligoland.
hell [hɛl] *adj* clear; (*Licht, Himmel*) bright; (*Farbe*) light; **~es Bier** ≈ lager; **von etw ~ begeistert sein** to be very enthusiastic about sth; **es wird** ~ it's getting light; **~blau** *adj* light blue; **~blond** *adj* ash-blond.
Helle (-) *f* clearness; brightness.
Heller (-s, -) *m* farthing; **auf ~ und Pfennig** (down) to the last penny.
hellhörig *adj* keen of hearing; (*Wand*) poorly soundproofed.
hellicht ['hɛllɪçt] (*getrennt* **hell-licht**) *adj:* **am ~en Tage** in broad daylight.
Helligkeit *f* clearness; brightness; lightness.
hell- *zW:* **~sehen** *vi:* **~sehen können** to be clairvoyant; **H~seher(in)** *m(f)* clairvoyant; **~wach** *adj* wide-awake.
Helm ['hɛlm] (-(e)s, -e) *m* helmet.
Helsinki ['hɛlzɪŋki] (-s) *nt* Helsinki.
Hemd [hɛmt] (-(e)s, -en) *nt* shirt; (*Unter~*) vest; **~bluse** *f* blouse.
Hemdenknopf *m* shirt button.
hemdsärmelig *adj* shirt-sleeved; (*fig: umg: salopp*) pally; (*Ausdrucksweise*) casual.
Hemisphäre [hemi'sfɛːrə] *f* hemisphere.
hemmen ['hɛmən] *vt* to check, hold up; **gehemmt sein** to be inhibited.
Hemmschuh *m* (*fig*) impediment.
Hemmung *f* check; (*PSYCH*) inhibition; (*Bedenken*) scruple.
hemmungslos *adj* unrestrained, without restraint.
Hengst [hɛŋst] (-es, -e) *m* stallion.
Henkel ['hɛŋkəl] (-s, -) *m* handle; **~krug** *m* jug;

~**mann** (*umg*) *m* (*Gefäß*) canteen.
henken ['hɛŋkən] *vt* to hang.
Henker (-s, -) *m* hangman.
Henne ['hɛnə] (-, -n) *f* hen.
Hepatitis [hepa'tiːtɪs] *f* (-, **Hepatitiden**) hepatitis.

================ *SCHLÜSSELWORT*

her [heːr] *adv* **1** (*Richtung*): **komm ~ zu mir** come here (to me); **von England ~** from England; **von weit ~** from a long way away; **~ damit!** hand it over!; **wo bist du ~?** where do you come from?; **wo hat er das ~?** where did he get that from?
2 (*Blickpunkt*): **von der Form ~** as far as the form is concerned
3 (*zeitlich*): **das ist 5 Jahre ~** that was 5 years ago; **ich kenne ihn von früher ~** I know him from before.

herab [hɛ'rap] *adv* down, downward(s); **~hängen** *unreg vi* to hang down; **~lassen** *unreg vt* to let down ♦ *vr* to condescend; **~lassend** *adj* condescending; **H~lassung** *f* condescension; **~sehen** *unreg vi:* **~sehen (auf +akk)** to look down (on); **~setzen** *vt* to lower, reduce; (*fig*) to belittle, disparage; **zu stark ~gesetzten Preisen** at greatly reduced prices; **H~setzung** *f* reduction; disparagement; **~stürzen** *vi* to fall off; (*Felsbrocken*) to fall down; **von etw ~stürzen** to fall off sth; to fall down from sth; **~würdigen** *vt* to belittle, disparage.
heran [hɛ'ran] *adv:* **näher ~!** come closer!; **~ zu mir!** come up to me!; **~bilden** *vt* to train; **~bringen** *unreg vt:* **~bringen (an +akk)** to bring up (to); **~fahren** *unreg vi:* **~fahren (an +akk)** to drive up (to); **~gehen** *unreg vi:* **an etw** *akk* **~gehen** (*an Problem, Aufgabe*) to tackle sth; **~kommen** *unreg vi:* **(an jdn/etw) ~kommen** to approach (sb/sth), come near ((to) sb/sth); **er läßt alle Probleme an sich ~kommen** he always adopts a wait-and-see attitude; **~machen** *vr:* **sich an jdn ~machen** to make up to sb; (*umg*) to approach sb; **~wachsen** *unreg vi* to grow up; **H~wachsende(r)** *f(m)* adolescent; **~winken** *vt* to beckon over; (*Taxi*) to hail; **~ziehen** *unreg vt* to pull nearer; (*aufziehen*) to raise; (*ausbilden*) to train; (*zu Hilfe holen*) to call in; (*Literatur*) to consult; **etw zum Vergleich ~ziehen** to use sth by way of comparison; **jdn zu etw ~ziehen** to call upon sb to help in sth.
herauf [hɛ'rauf] *adv* up, upward(s), up here; **~beschwören** *unreg vt* to conjure up, evoke; **~bringen** *unreg vt* to bring up; **~setzen** *vt* to increase; **~ziehen** *unreg vt* to draw *od* pull up ♦ *vi* to approach; (*Sturm*) to gather.
heraus [hɛ'raus] *adv* out; **nach vorn ~ wohnen** to live at the front (of the house); **~ mit der Sprache!** out with it!; **~arbeiten** *vt* to work

out; **~bekommen** *unreg vt* to get out; (*fig*) to find *od* figure out; (*Wechselgeld*) to get back; **~bringen** *unreg vt* to bring out; (*Geheimnis*) to elicit; **jdn/etw ganz groß ~bringen** (*umg*) to give sb/sth a big build-up; **aus ihm war kein Wort ~zubringen** they couldn't get a single word out of him; **~finden** *unreg vt* to find out; **~fordern** *vt* to challenge; (*provozieren*) to provoke; **H~forderung** *f* challenge; provocation; **~geben** *unreg vt* to give up, surrender; (*Geld*) to give back; (*Buch*) to edit; (*veröffentlichen*) to publish ♦ *vi* (*Wechselgeld geben*): **können Sie (mir) ~geben?** can you give me change?; **H~geber** (-s, -) *m* editor; (*Verleger*) publisher; **~gehen** *unreg vi:* **aus sich ~gehen** to come out of one's shell; **~halten** *unreg vr:* **sich aus etw ~halten** to keep out of sth; **~hängen** *unreg vt, vi* to hang out; **~holen** *vt:* **~holen (aus)** to get out (of); **~hören** *vt* (*wahrnehmen*) to hear; (*fühlen*): **~hören (aus)** to detect (in); **~kehren** *vt* (*fig*): **den Vorgesetzten ~kehren** to act the boss; **~kommen** *unreg vi* to come out; **dabei kommt nichts ~** nothing will come of it; **er kam aus dem Staunen nicht ~** he couldn't get over his astonishment; **es kommt auf dasselbe ~** it comes (down) to the same thing; **~nehmen** *unreg vt* to take out; **sich** *dat* **Freiheiten ~nehmen** to take liberties; **Sie nehmen sich zuviel ~** you're going too far; **~putzen** *vt:* **sich ~putzen** to get dressed up; **~reden** *vr* to talk one's way out of it (*umg*); **~reißen** *unreg vt* to tear out· (*Zahn, Baum*) to pull out; **~rücken** *vt* (*Geld*) to fork out, hand over; **mit etw ~rücken** (*fig*) to come out with sth; **~rutschen** *vi* to slip out; **~schlagen** *unreg vt* to knock out; (*fig*) to obtain; **~sein** *unreg vi:* **aus dem Gröbsten ~sein** to be over the worst; **~stellen** *vr:* **sich ~stellen (als)** to turn out (to be); **das muß sich erst ~stellen** that remains to be seen; **~strecken** *vt* to stick out; **~suchen** *vt:* **sich** *dat* **jdn/etw ~suchen** to pick out sb/sth; **~treten** *unreg vi:* **~treten (aus)** to come out (of); **~wachsen** *unreg vi:* **~wachsen aus** to grow out of; **~winden** *unreg vr* (*fig*): **sich aus etw ~winden** to wriggle out of sth; **~wollen** *vi:* **nicht mit etw ~wollen** (*umg: sagen wollen*) to not want to come out with sth; **~ziehen** *unreg vt* to pull out, extract.
herb [hɛrp] *adj* (slightly) bitter, acid; (*Wein*) dry; (*fig: schmerzlich*) bitter; (: *streng*) stern, austere.
herbei [hɛr'baɪ] *adv* (over) here; **~führen** *vt* to bring about; **~schaffen** *vt* to procure; **~sehnen** *vt* to long for.
herbemühen ['hɛːrbəmyːən] *vr* to take the trouble to come.
Herberge ['hɛrbɛrgə] (-, -n) *f* (*Jugend~ etc*) hostel.
Herbergsmutter *f* warden.

Herbergsvater m warden.
herbitten unreg vt to ask to come (here).
herbringen unreg vt to bring here.
Herbst [hɛrpst] (-(e)s, -e) m autumn, fall (US);
im ~ in autumn, in the fall (US); **h~lich** adj
autumnal.
Herd [heːrt] (-(e)s, -e) m cooker; (fig, MED)
focus, centre (BRIT), center (US).
Herde ['heːrdə] (-, -n) f herd; (Schaf~) flock.
Herdentrieb m (lit, fig: pej) herd instinct.
Herdplatte f (von Elektroherd) hotplate.
herein [hɛ'raɪn] adv in (here), here; **~!** come
in!; **~bitten** unreg vt to ask in; **~brechen** unreg
vi to set in; **~bringen** unreg vt to bring in;
~dürfen unreg vi to have permission to enter;
H~fall m letdown; **~fallen** unreg vi to be
caught, be taken in; **~fallen auf** +akk to fall
for; **~kommen** unreg vi to come in; **~lassen**
unreg vt to admit; **~legen** vt: **jdn ~legen** to
take sb in; **~platzen** vi to burst in;
~schneien (umg) vi to drop in; **~spazieren** vi:
~spaziert! come right in!
her- zW: **H~fahrt** f journey here; **~fallen**
unreg vi: **~fallen über** +akk to fall upon;
H~gang m course of events, circumstances
pl; **~geben** unreg vt to give, hand (over); **sich
zu etw ~geben** to lend one's name to sth;
das Thema gibt viel/nichts ~ there's a lot/
nothing to this topic; **~gebracht** adj: **in
~gebrachter Weise** in the traditional way;
~gehen unreg vi: **hinter jdm ~gehen** to follow
sb; **es geht hoch ~** there are a lot of
goings-on; **~haben** unreg (umg) vt: **wo hat er
das ~?** where did he get that from?;
~halten unreg vt to hold out; **~halten müssen**
(umg) to have to suffer; **~hören** vi to listen;
hör mal ~! listen here!
Hering ['heːrɪŋ] (-s, -e) m herring; (Zeltpflock)
(tent) peg.
herkommen unreg vi to come; **komm mal her!**
come here!
herkömmlich adj traditional.
Herkunft (-, -künfte) f origin.
Herkunftsland nt (COMM) country of origin.
her- zW: **~laufen** unreg vi: **~laufen hinter** +dat to
run after; **~leiten** vr to derive; **~machen** vr:
sich ~machen über +akk to set about od upon
♦ vt (umg): **viel ~machen** to look impressive.
Hermelin [hɛrmə'liːn] (-s, -e) m od nt ermine.
hermetisch [hɛr'meːtɪʃ] adj hermetic;
~ abgeriegelt completely sealed off.
her- zW: **~nach** adv afterwards; **~nehmen**
unreg vt: **wo soll ich das ~nehmen?** where am
I supposed to get that from?; **~nieder** adv
down.
Heroin [hero'iːn] (-s) nt heroin.
heroisch [he'roːɪʃ] adj heroic.
Herold ['heːrɔlt] (-(e)s, -e) m herald.
Herpes ['hɛrpɛs] m (-) (MED) herpes.
Herr [hɛr] (-(e)n, -en) m master; (Mann)
gentleman; (adliger, REL) Lord; (vor Namen)
Mr.; **mein ~!** sir!; **meine ~en!** gentlemen!;

Lieber ~ A, Sehr geehrter ~ A (in Brief) Dear
Mr. A; **„~en"** (Toilette) "gentlemen" (BRIT),
"men's room" (US); **die ~en der Schöpfung**
(hum: Männer) the gentlemen.
Herrchen (umg) nt (von Hund) master.
Herren- zW: **~bekanntschaft** f gentleman
friend; **~bekleidung** f menswear; **~besuch**
m gentleman visitor od visitors; **~doppel** nt
men's doubles; **~einzel** nt men's singles;
~haus nt mansion; **h~los** adj ownerless;
~magazin nt men's magazine.
Herrgott m: **~ noch mal!** (umg) damn it all!
Herrgottsfrühe f: **in aller ~** (umg) at the
crack of dawn.
herrichten ['heːrrɪçtən] vt to prepare.
Herrin f mistress.
herrisch adj domineering.
herrje [hɛr'jeː] interj goodness gracious!
herrjemine [hɛr'jeːmine] interj goodness
gracious!
herrlich adj marvellous (BRIT), marvelous
(US), splendid; **H~keit** f splendour (BRIT),
splendor (US), magnificence.
Herrschaft f power, rule; (Herr und Herrin)
master and mistress; **meine ~en!** ladies and
gentlemen!
herrschen ['hɛrʃən] vi to rule; (bestehen) to
prevail, be; **hier ~ ja Zustände!** things are in
a pretty state round here!
Herrscher(in) (-s, -) m(f) ruler.
Herrschsucht f domineeringness.
her- zW: **~rühren** vi to arise, originate;
~sagen vt to recite; **~sehen** unreg vi: **hinter
jdm/etw ~sehen** to follow sb/sth with one's
eyes; **~sein** unreg vi: **das ist schon 5 Jahre ~**
that was 5 years ago; **hinter jdm/etw ~sein**
to be after sb/sth; **~stammen** vi to descend
od come from; **~stellen** vt to make,
manufacture; (zustande bringen) to establish;
H~steller (-s, -) m manufacturer;
H~stellung f manufacture;
H~stellungskosten pl manufacturing costs
pl; **~tragen** unreg vt: **etw hinter jdm ~tragen**
to carry sth behind sb.
herüber [hɛ'ryːbər] adv over (here), across.
herum [hɛ'rʊm] adv about, (a)round; **um etw
~** around sth; **~ärgern** vr: **sich ~ärgern (mit)**
to get annoyed (with); **~blättern** vi:
~blättern in +dat to browse od flick through;
~doktern (umg) vi to fiddle od tinker about;
~drehen vi: **jdm das Wort im Mund ~drehen**
to twist sb's words; **~drücken** vr (vermeiden):
sich um etw ~drücken to dodge sth;
~fahren unreg vi to travel around; (mit Auto)
to drive around; (sich rasch umdrehen) to
spin (a)round; **~führen** vt to show around;
~gammeln (umg) vi to bum around; **~gehen**
unreg vi (~spazieren) to walk about; **um etw
~gehen** to walk od go round sth; **etw
~gehen lassen** to circulate sth; **~hacken** vi
(fig: umg): **auf jdm ~hacken** to pick on sb;
~irren vi to wander about; **~kommen** unreg

(*umg*) *vi:* **um etw ~kommen** to get out of sth; **er ist viel ~gekommen** he has been around a lot; **~kriegen** *vt* to bring *od* talk round; **~lungern** *vi* to lounge about; (*umg*) to hang around; **~quälen** *vr:* **sich mit Rheuma ~quälen** to be plagued by rheumatism; **~reißen** *unreg vt* to swing around (hard); **~schlagen** *unreg vr:* **sich mit etw ~schlagen** (*umg*) to tussle with sth; **~schleppen** *vt:* **etw mit sich ~schleppen** (*Sorge, Problem*) to be troubled by sth; (*Krankheit*) to have sth; **~sprechen** *unreg vr* to get around, be spread; **~stochern** (*umg*) *vi:* **im Essen ~stochern** to pick at one's food; **~treiben** *unreg vi, vr* to drift about; **H~treiber(in)** (**-s, -**) (*pej*) *m(f)* tramp; **~ziehen** *unreg vi, vr* to wander about.

herunter [hɛ'rʊntər] *adv* downward(s), down (there); **~gekommen** *adj* run-down; **~handeln** (*umg*) *vt* (*Preis*) to beat down; **~hängen** *unreg vi* to hang down; **~holen** *vt* to bring down; **~kommen** *unreg vi* to come down; (*fig*) to come down in the world; **~leiern** (*umg*) *vt* to reel off; **~machen** *vt* to take down; (*schlechtmachen*) to run down, knock; **~putzen** (*umg*) *vt:* **jdn ~putzen** to tear sb off a strip; **~sein** *unreg* (*umg*) *vi:* **mit den Nerven/der Gesundheit ~sein** to be at the end of one's tether/be run-down; **~spielen** *vt* to play down; **~wirtschaften** (*umg*) *vt* to bring to the brink of ruin.

hervor [hɛr'foːr] *adv* out, forth; **~brechen** *unreg vi* to burst forth, break out; **~bringen** *unreg vt* to produce; (*Wort*) to utter; **~gehen** *unreg vi* to emerge, result; **daraus geht ~, daß ...** from this it follows that ...; **~heben** *unreg vt* to stress; (*als Kontrast*) to set off; **~ragend** *adj* excellent; (*lit*) projecting; **~rufen** *unreg vt* to cause, give rise to; **~stechen** *unreg vi* (*lit, fig*) to stand out; **~stoßen** *unreg vt* (*Worte*) to gasp (out); **~treten** *unreg vi* to come out; **~tun** *unreg vr* to distinguish o.s.; (*umg: sich wichtig tun*) to show off; **sich mit etw ~tun** to show off sth.

Herz [hɛrts] (**-ens, -en**) *nt* heart; (*KARTEN: Farbe*) hearts *pl*; **mit ganzem ~en** wholeheartedly; **etw auf dem ~en haben** to have sth on one's mind; **sich** *dat* **etw zu ~en nehmen** to take sth to heart; **du sprichst mir aus dem ~en** that's just what I feel; **es liegt mir am ~en** I am very concerned about it; **seinem ~en Luft machen** to give vent to one's feelings; **sein ~ an jdn/etw hängen** to commit o.s. heart and soul to sb/sth; **ein ~ und eine Seele sein** to be the best of friends; **jdn/etw auf ~ und Nieren prüfen** to examine sb/sth very thoroughly; **~anfall** *m* heart attack; **~beschwerden** *pl* heart trouble *sing*.

herzen *vt* to caress, embrace.

Herzenslust *f:* **nach ~** to one's heart's content.

Herz- *zW:* **h~ergreifend** *adj* heart-rending;

h~erweichend *adj* heartrending; **~fehler** *m* heart defect; **h~haft** *adj* hearty.

herziehen ['hɛːrtsiːən] *vi:* **über jdn/etw ~** (*umg*) to pull sb/sth to pieces (*fig*).

Herz- *zW:* **~infarkt** *m* heart attack; **~klappe** *f* (heart) valve; **~klopfen** *nt* palpitation; **h~krank** *adj* suffering from a heart condition.

herzlich *adj* cordial ♦ *adv* (*sehr*): **~ gern!** with the greatest of pleasure!; **~en Glückwunsch** congratulations *pl*; **~e Grüße** best wishes; **H~keit** *f* cordiality.

herzlos *adj* heartless; **H~igkeit** *f* heartlessness.

Herzog ['hɛrtsoːk] (**-(e)s, ⁻e**) *m* duke; **~in** *f* duchess; **h~lich** *adj* ducal; **~tum** *nt* duchy.

Herz- *zW:* **~schlag** *m* heartbeat; (*MED*) heart attack; **~schrittmacher** *m* pacemaker; **h~zerreißend** *adj* heartrending.

Hesse ['hɛsə] (**-n, -n**) *m* Hessian.

Hessen ['hɛsən] (**-s**) *nt* Hesse.

Hessin *f* Hessian.

hessisch *adj* Hessian.

heterogen [hetero'geːn] *adj* heterogeneous.

heterosexuell [heteroze'ksuɛl] *adj* heterosexual.

Hetze ['hɛtsə] *f* (*Eile*) rush.

hetzen *vt* to hunt; (*verfolgen*) to chase ♦ *vi* (*eilen*) to rush; **jdn/etw auf jdn/etw ~** to set sb/sth on sb/sth; **~ gegen** to stir up feeling against; **~ zu** to agitate for.

Hetzerei [hɛtsə'raɪ] *f* agitation; (*Eile*) rush.

Hetzkampagne ['hɛtskampanjə] *f* smear campaign.

Heu [hɔʏ] (**-(e)s**) *nt* hay; **~boden** *m* hayloft.

Heuchelei [hɔʏçə'laɪ] *f* hypocrisy.

heucheln ['hɔʏçəln] *vt* to pretend, feign ♦ *vi* to be hypocritical.

Heuchler(in) [hɔʏçlər(ɪn)] (**-s, -**) *m(f)* hypocrite; **h~isch** *adj* hypocritical.

Heuer ['hɔʏər] (**-, -n**) *f* (*NAUT*) pay.

heuer *adv* this year.

heuern ['hɔʏərn] *vt* to sign on, hire.

Heugabel *f* pitchfork.

Heuhaufen *m* haystack.

heulen ['hɔʏlən] *vi* to howl; (*weinen*) to cry; **das ~de Elend bekommen** to get the blues.

heurig ['hɔʏrɪç] *adj* this year's.

Heuschnupfen *m* hay fever.

Heuschrecke *f* grasshopper; (*in heißen Ländern*) locust.

heute ['hɔʏtə] *adv* today; **~ abend/früh** this evening/morning; **~ morgen** this morning; **~ in einer Woche** a week today, today week; **von ~ auf morgen** (*fig: plötzlich*) overnight, from one day to the next; **das H~** today.

heutig ['hɔʏtɪç] *adj* today's; **unser ~es Schreiben** (*COMM*) our letter of today('s date).

heutzutage ['hɔʏtsutaːgə] *adv* nowadays.

Hexe ['hɛksə] (**-, -n**) *f* witch.

hexen *vi* to practise witchcraft; **ich kann**

doch nicht ~ I can't work miracles.
Hexen- zW: ~**häuschen** nt gingerbread house;
~**kessel** m (lit, fig) cauldron; ~**meister** m
wizard; ~**schuß** m lumbago.
Hexerei [hɛksə'raɪ] f witchcraft.
HG f abk = **Handelsgesellschaft.**
Hg. abk (= Herausgeber) ed.
hg. abk (= herausgegeben) ed.
HGB (-) nt abk (= Handelsgesetzbuch) statutes
of commercial law.
Hieb (-(e)s, -e) m blow; (Wunde) cut, gash;
(Stichelei) cutting remark; ~**e bekommen** to
get a thrashing.
hieb etc [hi:p] vb (veraltet) siehe **hauen.**
hieb- und stichfest adj (fig) watertight.
hielt etc [hi:lt] vb siehe **halten.**
hier [hi:r] adv here; ~ **spricht Dr. Müller** (TEL)
this is Dr Müller (speaking); **er ist von** ~
he's a local (man).
Hierarchie [hierar'çi:] f hierarchy.
hier- zW: ~**auf** adv thereupon; (danach) after
that; ~**aus** adv: ~**aus folgt, daß** ... from this
it follows that ...; ~**behalten** unreg vt to keep
here; ~**bei** adv (bei dieser Gelegenheit) on
this occasion; ~**bleiben** unreg vi to stay here;
~**durch** adv by this means; (örtlich) through
here; ~**her** adv this way, here; ~**hergehören**
vi to belong here; (fig: relevant sein) to be
relevant; ~**lassen** unreg vt to leave here;
~**mit** adv hereby; ~**mit erkläre ich** ... (form) I
hereby declare ...; ~**nach** adv hereafter;
~**von** adv about this, hereof; ~**von**
abgesehen apart from this; ~**zu** adv (dafür)
for this; (dazu) with this; (außerdem) in
addition to this, moreover; (zu diesem Punkt)
about this; ~**zulande** adv in this country.
hiesig ['hi:zɪç] adj of this place, local.
hieß etc [hi:s] vb siehe **heißen.**
Hi-Fi-Anlage ['haɪfianla:gə] f hi-fi set od
system.
High-Tech-Industrie ['haɪtɛkɪndʊs'tri:] f high
tech od hi-tech industry.
Hilfe ['hɪlfə] (-, -n) f help; (für Notleidende) aid;
Erste ~ first aid; **jdm** ~ **leisten** to help sb; ~**!**
help!; ~**leistung** f: **unterlassene** ~**leistung**
(JUR) denial of assistance; ~**stellung** f
(SPORT, fig) support.
Hilf- zW: **h**~**los** adj helpless; ~**losigkeit** f
helplessness; **h**~**reich** adj helpful.
Hilfs- zW: ~**aktion** f relief action, relief
measures pl; ~**arbeiter** m labourer (BRIT),
laborer (US); **h**~**bedürftig** adj needy;
h~**bereit** adj ready to help; ~**kraft** f
assistant, helper; ~**mittel** nt aid; ~**schule** f
school for backward children; ~**zeitwort** nt
auxiliary verb.
hilft [hɪlft] vb siehe **helfen.**
Himalaja [hi'ma:laja] (-s) m: **der** ~ the
Himalayas pl.
Himbeere ['hɪmbe:rə] (-, -n) f raspberry.
Himmel ['hɪməl] (-s, -) m sky; (REL, liter)
heaven; **um** ~**s willen** (umg) for Heaven's

sake; **zwischen** ~ **und Erde** in midair;
h~**angst** adj: **es ist mir h**~**angst** I'm scared
to death; ~**bett** nt four-poster bed; **h**~**blau**
adj sky-blue.
Himmelfahrt f Ascension.
Himmelfahrtskommando nt (MIL: umg)
suicide squad; (Unternehmen) suicide
mission.
Himmelreich nt (REL) Kingdom of Heaven.
himmelschreiend adj outrageous.
Himmelsrichtung f direction; **die vier** ~**en**
the four points of the compass.
himmelweit adj: **ein** ~**er Unterschied** a world
of difference.
himmlisch ['hɪmlɪʃ] adj heavenly.

═══════════════════ SCHLÜSSELWORT

hin [hɪn] adv **1** (Richtung): ~ **und zurück** there
and back; **einmal London** ~ **und zurück** a
return to London (BRIT), a roundtrip ticket
to London (US); ~ **und her** to and fro; **etw**
~ **und her überlegen** to turn sth over and
over in one's mind; **bis zur Mauer** ~ up to
the wall; **wo ist er** ~**?** where has he gone?;
nichts wie ~**!** (umg) let's go then!; **nach**
außen ~ (fig) outwardly; **Geld** ~, **Geld her**
money or no money
2 (auf ... ~): **auf meine Bitte** ~ at my request;
auf seinen Rat ~ on the basis of his advice;
auf meinen Brief ~ on the strength of my
letter
3: **mein Glück ist** ~ my happiness is gone;
~ **und wieder** (every) now and again.

hinab [hɪ'nap] adv down; ~**gehen** unreg vi to go
down; ~**sehen** unreg vi to look down.
hinarbeiten ['hɪnarbaɪtən] vi: **auf etw** akk ~
(auf Ziel) to work towards sth.
hinauf [hɪ'nauf] adv up; ~**arbeiten** vr to work
one's way up; ~**steigen** unreg vi to climb.
hinaus [hɪ'naus] adv out; **hinten/vorn** ~ at the
back/front; **darüber** ~ over and above this;
auf Jahre ~ for years to come; ~**befördern**
vt to kick or chuck out; ~**fliegen** unreg (umg)
vi to be kicked out; ~**führen** vi: **über etw** akk
~**führen** (lit, fig) to go beyond sth; ~**gehen**
unreg vi to go out; ~**gehen über** +akk to
exceed; ~**laufen** unreg vi to run out; ~**laufen**
auf +akk to come to, amount to; ~**schieben**
unreg vt to put off, postpone; ~**schießen** unreg
vi: **über das Ziel** ~**schießen** (fig) to overshoot
the mark; ~**wachsen** unreg vi: **er wuchs über**
sich selbst ~ he surpassed himself;
~**werfen** unreg vt to throw out; ~**wollen** vi to
want to go out; ~**wollen** hoch ~ to aim high;
~**wollen auf** +akk to drive at, get at; ~**ziehen**
unreg vt to draw out ♦ vr to be protracted;
~**zögern** vt to delay, put off ♦ vr to be
delayed, be put off.
hinbekommen unreg (umg) vt: **das hast du gut**
~ you've made a good job of it.
hinblättern (umg) vt (Geld) to fork out.

Hinblick ['hɪnblɪk] *m:* **in** *od* **im ~ auf** +*akk* in view of.

hinderlich ['hɪndərlɪç] *adj* awkward; **jds Karriere** *dat* **~ sein** to be a hindrance to sb's career.

hindern *vt* to hinder, hamper; **jdn an etw** *dat* **~** to prevent sb from doing sth.

Hindernis (**-ses, -se**) *nt* obstacle; **~lauf** *m,* **~rennen** *nt* steeplechase.

Hinderungsgrund *m* obstacle.

hindeuten ['hɪndɔytən] *vi:* **~ auf** +*akk* to point to.

Hinduismus [hɪndu'ɪsmʊs] *m* Hinduism.

hindurch [hɪn'dʊrç] *adv* through; across; (*zeitlich*) over.

hindürfen [hɪn'dʏrfən] *unreg vi:* **~** (**zu**) to be allowed to go (to).

hinein [hɪ'naɪn] *adv* in; **bis tief in die Nacht ~** well into the night; **~fallen** *unreg vi* to fall in; **~fallen in** +*akk* to fall into; **~finden** *unreg vr* (*fig: sich zurechtfinden*) to find one's feet; (*sich abfinden*) to come to terms with it; **~gehen** *unreg vi* to go in; **~gehen in** +*akk* to go into, enter; **~geraten** *unreg vi:* **~geraten in** +*akk* to get into; **~knien** *vr* (*fig: umg*): **sich in etw** *akk* **~knien** to get into sth; **~lesen** *unreg vt:* **etw in etw** *akk* **~lesen** to read sth into sth; **~passen** *vi* to fit in; **~passen in** +*akk* to fit into; **~prügeln** *vt:* **etw in jdn ~prügeln** to cudgel sth into sb; **~reden** *vi:* **jdm ~reden** to interfere in sb's affairs; **~stecken** *vt:* **Geld/Arbeit in etw** *akk* **~stecken** to put money/some work into sth; **~steigern** *vr* to get worked up; **~versetzen** *vr:* **sich in jdn ~versetzen** to put o.s. in sb's position; **~ziehen** *unreg vt:* **~ziehen** (**in** +*akk*) to pull in (to); **jdn in etw ~ziehen** (*in Konflikt, Gespräch*) to draw sb into sth.

hin- *zW:* **~fahren** *unreg vi* to go; to drive ♦ *vt* to take; to drive; **H~fahrt** *f* journey there; **~fallen** *unreg vi* to fall down; **~fällig** *adj* frail, decrepit; (*Regel etc*) unnecessary; **~fliegen** *unreg vi* to fly there; (*umg: ~fallen*) to fall over; **H~flug** *m* outward flight.

hing *etc* [hɪŋ] *vb siehe* **hängen**.

hin- *zW:* **H~gabe** *f* devotion; **mit H~gabe tanzen/singen** *etc* (*fig*) to dance/sing *etc* with abandon; **~geben** *unreg vr* +*dat* to give o.s. up to, devote o.s. to; **~gebungsvoll** ['hɪngeːbʊŋsfɔl] *adv* (*begeistert*) with abandon; (*lauschen*) raptly.

hingegen [hɪn'geːgən] *konj* however.

hin- *zW:* **~gehen** *unreg vi* to go; (*Zeit*) to pass; **gehst du auch ~?** are you going too?; **~gerissen** *adj:* **~gerissen sein** to be enraptured; **ich bin ganz ~- und hergerissen** (*ironisch*) that's absolutely great; **~halten** *unreg vt* to hold out; (*warten lassen*) to put off, stall; **H~haltetaktik** *f* stalling *od* delaying tactics *pl.*

hinhauen ['hɪnhaʊən] *unreg* (*umg*) *vi* (*klappen*) to work; (*ausreichen*) to do.

hinhören ['hɪnhøːrən] *vi* to listen.

hinken ['hɪŋkən] *vi* to limp; (*Vergleich*) to be unconvincing.

hin- *zW:* **~kommen** *unreg* (*umg*) *vi* (*auskommen*) to manage; (*: ausreichen, stimmen*) to be right; **~länglich** *adj* adequate ♦ *adv* adequately; **~legen** *vt* to put down ♦ *vr* to lie down; **sich der Länge nach ~legen** (*umg*) to fall flat; **~nehmen** *unreg vt* (*fig*) to put up with, take; **~reichen** *vi* to be adequate ♦ *vt:* **jdm etw ~reichen** to hand sb sth; **~reichend** *adj* adequate; (*genug*) sufficient; **H~reise** *f* journey out; **~reißen** *unreg vt* to carry away, enrapture; **sich ~reißen lassen, etw zu tun** to get carried away and do sth; **~reißend** *adj* (*Landschaft, Anblick*) enchanting; (*Schönheit, Mensch*) captivating; **~richten** *vt* to execute; **H~richtung** *f* execution; **~sehen** *unreg vi:* **bei genauerem H~sehen** on closer inspection.

hinsein ['hɪnzaɪn] *unreg* (*umg*) *vi* (*kaputt sein*) to have had it; (*Ruhe*) to be gone.

hin- *zW:* **~setzen** *vr* to sit down; **H~sicht** *f:* **in mancher** *od* **gewisser H~sicht** in some respects *od* ways; **~sichtlich** *präp* +*gen* with regard to; **~sollen** (*umg*) *vi:* **wo soll ich/das Buch ~?** where do I/does the book go?; **H~spiel** *nt* (*SPORT*) first leg; **~stellen** *vt* to put (down) ♦ *vr* to place o.s.

hinanstellen [hɪnt'|anʃtɛlən] *vt* (*fig*) to ignore.

hinten ['hɪntən] *adv* behind; (*rückwärtig*) at the back; **~ und vorn** (*fig: betrügen*) left, right and centre; **das reicht ~ und vorn nicht** that's nowhere near enough; **~dran** (*umg*) *adv* at the back; **~herum** *adv* round the back; (*fig*) secretly.

hinter ['hɪntər] *präp* (+*dat od akk*) behind; (*: nach*) after; **~ jdm hersein** to be after sb; **~ die Wahrheit kommen** to get to the truth; **sich ~ jdn stellen** to support sb; **etw ~ sich** *dat* **haben** (*zurückgelegt haben*) to have got through sth; **sie hat viel ~ sich** she has been through a lot; **H~achse** *f* rear axle; **H~bänkler** (**-s, -**) *m* (*POL: pej*) backbencher; **H~bein** *nt* hind leg; **sich auf die H~beine stellen** to get tough; **H~bliebene(r)** *f(m)* surviving relative; **~drein** *adv* afterwards.

hintere(r, s) *adj* rear, back.

hinter- *zW:* **~'einander** *adv* one after the other; **zwei Tage ~einander** two days running; **~fotzig** (*umg*) *adj* underhanded; **~fragen** *vt untr* to analyse; **H~gedanke** *m* ulterior motive; **~gehen** *unreg vt untr* to deceive; **H~grund** *m* background; **~gründig** *adj* cryptic, enigmatic; **H~grundprogramm** *nt* (*COMPUT*) background program; **H~halt** *m* ambush; **etw im H~halt haben** to have sth in reserve; **~hältig** *adj* underhand, sneaky; **~her** *adv* afterwards, after; **~hersein** *unreg vi:* **er ist ~her, daß ...** (*fig*) he sees to it that ...; **H~hof** *m* back yard; **H~kopf** *m* back of one's head; H~**land** *nt* hinterland; ~**lassen** *unreg vt untr* to leave; H~**lassenschaft** *f* (testator's) estate; ~**legen** *vt untr* to deposit; H~**legungsstelle** *f* depository; H~**list** *f* cunning, trickery; (*Handlung*) trick, dodge; ~**listig** *adj* cunning, crafty; H~**mann** (-(e)s, *pl* -**männer**) *m* person behind; **die** H~**männer des Skandals** the men behind the scandal.

Hintern ['hɪntərn] (-s, -) (*umg*) *m* bottom, backside; **jdm den** ~ **versohlen** to smack sb's bottom.

hinter- *zW:* H~**rad** *nt* back wheel; H~**radantrieb** *m* (*AUT*) rear-wheel drive; ~**rücks** *adv* from behind; H~**teil** *nt* behind; H~**treffen** *nt:* **ins** H~**treffen kommen** to lose ground; ~**treiben** *unreg vt untr* to prevent, frustrate; H~**treppe** *f* back stairs *pl;* H~**tür** *f* back door; (*fig: Ausweg*) escape, loophole; H~**wäldler** (-s, -) (*umg*) *m* backwoodsman, hillbilly (*bes US*); ~**ziehen** *unreg vt untr* (*Steuern*) to evade (paying).

hintun ['hɪntuːn] *unreg* (*umg*) *vt:* **ich weiß nicht, wo ich ihn ~ soll** (*fig*) I can't (quite) place him.

hinüber [hɪ'nyːbər] *adv* across, over; ~**gehen** *unreg vi* to go over *od* across.

hinunter [hɪ'nʊntər] *adv* down; ~**bringen** *unreg vt* to take down; ~**schlucken** *vt* (*lit, fig*) to swallow; ~**spülen** *vt* to flush away; (*Essen, Tablette*) to wash down; (*fig: Ärger*) to soothe; ~**steigen** *unreg vi* to descend.

Hinweg ['hɪnveːk] *m* journey out.

hinweg- [hɪn'vɛk] *zW:* ~**gehen** *unreg vi:* **über etw** *akk* ~**gehen** (*fig*) to pass over sth; ~**helfen** *unreg vi:* **jdm über etw** *akk* ~**helfen** to help sb to get over sth; ~**kommen** *unreg vi* (*fig*): **über etw** *akk* ~**kommen** to get over sth; ~**sehen** *unreg vi:* **darüber** ~**sehen, daß** ... to overlook the fact that ...; ~**setzen** *vr:* **sich** ~**setzen über** +*akk* to disregard.

Hinweis ['hɪnvaɪs] (-es, -e) *m* (*Andeutung*) hint; (*Anweisung*) instruction; (*Verweis*) reference; **sachdienliche** ~**e** relevant information.

hinweisen *unreg vi:* ~ **auf** +*akk* to point to; (*verweisen*) to refer to; **darauf** ~, **daß** ... to point out that ...; (*anzeigen*) to indicate that ...

Hinweisschild *nt* sign.

Hinweistafel *f* sign.

hinwerfen *unreg vt* to throw down; **eine hingeworfene Bemerkung** a casual remark.

hinwirken *vi:* **auf etw** *akk* ~ to work towards sth.

Hinz [hɪnts] *m:* ~ **und Kunz** (*umg*) every Tom, Dick and Harry.

hinziehen *unreg vr* (*fig*) to drag on.

hinzielen *vi:* ~ **auf** +*akk* to aim at.

hinzu [hɪn'tsuː] *adv* in addition; ~**fügen** *vt* to add; H~**fügung** *f:* **unter** H~**fügung von etw** (*form*) by adding sth; ~**kommen** *unreg vi:* **es**

kommt noch ~, daß ... there is also the fact that ...; ~**ziehen** *unreg vt* to consult.

Hiobsbotschaft ['hiːɔpsboːtʃaft] *f* bad news.

Hirn [hɪrn] (-(e)s, -e) *nt* brain(s); ~**gespinst** (-(e)s, -e) *nt* fantasy; ~**hautentzündung** *f* (*MED*) meningitis; h~**tot** *adj* braindead; h~**verbrannt** *adj* (*umg*) harebrained.

Hirsch [hɪrʃ] (-(e)s, -e) *m* stag.

Hirse ['hɪrzə] (-, -n) *f* millet.

Hirt ['hɪrt] (-en, -en) *m*, **Hirte** (-n, -n) *m* herdsman; (*Schaf~, fig*) shepherd.

Hirtin *f* herdswoman; (*Schaf~*) shepherdess.

hissen ['hɪsən] *vt* to hoist.

Historiker [hɪs'toːrikər] (-s, -) *m* historian.

historisch [hɪs'toːrɪʃ] *adj* historical.

Hit [hɪt] (-s, -s) *m* (*MUS, fig: umg*) hit; ~**parade** *f* hit parade.

Hitze ['hɪtsə] (-) *f* heat; h~**beständig** *adj* heat-resistant; h~**frei** *adj:* h~**frei haben** to have time off school/work because of excessive heat; ~**welle** *f* heat wave.

hitzig *adj* hot-tempered; (*Debatte*) heated.

Hitz- *zW:* ~**kopf** *m* hothead; h~**köpfig** *adj* fiery, hot-headed; ~**schlag** *m* heatstroke.

HIV-negativ *adj* HIV-negative.

HIV-positiv *adj* HIV-positive.

hl. *abk* = **heilig.**

H-Milch ['haːmɪlç] *f* long-life milk, UHT milk.

HNO-Arzt *m* ENT specialist.

hob *etc* [hoːp] *vb siehe* **heben.**

Hobby ['hɔbi] (-s, -s) *nt* hobby.

Hobel ['hoːbəl] (-s, -) *m* plane; ~**bank** *f* carpenter's bench.

hobeln *vt, vi* to plane.

Hobelspäne *pl* wood shavings *pl.*

hoch [hoːx] (*attrib* **hohe(r, s)**) *adj* high ♦ *adv:* **wenn es ~ kommt** (*umg*) at (the) most, at the outside; **das ist mir zu ~** (*umg*) that's above my head; **ein hohes Tier** (*umg*) a big fish; **es ging ~ her** (*umg*) we/they *etc* had a whale of a time; **~ und heilig versprechen** to promise faithfully.

Hoch (-s, -s) *nt* (*Ruf*) cheer; (*MET, fig*) high.

hoch- *zW:* ~**achten** *vt* to respect; H~**achtung** *f* respect, esteem; **mit vorzüglicher** H~**achtung** (*form: Briefschluß*) yours faithfully; ~**achtungsvoll** *adv* yours faithfully; ~**aktuell** *adj* highly topical; H~**amt** *nt* high mass; ~**arbeiten** *vr* to work one's way up; ~**begabt** *adj* extremely gifted; ~**betagt** *adj* very old, aged; H~**betrieb** *m* intense activity; (*COMM*) peak time; H~**betrieb haben** to be at one's *od* its busiest; ~**bringen** *unreg vt* to bring up; H~**burg** *f* stronghold; H~**deutsch** *nt* High German; ~**dotiert** *adj* highly paid; H~**druck** *m* high pressure; H~**ebene** *f* plateau; ~**empfindlich** *adj* highly sensitive; (*Film*) high-speed; ~**entwickelt** *adj attrib* (*Kultur, Land*) highly developed; (*Geräte, Methoden*) sophisticated; ~**erfreut** *adj* highly delighted; ~**fahren** *unreg vi* (*erschreckt*) to jump;

~**fliegend** adj ambitious; (fig) high-flown;
H~form f top form; **H~gebirge** nt high
mountains pl; **H~gefühl** nt elation; ~**gehen**
unreg (umg) vi (explodieren) to blow up;
(Bombe) to go off; **H~genuß** m great od
special treat; (großes Vergnügen) great
pleasure; ~**geschlossen** adj (Kleid etc) high-
necked; ~**gestellt** adj attrib (fig: Persönlichkeit)
high-ranking; **H~glanz** m high polish;
(PHOT) gloss; ~**gradig** adj intense, extreme;
~**halten** unreg vt to hold up; (fig) to uphold,
cherish; **H~haus** nt multi-storey building;
~**heben** unreg vt to lift (up); ~**kant** adv: jdn
~**kant hinauswerfen** (fig: umg) to chuck sb
out on his/her ear; ~**kommen** unreg vi (nach
oben) to come up; (fig: gesund werden) to get
back on one's feet; (beruflich, gesellschaftlich)
to come up in the world; **H~konjunktur** f
boom; ~**krempeln** vt to roll up; **H~land** nt
highlands pl; ~**leben** vi: jdn ~**leben lassen** to
give sb three cheers; **H~leistungssport** m
competitive sport; ~**modern** adj very
modern, ultra-modern; **H~mut** m pride;
~**mütig** adj proud, haughty; ~**näsig** adj
stuck-up, snooty; ~**nehmen** unreg vt to pick
up; jdn ~**nehmen** (umg: verspotten) to pull
sb's leg; **H~ofen** m blast furnace;
~**prozentig** adj (Alkohol) strong; **H~rechnung**
f projected result; **H~saison** f high season;
H~schätzung f high esteem.
Hochschulabschluß m degree.
Hochschulbildung f higher education.
Hochschule f college; (Universität)
university.
Hochschulreife f: er hat (die) ~ ≈ he's got his
A-levels (BRIT), he's graduated from high
school (US).
hoch- zW: ~**schwanger** adj heavily pregnant,
well advanced in pregnancy;
H~seefischerei f deep-sea fishing; **H~sitz** m
(Jagd) (raised) hide; **H~sommer** m middle
of summer; **H~spannung** f high tension;
~**spielen** vt (fig) to blow up; **H~sprache** f
standard language; ~**springen** unreg vi to
jump up; **H~sprung** m high jump.
höchst [høːçst] adv highly, extremely.
Hochstapler ['hoːxstaːplər] (-s, -) m swindler.
höchste(r, s) adj highest; (äußerste) extreme;
die ~ Instanz (JUR) the supreme court of
appeal.
höchstens adv at the most.
Höchstgeschwindigkeit f maximum speed.
Höchstgrenze f upper limit.
Hochstimmung f high spirits pl.
Höchst- zW: ~**leistung** f best performance;
(bei Produktion) maximum output;
h~persönlich adv personally, in person;
~**preis** m maximum price; ~**stand** m peak;
h~wahrscheinlich adv most probably.
Hoch- zW: ~**technologie** f high technology;
h~technologisch adj high-tech;
~**temperatur-Reaktor** m high-temperature

reactor; ~**tour** f: **auf ~touren laufen** od
arbeiten to be working flat out; **h~trabend**
adj pompous; ~**- und Tiefbau** m structural
and civil engineering; ~**verrat** m high
treason; ~**wasser** nt high water;
(Überschwemmung) floods pl; **h~wertig** adj
high-class, first-rate; ~**würden** m
Reverend; ~**zahl** f (MATH) exponent.
Hochzeit ['hɔxtsait] (-, -en) f wedding; **man
kann nicht auf zwei ~en tanzen** (Sprichwort)
you can't have your cake and eat it.
Hochzeitsreise f honeymoon.
Hochzeitstag m wedding day; (Jahrestag)
wedding anniversary.
hochziehen unreg vt (Rolladen, Hose) to pull
up; (Brauen) to raise.
Hocke ['hɔkə] (-, -n) f squatting position;
(beim Turnen) squat vault; (beim Skilaufen)
crouch.
hocken ['hɔkən] vi, vr to squat, crouch.
Hocker (-s, -) m stool.
Höcker ['hœkər] (-s, -) m hump.
Hockey ['hɔki] (-s) nt hockey.
Hoden ['hoːdən] (-s, -) m testicle.
Hodensack m scrotum.
Hof [hoːf] (-(e)s, ⸚e) m (Hinter~) yard;
(Bauern~) farm; (Königs~) court; **einem
Mädchen den ~ machen** (veraltet) to court a
girl.
hoffen ['hɔfən] vi: ~ (**auf** +akk) to hope (for).
hoffentlich adv I hope, hopefully.
Hoffnung ['hɔfnʊŋ] f hope; **jdm ~en machen**
to raise sb's hopes; **sich** dat **~en machen** to
have hopes; **sich** dat **keine ~en machen** not
to hold out any hope(s).
Hoffnungs- zW: **h~los** adj hopeless;
~**losigkeit** f hopelessness; ~**schimmer** m
glimmer of hope; **h~voll** adj hopeful.
höflich ['høːflıç] adj courteous, polite; **H~keit**
f courtesy, politeness.
hohe(r, s) ['hoːə(r, s)] adj siehe hoch.
Höhe ['høːə] (-, -n) f height; (An~) hill; **nicht
auf der ~ sein** (fig: umg) to feel below par;
ein Scheck in ~ von ... a cheque (BRIT) od
check (US) for the amount of ...; **das ist
doch die ~** (fig: umg) that's the limit; **er geht
immer gleich in die ~** (umg) he always flares
up; **auf der ~ der Zeit sein** to be up-to-date.
Hoheit ['hoːhait] f (POL) sovereignty; (Titel)
Highness.
Hoheits- zW: ~**gebiet** nt sovereign territory;
~**gewalt** f (national) jurisdiction;
~**gewässer** nt territorial waters pl;
~**zeichen** nt national emblem.
Höhen- zW: ~**angabe** f altitude reading; (auf
Karte) height marking; ~**flug** m: **geistiger
~flug** intellectual flight; ~**lage** f altitude;
~**luft** f mountain air; ~**messer** m altimeter;
~**sonne** f sun lamp; ~**unterschied** m
difference in altitude; ~**zug** m mountain
chain.
Höhepunkt m climax; (des Lebens) high

point.

höher *adj, adv* higher.

hohl [ho:l] *adj* hollow; (*umg: dumm*) hollow(-headed).

Höhle ['hø:lə] (-, -n) *f* cave; hole; (*Mund~*) cavity; (*fig, ZOOL*) den.

Hohl- *zW:* ~**heit** *f* hollowness; ~**kreuz** *nt* (*MED*) hollow back; ~**maß** *nt* measure of volume; ~**raum** *m* hollow space; (*Gebäude*) cavity; ~**saum** *m* hemstitch; ~**spiegel** *m* concave mirror.

Hohn [ho:n] (-(e)s) *m* scorn; **das ist der reinste** ~ it's sheer mockery.

höhnen ['hø:nən] *vt* to taunt, scoff at.

höhnisch *adj* scornful, taunting.

Hokuspokus [ho:kus'po:kus] (-) *m* (*Zauberformel*) hey presto; (*fig: Täuschung*) hocus-pocus.

hold [holt] *adj* charming, sweet.

holen ['ho:lən] *vt* to get, fetch; (*Atem*) to take; **jdn/etw** ~ **lassen** to send for sb/sth; **sich** *dat* **eine Erkältung** ~ to catch a cold.

Holland ['holant] (-s) *nt* Holland.

Holländer ['holɛndər] (-s, -) *m* Dutchman.

Holländerin *f* Dutchwoman, Dutch girl.

holländisch *adj* Dutch.

Hölle ['hœlə] (-, -n) *f* hell; **ich werde ihm die** ~ **heiß machen** (*umg*) I'll give him hell.

Höllenangst *f:* **eine** ~ **haben** to be scared to death.

Höllenlärm *m* infernal noise (*umg*).

höllisch ['hœlɪʃ] *adj* hellish, infernal.

Hologramm [holo'gram] (-s, -e) *nt* hologram.

holperig ['holpərɪç] *adj* rough, bumpy.

holpern ['holpərn] *vi* to jolt.

Holunder [ho'lundər] (-s, -) *m* elder.

Holz [holts] (-es, ⁻er) *nt* wood; **aus** ~ made of wood, wooden; **aus einem anderen/demselben** ~ **geschnitzt sein** (*fig*) to be cast in a different/the same mould; **gut** ~! (*Kegeln*) have a good game!; ~**bläser** *m* woodwind player.

hölzern ['hœltsərn] *adj* (*lit, fig*) wooden.

Holz- *zW:* ~**fäller** (-s, -) *m* lumberjack, woodcutter; ~**faserplatte** *f* (wood) fibreboard (*BRIT*) *od* fiberboard (*US*); **h~frei** *adj* (*Papier*) wood-free.

holzig *adj* woody.

Holz- *zW:* ~**klotz** *m* wooden block; ~**kohle** *f* charcoal; ~**kopf** *m* (*fig: umg*) blockhead, numbskull; ~**scheit** *nt* log; ~**schuh** *m* clog; ~**weg** *m* (*fig*) wrong track; ~**wolle** *f* fine wood shavings *pl*; ~**wurm** *m* woodworm.

Homecomputer ['houmkɔm'pju:tər] (-s, -) *m* home computer.

homogen [homo'ge:n] *adj* homogenous.

Homöopath [homøo'pa:t] (-en, -en) *m* homeopath.

Homöopathie [homøopa'ti:] *f* homeopathy, homeopathic medicine.

homosexuell [homozɛksu'ɛl] *adj* homosexual.

Honduras [hon'du:ras] (-) *nt* Honduras.

Hongkong [hoŋ'koŋ] (-s) *nt* Hong Kong.

Honig ['ho:nɪç] (-s, -e) *m* honey; ~**lecken** *nt* (*fig*): **das ist kein** ~**lecken** it's no picnic; ~**melone** *f* honeydew melon; ~**wabe** *f* honeycomb.

Honorar [hono'ra:r] (-s, -e) *nt* fee.

Honoratioren [honoratsi'o:rən] *pl* dignitaries *pl*.

honorieren [hono'ri:rən] *vt* to remunerate; (*Scheck*) to honour (*BRIT*), honor (*US*).

Hopfen ['hopfən] (-s, -) *m* hops *pl*; **bei ihm ist** ~ **und Malz verloren** (*umg*) he's a dead loss.

hoppla ['hopla] *interj* whoops.

hopsen ['hopsən] *vi* to hop.

Hörapparat *m* hearing aid.

hörbar *adj* audible.

horch [horç] *interj* listen.

horchen *vi* to listen; (*pej*) to eavesdrop.

Horcher (-s, -) *m* listener; eavesdropper.

Horde ['hordə] (-, -n) *f* horde.

hören ['hø:rən] *vt, vi* to hear; **auf jdn/etw** ~ to listen to sb/sth; **ich lasse von mir** ~ I'll be in touch; **etwas/nichts von sich** ~ **lassen** to get/not to get in touch; **H~** *nt:* **es verging ihm H~ und Sehen** (*umg*) he didn't know whether he was coming or going.

Hörensagen *nt:* **vom** ~ from hearsay.

Hörer (-s, -) *m* (*RUNDF*) listener; (*UNIV*) student; (*Telefon~*) receiver.

Hörfunk *m* radio.

Hörgerät *nt* hearing aid.

hörig ['hø:rɪç] *adj:* **sie ist ihm (sexuell)** ~ he has (sexual) power over her.

Horizont [hori'tsont] (-(e)s, -e) *m* horizon; **das geht über meinen** ~ (*fig*) that is beyond me.

horizontal [horitso'ta:l] *adj* horizontal.

Hormon [hor'mo:n] (-s, -e) *nt* hormone.

Hörmuschel *f* (*TEL*) earpiece.

Horn [horn] (-(e)s, ⁻er) *nt* horn; **ins gleiche** *od* **in jds** ~ **blasen** to chime in; **sich** *dat* **die Hörner abstoßen** (*umg*) to sow one's wild oats; ~**brille** *f* horn-rimmed spectacles *pl*.

Hörnchen ['hœrnçən] *nt* (*Gebäck*) croissant.

Hornhaut *f* horny skin; (*des Auges*) cornea.

Hornisse [hor'nɪsə] (-, -n) *f* hornet.

Hornochs(e) *m* (*fig: umg*) blockhead, idiot.

Horoskop [horo'sko:p] (-s, -e) *nt* horoscope.

Hör- *zW:* ~**rohr** *nt* ear trumpet; (*MED*) stethoscope; ~**saal** *m* lecture room; ~**spiel** *nt* radio play.

Horst [horst] (-(e)s, -e) *m* (*Nest*) nest; (*Adler~*) eyrie.

Hort [hort] (-(e)s, -e) *m* hoard; (*SCH*) nursery school; **h~en** *vt* to hoard.

Hörweite *f:* **in/außer** ~ within/out of hearing *od* earshot.

Hose ['ho:ze] (-, -n) *f* trousers *pl*, pants *pl* (*US*); **in die** ~ **gehen** (*umg*) to be a complete flop.

Hosen- *zW:* ~**anzug** *m* trouser suit, pantsuit (*US*); ~**boden** *m:* **sich auf den** ~**boden setzen** (*umg*) to get stuck in; ~**rock** *m*

culottes *pl*; ~**tasche** *f* trouser pocket;
~**träger** *pl* braces *pl* (*BRIT*), suspenders *pl*
(*US*).
Hostie ['hɔstiə] *f* (*REL*) host.
Hotel [ho'tɛl] (-**s**, -**s**) *nt* hotel; ~**fach** *nt* hotel
management; ~ **garni** *nt* bed and breakfast
hotel.
Hotelier [hotɛli'eː] (-**s**, -**s**) *m* hotelkeeper,
hotelier.
HR *abk* (= *Hessischer Rundfunk*) Hessen Radio.
Hr. *abk* (= *Herr*) Mr.
Hrsg. *abk* (= *Herausgeber*) ed.
hrsg. *abk* (= *herausgegeben*) ed.
Hub [huːp] (-**(e)s**, -**e**) *m* lift; (*TECH*) stroke.
hüben ['hyːbən] *adv* on this side, over here;
~ **und drüben** on both sides.
Hubraum *m* (*AUT*) cubic capacity.
hübsch [hypʃ] *adj* pretty, nice; **immer**
~ **langsam!** (*umg*) nice and easy.
Hubschrauber (-**s**, -) *m* helicopter.
Hucke ['hʊkə] (-, -**n**) *f:* **jdm die** ~ **vollhauen**
(*umg*) to give sb a good hiding.
huckepack ['hʊkəpak] *adv* piggy-back, pick-
a-back.
hudeln ['huːdəln] *vi* to be sloppy.
Huf ['huːf] (-**(e)s**, -**e**) *m* hoof; ~**eisen** *nt*
horseshoe; ~**nagel** *m* horseshoe nail.
Hüfte ['hyftə] (-, -**n**) *f* hip.
Hüftgürtel *m* girdle.
Hüfthalter *m* girdle.
Huftier *nt* hoofed animal.
Hügel ['hyːgəl] (-**s**, -) *m* hill.
hüg(e)lig *adj* hilly.
Huhn [huːn] (-**(e)s**, -**er**) *nt* hen; (*KOCH*)
chicken; **da lachen ja die Hühner** (*umg*) it's
enough to make a cat laugh; **er sah aus wie
ein gerupftes** ~ (*umg*) he looked as if he'd
been dragged through a hedge backwards.
Hühnchen ['hyːnçən] *nt* young chicken; **mit
jdm ein** ~ **zu rupfen haben** (*umg*) to have a
bone to pick with sb.
Hühner- *zW:* ~**auge** *nt* corn; ~**brühe** *f*
chicken broth; ~**klein** *nt* (*KOCH*) chicken
trimmings *pl*.
Huld [hʊlt] (-) *f* favour (*BRIT*), favor (*US*).
huldigen ['hʊldɪgən] *vi:* **jdm** ~ to pay homage
to sb.
Huldigung *f* homage.
Hülle ['hylə] (-, -**n**) *f* cover(ing); (*Zellophan~*)
wrapping; **in** ~ **und Fülle** galore; **die** ~**n
fallen lassen** (*fig*) to strip off.
hüllen *vt:* ~ (**in** +*akk*) to cover (with); to wrap
(in).
Hülse ['hylzə] (-, -**n**) *f* husk, shell.
Hülsenfrucht *f* pulse.
human [hu'maːn] *adj* humane.
humanistisch [huma'nɪstɪʃ] *adj:* ~**es
Gymnasium** *secondary school with bias on
Latin and Greek.*
humanitär [humani'tɛːr] *adj* humanitarian.
Humanität *f* humanity.
Humanmedizin *f* (human) medicine.

Hummel ['hʊməl] (-, -**n**) *f* bumblebee.
Hummer ['hʊmər] (-**s**, -) *m* lobster.
Humor [hu'moːr] (-**s**, -**e**) *m* humour (*BRIT*),
humor (*US*); ~ **haben** to have a sense of
humo(u)r; ~**ist(in)** *m(f)* humorist; **h~istisch**
adj humorous; **h~voll** *adj* humorous.
humpeln ['hʊmpəln] *vi* to hobble.
Humpen ['hʊmpən] (-**s**, -) *m* tankard.
Humus ['huːmʊs] (-) *m* humus.
Hund [hʊnt] (-**(e)s**, -**e**) *m* dog; **auf den**
~ **kommen, vor die** ~**e gehen** (*fig: umg*) to
go to the dogs; ~**e, die bellen, beißen nicht**
(*Sprichwort*) empty vessels make most noise
(*Sprichwort*); **er ist bekannt wie ein bunter** ~
(*umg*) everybody knows him.
Hunde- *zW:* **h~elend** (*umg*) *adj:* **mir ist
h~elend** I feel lousy; ~**hütte** *f* (dog)
kennel; ~**kuchen** *m* dog biscuit; ~**marke** *f*
dog licence disc, dog tag (*US*); **h~müde**
(*umg*) *adj* dog-tired.
hundert ['hʊndərt] *num* hundred; **H~** (-**s**, -**e**) *nt*
hundred; **H~e von Menschen** hundreds of
people.
Hunderter (-**s**, -) *m* hundred; (*umg:
Geldschein*) hundred (mark/pound/dollar *etc*
note).
hundert- *zW:* **H~jahrfeier** *f* centenary;
H~meterlauf *m* (*SPORT*): **der/ein
H~meterlauf** the/a hundred metres (*BRIT*)
od meters (*US*) *sing*; ~**prozentig** *adj, adv* one
hundred per cent.
hundertste(r, s) *adj* hundredth; **von H~n ins
Tausendste kommen** (*fig*) to get carried
away.
Hundesteuer *f* dog licence (*BRIT*) *od* license
(*US*) fee.
Hundewetter (*umg*) *nt* filthy weather.
Hündin ['hyndɪn] *f* bitch.
Hüne ['hyːnə] (-**n**, -**n**) *m:* **ein** ~ **von Mensch** a
giant of a man.
Hünengrab *nt* megalithic tomb.
Hunger ['hʊŋər] (-**s**) *m* hunger; ~ **haben** to be
hungry; **ich sterbe vor** ~ (*umg*) I'm starving;
~**lohn** *m* starvation wages *pl*.
hungern *vi* to starve.
Hungersnot *f* famine.
Hungerstreik *m* hunger strike.
Hungertuch *nt:* **am** ~ **nagen** (*fig*) to be
starving.
hungrig ['hʊŋrɪç] *adj* hungry.
Hunsrück ['hʊnsrʏk] *m* Hunsruck (Mountains
pl).
Hupe ['huːpə] (-, -**n**) *f* horn.
hupen *vi* to hoot, sound one's horn.
hupfen ['huːpfən] *vi* to hop, jump; **das ist
gehupft wie gesprungen** (*umg*) it's six of
one and half a dozen of the other.
hüpfen ['hypfən] *vi* = **hupfen.**
Hupkonzert (*umg*) *nt* hooting (of car horns).
Hürde ['hʏrdə] (-, -**n**) *f* hurdle; (*für Schafe*)
pen.
Hürdenlauf *m* hurdling.

Hure ['hu:rə] (-, -n) f whore.
Hurensohn (pej: umg!) m bastard (!), son of a bitch (!).
hurra [hʊ'ra:] interj hurray, hurrah.
hurtig ['hʊrtɪç] adj brisk, quick ♦ adv briskly, quickly.
huschen ['hʊʃən] vi to flit, scurry.
Husten ['hu:stən] (-s) m cough; **h~** vi to cough; **auf etw** akk **h~** (umg) not to give a damn for sth; **~anfall** m coughing fit; **~bonbon** m od nt cough drop; **~saft** m cough mixture.
Hut¹ [hu:t] (-(e)s, ̈-e) m hat; **unter einen ~ bringen** (umg) to reconcile; (Termine etc) to fit in.
Hut² [hu:t] (-) f care; **auf der ~ sein** to be on one's guard.
hüten ['hy:tən] vt to guard ♦ vr to watch out; **das Bett/Haus ~** to stay in bed/indoors; **sich ~, zu** to take care not to; **sich ~ vor** +dat to beware of; **ich werde mich ~**! not likely!
Hutschnur f: **das geht mir über die ~** (umg) that's going too far.
Hütte ['hʏtə] (-, -n) f hut; (Holz~, Block~) cabin; (Eisen~) forge; (umg: Wohnung) pad; (TECH: ~nwerk) iron and steel works.
Hüttenindustrie f iron and steel industry.
Hüttenkäse m cottage cheese.
Hüttenwerk nt iron and steel works.
hutzelig ['hʊtsəlɪç] adj shrivelled.
Hyäne [hy'ɛ:nə] (-, -n) f hyena.
Hyazinthe [hya'tsɪntə] (-, -n) f hyacinth.
Hydrant [hy'drant] m hydrant.
hydraulisch [hy'draʊlɪʃ] adj hydraulic.
Hydrierung [hy'dri:rʊŋ] f hydrogenation.
Hygiene [hygi'e:nə] (-) f hygiene.
hygienisch [hygi'e:nɪʃ] adj hygienic.
Hymne ['hʏmnə] (-, -n) f hymn, anthem.
hyper- ['hypɛr] präf hyper-.
Hypnose [hyp'no:zə] (-, -n) f hypnosis.
hypnotisch adj hypnotic.
Hypnotiseur [hypnoti'zø:r] m hypnotist.
hypnotisieren [hypnoti|zi:rən] vt to hypnotize.
Hypotenuse [hypote'nu:zə] (-, -n) f hypotenuse.
Hypothek [hypo'te:k] (-, -en) f mortgage; **eine ~ aufnehmen** to raise a mortgage; **etw mit einer ~ belasten** to mortgage sth.
Hypothese [hypo'te:zə] (-, -n) f hypothesis.
hypothetisch [hypo'te:tɪʃ] adj hypothetical.
Hysterie [hyste'ri:] f hysteria.
hysterisch [hʏs'te:rɪʃ] adj hysterical; **einen ~en Anfall bekommen** (fig) to have hysterics.

I, i

I, i [i:] nt I, i; **~ wie Ida** ≈ I for Isaac, I for Item (US); **das Tüpfelchen auf dem i** (fig) the final touch.
i. abk = **in, im**.
i.A. abk (= im Auftrag) p.p.
iberisch [i'be:rɪʃ] adj Iberian; **die ~e Halbinsel** the Iberian Peninsula.
IC (-) m abk = **Intercity-Zug**.
ICE m abk (= Intercity-Expreßzug) inter-city train.
ich [ɪç] pron I; **~ bin's!** it's me!; **I~ (-(s), -(s))** nt self; (PSYCH) ego; **I~-form** f first person; **I~-Roman** m novel in the first person.
Ideal [ide'a:l] (-s, -e) nt ideal; **i~** adj ideal; **~fall** m: **im ~fall** ideally.
Idealismus [idea'lɪsmʊs] m idealism.
Idealist(in) m(f) idealist.
idealistisch adj idealistic.
Idealvorstellung f ideal.
Idee [i'de:] (-, -n) f idea; (ein wenig) shade, trifle; **jdn auf die ~ bringen, etw zu tun** to give sb the idea of doing sth.
ideell [ide'ɛl] adj ideal.
identifizieren [identifi'tsi:rən] vt to identify.
identisch [i'dɛntɪʃ] adj identical.
Identität [idɛnti'tɛ:t] f identity.
Ideologe [ideo'lo:gə] (-n, -n) m ideologist.
Ideologie [ideolo'gi:] f ideology.
Ideologin [ideo'lo:gɪn] f ideologist.
ideologisch [ideo'lo:gɪʃ] adj ideological.
idiomatisch [idio'ma:tɪʃ] adj idiomatic.
Idiot [idi'o:t] (-en, -en) m idiot.
Idiotenhügel m (hum: umg) beginners' od nursery slope.
idiotensicher (umg) adj foolproof.
Idiotin f idiot.
idiotisch adj idiotic.
Idol [i'do:l] nt (-s, -e) idol.
idyllisch [i'dʏlɪʃ] adj idyllic.
IG abk (= Industriegewerkschaft) industrial trade union.
IGB (-) m abk (= Internationaler Gewerkschaftsbund) International Trades Union Congress.
Igel ['i:gəl] (-s, -) m hedgehog.
igitt(igitt) [i'gɪt(i'gɪt)] interj ugh!
Iglu ['i:glu] (-s, -s) m od nt igloo.
Ignorant [ɪgno'rant] (-en, -en) m ignoramus.
ignorieren [ɪgno'ri:rən] vt to ignore.
IHK f abk = **Industrie- und Handelskammer**.
ihm [i:m] dat von er, es pers pron (to) him, (to) it; **es ist ~ nicht gut** he doesn't feel well.

ihn [iːn] *akk von er pers pron* him; (*bei Tieren, Dingen*) it.
ihnen ['iːnən] *dat pl von sie pers pron* (to) them; (*nach Präpositionen*) them.
Ihnen *dat von Sie pers pron* (to) you; (*nach Präpositionen*) you.

════════════ *SCHLÜSSELWORT*

ihr [iːr] *pron* **1** (*nom pl*) you; ~ **seid es** it's you **2** (*dat von sie*) (to) her; (*bei Tieren, Dingen*) (to) it; **gib es** ~ give it to her; **er steht neben** ~ he is standing beside her
♦ *poss pron* **1** (*sing*) her; (: *bei Tieren, Dingen*) its; ~ **Mann** her husband **2** (*pl*) their; **die Bäume und** ~**e Blätter** the trees and their leaves.

Ihr *poss pron* your.
Ihre(r, s) *poss pron* yours; **tun Sie das** ~ (*geh*) you do your bit.
ihre(r, s) *poss pron* hers; (*eines Tieres*) its; (*von mehreren*) theirs; **sie taten das** ~ (*geh*) they did their bit.
ihrer ['iːrər] *gen von sie pers pron* (*sing*) of her; (*pl*) of them.
Ihrer *gen von Sie pers pron* of you.
ihrerseits *adv* for your part.
ihrerseits *adv* for her/their part.
ihresgleichen *pron* people like her/them; (*von Dingen*) others like it; **eine Frechheit, die** ~ **sucht!** an incredible cheek!
ihretwegen *adv* (*für sie*) for her/its/their sake; (*wegen ihr, ihnen*) on her/its/their account; **sie sagte,** ~ **könnten wir gehen** she said that, as far as she was concerned, we could go.
ihretwillen *adv:* **um** ~ for her/its/their sake.
ihrige ['iːrɪgə] *pron:* **der/die/das** ~ hers; its; theirs.
i.J. *abk* (= *im Jahre*) in (the year).
Ikone [i'koːnə] (-, -n) *f* icon.
IKRK *nt abk* (= *Internationales Komitee vom Roten Kreuz*) ICRC.
illegal ['ɪlegaːl] *adj* illegal.
illegitim ['ɪlegitiːm] *adj* illegitimate.
Illusion [ɪluzi'oːn] *f* illusion; **sich** *dat* ~**en machen** to delude o.s.
illusorisch [ɪlu'zoːrɪʃ] *adj* illusory.
Illustration [ɪlustratsi'oːn] *f* illustration.
illustrieren [ɪlus'triːrən] *vt* to illustrate.
Illustrierte (-n, -n) *f* picture magazine.
Iltis ['ɪltɪs] (-ses, -se) *m* polecat.
im [ɪm] = **in dem** ♦ *präp:* **etw** ~ **Liegen/Stehen tun** do sth lying down/standing up.
Image ['ɪmɪtʃ] (-(s), -s) *nt* image; ~**pflege** ['ɪmɪtʃpfleːgə] (*umg*) *f* image-building.
imaginär [imagi'nɛːr] *adj* imaginary.
Imbiß ['ɪmbɪs] (-sses, -sse) *m* snack; ~**halle** *f* snack bar; ~**stube** *f* snack bar.
imitieren [imi'tiːrən] *vt* to imitate.
Imker ['ɪmkər] (-s, -) *m* beekeeper.
immanent [ima'nɛnt] *adj* inherent, intrinsic.

Immatrikulation [ɪmatrikulatsi'oːn] *f* (*UNIV*) registration.
immatrikulieren [ɪmatriku'liːrən] *vi, vr* to register.
immer ['ɪmər] *adv* always; ~ **wieder** again and again; **etw** ~ **wieder tun** to keep on doing sth; ~ **noch** still; ~ **noch nicht** still not; **für** ~ forever; ~ **wenn ich ... every time I ...**; ~ **schöner** more and more beautiful; ~**trauriger** sadder and sadder; **was/wer (auch)** ~ whatever/whoever; ~**hin** *adv* all the same; ~**zu** *adv* all the time.
Immigrant(in) [ɪmi'grant(ɪn)] *m(f)* immigrant.
Immobilien [ɪmo'biːliən] *pl* real property (*BRIT*), real estate (*US*); (*in Zeitungs-annoncen*) property *sing*; ~**händler** *m*, ~**makler** *m* estate agent (*BRIT*), realtor (*US*).
immun [ɪ'muːn] *adj* immune.
immunisieren [ɪmuni'ziːrən] *vt* to immunize.
Immunität [ɪmuni'tɛːt] *f* immunity.
Immunschwäche *f* immunodeficiency.
Immunsystem *nt* immune system.
imperativ ['ɪmperatiːf] *adj:* ~**es Mandat** imperative mandate.
Imperativ (-s, -e) *m* imperative.
Imperfekt ['ɪmpɛrfɛkt] (-s, -e) *nt* imperfect (tense).
Imperialismus [ɪmperia'lɪsmʊs] *m* imperialism.
Imperialist [ɪmperia'lɪst] *m* imperialist; **i**~**isch** *adj* imperialistic.
impfen ['ɪmpfən] *vt* to vaccinate.
Impf- *zW:* ~**paß** *m* vaccination card; ~**schutz** *m* protection given by vaccination; ~**stoff** *m* vaccine; ~**ung** *f* vaccination; ~**zwang** *m* compulsory vaccination.
implizieren [ɪmpli'tsiːrən] *vt* to imply.
imponieren [ɪmpo'niːrən] *vi +dat* to impress.
Import [ɪm'pɔrt] (-(e)s, -e) *m* import.
Importeur [ɪmpɔr'tøːr] (-s, -e) *m* importer.
importieren [ɪmpɔr'tiːrən] *vt* to import.
imposant [ɪmpo'zant] *adj* imposing.
impotent ['ɪmpotɛnt] *adj* impotent.
Impotenz ['ɪmpotɛnts] *f* impotence.
imprägnieren [ɪmprɛ'gniːrən] *vt* to (water)proof.
Impressionismus [ɪmpresio'nɪsmʊs] *m* impressionism.
Impressum [ɪm'presʊm] (-s, -ssen) *nt* imprint; (*von Zeitung*) masthead.
Improvisation [ɪmprovizatsi'oːn] *f* improvisation.
improvisieren [ɪmprovi'ziːrən] *vt, vi* to improvise.
Impuls [ɪm'pʊls] (-es, -e) *m* impulse; **etw aus einem** ~ **heraus tun** to do sth on impulse.
impulsiv [ɪmpʊl'ziːf] *adj* impulsive.
imstande [ɪm'ʃtandə] *adj:* ~ **sein** to be in a position; (*fähig*) to be able; **er ist zu allem** ~ he's capable of anything.

========================= SCHLÜSSELWORT

in [ɪn] *präp +akk* **1** (*räumlich: wohin*) in, into;
~ **die Stadt** into town; ~ **die Schule gehen** to
go to school; ~ **die Hunderte gehen** to run
into (the) hundreds
2 (*zeitlich*): **bis** ~**s 20. Jahrhundert** into *od* up
to the 20th century
♦ *präp +dat* **1** (*räumlich: wo*) in; ~ **der Stadt** in
town; ~ **der Schule sein** to be at school; **es**
~ **sich haben** (*umg: Text*) to be tough;
(: *Drink*) to have quite a kick
2 (*zeitlich: wann*): ~ **diesem Jahr** this year;
(*in jenem Jahr*) in that year; **heute** ~ **zwei
Wochen** two weeks today.

inaktiv ['ɪn|aktiːf] *adj* inactive; (*Mitglied*) non-
active.
Inangriffnahme [ɪn'|angrɪfnaːmə] (-, -n) *f*
(*form*) commencement.
Inanspruchnahme [ɪn'|anʃpruxnaːmə] (-, -n) *f*:
~ (*+gen*) demands *pl* (on); **im Falle einer** ~ **der
Arbeitslosenunterstützung** (*form*) where
unemployment benefit has been sought.
Inbegriff ['ɪnbəgrɪf] *m* embodiment,
personification.
inbegriffen *adv* included.
Inbetriebnahme ['ɪnbətriːpnaːmə] (-, -n) *f*
(*form*) commissioning; (*von Gebäude,
U-Bahn etc*) inauguration.
inbrünstig ['ɪnbrʏnstɪç] *adj* ardent.
indem [ɪn'deːm] *konj* while; ~ **man etw macht**
(*dadurch*) by doing sth.
Inder(in) ['ɪndər(ɪn)] (-s, -) *m(f)* Indian.
indes(sen) [ɪn'dɛs(ən)] *adv* meanwhile ♦ *konj*
while.
Index ['ɪndɛks] (-(es), -e *od* **Indizes**) *m*: **auf dem**
~ **stehen** (*fig*) to be banned; ~**zahl** *f* index
number.
Indianer(in) [ɪndi'aːnər(ɪn)] (-s, -) *m(f)* (Red *od*
American) Indian.
indianisch *adj* (Red *od* American) Indian.
Indien ['ɪndiən] (-s) *nt* India.
indigniert [ɪndɪ'gniːrt] *adj* indignant.
Indikation [ɪndikatsi'oːn] *f*: **medizinische/
soziale** ~ medical/social grounds *pl* for the
termination of pregnancy.
Indikativ ['ɪndikatiːf] (-s, -e) *m* indicative.
indirekt ['ɪndirɛkt] *adj* indirect; ~**e Steuer**
indirect tax.
indisch ['ɪndɪʃ] *adj* Indian; **I**~**er Ozean** Indian
Ocean.
indiskret ['ɪndɪskreːt] *adj* indiscreet.
Indiskretion [ɪndɪskretsi'oːn] *f* indiscretion.
indiskutabel ['ɪndɪskutaːbəl] *adj* out of the
question.
indisponiert ['ɪndɪsponiːrt] *adj* (*geh*)
indisposed.
Individualist [ɪndividua'lɪst] *m* individualist.
Individualität [ɪndividuali'tɛt] *f* individuality.
individuell [ɪndividu'ɛl] *adj* individual; **etw**
~ **gestalten** to give sth a personal note.

Individuum [ɪndi'viːduʊm] (-s, -duen) *nt*
individual.
Indiz [ɪn'diːts] (-es, -ien) *nt* (*JUR*) clue; ~ **(für)**
sign (of).
Indizes ['ɪnditseːz] *pl von* **Index**.
Indizienbeweis *m* circumstantial evidence.
indizieren [ɪndi'tsiːrən] *vt, vi* (*COMPUT*) to
index.
Indochina ['ɪndo'çiːna] (-s) *nt* Indochina.
indogermanisch ['ɪndogɛr'maːnɪʃ] *adj* Indo-
Germanic, Indo-European.
indoktrinieren [ɪndɔktri'niːrən] *vt* to
indoctrinate.
Indonesien [ɪndo'neːziən] (-s) *nt* Indonesia.
Indonesier(in) (-s, -) *m(f)* Indonesian.
indonesisch [ɪndo'neːzɪʃ] *adj* Indonesian.
Indossament [ɪndɔsa'mɛnt] *nt* (*COMM*)
endorsement.
Indossant [ɪndɔ'sant] *m* endorser.
Indossat [ɪndɔ'saːt] (-en, -en) *m* endorsee.
indossieren *vt* to endorse.
industrialisieren [ɪndustriali'ziːrən] *vt* to
industrialize.
Industrialisierung *f* industrialization.
Industrie [ɪndus'triː] *f* industry; **in der**
~ **arbeiten** to be in industry; ~**gebiet** *nt*
industrial area; ~**gelände** *nt* industrial *od*
trading estate; ~**kaufmann** *m* industrial
manager.
industriell [ɪndustri'ɛl] *adj* industrial; ~**e
Revolution** industrial revolution.
Industrielle(r) *f(m)* industrialist.
Industrie- *zW*: ~**staat** *m* industrial nation; ~-
und Handelskammer *f* chamber of industry
and commerce; ~**zweig** *m* branch of
industry.
ineinander [ɪn|aɪ'nandər] *adv* in(to) one
another *od* each other; ~ **übergehen** to
merge (into each other); ~**greifen** *unreg vi*
(*lit*) to interlock; (*Zahnräder*) to mesh; (*fig:
Ereignisse etc*) to overlap.
Infanterie [ɪnfantə'riː] *f* infantry.
Infarkt [ɪn'farkt] (-(e)s, -e) *m* coronary
(thrombosis).
Infektion [ɪnfɛktsi'oːn] *f* infection.
Infektionsherd *m* focus of infection.
Infektionskrankheit *f* infectious disease.
Infinitiv ['ɪnfinitiːf] (-s, -e) *m* infinitive.
infizieren [ɪnfi'tsiːrən] *vt* to infect ♦ *vr*: **sich
(bei jdm)** ~ to be infected (by sb).
in flagranti [ɪn fla'granti] *adv* in the act, red-
handed.
Inflation [ɪnflatsi'oːn] *f* inflation.
inflationär [ɪnflatsio'nɛːr] *adj* inflationary.
Inflationsrate *f* rate of inflation.
inflatorisch [ɪnfla'toːrɪʃ] *adj* inflationary.
Info ['ɪnfo] (-s, -s) (*umg*) *nt* (information)
leaflet.
infolge [ɪn'fɔlgə] *präp +gen* as a result of, owing
to; ~**dessen** *adv* consequently.
Informatik [ɪnfɔr'maːtɪk] *f* information
studies *pl*.

Informatiker(in) (-s, -) *m(f)* computer scientist.

Information [ɪnfɔrmatsi'oːn] *f* information *no pl*; **Informationen** *pl* (*COMPUT*) data; **zu Ihrer ~ for your information.

Informationsabruf *m* (*COMPUT*) information retrieval.

Informationstechnik *f* information technology.

informativ [ɪnfɔrma'tiːf] *adj* informative.

informieren [ɪnfɔr'miːrən] *vt*: **~ (über** +*akk*) to inform (about) ♦ *vr*: **sich ~ (über** +*akk*) to find out (about).

Infrastruktur ['ɪnfraʃtruktuːr] *f* infrastructure.

Infusion [ɪnfuzi'oːn] *f* infusion.

Ing. *abk* = **Ingenieur.**

Ingenieur [ɪnʒeni'øːr] *m* engineer; **~schule** *f* school of engineering.

Ingwer ['ɪŋvər] (-s) *m* ginger.

Inh. *abk* (= *Inhaber(in)*) prop.; (= *Inhalt*) cont.

Inhaber(in) ['ɪnhaːbər(ɪn)] (-s, -) *m(f)* owner; (*COMM*) proprietor; (*Haus~*) occupier; (*Lizenz~*) licensee, holder; (*FIN*) bearer.

inhaftieren [ɪnhaf'tiːrən] *vt* to take into custody.

inhalieren [ɪnha'liːrən] *vt, vi* to inhale.

Inhalt ['ɪnhalt] (-(e)s, -e) *m* contents *pl*; (*eines Buchs etc*) content; (*MATH: Flächen~*) area; (: *Raum~*) volume; **i~lich** *adj* as regards content.

Inhalts- *zW*: **~angabe** *f* summary; **i~los** *adj* empty; **i~reich** *adj* full; **~verzeichnis** *nt* table of contents; (*COMPUT*) directory.

inhuman ['ɪnhumaːn] *adj* inhuman.

initialisieren [initsia:li'ziːrən] *vt* (*COMPUT*) to initialize.

Initialisierung *f* (*COMPUT*) initialization.

Initiative [initsia'tiːvə] *f* initiative; **die ~ ergreifen** to take the initiative.

Initiator(in) [initsi'aːtɔr(ɪn)] *m(f)* (*geh*) initiator.

Injektion [ɪnjɛktsi'oːn] *f* injection.

injizieren [ɪnji'tsiːrən] *vt* to inject; **jdm etw ~** to inject sb with sth.

Inka ['ɪŋka] (-(s), -s) *f(m)* Inca.

Inkaufnahme [ɪn'kaʊfnaːmə] *f* (*form*): **unter ~ finanzieller Verluste** accepting the inevitable financial losses.

inkl. *abk* (= *inklusive*) inc.

inklusive [ɪnklu'ziːvə] *präp* +*gen* inclusive of ♦ *adv* inclusive.

Inklusivpreis *m* all-in rate.

inkognito [ɪn'kɔgnito] *adv* incognito.

inkonsequent ['ɪnkɔnzekvɛnt] *adj* inconsistent.

inkorrekt ['ɪnkɔrɛkt] *adj* incorrect.

Inkrafttreten [ɪn'krafttreːtən] (-s) *nt* coming into force.

Inkubationszeit [ɪnkubatsi'oːnstsaɪt] *f* (*MED*) incubation period.

Inland ['ɪnlant] (-(e)s) *nt* (*GEOG*) inland; (*POL,*

COMM) home (country); **im ~ und Ausland** at home and abroad; **~flug** *m* domestic flight.

Inlandsporto *nt* inland postage.

inmitten [ɪn'mɪtən] *präp* +*gen* in the middle of; **~ von** amongst.

innehaben ['ɪnahaːbən] *unreg vt* to hold.

innehalten ['ɪnahaltən] *unreg vi* to pause, stop.

innen ['ɪnən] *adv* inside; **nach ~** inwards; **von ~** from the inside; **I~architekt** *m* interior designer; **I~aufnahme** *f* indoor photograph; **I~bahn** *f* (*SPORT*) inside lane; **I~dienst** *m*: **im I~dienst sein** to work in the office; **I~einrichtung** *f* (interior) furnishings *pl*; **I~leben** *nt* (*seelisch*) emotional life; (*umg: körperlich*) insides *pl*; **I~minister** *m* minister of the interior, Home Secretary (*BRIT*); **I~politik** *f* domestic policy; **~politisch** *adj* relating to domestic policy, domestic; **I~stadt** *f* town *od* city centre (*BRIT*) *od* center (*US*).

innerbetrieblich *adj* in-house; **etw ~ regeln** to settle sth within the company.

innerdeutsch *adj*: **~e(r) Handel** domestic trade in Germany.

Innere(s) *nt* inside; (*Mitte*) centre (*BRIT*), center (*US*); (*fig*) heart.

innere(r, s) *adj* inner; (*im Körper, inländisch*) internal.

Innereien [ɪnə'raɪən] *pl* innards *pl*.

inner- *zW*: **~halb** *adv* within; (*räumlich*) inside ♦ *prep* +*dat* within; inside; **~lich** *adj* internal; (*geistig*) inward; **I~lichkeit** *f* (*LITER*) inwardness; **~parteilich** *adj*: **~parteiliche Demokratie** democracy (with)in the party structure.

Innerste(s) *nt* heart; **bis ins ~ getroffen** hurt to the quick.

innerste(r, s) *adj* innermost.

innewohnen ['ɪnəvoːnən] *vi* +*dat* (*geh*) to be inherent in.

innig ['ɪnɪç] *adj* profound; (*Freundschaft*) intimate; **mein ~ster Wunsch** my dearest wish.

Innung ['ɪnʊŋ] *f* (trade) guild; **du blamierst die ganze ~** (*hum: umg*) you are letting the whole side down.

inoffiziell ['ɪnʔofitsiɛl] *adj* unofficial.

ins [ɪns] = **in das.**

Insasse ['ɪnzasə] (-n, -n) *m*, **Insassin** *f* (*einer Anstalt*) inmate; (*AUT*) passenger.

insbesondere [ɪnsbə'zɔndərə] *adv* (e)specially.

Inschrift ['ɪnʃrɪft] *f* inscription.

Insekt [ɪn'zɛkt] (-(e)s, -en) *nt* insect.

Insektenvertilgungsmittel *nt* insecticide.

Insel ['ɪnzəl] (-, -n) *f* island.

Inserat [ɪnze'raːt] (-(e)s, -e) *nt* advertisement.

Inserent [ɪnze'rɛnt] *m* advertiser.

inserieren [ɪnze'riːrən] *vt, vi* to advertise.

insgeheim [ɪnsgə'haɪm] *adv* secretly.

insgesamt [ɪnsgə'zamt] *adv* altogether, all in

all.

Insiderhandel m insider dealing od trading.

insofern [ɪnzoˈfɛrn] adv in this respect ♦ konj if; (deshalb) (and) so; ~ **als** in so far as.

insolvent [ˈɪnzɔlvɛnt] adj bankrupt, insolvent.

Insolvenz f (COMM) insolvency.

insoweit adv, konj = **insofern**.

in spe [ɪnˈʃpeː] (umg) adj: **unser Schwiegersohn** ~ our son-in-law to be, our future son-in-law.

Inspektion [ɪnspɛktsiˈoːn] f inspection; (AUT) service.

Inspektor(in) [ɪnˈspɛktɔr, -ˈtoːrɪn] (-s, -en) m(f) inspector.

Inspiration [ɪnspiratsiˈoːn] f inspiration.

inspirieren [ɪnspiˈriːrən] vt to inspire; **sich von etw** ~ **lassen** to get one's inspiration from sth.

inspizieren [ɪnspiˈtsiːrən] vt to inspect.

Installateur [ɪnstalaˈtøːr] m plumber; (Elektro~) electrician.

installieren [ɪnstaˈliːrən] vt to install (auch fig, COMPUT).

Instandhaltung [ɪnˈʃtanthaltʊŋ] f maintenance.

inständig [ɪnˈʃtɛndɪç] adj urgent; ~ **bitten** to beg.

Instandsetzung f overhaul; (eines Gebäudes) restoration.

Instanz [ɪnˈstants] f authority; (JUR) court; **Verhandlung in erster/zweiter** ~ first/ second court case.

Instanzenweg m official channels pl.

Instinkt [ɪnˈstɪŋkt] (-(e)s, -e) m instinct.

instinktiv [ɪnstɪŋkˈtiːf] adj instinctive.

Institut [ɪnstiˈtuːt] (-(e)s, -e) nt institute.

Institution [ɪnstitutsiˈoːn] f institution.

Instrument [ɪnstruˈmɛnt] nt instrument.

Insulin [ɪnzuˈliːn] (-s) nt insulin.

inszenieren [ɪnstseˈniːrən] vt to direct; (fig) to stage-manage.

Inszenierung f production.

intakt [ɪnˈtakt] adj intact.

Integralrechnung [ɪnteˈgraːlrɛçnʊŋ] f integral calculus.

Integration [ɪntegratsiˈoːn] f integration.

integrieren [ɪnteˈgriːrən] vt to integrate; **integrierte Gesamtschule** comprehensive school (BRIT).

Integrität [ɪntegriˈtɛːt] f integrity.

Intellekt [ɪntɛˈlɛkt] (-(e)s) m intellect.

intellektuell [ɪntɛlɛktuˈɛl] adj intellectual.

Intellektuelle(r) f(m) intellectual.

intelligent [ɪntɛliˈgɛnt] adj intelligent.

Intelligenz [ɪntɛliˈgɛnts] f intelligence; (Leute) intelligentsia pl; ~**quotient** m IQ, intelligence quotient.

Intendant [ɪntɛnˈdant] m director.

Intensität [ɪntɛnziˈtɛːt] f intensity.

intensiv [ɪntɛnˈziːf] adj intensive.

intensivieren [ɪntɛnziˈviːrən] vt to intensify.

Intensivkurs m intensive course.

Intensivstation f intensive care unit.

interaktiv adj (COMPUT) interactive.

Intercity-Zug [ɪntərˈsɪtitsuːk] m inter-city train.

interessant [ɪntereˈsant] adj interesting; **sich** ~ **machen** to attract attention.

interessanterweise adv interestingly enough.

Interesse [ɪnteˈrɛsə] (-s, -n) nt interest; ~ **haben an** +dat to be interested in.

Interessengebiet nt field of interest.

Interessengegensatz m clash of interests.

Interessent(in) [ɪntereˈsɛnt(ɪn)] m(f) interested party; **es haben sich mehrere** ~**en gemeldet** several people have shown interest.

Interessenvertretung f representation of interests; (Personen) group representing (one's) interests.

interessieren [ɪntereˈsiːrən] vt: **jdn (für etw** od **an etw** dat**)** ~ to interest sb (in sth) ♦ vr: **sich** ~ **für** to be interested in.

interessiert adj: **politisch** ~ interested in politics.

Interkontinentalrakete [ɪntərkɔntinɛnˈtaːlrakeːtə] f intercontinental missile.

intern [ɪnˈtɛrn] adj internal.

Internat [ɪntɛrˈnaːt] (-(e)s, -e) nt boarding school.

international [ɪntɛrnatsioˈnaːl] adj international.

Internatsschüler(in) m(f) boarder.

internieren [ɪntɛrˈniːrən] vt to intern.

Internierungslager nt internment camp.

Internist(in) m(f) internist.

Interpol [ˈɪntərpoːl] (-) f abk (= Internationale Polizei) Interpol.

Interpret [ɪntərˈpreːt] (-en, -en) m: **Lieder verschiedener** ~**en** songs by various singers.

Interpretation [ɪntərpretatsiˈoːn] f interpretation.

interpretieren [ɪntɛrpreˈtiːrən] vt to interpret.

Interpretin f siehe **Interpret**.

Interpunktion [ɪntɛrpʊŋktsiˈoːn] f punctuation.

Intervall [ɪntɛrˈval] (-s, -e) nt interval.

intervenieren [ɪntɛrveˈniːrən] vi to intervene.

Interview [ɪntərˈvjuː] (-s, -s) nt interview; **i~en** [-ˈvjuːən] vt to interview.

intim [ɪnˈtiːm] adj intimate; **I~bereich** m (ANAT) genital area.

Intimität [ɪntimiˈtɛːt] f intimacy.

Intimsphäre f: **jds** ~ **verletzen** to invade sb's privacy.

intolerant [ˈɪntolerant] adj intolerant.

intransitiv [ˈɪntranzitiːf] adj (GRAM) intransitive.

Intrige [ɪnˈtriːgə] (-, -n) f intrigue, plot.

intrinsisch [ɪnˈtrɪnzɪʃ] adj: ~**er Wert** intrinsic value.

introvertiert [ɪntrover'tiːrt] *adj:* ~ **sein** to be an introvert.
intuitiv [ɪntui'tiːf] *adj* intuitive.
intus ['ɪntʊs] *adj:* **etw ~ haben** (*umg: Wissen*) to have got sth into one's head; (*Essen, Trinken*) to have got sth down one (*umg*).
Invalide [ɪnva'liːdə] (-n, -n) *m* disabled person, invalid.
Invalidenrente *f* disability pension.
Invasion [ɪnvazi'oːn] *f* invasion.
Inventar [ɪnvɛn'taːr] (-s, -e) *nt* inventory; (*COMM*) assets and liabilities *pl.*
Inventur [ɪnvɛn'tuːr] *f* stocktaking; ~ **machen** to stocktake.
investieren [ɪnvɛs'tiːrən] *vt* to invest.
investiert *adj:* ~**es Kapital** capital employed.
Investition [ɪnvɛstitsi'oːn] *f* investment.
Investitionszulage *f* investment grant.
Investmentgesellschaft [ɪn'vɛstməntgəzɛlʃaft] *f* unit trust.
inwiefern [ɪnvi'fɛrn] *adv* how far, to what extent.
inwieweit [ɪnvi'vaɪt] *adv* how far, to what extent.
Inzest [ɪn'tsɛst] (-(e)s, -e) *m* incest *no pl.*
inzwischen [ɪn'tsvɪʃən] *adv* meanwhile.
IOK *nt abk* (= *Internationales Olympisches Komitee*) IOC.
Ion [i'oːn] (-s, -en) *nt* ion.
ionisch [i'oːnɪʃ] *adj* Ionian; I~**es Meer** Ionian Sea.
IQ *m abk* (= *Intelligenzquotient*) IQ.
i.R. *abk* (= *im Ruhestand*) retd.
IRA *f abk* (= *Irisch-Republikanische Armee*) IRA.
Irak [i'raːk] (-s) *m:* (**der**) ~ Iraq.
Iraker(in) (-s, -) *m(f)* Iraqi.
irakisch *adj* Iraqi.
Iran [i'raːn] (-s) *m:* (**der**) ~ Iran.
Iraner(in) (-s, -) *m(f)* Iranian.
iranisch *adj* Iranian.
irdisch ['ɪrdɪʃ] *adj* earthly; **den Weg alles Irdischen gehen** to go the way of all flesh.
Ire ['iːrə] (-n, -n) *m* Irishman; Irish boy; **die ~n** the Irish.
irgend ['ɪrgənt] *adv* at all; **wann/was/wer ~** whenever/whatever/whoever; ~ **jemand/ etwas** somebody/something; (*fragend, verneinend*) anybody/anything; ~**ein(e, s)** *adj* some, any; **haben Sie (sonst) noch ~einen Wunsch?** is there anything else you would like?; ~**eine(r, s)** *pron* (*Person*) somebody; (*Ding*) something; (*fragend, verneinend*) anybody/anything; **ich will nicht bloß ~ein(e)s** I don't want any old one; ~**einmal** *adv* sometime or other; (*fragend*) ever; ~**wann** *adv* sometime; ~**wer** (*umg*) *pron* somebody; (*fragend, verneinend*) anybody; ~**wie** *adv* somehow; ~**wo** *adv* somewhere (*BRIT*), someplace (*US*); (*fragend, verneinend, bedingend*) anywhere (*BRIT*), any place (*US*); ~**wohin** *adv* somewhere (*BRIT*), someplace (*US*); (*fragend, verneinend, bedingend*)

anywhere (*BRIT*), any place (*US*).
Irin ['iːrɪn] *f* Irishwoman; Irish girl.
Iris ['iːrɪs] (-, -) *f* iris.
irisch *adj* Irish; I~**e** See Irish Sea.
IRK *nt abk* (= *Internationales Rotes Kreuz*) IRC.
Irland ['ɪrlant] (-s) *nt* Ireland; (*Republik* ~) Eire.
Irländer ['ɪrlɛndər(ɪn)] (-s, -) *m* = **Ire**; ~**in** *f* = **Irin**.
Ironie [iro'niː] *f* irony.
ironisch [i'roːnɪʃ] *adj* ironic(al).
irre ['ɪrə] *adj* crazy, mad; ~ **gut** (*umg*) way out (*umg*); I~**(r)** *f(m)* lunatic; ~**führen** *vt* to mislead; I~**führung** *f* fraud.
irrelevant ['ɪrelevant] *adj:* ~ (**für**) irrelevant (for *od* to).
irremachen *vt* to confuse.
irren *vi* to be mistaken; (*umher~*) to wander, stray ♦ *vr* to be mistaken; **jeder kann sich mal** ~ anyone can make a mistake; I~**anstalt** *f* (*veraltet*) lunatic asylum; I~**haus** *nt:* **hier geht es zu wie im I~haus** (*umg*) this place is an absolute madhouse.
Irrfahrt ['ɪrfaːrt] *f* wandering.
irrig ['ɪrɪç] *adj* incorrect, wrong.
irritieren [ɪri'tiːrən] *vt* (*verwirren*) to confuse, muddle; (*ärgern*) to irritate.
Irr- *zW:* ~**licht** *nt* will-o'-the-wisp; ~**sinn** *m* madness; **so ein ~sinn, das zu tun** what a crazy thing to do!; i~**sinnig** *adj* mad, crazy; (*umg*) terrific; i~**sinnig komisch** incredibly funny; ~**tum** (-s, -tümer) *m* mistake, error; **im ~tum sein** to be wrong *od* mistaken; ~**tum!** wrong!; i~**tümlich** *adj* mistaken.
ISBN *f abk* (= *Internationale Standardbuchnummer*) ISBN.
Ischias ['ɪʃias] (-) *m od nt* sciatica.
Islam ['ɪslam] (-s) *m* Islam.
islamisch [ɪs'laːmɪʃ] *adj* Islamic.
Island ['iːslant] (-s) *nt* Iceland.
Isländer(in) ['iːslɛndər(ɪn)] (-s, -) *m(f)* Icelander.
isländisch *adj* Icelandic.
Isolation [izolatsi'oːn] *f* isolation; (*ELEK*) insulation; (*von Häftlingen*) solitary confinement.
Isolator [izo'laːtɔr] *m* insulator.
Isolierband *nt* insulating tape.
isolieren [izo'liːrən] *vt* to isolate; (*ELEK*) to insulate.
Isolierstation *f* (*MED*) isolation ward.
Isolierung *f* isolation; (*ELEK*) insulation.
Israel ['ɪsraeːl] (-s) *nt* Israel.
Israeli[1] [ɪsra'eːli] (-s, -s) *m* Israeli.
Israeli[2] [ɪsra'eːli] (-, -(s)) *f* Israeli.
israelisch *adj* Israeli.
ißt [ɪst] *vb siehe* **essen**.
ist [ɪst] *vb siehe* **sein**.
Istanbul ['ɪstambuːl] (-s) *nt* Istanbul.
Ist-Bestand *m* (*Geld*) cash in hand; (*Waren*) actual stock.
Italien [i'taːliən] (-s) *nt* Italy.

Italiener(in) [itali'e:nər(ın)] (**-s**, **-**) *m(f)* Italian.
italienisch *adj* Italian; **die ~e Schweiz**
Italian-speaking Switzerland.
i.V., I.V. *abk* (= *in Vertretung*) on behalf of;
(= *in Vollmacht*) by proxy.
IWF *m abk* (= *Internationaler Währungsfonds*)
IMF.

J, j

J, j [jɔt] *nt* J, j; **~ wie Julius** ≈ J for Jack, J
for Jig (*US*).

SCHLÜSSELWORT

ja [ja:] *adv* **1** yes; **haben Sie das gesehen? - ~**
did you see it? - yes(, I did); **ich glaube ~**
(yes) I think so; **zu allem ~ und amen sagen**
(*umg*) to accept everything without
question
2 (*fragend*) really; **ich habe gekündigt - ~?**
I've quit - have you?; **du kommst, ~?** you're
coming, aren't you?
3: sei ~ vorsichtig do be careful; **Sie wissen**
~, daß ... as you know, ...; **tu das ~ nicht!**
don't do that!; **sie ist ~ erst fünf** (after all)
she's only five; **Sie wissen ~, wie das so ist**
you know how it is; **ich habe es ~ gewußt** I
just knew it; **~, also ...** well you see ...

Jacht [jaxt] (**-**, **-en**) *f* yacht.
Jacke ['jakə] (**-**, **-n**) *f* jacket; (*Woll~*)
cardigan.
Jacketkrone ['dʒɛkɪtkro:nə] *f* (*Zahnkrone*)
jacket crown.
Jackett [ʒa'kɛt] (**-s**, **-s** *od* **-e**) *nt* jacket.
Jagd [ja:kt] (**-**, **-en**) *f* hunt; (*Jagen*) hunting;
~beute *f* kill; **~flugzeug** *nt* fighter; **~gewehr**
nt sporting gun; **~hund** *m* hunting dog;
~schein *m* hunting licence (*BRIT*) *od* license
(*US*); **~wurst** *f* smoked sausage.
jagen ['ja:gən] *vi* to hunt; (*eilen*) to race ♦ *vt* to
hunt; (*weg~*) to drive (off); (*verfolgen*) to
chase; **mit diesem Essen kannst**
du mich ~ (*umg*) I wouldn't touch that food
with a barge pole (*BRIT*) *od* ten-foot pole
(*US*).
Jäger ['jɛ:gər] (**-s**, **-**) *m* hunter; **~in** *f* huntress,
huntswoman; **~latein** (*umg*) *nt* hunters' tales
pl; **~schnitzel** *nt* (*KOCH*) *cutlet served with*
mushroom sauce.
jäh [jɛ:] *adj* abrupt, sudden; (*steil*) steep,
precipitous; **~lings** *adv* abruptly.
Jahr [ja:r] (**-(e)s**, **-e**) *nt* year; **im ~(e) 1066** in
(the year) 1066; **die sechziger ~e** the sixties
pl; **mit dreißig ~en** at the age of thirty; **in**
den besten ~en sein to be in the prime of
(one's) life; **nach ~ und Tag** after (many)
years; **zwischen den ~en** (*umg*) between
Christmas and New Year; **j~aus** *adv:* **j~aus,**
j~ein year in, year out; **~buch** *nt* annual,
year book.
jahrelang *adv* for years.
Jahres- *zW:* **~abonnement** *nt* annual
subscription; **~abschluß** *m* end of the year;
(*COMM*) annual statement of account;
~beitrag *m* annual subscription; **~bericht** *m*
annual report; **~hauptversammlung** *f*
(*COMM*) annual general meeting, AGM;
~karte *f* annual season ticket; **~tag** *m*
anniversary; **~umsatz** *m* (*COMM*) yearly
turnover; **~wechsel** *m* turn of the year;
~zahl *f* date, year; **~zeit** *f* season.
Jahr- *zW:* **~gang** *m* age group; (*von Wein*)
vintage; **er ist ~gang 1950** he was born in
1950; **~hundert** *nt* century; **~hundertfeier** *f*
centenary; **~hundertwende** *f* turn of the
century.
jährlich ['jɛ:rlɪç] *adj, adv* yearly; **zweimal ~**
twice a year.
Jahr- *zW:* **~markt** *m* fair; **~tausend** *nt*
millennium; **~zehnt** *nt* decade.
Jähzorn ['jɛ:tsɔrn] *m* hot temper.
jähzornig *adj* hot-tempered.
Jalousie [ʒalu'zi:] *f* venetian blind.
Jamaika [ja'maıka] (**-s**) *nt* Jamaica.
Jammer ['jamər] (**-s**) *m* misery; **es ist ein ~,**
daß ... it is a crying shame that ...
jämmerlich ['jɛmərlıç] *adj* wretched, pathetic;
J~keit *f* wretchedness.
jammern *vi* to wail ♦ *vt unpers:* **es jammert**
mich it makes me feel sorry.
jammerschade *adj:* **es ist ~** it is a crying
shame.
Jan. *abk* (= *Januar*) Jan.
Januar ['janua:r] (**-s**, **-e**) (*pl selten*) *m* January;
siehe auch **September.**
Japan ['ja:pan] (**-s**) *nt* Japan.
Japaner(in) [ja'pa:nər(ın)] (**-s**, **-**) *m(f)*
Japanese.
japanisch *adj* Japanese.
Jargon [ʒar'gõ:] (**-s**, **-s**) *m* jargon.
Jasager ['ja:za:gər] (**-s**, **-**) (*pej*) *m* yes man.
Jastimme *f* vote in favour (*BRIT*) *od* favor
(*US*) (of).
jäten ['jɛ:tən] *vt, vi* to weed.
Jauche ['jauxə] *f* liquid manure; **~grube** *f*
cesspool, cesspit.
jauchzen ['jauxtsən] *vi* to rejoice, shout (with
joy).
Jauchzer (**-s**, **-**) *m* shout of joy.
jaulen ['jaulən] *vi* to howl.
Jause ['jauzə] (*ÖSTERR*) *f* snack.
jawohl *adv* yes (of course).
Jawort *nt* consent; **jdm das ~ geben** to
consent to marry sb; (*bei Trauung*) to say "I
do".
Jazz [dʒæz] (**-**) *m* jazz; **~keller** *m* jazz club.

========================= *SCHLÜSSELWORT*

je [jeː] *adv* **1** (*jemals*) ever; **hast du so was ~ gesehen?** did you ever see anything like it?
2 (*jeweils*) every, each; **sie zahlten ~ 3 Mark** they paid 3 marks each
♦ *konj* **1**: **~ nach** depending on; **~ nachdem** it depends; **~ nachdem, ob** ... depending on whether ...
2: **~ eher, desto** *od* **um so besser** the sooner the better; **~ länger, ~ lieber** the longer the better.

Jeans [dʒiːnz] *pl* jeans *pl*; **~anzug** *m* denim suit.
jede(r, s) ['jeːdə(r, s)] *adj* (*einzeln*) each; (*von zweien*) either; (*~ von allen*) every ♦ *indef pron* (*einzeln*) each (one); (*~ von allen*) everyone, everybody; **ohne ~ Anstrengung** without any effort; **~r zweite** every other (one).
jedenfalls *adv* in any case.
jedermann *pron* everyone; **das ist nicht ~s Sache** it's not everyone's cup of tea.
jederzeit *adv* at any time.
jedesmal *adv* every time, each time.
jedoch [je'dɔx] *adv* however.
jeher ['jeːheːr] *adv:* **von ~** all along.
jein [jaɪn] *adv* (*hum*) yes no.
jemals ['jeːmaːls] *adv* ever.
jemand ['jeːmant] *indef pron* someone, somebody; (*bei Fragen, bedingenden Sätzen, Negation*) anyone, anybody.
Jemen ['jeːmən] (**-s**) *m* Yemen.
Jemenit(in) [jeme'niːt(ɪn)] (**-en, -en**) *m(f)* Yemeni.
jemenitisch *adj* Yemeni.
Jenaer Glas ® ['jeːnaərglaːs] *nt* heatproof glass, ≈ Pyrex ®.
jene(r, s) ['jeːnə(r, s)] *adj* that; (*pl*) those ♦ *pron* that one; (*pl*) those; (*der Vorherige, die Vorherigen*) the former.
jenseits ['jeːnzaɪts] *adv* on the other side ♦ *präp +gen* on the other side of, beyond; **J~** *nt:* **das J~** the hereafter, the beyond; **jdn ins J~ befördern** (*umg*) to send sb to kingdom come.
Jesus ['jeːzʊs] (**Jesu**) *m* Jesus; **~ Christus** Jesus Christ.
jetten ['dʒɛtən] (*umg*) *vi* to jet (*inf*).
jetzig ['jɛtsɪç] *adj* present.
jetzt [jɛtst] *adv* now; **~ gleich** right now.
jeweilig *adj* respective; **die ~e Regierung** the government of the day.
jeweils *adv:* **~ zwei zusammen** two at a time; **zu ~ 5 DM** at 5 marks each; **~ das erste** the first each time; **~ am Monatsletzten** on the last day of each month.
Jg. *abk* = **Jahrgang**.
Jh. *abk* (= *Jahrhundert*) cent.
jiddisch ['jɪdɪʃ] *adj* Yiddish.
Job [dʒɔp] (**-s, -s**) (*umg*) *m* job.

jobben ['dʒɔbən] (*umg*) *vi* to work, have a job.
Joch [jɔx] (**-(e)s, -e**) *nt* yoke.
Jochbein *nt* cheekbone.
Jockei ['dʒɔke] (**-s, -s**) *m* jockey.
Jod [joːt] (**-(e)s**) *nt* iodine.
jodeln ['joːdəln] *vi* to yodel.
joggen ['dʒɔgən] *vi* to jog.
Joghurt ['joːgʊrt] (**-s, -s**) *m od nt* yog(h)urt.
Johannisbeere [jo'hanɪsbeːrə] *f:* **rote ~** redcurrant; **schwarze ~** blackcurrant.
johlen ['joːlən] *vi* to yell.
Joint [dʒɔɪnt] (**-s, -s**) (*umg*) *m* joint.
Joint-venture ['dʒɔɪntventʃəʳ] (**-, -s**) *nt* joint venture.
Jolle ['jɔlə] (**-, -n**) *f* dinghy.
Jongleur [ʒõ'gløːr] (**-s, -e**) *m* juggler.
jonglieren [ʒõ'gliːrən] *vi* to juggle.
Joppe ['jɔpə] (**-, -n**) *f* jacket.
Jordanien [jɔr'daːniən] (**-s**) *nt* Jordan.
Jordanier(in) (**-s, -**) *m(f)* Jordanian.
jordanisch *adj* Jordanian.
Journalismus [ʒʊrna'lɪsmʊs] *m* journalism.
Journalist(in) [ʒʊrna'lɪst(ɪn)] *m(f)* journalist; **j~isch** *adj* journalistic.
Jubel ['juːbəl] (**-s**) *m* rejoicing; **~, Trubel, Heiterkeit** laughter and merriment; **~jahr** *nt:* **alle ~jahre (einmal)** (*umg*) once in a blue moon.
jubeln *vi* to rejoice.
Jubilar(in) [jubi'laːr(ɪn)] (**-s, -e**) *m(f)* person celebrating an anniversary.
Jubiläum [jubi'lɛːʊm] (**-s, Jubiläen**) *nt* jubilee; (*Jahrestag*) anniversary.
jucken ['jʊkən] *vi* to itch ♦ *vt:* **es juckt mich am Arm** my arm is itching; **das juckt mich** that's itchy; **das juckt mich doch nicht** (*umg*) I don't care.
Juckpulver *nt* itching powder.
Juckreiz *m* itch.
Judaslohn ['juːdasloːn] *m* (*liter*) blood money.
Jude ['juːdə] (**-n, -n**) *m* Jew.
Juden- *zW:* **~stern** *m* star of David; **~tum** (**-s**) *nt* (*die Juden*) Jewry; **~verfolgung** *f* persecution of the Jews.
Jüdin ['jyːdɪn] *f* Jewess.
jüdisch *adj* Jewish.
Judo ['juːdo] (**-(s)**) *nt* judo.
Jugend ['juːgənt] (**-**) *f* youth; **~amt** *nt* youth welfare department; **j~frei** *adj* suitable for young people; (*FILM*) U(-certificate), G (*US*); **~herberge** *f* youth hostel; **~hilfe** *f* youth welfare scheme; **~kriminalität** *f* juvenile crime; **j~lich** *adj* youthful; **~liche(r)** *f(m)* teenager, young person; **~liebe** *f* (*Geliebte(r)*) love of one's youth; **~richter** *m* juvenile court judge; **~schutz** *m* protection of children and young people; **~stil** *m* (*KUNST*) Art Nouveau; **~strafanstalt** *f* youth custody centre (*BRIT*); **~sünde** *f* youthful misdeed; **~zentrum** *nt* youth centre (*BRIT*) *od* center (*US*).
Jugoslawe [jugo'slaːvə] (**-n, -n**) *m* Yugoslav.

Jugoslawien [jugo'sla:viən] (**-s**) *nt*
Yugoslavia.
Jugoslawin [jugo'sla:vɪn] *f* Yugoslav.
jugoslawisch *adj* Yugoslav(ian).
Juli ['ju:li] (**-(s)**, **-s**) (*pl selten*) *m* July; *siehe auch*
September.
jun. *abk* (= *junior*) jun.
jung [juŋ] *adj* young.
Junge (**-n**, **-n**) *m* boy, lad ♦ *nt* young animal;
(*pl*) young *pl*.
Jünger ['jʏŋər] (**-s**, **-**) *m* disciple.
jünger *adj* younger.
Jungfer (**-**, **-n**) *f:* **alte** ~ old maid.
Jungfernfahrt *f* maiden voyage.
Jung- *zW:* ~**frau** *f* virgin; (*ASTROL*) Virgo;
~**geselle** *m* bachelor; ~**gesellin** *f* bachelor
girl; (*älter*) single woman.
Jüngling ['jʏŋlɪŋ] *m* youth.
Jungsozialist *m* (*BRD POL*) Young Socialist.
jüngst [jʏŋst] *adv* lately, recently.
jüngste(r, s) *adj* youngest; (*neueste*) latest;
das J~ Gericht the Last Judgement; **der
J~ Tag** Doomsday, the Day of Judgement.
Jungwähler(in) *m(f)* young voter.
Juni ['ju:ni] (**-(s)**, **-s**) (*pl selten*) *m* June; *siehe
auch* September.
Junior ['ju:niɔr] (**-s**, **-en**) *m* junior.
Junta ['xʊnta] (**-**, **-ten**) *f* (*POL*) junta.
jur. *abk* = **juristisch**.
Jura ['ju:ra] *no art* (*UNIV*) law.
Jurist(in) [ju'rɪst(ɪn)] *m(f)* jurist, lawyer;
(*Student*) law student; **j~isch** *adj* legal.
Juso ['ju:zo] (**-s**, **-s**) *m abk* = **Jungsozialist**.
just [jʊst] *adv* just.
Justiz [jʊs'ti:ts] (**-**) *f* justice; ~**beamte(r)** *m*
judicial officer; ~**irrtum** *m* miscarriage of
justice; ~**minister** *m* minister of justice;
~**mord** *m* judicial murder.
Juwel [ju've:l] (**-s**, **-en**) *m od nt* jewel.
Juwelier [juve'li:r] (**-s**, **-e**) *m* jeweller (*BRIT*),
jeweler (*US*); ~**geschäft** *nt* jeweller's (*BRIT*)
od jeweler's (*US*) (shop).
Jux [jʊks] (**-es**, **-e**) *m* joke, lark; **etw aus
~ tun/sagen** (*umg*) to do/say sth in fun.
jwd [jɔtve:'de:] *adv* (*hum*) in the back of
beyond.

K, k

K, k [ka:] *nt* K, k; ~ **wie Kaufmann** ≈ K for
King.
Kabarett [kaba'rɛt] (**-s**, **-e** *od* **-s**) *nt* cabaret;
~**ist(in)** [kabarɛ'tɪst(ɪn)] *m(f)* cabaret artiste.
Kabel ['ka:bəl] (**-s**, **-**) *nt* (*ELEK*) wire; (*stark*)
cable; ~**anschluß** *m:* ~**anschluß haben** to
have cable television; ~**fernsehen** *nt* cable
television.
Kabeljau ['ka:bəljau] (**-s**, **-e** *od* **-s**) *m* cod.
kabeln *vt, vi* to cable.
Kabelsalat (*umg*) *m* tangle of cable.
Kabine [ka'bi:nə] *f* cabin; (*Zelle*) cubicle.
Kabinett [kabi'nɛt] (**-s**, **-e**) *nt* (*POL*) cabinet;
(*kleines Zimmer*) small room ♦ *m high-quality
German white wine*.
Kachel ['kaxəl] (**-**, **-n**) *f* tile.
kacheln *vt* to tile.
Kachelofen *m* tiled stove.
Kacke ['kakə] (**-**, **-n**) (*umg!*) *f* crap (*!*).
Kadaver [ka'da:vər] (**-s**, **-**) *m* carcass.
Kader ['ka:dər] (**-s**, **-**) *m* (*MIL, POL*) cadre;
(*SPORT*) squad; (*DDR, SCHWEIZ: Fachleute*)
group of specialists; ~**schmiede** *f* (*POL:
umg*) institution *for the training of cadre
personnel*.
Kadett [ka'dɛt] (**-en**, **-en**) *m* cadet.
Käfer ['kɛ:fər] (**-s**, **-**) *m* beetle.
Kaff [kaf] (**-s**, **-s**) (*umg*) *nt* dump, hole.
Kaffee ['kafe] (**-s**, **-s**) *m* coffee; **zwei** ~, **bitte!**
two coffees, please; **das ist kalter** ~ (*umg*)
that's old hat; ~**kanne** *f* coffeepot; ~**klatsch**
m, ~**kränzchen** *nt* coffee circle; ~**löffel** *m*
coffee spoon; ~**maschine** *f* coffee maker;
~**mühle** *f* coffee grinder; ~**satz** *m* coffee
grounds *pl*; ~**tante** *f* (*hum*) coffee addict; (*in
Café*) old biddy; ~**wärmer** *m* cosy (*for
coffeepot*).
Käfig ['kɛ:fɪç] (**-s**, **-e**) *m* cage.
kahl [ka:l] *adj* bald; ~**fressen** *unreg vt* to strip
bare; ~**geschoren** *adj* shaven, shorn; **K~heit**
f baldness; ~**köpfig** *adj* bald-headed;
K~schlag *m* (*in Wald*) clearing.
Kahn [ka:n] (**-(e)s**, **-̈e**) *m* boat, barge.
Kai [kaɪ] (**-s**, **-e** *od* **-s**) *m* quay.
Kairo ['kaɪro] (**-s**) *nt* Cairo.
Kaiser ['kaɪzər] (**-s**, **-**) *m* emperor; ~**in** *f*
empress; **k~lich** *adj* imperial; ~**reich** *nt*
empire; ~**schmarren** ['kaɪzərʃmarən] *m*
(*KOCH*) sugared, cut-up pancake with
raisins; ~**schnitt** *m* (*MED*) Caesarean (*BRIT*)
od Cesarean (*US*) (section).
Kajak ['ka:jak] (**-s**, **-s**) *m or nt* kayak.

Kajüte [ka'jy:tə] (-, -n) *f* cabin.
Kakao [ka'ka:o] (-s, -s) *m* cocoa; **jdn durch den ~ ziehen** (*umg: veralbern*) to make fun of sb; (: *boshaft reden*) to run sb down.
Kakerlak ['ka:kərlak] (-en, -en) *m* cockroach.
Kaktee [kak'te:ə] (-, -n) *f* cactus.
Kaktus ['kaktʊs] (-, -se) *m* cactus.
Kalabrien [ka'la:briən] (-s) *nt* Calabria.
Kalauer ['ka:lauər] (-s, -) *m* corny joke; (*Wortspiel*) corny pun.
Kalb [kalp] (-(e)s, ̈er) *nt* calf; **k~en** ['kalbən] *vi* to calve; **~fleisch** *nt* veal.
Kalbsleder *nt* calf(skin).
Kalender [ka'lɛndər] (-s, -) *m* calendar; (*Taschen~*) diary.
Kali ['ka:li] (-s, -s) *nt* potash.
Kaliber [ka'li:bər] (-s, -) *nt* (*lit, fig*) calibre (*BRIT*), caliber (*US*).
Kalifornien [kali'fɔrniən] (-s) *nt* California.
Kalk [kalk] (-(e)s, -e) *m* lime; (*BIOL*) calcium; **~stein** *m* limestone.
Kalkül [kal'ky:l] (-s, -e) *m od nt* (*geh*) calculation.
Kalkulation [kalkulatsi'o:n] *f* calculation.
Kalkulator [kalku'la:tɔr] *m* cost accountant.
kalkulieren [kalku'li:rən] *vt* to calculate.
kalkuliert *adj:* **~es Risiko** calculated risk.
Kalkutta [kal'kʊta] (-s) *nt* Calcutta.
Kalorie [kalo'ri:] (-, -n) *f* calorie.
kalorienarm *adj* low-calorie.
kalt [kalt] *adj* cold; **mir ist (es) ~** I am cold; **~e Platte** cold meat; **der K~e Krieg** the Cold War; **etw ~ stellen** to put sth to chill; **die Wohnung kostet ~ 980 DM** the flat costs 980 DM without heating; **~bleiben** *unreg vi* to be unmoved; **~blütig** *adj* cold-blooded; (*ruhig*) cool; **K~blütigkeit** *f* cold-bloodedness; coolness.
Kälte ['kɛltə] (-) *f* coldness; (*Wetter*) cold; **~einbruch** *m* cold spell; **~grad** *m* degree of frost *od* below zero; **~welle** *f* cold spell.
kalt- *zW:* **~herzig** *adj* cold-hearted; **~lächelnd** *adv* (*ironisch*) cool as you please; **~machen** (*umg*) *vt* to do in; **K~miete** *f* rent exclusive of heating; **K~schale** *f* (*KOCH*) cold sweet soup; **~schnäuzig** *adj* cold, unfeeling; **~stellen** *vt* to chill; (*fig*) to leave out in the cold.
Kalzium ['kaltsiʊm] (-s) *nt* calcium.
kam *etc* [ka:m] *vb siehe* **kommen**.
Kambodscha [kam'bɔdʒa] *nt* Cambodia.
Kamel [ka'me:l] (-(e)s, -e) *nt* camel.
Kamera ['kamera] (-, -s) *f* camera; **~-Recorder** *m* camcorder.
Kamerad(in) [kamə'ra:t, -'ra:dɪn] (-en, -en) *m(f)* comrade, friend; **~schaft** *f* comradeship; **k~schaftlich** *adj* comradely.
Kameraführung *f* camera work.
Kameramann (-(e)s, *pl* **-männer**) *m* cameraman.
Kamerun ['kaməru:n] (-s) *nt* Cameroon.
Kamille [ka'mɪlə] (-, -n) *f* camomile.

Kamillentee *m* camomile tea.
Kamin [ka'mi:n] (-s, -e) *m* (*außen*) chimney; (*innen*) fireside; (*Feuerstelle*) fireplace; **~feger** (-s, -) *m* chimney sweep; **~kehrer** (-s, -) *m* chimney sweep.
Kamm [kam] (-(e)s, ̈e) *m* comb; (*Berg~*) ridge; (*Hahnen~*) crest; **alle/alles über einen ~ scheren** (*fig*) to lump everyone/ everything together.
kämmen ['kɛmən] *vt* to comb.
Kammer ['kamər] (-, -n) *f* chamber; (*Zimmer*) small bedroom; **~diener** *m* valet; **~jäger** *m* (*Schädlingsbekämpfer*) pest controller; **~musik** *f* chamber music; **~zofe** *f* chambermaid.
Kammstück *nt* (*KOCH*) shoulder.
Kampagne [kam'panjə] (-, -n) *f* campaign.
Kampf [kampf] (-(e)s, ̈e) *m* fight, battle; (*Wettbewerb*) contest; (*fig: Anstrengung*) struggle; **jdm/etw den ~ ansagen** (*fig*) to declare war on sb/sth; **k~bereit** *adj* ready for action.
kämpfen ['kɛmpfən] *vi* to fight; **ich habe lange mit mir ~ müssen, ehe ...** I had a long battle with myself before ...
Kampfer ['kampfər] (-s) *m* camphor.
Kämpfer(in) (-s, -) *m(f)* fighter, combatant.
Kampf- *zW:* **~flugzeug** *nt* fighter (aircraft); **~geist** *m* fighting spirit; **~handlung** *f* action; **~kunst** *f* martial arts *pl*; **k~los** *adj* without a fight; **k~lustig** *adj* pugnacious; **~platz** *m* battlefield; (*SPORT*) arena, stadium; **~sport** *m* martial art; **~richter** *m* (*SPORT*) referee.
Kampuchea [kampʊ'tʃe:a] (-s) *nt* Kampuchea.
Kanada ['kanada] (-s) *nt* Canada.
Kanadier(in) [ka'na:diər(ɪn)] (-s, -) *m(f)* Canadian.
kanadisch [ka'na:dɪʃ] *adj* Canadian.
Kanal [ka'na:l] (-s, **Kanäle**) *m* (*Fluß*) canal; (*Rinne*) channel; (*für Abfluß*) drain; **der ~** (*auch:* **der Ärmelkanal**) the (English) Channel.
Kanalinseln *pl* Channel Islands *pl*.
Kanalisation [kanalizatsi'o:n] *f* sewage system.
kanalisieren [kanali'zi:rən] *vt* to provide with a sewage system; (*fig: Energie etc*) to channel.
Kanaltunnel *m* Channel Tunnel.
Kanarienvogel [ka'na:riənfo:gəl] *m* canary.
Kanarische Inseln [ka'na:rɪʃə'ɪnzəln] *pl* Canary Islands *pl*, Canaries *pl*.
Kandare [kan'da:rə] (-, -n) *f:* **jdn an die ~ nehmen** (*fig*) to take sb in hand.
Kandidat(in) [kandi'da:t(ɪn)] (-en, -en) *m(f)* candidate; **jdn als ~en aufstellen** to nominate sb.
Kandidatur [kandida'tu:r] *f* candidature, candidacy.
kandidieren [kandi'di:rən] *vi* (*POL*) to stand, run.

kandiert [kan'diːrt] *adj* (*Frucht*) candied.
Kandis(zucker) ['kandɪs(tsʊkər)] (-) *m* rock candy.
Känguruh ['kɛŋguru] (-s, -s) *nt* kangaroo.
Kaninchen [ka'niːnçən] *nt* rabbit.
Kanister [ka'nɪstər] (-s, -) *m* can, canister.
kann [kan] *vb siehe* **können.**
Kännchen ['kɛnçən] *nt* pot; (*für Milch*) jug.
Kanne ['kanə] (-, -n) *f* (*Krug*) jug; (*Kaffee~*) pot; (*Milch~*) churn; (*Gieß~*) watering can.
Kannibale [kani'baːlə] (-n, -n) *m* cannibal.
kannte *etc* ['kantə] *vb siehe* **kennen.**
Kanon ['kaːnɔn] (-s, -s) *m* canon.
Kanone [ka'noːnə] (-, -n) *f* gun; (*HIST*) cannon; (*fig: Mensch*) ace; **das ist unter aller ~** (*umg*) that defies description.
Kanonenfutter (*umg*) *nt* cannon fodder.
Kant. *abk* = **Kanton.**
Kantate [kan'taːtə] (-, -n) *f* cantata.
Kante ['kantə] (-, -n) *f* edge; **Geld auf die hohe ~ legen** (*umg*) to put money by.
kantig ['kantɪç] *adj* (*Holz*) edged; (*Gesicht*) angular.
Kantine [kan'tiːnə] *f* canteen.
Kanton [kan'toːn] (-s, -e) *m* canton.
Kantor ['kantɔr] *m* choirmaster.
Kanu ['kaːnu] (-s, -s) *nt* canoe.
Kanzel ['kantsəl] (-, -n) *f* pulpit; (*AVIAT*) cockpit.
Kanzlei [kants'laɪ] *f* chancery; (*Büro*) chambers *pl.*
Kanzler ['kantslər] (-s, -) *m* chancellor.
Kap [kap] (-s, -s) *nt* cape; **das ~ der guten Hoffnung** the Cape of Good Hope.
Kapazität [kapatsi'tɛːt] *f* capacity; (*Fachmann*) authority.
Kapelle [ka'pɛlə] *f* (*Gebäude*) chapel; (*MUS*) band.
Kapellmeister(in) *m(f)* director of music; (*MIL, von Tanzkapelle etc*) bandmaster, bandleader.
Kaper ['kaːpər] (-, -n) *f* caper.
kapern *vt* to capture.
kapieren [ka'piːrən] (*umg*) *vt, vi* to understand.
Kapital [kapi'taːl] (-s, -e *od* -ien) *nt* capital; **aus etw ~ schlagen** (*pej: lit, fig*) to make capital out of sth; **~anlage** *f* investment; **~aufwand** *m* capital expenditure; **~ertrag** *m* capital gains *pl*; **~ertragssteuer** *f* capital gains tax; **~flucht** *f* flight of capital; **~gesellschaft** *f* (*COMM*) joint-stock company; **~güter** *pl* capital goods *pl*; **k~intensiv** *adj* capital-intensive.
Kapitalismus [kapita'lɪsmʊs] *m* capitalism.
Kapitalist [kapita'lɪst] *m* capitalist.
kapitalistisch *adj* capitalist.
Kapital- *zW*: **k~kräftig** *adj* wealthy; **~markt** *m* money market; **~verbrechen** *nt* serious crime; (*mit Todesstrafe*) capital crime.
Kapitän [kapi'tɛːn] (-s, -e) *m* captain.
Kapitel [ka'pɪtəl] (-s, -) *nt* chapter; **ein trauriges ~** (*Angelegenheit*) a sad story.

Kapitulation [kapitulatsi'oːn] *f* capitulation.
kapitulieren [kapitu'liːrən] *vi* to capitulate.
Kaplan [ka'plaːn] (-s, **Kapläne**) *m* chaplain.
Kappe ['kapə] (-, -n) *f* cap; (*Kapuze*) hood; **das nehme ich auf meine ~** (*fig: umg*) I'll take the responsibility for that.
kappen *vt* to cut.
Kapsel ['kapsəl] (-, -n) *f* capsule.
Kapstadt ['kapʃtat] *nt* Cape Town.
kaputt [ka'pʊt] (*umg*) *adj* smashed, broken; (*Person*) exhausted, knackered; **der Fernseher ist ~** the TV's not working; **ein ~er Typ** a bum; **~gehen** *unreg vi* to break; (*Schuhe*) to fall apart; (*Firma*) to go bust; (*Stoff*) to wear out; (*sterben*) to cop it (*umg*); **~lachen** *vr* to laugh o.s. silly; **~machen** *vt* to break; (*Mensch*) to exhaust, wear out; **~schlagen** *unreg vt* to smash.
Kapuze [ka'puːtsə] (-, -n) *f* hood.
Karabiner [kara'biːnər] (-s, -) *m* (*Gewehr*) carbine.
Karacho [ka'raxo] (-s) *nt*: **mit ~** (*umg*) hell for leather.
Karaffe [ka'rafə] (-, -n) *f* carafe; (*geschliffen*) decanter.
Karambolage [karambo'laːʒə] (-, -n) *f* (*Zusammenstoß*) crash.
Karamel [kara'mɛl] (-s) *m* caramel; **~bonbon** *m od nt* toffee.
Karat [ka'raːt] (-(e)s, -e) *nt* carat.
Karate (-s) *nt* karate.
Karawane [kara'vaːnə] (-, -n) *f* caravan.
Kardinal [kardi'naːl] (-s, **Kardinäle**) *m* cardinal; **~fehler** *m* cardinal error; **~zahl** *f* cardinal number.
Karenzzeit [ka'rɛntstsait] *f* waiting period.
Karfreitag [kaːr'fraitaːk] *m* Good Friday.
karg [kark] *adj* scanty, poor; (*Mahlzeit*) meagre (*BRIT*), meager (*US*); **etw ~ bemessen** to be mean with sth; **K~heit** *f* poverty, scantiness; meagreness (*BRIT*), meagerness (*US*).
kärglich ['kɛrklɪç] *adj* poor, scanty.
Kargo ['kargo] (-s, -s) *m* (*COMM*) cargo.
Karibik [ka'riːbɪk] (-) *f*: **die ~** the Caribbean.
karibisch *adj* Caribbean; **das K~e Meer** the Caribbean Sea.
kariert [ka'riːrt] *adj* (*Stoff*) checked (*BRIT*), checkered (*US*); (*Papier*) squared; **~ reden** (*umg*) to talk rubbish *od* nonsense.
Karies ['kaːries] (-) *f* caries.
Karikatur [karika'tuːr] *f* caricature; **~ist(in)** [karikatu'rɪst(ɪn)] *m(f)* cartoonist.
karikieren [kari'kiːrən] *vt* to caricature.
karitativ [karita'tiːf] *adj* charitable.
Karneval ['karnəval] (-s, -e *od* -s) *m* carnival.

> **Karneval** *is the name given to the days immediately before Lent when people gather to sing, dance, eat, drink and generally make merry before the fasting begins.* **Rosenmontag,** *the day before Shrove Tuesday, is the most*

important day of Karneval on the Rhine. Most firms take a day's holiday on that day to enjoy the parades and revelry. In South Germany Karneval is called Fasching.

Karnickel [kar'nıkəl] **(-s, -)** (*umg*) *nt* rabbit.
Kärnten ['kɛrntən] **(-s)** *nt* Carinthia.
Karo ['kaːro] **(-s, -s)** *nt* square; (*KARTEN*) diamonds; **~-As** *nt* ace of diamonds.
Karosse [ka'rɔsə] **(-, -n)** *f* coach, carriage.
Karosserie [karɔsə'riː] *f* (*AUT*) body(work).
Karotte [ka'rɔtə] **(-, -n)** *f* carrot.
Karpaten [kar'paːtən] *pl* Carpathians *pl*.
Karpfen ['karpfən] **(-s, -)** *m* carp.
Karre ['karə] **(-, -n)** *f* = **Karren**.
Karree [ka'reː] **(-s, -s)** *nt*: **einmal ums ~ gehen** (*umg*) to walk around the block.
karren ['karən] *vt* to cart, transport; **K~ (-s, -)** *m* cart, barrow; **den K~ aus dem Dreck ziehen** (*umg*) to get things sorted out.
Karriere [kari'ɛːrə] **(-, -n)** *f* career; **~ machen** to get on, get to the top; **~macher(in)** *m(f)* careerist.
Karsamstag [kaːr'zamstaːk] *m* Easter Saturday.
Karst [karst] **(-s, -e)** *m* (*GEOG, GEOL*) karst, *barren landscape*.
Karte ['kartə] **(-, -n)** *f* card; (*Land~*) map; (*Speise~*) menu; (*Eintritts~, Fahr~*) ticket; **mit offenen ~n spielen** (*fig*) to put one's cards on the table; **alles auf eine ~ setzen** to put all one's eggs in one basket.
Kartei [kar'taɪ] *f* card index; **~karte** *f* index card; **~leiche** (*umg*) *f* sleeping od nonactive member; **~schrank** *m* filing cabinet.
Kartell [kar'tɛl] **(-s, -e)** *nt* cartel; **~amt** *nt* monopolies commission; **~gesetzgebung** *f* anti-trust legislation.
Karten- *zW*: **~haus** *nt* (*lit, fig*) house of cards; **~legen** *nt* fortune-telling (*usiːig cards*); **~spiel** *nt* card game; (*Karten*) pack (*BRIT*) od deck (*US*) of cards; **~telefon** *nt* cardphone; **~vorverkauf** *m* advance sale of tickets.
Kartoffel [kar'tɔfəl] **(-, -n)** *f* potato; **~brei** *m* mashed potatoes *pl*; **~chips** *pl* potato crisps *pl* (*BRIT*), potato chips *pl* (*US*); **~püree** *nt* mashed potatoes *pl*; **~salat** *m* potato salad.
Karton [kar'tõː] **(-s, -s)** *m* cardboard; (*Schachtel*) cardboard box.
kartoniert [karto'niːrt] *adj* hardback.
Karussell [karu'sɛl] **(-s, -s)** *nt* roundabout (*BRIT*), merry-go-round.
Karwoche ['kaːrvɔxə] *f* Holy Week.
Karzinom [kartsi'noːm] **(-s, -e)** *nt* (*MED*) carcinoma.
Kasachstan [kazaxs'taːn] **(-s)** *nt* (*GEOG*) Kazakhstan.
Kaschemme [ka'ʃɛmə] **(-, -n)** *f* dive.
kaschieren [ka'ʃiːrən] *vt* to conceal, cover up.
Kaschmir ['kaʃmiːr] **(-s)** *nt* (*GEOG*) Kashmir.
Käse ['kɛːzə] **(-s, -)** *m* cheese; (*umg: Unsinn*) rubbish, twaddle; **~blatt** (*umg*) *nt* (local)

rag; **~glocke** *f* cheese cover; **~kuchen** *m* cheesecake.
Kaserne [ka'zɛrnə] **(-, -n)** *f* barracks *pl*.
Kasernenhof *m* parade ground.
käsig ['kɛːzıç] *adj* (*fig: umg: Gesicht, Haut*) pasty, pale; (*vor Schreck*) white; (*lit*) cheesy.
Kasino [ka'ziːno] **(-s, -s)** *nt* club; (*MIL*) officers' mess; (*Spiel~*) casino.
Kaskoversicherung ['kaskofɛrzıçərʊŋ] *f* (*AUT: Teil~*) ≈ third party, fire and theft insurance; (: *Voll~*) fully comprehensive insurance.
Kasper ['kaspər] **(-s, -)** *m* Punch; (*fig*) clown.
Kasperl(e)theater ['kaspərl(ə)teaːtər] *nt* Punch and Judy (show).
Kaspisches Meer ['kaspıʃəs'meːr] *nt* Caspian Sea.
Kasse ['kasə] **(-, -n)** *f* (*Geldkasten*) cashbox; (*in Geschäft*) till, cash register; (*Kino~, Theater~ etc*) box office; (*Kranken~*) health insurance; (*Spar~*) savings bank; **die ~ führen** to be in charge of the money; **jdn zur ~ bitten** to ask sb to pay up; **~ machen** to count the money; **getrennte ~ führen** to pay separately; **an der ~** (*in Geschäft*) at the (cash) desk; **gut bei ~ sein** to be in the money.
Kasseler ['kasələr] **(-s, -)** *nt* lightly smoked pork loin.
Kassen- *zW*: **~arzt** *m* ≈ National Health doctor (*BRIT*), panel doctor (*US*); **~bestand** *m* cash balance; **~führer** *m* (*COMM*) cashier; **~patient** *m* ≈ National Health patient (*BRIT*); **~prüfung** *f* audit; **~schlager** (*umg*) *m* (*THEAT etc*) box-office hit; (: *Ware*) big seller; **~sturz** *m*: **~sturz machen** to check one's money; **~wart** *m* (*von Klub etc*) treasurer; **~zettel** *m* sales slip.
Kasserolle [kasə'rɔlə] **(-, -n)** *f* casserole.
Kassette [ka'sɛtə] *f* small box; (*Tonband, PHOT*) cassette; (*COMPUT*) cartridge, cassette; (*Bücher~*) case.
Kassettenrecorder **(-s, -)** *m* cassette recorder.
Kassiber [ka'siːbər] **(-s, -)** *m* (*in Gefängnis*) secret message.
kassieren [ka'siːrən] *vt* (*Gelder etc*) to collect; (*umg: wegnehmen*) to take (away) ♦ *vi*: **darf ich ~?** would you like to pay now?
Kassierer(in) [ka'siːrər(ın)] **(-s, -)** *m(f)* cashier; (*von Klub*) treasurer.
Kastanie [kas'taːniə] *f* chestnut.
Kastanienbaum *m* chestnut tree.
Kästchen ['kɛstçən] *nt* small box, casket.
Kaste ['kastə] **(-, -n)** *f* caste.
Kasten ['kastən] **(-s, ⁻)** *m* box (*auch SPORT*), case; (*Truhe*) chest; **er hat was auf dem ~** (*umg*) he's brainy; **~form** *f* (*KOCH*) (square) baking tin (*BRIT*) od pan (*US*); **~wagen** *m* van.
kastrieren [kas'triːrən] *vt* to castrate.
Kat **(-, -s)** *m abk* (*AUT*) = **Katalysator**.

katalanisch [kata'la:nıʃ] *adj* Catalan.
Katalog [kata'lo:k] (-(e)s, -e) *m* catalogue (*BRIT*), catalog (*US*).
katalogisieren [katalogi'zi:rən] *vt* to catalogue (*BRIT*), catalog (*US*).
Katalysator [kataly'za:tɔr] *m* (*lit, fig*) catalyst; (*AUT*) catalytic converter; ~-**Auto** vehicle fitted with a catalytic converter.
Katapult [kata'pʊlt] (-(e)s, -e) *nt or m* catapult.
katapultieren [katapʊl'ti:rən] *vt* to catapult ♦ *vr* to catapult o.s.; (*Pilot*) to eject.
Katar ['ka:tar] *nt* Qatar.
Katarrh [ka'tar] (-s, -e) *m* catarrh.
Katasteramt [ka'tastəramt] *nt* land registry.
katastrophal [katastro'fa:l] *adj* catastrophic.
Katastrophe [kata'stro:fə] (-, -n) *f* catastrophe, disaster.
Katastrophen- *zW:* ~**alarm** *m* emergency alert; ~**gebiet** *nt* disaster area; ~**medizin** *f* medical treatment in disasters; ~**schutz** *m* disaster control.
Katechismus [kate'çısmʊs] *m* catechism.
Kategorie [katego'ri:] *f* category.
kategorisch [kate'go:rıʃ] *adj* categorical.
kategorisieren [kategori'zi:rən] *vt* to categorize.
Kater ['ka:tər] (-s, -) *m* tomcat; (*umg*) hangover; ~**frühstück** *nt* breakfast (of pickled herring etc) to cure a hangover.
kath. *abk* = **katholisch.**
Katheder [ka'te:dər] (-s, -) *nt* (*SCH*) teacher's desk; (*UNIV*) lectern.
Kathedrale [kate'dra:lə] (-, -n) *f* cathedral.
Katheter [ka'te:tər] (-s, -) *m* (*MED*) catheter.
Kathode [ka'to:də] (-, -n) *f* cathode.
Katholik(in) [kato'li:k(ın)] (-en, -en) *m(f)* Catholic.
katholisch [ka'to:lıʃ] *adj* Catholic.
Katholizismus [katoli'tsısmʊs] *m* Catholicism.
katzbuckeln ['katsbʊkəln] (*pej: umg*) *vi* to bow and scrape.
Kätzchen ['kɛtsçən] *nt* kitten.
Katze ['katsə] (-, -n) *f* cat; **die ~ im Sack kaufen** to buy a pig in a poke; **für die Katz** (*umg*) in vain, for nothing.
Katzen- *zW:* ~**auge** *nt* cat's-eye (*BRIT*); (*am Fahrrad*) rear light; ~**jammer** (*umg*) *m* hangover; ~**musik** *f* (*fig*) caterwauling; ~**sprung** (*umg*) *m* stone's throw, short distance; ~**tür** *f* cat flap; ~**wäsche** *f* a lick and a promise.
Kauderwelsch ['kaʊdərvɛlʃ] (-(s)) *nt* jargon; (*umg*) double Dutch (*BRIT*).
kauen ['kaʊən] *vt, vi* to chew.
kauern ['kaʊərn] *vi* to crouch.
Kauf [kaʊf] (-(e)s, Käufe) *m* purchase, buy; (~*en*) buying; **ein guter ~** a bargain; **etw in ~ nehmen** to put up with sth.
kaufen *vt* to buy; **dafür kann ich mir nichts ~** (*ironisch*) what use is that to me!
Käufer(in) ['kɔyfər(ın)] (-s, -) *m(f)* buyer.
Kauf- *zW:* ~**frau** *f* businesswoman;

(*Einzelhandelskauffrau*) shopkeeper; ~**haus** *nt* department store; ~**kraft** *f* purchasing power; ~**laden** *m* shop, store.
käuflich ['kɔyflıç] *adj* purchasable, for sale; (*pej*) venal ♦ *adv:* ~ **erwerben** to purchase.
Kauf- *zW:* ~**lust** *f* desire to buy things; (*BÖRSE*) buying; **k~lustig** *adj* interested in buying; ~**mann** (-(e)s, *pl* -**leute**) *m* businessman; (*Einzelhandelskaufmann*) shopkeeper; **k~männisch** *adj* commercial; **k~männischer Angestellter** clerk; ~**preis** *m* purchase price; ~**vertrag** *m* bill of sale; ~**willige(r)** *f(m)* potential buyer; ~**zwang** *m:* **kein/ohne ~zwang** no/without obligation.
Kaugummi ['kaʊgʊmi] *m* chewing gum.
Kaukasus ['kaʊkazʊs] *m:* **der ~** the Caucasus.
Kaulquappe ['kaʊlkvapə] (-, -n) *f* tadpole.
kaum [kaʊm] *adv* hardly, scarcely; **wohl ~, ich glaube ~** I hardly think so.
Kausalzusammenhang [kaʊ'za:ltsuzamənhaŋ] *m* causal connection.
Kaution [kaʊtsi'o:n] *f* deposit; (*JUR*) bail.
Kautschuk ['kaʊtʃʊk] (-s, -e) *m* India rubber.
Kauz [kaʊts] (-es, Käuze) *m* owl; (*fig*) queer fellow.
Kavalier [kava'li:r] (-s, -e) *m* gentleman.
Kavaliersdelikt *nt* peccadillo.
Kavallerie [kavalə'ri:] *f* cavalry.
Kavallerist [kavalə'rıst] *m* cavalryman.
Kaviar ['ka:viar] *m* caviar.
KB *nt abk* (= *Kilobyte*) KB, kbyte.
Kcal *abk* (= *Kilokalorie*) kcal.
keck [kɛk] *adj* daring, bold; **K~heit** *f* daring, boldness.
Kegel ['ke:gəl] (-s, -) *m* skittle; (*MATH*) cone; ~**bahn** *f* skittle alley, bowling alley; **k~förmig** *adj* conical.
kegeln *vi* to play skittles.
Kehle ['ke:lə] (-, -n) *f* throat; **er hat das in die falsche ~ bekommen** (*lit*) it went down the wrong way; (*fig*) he took it the wrong way; **aus voller ~** at the top of one's voice.
Kehl- *zW:* ~**kopf** *m* larynx; ~**kopfkrebs** *m* cancer of the throat; ~**laut** *m* guttural.
Kehre ['ke:rə] (-, -n) *f* turn(ing), bend.
kehren *vt, vi* (*wenden*) to turn; (*mit Besen*) to sweep; **sich an etw** *dat* **nicht ~** not to heed sth; **in sich** *akk* **gekehrt** (*versunken*) pensive; (*verschlossen*) introspective, introverted.
Kehricht (-s) *m* sweepings *pl*.
Kehr- *zW:* ~**maschine** *f* sweeper; ~**reim** *m* refrain; ~**seite** *f* reverse, other side; (*ungünstig*) wrong *od* bad side; **die ~seite der Medaille** the other side of the coin.
kehrtmachen *vi* to turn about, about-turn.
Kehrtwendung *f* about-turn.
keifen ['kaıfən] *vi* to scold, nag.
Keil [kaıl] (-(e)s, -e) *m* wedge; (*MIL*) arrowhead; **k~en** *vt* to wedge ♦ *vr* to fight.
Keilerei [kaılə'raı] (*umg*) *f* punch-up.
Keilriemen *m* (*AUT*) fan belt.
Keim [kaım] (-(e)s, -e) *m* bud; (*MED, fig*) germ;

etw im ~ **ersticken** to nip sth in the bud.
keimen *vi* to germinate.
Keim- *zW:* **k~frei** *adj* sterile; **k~tötend** *adj* antiseptic, germicidal; **~zelle** *f* (*fig*) nucleus.
kein(e) ['kaın(ə)] *pron* none ♦ *adj* no, not any; ~ **schlechte Idee** not a bad idea; ~ **Stunde/ drei Monate** (*nicht einmal*) less than an hour/three months.
keine(r, s) *indef pron* no one, nobody; (*von Gegenstand*) none.
keinerlei ['kaınər'laı] *adj attrib* no ... whatever.
keinesfalls *adv* on no account.
keineswegs *adv* by no means.
keinmal *adv* not once.
Keks [keːks] (**-es, -e**) *m od nt* biscuit (*BRIT*), cookie (*US*).
Kelch [kɛlç] (**-(e)s, -e**) *m* cup, goblet, chalice.
Kelle ['kɛlə] (**-, -n**) *f* ladle; (*Maurer~*) trowel.
Keller ['kɛlər] (**-s, -**) *m* cellar; **~assel** (**-, -n**) *f* woodlouse.
Kellerei [kɛlə'raı] *f* wine cellars *pl*; (*Firma*) wine producer.
Kellergeschoß *nt* basement.
Kellerwohnung *f* basement flat (*BRIT*) *od* apartment (*US*).
Kellner(in) ['kɛlnər(ın)] (**-s, -**) *m(f)* waiter, waitress.
kellnern (*umg*) *vi* to work as a waiter/ waitress (*BRIT*), wait on tables (*US*).
Kelte ['kɛltə] (**-n, -n**) *m* Celt.
Kelter (**-, -n**) *f* winepress; (*Obst~*) press.
keltern ['kɛltərn] *vt* to press.
Keltin ['kɛltın] *f* (female) Celt.
keltisch *adj* Celtic.
Kenia ['keːnia] (**-s**) *nt* Kenya.
kennen ['kɛnən] *unreg vt* to know; ~ **Sie sich schon?** do you know each other (already)?; **kennst du mich noch?** do you remember me?; **~lernen** *vt* to get to know; **sich ~lernen** to get to know each other; (*zum erstenmal*) to meet.
Kenner(in) (**-s, -**) *m(f):* ~ (**von** *od* **+gen**) connoisseur (of); expert (on).
Kennkarte *f* identity card.
kenntlich *adj* distinguishable, discernible; **etw ~ machen** to mark sth.
Kenntnis (**-, -se**) *f* knowledge *no pl*; **etw zur ~ nehmen** to note sth; **von etw ~ nehmen** to take notice of sth; **jdn in ~ setzen** to inform sb; **über ~se von etw verfügen** to be knowledgeable about sth.
Kenn- *zW:* **~wort** *nt* (*Chiffre*) code name; (*Losungswort*) password, code word; **~zeichen** *nt* mark, characteristic; **(amtliches/polizeiliches) ~zeichen** (*AUT*) number plate (*BRIT*), license plate (*US*); **k~zeichnen** *vt untr* to characterize; **k~zeichnenderweise** *adv* characteristically; **~ziffer** *f* (code) number; (*COMM*) reference number.
kentern ['kɛntərn] *vi* to capsize.

Keramik [ke'raːmɪk] (**-, -en**) *f* ceramics *pl*, pottery; (*Gegenstand*) piece of ceramic work *od* pottery.
Kerbe ['kɛrbə] (**-, -n**) *f* notch, groove.
Kerbel (**-s, -**) *m* chervil.
kerben *vt* to notch.
Kerbholz *nt:* **etw auf dem ~ haben** to have done sth wrong.
Kerker ['kɛrkər] (**-s, -**) *m* prison.
Kerl [kɛrl] (**-s, -e**) (*umg*) *m* chap, bloke (*BRIT*), guy; **du gemeiner ~!** you swine!
Kern [kɛrn] (**-(e)s, -e**) *m* (*Obst~*) pip, stone; (*Nuß~*) kernel; (*Atom~*) nucleus; (*fig*) heart, core; **~energie** *f* nuclear energy; **~fach** *nt* (*SCH*) core subject; **~familie** *f* nuclear family; **~forschung** *f* nuclear research; **~frage** *f* central issue; **~fusion** *f* nuclear fusion; **~gehäuse** *nt* core; **k~gesund** *adj* thoroughly healthy, fit as a fiddle.
kernig *adj* robust; (*Ausspruch*) pithy.
Kern- *zW:* **~kraftwerk** *nt* nuclear power station; **k~los** *adj* seedless, pipless; **~physik** *f* nuclear physics *sing*; **~reaktion** *f* nuclear reaction; **~reaktor** *m* nuclear reactor; **~schmelze** *f* meltdown; **~seife** *f* washing soap; **~spaltung** *f* nuclear fission; **~stück** *nt* (*fig*) main item; (*von Theorie etc*) central part, core; **~waffen** *pl* nuclear weapons *pl*; **k~waffenfrei** *adj* nuclear-free; **~zeit** *f* core time.
Kerze ['kɛrtsə] (**-, -n**) *f* candle; (*Zünd~*) plug.
Kerzen- *zW:* **k~gerade** *adj* straight as a die; **~halter** *m* candlestick; **~ständer** *m* candle-holder.
keß [kɛs] *adj* saucy.
Kessel ['kɛsəl] (**-s, -**) *m* kettle; (*von Lokomotive etc*) boiler; (*Mulde*) basin; (*GEOG*) depression; (*MIL*) encirclement; **~stein** *m* scale, fur (*BRIT*); **~treiben** *nt* (*fig*) witch-hunt.
Kette ['kɛtə] (**-, -n**) *f* chain; **jdn an die ~ legen** (*fig*) to tie sb down.
ketten *vt* to chain.
Ketten- *zW:* **~fahrzeug** *nt* tracked vehicle; **~hund** *m* watchdog; **~karussell** *nt* merry-go-round (*with gondolas on chains*); **~laden** *m* chain store; **~rauchen** *nt* chain smoking; **~reaktion** *f* chain reaction.
Ketzer(in) ['kɛtsər(ın)] (**-s, -**) *m(f)* heretic; **~ei** [kɛtsə'raı] *f* heresy; **k~isch** *adj* heretical.
keuchen ['kɔyçən] *vi* to pant, gasp.
Keuchhusten *m* whooping cough.
Keule ['kɔylə] (**-, -n**) *f* club; (*KOCH*) leg.
keusch [kɔyʃ] *adj* chaste; **K~heit** *f* chastity.
Kfm. *abk* = **Kaufmann.**
kfm. *abk* = **kaufmännisch.**
Kfz (**-(s), -(s)**) *f abk* = **Kraftfahrzeug.**
KG (**-, -s**) *f abk* = **Kommanditgesellschaft.**
kg *abk* (= *Kilogramm*) kg.
kHz *abk* (= *Kilohertz*) kHz.
Kibbuz [kı'buːts] (**-, Kibbuzim** *od* **-e**) *m* kibbutz.

kichern ['kıçərn] *vi* to giggle.
kicken ['kıkən] *vt, vi* (*Fußball*) to kick.
kidnappen ['kıtnɛpən] *vt* to kidnap.
Kidnapper(in) (-s, -) *m(f)* kidnapper.
Kiebitz ['ki:bıts] (-es, -e) *m* peewit.
Kiefer¹ ['ki:fər] (-s, -) *m* jaw.
Kiefer² ['ki:fər] (-, -n) *f* pine.
Kiefernholz *nt* pine(wood).
Kiefernzapfen *m* pine cone.
Kieferorthopäde *m* orthodontist.
Kieker ['ki:kər] (-s, -) *m:* **jdn auf dem ~ haben** (*umg*) to have it in for sb.
Kiel [ki:l] (-(e)s, -e) *m* (*Feder~*) quill; (*NAUT*) keel; ~**wasser** *nt* wake.
Kieme ['ki:mə] (-, -n) *f* gill.
Kies [ki:s] (-es, -e) *m* gravel; (*umg: Geld*) money, dough.
Kiesel ['ki:zəl] (-s, -) *m* pebble; ~**stein** *m* pebble.
Kiesgrube *f* gravel pit.
Kiesweg *m* gravel path.
Kiew ['ki:ɛf] (-s) *nt* Kiev.
kiffen ['kıfən] (*umg*) *vt* to smoke pot *od* grass.
Kilimandscharo [kiliman'dʒa:ro] (-s) *m* Kilimanjaro.
Killer ['kılər(ın)] (-s, -) (*umg*) *m* killer, murderer; (*gedungener*) hit man; ~**in** (*umg*) *f* killer, female murderer, murderess.
Kilo ['ki:lo] (-s, -(s)) *nt* kilo; ~**byte** [kilo'baıt] *nt* (*COMPUT*) kilobyte; ~**gramm** [kilo'gram] *nt* kilogram.
Kilometer [kilo'me:tər] *m* kilometre (*BRIT*), kilometer (*US*); ~**fresser** (*umg*) *m* long-haul driver; ~**geld** *nt* ≈ mileage (allowance); ~**stand** *m* ≈ mileage; ~**stein** *m* ≈ milestone; ~**zähler** *m* ≈ mileometer.
Kilowatt [kilo'vat] *nt* kilowatt.
Kimme ['kımə] (-, -n) *f* notch; (*Gewehr*) back sight.
Kind [kınt] (-(e)s, -er) *nt* child; **sich freuen wie ein ~** to be as pleased as Punch; **mit ~ und Kegel** (*hum: umg*) with the whole family; **von ~ auf** from childhood.
Kinderarzt *m* paediatrician (*BRIT*), pediatrician (*US*).
Kinderbett *nt* cot (*BRIT*), crib (*US*).
Kinderei [kındə'raı] *f* childishness.
Kindererziehung *f* bringing up of children; (*durch Schule*) education of children.
kinderfeindlich *adj* anti-children; (*Architektur, Planung*) not catering for children.
Kinderfreibetrag *m* child allowance.
Kindergarten *m* nursery school.

> A **Kindergarten** *is a nursery school for children aged between 3 and 6 years. The children sing, play and do handicrafts. They are not taught the three Rs at this stage. Most Kindergärten are financed by the town or the church and not by the state. Parents pay a monthly contribution towards the cost.*

Kinder- *zW:* ~**gärtner(in)** *m(f)* nursery-school teacher; ~**geld** *nt* child benefit (*BRIT*); ~**heim** *nt* children's home; ~**krankheit** *f* childhood illness; ~**laden** *m* (alternative) playgroup; ~**lähmung** *f* polio(myelitis); **k~leicht** *adj* childishly easy; **k~lieb** *adj* fond of children; ~**lied** *nt* nursery rhyme; **k~los** *adj* childless; ~**mädchen** *nt* nursemaid; ~**pflegerin** *f* child minder; **k~reich** *adj* with a lot of children; ~**schuh** *m:* **es steckt noch in den ~schuhen** (*fig*) it's still in its infancy; ~**spiel** *nt* child's play; **ein ~spiel sein** to be a doddle; ~**stube** *f:* **eine gute ~stube haben** to be well-mannered; ~**tagesstätte** *f* day-nursery; ~**teller** *m* children's dish; ~**wagen** *m* pram (*BRIT*), baby carriage (*US*); ~**zimmer** *nt* child's/children's room; (*für Kleinkinder*) nursery.
Kindes- *zW:* ~**alter** *nt* infancy; ~**beine** *pl:* **von ~beinen an** from early childhood; ~**mißhandlung** *f* child abuse.
Kind- *zW:* **k~gemäß** *adj* suitable for a child *od* children; ~**heit** *f* childhood; **k~isch** *adj* childish; **k~lich** *adj* childlike.
kindsköpfig *adj* childish.
Kinkerlitzchen ['kıŋkərlıtsçən] (*umg*) *pl* knick-knacks *pl.*
Kinn [kın] (-(e)s, -e) *nt* chin; ~**haken** *m* (*BOXEN*) uppercut; ~**lade** *f* jaw.
Kino ['ki:no] (-s, -s) *nt* cinema (*BRIT*), movies (*US*); ~**besucher** *m*, ~**gänger** *m* cinema-goer (*BRIT*), movie-goer (*US*); ~**programm** *nt* film programme (*BRIT*), movie program (*US*).
Kiosk [ki'ɔsk] (-(e)s, -e) *m* kiosk.
Kippe ['kıpə] (-, -n) *f* (*umg*) cigarette end; **auf der ~ stehen** (*fig*) to be touch and go.
kippen *vi* to topple over, overturn ♦ *vt* to tilt.
Kipper ['kıpər] (-s, -) *m* (*AUT*) tipper, dump(er) truck.
Kippschalter *m* rocker switch.
Kirche ['kırçə] (-, -n) *f* church.
Kirchen- *zW:* ~**chor** *m* church choir; ~**diener** *m* churchwarden; ~**fest** *nt* church festival; ~**lied** *nt* hymn; ~**schiff** *nt* (*Längsschiff*) nave; (*Querschiff*) transept; ~**steuer** *f* church tax; ~**tag** *m* church congress.
Kirch- *zW:* ~**gänger(in)** (-s, -) *m(f)* churchgoer; ~**hof** *m* churchyard; **k~lich** *adj* ecclesiastical; ~**turm** *m* church tower, steeple; ~**weih** *f* fair, kermis (*US*).
Kirgistan ['kırgista:n] (-s) *nt* (*GEOG*) Kirghizia.
Kirmes ['kırmɛs] (-, -sen) *f* (*Dialekt*) fair, kermis (*US*).
Kirschbaum ['kırʃbaum] *m* cherry tree; (*Holz*) cherry (wood).
Kirsche ['kırʃə] (-, -n) *f* cherry; **mit ihm ist nicht gut ~n essen** (*fig*) it's best not to tangle with him.
Kirschtorte *f:* **Schwarzwälder ~** Black Forest Gateau.

Kirschwasser *nt* kirsch.
Kissen ['kɪsən] (-s, -) *nt* cushion; (*Kopf~*) pillow; ~**bezug** *m* pillow case.
Kiste ['kɪstə] (-, -n) *f* box; (*Truhe*) chest; (*umg: Bett*) sack; (: *Fernsehen*) box (*BRIT*), tube (*US*).
Kita ['kɪta] *f abk* = **Kindertagesstätte**.
Kitsch [kɪtʃ] (-(e)s) *m* trash.
kitschig *adj* trashy.
Kitt [kɪt] (-(e)s, -e) *m* putty.
Kittchen (*umg*) *nt* clink.
Kittel (-s, -) *m* overall; (*von Arzt, Laborant etc*) (white) coat.
kitten *vt* to putty; (*fig*) to patch up.
Kitz [kɪts] (-es, -e) *nt* kid; (*Reh~*) fawn.
kitzelig ['kɪtsəlɪç] *adj* (*lit, fig*) ticklish.
kitzeln *vt, vi* to tickle.
Kiwi ['kiːvi] (-, -s) *f* kiwi fruit.
KKW (-, -s) *nt abk* = **Kernkraftwerk**.
Kl. *abk* (= *Klasse*) cl.
Klacks [klaks] (-es, -e) (*umg*) *m* (*von Kartoffelbrei, Sahne*) dollop; (*von Senf, Farbe etc*) blob.
Kladde ['kladə] (-, -n) *f* rough book; (*Block*) scribbling pad.
klaffen ['klafən] *vi* to gape.
kläffen ['klɛfən] *vi* to yelp.
Klage ['klaːgə] (-, -n) *f* complaint; (*JUR*) action; **eine ~ gegen jdn einreichen** *od* **erheben** to institute proceedings against sb; ~**lied** *nt*: **ein ~lied über jdn/etw anstimmen** (*fig*) to complain about sb/sth; ~**mauer** *f*: **die ~mauer** the Wailing Wall.
klagen *vi* (*weh~*) to lament, wail; (*sich beschweren*) to complain; (*JUR*) to take legal action; **jdm sein Leid/seine Not ~** to pour out one's sorrow/distress to sb.
Kläger(in) ['klɛːgər(ɪn)] (-s, -) *m(f)* (*JUR: im Zivilrecht*) plaintiff; (: *im Strafrecht*) prosecuting party; (: *in Scheidung*) petitioner.
Klageschrift *f* (*JUR*) charge; (*bei Scheidung*) petition.
kläglich ['klɛːklɪç] *adj* wretched.
Klamauk [kla'maʊk] (-s) (*umg*) *m* (*Alberei*) tomfoolery; (*im Theater*) slapstick.
Klamm [klam] (-, -en) *f* ravine.
klamm *adj* (*Finger*) numb; (*feucht*) damp.
Klammer ['klamər] (-, -n) *f* clamp; (*in Text*) bracket; (*Büro~*) clip; (*Wäsche~*) peg (*BRIT*), pin (*US*); (*Zahn~*) brace; ~ **auf/zu** open/close brackets.
klammern *vr*: **sich ~ an** *+akk* to cling to.
klammheimlich [klam'haɪmlɪç] (*umg*) *adj* secret ♦ *adv* on the quiet.
Klamotte [kla'mɔtə] (-, -n) *f* (*pej: Film etc*) rubbishy old film *etc*; **Klamotten** *pl* (*umg: Kleider*) clothes *pl*; (: *Zeug*) stuff.
Klampfe ['klampfə] (-, -n) (*umg*) *f* guitar.
klang *etc* [klaŋ] *vb siehe* **klingen**.
Klang (-(e)s, ¨e) *m* sound.
klangvoll *adj* sonorous.

Klappbett *nt* folding bed.
Klappe ['klapə] (-, -n) *f* valve; (*an Oboe etc*) key; (*FILM*) clapperboard; (*Ofen~*) damper; (*umg: Mund*) trap; **die ~ halten** to shut one's trap.
klappen *vi* (*Geräusch*) to click; (*Sitz etc*) to tip ♦ *vt* to tip ♦ *vi unpers* to work; **hat es mit den Karten/dem Job geklappt?** did you get the tickets/job O.K.?
Klappentext *m* blurb.
Klapper ['klapər] (-, -n) *f* rattle.
klapperig *adj* run-down, worn-out.
klappern *vi* to clatter, rattle.
Klapperschlange *f* rattlesnake.
Klapperstorch *m* stork; **er glaubt noch an den ~** he still thinks babies are found under the gooseberry bush.
Klapp- *zW*: ~**messer** *nt* jackknife; ~**rad** *nt* collapsible *od* folding bicycle; ~**stuhl** *m* folding chair; ~**tisch** *m* folding table.
Klaps [klaps] (-es, -e) *m* slap; **einen ~ haben** (*umg*) to have a screw loose; **k~en** *vt* to slap.
klar [klaːr] *adj* clear; (*NAUT*) ready to sail; (*MIL*) ready for action; **bei ~em Verstand sein** to be in full possession of one's faculties; **sich** *dat* **im ~en sein über** *+akk* to be clear about; **ins ~e kommen** to get clear.
Kläranlage *f* sewage plant; (*von Fabrik*) purification plant.
Klare(r) (*umg*) *m* schnapps.
klären *vt* (*Flüssigkeit*) to purify; (*Probleme*) to clarify ♦ *vr* to clear (itself) up.
Klarheit *f* clarity; **sich** *dat* **~ über etw** *akk* **verschaffen** to get sth straight.
Klarinette [klari'nɛtə] *f* clarinet.
klar- *zW*: ~**kommen** *unreg* (*umg*) *vi*: **mit jdm/ etw ~kommen** to be able to cope with sb/ sth; ~**legen** *vt* to clear up, explain; ~**machen** *vt* (*Schiff*) to get ready for sea; **jdm etw ~machen** to make sth clear to sb; ~**sehen** *unreg vi* to see clearly; **K~sichtfolie** *f* transparent film; ~**stellen** *vt* to clarify; **K~text** *m*: **im K~text** in clear; (*fig: umg*) ≈ in plain English.
Klärung ['klɛːrʊŋ] *f* purification; clarification.
klarwerden *unreg vr*: **sich** *dat* **über etw** *akk* **~** to get sth clear in one's mind.
Klasse ['klasə] (-, -n) *f* class; (*SCH*) class, form; (*auch*: **Steuer~**) bracket; (*Güter~*) grade.
klasse (*umg*) *adj* smashing.
Klassen- *zW*: ~**arbeit** *f* test; ~**bewußtsein** *nt* class-consciousness; ~**buch** *nt* (*SCH*) (class) register; ~**gesellschaft** *f* class society; ~**kamerad(in)** *m(f)* classmate; ~**kampf** *m* class conflict; ~**lehrer(in)** *m(f)* class teacher; **k~los** *adj* classless; ~**sprecher(in)** *m(f)* class spokesperson; ~**ziel** *nt*: **das ~ziel nicht erreichen** (*SCH*) not to reach the required standard (for the year); (*fig*) not to make the grade; ~**zimmer** *nt* classroom.
klassifizieren [klasifi'tsiːrən] *vt* to classify.

Klassifizierung f classification.
Klassik ['klasɪk] f (Zeit) classical period; (Stil) classicism; ~**er** (-s, -) m classic.
klassisch adj (lit, fig) classical.
Klassizismus [klasi'tsɪsmʊs] m classicism.
Klatsch [klatʃ] (-(e)s, -e) m smack, crack; (Gerede) gossip; ~**base** f gossip(monger).
klatschen vi (tratschen) to gossip; (Beifall spenden) to applaud, to clap ♦ vt: **(jdm) Beifall ~** to applaud od clap (sb).
Klatsch- zW: ~**mohn** m (corn) poppy; **k~naß** adj soaking wet; ~**spalte** f gossip column; ~**tante** (pej: umg) f gossip(monger).
klauben ['klaʊbən] vt to pick.
Klaue ['klaʊə] (-, -n) f claw; (umg: Schrift) scrawl.
klauen vt to claw; (umg) to pinch.
Klause ['klaʊzə] (-, -n) f cell; (von Mönch) hermitage.
Klausel ['klaʊzəl] (-, -n) f clause; (Vorbehalt) proviso.
Klausur [klaʊ'zuːr] f seclusion; ~**arbeit** f examination paper.
Klaviatur [klavia'tuːr] f keyboard.
Klavier [kla'viːr] (-s, -e) nt piano; ~**auszug** m piano score.
Klebeband nt adhesive tape.
Klebemittel nt glue.
kleben ['kleːbən] vt, vi: ~ **(an** +akk) to stick (to); **jdm eine ~** (umg) to belt sb one.
Klebezettel m gummed label.
klebrig adj sticky.
Klebstoff m glue.
Klebstreifen m adhesive tape.
kleckern ['klɛkərn] vi to slobber.
Klecks [klɛks] (-es, -e) m blot, stain; **k~en** vi to blot; (pej) to daub.
Klee [kleː] (-s) m clover; **jdn/etw über den grünen ~ loben** (fig) to praise sb/sth to the skies; ~**blatt** nt cloverleaf; (fig) trio.
Kleid [klaɪt] (-(e)s, -er) nt garment; (Frauen~) dress; **Kleider** pl clothes pl.
kleiden ['klaɪdən] vt to clothe, dress ♦ vr to dress; **jdn ~** to suit sb.
Kleider- zW: ~**bügel** m coat hanger; ~**bürste** f clothes brush; ~**schrank** m wardrobe; ~**ständer** m coat-stand.
kleidsam adj becoming.
Kleidung f clothing.
Kleidungsstück nt garment.
Kleie ['klaɪə] (-, -n) f bran.
klein [klaɪn] adj little, small; **haben Sie es nicht ~er?** haven't you got anything smaller?; **ein ~es Bier, ein K~es** (umg) ≈ half a pint, a half; **von ~ an** od **auf** (von Kindheit an) from childhood; (von Anfang an) from the very beginning; **das ~ere Übel** the lesser evil; **sein Vater war (ein) ~er Beamter** his father was a minor civil servant; **~ anfangen** to start off in a small way; **ein Wort ~ schreiben** to write a word with a small initial letter; **K~anzeige** f small ad

(BRIT), want ad (US); **Kleinanzeigen** pl classified advertising sing; **K~arbeit** f: **in zäher/mühseliger K~arbeit** with rigorous/ painstaking attention to detail; **K~asien** nt Asia Minor; **K~bürgertum** nt petite bourgeoisie; **K~bus** m minibus.
Kleine(r) f(m) little one.
klein- zW: **K~familie** f small family, nuclear family (SOZIOLOGIE); **K~format** nt small size; **im K~format** small-scale; **K~gedruckte(s)** nt small print; **K~geld** nt small change; **das nötige K~geld haben** (fig) to have the wherewithal (umg); ~**gläubig** adj of little faith; ~**hacken** vt to chop up; **K~holz** nt firewood; **K~holz aus jdm machen** to make mincemeat of sb.
Kleinigkeit f trifle; **wegen** od **bei jeder ~** for the slightest reason; **eine ~ essen** to have a bite to eat.
klein- zW: ~**kariert** adj: ~**kariert denken** to think small; **K~kind** nt infant; **K~kram** m details pl; **K~kredit** m personal loan; ~**kriegen** (umg) vt (gefügig machen) to bring into line; (unterkriegen) to get down; (körperlich) to tire out; ~**laut** adj dejected, quiet; ~**lich** adj petty, paltry; **K~lichkeit** f pettiness, paltriness; ~**mütig** adj fainthearted.
Kleinod ['klaɪnoːt] (-s, -odien) nt gem, jewel; (fig) treasure.
klein- zW: **K~rechner** m minicomputer; ~**schneiden** unreg vt to chop up; ~**schreiben** unreg vt: ~**geschrieben werden** (umg) to count for (very) little; **K~schreibung** f use of small initial letters; **K~stadt** f small town; ~**städtisch** adj provincial.
kleinstmöglich adj smallest possible.
Kleinwagen m small car.
Kleister ['klaɪstər] (-s, -) m paste.
kleistern vt to paste.
Klemme ['klɛmə] (-, -n) f clip; (MED) clamp; (fig) jam; **in der ~ sitzen** od **sein** (fig: umg) to be in a fix.
klemmen vt (festhalten) to jam; (quetschen) to pinch, nip ♦ vr to catch o.s.; (sich hineinzwängen) to squeeze o.s. ♦ vi (Tür) to stick, jam; **sich hinter jdn/etw ~** to get on to sb/get down to sth.
Klempner ['klɛmpnər] (-s, -) m plumber.
Kleptomanie [klɛptoma'niː] f kleptomania.
Kleriker ['kleːrikər] (-s, -) m cleric.
Klerus ['kleːrʊs] (-) m clergy.
Klette ['klɛtə] (-, -n) f burr; **sich wie eine ~ an jdn hängen** to cling to sb like a limpet.
Kletterer ['klɛtərər] (-s, -) m climber.
Klettergerüst nt climbing frame.
klettern vi to climb.
Kletterpflanze f creeper.
Kletterseil nt climbing rope.
Klettverschluß m Velcro ® fastener.
klicken ['klɪkən] vi to click.
Klient(in) [kli'ɛnt(ɪn)] m(f) client.

Klima ['kliːma] (-s, -s *od* -te) *nt* climate; ~**anlage** *f* air conditioning.
klimatisieren [klimati'ziːrən] *vt* to air-condition.
klimatisiert *adj* air-conditioned.
Klimawechsel *m* change of air.
Klimbim [klɪm'bɪm] (-s) (*umg*) *m* odds and ends *pl.*
klimpern ['klɪmpərn] *vi* to tinkle; (*auf Gitarre*) to strum.
Klinge ['klɪŋə] (-, -n) *f* blade, sword; **jdn über die ~ springen lassen** (*fig: umg*) to allow sb to run into trouble.
Klingel ['klɪŋəl] (-, -n) *f* bell; ~**beutel** *m* collection bag; ~**knopf** *m* bell push.
klingeln *vi* to ring; **es hat geklingelt** (*an Tür*) somebody just rang the doorbell, the doorbell just rang.
klingen ['klɪŋən] *unreg vi* to sound; (*Gläser*) to clink.
Klinik ['kliːnɪk] *f* clinic.
klinisch ['kliːnɪʃ] *adj* clinical.
Klinke ['klɪŋkə] (-, -n) *f* handle.
Klinker ['klɪŋkər] (-s, -) *m* clinker.
Klippe ['klɪpə] (-, -n) *f* cliff; (*im Meer*) reef; (*fig*) hurdle.
klippenreich *adj* rocky.
klipp und klar ['klɪp|ʊntklaːr] *adj* clear and concise.
Klips [klɪps] (-es, -e) *m* clip; (*Ohr~*) earring.
klirren ['klɪrən] *vi* to clank, jangle; (*Gläser*) to clink; ~**de Kälte** biting cold.
Klischee [klɪ'ʃeː] (-s, -s) *nt* (*Druckplatte*) plate, block; (*fig*) cliché; ~**vorstellung** *f* stereotyped idea.
Klitoris ['kliːtorɪs] (-, -) *f* clitoris.
Klo [kloː] (-s, -s) (*umg*) *nt* loo (*BRIT*), john (*US*).
Kloake [klo'aːkə] (-, -n) *f* sewer.
klobig ['kloːbɪç] *adj* clumsy.
Klon [kloːn] (-s, -e) *m* clone.
Klopapier (*umg*) *nt* toilet paper.
klopfen ['klɔpfən] *vi* to knock; (*Herz*) to thump ♦ *vt* to beat; **es klopft** somebody's knocking; **jdm auf die Finger ~** (*lit, fig*) to give sb a rap on the knuckles; **jdm auf die Schulter ~** to tap sb on the shoulder.
Klopfer (-s, -) *m* (*Teppich~*) beater; (*Tür~*) knocker.
Klöppel ['klœpəl] (-s, -) *m* (*von Glocke*) clapper.
klöppeln *vi* to make lace.
Klops [klɔps] (-es, -e) *m* meatball.
Klosett [klo'zɛt] (-s, -e *od* -s) *nt* lavatory, toilet; ~**brille** *f* toilet seat; ~**papier** *nt* toilet paper.
Kloß [kloːs] (-es, ̈-e) *m* (*Erd~*) clod; (*im Hals*) lump; (*KOCH*) dumpling.
Kloster ['kloːstər] (-s, ̈-) *nt* (*Männer~*) monastery; (*Frauen~*) convent; **ins ~ gehen** to become a monk/nun.
klösterlich ['kløːstərlɪç] *adj* monastic; convent *attr.*

Klotz [klɔts] (-es, ̈-e) *m* log; (*Hack~*) block; **jdm ein ~ am Bein sein** (*fig*) to be a millstone round sb's neck.
Klub [klʊp] (-s, -s) *m* club; ~**jacke** *f* blazer; ~**sessel** *m* easy chair.
Kluft [klʊft] (-, ̈-e) *f* cleft, gap; (*GEOG*) chasm; (*Uniform*) uniform; (*umg: Kleidung*) gear.
klug [kluːk] *adj* clever, intelligent; **ich werde daraus nicht ~** I can't make head or tail of it; **K~heit** *f* cleverness, intelligence; **K~scheißer** (*umg*) *m* smart-ass.
Klümpchen ['klʏmpçən] *nt* clot, blob.
klumpen ['klʊmpən] *vi* to go lumpy, clot.
Klumpen (-s, -) *m* (*KOCH*) lump; (*Erd~*) clod; (*Blut~*) clot; (*Gold~*) nugget.
Klumpfuß ['klʊmpfuːs] *m* club foot.
Klüngel ['klʏŋəl] (-s, -) (*umg*) *m* (*Clique*) clique.
Klunker ['klʊŋkər] (-s, -) (*umg*) *m* (*Schmuck*) rock(s *pl*).
km *abk* (= *Kilometer*) km.
km/h *abk* (= *Kilometer pro Stunde*) km/h.
knabbern ['knabərn] *vt, vi* to nibble; **an etw** *dat* ~ (*fig: umg*) to puzzle over sth.
Knabe ['knaːbə] (-n, -n) *m* boy.
knabenhaft *adj* boyish.
Knäckebrot ['knɛkəbroːt] *nt* crispbread.
knacken ['knakən] *vi* (*lit, fig*) to crack ♦ *vt* (*umg: Auto*) to break into.
knackfrisch (*umg*) *adj* oven-fresh, crispy-fresh.
knackig *adj* crisp.
Knacks [knaks] (-es, -e) *m*: **einen ~ weghaben** (*umg*) to be uptight about sth.
Knackwurst *f* type of frankfurter.
Knall [knal] (-(e)s, -e) *m* bang; (*Peitschen~*) crack; ~ **auf Fall** (*umg*) just like that; **einen ~ haben** (*umg*) to be crazy *od* crackers; ~**bonbon** *nt* cracker; ~**effekt** *m* surprise effect, spectacular effect; **k~en** *vi* to bang; to crack ♦ *vt*: **jdm eine k~en** (*umg*) to clout sb; ~**frosch** *m* jumping jack; **k~hart** (*umg*) *adj* really hard; (: *Worte*) hard-hitting; (: *Film*) brutal; (: *Porno*) hard-core; ~**kopf** (*umg*) *m* dickhead; **k~rot** *adj* bright red.
knapp [knap] *adj* tight; (*Geld*) scarce; (*kurz*) short; (*Mehrheit, Sieg*) narrow; (*Sprache*) concise; **meine Zeit ist ~ bemessen** I am short of time; **mit ~er Not** only just.
Knappe (-n, -n) *m* (*Edelmann*) young knight.
knapphalten *unreg vt*: **jdn ~ (mit)** to keep sb short (of).
Knappheit *f* tightness; scarcity; conciseness.
Knarre ['knarə] (-, -n) (*umg*) *f* (*Gewehr*) shooter.
knarren *vi* to creak.
Knast [knast] (-(e)s) (*umg*) *m* clink, can (*US*).
Knatsch [knatʃ] (-es) (*umg*) *m* trouble.
knattern ['knatərn] *vi* to rattle; (*Maschinengewehr*) to chatter.

Knäuel ['knɔyəl] (-s, -) m od nt (Woll~) ball; (Menschen~) knot.
Knauf [knauf] (-(e)s, Knäufe) m knob; (Schwert~) pommel.
Knauser ['knauzər] (-s, -) m miser.
knauserig adj miserly.
knausern vi to be mean.
knautschen ['knautʃən] vt, vi to crumple.
Knebel ['kne:bəl] (-s, -) m gag.
knebeln vt to gag; (NAUT) to fasten.
Knecht [kneçt] (-(e)s, -e) m servant; (auf Bauernhof) farm labourer (BRIT) od laborer (US).
knechten vt to enslave.
Knechtschaft f servitude.
kneifen ['knaifən] unreg vt to pinch ♦ vi to pinch; (sich drücken) to back out; **vor etw** dat ~ to dodge sth.
Kneifzange f pliers pl; (kleine) pincers pl.
Kneipe ['knaipə] (-, -n) (umg) f pub (BRIT), bar, saloon (US).
Kneippkur ['knaipku:r] f Kneipp cure, type of hydropathic treatment combined with diet, rest etc.
Knete ['kne:tə] (umg) f (Geld) dough.
kneten vt to knead; (Wachs) to mould (BRIT), mold (US).
Knetgummi m od nt Plasticine ®.
Knetmasse f Plasticine ®.
Knick [knik] (-(e)s, -e) m (Sprung) crack; (Kurve) bend; (Falte) fold.
knicken vt, vi (springen) to crack; (brechen) to break; (Papier) to fold; „**nicht** ~!" "do not bend"; **geknickt sein** to be downcast.
Knicks [kniks] (-es, -e) m curts(e)y; **k~en** vi to curts(e)y.
Knie [kni:] (-s, -) nt knee; **in die** ~ **gehen** to kneel; (fig) to be brought to one's knees; ~**beuge** (-, -n) f knee bend; ~**fall** m genuflection; ~**gelenk** nt knee joint; ~**kehle** f back of the knee.
knien vi to kneel ♦ vr: **sich in die Arbeit** ~ (fig) to get down to (one's) work.
Kniescheibe f kneecap.
Kniestrumpf m knee-length sock.
kniff etc [knif] vb siehe **kneifen**.
Kniff (-(e)s, -e) m (Zwicken) pinch; (Falte) fold; (fig) trick, knack.
kniffelig adj tricky.
knipsen ['knipsən] vt (Fahrkarte) to punch; (PHOT) to take a snap of, snap ♦ vi (PHOT) to take snaps/a snap.
Knirps [knirps] (-es, -e) m little chap; (®: Schirm) telescopic umbrella.
knirschen ['knirʃən] vi to crunch; **mit den Zähnen** ~ to grind one's teeth.
knistern ['knistərn] vi to crackle; (Papier, Seide) to rustle.
Knitterfalte f crease.
knitterfrei adj non-crease.
knittern vi to crease.
knobeln ['kno:bəln] vi (würfeln) to play dice;

(um eine Entscheidung) to toss for it.
Knoblauch ['kno:plaux] (-(e)s) m garlic.
Knöchel ['knœçəl] (-s, -) m knuckle; (Fuß~) ankle.
Knochen ['knɔxən] (-s, -) m bone; ~**arbeit** (umg) f hard work; ~**bau** m bone structure; ~**bruch** m fracture; ~**gerüst** nt skeleton; ~**mark** nt bone marrow.
knöchern ['knœçərn] adj bone.
knochig ['knɔxiç] adj bony.
Knödel ['knø:dəl] (-s, -) m dumpling.
Knolle ['knɔlə] (-, -n) f bulb.
Knopf [knɔpf] (-(e)s, ⁻e) m button; ~**druck** m touch of a button.
knöpfen ['knœpfən] vt to button.
Knopfloch nt buttonhole.
Knorpel ['knɔrpəl] (-s, -) m cartilage, gristle.
knorpelig adj gristly.
knorrig ['knɔriç] adj gnarled, knotted.
Knospe ['knɔspə] (-, -n) f bud.
knospen vi to bud.
knoten ['kno:tən] vt to knot; **K~** (-s, -) m knot; (Haar) bun; (BOT) node; (MED) lump.
Knotenpunkt m junction.
knuffen ['knufən] (umg) vt to cuff.
Knüller ['knylər] (-s, -) (umg) m hit; (Reportage) scoop.
knüpfen ['knypfən] vt to tie; (Teppich) to knot; (Freundschaft) to form.
Knüppel ['knypəl] (-s, -) m cudgel; (Polizei~) baton, truncheon; (AVIAT) (joy)stick; **jdm** ~ **zwischen die Beine werfen** (fig) to put a spoke in sb's wheel; **k~dick** (umg) adj very thick; (fig) thick and fast; ~**schaltung** f (AUT) floor-mounted gear change.
knurren ['knurən] vi (Hund) to snarl, growl; (Magen) to rumble; (Mensch) to mutter.
knusp(e)rig ['knusp(ə)riç] adj crisp; (Keks) crunchy.
knutschen ['knu:tʃən] (umg) vt to snog with ♦ vi, vr to snog.
k.o. adj (SPORT) knocked out; (fig: umg) whacked.
Koalition [koalitsi'o:n] f coalition.
Kobalt ['ko:balt] (-s) nt cobalt.
Kobold ['ko:bɔlt] (-(e)s, -e) m imp.
Kobra ['ko:bra] (-, -s) f cobra.
Koch [kɔx] (-(e)s, ⁻e) m cook; ~**buch** nt cookery book, cookbook; **k~echt** adj (Farbe) fast.
kochen vi to cook; (Wasser) to boil ♦ vt (Essen) to cook; **er kochte vor Wut** (umg) he was seething; **etw auf kleiner Flamme** ~ to simmer sth over a low heat.
Kocher (-s, -) m stove, cooker.
Köcher ['kœçər] (-s, -) m quiver.
Kochgelegenheit f cooking facilities pl.
Köchin ['kœçin] f cook.
Koch- zW: ~**kunst** f cooking; ~**löffel** m kitchen spoon; ~**nische** f kitchenette; ~**platte** f hotplate; ~**salz** nt cooking salt; ~**topf** m saucepan, pot; ~**wäsche** f washing

that can be boiled.

Kode [ko:t] (**-s, -s**) *m* code.

Köder ['kø:dər] (**-s, -**) *m* bait, lure.

ködern *vt* to lure, entice.

Koexistenz [koɛksɪs'tɛnts] *f* coexistence.

Koffein [kɔfe'i:n] (**-s**) *nt* caffeine; **k~frei** *adj* decaffeinated.

Koffer ['kɔfər] (**-s, -**) *m* suitcase; (*Schrank~*) trunk; **die ~ packen** (*lit, fig*) to pack one's bags; **~kuli** *m* (luggage) trolley (*BRIT*), cart (*US*); **~radio** *nt* portable radio; **~raum** *m* (*AUT*) boot (*BRIT*), trunk (*US*).

Kognak ['kɔnjak] (**-s, -s**) *m* brandy, cognac.

Kohl [ko:l] (**-(e)s, -e**) *m* cabbage.

Kohldampf (*umg*) *m:* **~ haben** to be famished.

Kohle ['ko:lə] (**-, -n**) *f* coal; (*Holz~*) charcoal; (*CHEM*) carbon; (*umg: Geld*): **die ~n stimmen** the money's right; **~hydrat** (**-(e)s, -e**) *nt* carbohydrate; **~kraftwerk** *nt* coal-fired power station.

kohlen ['ko:lən] (*umg*) *vi* to tell white lies.

Kohlen- *zW:* **~bergwerk** *nt* coal mine, pit, colliery (*BRIT*); **~dioxyd** (**-(e)s, -e**) *nt* carbon dioxide; **~grube** *f* coal mine, pit; **~händler** *m* coal merchant, coalman; **~säure** *f* carbon dioxide; **ein Getränk ohne ~säure** a non-fizzy *od* still drink; **~stoff** *m* carbon.

Kohlepapier *nt* carbon paper.

Köhler ['kø:lər] (**-s, -**) *m* charcoal burner.

Kohlestift *m* charcoal pencil.

Kohlezeichnung *f* charcoal drawing.

Kohl- *zW:* **k~(pech)rabenschwarz** *adj* (*Haar*) jet-black; (*Nacht*) pitch-black; **~rübe** *f* turnip; **k~schwarz** *adj* coal-black.

Koitus ['ko:itus] (**-, - od -se**) *m* coitus.

Koje ['ko:jə] (**-, -n**) *f* cabin; (*Bett*) bunk.

Kokain [koka'i:n] (**-s**) *nt* cocaine.

kokett [ko'kɛt] *adj* coquettish, flirtatious.

kokettieren [kokɛ'ti:rən] *vi* to flirt.

Kokosnuß ['ko:kɔsnʊs] *f* coconut.

Koks [ko:ks] (**-es, -e**) *m* coke.

Kolben ['kɔlbən] (**-s, -**) *m* (*Gewehr~*) butt; (*Keule*) club; (*CHEM*) flask; (*TECH*) piston; (*Mais~*) cob.

Kolchose [kɔl'ço:zə] (**-, -n**) *f* collective farm.

Kolik [ko:lik] *f* colic, gripe.

Kollaborateur(in) [kɔlabora'tø:r(ɪn)] *m(f)* (*POL*) collaborator.

Kollaps [kɔ'laps] (**-es, -e**) *m* collapse.

Kolleg [kɔl'e:k] (**-s, -s od -ien**) *nt* lecture course.

Kollege [kɔ'le:gə] (**-n, -n**) *m* colleague.

kollegial [kɔlegi'a:l] *adj* cooperative.

Kollegin [kɔ'le:gɪn] *f* colleague.

Kollegium *nt* board; (*SCH*) staff.

Kollekte [kɔ'lɛktə] (**-, -n**) *f* (*REL*) collection.

Kollektion [kɔlɛktsi'o:n] *f* collection; (*Sortiment*) range.

kollektiv [kɔlɛk'ti:f] *adj* collective.

Koller ['kɔlər] (**-s, -**) (*umg*) *m* (*Anfall*) funny mood; (*Wutanfall*) rage; (*Tropen~*,

Gefängnis~) madness.

kollidieren [kɔli'di:rən] *vi* to collide; (*zeitlich*) to clash.

Kollier [kɔli'e:] (**-s, -s**) *nt* necklet, necklace.

Kollision [kɔlizi'o:n] *f* collision; (*zeitlich*) clash.

Kollisionskurs *m:* **auf ~ gehen** (*fig*) to be heading for trouble.

Köln [kœln] (**-s**) *nt* Cologne.

Kölnischwasser *nt* eau de Cologne.

kolonial [koloni'a:l] *adj* colonial; **K~macht** *f* colonial power; **K~warenhändler** *m* grocer.

Kolonie [kolo'ni:] *f* colony.

kolonisieren [koloni'zi:rən] *vt* to colonize.

Kolonist(in) [kolo'nɪst(ɪn)] *m(f)* colonist.

Kolonne [ko'lɔnə] (**-, -n**) *f* column; (*von Fahrzeugen*) convoy.

Koloß [ko'lɔs] (**-sses, -sse**) *m* colossus.

kolossal [kolɔ'sa:l] *adj* colossal.

Kolumbianer(in) [kolumbi'a:nər(ɪn)] *m(f)* Columbian.

kolumbianisch *adj* Columbian.

Kolumbien [ko'lumbiən] (**-s**) *nt* Columbia.

Koma ['ko:ma] (**-s, -s od -ta**) *nt* (*MED*) coma.

Kombi ['kɔmbi] (**-s, -s**) *m* (*AUT*) estate (car) (*BRIT*), station wagon (*US*).

Kombination [kɔmbinatsi'o:n] *f* combination; (*Vermutung*) conjecture; (*Hemdhose*) combinations *pl*; (*AVIAT*) flying suit.

Kombinationsschloß *nt* combination lock.

kombinieren [kɔmbi'ni:rən] *vt* to combine ♦ *vi* to deduce, work out; (*vermuten*) to guess.

Kombiwagen *m* (*AUT*) estate (car) (*BRIT*), station wagon (*US*).

Kombizange *f* (pair of) pliers.

Komet [ko'me:t] (**-en, -en**) *m* comet.

kometenhaft *adj* (*fig: Aufstieg*) meteoric.

Komfort [kɔm'fo:r] (**-s**) *m* luxury; (*von Möbel etc*) comfort; (*von Wohnung*) amenities *pl*; (*von Auto*) luxury features *pl*; (*von Gerät*) extras *pl*.

komfortabel [kɔmfor'ta:bəl] *adj* comfortable.

Komik [ko:mɪk] *f* humour (*BRIT*), humor (*US*), comedy; **~er** (**-s, -**) *m* comedian.

komisch ['ko:mɪʃ] *adj* funny; **mir ist so ~** (*umg*) I feel funny *od* strange *od* odd; **~erweise** ['ko:mɪʃər'vaɪzə] *adv* funnily enough.

Komitee [komi'te:] (**-s, -s**) *nt* committee.

Komm. *abk* (= *Kommission*) comm.

Komma ['kɔma] (**-s, -s od -ta**) *nt* comma; (*MATH*) decimal point; **fünf ~ drei** five point three.

Kommandant [kɔman'dant] *m* commander, commanding officer.

Kommandeur [kɔman'dø:r] *m* commanding officer.

kommandieren [kɔman'di:rən] *vt* to command ♦ *vi* to command; (*Befehle geben*) to give orders.

Kommanditgesellschaft [kɔman'di:t-gəzɛlʃaft] *f* limited partnership.

Kommando [kɔ'mando] (-s, -s) nt command, order; (*Truppe*) detachment, squad; **auf ~** to order; **~brücke** f (*NAUT*) bridge; **~wirtschaft** f command economy.

kommen ['kɔmən] unreg vi to come; (*näher ~*) to approach; (*passieren*) to happen; (*gelangen, geraten*) to get; (*Blumen, Zähne, Tränen etc*) to appear; (*in die Schule, ins Gefängnis etc*) to go; **was kommt diese Woche im Kino?** what's on at the cinema this week? ♦ vi unpers: **es kam eins zum anderen** one thing led to another; **~ lassen** to send for; **in Bewegung ~** to start moving; **jdn besuchen ~** to come and visit sb; **das kommt davon!** see what happens?; **du kommst mir gerade recht** (*ironisch*) you're just what I need; **das kommt in den Schrank** that goes in the cupboard; **an etw** akk **~** (*berühren*) to touch sth; (*sich verschaffen*) to get hold of sth; **auf etw** akk **~** (*sich erinnern*) to think of sth; (*sprechen über*) to get onto sth; **das kommt auf die Rechnung** that goes onto the bill; **hinter etw** akk **~** (*herausfinden*) to find sth out; **zu sich ~** to come round od to; **zu etw ~** to acquire sth; **um etw ~** to lose sth; **nichts auf jdn/etw ~ lassen** to have nothing said against sb/sth; **jdm frech ~** to get cheeky with sb; **auf jeden vierten kommt ein Platz** there's one place to every fourth person; **mit einem Anliegen ~** to have a request (to make); **wer kommt zuerst?** who's first?; **wer zuerst kommt, mahlt zuerst** (*Sprichwort*) first come first served; **unter ein Auto ~** to be run over by a car; **das kommt zusammen auf 20 DM** that comes to 20 marks altogether; **und so kam es, daß ...** and that is how it happened that ...; **daher kommt es, daß ...** that's why ...

Kommen (-s) nt coming.

kommend adj (*Jahr, Woche, Generation*) coming; (*Ereignisse, Mode*) future; (*Trend*) upcoming; **(am) ~en Montag** next Monday.

Kommentar [kɔmɛn'taːr] m commentary; **kein ~** no comment; **k~los** adj without comment.

Kommentator [kɔmɛn'taːtɔr] m (*TV*) commentator.

kommentieren [kɔmɛn'tiːrən] vt to comment on; **kommentierte Ausgabe** annotated edition.

kommerziell [kɔmɛrtsi'ɛl] adj commercial.

Kommilitone [kɔmili'toːnə] (-n, -n) m, **Kommilitonin** f fellow student.

Kommiß [kɔ'mis] (-sses) m (life in the) army.

Kommissar [kɔmɪ'saːr] m police inspector.

Kommißbrot nt army bread.

Kommission [kɔmɪsi'oːn] f (*COMM*) commission; (*Ausschuß*) committee; **in ~ geben** to give (to a dealer) for sale on commission.

Kommode [kɔ'moːdə] (-, -n) f (chest of) drawers.

kommunal [kɔmu'naːl] adj local; (*von Stadt*) municipal; **K~abgaben** pl local rates and taxes pl; **K~politik** f local government politics; **K~verwaltung** f local government; **K~wahlen** pl local (government) elections pl.

Kommune [kɔ'muːnə] (-, -n) f commune.

Kommunikation [kɔmunɪkatsi'oːn] f communication.

Kommunion [kɔmuni'oːn] f communion.

Kommuniqué [kɔmyni'keː] (-s, -s) nt communiqué.

Kommunismus [kɔmu'nɪsmʊs] m communism.

Kommunist(in) [kɔmu'nɪst(ɪn)] m(f) communist; **k~isch** adj communist.

kommunizieren [kɔmuni'tsiːrən] vi to communicate; (*ECCL*) to receive communion.

Komödiant [komødi'ant] m comedian; **~in** f comedienne.

Komödie [ko'møːdiə] f comedy; **~ spielen** (*fig*) to put on an act.

Kompagnon [kɔmpan'jõː] (-s, -s) m (*COMM*) partner.

kompakt [kɔm'pakt] adj compact.

Kompaktanlage f (*RUNDF*) audio system.

Kompanie [kɔmpa'niː] f company.

Komparativ ['kɔmparatiːf] (-s, -e) m comparative.

Kompaß ['kɔmpas] (-sses, -sse) m compass.

kompatibel [kɔmpa'tiːbəl] adj (*auch COMPUT*) compatible.

Kompatibilität [kɔmpatibili'tɛːt] f (*auch COMPUT*) compatibility.

kompensieren [kɔmpɛn'ziːrən] vt to compensate for, offset.

kompetent [kɔmpe'tɛnt] adj competent.

Kompetenz f competence, authority; **~streitigkeiten** pl dispute over respective areas of responsibility.

komplett [kɔm'plɛt] adj complete.

komplex [kɔm'plɛks] adj complex; **K~** (-es, -e) m complex.

Komplikation [kɔmplikatsi'oːn] f complication.

Kompliment [kɔmpli'mɛnt] nt compliment.

Komplize [kɔm'pliːtsə] (-n, -n) m accomplice.

komplizieren [kɔmpli'tsiːrən] vt to complicate.

kompliziert adj complicated; (*MED: Bruch*) compound.

Komplizin [kɔm'pliːtsɪn] f accomplice.

Komplott [kɔm'plɔt] (-(e)s, -e) nt plot.

komponieren [kɔmpo'niːrən] vt to compose.

Komponist(in) [kɔmpo'nɪst(ɪn)] m(f) composer.

Komposition [kɔmpozitsi'oːn] f composition.

Kompost [kɔm'pɔst] (-(e)s, -e) m compost; **~haufen** m compost heap.

Kompott [kɔm'pɔt] (-(e)s, -e) nt stewed fruit.

Kompresse [kɔm'prɛsə] (-, -n) f compress.

Kompressor [kɔm'prɛsɔr] *m* compressor.
Kompromiß [kɔmpro'mɪs] **(-sses, -sse)** *m* compromise; **einen ~ schließen** to compromise; **k~bereit** *adj* willing to compromise; **~lösung** *f* compromise solution.
kompromittieren [kɔmprɔmɪ'tiːrən] *vt* to compromise.
Kondensation [kɔndɛnzatsi'oːn] *f* condensation.
Kondensator [kɔndɛn'zaːtɔr] *m* condenser.
kondensieren [kɔndɛn'ziːrən] *vt* to condense.
Kondensmilch *f* condensed milk.
Kondensstreifen *m* vapour (*BRIT*) *od* vapor (*US*) trail.
Kondition [kɔnditsi'oːn] *f* condition, shape; (*Durchhaltevermögen*) stamina.
Konditionalsatz [kɔnditsio'naːlzats] *m* conditional clause.
Konditionstraining *nt* fitness training.
Konditor [kɔn'diːtɔr] *m* pastry-cook.
Konditorei [kɔndito'raɪ] *f* cake shop; (*mit Café*) café.
kondolieren [kɔndo'liːrən] *vi:* **jdm ~ to** condole with sb, offer sb one's condolences.
Kondom [kɔn'doːm] **(-s, -e)** *m or nt* condom.
Konfektion [kɔnfɛktsi'oːn] *f* (production of) ready-to-wear *od* off-the-peg clothing.
Konfektionsgröße *f* clothes size.
Konfektionskleidung *f* ready-to-wear *od* off-the-peg clothing.
Konferenz [kɔnfe'rɛnts] *f* conference; (*Besprechung*) meeting; **~schaltung** *f* (*TEL*) conference circuit; (*RUNDF, TV*) television *od* radio link-up.
konferieren [kɔnfe'riːrən] *vi* to confer; to have a meeting.
Konfession [kɔnfɛsi'oːn] *f* religion; (*christlich*) denomination; **k~ell** [-'nɛl] *adj* denominational.
Konfessions- *zW:* **k~gebunden** *adj* denominational; **k~los** *adj* non-denominational; **~schule** *f* denominational school.
Konfetti [kɔn'fɛti] **(-(s))** *nt* confetti.
Konfiguration [kɔnfiguratsi'oːn] *f* (*COMPUT*) configuration.
Konfirmand(in) [kɔnfɪr'mant, -'mandɪn] *m(f)* candidate for confirmation.
Konfirmation [kɔnfɪrmatsi'oːn] *f* (*ECCL*) confirmation.
konfirmieren [kɔnfɪr'miːrən] *vt* to confirm.
konfiszieren [kɔnfɪs'tsiːrən] *vt* to confiscate.
Konfitüre [kɔnfi'tyːrə] **(-, -n)** *f* jam.
Konflikt [kɔn'flɪkt] **(-(e)s, -e)** *m* conflict; **~herd** *m* (*POL*) centre (*BRIT*) *od* center (*US*) of conflict; **~stoff** *m* cause of conflict.
konform [kɔn'fɔrm] *adj* concurring; **~ gehen** to be in agreement.
Konfrontation [kɔnfrɔntatsi'oːn] *f* confrontation.
konfrontieren [kɔnfrɔn'tiːrən] *vt* to confront.
konfus [kɔn'fuːs] *adj* confused.
Kongo ['kɔŋgo] **(-(s))** *m* Congo.

Kongreß [kɔn'grɛs] **(-sses, -sse)** *m* congress.
Kongruenz [kɔngru'ɛnts] *f* agreement, congruence.
König ['køːnɪç] **(-(e)s, -e)** *m* king.
Königin ['køːnɪgɪn] *f* queen.
königlich *adj* royal ♦ *adv:* **sich ~ amüsieren** (*umg*) to have the time of one's life.
Königreich *nt* kingdom.
Königtum ['køːnɪçtuːm] **(-(e)s, -tümer)** *nt* kingship; (*Reich*) kingdom.
konisch ['koːnɪʃ] *adj* conical.
Konj. *abk* (= *Konjunktiv*) conj.
Konjugation [kɔnjugatsi'oːn] *f* conjugation.
konjugieren [kɔnju'giːrən] *vt* to conjugate.
Konjunktion [kɔnjuŋktsi'oːn] *f* conjunction.
Konjunktiv ['kɔnjuŋktiːf] **(-s, -e)** *m* subjunctive.
Konjunktur [kɔnjuŋk'tuːr] *f* economic situation; (*Hoch~*) boom; **steigende/fallende ~** upward/downward economic trend; **~barometer** *nt* economic indicators *pl*; **~loch** *nt* temporary economic dip; **~politik** *f* policies aimed at preventing economic fluctuations.
konkav [kɔn'kaːf] *adj* concave.
konkret [kɔn'kreːt] *adj* concrete.
Konkurrent(in) [kɔnku'rɛnt(ɪn)] *m(f)* competitor.
Konkurrenz [kɔnku'rɛnts] *f* competition; **jdm ~ machen** (*COMM, fig*) to compete with sb; **k~fähig** *adj* competitive; **~kampf** *m* competition; (*umg*) rat race.
konkurrieren [kɔnku'riːrən] *vi* to compete.
Konkurs [kɔn'kurs] **(-es, -e)** *m* bankruptcy; **in ~ gehen** to go into receivership; **~ machen** (*umg*) to go bankrupt; **~verfahren** *nt* bankruptcy proceedings *pl*; **~verwalter** *m* receiver; (*von Gläubigern bevollmächtigt*) trustee.

SCHLÜSSELWORT

können ['kœnən] (*pt* **konnte,** *pp* **gekonnt** *od (als Hilfsverb)* **können**) *vt, vi* **1** to be able to; **ich kann es machen** I can do it, I am able to do it; **ich kann es nicht machen** I can't do it, I'm not able to do it; **ich kann nicht ...** I can't ..., I cannot ...; **was ~ Sie?** what can you do?; **ich kann nicht mehr** I can't go on; **ich kann nichts dafür** I can't help it; **du kannst mich (mal)!** (*umg*) get lost!
2 (*wissen, beherrschen*) to know; **~ Sie Deutsch?** can you speak German?; **er kann gut Englisch** he speaks English well; **sie kann keine Mathematik** she can't do mathematics
3 (*dürfen*) to be allowed to; **kann ich gehen?** can I go?; **könnte ich ...?** could I ...?; **kann ich mit?** (*umg*) can I come with you?
4 (*möglich sein*): **Sie könnten recht haben** you may be right; **das kann sein** that's possible; **kann sein** maybe.

Können (-s) nt ability.
Könner (-s, -) m expert.
Konnossement [kɔnɔsə'mɛnt] nt (Export) bill of lading.
konnte etc ['kɔntə] vb siehe **können.**
konsequent [kɔnze'kvɛnt] adj consistent; **ein Ziel ~ verfolgen** to pursue an objective single-mindedly.
Konsequenz [kɔnze'kvɛnts] f consistency; (Folgerung) conclusion; **die ~en tragen** to take the consequences; **(aus etw) die ~en ziehen** to take the appropriate steps.
konservativ [kɔnzɛrva'tiːf] adj conservative.
Konservatorium [kɔnzɛrva'toːriʊm] nt academy of music, conservatory.
Konserve [kɔn'zɛrvə] (-, -n) f tinned (BRIT) od canned food.
Konservenbüchse f, **Konservendose** f tin (BRIT), can.
konservieren [kɔnzɛr'viːrən] vt to preserve.
Konservierung f preservation.
Konservierungsstoff m preservative.
Konsole [kɔnzo:lə] f games console.
konsolidiert [kɔnzoli'diːrt] adj consolidated.
Konsolidierung f consolidation.
Konsonant [kɔnzo'nant] m consonant.
Konsortium [kɔn'zɔrtsiʊm] nt consortium, syndicate.
konspirativ [kɔnspira'tiːf] adj: **~e Wohnung** conspirators' hideaway.
konstant [kɔn'stant] adj constant.
Konstellation [kɔnstɛlatsi'oːn] f constellation; (fig) line-up; (von Faktoren etc) combination.
Konstitution [kɔnstitutsi'oːn] f constitution.
konstitutionell [kɔnstitutsio'nɛl] adj constitutional.
konstruieren [kɔnstru'iːrən] vt to construct.
Konstrukteur(in) [kɔnstrʊk'tøːr(ɪn)] m(f) designer.
Konstruktion [kɔnstrʊktsi'on] f construction.
Konstruktionsfehler m (im Entwurf) design fault; (im Aufbau) structural defect.
konstruktiv [kɔnstrʊk'tiːf] adj constructive.
Konsul ['kɔnzʊl] (-s, -n) m consul.
Konsulat [kɔnzʊ'laːt] (-(e)s, -e) nt consulate.
konsultieren [kɔnzʊl'tiːrən] vt to consult.
Konsum¹ [kɔn'zuːm] (-s) m consumption.
Konsum² ['kɔnzuːm] (-s, -s) m (Genossenschaft) cooperative society; (Laden) cooperative store, co-op (umg).
Konsumartikel m consumer article.
Konsument [kɔnzu'mɛnt] m consumer.
Konsumgesellschaft f consumer society.
konsumieren [kɔnzu'miːrən] vt to consume.
Konsumterror m pressures pl of a materialistic society.
Konsumzwang m compulsion to buy.
Kontakt [kɔn'takt] (-(e)s, -e) m contact; **mit jdm ~ aufnehmen** to get in touch with sb;

~anzeige f lonely hearts ad; **k~arm** adj unsociable; **k~freudig** adj sociable.
kontaktieren [kɔntak'tiːrən] vt to contact.
Kontakt- zW: **~linsen** pl contact lenses pl; **~mann** (-(e)s, pl -männer) m (Agent) contact; **~sperre** f ban on visits and letters (to a prisoner).
Konterfei ['kɔntərfaɪ] (-s, -s) nt likeness, portrait.
kontern ['kɔntərn] vt, vi to counter.
Konterrevolution ['kɔntərrevolutsioːn] f counter-revolution.
Kontinent [kɔnti'nɛnt] m continent.
Kontingent [kɔntɪŋ'gɛnt] (-(e)s, -e) nt quota; (Truppen~) contingent.
kontinuierlich [kɔntinu'iːrlɪç] adj continuous.
Kontinuität [kɔntinui'tɛːt] f continuity.
Konto ['kɔnto] (-s, **Konten**) nt account; **das geht auf mein ~** (umg: ich bin schuldig) I am to blame for this; (ich zahle) this is on me (umg); **~auszug** m statement (of account); **~inhaber(in)** m(f) account holder.
Kontor [kɔn'toːr] (-s, -e) nt office.
Kontorist(in) [kɔnto'rɪst(ɪn)] m(f) clerk, office worker.
Kontostand m bank balance.
kontra ['kɔntra] präp +akk against; (JUR) versus.
Kontra (-s, -s) nt (KARTEN) double; **jdm ~ geben** (fig) to contradict sb.
Kontrabaß m double bass.
Kontrahent [-'hɛnt] m contracting party; (Gegner) opponent.
Kontrapunkt m counterpoint.
Kontrast [kɔn'trast] (-(e)s, -e) m contrast.
Kontrollabschnitt m (COMM) counterfoil, stub.
Kontrollampe [kɔn'trɔllampə] (getrennt: Kontroll-lampe) f pilot lamp; (AUT: für Ölstand etc) warning light.
Kontrolle [kɔn'trɔlə] (-, -n) f control, supervision; (Paß~) passport control.
Kontrolleur [kɔntro'løːr] m inspector.
kontrollieren [kɔntro'liːrən] vt to control, supervise; (nachprüfen) to check.
Kontrollturm m control tower.
Kontroverse [kɔntro'vɛrzə] (-, -n) f controversy.
Kontur [kɔn'tuːr] f contour.
Konvention [kɔnvɛntsi'oːn] f convention.
Konventionalstrafe [kɔnvɛntsio'naːlʃtraːfə] f penalty od fine (for breach of contract).
konventionell [kɔnvɛntsio'nɛl] adj conventional.
Konversation [kɔnvɛrzatsi'oːn] f conversation.
Konversationslexikon nt encyclopaedia.
konvex [kɔn'vɛks] adj convex.
Konvoi ['kɔnvɔy] (-s, -s) m convoy.
Konzentrat [kɔntsɛn'traːt] (-s, -e) nt concentrate.
Konzentration [kɔntsɛntratsi'oːn] f

concentration.

Konzentrationsfähigkeit *f* power of concentration.

Konzentrationslager *nt* concentration camp.

konzentrieren [kɔntsɛn'triːrən] *vt, vr* to concentrate.

konzentriert *adj* concentrated ♦ *adv* (*zuhören, arbeiten*) intently.

Konzept [kɔn'tsɛpt] (-(e)s, -e) *nt* rough draft; (*Plan, Programm*) plan; (*Begriff, Vorstellung*) concept; **jdn aus dem ~ bringen** to confuse sb; **~papier** *nt* rough paper.

Konzern [kɔn'tsɛrn] (-s, -e) *m* combine.

Konzert [kɔn'tsɛrt] (-(e)s, -e) *nt* concert; (*Stück*) concerto; **~saal** *m* concert hall.

Konzession [kɔntsɛsi'oːn] *f* licence (*BRIT*), license (*US*); (*Zugeständnis*) concession; **die ~ entziehen** +*dat* (*COMM*) to disenfranchise.

Konzessionär [kɔntsɛsio'nɛːr] (-s, -e) *m* concessionaire.

konzessionieren [kɔntsɛsio'niːrən] *vt* to license.

Konzil [kɔn'tsiːl] (-s, -e *od* -ien) *nt* council.

konzipieren [kɔntsi'piːrən] *vt* to conceive; (*entwerfen*) to design.

kooperativ [ko|opera'tiːf] *adj* cooperative.

kooperieren [ko|ope'riːrən] *vi* to cooperate.

koordinieren [ko|ɔrdi'niːrən] *vt* to coordinate.

Kopenhagen [koːpən'haːgən] (-s) *nt* Copenhagen.

Kopf [kɔpf] (-(e)s, ⁼e) *m* head; **~ hoch!** chin up!; **~ an ~** shoulder to shoulder; (*SPORT*) neck and neck; **pro ~** per person *od* head; **~ oder Zahl?** heads or tails?; **jdm den ~ waschen** (*fig: umg*) to give sb a piece of one's mind; **jdm über den ~ wachsen** (*lit*) to outgrow sb; (*fig: Sorgen etc*) to be more than sb can cope with; **jdn vor den ~ stoßen** to antagonize sb; **sich** *dat* **an den ~ fassen** (*fig*) to be speechless; **sich** *dat* **über etw** *akk* **den ~ zerbrechen** to rack one's brains over sth; **sich** *dat* **etw durch den ~ gehen lassen** to think about sth; **sich** *dat* **etw aus dem ~ schlagen** to put sth out of one's mind; **... und wenn du dich auf den ~ stellst!** (*umg*) ... no matter what you say/do!; **er ist nicht auf den ~ gefallen** he's no fool; **~bahnhof** *m* terminus station; **~bedeckung** *f* headgear.

Köpfchen ['kœpfçən] *nt*: **~ haben** to be brainy.

köpfen ['kœpfən] *vt* to behead; (*Baum*) to lop; (*Ei*) to take the top off; (*Ball*) to head.

Kopf- *zW*: **~ende** *nt* head; **~haut** *f* scalp; **~hörer** *m* headphone; **~kissen** *nt* pillow; **k~lastig** *adj* (*fig*) completely rational; **k~los** *adj* panic-stricken; **~losigkeit** *f* panic; **k~rechnen** *vi* to do mental arithmetic; **~salat** *m* lettuce; **k~scheu** *adj*: **jdn k~scheu machen** to intimidate sb; **~schmerzen** *pl* headache *sing*; **~sprung** *m* header, dive; **~stand** *m* headstand; **~steinpflaster** *nt*: **eine Straße mit ~steinpflaster** a cobbled street;

~stütze *f* headrest; (*im Auto*) head restraint; **~tuch** *nt* headscarf; **k~über** *adv* head-first; **~weh** *nt* headache; **~zerbrechen** *nt*: **jdm ~zerbrechen machen** to give sb a lot of headaches.

Kopie [ko'piː] *f* copy.

kopieren [ko'piːrən] *vt* to copy.

Kopierer (-s, -) *m* (photo)copier.

Kopilot(in) ['koːpiloːt(ɪn)] *m(f)* co-pilot.

Koppel¹ ['kɔpəl] (-, -n) *f* (*Weide*) enclosure.

Koppel² ['kɔpəl] (-s, -) *nt* (*Gürtel*) belt.

koppeln *vt* to couple.

Koppelung *f* coupling.

Koppelungsmanöver *nt* docking manoeuvre (*BRIT*) *od* maneuver (*US*).

Koralle [ko'ralə] (-, -n) *f* coral.

Korallenkette *f* coral necklace.

Korallenriff *nt* coral reef.

Korb [kɔrp] (-(e)s, ⁼e) *m* basket; **jdm einen ~ geben** (*fig*) to turn sb down; **~ball** *m* basketball.

Körbchen ['kœrpçən] *nt* (*von Büstenhalter*) cup.

Korbstuhl *m* wicker chair.

Kord [kɔrt] (-(e)s, -e) *m* corduroy.

Kordel ['kɔrdəl] (-, -n) *f* cord, string.

Korea [ko'reːa] (-s) *nt* Korea.

Koreaner(in) (-s, -) *m(f)* Korean.

Korfu ['kɔrfu] (-s) *nt* Corfu.

Korinthe [ko'rɪntə] (-, -n) *f* currant.

Korinthenkacker [ko'rɪntənkakər] (-s, -) (*umg*) *m* fusspot, hair-splitter.

Kork [kɔrk] (-(e)s, -e) *m* cork.

Korken (-s, -) *m* stopper, cork; **~zieher** (-s, -) *m* corkscrew.

Korn¹ [kɔrn] (-(e)s, ⁼er) *nt* corn, grain; (*Gewehr*) sight; **etw aufs ~ nehmen** (*fig: umg*) to hit out at sth.

Korn² [kɔrn] (-, -s) *m* (*Kornbranntwein*) corn schnapps.

Kornblume *f* cornflower.

Körnchen ['kœrnçən] *nt* grain, granule.

körnig ['kœrnɪç] *adj* granular, grainy.

Kornkammer *f* granary.

Körnung ['kœrnʊŋ] *f* (*TECH*) grain size; (*PHOT*) granularity.

Körper ['kœrper] (-s, -) *m* body; **~bau** *m* build; **k~behindert** *adj* disabled; **~geruch** *m* body odour (*BRIT*) *od* odor (*US*); **~gewicht** *nt* weight; **~größe** *f* height; **~haltung** *f* carriage, deportment; **k~lich** *adj* physical; **k~liche Arbeit** manual work; **~pflege** *f* personal hygiene; **~schaft** *f* corporation; **~schaft des öffentlichen Rechts** public corporation *od* body; **~schaftssteuer** *f* corporation tax; **~sprache** *f* body language; **~teil** *m* part of the body; **~verletzung** *f* (*JUR*): **schwere ~verletzung** grievous bodily harm.

Korps [koːr] (-, -) *nt* (*MIL*) corps; (*UNIV*) students' club.

korpulent [kɔrpu'lɛnt] *adj* corpulent.

korrekt [kɔ'rɛkt] *adj* correct; **K~heit** *f*

correctness.
Korrektor(in) [kɔ'rɛktɔr, -'to:rɪn] (-s, -) m(f)
proofreader.
Korrektur [kɔrɛk'tu:r] f (eines Textes)
proofreading; (Text) proof; (SCH) marking,
correction; (bei etw) ~ lesen to proofread
(sth); ~fahne f (TYP) proof.
Korrespondent(in) [kɔrɛspɔn'dɛnt(ɪn)] m(f)
correspondent.
Korrespondenz [kɔrɛspɔn'dɛnts] f
correspondence; ~qualität f (Drucker) letter
quality.
korrespondieren [kɔrɛspɔn'di:rən] vi to
correspond.
Korridor ['kɔrido:r] (-s, -e) m corridor.
korrigieren [kɔri'gi:rən] vt to correct;
(Meinung, Einstellung) to change.
Korrosion [kɔrozi'o:n] f corrosion.
Korrosionsschutz m corrosion protection.
korrumpieren [kɔrʊm'pi:rən] vt (auch
COMPUT) to corrupt.
korrupt [kɔ'rʊpt] adj corrupt.
Korruption [kɔrʊptsi'o:n] f corruption.
Korsett [kɔr'zɛt] (-(e)s, -e) nt corset.
Korsika ['kɔrzika] (-s) nt Corsica.
Koseform ['ko:zəfɔrm] f pet form.
kosen vt to caress ♦ vi to bill and coo.
Kosename m pet name.
Kosewort nt term of endearment.
Kosmetik [kɔs'me:tɪk] f cosmetics pl.
Kosmetikerin f beautician.
kosmetisch adj cosmetic; (Chirurgie) plastic.
kosmisch ['kɔsmɪʃ] adj cosmic.
Kosmonaut [kɔsmo'naʊt] (-en, -en) m
cosmonaut.
Kosmopolit [kɔsmopo'li:t] (-en, -en) m
cosmopolitan; k~isch [-po'li:tiʃ] adj
cosmopolitan.
Kosmos ['kɔsmɔs] (-) m cosmos.
Kost [kɔst] (-) f (Nahrung) food; (Verpflegung)
board; ~ und Logis board and lodging.
kostbar adj precious; (teuer) costly,
expensive; K~keit f preciousness;
costliness, expensiveness; (Wertstück)
treasure.
Kosten pl cost(s); (Ausgaben) expenses pl; auf
~ von at the expense of; auf seine
~ kommen (fig) to get one's money's worth.
kosten vt to cost; (versuchen) to taste ♦ vi to
taste; koste es, was es wolle whatever the
cost.
Kosten- zW: ~anschlag m estimate;
k~deckend adj cost-effective; ~erstattung f
reimbursement of expenses; ~kontrolle f
cost control; k~los adj free (of charge); ~-
Nutzen-Analyse f cost-benefit analysis;
k~pflichtig adj: ein Auto k~pflichtig
abschleppen to tow away a car at the
owner's expense; ~stelle f (COMM) cost
centre (BRIT) od center (US); ~voranschlag
m (costs) estimate.
Kostgeld nt board.

köstlich ['kœstlɪç] adj precious; (Einfall)
delightful; (Essen) delicious; sich
~ amüsieren to have a marvellous time.
Kostprobe f taste; (fig) sample.
kostspielig adj expensive.
Kostüm [kɔs'ty:m] (-s, -e) nt costume;
(Damen~) suit; ~fest nt fancy-dress party.
kostümieren [kɔsty'mi:rən] vt, vr to dress up.
Kostümprobe f (THEAT) dress rehearsal.
Kostümverleih m costume agency.
Kot [ko:t] (-(e)s) m excrement.
Kotelett [kotə'lɛt] (-(e)s, -e od -s) nt cutlet,
chop.
Koteletten pl sideboards pl (BRIT), sideburns
pl (US).
Köter ['kø:tər] (-s, -) m cur.
Kotflügel m (AUT) wing.
kotzen ['kɔtsən] (umg!) vi to puke (!), throw
up; das ist zum K~ it makes you sick.
KP (-, -s) f abk (= Kommunistische Partei) C.P.
KPÖ (-) f abk (= Kommunistische Partei
Österreichs) Austrian Communist Party.
Kr. abk = **Kreis**.
Krabbe ['krabə] (-, -n) f shrimp.
krabbeln vi to crawl.
Krach [krax] (-(e)s, -s od -e) m crash;
(andauernd) noise; (umg: Streit) quarrel,
argument; ~ schlagen to make a fuss; k~en
vi to crash; (beim Brechen) to crack ♦ vr
(umg) to argue, quarrel.
krächzen ['krɛçtsən] vi to croak.
Kräcker ['krɛkər] (-s, -) m (KOCH) cracker.
kraft [kraft] präp +gen by virtue of.
Kraft (-, -̈e) f strength; (von Stimme, fig)
power, force; (Arbeits~) worker; mit
vereinten Kräften werden wir ... if we
combine our efforts we will ...; nach
(besten) Kräften to the best of one's
abilities; außer ~ sein (JUR: Geltung) to be
no longer in force; in ~ treten to come into
effect.
Kraft- zW: ~aufwand m effort; ~ausdruck m
swearword; ~brühe f beef tea.
Kräfteverhältnis ['krɛftəfɛrhɛltnɪs] nt (POL)
balance of power; (von Mannschaften etc)
relative strength.
Kraftfahrer m motor driver.
Kraftfahrzeug nt motor vehicle; ~brief m
(AUT) logbook (BRIT), motor-vehicle
registration certificate (US); ~schein m
(AUT) car licence (BRIT) od license (US);
~steuer f ≈ road tax.
kräftig ['krɛftɪç] adj strong; (Suppe, Essen)
nourishing; ~en ['krɛftɪgən] vt to strengthen.
Kraft- zW: k~los adj weak; powerless; (JUR)
invalid; ~meierei (umg) f showing off of
physical strength; ~probe f trial of
strength; ~rad nt motorcycle; ~stoff m fuel;
~training nt weight training; k~voll adj
vigorous; ~wagen m motor vehicle; ~werk
nt power station; ~werker m power station
worker.

Kragen ['kra:gən] (-s, -) m collar; **da ist mir der ~ geplatzt** (umg) I blew my top; **es geht ihm an den ~** (umg) he's in for it; **~weite** f collar size; **das ist nicht meine ~weite** (fig: umg) that's not my cup of tea.

Krähe ['krɛ:ə] (-, -n) f crow.

krähen vi to crow.

krakeelen [kra'ke:lən] (umg) vi to make a din.

krakelig ['kra:kəlɪç] (umg) adj (Schrift) scrawly, spidery.

Kralle ['kralə] (-, -n) f claw; (Vogel~) talon.

krallen vt to clutch; (krampfhaft) to claw.

Kram [kra:m] (-(e)s) m stuff, rubbish; **den ~ hinschmeißen** (umg) to chuck the whole thing; **k~en** vi to rummage; **~laden** (pej) m small shop.

Krampf [krampf] (-(e)s, ⁻e) m cramp; (zuckend) spasm; (Unsinn) rubbish; **~ader** f varicose vein; **k~haft** adj convulsive; (fig: Versuche) desperate.

Kran [kra:n] (-(e)s, ⁻e) m crane; (Wasser~) tap (BRIT), faucet (US).

Kranich ['kra:nɪç] (-s, -e) m (ZOOL) crane.

krank [kraŋk] adj ill, sick; **sich ~ melden** to let one's boss etc know that one is ill; (telefonisch) to phone in sick; (bes MIL) to report sick; **jdn ~ schreiben** to give sb a medical certificate; (bes MIL) to put sb on the sick list; **das macht mich ~!** (umg) it gets on my nerves!, it drives me round the bend!; **sich ~ stellen** to pretend to be ill, malinger.

Kranke(r) f(m) sick person, invalid; (Patient) patient.

kränkeln ['krɛŋkəln] vi to be in bad health.

kranken ['kraŋkən] vi: **an etw** dat **~** (fig) to suffer from sth.

kränken ['krɛŋkən] vt to hurt.

Kranken- zW: **~bericht** m medical report; **~besuch** m visit to a sick person; **~geld** nt sick pay; **~geschichte** f medical history; **~gymnastik** f physiotherapy; **~haus** nt hospital; **~kasse** f health insurance; **~pfleger** m orderly; (mit Schwesternausbildung) male nurse; **~pflegerin** f nurse; **~schein** m medical insurance certificate; **~schwester** f nurse; **~versicherung** f health insurance; **~wagen** m ambulance.

krankfeiern (umg) vi to be off sick; (vortäuschend) to skive (BRIT).

krankhaft adj diseased; (Angst etc) morbid; **sein Geiz ist schon ~** his meanness is almost pathological.

Krankheit f illness; disease; **nach langer schwerer ~** after a long serious illness.

Krankheitserreger m disease-causing agent.

kränklich ['krɛŋklɪç] adj sickly.

Kränkung f insult, offence (BRIT), offense (US).

Kranz [krants] (-es, ⁻e) m wreath, garland.

Kränzchen ['krɛntsçən] nt small wreath; (fig: Kaffee~) coffee circle.

Krapfen ['krapfən] (-s, -) m fritter; (Berliner) doughnut (BRIT), donut (US).

kraß [kras] adj crass; (Unterschied) extreme.

Krater ['kra:tər] (-s, -) m crater.

Kratzbürste ['kratsbʏrstə] f (fig) crosspatch.

Krätze ['krɛtsə] f (MED) scabies sing.

kratzen ['kratsən] vt, vi to scratch; (ab~): **etw von etw ~** to scrape sth off sth.

Kratzer (-s, -) m scratch; (Werkzeug) scraper.

Kraul [kraʊl] (-s) nt (auch: ~schwimmen) crawl; **k~en** vi (schwimmen) to do the crawl ♦ vt (streicheln) to tickle.

kraus [kraʊs] adj crinkly; (Haar) frizzy; (Stirn) wrinkled.

Krause ['kraʊzə] (-, -n) f frill, ruffle.

kräuseln ['krɔʏzəln] vt (Haar) to make frizzy; (Stoff) to gather; (Stirn) to wrinkle ♦ vr (Haar) to go frizzy; (Stirn) to wrinkle; (Wasser) to ripple.

Kraut [kraʊt] (-(e)s, Kräuter) nt plant; (Gewürz) herb; (Gemüse) cabbage; **dagegen ist kein ~ gewachsen** (fig) there's nothing anyone can do about that; **ins ~ schießen** (lit) to run to seed; (fig) to get out of control; **wie ~ und Rüben** (umg) extremely untidy.

Kräutertee ['krɔʏtərte:] m herb tea.

Krawall [kra'val] (-s, -e) m row, uproar.

Krawatte [kra'vatə] (-, -n) f tie.

kreativ [krea'ti:f] adj creative.

Kreativität [kreativi'tɛ:t] f creativity.

Kreatur [krea'tu:r] f creature.

Krebs [kre:ps] (-es, -e) m crab; (MED) cancer; (ASTROL) Cancer; **k~erregend** adj carcinogenic; **k~krank** adj suffering from cancer; **k~krank sein** to have cancer; **~kranke(r)** f(m) cancer victim; (Patient) cancer patient; **k~rot** adj red as a lobster.

Kredit [kre'di:t] (-(e)s, -e) m credit; (Darlehen) loan; (fig) standing; **~drosselung** f credit squeeze; **k~fähig** adj creditworthy; **~grenze** f credit limit; **~hai** (umg) m loan-shark; **~karte** f credit card; **~konto** nt credit account; **~politik** f lending policy; **k~würdig** adj creditworthy; **~würdigkeit** f creditworthiness, credit status.

Kreide ['kraɪdə] (-, -n) f chalk; **bei jdm (tief) in der ~ stehen** to be (deep) in debt to sb; **k~bleich** adj as white as a sheet.

Kreis [kraɪs] (-es, -e) m circle; (Stadt~ etc) district; **im ~ gehen** (lit, fig) to go round in circles; **(weite) ~e ziehen** (fig) to have (wide) repercussions; **weite ~e der Bevölkerung** wide sections of the population; **eine Feier im kleinen ~e** a celebration for a few close friends and relatives.

kreischen ['kraɪʃən] vi to shriek, screech.

Kreisel ['kraɪzəl] (-s, -) m top; (Verkehrs~) roundabout (BRIT), traffic circle (US).

kreisen ['kraɪzən] vi to spin; (fig: Gedanken, Gespräch): **~ um** to revolve around.

Kreis- zW: **k~förmig** adj circular; **~lauf** m

(MED) circulation; (fig: der Natur etc) cycle; ~**laufkollaps** m circulatory collapse; ~**laufstörungen** pl circulation trouble sing; ~**säge** f circular saw.

Kreißsaal ['kraɪszaːl] m delivery room.

Kreisstadt f ≈ county town.

Kreisverkehr m roundabout (BRIT), traffic circle (US).

Krematorium [krema'toːriʊm] nt crematorium.

Kreml ['kreːml] (-s) m: **der** ~ the Kremlin.

Krempe ['krɛmpə] (-, -n) f brim.

Krempel (-s) (umg) m rubbish.

krepieren [kre'piːrən] (umg) vi (sterben) to die, kick the bucket.

Krepp [krɛp] (-s, -s od -e) m crêpe.

Kreppapier (getrennt: Krepp-papier) nt crêpe paper.

Kreppsohle f crêpe sole.

Kresse ['krɛsə] (-, -n) f cress.

Kreta ['kreːta] (-s) nt Crete.

Kreter(in) [kreːtər(ɪn)] (-s, -) m(f) Cretan.

kretisch adj Cretan.

kreuz [krɔʏts] adj: ~ **und quer** all over.

Kreuz (-es, -e) nt cross; (ANAT) small of the back; (KARTEN) clubs; (MUS) sharp; (Autobahn~) intersection; **zu ~e kriechen** (fig) to eat humble pie, eat crow (US); **jdn aufs ~ legen** to throw sb on his back; (fig: umg) to take sb for a ride.

kreuzen vt to cross ♦ vr to cross; (Meinungen etc) to clash ♦ vi (NAUT) to cruise; **die Arme** ~ to fold one's arms.

Kreuzer (-s, -) m (Schiff) cruiser.

Kreuz- zW: ~**fahrt** f cruise; ~**feuer** nt (fig): **im** ~**feuer stehen** to be caught in the crossfire; ~**gang** m cloisters pl.

kreuzigen vt to crucify.

Kreuzigung f crucifixion.

Kreuzotter f adder.

Kreuzschmerzen pl backache sing.

Kreuzung f (Verkehrs~) crossing, junction; (Züchtung) cross.

Kreuz- zW: **k~unglücklich** adj absolutely miserable; ~**verhör** nt cross-examination; **ins ~verhör nehmen** to cross-examine; ~**weg** m crossroads; (REL) Way of the Cross; ~**worträtsel** nt crossword puzzle; ~**zeichen** nt sign of the cross; ~**zug** m crusade.

kribb(e)lig ['krɪb(ə)lɪç] (umg) adj fidgety; (kribbelnd) tingly.

kribbeln ['krɪbəln] vi (jucken) to itch; (prickeln) to tingle.

kriechen ['kriːçən] unreg vi to crawl, creep; (pej) to grovel, crawl.

Kriecher (-s, -) m crawler.

kriecherisch adj grovelling (BRIT), groveling (US).

Kriechspur f crawler lane (BRIT).

Kriechtier nt reptile.

Krieg [kriːk] (-(e)s, -e) m war; ~ **führen (mit** od **gegen)** to wage war (on).

kriegen ['kriːgən] (umg) vt to get.

Krieger (-s, -) m warrior; ~**denkmal** nt war memorial; **k~isch** adj warlike.

Kriegführung f warfare.

Kriegs- zW: ~**beil** nt: **das** ~**beil begraben** (fig) to bury the hatchet; ~**bemalung** f war paint; ~**dienstverweigerer** m conscientious objector; ~**erklärung** f declaration of war; ~**fuß** m: **mit jdm/etw auf** ~**fuß stehen** to be at loggerheads with sb/not to get on with sth; ~**gefangene(r)** f(m) prisoner of war; ~**gefangenschaft** f captivity; ~**gericht** nt court-martial; ~**rat** m council of war; ~**recht** nt (MIL) martial law; ~**schauplatz** m theatre (BRIT) od theater (US) of war; ~**schiff** nt warship; ~**schuld** f war guilt; ~**verbrecher** m war criminal; ~**versehrte(r)** f(m) person disabled in the war; ~**zustand** m state of war.

Krim [krɪm] f: **die** ~ the Crimea.

Krimi ['kriːmi] (-s, -s) (umg) m thriller.

kriminal [krimi'naːl] adj criminal; **K~beamte(r)** m detective; **K~film** m crime thriller od movie (bes US).

Kriminalität [kriminaliˈtɛːt] f criminality.

Kriminalpolizei f ≈ Criminal Investigation Department (BRIT), Federal Bureau of Investigation (US).

Kriminalroman m detective story.

kriminell [krimiˈnɛl] adj criminal.

Kriminelle(r) f(m) criminal.

Krimskrams ['krɪmskrams] (-es) (umg) m odds and ends pl.

Kringel ['krɪŋəl] (-s, -) m (der Schrift) squiggle; (KOCH) ring.

kringelig adj: **sich** ~ **lachen** (umg) to kill o.s. laughing.

Kripo ['kriːpo] (-, -s) f abk (= Kriminalpolizei) ≈ CID (BRIT), ≈ FBI (US).

Krippe ['krɪpə] (-, -n) f manger, crib; (Kinder~) crèche.

Krippenspiel nt nativity play.

Krippentod m cot death.

Krise ['kriːzə] (-, -n) f crisis.

kriseln vi: **es kriselt** there's a crisis looming, there is trouble brewing.

Krisen- zW: **k~fest** adj stable; ~**herd** m flash point; trouble spot; ~**stab** m action od crisis committee.

Kristall¹ [krɪsˈtal] (-s, -e) m crystal.

Kristall² (-s) nt (Glas) crystal; ~**zucker** m refined sugar crystals pl.

Kriterium [kriˈteːriʊm] nt criterion.

Kritik [kriˈtiːk] f criticism; (Zeitungs~) review, write-up; **an jdm/etw** ~ **üben** to criticize sb/sth; **unter aller** ~ **sein** (umg) to be beneath contempt.

Kritiker(in) ['kriːtikər(ɪn)] (-s, -) m(f) critic.

kritiklos adj uncritical.

kritisch ['kriːtɪʃ] adj critical.

kritisieren [kritiˈziːrən] vt, vi to criticize.

kritteln ['krɪtəln] vi to find fault, carp.

kritzeln ['krɪtsəln] *vt, vi* to scribble, scrawl.
Kroate [kro'aːtə] (-**n**, -**n**) *m* Croat.
Kroatien [kro'aːtsiən] (-**s**) *nt* Croatia.
Kroatin *f* Croat.
kroatisch *adj* Croatian.
kroch *etc* [krɔx] *vb siehe* **kriechen.**
Krokodil [kroko'diːl] (-**s**, -**e**) *nt* crocodile.
Krokodilstränen *pl* crocodile tears *pl.*
Krokus ['kroːkʊs] (-, - *od* -**se**) *m* crocus.
Krone ['kroːnə] (-, -**n**) *f* crown; (*Baum~*) top;
  einen in der ~ **haben** (*umg*) to be tipsy.
krönen ['krøːnən] *vt* to crown.
Kron- *zW:* ~**korken** *m* bottle top; ~**leuchter** *m*
  chandelier; ~**prinz** *m* crown prince.
Krönung ['krøːnʊŋ] *f* coronation.
Kronzeuge *m* (*JUR*) person who turns
  Queen's/King's (*BRIT*) *od* State's (*US*)
  evidence; (*Hauptzeuge*) principal witness.
Kropf [krɔpf] (-(**e**)**s**, ⁻**e**) *m* (*MED*) goitre (*BRIT*),
  goiter (*US*); (*von Vogel*) crop.
Krösus ['krøːzʊs] (-**ses**, -**se**) *m*: **ich bin doch**
  kein ~ (*umg*) I'm not made of money.
Kröte ['krøːtə] (-, -**n**) *f* toad; **Kröten** *pl* (*umg:*
  Geld) pennies *pl.*
Krs. *abk* = **Kreis.**
Krücke ['krʏkə] (-, -**n**) *f* crutch.
Krug [kruːk] (-(**e**)**s**, ⁻**e**) *m* jug; (*Bier~*) mug.
Krümel ['kryːməl] (-**s**, -) *m* crumb.
krümeln *vt, vi* to crumble.
krumm [krʊm] *adj* (*lit, fig*) crooked; (*kurvig*)
  curved; **sich** ~ **und schief lachen** (*umg*) to
  fall about laughing; **keinen Finger** ~ **machen**
  (*umg*) not to lift a finger; **ein** ~**es Ding**
  drehen (*umg*) to do something crooked;
  ~**beinig** *adj* bandy-legged.
krümmen ['krʏmːən] *vt* to bend ♦ *vr* to bend,
  curve.
krummlachen (*umg*) *vr* to laugh o.s. silly.
krummnehmen *unreg vt:* **jdm etw** ~ (*umg*) to
  take sth amiss.
Krümmung *f* bend, curve.
Krüppel ['krʏpəl] (-**s**, -) *m* cripple.
Kruste ['krʊstə] (-, -**n**) *f* crust.
Kruzifix [krutsi'fɪks] (-**es**, -**e**) *nt* crucifix.
Kt. *abk* = **Kanton.**
Kto. *abk* (= **Konto**) a/c.
Kuba ['kuːba] (-**s**) *nt* Cuba.
Kubaner(in) [ku'baːnər(ɪn)] (-**s**, -) *m(f)* Cuban.
kubanisch [ku'baːnɪʃ] *adj* Cuban.
Kübel ['kyːbəl] (-**s**, -) *m* tub; (*Eimer*) pail.
Kubik- [ku'biːk] *in zW* cubic; ~**meter** *m* cubic
  metre (*BRIT*) *od* meter (*US*).
Küche ['kʏçə] (-, -**n**) *f* kitchen; (*Kochen*)
  cooking, cuisine.
Kuchen ['kuːxən] (-**s**, -) *m* cake; ~**blech** *nt*
  baking tray; ~**form** *f* baking tin (*BRIT*) *od*
  pan (*US*); ~**gabel** *f* pastry fork.
Küchen- *zW:* ~**gerät** *nt* kitchen utensil;
  (*elektrisch*) kitchen appliance; ~**herd** *m*
  cooker, stove; ~**maschine** *f* food processor;
  ~**messer** *nt* kitchen knife; ~**schabe** *f*
  cockroach; ~**schrank** *m* kitchen cabinet.

Kuchenteig *m* cake mixture.
Kuckuck ['kʊkʊk] (-**s**, -**e**) *m* cuckoo; (*umg:*
  Siegel des Gerichtsvollziehers) bailiff's seal
  (*for distraint of goods*); **das weiß der** ~
  heaven (only) knows.
Kuckucksuhr *f* cuckoo clock.
Kuddelmuddel ['kʊdəlmʊdəl] (-**s**) (*umg*) *m od*
  nt mess.
Kufe ['kuːfə] (-, -**n**) *f* (*Faß~*) vat; (*Schlitten~*)
  runner; (*AVIAT*) skid.
Kugel ['kuːgəl] (-, -**n**) *f* ball; (*MATH*) sphere;
  (*MIL*) bullet; (*Erd~*) globe; (*SPORT*) shot; **eine**
  ruhige ~ **schieben** (*umg*) to have a cushy
  number; **k~förmig** *adj* spherical; ~**kopf** *m*
  (*Schreibmaschine*) golf ball;
  ~**kopfschreibmaschine** *f* golf-ball
  typewriter; ~**lager** *nt* ball bearing.
kugeln *vt* to roll; (*SPORT*) to bowl ♦ *vr* (*vor*
  Lachen) to double up.
Kugel- *zW:* **k~rund** *adj* (*Gegenstand*) round;
  (*umg: Person*) tubby; ~**schreiber** *m* ball-point
  (pen), Biro ®; **k~sicher** *adj* bulletproof;
  ~**stoßen** (-**s**) *nt* shot put.
Kuh [kuː] (-, ⁻**e**) *f* cow; ~**dorf** (*pej: umg*) *nt*
  one-horse town; ~**handel** (*pej: umg*) *m*
  horse-trading; ~**haut** *f*: **das geht auf keine**
  ~**haut** (*fig: umg*) that's absolutely
  incredible.
kühl [kyːl] *adj* (*lit, fig*) cool; **K~anlage** *f*
  refrigeration plant.
Kühle (-) *f* coolness.
kühlen *vt* to cool.
Kühler (-**s**, -) *m* (*AUT*) radiator; ~**haube** *f*
  (*AUT*) bonnet (*BRIT*), hood (*US*).
Kühl- *zW:* ~**flüssigkeit** *f* coolant; ~**haus** *nt*
  cold-storage depot; ~**raum** *m* cold-storage
  chamber; ~**schrank** *m* refrigerator;
  ~**tasche** *f* cool bag; ~**truhe** *f* freezer.
Kühlung *f* cooling.
Kühlwagen *m* (*EISENB, Lastwagen*)
  refrigerator van.
Kühlwasser *nt* coolant.
kühn [kyːn] *adj* bold, daring; **K~heit** *f*
  boldness.
Kuhstall *m* cow-shed.
k.u.k. *abk* (= *kaiserlich und königlich*) imperial
  and royal.
Küken ['kyːkən] (-**s**, -) *nt* chicken; (*umg:*
  Nesthäkchen) baby of the family.
kulant [ku'lant] *adj* obliging.
Kulanz [ku'lants] *f* accommodating attitude,
  generousness.
Kuli ['kuːli] (-**s**, -**s**) *m* coolie; (*umg:*
  Kugelschreiber) Biro ®.
kulinarisch [kuli'naːrɪʃ] *adj* culinary.
Kulisse [ku'lɪsə] (-, -**n**) *f* scene.
Kulissenschieber(in) *m(f)* stagehand.
Kulleraugen ['kʊləraʊgən] (*umg*) *pl* wide eyes
  pl.
kullern ['kʊlərn] *vi* to roll.
Kult [kʊlt] (-(**e**)**s**, -**e**) *m* worship, cult; **mit etw**
  ~ **treiben** to make a cult out of sth.

kultivieren [kʊlti'viːrən] vt to cultivate.
kultiviert adj cultivated, refined.
Kultstätte f place of worship.
Kultur [kʊl'tuːr] f culture; (Lebensform)
civilization; (des Bodens) cultivation;
~**banause** (umg) m philistine, low-brow;
~**betrieb** m culture industry; ~**beutel** m
toilet bag (BRIT), washbag.
kulturell [kʊltu'rɛl] adj cultural.
Kulturfilm m documentary film.
Kulturteil m (von Zeitung) arts section.
Kultusminister ['kʊltʊsmɪnɪstər] m minister
of education and the arts.
Kümmel ['kʏməl] (-s, -) m caraway seed;
(Branntwein) kümmel.
Kummer ['kʊmər] (-s) m grief, sorrow.
kümmerlich ['kʏmərlɪç] adj miserable,
wretched.
kümmern vr: **sich um jdn** ~ to look after sb
♦ vt to concern; **sich um etw** ~ to see to sth;
das kümmert mich nicht that doesn't worry
me.
Kumpan(in) [kʊm'paːn(ɪn)] (-s, -e) m(f) mate;
(pej) accomplice.
Kumpel ['kʊmpəl] (-s, -) (umg) m mate.
kündbar ['kʏntbaːr] adj redeemable,
recallable; (Vertrag) terminable.
Kunde¹ ['kʊndə] (-n, -n) m customer.
Kunde² ['kʊndə] (-, -n) f (Botschaft) news.
Kunden- zW: ~**beratung** f customer advisory
service; ~**dienst** m after-sales service;
~**fang** (pej) m: **auf** ~**fang sein** to be touting
for customers; ~**fänger** m tout (umg);
~**konto** nt charge account; ~**kreis** m
customers pl, clientele; ~**werbung** f
publicity (aimed at attracting custom or
customers).
Kund- zW: ~**gabe** f announcement; **k~geben**
unreg vt to announce; ~**gebung** f
announcement; (Versammlung) rally.
kundig adj expert, experienced.
kündigen ['kʏndɪgən] vi to give in one's notice
♦ vt to cancel; **jdm** ~ to give sb his notice;
zum 1. April ~ to give one's notice for April
1st; (Mieter) to give notice for April 1st; (bei
Mitgliedschaft) to cancel one's membership
as of April 1st; **(jdm) die Stellung** ~ to give
(sb) notice; **sie hat ihm die Freundschaft
gekündigt** she has broken off their
friendship.
Kündigung f notice.
Kündigungsfrist f period of notice.
Kündigungsschutz m protection against
wrongful dismissal.
Kundin f customer.
Kundschaft f customers pl, clientele.
Kundschafter (-s, -) m spy; (MIL) scout.
künftig ['kʏnftɪç] adj future ♦ adv in future.
Kunst [kʊnst] (-, ⁻e) f (auch SCH) art;
(Können) skill; **das ist doch keine** ~ it's easy;
mit seiner ~ **am Ende sein** to be at one's
wits' end; **das ist eine brotlose** ~ there's no

money in that; ~**akademie** f academy of
art; ~**druck** m art print; ~**dünger** m artificial
manure; ~**erziehung** f (SCH) art; ~**faser** f
synthetic fibre (BRIT) od fiber (US); ~**fehler**
m professional error; (weniger ernst) slip;
~**fertigkeit** f skilfulness (BRIT), skillfulness
(US); ~**flieger** m stunt flyer; ~**gerecht** adj
skilful (BRIT), skillful (US); ~**geschichte** f
history of art; ~**gewerbe** nt arts and crafts
pl; ~**griff** m trick, knack; ~**händler** m art
dealer; ~**harz** nt artificial resin; ~**leder** nt
artificial leather.
Künstler(in) ['kʏnstlər(ɪn)] (-s, -) m(f) artist;
k~isch adj artistic; ~**name** m pseudonym;
(von Schauspieler) stage name; ~**pech** (umg)
nt hard luck.
künstlich ['kʏnstlɪç] adj artificial; ~**e
Intelligenz** (COMPUT) artificial intelligence;
sich ~ **aufregen** (umg) to get all worked up
about nothing.
Kunst- zW: ~**sammler** m art collector; ~**seide**
f artificial silk; ~**stoff** m synthetic material;
~**stopfen** (-s) nt invisible mending; ~**stück**
nt trick; **das ist kein** ~**stück** (fig) there's
nothing to it; ~**turnen** nt gymnastics sing;
k~voll adj artistic; ~**werk** nt work of art.
kunterbunt ['kʊntərbʊnt] adj higgledy-
piggledy.
Kupfer ['kʊpfər] (-s, -) nt copper; ~**geld** nt
coppers pl.
kupfern adj copper ♦ vt (fig: umg) to
plagiarize, copy, imitate.
Kupferstich m copperplate engraving.
Kuppe ['kʊpə] (-, -n) f (Berg~) top; (Finger~)
tip.
Kuppel (-, -n) f cupola, dome.
Kuppelei [kʊpə'laɪ] f (JUR) procuring.
kuppeln vi (JUR) to procure; (AUT) to
declutch ♦ vt to join.
Kuppler ['kʊplər] (-s, -) m procurer; ~**in** f
procuress.
Kupplung f (auch TECH) coupling; (AUT etc)
clutch; **die** ~ **(durch)treten** to disengage the
clutch.
Kur [kuːr] (-, -en) f (im Kurort) (health) cure,
(course of) treatment; (Schlankheitskur) diet;
eine ~ **machen** to take a cure (in a health
resort).
Kür [kyːr] (-, -en) f (SPORT) free exercises pl.
Kuratorium [kura'toːrium] nt (Vereinigung)
committee.
Kurbel ['kʊrbəl] (-, -n) f crank, winder; (AUT)
starting handle; ~**welle** f crankshaft.
Kürbis ['kʏrbɪs] (-ses, -se) m pumpkin;
(exotisch) gourd.
Kurde ['kʊrdə] (-n, -n) m, **Kurdin** f Kurd.
Kurfürst ['kuːrfʏrst] m Elector, electoral
prince.
Kurgast m visitor (to a health resort).
Kurier [ku'riːr] (-s, -e) m courier, messenger.
kurieren [ku'riːrən] vt to cure.
kurios [kuri'oːs] adj curious, odd.

Kuriosität [kuriozi'tɛːt] *f* curiosity.
Kur- *zW:* ~**konzert** *nt* concert (*at a health resort*); ~**ort** *m* health resort; ~**pfuscher** *m* quack.
Kurs [kʊrs] (**-es, -e**) *m* course; (*FIN*) rate; **hoch im** ~ **stehen** (*fig*) to be highly thought of; **einen** ~ **besuchen** *od* **mitmachen** to attend a class; **harter/weicher** ~ (*POL*) hard/soft line; ~**änderung** *f* (*lit, fig*) change of course; ~**buch** *nt* timetable.
Kürschner(in) ['kyrʃnər(ɪn)] (**-s, -**) *m(f)* furrier.
kursieren [kʊr'ziːrən] *vi* to circulate.
kursiv *adv* in italics.
Kursnotierung *f* quotation.
Kursus ['kʊrzʊs] (**-, Kurse**) *m* course.
Kurswagen *m* (*EISENB*) through carriage.
Kurswert *m* (*FIN*) market value.
Kurtaxe *f* spa tax (*paid by visitors*).
Kurve ['kʊrvə] (**-, -n**) *f* curve; (*Straßen~*) bend; (*statistisch, Fieber~ etc*) graph; **die** ~ **nicht kriegen** (*umg*) not to get around to it.
kurvenreich *adj:* „~**e Strecke"** "bends".
kurvig *adj* (*Straße*) bendy.
kurz [kʊrts] *adj* short ♦ *adv:* ~ **und bündig** concisely; **zu** ~ **kommen** to come off badly; **den kürzeren ziehen** to get the worst of it; ~ **und gut** in short; **über** ~ **oder lang** sooner or later; **eine Sache** ~ **abtun** to dismiss sth out of hand; **sich** ~ **fassen** to be brief; **darf ich mal** ~ **stören?** could I just interrupt for a moment?
Kurzarbeit *f* short-time work.

> Kurzarbeit *is the term used to describe a shorter working week made necessary by a lack of work. It has been introduced in recent years as a preferable alternative to redundancy. It has to be approved by the* **Arbeitsamt**, *the job centre, which pays some compensation to the worker for loss of pay.*

kurzärm(e)lig *adj* short-sleeved.
kurzatmig *adj* (*fig*) feeble, lame; (*MED*) short-winded.
Kürze ['kyrtsə] (**-, -n**) *f* shortness, brevity.
kürzen *vt* to cut short; (*in der Länge*) to shorten; (*Gehalt*) to reduce.
kurzerhand ['kʊrtsər'hant] *adv* without further ado; (*entlassen*) on the spot.
kurz- *zW:* **K~fassung** *f* shortened version; ~**fristig** *adj* short-term; ~**fristige Verbindlichkeiten** current liabilities *pl*; ~**gefaßt** *adj* concise; **K~geschichte** *f* short story; ~**halten** *unreg vt* to keep short; ~**lebig** *adj* short-lived.
kürzlich ['kyrtslɪç] *adv* lately, recently.
Kurz- *zW:* ~**meldung** *f* news flash; ~**parker** *m* short-stay parker; ~**schluß** *m* (*ELEK*) short circuit; ~**schlußhandlung** *f* (*fig*) rash action; ~**schrift** *f* shorthand; **k~sichtig** *adj* short-sighted; ~**strecken-** *in zW* short-range;

~**streckenläufer(in)** *m(f)* sprinter; **k~treten** *unreg vi* (*fig: umg*) to go easy; **k~um** *adv* in a word.
Kürzung *f* cutback.
Kurzwaren *pl* haberdashery (*BRIT*), notions *pl* (*US*).
Kurzwelle *f* short wave.
kuschelig *adj* cuddly.
kuscheln ['kʊʃəln] *vr* to snuggle up.
kuschen ['kʊʃən] *vi, vr* (*Hund etc*) to get down; (*fig*) to knuckle under.
Kusine [ku'ziːnə] *f* cousin.
Kuß [kʊs] (**-sses, ⁻sse**) *m* kiss.
küssen ['kʏsən] *vt, vr* to kiss.
Küste ['kʏstə] (**-, -n**) *f* coast, shore.
Küsten- *zW:* ~**gewässer** *pl* coastal waters *pl*; ~**schiff** *nt* coaster; ~**wache** *f* coastguard (station).
Küster ['kʏstər] (**-s, -**) *m* sexton, verger.
Kutsche ['kʊtʃə] (**-, -n**) *f* coach, carriage.
Kutscher (**-s, -**) *m* coachman.
kutschieren [ku'tʃiːrən] *vi:* **durch die Gegend** ~ (*umg*) to drive around.
Kutte ['kʊtə] (**-, -n**) *f* cowl.
Kuvert [ku'vert] (**-s, -e** *od* **-s**) *nt* envelope; (*Gedeck*) cover.
Kuwait ['kuvaɪt] (**-s**) *nt* Kuwait.
KV *abk* (*MUS:* = *Köchelverzeichnis*): ~ **280** K. (number) 280.
KW *abk* (= *Kurzwelle*) SW.
kW *abk* (= *Kilowatt*) kW.
Kybernetik [kyber'neːtɪk] *f* cybernetics *sing*.
kybernetisch [kyber'neːtɪʃ] *adj* cybernetic.
KZ (**-s, -s**) *nt abk* = **Konzentrationslager**.

L, l

L, l¹ [ɛl] *nt* L, l; ~ **wie Ludwig** ≈ L for Lucy, L for Love (*US*).
l² [ɛl] *abk* (= *Liter*) l.
laben ['laːbən] *vt* to refresh ♦ *vr* to refresh o.s.; (*fig*): **sich an etw** *dat* ~ to relish sth.
labern ['laːbərn] (*umg*) *vi* to prattle (on) ♦ *vt* to talk.
labil [la'biːl] *adj* (*physisch: Gesundheit*) delicate; (: *Kreislauf*) poor; (*psychisch*) unstable.
Labor [la'boːr] (**-s, -e** *od* **-s**) *nt* lab(oratory).
Laborant(in) [labo'rant(ɪn)] *m(f)* lab(oratory) assistant.
Laboratorium [labora'toːrium] *nt* lab(oratory).
Labyrinth [laby'rɪnt] (**-s, -e**) *nt* labyrinth.
Lache ['laxə] (**-, -n**) *f* (*Wasser*) pool, puddle; (*umg: Gelächter*) laugh.
lächeln ['lɛçəln] *vi* to smile; **L~** (**-s**) *nt* smile.

lachen ['laxən] *vi* to laugh; **mir ist nicht zum L~ (zumute)** I'm in no laughing mood; **daß ich nicht lache!** (*umg*) don't make me laugh!; **das wäre doch gelacht** it would be ridiculous; **L~** *nt*: **dir wird das L~ schon noch vergehen!** you'll soon be laughing on the other side of your face.

Lacher (-s, -) *m*: **die ~ auf seiner Seite haben** to have the last laugh.

lächerlich ['lɛçərlɪç] *adj* ridiculous; **L~keit** *f* absurdity.

Lach- *zW*: **~gas** *nt* laughing gas; **l~haft** *adj* laughable; **~krampf** *m*: **einen ~krampf bekommen** to go into fits of laughter.

Lachs [laks] (-es, -e) *m* salmon.

Lachsalve ['laxzalvə] *f* burst *od* roar of laughter.

Lachsschinken *m* smoked, rolled fillet of ham.

Lack [lak] (-(e)s, -e) *m* lacquer, varnish; (*von Auto*) paint.

lackieren [la'ki:rən] *vt* to varnish; (*Auto*) to spray.

Lackierer [la'ki:rər] (-s, -) *m* varnisher.

Lackleder *nt* patent leather.

Lackmus ['lakmʊs] (-) *m od nt* litmus.

Lade ['la:də] (-, -n) *f* box, chest; **~baum** *m* derrick; **~fähigkeit** *f* load capacity; **~fläche** *f* load area; **~gewicht** *nt* tonnage; **~hemmung** *f*: **das Gewehr hat ~hemmung** the gun is jammed.

Laden ['la:dən] (-s, -̈) *m* shop; (*Fenster~*) shutter; (*umg: Betrieb*) outfit; **der ~ läuft** (*umg*) business is good.

laden ['la:dən] *unreg vt* (*Lasten, COMPUT*) to load; (*JUR*) to summon; (*ein~*) to invite; **eine schwere Schuld auf sich** *akk* **~** to place o.s. under a heavy burden of guilt.

Laden- *zW*: **~aufsicht** *f* shopwalker (*BRIT*), floorwalker (*US*); **~besitzer** *m* shopkeeper; **~dieb** *m* shoplifter; **~diebstahl** *m* shoplifting; **~hüter** (-s, -) *m* unsaleable item; **~preis** *m* retail price; **~schluß** *m*, **~schlußzeit** *f* closing time; **~tisch** *m* counter.

Laderampe *f* loading ramp.

Laderaum *m* (*NAUT*) hold.

lädieren [lɛ'di:rən] *vt* to damage.

lädt [lɛ:t] *vb siehe* **laden**.

Ladung ['la:dʊŋ] *f* (*Last*) cargo, load; (*Beladen*) loading; (*JUR*) summons; (*Ein~*) invitation; (*Spreng~*) charge.

lag *etc* [la:k] *vb siehe* **liegen**.

Lage ['la:gə] (-, -n) *f* position, situation; (*Schicht*) layer; **in der ~ sein** to be in a position; **eine gute/ruhige ~ haben** to be in a good/peaceful location; **Herr der ~ sein** to be in control of the situation; **~bericht** *m* report; (*MIL*) situation report; **~beurteilung** *f* situation assessment.

lagenweise *adv* in layers.

Lager ['la:gər] (-s, -) *nt* camp; (*COMM*) warehouse; (*Schlaf~*) bed; (*von Tier*) lair; (*TECH*) bearing; **etw auf ~ haben** to have sth in stock; **~arbeiter** *m* storehand; **~bestand** *m* stocks *pl*; **~feuer** *nt* camp fire; **~geld** *nt* storage (charges *pl*); **~haus** *nt* warehouse, store.

Lagerist(in) [la:gə'rɪst(ɪn)] *m(f)* storeman, storewoman.

lagern ['la:gərn] *vi* (*Dinge*) to be stored; (*Menschen*) to camp; (*auch vr: rasten*) to lie down ◊ *vt* to store; (*betten*) to lay down; (*Maschine*) to bed.

Lager- *zW*: **~raum** *m* storeroom; (*in Geschäft*) stockroom; **~schuppen** *m* store shed; **~stätte** *f* resting place.

Lagerung *f* storage.

Lagune [la'gu:nə] (-, -n) *f* lagoon.

lahm [la:m] *adj* lame; (*umg: langsam, langweilig*) dreary, dull; (*Geschäftsgang*) slow, sluggish; **eine ~e Ente sein** (*umg*) to have no zip; **~arschig** ['la:m|arʃɪç] (*umg*) *adj* bloody *od* damn (*!*) slow.

lahmen *vi* to be lame, limp.

lähmen ['lɛ:mən], **lahmlegen** ['la:mle:gən] *vt* to paralyse (*BRIT*), paralyze (*US*).

Lähmung *f* paralysis.

Lahn [la:n] (-) *f* (*Fluß*) Lahn.

Laib [laip] (-s, -e) *m* loaf.

Laich [laɪç] (-(e)s, -e) *m* spawn; **l~en** *vi* to spawn.

Laie ['laɪə] (-n, -n) *m* layman; (*fig, THEAT*) amateur.

laienhaft *adj* amateurish.

Lakai [la'kaɪ] (-en, -en) *m* lackey.

Laken ['la:kən] (-s, -) *nt* sheet.

Lakritze [la'krɪtsə] (-, -n) *f* liquorice.

lala ['la'la] (*umg*) *adv*: **so ~** so-so, not too bad.

lallen ['lalən] *vt, vi* to slur; (*Baby*) to babble.

Lama ['la:ma] (-s, -s) *nt* llama.

Lamelle [la'mɛlə] *f* lamella; (*ELEK*) lamina; (*TECH*) plate.

lamentieren [lamɛn'ti:rən] *vi* to lament.

Lametta [la'mɛta] (-s) *nt* tinsel.

Lamm [lam] (-(e)s, -̈er) *nt* lamb; **~fell** *nt* lambskin; **l~fromm** *adj* like a lamb; **~wolle** *f* lambswool.

Lampe ['lampə] (-, -n) *f* lamp.

Lampenfieber *nt* stage fright.

Lampenschirm *m* lampshade.

Lampion [lampi'õ:] (-s, -s) *m* Chinese lantern.

Land [lant] (-(e)s, -̈er) *nt* land; (*Nation, nicht Stadt*) country; (*Bundes~*) state; **auf dem ~(e)** in the country; **an ~ gehen** to go ashore; **endlich sehe ich ~** (*fig*) at last I can see the light at the end of the tunnel; **einen Auftrag an ~ ziehen** (*umg*) to land an order; **aus aller Herren Länder** from all over the world.

A **Land** (*plural* **Länder**) *is a member state of the* **BRD**. *There are 16 Länder, namely Baden-Württemberg, Bayern, Berlin, Brandenburg,*

Bremen, Hamburg, Hessen, Mecklenburg-Vorpommern, Niedersachsen, Nordrhein-Westfalen, Rheinland-Pfalz, Saarland, Sachsen, Sachsen-Anhalt, Schleswig-Holstein and Thüringen. Each Land has its own parliament and constitution.

Landarbeiter *m* farm *od* agricultural worker.

Landbesitz *m* landed property.

Landbesitzer *m* landowner.

Landebahn *f* runway.

Landeerlaubnis *f* permission to land.

landeinwärts [lant'|aɪnvɛrts] *adv* inland.

landen ['landən] *vt, vi* to land; **mit deinen Komplimenten kannst du bei mir nicht ~** your compliments won't get you anywhere with me.

Ländereien [lɛndə'raɪən] *pl* estates *pl.*

Länderspiel *nt* international (match).

Landes- *zW:* **~farben** *pl* national colours *pl* (*BRIT*) *od* colors *pl* (*US*); **~grenze** *f* (national) frontier; (*von Bundesland*) state boundary; **~innere(s)** *nt* inland region; **~kind** *nt* native of a German state; **~kunde** *f* regional studies *pl;* **~tracht** *f* national costume; **l~üblich** *adj* customary; **~verrat** *m* high treason; **~verweisung** *f* banishment; **~währung** *f* national currency; **l~weit** *adj* countrywide.

Landeverbot *nt* refusal of permission to land.

Land- *zW:* **~flucht** *f* emigration to the cities; **~gut** *nt* estate; **~haus** *nt* country house; **~karte** *f* map; **~kreis** *m* administrative region; **l~läufig** *adj* customary.

ländlich ['lɛntlɪç] *adj* rural.

Land- *zW:* **~rat** *m* head of administration of a Landkreis; **~schaft** *f* countryside; (*KUNST*) landscape; **die politische ~schaft** the political scene; **l~schaftlich** *adj* scenic; (*Besonderheiten*) regional.

Landsmann (-(e)s, *pl* **-leute**) *m* compatriot, fellow countryman.

Landsmännin *f* compatriot, fellow countrywoman.

Land- *zW:* **~straße** *f* country road; **~streicher** (-s, -) *m* tramp; **~strich** *m* region; **~tag** *m* (*POL*) regional parliament.

Landung ['landʊŋ] *f* landing.

Landungs- *zW:* **~boot** *nt* landing craft; **~brücke** *f* jetty, pier; **~stelle** *f* landing place.

Landurlaub *m* shore leave.

Landvermesser *m* surveyor.

landw. *abk* (= *landwirtschaftlich*) agricultural.

Land- *zW:* **~wirt** *m* farmer; **~wirtschaft** *f* agriculture; **~wirtschaft betreiben** to farm; **~zunge** *f* spit.

lang [laŋ] *adj* long; (*umg: Mensch*) tall ♦ *adv:* **~ anhaltender Beifall** prolonged applause; **hier wird mir die Zeit nicht ~** I won't get

bored here; **er machte ein ~es Gesicht** his face fell; **~ und breit** at great length; **~atmig** *adj* long-winded.

lange *adv* for a long time; (*dauern, brauchen*) a long time; **~ nicht so ...** not nearly as ...; **wenn der das schafft, kannst du das schon ~** if he can do it, you can do it easily.

Länge ['lɛŋə] (-, -n) *f* length; (*GEOG*) longitude; **etw der ~ nach falten** to fold sth lengthways; **etw in die ~ ziehen** to drag sth out (*umg*); **der ~ nach hinfallen** to fall flat (on one's face).

langen ['laŋən] *vi* (*ausreichen*) to do, suffice; (*fassen*): **~ nach** to reach for; **es langt mir** I've had enough; **jdm eine ~** (*umg*) to give sb a clip on the ear.

Längengrad *m* longitude.

Längenmaß *nt* linear measure.

langersehnt ['laŋ|ɛrzeːnt] *adj attrib* longed-for.

Langeweile *f* boredom.

lang- *zW:* **~fristig** *adj* long-term ♦ *adv* in the long term; (*planen*) for the long term; **~fristige Verbindlichkeiten** long-term liabilities *pl;* **~jährig** *adj* (*Freundschaft, Gewohnheit*) long-standing; (*Erfahrung, Verhandlungen*) many years of; (*Mitarbeiter*) of many years' standing; **L~lauf** *m* (*SKI*) cross-country skiing; **~lebig** *adj* long-lived; **~lebige Gebrauchsgüter** consumer durables *pl.*

länglich *adj* longish.

Langmut *f* forbearance, patience.

langmütig *adj* forbearing.

längs [lɛŋs] *präp* (*+gen od dat*) along ♦ *adv* lengthways.

langsam *adj* slow; **immer schön ~!** (*umg*) easy does it!; **ich muß jetzt ~ gehen** I must be getting on my way; **~ (aber sicher) reicht es mir** I've just about had enough; **L~keit** *f* slowness.

Langschläfer *m* late riser.

Langspielplatte *f* long-playing record.

längsseit(s) *adv* alongside ♦ *präp +gen* alongside.

längst [lɛŋst] *adv:* **das ist ~ fertig** that was finished a long time ago, that has been finished for a long time.

längste(r, s) *adj* longest.

Langstrecken- *in zW* long-distance; **~flugzeug** *nt* long-range aircraft.

Languste [laŋ'gʊstə] (-, -n) *f* crayfish, crawfish (*US*).

lang- *zW:* **~weilen** *vt untr* to bore ♦ *vr untr* to be *od* get bored; **L~weiler** (-s, -) *m* bore; **~weilig** *adj* boring, tedious; **L~welle** *f* long wave; **~wierig** *adj* lengthy, long-drawn-out.

Lanze ['lantsə] (-, -n) *f* lance.

Lanzette [lan'tsɛtə] *f* lancet.

Laos ['laːɔs] (-) *nt* Laos.

Laote [la'oːtə] (-n, -n,) *m*, **Laotin** *f* Laotian.

laotisch [la'oːtɪʃ] *adj* Laotian.

lapidar [lapi'daːr] *adj* terse, pithy.

Lappalie [la'pa:liə] f trifle.
Lappe ['lapə] (-n, -n) m Lapp, Laplander.
Lappen (-s, -) m cloth, rag; (ANAT) lobe; **jdm durch die ~ gehen** (umg) to slip through sb's fingers.
läppern ['lɛpərn] (umg) vr unpers: **es läppert sich zusammen** it (all) mounts up.
Lappin f Lapp, Laplander.
läppisch ['lɛpɪʃ] adj foolish.
Lappland ['laplant] (-s) nt Lapland.
Lappländer(in) ['laplɛndər(ɪn)] (-s, -) m(f) Lapp, Laplander.
lappländisch adj Lapp.
Lapsus ['lapsus] (-, -) m slip.
Laptop ['lɛptɔp] (-s, -s) m laptop.
Lärche ['lɛrçə] (-, -n) f larch.
Lärm [lɛrm] (-(e)s) m noise; **~belästigung** f noise nuisance; **l~en** vi to be noisy, make a noise.
Larve ['larfə] (-, -n) f mask; (BIOL) larva.
las etc [la:s] vb siehe **lesen**.
Lasagne [la'zanjə] pl lasagne sing.
lasch [laʃ] adj slack; (Geschmack) tasteless.
Lasche ['laʃə] (-, -n) f (Schuh~) tongue; (EISENB) fishplate.
Laser ['le:zər] (-s, -) m laser; **~drucker** m laser printer.

════════════ SCHLÜSSELWORT

lassen ['lasən] (pt **ließ**, pp **gelassen** od (als Hilfsverb) **lassen**) vt **1** (unter~) to stop; (momentan) to leave; **laß das (sein)!** don't (do it)!; (hör auf) stop it!; **laß mich!** leave me alone!; **~ wir das!** let's leave it; **er kann das Trinken nicht ~** he can't stop drinking; **tu, was du nicht ~ kannst!** if you must, you must!
2 (zurück~) to leave; **etw ~, wie es ist** to leave sth (just) as it is
3 (erlauben) to let, allow; **laß ihn doch** let him; **jdn ins Haus ~** to let sb into the house; **das muß man ihr ~** (zugestehen) you've got to grant her that
♦ vi: **laß mal, ich mache das schon** leave it, I'll do it
♦ Hilfsverb **1** (veran~): **etw machen ~** to have od get sth done; **jdn etw machen ~** to get sb to do sth; (durch Befehl usw) to make sb do sth; **er ließ mich warten** he kept me waiting; **mein Vater wollte mich studieren ~** my father wanted me to study; **sich dat etw schicken ~** to have sth sent (to one)
2 (zu~): **jdn etw wissen ~** to let sb know sth; **das Licht brennen ~** to leave the light on; **einen Bart wachsen ~** to grow a beard; **laß es dir gutgehen!** take care of yourself!
3: laß uns gehen let's go
♦ vr: **das läßt sich machen** that can be done; **es läßt sich schwer sagen** it's difficult to say.

lässig ['lɛsɪç] adj casual; **L~keit** f casualness.

läßlich ['lɛslɪç] adj pardonable, venial.
läßt [lɛst] vb siehe **lassen**.
Last [last] (-, -en) f load; (Trag~) burden; (NAUT, AVIAT) cargo; (meist pl: Gebühr) charge; **jdm zur ~ fallen** to be a burden to sb; **~auto** nt lorry (BRIT), truck.
lasten vi: **~ auf** +dat to weigh on.
Lastenaufzug m hoist, goods lift (BRIT) od elevator (US).
Lastenausgleichsgesetz nt law on financial compensation for losses suffered in WWII.
Laster ['lastər] (-s, -) nt vice ♦ m (umg) lorry (BRIT), truck.
Lästerer ['lɛstərər] (-s, -) m mocker; (Gottes~) blasphemer.
lasterhaft adj immoral.
lästerlich adj scandalous.
lästern ['lɛstərn] vt, vi (Gott) to blaspheme; (schlecht sprechen) to mock.
Lästerung f jibe; (Gottes~) blasphemy.
lästig ['lɛstɪç] adj troublesome, tiresome; **(jdm) ~ werden** to become a nuisance (to sb); (zum Ärgernis werden) to get annoying (to sb).
Last- zW: **~kahn** m barge; **~kraftwagen** m heavy goods vehicle; **~schrift** f debiting; (Eintrag) debit item; **~tier** nt beast of burden; **~träger** m porter; **~wagen** m lorry (BRIT), truck; **~zug** m truck and trailer.
Latein [la'taɪn] (-s) nt Latin; **mit seinem ~ am Ende sein** (fig) to be stumped (umg); **~amerika** nt Latin America; **l~amerikanisch** adj Latin-American; **l~isch** adj Latin.
latent [la'tɛnt] adj latent.
Laterne [la'tɛrnə] (-, -n) f lantern; (Straßen~) lamp, light.
Laternenpfahl m lamppost.
Latinum [la'ti:num] (-s) nt: **kleines/großes ~** ≈ Latin O-/A-level exams (BRIT).
Latrine [la'tri:nə] f latrine.
Latsche ['latʃə] (-, -n) f dwarf pine.
Latschen ['la:tʃən] (umg) m (Hausschuh) slipper; (pej: Schuh) worn-out shoe.
latschen (umg) vi (gehen) to wander, go; (lässig) to slouch.
Latte ['latə] (-, -n) f lath; (SPORT) goalpost; (quer) crossbar.
Lattenzaun m lattice fence.
Latz [lats] (-es, ⁻e) m bib; (Hosen~) front flap.
Lätzchen ['lɛtsçən] nt bib.
Latzhose f dungarees pl.
lau [lau] adj (Nacht) balmy; (Wasser) lukewarm; (fig: Haltung) half-hearted.
Laub [laup] (-(e)s) nt foliage; **~baum** m deciduous tree.
Laube ['laubə] (-, -n) f arbour (BRIT), arbor (US); (Gartenhäuschen) summerhouse.
Laub- zW: **~frosch** m tree frog; **~säge** f fretsaw; **~wald** m deciduous forest.
Lauch [laux] (-(e)s, -e) m leek.
Lauer ['lauər] f: **auf der ~ sein** od **liegen** to lie in wait.

lauern *vi* to lie in wait; (*Gefahr*) to lurk.
Lauf [lauf] (-(e)s, Läufe) *m* run; (*Wett~*) race; (*Entwicklung, ASTRON*) course; (*Gewehr~*) barrel; **im ~e des Gesprächs** during the conversation; **sie ließ ihren Gefühlen freien ~** she gave way to her feelings; **einer Sache** *dat* **ihren ~ lassen** to let sth take its course; **~bahn** *f* career; **eine ~bahn einschlagen** to embark on a career; **~bursche** *m* errand boy.
laufen ['laufən] *unreg vi* to run; (*umg: gehen*) to walk; (*Uhr*) to go; (*funktionieren*) to work; (*Elektrogerät: eingeschaltet sein*) to be on; (*gezeigt werden: Film, Stück*) to be on; (*Bewerbung, Antrag*) to be under consideration ♦ *vt* to run; **es lief mir eiskalt über den Rücken** a chill ran up my spine; **ihm läuft die Nase** he's got a runny nose; **die Dinge ~ lassen** to let things slide; **die Sache ist gelaufen** (*umg*) it's in the bag; **das Auto läuft auf meinen Namen** the car is in my name; **Ski/Schlittschuh/Rollschuh** *etc* **~** to ski/skate/rollerskate *etc.*
laufend *adj* running; (*Monat, Ausgaben*) current; **auf dem ~en sein/halten** to be/keep up to date; **am ~en Band** (*fig*) continuously; **~e Nummer** serial number; (*von Konto*) number; **~e Kosten** running costs *pl.*
laufenlassen *unreg vt* (*Person*) to let go.
Läufer ['lɔyfər] (-s, -) *m* (*Teppich, SPORT*) runner; (*Fußball*) half-back; (*Schach*) bishop.
Lauferei [laufə'rai] (*umg*) *f* running about.
Läuferin *f* (*SPORT*) runner.
Lauf- *zW*: **~feuer** *nt*: **sich wie ein ~feuer verbreiten** to spread like wildfire; **~kundschaft** *f* passing trade; **~masche** *f* run, ladder (*BRIT*); **~paß** *m*: **jdm den ~paß geben** (*umg*) to give sb his/her marching orders; **~schritt** *m*: **im ~schritt** at a run; **~stall** *m* playpen; **~steg** *m* catwalk.
läuft [lɔyft] *vb siehe* **laufen.**
Lauf- *zW*: **~werk** *nt* running gear; (*COMPUT*) drive; **~zeit** *f* (*von Wechsel, Vertrag*) period of validity; (*von Maschine*) life; **~zettel** *m* circular.
Lauge ['laugə] (-, -n) *f* soapy water; (*CHEM*) alkaline solution.
Laune ['launə] (-, -n) *f* mood, humour (*BRIT*), humor (*US*); (*Einfall*) caprice; (*schlechte ~*) temper.
launenhaft *adj* capricious, changeable.
launisch *adj* moody.
Laus [laus] (-, Läuse) *f* louse; **ihm ist (wohl) eine ~ über die Leber gelaufen** (*umg*) something's biting him; **~bub** *m* rascal, imp.
Lauschangriff *m*: **~ (gegen)** bugging operation (on).
lauschen ['lauʃən] *vi* to eavesdrop, listen in.
Lauscher(in) (-s, -) *m(f)* eavesdropper.
lauschig ['lauʃıç] *adj* snug.
Lausejunge (*umg*) *m* little devil; (*wohlwollend*) rascal.

lausen ['lauzən] *vt* to delouse; **ich denk', mich laust der Affe!** (*umg*) well blow me down!
lausig ['lauzıç] (*umg*) *adj* lousy; (*Kälte*) perishing ♦ *adv* awfully.
laut [laut] *adj* loud ♦ *adv* loudly; (*lesen*) aloud ♦ *präp* (*+gen od dat*) according to.
Laut (-(e)s, -e) *m* sound.
Laute ['lautə] (-, -n) *f* lute.
lauten ['lautən] *vi* to say; (*Urteil*) to be.
läuten ['lɔytən] *vt, vi* to ring, sound; **er hat davon (etwas) ~ hören** (*umg*) he has heard something about it.
lauter ['lautər] *adj* (*Wasser*) clear, pure; (*Wahrheit, Charakter*) honest ♦ *adj inv* (*Freude, Dummheit etc*) sheer ♦ *adv* (*nur*) nothing but, only; **L~keit** *f* purity; honesty, integrity.
läutern ['lɔytərn] *vt* to purify.
Läuterung *f* purification.
laut- *zW*: **~hals** *adv* at the top of one's voice; **~los** *adj* noiseless, silent; **~malend** *adj* onomatopoeic; **L~schrift** *f* phonetics *pl*; **L~sprecher** *m* loudspeaker; **L~sprecheranlage** *f*: **öffentliche L~sprecheranlage** public-address *od* PA system; **L~sprecherwagen** *m* loudspeaker van; **~stark** *adj* vociferous; **L~stärke** *f* (*RUNDF*) volume.
lauwarm ['lauvarm] *adj* (*lit, fig*) lukewarm.
Lava ['laːva] (-, **Laven**) *f* lava.
Lavendel [la'vɛndəl] (-s, -) *m* lavender.
Lawine [la'viːnə] *f* avalanche.
Lawinengefahr *f* danger of avalanches.
lax [laks] *adj* lax.
Layout ['leːaut] (-s, -s) *nt* layout.
Lazarett [latsa'rɛt] (-(e)s, -e) *nt* (*MIL*) hospital, infirmary.
Ldkrs. *abk* = **Landkreis.**
leasen ['liːzən] *vt* to lease.
Leasing ['liːzıŋ] (-s, -s) *nt* (*COMM*) leasing.
Lebehoch *nt* three cheers *pl.*
Lebemann (-(e)s, *pl* **-männer**) *m* man about town.
Leben ['leːbən] (-s, -) *nt* life; **am ~ sein/ bleiben** to be/stay alive; **ums ~ kommen** to die; **etw ins ~ rufen** to bring sth into being; **seines ~s nicht mehr sicher sein** to fear for one's life; **etw für sein ~ gern tun** to love doing sth.
leben *vt, vi* to live.
lebend *adj* living; **~es Inventar** livestock.
lebendig [le'bɛndıç] *adj* living, alive; (*lebhaft*) lively; **L~keit** *f* liveliness.
Lebens- *zW*: **~abend** *m* old age; **~alter** *nt* age; **~anschauung** *f* philosophy of life; **~art** *f* way of life; **I~bejahend** *adj* positive; **~dauer** *f* life (span); (*von Maschine*) life; **~erfahrung** *f* experience of life; **~erwartung** *f* life expectancy; **I~fähig** *adj* able to live; **I~froh** *adj* full of the joys of life; **~gefahr** *f*: **~gefahr!** danger!; **in ~gefahr** critically *od* dangerously ill; **I~gefährlich** *adj* dangerous; (*Krankheit, Verletzung*) critical; **~gefährte** *m*:

ihr ~**gefährte** the man she lives with; ~**gefährtin** *f:* **seine** ~**gefährtin** the woman he lives with; ~**größe** *f:* **in** ~**größe** life-size(d); ~**haltungskosten** *pl* cost of living *sing*; ~**inhalt** *m* purpose in life; ~**jahr** *nt* year of life; ~**künstler** *m* master in the art of living; ~**lage** *f* situation in life; **l~länglich** *adj* (*Strafe*) for life; ~**lauf** *m* curriculum vitae, CV; **l~lustig** *adj* cheerful, lively; ~**mittel** *pl* food *sing*; ~**mittelgeschäft** *nt* grocer's; ~**mittelvergiftung** *f* food poisoning; **l~müde** *adj* tired of life; ~**qualität** *f* quality of life; ~**raum** *m* (*POL*) Lebensraum; (*BIOL*) biosphere; ~**retter** *m* lifesaver; ~**standard** *m* standard of living; ~**stellung** *f* permanent post; ~**stil** *m* life style; ~**unterhalt** *m* livelihood; ~**versicherung** *f* life insurance; ~**wandel** *m* way of life; ~**weise** *f* way of life, habits *pl*; ~**weisheit** *f* maxim; (~*erfahrung*) wisdom; ~**wichtig** *adj* vital; ~**zeichen** *nt* sign of life; ~**zeit** *f* lifetime; **Beamter auf** ~**zeit** permanent civil servant.

Leber ['leːbər] (-, -n) *f* liver; **frei** *od* **frisch von der** ~ **weg reden** (*umg*) to speak out frankly; ~**fleck** *m* mole; ~**käse** *m* ≈ meat loaf; ~**tran** *m* cod-liver oil; ~**wurst** *f* liver sausage.

Lebewesen *nt* creature.

Lebewohl *nt* farewell, goodbye.

leb- *zW:* ~**haft** *adj* lively, vivacious; **L~haftigkeit** *f* liveliness, vivacity; **L~kuchen** *m* gingerbread; ~**los** *adj* lifeless; **L~tag** *m* (*fig*): **das werde ich mein L~tag nicht vergessen** I'll never forget that as long as I live; **L~zeiten** *pl:* **zu jds L~zeiten** (*Leben*) in sb's lifetime.

lechzen ['lɛçtsən] *vi:* **nach etw** ~ to long for sth.

leck [lɛk] *adj* leaky, leaking; **L~** (-(e)s, -e) *nt* leak.

lecken¹ *vi* (*Loch haben*) to leak.

lecken² *vt, vi* (*schlecken*) to lick.

lecker ['lɛkər] *adj* delicious, tasty; **L~bissen** *m* dainty morsel; **L~maul** *nt:* **ein L~maul sein** to enjoy one's food.

led. *abk* = **ledig**.

Leder ['leːdər] (-s, -) *nt* leather; (*umg: Fußball*) ball; ~**hose** *f* leather trousers *pl*; (*von Tracht*) leather shorts *pl*.

ledern *adj* leather.

Lederwaren *pl* leather goods *pl*.

ledig ['leːdɪç] *adj* single; **einer Sache** *gen* ~ **sein** to be free of sth; ~**lich** *adv* merely, solely.

leer [leːr] *adj* empty; (*Blick*) vacant.

Leere (-) *f* emptiness; **(eine) gähnende** ~ a gaping void.

leeren *vt* to empty ♦ *vr* to (become) empty.

leer- *zW:* ~**gefegt** *adj* (*Straße*) deserted; **L~gewicht** *nt* unladen weight; **L~gut** *nt* empties *pl*; **L~lauf** *m* (*AUT*) neutral; ~**stehend** *adj* empty; **L~taste** *f*

(*Schreibmaschine*) space-bar.

Leerung *f* emptying; (*POST*) collection.

legal [le'gaːl] *adj* legal, lawful.

legalisieren [legali'ziːrən] *vt* to legalize.

Legalität [legali'tɛːt] *f* legality; **(etwas) außerhalb der** ~ (*euph*) (slightly) outside the law.

Legasthenie [legaste'niː] *f* dyslexia.

Legastheniker(in) [legas'teːnikər(ɪn)] (-s, -) *m(f)* dyslexic.

Legebatterie *f* laying battery.

legen ['leːgən] *vt* to lay, put, place; (*Ei*) to lay ♦ *vr* to lie down; (*fig*) to subside; **sich ins Bett** ~ to go to bed.

Legende [le'gɛndə] (-, -n) *f* legend.

leger [le'ʒɛːr] *adj* casual.

legieren [le'giːrən] *vt* to alloy.

Legierung *f* alloy.

Legislative [legɪsla'tiːvə] *f* legislature.

Legislaturperiode [legɪsla'tuːrperioːdə] *f* parliamentary (*BRIT*) *od* congressional (*US*) term.

legitim [legi'tiːm] *adj* legitimate.

Legitimation [legitimatsi'oːn] *f* legitimation.

legitimieren [legiti'miːrən] *vt* to legitimate ♦ *vr* to prove one's identity.

Legitimität [legitimi'tɛːt] *f* legitimacy.

Lehm [leːm] (-(e)s, -e) *m* loam.

lehmig *adj* loamy.

Lehne ['leːnə] (-, -n) *f* arm; (*Rücken~*) back.

lehnen *vt, vr* to lean.

Lehnstuhl *m* armchair.

Lehr- *zW:* ~**amt** *nt* teaching profession; ~**befähigung** *f* teaching qualification; ~**brief** *m* indentures *pl*; ~**buch** *nt* textbook.

Lehre ['leːrə] (-, -n) *f* teaching, doctrine; (*beruflich*) apprenticeship; (*moralisch*) lesson; (*TECH*) gauge; **bei jdm in die** ~ **gehen** to serve one's apprenticeship with sb.

lehren *vt* to teach.

Lehrer(in) (-s, -) *m(f)* teacher; ~**ausbildung** *f* teacher training; ~**kollegium** *nt* teaching staff; ~**zimmer** *nt* staff room.

Lehr- *zW:* ~**gang** *m* course; ~**geld** *nt:* ~**geld für etw zahlen müssen** (*fig*) to pay dearly for sth; ~**jahre** *pl* apprenticeship *sing*; ~**kraft** *f* (*form*) teacher; ~**ling** *m* apprentice; trainee; ~**mittel** *nt* teaching aid; ~**plan** *m* syllabus; ~**probe** *f* demonstration lesson, crit (*umg*); **l~reich** *adj* instructive; ~**satz** *m* proposition; ~**stelle** *f* apprenticeship; ~**stuhl** *m* chair; ~**zeit** *f* apprenticeship.

Leib [laip] (-(e)s, -er) *m* body; **halt ihn mir vom** ~! keep him away from me!; **etw am eigenen** ~(**e**) **spüren** to experience sth for o.s.

leiben ['laibən] *vi:* **wie er leibt und lebt** to a T (*umg*).

Leibes- *zW:* ~**erziehung** *f* physical education; ~**kraft** *f:* **aus** ~**kraft schreien** *etc* to shout *etc* with all one's might; ~**übung** *f* physical exercise; ~**visitation** *f* body search.

Leibgericht *nt* favourite (*BRIT*) *od* favorite (*US*) meal.

Leib- *zW:* **l~haftig** *adj* personified; (*Teufel*) incarnate; **l~lich** *adj* bodily; (*Vater etc*) natural; **~rente** *f* life annuity; **~wache** *f* bodyguard.

Leiche ['laiçə] (-, -n) *f* corpse; **er geht über ~n** (*umg*) he'd stick at nothing.

Leichen- *zW:* **~beschauer** (-s, -) *m* doctor conducting a post-mortem; **~halle** *f* mortuary; **~hemd** *nt* shroud; **~träger** *m* bearer; **~wagen** *m* hearse.

Leichnam ['laiçnaːm] (-(e)s, -e) *m* corpse.

leicht [laiçt] *adj* light; (*einfach*) easy ♦ *adv:* **~ zerbrechlich** very fragile; **nichts ~er als das!** nothing (could be) simpler!; **L~athletik** *f* athletics *sing*; **~fallen** *unreg vi:* **jdm ~fallen** to be easy for sb; **~fertig** *adj* thoughtless; **~gläubig** *adj* gullible, credulous; **L~gläubigkeit** *f* gullibility, credulity; **~hin** *adv* lightly.

Leichtigkeit *f* easiness; **mit ~** with ease.

leicht- *zW:* **~lebig** *adj* easy-going; **~machen** *vt:* **es sich** *dat* **~machen** to make things easy for o.s.; (*nicht gewissenhaft sein*) to take the easy way out; **L~matrose** *m* ordinary seaman; **L~metall** *nt* light alloy; **~nehmen** *unreg vt* to take lightly; **L~sinn** *m* carelessness; **sträflicher L~sinn** criminal negligence; **~sinnig** *adj* careless; **~verletzt** *adj attrib* slightly injured.

Leid [lait] (-(e)s) *nt* grief, sorrow; **jdm sein ~ klagen** to tell sb one's troubles.

leid *adj:* **etw ~ haben** *od* **sein** to be tired of sth; **es tut mir/ihm ~** I am/he is sorry; **er/das tut mir ~** I am sorry for him/about it; **sie kann einem ~ tun** you can't help feeling sorry for her.

leiden ['laidən] *unreg vt* to suffer; (*erlauben*) to permit ♦ *vi* to suffer; **jdn/etw nicht ~ können** not to be able to stand sb/sth; **L~** (-s, -) *nt* suffering; (*Krankheit*) complaint.

Leidenschaft *f* passion; **l~lich** *adj* passionate.

Leidens- *zW:* **~genosse** *m*, **~genossin** *f* fellow sufferer; **~geschichte** *f:* **die ~geschichte (Christi)** (*REL*) Christ's Passion.

leider ['laidər] *adv* unfortunately; **ja, ~** yes, I'm afraid so; **~ nicht** I'm afraid not.

leidig ['laidiç] *adj* miserable, tiresome.

leidlich ['laitliç] *adj* tolerable ♦ *adv* tolerably.

Leidtragende(r) *f(m)* bereaved; (*Benachteiligter*) one who suffers.

Leidwesen *nt:* **zu jds ~** to sb's dismay.

Leier ['laiər] (-, -n) *f* lyre; (*fig*) old story.

Leierkasten *m* barrel organ.

leiern *vt* (*Kurbel*) to turn; (*umg: Gedicht*) to rattle off ♦ *vi* (*drehen*): **~ an** +*dat* to crank.

Leiharbeit *f* subcontracted labour; **~arbeiter(in)** *m(f)* subcontracted worker; **~bibliothek** *f*, **~bücherei** *f* lending library.

leihen ['laiən] *unreg vt* to lend; **sich** *dat* **etw ~** to borrow sth.

Leih- *zW:* **~gabe** *f* loan; **~gebühr** *f* hire charge; **~haus** *nt* pawnshop; **~mutter** *f* surrogate mother; **~schein** *m* pawn ticket; (*in der Bibliothek*) borrowing slip; **~unternehmen** *nt* hire service; (*Arbeitsmarkt*) temp service; **~wagen** *m* hired car (*BRIT*), rental car (*US*); **~weise** *adv* on loan.

Leim [laim] (-(e)s, -e) *m* glue; **jdm auf den ~ gehen** to be taken in by sb; **l~en** *vt* to glue.

Leine ['lainə] (-, -n) *f* line, cord; (*Hunde~*) leash, lead; **~ ziehen** (*umg*) to clear out.

Leinen (-s, -) *nt* linen; (*grob, segeltuchartig*) canvas; (*als Bucheinband*) cloth.

leinen *adj* linen.

Lein- *zW:* **~samen** *m* linseed; **~tuch** *nt* linen cloth; (*Bettuch*) sheet; **~wand** *f* (*KUNST*) canvas; (*FILM*) screen.

leise ['laizə] *adj* quiet; (*sanft*) soft, gentle; **mit ~r Stimme** in a low voice; **nicht die ~ste Ahnung haben** not to have the slightest (idea).

Leisetreter (*pej: umg*) *m* pussyfoot(er).

Leiste ['laistə] (-, -n) *f* ledge; (*Zier~*) strip; (*ANAT*) groin.

leisten ['laistən] *vt* (*Arbeit*) to do; (*Gesellschaft*) to keep; (*Ersatz*) to supply; (*vollbringen*) to achieve; **sich** *dat* **etw ~** to allow o.s. sth; (*sich gönnen*) to treat o.s. to sth; **sich** *dat* **etw ~ können** to be able to afford sth.

Leistenbruch *m* (*MED*) hernia, rupture.

Leistung *f* performance; (*gute*) achievement; (*eines Motors*) power; (*von Krankenkasse etc*) benefit; (*Zahlung*) payment.

Leistungs- *zW:* **~abfall** *m* (*in bezug auf Qualität*) drop in performance; (*in bezug auf Quantität*) drop in productivity; **~beurteilung** *f* performance appraisal; **~druck** *m* pressure; **l~fähig** *adj* efficient; **~fähigkeit** *f* efficiency; **~gesellschaft** *f* meritocracy; **~kurs** *m* (*SCH*) set; **l~orientiert** *adj* performance-orientated; **~prinzip** *nt* achievement principle; **~sport** *m* competitive sport; **~zulage** *f* productivity bonus.

Leitartikel *m* leader.

Leitbild *nt* model.

leiten ['laitən] *vt* to lead; (*Firma*) to manage; (*in eine Richtung*) to direct; (*ELEK*) to conduct; **sich von jdm/etw ~ lassen** (*lit, fig*) to (let o.s.) be guided by sb/sth.

leitend *adj* leading; (*Gedanke, Idee*) dominant; (*Stellung, Position*) managerial; (*Ingenieur, Beamter*) in charge; (*PHYS*) conductive; **~er Angestellter** executive.

Leiter¹ ['laitər] (-s, -) *m* leader, head; (*ELEK*) conductor.

Leiter² ['laitər] (-, -n) *f* ladder.

Leiterin *f* leader, head.

Leiterplatte *f* (*COMPUT*) circuit board.

Leit- *zW:* **~faden** *m* guide; **~fähigkeit** *f*

conductivity; ~**gedanke** m central idea;
~**motiv** nt leitmotiv; ~**planke** f crash
barrier; ~**spruch** m motto.
Leitung f (Führung) direction; (FILM, THEAT
etc) production; (von Firma) management;
directors pl; (Wasser~) pipe; (Kabel) cable;
eine lange ~ haben to be slow on the
uptake; **da ist jemand in der ~** (umg) there's
somebody else on the line.
Leitungs- zW: ~**draht** m wire; ~**mast** m
telegraph pole; ~**rohr** nt pipe; ~**wasser** nt
tap water.
Leitwerk nt (AVIAT) tail unit.
Leitzins m (FIN) base rate.
Lektion [lɛktsiˈoːn] f lesson; **jdm eine**
~ erteilen (fig) to teach sb a lesson.
Lektor(in) [ˈlɛktɔr, lɛkˈtoːrɪn] m(f) (UNIV)
lector; (Verlag) editor.
Lektüre [lɛkˈtyːrə] (-, -n) f (Lesen) reading;
(Lesestoff) reading matter.
Lende [ˈlɛndə] (-, -n) f loin.
Lendenbraten m roast sirloin.
Lendenstück nt fillet.
lenkbar [ˈlɛŋkbaːr] adj (Fahrzeug) steerable;
(Kind) manageable.
lenken vt to steer; (Kind) to guide; (Gespräch)
to lead; **~ auf** +akk (Blick, Aufmerksamkeit) to
direct at; (Verdacht) to throw on(to); (: auf
sich) to draw onto.
Lenkrad nt steering wheel.
Lenkstange f handlebars pl.
Lenkung f steering; (Führung) direction.
Lenz [lɛnts] (-es, -e) m (liter) spring; **sich** dat
einen (faulen) ~ machen (umg) to laze
about, swing the lead.
Leopard [leoˈpart] (-en, -en) m leopard.
Lepra [ˈleːpra] (-) f leprosy; ~**kranke(r)** f(m)
leper.
Lerche [ˈlɛrçə] (-, -n) f lark.
lernbegierig adj eager to learn.
lernbehindert adj educationally handicapped
(BRIT) od handicaped (US).
lernen vt to learn ♦ vi: **er lernt bei der Firma**
Braun he's training at Braun's.
Lernhilfe f educational aid.
lesbar [ˈleːsbaːr] adj legible.
Lesbierin [ˈlɛsbiərɪn] f lesbian.
lesbisch adj lesbian.
Lese [ˈleːzə] (-, -n) f (Wein~) harvest.
Lesebuch nt reading book, reader.
lesen unreg vt to read; (ernten) to gather, pick
♦ vi to read; ~/**schreiben** (COMPUT) to read/
write.
Leser(in) (-s, -) m(f) reader.
Leseratte [ˈleːzəratə] (umg) f bookworm.
Leser- zW: ~**brief** m reader's letter; „~**briefe**"
"letters to the editor"; ~**kreis** m readership;
l~lich adj legible.
Lese- zW: ~**saal** m reading room; ~**stoff** m
reading material; ~**zeichen** nt bookmark;
~**zirkel** m magazine club.
Lesotho [leˈzoːto] (-s) nt Lesotho.

Lesung [ˈleːzʊŋ] f (PARL) reading; (ECCL)
lesson.
lethargisch [leˈtargɪʃ] adj (MED, fig)
lethargic.
Lette [ˈlɛtə] (-n, -n) m, **Lettin** f Latvian.
lettisch adj Latvian.
Lettland [ˈlɛtlant] (-s) nt Latvia.
Letzt f: **zu guter ~** finally, in the end.
letzte(r, s) [ˈlɛtstə(r, s)] adj last; (neueste)
latest; **der L~ Wille** the last will and
testament; **bis zum ~n** to the utmost; **in ~r**
Zeit recently.
Letzte(s) nt: **das ist ja das ~!** (umg) that
really is the limit!
letztenmal adv: **zum ~** for the last time.
letztens adv lately.
letztere(r, s) adj the latter.
letztlich adv in the end.
Leuchte [ˈlɔʏçtə] (-, -n) f lamp, light; (umg:
Mensch) genius.
leuchten vi to shine, gleam.
Leuchter (-s, -) m candlestick.
Leucht- zW: ~**farbe** f fluorescent colour
(BRIT) od color (US); ~**feuer** nt beacon;
~**käfer** m glow-worm; ~**kugel** f flare;
~**pistole** f flare pistol; ~**rakete** f flare;
~**reklame** f neon sign; ~**röhre** f strip light;
~**turm** m lighthouse; ~**zifferblatt** nt
luminous dial.
leugnen [ˈlɔʏgnən] vt, vi to deny.
Leugnung f denial.
Leukämie [lɔʏkɛˈmiː] f leukaemia (BRIT),
leukemia (US).
Leukoplast ® [lɔʏkoˈplast] (-(e)s, -e) nt
Elastoplast ®.
Leumund [ˈlɔʏmʊnt] (-(e)s, -e) m reputation.
Leumundszeugnis nt character reference.
Leute [ˈlɔʏtə] pl people pl; **kleine ~** (fig)
ordinary people; **etw unter die ~ bringen**
(umg: Gerücht etc) to spread sth around.
Leutnant [ˈlɔʏtnant] (-s, -s od -e) m
lieutenant.
leutselig [ˈlɔʏtzeːlɪç] adj affable; **L~keit** f
affability.
Leviten [leˈviːtən] pl: **jdm die ~ lesen** (umg) to
haul sb over the coals.
lexikalisch [lɛksiˈkaːlɪʃ] adj lexical.
Lexikographie [lɛksikograˈfiː] f
lexicography.
Lexikon [ˈlɛksikɔn] (-s, Lexiken od Lexika) nt
encyclopedia.
lfd. abk = **laufend.**
Libanese [libaˈneːzə] (-n, -n) m, **Libanesin** f
Lebanese.
libanesisch adj Lebanese.
Libanon [ˈliːbanɔn] (-s) m: **der ~** the Lebanon.
Libelle [liˈbɛlə] (-, -n) f dragonfly; (TECH)
spirit level.
liberal [libeˈraːl] adj liberal.
Liberale(r) f(m) (POL) Liberal.
Liberalisierung [liberaliˈziːrʊŋ] f
liberalization.

Liberalismus [libera'lısmʊs] *m* liberalism.
Liberia [li'beːria] (**-s**) *nt* Liberia.
Liberianer(in) [liberi'aːnər(ın)] (**-s, -**) *m(f)* Liberian.
liberianisch *adj* Liberian.
Libero ['liːbero] (**-s, -s**) *m* (*FUSSBALL*) sweeper.
Libyen ['liːbyən] (**-s**) *nt* Libya.
Libyer(in) (**-s, -**) *m(f)* Libyan.
libyisch *adj* Libyan.
Licht [lıçt] (**-(e)s, -er**) *nt* light; ~ **machen** (*anschalten*) to turn on a light; (*anzünden*) to light a candle *etc*; **mir geht ein** ~ **auf** it's dawned on me; **jdn hinters** ~ **führen** (*fig*) to lead sb up the garden path.
licht *adj* light, bright.
Licht- *zW*: ~**bild** *nt* photograph; (*Dia*) slide; ~**blick** *m* cheering prospect; **l~empfindlich** *adj* sensitive to light.
lichten ['lıçtən] *vt* to clear; (*Anker*) to weigh ♦ *vr* (*Nebel*) to clear; (*Haar*) to thin.
lichterloh ['lıçtər'loː] *adv*: ~ **brennen** to blaze.
Licht- *zW*: ~**geschwindigkeit** *f* speed of light; ~**griffel** *m* (*COMPUT*) light pen; ~**hupe** *f* flashing of headlights; ~**jahr** *nt* light year; ~**maschine** *f* dynamo; ~**meß** (**-**) *f* Candlemas; ~**pause** *f* photocopy; (*bei Blaupausverfahren*) blueprint; ~**schalter** *m* light switch; **l~scheu** *adj* averse to light; (*fig: Gesindel*) shady.
Lichtung *f* clearing, glade.
Lid [liːt] (**-(e)s, -er**) *nt* eyelid; ~**schatten** *m* eyeshadow.
lieb [liːp] *adj* dear; (*viele*) ~**e Grüße, Deine Silvia** love, Silvia; **L~e Anna,** ~**er Klaus!** ... Dear Anna and Klaus, ...; **am** ~**sten lese ich Kriminalromane** best of all I like detective novels; **den** ~**en langen Tag** (*umg*) all the livelong day; **sich bei jdm** ~ **Kind machen** (*pej*) to suck up to sb (*umg*).
liebäugeln ['liːp|ɔygəln] *vi untr*: **mit dem Gedanken** ~, **etw zu tun** to toy with the idea of doing sth.
Liebe ['liːbə] (**-, -n**) *f* love; **l~bedürftig** *adj*: **l~bedürftig sein** to need love.
Liebelei *f* flirtation.
lieben ['liːbən] *vt* to love; (*weniger stark*) to like; **etw** ~**d gern tun** to love to do sth.
liebens- *zW*: ~**wert** *adj* loveable; ~**würdig** *adj* kind; ~**würdigerweise** *adv* kindly; **L~würdigkeit** *f* kindness.
lieber ['liːbər] *adv* rather, preferably; **ich gehe** ~ **nicht** I'd rather not go; **ich trinke** ~ **Wein als Bier** I prefer wine to beer; **bleib** ~ **im Bett** you'd better stay in bed.
Liebes- *zW*: ~**brief** *m* love letter; ~**dienst** *m* good turn; ~**kummer** *m:* ~**kummer haben** to be lovesick; ~**paar** *nt* courting couple, lovers *pl*; ~**roman** *m* romantic novel.
liebevoll *adj* loving.
lieb- *zW*: ~**gewinnen** *unreg vt* to get fond of; ~**haben** *unreg vt* to love; (*weniger stark*) to be

(*very*) fond of; **L~haber(in)** (**-s, -**) *m(f)* lover; (*Sammler*) collector; **L~haberei** *f* hobby; ~**kosen** *vt untr* to caress; ~**lich** *adj* lovely, charming; (*Duft, Wein*) sweet.
Liebling *m* darling.
Lieblings- *in zW* favourite (*BRIT*), favorite (*US*).
lieblos *adj* unloving.
Liebschaft *f* love affair.
Liechtenstein ['lıçtənʃtain] (**-s**) *nt* Liechtenstein.
Lied [liːt] (**-(e)s, -er**) *nt* song; (*ECCL*) hymn; **davon kann ich ein** ~ **singen** (*fig*) I could tell you a thing or two about that (*umg*).
Liederbuch *nt* songbook; (*REL*) hymn book.
liederlich ['liːdərlıç] *adj* slovenly; (*Lebenswandel*) loose, immoral; **L~keit** *f* slovenliness; immorality.
lief *etc* [liːf] *vb siehe* **laufen**.
Lieferant [liːfə'rant] *m* supplier.
Lieferanteneingang *m* tradesmen's entrance; (*von Warenhaus etc*) goods entrance.
lieferbar *adj* (*vorrätig*) available.
Lieferbedingungen *pl* terms of delivery.
Lieferfrist *f* delivery period.
liefern ['liːfərn] *vt* to deliver; (*versorgen mit*) to supply; (*Beweis*) to produce.
Lieferschein *m* delivery note.
Liefertermin *m* delivery date.
Lieferung *f* delivery; (*Versorgung*) supply.
Lieferwagen *m* (delivery) van, panel truck (*US*).
Lieferzeit *f* delivery period; ~ **6 Monate** delivery six months.
Liege ['liːgə] (**-, -n**) *f* bed; (*Camping-*) camp bed (*BRIT*), cot (*US*); ~**geld** *nt* (*Hafen, Flughafen*) demurrage.
liegen ['liːgən] *unreg vi* to lie; (*sich befinden*) to be (situated); **mir liegt nichts/viel daran** it doesn't matter to me/it matters a lot to me; **es liegt bei Ihnen, ob** ... it rests with you whether ...; **Sprachen** ~ **mir nicht** languages are not my line; **woran liegt es?** what's the cause?; **so, wie die Dinge jetzt** ~ as things stand at the moment; **an mir soll es nicht** ~, **wenn die Sache schiefgeht** it won't be my fault if things go wrong; ~**bleiben** *unreg vi* (*Person*) to stay in bed; (*nicht aufstehen*) to stay lying down; (*Ding*) to be left (behind); (*nicht ausgeführt werden*) to be left (undone); ~**lassen** *unreg vt* (*vergessen*) to leave behind; **L~schaft** *f* real estate.
Liege- *zW*: ~**platz** *m* (*auf Schiff, in Zug etc*) berth; (*Ankerplatz*) moorings *pl*; ~**sitz** *m* (*AUT*) reclining seat; ~**stuhl** *m* deck chair; ~**stütz** *m* (*SPORT*) press-up (*BRIT*), push-up (*US*); ~**wagen** *m* (*EISENB*) couchette car; ~**wiese** *f* lawn (for sunbathing).
lieh *etc* [liː] *vb siehe* **leihen**.
ließ *etc* [liːs] *vb siehe* **lassen**.
liest [liːst] *vb siehe* **lesen**.

Lift [lɪft] (-(e)s, -e od -s) m lift.
Liga ['liːga] (-, **Ligen**) f (SPORT) league.
liieren [li'iːrən] vt: **liiert sein** (Firmen etc) to be working together; (ein Verhältnis haben) to have a relationship.
Likör [li'køːr] (-s, -e) m liqueur.
lila ['liːla] adj inv purple; **L~** (-s, -s) nt (Farbe) purple.
Lilie ['liːliə] f lily.
Liliputaner(in) [lilipu'taːnər(ɪn)] (-s, -) m(f) midget.
Limit ['lɪmɪt] (-s, -s od -e) nt limit; (FIN) ceiling.
Limonade [limo'naːdə] (-, -n) f lemonade.
lind [lɪnt] adj gentle, mild.
Linde ['lɪndə] (-, -n) f lime tree, linden.
lindern ['lɪndərn] vt to alleviate, soothe.
Linderung f alleviation.
lindgrün adj lime green.
Lineal [line'aːl] (-s, -e) nt ruler.
linear [line'aːr] adj linear.
Linguist(in) [lɪŋgu'ɪst(ɪn)] m(f) linguist.
Linguistik f linguistics sing.
Linie ['liːniə] f line; **in erster ~** first and foremost; **auf die ~ achten** to watch one's figure; **fahren Sie mit der ~ 2** take the number 2 (bus etc).
Linien- zW: **~blatt** nt ruled sheet; **~bus** m service bus; **~flug** m scheduled flight; **~richter** m (SPORT) linesman; **l~treu** adj loyal to the (party) line.
liniieren [lini'iːrən] vt to line.
Linke ['lɪŋkə] (-, -n) f left side; left hand; (POL) left.
Linke(r) f(m) (POL) left-winger, leftie (pej).
linke(r, s) adj left; **~ Masche** purl; **das mache ich mit der ~n Hand** (umg) I can do that with my eyes shut.
linkisch adj awkward, gauche.
links adv left; to the left; **~ von mir** on od to my left; **~ von der Mitte** left of centre; **jdn ~ liegenlassen** (fig: umg) to ignore sb; **L~abbieger** m motorist/vehicle turning left; **L~außen** (-s, -) m (SPORT) outside left; **L~händer(in)** (-s, -) m(f) left-handed person; **L~kurve** f left-hand bend; **~lastig** adj: **~lastig sein** to list od lean to the left; **~radikal** adj (POL) radically left-wing; **L~rutsch** m (POL) swing to the left; **L~steuerung** f (AUT) left-hand drive; **L~verkehr** m driving on the left.
Linoleum [li'noːleum] (-s) nt lino(leum).
Linse ['lɪnzə] (-, -n) f lentil; (optisch) lens.
linsen (umg) vi to peak.
Lippe ['lɪpə] (-, -n) f lip.
Lippenbekenntnis nt lip service.
Lippenstift m lipstick.
Liquidation [likvidatsi'oːn] f liquidation.
Liquidationswert m break-up value.
Liquidator [likvi'daːtor] m liquidator.
liquid(e) [lik'viːt, lik'viːdə] adj (Firma) solvent.
liquidieren [likvi'diːrən] vt to liquidate.

Liquidität [likvidi'tɛːt] f liquidity.
lispeln ['lɪspəln] vi to lisp.
Lissabon ['lɪsabɔn] nt Lisbon.
List [lɪst] (-, -en) f cunning; (Plan) trick, ruse; **mit ~ und Tücke** (umg) with a lot of coaxing.
Liste ['lɪstə] (-, -n) f list.
Listenplatz m (POL) place on the party list.
Listenpreis m list price.
listig adj cunning, sly.
Litanei [lita'naɪ] f litany.
Litauen ['liːtauən] (-s) nt Lithuania.
Litauer(in) (-s, -) m(f) Lithuanian.
litauisch adj Lithuanian.
Liter ['liːtər] (-s, -) m od nt litre (BRIT), liter (US).
literarisch [lɪte'raːrɪʃ] adj literary.
Literatur [lɪtera'tuːr] f literature; **~preis** m award od prize for literature; **~wissenschaft** f literary studies pl.
literweise ['liːtərvaɪzə] adv (lit) by the litre (BRIT) od liter (US); (fig) by the gallon.
Litfaßsäule ['lɪtfaszɔylə] f advertising (BRIT) od advertizing (US) pillar.
Lithographie [litogra'fiː] f lithography.
litt etc [lɪt] vb siehe **leiden**.
Liturgie [litur'giː] f liturgy.
liturgisch [li'turgɪʃ] adj liturgical.
Litze ['lɪtsə] (-, -n) f braid; (ELEK) flex.
live [laɪf] adj, adv (RUNDF, TV) live.
Livree [li'vreː] (-, -n) f livery.
Lizenz [li'tsɛnts] f licence (BRIT), license (US); **~ausgabe** f licensed edition; **~gebühr** f licence fee; (im Verlagswesen) royalty.
LKW, Lkw (-(s), -(s)) m abk = **Lastkraftwagen**.
l.M. abk (= laufenden Monats) inst.
Lob [loːp] (-(e)s) nt praise.
Lobby ['lɔbi] (-, -s od **Lobbies**) f lobby.
loben ['loːbən] vt to praise; **das lob ich mir** that's what I like to see/hear etc).
lobenswert adj praiseworthy.
löblich ['løːplɪç] adj praiseworthy, laudable.
Loblied nt: **ein ~ auf jdn/etw singen** to sing sb's/sth's praises.
Lobrede f eulogy.
Loch [lɔx] (-(e)s, ⁻er) nt hole; **l~en** vt to punch holes in; **~er** (-s, -) m punch.
löcherig ['lœçərɪç] adj full of holes.
löchern (umg) vt: **jdn ~** to pester sb with questions.
Loch- zW: **~karte** f punch card; **~streifen** m punch tape; **~zange** f punch.
Locke ['lɔkə] (-, -n) f lock, curl.
locken vt to entice; (Haare) to curl.
lockend adj tempting.
Lockenwickler (-s, -) m curler.
locker ['lɔkər] adj loose; (Kuchen, Schaum) light; (umg) cool; **~lassen** unreg vi: **nicht ~lassen** not to let up.
lockern vt to loosen ♦ vr (Atmosphäre) to get more relaxed.
Lockerungsübung f loosening-up exercise;

(*zur Warmwerden*) limbering-up exercise.
lockig ['lɔkɪç] *adj* curly.
Lockmittel *nt* lure.
Lockruf *m* call.
Lockung *f* enticement.
Lockvogel *m* decoy, bait; **~angebot** *nt* (*COMM*) loss leader.
Lodenmantel ['lo:dənmantəl] *m* thick woollen coat.
lodern ['lo:dərn] *vi* to blaze.
Löffel ['lœfəl] (**-s, -**) *m* spoon.
löffeln *vt* to spoon.
löffelweise *adv* by the spoonful.
log *etc* [lo:k] *vb siehe* **lügen.**
Logarithmentafel [loga'rɪtmənta:fəl] *f* log(arithm) tables *pl.*
Logarithmus [loga'rɪtmʊs] *m* logarithm.
Loge ['lo:ʒə] (**-, -n**) *f* (*THEAT*) box; (*Freimaurer~*) (masonic) lodge; (*Pförtner~*) office.
logieren [lo'ʒi:rən] *vi* to lodge, stay.
Logik ['lo:gɪk] *f* logic.
Logis [lo'ʒi:] (**-, -**) *nt:* **Kost und ~** board and lodging.
logisch ['lo:gɪʃ] *adj* logical; (*umg: selbstverständlich*): **gehst du auch hin? - ~** are you going too? - of course.
logo ['logo] (*umg*) *interj* obvious!
Logopäde [logo'pɛ:də] (**-n, -n**) *m* speech therapist.
Logopädin [logo'pɛ:dɪn] *f* speech therapist.
Lohn [lo:n] (**-(e)s, ̈-e**) *m* reward; (*Arbeits~*) pay, wages *pl*; **~abrechnung** *f* wages slip; **~ausfall** *m* loss of earnings; **~büro** *nt* wages office; **~diktat** *nt* wage dictate; **~empfänger** *m* wage earner.
lohnen ['lo:nən] *vt* (*liter*): **jdm etw ~** to reward sb for sth ♦ *vr unpers* to be worth it.
lohnend *adj* worthwhile.
Lohn- *zW:* **~erhöhung** *f* wage increase, pay rise; **~forderung** *f* wage claim; **~fortzahlung** *f* continued payment of wages; **~fortzahlungsgesetz** *nt law on continued payment of wages*; **~gefälle** *nt* wage differential; **~kosten** *pl* labour (*BRIT*) *od* labor (*US*) costs; **~politik** *f* wages policy; **~runde** *f* pay round; **~steuer** *f* income tax; **~steuerjahresausgleich** *m* income tax return; **~steuerkarte** *f* (income) tax card; **~stopp** *m* pay freeze; **~streifen** *m* pay slip; **~tüte** *f* pay packet.
Lok [lɔk] (**-, -s**) *f abk* (= *Lokomotive*) loco (*umg*).
lokal [lo'ka:l] *adj* local.
Lokal (**-(e)s, -e**) *nt* pub(lic house) (*BRIT*).
Lokalblatt (*umg*) *nt* local paper.
lokalisieren [loka:li'zi:rən] *vt* to localize.
Lokalisierung *f* localization.
Lokalität [lokali'tɛ:t] *f* locality; (*Raum*) premises *pl.*
Lokal- *zW:* **~presse** *f* local press; **~teil** *m* (*Zeitung*) local section; **~termin** *m* (*JUR*)

visit to the scene of the crime.
Lokomotive [lokomo'ti:və] (**-, -n**) *f* locomotive.
Lokomotivführer *m* engine driver (*BRIT*), engineer (*US*).
Lombardei [lɔmbar'daɪ] *f* Lombardy.
London ['lɔndɔn] (**-s**) *nt* London.
Londoner *adj attrib* London.
Londoner(in) (**-s, -**) *m(f)* Londoner.
Lorbeer ['lɔrbe:r] (**-s, -en**) *m* (*lit, fig*) laurel; **~blatt** *nt* (*KOCH*) bay leaf.
Lore ['lo:rə] (**-, -n**) *f* (*MIN*) truck.
Los [lo:s] (**-es, -e**) *nt* (*Schicksal*) lot, fate; (*in der Lotterie*) lottery ticket; **das große ~ ziehen** (*lit, fig*) to hit the jackpot; **etw durch das ~ entscheiden** to decide sth by drawing lots.
los *adj* loose ♦ *adv:* **~!** go on!; **etw ~ sein** to be rid of sth; **was ist ~?** what's the matter?; **dort ist nichts/viel ~** there's nothing/a lot going on there; **ich bin mein ganzes Geld ~** (*umg*) I'm cleaned out; **irgendwas ist mit ihm ~** there's something wrong with him; **wir wollen früh ~** we want to be off early; **nichts wie ~!** let's get going; **~binden** *unreg vt* to untie; **~brechen** *unreg vi* (*Sturm, Gewitter*) to break.
losch *etc* [lɔʃ] *vb siehe* **löschen.**
Löschblatt ['lœʃblat] *nt* sheet of blotting paper.
löschen ['lœʃən] *vt* (*Feuer, Licht*) to put out, extinguish; (*Durst*) to quench; (*COMM*) to cancel; (*Tonband*) to erase; (*Fracht*) to unload; (*COMPUT*) to delete; (*Tinte*) to blot ♦ *vi* (*Feuerwehr*) to put out a fire; (*Papier*) to blot.
Lösch- *zW:* **~fahrzeug** *nt* fire engine; **~gerät** *nt* fire extinguisher; **~papier** *nt* blotting paper; **~taste** *f* (*COMPUT*) delete key.
Löschung *f* extinguishing; (*COMM*) cancellation; (*Fracht*) unloading.
lose ['lo:zə] *adj* loose.
Lösegeld *nt* ransom.
losen ['lo:zən] *vi* to draw lots.
lösen ['lø:zən] *vt* to loosen; (*Handbremse*) to release; (*Husten, Krampf*) to ease; (*Rätsel etc*) to solve; (*Verlobung*) to call off; (*CHEM*) to dissolve; (*Partnerschaft*) to break up; (*Fahrkarte*) to buy ♦ *vr* (*aufgehen*) to come loose; (*Schuß*) to go off; (*Zucker etc*) to dissolve; (*Problem, Schwierigkeit*) to (re)solve itself.
los- *zW:* **~fahren** *unreg vi* to leave; **~gehen** *unreg vi* to set out; (*anfangen*) to start; (*Bombe*) to go off; **jetzt geht's ~!** here we go!; **nach hinten ~gehen** (*umg*) to backfire; **auf jdn ~gehen** to go for sb; **~kaufen** *vt* (*Gefangene, Geiseln*) to pay ransom for; **~kommen** *unreg vi* (*sich befreien*) to free o.s.; **von etw ~kommen** to get away from sth; **~lassen** *unreg vt* (*Seil etc*) to let go of; **der Gedanke läßt mich nicht mehr ~** the thought haunts

me; ~**laufen** *unreg vi* to run off; ~**legen** (*umg*) *vi*: **nun leg mal** ~ **und erzähl(e) ...** now come on and tell me/us ...
löslich ['lø:slıç] *adj* soluble; **L~keit** *f* solubility.
loslösen *vt* to free ♦ *vr*: **sich (von etw)** ~ to detach o.s. (from sth).
losmachen *vt* to loosen; (*Boot*) to unmoor ♦ *vr* to get free.
Losnummer *f* ticket number.
los- *zW*: ~**sagen** *vr*: **sich von jdm/etw** ~**sagen** to renounce sb/sth; ~**schießen** *unreg vi*: **schieß** ~! (*fig: umg*) fire away!; ~**schrauben** *vt* to unscrew; ~**sprechen** *unreg vt* to absolve; ~**stürzen** *vi*: **auf jdn/etw** ~**stürzen** to pounce on sb/sth.
Losung ['lo:zʊŋ] *f* watchword, slogan.
Lösung ['lø:zʊŋ] *f* (*Lockermachen*) loosening; (*eines Rätsels, CHEM*) solution.
Lösungsmittel *nt* solvent.
loswerden *unreg vt* to get rid of.
losziehen *unreg vi* (*sich aufmachen*) to set out; **gegen jdn** ~ (*fig*) to run sb down.
Lot [lo:t] (**-(e)s, -e**) *nt* plumbline; (*MATH*) perpendicular; **im** ~ vertical; (*fig*) on an even keel; **die Sache ist wieder im** ~ things have been straightened out; **l~en** *vt* to plumb, sound.
löten ['lø:tən] *vt* to solder.
Lothringen ['lo:trıŋən] (**-s**) *nt* Lorraine.
Lötkolben *m* soldering iron.
Lotse ['lo:tsə] (**-n, -n**) *m* pilot; (*AVIAT*) air traffic controller.
lotsen *vt* to pilot; (*umg*) to lure.
Lotterie [lɔtə'ri:] *f* lottery.
Lotterleben ['lɔtərle:bən] (*umg*) *nt* dissolute life.
Lotto ['lɔto] (**-s, -s**) *nt* ≈ National Lottery.
Lottozahlen *pl* winning Lotto numbers *pl*.
Löwe ['lø:və] (**-n, -n**) *m* lion; (*ASTROL*) Leo.
Löwen- *zW*: ~**anteil** *m* lion's share; ~**maul** *nt*, ~**mäulchen** *nt* antirrhinum, snapdragon; ~**zahn** *m* dandelion.
Löwin ['lø:vın] *f* lioness.
loyal [loa'ja:l] *adj* loyal.
Loyalität [loajali'tɛ:t] *f* loyalty.
LP (**-, -s**) *f abk* (= *Langspielplatte*) LP.
LSD (**-(s)**) *nt abk* (= *Lysergsäurediäthylamid*) LSD.
lt. *abk* = **laut**.
Luchs [lʊks] (**-es, -e**) *m* lynx.
Lücke ['lʏkə] (**-, -n**) *f* gap; (*Gesetzes~*) loophole; (*in Versorgung*) break.
Lücken- *zW*: ~**büßer** (**-s, -**) *m* stopgap; **l~haft** *adj* full of gaps; (*Versorgung*) deficient; **l~los** *adj* complete.
lud *etc* [lu:t] *vb siehe* **laden**.
Luder ['lu:dər] (**-s, -**) (*pej*) *nt* (*Frau*) hussy; (*bedauernswert*) poor wretch.
Luft [lʊft] (**-, ̈-e**) *f*; (*Atem*) breath; **die** ~ **anhalten** (*lit*) to hold one's breath; **seinem Herzen** ~ **machen** to get everything off

one's chest; **in der** ~ **liegen** to be in the air; **dicke** ~ (*umg*) a bad atmosphere; (**frische**) ~ **schnappen** (*umg*) to get some fresh air; **in die** ~ **fliegen** (*umg*) to explode; **diese Behauptung ist aus der** ~ **gegriffen** this statement is (a) pure invention; **die** ~ **ist rein** (*umg*) the coast is clear; **jdn an die** (**frische**) ~ **setzen** (*umg*) to show sb the door; **er ist** ~ **für mich** I'm not speaking to him; **jdn wie** ~ **behandeln** to ignore sb; ~**angriff** *m* air raid; ~**aufnahme** *f* aerial photo; ~**ballon** *m* balloon; ~**blase** *f* air bubble; ~**brücke** *f* airlift; **l~dicht** *adj* airtight; ~**druck** *m* atmospheric pressure; **l~durchlässig** *adj* pervious to air.
lüften ['lʏftən] *vt* to air; (*Hut*) to lift, raise ♦ *vi* to let some air in.
Luft- *zW*: ~**fahrt** *f* aviation; ~**feuchtigkeit** *f* humidity; ~**fracht** *f* air cargo; **l~gekühlt** *adj* air-cooled; ~**gewehr** *nt* air rifle.
luftig *adj* (*Ort*) breezy; (*Raum*) airy; (*Kleider*) summery.
Luft- *zW*: ~**kissenfahrzeug** *nt* hovercraft; ~**krieg** *m* war in the air, aerial warfare; ~**kurort** *m* health resort; **l~leer** *adj*: **l~leerer Raum** vacuum; ~**linie** *f*: **in der** ~**linie** as the crow flies; ~**loch** *nt* air hole; (*AVIAT*) air pocket; ~**matratze** *f* Lilo ® (*BRIT*), air mattress; ~**pirat** *m* hijacker; ~**post** *f* airmail; ~**pumpe** *f* (*für Fahrrad*) (bicycle) pump; ~**raum** *m* air space; ~**röhre** *f* (*ANAT*) windpipe; ~**schlange** *f* streamer; ~**schloß** *nt* (*fig*) castle in the air; ~**schutz** *m* anti-aircraft defence (*BRIT*) *od* defense (*US*); ~**schutzbunker** *m*, ~**schutzkeller** *m* air-raid shelter; ~**sprung** *m* (*fig*): **einen** ~**sprung machen** to jump for joy.
Lüftung ['lʏftʊŋ] *f* ventilation.
Luft- *zW*: ~**veränderung** *f* change of air; ~**verkehr** *m* air traffic; ~**verschmutzung** *f* air pollution; ~**waffe** *f* air force; ~**weg** *m*: **etw auf dem** ~**weg befördern** to transport sth by air; ~**zufuhr** *f* air supply; ~**zug** *m* draught (*BRIT*), draft (*US*).
Lüge ['ly:gə] (**-, -n**) *f* lie; **jdn/etw** ~**n strafen** to give the lie to sb/sth.
lügen ['ly:gən] *unreg vi* to lie; **wie gedruckt** ~ (*umg*) to lie like mad.
Lügendetektor ['ly:gəndetɛktɔr] *m* lie detector.
Lügner(in) (**-s, -**) *m(f)* liar.
Luke ['lu:kə] (**-, -n**) *f* hatch; (*Dach~*) skylight.
lukrativ [lukra'ti:f] *adj* lucrative.
Lümmel ['lʏməl] (**-s, -**) *m* lout.
lümmeln *vr* to lounge (about).
Lump [lʊmp] (**-en, -en**) *m* scamp, rascal.
lumpen ['lʊmpən] *vt*: **sich nicht** ~ **lassen** not to be mean.
Lumpen (**-s, -**) *m* rag.
Lumpensammler *m* rag and bone man.
lumpig ['lʊmpıç] *adj* shabby; ~**e 10 Mark** (*umg*) 10 measly marks.

Lüneburger Heide ['lyːnəbʊrgər 'haɪdə] *f*
Lüneburg Heath.
Lunge ['lʊŋə] (-, -n) *f* lung.
Lungen- *zW:* ~**entzündung** *f* pneumonia;
l~krank *adj* suffering from a lung disease;
~**krankheit** *f* lung disease.
lungern ['lʊŋərn] *vi* to hang about.
Lunte ['lʊntə] (-, -n) *f* fuse; ~ **riechen** to smell
a rat.
Lupe ['luːpə] (-, -n) *f* magnifying glass; **unter**
die ~ nehmen (*fig*) to scrutinize.
lupenrein *adj* (*lit: Edelstein*) flawless.
Lupine [lu'piːnə] *f* lupin.
Lurch [lʊrç] (-(e)s, -e) *m* amphibian.
Lust [lʊst] (-, -e) *f* joy, delight; (*Neigung*)
desire; (*sexuell*) lust (*pej*); ~ **haben zu** *od* **auf**
etw *akk*/**etw zu tun** to feel like sth/doing
sth; **hast du ~?** how about it?; **er hat die**
~ daran verloren he has lost all interest in
it; **je nach ~ und Laune** just depending on
how I *od* you *etc* feel; **l~betont** *adj* pleasure-
orientated.
lüstern ['lʏstərn] *adj* lustful, lecherous.
Lustgefühl *nt* pleasurable feeling.
Lustgewinn *m* pleasure.
lustig ['lʊstɪç] *adj* (*komisch*) amusing, funny;
(*fröhlich*) cheerful; **sich über jdn/etw**
~ machen to make fun of sb/sth.
Lüstling *m* lecher.
Lust- *zW:* **l~los** *adj* unenthusiastic; ~**mord** *m*
sex(ual) murder; ~**prinzip** *nt* (*PSYCH*)
pleasure principle; ~**spiel** *nt* comedy;
l~wandeln *vi* to stroll about.
luth. *abk* =**lutherisch**
Lutheraner(in) [lʊtə'raːnər(ɪn)] *m(f)* Lutheran.
lutherisch ['lʊtərɪʃ] *adj* Lutheran.
lutschen ['lʊtʃən] *vt, vi* to suck; **am Daumen ~**
to suck one's thumb.
Lutscher (-s, -) *m* lollipop.
Luxemburg ['lʊksəmbʊrk] (-s) *nt*
Luxembourg.
Luxemburger(in) ['lʊksəmbʊrgər(ɪn)] (-s, -)
m(f) citizen of Luxembourg, Luxembourger.
luxemburgisch *adj* Luxembourgian.
luxuriös [lʊksuri'øːs] *adj* luxurious.
Luxus ['lʊksʊs] (-) *m* luxury; ~**artikel** *pl* luxury
goods *pl*; ~**ausführung** *f* de luxe model;
~**dampfer** *m* luxury cruise ship; ~**hotel** *nt*
luxury hotel; ~**steuer** *f* tax on luxuries.
LVA (-) *f abk* (= *Landesversicherungsanstalt*)
county insurance company.
LW *abk* (= *Langwelle*) LW.
Lycra ['lyːkra] (-(s)) *no pl nt* Lycra ®.
Lymphe ['lʏmfə] (-, -n) *f* lymph.
Lymphknoten *m* lymph(atic) gland.
lynchen ['lʏnçən] *vt* to lynch.
Lynchjustiz *f* lynch law.
Lyrik ['lyːrɪk] *f* lyric poetry; ~**er(in)** (-s, -) *m(f)*
lyric poet.
lyrisch ['lyːrɪʃ] *adj* lyrical.

M, m

M, m¹ [ɛm] *nt* M, m; ~ **wie Martha** ≈ M for
Mary, M for Mike (*US*).
m² *abk* (= *Meter*) m; (=*männlich*) m.
M. *abk* = *Monat.*
MA. *abk* = **Mittelalter.**
Maat [maːt] (-s, -e *od* -en) *m* (*NAUT*) (ship's)
mate.
Machart *f* make.
machbar *adj* feasible.
Mache (-) (*umg*) *f* show, sham; **jdn in der**
~ haben to be having a go at sb.

machen ['maxən] *vt* **1** to do; **was machst du**
da? what are you doing there?; **das ist nicht**
zu ~ that can't be done; **was ~ Sie**
(beruflich)? what do you do for a living?;
mach, daß du hier verschwindest! (you just)
get out of here!; **mit mir kann man's ja ~!**
(*umg*) the things I put up with!; **das läßt er**
nicht mit sich ~ he won't stand for that;
eine Prüfung ~ to take an exam
2 (*herstellen*) to make; **das Radio leiser ~** to
turn the radio down; **aus Holz gemacht**
made of wood; **das Essen ~** to get the meal;
Schluß ~ to finish (off)
3 (*verursachen: bewirken*) to make; **jdm Angst**
~ to make sb afraid; **das macht die Kälte** it's
the cold that does that
4 (*aus~*) to matter; **das macht nichts** that
doesn't matter; **die Kälte macht mir nichts** I
don't mind the cold
5 (*kosten: ergeben*) to be; **3 und 5 macht 8** 3
and 5 is *od* are 8; **was** *od* **wieviel macht das?**
how much does that come to?
6: was macht die Arbeit? how's the work
going?; **was macht dein Bruder?** how is your
brother doing?; **das Auto ~ lassen** to have
the car done; **mach's gut!** take care!; (*viel*
Glück) good luck!
♦ *vi:* **mach schnell!** hurry up!; **mach schon!**
come on!; **jetzt macht sie auf große Dame**
(*umg*) she's playing the lady now; **laß mich**
mal ~ (*umg*) let me do it; (*ich bringe das in*
Ordnung) I'll deal with it; **groß/klein ~** (*umg:*
Notdurft) to do a big/little job; **sich** *dat* **in die**
Hose ~ to wet o.s.; **ins Bett ~** to wet one's
bed; **das macht müde** it makes you tired; **in**
etw *dat* **~** to be *od* deal in sth
♦ *vr* to come along (nicely); **sich an etw** *akk*
~ to set about sth; **sich verständlich ~** to
make o.s. understood; **sich** *dat* **viel aus jdm/**

etw ~ to like sb/sth; **mach dir nichts daraus** don't let it bother you; **sich auf den Weg ~** to get going; **sich an etw** akk ~ to set about sth.

Machenschaften pl wheelings and dealings pl.

Macher (-s, -) (umg) m man of action.

macho ['matʃo] (umg) adj macho.

Macho (-s, -s) (umg) m macho type.

Macht [maxt] **(-, ⁻e)** f power; **mit aller ~** with all one's might; **an der ~ sein** to be in power; **alles in unserer ~ Stehende** everything in our power; **~ergreifung** f seizure of power; **~haber (-s, -)** m ruler.

mächtig ['mɛçtɪç] adj powerful, mighty; (umg: ungeheuer) enormous.

Macht- zW: **m~los** adj powerless; **~probe** f trial of strength; **~stellung** f position of power; **~wort** nt: **ein ~wort sprechen** to lay down the law.

Machwerk nt work; (schlechte Arbeit) botched-up job.

Macke ['makə] **(-, -n)** (umg) f (Tick, Knall) quirk; (Fehler) fault.

Macker (-s, -) (umg) m fellow, guy.

MAD (-) m abk (= Militärischer Abschirmdienst) ≈ MI5 (BRIT), CIA (US).

Madagaskar [mada'gaskar] **(-s)** nt Madagascar.

Mädchen ['mɛːtçən] nt girl; **ein ~ für alles** (umg) a dogsbody; (im Büro etc) a girl Friday; **m~haft** adj girlish; **~name** m maiden name.

Made ['maːdə] **(-, -n)** f maggot.

Madeira¹ [ma'deːra] **(-s)** nt (GEOG) Madeira.

Madeira² (-s, -s) m (Wein) Madeira.

Mädel ['mɛːdl] **(-s, -(s))** nt (Dialekt) lass, girl.

madig ['maːdɪç] adj maggoty; **jdm etw ~ machen** to spoil sth for sb.

Madrid [ma'drɪt] **(-s)** nt Madrid.

mag [maːk] vb siehe **mögen.**

Mag. abk = **Magister.**

Magazin [maga'tsiːn] **(-s, -e)** nt (Zeitschrift, am Gewehr) magazine; (Lager) storeroom; (Bibliotheks~) stockroom.

Magd [maːkt] **(-, ⁻e)** f maid(servant).

Magen ['maːgən] **(-s, - od ⁻)** m stomach; **jdm auf den ~ schlagen** (umg) to upset sb's stomach; (fig) to upset sb; **sich** dat **den ~ verderben** to upset one's stomach; **~bitter** m bitters pl; **~geschwür** nt stomach ulcer; **~schmerzen** pl stomach-ache sing; **~verstimmung** f stomach upset.

mager ['maːgər] adj lean; (dünn) thin; **M~keit** f leanness; thinness; **M~milch** f skimmed milk; **M~quark** m low-fat soft cheese; **M~sucht** f (MED) anorexia; **~süchtig** adj anorexic.

Magie [ma'giː] f magic.

Magier ['maːgiər] **(-s, -)** m magician.

magisch ['maːgɪʃ] adj magical.

Magister [ma'gɪstər] **(-s, -)** m (UNIV) M.A., Master of Arts.

Magistrat [magɪs'traːt] **(-(e)s, -e)** m municipal authorities pl.

Magnat [ma'gnaːt] **(-en, -en)** m magnate.

Magnet [ma'gneːt] **(-s od -en, -en)** m magnet; **~bahn** f magnetic railway; **~band** nt (COMPUT) magnetic tape; **m~isch** adj magnetic.

magnetisieren [magneti'ziːrən] vt to magnetize.

Magnetnadel f magnetic needle.

Magnettafel f magnetic board.

Mahagoni [maha'goːni] **(-s)** nt mahogany.

Mähdrescher (-s, -) m combine (harvester).

mähen ['mɛːən] vt, vi to mow.

Mahl [maːl] **(-(e)s, -e)** nt meal.

mahlen unreg vt to grind.

Mahlstein m grindstone.

Mahlzeit f meal ♦ interj enjoy your meal!

Mahnbrief m reminder.

Mähne ['mɛːnə] **(-, -n)** f mane.

mahnen ['maːnən] vt to remind; (warnend) to warn; (wegen Schuld) to demand payment from; **jdn zur Eile/Geduld** etc ~ (auffordern) to urge sb to hurry/be patient etc.

Mahn- zW: **~gebühr** f reminder fee; **~mal** nt memorial; **~schreiben** nt reminder.

Mahnung f admonition, warning; (Mahnbrief) reminder.

Mähre ['mɛːra] **(-, -n)** f mare.

Mähren ['mɛːrən] **(-s)** nt Moravia.

Mai [mai] **(-(e)s, -e)** (pl selten) m May; siehe auch September; **~baum** m maypole; **~bowle** f white wine punch (flavoured with woodruff); **~glöckchen** nt lily of the valley; **~käfer** m cockchafer.

Mailand ['mailant] **(-s)** nt Milan.

Main [main] **(-(e)s)** m (Fluß) Main.

Mais [mais] **(-es, -e)** m maize, corn (US); **~kolben** m corncob.

Majestät [majɛs'tɛːt] f majesty.

majestätisch adj majestic.

Majestätsbeleidigung f lese-majesty.

Major [ma'joːr] **(-s, -e)** m (MIL) major; (AVIAT) squadron leader.

Majoran [majo'raːn] **(-s, -e)** m marjoram.

makaber [ma'kaːbər] adj macabre.

Makedonien [make'doːniən] **(-s)** nt Macedonia.

makedonisch adj Macedonian.

Makel ['maːkəl] **(-s, -)** m blemish; (moralisch) stain; **ohne ~** flawless; **m~los** adj immaculate, spotless.

mäkeln ['mɛːkəln] vi to find fault.

Make-up [meːk'ʔap] **(-s, -s)** nt make-up; (flüssig) foundation.

Makkaroni [maka'roːni] pl macaroni sing.

Makler ['maːklər] **(-s, -)** m broker; (Grundstücks~) estate agent (BRIT), realtor (US); **~gebühr** f broker's commission, brokerage.

Makrele [ma'kre:lə] (-, -n) f mackerel.
Makro- in zW macro-.
Makrone [ma'kro:nə] (-, -n) f macaroon.
Makroökonomie f macroeconomics sing.
Mal [ma:l] (-(e)s, -e) nt mark, sign; (Zeitpunkt) time; **ein für alle** ~ once and for all; **mit einem** ~(e) all of a sudden.
mal adv times.
-mal suff -times.
Malaie [ma'laɪə] (-n, -n) m, **Malaiin** f Malay.
malaiisch adj Malayan.
Malawi [ma'la:vi] (-s) nt Malawi.
Malaysia [ma'laɪzia] (-s) nt Malaysia.
Malaysier(in) (-s, -) m(f) Malaysian.
malaysisch adj Malaysian.
Malediven [male'di:vən] pl: **die** ~ the Maldive Islands.
malen vt, vi to paint.
Maler (-s, -) m painter.
Malerei [ma:lə'raɪ] f painting.
malerisch adj picturesque.
Malkasten m paintbox.
Mallorca [ma'lɔrka] (-s) nt Majorca.
Mallorquiner(in) [malɔr'ki:nər(ɪn)] (-s, -) m(f) Majorcan.
mallorquinisch adj Majorcan.
malnehmen unreg vt, vi to multiply.
Malta ['malta] (-s) nt Malta.
Malteser(in) [mal'te:zər(ɪn)] (-s, -) m(f) Maltese.
Malteser-Hilfsdienst m ≈ St. John's Ambulance Brigade (BRIT).
maltesisch adj Maltese.
malträtieren [maltrɛ'ti:rən] vt to ill-treat, maltreat.
Malz [malts] (-es) nt malt; ~**bonbon** nt or m cough drop; ~**kaffee** m coffee substitute made from malt barley.
Mama ['mama:] (-, -s) (umg) f mum(my) (BRIT), mom(my) (US).
Mami ['mami] (-, -s) f = **Mama**.
Mammographie [mamɔgra'fi:] f (MED) mammography.
Mammut ['mamʊt] (-s, -e od -s) nt mammoth ♦ in zW mammoth, giant; ~**anlagen** pl (INDUSTRIE) mammoth plants.
mampfen ['mampfən] (umg) vt, vi to munch, chomp.
man [man] pron one, you, people pl; ~ **hat mir gesagt** ... I was told ...
managen ['mɛnɪdʒən] vt to manage; **ich manage das schon!** (umg) I'll fix it somehow!
Manager(in) (-s, -) m(f) manager.
manch [manç] pron: ~ **ein(e)** ... many a ...; ~ **eine(r)** many a person.
manche(r, s) adj many a; (pl) a number of ♦ pron some.
mancherlei [mançər'laɪ] adj inv various ♦ pron a variety of things.
manchmal adv sometimes.
Mandant(in) [man'dant(ɪn)] m(f) (JUR) client.

Mandarine [manda'ri:nə] f mandarin, tangerine.
Mandat [man'da:t] (-(e)s, -e) nt mandate; **sein** ~ **niederlegen** (PARL) to resign one's seat.
Mandel ['mandəl] (-, -n) f almond; (ANAT) tonsil; ~**entzündung** f tonsillitis.
Mandschurei (-) [mandʒu'raɪ] f: **die** ~ Manchuria.
Manege [ma'nɛ:ʒə] (-, -n) f ring, arena.
Mangel¹ ['maŋəl] (-, -n) f mangle; **durch die** ~ **drehen** (fig: umg) to put through it; (Prüfling etc) to put through the mill.
Mangel² ['maŋəl] (-s, ⁺) m lack; (Knappheit) shortage; (Fehler) defect, fault; ~ **an** +dat shortage of.
Mängelbericht ['mɛŋəlbərɪçt] m list of faults.
Mangelerscheinung f deficiency symptom.
mangelhaft adj poor; (fehlerhaft) defective, faulty; (Schulnote) unsatisfactory.
mangeln vi unpers: **es mangelt jdm an etw** dat sb lacks sth ♦ vt (Wäsche) to mangle.
mangels präp +gen for lack of.
Mangelware f scarce commodity.
Manie [ma'ni:] f mania.
Manier [ma'ni:r] (-) f manner; (Stil) style; (pej) mannerism.
Manieren pl manners pl; (pej) mannerisms pl.
manieriert [mani'ri:rt] adj mannered, affected.
manierlich adj well-mannered.
Manifest [mani'fɛst] (-es, -e) nt manifesto.
Maniküre [mani'ky:rə] (-, -n) f manicure.
maniküren vt to manicure.
Manipulation [manipulatsi'o:n] f manipulation; (Trick) manoeuvre (BRIT), maneuver (US).
manipulieren [manipu'li:rən] vt to manipulate.
Manko ['maŋko] (-s, -s) nt deficiency; (COMM) deficit.
Mann [man] (-(e)s, ⁺er od (NAUT) **Leute**) m man; (Ehe~) husband; (NAUT) hand; **pro** ~ per head; **mit** ~ **und Maus untergehen** to go down with all hands; (Passagierschiff) to go down with no survivors; **seinen** ~ **stehen** to hold one's own; **etw an den** ~ **bringen** (umg) to get rid of sth; **einen kleinen** ~ **im Ohr haben** (hum: umg) to be crazy.
Männchen ['mɛnçən] nt little man; (Tier) male; ~ **machen** (Hund) to (sit up and) beg.
Mannequin [manə'kɛ:] (-s, -s) nt fashion model.
Männersache ['mɛnərzaxə] f (Angelegenheit) man's business; (Arbeit) man's job.
mannigfaltig ['manɪçfaltɪç] adj various, varied; **M~keit** f variety.
männlich ['mɛnlɪç] adj (BIOL) male; (fig, GRAM) masculine.
Mannsbild nt (veraltet: pej) fellow.
Mannschaft f (SPORT, fig) team; (NAUT, AVIAT) crew; (MIL) other ranks pl.
Mannschaftsgeist m team spirit.
Mannsleute (umg) pl menfolk pl.

Mannweib (*pej*) *nt* mannish woman.
Manometer [mano'me:tər] *nt* (*TECH*) pressure gauge; ~! (*umg*) wow!
Manöver [ma'nø:vər] (-s, -) *nt* manoeuvre (*BRIT*), maneuver (*US*).
manövrieren [manø'vri:rən] *vt, vi* to manoeuvre (*BRIT*), maneuver (*US*).
Mansarde [man'zardə] (-, -n) *f* attic.
Manschette [man'ʃɛtə] *f* cuff; (*Papier~*) paper frill; (*TECH*) sleeve.
Manschettenknopf *m* cufflink.
Mantel ['mantəl] (-s, ⁻) *m* coat; (*TECH*) casing, jacket; ~**tarif** *m* general terms of employment; ~**tarifvertrag** *m* general agreement on conditions of employment.
Manuskript [manu'skrɪpt] (-(e)s, -e) *nt* manuscript.
Mappe ['mapə] (-, -n) *f* briefcase; (*Akten~*) folder.
Marathonlauf ['ma:ratɔnlaʊf] *m* marathon.
Märchen ['mɛːrçən] *nt* fairy tale; **m~haft** *adj* fabulous; ~**prinz** *m* prince charming.
Marder ['mardər] (-s, -) *m* marten.
Margarine [marga'ri:nə] *f* margarine.
Marge ['marʒə] (-, -n) *f* (*COMM*) margin.
Maria [ma'ri:a] (-) *f* Mary.
Marienbild *nt* picture of the Virgin Mary.
Marienkäfer *m* ladybird.
Marihuana [marihu'a:na] (-s) *nt* marijuana.
Marinade [mari'na:də] (-, -n) *f* (*KOCH*) marinade; (*Soße*) mayonnaise-based sauce.
Marine [ma'ri:nə] *f* navy; **m~blau** *adj* navy-blue.
marinieren [mari'ni:rən] *vt* to marinate.
Marionette [mario'nɛtə] *f* puppet.
Mark¹ [mark] (-, -) *f* (*Geld*) mark.
Mark² [mark] (-(e)s) *nt* (*Knochen~*) marrow; **jdn bis ins ~ treffen** (*fig*) to cut sb to the quick; **jdm durch ~ und Bein gehen** to go right through sb.
markant [mar'kant] *adj* striking.
Marke ['markə] (-, -n) *f* mark; (*Warensorte*) brand; (*Fabrikat*) make; (*Rabatt~*, *Brief~*) stamp; (*Essen(s)~*) luncheon voucher; (*aus Metall etc*) token, disc.
Marken- *zW:* ~**artikel** *m* proprietary article; ~**butter** *f* best quality butter; ~**zeichen** *nt* trademark.
Marketing ['markətɪŋ] (-s) *nt* marketing.
markieren [mar'ki:rən] *vt* to mark; (*umg*) to act ♦ *vi* (*umg*) to act it.
Markierung *f* marking.
markig ['markɪç] *adj* (*fig*) pithy.
Markise [mar'ki:zə] (-, -n) *f* awning.
Markstück *nt* one-mark piece.
Markt [markt] (-(e)s, ⁻e) *m* market; ~**analyse** *f* market analysis; ~**anteil** *m* market share; **m~fähig** *adj* marketable; ~**forschung** *f* market research; **m~gängig** *adj* marketable; **m~gerecht** *adj* geared to market requirements; ~**lücke** *f* gap in the market; ~**platz** *m* market place; ~**preis** *m* market

price; ~**wert** *m* market value; ~**wirtschaft** *f* market economy; **m~wirtschaftlich** *adj* free enterprise.
Marmelade [marmə'la:də] (-, -n) *f* jam.
Marmor ['marmɔr] (-s, -e) *m* marble.
marmorieren [marmo'ri:rən] *vt* to marble.
Marmorkuchen *m* marble cake.
marmorn *adj* marble.
Marokkaner(in) [marɔ'ka:nər(ɪn)] (-s, -) *m(f)* Moroccan.
marokkanisch *adj* Moroccan.
Marokko [ma'rɔko] (-s) *nt* Morocco.
Marone [ma'ro:nə] (-, -n) *f* chestnut.
Marotte [ma'rɔtə] (-, -n) *f* fad, quirk.
Marsch¹ [marʃ] (-, -en) *f* marsh.
Marsch² (-(e)s, ⁻e) *m* march; **jdm den ~ blasen** (*umg*) to give sb a rocket ♦ **m~** *interj* march; **m~ ins Bett!** off to bed with you!
Marschbefehl *m* marching orders *pl*.
marschbereit *adj* ready to move.
marschieren [mar'ʃi:rən] *vi* to march.
Marschverpflegung *f* rations *pl*; (*MIL*) field rations *pl*.
Marseille [mar'sɛːj] (-s) *nt* Marseilles.
Marsmensch ['marsmɛnʃ] *m* Martian.
Marter ['martər] (-, -n) *f* torment.
martern *vt* to torture.
Martinshorn ['martiːnshɔrn] *nt* siren (*of police etc*).
Märtyrer(in) ['mɛrtyrər(ɪn)] (-s, -) *m(f)* martyr.
Martyrium [mar'ty:riʊm] *nt* (*fig*) ordeal.
Marxismus [mar'ksɪsmʊs] *m* Marxism.
März [mɛrts] (-(es), -e) (*pl selten*) *m* March; *siehe auch* **September**.
Marzipan [martsi'pa:n] (-s, -e) *nt* marzipan.
Masche ['maʃə] (-, -n) *f* mesh; (*Strick~*) stitch; **das ist die neueste ~** that's the latest dodge; **durch die ~n schlüpfen** to slip through the net.
Maschendraht *m* wire mesh.
maschenfest *adj* runproof.
Maschine [ma'ʃi:nə] *f* machine; (*Motor*) engine.
maschinell [maʃi'nɛl] *adj* machine(-), mechanical.
Maschinen- *zW:* ~**ausfallzeit** *f* machine downtime; ~**bauer** *m* mechanical engineer; ~**führer** *m* machinist; **m~geschrieben** *adj* typewritten; ~**gewehr** *nt* machine gun; **m~lesbar** *adj* (*COMPUT*) machine-readable; ~**pistole** *f* submachine gun; ~**raum** *m* plant room; (*NAUT*) engine room; ~**saal** *m* machine shop; ~**schaden** *m* mechanical fault; ~**schlosser** *m* fitter; ~**schrift** *f* typescript; ~**sprache** *f* (*COMPUT*) machine language.
Maschinerie [maʃinə'ri:] *f* (*fig*) machinery.
maschineschreiben *unreg vi* to type.
Maschinist(in) [maʃi'nɪst(ɪn)] *m(f)* engineer.
Maser ['ma:zər] (-, -n) *f* grain.
Masern *pl* (*MED*) measles *sing*.

Maserung f grain(ing).
Maske ['maskə] (-, -n) f mask.
Maskenball m fancy-dress ball.
Maskenbildner(in) m(f) make-up artist.
Maskerade [maskə'raːdə] f masquerade.
maskieren [mas'kiːrən] vt to mask; (verkleiden) to dress up ♦ vr to disguise o.s., dress up.
Maskottchen [mas'kɔtçən] nt (lucky) mascot.
Maskulinum [masku'liːnum] (-s, **Maskulina**) nt (GRAM) masculine noun.
Masochist [mazɔ'xɪst] (-en, -en) m masochist.
Maß[1] [maːs] (-es, -e) nt measure; (Mäßigung) moderation; (Grad) degree, extent; **über alle ~en** (liter) extremely, beyond measure; **mit zweierlei ~ messen** (fig) to operate a double standard; **sich** dat **etw nach ~ anfertigen lassen** to have sth made to measure od order (US); **in besonderem ~e** especially; **das ~ ist voll** (fig) that's enough (of that).
Maß[2] (-, -(e)) f litre (BRIT) od liter (US) of beer.
maß etc vb siehe **messen**.
Massage [ma'saːʒə] (-, -n) f massage.
Massaker [ma'saːkər] (-s, -) nt massacre.
Maßanzug m made-to-measure suit.
Maßarbeit f (fig) neat piece of work.
Masse ['masə] (-, -n) f mass; **eine ganze ~** (umg) a great deal.
Maßeinheit f unit of measurement.
Massen- zW: **~artikel** m mass-produced article; **~blatt** nt tabloid; **~grab** nt mass grave; **m~haft** adj masses of; **~medien** pl mass media pl; **~produktion** f mass production; **~veranstaltung** f mass meeting; **~vernichtungswaffen** pl weapons of mass destruction od extermination; **~ware** f mass-produced article; **m~weise** adv in huge numbers.
Masseur [ma'søːr] m masseur.
Masseuse [ma'søːzə] f masseuse.
Maß- zW: **m~gebend** adj authoritative; **m~gebende Kreise** influential circles; **m~geblich** adj definitive; **m~geschneidert** adj (Anzug) made-to-measure, made-to-order (US), custom attrib (US); **m~halten** unreg vi to exercise moderation.
massieren [ma'siːrən] vt to massage; (MIL) to mass.
massig ['masɪç] adj massive; (umg) a massive amount of.
mäßig ['mɛːsɪç] adj moderate; **~en** ['mɛːsɪgən] vt to restrain, moderate; **sein Tempo ~en** to slacken one's pace; **M~keit** f moderation.
massiv [ma'siːf] adj solid; (fig) heavy, rough; **~ werden** (umg) to turn nasty; **M~ (-s, -e)** nt massif.
Maß- zW: **~krug** m tankard; **m~los** adj (Verschwendung, Essen, Trinken) excessive, immoderate; (Enttäuschung, Ärger etc) extreme; **~nahme** (-, -n) f measure, step; **m~regeln** vt untr to reprimand.
Maßstab m rule, measure; (fig) standard;

(GEOG) scale; **als ~ dienen** to serve as a model.
maßstab(s)getreu adj (true) to scale.
maßvoll adj moderate.
Mast [mast] (-(e)s, -e(n)) m mast; (ELEK) pylon.
Mastdarm m rectum.
mästen ['mɛstən] vt to fatten.
masturbieren [mastur'biːrən] vi to masturbate.
Material [materi'aːl] (-s, -ien) nt material(s); **~fehler** m material defect.
Materialismus [materia'lismus] m materialism.
Materialist(in) m(f) materialist; **m~isch** adj materialistic.
Materialkosten pl cost sing of materials.
Materialprüfung f material(s) control.
Materie [ma'teːriə] f matter, substance.
materiell [materi'ɛl] adj material.
Mathe ['matə] (-) f (SCH: umg) maths (BRIT), math (US).
Mathematik [matema'tiːk] f mathematics sing; **~er(in)** [mate'maːtɪkər(ɪn)] (-s, -) m(f) mathematician.
mathematisch [mate'maːtɪʃ] adj mathematical.
Matjeshering ['matjəsheːrɪŋ] (umg) m salted young herring.
Matratze [ma'tratsə] (-, -n) f mattress.
Matrixdrucker m dot-matrix printer.
Matrixzeichen nt matrix character.
Matrize [ma'triːtsə] (-, -n) f matrix; (zum Abziehen) stencil.
Matrose [ma'troːzə] (-n, -n) m sailor.
Matsch [matʃ] (-(e)s) m mud; (Schnee~) slush.
matschig adj muddy; slushy.
matt [mat] adj weak; (glanzlos) dull; (PHOT) matt; (SCHACH) mate; **jdn ~ setzen** (auch fig) to checkmate sb; **M~ (-s, -s)** nt (SCHACH) checkmate.
Matte ['matə] (-, -n) f mat; **auf der ~ stehen** (am Arbeitsplatz etc) to be in.
Mattigkeit f weakness; dullness.
Mattscheibe f (TV) screen; **~ haben** (umg) to be not quite with it.
Matura [ma'tuːra] (-) (ÖSTERR, SCHWEIZ) f = **Abitur**.
Mätzchen ['mɛtsçən] (umg) nt antics pl; **~ machen** to fool around.
mau [mau] (umg) adj poor, bad.
Mauer ['mauər] (-, -n) f wall; **~blümchen** (umg) nt (fig) wallflower.
mauern vi to build, lay bricks ♦ vt to build.
Mauer- zW: **~schwalbe** f swift; **~segler** m swift; **~werk** nt brickwork; (Stein) masonry.
Maul [maul] (-(e)s, **Mäuler**) nt mouth; **ein loses od lockeres ~ haben** (umg: frech sein) to be an impudent so-and-so; (: indiskret sein) to be a blabbermouth; **halt's ~!** (umg) shut your face (!); **darüber werden sich die Leute das ~ zerreißen** (umg) that will start people's tongues wagging; **dem Volk** od **den Leuten**

aufs ~ schauen (*umg*) to listen to what ordinary people say; **m~en** (*umg*) *vi* to grumble; **~esel** *m* mule; **~korb** *m* muzzle; **~sperre** *f* lockjaw; **~tier** *nt* mule; **~- und Klauenseuche** *f* (*Tiere*) foot-and-mouth disease.

Maulwurf *m* mole.

Maulwurfshaufen *m* molehill.

Maurer ['maʊrər] (**-s, -**) *m* bricklayer; **pünktlich wie die ~** (*hum*) super-punctual.

Mauretanien [maʊrə'taːniən] (**-s**) *nt* Mauritania.

Mauritius [maʊ'riːtsiʊs] (**-**) *nt* Mauritius.

Maus [maʊs] (**-, Mäuse**) *f* (*auch COMPUT*) mouse; **Mäuse** *pl* (*umg: Geld*) bread *sing*, dough *sing*.

mauscheln ['maʊʃəln] (*umg*) *vt, vi* (*manipulieren*) to fiddle.

mäuschenstill ['mɔysçən'ʃtɪl] *adj* very quiet.

Mausefalle *f* mousetrap.

mausen *vt* (*umg*) to pinch ♦ *vi* to catch mice.

mausern *vr* to moult (*BRIT*), molt (*US*).

maus(e)tot *adj* stone dead.

Maut [maʊt] (**-, -en**) *f* toll.

max. *abk* (= *maximal*) max.

maximal [maksi'maːl] *adj* maximum.

Maxime [ma'ksiːmə] (**-, -n**) *f* maxim.

maximieren [maksi'miːrən] *vt* to maximize.

Maximierung *f* (*WIRTS*) maximization.

Maximum ['maksimʊm] (**-s, Maxima**) *nt* maximum.

Mayonnaise [majɔ'nɛːzə] (**-, -n**) *f* mayonnaise.

Mazedonien [matse'doːniən] (**-s**) *nt* Macedonia.

Mäzen [mɛ'tseːn] (**-s, -e**) *m* (*gen*) patron, sponsor.

MdB *nt abk* (= *Mitglied des Bundestages*) member of the Bundestag, ≈ MP.

MdL *nt abk* (= *Mitglied des Landtages*) member of the Landtag.

m.E. *abk* (= *meines Erachtens*) in my opinion.

Mechanik [me'çaːnɪk] *f* mechanics *sing*; (*Getriebe*) mechanics *pl*; **~er** (**-s, -**) *m* mechanic, engineer.

mechanisch *adj* mechanical.

mechanisieren [meçani|ziːrən] *vt* to mechanize.

Mechanisierung *f* mechanization.

Mechanismus [meça'nɪsmʊs] *m* mechanism.

meckern ['mɛkərn] *vi* to bleat; (*umg*) to moan.

Mecklenburg ['meːklənbʊrk] (**-s**) *nt* Mecklenburg.

Mecklenburg-Vorpommern (**-s**) *nt* (state of) Mecklenburg-Vorpommern.

Medaille [me'daljə] (**-, -n**) *f* medal.

Medaillon [medal'jõː] (**-s, -s**) *nt* (*Schmuck*) locket.

Medien ['meːdiən] *pl* media *pl*; **~forschung** *f* media research.

Medikament [medika'mɛnt] *nt* medicine.

Meditation [meditatsi'oːn] *f* meditation.

meditieren [medi'tiːrən] *vi* to meditate.

Medium ['meːdiʊm] *nt* medium.

Medizin [medi'tsiːn] (**-, -en**) *f* medicine.

Mediziner(in) (**-s, -**) *m(f)* doctor; (*UNIV*) medic (*umg*).

medizinisch *adj* medical; **~-technische Assistentin** medical assistant.

Meer [meːr] (**-(e)s, -e**) *nt* sea; **am ~(e)** by the sea; **ans ~ fahren** to go to the sea(side); **~busen** *m* bay, gulf; **~enge** *f* straits *pl*.

Meeres- *zW*: **~früchte** *pl* seafood; **~klima** *nt* maritime climate; **~spiegel** *m* sea level.

Meer- *zW*: **~jungfrau** *f* mermaid; **~rettich** *m* horseradish; **~schweinchen** *nt* guinea pig; **~wasser** *nt* sea water.

Mega-, mega- [mɛga-] *in zW* mega-; **~byte** [mega'baɪt] *nt* megabyte; **~phon** [mega'foːn] (**-s, -e**) *nt* megaphone; **~watt** [mɛga'vat] *nt* megawatt.

Mehl [m'eːl] (**-(e)s, -e**) *nt* flour.

mehlig *adj* floury.

Mehlschwitze *f* (*KOCH*) roux.

mehr [meːr] *adv* more; **nie ~** never again, nevermore (*liter*); **es war niemand ~ da** there was no one left; **nicht ~ lange** not much longer; **M~aufwand** *m* additional expenditure; **M~belastung** *f* excess load; (*fig*) additional burden; **~deutig** *adj* ambiguous.

mehrere *indef pron* several; (*verschiedene*) various; **~s** several things.

mehrfach *adj* multiple; (*wiederholt*) repeated.

Mehrheit *f* majority.

Mehrheitsprinzip *nt* principle of majority rule.

Mehrheitswahlrecht *nt* first-past-the-post voting system.

mehr- *zW*: **~jährig** *adj attrib* of several years; **M~kosten** *pl* additional costs *pl*; **~malig** *adj* repeated; **~mals** *adv* repeatedly; **M~parteiensystem** *nt* multi-party system; **M~platzsystem** *nt* (*COMPUT*) multi-user system; **M~programmbetrieb** *m* (*COMPUT*) multiprogramming; **~sprachig** *adj* multilingual; **~stimmig** *adj* for several voices; **~stimmig singen** to harmonize; **M~wegflasche** *f* returnable bottle; **M~wertsteuer** *f* value added tax, VAT; **M~zahl** *f* majority; (*GRAM*) plural.

Mehrzweck- *in zW* multipurpose.

meiden ['maɪdən] *unreg vt* to avoid.

Meile ['maɪlə] (**-, -n**) *f* mile; **das riecht man drei ~n gegen den Wind** (*umg*) you can smell that a mile off.

Meilenstein *m* milestone.

meilenweit *adj* for miles.

mein [maɪn] *pron* my.

meine(r, s) *poss pron* mine.

Meineid ['maɪn|aɪt] *m* perjury.

meinen ['maɪnən] *vt* to think; (*sagen*) to say; (*sagen wollen*) to mean ♦ *vi* to think; **wie Sie ~!** as you wish; **damit bin ich gemeint** that refers to me; **das will ich** ~ I should think so.

meiner *gen von* **ich** ♦ *pron* of me.

meinerseits *adv* for my part.

meinesgleichen ['maɪnəs'glaɪçən] *pron* people like me.

meinetwegen ['maɪnət've:gən] *adv* (*für mich*) for my sake; (*wegen mir*) on my account; (*von mir aus*) as far as I'm concerned; (*ich habe nichts dagegen*) I don't care *od* mind.

meinetwillen ['maɪnət'vɪlən] *adv:* **um** ~ = **meinetwegen**.

meinige *pron:* **der/die/das** ~ mine.

meins [maɪns] *pron* mine.

Meinung ['maɪnʊŋ] *f* opinion; **meiner** ~ **nach** in my opinion; **einer** ~ **sein** to think the same; **jdm die** ~ **sagen** to give sb a piece of one's mind.

Meinungs- *zW:* ~**austausch** *m* exchange of views; ~**forscher(in)** *m(f)* pollster; ~**forschungsinstitut** *nt* opinion research institute; ~**freiheit** *f* freedom of speech; ~**umfrage** *f* opinion poll; ~**verschiedenheit** *f* difference of opinion.

Meise ['maɪzə] (-, -n) *f* tit(mouse); **eine** ~ **haben** (*umg*) to be crackers.

Meißel ['maɪsəl] (-s, -) *m* chisel.

meißeln *vt* to chisel.

meist [maɪst] *adj* most ♦ *adv* mostly; **M~begünstigungsklausel** *f* (*COMM*) most-favoured-nation clause; ~**bietend** *adj:* ~**bietend versteigern** to sell to the highest bidder.

meiste(r, s) *superl von* **viel.**

meistens *adv* mostly.

Meister ['maɪstər] (-s, -) *m* master; (*SPORT*) champion; **seinen** ~ **machen** to take one's master craftsman's diploma; **es ist noch kein** ~ **vom Himmel gefallen** (*Sprichwort*) no one is born an expert; ~**brief** *m* master craftsman's diploma; **m~haft** *adj* masterly.

Meisterin *f* (*auf einem Gebiet*) master, expert; (*SPORT*) (woman) champion.

meistern *vt* to master; **sein Leben** ~ to come to grips with one's life.

Meister- *zW:* ~**schaft** *f* mastery; (*SPORT*) championship; ~**stück** *nt* masterpiece; ~**werk** *nt* masterpiece.

meistgekauft *adj attrib* best-selling.

Mekka ['mɛka] (-s, -s) *nt* (*GEOG, fig*) Mecca.

Melancholie [melaŋko'li:] *f* melancholy.

melancholisch [melaŋ'ko:lɪʃ] *adj* melancholy.

Meldebehörde *f* registration authorities *pl.*

Meldefrist *f* registration period.

melden *vt* to report; (*registrieren*) to register ♦ *vr* to report; to register; (*SCH*) to put one's hand up; (*freiwillig*) to volunteer; (*auf etw, am Telefon*) to answer; **nichts zu** ~ **haben** (*umg*) to have no say; **wen darf ich** ~**?** who shall I say (is here)?; **sich** ~ **bei** to report to; to register with; **sich auf eine Anzeige** ~ to answer an advertisement; **es meldet sich**

niemand there's no answer; **sich zu Wort** ~ to ask to speak.

Meldepflicht *f* obligation to register with the police.

Meldestelle *f* registration office.

Meldung ['mɛldʊŋ] *f* announcement; (*Bericht*) report.

meliert [me'li:rt] *adj* mottled, speckled.

melken ['mɛlkən] *unreg vt* to milk.

Melodie [melo'di:] *f* melody, tune.

melodisch [me'lo:dɪʃ] *adj* melodious, tuneful.

melodramatisch [melodra'ma:tɪʃ] *adj* (*auch fig*) melodramatic.

Melone [me'lo:nə] (-, -n) *f* melon; (*Hut*) bowler (hat).

Membran [mɛm'bra:n] (-, -en) *f* (*TECH*) diaphragm; (*ANAT*) membrane.

Memme ['mɛmə] (-, -n) (*umg*) *f* cissy, yellow-belly.

Memoiren [memo'a:rən] *pl* memoirs *pl.*

Menge ['mɛŋə] (-, -n) *f* quantity; (*Menschen~*) crowd; (*große Anzahl*) lot (of); **jede** ~ (*umg*) masses *pl*, loads *pl.*

mengen *vt* to mix ♦ *vr:* **sich** ~ **in** +*akk* to meddle with.

Mengen- *zW:* ~**einkauf** *m* bulk buying; ~**lehre** *f* (*MATH*) set theory; ~**rabatt** *m* bulk discount.

Menorca [me'nɔrka] (-s) *nt* Menorca.

Mensa ['mɛnza] (-, -s *od* **Mensen**) *f* (*UNIV*) refectory (*BRIT*), commons (*US*).

Mensch [mɛnʃ] (-en, -en) *m* human being, man; (*Person*) person; **kein** ~ nobody; **ich bin auch nur ein** ~! I'm only human; ~ **ärgere dich nicht** *nt* (*Spiel*) ludo.

Menschen- *zW:* ~**alter** *nt* generation; ~**feind** *m* misanthrope; **m~freundlich** *adj* philanthropical; ~**gedenken** *nt:* **der kälteste Winter seit** ~**gedenken** the coldest winter in living memory; ~**handel** *m* slave trade; (*JUR*) trafficking in human beings; ~**kenner** *m* judge of human nature; ~**kenntnis** *f* knowledge of human nature; **m~leer** *adj* deserted; ~**liebe** *f* philanthropy; ~**masse** *f* crowd (of people); ~**menge** *f* crowd (of people); **m~möglich** *adj* humanly possible; ~**rechte** *pl* human rights *pl*; **m~scheu** *adj* shy; ~**schlag** (*umg*) *m* kind of people; ~**seele** *f:* **keine** ~**seele** (*fig*) not a soul.

Menschenskind *interj* good heavens!

Menschen- *zW:* **m~unwürdig** *adj* degrading; ~**verachtung** *f* contempt for human beings *od* of mankind; ~**verstand** *m:* **gesunder** ~**verstand** common sense; ~**würde** *f* human dignity; **m~würdig** *adj* (*Behandlung*) humane; (*Unterkunft*) fit for human habitation.

Mensch- *zW:* ~**heit** *f* humanity, mankind; **m~lich** *adj* human; (*human*) humane; ~**lichkeit** *f* humanity.

Menstruation [mɛnstruatsi'o:n] *f* menstruation.

Mentalität [mɛntali'tɛːt] *f* mentality.
Menü [me'nyː] **(-s, -s)** *nt* (*auch COMPUT*) menu; **m~gesteuert** *adj* (*COMPUT*) menu-driven.
Merkblatt *nt* instruction sheet *od* leaflet.
merken ['mɛrkən] *vt* to notice; **sich** *dat* **etw ~** to remember sth; **sich** *dat* **eine Autonummer ~** to make a (mental) note of a licence (*BRIT*) *od* license (*US*) number.
merklich *adj* noticeable.
Merkmal *nt* sign, characteristic.
merkwürdig *adj* odd.
meschugge [me'ʃʊgə] (*umg*) *adj* nuts, meshuga (*US*).
Meß- *zW:* **~band** *nt* tape measure; **m~bar** *adj* measurable; **~becher** *m* measuring cup.
Meßbuch *nt* missal.
Meßdiener *m* (*REL*) server, acolyte (*form*).
Messe ['mɛsə] **(-, -n)** *f* fair; (*ECCL*) mass; (*MIL*) mess; **auf der ~** at the fair; **~gelände** *nt* exhibition centre (*BRIT*) *od* center (*US*).
messen *unreg vt* to measure ♦ *vr* to compete.
Messer **(-s, -)** *nt* knife; **auf des ~s Schneide stehen** (*fig*) to hang in the balance; **jdm ins offene ~ laufen** (*fig*) to walk into a trap; **m~scharf** *adj* (*fig*): **m~scharf schließen** to conclude with incredible logic (*ironisch*); **~spitze** *f* knife point; (*in Rezept*) pinch; **~stecherei** *f* knife fight.
Messestadt *f* (town with an) exhibition centre (*BRIT*) *od* center (*US*).
Messestand *m* exhibition stand.
Meßgerät *nt* measuring device, gauge.
Meßgewand *nt* chasuble.
Messing ['mɛsɪŋ] **(-s)** *nt* brass.
Meßstab *m* (*AUT: Öl~ etc*) dipstick.
Messung *f* (*das Messen*) measuring; (*von Blutdruck*) taking; (*Meßergebnis*) measurement.
Meßwert *m* measurement; (*Ableseergebnis*) reading.
Metall [me'tal] **(-s, -e)** *nt* metal; **m~en** *adj* metallic; **m~isch** *adj* metallic; **m~verarbeitend** *adj*: **die m~verarbeitende Industrie** the metal-processing industry.
Metallurgie [metalur'giː] *f* metallurgy.
Metapher [me'tafər] **(-, -n)** *f* metaphor.
metaphorisch [meta'foːrɪʃ] *adj* metaphorical.
Metaphysik [metafy'ziːk] *f* metaphysics *sing*.
Metastase [meta'staːzə] **(-, -n)** *f* (*MED*) secondary growth.
Meteor [mete'oːr] **(-s, -e)** *m* meteor.
Meteorologe [meteoro'loːgə] **(-n, -n)** *m* meteorologist.
Meter ['meːtər] **(-s, -)** *m od nt* metre (*BRIT*), meter (*US*); **in 500 ~ Höhe** at a height of 500 metres; **~maß** *nt* tape measure; **~ware** *f* (*TEXTIL*) piece goods.
Methode [me'toːdə] **(-, -n)** *f* method.
Methodik [me'toːdɪk] *f* methodology.
methodisch [me'toːdɪʃ] *adj* methodical.
Metier [meti'eː] **(-s, -s)** *nt* (*hum*) job, profession.

metrisch ['meːtrɪʃ] *adj* metric, metrical.
Metropole [metro'poːlə] **(-, -n)** *f* metropolis.
Mettwurst ['mɛtvʊrst] *f* (smoked) pork/beef sausage.
Metzger ['mɛtsgər] **(-s, -)** *m* butcher.
Metzgerei [mɛtsgə'raɪ] *f* butcher's (shop).
Meuchelmord ['mɔʏçəlmɔrt] *m* assassination.
Meute ['mɔʏtə] **(-, -n)** *f* pack.
Meuterei [mɔʏtə'raɪ] *f* mutiny.
Meuterer **(-s, -)** *m* mutineer.
meutern *vi* to mutiny.
Mexikaner(in) [mɛksi'kaːnər(ɪn)] **(-s, -)** *m(f)* Mexican.
mexikanisch *adj* Mexican.
Mexiko ['mɛksiko] **(-s)** *nt* Mexico.
MEZ *abk* (= *mitteleuropäische Zeit*) C.E.T.
MFG *abk* = **Mitfahrgelegenheit.**
MG **(-(s), -(s))** *nt abk* = **Maschinengewehr.**
mg *abk* (= *Milligramm*) mg.
mhd. *abk* (= *mittelhochdeutsch*) MHG.
MHz *abk* (= *Megahertz*) MHz.
miauen [mi'aʊən] *vi* to miaow.
mich [mɪç] *akk von* **ich** ♦ *pron* me; (*reflexiv*) myself.
mick(e)rig ['mɪk(ə)rɪç] (*umg*) *adj* pathetic; (*altes Männchen*) puny.
mied *etc* [miːt] *vb siehe* **meiden.**
Miederwaren ['miːdərvaːrən] *pl* corsetry *sing*.
Mief [miːf] **(-s)** (*umg*) *m* fug; (*muffig*) stale air; (*Gestank*) stink, pong (*BRIT*).
miefig (*umg*) *adj* smelly, pongy (*BRIT*).
Miene ['miːnə] **(-, -n)** *f* look, expression; **gute ~ zum bösen Spiel machen** to grin and bear it.
Mienenspiel *nt* facial expressions *pl*.
mies [miːs] (*umg*) *adj* lousy.
Miese ['miːzə] (*umg*) *pl*: **in den ~n sein** to be in the red.
Miesmacher(in) (*umg*) *m(f)* killjoy.
Mietauto *nt* hired car (*BRIT*), rental car (*US*).
Miete ['miːtə] **(-, -n)** *f* rent; **zur ~ wohnen** to live in rented accommodation *od* accommodations (*US*).
mieten *vt* to rent; (*Auto*) to hire (*BRIT*), rent.
Mieter(in) **(-s, -)** *m(f)* tenant; **~schutz** *m* rent control.
Mietshaus *nt* tenement, block of flats (*BRIT*) *od* apartments (*US*).
Miet- *zW:* **~verhältnis** *nt* tenancy; **~vertrag** *m* tenancy agreement; **~wagen** *m* = **~auto**; **~wucher** *m* the charging of exorbitant rent(s).
Mieze ['miːtsə] **(-, -n)** (*umg*) *f* (*Katze*) pussy; (*Mädchen*) chick, bird (*BRIT*).
Migräne [mi'grɛːnə] **(-, -n)** *f* migraine.
Mikado [mi'kaːdo] **(-s)** *nt* (*Spiel*) pick-a-stick.
Mikro- ['miːkro] *in zW* micro-.
Mikrobe [mi'kroːbə] **(-, -n)** *f* microbe.
Mikro- *zW:* **~chip** *m* microchip; **~computer** *m* microcomputer; **~fiche** *m od nt* microfiche; **~film** *m* microfilm.

Mikrofon [mikro'fo:n] **(-s, e)** *nt* microphone.
Mikroökonomie *f* microeconomics *pl*.
Mikrophon [mikro'fo:n] **(-s, -e)** *nt*
microphone.
Mikroprozessor **(-s, -oren)** *m*
microprocessor.
Mikroskop [mikro'sko:p] **(-s, -e)** *nt*
microscope; **m~isch** *adj* microscopic.
Mikrowelle ['mi:krovɛlə] *f* microwave.
Mikrowellenherd *m* microwave (oven).
Milbe ['mɪlbə] **(-, -n)** *f* mite.
Milch [mɪlç] **(-)** *f* milk; (*Fisch~*) milt, roe;
~drüse *f* mammary gland; **~glas** *nt* frosted
glass.
milchig *adj* milky.
Milch- *zW:* **~kaffee** *m* white coffee;
~mixgetränk *nt* milk shake; **~pulver** *nt*
powdered milk; **~straße** *f* Milky Way;
~tüte *f* milk carton; **~zahn** *m* milk tooth.
mild [mɪlt] *adj* mild; (*Richter*) lenient;
(*freundlich*) kind, charitable.
Milde ['mɪldə] **(-, -n)** *f* mildness; leniency.
mildern *vt* to mitigate, soften; (*Schmerz*) to
alleviate; **~de Umstände** extenuating
circumstances.
Milieu [mili'ø:] **(-s, -s)** *nt* background,
environment; **m~geschädigt** *adj*
maladjusted.
militant [mili'tant] *adj* militant.
Militär [mili'tɛ:r] **(-s)** *nt* military, army;
~dienst *m* military service; **~gericht** *nt*
military court; **m~isch** *adj* military.
Militarismus [milita'rɪsmʊs] *m* militarism.
militaristisch *adj* militaristic.
Militärpflicht *f* (compulsory) military
service.
Mill. *abk* (= *Million(en)*) m.
Milli- *in zW* milli-.
Milliardär(in) [mɪliar'dɛ:r(ɪn)] **(-s, -e)** *m(f)*
multimillionaire.
Milliarde [mɪli'ardə] **(-, -n)** *f* milliard, billion
(*bes US*).
Millimeter *m* millimetre (*BRIT*), millimeter
(*US*); **~papier** *nt* graph paper.
Million [mɪli'o:n] **(-, -en)** *f* million.
Millionär(in) [mɪlio'nɛ:r(ɪn)] **(-s, -e)** *m(f)*
millionaire.
millionenschwer (*umg*) *adj* worth a few
million.
Milz [mɪlts] **(-, -en)** *f* spleen.
Mimik ['mi:mɪk] *f* mime.
Mimose [mi'mo:zə] **(-, -n)** *f* mimosa; (*fig*)
sensitive person.
minder ['mɪndər] *adj* inferior ♦ *adv* less;
~begabt *adj* less able; **~bemittelt** *adj*: **geistig
~bemittelt** (*ironisch*) intellectually
challenged.
Minderheit *f* minority.
Minderheitsbeteiligung *f* (*Aktien*) minority
interest.
Minderheitsregierung *f* minority
government.

minderjährig *adj* minor; **M~jährige(r)** *f(m)*
minor; **M~keit** *f* minority.
mindern *vt, vr* to decrease, diminish.
Minderung *f* decrease.
minder- *zW:* **~wertig** *adj* inferior;
M~wertigkeitsgefühl *nt* inferiority complex;
M~wertigkeitskomplex **(-es, -e)** *m*
inferiority complex.
Mindestalter *nt* minimum age.
Mindestbetrag *m* minimum amount.
mindeste(r, s) *adj* least.
mindestens *adv* at least.
Mindest- *zW:* **~lohn** *m* minimum wage;
~maß *nt* minimum; **~stand** *m* (*COMM*)
minimum stock; **~umtausch** *m* minimum
obligatory exchange.
Mine ['mi:nə] **(-, -n)** *f* mine; (*Bleistift~*) lead;
(*Kugelschreiber~*) refill.
Minenfeld *nt* minefield.
Minensuchboot *nt* minesweeper.
Mineral [mine'ra:l] **(-s, -e** *od* **-ien)** *nt* mineral;
m~isch *adj* mineral; **~ölsteuer** *f* tax on oil
and petrol (*BRIT*) *od* gasoline (*US*); **~wasser**
nt mineral water.
Miniatur [minia'tu:r] *f* miniature.
Minigolf ['mɪnigɔlf] *nt* miniature golf.
minimal [mini'ma:l] *adj* minimal.
Minimum ['mi:nimʊm] **(-s, Minima)** *nt*
minimum.
Minirock ['mɪnirɔk] *m* miniskirt.
Minister(in) [mi'nɪstər(ɪn)] **(-s, -)** *m(f)* (*POL*)
minister.
ministeriell [minɪsteri'ɛl] *adj* ministerial.
Ministerium [minɪs'te:rium] *nt* ministry.
Ministerpräsident(in) *m(f)* prime minister.
Minna ['mɪna] *f*: **jdn zur ~ machen** (*umg*) to
give sb a piece of one's mind.
minus ['mi:nʊs] *adv* minus; **M~ (-, -)** *nt* deficit;
M~pol *m* negative pole; **M~zeichen** *nt* minus
sign.
Minute [mi'nu:tə] **(-, -n)** *f* minute; **auf die
~ (genau od pünktlich)** (right) on the dot.
Minutenzeiger *m* minute hand.
Mio. *abk* (= *Million(en)*) m.
mir [mi:r] *dat von* **ich** ♦ *pron* (to) me; **von ~ aus!**
I don't mind; **wie du ~, so ich dir**
(*Sprichwort*) tit for tat (*umg*); (*als Drohung*)
I'll get my own back; **~ nichts, dir nichts**
just like that.
Mirabelle [mira'bɛlə] *f* mirabelle, *small
yellow plum.*
Misch- *zW:* **~batterie** *f* mixer tap; **~brot** *nt*
bread made from more than one kind of
flour; **~ehe** *f* mixed marriage.
mischen *vt* to mix; (*COMPUT: Datei, Text*) to
merge; (*Karten*) to shuffle ♦ *vi* (*Karten*) to
shuffle.
Misch- *zW:* **~konzern** *m* conglomerate; **~ling**
m half-caste; **~masch** (*umg*) *m* hotchpotch;
(*Essen*) concoction; **~pult** *nt* (*RUNDF, TV*)
mixing panel.
Mischung *f* mixture.

Mischwald *m* mixed (deciduous and coniferous) woodland.
miserabel [mizə'raːbəl] (*umg*) *adj* lousy; (*Gesundheit*) wretched; (*Benehmen*) dreadful.
Misere [mi'zeːrə] (-, -n) *f* (*von Leuten, Wirtschaft etc*) plight; (*von Hunger, Krieg etc*) misery, miseries *pl*.
Miß- *zW:* **m~achten** *vt untr* to disregard; **~achtung** *f* disregard; **~behagen** *nt* uneasiness; (*~fallen*) discontent; **~bildung** *f* deformity; **m~billigen** *vt untr* to disapprove of; **~billigung** *f* disapproval; **~brauch** *m* abuse; (*falscher Gebrauch*) misuse; **m~brauchen** *vt untr* to abuse; to misuse; (*vergewaltigen*) to assault; **jdn zu** *od* **für etw m~brauchen** to use sb for *od* to do sth; **m~deuten** *vt untr* to misinterpret.
missen *vt* to do without; (*Erfahrung*) to miss.
Mißerfolg *m* failure.
Mißernte *f* crop failure.
Missetat ['mɪsətaːt] *f* misdeed.
Missetäter *m* criminal; (*umg*) scoundrel.
Miß- *zW:* **m~fallen** *unreg vi untr:* **jdm m~fallen** to displease sb; **~fallen (-s)** *nt* displeasure; **~geburt** *f* freak; (*fig*) failure; **~geschick** *nt* misfortune; **m~glücken** *vi untr* to fail; **jdm m~glückt etw** sb. does not succeed with sth; **m~gönnen** *vt untr:* **jdm etw m~gönnen** to (be)grudge sb sth; **~griff** *m* mistake; **~gunst** *f* envy; **m~günstig** *adj* envious; **m~handeln** *vt untr* to ill-treat; **~handlung** *f* ill-treatment; **~helligkeit** *f:* **~helligkeiten haben** to be at variance.
Mission [mɪsi'oːn] *f* mission.
Missionar(in) [mɪsio'naːr(ɪn)] *m(f)* missionary.
Mißklang *m* discord.
Mißkredit *m* discredit.
mißlang etc [mɪs'laŋ] *vb siehe* **mißlingen**.
mißliebig *adj* unpopular.
mißlingen [mɪs'lɪŋən] *unreg vi untr* to fail; **M~ (-s)** *nt* failure.
mißlungen [mɪs'lʊŋən] *pp von* **mißlingen**.
Miß- *zW:* **~mut** *m* bad temper; **m~mutig** *adj* cross; **m~raten** *unreg vi untr* to turn out badly ♦ *adj* ill-bred; **~stand** *m* deplorable state of affairs; **~stimmung** *f* discord; (*~mut*) ill feeling.
mißt *vb siehe* **messen**.
Miß- *zW:* **m~trauen** *vi untr* to mistrust; **~trauen (-s)** *nt:* **~trauen (gegenüber)** distrust (of), suspicion (of); **~trauensantrag** *m* (*POL*) motion of no confidence; **~trauensvotum** *nt* (*POL*) vote of no confidence; **m~trauisch** *adj* distrustful, suspicious; **~verhältnis** *nt* disproportion; **m~verständlich** *adj* unclear; **~verständnis** *nt* misunderstanding; **m~verstehen** *unreg vt untr* to misunderstand.
Mißwahl, Misswahl ['mɪsvaːl] *f* beauty contest.
Mißwirtschaft *f* mismanagement.

Mist [mɪst] (-(e)s) *m* dung; (*umg*) rubbish; **~!** (*umg*) blast!; **das ist nicht auf seinem ~ gewachsen** (*umg*) he didn't think that up himself.
Mistel (-, -n) *f* mistletoe.
Mist- *zW:* **~gabel** *f* pitchfork (*used for shifting manure*); **~haufen** *m* dungheap; **~stück** (*umg!*) *nt*, **~vieh** (*umg!*) *nt* (*Mann*) bastard (*!*); (*Frau*) bitch (*!*).
mit [mɪt] *präp +dat* with; (*mittels*) by ♦ *adv* along, too; **~ der Bahn** by train; **~ dem nächsten Flugzeug/Bus kommen** to come on the next plane/bus; **~ Bleistift schreiben** to write in pencil; **~ Verlust** at a loss; **er ist ~ der Beste in der Gruppe** he is among the best in the group; **wie wär's ~ einem Bier?** (*umg*) how about a beer?; **~ 10 Jahren** at the age of 10; **wollen Sie ~?** do you want to come along?
Mitarbeit ['mɪtarbaɪt] *f* cooperation; **m~en** *vi:* **m~en (an** *+dat*) to cooperate (on), collaborate (on).
Mitarbeiter(in) *m(f)* (*an Projekt*) collaborator; (*Kollege*) colleague; (*Angestellter*) member of staff ♦ *pl* staff; **~stab** *m* staff.
mit- *zW:* **~bekommen** *unreg vt* to get *od* be given; (*umg: verstehen*) to get; **~bestimmen** *vi:* (*bei etw*) **~bestimmen** to have a say (in sth) ♦ *vt* to have an influence on; **M~bestimmung** *f* participation in decision-making; (*POL*) determination; **~bringen** *unreg vt* to bring along; **M~bringsel** ['mɪtbrɪŋzəl] (-s, -) *nt* (*Geschenk*) small present; (*Andenken*) souvenir; **M~bürger(in)** *m(f)* fellow citizen; **~denken** *unreg vi* to follow; **du hast ja ~gedacht!** good thinking!; **~dürfen** *unreg vi:* **wir durften nicht ~** we weren't allowed to go along; **M~eigentümer** *m* joint owner.
miteinander [mɪtaɪ'nandər] *adv* together, with one another.
miterleben *vt* to see, witness.
Mitesser ['mɪtɛsər] (-s, -) *m* blackhead.
mit- *zW:* **~fahren** *unreg vi:* (*mit jdm*) **~fahren** to go (with sb); (*auf Reise auch*) to go *od* travel (with sb); **M~fahrerzentrale** *f* agency for arranging lifts; **M~fahrgelegenheit** *f* lift; **~fühlen** *vi:* **~ jdm/etw ~fühlen** to sympathize with sb/sth; **~fühlend** *adj* sympathetic; **~führen** *vt* (*Papiere, Ware etc*) to carry (with one); (*Fluß*) to carry along; **~geben** *unreg vt* to give; **M~gefühl** *nt* sympathy; **~gehen** *unreg vi* to go *od* come along; **etw ~gehen lassen** (*umg*) to pinch sth; **~genommen** *adj* done in, in a bad way; **M~gift** *f* dowry.
Mitglied ['mɪtgliːt] *nt* member.
Mitgliedsbeitrag *m* membership fee, subscription.
Mitgliedschaft *f* membership.
mit- *zW:* **~haben** *unreg vt:* **etw ~haben** to have sth (with one); **~halten** *unreg vi* to keep up;

~**helfen** *vi unreg* to help, lend a hand; **bei etw** ~**helfen** to help with sth; **M**~**hilfe** *f* help, assistance; ~**hören** *vt* to listen in to; ~**kommen** *unreg vi* to come along; (*verstehen*) to keep up, follow; **M**~**läufer** *m* hanger-on; (*POL*) fellow traveller.

Mitleid *nt* sympathy; (*Erbarmen*) compassion.

Mitleidenschaft *f*: **in** ~ **ziehen** to affect.

mitleidig *adj* sympathetic.

mitleidslos *adj* pitiless, merciless.

mit- *zW:* ~**machen** *vt* to join in, take part in; (*umg: einverstanden sein*): **da macht mein Chef nicht** ~ my boss won't go along with that; **M**~**mensch** *m* fellow man; ~**mischen** (*umg*) *vi* (*sich beteiligen*): ~**mischen (in** +*dat od* **bei)** to be involved (in); (*sich einmischen*) to interfere (in); ~**nehmen** *unreg vt* to take along *od* away; (*anstrengen*) to wear out, exhaust; ~**genommen aussehen** to look the worse for wear; ~**reden** *vi* (*Meinung äußern*): (**bei etw**) ~**reden** to join in (sth); (~*bestimmen*) to have a say (in sth) ♦ *vt:* **Sie haben hier nichts** ~**zureden** this is none of your concern; ~**reißen** *vt unreg* to sweep away; (*fig: begeistern*) to carry away; ~**reißend** *adj* (*Rhythmus*) infectious; (*Reden*) rousing; (*Film, Fußballspiel*) thrilling, exciting.

mitsamt [mɪt'zamt] *präp* +*dat* together with.

mitschneiden *vt unreg* to record.

Mitschnitt ['mɪtʃnɪt] (**-(e)s, -e**) *m* recording.

mitschreiben *unreg vt* to write *od* take down ♦ *vi* to take notes.

Mitschuld *f* complicity.

mitschuldig *adj:* ~ (**an** +*dat*) implicated (in); (*an Unfall*) partly responsible (for).

Mitschuldige(r) *f(m)* accomplice.

mit- *zW:* **M**~**schüler(in)** *m(f)* schoolmate; ~**spielen** *vi* to join in, take part; **er hat ihr übel** *od* **hart** ~**gespielt** (*Schaden zufügen*) he has treated her badly; **M**~**spieler(in)** *m(f)* partner; **M**~**spracherecht** *nt* voice, say.

Mittag ['mɪtaːk] (**-(e)s, -e**) *m* midday, noon, lunchtime; ~ **machen** to take one's lunch hour; (**zu**) ~ **essen** to have lunch; **m**~ *adv* at lunchtime *od* noon; ~**essen** *nt* lunch, dinner.

mittags *adv* at lunchtime *od* noon.

Mittags- *zW:* ~**pause** *f* lunch break; ~**ruhe** *f* period of quiet (after lunch); (*in Geschäft*) midday closing; ~**schlaf** *m* early afternoon nap, siesta; ~**zeit** *f*: **während** *od* **in der** ~**zeit** at lunchtime.

Mittäter(in) ['mɪtːɛːtɐ(ɪn)] *m(f)* accomplice.

Mitte ['mɪtə] (**-, -n**) *f* middle; **aus unserer** ~ from our midst.

mitteilen ['mɪttaɪlən] *vt:* **jdm etw** ~ to inform sb of sth, communicate sth to sb ♦ *vr:* **sich (jdm)** ~ to communicate (with sb).

mitteilsam *adj* communicative.

Mitteilung *f* communication; **jdm (eine)** ~ **von etw machen** (*form*) to inform sb of sth; (*bekanntgeben*) to announce sth

to sb.

Mitteilungsbedürfnis *nt* need to talk to other people.

Mittel ['mɪtəl] (**-s, -**) *nt* means; (*Methode*) method; (*MATH*) average; (*MED*) medicine; **kein** ~ **unversucht lassen** to try everything; **als letztes** ~ as a last resort; **ein** ~ **zum Zweck** a means to an end; ~**alter** *nt* Middle Ages *pl*; **m**~**alterlich** *adj* medieval; ~**amerika** *nt* Central America (and the Caribbean); **m**~**amerikanisch** *adj* Central American; **m**~**bar** *adj* indirect; ~**ding** *nt* (*Mischung*) cross; ~**europa** *nt* Central Europe; ~**europäer(in)** *m(f)* Central European; **m**~**europäisch** *adj* Central European; **m**~**fristig** *adj* (*Finanzplanung, Kredite*) medium-term; ~**gebirge** *nt* low mountain range; **m**~**groß** *adj* medium-sized; **m**~**los** *adj* without means; ~**maß** *nt:* **das (gesunde)** ~**maß** the happy medium; **m**~**mäßig** *adj* mediocre, middling; ~**mäßigkeit** *f* mediocrity; ~**meer** *nt* Mediterranean (Sea); **m**~**prächtig** *adj* not bad; ~**punkt** *m* centre (*BRIT*), center (*US*); **im** ~**punkt stehen** to be centre-stage.

mittels *präp* +*gen* by means of.

Mittelschicht *f* middle class.

Mittelsmann (**-(e)s,** *pl* **Mittelsmänner** *od* **Mittelsleute**) *m* intermediary.

Mittel- *zW:* ~**stand** *m* middle class; ~**streckenrakete** *f* medium-range missile; ~**streifen** *m* central reservation (*BRIT*), median strip (*US*); ~**stufe** *f* (*SCH*) middle school (*BRIT*), junior high (*US*); ~**stürmer** *m* centre forward; ~**weg** *m* middle course; ~**welle** *f* (*RUNDF*) medium wave; ~**wert** *m* average value, mean.

mitten ['mɪtən] *adv* in the middle; ~ **auf der Straße/in der Nacht** in the middle of the street/night; ~**drin** *adv* (right) in the middle of it; ~**durch** *adv* (right) through the middle.

Mitternacht ['mɪtɐnaxt] *f* midnight.

mittlere(r, s) ['mɪtlərə(r, s)] *adj* middle; (*durchschnittlich*) medium, average; **der Mittlere Osten** the Middle East; **mittleres Management** middle management.

The **mittlere Reife** *is the standard certificate achieved at a* **Realschule** *on successful completion of 6 years' education there. If a pupil at a Realschule attains good results in several subjects he is allowed to enter the 11th class of a Gymnasium to study for the* **Abitur**.

---

mittlerweile ['mɪtlɐˈvaɪlə] *adv* meanwhile.

Mittwoch ['mɪtvɔx] (**-(e)s, -e**) *m* Wednesday; *siehe auch* **Dienstag**.

mittwochs *adv* on Wednesdays.

mitunter [mɪt'ʊntɐ] *adv* occasionally, sometimes.

mit- *zW:* ~**verantwortlich** *adj* also responsible; ~**verdienen** *vi* to (go out to) work as well;

M~verfasser m co-author; **M~verschulden** nt contributory negligence; **~wirken** vi: **(bei etw) ~wirken** to contribute (to sth); (*THEAT*) to take part (in sth); **M~wirkende(r)** f(m): **die M~wirkenden** (*THEAT*) the cast; **M~wirkung** f contribution; participation; **unter M~wirkung von** with the help of; **M~wisser** (**-s, -**) m: **M~wisser (einer Sache** gen) **sein** to be in the know (about sth); **jdn zum M~wisser machen** to tell sb (all) about it.

Mixer ['mɪksər] (**-s, -**) m (*Bar~*) cocktail waiter; (*Küchen~*) blender; (*Rührmaschine, RUNDF, TV*) mixer.

ml abk (= Milliliter) ml.

mm abk (= Millimeter) mm.

Mnemonik [mne'moːnɪk] f (*auch COMPUT*) mnemonic.

Möbel ['møːbəl] (**-s, -**) nt (piece of) furniture; **~packer** m removal man (*BRIT*), (furniture) mover (*US*); **~wagen** m furniture od removal van (*BRIT*), moving van (*US*).

mobil [mo'biːl] adj mobile; (*MIL*) mobilized.

Mobilfunk m cellular telephone service.

Mobiliar [mobili'aːr] (**-s, -e**) nt movable assets pl.

mobilisieren [mobili'ziːrən] vt (*MIL*) to mobilize.

Mobilmachung f mobilization.

Mobiltelefon nt (*TELEC*) mobile phone.

möbl. abk = möbliert.

möblieren [mø'bliːrən] vt to furnish; **möbliert wohnen** to live in furnished accommodation.

mochte etc ['mɔxtə] vb siehe **mögen**.

Möchtegern- ['mœçtəgɛrn] in zW (*ironisch*) would-be.

Modalität [modali'tɛːt] f (*von Plan, Vertrag etc*) arrangement.

Mode ['moːdə] (**-, -n**) f fashion; **~farbe** f in colour (*BRIT*) od color (*US*); **~heft** nt fashion magazine; **~journal** nt fashion magazine.

Modell [mo'dɛl] (**-s, -e**) nt model; **~eisenbahn** f model railway; (*als Spielzeug*) train set; **~fall** m textbook case.

modellieren [modɛ'liːrən] vt to model.

Modellversuch m (*bes SCH*) pilot scheme.

Modem ['moːdɛm] (**-s, -s**) nt (*COMPUT*) modem.

Modenschau f fashion show.

Modepapst m high priest of fashion.

Moder ['moːdər] (**-s**) m mustiness; (*Schimmel*) mildew.

moderat [mode'raːt] adj moderate.

Moderator(in) [mode'raːtor, -a'toːrɪn] m(f) presenter.

moderieren [mode'riːrən] vt, vi (*RUNDF, TV*) to present.

modern [mo'dɛrn] adj modern; (*modisch*) fashionable.

modernisieren [modɛrni'ziːrən] vt to modernize.

Mode- zW: **~schmuck** m fashion jewellery (*BRIT*) od jewelry (*US*); **~schöpfer(in)** m(f) fashion designer; **~wort** nt fashionable word.

modifizieren [modifi'tsiːrən] vt to modify.

modisch ['moːdɪʃ] adj fashionable.

Modul ['moːdʊl] (**-s, -n**) nt (*COMPUT*) module.

Modus ['moːdʊs] (**-, Modi**) m way; (*GRAM*) mood; (*COMPUT*) mode.

Mofa ['moːfa] (**-s, -s**) nt (= Motorfahrrad) small moped.

Mogadischu (**-s**) [moga'dɪʃu] nt Mogadishu.

mogeln ['moːgəln] (*umg*) vi to cheat.

================= *SCHLÜSSELWORT*

mögen ['møːgən] (*pt* **mochte**, *pp* **gemocht** od (*als Hilfsverb*) **mögen**) vt, vi to like; **magst du/ mögen Sie ihn?** do you like him?; **ich möchte ...** I would like ..., I'd like ...; **er möchte in die Stadt** he'd like to go into town; **ich möchte nicht, daß du ...** I wouldn't like you to ...; **ich mag nicht mehr** I've had enough; (*bin am Ende*) I can't take any more; **man möchte meinen, daß ...** you would think that ...

♦ *Hilfsverb* to like to; (*wollen*) to want; **möchtest du etwas essen?** would you like something to eat?; **sie mag nicht bleiben** she doesn't want to stay; **das mag wohl sein** that may very well be; **was mag das heißen?** what might that mean?; **Sie möchten zu Hause anrufen** could you please call home?

möglich ['møːklɪç] adj possible; **er tat sein ~stes** he did his utmost.

möglicherweise adv possibly.

Möglichkeit f possibility; **nach ~** if possible.

möglichst adv as ... as possible.

Mohammedaner(in) [mohame'daːnər(ɪn)] (**-s, -**) m(f) Mohammedan, Muslim.

Mohikaner [mohi'kaːnər] (**-s, -**) m: **der letzte ~** (*hum: umg*) the very last one.

Mohn [moːn] (**-(e)s, -e**) m (*~blume*) poppy; (*~samen*) poppy seed.

Möhre ['møːrə] (**-, -n**) f carrot.

Mohrenkopf ['moːrənkɔpf] m chocolate-covered marshmallow.

Mohrrübe f carrot.

mokieren [mo'kiːrən] vr: **sich über etw** akk **~** to make fun of sth.

Mokka ['mɔka] (**-s**) m mocha, *strong coffee*.

Moldau ['mɔldau] f: **die ~** the Vltava.

Moldawien [mɔl'daːviən] (**-s**) nt Moldavia.

moldawisch adj Moldavian.

Mole ['moːlə] (**-, -n**) f (*NAUT*) mole.

Molekül [mole'kyːl] (**-s, -e**) nt molecule.

molk etc [mɔlk] vb siehe **melken**.

Molkerei [mɔlkə'rai] f dairy; **~butter** f blended butter.

Moll [mɔl] (**-, -**) nt (*MUS*) minor (key).

mollig adj cosy; (*dicklich*) plump.

Molotowcocktail ['mo:lotɔfkɔkte:l] *m* Molotov cocktail.

Moment [mo'mɛnt] (-(e)s, -e) *m* moment ♦ *nt* factor, element; **im** ~ at the moment; ~ **mal!** just a minute!; **im ersten** ~ for a moment.

momentan [momɛn'taːn] *adj* momentary ♦ *adv* at the moment.

Monaco ['mo:nako] (-s) *nt* Monaco.

Monarch [mo'narç] (-en, -en) *m* monarch.

Monarchie [monar'çiː] *f* monarchy.

Monat ['mo:nat] (-(e)s, -e) *m* month; **sie ist im sechsten** ~ **(schwanger)** she's five months pregnant; **was verdient er im** ~? how much does he earn a month?

monatelang *adv* for months.

monatlich *adj* monthly.

Monats- *zW:* ~**blutung** *f* menstrual period; ~**karte** *f* monthly ticket; ~**rate** *f* monthly instalment (*BRIT*) *od* installment (*US*).

Mönch [mœnç] (-(e)s, -e) *m* monk.

Mond [mo:nt] (-(e)s, -e) *m* moon; **auf** *od* **hinter dem** ~ **leben** (*umg*) to be behind the times; ~**fähre** *f* lunar (excursion) module; ~**finsternis** *f* eclipse of the moon; **m**~**hell** *adj* moonlit; ~**landung** *f* moon landing; ~**schein** *m* moonlight; ~**sonde** *f* moon probe.

Monegasse [mone'gasə] (-n, -n) *m* Monegasque.

Monegassin [mone'gasɪn] *f* Monegasque.

monegassisch *adj* Monegasque.

Monetarismus [moneta'rɪsmʊs] *m* (*ECON*) monetarism.

Monetarist *m* monetarist.

Moneten [mo'ne:tən] (*umg*) *pl* (*Geld*) bread *sing*, dough *sing*.

Mongole [mɔŋ'go:lə] (-n, -n) *m* Mongolian, Mongol.

Mongolei [mɔŋgo'laɪ] *f:* **die** ~ Mongolia.

Mongolin *f* Mongolian, Mongol.

mongolisch [mɔŋ'go:lɪʃ] *adj* Mongolian.

mongoloid [mɔŋgolo'iːt] *adj* (*MED*) mongoloid.

monieren [mo'niːrən] *vt* to complain about ♦ *vi* to complain.

Monitor ['mo:nitɔr] *m* (*Bildschirm*) monitor.

Mono- [mono] *in zW* mono.

monogam [mono'ga:m] *adj* monogamous.

Monogamie [monogs'miː] *f* monogamy.

Monolog [mono'lo:k] (-s, -e) *m* monologue.

Monopol (-s, -e) *nt* monopoly.

monopolisieren [monopoli'ziːrən] *vt* to monopolize.

Monopolstellung *f* monopoly.

monoton [mono'to:n] *adj* monotonous.

Monotonie [monoto'niː] *f* monotony.

Monstrum ['mɔnstrʊm] (-s, Monstren) *nt* (*lit, fig*) monster; **ein** ~ **von einem/einer** ... a hulking great ...

Monsun [mɔn'zu:n] (-s, -e) *m* monsoon.

Montag ['mo:nta:k] (-(e)s, -e) *m* Monday; *siehe auch* **Dienstag.**

Montage [mɔn'ta:ʒə] (-, -n) *f* (*PHOT etc*) montage; (*TECH*) assembly; (*Einbauen*) fitting.

montags *adv* on Mondays.

Montanindustrie [mɔn'ta:nɪndʊstri:] *f* coal and steel industry.

Montblanc [mõ'blã:] *m* Mont Blanc.

Monte Carlo ['mɔntə 'karlo] (-s) *nt* Monte Carlo.

Montenegro [mɔnte'ne:gro] (-s) *nt* Montenegro.

Monteur [mɔn'tø:r] *m* fitter, assembly man.

montieren [mɔn'tiːrən] *vt* to assemble, set up.

Montur [mɔn'tu:r] (*umg*) *f* (*Spezialkleidung*) gear, rig-out.

Monument [monu'mɛnt] *nt* monument.

monumental [monumɛn'ta:l] *adj* monumental.

Moor [mo:r] (-(e)s, -e) *nt* moor; ~**bad** *nt* mud bath.

Moos [mo:s] (-es, -e) *nt* moss.

Moped ['mo:pɛt] (-s, -s) *nt* moped.

Mops [mɔps] (-es, ⁻e) *m* (*Hund*) pug.

Moral [mo'ra:l] (-, -en) *f* morality; (*einer Geschichte*) moral; (*Disziplin: von Volk, Soldaten*) morale; ~**apostel** *m* upholder of moral standards; **m**~**isch** *adj* moral; **einen** *od* **den** ~**ischen haben** (*umg*) to have (a fit of) the blues.

Moräne [mo'rɛ:nə] (-, -n) *f* moraine.

Morast [mo'rast] (-(e)s, -e) *m* morass, mire.

morastig *adj* boggy.

Mord [mɔrt] (-(e)s, -e) *m* murder; **dann gibt es** ~ **und Totschlag** (*umg*) there'll be hell to pay; ~**anschlag** *m* murder attempt.

Mörder ['mœrdər] (-s, -) *m* murderer; ~**in** *f* murderess.

mörderisch *adj* (*fig: schrecklich*) dreadful, terrible; (*Preise*) exorbitant; (*Konkurrenzkampf*) cut-throat ♦ *adv* (*umg: entsetzlich*) dreadfully, terribly.

Mordkommission *f* murder squad.

Mords- *zW:* ~**ding** (*umg*) *nt* whopper; ~**glück** (*umg*) *nt* amazing luck; ~**kerl** (*umg*) *m* (*verwegen*) hell of a guy; **m**~**mäßig** (*umg*) *adj* terrific, enormous; ~**schreck** (*umg*) *m* terrible fright.

Mord- *zW:* ~**verdacht** *m* suspicion of murder; ~**versuch** *m* murder attempt; ~**waffe** *f* murder weapon.

morgen ['mɔrgən] *adv* tomorrow; **bis** ~! see you tomorrow!; ~ **in acht Tagen** a week (from) tomorrow; ~ **um diese Zeit** this time tomorrow; ~ **früh** tomorrow morning; **M**~ (-s, -) *m* morning; (*Maß*) ≈ acre; **am M**~ in the morning; **guten M**~! good morning!

Morgen- *zW:* ~**grauen** *nt* dawn, daybreak; ~**mantel** *m* dressing gown; ~**rock** *m* dressing gown; ~**rot** *nt*, ~**röte** *f* dawn.

morgens *adv* in the morning; **von** ~ **bis abends** from morning to night.

Morgenstunde *f:* **Morgenstund(e) hat Gold**

im **Mund(e)** (*Sprichwort*) the early bird catches the worm (*Sprichwort*).

morgig ['mɔrgɪç] *adj* tomorrow's; **der ~e Tag** tomorrow.

Morphium ['mɔrfiʊm] *nt* morphine.

morsch [mɔrʃ] *adj* rotten.

Morsealphabet ['mɔrzə|alfabeːt] *nt* Morse code.

morsen *vi* to send a message by Morse code.

Mörser ['mœrzər] (-) *m* mortar (*auch MIL*).

Mörtel ['mœrtəl] (-s, -) *m* mortar.

Mosaik [moza'iːk] (-s, -en *od* -e) *nt* mosaic.

Mosambik [mosam'biːk] (-s) *nt* Mozambique.

Moschee [mɔ'ʃeː] (-, -n) *f* mosque.

Mosel[1] ['moːzəl] *f* (*GEOG*) Moselle.

Mosel[2] (-s, -) *m* (*auch:* **~wein**) Moselle (wine).

mosern ['moːzərn] (*umg*) *vi* to gripe, bellyache.

Moskau ['mɔskaʊ] (-s) *nt* Moscow.

Moskauer *adj* Moscow *attrib*.

Moskauer(in) (-s, -) *m(f)* Muscovite.

Moskito [mɔs'kiːto] (-s, -s) *m* mosquito.

Moslem ['mɔslɛm] (-s, -s) *m* Muslim.

moslemisch [mɔs'leːmɪʃ] *adj* Muslim.

Most [mɔst] (-(e)s, -e) *m* (unfermented) fruit juice; (*Apfelwein*) cider.

Motel [mo'tel] (-s, -s) *nt* motel.

Motiv [mo'tiːf] (-s, -e) *nt* motive; (*MUS*) theme.

Motivation [motivatsi'oːn] *f* motivation.

motivieren [moti'viːrən] *vt* to motivate.

Motivierung *f* motivation.

Motor ['moːtɔr] (-s, -en) *m* engine; (*bes ELEK*) motor; **~boot** *nt* motorboat.

Motorenöl *nt* engine oil.

Motorhaube *f* (*AUT*) bonnet (*BRIT*), hood (*US*).

motorisch *adj* (*PHYSIOLOGIE*) motor *attrib*.

motorisieren [motori'ziːrən] *vt* to motorize.

Motor- *zW:* **~rad** *nt* motorcycle; **~radfahrer** *m* motorcyclist; **~roller** *m* motor scooter; **~schaden** *m* engine trouble *od* failure; **~sport** *m* motor sport.

Motte ['mɔtə] (-, -n) *f* moth.

Motten- *zW:* **m~fest** *adj* mothproof; **~kiste** *f:* **etw aus der ~kiste hervorholen** (*fig*) to dig sth out; **~kugel** *f* mothball.

Motto ['mɔto] (-s, -s) *nt* motto.

motzen ['mɔtsən] (*umg*) *vi* to grouse, beef.

Mountain-Bike *nt* mountain bike.

Möwe ['møːvə] (-, -n) *f* seagull.

MP (-) *f abk* = **Maschinenpistole**.

Mrd. *abk* = **Milliarde(n)**.

MS *abk* (= *Motorschiff*) motor vessel, MV; (= *multiple Sklerose*) MS.

MTA (-, -s) *f abk* (= *medizinisch-technische Assistentin*) medical assistant.

mtl. *abk* = **monatlich**.

Mucke ['mʊkə] (-, -n) *f* (*meist pl*) caprice; (*von Ding*) snag, bug; **seine ~n haben** to be temperamental.

Mücke ['mʏkə] (-, -n) *f* midge, gnat; **aus einer ~ einen Elefanten machen** (*umg*) to make a mountain out of a molehill.

Muckefuck ['mʊkəfʊk] (-s) (*umg*) *m* coffee substitute.

mucken *vi:* **ohne zu ~** without a murmur.

Mückenstich *m* midge *od* gnat bite.

Mucks [mʊks] (-es, e) *m:* **keinen ~ sagen** not to make a sound; (*nicht widersprechen*) not to say a word.

mucksen (*umg*) *vr* to budge; (*Laut geben*) to open one's mouth.

mucksmäuschenstill ['mʊks'mɔysçənʃtɪl] (*umg*) *adj* (as) quiet as a mouse.

müde ['myːdə] *adj* tired; **nicht ~ werden, etw zu tun** never to tire of doing something.

Müdigkeit ['myːdɪçkaɪt] *f* tiredness; **nur keine ~ vorschützen!** (*umg*) don't (you) tell me you're tired.

Muff [mʊf] (-(e)s, -e) *m* (*Handwärmer*) muff.

Muffel (-s, -) (*umg*) *m* killjoy, sourpuss.

muffig *adj* (*Luft*) musty.

Mühe ['myːə] (-, -n) *f* trouble, pains *pl*; **mit Müh(e) und Not** with great difficulty; **sich** *dat* **~ geben** to go to a lot of trouble; **m~los** *adj* effortless, easy.

muhen ['muːən] *vi* to low, moo.

mühevoll *adj* laborious, arduous.

Mühle ['myːlə] (-, -n) *f* mill; (*Kaffee~*) grinder; (*~spiel*) nine men's morris.

Mühlrad *nt* millwheel.

Mühlstein *m* millstone.

Mühsal (-, -e) *f* tribulation.

mühsam *adj* arduous, troublesome ♦ *adv* with difficulty.

mühselig *adj* arduous, laborious.

Mulatte [mu'latə] (-, -n) *m* mulatto.

Mulattin *f* mulatto.

Mulde ['mʊldə] (-, -n) *f* hollow, depression.

Mull [mʊl] (-(e)s, -e) *m* thin muslin.

Müll [mʏl] (-(e)s) *m* refuse, rubbish, garbage (*US*); **~abfuhr** *f* refuse *od* garbage (*US*) collection; (*Leute*) dustmen *pl* (*BRIT*), garbage collectors *pl* (*US*); **~abladeplatz** *m* rubbish dump; **~beutel** *m* bin liner (*BRIT*), trashcan liner (*US*).

Mullbinde *f* gauze bandage.

Mülldeponie *f* waste disposal site, rubbish tip.

Mülleimer *m* rubbish bin (*BRIT*), garbage can (*US*).

Müller (-s, -) *m* miller.

Müll- *zW:* **~halde** *f*, **~haufen** *m* rubbish *od* garbage (*US*) heap; **~mann** (-(e)s, *pl* **~männer**) (*umg*) *m* dustman (*BRIT*), garbage collector (*US*); **~sack** *m* rubbish *od* garbage (*US*) bag; **~schlucker** *m* waste (*BRIT*) *od* garbage (*US*) disposal unit; **~tonne** *f* dustbin (*BRIT*), trashcan (*US*); **~verbrennung** *f* rubbish *od* garbage (*US*) incineration; **~verbrennungsanlage** *f* incinerator, incinerating plant; **~wagen** *m*

dustcart (*BRIT*), garbage truck (*US*).
mulmig ['mʊlmɪç] *adj* rotten; (*umg*)
uncomfortable; **jdm ist ~ sb** feels funny.
Multi ['mʊlti] (**-s, -s**) (*umg*) *m* multinational
(organization).
multi- *in zW* multi; **~lateral** *adj:* **~lateraler**
Handel multilateral trade; **~national** *adj*
multinational; **~nationaler Konzern**
multinational organization.
multiple Sklerose [mʊl'tiːplə skle'roːzə] *f*
multiple sclerosis.
multiplizieren [mʊltipli'tsiːrən] *vt* to multiply.
Mumie ['muːmiə] *f* (*Leiche*) mummy.
Mumm [mʊm] (**-s**) (*umg*) *m* gumption, nerve.
Mumps [mʊmps] (**-**) *m od f* mumps *sing*.
München ['mʏnçən] *nt* Munich.
Münch(e)ner(in) (**-s, -**) *m(f)* person from
Munich.
Mund [mʊnt] (**-(e)s, ⁻er**) *m* mouth; **den**
~ aufmachen (*fig: seine Meinung sagen*) to
speak up; **sie ist nicht auf den ~ gefallen**
(*umg*) she's never at a loss for words; **~art** *f*
dialect.
Mündel ['mʏndəl] (**-s, -**) *nt* (*JUR*) ward.
münden ['mʏndən] *vi:* **in etw** *akk* **~** to flow into
sth.
Mund- *zW:* **m~faul** *adj* uncommunicative;
m~gerecht *adj* bite-sized; **~geruch** *m* bad
breath; **~harmonika** *f* mouth organ.
mündig ['mʏndɪç] *adj* of age; **M~keit** *f*
majority.
mündlich ['mʏntlɪç] *adj* oral; **mündliche**
Prüfung oral (exam); **~e Verhandlung** (*JUR*)
hearing; **alles weitere ~!** let's talk about it
more when I see you.
Mund- *zW:* **~raub** *m* (*JUR*) theft of food for
personal consumption; **~stück** *nt*
mouthpiece; (*von Zigarette*) tip; **m~tot** *adj:*
jdn m~tot machen to muzzle sb.
Mündung ['mʏndʊŋ] *f* estuary; (*von Fluß,*
Rohr etc) mouth; (*Gewehr~*) muzzle.
Mund- *zW:* **~wasser** *nt* mouthwash; **~werk** *nt:*
ein großes ~werk haben to have a big
mouth; **~winkel** *m* corner of the mouth; **~-**
zu-~-Beatmung *f* mouth-to-mouth
resuscitation.
Munition [munitsi'oːn] *f* ammunition.
Munitionslager *nt* ammunition dump.
munkeln ['mʊŋkəln] *vi* to whisper, mutter;
man munkelt, daß ... there's a rumour
(*BRIT*) *od* rumor (*US*) that ...
Münster ['mʏnstər] (**-s, -**) *nt* minster.
munter ['mʊntər] *adj* lively; (*wach*) awake;
(*aufgestanden*) up and about; **M~keit** *f*
liveliness.
Münzanstalt *f* mint.
Münzautomat *m* slot machine.
Münze ['mʏntsə] (**-, -n**) *f* coin.
münzen *vt* to coin, mint; **auf jdn gemünzt**
sein to be aimed at sb.
Münzfernsprecher ['mʏntsfɛrnʃprɛçər] *m*
callbox (*BRIT*), pay phone (*US*).

Münzwechsler *m* change machine.
mürb(e) *adj* (*Gestein*) crumbly; (*Holz*) rotten;
(*Gebäck*) crisp; **jdn ~ machen** to wear sb
down.
Mürb(e)teig *m* shortcrust pastry.
Murmel ['mʊrməl] (**-, -n**) *f* marble.
murmeln *vt, vi* to murmur, mutter.
Murmeltier ['mʊrməltiːr] *nt* marmot; **schlafen**
wie ein ~ to sleep like a log.
murren ['mʊrən] *vi* to grumble, grouse.
mürrisch ['mʏrɪʃ] *adj* sullen.
Mus [muːs] (**-es, -e**) *nt* purée.
Muschel ['mʊʃəl] (**-, -n**) *f* mussel; (*~schale*)
shell; (*Telefon~*) receiver.
Muse ['muːzə] (**-, -n**) *f* muse.
Museum [mu'zeːʊm] (**-s, Museen**) *nt* museum.
museumsreif *adj:* **~ sein** to be almost a
museum piece.
Musik [mu'ziːk] *f* music; (*Kapelle*) band.
musikalisch [muziː'kaːlɪʃ] *adj* musical.
Musikbox *f* jukebox.
Musiker(in) ['muːzikər(ɪn)] (**-s, -**) *m(f)*
musician.
Musik- *zW:* **~hochschule** *f* music school;
~instrument *nt* musical instrument;
~kapelle *f* band; **~stück** *nt* piece of music;
~stunde *f* music lesson.
musisch ['muːzɪʃ] *adj* artistic.
musizieren [muzi'tsiːrən] *vi* to make music.
Muskat [mʊs'kaːt] (**-(e)s, -e**) *m* nutmeg.
Muskel ['mʊskəl] (**-s, -n**) *m* muscle;
~dystrophie *f* muscular dystrophy; **~kater**
m: **einen ~kater haben** to be stiff; **~paket**
(*umg*) *nt* muscleman; **~zerrung** (*umg*) *f*
pulled muscle.
Muskulatur [mʊskula'tuːr] *f* muscular
system.
muskulös [mʊsku'løːs] *adj* muscular.
Müsli ['myːsli] (**-s, -**) *nt* muesli.
Muß [mʊs] (**-**) *nt* necessity, must.
muß *vb siehe* **müssen.**
Muße ['muːsə] (**-**) *f* leisure.

═══════════════ *SCHLÜSSELWORT*

müssen ['mʏsən] (*pt* **mußte,** *pp* **gemußt** *od* (*als*
Hilfsverb) **müssen**) *vi* **1** (*Zwang*) must (*nur im*
Präsens), to have to; **ich muß es tun** I must
do it, I have to do it; **ich mußte es tun** I had
to do it; **er muß es nicht tun** he doesn't have
to do it; **muß ich?** must I?, do I have to?;
wann müßt ihr zur Schule? when do you
have to go to school?; **der Brief muß heute**
noch zur Post the letter must be posted
(*BRIT*) *od* mailed (*US*) today; **er hat gehen ~**
he (has) had to go; **muß das sein?** is that
really necessary?; **wenn es (unbedingt) sein**
muß if it's absolutely necessary; **ich muß**
mal (*umg*) I need to go to the loo (*BRIT*) *od*
bathroom (*US*).
2 (*sollen*): **das mußt du nicht tun!** you
oughtn't to *od* shouldn't do that; **das**
müßtest du eigentlich wissen you ought to

od you should know that; **Sie hätten ihn fragen** ~ you should have asked him **3: es muß geregnet haben** it must have rained; **es muß nicht wahr sein** it needn't be true.

Mußheirat (*umg*) *f* shotgun wedding.
müßig ['my:sɪç] *adj* idle; **M~gang** *m* idleness.
mußt [mʊst] *vb siehe* **müssen**.
mußte *etc* ['mʊstə] *vb siehe* **müssen**.
Muster ['mʊstər] (**-s, -**) *nt* model; (*Dessin*) pattern; (*Probe*) sample; ~ **ohne Wert** free sample; ~**beispiel** *nt* classic example; **m~gültig** *adj* exemplary; **m~haft** *adj* exemplary.
mustern *vt* (*betrachten, MIL*) to examine; (*Truppen*) to inspect.
Musterprozeß *m* test case.
Musterschüler *m* model pupil.
Musterung *f* (*von Stoff*) pattern; (*MIL*) inspection.
Mut [muːt] *m* courage; **nur ~!** cheer up!; **jdm ~ machen** to encourage sb; ~ **fassen** to pluck up courage.
mutig *adj* courageous.
mutlos *adj* discouraged, despondent.
mutmaßen *vt untr* to conjecture ♦ *vi untr* to conjecture.
mutmaßlich ['muːtmaːslɪç] *adj* presumed ♦ *adv* probably.
Mutprobe *f* test of courage.
Mutter¹ ['mʊtər] (**-, -n**) *f* (*Schrauben~*) nut.
Mutter² ['mʊtər] (**-, ⸚**) *f* mother; ~**freuden** *pl* the joys *pl* of motherhood; ~**gesellschaft** *f* (*COMM*) parent company; ~**kuchen** *m* (*ANAT*) placenta; ~**land** *nt* mother country; ~**leib** *m* womb.
mütterlich ['mʏtərlɪç] *adj* motherly.
mütterlicherseits *adv* on the mother's side.
Mutter- *zW:* ~**liebe** *f* motherly love; ~**mal** *nt* birthmark; ~**milch** *f* mother's milk.
Mutterschaft *f* motherhood.
Mutterschaftsgeld *nt* maternity benefit.
Mutterschaftsurlaub *m* maternity leave.
Mutter- *zW:* ~**schutz** *m* maternity regulations *pl*; **m~seelenallein** *adj* all alone; ~**sprache** *f* native language; ~**tag** *m* Mother's Day.
Mutti (**-, -s**) (*umg*) *f* mum(my) (*BRIT*), mom(my) (*US*).
mutwillig ['muːtvɪlɪç] *adj* malicious, deliberate.
Mütze ['mʏtsə] (**-, -n**) *f* cap.
MV *f abk* (= *Mitgliederversammlung*) general meeting.
MW *abk* (= *Mittelwelle*) MW.
MWSt, MwSt *abk* (= *Mehrwertsteuer*) VAT.
mysteriös [mysteri'øːs] *adj* mysterious.
Mystik ['mʏstɪk] *f* mysticism.
Mystiker(in) (**-s, -**) *m(f)* mystic.
mystisch ['mʏstɪʃ] *adj* mystical; (*rätselhaft*) mysterious.
Mythologie [mytolo'giː] *f* mythology.

Mythos ['myːtɔs] (**-, Mythen**) *m* myth.

N, n

N¹, n [ɛn] *nt* N, n; ~ **wie Nordpol** ≈ N for Nellie, N for Nan (*US*).
N² [ɛn] *abk* (= *Norden*) N.
na [na] *interj* well; ~ **gut** (*umg*) all right, OK; ~ **also!** (well,) there you are (then)!; ~ **so was!** well, I never!; ~ **und?** so what?
Nabel ['naːbəl] (**-s, -**) *m* navel; **der ~ der Welt** (*fig*) the hub of the universe; ~**schnur** *f* umbilical cord.

nach [naːx] *präp +dat* **1** (*örtlich*) to; ~ **Berlin** to Berlin; ~ **links/rechts** (to the) left/right; ~ **oben/hinten** up/back; **er ist schon ~ London abgefahren** he has already left for London
2 (*zeitlich*) after; **einer ~ dem anderen** one after the other; ~ **Ihnen!** after you!; **zehn (Minuten) ~ drei** ten (minutes) past *od* after (*US*) three
3 (*gemäß*) according to; ~ **dem Gesetz** according to the law; **die Uhr ~ dem Radio stellen** to put a clock right by the radio; **ihrer Sprache ~ (zu urteilen)** judging by her language; **dem Namen ~** judging by his/her name; ~ **allem, was ich weiß** as far as I know
♦ *adv:* **ihm ~!** after him!; ~ **und ~** gradually, little by little; ~ **wie vor** still.

nachäffen ['naːxɛfən] *vt* to ape.
nachahmen ['naːxaːmən] *vt* to imitate.
nachahmenswert *adj* exemplary.
Nachahmung *f* imitation; **etw zur ~ empfehlen** to recommend sth as an example.
Nachbar(in) ['naxbaːr(ɪn)] (**-s, -n**) *m(f)* neighbour (*BRIT*), neighbor (*US*); ~**haus** *nt:* **im ~haus** next door; **n~lich** *adj* neighbourly (*BRIT*), neighborly (*US*); ~**schaft** *f* neighbourhood (*BRIT*), neighborhood (*US*); ~**staat** *m* neighbouring (*BRIT*) *od* neighboring (*US*) state.
nach- *zW:* **N~behandlung** *f* (*MED*) follow-up treatment; ~**bestellen** *vt* to order again; **N~bestellung** *f* (*COMM*) repeat order; ~**beten** (*pej: umg*) *vt* to repeat parrot-fashion; ~**bezahlen** *vt* to pay; (*später*) to pay later; ~**bilden** *vt* to copy; **N~bildung** *f* imitation, copy; ~**blicken** *vi* to look *od* gaze after; ~**datieren** *vt* to postdate.

nachdem [naːxˈdeːm] *konj* after; (*weil*) since; **je ~ (ob)** it depends (whether).

nach- *zW:* **~denken** *unreg vi:* **über etw** *akk* **~denken** to think about sth; **darüber darf man gar nicht ~denken** it doesn't bear thinking about; **N~denken** *nt* reflection, meditation; **~denklich** *adj* thoughtful, pensive; **~denklich gestimmt sein** to be in a thoughtful mood.

Nachdruck [ˈnaːxdrʊk] *m* emphasis; (*TYP*) reprint, reproduction; **besonderen ~ darauf legen, daß ...** to stress *od* emphasize particularly that ...

nachdrücklich [ˈnaːxdrʏklɪç] *adj* emphatic; **~ auf etw** *dat* **bestehen** to insist firmly (up)on sth.

nacheifern [ˈnaːx|aɪfərn] *vi:* **jdm ~** to emulate sb.

nacheinander [naːx|aɪˈnandər] *adv* one after the other; **kurz ~** shortly after each other; **drei Tage ~** three days running, three days on the trot (*umg*).

nachempfinden [ˈnaːx|ɛmpfɪndən] *unreg vt:* **jdm etw ~** to feel sth with sb.

nacherzählen [ˈnaːx|ɛrtsɛːlən] *vt* to retell.

Nacherzählung *f* reproduction (of a story).

Nachf. *abk* = **Nachfolger**.

Nachfahr [ˈnaːxfaːr] (**-en, -en**) *m* descendant.

Nachfolge [ˈnaːxfɔlɡə] *f* succession; **die/jds ~ antreten** to succeed/succeed sb.

nachfolgen *vi* (*lit*): **jdm/etw ~** to follow sb/sth.

nachfolgend *adj* following.

Nachfolger(in) (**-s, -**) *m(f)* successor.

nachforschen *vt, vi* to investigate.

Nachforschung *f* investigation; **~en anstellen** to make enquiries.

Nachfrage [ˈnaːxfraːɡə] *f* inquiry; (*COMM*) demand; **es besteht eine rege ~** (*COMM*) there is a great demand; **danke der ~** (*form*) thank you for your concern; (*umg*) nice of you to ask; **n~mäßig** *adj* according to demand.

nachfragen *vi* to inquire.

nach- *zW:* **~fühlen** *vt* = **nachempfinden**; **~füllen** *vt* to refill; **~geben** *unreg vi* to give way, yield.

Nachgebühr *f* surcharge; (*POST*) excess postage.

Nachgeburt *f* afterbirth.

nachgehen [ˈnaːxɡeːən] *unreg vi* (+*dat*) to follow; (*erforschen*) to inquire (into); (*Uhr*) to be slow; **einer geregelten Arbeit ~** to have a steady job.

Nachgeschmack [ˈnaːxɡəʃmak] *m* aftertaste.

nachgiebig [ˈnaːxɡiːbɪç] *adj* soft, accommodating; **N~keit** *f* softness.

nachgrübeln [ˈnaːxɡryːbəln] *vi:* **über etw** *akk* **~** to think about sth; (*sich Gedanken machen*) to ponder on sth.

nachgucken [ˈnaːxɡʊkən] *vt, vi* = **nachsehen**.

nachhaken [ˈnaːxhaːkən] (*umg*) *vi* to dig

deeper.

Nachhall [ˈnaːxhal] *m* resonance.

nachhallen *vi* to resound.

nachhaltig [ˈnaːxhaltɪç] *adj* lasting; (*Widerstand*) persistent.

nachhängen [ˈnaːxhɛŋən] *unreg vi:* **seinen Erinnerungen ~** to lose o.s. in one's memories.

Nachhauseweg [naːxˈhauzəveːk] *m* way home.

nachhelfen [ˈnaːxhɛlfən] *unreg vi:* **jdm ~** to help *od* assist sb; **er hat dem Glück ein bißchen nachgeholfen** he engineered himself a little luck.

nachher [naːxˈheːr] *adv* afterwards; **bis ~** see you later!

Nachhilfe [ˈnaːxhɪlfə] *f* (*auch:* **~unterricht**) extra (private) tuition.

nachhinein [ˈnaːxhɪnaɪn] *adv:* **im ~** afterwards; (*rückblickend*) in retrospect.

Nachholbedarf *m:* **einen ~ an etw** *dat* **haben** to have a lot of sth to catch up on.

nachholen [ˈnaːxhoːlən] *vt* to catch up with; (*Versäumtes*) to make up for.

Nachkomme [ˈnaːxkɔmə] (**-, -n**) *m* descendant.

nachkommen *unreg vi* to follow; (*einer Verpflichtung*) to fulfil; **Sie können Ihr Gepäck ~ lassen** you can have your luggage sent on (after).

Nachkommenschaft *f* descendants *pl*.

Nachkriegs- [ˈnaːxkriːks] *in zW* postwar; **~zeit** *f* postwar period.

Nach- *zW:* **~laß** (**-lasses, -lässe**) *m* (*COMM*) discount, rebate; (*Erbe*) estate; **n~lassen** *unreg vt* (*Strafe*) to remit; (*Summe*) to take off; (*Schulden*) to cancel ♦ *vi* to decrease, ease off; (*Sturm*) to die down; (*schlechter werden*) to deteriorate; **er hat n~gelassen** he has got worse; **n~lässig** *adj* negligent, careless; **~lässigkeit** *f* negligence, carelessness; **~laßsteuer** *f* death duty; **~laßverwalter** *m* executor.

nachlaufen [ˈnaːxlaufən] *unreg vi:* **jdm ~** to run after *od* chase sb.

nachliefern [ˈnaːxliːfərn] *vt* (*später liefern*) to deliver at a later date; (*zuzüglich liefern*) to make a further delivery of.

nachlösen [ˈnaːxløːzən] *vi* to pay on the train/when one gets off; (*zur Weiterfahrt*) to pay the extra.

nachm. *abk* (= *nachmittags*) p.m.

nachmachen [ˈnaːxmaxən] *vt* to imitate, copy; (*fälschen*) to counterfeit; **jdm etw ~** to copy sth from sb; **das soll erst mal einer ~!** I'd like to see anyone else do that!

Nachmieter(in) [ˈnaːxmiːtər(ɪn)] *m(f):* **wir müssen einen ~ finden** we have to find someone to take over the flat *etc*.

Nachmittag [ˈnaːxmɪtaːk] *m* afternoon; **am ~** in the afternoon; **n~** *adv:* **gestern/heute n~** yesterday/this afternoon.

nachmittags adv in the afternoon.
Nachmittagsvorstellung f matinée (performance).
Nachn. abk = **Nachnahme.**
Nachnahme (-, -n) f cash on delivery (BRIT), collect on delivery (US); **per ~** C.O.D.
Nachname m surname.
Nachporto nt excess postage.
nachprüfbar ['na:xpry:fba:r] adj verifiable.
nachprüfen ['na:xpry:fən] vt to check, verify.
nachrechnen ['na:xrɛçnən] vt to check.
Nachrede ['na:xre:də] f: **üble ~** (JUR) defamation of character.
nachreichen ['na:xraɪçən] vt to hand in later.
Nachricht ['na:xrɪçt] (-, -en) f (piece of) news sing; (Mitteilung) message.
Nachrichten pl news sing; **~agentur** f news agency; **~dienst** m (MIL) intelligence service; **~satellit** m (tele)communications satellite; **~sperre** f news blackout; **~sprecher(in)** m(f) newsreader; **~technik** f telecommunications sing.
nachrücken ['na:xrʏkən] vi to move up.
Nachruf ['na:xru:f] m obituary (notice).
nachrüsten ['na:xrʏstən] vt (Kraftwerk etc) to modernize; (Auto etc) to refit; (Waffen) to keep up to date ♦ vi (MIL) to deploy new arms.
nachsagen ['na:xza:gən] vt to repeat; **jdm etw ~** to say sth of sb; **das lasse ich mir nicht ~!** I'm not having that said of me!
Nachsaison ['na:xzɛzõ:] f off season.
nachschenken ['na:xʃɛŋkən] vt, vi: **darf ich Ihnen noch (etwas) ~?** may I top up your glass?
nachschicken ['na:xʃɪkən] vt to forward.
nachschlagen ['na:xʃla:gən] unreg vt to look up ♦ vi: **jdm ~** to take after sb.
Nachschlagewerk nt reference book.
Nachschlüssel m master key.
nachschmeißen ['na:xʃmaɪsən] unreg (umg) vt: **das ist ja nachgeschmissen!** it's a real bargain!
Nachschrift ['na:xʃrɪft] f postscript.
Nachschub ['na:xʃu:p] m supplies pl; (Truppen) reinforcements pl.
nachsehen ['na:xze:ən] unreg vt (prüfen) to check ♦ vi (erforschen) to look and see; **jdm etw ~** to forgive sb sth; **jdm ~** to gaze after sb.
Nachsehen nt: **das ~ haben** to be left empty-handed.
nachsenden ['na:xzɛndən] unreg vt to send on, forward.
Nachsicht ['na:xzɪçt] (-) f indulgence, leniency.
nachsichtig adj indulgent, lenient.
Nachsilbe ['na:xzɪlbə] f suffix.
nachsitzen ['na:xzɪtsən] unreg vi (SCH) to be kept in.
Nachsorge ['na:xzɔrgə] f (MED) aftercare.
Nachspann ['na:xʃpan] m credits pl.

Nachspeise ['na:xʃpaɪzə] f dessert, sweet (BRIT).
Nachspiel ['na:xʃpi:l] nt epilogue; (fig) sequel.
nachspionieren ['na:xʃpioni:rən] (umg) vi: **jdm ~** to spy on sb.
nachsprechen ['na:xʃprɛçən] unreg vt: **(jdm) ~** to repeat (after sb).
nächst [nɛ:çst] präp +dat (räumlich) next to; (außer) apart from; **~beste(r, s)** adj first that comes along; (zweitbeste) next-best.
Nächste(r, s) f(m) neighbour (BRIT), neighbor (US).
nächste(r, s) adj next; (nächstgelegen) nearest; **aus ~r Nähe** from close by; (betrachten) at close quarters; **Ende ~n Monats** at the end of next month; **am ~n Tag** (the) next day; **bei ~r Gelegenheit** at the earliest opportunity; **in ~r Zeit** some time soon; **der ~ Angehörige** the next of kin.
nachstehen ['na:xʃte:ən] unreg vi: **jdm in nichts ~** to be sb's equal in every way.
nachstehend adj attrib following.
nachstellen ['na:xʃtɛlən] vi: **jdm ~** to follow sb; (aufdringlich umwerben) to pester sb.
Nächstenliebe f love for one's fellow men.
nächstens adv shortly, soon.
nächstliegend adj (lit) nearest; (fig) obvious.
nächstmöglich adj next possible.
nachsuchen ['na:xzu:xən] vi: **um etw ~** to ask od apply for sth.
Nacht [naxt] (-, ̈-e) f night; **gute ~!** good night!; **in der ~** at night; **in der ~ auf Dienstag** during Monday night; **in der ~ vom 12. zum 13. April** during the night of April 12th to 13th; **über ~** (auch fig) overnight; **bei ~ und Nebel** (umg) at dead of night; **sich dat die ~ um die Ohren schlagen** (umg) to stay up all night; (mit Feiern, arbeiten) to make a night of it.
nacht adv: **heute ~** tonight.
Nachtdienst m night duty.
Nachteil ['na:xtaɪl] m disadvantage; **im ~ sein** to be at a disadvantage.
nachteilig adj disadvantageous.
Nachtfalter m moth.
Nachthemd nt (Herren~) nightshirt; nightdress (BRIT), nightgown.
Nachtigall ['naxtɪgal] (-, -en) f nightingale.
Nachtisch ['na:xtɪʃ] m = **Nachspeise.**
Nachtleben nt night life.
nächtlich ['nɛçtlɪç] adj nightly.
Nacht- zW: **~lokal** nt night club; **~mensch** ['naxtmɛnʃ] m night person; **~portier** m night porter.
nach- zW: **N~trag** ['na:xtra:k] (-(e)s, -träge) m supplement; **~tragen** unreg vt (zufügen) to add; **jdm etw ~tragen** to carry sth after sb; (fig) to hold sth against sb; **~tragend** adj resentful; **~träglich** adj later, subsequent; (zusätzlich) additional ♦ adv later, subsequently; (zusätzlich) additionally;

~**trauern** *vi:* **jdm/etw** ~**trauern** to mourn the loss of sb/sth.
Nachtruhe ['naxtruːə] *f* sleep.
nachts *adv* by night.
Nachtschicht *f* night shift.
Nachtschwester *f* night nurse.
nachtsüber *adv* during the night.
Nacht- *zW:* ~**tarif** *m* off-peak tariff; ~**tisch** *m* bedside table; ~**topf** *m* chamber pot; ~**wache** *f* night watch; (*im Krankenhaus*) night duty; ~**wächter** *m* night watchman.
Nach- *zW:* ~**untersuchung** *f* checkup; **n**~**vollziehen** *unreg vt* to understand, comprehend; **n**~**wachsen** *unreg vi* to grow again; ~**wahl** *f* ≈ by-election (*bes BRIT*); ~**wehen** *pl* afterpains *pl*; (*fig*) aftereffects *pl*; **n**~**weinen** *vi* +*dat* to mourn ♦ *vt:* **dieser Sache** *dat* **weine ich keine Träne n**~ I won't shed any tears over that.
Nachweis ['naːxvaɪs] **(-es, -e)** *m* proof; **den** ~ **für etw erbringen** *od* **liefern** to furnish proof of sth; **n**~**bar** *adj* provable, demonstrable; **n**~**en** ['naːxvaɪzən] *unreg vt* to prove; **jdm etw n**~**en** to point sth out to sb; **n**~**lich** *adj* evident, demonstrable.
nach- *zW:* **N**~**welt** *f:* **die N**~**welt** posterity; ~**winken** *vi:* **jdm** ~**winken** to wave after sb; ~**wirken** *vi* to have aftereffects; **N**~**wirkung** *f* aftereffect; **N**~**wort** *nt* appendix; **N**~**wuchs** *m* offspring; (*beruflich etc*) new recruits *pl*; ~**zahlen** *vt, vi* to pay extra; ~**zählen** *vt* to count again; **N**~**zahlung** *f* additional payment; (*zurückdatiert*) back pay.
nachziehen ['naːxtsiːən] *unreg vt* (*Linie*) to go over; (*Lippen*) to paint; (*Augenbrauen*) to pencil in; (*hinterherziehen*): **etw** ~ to drag sth behind one.
Nachzügler (-s, -) *m* straggler.
Nackedei ['nakədaɪ] **(-(e)s, -e** *od* **-s)** *m* (*hum: umg: Kind*) little bare monkey.
Nacken ['nakən] **(-s, -)** *m* nape of the neck; **jdm im** ~ **sitzen** (*umg*) to breathe down sb's neck.
nackt [nakt] *adj* naked; (*Tatsachen*) plain, bare; **N**~**heit** *f* nakedness; **N**~**kultur** *f* nudism.
Nadel ['naːdəl] **(-, -n)** *f* needle; (*Steck*~) pin; ~**baum** *m* conifer; ~**kissen** *nt* pincushion; ~**öhr** *nt* eye of a needle; ~**wald** *m* coniferous forest.
Nagel ['naːgəl] **(-s, ̈)** *m* nail; **sich** *dat* **etw unter den** ~ **reißen** (*umg*) to pinch sth; **etw an den** ~ **hängen** (*fig*) to chuck sth in (*umg*); **Nägel mit Köpfen machen** (*umg*) to do the job properly; ~**bürste** *f* nailbrush; ~**feile** *f* nailfile; ~**haut** *f* cuticle; ~**lack** *m* nail varnish (*BRIT*) *od* polish; ~**lackentferner (-s, -)** *m* nail polish remover.
nageln *vt, vi* to nail.
nagelneu *adj* brand-new.
Nagelschere *f* nail scissors *pl*.
nagen ['naːgən] *vt, vi* to gnaw.
Nagetier ['naːgətiːr] *nt* rodent.

nah *adj* = **nahe**.
Nahaufnahme *f* close-up.
Nahe *f* (*Fluß*) Nahe.
nahe *adj* (*räumlich*) near(by); (*Verwandte*) near, close; (*Freunde*) close; (*zeitlich*) near, close ♦ *adv:* **von nah und fern** from near and far ♦ *präp* +*dat* near (to), close to; **von** ~**m** at close quarters; **der N**~ **Osten** the Middle East; **jdm zu** ~ **treten** (*fig*) to offend sb; **mit jdm** ~ **verwandt sein** to be closely related to sb.
Nähe ['nɛːə] **(-)** *f* nearness, proximity; (*Umgebung*) vicinity; **in der** ~ close by; at hand; **aus der** ~ from close to.
nahe- *zW:* ~**bei** *adv* nearby; ~**bringen** *unreg vt* +*dat* (*fig*): **jdm etw** ~**bringen** to bring sth home to sb; ~**gehen** *unreg vi:* **jdm** ~**gehen** to grieve sb; ~**kommen** *unreg vi:* **jdm** ~**kommen** to get close to sb; ~**legen** *vt:* **jdm etw** ~**legen** to suggest sth to sb; ~**liegen** *unreg vi* to be obvious; **der Verdacht liegt** ~, **daß ...** it seems reasonable to suspect that ...; ~**liegend** *adj* obvious.
nahen *vi, vr* to approach, draw near.
nähen ['nɛːən] *vt, vi* to sew.
näher *adj* nearer; (*Erklärung, Erkundigung*) more detailed ♦ *adv* nearer; in greater detail; **ich kenne ihn nicht** ~ I don't know him well.
Nähere(s) *nt* details *pl*, particulars *pl*.
Näherei [nɛːəˈraɪ] *f* sewing, needlework.
Naherholungsgebiet *nt* recreational area (*close to a centre of population*).
Näherin *f* seamstress.
näherkommen *unreg vi, vr* to get closer.
nähern *vr* to approach.
Näherungswert *m* approximate value.
nahe- *zW:* ~**stehen** *unreg vi:* **jdm** ~**stehen** to be close to sb; **einer Sache** ~**stehen** to sympathize with sth; ~**stehend** *adj* close; ~**zu** *adv* nearly.
Nähgarn *nt* thread.
Nahkampf *m* hand-to-hand fighting.
Nähkasten *m* workbox, sewing basket.
nahm *etc* [naːm] *vb siehe* **nehmen**.
Nähmaschine *f* sewing machine.
Nähnadel *f* (sewing) needle.
Nahost [naːˈɔst] *m:* **aus** ~ from the Middle East.
Nährboden *m* (*lit*) fertile soil; (*fig*) breeding ground.
nähren ['nɛːrən] *vt* to feed ♦ *vr* (*Person*) to feed o.s.; (*Tier*) to feed; **er sieht gut genährt aus** he looks well fed.
Nährgehalt ['nɛːrgəhalt] *m* nutritional value.
nahrhaft ['naːrhaft] *adj* (*Essen*) nourishing.
Nährstoffe *pl* nutrients *pl*.
Nahrung ['naːrʊŋ] *f* food; (*fig*) sustenance.
Nahrungs- *zW:* ~**aufnahme** *f:* **die** ~**aufnahme verweigern** to refuse food; ~**kette** *f* food chain; ~**mittel** *nt* food(stuff); ~**mittelindustrie** *f* food industry; ~**suche** *f* search

for food.

Nährwert *m* nutritional value.

Naht [na:t] (-, ⁻e) *f* seam; (*MED*) suture; (*TECH*) join; **aus allen Nähten platzen** (*umg*) to be bursting at the seams; **n~los** *adj* seamless; **n~los ineinander übergehen** to follow without a gap.

Nahverkehr *m* local traffic.

Nahverkehrszug *m* local train.

Nähzeug *nt* sewing kit, sewing things *pl*.

Nahziel *nt* immediate objective.

naiv [na'iːf] *adj* naïve.

Naivität [naivi'tɛːt] *f* naïveté, naïvety.

Name ['naːmə] (-ns, -n) *m* name; **im ~n von** on behalf of; **dem ~n nach müßte sie Deutsche sein** judging by her name she must be German; **die Dinge beim ~n nennen** (*fig*) to call a spade a spade; **ich kenne das Stück nur dem ~n nach** I've heard of the play but that's all.

namens *adv* by the name of.

Namensänderung *f* change of name.

Namenstag *m* name day, saint's day.

---

*In catholic areas of Germany the **Namenstag** is often a more important celebration than a birthday. It is the day dedicated to the saint after whom a person is called, and on that day the person receives presents and invites relatives and friends round to celebrate.*

---

namentlich ['naːməntlɪç] *adj* by name ♦ *adv* particularly, especially.

namhaft ['naːmhaft] *adj* (*berühmt*) famed, renowned; (*beträchtlich*) considerable; **~ machen** to name, identify.

Namibia [na'miːbia] (-s) *nt* Namibia.

nämlich ['nɛːmlɪç] *adv* that is to say, namely; (*denn*) since; **der/die/das ~e** the same.

nannte *etc* ['nantə] *vb siehe* **nennen**.

nanu [na'nuː] *interj* well I never!

Napalm [na'palm] (-s) *nt* napalm.

Napf [napf] (-(e)s, ⁻e) *m* bowl, dish; **~kuchen** *m* ≈ ring-shaped pound cake.

Narbe ['narbə] (-, -n) *f* scar.

narbig ['narbɪç] *adj* scarred.

Narkose [nar'koːzə] (-, -n) *f* anaesthetic (*BRIT*), anesthetic (*US*).

Narr [nar] (-en, -en) *m* fool; **jdn zum ~en halten** to make a fool of sb; **n~en** *vt* to fool.

Narrenfreiheit *f*: **sie hat bei ihm ~** he gives her (a) free rein.

Narrensicher *adj* foolproof.

Narrheit *f* foolishness.

Närrin ['nɛrɪn] *f* fool.

närrisch *adj* foolish, crazy; **die ~en Tage** *Fasching* and the period leading up to it.

Narzisse [nar'tsɪsə] (-, -n) *f* narcissus.

narzißtisch [nar'tsɪstɪʃ] *adj* narcissistic.

NASA ['naːza] (-) *f abk* (= *National Aeronautics and Space Administration*) NASA.

naschen ['naʃən] *vt* to nibble; (*heimlich*) to eat secretly ♦ *vi* to nibble sweet things; **~ von** *od* **an** +*dat* to nibble at.

naschhaft *adj* sweet-toothed.

Nase ['naːzə] (-, -n) *f* nose; **sich** *dat* **die ~ putzen** to wipe one's nose; (*sich schneuzen*) to blow one's nose; **jdm auf der ~ herumtanzen** (*umg*) to play sb up; **jdm etw vor der ~ wegschnappen** (*umg*) to just beat sb to sth; **die ~ voll haben** (*umg*) to have had enough; **jdm etw auf die ~ binden** (*umg*) to tell sb all about sth; **(immer) der ~ nachgehen** (*umg*) to follow one's nose; **jdn an der ~ herumführen** (*als Täuschung*) to lead sb by the nose; (*als Scherz*) to pull sb's leg.

Nasen- *zW*: **~bluten** (-s) *nt* nosebleed; **~loch** *nt* nostril; **~rücken** *m* bridge of the nose; **~tropfen** *pl* nose drops *pl*.

naseweis *adj* pert, cheeky; (*neugierig*) nosey.

Nashorn ['naːshɔrn] *nt* rhinoceros.

naß [nas] *adj* wet.

Nassauer ['nasaʊər] (-s, -) (*umg*) *m* scrounger.

Nässe ['nɛsə] (-) *f* wetness.

nässen *vt* to wet.

naßkalt *adj* wet and cold.

Naßrasur *f* wet shave.

Nation [natsi'oːn] *f* nation.

national [natsio'naːl] *adj* national; **N~elf** *f* international (football) team; **N~feiertag** *m* national holiday; **N~hymne** *f* national anthem.

nationalisieren [natsionali'ziːrən] *vt* to nationalize.

Nationalisierung *f* nationalization.

Nationalismus [natsiona'lɪsmʊs] *m* nationalism.

nationalistisch [natsiona'lɪstɪʃ] *adj* nationalistic.

Nationalität [natsionali'tɛːt] *f* nationality.

National- *zW*: **~mannschaft** *f* international team; **~sozialismus** *m* National Socialism; **~sozialist** *m* National Socialist.

NATO, Nato ['naːto] (-) *f abk*: **die ~** NATO.

Natrium ['naːtrium] (-s) *nt* sodium.

Natron ['naːtron] (-s) *nt* soda.

Natter ['natər] (-, -n) *f* adder.

Natur [na'tuːr] *f* nature; (*körperlich*) constitution; (*freies Land*) countryside; **das geht gegen meine ~** it goes against the grain.

Naturalien [natu'raːliən] *pl* natural produce *sing*; **in ~** in kind.

Naturalismus [natura'lɪsmʊs] *m* naturalism.

Naturell [natu'rɛl] (-s, -e) *nt* temperament, disposition.

Natur- *zW*: **~erscheinung** *f* natural phenomenon *od* event; **n~farben** *adj* natural-coloured (*BRIT*) *od* -colored (*US*); **~forscher** *m* natural scientist; **~freak** (-s, -s) (*umg*) *m* back-to-nature freak; **n~gemäß** *adj* natural; **~geschichte** *f* natural history; **~gesetz** *nt* law of nature; **n~getreu** *adj* true

to life; ~**heilverfahren** nt natural cure;
~**katastrophe** f natural disaster;
~**kostladen** m health food shop; ~**kunde** f
natural history; ~**lehrpfad** m nature trail.
natürlich [na'ty:rlıç] adj natural ◆ adv
naturally; **eines ~en Todes sterben** to die of
natural causes.
natürlicherweise [na'ty:rlıçər'vaızə] adv
naturally, of course.
Natürlichkeit f naturalness.
Natur- zW: ~**produkt** nt natural product;
n~rein adj natural, pure; ~**schutz** m: **unter
~schutz stehen** to be legally protected;
~**schutzgebiet** nt nature reserve (BRIT),
national park (US); ~**talent** nt natural
prodigy; **n~verbunden** adj nature-loving;
~**wissenschaft** f natural science;
~**wissenschaftler** m scientist; ~**zustand** m
natural state.
Nautik ['naʊtık] f nautical science,
navigation.
nautisch ['naʊtıʃ] adj nautical.
Navelorange ['na:vəlɔrã:ʒə] f navel orange.
Navigation [navigatsi'o:n] f navigation.
Navigationsfehler m navigational error.
Navigationsinstrumente pl navigation
instruments pl.
Nazi ['na:tsi] (-**s**, -**s**) m Nazi.
NB abk (= nota bene) NB.
n.Br. abk (= nördlicher Breite) northern
latitude.
NC m abk (= numerus clausus) siehe **Numerus.**
Nchf. abk = **Nachfolger.**
n.Chr. abk (= nach Christus) A.D.
NDR (-) m abk (= Norddeutscher Rundfunk)
North German Radio.
Neapel [ne'a:pəl] (-**s**) nt Naples.
Neapolitaner(in) [neapoli'ta:nər(ın)] (-**s**, -) m(f)
Neapolitan.
neapolitanisch [neapoli'ta:nıʃ] adj
Neapolitan.
Nebel ['ne:bəl] (-**s**, -) m fog, mist.
nebelig adj foggy, misty.
Nebel- zW: ~**leuchte** f (AUT) rear fog-light;
~**scheinwerfer** m fog-lamp; ~**schlußleuchte**
f (AUT) rear fog-light.
neben ['ne:bən] präp +akk next to ◆ präp +dat
next to; (außer) apart from, besides; ~**an**
[ne:bən|'an] adv next door; **N~anschluß** m
(TEL) extension; **N~ausgaben** pl incidental
expenses pl; ~**bei** [ne:bən'baı] adv at the
same time; (außerdem) additionally;
(beiläufig) incidentally; ~**bei bemerkt** od
gesagt by the way, incidentally; **N~beruf** m
second occupation; **er ist im N~beruf** ... he
has a second job as a ...; **N~beschäftigung** f
sideline; (Zweitberuf) extra job; **N~buhler(in)**
(-**s**, -) m(f) rival; ~**einander** [ne:bənaı'nandər]
adv side by side; ~**einanderlegen** vt to put
next to each other; **N~eingang** m side
entrance; **N~einkünfte** pl, **N~einnahmen** pl
supplementary income sing; **N~erscheinung**

f side effect; **N~fach** nt subsidiary subject;
N~fluß m tributary; **N~geräusch** nt (RUNDF)
atmospherics pl, interference; **N~handlung**
f (LITER) subplot; ~**her** [ne:bən'he:r] adv
(zusätzlich) besides; (gleichzeitig) at the same
time; (daneben) alongside; ~**herfahren** unreg
vi to drive alongside; **N~kläger** m (JUR) joint
plaintiff; **N~kosten** pl extra charges pl,
extras pl; **N~mann** (-(e)s, pl -männer) m: **Ihr
N~mann** the person next to you;
N~produkt nt by-product; **N~rolle** f minor
part; **N~sache** f trifle, side issue; ~**sächlich**
adj minor, peripheral; **N~saison** f low
season; **N~satz** m (GRAM) subordinate
clause; ~**stehend** adj: ~**stehende Abbildung**
illustration opposite; **N~straße** f side
street; **N~strecke** f (EISENB) branch od
local line; **N~verdienst** m secondary
income; **N~zimmer** nt adjoining room.
neblig ['ne:blıç] adj = **nebelig.**
nebst [ne:pst] präp +dat together with.
Necessaire [nesɛ'sɛ:r] (-**s**, -**s**) nt (Näh~)
needlework box; (Nagel~) manicure case.
Neckar ['nɛkar] (-**s**) m (Fluß) Neckar.
necken ['nɛkən] vt to tease.
Neckerei [nɛkə'raı] f teasing.
neckisch adj coy; (Einfall, Lied) amusing.
nee [ne:] (umg) adv no, nope.
Neffe ['nɛfə] (-**n**, -**n**) m nephew.
negativ ['ne:gati:f] adj negative; **N~** (-**s**, -**e**) nt
(PHOT) negative.
Neger ['ne:gər] (-**s**, -) m negro; ~**in** f negress;
~**kuß** m chocolate-covered marshmallow.
negieren [ne'gi:rən] vt (bestreiten) to deny;
(verneinen) to negate.
nehmen ['ne:mən] unreg vt, vi to take; **etw zu
sich ~** to take sth, partake of sth (liter); **jdm
etw ~** to take sth (away) from sb; **sich ernst
~** to take o.s. seriously; ~ **Sie sich doch
bitte** help yourself; **man nehme ...** (KOCH)
take ...; **wie man's nimmt** depending on
your point of view; **die Mauer nimmt einem
die ganze Sicht** the wall blocks the whole
view; **er ließ es sich** dat **nicht ~, es
persönlich zu tun** he insisted on doing it
himself.
Nehrung ['ne:rʊŋ] f (GEOG) spit (of land).
Neid [naıt] (-(**e**)**s**) m envy.
Neider ['naıdər] (-**s**, -) m envier.
Neidhammel (umg) m envious person.
neidisch adj envious, jealous.
Neige (-, -**n**) f (geh: Ende): **die Vorräte gehen
zur ~** the provisions are fast becoming
exhausted.
neigen ['naıgən] vt to incline, lean; (Kopf) to
bow ◆ vi: **zu etw ~** to tend to sth.
Neigung f (des Geländes) slope; (Tendenz)
tendency, inclination; (Vorliebe) liking;
(Zuneigung) affection.
Neigungswinkel m angle of inclination.
nein [naın] adv no.
Nelke ['nɛlkə] (-, -**n**) f carnation, pink;

(*Gewürz~*) clove.

nennen ['nɛnən] *unreg vt* to name; (*mit Namen*) to call; **das nenne ich Mut!** that's what I call courage!

nennenswert *adj* worth mentioning.

Nenner (**-s, -**) *m* denominator; **etw auf einen ~ bringen** (*lit, fig*) to reduce sth to a common denominator.

Nennung *f* naming.

Nennwert *m* nominal value; (*COMM*) par.

Neon ['ne:ɔn] (**-s**) *nt* neon.

Neo-Nazi [neo'na:tsi] *m* Neonazi.

Neon- *zW:* ~**licht** *nt* neon light; ~**reklame** *f* neon sign; ~**röhre** *f* neon tube.

Nepal ['ne:pal] (**-s**) *nt* Nepal.

Nepp [nɛp] (**-s**) (*umg*) *m:* **der reinste ~** daylight robbery, a rip-off.

Nerv [nɛrf] (**-s, -en**) *m* nerve; **die ~en sind mit ihm durchgegangen** he lost control, he snapped (*umg*); **jdm auf die ~en gehen** to get on sb's nerves.

nerven (*umg*) *vt:* **jdn ~** to get on sb's nerves.

Nerven- *zW:* ~**aufreibend** *adj* nerve-racking; ~**bündel** *nt* bundle of nerves; ~**gas** *nt* (*MIL*) nerve gas; ~**heilanstalt** *f* mental hospital; ~**klinik** *f* psychiatric clinic; **n~krank** *adj* mentally ill; ~**säge** (*umg*) *f* pain (in the neck); ~**schwäche** *f* neurasthenia; ~**system** *nt* nervous system; ~**zusammenbruch** *m* nervous breakdown.

nervig ['nɛrvɪç] (*umg*) *adj* exasperating, annoying.

nervös [nɛr'vø:s] *adj* nervous.

Nervosität [nɛrvozi'tɛ:t] *f* nervousness.

nervtötend *adj* nerve-racking; (*Arbeit*) soul-destroying.

Nerz [nɛrts] (**-es, -e**) *m* mink.

Nessel ['nɛsəl] (**-, -n**) *f* nettle; **sich in die ~n setzen** (*fig: umg*) to put o.s. in a spot.

Nest [nɛst] (**-(e)s, -er**) *nt* nest; (*umg: Ort*) dump; (*fig: Bett*) bed; (: *Schlupfwinkel*) hideout, lair; **da hat er sich ins warme ~ gesetzt** (*umg*) he's got it made; ~**beschmutzung** (*pej*) *f* running-down (*umg*) *od* denigration (of one's family/country).

nesteln *vi:* **an etw** +*dat* **~** to fumble *od* fiddle about with sth.

Nesthäkchen ['nɛsthɛ:kçən] *nt* baby of the family.

nett [nɛt] *adj* nice; **sei so ~ und räum auf!** would you mind clearing up?

netterweise ['nɛtər'vaɪzə] *adv* kindly.

netto *adv* net; **N~einkommen** *nt* net income; **N~gewicht** *nt* net weight; **N~gewinn** *m* net profit; **N~gewinnspanne** *f* net margin; **N~lohn** *m* take-home pay.

Netz [nɛts] (**-es, -e**) *nt* net; (*Gepäck~*) rack; (*Einkaufs~*) string bag; (*Spinnen~*) web; (*System, auch COMPUT*) network; (*Strom~*) mains *sing od pl;* **das soziale ~** the social security network; **jdm ins ~ gehen** (*fig*) to fall into sb's trap; ~**anschluß** *m* mains

connection; ~**haut** *f* retina; ~**karte** *f* (*EISENB*) runabout ticket (*BRIT*); ~**plantechnik** *f* network analysis; ~**spannung** *f* mains voltage.

neu [nɔy] *adj* new; (*Sprache, Geschichte*) modern; **der/die N~e** the new person, the newcomer; **seit ~estem** (since) recently; **~ schreiben** to rewrite, write again; **auf ein ~es!** (*Aufmunterung*) let's try again; **was gibt's N~es?** (*umg*) what's the latest?; **von ~em** (*von vorn*) from the beginning; (*wieder*) again; **sich ~ einkleiden** to buy o.s. a new set of clothes; **N~ankömmling** *m* newcomer; **N~anschaffung** *f* new purchase *od* acquisition; ~**artig** *adj* new kind of; **N~auflage** *f* new edition; **N~ausgabe** *f* new edition; **N~bau** (**-(e)s, -ten**) *m* new building; **N~bauwohnung** *f* newly-built flat; **N~bearbeitung** *f* revised edition; (*das Neubearbeiten*) revision, reworking; **N~druck** *m* reprint; **N~emission** *f* (*Aktien*) new issue.

neuerdings *adv* (*kürzlich*) (since) recently; (*von neuem*) again.

neueröffnet *adj attrib* newly-opened; (*wiedergeöffnet*) reopened.

Neuerscheinung *f* (*Buch*) new publication; (*Schallplatte*) new release.

Neuerung *f* innovation, new departure.

Neufassung *f* revised version.

Neufundland [nɔy'fʊntlant] *nt* Newfoundland; **Neufundländer(in)** (**-s, -**) *m(f)* Newfoundlander; **neufundländisch** *adj* Newfoundland *attrib.*

neugeboren *adj* newborn; **sich wie ~ fühlen** to feel (like) a new man/woman.

Neugier *f* curiosity.

Neugierde (**-**) *f:* **aus ~** out of curiosity.

neugierig *adj* curious.

Neuguinea [nɔygi'ne:a] (**-s**) *nt* New Guinea.

Neuheit *f* novelty; (*neuartige Ware*) new thing.

Neuigkeit *f* news *sing.*

neu- *zW:* **N~jahr** *nt* New Year; **N~land** *nt* virgin land; (*fig*) new ground; ~**lich** *adv* recently, the other day; **N~ling** *m* novice; ~**modisch** *adj* fashionable; (*pej*) newfangled; **N~mond** *m* new moon.

neun [nɔyn] *num* nine; **N~** (**-, -en**) *f* nine; **ach du grüne N~e!** (*umg*) well I'm blowed!

neunmalklug *adj* (*ironisch*) smart-aleck *attrib.*

neunzehn *num* nineteen.

neunzig *num* ninety.

Neureg(e)lung *f* adjustment.

neureich *adj* nouveau riche; **N~e(r)** *f(m)* nouveau riche.

Neurologie [nɔyrolo'gi:] *f* neurology.

neurologisch [nɔyro'lo:gɪʃ] *adj* neurological.

Neurose [nɔy'ro:zə] (**-, -n**) *f* neurosis.

Neurotiker(in) [nɔy'ro:tikər(ɪn)] (**-s, -**) *m(f)* neurotic.

neurotisch *adj* neurotic.

Neu- *zW:* ~**schnee** *m* fresh snow; ~**seeland** [nɔy'zeːlant] *nt* New Zealand; ~**seeländer(in)** (**-s**, **-**) *m(f)* New Zealander; **n~seeländisch** *adj* New Zealand *attrib;* **n~sprachlich** *adj:* **n~sprachliches Gymnasium** grammar school (*BRIT*) *od* high school (*bes US*) stressing modern languages.
neutral [nɔy'traːl] *adj* neutral.
neutralisieren [nɔytraliˈziːrən] *vt* to neutralize.
Neutralität [nɔytraliˈtɛːt] *f* neutrality.
Neutron ['nɔytrɔn] (**-s**, **-en**) *nt* neutron.
Neutrum ['nɔytrʊm] (**-s**, **Neutra** *od* **Neutren**) *nt* neuter.
Neu- *zW:* ~**wert** *m* purchase price; **n~wertig** *adj* as new; ~**zeit** *f* modern age; **n~zeitlich** *adj* modern, recent.
N.H. *abk* (= *Normalhöhenpunkt*) normal peak (level).
nhd. *abk* (= *neuhochdeutsch*) NHG.
Nicaragua [nika'raːgua] (**-s**) *nt* Nicaragua; ~**ner(in)** [nikaraguˈaːnər(ɪn)] (**-s**, **-**) *m(f)* Nicaraguan; **n~nisch** [nikaraguˈaːnɪʃ] *adj* Nicaraguan.

══════════ *SCHLÜSSELWORT*

nicht [nɪçt] *adv* **1** (*Verneinung*) not; **er ist es ~** it's not him, it isn't him; **er raucht ~** (*gerade*) he isn't smoking; (*gewöhnlich*) he doesn't smoke; **ich kann das ~ - ich auch ~** I can't do it - neither *od* nor can I; **es regnet ~ mehr** it's not raining any more; ~ **mehr als** no more than
2 (*Bitte, Verbot*): ~**!** don't!, no!; ~ **berühren!** do not touch!; ~ **doch!** don't!
3 (*rhetorisch*): **du bist müde, ~ (wahr)?** you're tired, aren't you?; **das ist schön, ~ (wahr)?** it's nice, isn't it?
4: was du ~ sagst! the things you say!
◆ *präf* non-.

Nicht- *zW:* ~**achtung** *f* disregard; ~**anerkennung** *f* repudiation; ~**angriffspakt** *m* non-aggression pact.
Nichte ['nɪçtə] (**-**, **-n**) *f* niece.
Nicht- *zW:* ~**einhaltung** *f* (+*gen*) non-compliance (with); ~**einmischung** *f* (*POL*) nonintervention; ~**gefallen** *nt:* **bei** ~**gefallen (zurück)** if not satisfied (return).
nichtig ['nɪçtɪç] *adj* (*ungültig*) null, void; (*wertlos*) futile; **N~keit** *f* nullity, invalidity; (*Sinnlosigkeit*) futility.
Nichtraucher *m* nonsmoker; **ich bin ~** I don't smoke.
nichtrostend *adj* stainless.
nichts [nɪçts] *pron* nothing; ~ **als** nothing but; ~ **da!** (*ausgeschlossen*) nothing doing (*umg*); ~ **wie raus/hin** *etc* (*umg*) let's get out/over there *etc* (on the double); **für ~ und wieder** ~ for nothing at all; **N~** (**-s**) *nt* nothingness; (*pej: Person*) nonentity; **n~ahnend** *adj* unsuspecting.

Nichtschwimmer (**-s**, **-**) *m* nonswimmer.
nichts- *zW:* ~**destotrotz** *adv* notwithstanding (*form*), nonetheless; ~**destoweniger** *adv* nevertheless; **N~nutz** (**-es**, **-e**) *m* good-for-nothing; ~**nutzig** *adj* worthless, useless; ~**sagend** *adj* meaningless; **N~tun** (**-s**) *nt* idleness.
Nichtzutreffende(s) *nt:* ~ **(bitte) streichen** (please) delete as applicable.
Nickel ['nɪkəl] (**-s**) *nt* nickel; ~**brille** *f* metal-rimmed glasses *pl.*
nicken ['nɪkən] *vi* to nod.
Nickerchen ['nɪkərçən] *nt* nap; **ein ~ machen** (*umg*) to have forty winks.
Nicki ['nɪki] (**-s**, **-s**) *m* velours pullover.
nie [niː] *adv* never; ~ **wieder** *od* **mehr** never again; ~ **und nimmer** never ever; **fast ~** hardly ever.
nieder ['niːdər] *adj* low; (*gering*) inferior ◆ *adv* down; ~**deutsch** *adj* (*LING*) Low-German; **N~gang** *m* decline; ~**gedrückt** *adj* depressed; ~**gehen** *unreg vi* to descend; (*AVIAT*) to come down; (*Regen*) to fall; (*Boxer*) to go down; ~**geschlagen** *adj* depressed, dejected; **N~geschlagenheit** *f* depression, dejection; **N~kunft** *f* (*veraltet*) delivery, giving birth; **N~lage** *f* defeat.
Niederlande ['niːdərlandə] *pl:* **die ~** the Netherlands *pl.*
Niederländer(in) ['niːdərlɛndər(ɪn)] (**-s**, **-**) *m(f)* Dutchman, Dutchwoman.
niederländisch *adj* Dutch, Netherlands *attrib.*
nieder- *zW:* ~**lassen** *unreg vr* (*sich setzen*) to sit down; (*an Ort*) to settle (down); (*Arzt, Rechtsanwalt*) to set up in practice; **N~lassung** *f* settlement; (*COMM*) branch; ~**legen** *vt* to lay down; (*Arbeit*) to stop; (*Amt*) to resign; ~**machen** *vt* to mow down; **N~österreich** *nt* Lower Austria; **N~rhein** *m* Lower Rhine; ~**rheinisch** *adj* Lower Rhine *attrib;* **N~sachsen** *nt* Lower Saxony; **N~schlag** *m* (*CHEM*) precipitate; (*Bodensatz*) sediment; (*MET*) precipitation (*form*), rainfall; (*BOXEN*) knockdown; **radioaktiver N~schlag** (radioactive) fallout; ~**schlagen** *unreg vt* (*Gegner*) to beat down; (*Gegenstand*) to knock down; (*Augen*) to lower; (*JUR: Prozeß*) to dismiss; (*Aufstand*) to put down ◆ *vr* (*CHEM*) to precipitate; **sich in etw** *dat* ~**schlagen** (*Erfahrungen etc*) to find expression in sth; ~**schlagsfrei** ['niːdərʃlaːksfraɪ] *adj* dry, without precipitation (*form*); ~**schmetternd** *adj* (*Nachricht, Ergebnis*) shattering; ~**schreiben** *unreg vt* to write down; **N~schrift** *f* transcription; ~**tourig** *adj* (*Motor*) low-revving; ~**trächtig** *adj* base, mean; **N~trächtigkeit** *f* despicable *od* malicious behaviour.
Niederung *f* (*GEOG*) depression.
niederwalzen ['niːdərvaltsən] *vt:* **jdn/etw ~**

(*umg*) to mow sb/sth down.

niederwerfen ['niːdərvɛrfən] *unreg vt* to throw down; (*fig*) to overcome; (*Aufstand*) to suppress.

niedlich ['niːtlɪç] *adj* sweet, nice, cute.

niedrig ['niːdrɪç] *adj* low; (*Stand*) lowly, humble; (*Gesinnung*) mean.

niemals ['niːmaːls] *adv* never.

niemand ['niːmant] *pron* nobody, no-one.

Niemandsland ['niːmantslant] *nt* no-man's-land.

Niere ['niːrə] (-, -n) *f* kidney; **künstliche** ~ kidney machine.

Nierenentzündung *f* kidney infection.

nieseln ['niːzəln] *vi* to drizzle.

Nieselregen *m* drizzle.

niesen ['niːzən] *vi* to sneeze.

Niespulver *nt* sneezing powder.

Niet [niːt] (-(e)s, -e) *m* (*TECH*) rivet.

Niete ['niːtə] (-, -n) *f* (*TECH*) rivet; (*Los*) blank; (*Reinfall*) flop; (*Mensch*) failure.

nieten *vt* to rivet.

Nietenhose *f* (pair of) studded jeans *pl*.

niet- und nagelfest (*umg*) *adj* nailed down.

Niger¹ ['niːgər] (-s) *nt* (*Staat*) Niger.

Niger² ['niːgər] (-s) *m* (*Fluß*) Niger.

Nigeria [ni'geːria] (-s) *nt* Nigeria; ~**ner(in)** [nigeri'aːnər(ɪn)] *m(f)* Nigerian; **n~nisch** [nigeˈriːanɪʃ] *adj* Nigerian.

Nihilismus [nihiˈlɪsmʊs] *m* nihilism.

Nihilist [nihiˈlɪst] *m* nihilist; **n~isch** *adj* nihilistic.

Nikolaus ['niːkolaʊs] (-, -e *od* (*hum: umg*) -läuse) *m* ≈ Santa Claus, Father Christmas.

Nikosia [nikoˈziːa] (-s) *nt* Nicosia.

Nikotin [nikoˈtiːn] (-s) *nt* nicotine; **n~arm** *adj* low-nicotine.

Nil [niːl] (-s) *m* Nile; ~**pferd** *nt* hippopotamus.

Nimbus ['nɪmbʊs] (-, -se) *m* (*Heiligenschein*) halo; (*fig*) aura.

nimmersatt ['nɪmərzat] *adj* insatiable; **N~** (-(e)s, -e) *m* glutton.

Nimmerwiedersehen (*umg*) *nt*: **auf ~!** I never want to see you again.

nimmt [nɪmt] *vb siehe* **nehmen.**

nippen ['nɪpən] *vt, vi* to sip.

Nippes ['nɪpəs] *pl* knick-knacks *pl*, bric-a-brac *sing*.

Nippsachen ['nɪpzaxən] *pl* knick-knacks *pl*.

nirgends ['nɪrgənts] *adv* nowhere; **überall und** ~ here, there and everywhere.

nirgendwo ['nɪrgəntvo] *adv* = **nirgends.**

nirgendwohin *adv* nowhere.

Nische ['niːʃə] (-, -n) *f* niche.

nisten ['nɪstən] *vi* to nest.

Nitrat [niˈtraːt] (-(e)s, -e) *nt* nitrate.

Niveau [niˈvoː] (-s, -s) *nt* level; **diese Schule hat ein hohes** ~ this school has high standards; **unter meinem** ~ beneath me.

Nivellierung [nivɛˈliːrʊŋ] *f* (*Ausgleichung*) levelling out.

nix [nɪks] (*umg*) *pron* = **nichts.**

Nixe ['nɪksə] (-, -n) *f* water nymph.

Nizza ['nɪtsa] (-s) *nt* Nice.

n.J. *abk* (= *nächsten Jahres*) next year.

n.M. *abk* (= *nächsten Monats*) next month.

NN *abk* (= *Normalnull*) m.s.l.

N.N. *abk* = **NN.**

NO *abk* (= *Nordost*) NE.

no. *abk* (= *netto*) net.

nobel ['noːbəl] *adj* (*großzügig*) generous; (*elegant*) posh (*umg*).

Nobelpreis [no'bɛlpraɪs] *m* Nobel prize; ~**träger(in)** *m(f)* Nobel prize winner.

═══════════════════════ *SCHLÜSSELWORT*

noch [nɔx] *adv* **1** (*weiterhin*) still; ~ **nicht** not yet; ~ **nie** never (yet); ~ **immer** *od* **immer** ~ still; **bleiben Sie doch** ~ stay a bit longer; **ich gehe kaum** ~ **aus** I hardly go out any more

2 (*in Zukunft*) still, yet; (*irgendwann einmal*) one day; **das kann** ~ **passieren** that might still happen; **er wird** ~ **kommen** he'll come (yet); **das wirst du** ~ **bereuen** you'll come to regret it (one day)

3 (*nicht später als*): ~ **vor einer Woche** only a week ago; ~ **am selben Tag** the very same day; ~ **im 19. Jahrhundert** as late as the 19th century; ~ **heute** today

4 (*zusätzlich*): **wer war** ~ **da?** who else was there?; ~ **einmal** once more, again; ~ **dreimal** three more times; ~ **einer** another one; **und es regnete auch** ~ and on top of that it was raining

5 (*bei Vergleichen*): ~ **größer** even bigger; **das ist** ~ **besser** that's better still; **und wenn es** ~ **so schwer ist** however hard it is

6: Geld ~ **und** ~ heaps (and heaps) of money; **sie hat** ~ **und** ~ **versucht, ...** she tried again and again to ...

♦ *konj*: **weder A** ~ **B** neither A nor B.

nochmal(s) *adv* again, once more.

nochmalig *adj* repeated.

Nockenwelle ['nɔkənvɛlə] *f* camshaft.

NOK *nt abk* (= *Nationales Olympisches Komitee*) National Olympic Committee.

Nom. *abk* = **Nominativ.**

Nominalwert [nomiˈnaːlveːrt] *m* (*FIN*) nominal *od* par value.

Nominativ ['noːminatiːf] (-s, -e) *m* nominative.

nominell [nomiˈnɛl] *adj* nominal.

nominieren [nomiˈniːrən] *vt* to nominate.

Nonne ['nɔnə] (-, -n) *f* nun.

Nonnenkloster *nt* convent.

Nonplusultra [nɔnplusˈ|ʊltra] (-s) *nt* ultimate.

Nord [nɔrt] (-s) *m* north; ~**afrika** ['nɔrt|aːfrika] *nt* North Africa; ~**amerika** *nt* North America; **n~amerikanisch** ['nɔrt|ameriˈkaːnɪʃ] *adj* North American.

nordd. *abk* = **norddeutsch.**

norddeutsch *adj* North German.

Norddeutschland *nt* North(ern) Germany.
Norden ['nɔrdən] *m* north.
Nord- *zW:* ~**england** *nt* the North of England;
~**irland** *nt* Northern Ireland, Ulster; **n~isch**
adj northern; **n~ische Kombination** (*SKI*)
nordic combination; ~**kap** *nt* North Cape;
~**korea** ['nɔrtko'reːa] *nt* North Korea.
nördlich ['nœrtlıç] *adj* northerly, northern
♦ *präp +gen* (to the) north of; **der** ~**e**
Polarkreis the Arctic Circle; **N~es Eismeer**
Arctic Ocean; ~ **von** north of.
Nord- *zW:* ~**licht** *nt* northern lights *pl*, aurora
borealis; ~**-Ostsee-Kanal** *m* Kiel Canal;
~**pol** *m* North Pole; ~**polargebiet** *nt* Arctic
(Zone).
Nordrhein-Westfalen ['nɔrtraınvɛst'faːlən]
(**-s**) *nt* North Rhine-Westphalia.
Nordsee *f* North Sea.
nordwärts *adv* northwards.
Nörgelei [nœrgə'laı] *f* grumbling.
nörgeln *vi* to grumble.
Nörgler(in) (**-s**, **-**) *m(f)* grumbler.
Norm [nɔrm] (**-**, **-en**) *f* norm; (*Leistungssoll*)
quota; (*Größenvorschrift*) standard
(specification).
normal [nɔr'maːl] *adj* normal; **bist du noch** ~?
(*umg*) have you gone mad?; **N~benzin** *nt*
two-star petrol (*BRIT veraltet*), regular gas
(*US*).
normalerweise *adv* normally.
Normalfall *m:* **im** ~ normally.
Normalgewicht *nt* normal weight; (*genormt*)
standard weight.
normalisieren [nɔrmali'ziːrən] *vt* to normalize
♦ *vr* to return to normal.
Normalzeit *f* (*GEOG*) standard time.
Normandie [nɔrman'diː] *f* Normandy.
normen *vt* to standardize.
Norwegen ['nɔrveːgən] (**-s**) *nt* Norway.
Norweger(in) (**-s**, **-**) *m(f)* Norwegian.
norwegisch *adj* Norwegian.
Nostalgie [nɔstal'giː] *f* nostalgia.
Not [noːt] (**-**, **⁻e**) *f* need; (*Mangel*) want;
(*Mühe*) trouble; (*Zwang*) necessity; **zur** ~ if
necessary; (*gerade noch*) just about; **wenn**
~ **am Mann ist** if you/they *etc* are short
(*umg*); (*im Notfall*) in an emergency; **er hat**
seine liebe ~ **mit ihr/damit** he really has
problems with her/it; **in seiner** ~ in his hour
of need.
Notar(in) [no'taːr(ın)] (**-s**, **-e**) *m(f)* notary;
n~iell *adj* notarial; **n~iell beglaubigt** attested
by a notary.
Not- *zW:* ~**arzt** *m* doctor on emergency call;
~**ausgang** *m* emergency exit; ~**behelf** *m*
stopgap; ~**bremse** *f* emergency brake;
~**dienst** *m:* ~**dienst haben** (*Apotheke*) to be
open 24 hours; (*Arzt*) to be on call;
n~dürftig *adj* scanty; (*behelfsmäßig*)
makeshift; **sich n~dürftig verständigen**
können to be abe to communicate to some
extent.

Note ['noːtə] (**-**, **-n**) *f* note; (*SCH*) mark (*BRIT*),
grade (*US*); **Noten** *pl* (*MUS*) music *sing*; **eine**
persönliche ~ a personal touch.
Noten- *zW:* ~**bank** *f* issuing bank; ~**blatt** *nt*
sheet of music; ~**schlüssel** *m* clef;
~**ständer** *m* music stand.
Not- *zW:* ~**fall** *m* (case of) emergency; **n~falls**
adv if need be; **n~gedrungen** *adj* necessary,
unavoidable; **etw n~gedrungen machen** to
be forced to do sth; ~**groschen** ['noːtgrɔʃən]
m nest egg.
notieren [no'tiːrən] *vt* to note; (*COMM*) to
quote.
Notierung *f* (*COMM*) quotation.
nötig ['nøːtıç] *adj* necessary ♦ *adv* (*dringend*):
etw ~ **brauchen** to need sth urgently; **etw**
~ **haben** to need sth; **das habe ich nicht** ~! I
can do without that!
nötigen *vt* to compel, force; ~**falls** *adv* if
necessary.
Nötigung *f* compulsion, coercion (*JUR*).
Notiz [no'tiːts] (**-**, **-en**) *f* note; (*Zeitungs*~)
item; ~ **nehmen** to take notice; ~**block** *m*
notepad; ~**buch** *nt* notebook; ~**zettel** *m* piece
of paper.
Not- *zW:* ~**lage** *f* crisis, emergency;
n~landen *vi* to make a forced *od* emergency
landing; ~**landung** *f* forced *od* emergency
landing; **n~leidend** *adj* needy; ~**lösung** *f*
temporary solution; ~**lüge** *f* white lie.
notorisch [no'toːrıʃ] *adj* notorious.
Not- *zW:* ~**ruf** *m* emergency call; ~**rufsäule** *f*
emergency telephone; **n~schlachten** *vt*
(*Tiere*) to destroy; ~**stand** *m* state of
emergency; ~**standsgebiet** *nt* (*wirtschaftlich*)
depressed area; (*bei Katastrophen*) disaster
area; ~**standsgesetz** *nt* emergency law;
~**unterkunft** *f* emergency accommodation;
~**verband** *m* emergency dressing; ~**wehr**
(**-**) *f* self-defence; **n~wendig** *adj* necessary;
~**wendigkeit** *f* necessity; ~**zucht** *f* rape.
Nov. *abk* (= *November*) Nov.
Novelle [no'vɛlə] (**-**, **-n**) *f* novella; (*JUR*)
amendment.
November [no'vɛmbər] (**-(s)**, **-**) *m* November;
siehe auch **September**.
Novum ['noːvum] (**-**, **Nova**) *nt* novelty.
NPD (**-**) *f abk* (= *Nationaldemokratische Partei*
Deutschlands) National Democratic Party.
Nr. *abk* (= *Nummer*) no.
NRW *abk* = **Nordrhein-Westfalen.**
NS *abk* = **Nachschrift; Nationalsozialismus.**
NS- *in zW* Nazi.
N.T. *abk* (= *Neues Testament*) N.T.
Nu [nuː] *m:* **im** ~ in an instant.
Nuance [ny'ãːsə] (**-**, **-n**) *f* nuance; (*Kleinigkeit*)
shade.
nüchtern [nʏçtərn] *adj* sober; (*Magen*) empty;
(*Urteil*) prudent; **N~heit** *f* sobriety.
Nudel ['nuːdəl] (**-**, **-n**) *f* noodle; (*umg: Mensch:*
dick) dumpling; (: : *komisch*) character;
~**holz** *nt* rolling pin.

Nugat ['nu:gat] (**-s, -s**) *m od nt* nougat.
nuklear [nukle'a:r] *adj attrib* nuclear.
null [nʊl] *num* zero; (*Fehler*) no; ~ **Uhr**
midnight; ~ **und nichtig** null and void; **N~**
(**-, -en**) *f* nought, zero; (*pej: Mensch*) dead
loss; **in N~ Komma nichts** (*umg*) in less than
no time; **die Stunde N~** the new starting
point; **gleich N~ sein** to be absolutely nil;
~**achtfünfzehn** (*umg*) *adj* run-of-the-mill;
N~diät *f* starvation diet; **N~(l)ösung** *f*
(*POL*) zero option; **N~punkt** *m* zero; **auf dem
N~punkt** at zero; **N~tarif** *m* (*für
Verkehrsmittel*) free travel; **zum N~tarif** free
of charge.
numerieren [nume'ri:rən] *vt* to number.
numerisch [nu'me:rɪʃ] *adj* numerical; ~**es
Tastenfeld** (*COMPUT*) numeric pad.
Numerus ['nu:merʊs] (**-, Numeri**) *m* (*GRAM*)
number; ~ **clausus** (*UNIV*) restricted entry.
Nummer ['nʊmər] (**-, -n**) *f* number; **auf
~ Sicher gehen** (*umg*) to play (it) safe.
Nummern- *zW:* ~**konto** *nt* numbered bank
account; ~**scheibe** *f* telephone dial;
~**schild** *nt* (*AUT*) number *od* license (*US*)
plate.
nun [nu:n] *adv* now ♦ *interj* well.
nur [nu:r] *adv* just, only; **nicht ~ ..., sondern
auch ...** not only ... but also ...; **alle, ~ ich
nicht** everyone but me; **ich hab' das ~ so
gesagt** I was just talking.
Nürnberg ['nʏrnbɛrk] (**-s**) *nt* Nuremberg.
nuscheln ['nʊʃəln] (*umg*) *vt, vi* to mutter,
mumble.
Nuß [nʊs] (**-, Nüsse**) *f* nut; **eine doofe ~** (*umg*)
a stupid twit; **eine harte ~** a hard nut (to
crack); ~**baum** *m* walnut tree; ~**knacker**
(**-s, -**) *m* nutcracker.
Nüster ['ny:stər] (**-, -n**) *f* nostril.
Nutte ['nʊtə] (**-, -n**) *f* tart (*BRIT*), hooker (*US*).
nutz [nʊts] *adj* = **nütze**; ~**bar** *adj:* ~**bar machen**
to utilize; **N~barmachung** *f* utilization;
~**bringend** *adj* profitable; **etw ~bringend
anwenden** to use sth to good effect, put sth
to good use.
nütze ['nʏtsə] *adj:* **zu nichts ~ sein** to be
useless.
nutzen *vi* to be of use ♦ *vt:* (**zu etw**) ~ to use
(for sth); **was nutzt es?** what's the use?,
what use is it?; **N~** (**-s**) *m* usefulness;
(*Gewinn*) profit; **von N~** useful.
nützen *vt, vi* = **nutzen**.
Nutz- *zW:* ~**fahrzeug** *nt farm od military
vehicle etc*; (*COMM*) commercial vehicle;
~**fläche** *f* us(e)able floor space; (*AGR*)
productive land; ~**last** *f* maximum load,
payload.
nützlich ['nʏtslɪç] *adj* useful; **N~keit** *f*
usefulness.
Nutz- *zW:* **n~los** *adj* useless; (*unnötig*)
needless; ~**losigkeit** *f* uselessness;
~**nießer** (**-s, -**) *m* beneficiary.
Nutzung *f* (*Gebrauch*) use; (*das Ausnutzen*)

exploitation.
NW *abk* (= *Nordwest*) NW.
Nylon ['naɪlɔn] (**-s**) *nt* nylon.
Nymphe ['nʏmfə] (**-, -n**) *f* nymph.

O, o

O¹, o [o:] *nt* O, o; ~ **wie Otto** ≈ O for Olive, O
for Oboe (*US*).
O² [o:] *abk* (= *Osten*) E.
o.ä. *abk* (= *oder ähnliche(s)*) or similar.
Oase [o'a:zə] (**-, -n**) *f* oasis.
OB (**-s, -s**) *m abk* = **Oberbürgermeister.**
ob [ɔp] *konj* if, whether; ~ **das wohl wahr ist?**
can that be true?; ~ **ich (nicht) lieber gehe?**
maybe I'd better go; (**so**) **tun als ~** (*umg*) to
pretend; **und ~!** you bet!
Obacht ['o:baxt] *f:* ~ **geben** to pay attention.
Obdach ['ɔpdax] (**-(e)s**) *nt* shelter, lodging;
o~los *adj* homeless; ~**losenasyl** *nt* hostel *od*
shelter for the homeless; ~**losenheim** *nt*
= **Obdachlosenasyl;** ~**lose(r)** *f(m)* homeless
person.
Obduktion [ɔpdʊktsi'o:n] *f* postmortem.
obduzieren [ɔpdu'tsi:rən] *vt* to do a
postmortem on.
O-Beine ['o:baɪnə] *pl* bow *od* bandy legs *pl*.
oben ['o:bən] *adv* above; (*in Haus*) upstairs;
(*am oberen Ende*) at the top; **nach ~** up; **von
~ down**; **siehe ~** see above; **ganz ~** right at
the top; ~ **ohne** topless; **die Abbildung
~ links** *od* **links ~** the illustration in the top
left-hand corner; **jdn von ~ herab
behandeln** to treat sb condescendingly; **jdn
von ~ bis unten ansehen** to look sb up and
down; **Befehl von ~** orders from above; **die
da ~** (*umg: die Vorgesetzten*) the powers that
be; ~**'an** *adv* at the top; ~**'auf** *adv* up above,
on the top ♦ *adj* (*munter*) in form; ~**'drein** *adv*
into the bargain; ~**erwähnt** *adj* above-
mentioned; ~**genannt** *adj* above-mentioned;
~**'hin** *adv* cursorily, superficially.
Ober ['o:bər] (**-s, -**) *m* waiter.
Ober- *zW:* ~**arm** *m* upper arm; ~**arzt** *m* senior
physician; ~**aufsicht** *f* supervision;
~**bayern** *nt* Upper Bavaria; ~**befehl** *m*
supreme command; ~**befehlshaber** *m*
commander-in-chief; ~**begriff** *m* generic
term; ~**bekleidung** *f* outer clothing; ~**bett**
nt quilt; ~**bürgermeister** *m* lord mayor;
~**deck** *nt* upper *od* top deck.
obere(r, s) *adj* upper; **die O~n** the bosses;
(*ECCL*) the superiors; **die ~n Zehntausend**
(*umg*) high society.
Ober- *zW:* ~**fläche** *f* surface; **o~flächlich** *adj*

superficial; **bei o~flächlicher Betrachtung** at a quick glance; **jdn (nur) o~flächlich kennen** to know sb (only) slightly; **~geschoß** *nt* upper storey *od* story (*US*); **im zweiten ~geschoß** on the second floor (*BRIT*), on the third floor (*US*); **o~halb** *adv* above ◊ *präp +gen* above; **~hand** *f* (*fig*): **die ~hand gewinnen (über** +akk) to get the upper hand (over); **~haupt** *nt* head, chief; **~haus** *nt* (*BRIT POL*) upper house, House of Lords, **~hemd** *nt* shirt; **~herrschaft** *f* supremacy, sovereignty.

Oberin *f* matron; (*ECCL*) Mother Superior.

Ober- *zW:* **o~irdisch** *adj* above ground; (*Leitung*) overhead; **~italien** *nt* Northern Italy; **~kellner** *m* head waiter; **~kiefer** *m* upper jaw; **~kommando** *nt* supreme command; **~körper** *m* upper part of body; **~lauf** *m:* **am ~lauf des Rheins** in the upper reaches of the Rhine; **~leitung** *f* (*ELEK*) overhead cable; **~licht** *nt* skylight; **~lippe** *f* upper lip; **~österreich** *nt* Upper Austria; **~prima** *f* final year of German secondary school; **~schenkel** *m* thigh; **~schicht** *f* upper classes *pl*; **~schule** *f* grammar school (*BRIT*), high school (*US*); **~schwester** *f* (*MED*) matron; **~seite** *f* top (side); **~sekunda** *f* seventh year of German secondary school.

Oberst ['o:bərst] (**-en** *od* **-s, -en** *od* **-e**) *m* colonel.

oberste(r, s) *adj* very top, topmost.

Ober- *zW:* **~stübchen** (*umg*) *nt:* **er ist nicht ganz richtig im ~stübchen** he's not quite right up top; **~stufe** *f* upper school; **~teil** *nt* upper part; **~tertia** *f* fifth year of German secondary school; **~wasser** *nt:* **~wasser haben/bekommen** to be/get on top (of things); **~weite** *f* bust *od* chest measurement.

obgleich [ɔp'glaɪç] *konj* although.

Obhut ['ɔphu:t] (**-**) *f* care, protection; **in jds ~** *dat* **sein** to be in sb's care.

obig ['o:bɪç] *adj* above.

Objekt [ɔp'jɛkt] (**-(e)s, -e**) *nt* object.

objektiv [ɔpjɛk'ti:f] *adj* objective.

Objektiv (**-s, -e**) *nt* lens *sing*.

Objektivität [ɔpjɛktivi'tɛ:t] *f* objectivity.

Oblate [o'bla:tə] (**-, -n**) *f* (*Gebäck*) wafer; (*ECCL*) host.

obligatorisch [obliga'to:rɪʃ] *adj* compulsory, obligatory.

Oboe [o'bo:ə] (**-, -n**) *f* oboe.

Obrigkeit ['o:brɪçkaɪt] *f* (*Behörden*) authorities *pl*, administration; (*Regierung*) government.

Obrigkeitsdenken *nt* acceptance of authority.

obschon [ɔp'ʃo:n] *konj* although.

Observatorium [ɔpzɛrva'to:riʊm] *nt* observatory.

obskur [ɔps'ku:r] *adj* obscure; (*verdächtig*) dubious.

Obst [o:pst] (**-(e)s**) *nt* fruit; **~bau** *m* fruit-growing; **~baum** *m* fruit tree; **~garten** *m* orchard; **~händler** *m* fruiterer (*BRIT*), fruit merchant; **~kuchen** *m* fruit tart; **~saft** *m* fruit juice; **~salat** *m* fruit salad.

obszön [ɔps'tsø:n] *adj* obscene.

Obszönität [ɔpstøni'tɛ:t] *f* obscenity.

Obus ['o:bʊs] (**-ses, -se**) (*umg*) *m* trolleybus.

obwohl [ɔp'vo:l] *konj* although.

Ochse ['ɔksə] (**-n, -n**) *m* ox; (*umg: Dummkopf*) twit; **er stand da wie der ~ vorm Berg** (*umg*) he stood there utterly bewildered.

ochsen (*umg*) *vt, vi* to cram, swot (*BRIT*).

Ochsenschwanzsuppe *f* oxtail soup.

Ochsenzunge *f* ox tongue.

Ocker ['ɔkər] (**-s, -**) *m od nt* ochre (*BRIT*), ocher (*US*).

öd [ø:t(ə)] *adj* = **öde**.

öde *adj* (*Land*) waste, barren; (*fig*) dull; **~ und leer** dreary and desolate.

Öde (**-, -n**) *f* desert, waste(land); (*fig*) tedium.

oder ['o:dər] *konj* or; **entweder ... ~** either ... or; **du kommst doch, ~?** you're coming, aren't you?

Ofen ['o:fən] (**-s, ⁻**) *m* oven; (*Heiz~*) fire, heater; (*Kohle~*) stove; (*Hoch~*) furnace; (*Herd*) cooker, stove; **jetzt ist der ~ aus** (*umg*) that does it!; **~rohr** *nt* stovepipe.

offen ['ɔfən] *adj* open; (*aufrichtig*) frank; (*Stelle*) vacant; (*Bein*) ulcerated; (*Haare*) loose; **~er Wein** wine by the carafe *od* glass; **auf ~er Strecke** (*Straße*) on the open road; (*EISENB*) between stations; **Tag der ~en Tür** open day (*BRIT*), open house (*US*); **~e Handelsgesellschaft** (*COMM*) general *od* ordinary (*US*) partnership; **seine Meinung ~ sagen** to speak one's mind; **ein ~es Wort mit jdm reden** to have a frank talk with sb; **~ gesagt** to be honest.

offenbar *adj* obvious; (*vermutlich*) apparently.

offenbaren [ɔfən'ba:rən] *vt* to reveal, manifest.

Offenbarung *f* (*REL*) revelation.

Offenbarungseid *m* (*JUR*) oath of disclosure.

offen- *zW:* **~bleiben** *unreg vi* (*Fenster*) to stay open; (*Frage, Entscheidung*) to remain open; **~halten** *unreg vt* to keep open; **O~heit** *f* candour (*BRIT*), candor (*US*), frankness; **~herzig** *adj* candid, frank; (*hum: Kleid*) revealing; **O~herzigkeit** *f* frankness; **~kundig** *adj* well-known; (*klar*) evident; **~lassen** *unreg vt* to leave open; **~sichtlich** *adj* evident, obvious.

offensiv [ɔfɛn'zi:f] *adj* offensive.

Offensive (**-, -n**) *f* offensive.

offenstehen *unreg vi* to be open; (*Rechnung*) to be unpaid; **es steht Ihnen offen, es zu tun** you are at liberty to do it; **die (ganze) Welt steht ihm offen** he has the (whole) world at his feet.

öffentlich ['œfəntlɪç] *adj* public; **die ~e Hand** (central/local) government; **Anstalt des ~en Rechts** public institution; **Ausgaben der ~en Hand** public spending *sing*.

Öffentlichkeit *f* (*Leute*) public; (*einer Versammlung etc*) public nature; **in aller ~** in public; **an die ~ dringen** to reach the public ear; **unter Ausschluß der ~** in secret; (*JUR*) in camera.

Öffentlichkeitsarbeit *f* public relations work.

öffentlich-rechtlich *adj attrib* (under) public law.

offerieren [ɔfe'riːrən] *vt* to offer.

Offerte [ɔ'fɛrtə] (-, -n) *f* offer.

offiziell [ɔfitsi'ɛl] *adj* official.

Offizier [ɔfi'tsiːr] (-s, -e) *m* officer.

Offizierskasino *nt* officers' mess.

öffnen ['œfnən] *vt, vr* to open; **jdm die Tür ~** to open the door for sb.

Öffner ['œfnər] (-s, -) *m* opener.

Öffnung ['œfnʊŋ] *f* opening.

Öffnungszeiten *pl* opening times *pl*.

Offsetdruck ['ɔfsɛtdrʊk] *m* offset (printing).

oft [ɔft] *adv* often.

öfter ['œftər] *adv* more often *od* frequently; **des ~en** quite frequently; **~ mal was Neues** (*umg*) variety is the spice of life (*Sprichwort*).

öfters *adv* often, frequently.

oftmals *adv* often, frequently.

o.G. *abk* (= *ohne Gewähr*) without liability.

OHG *f abk* (= *offene Handelsgesellschaft*) *siehe* **offen**.

ohne ['oːnə] *präp +akk, konj* without; **das Darlehen ist ~ weiteres bewilligt worden** the loan was granted without any problem; **das kann man nicht ~ weiteres voraussetzen** you can't just assume that automatically; **das ist nicht ~** (*umg*) it's not bad; **~ weiteres** without a second thought; (*sofort*) immediately; **~dies** *adv* anyway; **~einander** [oːnə|aɪˈnandər] *adv* without each other; **~gleichen** *adj* unsurpassed, without equal; **~hin** *adv* anyway, in any case; **es ist ~hin schon spät** it's late enough already.

Ohnmacht ['oːnmaxt] *f* faint; (*fig*) impotence; **in ~ fallen** to faint.

ohnmächtig ['oːnmɛçtɪç] *adj* in a faint, unconscious; (*fig*) weak, impotent; **sie ist ~** she has fainted; **~e Wut, ~er Zorn** helpless rage; **einer Sache** *dat* **~ gegenüberstehen** to be helpless in the face of sth.

Ohr [oːr] (-(e)s, -en) *nt* ear; (*Gehör*) hearing; **sich aufs ~ legen** *od* **hauen** (*umg*) to kip down; **jdm die ~en langziehen** (*umg*) to tweak sb's ear(s); **jdm in den ~en liegen** to keep on at sb; **jdn übers ~ hauen** (*umg*) to pull a fast one on sb; **auf dem ~ bin ich taub** (*fig*) nothing doing (*umg*); **schreib es dir hinter die ~en** (*umg*) will you (finally) get that into your (thick) head!; **bis über die** *od*

beide ~en verliebt sein to be head over heels in love; **viel um die ~en haben** (*umg*) to have a lot on (one's plate); **halt die ~en steif!** keep a stiff upper lip!

Öhr [øːr] (-(e)s, -e) *nt* eye.

Ohren- *zW:* **~arzt** *m* ear specialist; **o~betäubend** *adj* deafening; **~sausen** *nt* (*MED*) buzzing in one's ears; **~schmalz** *nt* earwax; **~schmerzen** *pl* earache *sing*; **~schützer** (-s, -) *m* earmuff.

Ohr- *zW:* **~feige** *f* slap on the face; (*als Strafe*) box on the ears; **o~feigen** *vt untr:* **jdn o~feigen** to slap sb's face; to box sb's ears; **ich könnte mich selbst o~feigen, daß ich das gemacht habe** I could kick myself for doing that; **~läppchen** *nt* ear lobe; **~ringe** *pl* earrings *pl*; **~wurm** *m* earwig; (*MUS*) catchy tune.

o.J. *abk* (= *ohne Jahr*) no year given.

okkupieren [ɔkuˈpiːrən] *vt* to occupy.

Öko- ['øko-] *in zW* eco-, ecological; **~laden** ['øːkolaːdən] *m* wholefood shop.

Ökologie [økoloˈgiː] *f* ecology.

ökologisch [økoˈloːgɪʃ] *adj* ecological, environmental.

Ökonometrie [økonomeˈtriː] *f* econometrics *pl*.

Ökonomie [økonoˈmiː] *f* economy; (*als Wissenschaft*) economics *sing*.

ökonomisch [økoˈnoːmɪʃ] *adj* economical.

Ökopaxe [økoˈpaksə] (-n, -n) (*umg*) *m* environmentalist.

Ökosystem ['øːkozysteːm] *nt* ecosystem.

Okt. *abk* (= *Oktober*) Oct.

Oktan [ɔkˈtaːn] (-s, -e) *nt* octane; **~zahl** *f* octane rating.

Oktave [ɔkˈtaːvə] (-, -n) *f* octave.

Oktober [ɔkˈtoːbər] (-(s), -) *m* October; *siehe auch* **September**.

> *The annual October beer festival, the* **Oktoberfest**, *takes place in Munich on a huge field where beer tents, roller coasters and many other amusements are set up. People sit at long wooden tables, drink beer from enormous litre beer mugs, eat pretzels and listen to brass bands. It is a great attraction for tourists and locals alike.*

ökumenisch [økuˈmeːnɪʃ] *adj* ecumenical.

Öl [øːl] (-(e)s, -e) *nt* oil; **auf ~ stoßen** to strike oil.

Öl- *zW:* **~baum** *m* olive tree; **ö~en** *vt* to oil; (*TECH*) to lubricate; **wie ein geölter Blitz** (*umg*) like greased lightning; **~farbe** *f* oil paint; **~feld** *nt* oilfield; **~film** *m* film of oil; **~heizung** *f* oil-fired central heating.

ölig *adj* oily.

Oligopol [oligoˈpoːl] (-s, -e) *nt* oligopoly.

oliv [oˈliːf] *adj* olive-green.

Olive [oˈliːvə] (-, -n) *f* olive.

Olivenöl *nt* olive oil.

Öljacke f oilskin jacket.
oll [ɔl] (*umg*) *adj* old; **das sind ~e Kamellen** that's old hat.
Öl- *zW:* **~meßstab** m dipstick; **~pest** f oil pollution; **~plattform** f oil rig; **~sardine** f sardine; **~scheich** m oil sheik; **~stand** m oil level; **~standanzeiger** m (*AUT*) oil level indicator; **~tanker** m oil tanker; **~teppich** m oil slick.
Ölung f oiling; (*ECCL*) anointment; **die Letzte ~** Extreme Unction.
Ölwanne f (*AUT*) sump (*BRIT*), oil pan (*US*).
Ölwechsel m oil change.
Olymp [o'lʏmp] (**-s**) m (*Berg*) Mount Olympus.
Olympiade [olʏmpi'aːdə] (**-**, **-n**) f Olympic Games *pl*.
Olympiasieger(in) [o'lʏmpiaziːgər(ɪn)] m(f) Olympic champion.
olympisch [o'lʏmpɪʃ] *adj* Olympic.
Ölzeug nt oilskins *pl*.
Oma ['oːma] (**-**, **-s**) (*umg*) f granny.
Oman [o'maːn] (**-s**) nt Oman.
Omelett [ɔm(ə)'lɛt] (**-(e)s**, **-s**) nt omelette (*BRIT*), omelet (*US*).
Omelette [ɔm(ə)'lɛt] f = **Omelett**.
Omen ['oːmɛn] (**-s**, **-** *od* **Omina**) nt omen.
Omnibus ['ɔmnibʊs] m (omni)bus.
Onanie [ona'niː] f masturbation.
onanieren vi to masturbate.
ondulieren [ɔndu'liːrən] vt, vi to crimp.
Onkel ['ɔŋkəl] (**-s**, **-**) m uncle.
OP m abk = **Operationssaal**.
Opa ['oːpa] (**-s**, **-s**) (*umg*) m grandpa.
Opal [o'paːl] (**-s**, **-e**) m opal.
Oper ['oːpər] (**-**, **-n**) f opera; (*Opernhaus*) opera house.
Operation [operatsi'oːn] f operation.
Operationssaal m operating theatre (*BRIT*) *od* theater (*US*).
operativ [opəra'tiːf] *adv* (*MED*): **eine Geschwulst ~ entfernen** to remove a growth by surgery.
Operette [ope'rɛtə] f operetta.
operieren [ope'riːrən] vt, vi to operate; **sich ~ lassen** to have an operation.
Opern- *zW:* **~glas** nt opera glasses *pl*; **~haus** nt opera house; **~sänger(in)** m(f) opera singer.
Opfer ['ɔpfər] (**-s**, **-**) nt sacrifice; (*Mensch*) victim; **~bereitschaft** f readiness to make sacrifices.
opfern vt to sacrifice.
Opferstock m (*ECCL*) offertory box.
Opferung f sacrifice; (*ECCL*) offertory.
Opium ['oːpiʊm] (**-s**) nt opium.
opponieren [ɔpo'niːrən] vi: **gegen jdn/etw ~** to oppose sb/sth.
opportun [ɔpɔr'tuːn] *adj* opportune; **O~ismus** [-'nɪsmʊs] m opportunism; **O~ist(in)** [-'nɪst(ɪn)] m(f) opportunist.
Opposition [ɔpozitsi'oːn] f opposition.
oppositionell [ɔpozitsio'nɛl] *adj* opposing.

Oppositionsführer m leader of the opposition.
optieren [ɔp'tiːrən] vi (*POL: form*): **~ für** to opt for.
Optik ['ɔptɪk] f optics *sing*.
Optiker(in) (**-s**, **-**) m(f) optician.
optimal [ɔpti'maːl] *adj* optimal, optimum.
Optimismus [ɔpti'mɪsmʊs] m optimism.
Optimist(in) [ɔpti'mɪst(ɪn)] m(f) optimist; **o~isch** *adj* optimistic.
optisch ['ɔptɪʃ] *adj* optical; **~e Täuschung** optical illusion.
Orakel [o'raːkəl] (**-s**, **-**) nt oracle.
Orange [o'rãːʒə] (**-**, **-n**) f orange; **o~** *adj* orange.
Orangeade [orã'ʒaːdə] (**-**, **-n**) f orangeade.
Orangeat [orã'ʒaːt] (**-s**, **-e**) nt candied peel.
Orangen- *zW:* **~marmelade** f marmalade; **~saft** m orange juice; **~schale** f orange peel.
Oratorium [ora'toːriʊm] nt (*MUS*) oratorio.
Orchester [ɔr'kɛstər] (**-s**, **-**) nt orchestra.
Orchidee [ɔrçi'deːə] (**-**, **-n**) f orchid.
Orden ['ɔrdən] (**-s**, **-**) m (*ECCL*) order; (*MIL*) decoration.
Ordensgemeinschaft f religious order.
Ordensschwester f nun.
ordentlich ['ɔrdəntlɪç] *adj* (*anständig*) decent, respectable; (*geordnet*) tidy, neat; (*umg: annehmbar*) not bad; (: *tüchtig*) real, proper; (*Leistung*) reasonable; **~es Mitglied** full member; **~er Professor** (full) professor; **eine ~e Tracht Prügel** a proper hiding; **~ arbeiten** to be a thorough and precise worker; **O~keit** f respectability; tidiness, neatness.
Order (**-**, **-s** *od* **-n**) f (*COMM: Auftrag*) order.
ordern vt (*COMM*) to order.
Ordinalzahl [ɔrdi'naːltsaːl] f ordinal number.
ordinär [ɔrdi'nɛːr] *adj* common, vulgar.
Ordinarius [ɔrdi'naːrius] (**-**, **Ordinarien**) m (*UNIV*): **~ (für)** professor (of).
ordnen ['ɔrdnən] vt to order, put in order.
Ordner (**-s**, **-**) m steward; (*COMM*) file.
Ordnung f order; (*Ordnen*) ordering; (*Geordnetsein*) tidiness; **geht in ~** (*umg*) that's all right *od* OK (*umg*); **~ schaffen, für ~ sorgen** to put things in order, tidy things up; **jdn zur ~ rufen** to call sb to order; **bei ihm muß alles seine ~ haben** (*räumlich*) he has to have everything in its proper place; (*zeitlich*) he has to do everything according to a fixed schedule; **das Kind braucht seine ~** the child needs a routine.
Ordnungs- *zW:* **~amt** nt ≈ town clerk's office; **o~gemäß** *adj* proper, according to the rules; **o~halber** *adv* as a matter of form; **~liebe** f tidiness, orderliness; **~strafe** f fine; **o~widrig** *adj* contrary to the rules, irregular; **~widrigkeit** f infringement (*of law or rule*); **~zahl** f ordinal number.
ORF (**-**) m abk = **Österreichischer Rundfunk**.

Organ [ɔr'gaːn] (-s, -e) nt organ; (*Stimme*) voice.
Organisation [ɔrganizatsi'oːn] f organization.
Organisationstalent nt organizing ability; (*Person*) good organizer.
Organisator [ɔrgani'zaːtɔr] m organizer.
organisch [ɔr'gaːnɪʃ] adj organic; (*Erkrankung, Leiden*) physical.
organisieren [ɔrgani'ziːrən] vt to organize, arrange; (*umg: beschaffen*) to acquire ♦ vr to organize.
Organismus [ɔrga'nɪsmʊs] m organism.
Organist [ɔrga'nɪst] m organist.
Organspender m donor (of an organ).
Organspenderausweis m donor card.
Organverpflanzung f transplantation (of an organ).
Orgasmus [ɔr'gasmʊs] m orgasm.
Orgel ['ɔrgəl] (-, -n) f organ; ~**pfeife** f organ pipe; **wie die ~pfeifen stehen** to stand in order of height.
Orgie ['ɔrgiə] f orgy.
Orient ['oːrient] (-s) m Orient, east; **der Vordere ~** the Near East.
Orientale [oːrien'taːlə] (-n, -n) m Oriental.
Orientalin [oːrien'taːlɪn] f Oriental.
orientalisch adj oriental.
orientieren [oːrien'tiːrən] vt (*örtlich*) to locate; (*fig*) to inform ♦ vr to find one's way od bearings; (*fig*) to inform o.s.
Orientierung [oːrien'tiːrʊŋ] f orientation; (*fig*) information; **die ~ verlieren** to lose one's bearings.
Orientierungssinn m sense of direction.

The **Orientierungsstufe** *is the name given to the first two years spent in a* **Realschule** *or* **Gymnasium**, *during which a child is assessed as to his or her suitability for that type of school. At the end of the two years it may be decided to transfer the child to a school more suited to his or her ability.*

original [origi'naːl] adj original; **~ Meißener Porzellan** genuine Meissen porcelain; **O~** (-s, -e) nt original; (*Mensch*) character; **O~ausgabe** f first edition; **O~fassung** f original version.
Originalität [originali'tɛːt] f originality.
Originalübertragung f live broadcast.
originell [origi'nɛl] adj original.
Orkan [ɔr'kaːn] (-(e)s, -e) m hurricane; **o~artig** adj (*Wind*) gale-force; (*Beifall*) thunderous.
Orkneyinseln ['ɔːknɪ|ɪnzəln] pl Orkney Islands pl, Orkneys pl.
Ornament [ɔrna'mɛnt] nt decoration, ornament.
ornamental [ɔrnamɛn'taːl] adj decorative, ornamental.
Ornithologe [ɔrnito'loːgə] (-n, -n) m ornithologist.
Ornithologin [ɔrnito'loːgɪn] f ornithologist.

Ort¹ [ɔrt] (-(e)s, -e) m place; **an ~ und Stelle** on the spot; **am ~** in the place; **am angegebenen ~** in the place quoted, loc. cit.; **~ der Handlung** (*THEAT*) scene of the action; **das ist höheren ~(e)s entschieden worden** (*hum: form*) the decision came from above.
Ort² [ɔrt] (-(e)s, ⁻er) m: **vor ~** at the (coal) face; (*auch fig*) on the spot.
Örtchen ['œrtçən] (*umg*) nt loo (*BRIT*), john (*US*).
orten vt to locate.
orthodox [ɔrto'dɔks] adj orthodox.
Orthographie [ɔrtogra'fiː] f spelling, orthography.
orthographisch [ɔrto'graːfɪʃ] adj orthographic.
Orthopäde [ɔrto'pɛːdə] (-n, -n) m orthopaedic (*BRIT*) od orthopedic (*US*) specialist, orthopaedist (*BRIT*), orthopedist (*US*).
Orthopädie [ɔrtope'diː] f orthopaedics sing (*BRIT*), orthopedics sing (*US*).
orthopädisch adj orthopaedic (*BRIT*), orthopedic (*US*).
örtlich ['œrtlɪç] adj local; **jdn ~ betäuben** to give sb a local anaesthetic (*BRIT*) od anesthetic (*US*); **Ö~keit** f locality; **sich mit den Ö~keiten vertraut machen** to get to know the place.
Ortsangabe f (name of the) town; **ohne ~** (*Buch*) no place of publication indicated.
ortsansässig adj local.
Ortschaft f village, small town; **geschlossene ~** built-up area.
Orts- zW: **o~fremd** adj nonlocal; **~fremde(r)** f(m) stranger; **~gespräch** nt local (phone) call; **~gruppe** f local branch od group; **~kenntnis** f: **(gute) ~kenntnisse haben** to know one's way around (well); **~krankenkasse** f: **Allgemeine ~krankenkasse** compulsory medical insurance scheme; **o~kundig** adj familiar with the place; **o~kundig sein** to know one's way around; **~name** m place name; **~netz** nt (*TEL*) local telephone exchange area; **~netzkennzahl** f (*TEL*) dialling (*BRIT*) od area (*US*) code; **~schild** nt place name sign; **~sinn** m sense of direction; **~tarif** m (*TEL*) charge for local calls; **~vorschriften** pl by(e)-laws pl; **~zeit** f local time; **~zuschlag** m (local) weighting allowance.
Ortung f locating.
öS. abk = **österreichischer Schilling**.
Öse ['øːzə] (-, -n) f loop; (*an Kleidung*) eye.
Oslo ['ɔslo] (-s) nt Oslo.
Ossi ['ɔsi] (-s, -s) (*umg*) m East German.

Ossi *is a colloquial and often derogatory word used to describe a German from the former DDR.*

öst. abk (= **österreichisch**) Aust.

Ost- *zW:* **~afrika** *nt* East Africa; **o~deutsch** *adj* East German; **~deutsche(r)** *f(m)* East German; **~deutschland** *nt* (*POL: früher*) East Germany; (*GEOG*) Eastern Germany.

Osten (-s) *m* east; **der Ferne ~** the Far East; **der Nahe ~** the Middle East, the Near East.

ostentativ [ɔstɛnta'tiːf] *adj* pointed, ostentatious.

Oster- *zW:* **~ei** *nt* Easter egg; **~fest** *nt* Easter; **~glocke** *f* daffodil; **~hase** *m* Easter bunny; **~insel** *f* Easter Island; **~marsch** *m* Easter demonstration; **~montag** *m* Easter Monday.

Ostern (-s, -) *nt* Easter; **frohe** *od* **fröhliche ~!** Happy Easter!; **zu ~** at Easter.

Österreich ['øːstəraɪç] (-s) *nt* Austria.

Österreicher(in) (-s, -) *m(f)* Austrian.

österreichisch *adj* Austrian.

Ostersonntag *m* Easter Day *od* Sunday.

Osteuropa *nt* East(ern) Europe.

osteuropäisch *adj* East European.

östlich ['œstlɪç] *adj* eastern, easterly.

Östrogen [œstro'geːn] (-s, -e) *nt* oestrogen (*BRIT*), estrogen (*US*).

Ost- *zW:* **~see** *f* Baltic Sea; **o~wärts** *adv* eastwards; **~wind** *m* east wind.

oszillieren [ɔstsɪ'liːrən] *vi* to oscillate.

Otter¹ ['ɔtər] (-s, -) *m* otter.

Otter² ['ɔtər] (-, -n) *f* (*Schlange*) adder.

ÖTV (-) *f* abk (= *Gewerkschaft öffentliche Dienste, Transport und Verkehr*) ≈ Transport and General Workers' Union.

Ouvertüre [uvɛr'tyːrə] (-, -n) *f* overture.

oval [o'vaːl] *adj* oval.

Ovation [ovatsi'oːn] *f* ovation.

Overall ['oʊvərɔːl] (-s, -s) *m* (*Schutzanzug*) overalls *pl*.

ÖVP (-) *f* abk (= *Österreichische Volkspartei*) Austrian People's Party.

Ovulation [ovulatsi'oːn] *f* ovulation.

Oxyd [ɔ'ksyːt] (-(e)s, -e) *nt* oxide.

oxydieren [ɔksy'diːrən] *vt, vi* to oxidize.

Oxydierung *f* oxidization.

Ozean ['oːtseaːn] (-s, -e) *m* ocean; **~dampfer** *m* (ocean-going) liner.

Ozeanien [otse'aːniən] (-s) *nt* Oceania.

ozeanisch [otse'aːnɪʃ] *adj* oceanic; (*Sprachen*) Oceanic.

Ozeanriese (*umg*) *m* ocean liner.

Ozon [o'tsoːn] (-s) *nt* ozone; **~loch** *nt* hole in the ozone layer; **~schicht** *f* ozone layer.

P, p

P, p [peː] *nt* P, p; **~ wie Peter** ≈ P for Peter.

P. *abk* = **Pastor; Pater.**

Paar [paːr] (-(e)s, -e) *nt* pair; (*Liebes~*) couple.

paar *adj inv:* **ein ~** a few; (*zwei oder drei*) a couple of.

paaren *vt, vr* (*Tiere*) to mate, pair.

Paar- *zW:* **~hufer** *pl* (*ZOOL*) cloven-hoofed animals *pl*; **~lauf** *m* pair skating; **p~mal** *adv:* **ein p~mal** a few times.

Paarung *f* combination; (*von Tieren*) mating.

paarweise *adv* in pairs; in couples.

Pacht [paxt] (-, -en) *f* lease; (*Entgelt*) rent; **p~en** *vt* to lease; **du hast das Sofa doch nicht für dich gepachtet** (*umg*) don't hog the sofa.

Pächter(in) ['pɛçtər(ɪn)] (-s, -) *m(f)* leaseholder; tenant.

Pachtvertrag *m* lease.

Pack¹ [pak] (-(e)s, -e *od* ⁻e) *m* bundle, pack.

Pack² [pak] (-(e)s) (*pej*) *nt* mob, rabble.

Päckchen ['pɛkçən] *nt* small package; (*Zigaretten*) packet; (*Post~*) small parcel.

Packeis *nt* pack ice.

Packen (-s, -) *m* bundle; (*fig: Menge*) heaps (of); **p~** *vt, vi* (*auch COMPUT*) to pack; (*fassen*) to grasp, seize; (*umg: schaffen*) to manage; (*fig: fesseln*) to grip; **p~ wir's!** (*umg: gehen*) let's go.

Packer(in) (-s, -) *m(f)* packer.

Packesel *m* pack mule; (*fig*) packhorse.

Packpapier *nt* brown paper, wrapping paper.

Packung *f* packet; (*Pralinen~*) box; (*MED*) compress.

Packzettel *m* (*COMM*) packing slip.

Pädagoge [pɛda'goːgə] (-n, -n) *m* educationalist.

Pädagogik *f* education.

Pädagogin [pɛda'goːgɪn] *f* educationalist.

pädagogisch *adj* educational, pedagogical; **P~e Hochschule** college of education.

Paddel ['padəl] (-s, -) *nt* paddle; **~boot** *nt* canoe.

paddeln *vi* to paddle.

pädophil [pɛdo'fiːl] *adj* paedophile (*BRIT*), pedophile (*US*).

Pädophilie [pɛdofi'liː] *f* paedophilia (*BRIT*), pedophilia (*US*).

paffen ['pafən] *vt, vi* to puff.

Page ['paːʒə] (-n, -n) *m* page(boy).

Pagenkopf *m* pageboy cut.

paginieren [pagi'niːrən] *vt* to paginate.

Paginierung *f* pagination.

Paillette [paɪ'jɛtə] *f* sequin.

Paket [pa'keːt] (-(e)s, -e) nt packet; (Post~)
parcel; ~**annahme** f parcels office;
~**ausgabe** f parcels office; ~**karte** f
dispatch note; ~**post** f parcel post;
~**schalter** m parcels counter.
Pakistan ['paːkɪstaːn] (-s) nt Pakistan.
Pakistaner(in) [pakɪs'taːnər(ɪn)] (-s, -) m(f)
Pakistani.
Pakistani [pakɪs'taːni] (-(s), -(s)) m Pakistani.
pakistanisch adj Pakistani.
Pakt [pakt] (-(e)s, -e) m pact.
Paläontologie [palɛɔntolo'giː] f
palaeontology (BRIT), paleontology (US).
Palast [pa'last] (-es, **Paläste**) m palace.
Palästina [palɛ'stiːna] (-s) nt Palestine.
Palästinenser(in) [palɛsti'nɛnzər(ɪn)] (-s, -)
m(f) Palestinian.
palästinensisch adj Palestinian.
Palaver [pa'laːvər] (-s, -) nt (auch fig: umg)
palaver.
Palette [pa'lɛtə] f palette; (fig) range; (Lade~)
pallet.
Palme ['palmə] (-, -n) f palm (tree); **jdn auf
die ~ bringen** (umg) to make sb see red.
Palmsonntag m Palm Sunday.
Pampelmuse ['pampəlmuːzə] (-, -n) f
grapefruit.
pampig ['pampɪç] (umg) adj (frech) fresh.
Panama ['panama] (-s) nt Panama; ~**kanal** m
Panama Canal.
Panflöte ['paːnfløːtə] f panpipes pl, Pan's
pipes pl.
panieren [pa'niːrən] vt (KOCH) to coat with
egg and breadcrumbs.
Paniermehl [pa'niːrmeːl] nt breadcrumbs pl.
Panik [pa'niːk] f panic; **nur keine ~!** don't
panic!; **in ~ ausbrechen** to panic.
Panikkäufe pl panic buying sing; ~**mache**
(umg) f panicmongering.
panisch ['paːnɪʃ] adj panic-stricken.
Panne ['panə] (-, -n) f (AUT etc) breakdown;
(Mißgeschick) slip; **uns ist eine ~ passiert**
we've boobed (BRIT) (umg) od goofed (US)
(umg).
Pannendienst m breakdown service.
Pannenhilfe f breakdown service.
Panorama [pano'raːma] (-s, -men) nt
panorama.
panschen ['panʃən] vi to splash about ♦ vt to
water down.
Panther ['pantər] (-s, -) m panther.
Pantoffel [pan'tɔfəl] (-s, -n) m slipper; ~**held**
(umg) m henpecked husband.
Pantomime [panto'miːmə] (-, -n) f mime.
Panzer ['pantsər] (-s, -) m armour (BRIT),
armor (US); (fig) shield; (Platte) armo(u)r
plate; (Fahrzeug) tank; ~**faust** f bazooka;
~**glas** nt bulletproof glass; ~**grenadier** m
armoured (BRIT) od armored (US)
infantryman.
panzern vt to armour (BRIT) od armor (US)
plate ♦ vr (fig) to arm o.s.

Panzerschrank m strongbox.
Panzerwagen m armoured (BRIT) od
armored (US) car.
Papa [pa'paː] (-s, -s) (umg) m dad(dy), pa.
Papagei [papa'gaɪ] (-s, -en) m parrot.
Papier [pa'piːr] (-s, -e) nt paper; (Wert~) share;
Papiere pl (identity) papers pl; (Urkunden)
documents pl; **seine ~e bekommen**
(entlassen werden) to get one's cards;
~**fabrik** f paper mill; ~**geld** nt paper money;
~**korb** m wastepaper basket; ~**kram** (umg) m
bumf (BRIT) (umg); ~**krieg** m red tape; ~**tüte**
f paper bag; ~**vorschub** m (Drucker) paper
advance.
Pappbecher m paper cup.
Pappdeckel (-, -n) m cardboard.
Pappe ['papə] f cardboard; **das ist nicht von
~** (umg) that is really something.
Pappeinband m pasteboard.
Pappel (-, -n) f poplar.
pappen (umg) vt, vi to stick.
Pappenheimer pl: **ich kenne meine ~** (umg) I
know you lot/that lot (inside out).
Pappenstiel (umg) m: **keinen ~ wert sein** not
to be worth a thing; **für einen ~ bekommen**
to get for a song.
papperlapapp [papərla'pap] interj rubbish!
pappig adj sticky.
Pappmaché [papma'ʃeː] (-s, -s) nt papier-
mâché.
Pappteller m paper plate.
Paprika ['paprika] (-s, -s) m (Gewürz) paprika;
(~schote) pepper; ~**schote** f pepper;
gefüllte ~schoten stuffed peppers.
Papst [paːpst] (-(e)s, ̈-e) m pope.
päpstlich ['pɛːpstlɪç] adj papal; ~**er als der
Papst sein** to be more Catholic than the
Pope.
Parabel [pa'raːbəl] (-, -n) f parable; (MATH)
parabola.
Parabolantenne [para'boːl|antɛnə] f (TV)
satellite dish.
Parade [pa'raːdə] (-, -n) f (MIL) parade,
review; (SPORT) parry; ~**beispiel** nt prime
example; ~**marsch** m march past; ~**schritt** m
goose step.
Paradies [para'diːs] (-es, -e) nt paradise;
p~isch adj heavenly.
Paradox [para'dɔks] (-es, -e) nt paradox; **p~**
adj paradoxical.
Paraffin [para'fiːn] (-s, -e) nt (CHEM: ~öl)
paraffin (BRIT), kerosene (US); (~wachs)
paraffin wax.
Paragraph [para'graːf] (-en, -en) m paragraph;
(JUR) section.
Paragraphenreiter (umg) m pedant.
Paraguay [paragu'aːi] (-s) nt Paraguay.
Paraguayer(in) [para'gua:jər(ɪn)] (-s, -) m(f)
Paraguayan.
paraguayisch adj Paraguayan.
parallel [para'leːl] adj parallel; ~ **schalten**
(ELEK) to connect in parallel.

Parallele (-, -n) *f* parallel.
Parameter [pa'ra:metər] *m* parameter.
paramilitärisch [paramili'tɛ:rɪʃ] *adj* paramilitary.
Paranuß ['pa:ranʊs] *f* Brazil nut.
paraphieren [para'fi:rən] *vt* (*Vertrag*) to initial.
Parasit [para'zi:t] (-en, -en) *m* (*lit, fig*) parasite.
parat [pa'ra:t] *adj* ready.
Pärchen ['pɛ:rçən] *nt* couple.
Parcours [par'ku:r] (-, -) *m* showjumping course; (*Sportart*) showjumping.
Pardon [par'dõ:] (-s) (*umg*) *m od nt:* ~!
(*Verzeihung*) sorry!; **kein ~ kennen** to be ruthless.
Parfüm [par'fy:m] (-s, -s *od* -e) *nt* perfume.
Parfümerie [parfymə'ri:] *f* perfumery.
Parfümflasche *f* scent bottle.
parfümieren [parfy'mi:rən] *vt* to scent, perfume.
parieren [pa'ri:rən] *vt* to parry ♦ *vi* (*umg*) to obey.
Paris [pa'ri:s] (-) *nt* Paris.
Pariser [pa'ri:zər] (-s, -) *m* Parisian; (*umg: Kondom*) rubber ♦ *adj attrib* Parisian, Paris *attrib*.
Pariserin *f* Parisian.
Parität [pari'tɛ:t] *f* parity; **p~isch** *adj:* **p~ische Mitbestimmung** equal representation.
Pariwert ['pa:rive:rt] *m* par value, parity.
Park [park] (-s, -s) *m* park.
Parka ['parka] (-(s), -s) *m* parka.
Parkanlage *f* park; (*um Gebäude*) grounds *pl*.
Parkbucht *f* parking bay.
parken *vt, vi* to park; „**P~ verboten!**" "No Parking".
Parkett [par'kɛt] (-(e)s, -e) *nt* parquet (floor); (*THEAT*) stalls *pl* (*BRIT*), orchestra (*US*).
Park- *zW:* **~haus** *nt* multistorey car park; **~lücke** *f* parking space; **~platz** *m* car park, parking lot (*US*); parking place; **~scheibe** *f* parking disc; **~uhr** *f* parking meter; **~verbot** *nt* parking ban.
Parlament [parla'mɛnt] *nt* parliament.
Parlamentarier [parlamɛn'ta:riər] (-s, -) *m* parliamentarian.
parlamentarisch *adj* parliamentary.
Parlaments- *zW:* **~ausschuß** *m* parliamentary committee; **~beschluß** *m* vote of parliament; **~ferien** *pl* recess *sing*; **~mitglied** *nt* Member of Parliament (*BRIT*), Congressman (*US*); **~sitzung** *f* sitting (of parliament).
Parodie [paro'di:] *f* parody.
parodieren *vt* to parody.
Parodontose [parodɔn'to:zə] (-, -n) *f* shrinking gums *pl*.
Parole [pa'ro:lə] (-, -n) *f* password; (*Wahlspruch*) motto.
Partei [par'tai] *f* party; (*im Mietshaus*) tenant, party (*form*); **für jdn ~ ergreifen** to take sb's side; **~buch** *nt* party membership book; **~führung** *f* party leadership; **~genosse** *m*

party member; **p~isch** *adj* partial, bias(s)ed; **p~lich** *adj* party *attrib*; **~linie** *f* party line; **p~los** *adj* neutral; **~nahme** (-, -n) *f* partisanship; **p~politisch** *adj* party political; **~programm** *nt* (party) manifesto; **~tag** *m* party conference; **~vorsitzende(r)** *f(m)* party leader.
Parterre [par'tɛr] (-s, -s) *nt* ground floor; (*THEAT*) stalls *pl* (*BRIT*), orchestra (*US*).
Partie [par'ti:] *f* part; (*Spiel*) game; (*Ausflug*) outing; (*Mann, Frau*) catch; (*COMM*) lot; **mit von der ~ sein** to join in.
partiell [partsi'ɛl] *adj* partial.
Partikel [par'ti:kəl] (-, -n) *f* particle.
Partisan(in) [parti'za:n(ɪn)] (-s *od* -en, -en) *m(f)* partisan.
Partitur [parti'tu:r] *f* (*MUS*) score.
Partizip [parti'tsi:p] (-s, -ien) *nt* participle; **~ Präsens/Perfekt** (*GRAM*) present/past participle.
Partner(in) ['partnər(ɪn)] (-s, -) *m(f)* partner; **~schaft** *f* partnership; (*Städtepartnerschaft*) twinning; **p~schaftlich** *adj* as partners; **~stadt** *f* twin town (*Brit*).
partout [par'tu:] *adv:* **er will ~ ins Kino gehen** he insists on going to the cinema.
Party ['pa:rti] (-, -s *od* **Parties**) *f* party.
Parzelle [par'tsɛlə] *f* plot, lot.
Pascha ['paʃa] (-s, -s) *m:* **wie ein ~** like Lord Muck (*BRIT*) (*umg*).
Paß [pas] (-sses, ⁻sse) *m* pass; (*Ausweis*) passport.
passabel [pa'sa:bəl] *adj* passable, reasonable.
Passage [pa'sa:ʒə] (-, -n) *f* passage; (*Ladenstraße*) arcade.
Passagier [pasa'ʒi:r] (-s, -e) *m* passenger; **~dampfer** *m* passenger steamer; **~flugzeug** *nt* airliner.
Passah(fest) ['pasa(fɛst)] *nt* (Feast of the) Passover.
Paßamt *nt* passport office.
Passant(in) [pa'sant(ɪn)] *m(f)* passer-by.
Paßbild *nt* passport photo(graph).
passé [pa'se:] *adj:* **diese Mode ist längst ~** this fashion went out long ago.
passen ['pasən] *vi* to fit; (*auf Frage, KARTEN*) to pass; **~ zu** (*Farbe etc*) to go with; **Sonntag paßt uns nicht** Sunday is no good for us; **die Schuhe ~ (mir) gut** the shoes are a good fit (for me); **zu jdm ~** (*Mensch*) to suit sb; **das paßt mir nicht** that doesn't suit me; **er paßt nicht zu dir** he's not right for you; **das könnte dir so ~!** (*umg*) you'd like that, wouldn't you?
passend *adj* suitable; (*zusammen~*) matching; (*angebracht*) fitting; (*Zeit*) convenient; **haben Sie es ~?** (*Geld*) have you got the right money?
Paßfoto *nt* passport photo(graph).
passierbar [pa'si:rba:r] *adj* passable; (*Fluß, Kanal*) negotiable.
passieren *vt* to pass; (*durch Sieb*) to strain ♦ *vi*

(*Hilfsverb sein*) to happen; **es ist ein Unfall passiert** there has been an accident.
Passierschein *m* pass, permit.
Passion [pasi'o:n] *f* passion.
passioniert [pasio:'ni:rt] *adj* enthusiastic, passionate.
Passionsfrucht *f* passion fruit.
Passionsspiel *nt* Passion Play.
Passionszeit *f* Passiontide.
passiv ['pasi:f] *adj* passive; **~es Rauchen** passive smoking; **P~** (**-s, -e**) *nt* passive.
Passiva [pa'si:va] *pl* (*COMM*) liabilities *pl*.
Passivität [pasivi'tɛ:t] *f* passiveness.
Passivposten *m* (*COMM*) debit entry.
Paß- *zW:* **~kontrolle** *f* passport control; **~stelle** *f* passport office; **~straße** *f* (mountain) pass; **~zwang** *m* requirement to carry a passport.
Paste ['pastə] (**-, -n**) *f* paste.
Pastell [pas'tɛl] (**-(e)s, -e**) *nt* pastel; **~farbe** *f* pastel colour (*BRIT*) *od* color (*US*); **p~farben** *adj* pastel-colo(u)red.
Pastete [pas'te:tə] (**-, -n**) *f* pie; (*Pastetchen*) vol-au-vent; (*: ungefüllt*) vol-au-vent case.
pasteurisieren [pastøri'zi:rən] *vt* to pasteurize.
Pastor ['pastɔr] *m* vicar; pastor, minister.
Pate ['pa:tə] (**-n, -n**) *m* godfather; **bei etw ~ gestanden haben** (*fig*) to be the force behind sth.
Patenkind *nt* godchild.
Patenstadt *f* twin town (*BRIT*).
patent [pa'tɛnt] *adj* clever.
Patent (**-(e)s, -e**) *nt* patent; (*MIL*) commission; **etw als** *od* **zum ~ anmelden** to apply for a patent on sth.
Patentamt *nt* patent office.
patentieren [patɛn'ti:rən] *vt* to patent.
Patent- *zW:* **~inhaber** *m* patentee; **~lösung** *f* (*fig*) patent remedy; **~schutz** *m* patent right; **~urkunde** *f* letters patent *pl*.
Pater ['pa:tər] (**-s, -** *od* **Patres**) *m* (*ECCL*) Father.
Paternoster [patər'nɔstər] (**-s, -**) *m* (*Aufzug*) paternoster.
pathetisch [pa'te:tɪʃ] *adj* emotional.
Pathologe [pato'lo:gə] (**-n, -n**) *m* pathologist.
Pathologin [pato'lo:gɪn] *f* pathologist.
pathologisch *adj* pathological.
Pathos ['pa:tɔs] (**-**) *nt* emotiveness, emotionalism.
Patience [pasi'ã:s] (**-, -n**) *f:* **~n legen** to play patience.
Patient(in) [patsi'ɛnt(ɪn)] *m(f)* patient.
Patin ['pa:tɪn] *f* godmother.
Patina ['pa:tina] (**-**) *f* patina.
Patriarch [patri'arç] (**-en, -en**) *m* patriarch.
patriarchalisch [patriar'ça:lɪʃ] *adj* patriarchal.
Patriot(in) [patri'o:t(ɪn)] (**-en, -en**) *m(f)* patriot; **p~isch** *adj* patriotic.
Patriotismus [patrio'tɪsmʊs] *m* patriotism.
Patron [pa'tro:n] (**-s, -e**) *m* patron; (*ECCL*)

patron saint.
Patrone (**-, -n**) *f* cartridge.
Patronenhülse *f* cartridge case.
Patronin *f* patroness; (*ECCL*) patron saint.
Patrouille [pa'trʊljə] (**-, -n**) *f* patrol.
patrouillieren [patrʊl'ji:rən] *vi* to patrol.
patsch [patʃ] *interj* splash!
Patsche (**-, -n**) (*umg*) *f* (*Händchen*) paw; (*Fliegen~*) swat; (*Feuer~*) beater; (*Bedrängnis*) mess, jam.
patschen *vi* to smack, slap; (*im Wasser*) to splash.
patschnaß *adj* soaking wet.
Patt [pat] (**-s, -s**) *nt* (*lit, fig*) stalemate.
patzen ['patsən] (*umg*) *vi* to boob (*BRIT*), goof (*US*).
patzig ['patsɪç] (*umg*) *adj* cheeky, saucy.
Pauke ['paʊkə] (**-, -n**) *f* kettledrum; **auf die ~ hauen** to live it up; **mit ~n und Trompeten durchfallen** (*umg*) to fail dismally.
pauken *vt, vi* (*SCH*) to swot (*BRIT*), cram.
Pauker (**-s, -**) (*umg*) *m* teacher.
pausbäckig ['paʊsbɛkɪç] *adj* chubby-cheeked.
pauschal [paʊ'ʃa:l] *adj* (*Kosten*) inclusive; (*einheitlich*) flat-rate *attrib*; (*Urteil*) sweeping; **die Werkstatt berechnet ~ pro Inspektion 250 DM** the garage has a flat rate of 250 marks per service.
Pauschale (**-, -n**) *f* flat rate; (*vorläufig geschätzter Betrag*) estimated amount.
Pauschal- *zW:* **~gebühr** *f* flat rate; **~preis** *m* all-in price; **~reise** *f* package tour; **~summe** *f* lump sum; **~versicherung** *f* comprehensive insurance.
Pause ['paʊzə] (**-, -n**) *f* break; (*THEAT*) interval; (*das Innehalten*) pause; (*MUS*) rest; (*Kopie*) tracing.
pausen *vt* to trace.
Pausen- *zW:* **~brot** *nt* sandwich (*to eat at break*); **~hof** *m* playground, schoolyard (*US*); **p~los** *adj* nonstop; **~zeichen** *nt* (*RUNDF*) call sign; (*MUS*) rest.
pausieren [paʊ'si:rən] *vi* to make a break.
Pauspapier ['paʊspapi:r] *nt* tracing paper.
Pavian ['pa:via:n] (**-s, -e**) *m* baboon.
Pazifik [pa'tsi:fɪk] (**-s**) *m* Pacific.
pazifisch *adj* Pacific; **der P~e Ozean** the Pacific (Ocean).
Pazifist(in) [patsi'fɪst(ɪn)] *m(f)* pacifist; **p~isch** *adj* pacifist.
PC *m abk* (= *Personalcomputer*) PC.
PDS *f abk* (= *Partei des Demokratischen Sozialismus*) German Socialist Party.

The **PDS** *(Partei des Demokratischen Sozialismus) was founded in 1989 as the successor of the SED, the former East German Communist Party. Its aims are the establishment of a democratic socialist society and to hold a position in the German political scene left of the* **SPD**.

Pech [pɛç] (-s, -e) *nt* pitch; (*fig*) bad luck; ~ **haben** to be unlucky; **die beiden halten zusammen wie ~ und Schwefel** (*umg*) the two are inseparable; ~ **gehabt!** tough! (*umg*); **p~schwarz** *adj* pitch-black; **~strähne** (*umg*) *f* unlucky patch; **~vogel** (*umg*) *m* unlucky person.

Pedal [pe'da:l] (-s, -e) *nt* pedal; **in die ~e treten** to pedal (hard).

Pedant [pe'dant] *m* pedant.

Pedanterie [pedantə'ri:] *f* pedantry.

pedantisch *adj* pedantic.

Peddigrohr ['pɛdiçro:r] *nt* cane.

Pediküre [pedi'ky:rə] (-, -n) *f* (*Fußpflege*) pedicure; (*Fußpflegerin*) chiropodist.

Pegel ['pe:gəl] (-s, -) *m* water gauge; (*Geräusch~*) noise level; **~stand** *m* water level.

peilen ['paɪlən] *vt* to get a fix on; **die Lage ~** (*umg*) to see how the land lies.

Pein [paɪn] (-) *f* agony, suffering.

peinigen *vt* to torture; (*plagen*) to torment.

peinlich *adj* (*unangenehm*) embarrassing, awkward, painful; (*genau*) painstaking; **in seinem Zimmer herrschte ~e Ordnung** his room was meticulously tidy; **er vermied es ~st, davon zu sprechen** he was at pains not to talk about it; **P~keit** *f* painfulness, awkwardness; (*Genauigkeit*) scrupulousness.

Peitsche ['paɪtʃə] (-, -n) *f* whip.

peitschen *vt* to whip; (*Regen*) to lash.

Peitschenhieb *m* lash.

Pekinese [peki'ne:zə] (-n, -n) *m* Pekinese, peke (*umg*).

Peking ['pe:kɪŋ] (-s) *nt* Peking.

Pelikan ['pe:lika:n] (-s, -e) *m* pelican.

Pelle ['pɛlə] (-, -n) *f* skin; **der Chef sitzt mir auf der ~** (*umg*) I've got the boss on my back.

pellen *vt* to skin, peel.

Pellkartoffeln *pl* jacket potatoes *pl*.

Pelz [pɛlts] (-es, -e) *m* fur.

Pendel ['pɛndəl] (-s, -) *nt* pendulum.

pendeln *vi* (*schwingen*) to swing (to and fro); (*Zug, Fähre etc*) to shuttle; (*Mensch*) to commute; (*fig*) to fluctuate.

Pendelverkehr *m* shuttle service; (*Berufsverkehr*) commuter traffic.

Pendler(in) ['pɛndlər(ɪn)] (-s, -) *m(f)* commuter.

penetrant [pene'trant] *adj* sharp; (*Person*) pushing; **das schmeckt/riecht ~ nach Knoblauch** it has a very strong taste/smell of garlic.

penibel [pe'ni:bəl] *adj* pernickety (*BRIT*) (*umg*), persnickety (*US*) (*umg*), precise.

Penis ['pe:nɪs] (-, -se) *m* penis.

Pennbruder ['pɛnbru:dər] (*umg*) *m* tramp (*BRIT*), hobo (*US*).

Penne (-, -n) (*umg*) *f* (*SCH*) school.

pennen (*umg*) *vi* to kip.

Penner (-s, -) (*pej: umg*) *m* tramp (*BRIT*), hobo (*US*).

Pension [pɛnzi'o:n] *f* (*Geld*) pension; (*Ruhestand*) retirement; (*für Gäste*) boarding house, guesthouse; **halbe/volle ~** half/full board; **in ~ gehen** to retire.

Pensionär(in) [pɛnzio'nɛ:r(ɪn)] (-s, -e) *m(f)* pensioner.

Pensionat (-(e)s, -e) *nt* boarding school.

pensionieren [pɛnzio'ni:rən] *vt* to pension (off); **sich ~ lassen** to retire.

pensioniert *adj* retired.

Pensionierung *f* retirement.

Pensions- *zW:* **p~berechtigt** *adj* entitled to a pension; **~gast** *m* boarder, paying guest; **p~reif** (*umg*) *adj* ready for retirement.

Pensum ['pɛnzʊm] (-s, **Pensen**) *nt* quota; (*SCH*) curriculum.

Peperoni [pepe'ro:ni] *pl* chillies *pl*.

per [pɛr] *präp +akk* by, per; (*pro*) per; (*bis*) by; ~ **Adresse** (*COMM*) care of, c/o; **mit jdm ~ du sein** (*umg*) to be on first-name terms with sb.

Perfekt ['pɛrfɛkt] (-(e)s, -e) *nt* perfect.

perfekt [pɛr'fɛkt] *adj* perfect; (*abgemacht*) settled; **die Sache ~ machen** to clinch the deal; **der Vertrag ist ~** the contract is all settled.

perfektionieren [pɛrfɛktsio'ni:rən] *vt* to perfect.

Perfektionismus [pɛrfɛktsio'nɪsmʊs] *m* perfectionism.

perforieren [pɛrfo'ri:rən] *vt* to perforate.

Pergament [pɛrga'mɛnt] *nt* parchment; **~papier** *nt* greaseproof paper (*BRIT*), wax(ed) paper (*US*).

Pergola ['pɛrgola] (-, **Pergolen**) *f* pergola, arbour (*BRIT*), arbor (*US*).

Periode [peri'o:də] (-, -n) *f* period; **0,33 ~** 0.33 recurring.

periodisch [peri'o:dɪʃ] *adj* periodic; (*dezimal*) recurring.

Peripherie [perife'ri:] *f* periphery; (*um Stadt*) outskirts *pl*; (*MATH*) circumference; **~gerät** *nt* (*COMPUT*) peripheral.

Perle ['pɛrlə] (-, -n) *f* (*lit, fig*) pearl; (*Glas~, Holz~, Tropfen~*) bead; (*veraltet: umg: Hausgehilfin*) maid.

perlen *vi* to sparkle; (*Tropfen*) to trickle.

Perlenkette *f* pearl necklace.

Perlhuhn *nt* guinea fowl.

Perlmutt ['pɛrlmʊt] (-s) *nt* mother-of-pearl.

Perlon ® ['pɛrlɔn] (-s) *nt* ≈ nylon.

Perlwein *m* sparkling wine.

perplex [pɛr'plɛks] *adj* dumbfounded.

Perser ['pɛrzər] (-s, -) *m* (*Person*) Persian; (*umg: Teppich*) Persian carpet.

Perserin *f* Persian.

Persianer [pɛrzi'a:nər] (-s, -) *m* Persian lamb (coat).

Persien ['pɛrziən] (-s) *nt* Persia.

Persiflage [pɛrzi'flaːʒə] (-, -n) f: ~ (+gen od auf +akk) pastiche (of), satire (on).

persisch adj Persian; **P~er Golf** Persian Gulf.

Person [pɛr'zoːn] (-, -en) f person; (pej: Frau) female; **sie ist Köchin und Haushälterin in einer** ~ she is cook and housekeeper rolled into one; **ich für meine** ~ personally I.

Personal [pɛrzo'naːl] (-s) nt personnel; (Bedienung) servants pl; ~**abbau** m staff cuts pl; ~**akte** f personal file; ~**angaben** pl particulars pl; ~**ausweis** m identity card; ~**bogen** m personal record; ~**büro** nt personnel (department); ~**chef** m personnel manager; ~**computer** m personal computer.

Personalien [pɛrzo'naːliən] pl particulars pl.

Personalität [pɛrzonali'tɛːt] f personality.

Personal- zW: ~**kosten** pl staff costs; ~**mangel** m staff shortage; ~**pronomen** nt personal pronoun; ~**reduzierung** f staff reduction.

personell [pɛrzo'nɛl] adj staff attrib; ~**e Veränderungen** changes in personnel.

Personen- zW: ~**aufzug** m lift, elevator (US); ~**beschreibung** f (personal) description; ~**gedächtnis** nt memory for faces; ~**gesellschaft** f partnership; ~**kraftwagen** m private motorcar, automobile (US); ~**kreis** m group of people; ~**kult** m personality cult; ~**schaden** m injury to persons; ~**verkehr** m passenger services pl; ~**waage** f scales pl; ~**zug** m stopping train; passenger train.

personifizieren [pɛrzonifi'tsiːrən] vt to personify.

persönlich [pɛr'zøːnlɪç] adj personal ♦ adv in person; personally; (auf Briefen) private (and confidential); ~ **haften** (COMM) to be personally liable; **P~keit** f personality; **P~keiten des öffentlichen Lebens** public figures.

Perspektive [pɛrspɛk'tiːvə] f perspective; **das eröffnet ganz neue** ~**n für uns** that opens new horizons for us.

Pers. Ref. abk (= Persönlicher Referent) personal representative.

Peru [pe'ruː] (-s) nt Peru.

Peruaner(in) [peru'aːnər(ɪn)] (-s, -) m(f) Peruvian.

peruanisch adj Peruvian.

Perücke [pe'rʏkə] (-, -n) f wig.

pervers [pɛr'vɛrs] adj perverse.

Perversität [pɛrvɛrzi'tɛːt] f perversity.

Pessar [pɛ'saːr] (-s, -e) nt pessary; (zur Empfängnisverhütung) cap, diaphragm.

Pessimismus [pɛsi'mɪsmʊs] m pessimism.

Pessimist(in) [pɛsi'mɪst(ɪn)] m(f) pessimist; **p~isch** adj pessimistic.

Pest [pɛst] (-) f plague; **jdn/etw wie die** ~ **hassen** (umg) to loathe (and detest) sb/sth.

Petersilie [petər'ziːliə] f parsley.

Petrochemie [petro:çe'miː] f petrochemistry.

Petrodollar [petro'dɔlar] m petrodollar.

Petroleum [pe'troːleʊm] (-s) nt paraffin (BRIT), kerosene (US).

petzen ['pɛtsən] (umg) vi to tell tales; **er petzt immer** he always tells.

Pf abk = **Pfennig.**

Pfad [pfaːt] (-(e)s, -e) m path; ~**finder** m Boy Scout; **er ist bei den** ~**findern** he's in the (Boy) Scouts; ~**finderin** f Girl Guide.

Pfaffe ['pfafə] (-n, -n) (pej) m cleric, parson.

Pfahl [pfaːl] (-(e)s, ⁼e) m post, stake; ~**bau** m pile dwelling.

Pfalz [pfalts] (-, -en) f (GEOG) Palatinate.

Pfälzer(in) ['pfɛltsər(ɪn)] (-s, -) m(f) person from the Palatinate.

pfälzisch adj Palatine, of the (Rhineland) Palatinate.

Pfand [pfant] (-(e)s, ⁼er) nt pledge, security; (Flaschen~) deposit; (im Spiel) forfeit; (fig: der Liebe etc) pledge; ~**brief** m bond.

pfänden ['pfɛndən] vt to seize, impound.

Pfänderspiel nt game of forfeits.

Pfand- zW: ~**haus** nt pawnshop; ~**leiher** (-s, -) m pawnbroker; ~**recht** nt lien; ~**schein** m pawn ticket.

Pfändung ['pfɛndʊŋ] f seizure, distraint (form).

Pfanne ['pfanə] (-, -n) f (frying) pan; **jdn in die** ~ **hauen** (umg) to tear a strip off sb.

Pfannkuchen m pancake; (Berliner) doughnut (BRIT), donut (US).

Pfarrei [pfar'raɪ] f parish.

Pfarrer (-s, -) m priest; (evangelisch) vicar; (von Freikirchen) minister.

Pfarrhaus nt vicarage.

Pfau [pfaʊ] (-(e)s, -en) m peacock.

Pfauenauge nt peacock butterfly.

Pfd. abk (= Pfund) ≈ lb.

Pfeffer ['pfɛfər] (-s, -) m pepper; **er soll bleiben, wo der** ~ **wächst!** (umg) he can take a running jump; ~**korn** nt peppercorn; ~**kuchen** m gingerbread; ~**minz** (-es, -e) nt peppermint; ~**minze** f peppermint (plant); ~**mühle** f pepper mill.

pfeffern vt to pepper; (umg: werfen) to fling; **gepfefferte Preise/Witze** steep prices/spicy jokes.

Pfeife ['pfaɪfə] (-, -n) f whistle; (Tabak~, Orgel~) pipe; **nach jds** ~ **tanzen** to dance to sb's tune.

pfeifen unreg vt, vi to whistle; **auf dem letzten Loch** ~ (umg: erschöpft sein) to be on one's last legs; (: finanziell) to be on one's beam ends; **ich pfeif(e) drauf!** (umg) I don't give a damn!; **P~stopfer** m tamper.

Pfeifer (-s, -) m piper.

Pfeifkonzert nt catcalls pl.

Pfeil [pfaɪl] (-(e)s, -e) m arrow.

Pfeiler ['pfaɪlər] (-s, -) m pillar, prop; (Brücken~) pier.

Pfennig ['pfɛnɪç] (-(e)s, -e) m pfennig (hundredth part of a mark); ~**absatz** m stiletto

heel; **~fuchser (-s, -)** (*umg*) *m* skinflint.
pferchen ['pfɛrçən] *vt* to cram, pack.
Pferd [pfeːrt] **(-(e)s, -e)** *nt* horse; **wie ein
~ arbeiten** (*umg*) to work like a Trojan; **mit
ihm kann man ~e stehlen** (*umg*) he's a great
sport; **auf das falsche/richtige ~ setzen** (*lit,
fig*) to back the wrong/right horse.
Pferde- *zW:* **~äpfel** *pl* horse droppings *pl od*
dung *sing;* **~fuß** *m:* **die Sache hat aber einen
~fuß** there's just one snag; **~rennen** *nt*
horse-race; (*Sportart*) horse-racing;
~schwanz *m* (*Frisur*) ponytail; **~stall** *m*
stable; **~stärke** *f* horsepower.
Pfiff **(-(e)s, -e)** *m* whistle; (*Kniff*) trick.
pfiff *etc* [pfɪf] *vb siehe* **pfeifen.**
Pfifferling ['pfɪfərlɪŋ] *m* yellow chanterelle;
keinen ~ wert not worth a thing.
pfiffig *adj* smart.
Pfingsten ['pfɪŋstən] **(-, -)** *nt* Whitsun.
Pfingstrose *f* peony.
Pfingstsonntag *m* Whit Sunday, Pentecost
(*REL*).
Pfirsich ['pfɪrzɪç] **(-s, -e)** *m* peach.
Pflanze ['pflantsə] **(-, -n)** *f* plant.
pflanzen *vt* to plant ♦ *vr* (*umg*) to plonk o.s.
Pflanzenfett *nt* vegetable fat.
Pflanzenschutzmittel *nt* pesticide.
pflanzlich *adj* vegetable.
Pflanzung *f* plantation.
Pflaster ['pflastər] **(-s, -)** *nt* plaster; (*Straßen~*)
pavement (*BRIT*), sidewalk (*US*); **ein teures
~** (*umg*) a pricey place; **ein heißes ~** a
dangerous *od* unsafe place; **p~müde** *adj*
dead on one's feet.
pflastern *vt* to pave.
Pflasterstein *m* paving stone.
Pflaume ['pflaumə] **(-, -n)** *f* plum; (*umg:
Mensch*) twit (*BRIT*).
Pflaumenmus *nt* plum jam.
Pflege ['pfleːgə] **(-, -n)** *f* care; (*von Idee*)
cultivation; (*Kranken~*) nursing; **jdn/etw in
~ nehmen** to look after sb/sth; **in ~ sein**
(*Kind*) to be fostered out; **p~bedürftig** *adj*
needing care; **~eltern** *pl* foster parents *pl*;
~fall *m* case for nursing; **~geld** *nt* (*für
~kinder*) boarding-out allowance; (*für
Kranke*) attendance allowance; **~heim** *nt*
nursing home; **~kind** *nt* foster child;
p~leicht *adj* easy-care; **~mutter** *f* foster
mother.
pflegen *vt* to look after; (*Kranke*) to nurse;
(*Beziehungen*) to foster ♦ *vi* (*gewöhnlich tun*):
sie pflegte zu sagen she used to say.
Pfleger **(-s, -)** *m* (*im Krankenhaus*) orderly;
(*voll qualifiziert*) male nurse; **~in** *f* nurse.
Pflegesatz *m* hospital and nursing charges
pl.
Pflegevater *m* foster father.
Pflegeversicherung *f* geriatric care
insurance.
Pflicht [pflɪçt] **(-, -en)** *f* duty; (*SPORT*)
compulsory section; **Rechte und ~en** rights

and responsibilities; **p~bewußt** *adj*
conscientious; **~bewußtsein** *nt* sense of
duty; **~fach** *nt* (*SCH*) compulsory subject;
~gefühl *nt* sense of duty; **p~gemäß** *adj*
dutiful **p~vergessen** *adj* irresponsible;
~versicherung *f* compulsory insurance.
Pflock [pflɔk] **(-(e)s, ⸚e)** *m* peg; (*für Tiere*)
stake.
pflog *etc* [pfloːk] *vb* (*veraltet*) *siehe* **pflegen.**
pflücken ['pflʏkən] *vt* to pick.
Pflug [pfluːk] **(-(e)s, ⸚e)** *m* plough (*BRIT*), plow
(*US*).
pflügen ['pflyːgən] *vt* to plough (*BRIT*), plow
(*US*).
Pflugschar *f* ploughshare (*BRIT*), plowshare
(*US*).
Pforte ['pfɔrtə] **(-, -n)** *f* (*Tor*) gate.
Pförtner ['pfœrtnər] **(-s, -)** *m* porter,
doorkeeper, doorman.
Pförtnerin *f* doorkeeper, porter.
Pfosten ['pfɔstən] **(-s, -)** *m* post; (*senkrechter
Balken*) upright.
Pfote ['pfoːtə] **(-, -n)** *f* paw; (*umg: Schrift*)
scrawl.
Pfropf [pfrɔpf] **(-(e)s, -e)** *m* (*Flaschen~*)
stopper; (*Blut~*) clot.
Pfropfen **(-s, -)** *m* = **Pfropf.**
pfropfen *vt* (*stopfen*) to cram; (*Baum*) to graft;
gepfropft voll crammed full.
pfui [pfʊi] *interj* ugh!; (*na na*) tut tut!; (*Buhruf*)
boo!; **~ Teufel!** (*umg*) ugh!, yuck!
Pfund [pfʊnt] **(-(e)s, -e)** *nt* (*Gewicht, FIN*)
pound; **das ~ sinkt** sterling *od* the pound is
falling.
pfundig (*umg*) *adj* great.
Pfundskerl ['pfʊntskerl] (*umg*) *m* great guy.
pfundweise *adv* by the pound.
pfuschen ['pfʊʃən] *vi* to bungle; (*einen Fehler
machen*) to slip up.
Pfuscher(in) ['pfʊʃər(ɪn)] **(-s, -)** (*umg*) *m(f)*
sloppy worker; (*Kur~*) quack.
Pfuscherei [pfʊʃəˈraɪ] (*umg*) *f* sloppy work;
(*Kur~*) quackery.
Pfütze ['pfʏtsə] **(-, -n)** *f* puddle.
PH **(-, -s)** *f abk* = **Pädagogische Hochschule.**
Phänomen [fɛnoˈmeːn] **(-s, -e)** *nt*
phenomenon; **p~al** [-ˈnaːl] *adj* phenomenal.
Phantasie [fantaˈziː] *f* imagination; **in seiner
~** in his mind; **~gebilde** *nt* (*Einbildung*)
figment of the imagination; **p~los** *adj*
unimaginative.
phantasieren [fantaˈziːrən] *vi* to fantasize;
(*MED*) to be delirious.
phantasievoll *adj* imaginative.
Phantast [fanˈtast] **(-en, -en)** *m* dreamer,
visionary.
phantastisch *adj* fantastic.
Phantom [fanˈtoːm] **(-s, -e)** *nt* (*Trugbild*)
phantom; **einem ~ nachjagen** (*fig*) to tilt at
windmills; **~bild** *nt* Identikit ® picture.
Pharisäer [fariˈzɛːər] **(-s, -)** *m* (*lit, fig*) pharisee.
Pharmazeut(in) [farmaˈtsɔʏt(ɪn)] **(-en, -en)**

m(f) pharmacist.
pharmazeutisch *adj* pharmaceutical.
Pharmazie *f* pharmacy, pharmaceutics *sing.*
Phase ['faːzə] (-, -n) *f* phase.
Philanthrop [filan'troːp] (-en, -en) *m* philanthropist; **p~isch** *adj* philanthropic.
Philharmoniker [fɪlhar'moːnikər] (-s, -) *m*: **die** ~ the philharmonic (orchestra) *sing.*
Philatelist(in) [filate'lɪst(ɪn)] (-en, -en) *m(f)* philatelist.
Philippine [fɪlɪ'piːnə] (-n, -n) *m* Filipino.
Philippinen *pl* Philippines *pl*, Philippine Islands *pl.*
Philippinin *f* Filipino.
philippinisch *adj* Filipino.
Philologe [filo'loːgə] (-n, -n) *m* philologist.
Philologie [filolo'giː] *f* philology.
Philologin *f* philologist.
Philosoph(in) [filo'zoːf(ɪn)] (-en, -en) *m(f)* philosopher.
Philosophie [filozo'fiː] *f* philosophy.
philosophieren [filozo'fiːrən] *vi*: ~ **(über** +*akk*) to philosophize (about).
philosophisch *adj* philosophical.
Phlegma ['flɛgma] (-s) *nt* lethargy.
phlegmatisch [flɛ'gmaːtɪʃ] *adj* lethargic.
Phobie [fo'biː] *f*: ~ **(vor** +*dat*) phobia (about).
Phonetik [fo'neːtɪk] *f* phonetics *sing.*
phonetisch *adj* phonetic.
Phonotypistin [fonoty'pɪstɪn] *f* audiotypist.
Phosphat [fɔs'faːt] (-(e)s, -e) *nt* phosphate.
Phosphor ['fɔsfɔr] (-s) *m* phosphorus.
phosphoreszieren [fɔsforɛs'tsiːrən] *vt* to phosphoresce.
Photo *etc* ['foːto] = **Foto** *etc.*
Phrase ['fraːzə] (-, -n) *f* phrase; (*pej*) hollow phrase; ~**n dreschen** (*umg*) to churn out one cliché after another.
pH-Wert [peː'haːveːrt] *m* pH value.
Physik [fy'ziːk] *f* physics *sing.*
physikalisch [fyzi'kaːlɪʃ] *adj* of physics.
Physiker(in) ['fyːzikər(ɪn)] (-s, -) *m(f)* physicist.
Physikum ['fyːzikʊm] (-s) *nt* (*UNIV*) preliminary examination in medicine.
Physiologe [fyzio'loːgə] (-n, -n) *m* physiologist.
Physiologie [fyziolo'giː] *f* physiology.
Physiologin *f* physiologist.
physisch ['fyːzɪʃ] *adj* physical.
Pianist(in) [pia'nɪst(ɪn)] *m(f)* pianist.
picheln ['pɪçəln] (*umg*) *vi* to booze.
Pickel ['pɪkəl] (-s, -) *m* pimple; (*Werkzeug*) pickaxe; (*Berg~*) ice axe.
pick(e)lig *adj* pimply.
picken ['pɪkən] *vt* to peck ♦ *vi*: ~ **(nach)** to peck (at).
Picknick ['pɪknɪk] (-s, -e *od* -s) *nt* picnic; ~ **machen** to have a picnic.
piekfein ['piːk'faɪn] (*umg*) *adj* posh.
Piemont [pie'mɔnt] (-s) *nt* Piedmont.
piepen ['piːpən] *vi* to chirp; (*Funkgerät etc*) to

bleep; **bei dir piept's wohl!** (*umg*) are you off your head?; **es war zum P~!** (*umg*) it was a scream!
piepsen ['piːpsən] *vi* = **piepen**.
Piepser (*umg*) *m* pager, paging device.
Piepsstimme *f* squeaky voice.
Piepton *m* bleep.
Pier [piːər] (-s, -s *od* -e) *m* jetty, pier.
piesacken ['piːzakən] (*umg*) *vt* to torment.
Pietät [pie'tɛːt] *f* piety; reverence; **p~los** *adj* impious, irreverent.
Pigment [pɪg'mɛnt] (-(e)s, -e) *nt* pigment.
Pik [piːk] (-s, -s) *nt* (*KARTEN*) spades; **einen** ~ **auf jdn haben** (*umg*) to have it in for sb.
pikant [pi'kant] *adj* spicy, piquant; (*anzüglich*) suggestive.
Pike (-, -n) *f*: **etw von der** ~ **auf lernen** (*fig*) to learn sth from the bottom up.
pikiert [pi'kiːrt] *adj* offended.
Pikkolo ['pɪkolo] (-s, -s) *m* trainee waiter; (*auch:* ~**flasche**) *quarter bottle of champagne*; (*MUS: auch:* ~**flöte**) piccolo.
Piktogramm [pɪkto'gram] *nt* pictogram.
Pilger(in) ['pɪlgər(ɪn)] (-s, -) *m(f)* pilgrim; ~**fahrt** *f* pilgrimage.
pilgern *vi* to make a pilgrimage; (*umg: gehen*) to wend one's way.
Pille ['pɪlə] (-, -n) *f* pill.
Pilot(in) [pi'loːt(ɪn)] (-en, -en) *m(f)* pilot; ~**enschein** *m* pilot's licence (*BRIT*) *od* license (*US*).
Pils [pɪls] (-, -) *nt* Pilsner (lager).
Pils(e)ner [pɪlz(ə)nər] (-s, -) *nt* Pilsner (lager).
Pilz [pɪlts] (-es, -e) *m* fungus; (*eßbar*) mushroom; (*giftig*) toadstool; **wie ~e aus dem Boden schießen** (*fig*) to mushroom; ~**krankheit** *f* fungal disease.
Pimmel ['pɪməl] (-s, -) (*umg*) *m* (*Penis*) willie.
pingelig ['pɪŋəlɪç] (*umg*) *adj* fussy.
Pinguin ['pɪŋguiːn] (-s, -e) *m* penguin.
Pinie ['piːniə] *f* pine.
Pinkel (-s, -) (*umg*) *m*: **ein feiner** *od* **vornehmer** ~ a swell, Lord Muck (*BRIT*) (*umg*).
pinkeln ['pɪŋkəln] (*umg*) *vi* to pee.
Pinnwand ['pɪnvant] *f* pinboard.
Pinsel ['pɪnzəl] (-s, -) *m* paintbrush.
pinseln (*umg*) *vt, vi* to paint; (*pej: malen*) to daub.
Pinte ['pɪntə] (-, -n) (*umg*) *f* (*Lokal*) boozer (*BRIT*).
Pinzette [pɪn'tsɛtə] *f* tweezers *pl.*
Pionier [pio'niːr] (-s, -e) *m* pioneer; (*MIL*) sapper, engineer; ~**arbeit** *f* pioneering work; ~**unternehmen** *nt* pioneer company.
Pipi [pi'piː] (-s, -s) *nt od m* (*Kindersprache*) wee(-wee).
Pirat [pi'raːt] (-en, -en) *m* pirate.
Piratensender *m* pirate radio station.
Pirsch [pɪrʃ] (-) *f* stalking.
pissen ['pɪsən] (*umg!*) *vi* to (have a) piss (*!*); (*regnen*) to piss down (*!*).
Pistazie [pɪs'taːtsiə] (-, -n) *f* pistachio.

Piste ['pɪstə] (-, -n) *f* (*SKI*) run, piste; (*AVIAT*) runway.

Pistole [pɪs'toːlə] (-, -n) *f* pistol; **wie aus der ~ geschossen** (*fig*) like a shot; **jdm die ~ auf die Brust setzen** (*fig*) to hold a pistol to sb's head.

pitsch(e)naß ['pɪtʃ(ə)'nas] (*umg*) *adj* soaking (wet).

Pizza ['pɪtsa] (-, -s) *f* pizza.

PKW *m abk* = **Pkw.**

Pkw (-(s), -(s)) *m abk* = **Personenkraftwagen.**

Pl. *abk* (= *Plural*) pl.; (= *Platz*) Sq.

Plackerei [plakə'raɪ] *f* drudgery.

plädieren [plɛ'diːrən] *vi* to plead.

Plädoyer [plɛdoa'jeː] (-s, -s) *nt* speech for the defence; (*fig*) plea.

Plage ['plaːgə] (-, -n) *f* plague; (*Mühe*) nuisance; **~geist** *m* pest, nuisance.

plagen *vt* to torment ♦ *vr* to toil, slave.

Plagiat [plagi'aːt] (-(e)s, -e) *nt* plagiarism.

Plakat [pla'kaːt] (-(e)s, -e) *nt* poster; (*aus Pappe*) placard.

plakativ [plaka'tiːf] *adj* striking, bold.

Plakatwand *f* hoarding, billboard (*US*).

Plakette [pla'kɛtə] (-, -n) *f* (*Abzeichen*) badge; (*Münze*) commemorative coin; (*an Wänden*) plaque.

Plan [plaːn] (-(e)s, ̈e) *m* plan; (*Karte*) map; **Pläne schmieden** to make plans; **nach ~ verlaufen** to go according to plan; **jdn auf den ~ rufen** (*fig*) to bring sb into the arena.

Plane (-, -n) *f* tarpaulin.

planen *vt* to plan; (*Mord etc*) to plot.

Planer(in) (-s, -) *m(f)* planner.

Planet [pla'neːt] (-en, -en) *m* planet.

Planetenbahn *f* orbit (of a planet).

planieren [pla'niːrən] *vt* to level off.

Planierraupe *f* bulldozer.

Planke ['plaŋkə] (-, -n) *f* plank.

Plänkelei [plɛŋkə'laɪ] *f* skirmish(ing).

plänkeln ['plɛŋkəln] *vi* to skirmish.

Plankton ['plaŋktɔn] (-s) *nt* plankton.

planlos *adj* (*Vorgehen*) unsystematic; (*Umherlaufen*) aimless.

planmäßig *adj* according to plan; (*methodisch*) systematic; (*EISENB*) scheduled.

Planschbecken ['planʃbɛkən] *nt* paddling pool.

planschen *vi* to splash.

Plansoll *nt* output target.

Planstelle *f* post.

Plantage [plan'taːʒə] (-, -n) *f* plantation.

Planung *f* planning.

Planwagen *m* covered wagon.

Planwirtschaft *f* planned economy.

Plappermaul (*umg*) *nt* (*Kind*) chatterbox.

plappern ['plapərn] *vi* to chatter.

plärren ['plɛrən] *vi* (*Mensch*) to cry, whine; (*Radio*) to blare.

Plasma ['plasma] (-s, **Plasmen**) *nt* plasma.

Plastik¹ ['plastɪk] *f* sculpture.

Plastik² ['plastɪk] (-s) *nt* (*Kunststoff*) plastic; **~folie** *f* plastic film; **~geschoß** *nt* plastic bullet; **~tüte** *f* plastic bag.

Plastilin [plasti'liːn] (-s) *nt* Plasticine ®.

plastisch ['plastɪʃ] *adj* plastic; **stell dir das ~ vor!** just picture it!

Platane [pla'taːnə] (-, -n) *f* plane (tree).

Platin ['plaːtiːn] (-s) *nt* platinum.

Platitüde [plati'tyːdə] (-, -n) *f* platitude.

platonisch [pla'toːnɪʃ] *adj* platonic.

platsch [platʃ] *interj* splash!

platschen *vi* to splash.

plätschern ['plɛtʃərn] *vi* to babble.

platschnaß *adj* drenched.

platt [plat] *adj* flat; (*umg: überrascht*) flabbergasted; (*fig: geistlos*) flat, boring; **einen P~en haben** to have a flat (*umg*), have a flat tyre (*BRIT*) *od* tire (*US*).

plattdeutsch *adj* Low German.

Platte (-, -n) *f* (*Speisen~, PHOT, TECH*) plate; (*Stein~*) flag; (*Kachel*) tile; (*Schall~*) record; **kalte ~** cold dish; **die ~ kenne ich schon** (*umg*) I've heard all that before.

Plätteisen *nt* iron.

plätten *vt, vi* to iron.

Platten- *zW:* **~leger** (-s, -) *m* paver; **~spieler** *m* record player; **~teller** *m* turntable.

Plattform *f* platform; (*fig: Grundlage*) basis.

Plattfuß *m* flat foot; (*Reifen*) flat tyre (*BRIT*) *od* tire (*US*).

Platz [plats] (-es, ̈e) *m* place; (*Sitz~*) seat; (*Raum*) space, room; (*in Stadt*) square; (*Sport~*) playing field; **~ machen** to get out of the way; **~ nehmen** to take a seat; **jdm ~ machen** to make room for sb; **auf ~ zwei** in second place; **fehl am ~e sein** to be out of place; **seinen ~ behaupten** to stand one's ground; **das erste Hotel am ~** the best hotel in town; **auf die Plätze, fertig, los!** (*beim Sport*) on your marks, get set, go!; **einen Spieler vom ~ stellen** *od* **verweisen** (*SPORT*) to send a player off; **~angst** *f* (*MED*) agoraphobia; (*umg*) claustrophobia; **~angst haben/bekommen** (*umg*) to feel/get claustrophobic; **~anweiser(in)** (-s, -) *m(f)* usher(ette).

Plätzchen ['plɛtsçən] *nt* spot; (*Gebäck*) biscuit.

platzen *vi* (*Hilfsverb sein*) to burst; (*Bombe*) to explode; (*Naht, Hose, Haut*) to split; (*umg: scheitern: Geschäft*) to fall through; (: *Freundschaft*) to break up; (: *Theorie, Verschwörung*) to collapse; (: *Wechsel*) to bounce; **vor Wut ~** (*umg*) to be bursting with anger.

Platz- *zW:* **~karte** *f* seat reservation; **~konzert** *nt* open-air concert; **~mangel** *m* lack of space; **~patrone** *f* blank cartridge; **~regen** *m* downpour; **~sparend** *adj* space-saving; **~verweis** *m* sending-off; **~wart** *m* (*SPORT*) groundsman (*BRIT*), groundskeeper (*US*); **~wunde** *f* cut.

Plauderei [plaudə'raɪ] *f* chat, conversation.

plaudern ['plaʊdərn] *vi* to chat, talk.

Plausch [plaʊʃ] (-(e)s, -e) *(umg)* *m* chat.

plausibel [plaʊ'ziːbəl] *adj* plausible.

Playback ['pleɪbæk] (-s, -s) *nt* (*Verfahren: Schallplatte*) double-tracking; (*TV*) miming.

plazieren [pla'tsiːrən] *vt* to place ♦ *vr* (*SPORT*) to be placed; (*TENNIS*) to be seeded; (*umg: sich setzen, stellen*) to plant o.s.

Plebejer(in) [ple'beːjər(ɪn)] (-s, -) *m(f)* plebeian.

plebejisch [ple'beːjɪʃ] *adj* plebeian.

pleite ['plaɪtə] *(umg)* *adj* broke; **P~** (-, -n) *f* bankruptcy; (*umg: Reinfall*) flop; **P~ machen** to go bust.

Pleitegeier *(umg)* *m* (*drohende Pleite*) vulture; (*Bankrotteur*) bankrupt.

plemplem [plɛm'plɛm] *(umg)* *adj* nuts.

Plenarsitzung [ple'naːrzɪtsʊŋ] *f* plenary session.

Plenum ['pleːnʊm] (-s, **Plenen**) *nt* plenum.

Pleuelstange ['plɔʏəlʃtaŋə] *f* connecting rod.

Plissee [plɪ'seː] (-s, -s) *nt* pleat.

Plombe ['plɔmbə] (-, -n) *f* lead seal; (*Zahn~*) filling.

plombieren [plɔm'biːrən] *vt* to seal; (*Zahn*) to fill.

Plotter ['plɔtər] (-s, -s) *m* (*COMPUT*) plotter.

plötzlich ['plœtslɪç] *adj* sudden ♦ *adv* suddenly; **~er Kindstod** SIDS= *sudden infant death syndrome.*

Pluderhose ['pluːdərhoːzə] *f* harem trousers *pl.*

plump [plʊmp] *adj* clumsy; (*Hände*) coarse; (*Körper*) shapeless; **~e Annäherungs- versuche** very obvious advances.

plumpsen *(umg)* *vi* to plump down, fall.

Plumpsklo(sett) *(umg)* *nt* earth closet.

Plunder ['plʊndər] (-s) *m* junk, rubbish.

Plundergebäck *nt* flaky pastry.

plündern ['plʏndərn] *vt* to plunder; (*Stadt*) to sack ♦ *vi* to plunder.

Plünderung ['plʏndərʊŋ] *f* plundering, sack, pillage.

Plural ['pluːraːl] (-s, -e) *m* plural; **im ~ stehen** to be (in the) plural.

pluralistisch [plura'lɪstɪʃ] *adj* pluralistic.

plus [plʊs] *adv* plus; **mit ~ minus null abschließen** (*COMM*) to break even; **P~** (-, -) *nt* plus; (*FIN*) profit; (*Vorteil*) advantage.

Plüsch [plyːʃ] (-(e)s, -e) *m* plush; **~tier** *nt* ≈ soft toy.

Plus- *zW:* **~pol** *m* (*ELEK*) positive pole; **~punkt** *m* (*SPORT*) point; (*fig*) point in sb's favour; **~quamperfekt** *nt* pluperfect.

Plutonium [plu'toːnium] (-s) *nt* plutonium.

PLZ *abk* = **Postleitzahl.**

Pneu [pnɔʏ] (-s, -s) *m abk* (= *Pneumatik*) tyre (*BRIT*), tire (*US*).

Po [poː] (-s, -s) *(umg)* *m* bum (*BRIT*), fanny (*US*).

Pöbel ['pøːbəl] (-s) *m* mob, rabble.

Pöbelei [pøːbə'laɪ] *f* vulgarity.

pöbelhaft *adj* low, vulgar.

pochen ['pɔxən] *vi* to knock; (*Herz*) to pound; **auf etw** *akk* **~** (*fig*) to insist on sth.

Pocken ['pɔkən] *pl* smallpox *sing.*

Pocken(schutz)impfung *f* smallpox vaccination.

Podest [po'dɛst] (-(e)s, -e) *nt od m* (*Sockel, fig*) pedestal; (*Podium*) platform.

Podium ['poːdium] *nt* podium.

Podiumsdiskussion *f* panel discussion.

Poesie [poe'ziː] *f* poetry.

Poet [po'eːt] (-en, -en) *m* poet; **p~isch** *adj* poetic.

pofen ['poːfən] *(umg)* *vi* to kip (*BRIT*), doss.

Pointe [po'ɛ̃tə] (-, -n) *f* point; (*eines Witzes*) punch line.

pointiert [poɛ̃'tiːrt] *adj* trenchant, pithy.

Pokal [po'kaːl] (-s, -e) *m* goblet; (*SPORT*) cup; **~spiel** *nt* cup tie.

Pökelfleisch ['pøːkəlflaɪʃ] *nt* salt meat.

pökeln *vt* (*Fleisch, Fisch*) to pickle, salt.

Poker ['poːkər] (-s) *nt* poker.

pokern ['poːkərn] *vi* to play poker.

Pol [poːl] (-s, -e) *m* pole; **der ruhende ~** (*fig*) the calming influence.

pol. *abk* = **politisch; polizeilich.**

polar [po'laːr] *adj* polar.

polarisieren [polari'ziːrən] *vt, vr* to polarize.

Polarkreis *m* polar circle; **nördlicher/ südlicher ~** Arctic/Antarctic Circle.

Polarstern *m* Pole Star.

Pole ['poːlə] (-n, -n) *m* Pole.

Polemik [po'leːmɪk] *f* polemics *sing.*

polemisch *adj* polemical.

polemisieren [polemi'ziːrən] *vi* to polemicize.

Polen ['poːlən] (-s) *nt* Poland.

Polente (-) (*veraltet: umg*) *f* cops *pl.*

Police [po'liːs(ə)] (-, -n) *f* insurance policy.

Polier [po'liːr] (-s, -e) *m* foreman.

polieren *vt* to polish.

Poliklinik [poli'kliːnɪk] *f* outpatients (department) *sing.*

Polin *f* Pole, Polish woman.

Politesse [poli'tɛsə] (-, -n) *f* (*Frau*) ≈ traffic warden (*BRIT*).

Politik [poli'tiːk] *f* politics *sing;* (*eine bestimmte*) policy; **in die ~ gehen** to go into politics; **eine ~ verfolgen** to pursue a policy.

Politiker(in) [po'liːtikər(ɪn)] (-s, -) *m(f)* politician.

politisch [po'liːtɪʃ] *adj* political.

politisieren [politi'ziːrən] *vi* to talk politics ♦ *vt* to politicize; **jdn ~** to make sb politically aware.

Politur [poli'tuːr] *f* polish.

Polizei [poli'tsaɪ] *f* police; **~aufsicht** *f:* **unter ~aufsicht stehen** to have to report regularly to the police; **~beamte(r)** *m* police officer; **p~lich** *adj* police *attrib;* **sich p~lich melden** to register with the police; **p~liches Führungszeugnis** *certificate of "no criminal record" issued by the police;* **~präsidium** *nt*

police headquarters *pl*; **~revier** *nt* police
station; **~spitzel** *m* police spy, informer;
~staat *m* police state; **~streife** *f* police
patrol; **~stunde** *f* closing time; **~wache** *f*
police station; **p~widrig** *adj* illegal.
Polizist(in) [poli'tsɪst(ɪn)] (**-en, -en**) *m(f)*
policeman/-woman.
Pollen ['pɔlən] (**-s, -**) *m* pollen.
poln. *abk* = polnisch.
polnisch ['pɔlnɪʃ] *adj* Polish.
Polohemd ['po:lohɛmt] *nt* polo shirt.
Polster ['pɔlstər] (**-s, -**) *nt* çushion; (~*ung*)
upholstery; (*in Kleidung*) padding; (*fig: Geld*)
reserves *pl*; **~er** (**-s, -**) *m* upholsterer;
~garnitur *f* three-piece suite; **~möbel** *pl*
upholstered furniture *sing*.
polstern *vt* to upholster; (*Kleidung*) to pad; **sie
ist gut gepolstert** (*umg*) she's well padded;
(: *finanziell*) she's not short of the odd penny.
Polsterung *f* upholstery.
Polterabend ['pɔltəra:bənt] *m party on the
eve of a wedding*.
poltern *vi* (*Krach machen*) to crash;
(*schimpfen*) to rant.
Polygamie [polyga'mi:] *f* polygamy.
Polynesien [poly'ne:ziən] (**-s**) *nt* Polynesia.
Polynesier(in) [poly'ne:ziər(ɪn)] (**-s, -**) *m(f)*
Polynesian.
polynesisch *adj* Polynesian.
Polyp [po'ly:p] (**-en, -en**) *m* polyp; (*umg*) cop;
Polypen *pl* (*MED*) adenoids *pl*.
Polytechnikum [poly'tɛçnikʊm]
(**-s, Polytechnika**) *nt* polytechnic, poly (*umg*).
Pomade [po'ma:də] *f* pomade.
Pommern ['pɔmərn] (**-s**) *nt* Pomerania.
Pommes frites [pɔm'frɪt] *pl* chips *pl* (*BRIT*),
French fried potatoes *pl* (*BRIT*), French fries
pl (*US*).
Pomp [pɔmp] (**-(e)s**) *m* pomp.
pompös [pɔm'pø:s] *adj* grandiose.
Pontius ['pɔntsiʊs] *m:* **von ~ zu Pilatus** from
pillar to post.
Pony ['pɔni] (**-s, -s**) *m* (*Frisur*) fringe (*BRIT*),
bangs *pl* (*US*) ♦ *nt* (*Pferd*) pony.
Pop [pɔp] (**-s**) *m* (*MUS*) pop; (*KUNST*) pop art.
Popelin [popə'li:n] (**-s, -e**) *m* poplin.
Popeline (**-, -n**) *f* poplin.
Popkonzert *nt* pop concert.
Popmusik *f* pop music.
Popo [po'po:] (**-s, -s**) (*umg*) *m* bottom, bum
(*BRIT*).
populär [popu'lɛ:r] *adj* popular.
Popularität [populari'tɛ:t] *f* popularity.
populärwissenschaftlich *adj* popular
science.
Pore ['po:rə] (**-, -n**) *f* pore.
Porno ['pɔrno] (**-s, no pl**) (*umg*) *m* porn.
Pornographie [pɔrnogra'fi:] *f* pornography.
pornographisch [pɔrno'gra:fɪʃ] *adj*
pornographic.
porös [po'rø:s] *adj* porous.
Porree ['pɔre] (**-s, -s**) *m* leek.

Portal [pɔr'ta:l] (**-s, -e**) *nt* portal.
Portefeuille [pɔrt(ə)'fø:j] (**-s, -s**) *nt* (*POL, FIN*)
portfolio.
Portemonnaie [pɔrtmɔ'nɛ:] (**-s, -s**) *nt* purse.
Portier [pɔrti'e:] (**-s, -s**) *m* porter; (*Pförtner*)
porter, doorkeeper, doorman.
Portion [pɔrtsi'o:n] *f* portion, helping; (*umg:
Anteil*) amount; **eine halbe ~** (*fig: umg:
Person*) a half-pint; **eine ~ Kaffee** a pot of
coffee.
Porto ['pɔrto] (**-s, -s od Porti**) *nt* postage;
~ zahlt Empfänger postage paid; **p~frei** *adj*
post-free, (postage) prepaid.
Porträt [pɔr'trɛ:] (**-s, -s**) *nt* portrait.
porträtieren [pɔrtrɛ'ti:rən] *vt* to paint (a
portrait of); (*fig*) to portray.
Portugal ['pɔrtugal] (**-s**) *nt* Portugal.
Portugiese [pɔrtu'gi:zə] (**-n, -n**) *m* Portuguese.
Portugiesin *f* Portuguese.
portugiesisch *adj* Portuguese.
Portwein ['pɔrtvain] *m* port.
Porzellan [pɔrtsɛ'la:n] (**-s, -e**) *nt* china,
porcelain; (*Geschirr*) china.
Posaune [po'zaʊnə] (**-, -n**) *f* trombone.
Pose ['po:zə] (**-, -n**) *f* pose.
posieren [po'zi:rən] *vi* to pose.
Position [pozitsi'o:n] *f* position; (*COMM: auf
Liste*) item.
Positionslichter *pl* navigation lights *pl*.
positiv ['po:ziti:f] *adj* positive; **~ zu etw
stehen** to be in favour (*BRIT*) *od* favor (*US*)
of sth; **P~** (**-s, -e**) *nt* (*PHOT*) positive.
Positur [pozi'tu:r] *f* posture, attitude; **sich in
~ setzen** *od* **stellen** to adopt a posture.
Posse ['pɔsə] (**-, -n**) *f* farce.
possessiv ['pɔsɛsi:f] *adj* possessive; **P~** (**-s, -e**)
nt possessive pronoun; **P~pronomen** (**-s, -e**)
nt possessive pronoun.
possierlich [pɔ'si:rlɪç] *adj* funny.
Post [pɔst] (**-, -en**) *f* post (office); (*Briefe*) post,
mail; **ist ~ für mich da?** are there any
letters for me?; **mit getrennter ~** under
separate cover; **etw auf die ~ geben** to post
(*BRIT*) *od* mail sth; **auf die od zur ~ gehen** to
go to the post office; **~amt** *nt* post office;
~anweisung *f* postal order (*BRIT*), money
order; **~bote** *m* postman (*BRIT*), mailman
(*US*).
Posten (**-s, -**) *m* post, position; (*COMM*) item;
(: *Warenmenge*) quantity, lot; (*auf Liste*)
entry; (*MIL*) sentry; (*Streik~*) picket;
~ beziehen to take up one's post; **nicht ganz
auf dem ~ sein** (*nicht gesund sein*) to be off-
colour (*BRIT*) *od* off-color (*US*).
Poster ['pɔstər] (**-s, -(s)**) *nt* poster.
Postf. *abk* (= *Postfach*) PO Box.
Post- *zW:* **~fach** *nt* post office box; **~karte** *f*
postcard; **p~lagernd** *adv* poste restante;
~leitzahl *f* postal code.
postmodern [pɔstmo'dɛrn] *adj* postmodern.
Post- *zW:* **~scheckkonto** *nt* Post Office Giro
account (*BRIT*); **~sparbuch** *nt* post office

savings book (*Brit*); ~**sparkasse** *f* post office savings bank; ~**stempel** *m* postmark; **p~wendend** *adv* by return (of post); ~**wertzeichen** *nt* (*form*) postage stamp; ~**wurfsendung** *f* direct mail advertising.

potent [po'tɛnt] *adj* potent; (*fig*) high-powered.

Potential [potɛntsi'aːl] (-s, -e) *nt* potential.

potentiell [potɛntsi'ɛl] *adj* potential.

Potenz [po'tɛnts] *f* power; (*eines Mannes*) potency.

potenzieren [potɛn'tsiːrən] *vt* (*MATH*) to raise to the power of.

Potpourri ['pɔtpuri] (-s, -s) *nt*: ~ (**aus**) (*MUS*) medley (of); (*fig*) assortment (of).

Pott [pɔt] (-(e)s, ⁻e) (*umg*) *m* pot; **p~häßlich** (*umg*) *adj* ugly as sin.

pp., ppa. *abk* (= *per procura*) p.p.

Präambel [prɛ'|ambəl] (-, -n) *f* (+*gen*) preamble (to).

Pracht [praxt] (-) *f* splendour (*BRIT*), splendor (*US*), magnificence; **es ist eine wahre** ~ it's (really) marvellous; ~**exemplar** *nt* beauty (*umg*); (*fig: Mensch*) fine specimen.

prächtig ['prɛçtɪç] *adj* splendid.

Prachtstück *nt* showpiece.

prachtvoll *adj* splendid, magnificent.

prädestinieren [predɛsti'niːrən] *vt* to predestine.

Prädikat [predi'kaːt] (-(e)s, -e) *nt* title; (*GRAM*) predicate; (*Zensur*) distinction; **Wein mit** ~ special quality wine.

Prag [praːk] (-s) *nt* Prague.

prägen ['prɛːgən] *vt* to stamp; (*Münze*) to mint; (*Ausdruck*) to coin; (*Charakter*) to form; (*kennzeichnen: Stadtbild*) to characterize; **das Erlebnis prägte ihn** the experience left its mark on him.

prägend *adj* having a forming *od* shaping influence.

pragmatisch [pra'gmaːtɪʃ] *adj* pragmatic.

prägnant [prɛ'gnant] *adj* concise, terse.

Prägnanz *f* conciseness, terseness.

Prägung ['prɛːguŋ] *f* minting; forming; (*Eigenart*) character, stamp.

prahlen ['praːlən] *vi* to boast, brag.

Prahlerei [praːlə'raɪ] *f* boasting.

prahlerisch *adj* boastful.

Praktik ['praktɪk] *f* practice.

praktikabel [praktɪ'kaːbəl] *adj* practicable.

Praktikant(in) [praktɪ'kant(ɪn)] *m(f)* trainee.

Praktikum (-s, **Praktika** *od* **Praktiken**) *nt* practical training.

praktisch ['praktɪʃ] *adj* practical, handy; ~**er Arzt** general practitioner; ~**es Beispiel** concrete example.

praktizieren [praktɪ'tsiːrən] *vt, vi* to practise (*BRIT*), practice (*US*).

Praline [pra'liːnə] *f* chocolate.

prall [pral] *adj* firmly rounded; (*Segel*) taut; (*Arme*) plump; (*Sonne*) blazing.

prallen *vi* to bounce, rebound; (*Sonne*) to blaze.

prallvoll *adj* full to bursting; (*Brieftasche*) bulging.

Prämie ['prɛːmiə] *f* premium; (*Belohnung*) award, prize.

prämienbegünstigt *adj* with benefit of premiums.

prämiensparen *vi* to save in a bonus scheme.

prämieren [prɛ'miːrən] *vt* to give an award to.

Pranger ['praŋər] (-s, -) *m* (*HIST*) pillory; **jdn an den** ~ **stellen** (*fig*) to pillory sb.

Pranke ['praŋkə] (-, -n) *f* (*Tier~: umg: Hand*) paw.

Präparat [prepa'raːt] (-(e)s, -e) *nt* (*BIOL*) preparation; (*MED*) medicine.

präparieren *vt* (*konservieren*) to preserve; (*MED: zerlegen*) to dissect.

Präposition [prepozitsi'oːn] *f* preposition.

Prärie [prɛ'riː] *f* prairie.

Präs. *abk* = **Präsens; Präsident.**

Präsens ['prɛːzɛns] (-) *nt* present tense.

präsent *adj: etw* ~ **haben** to have sth at hand.

präsentieren [prɛzɛn'tiːrən] *vt* to present.

Präsenzbibliothek *f* reference library.

Präservativ [prɛzɛrva'tiːf] (-s, -e) *nt* condom, sheath.

Präsident(in) [prɛzi'dɛnt(ɪn)] *m(f)* president; ~**schaft** *f* presidency; ~**schaftskandidat** *m* presidential candidate.

Präsidium [prɛ'ziːdiʊm] *nt* presidency, chairmanship; (*Polizei~*) police headquarters *pl*.

prasseln ['prasəln] *vi* (*Feuer*) to crackle; (*Hagel*) to drum; (*Wörter*) to rain down.

prassen ['prasən] *vi* to live it up.

Präteritum [prɛ'teːritʊm] (-s, **Präterita**) *nt* preterite.

Pratze ['pratsə] (-, -n) *f* paw.

Präventiv- [prɛvɛn'tiːf] *in zW* preventive.

Praxis ['praksɪs] (-, **Praxen**) *f* practice; (*Erfahrung*) experience; (*Behandlungsraum*) surgery; (*von Anwalt*) office; **die** ~ **sieht anders aus** the reality is different; **ein Beispiel aus der** ~ an example from real life.

Präzedenzfall [prɛtse'dɛntsfal] *m* precedent.

präzis [prɛ'tsiːs] *adj* precise.

Präzision [prɛtsizi'oːn] *f* precision.

PR-Chef *m* PR officer.

predigen ['preːdɪgən] *vt, vi* to preach.

Prediger (-s, -) *m* preacher.

Predigt ['preːdɪçt] (-, -en) *f* sermon.

Preis [praɪs] (-es, -e) *m* price; (*Sieges~*) prize; (*Auszeichnung*) award; **um keinen** ~ not at any price; **um jeden** ~ at all costs; ~**angebot** *nt* quotation; ~**ausschreiben** *nt* competition; ~**bindung** *f* price-fixing; ~**brecher** *m* (*Firma*) undercutter.

Preiselbeere *f* cranberry.

preisempfindlich *adj* price-sensitive.

preisen [praɪzən] *unreg vt* to praise; **sich glücklich ~** (*geh*) to count o.s. lucky.

Preis- *zW:* **~entwicklung** *f* price trend; **~erhöhung** *f* price increase; **~frage** *f* question of price; (*Wettbewerb*) prize question.

preisgeben *unreg vt* to abandon; (*opfern*) to sacrifice; (*zeigen*) to expose.

Preis- *zW:* **~gefälle** *nt* price gap; **p~gekrönt** *adj* prizewinning; **~gericht** *nt* jury; **p~günstig** *adj* inexpensive; **~index** *m* price index; **~krieg** *m* price war; **~lage** *f* price range; **p~lich** *adj* price *attr*, in price; **~liste** *f* price list, tariff; **~nachlaß** *m* discount; **~schild** *nt* price tag; **~spanne** *f* price range; **~sturz** *m* slump; **~träger** *m* prizewinner; **p~wert** *adj* inexpensive.

prekär [pre'kɛːr] *adj* precarious.

Prellbock [prɛlbɔk] *m* buffers *pl*.

prellen *vt* to bruise; (*fig*) to cheat, swindle.

Prellung *f* bruise.

Premiere [prəmɪ'ɛːrə] (*-, -n*) *f* premiere.

Premierminister(in) [prəmɪ'eːmɪnɪstər(ɪn)] *m(f)* prime minister, premier.

Presse [prɛsə] (*-, -n*) *f* press; **~agentur** *f* press *od* news agency; **~sausweis** *m* press pass; **~erklärung** *f* press release; **~freiheit** *f* freedom of the press; **~konferenz** *f* press conference; **~meldung** *f* press report.

pressen *vt* to press.

Presse- *zW:* **~sprecher(in)** *m(f)* spokesperson, press officer; **~stelle** *f* press office; **~verlautbarung** *f* press release.

pressieren [prɛ'siːrən] *vi* to be in a hurry; **es pressiert** it's urgent.

Preßluft [prɛslʊft] *f* compressed air; **~bohrer** *m* pneumatic drill.

Prestige [prɛs'tiːʒə] (*-s*) *nt* prestige; **~verlust** *m* loss of prestige.

Preuße [prɔʏsə] (*-n, -n*) *m* Prussian.

Preußen (*-s*) *nt* Prussia.

Preußin *f* Prussian.

preußisch *adj* Prussian.

prickeln [prɪkəln] *vi* to tingle; (*kitzeln*) to tickle; (*Bläschen bilden*) to sparkle, bubble ♦ *vt* to tickle.

pries *etc* [priːs] *vb siehe* **preisen**.

Priester [priːstər] (*-s, -*) *m* priest.

Priesterin *f* priestess.

Priesterweihe *f* ordination (to the priesthood).

Prima [priːma] (*-, Primen*) *f* *eighth and ninth year of German secondary school.*

prima *adj inv* first-class, excellent.

primär [pri'mɛːr] *adj* primary; **P~daten** *pl* primary data *pl*.

Primel [priːməl] (*-, -n*) *f* primrose.

primitiv [primi'tiːf] *adj* primitive.

Primzahl [priːmtsaːl] *f* prime (number).

Prinz [prɪnts] (*-en, -en*) *m* prince.

Prinzessin [prɪn'tsɛsɪn] *f* princess.

Prinzip [prɪn'tsiːp] (*-s, -ien*) *nt* principle; **aus ~**

on principle; **im ~** in principle.

prinzipiell [prɪntsi'piɛl] *adj* on principle.

prinzipienlos *adj* unprincipled.

Priorität [priori'tɛːt] *f* priority; **Prioritäten** *pl* (*COMM*) preference shares *pl*, preferred stock *sing* (*US*); **~en setzen** to establish one's priorities.

Prise [priːzə] (*-, -n*) *f* pinch.

Prisma [prɪsma] (*-s, Prismen*) *nt* prism.

privat [pri'vaːt] *adj* private; **jdn ~ sprechen** to speak to sb in private; **P~besitz** *m* private property; **P~dozent** *m* outside lecturer; **P~fernsehen** *nt* commercial television; **P~gespräch** *nt* private conversation; (*am Telefon*) private call.

privatisieren [privati'ziːrən] *vt* to privatize.

Privatschule *f* private school.

Privatwirtschaft *f* private sector.

Privileg [privi'leːk] (*-(e)s, -ien*) *nt* privilege.

Pro [proː] (*-*) *nt* pro.

pro *präp +akk* per; **~ Stück** each, apiece.

Probe [proːbə] (*-, -n*) *f* test; (*Teststück*) sample; (*THEAT*) rehearsal; **jdn auf die ~ stellen** to put sb to the test; **er ist auf ~ angestellt** he's employed for a probationary period; **zur ~** to try out; **~bohrung** *f* (*Öl*) exploration well; **~exemplar** *nt* specimen copy; **~fahrt** *f* test drive; **~lauf** *m* trial run.

proben *vt* to try; (*THEAT*) to rehearse.

Probe- *zW:* **~stück** *nt* specimen; **p~weise** *adv* on approval; **~zeit** *f* probation period.

probieren [pro'biːrən] *vt* to try; (*Wein, Speise*) to taste, sample ♦ *vi* to try; to taste.

Problem [pro'bleːm] (*-s, -e*) *nt* problem; **vor einem ~ stehen** to be faced with a problem.

Problematik [proble'maːtɪk] *f* problem.

problematisch [proble'maːtɪʃ] *adj* problematic.

problemlos *adj* problem-free.

Problemstellung *f* way of looking at a problem.

Produkt [pro'dʊkt] (*-(e)s, -e*) *nt* product; (*AGR*) produce *no pl*.

Produktion [prodʊktsi'oːn] *f* production.

Produktionsleiter *m* production manager.

Produktionsstätte *f* (*Halle*) shop floor.

produktiv [prodʊk'tiːf] *adj* productive.

Produktivität [prodʊktivi'tɛːt] *f* productivity.

Produzent [produ'tsɛnt] *m* manufacturer; (*FILM*) producer.

produzieren [produ'tsiːrən] *vt* to produce ♦ *vr* to show off.

Prof. [prof] *abk* (*= Professor*) Prof.

profan [pro'faːn] *adj* (*weltlich*) secular, profane; (*gewöhnlich*) mundane.

professionell [profɛsio'nɛl] *adj* professional.

Professor(in) [pro'fɛsɔr, profɛ'soːrɪn] *m(f)* professor; (*ÖSTERR: Gymnasiallehrer*) grammar school teacher (*BRIT*), high school teacher (*US*).

Professur [profɛ'suːr] *f:* **~ (für)** chair (of).

Profi ['proːfi] (-s, -s) *m abk* (= *Professional*) pro.

Profil [pro'fiːl] (-s, -e) *nt* profile; (*fig*) image; (*Querschnitt*) cross section; (*Längsschnitt*) vertical section; (*von Reifen, Schuhsohle*) tread.

profilieren [profi'liːrən] *vr* to create an image for o.s.

Profilsohle *f* sole with a tread.

Profit [pro'fiːt] (-(e)s, -e) *m* profit.

profitieren [profi'tiːrən] *vi:* ~ **(von)** to profit (from).

Profitmacherei (*umg*) *f* profiteering.

pro forma *adv* as a matter of form.

Pro-forma-Rechnung *f* pro forma invoice.

Prognose [pro'gnoːzə] (-, -e) *f* prediction, prognosis.

Programm [pro'gram] (-s, -e) *nt* programme (*BRIT*), program (*US*); (*COMPUT*) program; (*TV: Sender*) channel; (*Kollektion*) range; **nach** ~ as planned; **p~gemäß** *adj* according to plan; **~fehler** *m* (*COMPUT*) bug; **~hinweis** *m* (*RUNDF, TV*) programme (*BRIT*) *od* program (*US*) announcement.

programmieren [progra'miːrən] *vt* to programme (*BRIT*), program (*US*); (*COMPUT*) to program; **auf etw** *akk* **programmiert sein** (*fig*) to be geared to sth.

Programmierer(in) (-s, -) *m(f)* programmer.

Programmiersprache *f* (*COMPUT*) programming language.

Programmierung *f* (*COMPUT*) programming.

Programmvorschau *f* preview; (*FILM*) trailer.

progressiv [progrɛ'siːf] *adj* progressive.

Projekt [pro'jɛkt] (-(e)s, -e) *nt* project.

Projektleiter(in) *m(f)* project manager(ess).

Projektor [pro'jɛktɔr] *m* projector.

projizieren [proji'tsiːrən] *vt* to project.

proklamieren [prokla'miːrən] *vt* to proclaim.

Pro-Kopf-Einkommen *nt* per capita income.

Prokura [pro'kuːra] (-, **Prokuren**) *f* (*form*) power of attorney.

Prokurist(in) [proku'rɪst(ɪn)] *m(f)* attorney.

Prolet [pro'leːt] (-en, -en) *m* prole, pleb.

Proletariat [proletari'aːt] (-(e)s, -e) *nt* proletariat.

Proletarier [prole'taːriər] (-s, -) *m* proletarian.

Prolog [pro'loːk] (-(e)s, -e) *m* prologue.

Promenade [promə'naːdə] (-, -n) *f* promenade.

Promenadenmischung *f* (*hum*) mongrel.

Promille [pro'mɪlə] (-(s), -) (*umg*) *nt* alcohol level; **~grenze** *f* legal (alcohol) limit.

prominent [promi'nɛnt] *adj* prominent.

Prominenz [promi'nɛnts] *f* VIPs *pl.*

Promoter [pro'moːtər] (-s, -) *m* promoter.

Promotion [promotsi'oːn] *f* doctorate, Ph.D.

promovieren [promo'viːrən] *vi* to receive a doctorate *etc*.

prompt [prɔmpt] *adj* prompt.

Pronomen [pro'noːmɛn] (-s, -) *nt* pronoun.

Propaganda [propa'ganda] (-) *f* propaganda.

propagieren [propa'giːrən] *vt* to propagate.

Propangas [pro'paːngaːs] *nt* propane gas.

Propeller [pro'pɛlər] (-s, -) *m* propeller.

proper ['prɔpər] (*umg*) *adj* neat, tidy.

Prophet(in) [pro'feːt(ɪn)] (-en, -en) *m(f)* prophet(ess).

prophezeien [profe'tsaɪən] *vt* to prophesy.

Prophezeiung *f* prophecy.

prophylaktisch [profy'laktɪʃ] *adj* prophylactic (*form*), preventive.

Proportion [proportsi'oːn] *f* proportion.

proportional [proportsio'naːl] *adj* proportional; **P~schrift** *f* (*COMPUT*) proportional printing.

proportioniert [proportsio'niːrt] *adj:* **gut/ schlecht** ~ well/badly proportioned.

Proporz [pro'pɔrts] (-es, -e) *m* proportional representation.

Prosa ['proːza] (-) *f* prose.

prosaisch [pro'zaːɪʃ] *adj* prosaic.

prosit ['proːzɪt] *interj* cheers!; **P~ Neujahr!** happy New Year!

Prospekt [pro'spɛkt] (-(e)s, -e) *m* leaflet, brochure.

prost [proːst] *interj* cheers!

Prostata ['prɔstata] (-) *f* prostate gland.

Prostituierte [prostitu'iːrtə] (-, -n) *f* prostitute.

Prostitution [prostitutsi'oːn] *f* prostitution.

prot. [prot] *abk* = **protestantisch.**

Protektionismus [protɛktsio'nɪsmʊs] *m* protectionism.

Protektorat [protɛkto'raːt] (-(e)s, -e) *nt* (*Schirmherrschaft*) patronage; (*Schutzgebiet*) protectorate.

Protest [pro'tɛst] (-(e)s, -e) *m* protest.

Protestant(in) [protɛs'tant(ɪn)] *m(f)* Protestant; **p~isch** *adj* Protestant.

Protestbewegung *f* protest movement.

protestieren [protɛs'tiːrən] *vi* to protest.

Protestkundgebung *f* (protest) rally.

Prothese [pro'teːzə] (-, -n) *f* artificial limb; (*Zahn~*) dentures *pl.*

Protokoll [proto'kɔl] (-s, -e) *nt* register; (*Niederschrift*) record; (*von Sitzung*) minutes *pl*; (*diplomatisch*) protocol; (*Polizei~*) statement; (*Strafzettel*) ticket; (**das**) ~ **führen** (*bei Sitzung*) to take the minutes; (*bei Gericht*) to make a transcript of the proceedings; **etw zu** ~ **geben** to have sth put on record; (*bei Polizei*) to say sth in one's statement; **~führer** *m* secretary; (*JUR*) clerk (of the court).

protokollieren [protokɔ'liːrən] *vt* to take down; (*Bemerkung*) to enter in the minutes.

Proton ['proːton] (-s, -en) *nt* proton.

Prototyp *m* prototype.

Protz ['prɔts] (-es, -e) *m* swank; **p~en** *vi* to show off.

protzig *adj* ostentatious.

Proviant [provi'ant] (-s, -e) *m* provisions *pl*,

supplies *pl.*

Provinz [pro'vɪnts] (-, -en) *f* province; **das ist finsterste** ~ (*pej*) it's a cultural backwater.

provinziell [provɪn'tsiɛl] *adj* provincial.

Provision [provizi'oːn] *f* (*COMM*) commission.

provisorisch [provi'zoːrɪʃ] *adj* provisional.

Provisorium [provi'zoːriʊm] (-s, -ien) *nt* provisional arrangement.

Provokation [provokatsi'oːn] *f* provocation.

provokativ [provoka'tiːf] *adj* provocative, provoking.

provokatorisch [provoka'toːrɪʃ] *adj* provocative, provoking.

provozieren [provo'tsiːrən] *vt* to provoke.

Proz. *abk* (= *Prozent*) pc.

Prozedur [protse'duːr] *f* procedure; (*pej*) carry-on; **die** ~ **beim Zahnarzt** the ordeal at the dentist's.

Prozent [pro'tsɛnt] (-(e)s, -e) *nt* per cent, percentage; ~**rechnung** *f* percentage calculation; ~**satz** *m* percentage.

prozentual [protsɛntu'aːl] *adj* percentage; *attrib.*

Prozeß [pro'tsɛs] (-sses, -sse) *m* trial, case; (*Vorgang*) process; **es zum** ~ **kommen lassen** to go to court; **mit jdm/etw kurzen** ~ **machen** (*fig: umg*) to make short work of sb/sth; ~**anwalt** *m* barrister, counsel; ~**führung** *f* handling of a case.

prozessieren [protsɛ'siːrən] *vi:* ~ (**mit**) to bring an action (against), go to law (with *od* against).

Prozession [protsɛsi'oːn] *f* procession.

Prozeßkosten *pl* (legal) costs *pl.*

prüde ['pryːdə] *adj* prudish.

Prüderie [prydə'riː] *f* prudery.

prüfen ['pryːfən] *vt* to examine, test; (*nach*~) to check; (*erwägen*) to consider; (*Geschäftsbücher*) to audit; (*mustern*) to scrutinize.

Prüfer(in) (-s, -) *m(f)* examiner.

Prüfling *m* examinee.

Prüfstein *m* touchstone.

Prüfung *f* (*SCH, UNIV*) examination, exam; (*Über*~) checking; **eine** ~ **machen** to take *od* sit (*BRIT*) an exam(ination); **durch eine** ~ **fallen** to fail an exam(ination).

Prüfungs- *zW:* ~**ausschuß** *m* examining board; ~**kommission** *f* examining board; ~**ordnung** *f* exam(ination) regulations *pl.*

Prügel ['pryːgəl] (-s, -) *m* cudgel ♦ *pl* beating *sing.*

Prügelei [pryːgə'laɪ] *f* fight.

Prügelknabe *m* scapegoat.

prügeln *vt* to beat ♦ *vr* to fight.

Prügelstrafe *f* corporal punishment.

Prunk [prʊŋk] (-(e)s) *m* pomp, show; **p**~**voll** *adj* splendid, magnificent.

prusten ['pruːstən] (*umg*) *vi* to snort.

PS *abk* (= *Pferdestärke*) hp; (= *Postskript(um)*) PS.

Psalm [psalm] (-s, -en) *m* psalm.

PSchA *nt abk* (= *Postscheckamt*) National Giro Office.

pseudo- [psɔydo] *in zW* pseudo.

Psychiater [psy'çiaːtər] (-s, -) *m* psychiatrist.

Psychiatrie [psyçia'triː] *f* psychiatry.

psychiatrisch [psy'çiaːtrɪʃ] *adj* psychiatric; ~**e Klinik** mental *od* psychiatric hospital.

psychisch ['psyːçɪʃ] *adj* psychological; ~ **gestört** emotionally *od* psychologically disturbed.

Psychoanalyse [psyçoana'lyːzə] *f* psychoanalysis.

Psychologe [psyço'loːgə] (-n, -n) *m* psychologist.

Psychologie *f* psychology.

Psychologin *f* psychologist.

psychologisch *adj* psychological.

Psychotherapie *f* psychotherapy.

PTT (*SCHWEIZ*) *abk* (= *Post, Telefon, Telegraf*) *postal and telecommunication services.*

Pubertät [puber'tɛːt] *f* puberty.

publik [pu'bliːk] *adj:* ~ **werden** to become public knowledge.

Publikum ['puːblikʊm] (-s) *nt* audience; (*SPORT*) crowd; **das** ~ **in dieser Bar ist sehr gemischt** you get a very mixed group of people using this bar.

Publikumserfolg *m* popular success.

Publikumsverkehr *m:* „**heute kein** ~" "closed today for public business".

publizieren [publi'tsiːrən] *vt* to publish.

Pudding ['pʊdɪŋ] (-s, -e *od* -s) *m* blancmange; ~**pulver** *nt* custard powder.

Pudel ['puːdəl] (-s, -) *m* poodle; **das also ist des** ~**s Kern** (*fig*) that's what it's really all about.

pudelwohl (*umg*) *adj:* **sich** ~ **fühlen** to feel on top of the world.

Puder ['puːdər] (-s, -) *m* powder; ~**dose** *f* powder compact.

pudern *vt* to powder.

Puderzucker *m* icing sugar (*BRIT*), confectioner's sugar (*US*).

Puertoricaner(in) [pʊɛrtori'kaːnər(ɪn)] (-s, -) *m(f)* Puerto Rican.

puertoricanisch *adj* Puerto Rican.

Puerto Rico [pu'ɛrto'riːko] (-s) *nt* Puerto Rico.

Puff¹ [pʊf] (-(e)s, -e) *m* (*Wäsche*~) linen basket; (*Sitz*~) pouf.

Puff² (-(e)s, ⁻e) (*umg*) *m* (*Stoß*) push.

Puff³ (-s, -s) (*umg*) *m od nt* (*Bordell*) brothel.

Puffer (-s, -) *m* (*auch COMPUT*) buffer; ~**speicher** *m* (*COMPUT*) cache; ~**staat** *m* buffer state; ~**zone** *f* buffer zone.

Puffreis *m* puffed rice.

Pulle ['pʊlə] (-, -n) (*umg*) *f* bottle; **volle** ~ **fahren** (*umg*) to drive flat out.

Pulli ['pʊli] (-s, -s) (*umg*) *m* sweater, jumper (*BRIT*).

Pullover [pʊ'loːvər] (-s, -) *m* sweater, jumper (*BRIT*).

Pullunder [pʊ'lʊndər] (-s, -) *m* slipover.

Puls [pʊls] (-es, -e) m pulse; ~**ader** f artery; **sich** dat **die** ~**ader(n) aufschneiden** to slash one's wrists.
pulsieren [pʊl'ziːrən] vi to throb, pulsate.
Pult [pʊlt] (-(e)s, -e) nt desk.
Pulver ['pʊlfər] (-s, -) nt powder; ~**faß** nt powder keg; **(wie) auf einem** ~**faß sitzen** (fig) to be sitting on (top of) a volcano.
pulverig adj powdery.
pulverisieren [pʊlveri'ziːrən] vt to pulverize.
Pulverkaffee m instant coffee.
Pulverschnee m powdery snow.
pummelig ['pʊməlɪç] adj chubby.
Pump (-(e)s) (umg) m: **auf** ~ **kaufen** to buy on tick (BRIT) od credit.
Pumpe ['pʊmpə] (-, -n) f pump; (umg: Herz) ticker.
pumpen vt to pump; (umg) to lend; (: entleihen) to borrow.
Pumphose f knickerbockers pl.
puncto ['pʊŋkto] präp +gen: **in** ~ **X** where X is concerned.
Punkt [pʊŋkt] (-(e)s, -e) m point; (bei Muster) dot; (Satzzeichen) full stop, period (bes US); ~ **12 Uhr** at 12 o'clock on the dot; **nun mach aber mal einen** ~**!** (umg) come off it!; **p**~**gleich** adj (SPORT) level.
punktieren [pʊŋk'tiːrən] vt to dot; (MED) to aspirate.
pünktlich ['pʏŋktlɪç] adj punctual; **P**~**keit** f punctuality.
Punkt- zW: ~**matrix** f dot matrix; ~**richter** m (SPORT) judge; ~**sieg** m victory on points; ~**wertung** f points system; ~**zahl** f score.
Punsch [pʊnʃ] (-(e)s, -e) m (hot) punch.
Pupille [pu'pɪlə] (-, -n) f (im Auge) pupil.
Puppe ['pʊpə] (-, -n) f doll; (Marionette) puppet; (Insekten~) pupa, chrysalis; (Schaufenster~, MIL: Übungs~) dummy; (umg: Mädchen) doll, bird (bes BRIT).
Puppen- zW: ~**haus** nt doll's house, dollhouse (US); ~**spieler** m puppeteer; ~**stube** f (single-room) doll's house od dollhouse (US); ~**theater** nt puppet theatre (BRIT) od theater (US); ~**wagen** m doll's pram.
pupsen ['puːpsən] (umg) vi to make a rude noise/smell.
pur [puːr] adj pure; (völlig) sheer; (Whisky) neat.
Püree [py're:] (-s, -s) nt purée; (Kartoffel~) mashed potatoes pl.
Purpur ['pʊrpʊr] (-s) m crimson.
Purzelbaum ['pʊrtsəlbaʊm] m somersault.
purzeln vi to tumble.
Puste ['puːstə] (-) (umg) f puff; (fig) steam.
Pusteblume (umg) f dandelion.
Pustel ['pʊstəl] (-, -n) f pustule.
pusteln vi to puff, blow.
pusten ['puːstən] (umg) vi to puff.
Pute ['puːtə] (-, -n) f turkey hen.
Puter (-s, -) m turkey cock; **p**~**rot** adj scarlet.
Putsch [pʊtʃ] (-(e)s, -e) m revolt, putsch;

p~**en** vi to revolt; ~**ist** m rebel; ~**versuch** m attempted coup (d'état).
Putte ['pʊtə] (-, -n) f (KUNST) cherub.
Putz [pʊts] (-es) m (Mörtel) plaster, roughcast; **eine Mauer mit** ~ **verkleiden** to roughcast a wall.
putzen vt to clean; (Nase) to wipe, blow ♦ vr to clean o.s.; (veraltet: sich schmücken) to dress o.s. up.
Putzfrau f cleaning lady, charwoman (BRIT).
putzig adj quaint, funny.
Putzlappen m cloth.
putzmunter (umg) adj full of beans.
Putz- zW: ~**tag** m cleaning day; ~**teufel** (umg) m maniac for housework; ~**zeug** nt cleaning things pl.
Puzzle ['pasəl] (-s, -s) nt jigsaw (puzzle).
PVC [pe:fau'tse:] (-(s)) nt abk PVC.
Pygmäe [py'gmɛːə] (-n, -n) m Pygmy.
Pyjama [pi'dʒaːma] (-s, -s) m pyjamas pl (BRIT), pajamas pl (US).
Pyramide [pyra'miːdə] (-, -n) f pyramid.
Pyrenäen [pyre'nɛːən] pl: **die** ~ the Pyrenees pl.
Python ['pyːtɔn] (-s, -s) m python; ~**schlange** f python.

Q, q

Q, q [kuː] nt Q, q; ~ **wie Quelle** ≈ Q for Queen.
qcm abk (= Quadratzentimeter) cm².
qkm abk (= Quadratkilometer) km².
qm abk (= Quadratmeter) m².
quabb(e)lig ['kvab(ə)lɪç] adj wobbly; (Frosch) slimy.
Quacksalber ['kvakzalbər] (-s, -) m quack (doctor).
Quader ['kvaːdər] (-s, -) m square stone block; (MATH) cuboid.
Quadrat [kva'draːt] (-(e)s, -e) nt square; **q**~**isch** adj square; ~**latschen** pl (hum: umg: Schuhe) clodhoppers pl; ~**meter** m square metre (BRIT) od meter (US).
quadrieren [kva'driːrən] vt to square.
quaken ['kvaːkən] vi to croak; (Ente) to quack.
quäken ['kvɛːkən] vi to screech.
quäkend adj screeching.
Quäker(in) ['kvɛːkər] (-s, -) m(f) Quaker.
Qual [kvaːl] (-, -en) f pain, agony; (seelisch) anguish; **er machte ihr das Leben zur** ~ he made her life a misery.
quälen ['kvɛːlən] vt to torment ♦ vr (sich abmühen) to struggle; (geistig) to torment o.s.; ~**de Ungewißheit** agonizing uncertainty.

Quälerei [kvɛːləˈraɪ] *f* torture, torment.
Quälgeist (*umg*) *m* pest.
Qualifikation [kvalifikatsiˈoːn] *f* qualification.
qualifizieren [kvalifiˈtsiːrən] *vt* to qualify; (*einstufen*) to label ♦ *vr* to qualify.
qualifiziert *adj* (*Arbeiter, Nachwuchs*) qualified; (*Arbeit*) professional; (*POL: Mehrheit*) requisite.
Qualität [kvaliˈtɛːt] *f* quality; **von ausgezeichneter** ~ (of) top quality.
qualitativ [kvalitaˈtiːf] *adj* qualitative.
Qualitätskontrolle *f* quality control.
Qualitätsware *f* article of high quality.
Qualle [ˈkvalə] (-, -n) *f* jellyfish.
Qualm [kvalm] (-(e)s) *m* thick smoke.
qualmen *vt, vi* to smoke.
qualvoll [ˈkvaːlfɔl] *adj* painful; (*Schmerzen*) excruciating, agonizing.
Quantensprung *m* quantum leap.
Quantentheorie [ˈkvantənteoriː] *f* quantum theory.
Quantität [kvantiˈtɛːt] *f* quantity.
quantitativ [kvantitaˈtiːf] *adj* quantitative.
Quantum [ˈkvantʊm] (-s, Quanten) *nt* quantity, amount.
Quarantäne [karanˈtɛːnə] (-, -n) *f* quarantine.
Quark¹ [kvark] (-s) *m* curd cheese, quark; (*umg*) rubbish.
Quark² [kvark] (-s, -s) *nt* (*PHYS*) quark.
Quarta [ˈkvarta] (-, Quarten) *f* third year of German secondary school.
Quartal [kvarˈtaːl] (-s, -e) *nt* quarter (year); **Kündigung zum** ~ quarterly notice date.
Quartett [kvarˈtɛt] (-(e)s, -e) *nt* (*MUS*) quartet; (*KARTEN*) set of four cards; (: *Spiel*) ≈ happy families.
Quartier [kvarˈtiːr] (-s, -e) *nt* accommodation (*BRIT*), accommodations *pl* (*US*); (*MIL*) quarters *pl*; (*Stadt~*) district.
Quarz [kvaːrts] (-es, -e) *m* quartz.
quasi [ˈkvaːzi] *adv* virtually ♦ *präf* quasi.
quasseln [ˈkvasəln] (*umg*) *vi* to natter.
Quaste [ˈkvastə] (-, -n) *f* (*Troddel*) tassel; (*von Pinsel*) bristles *pl*.
Quästur [kvɛsˈtuːr] *f* (*UNIV*) bursary.
Quatsch [kvatʃ] (-es) (*umg*) *m* rubbish, hogwash; **hört doch endlich auf mit dem** ~! stop being so stupid!; ~ **machen** to mess about.
quatschen *vi* to chat, natter.
Quatschkopf (*umg*) *m* (*pej: Schwätzer*) windbag; (*Dummkopf*) twit (*BRIT*).
Quecksilber [ˈkvɛkzɪlbər] *nt* mercury.
Quelle [ˈkvɛlə] (-, -n) *f* spring; (*eines Flusses, COMPUT*) source; **an der** ~ **sitzen** (*fig*) to be well placed; **aus zuverlässiger** ~ from a reliable source.
quellen *vi* (*hervor~*) to pour *od* gush forth; (*schwellen*) to swell.
Quellenangabe *f* reference.
Quellsprache *f* source language.
Quengelei [kvɛŋəˈlaɪ] (*umg*) *f* whining.

quengelig (*umg*) *adj* whining.
quengeln (*umg*) *vi* to whine.
quer [kveːr] *adv* crossways, diagonally; (*rechtwinklig*) at right angles; ~ **auf dem Bett** across the bed; **Q~balken** *m* crossbeam; **Q~denker** *m* maverick.
Quere [ˈkveːrə] (-) *f*: **jdm in die** ~ **kommen** to cross sb's path.
quer- *zW*: ~**feldein** *adv* across country; **Q~feldeinrennen** *nt* cross-country; (*mit Motorrädern*) motocross; (*Radrennen*) cyclocross; **Q~flöte** *f* flute; **Q~format** *nt* oblong format; ~**gestreift** *adj attrib* horizontally striped; **Q~kopf** *m* awkward customer; ~**legen** *vr* (*fig: umg*) to be awkward; **Q~schiff** *nt* transept; **Q~schläger** (*umg*) *m* ricochet; **Q~schnitt** *m* cross section; ~**schnittsgelähmt** *adj* paraplegic, paralysed below the waist; **Q~schnittslähmung** *f* paraplegia; **Q~straße** *f* intersecting road; **Q~strich** *m* (horizontal) stroke *od* line; **Q~summe** *f* (*MATH*) sum of digits of a number; **Q~treiber** (-s, -) *m* obstructionist.
Querulant(in) [kveruˈlant(ɪn)] (-en, -en) *m(f)* grumbler.
Querverbindung *f* connection, link.
Querverweis *m* cross-reference.
quetschen [ˈkvɛtʃən] *vt* to squash, crush; (*MED*) to bruise ♦ *vr* (*sich klemmen*) to be caught; (*sich zwängen*) to squeeze (o.s.).
Quetschung *f* bruise, contusion (*form*).
Queue [køː] (-s, -s) *nt* (*BILLIARD*) cue.
quicklebendig [ˈkvɪkleˈbɛndɪç] (*umg*) *adj* (*Kind*) lively, active; (*ältere Person*) spry.
quieken [ˈkviːkən] *vi* to squeak.
quietschen [ˈkviːtʃən] *vi* to squeak.
quietschvergnügt [ˈkviːtʃfɛrɡnyːkt] (*umg*) *adj* happy as a sandboy.
quillt [kvɪlt] *vb siehe* **quellen**.
Quinta [ˈkvɪnta] (-, Quinten) *f* second year in German secondary school.
Quintessenz [ˈkvɪntɛsɛnts] *f* quintessence.
Quintett [kvɪnˈtɛt] (-(e)s, -e) *nt* quintet.
Quirl [kvɪrl] (-(e)s, -e) *m* whisk.
quirlig [ˈkvɪrlɪç] *adj* lively, frisky.
quitt [kvɪt] *adj* quits, even.
Quitte (-, -n) *f* quince.
quittieren [kvɪˈtiːrən] *vt* to give a receipt for; (*Dienst*) to leave.
Quittung *f* receipt; **er hat seine** ~ **bekommen** he's paid the penalty *od* price.
Quiz [kvɪs] (-, -) *nt* quiz.
quoll *etc* [kvɔl] *vb siehe* **quellen**.
Quote [ˈkvoːtə] (-, -n) *f* proportion; (*Rate*) rate.
Quotenregelung *f* quota system (*for ensuring adequate representation of women*).
Quotierung [kvoˈtiːrʊŋ] *f* (*COMM*) quotation.

$$R, r$$

R¹, r *nt* R, r; ~ **wie Richard** ≈ R for Robert, R for Roger (*US*).
R², r *abk* (= *Radius*) r.
r. *abk* (= *rechts*) r.
Rabatt [ra'bat] (-(e)s, -e) *m* discount.
Rabatte (-, -n) *f* flower bed, border.
Rabattmarke *f* trading stamp.
Rabatz [ra'bats] (-es) (*umg*) *m* row, din.
Rabe ['ra:bə] (-n, -n) *m* raven.
Rabenmutter *f* bad mother.
rabenschwarz *adj* pitch-black.
rabiat [rabi'a:t] *adj* furious.
Rache ['raxə] (-) *f* revenge, vengeance.
Rachen (-s, -) *m* throat.
rächen ['rɛçən] *vt* to avenge, revenge ♦ *vr* to take (one's) revenge; **das wird sich ~** you'll pay for that.
Rachitis [ra'xi:tɪs] (-) *f* rickets *sing.*
Rachsucht *f* vindictiveness.
rachsüchtig *adj* vindictive.
Racker ['rakər] (-s, -) *m* rascal, scamp.
Rad [ra:t] (-(e)s, ̈-er) *nt* wheel; (*Fahr~*) bike; **unter die Räder kommen** (*umg*) to fall into bad ways; **das fünfte ~ am Wagen sein** (*umg*) to be in the way.
Radar ['ra:da:r] (-s) *m od nt* radar; ~**falle** *f* speed trap; ~**kontrolle** *f* radar-controlled speed check.
Radau [ra'dau] (-s) (*umg*) *m* row; ~ **machen** to kick up a row; (*Unruhe stiften*) to cause trouble.
Raddampfer *m* paddle steamer.
radebrechen ['ra:dəbrɛçən] *vi untr:* **deutsch etc** ~ to speak broken German *etc.*
radeln *vi* (*Hilfsverb sein*) to cycle.
Rädelsführer ['rɛ:dəlsfy:rər] (-s, -) *m* ringleader.
Rad- *zW:* **r~fahren** *unreg vi* to cycle; ~**fahrer** *m* cyclist; (*pej: umg*) crawler; ~**fahrweg** *m* cycle track *od* path.
radieren [ra'di:rən] *vt* to rub out, erase; (*ART*) to etch.
Radiergummi *m* rubber (*BRIT*), eraser (*bes US*).
Radierung *f* etching.
Radieschen [ra'di:sçən] *nt* radish.
radikal [radi'ka:l] *adj* radical; ~ **gegen etw vorgehen** to take radical steps against sth.
Radikale(r) *f(m)* radical.
Radikalisierung [radikali'zi:rʊŋ] *f* radicalization.
Radikalkur (*umg*) *f* drastic remedy.

Radio ['ra:dio] (-s, -s) *nt* radio, wireless (*bes BRIT*); **im** ~ on the radio; **r~aktiv** *adj* radioactive; **r~aktiver Niederschlag** (radioactive) fallout; ~**aktivität** *f* radioactivity; ~**apparat** *m* radio (set); ~**recorder** *m* radio-cassette recorder.
Radium ['ra:diʊm] (-s) *nt* radium.
Radius ['ra:diʊs] (-, **Radien**) *m* radius.
Radkappe *f* (*AUT*) hub cap.
Radler(in) (-s, -) *m(f)* cyclist.
Rad- *zW:* ~**rennbahn** *f* cycling (race)track; ~**rennen** *nt* cycle race; (*Sportart*) cycle racing; ~**sport** *m* cycling.
RAF (-) *f abk* (= *Rote Armee Fraktion*) Red Army Faction.
raffen ['rafən] *vt* to snatch, pick up; (*Stoff*) to gather (up); (*Geld*) to pile up, rake in; (*umg: verstehen*) to catch on to.
Raffgier *f* greed, avarice.
Raffinade [rafi'na:də] *f* refined sugar.
Raffinesse [rafi'nɛsə] (-) *f* (*Feinheit*) refinement; (*Schlauheit*) cunning.
raffinieren [rafi'ni:rən] *vt* to refine.
raffiniert *adj* crafty, cunning; (*Zucker*) refined.
Rage ['ra:ʒə] (-) *f* (*Wut*) rage, fury.
ragen ['ra:gən] *vi* to tower, rise.
Rahm [ra:m] (-s) *m* cream.
Rahmen (-s, -) *m* frame(work); **aus dem** ~ **fallen** to go too far; **im** ~ **des Möglichen** within the bounds of possibility; **r~** *vt* to frame; ~**handlung** *f* (*LITER*) background story; ~**plan** *m* outline plan; ~**richtlinien** *pl* guidelines *pl.*
rahmig *adj* creamy.
Rakete [ra'ke:tə] (-, -n) *f* rocket; **ferngelenkte** ~ guided missile.
Raketenstützpunkt *m* missile base.
Rallye ['rali] (-, -s) *f* rally.
rammdösig ['ramdø:zɪç] (*umg*) *adj* giddy, dizzy.
rammen ['ramən] *vt* to ram.
Rampe ['rampə] (-, -n) *f* ramp.
Rampenlicht *nt* (*THEAT*) footlights *pl*; **sie möchte immer im** ~ **stehen** (*fig*) she always wants to be in the limelight.
ramponieren [rampo'ni:rən] (*umg*) *vt* to damage.
Ramsch [ramʃ] (-(e)s, -e) *m* junk.
ran [ran] (*umg*) *adv* = **heran.**
Rand [rant] (-(e)s, ̈-er) *m* edge; (*von Brille, Tasse etc*) rim; (*Hut~*) brim; (*auf Papier*) margin; (*Schmutz~, unter Augen*) ring; (*fig*) verge, brink; **außer** ~ **und Band** wild; **am** ~**e bemerkt** mentioned in passing; **am** ~**e der Stadt** on the outskirts of the town; **etw am** ~**e miterleben** to experience sth from the sidelines.
randalieren [randa'li:rən] *vi* to (go on the) rampage.
Rand- *zW:* ~**bemerkung** *f* marginal note; (*fig*) odd comment; ~**erscheinung** *f* unimportant side effect, marginal phenomenon; ~**figur** *f*

minor figure; ~**gebiet** nt (*GEOG*) fringe; (*POL*) border territory; (*fig*) subsidiary; ~**streifen** m (*der Straße*) verge (*BRIT*), berm (*US*); (*der Autobahn*) hard shoulder (*BRIT*), shoulder (*US*); r~**voll** adj full to the brim.

rang etc [raŋ] vb siehe **ringen**.

Rang (-(e)s, ⁻e) m rank; (*Stand*) standing; (*Wert*) quality; (*THEAT*) circle; **ein Mann ohne ~ und Namen** a man without any standing; **erster/zweiter ~** dress/upper circle.

Rangabzeichen nt badge of rank.

Rangälteste(r) m senior officer.

rangeln ['raŋəln] (*umg*) vi to scrap; (*um Posten*): ~ (**um**) to wrangle (for).

Rangfolge f order of rank (*bes MIL*).

Rangierbahnhof [rä'ʒiːrbaːnhoːf] m marshalling yard.

rangieren vt (*EISENB*) to shunt, switch (*US*)
♦ vi to rank, be classed.

Rangiergleis nt siding.

Rangliste f (*SPORT*) ranking list, rankings pl.

Rangordnung f hierarchy; (*MIL*) rank.

Rangunterschied m social distinction; (*MIL*) difference in rank.

rank [raŋk] adj: ~ **und schlank** (*liter*) slender and supple.

Ranke ['raŋkə] (-, -n) f tendril, shoot.

Ränke ['rɛŋkə] pl intrigues pl; ~**schmied** m (*liter*) intriguer.

ranken ['raŋkən] vr to trail, grow; **sich um etw ~** to twine around sth.

ränkevoll adj scheming.

ranklotzen ['raŋklɔtsən] (*umg*) vi to put one's nose to the grindstone.

ranlassen unreg (*umg*) vt: **jdn ~** to let sb have a go.

rann etc [ran] vb siehe **rinnen**.

rannte etc ['rantə] vb siehe **rennen**.

Ranzen ['rantsən] (-s, -) m satchel; (*umg: Bauch*) belly, gut.

ranzig ['rantsɪç] adj rancid.

Rappe ['rapə] (-n, -n) m black horse.

Rappel ['rapəl] (-s, -) (*umg*) m (*Fimmel*) craze; (*Wutanfall*): **einen ~ kriegen** to throw a fit.

Rappen ['rapən] (-s, -) (*SCHWEIZ*) m (*Geld*) centime, rappen.

Raps [raps] (-es, -e) m (*BOT*) rape; ~**öl** nt rapeseed oil.

rar [raːr] adj rare; **sich ~ machen** (*umg*) to stay away.

Rarität [rari'tɛːt] f rarity; (*Sammelobjekt*) curio.

rasant [ra'zant] adj quick, rapid.

rasch [raʃ] adj quick.

rascheln vi to rustle.

rasen ['raːzən] vi to rave; (*sich schnell bewegen*) to race.

Rasen (-s, -) m grass; (*gepflegt*) lawn.

rasend adj furious; ~**e Kopfschmerzen** a splitting headache.

Rasen- zW: ~**mäher** (-s, -) m lawnmower; ~**mähmaschine** f lawnmower; ~**platz** m lawn; ~**sprenger** m (lawn) sprinkler.

Raserei [raːzə'raɪ] f raving, ranting; (*Schnelle*) reckless speeding.

Rasier- zW: ~**apparat** m shaver; ~**creme** f shaving cream; r~**en** vt, vr to shave; ~**klinge** f razor blade; ~**messer** nt razor; ~**pinsel** m shaving brush; ~**seife** f shaving soap od stick; ~**wasser** nt aftershave.

raspeln ['raspəln] vt to grate; (*Holz*) to rasp.

Rasse ['rasə] (-, -n) f race; (*Tier~*) breed; ~**hund** m thoroughbred dog.

Rassel (-, -n) f rattle.

rasseln vi to rattle, clatter.

Rassenhaß m race od racial hatred.

Rassentrennung f racial segregation.

rassig ['rasɪç] adj (*Pferd, Auto*) sleek; (*Frau*) vivacious; (*Wein*) spirited, lively.

Rassismus [ra'sɪsmʊs] (-) m racialism, racism.

rassistisch [ra'sɪstɪʃ] adj racialist, racist.

Rast [rast] (-, -en) f rest; r~**en** vi to rest.

Raster ['rastər] (-s, -) m (*ARCHIT*) grid; (*PHOT: Gitter*) screen; (*TV*) raster; (*fig*) framework.

Rast- zW: ~**haus** nt (*AUT*) service area, services pl; ~**hof** m (motorway) motel; (*mit Tankstelle*) service area (*with a motel*); r~**los** adj tireless; (*unruhig*) restless; ~**platz** m (*AUT*) lay-by (*BRIT*); ~**stätte** f service area, services pl.

Rasur [ra'zuːr] f shave; (*das Rasieren*) shaving.

Rat [raːt] (-(e)s, -schläge) m (piece of) advice; **jdn zu ~e ziehen** to consult sb; **jdm mit ~ und Tat zur Seite stehen** to support sb in (both) word and deed; (**sich** dat) **keinen ~ wissen** not to know what to do.

rät [rɛːt] vb siehe **raten**.

Rate (-, -n) f instalment (*BRIT*), installment (*US*); **auf ~n kaufen** to buy on hire purchase (*BRIT*) od on the installment plan (*US*); **in ~n zahlen** to pay in instalments (*BRIT*) od installments (*US*).

raten unreg vt, vi to guess; (*empfehlen*): **jdm ~** to advise sb; **dreimal darfst du ~** I'll give you three guesses (*auch ironisch*).

ratenweise adv by instalments (*BRIT*) od installments (*US*).

Ratenzahlung f hire purchase (*BRIT*), installment plan (*US*).

Ratespiel nt guessing game; (*TV*) quiz; (: *Beruferaten etc*) panel game.

Ratgeber (-s, -) m adviser.

Rathaus nt town hall; (*einer Großstadt*) city hall (*bes US*).

ratifizieren [ratifi'tsiːrən] vt to ratify.

Ratifizierung f ratification.

Ration [ratsi'oːn] f ration.

rational [ratsio'naːl] adj rational.

rationalisieren [ratsionali'ziːrən] vt to rationalize.

rationell [ratsio'nɛl] *adj* efficient.
rationieren [ratsio'niːrən] *vt* to ration.
ratlos *adj* at a loss, helpless.
Ratlosigkeit *f* helplessness.
rätoromanisch [rɛtoro'maːnɪʃ] *adj* Rhaetian.
ratsam *adj* advisable.
Ratschlag *m* (piece of) advice.
Rätsel ['rɛːtsəl] (**-s,** -) *nt* puzzle; (*Wort~*)
  riddle; **vor einem ~ stehen** to be baffled;
  r~haft *adj* mysterious; **es ist mir r~haft** it's a
  mystery to me; **r~n** *vi* to puzzle; **~raten** *nt*
  guessing game.
Ratsherr *m* councillor (*BRIT*), councilor (*US*).
Ratskeller *m* town-hall restaurant.
ratsuchend *adj*: **sich ~ an jdn wenden** to turn
  to sb for advice.
Ratte ['ratə] (-, **-n**) *f* rat.
Rattenfänger (**-s,** -) *m* rat-catcher.
rattern ['ratərn] *vi* to rattle, clatter.
Raub [raup] (**-(e)s**) *m* robbery; (*Beute*) loot,
  booty; **~bau** *m* overexploitation; **~druck** *m*
  pirate(d) edition; **r~en** ['raubən] *vt* to rob;
  (*jdn*) to kidnap, abduct.
Räuber ['rɔybər] (**-s,** -) *m* robber; **r~isch** *adj*
  thieving.
Raub- *zW*: **~fisch** *m* predatory fish; **r~gierig**
  adj rapacious; **~kassette** *f* pirate cassette;
  ~mord *m* robbery with murder; **~tier** *nt*
  predator; **~überfall** *m* robbery with
  violence; **~vogel** *m* bird of prey.
Rauch [raux] (**-(e)s**) *m* smoke; **~abzug** *m*
  smoke outlet.
rauchen *vt, vi* to smoke; **mir raucht der Kopf**
  (*fig*) my head's spinning; „**R~ verboten**"
  "no smoking".
Raucher(in) (**-s,** -) *m(f)* smoker; **~abteil** *nt*
  (*EISENB*) smoker.
räuchern ['rɔyçərn] *vt* to smoke, cure.
Räucherspeck *m* ~ smoked bacon.
Räucherstäbchen *nt* joss stick.
Rauch- *zW*: **~fahne** *f* smoke trail; **~fang** *m*
  chimney hood; **~fleisch** *nt* smoked meat.
rauchig *adj* smoky.
Rauchschwaden *pl* drifts of smoke *pl*.
räudig ['rɔydıç] *adj* mangy.
rauf [rauf] (*umg*) *adv* = **herauf; hinauf.**
Raufbold (**-(e)s, -e**) *m* thug, hooligan.
raufen *vt* (*Haare*) to pull out ♦ *vi, vr* to fight.
Rauferei [raufə'rai] *f* brawl, fight.
rauflustig *adj* ready for a fight, pugnacious.
rauh [rau] *adj* rough, coarse; (*Wetter*) harsh; **in
  ~en Mengen** (*umg*) by the ton, galore;
  ~beinig *adj* rough-and-ready; **R~fasertapete**
  f woodchip paper; **~haarig** *adj* wire-haired;
  R~reif *m* hoarfrost.
Raum [raum] (**-(e)s, Räume**) *m* space; (*Zimmer,
  Platz*) room; (*Gebiet*) area; **eine Frage im
  ~ stehen lassen** to leave a question
  unresolved; **~ausstatter(in)** *m(f)* interior
  decorator.
räumen ['rɔymən] *vt* to clear; (*Wohnung, Platz*)
  to vacate, move out of; (*verlassen: Gebäude,

  Gebiet*) to evacuate; (*wegbringen*) to shift,
  move; (*in Schrank etc*) to put away.
Raum- *zW*: **~fähre** *f* space shuttle; **~fahrer** *m*
  astronaut; (*sowjetisch*) cosmonaut; **~fahrt** *f*
  space travel.
Raumfahrzeug ['raumfaːrtsɔyk] *nt* bulldozer;
  (*für Schnee*) snow-clearer.
Rauminhalt *m* cubic capacity, volume.
Raumkapsel *f* space capsule.
räumlich ['rɔymlıç] *adj* spatial; **R~keiten** *pl*
  premises *pl*.
Raum- *zW*: **~mangel** *m* lack of space; **~maß**
  nt unit of volume; cubic measurement;
  ~meter *m* cubic metre (*BRIT*) od meter (*US*);
  ~pflegerin *f* cleaner; **~schiff** *nt* spaceship;
  ~schiffahrt *f* space travel; **r~sparend** *adj*
  space-saving; **~station** *f* space station;
  ~transporter *m* space shuttle.
Räumung ['rɔymuŋ] *f* clearing (away); (*von
  Haus etc*) vacating; (*wegen Gefahr*)
  evacuation; (*unter Zwang*) eviction.
Räumungs- *zW*: **~befehl** *m* eviction order;
  ~klage *f* action for eviction; **~verkauf** *m*
  clearance sale.
raunen ['raunən] *vt, vi* to whisper.
Raupe ['raupə] (-, **-n**) *f* caterpillar;
  (*Raupenkette*) (caterpillar) track.
Raupenschlepper *m* caterpillar tractor.
raus [raus] (*umg*) *adv* = **heraus; hinaus.**
Rausch [rauʃ] (**-(e),** *pl* **Räusche**) *m*
  intoxication; **einen ~ haben** to be drunk.
rauschen *vi* (*Wasser*) to rush; (*Baum*) to
  rustle; (*Radio etc*) to hiss; (*Mensch*) to sweep,
  sail.
rauschend *adj* (*Beifall*) thunderous; (*Fest*)
  sumptuous.
Rauschgift *nt* drug; **~handel** *m* drug traffic;
  ~süchtige(r) *f(m)* drug addict.
rausfliegen *unreg* (*umg*) *vi* to be chucked out.
räuspern ['rɔyspərn] *vr* to clear one's throat.
Rausschmeißer ['rausʃmaisər] (**-s,** -) (*umg*) *m*
  bouncer.
Raute ['rautə] (-, **-n**) *f* diamond; (*MATH*)
  rhombus.
rautenförmig *adj* rhombic.
Razzia ['ratsia] (-, **Razzien**) *f* raid.
Reagenzglas [rea'gɛntsglaːs] *nt* test tube.
reagieren [rea'giːrən] *vi*: **~** (**auf** +*akk*) to react
  (to).
Reaktion [reaktsi'oːn] *f* reaction.
reaktionär [reaktsio'nɛːr] *adj* reactionary.
Reaktionsfähigkeit *f* reactions *pl*.
Reaktionsgeschwindigkeit *f* speed of
  reaction.
Reaktor [re'aktor] *m* reactor; **~kern** *m* reactor
  core; **~unglück** *nt* nuclear accident.
real [re'aːl] *adj* real, material; **R~einkommen**
  nt real income.
realisierbar [reali'ziːrbaːr] *adj* practicable,
  feasible.
Realismus [rea'lısmus] *m* realism.
Realist(in) [rea'lıst(ın)] *m(f)* realist; **r~isch** *adj*

realistic.
Realität [reali'tɛːt] *f* reality; **Realitäten** *pl* (*Gegebenheiten*) facts *pl*.
realitätsfremd *adj* out of touch with reality.
Realpolitik *f* political realism.
Realschule *f* ≈ middle school (*BRIT*), junior high school (*US*).

> The **Realschule** *is one of the choices of secondary schools available to a German schoolchild after the* **Grundschule**. *At the end of six years schooling in the Realschule pupils gain the* **mittlere Reife** *and usually go on to some kind of training or to a college of further education.*

Realzeit *f* real time.
Rebe ['reːbə] (-, -n) *f* vine.
Rebell(in) [re'bɛl(ɪn)] (-en, -en) *m(f)* rebel.
rebellieren [rebɛ'liːrən] *vi* to rebel.
Rebellion [rebɛli'oːn] *f* rebellion.
rebellisch [re'bɛlɪʃ] *adj* rebellious.
Rebensaft *m* wine.
Reb- [rep] *zW:* ~**huhn** *nt* partridge; ~**laus** *f* vine pest; ~**stock** *m* vine.
Rechen ['rɛçən] (-s, -) *m* rake; **r~** *vt, vi* to rake.
Rechen- *zW:* ~**aufgabe** *f* sum, mathematical problem; ~**fehler** *m* miscalculation; ~**maschine** *f* adding machine.
Rechenschaft *f* account; **jdm über etw** *akk* ~ **ablegen** to account to sb for sth; **jdn zur** ~ **ziehen (für)** to call sb to account (for *od* over); **jdm** ~ **schulden** to be accountable to sb.
Rechenschaftsbericht *m* report.
Rechenschieber *m* slide rule.
Rechenzentrum *nt* computer centre (*BRIT*) *od* center (*US*).
recherchieren [reʃɛr'ʃiːrən] *vt, vi* to investigate.
rechnen ['rɛçnən] *vt, vi* to calculate; (*veranschlagen*) to estimate, reckon; **jdn/etw zu etw** ~ to count sb/sth among sth; ~ **mit** to reckon with; ~ **auf** +*akk* to count on.
Rechnen *nt* arithmetic; (*bes SCH*) sums *pl*.
Rechner (-s, -) *m* calculator; (*COMPUT*) computer; **r~abhängig** *adj* (*COMPUT*) on line; **r~fern** *adj* (*COMPUT*) remote; **r~isch** *adj* arithmetical; **r~unabhängig** *adj* (*COMPUT*) off line.
Rechnung *f* calculation(s); (*COMM*) bill (*BRIT*), check (*US*); **auf eigene** ~ on one's own account; (**jdm**) **etw in** ~ **stellen** to charge (sb) for sth; **jdm/etw** ~ **tragen** to take sb/sth into account.
Rechnungs- *zW:* ~**aufstellung** *f* statement; ~**buch** *nt* account book; ~**hof** *m* ≈ Auditor-General's office (*BRIT*), audit division (*US*); ~**jahr** *nt* financial year; ~**prüfer** *m* auditor; ~**prüfung** *f* audit(ing).
recht [rɛçt] *adj* right ♦ *adv* (*vor Adjektiv*) really, quite; **das ist mir** ~ that suits me; **jetzt erst**

~ now more than ever; **alles, was** ~ **ist** (*empört*) fair's fair; (*anerkennend*) you can't deny it; **nach dem R~en sehen** to see that everything's O.K.; ~ **haben** to be right; **jdm** ~ **geben** to agree with sb, admit that sb is right; **du kommst gerade** ~, **um ...** you're just in time to ...; **gehe ich** ~ **in der Annahme, daß ...?** am I correct in assuming that ...?; ~ **herzlichen Dank** thank you very much indeed.
Recht (-(e)s, -e) *nt* right; (*JUR*) law; ~ **sprechen** to administer justice; **mit** *od* **zu** ~ rightly, justly; **von** ~**s wegen** by rights; **zu seinem** ~ **kommen** (*lit*) to gain one's rights; (*fig*) to come into one's own; **gleiches** ~ **für alle!** equal rights for all!
Rechte *f* right (hand); (*POL*) Right.
Rechte(r, s) *f(m)* (*POL*) right-winger ♦ *nt* right thing; **etwas/nichts** ~**s** something/nothing proper.
rechte(r, s) *adj* right; (*POL*) right-wing.
recht- *zW:* **R~eck** (-(e)s, -e) *nt* rectangle; ~**eckig** *adj* rectangular; ~**fertigen** *vt untr* to justify ♦ *vr untr* to justify o.s.; **R~fertigung** *f* justification; ~**haberisch** *adj* dogmatic; ~**lich** *adj* legal, lawful; ~**lich nicht zulässig** not permissible in law, illegal; ~**mäßig** *adj* legal, lawful.
rechts [rɛçts] *adv* od od to the right; ~ **stehen** *od* **sein** (*POL*) to be right-wing; ~ **stricken** to knit (plain); **R~abbieger** (-s, -) *m:* **die Spur für R~abbieger** the right-hand turn-off lane; **R~anspruch** *m:* **einen R~anspruch auf etw** *akk* **haben** to be legally entitled to sth; **R~anwalt** *m*, **R~anwältin** *f* lawyer, barrister; **R~außen** (-, -) *m* (*SPORT*) outside right; **R~beistand** *m* legal adviser.
rechtschaffen *adj* upright.
Rechtschreibung *f* spelling.
Rechts- *zW:* ~**drehung** *f* clockwise rotation; ~**extremismus** *m* right-wing extremism; ~**extremist** *m* right-wing extremist; ~**fall** *m* (law) case; ~**frage** *f* legal question; **r~gültig** *adj* legally valid; ~**händer(in)** (-s, -) *m(f)* right-handed person; **r~kräftig** *adj* valid, legal; ~**kurve** *f* right-hand bend; ~**lage** *f* legal position; **r~lastig** *adj* listing to the right; (*fig*) leaning to the right; ~**pflege** *f* administration of justice; ~**pfleger** *m* official with certain judicial powers.
Rechtsprechung ['rɛçtʃprɛçʊŋ] *f* (*Gerichtsbarkeit*) jurisdiction; (*richterliche Tätigkeit*) dispensation of justice.
Rechts- *zW:* **r~radikal** *adj* (*POL*) extreme right-wing; ~**schutz** *m* legal protection; ~**spruch** *m* verdict; ~**staat** *m* state under the rule of law; ~**streit** *m* lawsuit; ~**titel** *m* title; **r~verbindlich** *adj* legally binding; ~**verkehr** *m* driving on the right; ~**weg** *m:* **der** ~**weg ist ausgeschlossen** ≈ the judges' decision is final; **r~widrig** *adj* illegal; ~**wissenschaft** *f* jurisprudence.

rechtwinklig adj right-angled.
rechtzeitig adj timely ♦ adv in time.
Reck [rɛk] (-(e)s, -e) nt horizontal bar.
recken vt, vr to stretch.
recyceln [riːˈsaikəln] vt to recycle.
Recycling [riːˈsailkɪŋ] (-s) nt recycling.
Red. abk = **Redaktion**; (= Redakteur(in)) ed.
Redakteur(in) [redakˈtøːr(ɪn)] m(f) editor.
Redaktion [redaktsiˈoːn] f editing; (Leute) editorial staff; (Büro) editorial office(s pl).
Redaktionsschluß m time of going to press; (Einsendeschluß) copy deadline.
Rede [ˈreːdə] (-, -n) f speech; (Gespräch) talk; **jdn zur ~ stellen** to take sb to task; **eine ~ halten** to make a speech; **das ist nicht der ~ wert** it's not worth mentioning; **davon kann keine ~ sein** it's out of the question; **~freiheit** f freedom of speech; **r~gewandt** adj eloquent.
Reden (-s) nt talking, speech.
reden vi to talk, speak ♦ vt to say; (Unsinn etc) to talk; **(viel) von sich ~ machen** to become (very much) a talking point; **darüber läßt sich ~** that's a possibility; (über Preis, Bedingungen) I think we could discuss that; **er läßt mit sich ~** he could be persuaded; (in bezug auf Preis) he's open to offers; (gesprächsbereit) he's open to discussion.
Redensart f set phrase.
Redeschwall m torrent of words.
Redewendung f expression, idiom.
redlich [ˈreːtlɪç] adj honest; **R~keit** f honesty.
Redner(in) (-s, -) m(f) speaker, orator.
redselig [ˈreːtzeːlɪç] adj talkative, loquacious; **R~keit** f talkativeness, loquacity.
redundant [redʊnˈdant] adj redundant.
Redundanz [redʊnˈdants] (-) f redundancy.
reduzieren [reduˈtsiːrən] vt to reduce.
Reduzierung f reduction.
Reede [ˈreːdə] (-, -n) f protected anchorage.
Reeder (-s, -) m shipowner.
Reederei [reːdəˈrai] f shipping line od firm.
reell [reˈɛl] adj fair, honest; (Preis) fair; (COMM: Geschäft) sound; (MATH) real.
Reetdach [ˈreːtdax] nt thatched roof.
Ref. abk = **Referendar(in)**; **Referent(in)**.
Referat [refeˈraːt] (-(e)s, -e) nt report; (Vortrag) paper; (Gebiet) section; (VERWALTUNG: Ressort) department; **ein ~ halten** to present a seminar paper.
Referendar(in) [referɛnˈdaːr(ɪn)] m(f) trainee (in civil service); (Studien~) trainee teacher; (Gerichts~) articled clerk.
Referendum [refeˈrɛndʊm] (-s, Referenden) nt referendum.
Referent(in) [refeˈrɛnt(ɪn)] m(f) speaker; (Berichterstatter) reporter; (Sachbearbeiter) expert.
Referenz [refeˈrɛnts] f reference.
referieren [refeˈriːrən] vi: **~ über** +akk to speak od talk on.
reflektieren [reflɛkˈtiːrən] vt, vi to reflect;

~ auf +akk to be interested in.
Reflex [reˈflɛks] (-es, -e) m reflex; **~bewegung** f reflex action.
reflexiv [reflɛˈksiːf] adj (GRAM) reflexive.
Reform [reˈfɔrm] (-, -en) f reform.
Reformation [reformatsiˈoːn] f reformation.
Reformator [reforˈmaːtɔr] m reformer; **r~isch** adj reformatory, reforming.
reform- zW: **~bedürftig** adj in need of reform; **~freudig** adj avid for reform; **R~haus** nt health food shop.
reformieren [reforˈmiːrən] vt to reform.
Refrain [rəˈfrɛː] (-s, -s) m refrain, chorus.
Reg. abk (= Regierungs-) gov.; (= Register) reg.
Regal [reˈgaːl] (-s, -e) nt (book)shelves pl, bookcase; (TYP) stand, rack.
Regatta [reˈgata] (-, Regatten) f regatta.
Reg.-Bez. abk = **Regierungsbezirk**.
rege [ˈreːgə] adj lively, active; (Geschäft) brisk.
Regel [ˈreːgəl] (-, -n) f rule; (MED) period; **in der ~** as a rule; **nach allen ~n der Kunst** (fig) thoroughly; **sich** dat **etw zur ~ machen** to make a habit of sth; **r~los** adj irregular, unsystematic; **r~mäßig** adj regular; **~mäßigkeit** f regularity.
regeln vt to regulate, control; (Angelegenheit) to settle ♦ vr: **sich von selbst ~** to take care of itself; **gesetzlich geregelt sein** to be laid down by law.
regelrecht adj proper, thorough.
Regelung f regulation; settlement.
regelwidrig adj irregular, against the rules.
regen [ˈreːgən] vt to move ♦ vr to move, stir.
Regen (-s, -) m rain; **vom ~ in die Traufe kommen** (Sprichwort) to jump out of the frying pan into the fire (Sprichwort).
Regenbogen m rainbow; **~haut** f (ANAT) iris; **~presse** f trashy magazines pl.
regenerieren [regeneˈriːrən] vr (BIOL) to regenerate; (fig) to revitalize od regenerate o.s. od itself; (nach Anstrengung, Schock etc) to recover.
Regen- zW: **~guß** m downpour; **~mantel** m raincoat, mac(kintosh); **~menge** f rainfall; **~schauer** m shower (of rain); **~schirm** m umbrella.
Regent(in) [reˈgɛnt(ɪn)] m(f) regent.
Regentag m rainy day.
Regentropfen m raindrop.
Regentschaft f regency.
Regen- zW: **~wald** m (GEOG) rain forest; **~wetter** nt: **er macht ein Gesicht wie drei** od **sieben Tage ~wetter** (umg) he's got a face as long as a month of Sundays; **~wurm** m earthworm; **~zeit** f rainy season, rains pl.
Regie [reˈʒiː] f (FILM etc) direction; (THEAT) production; **unter der ~ von** directed od produced by; **~anweisung** f (stage) direction.
regieren [reˈgiːrən] vt, vi to govern, rule.

Regierung f government; (*Monarchie*) reign; **an die ~ kommen** to come to power.
Regierungs- zW: **~bezirk** m ≈ county (*BRIT, US*), region (*SCOT*); **~erklärung** f inaugural speech; (*in Großbritannien*) Queen's/King's Speech; **~sprecher** m government spokesman; **~vorlage** f government bill; **~wechsel** m change of government; **~zeit** f period in government; (*von König*) reign.
Regiment [regi'mɛnt] (**-s, -er**) nt regiment.
Region [regi'oːn] f region.
Regionalplanung [regio'naːlplaːnʊŋ] f regional planning.
Regionalprogramm nt (*RUNDF, TV*) regional programme (*BRIT*) od program (*US*).
Regisseur(in) [reʒɪ'søːr(ɪn)] m(f) director; (*THEAT*) (stage) producer.
Register [re'gɪstər] (**-s, -**) nt register; (*in Buch*) table of contents, index; **alle ~ ziehen** (*fig*) to pull out all the stops; **~führer** m registrar.
Registratur [regɪstra'tuːr] f registry, records office.
registrieren [regɪs'triːrən] vt to register; (*umg: zur Kenntnis nehmen*) to note.
Registrierkasse f cash register.
Regler ['reːglər] (**-s, -**) m regulator, governor.
reglos ['reːkloːs] adj motionless.
regnen ['reːgnən] vi unpers to rain ♦ vt unpers: **es regnet Glückwünsche** congratulations are pouring in; **es regnet in Strömen** it's pouring (with rain).
regnerisch adj rainy.
Regreß [re'grɛs] (**-sses, -sse**) m (*JUR*) recourse, redress; **~anspruch** m (*JUR*) claim for compensation.
regsam ['reːkzaːm] adj active.
regulär [regu'lɛːr] adj regular.
regulieren [regu'liːrən] vt to regulate; (*COMM*) to settle; **sich von selbst ~** to be self-regulating.
Regung ['reːgʊŋ] f motion; (*Gefühl*) feeling, impulse.
regungslos adj motionless.
Reh [reː] (**-(e)s, -e**) nt deer; (*weiblich*) roe deer.
rehabilitieren [rehabili'tiːrən] vt to rehabilitate; (*Ruf, Ehre*) to vindicate ♦ vr to rehabilitate (*form*) od vindicate o.s.
Rehabilitierung f rehabilitation.
Reh- zW: **~bock** m roebuck; **~braten** m roast venison; **~kalb** nt fawn; **~kitz** nt fawn.
Reibach ['raɪbax] (**-s**) m: **einen ~ machen** (*umg*) to make a killing.
Reibe ['raɪbə] (**-, -n**) f grater.
Reibeisen ['raɪp|aɪzən] nt grater.
Reibekuchen m (*KOCH*) ≈ potato waffle.
reiben unreg vt to rub; (*KOCH*) to grate.
Reiberei [raɪbə'raɪ] f friction no pl.
Reibfläche f rough surface.
Reibung f friction.
reibungslos adj smooth; **~ verlaufen** to go off smoothly.
Reich [raɪç] (**-(e)s, -e**) nt empire, kingdom;

(*fig*) realm; **das Dritte ~** the Third Reich.
reich adj rich ♦ adv: **eine ~ ausgestattete Bibliothek** a well-stocked library.
reichen vi to reach; (*genügen*) to be enough od sufficient ♦ vt to hold out; (*geben*) to pass, hand; (*anbieten*) to offer; **so weit das Auge reicht** as far as the eye can see; **jdm ~** (*genügen*) to be enough od sufficient for sb; **mir reichts!** I've had enough!
reich- zW: **~haltig** adj ample, rich; **~lich** adj ample, plenty of; **R~tum** (**-s, -tümer**) m wealth; **R~weite** f range; **jd ist in R~weite** sb is nearby.
reif [raɪf] adj ripe; (*Mensch, Urteil*) mature; **für etw ~ sein** (*umg*) to be ready for sth.
Reif¹ (**-(e)s**) m hoarfrost.
Reif² (**-(e)s, -e**) m (*Ring*) ring, hoop.
Reife (**-**) f ripeness; maturity; **mittlere ~** (*SCH*) first public examination in secondary school, ≈ O-Levels pl (*BRIT*).
Reifen (**-s, -**) m ring, hoop; (*Fahrzeug~*) tyre (*BRIT*), tire (*US*).
reifen vi to mature; (*Obst*) to ripen.
Reifen- zW: **~druck** m tyre (*BRIT*) od tire (*US*) pressure; **~panne** f puncture, flat; **~profil** nt tyre (*BRIT*) od tire (*US*) tread; **~schaden** m puncture, flat.
Reifeprüfung f school-leaving exam.
Reifezeugnis nt school-leaving certificate.
reiflich ['raɪflɪç] adj thorough, careful.
Reihe ['raɪə] (**-, -n**) f row; (*von Tagen etc: umg: Anzahl*) series sing; **eine ganze ~ (von)** (*unbestimmte Anzahl*) a whole lot (of); **der ~ nach** in turn; **er ist an der ~** it's his turn; **an die ~ kommen** to have one's turn; **außer der ~** out of turn; (*ausnahmsweise*) out of the usual way of things; **aus der ~ tanzen** (*fig: umg*) to be different; (*gegen Konventionen verstoßen*) to step out of line; **ich kriege heute nichts auf die ~** I can't get my act together today.
reihen vt to set in a row; to arrange in series; (*Perlen*) to string.
Reihen- zW: **~folge** f sequence; **alphabetische ~folge** alphabetical order; **~haus** nt terraced (*BRIT*) od row (*US*) house; **~untersuchung** f mass screening; **r~weise** adv (*in Reihen*) in rows; (*fig: in großer Anzahl*) by the dozen.
Reiher (**-s, -**) m heron.
reihum [raɪ'|ʊm] adv: **etw ~ gehen lassen** to pass sth around.
Reim [raɪm] (**-(e)s, -e**) m rhyme; **sich** dat **einen ~ auf etw** akk **machen** (*umg*) to make sense of sth; **r~en** vt to rhyme.
rein¹ [raɪn] (*umg*) adv = **herein; hinein**.
rein² [raɪn] adj pure; (*sauber*) clean ♦ adv purely; **das ist die ~ste Freude/der ~ste Hohn** etc it's pure od sheer joy/mockery etc; **etw ins ~e schreiben** to make a fair copy of sth; **etw ins ~e bringen** to clear sth up; **~en Tisch machen** (*fig*) to get things straight;

~ **unmöglich** (*umg: ganz, völlig*) absolutely impossible.
Rein- *in zW* (*COMM*) net(t).
Rein(e)machefrau *f* cleaning lady, charwoman (*BRIT*).
rein(e)weg (*umg*) *adv* completely, absolutely.
rein- *zW:* **R~fall** (*umg*) *m* let-down; (*Mißerfolg*) flop; **~fallen** *vi:* **auf jdn/etw ~fallen** to be taken in by sb/sth; **R~gewinn** *m* net profit; **R~heit** *f* purity; cleanliness.
reinigen ['raɪnɪgən] *vt* to clean; (*Wasser*) to purify.
Reiniger (**-s, -**) *m* cleaner.
Reinigung *f* cleaning; purification; (*Geschäft*) cleaner's; **chemische ~** dry-cleaning; (*Geschäft*) dry-cleaner's.
Reinigungsmittel *nt* cleansing agent.
rein- *zW:* **~lich** *adj* clean; **R~lichkeit** *f* cleanliness; **~rassig** *adj* pedigree; **~reiten** *unreg vt:* **jdn ~reiten** to get sb into a mess; **R~schrift** *f* fair copy; **R~vermögen** *nt* net assets *pl;* **~waschen** *unreg vr* to clear o.s.
Reis¹ [raɪs] (**-es, -e**) *m* rice.
Reis² [raɪs] (**-es, -er**) *nt* twig, sprig.
Reise ['raɪzə] (**-, -n**) *f* journey; (*Schiffs~*) voyage; **Reisen** *pl* travels *pl;* **gute ~!** bon voyage!, have a good journey!; **auf ~n sein** to be away (travelling (*BRIT*) *od* traveling (*US*)); **er ist viel auf ~n** he does a lot of travelling (*BRIT*) *od* traveling (*US*); **~andenken** *nt* souvenir; **~apotheke** *f* first-aid kit; **~bericht** *m* account of one's journey; (*Buch*) travel story; (*Film*) travelogue (*BRIT*), travelog (*US*); **~büro** *nt* travel agency; **~diplomatie** *f* shuttle diplomacy; **~erleichterungen** *pl* easing *sing* of travel restrictions; **r~fertig** *adj* ready to start; **~fieber** *nt* (*fig*) travel nerves *pl;* **~führer** *m* guide(book); (*Mensch*) (travel) guide; **~gepäck** *nt* luggage; **~gesellschaft** *f* party of travellers (*BRIT*) *od* travelers (*US*); **~kosten** *pl* travelling (*BRIT*) *od* traveling (*US*) expenses *pl;* **~leiter** *m* courier; **~lektüre** *f* reading for the journey; **~lust** *f* wanderlust.
reisen *vi* to travel; **~ nach** to go to.
Reisende(r) *f(m)* traveller (*BRIT*), traveler (*US*).
Reise- *zW:* **~paß** *m* passport; **~pläne** *pl* plans *pl* for a *od* the journey; **~proviant** *m* provisions *pl* for the journey; **~route** *f* itinerary; **~scheck** *m* traveller's cheque (*BRIT*), traveler's check (*US*); **~schreibmaschine** *f* portable typewriter; **~tasche** *f* travelling (*BRIT*) *od* traveling (*US*) bag *od* case; **~veranstalter** *m* tour operator; **~verkehr** *m* tourist *od* holiday traffic; **~wetter** *nt* holiday weather; **~ziel** *nt* destination.
Reisig ['raɪzɪç] (**-s**) *nt* brushwood.
Reißaus *m:* **~ nehmen** to run away, flee.
Reißbrett *nt* drawing board; **~stift** *m* drawing

reißen ['raɪsən] *unreg vt* to tear; (*ziehen*) to pull, drag; (*Witz*) to crack ♦ *vi* to tear; to pull, drag; **etw an sich ~** to snatch sth up; (*fig*) to take sth over; **sich um etw ~** to scramble for sth; **hin und her gerissen sein** (*fig*) to be torn; **wenn alle Stricke ~** (*fig: umg*) if the worst comes to the worst.
Reißen *nt* (*Gewichtheben: Disziplin*) snatch; (*umg: Glieder~*) ache.
reißend *adj* (*Fluß*) torrential; (*COMM*) rapid; **~en Absatz finden** to sell like hot cakes (*umg*).
Reißer (**-s, -**) (*umg*) *m* thriller; **r~isch** *adj* sensational.
Reiß- *zW:* **~leine** *f* (*AVIAT*) ripcord; **~nagel** *m* drawing pin (*BRIT*), thumbtack (*US*); **~schiene** *f* T-square; **~verschluß** *m* zip (fastener) (*BRIT*), zipper (*US*); **~wolf** *m* shredder; **durch den ~wolf geben** (*Dokumente*) to shred; **~zeug** *nt* geometry set; **~zwecke** *f* = Reißnagel.
reiten ['raɪtən] *unreg vt, vi* to ride.
Reiter (**-s, -**) *m* rider; (*MIL*) cavalryman, trooper.
Reiterei [raɪtə'raɪ] *f* cavalry.
Reiterin *f* rider.
Reit- *zW:* **~hose** *f* riding breeches *pl;* **~pferd** *nt* saddle horse; **~schule** *f* riding school; **~stiefel** *m* riding boot; **~turnier** *nt* horse show; **~weg** *m* bridle path; **~zeug** *nt* riding outfit.
Reiz [raɪts] (**-es, -e**) *m* stimulus; (*angenehm*) charm; (*Verlockung*) attraction.
reizbar *adj* irritable; **R~keit** *f* irritability.
reizen *vt* to stimulate; (*unangenehm*) to irritate; (*verlocken*) to appeal to, attract; (*KARTEN*) to bid ♦ *vi:* **zum Widerspruch ~** to invite contradiction.
reizend *adj* charming.
Reiz- *zW:* **~gas** *nt* tear gas, CS gas; **~husten** *m* chesty cough; **r~los** *adj* unattractive; **r~voll** *adj* attractive; **~wäsche** *f* sexy underwear; **~wort** *nt* emotive word.
rekapitulieren [rekapitu'li:rən] *vt* to recapitulate.
rekeln ['re:kəln] *vr* to stretch out; (*lümmeln*) to lounge *od* loll about.
Reklamation [reklamatsi'o:n] *f* complaint.
Reklame [re'kla:mə] (**-, -n**) *f* advertising; (*Anzeige*) advertisement; **mit etw ~ machen** (*pej*) to show off about sth; **für etw ~ machen** to advertise sth; **~trommel** *f:* **die ~trommel für jdn/etw rühren** (*umg*) to beat the (big) drum for sb/sth; **~wand** *f* notice (*BRIT*) *od* bulletin (*US*) board.
reklamieren [rekla'mi:rən] *vi* to complain ♦ *vt* to complain about; (*zurückfordern*) to reclaim.
rekonstruieren [rekɔnstru'i:rən] *vt* to reconstruct.
Rekonvaleszenz [rekɔnvalɛs'tsɛnts] *f*

convalescence.
Rekord [re'kɔrt] **(-(e)s, -e)** *m* record; **~leistung**
f record performance.
Rekrut [re'kruːt] **(-en, -en)** *m* recruit.
rekrutieren [rekru'tiːrən] *vt* to recruit ♦ *vr* to
be recruited.
Rektor ['rɛktɔr] *m* (*UNIV*) rector, vice-
chancellor; (*SCH*) head teacher (*BRIT*),
principal (*US*).
Rektorat [rɛktɔ'rat] **(-(e)s, -e)** *nt* rectorate,
vice-chancellorship; headship (*BRIT*),
principalship (*US*); (*Zimmer*) rector's *etc*
office.
Rektorin [rɛk'toːrɪn] *f* (*SCH*) head teacher
(*BRIT*), principal (*US*).
Rel. *abk* (= *Religion*) rel.
Relais [rə'lɛː] **(-, -)** *nt* relay.
Relation [relatsi'oːn] *f* relation.
relativ [rela'tiːf] *adj* relative.
Relativität [relativi'tɛːt] *f* relativity.
Relativpronomen *nt* (*GRAM*) relative
pronoun.
relevant [rele'vant] *adj* relevant.
Relevanz *f* relevance.
Relief [reli'ɛf] **(-s, -s)** *nt* relief.
Religion [religi'oːn] *f* religion.
Religions- *zW:* **~freiheit** *f* freedom of
worship; **~lehre** *f* religious education;
~unterricht *m* religious education.
religiös [religi'øːs] *adj* religious.
Relikt [re'lɪkt] **(-(e)s, -e)** *nt* relic.
Reling ['reːlɪŋ] **(-, -s)** *f* (*NAUT*) rail.
Reliquie [re'liːkviə] *f* relic.
Reminiszenz [reminɪs'tsɛnts] *f* reminiscence,
recollection.
Remis [rə'miː] **(-, - od -en)** *nt* (*SCHACH, SPORT*)
draw.
Remittende [remɪ'tɛndə] **(-, -n)** *f* (*COMM*)
return.
Remittent *m* (*FIN*) payee.
remittieren *vt* (*COMM: Waren*) to return;
(*Geld*) to remit.
Remmidemmi ['rɛmidɛmi] **(-s)** (*umg*) *nt*
(*Krach*) row, rumpus; (*Trubel*) rave-up.
Remoulade [remu'laːdə] **(-, -n)** *f* remoulade.
rempeln ['rɛmpəln] (*umg*) *vt* to jostle, elbow;
(*SPORT*) to barge into; (*foulen*) to push.
Ren [rɛn] **(-s, -s** *od* **-e)** *nt* reindeer.
Renaissance [rənɛ'sãːs] **(-, -n)** *f* (*HIST*)
renaissance; (*fig*) revival, rebirth.
Rendezvous [rãde'vuː] **(-, -)** *nt* rendezvous.
Rendite [rɛn'diːtə] **(-, -n)** *f* (*FIN*) yield, return
on capital.
Rennbahn *f* racecourse; (*AUT*) circuit,
racetrack.
rennen ['rɛnən] *unreg vt, vi* to run; race; **um die
Wette ~** to have a race; **R~ (-s, -)** *nt* running;
(*Wettbewerb*) race; **das R~ machen** (*lit, fig*) to
win (the race).
Renner (-s, -) (*umg*) *m* winner, worldbeater.
Renn- *zW:* **~fahrer** *m* racing driver (*BRIT*),
race car driver (*US*); **~pferd** *nt* racehorse;

~platz *m* racecourse; **~rad** *nt* racing cycle;
~sport *m* racing; **~wagen** *m* racing car
(*BRIT*), race car (*US*).
renommiert [renɔ'miːrt] *adj:* **~ (wegen)**
renowned (for), famous (for).
renovieren [reno'viːrən] *vt* to renovate.
Renovierung *f* renovation.
rentabel [rɛn'taːbəl] *adj* profitable, lucrative.
Rentabilität [rɛntabili'tɛːt] *f* profitability.
Rente ['rɛntə] **(-, -n)** *f* pension.
Renten- *zW:* **~basis** *f* annuity basis;
~empfänger *m* pensioner; **~papier** *nt* (*FIN*)
fixed-interest security; **~versicherung** *f*
pension scheme.
Rentier ['rɛntiːr] *nt* reindeer.
rentieren [rɛn'tiːrən] *vi, vr* to pay, be
profitable; **das rentiert (sich) nicht** it's not
worth it.
Rentner(in) ['rɛntnər(ɪn)] **(-s, -)** *m(f)* pensioner.
Reparation [reparatsi'oːn] *f* reparation.
Reparatur [repara'tuːr] *f* repairing; repair;
etw in ~ geben to have sth repaired;
r~bedürftig *adj* in need of repair;
~werkstatt *f* repair shop; (*AUT*) garage.
reparieren [repa'riːrən] *vt* to repair.
Repertoire [repɛrto'aːr] **(-s, -s)** *nt* repertoire.
Reportage [repɔr'taːʒə] **(-, -n)** *f* report.
Reporter(in) [re'pɔrtər(ɪn)] **(-s, -)** *m(f)*
reporter, commentator.
Repräsentant(in) [reprɛzɛn'tant(ɪn)] *m(f)*
representative.
repräsentativ [reprɛzɛnta'tiːf] *adj*
representative; (*Geschenk etc*) prestigious;
die ~en Pflichten eines Botschafters the
social duties of an ambassador.
repräsentieren [reprɛzɛn'tiːrən] *vt* to
represent ♦ *vi* to perform official duties.
Repressalien [reprɛ'saːliən] *pl* reprisals *pl*.
reprivatisieren [reprivati'ziːrən] *vt* to
denationalize.
Reprivatisierung *f* denationalization.
Reproduktion [reprodɔktsi'oːn] *f*
reproduction.
reproduzieren [reprodu'tsiːrən] *vt* to
reproduce.
Reptil [rɛp'tiːl] **(-s, -ien)** *nt* reptile.
Republik [repu'bliːk] *f* republic.
Republikaner [republi'kaːnər] **(-s, -)** *m*
republican.
republikanisch *adj* republican.
Requisiten *pl* (*THEAT*) props *pl*, properties *pl*
(*form*).
Reservat [rezɛr'vaːt] **(-(e)s, -e)** *nt* reservation.
Reserve [re'zɛrvə] **(-, -n)** *f* reserve; **jdn aus
der ~ locken** to bring sb out of his/her shell;
~rad *nt* (*AUT*) spare wheel; **~spieler** *m*
reserve; **~tank** *m* reserve tank.
reservieren [rezɛr'viːrən] *vt* to reserve.
reserviert *adj* (*Platz, Mensch*) reserved.
Reservist [rezɛr'vɪst] *m* reservist.
Reservoir [rezɛrvo'aːr] **(-s, -e)** *nt* reservoir.
Residenz [rezi'dɛnts] *f* residence, seat.

residieren [rezi'di:rən] *vi* to reside.
Resignation [rezɪgnatsi'o:n] *f* resignation.
resignieren [rezɪ'gni:rən] *vi* to resign.
resolut [rezo'lu:t] *adj* resolute.
Resolution [rezolutsi'o:n] *f* resolution;
  (*Bittschrift*) petition.
Resonanz [rezo'nants] *f* (*lit, fig*) resonance;
  ~**boden** *m* sounding board; ~**kasten** *m*
  soundbox.
Resopal ® [rezo'pa:l] (**-s**) *nt* Formica ®.
resozialisieren [rezotsiali'zi:rən] *vt* to
  rehabilitate.
Resozialisierung *f* rehabilitation.
Respekt [rɛ'spɛkt] (**-(e)s**) *m* respect; (*Angst*)
  fear; **bei allem** ~ **(vor jdm/etw)** with all due
  respect (to sb/for sth).
respektabel [rɛspɛk'ta:bəl] *adj* respectable.
respektieren [rɛspɛk'ti:rən] *vt* to respect.
respektlos *adj* disrespectful.
Respektsperson *f* person commanding
  respect.
respektvoll *adj* respectful.
Ressentiment [rɛsäti'mã:] (**-s, -s**) *nt*
  resentment.
Ressort [rɛ'so:r] (**-s, -s**) *nt* department; **in das**
  ~ **von jdm fallen** (*lit, fig*) to be sb's
  department.
Ressourcen [rɛ'sʊrsən] *pl* resources *pl*.
Rest [rɛst] (**-(e)s, -e**) *m* remainder, rest;
  (*Über~*) remains *pl*; **Reste** *pl* (*COMM*)
  remnants *pl*; **das hat mir den** ~ **gegeben**
  (*umg*) that finished me off.
Restaurant [rɛsto'rā:] (**-s, -s**) *nt* restaurant.
Restauration [rɛstauratsi'o:n] *f* restoration.
restaurieren [rɛstau'ri:rən] *vt* to restore.
Restaurierung *f* restoration.
Rest- *zW*: ~**betrag** *m* remainder, outstanding
  sum; **r~lich** *adj* remaining; **r~los** *adj*
  complete; ~**posten** *m* (*COMM*) remaining
  stock.
Resultat [rezʊl'ta:t] (**-(e)s, -e**) *nt* result.
Retorte [re'tɔrtə] (**-, -n**) *f* retort; **aus der** ~
  (*umg*) synthetic.
Retortenbaby *nt* test-tube baby.
retour [re'tu:r] *adv* (*veraltet*) back.
Retouren *pl* (*Waren*) returns *pl*.
retten ['rɛtən] *vt* to save, rescue ♦ *vr* to
  escape; **bist du noch zu** ~? (*umg*) are you
  out of your mind?; **sich vor etw** *dat* **nicht**
  mehr ~ **können** (*fig*) to be swamped with
  sth.
Retter(in) (**-s, -**) *m(f)* rescuer, saviour (*BRIT*),
  savior (*US*).
Rettich ['rɛtɪç] (**-s, -e**) *m* radish.
Rettung *f* rescue; (*Hilfe*) help; **seine letzte** ~
  his last hope.
Rettungs- *zW*: ~**aktion** *f* rescue operation;
  ~**boot** *nt* lifeboat; ~**dienst** *m* rescue service;
  ~**gürtel** *m* lifebelt, life preserver (*US*);
  r~los *adj* hopeless; ~**ring** *m*
  = **Rettungsgürtel**; ~**schwimmer** *m* lifesaver;
  (*am Strand*) lifeguard; ~**wagen** *m*
  ambulance.
Return-Taste [ri'tø:rntastə] *f* (*COMPUT*)
  return key.
retuschieren [retu'ʃi:rən] *vt* (*PHOT*) to
  retouch.
Reue ['rɔyə] (**-**) *f* remorse; (*Bedauern*) regret.
reuen *vt*: **es reut ihn** he regrets it, he is sorry
  about it.
reuig ['rɔyɪç] *adj* penitent.
reumütig *adj* remorseful; (*Sünder*) contrite.
Reuse ['rɔyzə] (**-, -n**) *f* fish trap.
Revanche [re'vã:ʃə] (**-, -n**) *f* revenge; (*SPORT*)
  return match.
revanchieren [revã'ʃi:rən] *vr* (*sich rächen*) to
  get one's own back, have one's revenge;
  (*erwidern*) to reciprocate, return the
  compliment.
Revers [re'vɛ:r] (**-, -**) *nt or m* lapel.
revidieren [revi'di:rən] *vt* to revise; (*COMM*) to
  audit.
Revier [re'vi:r] (**-s, -e**) *nt* district; (*MIN*:
  Kohlen~) (coal)mine; (*Jagd~*) preserve;
  (*Polizei~*) police station, station house (*US*);
  (*Dienstbereich*) beat (*BRIT*), precinct (*US*);
  (*MIL*) sick bay.
Revision [revizi'o:n] *f* revision; (*COMM*)
  auditing; (*JUR*) appeal.
Revisionsverhandlung *f* appeal hearing.
Revisor [re'vi:zor] (**-s, -en**) *m* (*COMM*) auditor.
Revolte [re'vɔltə] (**-, -n**) *f* revolt.
Revolution [revolutsi'o:n] *f* revolution.
revolutionär [revolutsio'nɛ:r] *adj*
  revolutionary.
Revolutionär(in) [revolutsio'nɛ:r(ɪn)] (**-s, -e**)
  m(f) revolutionary.
revolutionieren [revolutsio'ni:rən] *vt* to
  revolutionize.
Revoluzzer [revo'lutsər] (**-s, -**) (*pej*) *m* would-
  be revolutionary.
Revolver [re'vɔlvər] (**-s, -**) *m* revolver.
Revue [rə'vy:] (**-, -n**) *f*: **etw** ~ **passieren lassen**
  (*fig*) to pass sth in review.
Reykjavik ['raɪkjavi:k] (**-s**) *nt* Reykjavik.
Rezensent [retsen'zɛnt] *m* reviewer, critic.
rezensieren [retsen'zi:rən] *vt* to review.
Rezension *f* review.
Rezept [re'tsept] (**-(e)s, -e**) *nt* (*KOCH*) recipe;
  (*MED*) prescription.
Rezeption [retseptsi'o:n] *f* (*von Hotel:*
  Empfang) reception.
rezeptpflichtig *adj* available only on
  prescription.
Rezession [retsesi'o:n] *f* (*FIN*) recession.
rezitieren [retsi'ti:rən] *vt* to recite.
R-Gespräch ['ɛrgəʃprɛːç] *nt* (*TEL*) reverse
  charge call (*BRIT*), collect call (*US*).
Rh *abk* (= *Rhesus(faktor) positiv*) Rh positive.
rh *abk* (= *Rhesus(faktor) negativ*) Rh negative.
Rhabarber [ra'barbər] (**-s**) *m* rhubarb.
Rhein [raɪn] (**-(e)s**) *m* Rhine.
rhein. *abk* = **rheinisch**.
Rheingau *m* wine-growing area along the

Rhine.

Rheinhessen *nt* wine-growing area along the *Rhine.*

rheinisch *adj attrib* Rhenish, Rhineland.

Rheinland *nt* Rhineland.

Rheinländer(in) *m(f)* Rhinelander.

Rheinland-Pfalz *nt* Rhineland-Palatinate.

Rhesusfaktor ['re:zusfaktɔr] *m* rhesus factor.

Rhetorik [re'to:rɪk] *f* rhetoric.

rhetorisch [re'to:rɪʃ] *adj* rhetorical.

Rheuma ['rɔyma] (-s) *nt* rheumatism.

Rheumatismus [rɔyma'tɪsmʊs] *m* rheumatism.

Rhinozeros [ri'no:tserɔs] (- *od* -ses, -se) *nt* rhinoceros; (*umg: Dummkopf*) fool.

Rhld. *abk* = **Rheinland**.

Rhodesien [ro'de:ziən] (-s) *nt* Rhodesia.

Rhodos ['ro:dɔs] (-) *nt* Rhodes.

rhythmisch ['rytmɪʃ] *adj* rythmical.

Rhythmus *m* rhythm.

RIAS ['ri:as] (-) *m abk* (= *Rundfunk im amerikanischen Sektor (Berlin)*) broadcasting station in the former American sector of Berlin.

Richtantenne ['rɪçt|antɛnə] (-, -n) *f* directional aerial (*bes BRIT*) *od* antenna.

richten ['rɪçtən] *vt* to direct; (*Waffe*) to aim; (*einstellen*) to adjust; (*instand setzen*) to repair; (*zurechtmachen*) to prepare, get ready; (*adressieren: Briefe, Anfragen*) to address; (*Bitten, Forderungen*) to make; (*in Ordnung bringen*) to do, fix; (*bestrafen*) to pass judgement on ♦ *vr*: **sich ~ nach** to go by; **~ an** +*akk* to direct at; (*fig*) to direct to; (*Briefe etc*) to address to; (*Bitten etc*) to make to; **~ auf** +*akk* to aim at; **wir ~ uns ganz nach unseren Kunden** we are guided entirely by our customers' wishes.

Richter(in) (-s, -) *m(f)* judge; **sich zum ~ machen** (*fig*) to set (o.s.) up in judgement; **r~lich** *adj* judicial.

Richtgeschwindigkeit *f* recommended speed.

richtig *adj* right, correct; (*echt*) proper ♦ *adv* correctly, right; (*umg: sehr*) really; **der/die R~e** the right one *od* person; **das R~e** the right thing; **die Uhr geht ~** the clock is right; **R~keit** *f* correctness; **das hat schon seine R~keit** it's right enough; **~stellen** *vt* to correct; **R~stellung** *f* correction, rectification.

Richt- *zW*: **~linie** *f* guideline; **~preis** *m* recommended price; **~schnur** *f* (*fig: Grundsatz*) guiding principle.

Richtung *f* direction; (*Tendenz*) tendency, orientation; **in jeder ~** each way.

richtungweisend *adj*: **~ sein** to point the way (ahead).

rieb *etc* [ri:p] *vb siehe* **reiben**.

riechen ['ri:çən] *unreg vt, vi* to smell; **an etw** *dat* **~** to smell sth; **es riecht nach Gas** there's a smell of gas; **ich kann das/ihn nicht ~** (*umg*)

I can't stand it/him; das konnte ich doch nicht ~! (*umg*) how was I (supposed) to know?

Riecher (-s, -) *m*: **einen guten** *od* **den richtigen ~ für etw haben** (*umg*) to have a nose for sth.

Ried [ri:t] (-(e)s, -e) *nt* reed; (*Moor*) marsh.

rief *etc* [ri:f] *vb siehe* **rufen**.

Riege ['ri:gə] (-, -n) *f* team, squad.

Riegel ['ri:gəl] (-s, -) *m* bolt, bar; **einer Sache** *dat* **einen ~ vorschieben** (*fig*) to clamp down on sth.

Riemen ['ri:mən] (-s, -) *m* strap; (*Gürtel, TECH*) belt; (*NAUT*) oar; **sich am ~ reißen** (*fig: umg*) to get a grip on o.s.; **~antrieb** *m* belt drive.

Riese ['ri:zə] (-n, -n) *m* giant.

rieseln *vi* to trickle; (*Schnee*) to fall gently.

Riesen- *zW*: **~erfolg** *m* enormous success; **~gebirge** *nt* (*GEOG*) Sudeten Mountains *pl*; **r~groß** *adj*, **r~ haft** *adj* colossal, gigantic, huge; **~rad** *nt* big *od* Ferris wheel; **~schritt** *m*: **sich mit ~schritten nähern** (*fig*) to be drawing on apace; **~slalom** *m* (*SKI*) giant slalom.

riesig ['ri:zɪç] *adj* enormous, huge, vast.

Riesin *f* giantess.

riet *etc* [ri:t] *vb siehe* **raten**.

Riff [rɪf] (-(e)s, -e) *nt* reef.

rigoros [rigo'ro:s] *adj* rigorous.

Rille ['rɪlə] (-, -n) *f* groove.

Rind [rɪnt] (-(e)s, -er) *nt* ox; (*Kuh*) cow; (*KOCH*) beef; **Rinder** *pl* cattle *pl*; **vom ~** beef.

Rinde ['rɪndə] (-, -n) *f* rind; (*Baum~*) bark; (*Brot~*) crust.

Rinderbraten *m* roast beef.

Rinderwahn ['rɪndərva:n] *m* mad cow disease.

Rindfleisch *nt* beef.

Rindvieh *nt* cattle *pl*; (*umg*) blockhead, stupid oaf.

Ring [rɪŋ] (-(e)s, -e) *m* ring; **~buch** *nt* ring binder.

ringeln ['rɪŋəln] *vt* (*Pflanze*) to (en)twine; (*Schwanz etc*) to curl ♦ *vr* to go curly, curl; (*Rauch*) to curl up(wards).

Ringelnatter *f* grass snake.

Ringeltaube *f* wood pigeon.

ringen *unreg vi* to wrestle; **nach** *od* **um etw ~** (*streben*) to struggle for sth; **R~** (-s) *nt* wrestling.

Ringer (-s, -) *m* wrestler.

Ring- *zW*: **~finger** *m* ring finger; **r~förmig** *adj* ring-shaped; **~kampf** *m* wrestling bout; **~richter** *m* referee.

rings *adv*: **~ um** round; **~herum** *adv* round about.

Ringstraße *f* ring road.

ringsum(her) [rɪŋs'|ʊm, 'rɪŋs|ʊm'he:r] *adv* (*rundherum*) round about; (*überall*) all round.

Rinne ['rɪnə] (-, -n) *f* gutter, drain.

rinnen *unreg vi* to run, trickle.

Rinnsal (-s, -e) *nt* trickle of water.

Rinnstein *m* gutter.

Rippchen ['rɪpçən] *nt* small rib; cutlet.
Rippe ['rɪpə] (-, -n) *f* rib.
Rippen- *zW*: ~**fellentzündung** *f* pleurisy; ~**speer** *m od nt* (*KOCH*): **Kasseler** ~**speer** *slightly cured pork spare rib*; ~**stoß** *m* dig in the ribs.
Risiko ['riːziko] (-s, -s *od* **Risiken**) *nt* risk; **r**~**behaftet** *adj* fraught with risk; ~**investition** *f* sunk cost.
riskant [rɪs'kant] *adj* risky, hazardous.
riskieren [rɪs'kiːrən] *vt* to risk.
riß *etc* [rɪs] *vb siehe* **reißen**.
Riß (-sses, -sse) *m* tear; (*in Mauer, Tasse etc*) crack; (*in Haut*) scratch; (*TECH*) design.
rissig ['rɪsɪç] *adj* torn; cracked; scratched.
ritt *etc* [rɪt] *vb siehe* **reiten**.
Ritt (-(e)s, -e) *m* ride.
Ritter (-s, -) *m* knight; **jdn zum** ~ **schlagen** to knight sb; **arme** ~ *pl* (*KOCH*) sweet French toast, made with bread soaked in milk; **r**~**lich** *adj* chivalrous; ~**schlag** *m* knighting; ~**tum** (-s) *nt* chivalry; ~**zeit** *f* age of chivalry.
rittlings *adv* astride.
Ritual [ritu'aːl] (-s, -e *od* -ien) *nt* (*lit, fig*) ritual.
rituell [ritu'ɛl] *adj* ritual.
Ritus ['riːtʊs] (-, **Riten**) *m* rite.
Ritze ['rɪtsə] (-, -n) *f* crack, chink.
ritzen *vt* to scratch; **die Sache ist geritzt** (*umg*) it's all fixed up.
Rivale [ri'vaːlə] (-n, -n) *m*, **Rivalin** *f* rival.
rivalisieren [rivali'ziːrən] *vi:* **mit jdm** ~ to compete with sb.
Rivalität [rivali'tɛːt] *f* rivalry.
Riviera [rivi'eːra] (-) *f* Riviera.
Rizinusöl ['riːtsinʊsˌøːl] *nt* castor oil.
r.-k. *abk* (= *römisch-katholisch*) R.C.
Robbe ['rɔbə] (-, -n) *f* seal.
robben ['rɔbən] *vi* (*Hilfsverb sein: auch MIL*) to crawl (*using elbows*).
Robbenfang *m* seal hunting.
Robe ['roːbə] (-, -n) *f* robe.
Roboter ['rɔbɔtər] (-s, -) *m* robot; ~**technik** *f* robotics *sing*.
Robotik ['rɔbɔtɪk] *f* robotics *sing*.
robust [ro'bʊst] *adj* (*Mensch, Gesundheit*) robust; (*Material*) tough.
roch *etc* [rɔx] *vb siehe* **riechen**.
Rochade [rɔ'xaːdə] (-, -n) *f* (*SCHACH*): **die kleine/große** ~ castling king's side/queen's side.
röcheln ['rœçəln] *vi* to wheeze; (*Sterbender*) to give the death rattle.
Rock¹ [rɔk] (-(e)s, ⁼e) *m* skirt; (*Jackett*) jacket; (*Uniform*~) tunic.
Rock² [rɔk] (-(s), -(s)) *m* (*MUS*) rock; ~**musik** *f* rock music.
Rockzipfel *m*: **an Mutters** ~ **hängen** (*umg*) to cling to (one's) mother's skirts.
Rodel ['roːdəl] (-s, -) *m* toboggan; ~**bahn** *f* toboggan run.
rodeln *vi* to toboggan.

roden ['roːdən] *vt, vi* to clear.
Rogen ['roːgən] (-s, -) *m* roe.
Roggen ['rɔgən] (-s, -) *m* rye; ~**brot** *nt* rye bread; (*Vollkornbrot*) black bread.
roh [roː] *adj* raw; (*Mensch*) coarse, crude; ~**e Gewalt** brute force; **R**~**bau** *m* shell of a building; **R**~**eisen** *nt* pig iron; **R**~**fassung** *f* rough draft; **R**~**kost** *f* raw fruit and vegetables *pl*; **R**~**ling** *m* ruffian; **R**~**material** *nt* raw material; **R**~**öl** *nt* crude oil.
Rohr [roːr] (-(e)s, -e) *nt* pipe, tube; (*BOT*) cane; (*Schilf*) reed; (*Gewehr*~) barrel; ~**bruch** *m* burst pipe.
Röhre ['røːrə] (-, -n) *f* tube, pipe; (*RUNDF etc*) valve; (*Back*~) oven.
Rohr- *zW*: ~**geflecht** *nt* wickerwork; ~**leger** (-s, -) *m* plumber; ~**leitung** *f* pipeline; ~**post** *f* pneumatic post; ~**spatz** *m*: **schimpfen wie ein** ~**spatz** (*umg*) to curse and swear; ~**stock** *m* cane; ~**stuhl** *m* basket chair; ~**zucker** *m* cane sugar.
Rohseide *f* raw silk.
Rohstoff *m* raw material.
Rokoko ['rɔkoko] (-s) *nt* rococo.
Rollbahn *f* (*AVIAT*) runway.
Rolle ['rɔlə] (-, -n) *f* roll; (*THEAT, SOZIOLOGIE*) role; (*Garn*~ *etc*) reel, spool; (*Walze*) roller; (*Wäsche*~) mangle, wringer; **bei** *od* **in etw** *dat* **eine** ~ **spielen** to play a part in sth; **aus der** ~ **fallen** (*fig*) to forget o.s.; **keine** ~ **spielen** not to matter.
rollen *vi* to roll; (*AVIAT*) to taxi ♦ *vt* to roll; (*Wäsche*) to mangle, put through the wringer; **den Stein ins R**~ **bringen** (*fig*) to start the ball rolling.
Rollen- *zW*: ~**besetzung** *f* (*THEAT*) cast; ~**konflikt** *m* (*PSYCH*) role conflict; ~**spiel** *nt* role-play; ~**tausch** *m* exchange of roles; (*SOZIOLOGIE*) role reversal.
Roller (-s, -) *m* scooter; (*Welle*) roller.
Roll- *zW*: ~**feld** *nt* runway; ~**kragen** *m* roll *od* polo neck; ~**(l)aden** *m* shutter; ~**mops** *m* pickled herring.
Rollo ['rɔlo] (-, -s) *nt* (roller) blind.
Roll- *zW*: ~**schrank** *m* roll-fronted cupboard; ~**schuh** *m* roller skate; ~**schuhlaufen** *nt* roller skating; ~**splitt** *m* grit; ~**stuhl** *m* wheelchair; ~**treppe** *f* escalator.
Rom [roːm] (-s) *nt* Rome; **das sind Zustände wie im alten** ~ (*umg: unmoralisch*) it's disgraceful; (: *primitiv*) it's medieval (*umg*).
röm. *abk* = *römisch*.
Roman [ro'maːn] (-s, -e) *m* novel; (**jdm) einen ganzen** ~ **erzählen** (*umg*) to give (sb) a long rigmarole; ~**heft** *nt* pulp novel.
romanisch *adj* (*Volk, Sprache*) Romance; (*KUNST*) Romanesque.
Romanistik [roma'nɪstɪk] *f* (*UNIV*) Romance languages and literature.
Romanschreiber *m* novelist.
Romanschriftsteller *m* novelist.
Romantik [ro'mantɪk] *f* romanticism.

Romantiker(in) (-s, -) *m(f)* romanticist.
romantisch *adj* romantic.
Romanze [ro'mantsə] (-, -n) *f* romance.
Römer ['rø:mər] (-s, -) *m* wineglass; (*Mensch*) Roman; ~**topf** ® *m* (*KOCH*) ≈ (chicken) brick.
römisch ['rø:mɪʃ] *adj* Roman; ~**-katholisch** *adj* Roman Catholic.
röm.-kath. *abk* (= *römisch-katholisch*) R.C.
Rommé [rɔ'me:] (-s, -s) *nt* rummy.
röntgen ['rɛntgən] *vt* to X-ray; **R~aufnahme** *f* X-ray; **R~bild** *nt* X-ray; **R~strahlen** *pl* X-rays *pl*.
rosa ['ro:za] *adj inv* pink, rose(-coloured).
Rose ['ro:zə] (-, -n) *f* rose.
Rosé [ro'ze:] (-s, -s) *m* rosé.
Rosenkohl *m* Brussels sprouts *pl*.
Rosenkranz *m* rosary.
Rosenmontag *m* Monday of Shrovetide; *siehe auch* **Karneval**.
Rosette [ro'zɛtə] *f* rosette.
rosig ['ro:zɪç] *adj* rosy.
Rosine [ro'zi:nə] *f* raisin; **(große)** ~**n im Kopf haben** (*umg*) to have big ideas.
Rosmarin ['ro:smari:n] (-s) *m* rosemary.
Roß [rɔs] (-sses, -sse) *nt* horse, steed; **auf dem hohen** ~ **sitzen** (*fig*) to be on one's high horse; ~**kastanie** *f* horse chestnut; ~**kur** (*umg*) *f* kill-or-cure remedy.
Rost [rɔst] (-(e)s, -e) *m* rust; (*Gitter*) grill, gridiron; (*Bett~*) springs *pl*; ~**braten** *m* roast(ed) meat, roast; ~**bratwurst** *f* grilled *od* barbecued sausage.
rosten *vi* to rust.
rösten ['rø:stən] *vt* to roast; (*Brot*) to toast
rostfrei *adj* (*Stahl*) stainless.
rostig *adj* rusty.
Röstkartoffeln *pl* fried potatoes *pl*.
Rostschutz *m* rustproofing.
rot [ro:t] *adj* red; ~ **werden, einen** ~**en Kopf bekommen** to blush, go red; ~ **sehen** (*umg*) to see red, become angry; **die R~e Armee** the Red Army; **das R~e Kreuz** the Red Cross; **das R~e Meer** the Red Sea.
Rotation [rotatsi'o:n] *f* rotation.
rot- *zW:* ~**bäckig** *adj* red-cheeked; **R~barsch** *m* rosefish; ~**blond** *adj* strawberry blond.
Röte ['rø:tə] (-) *f* redness.
Röteln *pl* German measles *sing*.
röten *vt, vr* to redden.
rothaarig *adj* red-haired.
rotieren [ro'ti:rən] *vi* to rotate.
Rot- *zW:* ~**käppchen** *nt* Little Red Riding Hood; ~**kehlchen** *nt* robin; ~**kohl** *m* red cabbage; ~**kraut** *nt* red cabbage; ~**stift** *m* red pencil; ~**wein** *m* red wine.
Rotz [rɔts] (-es, -e) (*umg*) *m* snot; **r~frech** (*umg*) *adj* cocky; **r~näsig** (*umg*) *adj* snotty-nosed.
Rouge [ru:ʒ] (-s, -s) *nt* rouge.
Roulade [ru'la:də] (-, -n) *f* (*KOCH*) beef olive.
Roulett(e) [ru'lɛt(ə)] (-s, -s) *nt* roulette.

Route ['ru:tə] (-, -n) *f* route.
Routine [ru'ti:nə] *f* experience; (*Gewohnheit*) routine.
routiniert [ruti'ni:ərt] *adj* experienced.
Rowdy ['raʊdɪ] (-s, -s *od* **Rowdies**) *m* hooligan; (*zerstörerisch*) vandal; (*lärmend*) rowdy (type).
Ruanda [ru'anda] *nt* Rwanda.
ruandisch *adj* Rwandan.
rubbeln ['rʊbəln] (*umg*) *vt, vi* to rub.
Rübe ['ry:bə] (-, -n) *f* turnip; **gelbe** ~ carrot; **rote** ~ beetroot (*BRIT*), beet (*US*).
Rübenzucker *m* beet sugar.
Rubin [ru'bi:n] (-s, -e) *m* ruby.
Rubrik [ru'bri:k] *f* heading; (*Spalte*) column.
Ruck [rʊk] (-(e)s, -e) *m* jerk, jolt; **sich** *dat* **einen** ~ **geben** (*fig: umg*) to make an effort.
ruck *adv:* **das geht** ~, **zuck** it won't take a second.
Rückantwort *f* reply, answer; **um** ~ **wird gebeten** please reply.
ruckartig *adj:* **er stand** ~ **auf** he shot to his feet.
Rück- *zW:* ~**besinnung** *f* recollection; **r~bezüglich** *adj* reflexive; ~**blende** *f* flashback; **r~blenden** *vi* to flash back; ~**blick** *m:* **im** ~**blick auf etw** *akk* looking back on sth; **r~blickend** *adj* retrospective ♦ *adv* in retrospect; **r~datieren** *vt* to backdate.
Rücken (-s, -) *m* back; (*Berg~*) ridge; **jdm in den** ~ **fallen** (*fig*) to stab sb in the back.
rücken *vt, vi* to move.
Rücken- *zW:* ~**deckung** *f* backing; ~**lage** *f* supine position; ~**lehne** *f* back (of chair); ~**mark** *nt* spinal cord; ~**schwimmen** *nt* backstroke; ~**stärkung** *f* (*fig*) moral support; ~**wind** *m* following wind.
Rück- *zW:* ~**erstattung** *f* return, restitution; ~**fahrkarte** *f* return ticket (*BRIT*), round-trip ticket (*US*); ~**fahrt** *f* return journey; ~**fall** *m* relapse; **r~fällig** *adj* relapsed; **r~fällig werden** to relapse; ~**flug** *m* return flight; ~**frage** *f* question; **nach** ~**frage bei der zuständigen Behörde** ... after checking this with the appropriate authority ...; **r~fragen** *vi* to inquire; (*nachprüfen*) to check; ~**führung** *f* (*von Menschen*) repatriation, return; ~**gabe** *f* return; **gegen** ~**gabe** (+*gen*) on return (of); ~**gang** *m* decline, fall; **r~gängig** *adj:* **etw r~gängig machen** (*widerrufen*) to undo sth; (*Bestellung*) to cancel sth; ~**gewinnung** *f* recovery; (*von Land, Gebiet*) reclaiming; (*aus verbrauchten Stoffen*) recycling.
Rückgrat *nt* spine, backbone.
Rück- *zW:* ~**griff** *m* recourse; ~**halt** *m* backing; (*Einschränkung*) reserve; **r~haltlos** *adj* unreserved; ~**hand** *f* (*SPORT*) backhand; **r~kaufbar** *adj* redeemable; ~**kehr** (-, -en) *f* return; ~**koppelung** *f* feedback; ~**lage** *f* reserve, savings *pl*; ~**lauf** *m* reverse running; (*beim Tonband*)

rewind; (*von Maschinenteil*) return travel;
r~läufig *adj* declining, falling; **eine r~läufige
Entwicklung** a decline; **~licht** *nt* rear light;
r~lings *adv* from behind; (*rückwärts*)
backwards; **~meldung** *f* (*UNIV*)
reregistration; **~nahme (-, -n)** *f* taking
back; **~porto** *nt* return postage; **~reise** *f*
return journey; (*NAUT*) home voyage; **~ruf**
m recall.
Rucksack ['rʊkzak] *m* rucksack.
Rück- *zW:* **~schau** *f* reflection; **r~schauend**
adj = **rückblickend**; **~schlag** *m* setback;
~schluß *m* conclusion; **~schritt** *m*
retrogression; **r~schrittlich** *adj* reactionary;
(*Entwicklung*) retrograde; **~seite** *f* back;
(*von Münze etc*) reverse; **siehe ~seite** see
over(leaf); **r~setzen** *vt* (*COMPUT*) to reset.
Rücksicht *f* consideration; **~ nehmen auf**
+*akk* to show consideration for; **~nahme** *f*
consideration.
rücksichtslos *adj* inconsiderate; (*Fahren*)
reckless; (*unbarmherzig*) ruthless.
Rücksichtslosigkeit *f* lack of consideration;
(*beim Fahren*) recklessness;
(*Unbarmherzigkeit*) ruthlessness.
rücksichtsvoll *adj* considerate.
Rück- *zW:* **~sitz** *m* back seat; **~spiegel** *m*
(*AUT*) rear-view mirror; **~spiel** *nt* return
match; **~sprache** *f* further discussion *od*
talk; **~sprache mit jdm nehmen** to confer
with sb; **~stand** *m* arrears *pl*; (*Verzug*) delay;
r~ständig *adj* backward, out-of-date;
(*Zahlungen*) in arrears; **~stau** *m* (*AUT*)
tailback (*BRIT*), line of cars; **~stoß** *m*
recoil; **~strahler (-s, -)** *m* rear reflector;
~strom *m* (*von Menschen, Fahrzeugen*)
return; **~taste** *f* (*an Schreibmaschine*)
backspace key; **~tritt** *m* resignation;
~trittbremse *f* backpedal brake;
~trittsklausel *f* (*Vertrag*) escape clause;
~vergütung *f* repayment; (*COMM*) refund;
r~versichern *vt, vi* to reinsure ♦ *vr* to check
(up *od* back); **~versicherung** *f* reinsurance;
r~wärtig *adj* rear; **r~wärts** *adv* backward(s),
back; **~wärtsgang** *m* (*AUT*) reverse gear;
im ~wärtsgang fahren to reverse; **~weg** *m*
return journey, way back; **r~wirkend** *adj*
retroactive; **~wirkung** *f* repercussion; **eine
Zahlung mit ~wirkung vom ...** a payment
backdated to ...; **eine Gesetzesänderung mit
~wirkung vom ...** an amendment made
retrospective to ...; **~zahlung** *f* repayment;
~zieher (*umg*) *m:* **einen ~zieher machen** to
back out; **~zug** *m* retreat; **~zugsgefecht** *nt*
(*MIL, fig*) rearguard action.
rüde ['ry:də] *adj* blunt, gruff.
Rüde (-n, -n) *m* male dog.
Rudel ['ru:dəl] **(-s, -)** *nt* pack; (*von Hirschen*)
herd.
Ruder ['ru:dər] **(-s, -)** *nt* oar; (*Steuer*) rudder;
das ~ fest in der Hand haben (*fig*) to be in
control of the situation; **~boot** *nt* rowing

boat; **~er (-s, -)** *m* rower, oarsman.
rudern *vt, vi* to row; **mit den Armen ~** (*fig*) to
flail one's arms about.
Ruf [ru:f] **(-(e)s, -e)** *m* call, cry; (*Ansehen*)
reputation; (*UNIV: Berufung*) offer of a chair.
rufen *unreg vt, vi* to call; (*aus~*) to cry; **um Hilfe
~** to call for help; **das kommt mir wie
gerufen** that's just what I needed.
Rüffel ['ryfəl] **(-s, -)** (*umg*) *m* telling-off,
ticking-off.
Ruf- *zW:* **~mord** *m* character assassination;
~name *m* usual (first) name; **~nummer** *f*
(tele)phone number; **~säule** *f* (*für Taxi*)
telephone; (*an Autobahn*) emergency
telephone; **~zeichen** *nt* (*RUNDF*) call sign;
(*TEL*) ringing tone.
Rüge ['ry:gə] **(-, -n)** *f* reprimand, rebuke.
rügen *vt* to reprimand.
Ruhe ['ru:ə] **(-)** *f* rest; (*Ungestörtheit*) peace,
quiet; (*Gelassenheit, Stille*) calm; (*Schweigen*)
silence; **~! be quiet!, silence!; angenehme
~!** sleep well!; **~ bewahren** to stay cool *od*
calm; **das läßt ihm keine ~** he can't stop
thinking about it; **sich zur ~ setzen** to
retire; **die ~ weghaben** (*umg*) to be
unflappable; **immer mit der ~** (*umg*) don't
panic; **die letzte ~ finden** (*liter*) to be laid to
rest; **~lage** *f* (*von Mensch*) reclining
position; (*MED: bei Bruch*) immobile position;
r~los *adj* restless.
ruhen *vi* to rest; (*Verkehr*) to cease; (*Arbeit*) to
stop, cease; (*Waffen*) to be laid down;
(*begraben sein*) to lie, be buried.
Ruhe- *zW:* **~pause** *f* break; **~platz** *m* resting
place; **~stand** *m* retirement; **~stätte** *f:*
letzte ~stätte final resting place; **~störung**
f breach of the peace; **~tag** *m* closing day.
ruhig ['ru:ɪç] *adj* quiet; (*bewegungslos*) still;
(*Hand*) steady; (*gelassen, friedlich*) calm;
(*Gewissen*) clear; **tu das ~** feel free to do
that; **etw ~ mitansehen** (*gleichgültig*) to
stand by and watch sth; **du könntest ~ mal
etwas für mich tun!** it's about time you did
something for me!
Ruhm [ru:m] **(-(e)s)** *m* fame, glory.
rühmen ['ry:mən] *vt* to praise ♦ *vr* to boast.
rühmlich *adj* praiseworthy; (*Ausnahme*)
notable.
ruhmlos *adj* inglorious.
ruhmreich *adj* glorious.
Ruhr [ru:r] **(-)** *f* dysentery.
Rührei ['ry:r|aɪ] *nt* scrambled egg.
rühren *vt* (*lit, fig*) to move, stir (*auch KOCH*)
♦ *vr* (*lit, fig*) to move, stir ♦ *vi:* **~ von** to come
od stem from; **~ an** +*akk* to touch; (*fig*) to
touch on.
rührend *adj* touching, moving; **das ist ~ von
Ihnen** that is sweet of you.
Ruhrgebiet *nt* Ruhr (area).
rührig *adj* active, lively.
rührselig *adj* sentimental, emotional.
Rührung *f* emotion.

Ruin [ru'iːn] **(-s)** *m* ruin; **vor dem ~ stehen** to be on the brink *od* verge of ruin.

Ruine (-, -n) *f* (*lit, fig*) ruin.

ruinieren [ruiˈniːrən] *vt* to ruin.

rülpsen ['rʏlpsən] *vi* to burp, belch.

Rum [rom] **(-s, -s)** *m* rum.

rum (*umg*) *adv* = **herum**.

Rumäne [ruˈmɛːnə] **(-n, -n)** *m* Romanian.

Rumänien (-s) *nt* Romania.

Rumänin *f* Romanian.

rumänisch *adj* Romanian.

rumfuhrwerken ['romfuːrvɛrkən] (*umg*) *vt* to bustle around.

Rummel ['roməl] **(-s)** (*umg*) *m* hurly-burly; (*Jahrmarkt*) fair; **~platz** *m* fairground, fair.

rumoren [ruˈmoːrən] *vi* to be noisy, make a noise.

Rumpelkammer ['rompəlkamər] *f* junk room.

rumpeln *vi* to rumble; (*holpern*) to jolt.

Rumpf [rompf] **(-(e)s, ⁼e)** *m* trunk, torso; (*AVIAT*) fuselage; (*NAUT*) hull.

rümpfen ['rʏmpfən] *vt* (*Nase*) to turn up.

Rumtopf *m* soft fruit in rum.

rund [ront] *adj* round ♦ *adv* (*etwa*) around; **~ um etw** round sth; **jetzt geht's ~** (*umg*) this is where the fun starts; **wenn er das erfährt, geht's ~** (*umg*) there'll be a to-do when he finds out; **R~bogen** *m* Norman *od* Romanesque arch; **R~brief** *m* circular.

Runde ['rondə] **(-, -n)** *f* round; (*in Rennen*) lap; (*Gesellschaft*) circle; **die ~ machen** to do the rounds; (*herumgegeben werden*) to be passed round; **über die ~n kommen** (*SPORT, fig*) to pull through; **eine ~ spendieren** *od* **schmeißen** (*umg: Getränke*) to stand a round.

runden *vt* to make round ♦ *vr* (*fig*) to take shape.

rund- *zW:* **~erneuert** *adj* (*Reifen*) remoulded (*BRIT*), remolded (*US*); **R~fahrt** *f* (round) trip; **R~frage** *f:* **R~frage** (**unter** +*dat*) survey (of).

Rundfunk ['rontfoŋk] **(-(e)s)** *m* broadcasting; (*bes Hörfunk*) radio; (*~anstalt*) broadcasting corporation; **im ~** on the radio; **~anstalt** *f* broadcasting corporation; **~empfang** *m* reception; **~gebühr** *f* licence (*BRIT*), license (*US*); **~gerät** *nt* radio set; **~sendung** *f* broadcast, radio programme (*BRIT*) *od* program (*US*).

Rund- *zW:* **~gang** *m* (*Spaziergang*) walk; (*von Wachmann*) rounds *pl*; (*von Briefträger etc*) round; (*zur Besichtigung*): **~gang (durch)** tour (of); **r~heraus** *adv* straight out, bluntly; **r~herum** *adv* all round; (*fig: umg: völlig*) totally; **r~lich** *adj* plump, rounded; **~reise** *f* round trip; **~schreiben** *nt* (*COMM*) circular; **r~um** *adv* all around; (*fig*) completely.

Rundung *f* curve, roundness.

rundweg *adv* straight out.

runter ['rontər] (*umg*) *adv* = **herunter**; **hinunter**; **~würgen** (*umg*) *vt* (*Ärger*) to

swallow.

Runzel ['rontsəl] **(-, -n)** *f* wrinkle.

runz(e)lig *adj* wrinkled.

runzeln *vt* to wrinkle; **die Stirn ~** to frown.

Rüpel ['ryːpəl] **(-s, -)** *m* lout; **r~haft** *adj* loutish.

rupfen ['ropfən] *vt* to pluck; **wie ein gerupftes Huhn aussehen** to look like a shorn sheep.

Rupfen **(-s, -)** *m* sackcloth.

ruppig ['ropiç] *adj* rough, gruff.

Rüsche ['ryːʃə] **(-, -n)** *f* frill.

Ruß [ruːs] **(-es)** *m* soot.

Russe ['rosə] **(-n, -n)** *m* Russian.

Rüssel ['rʏsəl] **(-s, -)** *m* snout; (*Elefanten~*) trunk.

rußen *vi* to smoke; (*Ofen*) to be sooty.

rußig *adj* sooty.

Russin *f* Russian.

russisch *adj* Russian; **~e Eier** (*KOCH*) egg(s) mayonnaise.

Rußland **(-s)** *nt* Russia.

rüsten ['rʏstən] *vt, vi, vr* to prepare; (*MIL*) to arm.

rüstig ['rʏstiç] *adj* sprightly, vigorous; **R~keit** *f* sprightliness, vigour (*BRIT*), vigor (*US*).

rustikal [rostiˈkaːl] *adj:* **sich ~ einrichten** to furnish one's home in a rustic style.

Rüstung ['rʏstoŋ] *f* preparation; (*MIL*) arming; (*Ritter~*) armour (*BRIT*), armor (*US*); (*Waffen etc*) armaments *pl*.

Rüstungs- *zW:* **~gegner** *m* opponent of the arms race; **~industrie** *f* armaments industry; **~kontrolle** *f* arms control; **~wettlauf** *m* arms race.

Rüstzeug *nt* tools *pl*; (*fig*) capacity.

Rute ['ruːtə] **(-, -n)** *f* rod, switch.

Rutsch [rotʃ] **(-(e)s, -e)** *m* slide; (*Erd~*) landslide; **guten ~!** (*umg*) have a good New Year!; **~bahn** *f* slide.

rutschen *vi* to slide; (*aus~*) to slip; **auf dem Stuhl hin und her ~** to fidget around on one's chair.

rutschfest *adj* non-slip.

rutschig *adj* slippery.

rütteln ['rʏtəln] *vt, vi* to shake, jolt; **daran ist nicht zu ~** (*fig: umg: an Grundsätzen*) there's no doubt about that.

Rüttelschwelle *f* (*AUT*) rumble strips *pl*.

S, s

S¹, s¹ [ɛs] *nt* S, s; ~ **wie Samuel** ≈ S for Sugar.
S² [ɛs] *abk* (= *Süden*) S; (= *Seite*) p; (= *Schilling*) S.
s² *abk* (= *Sekunde*) sec.; (= *siehe*) v., vid.
SA (-) *f abk* (= *Sturmabteilung*) SA.
s.a. *abk* (= *siehe auch*) see also.
Saal [zaːl] (-(e)s, **Säle**) *m* hall; (*für Sitzungen etc*) room.
Saarland ['zaːrlant] (-s) *nt* Saarland.
Saat [zaːt] (-, **-en**) *f* seed; (*Pflanzen*) crop; (*Säen*) sowing; ~**gut** *nt* seed(s *pl*).
Sabbat ['zabat] (-s, **-e**) *m* sabbath.
sabbern ['zabərn] (*umg*) *vi* to dribble.
Säbel ['zɛːbəl] (-s, -) *m* sabre (*BRIT*), saber (*US*); ~**rasseln** *nt* sabre-rattling.
Sabotage [zabo'taːʒə] (-, -) *f* sabotage.
sabotieren [zabo'tiːrən] *vt* to sabotage.
Saccharin [zaxa'riːn] (-s) *nt* saccharin.
Sachanlagen ['zax|anlaːɡən] *pl* tangible assets *pl*.
Sachbearbeiter(in) *m(f)*: ~ **(für)** (*Beamter*) official in charge (of).
Sachbuch *nt* non-fiction book.
sachdienlich *adj* relevant, helpful.
Sache ['zaxə] (-, -n) *f* thing; (*Angelegenheit*) affair, business; (*Frage*) matter; (*Pflicht*) task; (*Thema*) subject; (*JUR*) case; (*Aufgabe*) job; (*Ideal*) cause; (*umg*: *km/h*): **mit 60/100** ~**n** ≈ at 40/60 (mph); **ich habe mir die** ~ **anders vorgestellt** I had imagined things differently; **er versteht seine** ~ he knows what he's doing; **das ist so eine** ~ (*umg*) it's a bit tricky; **mach keine** ~**n!** (*umg*) don't be daft!; **bei der** ~ **bleiben** (*bei Diskussion*) to keep to the point; **bei der** ~ **sein** to be with it (*umg*); **das ist** ~ **der Polizei** this is a matter for the police; **zur** ~ to the point; **das ist eine runde** ~ that is well-balanced *od* rounded-off.
Sachertorte ['zaxərtɔrtə] *f* rich *chocolate cake*, sachertorte.
Sach- *zW*: **s~gemäß** *adj* appropriate, suitable; ~**kenntnis** *f* (*in bezug auf Wissensgebiet*) knowledge of the/his *etc* subject; (*in bezug auf* ~*lage*) knowledge of the facts; **s~kundig** *adj* (well-)informed; **sich s~kundig machen** to inform oneself; ~**lage** *f* situation, state of affairs; ~**leistung** *f* payment in kind; **s~lich** *adj* matter-of-fact; (*Kritik etc*) objective; (*Irrtum, Angabe*) factual; **bleiben Sie bitte s~lich**

don't get carried away (*umg*); (*nicht persönlich werden*) please stay objective.
sächlich ['zɛxlıç] *adj* neuter.
Sachregister *nt* subject index.
Sachschaden *m* material damage.
Sachse ['zaksə] (-n, -n) *m* Saxon.
Sachsen (-s) *nt* Saxony; ~-**Anhalt** (-s) *nt* Saxony Anhalt.
Sächsin ['zɛksın] *f* Saxon.
sächsisch ['zɛksıʃ] *adj* Saxon.
sacht(e) *adv* softly, gently.
Sach- *zW*: ~**verhalt** (-(e)s, -e) *m* facts *pl* (of the case); **s~verständig** *adj* (*Urteil*) expert; (*Publikum*) informed; ~**verständige(r)** *f(m)* expert; ~**zwang** *m* force of circumstances.
Sack [zak] (-(e)s, **-e**) *m* sack; (*aus Papier, Plastik*) bag; (*ANAT, ZOOL*) sac; (*umg!: Hoden*) balls *pl* (*!*); (: *Kerl, Bursche*) bastard (*!*); **mit** ~ **und Pack** (*umg*) with bag and baggage.
sacken *vi* to sag, sink.
Sackgasse *f* cul-de-sac, dead-end street (*US*).
Sackhüpfen *nt* sack race.
Sadismus [za'dısmus] *m* sadism.
Sadist(in) [za'dıst(ın)] *m(f)* sadist; **s~isch** *adj* sadistic.
Sadomasochismus [zadomazɔ'xısmʊs] *m* sadomasochism.
säen ['zɛːən] *vt, vi* to sow; **dünn gesät** (*fig*) thin on the ground, few and far between.
Safari [za'faːri] (-, -s) *f* safari.
Safe [zeːf] (-s, -s) *m od nt* safe.
Saft [zaft] (-(e)s, **-e**) *m* juice; (*BOT*) sap; **ohne** ~ **und Kraft** (*fig*) wishy-washy (*umg*), effete.
saftig *adj* juicy; (*Grün*) lush; (*umg: Rechnung, Ohrfeige*) hefty; (*Brief, Antwort*) hard-hitting.
Saftladen (*pej: umg*) *m* rum joint.
saftlos *adj* dry.
Sage ['zaːɡə] (-, -n) *f* saga.
Säge ['zɛːɡə] (-, -n) *f* saw; ~**blatt** *nt* saw blade; ~**mehl** *nt* sawdust.
sagen ['zaːɡən] *vt, vi*: **(jdm etw)** ~ to say (sth to sb), tell (sb sth); **unter uns gesagt** between you and me (and the gatepost (*hum umg*)); **laß dir das gesagt sein** take it from me; **das hat nichts zu** ~ that doesn't mean anything; **sagt dir der Name etwas?** does the name mean anything to you?; **das ist nicht gesagt** that's by no means certain; **sage und schreibe** (whether you) believe it or not.
sägen *vt, vi* to saw; (*hum: umg: schnarchen*) to snore, saw wood (*US*).
sagenhaft *adj* legendary; (*umg*) great, smashing.
sagenumwoben *adj* legendary.
Sägespäne *pl* wood shavings *pl*.
Sägewerk *nt* sawmill.
sah *etc* [zaː] *vb siehe* **sehen**.
Sahara [za'haːra] *f* Sahara (Desert).
Sahne ['zaːnə] (-) *f* cream.
Saison [zɛ'zõː] (-, -s) *f* season.

saisonal [zɛzo'naːl] *adj* seasonal.
Saisonarbeiter *m* seasonal worker.
saisonbedingt *adj* seasonal.
Saite ['zaɪtə] (-, -n) *f* string; **andere ~n aufziehen** (*umg*) to get tough.
Saiteninstrument *nt* string(ed) instrument.
Sakko ['zako] (-s, -s) *m od nt* jacket.
Sakrament [zakra'mɛnt] *nt* sacrament.
Sakristei [zakrɪs'taɪ] *f* sacristy.
Salami [za'laːmi] (-, -s) *f* salami.
Salat [za'laːt] (-(e)s, -e) *m* salad; (*Kopf~*) lettuce; **da haben wir den ~!** (*umg*) now we're in a fine mess; **~besteck** *nt* salad servers *pl*; **~platte** *f* salad; **~soße** *f* salad dressing.
Salbe ['zalbə] (-, -n) *f* ointment.
Salbei ['zalbaɪ] (-s) *m* sage.
salben *vt* to anoint.
Salbung *f* anointing.
salbungsvoll *adj* unctuous.
saldieren [zal'diːrən] *vt* (*COMM*) to balance.
Saldo ['zaldo] (-s, **Salden**) *m* balance; **~übertrag** *m* balance brought *od* carried forward; **~vortrag** *m* balance brought *od* carried forward.
Säle ['zɛːlə] *pl von* **Saal**.
Salmiak [zalmi'ak] (-s) *m* sal ammoniac; **~geist** *m* liquid ammonia.
Salmonellen [zalmo'nɛlən] *pl* salmonellae *pl*.
Salon [za'lõː] (-s, -s) *m* salon; **~löwe** *m* lounge lizard.
salopp [za'lɔp] *adj* casual; (*Manieren*) slovenly; (*Sprache*) slangy.
Salpeter [zal'peːtər] (-s) *m* saltpetre (*BRIT*), saltpeter (*US*); **~säure** *f* nitric acid.
Salto ['zalto] (-s, -s *od* **Salti**) *m* somersault.
Salut [za'luːt] (-(e)s, -e) *m* salute.
salutieren [zalu'tiːrən] *vi* to salute.
Salve ['zalvə] (-, -n) *f* salvo.
Salz [zalts] (-es, -e) *nt* salt; **s~arm** *adj* (*KOCH*) low-salt; **~bergwerk** *nt* salt mine.
salzen *unreg vt* to salt.
salzig *adj* salty.
Salz- *zW:* **~kartoffeln** *pl* boiled potatoes *pl*; **~säule** *f:* **zur ~säule erstarren** (*fig*) to stand (as though) rooted to the spot; **~säure** *f* hydrochloric acid; **~stange** *f* pretzel stick; **~streuer** *m* salt cellar *od* shaker (*US*); **~wasser** *nt* salt water.
Sambia ['zambia] (-s) *nt* Zambia.
sambisch *adj* Zambian.
Samen ['zaːmən] (-s, -) *m* seed; (*ANAT*) sperm; **~bank** *f* sperm bank; **~handlung** *f* seed shop.
sämig ['zɛːmɪç] *adj* thick, creamy.
Sammel- *zW:* **~anschluß** *m* (*TEL*) private (branch) exchange; (*von Privathäusern*) party line; **~antrag** *m* composite motion; **~band** *m* anthology; **~becken** *nt* reservoir; (*fig*): **~becken (von)** melting pot (for); **~begriff** *m* collective term; **~bestellung** *f* collective order; **~büchse** *f* collecting tin;

~mappe *f* folder.
sammeln *vt* to collect ♦ *vr* to assemble, gather; (*sich konzentrieren*) to collect one's thoughts.
Sammelname *m* collective term.
Sammelnummer *f* (*TEL*) private exchange number, switchboard number.
Sammelsurium [zaməl'zuːrium] *nt* hotchpotch (*BRIT*), hodgepodge (*US*).
Sammler(in) (-s, -) *m(f)* collector.
Sammlung ['zamluŋ] *f* collection; (*Konzentration*) composure.
Samstag ['zamstaːk] *m* Saturday; *siehe auch* **Dienstag**.
samstags *adv* (on) Saturdays.
samt [zamt] *präp +dat* (along) with, together with; **~ und sonders** each and every one (of them); **S~** (-(e)s, -e) *m* velvet; **in S~ und Seide** (*liter*) in silks and satins.
Samthandschuh *m:* **jdn mit ~en anfassen** (*umg*) to handle sb with kid gloves.
sämtlich ['zɛmtlɪç] *adj* (*alle*) all (the); (*vollständig*) complete; **Schillers ~e Werke** the complete works of Schiller.
Sanatorium [zana'toːrium] *nt* sanatorium (*BRIT*), sanitarium (*US*).
Sand [zant] (-(e)s, -e) *m* sand; **das/die gibt's wie ~ am Meer** (*umg*) there are piles of it/ heaps of them; **im ~e verlaufen** to peter out.
Sandale [zan'daːlə] (-, -n) *f* sandal.
Sandbank *f* sandbank.
Sandelholz ['zandəlhɔlts] (-es) *nt* sandalwood.
sandig ['zandɪç] *adj* sandy.
Sand- *zW:* **~kasten** *m* sandpit; **~kastenspiele** *pl* (*MIL*) sand-table exercises *pl*; (*fig*) tactical manoeuvrings *pl* (*BRIT*) *od* maneuverings *pl* (*US*); **~kuchen** *m* Madeira cake; **~mann** *m*, **~männchen** *nt* (*in Geschichten*) sandman; **~papier** *nt* sandpaper; **~stein** *m* sandstone; **s~strahlen** *vt, vi untr* to sandblast
sandte *etc* ['zantə] *vb siehe* **senden**.
Sanduhr *f* hourglass; (*Eieruhr*) egg timer.
sanft [zanft] *adj* soft, gentle; **~mütig** *adj* gentle, meek.
sang *etc* [zaŋ] *vb siehe* **singen**.
Sänger(in) ['zɛŋər(ɪn)] (-s, -) *m(f)* singer.
sang- und klanglos (*umg*) *adv* without any ado, quietly.
Sani ['zani] (-s, -s) (*umg*) *m* = **Sanitäter**.
sanieren [za'niːrən] *vt* to redevelop; (*Betrieb*) to make financially sound; (*Haus*) to renovate ♦ *vr* to line one's pockets; (*Unternehmen*) to become financially sound.
Sanierung *f* redevelopment; renovation.
sanitär [zani'tɛːr] *adj* sanitary; **~e Anlagen** sanitation *sing*.
Sanitäter [zani'tɛːtər] (-s, -) *m* first-aid attendant; (*in Krankenwagen*) ambulance man; (*MIL*) (medical) orderly.
Sanitätsauto *nt* ambulance.
sank *etc* [zaŋk] *vb siehe* **sinken**.
Sanktion [zaŋktsi'oːn] *f* sanction.

sanktionieren [zaŋktsio'niːrən] *vt* to sanction.
sann *etc* [zan] *vb siehe* **sinnen.**
Saphir ['zaːfiːr] (**-s, -e**) *m* sapphire.
Sarde ['zardə] (**-n, -n**) *m* Sardinian.
Sardelle [zar'dɛlə] *f* anchovy.
Sardine [zar'diːnə] *f* sardine.
Sardinien [zar'diːniən] (**-s**) *nt* Sardinia.
Sardinier(in) (**-s, -**) *m(f)* Sardinian.
sardinisch *adj* Sardinian.
sardisch *adj* Sardinian.
Sarg [zark] (**-(e)s, ̈-e**) *m* coffin; ~**nagel** (*umg*) *m* (*Zigarette*) coffin nail.
Sarkasmus [zar'kasmʊs] *m* sarcasm.
sarkastisch [zar'kastɪʃ] *adj* sarcastic.
saß *etc* [zas] *vb siehe* **sitzen.**
Satan ['zaːtan] (**-s, -e**) *m* Satan; (*fig*) devil.
Satansbraten *m* (*hum: umg*) young devil.
Satellit [zatɛ'liːt] (**-en, -en**) *m* satellite.
Satelliten- *zW:* ~**antenne** *f* satellite dish; ~**fernsehen** *nt* satellite television; ~**foto** *nt* satellite picture; ~**schüssel** *f* satellite dish; ~**station** *f* space station.
Satin [za'tɛ̃ː] (**-s, -s**) *m* satin.
Satire [za'tiːrə] (**-, -n**) *f:* ~ (**auf** +*akk*) satire (on).
Satiriker [za'tiːrikər] (**-s, -**) *m* satirist.
satirisch [za'tiːrɪʃ] *adj* satirical.
satt [zat] *adj* full; (*Farbe*) rich, deep; (*blasiert, übersättigt*) well-fed; (*selbstgefällig*) smug; **jdn/etw ~ sein** *od* **haben** to be fed-up with sb/sth; **sich ~ hören/sehen an** +*dat* to see/ hear enough of; **sich ~ essen** to eat one's fill; ~ **machen** to be filling.
Sattel ['zatəl] (**-s, ̈-**) *m* saddle; (*Berg*) ridge; **s~fest** *adj* (*fig*) proficient.
satteln *vt* to saddle.
Sattelschlepper *m* articulated lorry (*BRIT*), artic (*BRIT umg*), semitrailer (*US*), semi (*US umg*).
Satteltasche *f* saddlebag; (*Gepäcktasche am Fahrrad*) pannier.
sättigen ['zɛtɪɡən] *vt* to satisfy; (*CHEM*) to saturate.
Sattler (**-s, -**) *m* saddler; (*Polsterer*) upholsterer.
Satz [zats] (**-es, ̈-e**) *m* (*GRAM*) sentence; (*Neben~, Adverbial~*) clause; (*Theorem*) theorem; (*der gesetzte Text*) type; (*MUS*) movement; (*COMPUT*) record; (*TENNIS, Briefmarken, Zusammengehöriges*) set; (*Kaffee~*) grounds *pl*; (*Boden~*) dregs *pl*; (*Spesen~*) allowance; (*COMM*) rate; (*Sprung*) jump; ~**bau** *m* sentence construction; ~**gegenstand** *m* (*GRAM*) subject; ~**lehre** *f* syntax; ~**teil** *m* constituent (of a sentence).
Satzung *f* statute, rule; (*Firma*) (memorandum and) articles of association.
satzungsgemäß *adj* statutory.
Satzzeichen *nt* punctuation mark.
Sau [zaʊ] (**-, Säue**) *f* sow; (*umg*) dirty pig; **die ~ rauslassen** (*fig: umg*) to let it all hang out.
sauber ['zaʊbər] *adj* clean; (*anständig*) honest, upstanding; (*umg: großartig*) fantastic, great; (: *ironisch*) fine; ~ **sein** (*Kind*) to be (potty-)trained; (*Hund etc*) to be house-trained; ~**halten** *unreg vt* to keep clean; **S~keit** *f* cleanness; (*einer Person*) cleanliness.
säuberlich ['zɔybərlɪç] *adv* neatly.
saubermachen *vt* to clean.
säubern *vt* to clean; (*POL etc*) to purge.
Säuberung *f* cleaning; purge.
Säuberungsaktion *f* cleaning-up operation; (*POL*) purge.
saublöd (*umg*) *adj* bloody (*BRIT!*) *od* damn (*!*) stupid.
Saubohne *f* broad bean.
Sauce ['zoːsə] (**-, -n**) *f* = **Soße.**
Sauciere [zosi'eːrə] (**-, -n**) *f* sauce boat.
Saudi- [zaʊdi-] *zW:* ~**araber(in)** *m(f)* Saudi; ~**Arabien** (**-s**) *nt* Saudi Arabia; **s~arabisch** *adj* Saudi(-Arabian).
sauer ['zaʊər] *adj* sour; (*CHEM*) acid; (*umg*) cross; **Saurer Regen** acid rain; ~ **werden** (*Milch, Sahne*) to go sour, turn; **jdm das Leben ~ machen** to make sb's life a misery; **S~braten** *m* braised beef (marinaded in vinegar), sauerbraten (*US*).
Sauerei [zaʊə'raɪ] (*umg*) *f* rotten state of affairs, scandal; (*Schmutz etc*) mess; (*Unanständigkeit*) obscenity.
Sauerkirsche *f* sour cherry.
Sauerkraut (**-(e)s**) *nt* sauerkraut, pickled cabbage.
säuerlich ['zɔyərlɪç] *adj* sourish, tart.
Sauer- *zW:* ~**milch** *f* sour milk; ~**stoff** *m* oxygen; ~**stoffgerät** *nt* breathing apparatus; ~**teig** *m* leaven.
saufen ['zaʊfən] *unreg* (*umg*) *vt, vi* to drink, booze; **wie ein Loch ~** (*umg*) to drink like a fish.
Säufer(in) ['zɔyfər(ɪn)] (**-s, -**) (*umg*) *m(f)* boozer, drunkard.
Sauferei [zaʊfə'raɪ] *f* drinking, boozing; (*Saufgelage*) booze-up.
Saufgelage (*pej: umg*) *nt* drinking bout, booze-up.
säuft [zɔyft] *vb siehe* **saufen.**
saugen ['zaʊɡən] *unreg vt, vi* to suck.
säugen ['zɔyɡən] *vt* to suckle.
Sauger ['zaʊɡər] (**-s, -**) *m* dummy (*BRIT*), pacifier (*US*); (*auf Flasche*) teat; (*Staub~*) vacuum cleaner, hoover ® (*BRIT*).
Säugetier *nt* mammal.
saugfähig *adj* absorbent.
Säugling *m* infant, baby.
Säuglingsschwester *f* infant nurse.
Sau- *zW:* ~**haufen** (*umg*) *m* bunch of layabouts; **s~kalt** (*umg*) *adj* bloody (*BRIT!*) *od* damn (*!*) cold; ~**klaue** (*umg*) *f* scrawl.
Säule ['zɔylə] (**-, -n**) *f* column, pillar.
Säulengang *m* arcade.
Saum [zaʊm] (**-(e)s, Säume**) *m* hem; (*Naht*) seam.

saumäßig (*umg*) *adj* lousy ♦ *adv* lousily.
säumen ['zɔʏmən] *vt* to hem; to seam ♦ *vi* to delay, hesitate.
säumig ['zɔʏmɪç] *adj* (*geh: Schuldner*) defaulting; (*Zahlung*) outstanding, overdue.
Sauna ['zaʊna] (-, -**s**) *f* sauna.
Säure ['zɔʏrə] (-, -**n**) *f* acid; (*Geschmack*) sourness, acidity; **s~beständig** *adj* acid-proof.
Sauregurkenzeit (-) *f* (*hum: umg*) bad time *od* period; (*in den Medien*) silly season.
säurehaltig *adj* acidic.
Saurier ['zaʊriər] (-**s**, -) *m* dinosaur.
Saus [zaʊs] (-**es**) *m*: **in ~ und Braus leben** to live like a lord.
säuseln ['zɔʏzəln] *vi* to murmur; (*Blätter*) to rustle ♦ *vt* to murmur.
sausen ['zaʊzən] *vi* to blow; (*umg: eilen*) to rush; (*Ohren*) to buzz; **etw ~ lassen** (*umg*) not to bother with sth.
Sau- *zW:* **~stall** (*umg*) *m* pigsty; **~wetter** (*umg*) *nt* bloody (*BRIT!*) *od* damn (*!*) awful weather; **s~wohl** (*umg*) *adj:* **ich fühle mich s~wohl** I feel bloody (*BRIT!*) *od* really good.
Saxophon [zakso'foːn] (-**s**, -**e**) *nt* saxophone.
SB *abk* = **Selbstbedienung**.
S-Bahn *f abk* (= *Schnellbahn*) *high-speed suburban railway od railroad* (*US*).
SBB *abk* (= *Schweizerische Bundesbahnen*) Swiss Railways.
s. Br. *abk* (= *südlicher Breite*) southern latitude.
Schabe ['ʃaːbə] (-, -**n**) *f* cockroach.
schaben *vt* to scrape.
Schaber (-**s**, -) *m* scraper.
Schabernack (-**(e)s**, -**e**) *m* trick, prank.
schäbig ['ʃɛːbɪç] *adj* shabby; (*Mensch*) mean; **S~keit** *f* shabbiness.
Schablone [ʃa'bloːnə] (-, -**n**) *f* stencil; (*Muster*) pattern; (*fig*) convention.
schablonenhaft *adj* stereotyped, conventional.
Schach [ʃax] (-**s**, -**s**) *nt* chess; (*Stellung*) check; **im ~ stehen** to be in check; **jdn in ~ halten** (*fig*) to stall sb; **~brett** *nt* chessboard.
schachern (*pej*) *vi:* **um etw ~** to haggle over sth.
Schach- *zW:* **~figur** *f* chessman; **s~matt** *adj* checkmate; **jdn s~matt setzen** (*lit*) to (check)mate sb; (*fig*) to snooker sb (*umg*); **~partie** *f* game of chess; **~spiel** *nt* game of chess.
Schacht [ʃaxt] (-**(e)s**, -̈**e**) *m* shaft.
Schachtel (-, -**n**) *f* box; (*pej: Frau*) bag, cow (*BRIT*); **~satz** *m* complicated *od* multi-clause sentence.
Schachzug *m* (*auch fig*) move.
schade ['ʃaːdə] *adj* a pity *od* shame ♦ *interj* (what a) pity *od* shame; **sich** *dat* **für etw zu ~ sein** to consider o.s. too good for sth; **um sie ist es nicht ~** she's no great loss.
Schädel ['ʃɛːdəl] (-**s**, -) *m* skull; **einen dicken**

~ haben (*fig: umg*) to be stubborn; **~bruch** *m* fractured skull.
Schaden (-**s**, -̈) *m* damage; (*Verletzung*) injury; (*Nachteil*) disadvantage; **zu ~ kommen** to suffer; (*physisch*) to be injured; **jdm ~ zufügen** to harm sb.
schaden ['ʃaːdən] *vi* +*dat* to hurt; **einer Sache ~** to damage sth.
Schaden- *zW:* **~ersatz** *m* compensation, damages *pl*; **~ersatz leisten** to pay compensation; **~ersatzanspruch** *m* claim for compensation; **s~ersatzpflichtig** *adj* liable for damages; **~freiheitsrabatt** *m* (*Versicherung*) no-claim(s) bonus; **~freude** *f* malicious delight; **s~froh** *adj* gloating.
schadhaft ['ʃaːthaft] *adj* faulty, damaged.
schädigen ['ʃɛːdɪɡən] *vt* to damage; (*Person*) to do harm to, harm.
Schädigung *f* damage; harm.
schädlich *adj:* **~ (für)** harmful (to); **S~keit** *f* harmfulness.
Schädling *m* pest.
Schädlingsbekämpfungsmittel *nt* pesticide.
schadlos ['ʃaːtloːs] *adj:* **sich ~ halten an** +*dat* to take advantage of.
Schadstoff (-**(e)s**, -**e**) *m* pollutant; **s~arm** *adj* low in pollutants; **s~haltig** *adj* containing pollutants.
Schaf [ʃaːf] (-**(e)s**, -**e**) *nt* sheep; (*umg: Dummkopf*) twit (*BRIT*), dope; **~bock** *m* ram.
Schäfchen ['ʃɛːfçən] *nt* lamb; **sein ~ ins Trockene bringen** (*Sprichwort*) to see o.s. all right (*umg*); **~wolken** *pl* cirrus clouds *pl*.
Schäfer ['ʃɛːfər] (-**s**, -) *m* shepherd; **~hund** *m* Alsatian (dog) (*BRIT*), German shepherd (dog) (*US*); **~in** *f* shepherdess.
Schaffen ['ʃafən] (-**s**) *nt* (creative) activity.
schaffen[1] *unreg vt* to create; (*Platz*) to make; **sich** *dat* **etw ~** to get o.s. sth; **dafür ist er wie geschaffen** he's just made for it.
schaffen[2] ['ʃafən] *vt* (*erreichen*) to manage, do; (*erledigen*) to finish; (*Prüfung*) to pass; (*transportieren*) to take ♦ *vi* (*tun*) to do; (*umg: arbeiten*) to work; **das ist nicht zu ~** that can't be done; **das hat mich geschafft** it took it out of me; (*nervlich*) it got on top of me; **ich habe damit nichts zu ~** that has nothing to do with me; **jdm (schwer) zu ~ machen** (*zusetzen*) to cause sb (a lot of) trouble; (*bekümmern*) to worry sb (a lot); **sich** *dat* **an etw** *dat* **zu ~ machen** to busy o.s. with sth.
Schaffensdrang *m* energy; (*von Künstler*) creative urge.
Schaffenskraft *f* creativity.
Schaffner(in) ['ʃafnər(ɪn)] (-**s**, -) *m(f)* (*Bus~*) conductor, conductress; (*EISENB*) guard (*BRIT*), conductor (*US*).
Schaffung *f* creation.
Schafskäse *m* sheep's *od* ewe's milk cheese.
Schaft [ʃaft] (-**(e)s**, -̈**e**) *m* shaft; (*von Gewehr*) stock; (*von Stiefel*) leg; (*BOT*) stalk; (*von*

Baum) tree trunk; ~**stiefel** *m* high boot.
Schakal [ʃaˈkaːl] (-**s**, -**e**) *m* jackal.
Schäker(in) [ˈʃɛːkər(ɪn)] (-**s**, -) *m(f)* flirt; (*Witzbold*) joker.
schäkern *vi* to flirt; to joke.
Schal [ʃaːl] (-**s**, -**s** *od* -**e**) *m* scarf.
schal *adj* flat; (*fig*) insipid.
Schälchen [ˈʃɛːlçən] *nt* bowl.
Schale [ˈʃaːlə] (-, -**n**) *f* skin; (*abgeschält*) peel; (*Nuß~, Muschel~, Eier~*) shell; (*Geschirr*) dish, bowl; **sich in** ~ **werfen** (*umg*) to get dressed up.
schälen [ˈʃɛːlən] *vt* to peel; to shell ♦ *vr* to peel.
Schalk [ʃalk] (-**s**, -**e** *od* -̈**e**) *m* (*veraltet*) joker.
Schall [ʃal] (-(**e**)**s**, -**e**) *m* sound; **Name ist** ~ **und Rauch** what's in a name?; **s~dämmend** *adj* sound-deadening; ~**dämpfer** *m* (*AUT*) silencer (*BRIT*), muffler (*US*); **s~dicht** *adj* soundproof.
schallen *vi* to (re)sound.
schallend *adj* resounding, loud.
Schall- *zW:* ~**geschwindigkeit** *f* speed of sound; ~**grenze** *f* sound barrier; ~**mauer** *f* sound barrier; ~**platte** *f* record.
schalt *etc* [ʃalt] *vb siehe* **schelten**.
Schaltbild *nt* circuit diagram.
Schaltbrett *nt* switchboard.
schalten [ˈʃaltən] *vt* to switch, turn ♦ *vi* (*AUT*) to change (gear); (*umg: begreifen*) to catch on; (*reagieren*) to react; **in Reihe/parallel** ~ (*ELEK*) to connect in series/in parallel; ~ **und walten** to do as one pleases.
Schalter (-**s**, -) *m* counter; (*an Gerät*) switch; ~**beamte(r)** *m* counter clerk; ~**stunden** *pl* hours of business *pl*.
Schalt- *zW:* ~**hebel** *m* switch; (*AUT*) gear lever (*BRIT*), gearshift (*US*); ~**jahr** *nt* leap year; ~**knüppel** *m* (*AUT*) gear lever (*BRIT*), gearshift (*US*); (*AVIAT, COMPUT*) joystick; ~**kreis** *m* (switching) circuit; ~**plan** *m* circuit diagram; ~**pult** *nt* control desk; ~**stelle** *f* (*fig*) coordinating point; ~**uhr** *f* time switch.
Schaltung *f* switching; (*ELEK*) circuit; (*AUT*) gear change.
Scham [ʃaːm] (-) *f* shame; (~*gefühl*) modesty; (*Organe*) private parts *pl*.
schämen [ˈʃɛːmən] *vr* to be ashamed.
Scham- *zW:* ~**gefühl** *nt* sense of shame; ~**haare** *pl* pubic hair *sing*; **s~haft** *adj* modest; bashful; ~**lippen** *pl* labia *pl*, lips *pl* of the vulva; **s~los** *adj* shameless; (*unanständig*) indecent; (*Lüge*) brazen, barefaced.
Schampus [ˈʃampʊs] (-, *no pl*) (*umg*) *m* champagne, champers (*BRIT*).
Schande [ˈʃandə] (-) *f* disgrace; **zu meiner** ~ **muß ich gestehen, daß** ... to my shame I have to admit that ...
schänden [ˈʃɛndən] *vt* to violate.
Schandfleck [ˈʃantflɛk] *m:* **er war der** ~ **der Familie** he was the disgrace of his family.

schändlich [ˈʃɛntlɪç] *adj* disgraceful, shameful; **S~keit** *f* disgracefulness, shamefulness.
Schandtat (*umg*) *f* escapade, shenanigan.
Schändung *f* violation, defilement.
Schank- *zW:* ~**erlaubnis** *f*, ~**konzession** *f* (publican's) licence (*BRIT*), excise license (*US*); ~**tisch** *m* bar.
Schanze [ˈʃantsə] (-, -**n**) *f* (*MIL*) fieldwork, earthworks *pl*; (*Sprung~*) ski jump.
Schar [ʃaːr] (-, -**en**) *f* band, company; (*Vögel*) flock; (*Menge*) crowd; **in** ~**en** in droves.
Scharade [ʃaˈraːdə] (-, -**n**) *f* charade.
scharen *vr* to assemble, rally.
scharenweise *adv* in droves.
scharf [ʃarf] *adj* sharp; (*Verstand, Augen*) keen; (*Kälte, Wind*) biting; (*Protest*) fierce; (*Ton*) piercing, shrill; (*Essen*) hot, spicy; (*Munition*) live; (*Maßnahmen*) severe; (*Bewachung*) close, tight; (*Geruch, Geschmack*) pungent, acrid; (*umg: geil*) randy (*BRIT*), horny; (*Film*) sexy, blue *attrib*; ~ **nachdenken** to think hard; ~ **aufpassen/zuhören** to pay close attention/listen closely; **etw** ~ **einstellen** (*Bild, Diaprojektor etc*) to bring sth into focus; **mit** ~**em Blick** (*fig*) with penetrating insight; **auf etw** *akk* ~ **sein** (*umg*) to be keen on sth; ~**e Sachen** (*umg*) hard stuff.
Scharfblick *m* (*fig*) penetration.
Schärfe [ˈʃɛrfə] (-, -**n**) *f* sharpness; (*Strenge*) rigour (*BRIT*), rigor (*US*); (*an Kamera, Fernsehen*) focus.
schärfen *vt* to sharpen.
Schärfentiefe *f* (*PHOT*) depth of focus.
Scharf- *zW:* **s~machen** (*umg*) *vt* to stir up; ~**richter** *m* executioner; ~**schießen** *nt* shooting with live ammunition; ~**schütze** *m* marksman, sharpshooter; ~**sinn** *m* astuteness, shrewdness; **s~sinnig** *adj* astute, shrewd.
Scharlach [ˈʃarlax] (-**s**, -**e**) *m* scarlet; (*Krankheit*) scarlet fever; ~**fieber** *nt* scarlet fever.
Scharlatan [ˈʃarlatan] (-**s**, -**e**) *m* charlatan.
Scharmützel [ʃarˈmʏtsəl] (-**s**, -) *nt* skirmish.
Scharnier [ʃarˈniːr] (-**s**, -**e**) *nt* hinge.
Schärpe [ˈʃɛrpə] (-, -**n**) *f* sash.
scharren [ˈʃarən] *vt, vi* to scrape, scratch.
Scharte [ˈʃartə] (-, -**n**) *f* notch, nick; (*Berg*) wind gap.
schartig [ˈʃartɪç] *adj* jagged.
Schaschlik [ˈʃaʃlɪk] (-**s**, -**s**) *m od nt* (shish) kebab.
Schatten [ˈʃatən] (-**s**, -) *m* shadow; (*schattige Stelle*) shade; **jdn/etw in den** ~ **stellen** (*fig*) to put sb/sth in the shade; ~**bild** *nt* silhouette; **s~haft** *adj* shadowy.
Schattenmorelle (-, -**n**) *f* morello cherry.
Schatten- *zW:* ~**riß** *m* silhouette; ~**seite** *f* shady side; (*von Planeten*) dark side; (*fig: Nachteil*) drawback; ~**wirtschaft** *f* black

economy.
schattieren [ʃa'tiːrən] *vt, vi* to shade.
Schattierung *f* shading.
schattig ['ʃatıç] *adj* shady.
Schatulle [ʃa'tʊlə] (-, -n) *f* casket; (*Geld~*) coffer.
Schatz [ʃats] (-es, ⁻e) *m* treasure; (*Person*) darling; ~**amt** *nt* treasury.
schätzbar ['ʃɛtsbaːr] *adj* assessable.
Schätzchen *nt* darling, love.
schätzen *vt* (*ab~*) to estimate; (*Gegenstand*) to value; (*würdigen*) to value, esteem; (*vermuten*) to reckon; **etw zu ~ wissen** to appreciate sth; **sich glücklich ~ to** consider o.s. lucky; ~**lernen** *vt* to learn to appreciate.
Schatzkammer *f* treasure chamber *od* vault.
Schatzmeister *m* treasurer.
Schätzung *f* estimate; estimation; valuation; **nach meiner ~ ...** I reckon that ...
schätzungsweise *adv* (*ungefähr*) approximately; (*so vermutet man*) it is thought.
Schätzwert *m* estimated value.
Schau [ʃaʊ] (-) *f* show; (*Ausstellung*) display, exhibition; **etw zur ~ stellen** to make a show of sth, show sth off; **eine ~ abziehen** (*umg*) to put on a show; ~**bild** *nt* diagram.
Schauder ['ʃaʊdər] (-s, -) *m* shudder; (*wegen Kälte*) shiver; **s~haft** *adj* horrible.
schaudern *vi* to shudder; (*wegen Kälte*) to shiver.
schauen ['ʃaʊən] *vi* to look; **da schau her!** well, well!
Schauer ['ʃaʊər] (-s, -) *m* (*Regen~*) shower; (*Schreck*) shudder; ~**geschichte** *f* horror story; **s~lich** *adj* horrific, spine-chilling; ~**märchen** (*umg*) *nt* horror story.
Schaufel ['ʃaʊfəl] (-, -n) *f* shovel; (*Kehricht~*) dustpan; (*von Turbine*) vane; (*NAUT*) paddle; (*TECH*) scoop.
schaufeln *vt* to shovel; (*Grab, Grube*) to dig ♦ *vi* to shovel.
Schaufenster *nt* shop window; ~**auslage** *f* window display; ~**bummel** *m* window-shopping (expedition); ~**dekorateur(in)** *m(f)* window dresser; ~**puppe** *f* display dummy.
Schaugeschäft *nt* show business.
Schaukasten *m* showcase.
Schaukel ['ʃaʊkəl] (-, -n) *f* swing.
schaukeln *vi* to swing, rock ♦ *vt* to rock; **wir werden das Kind** *od* **das schon ~** (*fig: umg*) we'll manage it.
Schaukelpferd *nt* rocking horse.
Schaukelstuhl *m* rocking chair.
Schaulustige(r) ['ʃaʊlʊstıgə(r)] *f(m)* onlooker.
Schaum [ʃaʊm] (-(e)s, Schäume) *m* foam; (*Seifen~*) lather; (*von Getränken*) froth; (*von Bier*) head; ~**bad** *nt* bubble bath.
schäumen ['ʃɔʏmən] *vi* to foam.
Schaumgummi *m* foam (rubber).
schaumig *adj* frothy, foamy.

Schaum- *zW:* ~**krone** *f* whitecap; ~**schläger** *m* (*fig*) windbag; ~**schlägerei** *f* (*fig: umg*) hot air; ~**stoff** *m* foam material; ~**wein** *m* sparkling wine.
Schauplatz *m* scene.
Schauprozeß *m* show trial.
schaurig *adj* horrific, dreadful.
Schauspiel *nt* spectacle; (*THEAT*) play.
Schauspieler(in) *m(f)* actor, actress; **s~isch** *adj* (*Können, Leistung*) acting.
schauspielern *vi untr* to act.
Schauspielhaus *nt* playhouse, theatre (*BRIT*), theater (*US*).
Schauspielschule *f* drama school.
Schausteller ['ʃaʊʃtɛlər] (-s, -) *m person who owns or runs a fairground ride/sideshow etc.*
Scheck [ʃɛk] (-s, -s) *m* cheque (*BRIT*), check (*US*); ~**buch** *nt*, ~**heft** *nt* cheque book (*BRIT*), check book (*US*).
scheckig *adj* dappled, piebald.
Scheckkarte *f* cheque (*BRIT*) *od* check (*US*) card, banker's card.
scheel [ʃeːl] (*umg*) *adj* dirty; **jdn ~ ansehen** to give sb a dirty look.
scheffeln ['ʃɛfəln] *vt* to amass.
Scheibe ['ʃaibə] (-, -n) *f* disc (*BRIT*), disk (*US*); (*Brot etc*) slice; (*Glas~*) pane; (*MIL*) target; (*Eishockey*) puck; (*Töpfer~*) wheel; (*umg: Schallplatte*) disc (*BRIT*), disk (*US*); **von ihm könntest du dir eine ~ abschneiden** (*fig: umg*) you could take a leaf out of his book.
Scheiben- *zW:* ~**bremse** *f* (*AUT*) disc brake; ~**kleister** *interj* (*euph: umg*) sugar!; ~**waschanlage** *f* (*AUT*) windscreen (*BRIT*) *od* windshield (*US*) washers *pl*; ~**wischer** *m* (*AUT*) windscreen (*BRIT*) *od* windshield (*US*) wiper.
Scheich [ʃaiç] (-s, -e *od* -s) *m* sheik(h).
Scheide ['ʃaidə] (-, -n) *f* sheath; (*ANAT*) vagina.
scheiden *unreg vt* to separate; (*Ehe*) to dissolve ♦ *vi* to depart; (*sich trennen*) to part ♦ *vr* (*Wege*) to divide; (*Meinungen*) to diverge; **sich ~ lassen** to get a divorce; **von dem Moment an waren wir (zwei) geschiedene Leute** (*umg*) after that it was the parting of the ways for us; **aus dem Leben ~** to depart this life.
Scheideweg *m* (*fig*) crossroads *sing.*
Scheidung *f* (*Ehe~*) divorce; **die ~ einreichen** to file a petition for divorce.
Scheidungsgrund *m* grounds *pl* for divorce.
Scheidungsklage *f* divorce suit.
Schein [ʃain] (-(e)s, -e) *m* light; (*An~*) appearance; (*Geld~*) (bank)note; (*Bescheinigung*) certificate; **den ~ wahren** to keep up appearances; **etw zum ~ tun** to pretend to do sth, make a pretence (*BRIT*) *od* pretense (*US*) of doing sth; **s~bar** *adj* apparent.
scheinen *unreg vi* to shine; (*Anschein haben*) to

seem.

Schein- zW: **s~heilig** adj hypocritical; **~tod** m apparent death; **~werfer (-s, -)** m floodlight; (THEAT) spotlight; (Suchscheinwerfer) searchlight; (AUT) headlight.

Scheiß [ʃaɪs] (-, no pl) (umg) m bullshit (!).

Scheiß- [ˈʃaɪs-] (umg) in zW bloody (BRIT!); **~dreck** (umg!) m shit (!), crap (!); **das geht dich einen ~dreck an** it's got bugger-all to do with you (!).

Scheiße [ˈʃaɪsə] (-) (umg!) f shit (!).

scheißegal (umg!) adj: **das ist mir doch ~!** I don't give a shit (!).

scheißen (umg!) vi to shit (!).

scheißfreundlich (pej: umg) adj as nice as pie (ironisch).

Scheißkerl (umg!) m bastard (!), son-of-a-bitch (US!).

Scheit [ʃaɪt] (-(e)s, -e od -er) nt log.

Scheitel [ˈʃaɪtəl] (-s, -) m top; (Haar) parting (BRIT), part (US).

scheiteln vt to part.

Scheitelpunkt m zenith, apex.

Scheiterhaufen [ˈʃaɪtərhaʊfən] m (funeral) pyre; (HIST: zur Hinrichtung) stake.

scheitern [ˈʃaɪtərn] vi to fail.

Schelle [ˈʃɛlə] (-, -n) f small bell.

schellen vi to ring; **es hat geschellt** the bell has gone.

Schellfisch [ˈʃɛlfɪʃ] m haddock.

Schelm [ʃɛlm] (-(e)s, -e) m rogue.

Schelmenroman m picaresque novel.

schelmisch adj mischievous, roguish.

Schelte [ˈʃɛltə] (-, -n) f scolding.

schelten unreg vt to scold.

Schema [ˈʃeːma] (-s, -s od -ta) nt scheme, plan; (Darstellung) schema; **nach ~ F** quite mechanically.

schematisch [ʃeˈmaːtɪʃ] adj schematic; (pej) mechanical.

Schemel [ˈʃeːməl] (-s, -) m (foot)stool.

schemenhaft adj shadowy.

Schenke (-, -n) f tavern, inn.

Schenkel [ˈʃɛŋkəl] (-s, -) m thigh; (MATH: von Winkel) side.

schenken [ˈʃɛŋkən] vt (lit, fig) to give; (Getränk) to pour; **ich möchte nichts geschenkt haben!** (lit) I don't want any presents!; (fig: bevorzugt werden) I don't want any special treatment!; **sich** dat **etw ~** (umg) to skip sth; **jdm etw ~** (erlassen) to let sb off sth; **ihm ist nie etwas geschenkt worden** (fig) he never had it easy; **das ist geschenkt!** (billig) that's a giveaway!; (nichts wert) that's worthless!

Schenkung f gift.

Schenkungsurkunde f deed of gift.

scheppern [ˈʃɛpərn] (umg) vi to clatter.

Scherbe [ˈʃɛrbə] (-, -n) f broken piece, fragment; (archäologisch) potsherd.

Schere [ˈʃeːrə] (-, -n) f scissors pl; (groß) shears pl; (ZOOL) pincer; (von Hummer, Krebs

etc) pincer, claw; **eine ~** a pair of scissors.

scheren unreg vt to cut; (Schaf) to shear; (stören) to bother ♦ vr (sich kümmern) to care; **scher dich (zum Teufel)!** get lost!

Scherenschleifer (-s, -) m knife grinder.

Scherenschnitt m silhouette.

Schererei [ʃeːrəˈraɪ] (umg) f bother, trouble.

Scherflein [ˈʃɛrflaɪn] nt mite, bit.

Scherz [ʃɛrts] (-es, -e) m joke; fun; **s~en** vi to joke; (albern) to banter; **~frage** f conundrum; **s~haft** adj joking, jocular.

Scheu [ʃɔʏ] (-) f shyness; (Ehrfurcht) awe; (Angst): **~ (vor** +dat) fear (of).

scheu [ʃɔʏ] adj shy.

Scheuche (-, -n) f scarecrow.

scheuchen [ˈʃɔʏçən] vt to scare (off).

scheuen vr: **sich ~ vor** +dat to be afraid of, shrink from ♦ vt to shun ♦ vi (Pferd) to shy; **weder Mühe noch Kosten ~** to spare neither trouble nor expense.

Scheuer [ˈʃɔʏər] (-, -n) f barn.

Scheuer- zW: **~bürste** f scrubbing brush; **~lappen** m floorcloth (BRIT), scrubbing rag (US); **~leiste** f skirting board.

scheuern vt to scour; (mit Bürste) to scrub ♦ vr: **sich** akk **(wund) ~** to chafe o.s.; **jdm eine ~** (umg) to clout sb one.

Scheuklappe f blinker.

Scheune [ˈʃɔʏnə] (-, -n) f barn.

Scheunendrescher (-s, -) m: **er frißt wie ein ~** he eats like a horse.

Scheusal [ˈʃɔʏzaːl] (-s, -e) nt monster.

scheußlich [ˈʃɔʏslɪç] adj dreadful, frightful; **S~keit** f dreadfulness.

Schi [ʃiː] m = Ski.

Schicht [ʃɪçt] (-, -en) f layer; (Klasse) class, level; (in Fabrik etc) shift; **~arbeit** f shift work.

schichten vt to layer, stack.

Schichtwechsel m change of shifts.

schick [ʃɪk] adj stylish, chic.

schicken vt to send ♦ vr: **sich ~ (in** +akk) to resign o.s. (to) ♦ vb unpers (anständig sein) to be fitting.

Schickeria [ʃɪkəˈriːa] f (ironisch) in-people pl.

Schicki(micki) [ˈʃɪkɪ(ˈmɪkɪ)] (-s, -s) (umg) m trendy.

schicklich adj proper, fitting.

Schicksal (-s, -e) nt fate.

schicksalhaft adj fateful.

Schicksalsschlag m great misfortune, blow.

Schickse [ˈʃɪksə] (-, -n) (umg) f floozy, shiksa (US).

Schiebedach nt (AUT) sunroof, sunshine roof.

schieben [ˈʃiːbən] unreg vt (auch Drogen) to push; (Schuld) to put; (umg: handeln mit) to traffic in; **die Schuld auf jdn ~** to put the blame on (to) sb; **etw vor sich** dat **her ~** (fig) to put sth off.

Schieber (-s, -) m slide; (Besteckteil) pusher; (Person) profiteer; (umg: Schwarzhändler)

black marketeer; (: *Waffen~*) gunrunner; (:
Drogen~) pusher.
Schiebetür *f* sliding door.
Schieblehre *f* (*MATH*) calliper (*BRIT*) *od*
caliper (*US*) rule.
Schiebung *f* fiddle; **das war doch ~** (*umg*)
that was rigged *od* a fix.
schied *etc* [ʃiːt] *vb siehe* **scheiden.**
Schieds- *zW*: **~gericht** *nt* court of arbitration;
~mann (-(e)s, *pl* -**männer**) *m* arbitrator;
~richter *m* referee, umpire; (*Schlichter*)
arbitrator; **s~richtern** *vi untr* to referee,
umpire; to arbitrate; **~spruch** *m*
(arbitration) award; **~verfahren** *nt*
arbitration.
schief [ʃiːf] *adj* crooked; (*Ebene*) sloping;
(*Turm*) leaning; (*Winkel*) oblique; (*Blick*) wry;
(*Vergleich*) distorted ♦ *adv* crookedly;
(*ansehen*) askance; **auf die ~e Bahn geraten**
(*fig*) to leave the straight and narrow; **etw**
~ stellen to slope sth.
Schiefer [ˈʃiːfər] (-s, -) *m* slate; **~dach** *nt* slate
roof; **~tafel** *f* (child's) slate.
schief- *zW*: **~gehen** *unreg* (*umg*) *vi* to go wrong;
es wird schon ~gehen! (*hum*) it'll be O.K.;
~lachen (*umg*) *vr* to kill o.s. laughing;
~liegen *unreg* (*umg*) *vi* to be wrong, be on the
wrong track (*umg*).
schielen [ˈʃiːlən] *vi* to squint; **nach etw ~** (*fig*)
to eye sth up.
schien *etc* [ʃiːn] *vb siehe* **scheinen.**
Schienbein *nt* shinbone.
Schiene [ˈʃiːnə] *f* rail; (*MED*) splint.
schienen *vt* to put in splints.
Schienenbus *m* railcar.
Schienenstrang *m* (*EISENB etc*) (section of)
track.
schier [ʃiːr] *adj* pure; (*fig*) sheer ♦ *adv* nearly,
almost.
Schießbude *f* shooting gallery.
Schießbudenfigur (*umg*) *f* clown, ludicrous
figure.
schießen [ˈʃiːsən] *unreg vi* to shoot; (*Salat etc*)
to run to seed ♦ *vt* to shoot; (*Ball*) to kick;
(*Geschoß*) to fire; **~ auf** +*akk* to shoot at; **aus**
dem Boden ~ (*lit, fig*) to spring *od* sprout up;
jdm durch den Kopf ~ (*fig*) to flash through
sb's mind.
Schießerei [ʃiːsəˈraɪ] *f* shoot-out, gun battle.
Schieß- *zW*: **~gewehr** *nt* (*hum*) gun; **~hund** *m*:
wie ein ~hund aufpassen (*umg*) to watch
like a hawk; **~platz** *m* firing range; **~pulver**
nt gunpowder; **~scharte** *f* embrasure;
~stand *m* rifle *od* shooting range.
Schiff [ʃɪf] (-(e)s, -e) *nt* ship, vessel; (*Kirchen~*)
nave; **s~bar** *adj* navigable; **~bau** *m*
shipbuilding; **~bruch** *m* shipwreck; **~bruch**
erleiden (*lit*) to be shipwrecked; (*fig*) to fail;
(*Unternehmen*) to founder; **s~brüchig** *adj*
shipwrecked.
Schiffchen *nt* small boat; (*WEBEN*) shuttle;
(*Mütze*) forage cap.

Schiffer (-s, -) *m* boatman, sailor; (*von*
Lastkahn) bargee.
Schiff- *zW*: **~(f)ahrt** *f* shipping; (*Reise*)
voyage; **~(f)ahrtslinie** *f* shipping route;
~schaukel *f* swing boat.
Schiffs- *zW*: **~junge** *m* cabin boy; **~körper** *m*
hull; **~ladung** *f* cargo, shipload; **~planke** *f*
gangplank; **~schraube** *f* ship's propeller.
Schiit [ʃiˈiːt] (-en, -en) *m* Shiite; **s~isch** *adj*
Shiite.
Schikane [ʃiˈkaːnə] (-, -n) *f* harassment; dirty
trick; **mit allen ~n** with all the trimmings;
das hat er aus reiner ~ gemacht he did it out
of sheer bloody-mindedness.
schikanieren [ʃikaˈniːrən] *vt* to harass;
(*Ehepartner*) to mess around; (*Mitschüler*) to
bully.
schikanös [ʃikaˈnøːs] *adj* (*Mensch*) bloody-
minded; (*Maßnahme etc*) harassing.
Schild¹ [ʃɪlt] (-(e)s, -e) *m* shield; (*Mützen~*)
peak, visor; **etwas im ~e führen** to be up to
something.
Schild² [ʃɪlt] (-(e)s, -er) *nt* sign; (*Namens~*)
nameplate; (*an Monument, Haus, Grab*)
plaque; (*Etikett*) label.
Schildbürger *m* duffer, blockhead.
Schilddrüse *f* thyroid gland.
schildern [ˈʃɪldərn] *vt* to describe; (*Menschen*
etc) to portray; (*skizzieren*) to outline.
Schilderung *f* description; portrayal.
Schildkröte *f* tortoise; (*Wasser~*) turtle.
Schildkrötensuppe *f* turtle soup.
Schilf [ʃɪlf] (-(e)s, -e) *nt*, **Schilfrohr** *nt*
(*Pflanze*) reed; (*Material*) reeds *pl*, rushes *pl*.
Schillerlocke [ˈʃɪlərlɔkə] *f* (*Gebäck*) cream
horn; (*Räucherfisch*) strip of smoked rock
salmon.
schillern [ˈʃɪlərn] *vi* to shimmer.
schillernd *adj* iridescent; (*fig: Charakter*)
enigmatic.
Schilling [ˈʃɪlɪŋ] (-s, - *od* (*Schillingstücke*) -e)
(*ÖSTERR*) *m* schilling.
schilt [ʃɪlt] *vb siehe* **schelten.**
Schimmel [ˈʃɪməl] (-s, -) *m* mould (*BRIT*),
mold (*US*); (*Pferd*) white horse.
schimm(e)lig *adj* mouldy (*BRIT*), moldy (*US*).
schimmeln *vi* to go mouldy (*BRIT*) *od* moldy
(*US*).
Schimmer [ˈʃɪmər] (-s) *m* glimmer; **keinen**
(blassen) ~ von etw haben (*umg*) not to
have the slightest idea about sth.
schimmern *vi* to glimmer; (*Seide, Perlen*) to
shimmer.
Schimpanse [ʃɪmˈpanzə] (-n, -n) *m*
chimpanzee.
Schimpf [ʃɪmpf] (-(e)s, -e) *m* disgrace; **mit**
~ und Schande in disgrace.
schimpfen [ˈʃɪmpfn] *vi* (*sich beklagen*) to grumble;
(*fluchen*) to curse.
Schimpfkanonade *f* barrage of abuse.
Schimpfwort *nt* term of abuse.
Schindel [ˈʃɪndəl] (-, -n) *f* shingle.

schinden ['ʃɪndən] *unreg vt* to maltreat, drive too hard ♦ *vr:* **sich ~ (mit)** to sweat and strain (at), toil away (at); **Eindruck ~** (*umg*) to create an impression.

Schinder (**-s**, **-**) *m* knacker; (*fig*) slave driver.

Schinderei [ʃɪndə'raɪ] *f* grind, drudgery.

Schindluder ['ʃɪntluːdər] *nt:* **mit etw ~ treiben** to muck *od* mess sth about; (*Vorrecht*) to abuse sth.

Schinken ['ʃɪŋkən] (**-s**, **-**) *m* ham; (*gekocht und geräuchert*) gammon; (*pej: umg: Theaterstück etc*) hackneyed and clichéd play *etc*; **~speck** *m* bacon.

Schippe ['ʃɪpə] (**-**, **-n**) *f* shovel; **jdn auf die ~ nehmen** (*fig: umg*) to pull sb's leg.

schippen *vt* to shovel.

Schirm [ʃɪrm] (**-(e)s**, **-e**) *m* (*Regen~*) umbrella; (*Sonnen~*) parasol, sunshade; (*Wand~, Bild~*) screen; (*Lampen~*) (lamp)shade; (*Mützen~*) peak; (*Pilz~*) cap; **~bildaufnahme** *f* X-ray; **~herr(in)** *m(f)* patron(ess); **~herrschaft** *f* patronage; **~mütze** *f* peaked cap; **~ständer** *m* umbrella stand.

Schiß *m:* **~ haben** (*umg*) to be shit scared (*!*).

schiß *etc* [ʃɪs] *vb siehe* **scheißen**.

schizophren [ʃitso'freːn] *adj* schizophrenic.

Schizophrenie [ʃitsofre'niː] *f* schizophrenia.

schlabbern ['ʃlabərn] (*umg*) *vt, vi* to slurp.

Schlacht [ʃlaxt] (**-**, **-en**) *f* battle.

schlachten *vt* to slaughter, kill.

Schlachtenbummler (*umg*) *m* visiting football fan.

Schlachter (**-s**, **-**) *m* butcher.

Schlacht- *zW:* **~feld** *nt* battlefield; **~fest** *nt* country feast at which freshly slaughtered meat is served; **~haus** *nt*, **~hof** *m* slaughterhouse, abattoir (*BRIT*); **~opfer** *nt* sacrifice; (*Mensch*) human sacrifice; **~plan** *m* battle plan; (*fig*) plan of action; **~ruf** *m* battle cry, war cry; **~schiff** *nt* battleship; **~vieh** *nt* animals *pl* kept for meat.

Schlacke ['ʃlakə] (**-**, **-n**) *f* slag.

schlackern (*umg*) *vi* to tremble; (*Kleidung*) to hang loosely, be baggy; **mit den Ohren ~** (*fig*) to be (left) speechless.

Schlaf [ʃlaːf] (**-(e)s**) *m* sleep; **um seinen ~ kommen** *od* **gebracht werden** to lose sleep; **~anzug** *m* pyjamas *pl* (*BRIT*), pajamas *pl* (*US*).

Schläfchen ['ʃlɛːfçən] *nt* nap.

Schläfe (**-**, **-n**) *f* (*ANAT*) temple.

schlafen *unreg vi* to sleep; (*umg: nicht aufpassen*) to be asleep; **bei jdm ~** to stay overnight with sb; **S~gehen** *nt* going to bed.

Schlafenszeit *f* bedtime.

Schläfer(in) ['ʃlɛːfər(ɪn)] (**-s**, **-**) *m(f)* sleeper.

schlaff [ʃlaf] *adj* slack; (*Haut*) loose; (*Muskeln*) flabby; (*energielos*) limp; (*erschöpft*) exhausted; **S~heit** *f* slackness; looseness; flabbiness; limpness; exhaustion.

Schlafgelegenheit *f* place to sleep.

Schlafittchen [ʃla'fɪtçən] (*umg*) *nt:* **jdn am** *od*

beim ~ nehmen to take sb by the scruff of the neck.

Schlaf- *zW:* **~krankheit** *f* sleeping sickness; **~lied** *nt* lullaby; **s~los** *adj* sleepless; **~losigkeit** *f* sleeplessness, insomnia; **~mittel** *nt* sleeping drug; (*fig, ironisch*) soporific; **~mütze** (*umg*) *f* dope.

schläfrig ['ʃlɛːfrɪç] *adj* sleepy.

Schlaf- *zW:* **~rock** *m* dressing gown; **Apfel im ~rock** baked apple in puff pastry; **~saal** *m* dormitory; **~sack** *m* sleeping bag.

schläft [ʃlɛːft] *vb siehe* **schlafen**.

Schlaf- *zW:* **~tablette** *f* sleeping pill; **s~trunken** *adj* drowsy, half-asleep; **~wagen** *m* sleeping car, sleeper; **s~wandeln** *vi untr* to sleepwalk; **~wandler(in)** (**-s**, **-**) *m(f)* sleepwalker; **~zimmer** *nt* bedroom.

Schlag [ʃlaːk] (**-(e)s**, **-̈e**) *m* (*lit, fig*) blow; (*auch MED*) stroke; (*Puls~, Herz~*) beat; (*ELEK*) shock; (*Blitz~*) bolt, stroke; (*Glocken~*) chime; (*Autotür*) car door; (*umg: Portion*) helping; (: *Art*) kind, type; **Schläge** *pl* (*Tracht Prügel*) beating *sing*; **~ acht Uhr** (*umg*) on the stroke of eight; **mit einem ~** all at once; **~ auf ~** in rapid succession; **die haben keinen ~ getan** (*umg*) they haven't done a stroke (of work); **ich dachte, mich trifft der ~** (*umg*) I was thunderstruck; **vom gleichen ~ sein** to be cast in the same mould (*BRIT*) *od* mold (*US*); (*pej*) to be tarred with the same brush; **ein ~ ins Wasser** (*umg*) a wash-out; **~abtausch** *m* (*BOXEN*) exchange of blows; (*fig*) (verbal) exchange; **~ader** *f* artery; **~anfall** *m* stroke; **s~artig** *adj* sudden, without warning; **~baum** *m* barrier; **~bohrer** *m* percussion drill.

schlagen ['ʃlaːgən] *unreg vt* to strike, hit; (*wiederholt ~, besiegen*) to beat; (*Glocke*) to ring; (*Stunde*) to strike; (*Kreis, Bogen*) to describe; (*Purzelbaum*) to do; (*Sahne*) to whip; (*Schlacht*) to fight; (*einwickeln*) to wrap ♦ *vi* to strike, hit; to beat; to ring; to strike ♦ *vr* to fight; **um sich ~** to lash out; **ein Ei in die Pfanne ~** to crack an egg into the pan; **eine geschlagene Stunde** a full hour; **na ja, ehe ich mich ~ lasse!** (*hum: umg*) I suppose you could twist my arm; **nach jdm ~** (*fig*) to take after sb; **sich gut ~** (*fig*) to do well; **sich nach links/Norden ~** to strike out to the left/(for the) north; **sich auf jds Seite** *akk* **~** to side with sb; (*die Fronten wechseln*) to go over to sb.

schlagend *adj* (*Beweis*) convincing; **~e Wetter** (*MIN*) firedamp.

Schlager ['ʃlaːgər] (**-s**, **-**) *m* (*MUS, fig*) hit.

Schläger ['ʃlɛːgər] (**-s**, **-**) *m* brawler; (*SPORT*) bat; (*TENNIS etc*) racket; (*GOLF*) club; (*Hockey~*) hockey stick.

Schlägerei [ʃlɛːgə'raɪ] *f* fight, punch-up.

Schlagersänger *m* pop singer.

Schlägertyp (*umg*) *m* thug.

Schlag- *zW:* **s~fertig** *adj* quick-witted;

~fertigkeit *f* ready wit, quickness of repartee; **~instrument** *nt* percussion instrument; **~kraft** *f* (*lit, fig*) power; (*MIL*) strike power; (*BOXEN*) punch(ing power); **s~kräftig** *adj* powerful; (*Beweise*) clear-cut; **~loch** *nt* pothole; **~obers** (-, -) (*ÖSTERR*) *nt*, **~rahm** *m*, **~sahne** *f* (whipped) cream; **~seite** *f* (*NAUT*) list; **~stock** *m* (*form*) truncheon (*BRIT*), nightstick (*US*).

schlägt [ʃlɛːkt] *vb siehe* **schlagen**.

Schlag- *zW:* **~wort** *nt* slogan, catch phrase; **~zeile** *f* headline; **~zeilen machen** (*umg*) to hit the headlines; **~zeug** *nt* drums *pl*; (*in Orchester*) percussion; **~zeuger** (-s, -) *m* drummer; percussionist.

schlaksig ['ʃlaːksɪç] (*umg*) *adj* gangling, gawky.

Schlamassel [ʃlaˈmasəl] (-s, -) (*umg*) *m* mess.

Schlamm [ʃlam] (-(e)s, -e) *m* mud.

schlammig *adj* muddy.

Schlampe ['ʃlampə] (-, -n) (*umg*) *f* slattern, slut.

schlampen (*umg*) *vi* to be sloppy.

Schlamperei [ʃlampəˈraɪ] (*umg*) *f* disorder, untidiness; (*schlechte Arbeit*) sloppy work.

schlampig (*umg*) *adj* slovenly, sloppy.

schlang *etc* [ʃlaŋ] *vb siehe* **schlingen**.

Schlange ['ʃlaŋə] (-, -n) *f* snake; (*Menschen~*) queue (*BRIT*), line (*US*); **~ stehen** to (form a) queue (*BRIT*), stand in line (*US*); **eine falsche ~** a snake in the grass.

schlängeln ['ʃlɛŋəln] *vr* to twist, wind; (*Fluß*) to meander.

Schlangen- *zW:* **~biß** *m* snake bite; **~gift** *nt* snake venom; **~linie** *f* wavy line.

schlank [ʃlaŋk] *adj* slim, slender; **S~heit** *f* slimness, slenderness; **S~heitskur** *f* diet.

schlapp [ʃlap] *adj* limp; (*locker*) slack; (*umg: energielos*) listless; (*nach Krankheit etc*) run-down.

Schlappe (-, -n) (*umg*) *f* setback.

Schlappen (-s, -) (*umg*) *m* slipper.

schlapp- *zW:* **S~heit** *f* limpness; slackness; **S~hut** *m* slouch hat; **~machen** (*umg*) *vi* to wilt, droop; **S~schwanz** (*pej: umg*) *m* weakling, softy.

Schlaraffenland [ʃlaˈrafənlant] *nt* land of milk and honey.

schlau [ʃlau] *adj* crafty, cunning; **ich werde nicht ~ aus ihm** I don't know what to make of him; **S~berger** (-s, -) (*umg*) *m* clever Dick.

Schlauch [ʃlaux] (-(e)s, Schläuche) *m* hose; (*in Reifen*) inner tube; (*umg: Anstrengung*) grind; **auf dem ~ stehen** (*umg*) to be in a jam *od* fix; **~boot** *nt* rubber dinghy.

schlauchen (*umg*) *vt* to tell on, exhaust.

schlauchlos *adj* (*Reifen*) tubeless.

Schläue ['ʃlɔʏə] (-) *f* cunning.

Schlaufe ['ʃlaufə] (-, -n) *f* loop; (*Aufhänger*) hanger.

Schlauheit *f* cunning.

Schlaukopf *m* clever Dick.

Schlawiner [ʃlaˈviːnər] (-s, -) *m* (*hum: umg*) villain, rogue.

schlecht [ʃlɛçt] *adj* bad; (*ungenießbar*) bad, off (*BRIT*) ♦ *adv:* **er kann ~ nein sagen** he finds it hard to say no, he can't say no; **jdm ist ~** sb feels sick *od* ill; **~ und recht** after a fashion; **auf jdn ~ zu sprechen sein** not to have a good word to say for sb; **er hat nicht ~ gestaunt** (*umg*) he wasn't half surprised.

schlechterdings *adv* simply.

schlecht- *zW:* **~gehen** *unreg vi unpers:* **jdm geht es ~** sb is in a bad way; **heute geht es ~** today is not very convenient; **S~heit** *f* badness; **~hin** *adv* simply; **der Dramatiker ~hin** THE playwright.

Schlechtigkeit *f* badness; (*Tat*) bad deed.

schlechtmachen *vt* to run down, denigrate.

schlecken ['ʃlɛkən] *vt, vi* to lick.

Schlegel ['ʃleːgəl] (-s, -) *m* (drum)stick; (*Hammer*) hammer; (*KOCH*) leg.

schleichen ['ʃlaɪçən] *unreg vi* to creep, crawl.

schleichend *adj* creeping; (*Krankheit, Gift*) insidious.

Schleichweg *m:* **auf ~en** (*fig*) on the quiet.

Schleichwerbung *f:* **eine ~** a plug.

Schleie ['ʃlaɪə] (-, -n) *f* tench.

Schleier ['ʃlaɪər] (-s, -) *m* veil; **~eule** *f* barn owl; **s~haft** (*umg*) *adj:* **jdm s~haft sein** to be a mystery to sb.

Schleife ['ʃlaɪfə] (-, -n) *f* (*auch COMPUT*) loop; (*Band*) bow; (*Kranz~*) ribbon.

schleifen¹ *vt* to drag; (*MIL: Festung*) to raze ♦ *vi* to drag; **die Kupplung ~ lassen** (*AUT*) to slip the clutch.

schleifen² *unreg vt* to grind; (*Edelstein*) to cut; (*MIL: Soldaten*) to drill.

Schleifmaschine *f* sander; (*in Fabrik*) grinding machine.

Schleifstein *m* grindstone.

Schleim [ʃlaɪm] (-(e)s, -e) *m* slime; (*MED*) mucus; (*KOCH*) gruel; **~haut** *f* mucous membrane.

schleimig *adj* slimy.

schlemmen ['ʃlɛmən] *vi* to feast.

Schlemmer(in) (-s, -) *m(f)* gourmet, bon vivant.

Schlemmerei [ʃlɛməˈraɪ] *f* feasting.

schlendern ['ʃlɛndərn] *vi* to stroll.

Schlendrian ['ʃlɛndriaːn] (-(e)s) *m* sloppy way of working.

Schlenker ['ʃlɛŋkər] (-s, -) *m* swerve.

schlenkern *vt, vi* to swing, dangle.

Schleppe ['ʃlɛpə] (-, -n) *f* train.

schleppen *vt* to drag; (*Auto, Schiff*) to tow; (*tragen*) to lug.

schleppend *adj* dragging; (*Bedienung, Abfertigung*) sluggish, slow.

Schlepper (-s, -) *m* tractor; (*Schiff*) tug.

Schleppkahn *m* (canal) barge.

Schlepptau *nt* towrope; **jdn ins ~ nehmen** (*fig*) to take sb in tow.

Schlesien ['ʃleːziən] (**-s**) *nt* Silesia.
Schlesier(in) (**-s, -**) *m(f)* Silesian.
schlesisch *adj* Silesian.
Schleswig-Holstein ['ʃleːsvɪç'hɔlʃtaɪn] (**-s**) *nt* Schleswig-Holstein.
Schleuder ['ʃlɔʏdər] (**-, -n**) *f* catapult; (*Wäsche~*) spin-dryer; (*Zentrifuge*) centrifuge; **~honig** *m* extracted honey.
schleudern *vt* to hurl; (*Wäsche*) to spin-dry ♦ *vi* (*AUT*) to skid; **ins S~ kommen** (*AUT*) to go into a skid; (*fig: umg*) to run into trouble.
Schleuder- *zW:* **~preis** *m* give-away price; **~sitz** *m* (*AVIAT*) ejector seat; (*fig*) hot seat; **~ware** *f* cut-price (*BRIT*) *od* cut-rate (*US*) goods *pl*.
schleunig ['ʃlɔʏnɪç] *adj* prompt, speedy; (*Schritte*) quick.
schleunigst *adv* straight away.
Schleuse ['ʃlɔʏzə] (**-, -n**) *f* lock; (*Schleusentor*) sluice.
schleusen *vt* (*Schiffe*) to pass through a lock, lock; (*Wasser*) to channel; (*Menschen*) to filter; (*fig: heimlich*) to smuggle.
Schlich (**-(e)s, -e**) *m* dodge, trick; **jdm auf die ~e kommen** to get wise to sb.
schlich *etc* [ʃlɪç] *vb siehe* **schleichen**.
schlicht [ʃlɪçt] *adj* simple, plain.
schlichten *vt* to smooth; (*beilegen*) to settle; (*Streit: vermitteln*) to mediate, arbitrate.
Schlichter(in) (**-s, -**) *m(f)* mediator, arbitrator.
Schlichtheit *f* simplicity, plainness.
Schlichtung *f* settlement; arbitration.
Schlick [ʃlɪk] (**-(e)s, -e**) *m* mud; (*Öl~*) slick.
schlief *etc* [ʃliːf] *vb siehe* **schlafen**.
Schließe ['ʃliːsə] (**-, -n**) *f* fastener.
schließen ['ʃliːsən] *unreg vt* to close, shut; (*beenden*) to close; (*Freundschaft, Bündnis, Ehe*) to enter into; (*COMPUT: Datei*) to close; (*folgern*): **~ (aus)** to infer (from) ♦ *vi, vr* to close, shut; **auf etw** *akk* **~ lassen** to suggest sth; **jdn/etw in sein Herz ~** to take sb/sth to one's heart; **etw in sich ~** to include sth; **„geschlossen"** "closed".
Schließfach *nt* locker.
schließlich *adv* finally; (**~ doch**) after all.
Schliff (**-(e)s, -e**) *m* cut(ting); (*fig*) polish; **einer Sache den letzten ~ geben** (*fig*) to put the finishing touch(es) to sth.
schliff *etc* [ʃlɪf] *vb siehe* **schleifen**.
schlimm [ʃlɪm] *adj* bad; **das war ~** that was terrible; **das ist halb so ~!** that's not so bad!; **~er** *adj* worse; **~ste(r, s)** *adj* worst.
schlimmstenfalls *adv* at (the) worst.
Schlinge ['ʃlɪŋə] (**-, -n**) *f* loop; (*an Galgen*) noose; (*Falle*) snare; (*MED*) sling.
Schlingel (**-s, -**) *m* rascal.
schlingen *unreg vt* to wind ♦ *vi* (*essen*) to bolt one's food, gobble.
schlingern *vi* to roll.
Schlingpflanze *f* creeper.
Schlips [ʃlɪps] (**-es, -e**) *m* tie, necktie (*US*);

sich auf den ~ getreten fühlen (*fig: umg*) to feel offended.
Schlitten ['ʃlɪtən] (**-s, -**) *m* sledge, sled; (*Pferde~*) sleigh; **mit jdm ~ fahren** (*umg*) to give sb a rough time; **~bahn** *f* toboggan run; **~fahren** (**-s**) *nt* tobogganing.
schlittern ['ʃlɪtərn] *vi* to slide; (*Wagen*) to skid.
Schlittschuh ['ʃlɪtʃuː] *m* skate; **~bahn** *f* skating rink; **~ laufen** to skate; **~läufer** *m* skater.
Schlitz [ʃlɪts] (**-es, -e**) *m* slit; (*für Münze*) slot; (*Hosen~*) flies *pl*; **s~äugig** *adj* slant-eyed; **s~en** *vt* to slit; **~ohr** *nt* (*fig*) sly fox.
schlohweiß ['ʃloː'vaɪs] *adj* snow-white.
Schlokal *nt* gourmet restaurant.
Schloß *etc* [ʃlɔs] *vb siehe* **schließen**.
Schloß (**-sses, ⁼sser**) *nt* lock, padlock; (*an Schmuck etc*) clasp; (*Bau*) castle; (*Palast*) palace; **ins ~ fallen** to lock (itself).
Schlosser ['ʃlɔsər] (**-s, -**) *m* (*Auto~*) fitter; (*für Schlüssel etc*) locksmith.
Schlosserei [ʃlɔsə'raɪ] *f* metal(working) shop.
Schloßhund *m:* **heulen wie ein ~** to howl one's head off.
Schlot [ʃloːt] (**-(e)s, -e**) *m* chimney; (*NAUT*) funnel.
schlottern ['ʃlɔtərn] *vi* to shake; (*vor Angst*) to tremble; (*Kleidung*) to be baggy.
Schlucht [ʃlʊxt] (**-, -en**) *f* gorge, ravine.
schluchzen ['ʃlʊxtsən] *vi* to sob.
Schluck [ʃlʊk] (**-(e)s, -e**) *m* swallow; (*größer*) gulp; (*kleiner*) sip; (*ein bißchen*) drop.
Schluckauf (**-s**) *m* hiccups *pl*.
schlucken *vt* to swallow; (*umg: Alkohol, Benzin*) to guzzle; (: *verschlingen*) to swallow up ♦ *vi* to swallow.
Schlucker (**-s, -**) (*umg*) *m:* **armer ~** poor devil.
Schluckimpfung *f* oral vaccination.
schlud(e)rig ['ʃluːdrɪç] (*umg*) *adj* slipshod.
schludern ['ʃluːdərn] (*umg*) *vi* to do slipshod work.
schlug *etc* [ʃluːk] *vb siehe* **schlagen**.
Schlummer ['ʃlʊmər] (**-s**) *m* slumber.
schlummern *vi* to slumber.
Schlund [ʃlʊnt] (**-(e)s, ⁼e**) *m* gullet; (*fig*) jaw.
schlüpfen ['ʃlʏpfən] *vi* to slip; (*Vogel etc*) to hatch (out).
Schlüpfer ['ʃlʏpfər] (**-s, -**) *m* panties *pl*, knickers *pl*.
Schlupfloch ['ʃlʊpflɔx] *nt* hole; (*Versteck*) hide-out; (*fig*) loophole.
schlüpfrig ['ʃlʏpfrɪç] *adj* slippery; (*fig*) lewd; **S~keit** *f* slipperiness; lewdness.
Schlupfwinkel *m* hiding place; (*fig*) quiet corner.
schlurfen ['ʃlʊrfən] *vi* to shuffle.
schlürfen ['ʃlʏrfən] *vt, vi* to slurp.
Schluß [ʃlʊs] (**-sses, ⁼sse**) *m* end; (*~folgerung*) conclusion; **am ~** at the end; **~ für heute!** that'll do for today; **~ jetzt!** that's enough

now!; ~ **machen mit** to finish with.
Schlüssel ['ʃlʏsəl] (**-s**, -) m (lit, fig) key;
(Schraub~) spanner, wrench; (MUS) clef;
~**bein** nt collarbone; ~**blume** f cowslip,
primrose; ~**bund** m bunch of keys;
~**erlebnis** nt (PSYCH) crucial experience;
~**kind** nt latchkey child; ~**loch** nt keyhole;
~**position** f key position; ~**wort** nt safe
combination; (COMPUT) keyword.
Schlußfolgerung f conclusion, inference.
Schlußformel f (in Brief) closing formula;
(bei Vertrag) final clause.
schlüssig ['ʃlʏsɪç] adj conclusive; **sich** dat
(**über etw** akk) ~ **sein** to have made up one's
mind (about sth).
Schluß- zW: ~**licht** nt rear light (BRIT),
taillight (US); (fig) tail ender; ~**strich** m (fig)
final stroke; **einen** ~**strich unter etw** akk
ziehen to consider sth finished; ~**verkauf** m
clearance sale; ~**wort** nt concluding words
pl.
Schmach [ʃmaːx] (-) f disgrace, ignominy.
schmachten ['ʃmaxtən] vi to languish; **nach**
jdm ~ to pine for sb.
schmächtig ['ʃmɛçtɪç] adj slight.
schmachvoll adj ignominious, humiliating.
schmackhaft ['ʃmakhaft] adj tasty; **jdm etw**
~ **machen** (fig) to make sth palatable to sb.
schmähen ['ʃmɛːən] vt to abuse, revile.
schmählich adj ignominious, shameful.
Schmähung f abuse.
schmal [ʃmaːl] adj narrow; (Person, Buch etc)
slender, slim; (karg) meagre (BRIT), meager
(US); ~**brüstig** adj narrow-chested.
schmälern ['ʃmɛːlərn] vt to diminish; (fig) to
belittle.
Schmalfilm m cine (BRIT) od movie (US) film.
Schmalspur f narrow gauge.
Schmalspur- (pej) in zW small-time.
Schmalz [ʃmalts] (-es, -e) nt dripping;
(Schweine~) lard; (fig) sentiment, schmaltz.
schmalzig adj (fig) schmaltzy, slushy.
schmarotzen [ʃma'rɔtsən] vi (BIOL) to be
parasitic; (fig) to sponge.
Schmarotzer (-s, -) m (auch fig) parasite.
Schmarren ['ʃmarən] (-s, -) m (ÖSTERR) small
pieces of pancake; (fig) rubbish, tripe.
schmatzen ['ʃmatsən] vi to eat noisily.
Schmaus [ʃmaʊs] (-es, **Schmäuse**) m feast;
s~en vi to feast.
schmecken ['ʃmɛkən] vt, vi to taste; **es**
schmeckt ihm he likes it; **schmeckt es**
Ihnen? is it good?, are you enjoying your
food od meal?; **das schmeckt nach mehr!**
(umg) it's very moreish (hum); **es sich**
~ **lassen** to tuck in.
Schmeichelei [ʃmaɪçə'laɪ] f flattery.
schmeichelhaft ['ʃmaɪçəlhaft] adj flattering.
schmeicheln vi to flatter.
Schmeichler(in) (-s, -) m(f) flatterer.
schmeißen ['ʃmaɪsən] unreg (umg) vt to throw,
chuck; (spendieren): **eine Runde** od **Lage** ~ to

stand a round.
Schmeißfliege f bluebottle.
Schmelz [ʃmɛlts] (-es, -e) m enamel; (Glasur)
glaze; (von Stimme) melodiousness; **s~bar**
adj fusible.
schmelzen unreg vt to melt; (Erz) to smelt ♦ vi
to melt.
Schmelz- zW: ~**hütte** f smelting works pl;
~**käse** m cheese spread; (in Scheiben)
processed cheese; ~**ofen** m melting
furnace; (für Erze) smelting furnace;
~**punkt** m melting point; ~**tiegel** m (lit, fig)
melting pot; ~**wasser** nt melted snow.
Schmerbauch ['ʃmeːrbaʊx] (umg) m paunch,
potbelly.
Schmerz [ʃmɛrts] (-es, -en) m pain; (Trauer)
grief no pl; ~**en haben** to be in pain;
s~empfindlich adj sensitive to pain.
schmerzen vt, vi to hurt.
Schmerzensgeld nt compensation.
Schmerz- zW: **s~haft** adj painful; **s~lich** adj
painful; **s~lindernd** adj pain-relieving;
s~los adj painless; ~**mittel** nt painkiller,
analgesic; **s~stillend** adj pain-killing,
analgesic; ~**tablette** f pain-killing tablet.
Schmetterling ['ʃmɛtərlɪŋ] m butterfly.
Schmetterlingsstil m (SCHWIMMEN)
butterfly stroke.
schmettern ['ʃmɛtərn] vt to smash; (Melodie)
to sing loudly, bellow out ♦ vi to smash
(SPORT); (Trompete) to blare.
Schmied [ʃmiːt] (-(e)s, -e) m blacksmith.
Schmiede ['ʃmiːdə] (-, -n) f smithy, forge;
~'**eisen** nt wrought iron.
schmieden vt to forge; (Pläne) to devise,
concoct.
schmiegen ['ʃmiːgən] vt to press, nestle ♦ vr:
sich ~ **an** +akk to cuddle up to, nestle up to.
schmiegsam ['ʃmiːkzaːm] adj flexible, pliable.
Schmiere ['ʃmiːrə] f grease; (THEAT)
greasepaint, make-up; (pej: schlechtes
Theater) fleapit; ~ **stehen** (umg) to be the
look-out.
schmieren vt to smear; (ölen) to lubricate,
grease; (bestechen) to bribe ♦ vi (schreiben)
to scrawl; **es läuft wie geschmiert** it's going
like clockwork; **jdm eine** ~ (umg) to clout sb
one.
Schmierenkomödiant (pej) m ham (actor).
Schmier- zW: ~**fett** nt grease; ~**fink** m messy
person; ~**geld** nt bribe; ~**heft** nt jotter.
schmierig adj greasy.
Schmiermittel nt lubricant.
Schmierseife f soft soap.
schmilzt [ʃmɪltst] vb siehe **schmelzen**.
Schminke ['ʃmɪŋkə] (-, -n) f make-up.
schminken vt, vr to make up.
schmirgeln ['ʃmɪrgəln] vt to sand (down).
Schmirgelpapier (-s) nt emery paper.
Schmiß (-sses, -sse) m (Narbe) duelling (BRIT)
od dueling (US) scar; (veraltet: Schwung)
dash, élan.

schmiß etc [ʃmɪs] vb siehe **schmeißen**.
Schmöker ['ʃmøːkər] (-s, -) (umg) m (trashy) old book.
schmökern vi to bury o.s. in a book; (umg) to browse.
schmollen ['ʃmɔlən] vi to pout; (gekränkt) to sulk.
schmollend adj sulky.
Schmollmund m pout.
schmolz etc [ʃmɔlts] vb siehe **schmelzen**.
Schmorbraten m stewed od braised meat.
schmoren ['ʃmoːrən] vt to braise.
Schmu [ʃmuː] (-s) (umg) m cheating.
Schmuck [ʃmʊk] (-(e)s, -e) m jewellery (BRIT), jewelry (US); (Verzierung) decoration.
schmücken ['ʃmʏkən] vt to decorate.
Schmuck- zW: **s~los** adj unadorned, plain; **~losigkeit** f simplicity; **~sachen** pl jewels pl, jewellery sing (BRIT), jewelry sing (US); **~stück** nt (Ring etc) piece of jewellery (BRIT) od jewelry (US); (fig: Prachtstück) gem.
schmudd(e)lig ['ʃmʊd(ə)lɪç] adj messy; (schmutzig) dirty; (schmierig, unsauber) filthy.
Schmuggel ['ʃmʊgəl] (-s) m smuggling.
schmuggeln vt, vi to smuggle.
Schmuggelware f contraband.
Schmuggler(in) (-s, -) m(f) smuggler.
schmunzeln ['ʃmʊntsəln] vi to smile benignly.
schmusen ['ʃmuːzən] (umg) vi (zärtlich sein) to cuddle; **mit jdm ~** to cuddle sb.
Schmutz [ʃmʊts] (-es) m dirt; (fig) filth; **s~en** vi to get dirty; **~fink** m filthy creature; **~fleck** m stain.
schmutzig adj dirty; **~e Wäsche waschen** (fig) to wash one's dirty linen in public.
Schnabel ['ʃnaːbəl] (-s, ̈) m beak, bill; (Ausguß) spout; (umg: Mund) mouth; **reden, wie einem der ~ gewachsen ist** to say exactly what comes into one's head; (unaffektiert) to talk naturally.
schnacken ['ʃnakən] (NORDD: umg) vi to chat.
Schnake ['ʃnaːkə] (-, -n) f crane fly; (Stechmücke) gnat.
Schnalle ['ʃnalə] (-, -n) f buckle; (an Handtasche, Buch) clasp.
schnallen vt to buckle.
schnalzen ['ʃnaltsən] vi to snap; (mit Zunge) to click.
Schnäppchen ['ʃnɛpçən] (umg) nt bargain, snip.
schnappen ['ʃnapən] vt to grab, catch; (umg: ergreifen) to snatch ♦ vi to snap.
Schnappschloß nt spring lock.
Schnappschuß m (PHOT) snapshot.
Schnaps [ʃnaps] (-es, ̈e) m schnapps; (umg: Branntwein) spirits pl; **~idee** (umg) f crackpot idea; **~leiche** (umg) f drunk.
schnarchen ['ʃnarçən] vi to snore.
schnattern ['ʃnatərn] vi to chatter; (zittern) to shiver.
schnauben ['ʃnaubən] vi to snort ♦ vr to blow one's nose.

schnaufen ['ʃnaufən] vi to puff, pant.
Schnaufer (-s, -) (umg) m breath.
Schnauzbart ['ʃnautsbaːrt] m moustache (BRIT), mustache (US).
Schnauze (-, -n) f snout, muzzle; (Ausguß) spout; (umg) gob; **auf die ~ fallen** (fig) to come a cropper (umg); **etw frei nach ~ machen** to do sth any old how.
Schnecke ['ʃnɛkə] (-, -n) f snail; (Nackt~) slug; (KOCH: Gebäck) ≈ Chelsea bun; **jdn zur ~ machen** (umg) to give sb a real bawling out.
Schneckenhaus nt snail's shell.
Schneckentempo (umg) nt: **im ~** at a snail's pace.
Schnee [ʃneː] (-s) m snow; (Ei~) beaten egg white; **~ von gestern** old hat; **water under the bridge**; **~ball** m snowball; **~besen** m (KOCH) whisk; **~fall** m snowfall; **~flocke** f snowflake; **~gestöber** nt snowstorm; **~glöckchen** nt snowdrop; **~grenze** f snowline; **~kette** f (AUT) snow chain; **~könig** m: **sich freuen wie ein ~könig** to be as pleased as Punch; **~mann** m snowman; **~pflug** m snowplough (BRIT), snowplow (US); **~regen** m sleet; **~schmelze** f thaw; **~treiben** nt driving snow; **~wehe** f snowdrift; **~wittchen** nt Snow White.
Schneid [ʃnait] (-(e)s) (umg) m pluck.
Schneidbrenner (-s, -) m (TECH) oxyacetylene cutter.
Schneide ['ʃnaidə] (-, -n) f edge; (Klinge) blade.
schneiden unreg vt to cut; (Film, Tonband) to edit; (kreuzen) to cross, intersect ♦ vr to cut o.s.; (umg: sich täuschen): **da hat er sich aber geschnitten!** he's very much mistaken; **die Luft ist zum S~** (fig: umg) the air is very bad.
schneidend adj cutting.
Schneider (-s, -) m tailor; **frieren wie ein ~** (umg) to be frozen to the marrow; **aus dem ~ sein** (fig) to be out of the woods.
Schneiderei [ʃnaidəˈrai] f tailor's shop; (einer Schneiderin) dressmaker's shop.
Schneiderin f dressmaker.
schneidern vt to make ♦ vi to be a tailor.
Schneidersitz (-es) m: **im ~ sitzen** to sit cross-legged.
Schneidezahn m incisor.
schneidig adj dashing; (mutig) plucky.
schneien ['ʃnaiən] vi to snow; **jdm ins Haus ~** (umg: Besuch) to drop in on sb; (: Rechnung, Brief) to come in the post (BRIT) od mail (US).
Schneise ['ʃnaizə] (-, -n) f (Wald~) clearing.
schnell [ʃnɛl] adj quick, fast ♦ adv quick(ly), fast; **das ging ~** that was quick; **S~boot** nt speedboat.
Schnelle (-) f: **etw auf die ~ machen** to do sth in a rush.
schnellen vi to shoot.

Schnellgericht nt (*JUR*) summary court; (*KOCH*) convenience food.
Schnellhefter m loose-leaf binder.
Schnelligkeit f speed.
Schnell- zW: ~**imbiß** m (*Essen*) (quick) snack; (*Raum*) snack bar; ~**kochtopf** m (*Dampfkochtopf*) pressure cooker; ~**reinigung** f express cleaner's.
schnellstens adv as quickly as possible.
Schnellstraße f expressway.
Schnellzug m fast od express train.
schneuzen ['ʃnɔʏtsən] vr to blow one's nose.
Schnickschnack ['ʃnɪkʃnak] (-(e)s) (*umg*) m twaddle.
Schnippchen ['ʃnɪpçən] nt: **jdm ein ~ schlagen** to play a trick on sb.
schnippeln ['ʃnɪpəln] (*umg*) vt to snip; (*mit Messer*) to hack ♦ vi: ~ **an** +dat to snip at; to hack at.
schnippen ['ʃnɪpən] vi: **mit den Fingern ~** to snap one's fingers.
schnippisch ['ʃnɪpɪʃ] adj sharp-tongued.
Schnipsel ['ʃnɪpsəl] (-s, -) (*umg*) m od nt scrap; (*Papier~*) scrap of paper.
Schnitt (-(e)s, -e) m cut(ting); (*~punkt*) intersection; (*Quer~*) (cross) section; (*Durch~*) average; (*~muster*) pattern; (*Ernte*) crop; (*an Buch*) (*umg*: *Gewinn*) profit; ~: **L. Schwarz** (*FILM*) editor - L. Schwarz; **im ~** on average.
schnitt etc [ʃnɪt] vb siehe **schneiden**.
Schnittblumen pl cut flowers pl.
Schnittbohnen pl French od green beans pl.
Schnitte (-, -n) f slice; (*belegt*) sandwich.
schnittfest adj (*Tomaten*) firm.
Schnittfläche f section.
schnittig ['ʃnɪtɪç] adj smart; (*Auto, Formen*) stylish.
Schnitt- zW: ~**lauch** m chive; ~**muster** nt pattern; ~**punkt** m (point of) intersection; ~**stelle** f (*COMPUT*) interface; ~**wunde** f cut.
Schnitzarbeit f wood carving.
Schnitzel (-s, -) nt scrap; (*KOCH*) escalope; ~**jagd** f paperchase.
schnitzen ['ʃnɪtsən] vt to carve.
Schnitzer (-s, -) m carver; (*umg*) blunder.
Schnitzerei ['ʃnɪtsə'raɪ] f wood carving.
schnodderig ['ʃnɔdərɪç] (*umg*) adj snotty.
schnöde ['ʃnøːdə] adj base, mean.
Schnorchel ['ʃnɔrçəl] (-s, -) m snorkel.
schnorcheln vi to go snorkelling.
Schnörkel ['ʃnœrkəl] (-s, -) m flourish; (*ARCHIT*) scroll.
schnorren ['ʃnɔrən] vt, vi to cadge (*BRIT*).
Schnorrer (-s, -) (*umg*) m cadger (*BRIT*).
Schnösel ['ʃnøːzəl] (-s, -) (*umg*) m snotty(-nosed) little upstart.
schnuckelig ['ʃnʊkəlɪç] (*umg*) adj (*gemütlich*) snug, cosy; (*Person*) sweet.
schnüffeln ['ʃnʏfəln] vi to sniff; (*fig*: *umg*: *spionieren*) to snoop around; **S~** nt (*von*

Klebstoff etc) glue-sniffing etc.
Schnüffler(in) (-s, -) m(f) snooper.
Schnuller ['ʃnʊlər] (-s, -) m dummy (*BRIT*), pacifier (*US*).
Schnulze ['ʃnʊltsə] (-, -n) (*umg*) f schmaltzy film/book/song.
Schnupfen ['ʃnʊpfən] (-s, -) m cold.
Schnupftabak m snuff.
schnuppe ['ʃnʊpə] (*umg*) adj: **jdm ~ sein** to be all the same to sb.
schnuppern ['ʃnʊpərn] vi to sniff.
Schnur [ʃnuːr] (-, ⁻e) f string; (*Kordel*) cord; (*ELEK*) flex.
Schnürchen ['ʃnyːrçən] nt: **es läuft** od **klappt (alles) wie am ~** everything's going like clockwork.
schnüren ['ʃnyːrən] vt to tie.
schnurgerade adj straight (as a die od an arrow).
Schnurrbart ['ʃnʊrbaːrt] m moustache (*BRIT*), mustache (*US*).
schnurren ['ʃnʊrən] vi to purr; (*Kreisel*) to hum.
Schnürschuh m lace-up (shoe).
Schnürsenkel m shoelace.
schnurstracks adv straight (away); ~ **auf jdn/etw zugehen** to make a beeline for sb/sth (*umg*).
schob etc [ʃoːp] vb siehe **schieben**.
Schock [ʃɔk] (-(e)s, -e) m shock; **unter ~ stehen** to be in (a state of) shock.
schocken (*umg*) vt to shock.
Schocker (-s, -) (*umg*) m shocking film/novel, shocker.
schockieren vt to shock, outrage.
Schöffe ['ʃœfə] (-n, -n) m lay magistrate.
Schöffengericht nt magistrates' court.
Schöffin f lay magistrate.
Schokolade [ʃoko'laːdə] (-, -n) f chocolate.
scholl etc [ʃɔl] vb siehe **schallen**.
Scholle ['ʃɔlə] (-, -n) f clod; (*Eis~*) ice floe; (*Fisch*) plaice.
Scholli ['ʃɔlɪ] (*umg*) m: **mein lieber ~!** (*drohend*) now look here!

═══════════ *SCHLÜSSELWORT*

schon [ʃoːn] adv **1** (*bereits*) already; **er ist ~ da** he's there/here already; he's already there/here; **ist er ~ da?** is he there/here yet?; **warst du ~ einmal dort?** have you ever been there?; **ich war ~ einmal dort** I've been there before; **das war ~ immer so** that has always been the case; **hast du ~ gehört?** have you heard?; **~ 1920** as early as 1920; **~ vor 100 Jahren** as far back as 100 years ago; **er wollte ~ die Hoffnung aufgeben, als ...** he was just about to give up hope when ...; **wartest du ~ lange?** have you been waiting (for) long?; **wie lang so oft** as so often (before); **was, ~ wieder?** what - again?
2 (*bestimmt*) all right; **du wirst ~ sehen**

you'll see (all right); **das wird ~ noch gutgehen** that should turn out OK (in the end)

3 (*bloß*) just; **allein ~ das Gefühl** ... just the very feeling ...; **~ der Gedanke** the mere *od* very thought; **wenn ich das ~ höre** I only have to hear that

4 (*einschränkend*): **ja ~, aber** ... yes (well), but ...

5: **das ist ~ möglich** that's quite possible; **~ gut** OK; **du weißt ~** you know; **komm ~** come on; **hör ~ auf damit!** will you stop that!; **was macht das ~, wenn ...?** what does it matter if ...?; **und wenn ~!** (*umg*) so what?

schön [ʃøːn] *adj* beautiful; (*Mann*) handsome; (*nett*) nice ♦ *adv*: **sich ganz ~ ärgern** to be very angry; **da hast du etwas S~es angerichtet** you've made a fine *od* nice mess; **~e Grüße** best wishes; **~en Dank** (many) thanks; **~ weich/warm** nice and soft/warm.

schonen ['ʃoːnən] *vt* to look after; (*jds Nerven*) to spare; (*Gegner, Kind*) to be easy on; (*Teppich, Füße*) to save ♦ *vr* to take it easy.

schonend *adj* careful, gentle; **jdm etw ~ beibringen** to break sth to sb gently.

Schoner ['ʃoːnər] (**-s, -**) *m* (*NAUT*) schooner; (*Sessel~*) cover.

Schönfärberei *f* (*fig*) glossing things over.

Schonfrist *f* period of grace.

Schöngeist *m* cultured person, aesthete (*BRIT*), esthete (*US*).

Schönheit *f* beauty.

Schönheits- *zW*: **~fehler** *m* blemish, flaw; **~operation** *f* cosmetic surgery; **~wettbewerb** *m* beauty contest.

Schonkost (**-**) *f* light diet.

schönmachen *vr* to make o.s. look nice.

Schönschrift *f*: **in ~** in one's best (hand)writing.

schöntun *unreg vi*: **jdm ~** (*schmeicheln*) to flatter *od* soft-soap sb, play up to sb.

Schonung *f* good care; (*Nachsicht*) consideration; (*Forst*) plantation of young trees.

schonungslos *adj* ruthless, harsh.

Schonzeit *f* close season.

Schopf [ʃɔpf] (**-(e)s, ¨e**) *m*: **eine Gelegenheit beim ~ ergreifen** *od* **fassen** to seize *od* grasp an opportunity with both hands.

schöpfen ['ʃœpfən] *vt* to scoop; (*Suppe*) to ladle; (*Mut*) to summon up; (*Luft*) to breathe in; (*Hoffnung*) to find.

Schöpfer (**-s, -**) *m* creator; (*Gott*) Creator; (*umg: Schöpfkelle*) ladle; **s~isch** *adj* creative.

Schöpfkelle *f* ladle.

Schöpflöffel *m* skimmer, scoop.

Schöpfung *f* creation.

Schoppen ['ʃɔpən] (**-s, -**) *m* (*Glas Wein*) glass of wine; **~wein** *m* wine by the glass.

schor *etc* [ʃoːr] *vb siehe* **scheren**.

Schorf [ʃɔrf] (**-(e)s, -e**) *m* scab.

Schorle ['ʃɔrlə] (**-, -n**) *f* spritzer, *wine and soda water or lemonade*.

Schornstein ['ʃɔrnʃtaɪn] *m* chimney; (*NAUT*) funnel; **~feger** (**-s, -**) *m* chimney sweep.

Schoß (**-es, ¨e**) *m* lap; (*Rock~*) coat tail; **im ~e der Familie** in the bosom of one's family.

schoß *etc* [ʃɔs] *vb siehe* **schießen**.

Schoßhund *m* lapdog.

Schößling ['ʃœslɪŋ] *m* (*BOT*) shoot.

Schote ['ʃoːtə] (**-, -n**) *f* pod.

Schotte ['ʃɔtə] (**-n, -n**) *m* Scot, Scotsman.

Schottenrock ['ʃɔtənrɔk] *m* kilt; (*für Frauen*) tartan skirt.

Schotter ['ʃɔtər] (**-s**) *m* gravel; (*im Straßenbau*) road metal; (*EISENB*) ballast.

Schottin ['ʃɔtɪn] *f* Scot, Scotswoman.

schottisch ['ʃɔtɪʃ] *adj* Scottish, Scots; **das ~e Hochland** the Scottish Highlands *pl*.

Schottland (**-s**) *nt* Scotland.

schraffieren [ʃra'fiːrən] *vt* to hatch.

schräg [ʃrɛːk] *adj* slanting; (*schief, geneigt*) sloping; (*nicht gerade od parallel*) oblique ♦ *adv*: **~ gedruckt** in italics; **etw ~ stellen** to put sth at an angle; **~ gegenüber** diagonally opposite.

Schräge ['ʃrɛːgə] (**-, -n**) *f* slant.

Schräg- *zW*: **~kante** *f* bevelled (*BRIT*) *od* beveled (*US*) edge; **~schrift** *f* italics *pl*; **~streifen** *m* bias binding; **~strich** *m* oblique stroke.

Schramme ['ʃramə] (**-, -n**) *f* scratch.

schrammen *vt* to scratch.

Schrank [ʃraŋk] (**-(e)s, ¨e**) *m* cupboard (*BRIT*), closet (*US*); (*Kleider~*) wardrobe.

Schranke (**-, -n**) *f* barrier; (*fig: Grenze*) limit; (*: Hindernis*) barrier; **jdn in seine ~n (ver)weisen** (*fig*) to put sb in his place.

schrankenlos *adj* boundless; (*zügellos*) unrestrained.

Schrankenwärter *m* (*EISENB*) level-crossing (*BRIT*) *od* grade-crossing (*US*) attendant.

Schrankkoffer *m* wardrobe trunk.

Schrankwand *f* wall unit.

Schraube ['ʃraʊbə] (**-, -n**) *f* screw.

schrauben *vt* to screw; **etw in die Höhe ~** (*fig: Preise, Rekorde*) to push sth up; (*: Ansprüche*) to raise sth.

Schraubenschlüssel *m* spanner (*BRIT*), wrench (*US*).

Schraubenzieher (**-s, -**) *m* screwdriver.

Schraubstock ['ʃraʊpʃtɔk] *m* (*TECH*) vice (*BRIT*), vise (*US*).

Schrebergarten ['ʃreːbərgartən] *m* allotment (*BRIT*).

Schreck [ʃrɛk] (**-(e)s, -e**) *m* fright; **o ~ laß nach** (*hum: umg*) for goodness' sake!

Schrecken (**-s, -**) *m* terror; (*Schreck*) fright; **s~** *vt* to frighten, scare ♦ *vi*: **aus dem Schlaf s~** to be startled out of one's sleep.

schreckensbleich *adj* as white as a sheet *od* ghost.

Schreckensherrschaft f (reign of) terror.
Schreck- zW: ~**gespenst** nt nightmare;
s~**haft** adj jumpy, easily frightened; s~**lich**
adj terrible, dreadful; s~**lich gerne**! (umg)
I'd absolutely love to; ~**schraube** (pej: umg)
f (old) battle-axe; ~**schuß** m shot fired in
the air; ~**sekunde** f moment of shock.
Schrei [ʃraɪ] (-(e)s, -e) m scream; (Ruf) shout;
der letzte ~ (umg) the latest thing, all the
rage.
Schreibbedarf m writing materials pl,
stationery.
Schreibblock m writing pad.
schreiben ['ʃraɪbən] unreg vt to write; (mit
Schreibmaschine) to type out; (berichten:
Zeitung etc) to say; (buchstabieren) to spell
♦ vi to write; to type; to say; to spell ♦ vr: **wie
schreibt sich das?** how is that spelt?; **S~**
(-s, -) nt letter, communication.
Schreiber(in) (-s, -) m(f) writer; (Büro~)
clerk.
Schreib- zW: s~**faul** adj lazy about writing
letters; ~**fehler** m spelling mistake; ~**kraft**
f typist; ~**maschine** f typewriter; ~**papier**
nt notepaper; ~**schrift** f running
handwriting; (TYP) script; ~**schutz** m
(COMPUT) write-protect; ~**stube** f orderly
room; ~**tisch** m desk; ~**tischtäter** m wire od
string puller.
Schreibung f spelling.
Schreib- zW: ~**unterlage** f pad; ~**waren** pl
stationery sing; ~**warengeschäft** nt
stationer's (shop) (BRIT), stationery store
(US); ~**weise** f spelling; (Stil) style;
s~**wütig** adj crazy about writing; ~**zentrale**
f typing pool; ~**zeug** nt writing materials pl.
schreien ['ʃraɪən] unreg vt, vi to scream; (rufen)
to shout; **es war zum S~** (umg) it was a
scream od a hoot; **nach etw** ~ (fig) to cry
out for sth.
schreiend adj (fig) glaring; (: Farbe) loud.
Schreihals (umg) m (Baby) bawler;
(Unruhestifter) noisy troublemaker.
Schreikrampf m screaming fit.
Schreiner ['ʃraɪnər] (-s, -) m joiner;
(Zimmermann) carpenter; (Möbel~)
cabinetmaker.
Schreinerei [ʃraɪnə'raɪ] f joiner's workshop.
schreiten ['ʃraɪtən] unreg vi to stride.
schrie etc [ʃriː] vb siehe **schreien**.
Schrieb (-(e)s, -e) (umg) m missive (hum).
schrieb etc [ʃriːp] vb siehe **schreiben**.
Schrift [ʃrɪft] (-, -en) f writing; (Hand~)
handwriting; (~art) script; (TYP) typeface;
(Buch) work; ~**art** f (Hand~) script; (TYP)
typeface; ~**bild** nt script; (COMPUT)
typeface; ~**deutsch** nt written German;
~**führer** m secretary; s~**lich** adj written ♦ adv
in writing; **das kann ich Ihnen** s~**lich geben**
(fig: umg) I can tell you that for free;
~**probe** f (Hand~) specimen of one's
handwriting; ~**satz** m (TYP) fount (BRIT),

font (US); ~**setzer** m compositor; ~**sprache** f
written language.
Schriftsteller(in) (-s, -) m(f) writer; s~**isch** adj
literary.
Schrift- zW: ~**stück** nt document; ~**verkehr** m
correspondence; ~**wechsel** m
correspondence.
schrill [ʃrɪl] adj shrill; ~**en** vi (Stimme) to
sound shrilly; (Telefon) to ring shrilly.
Schritt (-(e)s, -e) m step; (Gangart) walk;
(Tempo) pace; (von Hose) crotch, crutch
(BRIT); **auf** ~ **und Tritt** (lit, fig) wherever od
everywhere one goes; „~ **fahren"** "dead
slow"; **mit zehn** ~**en Abstand** at a distance
of ten paces; **den ersten** ~ **tun** (fig) to make
the first move; (: etw beginnen) to take the
first step.
schritt etc [ʃrɪt] vb siehe **schreiten**.
Schritt- zW: ~**macher** m pacemaker;
~(t)**empo** nt: **im** ~(t)**empo** at a walking pace;
s~**weise** adv gradually, little by little.
schroff [ʃrɔf] adj steep; (zackig) jagged; (fig)
brusque; (ungeduldig) abrupt.
schröpfen ['ʃrœpfən] vt (fig) to fleece.
Schrot [ʃroːt] (-(e)s, -e) m od nt (Blei) (small)
shot; (Getreide) coarsely ground grain,
groats pl; ~**flinte** f shotgun.
Schrott [ʃrɔt] (-(e)s, -e) m scrap metal; **ein
Auto zu** ~ **fahren** to write off a car;
~**händler** m scrap merchant; ~**haufen** m
scrap heap; s~**reif** adj ready for the scrap
heap; ~**wert** m scrap value.
schrubben ['ʃrʊbən] vt to scrub.
Schrubber (-s, -) m scrubbing brush.
Schrulle ['ʃrʊlə] (-, -n) f eccentricity, quirk.
schrullig adj cranky.
schrumpfen ['ʃrʊmpfən] vi (Hilfsverb sein) to
shrink; (Apfel) to shrivel; (Leber, Niere) to
atrophy.
Schub [ʃuːp] (-(e)s, -̈e) m (Stoß) push, shove;
(Gruppe, Anzahl) batch; ~**fach** nt drawer;
~**karren** m wheelbarrow; ~**lade** f drawer.
Schubs [ʃuːps] (-es, -e) (umg) m shove, push;
s~**en** (umg) vt, vi to shove, push.
schüchtern ['ʃʏçtərn] adj shy; **S~heit** f
shyness.
schuf etc [ʃuːf] vb siehe **schaffen**.
Schuft [ʃʊft] (-(e)s, -e) m scoundrel.
schuften (umg) vi to graft, slave away.
Schuh [ʃuː] (-(e)s, -e) m shoe; **jdm etw in die**
~**e schieben** (fig: umg) to put the blame for
sth on sb; **wo drückt der** ~? (fig) what's
troubling you?; ~**band** nt shoelace; ~**creme** f
shoe polish; ~**größe** f shoe size; ~**löffel** m
shoehorn; ~**macher** m shoemaker; ~**werk** nt
footwear.
Schukosteckdose ® ['ʃuːkoʃtɛkdoːzə] f
safety socket.
Schukostecker ® m safety plug.
Schul- zW: ~**aufgaben** pl homework sing;
~**bank** f: **die** ~**bank drücken** (umg) to go to
school; ~**behörde** f education authority;

~**besuch** m school attendance; ~**buch** nt schoolbook; ~**buchverlag** m educational publisher.

Schuld [ʃʊlt] (-, -en) f guilt; (FIN) debt; (Verschulden) fault; **jdm die ~ geben** od **zuschieben** to blame sb; **ich bin mir keiner ~ bewußt** I'm not aware of having done anything wrong; ~ **und Sühne** crime and punishment; **ich stehe tief in seiner ~** (fig) I'm deeply indebted to him; ~**en machen** to run up debts; **s~** adj: **s~ sein** od **haben (an** +dat) to be to blame (for); **er ist** od **hat s~** it's his fault; **jdm s~ geben** to blame sb.

schuldbewußt adj (Mensch) feeling guilty; (Miene) guilty.

schulden ['ʃʊldən] vt to owe.

schuldenfrei adj free from debt.

Schuldgefühl nt feeling of guilt.

schuldhaft adj (JUR) culpable.

Schuldienst (-(e)s) m (school)teaching.

schuldig adj guilty; (gebührend) due; **an etw** dat ~ **sein** to be guilty of sth; **jdm etw ~ sein** od **bleiben** to owe sb sth; **jdn ~ sprechen** to find sb guilty; ~ **geschieden sein** to be the guilty party in a divorce; **S~keit** f duty.

schuldlos adj innocent, blameless.

Schuldner(in) (-s, -) m(f) debtor.

Schuld- zW: ~**prinzip** nt (JUR) principle of the guilty party; ~**schein** m promissory note, IOU; ~**spruch** m verdict of guilty.

Schule ['ʃuːlə] (-, -n) f school; **auf** od **in der ~** at school; **in die ~ kommen/gehen** to start school/go to school; ~ **machen** (fig) to become the accepted thing.

schulen vt to train, school.

Schüler(in) ['ʃyːlər(ɪn)] (-s, -) m(f) pupil; ~**ausweis** m (school) student card; ~**lotse** m pupil acting as a road-crossing warden; ~**mitverwaltung** f school od student council.

Schul- zW: ~**ferien** pl school holidays pl (BRIT) od vacation sing (US); ~**fernsehen** nt schools' od educational television; **s~frei** adj: **die Kinder haben morgen s~frei** the children don't have to go to school tomorrow; ~**funk** m schools' broadcasts pl; ~**geld** nt school fees pl, tuition (US); ~**heft** nt exercise book; ~**hof** m playground, schoolyard.

schulisch ['ʃuːlɪʃ] adj (Leistungen, Probleme) at school; (Angelegenheiten) school attrib.

Schul- zW: ~**jahr** nt school year; ~**junge** m schoolboy; ~**kind** nt schoolchild; ~**leiter** m headmaster (bes BRIT), principal; ~**leiterin** f headmistress (bes BRIT), principal; ~**mädchen** nt schoolgirl; ~**medizin** f orthodox medicine; ~**pflicht** f compulsory school attendance; **s~pflichtig** adj of school age; ~**reife** f: **die ~reife haben** to be ready to go to school; ~**schiff** nt (NAUT) training ship; ~**sprecher(in)** m(f) head boy/girl (BRIT); ~**stunde** f period, lesson; ~**tasche** f school bag.

Schulter ['ʃʊltər] (-, -n) f shoulder; **auf die leichte ~ nehmen** to take lightly; ~**blatt** nt shoulder blade.

schultern vt to shoulder.

Schultüte f bag of sweets given to children on the first day at school.

Schulung f education, schooling.

Schul- zW: ~**weg** m way to school; ~**wesen** nt educational system; ~**zeugnis** nt school report.

schummeln ['ʃʊməln] (umg) vi: **(bei etw) ~** to cheat (at sth).

schumm(e)rig ['ʃʊm(ə)rɪç] adj (Beleuchtung) dim; (Raum) dimly-lit.

Schund (-(e)s) m trash, garbage.

schund etc [ʃʊnt] vb siehe **schinden**.

Schundroman m trashy novel.

Schupo ['ʃuːpo] (-s, -s) m abk (veraltet: = Schutzpolizist) cop.

Schuppe ['ʃʊpə] (-, -n) f scale; **Schuppen** pl (Haarschuppen) dandruff.

Schuppen (-s, -) m shed; (umg: übles Lokal) dive; siehe auch **Schuppe**.

schuppen vt to scale ♦ vr to peel.

schuppig ['ʃʊpɪç] adj scaly.

Schur [ʃuːr] (-, -en) f shearing.

Schüreisen nt poker.

schüren ['ʃyːrən] vt to rake; (fig) to stir up.

schürfen ['ʃʏrfən] vt, vi to scrape, scratch; (MIN) to prospect; to dig.

Schürfung f abrasion; (MIN) prospecting.

Schürhaken m poker.

Schurke ['ʃʊrkə] (-n, -n) m rogue.

Schurwolle f: „**reine ~**" "pure new wool".

Schurz [ʃʊrts] (-es, -e) m apron.

Schürze ['ʃʏrtsə] (-, -n) f apron.

Schürzenjäger (umg) m philanderer, one for the girls.

Schuß [ʃʊs] (-sses, ⁻sse) m shot; (FUSSBALL) kick; (Spritzer: von Wein, Essig etc) dash; (WEBEN) weft; **(gut) in ~ sein** (umg) to be in good shape od nick; (Mensch) to be in form; **etw in ~ halten** to keep sth in good shape; **weitab vom ~ sein** (fig: umg) to be miles from where the action is; **der goldene ~** ≈ a lethal dose of a drug; **ein ~ in den Ofen** (umg) a complete waste of time, a failure; ~**bereich** m effective range.

Schüssel ['ʃʏsəl] (-, -n) f bowl, basin; (Servier~, umg: Satelliten~) dish; (Wasch~) basin.

schusselig ['ʃʊsəlɪç] (umg) adj (zerstreut) scatterbrained, muddle-headed (umg).

Schuß- zW: ~**linie** f line of fire; ~**verletzung** f bullet wound; ~**waffe** f firearm; ~**waffengebrauch** m (form) use of firearms; ~**wechsel** m exchange of shots; ~**weite** f range (of fire).

Schuster ['ʃuːstər] (-s, -) m cobbler, shoemaker.

Schutt [ʃʊt] (-(e)s) m rubbish; (Bau~) rubble; „**~ abladen verboten**" "no tipping";

~**abladeplatz** *m* refuse dump.
Schüttelfrost *m* shivering.
schütteln ['ʃʏtəln] *vt* to shake ♦ *vr* to shake
o.s.; **sich vor Kälte** ~ to shiver with cold;
sich vor Ekel ~ to shudder with *od* in
disgust.
schütten ['ʃʏtən] *vt* to pour; (*Zucker, Kies etc*)
to tip; (*ver~*) to spill ♦ *vi unpers* to pour
(down).
schütter *adj* (*Haare*) sparse, thin.
Schutthalde *f* dump.
Schutthaufen *m* heap of rubble.
Schutz [ʃʊts] (*-es*) *m* protection;
(*Unterschlupf*) shelter; **jdn in** ~ **nehmen** to
stand up for sb; ~**anzug** *m* overalls *pl*;
s~bedürftig *adj* in need of protection;
~**befohlene(r)** *f(m)* charge; ~**blech** *nt*
mudguard; ~**brief** *m* (*Versicherung*)
(international) travel cover; ~**brille** *f*
goggles *pl*.
Schütze ['ʃʏtsə] (*-n, -n*) *m* gunman; (*Gewehr~*)
rifleman; (*Scharf~, Sport~*) marksman;
(*ASTROL*) Sagittarius.
schützen ['ʃʏtsən] *vt* to protect ♦ *vr* to protect
o.s.; (**sich**) ~ **vor** *+dat od* **gegen** to protect
(o.s.) from *od* against; **gesetzlich geschützt**
registered; **urheberrechtlich geschützt**
protected by copyright; **vor Nässe** ~! keep
dry.
Schützenfest *nt fair featuring shooting
matches.*
Schutzengel *m* guardian angel.
Schützen- *zW:* ~**graben** *m* trench; ~**hilfe** *f*
(*fig*) support; ~**verein** *m* shooting
club.
Schutz- *zW:* ~**gebiet** *nt* protectorate;
(*Naturschutzgebiet*) reserve; ~**gebühr** *f*
(token) fee; ~**haft** *f* protective custody;
~**heilige(r)** *f(m)* patron saint; ~**helm** *m* safety
helmet; ~**impfung** *f* immunization.
Schützling ['ʃʏtslɪŋ] *m* protégé; (*bes Kind*)
charge.
Schutz- *zW:* **s~los** *adj* defenceless (*BRIT*),
defenseless (*US*); ~**mann** (*-(e)s, pl* -**leute**
od -**männer**) *m* policeman; ~**marke** *f*
trademark; ~**maßnahme** *f* precaution;
~**patron** *m* patron saint; ~**schirm** *m* (*TECH*)
protective screen; ~**umschlag** *m* (book)
jacket; ~**verband** *m* (*MED*) protective
bandage *od* dressing; ~**vorrichtung** *f* safety
device.
Schw. *abk* = **Schwester.**
schwabbelig ['ʃvab(ə)lɪç] (*umg*) *adj*
(*Körperteil*) flabby; (: *Gelee*) wobbly.
Schwabe ['ʃvaːbə] (*-n, -n*) *m* Swabian.
Schwaben (*-s*) *nt* Swabia.
Schwäbin ['ʃvɛːbɪn] *f* Swabian.
schwäbisch ['ʃvɛːbɪʃ] *adj* Swabian.
schwach [ʃvax] *adj* weak, feeble; (*Gedächtnis,
Gesundheit*) poor; (*Hoffnung*) faint; ~ **werden**
to weaken; **das ist ein** ~**es Bild** (*umg*) *od* **eine**
~**e Leistung** (*umg*) that's a poor show; **ein**

~**er Trost** cold *od* small comfort; **mach mich
nicht** ~! (*umg*) don't say that!; **auf** ~**en
Beinen** *od* **Füßen stehen** (*fig*) to be on shaky
ground; (: *Theorie*) to be shaky.
Schwäche ['ʃvɛçə] (*-, -n*) *f* weakness.
schwächen *vt* to weaken.
schwach- *zW:* **S~heit** *f* weakness; **S~kopf**
(*umg*) *m* dimwit, idiot; ~**köpfig** *adj* silly, daft
(*BRIT*).
schwächlich *adj* weakly, delicate.
Schwächling *m* weakling.
Schwach- *zW:* ~**sinn** *m* (*MED*) mental
deficiency, feeble-mindedness (*veraltet*);
(*umg: Quatsch*) rubbish; (*fig: umg: unsinnige
Tat*) idiocy; **s~sinnig** *adj* mentally deficient;
(*Idee*) idiotic; ~**stelle** *f* weak point; ~**strom**
m weak current.
Schwächung ['ʃvɛçʊŋ] *f* weakening.
Schwaden ['ʃvaːdən] (*-s, -*) *m* cloud.
schwafeln ['ʃvaːfəln] (*umg*) *vi* to blather,
drivel; (*in einer Prüfung*) to waffle.
Schwager ['ʃvaːgər] (*-s, ̈-*) *m* brother-in-law.
Schwägerin ['ʃvɛːgərɪn] *f* sister-in-law.
Schwalbe ['ʃvalbə] (*-, -n*) *f* swallow.
Schwall [ʃval] (*-(e)s, -e*) *m* surge; (*Worte*)
flood, torrent.
Schwamm (*-(e)s, ̈-e*) *m* sponge; (*Pilz*) fungus;
~ **drüber!** (*umg*) (let's) forget it!
schwamm *etc* [ʃvam] *vb siehe* **schwimmen**.
schwammig *adj* spongy; (*Gesicht*) puffy;
(*vage: Begriff*) woolly (*BRIT*), wooly (*US*).
Schwan [ʃvaːn] (*-(e)s, ̈-e*) *m* swan.
schwand *etc* [ʃvant] *vb siehe* **schwinden**.
schwanen *vi unpers:* **jdm schwant es** sb has a
foreboding *od* forebodings; **jdm schwant
etwas** sb senses something might happen.
schwang *etc* [ʃvaŋ] *vb siehe* **schwingen**.
schwanger ['ʃvaŋər] *adj* pregnant.
schwängern ['ʃvɛŋərn] *vt* to make pregnant.
Schwangerschaft *f* pregnancy.
Schwangerschaftsabbruch *m* termination
of pregnancy, abortion.
Schwank [ʃvaŋk] (*-(e)s, ̈-e*) *m* funny story;
(*LITER*) merry *od* comical tale; (*THEAT*)
farce.
schwanken *vi* to sway; (*taumeln*) to stagger,
reel; (*Preise, Zahlen*) to fluctuate; (*zögern*) to
hesitate; (*Überzeugung etc*) to begin to
waver; **ins S~ kommen** (*Baum, Gebäude etc*)
to start to sway; (*Preise, Kurs etc*) to start to
fluctuate *od* vary.
Schwankung *f* fluctuation.
Schwanz [ʃvants] (*-es, ̈-e*) *m* tail; (*umg!:
Penis*) prick (*!*); **kein** ~ (*umg*) not a (blessed)
soul.
schwänzen ['ʃvɛntsən] (*umg*) *vt* (*Stunde,
Vorlesung*) to skip ♦ *vi* to play truant.
Schwänzer ['ʃvɛntsər] (*-s, -*) (*umg*) *m* truant.
schwappen ['ʃvapən] *vi* (*über~*) to splash,
slosh.
Schwarm [ʃvarm] (*-(e)s, ̈-e*) *m* swarm; (*umg*)
heart-throb, idol.

schwärmen ['ʃvɛrmən] vi to swarm; ~ **für** to be mad od wild about.
Schwärmerei [ʃvɛrmə'raɪ] f enthusiasm.
schwärmerisch adj impassioned, effusive.
Schwarte ['ʃvartə] (-, -n) f hard skin; (*Speck~*) rind; (*umg: Buch*) tome (*hum*).
Schwartenmagen (-s) m (*KOCH*) brawn.

schwarz [ʃvarts] adj black; (*umg: ungesetzlich*) illicit; (*: katholisch*) Catholic, Papist (*pej*); (*POL*) Christian Democrat; **ins S~e treffen** (*lit, fig*) to hit the bull's-eye; **das S~e Brett** the notice (*BRIT*) od bulletin (*US*) board; ~**e Liste** blacklist; ~**es Loch** black hole; **das S~e Meer** the Black Sea; **S~er Peter** (*KARTEN*) *children's card game*; **jdm den S~en Peter zuschieben** (*fig: die Verantwortung abschieben*) to pass the buck to sb (*umg*); **sich ~ ärgern** to get extremely annoyed; **dort wählen alle ~** they all vote conservative there; **in den ~en Zahlen** in the black; **S~arbeit** f illicit work, moonlighting; **S~arbeiter** m moonlighter; **S~brot** nt (*Pumpernickel*) black bread, pumpernickel; (*braun*) brown rye bread.
Schwärze ['ʃvɛrtsə] (-, -n) f blackness; (*Farbe*) blacking; (*Drucker~*) printer's ink.
Schwarze(r) f(m) (*Neger*) black; (*umg: Katholik*) Papist; (*POL: umg*) Christian Democrat.
schwärzen vt to blacken.
Schwarz- zW: **s~fahren** unreg vi to travel without paying; (*ohne Führerschein*) to drive without a licence (*BRIT*) od license (*US*); ~**fahrer** m (*Bus etc*) fare dodger (*umg*); ~**handel** m black market (trade); ~**händler** m black-market operator; **s~hören** vi to listen to the radio without a licence (*BRIT*) od license (*US*).
schwärzlich ['ʃvɛrtslɪç] adj blackish, darkish.
Schwarz- zW: **s~malen** vi to be pessimistic ♦ vt to be pessimistic about; ~**markt** m black market; **s~sehen** unreg (*umg*) vi to see the gloomy side of things; (*TV*) to watch TV without a licence (*BRIT*) od license (*US*); ~**seher** m pessimist; (*TV*) viewer without a licence (*BRIT*) od license (*US*); ~**wald** m Black Forest; ~**wälder Kirschtorte** f Black Forest gâteau; **s~weiß** adj black and white; ~**weiß-** in zW black and white; ~**wurzel** f (*KOCH*) salsify.
Schwatz [ʃvats] (-es, -e) m chat.
schwatzen ['ʃvatsən] vi to chat; (*schnell, unaufhörlich*) to chatter; (*über belanglose Dinge*) to prattle; (*Unsinn reden*) to blether (*umg*).
schwätzen ['ʃvɛtsən] vi = **schwatzen**.
Schwätzer(in) ['ʃvɛtsər(ɪn)] (-s, -) m(f) chatterbox; (*Schwafler*) gasbag (*umg*); (*Klatschbase*) gossip.
schwatzhaft adj talkative, gossipy.
Schwebe ['ʃveːbə] f: **in der ~** (*fig*) in abeyance; (*JUR, COMM*) pending.

Schwebebahn f overhead railway (*BRIT*) od railroad (*US*).
Schwebebalken m (*SPORT*) beam.
schweben vi to drift, float; (*hoch*) to soar; (*unentschieden sein*) to be in the balance; **es schwebte mir vor Augen** (*Bild*) I saw it in my mind's eye.
schwebend adj (*TECH, CHEM*) suspended; (*fig*) undecided, unresolved; ~**es Verfahren** (*JUR*) pending case.
schwed. abk = **schwedisch**.
Schwede ['ʃveːdə] (-n, -n) m Swede.
Schweden (-s) nt Sweden.
Schwedin ['ʃveːdɪn] f Swede.
schwedisch adj Swedish.
Schwefel ['ʃveːfəl] (-s) m sulphur (*BRIT*), sulfur (*US*); ~**dioxid** nt sulphur dioxide.
schwefelig adj sulphurous (*BRIT*), sulfurous (*US*).
Schwefelsäure f sulphuric (*BRIT*) od sulfuric (*US*) acid.
Schweif [ʃvaɪf] (-(e)s, -e) m tail.
schweifen vi to wander, roam.
Schweigegeld nt hush money.
Schweigeminute f one minute('s) silence.
schweigen ['ʃvaɪgən] unreg vi to be silent; (*still sein*) to keep quiet; **kannst du ~?** can you keep a secret?; **ganz zu ~ von ...** to say nothing of ...; **S~** (-s) nt silence.
schweigend adj silent.
Schweigepflicht f pledge of secrecy; (*von Anwalt etc*) requirement of confidentiality.
schweigsam ['ʃvaɪkzaːm] adj silent; (*als Charaktereigenschaft*) taciturn; **S~keit** f silence; taciturnity.
Schwein [ʃvaɪn] (-(e)s, -e) nt pig; (*fig: umg*) (good) luck; **kein ~** (*umg*) nobody, not a single person.
Schweine- zW: ~**braten** m joint of pork; (*gekocht*) roast pork; ~**fleisch** nt pork; ~**geld** (*umg*) nt: **ein ~geld** a packet; ~**hund** (*umg*) m stinker, swine.
Schweinerei [ʃvaɪnə'raɪ] f mess; (*Gemeinheit*) dirty trick; **so eine ~!** (*umg*) how disgusting!
Schweineschmalz nt dripping; (*als Kochfett*) lard.
Schweinestall m pigsty.
schweinisch adj filthy.
Schweinsleder nt pigskin.
Schweinsohr nt pig's ear; (*Gebäck*) (kidney-shaped) pastry.
Schweiß [ʃvaɪs] (-es) m sweat, perspiration; ~**band** nt sweatband.
Schweißbrenner (-s, -) m (*TECH*) welding torch.
schweißen vt, vi to weld.
Schweißer (-s, -) m welder.
Schweiß- zW: ~**füße** pl sweaty feet pl; ~**naht** f weld; **s~naß** adj sweaty.
Schweiz [ʃvaɪts] f: **die ~** Switzerland.
schweiz. abk = **schweizerisch**.

Schweizer ['ʃvaitsər] (-s, -) *m* Swiss ♦ *adj attrib*
Swiss; ~**deutsch** *nt* Swiss German; ~**in** *f*
Swiss; **s~isch** *adj* Swiss.
schwelen ['ʃveːlən] *vi* to smoulder (*BRIT*),
smolder (*US*).
schwelgen ['ʃvɛlgən] *vi* to indulge o.s.; ~ **in**
+*dat* to indulge in.
Schwelle ['ʃvɛlə] (-, -n) *f* (*auch fig*) threshold;
(*EISENB*) sleeper (*BRIT*), tie (*US*).
schwellen *unreg vi* to swell.
Schwellenland *nt* threshold country.
Schwellung *f* swelling.
Schwemme ['ʃvɛmə] *f*: **eine ~ an** +*dat* a glut
of.
schwemmen ['ʃvɛmən] *vt* (*treiben: Sand etc*)
to wash.
Schwengel ['ʃvɛŋəl] (-s, -) *m* pump handle;
(*Glocken~*) clapper.
Schwenk [ʃvɛŋk] (-(e)s, -s) *m* (*FILM*) pan,
panning shot.
Schwenkarm *m* swivel arm.
schwenkbar *adj* swivel-mounted.
schwenken *vt* to swing; (*Kamera*) to pan;
(*Fahne*) to wave; (*Kartoffeln*) to toss;
(*abspülen*) to rinse ♦ *vi* to turn, swivel; (*MIL*)
to wheel.
Schwenkung *f* turn; (*MIL*) wheel.
schwer [ʃveːr] *adj* heavy; (*schwierig*) difficult,
hard; (*schlimm*) serious, bad ♦ *adv* (*sehr*)
very (much); (*verletzt etc*) seriously, badly;
~ **erkältet sein** to have a heavy cold; **er lernt**
~ he's a slow learner; **er ist ~ in Ordnung**
(*umg*) he's a good bloke (*BRIT*) *od* guy;
~ **hören** to be hard of hearing; **S~arbeiter** *m*
labourer (*BRIT*), laborer (*US*);
S~behinderte(r) *f(m)*, **S~beschädigte(r)** *f(m)*
(*veraltet*) severely handicapped person.
Schwere (-, -n) *f* weight; heaviness; (*PHYS*)
gravity; **s~los** *adj* weightless; ~**losigkeit** *f*
weightlessness.
schwer- *zW*: ~**erziehbar** *adj* maladjusted;
~**fallen** *unreg vi*: **jdm ~fallen** to be difficult for
sb; ~**fällig** *adj* (*auch Stil*) ponderous; (*Gang*)
clumsy, awkward; (*Verstand*) slow;
S~gewicht *nt* heavyweight; (*fig*) emphasis;
~**gewichtig** *adj* heavyweight; ~**hörig** *adj*
hard of hearing; **S~industrie** *f* heavy
industry; **S~kraft** *f* gravity; **S~kranke(r)**
f(m) person who is seriously ill; ~**lich** *adv*
hardly; ~**machen** *vt*: **jdm/sich etw ~machen**
to make sth difficult for sb/o.s.; **S~metall** *nt*
heavy metal; ~**mütig** *adj* melancholy;
~**nehmen** *unreg vt* to take to heart; **S~punkt**
m centre (*BRIT*) *od* center (*US*) of gravity;
(*fig*) emphasis, crucial point; **S~punktstreik**
m pinpoint strike; ~**reich** (*umg*) *adj attrib*
stinking rich.
Schwert [ʃveːrt] (-(e)s, -er) *nt* sword; ~**lilie** *f*
iris.
schwer- *zW*: ~**tun** *unreg vi*: **sich** *dat od akk* ~**tun**
to have difficulties; **S~verbrecher** *m*
criminal; ~**verdaulich** *adj* indigestible; (*fig*)

heavy; ~**verdient** *adj attrib* (*Geld*) hard-
earned; ~**verletzt** *adj* seriously *od* badly
injured; **S~verletzte(r)** *f(m)* serious
casualty; ~**verwundet** *adj* seriously
wounded; ~**wiegend** *adj* weighty,
important.
Schwester ['ʃvɛstər] (-, -n) *f* sister; (*MED*)
nurse; **s~lich** *adj* sisterly.
schwieg *etc* [ʃviːk] *vb siehe* **schweigen**.
Schwieger- *zW*: ~**eltern** *pl* parents-in-law *pl*;
~**mutter** *f* mother-in-law; ~**sohn** *m* son-in-
law; ~**tochter** *f* daughter-in-law; ~**vater** *m*
father-in-law.
Schwiele ['ʃviːlə] (-, -n) *f* callus.
schwierig ['ʃviːrɪç] *adj* difficult, hard; **S~keit** *f*
difficulty; **S~keitsgrad** *m* degree of
difficulty.
schwillt [ʃvɪlt] *vb siehe* **schwellen**.
Schwimmbad *nt* swimming baths *pl*.
Schwimmbecken *nt* swimming pool.
schwimmen *unreg vi* to swim; (*treiben, nicht
sinken*) to float; (*fig: unsicher sein*) to be all at
sea; **im Geld ~** (*umg*) to be rolling in money;
mir schwimmt es vor den Augen I feel
dizzy.
Schwimmer (-s, -) *m* swimmer; (*ANGELN*)
float.
Schwimmerin *f* swimmer.
Schwimm- *zW*: ~**flosse** *f* (*von Taucher*)
flipper; ~**haut** *f* (*ORNITHOLOGIE*) web;
~**lehrer** *m* swimming instructor; ~**sport** *m*
swimming; ~**weste** *f* life jacket.
Schwindel ['ʃvɪndəl] (-s) *m* dizziness; (*Betrug*)
swindle, fraud; (*Zeug*) stuff; **s~erregend** *adj*:
in s~erregender Höhe at a dizzy height;
s~frei *adj* free from giddiness.
schwindeln *vi* (*umg: lügen*) to fib; **mir
schwindelt** I feel dizzy; **jdm schwindelt es**
sb feels dizzy.
schwinden ['ʃvɪndən] *unreg vi* to disappear;
(*Kräfte*) to fade, fail; (*sich verringern*) to
decrease.
Schwindler (-s, -) *m* swindler; (*Hochstapler*)
con man, fraud; (*Lügner*) liar.
schwindlig *adj* dizzy; **mir ist ~** I feel dizzy.
Schwindsucht *f* (*veraltet*) consumption.
schwingen ['ʃvɪŋən] *unreg vt* to swing; (*Waffe
etc*) to brandish ♦ *vi* to swing; (*vibrieren*) to
vibrate; (*klingen*) to sound.
Schwinger (-s, -) *m* (*BOXEN*) swing.
Schwingtor *nt* up-and-over door.
Schwingtür *f* swing door(s *pl*) (*BRIT*),
swinging door(s *pl*) (*US*).
Schwingung *f* vibration; (*PHYS*) oscillation.
Schwips [ʃvɪps] (-es, -e) *m*: **einen ~ haben** to
be tipsy.
schwirren ['ʃvɪrən] *vi* to buzz.
Schwitze ['ʃvɪtsə] (-, -n) *f* (*KOCH*) roux.
schwitzen *vi* to sweat, perspire.
schwofen ['ʃvoːfən] (*umg*) *vi* to dance.
schwoll *etc* [ʃvɔl] *vb siehe* **schwellen**.
schwören ['ʃvøːrən] *unreg vt, vi* to swear; **auf**

jdn/etw ~ (*fig*) to swear by sb/sth.
schwul [ʃvuːl] (*umg*) *adj* gay, queer (*pej*).
schwül [ʃvyːl] *adj* sultry, close.
Schwule(r) (*umg*) *m* gay, queer (*pej*), fag (*US pej*).
Schwüle (-) *f* sultriness, closeness.
Schwulität [ʃvuliˈtɛːt] (*umg*) *f* trouble, difficulty.
Schwulst [ʃvʊlst] (-(e)s) *m* bombast.
schwülstig [ˈʃvʏlstɪç] *adj* pompous.
Schwund [ʃvʊnt] (-(e)s) *m* (+*gen*) decrease (in), decline (in), dwindling (of); (*MED*) atrophy; (*Schrumpfen*) shrinkage.
Schwung [ʃvʊŋ] (-(e)s, ⁻e) *m* swing; (*Triebkraft*) momentum; (*fig: Energie*) verve, energy; (*umg: Menge*) batch; **in ~ sein** (*fig*) to be in full swing; **~ in die Sache bringen** (*umg*) to liven things up; **s~haft** *adj* brisk, lively; **~rad** *nt* flywheel; **s~voll** *adj* vigorous.
Schwur (-(e)s, ⁻e) *m* oath.
schwur *etc* [ʃvuːr] *vb siehe* **schwören**.
Schwurgericht *nt* court with a jury.
SDR (-) *m abk* (= *Süddeutscher Rundfunk*) South German Radio.
sechs [zɛks] *num* six; **S~eck** *nt* hexagon; **~hundert** *num* six hundred.
sechste(r, s) *adj* sixth.
Sechstel [ˈzɛkstəl] (-s, -) *nt* sixth.
sechzehn [ˈzɛçtseːn] *num* sixteen.
sechzig [ˈzɛçtsɪç] *num* sixty.
See¹ [zeː] (-, -n) *f* sea; **an der ~** by the sea, at the seaside; **in ~ stechen** to put to sea; **auf hoher ~** on the high seas.
See² [zeː] (-s, -n) *m* lake.
See- *zW:* **~bad** *nt* seaside resort; **~bär** *m* (*hum: umg*) seadog; (*ZOOL*) fur seal; **~fahrt** *f* seafaring; (*Reise*) voyage; **s~fest** *adj* (*Mensch*) not subject to seasickness; **~gang** *m* (motion of the) sea; **~gras** *nt* seaweed; **~hund** *m* seal; **~igel** *m* sea urchin; **~karte** *f* chart; **s~krank** *adj* seasick; **~krankheit** *f* seasickness; **~lachs** *m* rock salmon.
Seele [ˈzeːlə] (-, -n) *f* soul; (*Mittelpunkt*) life and soul; **jdm aus der ~ sprechen** to express exactly what sb feels; **das liegt mir auf der ~** it weighs heavily on my mind; **eine ~ von Mensch** an absolute dear.
Seelen- *zW:* **~amt** *nt* (*REL*) requiem; **~friede(n)** *m* peace of mind; **~heil** *nt* salvation of one's soul; (*fig*) spiritual welfare; **~ruhe** *f*: **in aller ~ruhe** calmly; (*kaltblütig*) as cool as you please; **s~ruhig** *adv* calmly.
Seeleute [ˈzeːlɔytə] *pl* seamen *pl*.
Seel- *zW:* **s~isch** *adj* mental; (*REL*) spiritual; (*Belastung*) emotional; **~sorge** *f* pastoral duties *pl*; **~sorger** (-s, -) *m* clergyman.
See- *zW:* **~macht** *f* naval power; **~mann** (-(e)s, *pl* **-leute**) *m* seaman, sailor; **~meile** *f* nautical mile.
Seengebiet [ˈzeːəngəbiːt] *nt* lakeland district.
See- *zW:* **~not** *f*: **in ~not** (*Schiff etc*) in

distress; **~pferd(chen)** *nt* sea horse; **~räuber** *m* pirate; **~recht** *nt* maritime law; **~rose** *f* waterlily; **~stern** *m* starfish; **~tang** *m* seaweed; **s~tüchtig** *adj* seaworthy; **~versicherung** *f* marine insurance; **~weg** *m* sea route; **auf dem ~weg** by sea; **~zunge** *f* sole.
Segel [ˈzeːgəl] (-s, -) *nt* sail; **mit vollen ~n** under full sail *od* canvas; (*fig*) with gusto; **die ~ streichen** (*fig*) to give in; **~boot** *nt* yacht; **~fliegen** (-s) *nt* gliding; **~flieger** *m* glider pilot; **~flugzeug** *nt* glider.
segeln *vt, vi* to sail; **durch eine Prüfung ~** (*umg*) to flop in an exam, fail (in) an exam.
Segel- *zW:* **~schiff** *nt* sailing vessel; **~sport** *m* sailing; **~tuch** *nt* canvas.
Segen [ˈzeːgən] (-s, -) *m* blessing.
segensreich *adj* beneficial.
Segler [ˈzeːglər] (-s, -) *m* sailor, yachtsman; (*Boot*) sailing boat.
Seglerin *f* yachtswoman.
segnen [ˈzeːgnən] *vt* to bless.
sehen [ˈzeːən] *unreg vt, vi* to see; (*in bestimmte Richtung*) to look; (*Fernsehsendung*) to watch; **sieht man das?** does it show?; **man('s) mal wieder!** that's typical!; **du siehst das nicht richtig** you've got it wrong; **so gesehen** looked at in this way; **sich ~ lassen** to put in an appearance, appear; **das neue Rathaus kann sich ~ lassen** the new town hall is certainly something to be proud of; **siehe oben/unten** see above/below; **da kann man mal ~** that just shows (you) *od* just goes to show (*umg*); **mal ~!** we'll see; **darauf ~, daß ...** to make sure (that) ...; **jdn kommen ~** to see sb coming.
sehenswert *adj* worth seeing.
Sehenswürdigkeiten *pl* sights *pl* (of a town).
Seher (-s, -) *m* seer.
Sehfehler *m* sight defect.
Sehkraft *f* (eye)sight.
Sehne [ˈzeːnə] (-, -n) *f* sinew; (*an Bogen*) string.
sehnen *vr*: **sich ~ nach** to long *od* yearn for.
Sehnenscheidenentzündung *f* (*MED*) tendovaginitis.
Sehnerv *m* optic nerve.
sehnig *adj* sinewy.
sehnlich *adj* ardent.
Sehnsucht *f* longing.
sehnsüchtig *adj* longing; (*Erwartung*) eager.
sehnsuchtsvoll *adv* longingly, yearningly.
sehr [zeːr] *adv* (*vor adj, adv*) very; (*mit Verben*) a lot, (very) much; **zu ~** too much; **er ist ~ dafür/dagegen** he is all for it/very much against it; **wie ~ er sich auch bemühte ...** however much he tried ...
Sehvermögen [ˈzeːfɛrmøːgən] (-s) *nt* powers *pl* of vision.
seicht [zaɪçt] *adj* (*lit, fig*) shallow.
seid [zaɪt] *vb siehe* **sein**.
Seide [ˈzaɪdə] (-, -n) *f* silk.

Seidel (-s, -) *nt* tankard, beer mug.
seiden *adj* silk; **S~papier** *nt* tissue paper.
seidig ['zaɪdɪç] *adj* silky.
Seife ['zaɪfə] (-, -n) *f* soap.
Seifen- *zW:* **~blase** *f* soap bubble; (*fig*)
bubble; **~lauge** *f* soapsuds *pl*; **~schale** *f*
soap dish; **~schaum** *m* lather.
seifig ['zaɪfɪç] *adj* soapy.
seihen ['zaɪən] *vt* to strain, filter.
Seil [zaɪl] (-(e)s, -e) *nt* rope; (*Kabel*) cable;
~bahn *f* cable railway; **~hüpfen** (-s) *nt*
skipping; **~springen** (-s) *nt* skipping;
~tänzer(in) *m(f)* tightrope walker; **~zug** *m*
tackle.

═══════════════════ *SCHLÜSSELWORT*

sein [zaɪn] (*pt* **war**, *pp* **gewesen**) *vi* **1** to be; **ich
bin** I am; **du bist** you are; **er/sie/es ist** he/
she/it is; **wir sind/ihr seid/sie sind** we/you/
they are; **wir waren** we were; **wir sind
gewesen** we have been
2: seien Sie nicht böse don't be angry; **sei so
gut und ...** be so kind as to ...; **das wäre gut**
that would *od* that'd be a good thing; **wenn
ich Sie wäre** if I were *od* was you; **das wär's**
that's all, that's it; **morgen bin ich in Rom**
tomorrow I'll *od* I will *od* I shall be in
Rome; **waren Sie mal in Rom?** have you
ever been to Rome?
3: wie ist das zu verstehen? how is that to be
understood?; **er ist nicht zu ersetzen** he
cannot be replaced; **mit ihr ist nicht zu
reden** you can't talk to her
4: mir ist kalt I'm cold; **mir ist, als hätte ich
ihn früher schon einmal gesehen** I've a
feeling I've seen him before; **was ist?**
what's the matter?, what is it?; **ist was?** is
something the matter?; **es sei denn(, daß ...)**
unless ...; **wie dem auch sei** be that as it
may; **wie wäre es mit ...?** how *od* what about
...?; **laß das ~!** stop that!; **es ist an dir, zu ...**
it's up to you to ...; **was sind Sie (beruflich)?**
what do you do?; **das kann schon ~** that
may well be
♦ *pron* his; (*bei Dingen*) its.

Sein (-s) *nt:* **~ oder Nichtsein** to be or not to
be.
seine(r, s) *poss pron* his; its; **er ist gut ~ zwei
Meter** (*umg*) he's a good two metres (*BRIT*)
od meters (*US*); **die S~n** (*geh*) his family,
his people; **jedem das S~** to each his own.
seiner *gen von* **er**, **es** ♦ *pron* of him; of it.
seinerseits *adv* for his part.
seinerzeit *adv* in those days, formerly.
seinesgleichen *pron* people like him.
seinetwegen *adv* (*für ihn*) for his sake;
(*wegen ihm*) on his account; (*von ihm aus*) as
far as he is concerned.
seinetwillen *adv:* **um ~ = seinetwegen**.
seinige *pron:* **der/die/das ~** his.
seinlassen *unreg vt:* **etw ~** (*aufhören*) to stop

(doing) sth; (*nicht tun*) to drop sth, leave sth.
Seismograph [zaɪsmo'graːf] (-en, -en) *m*
seismograph.
seit [zaɪt] *präp +dat* since; (*Zeitdauer*) for, in
(*bes US*) ♦ *konj* since; **er ist ~ einer Woche
hier** he has been here for a week; **~ langem**
for a long time; **~dem** *adv, konj* since.
Seite ['zaɪtə] (-, -n) *f* side; (*Buch~*) page; (*MIL*)
flank; **~ an ~** side by side; **jdm zur ~ stehen**
(*fig*) to stand by sb's side; **jdn zur ~ nehmen**
to take sb aside *od* on one side; **auf der
einen ~ ..., auf der anderen (~) ...** on the one
hand ..., on the other (hand) ...; **einer Sache**
dat **die beste ~ abgewinnen** to make the
best *od* most of sth.
seiten *präp +gen:* **auf** *od* **von ~** on the part of.
Seiten- *zW:* **~ansicht** *f* side view; **~hieb** *m*
(*fig*) passing shot, dig; **s~lang** *adj* several
pages long, going on for pages; **~ruder** *nt*
(*AVIAT*) rudder.
seitens *präp +gen* on the part of.
Seiten- *zW:* **~schiff** *nt* aisle; **~sprung** *m*
extramarital escapade; **~stechen** *nt* (a)
stitch; **~straße** *f* side road; **~streifen** *m*
(*der Straße*) verge (*BRIT*), berm (*US*); (*der
Autobahn*) hard shoulder (*BRIT*), shoulder
(*US*); **s~verkehrt** *adj* the wrong way round;
~wagen *m* sidecar; **~wind** *m* crosswind;
~zahl *f* page number; (*Gesamtzahl*) number
of pages.
seit- *zW:* **~her** [zaɪt'heːr] *adv, konj* since (then);
~lich *adv* on one/the side ♦ *adj* side *attrib*;
~wärts *adv* sideways.
sek, Sek. *abk* (= *Sekunde*) sec.
Sekretär [zekre'tɛːr] *m* secretary; (*Möbel*)
bureau.
Sekretariat [zekretari'aːt] (-(e)s, -e) *nt*
secretary's office, secretariat.
Sekretärin *f* secretary.
Sekt [zɛkt] (-(e)s, -e) *m* sparkling wine.
Sekte (-, -n) *f* sect.
Sektor ['zɛktɔr] *m* sector; (*Sachgebiet*) field.
Sekunda [ze'kʊnda] (-, **Sekunden**) *f* (*SCH:
Unter~/Ober~*) sixth/seventh year of German
secondary school.
sekundär [zekʊn'dɛːr] *adj* secondary;
S~literatur *f* secondary literature.
Sekunde [ze'kʊnda] (-, -n) *f* second.
Sekunden- *zW:* **~kleber** *m* superglue;
~schnelle *f:* **in ~schnelle** in a matter of
seconds; **~zeiger** *m* second hand.
sel. *abk* = **selig**.
selber ['zɛlbər] *demon pron* = **selbst**; **S~machen**
nt do-it-yourself, DIY (*BRIT*); (*von Kleidern
etc*) making one's own.
Selbst [zɛlpst] (-) *nt* self.

═══════════════════ *SCHLÜSSELWORT*

selbst [zɛlpst] *pron* **1: ich/er/wir ~** I myself/he
himself/we ourselves; **sie ist die Tugend ~**
she's virtue itself; **er braut sein Bier ~** he
brews his own beer; **das muß er ~ wissen**

it's up to him; **wie geht's? - gut, und ~?** how are things? - fine, and yourself?
2 (*ohne Hilfe*) alone, on my/his/one's *etc* own; **von ~** by itself; **er kam von ~** he came of his own accord; **~ ist der Mann/die Frau!** self-reliance is the name of the game (*umg*) ♦ *adv* even; **~ wenn** even if; **~ Gott** even God (himself).

Selbstachtung *f* self-respect.

selbständig ['zɛlpʃtɛndɪç] *adj* independent; **sich ~ machen** (*beruflich*) to set up on one's own, start one's own business; **S~keit** *f* independence.

Selbst- *zW:* **~anzeige** *f:* **~anzeige erstatten** to come forward oneself; **der Dieb hat ~anzeige erstattet** the thief has come forward; **~auslöser** *m* (*PHOT*) delayed-action shutter release; **~bedienung** *f* self-service; **~befriedigung** *f* masturbation; (*fig*) self-gratification; **~beherrschung** *f* self-control; **~bestätigung** *f* self-affirmation; **s~bewußt** *adj* self-confident; (*selbstsicher*) self-assured; **~bewußtsein** *nt* self-confidence; **~bildnis** *nt* self-portrait; **~erhaltung** *f* self-preservation; **~erkenntnis** *f* self-knowledge; **~fahrer** *m* (*AUT*): **Autovermietung für ~fahrer** self-drive car hire (*BRIT*) *od* rental; **s~gefällig** *adj* smug, self-satisfied; **s~gemacht** *adj* home-made; **s~gerecht** *adj* self-righteous; **~gespräch** *nt* conversation with o.s.; **s~gestrickt** *adj* hand-knitted; (*umg: Methode etc*) homespun, amateurish; **s~gewiß** *adj* confident; **s~herrlich** *adj* high-handed; (*selbstgerecht*) self-satisfied; **~hilfe** *f* self-help; **zur ~hilfe greifen** to take matters into one's own hands; **s~klebend** *adj* self-adhesive; **~kostenpreis** *m* cost price; **s~los** *adj* unselfish, selfless; **~mord** *m* suicide; **~mörder(in)** *m(f)* (*Person*) suicide; **s~mörderisch** *adj* suicidal; **s~sicher** *adj* self-assured; **~sicherheit** *f* self-assurance; **~studium** *nt* private study; **s~süchtig** *adj* selfish; **s~tätig** *adj* automatic; **~überwindung** *f* willpower; **s~verdient** *adj:* **s~verdientes Geld** money one has earned o.s.; **s~vergessen** *adj* absent-minded; (*Blick*) faraway; **s~verschuldet** *adj:* **wenn der Unfall s~verschuldet ist** if there is personal responsibility for the accident; **~versorger** *m:* **~versorger sein** to be self-sufficient *od* self-reliant; **Urlaub für ~versorger** self-catering holiday.

selbstverständlich *adj* obvious ♦ *adv* naturally; **ich halte das für ~** I take that for granted.

Selbstverständlichkeit *f* (*Unbefangenheit*) naturalness; (*natürliche Voraussetzung*) matter of course.

Selbst- *zW:* **~verständnis** *nt:* **nach seinem eigenen ~verständnis** as he sees himself;

~verteidigung *f* self-defence (*BRIT*), self-defense (*US*); **~vertrauen** *nt* self-confidence; **~verwaltung** *f* autonomy, self-government; **~wählferndienst** *m* (*TEL*) automatic dialling service, subscriber trunk dialling (*BRIT*), STD (*BRIT*), direct distance dialing (*US*); **~wertgefühl** *nt* feeling of one's own worth *od* value, self-esteem; **s~zufrieden** *adj* self-satisfied; **~zweck** *m* end in itself.

selig ['ze:lɪç] *adj* happy, blissful; (*REL*) blessed; (*tot*) late; **S~keit** *f* bliss.

Sellerie ['zɛləriː] (**-s, -(s)** *od* **-, -n**) *m od f* celery.

selten ['zɛltən] *adj* rare ♦ *adv* seldom, rarely; **S~heit** *f* rarity; **S~heitswert** (**-(e)s**) *m* rarity value.

Selterswasser ['zɛltərsvasər] *nt* soda water.

seltsam ['zɛltzaːm] *adj* curious, strange.

seltsamerweise *adv* curiously, strangely.

Seltsamkeit *f* strangeness.

Semester [ze'mɛstər] (**-s, -**) *nt* semester; **ein älteres ~** a senior student.

Semi- [zemi] *in zW* semi-.

Semikolon [-'koːlɔn] (**-s, -s**) *nt* semicolon.

Seminar [zemi'naːr] (**-s, -e**) *nt* seminary; (*Kurs*) seminar; (*UNIV: Ort*) department building.

semitisch [ze'miːtɪʃ] *adj* Semitic.

Semmel ['zɛməl] (**-, -n**) *f* roll; **~brösel(n)** *pl* breadcrumbs *pl*; **~knödel** (*SÜDD, ÖSTERR*) *m* bread dumpling.

sen. *abk* (= *senior*) sen.

Senat [ze'naːt] (**-(e)s, -e**) *m* senate.

Sendebereich *m* transmission range.

Sendefolge *f* (*Serie*) series.

senden¹ *unreg vt* to send.

senden² *vt, vi* (*RUNDF, TV*) to transmit, broadcast.

Sendenetz *nt* network.

Sendepause *f* (*RUNDF, TV*) interval.

Sender (**-s, -**) *m* station; (*Anlage*) transmitter.

Sende- *zW:* **~reihe** *f* series (of broadcasts); **~schluß** *m* (*RUNDF, TV*) closedown; **~station** *f* transmitting station; **~stelle** *f* transmitting station; **~zeit** *f* broadcasting time, air time.

Sendung ['zɛndʊŋ] *f* consignment; (*Aufgabe*) mission; (*RUNDF, TV*) transmission; (*Programm*) programme (*BRIT*), program (*US*).

Senegal ['zeːnegal] (**-s**) *nt* Senegal.

Senf [zɛnf] (**-(e)s, -e**) *m* mustard; **seinen ~ dazugeben** (*umg*) to put one's oar in; **~korn** *nt* mustard seed.

sengen ['zɛŋən] *vt* to singe ♦ *vi* to scorch.

senil [ze'niːl] (*pej*) *adj* senile.

Senior ['zeːniɔr] (**-s, -en**) *m* (*Rentner*) senior citizen; (*Geschäftspartner*) senior partner.

Seniorenpaß [zeni'oːrənpas] *m* senior citizen's travel pass (*BRIT*).

Senkblei ['zɛŋkblaɪ] *nt* plumb.

Senke (-, -n) *f* depression.
Senkel (-s, -) *m* (shoe)lace.
senken *vt* to lower; (*Kopf*) to bow; (*TECH*) to sink ♦ *vr* to sink; (*Stimme*) to drop.
Senk- *zW:* ~**fuß** *m* flat foot; ~**grube** *f* cesspit; **s~recht** *adj* vertical, perpendicular; ~**rechte** *f* perpendicular; ~**rechtstarter** *m* (*AVIAT*) vertical takeoff plane; (*fig: Person*) high-flier.
Senner(in) ['zɛnər(ɪn)] (-s, -) *m(f)* (*Alpine*) dairyman, dairymaid.
Sensation [zɛnzatsi'oːn] *f* sensation.
sensationell [zɛnzatsio'nɛl] *adj* sensational.
Sensationsblatt *nt* sensational paper.
Sensationssucht *f* sensationalism.
Sense ['zɛnzə] (-, -n) *f* scythe; **dann ist** ~! (*umg*) that's the end!
sensibel [zɛn'ziːbəl] *adj* sensitive.
sensibilisieren [zɛnzibili'ziːrən] *vt* to sensitize.
Sensibilität [zɛnzibili'tɛːt] *f* sensitivity.
sentimental [zɛntimɛn'taːl] *adj* sentimental.
Sentimentalität [zɛntimentali'tɛːt] *f* sentimentality.
separat [zepa'raːt] *adj* separate; (*Wohnung, Zimmer*) self-contained.
Sept. *abk* (= *September*) Sept.
September [zɛp'tɛmbər] (-(s), -) *m* September; **im** ~ in September; **im Monat** ~ in the month of September; **heute ist der zweite** ~ today is the second of September *od* September second (*US*); (*geschrieben*) today is 2nd September; **in diesem** ~ this September; **Anfang/Ende/Mitte** ~ at the beginning/end/in the middle of September.
septisch ['zɛptɪʃ] *adj* septic.
sequentiell [zekvɛntsi'ɛl] *adj* (*COMPUT*) sequential; ~**er Zugriff** sequential access.
Sequenz [ze'kvɛnts] *f* sequence.
Serbe ['zɛrbə] (-n, -n) *m* Serbian.
Serbien (-s) *nt* Serbia.
Serbin *f* Serbian.
serbisch *adj* Serbian.
Serbokroatisch(e) *nt* Serbo-Croat.
Serie ['zeːriə] *f* series.
seriell [zeri'ɛl] *adj* (*COMPUT*) serial; ~**e Daten** serial data *pl*; ~**er Anschluß** serial port; ~**er Drucker** serial printer.
Serien- *zW:* ~**anfertigung** *f*, ~**herstellung** *f* series production; **s~mäßig** *adj* (*Ausstattung*) standard; (*Herstellung*) series *attrib* ♦ *adv* (*herstellen*) in series; ~**nummer** *f* serial number; **s~weise** *adv* in series.
seriös [zeri'øːs] *adj* serious; (*anständig*) respectable.
Serpentine [zɛrpɛn'tiːnə] *f* hairpin (bend).
Serum ['zeːrʊm] (-s, Seren) *nt* serum.
Service¹ [zɛr'viːs] (-(s), -) *nt* (*Gläser~*) set; (*Geschirr*) service.
Service² ['søːvɪs] (-, -s) *m* (*COMM, SPORT*) service.
servieren [zɛr'viːrən] *vt, vi* to serve.

Serviererin [zɛr'viːrərɪn] *f* waitress.
Servierwagen *m* trolley.
Serviette [zɛrvi'ɛtə] *f* napkin, serviette.
Servolenkung ['zɛrvo-] *f* power steering.
Servomotor *m* servo motor.
Servus ['zɛrvʊs] (*ÖSTERR, SÜDD*) *interj* hello; (*beim Abschied*) goodbye, so long (*umg*).
Sesam ['zeːzam] (-s, -s) *m* sesame.
Sessel ['zɛsəl] (-s, -) *m* armchair; ~**lift** *m* chairlift.
seßhaft ['zɛshaft] *adj* settled; (*ansässig*) resident.
Set [zɛt] (-s, -s) *nt od m* set; (*Deckchen*) tablemat.
setzen ['zɛtsən] *vt* to put, place, set; (*Baum etc*) to plant; (*Segel, TYP*) to set ♦ *vr* (*Platz nehmen*) to sit down; (*Kaffee, Tee*) to settle ♦ *vi* to leap; (*wetten*) to bet; (*TYP*) to set; **jdm ein Denkmal** ~ to build a monument to sb; **sich zu jdm** ~ to sit with sb.
Setzer ['zɛtsər] (-s, -) *m* (*TYP*) typesetter.
Setzerei [zɛtsə'raɪ] *f* caseroom; (*Firma*) typesetting firm.
Setz- *zW:* ~**kasten** *m* (*TYP*) case; (*an Wand*) ornament shelf; ~**ling** *m* young plant; ~**maschine** *f* (*TYP*) typesetting machine.
Seuche ['zɔʏçə] (-, -n) *f* epidemic.
Seuchengebiet *nt* infected area.
seufzen ['zɔʏftsən] *vt, vi* to sigh.
Seufzer ['zɔʏftsər] (-s, -) *m* sigh.
Sex [zɛks] (-(es)) *m* sex.
Sexta ['zɛksta] (-, Sexten) *f* first year of German secondary school.
Sexualerziehung [zɛksu'aːlɛrtsiːʊŋ] *f* sex education.
Sexualität [zɛksuali'tɛːt] *f* sex, sexuality.
Sexual- *zW:* ~**kunde** [zɛksu'aːlkʊndə] *f* sex education; ~**leben** *nt* sex life; ~**objekt** *nt* sex object.
sexuell [zɛksu'ɛl] *adj* sexual.
Seychellen [ze'ʃɛlən] *pl* Seychelles *pl*.
sezieren [ze'tsiːrən] *vt* to dissect.
SFB (-) *m abk* (= *Sender Freies Berlin*) Radio Free Berlin.
Sfr, sFr *abk* (= *Schweizer Franken*) sfr.
Shampoo [ʃam'puː] (-s, -s) *nt* shampoo.
Shetlandinseln ['ʃɛtlant|ɪnzəln] *pl* Shetland, Shetland Isles *pl*.
Shorts [ʃɔːrts] *pl* shorts *pl*.
Showmaster ['ʃoʊmaːstər] (-s, -) *m* compère, MC.
siamesisch [zia'meːzɪʃ] *adj:* ~**e Zwillinge** Siamese twins.
Siamkatze *f* Siamese (cat).
Sibirien [zi'biːriən] (-s) *nt* Siberia.
sibirisch *adj* Siberian.

═══════════ *SCHLÜSSELWORT*

sich [zɪç] *pron* **1** (*akk*): **er/sie/es** ... ~ he/she/it ... himself/herself/itself; **sie** *pl*/**man** ... ~ they/ one ... themselves/oneself; **Sie** ... ~ you ... yourself/yourselves *pl*; ~ **wiederholen** to repeat oneself/itself

2 (*dat*): **er/sie/es ... ~** he/she/it ... to himself/herself/itself; **sie** *pl*/**man ... ~** they/one ... to themselves/oneself; **Sie ... ~** you ... to yourself/yourselves *pl*; **sie hat ~ einen Pullover gekauft** she bought herself a jumper; **~ die Haare waschen** to wash one's hair

3 (*mit Präposition*): **haben Sie Ihren Ausweis bei ~?** do you have your pass on you?; **er hat nichts bei ~** he's got nothing on him; **sie bleiben gern unter ~** they keep themselves to themselves

4 (*einander*) each other, one another; **sie bekämpfen ~** they fight each other *od* one another.

5: **dieses Auto fährt ~ gut** this car drives well; **hier sitzt es ~ gut** it's good to sit here.

Sichel ['zɪçəl] (-, -n) *f* sickle; (*Mond~*) crescent.

sicher ['zɪçər] *adj* safe; (*gewiß*) certain; (*Hand, Job*) steady; (*zuverlässig*) secure, reliable; (*selbst~*) confident; (*Stellung*) secure ♦ *adv* (*natürlich*): **du hast dich ~ verrechnet** you must have counted wrongly; **vor jdm/etw ~ sein** to be safe from sb/sth; **sich** *dat* **einer Sache/jds ~ sein** to be sure of sth/sb; **~ ist ~** you can't be too sure.

sichergehen *unreg vi* to make sure.

Sicherheit ['zɪçərhaɪt] *f* safety; (*auch FIN*) security; (*Gewißheit*) certainty; (*Selbst~*) confidence; **die öffentliche ~** public security; **~ im Straßenverkehr** road safety; **~ leisten** (*COMM*) to offer security.

Sicherheits- *zW*: **~abstand** *m* safe distance; **~bestimmungen** *pl* safety regulations *pl*; (*betrieblich, POL etc*) security controls *pl*; **~einrichtungen** *pl* security equipment *sing*, security devices *pl*; **~glas** *nt* safety glass; **~gurt** *m* seat belt; **s~halber** *adv* to be on the safe side; **~nadel** *f* safety pin; **~rat** *m* Security Council; **~schloß** *nt* safety lock; **~spanne** *f* (*COMM*) margin of safety; **~verschluß** *m* safety clasp; **~vorkehrung** *f* safety precaution.

sicherlich *adv* certainly, surely.

sichern *vt* to secure; (*schützen*) to protect; (*Bergsteiger etc*) to belay; (*Waffe*) to put the safety catch on; (*COMPUT: Daten*) to back up; **jdm/sich etw ~** to secure sth for sb/for o.s.

sicherstellen *vt* to impound; (*garantieren*) to guarantee.

Sicherung *f* (*Sichern*) securing; (*Vorrichtung*) safety device; (*an Waffen*) safety catch; (*ELEK*) fuse; **da ist (bei) ihm die ~ durchgebrannt** (*fig: umg*) he blew a fuse.

Sicherungskopie *f* backup copy.

Sicht [zɪçt] (-) *f* sight; (*Aus~*) view; (*Sehweite*) visibility; **auf** *od* **nach ~** (*FIN*) at sight; **auf lange ~** on a long-term basis; **s~bar** *adj*

visible; **~barkeit** *f* visibility.

sichten *vt* to sight; (*auswählen*) to sort out; (*ordnen*) to sift through.

Sicht- *zW*: **s~lich** *adj* evident, obvious; **~verhältnisse** *pl* visibility *sing*; **~vermerk** *m* visa; **~weite** *f* visibility; **außer ~weite** out of sight.

sickern ['zɪkərn] *vi* (*Hilfsverb sein*) to seep; (*in Tropfen*) to drip.

Sie [ziː] *nom, akk pron* you.

sie *pron* (*sing: nom*) she; (: *akk*) her; (*pl: nom*) they; (: *akk*) them.

Sieb [ziːp] (-(e)s, -e) *nt* sieve; (*KOCH*) strainer; (*Gemüse~*) colander.

sieben[1] ['ziːbən] *vt* to sieve, sift; (*Flüssigkeit*) to strain ♦ *vi*: **bei der Prüfung wird stark gesiebt** (*fig: umg*) the exam will weed a lot of people out.

sieben[2] ['ziːbən] *num* seven; **S~gebirge** *nt*: **das S~gebirge** the Seven Mountains *pl* (*near Bonn*); **~hundert** *num* seven hundred; **S~meter** *m* (*SPORT*) penalty; **S~sachen** *pl* belongings *pl*; **S~schläfer** *m* (*ZOOL*) dormouse.

siebte(r, s) ['ziːptə(r, s)] *adj* seventh.

Siebtel (-s, -) *nt* seventh.

siebzehn ['ziːptseːn] *num* seventeen.

siebzig ['ziːptsɪç] *num* seventy.

siedeln ['ziːdəln] *vi* to settle.

sieden ['ziːdən] *vt, vi* to boil.

Siedepunkt *m* boiling point.

Siedler (-s, -) *m* settler.

Siedlung *f* settlement; (*Häuser~*) housing estate (*BRIT*) *od* development (*US*).

Sieg [ziːk] (-(e)s, -e) *m* victory.

Siegel ['ziːgəl] (-s, -) *nt* seal; **~lack** *m* sealing wax; **~ring** *m* signet ring.

siegen ['ziːgən] *vi* to be victorious; (*SPORT*) to win; **über jdn/etw ~** (*fig*) to triumph over sb/sth; (*in Wettkampf*) to beat sb/sth.

Sieger(in) (-s, -) *m(f)* victor; (*SPORT etc*) winner; **~ehrung** *f* (*SPORT*) presentation ceremony.

siegessicher *adj* sure of victory.

Siegeszug *m* triumphal procession.

siegreich *adj* victorious.

siehe ['ziːə] *Imperativ* see; (**~ da**) behold.

siehst [ziːst] *vb siehe* **sehen.**

sieht [ziːt] *vb siehe* **sehen.**

Siel [ziːl] (-(e)s, -e) *nt od m* (*Schleuse*) sluice; (*Abwasserkanal*) sewer.

siezen ['ziːtsən] *vt* to address as "Sie"; *siehe auch* **duzen.**

Signal [zɪ'gnaːl] (-s, -e) *nt* signal; **~anlage** *f* signals *pl*, set of signals.

signalisieren [zɪgnali'ziːrən] *vt* (*lit, fig*) to signal.

Signatur [zɪgna'tuːr] *f* signature; (*Bibliotheks~*) shelf mark.

Silbe ['zɪlbə] (-, -n) *f* syllable; **er hat es mit keiner ~ erwähnt** he didn't say a word about it.

Silber ['zɪlbər] **(-s)** *nt* silver; ~**bergwerk** *nt* silver mine; ~**blick** *m*: **einen** ~**blick haben** to have a slight squint; ~**hochzeit** *f* silver wedding.

silbern *adj* silver.

Silberpapier *nt* silver paper.

Silhouette [zilu'ɛtə] *f* silhouette.

Silikonchip [zili'koːntʃɪp] *m* silicon chip.

Silikonplättchen [zili'koːnplɛtçən] *nt* silicon chip.

Silo ['ziːlo] **(-s, -s)** *nt od m* silo.

Silvester [zɪl'vɛstər] **(-s, -)** *m or nt* New Year's Eve, Hogmanay (*SCOT*).

Silvester is the German name for New Year's Eve. Although not an official holiday most businesses close early and shops shut at midday. Most Germans celebrate in the evening, and at midnight they let off fireworks and rockets; the revelry usually lasts until the early hours of the morning.

Simbabwe [zɪm'baːbvə] **(-s)** *nt* Zimbabwe.

simpel ['zɪmpəl] *adj* simple; **S~ (-s, -)** (*umg*) *m* simpleton.

Sims [zɪms] **(-es, -e)** *nt od m* (*Kamin~*) mantelpiece; (*Fenster~*) (window)sill.

Simulant(in) [zimu'lant(ɪn)] **(-en, -en)** *m(f)* malingerer.

simulieren [zimu'liːrən] *vt* to simulate; (*vortäuschen*) to feign ♦ *vi* to feign illness.

simultan [zimʊl'taːn] *adj* simultaneous; **S~dolmetscher** *m* simultaneous interpreter.

sind [zɪnt] *vb siehe* **sein**.

Sinfonie [zɪnfo'niː] *f* symphony.

Singapur ['zɪŋgapuːr] **(-s)** *nt* Singapore.

singen ['zɪŋən] *unreg vt, vi* to sing.

Single¹ ['sɪŋgəl] **(-s, -s)** *m* (*Alleinlebender*) single person.

Single² ['sɪŋgəl] **(-, -s)** *f* (*MUS*) single.

Singsang *m* (*Gesang*) monotonous singing.

Singstimme *f* vocal part.

Singular ['zɪŋgulaːr] *m* singular.

Singvogel ['zɪŋfoːgəl] *m* songbird.

sinken ['zɪŋkən] *unreg vi* to sink; (*Boden, Gebäude*) to subside; (*Fundament*) to settle; (*Preise etc*) to fall, go down; **den Mut/die Hoffnung** ~ **lassen** to lose courage/hope.

Sinn [zɪn] **(-(e)s, -e)** *m* mind; (*Wahrnehmungs~*) sense; (*Bedeutung*) sense, meaning; **im** ~**e des Gesetzes** according to the spirit of the law; ~ **für etw** sense of sth; **im** ~**e des Verstorbenen** in accordance with the wishes of the deceased; **von** ~**en sein** to be out of one's mind; **das ist nicht der** ~ **der Sache** that is not the point; **das hat keinen** ~ there is no point in that; ~**bild** *nt* symbol; **s~bildlich** *adj* symbolic.

sinnen *unreg vi* to ponder; **auf etw** *akk* ~ to contemplate sth.

Sinnenmensch *m* sensualist.

Sinnes- *zW:* ~**organ** *nt* sense organ; ~**täuschung** *f* illusion; ~**wandel** *m* change of mind.

sinngemäß *adj* faithful; (*Wiedergabe*) in one's own words.

sinnig *adj* apt; (*ironisch*) clever.

Sinn- *zW:* **s~lich** *adj* sensual, sensuous; (*Wahrnehmung*) sensory; ~**lichkeit** *f* sensuality; **s~los** *adj* senseless, meaningless; **s~los betrunken** blind drunk; ~**losigkeit** *f* senselessness, meaninglessness; **s~verwandt** *adj* synonymous; **s~voll** *adj* meaningful; (*vernünftig*) sensible.

Sinologe [zino'loːgə] **(-n, -n)** *m* Sinologist.

Sinologin *f* Sinologist.

Sintflut ['zɪntfluːt] *f* Flood; **nach uns die** ~ (*umg*) it doesn't matter what happens after we've gone; **s~artig** *adj*: **s~artige Regenfälle** torrential rain *sing*.

Sinus ['ziːnus] **(-, - *od* -se)** *m* (*ANAT*) sinus; (*MATH*) sine.

Siphon [zi'föː] **(-s, -s)** *m* siphon.

Sippe ['zɪpə] **(-, -n)** *f* (extended) family; (*umg: Verwandtschaft*) clan.

Sippschaft ['zɪpʃaft] (*pej*) *f* tribe; (*Bande*) gang.

Sirene [zi'reːnə] **(-, -n)** *f* siren.

Sirup ['ziːrup] **(-s, -e)** *m* syrup.

Sit-in [sɪt'ˈɪn] **(-(s), -s)** *nt*: **ein** ~ **machen** to stage a sit-in.

Sitte ['zɪtə] **(-, -n)** *f* custom; **Sitten** *pl* morals *pl*; **was sind denn das für** ~**n?** what sort of way is that to behave?

Sitten- *zW:* ~**polizei** *f* vice squad; ~**strolch** (*umg*) *m* sex fiend; ~**wächter** *m* (*ironisch*) guardian of public morals; **s~widrig** *adj* (*form*) immoral.

Sittich ['zɪtɪç] **(-(e)s, -e)** *m* parakeet.

Sitt- *zW:* **s~lich** *adj* moral; ~**lichkeit** *f* morality; ~**lichkeitsverbrechen** *nt* sex offence (*BRIT*) *od* offense (*US*); **s~sam** *adj* modest, demure.

Situation [zituatsi'oːn] *f* situation.

situiert [zitu'iːrt] *adj*: **gut** ~ **sein** to be well off.

Sitz [zɪts] **(-es, -e)** *m* seat; (*von Firma, Verwaltung*) headquarters *pl*; **der Anzug hat einen guten** ~ the suit sits well.

sitzen *unreg vi* to sit; (*Bemerkung, Schlag*) to strike home; (*Gelerntes*) to have sunk in; (*umg: im Gefängnis* ~) to be inside; **locker** ~ to be loose; ~ **Sie bequem?** are you comfortable?; **einen** ~ **haben** (*umg*) to have had one too many; **er sitzt im Kultusministerium** (*umg: sein*) he's in the Ministry of Education; ~ **bleiben** to remain seated.

sitzenbleiben *unreg vi* (*SCH*) to have to repeat a year; **auf etw** *dat* ~ to be lumbered with sth.

sitzend *adj* (*Tätigkeit*) sedentary.

sitzenlassen *unreg vt* (*SCH*) to keep down a year; (*Mädchen*) to jilt; (*Wartenden*) to stand up; **etw auf sich** *dat* ~ to take sth lying down.

Sitz- *zW:* ~**fleisch** (*umg*) *nt:* ~**fleisch haben** to be able to sit still; ~**gelegenheit** *f* seats *pl;* ~**ordnung** *f* seating plan; ~**platz** *m* seat; ~**streik** *m* sit-down strike.

Sitzung *f* meeting.

Sizilianer(in) [zitsili'a:nər(ın)] (**-s, -**) *m(f)* Sicilian.

sizilianisch *adj* Sicilian.

Sizilien [zi'tsi:liən] (**-s**) *nt* Sicily.

Skala ['ska:la] (**-, Skalen**) *f* scale; (*fig*) range.

Skalpell [skal'pɛl] (**-s, -e**) *nt* scalpel.

skalpieren [skal'pi:rən] *vt* to scalp.

Skandal [skan'da:l] (**-s, -e**) *m* scandal.

skandalös [skanda'lø:s] *adj* scandalous.

Skandinavien [skandi'na:viən] (**-s**) *nt* Scandinavia.

Skandinavier(in) (**-s, -**) *m(f)* Scandinavian.

skandinavisch *adj* Scandinavian.

Skat [ska:t] (**-(e)s, -e** *od* **-s**) *m* (*KARTEN*) skat.

Skelett [ske'lɛt] (**-(e)s, -e**) *nt* skeleton.

Skepsis ['skɛpsıs] (**-**) *f* scepticism (*BRIT*), skepticism (*US*).

skeptisch ['skɛptıʃ] *adj* sceptical (*BRIT*), skeptical (*US*).

Ski [ʃi:] (**-s, -er**) *m* ski; ~ **laufen** *od* **fahren** to ski; ~**fahrer** *m* skier; ~**hütte** *f* ski hut *od* lodge (*US*); ~**läufer** *m* skier; ~**lehrer** *m* ski instructor; ~**lift** *m* ski lift; ~**springen** *nt* ski jumping; ~**stiefel** *m* ski boot; ~**stock** *m* ski pole.

Skizze ['skıtsə] (**-, -n**) *f* sketch.

skizzieren [skı'tsi:rən] *vt* to sketch; (*fig: Plan etc*) to outline ♦ *vi* to sketch.

Sklave ['skla:və] (**-n, -n**) *m* slave.

Sklaventreiber (**-s, -**) (*pej*) *m* slave-driver.

Sklaverei [skla:və'raı] *f* slavery.

Sklavin *f* slave.

sklavisch *adj* slavish.

Skonto ['skonto] (**-s, -s**) *nt od m* discount.

Skorbut [skor'bu:t] (**-(e)s**) *m* scurvy.

Skorpion [skorpi'o:n] (**-s, -e**) *m* scorpion; (*ASTROL*) Scorpio.

Skrupel ['skru:pəl] (**-s, -**) *m* scruple; **s~los** *adj* unscrupulous.

Skulptur [skulp'tu:r] *f* sculpture.

skurril [sku'ri:l] *adj* (*geh*) droll, comical.

Slalom ['sla:lom] (**-s, -s**) *m* slalom.

Slawe ['sla:və] (**-n, -n**) *m* Slav.

Slawin *f* Slav.

slawisch *adj* Slavonic, Slavic.

Slip [slıp] (**-s, -s**) *m* (pair of) briefs *pl.*

Slowake [slo'va:kə] (**-n, -n**) *m* Slovak.

Slowakei [slova'kaı] *f* Slovakia.

Slowakin *f* Slovak.

Slowakisch [slo'va:kıʃ] *nt* (*LING*) Slovak; **s~** *adj* Slovak.

Slowenien [slo've:niən] (**-s**) *nt* Slovenia.

slowenisch *adj* Slovene.

S.M. *abk* (= *Seine Majestät*) H.M.

Smaragd [sma'rakt] (**-(e)s, -e**) *m* emerald.

Smoking ['smo:kıŋ] (**-s, -s**) *m* dinner jacket (*BRIT*), tuxedo (*US*).

SMV (**-, -s**) *f abk* = **Schülermitverwaltung.**

Snob [snɔp] (**-s, -s**) *m* snob.

SO *abk* (= *Südost(en)*) SE.

═══════════════════ *SCHLÜSSELWORT*

so [zo:] *adv* **1** (*sosehr*) so; ~ **groß/schön** *etc* so big/nice *etc;* ~ **groß/schön wie** ... as big/nice as ...; **das hat ihn** ~ **geärgert, daß** ... that annoyed him so much that ...

2 (*auf diese Weise*) like this; **mach es nicht** ~ don't do it like that; ~ **oder** ~ (in) one way or the other; ... **oder** ~ or something (like that); **und** ~ **weiter** and so on; ~ **ein** ... such a ...; ~ **einer wie ich** somebody like me; ~ **(et)was** something like this/that; **na** ~ **was!** well I never!; **das ist gut** ~ that's fine; **sie ist nun einmal** ~ that's just the way she is; **das habe ich nur** ~ **gesagt** I didn't really mean it

3 (*umg: umsonst*): **ich habe es** ~ **bekommen** I got it for nothing

4 (*als Füllwort: nicht übersetzt*): ~ **mancher** a number of people *pl*

♦ *konj:* ~ **daß** so that; ~ **wie es jetzt ist** as things are at the moment

♦ *interj:* ~**?** really?; ~**, das wär's** right, that's it then.

s.o. *abk* (= *siehe oben*) see above.

sobald [zo'balt] *konj* as soon as.

Söckchen [zœkçən] *nt* ankle sock.

Socke ['zɔkə] (**-, -n**) *f* sock; **sich auf die ~n machen** (*umg*) to get going.

Sockel ['zɔkəl] (**-s, -**) *m* pedestal, base.

Sodawasser ['zo:davasər] *nt* soda water.

Sodbrennen ['zo:tbrɛnən] (**-s**) *nt* heartburn.

Sodomie [zodo'mi:] *f* bestiality.

soeben [zo'|e:bən] *adv* just (now).

Sofa ['zo:fa] (**-s, -s**) *nt* sofa.

Sofabett *nt* sofa bed, bed settee.

sofern [zo'fɛrn] *konj* if, provided (that).

soff *etc* [zɔf] *vb siehe* **saufen.**

sofort [zo'fort] *adv* immediately, at once; **(ich) komme** ~**!** (I'm) just coming!; **S~hilfe** *f* emergency relief *od* aid; **S~hilfegesetz** *nt* law on emergency aid.

sofortig *adj* immediate.

Sofortmaßnahme *f* immediate measure.

Softeis ['sɔft|aıs] (**-es**) *nt* soft ice-cream.

Softie ['zɔfti:] (**-s, -s**) (*umg*) *m* softy.

Software ['zɔftwɛ:ər] (**-, -s**) *f* software; **s~kompatibel** *adj* software compatible; ~**paket** *nt* software package.

Sog (**-(e)s, -e**) *m* suction; (*von Strudel*) vortex; (*fig*) maelstrom.

sog *etc* [zo:k] *vb siehe* **saugen.**

sog. *abk* = **sogenannt.**

sogar [zo'ga:r] *adv* even.

sogenannt ['zo:gənant] *adj* so-called.

sogleich [zo'glaıç] *adv* straight away, at once.

Sogwirkung f suction; (fig) knock-on effect.
Sohle ['zo:lə] (-, -n) f (Fuß~) sole; (Tal~ etc) bottom; (MIN) level; **auf leisen ~n** (fig) softly, noiselessly.
Sohn [zo:n] (-(e)s, ̈-e) m son.
Sojasoße ['zo:jazo:sə] f soy od soya sauce.
solang(e) konj as od so long as.
Solar- [zo'la:r] in zW solar; **~energie** f solar energy.
Solarium [zo'la:riʊm] nt solarium.
Solbad ['zo:lba:t] nt saltwater bath.
solch [zɔlç] adj inv such.
solche(r, s) adj such; **ein ~r Mensch** such a person.
Sold [zɔlt] (-(e)s, -e) m pay.
Soldat [zɔl'da:t] (-en, -en) m soldier; **s~isch** adj soldierly.
Söldner ['zœldnər] (-s, -) m mercenary.
Sole ['zo:lə] (-, -n) f brine, salt water.
Solei ['zo:laɪ] nt pickled egg.
Soli ['zo:li] pl von Solo.
solid(e) [zo'li:d(ə)] adj solid; (Arbeit, Wissen) sound; (Leben, Person) staid, respectable.
solidarisch [zoli'da:rɪʃ] adj in od with solidarity; **sich ~ erklären** to declare one's solidarity.
solidarisieren [zolidari'zi:rən] vr: **sich ~ mit** to show (one's) solidarity with.
Solidarität [zolidari'tɛ:t] f solidarity.
Solidaritätsstreik m sympathy strike.
Solist(in) [zo'lɪst(ɪn)] m(f) (MUS) soloist.
Soll [zɔl] (-(s), -(s)) nt (FIN) debit (side); (Arbeitsmenge) quota, target; **~ und Haben** debit and credit.
soll vb siehe **sollen**.

=================== *SCHLÜSSELWORT*

sollen ['zɔlən] (pt **sollte**, pp **gesollt** od (als Hilfsverb) **sollen**) Hilfsverb **1** (Pflicht, Befehl) be supposed to; **du hättest nicht gehen ~** you shouldn't have gone, you oughtn't to have gone; **er sollte eigentlich morgen kommen** he was supposed to come tomorrow; **soll ich?** shall I?; **soll ich dir helfen?** shall I help you?; **sag ihm, er soll warten** tell him he's to wait; **was soll ich machen?** what should I do?; **mir soll es gleich sein** it's all the same to me; **er sollte sie nie wiedersehen** he was never to see her again
2 (Vermutung): **sie soll verheiratet sein** she's said to be married; **was soll das heißen?** what's that supposed to mean?; **man sollte glauben, daß ...** you would think that ...; **sollte das passieren, ...** if that should happen ...
♦ vt, vi: **was soll das?** what's all this about od in aid of?; **das sollst du nicht** you shouldn't do that; **was soll's?** what the hell!

sollte etc ['zɔltə] vb siehe **sollen**.
Solo ['zo:lo] (-s, -s od Soli) nt solo.
solo adv (MUS) solo; (fig: umg) on one's own,

alone.
solvent [zɔl'vɛnt] adj (FIN) solvent.
Solvenz [zɔl'vɛnts] f (FIN) solvency.
Somalia [zo'ma:lia] (-s) nt Somalia.
somit [zo'mɪt] konj and so, therefore.
Sommer ['zɔmər] (-s, -) m summer; **~ wie Winter** all year round; **~ferien** pl summer holidays pl (BRIT) od vacation sing (US); (JUR, PARL) summer recess sing; **s~lich** adj summer attrib; (sommerartig) summery; **~loch** nt silly season; **~reifen** m normal tyre (BRIT) od tire (US); **~schlußverkauf** m summer sale; **~semester** nt (UNIV) summer semester (bes US), ≈ summer term (BRIT); **~sprossen** pl freckles pl; **~zeit** f summertime.
Sonate [zo'na:tə] (-, -n) f sonata.
Sonde ['zɔndə] (-, -n) f probe.
Sonder- ['zɔndər] in zW special; **~anfertigung** f special model; **~angebot** nt special offer; **~ausgabe** f special edition; **s~bar** adj strange, odd; **~beauftragte(r)** f(m) (POL) special emissary; **~beitrag** m (special) feature; **~fahrt** f special trip; **~fall** m special case; **s~gleichen** adj inv without parallel, unparalleled; **eine Frechheit s~gleichen** the height of cheek; **s~lich** adj particular; (außergewöhnlich) remarkable; (eigenartig) peculiar; **~ling** m eccentric; **~marke** f special issue (stamp); **~müll** m dangerous waste.
sondern konj but ♦ vt to separate; **nicht nur ..., ~ auch** not only ..., but also.
Sonder- zW: **~preis** m special price; **~regelung** f special provision; **~schule** f special school; **~vergünstigungen** pl perquisites pl, perks pl (bes BRIT); **~wünsche** pl special requests pl; **~zug** m special train.
sondieren [zɔn'di:rən] vt to suss out; (Gelände) to scout out.
Sonett [zo'nɛt] (-(e)s, -e) nt sonnet.
Sonnabend ['zɔn|a:bənt] m Saturday; siehe auch **Dienstag**.
Sonne ['zɔnə] (-, -n) f sun; **an die ~ gehen** to go out in the sun.
sonnen vr to sun o.s.; **sich in etw** dat **~** (fig) to bask in sth.
Sonnen- zW: **~aufgang** m sunrise; **s~baden** vi to sunbathe; **~blume** f sunflower; **~brand** m sunburn; **~brille** f sunglasses pl; **~creme** f suntan lotion; **~energie** f solar energy; **~finsternis** f solar eclipse; **~fleck** m sunspot; **s~gebräunt** adj suntanned; **s~klar** adj crystal-clear; **~kollektor** m solar panel; **~kraftwerk** nt solar power station; **~milch** f suntan lotion; **~öl** nt suntan oil; **~schein** m sunshine; **~schirm** m sunshade; **~schutzmittel** nt sunscreen; **~stich** m sunstroke; **du hast wohl einen ~stich!** (hum: umg) you must have been out in the sun too long!; **~system** nt solar system; **~uhr** f

sundial; ~**untergang** m sunset; ~**wende** f solstice.

sonnig ['zɔnɪç] adj sunny.

Sonntag ['zɔnta:k] m Sunday; siehe auch Dienstag.

sonntäglich adj attrib: ~ **gekleidet** dressed in one's Sunday best.

sonntags adv (on) Sundays.

Sonntagsdienst m: ~ **haben** (Apotheke) to be open on Sundays.

Sonntagsfahrer (pej) m Sunday driver.

sonst [zɔnst] adv otherwise; (mit pron, in Fragen) else; (zu anderer Zeit) at other times; (gewöhnlich) usually, normally ♦ konj otherwise; **er denkt, er ist ~ wer** (umg) he thinks he's somebody special; ~ **geht's dir gut?** (ironisch: umg) are you feeling okay?; **wenn ich Ihnen ~ noch behilflich sein kann** if I can help you in any other way; ~ **noch etwas?** anything else?; ~ **nichts** nothing else.

sonstig adj other; „**S~es**" "other".

sonst- zW: ~**jemand** (umg) pron anybody (at all); ~**was** (umg) pron: **da kann ja** ~**was passieren** anything could happen; ~**wo** (umg) adv somewhere else; ~**woher** (umg) adv from somewhere else; ~**wohin** (umg) adv somewhere else.

sooft [zo'|ɔft] konj whenever.

Sopran [zo'pra:n] (-s, -e) m soprano (voice).

Sopranistin [zopra'nɪstɪn] f soprano (singer).

Sorge ['zɔrgə] (-, -n) f care, worry; **dafür ~ tragen, daß** ... (geh) to see to it that ...

sorgen vi: **für jdn ~** to look after sb ♦ vr: **sich ~ (um)** to worry (about); **für etw ~** to take care of od see to sth; **dafür ~, daß** ... to see to it that ...; **dafür ist gesorgt** that's taken care of.

Sorgen- zW: **s~frei** adj carefree; ~**kind** nt problem child; **s~voll** adj troubled, worried.

Sorgerecht (-(e)s) nt custody (of a child).

Sorgfalt ['zɔrkfalt] (-) f care(fulness); **viel ~ auf etw** akk **verwenden** to take a lot of care over sth.

sorgfältig adj careful.

sorglos adj careless; (ohne Sorgen) carefree.

sorgsam adj careful.

Sorte ['zɔrtə] (-, -n) f sort; (Waren~) brand; **Sorten** pl (FIN) foreign currency sing.

sortieren [zɔr'ti:rən] vt to sort (out); (COMPUT) to sort.

Sortiermaschine f sorting machine.

Sortiment [zɔrti'mɛnt] nt assortment.

SOS [ɛs|o:'|ɛs] nt abk SOS.

sosehr [zo'ze:r] konj as much as.

soso [zo'zo:] interj: ~! I see!; (erstaunt) well, well!; (drohend) well!

Soße ['zo:sə] (-, -n) f sauce; (Braten~) gravy.

Souffleur [zu'flø:r] m prompter.

Souffleuse [zu'flø:zə] f prompter.

soufflieren [zu'fli:rən] vt, vi to prompt.

soundso ['zo:|ʊnt'zo:] adv: ~ **lange** for such and such a time.

soundsoviele(r, s) adj: **am S~n** (Datum) on such and such a date.

Souterrain [zute'rɛ:] (-s, -s) nt basement.

Souvenir [zuvə'ni:r] (-s, -s) nt souvenir.

souverän [zuvə'rɛ:n] adj sovereign; (überlegen) superior; (fig) supremely good.

soviel [zo'fi:l] konj as far as ♦ pron: ~ **(wie)** as much (as); **rede nicht** ~ don't talk so much.

soweit [zo'vait] konj as far as ♦ adv: ~ **sein** to be ready; ~ **wie** od **als möglich** as far as possible; **ich bin** ~ **zufrieden** by and large I'm quite satisfied; **es ist bald** ~ it's nearly time.

sowenig [zo've:nɪç] adv: ~ **(wie)** no more (than), not any more (than) ♦ konj however little; ~ **wie möglich** as little as possible.

sowie [zo'vi:] konj (sobald) as soon as; (ebenso) as well as.

sowieso [zovi'zo:] adv anyway.

Sowjetbürger m (früher) Soviet citizen.

sowjetisch [zɔ'vjetɪʃ] adj (früher) Soviet.

Sowjet- zW (früher): ~**republik** f Soviet Republic; ~**russe** m Soviet Russian; ~**union** f Soviet Union.

sowohl [zo'vo:l] konj: ~ ... **als** od **wie auch** ... both ... and ...

soz. abk = sozial; sozialistisch.

sozial [zotsi'a:l] adj social; ~ **eingestellt** public-spirited; ~**er Wohnungsbau** public-sector housing (programme); **S~abbau** m public-spending cuts pl; **S~abgaben** pl National Insurance contributions pl (BRIT), Social Security contributions pl (US); **S~amt** nt (social) welfare office; **S~arbeiter** m social worker; **S~beruf** m caring profession; **S~demokrat** m social democrat; **S~hilfe** f welfare (aid).

Sozialisation [zotsializatsi'o:n] f (PSYCH, SOZIOLOGIE) socialization.

sozialisieren [zotsiali'zi:rən] vt to socialize.

Sozialismus [zotsia'lɪsmʊs] m socialism.

Sozialist(in) [zotsia'lɪst(ɪn)] m(f) socialist.

sozialistisch adj socialist.

Sozial- zW: ~**kunde** f social studies sing; ~**leistungen** pl social security contributions (from the state and employer); ~**plan** m redundancy payments scheme; ~**politik** f social welfare policy; ~**produkt** nt (gross od net) national product; ~**staat** m welfare state; ~**versicherung** f national insurance (BRIT), social security (US); ~**wohnung** f ≈ council flat (BRIT), state-subsidized apartment.

A **Sozialwohnung** is a council house or flat let at a fairly low rent to people on low incomes. They are built from public funds (in 1993 there was a cash injection of DM 2 million into this housing fund). People applying for a Sozialwohnung have to prove their entitlement.

Soziologe [zotsio'lo:gə] (-n, -n) *m* sociologist.
Soziologie [zotsiolo'gi:] *f* sociology.
Soziologin [zotsio'lo:gɪn] *f* sociologist.
soziologisch [zotsio'lo:gɪʃ] *adj* sociological.
Sozius ['zo:tsiʊs] (-, -se) *m* (*COMM*) partner; (*Motorrad*) pillion rider; ~**sitz** *m* pillion (seat).
sozusagen [zotsu'za:gən] *adv* so to speak. ›
Spachtel ['ʃpaxtəl] (-s, -) *m* spatula.
spachteln *vt* (*Mauerfugen, Ritzen*) to fill (in) ♦ *vi* (*umg: essen*) to tuck in.
Spagat [ʃpa'ga:t] (-s, -e) *m od nt* splits *pl*.
Spaghetti [ʃpa'gɛti] *pl* spaghetti *sing*.
spähen ['ʃpɛːən] *vi* to peep, peek.
Spalier [ʃpa'li:r] (-s, -e) *nt* (*Gerüst*) trellis; (*Leute*) guard of honour (*BRIT*) *od* honor (*US*); ~ **stehen, ein ~ bilden** to form a guard of honour (*BRIT*) *or* honor (*US*).
Spalt [ʃpalt] (-(e)s, -e) *m* crack; (*Tür~*) chink; (*fig: Kluft*) split.
Spalte (-, -n) *f* crack, fissure; (*Gletscher~*) crevasse; (*in Text*) column.
spalten *vt, vr* (*lit, fig*) to split.
Spaltung *f* splitting.
Span [ʃpa:n] (-(e)s, -̈e) *m* shaving.
Spanferkel *nt* sucking pig.
Spange ['ʃpaŋə] (-, -n) *f* clasp; (*Haar~*) hair slide; (*Schnalle*) buckle; (*Arm~*) bangle.
Spaniel ['ʃpa:niəl] (-s, -s) *m* spaniel.
Spanien ['ʃpa:niən] (-s) *nt* Spain.
Spanier(in) (-s, -) *m(f)* Spaniard.
spanisch *adj* Spanish; **das kommt mir ~ vor** (*umg*) that seems odd to me; ~**e Wand** (folding) screen.
Spann (-(e)s, -e) *m* instep.
spann *etc* [ʃpan] *vb siehe* **spinnen**.
Spannbeton (-s) *m* prestressed concrete.
Spanne (-, -n) *f* (*Zeit~*) space; (*Differenz*) gap; *siehe auch* **Spann**.
spannen *vt* (*straffen*) to tighten, tauten; (*befestigen*) to brace ♦ *vi* to be tight.
spannend *adj* exciting, gripping; **mach's nicht so ~!** (*umg*) don't keep me *etc* in suspense.
Spanner (-s, -) (*umg*) *m* (*Voyeur*) peeping Tom.
Spannkraft *f* elasticity; (*fig*) energy.
Spannung *f* tension; (*ELEK*) voltage; (*fig*) suspense; (*unangenehm*) tension.
Spannungsgebiet *nt* (*POL*) flashpoint, area of tension.
Spannungsprüfer *m* voltage detector.
Spannweite *f* (*von Flügeln, AVIAT*) (wing)span.
Spanplatte *f* chipboard.
Sparbuch *nt* savings book.
Sparbüchse *f* moneybox.
sparen ['ʃpa:rən] *vt, vi* to save; **sich** *dat* **etw ~** to save o.s. sth; (*Bemerkung*) to keep sth to o.s.; **mit etw ~** to be sparing with sth; **an etw** *dat* **~** to economize on sth.
Sparer(in) (-s, -) *m(f)* (*bei Bank etc*) saver.

Sparflamme *f* low flame; **auf ~** (*fig: umg*) just ticking over.
Spargel ['ʃpargəl] (-s, -) *m* asparagus.
Spar- *zW:* ~**groschen** *m* nest egg; ~**kasse** *f* savings bank; ~**konto** *nt* savings account.
spärlich ['ʃpɛːrlɪç] *adj* meagre (*BRIT*), meager (*US*); (*Bekleidung*) scanty; (*Beleuchtung*) poor.
Spar- *zW:* ~**maßnahme** *f* economy measure; ~**packung** *f* economy size; **s~sam** *adj* economical, thrifty; **s~sam im Verbrauch** economical; ~**samkeit** *f* thrift, economizing; ~**schwein** *nt* piggy bank.
Sparte ['ʃpartə] (-, -n) *f* field; (*COMM*) line of business; (*PRESSE*) column.
Sparvertrag *m* savings agreement.
Spaß [ʃpa:s] (-es, -̈e) *m* joke; (*Freude*) fun; ~ **muß sein** there's no harm in a joke; **jdm ~ machen** to be fun (for sb); **s~en** *vi* to joke; **mit ihm ist nicht zu s~en** you can't take liberties with him.
spaßeshalber *adv* for the fun of it.
spaßig *adj* funny, droll.
Spaß- *zW:* ~**macher** *m* joker, funny man; ~**verderber** (-s, -) *m* spoilsport; ~**vogel** *m* joker.
Spastiker(in) ['ʃpastikər(ɪn)] *m(f)* (*MED*) spastic.
spät [ʃpɛːt] *adj, adv* late; **heute abend wird es ~** it'll be a late night tonight.
Spaten ['ʃpa:tən] (-s, -) *m* spade; ~**stich** *m*: **den ersten ~stich tun** to turn the first sod.
Spätentwickler *m* late developer.
später *adj, adv* later; **an ~ denken** to think of the future; **bis ~!** see you later!
spätestens *adv* at the latest.
Spätlese *f* late vintage.
Spatz [ʃpats] (-en, -en) *m* sparrow.
spazieren [ʃpa'tsi:rən] *vi* (*Hilfsverb sein*) to stroll; ~**fahren** *unreg vi* to go for a drive; ~**gehen** *unreg vi* to go for a walk.
Spazier- *zW:* ~**gang** *m* walk; **einen ~gang machen** to go for a walk; ~**gänger(in)** *m(f)* stroller; ~**stock** *m* walking stick; ~**weg** *m* path, walk.
SPD (-) *f abk* (= *Sozialdemokratische Partei Deutschlands*) German Social Democratic Party.

The SPD (Sozialdemokratische Partei Deutschlands), the German Social Democratic Party, was newly formed in 1945. It is the largest political party in Germany. It shared in the government with the CDU/CSU from 1966-69 and governed from 1969-82 along with the FDP in a socialist-liberal coalition.

Specht [ʃpɛçt] (-(e)s, -e) *m* woodpecker.
Speck [ʃpɛk] (-(e)s, -e) *m* bacon; **mit ~ fängt man Mäuse** (*Sprichwort*) you need a sprat to catch a mackerel; **'ran an den ~** (*umg*) let's get stuck in.

Spediteur [ʃpedi'tøːr] *m* carrier; (*Möbel~*) furniture remover.
Spedition [ʃpeditsi'oːn] *f* carriage; (*~sfirma*) road haulage contractor; (*Umzugsfirma*) removal (*BRIT*) *od* moving (*US*) firm.
Speer [ʃpeːr] (**-(e)s, -e**) *m* spear; (*SPORT*) javelin; **~werfen** *nt:* **das ~werfen** throwing the javelin.
Speiche ['ʃpaɪçə] (**-, -n**) *f* spoke.
Speichel ['ʃpaɪçəl] (**-s**) *m* saliva, spit(tle); **~lecker** (*pej: umg*) *m* bootlicker.
Speicher ['ʃpaɪçər] (**-s, -**) *m* storehouse; (*Dach~*) attic, loft; (*Korn~*) granary; (*Wasser~*) tank; (*TECH*) store; (*COMPUT*) memory; **~auszug** *m* (*COMPUT*) dump.
speichern *vt* (*auch COMPUT*) to store.
speien ['ʃpaɪən] *unreg vt, vi* to spit; (*erbrechen*) to vomit; (*Vulkan*) to spew.
Speise ['ʃpaɪzə] (**-, -n**) *f* food; **kalte und warme ~n** hot and cold meals; **~eis** *nt* ice-cream; **~fett** *nt* cooking fat; **~kammer** *f* larder, pantry; **~karte** *f* menu.
speisen *vt* to feed; to eat ♦ *vi* to dine.
Speise- *zW:* **~öl** *nt* salad oil; (*zum Braten*) cooking oil; **~röhre** *f* (*ANAT*) gullet, oesophagus (*BRIT*), esophagus (*US*); **~saal** *m* dining room; **~wagen** *m* dining car; **~zettel** *m* menu.
Spektakel [ʃpɛk'taːkəl] (**-s, -**) *m* (*umg: Lärm*) row ♦ *nt* (**-s, -**) spectacle.
spektakulär [ʃpɛktaku'lɛːr] *adj* spectacular.
Spektrum ['ʃpɛktrʊm] (**-s, -tren**) *nt* spectrum.
Spekulant(in) [ʃpeku'lant(ɪn)] *m(f)* speculator.
Spekulation [ʃpekulatsi'oːn] *f* speculation.
Spekulatius [ʃpeku'laːtsiʊs] (**-, -**) *m* spiced biscuit (*BRIT*) *od* cookie (*US*).
spekulieren [ʃpeku'liːrən] *vi* (*fig*) to speculate; **auf etw** *akk* **~** to have hopes of sth.
Spelunke [ʃpe'lʊŋkə] (**-, -n**) *f* dive.
spendabel [ʃpɛn'daːbəl] (*umg*) *adj* generous, open-handed.
Spende ['ʃpɛndə] (**-, -n**) *f* donation.
spenden *vt* to donate, give; **S~konto** *nt* donations account; **S~waschanlage** *f* donation-laundering organization.
Spender(in) (**-s, -**) *m(f)* donator; (*MED*) donor.
spendieren [ʃpɛn'diːrən] *vt* to pay for, buy; **jdm etw ~** to treat sb to sth, stand sb sth.
Sperling ['ʃpɛrlɪŋ] *m* sparrow.
Sperma ['ʃpɛrma] (**-s, Spermen**) *nt* sperm.
sperrangelweit ['ʃpɛr'aŋəl'vaɪt] *adj* wide-open.
Sperrbezirk *m* no-go area.
Sperre (**-, -n**) *f* barrier; (*Verbot*) ban; (*Polizei~*) roadblock.
sperren ['ʃpɛrən] *vt* to block; (*COMM: Konto*) to freeze; (*COMPUT: Daten*) to disable; (*SPORT*) to suspend, bar; (: *vom Ball*) to obstruct; (*einschließen*) to lock; (*verbieten*) to ban ♦ *vr* to baulk, jibe, jib.
Sperr- *zW:* **~feuer** *nt* (*MIL, fig*) barrage; **~frist** *f* (*auch JUR*) waiting period; (*SPORT*)

(period of) suspension; **~gebiet** *nt* prohibited area; **~gut** *nt* bulky freight; **~holz** *nt* plywood.
sperrig *adj* bulky.
Sperr- *zW:* **~konto** *nt* blocked account; **~müll** *m* bulky refuse; **~sitz** *m* (*THEAT*) stalls *pl* (*BRIT*), orchestra (*US*); **~stunde** *f* closing time; **~zeit** *f* closing time; **~zone** *f* exclusion zone.
Spesen ['ʃpeːzən] *pl* expenses *pl*; **~abrechnung** *f* expense account.
Spessart ['ʃpɛsart] (**-s**) *m* Spessart (Mountains *pl*).
Spezi ['ʃpeːtsi] (**-s, -s**) (*umg*) *m* pal, mate (*BRIT*).
Spezial- [ʃpetsi'aːl] *in zW* special; **s~angefertigt** *adj* custom-built; **~ausbildung** *f* specialized training.
spezialisieren [ʃpetsiali'ziːrən] *vr* to specialize.
Spezialisierung *f* specialization.
Spezialist(in) [ʃpetsia'lɪst(ɪn)] *m(f):* **~ (für)** specialist (in).
Spezialität [ʃpetsiali'tɛːt] *f* speciality (*BRIT*), specialty (*US*).
speziell [ʃpetsi'ɛl] *adj* special.
Spezifikation [ʃpetsifikatsi'oːn] *f* specification.
spezifisch [ʃpe'tsiːfɪʃ] *adj* specific.
Sphäre ['sfɛːrə] (**-, -n**) *f* sphere.
spicken ['ʃpɪkən] *vt* to lard ♦ *vi* (*SCH*) to copy, crib.
Spickzettel *m* (*SCH: umg*) crib.
spie *etc* [ʃpiː] *vb siehe* **speien**.
Spiegel ['ʃpiːgəl] (**-s, -**) *m* mirror; (*Wasser~*) level; (*MIL*) tab; **~bild** *nt* reflection; **s~bildlich** *adj* reversed.
Spiegelei ['ʃpiːgəl|aɪ] *nt* fried egg.
spiegeln *vt* to mirror, reflect ♦ *vr* to be reflected ♦ *vi* to gleam; (*wider~*) to be reflective.
Spiegelreflexkamera *f* reflex camera.
Spiegelschrift *f* mirror writing.
Spiegelung *f* reflection.
spiegelverkehrt *adj* in mirror image.
Spiel [ʃpiːl] (**-(e)s, -e**) *nt* game; (*Schau~*) play; (*Tätigkeit*) play(ing); (*KARTEN*) pack (*BRIT*), deck (*US*); (*TECH*) (free) play; **leichtes ~ (bei** *od* **mit jdm) haben** to have an easy job of it (with sb); **die Hand** *od* **Finger im ~ haben** to have a hand in affairs; **jdn/etw aus dem ~ lassen** to leave sb/sth out of it; **auf dem ~(e) stehen** to be at stake; **~automat** *m* gambling machine; (*zum Geldgewinnen*) fruit machine (*BRIT*); **~bank** *f* casino; **~dose** *f* musical box (*BRIT*), music box (*US*).
spielen *vt, vi* to play; (*um Geld*) to gamble; (*THEAT*) to perform, act; **was wird hier gespielt?** (*umg*) what's going on here?
spielend *adv* easily.
Spieler(in) (**-s, -**) *m(f)* player; (*um Geld*)

gambler.
Spielerei [ʃpiːlǝˈraɪ] *f* (*Kinderspiel*) child's play.
spielerisch *adj* playful; (*Leichtigkeit*) effortless; **~es Können** skill as a player; (*THEAT*) acting ability.
Spiel- *zW:* **~feld** *nt* pitch, field; **~film** *m* feature film; **~geld** *nt* (*Einsatz*) stake; (*unechtes Geld*) toy money; **~karte** *f* playing card; **~mannszug** *m* (brass) band; **~plan** *m* (*THEAT*) programme (*BRIT*), program (*US*); **~platz** *m* playground; **~raum** *m* room to manoeuvre (*BRIT*) *od* maneuver (*US*), scope; **~regel** *f* (*lit, fig*) rule of the game; **~sachen** *pl* toys *pl*; **~show** *f* gameshow; **~stand** *m* score; **~straße** *f* play street; **~sucht** *f* addiction to gambling; **~verderber** (**-s, -**) *m* spoilsport; **~waren** *pl* toys *pl*; **~zeit** *f* (*Saison*) season; (*~dauer*) playing time; **~zeug** *nt* toy; (*~sachen*) toys *pl*.
Spieß [ʃpiːs] (**-es, -e**) *m* spear; (*Brat~*) spit; (*MIL: umg*) sarge; **den ~ umdrehen** (*fig*) to turn the tables; **wie am ~(e) schreien** (*umg*) to squeal like a stuck pig; **~braten** *m* joint roasted on a spit.
Spießbürger (**-s, -**) *m* bourgeois.
Spießer (**-s, -**) *m* bourgeois.
Spikes [spaɪks] *pl* (*SPORT*) spikes *pl*; (*AUT*) studs *pl*; **~reifen** *m* studded tyre (*BRIT*) *od* tire (*US*).
Spinat [ʃpiˈnaːt] (**-(e)s, -e**) *m* spinach.
Spind [ʃpɪnt] (**-(e)s, -e**) *m od nt* locker.
spindeldürr [ʃpɪndǝlˈdyr] (*pej*) *adj* spindly, thin as a rake.
Spinne [ˈʃpɪnǝ] (**-, -n**) *f* spider; **s~feind** (*umg*) *adj:* **sich od einander** *dat* **s~feind sein** to be deadly enemies.
spinnen *unreg vt* to spin ♦ *vi* (*umg*) to talk rubbish; (*verrückt*) to be crazy *od* mad; **ich denk' ich spinne** (*umg*) I don't believe it.
Spinnengewebe *nt* cobweb.
Spinner(in) (**-s, -**) *m(f)* (*fig: umg*) screwball, crackpot.
Spinnerei [ʃpɪnǝˈraɪ] *f* spinning mill.
Spinn- *zW:* **~gewebe** *nt* cobweb; **~rad** *nt* spinning wheel; **~webe** *f* cobweb.
Spion [ʃpiˈoːn] (**-s, -e**) *m* spy; (*in Tür*) spyhole.
Spionage [ʃpioˈnaːʒǝ] (**-**) *f* espionage; **~abwehr** *f* counterintelligence; **~satellit** *m* spy satellite.
spionieren [ʃpioˈniːrǝn] *vi* to spy.
Spionin *f* (woman) spy.
Spirale [ʃpiˈraːlǝ] (**-, -n**) *f* spiral; (*MED*) coil.
Spirituosen [ʃpirituˈoːzǝn] *pl* spirits *pl*.
Spiritus [ˈʃpiːritʊs] (**-, -se**) *m* (methylated) spirits *pl*; **~kocher** *m* spirit stove.
Spitz [ʃpɪts] (**-es, -e**) *m* (*Hund*) spitz.
spitz *adj* pointed; (*Winkel*) acute; (*fig: Zunge*) sharp; (: *Bemerkung*) caustic.
Spitz- *zW:* **s~bekommen** *unreg vt:* **etw s~bekommen** (*umg*) to get wise to sth; **~bogen** *m* pointed arch; **~bube** *m* rogue.

Spitze (**-, -n**) *f* point, tip; (*Berg~*) peak; (*Bemerkung*) taunt; (*fig: Stichelei*) dig; (*erster Platz*) lead, top; (*meist pl: Gewebe*) lace; (*umg: prima*) great; **etw auf die ~ treiben** to carry sth too far.
Spitzel (**-s, -**) *m* police informer.
spitzen *vt* to sharpen; (*Lippen, Mund*) to purse; (*lit, fig: Ohren*) to prick up.
Spitzen- *in zW* top; (*Leistung*) top performance; **~lohn** *m* top wages *pl*; **~marke** *f* brand leader; **s~mäßig** *adj* really great; **~position** *f* leading position; **~reiter** *m* (*SPORT*) leader; (*fig: Kandidat*) front runner; (*Ware*) top seller; (*Schlager*) number one; **~sportler** *m* top-class sportsman; **~verband** *m* leading organization.
Spitzer (**-s, -**) *m* sharpener.
spitzfindig *adj* (over)subtle.
Spitzmaus *f* shrew.
Spitzname *m* nickname.
Spleen [ʃpliːn] (**-s, -e** *od* **-s**) *m* (*Angewohnheit*) crazy habit; (*Idee*) crazy idea; (*Fimmel*) obsession.
Splitt [ʃplɪt] (**-s, -e**) *m* stone chippings *pl*; (*Streumittel*) grit.
Splitter (**-s, -**) *m* splinter; **~gruppe** *f* (*POL*) splinter group; **s~nackt** *adj* stark naked.
SPÖ (**-**) *f abk* (= *Sozialistische Partei Österreichs*) Austrian Socialist Party.
sponsern [ˈʃpɔnzǝrn] *vt* to sponsor.
Sponsor [ˈʃpɔnzɔr] (**-s, -en**) *m* sponsor.
spontan [ʃpɔnˈtaːn] *adj* spontaneous.
sporadisch [ʃpoˈraːdɪʃ] *adj* sporadic.
Sporen [ˈʃpoːrǝn] *pl* (*auch BOT, ZOOL*) spurs *pl*.
Sport [ʃpɔrt] (**-(e)s, -e**) *m* sport; (*fig*) hobby; **treiben Sie ~?** do you do any sport?; **~abzeichen** *nt* sports certificate; **~artikel** *pl* sports equipment *sing*; **~fest** *nt* sports gala; (*SCH*) sports day (*BRIT*); **~geist** *m* sportsmanship; **~halle** *f* sports hall; **~klub** *m* sports club; **~lehrer** *m* games *od* P.E. teacher.
Sportler(in) (**-s, -**) *m(f)* sportsman, sportswoman.
Sport- *zW:* **s~lich** *adj* sporting; (*Mensch*) sporty; (*durchtrainiert*) athletic; (*Kleidung*) smart but casual; **~medizin** *f* sports medicine; **~platz** *m* playing *od* sports field; **~schuh** *m* sports shoe; (*sportlicher Schuh*) casual shoe.
Sportsfreund *m* (*fig: umg*) buddy.
Sport- *zW:* **~verein** *m* sports club; **~wagen** *m* sports car; **~zeug** *nt* sports gear.
Spot [spɔt] (**-s, -s**) *m* commercial, advertisement.
Spott [ʃpɔt] (**-(e)s**) *m* mockery, ridicule; **s~billig** *adj* dirt-cheap; **s~en** *vi* to mock; **s~en über** +*akk* to mock (at), ridicule; **das s~et jeder Beschreibung** that simply defies description.
spöttisch [ˈʃpœtɪʃ] *adj* mocking.
Spottpreis *m* ridiculously low price.

sprach *etc* [ʃpraːx] *vb siehe* **sprechen.**
sprachbegabt *adj* good at languages.
Sprache (-, -n) *f* language; **heraus mit der ~!**
(*umg*) come on, out with it!; **zur ~ kommen**
to be mentioned; **in französischer ~** in
French.
Sprachenschule *f* language school.
Sprach- *zW:* **~fehler** *m* speech defect;
~fertigkeit *f* fluency; **~führer** *m* phrase
book; **~gebrauch** *m* (linguistic) usage;
~gefühl *nt* feeling for language;
~kenntnisse *pl:* **mit englischen ~kenntnissen**
with a knowledge of English; **~kurs** *m*
language course; **~labor** *nt* language
laboratory; **s~lich** *adj* linguistic; **s~los** *adj*
speechless; **~rohr** *nt* megaphone; (*fig*)
mouthpiece; **~störung** *f* speech disorder;
~wissenschaft *f* linguistics *sing.*
sprang *etc* [ʃpraŋ] *vb siehe* **springen.**
Spray [spreː] (-s, -s) *m od nt* spray; **~dose** *f*
aerosol (can), spray.
sprayen *vt, vi* to spray.
Sprechanlage *f* intercom.
Sprechblase *f* speech balloon.
sprechen [ˈʃprɛçən] *unreg vi* to speak, talk ♦ *vt*
to say; (*Sprache*) to speak; (*Person*) to speak
to; **mit jdm ~** to speak *od* talk to sb; **das**
spricht für ihn that's a point in his favour;
frei ~ to extemporize; **nicht gut auf jdn zu**
~ sein to be on bad terms with sb; **es spricht**
vieles dafür, daß ... there is every reason to
believe that ...; **hier spricht man Spanisch**
Spanish spoken; **wir ~ uns noch!** you
haven't heard the last of this!
Sprecher(in) (-s, -) *m(f)* speaker; (*für Gruppe*)
spokesman, spokeswoman; (*RUNDF, TV*)
announcer.
Sprech- *zW:* **~funkgerät** *nt* radio telephone;
~rolle *f* speaking part; **~stunde** *f*
consultation (hour); (*von Arzt*) (doctor's)
surgery (*BRIT*); **~stundenhilfe** *f* (doctor's)
receptionist; **~zimmer** *nt* consulting room,
surgery (*BRIT*).
spreizen [ˈʃpraɪtsən] *vt* to spread ♦ *vr* to put on
airs.
Sprengarbeiten *pl* blasting operations *pl.*
sprengen [ˈʃprɛŋən] *vt* to sprinkle; (*mit*
Sprengstoff) to blow up; (*Gestein*) to blast;
(*Versammlung*) to break up.
Spreng- *zW:* **~kopf** *m* warhead; **~ladung** *f*
explosive charge; **~satz** *m* explosive
device; **~stoff** *m* explosive(s *pl*);
~stoffanschlag *m* bomb attack.
Spreu [ʃprɔʏ] (-) *f* chaff.
spricht [ʃprɪçt] *vb siehe* **sprechen.**
Sprichwort *nt* proverb.
sprichwörtlich *adj* proverbial.
sprießen [ˈʃpriːsən] *vi* (*aus der Erde*) to spring
up; (*Knospen*) to sprout.
Springbrunnen *m* fountain.
springen [ˈʃprɪŋən] *unreg vi* to jump, leap;
(*Glas*) to crack; (*mit Kopfsprung*) to dive; **etw**

~ lassen (*umg*) to fork out for sth.
springend *adj:* **der ~e Punkt** the crucial
point.
Springer (-s, -) *m* jumper; (*SCHACH*) knight.
Springreiten *nt* show jumping.
Springseil *nt* skipping rope.
Sprinkler [ˈʃprɪŋklər] (-s, -) *m* sprinkler.
Sprit [ʃprɪt] (-(e)s, -e) (*umg*) *m* petrol (*BRIT*),
gas(oline) (*US*), fuel.
Spritzbeutel *m* icing bag.
Spritze [ˈʃprɪtsə] (-, -n) *f* syringe; (*Injektion*)
injection; (*an Schlauch*) nozzle.
spritzen *vt* to spray; (*Wein*) to dilute with
soda water/lemonade; (*MED*) to inject ♦ *vi* to
splash; (*heißes Fett*) to spit; (*heraus~*) to
spurt; (*aus einer Tube etc*) to squirt; (*MED*) to
give injections.
Spritzer (-s, -) *m* (*Farb~, Wasser~*) splash.
Spritzpistole *f* spray gun.
Spritztour (*umg*) *f* spin.
spröde [ˈʃprøːdə] *adj* brittle; (*Person*)
reserved; (*Haut*) rough.
Sproß (-sses, -sse) *m* shoot.
sproß *etc* [ʃprɔs] *vb siehe* **sprießen.**
Sprosse [ˈʃprɔsə] (-, -n) *f* rung.
Sprossenwand *f* (*SPORT*) wall bars *pl.*
Sprößling [ˈʃprœslɪŋ] *m* offspring *no pl.*
Spruch [ʃprʊx] (-(e)s, ⁻e) *m* saying, maxim;
(*JUR*) judgement; **Sprüche klopfen** (*umg*) to
talk fancy; **~band** *nt* banner.
Sprüchemacher [ˈʃprʏçəmaxər] (*umg*) *m*
patter-merchant.
spruchreif *adj:* **die Sache ist noch nicht ~** it's
not definite yet.
Sprudel [ˈʃpruːdəl] (-s, -) *m* mineral water;
(*süß*) lemonade.
sprudeln *vi* to bubble.
Sprüh- *zW:* **~dose** *f* aerosol (can); **s~en** *vi* to
spray; (*fig*) to sparkle ♦ *vt* to spray; **~regen**
m drizzle.
Sprung [ʃprʊŋ] (-(e)s, ⁻e) *m* jump;
(*schwungvoll, fig: Gedanken~*) leap; (*Riß*)
crack; **immer auf dem ~ sein** (*umg*) to be
always on the go; **jdm auf die Sprünge**
helfen (*wohlwollend*) to give sb a (helping)
hand; **auf einen ~ bei jdm vorbeikommen**
(*umg*) to drop in to see sb; **damit kann man**
keine großen Sprünge machen (*umg*) you
can't exactly live it up on that; **~brett** *nt*
springboard; **~feder** *f* spring; **s~haft** *adj*
erratic; (*Aufstieg*) rapid; **~schanze** *f* ski
jump; **~turm** *m* diving platform.
Spucke [ˈʃpʊkə] (-) *f* spit.
spucken *vt, vi* to spit; **in die Hände ~** (*fig*) to
roll up one's sleeves.
Spucknapf *m* spittoon.
Spucktüte *f* sickbag.
Spuk [ʃpuːk] (-(e)s, -e) *m* haunting; (*fig*)
nightmare; **s~en** *vi* to haunt; **hier s~t es** this
place is haunted.
Spülbecken [ˈʃpyːlbɛkən] *nt* sink.
Spule [ˈʃpuːlə] (-, -n) *f* spool; (*ELEK*) coil.

Spüle ['ʃpyːlə] (-, -n) f (kitchen) sink.
spülen vt to rinse; (Geschirr) to wash, do; (Toilette) to flush ♦ vi to rinse; to wash up (BRIT), do the dishes; to flush; **etw an Land ~** to wash sth ashore.
Spül- zW: **~maschine** f dishwasher; **~mittel** nt washing-up liquid (BRIT), dish-washing liquid; **~stein** m sink.
Spülung f rinsing; (Wasser~) flush; (MED) irrigation.
Spund [ʃpʊnt] (-(e)s, -e) m: **junger ~** (veraltet: umg) young pup.
Spur [ʃpuːr] (-, -en) f trace; (Fuß~, Rad~, Tonband~) track; (Fährte) trail; (Fahr~) lane; **jdm auf die ~ kommen** to get onto sb; **(seine) ~en hinterlassen** (fig) to leave its mark; **keine ~** (umg) not/nothing at all.
spürbar adj noticeable, perceptible.
spuren (umg) vi to obey; (sich fügen) to toe the line.
spüren ['ʃpyːrən] vt to feel; **etw zu ~ bekommen** (lit) to feel sth; (fig) to feel the (full) force of sth.
Spurenelement nt trace element.
Spurensicherung f securing of evidence.
Spürhund m tracker dog; (fig) sleuth.
spurlos adv without (a) trace; **~ an jdm vorübergehen** to have no effect on sb.
Spurt [ʃpʊrt] (-(e)s, -s od -e) m spurt.
spurten vi (Hilfsverb sein: SPORT) to spurt; (umg: rennen) to sprint.
Squash [skvɔʃ] (-) nt (SPORT) squash.
sputen ['ʃpuːtən] vr to make haste.
SS (-) f abk (= Schutzstaffel) SS ♦ nt abk = Sommersemester.
s. S. abk (= siehe Seite) see p.
SSV abk = Sommerschlußverkauf.
st abk (= Stunde) h.
St. abk = Stück; (= Stunde) h.; (= Sankt) St.
Staat [ʃtaːt] (-(e)s, -en) m state; (Prunk) show; (Kleidung) finery; **mit etw ~ machen** to show off od parade sth.
staatenlos adj stateless.
staatl. abk = staatlich.
staatlich adj state attrib; state-run ♦ adv: **~ geprüft** state-certified.
Staats- zW: **~affäre** f (lit) affair of state; (fig) major operation; **~angehörige(r)** f(m) national; **~angehörigkeit** f nationality; **~anleihe** f government bond; **~anwalt** m public prosecutor; **~bürger** m citizen; **~dienst** m civil service; **s~eigen** adj state-owned; **~eigentum** nt public ownership; **~examen** nt (UNIV) degree; **s~feindlich** adj subversive; **~geheimnis** nt (lit, fig hum) state secret; **~haushalt** m budget; **~kosten** pl public expenses pl; **~mann** (-(e)s, pl -männer) m statesman; **s~männisch** adj statesmanlike; **~oberhaupt** nt head of state; **~schuld** f (FIN) national debt; **~sekretär** m secretary of state; **~streich** m coup (d'état); **~verschuldung** f national

debt.
Stab [ʃtaːp] (-(e)s, ̈-e) m rod; (für ~hochsprung) pole; (für Staffellauf) baton; (Gitter~) bar; (Menschen) staff; (von Experten) panel.
Stäbchen ['ʃtɛːpçən] nt (Eß~) chopstick.
Stabhochsprung m pole vault.
stabil [ʃtaˈbiːl] adj stable; (Möbel) sturdy.
Stabilisator [ʃtabiliˈzaːtɔr] m stabilizer.
stabilisieren [ʃtabiliˈziːrən] vt to stabilize.
Stabilisierung f stabilization.
Stabilität [ʃtabiliˈtɛːt] f stability.
Stabreim m alliteration.
Stabsarzt m (MIL) captain in the medical corps.
stach etc [ʃtaːx] vb siehe **stechen**.
Stachel ['ʃtaxəl] (-s, -n) m spike; (von Tier) spine; (von Insekten) sting; **~beere** f gooseberry; **~draht** m barbed wire.
stach(e)lig adj prickly.
Stachelschwein nt porcupine.
Stadion ['ʃtaːdiɔn] (-s, Stadien) nt stadium.
Stadium ['ʃtaːdiʊm] nt stage, phase.
Stadt [ʃtat] (-, ̈-e) f town; (Groß~) city; (~verwaltung) (town/city) council; **~bad** nt municipal swimming baths pl; **s~bekannt** adj known all over town; **~bezirk** m municipal district.
Städtchen ['ʃtɛːtçən] nt small town.
Städtebau (-(e)s) m town planning.
Städter(in) (-s, -) m(f) town/city dweller, townie.
Stadtgespräch nt: **(das) ~ sein** to be the talk of the town.
Stadtguerilla f urban guerrilla.
städtisch adj municipal; (nicht ländlich) urban.
Stadt- zW: **~kasse** f town/city treasury; **~kern** m = Stadtzentrum; **~kreis** m town/city borough; **~mauer** f city wall(s pl); **~mitte** f town/city centre (BRIT) od center (US); **~park** m municipal park; **~plan** m street map; **~rand** m outskirts pl; **~rat** m (Behörde) (town/city) council; **~streicher** m street vagrant; **~streicherin** f bag lady; **~teil** m district, part of town; **~verwaltung** f (Behörde) municipal authority; **~viertel** m district od part of a town; **~zentrum** nt town/city centre (BRIT) od center (US).
Staffel ['ʃtafəl] (-, -n) f rung; (SPORT) relay (team); (AVIAT) squadron.
Staffelei [ʃtafəˈlaɪ] f easel.
Staffellauf m relay race.
staffeln vt to graduate.
Staffelung f graduation.
Stagnation [ʃtagnatsiˈoːn] f stagnation.
stagnieren [ʃtaˈgniːrən] vi to stagnate.
Stahl (-(e)s, ̈-e) m steel.
stahl etc [ʃtaːl] vb siehe **stehlen**.
Stahlhelm m steel helmet.
stak etc [ʃtaːk] vb siehe **stecken**.
Stall [ʃtal] (-(e)s, ̈-e) m stable; (Kaninchen~) hutch; (Schweine~) sty; (Hühner~) henhouse.

Stallung f stables pl.

Stamm [ʃtam] (-(e)s, ⁻e) m (Baum~) trunk; (Menschen~) tribe; (GRAM) stem; (Bakterien~) strain; ~**aktie** f ordinary share, common stock (US); ~**baum** m family tree; (von Tier) pedigree; ~**buch** nt book of family events with legal documents, ≈ family bible.

stammeln vt, vi to stammer.

stammen vi: ~ **von** od **aus** to come from.

Stamm- zW: ~**form** f base form; ~**gast** m regular (customer); ~**halter** m son and heir.

stämmig ['ʃtɛmɪç] adj sturdy; (Mensch) stocky; **S~keit** f sturdiness; stockiness.

Stamm- zW: ~**kapital** nt (FIN) ordinary share od common stock (US) capital; ~**kunde** m, ~**kundin** f regular (customer); ~**lokal** nt café/restaurant etc; (Kneipe) local (BRIT); ~**platz** m usual seat; ~**tisch** m (Tisch in Gasthaus) table reserved for the regulars.

stampfen ['ʃtampfən] vi to stamp; (stapfen) to tramp ♦ vt (mit Stampfer) to mash.

Stampfer (-s, -) m (Stampfgerät) masher.

Stand (-(e)s, ⁻e) m position; (Wasser~, Benzin~ etc) level; (Zähler~ etc) reading; (Stehen) standing position; (Zustand) state; (Spiel~) score; (Messe~ etc) stand; (Klasse) class; (Beruf) profession; **bei jdm** od **gegen jdn einen schweren ~ haben** (fig) to have a hard time of it with sb; **etw auf den neuesten ~ bringen** to bring sth up to date.

stand etc [ʃtant] vb siehe **stehen**.

Standard ['ʃtandart] (-s, -s) m standard; ~**ausführung** f standard design.

standardisieren [ʃtandardi'ziːrən] vt to standardize.

Standarte (-, -n) f (MIL, POL) standard.

Standbild nt statue.

Ständchen ['ʃtɛntçən] nt serenade.

Ständer (-s, -) m stand.

Standes- zW: ~**amt** nt registry office (BRIT), city/county clerk's office (US); **s~amtlich** adj: **s~amtliche Trauung** registry office wedding (BRIT), civil marriage ceremony; ~**beamte(r)** m registrar; ~**bewußtsein** nt status consciousness; ~**dünkel** m snobbery; **s~gemäß** adj, adv according to one's social position; ~**unterschied** m social difference.

Stand- zW: **s~fest** adj (Tisch, Leiter) stable, steady; (fig) steadfast; **s~haft** adj steadfast; ~**haftigkeit** f steadfastness; **s~halten** vi: (jdm/etw) **s~halten** to stand firm (against sb/sth), resist (sb/sth).

ständig ['ʃtɛndɪç] adj permanent; (ununterbrochen) constant, continual.

Stand- zW: ~**licht** nt sidelights pl (BRIT), parking lights pl (US); ~**ort** m location; (MIL) garrison; ~**pauke** (umg) f: **jdm eine ~pauke halten** to give sb a lecture; ~**punkt** m standpoint; **s~rechtlich** adj: **s~rechtlich erschießen** to put before a firing squad;

~**spur** f (AUT) hard shoulder (BRIT), berm (US).

Stange ['ʃtaŋə] (-, -n) f stick; (Stab) pole; (Quer~) bar; (Zigaretten) carton; **von der ~** (COMM) off the peg (BRIT) od rack (US); **eine ~ Geld** quite a packet; **jdm die ~ halten** (umg) to stick up for sb; **bei der ~ bleiben** (umg) to stick at od to sth.

Stangenbohne f runner bean.

Stangenbrot nt French bread; (Laib) French stick (loaf).

stank etc [ʃtaŋk] vb siehe **stinken**.

stänkern ['ʃtɛŋkərn] (umg) vi to stir things up.

Stanniol [ʃtani'oːl] (-s, -e) nt tinfoil.

Stanze ['ʃtantsə] (-, -n) f stanza; (TECH) stamp.

stanzen vt to stamp; (Löcher) to punch.

Stapel ['ʃtaːpəl] (-s, -) m pile; (NAUT) stocks pl; ~**lauf** m launch.

stapeln vt to pile (up).

Stapelverarbeitung f (COMPUT) batch processing.

stapfen ['ʃtapfən] vi to trudge, plod.

Star¹ [ʃtaːr] (-(e)s, -e) m starling; **grauer/grüner ~** (MED) cataract/glaucoma.

Star² [ʃtaːr] (-s, -s) m (Film~ etc) star.

starb etc [ʃtarp] vb siehe **sterben**.

stark [ʃtark] adj strong; (heftig, groß) heavy; (Maßangabe) thick; (umg: hervorragend) great ♦ adv very; (beschädigt etc) badly; (vergrößert, verkleinert) greatly; **das ist ein ~es Stück!** (umg) that's a bit much!; **sich für etw ~ machen** (umg) to stand up for sth; **er ist ~ erkältet** he has a bad cold.

Stärke ['ʃtɛrkə] (-, -n) f strength (auch fig); heaviness; thickness; (von Mannschaft) size; (KOCH, Wäsche~) starch; ~**mehl** nt (KOCH) thickening agent.

stärken vt (lit, fig) to strengthen; (Wäsche) to starch; (Selbstbewußtsein) to boost; (Gesundheit) to improve; (erfrischen) to fortify ♦ vi to be fortifying; ~**des Mittel** tonic.

Starkstrom m heavy current.

Stärkung ['ʃtɛrkʊŋ] f strengthening; (Essen) refreshment.

Stärkungsmittel nt tonic.

starr [ʃtar] adj stiff; (unnachgiebig) rigid; (Blick) staring.

starren vi to stare; ~ **vor** +dat od **von** (voll von) to be covered in; (Waffen) to be bristling with; **vor sich** akk **hin ~** to stare straight ahead.

starr- zW: **S~heit** f rigidity; ~**köpfig** adj stubborn; **S~sinn** m obstinacy.

Start [ʃtart] (-(e)s, -e) m start; (AVIAT) takeoff; ~**automatik** f (AUT) automatic choke; ~**bahn** f runway; **s~en** vi to start; (AVIAT) to take off ♦ vt to start; ~**er** (-s, -) m starter; ~**erlaubnis** f takeoff clearance; ~**hilfe** f (AVIAT) rocket-assisted takeoff; (fig) initial aid; **jdm ~hilfe geben** to help sb get off the ground; ~**hilfekabel** *nt* jump leads *pl* (*BRIT*), jumper cables *pl* (*US*); **s~klar** *adj* (*AVIAT*) clear for takeoff; (*SPORT*) ready to start; ~**kommando** *nt* (*SPORT*) starting signal; ~**zeichen** *nt* start signal.

Stasi ['ʃtaːzi] (-**s**) (*umg*) *f abk* (*früher*: = *Staatssicherheitsdienst der DDR*) Stasi.

> **Stasi**, *an abbreviation of*
> *Staatssicherheitsdienst, the* **DDR** *secret*
> *service, was founded in 1950 and disbanded in*
> *1989. The Stasi organized an extensive spy*
> *network of full-time and part-time workers*
> *who often held positions of trust in both the*
> *DDR and the* **BRD**. *They held personal files on*
> *6 million people.*

Station [ʃtatsi'oːn] *f* station; (*Kranken~*) hospital ward; (*Haltestelle*) stop; ~ **machen** to stop off.

stationär [ʃtatsio'nɛːr] *adj* stationary; (*MED*) in-patient *attrib*.

stationieren [ʃtatsio'niːrən] *vt* to station; (*Atomwaffen etc*) to deploy.

Stations- *zW:* ~**arzt** *m* ward doctor; ~**ärztin** *f* ward doctor; ~**vorsteher** *m* (*EISENB*) stationmaster.

statisch ['ʃtaːtɪʃ] *adj* static.

Statist(in) [ʃta'tɪst(ɪn)] *m(f)* (*FILM*) extra; (*THEAT*) supernumerary.

Statistik *f* statistic; (*Wissenschaft*) statistics *sing*.

Statistiker(in) (-**s**, -) *m(f)* statistician.

statistisch *adj* statistical.

Stativ [ʃta'tiːf] (-**s**, -**e**) *nt* tripod.

Statt [ʃtat] (-) *f* place.

statt *konj* instead of ♦ *präp* (+*dat od gen*) instead of; ~ **dessen** instead.

Stätte ['ʃtɛtə] (-, -**n**) *f* place.

statt- *zW:* ~**finden** *unreg vi* to take place; ~**haft** *adj* admissible; **S~halter** *m* governor; ~**lich** *adj* imposing, handsome; (*Bursche*) strapping; (*Sammlung*) impressive; (*Familie*) large; (*Summe*) handsome.

Statue ['ʃtaːtuə] (-, -**n**) *f* statue.

Statur [ʃta'tuːr] *f* build.

Status ['ʃtaːtʊs] (-, -) *m* status; ~**symbol** *nt* status symbol.

Statuten [ʃta'tuːtən] *pl* by(e)-law(s *pl*).

Stau [ʃtaʊ] (-(**e**)**s**, -**e**) *m* blockage; (*Verkehrs~*) (traffic) jam.

Staub [ʃtaʊp] (-(**e**)**s**) *m* dust; ~ **wischen** to dust; **sich aus dem ~ machen** (*umg*) to clear off.

stauben ['ʃtaʊbən] *vi* to be dusty.

Staubfaden *m* (*BOT*) stamen.

staubig ['ʃtaʊbɪç] *adj* dusty.

Staub- *zW:* ~**lappen** *m* duster; ~**lunge** *f* (*MED*) dust on the lung; **s~saugen** (*pp* **s~gesaugt**) *vi untr* to vacuum; ~**sauger** *m* vacuum cleaner; ~**tuch** *nt* duster.

Staudamm *m* dam.

Staude ['ʃtaʊdə] (-, -**n**) *f* shrub.

stauen ['ʃtaʊən] *vt* (*Wasser*) to dam up; (*Blut*) to stop the flow of ♦ *vr* (*Wasser*) to become dammed up; (*MED, Verkehr*) to become congested; (*Menschen*) to collect together; (*Gefühle*) to build up.

staunen ['ʃtaʊnən] *vi* to be astonished; **da kann man nur noch ~** it's just amazing; **S~** (-**s**) *nt* amazement.

Stausee ['ʃtaʊzeː] *m* reservoir; artificial lake.

Stauung ['ʃtaʊʊŋ] *f* (*von Wasser*) damming-up; (*von Blut, Verkehr*) congestion.

Std., Stde. *abk* (= *Stunde*) h.

stdl. *abk* = **stündlich**.

Steak [ʃteːk] (-**s**, -**s**) *nt* steak.

Stechen ['ʃtɛçən] (-**s**, -) *nt* (*SPORT*) play-off; (*Springreiten*) jump-off; (*Schmerz*) sharp pain.

stechen *unreg vt* (*mit Nadel etc*) to prick; (*mit Messer*) to stab; (*mit Finger*) to poke; (*Biene etc*) to sting; (*Mücke*) to bite; (*KARTEN*) to take; (*KUNST*) to engrave; (*Torf, Spargel*) to cut ♦ *vi* (*Sonne*) to beat down; (*mit Stechkarte*) to clock in ♦ *vr:* **sich** *akk od dat* **in den Finger ~** to prick one's finger; **es sticht** it is prickly; **in See ~** to put to sea.

stechend *adj* piercing, stabbing; (*Geruch*) pungent.

Stech- *zW:* ~**ginster** *m* gorse; ~**karte** *f* clocking-in card; ~**mücke** *f* gnat; ~**palme** *f* holly; ~**uhr** *f* time clock.

Steck- *zW:* ~**brief** *m* "wanted" poster; **s~brieflich** *adv:* **s~brieflich gesucht werden** to be wanted; ~**dose** *f* (wall) socket.

stecken ['ʃtɛkən] *vt* to put; (*einführen*) to insert; (*Nadel*) to stick; (*Pflanzen*) to plant; (*beim Nähen*) to pin ♦ *vi* (*auch unreg*) to be; (*festsitzen*) to be stuck; (*Nadeln*) to stick; **etw in etw** *akk* ~ (*umg: Geld, Mühe*) to put sth into sth; (: *Zeit*) to devote sth to sth; **der Schlüssel steckt** the key is in the lock; **wo steckt er?** where has he got to?; **zeigen, was in einem steckt** to show what one is made of; ~**bleiben** *unreg vi* to get stuck; ~**lassen** *unreg vt* to leave in.

Steckenpferd *nt* hobbyhorse.

Stecker (-**s**, -) *m* (*ELEK*) plug.

Steck- *zW:* ~**nadel** *f* pin; ~**rübe** *f* swede, turnip; ~**schlüssel** *m* box spanner (*BRIT*) *od* wrench (*US*); ~**zwiebel** *f* bulb.

Steg [ʃteːk] (-(**e**)**s**, -**e**) *m* small bridge; (*Anlege~*) landing stage.

Stegreif *m:* **aus dem ~** just like that.

Stehaufmännchen ['ʃteːʔaʊfmɛnçən] *nt* (*Spielzeug*) tumbler.

stehen ['ʃteːən] *unreg vi* to stand; (*sich befinden*) to be; (*in Zeitung*) to say; (*angehalten haben*) to have stopped ♦ *vi unpers:* **es steht schlecht um ...** things are bad for ... ♦ *vr:* **sich gut/schlecht ~** to be well-off/badly off; **zu jdm/etw ~** to stand by sb/ sth; **jdm ~** to suit sb; **ich tue, was in meinen**

Kräften steht I'll do everything I can; **es steht 2:1 für München** the score is 2-1 to Munich; **mit dem Dativ ~** (*GRAM*) to take the dative; **auf Betrug steht eine Gefängnisstrafe** the penalty for fraud is imprisonment; **wie ~ Sie dazu?** what are your views on that?; **wie steht's?** how are things?; (*SPORT*) what's the score?; **wie steht es damit?** how about it?; **~bleiben** *unreg vi* (*Uhr*) to stop; (*Zeit*) to stand still; (*Auto, Zug*) to stand; (*Fehler*) to stay as it is; (*Verkehr, Produktion etc*) to come to a standstill *od* stop.

stehend *adj attrib* (*Fahrzeug*) stationary; (*Gewässer*) stagnant; (*ständig: Heer*) regular.

stehenlassen *unreg vt* to leave; (*Bart*) to grow; **alles stehen- und liegenlassen** to drop everything.

Stehlampe *f* standard lamp (*BRIT*), floor lamp (*US*).

stehlen ['ʃteːlən] *unreg vt* to steal.

Stehplatz *m*: **ein ~ kostet 10 Mark** a standing ticket costs 10 marks.

Stehvermögen *nt* staying power, stamina.

Steiermark ['ʃtaɪrmark] *f*: **die ~** Styria.

steif [ʃtaɪf] *adj* stiff; **~ und fest auf etw** *dat* **beharren** to insist stubbornly on sth.

Steifftier® ['ʃtaɪftiːr] *nt soft toy animal*.

Steifheit *f* stiffness.

Steigbügel ['ʃtaɪkbyːgəl] *m* stirrup.

steigen *unreg vi* to rise; (*klettern*) to climb ♦ *vt* (*Treppen, Stufen*) to climb (up); **das Blut stieg ihm in den Kopf** the blood rushed to his head; **~ in** +*akk*/**auf** +*akk* to get in/on.

Steiger (-s, -) *m* (*MIN*) pit foreman.

steigern *vt* to raise; (*GRAM*) to compare ♦ *vi* (*Auktion*) to bid ♦ *vr* to increase.

Steigerung *f* raising; (*GRAM*) comparison.

Steigung *f* incline, gradient, rise.

steil [ʃtaɪl] *adj* steep; **S~hang** *m* steep slope; **S~paß** *m* (*SPORT*) through ball.

Stein [ʃtaɪn] (-(e)s, -e) *m* stone; (*in Uhr*) jewel; **mir fällt ein ~ vom Herzen!** (*fig*) that's a load off my mind!; **bei jdm einen ~ im Brett haben** (*fig: umg*) to be well in with sb; **jdm ~e in den Weg legen** to make things difficult for sb; **~adler** *m* golden eagle; **s~alt** *adj* ancient; **~bock** *m* (*ASTROL*) Capricorn; **~bruch** *m* quarry.

steinern *adj* (made of) stone; (*fig*) stony.

Stein- *zW*: **~erweichen** *nt*: **zum ~erweichen weinen** to cry heartbreakingly; **~garten** *m* rockery; **~gut** *nt* stoneware; **s~hart** *adj* hard as stone.

steinig *adj* stony.

steinigen *vt* to stone.

Stein- *zW*: **~kohle** *f* mineral coal; **~metz** (-es, -e) *m* stonemason; **s~reich** (*umg*) *adj* stinking rich; **~schlag** *m*: „**Achtung ~schlag**" "danger - falling stones"; **~wurf** *m* (*fig*) stone's throw; **~zeit** *f* Stone Age.

Steiß [ʃtaɪs] (-es, -e) *m* rump; **~bein** *nt* (*ANAT*) coccyx.

Stelle ['ʃtɛlə] (-, -n) *f* place; (*Arbeit*) post, job; (*Amt*) office; (*Abschnitt*) passage; (*Text~, bes beim Zitieren*) reference; **drei ~n hinter dem Komma** (*MATH*) three decimal places; **eine freie** *od* **offene ~** a vacancy; **an dieser ~ in** this place, here; **an anderer ~** elsewhere; **nicht von der ~ kommen** not to make any progress; **auf der ~** (*fig: sofort*) on the spot.

stellen *vt* to put; (*Uhr etc*) to set; (*zur Verfügung ~*) to supply; (*fassen: Dieb*) to apprehend; (*Antrag, Forderung*) to make; (*Aufnahme*) to pose; (*arrangieren: Szene*) to arrange ♦ *vr* (*sich auf~*) to stand; (*sich einfinden*) to present o.s.; (*bei Polizei*) to give o.s. up; (*vorgeben*) to pretend (to be); **das Radio lauter/leiser ~** to turn the radio up/ down; **auf sich** *akk* **selbst gestellt sein** (*fig*) to have to fend for o.s.; **sich hinter jdn/etw ~** (*fig*) to support sb/sth; **sich einer Herausforderung ~** to take up a challenge; **sich zu etw ~** to have an opinion of sth.

Stellen- *zW*: **~angebot** *nt* offer of a post; (*in Zeitung*): „**~angebote**" "vacancies"; **~anzeige** *f* job advertisement *od* ad (*umg*); **~gesuch** *nt* application for a post; „**~gesuche**" "situations wanted"; **~markt** *m* job market; (*in Zeitung*) appointments section; **~nachweis** *m* employment agency; **~vermittlung** *f* employment agency; **s~weise** *adv* in places; **~wert** *m* (*fig*) status.

Stellung *f* position; (*MIL*) line; **~ nehmen zu** to comment on.

Stellungnahme *f* comment.

stellungslos *adj* unemployed.

stellv. *abk* = **stellvertretend**.

Stell- *zW*: **s~vertretend** *adj* deputy *attrib*, acting *attrib*; **~vertreter** *m* (*von Amts wegen*) deputy, representative; **~werk** *nt* (*EISENB*) signal box.

Stelze ['ʃtɛltsə] (-, -n) *f* stilt.

stelzen (*umg*) *vi* to stalk.

Stemmbogen *m* (*SKI*) stem turn.

Stemmeisen *nt* crowbar.

stemmen ['ʃtɛmən] *vt* to lift (up); (*drücken*) to press; **sich ~ gegen** (*fig*) to resist, oppose.

Stempel ['ʃtɛmpəl] (-s, -) *m* stamp; (*Post~*) postmark; (*TECH: Präge~*) die; (*BOT*) pistil; **~gebühr** *f* stamp duty; **~kissen** *nt* inkpad.

stempeln *vt* to stamp; (*Briefmarke*) to cancel ♦ *vi* (*umg: Stempeluhr betätigen*) to clock in/ out; **~ gehen** (*umg*) to be *od* go on the dole (*BRIT*) *od* on welfare (*US*).

Stengel ['ʃtɛŋəl] (-s, -) *m* stalk; **vom ~ fallen** (*umg: überrascht sein*) to be staggered.

Steno ['ʃteno] (*umg*) *f* shorthand; **~gramm** [-'gram] *nt* text in shorthand; **~graph(in)** [-graːf(ɪn)] *m(f)* (*im Büro*) shorthand secretary; **~graphie** [-graˈfiː] *f* shorthand; **s~graphieren** [-graˈfiːrən] *vt, vi* to write (in) shorthand; **~typist(in)** [-tyˈpɪst(ɪn)] *m(f)*

shorthand typist (*BRIT*), stenographer (*US*).
Steppdecke *f* quilt.
Steppe (-, -n) *f* steppe.
steppen ['ʃtɛpən] *vt* to stitch ♦ *vi* to tap-dance.
Steptanz *m* tap-dance.
Sterbe- *zW:* **~bett** *nt* deathbed; **~fall** *m* death;
~hilfe *f* euthanasia; **~kasse** *f* death benefit
fund.
sterben ['ʃtɛrbən] *unreg vi* to die; **an einer**
Krankheit/Verletzung **~** to die of an illness/
from an injury; **er ist für mich gestorben**
(*fig: umg*) he might as well be dead.
Sterben *nt:* **im** **~** **liegen** to be dying.
sterbenslangweilig (*umg*) *adj* deadly boring.
Sterbenswörtchen (*umg*) *nt:* **er hat kein**
~ **gesagt** he didn't say a word.
Sterbeurkunde *f* death certificate.
sterblich ['ʃtɛrplɪç] *adj* mortal; **S~keit** *f*
mortality; **S~keitsziffer** *f* death rate.
stereo- ['ʃteːreo] *in zW* stereo(-); **S~anlage** *f*
stereo unit; **~typ** *adj* stereotyped.
steril [ʃteˈriːl] *adj* sterile.
sterilisieren [ʃterili'ziːrən] *vt* to sterilize.
Sterilisierung *f* sterilization.
Stern [ʃtɛrn] (-(e)s, -e) *m* star; **das steht (noch)**
in den **~en** (*fig*) it's in the lap of the gods;
~bild *nt* constellation; **~chen** *nt* asterisk;
~enbanner *nt* Stars and Stripes *sing*;
s~hagelvoll (*umg*) *adj* legless; **~schnuppe**
(-, -n) *f* meteor, falling star; **~stunde** *f*
historic moment; **~warte** *f* observatory;
~zeichen *nt* (*ASTROL*) sign of the zodiac.
stet [ʃteːt] *adj* steady.
Stethoskop [ʃteto'skoːp] (-(e)s, -e) *nt*
stethoscope.
stetig *adj* constant, continual; (*MATH:*
Funktion) continuous.
stets *adv* continually, always.
Steuer[1] ['ʃtɔʏər] (-s, -) *nt* (*NAUT*) helm;
(**~ruder**) rudder; (*AUT*) steering wheel; **am**
~ **sitzen** (*AUT*) to be at the wheel; (*AVIAT*) to
be at the controls.
Steuer[2] (-, -n) *f* tax.
Steuer- *zW:* **~befreiung** *f* tax exemption;
s~begünstigt *adj* (*Investitionen, Hypothek*)
tax-deductible; (*Waren*) taxed at a lower
rate; **~berater(in)** *m(f)* tax consultant;
~bescheid *m* tax assessment; **~bord** *nt*
starboard; **~erhöhung** *f* tax increase;
~erklärung *f* tax return; **s~frei** *adj* tax-free;
~freibetrag *m* tax allowance;
~hinterziehung *f* tax evasion; **~jahr** *nt*
fiscal *od* tax year; **~karte** *f* tax notice;
~klasse *f* tax group; **~knüppel** *m*
control column; (*AVIAT, COMPUT*)
joystick; **s~lich** *adj* tax *attrib*; **~mann**
(-(e)s, *pl* **-männer** *od* **-leute**) *m* helmsman.
steuern *vt* to steer; (*Flugzeug*) to pilot;
(*Entwicklung, Tonstärke*) to control ♦ *vi* to
steer; (*in Flugzeug etc*) to be at the controls;
(*bei Entwicklung etc*) to be in control.
Steuer- *zW:* **~nummer** *f* ≈ National

Insurance Number (*BRIT*), Social Security
Number (*US*); **~paradies** *nt* tax haven;
s~pflichtig *adj* taxable; (*Person*) liable to pay
tax; **~progression** *f* progressive taxation;
~prüfung *f* tax inspector's investigation;
~rad *nt* steering wheel; **~rückvergütung** *f*
tax rebate; **~senkung** *f* tax cut.
Steuerung *f* steering (*auch AUT*); piloting;
control; (*Vorrichtung*) controls *pl*;
automatische **~** (*AVIAT*) autopilot; (*TECH*)
automatic steering (device).
Steuer- *zW:* **~vergünstigung** *f* tax relief;
~zahler *m* taxpayer; **~zuschlag** *m* additional
tax.
Steward ['stjuːərt] (-s, -s) *m* steward.
Stewardeß ['stjuːərdɛs] (-, -essen) *f*
stewardess.
StGB (-s) *nt abk* = **Strafgesetzbuch.**
stibitzen [ʃti'bɪtsən] (*umg*) *vt* to pilfer, pinch
(*umg*).
Stich [ʃtɪç] (-(e)s, -e) *m* (*Insekten~*) sting;
(*Messer~*) stab; (*beim Nähen*) stitch;
(*Färbung*) tinge; (*KARTEN*) trick; (*ART*)
engraving; (*fig*) pang; **ein** **~** **ins Rote** a tinge
of red; **einen** **~** **haben** (*umg: Eßwaren*) to be
bad *od* off (*BRIT*); (: *Mensch: verrückt sein*) to
be nuts; **jdn im** **~** **lassen** to leave sb in the
lurch.
Stichel (-s, -) *m* engraving tool, style.
Stichelei [ʃtɪçə'laɪ] *f* jibe, taunt.
sticheln *vi* (*fig*) to jibe; (*pej: umg*) to make
snide remarks.
Stich- *zW:* **~flamme** *f* tongue of flame;
s~haltig *adj* valid; (*Beweis*) conclusive;
~probe *f* spot check.
sticht [ʃtɪçt] *vb siehe* **stechen.**
Stichtag *m* qualifying date.
Stichwahl *f* final ballot.
Stichwort *nt* (*pl* **-worte**) cue; (: *für Vortrag*)
note; (*pl* **-wörter**: *in Wörterbuch*) headword;
~katalog *m* classified catalogue (*BRIT*) *od*
catalog (*US*); **~verzeichnis** *nt* index.
Stichwunde *f* stab wound.
sticken ['ʃtɪkən] *vt, vi* to embroider.
Stickerei [ʃtɪkə'raɪ] *f* embroidery.
stickig *adj* stuffy, close.
Stickstoff (-(e)s) *m* nitrogen.
stieben ['ʃtiːbən] *vi* (*geh: sprühen*) to fly.
Stief- ['ʃtiːf] *in zW* step-.
Stiefel ['ʃtiːfəl] (-s, -) *m* boot; (*Trinkgefäß*)
large boot-shaped beer glass.
Stief- *zW:* **~kind** *nt* stepchild; (*fig*) Cinderella;
~mutter *f* stepmother; **~mütterchen** *nt*
pansy; **s~mütterlich** *adj* (*fig*): **jdn/etw**
s~mütterlich behandeln to pay little
attention to sb/sth; **~vater** *m* stepfather.
stieg *etc* [ʃtiːk] *vb siehe* **steigen.**
Stiege ['ʃtiːgə] (-, -n) *f* staircase.
Stieglitz ['ʃtiːglɪts] (-es, -e) *m* goldfinch.
stiehlt [ʃtiːlt] *vb siehe* **stehlen.**
Stiel [ʃtiːl] (-(e)s, -e) *m* handle; (*BOT*) stalk.
Stielaugen *pl* (*fig: umg*): **er machte** **~** his eyes

(nearly) popped out of his head.
Stier (-(e)s, -e) *m* bull; (*ASTROL*) Taurus.
stier [ʃtiːr] *adj* staring, fixed.
stieren *vi* to stare.
Stierkampf *m* bullfight.
stieß *etc* [ʃtiːs] *vb siehe* **stoßen.**
Stift [ʃtɪft] (-(e)s, -e) *m* peg; (*Nagel*) tack;
(*Bunt~*) crayon; (*Blei~*) pencil; (*umg:
Lehrling*) apprentice (boy).
stiften *vt* to found; (*Unruhe*) to cause;
(*spenden*) to contribute; **~gehen** *unreg* (*umg*)
vi to hop it.
Stifter(in) (-s, -) *m(f)* founder.
Stiftung *f* donation; (*Organisation*)
foundation.
Stiftzahn *m* post crown.
Stil [ʃtiːl] (-(e)s, -e) *m* style; (*Eigenart*) way,
manner; **~blüte** *f* howler; **~bruch** *m* stylistic
incongruity.
stilistisch [ʃtiˈlɪstɪʃ] *adj* stylistic.
still [ʃtɪl] *adj* quiet; (*unbewegt*) still; (*heimlich*)
secret; **ich dachte mir im ~en** I thought to
myself; **er ist ein ~es Wasser** he's a deep
one; **~er Teilhaber** (*COMM*) sleeping (*BRIT*)
od silent (*US*) partner; **der S~e Ozean** the
Pacific (Ocean).
Stille (-, -n) *f* quietness; stillness; **in aller ~**
quietly.
Stilleben *nt siehe* **Still(l)eben.**
Stillegung *f siehe* **Still(l)egung.**
stillen *vt* to stop; (*befriedigen*) to satisfy;
(*Säugling*) to breast-feed.
still- *zW:* **~gestanden** *interj* attention!;
S~halteabkommen *nt* (*FIN, fig*) moratorium;
~halten *unreg vi* to keep still; **S~(l)eben** *nt*
still life; **~(l)egen** *vt* to close down;
S~(l)egung *f* (*Betrieb*) shut-down, closure;
~(l)iegen *unreg vi* (*außer Betrieb sein*) to be
shut down; (*lahmliegen*) to be at a standstill;
S~schweigen *nt* silence; **~schweigen** *unreg*
vi to be silent; **~schweigend** *adj* silent;
(*Einverständnis*) tacit ♦ *adv* silently; tacitly;
S~stand *m* standstill; **~stehen** *unreg vi* to
stand still.
Stilmöbel *pl* reproduction *od* (*antik*) period
furniture *sing.*
stilvoll *adj* stylish.
Stimm- *zW:* **~abgabe** *f* voting; **~bänder** *pl*
vocal cords *pl*; **s~berechtigt** *adj* entitled to
vote; **~bruch** *m:* **er ist im ~bruch** his voice is
breaking.
Stimme [ˈʃtɪmə] (-, -n) *f* voice; (*Wahl~*) vote;
(*MUS: Rolle*) part; **mit leiser/lauter ~** in a
soft/loud voice; **seine ~ abgeben** to vote.
stimmen *vi* (*richtig sein*) to be right; (*wählen*)
to vote ♦ *vt* (*Instrument*) to tune; **stimmt so!**
that's all right; **für/gegen etw ~** to vote
for/against sth; **jdn traurig ~** to make sb
feel sad.
Stimmen- *zW:* **~gewirr** *nt* babble of voices;
~gleichheit *f* tied vote; **~mehrheit** *f*
majority (of votes).

Stimm- *zW:* **~enthaltung** *f* abstention;
~gabel *f* tuning fork; **s~haft** *adj* voiced.
stimmig *adj* harmonious.
Stimm- *zW:* **s~los** *adj* (*LING*) unvoiced;
~recht *nt* right to vote; **s~rechtslos** *adj:*
s~rechtslose Aktien "A" shares.
Stimmung *f* mood; (*Atmosphäre*)
atmosphere; (*Moral*) morale; **in ~ kommen**
to liven up; **~ gegen/für jdn/etw machen** to
stir up (public) opinion against/in favour of
sb/sth.
Stimmungs- *zW:* **~kanone** (*umg*) *f* life and
soul of the party; **~mache** (*pej*) *f* cheap
propaganda; **s~voll** *adj* (*Atmosphäre*)
enjoyable; (*Gedicht*) full of atmosphere.
Stimmzettel *m* ballot paper.
stinken [ˈʃtɪŋkən] *unreg vi* to stink; **die Sache
stinkt mir** (*umg*) I'm fed-up to the back
teeth (with it).
Stink- *zW:* **s~faul** (*umg*) *adj* bone-lazy;
s~langweilig (*umg*) *adj* deadly boring; **~tier**
nt skunk; **~wut** (*umg*) *f:* **eine ~wut (auf jdn)
haben** to be livid (with sb).
Stipendium [ʃtiˈpɛndium] *nt* grant; (*als
Auszeichnung*) scholarship.
Stippvisite [ˈʃtɪpviˈziːtə] (*umg*) *f* flying visit.
stirbt [ʃtɪrpt] *vb siehe* **sterben.**
Stirn [ʃtɪrn] (-, -en) *f* forehead, brow;
(*Frechheit*) impudence; **die ~ haben zu ...** to
have the nerve to ...; **~band** *nt* headband;
~höhle *f* sinus; **~runzeln** (-s) *nt* frown.
stob *etc* [ʃtoːp] *vb siehe* **stieben.**
stöbern [ˈʃtøːbərn] *vi* to rummage.
stochern [ˈʃtɔxərn] *vi* to poke (about).
Stock¹ [ʃtɔk] (-(e)s, ̈-e) *m* stick; (*Rohr~*) cane;
(*Zeige~*) pointer; (*BOT*) stock; **über ~ und
Stein** up hill and down dale.
Stock² [ʃtɔk] (-(e)s, - *od* -werke) *m* storey
(*BRIT*), story (*US*); **im ersten ~** on the first
(*BRIT*) *od* second (*US*) floor.
stock- *in zW* (*vor adj: umg*) completely.
Stöckelschuh [ˈʃtœkəlʃuː] *m* stiletto-heeled
shoe.
stocken *vi* to stop, pause; (*Arbeit, Entwicklung*)
to make no progress; (*im Satz*) to break off;
(*Verkehr*) to be held up.
stockend *adj* halting.
stockfinster (*umg*) *adj* pitch-dark.
Stockholm [ˈʃtɔkhɔlm] (-s) *nt* Stockholm.
stocksauer (*umg*) *adj* pissed-off (*!*).
stocktaub *adj* stone-deaf.
Stockung *f* stoppage.
Stockwerk *nt* storey (*BRIT*), story (*US*), floor.
Stoff [ʃtɔf] (-(e)s, -e) *m* (*Gewebe*) material,
cloth; (*Materie*) matter; (*von Buch etc*)
subject (matter); (*umg: Rauschgift*) dope.
Stoffel (-s, -) (*pej: umg*) *m* lout, boor.
Stoff- *zW:* **s~lich** *adj* with regard to subject
matter; **~rest** *m* remnant; **~tier** *nt* soft toy;
~wechsel *m* metabolism.
stöhnen [ˈʃtøːnən] *vi* to groan.
stoisch [ˈʃtoːɪʃ] *adj* stoical.

Stola ['ʃtoːla] (-, **Stolen**) *f* stole.
Stollen ['ʃtɔlən] (**-s**, **-**) *m* (*MIN*) gallery; (*KOCH*) stollen, *cake eaten at Christmas*; (*von Schuhen*) stud.
stolpern ['ʃtɔlpərn] *vi* to stumble, trip; (*fig: zu Fall kommen*) to come a cropper (*umg*).
stolz [ʃtɔlts] *adj* proud; (*imposant: Bauwerk*) majestic; (*ironisch: Preis*) princely; **S~** (**-es**) *m* pride.
stolzieren [ʃtɔl'tsiːrən] *vi* to strut.
stopfen ['ʃtɔpfən] *vt* (*hinein~*) to stuff; (*voll~*) to fill (up); (*nähen*) to darn ♦ *vi* (*MED*) to cause constipation; **jdm das Maul ~** (*umg*) to silence sb.
Stopfgarn *nt* darning thread.
Stopp [ʃtɔp] (**-s**, **-s**) *m* stop, halt; (*Lohn~*) freeze.
Stoppel ['ʃtɔpəl] (**-**, **-n**) *f* stubble.
stoppen *vt* to stop; (*mit Uhr*) to time ♦ *vi* to stop.
Stoppschild *nt* stop sign.
Stoppuhr *f* stopwatch.
Stöpsel ['ʃtœpsəl] (**-s**, **-**) *m* plug; (*für Flaschen*) stopper.
Stör [ʃtøːr] (**-s**, **-e**) *m* sturgeon.
Störaktion *f* disruptive action.
störanfällig *adj* susceptible to interference *od* breakdown.
Storch [ʃtɔrç] (**-(e)s**, **~e**) *m* stork.
Store [ʃtoːr] (**-s**, **-s**) *m* net curtain.
stören ['ʃtøːrən] *vt* to disturb; (*behindern, RUNDF*) to interfere with ♦ *vr*: **sich an etw** *dat* ~ to let sth bother one ♦ *vi* to get in the way; **was mich an ihm/daran stört** what I don't like about him/it; **stört es Sie, wenn ich rauche?** do you mind if I smoke?; **ich möchte nicht ~** I don't want to be in the way.
störend *adj* disturbing, annoying.
Störenfried (**-(e)s**, **-e**) *m* troublemaker.
Störfall *m* (*in Kraftwerk etc*) malfunction, accident.
stornieren [ʃtɔr'niːrən] *vt* (*COMM: Auftrag*) to cancel; (: *Buchungsfehler*) to reverse.
Storno ['ʃtɔrno] (**-s**) *m od nt* (*COMM: von Buchungsfehler*) reversal; (: *von Auftrag*) cancellation (*BRIT*), cancelation (*US*).
störrisch ['ʃtœrɪʃ] *adj* stubborn, perverse.
Störsender *m* jammer, jamming transmitter.
Störung *f* disturbance; interference; (*TECH*) fault; (*MED*) disorder.
Störungsstelle *f* (*TEL*) faults service.
Stoß [ʃtoːs] (**-es**, **~e**) *m* (*Schub*) push; (*leicht*) poke; (*Schlag*) blow; (*mit Schwert*) thrust; (*mit Ellbogen*) nudge; (*mit Fuß*) kick; (*Erd~*) shock; (*Haufen*) pile; **seinem Herzen einen ~ geben** to pluck up courage; **~dämpfer** *m* shock absorber.
•**Stößel** ['ʃtøːsəl] (**-s**, **-**) *m* pestle; (*AUT: Ventil~*) tappet.
stoßen *unreg vt* (*mit Druck*) to shove, push; (*mit*

Schlag) to knock, bump; (*mit Ellbogen*) to nudge; (*mit Fuß*) to kick; (*mit Schwert*) to thrust; (*an~: Kopf etc*) to bump; (*zerkleinern*) to pulverize ♦ *vr* to get a knock ♦ *vi*: **~ an** *od* **auf** +*akk* to bump into; (*finden*) to come across; (*angrenzen*) to be next to; **sich ~ an** +*dat* (*fig*) to take exception to; **zu jdm ~** to meet up with sb.
Stoßgebet *nt* quick prayer.
Stoßstange *f* (*AUT*) bumper.
stößt [ʃtøːst] *vb siehe* **stoßen**.
Stoß- *zW*: **~verkehr** *m* rush-hour traffic; **~zahn** *m* tusk; **~zeit** *f* (*im Verkehr*) rush hour; (*in Geschäft etc*) peak period.
Stotterer (**-s**, **-**) *m* stutterer.
Stotterin *f* stutterer.
stottern ['ʃtɔtərn] *vt, vi* to stutter.
Stövchen *f* ['ʃtøːfçən] *nt* (teapot- *etc*) warmer.
StPO *abk* = **Strafprozeßordnung**.
Str. *abk* (= *Straße*) St.
stracks [ʃtraks] *adv* straight.
Straf- *zW*: **~anstalt** *f* penal institution; **~arbeit** *f* (*SCH*) lines *pl*, punishment exercise; **~bank** *f* (*SPORT*) penalty bench; **s~bar** *adj* punishable; **sich s~bar machen** to commit an offence (*BRIT*) *od* offense (*US*); **~barkeit** *f* criminal nature.
Strafe ['ʃtraːfə] (**-**, **-n**) *f* punishment; (*JUR*) penalty; (*Gefängnis~*) sentence; (*Geld~*) fine; **... bei ~ verboten ...** forbidden; **100 Dollar ~ zahlen** to pay a $100 fine; **er hat seine ~ weg** (*umg*) he's had his punishment.
strafen *vt, vi* to punish; **mit etw gestraft sein** to be cursed with sth.
strafend *adj attrib* punitive; (*Blick*) reproachful.
straff [ʃtraf] *adj* tight; (*streng*) strict; (*Stil etc*) concise; (*Haltung*) erect.
straffällig ['ʃtraːfɛlɪç] *adj*: **~ werden** to commit a criminal offence (*BRIT*) *od* offense (*US*).
straffen *vt* to tighten.
Straf- *zW*: **s~frei** *adj*: **s~frei ausgehen** to go unpunished; **~gefangene(r)** *f(m)* prisoner, convict; **~gesetzbuch** *nt* penal code; **~kolonie** *f* penal colony.
sträflich ['ʃtrɛːflɪç] *adj* criminal ♦ *adv* (*vernachlässigen etc*) criminally.
Sträfling *m* convict.
Straf- *zW*: **~mandat** *nt* ticket; **~maß** *nt* sentence; **s~mildernd** *adj* mitigating; **~porto** *nt* excess postage (charge); **~predigt** *f* severe lecture; **~prozeßordnung** *f* code of criminal procedure; **~raum** *m* (*SPORT*) penalty area; **~recht** *nt* criminal law; **s~rechtlich** *adj* criminal; **~stoß** *m* (*SPORT*) penalty (kick); **~tat** *f* punishable act; **s~versetzen** *vt untr* (*Beamte*) to transfer for disciplinary reasons; **~vollzug** *m* penal system; **~zettel** (*umg*) *m* ticket.
Strahl [ʃtraːl] (**-(e)s**, **-en**) *m* ray, beam;

(*Wasser~*) jet.
strahlen *vi* (*Kernreaktor*) to radiate; (*Sonne, Licht*) to shine; (*fig*) to beam.
Strahlenbehandlung *f* radiotherapy.
Strahlenbelastung *f* (effects of) radiation.
strahlend *adj* (*Wetter*) glorious; (*Lächeln, Schönheit*) radiant.
Strahlen- *zW:* **~dosis** *f* radiation dose; **s~geschädigt** *adj* suffering from radiation damage; **~opfer** *nt* victim of radiation; **~schutz** *m* radiation protection; **~therapie** *f* radiotherapy.
Strahlung *f* radiation.
Strähnchen ['ʃtrɛːnçən] *pl* strands (of hair); (*gefärbt*) highlights.
Strähne ['ʃtrɛːnə] (-, -n) *f* strand.
strähnig *adj* (*Haar*) straggly.
stramm [ʃtram] *adj* tight; (*Haltung*) erect; (*Mensch*) robust; **~stehen** *unreg vi* (*MIL*) to stand to attention.
Strampelhöschen *nt* rompers *pl*.
strampeln ['ʃtrampəln] *vi* to kick (about), fidget.
Strand [ʃtrant] (-(e)s, ⁻e) *m* shore; (*Meeres~*) beach; **am ~** on the beach; **~bad** *nt* open-air swimming pool; (*Badeort*) bathing resort.
stranden ['ʃtrandən] *vi* to run aground; (*fig: Mensch*) to fail.
Strandgut *nt* flotsam and jetsam.
Strandkorb *m* beach chair.
Strang [ʃtraŋ] (-(e)s, ⁻e) *m* (*Nerven~, Muskel~*) cord; (*Schienen~*) track; **über die Stränge schlagen** to run riot (*umg*); **an einem ~ ziehen** (*fig*) to be in the same boat.
strangulieren [ʃtraŋguˈliːrən] *vt* to strangle.
Strapaze [ʃtraˈpaːtsə] (-, -n) *f* strain.
strapazieren [ʃtrapaˈtsiːrən] *vt* (*Material*) to be hard on, punish; (*jdn*) to be a strain on; (*erschöpfen*) to wear out, exhaust.
strapazierfähig *adj* hard-wearing.
strapaziös [ʃtrapatsiˈøːs] *adj* exhausting, tough.
Straßburg ['ʃtraːsburk] (-s) *nt* Strasbourg.
Straße ['ʃtraːsə] (-, -n) *f* road; (*in Stadt, Dorf*) street; **auf der ~** in the street; **auf der ~ liegen** (*fig: umg*) to be out of work; **auf die ~ gesetzt werden** (*umg*) to be turned out (onto the streets).
Straßen- *zW:* **~bahn** *f* tram (*BRIT*), streetcar (*US*); **~bauarbeiten** *pl* roadworks *pl* (*BRIT*), roadwork *sing* (*US*); **~beleuchtung** *f* street lighting; **~feger** (-s, -) *m* roadsweeper; **~glätte** *f* slippery road surface; **~junge** (*pej*) *m* street urchin; **~karte** *f* road map; **~kehrer** (-s, -) *m* roadsweeper; **~kind** *nt* child of the streets; **~kreuzer** (*umg*) *m* limousine; **~mädchen** *nt* streetwalker; **~rand** *m* road side; **~sperre** *f* roadblock; **~überführung** *f* footbridge; **~verkehr** *m* road traffic; **~verkehrsordnung** *f* Highway Code (*BRIT*); **~zustandsbericht** *m* road report.

Stratege [ʃtraˈteːgə] (-n, -n) *m* strategist.
Strategie [ʃtrateˈgiː] *f* strategy.
strategisch *adj* strategic.
Stratosphäre [ʃtratoˈsfɛːrə] (-) *f* stratosphere.
sträuben ['ʃtrɔybən] *vt* to ruffle ♦ *vr* to bristle; (*Mensch*): **sich (gegen etw) ~** to resist (sth).
Strauch [ʃtraux] (-(e)s, Sträucher) *m* bush, shrub.
straucheln ['ʃtrauxəln] *vi* to stumble, stagger.
Strauß¹ [ʃtraus] (-es, Sträuße) *m* (*Blumen~*) bouquet, bunch.
Strauß² [ʃtraus] (-es, -e) *m* ostrich.
Strebe ['ʃtreːbə] (-, -n) *f* strut.
Strebebalken *m* buttress.
streben *vi* to strive, endeavour (*BRIT*), endeavor (*US*); **~ nach** to strive for; **~ zu** *od* **nach** (*sich bewegen*) to make for.
Strebepfeiler *m* buttress.
Streber (-s, -) *m* (*pej*) pushy person; (*SCH*) swot (*BRIT*).
strebsam *adj* industrious; **S~keit** *f* industry.
Strecke ['ʃtrɛkə] (-, -n) *f* stretch; (*Entfernung*) distance; (*EISENB, MATH*) line; **auf der ~ Paris-Brüssel** on the way from Paris to Brussels; **auf der ~ bleiben** (*fig*) to fall by the wayside; **zur ~ bringen** (*Jagd*) to bag.
strecken *vt* to stretch; (*Waffen*) to lay down; (*KOCH*) to eke out ♦ *vr* to stretch (o.s.).
streckenweise *adv* in parts.
Streich [ʃtraiç] (-(e)s, -e) *m* trick, prank; (*Hieb*) blow; **jdm einen ~ spielen** (*Person*) to play a trick on sb.
streicheln *vt* to stroke.
streichen *unreg vt* (*berühren*) to stroke; (*auftragen*) to spread; (*anmalen*) to paint; (*durch~*) to delete; (*nicht genehmigen*) to cancel; (*Schulden*) to write off; (*Zuschuß etc*) to cut ♦ *vi* (*berühren*) to brush past; (*schleichen*) to prowl; **etw glatt ~** to smooth sth (out).
Streicher *pl* (*MUS*) strings *pl*.
Streich- *zW:* **~holz** *nt* match; **~holzschachtel** *f* matchbox; **~instrument** *nt* string(ed) instrument; **~käse** *m* cheese spread.
Streifband *nt* wrapper; **~zeitung** *f* newspaper sent at printed paper rate.
Streife (-, -n) *f* patrol.
streifen ['ʃtraifən] *vt* (*leicht berühren*) to brush against, graze; (*Blick*) to skim over; (*Thema, Problem*) to touch on; (*ab~*) to take off ♦ *vi* (*gehen*) to roam.
Streifen (-s, -) *m* (*Linie*) stripe; (*Stück*) strip; (*Film*) film.
Streifendienst *m* patrol duty.
Streifenwagen *m* patrol car.
Streifschuß *m* graze, grazing shot.
Streifzug *m* scouting trip; (*Bummel*) expedition; (*fig: kurzer Überblick*): **~ (durch)** brief survey (of).
Streik [ʃtraik] (-(e)s, -s) *m* strike; **in den ~ treten** to come out on strike, strike;

~**brecher** *m* blackleg (*BRIT*), strikebreaker;
s~en *vi* to strike; **der Computer s~t** the
computer's packed up (*umg*), the
computer's on the blink (*umg*); **da s~e ich**
(*umg*) I refuse!; ~**kasse** *f* strike fund;
~**maßnahmen** *pl* industrial action *sing*;
~**posten** *m* (peaceful) picket.

Streit [ʃtraıt] (-(e)s, -e) *m* argument;
(*Auseinandersetzung*) dispute.

streiten *unreg vi, vr* to argue; to dispute;
darüber läßt sich ~ that's debatable.

Streitfrage *f* point at issue.

Streitgespräch *nt* debate.

streitig *adj*: **jdm etw ~ machen** to dispute sb's
right to sth; **S~keiten** *pl* quarrel *sing*, dispute
sing.

Streit- *zW*: ~**kräfte** *pl* (*MIL*) armed forces *pl*;
s~lustig *adj* quarrelsome; ~**punkt** *m*
contentious issue; ~**sucht** *f*
quarrelsomeness.

streng [ʃtrɛŋ] *adj* severe; (*Lehrer, Maßnahme*)
strict; (*Geruch etc*) sharp; ~ **geheim** top-
secret; ~ **verboten!** strictly prohibited.

Strenge (-) *f* severity; strictness; sharpness.

strenggenommen *adv* strictly speaking.

strenggläubig *adj* strict.

strengstens *adv* strictly.

Streß [ʃtrɛs] (-sses, -sse) *m* stress.

stressen *vt* to put under stress.

streßfrei *adj* without stress.

stressig *adj* stressful.

Streu [ʃtrɔʏ] (-, -en) *f* litter, bed of straw.

streuen *vt* to strew, scatter, spread ♦ *vi* (*mit
Streupulver*) to grit; (*mit Salz*) to put down
salt.

Streuer (-s, -) *m* shaker; (*Salz~*) cellar;
(*Pfeffer~*) pot.

Streufahrzeug *nt* gritter (*BRIT*), sander.

streunen *vi* to roam about; (*Hund, Katze*) to
stray.

Streupulver (-s) *nt* grit *od* sand for road.

Streuselkuchen [ʃtrɔʏzəlkuːxən] *m cake with
crumble topping.*

Streuung *f* dispersion; (*Statistik*) mean
variation; (*PHYS*) scattering.

Strich (-(e)s, -e) *m* (*Linie*) line; (*Feder~,
Pinsel~*) stroke; (*von Geweben*) nap; (*von
Fell*) pile; (*Quer~*) dash; (*Schräg~*) oblique,
slash (*bes US*); **einen ~ machen durch** (*lit*) to
cross out; (*fig*) to foil; **jdm einen ~ durch die
Rechnung machen** to thwart *od* foil sb's
plans; **einen ~ unter etw** *akk* **machen** (*fig*) to
forget sth; **nach ~ und Faden** (*umg*) good
and proper; **auf den ~ gehen** (*umg*) to walk
the streets; **jdm gegen den ~ gehen** to rub
sb up the wrong way.

strich *etc* [ʃtrıç] *vb siehe* **streichen**.

Strichcode *m* = **Strichkode**.

Stricheinteilung *f* calibration.

stricheln [ʃtrıçəln] *vt*: **eine gestrichelte Linie** a
broken line.

Strich- *zW*: ~**junge** (*umg*) *m* male prostitute;

~**kode** *m* bar code (*BRIT*), universal product
code (*US*); ~**mädchen** *nt* streetwalker;
~**punkt** *m* semicolon; **s~weise** *adv* here and
there; **s~weise Regen** (*MET*) rain in places.

Strick [ʃtrık] (-(e)s, -e) *m* rope; **jdm aus etw
einen ~ drehen** to use sth against sb.

stricken *vt, vi* to knit.

Strick- *zW*: ~**jacke** *f* cardigan; ~**leiter** *f* rope
ladder; ~**nadel** *f* knitting needle; ~**waren**
pl knitwear *sing*.

striegeln [ʃtriːɡəln] (*umg*) *vr* to spruce o.s.
up.

Strieme [ʃtriːmə] (-, -n) *f* weal.

strikt [strıkt] *adj* strict.

Strippe [ʃtrıpə] (-, -n) *f* (*TEL: umg*): **jdn an der
~ haben** to have sb on the line.

Stripper(in) (-s, -) *m(f)* stripper.

stritt *etc* [ʃtrıt] *vb siehe* **streiten**.

strittig [ʃtrıtıç] *adj* disputed, in dispute.

Stroh [ʃtroː] (-(e)s) *nt* straw; ~**blume** *f*
everlasting flower; ~**dach** *nt* thatched roof;
s~dumm (*umg*) *adj* thick; ~**feuer** *nt*: **ein
~feuer sein** (*fig*) to be a passing fancy;
~**halm** *m* (drinking) straw; ~**mann**
(-(e)s, *pl* -**männer**) *m* (*COMM*) dummy;
~**witwe** *f* grass widow; ~**witwer** *m* grass
widower.

Strolch [ʃtrɔlç] (-(e)s, -e) (*pej*) *m* rogue, rascal.

Strom [ʃtroːm] (-(e)s, -e) *m* river; (*fig*)
stream; (*ELEK*) current; **unter ~ stehen**
(*ELEK*) to be live; (*fig*) to be excited; **der
Wein floß in Strömen** the wine flowed like
water; **in Strömen regnen** to be pouring
with rain; **s~abwärts** *adv* downstream;
~**anschluß** *m*: ~**anschluß haben** to be
connected to the electricity mains;
s~aufwärts *adv* upstream; ~**ausfall** *m* power
failure.

strömen [ʃtrøːmən] *vi* to stream, pour.

Strom- *zW*: ~**kabel** *nt* electric cable; ~**kreis** *m*
(electrical) circuit; **s~linienförmig** *adj*
streamlined; ~**netz** *nt* power supply
system; ~**rechnung** *f* electricity bill;
~**schnelle** *f* rapids *pl*; ~**sperre** *f* power cut;
~**stärke** *f* amperage.

Strömung [ʃtrøːmʊŋ] *f* current.

Stromzähler *m* electricity meter.

Strophe [ʃtroːfə] (-, -n) *f* verse.

strotzen [ʃtrɔtsən] *vi*: ~ **vor** +*dat od* **von** to
abound in, be full of.

Strudel [ʃtruːdəl] (-s, -) *m* whirlpool, vortex;
(*KOCH*) strudel.

strudeln *vi* to swirl, eddy.

Struktur [ʃtrʊktuːr] *f* structure.

strukturell [ʃtrʊkturɛl] *adj* structural.

strukturieren [ʃtrʊkturiːrən] *vt* to structure.

Strumpf [ʃtrʊmpf] (-(e)s, -e) *m* stocking;
~**band** *nt* garter; ~**halter** *m* suspender
(*BRIT*), garter (*US*); ~**hose** *f* (pair of) tights
pl (*BRIT*) *od* pantihose *pl* (*US*).

Strunk [ʃtrʊŋk] (-(e)s, -e) *m* stump.

struppig [ʃtrʊpıç] *adj* shaggy, unkempt.

Stube ['ʃtuːbə] (-, -n) f room; **die gute ~** (*veraltet*) the parlour (*BRIT*) od parlor (*US*).

Stuben- zW: **~arrest** m confinement to one's room; (*MIL*) confinement to quarters; **~fliege** f (common) housefly; **~hocker** (*umg*) m stay-at-home; **s~rein** adj housetrained.

Stuck [ʃtʊk] (-(e)s) m stucco.

Stück [ʃtʏk] (-(e)s, -e) nt piece; (*etwas*) bit; (*THEAT*) play; **am ~** in one piece; **das ist ein starkes ~!** (*umg*) that's a bit much!; **große ~ auf jdn halten** to think highly of sb; **~arbeit** f piecework; **~gut** nt (*EISENB*) parcel service; **~kosten** pl unit cost sing; **~lohn** m piecework rates pl; **s~weise** adv bit by bit, piecemeal; (*COMM*) individually; **~werk** nt bits and pieces pl.

Student(in) [ʃtuˈdɛnt(ɪn)] m(f) student.

Studenten- zW: **~ausweis** m student card; **~futter** nt nuts and raisins pl; **~werk** nt student administration; **~wohnheim** nt hall of residence (*BRIT*), dormitory (*US*).

studentisch adj student attrib.

Studie ['ʃtuːdiə] f study.

Studien- zW: **~beratung** f course guidance service; **~buch** nt (*UNIV*) book in which the courses one has attended are entered; **~fahrt** f study trip; **~platz** m university place; **~rat** m, **~rätin** f teacher at a secondary (*BRIT*) od high (*US*) school.

studieren [ʃtuˈdiːrən] vt, vi to study; **bei jdm ~** to study under sb.

Studio ['ʃtuːdio] (-s, -s) nt studio.

Studium ['ʃtuːdiʊm] nt studies pl.

Stufe ['ʃtuːfə] (-, -n) f step; (*Entwicklungs~*) stage; (*Niveau*) level.

Stufen- zW: **~heck** nt (*AUT*) notchback; **~leiter** f (fig) ladder; **s~los** adj (*TECH*) infinitely variable; **s~los verstellbar** continuously adjustable; **~plan** m graduated plan; **~schnitt** m (*Frisur*) layered cut; **s~weise** adv gradually.

Stuhl [ʃtuːl] (-(e)s, ⸚e) m chair; **zwischen zwei Stühlen sitzen** (fig) to fall between two stools.

Stuhlgang m bowel movement.

Stukkateur [ʃtʊkaˈtøːr] m (ornamental) plasterer.

stülpen ['ʃtʏlpən] vt (*bedecken*) to put; **etw über etw** akk **~** to put sth over sth; **den Kragen nach oben ~** to turn up one's collar.

stumm [ʃtʊm] adj silent; (*MED*) dumb.

Stummel (-s, -) m stump; (*Zigaretten~*) stub.

Stummfilm m silent film (*BRIT*) od movie (*US*).

Stümper(in) ['ʃtʏmpər(ɪn)] (-s, -) m(f) incompetent, duffer; **s~haft** adj bungling, incompetent.

stümpern (*umg*) vi to bungle.

Stumpf [ʃtʊmpf] (-(e)s, ⸚e) m stump; **etw mit ~ und Stiel ausrotten** to eradicate sth root and branch.

stumpf adj blunt; (*teilnahmslos, glanzlos*) dull; (*Winkel*) obtuse.

Stumpfsinn (-(e)s) m tediousness.

stumpfsinnig adj dull.

Stunde ['ʃtʊndə] (-, -n) f hour; (*Augenblick, Zeitpunkt*) time; (*SCH*) lesson, period (*BRIT*); **~ um ~** hour after hour; **80 Kilometer in der ~ ≈** 50 miles per hour.

stunden vt: **jdm etw ~** to give sb time to pay sth.

Stunden- zW: **~geschwindigkeit** f average speed (per hour); **~kilometer** pl kilometres (*BRIT*) od kilometers (*US*) per hour; **s~lang** adj for hours; **~lohn** m hourly wage; **~plan** m timetable; **s~weise** adv by the hour; (*stündlich*) every hour.

stündlich ['ʃtʏntlɪç] adj hourly.

Stunk [ʃtʊŋk] (-s, no pl) m: **~ machen** (*umg*) to kick up a stink.

stupide [ʃtuˈpiːdə] adj mindless.

Stups [ʃtʊps] (-es, -e) (*umg*) m push.

stupsen vt to nudge.

Stupsnase f snub nose.

stur [ʃtuːr] adj obstinate, stubborn; (*Nein, Arbeiten*) dogged; **er fuhr ~ geradeaus** he just carried straight on; **sich ~ stellen, auf ~ stellen** (*umg*) to dig one's heels in; **ein ~er Bock** (*umg*) a pig-headed fellow.

Sturm [ʃtʊrm] (-(e)s, ⸚e) m storm; (*Wind*) gale; (*MIL etc*) attack, assault; **~ läuten** to keep one's finger on the doorbell; **gegen etw ~ laufen** (fig) to be up in arms against sth.

stürmen ['ʃtʏrmən] vi (*Wind*) to blow hard, to rage; (*rennen*) to storm ♦ vt (*MIL, fig*) to storm ♦ vi unpers: **es stürmt** there's a gale blowing.

Stürmer (-s, -) m (*SPORT*) forward.

sturmfrei adj (*MIL*) unassailable; **eine ~e Bude** (*umg*) a room free from disturbance.

stürmisch adj stormy; (fig) tempestuous; (*Entwicklung*) rapid; (*Liebhaber*) passionate; (*Beifall*) tumultuous; **nicht so ~** take it easy.

Sturm- zW: **~schritt** m (*MIL, fig*): **im ~schritt** at the double; **~warnung** f gale warning; **~wind** m gale.

Sturz [ʃtʊrts] (-es, ⸚e) m fall; (*POL*) overthrow; (*in Temperatur, Preis*) drop.

stürzen ['ʃtʏrtsən] vt (*werfen*) to hurl; (*POL*) to overthrow; (*umkehren*) to overturn ♦ vr to rush; (*hinein~*) to plunge ♦ vi to fall; (*AVIAT*) to dive; (*rennen*) to dash; **jdn ins Unglück ~** to bring disaster upon sb; **„nicht ~"** "this side up"; **sich auf jdn/etw ~** to pounce on sb/sth; **sich in Unkosten ~** to go to great expense.

Sturzflug m nose dive.

Sturzhelm m crash helmet.

Stuß [ʃtʊs] (**Stusses**) (*umg*) m nonsense, rubbish.

Stute ['ʃtuːtə] (-, -n) f mare.

Stuttgart ['ʃtʊtgart] (-s) nt Stuttgart.

Stützbalken m brace, joist.

Stütze ['ʃtʏtsə] (-, -n) _f_ support; (_Hilfe_) help; **die ~n der Gesellschaft** the pillars of society.

stutzen ['ʃtʊtsən] _vt_ to trim; (_Ohr, Schwanz_) to dock; (_Flügel_) to clip ♦ _vi_ to hesitate; (_argwöhnisch werden_) to become suspicious.

stützen _vt_ (_lit, fig_) to support; (_Ellbogen etc_) to prop up ♦ _vr:_ **sich auf jdn/etw ~** (_lit_) to lean on sb/sth; (_Beweise, Theorie_) to be based on sb/sth.

stutzig _adj_ perplexed, puzzled; (_mißtrauisch_) suspicious.

Stützmauer _f_ supporting wall.

Stützpunkt _m_ point of support; (_von Hebel_) fulcrum; (_MIL, fig_) base.

Stützungskäufe _pl_ (_FIN_) support buying _sing._

StVO _abk_ = **Straßenverkehrsordnung.**

stylen ['staɪlən] _vt_ to style; (_Wohnung_) to design.

Styling ['staɪlɪŋ] (-s, _no pl_) _nt_ styling.

Styropor® [ʃtyro'poːr] (-s) _nt_ (expanded) polystyrene.

s.u. _abk_ (= _siehe unten_) see below.

Suaheli [zua'heːli] (-(s)) _nt_ Swahili.

Subjekt [zʊp'jɛkt] (-(e)s, -e) _nt_ subject; (_pej: Mensch_) character (_umg_).

subjektiv [zʊpjɛk'tiːf] _adj_ subjective.

Subjektivität [zʊpjɛktivi'tɛːt] _f_ subjectivity.

Subkultur ['zʊpkʊltuːr] _f_ subculture.

sublimieren [zubli'miːrən] _vt_ (_CHEM, PSYCH_) to sublimate.

Submissionsangebot [zʊpmɪsi'oːns-|aŋgəboːt] _nt_ sealed-bid tender.

Subroutine ['zʊprutiːnə] _f_ (_COMPUT_) subroutine.

Subskription [zʊpskrɪptsi'oːn] _f_ subscription.

Substantiv [zʊpstan'tiːf] (-s, -e) _nt_ noun.

Substanz [zʊp'stants] _f_ substance; **von der ~ zehren** to live on one's capital.

subtil [zʊp'tiːl] _adj_ subtle.

subtrahieren [zʊptra'hiːrən] _vt_ to subtract.

subtropisch ['zʊptroːpɪʃ] _adj_ subtropical.

Subunternehmer _m_ subcontractor.

Subvention [zʊpvɛntsi'oːn] _f_ subsidy.

subventionieren [zʊpvɛntsio'niːrən] _vt_ to subsidize.

subversiv [zʊpvɛr'ziːf] _adj_ subversive.

Suchaktion _f_ search.

Suchdienst _m_ missing persons tracing service.

Suche (-, -n) _f_ search.

suchen ['zuːxən] _vt_ to look for, seek; (_versuchen_) to try ♦ _vi_ to seek, search; **du hast hier nichts zu ~** you have no business being here; **nach Worten ~** to search for words; (_sprachlos sein_) to be at a loss for words; **such!** (_zu Hund_) seek!, find!; **~ und ersetzen** (_COMPUT_) search and replace.

Sucher (-s, -) _m_ seeker, searcher; (_PHOT_) viewfinder.

Suchmeldung _f_ missing _od_ wanted person announcement.

Suchscheinwerfer _m_ searchlight.

Sucht [zʊxt] (-, -̈e) _f_ mania; (_MED_) addiction; **~droge** _f_ addictive drug; **s~erzeugend** _adj_ addictive.

süchtig ['zʏçtɪç] _adj_ addicted.

Süchtige(r) _f(m)_ addict.

Süd [zyːt] (-(e)s) _m_ south; **~afrika** _nt_ South Africa; **~amerika** _nt_ South America.

Sudan [zu'daːn] (-s) _m:_ **der ~** the Sudan.

Sudanese [zuda'neːzə] (-n, -n) _m_ Sudanese.

Sudanesin _f_ Sudanese.

südd. _abk_ = **süddeutsch.**

süddeutsch _adj_ South German.

Süddeutschland _nt_ South(ern) Germany.

Süden ['zyːdən] (-s) _m_ south.

Süd- _zW:_ **~europa** _nt_ Southern Europe; **~früchte** _pl_ Mediterranean fruit; **~korea** _nt_ South Korea; **s~ländisch** _adj_ southern; (_italienisch, spanisch etc_) Latin; **s~lich** _adj_ southern; **s~lich von** (to the) south of; **~ostasien** _nt_ South-East Asia; **~pol** _m_ South Pole; **~polarmeer** _nt_ Antarctic Ocean; **~see** _f_ South Seas _pl_, South Pacific; **~tirol** _nt_ South Tyrol; **s~wärts** _adv_ southwards; **~westafrika** _nt_ South West Africa, Namibia.

Sueskanal ['zuːɛskanaːl] (-s) _m_ Suez Canal.

Suff [zʊf] _m:_ **etw im ~ sagen** (_umg_) to say sth while under the influence.

süffig ['zʏfɪç] _adj_ (_Wein_) very drinkable.

süffisant [zʏfi'zant] _adj_ smug.

suggerieren [zʊge'riːrən] _vt_ to suggest.

Suggestivfrage [zʊgɛs'tiːffraːgə] _f_ suggestive question.

suhlen ['zuːlən] _vr_ (_lit, fig_) to wallow.

Sühne ['zyːnə] (-, -n) _f_ atonement, expiation.

sühnen _vt_ to atone for, expiate.

Sühnetermin _m_ (_JUR_) conciliatory hearing.

Suite ['sviːtə] _f_ suite.

Sulfat [zʊl'faːt] (-(e)s, -e) _nt_ sulphate (_BRIT_), sulfate (_US_).

Sultan ['zʊltan] (-s, -e) _m_ sultan.

Sultanine [zʊlta'niːnə] _f_ sultana.

Sülze ['zʏltsə] (-, -n) _f_ brawn (_BRIT_), headcheese (_US_); (_Aspik_) aspic.

summarisch [zu'maːrɪʃ] _adj_ summary.

Sümmchen ['zʏmçən] _nt:_ **ein hübsches ~** a tidy sum.

Summe (-, -n) _f_ sum, total.

summen _vi_ to buzz ♦ _vt_ (_Lied_) to hum.

Summer (-s, -) _m_ buzzer.

summieren [zʊ'miːrən] _vt_ to add up ♦ _vr_ to mount up.

Sumpf [zʊmpf] (-(e)s, -̈e) _m_ swamp, marsh.

sumpfig _adj_ marshy.

Sund [zʊnt] (-(e)s, -e) _m_ sound, straits _pl._

Sünde ['zʏndə] (-, -n) _f_ sin.

Sünden- _zW:_ **~bock** _m_ (_fig_) scapegoat; **~fall** _m_ (_REL_) Fall; **~register** _nt_ (_fig_) list of sins.

Sünder(in) (-s, -) _m(f)_ sinner.

sündhaft _adj_ (_lit_) sinful; (_fig: umg: Preise_) wicked.

sündigen ['zʏndɪgən] _vi_ to sin; (_hum_) to

indulge; ~ **an** +*dat* to sin against.
Super ['zuːpər] (**-s**) *nt* (*Benzin*) four-star
(petrol) (*BRIT*), premium (*US*).
super (*umg*) *adj* super ♦ *adv* incredibly well.
Superlativ ['zuːpərlatiːf] (**-s, -e**) *m* superlative.
Supermarkt *m* supermarket.
Superstar *m* superstar.
Suppe ['zupə] (**-, -n**) *f* soup; (*mit Einlage*)
broth; (*klare Brühe*) bouillon; (*fig: umg: Nebel*)
peasouper (*BRIT*), pea soup (*US*); **jdm die**
~ **versalzen** (*umg*) to put a spoke in sb's
wheel.
Suppen- *zW:* ~**fleisch** *nt* meat for making
soup; ~**grün** *nt herbs and vegetables for
making soup;* ~**kasper** (*umg*) *m* poor eater;
~**teller** *m* soup plate.
Surfbrett ['zøːrfbrɛt] *nt* surfboard.
surfen ['zøːrfən] *vi* to surf.
Surfer(in) *m(f)* surfer.
Surrealismus [zʊreaˈlɪsmʊs] *m* surrealism.
surren ['zʊrən] *vi* to buzz; (*Insekt*) to hum.
Surrogat [zʊroˈgaːt] (**-(e)s, -e**) *nt* substitute,
surrogate.
suspekt [zʊsˈpɛkt] *adj* suspect.
suspendieren [zʊspɛnˈdiːrən] *vt:* ~ **(von)** to
suspend (from).
Suspendierung *f* suspension.
süß [zyːs] *adj* sweet.
Süße (**-**) *f* sweetness.
süßen *vt* to sweeten.
Süßholz *nt:* ~ **raspeln** (*fig*) to turn on the
blarney.
Süßigkeit *f* sweetness; (*Bonbon etc*) sweet
(*BRIT*), candy (*US*).
süß- *zW:* ~**lich** *adj* sweetish; (*fig*) sugary;
~**sauer** *adj* sweet-and-sour; (*fig: gezwungen:
Lächeln*) forced; (*Gurken etc*) pickled; (*Miene*)
artificially friendly; **S**~**speise** *f* pudding,
sweet (*BRIT*); **S**~**stoff** *m* sweetener;
S~**waren** *pl* confectionery *sing;* **S**~**wasser** *nt*
fresh water.
SV (**-**) *m abk* = **Sportverein.**
SW *abk* (= *Südwest(en)*) SW.
Swasiland ['svaːzilant] (**-s**) *nt* Swaziland.
SWF (**-**) *m abk* (= *Südwestfunk*) South West
German Radio.
Sylvester [zylˈvɛstər] (**-s, -**) *nt* = **Silvester.**
Symbol [zymˈboːl] (**-s, -e**) *nt* symbol.
Symbolik *f* symbolism.
symbolisch *adj* symbolic(al).
symbolisieren [zymboliˈziːrən] *vt* to
symbolize.
Symmetrie [zymeˈtriː] *f* symmetry; ~**achse** *f*
symmetric axis.
symmetrisch [zyˈmeːtrɪʃ] *adj* symmetrical.
Sympathie [zympaˈtiː] *f* liking; sympathy; **er
hat sich** *dat* **alle** ~**(n) verscherzt** he has
turned everyone against him;
~**kundgebung** *f* demonstration of support;
~**streik** *m* sympathy strike.
Sympathisant(in) *m(f)* sympathizer.
sympathisch [zymˈpaːtɪʃ] *adj* likeable,

congenial; **er ist mir** ~ I like him.
sympathisieren [zympatiˈziːrən] *vi* to
sympathize.
Symphonie [zymfoˈniː] *f* symphony.
Symptom [zympˈtoːm] (**-s, -e**) *nt* symptom.
symptomatisch [zymptoˈmaːtɪʃ] *adj*
symptomatic.
Synagoge [zynaˈgoːgə] (**-, -n**) *f* synagogue.
synchron [zynˈkroːn] *adj* synchronous;
S~**getriebe** *nt* synchromesh gearbox (*BRIT*)
od transmission (*US*).
synchronisieren [zynkroniˈziːrən] *vt* to
synchronize; (*Film*) to dub.
Synchronschwimmen *nt* synchronized
swimming.
Syndikat [zyndiˈkaːt] (**-(e)s, -e**) *nt* combine,
syndicate.
Syndrom [zynˈdroːm] (**-s, -e**) *nt* syndrome.
Synkope [zynˈkoːpə] (**-, -n**) *f* (*MUS*)
syncopation.
Synode [zyˈnoːdə] (**-, -n**) *f* (*REL*) synod.
Synonym [zynoˈnyːm] (**-s, -e**) *nt* synonym; **s**~
adj synonymous.
Syntax ['zyntaks] (**-, -en**) *f* syntax.
Synthese [zynˈteːzə] (**-, -n**) *f* synthesis.
synthetisch *adj* synthetic.
Syphilis ['zyːfilɪs] (**-**) *f* syphilis.
Syrer(in) ['zyːrər(ɪn)] (**-s, -**) *m(f)* Syrian.
Syrien (**-s**) *nt* Syria.
syrisch *adj* Syrian.
System [zysˈteːm] (**-s, -e**) *nt* system; ~**analyse**
f systems analysis; ~**analytiker(in)** *m(f)*
systems analyst.
Systematik *f* system.
systematisch [zysteˈmaːtɪʃ] *adj* systematic.
systematisieren [zystematiˈziːrən] *vt* to
systematize.
System- *zW:* ~**kritiker** *m* critic of the system;
~**platte** *f* (*COMPUT*) system disk; ~**zwang**
m obligation to conform (to the system).
Szenarium [stseˈnaːriʊm] *nt* scenario.
Szene ['stseːnə] (**-, -n**) *f* scene; **sich in der**
~ **auskennen** (*umg*) to know the scene; **sich
in** ~ **setzen** to play to the gallery.
Szenenwechsel *m* scene change.
Szenerie [stsenəˈriː] *f* scenery.

T, t

T, t¹ [te:] *nt* T, t; ~ **wie Theodor** ≈ T for Tommy.
t² *abk* (= *Tonne*) t.
Tabak ['ta:bak] (**-s, -e**) *m* tobacco; ~**laden** *m* tobacconist's (*BRIT*), tobacco store (*US*).
tabellarisch [tabε'la:rɪʃ] *adj* tabular.
Tabelle (**-, -n**) *f* table.
Tabellenführer *m* (*SPORT*) top of the table, league leader.
Tabernakel [tabεr'na:kəl] (**-s, -**) *nt* tabernacle.
Tabl. *abk* = **Tablette(n)**.
Tablett (**-(e)s, -s** *od* **-e**) *nt* tray.
Tablette [ta'blεtə] (**-, -n**) *f* tablet, pill.
Tabu [ta'bu:] (**-s, -s**) *nt* taboo.
tabuisieren [tabui'zi:rən] *vt* to make taboo.
Tabulator [tabu'la:tɔr] *m* tabulator, tab (*umg*).
tabulieren *vt* to tab.
Tacho ['taxo] (**-s, -s**) (*umg*) *m* speedo (*BRIT*).
Tachometer [taxo'me:tər] (**-s, -**) *m* (*AUT*) speedometer.
Tadel ['ta:dəl] (**-s, -**) *m* censure, scolding; (*Fehler*) fault; (*Makel*) blemish; **t~los** *adj* faultless, irreproachable.
tadeln *vt* to scold.
tadelnswert *adj* blameworthy.
Tadschikistan [ta'dʒi:kista:n] (**-s**) *nt* Tajikistan.
Tafel ['ta:fəl] (**-, -n**) *f* (*form: festlicher Speisetisch, MATH*) table; (*Festmahl*) meal; (*Anschlag~*) board; (*Wand~*) blackboard; (*Schiefer~*) slate; (*Gedenk~*) plaque; (*Illustration*) plate; (*Schalt~*) panel; (*Schokoladen~ etc*) bar; **t~fertig** *adj* ready to serve.
täfeln ['tε:fəln] *vt* to panel.
Tafelöl *nt* cooking oil; salad oil.
Täfelung *f* panelling (*BRIT*), paneling (*US*).
Tafelwasser *nt* table water.
Taft [taft] (**-(e)s, -e**) *m* taffeta.
Tag [ta:k] (**-(e)s, -e**) *m* day; (*Tageslicht*) daylight; **am** ~ during the day; **für** *od* **auf ein paar** ~**e** for a few days; **in den** ~ **hinein leben** to take each day as it comes; **bei** ~**(e)** (*ankommen*) while it's light; (*arbeiten, reisen*) during the day; **unter** ~**e** (*MIN*) underground; **über** ~**e** (*MIN*) on the surface; **an den** ~ **kommen** to come to light; **er legte großes Interesse an den** ~ he showed great interest; **auf den** ~ (**genau**) to the day; **auf seine alten** ~**e** at his age; **guten** ~! good morning/afternoon!; **t~aus** *adv:* **t~aus, t~ein** day in, day out; ~**dienst** *m* day duty.
Tage- *zW:* ~**bau** *m* (*MIN*) open-cast mining; ~**buch** *nt* diary; ~**dieb** *m* idler; ~**geld** *nt* daily allowance; **t~lang** *adv* for days.
tagen *vi* to sit, meet ♦ *vi unpers:* **es tagt** dawn is breaking.
Tages- *zW:* ~**ablauf** *m* daily routine; ~**anbruch** *m* dawn; ~**ausflug** *m* day trip; ~**decke** *f* bedspread; ~**fahrt** *f* day trip; ~**karte** *f* (*Eintrittskarte*) day ticket; (*Speisekarte*) menu of the day; ~**kasse** *f* (*COMM*) day's takings *pl*; (*THEAT*) box office; ~**licht** *nt* daylight; ~**mutter** *f* child minder; ~**ordnung** *f* agenda; **an der** ~**ordnung sein** (*fig*) to be the order of the day; ~**rückfahrkarte** *f* day return (ticket); ~**satz** *m* daily rate; ~**schau** *f* (*TV*) television news (programme (*BRIT*) *od* program (*US*)); ~**stätte** *f* day nursery (*BRIT*), daycare center (*US*); ~**wert** *m* (*FIN*) present value; ~**zeit** *f* time of day; **zu jeder** ~**- und Nachtzeit** at all hours of the day and night; ~**zeitung** *f* daily (paper).
tägl. *abk* = **täglich**.
täglich ['tε:klɪç] *adj, adv* daily; **einmal** ~ once a day.
tags [ta:ks] *adv:* ~ **darauf** *od* **danach** the next *od* following day; ~**über** *adv* during the day.
tagtäglich *adj* daily ♦ *adv* every (single) day.
Tagung *f* conference.
Tagungsort *m* venue (of a conference).
Tahiti [ta'hi:ti] (**-s**) *nt* Tahiti.
Taifun [taɪ'fu:n] (**-s, -e**) *m* typhoon.
Taille ['taljə] (**-, -n**) *f* waist.
tailliert [ta'ji:rt] *adj* waisted, gathered at the waist.
Taiwan ['taɪvan] (**-s**) *nt* Taiwan.
Takel ['ta:kəl] (**-s, -**) *nt* tackle.
takeln ['ta:kəln] *vt* to rig.
Takt [takt] (**-(e)s, -e**) *m* tact; (*MUS*) time; ~**gefühl** *nt* tact.
Taktik *f* tactics *pl*.
Taktiker(in) *m(f)* tactician.
taktisch *adj* tactical.
Takt- *zW:* **t~los** *adj* tactless; ~**losigkeit** *f* tactlessness; ~**stock** *m* (conductor's) baton; ~**strich** *m* (*MUS*) bar (line); **t~voll** *adj* tactful.
Tal [ta:l] (**-(e)s, ⁻er**) *nt* valley.
Talar [ta'la:r] (**-s, -e**) *m* (*JUR*) robe; (*UNIV*) gown.
Talbrücke *f* bridge over a valley.
Talent [ta'lεnt] (**-(e)s, -e**) *nt* talent.
talentiert [talεn'ti:rt] *adj* talented, gifted.
Talfahrt *f* descent; (*fig*) decline.
Talg [talk] (**-(e)s, -e**) *m* tallow.
Talgdrüse *f* sebaceous gland.
Talisman ['ta:lɪsman] (**-s, -e**) *m* talisman.
Tal- *zW:* ~**sohle** *f* bottom of a valley; ~**sperre** *f* dam; **t~wärts** *adv* down to the valley.
Tamburin [tambu'ri:n] (**-s, -e**) *nt* tambourine.
Tamile [ta'mi:lə] (**-n, -n**) *m*, **Tamilin** *f* Tamil.
tamilisch *adj* Tamil.

Tampon ['tampɔn] (-s, -s) *m* tampon.
Tamtam [tam'tam] (-s, -s) *nt* (*MUS*) tomtom; (*umg: Wirbel*) fuss, ballyhoo; (*Lärm*) din.
Tang [taŋ] (-(e)s, -e) *m* seaweed.
Tangente [taŋ'gɛntə] (-, -n) *f* tangent.
Tanger ['taŋər] (-s) *nt* Tangier(s).
tangieren [taŋ'giːrən] *vt* (*Problem*) to touch on; (*fig*) to affect.
Tank [taŋk] (-s, -s) *m* tank.
tanken *vt* (*Wagen etc*) to fill up with petrol (*BRIT*) *od* gas (*US*); (*Benzin etc*) to fill up with; (*AVIAT*) to (re)fuel; (*umg: frische Luft, neue Kräfte*) to get ♦ *vi* to fill up (with petrol *od* gas); to (re)fuel.
Tanker (-s, -) *m* tanker.
Tank- *zW:* ~**laster** *m* tanker; ~**schiff** *nt* tanker; ~**stelle** *f* petrol (*BRIT*) *od* gas (*US*) station; ~**uhr** *f* fuel gauge; ~**verschluß** *m* fuel cap; ~**wart** *m* petrol pump (*BRIT*) *od* gas station (*US*) attendant.
Tanne ['tanə] (-, -n) *f* fir.
Tannenbaum *m* fir tree.
Tannenzapfen *m* fir cone.
Tansania [tan'zaːnia] (-s) *nt* Tanzania.
Tante ['tantə] (-, -n) *f* aunt; ~**-Emma-Laden** (*umg*) *m* corner shop.
Tantieme [tãti'eːmə] (-, -n) *f* fee; (*für Künstler etc*) royalty.
Tanz [tants] (-es, ̈-e) *m* dance.
tänzeln ['tɛntsəln] *vi* to dance along.
tanzen *vt, vi* to dance.
Tänzer(in) (-s, -) *m(f)* dancer.
Tanz- *zW:* ~**fläche** *f* (dance) floor; ~**lokal** *nt* café/restaurant with dancing; ~**schule** *f* dancing school.
Tapet (*umg*) *nt:* **etw aufs** ~ **bringen** to bring sth up.
Tapete [ta'peːtə] (-, -n) *f* wallpaper.
Tapetenwechsel *m* (*fig*) change of scenery.
tapezieren [tape'tsiːrən] *vt* to (wall)paper.
Tapezierer (-s, -) *m* (interior) decorator.
tapfer ['tapfər] *adj* brave; **sich** ~ **schlagen** (*umg*) to put on a brave show; **T~keit** *f* courage, bravery.
tappen ['tapən] *vi* to walk uncertainly *od* clumsily; **im dunkeln** ~ (*fig*) to grope in the dark.
täppisch ['tɛpɪʃ] *adj* clumsy.
Tara ['taːra] (-, **Taren**) *f* tare.
Tarantel [ta'rantəl] (-, -n) *f:* **wie von der** ~ **gestochen** as if stung by a bee.
Tarif [ta'riːf] (-s, -e) *m* tariff, (scale of) fares/charges; **nach/über/unter** ~ **bezahlen** to pay according to/above/below the (union) rate(s); ~**autonomie** *f* free collective bargaining; ~**gruppe** *f* grade; **t~lich** *adj* agreed, union; ~**lohn** *m* standard wage rate; ~**ordnung** *f* wage *od* salary scale; ~**partner** *m:* **die** ~**partner** union and management; ~**vereinbarung** *f* labour (*BRIT*) *od* labor (*US*) agreement; ~**verhandlungen** *pl* collective bargaining *sing*; ~**vertrag** *m* pay agreement.

tarnen ['tarnən] *vt* to camouflage; (*Person, Absicht*) to disguise.
Tarnfarbe *f* camouflage paint.
Tarnmanöver *nt* (*lit, fig*) feint, covering ploy.
Tarnung *f* camouflaging; disguising.
Tarock [ta'rɔk] (-s, s) *m od nt* tarot.
Tasche ['taʃə] (-, -n) *f* pocket; (*Hand~*) handbag; **in die eigene** ~ **wirtschaften** to line one's own pockets; **jdm auf der** ~ **liegen** (*umg*) to live off sb.
Taschen- *zW:* ~**buch** *nt* paperback; ~**dieb** *m* pickpocket; ~**geld** *nt* pocket money; ~**lampe** *f* (electric) torch, flashlight (*US*); ~**messer** *nt* penknife; ~**rechner** *m* pocket calculator; ~**spieler** *m* conjurer; ~**tuch** *nt* handkerchief.
Tasmanien [tas'maːniən] (-s) *nt* Tasmania.
Tasse ['tasə] (-, -n) *f* cup; **er hat nicht alle** ~**n im Schrank** (*umg*) he's not all there.
Tastatur [tasta'tuːr] *f* keyboard.
Taste ['tastə] (-, -n) *f* push-button control; (*an Schreibmaschine*) key.
tasten *vt* to feel, touch; (*drücken*) to press ♦ *vi* to feel, grope ♦ *vr* to feel one's way.
Tastentelefon *nt* push-button telephone.
Tastsinn *m* sense of touch.
Tat (-, -en) *f* act, deed, action; **in der** ~ indeed, as a matter of fact; **etw in die** ~ **umsetzen** to put sth into action.
tat *etc* [taːt] *vb siehe* **tun.**
Tatbestand *m* facts *pl* of the case.
Tatendrang *m* energy.
tatenlos *adj* inactive.
Täter(in) ['tɛːtər(ɪn)] (-s, -) *m(f)* perpetrator, culprit; ~**schaft** *f* guilt.
tätig *adj* active; ~**er Teilhaber** active partner; **in einer Firma** ~ **sein** to work for a firm.
tätigen *vt* (*COMM*) to conclude; (*geh: Einkäufe, Anruf*) to make.
Tätigkeit *f* activity; (*Beruf*) occupation.
Tätigkeitsbereich *m* field of activity.
tatkräftig *adj* energetic; (*Hilfe*) active.
tätlich *adj* violent; **T~keit** *f* violence; **es kam zu T~keiten** there were violent scenes.
Tatort (-(e)s, -e) *m* scene of the crime.
tätowieren [tɛto'viːrən] *vt* to tattoo.
Tätowierung *f* tattooing; (*Ergebnis*) tattoo.
Tatsache *f* fact; **jdn vor vollendete** ~**n stellen** to present sb with a fait accompli.
Tatsachenbericht *m* documentary (report).
tatsächlich *adj* actual ♦ *adv* really.
tatverdächtig *adj* suspected.
Tatze ['tatsə] (-, -n) *f* paw.
Tau[1] [tau] (-(e)s, -e) *nt* rope.
Tau[2] (-(e)s) *m* dew.
taub [taup] *adj* deaf; (*Nuß*) hollow; **sich** ~ **stellen** to pretend not to hear.
Taube ['taubə] (-, -n) *f* (*ZOOL*) pigeon; (*fig*) dove.
Taubenschlag *m* dovecote; **hier geht es zu wie im** ~ (*fig: umg*) it's like Waterloo Station here (*BRIT*), it's like Grand Central Station

here (US).

Taubheit f deafness.

taubstumm adj deaf-mute.

tauchen ['tauxən] vt to dip ♦ vi to dive; (NAUT) to submerge.

Taucher (-s, -) m diver; ~**anzug** m diving suit.

Tauchsieder (-s, -) m portable immersion heater.

Tauchstation f: **auf** ~ **gehen** (U-Boot) to dive.

tauen ['tauən] vt, vi to thaw ♦ vi unpers: **es taut** it's thawing.

Taufbecken nt font.

Taufe ['taufə] (-, -n) f baptism.

taufen vt to baptize; (nennen) to christen.

Tauf- zW: ~**name** m Christian name; ~**pate** m godfather; ~**patin** f godmother; ~**schein** m certificate of baptism.

taugen ['taugən] vi to be of use; ~ **für** to do od be good for; **nicht** ~ to be no good od useless.

Taugenichts (-es, -e) m good-for-nothing.

tauglich ['tauklıç] adj suitable; (MIL) fit (for service); **T~keit** f suitability; fitness.

Taumel ['tauməl] (-s) m dizziness; (fig) frenzy.

taumelig adj giddy, reeling.

taumeln vi to reel, stagger.

Taunus ['taunus] (-) m Taunus (Mountains pl).

Tausch [tauʃ] (-(e)s, -e) m exchange; **einen guten/schlechten** ~ **machen** to get a good/ bad deal.

tauschen vt to exchange, swap ♦ vi: **ich möchte nicht mit ihm** ~ I wouldn't like to be in his place.

täuschen ['tɔyʃən] vt to deceive ♦ vi to be deceptive ♦ vr to be wrong; **wenn mich nicht alles täuscht** unless I'm completely wrong.

täuschend adj deceptive.

Tauschhandel m barter.

Täuschung f deception; (optisch) illusion.

Täuschungsmanöver nt (SPORT) feint; (fig) ploy.

tausend ['tauzənt] num a od one thousand; **T~** (-, -en) f (Zahl) thousand.

Tausender (-s, -) m (Geldschein) thousand.

Tausendfüßler (-s, -) m centipede.

Tau- zW: ~**tropfen** m dew drop; ~**wetter** nt thaw; ~**ziehen** nt tug-of-war.

Taxe ['taksə] (-, -n) f taxi, cab.

Taxi ['taksi] (-(s), -(s)) nt taxi, cab.

taxieren [ta'ksi:rən] vt (Preis, Wert) to estimate; (Haus, Gemälde) to value; (mustern) to look up and down.

Taxi- zW: ~**fahrer** m taxi driver; ~**stand** m taxi rank (BRIT) od stand (US).

Tb, Tbc f abk (= Tuberkulose) TB.

Teamarbeit ['ti:m|arbaɪt] f teamwork.

Technik ['tɛçnɪk] f technology; (Methode, Kunstfertigkeit) technique.

Techniker(in) (-s, -) m(f) technician.

technisch adj technical; **T~e Hochschule** ≈ polytechnic.

Technologie [tɛçnolo'gi:] f technology.

technologisch [tɛçno'lo:gɪʃ] adj technological.

Techtelmechtel [tɛçtəl'mɛçtəl] (-s, -) (umg) nt (Liebschaft) affair, carry-on.

TEE abk (= Trans-Europ-Express) Trans-Europe-Express.

Tee [te:] (-s, -s) m tea; ~**beutel** m tea bag; ~**kanne** f teapot; ~**licht** nt night-light; ~**löffel** m teaspoon; ~**mischung** f blend of tea.

Teer [te:r] (-(e)s, -e) m tar; **t~en** vt to tar.

Teesieb nt tea strainer.

Teewagen m tea trolley.

Teflon ® ['tɛfloːn] (-s) nt Teflon ®.

Teheran ['te:həra:n] (-s) nt Teheran.

Teich [taɪç] (-(e)s, -e) m pond.

Teig [taɪk] (-(e)s, -e) m dough.

teigig ['taɪgɪç] adj doughy.

Teigwaren pl pasta sing.

Teil [taɪl] (-(e)s, -e) m od nt part; (Anteil) share ♦ nt (Bestand~) component, part; (Ersatz~) spare (part); **zum** ~ partly; **ich für mein(en)** ~ ... I, for my part ...; **sich** dat **sein** ~ **denken** (umg) to draw one's own conclusions; **er hat sein(en)** ~ **dazu beigetragen** he did his bit od share; **t~bar** adj divisible; ~**betrag** m instalment (BRIT), installment (US); ~**chen** nt (atomic) particle.

teilen vt to divide; (mit jdm) to share ♦ vr to divide; (in Gruppen) to split up.

Teil- zW: **t~entrahmt** adj semi-skimmed; ~**gebiet** nt (Bereich) branch; (räumlich) area; **t~haben** unreg vi: **an etw** dat **t~haben** to share in sth; ~**haber** (-s, -) m partner; ~**kaskoversicherung** f third party, fire and theft insurance.

Teilnahme (-, -n) f participation; (Mitleid) sympathy; **jdm seine herzliche** ~ **aussprechen** to offer sb one's heartfelt sympathy.

teilnahmslos adj disinterested, apathetic.

teilnehmen unreg vi: **an etw** dat ~ to take part in sth.

Teilnehmer(in) (-s, -) m(f) participant.

teils adv partly.

Teilschaden m partial loss.

Teilstrecke f stage; (von Straße) stretch; (bei Bus etc) fare stage.

Teilung f division.

Teil- zW: **t~weise** adv partially, in part; ~**zahlung** f payment by instalments (BRIT) od installments (US); ~**zeitarbeit** f part-time job od work.

Teint [tɛ̃:] (-s, -s) m complexion.

Telebrief ['te:lebri:f] m facsimile, fax.

Telefax ['te:lefaks] (-) nt telefax.

Telefon [tele'fo:n] (-s, -e) nt (tele)phone; **ans** ~ **gehen** to answer the phone; ~**amt** nt telephone exchange; ~**anruf** m (tele)phone call.

Telefonat [telefo'na:t] (-(e)s, -e) nt (tele)phone call.

Telefon- zW: **~buch** nt (tele)phone directory;
~gebühr f call charge; (*Grundgebühr*)
(tele)phone rental; **~gespräch** nt
(tele)phone call; **~häuschen** (*umg*) nt
= **Telefonzelle.**

telefonieren [telefo'niːrən] vi to (tele)phone;
bei jdm ~ to use sb's phone; **mit jdm ~** to
speak to sb on the phone.

telefonisch [tele'foːnɪʃ] adj telephone;
(*Benachrichtigung*) by telephone; **ich bin ~ zu
erreichen** I can be reached by phone.

Telefonist(in) [telefo'nɪst(ɪn)] m(f) telephonist.

Telefon- zW: **~karte** f phone card; **~nummer**
f (tele)phone number; **~seelsorge** f: **die
~seelsorge** ≈ the Samaritans; **~verbindung**
f telephone connection; **~zelle** f telephone
box (*BRIT*) od booth (*US*), callbox (*BRIT*);
~zentrale f telephone exchange.

Telegraf [tele'graːf] (**-en, -en**) m telegraph.

Telegrafenleitung f telegraph line.

Telegrafenmast m telegraph pole.

Telegrafie [telegra'fiː] f telegraphy.

telegrafieren [telegra'fiːrən] vt, vi to
telegraph, cable, wire.

telegrafisch [tele'graːfɪʃ] adj telegraphic; **jdm
~ Geld überweisen** to cable sb money.

Telegramm [tele'gram] (**-s, -e**) nt telegram,
cable; **~adresse** f telegraphic address;
~formular nt telegram form.

Telegraph m = **Telegraf.**

Telekolleg ['teːləkɔlek] nt ≈ Open University
(*BRIT*).

Teleobjektiv ['teːlə|ɔpjɛktiːf] nt telephoto
lens.

Telepathie [telepa'tiː] f telepathy.

telepathisch [tele'paːtɪʃ] adj telepathic.

Telephon nt = **Telefon.**

Teleskop [tele'skoːp] (**-s, -e**) nt telescope.

Telespiel nt video game.

Telex ['teːlɛks] (**-, -(e)**) nt telex.

Teller ['tɛlər] (**-s, -**) m plate.

Tempel ['tɛmpəl] (**-s, -**) m temple.

Temperafarbe ['tɛmperafarbə] f distemper.

Temperament [tɛmpera'mɛnt] nt
temperament; (*Schwung*) vivacity, vitality;
sein ~ ist mit ihm durchgegangen he went
over the top; **t~los** adj spiritless; **t~voll** adj
high-spirited, lively.

Temperatur [tɛmpera'tuːr] f temperature;
erhöhte ~ haben to have a temperature.

Tempo¹ ['tɛmpo] (**-s, -s**) nt speed, pace; **~!**
get a move on!

Tempo² ['tɛmpo] (**-s, Tempi**) nt (*MUS*) tempo;
das ~ angeben (*fig*) to set the pace; **~limit** nt
speed limit.

temporär [tɛmpo'rɛːr] adj temporary.

Tempotaschentuch ® nt paper
handkerchief.

Tendenz [tɛn'dɛnts] f tendency; (*Absicht*)
intention.

tendenziell [tɛndɛntsi'ɛl] adj: **nur ~e
Unterschiede** merely differences in

emphasis.

tendenziös [tɛndɛntsi'øːs] adj bias(s)ed,
tendentious.

tendieren [tɛn'diːrən] vi: **zu etw ~** to show a
tendency to(wards) sth, incline to(wards)
sth.

Teneriffa [tene'rɪfa] (**-s**) nt Tenerife.

Tenne ['tɛnə] (**-, -n**) f threshing floor.

Tennis ['tɛnɪs] (**-**) nt tennis; **~platz** m tennis
court; **~schläger** m tennis racket; **~spieler** m
tennis player.

Tenor [te'noːr] (**-s, ̈-e**) m tenor.

Teppich ['tɛpɪç] (**-s, -e**) m carpet; **~boden** m
wall-to-wall carpeting; **~kehrmaschine** f
carpet sweeper; **~klopfer** m carpet beater.

Termin [tɛr'miːn] (**-s, -e**) m (*Zeitpunkt*) date;
(*Frist*) deadline; (*Arzt~ etc*) appointment;
(*JUR: Verhandlung*) hearing; **sich** dat **einen
~ geben lassen** to make an appointment;
t~gerecht adj on schedule.

terminieren [tɛrmi'niːrən] vt (*befristen*) to
limit; (*festsetzen*) to set a date for.

Terminkalender m diary, appointments
book.

Terminologie [tɛrminolo'giː] f terminology.

Termite [tɛr'miːtə] (**-, -n**) f termite.

Terpentin [tɛrpɛn'tiːn] (**-s, -e**) nt turpentine,
turps sing.

Terrain [tɛ'rɛ̃ː] (**-s, -s**) nt land, terrain; (*fig*)
territory; **das ~ sondieren** (*MIL*) to
reconnoitre the terrain; (*fig*) to see how the
land lies.

Terrasse [tɛ'rasə] (**-, -n**) f terrace.

Terrine [tɛ'riːnə] f tureen.

territorial [tɛritori'aːl] adj territorial.

Territorium [tɛri'toːriʊm] nt territory.

Terror ['tɛrɔr] (**-s**) m terror; (*~herrschaft*)
reign of terror; **blanker ~** sheer terror;
~anschlag m terrorist attack.

terrorisieren [tɛrori'ziːrən] vt to terrorize.

Terrorismus [tɛro'rɪsmʊs] m terrorism.

Terrorist(in) [tɛro'rɪst(ɪn)] m(f) terrorist.

terroristisch [tɛro'rɪstɪʃ] adj terrorist attr.

Terrororganisation f terrorist organization.

Tertia ['tɛrtsia] (**-, Tertien**) f (*SCH: Unter~/
Ober~*) *fourth/fifth year of German
secondary school.*

Terz [tɛrts] (**-, -en**) f (*MUS*) third.

Terzett [tɛr'tsɛt] (**-(e)s, -e**) nt (*MUS*) trio.

Tesafilm ® ['teːzafɪlm] m Sellotape ® (*BRIT*),
Scotch tape ® (*US*).

Test [tɛst] (**-s, -s**) m test.

Testament [tɛsta'mɛnt] nt will, testament;
(*REL*) Testament; **Altes/Neues ~** Old/New
Testament.

testamentarisch [tɛstamɛn'taːrɪʃ] adj
testamentary.

Testamentsvollstrecker(in) (**-s, -**) m(f)
executor (of a will).

Testat [tɛs'taːt] (**-(e)s, -e**) nt certificate.

Testator [tɛs'taːtɔr] m testator.

Test- zW: **~bild** nt (*TV*) test card; **t~en** vt to

test; ~**fall** m test case; ~**person** f subject (of a test); ~**stoppabkommen** nt nuclear test ban agreement.

Tetanus ['te:tanʊs] (-) m tetanus; ~**impfung** f (anti-)tetanus injection.

teuer ['tɔyər] adj dear, expensive; **teures Geld** good money; **das wird ihn ~ zu stehen kommen** (fig) that will cost him dear.

Teuerung f increase in prices.

Teuerungszulage f cost-of-living bonus.

Teufel ['tɔyfəl] (-s, -) m devil; **den ~ an die Wand malen** (schwarzmalen) to imagine the worst; (Unheil heraufbeschwören) to tempt fate od providence; **in ~s Küche kommen** to get into a mess; **jdn zum ~ jagen** (umg) to send sb packing.

Teufelei [tɔyfə'laɪ] f devilment.

Teufels- zW: ~**austreibung** f exorcism; ~**brut** (umg) f devil's brood; ~**kreis** m vicious circle.

teuflisch ['tɔyflɪʃ] adj fiendish, diabolic.

Text [tɛkst] (-(e)s, -e) m text; (Lieder~) words pl; (: von Schlager) lyrics pl; ~**dichter** m songwriter; **t~en** vi to write the words.

textil [tɛks'ti:l] adj textile; **T~branche** f textile trade.

Textilien pl textiles pl.

Textilindustrie f textile industry.

Textilwaren pl textiles pl.

Textstelle f passage.

Textverarbeitungssystem nt word processor.

TH (-, -s) f abk (= Technische Hochschule) siehe **technisch**.

Thailand ['taɪlant] (-s) nt Thailand.

Thailänder(in) ['taɪlɛndər(ɪn)] (-s, -) m(f) Thai.

Theater [te'a:tər] (-s, -) nt theatre (BRIT), theater (US); (umg) fuss; **(ein) ~ machen** to make a (big) fuss; ~ **spielen** to act; (fig) to put on an act; ~**besucher** m playgoer; ~**kasse** f box office; ~**stück** nt (stage) play.

theatralisch [tea'tra:lɪʃ] adj theatrical.

Theke ['te:kə] (-, -n) f (Schanktisch) bar; (Ladentisch) counter.

Thema ['te:ma] (-s, Themen od -ta) nt (MUS, Leitgedanke) theme; topic, subject; **beim ~ bleiben/vom ~ abschweifen** to stick to/ wander off the subject.

thematisch [te'ma:tɪʃ] adj thematic.

Themenkreis m topic.

Themenpark m theme park.

Themse ['tɛmzə] f: **die ~** the Thames.

Theologe [teo'lo:gə] (-n, -n) m theologian.

Theologie [teolo'gi:] f theology.

Theologin f theologian.

theologisch [teo'lo:gɪʃ] adj theological.

Theoretiker(in) [teo're:tikər(ɪn)] (-s, -) m(f) theorist.

theoretisch adj theoretical; ~ **gesehen** in theory, theoretically.

Theorie [teo'ri:] f theory.

Therapeut [tera'pɔyt] (-en, -en) m therapist.

therapeutisch adj therapeutic.

Therapie [tera'pi:] f therapy.

Thermalbad [tɛr'ma:lba:t] nt thermal bath; (Badeort) thermal spa.

Thermalquelle f thermal spring.

Thermometer [tɛrmo'me:tər] (-s, -) nt thermometer.

Thermosflasche ® ['tɛrmɔsflaʃə] f Thermos ® flask.

Thermostat [tɛrmo'sta:t] (-(e)s od -en, -e(n)) m thermostat.

These ['te:zə] (-, -n) f thesis.

Thrombose [trɔm'bo:sə] (-, -n) f thrombosis.

Thron [tro:n] (-(e)s, -e) m throne; ~**besteigung** f accession (to the throne).

thronen vi to sit enthroned; (fig) to sit in state.

Thronerbe m heir to the throne.

Thronfolge f succession (to the throne).

Thunfisch ['tu:nfɪʃ] m tuna (fish).

Thüringen ['ty:rɪŋən] (-s) nt Thuringia.

Thymian ['ty:mia:n] (-s, -e) m thyme.

Tibet ['ti:bet] (-s) nt Tibet.

Tick [tɪk] (-(e)s, -s) m tic; (Eigenart) quirk; (Fimmel) craze.

ticken vi to tick; **nicht richtig ~** (umg) to be off one's rocker.

Ticket ['tɪkət] (-s, -s) nt ticket.

tief [ti:f] adj deep; (~sinnig) profound; (Ausschnitt, Ton) low; ~**er Teller** soup plate; **bis ~ in die Nacht hinein** late into the night; **T~** (-s, -s) nt (MET) depression; (fig) low; **T~bau** m civil engineering (at or below ground level); **T~druck** m (MET) low pressure.

Tiefe (-, -n) f depth.

Tiefebene ['ti:fe:bənə] f plain.

Tiefenpsychologie f depth psychology.

Tiefenschärfe f (PHOT) depth of focus.

tief- zW: ~**ernst** adj very grave od solemn; **T~flug** m low-level od low-altitude flight; **T~gang** m (NAUT) draught (BRIT), draft (US); (geistig) depth; **T~garage** f underground car park (BRIT) od parking lot (US); ~**gekühlt** adj frozen; ~**greifend** adj far-reaching; **T~kühlfach** nt freezer compartment; **T~kühlkost** f frozen food; **T~kühltruhe** f freezer, deep freezer (US); **T~lader** (-s, -) m low-loader; **T~land** nt lowlands pl; **T~parterre** f basement; **T~punkt** m low point; (fig) low ebb; **T~schlag** m (BOXEN, fig) blow below the belt; ~**schürfend** adj profound; **T~see** f deep parts of the sea; **T~sinn** m profundity; ~**sinnig** adj profound; (umg) melancholy; **T~stand** m low level; ~**stapeln** vi to be overmodest; **T~start** m (SPORT) crouch start.

Tiefstwert m minimum od lowest value.

Tiegel ['ti:gəl] (-s, -) m saucepan; (CHEM) crucible.

Tier [ti:r] (-(e)s, -e) nt animal; ~**arzt** m, ~**ärztin**

f vet(erinary surgeon) (*BRIT*), veterinarian (*US*); ~**freund** *m* animal lover; ~**garten** *m* zoo, zoological gardens *pl*; ~**handlung** *f* pet shop (*BRIT*) *od* store (*US*); **t~isch** *adj* animal *attrib*; (*lit, fig*) brutish; (*fig: Ernst etc*) deadly; ~**kreis** *m* zodiac; ~**kunde** *f* zoology; **t~lieb** *adj*, **t~liebend** *adj* fond of animals; ~**quälerei** *f* cruelty to animals; ~**reich** *nt* animal kingdom; ~**schutz** *m* protection of animals; ~**schutzverein** *m* society for the prevention of cruelty to animals; ~**versuch** *m* animal experiment; ~**welt** *f* animal kingdom.

Tiger ['tiːɡər] (-**s**, -) *m* tiger; ~**in** *f* tigress.

tilgen ['tɪlɡən] *vt* to erase; (*Sünden*) to expiate; (*Schulden*) to pay off.

Tilgung *f* erasing, blotting out; expiation; repayment.

Tilgungsfonds *m* (*COMM*) sinking fund.

tingeln ['tɪŋɡəln] (*umg*) *vi* to appear in small night clubs.

Tinktur [tɪŋk'tuːr] *f* tincture.

Tinte ['tɪntə] (-, -**n**) *f* ink.

Tinten- *zW:* ~**faß** *nt* inkwell; ~**fisch** *m* cuttlefish; (*achtarmig*) octopus; ~**fleck** *m* ink stain *od* blot; ~**stift** *m* indelible pencil; ~**strahldrucker** *m* ink-jet printer.

Tip [tɪp] (-**s**, -**s**) *m* (*SPORT, BÖRSE*) tip; (*Andeutung*) hint; (*an Polizei*) tip-off.

Tippelbruder (*umg*) *m* tramp, gentleman of the road (*BRIT*), hobo (*US*).

tippen ['tɪpən] *vi* to tap, touch; (*umg: schreiben*) to type; (*im Lotto etc*) to bet ♦ *vt* to type; to bet; **auf jdn** ~ (*umg: raten*) to tip sb, put one's money on sb (*fig*).

Tippfehler (*umg*) *m* typing error.

Tippse (-, -**n**) (*umg*) *f* typist.

tipptopp ['tɪp'tɔp] (*umg*) *adj* tiptop.

Tippzettel *m* (pools) coupon.

Tirade [ti'raːdə] (-, -**n**) *f* tirade.

Tirol [ti'roːl] (-**s**) *nt* the Tyrol.

Tiroler(in) (-**s**, -) *m(f)* Tyrolese, Tyrolean.

tirolerisch *adj* Tyrolese, Tyrolean.

Tisch [tɪʃ] (-(**e**)**s**, -**e**) *m* table; **bitte zu** ~! lunch *od* dinner is served; **bei** ~ at table; **vor/nach** ~ before/after eating; **unter den** ~ **fallen** (*fig*) to be dropped; ~**decke** *f* tablecloth.

Tischler (-**s**, -) *m* carpenter, joiner.

Tischlerei [tɪʃlə'raɪ] *f* joiner's workshop; (*Arbeit*) carpentry, joinery.

Tischlerhandwerk *nt* cabinetmaking.

tischlern *vi* to do carpentry *etc*.

Tisch- *zW:* ~**nachbar** *m* neighbour (*BRIT*) *od* neighbor (*US*) (at table); ~**rechner** *m* desk calculator; ~**rede** *f* after-dinner speech; ~**tennis** *nt* table tennis; ~**tuch** *nt* tablecloth.

Titel ['tiːtəl] (-**s**, -) *m* title; ~**anwärter** *m* (*SPORT*) challenger; ~**bild** *nt* cover (picture); (*von Buch*) frontispiece; ~**geschichte** *f* headline story; ~**rolle** *f* title role; ~**seite** *f* cover; (*Buch~*) title page; ~**verteidiger** *m* defending champion, title holder.

Titte ['tɪtə] (-, -**n**) (*umg*) *f* (*weibliche Brust*) boob, tit (*umg*).

titulieren [titu'liːrən] *vt* to entitle; (*anreden*) to address.

tja [tja] *interj* well!

Toast [toːst] (-(**e**)**s**, -**s** *od* -**e**) *m* toast.

toasten *vi* to drink a toast ♦ *vt* (*Brot*) to toast; **auf jdn** ~ to toast sb, drink a toast to sb.

Toaster (-**s**, -) *m* toaster.

toben ['toːbən] *vi* to rage; (*Kinder*) to romp about.

tob- *zW:* **T~sucht** *f* raving madness; ~**süchtig** *adj* maniacal; **T~suchtsanfall** *m* maniacal fit.

Tochter ['tɔxtər] (-, -̈) *f* daughter; ~**gesellschaft** *f* subsidiary (company).

Tod [toːt] (-(**e**)**s**, -**e**) *m* death; **zu** ~**e betrübt sein** to be in the depths of despair; **eines natürlichen/gewaltsamen** ~**es sterben** to die of natural causes/die a violent death; **t~ernst** (*umg*) *adj* deadly serious ♦ *adv* in dead earnest.

Todes- *zW:* ~**angst** *f* mortal fear; ~**ängste ausstehen** (*umg*) to be scared to death; ~**anzeige** *f* obituary (notice); ~**fall** *m* death; ~**kampf** *m* death throes *pl*; ~**opfer** *nt* death, casualty, fatality; ~**qualen** *pl:* ~**qualen ausstehen** (*fig*) to suffer agonies; ~**stoß** *m* deathblow; ~**strafe** *f* death penalty; ~**tag** *m* anniversary of death; ~**ursache** *f* cause of death; ~**urteil** *nt* death sentence; ~**verachtung** *f* utter disgust.

Todfeind *m* deadly *od* mortal enemy.

todkrank *adj* dangerously ill.

tödlich ['tøːtlɪç] *adj* fatal; (*Gift*) deadly, lethal.

tod- *zW:* ~**müde** *adj* dead tired; ~**schick** (*umg*) *adj* smart, classy; ~**sicher** (*umg*) *adj* absolutely *od* dead certain; **T~sünde** *f* deadly sin; ~**traurig** *adj* extremely sad.

Tofu ['toːfu] (-(**s**)) *m* tofu.

Togo ['toːɡo] (-**s**) *nt* Togo.

Toilette [toa'lɛtə] *f* toilet, lavatory (*BRIT*), john (*US*); (*Frisiertisch*) dressing table; (*Kleidung*) outfit; **auf die** ~ **gehen/auf der** ~ **sein** to go to/be in the toilet.

Toiletten- *zW:* ~**artikel** *pl* toiletries *pl*, toilet articles *pl*; ~**papier** *nt* toilet paper; ~**tisch** *m* dressing table.

toi, toi, toi ['tɔy'tɔy'tɔy] (*umg*) *interj* good luck; (*unberufen*) touch wood.

Tokio ['toːkjo] (-**s**) *nt* Tokyo.

tolerant [tole'rant] *adj* tolerant.

Toleranz *f* tolerance.

tolerieren [tole'riːrən] *vt* to tolerate.

toll [tɔl] *adj* mad; (*Treiben*) wild; (*umg*) terrific.

tollen *vi* to romp.

toll- *zW:* **T~heit** *f* madness, wildness; **T~kirsche** *f* deadly nightshade; ~**kühn** *adj* daring; **T~wut** *f* rabies.

Tölpel ['tœlpəl] (-**s**, -) *m* oaf, clod.

Tomate [to'maːtə] (-, -**n**) *f* tomato; **du treulose** ~! (*umg*) you're a fine friend!

Tomatenmark (-(e)s) *nt* tomato purée.
Tombola ['tɔmbola] (-, -s *od* **Tombolen**) *f* tombola.
Ton¹ [toːn] (-(e)s, -e) *m* (*Erde*) clay.
Ton² [toːn] (-(e)s, ⁼e) *m* (*Laut*) sound; (*MUS*) note; (*Redeweise*) tone; (*Farb~*, *Nuance*) shade; (*Betonung*) stress; **keinen ~ herausbringen** not to be able to say a word; **den ~ angeben** (*MUS*) to give an A; (*fig: Mensch*) to set the tone; **~abnehmer** *m* pick-up; **t~angebend** *adj* leading; **~arm** *m* pick-up arm; **~art** *f* (musical) key; **~band** *nt* tape; **~bandaufnahme** *f* tape recording; **~bandgerät** *nt* tape recorder.
tönen ['tøːnən] *vi* to sound ♦ *vt* to shade; (*Haare*) to tint.
tönern ['tøːnərn] *adj* clay.
Ton- *zW:* **~fall** *m* intonation; **~film** *m* sound film; **~höhe** *f* pitch.
Tonika ['toːnika] (-, -iken) *f* (*MUS*) tonic.
Tonikum (-s, -ika) *nt* (*MED*) tonic.
Ton- *zW:* **~ingenieur** *m* sound engineer; **~kopf** *m* recording head; **~künstler** *m* musician; **~leiter** *f* (*MUS*) scale; **t~los** *adj* soundless.
Tonne ['tɔnə] (-, -n) *f* barrel; (*Maß*) ton.
Ton- *zW:* **~spur** *f* soundtrack; **~taube** *f* clay pigeon; **~waren** *pl* pottery *sing*, earthenware *sing*.
Topf [tɔpf] (-(e)s, ⁼e) *m* pot; **alles in einen ~ werfen** (*fig*) to lump everything together; **~blume** *f* pot plant.
Töpfer(in) ['tœpfər(ɪn)] (-s, -) *m(f)* potter.
Töpferei [tœpfə'raɪ] *f* (*Töpferware*) pottery; (*Werkstatt*) pottery, potter's workshop.
töpfern *vi* to do pottery.
Töpferscheibe *f* potter's wheel.
topfit ['tɔp'fɪt] *adj* in top form.
Topflappen *m* ovencloth.
topographisch [topo'graːfɪʃ] *adj* topographic.
topp [tɔp] *interj* O.K.
Tor¹ [toːr] (-en, -en) *m* fool.
Tor² (-(e)s, -e) *nt* gate; (*SPORT*) goal; **~bogen** *m* archway; **~einfahrt** *f* entrance gate.
Toresschluß *m:* (*kurz*) **vor ~** right at the last minute.
Torf [tɔrf] (-(e)s) *m* peat; **~stechen** *nt* peat-cutting.
Torheit *f* foolishness; (*törichte Handlung*) foolish deed.
Torhüter (-s, -) *m* goalkeeper.
töricht ['tøːrɪçt] *adj* foolish.
torkeln ['tɔrkəln] *vi* to stagger, reel.
torpedieren [tɔrpe'diːrən] *vt* (*lit, fig*) to torpedo.
Torpedo [tɔr'peːdo] (-s, -s) *m* torpedo.
Torschlußpanik ['toːrʃluspaːnɪk] (*umg*) *f* (*von Unverheirateten*) *fear of being left on the shelf.*
Torte ['tɔrtə] (-, -n) *f* cake; (*Obst~*) flan, tart.
Tortenguß *m* glaze.
Tortenheber *m* cake slice.

Tortur [tɔr'tuːr] *f* ordeal.
Torverhältnis *nt* goal average.
Torwart (-(e)s, -e) *m* goalkeeper.
tosen ['toːzən] *vi* to roar.
Toskana [tɔs'kaːna] *f* Tuscany.
tot [toːt] *adj* dead; **er war auf der Stelle ~** he died instantly; **der ~e Winkel** the blind spot; **einen ~en Punkt haben** to be at one's lowest; **das T~e Meer** the Dead Sea.
total [to'taːl] *adj* total; **T~ausverkauf** *m* clearance sale.
totalitär [totali'tɛːr] *adj* totalitarian.
Totaloperation *f* extirpation; (*von Gebärmutter*) hysterectomy.
Totalschaden *m* (*AUT*) complete write-off.
totarbeiten *vr* to work o.s. to death.
totärgern (*umg*) *vr* to get really annoyed.
Tote(r) *f(m)* dead person.
töten ['tøːtən] *vt*, *vi* to kill.
Toten- *zW:* **~bett** *nt* deathbed; **t~blaß** *adj* deathly pale, white as a sheet; **~gräber** (-s, -) *m* gravedigger; **~hemd** *nt* shroud; **~kopf** *m* skull; **~messe** *f* requiem mass; **~schein** *m* death certificate; **~stille** *f* deathly silence; **~tanz** *m* danse macabre; **~wache** *f* wake.
tot- *zW:* **~fahren** *unreg vt* to run over; **~geboren** *adj* stillborn; **~kriegen** (*umg*) *vt:* **nicht ~zukriegen sein** to go on for ever; **~lachen** (*umg*) *vr* to laugh one's head off.
Toto ['toːto] (-s, -s) *m od nt* ≈ pools *pl*; **~schein** *m* ≈ pools coupon.
tot- *zW:* **~sagen** *vt:* **jdn ~sagen** to say that sb is dead; **T~schlag** *m* (*JUR*) manslaughter, second degree murder (*US*); **~schlagen** *unreg vt* (*lit, fig*) to kill; **T~schläger** *m* (*Waffe*) cosh (*BRIT*), blackjack (*US*); **~schweigen** *unreg vt* to hush up; **~stellen** *vr* to pretend to be dead; **~treten** *unreg vt* to trample to death.
Tötung ['tøːtʊŋ] *f* killing.
Toupet [tu'peː] (-s, -s) *nt* toupee.
toupieren [tu'piːrən] *vt* to backcomb.
Tour [tuːr] (-, -en) *f* tour, trip; (*Umdrehung*) revolution; (*Verhaltensart*) way; **auf ~en kommen** (*AUT*) to reach top speed; (*fig*) to get into top gear; **auf vollen ~en laufen** (*lit*) to run at full speed; (*fig*) to be in full swing; **auf die krumme ~** by dishonest means; **in einer ~** incessantly.
Tourenzahl *f* number of revolutions.
Tourenzähler *m* rev counter.
Tourismus [tu'rɪsmʊs] *m* tourism.
Tourist(in) *m(f)* tourist.
Touristenklasse *f* tourist class.
Touristik [tu'rɪstɪk] *f* tourism.
touristisch *adj* tourist *attr*.
Tournee [tʊr'neː] (-, -s *od* -n) *f* (*THEAT etc*) tour; **auf ~ gehen** to go on tour.
Trab [traːp] (-(e)s) *m* trot; **auf ~ sein** (*umg*) to be on the go.
Trabant [tra'bant] *m* satellite.

Trabantenstadt f satellite town.
traben ['tra:bən] vi to trot.
Tracht [traxt] (-, -en) f (Kleidung) costume,
dress; **eine ~ Prügel** a sound thrashing.
trachten vi to strive, endeavour (BRIT),
endeavor (US); **danach ~, etw zu tun** to
strive to do sth; **jdm nach dem Leben ~** to
seek to kill sb.
trächtig ['trɛçtɪç] adj (Tier) pregnant.
Tradition [traditsi'o:n] f tradition.
traditionell [traditsio:'nɛl] adj traditional.
traf etc [tra:f] vb siehe **treffen**.
Tragbahre f stretcher.
tragbar adj (Gerät) portable; (Kleidung)
wearable; (erträglich) bearable.
träge ['trɛ:gə] adj sluggish, slow; (PHYS) inert.
tragen ['tra:gən] unreg vt to carry; (Kleidung,
Brille) to wear; (Namen, Früchte) to bear;
(erdulden) to endure ♦ vi (schwanger sein) to
be pregnant; (Eis) to hold; **schwer an etw** dat
~ (lit) to have a job carrying sth; (fig) to find
sth hard to bear; **zum T~ kommen** to come
to fruition; (nützlich werden) to come in
useful.
tragend adj (Säule, Bauteil) load-bearing;
(Idee, Motiv) fundamental.
Träger ['trɛ:gər] (-s, -) m carrier; wearer;
bearer; (Ordens~) holder; (an Kleidung)
(shoulder) strap; (Körperschaft etc) sponsor;
(Holz~, Beton~) (supporting) beam; (Stahl~,
Eisen~) girder; (TECH: Stütze von Brücken etc)
support.
Trägerin f (Person) siehe **Träger**.
Träger- zW: **~kleid** nt pinafore dress (BRIT),
jumper (US); **~rakete** f launch vehicle;
~rock m skirt with shoulder straps.
Tragetasche f carrier bag (BRIT), carry-all
(US).
Trag- zW: **~fähigkeit** f load-bearing capacity;
~fläche f (AVIAT) wing; **~flügelboot** nt
hydrofoil.
Trägheit ['trɛ:khaɪt] f laziness; (PHYS)
inertia.
Tragik ['tra:gɪk] f tragedy.
tragikomisch [tragi'ko:mɪʃ] adj tragi-comic.
tragisch adj tragic; **etw ~ nehmen** (umg) to
take sth to heart.
Traglast f load.
Tragödie [tra'gø:diə] f tragedy.
trägt [trɛ:kt] vb siehe **tragen**.
Tragweite f range; (fig) scope; **von großer
~ sein** to have far-reaching consequences.
Tragwerk nt wing assembly.
Trainer(in) ['trɛ:nər(ɪn)] (-s, -) m(f) (SPORT)
trainer, coach; (FUSSBALL) manager.
trainieren [trɛ'ni:rən] vt to train; (Übung) to
practise (BRIT), practice (US) ♦ vi to train;
Fußball ~ to do football practice.
Training (-s, -s) nt training.
Trainingsanzug m track suit.
Trakt [trakt] (-(e)s, -e) m (Gebäudeteil) section;
(Flügel) wing.

Traktat [trak'ta:t] (-(e)s, -e) m od nt
(Abhandlung) treatise; (Flugschrift, religiöse
Schrift) tract.
traktieren (umg) vt (schlecht behandeln) to
maltreat; (quälen) to torment.
Traktor ['traktɔr] m tractor; (von Drucker)
tractor feed.
trällern ['trɛlərn] vt, vi to warble; (Vogel) to
trill, warble.
trampeln ['trampəln] vt to trample;
(abschütteln) to stamp ♦ vi to stamp.
Trampelpfad m track, path.
Trampeltier nt (ZOOL) (Bactrian) camel; (fig:
umg) clumsy oaf.
trampen ['trɛmpən] vi to hitchhike.
Tramper(in) [trɛmpər(ɪn)] (-s, -) m(f)
hitchhiker.
Trampolin [trampo'li:n] (-s, -e) nt trampoline.
Tranchierbesteck nt pair of carvers,
carvers pl.
tranchieren [trã'ʃi:rən] vt to carve.
Träne ['trɛ:nə] (-, -n) f tear.
tränen vi to water.
Tränengas nt tear gas.
tranig ['tra:nɪç] (umg) adj slow, sluggish.
trank etc [traŋk] vb siehe **trinken**.
Tränke ['trɛŋkə] (-, -n) f watering place.
tränken vt (naß machen) to soak; (Tiere) to
water.
Transaktion [transˌaktsi'o:n] f transaction.
Transformator [transfɔr'ma:tɔr] m
transformer.
Transfusion [transfuzi'o:n] f transfusion.
Transistor [tran'zɪstɔr] m transistor.
transitiv ['tranziti:f] adj transitive.
Transitverkehr [tran'zi:tfɛrke:r] m transit
traffic.
transparent [transpa'rɛnt] adj transparent; **T~**
(-(e)s, -e) nt (Bild) transparency;
(Spruchband) banner.
transpirieren [transpi'ri:rən] vi to perspire.
Transplantation [transplantatsi'o:n] f
transplantation; (Haut~) graft(ing).
Transport [trans'pɔrt] (-(e)s, -e) m transport;
(Fracht) consignment, shipment; **t~fähig** adj
moveable.
transportieren [transpɔr'ti:rən] vt to
transport.
Transport- zW: **~kosten** pl transport charges
pl, carriage sing; **~mittel** nt means sing of
transport; **~unternehmen** nt carrier.
transsexuell [transzɛksu'ɛl] adj transsexual.
transusig ['transˌu:zɪç] (umg) adj sluggish.
Transvestit [transvɛs'ti:t] (-en, -en) m
transvestite.
Trapez [tra'pe:ts] (-es, -e) nt trapeze; (MATH)
trapezium.
Trara [tra'ra:] (-s) nt: **mit viel ~ (um)** (fig: umg)
with a great hullabaloo (about).
trat etc [tra:t] vb siehe **treten**.
Tratsch [tra:tʃ] (-(e)s) (umg) m gossip.
tratschen ['tra:tʃən] (umg) vi to gossip.

Tratte ['tratə] (-, -n) *f* (*FIN*) draft.
Traube ['traubə] (-, -n) *f* grape; (*ganze Frucht*) bunch (of grapes).
Traubenlese *f* grape harvest.
Traubenzucker *m* glucose.
trauen ['trauən] *vi +dat* to trust ◊ *vr* to dare ◊ *vt* to marry; **jdm/etw** ~ to trust sb/sth.
Trauer ['trauər] (-) *f* sorrow; (*für Verstorbenen*) mourning; **~fall** *m* death, bereavement; **~feier** *f* funeral service; **~flor** (-s, -e) *m* black ribbon; **~gemeinde** *f* mourners *pl*; **~marsch** *m* funeral march.
trauern *vi* to mourn; **um jdn** ~ to mourn (for) sb.
Trauer- *zW:* **~rand** *m* black border; **~spiel** *nt* tragedy; **~weide** *f* weeping willow.
Traufe ['traufə] (-, -n) *f* eaves *pl*.
träufeln ['trɔyfəln] *vt, vi* to drip.
traulich ['trauliç] *adj* cosy, intimate.
Traum [traum] (-(e)s, **Träume**) *m* dream; **aus der** ~! it's all over!
Trauma (-s, -men) *nt* trauma.
traumatisieren [traumati'ziːrən] *vt* to traumatize.
Traumbild *nt* vision.
Traumdeutung *f* interpretation of dreams.
träumen ['trɔymən] *vt, vi* to dream; **das hätte ich mir nicht** ~ **lassen** I'd never have thought it possible.
Träumer(in) (-s, -) *m(f)* dreamer.
Träumerei [trɔymə'rai] *f* dreaming.
träumerisch *adj* dreamy.
traumhaft *adj* dreamlike; (*fig*) wonderful.
Traumtänzer *m* dreamer.
traurig ['trauriç] *adj* sad; **T~keit** *f* sadness.
Trauring *m* wedding ring.
Trauschein *m* marriage certificate.
Trauung *f* wedding ceremony.
Trauzeuge *m* witness (to a marriage).
treffen ['trɛfən] *unreg vt* to strike, hit; (*Bemerkung*) to hurt; (*begegnen*) to meet; (*Entscheidung etc*) to make; (*Maßnahmen*) to take ◊ *vi* to hit ◊ *vr* to meet; **er hat es gut getroffen** he did well; **er fühlte sich getroffen** he took it personally; ~ **auf** *+akk* to come across, meet; **es traf sich, daß** ... it so happened that ...; **es trifft sich gut** it's convenient.
Treffen (-s, -) *nt* meeting.
treffend *adj* pertinent, apposite.
Treffer (-s, -) *m* hit; (*Tor*) goal; (*Los*) winner.
trefflich *adj* excellent.
Treffpunkt *m* meeting place.
Treibeis *nt* drift ice.
treiben ['traibən] *unreg vt* to drive; (*Studien etc*) to pursue; (*SPORT*) to do, go in for ◊ *vi* (*Schiff etc*) to drift; (*Pflanzen*) to sprout; (*KOCH: aufgehen*) to rise; (*Medikamente*) to be diuretic; **die ~de Kraft** (*fig*) the driving force; **Handel mit etw/jdm** ~ to trade in sth/with sb; **es zu weit** ~ to go too far; **Unsinn** ~ to fool around; **T~** (-s) *nt* activity.

Treib- *zW:* **~gut** *nt* flotsam and jetsam; **~haus** *nt* greenhouse; **~hauseffekt** *m* greenhouse effect; **~hausgas** *nt* greenhouse gas; **~jagd** *f* shoot (*in which game is sent up*); (*fig*) witchhunt; **~sand** *m* quicksand; **~stoff** *m* fuel.
Trend [trɛnt] (-s, -s) *m* trend; **~wende** *f* new trend.
trennbar *adj* separable.
trennen ['trɛnən] *vt* to separate; (*teilen*) to divide ◊ *vr* to separate; **sich** ~ **von** to part with.
Trennschärfe *f* (*RUNDF*) selectivity.
Trennung *f* separation.
Trennungsstrich *m* hyphen.
Trennwand *f* partition (wall).
treppab *adv* downstairs.
treppauf *adv* upstairs.
Treppe ['trɛpə] (-, -n) *f* stairs *pl*, staircase; (*im Freien*) steps *pl*; **eine** ~ a staircase, a flight of stairs *od* steps; **sie wohnt zwei ~n hoch/höher** she lives two flights up/higher up.
Treppengeländer *nt* banister.
Treppenhaus *nt* staircase.
Tresen ['treːzən] (-s, -) *m* (*Theke*) bar; (*Ladentisch*) counter.
Tresor [tre'zoːr] (-s, -e) *m* safe.
Tretboot *nt* pedal boat, pedalo.
treten ['treːtən] *unreg vi* to step; (*Tränen, Schweiß*) to appear ◊ *vt* (*mit Fußtritt*) to kick; (*nieder~*) to tread, trample; ~ **nach** to kick at; ~ **in** *+akk* to step in(to); **in Verbindung** ~ to get in contact; **in Erscheinung** ~ to appear; **der Fluß trat über die Ufer** the river overflowed its banks; **in Streik** ~ to go on strike.
Treter ['treːtər] (*umg*) *pl* (*Schuhe*) casual shoes *pl*.
Tretmine *f* (*MIL*) (anti-personnel) mine.
Tretmühle *f* (*fig*) daily grind.
treu [trɔy] *adj* faithful, true; **~doof** (*umg*) *adj* naïve.
Treue (-) *f* loyalty, faithfulness.
Treuhand (*umg*) *f*, **Treuhandanstalt** *f* trustee organization (*overseeing the privatization of former GDR state-owned firms*).

The **Treuhandanstalt** *is an organization set up in 1990 to take over the nationally-owned companies of the former* **DDR** *and to break them down into smaller units and to privatize them. It is based in Berlin and has nine branches. Many companies have been closed down by the Treuhandanstalt because of their outdated equipment and inability to compete with the western firms. This has resulted in rising unemployment.*

Treuhänder (-s, -) *m* trustee.
Treuhandgesellschaft *f* trust company.
treu- *zW:* **~herzig** *adj* innocent; **~lich** *adv*

faithfully; ~los adj faithless; ~los an jdm handeln to fail sb.

Triathlon ['triːatlɔn] (-s, -s) nt triathlon.

Tribüne [tri'byːnə] (-, -n) f grandstand; (Redner~) platform.

Tribut [tri'buːt] (-(e)s, -e) m tribute.

Trichter ['trɪçtər] (-s, -) m funnel; (Bomben~) crater.

Trick [trɪk] (-s, -e od -s) m trick; ~film m cartoon.

Trieb (-(e)s, -e) m urge, drive; (Neigung) inclination; (BOT) shoot.

trieb etc [triːp] vb siehe **treiben**.

Trieb- zW: ~feder f (fig) motivating force; t~haft adj impulsive; ~kraft f (fig) drive; ~täter m sex offender; ~wagen m (EISENB) railcar; ~werk nt engine.

triefen ['triːfən] vi to drip.

trifft [trɪft] vb siehe **treffen**.

triftig ['trɪftɪç] adj convincing; (Grund etc) good.

Trigonometrie [trigonome'triː] f trigonometry.

Trikot [tri'koː] (-s, -s) nt vest; (SPORT) shirt ♦ m (Gewebe) tricot.

Triller ['trɪlər] (-s, -) m (MUS) trill.

trillern vi to trill, warble.

Trillerpfeife f whistle.

Trilogie [trilo'giː] f trilogy.

Trimester [tri'mɛstər] (-s, -) nt term.

Trimm-Aktion f keep-fit campaign.

Trimm-dich-Pfad m keep-fit trail.

trimmen vt (Hund) to trim; (umg: Mensch, Tier) to teach, train ♦ vr to keep fit.

trinkbar adj drinkable.

trinken ['trɪŋkən] unreg vt, vi to drink.

Trinker(in) (-s, -) m(f) drinker.

Trink- zW: t~fest adj: ich kann nicht sehr t~fest I can't hold my drink very well; ~geld nt tip; ~halle f (Kiosk) refreshment kiosk; ~halm m (drinking) straw; ~milch f milk; ~spruch m toast; ~wasser nt drinking water.

Trio ['triːo] (-s, -s) nt trio.

trippeln ['trɪpəln] vi to toddle.

Tripper ['trɪpər] (-s, -) m gonorrhoea (BRIT), gonorrhea (US).

trist [trɪst] adj dreary, dismal; (Farbe) dull.

tritt [trɪt] vb siehe **treten**.

Tritt (-(e)s, -e) m step; (Fuß~) kick.

Trittbrett nt (EISENB) step; (AUT) running board.

Trittleiter f stepladder.

Triumph [tri'ʊmf] (-(e)s, -e) m triumph; ~bogen m triumphal arch.

triumphieren [triʊm'fiːrən] vi to triumph; (jubeln) to exult.

trivial [trivi'aːl] adj trivial; T~literatur f light fiction.

trocken ['trɔkən] adj dry; sich ~ rasieren to use an electric razor; T~automat m tumble dryer; T~dock nt dry dock; T~eis nt dry ice;

T~element nt dry cell; T~haube f hairdryer; T~heit f dryness; ~legen vt (Sumpf) to drain; (Kind) to put a clean nappy (BRIT) od diaper (US) on; T~milch f dried milk; T~zeit f (Jahreszeit) dry season.

trocknen vt, vi to dry.

Trockner (-s, -) m dryer.

Troddel ['trɔdəl] (-, -n) f tassel.

Trödel ['trøːdəl] (-s) (umg) m junk; ~markt m flea market.

trödeln (umg) vi to dawdle.

Trödler (-s, -) m secondhand dealer.

Trog (-(e)s, ̈-e) m trough.

trog etc [troːk] vb siehe **trügen**.

trollen ['trɔlən] (umg) vr to push off.

Trommel ['trɔməl] (-, -n) f drum; die ~ rühren (fig: umg) to drum up support; ~fell nt eardrum; ~feuer nt drumfire, heavy barrage.

trommeln vt, vi to drum.

Trommelrevolver m revolver.

Trommelwaschmaschine f tumble-action washing machine.

Trommler(in) ['trɔmlər(ɪn)] (-s, -) m(f) drummer.

Trompete [trɔm'peːtə] (-, -n) f trumpet.

Trompeter (-s, -) m trumpeter.

Tropen ['troːpən] pl tropics pl; t~beständig adj suitable for the tropics; ~helm m topee, sun helmet.

Tropf¹ [trɔpf] (-(e)s, ̈-e) (umg) m rogue; armer ~ poor devil.

Tropf² (-(e)s) (umg) m (MED: Infusion) drip (umg); am ~ hängen to be on a drip.

tröpfeln ['trœpfəln] vi to drip, trickle.

Tropfen (-s, -) m drop; ein guter od edler ~ a good wine; ein ~ auf den heißen Stein (fig: umg) a drop in the ocean.

tropfen vt, vi to drip ♦ vi unpers: es tropft a few raindrops are falling.

tropfenweise adv in drops.

tropfnaß adj dripping wet.

Tropfsteinhöhle f stalactite cave.

Trophäe [tro'fɛːə] (-, -n) f trophy.

tropisch ['troːpɪʃ] adj tropical.

Trost [troːst] (-es) m consolation, comfort; t~bedürftig adj in need of consolation.

trösten ['trøːstən] vt to console, comfort.

Tröster(in) (-s, -) m(f) comfort(er).

tröstlich adj comforting.

trost- zW: ~los adj bleak; (Verhältnisse) wretched; T~pflaster nt (fig) consolation; T~preis m consolation prize; ~reich adj comforting.

Tröstung ['trøːstʊŋ] f comfort, consolation.

Trott [trɔt] (-(e)s, -e) m trot; (Routine) routine.

Trottel (-s, -) (umg) m fool, dope.

trotten vi to trot.

Trottoir [trɔto'aːr] (-s, -s od -e) nt (veraltet) pavement (BRIT), sidewalk (US).

trotz [trɔts] präp (+gen od dat) in spite of.

Trotz (-es) m pig-headedness; etw aus ~ tun

to do sth just to show them; **jdm zum ~ in defiance of sb.**
Trotzalter *nt* obstinate phase.
trotzdem *adv* nevertheless ♦ *konj* although.
trotzen *vi* +*dat* to defy; (*der Kälte, dem Klima etc*) to withstand; (*der Gefahr*) to brave; (*trotzig sein*) to be awkward.
trotzig *adj* defiant; (*Kind*) difficult, awkward.
Trotzkopf *m* obstinate child.
Trotzreaktion *f* fit of pique.
trüb [tryːp] *adj* dull; (*Flüssigkeit, Glas*) cloudy; (*fig*) gloomy; **~e Tasse** (*umg*) drip.
Trubel ['truːbəl] (**-s**) *m* hurly-burly.
trüben ['tryːbən] *vt* to cloud ♦ *vr* to become clouded.
Trübheit *f* dullness; cloudiness; gloom.
Trübsal (**-, -e**) *f* distress; **~ blasen** (*umg*) to mope.
trüb- *zW:* **~selig** *adj* sad, melancholy; **T~sinn** *m* depression; **~sinnig** *adj* depressed, gloomy.
trudeln ['truːdəln] *vi* (*AVIAT*) to (go into a) spin.
Trüffel ['tryfəl] (**-, -n**) *f* truffle.
Trug (**-(e)s**) *m* (*liter*) deception; (*der Sinne*) illusion.
trug *etc* [truːk] *vb siehe* **tragen.**
trügen ['tryːgən] *unreg vt* to deceive ♦ *vi* to be deceptive; **wenn mich nicht alles trügt** unless I am very much mistaken.
trügerisch *adj* deceptive.
Trugschluß ['truːgʃlʊs] *m* false conclusion.
Truhe ['truːə] (**-, -n**) *f* chest.
Trümmer ['trymər] *pl* wreckage *sing*; (*Bau~*) ruins *pl*; **~feld** *nt* expanse of rubble *od* ruins; (*fig*) scene of devastation; **~frauen** *pl* (*German*) *women who cleared away the rubble after the war*; **~haufen** *m* heap of rubble.
Trumpf [trʊmpf] (**-(e)s, ¨e**) *m* (*lit, fig*) trump; **t~en** *vt, vi* to trump.
Trunk [trʊŋk] (**-(e)s, ¨e**) *m* drink.
trunken *adj* intoxicated; **T~bold** (**-(e)s, -e**) *m* drunkard; **T~heit** *f* intoxication; **T~heit am Steuer** drink-driving.
Trunksucht *f* alcoholism.
Trupp [trʊp] (**-s, -s**) *m* troop.
Truppe (**-, -n**) *f* troop; (*Waffengattung*) force; (*Schauspiel~*) troupe; **nicht von der schnellen ~ sein** (*umg*) to be slow.
Truppen *pl* troops *pl*; **~abbau** *m* cutback in troop numbers; **~führer** *m* (military) commander; **~teil** *m* unit; **~übungsplatz** *m* training area.
Trust [trast] (**-(e)s, -e** *od* **-s**) *m* trust.
Truthahn ['truːthaːn] *m* turkey.
Tschad [tʃat] (**-s**) *m*: **der ~** Chad.
Tscheche ['tʃɛçə] (**-n, -n**) *m*, **Tschechin** *f* Czech.
tschechisch *adj* Czech; **die T~e Republik** the Czech Republic.
Tschechoslowakei [tʃɛçoslo'va:'kaɪ] *f*

(*früher*): **die ~** Czechoslovakia.
tschüs [tʃʏs] (*umg*) *interj* cheerio (*BRIT*), so long (*US*).
T-Shirt ['tiːʃəːt] (**-s, -s**) *nt* T-shirt.
TU (**-**) *f abk* (= *Technische Universität*) ≈ polytechnic.
Tuba ['tuːba] (**-, Tuben**) *f* (*MUS*) tuba.
Tube ['tuːbə] (**-, -n**) *f* tube.
Tuberkulose [tubɛrkuˈloːzə] (**-, -n**) *f* tuberculosis.
Tuch [tuːx] (**-(e)s, ¨er**) *nt* cloth; (*Hals~*) scarf; (*Kopf~*) (head)scarf; (*Hand~*) towel; **~fühlung** *f* physical contact.
tüchtig ['tʏçtɪç] *adj* efficient; (*fähig*) able, capable; (*umg: kräftig*) good, sound; **etwas T~es lernen/werden** (*umg*) to get a proper training/job; **T~keit** *f* efficiency; ability.
Tücke ['tʏkə] (**-, -n**) *f* (*Arglist*) malice; (*Trick*) trick; (*Schwierigkeit*) difficulty, problem; **seine ~n haben** to be temperamental.
tückisch *adj* treacherous; (*böswillig*) malicious.
tüfteln ['tʏftəln] (*umg*) *vi* to puzzle; (*basteln*) to fiddle about.
Tugend ['tuːgənt] (**-, -en**) *f* virtue; **t~haft** *adj* virtuous.
Tüll [tʏl] (**-s, -e**) *m* tulle.
Tülle (**-, -n**) *f* spout.
Tulpe ['tʊlpə] (**-, -n**) *f* tulip.
tummeln ['tʊməln] *vr* to romp (about); (*sich beeilen*) to hurry.
Tummelplatz *m* play area; (*fig*) hotbed.
Tumor ['tuːmɔr] (**-s, -e**) *m* tumour (*BRIT*), tumor (*US*).
Tümpel ['tʏmpəl] (**-s, -**) *m* pond.
Tumult [tuˈmʊlt] (**-(e)s, -e**) *m* tumult.
tun [tuːn] *unreg vt* (*machen*) to do; (*legen*) to put ♦ *vi* to act ♦ *vr*: **es tut sich etwas/viel** something/a lot is happening; **jdm etw ~ to** do sth to sb; **etw tut es auch** sth will do; **das tut nichts** that doesn't matter; **das tut nichts zur Sache** that's neither here nor there; **du kannst ~ und lassen, was du willst** you can do as you please; **so ~, als ob** to act as if; **zu ~ haben** (*beschäftigt sein*) to be busy, have things *od* something to do.
Tünche ['tʏnçə] (**-, -n**) *f* whitewash.
tünchen *vt* to whitewash.
Tunesien [tuˈneːziən] (**-s**) *nt* Tunisia.
Tunesier(in) (**-s, -**) *m(f)* Tunisian.
tunesisch *adj* Tunisian.
Tunke ['tʊŋkə] (**-, -n**) *f* sauce.
tunken *vt* to dip, dunk.
tunlichst ['tuːnlɪçst] *adv* if at all possible; **~ bald** as soon as possible.
Tunnel ['tʊnəl] (**-s, -s** *od* **-**) *m* tunnel.
Tunte ['tʊntə] (**-, -n**) (*pej: umg*) *f* fairy (*pej*).
Tüpfel ['tʏpfəl] (**-s, -**) *m* dot; **~chen** *nt* (small) dot.
tüpfeln ['tʏpfəln] *vt* to dab.
tupfen ['tʊpfən] *vt* to dab; (*mit Farbe*) to dot; **T~** (**-s, -**) *m* dot, spot.

Tupfer (-s, -) *m* swab.
Tür [tyːr] (-, -en) *f* door; **an die ~ gehen** to answer the door; **zwischen ~ und Angel** in passing; **Weihnachten steht vor der ~** (*fig*) Christmas is just around the corner; **mit der ~ ins Haus fallen** (*umg*) to blurt it *od* things out; **~angel** *f* (door) hinge.
Turbine [tʊrˈbiːnə] *f* turbine.
turbulent [tʊrbuˈlɛnt] *adj* turbulent.
Türke [ˈtʏrkə] (-n, -n) *m* Turk.
Türkei [tʏrˈkaɪ] *f*: **die ~** Turkey.
Türkin *f* Turk.
Türkis [tʏrˈkiːs] (-es, -e) *m* turquoise; **t~** *adj* turquoise.
türkisch *adj* Turkish.
Türklinke *f* door handle.
Turm [tʊrm] (-(e)s, ⁻e) *m* tower; (*Kirch~*) steeple; (*Sprung~*) diving platform; (*SCHACH*) castle, rook.
türmen [ˈtʏrmən] *vr* to tower up ♦ *vt* to heap up ♦ *vi* (*umg*) to scarper, bolt.
Turmuhr *f* clock (on a tower); (*Kirch~*) church clock.
Turnanzug *m* gym costume.
turnen [ˈtʊrnən] *vi* to do gymnastic exercises; (*herumklettern*) (*Kind*) to romp ♦ *vt* to perform; **T~** (-s) *nt* gymnastics *sing*; (*SCH*) physical education, P.E.
Turner(in) (-s, -) *m(f)* gymnast.
Turnhalle *f* gym(nasium).
Turnhose *f* gym shorts *pl*.
Turnier [tʊrˈniːr] (-s, -e) *nt* tournament.
Turn- *zW*: **~lehrer(in)** *m(f)* gym *od* PE teacher; **~schuh** *m* gym shoe; **~stunde** *f* gym *od* PE lesson.
Turnus [ˈtʊrnʊs] (-, -se) *m* rota; **im ~** in rotation.
Turnverein *m* gymnastics club.
Turnzeug *nt* gym kit.
Türöffner *m* buzzer.
turteln [ˈtʊrtəln] (*umg*) *vi* to bill and coo; (*fig*) to whisper sweet nothings.
Tusch [tʊʃ] (-(e)s, -e) *m* (*MUS*) flourish.
Tusche [ˈtʊʃə] (-, -n) *f* Indian ink.
tuscheln [ˈtʊʃəln] *vt, vi* to whisper.
Tuschkasten *m* paintbox.
Tussi [ˈtʊsɪ] (-, -s) (*umg*) *f* (*Frau, Freundin*) bird (*BRIT*), chick (*US*).
tust [tuːst] *vb siehe* **tun**.
tut [tuːt] *vb siehe* **tun**.
Tüte [ˈtyːtə] (-, -n) *f* bag; **in die ~ blasen** (*umg*) to be breathalyzed; **das kommt nicht in die ~!** (*umg*) no way!
tuten [ˈtuːtən] *vi* (*AUT*) to hoot (*BRIT*), honk (*US*); **von T~ und Blasen keine Ahnung haben** (*umg*) not to have a clue.
TÜV [tʏf] *m abk* (= *Technischer Überwachungs-Verein*) ≈ MOT (*BRIT*); **durch den ~ kommen** (*AUT*) to pass its test *od* MOT (*Brit*).

> The **TÜV** (= *Technischer Überwachungs-Verein*) *is the organization responsible for checking the safety of machinery, particularly vehicles. Cars over three years old have to be examined every two years for their safety and for their exhaust emissions. The TÜV is the German equivalent of the MOT.*

TV (-) *nt abk* (= *Television*) TV ♦ *m abk* = **Turnverein**.
Twen [tvɛn] (-(s), -s) *m* person in his/her twenties.
Typ [tyːp] (-s, -en) *m* type.
Type (-, -n) *f* (*TYP*) type.
Typenrad *nt* (*Drucker*) daisywheel; **~drucker** *m* daisywheel printer.
Typhus [ˈtyːfʊs] (-) *m* typhoid (fever).
typisch [ˈtyːpɪʃ] *adj*: **~ (für)** typical (of).
Tyrann [tyˈran] (-en, -en) *m(f)* tyrant.
Tyrannei [tyraˈnaɪ] *f* tyranny.
Tyrannin *f* tyrant.
tyrannisch *adj* tyrannical.
tyrannisieren [tyraniˈziːrən] *vt* to tyrannize.
tyrrhenisch [tyˈreːnɪʃ] *adj* Tyrrhenian; **T~es Meer** Tyrrhenian Sea.

U, u

U, u [uː] *nt* U, u; **~ wie Ulrich** ≈ U for Uncle.
u. *abk* = **und**.
u.a. *abk* (= *und andere(s)*) and others; (= *unter anderem*) amongst other things.
u.ä. *abk* (= *und ähnliche(s)*) and similar.
u.A.w.g. *abk* (= *um Antwort wird gebeten*) R.S.V.P.
U-Bahn [ˈuːbaːn] *f abk* (= *Untergrundbahn*) underground (*BRIT*), subway (*US*).
übel [ˈyːbəl] *adj* bad; **jdm ist ~** sb feels sick; **Ü~** (-s, -) *nt* evil; (*Krankheit*) disease; **zu allem Ü~ ...** to make matters worse ...; **~gelaunt** *adj attrib* bad-tempered, sullen; **Ü~keit** *f* nausea; **~nehmen** *unreg vt*: **jdm eine Bemerkung** *etc* **~nehmen** to be offended at sb's remark *etc*; **Ü~stand** *m* bad state of affairs; **Ü~täter** *m* wrongdoer; **~wollend** *adj* malevolent.
üben [ˈyːbən] *vt, vi, vr* to practise (*BRIT*), practice (*US*); (*Gedächtnis, Muskeln*) to exercise; **Kritik an etw** *dat* **~** to criticize sth.

SCHLÜSSELWORT

über [ˈyːbər] *präp +dat* **1** (*räumlich*) over, above; **zwei Grad ~ Null** two degrees above zero **2** (*zeitlich*) over; **~ der Arbeit einschlafen** to

fall asleep over one's work
♦ *präp +akk* **1** (*räumlich*) over; (*hoch* ~) above; (*quer* ~) across; **er lachte ~ das ganze Gesicht** he was beaming all over his face; **Macht ~ jdn haben** to have power over sb **2** (*zeitlich*) over; **~ Weihnachten** over Christmas; **~ kurz oder lang** sooner or later **3** (*auf dem Wege*) via; **nach Köln ~ Aachen** to Cologne via Aachen; **ich habe es ~ die Auskunft erfahren** I found out from information **4** (*betreffend*) about; **ein Buch ~ ...** a book about *od* on ...; **~ jdn/etw lachen** to laugh about *od* at sb/sth; **ein Scheck ~ 200 Mark** a cheque for 200 marks **5**: **Fehler ~ Fehler** mistake after mistake ♦ *adv* **1** (*mehr als*) over, more than; **Kinder ~ 12 Jahren** children over *od* above 12 years of age; **sie liebt ihn ~ alles** she loves him more than anything **2**: **~ und ~** over and over; **den ganzen Tag/die ganze Zeit ~** all day long/all the time; **jdm in etw** *dat* **~ sein** to be superior to sb in sth.

überall [yːbər'|al] *adv* everywhere; **~hin** *adv* everywhere.

überaltert [yːbər'|altərt] *adj* obsolete.

Überangebot ['yːbər|angəboːt] *nt*: **~ (an +***dat***)** surplus (of).

überanstrengen [yːbər'|anʃtrɛŋən] *vt untr* to overexert ♦ *vr untr* to overexert o.s.

überantworten [yːbər'|antvɔrtən] *vt untr* to hand over, deliver (up).

überarbeiten [yːbər'|arbaɪtən] *vt untr* to revise, rework ♦ *vr untr* to overwork (o.s.).

überaus ['yːbər|aʊs] *adv* exceedingly.

überbacken [yːbər'bakən] *unreg vt untr* to put in the oven/under the grill.

Überbau ['yːbərbaʊ] *m* (*Gebäude, Philosophie*) superstructure.

überbeanspruchen ['yːbərbə|anʃpruxən] *vt untr* (*Menschen, Körper, Maschine*) to overtax.

überbelichten ['yːbərbəlɪçtən] *vt untr* (*PHOT*) to overexpose.

Überbesetzung ['yːbərbəzɛtsʊŋ] *f* overmanning.

überbewerten ['yːbərbəveːrtən] *vt untr* (*fig*) to overrate; (*Äußerungen*) to attach too much importance to.

überbieten [yːbər'biːtən] *unreg vt untr* to outbid; (*übertreffen*) to surpass; (*Rekord*) to break ♦ *vr untr*: **sich in etw** *dat* **(gegenseitig) ~** to vie with each other in sth.

Überbleibsel ['yːbərblaɪpsəl] (**-s, -**) *nt* residue, remainder.

Überblick ['yːbərblɪk] *m* view; (*fig: Darstellung*) survey, overview; (*Fähigkeit*): **~ (über +***akk***)** overall view (of), grasp (of); **den ~ verlieren** to lose track (of things); **sich** *dat* **einen ~ verschaffen** to get a general idea.

überblicken [yːbər'blɪkən] *vt untr* to survey;

(*fig*) to see; (: *Lage etc*) to grasp.

überbringen [yːbər'brɪŋən] *unreg vt untr* to deliver, hand over.

Überbringer (**-s, -**) *m* bearer.

Überbringung *f* delivery.

überbrücken [yːbər'brʏkən] *vt untr* to bridge.

Überbrückung *f*: **100 Mark zur ~** 100 marks to tide me/him *etc* over.

Überbrückungskredit *m* bridging loan.

überbuchen ['yːbərbuːxən] *vt* to overbook.

überdauern [yːbər'daʊərn] *vt untr* to outlast.

überdenken [yːbər'dɛŋkən] *unreg vt untr* to think over.

überdies [yːbər'diːs] *adv* besides.

überdimensional ['yːbərdimɛnzionaːl] *adj* oversize.

Überdosis ['yːbərdoːzɪs] *f* overdose, OD (*umg*); (*zu große Zumessung*) excessive amount.

überdrehen [yːbər'dreːən] *vt untr* (*Uhr etc*) to overwind.

überdreht *adj*: **~ sein** (*fig*) to be hyped up, be overexcited.

Überdruck ['yːbərdrʊk] *m* (*TECH*) excess pressure.

Überdruß ['yːbərdrʊs] (**-sses**) *m* weariness; **bis zum ~** ad nauseam.

überdrüssig ['yːbərdrʏsɪç] *adj +gen* tired of, sick of.

überdurchschnittlich ['yːbərdʊrçʃnɪtlɪç] *adj* above-average ♦ *adv* exceptionally.

übereifrig ['yːbər|aɪfrɪç] *adj* overzealous.

übereignen [yːbər'|aɪgnən] *vt untr*: **jdm etw ~** (*geh*) to make sth over to sb.

übereilen [yːbər'|aɪlən] *vt untr* to hurry.

übereilt *adj* (over)hasty.

übereinander [yːbər|aɪ'nandər] *adv* one upon the other; (*sprechen*) about each other; **~schlagen** *unreg vt* (*Arme*) to fold; (*Beine*) to cross.

übereinkommen [yːbər'|aɪnkɔmən] *unreg vi* to agree.

Übereinkunft [yːbər'|aɪnkʊnft] (**-, -künfte**) *f* agreement.

übereinstimmen [yːbər'|aɪnʃtɪmən] *vi* to agree; (*Angaben, Meßwerte etc*) to tally; (*mit Tatsachen*) to fit.

Übereinstimmung *f* agreement.

überempfindlich ['yːbər|ɛmpfɪntlɪç] *adj* hypersensitive.

überfahren¹ ['yːbərfaːrən] *unreg vt* to take across ♦ *vi* to cross, go across.

überfahren² [yːbər'faːrən] *unreg vt untr* (*AUT*) to run over; (*fig*) to walk all over.

Überfahrt ['yːbərfaːrt] *f* crossing.

Überfall ['yːbərfal] *m* (*Bank~, MIL*) raid; (*auf jdn*) assault.

überfallen [yːbər'falən] *unreg vt untr* to attack; (*Bank*) to raid; (*besuchen*) to drop in on, descend (up)on.

überfällig ['yːbərfɛlɪç] *adj* overdue.

Überfallkommando *nt* flying squad.

überfliegen [y:bər'fli:gən] *unreg vt untr* to fly over, overfly; (*Buch*) to skim through.

Überflieger *m* (*fig*) high-flier.

überflügeln [y:bər'fly:gəln] *vt untr* to outdo.

Überfluß ['y:bərflus] *m:* ~ (**an** +*dat*) (super)abundance (of), excess (of); **zu allem** *od* **zum** ~ (*unnötigerweise*) superfluously; (*obendrein*) to crown it all (*umg*); ~**gesellschaft** *f* affluent society.

überflüssig ['y:bərflysıç] *adj* superfluous.

überfluten [y:bər'flu:tən] *vt untr* (*lit*) to flood; (*fig*) to flood, inundate.

überfordern [y:bər'fɔrdərn] *vt untr* to demand too much of; (*Kräfte etc*) to overtax.

überfragt [y:bər'fra:kt] *adj:* **da bin ich** ~ there you've got me, you've got me there.

überführen[1] ['y:bərfy:rən] *vt* to transfer; (*Leiche etc*) to transport.

überführen[2] [y:bər'fy:rən] *vt untr* (*Täter*) to have convicted.

Überführung *f* (*siehe vbs*) transfer; transport; conviction; (*Brücke*) bridge, overpass.

überfüllt [y:bər'fylt] *adj* overcrowded; (*Kurs*) oversubscribed.

Übergabe ['y:bərga:bə] *f* handing over; (*MIL*) surrender.

Übergang ['y:bərgaŋ] *m* crossing; (*Wandel, Überleitung*) transition.

Übergangs- *zW:* ~**erscheinung** *f* transitory phenomenon; ~**finanzierung** *f* (*FIN*) accommodation; **ü**~**los** *adj* without a transition; ~**lösung** *f* provisional solution, stopgap; ~**stadium** *nt* state of transition; ~**zeit** *f* transitional period.

übergeben [y:bər'ge:bən] *unreg vt untr* to hand over; (*MIL*) to surrender ♦ *vr untr* to be sick; **dem Verkehr** ~ to open to traffic.

übergehen[1] ['y:bərge:ən] *unreg vi* (*Besitz*) to pass; (*zum Feind etc*) to go over, defect; (*überwechseln*): (**zu etw**) ~ to go on (to sth); ~ **in** +*akk* to turn into.

übergehen[2] [y:bər'ge:ən] *unreg vt untr* to pass over, omit.

übergeordnet ['y:bərgə|ɔrdnət] *adj* (*Behörde*) higher.

Übergepäck ['y:bərgəpɛk] *nt* excess baggage.

übergeschnappt ['y:bərgəʃnapt] (*umg*) *adj* crazy.

Übergewicht ['y:bərgəvɪçt] *nt* excess weight; (*fig*) preponderance.

übergießen [y:bər'gi:sən] *unreg vt untr* to pour over; (*Braten*) to baste.

überglücklich ['y:bərglyklıç] *adj* overjoyed.

übergreifen ['y:bərgraıfən] *unreg vi:* ~ **(auf** +*akk*) (*auf Rechte etc*) to encroach (on); (*Feuer, Streik, Krankheit etc*) to spread (to); **ineinander** ~ to overlap.

übergroß ['y:bərgro:s] *adj* outsize, huge.

Übergröße ['y:bərgrø:sə] *f* oversize.

überhaben ['y:bərha:bən] *unreg* (*umg*) *vt* to be fed up with.

überhandnehmen [y:bər'hantne:mən] *unreg vi* to gain the ascendancy.

überhängen ['y:bərhɛŋən] *unreg vi* to overhang.

überhäufen [y:bər'hɔyfən] *vt untr:* **jdn mit Geschenken/Vorwürfen** ~ to heap presents/reproaches on sb.

überhaupt [y:bər'haupt] *adv* at all; (*im allgemeinen*) in general; (*besonders*) especially; ~ **nicht** not at all; **wer sind Sie** ~? who do you think you are?

überheblich [y:bər'he:plıç] *adj* arrogant; **Ü**~**keit** *f* arrogance.

überhöht [y:bər'hø:t] *adj* (*Forderungen, Preise*) exorbitant, excessive.

überholen [y:bər'ho:lən] *vt untr* to overtake; (*TECH*) to overhaul.

Überholspur *f* overtaking lane.

überholt *adj* out-of-date, obsolete.

Überholverbot [y:bər'ho:lfɛrbo:t] *nt* overtaking (*BRIT*) *od* passing ban.

überhören [y:bər'hø:rən] *vt untr* to not hear; (*absichtlich*) to ignore; **das möchte ich überhört haben!** (I'll pretend) I didn't hear that!

Über-Ich ['y:bər|ıç] (**-s**) *nt* superego.

überirdisch ['y:bər|ırdıʃ] *adj* supernatural, unearthly.

überkapitalisieren ['y:bərkapitali'zi:rən] *vt untr* to overcapitalize.

überkochen ['y:bərkɔxən] *vi* to boil over.

überkompensieren ['y:bərkɔmpɛnzi:rən] *vt untr* to overcompensate for.

überladen [y:bər'la:dən] *unreg vt untr* to overload ♦ *adj* (*fig*) cluttered.

überlassen [y:bər'lasən] *unreg vt untr:* **jdm etw** ~ to leave sth to sb ♦ *vr untr:* **sich einer Sache** *dat* ~ to give o.s. over to sth; **das bleibt Ihnen** ~ that's up to you; **jdn sich** *dat* **selbst** ~ to leave sb to his/her own devices.

überlasten [y:bər'lastən] *vt untr* to overload; (*jdn*) to overtax.

überlaufen[1] ['y:bərlaufən] *unreg vi* (*Flüssigkeit*) to flow over; (*zum Feind etc*) to go over, defect.

überlaufen[2] [y:bər'laufən] *unreg vt untr* (*Schauer etc*) to come over ♦ *adj* overcrowded; ~ **sein** to be inundated *od* besieged.

Überläufer ['y:bərlɔyfər] *m* deserter.

überleben [y:bər'le:bən] *vt untr* to survive.

Überlebende(r) *f(m)* survivor.

überlebensgroß *adj* larger-than-life.

überlegen [y:bər'le:gən] *vt untr* to consider ♦ *adj* superior; **ich habe es mir anders** *od* **noch einmal überlegt** I've changed my mind; **Ü**~**heit** *f* superiority.

Überlegung *f* consideration, deliberation.

überleiten ['y:bərlaıtən] *vt* (*Abschnitt etc*): ~ **in** +*akk* to link up with.

überlesen [y:bər'le:zən] *unreg vt untr* (*übersehen*) to overlook, miss.

überliefern [yːbər'liːfərn] vt untr to hand down, transmit.

Überlieferung f tradition; **schriftliche ~en** (written) records.

überlisten [yːbər'lɪstən] vt untr to outwit.

überm ['yːbərm] = **über dem**.

Übermacht ['yːbərmaxt] f superior force, superiority.

übermächtig ['yːbərmɛçtɪç] adj superior (in strength); (Gefühl etc) overwhelming.

übermannen [yːbər'manən] vt untr to overcome.

Übermaß ['yːbərmaːs] nt: ~ **(an** +dat) excess (of).

übermäßig ['yːbərmɛːsɪç] adj excessive.

Übermensch ['yːbərmɛnʃ] m superman; **ü~lich** adj superhuman.

übermitteln [yːbər'mɪtəln] vt untr to convey.

übermorgen ['yːbərmɔrgən] adv the day after tomorrow.

Übermüdung [yːbər'myːdʊŋ] f overtiredness.

Übermut ['yːbərmuːt] m exuberance.

übermütig ['yːbərmyːtɪç] adj exuberant, high-spirited; ~ **werden** to get overconfident.

übernächste(r, s) ['yːbərnɛːçstə(r, s)] adj next ... but one; (Woche, Jahr etc) after next.

übernachten [yːbər'naxtən] vi untr: **(bei jdm)** ~ to spend the night (at sb's place).

übernächtigt [yːbər'nɛçtɪçt] adj sleepy, tired.

Übernachtung f: ~ **mit Frühstück** bed and breakfast.

Übernahme ['yːbərnaːmə] (-, -n) f taking over od on; (von Verantwortung) acceptance; ~**angebot** nt takeover bid.

übernatürlich ['yːbərnatyːrlɪç] adj supernatural.

übernehmen [yːbər'neːmən] unreg vt untr to take on, accept; (Amt, Geschäft) to take over ♦ vr untr to take on too much; (sich überanstrengen) to overdo it.

überparteilich ['yːbərpartaɪlɪç] adj (Zeitung) independent; (Amt, Präsident etc) above party politics.

überprüfen [yːbər'pryːfən] vt untr to examine, check; (POL: jdn) to screen.

Überprüfung f examination.

überqueren [yːbər'kveːrən] vt untr to cross.

überragen [yːbər'raːgən] vt untr to tower above; (fig) to surpass.

überragend adj outstanding; (Bedeutung) paramount.

überraschen [yːbər'raʃən] vt untr to surprise.

Überraschung f surprise.

überreden [yːbər'reːdən] vt untr to persuade; **jdn zu etw** ~ to talk sb into sth.

Überredungskunst f powers pl of persuasion.

überregional ['yːbərregioinaːl] adj national; (Zeitung, Sender) nationwide.

überreichen [yːbər'raɪçən] vt untr to hand over; (feierlich) to present.

überreichlich adj (more than) ample.

überreizt [yːbər'raɪtst] adj overwrought.

Überreste ['yːbərrɛstə] pl remains pl, remnants pl.

überrumpeln [yːbər'rʊmpəln] vt untr to take by surprise; (umg: überwältigen) to overpower.

überrunden [yːbər'rʊndən] vt untr (SPORT) to lap.

übers ['yːbərs] = **über das**.

übersättigen [yːbər'zɛtɪgən] vt untr to satiate.

Überschall- ['yːbərʃal] in zW supersonic; ~**flugzeug** nt supersonic jet; ~**geschwindigkeit** f supersonic speed.

überschatten [yːbər'ʃatən] vt untr to overshadow.

überschätzen [yːbər'ʃɛtsən] vt untr, vr untr to overestimate.

überschaubar [yːbər'ʃaʊbaːr] adj (Plan) easily comprehensible, clear.

überschäumen ['yːbərʃɔʏmən] vi to froth over; (fig) to bubble over.

überschlafen [yːbər'ʃlaːfən] unreg vt untr (Problem) to sleep on.

Überschlag ['yːbərʃlaːk] m (FIN) estimate; (SPORT) somersault.

überschlagen¹ [yːbər'ʃlaːgən] unreg vt untr (berechnen) to estimate; (auslassen: Seite) to omit ♦ vr untr to somersault; (Stimme) to crack; (AVIAT) to loop the loop ♦ adj lukewarm, tepid.

überschlagen² ['yːbərʃlaːgən] unreg vt (Beine) to cross; (Arme) to fold ♦ vi (Hilfsverb sein: Wellen) to break; (: Funken) to flash over; **in etw** akk ~ (Stimmung etc) to turn into sth.

überschnappen ['yːbərʃnapən] vi (Stimme) to crack; (umg: Mensch) to flip one's lid.

überschneiden [yːbər'ʃnaɪdən] unreg vr untr (lit, fig) to overlap; (Linien) to intersect.

überschreiben [yːbər'ʃraɪbən] unreg vt untr to provide with a heading; (COMPUT) to overwrite; **jdm etw** ~ to transfer od make over sth to sb.

überschreiten [yːbər'ʃraɪtən] unreg vt untr to cross over; (fig) to exceed; (verletzen) to transgress.

Überschrift ['yːbərʃrɪft] f heading, title.

überschuldet [yːbər'ʃʊldət] adj heavily in debt; (Grundstück) heavily mortgaged.

Überschuß ['yːbərʃʊs] m: ~ **(an** +dat) surplus (of).

überschüssig ['yːbərʃʏsɪç] adj surplus, excess.

überschütten [yːbər'ʃʏtən] vt untr: **jdn/etw mit etw** ~ (lit) to pour sth over sb/sth; **jdn mit etw** ~ (fig) to shower sb with sth.

Überschwang ['yːbərʃvaŋ] m exuberance.

überschwappen ['yːbərʃvapən] vi to splash over.

überschwemmen [yːbər'ʃvɛmən] vt untr to flood.

Überschwemmung f flood.

überschwenglich ['y:bərʃvɛŋlɪç] adj effusive; Ü~keit f effusion.

Übersee ['y:bərze:] f: nach/in ~ overseas.

überseeisch adj overseas.

übersehbar [y:bər'ze:ba:r] adj (fig: Folgen, Zusammenhänge etc) clear; (Kosten, Dauer etc) assessable.

übersehen [y:bər'ze:ən] unreg vt untr to look (out) over; (fig: Folgen) to see, get an overall view of; (: nicht beachten) to overlook.

übersenden [y:bər'zɛndən] unreg vt untr to send, forward.

übersetzen¹ [y:bər'zɛtsən] vt untr, vi untr to translate.

übersetzen² ['y:bərzɛtsən] vi (Hilfsverb sein) to cross.

Übersetzer(in) [y:bər'zɛtsər(ın)] (-s, -) m(f) translator.

Übersetzung [y:bər'zɛtsʊŋ] f translation; (TECH) gear ratio.

Übersicht ['y:bərzɪçt] f overall view; (Darstellung) survey; die ~ verlieren to lose track; ü~lich adj clear; (Gelände) open; ~lichkeit f clarity, lucidity.

übersiedeln¹ ['y:bərzi:dəln] vi to move.

übersiedeln² [y:bər'zi:dəln] vi untr to move.

überspannen [y:bər'ʃpanən] vt untr (zu sehr spannen) to overstretch; (überdecken) to cover.

überspannt adj eccentric; (Idee) wild, crazy; Ü~heit f eccentricity.

überspielen [y:bər'ʃpi:lən] vt untr (verbergen) to cover (up); (übertragen: Aufnahme) to transfer.

überspitzt [y:bər'ʃpɪtst] adj exaggerated.

überspringen [y:bər'ʃprɪŋən] unreg vt untr to jump over; (fig) to skip.

übersprudeln ['y:bərʃpru:dəln] vi to bubble over.

überstehen¹ [y:bər'ʃte:ən] unreg vt untr to overcome, get over; (Winter etc) to survive, get through.

überstehen² ['y:bərʃte:ən] unreg vi to project.

übersteigen [y:bər'ʃtaɪgən] unreg vt untr to climb over; (fig) to exceed.

übersteigert [y:bər'ʃtaɪgərt] adj excessive.

überstimmen [y:bər'ʃtɪmən] vt untr to outvote.

überstrapazieren ['y:bərʃtrapatsi:rən] vt untr to wear out ♦ vr to wear o.s. out.

überstreifen ['y:bərʃtraɪfən] vt: (sich dat) etw ~ to slip sth on.

überströmen¹ [y:bər'ʃtrø:mən] vt untr: von Blut überströmt sein to be streaming with blood.

überströmen² ['y:bərʃtrø:mən] vi (lit, fig): ~ (vor +dat) to overflow (with).

Überstunden ['y:bərʃtʊndən] pl overtime sing.

überstürzen [y:bər'ʃtʏrtsən] vt untr to rush ♦ vr untr to follow (one another) in rapid succession.

überstürzt adj (over)hasty.

übertariflich ['y:bərtarifliç] adj, adv above the agreed od union rate.

übertölpen [y:bər'tœlpən] vt untr to dupe.

übertönen [y:bər'tø:nən] vt untr to drown (out).

Übertrag ['y:bərtra:k] (-(e)s, -träge) m (COMM) amount brought forward.

übertragbar [y:bər'tra:kba:r] adj transferable; (MED) infectious.

übertragen [y:bər'tra:gən] unreg vt untr to transfer; (RUNDF) to broadcast; (anwenden: Methode) to apply; (übersetzen) to render; (Krankheit) to transmit ♦ vr untr to spread ♦ adj figurative; ~ auf +akk to transfer to; to apply to; sich ~ auf +akk to spread to; jdm etw ~ to assign sth to sb; (Verantwortung etc) to give sb sth od sth to sb.

Übertragung f (siehe vb) transference; broadcast; rendering; transmission.

übertreffen [y:bər'trɛfən] unreg vt untr to surpass.

übertreiben [y:bər'traɪbən] unreg vt untr to exaggerate; man kann es auch ~ you can overdo things.

Übertreibung f exaggeration.

übertreten¹ [y:bər'tre:tən] unreg vt untr to cross; (Gebot etc) to break.

übertreten² ['y:bərtre:tən] unreg vi (über Linie, Gebiet) to step (over); (SPORT) to overstep; (zu anderem Glauben) to be converted; ~ (in +akk) (POL) to go over (to).

Übertretung [y:bər'tre:tʊŋ] f violation, transgression.

übertrieben [y:bər'tri:bən] adj exaggerated, excessive.

Übertritt ['y:bərtrɪt] m (zu anderem Glauben) conversion; (bes zu anderer Partei) defection.

übertrumpfen [y:bər'trʊmpfən] vt untr to outdo; (KARTEN) to overtrump.

übertünchen [y:bər'tʏnçən] vt untr to whitewash; (fig) to cover up, whitewash.

übervölkert [y:bər'fœlkərt] adj overpopulated.

übervoll ['y:bərfɔl] adj overfull.

übervorteilen [y:bər'fɔrtaɪlən] vt untr to dupe, cheat.

überwachen [y:bər'vaxən] vt untr to supervise; (Verdächtigen) to keep under surveillance.

Überwachung f supervision; surveillance.

überwältigen [y:bər'vɛltɪgən] vt untr to overpower.

überwältigend adj overwhelming.

überwechseln ['y:bərvɛksəln] vi: ~ (in +akk) to move (to); (zu Partei etc): ~ (zu) to go over (to).

überweisen [y:bər'vaɪzən] unreg vt untr to transfer; (Patienten) to refer.

Überweisung f transfer; (von Patient) referral.

überwerfen¹ ['y:bərvɛrfən] unreg vt (Kleidungsstück) to put on; (sehr rasch) to throw on.

überwerfen² [y:bər'vɛrfən] unreg vr untr: sich

(mit jdm) ~ to fall out (with sb).
überwiegen [y:bər'vi:gən] *unreg vi untr* to predominate.
überwiegend *adj* predominant.
überwinden [y:bər'vɪndən] *unreg vt untr* to overcome ♦ *vr untr:* **sich ~, etw zu tun to** make an effort to do sth, bring o.s. to do sth.
Überwindung *f* overcoming; (*Selbst ~*) effort of will.
überwintern [y:bər'vɪntərn] *vi untr* to (spend the) winter; (*umg: Winterschlaf halten*) to hibernate.
Überwurf ['y:bərvʊrf] *m* wrap.
Überzahl ['y:bərtsa:l] *f* superior numbers *pl*, superiority; **in der ~ sein** to be numerically superior.
überzählig ['y:bərtsɛ:lɪç] *adj* surplus.
überzeugen [y:bər'tsɔygən] *vt untr* to convince.
überzeugend *adj* convincing.
überzeugt *adj attrib* (*Anhänger etc*) dedicated; (*Vegetarier*) strict; (*Christ, Moslem*) devout.
Überzeugung *f* conviction; **zu der ~ gelangen, daß ...** to become convinced that ...
Überzeugungskraft *f* power of persuasion.
überziehen¹ ['y:bərtsi:ən] *unreg vt* to put on.
überziehen² [y:bər'tsi:ən] *unreg vt untr* to cover; (*Konto*) to overdraw; (*Redezeit etc*) to overrun ♦ *vr untr* (*Himmel*) to cloud over; **ein Bett frisch ~** to change a bed, change the sheets (on a bed).
Überziehungskredit *m* overdraft.
überzüchten [y:bər'tsʏçtən] *vt untr* to overbreed.
Überzug ['y:bərtsu:k] *m* cover; (*Belag*) coating.
üblich ['y:plɪç] *adj* usual; **allgemein ~ sein** to be common practice.
U-Boot ['u:bo:t] *nt* U-boat, submarine.
übrig ['y:brɪç] *adj* remaining; **für jdn etwas ~ haben** (*umg*) to be fond of sb; **die ~en** the others; **das ~e** the rest; **im ~en** besides; **~bleiben** *unreg vi* to remain, be left (over).
übrigens ['y:brɪgəns] *adv* besides; (*nebenbei bemerkt*) by the way.
übriglassen ['y:brɪglasən] *unreg vt* to leave (over); **einiges/viel zu wünschen ~** (*umg*) to leave something/a lot to be desired.
Übung ['y:bʊŋ] *f* practice; (*Turn~, Aufgabe etc*) exercise; **~ macht den Meister** (*Sprichwort*) practice makes perfect.
Übungsarbeit *f* (*SCH*) mock test.
Übungsplatz *m* training ground; (*MIL*) drill ground.
u.d.M. *abk* (= *unter dem Meeresspiegel*) below sea level.
ü.d.M. *abk* (= *über dem Meeresspiegel*) above sea level.
u.E. *abk* (= *unseres Erachtens*) in our opinion.
Ufer ['u:fər] (*-s, -*) *nt* bank; (*Meeres~*) shore; **~befestigung** *f* embankment; **u~los** *adj*

endless; (*grenzenlos*) boundless; **ins u~lose gehen** (*Kosten*) to go up and up; (*Debatte etc*) to go on forever.
UFO, Ufo ['u:fo] (*-(s), -s*) *nt abk* (= *unbekanntes Flugobjekt*) UFO, ufo.
Uganda [u'ganda] (*-s*) *nt* Uganda.
Ugander(in) (*-s, -*) *m(f)* Ugandan.
ugandisch *adj* Ugandan.
U-Haft ['u:haft] *f abk* = **Untersuchungshaft**.
Uhr [u:r] (*-, -en*) *f* clock; (*Armband~*) watch; **wieviel ~ ist es?** what time is it?; **um wieviel ~?** at what time?; **1 ~** 1 o'clock; **20 ~** 8 o'clock, 20.00 (twenty hundred) hours; **~band** *nt* watchstrap; **~(en)gehäuse** *nt* clock case; watch case; **~kette** *f* watch chain; **~macher** *m* watchmaker; **~werk** *nt* (*auch fig*) clockwork mechanism; **~zeiger** *m* hand; **~zeigersinn** *m:* **im ~zeigersinn** clockwise; **entgegen dem ~zeigersinn** anticlockwise; **~zeit** *f* time (of day).
Uhu ['u:hu] (*-s, -s*) *m* eagle owl.
Ukraine [ukra'i:nə] *f* Ukraine.
Ukrainer(in) [ukra'i:nər(ɪn)] (*-s, -*) *m(f)* Ukrainian.
ukrainisch *adj* Ukrainian.
UKW *abk* (= *Ultrakurzwelle*) VHF.
Ulk [ʊlk] (*-s, -e*) *m* lark.
ulkig ['ʊlkɪç] *adj* funny.
Ulme ['ʊlmə] (*-, -n*) *f* elm.
Ulster ['ʊlstər] (*-s*) *nt* Ulster.
Ultimatum [ulti'ma:tʊm] (*-s, Ultimaten*) *nt* ultimatum; **jdm ein ~ stellen** to give sb an ultimatum.
Ultra- *zW:* **~kurzwelle** *f* very high frequency; **~leichtflugzeug** *nt* microlight; **~schall** *m* (*PHYS*) ultrasound; **u~violett** *adj* ultraviolet.

══════ *SCHLÜSSELWORT*

um [ʊm] *präp +akk* **1** (*~ herum*) (a)round; **~ Weihnachten** around Christmas; **er schlug ~ sich** he hit about him
2 (*mit Zeitangabe*) at; **~ acht (Uhr)** at eight (o'clock)
3 (*mit Größenangabe*) by; **etw ~ 4 cm kürzen** to shorten sth by 4 cm; **~ 10% teurer** 10% more expensive; **~ vieles besser** better by far; **~ nichts besser** not in the least bit better; **~ so besser** so much the better; **~ so mehr, als ...** all the more considering ...
4: der Kampf ~ den Titel the battle for the title; **~ Geld spielen** to play for money; **es geht ~ das Prinzip** it's a question of principle; **Stunde ~ Stunde** hour after hour; **Auge ~ Auge** an eye for an eye
♦ *präp +gen:* **~ ... willen** for the sake of ...; **~ Gottes willen** for goodness *od* (*stärker*) God's sake
♦ *konj:* **~ ... zu** (in order) to ...; **zu klug, ~ zu ...** too clever to ...; **~ so besser/schlimmer** so much the better/worse
♦ *adv* **1** (*ungefähr*) about; **~ (die) 30 Leute** about *od* around 30 people

2 (*vorbei*): **die zwei Stunden sind** ~ the two hours are up.

umadressieren ['ʊm|adrɛsiːrən] *vt untr* to readdress.

umändern ['ʊm|ɛndərn] *vt* to alter.

Umänderung *f* alteration.

umarbeiten ['ʊm|arbaɪtən] *vt* to remodel; (*Buch etc*) to revise, rework.

umarmen [ʊm'|armən] *vt untr* to embrace.

Umbau ['ʊmbaʊ] (**-(e)s, -e** *od* **-ten**) *m* reconstruction, alteration(s *pl*).

umbauen ['ʊmbaʊən] *vt* to rebuild, reconstruct.

umbenennen ['ʊmbənɛnən] *unreg vt untr* to rename.

umbesetzen ['ʊmbəzɛtsən] *vt untr* (*THEAT*) to recast; (*Mannschaft*) to change; (*Posten, Stelle*) to find someone else for.

umbiegen ['ʊmbiːgən] *unreg vt* to bend (over).

umbilden ['ʊmbɪldən] *vt* to reorganize; (*POL: Kabinett*) to reshuffle.

umbinden[1] ['ʊmbɪndən] *unreg vt* (*Krawatte etc*) to put on.

umbinden[2] [ʊm'bɪndən] *unreg vt untr*: **etw mit etw** ~ to tie sth round sth.

umblättern ['ʊmblɛtərn] *vt* to turn over.

umblicken ['ʊmblɪkən] *vr* to look around.

umbringen ['ʊmbrɪŋən] *unreg vt* to kill.

Umbruch ['ʊmbrʊx] *m* radical change; (*TYP*) make-up (into page).

umbuchen ['ʊmbuːxən] *vi* to change one's reservation *od* flight *etc* ♦ *vt* to change.

umdenken ['ʊmdɛŋkən] *unreg vi* to adjust one's views.

umdisponieren ['ʊmdɪsponiːrən] *vi untr* to change one's plans.

umdrängen [ʊm'drɛŋən] *vt untr* to crowd round.

umdrehen ['ʊmdreːən] *vt* to turn (round); (*Hals*) to wring ♦ *vr* to turn (round); **jdm den Arm** ~ to twist sb's arm.

Umdrehung *f* turn; (*PHYS*) revolution, rotation.

umeinander [ʊm|aɪ'nandər] *adv* round one another; (*füreinander*) for one another.

umerziehen ['ʊm|ɛrtsiːən] *unreg vt* (*POL: euph*): **jdn (zu etw)** ~ to re-educate sb (to become sth).

umfahren[1] ['ʊmfaːrən] *unreg vt* to run over.

umfahren[2] [ʊm'faːrən] *unreg vt untr* to drive round; (*die Welt*) to sail round.

umfallen ['ʊmfalən] *unreg vi* to fall down *od* over; (*fig: umg: nachgeben*) to give in.

Umfang ['ʊmfaŋ] *m* extent; (*von Buch*) size; (*Reichweite*) range; (*Fläche*) area; (*MATH*) circumference; **in großem** ~ on a large scale; **u~reich** *adj* extensive; (*Buch etc*) voluminous.

umfassen [ʊm'fasən] *vt untr* to embrace; (*umgeben*) to surround; (*enthalten*) to include.

umfassend *adj* comprehensive; (*umfangreich*) extensive.

Umfeld ['ʊmfɛlt] *nt*: **zum** ~ **von etw gehören** to be associated with sth.

umformatieren ['ʊmfɔrmatiːrən] *vt untr* (*COMPUT*) to reformat.

umformen ['ʊmfɔrmən] *vi* to transform.

Umformer (**-s, -**) *m* (*ELEK*) converter.

umformulieren ['ʊmfɔrmuliːrən] *vt untr* to redraft.

Umfrage ['ʊmfraːgə] *f* poll; ~ **halten** to ask around.

umfüllen ['ʊmfʏlən] *vt* to transfer; (*Wein*) to decant.

umfunktionieren ['ʊmfʊŋktsioniːrən] *vt untr* to convert.

umg *abk* (= *umgangssprachlich*) colloquial.

Umgang ['ʊmgaŋ] *m* company; (*mit jdm*) dealings *pl*; (*Behandlung*) dealing.

umgänglich ['ʊmgɛŋlɪç] *adj* sociable.

Umgangs- *zW*: ~**formen** *pl* manners *pl*; ~**sprache** *f* colloquial language; **u~sprachlich** *adj* colloquial.

umgeben [ʊm'geːbən] *unreg vt untr* to surround.

Umgebung *f* surroundings *pl*; (*Milieu*) environment; (*Personen*) people in one's circle; **in der näheren/weiteren** ~ **Münchens** on the outskirts/in the environs of Munich.

umgehen[1] ['ʊmgeːən] *unreg vi* to go (a)round; **im Schlosse** ~ to haunt the castle; **mit jdm/ etw** ~ **können** to know how to handle sb/sth; **mit jdm grob** *etc* ~ to treat sb roughly *etc*; **mit Geld sparsam** ~ to be careful with one's money.

umgehen[2] [ʊm'geːən] *unreg vt untr* to bypass; (*MIL*) to outflank; (*Gesetz, Vorschrift etc*) to circumvent; (*vermeiden*) to avoid.

umgehend *adj* immediate.

Umgehung *f* (*siehe vb*) bypassing; outflanking; circumvention; avoidance.

Umgehungsstraße *f* bypass.

umgekehrt ['ʊmgəkeːrt] *adj* reverse(d); (*gegenteilig*) opposite ♦ *adv* the other way around; **und** ~ and vice versa.

umgestalten ['ʊmgəʃtaltən] *vt untr* to alter; (*reorganisieren*) to reorganize; (*umordnen*) to rearrange.

umgewöhnen ['ʊmgəvøːnən] *vr* to readapt.

umgraben ['ʊmgraːbən] *unreg vt* to dig up.

umgruppieren ['ʊmgrʊpiːrən] *vt untr* to regroup.

Umhang ['ʊmhaŋ] *m* wrap, cape.

umhängen ['ʊmhɛŋən] *vt* (*Bild*) to hang somewhere else; **jdm etw** ~ to put sth on sb.

Umhängetasche *f* shoulder bag.

umhauen ['ʊmhaʊən] *vt* to fell; (*fig*) to bowl over.

umher [ʊm'heːr] *adv* about, around; ~**gehen** *unreg vi* to walk about; ~**irren** *vi* to wander around; (*Blick, Augen*) to roam about; ~**reisen** *vi* to travel about; ~**schweifen** *vi* to roam about; **~ziehen** *unreg vi* to wander from place to place.

umhinkönnen [ʊm'hɪnkœnən] *unreg vi:* **ich kann nicht umhin, das zu tun** I can't help doing it.

umhören ['ʊmhøːrən] *vr* to ask around.

umkämpfen [ʊm'kɛmpfən] *vt untr* (*Entscheidung*) to dispute; (*Wahlkreis, Sieg*) to contest.

Umkehr ['ʊmkeːr] (-) *f* turning back; (*Änderung*) change.

umkehren *vi* to turn back; (*fig*) to change one's ways ♦ *vt* to turn round, reverse; (*Tasche etc*) to turn inside out; (*Gefäß etc*) to turn upside down.

umkippen ['ʊmkɪpən] *vt* to tip over ♦ *vi* to overturn; (*umg: ohnmächtig werden*) to keel over; (*fig: Meinung ändern*) to change one's mind.

umklammern [ʊm'klamərn] *vt untr* (*mit Händen*) to clasp; (*festhalten*) to cling to.

umklappen ['ʊmklapən] *vt* to fold down.

Umkleidekabine ['ʊmklaɪdəkabiːnə] *f* changing cubicle (*BRIT*), dressing room (*US*).

Umkleideraum ['ʊmklaɪdəraʊm] *m* changing room; (*US, THEAT*) dressing room.

umknicken ['ʊmknɪkən] *vt* (*Papier*) to fold (over) ♦ *vi:* **mit dem Fuß ~** to twist one's ankle.

umkommen ['ʊmkɔmən] *unreg vi* to die, perish; (*Lebensmittel*) to go bad.

Umkreis ['ʊmkraɪs] *m* neighbourhood (*BRIT*), neighborhood (*US*); **im ~ von** within a radius of.

umkreisen [ʊm'kraɪzən] *vt untr* to circle (round); (*Satellit*) to orbit.

umkrempeln ['ʊmkrɛmpəln] *vt* to turn up; (*mehrmals*) to roll up; (*umg: Betrieb*) to shake up.

umladen ['ʊmlaːdən] *unreg vt* to transfer, reload.

Umlage ['ʊmlaːgə] *f* share of the costs.

Umlauf *m* (*Geld~*) circulation; (*von Gestirn*) revolution; (*Schreiben*) circular; **in ~ bringen** to circulate; **~bahn** *f* orbit.

umlaufen ['ʊmlaʊfən] *unreg vi* to circulate.

Umlaufkapital *nt* working capital.

Umlaufvermögen *nt* current assets *pl*.

Umlaut ['ʊmlaʊt] *m* umlaut.

umlegen ['ʊmleːgən] *vt* to put on; (*verlegen*) to move, shift; (*Kosten*) to share out; (*umkippen*) to tip over; (*umg: töten*) to bump off.

umleiten ['ʊmlaɪtən] *vt* to divert.

Umleitung *f* diversion.

umlernen ['ʊmlɛrnən] *vi* to learn something new; (*fig*) to adjust one's views.

umliegend ['ʊmliːgənt] *adj* surrounding.

ummelden ['ʊmmɛldən] *vt, vr:* **jdn/sich ~ to** notify (the police of) a change in sb's/one's address.

Umnachtung [ʊm'naxtʊŋ] *f* mental derangement.

umorganisieren ['ʊm|ɔrganiziːrən] *vt untr* to reorganize.

umpflanzen ['ʊmpflantsən] *vt* to transplant.

umquartieren ['ʊmkvartiːrən] *vt untr* to move; (*Truppen*) to requarter.

umrahmen [ʊm'raːmən] *vt untr* to frame.

umranden [ʊm'randən] *vt untr* to border, edge.

umräumen ['ʊmrɔʏmən] *vt* (*anders anordnen*) to rearrange ♦ *vi* to rearrange things, move things around.

umrechnen ['ʊmrɛçnən] *vt* to convert.

Umrechnung *f* conversion.

Umrechnungskurs *m* rate of exchange.

umreißen [ʊm'raɪsən] *unreg vt untr* to outline.

umrennen ['ʊmrɛnən] *unreg vt* to (run into and) knock down.

umringen [ʊm'rɪŋən] *vt untr* to surround.

Umriß ['ʊmrɪs] *m* outline.

umrühren ['ʊmryːrən] *vt, vi* to stir.

umrüsten ['ʊmrystən] *vt* (*TECH*) to adapt; (*MIL*) to re-equip; **~ auf** *+akk* to adapt to.

ums [ʊms] = **um das.**

umsatteln ['ʊmzatəln] (*umg*) *vi* to change one's occupation, switch jobs.

Umsatz ['ʊmzats] *m* turnover; **~beteiligung** *f* commission; **~einbuße** *f* loss of profit; **~steuer** *f* turnover tax.

umschalten ['ʊmʃaltən] *vt* to switch ♦ *vi* to push/pull a lever; (*auf anderen Sender*): **~ (auf** *+akk*) to change over (to); (*AUT*): **~ in** *+akk* to change (*BRIT*) *od* shift into; **„wir schalten jetzt um nach Hamburg"** "and now we go over to Hamburg".

Umschalttaste *f* shift key.

Umschau *f* look(ing) round; **~ halten nach** to look around for.

umschauen ['ʊmʃaʊən] *vr* to look round.

Umschlag ['ʊmʃlaːk] *m* cover; (*Buch~*) jacket, cover; (*MED*) compress; (*Brief~*) envelope; (*Gütermenge*) volume of traffic; (*Wechsel*) change; (*von Hose*) turn-up (*BRIT*), cuff (*US*).

umschlagen ['ʊmʃlaːgən] *unreg vi* to change; (*NAUT*) to capsize ♦ *vt* to knock over; (*Ärmel*) to turn up; (*Seite*) to turn over; (*Waren*) to transfer.

Umschlag- *zW:* **~hafen** *m* port of transshipment; **~platz** *m* (*COMM*) distribution centre (*BRIT*) *od* center (*US*); **~seite** *f* cover page.

umschlingen [ʊm'ʃlɪŋən] *unreg vt untr* (*Pflanze*) to twine around; (*jdn*) to embrace.

umschreiben[1] ['ʊmʃraɪbən] *unreg vt* (*neu ~*) to rewrite; (*übertragen*) to transfer; **~ auf** *+akk* to transfer to.

umschreiben[2] [ʊm'ʃraɪbən] *unreg vt untr* to paraphrase; (*abgrenzen*) to circumscribe, define.

Umschuldung [ʊm'ʃʊldʊŋ] *f* rescheduling (of debts).

umschulen ['ʊmʃuːlən] *vt* to retrain; (*Kind*) to

send to another school.

umschwärmen ['ʊmˈʃvɛrmən] *vt untr* to swarm round; (*fig*) to surround, idolize.

Umschweife ['ʊmʃvaifə] *pl:* **ohne ~ without** beating about the bush, straight out.

umschwenken ['ʊmʃvɛŋkən] *vi* (*Kran*) to swing out; (*fig*) to do an about-turn (*BRIT*) *od* about-face (*US*); (*Wind*) to veer.

Umschwung ['ʊmʃvʊŋ] *m* (*GYMNASTIK*) circle; (*fig: ins Gegenteil*) change (around).

umsegeln [ʊmˈzeːgəln] *vt untr* to sail around; (*Erde*) to circumnavigate.

umsehen ['ʊmzeːən] *unreg vr* to look around *od* about; (*suchen*): **sich ~ (nach)** to look out (for); **ich möchte mich nur mal ~** (*in Geschäft*) I'm just looking.

umseitig ['ʊmzaitɪç] *adv* overleaf.

umsetzen ['ʊmzɛtsən] *vt* (*Waren*) to turn over ♦ *vr* (*Schüler*) to change places; **etw in die Tat ~** to translate sth into action.

Umsicht ['ʊmzɪçt] *f* prudence, caution.

umsichtig *adj* prudent, cautious.

umsiedeln ['ʊmziːdəln] *vt* to resettle.

Umsiedler(in) (**-s, -**) *m(f)* resettler.

umsonst [ʊmˈzɔnst] *adv* in vain; (*gratis*) for nothing.

umspringen ['ʊmʃprɪŋən] *unreg vi* to change; **mit jdm ~** to treat sb badly.

Umstand ['ʊmʃtant] *m* circumstance; **Umstände** *pl* (*fig: Schwierigkeiten*) fuss *sing*; **in anderen Umständen sein** to be pregnant; **Umstände machen** to go to a lot of trouble; **den Umständen entsprechend** much as one would expect (under the circumstances); **die näheren Umstände** further details; **unter Umständen** possibly; **mildernde Umstände** (*JUR*) extenuating circumstances.

umständehalber *adv* owing to circumstances.

umständlich ['ʊmʃtɛntlɪç] *adj* (*Methode*) cumbersome, complicated; (*Ausdrucksweise, Erklärung*) long-winded; (*ungeschickt*) ponderous; **etw ~ machen** to make heavy weather of (doing) sth.

Umstandskleid *nt* maternity dress.

Umstandswort *nt* adverb.

umstehend ['ʊmʃteːənt] *adj attrib* (*umseitig*) overleaf; **die U~en** *pl* the bystanders *pl*.

Umsteigekarte *f* transfer ticket.

umsteigen ['ʊmʃtaigən] *unreg vi* (*EISENB*) to change; (*fig: umg*): **~ (auf** +*akk*) to change over (to), switch (over) (to).

umstellen[1] ['ʊmʃtɛlən] *vt* (*an anderen Ort*) to change round, rearrange; (*TECH*) to convert ♦ *vr:* **sich ~ (auf** +*akk*) to adapt o.s. (to).

umstellen[2] [ʊmˈʃtɛlən] *vt untr* to surround.

Umstellung *f* change; (*Umgewöhnung*) adjustment; (*TECH*) conversion.

umstimmen ['ʊmʃtɪmən] *vt* (*MUS*) to retune; **jdn ~** to make sb change his mind.

umstoßen ['ʊmʃtoːsən] *unreg vt* (*lit*) to overturn; (*Plan etc*) to change, upset.

umstritten [ʊmˈʃtrɪtən] *adj* disputed; (*fraglich*) controversial.

Umsturz ['ʊmʃtʊrts] *m* overthrow.

umstürzen ['ʊmʃtʏrtsən] *vt* (*umwerfen*) to overturn ♦ *vi* to collapse, fall down; (*Wagen*) to overturn.

umstürzlerisch *adj* revolutionary.

Umtausch ['ʊmtauʃ] *m* exchange; **diese Waren sind vom ~ ausgeschlossen** these goods cannot be exchanged.

umtauschen *vt* to exchange.

Umtriebe ['ʊmtriːbə] *pl* machinations *pl*, intrigues *pl*.

umtun ['ʊmtuːn] *unreg vr:* **sich nach etw ~** to look for sth.

umverteilen ['ʊmfɛrtailən] *vt untr* to redistribute.

umwälzend ['ʊmvɛltsənt] *adj* (*fig*) radical; (*Veränderungen*) sweeping; (*Ereignisse*) revolutionary.

Umwälzung *f* (*fig*) radical change.

umwandeln ['ʊmvandəln] *vt* to change, convert; (*ELEK*) to transform.

umwechseln ['ʊmvɛksəln] *vt* to change.

Umweg ['ʊmveːk] *m* detour; (*fig*) roundabout way.

Umwelt ['ʊmvɛlt] *f* environment; **~auto** (*umg*) *nt* environment-friendly vehicle; **~belastung** *f* environmental pollution; **~bewußtsein** *nt* environmental awareness; **u~freundlich** *adj* environment-friendly; **~kriminalität** *f* crimes *pl* against the environment; **~ministerium** *nt* Ministry of the Environment; **u~schädlich** *adj* harmful to the environment; **~schutz** *m* environmental protection; **~schützer** (**-s, -**) *m* environmentalist; **~verschmutzung** *f* pollution (of the environment).

umwenden ['ʊmvɛndən] *unreg vt, vr* to turn (round).

umwerben [ʊmˈvɛrbən] *unreg vt untr* to court, woo.

umwerfen ['ʊmvɛrfən] *unreg vt* (*lit*) to upset, overturn; (*Mantel*) to throw on; (*fig: erschüttern*) to upset, throw.

umwerfend (*umg*) *adj* fantastic.

umziehen ['ʊmtsiːən] *unreg vt, vr* to change ♦ *vi* to move.

umzingeln [ʊmˈtsɪŋəln] *vt untr* to surround, encircle.

Umzug ['ʊmtsuːk] *m* procession; (*Wohnungs~*) move, removal.

UN *pl abk* (= *United Nations*): **die ~** the UN *sing*.

un- *zW:* **~abänderlich** *adj* irreversible, unalterable; **~abänderlich feststehen** to be absolutely certain; **~abdingbar** *adj* indispensable, essential; (*Recht*) inalienable; **~abhängig** *adj* independent; **U~abhängigkeit** *f* independence; **~abkömmlich** *adj* indispensable; **zur Zeit ~abkömmlich** not free at the moment;

~**ablässig** *adj* incessant, constant;
~**absehbar** *adj* immeasurable; (*Folgen*)
unforeseeable; (*Kosten*) incalculable;
~**absichtlich** *adj* unintentional; ~**abwendbar**
adj inevitable.
unachtsam ['ʊn|axtzaːm] *adj* careless; **U~keit**
f carelessness.
un- *zW:* ~**anfechtbar** *adj* indisputable;
~**angebracht** *adj* uncalled-for;
~**angefochten** *adj* unchallenged; (*Testament,
Wahlkandidat, Urteil*) uncontested;
~**angemeldet** *adj* unannounced; (*Besucher*)
unexpected; ~**angemessen** *adj* inadequate;
~**angenehm** *adj* unpleasant; (*peinlich*)
embarrassing; ~**angepaßt** *adj*
nonconformist; **U~annehmlichkeit** *f*
inconvenience; **Unannehmlichkeiten** *pl*
trouble *sing;* ~**ansehnlich** *adj* unsightly;
~**anständig** *adj* indecent, improper;
U~anständigkeit *f* indecency, impropriety;
~**antastbar** *adj* inviolable, sacrosanct.
unappetitlich ['ʊn|apetiːtlɪç] *adj* unsavoury
(*BRIT*), unsavory (*US*).
Unart ['ʊn|aːrt] *f* bad manners *pl;*
(*Angewohnheit*) bad habit.
unartig *adj* naughty, badly behaved.
un- *zW:* ~**aufdringlich** *adj* unobtrusive;
(*Parfüm*) discreet; (*Mensch*) unassuming;
~**auffällig** *adj* unobtrusive; (*Kleidung*)
inconspicuous; ~**auffindbar** *adj* not to be
found; ~**aufgefordert** *adj* unsolicited ♦ *adv*
unasked, spontaneously; ~**aufgefordert
zugesandte Manuskripte** unsolicited
manuscripts; ~**aufhaltsam** *adj* irresistible;
~**aufhörlich** *adj* incessant, continuous;
~**aufmerksam** *adj* inattentive; ~**aufrichtig**
adj insincere.
un- *zW:* ~**ausbleiblich** *adj* inevitable,
unavoidable; ~**ausgeglichen** *adj* volatile;
~**ausgegoren** *adj* immature; (*Idee, Plan*)
half-baked; ~**ausgesetzt** *adj* incessant,
constant; ~**ausgewogen** *adj* unbalanced;
~**aussprechlich** *adj* inexpressible;
~**ausstehlich** *adj* intolerable; ~**ausweichlich**
adj inescapable, ineluctable.
unbändig ['ʊnbɛndɪç] *adj* extreme, excessive.
unbarmherzig ['ʊnbarmhɛrtsɪç] *adj* pitiless,
merciless.
unbeabsichtigt ['ʊnbə|apzɪçtɪçt] *adj*
unintentional.
unbeachtet ['ʊnbə|axtət] *adj* unnoticed;
(*Warnung*) ignored.
unbedacht ['ʊnbədaxt] *adj* rash.
unbedarft ['ʊnbədarft] (*umg*) *adj* clueless.
unbedenklich ['ʊnbədɛŋklɪç] *adj* unhesitating;
(*Plan*) unobjectionable ♦ *adv* without
hesitation.
unbedeutend ['ʊnbədɔʏtənt] *adj* insignificant,
unimportant; (*Fehler*) slight.
unbedingt ['ʊnbədɪŋt] *adj* unconditional ♦ *adv*
absolutely; **mußt du ~ gehen?** do you really
have to go?; **nicht ~** not necessarily.

unbefangen ['ʊnbəfaŋən] *adj* impartial,
unprejudiced; (*ohne Hemmungen*)
uninhibited; **U~heit** *f* impartiality;
uninhibitedness.
unbefriedigend ['ʊnbəfriːdɪgənd] *adj*
unsatisfactory.
unbefriedigt ['ʊnbəfriːdɪçt] *adj* unsatisfied;
(*unzufrieden*) dissatisfied; (*unerfüllt*)
unfulfilled.
unbefristet ['ʊnbəfrɪstət] *adj* permanent.
unbefugt ['ʊnbəfuːkt] *adj* unauthorized; **U~en
ist der Eintritt verboten** no admittance to
unauthorized persons.
unbegabt ['ʊnbəgaːpt] *adj* untalented.
unbegreiflich [ʊnbə'ɡraɪflɪç] *adj*
inconceivable.
unbegrenzt ['ʊnbəɡrɛntst] *adj* unlimited.
unbegründet ['ʊnbəɡrʏndət] *adj* unfounded.
Unbehagen ['ʊnbəhaːɡən] *nt* discomfort.
unbehaglich ['ʊnbəhaːklɪç] *adj*
uncomfortable; (*Gefühl*) uneasy.
unbeherrscht ['ʊnbəhɛrʃt] *adj* uncontrolled;
(*Mensch*) lacking self-control.
unbeholfen ['ʊnbəhɔlfən] *adj* awkward,
clumsy; **U~heit** *f* awkwardness,
clumsiness.
unbeirrt ['ʊnbə|ɪrt] *adj* imperturbable.
unbekannt ['ʊnbəkant] *adj* unknown; ~**e
Größe** (*MATH, fig*) unknown quantity.
unbekannterweise *adv:* **grüß(e) sie ~ von
mir** give her my regards although I don't
know her.
unbekümmert ['ʊnbəkʏmərt] *adj*
unconcerned.
unbelehrbar [ʊnbə'leːrbaːr] *adj* fixed in one's
views; (*Rassist etc*) dyed-in-the-wool *attrib.*
unbeliebt ['ʊnbəliːpt] *adj* unpopular; **U~heit** *f*
unpopularity.
unbemannt ['ʊnbəmant] *adj* (*Raumflug*)
unmanned; (*Flugzeug*) pilotless.
unbemerkt ['ʊnbəmɛrkt] *adj* unnoticed.
unbenommen [ʊnbə'nɔmən] *adj* (*form*): **es
bleibt** *od* **ist Ihnen ~, zu ...** you are at liberty
to ...
unbequem ['ʊnbəkveːm] *adj* (*Stuhl*)
uncomfortable; (*Mensch*) bothersome;
(*Regelung*) inconvenient.
unberechenbar [ʊnbə'rɛçənbaːr] *adj*
incalculable; (*Mensch, Verhalten*)
unpredictable.
unberechtigt ['ʊnbərɛçtɪçt] *adj* unjustified;
(*nicht erlaubt*) unauthorized.
unberücksichtigt [ʊnbə'rʏkzɪçtɪçt] *adj:* **etw
~ lassen** not to consider sth.
unberufen [ʊnbə'ruːfən] *interj* touch wood!
unberührt ['ʊnbəryːrt] *adj* untouched; (*Natur*)
unspoiled; **sie ist noch ~** she is still a virgin.
unbeschadet [ʊnbə'ʃaːdət] *präp +gen* (*form*)
regardless of.
unbescheiden ['ʊnbəʃaɪdən] *adj*
presumptuous.
unbescholten ['ʊnbəʃɔltən] *adj* respectable;

(*Ruf*) spotless.
unbeschrankt ['ʊnbəʃraŋkt] *adj*
(*Bahnübergang*) unguarded.
unbeschränkt [ʊnbə'ʃrɛŋkt] *adj* unlimited.
unbeschreiblich [ʊnbə'ʃraɪplɪç] *adj*
indescribable.
unbeschwert ['ʊnbəʃveːrt] *adj* (*sorgenfrei*)
carefree; (*Melodien*) light.
unbesehen [ʊnbə'zeːən] *adv* indiscriminately;
(*ohne es anzusehen*) without looking at it.
unbesonnen ['ʊnbəzɔnən] *adj* unwise, rash,
imprudent.
unbesorgt ['ʊnbəzɔrkt] *adj* unconcerned; **Sie
können ganz ~ sein** you can set your mind
at rest.
unbespielt ['ʊnbəʃpiːlt] *adj* (*Kassette*) blank.
unbest. *abk* = **unbestimmt**.
unbeständig ['ʊnbəʃtɛndɪç] *adj* (*Mensch*)
inconstant; (*Wetter*) unsettled; (*Lage*)
unstable.
unbestechlich [ʊnbə'ʃtɛçlɪç] *adj*
incorruptible.
unbestimmt ['ʊnbəʃtɪmt] *adj* indefinite;
(*Zukunft*) uncertain; **U~heit** *f* vagueness.
unbestritten ['ʊnbəʃtrɪtən] *adj* undisputed.
unbeteiligt [ʊnbə'taɪlɪçt] *adj* unconcerned;
(*uninteressiert*) indifferent.
unbeugsam ['ʊnbɔʏkzaːm] *adj* stubborn,
inflexible; (*Wille*) unbending.
unbewacht ['ʊnbəvaxt] *adj* unguarded,
unwatched.
unbewaffnet ['ʊnbəvafnət] *adj* unarmed.
unbeweglich ['ʊnbəveːklɪç] *adj* immovable.
unbewegt *adj* motionless; (*fig: unberührt*)
unmoved.
unbewohnt ['ʊnbəvoːnt] *adj* (*Gegend*)
uninhabited; (*Haus*) unoccupied.
unbewußt ['ʊnbəvʊst] *adj* unconscious.
unbezahlbar [ʊnbə'tsaːlbaːr] *adj* prohibitively
expensive; (*fig*) priceless; (*nützlich*)
invaluable.
unbezahlt ['ʊnbətsaːlt] *adj* unpaid.
unblutig ['ʊnbluːtɪç] *adj* bloodless.
unbrauchbar ['ʊnbrauxbaːr] *adj* (*nutzlos*)
useless; (*Gerät*) unusable; **U~keit** *f*
uselessness.
unbürokratisch ['ʊnbyrokratɪʃ] *adj* without
any red tape.
und [ʊnt] *konj* and; **~ so weiter** and so on.
Undank ['ʊndaŋk] *m* ingratitude; **u~bar** *adj*
ungrateful; **~barkeit** *f* ingratitude.
undefinierbar [ʊndefi'niːrbaːr] *adj* indefinable.
undenkbar [ʊn'dɛŋkbaːr] *adj* inconceivable.
undeutlich ['ʊndɔʏtlɪç] *adj* indistinct; (*Schrift*)
illegible; (*Ausdrucksweise*) unclear.
undicht ['ʊndɪçt] *adj* leaky.
undifferenziert ['ʊndɪfərɛntsiːrt] *adj*
simplistic.
Unding ['ʊndɪŋ] *nt* absurdity.
unduldsam ['ʊndʊldsaːm] *adj* intolerant.
un- *zW:* **~durchdringlich** *adj* (*Urwald*)
impenetrable; (*Gesicht*) inscrutable;

~durchführbar *adj* impracticable;
~durchlässig *adj* impervious; (*wasser~*)
waterproof, impermeable; **~durchschaubar**
adj inscrutable; **~durchsichtig** *adj* opaque;
(*Motive*) obscure; (*fig: pej: Mensch, Methoden*)
devious.
uneben ['ʊneːbən] *adj* uneven.
unecht ['ʊn|ɛçt] *adj* artificial, fake; (*pej:
Freundschaft, Lächeln*) false.
unehelich ['ʊn|eːəlɪç] *adj* illegitimate.
uneigennützig ['ʊn|aɪɡənnʏtsɪç] *adj* unselfish.
uneinbringlich [ʊn|aɪn'brɪŋlɪç] *adj:* **~e
Forderungen** (*COMM*) bad debts *pl*.
uneingeschränkt ['ʊn|aɪŋɡəʃrɛŋkt] *adj*
absolute, total; (*Rechte, Handel*)
unrestricted; (*Zustimmung*) unqualified.
uneinig ['ʊn|aɪnɪç] *adj* divided; **~ sein** to
disagree; **U~keit** *f* discord, dissension.
uneinnehmbar [ʊn|aɪn'neːmbaːr] *adj*
impregnable.
uneins ['ʊn|aɪns] *adj* at variance, at odds.
unempfänglich ['ʊn|ɛmpfɛŋlɪç] *adj:* **~ (für)** not
susceptible (to).
unempfindlich ['ʊn|ɛmpfɪntlɪç] *adj*
insensitive; **U~keit** *f* insensitivity.
unendlich [ʊn'|ɛntlɪç] *adj* infinite ♦ *adv*
endlessly; (*fig: sehr*) terribly; **U~keit** *f*
infinity.
un- *zW:* **~entbehrlich** *adj* indispensable;
~entgeltlich *adj* free (of charge);
~entschieden *adj* undecided; **~entschieden
enden** (*SPORT*) to end in a draw;
~entschlossen *adj* undecided; (*entschlußlos*)
irresolute; **~entwegt** *adj* unswerving;
(*unaufhörlich*) incessant.
un- *zW:* **~erbittlich** *adj* unyielding, inexorable;
~erfahren *adj* inexperienced; **~erfreulich** *adj*
unpleasant; **U~erfreuliches** (*schlechte
Nachrichten*) bad news *sing*; (*Übles*) bad
things *pl*; **~erfüllt** *adj* unfulfilled; **~ergiebig**
adj (*Quelle, Thema*) unproductive; (*Ernte,
Nachschlagewerk*) poor; **~ergründlich** *adj*
unfathomable; **~erheblich** *adj* unimportant;
~erhört *adj* unheard-of; (*unverschämt*)
outrageous; (*Bitte*) unanswered; **~erläßlich**
adj indispensable; **~erlaubt** *adj*
unauthorized; **~erledigt** *adj* unfinished;
(*Post*) unanswered; (*Rechnung*) outstanding;
(*schwebend*) pending; **~ermeßlich** *adj*
immeasurable, immense; **~ermüdlich** *adj*
indefatigable; **~ersättlich** *adj* insatiable;
~erschlossen *adj* (*Land*) undeveloped;
(*Boden*) unexploited; (*Vorkommen, Markt*)
untapped; **~erschöpflich** *adj* inexhaustible;
~erschrocken *adj* intrepid, courageous;
~erschütterlich *adj* unshakeable;
~erschwinglich *adj* (*Preis*) prohibitive;
~ersetzlich *adj* irreplaceable; **~erträglich** *adj*
unbearable; (*Frechheit*) insufferable;
~erwartet *adj* unexpected; **~erwünscht** *adj*
undesirable, unwelcome; **~erzogen** *adj* ill-
bred, rude.

unfähig ['ʊnfɛːɪç] *adj* incapable; *(attrib)* incompetent; **zu etw ~ sein** to be incapable of sth; **U~keit** *f* inability; incompetence.

unfair ['ʊnfɛːr] *adj* unfair.

Unfall ['ʊnfal] *m* accident; **~flucht** *f* hit-and-run (driving); **~opfer** *nt* casualty; **~station** *f* emergency ward; **~stelle** *f* scene of the accident; **~versicherung** *f* accident insurance; **~wagen** *m* car involved in an accident; *(umg: Rettungswagen)* ambulance.

unfaßbar [ʊn'fasbaːr] *adj* inconceivable.

unfehlbar [ʊn'feːlbaːr] *adj* infallible ♦ *adv* without fail; **U~keit** *f* infallibility.

unfertig ['ʊnfɛrtɪç] *adj* unfinished, incomplete; *(Mensch)* immature.

unflätig ['ʊnflɛːtɪç] *adj* rude.

unfolgsam ['ʊnfɔlkzaːm] *adj* disobedient.

unförmig ['ʊnfœrmɪç] *adj* *(formlos)* shapeless; *(groß)* cumbersome; *(Füße, Nase)* unshapely.

unfrankiert ['ʊnfraŋkiːrt] *adj* unfranked.

unfrei ['ʊnfraɪ] *adj* not free.

unfreiwillig *adj* involuntary.

unfreundlich ['ʊnfrɔʏntlɪç] *adj* unfriendly; **U~keit** *f* unfriendliness.

Unfriede(n) ['ʊnfriːdə(n)] *m* dissension, strife.

unfruchtbar ['ʊnfrʊxtbaːr] *adj* infertile; *(Gespräche)* fruitless; **U~keit** *f* infertility; fruitlessness.

Unfug ['ʊnfuːk] (**-s**) *m* *(Benehmen)* mischief; *(Unsinn)* nonsense; **grober ~** *(JUR)* gross misconduct.

Ungar(in) ['ʊŋgar(ɪn)] (**-n, -n**) *m(f)* Hungarian; **u~isch** *adj* Hungarian.

Ungarn (**-s**) *nt* Hungary.

ungeachtet ['ʊngəˌaxtət] *präp +gen* notwithstanding.

ungeahndet ['ʊngəˌaːndət] *adj* *(JUR)* unpunished.

ungeahnt ['ʊngəˌaːnt] *adj* unsuspected, undreamt-of.

ungebeten ['ʊngəbeːtən] *adj* uninvited.

ungebildet ['ʊngəbɪldət] *adj* uncultured; *(ohne Bildung)* uneducated.

ungeboren ['ʊngəboːrən] *adj* unborn.

ungebräuchlich ['ʊngəbrɔʏçlɪç] *adj* unusual, uncommon.

ungebraucht ['ʊngəbrauxt] *adj* unused.

ungebührlich ['ʊngəbyːrlɪç] *adj*: **sich ~ aufregen** to get unduly excited.

ungebunden ['ʊngəbʊndən] *adj* *(Buch)* unbound; *(Leben)* (fancy-)free; *(ohne festen Partner)* unattached; *(POL)* independent.

ungedeckt ['ʊngədɛkt] *adj* *(schutzlos)* unprotected; *(Scheck)* uncovered.

Ungeduld ['ʊngədʊlt] *f* impatience.

ungeduldig ['ʊngədʊldɪç] *adj* impatient.

ungeeignet ['ʊngəˌaɪgnət] *adj* unsuitable.

ungefähr ['ʊngəfɛːr] *adj* rough, approximate ♦ *adv* roughly, approximately; **so ~!** more or less!; **das kommt nicht von ~** that's hardly surprising.

ungefährlich ['ʊngəfɛːrlɪç] *adj* not dangerous, harmless.

ungehalten ['ʊngəhaltən] *adj* indignant.

ungeheuer ['ʊngəhɔʏər] *adj* huge ♦ *adv (umg)* enormously; **U~** (**-s, -**) *nt* monster; **~lich** [ʊngə'hɔʏərlɪç] *adj* monstrous.

ungehindert ['ʊngəhɪndərt] *adj* unimpeded.

ungehobelt ['ʊngəhoːbəlt] *adj* *(fig)* uncouth.

ungehörig ['ʊngəhøːrɪç] *adj* impertinent, improper; **U~keit** *f* impertinence.

ungehorsam ['ʊngəhoːrzaːm] *adj* disobedient; **U~** *m* disobedience.

ungeklärt ['ʊngəklɛːrt] *adj* not cleared up; *(Rätsel)* unsolved; *(Abwasser)* untreated.

ungekürzt ['ʊngəkyrtst] *adj* not shortened; *(Film)* uncut.

ungeladen ['ʊngəlaːdən] *adj* not loaded; *(ELEK)* uncharged; *(Gast)* uninvited.

ungelegen ['ʊngəleːgən] *adj* inconvenient; **komme ich (Ihnen) ~?** is this an inconvenient time for you?

ungelernt ['ʊngəlɛrnt] *adj* unskilled.

ungelogen ['ʊngəloːgən] *adv* really, honestly.

ungemein ['ʊngəmaɪn] *adj* immense.

ungemütlich ['ʊngəmyːtlɪç] *adj* uncomfortable; *(Person)* disagreeable; **er kann ~ werden** he can get nasty.

ungenau ['ʊngənau] *adj* inaccurate.

Ungenauigkeit *f* inaccuracy.

ungeniert ['ʊnʒeniːrt] *adj* free and easy; *(bedenkenlos, taktlos)* uninhibited ♦ *adv* without embarrassment, freely.

ungenießbar ['ʊngəniːsbaːr] *adj* inedible; *(nicht zu trinken)* undrinkable; *(umg)* unbearable.

ungenügend ['ʊngənyːgənt] *adj* insufficient, inadequate; *(SCH)* unsatisfactory.

ungenutzt ['ʊngənʊtst] *adj*: **eine Chance ~ lassen** to miss an opportunity.

ungepflegt ['ʊngəpfleːkt] *adj* *(Garten etc)* untended; *(Person)* unkempt; *(Hände)* neglected.

ungerade ['ʊngəraːdə] *adj* odd, uneven *(US)*.

ungerecht ['ʊngərɛçt] *adj* unjust.

ungerechtfertigt *adj* unjustified.

Ungerechtigkeit *f* unfairness, injustice.

ungeregelt ['ʊngəreːgəlt] *adj* irregular.

ungereimt ['ʊngəraɪmt] *adj* *(Verse)* unrhymed; *(fig)* inconsistent.

ungern ['ʊngern] *adv* unwillingly, reluctantly.

ungerufen ['ʊngəruːfən] *adj* without being called.

ungeschehen ['ʊngəʃeːən] *adj*: **~ machen** to undo.

Ungeschicklichkeit ['ʊngəʃɪklɪçkaɪt] *f* clumsiness.

ungeschickt *adj* awkward, clumsy.

ungeschliffen ['ʊngəʃlɪfən] *adj* *(Edelstein)* uncut; *(Messer etc)* blunt; *(fig: Benehmen)* uncouth.

ungeschmälert ['ʊngəʃmɛːlərt] *adj* undiminished.

ungeschminkt ['ʊngəʃmɪŋkt] *adj* without

make-up; (*fig*) unvarnished.
ungeschoren ['ʊngəʃoːrən] *adj:* **jdn ~ lassen**
(*umg*) to spare sb; (*ungestraft*) to let sb off.
ungesetzlich ['ʊngəzɛtslɪç] *adj* illegal.
ungestempelt ['ʊngəʃtɛmpəlt] *adj* (*Briefmarke*)
unfranked, mint.
ungestört ['ʊngəʃtøːrt] *adj* undisturbed.
ungestraft ['ʊngəʃtraːft] *adv* with impunity.
ungestüm ['ʊngəʃtyːm] *adj* impetuous; **U~**
(-(e)s) *nt* impetuosity.
ungesund ['ʊngəzʊnt] *adj* unhealthy.
ungetrübt ['ʊngətryːpt] *adj* clear; (*fig*)
untroubled; (*Freude*) unalloyed.
Ungetüm ['ʊngətyːm] **(-(e)s, -e)** *nt* monster.
ungeübt ['ʊngə|yːpt] *adj* unpractised (*BRIT*),
unpracticed (*US*); (*Mensch*) out of practice.
ungewiß ['ʊngəvɪs] *adj* uncertain; **U~heit** *f*
uncertainty.
ungewöhnlich ['ʊngəvøːnlɪç] *adj* unusual.
ungewohnt ['ʊngəvoːnt] *adj* unusual.
ungewollt ['ʊngəvɔlt] *adj* unintentional.
Ungeziefer ['ʊngətsiːfər] **(-s)** *nt* vermin *pl*.
ungezogen ['ʊngətsoːgən] *adj* rude,
impertinent; **U~heit** *f* rudeness,
impertinence.
ungezwungen ['ʊngətsvʊŋən] *adj* natural,
unconstrained.
ungläubig ['ʊnglɔybɪç] *adj* unbelieving; **ein**
~er Thomas a doubting Thomas; **die U~en**
the infidel(s *pl*).
unglaublich [ʊn'glaʊplɪç] *adj* incredible.
unglaubwürdig ['ʊnglaʊpvyrdɪç] *adj*
untrustworthy, unreliable; (*Geschichte*)
improbable; **sich ~ machen** to lose
credibility.
ungleich ['ʊnglaɪç] *adj* dissimilar; (*Mittel,*
Waffen) unequal ♦ *adv* incomparably; **~artig**
adj different; **U~behandlung** *f* (*von Frauen,*
Ausländern) unequal treatment; **U~heit** *f*
dissimilarity; inequality; **~mäßig** *adj*
uneven; (*Atemzüge, Gesichtszüge, Puls*)
irregular.
Unglück ['ʊnglʏk] *nt* misfortune; (*Pech*) bad
luck; (*~sfall*) calamity, disaster; (*Verkehrs~*)
accident; **zu allem ~** to make matters
worse; **u~lich** *adj* unhappy; (*erfolglos*)
unlucky; (*unerfreulich*) unfortunate;
u~licherweise *adv* unfortunately; **u~selig** *adj*
calamitous; (*Person*) unfortunate.
Unglücksfall *m* accident, mishap.
Unglücksrabe (*umg*) *m* unlucky thing.
Ungnade ['ʊngnaːdə] *f:* **bei jdm in ~ fallen** to
fall out of favour (*BRIT*) *od* favor (*US*) with
sb.
ungültig ['ʊngʏltɪç] *adj* invalid; **etw für**
~ erklären to declare sth null and void;
U~keit *f* invalidity.
ungünstig ['ʊngʏnstɪç] *adj* unfavourable
(*BRIT*), unfavorable (*US*); (*Termin*)
inconvenient; (*Augenblick, Wetter*) bad; (*nicht*
preiswert) expensive.
ungut ['ʊnguːt] *adj* (*Gefühl*) uneasy; **nichts für**

~! no offence!
unhaltbar ['ʊnhaltbaːr] *adj* untenable.
unhandlich ['ʊnhantlɪç] *adj* unwieldy.
Unheil ['ʊnhaɪl] *nt* evil; (*Unglück*) misfortune;
~ anrichten to cause mischief.
unheilbar [ʊn'haɪlbaːr] *adj* incurable.
unheilbringend *adj* fatal, fateful.
unheilvoll *adj* disastrous.
unheimlich ['ʊnhaɪmlɪç] *adj* weird, uncanny
♦ *adv* (*umg*) tremendously; **das/er ist mir ~**
it/he gives me the creeps (*umg*).
unhöflich ['ʊnhøːflɪç] *adj* impolite; **U~keit** *f*
impoliteness.
unhörbar [ʊn'høːrbaːr] *adj* silent; (*Frequenzen*)
inaudible.
unhygienisch ['ʊnhygieːnɪʃ] *adj* unhygienic.
Uni ['ʊni] **(-, -s)** (*umg*) *f* university.
uni ['yniː] *adj* self-coloured (*BRIT*), self-
colored (*US*).
Uniform [uni'fɔrm] **(-, -en)** *f* uniform.
uniformiert [unifɔr'miːrt] *adj* uniformed.
Unikum ['uːnɪkʊm] **(-s, -s** *od* **Unika)** (*umg*) *nt*
real character.
uninteressant ['ʊn|ɪntɛrɛsant] *adj*
uninteresting.
uninteressiert ['ʊn|ɪntərɛ'siːrt] *adj:* **~ (an** +*dat*)
uninterested (in), not interested (in).
Union [uni'oːn] *f* union.
Unionsparteien *pl* (*BRD POL*) CDU and CSU
parties *pl*.
universal [univɛr'zaːl] *adj* universal.
universell [univɛr'zɛl] *adj* universal.
Universität [univɛrzi'tɛːt] *f* university; **auf**
die ~ gehen, die ~ besuchen to go to
university.
Universum [uni'vɛrzʊm] **(-s)** *nt* universe.
unkenntlich ['ʊnkɛntlɪç] *adj* unrecognizable;
U~keit *f:* **bis zur U~keit** beyond recognition.
Unkenntnis ['ʊnkɛntnɪs] *f* ignorance.
unklar ['ʊnklaːr] *adj* unclear; **im ~en sein über**
+*akk* to be in the dark about; **U~heit** *f*
unclarity; (*Unentschiedenheit*) uncertainty.
unklug ['ʊnkluːk] *adj* unwise.
unkompliziert ['ʊnkɔmplitsiːrt] *adj*
straightforward, uncomplicated.
unkontrolliert ['ʊnkɔntrɔliːrt] *adj* unchecked.
unkonzentriert ['ʊnkɔntsɛntriːrt] *adj* lacking
in concentration.
Unkosten ['ʊnkɔstən] *pl* expense(s *pl*); **sich in**
~ stürzen (*umg*) to go to a lot of expense.
Unkraut ['ʊnkraʊt] *nt* weed; weeds *pl*;
~ vergeht nicht (*Sprichwort*) it would take
more than that to finish me/him *etc* off;
~vertilgungsmittel *nt* weedkiller.
unlängst ['ʊnlɛŋst] *adv* not long ago.
unlauter ['ʊnlaʊtər] *adj* unfair.
unleserlich ['ʊnleːzərlɪç] *adj* illegible.
unleugbar ['ʊnlɔykbaːr] *adj* undeniable,
indisputable.
unlogisch ['ʊnloːgɪʃ] *adj* illogical.
unlösbar [ʊn'løːsbaːr] *adj* insoluble.
unlöslich [ʊn'løːslɪç] *adj* insoluble.

Unlust ['ʊnlʊst] *f* lack of enthusiasm.
unlustig *adj* unenthusiastic ♦ *adv* without enthusiasm.
unmännlich ['ʊnmɛnlɪç] *adj* unmanly.
Unmasse ['ʊnmasə] (*umg*) *f* load.
unmäßig ['ʊnmɛːsɪç] *adj* immoderate.
Unmenge ['ʊnmɛŋə] *f* tremendous number, vast number.
Unmensch ['ʊnmɛnʃ] *m* ogre, brute; **u~lich** *adj* inhuman, brutal; (*ungeheuer*) awful.
unmerklich [ʊn'mɛrklɪç] *adj* imperceptible.
unmißverständlich ['ʊnmɪsfɛrʃtɛntlɪç] *adj* unmistakable.
unmittelbar ['ʊnmɪtəlbaːr] *adj* immediate; **~er Kostenaufwand** direct expense.
unmöbliert ['ʊnmøbliːrt] *adj* unfurnished.
unmöglich ['ʊnmøːklɪç] *adj* impossible; **ich kann es ~ tun** I can't possibly do it; **~ aussehen** (*umg*) to look ridiculous; **U~keit** *f* impossibility.
unmoralisch ['ʊnmoraːlɪʃ] *adj* immoral.
unmotiviert ['ʊnmotiviːrt] *adj* unmotivated.
unmündig ['ʊnmʏndɪç] *adj* (*minderjährig*) underage.
Unmut ['ʊnmuːt] *m* ill humour (*BRIT*) od humor (*US*).
unnachahmlich ['ʊnnaːx|aːmlɪç] *adj* inimitable.
unnachgiebig ['ʊnnaːxgiːbɪç] *adj* unyielding.
unnahbar [ʊn'naːbaːr] *adj* unapproachable.
unnatürlich ['ʊnnatyːrlɪç] *adj* unnatural.
unnormal ['ʊnnɔrmaːl] *adj* abnormal.
unnötig ['ʊnnøːtɪç] *adj* unnecessary.
unnötigerweise *adv* unnecessarily.
unnütz ['ʊnnʏts] *adj* useless.
UNO ['uːno] *f abk* (= *United Nations Organization*): **die ~** the UN.
unordentlich ['ʊn|ɔrdəntlɪç] *adj* untidy.
Unordnung ['ʊn|ɔrdnʊŋ] *f* disorder; (*Durcheinander*) mess.
unorganisiert ['ʊn|ɔrganiziːrt] *adj* disorganized.
unparteiisch ['ʊnpartaɪɪʃ] *adj* impartial.
Unparteiische(r) *f(m)* umpire; (*FUSSBALL*) referee.
unpassend ['ʊnpasənt] *adj* inappropriate; (*Zeit*) inopportune.
unpäßlich ['ʊnpɛslɪç] *adj* unwell.
unpersönlich ['ʊnpɛrzøːnlɪç] *adj* impersonal.
unpolitisch ['ʊnpoliːtɪʃ] *adj* apolitical.
unpraktisch ['ʊnpraktɪʃ] *adj* impractical, unpractical.
unproduktiv ['ʊnprodʊktiːf] *adj* unproductive.
unproportioniert ['ʊnprɔpɔrtsioniːrt] *adj* out of proportion.
unpünktlich ['ʊnpʏŋktlɪç] *adj* unpunctual.
unqualifiziert ['ʊnkvalifitsiːrt] *adj* unqualified; (*Äußerung*) incompetent.
unrasiert ['ʊnraziːrt] *adj* unshaven.
Unrat ['ʊnraːt] (-(e)s) *m* (*geh*) refuse; (*fig*) filth.
unrationell ['ʊnratsionɛl] *adj* inefficient.

unrecht ['ʊnrɛçt] *adj* wrong; **das ist mir gar nicht so ~** I don't really mind; **U~** *nt* wrong; **zu U~** wrongly; **nicht zu U~** not without good reason; **U~ haben, im U~ sein** to be wrong.
unrechtmäßig *adj* unlawful, illegal.
unredlich ['ʊnreːtlɪç] *adj* dishonest; **U~keit** *f* dishonesty.
unreell ['ʊnreːl] *adj* unfair; (*unredlich*) dishonest; (*Preis*) unreasonable.
unregelmäßig ['ʊnreːgəlmɛːsɪç] *adj* irregular; **U~keit** *f* irregularity.
unreif ['ʊnraɪf] *adj* (*Obst*) unripe; (*fig*) immature.
Unreife *f* immaturity.
unrein ['ʊnraɪn] *adj* not clean; (*Ton, Gedanken, Taten*) impure; (*Atem, Haut*) bad.
unrentabel ['ʊnrɛntaːbəl] *adj* unprofitable.
unrichtig ['ʊnrɪçtɪç] *adj* incorrect, wrong.
Unruh ['ʊnruː] (-, -en) *f* (*von Uhr*) balance.
Unruhe (-, -n) *f* unrest; **~herd** *m* trouble spot; **~stifter** *m* troublemaker.
unruhig *adj* restless; (*nervös*) fidgety; (*belebt*) noisy; (*Schlaf*) fitful; (*Zeit etc, Meer*) troubled.
unrühmlich ['ʊnryːmlɪç] *adj* inglorious.
uns [ʊns] *pron akk, dat von* **wir** us; (*reflexiv*) ourselves.
unsachgemäß ['ʊnzaxgəmɛːs] *adj* improper.
unsachlich ['ʊnzaxlɪç] *adj* not to the point, irrelevant; (*persönlich*) personal.
unsagbar [ʊn'zaːkbaːr] *adj* indescribable.
unsäglich [ʊn'zɛːklɪç] *adj* indescribable.
unsanft ['ʊnzanft] *adj* rough.
unsauber ['ʊnzaʊbər] *adj* (*schmutzig*) dirty; (*fig*) crooked; (: *Klang*) impure.
unschädlich ['ʊnʃɛːtlɪç] *adj* harmless; **jdn/etw ~ machen** to render sb/sth harmless.
unscharf ['ʊnʃarf] *adj* indistinct; (*Bild etc*) out of focus, blurred.
unscheinbar ['ʊnʃaɪnbaːr] *adj* insignificant; (*Aussehen, Haus etc*) unprepossessing.
unschlagbar [ʊn'ʃlaːkbaːr] *adj* invincible.
unschlüssig ['ʊnʃlʏsɪç] *adj* undecided.
unschön ['ʊnʃøːn] *adj* unsightly; (*lit, fig: Szene*) ugly; (*Vorfall*) unpleasant.
Unschuld ['ʊnʃʊlt] *f* innocence.
unschuldig ['ʊnʃʊldɪç] *adj* innocent.
Unschuldsmiene *f* innocent expression.
unschwer ['ʊnʃveːr] *adv* easily, without difficulty.
unselbständig ['ʊnzɛlpʃtɛndɪç] *adj* dependent, over-reliant on others.
unselig ['ʊnzeːlɪç] *adj* unfortunate; (*verhängnisvoll*) ill-fated.
unser ['ʊnzər] *poss pron* our ♦ *pron gen von* **wir** of us.
unsere(r, s) *poss pron* ours; **wir tun das U~** (*geh*) we are doing our bit.
unsereiner *pron* the likes of us.
unsereins *pron* the likes of us.

unser(er)seits ['ʊnzər(ər)'zaɪts] *adv* on our part.
uneresgleichen *pron* the likes of us.
unserige(r, s) *poss pron:* **der/die/das ~** ours.
unseriös ['ʊnzeriøːs] *adj* (*unehrlich*) not straight, untrustworthy.
unsertwegen ['ʊnzərt'veːɡən] *adv* (*für uns*) for our sake; (*wegen uns*) on our account.
unsertwillen ['ʊnzərt'vɪlən] *adv:* **um ~** = **unsertwegen.**
unsicher ['ʊnzɪçər] *adj* uncertain; (*Mensch*) insecure; **die Gegend ~ machen** (*fig: umg*) to knock about the district; **U~heit** *f* uncertainty; insecurity.
unsichtbar ['ʊnzɪçtbaːr] *adj* invisible; **U~keit** *f* invisibility.
Unsinn ['ʊnzɪn] *m* nonsense.
unsinnig *adj* nonsensical.
Unsitte ['ʊnzɪtə] *f* deplorable habit.
unsittlich ['ʊnzɪtlɪç] *adj* indecent; **U~keit** *f* indecency.
unsolide ['ʊnzoliːdə] *adj* (*Mensch, Leben*) loose; (*Firma*) unreliable.
unsozial ['ʊnzotsiaːl] *adj* (*Verhalten*) antisocial; (*Politik*) unsocial.
unsportlich ['ʊnʃpɔrtlɪç] *adj* not sporty; (*Verhalten*) unsporting.
unsre *etc* ['ʊnzrə] *poss pron* = **unsere** *etc; siehe auch* **unser.**
unsrige(r, s) ['ʊnzrɪɡə(r, s)] *poss pron* = **unserige.**
unsterblich ['ʊnʃtɛrplɪç] *adj* immortal; **U~keit** *f* immortality.
unstet ['ʊnʃteːt] *adj* (*Mensch*) restless; (*wankelmütig*) changeable; (*Leben*) unsettled.
Unstimmigkeit ['ʊnʃtɪmɪçkaɪt] *f* inconsistency; (*Streit*) disagreement.
Unsumme ['ʊnzʊmə] *f* vast sum.
unsympathisch ['ʊnzʏmpaːtɪʃ] *adj* unpleasant; **er ist mir ~** I don't like him.
untad(e)lig ['ʊntaːd(ə)lɪç] *adj* impeccable; (*Mensch*) beyond reproach.
Untat ['ʊntaːt] *f* atrocity.
untätig ['ʊntɛːtɪç] *adj* idle.
untauglich ['ʊntaʊklɪç] *adj* unsuitable; (*MIL*) unfit; **U~keit** *f* unsuitability; unfitness.
unteilbar ['ʊn'taɪlbaːr] *adj* indivisible.
unten ['ʊntən] *adv* below; (*im Haus*) downstairs; (*an der Treppe etc*) at the bottom; **siehe ~** see below; **nach ~** down; **~ am Berg** *etc* at the bottom of the mountain *etc*; **er ist bei mir ~ durch** (*umg*) I'm through with him; **~an** *adv* (*am unteren Ende*) at the far end; (*lit, fig*) at the bottom; **~genannt** *adj* undermentioned.

=============== *SCHLÜSSELWORT*

unter ['ʊntər] *präp +dat* **1** (*räumlich*) under; (*drunter*) underneath, below
2 (*zwischen*) among(st); **sie waren ~ sich** they were by themselves; **einer ~ ihnen** one of them; **~ anderem** among other things

♦ *präp +akk* under, below
♦ *adv* (*weniger als*) under; **Mädchen ~ 18 Jahren** girls under *od* less than 18 (years of age).

Unter- *zW:* **~abteilung** *f* subdivision; **~arm** *m* forearm; **u~belegt** *adj* (*Kurs*) undersubscribed; (*Hotel etc*) not full.
unterbelichten ['ʊntərbəlɪçtən] *vt untr* (*PHOT*) to underexpose.
Unterbeschäftigung ['ʊntərbəʃɛːftɪɡʊŋ] *f* underemployment.
unterbesetzt ['ʊntərbəzɛtst] *adj* understaffed.
Unterbewußtsein ['ʊntərbəvʊstzaɪn] *nt* subconscious.
unterbezahlt ['ʊntərbətsaːlt] *adj* underpaid.
unterbieten [ʊntər'biːtən] *unreg vt untr* (*COMM*) to undercut; (*fig*) to surpass.
unterbinden [ʊntər'bɪndən] *unreg vt untr* to stop, call a halt to.
unterbleiben [ʊntər'blaɪbən] *unreg vi untr* (*aufhören*) to stop; (*versäumt werden*) to be omitted.
Unterbodenschutz [ʊntər'boːdənʃʊts] *m* (*AUT*) underseal.
unterbrechen [ʊntər'brɛçən] *unreg vt untr* to interrupt.
Unterbrechung *f* interruption.
unterbreiten [ʊntər'braɪtən] *vt untr* (*Plan*) to present.
unterbringen ['ʊntərbrɪŋən] *unreg vt* (*in Koffer*) to stow; (*in Zeitung*) to place; (*Person: in Hotel etc*) to accommodate, put up; (: *beruflich*): **~ (bei)** to fix up (with).
unterbuttern ['ʊntərbʊtərn] (*umg*) *vt* (*zuschießen*) to throw in; (*unterdrücken*) to ride roughshod over.
unterderhand [ʊntərder'hant] *adv* secretly; (*verkaufen*) privately.
unterdessen [ʊntər'dɛsən] *adv* meanwhile.
Unterdruck ['ʊntərdrʊk] *m* (*TECH*) below atmospheric pressure.
unterdrücken [ʊntər'drʏkən] *vt untr* to suppress; (*Leute*) to oppress.
untere(r, s) ['ʊntərə(r, s)] *adj* lower.
untereinander [ʊntər|aɪ'nandər] *adv* (*gegenseitig*) each other; (*miteinander*) among themselves *etc.*
unterentwickelt ['ʊntər|ɛntvɪkəlt] *adj* underdeveloped.
unterernährt ['ʊntər|ɛrnɛːrt] *adj* undernourished.
Unterernährung *f* malnutrition.
Unterfangen [ʊntər'faŋən] *nt* undertaking.
Unterführung [ʊntər'fyːrʊŋ] *f* subway, underpass.
Untergang ['ʊntərɡaŋ] *m* (down)fall, decline; (*NAUT*) sinking; (*von Gestirn*) setting; **dem ~ geweiht sein** to be doomed.
untergeben [ʊntər'ɡeːbən] *adj* subordinate.
Untergebene(r) *f(m)* subordinate.
untergehen ['ʊntərɡeːən] *unreg vi* to go down;

(*Sonne*) to set, go down; (*Staat*) to fall; (*Volk*) to perish; (*Welt*) to come to an end; (*im Lärm*) to be drowned.

untergeordnet ['ʊntərgəˌɔrdnət] *adj* (*Dienststelle*) subordinate; (*Bedeutung*) secondary.

Untergeschoß ['ʊntərgəʃɔs] *nt* basement.

Untergewicht ['ʊntərgəvɪçt] *nt:* **(10 Kilo)** ~ **haben** to be (10 kilos) underweight.

untergliedern [ʊntər'gli:dərn] *vt untr* to subdivide.

untergraben [ʊntər'gra:bən] *unreg vt untr* to undermine.

Untergrund ['ʊntərgrʊnt] *m* foundation; (*POL*) underground; ~**bahn** *f* underground (*BRIT*), subway (*US*); ~**bewegung** *f* underground (movement).

unterhaken ['ʊntərha:kən] *vr:* **sich bei jdm** ~ to link arms with sb.

unterhalb ['ʊntərhalp] *präp +gen* below ♦ *adv* below; ~ **von** below.

Unterhalt ['ʊntərhalt] *m* maintenance; **seinen** ~ **verdienen** to earn one's living.

unterhalten [ʊntər'haltən] *unreg vt untr* to maintain; (*belustigen*) to entertain; (*versorgen*) to support; (*Geschäft, Kfz*) to run; (*Konto*) to have ♦ *vr untr* to talk; (*sich belustigen*) to enjoy o.s.

unterhaltend, unterhaltsam [ʊntər'haltza:m] *adj* entertaining.

Unterhaltskosten *pl* maintenance costs *pl*.

Unterhaltszahlung *f* maintenance payment.

Unterhaltung *f* maintenance; (*Belustigung*) entertainment, amusement; (*Gespräch*) talk.

Unterhaltungskosten *pl* running costs *pl*.

Unterhaltungsmusik *f* light music.

Unterhändler ['ʊntərhɛntlər] *m* negotiator.

Unterhaus ['ʊntərhaus] *nt* House of Commons (*BRIT*), House of Representatives (*US*), Lower House.

Unterhemd ['ʊntərhɛmt] *nt* vest (*BRIT*), undershirt (*US*).

unterhöhlen [ʊntər'hø:lən] *vt untr* (*lit, fig*) to undermine.

Unterholz ['ʊntərhɔlts] *nt* undergrowth.

Unterhose ['ʊntərho:zə] *f* underpants *pl*.

unterirdisch ['ʊntərˌɪrdɪʃ] *adj* underground.

unterjubeln ['ʊntərjubəln] (*umg*) *vt:* **jdm etw** ~ to palm sth off on sb.

unterkapitalisiert ['ʊntərkapitali'zi:rt] *adj* undercapitalized.

unterkellern [ʊntər'kɛlərn] *vt untr* to build with a cellar.

Unterkiefer ['ʊntərki:fər] *m* lower jaw.

unterkommen ['ʊntərkɔmən] *unreg vi* to find shelter; (*Stelle finden*) to find work; **das ist mir noch nie untergekommen** I've never met with that; **bei jdm** ~ to stay at sb's (place).

unterkriegen ['ʊntərkri:gən] (*umg*) *vt:* **sich nicht** ~ **lassen** not to let things get one

down.

unterkühlt [ʊntər'ky:lt] *adj* (*Körper*) affected by hypothermia; (*fig: Mensch, Atmosphäre*) cool.

Unterkunft ['ʊntərkʊnft] (-, -**künfte**) *f* accommodation (*BRIT*), accommodations *pl* (*US*); ~ **und Verpflegung** board and lodging.

Unterlage ['ʊntərla:gə] *f* foundation; (*Beleg*) document; (*Schreib*~ *etc*) pad.

unterlassen [ʊntər'lasən] *unreg vt untr* (*versäumen*) to fail to do; (*sich enthalten*) to refrain from.

unterlaufen [ʊntər'laufən] *unreg vi untr* to happen ♦ *adj:* **mit Blut** ~ suffused with blood; (*Augen*) bloodshot; **mir ist ein Fehler** ~ I made a mistake.

unterlegen¹ ['ʊntərle:gən] *vt* to lay *od* put under.

unterlegen² [ʊntər'le:gən] *adj* inferior; (*besiegt*) defeated.

Unterleib ['ʊntərlaip] *m* abdomen.

unterliegen [ʊntər'li:gən] *unreg vi untr +dat* to be defeated *od* overcome (by); (*unterworfen sein*) to be subject (to).

Unterlippe ['ʊntərlɪpə] *f* bottom *od* lower lip.

unterm = unter dem.

untermalen [ʊntər'ma:lən] *vt untr* (*mit Musik*) to provide with background music.

Untermalung *f:* **musikalische** ~ background music.

untermauern [ʊntər'mauərn] *vt untr* (*Gebäude, fig*) to underpin.

Untermiete ['ʊntərmi:tə] *f* subtenancy; **bei jdm zur** ~ **wohnen** to rent a room from sb.

Untermieter(in) *m(f)* lodger.

untern = unter den.

unternehmen [ʊntər'ne:mən] *unreg vt untr* to do; (*durchführen*) to undertake; (*Versuch, Reise*) to make; **U~** (-**s**, -) *nt* undertaking, enterprise (*auch COMM*); (*Firma*) business.

unternehmend *adj* enterprising, daring.

Unternehmensberater *m* management consultant.

Unternehmensplanung *f* corporate planning, management planning.

Unternehmer(in) [ʊntər'ne:mər(ɪn)] (-**s**, -) *m(f)* (business) employer; (*alten Stils*) entrepreneur; ~**verband** *m* employers' association.

Unternehmungsgeist *m* spirit of enterprise.

unternehmungslustig *adj* enterprising.

Unteroffizier ['ʊntərˌɔfɪtsi:r] *m* noncommissioned officer, NCO.

unterordnen ['ʊntərˌɔrdnən] *vt:* ~ (+*dat*) to subordinate (to).

Unterordnung *f* subordination.

Unterprima ['ʊntərpri:ma] *f eighth year of German secondary school.*

Unterprogramm ['ʊntərprogram] *nt* (*COMPUT*) subroutine.

Unterredung [ʊntər're:dʊŋ] *f* discussion,

talk.

Unterricht ['ʊntərrɪçt] (-(e)s) m teaching; (Stunden) lessons pl; jdm ~ **(in etw** dat) **geben** to teach sb (sth).

unterrichten [ʊntər'rɪçtən] vt untr to instruct; (SCH) to teach ♦ vr untr: **sich** ~ **(über** +akk) to inform o.s. (about), obtain information (about).

Unterrichts- zW: ~**gegenstand** m topic, subject; ~**methode** f teaching method; ~**stoff** m teaching material; ~**stunde** f lesson; ~**zwecke** pl: **zu** ~**zwecken** for teaching purposes.

Unterrock ['ʊntərrɔk] m petticoat, slip.

unters = **unter das.**

untersagen [ʊntər'zaːgən] vt untr to forbid; **jdm etw** ~ to forbid sb to do sth.

Untersatz ['ʊntərzats] m mat; (für Blumentöpfe etc) base.

unterschätzen [ʊntər'ʃɛtsən] vt untr to underestimate.

unterscheiden [ʊntər'ʃaɪdən] unreg vt untr to distinguish ♦ vr untr to differ.

Unterscheidung f (Unterschied) distinction; (Unterscheiden) differentiation.

Unterschenkel ['ʊntərʃɛŋkəl] m lower leg.

Unterschicht ['ʊntərʃɪçt] f lower class.

unterschieben ['ʊntərʃiːbən] unreg vt (fig): **jdm etw** ~ to foist sth on sb.

Unterschied ['ʊntərʃiːt] (-(e)s, -e) m difference, distinction; **im** ~ **zu** as distinct from; **u~lich** adj varying, differing; (diskriminierend) discriminatory.

unterschiedslos adv indiscriminately.

unterschlagen [ʊntər'ʃlaːgən] unreg vt untr to embezzle; (verheimlichen) to suppress.

Unterschlagung f embezzlement; (von Briefen, Beweis) withholding.

Unterschlupf ['ʊntərʃlʊpf] (-(e)s, -schlüpfe) m refuge.

unterschlüpfen ['ʊntərʃlʏpfən] (umg) vi to take cover od shelter; (Versteck finden): **(bei jdm)** ~ to hide out (at sb's) (umg).

unterschreiben [ʊntər'ʃraɪbən] unreg vt untr to sign.

Unterschrift ['ʊntərʃrɪft] f signature; (Bild~) caption.

unterschwellig ['ʊntərʃvɛlɪç] adj subliminal.

Unterseeboot ['ʊntərzeːboːt] nt submarine.

Unterseite ['ʊntərzaɪtə] f underside.

Untersekunda ['ʊntərzekunda] f sixth year of German secondary school.

Untersetzer ['ʊntərzɛtsər] m tablemat; (für Gläser) coaster.

untersetzt [ʊntər'zɛtst] adj stocky.

unterste(r, s) ['ʊntərstə(r, s)] adj lowest, bottom.

unterstehen[1] [ʊntər'ʃteːən] unreg vi untr +dat to be under ♦ vr untr to dare.

unterstehen[2] ['ʊntərʃteːən] unreg vi to shelter.

unterstellen[1] [ʊntər'ʃtɛlən] vt untr to subordinate; (fig) to impute; **jdm/etw unterstellt sein** to be under sb/sth; (in Firma) to report to sb/sth.

unterstellen[2] ['ʊntərʃtɛlən] vt (Auto) to garage, park ♦ vr to take shelter.

Unterstellung f (falsche Behauptung) misrepresentation; (Andeutung) insinuation.

unterstreichen [ʊntər'ʃtraɪçən] unreg vt untr (lit, fig) to underline.

Unterstufe ['ʊntərʃtuːfə] f lower grade.

unterstützen [ʊntər'ʃtʏtsən] vt untr to support.

Unterstützung f support, assistance.

untersuchen [ʊntər'zuːxən] vt untr (MED) to examine; (Polizei) to investigate; **sich ärztlich** ~ **lassen** to have a medical (BRIT) od physical (US) (examination), have a check-up.

Untersuchung f examination; investigation, inquiry.

Untersuchungs- zW: ~**ausschuß** m committee of inquiry; ~**ergebnis** nt (JUR) findings pl; (MED) result of an examination; ~**haft** f custody; **in** ~**haft sein** to be remanded in custody; ~**richter** m examining magistrate.

Untertagebau [ʊntər'taːgəbau] m underground mining.

Untertan ['ʊntərtaːn] (-s, -en) m subject.

untertänig ['ʊntərtɛːnɪç] adj submissive, humble.

Untertasse ['ʊntərtasə] f saucer.

untertauchen ['ʊntərtauxən] vi to dive; (fig) to disappear, go underground.

Unterteil ['ʊntərtaɪl] nt od m lower part, bottom.

unterteilen [ʊntər'taɪlən] vt untr to divide up.

Untertertia ['ʊntərtɛrtsia] f fourth year of German secondary school.

Untertitel ['ʊntərtiːtəl] m subtitle; (für Bild) caption.

unterwandern [ʊntər'vandərn] vt untr to infiltrate.

Unterwäsche ['ʊntərvɛʃə] f underwear.

unterwegs [ʊntər'veːks] adv on the way; (auf Reisen) away.

unterweisen [ʊntər'vaɪzən] unreg vt untr to instruct.

Unterwelt ['ʊntərvɛlt] f (lit, fig) underworld.

unterwerfen [ʊntər'vɛrfən] unreg vt untr to subject; (Volk) to subjugate ♦ vr untr to submit.

unterwürfig [ʊntər'vʏrfɪç] adj obsequious.

unterzeichnen [ʊntər'tsaɪçnən] vt untr to sign.

Unterzeichner m signatory.

unterziehen [ʊntər'tsiːən] unreg vt untr +dat to subject ♦ vr untr +dat to undergo; (einer Prüfung) to take.

Untiefe ['ʊntiːfə] f shallow.

Untier ['ʊntiːr] nt monster.

untragbar [ʊn'traːkbaːr] adj intolerable, unbearable.

untreu ['ʊntrɔy] adj unfaithful; **sich** dat **selbst**

~ **werden** to be untrue to o.s.
Untreue *f* unfaithfulness.
untröstlich [ʊn'trøːstlɪç] *adj* inconsolable.
Untugend ['ʊntuːɡənt] *f* vice; (*Angewohnheit*)
bad habit.
un- *zW:* ~**überbrückbar** *adj* (*fig: Gegensätze etc*)
irreconcilable; (*Kluft*) unbridgeable;
~**überlegt** *adj* ill-considered ♦ *adv* without
thinking; ~**übersehbar** *adj* (*Schaden etc*)
incalculable; (*Menge*) vast, immense;
(*auffällig: Fehler etc*) obvious; ~**übersichtlich**
adj (*Gelände*) broken; (*Kurve*) blind; (*System,
Plan*) confused; ~**übertroffen** *adj*
unsurpassed.
un- *zW:* ~**umgänglich** *adj* indispensable, vital;
~**umstößlich** *adj* (*Tatsache*) incontrovertible;
(*Entschluß*) irrevocable; ~**umstritten** *adj*
undisputed; ~**umwunden** [-ʊm'vʊndən] *adj*
candid ♦ *adv* straight out.
ununterbrochen ['ʊn|ʊntərbrɔxən] *adj*
uninterrupted.
un- *zW:* ~**veränderlich** *adj* unchangeable;
~**verantwortlich** *adj* irresponsible;
(~*entschuldbar*) inexcusable;
~**verarbeitet** *adj* (*lit, fig*) raw; ~**veräußerlich**
[-fɛr'ɔysərlɪç] *adj* inalienable; (*Besitz*)
unmarketable; ~**verbesserlich** *adj*
incorrigible; ~**verbindlich** *adj* not binding;
(*Antwort*) curt ♦ *adv* (*COMM*) without
obligation; ~**verbleit** [-fɛrblaɪt] *adj* (*Benzin*)
unleaded; ~**verblümt** [-fɛr'blyːmt] *adj* plain,
blunt ♦ *adv* plainly, bluntly; ~**verdaulich** *adj*
indigestible; ~**verdorben** *adj* unspoilt;
~**verdrossen** *adj* undeterred; (~*ermüdlich*)
untiring; ~**vereinbar** *adj* incompatible;
~**verfälscht** [-fɛrfɛlʃt] *adj* (*auch fig*)
unadulterated; (*Dialekt*) pure; (*Natürlichkeit*)
unaffected; ~**verfänglich** *adj* harmless;
~**verfroren** *adj* impudent; ~**vergänglich** *adj*
immortal; (*Eindruck, Erinnerung*) everlasting;
~**vergeßlich** *adj* unforgettable;
~**vergleichlich** *adj* unique, incomparable;
~**verhältnismäßig** *adv* disproportionately;
(*übermäßig*) excessively; ~**verheiratet** *adj*
unmarried; ~**verhofft** *adj* unexpected;
~**verhohlen** [-fɛrhoːlən] *adj* open, uncon-
cealed; ~**verkäuflich** *adj:* „~**verkäuflich**"
"not for sale"; ~**verkennbar** *adj*
unmistakable; ~**verletzlich** *adj* (*fig: Rechte*)
inviolable; (*lit*) invulnerable; ~**verletzt** *adj*
uninjured; ~**vermeidlich** *adj* unavoidable;
~**vermittelt** *adj* (*plötzlich*) sudden,
unexpected; **U~vermögen** *nt* inability;
~**vermutet** *adj* unexpected; ~**vernünftig** *adj*
foolish; ~**verrichtet** *adj:* ~**verrichteter Dinge**
empty-handed; ~**verschämt** *adj* impudent;
U~verschämtheit *f* impudence, insolence;
~**verschuldet** *adj* occurring through no fault
of one's own; ~**versehens** *adv* all of a
sudden; ~**versehrt** [-fɛrzeːrt] *adj* uninjured;
~**versöhnlich** *adj* irreconcilable;
U~verstand *m* lack of judgement; (*Torheit*)

folly; ~**verständlich** *adj* unintelligible;
~**versucht** *adj:* **nichts** ~**versucht lassen** to try
everything; ~**verträglich** *adj* quarrelsome;
(*Meinungen, MED*) incompatible;
~**verwechselbar** *adj* unmistakable,
distinctive; ~**verwüstlich** *adj* indestructible;
(*Mensch*) irrepressible; ~**verzeihlich** *adj*
unpardonable; ~**verzinslich** *adj* interest-
free; ~**verzüglich** [-fɛr'tsyːklɪç] *adj*
immediate; ~**vollendet** *adj* unfinished;
~**vollkommen** *adj* imperfect; ~**vollständig**
adj incomplete; ~**vorbereitet** *adj* unprepared;
~**voreingenommen** *adj* unbiased;
~**vorhergesehen** *adj* unforeseen;
~**vorsichtig** *adj* careless, imprudent;
~**vorstellbar** *adj* inconceivable; ~**vorteilhaft**
adj disadvantageous.
unwahr ['ʊnvaːr] *adj* untrue; ~**haftig** *adj*
untruthful; **U~heit** *f* untruth; **die U~heit
sagen** not to tell the truth; ~**scheinlich** *adj*
improbable, unlikely ♦ *adv* (*umg*) incredibly;
U~scheinlichkeit *f* improbability,
unlikelihood.
unwegsam ['ʊnveːkzaːm] *adj* (*Gelände etc*)
rough.
unweigerlich [ʊn'vaɪɡərlɪç] *adj* unquestioning
♦ *adv* without fail.
unweit ['ʊnvaɪt] *präp* +*gen* not far from ♦ *adv*
not far.
Unwesen ['ʊnveːzən] *nt* nuisance; (*Unfug*)
mischief; **sein ~ treiben** to wreak havoc;
(*Mörder etc*) to be at large.
unwesentlich *adj* inessential, unimportant;
~ **besser** marginally better.
Unwetter ['ʊnvɛtər] *nt* thunderstorm.
unwichtig ['ʊnvɪçtɪç] *adj* unimportant.
un- *zW:* ~**widerlegbar** *adj* irrefutable;
~**widerruflich** *adj* irrevocable;
~**widerstehlich** [-viːdər'ʃteːlɪç] *adj*
irresistible.
unwiederbringlich [ʊnviːdər'brɪŋlɪç] *adj* (*geh*)
irretrievable.
Unwille(n) ['ʊnvɪlə(n)] *m* indignation.
unwillig *adj* indignant; (*widerwillig*) reluctant.
unwillkürlich ['ʊnvɪlkyːrlɪç] *adj* involuntary
♦ *adv* instinctively; (*lachen*) involuntarily.
unwirklich ['ʊnvɪrklɪç] *adj* unreal.
unwirksam ['ʊnvɪrkzaːm] *adj* ineffective.
unwirsch ['ʊnvɪrʃ] *adj* cross, surly.
unwirtlich ['ʊnvɪrtlɪç] *adj* inhospitable.
unwirtschaftlich ['ʊnvɪrtʃaftlɪç] *adj*
uneconomical.
unwissend ['ʊnvɪsənt] *adj* ignorant.
Unwissenheit *f* ignorance.
unwissenschaftlich *adj* unscientific.
unwissentlich *adv* unwittingly,
unknowingly.
unwohl ['ʊnvoːl] *adj* unwell, ill; **U~sein (-s)** *nt*
indisposition.
unwürdig ['ʊnvyrdɪç] *adj* unworthy.
Unzahl ['ʊntsaːl] *f:* **eine ~ von ...** a whole host
of ...

unzählig [ʊn'tsɛːlɪç] *adj* innumerable, countless.

unzeitgemäß ['ʊntsaɪtgəmɛːs] *adj* (*altmodisch*) old-fashioned.

un- *zW:* ~**zerbrechlich** *adj* unbreakable; ~**zerreißbar** *adj* untearable; ~**zerstörbar** *adj* indestructible; ~**zertrennlich** *adj* inseparable.

Unzucht ['ʊntsʊxt] *f* sexual offence.

unzüchtig ['ʊntsʏçtɪç] *adj* immoral.

un- *zW:* ~**zufrieden** *adj* dissatisfied; **U**~**zufriedenheit** *f* discontent; ~**zugänglich** *adj* (*Gegend*) inaccessible; (*Mensch*) inapproachable; ~**zulänglich** *adj* inadequate; ~**zulässig** *adj* inadmissible; ~**zumutbar** *adj* unreasonable; ~**zurechnungsfähig** *adj* irresponsible; **jdn für** ~**zurechnungsfähig erklären lassen** (*JUR*) to have sb certified (insane); ~**zusammenhängend** *adj* disconnected; (*Äußerung*) incoherent; ~**zustellbar** *adj:* **falls** ~**zustellbar, bitte an Absender zurück** if undelivered, please return to sender; ~**zutreffend** *adj* incorrect; „~**zutreffendes bitte streichen"** "delete as applicable"; ~**zuverlässig** *adj* unreliable.

unzweckmäßig ['ʊntsvɛkmɛːsɪç] *adj* (*nicht ratsam*) inadvisable; (*unpraktisch*) impractical; (*ungeeignet*) unsuitable.

unzweideutig ['ʊntsvaɪdɔʏtɪç] *adj* unambiguous.

unzweifelhaft ['ʊntsvaɪfəlhaft] *adj* indubitable.

üppig ['ʏpɪç] *adj* (*Frau*) curvaceous; (*Essen*) sumptuous, lavish; (*Vegetation*) luxuriant, lush; (*Haar*) thick.

Ur- ['uːr] *in zW:* original.

Urabstimmung ['uːrʔapʃtɪmʊŋ] *f* ballot.

Ural [u'raːl] (**-s**) *m:* **der** ~ the Ural mountains *pl*, the Urals *pl*; ~**gebirge** *nt* Ural mountains.

uralt ['uːrʔalt] *adj* ancient, very old.

Uran [u'raːn] (**-s**) *nt* uranium.

Uraufführung *f* first performance.

urbar *adj:* **die Wüste/Land** ~ **machen** to reclaim the desert/cultivate land.

Urdu ['ʊrdu] (**-**) *nt* Urdu.

Ur- *zW:* ~**einwohner** *m* original inhabitant; ~**eltern** *pl* ancestors *pl*; ~**enkel(in)** *m(f)* great-grandchild; ~**fassung** *f* original version; ~**großmutter** *f* great-grandmother; ~**großvater** *m* great-grandfather.

Urheber (**-s**, **-**) *m* originator; (*Autor*) author; ~**recht** *nt:* ~**recht (an** +*dat*) copyright (on); **u**~**rechtlich** *adv:* **u**~**rechtlich geschützt** copyright.

urig ['uːrɪç] (*umg*) *adj* (*Mensch, Atmosphäre*) earthy.

Urin [u'riːn] (**-s**, **-e**) *m* urine.

urkomisch *adj* incredibly funny.

Urkunde *f* document; (*Kauf*~) deed.

urkundlich ['uːrkʊntlɪç] *adj* documentary.

urladen ['uːrlaːdən] *vt* (*COMPUT*) to boot.

Urlader *m* (*COMPUT*) bootstrap.

Urlaub ['uːrlaʊp] (**-(e)s**, **-e**) *m* holiday(s *pl*) (*BRIT*), vacation (*US*); (*MIL etc*) leave; ~**er** (**-s**, **-**) *m* holiday-maker (*BRIT*), vacationer (*US*).

Urlaubs- *zW:* ~**geld** *nt* holiday (*BRIT*) *od* vacation (*US*) money; ~**ort** *m* holiday (*BRIT*) *od* vacation (*US*) resort; **u**~**reif** *adj* in need of a holiday (*BRIT*) *od* vacation (*US*).

Urmensch *m* primitive man.

Urne ['ʊrnə] (**-**, **-n**) *f* urn; **zur** ~ **gehen** to go to the polls.

urplötzlich ['uːr'plœtslɪç] (*umg*) *adv* all of a sudden.

Ursache ['uːrzaxə] *f* cause; **keine** ~**!** (*auf Dank*) don't mention it, you're welcome; (*auf Entschuldigung*) that's all right.

ursächlich ['uːrzɛçlɪç] *adj* causal.

Urschrei ['uːrʃraɪ] *m* (*PSYCH*) primal scream.

Ursprung ['uːrʃprʊŋ] *m* origin, source; (*von Fluß*) source.

ursprünglich ['uːrʃprʏŋlɪç] *adj* original ♦ *adv* originally.

Ursprungsland *nt* (*COMM*) country of origin.

Ursprungszeugnis *nt* certificate of origin.

Urteil ['ʊrtaɪl] (**-s**, **-e**) *nt* opinion; (*JUR*) sentence, judgement; **sich** *dat* **ein** ~ **über etw** *akk* **erlauben** to pass judgement on sth; **ein** ~ **über etw** *akk* **fällen** to pass judgement on sth; **u**~**en** *vi* to judge.

Urteilsbegründung *f* (*JUR*) opinion.

Urteilsspruch *m* sentence; verdict.

Urtrieb ['uːrtriːp] (**-(e)s**) *m* basic drive.

Uruguay [uru'guaːi] (**-s**) *nt* Uruguay.

Uruguayer(in) (**-s**, **-**) *m(f)* Uruguayan.

uruguayisch *adj* Uruguayan.

Ur- *zW:* ~**wald** *m* jungle; **u**~**wüchsig** *adj* natural; (*Landschaft*) unspoilt; (*Humor*) earthy; ~**zeit** *f* prehistoric times *pl*.

USA [uː'ɛs'aː] *pl abk:* **die** ~ the USA *sing*.

Usbekistan [ʊs'beːkistaːn] (**-s**) *nt* Uzbekistan.

usw. *abk* (= *und so weiter*) etc.

Utensilien [uten'ziːliən] *pl* utensils *pl*.

Utopie [uto'piː] *f* pipe dream.

utopisch [u'toːpɪʃ] *adj* utopian.

u.U. *abk* (= *unter Umständen*) possibly.

UV *abk* (= *ultraviolett*) U.V.

u.v.a. *abk* (= *und viele(s) andere*) and much/many more.

u.v.a.m. *abk* (= *und viele(s) andere mehr*) and much/many more.

u.W. *abk* (= *unseres Wissens*) to our knowledge.

Ü-Wagen *m* (*RUNDF, TV*) outside broadcast vehicle.

uzen ['uːtsən] (*umg*) *vt, vi* to tease, kid.

u.zw. *abk* = **und zwar**.

V, v

V¹, v [faʊ] *nt* V, v; ~ **wie Viktor** ≈ V for Victor.

V² [faʊ] *abk* (= *Volt*) v.

VAE *pl abk* (= *Vereinigte Arabische Emirate*) UAE.

vag(e) *adj* vague.

Vagina [va'giːna] (-, **Vaginen**) *f* vagina.

Vakuum ['vaːkuʊm] (-s, **Vakua** *od* **Vakuen**) *nt* vacuum; **v~verpackt** *adj* vacuum-packed.

Vandalismus [vanda'lɪsmʊs] *m* vandalism.

Vanille [va'nɪljə] (-) *f* vanilla; **~zucker** *m* vanilla sugar.

Vanillinzucker *m* vanilla sugar.

variabel [vari'aːbəl] *adj:* **variable Kosten** variable costs.

Variable [vari'aːblə] (-, **-n**) *f* variable.

Variante [vari'antə] (-, **-n**) *f:* ~ **(zu)** variant (on).

Variation [variatsi'oːn] *f* variation.

variieren [vari'iːrən] *vt, vi* to vary.

Vase ['vaːzə] (-, **-n**) *f* vase.

Vater ['faːtər] (-s, ⸚) *m* father; ~ **Staat** (*umg*) the State; **~land** *nt* native country; (*bes Deutschland*) Fatherland; **~landsliebe** *f* patriotism.

väterlich ['fɛːtərlɪç] *adj* fatherly.

väterlicherseits *adv* on the father's side.

Vaterschaft *f* paternity.

Vaterschaftsklage *f* paternity suit.

Vaterstelle *f:* ~ **bei jdm vertreten** to take the place of sb's father.

Vaterunser (-s, -) *nt* Lord's Prayer.

Vati ['faːti] (-s, -s) (*umg*) *m* dad(dy).

Vatikan [vati'kaːn] (-s) *m* Vatican.

V-Ausschnitt ['faʊaʊsʃnɪt] *m* V-neck.

VB *abk* (= *Verhandlungsbasis*) o.i.r.o.

v. Chr. *abk* (= *vor Christus*) B.C.

Vegetarier(in) [vege'taːriər(ɪn)] (-s, -) *m(f)* vegetarian.

vegetarisch *adj* vegetarian.

Vegetation [vegetatsi'oːn] *f* vegetation.

vegetativ [vegeta'tiːf] *adj* (*BIOL*) vegetative; (*MED*) autonomic.

vegetieren [vege'tiːrən] *vi* to vegetate; (*kärglich leben*) to eke out a bare existence.

Vehikel [ve'hiːkəl] (-s, -) (*pej: umg*) *nt* boneshaker.

Veilchen ['faɪlçən] *nt* violet; (*umg: blaues Auge*) shiner, black eye.

Velours (-, -) *nt* suede; **~leder** *nt* suede.

Vene ['veːnə] (-, **-n**) *f* vein.

Venedig [ve'neːdɪç] (-s) *nt* Venice.

Venezianer(in) [venetsi'aːnər(ɪn)] (-s, -) *m(f)* Venetian.

venezianisch [venetsi'aːnɪʃ] *adj* Venetian.

Venezolaner(in) [venetso'laːnər(ɪn)] (-s, -) *m(f)* Venezuelan.

venezolanisch *adj* Venezuelan.

Venezuela [venetsu'eːla] (-s) *nt* Venezuela.

Ventil [vɛn'tiːl] (-s, **-e**) *nt* valve.

Ventilator [vɛnti'laːtor] *m* ventilator.

verabreden [fɛr'|apreːdən] *vt* to arrange; (*Termin*) to agree upon ♦ *vr* to arrange to meet; **sich (mit jdm)** ~ to arrange to meet (sb); **schon verabredet sein** to have a prior engagement (*form*), have something else on.

Verabredung *f* arrangement; (*Treffen*) appointment; **ich habe eine** ~ I'm meeting somebody.

verabreichen [fɛr'|apraɪçən] *vt* (*Tracht Prügel etc*) to give; (*Arznei*) to administer (*form*).

verabscheuen [fɛr'|apʃɔʏən] *vt* to detest, abhor.

verabschieden [fɛr'|apʃiːdən] *vt* (*Gäste*) to say goodbye to; (*entlassen*) to discharge; (*Gesetz*) to pass ♦ *vr:* **sich** ~ **(von)** to take one's leave (of).

Verabschiedung *f* (*von Beamten etc*) discharge; (*von Gesetz*) passing.

verachten [fɛr'|axtən] *vt* to despise; **nicht zu** ~ (*umg*) not to be scoffed at.

verächtlich [fɛr'|ɛçtlɪç] *adj* contemptuous; (*verachtenswert*) contemptible; **jdn** ~ **machen** to run sb down.

Verachtung *f* contempt; **jdn mit** ~ **strafen** to treat sb with contempt.

veralbern [fɛr'|albərn] (*umg*) *vt* to make fun of.

verallgemeinern [fɛr|algə'maɪnərn] *vt* to generalize.

Verallgemeinerung *f* generalization.

veralten [fɛr'|altən] *vi* to become obsolete *od* out-of-date.

Veranda [ve'randa] (-, **Veranden**) *f* veranda.

veränderlich [fɛr'|ɛndərlɪç] *adj* variable; (*Wetter*) changeable; **V~keit** *f* variability; changeability.

verändern *vt, vr* to change.

Veränderung *f* change; **eine berufliche** ~ a change of job.

verängstigen [fɛr'|ɛŋstɪgən] *vt* (*erschrecken*) to frighten; (*einschüchtern*) to intimidate.

verankern [fɛr'|aŋkərn] *vt* (*NAUT, TECH*) to anchor; (*fig*): ~ **(in** +*dat*) to embed (in).

veranlagen [fɛr'|anlaːgən] *vt:* **etw** ~ **(mit)** to assess sth (at).

veranlagt *adj:* **praktisch** ~ **sein** to be practically minded; **zu** *od* **für etw** ~ **sein** to be cut out for sth.

Veranlagung *f* disposition, aptitude.

veranlassen [fɛr'|anlasən] *vt* to cause; **Maßnahmen** ~ to take measures; **sich veranlaßt sehen** to feel prompted; **etw** ~ **to** arrange for sth; (*befehlen*) to order sth.

Veranlassung *f* cause; motive; **auf jds** ~ *akk* **(hin)** at sb's instigation.
veranschaulichen [fɛr'|anʃaʊlɪçən] *vt* to illustrate.
veranschlagen [fɛr'|anʃla:gən] *vt* to estimate.
veranstalten [fɛr'|anʃtaltən] *vt* to organize, arrange.
Veranstalter(in) (-s, -) *m(f)* organizer; (*COMM: von Konzerten etc*) promoter.
Veranstaltung *f* (*Veranstalten*) organizing; (*Veranstaltetes*) event; (*feierlich, öffentlich*) function.
verantworten [fɛr'|antvɔrtən] *vt* to accept responsibility for; (*Folgen etc*) to answer for ♦ *vr* to justify o.s.; **etw vor jdm** ~ to answer to sb for sth.
verantwortlich *adj* responsible.
Verantwortung *f* responsibility; **jdn zur** ~ **ziehen** to call sb to account.
verantwortungs- *zW:* ~**bewußt** *adj* responsible; **V~gefühl** *nt* sense of responsibility; ~**los** *adj* irresponsible; ~**voll** *adj* responsible.
verarbeiten [fɛr'|arbaɪtən] *vt* to process; (*geistig*) to assimilate; (*Erlebnis etc*) to digest; **etw zu etw** ~ to make sth into sth; ~**de Industrie** processing industries *pl*.
verarbeitet *adj:* **gut** ~ (*Kleid etc*) well finished.
Verarbeitung *f* processing; assimilation.
verärgern [fɛr'|ɛrgərn] *vt* to annoy.
verarmen [fɛr'|armən] *vi* (*lit, fig*) to become impoverished.
verarschen [fɛr'|arʃən] (*umg!*) *vt:* **jdn** ~ to take the mickey out of sb.
verarzten [fɛr'|a:rtstən] *vt* to fix up (*umg*).
verausgaben [fɛr'|aʊsga:bən] *vr* to run out of money; (*fig*) to exhaust o.s.
veräußern [fɛr'|ɔʏsərn] *vt* (*form: verkaufen*) to dispose of.
Verb [vɛrp] (-s, -en) *nt* verb.
Verb. *abk* (= *Verband*) assoc.
Verband [fɛr'bant] (-(e)s, ⁻e) *m* (*MED*) bandage, dressing; (*Bund*) association, society; (*MIL*) unit.
verband *etc vb siehe* **verbinden**.
Verband- *zW:* ~**(s)kasten** *m* medicine chest, first-aid box; ~**(s)päckchen** *nt* gauze bandage; ~**stoff** *m*, ~**zeug** *nt* bandage, dressing material.
verbannen [fɛr'banən] *vt* to banish.
Verbannung *f* exile.
verbarrikadieren [fɛrbarika'di:rən] *vt* to barricade ♦ *vr* to barricade o.s. in.
verbauen [fɛr'baʊən] *vt:* **sich** *dat* **alle Chancen** ~ to spoil one's chances.
verbergen [fɛr'bɛrgən] *unreg vt, vr:* **(sich)** ~ **(vor** +*dat*) to hide (from).
verbessern [fɛr'bɛsərn] *vt* to improve; (*berichtigen*) to correct ♦ *vr* to improve; to correct o.s.
verbessert *adj* revised; improved; **eine neue,** ~**e Auflage** a new revised edition.

Verbesserung *f* improvement; correction.
verbeugen [fɛr'bɔʏgən] *vr* to bow.
Verbeugung *f* bow.
verbiegen [fɛr'bi:gən] *unreg vi* to bend.
verbiestert [fɛr'bi:stərt] (*umg*) *adj* crotchety.
verbieten [fɛr'bi:tən] *unreg vt* to forbid; (*amtlich*) to prohibit; (*Zeitung, Partei*) to ban; **jdm etw** ~ to forbid sb to do sth.
verbilligen [fɛr'bɪlɪgən] *vt* to reduce (the price of) ♦ *vr* to become cheaper, go down.
verbinden [fɛr'bɪndən] *unreg vt* to connect; (*kombinieren*) to combine; (*MED*) to bandage ♦ *vr* to combine (*auch CHEM*), join (together); **jdm die Augen** ~ to blindfold sb.
verbindlich [fɛr'bɪntlɪç] *adj* binding; (*freundlich*) obliging; ~ **zusagen** to accept definitely; **V~keit** *f* obligation; (*Höflichkeit*) civility; **Verbindlichkeiten** *pl* (*JUR*) obligations *pl*; (*COMM*) liabilities *pl*.
Verbindung *f* connection; (*Zusammensetzung*) combination; (*CHEM*) compound; (*UNIV*) club; (*TEL: Anschluß*) line; **mit jdm in** ~ **stehen** to be in touch *od* contact with sb; ~ **mit jdm aufnehmen** to contact sb.
Verbindungsmann (-(e)s, *pl* -**männer** *od* -**leute**) *m* intermediary; (*Agent*) contact.
verbissen [fɛr'bɪsən] *adj* grim; (*Arbeiter*) dogged; **V~heit** *f* grimness; doggedness.
verbitten [fɛr'bɪtən] *unreg vt:* **sich** *dat* **etw** ~ not to tolerate sth, not to stand for sth.
verbittern [fɛr'bɪtərn] *vt* to embitter ♦ *vi* to get bitter.
verblassen [fɛr'blasən] *vi* to fade.
Verbleib [fɛr'blaɪp] (-(e)s) *m* whereabouts.
verbleiben [fɛr'blaɪbən] *unreg vi* to remain; **wir sind so verblieben, daß wir ...** we agreed to ...
verbleit [fɛr'blaɪt] *adj* leaded.
Verblendung [fɛr'blɛnduŋ] *f* (*fig*) delusion.
verblöden [fɛr'blø:dən] *vi* (*Hilfsverb sein*) to get stupid.
verblüffen [fɛr'blʏfən] *vt* to amaze; (*verwirren*) to baffle.
Verblüffung *f* stupefaction.
verblühen [fɛr'bly:ən] *vi* to wither, fade.
verbluten [fɛr'blu:tən] *vi* to bleed to death.
verbohren [fɛr'bo:rən] (*umg*) *vr:* **sich in etw** *akk* ~ to become obsessed with sth.
verbohrt *adj* (*Haltung*) stubborn, obstinate.
verborgen [fɛr'bɔrgən] *adj* hidden; ~**e Mängel** latent defects *pl*.
Verbot [fɛr'bo:t] (-(e)s, -e) *nt* prohibition, ban.
verboten *adj* forbidden; **Rauchen** ~**!** no smoking; **er sah** ~ **aus** (*umg*) he looked a real sight.
verbotenerweise *adv* though it is forbidden.
Verbotsschild *nt* prohibitory sign.
verbrämen [fɛr'brɛ:mən] *vt* (*fig*) to gloss over; (*Kritik*): ~ **(mit)** to veil (in).
Verbrauch [fɛr'braʊx] (-(e)s) *m* consumption.
verbrauchen *vt* to use up; **der Wagen**

verbraucht 10 Liter Benzin auf 100 km the car does 10 kms to the litre (*BRIT*) *od* liter (*US*).

Verbraucher(in) (-s, -) *m(f)* consumer; **~markt** *m* hypermarket; **v~nah** *adj* consumer-friendly; **~schutz** *m* consumer protection; **~verband** *m* consumer council.

Verbrauchsgüter *pl* consumer goods *pl*.

verbraucht *adj* used up, finished; (*Luft*) stale; (*Mensch*) worn-out.

Verbrechen [fɛr'brɛçən] **(-s, -)** *nt* crime.

Verbrecher(in) (-s, -) *m(f)* criminal; **v~isch** *adj* criminal; **~kartei** *f* file of offenders, ≈ rogues' gallery; **~tum (-s)** *nt* criminality.

verbreiten [fɛr'braɪtən] *vt* to spread; (*Licht*) to shed; (*Wärme, Ruhe*) to radiate ♦ *vr* to spread; **eine (weit) verbreitete Ansicht** a widely held opinion; **sich über etw** *akk* **~** to expound on sth.

verbreitern [fɛr'braɪtərn] *vt* to broaden.

Verbreitung *f* spread(ing); shedding; radiation.

verbrennbar *adj* combustible.

verbrennen [fɛr'brɛnən] *unreg vt* to burn; (*Leiche*) to cremate; (*versengen*) to scorch; (*Haar*) to singe; (*verbrühen*) to scald.

Verbrennung *f* burning; (*in Motor*) combustion; (*von Leiche*) cremation.

Verbrennungsanlage *f* incineration plant.

Verbrennungsmotor *m* internal-combustion engine.

verbriefen [fɛr'briːfən] *vt* to document.

verbringen [fɛr'brɪŋən] *unreg vt* to spend.

Verbrüderung [fɛr'bryːdərʊŋ] *f* fraternization.

verbrühen [fɛr'bryːən] *vt* to scald.

verbuchen [fɛr'buːxən] *vt* (*FIN*) to register; (*Erfolg*) to enjoy; (*Mißerfolg*) to suffer.

verbummeln [fɛr'bʊməln] (*umg*) *vt* (*verlieren*) to lose; (*Zeit*) to waste, fritter away; (*Verabredung*) to miss.

verbunden [fɛr'bʊndən] *adj* connected; **jdm ~ sein** to be obliged *od* indebted to sb; **ich/ er ist war falsch ~** (*TEL*) it was a wrong number.

verbünden [fɛr'byndən] *vr* to form an alliance.

Verbundenheit *f* bond, relationship.

Verbündete(r) *f(m)* ally.

Verbundglas [fɛr'bʊntglaːs] *nt* laminated glass.

verbürgen [fɛr'byrgən] *vr:* **sich ~ für** to vouch for; **ein verbürgtes Recht** an established right.

verbüßen [fɛr'byːsən] *vt:* **eine Strafe ~** to serve a sentence.

verchromt [fɛr'kroːmt] *adj* chromium-plated.

Verdacht [fɛr'daxt] **(-(e)s)** *m* suspicion; **~ schöpfen (gegen jdn)** to become suspicious (of sb); **jdn in ~ haben** to suspect sb; **es besteht ~ auf Krebs** *akk* cancer is suspected.

verdächtig *adj* suspicious.

verdächtigen [fɛr'dɛçtɪgən] *vt* to suspect.

Verdächtigung *f* suspicion.

verdammen [fɛr'damən] *vt* to damn, condemn.

Verdammnis (-) *f* perdition, damnation.

verdammt (*umg*) *adj, adv* damned; **~ noch mal!** bloody hell (*!*), damn (*!*).

verdampfen [fɛr'dampfən] *vt, vi* (*vi Hilfsverb sein*) to vaporize; (*KOCH*) to boil away.

verdanken [fɛr'daŋkən] *vt:* **jdm etw ~** to owe sb sth.

verdarb *etc* [fɛr'darp] *vb siehe* **verderben.**

verdattert [fɛr'datərt] (*umg*) *adj, adv* flabbergasted.

verdauen [fɛr'dauən] *vt* (*lit, fig*) to digest ♦ *vi* (*lit*) to digest.

verdaulich [fɛr'daulɪç] *adj* digestible; **das ist schwer ~** that is hard to digest.

Verdauung *f* digestion.

Verdauungsspaziergang *m* constitutional.

Verdauungsstörung *f* indigestion.

Verdeck [fɛr'dɛk] **(-(e)s, -e)** *nt* (*AUT*) soft top; (*NAUT*) deck.

verdecken *vt* to cover (up); (*verbergen*) to hide.

verdenken [fɛr'dɛŋkən] *unreg vt:* **jdm etw ~** to blame sb for sth, hold sth against sb.

verderben [fɛr'dɛrbən] *unreg vt* to spoil; (*schädigen*) to ruin; (*moralisch*) to corrupt ♦ *vi* (*Essen*) to spoil, rot; (*Mensch*) to go to the bad; **es mit jdm ~** to get into sb's bad books.

Verderben (-s) *nt* ruin.

verderblich *adj* (*Einfluß*) pernicious; (*Lebensmittel*) perishable.

verderbt *adj* (*veraltet*) depraved; **V~heit** *f* depravity.

verdeutlichen [fɛr'dɔytlɪçən] *vt* to make clear.

verdichten [fɛr'dɪçtən] *vt* (*PHYS, fig*) to compress ♦ *vr* to thicken; (*Verdacht, Eindruck*) to deepen.

verdienen [fɛr'diːnən] *vt* to earn; (*moralisch*) to deserve ♦ *vi* (*Gewinn machen*): **~ (an +dat)** to make (a profit) (on).

Verdienst [fɛr'diːnst] **(-(e)s, -e)** *m* earnings *pl* ♦ *nt* merit; (*Dank*) credit; (*Leistung*): **~ (um)** service (to), contribution (to); **v~voll** *adj* commendable.

verdient [fɛr'diːnt] *adj* well-earned; (*Person*) of outstanding merit; (*Lohn, Strafe*) rightful; **sich um etw ~ machen** to do a lot for sth.

verdirbst [fɛr'dɪrpst] *vb siehe* **verderben.**

verdirbt [fɛr'dɪrpt] *vb siehe* **verderben.**

verdonnern [fɛr'dɔnərn] (*umg*) *vt* (*zu Haft etc*): **~ (zu)** to sentence (to); **jdn zu etw ~** to order sb to do sth.

verdoppeln [fɛr'dɔpəln] *vt* to double.

Verdopp(e)lung *f* doubling.

verdorben [fɛr'dɔrbən] *pp von* **verderben** ♦ *adj* spoilt; (*geschädigt*) ruined; (*moralisch*) corrupt.

verdorren [fɛr'dɔrən] *vi* to wither.
verdrängen [fɛr'drɛŋən] *vt* to oust; (*auch PHYS*) to displace; (*PSYCH*) to repress.
Verdrängung *f* displacement; (*PSYCH*) repression.
verdrehen [fɛr'dreːən] *vt* (*lit, fig*) to twist; (*Augen*) to roll; **jdm den Kopf ~** (*fig*) to turn sb's head.
verdreht (*umg*) *adj* crazy; (*Bericht*) confused.
verdreifachen [fɛr'draɪfaxən] *vt* to treble.
verdrießen [fɛr'driːsən] *unreg vt* to annoy.
verdrießlich [fɛr'driːslɪç] *adj* peevish, annoyed.
verdroß *etc* [fɛr'drɔs] *vb siehe* **verdrießen**.
verdrossen [fɛr'drɔsən] *pp von* **verdrießen ♦** *adj* cross, sulky.
verdrücken [fɛr'drʏkən] (*umg*) *vt* to put away, eat **♦** *vr* to disappear.
Verdruß [fɛr'drʊs] (**-sses, -sse**) *m* frustration; **zu jds ~** to sb's annoyance.
verduften [fɛr'dʊftən] *vi* to evaporate; (*umg*) to disappear.
verdummen [fɛr'dʊmən] *vt* to make stupid **♦** *vi* to grow stupid.
verdunkeln [fɛr'dʊŋkəln] *vt* to darken; (*fig*) to obscure **♦** *vr* to darken.
Verdunk(e)lung *f* blackout; (*fig*) obscuring.
verdünnen [fɛr'dʏnən] *vt* to dilute.
Verdünner (**-s, -**) *m* thinner.
verdünnisieren [fɛrdʏni'ziːrən] (*umg*) *vr* to make o.s. scarce.
verdunsten [fɛr'dʊnstən] *vi* to evaporate.
verdursten [fɛr'dʊrstən] *vi* to die of thirst.
verdutzt [fɛr'dʊtst] *adj* nonplussed (*BRIT*), nonplused (*US*), taken aback.
verebben [fɛr'|ɛbən] *vi* to subside.
veredeln [fɛr'|eːdəln] *vt* (*Metalle, Erdöl*) to refine; (*Fasern*) to finish; (*BOT*) to graft.
verehren [fɛr'|eːrən] *vt* to venerate, worship (*auch REL*); **jdm etw ~** to present sb with sth.
Verehrer(in) (**-s, -**) *m(f)* admirer, worshipper (*BRIT*), worshiper (*US*).
verehrt *adj* esteemed; **(sehr) ~e Anwesende/ ~es Publikum** Ladies and Gentlemen.
Verehrung *f* respect; (*REL*) worship.
vereidigen [fɛr'|aɪdɪgən] *vt* to put on oath; **jdn auf etw** *akk* **~** to make sb swear on sth.
Vereidigung *f* swearing in.
Verein [fɛr'|aɪn] (**-(e)s, -e**) *m* club, association; **ein wohltätiger ~** a charity.
vereinbar *adj* compatible.
vereinbaren [fɛr'|aɪnbaːrən] *vt* to agree upon.
Vereinbarkeit *f* compatibility.
Vereinbarung *f* agreement.
vereinfachen [fɛr'|aɪnfaxən] *vt* to simplify.
Vereinfachung *f* simplification.
vereinheitlichen [fɛr'|aɪnhaɪtlɪçən] *vt* to standardize.
vereinigen [fɛr'|aɪnɪgən] *vt, vr* to unite.
vereinigt [fɛr'|aɪnɪçt] *adj* united; **V~e Arabische Emirate** *pl* United Arab Emirates;

V~es Königreich *nt* United Kingdom; **V~e Staaten** *pl* United States.
Vereinigung *f* union; (*Verein*) association.
vereinnahmen [fɛr'|aɪnnaːmən] *vt* (*geh*) to take; **jdn ~** (*fig*) to make demands on sb.
vereinsamen [fɛr'|aɪnzaːmən] *vi* to become lonely.
vereint [fɛr'|aɪnt] *adj* united; **V~e Nationen** *pl* United Nations.
vereinzelt [fɛr'|aɪntsəlt] *adj* isolated.
vereisen [fɛr'|aɪzən] *vi* to freeze, ice over **♦** *vt* (*MED*) to freeze.
vereiteln [fɛr'|aɪtəln] *vt* to frustrate.
vereitern [fɛr'|aɪtərn] *vi* to suppurate, fester.
Verelendung [fɛr'|eːlɛndʊŋ] *f* impoverishment.
verenden [fɛr'|ɛndən] *vi* to perish, die.
verengen [fɛr'|ɛŋən] *vr* to narrow.
vererben [fɛr'|ɛrbən] *vt* to bequeath; (*BIOL*) to transmit **♦** *vr* to be hereditary.
vererblich [fɛr'|ɛrplɪç] *adj* hereditary.
Vererbung *f* bequeathing; (*BIOL*) transmission; **das ist ~** (*umg*) it's hereditary.
verewigen [fɛr'|eːvɪgən] *vt* to immortalize **♦** *vr* (*umg*) to leave one's name.
Verf. *abk* = **Verfasser**.
verfahren [fɛr'faːrən] *unreg vi* to act **♦** *vr* to get lost **♦** *adj* tangled; **~ mit** to deal with.
Verfahren (**-s, -**) *nt* procedure; (*TECH*) process; (*JUR*) proceedings *pl*.
Verfahrenstechnik *f* (*Methode*) process.
Verfahrensweise *f* procedure.
Verfall [fɛr'fal] (**-(e)s**) *m* decline; (*von Haus*) dilapidation; (*FIN*) expiry.
verfallen *unreg vi* to decline; (*Haus*) to be falling down; (*FIN*) to lapse **♦** *adj* (*Gebäude*) dilapidated, ruined; (*Karten, Briefmarken*) invalid; (*Strafe*) lapsed; (*Paß*) expired; **~ in** *+akk* to lapse into; **~ auf** *+akk* to hit upon; **einem Laster ~ sein** to be addicted to a vice; **jdm völlig ~ sein** to be completely under sb's spell.
Verfallsdatum *nt* expiry date; (*der Haltbarkeit*) best-before date.
verfänglich [fɛr'fɛŋlɪç] *adj* awkward, tricky; (*Aussage, Beweismaterial etc*) incriminating; (*gefährlich*) dangerous.
verfärben [fɛr'fɛrbən] *vr* to change colour (*BRIT*) *od* color (*US*).
verfassen [fɛr'fasən] *vt* to write; (*Gesetz, Urkunde*) to draw up.
Verfasser(in) (**-s, -**) *m(f)* author, writer.
Verfassung *f* constitution (*auch POL*); (*körperlich*) state of health; (*seelisch*) state of mind; **sie ist in guter/schlechter ~** she is in good/bad shape.
Verfassungs- *zW*: **v~feindlich** *adj* anticonstitutional; **~gericht** *nt* constitutional court; **v~mäßig** *adj* constitutional; **~schutz** *m* (*Aufgabe*) defence of the constitution; (*Amt*) office responsible for defending the

constitution; ~**schützer(in)** *m(f)* defender of the constitution; **v~widrig** *adj* unconstitutional.

verfaulen [fɛr'faʊlən] *vi* to rot.

verfechten [fɛr'fɛçtən] *unreg vt* to defend; (*Lehre*) to advocate.

Verfechter(in) [fɛr'fɛçtər(ɪn)] (**-s, -**) *m(f)* champion; defender.

verfehlen [fɛr'fe:lən] *vt* to miss; **das Thema** ~ to be completely off the subject.

verfehlt *adj* unsuccessful; (*unangebracht*) inappropriate; **etw für** ~ **halten** to regard sth as mistaken.

Verfehlung *f* (*Vergehen*) misdemeanour (*BRIT*), misdemeanor (*US*); (*Sünde*) transgression.

verfeinern [fɛr'faɪnərn] *vt* to refine.

Verfettung [fɛr'fɛtʊŋ] *f* (*von Organ, Muskeln*) fatty degeneration.

verfeuern [fɛr'fɔʏərn] *vt* to burn; (*Munition*) to fire; (*umg*) to use up.

verfilmen [fɛr'fɪlmən] *vt* to film, make a film of.

Verfilmung *f* film (version).

Verfilzung [fɛr'fɪltsʊŋ] *f* (*fig: von Firmen, Parteien*) entanglements *pl*.

verflachen [fɛr'flaxən] *vi* to flatten out; (*fig: Diskussion*) to become superficial.

verfliegen [fɛr'fli:gən] *unreg vi* to evaporate; (*Zeit*) to pass, fly ♦ *vr* to stray (past).

verflixt [fɛr'flɪkst] (*umg*) *adj, adv* darned.

verflossen [fɛr'flɔsən] *adj* past, former.

verfluchen [fɛr'flu:xən] *vt* to curse.

verflüchtigen [fɛr'flʏçtɪgən] *vr* to evaporate; (*Geruch*) to fade.

verflüssigen [fɛr'flʏsɪgən] *vr* to become liquid.

verfolgen [fɛr'fɔlgən] *vt* to pursue; (*gerichtlich*) to prosecute; (*grausam, bes POL*) to persecute.

Verfolger(in) (**-s, -**) *m(f)* pursuer.

Verfolgte(r) *f(m)* (*politisch*) victim of persecution.

Verfolgung *f* pursuit; persecution; **strafrechtliche** ~ prosecution.

Verfolgungswahn *m* persecution mania.

verfrachten [fɛr'fraxtən] *vt* to ship.

verfremden [fɛr'frɛmdən] *vt* to alienate, distance.

verfressen [fɛr'frɛsən] (*umg*) *adj* greedy.

verfrüht [fɛr'fry:t] *adj* premature.

verfügbar *adj* available.

verfügen [fɛr'fy:gən] *vt* to direct, order ♦ *vr* to proceed ♦ *vi*: ~ **über** +*akk* to have at one's disposal; **über etw** *akk* **frei** ~ **können** to be able to do as one wants with sth.

Verfügung *f* direction, order; (*JUR*) writ; **zur** ~ at one's disposal; **jdm zur** ~ **stehen** to be available to sb.

Verfügungsgewalt *f* (*JUR*) right of disposal.

verführen [fɛr'fy:rən] *vt* to tempt; (*sexuell*) to

seduce; (*die Jugend, das Volk etc*) to lead astray.

Verführer *m* tempter; seducer.

Verführerin *f* temptress; seductress.

verführerisch *adj* seductive.

Verführung *f* seduction; (*Versuchung*) temptation.

Vergabe [fɛr'ga:bə] *f* (*von Arbeiten*) allocation; (*von Stipendium, Auftrag etc*) award.

vergällen [fɛr'gɛlən] *vt* (*geh*): **jdm die Freude/ das Leben** ~ to spoil sb's fun/sour sb's life.

vergaloppieren [fɛrgalɔ'pi:rən] (*umg*) *vr* (*sich irren*) to be on the wrong track.

vergammeln [fɛr'gaməln] (*umg*) *vi* to go to seed; (*Nahrung*) to go off; (*Zeit*) to waste.

vergangen [fɛr'gaŋən] *adj* past; **V~heit** *f* past; **V~heitsbewältigung** *f* coming to terms with the past.

vergänglich [fɛr'gɛŋlɪç] *adj* transitory; **V~keit** *f* transitoriness, impermanence.

vergasen [fɛr'ga:zən] *vt* to gasify; (*töten*) to gas.

Vergaser (**-s, -**) *m* (*AUT*) carburettor (*BRIT*), carburetor (*US*).

vergaß *etc* [fɛr'ga:s] *vb siehe* **vergessen**.

vergeben [fɛr'ge:bən] *unreg vt* to forgive; (*weggeben*) to give away; (*fig: Chance*) to throw away; (*Auftrag, Preis*) to award; (*Studienplätze, Stellen*) to allocate; **jdm (etw)** ~ to forgive sb (sth); ~ **an** +*akk* to award to; to allocate to; ~ **sein** to be occupied; (*umg: Mädchen*) to be spoken for.

vergebens *adv* in vain.

vergeblich [fɛr'ge:plɪç] *adv* in vain ♦ *adj* vain, futile.

Vergebung *f* forgiveness.

vergegenwärtigen [fɛrge:gən'vɛrtɪgən] *vr*: **sich** *dat* **etw** ~ to visualize sth; (*erinnern*) to recall sth.

vergehen [fɛr'ge:ən] *unreg vi* to pass by *od* away ♦ *vr* to commit an offence (*BRIT*) *od* offense (*US*); **vor Angst** ~ to be scared to death; **jdm vergeht etw** sb loses sth; **sich an jdm** ~ to (sexually) assault sb; **V~** (**-s, -**) *nt* offence (*BRIT*), offense (*US*).

vergeigen [fɛr'gaɪgən] (*umg*) *vt* to cock up.

vergeistigt [fɛr'gaɪstɪçt] *adj* spiritual.

vergelten [fɛr'gɛltən] *unreg vt*: **jdm etw** ~ to pay sb back for sth, repay sb for sth.

Vergeltung *f* retaliation, reprisal.

Vergeltungsmaßnahme *f* retaliatory measure.

Vergeltungsschlag *m* (*MIL*) reprisal.

vergesellschaften [fɛrgə'zɛlʃaftən] *vt* (*POL*) to nationalize.

vergessen [fɛr'gɛsən] *unreg vt* to forget; **V~heit** *f* oblivion; **in V~heit geraten** to fall into oblivion.

vergeßlich [fɛr'gɛslɪç] *adj* forgetful; **V~keit** *f* forgetfulness.

vergeuden [fɛr'gɔʏdən] *vt* to squander, waste.

vergewaltigen [fɛrgə'valtɪgən] vt to rape; (fig) to violate.

Vergewaltigung f rape.

vergewissern [fɛrgə'vɪsərn] vr to make sure; **sich einer Sache** gen od **über etw** akk ~ to make sure of sth.

vergießen [fɛr'giːsən] unreg vt to shed.

vergiften [fɛr'gɪftən] vt to poison.

Vergiftung f poisoning.

vergilbt [fɛr'gɪlpt] adj yellowed.

Vergißmeinnicht [fɛr'gɪsmaɪnnɪçt] (-(e)s, -e) nt forget-me-not.

vergißt [fɛr'gɪst] vb siehe **vergessen**.

vergittert [fɛr'gɪtərt] adj: ~**e Fenster** barred windows.

verglasen [fɛr'glaːzən] vt to glaze.

Vergleich [fɛr'glaɪç] (-(e)s, -e) m comparison; (JUR) settlement; **einen ~ schließen** (JUR) to reach a settlement; **in keinem ~ zu etw stehen** to be out of all proportion to sth; **im ~ mit** od **zu** compared with od to; **v~bar** adj comparable.

vergleichen unreg vt to compare ♦ vr (JUR) to reach a settlement.

vergleichsweise adv comparatively.

verglühen [fɛr'glyːən] vi (Feuer) to die away; (Draht) to burn out; (Raumkapsel, Meteor etc) to burn up.

vergnügen [fɛr'gnyːgən] vr to enjoy od amuse o.s.; **V~** (-s, -) nt pleasure; **das war ein teures V~** (umg) that was an expensive bit of fun; **viel V~!** enjoy yourself!

vergnüglich adj enjoyable.

vergnügt [fɛr'gnyːkt] adj cheerful.

Vergnügung f pleasure, amusement.

Vergnügungs- zW: ~**park** m amusement park; **v~süchtig** adj pleasure-loving; ~**viertel** nt entertainments district.

vergolden [fɛr'gɔldən] vt to gild.

vergönnen [fɛr'gœnən] vt to grant.

vergöttern [fɛr'gœtərn] vt to idolize.

vergraben [fɛr'graːbən] unreg vt to bury.

vergrämt [fɛr'grɛːmt] adj (Gesicht) troubled.

vergreifen [fɛr'graɪfən] unreg vr: **sich an jdm ~** to lay hands on sb; **sich an etw** dat ~ to misappropriate sth; **sich im Ton ~** to say the wrong thing.

vergriffen [fɛr'grɪfən] adj (Buch) out of print; (Ware) out of stock.

vergrößern [fɛr'grøːsərn] vt to enlarge; (mengenmäßig) to increase; (Lupe) to magnify.

Vergrößerung f enlargement; increase; magnification.

Vergrößerungsglas nt magnifying glass.

vergünstigt adj (Lage) improved; (Preis) reduced.

Vergünstigung [fɛr'gynstɪguŋ] f concession; (Vorteil) privilege.

vergüten [fɛr'gyːtən] vt: **jdm etw ~** to compensate sb for sth; (Arbeit, Leistung) to pay sb for sth.

Vergütung f compensation; payment.

verh. abk = **verheiratet**.

verhaften [fɛr'haftən] vt to arrest.

Verhaftete(r) f(m) prisoner.

Verhaftung f arrest.

verhallen [fɛr'halən] vi to die away.

verhalten [fɛr'haltən] unreg vr (Sache) to be, stand; (sich benehmen) to behave; (MATH) to be in proportion to ♦ vr unpers: **wie verhält es sich damit?** (wie ist die Lage?) how do things stand?; (wie wird das gehandhabt?) how do you go about it? ♦ adj restrained; **sich ruhig ~** to keep quiet; (sich nicht bewegen) to keep still; **wenn sich das so verhält ...** if that is the case ...; **V~** (-s) nt behaviour (BRIT), behavior (US).

Verhaltens- zW: ~**forschung** f behavioural (BRIT) od behavioral (US) science; **v~gestört** adj disturbed; ~**maßregel** f rule of conduct.

Verhältnis [fɛr'hɛltnɪs] (-ses, -se) nt relationship; (Liebes~) affair; (MATH) proportion, ratio; (Einstellung): ~ (zu) attitude (to); **Verhältnisse** pl (Umstände) conditions pl; **aus was für ~sen kommt er?** what sort of background does he come from?; **für klare ~se sorgen, klare ~se schaffen** to get things straight; **über seine ~se leben** to live beyond one's means; **v~mäßig** adj relative, comparative ♦ adv relatively, comparatively; ~**wahl** f proportional representation; ~**wahlrecht** nt (system of) proportional representation.

verhandeln [fɛr'handəln] vi to negotiate; (JUR) to hold proceedings ♦ vt to discuss; (JUR) to hear; **über etw** akk ~ to negotiate sth od about sth.

Verhandlung f negotiation; (JUR) proceedings pl; ~**en führen** to negotiate.

Verhandlungspaket nt (COMM) package deal.

Verhandlungstisch m negotiating table.

verhangen [fɛr'haŋən] adj overcast.

verhängen [fɛr'hɛŋən] vt (fig) to impose, inflict.

Verhängnis [fɛr'hɛŋnɪs] (-ses, -se) nt fate; **jdm zum ~ werden** to be sb's undoing; **v~voll** adj fatal, disastrous.

verharmlosen [fɛr'harmloːzən] vt to make light of, play down.

verharren [fɛr'harən] vi to remain; (hartnäckig) to persist.

verhärten [fɛr'hɛrtən] vr to harden.

verhaspeln [fɛr'haspəln] (umg) vr to get into a muddle od tangle.

verhaßt [fɛr'hast] adj odious, hateful.

verhätscheln [fɛr'hɛːtʃəln] vt to spoil, pamper.

Verhau [fɛr'hau] (-(e)s, -e) m (zur Absperrung) barrier; (Käfig) coop.

verhauen unreg (umg) vt (verprügeln) to beat up; (Prüfung etc) to muff.

verheben [fɛr'heːbən] *unreg vr* to hurt o.s. lifting sth.

verheerend [fɛr'heːrənt] *adj* disastrous, devastating.

verhehlen [fɛr'heːlən] *vt* to conceal.

verheilen [fɛr'haılən] *vi* to heal.

verheimlichen [fɛr'haımlıçən] *vt:* (jdm) etw ~ to keep sth secret (from sb).

verheiratet [fɛr'haıraːtət] *adj* married.

verheißen [fɛr'haısən] *unreg vt:* jdm etw ~ to promise sb sth.

verheißungsvoll *adj* promising.

verheizen [fɛr'haıtsən] *vt* to burn, use as fuel.

verhelfen [fɛr'hɛlfən] *unreg vi:* jdm zu etw ~ to help sb to get sth.

verherrlichen [fɛr'hɛrlıçən] *vt* to glorify.

verheult [fɛr'hɔylt] *adj (Augen, Gesicht)* puffy *(from crying).*

verhexen [fɛr'hɛksən] *vt* to bewitch; **es ist wie verhext** it's jinxed.

verhindern [fɛr'hındərn] *vt* to prevent; **verhindert sein** to be unable to make it; **das läßt sich leider nicht** ~ it can't be helped, unfortunately; **ein verhinderter Politiker** *(umg)* a would-be politician.

Verhinderung *f* prevention.

verhöhnen [fɛr'høːnən] *vt* to mock, sneer at.

verhohnepipeln [fɛr'hoːnəpiːpəln] *(umg) vt* to send up *(BRIT)*, ridicule.

verhökern [fɛr'høːkərn] *(umg) vt* to turn into cash.

Verhör [fɛr'høːr] *(-(e)s, -e) nt* interrogation; *(gerichtlich)* (cross-)examination.

verhören *vt* to interrogate; to (cross-) examine ♦ *vr* to mishear.

verhüllen [fɛr'hylən] *vt* to veil; *(Haupt, Körperteil)* to cover.

verhungern [fɛr'hʊŋərn] *vi* to starve, die of hunger.

verhunzen [fɛr'hʊntsən] *(umg) vt* to ruin.

verhüten [fɛr'hyːtən] *vt* to prevent, avert.

Verhütung *f* prevention.

Verhütungsmittel *nt* contraceptive.

verifizieren [verifi'tsiːrən] *vt* to verify.

verinnerlichen [fɛr'|ınərlıçən] *vt* to internalize.

verirren [fɛr'|ırən] *vr* to get lost, lose one's way, *(fig)* to go astray; *(Tier, Kugel)* to stray.

verjagen [fɛr'jaːgən] *vt* to drive away *od* out.

verjähren [fɛr'jɛːrən] *vi* to come under the statute of limitations; *(Anspruch)* to lapse.

Verjährungsfrist *f* limitation period.

verjubeln [fɛr'juːbəln] *(umg) vt (Geld)* to blow.

verjüngen [fɛr'jʏŋən] *vt* to rejuvenate ♦ *vr* to taper.

verkabeln [fɛr'kaːbəln] *vt (TV)* to link up to the cable network.

Verkabelung *f (TV)* linking up to the cable network.

verkalken [fɛr'kalkən] *vi* to calcify; *(umg)* to become senile.

verkalkulieren [fɛrkalku'liːrən] *vr* to miscalculate.

verkannt [fɛr'kant] *adj* unappreciated.

verkatert [fɛr'kaːtərt] *(umg) adj* hung over.

Verkauf [fɛr'kauf] *m* sale; **zum** ~ **stehen** to be up for sale.

verkaufen *vt, vi* to sell; **"zu** ~**"** "for sale".

Verkäufer(in) [fɛr'kɔyfər(ın)] *(-s, -) m(f)* seller; *(im Außendienst)* salesman, saleswoman; *(in Laden)* shop assistant *(BRIT)*, sales clerk *(US)*.

verkäuflich [fɛr'kɔyflıç] *adj* saleable.

Verkaufs- *zW:* ~**abteilung** *f* sales department; ~**automat** *m* slot machine; ~**bedingungen** *pl (COMM)* terms and conditions of sale; ~**kampagne** *f* sales drive; ~**leiter** *m* sales manager; **v**~**offen** *adj:* **v**~**offener Samstag** *Saturday on which the shops are open all day;* ~**schlager** *m* big seller; ~**stelle** *f* outlet; ~**tüchtigkeit** *f* salesmanship.

Verkehr [fɛr'keːr] *(-s, -e) m* traffic; *(Umgang, bes sexuell)* intercourse; *(Umlauf)* circulation; **aus dem** ~ **ziehen** to withdraw from service; **für den** ~ **freigeben** *(Straße etc)* to open to traffic; *(Transportmittel)* to bring into service.

verkehren *vi (Fahrzeug)* to ply, run ♦ *vt, vr* to turn, transform; ~ **mit** to associate with; **mit jdm brieflich** *od* **schriftlich** ~ *(form)* to correspond with sb; **bei jdm** ~ to visit sb regularly.

Verkehrs- *zW:* ~**ampel** *f* traffic lights *pl;* ~**amt** *nt* tourist (information) office; ~**aufkommen** *nt* volume of traffic; **v**~**beruhigt** *adj* traffic-calmed; ~**beruhigung** *f* traffic-calming; ~**betriebe** *pl* transport services *pl;* ~**delikt** *nt* traffic offence *(BRIT) od* violation *(US);* ~**erziehung** *f* road safety training; **v**~**günstig** *adj* convenient; ~**insel** *f* traffic island; ~**knotenpunkt** *m* traffic junction; ~**mittel** *nt:* **öffentliche/private** ~**mittel** public/private transport *sing;* ~**schild** *nt* road sign; **v**~**sicher** *adj (Fahrzeug)* roadworthy; ~**sicherheit** *f* road safety; ~**stockung** *f* traffic jam, stoppage; ~**sünder** *(umg) m* traffic offender; ~**teilnehmer** *m* road user; **v**~**tüchtig** *adj (Fahrzeug)* roadworthy; *(Mensch)* fit to drive; ~**unfall** *m* traffic accident; ~**verein** *m* tourist information office; **v**~**widrig** *adj* contrary to traffic regulations; ~**zeichen** *nt* road sign.

verkehrt *adj* wrong; *(umgekehrt)* the wrong way round.

verkennen [fɛr'kɛnən] *unreg vt* to misjudge; *(unterschätzen)* to underestimate.

Verkettung [fɛr'kɛtʊŋ] *f:* **eine** ~ **unglücklicher Umstände** an unfortunate chain of events.

verklagen [fɛr'klaːgən] *vt* to take to court.

verklappen [fɛr'klapən] *vt* to dump (at sea).

verklären [fɛr'klɛːrən] *vt* to transfigure; **verklärt lächeln** to smile radiantly.

verklausulieren [fɛrklauzu'liːrən] *vt* (*Vertrag*) to hedge in with (restrictive) clauses.

verkleben [fɛr'kleːbən] *vt* to glue up, stick ♦ *vi* to stick together.

verkleiden [fɛr'klaidən] *vt* to disguise; (*kostümieren*) to dress up; (*Schacht, Tunnel*) to line; (*vertäfeln*) to panel; (*Heizkörper*) to cover in ♦ *vr* to disguise o.s.; to dress up.

Verkleidung *f* disguise; (*ARCHIT*) panelling (*BRIT*), paneling (*US*).

verkleinern [fɛr'klainərn] *vt* to make smaller, reduce in size.

verklemmt [fɛr'klɛmt] *adj* (*fig*) inhibited.

verklickern [fɛr'klikərn] (*umg*) *vt*: **jdm etw** ~ to make sth clear to sb.

verklingen [fɛr'kliŋən] *unreg vi* to die away.

verknacksen [fɛr'knaksən] (*umg*) *vt*: **sich** *dat* **den Fuß** ~ to twist one's ankle.

verknallen [fɛr'knalən] (*umg*) *vr*: **sich in jdn** ~ to fall for sb.

verkneifen [fɛr'knaifən] (*umg*) *vt*: **sich** *dat* **etw** ~ to stop o.s. from doing sth; **ich konnte mir das Lachen nicht** ~ I couldn't help laughing.

verknöchert [fɛr'knœçərt] *adj* (*fig*) fossilized.

verknüpfen [fɛr'knypfən] *vt* to tie (up), knot; (*fig*) to connect.

Verknüpfung *f* connection.

verkochen [fɛr'kɔxən] *vt, vi* (*Flüssigkeit*) to boil away.

verkohlen [fɛr'koːlən] *vi* to carbonize ♦ *vt* to carbonize; (*umg*): **jdn** ~ to have sb on.

verkommen [fɛr'kɔmən] *unreg vi* to deteriorate, decay; (*Mensch*) to go downhill, come down in the world ♦ *adj* (*moralisch*) dissolute, depraved; **V~heit** *f* depravity.

verkorksen [fɛr'kɔrksən] (*umg*) *vt* to ruin, mess up.

verkörpern [fɛr'kœrpərn] *vt* to embody, personify.

verköstigen [fɛr'kœstɪgən] *vt* to feed.

verkrachen [fɛr'kraxən] (*umg*) *vr*: **sich (mit jdm)** ~ to fall out (with sb).

verkracht (*umg*) *adj* (*Leben*) ruined.

verkraften [fɛr'kraftən] *vt* to cope with.

verkrampfen [fɛr'krampfən] *vr* (*Muskeln*) to go tense.

verkrampft [fɛr'krampft] *adj* (*fig*) tense.

verkriechen [fɛr'kriːçən] *unreg vr* to creep away, creep into a corner.

verkrümeln [fɛr'kryːməln] (*umg*) *vr* to disappear.

verkrümmt [fɛr'krymt] *adj* crooked.

Verkrümmung *f* bend, warp; (*ANAT*) curvature.

verkrüppelt [fɛr'krypəlt] *adj* crippled.

verkrustet [fɛr'krʊstət] *adj* encrusted.

verkühlen [fɛr'kyːlən] *vr* to get a chill.

verkümmern [fɛr'kymərn] *vi* to waste away; **emotionell/geistig** ~ to become emotionally/intellectually stunted.

verkünden [fɛr'kyndən] *vt* to proclaim; (*Urteil*) to pronounce.

verkündigen [fɛr'kyndɪgən] *vt* to proclaim; (*ironisch*) to announce; (*Evangelium*) to preach.

verkuppeln [fɛr'kʊpəln] *vt*: **jdn an jdn** ~ (*Zuhälter*) to procure sb for sb.

verkürzen [fɛr'kyrtsən] *vt* to shorten; (*Wort*) to abbreviate; **sich** *dat* **die Zeit** ~ to while away the time; **verkürzte Arbeitszeit** shorter working hours *pl*.

Verkürzung *f* shortening; abbreviation.

Verl. *abk* (= *Verlag*) publ.

verladen [fɛr'laːdən] *unreg vt* to load.

Verlag [fɛr'laːk] (**-(e)s, -e**) *m* publishing firm.

verlagern [fɛr'laːgərn] *vt, vr* (*lit, fig*) to shift.

Verlagsanstalt *f* publishing firm.

Verlagswesen *nt* publishing.

verlangen [fɛr'laŋən] *vt* to demand; (*wollen*) to want ♦ *vi*: ~ **nach** to ask for; **Sie werden am Telefon verlangt** you are wanted on the phone; ~ **Sie Herrn X** ask for Mr X; **V~** (**-s, -**) *nt*: **V~** (**nach**) desire (for); **auf jds V~** *akk* (**hin**) at sb's request.

verlängern [fɛr'lɛŋərn] *vt* to extend; (*länger machen*) to lengthen; (*zeitlich*) to prolong; (*Paß, Abonnement etc*) to renew; **ein verlängertes Wochenende** a long weekend.

Verlängerung *f* extension; (*SPORT*) extra time.

Verlängerungsschnur *f* extension cable.

verlangsamen [fɛr'laŋzaːmən] *vt, vr* to decelerate, slow down.

Verlaß [fɛr'las] *m*: **auf ihn/das ist kein** ~ he/it cannot be relied upon.

verlassen [fɛr'lasən] *unreg vt* to leave ♦ *vr*: **sich** ~ **auf** +*akk* to depend on ♦ *adj* desolate; (*Mensch*) abandoned; **einsam und** ~ so all alone; **V~heit** *f* loneliness (*BRIT*), lonesomeness (*US*).

verläßlich [fɛr'lɛslɪç] *adj* reliable.

Verlauf [fɛr'lauf] *m* course; **einen guten/ schlechten** ~ **nehmen** to go well/badly.

verlaufen *unreg vi* (*zeitlich*) to pass; (*Farben*) to run ♦ *vr* to get lost; (*Menschenmenge*) to disperse.

Verlautbarung *f* announcement.

verlauten [fɛr'lautən] *vi*: **etw** ~ **lassen** to disclose sth; **wie verlautet** as reported.

verleben [fɛr'leːbən] *vt* to spend.

verlebt [fɛr'leːpt] *adj* dissipated, worn-out.

verlegen [fɛr'leːgən] *vt* to move; (*verlieren*) to mislay; (*Kabel, Fliesen etc*) to lay; (*Buch*) to publish; (*verschieben*): ~ (**auf** +*akk*) to postpone (until) ♦ *vr*: **sich auf etw** *akk* ~ to resort to sth ♦ *adj* embarrassed; **nicht** ~ **um** never at a loss for; **V~heit** *f* embarrassment; (*Situation*) difficulty, scrape.

Verleger [fɛr'leːgər] (**-s, -**) *m* publisher.

verleiden [fɛr'laidən] *vt*: **jdm etw** ~ to put sb off sth.

Verleih [fɛr'lai] (**-(e)s, -e**) *m* hire service; (*das ~en*) renting (out), hiring (out) (*BRIT*);

(*Film~*) distribution.

verleihen *unreg vt:* **etw (an jdn)** ~ to lend sth (to sb), lend (sb) sth; (*gegen Gebühr*) to rent sth (out) (to sb), hire sth (out) (to sb) (*BRIT*); (*Kraft, Anschein*) to confer sth (on sb), bestow sth (on sb); (*Preis, Medaille*) to award sth (to sb), award (sb) sth.

Verleiher (**-s, -**) *m* hire (*BRIT*) *od* rental firm; (*von Filmen*) distributor; (*von Büchern*) lender.

Verleihung *f* lending; (*von Kraft etc*) bestowal; (*von Preis*) award.

verleiten [fɛr'laɪtən] *vt* to lead astray; ~ **zu** to talk into, tempt into.

verlernen [fɛr'lɛrnən] *vt* to forget, unlearn.

verlesen [fɛr'leːzən] *unreg vt* to read out; (*aussondern*) to sort out ♦ *vr* to make a mistake in reading.

verletzbar *adj* vulnerable.

verletzen [fɛr'lɛtsən] *vt* (*lit, fig*) to injure, hurt; (*Gesetz etc*) to violate.

verletzend *adj* (*fig: Worte*) hurtful.

verletzlich *adj* vulnerable.

Verletzte(r) *f(m)* injured person.

Verletzung *f* injury; (*Verstoß*) violation, infringement.

verleugnen [fɛr'lɔʏgnən] *vt* to deny; (*Menschen*) to disown; **er läßt sich immer** ~ he always pretends not to be there.

Verleugnung *f* denial.

verleumden [fɛr'lɔʏmdən] *vt* to slander; (*schriftlich*) to libel.

verleumderisch *adj* slanderous; libellous (*BRIT*), libelous (*US*).

Verleumdung *f* slander; libel.

verlieben *vr:* **sich** ~ (**in** *+akk*) to fall in love (with).

verliebt [fɛr'liːpt] *adj* in love; **V~heit** *f* being in love.

verlieren [fɛr'liːrən] *unreg vt, vi* to lose ♦ *vr* to get lost; (*verschwinden*) to disappear; **das/er hat hier nichts verloren** (*umg*) that/he has no business to be here.

Verlierer(in) (**-s, -**) *m(f)* loser.

Verlies [fɛr'liːs] (**-es, -e**) *nt* dungeon.

verloben [fɛr'loːbən] *vr:* **sich** ~ (**mit**) to get engaged (to); **verlobt sein** to be engaged.

Verlobte(r) [fɛr'loːptə(r)] *f(m):* **mein** ~**r** my fiancé; **meine** ~ my fiancée.

Verlobung *f* engagement.

verlocken [fɛr'lɔkən] *vt* to entice, lure.

verlockend *adj* (*Angebot, Idee*) tempting.

Verlockung *f* temptation, attraction.

verlogen [fɛr'loːgən] *adj* untruthful; (*Komplimente, Versprechungen*) false; (*Moral, Gesellschaft*) hypocritical; **V~heit** *f* untruthfulness.

verlor *etc* [fɛr'loːr] *vb siehe* **verlieren**.

verloren *pp von* **verlieren** ♦ *adj* lost; (*Eier*) poached; **der** ~**e Sohn** the prodigal son; **auf** ~**em Posten kämpfen** *od* **stehen** to be fighting a losing battle; **etw** ~ **geben** to give

sth up for lost; ~**gehen** *unreg vi* to get lost; **an ihm ist ein Sänger** ~**gegangen** he would have made a (good) singer.

verlöschen [fɛr'lœʃən] *vi* (*Hilfsverb sein*) to go out; (*Inschrift, Farbe, Erinnerung*) to fade.

verlosen [fɛr'loːzən] *vt* to raffle (off), draw lots for.

Verlosung *f* raffle, lottery.

verlottern [fɛr'lɔtərn] (*umg*) *vi* to go to the dogs.

verludern [fɛr'luːdərn] (*umg*) *vi* to go to the dogs.

Verlust [fɛr'lʊst] (**-(e)s, -e**) *m* loss; (*MIL*) casualty; **mit** ~ **verkaufen** to sell at a loss; ~**anzeige** *f* "lost" notice; ~**geschäft** *nt:* **das war ein** ~**geschäft** I/he *etc* made a loss; ~**zeit** *f* (*INDUSTRIE*) waiting time.

vermachen [fɛr'maxən] *vt* to bequeath, leave.

Vermächtnis [fɛr'mɛçtnɪs] (**-ses, -se**) *nt* legacy.

vermählen [fɛr'mɛːlən] *vr* to marry.

Vermählung *f* wedding, marriage.

vermarkten [fɛr'marktən] *vt* to market; (*fig: Persönlichkeit*) to promote.

Vermarktung [fɛr'marktʊŋ] *f* marketing.

vermasseln [fɛr'masəln] (*umg*) *vt* to mess up.

vermehren [fɛr'meːrən] *vt, vr* to multiply; (*Menge*) to increase.

Vermehrung *f* multiplying; increase.

vermeiden [fɛr'maɪdən] *unreg vt* to avoid.

vermeidlich *adj* avoidable.

vermeintlich [fɛr'maɪntlɪç] *adj* supposed.

vermengen [fɛr'mɛŋən] *vt* to mix; (*fig*) to mix up, confuse.

Vermenschlichung [fɛr'mɛnʃlɪçʊŋ] *f* humanization.

Vermerk [fɛr'mɛrk] (**-(e)s, -e**) *m* note; (*in Ausweis*) endorsement.

vermerken *vt* to note.

vermessen [fɛr'mɛsən] *unreg vt* to survey ♦ *vr* (*falsch messen*) to measure incorrectly ♦ *adj* presumptuous, bold; **V~heit** *f* presumptuousness.

Vermessung *f* survey(ing).

Vermessungsamt *nt* land survey(ing) office.

Vermessungsingenieur *m* land surveyor.

vermiesen [fɛr'miːzən] (*umg*) *vt* to spoil.

vermieten [fɛr'miːtən] *vt* to let (*BRIT*), rent (out); (*Auto*) to hire out, rent.

Vermieter(in) (**-s, -**) *m(f)* landlord, landlady.

Vermietung *f* letting, renting (out); (*von Autos*) hiring (out), rental.

vermindern [fɛr'mɪndərn] *vt, vr* to lessen, decrease.

Verminderung *f* reduction.

verminen [fɛr'miːnən] *vt* to mine.

vermischen [fɛr'mɪʃən] *vt, vr* to mix; (*Teesorten etc*) to blend; **vermischte Schriften** miscellaneous writings.

vermissen [fɛr'mɪsən] *vt* to miss; **vermißt sein, als vermißt gemeldet sein** to be reported missing; **wir haben dich bei der Party vermißt** we didn't see you at the party.

Vermißte(r) *f(m)* missing person.

Vermißtenanzeige *f* missing persons report.

vermitteln [fɛr'mɪtəln] *vi* to mediate ♦ *vt* to arrange; (*Gespräch*) to connect; (*Stelle*) to find; (*Gefühl, Bild, Idee etc*) to convey; (*Wissen*) to impart; **~de Worte** conciliatory words; **jdm etw ~** to help sb to obtain sth; (*Stelle*) to find sth for sb.

Vermittler(in) [fɛr'mɪtlər(ɪn)] (**-s, -**) *m(f)* (*COMM*) agent; (*Schlichter*) mediator.

Vermittlung *f* procurement; (*Stellen~*) agency; (*TEL*) exchange; (*Schlichtung*) mediation.

Vermittlungsgebühr *f* commission.

vermögen [fɛr'møːgən] *unreg vt* to be capable of; **~ zu** to be able to; **V~** (**-s, -**) *nt* wealth; (*Fähigkeit*) ability; **mein ganzes V~ besteht aus ...** my entire assets consist of ...; **ein V~ kosten** to cost a fortune.

vermögend *adj* wealthy.

Vermögens- *zW:* **~steuer** *f* property tax, wealth tax; **~wert** *m* asset; **v~wirksam** *adj:* **sein Geld v~wirksam anlegen** to invest one's money profitably; **v~wirksame Leistungen** *employers' contributions to tax-deductible savings scheme.*

vermummen [fɛr'mʊmən] *vr* to wrap up (warm); (*sich verkleiden*) to disguise.

Vermummungsverbot (**-(e)s**) *nt law against disguising o.s. at demonstrations.*

vermurksen [fɛr'mʊrksən] (*umg*) *vt* to make a mess of.

vermuten [fɛr'muːtən] *vt* to suppose; (*argwöhnen*) to suspect.

vermutlich *adj* supposed, presumed ♦ *adv* probably.

Vermutung *f* supposition; suspicion; **die ~ liegt nahe, daß ...** there are grounds for assuming that ...

vernachlässigen [fɛr'naːxlɛsɪgən] *vt* to neglect ♦ *vr* to neglect o.s. *od* one's appearance.

Vernachlässigung *f* neglect.

vernarben [fɛr'narbən] *vi* to heal up.

vernarren [fɛr'narən] (*umg*) *vr:* **in jdn/etw vernarrt sein** to be crazy about sb/sth.

vernaschen [fɛr'naʃən] *vt* (*Geld*) to spend on sweets; (*umg: Mädchen, Mann*) to make it with.

vernehmen [fɛr'neːmən] *unreg vt* to hear, perceive; (*erfahren*) to learn; (*JUR*) to (cross-)examine; (*Polizei*) to question; **V~** *nt:* **dem V~ nach** from what I/we *etc* hear.

vernehmlich *adj* audible.

Vernehmung *f* (cross-)examination.

vernehmungsfähig *adj* in a condition to be (cross-)examined.

verneigen [fɛr'naɪgən] *vr* to bow.

verneinen [fɛr'naɪnən] *vt* (*Frage*) to answer in the negative; (*ablehnen*) to deny; (*GRAM*) to negate.

verneinend *adj* negative.

Verneinung *f* negation.

vernichten [fɛr'nɪçtən] *vt* to destroy, annihilate.

vernichtend *adj* (*fig*) crushing; (*Blick*) withering; (*Kritik*) scathing.

Vernichtung *f* destruction, annihilation.

Vernichtungsschlag *m* devastating blow.

verniedlichen [fɛr'niːtlɪçən] *vt* to play down.

Vernunft [fɛr'nʊnft] (**-**) *f* reason; **~ annehmen** to see reason; **~ehe** *f*, **~heirat** *f* marriage of convenience.

vernünftig [fɛr'nʏnftɪç] *adj* sensible, reasonable.

Vernunftmensch *m* rational person.

veröden [fɛr'|øːdən] *vi* to become desolate ♦ *vt* (*MED*) to remove.

veröffentlichen [fɛr'|œfəntlɪçən] *vt* to publish.

Veröffentlichung *f* publication.

verordnen [fɛr'|ɔrdnən] *vt* (*MED*) to prescribe.

Verordnung *f* order, decree; (*MED*) prescription.

verpachten [fɛr'paxtən] *vt* to lease (out).

verpacken [fɛr'pakən] *vt* to pack; (*verbrauchergerecht*) to package; (*einwickeln*) to wrap.

Verpackung *f* packing; packaging; wrapping.

verpassen [fɛr'pasən] *vt* to miss; **jdm eine Ohrfeige ~** (*umg*) to give sb a clip round the ear.

verpatzen [fɛr'patsən] (*umg*) *vt* to spoil, mess up.

verpennen [fɛr'pɛnən] (*umg*) *vi, vr* to oversleep.

verpesten [fɛr'pɛstən] *vt* to pollute.

verpetzen [fɛr'pɛtsən] (*umg*) *vt:* **jdn ~ (bei)** to tell on sb (to).

verpfänden [fɛr'pfɛndən] *vt* to pawn; (*JUR*) to mortgage.

verpfeifen [fɛr'pfaɪfən] *unreg* (*umg*) *vt:* **jdn ~ (bei)** to grass on sb (to).

verpflanzen [fɛr'pflantsən] *vt* to transplant.

Verpflanzung *f* transplanting; (*MED*) transplant.

verpflegen [fɛr'pfleːgən] *vt* to feed, cater for (*BRIT*).

Verpflegung *f* catering; (*Kost*) food; (*in Hotel*) board.

verpflichten [fɛr'pflɪçtən] *vt* to oblige, bind; (*anstellen*) to engage ♦ *vr* to undertake; (*MIL*) to sign on ♦ *vi* to carry obligations; **jdm verpflichtet sein** to be under an obligation to sb; **sich zu etw ~** to commit o.s. to doing sth; **jdm zu Dank verpflichtet sein** to be obliged to sb.

verpflichtend *adj* (*Zusage*) binding.

Verpflichtung *f* obligation; (*Aufgabe*) duty.

verpfuschen [fɛr'pfʊʃən] (*umg*) *vt* to bungle,

make a mess of.

verplanen [fɛr'plaːnən] *vt* (*Zeit*) to book up; (*Geld*) to budget.

verplappern [fɛr'plapərn] (*umg*) *vr* to open one's big mouth.

verplempern [fɛr'plɛmpərn] (*umg*) *vt* to waste.

verpönt [fɛr'pøːnt] *adj:* ~ **(bei)** frowned upon (by).

verprassen [fɛr'prasən] *vt* to squander.

verprügeln [fɛr'pryːgəln] (*umg*) *vt* to beat up.

verpuffen [fɛr'pufən] *vi* to (go) pop; (*fig*) to fall flat.

Verputz [fɛr'puts] *m* plaster; (*Rauhputz*) roughcast; **v~en** *vt* to plaster; (*umg: Essen*) to put away.

verqualmen [fɛr'kvalmən] *vt* (*Zimmer*) to fill with smoke.

verquollen [fɛr'kvɔlən] *adj* swollen; (*Holz*) warped.

verrammeln [fɛr'raməln] *vt* to barricade.

Verrat [fɛr'raːt] (-(e)s) *m* treachery; (*POL*) treason; ~ **an jdm üben** to betray sb.

verraten *unreg vt* to betray; (*fig: erkennen lassen*) to show; (*Geheimnis*) to divulge ♦ *vr* to give o.s. away.

Verräter(in) [fɛr'rɛːtər(ɪn)] (-s, -) *m(f)* traitor, traitress; **v~isch** *adj* treacherous.

verrauchen [fɛr'rauxən] *vi* (*fig: Zorn*) to blow over.

verrechnen [fɛr'rɛçnən] *vt:* ~ **mit** to set off against ♦ *vr* to miscalculate.

Verrechnung *f:* **nur zur** ~ (*auf Scheck*) a/c payee only.

Verrechnungsscheck *m* crossed cheque (*BRIT*).

verregnet [fɛr'reːgnət] *adj* rainy, spoilt by rain.

verreisen [fɛr'raizən] *vi* to go away (on a journey); **er ist geschäftlich verreist** he's away on business.

verreißen [fɛr'raisən] *unreg vt* to pull to pieces.

verrenken [fɛr'rɛŋkən] *vt* to contort; (*MED*) to dislocate; **sich** *dat* **den Knöchel** ~ to sprain one's ankle.

Verrenkung *f* contortion; (*MED*) dislocation.

verrennen [fɛr'rɛnən] *unreg vr:* **sich in etw** *akk* ~ to get stuck on sth.

verrichten [fɛr'rɪçtən] *vt* (*Arbeit*) to do, perform.

verriegeln [fɛr'riːgəln] *vt* to bolt.

verringern [fɛr'rɪŋərn] *vt* to reduce ♦ *vr* to decrease.

Verringerung *f* reduction; decrease.

verrinnen [fɛr'rɪnən] *unreg vi* to run out *od* away; (*Zeit*) to elapse.

Verriß [fɛr'rɪs] *m* slating review.

verrohen [fɛr'roːən] *vi* to become brutalized.

verrosten [fɛr'rɔstən] *vi* to rust.

verrotten [fɛr'rɔtən] *vi* to rot.

verrucht [fɛr'ruːxt] *adj* despicable; (*verrufen*) disreputable.

verrücken [fɛr'rykən] *vt* to move, shift.

verrückt *adj* crazy, mad; **V~e(r)** *f(m)* lunatic; **V~heit** *f* madness, lunacy.

Verruf [fɛr'ruːf] *m:* **in** ~ **geraten/bringen** to fall/bring into disrepute.

verrufen *adj* disreputable.

verrutschen [fɛr'rʊtʃən] *vi* to slip.

Vers [fɛrs] (-es, -e) *m* verse.

versacken [fɛr'zakən] *vi* (*lit*) to sink; (*fig: umg: herunterkommen*) to go downhill; (: *lange zechen*) to get involved in a booze-up (*BRIT*) *od* a drinking spree.

versagen [fɛr'zaːgən] *vt:* **jdm/sich etw** ~ to deny sb/o.s. sth ♦ *vi* to fail; **V~** (-s) *nt* failure; **menschliches V~** human error.

Versager (-s, -) *m* failure.

versalzen [fɛr'zaltsən] *vt* to put too much salt in; (*fig*) to spoil.

versammeln [fɛr'zaməln] *vt, vr* to assemble, gather.

Versammlung *f* meeting, gathering.

Versammlungsfreiheit *f* freedom of assembly.

Versand [fɛr'zant] (-(e)s) *m* dispatch; (~*abteilung*) dispatch department; ~**bahnhof** *m* dispatch station; ~**haus** *nt* mail-order firm; ~**kosten** *pl* transport(ation) costs *pl*; ~**weg** *m:* **auf dem** ~**weg** by mail order.

versäumen [fɛr'zɔymən] *vt* to miss; (*Pflicht*) to neglect; (*Zeit*) to lose.

Versäumnis (-ses, -se) *nt* neglect; (*Unterlassung*) omission.

verschachern [fɛr'ʃaxərn] (*umg*) *vt* to sell off.

verschachtelt [fɛr'ʃaxtəlt] *adj* (*Satz*) complex.

verschaffen [fɛr'ʃafən] *vt:* **jdm/sich etw** ~ to get *od* procure sth for sb/o.s.

verschämt [fɛr'ʃɛːmt] *adj* bashful.

verschandeln [fɛr'ʃandəln] (*umg*) *vt* to spoil.

verschanzen [fɛr'ʃantsən] *vr:* **sich hinter etw** *dat* ~ to dig in behind sth; (*fig*) to take refuge behind sth.

verschärfen [fɛr'ʃɛrfən] *vt* to intensify; (*Lage*) to aggravate; (*strenger machen: Kontrollen, Gesetze*) to tighten up ♦ *vr* to intensify; to become aggravated; to become tighter.

Verschärfung *f* intensification; (*der Lage*) aggravation; (*von Kontrollen etc*) tightening.

verscharren [fɛr'ʃarən] *vt* to bury.

verschätzen [fɛr'ʃɛtsən] *vr* to miscalculate.

verschenken [fɛr'ʃɛŋkən] *vt* to give away.

verscherzen [fɛr'ʃɛrtsən] *vt:* **sich** *dat* **etw** ~ to lose sth, throw sth away.

verscheuchen [fɛr'ʃɔyçən] *vt* to frighten away.

verschicken [fɛr'ʃɪkən] *vt* to send off; (*Sträfling*) to transport.

verschieben [fɛr'ʃiːbən] *unreg vt* to shift; (*EISENB*) to shunt; (*Termin*) to postpone; (*umg: Waren, Devisen*) to traffic in.

Verschiebung *f* shift, displacement; shunting; postponement.

verschieden [fɛr'ʃiːdən] *adj* different; **das ist**

ganz ~ (*wird* ~ *gehandhabt*) that varies, that just depends; **sie sind** ~ **groß** they are of different sizes; ~**artig** *adj* various, of different kinds; **zwei so** ~**artige** ... two such differing ...; ~**e** *pron pl* various people; various things *pl*; ~**es** *pron* various things *pl*; **etwas V**~**es** something different; **V**~**heit** *f* difference.

verschiedentlich *adv* several times.

verschiffen [fɛr'ʃɪfən] *vt* to ship; (*Sträfling*) to transport.

verschimmeln [fɛr'ʃɪməln] *vi* (*Nahrungsmittel*) to go mouldy (*BRIT*) *od* moldy (*US*); (*Leder, Papier etc*) to become mildewed.

verschlafen [fɛr'ʃlaːfən] *unreg vt* to sleep through; (*fig: versäumen*) to miss ♦ *vi, vr* to oversleep ♦ *adj* sleepy.

Verschlag [fɛr'ʃlaːk] *m* shed.

verschlagen [fɛr'ʃlaːgən] *unreg vt* to board up; (*TENNIS*) to hit out of play; (*Buchseite*) to lose ♦ *adj* cunning; **jdm den Atem** ~ to take sb's breath away; **an einen Ort** ~ **werden** to wind up in a place.

verschlampen [fɛr'ʃlampən] *vi* (*Hilfsverb sein: Mensch*) to go to seed (*umg*) ♦ *vt* to lose, mislay.

verschlechtern [fɛr'ʃlɛçtərn] *vt* to make worse ♦ *vr* to deteriorate, get worse; (*gehaltlich*) to take a lower-paid job.

Verschlechterung *f* deterioration.

Verschleierung [fɛr'ʃlaɪərʊŋ] *f* veiling; (*fig*) concealment; (*MIL*) screening.

Verschleierungstaktik *f* smoke-screen tactics *pl*.

Verschleiß [fɛr'ʃlaɪs] (**-es, -e**) *m* wear and tear.

verschleißen *unreg vt, vi, vr* to wear out.

verschleppen [fɛr'ʃlɛpən] *vt* to carry off, abduct; (*zeitlich*) to drag out, delay; (*verbreiten: Seuche*) to spread.

verschleudern [fɛr'ʃlɔydərn] *vt* to squander; (*COMM*) to sell dirt-cheap.

verschließbar *adj* lockable.

verschließen [fɛr'ʃliːsən] *unreg vt* to lock ♦ *vr:* **sich einer Sache** *dat* ~ to close one's mind to sth.

verschlimmern [fɛr'ʃlɪmərn] *vt* to make worse, aggravate ♦ *vr* to get worse, deteriorate.

Verschlimmerung *f* deterioration.

verschlingen [fɛr'ʃlɪŋən] *unreg vt* to devour, swallow up; (*Fäden*) to twist.

verschliß *etc* [fɛr'ʃlɪs] *vb siehe* **verschleißen**.

verschlissen [fɛr'ʃlɪsən] *pp von* **verschleißen** ♦ *adj* worn(-out).

verschlossen [fɛr'ʃlɔsən] *adj* locked; (*fig*) reserved; (*schweigsam*) tight-lipped; **V**~**heit** *f* reserve.

verschlucken [fɛr'ʃlʊkən] *vt* to swallow ♦ *vr* to choke.

Verschluß [fɛr'ʃlʊs] *m* lock; (*von Kleid etc*) fastener; (*PHOT*) shutter; (*Stöpsel*) plug;

unter ~ **halten** to keep under lock and key.

verschlüsseln [fɛr'ʃlʏsəln] *vt* to encode.

verschmachten [fɛr'ʃmaxtən] *vi:* ~ (**vor** +*dat*) to languish (for); **vor Durst** ~ to be dying of thirst.

verschmähen [fɛr'ʃmɛːən] *vt* to scorn, disdain.

verschmelzen [fɛr'ʃmɛltsən] *unreg vt, vi* to merge, blend.

verschmerzen [fɛr'ʃmɛrtsən] *vt* to get over.

verschmiert [fɛr'ʃmiːrt] *adj* (*Hände*) smeary; (*Schminke*) smudged.

verschmitzt [fɛr'ʃmɪtst] *adj* mischievous.

verschmutzen [fɛr'ʃmʊtsən] *vt* to soil; (*Umwelt*) to pollute.

verschnaufen [fɛr'ʃnaʊfən] (*umg*) *vi, vr* to have a breather.

verschneiden [fɛr'ʃnaɪdən] *vt* (*Whisky etc*) to blend.

verschneit [fɛr'ʃnaɪt] *adj* covered in snow, snowed up.

Verschnitt [fɛr'ʃnɪt] *m* (*von Whisky etc*) blend.

verschnörkelt [fɛr'ʃnœrkəlt] *adj* ornate.

verschnupft [fɛr'ʃnʊpft] (*umg*) *adj:* ~ **sein** to have a cold; (*beleidigt*) to be peeved (*umg*).

verschnüren [fɛr'ʃnyːrən] *vt* to tie up.

verschollen [fɛr'ʃɔlən] *adj* lost, missing.

verschonen [fɛr'ʃoːnən] *vt:* **jdn mit etw** ~ to spare sb sth; **von etw verschont bleiben** to escape sth.

verschönern [fɛr'ʃøːnərn] *vt* to decorate; (*verbessern*) to improve.

verschossen [fɛr'ʃɔsən] *adj:* ~ **sein** (*fig: umg*) to be in love.

verschränken [fɛr'ʃrɛŋkən] *vt* to cross; (*Arme*) to fold.

verschreckt [fɛr'ʃrɛkt] *adj* frightened, scared.

verschreiben [fɛr'ʃraɪbən] *unreg vt* (*Papier*) to use up; (*MED*) to prescribe ♦ *vr* to make a mistake (in writing); **sich einer Sache** *dat* ~ to devote o.s. to sth.

verschrie(e)n [fɛr'ʃriː(ə)n] *adj* notorious.

verschroben [fɛr'ʃroːbən] *adj* eccentric, odd.

verschrotten [fɛr'ʃrɔtən] *vt* to scrap.

verschüchtert [fɛr'ʃʏçtərt] *adj* subdued, intimidated.

verschulden [fɛr'ʃʊldən] *vt* to be guilty of ♦ *vi* (*in Schulden geraten*) to get into debt; **V**~ (**-s**) *nt* fault.

verschuldet *adj* in debt.

Verschuldung *f* debts *pl*.

verschütten [fɛr'ʃʏtən] *vt* to spill; (*zuschütten*) to fill; (*unter Trümmern*) to bury.

verschwand *etc* [fɛr'ʃvant] *vb siehe* **verschwinden**.

verschweigen [fɛr'ʃvaɪgən] *unreg vt* to keep secret; **jdm etw** ~ to keep sth from sb.

verschwenden [fɛr'ʃvɛndən] *vt* to squander.

Verschwender(in) (**-s, -**) *m(f)* spendthrift; **v**~**isch** *adj* wasteful; (*Leben*) extravagant.

Verschwendung *f* waste.

verschwiegen [fɛr'ʃviːgən] *adj* discreet; (*Ort*)

secluded; **V~heit** f discretion; seclusion; **zur V~heit verpflichtet** bound to secrecy.

verschwimmen [fɛr'ʃvɪmən] *unreg vi* to grow hazy, become blurred.

verschwinden [fɛr'ʃvɪndən] *unreg vi* to disappear, vanish; **verschwinde!** clear off! (*umg*); **V~** (**-s**) *nt* disappearance.

verschwindend *adj* (*Anzahl, Menge*) insignificant.

verschwitzen [fɛr'ʃvɪtsən] *vt* to stain with sweat; (*umg*) to forget.

verschwitzt *adj* (*Kleidung*) sweat-stained; (*Mensch*) sweaty.

verschwommen [fɛr'ʃvɔmən] *adj* hazy, vague.

verschworen [fɛr'ʃvoːrən] *adj* (*Gesellschaft*) sworn.

verschwören [fɛr'ʃvøːrən] *unreg vr* to conspire, plot.

Verschwörer(in) (**-s**, **-**) *m(f)* conspirator.

Verschwörung f conspiracy, plot.

verschwunden [fɛr'ʃvʊndən] *pp von* **verschwinden** ♦ *adj* missing.

versehen [fɛr'zeːən] *unreg vt* to supply, provide; (*Pflicht*) to carry out; (*Amt*) to fill; (*Haushalt*) to keep ♦ *vr* (*fig*) to make a mistake; **ehe er (es) sich ~ hatte** ... before he knew it ...; **V~** (**-s**, **-**) *nt* oversight; **aus V~** by mistake.

versehentlich *adv* by mistake.

Versehrte(r) [fɛr'zeːrtə(r)] *f(m)* disabled person.

verselbstständigen [fɛr'zɛlpʃtɛndɪgən] *vr* to become independent.

versenden [fɛr'zɛndən] *unreg vt* to send; (*COMM*) to forward.

versengen [fɛr'zɛŋən] *vt* to scorch; (*Feuer*) to singe; (*umg: verprügeln*) to wallop.

versenken [fɛr'zɛŋkən] *vt* to sink ♦ *vr:* **sich ~ in** +*akk* to become engrossed in.

versessen [fɛr'zɛsən] *adj:* **~ auf** +*akk* mad about, hellbent on.

versetzen [fɛr'zɛtsən] *vt* to transfer; (*verpfänden*) to pawn; (*umg: vergeblich warten lassen*) to stand up; (*nicht geradlinig anordnen*) to stagger; (*SCH: in höhere Klasse*) to move up ♦ *vr:* **sich in jdn** *od* **in jds Lage ~** to put o.s. in sb's place; **jdm einen Tritt/ Schlag ~** to kick/hit sb; **etw mit etw ~** to mix sth with sth; **jdm einen Stich ~** (*fig*) to cut sb to the quick, wound sb (deeply); **jdn in gute Laune ~** to put sb in a good mood.

Versetzung f transfer; **seine ~ ist gefährdet** (*SCH*) he's in danger of having to repeat a year.

verseuchen [fɛr'zɔʏçən] *vt* to contaminate.

Versicherer (**-s**, **-**) *m* insurer; (*bei Schiffen*) underwriter.

versichern [fɛr'zɪçərn] *vt* to assure; (*mit Geld*) to insure ♦ *vr:* **sich ~** +*gen* to make sure of.

Versicherte(r) *f(m)* insured.

Versicherung f assurance; insurance.

Versicherungs- *zW:* **~beitrag** *m* insurance premium; (*bei staatlicher Versicherung etc*) social security contribution; **~gesellschaft** f insurance company; **~nehmer** (**-s**, **-**) *m* (*form*) insured, policy holder; **~police** f insurance policy; **~schutz** *m* insurance cover; **~summe** f sum insured; **~träger** *m* insurer.

versickern [fɛr'zɪkərn] *vi* to seep away; (*fig: Interesse etc*) to peter out.

versiegeln [fɛr'ziːgəln] *vt* to seal (up).

versiegen [fɛr'ziːgən] *vi* to dry up.

versiert [vɛr'ziːrt] *adj:* **in etw** *dat* **~ sein** to be experienced *od* well versed in sth.

versilbert [fɛr'zɪlbərt] *adj* silver-plated.

versinken [fɛr'zɪŋkən] *unreg vi* to sink; **ich hätte im Boden** *od* **vor Scham ~ mögen** I wished the ground would swallow me up.

versinnbildlichen [fɛr'zɪnbɪltlɪçən] *vt* to symbolize.

Version [vɛrzi'oːn] f version.

Versmaß ['fɛrsmaːs] *nt* metre (*BRIT*), meter (*US*).

versohlen [fɛr'zoːlən] (*umg*) *vt* to belt.

versöhnen [fɛr'zøːnən] *vt* to reconcile ♦ *vr* to become reconciled.

versöhnlich *adj* (*Ton, Worte*) conciliatory; (*Ende*) happy.

Versöhnung f reconciliation.

versonnen [fɛr'zɔnən] *adj* (*Gesichtsausdruck*) pensive, thoughtful; (*träumerisch: Blick*) dreamy.

versorgen [fɛr'zɔrgən] *vt* to provide, supply; (*Familie etc*) to look after ♦ *vr* to look after o.s.

Versorger(in) (**-s**, **-**) *m(f)* (*Ernährer*) provider, breadwinner; (*Belieferer*) supplier.

Versorgung f provision; (*Unterhalt*) maintenance; (*Alters~ etc*) benefit, assistance.

Versorgungs- *zW:* **~amt** *nt* pension office; **~betrieb** *m* public utility; **~netz** *nt* (*Wasserversorgung etc*) (supply) grid; (*von Waren*) supply network.

verspannen [fɛr'ʃpanən] *vr* (*Muskeln*) to tense up.

verspäten [fɛr'ʃpɛːtən] *vr* to be late.

verspätet *adj* late.

Verspätung f delay; **~ haben** to be late; **mit zwanzig Minuten ~** twenty minutes late.

versperren [fɛr'ʃpɛrən] *vt* to bar, obstruct.

verspielen [fɛr'ʃpiːlən] *vt, vi* to lose; (**bei jdm**) **verspielt haben** to have had it (as far as sb is concerned).

verspielt [fɛr'ʃpiːlt] *adj* playful.

versponnen [fɛr'ʃpɔnən] *adj* crackpot.

verspotten [fɛr'ʃpɔtən] *vt* to ridicule, scoff at.

versprach *etc* [fɛr'ʃprax] *vb siehe* **versprechen**.

versprechen [fɛr'ʃprɛçən] *unreg vt* to promise ♦ *vr* (*etwas Nicht-Gemeintes sagen*) to make a slip of the tongue; **sich** *dat* **etw von etw ~** to expect sth from sth; **V~** (**-s**, **-**) *nt* promise.

Versprecher (-s, -) (*umg*) *m* slip (of the tongue).
verspricht [fɛr'ʃprɪçt] *vb siehe* **versprechen**.
verspüren [fɛr'ʃpyːrən] *vt* to feel, be conscious of.
verstaatlichen [fɛr'ʃtaːtlɪçən] *vt* to nationalize.
verstaatlicht *adj:* ~**er Industriezweig** nationalized industry.
Verstaatlichung *f* nationalization.
Verstand [fɛr'ʃtant] *m* intelligence; (*Intellekt*) mind; (*Fähigkeit zu denken*) reason; **den** ~ **verlieren** to go out of one's mind; **über jds** ~ *akk* **gehen** to be beyond sb.
verstand *etc vb siehe* **verstehen**.
verstanden [fɛr'ʃtandən] *pp von* **verstehen**.
verstandesmäßig *adj* rational.
verständig [fɛr'ʃtɛndɪç] *adj* sensible.
verständigen [fɛr'ʃtɛndɪɡən] *vt* to inform ♦ *vr* to communicate; (*sich einigen*) to come to an understanding.
Verständigkeit *f* good sense.
Verständigung *f* communication; (*Benachrichtigung*) informing; (*Einigung*) agreement.
verständlich [fɛr'ʃtɛntlɪç] *adj* understandable, comprehensible; (*hörbar*) audible; **sich** ~ **machen** to make o.s. understood; (*sich klar ausdrücken*) to make o.s. clear.
verständlicherweise *adv* understandably (enough).
Verständlichkeit *f* clarity, intelligibility.
Verständnis (-ses, -se) *nt* understanding; **für etw kein** ~ **haben** to have no understanding *od* sympathy for sth; (*für Kunst etc*) to have no appreciation of sth; **v~los** *adj* uncomprehending; **v~voll** *adj* understanding, sympathetic.
verstärken [fɛr'ʃtɛrkən] *vt* to strengthen; (*Ton*) to amplify; (*erhöhen*) to intensify ♦ *vr* to intensify.
Verstärker (-s, -) *m* amplifier.
Verstärkung *f* strengthening; (*Hilfe*) reinforcements *pl*; (*von Ton*) amplification.
verstaubt [fɛr'ʃtaupt] *adj* dusty; (*fig: Ansichten*) fuddy-duddy (*umg*).
verstauchen [fɛr'ʃtauxən] *vt* to sprain.
verstauen [fɛr'ʃtauən] *vt* to stow away.
Versteck [fɛr'ʃtɛk] (-(e)s, -e) *nt* hiding (place).
verstecken *vt, vr* to hide.
versteckt *adj* hidden; (*Tür*) concealed; (*fig: Lächeln, Blick*) furtive; (*Andeutung*) veiled.
verstehen [fɛr'ʃteːən] *unreg vt, vi* to understand; (*können, beherrschen*) to know ♦ *vr* (*auskommen*) to get on; **das ist nicht wörtlich zu** ~ that isn't to be taken literally; **das versteht sich von selbst** that goes without saying; **die Preise** ~ **sich einschließlich Lieferung** prices are inclusive of delivery; **sich auf etw** *akk* ~ to be an expert at sth.
versteifen [fɛr'ʃtaifən] *vt* to stiffen, brace ♦ *vr*

(*fig*): **sich** ~ **auf** *+akk* to insist on.
versteigen [fɛr'ʃtaigən] *unreg vr:* **sie hat sich zu der Behauptung verstiegen, daß** ... she presumed to claim that ...
versteigern [fɛr'ʃtaigərn] *vt* to auction.
Versteigerung *f* auction.
verstellbar *adj* adjustable, variable.
verstellen [fɛr'ʃtɛlən] *vt* to move, shift; (*Uhr*) to adjust; (*versperren*) to block; (*fig*) to disguise ♦ *vr* to pretend, put on an act.
Verstellung *f* pretence (*BRIT*), pretense (*US*).
versteuern [fɛr'ʃtɔyərn] *vt* to pay tax on; **zu** ~ taxable.
verstiegen [fɛr'ʃtiːɡən] *adj* exaggerated.
verstimmt [fɛr'ʃtɪmt] *adj* out of tune; (*fig*) cross, put out; (: *Magen*) upset.
Verstimmung *f* (*fig*) disgruntled state, peevishness.
verstockt [fɛr'ʃtɔkt] *adj* stubborn; **V~heit** *f* stubbornness.
verstohlen [fɛr'ʃtoːlən] *adj* stealthy.
verstopfen [fɛr'ʃtɔpfən] *vt* to block, stop up; (*MED*) to constipate.
Verstopfung *f* obstruction; (*MED*) constipation.
verstorben [fɛr'ʃtɔrbən] *adj* deceased, late.
Verstorbene(r) *f(m)* deceased.
verstört [fɛr'ʃtøːrt] *adj* (*Mensch*) distraught.
Verstoß [fɛr'ʃtoːs] *m:* ~ **(gegen)** infringement (of), violation (of).
verstoßen *unreg vt* to disown, reject ♦ *vi:* ~ **gegen** to offend against.
Verstrebung [fɛr'ʃtreːbʊŋ] *f* (*Strebebalken*) support(ing beam).
verstreichen [fɛr'ʃtraiçən] *unreg vt* to spread ♦ *vi* to elapse; (*Zeit*) to pass (by); (*Frist*) to expire.
verstreuen [fɛr'ʃtrɔyən] *vt* to scatter (about).
verstricken [fɛr'ʃtrɪkən] *vt* (*fig*) to entangle, ensnare ♦ *vr:* **sich** ~ **in** *+akk* to get entangled in.
verströmen [fɛr'ʃtrøːmən] *vt* to exude.
verstümmeln [fɛr'ʃtymələn] *vt* to maim, mutilate (*auch fig*).
verstummen [fɛr'ʃtʊmən] *vi* to go silent; (*Lärm*) to die away.
Versuch [fɛr'zuːx] (-(e)s, -e) *m* attempt; (*CHEM etc*) experiment; **das käme auf einen** ~ **an** we'll have to have a try.
versuchen *vt* to try; (*verlocken*) to tempt ♦ *vr:* **sich an etw** *dat* ~ to try one's hand at sth.
Versuchs- *zW:* ~**anstalt** *f* research institute; ~**bohrung** *f* experimental drilling; ~**kaninchen** *nt* guinea pig; ~**objekt** *nt* test object; (*fig: Mensch*) guinea pig; ~**reihe** *f* series of experiments; **v~weise** *adv* tentatively.
Versuchung *f* temptation.
versumpfen [fɛr'zʊmpfən] *vi* (*Gebiet*) to become marshy; (*fig: umg*) to go to pot; (*lange zechen*) to get involved in a booze-up

(*BRIT*) *od* drinking spree (*US*).

versündigen [fɛr'zʏndɪgən] *vr* (*geh*): **sich an jdm/etw** ~ to sin against sb/sth.

versunken [fɛr'zuŋkən] *adj* sunken; ~ **sein in** +*akk* to be absorbed *od* engrossed in; **V~heit** *f* absorption.

versüßen [fɛr'zyːsən] *vt*: **jdm etw** ~ (*fig*) to make sth more pleasant for sb.

vertagen [fɛr'taːgən] *vt, vi* to adjourn.

Vertagung *f* adjournment.

vertauschen [fɛr'tauʃən] *vt* to exchange; (*versehentlich*) to mix up; **vertauschte Rollen** reversed roles.

verteidigen [fɛr'taɪdɪgən] *vt* to defend ♦ *vr* to defend o.s.; (*vor Gericht*) to conduct one's own defence (*BRIT*) *od* defense (*US*).

Verteidiger(in) (**-s, -**) *m(f)* defender; (*Anwalt*) defence (*BRIT*) *od* defense (*US*) lawyer.

Verteidigung *f* defence (*BRIT*), defense (*US*).

Verteidigungsfähigkeit *f* ability to defend.

Verteidigungsminister *m* Minister of Defence (*BRIT*), Defense Secretary (*US*).

verteilen [fɛr'taɪlən] *vt* to distribute; (*Rollen*) to assign; (*Salbe*) to spread.

Verteiler (**-s, -**) *m* (*COMM, AUT*) distributor.

Verteilung *f* distribution.

Verteuerung [fɛr'tɔʏərʊŋ] *f* increase in price.

verteufeln [fɛr'tɔʏfəln] *vt* to condemn.

verteufelt (*umg*) *adj* awful, devilish ♦ *adv* awfully, devilishly.

vertiefen [fɛr'tiːfən] *vt* to deepen; (*SCH*) to consolidate ♦ *vr*: **sich in etw** *akk* ~ to become engrossed *od* absorbed in sth.

Vertiefung *f* depression.

vertikal [vɛrti'kaːl] *adj* vertical.

vertilgen [fɛr'tɪlgən] *vt* to exterminate; (*umg*) to eat up, consume.

Vertilgungsmittel *nt* weedkiller; (*Insekten~*) pesticide.

vertippen [fɛr'tɪpən] *vr* to make a typing mistake.

vertonen [fɛr'toːnən] *vt* to set to music; (*Film etc*) to add a soundtrack to.

vertrackt [fɛr'trakt] *adj* awkward, tricky, complex.

Vertrag [fɛr'traːk] (**-(e)s, ̈-e**) *m* contract, agreement; (*POL*) treaty.

vertragen [fɛr'traːgən] *unreg vt* to tolerate, stand ♦ *vr* to get along; (*sich aussöhnen*) to become reconciled; **viel** ~ **können** (*umg: Alkohol*) to be able to hold one's drink; **sich mit etw** ~ (*Nahrungsmittel, Farbe*) to go with sth; (*Aussage, Verhalten*) to be consistent with sth.

vertraglich *adj* contractual.

verträglich [fɛr'trɛːklɪç] *adj* good-natured; (*Speisen*) easily digested; (*MED*) easily tolerated; **V~keit** *f* good nature; digestibility.

Vertrags- *zW*: ~**bruch** *m* breach of contract;

v~brüchig *adj* in breach of contract; **v~fähig** *adj* (*JUR*) competent to contract; **v~mäßig** *adj, adv* (as) stipulated, according to contract; ~**partner** *m* party to a contract; ~**spieler** *m* (*SPORT*) player under contract; **v~widrig** *adj, adv* contrary to contract.

vertrauen [fɛr'trauən] *vi*: **jdm** ~ to trust sb; ~ **auf** +*akk* to rely on; **V~** (**-s**) *nt* confidence; **jdn ins V~ ziehen** to take sb into one's confidence; **V~ zu jdm fassen** to gain confidence in sb.

vertrauenerweckend *adj* inspiring trust.

Vertrauens- *zW*: ~**mann** (**-(e)s**, *pl* -**männer** *od* -**leute**) *m* intermediary; ~**sache** *f* (*vertrauliche Angelegenheit*) confidential matter; (*Frage des Vertrauens*) question of trust; **v~selig** *adj* trusting; **v~voll** *adj* trustful; ~**votum** *nt* (*PARL*) vote of confidence; **v~würdig** *adj* trustworthy.

vertraulich [fɛr'traulɪç] *adj* familiar; (*geheim*) confidential; **V~keit** *f* familiarity; confidentiality.

verträumt [fɛr'trɔʏmt] *adj* dreamy; (*Städtchen etc*) sleepy.

vertraut [fɛr'traut] *adj* familiar; **sich mit dem Gedanken** ~ **machen, daß** ... to get used to the idea that ...

Vertraute(r) *f(m)* confidant(e), close friend.

Vertrautheit *f* familiarity.

vertreiben [fɛr'traɪbən] *unreg vt* to drive away; (*aus Land*) to expel; (*COMM*) to sell; (*Zeit*) to pass.

Vertreibung *f* expulsion.

vertretbar *adj* justifiable; (*Theorie, Argument*) tenable.

vertreten [fɛr'treːtən] *unreg vt* to represent; (*Ansicht*) to hold, advocate; (*ersetzen*) to replace; (*Kollegen*) to cover for; (*COMM*) to be the agent for; **sich** *dat* **die Beine** ~ to stretch one's legs.

Vertreter(in) (**-s, -**) *m(f)* representative; (*Verfechter*) advocate; (*COMM: Firma*) agent; ~**provision** *f* agent's commission.

Vertretung *f* representation; advocacy; **die** ~ **übernehmen (für)** to stand in (for).

Vertretungsstunde *f* (*SCH*) cover lesson.

Vertrieb [fɛr'triːp] (**-(e)s, -e**) *m* marketing; **den** ~ **für eine Firma haben** to have the (selling) agency for a firm.

Vertriebene(r) [fɛr'triːbənə] *f(m)* exile.

Vertriebskosten *pl* marketing costs *pl*.

vertrocknen [fɛr'trɔknən] *vi* to dry up.

vertrödeln [fɛr'trøːdəln] (*umg*) *vt* to fritter away.

vertrösten [fɛr'trøːstən] *vt* to put off.

vertun [fɛr'tuːn] *unreg vt* to waste ♦ *vr* (*umg*) to make a mistake.

vertuschen [fɛr'tuʃən] *vt* to hush *od* cover up.

verübeln [fɛr'yːbəln] *vt*: **jdm etw** ~ to be cross *od* offended with sb on account of sth.

verüben [fɛr'yːbən] *vt* to commit.

verulken [fɛr'ʊlkən] (*umg*) *vt* to make fun of.

verunglimpfen [fɛr'|ʊnglɪmpfən] *vt* to disparage.

verunglücken [fɛr'|ʊnglʏkən] *vi* to have an accident; (*fig: umg: mißlingen*) to go wrong; **tödlich** ~ to be killed in an accident.

Verunglückte(r) *f(m)* accident victim.

verunreinigen [fɛr'|ʊnraɪnɪgən] *vt* to soil; (*Umwelt*) to pollute.

verunsichern [fɛr'|ʊnzɪçərn] *vt* to rattle (*fig*).

verunstalten [fɛr'|ʊnʃtaltən] *vt* to disfigure; (*Gebäude etc*) to deface.

veruntreuen [fɛr'|ʊntrɔyən] *vt* to embezzle.

verursachen [fɛr'|uːrzaxən] *vt* to cause.

verurteilen [fɛr'|uːrtaɪlən] *vt* to condemn; (*zu Strafe*) to sentence; (*für schuldig befinden*): **jdn** ~ **(für)** to convict sb (of).

Verurteilung *f* condemnation; (*JUR*) sentence; conviction.

vervielfachen [fɛr'fiːlfaxən] *vt* to multiply.

vervielfältigen [fɛr'fiːlfɛltɪgən] *vt* to duplicate, copy.

Vervielfältigung *f* duplication, copying.

vervollkommnen [fɛr'fɔlkɔmnən] *vt* to perfect.

vervollständigen [fɛr'fɔlʃtɛndɪgən] *vt* to complete.

verw. *abk* = **verwitwet**.

verwachsen [fɛr'vaksən] *adj* (*Mensch*) deformed; (*verkümmert*) stunted; (*überwuchert*) overgrown.

verwackeln [fɛr'vakəln] *vt* (*Photo*) to blur.

verwählen [fɛr'vɛːlən] *vr* (*TEL*) to dial the wrong number.

verwahren [fɛr'vaːrən] *vt* to keep (safe) ♦ *vr* to protest.

verwahrlosen *vi* to become neglected; (*moralisch*) to go to the bad.

verwahrlost *adj* neglected; (*moralisch*) wayward.

Verwahrung *f* (*von Geld etc*) keeping; (*von Täter*) custody, detention; **jdn in** ~ **nehmen** to take sb into custody.

verwaist [fɛr'vaɪst] *adj* orphaned.

verwalten [fɛr'valtən] *vt* to manage; (*Behörde*) to administer.

Verwalter(in) **(-s, -)** *m(f)* administrator; (*Vermögens*~) trustee.

Verwaltung *f* management; administration.

Verwaltungs- *zW:* ~**apparat** *m* administrative machinery; ~**bezirk** *m* administrative district; ~**gericht** *nt* Administrative Court.

verwandeln [fɛr'vandəln] *vt* to change, transform ♦ *vr* to change.

Verwandlung *f* change, transformation.

verwandt [fɛr'vant] *adj:* ~ **(mit)** related (to); **geistig** ~ **sein** (*fig*) to be kindred spirits.

Verwandte(r) *f(m)* relative, relation.

Verwandtschaft *f* relationship; (*Menschen*) relatives *pl*, relations *pl*; (*fig*) affinity.

verwarnen [fɛr'varnən] *vt* to caution.

Verwarnung *f* caution.

verwaschen [fɛr'vaʃən] *adj* faded; (*fig*) vague.

verwässern [fɛr'vɛsərn] *vt* to dilute, water down.

verwechseln [fɛr'vɛksəln] *vt:* ~ **mit** to confuse with; **zum V**~ **ähnlich** as like as two peas.

Verwechslung *f* confusion, mixing up; **das muß eine** ~ **sein** there must be some mistake.

verwegen [fɛr've:gən] *adj* daring, bold; **V**~**heit** *f* daring, audacity, boldness.

verwehren [fɛr've:rən] *vt* (*geh*): **jdm etw** ~ to refuse *od* deny sb sth.

Verwehung [fɛr've:ʊŋ] *f* (*Schnee*~) snowdrift; (*Sand*~) sanddrift.

verweichlichen [fɛr'vaɪçlɪçən] *vt* to mollycoddle.

verweichlicht *adj* effeminate, soft.

verweigern [fɛr'vaɪgərn] *vt:* **jdm etw** ~ to refuse sb sth; **den Gehorsam/die Aussage** ~ to refuse to obey/testify.

Verweigerung *f* refusal.

verweilen [fɛr'vaɪlən] *vi* to stay; (*fig*): ~ **bei** to dwell on.

verweint [fɛr'vaɪnt] *adj* (*Augen*) swollen with tears *od* with crying; (*Gesicht*) tear-stained.

Verweis [fɛr'vaɪs] **(-es, -e)** *m* reprimand, rebuke; (*Hinweis*) reference.

verweisen [fɛr'vaɪzən] *unreg vt* to refer; **jdn auf etw** *akk*/**an jdn** ~ (*hinweisen*) to refer sb to sth/sb; **jdn vom Platz** *od* **des Spielfeldes** ~ (*SPORT*) to send sb off; **jdn von der Schule** ~ to expel sb (from school); **jdn des Landes** ~ to deport sb.

Verweisung *f* reference; (*Landes*~) deportation.

verwelken [fɛr'vɛlkən] *vi* to fade; (*Blumen*) to wilt.

verweltlichen [fɛr'vɛltlɪçən] *vt* to secularize.

verwendbar [fɛr'vɛndbaːr] *adj* usable.

verwenden [fɛr'vɛndən] *unreg vt* to use; (*Mühe, Zeit, Arbeit*) to spend ♦ *vr* to intercede.

Verwendung *f* use.

Verwendungsmöglichkeit *f* (possible) use.

verwerfen [fɛr'vɛrfən] *unreg vt* to reject; (*Urteil*) to quash; (*kritisieren: Handlungsweise*) to condemn.

verwerflich [fɛr'vɛrflɪç] *adj* reprehensible.

verwertbar *adj* usable.

verwerten [fɛr've:rtən] *vt* to utilize.

Verwertung *f* utilization.

verwesen [fɛr've:zən] *vi* to decay.

Verwesung *f* decomposition.

verwickeln [fɛr'vɪkəln] *vt* to tangle (up); (*fig*) to involve ♦ *vr* to get tangled (up); **jdn** ~ **in** +*akk* to involve sb in, get sb involved in; **sich** ~ **in** +*akk* to get involved in.

verwickelt *adj* involved.

Verwicklung *f* entanglement, complication.

verwildern [fɛr'vɪldərn] *vi* to run wild.

verwildert *adj* wild; (*Garten*) overgrown; (*jds Aussehen*) unkempt.

verwinden [fɛr'vɪndən] _unreg vt_ to get over.
verwirken [fɛr'vɪrkən] _vt (geh)_ to forfeit.
verwirklichen [fɛr'vɪrklɪçən] _vt_ to realize, put
into effect.
Verwirklichung _f_ realization.
verwirren [fɛr'vɪrən] _vt_ to tangle (up); (_fig_) to
confuse.
Verwirrspiel _nt_ confusing tactics _pl._
Verwirrung _f_ confusion.
verwischen [fɛr'vɪʃən] _vt (verschmieren)_ to
smudge; (_lit, fig: Spuren_) to cover over; (_fig:
Erinnerungen_) to blur.
verwittern [fɛr'vɪtərn] _vi_ to weather.
verwitwet [fɛr'vɪtvət] _adj_ widowed.
verwöhnen [fɛr'vøːnən] _vt_ to spoil, pamper.
Verwöhnung _f_ spoiling, pampering.
verworfen [fɛr'vɔrfən] _adj_ depraved; **V~heit** _f_
depravity.
verworren [fɛr'vɔrən] _adj_ confused.
verwundbar [fɛr'vʊntbaːr] _adj_ vulnerable.
verwunden [fɛr'vʊndən] _vt_ to wound.
verwunderlich [fɛr'vʊndərlɪç] _adj_ surprising;
(_stärker_) astonishing.
verwundern _vt_ to astonish ♦ _vr:_ **sich ~ über**
+akk to be astonished at.
Verwunderung _f_ astonishment.
Verwundete(r) _f(m)_ injured person; **die ~n**
the injured; (_MIL_) the wounded.
Verwundung _f_ wound, injury.
verwünschen [fɛr'vʏnʃən] _vt_ to curse.
verwurzelt [fɛr'vʊrtsəlt] _adj:_ **(fest) in etw** _dat_
_od_ **mit etw ~** (_fig_) deeply rooted in sth.
verwüsten [fɛr'vyːstən] _vt_ to devastate.
Verwüstung _f_ devastation.
Verz. _abk =_ **Verzeichnis.**
verzagen [fɛr'tsaːgən] _vi_ to despair.
verzagt [fɛr'tsaːkt] _adj_ disheartened.
verzählen [fɛr'tsɛːlən] _vr_ to miscount.
verzahnen [fɛr'tsaːnən] _vt_ to dovetail;
(_Zahnräder_) to cut teeth in.
verzapfen [fɛr'tsapfən] (_umg_) _vt:_ **Unsinn ~** to
talk nonsense.
verzaubern [fɛr'tsaʊbərn] _vt (lit)_ to cast a
spell on; (_fig: jdn_) to enchant.
verzehren [fɛr'tseːrən] _vt_ to consume.
verzeichnen [fɛr'tsaɪçnən] _vt_ to list;
(_Niederlage, Verlust_) to register.
Verzeichnis **(-ses, -se)** _nt_ list, catalogue
(_BRIT_), catalog (_US_); (_in Buch_) index;
(_COMPUT_) directory.
verzeihen [fɛr'tsaɪən] _unreg vt, vi_ to forgive;
jdm etw ~ to forgive sb (for) sth; **~ Sie!**
excuse me!
verzeihlich _adj_ pardonable.
Verzeihung _f_ forgiveness, pardon; **~!**
sorry!, excuse me!; (**jdn) um ~ bitten** to
apologize (to sb).
verzerren [fɛr'tseːrən] _vt_ to distort; (_Sehne,
Muskel_) to strain, pull.
verzetteln [fɛr'tsɛtəln] _vr_ to waste a lot of
time.
Verzicht [fɛr'tsɪçt] **(-(e)s, -e)** _m:_ **~ (auf** _+akk_)

renunciation (of); **v~en** _vi:_ **v~en auf** _+akk_ to
forego, give up.
verziehen [fɛr'tsiːən] _unreg vi (Hilfsverb sein)_ to
move ♦ _vt_ to put out of shape; (_Kind_) to spoil;
(_Pflanzen_) to thin out ♦ _vr_ to go out of shape;
(_Gesicht_) to contort; (_verschwinden_) to
disappear; **verzogen** (_Vermerk_) no longer at
this address; **keine Miene ~** not to turn a
hair; **das Gesicht ~** to pull a face.
verzieren [fɛr'tsiːrən] _vt_ to decorate.
Verzierung _f_ decoration.
verzinsen [fɛr'tsɪnzən] _vt_ to pay interest on.
verzinslich _adj:_ **(fest) ~ sein** to yield (a fixed
rate of) interest.
verzogen [fɛr'tsoːgən] _adj (Kind)_ spoilt; _siehe
auch_ **verziehen.**
verzögern [fɛr'tsøːgərn] _vt_ to delay.
Verzögerung _f_ delay.
Verzögerungstaktik _f_ delaying tactics _pl._
verzollen [fɛr'tsɔlən] _vt_ to pay duty on; **haben
Sie etwas zu ~?** have you anything to
declare?
verzücken [fɛr'tsʏkən] _vt_ to send into
ecstasies, enrapture.
Verzug [fɛr'tsuːk] _m_ delay; (_FIN_) arrears _pl;_
mit etw in ~ geraten to fall behind with sth.
verzweifeln [fɛr'tsvaɪfəln] _vi_ to despair.
verzweifelt _adj_ desperate.
Verzweiflung _f_ despair.
verzweigen [fɛr'tsvaɪgən] _vr_ to branch out.
verzwickt [fɛr'tsvɪkt] (_umg_) _adj_ awkward,
complicated.
Vesper ['fɛspər] **(-, -n)** _f_ vespers _pl._
Vesuv [ve'zuːf] **(-(s))** _m_ Vesuvius.
Veto ['veːto] **(-s, -s)** _nt_ veto.
Vetter ['fɛtər] **(-s, -n)** _m_ cousin.
vgl. _abk (= vergleiche)_ cf.
v.H. _abk (= vom Hundert)_ pc.
VHS **(-)** _f abk =_ **Volkshochschule.**
Viadukt [via'dʊkt] **(-(e)s, -e)** _m_ viaduct.
Vibrator [vi'braːtɔr] _m_ vibrator.
vibrieren [vi'briːrən] _vi_ to vibrate.
Video ['viːdeo] **(-s, -s)** _nt_ video; **~aufnahme** _f_
video (recording); **~kamera** _f_ video
camera; **~recorder** _m_ video recorder; **~spiel**
_nt_ video game; **~text** _m_ teletext.
Vieh [fiː] **(-(e)s)** _nt_ cattle _pl;_ (_Nutztiere_)
livestock; (_umg: Tier_) animal; **v~isch** _adj_
bestial; **~zucht** _f_ (live)stock _od_ cattle
breeding.
viel [fiːl] _adj_ a lot of, much ♦ _adv_ a lot, much; **in
~em** in many respects; **noch (ein)mal so ~**
(_Zeit etc_) as much (time _etc_) again; **einer zu
~** one too many; **~ zuwenig** much too little;
~beschäftigt _adj attrib_ very busy; **~e** _pl_ a lot
of, many; **gleich ~e (Angestellte/Anteile** _etc_)
the same number (of employees/shares _etc_).
vielerlei _adj_ a great variety of.
vielerorts _adv_ in many places.
viel- _zW:_ **~fach** _adj, adv_ many times; **auf
~fachen Wunsch** at the request of many
people; **V~fache(s)** _nt (MATH)_ multiple; **um**

ein V~faches many times over; **V~falt** (-) f variety; **~fältig** adj varied, many-sided; **V~fraß** m glutton; **~geprüft** adj attrib (hum) sorely tried.

vielleicht [fi'laiçt] adv perhaps; (in Bitten) by any chance; **du bist ~ ein Idiot!** (umg) you really are an idiot!

viel- zW: **~mal(s)** adv many times; **danke ~mals** many thanks; **ich bitte ~mals um Entschuldigung!** I do apologize!; **~mehr** adv rather, on the contrary; **~sagend** adj significant; **~schichtig** adj (fig) complex; **~seitig** adj many-sided; (Ausbildung) all-round attrib; (Interessen) varied; (Mensch, Gerät) versatile; **~versprechend** adj promising; **V~völkerstaat** m multinational state.

vier [fi:r] num four; **alle ~e von sich strecken** (umg) to stretch out; **V~beiner** m (hum) four-legged friend; **V~eck** (-(e)s, -e) nt four-sided figure; (gleichseitig) square; **~eckig** adj four-sided; square; **~hundert** num four hundred; **~kant** adj, adv (NAUT) square; **~köpfig** adj: **eine ~köpfige Familie** a family of four; **V~mächteabkommen** nt four-power agreement.

viert adj: **wir gingen zu ~** four of us went.

Viertaktmotor m four-stroke engine.

vierte(r, s) ['fi:rtə(r, s)] adj fourth.

vierteilen vt to quarter.

Viertel ['firtəl] (-s, -) nt quarter; **ein ~ Leberwurst** a quarter of liver sausage; **~finale** nt quarter finals pl; **~jahr** nt three months pl, quarter (COMM, FIN); **~jahresschrift** f quarterly; **v~jährlich** adj quarterly; **~note** f crotchet (BRIT), quarter note (US); **~stunde** f quarter of an hour.

vier- zW: **~türig** adj four-door attr; **V~waldstättersee** m Lake Lucerne; **~zehn** ['firtse:n] num fourteen; **in ~zehn Tagen** in a fortnight (BRIT), in two weeks (US); **~zehntägig** adj fortnightly; **~zehnte(r, s)** adj fourteenth.

vierzig ['firtsiç] num forty; **V~stundenwoche** f forty-hour week.

Vierzimmerwohnung f four-room flat (BRIT) od apartment (US).

Vietnam [viet'nam] (-s) nt Vietnam.

Vietnamese [viɛtna'me:zə] (-n, -n) m, **Vietnamesin** f Vietnamese.

vietnamesisch adj Vietnamese.

Vikar [vi'ka:r] (-s, -e) m curate.

Villa ['vila] (-, Villen) f villa.

Villenviertel nt (prosperous) residential area.

violett [vio'lɛt] adj violet.

Violinbogen m violin bow.

Violine [vio'li:nə] (-, -n) f violin.

Violinkonzert nt violin concerto.

Violinschlüssel m treble clef.

virtuell [virtu'ɛl] adj (COMPUT) virtual; **~e Realität** virtual reality.

virtuos [virtu'o:s] adj virtuoso attrib.

Virtuose [virtu'o:zə] (-n, -n) m virtuoso.

Virtuosin [virtu'o:zin] f virtuoso.

Virtuosität [virtuozi'tɛt] f virtuosity.

Virus ['vi:rus] (-, Viren) m od nt (also COMPUT) virus.

Virus- in zW viral; **~infektion** f virus infection.

Visage [vi'za:ʒə] (-, -n) (pej) f face, (ugly) mug (umg).

Visagist(in) [viza'ʒist(in)] m(f) make-up artist.

vis-à-vis [viza'vi:] adv (veraltet): **~ (von)** opposite (to) ♦ präp +dat opposite (to).

Visier [vi'zi:r] (-s, -e) nt gunsight; (am Helm) visor.

Vision [vizi'o:n] f vision.

Visite [vi'zi:tə] (-, -n) f (MED) visit.

Visitenkarte f visiting card.

visuell [vizu'ɛl] adj visual.

Visum ['vi:zum] (-s, Visa od Visen) nt visa; **~zwang** m obligation to hold a visa.

vital [vi'ta:l] adj lively, full of life; (lebenswichtig) vital.

Vitamin [vita'mi:n] (-s, -e) nt vitamin; **~mangel** m vitamin deficiency.

Vitrine [vi'tri:nə] (-, -n) f (Schrank) glass cabinet; (Schaukasten) showcase, display case.

Vivisektion [vivizɛktsi'o:n] f vivisection.

Vize ['fi:tsə] m (umg) number two; (: **~meister**) runner-up ♦ in zW vice-.

v.J. abk (= vorigen Jahres) of the previous od last year.

Vlies [fli:s] (-es, -e) nt fleece.

v.M. abk (= vorigen Monats) ult.

V-Mann m abk = **Verbindungsmann**; **Vertrauensmann.**

VN pl abk (= Vereinte Nationen) UN.

VO abk = **Verordnung.**

Vogel ['fo:gəl] (-s, ⸚) m bird; **einen ~ haben** (umg) to have bats in the belfry; **den ~ abschießen** (umg) to surpass everyone (ironisch); **~bauer** m birdcage; **~beerbaum** m rowan (tree); **~dreck** m bird droppings pl; **~perspektive** f bird's-eye view; **~schau** f bird's-eye view; **~scheuche** f scarecrow; **~schutzgebiet** nt bird sanctuary; **~-Strauß-Politik** f head-in-the-sand policy.

Vogesen [vo'ge:zən] pl Vosges pl.

Vokabel [vo'ka:bəl] (-, -n) f word.

Vokabular [vokabu'la:r] (-s, -e) nt vocabulary.

Vokal [vo'ka:l] (-s, -e) m vowel.

Volk [fɔlk] (-(e)s, ⸚er) nt people; (Nation) nation; **etw unters ~ bringen** (Nachricht) to spread sth.

Völker- zW: **~bund** m League of Nations; **~kunde** f ethnology; **~mord** m genocide; **~recht** nt international law; **v~rechtlich** adj according to international law; **~verständigung** f international understanding; **~wanderung** f migration.

Volks- zW: **~abstimmung** f referendum;

~**armee** f People's Army; ~**begehren** nt petition for a referendum; ~**deutsche(r)** f(m) ethnic German; **v~eigen** adj (DDR) nationally-owned; ~**feind** m enemy of the people; ~**fest** nt popular festival; (Jahrmarkt) fair.

Volkshochschule f adult education classes pl.

The **Volkshochschule** *(VHS) is an institution which offers Adult Education classes. No set qualifications are necessary to attend. For a small fee adults can attend both vocational and non-vocational classes in the day-time or evening.*

Volks- zW: ~**lauf** m fun run; ~**lied** nt folk song; ~**mund** m vernacular; ~**polizei** f (DDR) People's Police; ~**republik** f people's republic; ~**schule** f ≈ primary school (BRIT), elementary school (US); ~**seuche** f epidemic; ~**stamm** m tribe; ~**stück** nt folk play in dialect; ~**tanz** m folk dance; ~**trauertag** m ≈ Remembrance Day (BRIT), Memorial Day (US); **v~tümlich** adj popular; ~**wirtschaft** f national economy; (Fach) economics sing, political economy; ~**wirtschaftler** m economist; ~**zählung** f (national) census.

voll [fɔl] adj full ♦ adv.fully; **jdn für ~ nehmen** (umg) to take sb seriously; **aus dem ~en schöpfen** to draw on unlimited resources; **in ~er Größe** (Bild) life-size(d); (bei plötzlicher Erscheinung etc) large as life; ~ **sein** (umg: satt) to be full (up); (: betrunken) to be plastered; ~ **und ganz** completely.

vollauf [fɔl'|aʊf] adv amply; ~ **zu tun haben** to have quite enough to do.

voll- zW: **V~bad** nt (proper) bath; **V~bart** m full beard; **V~beschäftigung** f full employment; **V~besitz** m: **im V~besitz** +gen in full possession of; **V~blut** nt thoroughbred; ~**blütig** adj full-blooded; **V~bremsung** f emergency stop; ~**bringen** unreg vt untr to accomplish; **V~dampf** m (NAUT): **mit V~dampf** at full steam; ~**enden** vt untr to finish, complete; ~**endet** adj (vollkommen) perfect; (Tänzer etc) accomplished; ~**ends** adv completely; **V~endung** f completion.

voller adj fuller; ~ **Flecken/Ideen** full of stains/ideas.

Völlerei [fœlə'raɪ] f gluttony.

Volleyball ['vɔlibal] (-(e)s) m volleyball.

voll- zW: ~**fett** adj full-fat; **V~gas** nt: **mit V~gas** at full throttle; **V~gas geben** to step on it.

völlig ['fœlɪç] adj complete ♦ adv completely.

voll- zW: ~**jährig** adj of age; **V~kaskoversicherung** f fully comprehensive insurance; ~**kommen** adj perfect; (völlig) complete, absolute;

V~kommenheit f perfection; **V~kornbrot** nt wholemeal (BRIT) od whole-wheat (US) bread; ~**(l)aufen** unreg vi: **etw ~(l)aufen lassen** to fill sth up; ~**machen** vt to fill (up); **V~macht** f authority, power of attorney; **V~matrose** m able-bodied seaman; **V~milch** f full-cream milk; **V~mond** m full moon; **V~narkose** f general anaesthetic (BRIT) od anesthetic (US); **V~pension** f full board; ~**schlank** adj plump, stout; ~**schreiben** unreg vt (Heft, Seite) to fill; (Tafel) to cover (with writing); ~**ständig** adj complete; ~**strecken** vt untr to execute; ~**tanken** vt, vi to fill up; **V~treffer** m (lit, fig) bull's-eye; **V~versammlung** f general meeting; **V~waise** f orphan; ~**wertig** adj full attrib; (Stellung) equal; **V~wertkost** f wholefoods pl; ~**zählig** adj complete; (anwesend) in full number; ~**ziehen** unreg vt untr to carry out ♦ vr untr to happen; **V~zug** m execution.

Volontär(in) [volɔn'tɛːr(ɪn)] (-s, -e) m(f) trainee.

Volt [vɔlt] (- od -(e)s, -) nt volt.

Volumen [vo'luːmən] (-s, - od Volumina) nt volume.

vom [fɔm] = **von dem**.

═══════════════════════ *SCHLÜSSELWORT*

von [fɔn] präp +dat **1** (Ausgangspunkt) from; ~ ... **bis** from ... to; ~ **morgens bis abends** from morning till night; ~ ... **nach** ... from ... to ...; ~ ... **an** from ...; ~ ... **aus** from ...; ~ **dort aus** from there; **etw** ~ **sich aus tun** to do sth of one's own accord; ~ **mir aus** (umg) if you like, I don't mind; ~ **wo/wann** ...? where/when ... from?

2 (Ursache, im Passiv) by; **ein Gedicht** ~ **Schiller** a poem by Schiller; ~ **etw müde** tired from sth

3 (als Genitiv) of; **ein Freund** ~ **mir** a friend of mine; **nett** ~ **dir** nice of you; **jeweils zwei** ~ **zehn** two out of every ten

4 (über) about; **er erzählte vom Urlaub** he talked about his holiday

5: ~ **wegen!** (umg) no way!

---

voneinander adv from each other.

vonstatten [fɔn'ʃtatən] adv: ~ **gehen** to proceed, go.

═══════════════════════ *SCHLÜSSELWORT*

vor [foːr] präp +dat **1** (räumlich) in front of

2 (zeitlich, Reihenfolge) before; **ich war** ~ **ihm da** I was there before him; **X kommt** ~ **Y** X comes before Y; ~ **zwei Tagen** two days ago; **5 (Minuten)** ~ **4** 5 (minutes) to 4; ~ **kurzem** a little while ago

3 (Ursache) with; ~ **Wut/Liebe** with rage/love; ~ **Hunger sterben** to die of hunger; ~ **lauter Arbeit** because of work

4: ~ **allem**, ~ **allen Dingen** above all ♦ präp +akk (räumlich) in front of; ~ **sich hin**

summen to hum to oneself
♦ *adv:* ~ **und zurück** backwards and forwards.

Vor- *zW:* ~**abdruck** *m* preprint; ~**abend** *m* evening before, eve; ~**ahnung** *f* presentiment, premonition.

voran [fo'ran] *adv* before, ahead; ~**bringen** *unreg vt* to make progress with; ~**gehen** *unreg vi* to go ahead; **einer Sache** *dat* ~**gehen** to precede sth; ~**gehend** *adj* previous; ~**kommen** *unreg vi* to make progress, come along.

Voranschlag ['fo:r|anʃla:k] *m* estimate.

voranstellen [fo'ranʃtɛlən] *vt +dat* to put in front (of); (*fig*) to give precedence (over).

Vorarbeiter ['fo:r|arbaɪtər] *m* foreman.

voraus [fo'raus] *adv* ahead; (*zeitlich*) in advance; **jdm** ~ **sein** to be ahead of sb; **im** ~ in advance; ~**bezahlen** *vt* to pay in advance; ~**gehen** *unreg vi* to go (on) ahead; (*fig*) to precede; ~**haben** *unreg vt:* **jdm etw** ~**haben** to have the edge on sb in sth; **V**~**sage** *f* prediction; ~**sagen** *vt* to predict; ~**sehen** *unreg vt* to foresee; ~**setzen** *vt* to assume; (*sicher annehmen*) to take for granted; (*erfordern: Kenntnisse, Geduld*) to require, demand; ~**gesetzt, daß** ... provided that ...; **V**~**setzung** *f* requirement, prerequisite; **unter der V**~**setzung, daß** ... on condition that ...; **V**~**sicht** *f* foresight; **aller V**~**sicht nach** in all probability; **in der V**~**sicht, daß** ... anticipating that ...; ~**sichtlich** *adv* probably; **V**~**zahlung** *f* advance payment.

Vorbau ['fo:rbau] (-(e)s, -ten) *m* porch; (*Balkon*) balcony.

vorbauen ['fo:rbauən] *vt* to build up in front ♦ *vi +dat* to take precautions (against).

Vorbedacht ['fo:rbədaxt] *m:* **mit/ohne** ~ (*Überlegung*) with/without due consideration; (*Absicht*) intentionally/ unintentionally.

Vorbedingung ['fo:rbədɪŋuŋ] *f* precondition.

Vorbehalt ['fo:rbəhalt] *m* reservation, proviso; **unter dem** ~, **daß** ... with the reservation that ...

vorbehalten *unreg vt:* **sich/jdm etw** ~ to reserve sth (for o.s.)/for sb; **alle Rechte** ~ all rights reserved.

vorbehaltlich *präp +gen* (*form*) subject to.

vorbehaltlos *adj* unconditional ♦ *adv* unconditionally.

vorbei [fɔr'baɪ] *adv* by, past; **aus und** ~ over and done with; **damit ist es nun** ~ that's all over now; ~**bringen** *unreg* (*umg*) *vt* to drop off; ~**gehen** *unreg vi* to pass by, go past; ~**kommen** *unreg vi:* **bei jdm** ~**kommen** to drop *od* call in on sb; ~**reden** *vi:* **an etw** *dat* ~**reden** to talk around sth.

vorbelastet ['fo:rbəlastət] *adj* (*fig*) handicapped (*BRIT*), handicaped (*US*).

Vorbemerkung ['fo:rbəmɛrkuŋ] *f*

introductory remark.

vorbereiten ['fo:rbəraɪtən] *vt* to prepare.

Vorbereitung *f* preparation.

vorbestellen ['fo:rbəʃtɛlən] *vt* to book (in advance), reserve.

Vorbestellung *f* advance booking.

vorbestraft ['fo:rbəʃtraft] *adj* previously convicted, with a record.

Vorbeugehaft *f* preventive custody.

vorbeugen ['fo:rbɔygən] *vt, vr* to lean forward ♦ *vi +dat* to prevent.

vorbeugend *adj* preventive.

Vorbeugung *f* prevention; **zur** ~ **gegen** for the prevention of.

Vorbild ['fo:rbɪlt] *nt* model; **sich** *dat* **jdn zum** ~ **nehmen** to model o.s. on sb; **v**~**lich** *adj* model, ideal.

Vorbildung ['fo:rbɪlduŋ] *f* educational background.

Vorbote ['fo:rbo:tə] *m* (*fig*) herald.

vorbringen ['fo:rbrɪŋən] *unreg vt* to voice; (*Meinung etc*) to advance, state; (*umg: nach vorne*) to bring to the front.

vordatieren ['fo:rdati:rən] *vt* (*Schreiben*) to postdate.

Vorder- *zW:* ~**achse** *f* front axle; ~**ansicht** *f* front view; ~**asien** *nt* Near East.

vordere(r, s) *adj* front.

Vorder- *zW:* ~**grund** *m* foreground; **im** ~**grund stehen** (*fig*) to be to the fore; ~**grundprogramm** *nt* (*COMPUT*) foreground program; **v**~**hand** *adv* for the present; ~**mann** (-(e)s, *pl* -**männer**) *m* man in front; **jdn auf** ~**mann bringen** (*umg*) to get sb to shape up; ~**seite** *f* front (side); ~**sitz** *m* front seat.

vorderste(r, s) *adj* front.

vordrängen ['fo:rdrɛŋən] *vr* to push to the front.

vordringen ['fo:rdrɪŋən] *unreg vi:* **bis zu jdm/ etw** ~ to get as far as sb/sth.

vordringlich *adj* urgent.

Vordruck ['fo:rdruk] *m* form.

vorehelich ['fo:r|e:əlɪç] *adj* premarital.

voreilig ['fo:r|aɪlɪç] *adj* hasty, rash; ~**e Schlüsse ziehen** to jump to conclusions.

voreinander [fo:r|aɪ'nandər] *adv* (*räumlich*) in front of each other; (*einander gegenüber*) face to face.

voreingenommen ['fo:r|aɪngənɔmən] *adj* bias(s)ed; **V**~**heit** *f* bias.

voreingestellt ['fo:r|aɪngəʃtɛlt] *adj:* ~**er Parameter** (*COMPUT*) default (parameter).

vorenthalten ['fo:r|ɛnthaltən] *unreg vt:* **jdm etw** ~ to withhold sth from sb.

Vorentscheidung ['fo:r|ɛntʃaɪduŋ] *f* preliminary decision.

vorerst ['fo:r|e:rst] *adv* for the moment *od* present.

Vorfahr ['fo:rfa:r] (-en, -en) *m* ancestor.

vorfahren *unreg vi* to drive (on) ahead; (*vors Haus etc*) to drive up.

Vorfahrt *f* (*AUT*) right of way;
„~ **(be)achten"** "give way" (*BRIT*), "yield"
(*US*).
Vorfahrts- *zW:* ~**regel** *f* rule of right of way;
~**schild** *nt* "give way" (*BRIT*) *od* "yield" (*US*)
sign; ~**straße** *f* major road.
Vorfall ['fo:rfal] *m* incident.
vorfallen *unreg vi* to occur.
Vorfeld ['fo:rfɛlt] *nt* (*fig*): im ~ (+*gen*) in the
run-up (to).
Vorfilm ['fo:rfɪlm] *m* short.
vorfinden ['fo:rfɪndən] *unreg vt* to find.
Vorfreude ['fo:rfrɔydə] *f* anticipation.
vorfühlen ['fo:rfy:lən] *vi* (*fig*) to put out
feelers.
vorführen ['fo:rfy:rən] *vt* to show, display,
(*Theaterstück, Kunststücke*): (jdm) etw ~ to
perform sth (to *od* in front of sb); **dem
Gericht** ~ to bring before the court.
Vorgabe ['fo:rga:bə] *f* (*SPORT*) handicap.
Vorgang ['fo:rgaŋ] *m* (*Ereignis*) event; (*Ablauf*)
course of events; (*CHEM etc*) process.
Vorgänger(in) ['fo:rgɛŋər(ɪn)] (*-s, -*) *m(f)*
predecessor.
vorgaukeln ['fo:rgaʊkəln] *vt:* jdm etw ~ to
lead sb to believe in sth.
vorgeben ['fo:rge:bən] *unreg vt* to pretend, use
as a pretext; (*SPORT*) to give an advantage
od a start of.
Vorgebirge ['fo:rgəbɪrgə] *nt* foothills *pl*.
vorgefaßt ['fo:rgəfast] *adj* preconceived.
vorgefertigt ['fo:rgəfɛrtɪçt] *adj* prefabricated.
Vorgefühl ['fo:rgəfy:l] *nt* anticipation; (*etwas
Böses*) presentiment.
vorgehen ['fo:rge:ən] *unreg vi* (*voraus*) to go
(on) ahead; (*nach vorn*) to go forward;
(*handeln*) to act, proceed; (*Uhr*) to be fast;
(*Vorrang haben*) to take precedence;
(*passieren*) to go on.
Vorgehen (*-s*) *nt* action.
Vorgehensweise *f* proceedings *pl*.
vorgerückt ['fo:rgərʏkt] *adj* (*Stunde*) late;
(*Alter*) advanced.
Vorgeschichte ['fo:rgəʃɪçtə] *f* prehistory;
(*von Fall, Krankheit*) past history.
Vorgeschmack ['fo:rgəʃmak] *m* foretaste.
Vorgesetzte(r) ['fo:rgəzɛtstə(r)] *f(m)* superior.
vorgestern ['fo:rgɛstərn] *adv* the day before
yesterday; **von** ~ (*fig*) antiquated.
vorgreifen ['fo:rgraɪfən] *unreg vi +dat* to
anticipate; **jdm** ~ to forestall sb.
vorhaben ['fo:rha:bən] *unreg vt* to intend; **hast
du schon was vor?** have you got anything
on?
Vorhaben (*-s, -*) *nt* intention.
Vorhalle ['fo:rhalə] *f* (*Diele*) entrance hall;
(*von Parlament*) lobby.
vorhalten ['fo:rhaltən] *unreg vt* to hold *od* put
up ♦ *vi* to last; **jdm etw** ~ to reproach sb for
sth.
Vorhaltung *f* reproach.
Vorhand ['fo:rhant] *f* forehand.

vorhanden [fo:r'handən] *adj* existing;
(*erhältlich*) available; **V~sein** (*-s*) *nt*
existence, presence.
Vorhang ['fo:rhaŋ] *m* curtain.
Vorhängeschloß ['fo:rhɛŋəʃlɔs] *nt* padlock.
Vorhaut ['fo:rhaʊt] *f* (*ANAT*) foreskin.
vorher [fo:r'he:r] *adv* before(hand);
~**bestimmen** *vt* (*Schicksal*) to preordain;
~**gehen** *unreg vi* to precede.
vorherig [fo:r'he:rɪç] *adj* previous.
Vorherrschaft ['fo:rhɛrʃaft] *f* predominance,
supremacy.
vorherrschen *vi* to predominate.
vorher- *zW:* **V~sage** *f* forecast; ~**sagen** *vt* to
forecast, predict; ~**sehbar** *adj* predictable;
~**sehen** *unreg vt* to foresee.
vorhin [fo:r'hɪn] *adv* not long ago, just now.
vorhinein ['fo:rhɪnaɪn] *adv:* im ~ beforehand.
Vorhof ['fo:rho:f] *m* forecourt.
vorig ['fo:rɪç] *adj* previous, last.
Vorjahr ['fo:rja:r] *nt* previous year, year
before.
vorjährig ['fo:rjɛ:rɪç] *adj* of the previous year.
vorjammern ['fo:rjamərn] *vt, vi:* jdm (etwas) ~
to moan to sb (about sth).
Vorkämpfer(in) ['fo:rkɛmpfər(ɪn)] *m(f)*
pioneer.
Vorkaufsrecht ['fo:rkaʊfsrɛçt] *nt* option to
buy.
Vorkehrung ['fo:rke:rʊŋ] *f* precaution.
Vorkenntnis ['fo:rkɛntnɪs] *f* previous
knowledge.
vorknöpfen ['fo:rknœpfən] *vt* (*fig: umg*): **sich**
dat jdn ~ to take sb to task.
vorkommen ['fo:rkɔmən] *unreg vi* to come
forward; (*geschehen, sich finden*) to occur;
(*scheinen*) to seem (to be); **so was soll** ~!
that's life!; **sich** *dat* **dumm** *etc* ~ to feel
stupid *etc*.
Vorkommen *nt* occurrence; (*MIN*) deposit.
Vorkommnis ['fo:rkɔmnɪs] (*-ses, -se*) *nt*
occurrence.
Vorkriegs- ['fo:rkri:ks] *in zW* pre-war.
vorladen ['fo:rla:dən] *unreg vt* (*bei Gericht*) to
summons.
Vorladung *f* summons.
Vorlage ['fo:rla:gə] *f* model, pattern; (*das
Vorlegen*) presentation; (*von Beweismaterial*)
submission; (*Gesetzes~*) bill; (*SPORT*) pass.
vorlassen ['fo:rlasən] *unreg vt* to admit;
(*überholen lassen*) to let pass; (*vorgehen
lassen*) to allow to go in front.
Vorlauf ['fo:rlaʊf] *m* (preliminary) heat (*of
running event*).
Vorläufer *m* forerunner.
vorläufig ['fo:rlɔyfɪç] *adj* temporary;
(*provisorisch*) provisional.
vorlaut ['fo:rlaʊt] *adj* impertinent, cheeky.
Vorleben ['fo:rle:bən] *nt* past (life).
vorlegen ['fo:rle:gən] *vt* to put in front,
present; (*Beweismaterial etc*) to produce,
submit; **jdm etw** ~ to put sth before sb.

Vorleger (-s, -) *m* mat.
Vorleistung ['fo:rlaistʊŋ] *f* (*FIN*: *Vorausbezahlung*) advance (payment); (*Vorarbeit*) preliminary work; (*POL*) prior concession.
vorlesen ['fo:rle:zən] *unreg vt* to read (out).
Vorlesung *f* (*UNIV*) lecture.
Vorlesungsverzeichnis *nt* lecture timetable.
vorletzte(r, s) ['fo:rlɛtstə(r, s)] *adj* last but one, penultimate.
Vorliebe ['fo:rli:bə] *f* preference, special liking; **etw mit ~ tun** to particularly like doing sth.
vorliebnehmen [fo:r'li:pne:mən] *unreg vi*: **~ mit** to make do with.
vorliegen ['fo:rli:gən] *unreg vi* to be (here); **etw liegt jdm vor** sb has sth; **etw liegt gegen jdn vor** sb is charged with sth.
vorliegend *adj* present, at issue.
vorm. *abk* (= *vormittags*) a.m.; (= *vormals*) formerly.
vormachen ['fo:rmaxən] *vt*: **jdm etw ~** to show sb how to do sth; **jdm etwas ~** (*fig*) to fool sb; **mach mir doch nichts vor** don't try and fool me.
Vormachtstellung ['fo:rmaxtʃtɛlʊŋ] *f* supremacy.
vormals ['fo:rmals] *adv* formerly.
Vormarsch ['fo:rmarʃ] *m* advance.
vormerken ['fo:rmɛrkən] *vt* to book; (*notieren*) to make note of; (*bei Bestellung*) to take an order for.
Vormittag ['fo:rmita:k] *m* morning; **am ~** in the morning.
vormittags *adv* in the morning, before noon.
Vormund ['fo:rmʊnt] (-(e)s, -e *od* -münder) *m* guardian.
vorn [fɔrn] *adv* in front; **von ~ anfangen** to start at the beginning; **nach ~** to the front; **er betrügt sie von ~ bis hinten** he deceives her right, left and centre.
Vorname ['fo:rna:mə] *m* first *od* Christian name.
vornan [fɔrn'|an] *adv* at the front.
vorne ['fɔrnə] = **vorn**.
vornehm ['fo:rne:m] *adj* distinguished; (*Manieren etc*) refined; (*Kleid*) elegant; **in ~en Kreisen** in polite society.
vornehmen *unreg vt* (*fig*) to carry out; **sich dat etw ~** to start on sth; (*beschließen*) to decide to do sth; **sich dat zuviel ~** to take on too much; **sich dat jdn ~** to tell sb off.
vornehmlich *adv* chiefly, specially.
vorn(e)weg ['fɔrn(ə)vɛk] *adv* in front; (*als erstes*) first.
vornherein ['fɔrnhɛrain] *adv*: **von ~** from the start.
Vorort ['fo:r|ɔrt] *m* suburb; **~zug** *m* commuter train.
vorprogrammiert ['fo:rprogrami:rt] *adj* (*Erfolg, Antwort*) automatic.

Vorrang ['fo:rraŋ] *m* precedence, priority.
vorrangig *adj* of prime importance, primary.
Vorrat ['fo:rra:t] *m* stock, supply; **solange der ~ reicht** (*COMM*) while stocks last.
vorrätig ['fo:rrɛ:tiç] *adj* in stock.
Vorratskammer *f* store cupboard; (*für Lebensmittel*) larder.
Vorraum *m* anteroom; (*Büro*) outer office.
vorrechnen ['fo:rrɛçnən] *vt*: **jdm etw ~** to calculate sth for sb; (*als Kritik*) to point sth out to sb.
Vorrecht ['fo:rrɛçt] *nt* privilege.
Vorrede ['fo:rre:də] *f* introductory speech; (*THEAT*) prologue (*BRIT*), prolog (*US*).
Vorrichtung ['fo:rriçtʊŋ] *f* device, gadget.
vorrücken ['fo:rrʏkən] *vi* to advance ♦ *vt* to move forward.
Vorruhestand ['fo:rru:əʃtant] *m* early retirement.
Vorrunde ['fo:rrʊndə] *f* (*SPORT*) preliminary round.
Vors. *abk* = **Vorsitzende(r)**.
vorsagen ['fo:rza:gən] *vt* to recite; (*SCH*: *zuflüstern*) to tell secretly, prompt.
Vorsaison ['fo:rzɛzõ:] *f* early season, low season.
Vorsatz ['fo:rzats] *m* intention; (*JUR*) intent; **einen ~ fassen** to make a resolution.
vorsätzlich ['fo:rzɛtsliç] *adj* intentional; (*JUR*) premeditated ♦ *adv* intentionally.
Vorschau ['fo:rʃau] *f* (*RUNDF, TV*) (programme (*BRIT*) *od* program (*US*) preview; (*Film*) trailer.
Vorschein ['fo:rʃain] *m*: **zum ~ kommen** (*lit*: *sichtbar werden*) to appear; (*fig*: *entdeckt werden*) to come to light.
vorschieben ['fo:rʃi:bən] *unreg vt* to push forward; (*vor etw*) to push across; (*fig*) to put forward as an excuse; **jdn ~** to use sb as a front.
vorschießen ['fo:rʃi:sən] *unreg* (*umg*) *vt*: **jdm Geld ~** to advance sb money.
Vorschlag ['fo:rʃla:k] *m* suggestion, proposal.
vorschlagen ['fo:rʃla:gən] *unreg vt* to suggest, propose.
Vorschlaghammer *m* sledgehammer.
vorschnell ['fo:rʃnɛl] *adj* hasty, too quick.
vorschreiben ['fo:rʃraibən] *unreg vt* (*Dosis*) to prescribe; (*befehlen*) to specify; (**jdm**) **etw ~** (*lit*) to write sth out (for sb); **ich lasse mir nichts ~** I won't be dictated to.
Vorschrift ['fo:rʃrift] *f* regulation(s *pl*), rule(s *pl*); (*Anweisungen*) instruction(s *pl*); **jdm ~en machen** to give sb orders; **Dienst nach ~** work-to-rule (*BRIT*), slowdown (*US*).
vorschriftsmäßig *adv* as per regulations/instructions.
Vorschub ['fo:rʃu:p] *m*: **jdm/einer Sache ~ leisten** to encourage sb/sth.
Vorschule ['fo:rʃu:lə] *f* nursery school.
vorschulisch ['fo:rʃu:liʃ] *adj* preschool *attr*.
Vorschuß ['fo:rʃʊs] *m* advance.

vorschützen ['foːrʃʏtsən] vt to put forward as a pretext; (Unwissenheit) to plead.

vorschweben ['foːrʃveːbən] vi: **jdm schwebt etw vor** sb has sth in mind.

vorsehen ['foːrzeːən] unreg vt to provide for; (planen) to plan ♦ vr to take care, be careful.

Vorsehung f providence.

vorsetzen ['foːrzɛtsən] vt to move forward; (davorsetzen): ~ **vor** +akk to put in front of; (anbieten): **jdm etw** ~ to offer sb sth.

Vorsicht ['foːrzɪçt] f caution, care; ~**!** look out!, take care!; (auf Schildern) caution!, danger!; ~**, Stufe!** mind the step!; **etw mit** ~ **genießen** (umg) to take sth with a pinch of salt.

vorsichtig adj cautious, careful.

vorsichtshalber adv just in case.

Vorsichtsmaßnahme f precaution.

Vorsilbe ['foːrzɪlbə] f prefix.

vorsintflutlich ['foːrzɪntfluːtlɪç] (umg) adj antiquated.

Vorsitz ['foːrzɪts] m chair(manship); **den** ~ **führen** to chair the meeting.

Vorsitzende(r) f(m) chairman/-woman, chair(person).

Vorsorge ['foːrzɔrgə] f precaution(s pl); (Fürsorge) provision(s pl).

vorsorgen vi: ~ **für** to make provision(s pl) for.

Vorsorgeuntersuchung ['foːrzɔrgə-ǀʊntərzuːxʊŋ] f medical check-up.

vorsorglich ['foːrzɔrklɪç] adv as a precaution.

Vorspann ['voːrʃpan] m (FILM, TV) opening credits pl; (PRESSE) opening paragraph.

vorspannen vt (Pferde) to harness.

Vorspeise ['foːrʃpaɪzə] f hors d'œuvre, starter.

Vorspiegelung ['foːrʃpiːgəlʊŋ] f: **das ist (eine)** ~ **falscher Tatsachen** it's all sham.

Vorspiel ['foːrʃpiːl] nt prelude; (bei Geschlechtsverkehr) foreplay.

vorspielen vt: **jdm etw** ~ (MUS) to play sth to sb; (THEAT) to act sth to sb; (fig) to act out a sham of sth in front of sb.

vorsprechen ['foːrʃprɛçən] unreg vt to say out loud; (vortragen) to recite ♦ vi (THEAT) to audition; **bei jdm** ~ to call on sb.

vorspringend ['foːrʃprɪŋənt] adj projecting; (Nase, Kinn) prominent.

Vorsprung ['foːrʃprʊŋ] m projection; (Fels~) ledge; (fig) advantage, start.

Vorstadt ['foːrʃtat] f suburbs pl.

Vorstand ['foːrʃtant] m executive committee; (COMM) board (of directors); (Person) director; (Leiter) head.

Vorstandssitzung f (von Firma) board meeting.

Vorstandsvorsitzende(r) f(m) chairperson.

vorstehen ['foːrʃteːən] unreg vi to project; **einer Sache** dat ~ (fig) to be the head of sth.

Vorsteher(in) (-s, -) m(f) (von Abteilung) head; (von Gefängnis) governor; (Bahnhofs~)

stationmaster.

vorstellbar adj conceivable.

vorstellen ['foːrʃtɛlən] vt to put forward; (vor etw) to put in front; (bekannt machen) to introduce; (darstellen) to represent ♦ vr to introduce o.s.; (bei Bewerbung) to go for an interview; **sich** dat **etw** ~ to imagine sth; **stell dir das nicht so einfach vor** don't think it's so easy.

Vorstellung f (Bekanntmachen) introduction; (THEAT etc) performance; (Gedanke) idea, thought.

Vorstellungsgespräch nt interview.

Vorstellungsvermögen nt powers of imagination pl.

Vorstoß ['foːrʃtoːs] m advance; (fig: Versuch) attempt.

vorstoßen unreg vt, vi to push forward.

Vorstrafe ['foːrʃtraːfə] f previous conviction.

vorstrecken ['foːrʃtrɛkən] vt to stretch out; (Geld) to advance.

Vorstufe ['foːrʃtuːfə] f first step(s pl).

Vortag ['foːrtak] m: **am** ~ **einer Sache** gen on the day before sth.

vortasten ['foːrtastən] vr: **sich langsam zu etw** ~ to approach sth carefully.

vortäuschen ['foːrtɔʏʃən] vt to pretend, feign.

Vortäuschung f: **unter** ~ **falscher Tatsachen** under false pretences (BRIT) od pretenses (US).

Vorteil ['foːrtaɪl] (-s, -e) m: ~ **(gegenüber)** advantage (over); **im** ~ **sein** to have the advantage; **die Vor- und Nachteile** the pros and cons; **v~haft** adj advantageous; (Kleider) flattering; (Geschäft) lucrative.

Vortr. abk = Vortrag.

Vortrag ['foːrtraːk] (-(e)s, Vorträge) m talk, lecture; (~sart) delivery; (von Gedicht) rendering; (COMM) balance carried forward; **einen** ~ **halten** to give a lecture od talk.

vortragen ['foːrtraːgən] unreg vt to carry forward (auch COMM); (fig) to recite; (Rede) to deliver; (Lied) to perform; (Meinung etc) to express.

Vortragsabend m lecture evening; (mit Musik) recital; (mit Gedichten) poetry reading.

Vortragsreihe f series of lectures.

vortrefflich [foːrˈtrɛflɪç] adj excellent.

vortreten ['foːrtreːtən] unreg vi to step forward; (Augen etc) to protrude.

Vortritt ['foːrtrɪt] m: **jdm den** ~ **lassen** (lit, fig) to let sb go first.

vorüber [foˈryːbər] adv past, over; ~**gehen** unreg vi to pass (by); ~**gehen an** +dat (fig) to pass over; ~**gehend** adj temporary, passing.

Voruntersuchung ['foːrǀʊntərzuːxʊŋ] f (MED) preliminary examination; (JUR) preliminary investigation.

Vorurteil ['foːrǀʊrtaɪl] nt prejudice.

vorurteilsfrei adj unprejudiced, open-minded.

Vorverkauf ['foːrfɛrkaʊf] *m* advance booking.
Vorverkaufsstelle *f* advance booking office.
vorverlegen ['foːrfɛrleːgən] *vt* (*Termin*) to bring forward.
Vorw. *abk* = **Vorwort**.
vorwagen ['foːrvaːgən] *vr* to venture forward.
Vorwahl ['foːrvaːl] *f* preliminary election; (*TEL*) dialling (*BRIT*) *od* dial (*US*) code.
Vorwand ['foːrvant] (-(**e**)**s**, **Vorwände**) *m* pretext.
Vorwarnung ['foːrvarnʊŋ] *f* (advance) warning.
vorwärts ['foːrvɛrts] *adv* forward; ~**!** (*umg*) let's go!; (*MIL*) forward march!; **V**~**gang** *m* (*AUT etc*) forward gear; ~**gehen** *unreg vi* to progress; ~**kommen** *unreg vi* to get on, make progress.
Vorwäsche *f* prewash.
Vorwaschgang *m* prewash.
vorweg [foːr'vɛk] *adv* in advance; **V**~**nahme** (-, -**n**) *f* anticipation; ~**nehmen** *unreg vt* to anticipate.
vorweisen ['foːrvaɪzən] *unreg vt* to show, produce.
vorwerfen ['foːrvɛrfən] *unreg vt*: **jdm etw** ~ to reproach sb for sth, accuse sb of sth; **sich** *dat* **nichts vorzuwerfen haben** to have nothing to reproach o.s. with; **das wirft er mir heute noch vor** he still holds it against me; **Tieren/Gefangenen etw** ~ (*lit*) to throw sth down for the animals/prisoners.
vorwiegend ['foːrviːgənt] *adj* predominant ♦ *adv* predominantly.
vorwitzig *adj* saucy, cheeky.
Vorwort ['foːrvɔrt] (-(**e**)**s**, -**e**) *nt* preface.
Vorwurf ['foːrvʊrf] (-(**e**)**s**, -̈**e**) *m* reproach; **jdm/sich Vorwürfe machen** to reproach sb/o.s.
vorwurfsvoll *adj* reproachful.
Vorzeichen ['foːrtsaɪçən] *nt* (*Omen*) omen; (*MED*) early symptom; (*MATH*) sign.
vorzeigen ['foːrtsaɪgən] *vt* to show, produce.
Vorzeit ['foːrtsaɪt] *f* prehistoric times *pl*.
vorzeitig *adj* premature.
vorziehen ['foːrtsiːən] *unreg vt* to pull forward; (*Gardinen*) to draw; (*zuerst behandeln, abfertigen*) to give priority to; (*lieber haben*) to prefer.
Vorzimmer ['foːrtsɪmər] *nt* anteroom; (*Büro*) outer office.
Vorzug ['foːrtsuːk] *m* preference; (*gute Eigenschaft*) merit, good quality; (*Vorteil*) advantage; (*EISENB*) relief train; **einer Sache** *dat* **den** ~ **geben** (*form*) to prefer sth; (*Vorrang geben*) to give sth precedence.
vorzüglich [foːr'tsyːklɪç] *adj* excellent, first-rate.
Vorzugsaktien *pl* preference shares (*BRIT*), preferred stock (*US*).
vorzugsweise *adv* preferably; (*hauptsächlich*) chiefly.

Votum ['voːtʊm] (-**s**, **Voten**) *nt* vote.
Voyeur [voa'jøːr] (-**s**, -**e**) *m* voyeur.
Voyeurismus [voajø'rɪsmʊs] *m* voyeurism.
v.T. *abk* (= *vom Tausend*) per thousand.
vulgär [vʊl'gɛːr] *adj* vulgar.
Vulkan [vʊl'kaːn] (-**s**, -**e**) *m* volcano; ~**ausbruch** *m* volcanic eruption.
vulkanisieren [vʊlkani'ziːrən] *vt* to vulcanize.
v.u.Z. *abk* (= *vor unserer Zeitrechnung*) B.C.

$$W, w$$

W, w [veː] *nt* W, w; ~ **wie Wilhelm** ≈ W for William.
W. *abk* (= *West(en)*) W.
w. *abk* = **wenden; werktags; westlich;** (= *weiblich*) f.
Waage ['vaːgə] (-, -**n**) *f* scales *pl*; (*ASTROL*) Libra; **sich** *dat* **die** ~ **halten** (*fig*) to balance one another; **w**~**recht** *adj* horizontal.
Waagschale *f* (scale) pan; (**schwer**) **in die** ~ **fallen** (*fig*) to carry weight.
wabb(e)lig ['vab(ə)lɪç] *adj* wobbly.
Wabe ['vaːbə] (-, -**n**) *f* honeycomb.
wach [vax] *adj* awake; (*fig*) alert; ~ **werden** to wake up.
Wachablösung *f* changing of the guard; (*Mensch*) relief guard; (*fig: Regierungswechsel*) change of government.
Wache (-, -**n**) *f* guard, watch; ~ **halten** to keep watch; ~ **stehen** *od* **schieben** (*umg*) to be on guard (duty).
wachen *vi* to be awake; (*Wache halten*) to keep watch; **bei jdm** ~ to sit up with sb.
wachhabend *adj attrib* duty.
Wachhund *m* watchdog, guard dog; (*fig*) watchdog.
Wacholder [va'xɔldər] (-**s**, -) *m* juniper.
wachrütteln ['vaxrʏtəln] *vt* (*fig*) to (a)rouse.
Wachs [vaks] (-**es**, -**e**) *nt* wax.
wachsam ['vaxzaːm] *adj* watchful, vigilant, alert; **W**~**keit** *f* vigilance.
wachsen¹ *unreg vi* to grow.
wachsen² *vt* (*Skier*) to wax.
Wachsfigurenkabinett *nt* waxworks (exhibition).
Wachs(mal)stift *m* wax crayon.
wächst [vɛkst] *vb siehe* **wachsen¹**.
Wachstuch ['vakstuːx] *nt* oilcloth.
Wachstum ['vakstuːm] (-**s**) *nt* growth.
Wachstums- *zW:* ~**branche** *f* growth industry; ~**grenze** *f* limits of growth; **w**~**hemmend** *adj* growth-inhibiting; ~**rate** *f* growth rate; ~**schmerzen** *pl* growing pains; ~**störung** *f* disturbance of growth.

Wachtel ['vaxtəl] (-, -n) f quail.
Wächter ['vɛçtər] (-s, -) m guard; (*Park~*) warden, keeper; (*Museums~, Parkplatz~*) attendant.
Wachtmeister m officer.
Wachtposten m guard, sentry.
Wach(t)turm m watchtower.
Wach- und Schließgesellschaft f security corps.
wack(e)lig adj shaky, wobbly; **auf ~en Beinen stehen** to be wobbly on one's legs; (*fig*) to be unsteady.
Wackelkontakt m loose connection.
wackeln vi to shake; (*fig: Position*) to be shaky; **mit den Hüften/Schwanz ~** to wiggle one's hips/wag its tail.
wacker ['vakər] adj valiant, stout; **sich ~ schlagen** (*umg*) to put up a brave fight.
Wade ['va:də] (-, -n) f (*ANAT*) calf.
Waffe ['vafə] (-, -n) f weapon; **jdn mit seinen eigenen ~n schlagen** (*fig*) to beat sb at his own game.
Waffel ['vafəl] (-, -n) f waffle; (*Eis~*) wafer.
Waffen- zW: **~gewalt** f: **mit ~gewalt** by force of arms; **~lager** nt (*von Armee*) ordnance depot; (*von Terroristen*) cache; **~schein** m firearms od gun licence (*BRIT*), firearms license (*US*); **~schmuggel** m gunrunning, arms smuggling; **~stillstand** m armistice, truce.
Wagemut ['va:gəmu:t] m daring.
Wagen ['va:gən] (-s, -) m vehicle; (*Auto*) car, automobile (*US*); (*EISENB*) car, carriage (*BRIT*); (*Pferde~*) wag(g)on, cart.
wagen vt to venture, dare.
Wagen- zW: **~führer** m driver; **~heber** (-s, -) m jack; **~park** m fleet of cars; **~rückholtaste** f (*Schreibmaschine*) carriage return (key); **~rücklauf** m carriage return.
Waggon [va'gõ:] (-s, -s) m wag(g)on; (*Güter~*) goods van (*BRIT*), freight truck (*US*).
waghalsig ['va:khalzıç] adj foolhardy.
Wagnis ['va:knıs] (-ses, -se) nt risk.
Wahl [va:l] (-, -en) f choice; (*POL*) election; **erste ~** (*Qualität*) top quality; (*Gemüse, Eier*) grade one; **zweite ~** (*COMM*) seconds pl; **aus freier ~** of one's own free choice; **wer die ~ hat, hat die Qual** (*Sprichwort*) he is od you are etc spoilt for choice; **die ~ fiel auf ihn** he was chosen; **sich zur ~ stellen** (*POL etc*) to stand (*BRIT*) od run (for parliament etc).
wählbar adj eligible.
Wahl- zW: **w~berechtigt** adj entitled to vote; **~beteiligung** f poll, turnout; **~bezirk** m (*POL*) ward.
wählen ['vɛ:lən] vt to choose; (*POL*) to elect, vote for; (*TEL*) to dial ♦ vi to choose; (*POL*) to vote; (*TEL*) to dial.
Wähler(in) (-s, -) m(f) voter; **~abwanderung** f voter drift; **w~isch** adj fastidious, particular; **~schaft** f electorate.
Wahl- zW: **~fach** nt optional subject; **w~frei**

adj: **w~freier Zugriff** (*COMPUT*) random access; **~gang** m ballot; **~geschenk** nt preelection vote-catching gimmick; **~heimat** f country of adoption; **~helfer** m (*im ~kampf*) election assistant; (*bei der ~*) polling officer; **~kabine** f polling booth; **~kampf** m election campaign; **~kreis** m constituency; **~leiter** m returning officer; **~liste** f electoral register; **~lokal** nt polling station; **w~los** adv at random; (*nicht wählerisch*) indiscriminately; **~recht** nt franchise; **allgemeines ~recht** universal franchise; **das aktive ~recht** the right to vote; **das passive ~recht** eligibility (for political office); **~spruch** m motto; **~urne** f ballot box; **w~weise** adv alternatively.
Wählzeichen nt (*TEL*) dialling tone (*BRIT*), dial tone (*US*).
Wahn [va:n] (-(e)s) m delusion; **~sinn** m madness; **w~sinnig** adj insane, mad ♦ adv (*umg*) incredibly; **w~witzig** adj crazy attrib ♦ adv terribly.
wahr [va:r] adj true; **da ist (et)was W~es dran** there's some truth in that.
wahren vt to maintain, keep.
währen ['vɛ:rən] vi to last.
während präp +gen during ♦ konj while; **~dessen** adv meanwhile.
wahr- zW: **~haben** unreg vt: **etw nicht ~haben wollen** to refuse to admit sth; **~haft** adv (*tatsächlich*) truly; **~haftig** adj true, real ♦ adv really.
Wahrheit f truth; **die ~ sagen** to tell the truth.
wahrheitsgetreu adj (*Bericht*) truthful; (*Darstellung*) faithful.
wahrnehmen unreg vt to perceive; (*Frist*) to observe; (*Veränderungen etc*) to be aware of; (*Gelegenheit*) to take; (*Interessen, Rechte*) to look after.
Wahrnehmung f perception; observing; awareness; taking; looking after.
wahrsagen vi to predict the future, tell fortunes.
Wahrsager m fortune-teller.
wahrscheinlich [va:r'ʃaɪnlıç] adj probable ♦ adv probably; **W~keit** f probability; **aller W~keit nach** in all probability.
Währung ['vɛ:rʊŋ] f currency.
Währungs- zW: **~einheit** f monetary unit; **~politik** f monetary policy; **~reserven** pl official reserves pl; **~union** f monetary union.
Wahrzeichen nt (*Gebäude, Turm etc*) symbol; (*von Stadt, Verein*) emblem.
Waise ['vaɪzə] (-, -n) f orphan.
Waisen- zW: **~haus** nt orphanage; **~kind** nt orphan; **~knabe** m: **gegen dich ist er ein ~knabe** (*umg*) he's no match for you; **~rente** f orphan's allowance.
Wal [va:l] (-(e)s, -e) m whale.
Wald [valt] (-(e)s, ̈-er) m wood(s pl); (*groß*)

forest; **~brand** m forest fire.
Wäldchen ['vɛltçən] nt copse, grove.
Waldhorn nt (MUS) French horn.
waldig ['valdɪç] adj wooded.
Wald- zW: **~lehrpfad** m nature trail; **~meister** m (BOT) woodruff; **~sterben** nt loss of trees due to pollution.
Wald- und Wiesen- (umg) in zW common-or-garden.
Waldweg m woodland od forest path.
Wales [weɪlz] nt Wales.
Walfang ['va:lfaŋ] m whaling.
Walfisch ['valfɪʃ] m whale.
Waliser(in) [va'li:zər(ɪn)] (-s, -) m(f) Welshman, Welshwoman.
walisisch adj Welsh.
Walkman ® ['wɔ:kman] (-s, Walkmen) m Walkman ®, personal stereo.
Wall [val] (-(e)s, ⁻e) m embankment; (Bollwerk) rampart.
wallfahren vi untr to go on a pilgrimage.
Wallfahrer(in) m(f) pilgrim.
Wallfahrt f pilgrimage.
Wallis ['valɪs] (-) nt: **das** ~ Valais.
Wallone [va'lo:nə] (-n, -n) m, **Wallonin** f Walloon.
Walnuß ['valnʊs] f walnut.
Walroß ['valrɔs] nt walrus.
walten ['valtən] vi (geh): **Vernunft** ~ **lassen** to let reason prevail.
Walzblech (-(e)s) nt sheet metal.
Walze ['valtsə] (-, -n) f (Gerät) cylinder; (Fahrzeug) roller.
walzen vt to roll (out).
wälzen ['vɛltsən] vt to roll (over); (Bücher) to hunt through; (Probleme) to deliberate on ♦ vr to wallow; (vor Schmerzen) to roll about; (im Bett) to toss and turn.
Walzer ['valtsər] (-s, -) m waltz.
Wälzer ['vɛltsər] (-s, -) (umg) m tome.
Wampe ['vampə] (-, -n) (umg) f paunch.
Wand (-, ⁻e) f wall; (Trenn~) partition; (Berg~) precipice; (Fels~) (rock) face; (fig) barrier; **weiß wie die** ~ as white as a sheet; **jdn an die** ~ **spielen** to put sb in the shade; (SPORT) to outplay sb.
wand etc [vant] vb siehe **winden**.
Wandel ['vandəl] (-s) m change; **w~bar** adj changeable, variable.
Wandelhalle f foyer.
wandeln vt, vr to change ♦ vi (gehen) to walk.
Wanderausstellung f touring exhibition.
Wanderbühne f touring theatre (BRIT) od theater (US).
Wanderer (-s, ⁻) m hiker, rambler.
Wanderin f hiker, rambler.
Wanderkarte f hiker's map.
Wanderlied nt hiking song.
wandern vi to hike; (Blick) to wander; (Gedanken) to stray; (umg: in den Papierkorb etc) to land.
Wanderpreis m challenge trophy.

Wanderschaft f travelling (BRIT), traveling (US).
Wanderung f walk, hike; (von Tieren, Völkern) migration.
Wanderweg m trail, (foot)path.
Wandgemälde nt mural.
Wandlung f change; (völlige Um~) transformation; (REL) transubstantiation.
Wand- zW: **~malerei** f mural painting; **~schirm** m (folding) screen; **~schrank** m cupboard.
wandte etc ['vantə] vb siehe **wenden**.
Wandteppich m tapestry.
Wandverkleidung f panelling.
Wange ['vaŋə] (-, -n) f cheek.
wankelmütig ['vaŋkəlmy:tɪç] adj fickle, inconstant.
wanken ['vankən] vi to stagger; (fig) to waver.
wann [van] adv when; **seit** ~ **bist/hast du ...?** how long have you been/have you had ...?
Wanne ['vanə] (-, -n) f tub.
Wanze ['vantsə] (-, -n) f (ZOOL, Abhörgerät) bug.
Wappen ['vapən] (-s, -) nt coat of arms, crest; **~kunde** f heraldry.
wappnen vr (fig) to prepare o.s.; **gewappnet sein** to be forearmed.
war etc [va:r] vb siehe **sein**.
warb etc [varp] vb siehe **werben**.
Ware ['va:rə] (-, -n) f ware; **Waren** pl goods pl.
wäre etc ['vɛ:rə] vb siehe **sein**.
Waren- zW: **~bestand** m stock; **~haus** nt department store; **~lager** nt stock, store; **~muster** nt sample; **~probe** f sample; **~rückstände** pl backlog sing; **~sendung** f trade sample (sent by post); **~zeichen** nt trademark.
warf etc [varf] vb siehe **werfen**.
warm [varm] adj warm; (Essen) hot; (umg: homosexuell) queer; **mir ist** ~ I'm warm; **mit jdm** ~ **werden** (umg) to get close to sb.
Wärme ['vɛrmə] (-, -n) f warmth; **10 Grad** ~ 10 degrees above zero.
wärmen vt, vr to warm (up), heat (up).
Wärmflasche f hot-water bottle.
warm- zW: **W~front** f (MET) warm front; **~halten** unreg vr: **sich dat jdn ~ halten** (fig) to keep in with sb; **~herzig** adj warm-hearted; **~laufen** unreg vi (AUT) to warm up; **W~wassertank** m hot-water tank.
Warnblinkanlage f (AUT) hazard warning lights pl.
Warndreieck nt warning triangle.
warnen ['varnən] vt to warn.
Warnstreik m token strike.
Warnung f warning.
Warschau ['varʃaʊ] (-s) nt Warsaw; **~er Pakt** m Warsaw Pact.
Warte (-, -n) f observation point; (fig) viewpoint.
warten ['vartən] vi to wait ♦ vt (Auto, Maschine) to service; ~ **auf** +akk to wait for;

auf sich ~ lassen to take a long time; **warte mal**! wait a minute!; (*überlegend*) let me see; **mit dem Essen auf jdn ~** to wait for sb before eating.

Wärter(in) ['vɛrtər(ɪn)] (**-s, -**) *m(f)* attendant.

Wartesaal *m* (*EISENB*) waiting room.

Wartezimmer *nt* (*bes beim Arzt*) waiting room.

Wartung *f* (*von Auto, Maschine*) servicing; **~ und Instandhaltung** maintenance.

warum [va'rʊm] *adv* why; **~ nicht gleich so!** that's better.

Warze ['vartsə] (**-, -n**) *f* wart.

was [vas] *pron* what; (*umg: etwas*) something; **das, ~ ...** that which ...; **~ für ...?** what sort *od* kind of ...?

Wasch- *zW:* **~anlage** *f* (*für Autos*) car wash; **w~bar** *adj* washable; **~becken** *nt* washbasin.

Wäsche ['vɛʃə] (**-, -n**) *f* wash(ing); (*Bett~*) linen; (*Unter~*) underwear; **dumm aus der ~ gucken** (*umg*) to look stupid.

waschecht *adj* (*Farbe*) fast; (*fig*) genuine.

Wäsche- *zW:* **~klammer** *f* clothes peg (*BRIT*), clothespin (*US*); **~korb** *m* dirty clothes basket; **~leine** *f* washing line (*BRIT*), clothes line (*US*).

waschen ['vaʃən] *unreg vt, vi* to wash ♦ *vr* to (have a) wash; **sich** *dat* **die Hände ~** to wash one's hands; **~ und legen** (*Haare*) to shampoo and set.

Wäscherei [vɛʃə'raɪ] *f* laundry.

Wascheschleuder *f* spin-dryer.

Wasch- *zW:* **~gang** *m* stage of the washing programme (*BRIT*) *od* program (*US*); **~küche** *f* laundry room; **~lappen** *m* face cloth *od* flannel (*BRIT*), washcloth (*US*); (*umg*) softy; **~maschine** *f* washing machine; **w~maschinenfest** *adj* machine-washable; **~mittel** *nt* detergent; **~pulver** *nt* washing powder; **~salon** *m* Launderette ® (*BRIT*), Laundromat ® (*US*).

wäscht [vɛʃt] *vb siehe* **waschen**.

Waschtisch *m* washstand.

Washington ['wɔʃɪŋtən] (**-s**) *nt* Washington.

Wasser[1] ['vasər] (**-s, -**) *nt* water; **dort wird auch nur mit ~ gekocht** (*fig*) they're no different from anybody else (there); **ins ~ fallen** (*fig*) to fall through; **mit allen ~n gewaschen sein** (*umg*) to be a shrewd customer; **~ lassen** (*euph*) to pass water; **jdm das ~ abgraben** (*fig*) to take the bread from sb's mouth, take away sb's livelihood.

Wasser[2] (**-s, ÷**) *nt* (*Flüssigkeit*) water; (*MED*) lotion; (*Parfüm*) cologne; (*Mineral~*) mineral water.

wasserabstoßend *adj* water-repellent.

Wässerchen *nt:* **er sieht aus, als ob er kein ~ trüben könnte** he looks as if butter wouldn't melt in his mouth.

Wasser- *zW:* **w~dicht** *adj* watertight; (*Stoff, Uhr*) waterproof; **~fall** *m* waterfall; **~farbe** *f* watercolour (*BRIT*), watercolor (*US*);

w~gekühlt *adj* (*AUT*) water-cooled; **~graben** *m* (*SPORT*) water jump; (*um Burg*) moat; **~hahn** *m* tap, faucet (*US*).

wässerig ['vɛsərɪç] *adj* watery.

Wasser- *zW:* **~kessel** *m* kettle; (*TECH*) boiler; **~kraftwerk** *nt* hydroelectric power station; **~leitung** *f* water pipe; (*Anlagen*) plumbing; **~mann** *m* (*ASTROL*) Aquarius.

wassern *vi* to land on the water.

wässern ['vɛsərn] *vt, vi* to water.

Wasser- *zW:* **~scheide** *f* watershed; **w~scheu** *adj* afraid of water; **~schutzpolizei** *f* (*auf Flüssen*) river police; (*im Hafen*) harbour (*BRIT*) *od* harbor (*US*) police; (*auf der See*) coastguard service; **~ski** *nt* water-skiing; **~spiegel** *m* (*Oberfläche*) surface of the water; (*~stand*) water level; **~stand** *m* water level; **~stoff** *m* hydrogen; **~stoffbombe** *f* hydrogen bomb; **~verbrauch** *m* water consumption; **~waage** *f* spirit level; **~welle** *f* shampoo and set; **~werfer** (**-s, -**) *m* water cannon; **~werk** *nt* waterworks; **~zeichen** *nt* watermark.

waten ['va:tən] *vi* to wade.

watscheln ['va:tʃəln] *vi* to waddle.

Watt[1] [vat] (**-(e)s, -en**) *nt* mud flats *pl*.

Watt[2] (**-s, -**) *nt* (*ELEK*) watt.

Watte (**-, -n**) *f* cotton wool (*BRIT*), absorbent cotton (*US*).

Wattenmeer (**-(e)s**) *nt* mud flats *pl*.

Wattestäbchen *nt* cotton(-wool) swab.

wattieren [va'ti:rən] *vt* to pad.

WC [ve:'tse:] (**-s, -s**) *nt abk* (= *Wasserklosett*) WC.

WDR (**-**) *m abk* (= *Westdeutscher Rundfunk*) *West German Radio*.

weben ['ve:bən] *unreg vt* to weave.

Weber(in) (**-s, -**) *m(f)* weaver.

Weberei [ve:bə'raɪ] *f* (*Betrieb*) weaving mill.

Webstuhl ['ve:pʃtu:l] *m* loom.

Wechsel ['vɛksəl] (**-s, -**) *m* change; (*Geld~*) exchange; (*COMM*) bill of exchange; **~bäder** *pl* alternating hot and cold baths *pl*; **~beziehung** *f* correlation; **~forderungen** *pl* (*COMM*) bills receivable *pl*; **~geld** *nt* change; **w~haft** *adj* (*Wetter*) variable; **~inhaber** *m* bearer; **~jahre** *pl* change of life, menopause; **in die ~jahre kommen** to start the change; **~kurs** *m* rate of exchange; **~kursmechanismus** *m* Exchange Rate Mechanism, ERM.

wechseln *vt* to change; (*Blicke*) to exchange ♦ *vi* to change; (*einander ablösen*) to alternate.

wechselnd *adj* changing; (*Stimmungen*) changeable; (*Winde, Bewölkung*) variable.

Wechsel- *zW:* **w~seitig** *adj* reciprocal; **~sprechanlage** *f* two-way intercom; **~strom** *m* alternating current; **~stube** *f* currency exchange, bureau de change; **~verbindlichkeiten** *pl* bills payable *pl*; **w~weise** *adv* alternately; **~wirkung** *f* interaction.

wecken ['vɛkən] *vt* to wake (up); (*fig*) to arouse; (*Bedarf*) to create; (*Erinnerungen*) to revive.

Wecker (-s, -) *m* alarm clock; **jdm auf den ~ fallen** (*umg*) to get on sb's nerves.

Weckglas ® *nt* preserving jar.

Weckruf *m* (*TEL*) alarm call.

wedeln ['veːdəln] *vi* (*mit Schwanz*) to wag; (*mit Fächer*) to fan; (*SKI*) to wedel.

weder ['veːdər] *konj* neither; **~ ... noch ...** neither ... nor ...

Weg [veːk] (-(e)s, -e) *m* way; (*Pfad*) path; (*Route*) route; **sich auf den ~ machen** to be on one's way; **jdm aus dem ~ gehen** to keep out of sb's way; **jdm nicht über den ~ trauen** (*fig*) not to trust sb an inch; **den ~ des geringsten Widerstandes gehen** to follow the line of least resistance; **etw in die ~e leiten** to arrange sth; **jdm Steine in den ~ legen** (*fig*) to put obstacles in sb's way.

weg [vɛk] *adv* away, off; **über etw** *akk* **~ sein** to be over sth; **er war schon ~** he had already left; **nichts wie** *od* **nur ~ von hier!** let's get out of here!; **~ damit!** (*mit Schere etc*) put it/them away!; **Finger ~!** hands off!

Wegbereiter (-s, -) *m* pioneer.

wegblasen *unreg vt* to blow away; **wie weggeblasen sein** (*fig*) to have vanished.

wegbleiben *unreg vi* to stay away; **mir bleibt die Spucke weg!** (*umg*) I am absolutely flabbergasted!

wegen ['veːgən] *präp +gen od* (*umg*) *+dat* because of; **von ~!** you must be joking!

weg- *zW:* **~fahren** *unreg vi* to drive away; (*abfahren*) to leave; **~fallen** *unreg vi* to be left out; (*Ferien, Bezahlung*) to be cancelled; (*aufhören*) to cease; **~gehen** *unreg vi* to go away, leave; (*umg: Ware*) to sell; **~hören** *vi* to turn a deaf ear; **~jagen** *vt* to chase away; **~kommen** *unreg vi:* (**bei etw**) **gut/schlecht ~kommen** (*umg*) to come off well/badly (with sth); **~lassen** *unreg vt* to leave out; **~laufen** *unreg vi* to run away *od* off; **das läuft (dir) nicht ~!** (*fig hum*) that can wait; **~legen** *vt* to put aside; **~machen** (*umg*) *vt* to get rid of; **~müssen** *unreg* (*umg*) *vi* to have to go; **~nehmen** *unreg vt* to take away.

Wegrand ['veːkrant] *m* wayside.

weg- *zW:* **~räumen** *vt* to clear away; **~schaffen** *vt* to clear away; **~schließen** *unreg vt* to lock away; **~schnappen** *vt:* (**jdm**) **etw ~schnappen** to snatch sth away (from sb); **~stecken** *vt* to put away; (*umg: verkraften*) to cope with; **~treten** *unreg vi* (*MIL*): **~treten!** dismiss!; **geistig ~getreten sein** (*umg: geistesabwesend*) to be away with the fairies; **~tun** *unreg vt* to put away.

wegweisend ['veːgvaɪzənt] *adj* pioneering *attrib*, revolutionary.

Wegweiser ['veːgvaɪzər] (-s, -) *m* road sign,

signpost; (*fig: Buch etc*) guide.

Wegwerf- ['vɛkvɛrf] *in zW* disposable.

weg- *zW:* **~werfen** *unreg vt* to throw away; **~werfend** *adj* disparaging; **W~werfgesellschaft** *f* throw-away society; **~wollen** *unreg vi* (*verreisen*) to want to go away; **~ziehen** *unreg vi* to move away.

weh [veː] *adj* sore; **~ tun** to hurt, be sore; **jdm/sich ~ tun** to hurt sb/o.s.

Wehe ['veːə] (-, -n) *f* drift.

wehe *interj:* **~, wenn du ...** you'll regret it if you ...; **~ dir!** you dare!

Wehen *pl* (*MED*) contractions *pl*; **in den ~ liegen** to be in labour (*BRIT*) *od* labor (*US*).

wehen *vt, vi* to blow; (*Fahnen*) to flutter.

weh- *zW:* **~klagen** *vi untr* to wail; **~leidig** *adj* oversensitive to pain; (*jammernd*) whiny, whining; **W~mut** *f* melancholy; **~mütig** *adj* melancholy.

Wehr¹ [veːr] (-(e)s, -e) *nt* weir.

Wehr² [veːr] (-, -en) *f* (*Feuer~*) fire brigade (*BRIT*) *od* department (*US*) ♦ *in zW* defence (*BRIT*), defense (*US*); **sich zur ~ setzen** to defend o.s.

Wehrdienst *m* military service.

Wehrdienst *is military service which is still compulsory in Germany. All young men receive their call-up papers at 18 and all who are pronounced physically fit are required to spend one year in the* **Bundeswehr**. *Conscientious objectors are allowed to do* **Zivildienst** *as an alternative, on attending a hearing and presenting their case.*

Wehrdienstverweigerer *m* ≈ conscientious objector.

wehren *vr* to defend o.s.

Wehr- *zW:* **w~los** *adj* defenceless (*BRIT*), defenseless (*US*); **jdm w~los ausgeliefert sein** to be at sb's mercy; **~macht** *f* armed forces *pl*; **~pflicht** *f* conscription; **w~pflichtig** *adj* liable for military service; **~übung** *f* reserve duty training exercise.

Wehwehchen (*umg*) *nt* (minor) complaint.

Weib [vaɪp] (-(e)s, -er) *nt* woman, female (*pej*).

Weibchen *nt* (*Ehefrau*) little woman; (*ZOOL*) female.

weibisch ['vaɪbɪʃ] *adj* effeminate.

weiblich *adj* feminine.

weich [vaɪç] *adj* soft; (*Ei*) soft-boiled; **~e Währung** soft currency.

Weiche (-, -n) *f* (*EISENB*) points *pl*; **die ~n stellen** (*lit*) to switch the points; (*fig*) to set the course.

weichen *unreg vi* to yield, give way; **(nicht) von jdm** *od* **von jds Seite ~** (not) to leave sb's side.

Weichensteller (-s, -) *m* pointsman.

weich- *zW:* **W~heit** *f* softness; **W~käse** *m* soft cheese; **~lich** *adj* soft, namby-pamby; **W~ling** *m* wimp; **W~spüler** (-s, -) *m* fabric

conditioner; **W~teile** *pl* soft parts *pl*; **W~tier** *nt* mollusc (*BRIT*), mollusk (*US*).
Weide ['vaɪdə] (-, -n) *f* (*Baum*) willow; (*Gras*) pasture.
weiden *vi* to graze ♦ *vr*: **sich an etw** *dat* ~ **to** delight in sth.
Weidenkätzchen *nt* willow catkin.
weidlich ['vaɪtlɪç] *adv* thoroughly.
weigern ['vaɪgərn] *vr* to refuse.
Weigerung ['vaɪgəruŋ] *f* refusal.
Weihe ['vaɪə] (-, -n) *f* consecration; (*Priester~*) ordination.
weihen *vt* to consecrate; (*widmen*) to dedicate; **dem Untergang geweiht** (*liter*) doomed.
Weiher (-s, -) *m* pond.
Weihnachten (-) *nt* Christmas; **fröhliche ~!** happy *od* merry Christmas!; **w~** *vi unpers*: **es weihnachtet sehr** (*poetisch, ironisch*) Christmas is very much in evidence.
weihnachtlich *adj* Christmas(sy).
Weihnachts- *zW*: **~abend** *m* Christmas Eve; **~baum** *m* Christmas tree; **~geld** *nt* Christmas bonus; **~geschenk** *nt* Christmas present; **~lied** *nt* Christmas carol; **~mann** *m* Father Christmas (*BRIT*), Santa Claus.
Weihnachtsmarkt *m* Christmas fair.

> The **Weihnachtsmarkt** *is a market held in most large towns in Germany in the weeks prior to Christmas. People visit it to buy presents, toys and Christmas decorations, and to enjoy the festive atmosphere. Food and drink associated with the Christmas festivities can also be eaten and drunk there, for example, gingerbread and mulled wine.*

Weihnachtstag *m*: **(erster)** ~ Christmas day; **zweiter** ~ Boxing Day (*BRIT*).
Weihrauch *m* incense.
Weihwasser *nt* holy water.
weil [vaɪl] *konj* because.
Weile ['vaɪlə] (-) *f* while, short time.
Weiler ['vaɪlər] (-s, -) *m* hamlet.
Weimarer Republik ['vaɪmarər repu'bliːk] *f* Weimar Republic.
Wein [vaɪn] (-(e)s, -e) *m* wine; (*Pflanze*) vine; **jdm reinen** ~ **einschenken** (*fig*) to tell sb the truth; **~bau** *m* cultivation of vines; **~bauer** *m* wine-grower; **~beere** *f* grape; **~berg** *m* vineyard; **~bergschnecke** *f* snail; **~brand** *m* brandy.
weinen *vt, vi* to cry; **das ist zum W~** it's enough to make you cry *od* weep.
weinerlich *adj* tearful.
Wein- *zW*: **~gegend** *f* wine-growing area; **~geist** *m* (ethyl) alcohol; **~glas** *nt* wine glass; **~gut** *nt* wine-growing estate; **~karte** *f* wine list.
Weinkrampf *m* crying fit.
Wein- *zW*: **~lese** *f* vintage; **~probe** *f* wine tasting; **~rebe** *f* vine; **w~rot** *adj* (*Farbe*)

claret; **w~selig** *adj* merry with wine; **~stein** *m* tartar; **~stock** *m* vine; **~stube** *f* wine bar; **~traube** *f* grape.
weise ['vaɪzə] *adj* wise.
Weise (-, -n) *f* manner, way; (*Lied*) tune; **auf diese** ~ in this way.
Weise(r) *f(m)* wise man, wise woman, sage.
weisen *unreg vt* to show; **etw (weit) von sich** ~ (*fig*) to reject sth (emphatically).
Weisheit ['vaɪshaɪt] *f* wisdom.
Weisheitszahn *m* wisdom tooth.
weismachen ['vaɪsmaxən] *vt*: **er wollte uns** ~, **daß** ... he would have us believe that ...
weiß¹ [vaɪs] *vb siehe* **wissen**.
weiß² *adj* white; **W~blech** *nt* tin plate; **W~brot** *nt* white bread; **~en** *vt* to whitewash; **W~glut** *f* (*TECH*) incandescence; **jdn zur W~glut bringen** (*fig*) to make sb see red; **W~kohl** *m* (white) cabbage.
Weißrußland *nt* B(y)elorussia.
weißt [vaɪst] *vb siehe* **wissen**.
Weiß- *zW*: **~waren** *pl* linen *sing*; **~wein** *m* white wine; **~wurst** *f* veal sausage.
Weisung ['vaɪzuŋ] *f* instruction.
weit [vaɪt] *adj* wide; (*Begriff*) broad; (*Reise, Wurf*) long ♦ *adv* far; **in** ~**er Ferne** in the far distance; **wie** ~ **ist es** ...? how far is it ...?; **das geht zu** ~ that's going too far; ~ **und breit** for miles around; ~ **gefehlt!** far from it; **es so** ~ **bringen, daß** ... to bring it about that ...; ~ **zurückliegen** to be far behind; **von** ~**em** from a long way off; **~ab** *adv*: **~ab von** far (away) from; **~aus** *adv* by far; **W~blick** *m* (*fig*) far-sightedness; **~blickend** *adj* far-seeing.
Weite (-, -n) *f* width; (*Raum*) space; (*von Entfernung*) distance.
weiten *vt, vr* to widen.
weiter ['vaɪtər] *adj* wider; (*zusätzlich*) further ♦ *adv* further; **wenn es** ~ **nichts ist** ... well, if that's all (it is), ...; **das hat** ~ **nichts zu sagen** that doesn't really matter; **immer** ~ on and on; (*Anweisung*) keep on (going); ~ **nichts/ niemand** nothing/nobody else; **~arbeiten** *vi* to go on working; **~bilden** *vr* to continue one's studies; **W~bildung** *f* further education.
Weitere(s) *nt* further details *pl*; **bis auf w~s** for the time being; **ohne w~s** without further ado, just like that.
weiter- *zW*: **~empfehlen** *unreg vt* to recommend (to others); **~erzählen** *vt* (*Geheimnis*) to pass on; **W~fahrt** *f* continuation of the journey; **~führend** *adj* (*Schule*) secondary (*BRIT*), high (*US*); **~gehen** *unreg vi* to go on; **~hin** *adv*: **etw** ~**hin tun** to go on doing sth; **~kommen** *unreg vi*: **nicht ~kommen** (*fig*) to be bogged down; **~leiten** *vt* to pass on; **~machen** *vt, vi* to continue; **~reisen** *vi* to continue one's journey; **~sagen** *vt*: **nicht** ~**sagen!** don't tell

anyone!; ~**sehen** *unreg vi:* **dann sehen wir** ~ then we'll see; ~**verarbeiten** *vt* to process; ~**wissen** *unreg vi:* **nicht (mehr)** ~**wissen** (*verzweifelt sein*) to be at one's wits' end.

weit- *zW:* ~**gehend** *adj* considerable ♦ *adv* largely; ~**hergeholt** *adj attrib* far-fetched; ~**hin** *adv* widely; (~*gehend*) to a large extent; ~**läufig** *adj* (*Gebäude*) spacious; (*Erklärung*) lengthy; (*Verwandter*) distant; ~**reichend** *adj* (*fig*) far-reaching; ~**schweifig** *adj* long-winded; ~**sichtig** *adj* (*lit*) long-sighted (*BRIT*), far-sighted (*US*); (*fig*) far-sighted; **W~sprung** *m* long jump; ~**verbreitet** *adj* widespread; ~**verzweigt** *adj attrib* (*Straßensystem*) extensive; **W~winkelobjektiv** *nt* (*PHOT*) wide-angle lens.

Weizen ['vaɪtsən] (**-s, -**) *m* wheat; ~**bier** *nt* light, fizzy wheat beer; ~**keime** *pl* (*KOCH*) wheatgerm *sing*.

welch [vɛlç] *pron:* ~ **ein(e)** ... what a ...

=============== *SCHLÜSSELWORT* ===============

welche(r, s) *interrog pron* which; ~**r von beiden?** which (one) of the two?; ~**n hast du genommen?** which (one) did you take?; ~ **Freude!** what joy!
♦ *indef pron* some; (*in Fragen*) any; **ich habe** ~ I have some; **haben Sie** ~? do you have any?
♦ *rel pron* (*bei Menschen*) who; (*bei Sachen*) which, that; ~**(r, s) auch immer** whoever/ whichever/whatever.

―――――――――――――――――――――

welk [vɛlk] *adj* withered; ~**en** *vi* to wither.
Wellblech *nt* corrugated iron.
Welle ['vɛlə] (**-, -n**) *f* wave; (*TECH*) shaft; **(hohe)** ~**n schlagen** (*fig*) to create (quite) a stir.
Wellen- *zW:* ~**bereich** *m* waveband; ~**brecher** *m* breakwater; ~**gang** *m:* **starker** ~**gang** heavy sea(s) *od* swell; ~**länge** *f* (*lit, fig*) wavelength; **mit jdm auf einer** ~**länge sein** (*fig*) to be on the same wavelength as sb; ~**linie** *f* wavy line.
Wellensittich *m* budgerigar.
Wellpappe *f* corrugated cardboard.
Welpe ['vɛlpə] (**-n, -n**) *m* pup, whelp; (*von Wolf etc*) cub.
Welt [vɛlt] (**-, -en**) *f* world; **aus der** ~ **schaffen** to eliminate; **in aller** ~ all over the world; **vor aller** ~ in front of everybody; **auf die** ~ **kommen** to be born; ~**all** *nt* universe; ~**anschauung** *f* philosophy of life; **w~berühmt** *adj* world-famous; **w~bewegend** *adj* world-shattering; ~**bild** *nt* conception of the world; (*jds Ansichten*) philosophy.
Weltenbummler(in) *m(f)* globetrotter.
Weltergewicht ['vɛltərgəviçt] *nt* (*SPORT*) welterweight.
weltfremd *adj* unworldly.

Weltgesundheitsorganisation *f* World Health Organization.
Welt- *zW:* **w~gewandt** *adj* sophisticated; ~**kirchenrat** *m* World Council of Churches; ~**krieg** *m* world war; **w~lich** *adj* worldly; (*nicht kirchlich*) secular; ~**literatur** *f* world literature; ~**macht** *f* world power; **w~männisch** *adj* sophisticated; ~**meister** *m* world champion; ~**meisterschaft** *f* world's (*US*) championship; (*FUSSBALL etc*) World Cup; ~**rang** *m:* **von** ~**rang** world-famous; ~**raum** *m* space; ~**raumforschung** *f* space research; ~**raumstation** *f* space station; ~**reise** *f* trip round the world; ~**ruf** *m* world-wide reputation; ~**sicherheitsrat** *m* (*POL*) United Nations Security Council; ~**stadt** *f* metropolis; ~**untergang** *m* (*lit, fig*) end of the world; **w~weit** *adj* world-wide; ~**wirtschaft** *f* world economy; ~**wirtschaftskrise** *f* world economic crisis; ~**wunder** *nt* wonder of the world.
wem [ve:m] *dat von* **wer** ♦ *pron* to whom.
wen [ve:n] *akk von* **wer** ♦ *pron* whom.
Wende ['vɛndə] (**-, -n**) *f* turn; (*Veränderung*) change; **die** ~ (*POL*) (the) reunification (of Germany); ~**kreis** *m* (*GEOG*) tropic; (*AUT*) turning circle.
Wendeltreppe *f* spiral staircase.
wenden *unreg vt, vi, vr* to turn; **bitte** ~**!** please turn over; **sich an jdn** ~ to go/come to sb.
Wendepunkt *m* turning point.
wendig *adj* (*lit, fig*) agile; (*Auto etc*) manoeuvrable (*BRIT*), maneuverable (*US*).
Wendung *f* turn; (*Rede~*) idiom.
wenig ['ve:nɪç] *adj, adv* little; **ein** ~ a little; **er hat zu** ~ **Geld** he doesn't have enough money; **ein Exemplar zu** ~ one copy too few.
wenige ['ve:nɪgə] *pl* few *pl*; **in** ~**n Tagen** in (just) a few days.
weniger *adj* less; (*mit pl*) fewer ♦ *adv* less.
Wenigkeit *f* trifle; **meine** ~ (*umg*) little me.
wenigste(r, s) *adj* least.
wenigstens *adv* at least.
wenn [vɛn] *konj* if; (*zeitlich*) when; ~ **auch** ... even if ...; ~ **ich doch** ... if only I ...; ~ **wir erst die neue Wohnung haben** once we get the new flat.
Wenn *nt:* **ohne** ~ **und Aber** unequivocally.
wennschon *adv:* **na** ~ so what?; ~**, dennschon!** in for a penny, in for a pound!
wer [ve:r] *pron* who.
Werbe- *zW:* ~**agentur** *f* advertising agency; ~**aktion** *f* advertising campaign; ~**antwort** *f* business reply card; ~**fernsehen** *nt* commercial television; ~**film** *m* promotional film; ~**geschenk** *nt* promotional gift, freebie (*umg*); (*zu Gekauftem*) free gift; ~**grafiker(in)** *m(f)* commercial artist; ~**kampagne** *f* advertising campaign.
werben ['vɛrbən] *unreg vt* to win; (*Mitglied*) to recruit ♦ *vi* to advertise; **um jdn/etw** ~ to

try to win sb/sth; **für jdn/etw** ~ to promote
sb/sth.

Werbe- *zW:* **~spot** *m* commercial; **~texter**
(-s, -) *m* copywriter; **~trommel** *f:* **die**
~trommel (für etw) rühren (*umg*) to beat the
big drum (for sth); **w~wirksam** *adj:*
w~wirksam sein to be good publicity.

Werbung *f* advertising; (*von Mitgliedern*)
recruitment; (*TV etc: Werbeblock*)
commercial break; ~ **um jdn/etw**
promotion of sb/sth.

Werbungskosten *pl* professional *od*
business expenses *pl*.

Werdegang ['ve:rdəgaŋ] *m* development;
(*beruflich*) career.

=========== *SCHLÜSSELWORT*

werden ['ve:rdən] *unreg* (*pt* **wurde**, *pp*
geworden *od* (*bei Passiv*) **worden**) *vi* to
become; **was ist aus ihm/aus der Sache**
geworden? what became of him/it; **es ist**
nichts/gut geworden it came to nothing/
turned out well; **es wird Nacht/Tage** it's
getting dark/light; **es wird bald ein Jahr,**
daß ... it's almost a year since ...; **er wird am**
8. Mai 36 he will be 36 on the 8th May; **mir**
wird kalt I'm getting cold; **mir wird schlecht**
I feel ill; **Erster** ~ to come *od* be first; **das**
muß anders ~ that will have to change;
rot/zu Eis ~ to turn red/to ice; **was willst du**
(mal) ~**?** what do you want to be?; **die Fotos**
sind gut geworden the photos turned out
well

♦ *Hilfsverb* **1** (*bei Futur*): **er wird es tun** he will
od he'll do it; **er wird das nicht tun** he will
not *od* he won't do it; **es wird gleich regnen**
it's going to rain any moment

2 (*bei Konjunktiv*): **ich würde ...** I would ...; **er**
würde gern ... he would *od* he'd like to ...; **ich**
würde lieber I would *od* I'd rather ...

3 (*bei Vermutung*): **sie wird in der Küche sein**
she will be in the kitchen

4 (*bei Passiv*): **gebraucht** ~ to be used; **er ist**
erschossen worden he has *od* he's been
shot; **mir wurde gesagt, daß** I was told that
...

werdend *adj:* **~e Mutter** expectant mother.

werfen ['vɛrfən] *unreg vt* to throw ♦ *vi* (*Tier*) to
have its young; „**nicht** ~" "handle with
care".

Werft [vɛrft] **(-, -en)** *f* shipyard; (*für*
Flugzeuge) hangar.

Werk [vɛrk] **(-(e)s, -e)** *nt* work; (*Tätigkeit*) job;
(*Fabrik, Mechanismus*) works *pl*; **ans** ~ **gehen**
to set to work; **das ist sein** ~ this is his
doing; **ab** ~ (*COMM*) ex works.

werkeln ['vɛrkəln] (*umg*) *vi* to potter about
(*BRIT*), putter around (*US*).

Werken (-s) *nt* (*SCH*) handicrafts *pl*.

Werkschutz *m* works security service.

Werksgelände *nt* factory premises *pl*.

Werk- *zW:* **~statt (-, -stätten)** *f* workshop;
(*AUT*) garage; **~stoff** *m* material; **~student**
m self-supporting student; **~tag** *m* working
day; **w~tags** *adv* on working days; **w~tätig**
adj working; **~zeug** *nt* tool; **~zeugkasten** *m*
toolbox; **~zeugmaschine** *f* machine tool;
~zeugschrank *m* tool chest.

Wermut ['ve:rmu:t] **(-(e)s, -s)** *m* wormwood;
(*Wein*) vermouth.

Wermutstropfen *m* (*fig*) drop of bitterness.

Wert [ve:rt] **(-(e)s, -e)** *m* worth; (*FIN*) value;
~ **legen auf** +*akk* to attach importance to; **es**
hat doch keinen ~ it's useless; **im ~e von** to
the value of.

wert [ve:rt] *adj* worth; (*geschätzt*) dear;
(*würdig*) worthy; **das ist nichts/viel** ~ it's not
worth anything/it's worth a lot; **das ist es/er**
mir ~ it's/he's worth that to me; **ein Auto ist**
viel ~ (*nützlich*) a car is very useful.

Wertangabe *f* declaration of value.

wertbeständig *adj* stable in value.

werten *vt* to rate; (*beurteilen*) to judge;
(*SPORT: als gültig* ~) to allow; ~ **als** to rate
as; to judge to be.

Wert- *zW:* **~gegenstand** *m* article of value;
w~los *adj* worthless; **~losigkeit** *f*
worthlessness; **~maßstab** *m* standard;
~papier *nt* security; **~steigerung** *f*
appreciation.

Wertung *f* (*SPORT*) score.

Wert- *zW:* **w~voll** *adj* valuable; **~vorstellung** *f*
moral concept; **~zuwachs** *m* appreciation.

Wesen ['ve:zən] **(-s, -)** *nt* (*Geschöpf*) being;
(*Natur, Character*) nature.

wesentlich *adj* significant; (*beträchtlich*)
considerable; **im ~en** essentially; (*im*
großen) in the main.

weshalb [vɛs'halp] *adv* why.

Wespe ['vɛspə] **(-, -n)** *f* wasp.

wessen ['vɛsən] *gen von* **wer** ♦ *pron* whose.

Wessi ['vɛsɪ] **(-s, -s)** (*umg*) *m* West German.

A *Wessi* is a colloquial and often derogatory
word used to describe a German from the
former West Germany. The expression
'Besserwessi' is used by East Germans to
describe a West German who is considered to
be a know-all.

West- *zW:* **w~deutsch** *adj* West German;
~deutsche(r) *f(m)* West German;
~deutschland *nt* (*POL: früher*) West
Germany; (*GEOG*) Western Germany.

Weste ['vɛstə] **(-, -n)** *f* waistcoat, vest (*US*);
eine reine ~ **haben** (*fig*) to have a clean
slate.

Westen (-s) *m* west.

Westentasche *f:* **etw wie seine** ~ **kennen**
(*umg*) to know sth like the back of one's
hand.

Westerwald ['vɛstərvalt] **(-s)** *m* Westerwald
(Mountains *pl*).

Westeuropa nt Western Europe.
westeuropäisch ['vɛst|ɔyro'pɛːɪʃ] adj
West(ern) European; ~**e Zeit** Greenwich
Mean Time.
Westfale [vɛst'faːlə] (**-n, -n**) m Westphalian.
Westfalen (**-s**) nt Westphalia.
Westfälin [vɛst'fɛːlɪn] f Westphalian.
westfälisch adj Westphalian.
Westindien ['vɛst|ɪndɪən] (**-s**) nt West Indies
pl.
westindisch adj West Indian; **die** ~**en Inseln**
the West Indies.
west- zW: ~**lich** adj western ◆ adv to the west;
W~**mächte** pl (POL: früher): **die W**~**mächte**
the Western powers pl; ~**wärts** adv
westwards.
weswegen [vɛs've:gən] adv why.
wett [vɛt] adj even; ~ **sein** to be quits.
Wettbewerb m competition.
Wettbewerbsbeschränkung f restraint of
trade.
wettbewerbsfähig adj competitive.
Wette (**-, -n**) f bet, wager; **um die** ~ **laufen** to
run a race (with each other).
Wetteifer m rivalry.
wetteifern vi untr: **mit jdm um etw wetteifern**
to compete with sb for sth.
wetten ['vɛtən] vt, vi to bet; **so haben wir nicht**
gewettet! that's not part of the bargain!
Wetter ['vɛtər] (**-s, -**) nt weather; (MIN) air;
~**amt** nt meteorological office; ~**aussichten**
pl weather outlook sing; ~**bericht** m weather
report; ~**dienst** m meteorological service;
w~**fest** adj weatherproof; **w**~**fühlig** adj
sensitive to changes in the weather; ~**karte**
f weather chart; ~**lage** f (weather)
situation.
wettern ['vɛtərn] vi to curse and swear.
Wetter- zW: ~**umschlag** m sudden change in
the weather; ~**vorhersage** f weather
forecast; ~**warte** f weather station;
w~**wendisch** adj capricious.
Wett- zW: ~**kampf** m contest; ~**lauf** m race;
ein ~**lauf mit der Zeit** a race against time.
wettmachen vt to make good.
Wett- zW: ~**rüsten** nt arms race; ~**spiel** nt
match; ~**streit** m contest.
wetzen ['vɛtsən] vt to sharpen ◆ vi (umg) to
scoot.
WEU f abk (= Westeuropäische Union) WEU.
WEZ abk (= westeuropäische Zeit) GMT.
WG abk = **Wohngemeinschaft**.
Whisky ['vɪski] (**-s, -s**) m whisky (BRIT),
whiskey (US, Ireland).
WHO (**-**) f abk (= World Health Organization)
WHO.
wich etc [vɪç] vb siehe **weichen**.
wichsen ['vɪksən] vt (Schuhe) to polish ◆ vi
(umg!: onanieren) to jerk od toss off (!).
Wichser (umg!) m wanker (!).
Wicht [vɪçt] (**-(e)s, -e**) m titch; (pej) worthless
creature.

wichtig adj important; **sich selbst/etw (zu)**
~ **nehmen** to take o.s./sth (too) seriously;
W~**keit** f importance; **W**~**tuer(in)** (pej) m(f)
pompous ass (umg).
Wicke ['vɪkə] (**-, -n**) f (BOT) vetch; (Garten~)
sweet pea.
Wickelkleid nt wrap-around dress.
wickeln ['vɪkəln] vt to wind; (Haare) to set;
(Kind) to change; **da bist du schief gewickelt!**
(fig: umg) you're very much mistaken; **jdn/**
etw in etw akk ~ to wrap sb/sth in sth.
Wickeltisch m baby's changing table.
Widder ['vɪdər] (**-s, -**) m ram; (ASTROL) Aries.
wider ['vi:dər] präp +akk against.
widerfahren unreg vi untr: **jdm widerfahren** to
happen to sb.
Widerhaken ['vi:dərhaːkən] m barb.
Widerhall ['vi:dərhal] m echo; **keinen** ~ **(bei**
jdm) finden (Interesse) to meet with no
response (from sb).
widerlegen vt untr to refute.
widerlich ['vi:dərlɪç] adj disgusting, repulsive;
W~**keit** f repulsiveness.
widerrechtlich adj unlawful.
Widerrede f contradiction; **keine** ~**!** don't
argue!
Widerruf ['vi:dərruːf] m retraction;
countermanding; **bis auf** ~ until revoked.
widerrufen unreg vt untr to retract;
(Anordnung) to revoke; (Befehl) to
countermand.
Widersacher(in) ['vi:dərzaxər(ɪn)] (**-s, -**) m(f)
adversary.
widersetzen vr untr: **sich jdm widersetzen** to
oppose sb; (der Polizei) to resist sb; **sich einer**
Sache widersetzen to oppose sth; (einem
Befehl) to refuse to comply with sth.
widerspenstig ['vi:dərʃpɛnstɪç] adj wilful
(BRIT), willful (US); **W**~**keit** f wilfulness
(BRIT), willfulness (US).
widerspiegeln ['vi:dərʃpiːgəln] vt to reflect.
widersprechen unreg vi untr: **jdm**
widersprechen to contradict sb.
widersprechend adj contradictory.
Widerspruch ['vi:dərʃprʊx] m contradiction;
ein ~ **in sich** a contradiction in terms.
widersprüchlich ['vi:dərʃpryçlɪç] adj
contradictory, inconsistent.
widerspruchslos adv without arguing.
Widerstand ['vi:dərʃtant] m resistance; **der**
Weg des geringsten ~**es** the line of least
resistance; **jdm/etw** ~ **leisten** to resist sb/
sth.
Widerstands- zW: ~**bewegung** f resistance
(movement); **w**~**fähig** adj resistant, tough;
w~**los** adj unresisting.
widerstehen unreg vi untr: **jdm/etw**
widerstehen to withstand sb/sth.
widerstreben vi untr: **es widerstrebt mir, so**
etwas zu tun I am reluctant to do anything
like that.
widerstrebend adj reluctant; (gegensätzlich)

conflicting.

Wider- *zW:* **~streit** *m* conflict; **w~wärtig** *adj* nasty, horrid; **~wille** *m:* **~wille (gegen)** aversion (to); (*Abneigung*) distaste (for); (*~streben*) reluctance; **w~willig** *adj* unwilling, reluctant; **~worte** *pl* answering back *sing.*

widmen ['vɪtmən] *vt* to dedicate ♦ *vr* to devote o.s.

Widmung *f* dedication.

widrig ['viːdrɪç] *adj* (*Umstände*) adverse; (*Mensch*) repulsive.

═══════════ *SCHLÜSSELWORT*

wie [viː] *adv* how; **~ groß/schnell?** how big/fast?; **~ wär's?** how about it?; **~ wär's mit einem Whisky?** (*umg*) how about a whisky?; **~ nennt man das?** what is that called?; **~ ist er?** what's he like?; **~ gut du das kannst!** you're very good at it; **~ bitte?** pardon? (*BRIT*), pardon me? (*US*); (*entrüstet*) I beg your pardon!; **und ~!** and how!

♦ *konj* **1** (*bei Vergleichen*): **so schön ~** ... as beautiful as ...; **~ ich schon sagte** as I said; **~ noch nie** as never before; **~ du** like you; **singen ~ ein** ... to sing like a ...; **~ (zum Beispiel)** such as (for example)

2 (*zeitlich*): **~ er das hörte, ging er** when he heard that he left; **er hörte, ~ der Regen fiel** he heard the rain falling.

wieder ['viːdər] *adv* again; **~ da sein** to be back (again); **gehst du schon ~?** are you off again?; **~ ein(e)** ... another ...; **das ist auch ~ wahr** that's true enough; **da sieht man mal** ... it just shows ...

wieder- *zW:* **W~aufbau** [-'|aufbau] *m* rebuilding; **~aufbereiten** *vt* to recycle; (*Atommüll*) to reprocess; **W~aufbereitungsanlage** *f* reprocessing plant; **W~aufnahme** [-'|aufnaːmə] *f* resumption; **~aufnehmen** *unreg vt* to resume; (*Gedanken, Hobby*) to take up again; (*Thema*) to revert to; (*JUR: Verfahren*) to reopen; **~bekommen** *unreg vt* to get back; **~beleben** *vt* to revive; **~bringen** *unreg vt* to bring back; **~erkennen** *unreg vt* to recognize; **W~erstattung** *f* reimbursement; **~finden** *unreg vt* (*fig: Selbstachtung etc*) to regain.

Wiedergabe *f* (*von Rede, Ereignis*) account; (*Wiederholung*) repetition; (*Darbietung*) performance; (*Reproduktion*) reproduction; **~gerät** *nt* playback unit.

wieder- *zW:* **~geben** *unreg vt* (*zurückgeben*) to return; (*Erzählung etc*) to repeat; (*Gefühle etc*) to convey; **W~geburt** *f* rebirth; **~gutmachen** [-'guːtmaxən] *vt* to make up for; (*Fehler*) to put right; **W~gutmachung** *f* reparation; **~herstellen** *vt* to restore.

wiederholen *vt untr* to repeat.

wiederholt *adj:* **zum ~en Male** once again.

Wiederholung *f* repetition.

Wiederholungstäter(in) *m(f)* (*JUR*) second-time offender; (*mehrmalig*) persistent offender.

wieder- *zW:* **W~hören** *nt:* **auf W~hören** (*TEL*) goodbye; **~käuen** *vi* to ruminate ♦ *vt* to ruminate; (*fig: umg*) to go over again and again; **W~kehr** (-) *f* return; (*von Vorfall*) repetition, recurrence; **~kehrend** *adj* recurrent; **W~kunft** (-, ¨e) *f* return; **~sehen** *unreg vt* to see again; **auf W~sehen** goodbye; **~um** *adv* again; (*seinerseits etc*) in turn; (*andererseits*) on the other hand; **~vereinigen** *vt* to reunite; **W~vereinigung** *f* reunification; **W~verkäufer** *m* distributor; **W~wahl** *f* re-election.

Wiege ['viːgə] (-, -n) *f* cradle.

wiegen¹ *vt* (*schaukeln*) to rock; (*Kopf*) to shake.

wiegen² *unreg vt, vi* to weigh; **schwer ~** (*fig*) to carry a lot of weight; (*Irrtum*) to be serious.

wiehern ['viːərn] *vi* to neigh, whinny.

Wien [viːn] (-s) *nt* Vienna.

Wiener(in) (-, -) *m(f)* Viennese ♦ *adj attrib* Viennese; **~ Schnitzel** Wiener schnitzel.

wies *etc* [viːs] *vb siehe* **weisen.**

Wiese ['viːzə] (-, -n) *f* meadow.

Wiesel ['viːzəl] (-s, -) *nt* weasel; **schnell** *od* **flink wie ein ~** quick as a flash.

wieso [viˈzoː] *adv* why.

wieviel [viˈfiːl] *adv* how much; **~ Menschen** how many people; **~mal** *adv* how often.

wievielte(r, s) *adj:* **zum ~n Mal?** how many times?; **den W~n haben wir?** what's the date?; **an ~r Stelle?** in what place?; **der ~ Besucher war er?** how many visitors were there before him?

wieweit [viˈvaɪt] *adv* to what extent.

Wikinger ['viːkɪŋər] (-s, -) *m* Viking.

wild [vɪlt] *adj* wild; **~er Streik** unofficial strike; **in ~er Ehe leben** (*veraltet, hum*) to live in sin; **~ entschlossen** (*umg*) dead set.

Wild (-(e)s) *nt* game.

Wild- *zW:* **~bahn** *f:* **in freier ~bahn** in the wild; **~bret** *nt* game; (*von Rotwild*) venison; **~dieb** *m* poacher.

Wilde(r) ['vɪldə(r)] *f(m)* savage.

wildern ['vɪldərn] *vi* to poach.

wild- *zW:* **W~fang** *m* little rascal; **~fremd** ['vɪlt'frɛmt] (*umg*) *adj* quite strange *od* unknown; **W~heit** *f* wildness; **W~leder** *nt* suede.

Wildnis (-, -se) *f* wilderness.

Wild- *zW:* **~schwein** *nt* (wild) boar; **~wechsel** *m:* „**~wechsel**" "wild animals"; **~westroman** *m* western.

will [vɪl] *vb siehe* **wollen.**

Wille ['vɪlə] (-ns, -n) *m* will; **jdm seinen ~n lassen** to let sb have his own way; **seinen eigenen ~n haben** to be self-willed.

willen *präp +gen:* **um ... ~** for the sake of ...

willenlos *adj* weak-willed.

willens *adj* (*geh*): ~ **sein** to be willing.
willensstark *adj* strong-willed.
willentlich ['vɪləntlɪç] *adj* wilful (*BRIT*), willful (*US*), deliberate.
willig *adj* willing.
willkommen [vɪl'kɔmən] *adj* welcome; **jdn** ~ **heißen** to welcome sb; **herzlich** ~ **(in** +*dat*) welcome (to); **W**~ (-**s**, -) *nt* welcome.
willkürlich *adj* arbitrary; (*Bewegung*) voluntary.
willst [vɪlst] *vb siehe* **wollen**.
Wilna ['vɪlna] (-**s**) *nt* Vilnius.
wimmeln ['vɪməln] *vi*: ~ (**von**) to swarm (with).
wimmern ['vɪmərn] *vi* to whimper.
Wimper ['vɪmpər] (-, -**n**) *f* eyelash; **ohne mit der** ~ **zu zucken** (*fig*) without batting an eyelid.
Wimperntusche *f* mascara.
Wind [vɪnt] (-(**e**)**s**, -**e**) *m* wind; **den Mantel** *od* **das Fähnchen nach dem** ~ **hängen** to trim one's sails to the wind; **etw in den** ~ **schlagen** to turn a deaf ear to sth.
Windbeutel *m* cream puff; (*fig*) windbag.
Winde ['vɪndə] (-, -**n**) *f* (*TECH*) winch, windlass; (*BOT*) bindweed.
Windel ['vɪndəl] (-, -**n**) *f* nappy (*BRIT*), diaper (*US*).
windelweich *adj*: **jdn** ~ **schlagen** (*umg*) to beat the living daylights out of sb.
winden¹ ['vɪndən] *vi unpers* to be windy.
winden² *unreg vt* to wind; (*Kranz*) to weave; (*ent*~) to twist ♦ *vr* to wind; (*Person*) to writhe; (*fig: ausweichen*) to try to wriggle out.
Windenergie *f* wind power.
Windeseile *f*: **sich in** *od* **mit Windeseile verbreiten** to spread like wildfire.
Windhose *f* whirlwind.
Windhund *m* greyhound; (*Mensch*) fly-by-night.
windig ['vɪndɪç] *adj* windy; (*fig*) dubious.
Wind- *zW*: ~**jacke** *f* windcheater, windbreaker (*US*); ~**kanal** *m* (*TECH*) wind tunnel; ~**kraft** *f* wind power; ~**kraftanlage** *f* wind power station; ~**mühle** *f* windmill; **gegen** ~**mühlen (an)kämpfen** (*fig*) to tilt at windmills; ~**park** *m* wind farm.
Windpocken *pl* chickenpox *sing*.
Wind- *zW*: ~**rose** *f* (*NAUT*) compass card; (*MET*) wind rose; ~**schatten** *m* lee; (*von Fahrzeugen*) slipstream; ~**schutzscheibe** *f* (*AUT*) windscreen (*BRIT*), windshield (*US*); ~**stärke** *f* wind force; **w**~**still** *adj* (*Tag*) windless; **es ist w**~**still** there's no wind; ~**stille** *f* calm; ~**stoß** *m* gust of wind; ~**surfen** *nt* windsurfing.
Windung *f* (*von Weg, Fluß etc*) meander; (*von Schlange, Spule*) coil; (*von Schraube*) thread.
Wink [vɪŋk] (-(**e**)**s**, -**e**) *m* (*mit Kopf*) nod; (*mit Hand*) wave; (*Tip, Hinweis*) hint; **ein** ~ **mit dem Zaunpfahl** a broad hint.

Winkel ['vɪŋkəl] (-**s**, -) *m* (*MATH*) angle; (*Gerät*) set square; (*in Raum*) corner; ~**advokat** (*pej*) *m* incompetent lawyer; ~**messer** *m* protractor; ~**zug** *m*: **mach keine** ~**züge** stop evading the issue.
winken ['vɪŋkən] *vt, vi* to wave; **dem Sieger winkt eine Reise nach Italien** the (lucky) winner will receive a trip to Italy.
winseln ['vɪnzəln] *vi* to whine.
Winter ['vɪntər] (-**s**, -) *m* winter; ~**garten** *m* conservatory; **w**~**lich** *adj* wintry; ~**reifen** *m* winter tyre (*BRIT*) *od* tire (*US*); ~**schlaf** *m* (*ZOOL*) hibernation; ~**schlußverkauf** *m* winter sale; ~**semester** *nt* (*UNIV*) winter semester (*bes US*), ≈ autumn term (*BRIT*); ~**spiele** *pl*: **(Olympische)** ~**spiele** Winter Olympics *pl*; ~**sport** *m* winter sports *pl*.
Winzer(in) ['vɪntsər(ɪn)] (-**s**, -) *m(f)* wine-grower.
winzig ['vɪntsɪç] *adj* tiny.
Wipfel ['vɪpfəl] (-**s**, -) *m* treetop.
Wippe ['vɪpə] (-, -**n**) *f* seesaw.
wir [viːr] *pron* we; ~ **alle** all of us, we all.
Wirbel ['vɪrbəl] (-**s**, -) *m* whirl, swirl; (*Trubel*) hurly-burly; (*Aufsehen*) fuss; (*ANAT*) vertebra; ~ **um jdn/etw machen** to make a fuss about sb/sth.
wirbellos *adj* (*ZOOL*) invertebrate.
wirbeln *vi* to whirl, swirl.
Wirbel- *zW*: ~**säule** *f* spine; ~**tier** *nt* vertebrate; ~**wind** *m* whirlwind.
wirbst *vb siehe* **werben**.
wirbt [vɪrpt] *vb siehe* **werben**.
wird [vɪrt] *vb siehe* **werden**.
wirfst *vb siehe* **werfen**.
wirft [vɪrft] *vb siehe* **werfen**.
wirken ['vɪrkən] *vi* to have an effect; (*erfolgreich sein*) to work; (*scheinen*) to seem ♦ *vt* (*Wunder*) to work; **etw auf sich** *akk* ~ **lassen** to take sth in.
wirklich ['vɪrklɪç] *adj* real; **W**~**keit** *f* reality; ~**keitsgetreu** *adj* realistic.
wirksam ['vɪrkzaːm] *adj* effective; **W**~**keit** *f* effectiveness.
Wirkstoff *m* active substance.
Wirkung ['vɪrkʊŋ] *f* effect.
Wirkungs- *zW*: ~**bereich** *m* field (of activity *od* interest *etc*); (*Domäne*) domain; **w**~**los** *adj* ineffective; **w**~**los bleiben** to have no effect; **w**~**voll** *adj* effective.
wirr [vɪr] *adj* confused; (*unrealistisch*) wild; (*Haare etc*) tangled.
Wirren *pl* disturbances *pl*.
Wirrwarr ['vɪrvar] (-**s**) *m* disorder, chaos; (*von Stimmen*) hubbub; (*von Fäden, Haaren etc*) tangle.
Wirsing(kohl) ['vɪrzɪŋ(koːl)] (-**s**) *m* savoy cabbage.
wirst [vɪrst] *vb siehe* **werden**.
Wirt(in) [vɪrt(ɪn)] (-(**e**)**s**, -**e**) *m(f)* landlord, landlady.
Wirtschaft ['vɪrtʃaft] *f* (*Gaststätte*) pub;

(*Haushalt*) housekeeping; (*eines Landes*) economy; (*Geschäftsleben*) industry and commerce; (*umg: Durcheinander*) mess; **w~en** *vi* (*sparsam sein*): **gut w~en können** to be economical; **~er** *m* (*Verwalter*) manager; **~erin** *f* (*im Haushalt, Heim etc*) housekeeper; **w~lich** *adj* economical; (*POL*) economic; **~lichkeit** *f* economy; (*von Betrieb*) viability.

Wirtschafts- *zW:* **~geld** *nt* housekeeping (money); **~geographie** *f* economic geography; **~hilfe** *f* economic aid; **~krise** *f* economic crisis; **~minister** *m* minister of economic affairs; **~ordnung** *f* economic system; **~politik** *f* economic policy; **~prüfer** *m* chartered accountant (*BRIT*), certified public accountant (*US*); **~spionage** *f* industrial espionage; **~wachstum** *nt* economic growth; **~wissenschaft** *f* economics *sing*; **~wunder** *nt* economic miracle; **~zweig** *m* branch of industry.

Wirtshaus *nt* inn.
Wisch [vɪʃ] (**-(e)s, -e**) *m* scrap of paper.
wischen *vt* to wipe.
Wischer (**-s, -**) *m* (*AUT*) wiper.
Wischiwaschi [vɪʃiːˈvaʃiː] (**-s**) (*pej: umg*) *nt* drivel.
Wisent [ˈviːzɛnt] (**-s, -e**) *m* bison.
WiSo [ˈvɪzo] *abk* (= *Wirtschafts- und Sozialwissenschaften*) economics and social sciences.
wispern [ˈvɪspərn] *vt, vi* to whisper.
Wiss. *abk* = **Wissenschaft**.
wiss. *abk* = **wissenschaftlich**.
Wißbegier(de) [ˈvɪsbəgiːr(də)] *f* thirst for knowledge.
wißbegierig *adj* eager for knowledge.
wissen [ˈvɪsən] *unreg vt, vi* to know; **von jdm/ etw nichts ~ wollen** not to be interested in sb/sth; **sie hält sich für wer weiß wie klug** (*umg*) she doesn't half think she's clever; **gewußt wie/wo!** *etc* sheer brilliance!; **ich weiß seine Adresse nicht mehr** (*sich erinnern*) I can't remember his address; **W~ (-s)** *nt* knowledge; **etw gegen (sein) besseres W~ tun** to do sth against one's better judgement; **nach bestem W~ und Gewissen** to the best of one's knowledge and belief.
Wissenschaft [ˈvɪsənʃaft] *f* science.
Wissenschaftler(in) (**-s, -**) *m(f)* scientist; (*Geistes~*) academic.
wissenschaftlich *adj* scientific; **W~er Assistent** assistant lecturer.
wissenswert *adj* worth knowing.
wissentlich *adj* knowing.
wittern [ˈvɪtərn] *vt* to scent; (*fig*) to suspect.
Witterung *f* weather; (*Geruch*) scent.
Witwe [ˈvɪtvə] (**-, -n**) *f* widow.
Witwer (**-s, -**) *m* widower.
Witz [vɪts] (**-es, -e**) *m* joke; **der ~ an der Sache ist, daß ...** the great thing about it is that ...; **~bold** (**-(e)s, -e**) *m* joker.

witzeln *vi* to joke.
witzig *adj* funny.
witzlos (*umg*) *adj* (*unsinnig*) pointless, futile.
WM (**-**) *f abk* = **Weltmeisterschaft**.
wo [vo:] *adv* where; (*umg: irgend~*) somewhere ♦ *konj* (*wenn*) if; **im Augenblick, ~ ...** the moment (that) ...; **die Zeit, ~ ...** the time when ...
woanders [vo:ˈ|andərs] *adv* elsewhere.
wob *etc* [vo:p] *vb siehe* **weben**.
wobei [vo:ˈbaɪ] *adv* (*rel*) ... in/by/with which; (*interrog*) how; what ... in/by/with; **~ mir gerade einfällt ...** which reminds me ...
Woche [ˈvɔxə] (**-, -n**) *f* week.
Wochenbett *nt*: **im ~ sterben** to die in childbirth.
Wochen- *zW:* **~ende** *nt* weekend; **~endhaus** *nt* weekend house; **~karte** *f* weekly ticket; **w~lang** *adj* lasting weeks ♦ *adv* for weeks; **~schau** *f* newsreel; **~tag** *m* weekday.
wöchentlich [ˈvœçəntlɪç] *adj, adv* weekly.
Wochenzeitung *f* weekly (paper).
Wöchnerin [ˈvœçnərɪn] *f* *woman who has recently given birth*.
wodurch [vo:ˈdurç] *adv* (*rel*) through which; (*interrog*) what ... through.
wofür [vo:ˈfyːr] *adv* (*rel*) for which; (*interrog*) what ... for.
Wodka [ˈvɔtka] (**-s, -s**) *m* vodka.
wog *etc* [vo:k] *vb siehe* **wiegen²**.
Woge [ˈvo:gə] (**-, -n**) *f* wave.
wogegen [vo:ˈge:gən] *adv* (*rel*) against which; (*interrog*) what ... against.
wogen *vi* to heave, surge.
woher [vo:ˈheːr] *adv* where ... from; **~ kommt es eigentlich, daß ...?** how is it that ...?
wohin [vo:ˈhɪn] *adv* where ... to; **~ man auch schaut** wherever you look.
wohingegen *konj* whereas, while.
Wohl (**-(e)s**) *nt* welfare; **zum ~!** cheers!

=================================== *SCHLÜSSELWORT*

wohl [vo:l] *adv* **1** well; (*behaglich*) at ease, comfortable; **sich ~ fühlen** (*zufrieden*) to feel happy; (*gesundheitlich*) to feel well; **bei dem Gedanken ist mir nicht ~** I'm not very happy at the thought; **~ oder übel** whether one likes it or not; **er weiß das sehr ~** he knows that perfectly well
2 (*wahrscheinlich*) probably; (*vermutlich*) I suppose; (*gewiß*) certainly; (*vielleicht*) perhaps; **sie ist ~ zu Hause** she's probably at home; **sie wird ~ das Haus verkaufen** I suppose *od* presumably she's going to sell the house; **das ist doch ~ nicht dein Ernst!** surely you're not serious!; **das mag ~ sein** that may well be; **ob das ~ stimmt?** I wonder if that's true.

wohl- *zW:* **~auf** [vo:lˈ|auf] *adj* well, in good health; **W~befinden** *nt* well-being; **W~behagen** *nt* comfort; **~behalten** *adj* safe and sound; **W~ergehen** nt welfare; **W~fahrt** f welfare; **W~fahrtsstaat** m welfare state; **W~gefallen** nt: **sich in W~gefallen auflösen** (hum: Gegenstände, Probleme) to vanish into thin air; (zerfallen) to fall apart; **~gemeint** adj well-intentioned; **~gemerkt** adv mark you; **~habend** adj wealthy.

wohlig adj contented; (gemütlich) comfortable.

wohl- zW: **W~klang** m melodious sound; **~meinend** adj well-meaning; **~schmeckend** adj delicious; **W~stand** m prosperity; **W~standsgesellschaft** f affluent society; **W~tat** f (Gefallen) favour (BRIT), favor (US); (gute Tat) good deed; (Erleichterung) relief; **W~täter** m benefactor; **~tätig** adj charitable; **W~tätigkeit** f charity; **~tuend** adj pleasant; **~tun** unreg vi: **jdm ~tun** to do sb good; **~verdient** adj (Ruhe) well-earned; (Strafe) well-deserved; **~weislich** adv prudently; **W~wollen** (-s) nt good will; **~wollend** adj benevolent.

Wohnblock ['vo:nblɔk] (-s, -s) m block of flats (BRIT), apartment house (US).

wohnen ['vo:nən] vi to live.

wohn- zW: **W~fläche** f living space; **W~geld** nt housing benefit; **W~gemeinschaft** f people sharing a flat (BRIT) od apartment (US); (von Hippies) commune; **~haft** adj resident; **W~heim** nt (für Studenten) hall (of residence), dormitory (US); (für Senioren) home; (bes für Arbeiter) hostel; **W~komfort** m: **mit sämtlichem W~komfort** with all mod cons (BRIT); **~lich** adj comfortable; **W~mobil** nt motor caravan (BRIT), motor home (US); **W~ort** m domicile; **W~silo** nt concrete block of flats (BRIT) od apartment block (US); **W~sitz** m place of residence; **ohne festen W~sitz** of no fixed abode.

Wohnung f house; (Etagen~) flat (BRIT), apartment (US).

Wohnungs- zW: **~amt** nt housing office; **~bau** m house-building; **~markt** m housing market; **~not** f housing shortage.

wohn- zW: **W~viertel** nt residential area; **W~wagen** m caravan (BRIT), trailer (US); **W~zimmer** nt living room.

wölben ['vœlbən] vt, vr to curve.

Wölbung f curve.

Wolf [vɔlf] (-(e)s, ⁻e) m wolf; (TECH) shredder; (Fleisch~) mincer (BRIT), grinder (US).

Wölfin ['vœlfɪn] f she-wolf.

Wolke ['vɔlkə] (-, -n) f cloud; **aus allen ~n fallen** (fig) to be flabbergasted (umg).

Wolken- zW: **~bruch** m cloudburst; **w~bruchartig** adj torrential; **~kratzer** m skyscraper; **~kuckucksheim** nt cloud-cuckoo-land (BRIT), cloudland (US); **w~los** adj cloudless.

wolkig ['vɔlkɪç] adj cloudy.

Wolle ['vɔlə] (-, -n) f wool; **sich mit jdm in die**

~ kriegen (fig: umg) to start squabbling with sb.

════════════════ SCHLÜSSELWORT

wollen¹ ['vɔlən] unreg (pt **wollte**, pp **gewollt** od (als Hilfsverb) **wollen**) vt, vi to want; **ich will nach Hause** I want to go home; **er will nicht** he doesn't want to; **sie wollte das nicht** she didn't want it; **wenn du willst** if you like; **ich will, daß du mir zuhörst** I want you to listen to me; **oh, das hab ich nicht gewollt** oh, I didn't mean to do that; **ich weiß nicht, was er will** (verstehe ihn nicht) I don't know what he's on about

♦ Hilfsverb: **er will ein Haus kaufen** he wants to buy a house; **ich wollte, ich wäre ...** I wish I were ...; **etw gerade tun ~** to be just about to od going to do sth; **und so jemand** od **etwas will Lehrer sein!** (umg) and he calls himself a teacher!; **das will alles gut überlegt sein** that needs a lot of thought.

wollen² adj woollen (BRIT), woolen (US).
Wollsachen pl wool(l)ens pl.
wollüstig ['vɔlʏstɪç] adj lusty, sensual.
wo- zW: **~mit** [vo'mɪt] adv (rel) with which; (interrog) what ... with; **~mit kann ich dienen?** what can I do for you?; **~möglich** [vo'mø:klɪç] adv probably, I suppose; **~nach** [vo'na:x] adv (rel) after/for which; (interrog) what ... after.
Wonne ['vɔnə] (-, -n) f joy, bliss.
woran [vo'ran] adv (rel) on/at which; (interrog) what ... on/at; **~ liegt das?** what's the reason for it?
worauf [vo'rauf] adv (rel) on which; (interrog) what ... on; (zeitlich) whereupon; **~ du dich verlassen kannst** of that you can be sure.
woraus [vo'raus] adv (rel) from/out of which; (interrog) what ... from/out of.
worin [vo'rɪn] adv (rel) in which; (interrog) what ... in.
Wort [vɔrt] (-(e)s, ⁻er od -e) nt word; **jdm beim ~ nehmen** to take sb at his word; **ein ernstes ~ mit jdm reden** to have a serious talk with sb; **man kann sein eigenes ~ nicht (mehr) verstehen** man can't hear yourself speak; **jdm aufs ~ gehorchen** to obey sb's every word; **zu ~ kommen** to get a chance to speak; **jdm das ~ erteilen** to allow sb to speak; **~art** f (GRAM) part of speech; **w~brüchig** adj not true to one's word.
Wörtchen nt: **da habe ich wohl ein ~ mitzureden** (umg) I think I have some say in that.
Wörterbuch ['vœrtərbu:x] nt dictionary.
Wort- zW: **~fetzen** pl snatches pl of conversation; **~führer** m spokesman; **w~getreu** adj true to one's word; (Übersetzung) literal; **w~gewaltig** adj eloquent; **w~karg** adj taciturn; **~laut** m wording; **im ~laut** verbatim.

wörtlich ['vœrtlıç] *adj* literal.
Wort- *zW:* **w~los** *adj* mute; **~meldung** *f:* **wenn es keine weiteren ~meldungen gibt, ...** if nobody else wishes to speak ...; **w~reich** *adj* wordy, verbose; **~schatz** *m* vocabulary; **~spiel** *nt* play on words, pun; **~wechsel** *m* dispute; **w~wörtlich** *adj* word-for-word ♦ *adv* quite literally.
worüber [vo'ry:bər] *adv* (*rel*) over/about which; (*interrog*) what ... over/about.
worum [vo'rʊm] *adv* (*rel*) about/round which; (*interrog*) what ... about/round; **~ handelt es sich?** what's it about?
worunter [vo'rʊntər] *adv* (*rel*) under which; (*interrog*) what ... under.
wo- *zW:* **~von** [vo'fɔn] *adv* (*rel*) from which; (*interrog*) what ... from; **~vor** [vo'fɔr] *adv* (*rel*) in front of/before which; (*interrog*) in front of/before what; **~zu** [vo'tsu] *adv* (*rel*) to/for which; (*interrog*) what ... for/to; (*warum*) why; **~zu soll das gut sein?** what's the point of that?
Wrack [vrak] (*-*(*e*)*s, -s*) *nt* wreck.
wrang *etc* [vraŋ] *vb siehe* **wringen**.
wringen ['vrıŋən] *unreg vt* to wring.
WS *abk* = **Wintersemester**.
WSV *abk* = **Winterschlußverkauf**.
Wucher ['vu:xər] (*-s*) *m* profiteering; **~er** (*-s, -*) *m*, **~in** *f* profiteer; **w~isch** *adj* profiteering.
wuchern *vi* (*Pflanzen*) to grow wild.
Wucherpreis *m* exorbitant price.
Wucherung *f* (*MED*) growth.
Wuchs (*-es*) [vu:ks] *m* (*Wachstum*) growth; (*Statur*) build.
wuchs *etc vb siehe* **wachsen¹**.
Wucht [vʊxt] (*-*) *f* force.
wuchtig *adj* massive, solid.
wühlen ['vy:lən] *vi* to scrabble; (*Tier*) to root; (*Maulwurf*) to burrow; (*umg: arbeiten*) to slave away ♦ *vt* to dig.
Wühlmaus *f* vole.
Wühltisch *m* (*in Kaufhaus*) bargain counter.
Wulst [vʊlst] (*-es, -̈e*) *m* bulge; (*an Wunde*) swelling.
wulstig *adj* bulging; (*Rand, Lippen*) thick.
wund [vʊnt] *adj* sore; **sich** *dat* **die Füße ~ laufen** (*lit*) to get sore feet from walking; (*fig*) to walk one's legs off; **ein ~er Punkt** a sore point; **W~brand** *m* gangrene.
Wunde ['vʊndə] (*-, -n*) *f* wound; **alte ~n wieder aufreißen** (*fig*) to open up old wounds.
wunder ['vʊndər] *adv:* **meine Eltern denken ~ was passiert ist** my parents think goodness knows what has happened.
Wunder (*-s, -*) *nt* miracle; **es ist kein ~** it's no wonder; **w~bar** *adj* wonderful, marvellous (*BRIT*), marvelous (*US*); **~kerze** *f* sparkler; **~kind** *nt* child prodigy; **w~lich** *adj* odd, peculiar.
wundern *vt* to surprise ♦ *vr:* **sich ~ über** +*akk*

to be surprised at.
Wunder- *zW:* **w~schön** *adj* beautiful; **~tüte** *f* lucky bag; **w~voll** *adj* wonderful.
Wundfieber (*-s*) *nt* traumatic fever.
Wundstarrkrampf ['vʊntʃtarkrampf] *m* tetanus, lockjaw.
Wunsch [vʊnʃ] (*-*(*e*)*s, -̈e*) *m* wish; **haben Sie (sonst) noch einen ~?** (*beim Einkauf etc*) is there anything else you'd like?; **auf jds (besonderen/ausdrücklichen) ~ hin** at sb's (special/express) request; **~denken** *nt* wishful thinking.
Wünschelrute ['vynʃəlru:tə] *f* divining rod.
wünschen ['vynʃən] *vt* to wish ♦ *vi:* **zu ~/viel zu ~ übrig lassen** to leave something/a great deal to be desired; **sich** *dat* **etw ~** to want sth, wish for sth; **was ~ Sie?** (*in Geschäft*) what can I do for you?; (*in Restaurant*) what would you like?
wünschenswert *adj* desirable.
Wunsch- *zW:* **~kind** *nt* planned child; **~konzert** *nt* (*RUNDF*) musical request programme (*BRIT*) *od* program (*US*); **w~los** *adj:* **w~los glücklich** perfectly happy; **~traum** *m* dream; (*unrealistisch*) pipe dream; **~zettel** *m* list of things one would like.
wurde *etc* [vʊrdə] *vb siehe* **werden**.
Würde ['vyrdə] (*-, -n*) *f* dignity; (*Stellung*) honour (*BRIT*), honor (*US*); **unter aller ~ sein** to be beneath contempt.
Würdenträger *m* dignitary.
würdevoll *adj* dignified.
würdig ['vyrdıç] *adj* worthy; (*würdevoll*) dignified.
würdigen ['vyrdıgən] *vt* to appreciate; **etw zu ~ wissen** to appreciate sth; **jdn keines Blickes ~** not to so much as look at sb.
Wurf [vʊrf] (*-*(*e*)*s, -̈e*) *m* throw; (*Junge*) litter.
Würfel ['vyrfəl] (*-s, -*) *m* dice; (*MATH*) cube; **die ~ sind gefallen** the die is cast; **~becher** *m* (dice) cup.
würfeln *vi* to play dice ♦ *vt* to dice.
Würfelspiel *nt* game of dice.
Würfelzucker *m* lump sugar.
Wurf- *zW:* **~geschoß** *nt* projectile; **~sendung** *f* circular; **~sendungen** *pl* (*Reklame*) junk mail.
Würgegriff (*-*(*e*)*s*) *m* (*lit, fig*) stranglehold.
würgen ['vyrgən] *vt, vi* to choke; **mit Hängen und W~** by the skin of one's teeth.
Wurm [vʊrm] (*-*(*e*)*s, -̈er*) *m* worm; **da steckt der ~ drin** (*fig: umg*) there's something wrong somewhere; (*verdächtig*) there's something fishy about it (*umg*).
wurmen (*umg*) *vt* to rile, nettle.
Wurmfortsatz *m* (*MED*) appendix.
wurmig *adj* worm-eaten.
wurmstichig *adj* worm-ridden.
Wurst [vʊrst] (*-, -̈e*) *f* sausage; **das ist mir ~** (*umg*) I don't care, I don't give a damn; **jetzt geht es um die ~** (*fig: umg*) the moment of truth has come.

Würstchen ['vʏrstçən] *nt* frankfurter, hot dog sausage; ~**bude** *f*, ~**stand** *m* hot dog stall.
Württemberg ['vʏrtəmbɛrk] *nt* Württemberg.
Würze ['vʏrtsə] (-, -n) *f* seasoning.
Wurzel ['vʊrtsəl] (-, -n) *f* root; ~**n schlagen** (*lit*) to root; (*fig*) to put down roots; **die ~ aus 4 ist 2** (*MATH*) the square root of 4 is 2.
würzen *vt* to season; (*würzig machen*) to spice.
würzig *adj* spicy.
wusch *etc* [vuːʃ] *vb siehe* **waschen.**
wußte *etc* ['vʊstə] *vb siehe* **wissen.**
Wust [vuːst] (-(e)s) (*umg*) *m* (*Durcheinander*) jumble; (*Menge*) pile.
wüst [vyːst] *adj* untidy, messy; (*ausschweifend*) wild; (*öde*) waste; (*umg: heftig*) terrible; **jdn ~ beschimpfen** to use vile language to sb.
Wüste (-, -n) *f* desert; **die ~ Gobi** the Gobi Desert; **jdn in die ~ schicken** (*fig*) to send sb packing.
Wut [vuːt] (-) *f* rage, fury; **eine ~ (auf jdn/etw) haben** to be furious (with sb/sth); ~**anfall** *m* fit of rage.
wüten ['vyːtən] *vi* to rage.
wütend *adj* furious, enraged.
wutentbrannt *adj* furious, enraged.
Wz *abk* (= *Warenzeichen*) ®.

===== **X, x**

X, x [ɪks] *nt* X, x; ~ **wie Xanthippe** ≈ X for Xmas; **jdm ein ~ für ein U vormachen** to put one over on sb (*umg*).
X-Beine ['ɪksbaɪnə] *pl* knock-knees *pl*.
x-beliebig [ɪksbə'liːbɪç] *adj* any (... whatever).
Xerographie [kserogra'fiː] *f* xerography.
xerokopieren [kseroko'piːrən] *vt* to xerox, photocopy.
x-fach ['ɪksfax] *adj*: **die ~e Menge** (*MATH*) n times the amount.
x-mal ['ɪksmaːl] *adv* any number of times, n times.
x-te ['ɪkstə] *adj* (*MATH: umg*) nth; **zum ~n Male** (*umg*) for the nth *od* umpteenth time.
Xylophon [ksylo'foːn] (-s, -e) *nt* xylophone.

===== **Y, y**

Y, y ['ʏpsilɔn] *nt* Y, y; ~ **wie Ypsilon** ≈ Y for Yellow, Y for Yoke (*US*).
Yen [jɛn] (-(s), -(s)) *m* yen.
Yoga ['joːga] (-(s)) *m od nt* yoga.
Ypsilon ['ʏpsilɔn] (-(s), -s) *nt* the letter Y.

===== **Z, z**

Z, z [tsɛt] *nt* Z, z; ~ **wie Zacharias** ≈ Z for Zebra.
Zack [tsak] *m*: **auf ~ sein** (*umg*) to be on the ball.
Zacke ['tsakə] (-, -n) *f* point; (*Berg~*) jagged peak; (*Gabel~*) prong; (*Kamm~*) tooth.
zackig ['tsakıç] *adj* jagged; (*umg*) smart; (: *Tempo*) brisk.
zaghaft ['tsaːkhaft] *adj* timid.
Zaghaftigkeit *f* timidity.
Zagreb ['zaːgrɛp] (-s) *nt* Zagreb.
zäh [tsɛː] *adj* tough; (*Mensch*) tenacious; (*Flüssigkeit*) thick; (*schleppend*) sluggish; ~**flüssig** *adj* viscous; (*Verkehr*) slow-moving.
Zähigkeit *f* toughness; tenacity.
Zahl [tsaːl] (-, -en) *f* number.
zahlbar *adj* payable.
zahlen *vt, vi* to pay; ~ **bitte!** the bill *od* check (*US*) please!
zählen ['tsɛːlən] *vt* to count ♦ *vi* (*sich verlassen*): ~ **auf** +*akk* to count on; **seine Tage sind gezählt** his days are numbered; ~ **zu** to be numbered among.
Zahlen- *zW*: ~**angabe** *f* figure; ~**kombination** *f* combination of figures; **z~mäßig** *adj* numerical; ~**schloß** *nt* combination lock.
Zahler (-s, -) *m* payer.
Zähler (-s, -) *m* (*TECH*) meter; (*MATH*) numerator; ~**stand** *m* meter reading.
Zahl- *zW*: ~**grenze** *f* fare stage; ~**karte** *f* transfer form; **z~los** *adj* countless; ~**meister** *m* (*NAUT*) purser; **z~reich** *adj* numerous; ~**tag** *m* payday.
Zahlung *f* payment; **in ~ geben/nehmen** to give/take in part exchange.
Zahlungs- *zW*: ~**anweisung** *f* transfer order; ~**aufforderung** *f* request for payment;

z~fähig adj solvent; **~mittel** nt means sing of payment; (*Münzen, Banknoten*) currency; **~rückstände** pl arrears pl; **z~unfähig** adj insolvent; **~verzug** m default.

Zahlwort nt numeral.

zahm [tsa:m] adj tame.

zähmen ['tsɛ:mən] vt to tame; (*fig*) to curb.

Zahn [tsa:n] (-(e)s, ̈-e) m tooth; **die dritten Zähne** (*umg*) false teeth pl; **einen ~ draufhaben** (*umg: Geschwindigkeit*) to be going like the clappers (*BRIT*) od like crazy (*US*); **jdm auf den ~ fühlen** (*fig*) to sound sb out; **einen ~ zulegen** (*fig*) to get a move on; **~arzt** m, **~ärztin** f dentist; **~belag** m plaque; **~bürste** f toothbrush; **~creme** f toothpaste; **z~en** vi to teethe; **~ersatz** m denture; **~fäule** (-) f tooth decay, caries sing; **~fleisch** nt gums pl; **auf dem ~fleisch gehen** (*fig: umg*) to be all in, be at the end of one's tether; **z~los** adj toothless; **~medizin** f dentistry; **~pasta** f, **~paste** f toothpaste; **~rad** nt cog(wheel); **~radbahn** f rack railway; **~schmelz** m (tooth) enamel; **~schmerzen** pl toothache sing; **~seide** f dental floss; **~spange** f brace; **~stein** m tartar; **~stocher** (-s, -) m toothpick; **~techniker(in)** m(f) dental technician; **~weh** nt toothache.

Zaire [za'i:r] (-s) nt Zaire.

Zange ['tsaŋə] (-, -n) f pliers pl; (*Zucker~ etc*) tongs pl; (*Beiß~, ZOOL*) pincers pl; (*MED*) forceps pl; **jdn in die ~ nehmen** (*fig*) to put the screws on sb (*umg*).

Zangengeburt f forceps delivery.

Zankapfel m bone of contention.

zanken ['tsaŋkən] vi, vr to quarrel.

zänkisch ['tsɛŋkɪʃ] adj quarrelsome.

Zäpfchen ['tsɛpfçən] nt (*ANAT*) uvula; (*MED*) suppository.

Zapfen ['tsapfən] (-s, -) m plug; (*BOT*) cone; (*Eis~*) icicle.

zapfen vt to tap.

Zapfenstreich m (*MIL*) tattoo.

Zapfsäule f petrol (*BRIT*) od gas (*US*) pump.

zappelig ['tsapəlɪç] adj wriggly; (*unruhig*) fidgety.

zappeln ['tsapəln] vi to wriggle; to fidget; **jdn ~ lassen** (*fig: umg*) to keep sb in suspense.

Zar [tsa:r] (-en, -en) m tzar, czar.

zart [tsart] adj (*weich, leise*) soft; (*Braten etc*) tender; (*fein, schwächlich*) delicate; **~besaitet** adj attrib highly sensitive; **~bitter** adj (*Schokolade*) plain (*BRIT*), bittersweet (*US*); **Z~gefühl** nt tact; **Z~heit** f softness; tenderness; delicacy.

zärtlich ['tsɛ:rtlɪç] adj tender, affectionate; **Z~keit** f tenderness; **Zärtlichkeiten** pl caresses pl.

Zäsur [tsɛ'zu:r] f caesura; (*fig*) break.

Zauber ['tsaubər] (-s, -) m magic; (*~bann*) spell; **fauler ~** (*umg*) humbug.

Zauberei [tsaubə'raɪ] f magic.

Zauberer (-s, -) m magician; (*Zauberkünstler*) conjurer.

Zauber- zW: **z~haft** adj magical, enchanting; **~in** f magician; conjurer; **~künstler** m conjurer; **~kunststück** nt conjuring trick; **~mittel** nt magical cure; (*Trank*) magic potion.

zaubern vi to conjure, do magic.

Zauberspruch m (magic) spell.

Zauberstab m magic wand.

zaudern ['tsaudərn] vi to hesitate.

Zaum [tsaum] (-(e)s, Zäume) m bridle; **etw im ~ halten** to keep sth in check.

Zaun [tsaun] (-(e)s, Zäune) m fence; **vom ~ brechen** (*fig*) to start; **~gast** m (*Person*) mere onlooker; **~könig** m wren.

z.B. abk (= *zum Beispiel*) e.g.

z.d.A. abk (= *zu den Akten*) to be filed.

The **ZDF** *(Zweites Deutsches Fernsehen) is the second German television channel. It was founded in 1961 and is based in Mainz. It is financed by licence fees and advertising. About 40% of its transmissions are news and education programmes.*

Zebra ['tse:bra] (-s, -s) nt zebra; **~streifen** m pedestrian crossing (*BRIT*), crosswalk (*US*).

Zeche ['tsɛçə] (-, -n) f (*Rechnung*) bill, check (*US*); (*Bergbau*) mine.

zechen vi to booze (*umg*).

Zechprellerei [tsɛçprɛlə'raɪ] f skipping payment in restaurants etc.

Zecke ['tsɛkə] (-, -n) f tick.

Zeder ['tse:dər] (-, -n) f cedar.

Zeh [tse:] (-s, -en) m toe.

Zehe ['tse:ə] (-, -n) f toe; (*Knoblauch~*) clove.

Zehenspitze f: **auf ~n** on tiptoe.

zehn [tse:n] num ten.

Zehnerpackung f packet of ten.

Zehnfingersystem nt touch-typing method.

Zehnkampf m (*SPORT*) decathlon.

zehnte(r, s) adj tenth.

Zehntel (-s, -) nt tenth (part).

zehren ['tse:rən] vi: **an jdm/etw ~** (*an Mensch, Kraft*) to wear sb/sth out.

Zeichen ['tsaɪçən] (-s, -) nt sign; (*COMPUT*) character; **jdm ein ~ geben** to give sb a signal; **unser/Ihr ~** (*COMM*) our/your reference; **~block** m sketch pad; **~code** m (*COMPUT*) character code; **~erklärung** f key; (*auf Karten*) legend; **~folge** f (*COMPUT*) string; **~kette** f (*COMPUT*) character string; **~satz** m (*COMPUT*) character set; **~setzung** f punctuation; **~trickfilm** m (animated) cartoon.

zeichnen vt to draw; (*kenn~*) to mark; (*unter~*) to sign ♦ vi to draw; to sign.

Zeichner(in) (-s, -) m(f) artist; **technischer ~** draughtsman (*BRIT*), draftsman (*US*).

Zeichnung f drawing; (*Markierung*) markings pl.

zeichnungsberechtigt *adj* authorized to sign.

Zeigefinger *m* index finger.

zeigen ['tsaɪgən] *vt* to show ♦ *vi* to point ♦ *vr* to show o.s.; ~ **auf** +*akk* to point to; **es wird sich** ~ time will tell; **es zeigte sich, daß** ... it turned out that ...

Zeiger (-s, -) *m* pointer; (*Uhr~*) hand.

Zeile ['tsaɪlə] (-, -n) *f* line; (*Häuser~*) row.

Zeilen- *zW:* ~**abstand** *m* line spacing; ~**ausrichtung** *f* justification; ~**drucker** *m* line printer; ~**umbruch** *m* (*COMPUT*) wraparound; ~**vorschub** *m* (*COMPUT*) line feed.

zeit [tsaɪt] *präp* +*gen:* ~ **meines Lebens** in my lifetime.

Zeit (-, -en) *f* time; (*GRAM*) tense; **zur** ~ at the moment; **sich** *dat* ~ **lassen** to take one's time; **eine Stunde** ~ **haben** to have an hour (to spare); **sich** *dat* **für jdn/etw** ~ **nehmen** to devote time to sb/sth; **von** ~ **zu** ~ from time to time; **in letzter** ~ recently; **nach** ~ **bezahlt werden** to be paid by the hour; **zu der** ~, **als** ... (at the time) when ...

Zeit- *zW:* ~**alter** *nt* age; ~**ansage** *f* (*RUNDF*) time check; (*TEL*) speaking clock; ~**arbeit** *f* temporary work; ~**aufwand** *m* time (*needed for a task*); ~**bombe** *f* time bomb; ~**druck** *m:* **unter** ~**druck stehen** to be under pressure; ~**geist** *m* spirit of the times; **z~gemäß** *adj* in keeping with the times; ~**genosse** *m* contemporary; **z~genössisch** ['tsaɪtgənœsɪʃ] *adj* contemporary.

zeitig *adj, adv* early.

Zeit- *zW:* ~**karte** *f* season ticket; **z~kritisch** *adj* (*Aufsatz*) commenting on contemporary issues; ~**lang** *f:* **eine** ~**lang** a while, a time; **z~lebens** *adv* all one's life; **z~lich** *adj* temporal ♦ *adv:* **das kann sie z~lich nicht einrichten** she can't find (the) time for that; **das** ~**liche segnen** (*euph*) to depart this life; **z~los** *adj* timeless; ~**lupe** *f* slow motion; ~**lupentempo** *nt:* **im** ~**lupentempo** at a snail's pace; ~**not** *f:* **in** ~**not geraten** to run short of time; ~**plan** *m* schedule; ~**punkt** *m* moment, point in time; ~**raffer** (-s) *m* time-lapse photography; **z~raubend** *adj* time-consuming; ~**raum** *m* period; ~**rechnung** *f* time, era; **nach/vor unserer** ~**rechnung** A.D./B.C.; ~**schrift** *f* periodical; ~**tafel** *f* chronological table.

Zeitung *f* newspaper.

Zeitungs- *zW:* ~**anzeige** *f* newspaper advertisement; ~**ausschnitt** *m* press cutting; ~**händler** *m* newsagent (*BRIT*), newsdealer (*US*); ~**papier** *nt* newsprint.

Zeit- *zW:* ~**verschwendung** *f* waste of time; ~**vertreib** *m* pastime, diversion; **z~weilig** *adj* temporary; **z~weise** *adv* for a time; ~**wort** *nt* verb; ~**zeichen** *nt* (*RUNDF*) time signal; ~**zone** *f* time zone; ~**zünder** *m* time fuse.

Zelle ['tsɛlə] (-, -n) *f* cell; (*Telefon~*) callbox

(*BRIT*), booth.

Zellkern *m* cell, nucleus.

Zellophan [tsɛlo'faːn] (-s) *nt* cellophane.

Zellstoff *m* cellulose.

Zellteilung *f* cell division.

Zelt [tsɛlt] (-(e)s, -e) *nt* tent; **seine** ~**e aufschlagen/abbrechen** to settle down/pack one's bags; ~**bahn** *f* groundsheet; **z~en** *vi* to camp; ~**lager** *nt* camp; ~**platz** *m* camp site.

Zement [tse'mɛnt] (-(e)s, -e) *m* cement.

zementieren [tsemɛn'tiːrən] *vt* to cement.

Zementmaschine *f* cement mixer.

Zenit [tse'niːt] (-(e)s) *m* (*lit, fig*) zenith.

zensieren [tsɛn'ziːrən] *vt* to censor; (*SCH*) to mark.

Zensur [tsɛn'zuːr] *f* censorship; (*SCH*) mark.

Zensus ['tsɛnzʊs] (-, -) *m* census.

Zentimeter [tsɛnti'meːtər] *m od nt* centimetre (*BRIT*), centimeter (*US*); ~**maß** *nt* (metric) tape measure.

Zentner ['tsɛntnər] (-s, -) *m* hundredweight.

zentral [tsɛn'traːl] *adj* central.

Zentrale (-, -n) *f* central office; (*TEL*) exchange.

Zentraleinheit *f* (*COMPUT*) central processing unit.

Zentralheizung *f* central heating.

zentralisieren [tsɛntrali'ziːrən] *vt* to centralize.

Zentralverriegelung *f* (*AUT*) central locking.

Zentrifugalkraft [tsɛntrifu'gaːlkraft] *f* centrifugal force.

Zentrifuge [tsɛntri'fuːgə] (-, -n) *f* centrifuge; (*für Wäsche*) spin-dryer.

Zentrum ['tsɛntrʊm] (-s, Zentren) *nt* centre (*BRIT*), center (*US*).

Zepter ['tsɛptər] (-s, -) *nt* sceptre (*BRIT*), scepter (*US*).

zerbrechen *unreg vt, vi* to break.

zerbrechlich *adj* fragile.

zerbröckeln [tsɛr'brœkəln] *vt, vi* to crumble (to pieces).

zerdeppern [tsɛr'dɛpərn] *vt* to smash.

zerdrücken *vt* to squash; to crush; (*Kartoffeln*) to mash.

Zeremonie [tseremo'niː] *f* ceremony.

Zeremoniell [tseremoni'ɛl] (-s, -e) *nt* ceremonial.

zerfahren *adj* scatterbrained, distracted.

Zerfall *m* decay, disintegration; (*von Kultur, Gesundheit*) decline; **z~en** *unreg vi* to disintegrate, decay; (*sich gliedern*): **z~en in** +*akk* to fall into.

zerfetzen [tsɛr'fɛtsən] *vt* to tear to pieces.

zerfleischen [tsɛr'flaɪʃən] *vt* to tear to pieces.

zerfließen *unreg vi* to dissolve, melt away.

zerfressen *unreg vt* to eat away; (*Motten, Mäuse etc*) to eat.

zergehen *unreg vi* to melt, dissolve.

zerkleinern [tsɛr'klaɪnərn] *vt* to reduce to small pieces.

zerklüftet [tsɛr'klʏftət] *adj:* **tief ~es Gestein** deeply fissured rock.

zerknirscht [tsɛr'knɪrʃt] *adj* overcome with remorse.

zerknüllen [tsɛr'knʏlən] *vt* to crumple up.

zerlaufen *unreg vi* to melt.

zerlegbar [tsɛr'leːkbaːr] *adj* able to be dismantled.

zerlegen *vt* to take to pieces; (*Fleisch*) to carve; (*Satz*) to analyse.

zerlumpt [tsɛr'lʊmpt] *adj* ragged.

zermalmen [tsɛr'malmən] *vt* to crush.

zermürben [tsɛr'mʏrbən] *vt* to wear down.

zerpflücken *vt* (*lit, fig*) to pick to pieces.

zerplatzen *vi* to burst.

zerquetschen *vt* to squash.

Zerrbild ['tsɛrbɪlt] *nt* (*fig*) caricature, distorted picture.

zerreden *vt* (*Problem*) to flog to death.

zerreiben *unreg vt* to grind down.

zerreißen *unreg vt* to tear to pieces ♦ *vi* to tear, rip.

Zerreißprobe *f* (*lit*) pull test; (*fig*) real test.

zerren ['tsɛrən] *vt* to drag ♦ *vi:* ~ (**an** +*dat*) to tug (at).

zerrinnen *unreg vi* to melt away; (*Geld*) to disappear.

zerrissen [tsɛr'rɪsən] *pp von* **zerreißen** ♦ *adj* torn, tattered; **Z~heit** *f* tattered state; (*POL*) disunion, discord; (*innere*) disintegration.

Zerrspiegel ['tsɛrʃpiːgəl] *m* (*lit*) distorting mirror; (*fig*) travesty.

Zerrung *f:* **eine** ~ a pulled ligament/muscle.

zerrütten [tsɛr'rʏtən] *vt* to wreck, destroy.

zerrüttet *adj* wrecked, shattered.

Zerrüttungsprinzip *nt* (*bei Ehescheidung*) principle of irretrievable breakdown.

zerschellen [tsɛr'ʃɛlən] *vi* (*Schiff, Flugzeug*) to be smashed to pieces.

zerschießen *unreg vt* to shoot to pieces.

zerschlagen *unreg vt* to shatter, smash; (*fig: Opposition*) to crush; (*: Vereinigung*) to break up ♦ *vr* to fall through.

zerschleißen [tsɛr'ʃlaɪsən] *unreg vt, vi* to wear out.

zerschmelzen *unreg vi* to melt.

zerschmettern *unreg vt* to shatter; (*Feind*) to crush ♦ *vi* to shatter.

zerschneiden *unreg vt* to cut up.

zersetzen *vt, vr* to decompose, dissolve.

zersetzend *adj* (*fig*) subversive.

zersplittern [tsɛr'ʃplɪtərn] *vt, vi* to split (into pieces); (*Glas*) to shatter.

zerspringen *unreg vi* to shatter ♦ *vi* (*fig*) to burst.

zerstäuben [tsɛr'ʃtɔybən] *vt* to spray.

Zerstäuber (**-s, -**) *m* atomizer.

zerstören *vt* to destroy.

Zerstörer (**-s, -**) *m* (*NAUT*) destroyer.

Zerstörung *f* destruction.

Zerstörungswut *f* destructive mania.

zerstoßen *unreg vt* to pound, pulverize.

zerstreiten *unreg vr* to fall out, break up.

zerstreuen *vt* to disperse, scatter; (*Zweifel etc*) to dispel ♦ *vr* (*sich verteilen*) to scatter; (*fig*) to be dispelled; (*sich ablenken*) to take one's mind off things.

zerstreut *adj* scattered; (*Mensch*) absent-minded; **Z~heit** *f* absent-mindedness.

Zerstreuung *f* dispersion; (*Ablenkung*) diversion.

zerstritten *adj:* **mit jdm zerstritten sein** to be on very bad terms with sb.

zerstückeln [tsɛr'ʃtʏkəln] *vt* to cut into pieces.

zerteilen *vt* to divide into parts.

Zertifikat [tsɛrtifi'kaːt] (**-(e)s, -e**) *nt* certificate.

zertreten *unreg vt* to crush underfoot.

zertrümmern [tsɛr'trʏmərn] *vt* to shatter; (*Gebäude etc*) to demolish.

zerwühlen *vt* to ruffle up, tousle; (*Bett*) to rumple (up).

Zerwürfnis [tsɛr'vʏrfnɪs] (**-ses, -se**) *nt* dissension, quarrel.

zerzausen [tsɛr'tsauzən] *vt* (*Haare*) to ruffle up, tousle.

zetern ['tseːtərn] (*pej*) *vi* to clamour (*BRIT*), clamor (*US*); (*keifen*) to scold.

Zettel ['tsɛtəl] (**-s, -**) *m* piece *od* slip of paper; (*Notiz~*) note; (*Formular*) form; „*~* **ankleben verboten**" "stick no bills"; **~kasten** *m* card index (box); **~wirtschaft** (*pej*) *f:* **eine ~wirtschaft haben** to have bits of paper everywhere.

Zeug [tsɔyk] (**-(e)s, -e**) (*umg*) *nt* stuff; (*Ausrüstung*) gear; **dummes** ~ (stupid) nonsense; **das** ~ **haben zu** to have the makings of; **sich ins** ~ **legen** to put one's shoulder to the wheel; **was das** ~ **hält** for all one is worth; **jdm am** ~ **flicken** to find fault with sb.

Zeuge ['tsɔygə] (**-n, -n**) *m* witness.

zeugen *vi* to bear witness, testify ♦ *vt* (*Kind*) to father; **es zeugt von ...** it testifies to ...

Zeugenaussage *f* evidence.

Zeugenstand *m* witness box (*BRIT*) *od* stand (*US*).

Zeugin *f* witness.

Zeugnis ['tsɔygnɪs] (**-ses, -se**) *nt* certificate; (*SCH*) report; (*Referenz*) reference; (*Aussage*) evidence, testimony; ~ **geben von** to be evidence of, testify to; **~konferenz** *f* (*SCH*) *staff meeting to decide on marks etc*.

Zeugung ['tsɔygʊŋ] *f* procreation.

zeugungsunfähig *adj* sterile.

ZH *abk* = **Zentralheizung**.

z.H., z.Hd. *abk* (= *zu Händen*) att., attn.

Zicken ['tsɪkən] (*umg*) *pl:* ~ **machen** to make trouble.

zickig *adj* (*albern*) silly; (*prüde*) prudish.

Zickzack ['tsɪktsak] (**-(e)s, -e**) *m* zigzag.

Ziege ['tsiːgə] (**-, -n**) *f* goat; (*pej: umg: Frau*) cow (!).

Ziegel ['tsiːgəl] (**-s, -**) *m* brick; (*Dach~*) tile.

Ziegelei [tsiːgə'laɪ] *f* brickworks.

Ziegelstein *m* brick.
Ziegenbock *m* billy goat.
Ziegenleder *nt* kid.
Ziegenpeter *m* mumps *sing.*
Ziehbrunnen *m* well.
ziehen ['tsi:ən] *unreg vt* to draw; (*zerren*) to
pull; (*SCHACH etc*) to move; (*züchten*) to rear
♦ *vi* to draw; (*um~, wandern*) to move;
(*Rauch, Wolke etc*) to drift; (*reißen*) to pull
♦ *vb unpers:* **es zieht** there is a draught (*BRIT*)
od draft (*US*), it's draughty (*BRIT*) *od* drafty
(*US*) ♦ *vr* (*Gummi*) to stretch; (*Grenze etc*) to
run; (*Gespräche etc*) to be drawn out; **etw nach
sich ~** to lead to sth, entail sth; **etw ins
Lächerliche ~** to ridicule sth; **so was zieht
bei mir nicht** I don't like that sort of thing;
zu jdm ~ to move in with sb; **mir zieht's im
Rücken** my back hurts; **Z~** (**-s, -**) *nt*
(*Schmerz*) ache; (*im Unterleib*) dragging pain.
Ziehharmonika ['tsi:harmo:nika] *f*
concertina.
Ziehung ['tsi:ʊŋ] *f* (*Los~*) drawing.
Ziel [tsi:l] (**-(e)s, -e**) *nt* (*einer Reise*) destination;
(*SPORT*) finish; (*MIL*) target; (*Absicht*) goal,
aim; **jdm/sich ein ~ stecken** to set sb/o.s. a
goal; **am ~ sein** to be at one's destination;
(*fig*) to have reached one's goal; **über das
~ hinausschießen** (*fig*) to overshoot the
mark; **z~bewußt** *adj* purposeful; **z~en** *vi:*
z~en (auf +*akk*) to aim (at); **~fernrohr** *nt*
telescopic sight; **~foto** *nt* (*SPORT*) photo-
finish, photograph; **~gruppe** *f* target group;
~linie *f* (*SPORT*) finishing line; **z~los** *adj*
aimless; **~ort** *m* destination; **~scheibe** *f*
target; **z~strebig** *adj* purposeful.
ziemen ['tsi:mən] *vr unpers* (*geh*): **das ziemt
sich nicht (für dich)** it is not proper (for
you).
ziemlich ['tsi:mlɪç] *adj attrib* (*Anzahl*) fair ♦ *adv*
quite, pretty (*umg*); (*beinahe*) almost,
nearly; **eine ~e Anstrengung** quite an
effort; **~ lange** quite a long time; **~ fertig**
almost *od* nearly ready.
Zierde ['tsi:rdə] (**-, -n**) *f* ornament,
decoration; (*Schmuckstück*) adornment.
zieren ['tsi:rən] *vr* to act coy.
Zierleiste *f* border; (*an Wand, Möbeln*)
moulding (*BRIT*), molding (*US*); (*an Auto*)
trim.
zierlich *adj* dainty; **Z~keit** *f* daintiness.
Zierstrauch *m* flowering shrub.
Ziffer ['tsɪfər] (**-, -n**) *f* figure, digit; **römische/
arabische ~n** roman/arabic numerals;
~blatt *nt* dial, (clock *od* watch) face.
zig [tsɪk] (*umg*) *adj* umpteen.
Zigarette [tsiga'rɛtə] *f* cigarette.
Zigaretten- *zW:* **~automat** *m* cigarette
machine; **~pause** *f* break for a cigarette;
~schachtel *f* cigarette packet *od* pack (*US*);
~spitze *f* cigarette holder.
Zigarillo [tsiga'rɪlo] (**-s, -s**) *nt od m* cigarillo.
Zigarre [tsi'garə] (**-, -n**) *f* cigar.

Zigeuner(in) [tsi'gɔʏnər(ɪn)] (**-s, -**) *m(f)* gipsy;
~schnitzel *nt* (*KOCH*) cutlet served in a spicy
sauce with green and red peppers;
~sprache *f* Romany, Romany *od* Gypsy
language.
Zimmer ['tsɪmər] (**-s, -**) *nt* room; **~antenne** *f*
indoor aerial; **~decke** *f* ceiling; **~lautstärke**
f reasonable volume; **~mädchen** *nt*
chambermaid; **~mann** (**-(e)s,** *pl* **-leute**) *m*
carpenter.
zimmern *vt* to make from wood.
Zimmer- *zW:* **~nachweis** *m* accommodation
service; **~pflanze** *f* indoor plant;
~vermittlung *f* accommodation (*BRIT*) *od*
accommodations (*US*) service.
zimperlich ['tsɪmpərlɪç] *adj* squeamish;
(*pingelig*) fussy, finicky.
Zimt [tsɪmt] (**-(e)s, -e**) *m* cinnamon; **~stange** *f*
cinnamon stick.
Zink [tsɪŋk] (**-(e)s**) *nt* zinc.
Zinke (**-, -n**) *f* (*Gabel~*) prong; (*Kamm~*)
tooth.
Zinken (**-s, -**) (*umg*) *m* (*Nase*) hooter.
zinken *vt* (*Karten*) to mark.
Zinksalbe *f* zinc ointment.
Zinn [tsɪn] (**-(e)s**) *nt* (*Element*) tin; (*in ~waren*)
pewter; **~becher** *m* pewter tankard.
zinnoberrot [tsɪn'no:bərrot] *adj* vermilion.
Zinnsoldat *m* tin soldier.
Zinnwaren *pl* pewter *sing.*
Zins [tsɪns] (**-es, -en**) *m* interest.
Zinseszins *m* compound interest.
Zins- *zW:* **~fuß** *m* rate of interest; **z~los** *adj*
interest-free; **~satz** *m* rate of interest.
Zionismus [tsio'nɪsmʊs] *m* Zionism.
Zipfel ['tsɪpfəl] (**-s, -**) *m* corner; (*von Land*) tip;
(*Hemd~*) tail; (*Wurst~*) end; **~mütze** *f*
pointed cap.
zirka ['tsɪrka] *adv* (round) about.
Zirkel ['tsɪrkəl] (**-s, -**) *m* circle; (*MATH*) pair of
compasses; **~kasten** *m* geometry set.
zirkulieren [tsɪrku'li:rən] *vi* to circulate.
Zirkus ['tsɪrkʊs] (**-, -se**) *m* circus; (*umg: Getue*)
fuss, to-do.
zirpen ['tsɪrpən] *vi* to chirp, cheep.
Zirrhose [tsɪ'ro:zə] (**-, -n**) *f* cirrhosis.
zischeln ['tsɪʃəln] *vt, vi* to whisper.
zischen ['tsɪʃən] *vi* to hiss; (*Limonade*) to fizz;
(*Fett*) to sizzle.
Zitat [tsi'ta:t] (**-(e)s, -e**) *nt* quotation, quote.
zitieren [tsi'ti:rən] *vt* to quote; (*vorladen,
rufen*): **~ (vor** +*akk*) to summon (before).
Zitronat [tsitro'na:t] (**-(e)s, -e**) *nt* candied
lemon peel.
Zitrone [tsi'tro:nə] (**-, -n**) *f* lemon.
Zitronen- *zW:* **~limonade** *f* lemonade; **~saft**
m lemon juice; **~säure** *f* citric acid;
~scheibe *f* lemon slice.
zitt(e)rig ['tsɪt(ə)rɪç] *adj* shaky.
zittern ['tsɪtərn] *vi* to tremble; **vor jdm ~** to be
terrified of sb.
Zitze ['tsɪtsə] (**-, -n**) *f* teat, dug.

Zivi ['tsivi] (-s, -s) m abk = **Zivildienstleistender.**
zivil [tsi'vi:l] adj civilian; (anständig) civil; (Preis) moderate; ~er Ungehorsam civil disobedience; Z~ (-s) nt plain clothes pl; (MIL) civilian clothing; Z~bevölkerung f civilian population; Z~courage f courage of one's convictions.
Zivildienst m alternative service (for conscientious objectors).

> A young German has to complete his 15 months' **Zivildienst** or community service if he has opted out of military service as a conscientious objector. This service is usually done in a hospital or old-people's home. About 18% of young Germans choose to do this as an alternative to the **Wehrdienst**, although it lasts three months longer.

Zivildienstleistender m conscientious objector doing alternative community service.
Zivilisation [tsivilizatsi'o:n] f civilization.
Zivilisationserscheinung f phenomenon of civilization.
Zivilisationskrankheit f disease of civilized man.
zivilisieren [tsivili'zi:rən] vt to civilize.
zivilisiert adj civilized.
Zivilist [tsivi'lıst] m civilian.
Zivilrecht nt civil law.
ZK (-s, -s) nt abk (= Zentralkomitee) central committee.
Zobel ['tso:bəl] (-s, -) m (auch: ~pelz) sable (fur).
Zofe ['tso:fə] (-, -n) f lady's maid; (von Königin) lady-in-waiting.
zog etc [tso:k] vb siehe ziehen.
zögern ['tsø:gərn] vi to hesitate.
Zölibat [tsøli'ba:t] (-(e)s) nt od m celibacy.
Zoll¹ [tsɔl] (-(e)s, -) m (Maß) inch.
Zoll² (-(e)s, ̈e) m customs pl; (Abgabe) duty; ~abfertigung f customs clearance; ~amt nt customs office; ~beamte(r) m customs official; ~erklärung f customs declaration; z~frei adj duty-free; ~gutlager nt bonded warehouse; ~kontrolle f customs (check); z~pflichtig adj liable to duty, dutiable.
Zollstock m inch rule.
Zone ['tso:nə] (-, -n) f zone; (von Fahrkarte) fare stage.
Zoo [tso:] (-s, -s) m zoo; ~handlung f pet shop.
Zoologe [tsoo'lo:gə] (-n, -n) m zoologist.
Zoologie f zoology.
Zoologin f zoologist.
zoologisch adj zoological.
Zoom [zu:m] (-s, -s) nt zoom shot; (Objektiv) zoom lens.
Zopf [tsɔpf] (-(e)s, ̈e) m plait; pigtail; **alter** ~ antiquated custom.
Zorn [tsɔrn] (-(e)s) m anger.

zornig adj angry.
Zote ['tso:tə] (-, -n) f smutty joke/remark.
zottig ['tsɔtıç] adj shaggy.
ZPO abk (= Zivilprozeßordnung) ≈ General Practice Act (US).
z.T. abk = zum Teil.

zu [tsu:] präp +dat **1** (örtlich) to; ~m Bahnhof/Arzt gehen to go to the station/doctor; ~r Schule/Kirche gehen to go to school/church; sollen wir ~ Euch gehen? shall we go to your place?; sie sah ~ ihm hin she looked towards him; ~m Fenster herein through the window; ~ meiner Linken to od on my left

2 (zeitlich) at; ~ Ostern at Easter; bis ~m 1. Mai until May 1st; (nicht später als) by May 1st; ~ meiner Zeit in my time

3 (Zusatz) with; Wein ~m Essen trinken to drink wine with one's meal; sich ~ jdm setzen to sit down beside sb; setz dich doch ~ uns (come and) sit with us; Anmerkungen ~ etw notes on sth

4 (Zweck) for; Wasser ~m Waschen water for washing; Papier ~m Schreiben paper to write on; etw ~m Geburtstag bekommen to get sth for one's birthday; es ist ~ seinem Besten it's for his own good

5 (Veränderung) into; ~ etw werden to turn into sth; jdn ~ etw machen to make sb (into) sth; ~ Asche verbrennen to burn to ashes

6 (mit Zahlen): 3 ~ 2 (SPORT) 3-2; das Stück ~ 2 Mark at 2 marks each; ~m ersten Mal for the first time

7: ~ meiner Freude etc to my joy etc; ~m Glück luckily; ~ Fuß on foot; es ist ~m Weinen it's enough to make you cry

♦ konj to; etw ~ essen sth to eat; um besser sehen ~ können in order to see better; ohne es ~ wissen without knowing it; noch ~ bezahlende Rechnungen outstanding bills

♦ adv **1** (allzu) too; ~ sehr too much

2 (örtlich) toward(s); er kam auf mich ~ he came towards od up to me

3 (geschlossen) shut; closed; die Geschäfte haben ~ the shops are closed; auf/zu (Wasserhahn etc) on/off

4 (umg: los): nur ~! just keep at it!; mach ~! hurry up!

zuallererst adv first of all.
zuallerletzt adv last of all.
zubauen ['tsu:bauən] vt (Lücke) to fill in; (Platz, Gebäude) to build up.
Zubehör ['tsu:bəhø:r] (-(e)s, -e) nt accessories pl.
Zuber ['tsu:bər] (-s, -) m tub.
zubereiten ['tsu:bəraıtən] vt to prepare.
zubilligen ['tsu:bılıgən] vt to grant.
zubinden ['tsu:bındən] unreg vt to tie up; **jdm**

die Augen ~ to blindfold sb.
zubleiben ['tsuːblaɪbən] *unreg vi* to stay shut.
zubringen ['tsuːbrɪŋən] *unreg vt* to spend;
(*herbeibringen*) to bring, take; (*umg: Tür*) to
get shut.
Zubringer **(-s, -)** *m* (*TECH*) feeder, conveyor;
(*Verkehrsmittel*) shuttle; (*zum Flughafen*)
airport bus; ~**(bus)** *m* shuttle (bus); ~**straße**
f slip road (*BRIT*), entrance ramp (*US*).
Zucchini [tsʊˈkiːniː] *pl* courgettes *pl* (*BRIT*),
zucchini(s) *pl* (*US*).
Zucht [tsʊxt] **(-, -en)** *f* (*von Tieren*) breeding;
(*von Pflanzen*) cultivation; (*Rasse*) breed;
(*Erziehung*) raising; (*Disziplin*) discipline;
~**bulle** *m* breeding bull.
züchten ['tsʏçtən] *vt* (*Tiere*) to breed;
(*Pflanzen*) to cultivate, grow.
Züchter(in) **(-s, -)** *m(f)* breeder; grower.
Zuchthaus *nt* prison, penitentiary (*US*).
Zuchthengst *m* stallion, stud.
züchtig ['tsʏçtɪç] *adj* modest, demure.
züchtigen ['tsʏçtɪgən] *vt* to chastise.
Züchtigung *f* chastisement; **körperliche** ~
corporal punishment.
Zuchtperle *f* cultured pearl.
Züchtung *f* (*von Tieren*) breeding; (*von
Pflanzen*) cultivation; (*Zuchtart: von Tier*)
breed; (: *von Pflanze*) strain.
zucken ['tsʊkən] *vi* to jerk, twitch; (*Strahl etc*)
to flicker ♦ *vt* to shrug; **der Schmerz zuckte
(mir) durch den ganzen Körper** the pain shot
right through my body.
zücken ['tsʏkən] *vt* (*Schwert*) to draw;
(*Geldbeutel*) to pull out.
Zucker ['tsʊkər] **(-s, -)** *m* sugar; (*MED*)
diabetes; ~ **haben** (*umg*) to be a diabetic;
~**dose** *f* sugar bowl; ~**erbse** *f* mangetout
(*BRIT*), sugar pea (*US*); ~**guß** *m* icing; ~**hut**
m sugar loaf; **z**~**krank** *adj* diabetic;
~**krankheit** *f* diabetes *sing*; ~**lecken** *nt*: **das
ist kein** ~**lecken** it's no picnic.
zuckern *vt* to sugar.
Zucker- *zW*: ~**rohr** *nt* sugar cane; ~**rübe** *f*
sugar beet; ~**spiegel** *m* (*MED*) (blood) sugar
level; **z**~**süß** *adj* sugary; ~**watte** *f* candy
floss (*BRIT*), cotton candy (*US*).
Zuckung *f* convulsion, spasm; (*leicht*) twitch.
zudecken ['tsuːdɛkən] *vt* to cover (up); (*im
Bett*) to tuck up *od* in.
zudem [tsuˈdeːm] *adv* in addition (to this).
zudrehen ['tsuːdreːən] *vt* to turn off.
zudringlich ['tsuːdrɪŋlɪç] *adj* forward, pushy;
(*Nachbar etc*) intrusive; ~ **werden** to make
advances; **Z**~**keit** *f* forwardness;
intrusiveness.
zudrücken ['tsuːdrʏkən] *vt* to close; **jdm die
Kehle** ~ to throttle sb; **ein Auge** ~ to turn a
blind eye.
zueinander [tsuˈaɪˈnandər] *adv* to one other;
(*in Verbverbindung*) together.
zuerkennen ['tsuːˈɛrkɛnən] *unreg vt*: **jdm etw** ~
to award sth to sb, award sb sth.

zuerst [tsuˈʔeːrst] *adv* first; (*zu Anfang*) at first;
~ **einmal** first of all.
Zufahrt ['tsuːfaːrt] *f* approach; „**keine** ~ **zum
Krankenhaus**" "no access to hospital".
Zufahrtsstraße *f* approach road; (*von
Autobahn etc*) slip road (*BRIT*), entrance
ramp (*US*).
Zufall ['tsuːfal] *m* chance; (*Ereignis*)
coincidence; **durch** ~ by accident; **so ein** ~!
what a coincidence!
zufallen *unreg vi* to close, shut; (*Anteil,
Aufgabe*): **jdm** ~ to fall to sb.
zufällig ['tsuːfɛlɪç] *adj* chance ♦ *adv* by chance;
(*in Frage*) by any chance.
Zufallstreffer *m* fluke.
zufassen ['tsuːfasən] *vi* (*zugreifen*) to take hold
(of it *od* them); (*fig: schnell handeln*) to seize
the opportunity; (*helfen*) to lend a hand.
zufliegen ['tsuːfliːgən] *unreg vi*: **ihm fliegt alles
nur so zu** (*fig*) everything comes so easily to
him.
Zuflucht ['tsuːflʊxt] *f* recourse; (*Ort*) refuge;
zu etw ~ **nehmen** (*fig*) to resort to sth.
Zufluchtsort *m*, **Zufluchtsstätte** *f* place of
refuge.
Zufluß ['tsuːflʊs] *m* (*Zufließen*) inflow, influx;
(*GEOG*) tributary; (*COMM*) supply.
zufolge [tsuˈfɔlgə] *präp* +*dat od* +*gen* judging by;
(*laut*) according to; (*aufgrund*) as a result of.
zufrieden [tsuˈfriːdən] *adj* content(ed); **er ist
mit nichts** ~ nothing pleases him; ~**geben**
unreg vr: **sich mit etw** ~**geben** to be satisfied
with sth; **Z**~**heit** *f* contentedness;
(*Befriedigtsein*) satisfaction; ~**lassen** *unreg vt*:
laß mich damit ~! (*umg*) shut up about it!;
~**stellen** *vt* to satisfy; ~**stellend** *adj*
satisfactory.
zufrieren ['tsuːfriːrən] *unreg vi* to freeze up *od*
over.
zufügen ['tsuːfyːgən] *vt* to add; (*Leid etc*): **jdm
etw** ~ to cause sb sth.
Zufuhr ['tsuːfuːr] **(-, -en)** *f* (*Herbeibringen*)
supplying; (*MET*) influx; (*MIL*) supplies *pl*.
zuführen ['tsuːfyːrən] *vt* (*bringen*) to bring;
(*transportieren*) to convey; (*versorgen*) to
supply ♦ *vi*: **auf etw** *akk* ~ to lead to sth.
Zug [tsuːk] **(-(e)s, ̈-e)** *m* (*Eisenbahn*~) train;
(*Luft*~) draught (*BRIT*), draft (*US*); (*Ziehen*)
pull(ing); (*Gesichts*~) feature; (*SCHACH etc*)
move; (*Klingel*~) pull; (*Schrift*~, *beim
Schwimmen*) stroke; (*Atem*~) breath;
(*Charakter*~) trait; (*an Zigarette*) puff, pull,
drag; (*Schluck*) gulp; (*Menschengruppe*)
procession; (*von Vögeln*) migration; (*MIL*)
platoon; **etw in vollen Zügen genießen** to
enjoy sth to the full; **in den letzten Zügen
liegen** (*umg*) to be at one's last gasp; **im** ~**(e)**
+*gen* (*im Verlauf*) in the course of; ~ **um** ~
(*fig*) step by step; **zum** ~**(e) kommen** (*umg*)
to get a look-in; **etw in groben Zügen
darstellen** *od* **umreißen** to outline sth; **das
war kein schöner** ~ **von dir** that wasn't nice

of you.

Zugabe ['tsu:ga:bə] *f* extra; (*in Konzert etc*) encore.

Zugabteil *nt* train compartment.

Zugang ['tsu:gaŋ] *m* entrance; (*Zutritt, fig*) access.

zugänglich ['tsu:gɛŋlıç] *adj* accessible; (*öffentliche Einrichtungen*) open; (*Mensch*) approachable.

Zugbegleiter *m* (*EISENB*) guard (*BRIT*), conductor (*US*).

Zugbrücke *f* drawbridge.

zugeben ['tsu:ge:bən] *unreg vt* (*beifügen*) to add, throw in; (*zugestehen*) to admit; (*erlauben*) to permit; **zugegeben ...** granted ...

zugegebenermaßen ['tsu:gegə:bənər'ma:sən] *adv* admittedly.

zugegen [tsu'ge:gən] *adv* (*geh*): ~ **sein** to be present.

zugehen ['tsu:ge:ən] *unreg vi* (*schließen*) to shut ♦ *vi unpers* (*sich ereignen*) to go on, happen; **auf jdn/etw** ~ to walk towards sb/ sth; **dem Ende** ~ to be finishing; **er geht schon auf die Siebzig zu** he's getting on for seventy; **hier geht es nicht mit rechten Dingen zu** there's something odd going on here; **dort geht es ... zu** things are ... there.

Zugehörigkeit ['tsu:gəhø:rıçkaıt] *f*: ~ (**zu**) membership (of), belonging (to).

Zugehörigkeitsgefühl *nt* feeling of belonging.

zugeknöpft ['tsu:gəknœpft] (*umg*) *adj* reserved, stand-offish.

Zügel ['tsy:gəl] (**-s, -**) *m* rein, reins *pl*; (*fig*) rein, curb; **die ~ locker lassen** to slacken one's hold on the reins; **die ~ locker lassen bei** (*fig*) to give free rein to.

zugelassen ['tsu:gəlasən] *adj* authorized; (*Heilpraktiker*) registered; (*Kfz*) licensed.

zügellos *adj* unrestrained; (*sexuell*) licentious.

Zügellosigkeit *f* lack of restraint; licentiousness.

zügeln *vt* to curb; (*Pferd*) to rein in.

zugesellen *vr*: **sich jdm** ~ to join sb, join up with sb.

Zugeständnis ['tsu:gəʃtɛntnıs] (**-ses, -se**) *nt* concession; **~se machen** to make allowances.

zugestehen *unreg vt* to admit; (*Rechte*) to concede.

zugetan ['tsu:gəta:n] *adj*: **jdm/etw** ~ **sein** to be fond of sb/sth.

Zugewinn (**-(e)s**) *m* (*JUR*) *property acquired during marriage.*

Zugezogene(r) ['tsu:gətso:gənə(r)] *f(m)* newcomer.

Zugführer *m* (*EISENB*) chief guard (*BRIT*) *od* conductor (*US*); (*MIL*) platoon commander.

zugig *adj* draughty (*BRIT*), drafty (*US*).

zügig ['tsy:gıç] *adj* speedy, swift.

zugkräftig *adj* (*fig: Werbetext, Titel*) eye-catching; (*Schauspieler*) crowd-pulling *attr*, popular.

zugleich [tsu'glaıç] *adv* (*zur gleichen Zeit*) at the same time; (*ebenso*) both.

Zugluft *f* draught (*BRIT*), draft (*US*).

Zugmaschine *f* traction engine, tractor.

zugreifen ['tsu:graıfən] *unreg vi* to seize *od* grab it/them; (*helfen*) to help; (*beim Essen*) to help o.s.

Zugriff ['tsu:grıf] *m* (*COMPUT*) access; **sich dem ~ der Polizei entziehen** (*fig*) to evade justice.

zugrunde [tsu'grondə] *adv*: ~ **gehen** to collapse; (*Mensch*) to perish; **er wird daran nicht ~ gehen** he'll survive; (*finanziell*) it won't ruin him; **einer Sache** *dat* **etw ~ legen** to base sth on sth; **einer Sache** *dat* ~ **liegen** to be based on sth; ~ **richten** to ruin, destroy.

zugunsten [tsu'gunstən] *präp +gen od +dat* in favour (*BRIT*) *od* favor (*US*) of.

zugute [tsu'gu:tə] *adv*: **jdm etw ~ halten** to concede sth to sb; **jdm ~ kommen** to be of assistance to sb.

Zug- *zW*: **~verbindung** *f* train connection; **~vogel** *m* migratory bird; **~zwang** *m* (*SCHACH*) zugzwang; **unter ~zwang stehen** (*fig*) to be in a tight spot.

zuhalten ['tsu:haltən] *unreg vt* to hold shut ♦ *vi*: **auf jdn/etw** ~ to make for sb/sth; **sich** *dat* **die Nase** ~ to hold one's nose.

Zuhälter ['tsu:hɛltər] (**-s, -**) *m* pimp.

zuhause [tsu'haʊzə] *adv* at home.

Zuhause (**-s**) *nt* home.

Zuhilfenahme [tsu'hılfəna:mə] *f*: **unter ~ von** with the help of.

zuhören ['tsu:hø:rən] *vi* to listen.

Zuhörer (**-s, -**) *m* listener; **~schaft** *f* audience.

zujubeln ['tsu:ju:bəln] *vi*: **jdm** ~ to cheer sb.

zukehren ['tsu:ke:rən] *vt* (*zuwenden*) to turn.

zuklappen ['tsu:klapən] *vt* (*Buch, Deckel*) to close ♦ *vi* (*Hilfsverb sein: Tür etc*) to click shut.

zukleben ['tsu:kle:bən] *vt* to paste up.

zukneifen ['tsu:knaıfən] *vt* (*Augen*) to screw up; (*Mund*) to shut tight(ly).

zuknöpfen ['tsu:knœpfən] *vt* to button (up), fasten (up).

zukommen ['tsu:kɔmən] *unreg vi* to come up; **auf jdn** ~ to come up to sb; **jdm** ~ (*sich gehören*) to be fitting for sb; **diesem Treffen kommt große Bedeutung zu** this meeting is of the utmost importance; **jdm etw** ~ **lassen** to give sb sth; **die Dinge auf sich** *akk* ~ **lassen** to take things as they come.

Zukunft ['tsu:kunft] (**-, no pl**) *f* future.

zukünftig ['tsu:kynftıç] *adj* future ♦ *adv* in future; **mein ~er Mann** my husband-to-be.

Zukunfts- *zW*: **~aussichten** *pl* future prospects *pl*; **~musik** (*umg*) *f* wishful thinking; **~roman** *m* science-fiction novel;

z~trächtig adj promising for the future;
z~weisend adj trend-setting.
Zulage ['tsu:la:gə] f bonus.
zulande [tsu'landə] adv: **bei uns ~** in our
country.
zulangen ['tsu:laŋən] (umg) vi (Dieb, beim
Essen) to help o.s.
zulassen ['tsu:lasən] unreg vt (hereinlassen) to
admit; (erlauben) to permit; (Auto) to
license; (umg: nicht öffnen) to keep shut.
zulässig ['tsu:lɛsɪç] adj permissible,
permitted; **~e Höchstgeschwindigkeit**
(upper) speed limit.
Zulassung f (amtlich) authorization; (von Kfz)
licensing; (als praktizierender Arzt)
registration.
Zulauf m: **großen ~ haben** (Geschäft) to be
very popular.
zulaufen ['tsu:laufən] unreg vi: **~ auf** +akk to run
towards; **jdm ~** (Tier) to adopt sb; **spitz ~** to
come to a point.
zulegen ['tsu:le:gən] vt to add; (Geld) to put in;
(Tempo) to accelerate, quicken; (schließen)
to cover over; **sich** dat **etw ~** (umg) to get
oneself sth.
zuleide [tsu'laɪdə] adj: **jdm etw ~ tun** to harm
sb.
zuleiten ['tsu:laɪtən] vt (Wasser) to supply;
(schicken) to send.
Zuleitung f (TECH) supply.
zuletzt [tsu'lɛtst] adv finally, at last; **wir**
blieben bis ~ we stayed to the very end;
nicht ~ wegen not least because of.
zuliebe [tsu'li:bə] adv: **jdm ~** (in order) to
please sb.
Zulieferbetrieb ['tsu:li:fərbətri:p] m (COMM)
supplier.
zum [tsʊm] = **zu dem**; **~ dritten Mal** for the
third time; **~ Scherz** as a joke; **~ Trinken**
for drinking; **bis ~ 15. April** until 15th April;
(nicht später als) by 15th April; **~ ersten**
Mal(e) for the first time; **es ist ~ Weinen** it's
enough to make you (want to) weep;
~ Glück luckily.
zumachen ['tsu:maxən] vt to shut; (Kleidung)
to do up, fasten ♦ vi to shut; (umg) to hurry
up.
zumal [tsu'ma:l] konj especially (as).
zumeist [tsu'maɪst] adv mostly.
zumessen ['tsu:mɛsən] unreg vt (+dat) (Zeit) to
allocate (for); (Bedeutung) to attach (to).
zumindest [tsu'mɪndəst] adv at least.
zumutbar [tsu'mu:tba:r] adj reasonable.
zumute [tsu'mu:tə] adv: **wie ist ihm ~?** how
does he feel?
zumuten ['tsu:mu:tən] vt: **(jdm) etw ~** to
expect od ask sth (of sb); **sich** dat **zuviel ~** to
take on too much.
Zumutung f unreasonable expectation od
demand; (Unverschämtheit) impertinence;
das ist eine ~! that's a bit much!
zunächst [tsu'nɛ:çst] adv first of all; **~ einmal**

to start with.
zunageln ['tsu:na:gəln] vt (Fenster etc) to nail
up; (Kiste etc) to nail down.
zunähen ['tsu:nɛ:ən] vt to sew up.
Zunahme ['tsu:na:mə] (-, -n) f increase.
Zuname ['tsu:na:mə] m surname.
zünden ['tsyndən] vi (Feuer) to light, ignite;
(Motor) to fire; (fig) to kindle enthusiasm
♦ vt to ignite; (Rakete) to fire.
zündend adj fiery.
Zünder (-s, -) m fuse; (MIL) detonator.
Zünd- zW: **~holz** nt match; **~kabel** nt (AUT)
plug lead; **~kerze** f (AUT) spark(ing) plug;
~plättchen nt cap; **~schlüssel** m ignition
key; **~schnur** f fuse wire; **~stoff** m fuel;
(fig) dynamite.
Zündung f ignition.
zunehmen ['tsu:ne:mən] unreg vi to increase,
grow; (Mensch) to put on weight.
zunehmend adj: **mit ~em Alter** with
advancing age.
zuneigen ['tsu:naɪgən] vi to incline, lean; **sich**
dem Ende ~ to draw to a close; **einer**
Auffassung ~ to incline towards a view; **jdm**
zugeneigt sein to be attracted to sb.
Zuneigung f affection.
Zunft [tsʊnft] (-, ̈-e) f guild.
zünftig ['tsynftɪç] adj (Arbeit) professional;
(umg: ordentlich) proper, real.
Zunge ['tsʊŋə] f tongue; (Fisch) sole; **böse ~n**
behaupten, ... malicious gossip has it ...
züngeln ['tsyŋəln] vi (Flammen) to lick.
Zungenbrecher m tongue-twister.
zungenfertig adj glib.
Zünglein ['tsyŋlaɪn] nt: **das ~ an der Waage**
sein (fig) to tip the scales.
zunichte [tsu'nɪçtə] adv: **~ machen** to ruin,
destroy; **~ werden** to come to nothing.
zunutze [tsu'nʊtsə] adv: **sich** dat **etw ~ machen**
to make use of sth.
zuoberst [tsu'|o:bərst] adv at the top.
zuordnen ['tsu:|ɔrdnən] vt to assign.
zupacken ['tsu:pakən] (umg) vi (zugreifen) to
make a grab for it; (bei der Arbeit) to get
down to it; **mit ~** (helfen) to give me/them
etc a hand.
zupfen ['tsʊpfən] vt to pull, pick, pluck;
(Gitarre) to pluck.
zur [tsu:r] = **zu der**.
zurechnungsfähig ['tsu:rɛçnʊŋsfɛ:ɪç] adj
(JUR) responsible, of sound mind; **Z~keit** f
responsibility, accountability.
zurecht- zW: **~biegen** unreg vt to bend into
shape; (fig) to twist; **~finden** unreg vr to find
one's way (about); **~kommen** unreg vi
(rechtzeitig kommen) to come in time;
(schaffen) to cope; (finanziell) to manage;
~legen vt to get ready; (Ausrede etc) to have
ready; **~machen** vt to prepare ♦ vr to get
ready; (sich schminken) to put on one's
make-up; **~weisen** unreg vt to reprimand;
Z~weisung f reprimand, rebuff.

zureden ['tsuːreːdən] *vi:* **jdm** ~ to persuade sb, urge sb.

zureiten ['tsuraɪtən] *unreg vt* (*Pferd*) to break in.

Zürich ['tsyːrɪç] (**-s**) *nt* Zurich.

zurichten ['tsuːrɪçtən] *vt* (*Essen*) to prepare; (*beschädigen*) to batter, bash up.

zürnen ['tsʏrnən] *vi:* **jdm** ~ to be angry with sb.

zurück [tsu'rʏk] *adv* back; (*mit Zahlungen*) behind; (*fig: ~geblieben: von Kind*) backward; ~! get back!; ~**behalten** *unreg vt* to keep back; **er hat Schäden** ~**behalten** he suffered lasting damage; ~**bekommen** *unreg vt* to get back; ~**bezahlen** *vt* to repay, pay back; ~**bleiben** *unreg vi* (*Mensch*) to remain behind; (*nicht nachkommen*) to fall behind, lag; (*Schaden*) to remain; ~**bringen** *unreg vt* to bring back; ~**datieren** *vt* to backdate; ~**drängen** *vt* (*Gefühle*) to repress; (*Feind*) to push back; ~**drehen** *vt* to turn back; ~**erobern** *vt* to reconquer; ~**erstatten** *vt* to refund; ~**fahren** *unreg vi* to travel back; (*vor Schreck*) to recoil ♦ *vt* to drive back; ~**fallen** *unreg vi* to fall back; (*in Laster*) to relapse; (*in Leistungen*) to fall behind; (*an Besitzer*): ~**fallen an** *+akk* to revert to; ~**finden** *unreg vi* to find one's way back; ~**fordern** *vt* to demand back; ~**führen** *vt* to lead back; **etw auf etw** *akk* ~**führen** to trace sth back to sth; ~**geben** *unreg vt* to give back; (*antworten*) to retort with; ~**geblieben** *adj* retarded; ~**gehen** *unreg vi* to go back; (*fallen*) to go down, fall; (*zeitlich*): ~**gehen (auf** *+akk*) to date back (to); **Waren** ~**gehen lassen** to send back goods; ~**gezogen** *adj* retired, withdrawn; ~**greifen** *unreg vi:* ~**greifen (auf** *+akk*) (*fig*) to fall back (upon); (*zeitlich*) to go back (to); ~**halten** *unreg vt* to hold back; (*Mensch*) to restrain; (*hindern*) to prevent ♦ *vr* (*reserviert sein*) to be reserved; (*im Essen*) to hold back; (*im Hintergrund bleiben*) to keep in the background; (*bei Verhandlung*) to keep a low profile; ~**haltend** *adj* reserved; **Z**~**haltung** *f* reserve; ~**holen** *vt* (*COMPUT: Daten*) to retrieve; ~**kehren** *vi* to return; ~**kommen** *unreg vi* to come back; **auf etw** *akk* ~**kommen** to return to sth; ~**lassen** *unreg vt* to leave behind; ~**legen** *vt* to put back; (*Geld*) to put by; (*reservieren*) to keep back; (*Strecke*) to cover ♦ *vr* to lie back; ~**liegen** *unreg vi:* **der Unfall liegt etwa eine Woche** ~ the accident was about a week ago; ~**nehmen** *unreg vt* to take back; ~**reichen** *vi* (*Tradition etc*): ~**reichen (in** *+akk*) to go back (to); ~**rufen** *unreg vt, vi* to call back; **etw ins Gedächtnis** ~**rufen** to recall sth; ~**schrauben** *vt:* **seine Ansprüche** ~**schrauben** to lower one's sights; ~**schrecken** *vi:* ~**schrecken vor** *+dat* to shrink from; **vor nichts** ~**schrecken** to stop at nothing; ~**setzen** *vt* to put back; (*im Preis*) to reduce;

(*benachteiligen*) to put at a disadvantage ♦ *vi* (*mit Fahrzeug*) to reverse, back; ~**stecken** *vt* to put back ♦ *vi* (*fig*) to moderate one's wishes; ~**stellen** *vt* to put back, replace; (*aufschieben*) to put off, postpone; (*MIL*) to turn down; (*Interessen*) to defer; (*Ware*) to keep; **persönliche Interessen hinter etw** *dat* ~**stellen** to put sth before one's personal interests; ~**stoßen** *unreg vt* to repulse; ~**stufen** *vt* to downgrade; ~**treten** *unreg vi* to step back; (*vom Amt*) to retire; (*von einem Vertrag etc*): ~**treten (von)** to withdraw (from); **gegenüber** *od* **hinter etw** *dat* ~**treten** to diminish in importance in view of sth; **bitte** ~**treten!** stand back, please!; ~**verfolgen** *vt* (*fig*) to trace back; ~**versetzen** *vt* (*in alten Zustand*): ~**versetzen (in** *+akk*) to restore (to) ♦ *vr:* **sich** ~**versetzen (in** *+akk*) to think back (to); ~**weichen** *unreg vi:* ~**weichen (vor** *+dat*) to shrink back (from); ~**weisen** *unreg vt* to turn down; (*Mensch*) to reject; ~**werfen** *unreg vt* (*Ball, Kopf*) to throw back; (*Strahlen, Schall*) to reflect; (*fig: Feind*) to repel; (: *wirtschaftlich*): ~**werfen (um)** to set back (by); ~**zahlen** *vt* to pay back, repay; **Z**~**zahlung** *f* repayment; ~**ziehen** *unreg vt* to pull back; (*Angebot*) to withdraw ♦ *vr* to retire.

Zuruf ['tsuːruːf] *m* shout, cry.

zus. *abk* = **zusammen; zusätzlich**.

Zusage ['tsuːzaːgə] *f* promise; (*Annahme*) consent.

zusagen *vt* to promise ♦ *vi* to accept; **jdm etw auf den Kopf** ~ (*umg*) to tell sb sth outright; **jdm** ~ (*gefallen*) to appeal to *od* please sb.

zusammen [tsu'zamən] *adv* together; **Z**~**arbeit** *f* cooperation; ~**arbeiten** *vi* to cooperate; **Z**~**ballung** *f* accumulation; ~**bauen** *vt* to assemble; ~**beißen** *unreg vt* (*Zähne*) to clench; ~**bleiben** *unreg vi* to stay together; ~**brauen** (*umg*) *vt* to concoct ♦ *vr* (*Gewitter, Unheil etc*) to be brewing; ~**brechen** *unreg vi* (*Hilfsverb sein*) to collapse; (*Mensch*) to break down, collapse; (*Verkehr etc*) to come to a standstill; ~**bringen** *unreg vt* to bring *od* get together; (*Geld*) to get; (*Sätze*) to put together; **Z**~**bruch** *m* collapse; (*COMPUT*) crash; ~**fahren** *unreg vi* to collide; (*erschrecken*) to start; ~**fallen** *unreg vi* (*einstürzen*) to collapse; (*Ereignisse*) to coincide; ~**fassen** *vt* to summarize; (*vereinigen*) to unite; ~**fassend** *adj* summarizing ♦ *adv* to summarize; **Z**~**fassung** *f* summary, résumé; ~**finden** *unreg vi, vr* to meet (together); ~**fließen** *unreg vi* to flow together, meet; **Z**~**fluß** *m* confluence; ~**fügen** *vt* to join (together), unite; ~**führen** *vt* to bring together; (*Familie*) to reunite; ~**gehören** *vi* to belong together; (*Paar*) to match; **Z**~**gehörigkeitsgefühl** *nt* sense of belonging; ~**gesetzt** *adj* compound, composite; ~**gewürfelt** *adj* motley; ~**halten**

unreg vt to hold together ♦ *vi* to hold together; (*Freunde, fig*) to stick together; **Z~hang** *m* connection; **im/aus dem Z~hang** in/out of context; **etw aus dem Z~hang reißen** to take sth out of its context; **~hängen** *unreg vi* to be connected *od* linked; **~hängend** *adj* (*Erzählung*) coherent; **~hang(s)los** *adj* incoherent; **~klappbar** *adj* folding, collapsible; **~klappen** *vt* (*Messer etc*) to fold ♦ *vi* (*umg: Mensch*) to flake out; **~knüllen** *vt* to crumple up; **~kommen** *unreg vi* to meet, assemble; (*sich ereignen*) to occur at once *od* together; **~kramen** *vt* to gather (together); **Z~kunft** (-, -künfte) *f* meeting; **~laufen** *unreg vi* to run *od* come together; (*Straßen, Flüsse etc*) to converge, meet; (*Farben*) to run into one another; **~legen** *vt* to put together; (*stapeln*) to pile up; (*falten*) to fold; (*verbinden*) to combine, unite; (*Termine, Feste*) to combine; (*Geld*) to collect; **~nehmen** *unreg vt* to summon up ♦ *vr* to pull o.s. together; **alles ~genommen** all in all; **~passen** *vi* to go well together, match; **Z~prall** *m* (*lit*) collision; (*fig*) clash; **~prallen** *vi* (*Hilfsverb sein*) to collide; **~reimen** (*umg*) *vt:* **das kann ich mir nicht ~reimen** I can't make head nor tail of this; **~reißen** *unreg vr* to pull o.s. together; **~rotten** *unreg* (*pej*) *vr* to gang up; **~schlagen** *unreg vt* (*jdn*) to beat up; (*Dinge*) to smash up; (*falten*) to fold; (*Hände*) to clap; (*Hacken*) to click; **~schließen** *unreg vt, vr* to join (together); **Z~schluß** *m* amalgamation; **~schmelzen** *unreg vi* (*verschmelzen*) to fuse; (*zerschmelzen*) to melt (away); (*Anzahl*) to dwindle; **~schrecken** *unreg vi* to start; **~schreiben** *unreg vt* to write together; (*Bericht*) to put together; **~schrumpfen** *vi* (*Hilfsverb sein*) to shrink, shrivel up; **Z~sein** (-s) *nt* get-together; **~setzen** *vt* to put together ♦ *vr:* **sich ~setzen aus** to consist of; **Z~setzung** *f* composition; **Z~spiel** *nt* teamwork; (*von Kräften etc*) interaction; **~stellen** *vt* to put together; **Z~stellung** *f* list; (*Vorgang*) compilation; **Z~stoß** *m* collision; **~stoßen** *unreg vi* (*Hilfsverb sein*) to collide; **~strömen** *vi* (*Hilfsverb sein: Menschen*) to flock together; **~tragen** *unreg vt* to collect; **Z~treffen** *nt* meeting; (*Zufall*) coincidence; **~treffen** *unreg vi* (*Hilfsverb sein*) to coincide; (*Menschen*) to meet; **~treten** *unreg vi* (*Verein etc*) to meet; **~wachsen** *unreg vi* to grow together; **~wirken** *vi* to combine; **~zählen** *vt* to add up; **~ziehen** *unreg vt* (*verengern*) to draw together; (*vereinigen*) to bring together; (*addieren*) to add up ♦ *vr* to shrink; (*sich bilden*) to form, develop; **~zucken** *vi* (*Hilfsverb sein*) to start.

Zusatz ['tsu:zats] *m* addition; **~antrag** *m* (*POL*) amendment; **~gerät** *nt* attachment.
zusätzlich ['tsu:zɛtslɪç] *adj* additional.
Zusatzmittel *nt* additive.

zuschauen ['tsu:ʃauən] *vi* to watch, look on.
Zuschauer (-s, -) *m* spectator ♦ *pl* (*THEAT*) audience *sing.*
zuschicken ['tsu:ʃɪkən] *vt:* **jdm etw ~** to send *od* forward sth to sb.
zuschießen ['tsu:ʃi:sən] *unreg vt* to fire; (*Geld*) to put in ♦ *vi:* **~ auf** *+akk* to rush towards.
Zuschlag ['tsu:ʃla:k] *m* extra charge; (*Erhöhung*) surcharge; (*EISENB*) supplement.
zuschlagen ['tsu:ʃla:gən] *unreg vt* (*Tür*) to slam; (*Ball*) to hit; (*bei Auktion*) to knock down; (*Steine etc*) to knock into shape ♦ *vi* (*Fenster, Tür*) to shut; (*Mensch*) to hit, punch.
zuschlagfrei *adj* (*EISENB*) not subject to a supplement.
zuschlagpflichtig *adj* subject to surcharge.
Zuschlagskarte *f* (*EISENB*) supplementary ticket.
zuschließen ['tsu:ʃli:sən] *unreg vt* to lock (up).
zuschmeißen ['tsu:ʃmaisən] *unreg* (*umg*) *vt* to slam, bang shut.
zuschmieren ['tsu:ʃmi:rən] *vt* to smear over; (*Löcher*) to fill in.
zuschneiden ['tsu:ʃnaidən] *unreg vt* to cut to size; (*NÄHEN*) to cut out; **auf etw** *akk* **zugeschnitten sein** (*fig*) to be geared to sth.
zuschnüren ['tsu:ʃny:rən] *vt* to tie up; **die Angst schnürte ihm die Kehle zu** (*fig*) he was choked with fear.
zuschrauben ['tsu:ʃraubən] *vt* to screw shut.
zuschreiben ['tsu:ʃraibən] *unreg vt* (*fig*) to ascribe, attribute; (*COMM*) to credit; **das hast du dir selbst zuzuschreiben** you've only got yourself to blame.
Zuschrift ['tsu:ʃrɪft] *f* letter, reply.
zuschulden [tsu'ʃuldən] *adv:* **sich** *dat* **etw ~ kommen lassen** to make o.s. guilty of sth.
Zuschuß ['tsu:ʃus] *m* subsidy.
Zuschußbetrieb *m* loss-making concern.
zuschütten ['tsu:ʃʏtən] *vt* to fill up.
zusehen ['tsu:ze:ən] *unreg vi* to watch; (*dafür sorgen*) to take care; (*etw dulden*) to sit back (and watch); **jdm/etw ~** to watch sb/sth.
zusehends *adv* visibly.
zusein ['tsu:zain] *unreg vi* to be closed.
zusenden ['tsu:zɛndən] *unreg vt* to forward, send on.
zusetzen ['tsu:zɛtsən] *vt* (*beifügen*) to add; (*Geld*) to lose ♦ *vi:* **jdm ~** to harass sb; (*Krankheit*) to take a lot out of sb; (*unter Druck setzen*) to lean on sb (*umg*); (*schwer treffen*) to hit sb hard.
zusichern ['tsu:zɪçərn] *vt:* **jdm etw ~** to assure sb of sth.
Zusicherung *f* assurance.
zusperren ['tsu:ʃpɛrən] *vt* to bar.
zuspielen ['tsu:ʃpi:lən] *vt, vi* to pass; **jdm etw ~** to pass sth to sb; (*fig*) to pass sth on to sb; **etw der Presse ~** to leak sth to the press.
zuspitzen ['tsu:ʃpɪtsən] *vt* to sharpen ♦ *vr* (*Lage*) to become critical.
zusprechen ['tsu:ʃprɛçən] *unreg vt*

(*zuerkennen*): **jdm etw** ~ to award sb sth, award sth to sb ♦ *vi:* **jdm** ~ to speak to sb; **jdm Trost** ~ to comfort sb; **dem Essen/ Alkohol** ~ to eat/drink a lot.

Zuspruch ['tsuːʃprʊx] *m* encouragement; (*Anklang*) popularity.

Zustand ['tsuːʃtant] *m* state, condition; **in gutem/schlechtem** ~ in good/poor condition; (*Haus*) in good/bad repair; **Zustände bekommen** *od* **kriegen** (*umg*) to have a fit.

zustande [tsuˈʃtandə] *adv:* ~ **bringen** to bring about; ~ **kommen** to come about.

zuständig ['tsuːʃtɛndɪç] *adj* competent, responsible; **Z~keit** *f* competence, responsibility; **Z~keitsbereich** *m* area of responsibility.

zustatten [tsuˈʃtatən] *adj:* **jdm** ~ **kommen** (*geh*) to come in useful for sb.

zustehen ['tsuːʃteːən] *unreg vi:* **jdm** ~ to be sb's right.

zusteigen ['tsuːʃtaɪɡən] *unreg vi:* **noch jemand zugestiegen?** (*in Zug*) any more tickets?

zustellen ['tsuːʃtɛlən] *vt* (*verstellen*) to block; (*Post etc*) to send.

Zustellung *f* delivery.

zusteuern ['tsuːʃtɔyərn] *vi:* **auf etw** *akk* ~ to head for sth; (*beim Gespräch*) to steer towards sth ♦ *vt* (*beitragen*) to contribute.

zustimmen ['tsuːʃtɪmən] *vi* to agree.

Zustimmung *f* agreement; (*Einwilligung*) consent; **allgemeine** ~ **finden** to meet with general approval.

zustoßen ['tsuːʃtoːsən] *unreg vi* (*fig*): **jdm** ~ to happen to sb.

Zustrom ['tsuːʃtroːm] *m* (*fig: Menschenmenge*) stream (of visitors *etc*); (*hineinströmend*) influx; (*MET*) inflow.

zustürzen ['tsuːʃtyrtsən] *vi:* **auf jdn/etw** ~ to rush up to sb/sth.

zutage [tsuˈtaːɡə] *adv:* ~ **bringen** to bring to light; ~ **treten** to come to light.

Zutaten ['tsuːtaːtən] *pl* ingredients *pl*; (*fig*) accessories *pl*.

zuteil [tsuˈtaɪl] *adv* (*geh*): **jdm wird etw** ~ sb is granted sth, sth is granted to sb.

zuteilen ['tsuːtaɪlən] *vt* to allocate, assign.

zutiefst [tsuˈtiːfst] *adv* deeply.

zutragen ['tsuːtraːɡən] *unreg vt:* **jdm etw** ~ to bring sb sth, bring sth to sb ♦ *vt* (*Klatsch*) to tell sb sth ♦ *vr* to happen.

zuträglich ['tsuːtrɛːklɪç] *adj* beneficial.

zutrauen ['tsuːtrauən] *vt:* **jdm etw** ~ to credit sb with sth; **sich** *dat* **nichts** ~ to have no confidence in o.s.; **jdm viel** ~ to think a lot of sb; **jdm wenig** ~ not to think much of sb; **Z~** (-**s**) *nt:* **Z~** (**zu**) trust (in); **zu jdm Z~ fassen** to begin to trust sb.

zutraulich *adj* trusting; (*Tier*) friendly; **Z~keit** *f* trust.

zutreffen ['tsuːtrɛfən] *unreg vi* to be correct; (*gelten*) to apply.

zutreffend *adj* (*richtig*) accurate; **Z~es bitte unterstreichen** please underline where applicable.

zutrinken ['tsuːtrɪŋkən] *unreg vi:* **jdm** ~ to drink to sb.

Zutritt ['tsuːtrɪt] *m* access; (*Einlaß*) admittance; **kein** ~, ~ **verboten** no admittance.

zutun ['tsuːtuːn] *unreg vt* to add; (*schließen*) to shut.

Zutun (-**s**) *nt* assistance.

zuunterst [tsuˈʔʊntərst] *adv* right at the bottom.

zuverlässig ['tsuːfɛrlɛsɪç] *adj* reliable; **Z~keit** *f* reliability.

Zuversicht ['tsuːfɛrzɪçt] (-) *f* confidence; **z~lich** *adj* confident; **Z~lichkeit** *f* confidence.

zuviel [tsuˈfiːl] *adv* too much; (*umg: zu viele*) too many; **er kriegt** ~ (*umg*) he gets annoyed.

zuvor [tsuˈfoːr] *adv* before, previously.

zuvorderst [tsuˈfɔrdərst] *adv* right at the front.

zuvorkommen *unreg vi +dat* to anticipate; (*Gefahr etc*) to forestall; **jdm** ~ to beat sb to it.

zuvorkommend *adj* courteous; (*gefällig*) obliging.

Zuwachs ['tsuːvaks] (-**es**) *m* increase, growth; (*umg*) addition.

zuwachsen *unreg vi* to become overgrown; (*Wunde*) to heal (up).

Zuwachsrate *f* rate of increase.

zuwandern ['tsuːvandərn] *vi* to immigrate.

zuwege [tsuˈveːɡə] *adv:* **etw** ~ **bringen** to accomplish sth; **mit etw** ~ **kommen** to manage sth; **gut** ~ **sein** to be (doing) well.

zuweilen [tsuˈvaɪlən] *adv* at times, now and then.

zuweisen ['tsuːvaɪzən] *unreg vt* to assign, allocate.

zuwenden ['tsuːvɛndən] *unreg vt +dat* to turn towards ♦ *vr +dat* to turn to; (*sich widmen*) to devote o.s. to; **jdm seine Aufmerksamkeit** ~ to give sb one's attention.

Zuwendung *f* (*Geld*) financial contribution; (*Liebe*) love and care.

zuwenig [tsuˈveːnɪç] *adv* too little; (*umg: zu wenige*) too few.

zuwerfen ['tsuːvɛrfən] *unreg vt:* **jdm etw** ~ to throw sth to sb, throw sb sth.

zuwider [tsuˈviːdər] *adv:* **etw ist jdm** ~ sb loathes sth, sb finds sth repugnant ♦ *präp +dat* contrary to; ~**handeln** *vi +dat* to act contrary to; **einem Gesetz** ~**handeln** to contravene a law; **Z~handlung** *f* contravention; ~**laufen** *unreg vi:* **einer Sache** *dat* ~**laufen** to run counter to sth.

zuz. *abk* = **zuzüglich**.

zuzahlen [tsuˈtsaːlən] *vt:* **10 Mark** ~ to pay another 10 marks.

zuziehen ['tsuːtsiːən] *unreg vt* (*schließen:*

Vorhang) to draw, close; (*herbeirufen: Experten*) to call in ♦ *vi* to move in, come; **sich** *dat* **etw** ~ (*Krankheit*) to catch sth; (*Zorn*) to incur sth; **sich** *dat* **eine Verletzung** ~ (*form*) to sustain an injury.

Zuzug ['tsu:tsuk] (-(e)s) *m* (*Zustrom*) influx; (*von Familie etc*): ~ **nach** move to.

zuzüglich ['tsu:tsy:klıç] *präp +gen* plus, with the addition of.

zuzwinkern ['tsu:tsvınkərn] *vi:* **jdm** ~ to wink at sb.

ZVS *f abk* (= *Zentralstelle für die Vergabe von Studienplätzen*) *central body organizing the granting of places at university*.

Zwang (-(e)s, ̈e) *m* compulsion; (*Gewalt*) coercion; **gesellschaftliche Zwänge** social constraints; **tu dir keinen** ~ **an** don't feel you have to be polite.

zwang *etc* [tsvaŋ] *vb siehe* **zwingen**.

zwängen ['tsvɛŋən] *vt, vr* to squeeze.

Zwang- *zW:* **z~haft** *adj* compulsive; **z~los** *adj* informal; **~losigkeit** *f* informality.

Zwangs- *zW:* **~abgabe** *f* (*COMM*) compulsory levy; **~arbeit** *f* forced labour (*BRIT*) *od* labor (*US*); **~ernährung** *f* force-feeding; **~jacke** *f* straitjacket; **~lage** *f* predicament, tight corner; **z~läufig** *adj* inevitable; **~maßnahme** *f* compulsory measure; (*POL*) sanction; **~vollstreckung** *f* execution; **~vorstellung** *f* (*PSYCH*) obsession; **z~weise** *adv* compulsorily.

zwanzig ['tsvantsıç] *num* twenty.

zwanzigste(r, s) *adj* twentieth.

zwar [tsva:r] *adv* to be sure, indeed; **das ist** ~ **..., aber ...** that may be ... but ...; **und** ~ **in** fact, actually; **und** ~ **am Sonntag** on Sunday to be precise; **und** ~ **so schnell, daß ...** in fact so quickly that ...

Zweck [tsvɛk] (-(e)s, -e) *m* purpose, aim; **es hat keinen** ~, **darüber zu reden** there is no point (in) talking about it; **z~dienlich** *adj* practical; (*nützlich*) useful; **z~dienliche Hinweise** (any) relevant information.

Zwecke (-, -n) *f* hobnail; (*Heft~*) drawing pin (*BRIT*), thumbtack (*US*).

Zweck- *zW:* **z~entfremden** *vt untr* to use for another purpose; **~entfremdung** *f* misuse; **z~frei** *adj* (*Forschung etc*) pure; **z~los** *adj* pointless; **z~mäßig** *adj* suitable, appropriate; **~mäßigkeit** *f* suitability.

zwecks *präp +gen* (*form*) for (the purpose of).

zweckwidrig *adj* unsuitable.

zwei [tsvaı] *num* two; **Z~bettzimmer** *nt* twin-bedded room; **~deutig** *adj* ambiguous; (*unanständig*) suggestive; **Z~drittelmehrheit** *f* (*PARL*) two-thirds majority; **~eiig** *adj* (*Zwillinge*) non-identical.

zweierlei ['tsvaıər'laı] *adj* two kinds *od* sorts of; ~ **Stoff** two different kinds of material; ~ **zu tun haben** to have two different things to do.

zweifach *adj* double.

Zweifel ['tsvaıfəl] (-s, -) *m* doubt; **ich bin mir darüber im** ~ I'm in two minds about it; **z~haft** *adj* doubtful, dubious; **z~los** *adj* doubtless.

zweifeln *vi:* (**an etw** *dat*) ~ to doubt (sth).

Zweifelsfall *m:* **im** ~ in case of doubt.

Zweifrontenkrieg *m* war(fare) on two fronts.

Zweig [tsvaık] (-(e)s, -e) *m* branch; **~geschäft** *nt* (*COMM*) branch.

zweigleisig ['tsvaıglaızıç] *adj:* ~ **argumentieren** to argue along two different lines.

Zweigstelle *f* branch (office).

zwei- *zW:* **~händig** *adj* two-handed; (*MUS*) for two hands; **Z~heit** *f* duality; **~hundert** *num* two hundred; **Z~kampf** *m* duel; **~mal** *adv* twice; **das lasse ich mir nicht ~mal sagen** I don't have to be told twice; **~motorig** *adj* twin-engined; **~reihig** *adj* (*Anzug*) double-breasted; **Z~samkeit** *f* togetherness; **~schneidig** *adj* (*fig*) double-edged; **Z~sitzer** (-s, -) *m* two-seater; **~sprachig** *adj* bilingual; **~spurig** *adj* (*AUT*) two-lane; **Z~spur(tonband)gerät** *nt* twin-track (tape) recorder; **~stellig** *adj* (*Zahl*) two-digit *attrib*, with two digits; **~stimmig** *adj* for two voices.

zweit [tsvaıt] *adv:* **zu** ~ (*in Paaren*) in twos.

Zweitaktmotor *m* two-stroke engine.

zweitbeste(r, s) *adj* second best.

zweite(r, s) *adj* second; **Bürger** ~**r Klasse** second-class citizen(s *pl*).

zweiteilig ['tsvaıtaılıç] *adj* (*Buch, Film etc*) in two parts; (*Kleidung*) two-piece.

zweitens *adv* secondly.

zweit- *zW:* **~größte(r, s)** *adj* second largest; **~klassig** *adj* second-class; **~letzte(r, s)** *adj* last but one, penultimate; **~rangig** *adj* second-rate; **Z~schlüssel** *m* duplicate key; **Z~stimme** *f* second vote; *siehe auch* **Erststimme**.

zweitürig ['tsvaıty:rıç] *adj* two-door.

Zweitwagen *m* second car.

Zweitwohnung *f* second home.

zweizeilig *adj* two-lined; (*TYP: Abstand*) double-spaced.

Zweizimmerwohnung *f* two-room(ed) flat (*BRIT*) *od* apartment (*US*).

Zwerchfell ['tsvɛrçfɛl] *nt* diaphragm.

Zwerg(in) [tsvɛrk, 'tsvɛrgın] (-(e)s, -e) *m(f)* dwarf; (*fig: Knirps*) midget; **~schule** (*umg*) *f* village school.

Zwetschge ['tsvɛtʃgə] (-, -n) *f* plum.

Zwickel ['tsvıkəl] (-s, -) *m* gusset.

zwicken ['tsvıkən] *vt* to pinch, nip.

Zwickmühle ['tsvıkmy:lə] *f:* **in der** ~ **sitzen** (*fig*) to be in a dilemma.

Zwieback ['tsvi:bak] (-(e)s, -e *od* -bäcke) *m* rusk.

Zwiebel ['tsvi:bəl] (-, -n) *f* onion; (*Blumen~*) bulb; **z~artig** *adj* bulbous; **~turm** *m* (tower with an) onion dome.

Zwie- *zw:* ~**gespräch** *nt* dialogue (*BRIT*), dialog (*US*); ~**licht** *nt* twilight; **ins** ~**licht geraten sein** (*fig*) to appear in an unfavourable (*BRIT*) *od* unfavorable (*US*) light; **z**~**lichtig** *adj* shady, dubious; ~**spalt** *m* conflict; (*zwischen Menschen*) rift, gulf; **z**~**spältig** *adj* (*Gefühle*) conflicting; (*Charakter*) contradictory; ~**tracht** *f* discord, dissension.

Zwilling ['tsvɪlɪŋ] (-s, -e) *m* twin; **Zwillinge** *pl* (*ASTROL*) Gemini.

zwingen ['tsvɪŋən] *unreg vt* to force.

zwingend *adj* (*Grund etc*) compelling; (*logisch notwendig*) necessary; (*Schluß, Beweis*) conclusive.

Zwinger (-s, -) *m* (*Käfig*) cage; (*Hunde*~) run.

zwinkern ['tsvɪŋkərn] *vi* to blink; (*absichtlich*) to wink.

Zwirn [tsvɪrn] (-(e)s, -e) *m* thread.

zwischen ['tsvɪʃən] *präp* (*+akk od dat*) between; (*bei mehreren*) among; **Z**~**aufenthalt** *m* stopover; **Z**~**bemerkung** *f* (*incidental*) remark; **Z**~**bilanz** *f* (*COMM*) interim balance; ~**blenden** *vt* (*FILM, RUNDF, TV*) to insert; **Z**~**ding** *nt* cross; **Z**~**dividende** *f* interim dividend; ~**durch** *adv* in between; (*räumlich*) here and there; **Z**~**ergebnis** *nt* intermediate result; **Z**~**fall** *m* incident; **Z**~**frage** *f* question; **Z**~**größe** *f* in-between size; **Z**~**handel** *m* wholesaling; **Z**~**händler** *m* middleman, agent; **Z**~**lagerung** *f* temporary storage; **Z**~**landung** *f* (*AVIAT*) stopover; **Z**~**lösung** *f* temporary solution; ~**mahlzeit** *f* snack (*between meals*); ~**menschlich** *adj* interpersonal; **Z**~**prüfung** *f* intermediate examination; **Z**~**raum** *m* gap, space; **Z**~**ruf** *m*

interjection, interruption; **Zwischenrufe** *pl* heckling *sing*; **Z**~**saison** *f* low season; **Z**~**spiel** *nt* (*THEAT, fig*) interlude; (*MUS*) intermezzo; ~**staatlich** *adj* interstate; (*international*) international; **Z**~**station** *f* intermediate station; **Z**~**stecker** *m* (*ELEK*) adapter; **Z**~**stück** *nt* connecting piece; **Z**~**summe** *f* subtotal; **Z**~**wand** *f* partition; **Z**~**zeit** *f* interval; **in der Z**~**zeit** in the interim, meanwhile; **Z**~**zeugnis** *nt* (*SCH*) interim report.

Zwist [tsvɪst] (-es, -e) *m* dispute.

zwitschern ['tsvɪtʃərn] *vt, vi* to twitter, chirp; **einen** ~ (*umg*) to have a drink.

Zwitter ['tsvɪtər] (-s, -) *m* hermaphrodite.

zwo [tsvoː] *num* (*TEL, MIL*) two.

zwölf [tsvœlf] *num* twelve; **fünf Minuten vor** ~ (*fig*) at the eleventh hour.

Zwölffingerdarm (-(e)s) *m* duodenum.

Zyankali [tsyaːn'kaːli] (-s) *nt* (*CHEM*) potassium cyanide.

Zyklon [tsy'kloːn] (-s, -e) *m* cyclone.

Zyklus ['tsyːklʊs] (-, **Zyklen**) *m* cycle.

Zylinder [tsi'lɪndər] (-s, -) *m* cylinder; (*Hut*) top hat; **z**~**förmig** *adj* cylindrical.

Zyniker(in) ['tsyːnikər(ɪn)] (-s, -) *m(f)* cynic.

zynisch ['tsyːnɪʃ] *adj* cynical.

Zynismus [tsy'nɪsmʊs] *m* cynicism.

Zypern ['tsyːpərn] (-s) *nt* Cyprus.

Zypresse [tsy'prɛsə] (-, -n) *f* (*BOT*) cypress.

Zypriot(in) [tsypri'oːt(ɪn)] (-en, -en) *m(f)* Cypriot.

zypriotisch *adj* Cypriot, Cyprian.

zyprisch ['tsyːprɪʃ] *adj* Cypriot, Cyprian.

Zyste ['tsʏstə] (-, -n) *f* cyst.

z.Z(t). *abk* = **zur Zeit**.

English–German

Englisch–Deutsch

A, a

A¹, a [eɪ] n (letter) A nt, a nt; (SCOL) ≈ Eins f, Sehr gut nt; ~ **for Andrew,** (US) ~ **for Able** ≈ A wie Anton; ~ **road** (BRIT: AUT) Hauptverkehrsstraße f; ~ **shares** (BRIT: STOCK EXCHANGE) stimmrechtslose Aktien pl.

A² [eɪ] n (MUS) A nt, a nt.

a [ə] (before vowel or silent h: **an**) indef art **1** ein; (before feminine noun) eine; ~ **book** ein Buch; ~ **lamp** eine Lampe; **she's** ~ **doctor** sie ist Ärztin; **I haven't got** ~ **car** ich habe kein Auto; ~ **hundred/thousand** etc **pounds** einhundert/eintausend etc Pfund
2 (in expressing ratios, prices etc) pro; **3** ~ **day/week** 3 pro Tag/Woche, 3 am Tag/in der Woche; **10 km an hour** 10 km pro Stunde.

a. abbr = **acre.**
AA n abbr (BRIT: = Automobile Association) Autofahrerorganisation, ≈ ADAC m; (US: = Associate in/of Arts) akademischer Grad für Geisteswissenschaftler; (= Alcoholics Anonymous) Anonyme Alkoholiker pl, AA pl; = **anti-aircraft.**
AAA n abbr (= American Automobile Association) Autofahrerorganisation, ≈ ADAC m; (BRIT: = Amateur Athletics Association) Leichtathletikverband der Amateure.
A & R n abbr (MUS: = artists and repertoire): ~ **person** Talentsucher(in) m(f).
AAUP n abbr (= American Association of University Professors) Verband amerikanischer Universitätsprofessoren.
AB abbr (BRIT) = **able-bodied seaman;** (CANADA: = Alberta).
abaci ['æbəsaɪ] npl of **abacus.**
aback [ə'bæk] adv: **to be taken** ~ verblüfft sein.

abacus ['æbəkəs] (pl **abaci**) n Abakus m.
abandon [ə'bændən] vt verlassen; (child) aussetzen; (give up) aufgeben ♦ n (wild behaviour): **with** ~ selbstvergessen; **to** ~ **ship** das Schiff verlassen.
abandoned [ə'bændənd] adj verlassen; (child) ausgesetzt; (unrestrained) selbstvergessen.
abase [ə'beɪs] vt: **to** ~ **o.s.** sich erniedrigen; **to** ~ **o.s. so far as to do sth** sich dazu erniedrigen, etw zu tun.
abashed [ə'bæʃt] adj verlegen.
abate [ə'beɪt] vi nachlassen, sich legen.
abatement [ə'beɪtmənt] n: **noise** ~ **society** Gesellschaft f zur Lärmbekämpfung.
abattoir ['æbətwɑː*] (BRIT) n Schlachthof m.
abbey ['æbɪ] n Abtei f.
abbot ['æbət] n Abt m.
abbreviate [ə'briːvɪeɪt] vt abkürzen; (essay etc) kürzen.
abbreviation [əbriːvɪ'eɪʃən] n Abkürzung f.
ABC n abbr (= American Broadcasting Companies) Fernsehsender.
abdicate ['æbdɪkeɪt] vt verzichten auf +acc ♦ vi (monarch) abdanken.
abdication [æbdɪ'keɪʃən] n (see vb) Verzicht m; Abdankung f.
abdomen ['æbdəmɛn] n Unterleib m.
abdominal [æb'dɒmɪnl] adj (pain etc) Unterleibs-.
abduct [æb'dʌkt] vt entführen.
abduction [æb'dʌkʃən] n Entführung f.
Aberdonian [æbə'dəʊnɪən] adj (GEOG) Aberdeener inv ♦ n Aberdeener(in) m(f).
aberration [æbə'reɪʃən] n Anomalie f; **in a moment of mental** ~ in einem Augenblick geistiger Verwirrung.
abet [ə'bɛt] vt see **aid.**
abeyance [ə'beɪəns] n: **in** ~ (law) außer Kraft; (matter) ruhend.
abhor [əb'hɔː*] vt verabscheuen.
abhorrent [əb'hɔrənt] adj abscheulich.
abide [ə'baɪd] vt: **I can't** ~ **it/him** ich kann es/

ihn nicht ausstehen.

▶**abide by** *vt fus* sich halten an +*acc.*

abiding [ə'baɪdɪŋ] *adj* (*memory, impression*) bleibend.

ability [ə'bɪlɪtɪ] *n* Fähigkeit *f*; **to the best of my** ~ so gut ich es kann.

abject ['æbdʒɛkt] *adj* (*poverty*) bitter; (*apology*) demütig; (*coward*) erbärmlich.

ablaze [ə'bleɪz] *adj* in Flammen; ~ **with light** hell erleuchtet.

able ['eɪbl] *adj* fähig; **to be** ~ **to do sth** etw tun können.

able-bodied ['eɪbl'bɔdɪd] *adj* kräftig; ~ **seaman** (*BRIT*) Vollmatrose *m.*

ablutions [ə'bluːʃənz] *npl* Waschungen *pl.*

ably ['eɪblɪ] *adv* gekonnt.

ABM *n abbr* (= *antiballistic missile*) Anti-Raketen-Rakete *f.*

abnormal [æb'nɔːməl] *adj* abnorm; (*child*) anormal.

abnormality [æbnɔː'mælɪtɪ] *n* Abnormität *f.*

aboard [ə'bɔːd] *adv* (*NAUT, AVIAT*) an Bord ♦ *prep* an Bord +*gen*; ~ **the train/bus** im Zug/Bus.

abode [ə'bəud] *n* (*LAW*): **of no fixed** ~ ohne festen Wohnsitz.

abolish [ə'bɔlɪʃ] *vt* abschaffen.

abolition [æbə'lɪʃən] *n* Abschaffung *f.*

abominable [ə'bɔmɪnəbl] *adj* scheußlich.

abominably [ə'bɔmɪnəblɪ] *adv* scheußlich.

Aborigine [æbə'rɪdʒɪnɪ] *n* Ureinwohner(in) *m(f)* Australiens.

abort [ə'bɔːt] *vt* abtreiben; (*MED: miscarry*) fehlgebären; (*COMPUT*) abbrechen.

abortion [ə'bɔːʃən] *n* Abtreibung *f*; (*miscarriage*) Fehlgeburt *f*; **to have an** ~ abtreiben lassen.

abortionist [ə'bɔːʃənɪst] *n* Abtreibungshelfer(in) *m(f).*

abortive [ə'bɔːtɪv] *adj* mißlungen.

abound [ə'baund] *vi* im Überfluß vorhanden sein; **to** ~ **in** *or* **with** reich sein an +*dat.*

═══════════════════════ **KEYWORD**

about [ə'baut] *adv* **1** (*approximately*) etwa, ungefähr; ~ **a hundred/thousand** *etc* etwa hundert/tausend *etc*; **at** ~ **2 o'clock** etwa um 2 Uhr; **I've just** ~ **finished** ich bin gerade fertig

2 (*referring to place*) herum; **to run/walk** *etc* ~ herumlaufen/-gehen *etc*; **is Paul** ~? ist Paul da?

3: **to be** ~ **to do sth** im Begriff sein, etw zu tun; **he was** ~ **to cry** er fing fast an zu weinen; **she was** ~ **to leave/wash the dishes** sie wollte gerade gehen/das Geschirr spülen

♦ *prep* **1** (*relating to*) über +*acc*; **what is it** ~? worum geht es?; (*book etc*) wovon handelt es?; **we talked** ~ **it** wir haben darüber geredet; **what** *or* **how** ~ **going to the cinema?** wollen wir ins Kino gehen?

2 (*referring to place*) um ... herum; **to walk** ~ **the town** durch die Stadt gehen; **her clothes were scattered** ~ **the room** ihre Kleider waren über das ganze Zimmer verstreut.

about-face [ə'baut'feɪs] (*US*) *n* = **about-turn.**

about-turn [ə'baut'təːn] (*BRIT*) *n* Kehrtwendung *f.*

above [ə'bʌv] *adv* oben; (*greater, more*) darüber ♦ *prep* über +*dat*; **to cost** ~ **£10** mehr als £10 kosten; **mentioned** ~ obengenannt; **he's not** ~ **a bit of blackmail** er ist sich *dat* nicht zu gut für eine kleine Erpressung; ~ **all** vor allem.

above board *adj* korrekt.

abrasion [ə'breɪʒən] *n* Abschürfung *f.*

abrasive [ə'breɪzɪv] *adj* (*substance*) Scheuer-; (*person, manner*) aggressiv.

abreast [ə'brɛst] *adv* nebeneinander; **three** ~ zu dritt nebeneinander; **to keep** ~ **of** (*fig*) auf dem laufenden bleiben mit.

abridge [ə'brɪdʒ] *vt* kürzen.

abroad [ə'brɔːd] *adv* (*be*) im Ausland; (*go*) ins Ausland; **there is a rumour** ~ **that ...** (*fig*) ein Gerücht geht um *or* kursiert, daß ...

abrupt [ə'brʌpt] *adj* abrupt; (*person, behaviour*) schroff.

abruptly [ə'brʌptlɪ] *adv* abrupt.

abscess ['æbsɪs] *n* Abszeß *m.*

abscond [əb'skɔnd] *vi*: **to** ~ **with** sich davonmachen mit; **to** ~ (**from**) fliehen (aus).

abseil ['æbseɪl] *vi* sich abseilen.

absence ['æbsəns] *n* Abwesenheit *f*; **in the** ~ **of** (*person*) in Abwesenheit +*gen*; (*thing*) in Ermangelung +*gen.*

absent ['æbsənt] *adj* abwesend, nicht da ♦ *vt*: **to** ~ **o.s. from** fernbleiben +*dat*; **to be** ~ fehlen; **to be** ~ **without leave** (*MIL*) sich unerlaubt von der Truppe entfernen.

absentee [æbsən'tiː] *n* Abwesende(r) *f(m).*

absenteeism [æbsən'tiːɪzəm] *n* (*from school*) Schwänzen *nt*; (*from work*) Nichterscheinen *nt* am Arbeitsplatz.

absent-minded ['æbsənt'maɪndɪd] *adj* zerstreut.

absent-mindedly ['æbsənt'maɪndɪdlɪ] *adv* zerstreut; (*look*) abwesend.

absent-mindedness ['æbsənt'maɪndɪdnɪs] *n* Zerstreutheit *f.*

absolute ['æbsəluːt] *adj* absolut; (*power*) uneingeschränkt.

absolutely [æbsə'luːtlɪ] *adv* absolut; (*agree*) vollkommen; ~! genau!

absolution [æbsə'luːʃən] *n* Lossprechung *f.*

absolve [əb'zɔlv] *vt*: **to** ~ **sb (from)** jdn lossprechen (von); (*responsibility*) jdn entbinden (von).

absorb [əb'zɔːb] *vt* aufnehmen (*also fig*); (*light, heat*) absorbieren; (*group, business*) übernehmen; **to be** ~**ed in a book** in ein Buch vertieft sein.

absorbent [əb'zɔːbənt] adj saugfähig.
absorbent cotton (US) n Watte f.
absorbing [əb'zɔːbɪŋ] adj saugfähig; (book, film, work etc) fesselnd.
absorption [əb'sɔːpʃən] n (see vb) Aufnahme f; Absorption f; Übernahme f; (interest) Faszination f.
abstain [əb'steɪn] vi (voting) sich (der Stimme) enthalten; **to ~ (from)** (eating, drinking etc) sich enthalten (+gen).
abstemious [əb'stiːmɪəs] adj enthaltsam.
abstention [əb'stɛnʃən] n (Stimm)enthaltung f.
abstinence ['æbstɪnəns] n Enthaltsamkeit f.
abstract ['æbstrækt] adj abstrakt ♦ n (summary) Zusammenfassung f ♦ vt: **to ~ sth (from)** (summarize) etw entnehmen (aus); (remove) etw entfernen (aus).
abstruse [æb'struːs] adj abstrus.
absurd [əb'sɜːd] adj absurd.
absurdity [əb'sɜːdɪtɪ] n Absurdität f.
ABTA ['æbtə] n abbr (= Association of British Travel Agents) Verband der Reiseveranstalter.
Abu Dhabi ['æbuː'dɑːbɪ] n (GEOG) Abu Dhabi nt.
abundance [ə'bʌndəns] n Reichtum m; **an ~ of** eine Fülle von; **in ~** in Hülle und Fülle.
abundant [ə'bʌndənt] adj reichlich.
abundantly [ə'bʌndəntlɪ] adv reichlich; **~ clear** völlig klar.
abuse [ə'bjuːs] n (insults) Beschimpfungen pl; (ill-treatment) Mißhandlung f; (misuse) Mißbrauch m ♦ vt (see n) beschimpfen; mißhandeln; mißbrauchen; **to be open to ~** sich leicht mißbrauchen lassen.
abuser [ə'bjuːzə*] n (drug abuser) jd, der Drogen mißbraucht; (child abuser) jd, der Kinder mißbraucht oder mißhandelt.
abusive [ə'bjuːsɪv] adj beleidigend.
abysmal [ə'bɪzməl] adj entsetzlich; (ignorance etc) grenzenlos.
abysmally [ə'bɪzməlɪ] adv (see adj) entsetzlich; grenzenlos.
abyss [ə'bɪs] n Abgrund m.
AC abbr = **alternating current**; (US: = athletic club) ≈ SV m.
a/c abbr (BANKING etc) = **account**; (= account current) Girokonto nt.
academic [ækə'dɛmɪk] adj akademisch (also pej); (work) wissenschaftlich; (person) intellektuell ♦ n Akademiker(in) m(f).
academic year n (university year) Universitätsjahr nt; (school year) Schuljahr nt.
academy [ə'kædəmɪ] n Akademie f; (school) Hochschule f; **~ of music** Musikhochschule f; **military/naval ~** Militär-/Marineakademie f.
ACAS ['eɪkæs] (BRIT) n abbr (= Advisory, Conciliation and Arbitration Service) Schlichtungsstelle für Arbeitskonflikte.

accede [æk'siːd] vi: **to ~ to** zustimmen +dat.
accelerate [æk'sɛləreɪt] vt beschleunigen ♦ vi (AUT) Gas geben.
acceleration [æksɛlə'reɪʃən] n Beschleunigung f.
accelerator [æk'sɛləreɪtə*] n Gaspedal nt.
accent ['æksɛnt] n Akzent m; (fig: emphasis, stress) Betonung f; **to speak with an Irish ~** mit einem irischen Akzent sprechen; **to have a strong ~** einen starken Akzent haben.
accentuate [æk'sɛntjueɪt] vt betonen; (need, difference etc) hervorheben.
accept [ək'sɛpt] vt annehmen; (fact, situation) sich abfinden mit; (risk) in Kauf nehmen; (responsibility) übernehmen; (blame) auf sich acc nehmen.
acceptable [ək'sɛptəbl] adj annehmbar.
acceptance [ək'sɛptəns] n Annahme f; **to meet with general ~** allgemeine Anerkennung finden.
access ['æksɛs] n Zugang m ♦ vt (COMPUT) zugreifen auf +dat; **the burglars gained ~ through a window** die Einbrecher gelangten durch ein Fenster hinein.
accessible [æk'sɛsəbl] adj erreichbar; (knowledge, art etc) zugänglich.
accession [æk'sɛʃən] n Antritt m; (of monarch) Thronbesteigung f; (to library) Neuanschaffung f.
accessory [æk'sɛsərɪ] n Zubehörteil nt; (DRESS) Accessoire nt; (LAW): **~ to** Mitschuldige(r) f(m) an +dat; **accessories** npl Zubehör nt; **toilet accessories** (BRIT) Toilettenartikel pl.
access road n Zufahrt(sstraße) f.
access time n (COMPUT) Zugriffszeit f.
accident ['æksɪdənt] n Zufall m; (mishap, disaster) Unfall m; **to meet with** or **to have an ~** einen Unfall haben, verunglücken; **~s at work** Arbeitsunfälle pl; **by ~** zufällig.
accidental [æksɪ'dɛntl] adj zufällig; (death, damage) Unfall-.
accidentally [æksɪ'dɛntəlɪ] adv zufällig.
accident insurance n Unfallversicherung f.
accident-prone ['æksɪdənt'prəun] adj vom Pech verfolgt.
acclaim [ə'kleɪm] n Beifall m ♦ vt: **to be ~ed for one's achievements** für seine Leistungen gefeiert werden.
acclamation [æklə'meɪʃən] n Anerkennung f; (applause) Beifall m.
acclimate [ə'klaɪmət] (US) vt = **acclimatize**.
acclimatize [ə'klaɪmətaɪz], (US) **acclimate** [ə'klaɪmɪt] vt: **to become ~d** sich akklimatisieren; **to become ~d to** sich gewöhnen an +acc.
accolade ['ækəleɪd] n (fig) Auszeichnung f.
accommodate [ə'kɔmədeɪt] vt unterbringen; (subj: car, hotel etc) Platz bieten +dat; (oblige, help) entgegenkommen +dat; **to ~ one's plans to** seine Pläne anpassen an +acc.

accommodating [əˈkɔmədeɪtɪŋ] *adj* entgegenkommend.

accommodation [əkɔməˈdeɪʃən] *n* Unterkunft *f*; **accommodations** (*US*) *npl* Unterkunft *f*; **have you any ~?** haben Sie eine Unterkunft?; **"~ to let"** „Zimmer zu vermieten"; **they have ~ for 500** sie können 500 Personen unterbringen; **the hall has seating ~ for 600** (*BRIT*) in dem Saal können 600 Personen sitzen.

accompaniment [əˈkʌmpənɪmənt] *n* Begleitung *f*.

accompanist [əˈkʌmpənɪst] *n* Begleiter(in) *m(f)*.

accompany [əˈkʌmpənɪ] *vt* begleiten.

accomplice [əˈkʌmplɪs] *n* Komplize *m*, Komplizin *f*.

accomplish [əˈkʌmplɪʃ] *vt* vollenden; (*achieve*) erreichen.

accomplished [əˈkʌmplɪʃt] *adj* ausgezeichnet.

accomplishment [əˈkʌmplɪʃmənt] *n* Vollendung *f*; (*achievement*) Leistung *f*; (*skill: gen pl*) Fähigkeit *f*.

accord [əˈkɔːd] *n* Übereinstimmung *f*; (*treaty*) Vertrag *m* ♦ *vt* gewähren; **of his own ~** freiwillig; **with one ~** geschlossen; **to be in ~** übereinstimmen.

accordance [əˈkɔːdəns] *n*: **in ~ with** in Übereinstimmung mit.

according [əˈkɔːdɪŋ] *prep*: **~ to** zufolge +*dat*; **~ to plan** wie geplant.

accordingly [əˈkɔːdɪŋlɪ] *adv* entsprechend; (*as a result*) folglich.

accordion [əˈkɔːdɪən] *n* Akkordeon *nt*.

accost [əˈkɔst] *vt* ansprechen.

account [əˈkaunt] *n* (*COMM: bill*) Rechnung *f*; (*in bank, department store*) Konto *nt*; (*report*) Bericht *m*; **accounts** *npl* (*COMM*) Buchhaltung *f*; (*BOOKKEEPING*) (Geschäfts)bücher *pl*; **"~ payee only"** (*BRIT*) „nur zur Verrechnung"; **to keep an ~ of** Buch führen über +*acc*; **to bring sb to ~ for sth/for having embezzled £50,000** jdn für etw/für die Unterschlagung von £50.000 zur Rechenschaft ziehen; **by all ~s** nach allem, was man hört; **of no ~** ohne Bedeutung; **on ~** auf Kredit; **to pay £5 on ~** eine Anzahlung von £5 leisten; **on no ~** auf keinen Fall; **on ~ of** wegen +*gen*; **to take into ~, take ~ of** berücksichtigen.

▶**account for** *vt fus* erklären; (*expenditure*) Rechenschaft ablegen für; (*represent*) ausmachen; **all the children were ~ed for** man wußte, wo alle Kinder waren; **4 people are still not ~ed for** 4 Personen werden immer noch vermißt.

accountability [əˈkauntəˈbɪlɪtɪ] *n* Verantwortlichkeit *f*.

accountable [əˈkauntəbl] *adj*: **~ (to)** verantwortlich (gegenüber +*dat*); **to be held ~ for sth** für etw verantwortlich gemacht werden.

accountancy [əˈkauntənsɪ] *n* Buchhaltung *f*.

accountant [əˈkauntənt] *n* Buchhalter(in) *m(f)*.

accounting [əˈkauntɪŋ] *n* Buchhaltung *f*.

accounting period *n* Abrechnungszeitraum *m*.

account number *n* Kontonummer *f*.

accounts payable *npl* Verbindlichkeiten *pl*.

accounts receivable *npl* Forderungen *pl*.

accredited [əˈkrɛdɪtɪd] *adj* anerkannt.

accretion [əˈkriːʃən] *n* Ablagerung *f*.

accrue [əˈkruː] *vi* sich ansammeln; **to ~ to** zufließen +*dat*.

accrued interest *n* aufgelaufene Zinsen *pl*.

accumulate [əˈkjuːmjuleɪt] *vt* ansammeln ♦ *vi* sich ansammeln.

accumulation [əkjuːmjuˈleɪʃən] *n* Ansammlung *f*.

accuracy [ˈækjurəsɪ] *n* Genauigkeit *f*.

accurate [ˈækjurɪt] *adj* genau.

accurately [ˈækjurɪtlɪ] *adv* genau; (*answer*) richtig.

accusation [ækjuˈzeɪʃən] *n* Vorwurf *m*; (*instance*) Beschuldigung *f*; (*LAW*) Anklage *f*.

accusative [əˈkjuːzətɪv] *n* Akkusativ *m*.

accuse [əˈkjuːz] *vt*: **to ~ sb (of sth)** jdn (einer Sache *gen*) beschuldigen; (*LAW*) jdn (wegen etw *dat*) anklagen.

accused [əˈkjuːzd] *n* (*LAW*): **the ~** der/die Angeklagte.

accuser [əˈkjuːzə*] *n* Ankläger(in) *m(f)*.

accusing [əˈkjuːzɪŋ] *adj* anklagend.

accustom [əˈkʌstəm] *vt* gewöhnen; **to ~ o.s. to sth** sich an etw *acc* gewöhnen.

accustomed [əˈkʌstəmd] *adj* gewohnt; (*in the habit*): **~ to** gewohnt an +*acc*.

AC/DC *abbr* (= *alternating current/direct current*) WS/GS.

ACE [eɪs] *n abbr* (= *American Council on Education*) akademischer Verband für das Erziehungswesen.

ace [eɪs] *n* As *nt*.

acerbic [əˈsɔːbɪk] *adj* scharf.

acetate [ˈæsɪteɪt] *n* Acetat *nt*.

ache [eɪk] *n* Schmerz *m* ♦ *vi* schmerzen, weh tun; (*yearn*): **to ~ to do sth** sich danach sehnen, etw zu tun; **I've got (a) stomach ~** ich habe Magenschmerzen; **I'm aching all over** mir tut alles weh; **my head ~s** mir tut der Kopf weh.

achieve [əˈtʃiːv] *vt* (*aim, result*) erreichen; (*success*) erzielen; (*victory*) erringen.

achievement [əˈtʃiːvmənt] *n* (*act of achieving*) Erreichen *nt*; (*success, feat*) Leistung *f*.

Achilles heel [əˈkɪliːz-] *n* Achillesferse *f*.

acid [ˈæsɪd] *adj* sauer ♦ *n* (*CHEM*) Säure *f*; (*inf: LSD*) Acid *nt*.

Acid House *n* Acid House *nt*, *elektronische Funk-Diskomusik*.

acidic [əˈsɪdɪk] *adj* sauer.

acidity [əˈsɪdɪtɪ] *n* Säure *f*.

acid rain *n* saurer Regen *m*.

acid test *n* (*fig*) Feuerprobe *f*.

acknowledge [ək'nɔlɪdʒ] vt (also: ~ **receipt of**) den Empfang +gen bestätigen; (fact) zugeben; (situation) zur Kenntnis nehmen; (person) grüßen.

acknowledgement [ək'nɔlɪdʒmənt] n Empfangsbestätigung f; **acknowledgements** npl (in book) ≈ Danksagung f.

ACLU n abbr (= American Civil Liberties Union) Bürgerrechtsverband.

acme ['ækmɪ] n Gipfel m, Höhepunkt m.

acne ['æknɪ] n Akne f.

acorn ['eɪkɔːn] n Eichel f.

acoustic [ə'kuːstɪk] adj akustisch.

acoustic coupler n (COMPUT) Akustikkoppler m.

acoustics [ə'kuːstɪks] n Akustik f.

acoustic screen n Trennwand f zur Schalldämpfung.

acquaint [ə'kweɪnt] vt: **to** ~ **sb with sth** jdn mit etw vertraut machen; **to be** ~**ed with** (person) bekannt sein mit; (fact) vertraut sein mit.

acquaintance [ə'kweɪntəns] n Bekannte(r) f(m); (with person) Bekanntschaft f; (with subject) Kenntnis f; **to make sb's** ~ jds Bekanntschaft machen.

acquiesce [ækwɪ'ɛs] vi einwilligen; **to** ~ **(to)** (demand, arrangement, request) einwilligen (in +acc).

acquire [ə'kwaɪə*] vt erwerben; (interest) entwickeln; (habit) annehmen.

acquired [ə'kwaɪəd] adj erworben; **whisky is an** ~ **taste** man muß sich an Whisky erst gewöhnen.

acquisition [ækwɪ'zɪʃən] n (see vb) Erwerb m, Entwicklung f, Annahme f; (thing acquired) Errungenschaft f.

acquisitive [ə'kwɪzɪtɪv] adj habgierig; **the** ~ **society** die Erwerbsgesellschaft.

acquit [ə'kwɪt] vt freisprechen; **to** ~ **o.s. well** seine Sache gut machen.

acquittal [ə'kwɪtl] n Freispruch m.

acre ['eɪkə*] n Morgen m.

acreage ['eɪkərɪdʒ] n Fläche f.

acrid ['ækrɪd] adj bitter; (smoke, fig) beißend.

acrimonious [ækrɪ'məunɪəs] adj bitter; (dispute) erbittert.

acrimony ['ækrɪmənɪ] n Erbitterung f.

acrobat ['ækrəbæt] n Akrobat(in) m(f).

acrobatic [ækrə'bætɪk] adj akrobatisch.

acrobatics [ækrə'bætɪks] npl Akrobatik f.

acronym ['ækrənɪm] n Akronym nt.

Acropolis [ə'krɔpəlɪs] n: **the** ~ (GEOG) die Akropolis.

across [ə'krɔs] prep über +acc; (on the other side of) auf der anderen Seite +gen ♦ adv (direction) hinüber, herüber; (measurement) breit; **to take sb** ~ **the road** jdn über die Straße bringen; **a road** ~ **the wood** eine Straße durch den Wald; **the lake is 12 km** ~ der See ist 12 km breit; ~ **from** gegenüber +dat; **to get sth** ~ **(to sb)** (jdm) etw

klarmachen.

acrylic [ə'krɪlɪk] adj (acid, paint, blanket) Acryl- ♦ n Acryl nt; **acrylics** npl: **he paints in** ~**s er malt mit Acrylfarbe.**

ACT n abbr (= American College Test) Eignungstest für Studienbewerber.

act [ækt] n Tat f; (of play) Akt m; (in a show etc) Nummer f; (LAW) Gesetz nt ♦ vi handeln; (behave) sich verhalten; (have effect) wirken; (THEAT) spielen ♦ vt spielen; **it's only an** ~ es ist nur Schau; ~ **of God** (LAW) höhere Gewalt f; **to be in the** ~ **of doing sth** dabei sein, etw zu tun; **to catch sb in the** ~ jdn auf frischer Tat ertappen; **to** ~ **the fool** (BRIT) herumalbern; **he is only** ~**ing er tut (doch) nur so; to** ~ **as fungieren als; it** ~**s as a deterrent es dient zur Abschreckung.**

▶**act on** vt: **to** ~ **on sth** (take action) auf etw +acc hin handeln.

▶**act out** vt (event) durchspielen; (fantasies) zum Ausdruck bringen.

acting ['æktɪŋ] adj stellvertretend ♦ n (profession) Schauspielkunst f; (activity) Spielen nt; ~ **in my capacity as chairman** ... in meiner Eigenschaft als Vorsitzender ...

action ['ækʃən] n Tat f; (motion) Bewegung f; (MIL) Kampf m, Gefecht nt; (LAW) Klage f; **to bring an** ~ **against sb** (LAW) eine Klage gegen jdn anstrengen; **killed in** ~ (MIL) gefallen; **out of** ~ (person) nicht einsatzfähig; (thing) außer Betrieb; **to take** ~ etwas unternehmen; **to put a plan into** ~ einen Plan in die Tat umsetzen.

action replay n (TV) Wiederholung f.

activate ['æktɪveɪt] vt in Betrieb setzen; (CHEM, PHYS) aktivieren.

active ['æktɪv] adj aktiv; (volcano) tätig; **to play an** ~ **part in sth** sich aktiv an etw dat beteiligen.

active duty (US) n (MIL) Einsatz m.

actively ['æktɪvlɪ] adv aktiv; (dislike) offen.

active partner n (COMM) tätiger Teilhaber m.

active service (BRIT) n (MIL) Einsatz m.

active suspension n (AUT) aktives or computergesteuertes Fahrwerk nt.

activist ['æktɪvɪst] n Aktivist(in) m(f).

activity [æk'tɪvɪtɪ] n Aktivität f; (pastime, pursuit) Betätigung f.

actor ['æktə*] n Schauspieler m.

actress ['æktrɪs] n Schauspielerin f.

actual ['æktjuəl] adj wirklich; (emphatic use) eigentlich.

actually ['æktjuəlɪ] adv wirklich; (in fact) tatsächlich; (even) sogar.

actuary ['æktjuərɪ] n Aktuar m.

actuate ['æktjueɪt] vt auslösen.

acuity [ə'kjuːɪtɪ] n Schärfe f.

acumen ['ækjumən] n Scharfsinn m; **business** ~ Geschäftssinn m.

acupuncture ['ækjupʌŋktʃə*] n Akupunktur f.

acute [ə'kjuːt] adj akut; (anxiety) heftig; (mind,

scharf; (*person*) scharfsinnig; (*MATH: angle*)
spitz; (*LING*): ~ **accent** Akut *m*.
AD *adv abbr* (= *Anno Domini*) n. Chr. ♦ *n abbr*
(*US: MIL*) = **active duty.**
ad [æd] (*inf*) *n abbr* = **advertisement.**
adage ['ædɪdʒ] *n* Sprichwort *nt*.
adamant ['ædəmənt] *adj*: **to be ~ that ...**
darauf bestehen, daß ...; **to be ~ about sth**
auf etw *dat* bestehen.
Adam's apple ['ædəmz-] *n* Adamsapfel *m*.
adapt [ə'dæpt] *vt* anpassen; (*novel etc*)
bearbeiten ♦ *vi*: **to ~ (to)** sich anpassen (an
+*acc*).
adaptability [ədæptə'bɪlɪtɪ] *n* Anpassungs-
fähigkeit *f*.
adaptable [ə'dæptəbl] *adj* anpassungsfähig;
(*device*) vielseitig.
adaptation [ædæp'teɪʃən] *n* (*of novel etc*)
Bearbeitung *f*; (*of machine etc*) Umstellung *f*.
adapter [ə'dæptə*] *n* (*ELEC*) Adapter *m*; (: *for*
several plugs) Mehrfachsteckdose *f*.
adaptor [ə'dæptə*] *n* = **adapter.**
ADC *n abbr* (*MIL*) = **aide-de-camp;** (*US:* = *Aid*
to Dependent Children) Beihilfe *für*
sozialschwache Familien.
add [æd] *vt* hinzufügen; (*figures: also:* ~ **up**)
zusammenzählen ♦ *vi*: **to ~ to** (*increase*)
beitragen zu.
►**add on** *vt* (*amount*) dazurechnen; (*room*)
anbauen.
►**add up** *vt* (*figures*) zusammenzählen ♦ *vi*
(*fig*): **it doesn't ~ up** es ergibt keinen Sinn; **it**
doesn't ~ up to much (*fig*) das ist nicht
berühmt (*inf*).
addenda [ə'dɛndə] *npl of* **addendum.**
addendum [ə'dɛndəm] (*pl* **addenda**) *n*
Nachtrag *m*.
adder ['ædə*] *n* Kreuzotter *f*, Viper *f*.
addict ['ædɪkt] *n* Süchtige(r) *f(m)*; (*enthusiast*)
Anhänger(in) *m(f)*.
addicted [ə'dɪktɪd] *adj*: **to be ~ to drugs/drink**
drogensüchtig/alkoholsüchtig sein; **to be**
~ **to football** (*fig*) ohne Fußball nicht mehr
leben können.
addiction [ə'dɪkʃən] *n* Sucht *f*.
addictive [ə'dɪktɪv] *adj*: **to be ~** (*drug*) süchtig
machen; (*activity*) zur Sucht werden können.
adding machine ['ædɪŋ-] *n* Addiermaschine
f.
Addis Ababa ['ædɪs'æbəbə] *n* (*GEOG*) Addis
Abeba *nt*.
addition [ə'dɪʃən] *n* (*adding up*)
Zusammenzählen *nt*; (*thing added*) Zusatz *m*;
(: *to payment, bill*) Zuschlag *m*; (: *to building*)
Anbau *m*; **in ~ (to)** zusätzlich (zu).
additional [ə'dɪʃənl] *adj* zusätzlich.
additive ['ædɪtɪv] *n* Zusatz *m*.
addled ['ædld] *adj* (*BRIT: egg*) faul; (*brain*)
verwirrt.
address [ə'drɛs] *n* Adresse *f*; (*speech*)
Ansprache *f* ♦ *vt* adressieren; (*speak to:*
person) ansprechen; (: *audience*) sprechen

zu; **form of ~** (*Form f der*) Anrede *f*; **what**
form of ~ do you use for ...? wie redet man
... an?; **absolute/relative ~** (*COMPUT*)
absolute/relative Adresse; **to ~ (o.s. to)**
(*problem*) sich befassen mit.
address book *n* Adreßbuch *nt*.
addressee [ædrɛ'siː] *n* Empfänger(in) *m(f)*.
Aden ['eɪdən] *n* (*GEOG*): **Gulf of ~** Golf *m* von
Aden.
adenoids ['ædɪnɔɪdz] *npl* Rachenmandeln *pl*.
adept ['ædɛpt] *adj*: **to be ~ at** gut sein in +*dat*.
adequacy ['ædɪkwəsɪ] *n* (*of resources*)
Adäquatheit *f*; (*of performance, proposals etc*)
Angemessenheit *f*.
adequate ['ædɪkwɪt] *adj* ausreichend,
adäquat; (*satisfactory*) angemessen.
adequately ['ædɪkwɪtlɪ] *adv* ausreichend;
(*satisfactorily*) zufriedenstellend.
adhere [əd'hɪə*] *vi*: **to ~ to** haften an +*dat*; (*fig:*
abide by) sich halten an +*acc*; (: *hold to*)
festhalten an +*dat*.
adhesion [əd'hiːʒən] *n* Haften *nt*, Haftung *f*.
adhesive [əd'hiːzɪv] *adj* klebend, Klebe- ♦ *n*
Klebstoff *m*.
adhesive tape *n* (*BRIT*) Klebstreifen *m*; (*US:*
MED) Heftpflaster *nt*.
ad hoc [æd'hɔk] *adj* (*committee, decision*) Ad-
hoc- ♦ *adv* ad hoc.
ad infinitum ['ædɪnfɪ'naɪtəm] *adv* ad infinitum.
adjacent [ə'dʒeɪsənt] *adj*: ~ **to** neben +*dat*.
adjective ['ædʒɛktɪv] *n* Adjektiv *nt*,
Eigenschaftswort *nt*.
adjoin [ə'dʒɔɪn] *vt*: **the hotel ~ing the station**
das Hotel neben dem Bahnhof.
adjoining [ə'dʒɔɪnɪŋ] *adj* benachbart, Neben-.
adjourn [ə'dʒəːn] *vt* vertagen ♦ *vi* sich
vertagen; **to ~ a meeting till the following**
week eine Besprechung auf die nächste
Woche vertagen; **they ~ed to the pub** (*BRIT:*
inf) sie begaben sich in die Kneipe.
adjournment [ə'dʒəːnmənt] *n* Unterbrechung
f.
Adjt. *abbr* (*MIL*) = **adjutant.**
adjudicate [ə'dʒuːdɪkeɪt] *vt* (*contest*)
Preisrichter sein bei; (*claim*) entscheiden
♦ *vi* entscheiden; **to ~ on** urteilen über +*dat*.
adjudication [ədʒuːdɪ'keɪʃən] *n* Entscheidung
f.
adjudicator [ə'dʒuːdɪkeɪtə*] *n* Schiedsrich-
ter(in) *m(f)*; (*in contest*) Preisrichter(in) *m(f)*.
adjust [ə'dʒʌst] *vt* anpassen; (*change*) ändern;
(*clothing*) zurechtrücken; (*machine etc*)
einstellen; (*INSURANCE*) regulieren ♦ *vi*: **to**
~ **(to)** sich anpassen (an +*acc*).
adjustable [ə'dʒʌstəbl] *adj* verstellbar.
adjuster [ə'dʒʌstə*] *n see* **loss.**
adjustment [ə'dʒʌstmənt] *n* Anpassung *f*; (*to*
machine) Einstellung *f*.
adjutant ['ædʒətənt] *n* Adjutant *m*.
ad-lib [æd'lɪb] *vi, vt* improvisieren ♦ *adv*: **ad lib**
aus dem Stegreif.
adman ['ædmæn] (*inf: irreg: like* **man**) *n*

Werbefachmann m.

admin ['ædmɪn] (*inf*) *n abbr* = **administration**.

administer [ad'mɪnɪstə*] *vt* (*country, department*) verwalten; (*justice*) sprechen; (*oath*) abnehmen; (*MED: drug*) verabreichen.

administration [ədmɪnɪs'treɪʃən] *n* (*management*) Verwaltung *f*; (*government*) Regierung *f*; **the A~** (*US*) die Regierung.

administrative [ad'mɪnɪstrativ] *adj* (*department, reform etc*) Verwaltungs-.

administrator [ad'mɪnɪstreɪtə*] *n* Verwaltungsbeamte(r) *f(m)*.

admirable ['ædmərəbl] *adj* bewundernswert.

admiral ['ædmərəl] *n* Admiral *m*.

Admiralty ['ædmərəltɪ] (*BRIT*) *n*: **the ~** (*also:* **the ~ Board**) das Marineministerium.

admiration [ædmə'reɪʃən] *n* Bewunderung *f*; **to have great ~ for sb/sth** jdn/etw sehr bewundern.

admire [ad'maɪə*] *vt* bewundern.

admirer [ad'maɪərə*] *n* (*suitor*) Verehrer *m*; (*fan*) Bewunderer *m*, Bewunderin *f*.

admiring [ad'maɪərɪŋ] *adj* bewundernd.

admissible [ad'mɪsəbl] *adj* (*evidence, as evidence*) zulässig.

admission [ad'mɪʃən] *n* (*admittance*) Zutritt *m*; (*to exhibition, night club etc*) Einlaß *m*; (*to club, hospital*) Aufnahme *f*; (*entry fee*) Eintritt(spreis) *m*; (*confession*) Geständnis *nt*; "**~ free**", "**free ~**" „Eintritt frei"; **by his own ~** nach eigenem Eingeständnis.

admit [ad'mɪt] *vt* (*confess*) gestehen; (*permit to enter*) einlassen; (*to club, hospital*) aufnehmen; (*responsibility etc*) anerkennen; "**children not ~ted**" „kein Zutritt für Kinder"; **this ticket ~s two** diese Karte ist für zwei Personen; **I must ~ that** ... ich muß zugeben, daß ...; **to ~ defeat** sich geschlagen geben.

▶**admit of** *vt fus* (*interpretation etc*) erlauben.

▶**admit to** *vt fus* (*murder etc*) gestehen.

admittance [ad'mɪtəns] *n* Zutritt *m*; "**no ~**" „kein Zutritt".

admittedly [ad'mɪtɪdlɪ] *adv* zugegebenermaßen.

admonish [ad'mɔnɪʃ] *vt* ermahnen.

ad nauseam [æd'nɔːsɪæm] *adv* (*talk*) endlos; (*repeat*) bis zum Gehtnichtmehr (*inf*).

ado [a'duː] *n*: **without (any) more ~** ohne weitere Umstände.

adolescence [ædəu'lɛsns] *n* Jugend *f*.

adolescent [ædəu'lɛsnt] *adj* heranwachsend; (*remark, behaviour*) pubertär ♦ *n* Jugendliche(r) *f(m)*.

adopt [a'dɔpt] *vt* adoptieren; (*POL: candidate*) aufstellen; (*policy, attitude, accent*) annehmen.

adopted [a'dɔptɪd] *adj* (*child*) adoptiert.

adoption [a'dɔpʃən] *n* (*see vb*) Adoption *f*; Aufstellung *f*; Annahme *f*.

adoptive [a'dɔptɪv] *adj* (*parents etc*) Adoptiv-; **~ country** Wahlheimat *f*.

adorable [a'dɔːrəbl] *adj* entzückend.

adoration [ædə'reɪʃən] *n* (*of person*) Verehrung *f*.

adore [a'dɔː*] *vt* (*person*) verehren; (*film, activity etc*) schwärmen für.

adoring [a'dɔːrɪŋ] *adj* (*fans etc*) ihn/sie bewundernd; (*husband/wife*) sie/ihn innig liebend.

adoringly [a'dɔːrɪŋlɪ] *adv* (*look, gaze*) bewundernd.

adorn [a'dɔːn] *vt* schmücken.

adornment [a'dɔːnmənt] *n* Schmuck *m*.

ADP *n abbr* = **automatic data processing**.

adrenalin [a'drɛnəlɪn] *n* Adrenalin *nt*; **it gets the ~ going** das bringt einen in Fahrt.

Adriatic [eɪdrɪ'ætɪk] *n*: **the ~ (Sea)** (*GEOG*) die Adria, das Adriatische Meer.

adrift [a'drɪft] *adv* (*NAUT*) treibend; (*fig*) ziellos; **to be ~** (*NAUT*) treiben; **to come ~** (*boat*) sich losmachen; (*fastening etc*) sich lösen.

adroit [a'drɔɪt] *adj* gewandt.

adroitly [a'drɔɪtlɪ] *adv* gewandt.

ADT (*US*) *abbr* (= *Atlantic Daylight Time*) atlantische Sommerzeit.

adulation [ædju'leɪʃən] *n* Verherrlichung *f*.

adult ['ædʌlt] *n* Erwachsene(r) *f(m)* ♦ *adj* erwachsen; (*animal*) ausgewachsen; (*literature etc*) für Erwachsene.

adult education *n* Erwachsenenbildung *f*.

adulterate [a'dʌltəreɪt] *vt* verunreinigen; (*with water*) panschen.

adulterer [a'dʌltərə*] *n* Ehebrecher *m*.

adulteress [a'dʌltərɪs] *n* Ehebrecherin *f*.

adultery [a'dʌltərɪ] *n* Ehebruch *m*.

adulthood [a'dʌlthud] *n* Erwachsenenalter *nt*.

advance [ad'vɑːns] *n* (*movement*) Vorrücken *nt*; (*progress*) Fortschritt *m*; (*money*) Vorschuß *m* ♦ *vt* (*money*) vorschießen; (*theory, idea*) vorbringen ♦ *vi* (*move forward*) vorrücken; (*make progress*) Fortschritte machen ♦ *adj*: **~ booking** Vorverkauf *m*; **to make ~s (to sb)** Annäherungsversuche (bei jdm) machen; **in ~** im voraus; **to give sb ~ notice** jdm frühzeitig Bescheid sagen; **to give sb ~ warning** jdn vorwarnen.

advanced [ad'vɑːnst] *adj* (*SCOL: studies*) für Fortgeschrittene; (*country*) fortgeschritten; (*child*) weit entwickelt; (*ideas*) fortschrittlich; **~ in years** in fortgeschrittenem Alter.

advancement [ad'vɑːnsmənt] *n* (*improvement*) Förderung *f*; (*in job, rank*) Aufstieg *m*.

advantage [ad'vɑːntɪdʒ] *n* Vorteil *m*; **to take ~ of** ausnutzen; (*opportunity*) nutzen; **it's to our ~ (to)** es ist für uns von Vorteil(, wenn wir).

advantageous [ædvən'teɪdʒəs] *adj*: **~ (to)** vorteilhaft (für), von Vorteil (für).

advent ['ædvənt] *n* (*of innovation*) Aufkommen *nt*; (*REL*): **A~** Advent *m*.

Advent calendar *n* Adventskalender *m*.

adventure [əd'vɛntʃəʳ] n Abenteuer nt.
adventure playground n
Abenteuerspielplatz m.
adventurous [əd'vɛntʃərəs] adj
abenteuerlustig; (bold) mutig.
adverb ['ædvə:b] n Adverb nt.
adversarial [ædvə'sɛərɪəl] adj (relationship)
konfliktreich.
adversary ['ædvəsərɪ] n Widersacher(in) m(f).
adverse ['ædvə:s] adj ungünstig; in
~ **circumstances** unter widrigen
Umständen; ~ **to** ablehnend gegenüber +dat.
adversity [əd'və:sɪtɪ] n Widrigkeit f.
advert ['ædvə:t] (BRIT) n abbr = **advertisement**.
advertise ['ædvətaɪz] vi (COMM) werben;
(in newspaper) annoncieren, inserieren
♦ vt (product, event) werben für; (job)
ausschreiben; **to** ~ **for** (staff, accommodation
etc) (per Anzeige) suchen.
advertisement [əd'və:tɪsmənt] n (COMM)
Werbung f, Reklame f; (in classified ads)
Anzeige f, Inserat nt.
advertiser ['ædvətaɪzəʳ] n (in newspaper)
Inserent(in) m(f); (on television etc) Firma,
die im Fernsehen etc wirbt.
advertising ['ædvətaɪzɪŋ] n Werbung f.
advertising agency n Werbeagentur f.
advertising campaign n Werbekampagne f.
advice [əd'vaɪs] n Rat m; (notification)
Benachrichtigung f, Avis m or nt (COMM); **a
piece of** ~ ein Rat(schlag); **to ask sb for** ~
jdn um Rat fragen; **to take legal** ~ einen
Rechtsanwalt zu Rate ziehen.
advice note (BRIT) n (COMM) Avis m or nt.
advisable [əd'vaɪzəbl] adj ratsam.
advise [əd'vaɪz] vt (person) raten +dat;
(company etc) beraten; **to** ~ **sb of sth** jdn
von etw in Kenntnis setzen; **to** ~ **against sth**
von etw abraten; **to** ~ **against doing sth**
davon abraten, etw zu tun; **you would be
well-/ill-**~**d to go** Sie wären gut/schlecht
beraten, wenn Sie gingen.
advisedly [əd'vaɪzɪdlɪ] adv bewußt.
adviser [əd'vaɪzəʳ] n Berater(in) m(f).
advisor [əd'vaɪzəʳ] n = **adviser**.
advisory [əd'vaɪzərɪ] adj beratend,
Beratungs-; **in an** ~ **capacity** in beratender
Funktion.
advocate ['ædvəkɪt] vt befürworten ♦ n (LAW)
(Rechts)anwalt m, (Rechts)anwältin f;
(supporter, upholder): ~ **of** Befürworter(in)
m(f) +gen; **to be an** ~ **of sth** etw befürworten.
advt. abbr = **advertisement**.
AEA (BRIT) n abbr (= Atomic Energy Authority)
britische Atomenergiebehörde.
AEC (US) n abbr (= Atomic Energy Commission)
amerikanische Atomenergiebehörde.
AEEU (BRIT) n abbr (= Amalgamated
Engineering and Electrical Union)
Gewerkschaft der Ingenieure und
Elektriker.
Aegean [iː'dʒiːən] n: **the** ~ **(Sea)** (GEOG) die

Ägäis, das Ägäische Meer.
aegis ['iːdʒɪs] n: **under the** ~ **of** unter der
Schirmherrschaft +gen.
aeon ['iːən] n Äon m, Ewigkeit f.
aerial ['ɛərɪəl] n Antenne f ♦ adj (view,
bombardment etc) Luft-.
aero... [ɛərə(ʊ)] pref Luft-.
aerobatics ['ɛərəʊ'bætɪks] npl fliegerische
Kunststücke pl.
aerobics [ɛə'rəʊbɪks] n Aerobic nt.
aerodrome ['ɛərədrəʊm] (BRIT) n Flugplatz m.
aerodynamic ['ɛərəʊdaɪ'næmɪk] adj
aerodynamisch.
aeronautics [ɛərə'nɔːtɪks] n Luftfahrt f,
Aeronautik f.
aeroplane ['ɛərəpleɪn] (BRIT) n Flugzeug nt.
aerosol ['ɛərəsɔl] n Sprühdose f.
aerospace industry ['ɛərəuspeɪs-] n
Raumfahrtindustrie f.
aesthetic [iːs'θɛtɪk] adj ästhetisch.
aesthetically [iːs'θɛtɪklɪ] adv ästhetisch.
afar [ə'fɑːʳ] adv: **from** ~ aus der Ferne.
AFB (US) n abbr (= Air Force Base)
Luftwaffenstützpunkt m.
AFDC (US) n abbr (= Aid to Families with
Dependent Children) Beihilfe für
sozialschwache Familien.
affable ['æfəbl] adj umgänglich, freundlich.
affair [ə'fɛəʳ] n Angelegenheit f; (romance: also:
love ~) Verhältnis nt; **affairs** npl Geschäfte
pl.
affect [ə'fɛkt] vt (influence) sich auswirken
auf +acc; (subj: disease) befallen; (move
deeply) bewegen; (concern) betreffen; (feign)
vortäuschen; **to be** ~**ed by sth** von etw
beeinflußt werden.
affectation [æfɛk'teɪʃən] n Affektiertheit f.
affected [ə'fɛktɪd] adj affektiert.
affection [ə'fɛkʃən] n Zuneigung f.
affectionate [ə'fɛkʃənɪt] adj liebevoll,
zärtlich; (animal) anhänglich.
affectionately [ə'fɛkʃənɪtlɪ] adv liebevoll,
zärtlich.
affidavit [æfɪ'deɪvɪt] n (LAW) eidesstattliche
Erklärung f.
affiliated [ə'fɪlieɪtɪd] adj angeschlossen.
affinity [ə'fɪnɪtɪ] n: **to have an** ~ **with** or **for**
sich verbunden fühlen mit; (resemblance):
to have an ~ **with** verwandt sein mit.
affirm [ə'fə:m] vt versichern; (profess) sich
bekennen zu.
affirmation [æfə'meɪʃən] n (of facts)
Bestätigung f; (of beliefs) Bekenntnis nt.
affirmative [ə'fə:mətɪv] adj bejahend ♦ n: **to
reply in the** ~ mit „ja" antworten.
affix [ə'fɪks] vt aufkleben.
afflict [ə'flɪkt] vt quälen; (misfortune)
heimsuchen.
affliction [ə'flɪkʃən] n Leiden nt.
affluence ['æfluəns] n Wohlstand m.
affluent ['æfluənt] adj wohlhabend; **the
** ~ **society** die Wohlstandsgesellschaft.

afford [ə'fɔːd] *vt* sich *dat* leisten; (*time*) aufbringen; (*provide*) bieten; **can we ~ a car?** können wir uns ein Auto leisten?; **I can't ~ the time** ich habe einfach nicht die Zeit.

affordable [ə'fɔːdəbl] *adj* erschwinglich.

affray [ə'freɪ] (*BRIT*) *n* Schlägerei *f*.

affront [ə'frʌnt] *n* Beleidigung *f*.

affronted [ə'frʌntɪd] *adj* beleidigt.

Afghan ['æfgæn] *adj* afghanisch ♦ *n* Afghane *m*, Afghanin *f*.

Afghanistan [æf'gænɪstæn] *n* Afghanistan *nt*.

afield [ə'fiːld] *adv*: **far ~** weit fort; **from far ~** aus weiter Ferne.

AFL-CIO *n abbr* (= *American Federation of Labor and Congress of Industrial Organizations*) amerikanischer Gewerkschafts-Dachverband.

afloat [ə'fləʊt] *adv* auf dem Wasser ♦ *adj*: **to be ~** schwimmen; **to stay ~** sich über Wasser halten; **to keep/get a business ~** ein Geschäft über Wasser halten/auf die Beine stellen.

afoot [ə'fʊt] *adv*: **there is something ~** da ist etwas im Gang.

aforementioned [ə'fɔːmenʃənd] *adj* obenerwähnt.

aforesaid [ə'fɔːsɛd] *adj* = aforementioned.

afraid [ə'freɪd] *adj* ängstlich; **to be ~ of** Angst haben vor +*dat*; **to be ~ of doing sth** *or* **to do sth** Angst davor haben, etw zu tun; **I am ~ that** ... leider ...; **I am ~ so/not** leider ja/nein.

afresh [ə'frɛʃ] *adv* von neuem, neu.

Africa ['æfrɪkə] *n* Afrika *nt*.

African ['æfrɪkən] *adj* afrikanisch ♦ *n* Afrikaner(in) *m(f)*.

Afrikaans [æfrɪ'kɑːns] *n* Afrikaans *nt*.

Afrikaner [æfrɪ'kɑːnəʳ] *n* Afrika(a)nder(in) *m(f)*.

Afro-American ['æfrəʊə'mɛrɪkən] *adj* afroamerikanisch.

AFT (*US*) *n abbr* (= *American Federation of Teachers*) Lehrergewerkschaft.

aft [ɑːft] *adv* (*be*) achtern; (*go*) nach achtern.

after ['ɑːftəʳ] *prep* nach +*dat*; (*of place*) hinter +*dat* ♦ *adv* danach ♦ *conj* nachdem; **~ dinner** nach dem Essen; **the day ~ tomorrow** übermorgen; **what are you ~?** was willst du; **who are you ~?** wen suchst du?; **the police are ~ him** die Polizei ist hinter ihm her; **to name sb ~ sb** jdn nach jdm nennen; **it's twenty ~ eight** (*US*) es ist zwanzig nach acht; **to ask ~ sb** nach jdm fragen; **~ all** schließlich; **~ you!** nach Ihnen!; **~ he left** nachdem er gegangen war; **~ having shaved** nachdem er sich rasiert hatte.

afterbirth ['ɑːftəbɜːθ] *n* Nachgeburt *f*.

aftercare ['ɑːftəkɛəʳ] (*BRIT*) *n* Nachbehandlung *f*.

aftereffects ['ɑːftərɪfɛkts] *npl* Nachwirkungen *pl*.

afterlife·['ɑːftəlaɪf] *n* Leben *nt* nach dem Tod.

aftermath ['ɑːftəmɑːθ] *n* Auswirkungen *pl*; **in the ~ of** nach +*dat*.

afternoon ['ɑːftə'nuːn] *n* Nachmittag *m*.

afters ['ɑːftəz] (*BRIT: inf*) *n* Nachtisch *m*.

after-sales service [ɑːftə'seɪlz-] (*BRIT*) *n* Kundendienst *m*.

aftershave (lotion) ['ɑːftəʃeɪv-] *n* Rasierwasser *nt*.

aftershock ['ɑːftəʃɔk] *n* Nachbeben *nt*.

aftertaste ['ɑːftəteɪst] *n* Nachgeschmack *m*.

afterthought ['ɑːftəθɔːt] *n*: **as an ~** nachträglich; **I had an ~** mir ist noch etwas eingefallen.

afterwards, (*US*) **afterward** ['ɑːftəwəd(z)] *adv* danach.

again [ə'gɛn] *adv* (*once more*) noch einmal; (*repeatedly*) wieder; **not him ~!** nicht schon wieder er!; **to do sth ~** etw noch einmal tun; **to begin ~** noch einmal anfangen; **to see ~** wieder sehen; **he's opened it ~** er hat er schon wieder geöffnet; **~ and ~** immer wieder; **now and ~** ab und zu, hin und wieder.

against [ə'gɛnst] *prep* gegen +*acc*; (*leaning on*) an +*acc*; (*compared to*) gegenüber +*dat*; **~ a blue background** vor einem blauen Hintergrund; **(as) ~** gegenüber +*dat*.

age [eɪdʒ] *n* Alter *nt*; (*period*) Zeitalter *nt* ♦ *vi* altern, alt werden ♦ *vt* alt machen; **what ~ is he?** wie alt ist er?; **20 years of ~** 20 Jahre alt; **under ~** minderjährig; **to come of ~** mündig werden; **it's been ~s since** ... es ist ewig her, seit ...

aged¹ [eɪdʒd] *adj*: **~ ten** zehn Jahre alt, zehnjährig.

aged² ['eɪdʒɪd] *npl*: **the ~** die Alten *pl*.

age group *n* Altersgruppe *f*; **the 40 to 50 ~** die Gruppe der Vierzig- bis Fünfzigjährigen.

ageing ['eɪdʒɪŋ] *adj* (*person, population*) alternd; (*thing*) älter werdend; (*system, technology*) veraltend.

ageless ['eɪdʒlɪs] *adj* zeitlos.

age limit *n* Altersgrenze *f*.

agency ['eɪdʒənsɪ] *n* Agentur *f*; (*government body*) Behörde *f*; **through** *or* **by the ~ of** durch die Vermittlung von.

agenda [ə'dʒɛndə] *n* Tagesordnung *f*.

agent ['eɪdʒənt] *n* (*COMM*) Vertreter(in) *m(f)*; (*representative, spy*) Agent(in) *m(f)*; (*CHEM*) Mittel *nt*; (*fig*) Kraft *f*.

aggravate ['ægrəveɪt] *vt* verschlimmern; (*inf: annoy*) ärgern.

aggravating ['ægrəveɪtɪŋ] (*inf*) *adj* ärgerlich.

aggravation [ægrə'veɪʃən] (*inf*) *n* Ärger *m*.

aggregate ['ægrɪgɪt] *n* Gesamtmenge *f* ♦ *vt* zusammenzählen; **on ~** (*SPORT*) nach Toren.

aggression [ə'grɛʃən] *n* Aggression *f*.

aggressive [ə'grɛsɪv] *adj* aggressiv.

aggressiveness [ə'grɛsɪvnɪs] *n* Aggressivität

f.

aggressor [ə'grɛsə'] *n* Aggressor(in) *m(f)*, Angreifer(in) *m(f)*.

aggrieved [ə'griːvd] *adj* verärgert.

aggro ['ægrəu] (*BRIT: inf*) *n* (*hassle*) Ärger *m*, Theater *nt*; (*aggressive behaviour*) Aggressivität *f*.

aghast [ə'gɑːst] *adj* entsetzt.

agile ['ædʒaɪl] *adj* beweglich, wendig.

agility [ə'dʒɪlɪtɪ] *n* Beweglichkeit *f*, Wendigkeit *f*; (*of mind*) (geistige) Beweglichkeit *f*.

agitate ['ædʒɪteɪt] *vt* aufregen; (*liquid: stir*) aufrühren; (: *shake*) schütteln ♦ *vi*: **to ~ for/ against sth** für/gegen etw agitieren.

agitated ['ædʒɪteɪtɪd] *adj* aufgeregt.

agitator ['ædʒɪteɪtə'] *n* Agitator(in) *m(f)*.

AGM *n abbr* (= *annual general meeting*) JHV *f*.

agnostic [æg'nɔstɪk] *n* Agnostiker(in) *m(f)*.

ago [ə'gəu] *adv*: **2 days ~** vor 2 Tagen; **not long ~** vor kurzem; **as long ~ as 1960** schon 1960; **how long ~?** wie lange ist das her?

agog [ə'gɔg] *adj* gespannt.

agonize ['ægənaɪz] *vi*: **to ~ over sth** sich *dat* den Kopf über etw *acc* zermartern.

agonizing ['ægənaɪzɪŋ] *adj* qualvoll; (*pain etc*) quälend.

agony ['ægənɪ] *n* (*pain*) Schmerz *m*; (*torment*) Qual *f*; **to be in ~** Qualen leiden.

agony aunt (*BRIT: inf*) *n* Briefkastentante *f*.

agony column *n* Kummerkasten *m*.

agree [ə'griː] *vt* (*price, date*) vereinbaren ♦ *vi* übereinstimmen; (*consent*) zustimmen; **to ~ with sb** (*subj: person*) jdm zustimmen; (: *food*) jdm bekommen; **to ~ to sth** einer Sache *dat* zustimmen; **to ~ to do sth** sich bereit erklären, etw zu tun; **to ~ on sth** sich auf etw *acc* einigen; **to ~ that** (*admit*) zugeben, daß; **garlic doesn't ~ with me** Knoblauch vertrage ich nicht; **it was ~d that ...** es wurde beschlossen, daß ...; **they ~d on this** sie haben sich in diesem Punkt geeinigt; **they ~d on going** sie einigten sich darauf, zu gehen; **they ~d on a price** sie vereinbarten einen Preis.

agreeable [ə'griːəbl] *adj* angenehm; (*willing*) einverstanden; **are you ~ to this?** sind Sie hiermit einverstanden?

agreed [ə'griːd] *adj* vereinbart; **to be ~** sich *dat* einig sein.

agreement [ə'griːmənt] *n* (*concurrence*) Übereinstimmung *f*; (*consent*) Zustimmung *f*; (*arrangement*) Abmachung *f*; (*contract*) Vertrag *m*; **to be in ~ (with sb)** (mit jdm) einer Meinung sein; **by mutual ~** in gegenseitigem Einverständnis.

agricultural [ægrɪ'kʌltʃərəl] *adj* landwirtschaftlich; (*show*) Landwirtschafts-.

agriculture ['ægrɪkʌltʃə'] *n* Landwirtschaft *f*.

aground [ə'graund] *adv*: **to run ~** auf Grund laufen.

ahead [ə'hɛd] *adv* vor uns/ihnen *etc*; **~ of** (*in advance of*) vor +*dat*; **to be ~ of sb** (*in progress, ranking*) vor jdm liegen; **to be ~ of schedule** schneller als geplant vorankommen; **~ of time** zeitlich voraus; **to arrive ~ of time** zu früh ankommen; **go right or straight ~** gehen/fahren Sie geradeaus; **go ~!** (*fig*) machen Sie nur!, nur zu!; **they were (right) ~ of us** sie waren (genau) vor uns.

AI *n abbr* (= *Amnesty International*) AI *no art*; (*COMPUT*) = **artificial intelligence**.

AIB (*BRIT*) *n abbr* (= *Accident Investigation Bureau*) *Untersuchungsstelle für Unglücksfälle*.

AID *n abbr* (= *artificial insemination by donor*) *künstliche Besamung durch Samenspender*; (*US*: = *Agency for International Development*) *Abteilung zur Koordination von Entwicklungshilfe und Außenpolitik*.

aid [eɪd] *n* Hilfe *f*; (*to less developed country*) Entwicklungshilfe *f*; (*device*) Hilfsmittel *nt* ♦ *vt* (*help*) helfen, unterstützen; **with the ~ of** mit Hilfe von; **in ~ of** zugunsten +*gen*; **to ~ and abet** Beihilfe leisten; *see also* **hearing aid**.

aide [eɪd] *n* Berater(in) *m(f)*; (*MIL*) Adjutant *m*.

aide-de-camp ['eɪddə'kɔŋ] *n* (*MIL*) Adjutant *m*.

AIDS [eɪdz] *n abbr* (= *acquired immune deficiency syndrome*) AIDS *nt*.

AIH *n abbr* (= *artificial insemination by husband*) *künstliche Besamung durch den Ehemann/ Partner*.

ailing ['eɪlɪŋ] *adj* kränklich; (*economy, industry etc*) krank.

ailment ['eɪlmənt] *n* Leiden *nt*.

aim [eɪm] *vt*: **to ~ at** (*gun, missile, camera*) richten auf +*acc*; (*blow*) zielen auf +*acc*; (*remark*) richten an +*acc* ♦ *vi* (*also*: **take ~**) zielen ♦ *n* (*objective*) Ziel *nt*; (*in shooting*) Zielsicherheit *f*; **to ~ at** zielen auf +*acc*; (*objective*) anstreben +*acc*; **to ~ to do sth** vorhaben, etw zu tun.

aimless ['eɪmlɪs] *adj* ziellos.

aimlessly ['eɪmlɪslɪ] *adv* ziellos.

ain't [eɪnt] (*inf*) = **am not**; **aren't**; **isn't**.

air [ɛə'] *n* Luft *f*; (*tune*) Melodie *f*; (*appearance*) Auftreten *nt*; (*demeanour*) Haltung *f*; (*of house etc*) Atmosphäre *f* ♦ *vt* lüften; (*grievances, views*) Luft machen +*dat*; (*knowledge*) zur Schau stellen; (*ideas*) darlegen ♦ *cpd* Luft-; **into the ~** in die Luft; **by ~** mit dem Flugzeug; **to be on the ~** (*RADIO, TV: programme*) gesendet werden; (: *station*) senden; (: *person*) auf Sendung sein.

air base *n* Luftwaffenstützpunkt *m*.

air bed (*BRIT*) *n* Luftmatratze *f*.

airborne ['ɛəbɔːn] *adj* in der Luft; (*plane, particles*) in der Luft befindlich; (*troops*)

Luftlande-.
air cargo n Luftfracht f.
air-conditioned ['ɛəkən'dɪʃənd] adj klimatisiert.
air conditioning n Klimaanlage f.
air-cooled ['ɛəkuːld] adj (engine) luftgekühlt.
aircraft ['ɛəkrɑːft] n inv Flugzeug nt.
aircraft carrier n Flugzeugträger m.
air cushion n Luftkissen nt.
airfield ['ɛəfiːld] n Flugplatz m.
Air Force n Luftwaffe f.
air freight n Luftfracht f.
air freshener n Raumspray nt.
air gun n Luftgewehr nt.
air hostess (BRIT) n Stewardeß f.
airily ['ɛərɪlɪ] adv leichtfertig.
airing ['ɛərɪŋ] n: **to give an ~ to** (fig: ideas) darlegen; (: views) Luft machen +dat.
air letter (BRIT) n Luftpostbrief m.
airlift ['ɛəlɪft] n Luftbrücke f.
airline ['ɛəlaɪn] n Fluggesellschaft f.
airliner ['ɛəlaɪnə'] n Verkehrsflugzeug nt.
airlock ['ɛəlɔk] n (in pipe etc) Luftblase f; (compartment) Luftschleuse f.
air mail n: **by ~** per or mit Luftpost.
air mattress n Luftmatratze f.
airplane ['ɛəpleɪn] (US) n Flugzeug nt.
air pocket n Luftloch nt.
airport ['ɛəpɔːt] n Flughafen m.
air raid n Luftangriff m.
air rifle n Luftgewehr nt.
airsick ['ɛəsɪk] adj luftkrank.
airspace ['ɛəspeɪs] n Luftraum m.
airspeed ['ɛəspiːd] n Fluggeschwindigkeit f.
airstrip ['ɛəstrɪp] n Start- und Lande-Bahn f.
air terminal n Terminal m or nt.
airtight ['ɛətaɪt] adj luftdicht.
airtime ['ɛətaɪm] n (RADIO, TV) Sendezeit f.
air-traffic control ['ɛətræfɪk-] n Flugsicherung f.
air-traffic controller ['ɛətræfɪk-] n Fluglotse m.
air waybill n Luftfrachtbrief m.
airy ['ɛərɪ] adj luftig; (casual) lässig.
aisle [aɪl] n Gang m; (section of church) Seitenschiff nt.
ajar [ə'dʒɑː'] adj angelehnt.
AK (US) abbr (= Alaska).
a.k.a. abbr (= also known as) alias.
akin [ə'kɪn] adj: **~ to** ähnlich +dat.
AL (US) abbr (POST: = Alabama).
ALA n abbr (= American Library Association) akademischer Verband für das Bibliothekswesen.
Ala. (US) abbr (POST: = Alabama).
alabaster ['æləbɑːstə'] n Alabaster m.
à la carte adv à la carte.
alacrity [ə'lækrɪtɪ] n Bereitwilligkeit f; **with ~** ohne zu zögern.
alarm [ə'lɑːm] n (anxiety) Besorgnis f; (in shop, bank) Alarmanlage f ♦ vt (worry) beunruhigen; (frighten) erschrecken.

alarm call n Weckruf m.
alarm clock n Wecker m.
alarmed [ə'lɑːmd] adj beunruhigt; **don't be ~** erschrecken Sie nicht.
alarming [ə'lɑːmɪŋ] adj (worrying) beunruhigend; (frightening) erschreckend.
alarmingly [ə'lɑːmɪŋlɪ] adv erschreckend.
alarmist [ə'lɑːmɪst] n Panikmacher(in) m(f).
alas [ə'læs] excl leider.
Alaska [ə'læskə] n Alaska nt.
Albania [æl'beɪnɪə] n Albanien nt.
Albanian [æl'beɪnɪən] adj albanisch ♦ n (LING) Albanisch nt.
albatross ['ælbətrɔs] n Albatros m.
albeit [ɔːl'biːɪt] conj wenn auch.
album ['ælbəm] n Album nt.
albumen ['ælbjumɪn] n Albumen nt.
alchemy ['ælkɪmɪ] n Alchimie f, Alchemie f.
alcohol ['ælkəhɔl] n Alkohol m.
alcoholic [ælkə'hɔlɪk] adj alkoholisch ♦ n Alkoholiker(in) m(f).
alcoholism ['ælkəhɔlɪzəm] n Alkoholismus m.
alcove ['ælkəuv] n Alkoven m, Nische f.
Ald. abbr = **alderman**.
alderman ['ɔːldəmən] (irreg: like **man**) n ≈ Stadtrat m.
ale [eɪl] n Ale nt.
alert [ə'lɜːt] adj aufmerksam ♦ n Alarm m ♦ vt alarmieren; **to be ~ to** (danger, opportunity) sich dat bewußt sein +gen; **to be on the ~** wachsam sein; **to ~ sb (to sth)** jdn (vor etw dat) warnen.
Aleutian Islands [ə'luːʃən-] npl Aleuten pl.
A level (BRIT) n ≈ Abschluß m der Sekundarstufe 2, Abitur nt.
Alexandria [ælɪg'zɑːndrɪə] n Alexandria nt.
alfresco [æl'frɛskəu] adj, adv im Freien.
algebra ['ældʒɪbrə] n Algebra f.
Algeria [æl'dʒɪərɪə] n Algerien nt.
Algerian [æl'dʒɪərɪən] adj algerisch ♦ n Algerier(in) m(f).
Algiers [æl'dʒɪəz] n Algier nt.
algorithm ['ælgərɪðəm] n Algorithmus m.
alias ['eɪlɪəs] adv alias ♦ n Deckname m.
alibi ['ælɪbaɪ] n Alibi nt.
alien ['eɪlɪən] n Ausländer(in) m(f); (extraterrestrial) außerirdisches Wesen nt ♦ adj: **~ (to)** fremd (+dat).
alienate ['eɪlɪəneɪt] vt entfremden; (antagonize) befremden.
alienation [eɪlɪə'neɪʃən] n Entfremdung f.
alight [ə'laɪt] adj brennend; (eyes, expression) leuchtend ♦ vi (bird) sich niederlassen; (passenger) aussteigen.
align [ə'laɪn] vt ausrichten.
alignment [ə'laɪnmənt] n Ausrichtung f; **it's out of ~ (with)** es ist nicht richtig ausgerichtet (nach).
alike [ə'laɪk] adj ähnlich ♦ adv (similarly) ähnlich; (equally) gleich; **to look ~** sich dat ähnlich sehen; **winter and summer ~** Sommer wie Winter.

alimony ['ælɪmənɪ] n Unterhalt m.
alive [ə'laɪv] adj (living) lebend; (lively) lebendig; (active) lebhaft; ~ **with** erfüllt von; **to be** ~ **to sth** sich dat einer Sache gen bewußt sein.
alkali ['ælkəlaɪ] n Base f, Lauge f.
alkaline ['ælkəlaɪn] adj basisch, alkalisch.

================= KEYWORD

all [ɔːl] adj alle(r, s); ~ **day/night** den ganzen Tag/die ganze Nacht (über); ~ **men are equal** alle Menschen sind gleich; ~ **five came** alle fünf kamen; ~ **the books** die ganzen Bücher, alle Bücher; ~ **the food** das ganze Essen; ~ **the time** die ganze Zeit (über); ~ **his life** sein ganzes Leben (lang)
♦ pron **1** alles; **I ate it** ~, **I ate** ~ **of it** ich habe alles gegessen; ~ **of us/the boys went** wir alle/alle Jungen gingen; **we** ~ **sat down** wir setzten uns alle; **is that** ~? ist das alles?; (in shop) sonst noch etwas?
2 (in phrases): **above** ~ vor allem; **after** ~ schließlich; ~ **in** ~ alles in allem
♦ adv ganz; ~ **alone** ganz allein; **it's not as hard as** ~ **that** so schwer ist es nun auch wieder nicht; ~ **the more/the better** um so mehr/besser; ~ **but** (all except for) alle außer; (almost) fast; **the score is 2** ~ der Spielstand ist 2 zu 2.

allay [ə'leɪ] vt (fears) zerstreuen.
all clear n Entwarnung f.
allegation [ælɪ'geɪʃən] n Behauptung f.
allege [ə'lɛdʒ] vt behaupten; **he is** ~**d to have said that** ... er soll angeblich gesagt haben, daß ...
alleged [ə'lɛdʒd] adj angeblich.
allegedly [ə'lɛdʒɪdlɪ] adv angeblich.
allegiance [ə'liːdʒəns] n Treue f.
allegory ['ælɪgərɪ] n Allegorie f.
all-embracing ['ɔːlɪm'breɪsɪŋ] adj (all)umfassend.
allergic [ə'lɜːdʒɪk] adj (rash, reaction) allergisch; (person): ~ **to** allergisch gegen.
allergy ['ælədʒɪ] n Allergie f.
alleviate [ə'liːvɪeɪt] vt lindern.
alley ['ælɪ] n Gasse f.
alleyway ['ælɪweɪ] n Durchgang m.
alliance [ə'laɪəns] n Bündnis nt.
allied ['ælaɪd] adj verbündet, alliiert; (products, industries) verwandt.
alligator ['ælɪgeɪtə'] n Alligator m.
all-important ['ɔːlɪm'pɔːtənt] adj entscheidend, äußerst wichtig.
all in (BRIT) adv inklusive.
all-in ['ɔːlɪn] (BRIT) adj (price) Inklusiv-.
all-in wrestling n (esp BRIT) Freistilringen nt.
alliteration [əlɪtə'reɪʃən] n Alliteration f.
all-night ['ɔːl'naɪt] adj (café, cinema) die ganze Nacht geöffnet; (party) die ganze Nacht dauernd.

allocate ['æləkeɪt] vt zuteilen.
allocation [æləu'keɪʃən] n Verteilung f; (of money, resources) Zuteilung f.
allot [ə'lɒt] vt: **to** ~ (**to**) zuteilen (+dat); **in the** ~**ed time** in der vorgesehenen Zeit.
allotment [ə'lɒtmənt] n (share) Anteil m; (garden) Schrebergarten m.
all-out ['ɔːlaut] adj (effort, dedication etc) äußerste(r, s); (strike) total ♦ adv: **all out** mit aller Kraft; **to go all out for** sein Letztes or Äußerstes geben für.
allow [ə'lau] vt erlauben; (behaviour) zulassen; (sum, time) einplanen; (claim, goal) anerkennen; (concede): **to** ~ **that** annehmen, daß; **to** ~ **sb to do sth** jdm erlauben, etw zu tun; **he is** ~**ed to** ... er darf ...; **smoking is not** ~**ed** Rauchen ist nicht gestattet; **we must** ~ **3 days for the journey** wir müssen für die Reise 3 Tage einplanen.
▸**allow for** vt fus einplanen, berücksichtigen.
allowance [ə'lauəns] n finanzielle Unterstützung f; (welfare payment) Beihilfe f; (pocket money) Taschengeld nt; (tax allowance) Freibetrag m; **to make** ~**s for** (person) Zugeständnisse machen für; (thing) berücksichtigen.
alloy ['ælɔɪ] n Legierung f.
all right adv (well) gut; (correctly) richtig; (as answer) okay, in Ordnung.
all-rounder [ɔːl'raundə'] n Allrounder m; (athlete etc) Allroundsportler(in) m(f).
allspice ['ɔːlspaɪs] n Piment m or nt.
all-time ['ɔːl'taɪm] adj aller Zeiten.
allude [ə'luːd] vi: **to** ~ **to** anspielen auf +acc.
alluring [ə'ljuərɪŋ] adj verführerisch.
allusion [ə'luːʒən] n Anspielung f.
alluvium [ə'luːvɪəm] n Anschwemmung f.
ally ['ælaɪ] n Verbündete(r) f(m); (during wars) Alliierte(r) f(m) ♦ vt: **to** ~ **o.s. with** sich verbünden mit.
almighty [ɔːl'maɪtɪ] adj allmächtig; (tremendous) mächtig.
almond ['aːmənd] n Mandel f; (tree) Mandelbaum m.
almost ['ɔːlməust] adv fast, beinahe; **he** ~ **fell** er wäre beinahe gefallen.
alms [aːmz] npl Almosen pl.
aloft [ə'lɒft] adv (hold, carry) empor.
alone [ə'ləun] adj, adv allein; **to leave sb** ~ jdn in Ruhe lassen; **to leave sth** ~ die Finger von etw lassen; **let** ~ ... geschweige denn ...
along [ə'lɒŋ] prep entlang +acc ♦ adv: **is he coming** ~ **with us?** kommt er mit?; **he was hopping/limping** ~ er hüpfte/humpelte daher; ~ **with** (together with) zusammen mit; **all** ~ (all the time) die ganze Zeit.
alongside [ə'lɒŋ'saɪd] prep neben +dat; (ship) längsseits +gen ♦ adv (come) nebendran; (be) daneben; **we brought our boat** ~ wir brachten unser Boot heran; **a car drew up** ~ ein Auto fuhr neben mich/ihn etc heran.
aloof [ə'luːf] adj unnahbar ♦ adv: **to stand** ~

abseits stehen.
aloofness [ə'luːfnɪs] n Unnahbarkeit f.
aloud [ə'laud] adv laut.
alphabet ['ælfəbɛt] n Alphabet nt.
alphabetical [ælfə'bɛtɪkl] adj alphabetisch; **in ~ order** in alphabetischer Reihenfolge.
alphanumeric ['ælfənjuː'mɛrɪk] adj alphanumerisch.
alpine ['ælpaɪn] adj alpin, Alpen-.
Alps [ælps] npl: **the ~** die Alpen.
already [ɔːl'rɛdɪ] adv schon.
alright ['ɔːl'raɪt] (BRIT) adv = **all right.**
Alsace ['ælsæs] n Elsaß nt.
Alsatian [æl'seɪʃən] (BRIT) n (dog) Schäferhund m.
also ['ɔːlsəu] adv (too) auch; (moreover) außerdem.
altar ['ɔltə*] n Altar m.
alter ['ɔltə*] vt ändern; (clothes) umändern ♦ vi sich (ver)ändern.
alteration [ɔltə'reɪʃən] n Änderung f; (to clothes) Umänderung f; (to building) Umbau m; **alterations** npl (SEWING) Änderungen pl; (ARCHIT) Umbau m.
altercation [ɔltə'keɪʃən] n Auseinandersetzung f.
alternate [adj ɔl'təːnɪt, vi 'ɔltəneɪt] adj abwechselnd; (US: alternative: plans etc) Alternativ- ♦ vi: **to ~ (with)** sich abwechseln (mit); **on ~ days** jeden zweiten Tag.
alternately [ɔl'təːnɪtlɪ] adv abwechselnd.
alternating current ['ɔltəneɪtɪŋ-] n Wechselstrom m.
alternative [ɔl'təːnətɪv] adj alternativ; (solution etc) Alternativ- ♦ n Alternative f.
alternative energy n Alternativenergie f.
alternatively [ɔl'təːnətɪvlɪ] adv: **~ one could ...** oder man könnte ...
alternative medicine n Alternativmedizin f.
alternative society n Alternativgesellschaft f.
alternator ['ɔltəːneɪtə*] n (AUT) Lichtmaschine f.
although [ɔːl'ðəu] conj obwohl.
altitude ['æltɪtjuːd] n Höhe f.
alto ['æltəu] n Alt m.
altogether [ɔːltə'gɛðə*] adv ganz; (on the whole, in all) im ganzen, insgesamt; **how much is that ~?** was macht das zusammen?
altruism ['æltruɪzəm] n Altruismus m.
altruistic [æltru'ɪstɪk] adj uneigennützig, altruistisch.
aluminium [ælju'mɪnɪəm], (US) **aluminum** [ə'luːmɪnəm] n Aluminium nt.
always ['ɔːlweɪz] adv immer; **we can ~ ...** (if all else fails) wir können ja auch ...
Alzheimer's (disease) n (MED) Alzheimer-Krankheit f.
AM abbr (= amplitude modulation) AM, ≈ MW.
am [æm] vb see **be.**
a.m. adv abbr (= ante meridiem) morgens; (later) vormittags.

AMA n abbr (= American Medical Association) Medizinerverband.
amalgam [ə'mælgəm] n Amalgam nt; (fig) Mischung f.
amalgamate [ə'mælgəmeɪt] vi, vt fusionieren.
amalgamation [əmælgə'meɪʃən] n Fusion f.
amass [ə'mæs] vt anhäufen; (evidence) zusammentragen.
amateur ['æmətə*] n Amateur m ♦ adj (SPORT: player, athlete) Amateur-; **~ dramatics** Laientheater nt.
amateurish ['æmətərɪʃ] adj (pej) dilettantisch, stümperhaft.
amaze [ə'meɪz] vt erstaunen; **to be ~d (at)** erstaunt sein (über +acc).
amazement [ə'meɪzmənt] n Erstaunen nt.
amazing [ə'meɪzɪŋ] adj erstaunlich; (bargain, offer) sensationell.
amazingly [ə'meɪzɪŋlɪ] adv erstaunlich.
Amazon ['æməzən] n (river) Amazonas m; (MYTHOLOGY) Amazone f; **the ~ basin** das Amazonastiefland; **the ~ jungle** der Amazonas-Regenwald.
Amazonian [æmə'zəunɪən] adj amazonisch.
ambassador [æm'bæsədə*] n Botschafter(in) m(f).
amber ['æmbə*] n Bernstein m; **at ~** (BRIT: traffic lights) auf Gelb; (: move off) bei Gelb.
ambidextrous [æmbɪ'dɛkstrəs] adj beidhändig.
ambience ['æmbɪəns] n Atmosphäre f.
ambiguity [æmbɪ'gjuɪtɪ] n Zweideutigkeit f; (lack of clarity) Unklarheit f.
ambiguous [æm'bɪgjuəs] adj zweideutig; (not clear) unklar.
ambition [æm'bɪʃən] n Ehrgeiz m; (desire) Ambition f; **to achieve one's ~** seine Ambitionen erfüllen.
ambitious [æm'bɪʃəs] adj ehrgeizig.
ambivalence [æm'bɪvələns] n Ambivalenz f.
ambivalent [æm'bɪvələnt] adj ambivalent.
amble ['æmbl] vi schleudern.
ambulance ['æmbjuləns] n Krankenwagen m.
ambulanceman ['æmbjulənsmən] (irreg: like man) n Sanitäter m.
ambush ['æmbuʃ] n Hinterhalt m; (attack) Überfall m aus dem Hinterhalt ♦ vt (aus dem Hinterhalt) überfallen.
ameba [ə'miːbə] (US) n = **amoeba.**
ameliorate [ə'miːlɪəreɪt] vt verbessern.
amen ['ɑːmɛn] excl amen.
amenable [ə'miːnəbl] adj: **~ to** zugänglich +dat; (to flattery etc) empfänglich für; **~ to the law** dem Gesetz verantwortlich.
amend [ə'mɛnd] vt ändern; (habits, behaviour) bessern.
amendment [ə'mɛndmənt] n Änderung f; (to law) Amendement nt.
amends [ə'mɛndz] npl: **to make ~** es wiedergutmachen; **to make ~ for sth** etw wiedergutmachen.
amenities [ə'miːnɪtɪz] npl Einkaufs-, Unter-

haltungs- und Transportmöglichkeiten.
amenity [ə'miːnɪtɪ] *n* (Freizeit)einrichtung *f*.
America [ə'mɛrɪkə] *n* Amerika *nt*.
American [ə'mɛrɪkən] *adj* amerikanisch ♦ *n* Amerikaner(in) *m(f)*.
Americanize [ə'mɛrɪkənaɪz] *vt* amerikanisieren.
amethyst ['æmɪθɪst] *n* Amethyst *m*.
Amex ['æmɛks] *n abbr* (= *American Stock Exchange*) *US-Börse;* (= *American Express* ®) *Kreditkarte.*
amiable ['eɪmɪəbl] *adj* liebenswürdig.
amiably ['eɪmɪəblɪ] *adv* liebenswürdig.
amicable ['æmɪkəbl] *adj* freundschaftlich; (*settlement*) gütlich.
amicably ['æmɪkəblɪ] *adv* (*part, discuss*) in aller Freundschaft; (*settle*) gütlich.
amid(st) [ə'mɪd(st)] *prep* inmitten +gen.
amiss [ə'mɪs] *adj, adv:* **to take sth** ~ etw übelnehmen; **there's something** ~ da stimmt irgend etwas nicht.
ammeter ['æmɪtə*] *n* Amperemeter *nt*.
ammo ['æməu] (*inf*) *n abbr* = **ammunition**.
ammonia [ə'məunɪə] *n* Ammoniak *nt*.
ammunition [æmju'nɪʃən] *n* Munition *f*.
ammunition dump *n* Munitionslager *nt*.
amnesia [æm'niːzɪə] *n* Amnesie *f*, Gedächtnisschwund *m*.
amnesty ['æmnɪstɪ] *n* Amnestie *f*; **to grant an** ~ **to** amnestieren.
Amnesty International *n* Amnesty International *no art*.
amoeba, (*US*) **ameba** [ə'miːbə] *n* Amöbe *f*.
amok [ə'mɔk] *adv:* **to run** ~ Amok laufen.
among(st) [ə'mʌŋ(st)] *prep* unter +dat.
amoral [æ'mɔrəl] *adj* unmoralisch.
amorous ['æmərəs] *adj* amourös.
amorphous [ə'mɔːfəs] *adj* formlos, gestaltlos.
amortization [əmɔːtaɪ'zeɪʃən] *n* Amortisation *f*.
amount [ə'maunt] *n* (*quantity*) Menge *f*; (*sum of money*) Betrag *m*; (*total*) Summe *f*; (*of bill etc*) Höhe *f* ♦ *vi:* **to** ~ **to** (*total*) sich belaufen auf +acc; (*be same as*) gleichkommen +dat; **the total** ~ (*of money*) die Gesamtsumme.
amp(ère) ['æmp(ɛə*)] *n* Ampere *nt*; **a 3** ~ **fuse** eine Sicherung von 3 Ampere; **a 13** ~ **plug** ein Stecker mit einer Sicherung von 13 Ampere.
ampersand ['æmpəsænd] *n* Et-Zeichen *nt*, Und-Zeichen *nt*.
amphetamine [æm'fɛtəmiːn] *n* Amphetamin *nt*.
amphibian [æm'fɪbɪən] *n* Amphibie *f*.
amphibious [æm'fɪbɪəs] *adj* amphibisch; (*vehicle*) Amphibien-.
amphitheatre, (*US*) **amphitheater** ['æmfɪθɪətə*] *n* Amphitheater *nt*.
ample ['æmpl] *adj* (*large*) üppig; (*abundant*) reichlich; (*enough*) genügend; **this is** ~ das ist reichlich; **to have** ~ **time/room** genügend Zeit/Platz haben.

amplifier ['æmplɪfaɪə*] *n* Verstärker *m*.
amplify ['æmplɪfaɪ] *vt* verstärken; (*expand: idea etc*) genauer ausführen.
amply ['æmplɪ] *adv* reichlich.
ampoule, (*US*) **ampule** ['æmpuːl] *n* Ampulle *f*.
amputate ['æmpjuteɪt] *vt* amputieren.
amputation [æmpju'teɪʃən] *n* Amputation *f*.
amputee [æmpju'tiː] *n* Amputierte(r) *f(m)*.
Amsterdam ['æmstədæm] *n* Amsterdam *nt*.
amt *abbr* = **amount**.
amuck [ə'mʌk] *adv* = **amok**.
amuse [ə'mjuːz] *vt* (*entertain*) unterhalten; (*make smile*) amüsieren, belustigen; **to** ~ **o.s. with sth/by doing sth** sich die Zeit mit etw vertreiben/damit vertreiben, etw zu tun; **to be** ~**d at** sich amüsieren über +acc; **he was not** ~**d** er fand das gar nicht komisch *or* zum Lachen.
amusement [ə'mjuːzmənt] *n* (*mirth*) Vergnügen *nt*; (*pleasure*) Unterhaltung *f*; (*pastime*) Zeitvertreib *m*; **much to my** ~ zu meiner großen Belustigung.
amusement arcade *n* Spielhalle *f*.
amusement park *n* Vergnügungspark *m*.
amusing [ə'mjuːzɪŋ] *adj* amüsant, unterhaltsam.
an [æn, ən] *indef art see* **a**.
ANA *n abbr* (= *American Newspaper Association*) *amerikanischer Zeitungsverband;* (= *American Nurses Association*) *Verband amerikanischer Krankenschwestern und Krankenpfleger.*
anachronism [ə'nækrənɪzəm] *n* Anachronismus *m*.
anaemic, (*US*) **anemia** [ə'niːmɪə] *n* Anämie *f*.
anaemic, (*US*) **anemic** [ə'niːmɪk] *adj* blutarm.
anaesthetic, (*US*) **anesthetic** [ænɪs'θɛtɪk] *n* Betäubungsmittel *nt*; **under (the)** ~ unter Narkose; **local** ~ örtliche Betäubung *f*; **general** ~ Vollnarkose *f*.
anaesthetist [æ'niːsθɪtɪst] *n* Anästhesist(in) *m(f)*.
anagram ['ænəgræm] *n* Anagramm *nt*.
anal ['eɪnl] *adj* anal, Anal-.
analgesic [ænæl'dʒiːsɪk] *adj* schmerzstillend ♦ *n* Schmerzmittel *nt*, schmerzstillendes Mittel *nt*.
analogous [ə'næləgəs] *adj:* ~ (**to** *or* **with**) analog (zu).
analogue, (*US*) **analog** ['ænəlɔg] *adj* (*watch, computer*) Analog-.
analogy [ə'nælədʒɪ] *n* Analogie *f*; **to draw an** ~ **between** eine Analogie herstellen zwischen +dat; **by** ~ durch einen Analogieschluß.
analyse, (*US*) **analyze** ['ænəlaɪz] *vt* analysieren; (*CHEM, MED*) untersuchen; (*person*) psychoanalytisch behandeln.
analyses [ə'næləsiːz] *npl of* **analysis**.
analysis [ə'næləsɪs] (*pl* **analyses**) *n* (*see vb*) Analyse *f*; Untersuchung *f*; Psychoanalyse *f*;

in the last ~ letzten Endes.
analyst ['ænəlɪst] n Analytiker(in) m(f); (US)
Psychoanalytiker(in) m(f).
analytic(al) [ænə'lɪtɪk(l)] adj analytisch.
analyze ['ænəlaɪz] (US) vt = **analyse**.
anarchic [æ'nɑːkɪk] adj anarchisch.
anarchist ['ænəkɪst] adj anarchistisch ♦ n
Anarchist(in) m(f).
anarchy ['ænəkɪ] n Anarchie f.
anathema [ə'næθɪmə] n: **that is** ~ **to him** das
ist ihm ein Greuel.
anatomical [ænə'tɔmɪkl] adj anatomisch.
anatomy [ə'nætəmɪ] n Anatomie f; (body)
Körper m.
ANC n abbr (= African National Congress) ANC
m.
ancestor ['ænsɪstə*] n Vorfahr(in) m(f).
ancestral [æn'sɛstrəl] adj angestammt;
~ **home** Stammsitz m.
ancestry ['ænsɪstrɪ] n Abstammung f.
anchor ['æŋkə*] n Anker m ♦ vi (also: **to drop**
~) ankern, vor Anker gehen ♦ vt (fig): **to**
~ **sth to** etw verankern in +dat; **to weigh** ~
den Anker lichten.
anchorage ['æŋkərɪdʒ] n Ankerplatz m.
anchorman [æŋkəmæn] (irreg: like **man**) n (TV,
RADIO) ≈ Moderator m.
anchorwoman [æŋkəwʊmən] (irreg: like
woman) n (TV, RADIO) ≈ Moderatorin f.
anchovy ['æntʃəvɪ] n Sardelle f, An(s)chovis f.
ancient ['eɪnʃənt] adj alt; (person, car) uralt.
ancient monument n historisches Denkmal
nt.
ancillary [æn'sɪlərɪ] adj Hilfs-.
and [ænd] conj und; ~ **so on** und so weiter; **try**
~ **come please** bitte versuche zu kommen;
better ~ **better** immer besser.
Andes ['ændiːz] npl: **the** ~ die Anden pl.
Andorra [æn'dɔːrə] n Andorra nt.
anecdote ['ænɪkdəʊt] n Anekdote f.
anemia etc [ə'niːmɪə] (US) = **anaemia** etc.
anemone [ə'nɛmənɪ] n (BOT) Anemone f,
Buschwindröschen nt.
anesthetic etc [ænɪs'θɛtɪk] (US) = **anaesthetic**
etc.
anew [ə'njuː] adv von neuem.
angel ['eɪndʒəl] n Engel m.
angel dust (inf) n als halluzinogene Droge
mißbrauchtes Medikament.
angelic [æn'dʒɛlɪk] adj engelhaft.
anger ['æŋgə*] n Zorn m ♦ vt ärgern; (enrage)
erzürnen; **red with** ~ rot vor Wut.
angina [æn'dʒaɪnə] n Angina pectoris f.
angle ['æŋgl] n Winkel m; (viewpoint): **from**
their ~ von ihrem Standpunkt aus ♦ vi: **to**
~ **for** (invitation) aussein auf +acc;
(compliments) fischen nach ♦ vt: **to** ~ **sth**
towards or **to** etw ausrichten auf +acc.
angler ['æŋglə*] n Angler(in) m(f).
Anglican ['æŋglɪkən] adj anglikanisch ♦ n
Anglikaner(in) m(f).
anglicize ['æŋglɪsaɪz] vt anglisieren.

angling ['æŋglɪŋ] n Angeln nt.
Anglo- ['æŋgləʊ] pref Anglo-, anglo-.
Anglo-German ['æŋgləʊ'dʒɜːmən] adj
englisch-deutsch.
Anglo-Saxon ['æŋgləʊ'sæksən] adj
angelsächsisch ♦ n Angelsachse m,
Angelsächsin f.
Angola [æŋ'gəʊlə] n Angola nt.
Angolan [æŋ'gəʊlən] adj angolanisch ♦ n
Angolaner(in) m(f).
angrily ['æŋgrɪlɪ] adv verärgert.
angry ['æŋgrɪ] adj verärgert; (wound)
entzündet; **to be** ~ **with sb** auf jdn böse
sein; **to be** ~ **at sth** über etw acc verärgert
sein; **to get** ~ wütend werden; **to make sb** ~
jdn wütend machen.
anguish ['æŋgwɪʃ] n Qual f.
anguished ['æŋgwɪʃt] adj gequält.
angular ['æŋgjʊlə*] adj eckig; (features) kantig.
animal ['ænɪml] n Tier nt; (living creature)
Lebewesen nt; (pej: person) Bestie f ♦ adj
tierhaft; (attraction etc) animalisch.
animal spirits npl Vitalität f.
animate [vt 'ænɪmeɪt, adj 'ænɪmɪt] vt beleben
♦ adj lebend.
animated ['ænɪmeɪtɪd] adj lebhaft; (film)
Zeichentrick-.
animation [ænɪ'meɪʃən] n (liveliness)
Lebhaftigkeit f; (film) Animation f.
animosity [ænɪ'mɔsɪtɪ] n Feindseligkeit f.
aniseed ['ænɪsiːd] n Anis m.
Ankara ['æŋkərə] n Ankara nt.
ankle ['æŋkl] n Knöchel m.
ankle sock (BRIT) n Söckchen nt.
annex ['ænɛks] n (also: ~**e**: BRIT) Anhang m;
(building) Nebengebäude nt; (extension)
Anbau m ♦ vt (take over) annektieren.
annexation [ænɛk'seɪʃən] n Annexion f.
annihilate [ə'naɪəleɪt] vt (also fig) vernichten.
annihilation [ənaɪə'leɪʃən] n Vernichtung f.
anniversary [ænɪ'vɜːsərɪ] n Jahrestag m.
anno Domini adv Anno Domini, nach
Christus.
annotate ['ænəʊteɪt] vt kommentieren.
announce [ə'naʊns] vt ankündigen; (birth,
death etc) anzeigen; **he** ~**d that he wasn't**
going er verkündete, daß er nicht gehen
würde.
announcement [ə'naʊnsmənt] n
Ankündigung f; (official) Bekanntmachung f;
(of birth, death etc) Anzeige f; **I'd like to make**
an ~ ich möchte etwas bekanntgeben.
announcer [ə'naʊnsə*] n Ansager(in) m(f).
annoy [ə'nɔɪ] vt ärgern; **to be** ~**ed (at sth/**
with sb) sich über (etw/jdn) ärgern; **don't**
get ~**ed!** reg' dich nicht auf!
annoyance [ə'nɔɪəns] n Ärger m.
annoying [ə'nɔɪɪŋ] adj ärgerlich; (person,
habit) lästig.
annual ['ænjʊəl] adj jährlich; (income) Jahres-
♦ n (BOT) einjährige Pflanze f; (book)
Jahresband m.

annual general meeting (*BRIT*) *n* Jahreshauptversammlung *f*.

annually ['ænjuəlɪ] *adv* jährlich.

annual report *n* Geschäftsbericht *m*.

annuity [ə'njuːɪtɪ] *n* Rente *f*; **life** ~ Rente *f* auf Lebenszeit.

annul [ə'nʌl] *vt* annullieren; (*law*) aufheben.

annulment [ə'nʌlmənt] *n* (*see vb*) Annullierung *f*; Aufhebung *f*.

annum ['ænəm] *n see* **per**.

Annunciation [ənʌnsɪ'eɪʃən] *n* Mariä Verkündigung *f*.

anode ['ænəud] *n* Anode *f*.

anodyne ['ænədaɪn] (*fig*) *n* Wohltat *f* ♦ *adj* schmerzlos.

anoint [ə'nɔɪnt] *vt* salben.

anomalous [ə'nɔmələs] *adj* anomal.

anomaly [ə'nɔmәlɪ] *n* Anomalie *f*.

anon. [ə'nɔn] *abbr* = **anonymous**.

anonymity [ænə'nɪmɪtɪ] *n* Anonymität *f*.

anonymous [ə'nɔnɪməs] *adj* anonym.

anorak ['ænəræk] *n* Anorak *m*.

anorexia [ænə'rɛksɪə] *n* Magersucht *f*, Anorexie *f*.

anorexic [ænə'rɛksɪk] *adj* magersüchtig.

another [ə'nʌðə˙] *pron* (*additional*) noch eine(r, s); (*different*) ein(e) andere(r, s) ♦ *adj*: ~ **book** (*one more*) noch ein Buch; (*a different one*) ein anderes Buch; ~ **drink?** noch etwas zu trinken?; **in** ~ **5 years** in weiteren 5 Jahren; *see also* **one**.

ANSI [eɪɛnɛs'aɪ] *n abbr* (= *American National Standards Institute*) *amerikanischer Normenausschuß*.

answer ['ɑːnsə˙] *n* Antwort *f*; (*to problem*) Lösung *f* ♦ *vi* antworten; (*TEL*) sich melden ♦ *vt* (*reply to: person*) antworten +*dat*; (: *letter, question*) beantworten; (*problem*) lösen; (*prayer*) erhören; **in** ~ **to your letter** in Beantwortung Ihres Schreibens; **to** ~ **the phone** ans Telefon gehen; **to** ~ **the bell** *or* **the door** die Tür aufmachen.

►**answer back** *vi* widersprechen; (*child*) frech sein.

►**answer for** *vt fus* (*person*) verantwortlich sein für, sich verbürgen für.

►**answer to** *vt fus* (*description*) entsprechen +*dat*.

answerable ['ɑːnsərəbl] *adj*: **to be** ~ **to sb for sth** jdm gegenüber für etw verantwortlich sein; **I am** ~ **to no-one** ich brauche mich vor niemandem zu verantworten.

answering machine ['ɑːnsərɪŋ-] *n* Anrufbeantworter *m*.

ant [ænt] *n* Ameise *f*.

ANTA *n abbr* (= *American National Theater and Academy*) *Nationaltheater und Schauspielerakademie*.

antagonism [æn'tægənɪzəm] *n* Feindseligkeit *f*, Antagonismus *m*.

antagonist [æn'tægənɪst] *n* Gegner(in) *m(f)*, Antagonist(in) *m(f)*.

antagonistic [æntægə'nɪstɪk] *adj* feindselig.

antagonize [æn'tægənaɪz] *vt* gegen sich aufbringen.

Antarctic [ænt'ɑːktɪk] *n*: **the** ~ die Antarktis.

Antarctica [ænt'ɑːktɪkə] *n* Antarktik *f*.

Antarctic Circle *n*: **the** ~ der südliche Polarkreis.

Antarctic Ocean *n*: **the** ~ das Südpolarmeer.

ante ['æntɪ] *n*: **to up the** ~ den Einsatz erhöhen.

ante... ['æntɪ] *pref* vor-.

anteater ['æntiːtə˙] *n* Ameisenbär *m*.

antecedent [æntɪ'siːdənt] *n* Vorläufer *m*; (*of living creature*) Vorfahr *m*; **antecedents** *npl* Herkunft *f*.

antechamber ['æntɪtʃeɪmbə˙] *n* Vorzimmer *nt*.

antelope ['æntɪləup] *n* Antilope *f*.

antenatal ['æntɪ'neɪtl] *adj* vor der Geburt, Schwangerschafts-.

antenatal clinic *n* Sprechstunde *f* für werdende Mütter.

antenna [æn'tɛnə] (*pl* ~**e**) *n* (*of insect*) Fühler *m*; (*RADIO, TV*) Antenne *f*.

antennae [æn'tɛniː] *npl of* **antenna**.

anteroom ['æntɪrum] *n* Vorzimmer *nt*.

anthem ['ænθəm] *n*: **national** ~ Nationalhymne *f*.

ant hill *n* Ameisenhaufen *m*.

anthology [æn'θɔlədʒɪ] *n* Anthologie *f*.

anthropologist [ænθrə'pɔlədʒɪst] *n* Anthropologe *m*, Anthropologin *f*.

anthropology [ænθrə'pɔlədʒɪ] *n* Anthropologie *f*.

anti... ['æntɪ] *pref* Anti-, anti-.

anti-aircraft ['æntɪ'ɛəkrɑːft] *adj* (*gun, rocket*) Flugabwehr-.

anti-aircraft defence *n* Luftverteidigung *f*.

antiballistic ['æntɪbə'lɪstɪk] *adj* (*missile*) Anti-Raketen-.

antibiotic ['æntɪbaɪ'ɔtɪk] *n* Antibiotikum *nt*.

antibody ['æntɪbɔdɪ] *n* Antikörper *m*.

anticipate [æn'tɪsɪpeɪt] *vt* erwarten; (*foresee*) vorhersehen; (*look forward to*) sich freuen auf +*acc*; (*forestall*) vorwegnehmen; **this is worse than I** ~**d** es ist schlimmer, als ich erwartet hatte; **as** ~**d** wie erwartet.

anticipation [æntɪsɪ'peɪʃən] *n* Erwartung *f*; (*eagerness*) Vorfreude *f*; **thanking you in** ~ vielen Dank im voraus.

anticlimax ['æntɪ'klaɪmæks] *n* Enttäuschung *f*.

anticlockwise ['æntɪ'klɔkwaɪz] (*BRIT*) *adv* gegen den Uhrzeigersinn.

antics ['æntɪks] *npl* Mätzchen *pl*; (*of politicians etc*) Gehabe *nt*.

anticyclone ['æntɪ'saɪkləun] *n* Hoch(druckgebiet) *nt*.

antidote ['æntɪdəut] *n* Gegenmittel *nt*.

antifreeze ['æntɪfriːz] *n* Frostschutzmittel *nt*.

antihistamine ['æntɪ'hɪstəmɪn] *n* Antihistamin(ikum) *nt*.

Antilles [æn'tɪliːz] *npl*: **the** ~ die Antillen *pl*.

antipathy [æn'tɪpəθɪ] *n* Antipathie *f*,

Abneigung *f*.
antiperspirant ['æntɪ'pəːspɪrənt] *n*
Antitranspirant *nt*.
Antipodean [æntɪpə'diːən] *adj* antipodisch.
Antipodes [æn'tɪpədiːz] *npl*: **the** ~ Australien
und Neuseeland *nt*.
antiquarian [æntɪ'kwɛərɪən] *n* (*collector*)
Antiquitätensammler(in) *m(f)*; (*seller*)
Antiquitätenhändler(in) *m(f)* ♦ *adj*:
~ **bookshop** Antiquariat *nt*.
antiquated ['æntɪkweɪtɪd] *adj* antiquiert.
antique [æn'tiːk] *n* Antiquität *f* ♦ *adj* antik.
antique dealer *n* Antiquitätenhändler(in)
m(f).
antique shop *n* Antiquitätenladen *m*.
antiquity [æn'tɪkwɪtɪ] *n* (*period*) Antike *f*;
antiquities *npl* (*objects*) Altertümer *pl*.
anti-Semitic ['æntɪsɪ'mɪtɪk] *adj* antisemitisch.
anti-Semitism ['æntɪ'sɛmɪtɪzəm] *n*
Antisemitismus *m*.
antiseptic [æntɪ'sɛptɪk] *n* Antiseptikum *nt*
♦ *adj* antiseptisch.
antisocial ['æntɪ'səuʃəl] *adj* unsozial; (*person*)
ungesellig.
antitank ['æntɪ'tæŋk] *adj* (*gun, fire*)
Panzerabwehr-.
antitheses [æn'tɪθɪsiːz] *npl of* **antithesis**.
antithesis [æn'tɪθɪsɪs] (*pl* **antitheses**) *n*
Gegensatz *m*; **she's the** ~ **of a good cook** sie
ist das genaue Gegenteil einer guten
Köchin.
antitrust ['æntɪ'trʌst] (*US*) *adj*: ~ **legislation**
Kartellgesetzgebung *f*.
antlers ['æntləz] *npl* Geweih *nt*.
Antwerp ['æntwəːp] *n* Antwerpen *nt*.
anus ['eɪnəs] *n* After *m*.
anvil ['ænvɪl] *n* Amboß *m*.
anxiety [æŋ'zaɪətɪ] *n* (*worry*) Sorge *f*; (*MED*)
Angstzustand *m*; (*eagerness*): ~ **to do sth**
Verlangen (danach), etw zu tun.
anxious ['æŋkʃəs] *adj* (*worried*) besorgt;
(*situation*) angsteinflößend; (*question,
moments*) bang(e); (*keen*): **to be** ~ **to do sth**
etw unbedingt tun wollen; **I'm very** ~ **about
you** ich mache mir große Sorgen um dich.
anxiously ['æŋkʃəslɪ] *adv* besorgt.

═══════════════════════ *KEYWORD*

any ['ɛnɪ] *adj* **1** (*in questions etc*): **have you**
~ **butter/children?** haben Sie Butter/
Kinder?; **if there are** ~ **tickets left** falls noch
Karten da sind
2 (*with negative*) kein(e); **I haven't**
~ **money/books** ich habe kein Geld/keine
Bücher
3 (*no matter which*) irgendein(e); **choose**
~ **book you like** nehmen Sie irgendein Buch
or ein beliebiges Buch
4 (*in phrases*): **in** ~ **case** in jedem Fall; ~ **day
now** jeden Tag; **at** ~ **moment** jeden
Moment; **at** ~ **rate** auf jeden Fall; ~ **time** (*at
any moment*) jeden Moment; (*whenever*)

jederzeit
♦ *pron* **1** (*in questions etc*) **have you got** ~?
haben Sie welche?; **can** ~ **of you sing?** kann
(irgend)einer von euch singen?
2 (*with negative*) **I haven't** ~ (**of them**) ich
habe keine (davon)
3 (*no matter which one(s)*) egal welche; **take**
~ **of those books (you like)** nehmen Sie
irgendwelche von diesen Büchern
♦ *adv* **1** (*in questions etc*): **do you want**
~ **more soup/sandwiches?** möchtest du
noch Suppe/Butterbrote?; **are you feeling**
~ **better?** geht es Ihnen etwas besser?
2 (*with negative*): **I can't hear him** ~ **more** ich
kann ihn nicht mehr hören; **don't wait**
~ **longer** warte nicht noch länger.

anybody ['ɛnɪbɔdɪ] *pron* = **anyone**.

═══════════════════════ *KEYWORD*

anyhow ['ɛnɪhau] *adv* **1** (*at any rate*) sowieso,
ohnehin; **I shall go** ~ ich gehe auf jeden Fall
2 (*haphazard*): **do it** ~ **you like** machen Sie
es, wie Sie wollen.

═══════════════════════ *KEYWORD*

anyone ['ɛnɪwʌn] *pron* **1** (*in questions etc*)
(irgend) jemand; **can you see** ~? siehst du
jemanden?
2 (*with negative*) keine(r); **I can't see** ~ ich
kann keinen *or* niemanden sehen
3 (*no matter who*) jede(r); ~ **could do it** das
kann jeder.

anyplace ['ɛnɪpleɪs] (*US*) *adv* = **anywhere**.

═══════════════════════ *KEYWORD*

anything ['ɛnɪθɪŋ] *pron* **1** (*in questions etc*)
(irgend) etwas; **can you see** ~? kannst du
etwas sehen?
2 (*with negative*) nichts; **I can't see** ~ ich
kann nichts sehen
3 (*no matter what*) irgend etwas; **you can say**
~ **you like** du kannst sagen, was du willst;
~ **between 15 and 20 pounds** (ungefähr)
zwischen 15 und 20 Pfund.

═══════════════════════ *KEYWORD*

anyway ['ɛnɪweɪ] *adv* **1** (*at any rate*) sowieso,
ohnehin; **I shall go** ~ ich gehe auf jeden Fall
2 (*besides*): ~, **I can't come** jedenfalls kann
ich nicht kommen; **why are you phoning,** ~?
warum rufst du überhaupt *or* eigentlich an?

═══════════════════════ *KEYWORD*

anywhere ['ɛnɪwɛəˑ] *adv* **1** (*in questions etc*)
irgendwo; **can you see him** ~? kannst du ihn
irgendwo sehen?
2 (*with negative*) nirgendwo, nirgends; **I can't**

see him ~ ich kann ihn nirgendwo *or* nirgends sehen **3** (*no matter where*) irgendwo; **put the books down** ~ legen Sie die Bücher irgendwohin.

Anzac ['ænzæk] *n abbr* (= *Australia-New Zealand Army Corps*) (*soldier*) australischer/ neuseeländischer Soldat *m*.

Anzac Day, *der 25. April, ist in Australien und Neuseeland ein Feiertag zum Gedenken an die Landung der australischen und neuseeländischen Truppen in Gallipoli im ersten Weltkrieg (1915).*

apace [ə'peɪs] *adv:* **to continue** ~ (*negotiations, preparations etc*) rasch vorangehen.

apart [ə'pɑːt] *adv* (*be*) entfernt; (*move*) auseinander; (*aside*) beiseite; (*separately*) getrennt; **10 miles** ~ 10 Meilen voneinander entfernt; **a long way** ~ weit auseinander; **they are living** ~ sie leben getrennt; **with one's legs** ~ mit gespreizten Beinen; **to take** ~ auseinandernehmen; ~ **from** (*excepting*) abgesehen von; (*in addition*) außerdem.

apartheid [ə'pɑːteɪt] *n* Apartheid *f*.

apartment [ə'pɑːtmənt] *n* (*US: flat*) Wohnung *f*; (*room*) Raum *m*, Zimmer *nt*.

apartment building (*US*) *n* Wohnblock *m*.

apathetic [æpə'θetɪk] *adj* apathisch, teilnahmslos.

apathy ['æpəθɪ] *n* Apathie *f*, Teilnahmslosigkeit *f*.

APB (*US*) *n abbr* (= *all points bulletin*) polizeiliche Fahndung.

ape [eɪp] *n* (Menschen)affe *m* ♦ *vt* nachahmen.

Apennines ['æpənaɪnz] *npl:* **the** ~ die Apenninen *pl*, der Appenin.

apéritif *n* Aperitif *m*.

aperture ['æpətʃuəʳ] *n* Öffnung *f*; (*PHOT*) Blende *f*.

APEX ['eɪpɛks] *n abbr* (*AVIAT, RAIL:* = *advance purchase excursion*) APEX.

apex ['eɪpɛks] *n* Spitze *f*.

aphid ['æfɪd] *n* Blattlaus *f*.

aphorism ['æfərɪzəm] *n* Aphorismus *m*.

aphrodisiac [æfrəʊ'dɪzɪæk] *adj* aphrodisisch ♦ *n* Aphrodisiakum *nt*.

API *n abbr* (= *American Press Institute*) amerikanischer Presseverband.

apiece [ə'piːs] *adv* (*each person*) pro Person; (*each thing*) pro Stück.

aplomb [ə'plɔm] *n* Gelassenheit *f*.

APO (*US*) *n abbr* (= *Army Post Office*) Poststelle der Armee.

apocalypse [ə'pɔkəlɪps] *n* Apokalypse *f*.

apolitical [eɪpə'lɪtɪkl] *adj* apolitisch.

apologetic [əpɔlə'dʒetɪk] *adj* entschuldigend; **to be very** ~ (**about sth**) sich (wegen etw *gen*) sehr entschuldigen.

apologize [ə'pɔlədʒaɪz] *vi:* **to** ~ (**for sth to sb**) sich (für etw bei jdm) entschuldigen.

apology [ə'pɔlədʒɪ] *n* Entschuldigung *f*; **to send one's apologies** sich entschuldigen lassen; **please accept my apologies** ich bitte um Verzeihung.

apoplectic [æpə'plɛktɪk] *adj* (*MED*) apoplektisch; (*fig*): **to be** ~ **with rage** vor Wut fast platzen.

apoplexy ['æpəplɛksɪ] *n* Schlaganfall *m*.

apostle [ə'pɔsl] *n* Apostel *m*.

apostrophe [ə'pɔstrəfɪ] *n* Apostroph *m*, Auslassungszeichen *nt*.

apotheosis [əpɔθɪ'əʊsɪs] *n* Apotheose *f*.

appal [ə'pɔːl] *vt* entsetzen; **to be** ~**led by** entsetzt sein über +*acc*.

Appalachian Mountains [æpə'leɪʃən-] *npl:* **the** ~ die Appalachen *pl*.

appalling [ə'pɔːlɪŋ] *adj* entsetzlich; **she's an** ~ **cook** sie kann überhaupt nicht kochen.

apparatus [æpə'reɪtəs] *n* Gerät *nt*; (*in gymnasium*) Geräte *pl*; (*of organization*) Apparat *m*; **a piece of** ~ ein Gerät *nt*.

apparel [ə'pærəl] (*US*) *n* Kleidung *f*.

apparent [ə'pærənt] *adj* (*seeming*) scheinbar; (*obvious*) offensichtlich; **it is** ~ **that** ... es ist klar, daß ...

apparently [ə'pærəntlɪ] *adv* anscheinend.

apparition [æpə'rɪʃən] *n* Erscheinung *f*.

appeal [ə'piːl] *vi* (*LAW*) Berufung einlegen ♦ *n* (*LAW*) Berufung *f*; (*plea*) Aufruf *m*; (*charm*) Reiz *m*; **to** ~ (**to sb**) **for** (jdn) bitten um; **to** ~ **to** (*be attractive to*) gefallen +*dat*; **it doesn't** ~ **to me** es reizt mich nicht; **right of** ~ (*LAW*) Berufungsrecht *nt*; **on** ~ (*LAW*) in der Berufung.

appealing [ə'piːlɪŋ] *adj* ansprechend; (*touching*) rührend.

appear [ə'pɪəʳ] *vi* erscheinen; (*seem*) scheinen; **to** ~ **on TV/in "Hamlet"** im Fernsehen/in „Hamlet" auftreten; **it would** ~ **that** ... anscheinend ...

appearance [ə'pɪərəns] *n* Erscheinen *nt*; (*look*) Aussehen *nt*; (*in public, on TV*) Auftritt *m*; **to put in** *or* **make an** ~ sich sehen lassen; **in** *or* **by order of** ~ (*THEAT etc*) in der Reihenfolge ihres Auftritts; **to keep up** ~**s** den (äußeren) Schein wahren; **to all** ~**s** allem Anschein nach.

appease [ə'piːz] *vt* beschwichtigen.

appeasement [ə'piːzmənt] *n* Beschwichtigung *f*.

append [ə'pɛnd] *vt* (*COMPUT*) anhängen.

appendage [ə'pɛndɪdʒ] *n* Anhängsel *nt*.

appendices [ə'pɛndɪsiːz] *npl of* **appendix**.

appendicitis [əpɛndɪ'saɪtɪs] *n* Blinddarmentzündung *f*.

appendix [ə'pɛndɪks] (*pl* **appendices**) *n* (*ANAT*) Blinddarm *m*; (*to publication*) Anhang *m*; **to have one's** ~ **out** sich *dat* den Blinddarm herausnehmen lassen.

appetite ['æpɪtaɪt] *n* Appetit *m*; (*fig*) Lust *f*; **that walk has given me an** ~ von dem

Spaziergang habe ich Appetit bekommen.
appetizer ['æpɪtaɪzə'] n (food) Appetithappen m; (drink) appetitanregendes Getränk nt.
appetizing ['æpɪtaɪzɪŋ] adj appetitanregend.
applaud [ə'plɔːd] vi applaudieren, klatschen ♦ vt (actor etc) applaudieren +dat, Beifall spenden or klatschen +dat; (action, attitude) loben; (decision) begrüßen.
applause [ə'plɔːz] n Applaus m, Beifall m.
apple ['æpl] n Apfel m; **he's the ~ of her eye** er ist ihr ein und alles.
apple tree n Apfelbaum m.
apple turnover n Apfeltasche f.
appliance [ə'plaɪəns] n Gerät nt.
applicable [ə'plɪkəbl] adj: ~ **(to)** anwendbar (auf +acc); (on official forms) zutreffend (auf +acc); **the law is ~ from January** das Gesetz gilt ab Januar.
applicant ['æplɪkənt] n Bewerber(in) m(f).
application [æplɪ'keɪʃən] n (for job) Bewerbung f; (for grant etc) Antrag m; (hard work) Fleiß m; (applying: of paint etc) Auftragen nt; **on ~** auf Antrag.
application form n (for a job) Bewerbungsformular nt; (for a grant etc) Antragsformular nt.
application program n (COMPUT) Anwendungsprogramm nt.
applications package n (COMPUT) Anwendungspaket nt.
applied [ə'plaɪd] adj angewandt.
apply [ə'plaɪ] vt anwenden; (paint etc) auftragen ♦ vi: **to ~ (to)** (be applicable) gelten (für); **to ~ the brakes** die Bremse betätigen, bremsen; **to ~ o.s. to sth** sich bei etw anstrengen; **to ~ to** (ask) sich wenden an +acc; **to ~ for** (permit, grant) beantragen; (job) sich bewerben um.
appoint [ə'pɔɪnt] vt ernennen; (date, place) festlegen, festsetzen.
appointed [ə'pɔɪntɪd] adj: **at the ~ time** zur festgesetzten Zeit.
appointee [əpɔɪn'tiː] n Ernannte(r) f(m).
appointment [ə'pɔɪntmənt] n Ernennung f; (post) Stelle f; (arranged meeting) Termin m; **to make an ~ (with sb)** einen Termin (mit jdm) vereinbaren; **by ~** nach Anmeldung, mit Voranmeldung.
apportion [ə'pɔːʃən] vt aufteilen; (blame) zuweisen; **to ~ sth to sb** jdm etw zuteilen.
apposition [æpə'zɪʃən] n Apposition f, Beifügung f; **A is in ~ to B** A ist eine Apposition zu B.
appraisal [ə'preɪzl] n Beurteilung f.
appraise [ə'preɪz] vt beurteilen.
appreciable [ə'priːʃəbl] adj merklich, deutlich.
appreciably [ə'priːʃəblɪ] adv merklich.
appreciate [ə'priːʃɪeɪt] vt (like) schätzen; (be grateful for) zu schätzen wissen; (understand) verstehen; (be aware of) sich dat bewußt sein +gen ♦ vi (COMM: currency, shares) im Wert

steigen; **I ~ your help** ich weiß Ihre Hilfe zu schätzen.
appreciation [əpriːʃɪ'eɪʃən] n (enjoyment) Wertschätzung f; (understanding) Verständnis nt; (gratitude) Dankbarkeit f; (COMM: in value) (Wert)steigerung f.
appreciative [ə'priːʃɪətɪv] adj dankbar; (comment) anerkennend.
apprehend [æprɪ'hɛnd] vt (arrest) festnehmen; (understand) verstehen.
apprehension [æprɪ'hɛnʃən] n (fear) Besorgnis f; (arrest) Festnahme f.
apprehensive [æprɪ'hɛnsɪv] adj ängstlich; **to be ~ about sth** sich dat Gedanken or Sorgen um etw machen.
apprentice [ə'prɛntɪs] n Lehrling m, Auszubildende(r) f(m) ♦ vt: **to be ~d to sb** bei jdm in der Lehre sein.
apprenticeship [ə'prɛntɪsʃɪp] n Lehre f, Lehrzeit f; **to serve one's ~** seine Lehre machen.
appro. ['æprəu] (BRIT: inf) abbr (COMM: = approval): **on ~** zur Ansicht.
approach [ə'prəutʃ] vi sich nähern; (event) nahen ♦ vt (come to) sich nähern +dat; (ask, apply to: person) herantreten an +acc, ansprechen; (situation, problem) herangehen an +acc, angehen ♦ n (advance) (Heran)nahen nt; (access) Zugang m; (: of vehicles) Zufahrt f; (to problem etc) Ansatz m; **to ~ sb about sth** jdn wegen etw ansprechen.
approachable [ə'prəutʃəbl] adj (person) umgänglich; (place) zugänglich.
approach road n Zufahrtsstraße f.
approbation [æprə'beɪʃən] n Zustimmung f.
appropriate [adj ə'prəuprɪɪt, vt ə'prəuprɪeɪt] adj (apt) angebracht; (relevant) entsprechend ♦ vt sich dat aneignen; **it would not be ~ for me to comment** es wäre nicht angebracht, wenn ich mich dazu äußern würde.
appropriately [ə'prəuprɪɪtlɪ] adv entsprechend.
appropriation [əprəuprɪ'eɪʃən] n Zuteilung f, Zuweisung f.
approval [ə'pruːvəl] n (approbation) Zustimmung f, Billigung f; (permission) Einverständnis f; **to meet with sb's ~** jds Zustimmung or Beifall finden; **on ~** (COMM) zur Probe.
approve [ə'pruːv] vt billigen; (motion, decision) annehmen.
► **approve of** vt fus etwas halten von; **I don't ~ of it/him** ich halte nichts davon/von ihm.
approved school [ə'pruːvd-] (BRIT) n Erziehungsheim nt.
approvingly [ə'pruːvɪŋlɪ] adv zustimmend.
approx. abbr = **approximately**.
approximate [adj ə'prɔksɪmɪt, vb ə'prɔksɪmeɪt] adj ungefähr ♦ vt, vi: **to ~ (to)** nahekommen +dat.
approximately [ə'prɔksɪmɪtlɪ] adv ungefähr.
approximation [ə'prɔksɪ'meɪʃən] n

Annäherung *f.*
APR *n abbr* (= *annual(ized) percentage rate*)
Jahreszinssatz *m.*
Apr. *abbr* = **April.**
apricot ['eɪprɪkɔt] *n* Aprikose *f.*
April ['eɪprəl] *n* April *m;* ~ **fool!** April, April!;
see also **July.**
apron ['eɪprən] *n* Schürze *f;* (*AVIAT*) Vorfeld *nt.*
apse [æps] *n* Apsis *f.*
APT (*BRIT*) *n abbr* (= *Advanced Passenger Train*)
Hochgeschwindigkeitszug *m.*
Apt. *abbr* = **apartment.**
apt [æpt] *adj* (*suitable*) passend, treffend;
(*likely*): **to be** ~ **to do sth** dazu neigen, etw
zu tun.
aptitude ['æptɪtjuːd] *n* Begabung *f.*
aptitude test *n* Eignungstest *m.*
aptly ['æptlɪ] *adv* passend, treffend.
aqualung ['ækwəlʌŋ] *n* Tauchgerät *nt.*
aquarium [ə'kwɛərɪəm] *n* Aquarium *nt.*
Aquarius [ə'kwɛərɪəs] *n* Wassermann *m;* **to be**
~ (ein) Wassermann sein.
aquatic [ə'kwætɪk] *adj* (*plants etc*) Wasser-;
(*life*) im Wasser.
aqueduct ['ækwɪdʌkt] *n* Aquädukt *m or nt.*
AR (*US*) *abbr* (*POST:* = *Arkansas*).
ARA (*BRIT*) *n abbr* (= *Associate of the Royal
Academy*) Qualifikationsnachweis im
künstlerischen Bereich.
Arab ['ærəb] *adj* arabisch ♦ *n* Araber(in) *m(f).*
Arabia [ə'reɪbɪə] *n* Arabien *nt.*
Arabian [ə'reɪbɪən] *adj* arabisch.
Arabian Desert *n:* **the** ~ die Arabische
Wüste.
Arabian Sea *n:* **the** ~ das Arabische Meer.
Arabic ['ærəbɪk] *adj* arabisch ♦ *n* (*LING*)
Arabisch *nt.*
arable ['ærəbl] *adj* (*land*) bebaubar; ~ **farm**
Bauernhof, der ausschließlich Ackerbau
betreibt.
ARAM (*BRIT*) *n abbr* (= *Associate of the Royal
Academy of Music*) Qualifikationsnachweis
in Musik.
arbiter ['ɑːbɪtə*] *n* Vermittler *m.*
arbitrary ['ɑːbɪtrərɪ] *adj* willkürlich.
arbitrate ['ɑːbɪtreɪt] *vi* vermitteln.
arbitration [ɑːbɪ'treɪʃən] *n* Schlichtung *f;* **the
dispute went to** ~ der Streit wurde vor eine
Schlichtungskommission gebracht.
arbitrator ['ɑːbɪtreɪtə*] *n* Vermittler(in) *m(f);*
(*INDUSTRY*) Schlichter(in) *m(f).*
ARC *n abbr* (= *American Red Cross*) ≈ DRK *nt.*
arc [ɑːk] *n* Bogen *m.*
arcade [ɑː'keɪd] *n* Arkade *f;* (*shopping mall*)
Passage *f.*
arch [ɑːtʃ] *n* Bogen *m;* (*of foot*) Gewölbe *nt* ♦ *vt*
(*back*) krümmen ♦ *adj* schelmisch ♦ *pref*
Erz-.
archaeological [ɑːkɪə'lɔdʒɪkl] *adj*
archäologisch.
archaeologist [ɑːkɪ'ɔlədʒɪst] *n* Archäologe *m,*
Archäologin *f.*

archaeology, (*US*) **archeology** [ɑːkɪ'ɔlədʒɪ] *n*
Archäologie *f.*
archaic [ɑː'keɪɪk] *adj* altertümlich; (*language*)
veraltet, archaisch.
archangel ['ɑːkeɪndʒəl] *n* Erzengel *m.*
archbishop [ɑːtʃ'bɪʃəp] *n* Erzbischof *m.*
archenemy ['ɑːtʃ'ɛnəmɪ] *n* Erzfeind(in) *m(f).*
archeology *etc* [ɑːkɪ'ɔlədʒɪ] (*US*)
= **archaeology** *etc.*
archery ['ɑːtʃərɪ] *n* Bogenschießen *nt.*
archetypal ['ɑːkɪtaɪpəl] *adj* (*arche*)typisch.
archetype ['ɑːkɪtaɪp] *n* Urbild *nt,* Urtyp *m.*
archipelago [ɑːkɪ'pɛlɪgəu] *n* Archipel *m.*
architect ['ɑːkɪtɛkt] *n* Architekt(in) *m(f).*
architectural [ɑːkɪ'tɛktʃərəl] *adj*
architektonisch.
architecture ['ɑːkɪtɛktʃə*] *n* Architektur *f.*
archive file *n* (*COMPUT*) Archivdatei *f.*
archives ['ɑːkaɪvz] *npl* Archiv *nt.*
archivist ['ɑːkɪvɪst] *n* Archivar(in) *m(f).*
archway ['ɑːtʃweɪ] *n* Torbogen *m.*
ARCM (*BRIT*) *n abbr* (= *Associate of the Royal
College of Music*) Qualifikationsnachweis in
Musik.
Arctic ['ɑːktɪk] *adj* arktisch ♦ *n:* **the** ~ die
Arktis.
Arctic Circle *n:* **the** ~ der nördliche
Polarkreis.
Arctic Ocean *n:* **the** ~ das Nordpolarmeer.
ARD (*US*) *n abbr* (*MED:* = *acute respiratory
disease*) akute Erkrankung der Atemwege.
ardent ['ɑːdənt] *adj* leidenschaftlich; (*admirer*)
glühend.
ardour, (*US*) **ardor** ['ɑːdə*] *n* Leidenschaft *f.*
arduous ['ɑːdjuəs] *adj* mühsam.
are [ɑː*] *vb see* **be.**
area ['ɛərɪə] *n* Gebiet *nt;* (*GEOM etc*) Fläche *f;*
(*dining area etc*) Bereich *m;* **in the London** ~
im Raum London.
area code (*US*) *n* Vorwahl(nummer) *f.*
arena [ə'riːnə] *n* Arena *f.*
aren't [ɑːnt] = **are not.**
Argentina [ɑːdʒən'tiːnə] *n* Argentinien *nt.*
Argentinian [ɑːdʒən'tɪnɪən] *adj* argentinisch
♦ *n* Argentinier(in) *m(f).*
arguable ['ɑːgjuəbl] *adj:* **it is** ~ **whether ...** es
ist (noch) die Frage, ob ...; **it is** ~ **that ...**
man kann (wohl) sagen, daß ...
arguably ['ɑːgjuəblɪ] *adv* wohl; **it is** ~ **...** es
dürfte wohl ... sein.
argue ['ɑːgjuː] *vi* (*quarrel*) sich streiten;
(*reason*) diskutieren ♦ *vt* (*debate*)
diskutieren, erörtern; **to** ~ **that ...** den
Standpunkt vertreten, daß ...; **to** ~ **about**
sth sich über etw *acc* streiten; **to** ~ **for/
against sth** sich für/gegen etw aussprechen.
argument ['ɑːgjumənt] *n* (*reasons*) Argument
nt; (*quarrel*) Streit *m,* Auseinandersetzung *f;*
(*debate*) Diskussion *f;* ~ **for/against**
Argument für/gegen; **to have an** ~ sich
streiten.
argumentative [ɑːgjuˈmɛntətɪv] *adj*

streitlustig.
aria ['ɑːrɪə] n Arie f.
ARIBA [[ə'riːbə]] (BRIT) n abbr (= Associate of
the Royal Institute of British Architects)
Qualifikationsnachweis in Architektur.
arid ['ærɪd] adj (land) dürr; (subject) trocken.
aridity [ə'rɪdɪtɪ] n Dürre f, Trockenheit f.
Aries ['ɛərɪz] n Widder m; **to be** ~ (ein)
Widder sein.
arise [ə'raɪz] (pt **arose**, pp **arisen**) vi (difficulty
etc) sich ergeben; (question) sich stellen; **to**
~ **from** sich ergeben aus, herrühren von;
should the need ~ falls es nötig wird.
arisen [ə'rɪzn] pp of **arise**.
aristocracy [ærɪs'tɔkrəsɪ] n Aristokratie f,
Adel m.
aristocrat ['ærɪstəkræt] n Aristokrat(in) m(f),
Ad(e)lige(r) f(m).
aristocratic [ærɪstə'krætɪk] n aristokratisch,
ad(e)lig.
arithmetic [ə'rɪθmətɪk] n Rechnen nt;
(calculation) Rechnung f.
arithmetical [ærɪθ'mɛtɪkl] adj rechnerisch,
arithmetisch.
Ariz. (US) abbr (POST: = Arizona).
ark [ɑːk] n: **Noah's A**~ die Arche Noah.
arm [ɑːm] n Arm m; (of clothing) Ärmel m; (of
chair) Armlehne f; (of organization etc) Zweig
m ♦ vt bewaffnen; **arms** npl (weapons) Waffen
pl; (HERALDRY) Wappen nt.
armaments ['ɑːməmənts] npl (weapons)
(Aus)rüstung f.
armband ['ɑːmbænd] n Armbinde f.
armchair ['ɑːmtʃɛə*] n Sessel m, Lehnstuhl m.
armed [ɑːmd] adj bewaffnet; **the** ~ **forces** die
Streitkräfte pl.
armed robbery n bewaffneter Raubüberfall
m.
Armenia [ɑː'miːnɪə] n Armenien nt.
Armenian [ɑː'miːnɪən] adj armenisch ♦ n
Armenier(in) m(f); (LING) Armenisch nt.
armful ['ɑːmful] n Armvoll m.
armistice ['ɑːmɪstɪs] n Waffenstillstand m.
armour, (US) **armor** ['ɑːmə*] n (HIST)
Rüstung f; (also: ~-**plating**) Panzerplatte f;
(MIL: tanks) Panzerfahrzeuge pl.
armoured car ['ɑːməd-] n Panzerwagen m.
armoury ['ɑːmərɪ] n (storeroom) Waffenlager
nt.
armpit ['ɑːmpɪt] n Achselhöhle f.
armrest ['ɑːmrɛst] n Armlehne f.
arms control [ɑːmz-] n Rüstungskontrolle f.
arms race [ɑːmz-] n: **the** ~ das Wettrüsten.
army ['ɑːmɪ] n Armee f, Heer nt; (fig: host)
Heer.
aroma [ə'rəumə] n Aroma nt, Duft m.
aromatherapy [ərəumə'θɛrəpɪ] n
Aromatherapie f.
aromatic [ærə'mætɪk] adj aromatisch,
duftend.
arose [ə'rəuz] pt of **arise**.
around [ə'raund] adv (about) herum; (in the

area) in der Nähe ♦ prep (encircling) um ...
herum; (near) in der Nähe von; (fig: about:
dimensions) etwa; (: : time) gegen; (: : date)
um; **is he** ~? ist er da?; ~ **£5** um die £5, etwa
£5; ~ **3 o'clock** gegen 3 Uhr.
arousal [ə'rauzəl] n (sexual) Erregung f; (of
feelings, interest) Weckung f.
arouse [ə'rauz] vt (feelings, interest) wecken.
arpeggio [ɑː'pɛdʒɪəu] n Arpeggio nt.
arrange [ə'reɪndʒ] vt (meeting etc)
vereinbaren; (tour etc) planen; (books etc)
anordnen; (flowers) arrangieren; (MUS)
arrangieren, bearbeiten ♦ vi: **we have** ~**d for
a car to pick you up** wir haben veranlaßt,
daß Sie mit dem Auto abgeholt werden; **it
was** ~**d that** ... es wurde vereinbart, daß ...;
to ~ **to do sth** vereinbaren or ausmachen,
etw zu tun.
arrangement [ə'reɪndʒmənt] n (agreement)
Vereinbarung f; (layout) Anordnung f; (MUS)
Arrangement nt, Bearbeitung f;
arrangements npl Pläne pl; (preparations)
Vorbereitungen pl; **to come to an** ~ **with sb**
eine Regelung mit jdm treffen; **home
deliveries by** ~ nach Vereinbarung
Lieferung ins Haus; **I'll make** ~**s for you to
be met** ich werde veranlassen, daß Sie
abgeholt werden.
arrant ['ærənt] adj (coward, fool etc) Erz-;
(nonsense) total.
array [ə'reɪ] n: **an** ~ **of** (things) eine Reihe von;
(people) Aufgebot an +dat; (MATH, COMPUT)
(Daten)feld nt.
arrears [ə'rɪəz] npl Rückstand m; **to be in** ~
with one's rent mit seiner Miete im
Rückstand sein.
arrest [ə'rɛst] vt (person) verhaften; (sb's
attention) erregen ♦ n Verhaftung f; **under** ~
verhaftet.
arresting [ə'rɛstɪŋ] adj (fig) atemberaubend.
arrival [ə'raɪvl] n Ankunft f; (COMM: of goods)
Sendung f; **new** ~ (person) Neuankömmling
m; (baby) Neugeborene(s) nt.
arrive [ə'raɪv] vi ankommen.
▶**arrive at** vt fus (fig: conclusion) kommen zu;
(: situation) es bringen zu.
arrogance ['ærəgəns] n Arroganz f,
Überheblichkeit f.
arrogant ['ærəgənt] adj arrogant, überheblich.
arrow ['ærəu] n Pfeil m.
arse [ɑːs] (BRIT: inf!) n Arsch m (!).
arsenal ['ɑːsɪnl] n Waffenlager nt; (stockpile)
Arsenal nt.
arsenic ['ɑːsnɪk] n Arsen nt.
arson ['ɑːsn] n Brandstiftung f.
art [ɑːt] n Kunst f; **Arts** npl (SCOL)
Geisteswissenschaften pl; **work of** ~
Kunstwerk nt.
artefact ['ɑːtɪfækt] n Artefakt nt.
arterial [ɑː'tɪərɪəl] adj arteriell; ~ **road**
Fernverkehrsstraße f; ~ **line** (RAIL)
Hauptstrecke f.

artery ['ɑːtərɪ] n Arterie f, Schlagader f; (fig) Verkehrsader f.

artful ['ɑːtful] adj raffiniert.

art gallery n Kunstgalerie f.

arthritic [ɑː'θrɪtɪk] adj arthritisch.

arthritis [ɑː'θraɪtɪs] n Arthritis f.

artichoke ['ɑːtɪtʃəuk] n (also: globe ~) Artischocke f; (also: Jerusalem ~) Topinambur m.

article ['ɑːtɪkl] n Artikel m; (object, item) Gegenstand m; **articles** (BRIT) npl (LAW) (Rechts)referendarzeit f; ~ **of clothing** Kleidungsstück nt.

articles of association npl (COMM) Gesellschaftsvertrag m.

articulate [adj ɑː'tɪkjulɪt, vt, vi ɑː'tɪkjuleɪt] adj (speech, writing) klar; (speaker) redegewandt ♦ vt darlegen ♦ vi artikulieren; **to be ~** (person) sich gut ausdrücken können.

articulated lorry (BRIT) n Sattelschlepper m.

artifice ['ɑːtɪfɪs] n List f.

artificial [ɑːtɪ'fɪʃəl] adj künstlich; (manner) gekünstelt; **to be ~** (person) gekünstelt or unnatürlich wirken.

artificial insemination [-ɪnsɛmɪ'neɪʃən] n künstliche Besamung f.

artificial intelligence n künstliche Intelligenz f.

artificial respiration n künstliche Beatmung f.

artillery [ɑː'tɪlərɪ] n Artillerie f.

artisan ['ɑːtɪzæn] n Handwerker m.

artist ['ɑːtɪst] n Künstler(in) m(f).

artistic [ɑː'tɪstɪk] adj künstlerisch.

artistry ['ɑːtɪstrɪ] n künstlerisches Geschick nt.

artless ['ɑːtlɪs] adj arglos.

art school n Kunstakademie f, Kunsthochschule f.

artwork ['ɑːtwɜːk] n (for advert etc, material for printing) Druckvorlage f; (in book) Bildmaterial nt.

ARV n abbr (BIBLE: = American Revised Version) amerikanische revidierte Bibelübersetzung.

AS (US) n abbr (= Associate in/of Science) akademischer Grad in Naturwissenschaften ♦ abbr (POST: = American Samoa).

════════════════ KEYWORD

as [æz] conj **1** (referring to time) als; ~ **the years went by** mit den Jahren; **he came in ~ I was leaving** als er hereinkam, ging ich gerade; ~ **from tomorrow** ab morgen

2 (in comparisons): ~ **big** ~ so groß wie; **twice** ~ **big** ~ zweimal so groß wie; ~ **much/many** ~ soviel/so viele wie; ~ **soon** ~ sobald; **much** ~ **I admire her** ... so sehr ich sie auch bewundere ...

3 (since, because) da, weil; ~ **you can't come I'll go without you** da du nicht mitkommen

kannst, gehe ich ohne dich

4 (referring to manner, way) wie; **do** ~ **you wish** mach, was du willst; ~ **she said** wie sie sagte; **he gave it to me** ~ **a present** er gab es mir als Geschenk; ~ **it were** sozusagen

5 (in the capacity of) als; **he works** ~ **a driver** er arbeitet als Fahrer

6 (concerning): ~ **for** or **to that** was das betrifft or angeht

7: ~ **if** or **though** als ob; see also **long, such, well**.

ASA n abbr (= American Standards Association) amerikanischer Normenausschuß.

a.s.a.p. adv abbr (= as soon as possible) baldmöglichst.

asbestos [æz'bɛstəs] n Asbest m.

ascend [ə'sɛnd] vt hinaufsteigen; (throne) besteigen.

ascendancy [ə'sɛndənsɪ] n Vormachtstellung f; ~ **over sb** Vorherrschaft über jdn.

ascendant [ə'sɛndənt] n: **to be in the** ~ im Aufstieg begriffen sein.

ascension [ə'sɛnʃən] n: **the A**~ (REL) die Himmelfahrt f (Christi).

Ascension Island n Ascension nt.

ascent [ə'sɛnt] n Aufstieg m.

ascertain [æsə'teɪn] vt feststellen.

ascetic [ə'sɛtɪk] adj asketisch.

asceticism [ə'sɛtɪsɪzəm] n Askese f.

ASCII ['æskiː] n abbr (COMPUT: = American Standard Code for Information Interchange) ASCII.

ascribe [ə'skraɪb] vt: **to** ~ **sth to** etw zuschreiben +dat; (cause) etw zurückführen auf +acc.

ASCU (US) n abbr (= Association of State Colleges and Universities) Verband staatlicher Bildungseinrichtungen.

ASEAN ['æsɪæn] n abbr (= Association of Southeast Asian Nations) ASEAN f (Gemeinschaft südostasiatischer Staaten).

ASH [æʃ] (BRIT) n abbr (= Action on Smoking and Health) Anti-Raucher-Initiative.

ash [æʃ] n Asche f; (wood, tree) Esche f.

ashamed [ə'ʃeɪmd] adj beschämt; **to be ~ of** sich schämen für; **to be ~ of o.s. for having done sth** sich schämen, daß man etw getan hat.

A shares npl stimmrechtslose Aktien pl.

ashen ['æʃən] adj (face) aschfahl.

ashore [ə'ʃɔː] adv an Land.

ashtray ['æʃtreɪ] n Aschenbecher m.

Ash Wednesday n Aschermittwoch m.

Asia ['eɪʃə] n Asien nt.

Asia Minor n Kleinasien nt.

Asian ['eɪʃən] adj asiatisch ♦ n Asiat(in) m(f).

Asiatic [eɪsɪ'ætɪk] adj asiatisch.

aside [ə'saɪd] adv zur Seite; (take) beiseite ♦ n beiseite gesprochene Worte pl; **to brush objections** ~ Einwände beiseite schieben.

aside from prep außer +dat.

ask [ɑːsk] vt fragen; (invite) einladen; **to ~ sb to do sth** jdn bitten, etw zu tun; **to ~ (sb) sth** (jdn) etw fragen; **to ~ sb a question** jdm eine Frage stellen; **to ~ sb the time** jdn nach der Uhrzeit fragen; **to ~ sb about sth** jdn nach etw fragen; **to ~ sb out to dinner** jdn zum Essen einladen.
►**ask after** vt fus fragen nach.
►**ask for** vt fus bitten um; (trouble) haben wollen; **it's just ~ing for trouble/it** das kann ja nicht gutgehen.

askance [əˈskɑːns] adv: **to look ~ at sb** jdn mißtrauisch ansehen; **to look ~ at sth** etw mit Mißtrauen betrachten.

askew [əˈskjuː] adv schief.

asking price [ˈɑːskɪŋ-] n: **the ~** der geforderte Preis.

asleep [əˈsliːp] adj schlafend; **to be ~** schlafen; **to fall ~** einschlafen.

ASLEF [ˈæzlɛf] (BRIT) n abbr (= Associated Society of Locomotive Engineers and Firemen) Eisenbahnergewerkschaft.

asp [æsp] n Natter f.

asparagus [əsˈpærəgəs] n Spargel m.

asparagus tips npl Spargelspitzen pl.

ASPCA n abbr (= American Society for the Prevention of Cruelty to Animals) Tierschutzverein.

aspect [ˈæspɛkt] n (of subject) Aspekt m; (of building etc) Lage f; (quality, air) Erscheinung f; **to have a south-westerly ~** nach Südwesten liegen.

aspersions [əsˈpɜːʃənz] npl: **to cast ~ on** sich abfällig äußern über +acc.

asphalt [ˈæsfælt] n Asphalt m.

asphyxiate [æsˈfɪksɪeɪt] vt ersticken.

asphyxiation [æsfɪksɪˈeɪʃən] n Erstickung f.

aspirate [ˈæspəreɪt] vt aspirieren, behauchen.

aspirations [æspəˈreɪʃənz] npl Hoffnungen pl; **to have ~ to(wards)** sth etw anstreben.

aspire [əsˈpaɪə*] vi: **to ~ to** streben nach.

aspirin [ˈæsprɪn] n Kopfschmerztablette f, Aspirin ® nt.

aspiring [əsˈpaɪərɪŋ] adj aufstrebend.

ass [æs] n (also fig) Esel m; (US: inf!) Arsch! m.

assail [əˈseɪl] vt angreifen; (fig): **to be ~ed by doubts** von Zweifeln geplagt werden.

assailant [əˈseɪlənt] n Angreifer(in) m(f).

assassin [əˈsæsɪn] n Attentäter(in) m(f).

assassinate [əˈsæsɪneɪt] vt ermorden, ein Attentat verüben auf +acc.

assassination [əsæsɪˈneɪʃən] n Ermordung f, (geglücktes) Attentat nt.

assault [əˈsɔːlt] n Angriff m ♦ vt angreifen; (sexually) vergewaltigen; **~ and battery** (LAW) Körperverletzung f.

assemble [əˈsɛmbl] vt versammeln; (car, machine) montieren; (furniture etc) zusammenbauen ♦ vi sich versammeln.

assembly [əˈsɛmblɪ] n Versammlung f; (of car, machine) Montage f; (of furniture) Zusammenbau m.

assembly language n (COMPUT) Assemblersprache f.

assembly line n Fließband nt.

assent [əˈsɛnt] n Zustimmung f ♦ vi: **to ~ (to)** zustimmen (+dat).

assert [əˈsɜːt] vt behaupten; (innocence) beteuern; (authority) geltend machen; **to ~ o.s.** sich durchsetzen.

assertion [əˈsɜːʃən] n Behauptung f.

assertive [əˈsɜːtɪv] adj (person) selbstbewußt; (manner) bestimmt.

assess [əˈsɛs] vt (situation) einschätzen; (abilities etc) beurteilen; (tax) festsetzen; (damages, property etc) schätzen.

assessment [əˈsɛsmənt] n (see vt) Einschätzung f; Beurteilung f; Festsetzung f; Schätzung f.

assessor [əˈsɛsə*] n (LAW: expert) Gutachter(in) m(f).

asset [ˈæsɛt] n Vorteil m; (person) Stütze f; **assets** npl (property, funds) Vermögen nt; (COMM) Aktiva pl.

asset-stripping [ˈæsɛtˈstrɪpɪŋ] n (COMM) Aufkauf von finanziell gefährdeten Firmen und anschließender Verkauf ihrer Vermögenswerte.

assiduous [əˈsɪdjuəs] adj gewissenhaft.

assign [əˈsaɪn] vt: **to ~ (to)** (date) zuweisen (+dat); (task) übertragen (+dat); (person) einteilen (für); (cause) zuschreiben (+dat); (meaning) zuordnen (+dat); **to ~ sb to do sth** jdn damit beauftragen, etw zu tun.

assignment [əˈsaɪnmənt] n Aufgabe f.

assimilate [əˈsɪmɪleɪt] vt aufnehmen; (immigrants) integrieren.

assimilation [əsɪmɪˈleɪʃən] n (see vt) Aufnahme f; Integration f.

assist [əˈsɪst] vt helfen; (with money etc) unterstützen.

assistance [əˈsɪstəns] n Hilfe f; (with money etc) Unterstützung f.

assistant [əˈsɪstənt] n Assistent(in) m(f); (BRIT: also: **shop ~**) Verkäufer(in) m(f).

assistant manager n stellvertretender Geschäftsführer m, stellvertretende Geschäftsführerin f.

assizes [əˈsaɪzɪz] (BRIT) npl Gerichtstage pl.

associate [adj, n əˈsəʊʃɪɪt, vt, vi əˈsəʊʃɪeɪt] adj (director) assoziiert; (member, professor) außerordentlich ♦ n (at work) Kollege m, Kollegin f ♦ vt in Verbindung bringen ♦ vi: **to ~ with sb** mit jdm verkehren.

associated company [əˈsəʊʃɪeɪtɪd-] n Partnerfirma f.

association [əsəʊsɪˈeɪʃən] n (group) Verband m; (involvement) Verbindung f; (PSYCH) Assoziation f; **in ~ with** in Zusammenarbeit mit.

association football n Fußball m.

assorted [əˈsɔːtɪd] adj gemischt; (various) diverse(r, s); **in ~ sizes** in verschiedenen Größen.

assortment [ə'sɔːtmənt] n Mischung f; (of books, people etc) Ansammlung f.

Asst abbr = **assistant**.

assuage [ə'sweɪdʒ] vt (grief, pain) lindern; (thirst, appetite) stillen, befriedigen.

assume [ə'sjuːm] vt annehmen; (responsibilities etc) übernehmen.

assumed name [ə'sjuːmd-] n Deckname m.

assumption [ə'sʌmpʃən] n Annahme f; (of power etc) Übernahme f; **on the ~ that ...** vorausgesetzt, daß ...

assurance [ə'ʃuərəns] n Versicherung f; (promise) Zusicherung f; (confidence) Zuversicht f; **I can give you no ~s** ich kann Ihnen nichts versprechen.

assure [ə'ʃuə'] vt versichern; (guarantee) sichern.

assured [ə'ʃuəd] n (BRIT) Versicherte(r) f(m) ♦ adj sicher.

AST (US) abbr (= Atlantic Standard Time) Ortszeit in Ostkanada.

asterisk ['æstərɪsk] n Sternchen nt.

astern [ə'stəːn] adv achtern.

asteroid ['æstərɔɪd] n Asteroid m.

asthma ['æsmə] n Asthma nt.

asthmatic [æs'mætɪk] adj asthmatisch ♦ n Asthmatiker(in) m(f).

astigmatism [ə'stɪgmətɪzəm] n Astigmatismus m.

astir [ə'stəː'] adv: **to be ~** (out of bed) auf sein.

astonish [ə'stɔnɪʃ] vt erstaunen.

astonishing [ə'stɔnɪʃɪŋ] adj erstaunlich; **I find it ~ that ...** es überrascht mich, daß ...

astonishingly [ə'stɔnɪʃɪŋlɪ] adv erstaunlich; **~, ...** erstaunlicherweise ...

astonishment [ə'stɔnɪʃmənt] n Erstaunen nt.

astound [ə'staund] vt verblüffen, sehr erstaunen.

astounded [ə'staundɪd] adj (höchst) erstaunt.

astounding [ə'staundɪŋ] adj erstaunlich.

astray [ə'streɪ] adv: **to go ~** (letter) verlorengehen; (fig) auf Abwege geraten; **to lead ~** auf Abwege bringen; **to go ~ in one's calculations** sich verrechnen.

astride [ə'straɪd] adv (sit, ride) rittlings; (stand) breitbeinig ♦ prep rittlings auf +dat; breitbeinig über +dat.

astringent [əs'trɪndʒənt] adj adstringierend; (fig: caustic) ätzend, beißend ♦ n Adstringens nt.

astrologer [əs'trɔlədʒə'] n Astrologe m, Astrologin f.

astrology [əs'trɔlədʒɪ] n Astrologie f.

astronaut ['æstrənɔːt] n Astronaut(in) m(f).

astronomer [əs'trɔnəmə'] n Astronom(in) m(f).

astronomical [æstrə'nɔmɪkl] adj (also fig) astronomisch.

astronomy [əs'trɔnəmɪ] n Astronomie f.

astrophysics ['æstrəu'fɪzɪks] n Astrophysik f.

astute [əs'tjuːt] adj scharfsinnig; (operator, behaviour) geschickt.

asunder [ə'sʌndə'] adv: **to tear ~**

auseinanderreißen.

ASV n abbr (BIBLE: = American Standard Version) amerikanische Standard-Bibelübersetzung.

asylum [ə'saɪləm] n Asyl nt; (mental hospital) psychiatrische Klinik f; **to seek political ~** um (politisches) Asyl bitten.

asymmetrical [eɪsɪ'mɛtrɪkl] adj asymmetrisch.

═══════════════════════════════ *KEYWORD*

at [æt] prep **1** (referring to position, direction) an +dat, in +dat; **~ the top** an der Spitze; **~ home** zu Hause; **~ school** in der Schule; **~ the baker's** beim Bäcker; **to look ~ sth** auf etw acc blicken

2 (referring to time): **~ 4 o'clock** um 4 Uhr; **~ night/dawn** bei Nacht/Tagesanbruch; **~ Christmas** zu Weihnachten; **~ times** zuweilen

3 (referring to rates, speed etc): **~ £2 a kilo** zu £2 pro Kilo; **two ~ a time** zwei auf einmal; **~ 50 km/h** mit 50 km/h

4 (referring to activity): **to be ~ work** (in office etc) auf der Arbeit sein; **to play ~ cowboys** Cowboy spielen; **to be good ~ sth** gut in etw dat sein

5 (referring to cause): **shocked/surprised/annoyed ~ sth** schockiert/überrascht/verärgert über etw acc; **I went ~ his suggestion** ich ging auf seinen Vorschlag hin

6: **not ~ all** (in answer to question) überhaupt nicht, ganz und gar nicht; (in answer to thanks) nichts zu danken, keine Ursache; **I'm not ~ all tired** ich bin überhaupt nicht müde; **anything ~ all** irgend etwas.

───

ate [eɪt] pt of **eat**.

atheism ['eɪθiːɪzəm] n Atheismus m.

atheist ['eɪθiːɪst] n Atheist(in) m(f).

Athenian [ə'θiːnɪən] adj Athener ♦ n Athener(in) m(f).

Athens ['æθɪnz] n Athen nt.

athlete ['æθliːt] n Athlet(in) m(f).

athletic [æθ'lɛtɪk] adj sportlich; (muscular) athletisch.

athletics [æθ'lɛtɪks] n Leichtathletik f.

Atlantic [ət'læntɪk] adj atlantisch; (coast etc) Atlantik- ♦ n: **the ~ (Ocean)** der Atlantik.

atlas ['ætləs] n Atlas m.

Atlas Mountains npl: **the ~** der Atlas, das Atlas-Gebirge.

ATM abbr (= automated telling machine) Geldautomat m.

atmosphere ['ætməsfɪə'] n Atmosphäre f; (air) Luft f.

atmospheric [ætməs'fɛrɪk] adj atmosphärisch.

atmospherics [ætməs'fɛrɪks] npl atmosphärische Störungen pl.

atoll ['ætɔl] n Atoll nt.

atom ['ætəm] n Atom nt.
atomic [ə'tɔmɪk] adj atomar; (energy, weapons) Atom-.
atom(ic) bomb n Atombombe f.
atomizer ['ætəmaɪzə'] n Zerstäuber m.
atone [ə'təun] vi: **to ~ for** büßen für.
atonement [ə'təunmənt] n Buße f.
A to Z ® n Stadtplan m.
ATP n abbr (= Association of Tennis Professionals) Tennis-Profiverband.
atrocious [ə'trəuʃəs] adj grauenhaft.
atrocity [ə'trɔsɪtɪ] n Greueltat f.
atrophy ['ætrəfɪ] n Schwund m, Atrophie f ♦ vt schwinden lassen ♦ vi schwinden, verkümmern.
attach [ə'tætʃ] vt befestigen; (document, letter) anheften, beiheften; (employee, troops) zuteilen; (importance etc) beimessen; **to be ~ed to sb/sth** (like) an jdm/etw hängen; (be connected with) mit jdm/etw zu tun haben; **the ~ed letter** der beiliegende Brief.
attaché [ə'tæʃeɪ] n Attaché m.
attaché case n Aktenkoffer m.
attachment [ə'tætʃmənt] n (tool) Zubehörteil nt; (love): **~ (to sb)** Zuneigung f (zu jdm).
attack [ə'tæk] vt angreifen; (subj: criminal) überfallen; (task, problem etc) in Angriff nehmen ♦ n (also fig) Angriff m; (on sb's life) Anschlag m; (of illness) Anfall m; **heart ~** Herzanfall m, Herzinfarkt m.
attacker [ə'tækə'] n Angreifer(in) m(f).
attain [ə'teɪn] vt (also: **~ to**) erreichen; (knowledge) erlangen.
attainments [ə'teɪnmənts] npl Fähigkeiten pl.
attempt [ə'tɛmpt] n Versuch m ♦ vt versuchen; **to make an ~ on sb's life** einen Anschlag auf jdn verüben.
attempted [ə'tɛmptɪd] adj versucht; **~ murder/suicide** Mord-/Selbstmordversuch m; **~ theft** versuchter Diebstahl.
attend [ə'tɛnd] vt besuchen; (patient) behandeln.
▶**attend to** vt fus sich kümmern um; (needs) nachkommen +dat; (customer) bedienen.
attendance [ə'tɛndəns] n Anwesenheit f; (people present) Besucherzahl f; (SPORT) Zuschauerzahl f.
attendant [ə'tɛndənt] n (helper) Begleiter(in) m(f); (in garage) Tankwart m; (in museum) Aufseher(in) m(f) ♦ adj damit verbunden.
attention [ə'tɛnʃən] n Aufmerksamkeit f; (care) Fürsorge f ♦ excl (MIL) Achtung!; **attentions** npl (acts of courtesy) Aufmerksamkeiten pl; **for the ~ of ...** zu Händen von ...; **it has come to my ~ that ...** ich bin darauf aufmerksam geworden, daß ...; **to stand to** or **at ~** (MIL) stillstehen.
attentive [ə'tɛntɪv] adj aufmerksam.
attentively [ə'tɛntɪvlɪ] adv aufmerksam.
attenuate [ə'tɛnjueɪt] vt abschwächen ♦ vi schwächer werden.

attest [ə'tɛst] vt, vi: **to ~ (to)** bezeugen.
attic ['ætɪk] n Dachboden m.
attire [ə'taɪə'] n Kleidung f.
attitude ['ætɪtjuːd] n (posture, manner) Haltung f; (mental): **~ to** or **towards** Einstellung f zu.
attorney [ə'təːnɪ] n (US: lawyer) (Rechts)anwalt m, (Rechts)anwältin f; (having proxy) Bevollmächtigte(r) f(m); **power of ~** Vollmacht f.
Attorney General n (BRIT) ≈ Justizminister(in) m(f); (US) ≈ Generalbundesanwalt m, Generalbundesanwältin f.
attract [ə'trækt] vt (draw) anziehen; (interest) auf sich acc lenken; (attention) erregen.
attraction [ə'trækʃən] n Anziehungskraft f; (of house, city) Reiz m; (gen pl: amusements) Attraktion f; (fig) **to feel an ~ towards sb/ sth** sich von jdm/etw angezogen fühlen.
attractive [ə'træktɪv] adj attraktiv; (price, idea, offer) verlockend, reizvoll.
attribute [n 'ætrɪbjuːt, vt ə'trɪbjuːt] n Eigenschaft f ♦ vt: **to ~ sth to** (cause) etw zurückführen auf +acc; (poem, painting) etw zuschreiben +dat; (quality) etw beimessen +dat.
attribution [ætrɪ'bjuːʃən] n (see vt) Zurückführung f; Zuschreibung f; Beimessung f.
attrition [ə'trɪʃən] n: **war of ~** Zermürbungskrieg m.
Atty. Gen. abbr = **Attorney General.**
ATV n abbr (= all-terrain vehicle) Geländefahrzeug nt.
atypical [eɪ'tɪpɪkl] adj atypisch.
aubergine ['əubəʒiːn] n Aubergine f; (colour) Aubergine nt.
auburn ['ɔːbən] adj rotbraun.
auction ['ɔːkʃən] n (also: **sale by ~**) Versteigerung f, Auktion f ♦ vt versteigern.
auctioneer [ɔːkʃə'nɪə'] n Versteigerer m.
auction room n Auktionssaal m.
audacious [ɔː'deɪʃəs] adj wagemutig, kühn.
audacity [ɔː'dæsɪtɪ] n Kühnheit f, Verwegenheit f; (pej: impudence) Dreistigkeit f.
audible ['ɔːdɪbl] adj hörbar.
audience ['ɔːdɪəns] n Publikum nt; (RADIO) Zuhörer pl; (TV) Zuschauer pl; (with queen etc) Audienz f.
audiotypist ['ɔːdɪəutaɪpɪst] n Phonotypist(in) m(f).
audiovisual ['ɔːdɪəu'vɪzjuəl] adj audiovisuell.
audiovisual aid n audiovisuelles Lehrmittel nt.
audit ['ɔːdɪt] vt (COMM) prüfen ♦ n Buchprüfung f, Rechnungsprüfung f.
audition [ɔː'dɪʃən] n Vorsprechprobe f ♦ vi: **to ~ (for)** vorsprechen (für).
auditor ['ɔːdɪtə'] n Buchprüfer(in) m(f), Rechnungsprüfer(in) m(f).
auditorium [ɔːdɪ'tɔːrɪəm] n (building) Auditorium nt; (audience area)

Zuschauerraum *m*.

Aug. *abbr* = **August**.

augment [ɔːgˈment] *vt* vermehren; (*income, diet*) verbessern.

augur [ˈɔːgə'] *vi:* **it ~s well** das ist ein gutes Zeichen *or* Omen.

August [ˈɔːgəst] *n* August *m*; *see also* **July**.

august [ɔːˈgʌst] *adj* erhaben.

aunt [ɑːnt] *n* Tante *f*.

auntie [ˈɑːntɪ] *n dimin of* **aunt**.

aunty [ˈɑːntɪ] *n dimin of* **aunt**.

au pair [ˈəuˈpɛə'] *n* (*also:* ~ **girl**) Au-Pair (-Mädchen) *nt*.

aura [ˈɔːrə] *n* Aura *f*.

auspices [ˈɔːspɪsɪz] *npl:* **under the ~ of** unter der Schirmherrschaft +*gen*.

auspicious [ɔːsˈpɪʃəs] *adj* verheißungsvoll; (*opening, start*) vielversprechend.

austere [ɔsˈtɪə'] *adj* streng; (*room, decoration*) schmucklos; (*person, lifestyle*) asketisch.

austerity [ɔsˈtɛrɪtɪ] *n* Strenge *f*; (*of room etc*) Schmucklosigkeit *f*; (*hardship*) Entbehrung *f*.

Australasia [ɔːstrəˈleɪzɪə] *n* Australien und Ozeanien *nt*.

Australasian [ɔːstrəˈleɪzɪən] *adj* ozeanisch, südwestpazifisch.

Australia [ɔsˈtreɪlɪə] *n* Australien *nt*.

Australian [ɔsˈtreɪlɪən] *adj* australisch ♦ *n* Australier(in) *m(f)*.

Austria [ˈɔstrɪə] *n* Österreich *nt*.

Austrian [ˈɔstrɪən] *adj* österreichisch ♦ *n* Österreicher(in) *m(f)*.

AUT (*BRIT*) *n abbr* (= *Association of University Teachers*) *Gewerkschaft der Universitätsdozenten*.

authentic [ɔːˈθentɪk] *adj* authentisch.

authenticate [ɔːˈθentɪkeɪt] *vt* beglaubigen.

authenticity [ɔːθenˈtɪsɪtɪ] *n* Echtheit *f*.

author [ˈɔːθə'] *n* (*of text*) Verfasser(in) *m(f)*; (*profession*) Autor(in) *m(f)*, Schriftsteller(in) *m(f)*; (*creator*) Urheber(in) *m(f)*; (: *of plan*) Initiator(in) *m(f)*.

authoritarian [ɔːθɔrɪˈtɛərɪən] *adj* autoritär.

authoritative [ɔːˈθɔrɪtətɪv] *adj* (*person, manner*) bestimmt, entschieden; (*source, account*) zuverlässig; (*study, treatise*) maßgeblich, maßgebend.

authority [ɔːˈθɔrɪtɪ] *n* Autorität *f*; (*government body*) Behörde *f*, Amt *nt*; (*official permission*) Genehmigung *f*; **the authorities** *npl* (*ruling body*) die Behörden *pl*; **to have the ~ to do sth** befugt sein, etw zu tun.

authorization [ɔːθəraɪˈzeɪʃən] *n* Genehmigung *f*.

authorize [ˈɔːθəraɪz] *vt* genehmigen; **to ~ sb to do sth** jdn ermächtigen, etw zu tun.

authorized capital [ˈɔːθəraɪzd-] *n* autorisiertes Aktienkapital *nt*.

authorship [ˈɔːθəʃɪp] *n* Autorschaft *f*, Verfasserschaft *f*.

autistic [ɔːˈtɪstɪk] *adj* autistisch.

auto [ˈɔːtəu] (*US*) *n* Auto *nt*, Wagen *m*.

autobiographical [ˈɔːtəbaɪəˈgræfɪkl] *adj* autobiographisch.

autobiography [ɔːtəbaɪˈɔgrəfɪ] *n* Autobiographie *f*.

autocratic [ɔːtəˈkrætɪk] *adj* autokratisch.

Autocue ® [ˈɔːtəukjuː] *n* Teleprompter *m*.

autograph [ˈɔːtəgrɑːf] *n* Autogramm *nt* ♦ *vt* signieren.

autoimmune [ɔːtəuɪˈmjuːn] *adj* (*disease*) Autoimmun-.

automat [ˈɔːtəmæt] *n* Automat *m*; (*US*) Automatenrestaurant *nt*.

automata [ɔːˈtɔmətə] *npl of* **automaton**.

automate [ˈɔːtəmeɪt] *vt* automatisieren.

automatic [ɔːtəˈmætɪk] *adj* automatisch ♦ *n* (*gun*) automatische Waffe; (*washing machine*) Waschautomat *m*; (*car*) Automatikwagen *m*.

automatically [ɔːtəˈmætɪklɪ] *adv* automatisch.

automatic data processing *n* automatische Datenverarbeitung *f*.

automation [ɔːtəˈmeɪʃən] *n* Automatisierung *f*.

automaton [ɔːˈtɔmətən] (*pl* **automata**) *n* Roboter *m*.

automobile [ˈɔːtəməbiːl] (*US*) *n* Auto(mobil) *nt*.

autonomous [ɔːˈtɔnəməs] *adj* autonom.

autonomy [ɔːˈtɔnəmɪ] *n* Autonomie *f*.

autopsy [ˈɔːtɔpsɪ] *n* Autopsie *f*.

autumn [ˈɔːtəm] *n* Herbst *m*; **in ~** im Herbst.

autumnal [ɔːˈtʌmnəl] *adj* herbstlich.

auxiliary [ɔːgˈzɪlɪərɪ] *adj* (*tool, verb*) Hilfs- ♦ *n* (*assistant*) Hilfskraft *f*.

AV *n abbr* (*BIBLE:* = *Authorized Version*) *englische Bibelübersetzung von 1611* ♦ *abbr* = **audiovisual**.

Av. *abbr* = **avenue**.

avail [əˈveɪl] *vt:* **to ~ o.s. of** Gebrauch machen von ♦ *n:* **to no ~** vergeblich, erfolglos.

availability [əveɪləˈbɪlɪtɪ] *n* Erhältlichkeit *f*; (*of staff*) Vorhandensein *nt*.

available [əˈveɪləbl] *adj* erhältlich; (*person: unoccupied*) frei, abkömmlich; (: *unattached*) zu haben; (*time*) frei, verfügbar; **every ~ means** alle verfügbaren Mittel; **is the manager ~?** ist der Geschäftsführer zu sprechen?; **to make sth ~ to sb** jdm etw zur Verfügung stellen.

avalanche [ˈævəlɑːnʃ] *n* (*also fig*) Lawine *f*.

avant-garde [ˈævãŋˈgɑːd] *adj* avantgardistisch.

avarice [ˈævərɪs] *n* Habsucht *f*.

avaricious [ævəˈrɪʃəs] *adj* habsüchtig.

avdp. *abbr* (= *avoirdupois*) *Handelsgewicht*.

Ave *abbr* = **avenue**.

avenge [əˈvendʒ] *vt* rächen.

avenue [ˈævənjuː] *n* Straße *f*; (*drive*) Auffahrt *f*; (*means*) Weg *m*.

average [ˈævərɪdʒ] *n* Durchschnitt *m* ♦ *adj* durchschnittlich, Durchschnitts- ♦ *vt* (*reach an average of*) einen Durchschnitt erreichen von; **on** ~ im Durchschnitt, durchschnittlich; **above/below (the)** ~ über/unter dem Durchschnitt.

▶**average out** vi: to ~ out at durchschnittlich ausmachen.

averse [ə'vɜːs] adj: **to be** ~ **to sth/doing sth** eine Abneigung gegen etw haben/dagegen haben, etw zu tun; **I wouldn't be** ~ **to a drink** ich hätte nichts gegen einen Drink.

aversion [ə'vɜːʃən] n Abneigung f; **to have an** ~ **to sb/sth** eine Abneigung gegen jdn/etw haben.

avert [ə'vɜːt] vt (prevent) verhindern; (ward off) abwehren; (turn away) abwenden.

aviary ['eɪvɪərɪ] n Vogelhaus nt.

aviation [eɪvɪ'eɪʃən] n Luftfahrt f.

avid ['ævɪd] adj begeistert, eifrig.

avidly ['ævɪdlɪ] adv begeistert, eifrig.

avocado [ævə'kɑːdəu] (BRIT) n (also: ~ **pear**) Avocado f.

avoid [ə'vɔɪd] vt (person, obstacle) ausweichen +dat; (trouble) vermeiden; (danger) meiden.

avoidable [ə'vɔɪdəbl] adj vermeidbar.

avoidance [ə'vɔɪdəns] n (of tax) Umgehung f; (of issue) Vermeidung f.

avowed [ə'vaud] adj erklärt.

AVP (US) n abbr (= assistant vice president) stellvertretender Vizepräsident.

avuncular [ə'vʌŋkjulə*] adj onkelhaft.

AWACS ['eɪwæks] n abbr (= airborne warning and control system) AWACS.

await [ə'weɪt] vt warten auf +acc; ~**ing attention/delivery** zur Bearbeitung/ Lieferung bestimmt; **long** ~**ed** langersehnt.

awake [ə'weɪk] (pt **awoke**, pp **awoken** or **awaked**) adj wach ♦ vt wecken ♦ vi erwachen, aufwachen; ~ **to** sich dat bewußt werden +gen.

awakening [ə'weɪknɪŋ] n (also fig) Erwachen nt.

award [ə'wɔːd] n Preis m; (for bravery) Auszeichnung f; (damages) Entschädigung(ssumme) f ♦ vt (prize) verleihen; (damages) zusprechen.

aware [ə'wɛə*] adj: ~ **(of)** bewußt +gen; **to become** ~ **of** sich dat bewußt werden +gen; **to become** ~ **that** ... sich dat bewußt werden, daß ...; **politically/socially** ~ politik-/ sozialbewußt; **I am fully** ~ **that** es ist mir völlig klar or bewußt, daß.

awareness [ə'wɛənɪs] n Bewußtsein nt; **to develop people's** ~ **of sth** den Menschen etw zu Bewußtsein bringen.

awash [ə'wɔʃ] adj (also fig) überflutet.

away [ə'weɪ] adv weg, fort; (position) entfernt; **two kilometres** ~ zwei Kilometer entfernt; **two hours** ~ **by car** zwei Autostunden entfernt; **the holiday was two weeks** ~ es war noch zwei Wochen bis zum Urlaub; **he's** ~ **for a week** er ist eine Woche nicht da; **he's** ~ **in Milan** er ist in Mailand; **to take** ~ **(from)** (remove) entfernen (von); (subtract)

abziehen (von); **to work/pedal** etc ~ unablässig arbeiten/strampeln etc; **to fade** ~ (colour, light) verblassen; (sound) verhallen; (enthusiasm) schwinden.

away game n Auswärtsspiel nt.

awe [ɔː] n Ehrfurcht f.

awe-inspiring ['ɔːɪnspaɪərɪŋ] adj ehrfurchtgebietend.

awesome ['ɔːsəm] adj ehrfurchtgebietend; (fig: inf) überwältigend.

awe-struck ['ɔːstrʌk] adj von Ehrfurcht ergriffen.

awful ['ɔːfəl] adj furchtbar, schrecklich; **an** ~ **lot (of)** furchtbar viel(e).

awfully ['ɔːfəlɪ] adv furchtbar, schrecklich.

awhile [ə'waɪl] adv eine Weile.

awkward ['ɔːkwəd] adj (clumsy) unbeholfen; (inconvenient, difficult) ungünstig; (embarrassing) peinlich.

awkwardness ['ɔːkwədnɪs] n (see adj) Unbeholfenheit f; Ungünstigkeit f; Peinlichkeit f.

awl [ɔːl] n Ahle f, Pfriem m.

awning ['ɔːnɪŋ] n (of tent, caravan) Vordach nt; (of shop etc) Markise f.

awoke [ə'wəuk] pt of **awake**.

awoken [ə'wəukən] pp of **awake**.

AWOL ['eɪwɔl] abbr (MIL: = absent without leave) see **absent**.

awry [ə'raɪ] adv: **to be** ~ (clothes) schief sitzen; **to go** ~ schiefgehen.

axe, (US) **ax** [æks] n Axt f, Beil nt ♦ vt (employee) entlassen; (project, jobs etc) streichen; **to have an** ~ **to grind** (fig) ein persönliches Interesse haben.

axes[1] ['æksɪz] npl of **ax(e)**.

axes[2] ['æksiːz] npl of **axis**.

axiom ['æksɪəm] n Axiom nt, Grundsatz m.

axiomatic [æksɪəu'mætɪk] adj axiomatisch.

axis ['æksɪs] (pl **axes**[2]) n Achse f.

axle ['æksl] n (also: ~**tree**) Achse f.

aye [aɪ] excl (yes) ja ♦ n: **the** ~**s** die Jastimmen pl.

AYH n abbr (= American Youth Hostels) Jugendherbergsverband, ≈ DJHV m.

AZ (US) abbr (POST: = Arizona).

azalea [ə'zeɪlɪə] n Azalee f.

Azerbaijan [æzəbaɪ'dʒɑːn] n Aserbaidschan nt.

Azerbaijani [æzəbaɪ'dʒɑːnɪ], **Azeri** [ə'zeərɪ] adj aserbaidschanisch ♦ n Aserbaidschaner(in) m(f).

Azores [ə'zɔːz] npl: **the** ~ die Azoren pl.

AZT n abbr (= azidothymidine) AZT nt.

Aztec ['æztɛk] adj aztekisch ♦ n Azteke m, Aztekin f.

azure ['eɪʒə*] adj azurblau, tiefblau.

B, b

B¹, b [biː] n (*letter*) B nt, b nt; (*SCOL*) ≈ Zwei f, Gut nt; ~ **for Benjamin,** (*US*) ~ **for Baker** ≈ B wie Bertha; ~ **road** (*BRIT*) Landstraße f.

B² [biː] n (*MUS*) H nt, h nt.

b. abbr = **born.**

BA n abbr (= *Bachelor of Arts*) see **bachelor;** (= *British Academy*) Verband zur Förderung der Künste und Geisteswissenschaften.

babble ['bæbl] vi schwatzen; (*baby*) plappern; (*brook*) plätschern ♦ n: **a ~ of voices** ein Stimmengewirr nt.

babe [beɪb] n (*liter*) Kindlein nt; (*esp US: address*) Schätzchen nt; ~ **in arms** Säugling m.

baboon [bə'buːn] n Pavian m.

baby ['beɪbɪ] n Baby nt; (*US: inf: darling*) Schatz m, Schätzchen nt.

baby carriage (*US*) n Kinderwagen m.

baby grand n (*also:* ~ **piano**) Stutzflügel m.

babyhood ['beɪbɪhud] n frühe Kindheit f.

babyish ['beɪbɪɪʃ] adj kindlich.

baby-minder ['beɪbɪ'maɪndə'] (*BRIT*) n Tagesmutter f.

baby-sit ['beɪbɪsɪt] vi babysitten.

baby-sitter ['beɪbɪsɪtə'] n Babysitter(in) m(f).

bachelor ['bætʃələ'] n Junggeselle m; **B~ of Arts/Science (degree)** ≈ Magister m der philosophischen Fakultät/der Naturwissenschaften.

bachelorhood ['bætʃələhud] n Junggesellentum nt.

bachelor party (*US*) n Junggesellenparty f.

Bachelor's Degree ist der akademische Grad, den man nach drei- oder vierjährigem erfolgreich abgeschlossenem Universitätsstudium erhält. Die am häufigsten verliehenen Grade sind **BA** (*Bachelor of Arts = Magister der Geisteswissenschaften*), **BSc** (*Bachelor of Science = Magister der Naturwissenschaften*), **BEd** (*Bachelor of Education = Magister der Erziehungswissenschaften*) und **LLB** (*Bachelor of Laws = Magister der Rechtswissenschaften*). Siehe auch **master's degree, doctorate.**

---

back [bæk] n Rücken m; (*of house, page*) Rückseite f; (*of chair*) (Rücken)lehne f; (*of train*) Ende nt; (*FOOTBALL*) Verteidiger m ♦ vt (*candidate: also:* ~ **up**) unterstützen; (*horse*) setzen or wetten auf +acc; (*car*) zurücksetzen, zurückfahren ♦ vi (*also:* ~ **up:** *person*) rückwärts gehen; (*car etc*)

zurücksetzen, zurückfahren ♦ cpd (*payment, rent*) ausstehend ♦ adv hinten; **in the ~** (*of the car*) hinten (im Auto); **at the ~ of the book/crowd/audience** hinten im Buch/in der Menge/im Publikum; ~ **to front** verkehrt herum; **to break the ~ of a job** (*BRIT*) mit einer Arbeit über den Berg sein; **to have one's ~ to the wall** (*fig*) in die Enge getrieben sein; ~ **room** Hinterzimmer nt; ~ **garden** Garten m (hinter dem Haus); ~ **seat** (*AUT*) Rücksitz m; **to take a ~ seat** (*fig*) sich zurückhalten; ~ **wheels** Hinterräder pl; **he's ~** er ist zurück or wieder da; **throw the ball** ~ wirf den Ball zurück; **he called** ~ er rief zurück; **he ran** ~ er rannte zurück; **when will you be ~?** wann kommen Sie wieder?; **can I have it ~?** kann ich es zurückhaben or wiederhaben?

▶**back down** vi nachgeben.

▶**back on to** vt fus: **the house ~s on to the golf course** das Haus grenzt hinten an den Golfplatz an.

▶**back out** vi (*of promise*) einen Rückzieher machen.

▶**back up** vt (*support*) unterstützen; (*COMPUT*) sichern.

backache ['bækeɪk] n Rückenschmerzen pl.

Back bench bezeichnet im britischen Unterhaus die am weitesten vom Mittelgang entfernten Bänke, im Gegensatz zur **front bench**. Auf diesen hinteren Bänken sitzen diejenigen Unterhausabgeordneten (auch backbenchers genannt), die kein Regierungsamt bzw. keine wichtige Stellung in der Opposition innehaben.

---

backbencher ['bæk'bentʃə'] (*BRIT*) n Abgeordnete(r) f(m) (*in den hinteren Reihen im britischen Parlament*), Hinterbänkler(in) m(f) (*pej*); see also **back bench.**

backbiting ['bækbaɪtɪŋ] n Lästern nt.

backbone ['bækbəʊn] n (*also fig*) Rückgrat nt.

backchat ['bæktʃæt] (*BRIT: inf*) n Widerrede f.

backcloth ['bækklɒθ] (*BRIT*) n Hintergrund m.

backcomb ['bækkəʊm] (*BRIT*) vt toupieren.

backdate [bæk'deɪt] vt (zu)rückdatieren; ~**d pay rise** rückwirkend geltende Gehaltserhöhung f.

backdrop ['bækdrɒp] n = **backcloth.**

backer ['bækə'] n (*COMM*) Geldgeber m.

backfire [bæk'faɪə'] vi (*AUT*) Fehlzündungen haben; (*plans*) ins Auge gehen.

backgammon ['bækgæmən] n Backgammon nt.

background ['bækgraʊnd] n Hintergrund m; (*basic knowledge*) Grundkenntnisse pl; (*experience*) Erfahrung f ♦ cpd (*music*) Hintergrund-; **family ~** Herkunft f, ~ **noise** Geräuschkulisse f; ~ **reading** vertiefende Lektüre f.

backhand ['bækhænd] n (*TENNIS: also:*

~ **stroke**) Rückhand *f*.
backhanded ['bæk'hændɪd] *adj* (*fig: compliment*) zweifelhaft.
backhander ['bæk'hændə*] (*BRIT*) *n* Schmiergeld *nt*.
backing ['bækɪŋ] *n* (*fig, COMM*) Unterstützung *f*; (*MUS*) Begleitung *f*.
backlash ['bæklæʃ] *n* (*fig*) Gegenreaktion *f*.
backlog ['bæklɔg] *n:* **to have a ~ of work** mit der Arbeit im Rückstand sein.
back number *n* alte Ausgabe *f or* Nummer *f*.
backpack ['bækpæk] *n* Rucksack *m*.
backpacker ['bækpækə*] *n* Rucksack-tourist(in) *m(f)*.
back pay *n* Nachzahlung *f*.
back-pedal ['bækpedl] *vi* (*fig*) einen Rückzieher machen.
back-seat driver *n* Mitfahrer, der dem Fahrer dazwischenredet.
backside ['bæksaɪd] (*inf*) *n* Hintern *m*.
backslash ['bækslæʃ] *n* Backslash *m*.
backslide ['bækslaɪd] *vi* rückfällig werden.
backspace ['bækspeɪs] *vi* (*in typing*) die Rücktaste betätigen.
backstage [bæk'steɪdʒ] *adv* (*THEAT*) hinter den Kulissen; (: *in dressing-room area*) in der Garderobe.
backstreet ['bækstriːt] *n* Seitenstraße *f* ♦ *cpd:* ~ **abortionist** Engelmacher(in) *m(f)*.
backstroke ['bækstrəuk] *n* Rückenschwimmen *nt*.
backtrack ['bæktræk] *vi* (*fig*) einen Rückzieher machen.
backup ['bækʌp] *adj* (*train, plane*) Entlastungs-; (*COMPUT: copy etc*) Sicherungs- ♦ *n* (*support*) Unterstützung *f*; (*COMPUT: also:* ~ **disk**, ~ **file**) Sicherungskopie *f*, Backup *nt*.
backward ['bækwəd] *adj* (*movement*) Rückwärts-; (*person*) zurückgeblieben; (*country*) rückständig; ~ **and forward movement** Vor- und Zurückbewegung *f*; ~ **step/glance** Blick *m*/Schritt *m* zurück.
backwards ['bækwədz] *adv* rückwärts; (*read*) von hinten nach vorne; (*fall*) nach hinten; (*in time*) zurück; **to know sth** ~ *or* (*US*) ~ **and forwards** etw in- und auswendig kennen.
backwater ['bækwɔːtə*] *n* (*fig*) Kaff *nt*.
back yard *n* Hinterhof *m*.
bacon ['beɪkən] *n* (Frühstücks)speck *m*, (Schinken)speck *m*.
bacteria [bæk'tɪərɪə] *npl* Bakterien *pl*.
bacteriology [bæktɪərɪ'ɔlədʒɪ] *n* Bakteriologie *f*.
bad [bæd] *adj* schlecht; (*naughty*) unartig, ungezogen; (*mistake, accident, injury*) schwer; **his ~ leg** sein schlimmes Bein; **to go ~** verderben, schlecht werden; **to have a ~ time of it** es schwer haben; **I feel ~ about it** es tut mir leid; **in ~ faith** mit böser Absicht.
bad debt *n* uneinbringliche Forderung *f*.

baddy {'bædɪ} (*inf*) *n* Bösewicht *m*.
bade [bæd] *pt of* **bid**.
badge [bædʒ] *n* Plakette *f*; (*stick-on*) Aufkleber *m*; (*fig*) Merkmal *nt*.
badger ['bædʒə*] *n* Dachs *m* ♦ *vt* zusetzen +*dat*.
badly ['bædlɪ] *adv* schlecht; ~ **wounded** schwer verletzt; **he needs it** ~ er braucht es dringend; **things are going** ~ es sieht schlecht *or* nicht gut aus; **to be** ~ **off (for money)** wenig Geld haben.
bad-mannered ['bæd'mænəd] *adj* ungezogen, unhöflich.
badminton ['bædmɪntən] *n* Federball *m*.
bad-tempered ['bæd'tɛmpəd] *adj* schlecht gelaunt; (*by nature*) übellaunig.
baffle ['bæfl] *vt* verblüffen.
baffling ['bæflɪŋ] *adj* rätselhaft, verwirrend.
bag [bæg] *n* Tasche *f*; (*made of paper, plastic*) Tüte *f*; (*handbag*) (Hand)tasche *f*; (*satchel*) Schultasche *f*; (*case*) Reisetasche *f*; (*of hunter*) Jagdbeute *f*; (*pej: woman*) Schachtel *f*; ~**s of** (*inf: lots of*) jede Menge; **to pack one's** ~**s** die Koffer packen; ~**s under the eyes** Ringe *pl* unter den Augen.
bagful ['bægful] *n:* **a** ~ **of** eine Tasche/Tüte voll.
baggage ['bægɪdʒ] *n* Gepäck *nt*.
baggage car (*US*) *n* Gepäckwagen *m*.
baggage claim *n* Gepäckausgabe *f*.
baggy ['bægɪ] *adj* weit; (*out of shape*) ausgebeult.
Baghdad [bæg'dæd] *n* Bagdad *nt*.
bag lady (*esp US*) *n* Stadtstreicherin *f*.
bagpipes ['bægpaɪps] *npl* Dudelsack *m*.
bag-snatcher ['bægsnætʃə*] (*BRIT*) *n* Handtaschendieb(in) *m(f)*.
Bahamas [bə'hɑːməz] *npl:* **the** ~ die Bahamas *pl*, die Bahamainseln *pl*.
Bahrain [bɑː'reɪn] *n* Bahrain *nt*.
bail [beɪl] *n* (*LAW: payment*) Kaution *f*; (: *release*) Freilassung *f* gegen Kaution ♦ *vt* (*prisoner*) gegen Kaution freilassen; (*boat: also:* ~ **out**) ausschöpfen; **to be on** ~ gegen Kaution freigelassen sein; **to be released on** ~ gegen Kaution freigelassen werden; *see also* **bale**.
▶**bail out** *vt* (*prisoner*) gegen Kaution freibekommen; (*firm, friend*) aus der Patsche helfen +*dat*.
bailiff ['beɪlɪf] *n* (*LAW: BRIT*) Gerichtsvollzieher(in) *m(f)*; (: *US*) Gerichtsdiener(in) *m(f)*; (*BRIT: factor*) (Guts)verwalter(in) *m(f)*.
bait [beɪt] *n* Köder *m* ♦ *vt* (*hook, trap*) mit einem Köder versehen; (*tease*) necken.
baize [beɪz] *n* Flausch *m*; **green** ~ Billardtuch *nt*.
bake [beɪk] *vt* backen; (*clay etc*) brennen ♦ *vi* backen.
baked beans [beɪkt-] *npl* gebackene Bohnen *pl* (in Tomatensauce).
baker ['beɪkə*] *n* Bäcker(in) *m(f)*.

baker's dozen *n* dreizehn (Stück).
bakery ['beɪkərɪ] *n* Bäckerei *f*.
baking ['beɪkɪŋ] *n* Backen *nt*; (*batch*) Ofenladung *f* ♦ *adj* (*inf: hot*) wie im Backofen.
baking powder *n* Backpulver *nt*.
baking tin *n* Backform *f*.
baking tray *n* Backblech *nt*.
balaclava [bælə'klɑːvə] *n* (*also:* ~ **helmet**) Kapuzenmütze *f*.
balance ['bæləns] *n* (*equilibrium*) Gleichgewicht *nt*; (*COMM: sum*) Saldo *m*; (*remainder*) Restbetrag *m*; (*scales*) Waage *f* ♦ *vt* ausgleichen; (*AUT: wheels*) auswuchten; (*pros and cons*) (gegeneinander) abwägen; **on** ~ alles in allem; ~ **of trade/payments** Handels-/Zahlungsbilanz *f*; ~ **carried forward** *or* **brought forward** (*COMM*) Saldovortrag *m*, Saldoübertrag *m*; **to** ~ **the books** (*COMM*) die Bilanz ziehen *or* machen.
balanced ['bælənst] *adj* ausgeglichen; (*report*) ausgewogen.
balance sheet *n* Bilanz *f*.
balance wheel *n* Unruh *f*.
balcony ['bælkənɪ] *n* Balkon *m*; (*in theatre*) oberster Rang *m*.
bald [bɔːld] *adj* kahl; (*tyre*) abgefahren; (*statement*) knapp.
baldness ['bɔːldnɪs] *n* Kahlheit *f*.
bale [beɪl] *n* (*AGR*) Bündel *nt*; (*of papers etc*) Packen *m*.
▶**bale out** *vi* (*of a plane*) abspringen ♦ *vt* (*water*) schöpfen; (*boat*) ausschöpfen.
Balearic Islands [bælɪ'ærɪk-] *npl:* **the** ~ die Balearen *pl*.
baleful ['beɪlful] *adj* böse.
balk [bɔːk] *vi:* **to** ~ (**at**) (*subj: person*) zurückschrecken (vor +*dat*); (*: horse*) scheuen (vor +*dat*).
Balkan ['bɔːlkən] *adj* (*countries etc*) Balkan- ♦ *n:* **the** ~**s** der Balkan, die Balkanländer *pl*.
ball [bɔːl] *n* Ball *m*; (*of wool, string*) Knäuel *m or nt*; **to set the** ~ **rolling** (*fig*) den Stein ins Rollen bringen; **to play** ~ (**with sb**) (*fig*) (mit jdm) mitspielen; **to be on the** ~ (*fig: competent*) am Ball sein; (*: alert*) auf Draht *or* Zack sein; **the** ~ **is in their court** (*fig*) sie sind am Ball.
ballad ['bæləd] *n* Ballade *f*.
ballast ['bæləst] *n* Ballast *m*.
ball bearing *npl* Kugellager *nt*; (*individual ball*) Kugellagerkugel *f*.
ball cock *n* Schwimmerhahn *m*.
ballerina [bælə'riːnə] *n* Ballerina *f*.
ballet ['bæleɪ] *n* Ballett *nt*.
ballet dancer *n* Balletttänzer(in) *m(f)*.
ballistic [bə'lɪstɪk] *adj* ballistisch.
ballistic missile *n* Raketengeschoß *nt*.
ballistics [bə'lɪstɪks] *n* Ballistik *f*.
balloon [bə'luːn] *n* (*Luft*)ballon *m*; (*hot air balloon*) Heißluftballon *m*; (*in comic strip*) Sprechblase *f*.

balloonist [bə'luːnɪst] *n* Ballonfahrer(in) *m(f)*.
ballot ['bælət] *n* (geheime) Abstimmung *f*.
ballot box *n* Wahlurne *f*.
ballot paper *n* Stimmzettel *m*.
ballpark ['bɔːlpɑːk] (*US*) *n* (*SPORT*) Baseballstadion *nt*.
ballpark figure (*inf*) *n* Richtzahl *f*.
ballpoint (pen) ['bɔːlpɔɪnt(-)] *n* Kugelschreiber *m*.
ballroom ['bɔːlrum] *n* Tanzsaal *m*.
balls [bɔːlz] (*inf!*) *npl* (*testicles*) Eier *pl* (*!*); (*courage*) Schneid *m*, Mumm *m* ♦ *excl* red keinen Scheiß! (*!*).
balm [bɑːm] *n* Balsam *m*.
balmy ['bɑːmɪ] *adj* (*breeze*) sanft; (*air*) lau, lind; (*BRIT: inf*) = **barmy**.
BALPA ['bælpə] *n abbr* (= *British Airline Pilots' Association*) Flugpilotengewerkschaft.
balsam ['bɔːlsəm] *n* Balsam *m*.
balsa (wood) ['bɔːlsə-] *n* Balsaholz *nt*.
Baltic ['bɔːltɪk] *n:* **the** ~ (**Sea**) die Ostsee.
balustrade [bæləs'treɪd] *n* Balustrade *f*.
bamboo [bæm'buː] *n* Bambus *m*.
bamboozle [bæm'buːzl] (*inf*) *vt* hereinlegen; **to** ~ **sb into doing sth** jdn durch Tricks dazu bringen, etw zu tun.
ban [bæn] *n* Verbot *nt* ♦ *vt* verbieten; **he was** ~**ned from driving** (*BRIT*) ihm wurde Fahrverbot erteilt.
banal [bə'nɑːl] *adj* banal.
banana [bə'nɑːnə] *n* Banane *f*.
band [bænd] *n* (*group*) Gruppe *f*, Schar *f*; (*MUS: jazz, rock etc*) Band *f*; (*: military etc*) (Musik)kapelle *f*; (*strip, range*) Band *nt*; (*stripe*) Streifen *m*.
▶**band together** *vi* sich zusammenschließen.
bandage ['bændɪdʒ] *n* Verband *m* ♦ *vt* verbinden.
Band-Aid ® ['bændeɪd] (*US*) *n* Heftpflaster *nt*.
B & B *n abbr* = **bed and breakfast**.
bandit ['bændɪt] *n* Bandit *m*.
bandstand ['bændstænd] *n* Musikpavillion *m*.
bandwagon ['bændwægən] *n:* **to jump on the** ~ (*fig*) auf den fahrenden Zug aufspringen.
bandy ['bændɪ] *vt* (*jokes*) sich erzählen; (*ideas*) diskutieren; (*insults*) sich an den Kopf werfen.
▶**bandy about** *vt* (*word, expression*) immer wieder gebrauchen; (*name*) immer wieder nennen.
bandy-legged ['bændɪ'lɛgɪd] *adj* O-beinig.
bane [beɪn] *n:* **it/he is the** ~ **of my life** das/er ist noch mal mein Ende.
bang [bæŋ] *n* (*of door*) Knallen *nt*; (*of gun, exhaust*) Knall *m*; (*blow*) Schlag *m* ♦ *excl* peng ♦ *vt* (*door*) zuschlagen, zuknallen; (*one's head etc*) sich *dat* stoßen +*acc* ♦ *vi* knallen ♦ *adv:* **to be** ~ **on time** (*BRIT: inf*) auf die Sekunde pünktlich sein; **to** ~ **at the door** gegen die Tür hämmern; **to** ~ **into sth** sich an etw *dat* stoßen.
banger ['bæŋə*] (*BRIT: inf*) *n* (*car: also:* **old** ~)

Klapperkiste *f*; (*sausage*) Würstchen *nt*; (*firework*) Knallkörper *m*.
Bangkok [bæŋ'kɔk] *n* Bangkok *nt*.
Bangladesh [bæŋglə'deʃ] *n* Bangladesch *nt*.
bangle ['bæŋgl] *n* Armreif(en) *m*.
bangs [bæŋz] (*US*) *npl* (*fringe*) Pony *m*.
banish ['bænɪʃ] *vt* verbannen.
banister(s) ['bænɪstə(z)] *n(pl)* Geländer *nt*.
banjo ['bændʒəu] (*pl* ~**es** *or* ~**s**) *n* Banjo *nt*.
bank [bæŋk] *n* Bank *f*; (*of river, lake*) Ufer *nt*; (*of earth*) Wall *m*; (*of switches*) Reihe *f* ♦ *vi* (*AVIAT*) sich in die Kurve legen; (*COMM*): **they ~ with Pitt's** sie haben ihr Konto bei Pitt's.
►**bank on** *vt fus* sich verlassen auf +*acc*.
bank account *n* Bankkonto *nt*.
bank balance *n* Kontostand *m*.
bank card *n* Scheckkarte *f*.
bank charges (*BRIT*) *npl* Kontoführungsgebühren *pl*.
bank draft *n* Bankanweisung *f*.
banker ['bæŋkə*] *n* Bankier *m*.
banker's card (*BRIT*) *n* = **bank card**.
banker's order (*BRIT*) *n* Dauerauftrag *m*.
bank giro *n* Banküberweisung *f*.
bank holiday (*BRIT*) *n* (öffentlicher) Feiertag *m*.

Als **bank holiday** *wird in Großbritannien ein gesetzlicher Feiertag bezeichnet, an dem die Banken geschlossen sind. Die meisten dieser Feiertage, abgesehen von Weihnachten und Ostern, fallen auf Montage im Mai und August. An diesen langen Wochenenden (bank holiday weekends) fahren viele Briten in Urlaub, so daß dann auf den Straßen, Flughäfen und bei der Bahn sehr viel Betrieb ist.*

---

banking ['bæŋkɪŋ] *n* Bankwesen *nt*.
banking hours *npl* Schalterstunden *pl*.
bank loan *n* Bankkredit *m*.
bank manager *n* Filialleiter(in) *m(f)* (einer Bank).
banknote ['bæŋknəut] *n* Geldschein *m*, Banknote *f*.
bank rate *n* Diskontsatz *m*.
bankrupt ['bæŋkrʌpt] *adj* bankrott ♦ *n* Bankrotteur(in) *m(f)*; **to go ~** Bankrott machen.
bankruptcy ['bæŋkrʌptsɪ] *n* (*COMM, fig*) Bankrott *m*.
bank statement *n* Kontoauszug *m*.
banner ['bænə*] *n* Banner *nt*; (*in demonstration*) Spruchband *nt*.
banner headline *n* Schlagzeile *f*.
bannister(s) ['bænɪstə(z)] *n(pl)* = **banister(s)**.
banns [bænz] *npl* Aufgebot *nt*.
banquet ['bæŋkwɪt] *n* Bankett *nt*.
bantamweight ['bæntəmweɪt] *n* Bantamgewicht *nt*.
banter ['bæntə*] *n* Geplänkel *nt*.
BAOR *n abbr* (= *British Army of the Rhine*)

britische Rheinarmee.
baptism ['bæptɪzəm] *n* Taufe *f*.
Baptist ['bæptɪst] *n* Baptist(in) *m(f)*.
baptize [bæp'taɪz] *vt* taufen.
bar [bɑː*] *n* (*for drinking*) Lokal *nt*; (*counter*) Theke *f*; (*rod*) Stange *f*; (*on window etc*) (Gitter)stab *m*; (*slab: of chocolate*) Tafel *f*; (*fig: obstacle*) Hindernis *nt*; (*prohibition*) Verbot *nt*; (*MUS*) Takt *m* ♦ *vt* (*road*) blockieren, versperren; (*window*) verriegeln; (*person*) ausschließen; (*activity*) verbieten; ~ **of soap** Stück *nt* Seife; **behind** ~**s** hinter Gittern; **the B~** (*LAW*) die Anwaltschaft; ~ **none** ohne Ausnahme.
Barbados [bɑː'beɪdɔs] *n* Barbados *nt*.
barbaric [bɑː'bærɪk] *adj* barbarisch.
barbarous ['bɑːbərəs] *adj* barbarisch.
barbecue ['bɑːbɪkjuː] *n* Grill *m*; (*meal, party*) Barbecue *nt*.
barbed wire ['bɑːbd-] *n* Stacheldraht *m*.
barber ['bɑːbə*] *n* (Herren)friseur *m*.
barbiturate [bɑː'bɪtjurɪt] *n* Schlafmittel *nt*, Barbiturat *nt*.
Barcelona [bɑːsə'ləunə] *n* Barcelona *nt*.
bar chart *n* Balkendiagramm *nt*.
bar code *n* Strichkode *m*.
bare [beə*] *adj* nackt; (*trees, countryside*) kahl; (*minimum*) absolut ♦ *vt* entblößen; (*teeth*) blecken; **the ~ essentials, the ~ necessities** das Allernotwendigste; **to ~ one's soul** sein Innerstes entblößen.
bareback ['beəbæk] *adv* ohne Sattel.
barefaced ['beəfeɪst] *adj* (*fig*) unverfroren, schamlos.
barefoot ['beəfut] *adj* barfüßig ♦ *adv* barfuß.
bareheaded [beə'hedɪd] *adj* barhäuptig ♦ *adv* ohne Kopfbedeckung.
barely ['beəlɪ] *adv* kaum.
Barents Sea ['bærənts-] *n*: **the ~** die Barentssee.
bargain ['bɑːgɪn] *n* (*deal*) Geschäft *nt*; (*transaction*) Handel *m*; (*good offer*) Sonderangebot *nt*; (*good buy*) guter Kauf *m* ♦ *vi*: **to ~ (with sb)** (mit jdm) verhandeln; (*haggle*) (mit jdm) handeln; **into the ~** obendrein.
►**bargain for** *vt fus*: **he got more than he ~ed for** er bekam mehr, als er erwartet hatte.
bargaining ['bɑːgənɪŋ] *n* Verhandeln *nt*.
bargaining position *n* Verhandlungsposition *f*.
barge [bɑːdʒ] *n* Lastkahn *m*, Frachtkahn *m*.
►**barge in** *vi* (*enter*) hereinplatzen; (*interrupt*) unterbrechen.
►**barge into** *vt fus* (*place*) hereinplatzen; (*person*) anrempeln.
bargepole ['bɑːdʒpəul] *n*: **I wouldn't touch it with a ~** (*fig*) das würde ich nicht mal mit der Kneifzange anfassen.
baritone ['bærɪtəun] *n* Bariton *m*.
barium meal ['beərɪəm-] *n* Kontrastbrei *m*.
bark [bɑːk] *n* (*of tree*) Rinde *f*; (*of dog*) Bellen

nt ♦ _vi_ bellen; **she's ~ing up the wrong tree**
(_fig_) sie ist auf dem Holzweg.
barley ['bɑːlɪ] _n_ Gerste _f_.
barley sugar _n_ Malzbonbon _nt or m_.
barmaid ['bɑːmeɪd] _n_ Bardame _f_.
barman ['bɑːmən] (_irreg: like_ **man**) _n_ Barmann
_m_.
barmy ['bɑːmɪ] (_BRIT: inf_) _adj_ bekloppt.
barn [bɑːn] _n_ Scheune _f_.
barnacle ['bɑːnəkl] _n_ Rankenfußkrebs _m_.
barn owl _n_ Schleiereule _f_.
barometer [bə'rɒmɪtə*] _n_ Barometer _nt_.
baron [~'bærən] _n_ Baron _m_; **industrial** ~
Industriemagnat _m_; **press** ~ Pressezar _m_.
baroness ['bærənɪs] _n_ (_baron's wife_) Baronin _f_;
(_baron's daughter_) Baroneß _f_, Baronesse _f_.
baronet ['bærənɪt] _n_ Baronet _m_.
barracking ['bærəkɪŋ] _n_ Buhrufe _pl_.
barracks ['bærəks] _npl_ Kaserne _f_.
barrage ['bærɑːʒ] _n_ (_MIL_) Sperrfeuer _nt_; (_dam_)
Staustufe _f_; (_fig: of criticism, questions etc_)
Hagel _m_.
barrel ['bærəl] _n_ Faß _nt_; (_of oil_) Barrel _nt_; (_of
gun_) Lauf _m_.
barrel organ _n_ Drehorgel _f_.
barren ['bærən] _adj_ unfruchtbar.
barricade [bærɪ'keɪd] _n_ Barrikade _f_ ♦ _vt_ (_road,
entrance_) verbarrikadieren; **to ~ o.s. (in)**
sich verbarrikadieren.
barrier ['bærɪə*] _n_ (_at frontier, entrance_)
Schranke _f_; (_BRIT: also:_ **crash ~**) Leitplanke _f_;
(_fig_) Barriere _f_; (: _to progress etc_) Hindernis
_nt_.
barrier cream (_BRIT_) _n_ Hautschutzcreme _f_.
barring ['bɑːrɪŋ] _prep_ außer im Falle +_gen_.
barrister ['bærɪstə*] (_BRIT_) _n_ Rechtsanwalt _m_,
Rechtsanwältin _f_.

Barrister _oder_ barrister-at-law _ist in England die_
Bezeichnung für einen Rechtsanwalt, der seine
Klienten vor allem vor Gericht vertritt; im
Gegensatz zum solicitor, _der nicht vor Gericht_
auftritt, sondern einen barrister mit dieser
Aufgabe beauftragt.

---

barrow ['bærəu] _n_ Schubkarre _f_, Schubkarren
_m_; (_cart_) Karren _m_.
bar stool _n_ Barhocker _m_.
Bart. (_BRIT_) _abbr_ = **baronet**.
bartender ['bɑːtɛndə*] (_US_) _n_ Barmann _m_.
barter ['bɑːtə*] _n_ Tauschhandel _m_ ♦ _vt_: **to**
~ sth for sth etw gegen etw tauschen.
base [beɪs] _n_ (_of tree etc_) Fuß _m_; (_of cup, box
etc_) Boden _m_; (_foundation_) Grundlage _f_;
(_centre_) Stützpunkt _m_, Standort _m_; (_for
organization_) Sitz _m_ ♦ _adj_ gemein,
niederträchtig ♦ _vt_: **to ~ sth on** etw gründen
_or_ basieren auf +_acc_; **to be ~d at** (_troops_)
stationiert sein in +_dat_; (_employee_) arbeiten
in +_dat_; **I'm ~d in London** ich wohne in
London; **a Paris-~d firm** eine Firma mit Sitz
in Paris; **coffee-~d** auf Kaffeebasis.

baseball ['beɪsbɔːl] _n_ Baseball _m_.
baseboard ['beɪsbɔːd] (_US_) _n_ Fußleiste _f_.
base camp _n_ Basislager _nt_,
Versorgungslager _nt_.
Basel [bɑːl] _n_ = **Basle**.
baseline ['beɪslaɪn] _n_ (_TENNIS_) Grundlinie _f_;
(_fig: standard_) Ausgangspunkt _m_.
basement ['beɪsmənt] _n_ Keller _m_.
base rate _n_ Eckzins _m_, Leitzins _m_.
bases¹ ['beɪsɪz] _npl of_ **base**.
bases² ['beɪsiːz] _npl of_ **basis**.
bash [bæʃ] (_inf_) _vt_ schlagen, hauen ♦ _n_: **I'll**
have a ~ (at it) (_BRIT_) ich probier's mal.
▶**bash up** _vt_ (_car_) demolieren; (_BRIT: person_)
vermöbeln.
bashful ['bæʃful] _adj_ schüchtern.
bashing ['bæʃɪŋ] (_inf_) _n_ Prügel _pl_; **Paki-/**
queer-~ Überfälle _pl_ auf Pakistaner/
Schwule.
BASIC ['beɪsɪk] _n_ (_COMPUT_) BASIC _nt_.
basic ['beɪsɪk] _adj_ (_method, needs etc_) Grund-;
(_principles_) grundlegend; (_problem_)
grundsätzlich; (_knowledge_) elementar;
(_facilities_) primitiv.
basically ['beɪsɪklɪ] _adv_ im Grunde.
basic rate _n_ Eingangssteuersatz _m_.
basics ['beɪsɪks] _npl_: **the ~** das Wesentliche.
basil ['bæzl] _n_ Basilikum _nt_.
basin ['beɪsn] _n_ Gefäß _nt_; (_BRIT: for food_)
Schüssel _f_; (_also:_ **wash ~**) (Wasch)becken _nt_;
(_of river, lake_) Becken _nt_.
basis ['beɪsɪs] (_pl_ **bases**) _n_ Basis _f_, Grundlage _f_;
on a part-time ~ stundenweise; **on a trial ~**
zur Probe; **on the ~ of what you've said** auf
Grund dessen, was Sie gesagt haben.
bask [bɑːsk] _vi_: **to ~ in the sun** sich sonnen.
basket ['bɑːskɪt] _n_ Korb _m_; (_smaller_) Körbchen
_nt_.
basketball ['bɑːskɪtbɔːl] _n_ Basketball _m_.
basketball player _n_ Basketballspieler(in)
_m(f)_.
Basle [bɑːl] _n_ Basel _nt_.
basmati rice [bɑz'mætɪ-] _n_ Basmatireis _m_.
Basque [bæsk] _adj_ baskisch ♦ _n_ Baske _m_,
Baskin _f_.
bass [beɪs] _n_ Baß _m_.
bass clef _n_ Baßschlüssel _m_.
bassoon [bə'suːn] _n_ Fagott _nt_.
bastard ['bɑːstəd] _n_ uneheliches Kind _nt_; (_inf!_)
Arschloch _nt_ (!).
baste [beɪst] _vt_ (_CULIN_) (mit Fett und
Bratensaft) begießen; (_SEWING_) heften,
reihen.
bastion ['bæstɪən] _n_ Bastion _f_.
bat [bæt] _n_ (_ZOOL_) Fledermaus _f_; (_for cricket,
baseball etc_) Schlagholz _nt_; (_BRIT: for table
tennis_) Schläger _m_ ♦ _vt_: **he didn't ~ an eyelid**
er hat nicht mit der Wimper gezuckt; **off**
one's own ~ auf eigene Faust.
batch [bætʃ] _n_ (_of bread_) Schub _m_; (_of letters,
papers_) Stoß _m_, Stapel _m_; (_of applicants_)
Gruppe _f_; (_of work_) Schwung _m_; (_of goods_)

Ladung f, Sendung f.
batch processing n (COMPUT)
Stapelverarbeitung f.
bated ['beɪtɪd] adj: **with ~ breath** mit
angehaltenem Atem.
bath [bɑ:θ] n Bad nt; (bathtub) (Bade)wanne f
♦ vt baden; **to have a ~** baden, ein Bad
nehmen; see also **baths.**
bathe [beɪð] vi, vt (also fig) baden.
bather ['beɪðə'] n Badende(r) f(m).
bathing ['beɪðɪŋ] n Baden nt.
bathing cap n Bademütze f, Badekappe f.
bathing costume, (US) **bathing suit** n
Badeanzug m.
bath mat n Badematte f, Badevorleger m.
bathrobe ['bɑ:rəub] n Bademantel m.
bathroom ['bɑ:θrum] n Bad(ezimmer) nt.
baths [bɑ:ðz] npl (also: **swimming ~**)
(Schwimm)bad nt.
bath towel n Badetuch nt.
bathtub ['bɑ:θtʌb] n (Bade)wanne f.
batman ['bætmən] (irreg: like **man**) (BRIT) n
(MIL) (Offiziers)bursche m.
baton ['bætən] n (MUS) Taktstock m;
(ATHLETICS) Staffelholz nt; (policeman's)
Schlagstock m.
battalion [bə'tælɪən] n Bataillon nt.
batten ['bætn] n Leiste f, Latte f; (NAUT: on
sail) Segellatte f.
▶**batten down** vt (NAUT): **to ~ down the
hatches** die Luken dicht machen.
batter ['bætə'] vt schlagen, mißhandeln; (subj:
rain) schlagen; (wind) rütteln ♦ n (CULIN)
Teig m; (for frying) (Ausback)teig m.
battered ['bætəd] adj (hat, pan) verbeult;
~ wife mißhandelte Ehefrau; **~ child**
mißhandeltes Kind.
battering ram ['bætərɪŋ-] n Rammbock m.
battery ['bætərɪ] n Batterie f; (of tests,
reporters) Reihe f.
battery charger n (Batterie)ladegerät nt.
battery farming n Batteriehaltung f.
battle ['bætl] n (MIL) Schlacht f; (fig) Kampf m
♦ vi kämpfen; **that's half the ~** damit ist
schon viel gewonnen; **it's a losing ~, we're
fighting a losing ~** (fig) es ist ein
aussichtsloser Kampf.
battledress ['bætldrɛs] n Kampfanzug m.
battlefield ['bætlfi:ld] n Schlachtfeld nt.
battlements ['bætlmənts] npl Zinnen pl.
battleship ['bætlʃɪp] n Schlachtschiff nt.
batty ['bætɪ] (inf) adj verrückt.
bauble ['bɔ:bl] n Flitter m.
baud [bɔ:d] n (COMPUT) Baud nt.
baud rate n (COMPUT) Baudrate f.
baulk [bɔ:lk] vi = **balk.**
bauxite ['bɔ:ksaɪt] n Bauxit m.
Bavaria [bə'vɛərɪə] n Bayern nt.
Bavarian [bə'vɛərɪən] adj bay(e)risch ♦ n
Bayer(in) m(f).
bawdy ['bɔ:dɪ] adj derb, obszön.
bawl [bɔ:l] vi brüllen, schreien.

bay [beɪ] n Bucht f; (BRIT: for parking)
Parkbucht f; (: for loading) Ladeplatz m;
(horse) Braune(r) m; **to hold sb at ~** jdn in
Schach halten.
bay leaf n Lorbeerblatt nt.
bayonet ['beɪənɪt] n Bajonett nt.
bay tree n Lorbeerbaum m.
bay window n Erkerfenster nt.
bazaar [bə'zɑ:'] n Basar m.
bazooka [bə'zu:kə] n Panzerfaust f.
BB (BRIT) n abbr (= Boys' Brigade)
Jugendorganisation für Jungen.
BBB (US) n abbr (= Better Business Bureau)
amerikanische Verbraucherbehörde.
BBC n abbr BBC f.

BBC (Abkürzung für British Broadcasting
Corporation) ist die staatliche britische
Rundfunk- und Fernsehanstalt. Die
Fernsehsender BBC1 und BBC2 bieten beide
ein umfangreiches Fernsehprogramm, wobei
BBC1 mehr Sendungen von allgemeinem
Interesse wie z.B. leichte Unterhaltung, Sport,
Aktuelles, Kinderprogramme und
Außenübertragungen zeigt. BBC2
berücksichtigt Reisesendungen, Drama, Musik
und internationale Filme. Die 5 landesweiten
Radiosender bieten von Popmusik bis Kricket
etwas für jeden Geschmack; dazu gibt es noch
37 regionale Radiosender. Der BBC World
Service ist auf der ganzen Welt auf Englisch
oder in einer von 35 anderen Sprachen zu
empfangen. Finanziert wird die BBC vor allem
durch Fernsehgebühren und ins Ausland
verkaufte Sendungen. Obwohl die BBC dem
Parlament verantwortlich ist, werden die
Sendungen nicht vom Staat kontrolliert.

BC adv abbr (= before Christ) v. Chr. ♦ abbr
(CANADA: = British Columbia) Britisch-
Kolumbien nt.
BCG n abbr (= bacille Calmette-Guérin) BCG m.
BD n abbr (= Bachelor of Divinity)
akademischer Grad in Theologie.
B/D abbr = bank draft.
BDS n abbr (= Bachelor of Dental Surgery)
akademischer Grad in Zahnmedizin.
B/E abbr = bill of exchange.

══════════ KEYWORD

be [bi:] (pt **was, were,** pp **been**) aux vb **1** (with
present participle: forming continuous tenses):
what are you doing? was machst du?; **it is
raining** es regnet; **have you been to Rome?**
waren Sie schon einmal in Rom?
2 (with pp: forming passives) werden; **to
~ killed** getötet werden; **the box had been
opened** die Kiste war geöffnet worden
3 (in tag questions): **he's good-looking, isn't
he?** er sieht gut aus, nicht (wahr)?; **she's
back again, is she?** sie ist wieder da, oder?
4 (+ to + infinitive): **the house is to ~ sold** das

Haus soll verkauft werden; **he's not to open it** er darf es nicht öffnen
♦ *vb + complement* **1** sein; **I'm tired/English** ich bin müde/Engländer(in); **I'm hot/cold** mir ist heiß/kalt; **2 and 2 are 4** 2 und 2 ist *or* macht 4; **she's tall/pretty** sie ist groß/hübsch; ~ **careful/quiet** sei vorsichtig/ruhig
2 (*of health*): **how are you?** wie geht es Ihnen?
3 (*of age*): **how old are you?** wie alt bist du?; **I'm sixteen (years old)** ich bin sechzehn (Jahre alt)
4 (*cost*) kosten; **how much was the meal?** was hat das Essen gekostet?; **that'll** ~ **5 pounds please** das macht 5 Pfund, bitte
♦ *vi* **1** (*exist, occur etc*) sein; **there is/are** es gibt; **is there a God?** gibt es einen Gott?; ~ **that as it may** wie dem auch sei; **so** ~ **it** gut (und schön)
2 (*referring to place*) sein, liegen; **Edinburgh is in Scotland** Edinburgh liegt *or* ist in Schottland; **I won't** ~ **here tomorrow** morgen bin ich nicht da
3 (*referring to movement*) sein; **where have you been?** wo warst du?
♦ *impers vb* **1** (*referring to time, distance, weather*) sein; **it's 5 o'clock** es ist 5 Uhr; **it's 10 km to the village** es sind 10 km bis zum Dorf; **it's too hot/cold** es ist zu heiß/kalt
2 (*emphatic*): **it's only me** ich bin's nur; **it's only the postman** es ist nur der Briefträger.

beach [biːtʃ] *n* Strand *m* ♦ *vt* (*boat*) auf (den) Strand setzen.
beach buggy *n* Strandbuggy *m*.
beachcomber ['biːtʃkəumə*] *n* Strandgutsammler *m*.
beachwear ['biːtʃwɛə*] *n* Strandkleidung *f*.
beacon ['biːkən] *n* Leuchtfeuer *nt*; (*marker*) Bake *f*; (*also:* **radio** ~) Funkfeuer *nt*.
bead [biːd] *n* Perle *f*; **beads** *npl* (*necklace*) Perlenkette *f*.
beady ['biːdɪ] *adj:* ~ **eyes** Knopfaugen *pl*.
beagle ['biːgl] *n* Beagle *m*.
beak [biːk] *n* Schnabel *m*.
beaker ['biːkə*] *n* Becher *m*.
beam [biːm] *n* (*ARCHIT*) Balken *m*; (*of light*) Strahl *m*; (*RADIO*) Leitstrahl *m* ♦ *vi* (*smile*) strahlen ♦ *vt* ausstrahlen, senden; **to** ~ **at sb** jdn anstrahlen; **to drive on full** *or* **main** *or* **high** ~ mit Fernlicht fahren.
beaming ['biːmɪŋ] *adj* strahlend.
bean [biːn] *n* Bohne *f*; **runner** ~ Stangenbohne *f*; **broad** ~ dicke Bohne; **coffee** ~ Kaffeebohne *f*.
beanpole ['biːnpəul] *n* (*lit, fig*) Bohnenstange *f*.
beanshoots ['biːnʃuːts] *npl* Sojabohnensprossen *pl*.
beansprouts ['biːnsprauts] *npl* = **beanshoots**.
bear [bɛə*] (*pt* **bore**, *pp* **borne**) *n* Bär *m*; (*STOCK EXCHANGE*) Baissier *m* ♦ *vt* tragen; (*tolerate, endure*) ertragen; (*examination*) standhalten +*dat*; (*traces, signs*) aufweisen, zeigen; (*COMM: interest*) tragen, bringen; (*produce: children*) gebären; (: *fruit*) tragen ♦ *vi:* **to** ~ **right/left** (*AUT*) sich rechts/links halten; **to** ~ **the responsibility of** die Verantwortung tragen für; **to** ~ **comparison with** einem Vergleich standhalten mit; **I can't** ~ **him** ich kann ihn nicht ausstehen; **to bring pressure to** ~ **on sb** Druck auf jdn ausüben.
▶**bear out** *vt* (*person, suspicions etc*) bestätigen.
▶**bear up** *vi* Haltung bewahren; **he bore up well** er hat sich gut gehalten.
▶**bear with** *vt fus* Nachsicht haben mit; ~ **me a minute** bitte gedulden Sie sich einen Moment.
bearable ['bɛərəbl] *adj* erträglich.
beard [bɪəd] *n* Bart *m*.
bearded ['bɪədɪd] *adj* bärtig.
bearer ['bɛərə*] *n* (*of letter, news*) Überbringer(in) *m(f)*; (*of cheque, passport, title etc*) Inhaber(in) *m(f)*.
bearing ['bɛərɪŋ] *n* (*posture*) Haltung *f*; (*air*) Auftreten *nt*; (*connection*) Bezug *m*; (*TECH*) Lager *nt*; **bearings** *npl* (*also:* **ball** ~**s**) Kugellager *nt*; **to take a** ~ **with a compass** den Kompaßkurs feststellen; **to get one's** ~**s** sich zurechtfinden.
beast [biːst] *n* (*animal*) Tier *nt*; (*inf: person*) Biest *nt*.
beastly ['biːstlɪ] *adj* scheußlich.
beat [biːt] (*pt* **beat**, *pp* **beaten**) *n* (*of heart*) Schlag *m*; (*MUS*) Takt *m*; (*of policeman*) Revier *nt* ♦ *vt* schlagen; (*record*) brechen ♦ *vi* schlagen; **to** ~ **time** den Takt schlagen; **to** ~ **it** (*inf*) abhauen, verschwinden; **that** ~**s everything** das ist doch wirklich der Gipfel *or* die Höhe; **to** ~ **about the bush** um den heißen Brei herumreden; **off the** ~**en track** abgelegen.
▶**beat down** *vt* (*door*) einschlagen; (*price*) herunterhandeln; (*seller*) einen niedrigeren Preis aushandeln mit ♦ *vi* (*rain*) herunterprasseln; (*sun*) herunterbrennen.
▶**beat off** *vt* (*attack, attacker*) abwehren.
▶**beat up** *vt* (*person*) zusammenschlagen; (*mixture, eggs*) schlagen.
beater ['biːtə*] *n* (*for eggs, cream*) Schneebesen *m*.
beating ['biːtɪŋ] *n* Schläge *pl*, Prügel *pl*; **to take a** ~ (*fig*) eine Schlappe einstecken.
beat-up ['biːt'ʌp] (*inf*) *adj* zerbeult, ramponiert.
beautician [bjuːˈtɪʃən] *n* Kosmetiker(in) *m(f)*.
beautiful ['bjuːtɪful] *adj* schön.
beautifully ['bjuːtɪflɪ] *adv* (*play, sing, drive etc*) hervorragend; (*quiet, empty etc*) schön.
beautify ['bjuːtɪfaɪ] *vt* verschönern.
beauty ['bjuːtɪ] *n* Schönheit *f*; (*fig: attraction*) Schöne *nt*; **the** ~ **of it is that ...** das Schöne

daran ist, daß ...
beauty contest n Schönheitswettbewerb m.
beauty queen n Schönheitskönigin f.
beauty salon n Kosmetiksalon m.
beauty sleep n (Schönheits)schlaf m.
beauty spot (BRIT) n besonders schöner Ort m.
beaver ['biːvə*] n Biber m.
becalmed [bɪ'kɑːmd] adj: **to be ~** (sailing ship) in eine Flaute geraten.
became [bɪ'keɪm] pt of **become**.
because [bɪ'kɔz] conj weil; **~ of** wegen +gen or (inf) +dat.
beck [bɛk] n: **to be at sb's ~ and call** nach jds Pfeife tanzen.
beckon ['bɛkən] vt (also: **~ to**) winken ♦ vi locken.
become [bɪ'kʌm] (irreg: like **come**) vi werden; **it became known that** es wurde bekannt, daß; **what has ~ of him?** was ist aus ihm geworden?
becoming [bɪ'kʌmɪŋ] adj (behaviour) schicklich; (clothes) kleidsam.
BECTU ['bɛktu] (BRIT) n abbr (= Broadcasting, Entertainment, Cinematographic and Theatre Union) Gewerkschaft für Beschäftigte in der Unterhaltungsindustrie.
BEd n abbr (= Bachelor of Education) akademischer Grad im Erziehungswesen.
bed [bɛd] n Bett nt; (of coal) Flöz nt; (of clay) Schicht f; (of river) (Fluß)bett nt; (of sea) (Meeres)boden m, (Meeres)grund m; (of flowers) Beet nt; **to go to ~** ins or zu Bett gehen.
▶**bed down** vi sein Lager aufschlagen.
bed and breakfast n (place) (Frühstücks)pension f; (terms) Übernachtung f mit Frühstück.

> Bed and Breakfast bedeutet 'Übernachtung mit Frühstück', wobei sich dies in Großbritannien nicht auf Hotels, sondern auf kleinere Pensionen, Privathäuser und Bauernhöfe bezieht, wo man wesentlich preisgünstiger übernachten kann als in Hotels. Oft wird für Bed and Breakfast, auch **B & B** genannt, durch ein entsprechendes Schild im Garten oder an der Einfahrt geworben.

bedbug ['bɛdbʌg] n Wanze f.
bedclothes ['bɛdkləʊðz] npl Bettzeug nt.
bedding ['bɛdɪŋ] n Bettzeug nt.
bedevil [bɪ'dɛvl] vt (person) heimsuchen; (plans) komplizieren; **to be ~led by misfortune/bad luck** vom Schicksal/Pech verfolgt sein.
bedfellow ['bɛdfɛləʊ] n: **they are strange ~s** (fig) sie sind ein merkwürdiges Gespann.
bedlam ['bɛdləm] n Chaos nt.
bedpan ['bɛdpæn] n Bettpfanne f, Bettschüssel f.
bedpost ['bɛdpəʊst] n Bettpfosten m.

bedraggled [bɪ'drægld] adj (wet) triefnaß, tropfnaß; (dirty) verdreckt.
bedridden ['bɛdrɪdn] adj bettlägerig.
bedrock ['bɛdrɔk] n (fig) Fundament nt; (GEOG) Grundgebirge nt, Grundgestein nt.
bedroom ['bɛdrum] n Schlafzimmer nt.
Beds [bɛdz] (BRIT) abbr (POST: = Bedfordshire).
bed settee n Sofabett nt.
bedside ['bɛdsaɪd] n: **at sb's ~** an jds Bett; **~ lamp** Nachttischlampe f; **~ book** Bettlektüre f.
bedsit(ter) ['bɛdsɪt(ə*)] (BRIT) n möbliertes Zimmer nt.
bedspread ['bɛdsprɛd] n Tagesdecke f.
bedtime ['bɛdtaɪm] n Schlafenszeit f; **it's ~** es ist Zeit, ins Bett zu gehen.
bee [biː] n Biene f; **to have a ~ in one's bonnet about cleanliness** einen Sauberkeitsfimmel or Sauberkeitstick haben.
beech [biːtʃ] n Buche f.
beef [biːf] n Rind(fleisch) nt; **roast ~** Rinderbraten m.
▶**beef up** (inf) vt aufmotzen; (essay) auswalzen.
beefburger ['biːfbəːgə*] n Hamburger m.
beefeater ['biːfiːtə*] n Beefeater m.
beehive ['biːhaɪv] n Bienenstock m.
beekeeping ['biːkiːpɪŋ] n Bienenzucht f, Imkerei f.
beeline ['biːlaɪn] n: **to make a ~ for** schnurstracks zugehen auf +acc.
been [biːn] pp of **be**.
beep [biːp] (inf) n Tut(tut) nt ♦ vi tuten ♦ vt: **to ~ one's horn** hupen.
beer [bɪə*] n Bier nt.
beer belly (inf) n Bierbauch m.
beer can n Bierdose f.
beet [biːt] n Rübe f; (US: also: **red ~**) rote Bete f.
beetle ['biːtl] n Käfer m.
beetroot ['biːtruːt] (BRIT) n rote Bete f.
befall [bɪ'fɔːl] (irreg: like **fall**) vi sich zutragen ♦ vt widerfahren +dat.
befit [bɪ'fɪt] vt sich gehören für.
before [bɪ'fɔː*] prep vor +dat; (with movement) vor +acc ♦ conj bevor ♦ adv (time) vorher; (space) davor; **~ going** bevor er/sie etc geht/ging; **~ she goes** bevor sie geht; **the week ~** die Woche davor; **I've never seen it ~** ich habe es noch nie gesehen.
beforehand [bɪ'fɔːhænd] adv vorher.
befriend [bɪ'frɛnd] vt sich annehmen +gen.
befuddled [bɪ'fʌdld] adj: **to be ~** verwirrt sein.
beg [bɛg] vi betteln ♦ vt (food, money) betteln um; (favour, forgiveness etc) bitten um; **to ~ for** (food etc) betteln um; (forgiveness, mercy etc) bitten um; **to ~ sb to do sth** jdn bitten, etw zu tun; **I ~ your pardon** (apologizing) entschuldigen Sie bitte; (: not hearing) (wie) bitte?; **to ~ the question** der Frage ausweichen; see also **pardon**.

began [bɪ'gæn] *pt of* **begin**.

beggar ['begə*] *n* Bettler(in) *m(f)*.

begin [bɪ'gɪn] (*pt* **began**, *pp* **begun**) *vt, vi* beginnen, anfangen; **to ~ doing** *or* **to do sth** anfangen, etw zu tun; **~ning (from) Monday** ab Montag; **I can't ~ to thank you** ich kann Ihnen gar nicht genug danken; **we'll have soup to ~ with** als Vorspeise hätten wir gern Suppe; **to ~ with, I'd like to know ...** zunächst einmal möchte ich wissen, ...

beginner [bɪ'gɪnə*] *n* Anfänger(in) *m(f)*.

beginning [bɪ'gɪnɪŋ] *n* Anfang *m*; **right from the ~** von Anfang an.

begrudge [bɪ'grʌdʒ] *vt*: **to ~ sb sth** jdm etw mißgönnen *or* nicht gönnen.

beguile [bɪ'gaɪl] *vt* betören.

beguiling [bɪ'gaɪlɪŋ] *adj* (*charming*) verführerisch; (*deluding*) betörend.

begun [bɪ'gʌn] *pp of* **begin**.

behalf [bɪ'hɑːf] *n*: **on ~ of**, (*US*) **in ~ of** (*as representative of*) im Namen von; (*for benefit of*) zugunsten von; **on my/his ~** in meinem/ seinem Namen; zu meinen/seinen Gunsten.

behave [bɪ'heɪv] *vi* (*person*) sich verhalten, sich benehmen; (*thing*) funktionieren; (*also:* **~ o.s.**) sich benehmen.

behaviour, (*US*) **behavior** [bɪ'heɪvjə*] *n* Verhalten *nt*; (*manner*) Benehmen *nt*.

behead [bɪ'hed] *vt* enthaupten.

beheld [bɪ'held] *pt, pp of* **behold**.

behind [bɪ'haɪnd] *prep* hinter ♦ *adv* (*at/towards the back*) hinten ♦ *n* (*buttocks*) Hintern *m*, Hinterteil *nt*; **~ the scenes** (*fig*) hinter den Kulissen; **we're ~ them in technology** auf dem Gebiet der Technologie liegen wir hinter ihnen zurück; **to be ~** (*schedule*) im Rückstand *or* Verzug sein; **to leave/stay ~** zurücklassen/-bleiben.

behold [bɪ'həuld] (*irreg: like* **hold**) *vt* sehen, erblicken.

beige [beɪʒ] *adj* beige.

Beijing ['beɪ'dʒɪŋ] *n* Peking *nt*.

being ['biːɪŋ] *n* (*creature*) (Lebe)wesen *nt*; (*existence*) Leben *nt*, (Da)sein *nt*; **to come into ~** entstehen.

Beirut [beɪ'ruːt] *n* Beirut *nt*.

Belarus [belə'rus] *n* Weißrußland *nt*.

Belarussian *adj* belarussisch, weißrussisch ♦ *n* Weißrusse *m*, Weißrussin *f*; (*LING*) Weißrussisch *nt*.

belated [bɪ'leɪtɪd] *adj* verspätet.

belch [beltʃ] *vi* rülpsen ♦ *vt* (*also:* **belch out:** *smoke etc*) ausstoßen.

beleaguered [bɪ'liːgɪd] *adj* (*city*) belagert; (*army*) eingekesselt; (*fig*) geplagt.

Belfast ['belfɑːst] *n* Belfast *nt*.

belfry ['belfrɪ] *n* Glockenstube *f*.

Belgian ['beldʒən] *adj* belgisch ♦ *n* Belgier(in) *m(f)*.

Belgium ['beldʒəm] *n* Belgien *nt*.

Belgrade [bel'greɪd] *n* Belgrad *nt*.

belie [bɪ'laɪ] *vt* (*contradict*) im Widerspruch stehen zu; (*give false impression of*) hinwegtäuschen über +*acc*; (*disprove*) widerlegen, Lügen strafen.

belief [bɪ'liːf] *n* Glaube *m*; (*opinion*) Überzeugung *f*; **it's beyond ~** es ist unglaublich *or* nicht zu glauben; **in the ~ that** im Glauben, daß.

believable [bɪ'liːvəbl] *adj* glaubhaft.

believe [bɪ'liːv] *vt* glauben ♦ *vi* (an Gott) glauben; **he is ~d to be abroad** es heißt, daß er im Ausland ist; **to ~ in** (*God, ghosts*) glauben an +*acc*; (*method etc*) Vertrauen haben zu; **I don't ~ in corporal punishment** ich halte nicht viel von der Prügelstrafe.

believer [bɪ'liːvə*] *n* (*in idea, activity*) Anhänger(in) *m(f)*; (*REL*) Gläubige(r) *f(m)*; **she's a great ~ in healthy eating** sie ist sehr für eine gesunde Ernährung.

belittle [bɪ'lɪtl] *vt* herabsetzen.

Belize [be'liːz] *n* Belize *nt*.

bell [bel] *n* Glocke *f*, (*small*) Glöckchen *nt*, Schelle *f*; (*on door*) Klingel *f*; **that rings a ~** (*fig*) das kommt mir bekannt vor.

bell-bottoms ['belbɒtəmz] *npl* Hose *f* mit Schlag.

bellboy ['belbɔɪ] (*BRIT*) *n* Page *m*, Hoteljunge *m*.

bellhop ['belhɒp] (*US*) *n* = **bellboy**.

belligerence [bɪ'lɪdʒərəns] *n* Angriffslust *f*.

belligerent [bɪ'lɪdʒərənt] *adj* angriffslustig.

bellow ['beləu] *vi, vt* brüllen.

bellows ['beləuz] *npl* Blasebalg *m*.

bell push (*BRIT*) *n* Klingel *f*.

belly ['belɪ] *n* Bauch *m*.

bellyache ['belɪeɪk] (*inf*) *n* Bauchschmerzen *pl* ♦ *vi* murren.

bellybutton ['belɪbʌtn] *n* Bauchnabel *m*.

bellyful ['belɪful] (*inf*) *n*: **I've had a ~ of that** davon habe ich die Nase voll.

belong [bɪ'lɒŋ] *vi*: **to ~ to** (*person*) gehören +*dat*; (*club etc*) angehören +*dat*; **this book ~s here** dieses Buch gehört hierher.

belongings [bɪ'lɒŋɪŋz] *npl* Sachen *pl*, Habe *f*; **personal ~** persönlicher Besitz *m*, persönliches Eigentum *nt*.

Belorussia [beleu'rʌʃə] *n* Weißrußland *nt*.

Belorussian [beleu'rʌʃən] *adj, n* = **Belarussian**.

beloved [bɪ'lʌvɪd] *adj* geliebt ♦ *n* Geliebte(r) *f(m)*.

below [bɪ'ləu] *prep* (*beneath*) unterhalb +*gen*; (*less than*) unter +*dat* ♦ *adv* (*beneath*) unten; **see ~** siehe unten; **temperatures ~ normal** Temperaturen unter dem Durchschnitt.

belt [belt] *n* Gürtel *m*; (*TECH*) (Treib)riemen *m* ♦ *vt* schlagen ♦ *vi* (*BRIT: inf*): **to ~ along** rasen; **to ~ down/into** hinunter-/ hineinrasen; **industrial ~** Industriegebiet *nt*.

▶**belt out** *vt* (*song*) schmettern.

▶**belt up** (*BRIT: inf*) *vi* den Mund *or* die Klappe halten.

beltway ['beltweɪ] (*US*) *n* Umgehungsstraße *f*, Ringstraße *f*; (*motorway*)

Umgehungsautobahn f.
bemoan [bɪ'məʊn] vt beklagen.
bemused [bɪ'mjuːzd] adj verwirrt.
bench [bentʃ] n Bank f; (work bench)
Werkbank f; **the B~** (LAW: judges) die
Richter pl, der Richterstand.
benchmark ['bentʃmɑːk] n (fig) Maßstab m.
bend [bend] (pt, pp **bent**) vt (leg, arm) beugen;
(pipe) biegen ♦ vi (person) sich beugen ♦ n
(BRIT: in road) Kurve f; (in pipe, river)
Biegung f; **bends** npl (MED): **the ~s** die
Taucherkrankheit.
►**bend down** vi sich bücken.
►**bend over** vi sich bücken.
beneath [bɪ'niːθ] prep unter +dat ♦ adv
darunter.
benefactor ['benɪfæktə*] n Wohltäter m.
benefactress ['benɪfæktrɪs] n Wohltäterin f.
beneficial [benɪ'fɪʃəl] adj (effect) nützlich;
(influence) vorteilhaft; **~ (to)** gut (für).
beneficiary [benɪ'fɪʃərɪ] n (LAW)
Nutznießer(in) m(f).
benefit ['benɪfɪt] n (advantage) Vorteil m;
(money) Beihilfe f; (also: **~ concert, ~ match**)
Benefizveranstaltung f ♦ vt nützen +dat,
zugute kommen +dat ♦ vi: **he'll ~ from it** er
wird davon profitieren.
Benelux ['benɪlʌks] n die Beneluxstaaten pl.
benevolent [bɪ'nevələnt] adj wohlwollend;
(organization) Wohltätigkeits-.
BEng n abbr (= Bachelor of Engineering)
akademischer Grad für Ingenieure.
benign [bɪ'naɪn] adj gütig; (MED) gutartig.
bent [bent] pt, pp of **bend** ♦ n Neigung f ♦ adj
(wire, pipe) gebogen; (inf: dishonest) korrupt;
(: pej: homosexual) andersrum; **to be ~ on**
entschlossen sein zu.
bequeath [bɪ'kwiːð] vt vermachen.
bequest [bɪ'kwest] n Vermächtnis nt, Legat nt.
bereaved [bɪ'riːvd] adj leidtragend ♦ npl: **the ~**
die Hinterbliebenen pl.
bereavement [bɪ'riːvmənt] n schmerzlicher
Verlust m.
bereft [bɪ'reft] adj: **~ of** beraubt +gen.
beret ['bereɪ] n Baskenmütze f.
Bering Sea ['beɪrɪŋ-] n: **the ~** das
Beringmeer.
berk [bɜːk] (inf) n Dussel m.
Berks [bɑːks] (BRIT) abbr (POST: = Berkshire).
Berlin [bɜː'lɪn] n Berlin nt; **East/West ~**
(formerly) Ost-/Westberlin nt.
berm [bɜːm] (US) n Seitenstreifen m.
Bermuda [bə'mjuːdə] n Bermuda nt, die
Bermudinseln pl.
Bermuda shorts npl Bermudashorts pl.
Bern [bɜːn] n Bern nt.
berry ['berɪ] n Beere f.
berserk [bə'sɜːk] adj: **to go ~** wild werden.
berth [bɜːθ] n (bed) Bett nt; (on ship) Koje f;
(on train) Schlafwagenbett nt; (for ship)
Liegeplatz m ♦ vi anlegen; **to give sb a wide
~** (fig) einen großen Bogen um jdn machen.

beseech [bɪ'siːtʃ] (pt, pp **besought**) vt anflehen.
beset [bɪ'set] (pt, pp **beset**) vt (subj: difficulties)
bedrängen; (: fears, doubts) befallen; **~ with**
(problems, dangers etc) voller +dat.
beside [bɪ'saɪd] prep neben +dat; (with
movement) neben +acc; **to be ~ o.s.** außer
sich sein; **that's ~ the point** das hat damit
nichts zu tun.
besides [bɪ'saɪdz] adv außerdem ♦ prep außer
+dat.
besiege [bɪ'siːdʒ] vt belagern; (fig) belagern,
bedrängen.
besmirch [bɪ'smɜːtʃ] vt besudeln.
besotted [bɪ'sɒtɪd] (BRIT) adj: **~ with** vernarrt
in +acc.
besought [bɪ'sɔːt] pt, pp of **beseech**.
bespectacled [bɪ'spektɪkld] adj bebrillt.
bespoke [bɪ'spəʊk] (BRIT) adj (garment)
maßgeschneidert; (suit) Maß-; **~ tailor**
Maßschneider m.
best [best] adj beste(r, s) ♦ adv am besten ♦ n:
at ~ bestenfalls; **the ~ thing to do is ...** das
beste ist ...; **the ~ part of** der größte Teil
+gen; **to make the ~ of sth** das Beste aus etw
machen; **to do one's ~** sein Bestes tun; **to
the ~ of my knowledge** meines Wissens; **to
the ~ of my ability** so gut ich kann; **he's not
exactly patient at the ~ of times** er ist schon
normalerweise ziemlich ungeduldig.
bestial ['bestɪəl] adj bestialisch.
best man n Trauzeuge m (des Bräutigams).
bestow [bɪ'stəʊ] vt schenken; **to ~ sth on sb**
(honour, praise) jdm etw zuteil werden
lassen; (title) jdm etw verleihen.
best seller n Bestseller m.
bet [bet] (pt, pp **bet** or **betted**) n Wette f ♦ vi
wetten ♦ vt: **to ~ sb sth** mit jdm um etw
wetten; **it's a safe ~** (fig) es ist so gut wie
sicher; **to ~ money on sth** Geld auf etw acc
setzen.
Bethlehem ['beθlɪhem] n Bethlehem nt.
betray [bɪ'treɪ] vt verraten; (trust, confidence)
mißbrauchen.
betrayal [bɪ'treɪəl] n Verrat m.
better ['betə*] adj, adv besser ♦ vt verbessern
♦ n: **to get the ~ of sb** jdn unterkriegen;
(curiosity) über jdn siegen; **I had ~ go** ich
gehe jetzt (wohl) besser; **you had ~ do it**
tun Sie es lieber; **he thought ~ of it** er
überlegte es sich dat anders; **to get ~** (ill)
gesund werden; **that's ~!** so ist es besser!; **a
change for the ~** eine Wendung zum Guten.
better off adj (wealthier) besser gestellt;
(more comfortable etc) besser dran; (fig):
you'd be ~ this way so wäre es besser für
Sie.
betting ['betɪŋ] n Wetten nt.
betting shop (BRIT) n Wettbüro nt.
between [bɪ'twiːn] prep zwischen +dat; (with
movement) zwischen +acc; (amongst) unter
+acc or dat ♦ adv dazwischen; **the road ~ here
and London** die Straße zwischen hier und

London; **we only had £5** ~ **us** wir hatten zusammen nur £5.

bevel ['bɛvəl] n (also: ~ **edge**) abgeschrägte Kante f.

bevelled ['bɛvəld] adj: **a** ~ **edge** eine Schrägkante, eine abgeschrägte Kante.

beverage ['bɛvərɪdʒ] n Getränk nt.

bevy ['bɛvɪ] n: **a** ~ **of** eine Schar +gen.

bewail [bɪ'weɪl] vt beklagen.

beware [bɪ'wɛə*] vi: **to** ~ **(of)** sich in acht nehmen (vor +dat); **"~ of the dog"** „Vorsicht, bissiger Hund".

bewildered [bɪ'wɪldəd] adj verwirrt.

bewildering [bɪ'wɪldrɪŋ] adj verwirrend.

bewitching [bɪ'wɪtʃɪŋ] adj bezaubernd, hinreißend.

beyond [bɪ'jɔnd] prep (in space) jenseits +gen; (exceeding) über +acc ... hinaus; (after) nach; (above) über +dat ♦ adv (in space) dahinter; (in time) darüber hinaus; **it is** ~ **doubt** es steht außer Zweifel; ~ **repair** nicht mehr zu reparieren; **it is** ~ **my understanding** es übersteigt mein Begriffsvermögen; **it's** ~ **me** das geht über meinen Verstand.

b/f abbr (COMM: = brought forward) Übertr.

BFPO n abbr (= British Forces Post Office) Postbehörde der britischen Armee.

bhp n abbr (AUT: = brake horsepower) Bremsleistung f.

bi... [baɪ] pref Bi-, bi-.

biannual [baɪ'ænjuəl] adj zweimal jährlich.

bias ['baɪəs] n (prejudice) Vorurteil nt; (preference) Vorliebe f.

bias(s)ed ['baɪəst] adj voreingenommen; **to be** ~ **against** voreingenommen sein gegen.

biathlon [baɪ'æθlən] n Biathlon nt.

bib [bɪb] n Latz m.

Bible ['baɪbl] n Bibel f.

biblical ['bɪblɪkl] adj biblisch.

bibliography [bɪblɪ'ɔgrəfɪ] n Bibliographie f.

bicarbonate of soda [baɪ'kɑːbənɪt-] n Natron nt.

bicentenary [baɪsɛn'tiːnərɪ] n Zweihundertjahrfeier f.

bicentennial [baɪsɛn'tɛnɪəl] (US) n = bicentenary.

biceps ['baɪsɛps] n Bizeps m.

bicker ['bɪkə*] vi sich zanken.

bickering ['bɪkərɪŋ] n Zankerei f.

bicycle ['baɪsɪkl] n Fahrrad nt.

bicycle path n (Fahr)radweg m.

bicycle pump n Luftpumpe f.

bicycle track n (Fahr)radweg m.

bid [bɪd] n (pt **bade** or **bid**, pp **bidden** or **bid**) n (at auction) Gebot nt; (in tender) Angebot nt; (attempt) Versuch m ♦ vi bieten; (CARDS) bieten, reizen ♦ vt bieten; **to** ~ **sb good day** jdm einen guten Tag wünschen.

bidder ['bɪdə*] n: **the highest** ~ der/die Höchstbietende or Meistbietende.

bidding ['bɪdɪŋ] n Steigern nt, Bieten nt; (order, command): **to do sb's** ~ tun, was jd

einem sagt.

bide [baɪd] vt: **to** ~ **one's time** den rechten Augenblick abwarten.

bidet ['biːdeɪ] n Bidet nt.

bidirectional ['baɪdɪ'rɛkʃənl] adj (COMPUT) bidirektional.

biennial [baɪ'ɛnɪəl] adj zweijährlich ♦ n zweijährige Pflanze f.

bier [bɪə*] n Bahre f.

bifocals [baɪ'fəuklz] npl Bifokalbrille f.

big [bɪg] adj groß; **to do things in a** ~ **way** alles im großen Stil tun.

bigamist ['bɪgəmɪst] n Bigamist(in) m(f).

bigamous ['bɪgəməs] adj bigamistisch.

bigamy ['bɪgəmɪ] n Bigamie f.

big dipper [-'dɪpə*] n Achterbahn f.

big end n (AUT) Pleuelfuß m, Schubstangenkopf m.

biggish ['bɪgɪʃ] adj ziemlich groß.

bigheaded ['bɪg'hɛdɪd] adj eingebildet.

big-hearted ['bɪg'hɑːtɪd] adj großherzig.

bigot ['bɪgət] n Eiferer m; (about religion) bigotter Mensch m.

bigoted ['bɪgətɪd] adj (see n) eifernd; bigott.

bigotry ['bɪgətrɪ] n (see n) eifernde Borniertheit f; Bigotterie f.

big toe n große Zehe f.

big top n Zirkuszelt nt.

big wheel n Riesenrad nt.

bigwig ['bɪgwɪg] (inf) n hohes Tier nt.

bike [baɪk] n (Fahr)rad nt; (motorcycle) Motorrad m.

bikini [bɪ'kiːnɪ] n Bikini m.

bilateral [baɪ'lætərəl] adj bilateral.

bile [baɪl] n Galle(nflüssigkeit) f; (fig: invective) Beschimpfungen pl.

bilingual [baɪ'lɪŋwəl] adj zweisprachig.

bilious ['bɪlɪəs] adj unwohl; (fig: colour) widerlich; **he felt** ~ ihm war schlecht or übel.

bill [bɪl] n Rechnung f; (POL) (Gesetz)entwurf m, (Gesetzes)vorlage f; (US: banknote) Banknote f, (Geld)schein m; (of bird) Schnabel m ♦ vt (item) in Rechnung stellen, berechnen; (customer) eine Rechnung ausstellen +dat; **"post no** ~**s"** „Plakate ankleben verboten"; **on the** ~ (THEAT) auf dem Programm; **to fit** or **fill the** ~ (fig) der/die/das richtige sein; ~ **of exchange** Wechsel m, Tratte f; ~ **of fare** Speisekarte f; ~ **of lading** Seefrachtbrief m, Konnossement nt; ~ **of sale** Verkaufsurkunde f.

billboard ['bɪlbɔːd] n Reklametafel f.

billet ['bɪlɪt] (MIL) n Quartier nt ♦ vt einquartieren.

billfold ['bɪlfəuld] (US) n Brieftasche f.

billiards ['bɪljədz] n Billard nt.

billion ['bɪljən] n (BRIT) Billion f; (US) Milliarde f.

billionaire [bɪljə'nɛə*] n Milliardär(in) m(f).

billow ['bɪləu] n (of smoke) Schwaden m ♦ vi

(*smoke*) in Schwaden aufsteigen; (*sail*) sich blähen.

billy goat ['bɪlɪ-] *n* Ziegenbock *m*.

bimbo ['bɪmbəu] (*inf: pej*) *n* (*woman*) Puppe *f*, Häschen *nt*.

bin [bɪn] *n* (*BRIT*) Mülleimer *m*; (*container*) Behälter *m*.

binary ['baɪnərɪ] *adj* binär.

bind [baɪnd] (*pt, pp* **bound**) *vt* binden; (*tie together: hands and feet*) fesseln; (*constrain, oblige*) verpflichten ♦ *n* (*inf: nuisance*) Last *f*.
►**bind over** *vt* rechtlich verpflichten.
►**bind up** *vt* (*wound*) verbinden; **to be bound up in** sehr beschäftigt sein mit; **to be bound up with** verbunden *or* verknüpft sein mit.

binder ['baɪndə⁎] *n* (*file*) Hefter *m*; (*for magazines*) Mappe *f*.

binding ['baɪndɪŋ] *adj* bindend, verbindlich ♦ *n* (*of book*) Einband *m*.

binge [bɪndʒ] (*inf*) *n:* **to go on a ~** auf eine Sauftour gehen.

bingo ['bɪŋgəu] *n* Bingo *nt*.

bin liner *n* Müllbeutel *m*.

binoculars [bɪˈnɔkjuləz] *npl* Fernglas *nt*.

biochemistry [baɪəˈkɛmɪstrɪ] *n* Biochemie *f*.

biodegradable ['baɪəudɪˈgreɪdəbl] *adj* biologisch abbaubar.

biodiversity ['baɪəudaɪˈvəːsɪtɪ] *n* biologische Vielfalt *f*.

biofuel *n* Biotreibstoff *m*.

biographer [baɪˈɔgrəfə⁎] *n* Biograph(in) *m(f)*.

biographic(al) [baɪəˈgræfɪk(l)] *adj* biographisch.

biography [baɪˈɔgrəfɪ] *n* Biographie *f*.

biological [baɪəˈlɔdʒɪkl] *adj* biologisch.

biological clock *n* biologische Uhr *f*.

biologist [baɪˈɔlədʒɪst] *n* Biologe *m*, Biologin *f*.

biology [baɪˈɔlədʒɪ] *n* Biologie *f*.

biophysics ['baɪəuˈfɪzɪks] *n* Biophysik *f*.

biopic ['baɪəupɪk] *n* Filmbiographie *f*.

biopsy ['baɪɔpsɪ] *n* Biopsie *f*.

biosphere ['baɪəsfɪə] *n* Biosphäre *f*.

biotechnology ['baɪəutɛkˈnɔlədʒɪ] *n* Biotechnik *f*.

biped ['baɪpɛd] *n* Zweifüßer *m*.

birch [bəːtʃ] *n* Birke *f*.

bird [bəːd] *n* Vogel *m*; (*BRIT: inf: girl*) Biene *f*.

bird of prey *n* Raubvogel *m*.

bird's-eye view ['bəːdzaɪ-] *n* Vogelperspektive *f*; (*overview*) Überblick *m*.

bird-watcher ['bəːdwɔtʃə⁎] *n* Vogelbeobachter(in) *m(f)*.

Biro ® ['baɪərəu] *n* Kugelschreiber *m*, Kuli *m* (*inf*).

birth [bəːθ] *n* Geburt *f*; **to give ~ to** (*subj: woman*) gebären, entbunden werden von; (*: animal*) werfen.

birth certificate *n* Geburtsurkunde *f*.

birth control *n* Geburtenkontrolle *f*, Geburtenregelung *f*.

birthday ['bəːθdeɪ] *n* Geburtstag *m* ♦ *cpd* Geburtstags-; *see also* **happy**.

birthmark ['bəːθmɑːk] *n* Muttermal *nt*.

birthplace ['bəːθpleɪs] *n* Geburtsort *m*; (*house*) Geburtshaus *nt*; (*fig*) Entstehungsort *m*.

birth rate ['bəːθreɪt] *n* Geburtenrate *f*, Geburtenziffer *f*.

Biscay ['bɪskeɪ] *n:* **the Bay of ~** der Golf von Biskaya.

biscuit ['bɪskɪt] *n* (*BRIT*) Keks *m or nt*; (*US*) Brötchen *nt*.

bisect [baɪˈsɛkt] *vt* halbieren.

bisexual ['baɪˈsɛksjuəl] *adj* bisexuell ♦ *n* Bisexuelle(r) *f(m)*.

bishop ['bɪʃəp] *n* (*REL*) Bischof *m*; (*CHESS*) Läufer *m*.

bistro ['biːstrəu] *n* Bistro *nt*.

bit [bɪt] *pt of* **bite** ♦ *n* (*piece*) Stück *nt*; (*of drill*) (Bohr)einsatz *m*, Bohrer *m*; (*of plane*) (Hobel)messer *nt*; (*COMPUT*) Bit *nt*; (*of horse*) Gebiß *nt*; (*US*): **two/four/six ~s** 25/50/75 Cent(s); **a ~ of** ein bißchen; **a ~ mad** ein bißchen verrückt; **a ~ dangerous** etwas gefährlich; **~ by ~** nach und nach; **to come to ~s** kaputtgehen; **bring all your ~s and pieces** bringen Sie Ihre (Sieben)sachen mit; **to do one's ~** sein(en) Teil tun *or* beitragen.

bitch [bɪtʃ] *n* (*dog*) Hündin *f*; (*inf!: woman*) Miststück *nt*.

bite [baɪt] (*pt* **bit**, *pp* **bitten**) *vt, vi* beißen; (*subj: insect etc*) stechen ♦ *n* (*insect bite*) Stich *m*; (*mouthful*) Bissen *m*; **to ~ one's nails** an seinen Nägeln kauen; **let's have a ~ (to eat)** (*inf*) laßt uns eine Kleinigkeit essen.

biting ['baɪtɪŋ] *adj* (*wind*) schneidend; (*wit*) scharf.

bit part *n* kleine Nebenrolle *f*.

bitten ['bɪtn] *pp of* **bite**.

bitter ['bɪtə⁎] *adj* bitter; (*person*) verbittert; (*wind, weather*) bitterkalt, eisig; (*criticism*) scharf ♦ *n* (*BRIT: beer*) halbdunkles obergäriges Bier; **to the ~ end** bis zum bitteren Ende.

bitterly ['bɪtəlɪ] *adv* (*complain, weep*) bitterlich; (*oppose*) erbittert; (*criticize*) scharf; (*disappointed*) bitter; (*jealous*) sehr; **it's ~ cold** es ist bitter kalt.

bitterness ['bɪtənɪs] *n* Bitterkeit *f*.

bittersweet ['bɪtəswiːt] *adj* bittersüß.

bitty ['bɪtɪ] (*BRIT: inf*) *adj* zusammengestoppelt, zusammengestückelt.

bitumen ['bɪtjumɪn] *n* Bitumen *nt*.

bivouac ['bɪvuæk] *n* Biwak *nt*.

bizarre [bɪˈzɑː⁎] *adj* bizarr.

bk *abbr* = **bank**; **book**.

BL *n abbr* (= *Bachelor of Law*) akademischer Grad für Juristen; (= *Bachelor of Letters*) *akademischer Grad für Literaturwissenschaftler*; (*US:* = *Bachelor of Literature*) akademischer Grad für Literaturwissenschaftler.

b.l. *abbr* = **bill of lading**.

blab [blæb] (*inf*) *vi* quatschen.

black [blæk] *adj* schwarz ♦ *vt* (*BRIT: INDUSTRY*)

boykottieren ♦ *n* Schwarz *nt*; (*person*): **B**~ Schwarze(r) *f(m)*; **to give sb a ~ eye** jdm ein blaues Auge schlagen; **~ and blue** grün und blau; **there it is in ~ and white** (*fig*) da steht es schwarz auf weiß; **to be in the ~** in den schwarzen Zahlen sein.

▶**black out** *vi* (*faint*) ohnmächtig werden.

black belt *n* (*US*) *Gebiet in den Südstaaten der USA, das vorwiegend von Schwarzen bewohnt wird*; (*JUDO*) schwarzer Gürtel *m*.

blackberry ['blækbərı] *n* Brombeere *f*.

blackbird ['blækbə:d] *n* Amsel *f*.

blackboard ['blækbɔ:d] *n* Tafel *f*.

black box *n* (*AVIAT*) Flugschreiber *m*.

black coffee *n* schwarzer Kaffee *m*.

Black Country (*BRIT*) *n:* **the ~** *Industriegebiet in den englischen Midlands*.

blackcurrant ['blæk'kʌrənt] *n* Johannisbeere *f*.

black economy *n:* **the ~** die Schattenwirtschaft.

blacken ['blækn] *vt:* **to ~ sb's name/reputation** (*fig*) jdn verunglimpfen.

Black Forest *n:* **the ~** der Schwarzwald.

blackhead ['blækhed] *n* Mitesser *m*.

black hole *n* schwarzes Loch *nt*.

black ice *n* Glatteis *nt*.

blackjack ['blækdʒæk] *n* (*CARDS*) Siebzehnundvier *nt*; (*US: truncheon*) Schlagstock *m*.

blackleg ['blækleg] (*BRIT*) *n* Streikbrecher(in) *m(f)*.

blacklist ['blæklıst] *n* schwarze Liste *f* ♦ *vt* auf die schwarze Liste setzen.

blackmail ['blækmeıl] *n* Erpressung *f* ♦ *vt* erpressen.

blackmailer ['blækmeılə'] *n* Erpresser(in) *m(f)*.

black market *n* Schwarzmarkt *m*.

blackout ['blækaut] *n* (*in wartime*) Verdunkelung *f*; (*power cut*) Stromausfall *m*; (*TV, RADIO*) Ausfall *m*; (*faint*) Ohnmachtsanfall *m*.

black pepper *n* schwarzer Pfeffer *m*.

Black Sea *n:* **the ~** das Schwarze Meer.

black sheep *n* (*fig*) schwarzes Schaf *nt*.

blacksmith ['blæksmıθ] *n* Schmied *m*.

black spot *n* (*AUT*) Gefahrenstelle *f*; (*for unemployment etc*) *Gebiet, in dem ein Problem besonders ausgeprägt ist*.

bladder ['blædə'] *n* Blase *f*.

blade [bleıd] *n* (*of knife etc*) Klinge *f*; (*of oar, propeller*) Blatt *nt*; **a ~ of grass** ein Grashalm *m*.

blame [bleım] *n* Schuld *f* ♦ *vt:* **to ~ sb for sth** jdm die Schuld an etw *dat* geben; **to be to ~** schuld daran haben *or* sein; **who's to ~?** wer hat *or* ist schuld?; **I'm not to ~** es ist nicht meine Schuld.

blameless ['bleımlıs] *adj* schuldlos.

blanch [blɑːntʃ] *vi* blaß werden ♦ *vt* (*CULIN*) blanchieren.

blancmange [blə'mɔnʒ] *n* Pudding *m*.

bland [blænd] *adj* (*taste, food*) fade.

blank [blæŋk] *adj* (*paper*) leer, unbeschrieben; (*look*) ausdruckslos ♦ *n* (*on form*) Lücke *f*; (*cartridge*) Platzpatrone *f*; **my mind was a ~** ich hatte ein Brett vor dem Kopf; **we drew a ~** (*fig*) wir hatten kein Glück.

blank cheque *n* Blankoscheck *m*; **to give sb a ~ to do sth** (*fig*) jdm freie Hand geben, etw zu tun.

blanket ['blæŋkıt] *n* Decke *f* ♦ *adj* (*statement*) pauschal; (*agreement*) Pauschal-.

blanket cover *n* (*INSURANCE*) umfassende Versicherung *f*.

blare [blɛə'] *vi* (*brass band*) schmettern; (*horn*) tuten; (*radio*) plärren.

▶**blare out** *vi* (*radio, stereo*) plärren.

blarney ['blɑːnı] *n* Schmeichelei *f*.

blasé ['blɑːzeı] *adj* blasiert.

blaspheme [blæs'fiːm] *vi* Gott lästern.

blasphemous ['blæsfıməs] *adj* lästerlich, blasphemisch.

blasphemy ['blæsfımı] *n* (Gottes)lästerung *f*, Blasphemie *f*.

blast [blɑːst] *n* (*of wind*) Windstoß *m*; (*of whistle*) Trillern *nt*; (*shock wave*) Druckwelle *f*; (*of air, steam*) Schwall *m*; (*of explosive*) Explosion *f* ♦ *vt* (*blow up*) sprengen ♦ *excl* (*BRIT: inf*) verdammt!, so ein Mist!; **at full ~** (*play music*) mit voller Lautstärke; (*move, work*) auf Hochtouren.

▶**blast off** *vi* (*SPACE*) abheben, starten.

blast furnace *n* Hochofen *m*.

blastoff ['blɑːstɔf] *n* (*SPACE*) Abschuß *m*.

blatant ['bleıtənt] *adj* offensichtlich.

blatantly ['bleıtəntlı] *adv* (*lie*) unverfroren; **it's ~ obvious** es ist überdeutlich.

blaze [bleız] *n* (*fire*) Feuer *nt*, Brand *m*; (*fig: of colour*) Farbenpracht *f*; (: *of glory*) Glanz *m* ♦ *vi* (*fire*) lodern; (*guns*) feuern; (*fig: eyes*) glühen ♦ *vt:* **to ~ a trail** (*fig*) den Weg bahnen; **in a ~ of publicity** mit viel Publicity.

blazer ['bleızə'] *n* Blazer *m*.

bleach [bliːtʃ] *n* (*also:* **household ~**) ≈ Reinigungsmittel *nt* ♦ *vt* bleichen.

bleached [bliːtʃt] *adj* gebleicht.

bleachers ['bliːtʃəz] (*US*) *npl* unüberdachte Zuschauertribüne *f*.

bleak [bliːk] *adj* (*countryside*) öde; (*weather, situation*) trostlos; (*prospect*) trüb; (*expression, voice*) deprimiert.

bleary-eyed ['blıərı'aıd] *adj* triefäugig.

bleat [bliːt] *vi* (*goat*) meckern; (*sheep*) blöken ♦ *n* Meckern *nt*; Blöken *nt*.

bled [bled] *pt, pp of* **bleed**.

bleed [bliːd] (*pt, pp* **bled**) *vi* bluten; (*colour*) auslaufen ♦ *vt* (*brakes, radiator*) entlüften; **my nose is ~ing** ich habe Nasenbluten.

bleep [bliːp] *n* Piepton *m* ♦ *vi* piepen ♦ *vt* (*doctor etc*) rufen, anpiepen (*inf*).

bleeper ['bliːpə'] *n* Piepser *m* (*inf*), Funkrufempfänger *m*.

blemish ['blemɪʃ] n Makel m.

blend [blend] n Mischung f ♦ vt (CULIN) mischen, mixen; (colours, styles, flavours etc) vermischen ♦ vi (colours etc: also: ~ **in**) harmonieren.

blender ['blendə'] n (CULIN) Mixer m.

bless [bles] (pt, pp **blessed** or **blest**) vt segnen; **to be ~ed with** gesegnet sein mit; ~ **you!** (after sneeze) Gesundheit!

blessed ['blesɪd] adj heilig; (happy) selig; **it rains every ~ day** (inf) es regnet aber auch jeden Tag.

blessing ['blesɪŋ] n (approval) Zustimmung f; (REL, fig) Segen m; **to count one's ~s** von Glück sagen können; **it was a ~ in disguise** es war schließlich doch ein Segen.

blew [bluː] pt of **blow**.

blight [blaɪt] vt zerstören; (hopes) vereiteln; (life) verderben ♦ n (of plants) Brand m.

blimey ['blaɪmɪ] (BRIT: inf) excl Mensch!

blind [blaɪnd] adj blind ♦ n (for window) Rollo nt, Rouleau nt; (also: **Venetian ~**) Jalousie f ♦ vt blind machen; (dazzle) blenden; (deceive: with facts etc) verblenden; **the blind** npl (blind people) die Blinden pl; **to turn a ~ eye (on or to)** ein Auge zudrücken (bei); **to be ~ to sth** (fig) blind für etw sein.

blind alley n (fig) Sackgasse f.

blind corner (BRIT) n unübersichtliche Ecke f.

blind date n Rendezvous nt mit einem/einer Unbekannten.

blinders ['blaɪndəz] (US) npl = **blinkers**.

blindfold ['blaɪndfəʊld] n Augenbinde f ♦ adj, adv mit verbundenen Augen ♦ vt die Augen verbinden +dat.

blinding ['blaɪndɪŋ] adj (dazzling) blendend; (remarkable) bemerkenswert.

blindly ['blaɪndlɪ] adv (without seeing) wie blind; (without thinking) blindlings.

blindness ['blaɪndnɪs] n Blindheit f.

blind spot n (AUT) toter Winkel m; (fig: weak spot) schwacher Punkt m.

blink [blɪŋk] vi blinzeln; (light) blinken ♦ n: **the TV's on the ~** (inf) der Fernseher ist kaputt.

blinkers ['blɪŋkəz] npl Scheuklappen pl.

blinking ['blɪŋkɪŋ] (BRIT: inf) adj: **this ~ ...** diese(r, s) verflixte ...

blip [blɪp] n (on radar screen) leuchtender Punkt m; (in a straight line) Ausschlag m; (fig) (zeitweilige) Abweichung f.

bliss [blɪs] n Glück nt, Seligkeit f.

blissful ['blɪsful] adj (event, day) herrlich; (smile) selig; **a ~ sigh** ein wohliger Seufzer m; **in ~ ignorance** in herrlicher Ahnungslosigkeit.

blissfully ['blɪsfəlɪ] adv selig; ~ **happy** überglücklich; ~ **unaware of ...** ohne auch nur zu ahnen, daß ...

blister ['blɪstə'] n Blase f ♦ vi (paint) Blasen werfen.

blithely ['blaɪðlɪ] adv (unconcernedly) unbekümmert, munter; (joyfully) fröhlich.

blithering ['blɪðərɪŋ] (inf) adj: **this ~ idiot** dieser Trottel.

BLit(t) n abbr (= Bachelor of Literature; Bachelor of Letters) akademischer Grad für Literaturwissenschaftler.

blitz [blɪts] n (MIL) Luftangriff m; **to have a ~ on sth** (fig) einen Großangriff auf etw acc starten.

blizzard ['blɪzəd] n Schneesturm m.

BLM (US) n abbr (= Bureau of Land Management) Behörde zur Verwaltung von Grund und Boden.

bloated ['bləʊtɪd] adj aufgedunsen; (full) (über)satt.

blob [blɒb] n Tropfen m; (sth indistinct) verschwommener Fleck m.

bloc [blɒk] n Block m; **the Eastern ~** (HIST) der Ostblock.

block [blɒk] n Block m; (toy) Bauklotz m; (in pipes) Verstopfung f ♦ vt blockieren; (progress) aufhalten; (COMPUT) blocken; ~ **of flats** (BRIT) Wohnblock m; **3 ~s from here** 3 Blocks or Straßen weiter; **mental ~** geistige Sperre f, Mattscheibe f (inf); ~ **and tackle** Flaschenzug m.

▶**block up** vt, vi verstopfen.

blockade [blɒ'keɪd] n Blockade f ♦ vt blockieren.

blockage ['blɒkɪdʒ] n Verstopfung f.

block booking n Gruppenbuchung f.

blockbuster ['blɒkbʌstə'] n Knüller m.

block capitals npl Blockschrift f.

blockhead ['blɒkhed] (inf) n Dummkopf m.

block letters npl Blockschrift f.

block release (BRIT) n blockweise Freistellung von Auszubildenden zur Weiterbildung.

block vote (BRIT) n Stimmenblock m.

bloke [bləʊk] (BRIT: inf) n Typ m.

blond(e) [blɒnd] adj blond ♦ n: ~ (woman) Blondine f.

blood [blʌd] n Blut nt; **new ~** (fig) frisches Blut nt.

blood bank n Blutbank f.

blood bath n Blutbad nt.

blood count n Blutbild nt.

bloodcurdling ['blʌdkəːdlɪŋ] adj grauenerregend.

blood donor n Blutspender(in) m(f).

blood group n Blutgruppe f.

bloodhound ['blʌdhaund] n Bluthund m.

bloodless ['blʌdlɪs] adj (victory) unblutig; (pale) blutleer.

blood-letting ['blʌdletɪŋ] n (also fig) Aderlaß m.

blood poisoning n Blutvergiftung f.

blood pressure n Blutdruck m; **to have high/low ~** hohen/niedrigen Blutdruck haben.

bloodshed ['blʌdʃed] n Blutvergießen nt.

bloodshot ['blʌdʃɒt] adj (eyes)

blutunterlaufen.
blood sport n Jagdsport m (und andere
Sportarten, bei denen Tiere getötet werden).
bloodstained ['blʌdsteɪnd] adj blutbefleckt.
bloodstream ['blʌdstriːm] n Blut nt,
Blutkreislauf m.
blood test n Blutprobe f.
bloodthirsty ['blʌdθəːstɪ] adj blutrünstig.
blood transfusion n Blutübertragung f,
(Blut)transfusion f.
blood type n Blutgruppe f.
blood vessel n Blutgefäß nt.
bloody ['blʌdɪ] adj blutig; (BRIT: inf!): this ~ ...
diese(r, s) verdammte ...; ~ **strong** (inf!)
verdammt stark; ~ **good** (inf!) echt gut.
bloody-minded ['blʌdɪ'maɪndɪd] (BRIT: inf) adj
stur.
bloom [bluːm] n Blüte f ♦ vi blühen; **to be in** ~
in Blüte stehen.
blooming ['bluːmɪŋ] (BRIT: inf) adj: **this** ~ ...
diese(r, s) verflixte ...
blossom ['blɔsəm] n Blüte f ♦ vi blühen; (fig):
to ~ **into** erblühen or aufblühen zu.
blot [blɔt] n Klecks m; (fig: on name etc) Makel
m ♦ vt (liquid) aufsaugen; (make blot on)
beklecksen; **to be a** ~ **on the landscape** ein
Schandfleck in der Landschaft sein; **to**
~ **one's copy book** (fig) sich unmöglich
machen.
▶**blot out** vt (view) verdecken; (memory)
auslöschen.
blotchy ['blɔtʃɪ] adj fleckig.
blotter ['blɔtə*] n (Tinten)löscher m.
blotting paper ['blɔtɪŋ-] n Löschpapier nt.
blotto ['blɔtəu] (inf) adj (drunk) sternhagelvoll.
blouse [blauz] n Bluse f.
blow [bləu] (pt **blew**, pp **blown**) n (also fig)
Schlag m ♦ vi (wind) wehen; (person) blasen
♦ vt (subj: wind) wehen; (instrument, whistle)
blasen; (fuse) durchbrennen lassen; **to come
to** ~s handgreiflich werden; **to** ~ **off course**
(ship) vom Kurs abgetrieben werden; **to**
~ **one's nose** sich dat die Nase putzen; **to**
~ **a whistle** pfeifen.
▶**blow away** vt wegblasen ♦ vi wegfliegen.
▶**blow down** vt umwehen.
▶**blow off** vt wegwehen ♦ vi wegfliegen.
▶**blow out** vi ausgehen.
▶**blow over** vi sich legen.
▶**blow up** vi ausbrechen ♦ vt (bridge) in die
Luft jagen; (tyre) aufblasen; (PHOT)
vergrößern.
blow-dry ['bləudraɪ] vt fönen ♦ n: **to have a** ~
sich fönen lassen.
blowlamp ['bləulæmp] (BRIT) n Lötlampe f.
blown [bləun] pp of **blow**.
blowout ['bləuaut] n Reifenpanne f; (inf: big
meal) Schlemmerei f; (of oil-well)
Ölausbruch m.
blowtorch ['bləutɔːtʃ] n = **blowlamp**.
blow-up ['bləuʌp] n Vergrößerung f.
blowzy ['blauzɪ] (BRIT) adj schlampig.

BLS (US) n abbr (= Bureau of Labor Statistics)
Amt für Arbeitsstatistik.
blubber ['blʌbə*] n Walfischspeck m ♦ vi (pej)
heulen.
bludgeon ['blʌdʒən] vt niederknüppeln; (fig):
to ~ **sb into doing sth** jdm so lange
zusetzen, bis er etw tut.
blue [bluː] adj blau; (depressed) deprimiert,
niedergeschlagen ♦ n: **out of the** ~ (fig) aus
heiterem Himmel; **blues** n (MUS): **the** ~s
der Blues; ~ **film** Pornofilm m; ~ **joke**
schlüpfriger Witz m; (only) **once in a**
~ **moon** (nur) alle Jubeljahre einmal; **to
have the** ~s deprimiert or
niedergeschlagen sein.
blue baby n Baby nt mit angeborenem
Herzfehler.
bluebell ['bluːbɛl] n Glockenblume f.
bluebottle ['bluːbɔtl] n Schmeißfliege f.
blue cheese n Blauschimmelkäse m.
blue-chip ['bluːtʃɪp] adj: ~ **investment** sichere
Geldanlage f.
blue-collar worker ['bluːkɔlə*-] n
Arbeiter(in) m(f).
blue jeans npl (Blue)jeans pl.
blueprint ['bluːprɪnt] n (fig): **a** ~ **(for)** ein Plan
m or Entwurf m (für).
bluff [blʌf] vi bluffen ♦ n Bluff m; (cliff) Klippe
f, (promontory) Felsvorsprung m; **to call sb's**
~ es darauf ankommen lassen.
blunder ['blʌndə*] n (dummer) Fehler m ♦ vi
einen (dummen) Fehler machen; **to** ~ **into**
sb mit jdm zusammenstoßen; **to** ~ **into sth**
in etw acc (hinein)tappen.
blunt [blʌnt] adj stumpf; (person) direkt; (talk)
unverblümt ♦ vt stumpf machen;
~ **instrument** (LAW) stumpfer Gegenstand
m.
bluntly ['blʌntlɪ] adv (speak) unverblümt.
bluntness ['blʌntnɪs] n (of person) Direktheit
f.
blur [bləː*] n (shape) verschwommener Fleck
m; (scene etc) verschwommenes Bild nt;
(memory) verschwommene Erinnerung f
♦ vt (vision) trüben; (distinction) verwischen.
blurb [bləːb] n Informationsmaterial nt.
blurred [bləːd] adj (photograph, TV picture etc)
verschwommen; (distinction) verwischt.
blurt out [bləːt-] vt herausplatzen mit.
blush [blʌʃ] vi erröten ♦ n Röte f.
blusher ['blʌʃə*] n Rouge nt.
bluster ['blʌstə*] n Toben nt, Geschrei n ♦ vi
toben.
blustering ['blʌstərɪŋ] adj polternd.
blustery ['blʌstərɪ] adj stürmisch.
Blvd abbr = **boulevard**.
BM n abbr (= British Museum) Britisches
Museum nt; (= Bachelor of Medicine)
akademischer Grad für Mediziner.
BMA n abbr (= British Medical Association)
Dachverband der Ärzte.
BMJ n abbr (= British Medical Journal) vom

BMA herausgegebene Zeitschrift.
BMus *n abbr* (= *Bachelor of Music*) *akademischer Grad für Musikwissenschaftler.*
BMX *n abbr* (= *bicycle motocross*): ~ **bike** BMX-Rad *nt.*
BO *n abbr* (*inf:* = *body odour*) Körpergeruch *m*; (*US*) = **box office.**
boar [bɔːʳ] *n* (*male pig*) Eber *m*; (*wild pig*) Keiler *m.*
board [bɔːd] *n* Brett *nt*; (*cardboard*) Pappe *f*; (*committee*) Ausschuß *m*; (*in firm*) Vorstand *m* ♦ *vt* (*ship*) an Bord +*gen* gehen; (*train*) einsteigen in +*acc*; **on** ~ (*NAUT, AVIAT*) an Bord; **full/half** ~ (*BRIT*) Voll-/Halbpension *f*; ~ **and lodging** Unterkunft und Verpflegung *f*; **to go by the** ~ (*fig*) unter den Tisch fallen; **above** ~ (*fig*) korrekt; **across the** ~ (*fig*) allgemein; (: *criticize, reject*) pauschal.
▶**board up** *vt* mit Brettern vernageln.
boarder [ˈbɔːdəʳ] *n* Internatsschüler(in) *m(f).*
board game *n* Brettspiel *nt.*
boarding card [ˈbɔːdɪŋ-] *n* (*AVIAT, NAUT*) = **boarding pass.**
boarding house [ˈbɔːdɪŋ-] *n* Pension *f.*
boarding party [ˈbɔːdɪŋ-] *n* (*NAUT*) Enterkommando *nt.*
boarding pass [ˈbɔːdɪŋ-] *n* Bordkarte *f.*
boarding school [ˈbɔːdɪŋ-] *n* Internat *nt.*
board meeting *n* Vorstandssitzung *f.*
boardroom [ˈbɔːdruːm] *n* Sitzungssaal *m.*
boardwalk [ˈbɔːdwɔːk] (*US*) *n* Holzsteg *m.*
boast [bəust] *vi* prahlen ♦ *vt* (*fig: possess*) sich rühmen +*gen*, besitzen; **to** ~ **about** *or* **of** prahlen mit.
boastful [ˈbəustful] *adj* prahlerisch.
boastfulness [ˈbəustfulnıs] *n* Prahlerei *f.*
boat [bəut] *n* Boot *nt*; (*ship*) Schiff *nt*; **to go by** ~ mit dem Schiff fahren; **to be in the same** ~ (*fig*) in einem Boot *or* im gleichen Boot sitzen.
boater [ˈbəutəʳ] *n* steifer Strohhut *m*, Kreissäge *f* (*inf*).
boating [ˈbəutɪŋ] *n* Bootfahren *nt.*
boat people *npl* Bootsflüchtlinge *pl.*
boatswain [ˈbəusn] *n* Bootsmann *m.*
bob [bob] *vi* (*also:* ~ **up and down**) sich auf und ab bewegen ♦ *n* (*BRIT: inf*) = **shilling.**
▶**bob up** *vi* auftauchen.
bobbin [ˈbobın] *n* Spule *f.*
bobby [ˈbobı] (*BRIT: inf*) *n* Bobby *m*, Polizist *m.*
bobsleigh [ˈbobsleı] *n* Bob *m.*
bode [bəud] *vi:* **to** ~ **well/ill (for)** ein gutes/ schlechtes Zeichen sein (für).
bodice [ˈbodıs] *n* (*of dress*) Oberteil *nt.*
bodily [ˈbodılı] *adj* körperlich; (*needs*) leiblich ♦ *adv* (*lift, carry*) mit aller Kraft.
body [ˈbodı] *n* Körper *m*; (*corpse*) Leiche *f*; (*main part*) Hauptteil *m*; (*of car*) Karosserie *f*; (*of plane*) Rumpf *m*; (*group*) Gruppe *f*; (*organization*) Organ *nt*; **ruling** ~ amtierendes Organ; **in a** ~ geschlossen; **a**

~ **of facts** Tatsachenmaterial *nt.*
body blow *n* (*fig: setback*) schwerer Schlag *m.*
body building *n* Bodybuilding *nt.*
body double *n* (*FILM, TV*) Double *für Szenen, in denen Körperpartien in Nahaufnahme gezeigt werden.*
bodyguard [ˈbodıgɑːd] *n* (*group*) Leibwache *f*; (*one person*) Butzemann *m*, Leibwächter *m.*
body language *n* Körpersprache *f.*
body repairs *npl* (*AUT*) Karosseriearbeiten *pl.*
body search *n* Leibesvisitation *f.*
body stocking *n* Body(stocking) *m.*
bodywork [ˈbodıwɔːk] *n* Karosserie *f.*
boffin [ˈbofın] (*BRIT*) *n* Fachidiot *m.*
bog [bog] *n* Sumpf *m* ♦ *vt:* **to get** ~**ged down** (*fig*) sich verzetteln.
bogey [ˈbəugı] *n* Schreckgespenst *nt*; (*also:* ~**man**) Butzemann *m*, Schwarzer Mann *m.*
boggle [ˈbogl] *vi:* **the mind** ~**s** das ist nicht *or* kaum auszumalen.
bogie [ˈbəugı] *n* Drehgestell *nt*; (*trolley*) Draisine *f.*
Bogotá [bəugəˈtaː] *n* Bogotá *nt.*
bogus [ˈbəugəs] *adj* (*workman etc*) falsch; (*claim*) erfunden.
Bohemia [bəuˈhiːmıə] *n* Böhmen *nt.*
Bohemian [bəuˈhiːmıən] *adj* böhmisch ♦ *n* Böhme *m*, Böhmin *f*; (*also:* **b~**) Bohemien *m.*
boil [bɔıl] *vt, vi* kochen ♦ *n* (*MED*) Furunkel *nt or m*; **to come to the** (*BRIT*) *or* **a** (*US*) ~ zu kochen anfangen.
▶**boil down to** *vt fus* (*fig*) hinauslaufen auf +*acc.*
▶**boil over** *vi* überkochen.
boiled egg [bɔıld-] *n* gekochtes Ei *nt.*
boiled potatoes *npl* Salzkartoffeln *pl.*
boiler [ˈbɔıləʳ] *n* Boiler *m.*
boiler suit (*BRIT*) *n* Overall *m.*
boiling [ˈbɔılıŋ] *adj:* **I'm** ~ (**hot**) (*inf*) mir ist fürchterlich heiß; **it's** ~ es ist eine Affenhitze (*inf*).
boiling point *n* Siedepunkt *m.*
boil-in-the-bag [bɔılınðəˈbæg] *adj* (*meals*) Kochbeutel-.
boisterous [ˈbɔıstərəs] *adj* ausgelassen.
bold [bəuld] *adj* (*brave*) mutig; (*pej: cheeky*) dreist; (*pattern, colours*) kräftig.
boldly [ˈbəuldlı] *adv* (*see adj*) mutig; dreist; kräftig.
boldness [ˈbəuldnıs] *n* Mut *m*; (*cheekiness*) Dreistigkeit *f.*
bold type *n* Fettdruck *m.*
Bolivia [bəˈlıvıə] *n* Bolivien *nt.*
Bolivian [bəˈlıvıən] *adj* bolivisch, bolivianisch ♦ *n* Bolivier(in) *m(f)*, Bolivianer(in) *m(f).*
bollard [ˈboləd] (*BRIT*) *n* Poller *m.*
bolshy [ˈbolʃı] (*BRIT: inf*) *adj* (*stroppy*) pampig.
bolster [ˈbəulstəʳ] *n* Nackenrolle *f.*
▶**bolster up** *vt* stützen; (*case*) untermauern.
bolt [bəult] *n* Riegel *m*; (*with nut*) Schraube *f*;

(*of lightning*) Blitz(strahl) *m* ♦ *vt* (*door*) verriegeln; (*also:* ~ **together**) verschrauben; (*food*) hinunterschlingen ♦ *vi* (*run away: person*) weglaufen; (: *horse*) durchgehen ♦ *adv:* ~ **upright** kerzengerade; **a** ~ **from the blue** (*fig*) ein Blitz aus heiterem Himmel.

bomb [bɔm] *n* Bombe *f* ♦ *vt* bombardieren; (*plant bomb in or near*) einen Bombenanschlag verüben auf +acc.

bombard [bɔm'baːd] *vt* (*also fig*) bombardieren.

bombardment [bɔm'baːdmənt] *n* Bombardierung *f*, Bombardement *nt*.

bombastic [bɔm'bæstɪk] *adj* bombastisch.

bomb disposal *n:* ~ **unit** Bombenräumkommando *nt;* ~ **expert** Bombenräumexperte *m*, Bombenräumexpertin *f*.

bomber ['bɔmə*] *n* Bomber *m;* (*terrorist*) Bombenattentäter(in) *m(f)*.

bombing ['bɔmɪŋ] *n* Bombenangriff *m*.

bomb scare *n* Bombenalarm *m*.

bombshell ['bɔmʃɛl] *n* (*fig: revelation*) Bombe *f*.

bomb site *n* Trümmergrundstück *nt*.

bona fide ['bəʊnə'faɪdɪ] *adj* echt; ~ **offer** Angebot *nt* auf Treu und Glauben.

bonanza [bə'nænzə] *n* (*ECON*) Boom *m*.

bond [bɔnd] *n* Band *nt*, Bindung *f*; (*FIN*) festverzinsliches Wertpapier *nt*, Bond *m;* (*COMM*): **in** ~ unter Zollverschluß.

bondage ['bɔndɪdʒ] *n* Sklaverei *f*.

bonded warehouse ['bɔndɪd] *n* Zollager *nt*.

bone [bəʊn] *n* Knochen *m;* (*of fish*) Gräte *f* ♦ *vt* (*meat*) die Knochen herauslösen aus; (*fish*) entgräten; **I've got a** ~ **to pick with you** ich habe mit Ihnen (noch) ein Hühnchen zu rupfen.

bone china *n* ≈ feines Porzellan *nt*.

bone-dry ['bəʊn'draɪ] *adj* knochentrocken.

bone idle *adj* stinkfaul.

bone marrow *n* Knochenmark *nt*.

boner ['bəʊnə*] (*US*) *n* Schnitzer *m*.

bonfire ['bɔnfaɪə*] *n* Feuer *nt*.

bonk [bɔŋk] (*inf*) *vt, vi* (*have sex (with)*) bumsen.

bonkers ['bɔŋkəz] (*BRIT: inf*) *adj* (*mad*) verrückt.

Bonn [bɔn] *n* Bonn *nt*.

bonnet ['bɔnɪt] *n* Haube *f*, (*for baby*) Häubchen *nt;* (*BRIT: of car*) Motorhaube *f*.

bonny ['bɔnɪ] (*SCOT, Northern English*) *adj* schön, hübsch.

bonus ['bəʊnəs] *n* Prämie *f*; (*on wages*) Zulage *f*; (*at Christmas*) Gratifikation *f*; (*fig: additional benefit*) Plus *nt*.

bony ['bəʊnɪ] *adj* knochig; (*MED*) knöchern; (*tissue*) knochenartig; (*meat*) mit viel Knochen; (*fish*) mit viel Gräten.

boo [buː] *excl* buh ♦ *vt* auspfeifen, ausbuhen.

boob [buːb] (*inf*) *n* (*breast*) Brust *f*; (*BRIT: mistake*) Schnitzer *m*.

booby prize ['buːbɪ-] *n* Scherzpreis für den schlechtesten Teilnehmer.

booby trap ['buːbɪ-] *n* versteckte Bombe *f*; (*fig: joke etc*) als Schabernack versteckt angebrachte Falle.

booby-trapped ['buːbɪtræpt] *adj:* **a** ~ **car** ein Auto, in dem eine Bombe versteckt ist.

book [buk] *n* Buch *nt;* (*of stamps, tickets*) Heftchen *nt* ♦ *vt* bestellen; (*seat, room*) buchen, reservieren lassen; (*subj: traffic warden, policeman*) aufschreiben; (: *referee*) verwarnen; **books** *npl* (*COMM: accounts*) Bücher *pl;* **to keep the** ~**s** die Bücher führen; **by the** ~ nach Vorschrift; **to throw the** ~ **at sb** jdn nach allen Regeln der Kunst fertigmachen.

▶**book in** (*BRIT*) *vi* sich eintragen.

▶**book up** *vt:* **all seats are** ~**ed up** es ist bis auf den letzten Platz ausverkauft; **the hotel is** ~**ed up** das Hotel ist ausgebucht.

bookable ['bukəbl] *adj:* **all seats are** ~ Karten für alle Plätze können vorbestellt werden.

bookcase ['bukkeɪs] *n* Bücherregal *nt*.

book ends *npl* Bücherstützen *pl*.

booking ['bukɪŋ] (*BRIT*) *n* Bestellung *f*; (*of seat, room*) Buchung *f*, Reservierung *f*.

booking office (*BRIT*) *n* (*RAIL*) Fahrkartenschalter *m;* (*THEAT*) Vorverkaufsstelle *f*, Vorverkaufskasse *f*.

book-keeping ['buk'kiːpɪŋ] *n* Buchhaltung *f*, Buchführung *f*.

booklet ['buklɪt] *n* Broschüre *f*.

bookmaker ['bukmeɪkə*] *n* Buchmacher *m*.

bookseller ['buksɛlə*] *n* Buchhändler(in) *m(f)*.

bookshelf ['bukʃɛlf] *n* Bücherbord *nt;* **bookshelves** *npl* Bücherregal *nt*.

bookshop ['bukʃɔp] *n* Buchhandlung *f*.

bookstall ['bukstɔːl] *n* Bücher- und Zeitungskiosk *m*.

book store *n* = bookshop.

book token *n* Buchgutschein *m*.

book value *n* Buchwert *m*, Bilanzwert *m*.

bookworm ['bukwəːm] *n* (*fig*) Bücherwurm *m*.

boom [buːm] *n* Donnern *nt*, Dröhnen *nt;* (*in prices, population etc*) rapider Anstieg *m;* (*ECON*) Hochkonjunktur *f*; (*busy period*) Boom *m* ♦ *vi* (*guns*) donnern; (*thunder*) hallen; (*voice*) dröhnen; (*business*) florieren.

boomerang ['buːməræŋ] *n* Bumerang *m* ♦ *vi* (*fig*) einen Bumerangeffekt haben; **to** ~ **on sb** sich für jdn als Bumerang erweisen.

boom town *n* Goldgräberstadt *f*.

boon [buːn] *n* Segen *m*.

boorish ['buərɪʃ] *adj* rüpelhaft.

boost [buːst] *n* Auftrieb *m* ♦ *vt* (*confidence*) stärken; (*sales, economy etc*) ankurbeln; **to give a** ~ **to sb/sb's spirits** jdm Auftrieb geben.

booster ['buːstə*] *n* (*MED*) Wiederholungsimpfung *f*; (*TV*) Zusatzgleichrichter *m;* (*ELEC*) Puffersatz *m;* (*also:* ~ **rocket**) Booster *m*, Startrakete *f*.

booster seat n (AUT) Sitzerhöhung f.
boot [buːt] n Stiefel m; (ankle boot) hoher
Schuh m; (BRIT: of car) Kofferraum m ♦ vt
(COMPUT) laden; ... **to ~** (in addition)
obendrein ...; **to give sb the ~** (inf) jdn
rauswerfen or rausschmeißen.
booth [buːð] n (at fair) Bude f, Stand m;
(telephone booth) Zelle f; (voting booth)
Kabine f.
bootleg ['buːtlɛg] adj (alcohol) schwarz
gebrannt; (fuel) schwarz hergestellt; (tape
etc) schwarz mitgeschnitten.
bootlegger ['buːtlɛgə*] n Bootlegger m,
Schwarzhändler m.
booty ['buːtɪ] n Beute f.
booze [buːz] (inf) n Alkohol m ♦ vi saufen.
boozer ['buːzə*] (inf) n (person) Säufer(in) m(f);
(BRIT: pub) Kneipe f.
border ['bɔːdə*] n Grenze f; (for flowers)
Rabatte f; (on cloth etc) Bordüre f ♦ vt (road)
säumen; (another country: also: ~ **on**) grenzen
an +acc; **Borders** n: **the B~s** das Grenzgebiet
zwischen England und Schottland.
▶**border on** vt fus (fig) grenzen an +acc.
borderline ['bɔːdəlaɪn] n (fig): **on the ~** an der
Grenze.
borderline case n Grenzfall m.
bore [bɔː*] pt of **bear** ♦ vt bohren; (person)
langweilen ♦ n Langweiler m; (of gun)
Kaliber nt; **to be ~d** sich langweilen; **he's
~d to tears** or **~d to death** or **~d stiff** er
langweilt sich zu Tode.
boredom ['bɔːdəm] n Langeweile f; (boring
quality) Langweiligkeit f.
boring ['bɔːrɪŋ] adj langweilig.
born [bɔːn] adj: **to be ~** geboren werden; **I was
~ in 1960** ich bin or wurde 1960 geboren;
~ blind blind geboren, von Geburt (an)
blind; **a ~ comedian** ein geborener
Komiker.
born-again [bɔːnə'gɛn] adj wiedergeboren.
borne [bɔːn] pp of **bear**.
Borneo ['bɔːnɪəu] n Borneo nt.
borough ['bʌrə] n Bezirk m, Stadtgemeinde f.
borrow ['bɔrəu] vt: **to ~ sth** etw borgen, sich
dat etw leihen; (from library) sich dat etw
ausleihen; **may I ~ your car?** kann ich
deinen Wagen leihen?
borrower ['bɔrəuə*] n (of loan etc)
Kreditnehmer(in) m(f).
borrowing ['bɔrəuɪŋ] n Kreditaufnahme f.
borstal ['bɔːstl] (BRIT) n (formerly)
Besserungsanstalt f.
Bosnia ['bɔznɪə] n Bosnien nt.
Bosnia-Herzegovina n Bosnien-
Herzegowina nt.
Bosnian ['bɔznɪən] adj bosnisch ♦ n
Bosnier(in) m(f).
bosom ['buzəm] n Busen m; (fig: of family)
Schoß m.
bosom friend n Busenfreund(in) m(f).
boss [bɔs] n Chef(in) m(f); (leader) Boß m ♦ vt

(also: ~ **around**, ~ **about**) herumkommandieren; **stop ~ing everyone about!**
hör auf mit dem ständigen
Herumkommandieren!
bossy ['bɔsɪ] adj herrisch.
bosun ['bəusn] n Bootsmann m.
botanical [bə'tænɪkl] adj botanisch.
botanist ['bɔtənɪst] n Botaniker(in) m(f).
botany ['bɔtənɪ] n Botanik f.
botch [bɔtʃ] vt (also: ~ **up**) verpfuschen.
both [bəuθ] adj beide ♦ pron beide; (two
different things) beides ♦ adv: ~ **A and B**
sowohl A als auch B; ~ (**of them**) (alle)
beide; ~ **of us went, we ~ went** wir gingen
beide; **they sell ~ the fabric and the finished
curtains** sie verkaufen sowohl den Stoff als
auch die fertigen Vorhänge.
bother ['bɔðə*] vt Sorgen machen +dat;
(disturb) stören ♦ vi (also: ~ **o.s.**) sich dat
Sorgen or Gedanken machen ♦ n (trouble)
Mühe f; (nuisance) Plage f ♦ excl Mist! (inf);
don't ~ phoning du brauchst nicht
anzurufen; **I'm sorry to ~ you** es tut mir
leid, daß ich Sie belästigen muß; **I can't be
~ed** ich habe keine Lust; **please don't ~**
bitte machen Sie sich keine Umstände;
don't ~! laß es!; **it is a ~ to have to shave
every morning** es ist wirklich lästig, sich
jeden Morgen rasieren zu müssen; **it's no ~**
es ist kein Problem.
Botswana [bɔt'swaːnə] n Botswana nt.
bottle ['bɔtl] n Flasche f; (BRIT: inf: courage)
Mumm m ♦ vt in Flaschen abfüllen; (fruit)
einmachen; **a ~ of wine/milk** eine Flasche
Wein/Milch; **wine/milk ~** Wein-/
Milchflasche f.
▶**bottle up** vt in sich dat aufstauen.
bottle bank n Altglascontainer m.
bottle-fed ['bɔtlfɛd] adj mit der Flasche
ernährt.
bottleneck ['bɔtlnɛk] n (also fig) Engpaß m.
bottle-opener ['bɔtləupnə*] n Flaschenöffner
m.
bottom ['bɔtəm] n Boden m; (buttocks)
Hintern m; (of page, list) Ende nt; (of chair)
Sitz m; (of mountain, tree) Fuß m ♦ adj (lower)
untere(r, s); (last) unterste(r, s); **at the ~ of**
unten an/in +dat; **at the ~ of the page/list**
unten auf der Seite/Liste; **to be at the ~ of
the class** der/die Letzte in der Klasse sein;
to get to the ~ of sth (fig) einer Sache dat
auf den Grund kommen.
bottomless ['bɔtəmlɪs] adj (fig)
unerschöpflich.
bottom line n (of accounts) Saldo m; (fig):
that's the ~ (of it) (what it amounts to) darauf
läuft es im Endeffekt hinaus.
botulism ['bɔtjulɪzəm] n Botulismus m,
Nahrungsmittelvergiftung f.
bough [bau] n Ast m.
bought [bɔːt] pt, pp of **buy**.
boulder ['bəuldə*] n Felsblock m.

boulevard ['buːləvɑːd] *n* Boulevard *m*.

bounce [bauns] *vi* (auf)springen; (*cheque*) platzen ♦ *vt* (*ball*) (auf)springen lassen; (*signal*) reflektieren ♦ *n* Aufprall *m*; **he's got plenty of ~** (*fig*) er hat viel Schwung.

bouncer ['baunsəʳ] (*inf*) *n* Rausschmeißer *m*.

bouncy castle ['baunsı-] *n aufblasbare Spielfläche in Form eines Schlosses, auf dem Kinder herumspringen können.*

bound [baund] *pt, pp of* **bind** ♦ *n* Sprung *m*; (*gen pl: limit*) Grenze *f* ♦ *vi* springen ♦ *vt* begrenzen ♦ *adj:* ~ **by** gebunden durch; **to be** ~ **to do sth** (*obliged*) verpflichtet sein, etw zu tun; (*very likely*) etw bestimmt tun; **he's** ~ **to fail** es kann ihm ja gar nicht gelingen; ~ **for** nach; **the area is out of ~s** das Betreten des Gebiets ist verboten.

boundary ['baundrı] *n* Grenze *f*.

boundless ['baundlıs] *adj* grenzenlos.

bountiful ['bauntıful] *adj* großzügig; (*God*) gütig; (*supply*) reichlich.

bounty ['bauntı] *n* Freigebigkeit *f*; (*reward*) Kopfgeld *nt*.

bounty hunter *n* Kopfgeldjäger *m*.

bouquet ['bukeı] *n* (Blumen)strauß *m*; (*of wine*) Bukett *nt*, Blume *f*.

bourbon ['buəbən] (*US*) *n* (*also:* ~ **whiskey**) Bourbon *m*.

bourgeois ['buəʒwɑː] *adj* bürgerlich, spießig (*pej*) ♦ *n* Bürger(in) *m(f)*, Bourgeois *m*.

bout [baut] *n* Anfall *m*; (*BOXING etc*) Kampf *m*.

boutique [buːˈtiːk] *n* Boutique *f*.

bow¹ [bəu] *n* Schleife *f*; (*weapon, MUS*) Bogen *m*.

bow² [bau] *n* Verbeugung *f*; (*NAUT: also:* ~**s**) Bug *m* ♦ *vi* sich verbeugen; (*yield:*) **to** ~ **to** *or* **before** sich beugen +*dat*; **to** ~ **to the inevitable** sich in das Unvermeidliche fügen.

bowels ['bauəlz] *npl* Darm *m*; (*of the earth etc*) Innere *nt*.

bowl [bəul] *n* Schüssel *f*; (*shallower*) Schale *f*; (*ball*) Kugel *f*; (*of pipe*) Kopf *m*; (*US: stadium*) Stadion *nt* ♦ *vi* werfen.

▶**bowl over** *vt* (*fig*) überwältigen.

bow-legged ['bəuˈlɛgıd] *adj* O-beinig.

bowler ['bəuləʳ] *n* Werfer(in) *m(f)*; (*BRIT: also:* ~ **hat**) Melone *f*.

bowling ['bəulıŋ] *n* Kegeln *nt*; (*on grass*) Bowling *nt*.

bowling alley *n* Kegelbahn *f*.

bowling green *n* Bowlingrasen *m*.

bowls [bəulz] *n* Bowling *nt*.

bow tie [bəu-] *n* Fliege *f*.

box [bɒks] *n* Schachtel *f*; (*cardboard box*) Karton *m*; (*crate*) Kiste *f*; (*THEAT*) Loge *f*; (*BRIT: AUT*) *gelb schraffierter Kreuzungsbereich*; (*on form*) Feld *nt* ♦ *vt* (in eine Schachtel *etc*) verpacken; (*fighter*) boxen ♦ *vi* boxen; **to** ~ **sb's ears** jdm eine Ohrfeige geben.

▶**box in** *vt* einkeilen.

▶**box off** *vt* abtrennen.

boxer ['bɒksəʳ] *n* (*person, dog*) Boxer *m*.

box file *n* Sammelordner *m*.

boxing ['bɒksıŋ] *n* Boxen *nt*.

Boxing Day (*BRIT*) *n* zweiter Weihnachts(feier)tag *m*.

Boxing Day *ist ein Feiertag in Großbritannien. Wenn Weihnachten auf ein Wochenende fällt, wird der Feiertag am nächsten darauffolgenden Wochentag nachgeholt. Der Name geht auf einen alten Brauch zurück; früher erhielten Händler und Lieferanten an diesem Tag ein Geschenk, die sogenannte Christmas Box.*

---

boxing gloves *npl* Boxhandschuhe *pl*.

boxing ring *n* Boxring *m*.

box number *n* Chiffre *f*.

box office *n* Kasse *f*.

boxroom ['bɒksrum] *n* Abstellraum *m*.

boy [bɔı] *n* Junge *m*.

boycott ['bɔıkɒt] *n* Boykott *m* ♦ *vt* boykottieren.

boyfriend ['bɔıfrɛnd] *n* Freund *m*.

boyish ['bɔııʃ] *adj* jungenhaft; (*woman*) knabenhaft.

boy scout *n* Pfadfinder *m*.

Bp *abbr* = **bishop**.

BR *abbr* = **British Rail**.

bra [brɑː] *n* BH *m*.

brace [breıs] *n* (*on teeth*) (Zahn)klammer *f*, (Zahn)spange *f*; (*tool*) (Hand)bohrer *m*; (*also:* ~ **bracket**) geschweifte Klammer *f* ♦ *vt* spannen; **braces** *npl* (*BRIT*) Hosenträger *pl*; **to** ~ **o.s.** (*for weight*) sich stützen; (*for shock*) sich innerlich vorbereiten.

bracelet ['breıslıt] *n* Armband *nt*.

bracing ['breısıŋ] *adj* belebend.

bracken ['brækən] *n* Farn *m*.

bracket ['brækıt] *n* Träger *m*; (*group, range*) Gruppe *f*, (*also:* **round** ~) (runde) Klammer *f*; (*also:* **brace** ~) geschweifte Klammer *f*; (*also:* **square** ~) eckige Klammer *f* ♦ *vt* (*also:* ~ **together**) zusammenfassen; (*word, phrase*) einklammern; **income** ~ Einkommensgruppe *f*; **in** ~**s** in Klammern.

brackish ['brækıʃ] *adj* brackig.

brag [bræg] *vi* prahlen.

braid [breıd] *n* Borte *f*; (*of hair*) Zopf *m*.

Braille [breıl] *n* Blindenschrift *f*, Brailleschrift *f*.

brain [breın] *n* Gehirn *nt*; **brains** *npl* (*CULIN*) Hirn *nt*; (*intelligence*) Intelligenz *f*; **he's got** ~**s** er hat Köpfchen *or* Grips.

brainchild ['breıntʃaıld] *n* Geistesprodukt *nt*.

braindead ['breındɛd] *adj* hirntot; (*inf*) hirnlos.

brain drain *n:* **the** ~ *die Abwanderung von Wissenschaftlern, Akademikern etc.*

brainless ['breınlıs] *adj* dumm.

brainstorm ['breınstɔːm] *n* (*fig*) Anfall *m* geistiger Umnachtung; (*US: brain wave*)

Geistesblitz m.

brainwash ['breɪnwɔʃ] vt einer Gehirnwäsche dat unterziehen.

brain wave n Geistesblitz m.

brainy ['breɪnɪ] adj intelligent.

braise [breɪz] vt schmoren.

brake [breɪk] n Bremse f ♦ vi bremsen.

brake fluid n Bremsflüssigkeit f.

brake light n Bremslicht nt.

brake pedal n Bremspedal nt.

bramble ['bræmbl] n Brombeerstrauch m; (fruit) Brombeere f.

bran [bræn] n Kleie f.

branch [brɑːntʃ] n Ast m; (of family, organization) Zweig m; (COMM) Filiale f, Zweigstelle f; (: bank, company etc) Geschäftsstelle f ♦ vi sich gabeln.

►**branch out** vi (fig): **to ~ out into** seinen (Geschäfts)bereich erweitern auf +acc.

branch line n (RAIL) Zweiglinie f, Nebenlinie f.

branch manager n Zweigstellenleiter(in) m(f), Filialleiter(in) m(f).

brand [brænd] n (also: ~ **name**) Marke f; (fig: type) Art f ♦ vt mit einem Brandzeichen kennzeichnen; (fig: pej): **to ~ sb a communist** jdn als Kommunist brandmarken.

brandish ['brændɪʃ] vt schwingen.

brand name n Markenname m.

brand-new ['brænd'njuː] adj nagelneu, brandneu.

brandy ['brændɪ] n Weinbrand m.

brash [bræʃ] adj dreist.

Brasilia [brə'zɪlɪə] n Brasilia nt.

brass [brɑːs] n Messing nt; **the ~** (MUS) die Blechbläser pl.

brass band n Blaskapelle f.

brassière ['bræsɪə*] n Büstenhalter m.

brass tacks npl: **to get down to ~** zur Sache kommen.

brassy ['brɑːsɪ] adj (colour) messingfarben; (sound) blechern; (appearance, behaviour) auffällig.

brat [bræt] (pej) n Balg m or nt, Gör nt.

bravado [brə'vɑːdəu] n Draufgängertum nt.

brave [breɪv] adj mutig; (attempt, smile) tapfer ♦ n (indianischer) Krieger m ♦ vt trotzen +dat.

bravely ['breɪvlɪ] adv (see adj) mutig; tapfer.

bravery ['breɪvərɪ] n (see adj) Mut m; Tapferkeit f.

bravo [brɑː'vəu] excl bravo.

brawl [brɔːl] n Schlägerei f ♦ vi sich schlagen.

brawn [brɔːn] n Muskeln pl; (meat) Schweinskopfsülze f.

brawny ['brɔːnɪ] adj muskulös, kräftig.

bray [breɪ] vi schreien ♦ n (Esels)schrei m.

brazen ['breɪzn] adj unverschämt, dreist; (lie) schamlos ♦ vt: **to ~ it out** durchhalten.

brazier ['breɪzɪə*] n (container) Kohlenbecken nt.

Brazil [brə'zɪl] n Brasilien nt.

Brazilian [brə'zɪljən] adj brasilianisch ♦ n Brasilianer(in) m(f).

Brazil nut n Paranuß f.

breach [briːtʃ] vt (defence) durchbrechen; (wall) eine Bresche schlagen in +acc ♦ n (gap) Bresche f; (estrangement) Bruch m; (breaking): **~ of contract** Vertragsbruch m; **~ of the peace** öffentliche Ruhestörung f; **~ of trust** Vertrauensbruch m.

bread [brɛd] n Brot nt; (inf: money) Moos nt, Kies m; **to earn one's daily ~** sein Brot verdienen; **to know which side one's ~ is buttered (on)** wissen, wo etwas zu holen ist.

bread and butter n Butterbrot nt; (fig) Broterwerb m.

bread bin (BRIT) n Brotkasten m.

breadboard ['brɛdbɔːd] n Brot(schneide)brett nt; (COMPUT) Leiterplatte f.

bread box (US) n Brotkasten m.

breadcrumbs ['brɛdkrʌmz] npl Brotkrumen pl; (CULIN) Paniermehl nt.

breadline ['brɛdlaɪn] n: **to be on the ~** nur das Allernotwendigste zum Leben haben.

breadth [brɛtθ] n (also fig) Breite f.

breadwinner ['brɛdwɪnə*] n Ernährer(in) m(f).

break [breɪk] (pt **broke**, pp **broken**) vt zerbrechen; (leg, arm) sich dat brechen; (promise, record) brechen; (law) verstoßen gegen ♦ vi zerbrechen, kaputtgehen; (storm) losbrechen; (weather) umschlagen; (dawn) anbrechen; (story, news) bekanntwerden ♦ n Pause f; (gap) Lücke f; (fracture) Bruch m; (chance) Chance f, Gelegenheit f; (holiday) Urlaub m; **to ~ the news to sb** es jdm sagen; **to ~ even** seine (Un)kosten decken; **to ~ with sb** mit jdm brechen, sich von jdm trennen; **to ~ free** or **loose** sich losreißen; **to take a ~** (eine) Pause machen; **without a ~** ohne Unterbrechung or Pause, ununterbrochen; **a lucky ~** ein Durchbruch m.

►**break down** vt (figures, data) aufschlüsseln; (door etc) einrennen ♦ vi (car) eine Panne haben; (machine) kaputtgehen; (person, resistance) zusammenbrechen; (talks) scheitern.

►**break in** vt (horse) zureiten ♦ vi einbrechen; (interrupt) unterbrechen.

►**break into** vt fus einbrechen in +acc.

►**break off** vi abbrechen ♦ vt (talks) abbrechen; (engagement) lösen.

►**break open** vt, vi aufbrechen.

►**break out** vi ausbrechen; **to ~ out in spots/a rash** Pickel/einen Ausschlag bekommen.

►**break through** vi: **the sun broke through** die Sonne kam durch ♦ vt fus durchbrechen.

►**break up** vi (ship) zerbersten; (crowd, meeting, partnership) sich auflösen; (marriage) scheitern; (friends) sich trennen; (SCOL) in die Ferien gehen ♦ vt zerbrechen; (journey, *fight etc)* unterbrechen; *(meeting)* auflösen; *(marriage)* zerstören.

breakable ['breɪkəbl] *adj* zerbrechlich ♦ *n:* ~s zerbrechliche Ware *f.*

breakage ['breɪkɪdʒ] *n* Bruch *m;* **to pay for** ~s für zerbrochene Ware *or* für Bruch bezahlen.

breakaway ['breɪkəweɪ] *adj (group etc)* Splitter-.

break dancing *n* Breakdance *m.*

breakdown ['breɪkdaun] *n (AUT)* Panne *f; (in communications)* Zusammenbruch *m; (of marriage)* Scheitern *nt; (also:* **nervous** ~*)* (Nerven)zusammenbruch *m; (of statistics)* Aufschlüsselung *f.*

breakdown service *(BRIT) n* Pannendienst *m.*

breakdown van *(BRIT) n* Abschleppwagen *m.*

breaker ['breɪkə*] *n (wave)* Brecher *m.*

breakeven ['breɪk'iːvn] *cpd:* ~ **chart** Gewinnschwellen-Diagramm *nt;* ~ **point** Gewinnschwelle *f.*

breakfast ['brɛkfəst] *n* Frühstück *nt* ♦ *vi* frühstücken.

breakfast cereal *n* Getreideflocken *pl.*

break-in ['breɪkɪn] *n* Einbruch *m.*

breaking and entering ['breɪkɪŋən'ɛntrɪŋ] *n (LAW)* Einbruch *m.*

breaking point ['breɪkɪŋ-] *n (fig):* **to reach** ~ völlig am Ende sein.

breakthrough ['breɪkθruː] *n* Durchbruch *m.*

break-up ['breɪkʌp] *n (of partnership)* Auflösung *f; (of marriage)* Scheitern *nt.*

break-up value *n (COMM)* Liquidationswert *m.*

breakwater ['breɪkwɔːtə*] *n* Wellenbrecher *m.*

breast [brɛst] *n* Brust *f; (of meat)* Brust *f,* Bruststück *nt.*

breast-feed ['brɛstfiːd] *(irreg: like* **feed)** *vt, vi* stillen.

breast pocket *n* Brusttasche *f.*

breaststroke ['brɛststrəuk] *n* Brustschwimmen *nt.*

breath [brɛθ] *n* Atem *m; (a breath)* Atemzug *m;* **to go out for a** ~ **of air** an die frische Luft gehen, frische Luft schnappen gehen; **out of** ~ außer Atem, atemlos; **to get one's** ~ **back** wieder zu Atem kommen.

breathalyse ['brɛθəlaɪz] *vt* blasen lassen *(inf).*

Breathalyser ® ['brɛθəlaɪzə*] *n* Promillemesser *m.*

breathe [briːð] *vt, vi* atmen; **I won't** ~ **a word about it** ich werde kein Sterbenswörtchen darüber sagen.

▶**breathe in** *vt, vi* einatmen.

▶**breathe out** *vt, vi* ausatmen.

breather ['briːðə*] *n* Atempause *f,* Verschnaufpause *f.*

breathing ['briːðɪŋ] *n* Atmung *f.*

breathing space *n (fig)* Atempause *f,* Ruhepause *f.*

breathless ['brɛθlɪs] *adj* atemlos, außer Atem; *(MED)* an Atemnot leidend; **I was** ~ **with**

excitement die Aufregung verschlug mir den Atem.

breathtaking ['brɛθteɪkɪŋ] *adj* atemberaubend.

breath test *n* Atemalkoholtest *m.*

bred [brɛd] *pt, pp of* **breed.**

-bred *suff:* **well/ill-**~ gut/schlecht erzogen.

breed [briːd] *(pt, pp* **bred)** *vt* züchten; *(fig: give rise to)* erzeugen; *(: : hate, suspicion)* hervorrufen ♦ *vi* Junge haben ♦ *n* Rasse *f; (type, class)* Art *f.*

breeder ['briːdə*] *n* Züchter(in) *m(f); (also:* ~ **reactor)** Brutreaktor *m,* Brüter *m.*

breeding ['briːdɪŋ] *n* Erziehung *f.*

breeding ground *n (also fig)* Brutstätte *f.*

breeze [briːz] *n* Brise *f.*

breeze block *(BRIT) n* Ytong ® *m.*

breezy ['briːzɪ] *adj (manner, tone)* munter; *(weather)* windig.

Breton ['brɛtən] *adj* bretonisch ♦ *n* Bretone *m,* Bretonin *f.*

brevity ['brɛvɪtɪ] *n* Kürze *f.*

brew [bruː] *vt (tea)* aufbrühen, kochen; *(beer)* brauen ♦ *vi (tea)* ziehen; *(beer)* gären; *(storm, fig)* sich zusammenbrauen.

brewer ['bruːə*] *n* Brauer *m.*

brewery ['bruːərɪ] *n* Brauerei *f.*

briar ['braɪə*] *n* Dornbusch *m; (wild rose)* wilde Rose *f.*

bribe [braɪb] *n* Bestechungsgeld *nt* ♦ *vt* bestechen; **to** ~ **sb to do sth** jdn bestechen, damit er etw tut.

bribery ['braɪbərɪ] *n* Bestechung *f.*

bric-a-brac ['brɪkəbræk] *n* Nippes *pl,* Nippsachen *pl.*

brick [brɪk] *n* Ziegelstein *m,* Backstein *m; (of ice cream)* Block *m.*

bricklayer ['brɪkleɪə*] *n* Maurer(in) *m(f).*

brickwork ['brɪkwəːk] *n* Mauerwerk *nt.*

bridal ['braɪdl] *adj (gown, veil etc)* Braut-.

bride [braɪd] *n* Braut *f.*

bridegroom ['braɪdgruːm] *n* Bräutigam *m.*

bridesmaid ['braɪdzmeɪd] *n* Brautjungfer *f.*

bridge [brɪdʒ] *n* Brücke *f; (NAUT)* (Kommando)brücke *f; (of nose)* Sattel *m; (CARDS)* Bridge *nt* ♦ *vt (river)* eine Brücke schlagen *or* bauen über *+acc; (fig)* überbrücken.

bridging loan ['brɪdʒɪŋ-] *(BRIT) n* Überbrückungskredit *m.*

bridle ['braɪdl] *n* Zaum *m* ♦ *vt* aufzäumen ♦ *vi:* **to** ~ **(at)** sich entrüstet wehren (gegen).

bridle path *n* Reitweg *m.*

brief [briːf] *adj* kurz ♦ *n (LAW)* Auftrag *m; (task)* Aufgabe *f* ♦ *vt* instruieren; *(MIL etc):* **to** ~ **sb (about)** jdn instruieren (über *+acc);* **briefs** *npl* Slip *m;* **in** ~ ... kurz (gesagt) ...

briefcase ['briːfkeɪs] *n* Aktentasche *f.*

briefing ['briːfɪŋ] *n* Briefing *nt,* Lagebespechung *f.*

briefly ['briːflɪ] *adv* kurz; **to glimpse sth** ~ einen flüchtigen Blick von etw erhaschen.

Brig. abbr = **brigadier.**
brigade [brɪ'geɪd] n Brigade f.
brigadier [brɪgə'dɪə*] n Brigadegeneral m.
bright [braɪt] adj (light, room) hell; (weather) heiter; (clever) intelligent; (lively) heiter, fröhlich; (colour) leuchtend; (outlook, future) glänzend; **to look on the ~ side** die Dinge von der positiven Seite betrachten.
brighten ['braɪtn] (also: ~ **up**) vt aufheitern; (event) beleben ♦ vi (weather, face) sich aufheitern; (person) fröhlicher werden; (prospects) sich verbessern.
brightly ['braɪtlɪ] adv (shine) hell; (smile) fröhlich; (talk) heiter.
brill [brɪl] (BRIT: inf) adj toll.
brilliance ['brɪljəns] n Strahlen nt; (of person) Genialität f, Brillanz f; (of talent, skill) Großartigkeit f.
brilliant ['brɪljənt] adj strahlend; (person, idea) genial, brillant; (career) großartig; (inf: holiday etc) phantastisch.
brilliantly ['brɪljəntlɪ] adv (see adj) strahlend; genial, brillant; großartig; phantastisch.
brim [brɪm] n Rand m; (of hat) Krempe f.
brimful ['brɪm'ful] adj: ~ (**of**) randvoll (mit); (fig) voll (von).
brine [braɪn] n Lake f.
bring [brɪŋ] (pt, pp **brought**) vt bringen; (with you) mitbringen; **to ~ sth to an end** etw zu Ende bringen; **I can't ~ myself to fire him** ich kann es nicht über mich bringen, ihn zu entlassen.
►**bring about** vt herbeiführen.
►**bring back** vt (restore) wieder einführen; (return) zurückbringen.
►**bring down** vt (government) zu Fall bringen; (plane) herunterholen; (price) senken.
►**bring forward** vt (meeting) vorverlegen; (proposal) vorbringen; (BOOKKEEPING) übertragen.
►**bring in** vt (money) (ein)bringen; (include) einbeziehen; (person) einschalten; (legislation) einbringen; (verdict) fällen.
►**bring off** vt (plan) durchführen; (deal) zustande bringen.
►**bring out** vt herausholen; (meaning, book, album) herausbringen.
►**bring round** vt (after faint) wieder zu Bewußtsein bringen.
►**bring up** vt heraufbringen; (educate) erziehen; (question, subject) zur Sprache bringen; (food) erbrechen.
bring-and-buy sale n Basar m (wo mitgebrachte Sachen verkauft werden).
brink [brɪŋk] n Rand m; **on the ~ of doing sth** nahe daran, etw zu tun; **she was on the ~ of tears** sie war den Tränen nahe.
brisk [brɪsk] adj (abrupt: person, tone) forsch; (pace) flott; (trade) lebhaft, rege; **to go for a ~ walk** einen ordentlichen Spaziergang machen; **business is ~** das Geschäft ist

rege.
bristle ['brɪsl] n Borste f; (of beard) Stoppel f ♦ vi zornig werden; **bristling with** strotzend von.
bristly ['brɪslɪ] adj borstig; (chin) stoppelig.
Brit [brɪt] (inf) n abbr (= British person) Brite m, Britin f.
Britain ['brɪtən] n (also: **Great ~**) Großbritannien nt.
British ['brɪtɪʃ] adj britisch ♦ npl: **the ~** die Briten pl.
British Isles npl: **the ~** die Britischen Inseln.
British Rail n britische Eisenbahngesellschaft.
British Summer Time n britische Sommerzeit f.
Briton ['brɪtən] n Brite m, Britin f.
Brittany ['brɪtənɪ] n die Bretagne.
brittle ['brɪtl] adj spröde; (glass) zerbrechlich; (bones) schwach.
Br(o). abbr (REL) = **brother.**
broach [brəutʃ] vt (subject) anschneiden.
broad [brɔːd] adj breit; (general) allgemein; (accent) stark ♦ n (US: inf) Frau f; **in ~ daylight** am hellichten Tag; ~ **hint** deutlicher Wink m.
broad bean n dicke Bohne f, Saubohne f.
broadcast ['brɔːdkɑːst] (pt, pp **broadcast**) n Sendung f ♦ vt, vi senden.
broadcaster ['brɔːdkɑːstə*] n (RADIO, TV) Rundfunk-/Fernsehpersönlichkeit f.
broadcasting ['brɔːdkɑːstɪŋ] n (RADIO) Rundfunk m; (TV) Fernsehen nt.
broadcasting station n (RADIO) Rundfunkstation f; (TV) Fernsehstation f.
broaden ['brɔːdn] vt erweitern ♦ vi breiter werden, sich verbreitern; **to ~ one's mind** seinen Horizont erweitern.
broadly ['brɔːdlɪ] adv (in general terms) in großen Zügen; ~ **speaking** allgemein or generell gesagt.
broad-minded ['brɔːd'maɪndɪd] adj tolerant.
broadsheet ['brɔːdʃiːt] n (newspaper) großformatige Zeitung.
broccoli ['brɔkəlɪ] n Brokkoli pl, Spargelkohl m.
brochure ['brəuʃjuə*] n Broschüre f.
brogue [brəug] n Akzent m; (shoe) fester Schuh m.
broil [brɔɪl] (US) vt grillen.
broiler ['brɔɪlə*] n Brathähnchen nt.
broke [brəuk] pt of **break** ♦ adj (inf) pleite; **to go ~** pleite gehen.
broken ['brəukn] pp of **break** ♦ adj zerbrochen; (machine: also: ~ **down**) kaputt; (promise, vow) gebrochen; **a ~ leg** ein gebrochenes Bein; **a ~ marriage** eine gescheiterte Ehe; **a ~ home** zerrüttete Familienverhältnisse pl; **in ~ English/German** in gebrochenem Englisch/Deutsch.
broken-down ['brəukn'daun] adj kaputt; (house) baufällig.

brokenhearted [brəʊkn'haːtɪd] *adj* untröstlich.

broker ['brəʊkə•] *n* Makler(in) *m(f)*.

brokerage ['brəʊkrɪdʒ] *n* (*commission*) Maklergebühr *f*; (*business*) Maklergeschäft *nt*.

brolly ['brɒlɪ] (*BRIT: inf*) *n* (Regen)schirm *m*.

bronchitis [brɒŋ'kaɪtɪs] *n* Bronchitis *f*.

bronze [brɒnz] *n* Bronze *f*.

bronzed [brɒnzd] *adj* braun, (sonnen)gebräunt.

brooch [brəʊtʃ] *n* Brosche *f*.

brood [bruːd] *n* Brut *f* ♦ *vi* (*hen*) brüten; (*person*) grübeln.

▶**brood on** *vt fus* nachgrübeln über +*acc*.

▶**brood over** *vt fus* = brood on.

broody ['bruːdɪ] *adj* (*person*) grüblerisch; (*hen*) brütig.

brook [bruk] *n* Bach *m*.

broom [brum] *n* Besen *m*; (*BOT*) Ginster *m*.

broomstick ['brumstɪk] *n* Besenstiel *m*.

Bros. *abbr* (*COMM*: = *brothers*) Gebr.

broth [brɒθ] *n* Suppe *f*, Fleischbrühe *f*.

brothel ['brɒθl] *n* Bordell *nt*.

brother ['brʌðə•] *n* Bruder *m*; (*in trade union, society etc*) Kollege *m*.

brotherhood ['brʌðəhud] *n* Brüderlichkeit *f*.

brother-in-law ['brʌðərɪn'lɔː] *n* Schwager *m*.

brotherly ['brʌðəlɪ] *adj* brüderlich.

brought [brɔːt] *pt, pp of* bring.

brought forward *adj* (*COMM*) vorgetragen.

brow [brau] *n* Stirn *f*; (*eyebrow*) (Augen)braue *f*; (*of hill*) (Berg)kuppe *f*.

browbeat ['braubiːt] *vt*: **to ~ sb (into doing sth)** jdn (so) unter Druck setzen(, daß er etw tut).

brown [braun] *adj* braun ♦ *n* Braun *nt* ♦ *vt* (*CULIN*) (an)bräunen; **to go ~** braun werden.

brown bread *n* Graubrot *nt*, Mischbrot *nt*.

Brownie ['braunɪ] *n* (*also*: **~ Guide**) Wichtel *m*.

brownie ['braunɪ] (*US*) *n* kleiner Schokoladenkuchen.

brown paper *n* Packpapier *nt*.

brown rice *n* Naturreis *m*.

brown sugar *n* brauner Zucker *m*.

browse [brauz] *vi* (*in shop*) sich umsehen; (*animal*) weiden; (: *deer*) äsen ♦ *n*: **to have a ~ (around)** sich umsehen; **to ~ through a book** in einem Buch schmökern.

bruise [bruːz] *n* blauer Fleck *m*, Bluterguß *m*; (*on fruit*) Druckstelle *f* ♦ *vt* (*arm, leg etc*) sich *dat* stoßen; (*person*) einen blauen Fleck schlagen; (*fruit*) beschädigen ♦ *vi* (*fruit*) eine Druckstelle bekommen; **to ~ one's arm** sich *dat* den Arm stoßen, sich *dat* einen blauen Fleck am Arm holen.

bruising ['bruːzɪŋ] *adj* (*experience, encounter*) schmerzhaft ♦ *n* Quetschung *f*.

Brum [brʌm] (*BRIT: inf*) *n abbr* (= *Birmingham*).

Brummie ['brʌmɪ] (*inf*) *n aus Birmingham stammende oder dort wohnhafte Person*,

Birminghamer(in) *m(f)*.

brunch [brʌntʃ] *n* Brunch *m*.

brunette [bruː'nɛt] *n* Brünette *f*.

brunt [brʌnt] *n*: **to bear the ~ of** die volle Wucht +*gen* tragen.

brush [brʌʃ] *n* Bürste *f*; (*for painting, shaving etc*) Pinsel *m*; (*quarrel*) Auseinandersetzung *f* ♦ *vt* fegen; (*groom*) bürsten; (*teeth*) putzen; (*also*: **~ against**) streifen; **to have a ~ with sb** (*verbally*) sich mit jdm streiten; (*physically*) mit jdm aneinandergeraten; **to have a ~ with the police** mit der Polizei aneinandergeraten.

▶**brush aside** *vt* abtun.

▶**brush past** *vt* streifen.

▶**brush up** *vt* auffrischen.

brushed [brʌʃt] *adj* (*steel, chrome etc*) gebürstet; (*denim etc*) aufgerauht; **~ nylon** Nylon-Velours *m*.

brushoff ['brʌʃɔf] (*inf*) *n*: **to give sb the ~** jdm eine Abfuhr erteilen.

brushwood ['brʌʃwud] *n* Reisig *nt*.

brusque [bruːsk] *adj* brüsk; (*tone*) schroff.

Brussels ['brʌslz] *n* Brüssel *nt*.

Brussels sprouts *npl* Rosenkohl *m*.

brutal ['bruːtl] *adj* brutal.

brutality [bruː'tælɪtɪ] *n* Brutalität *f*.

brutalize ['bruːtəlaɪz] *vt* brutalisieren; (*illtreat*) brutal behandeln.

brute [bruːt] *n* brutaler Kerl *m*; (*animal*) Tier *nt* ♦ *adj*: **by ~ force** mit roher Gewalt.

brutish ['bruːtɪʃ] *adj* tierisch.

BS (*US*) *n abbr* (= *Bachelor of Science*) *akademischer Grad für Naturwissenschaftler*.

bs *abbr* = bill of sale.

BSA *n abbr* (= *Boy Scouts of America*) *amerikanische Pfadfinderorganisation*.

BSc *abbr* (= *Bachelor of Science*) *akademischer Grad für Naturwissenschaftler*.

BSE *n abbr* (= *bovine spongiform encephalopathy*) BSE *f*.

BSI *n abbr* (= *British Standards Institution*) *britischer Normenausschuß*.

BST *abbr* = British Summer Time.

Bt (*BRIT*) *abbr* = baronet.

btu *n abbr* (= *British thermal unit*) *britische Wärmeeinheit*.

bubble ['bʌbl] *n* Blase *f* ♦ *vi* sprudeln; (*sparkle*) perlen; (*fig: person*) übersprudeln.

bubble bath *n* Schaumbad *nt*.

bubble gum *n* Bubble-Gum *m*.

bubble-jet printer *n* Bubble-Jet-Drucker *m*.

bubble pack *n* (Klar)sichtpackung *f*.

bubbly ['bʌblɪ] *adj* (*person*) lebendig; (*liquid*) sprudelnd ♦ *n* (*inf: champagne*) Schampus *m*.

Bucharest [buːkə'rɛst] *n* Bukarest *nt*.

buck [bʌk] *n* (*rabbit*) Rammler *m*; (*deer*) Bock *m*; (*US: inf*) Dollar *m* ♦ *vi* bocken; **to pass the ~** die Verantwortung abschieben; **to pass the ~ to sb** jdm die Verantwortung zuschieben.

►**buck up** vi (cheer up) aufleben ♦ vt: **to ~ one's ideas up** sich zusammenreißen.
bucket ['bʌkɪt] n Eimer m ♦ vi (BRIT: inf): **the rain is ~ing (down)** es gießt or schüttet (wie aus Kübeln).

Buckingham Palace ist die offizielle Londoner Residenz der britischen Monarchen und liegt am St James Park. Der Palast wurde 1703 für den Herzog von Buckingham erbaut, 1762 von Georg III gekauft, zwischen 1821 und 1836 von John Nash umgebaut, und Anfang des 20. Jahrhunderts teilweise neu gestaltet. Teile des Buckingham Palace sind heute der Öffentlichkeit zugänglich.

buckle ['bʌkl] n Schnalle f ♦ vt zuschnallen; (wheel) verbiegen ♦ vi sich verbiegen.
►**buckle down** vi sich dahinterklemmen; **to ~ down to sth** sich hinter etw acc klemmen.
Bucks [bʌks] (BRIT) abbr (POST: = Buckinghamshire).
bud [bʌd] n Knospe f ♦ vi knospen, Knospen treiben.
Budapest [bju:də'pɛst] n Budapest nt.
Buddha ['budə] n Buddha m.
Buddhism ['budɪzəm] n Buddhismus m.
Buddhist ['budɪst] adj buddhistisch ♦ n Buddhist(in) m(f).
budding ['bʌdɪŋ] adj angehend.
buddy ['bʌdɪ] (US) n Kumpel m.
budge [bʌdʒ] vt (von der Stelle) bewegen; (fig) zum Nachgeben bewegen ♦ vi sich von der Stelle rühren; (fig) nachgeben.
budgerigar ['bʌdʒərɪɡɑ:*] n Wellensittich m.
budget ['bʌdʒɪt] n Budget nt, Etat m, Haushalt m ♦ vi haushalten, wirtschaften; **I'm on a tight ~** ich habe nicht viel Geld zur Verfügung; **she works out her ~ every month** sie macht (sich dat) jeden Monat einen Haushaltsplan; **to ~ for sth** etw kostenmäßig einplanen.
budgie ['bʌdʒɪ] n = budgerigar.
Buenos Aires ['bweɪnɔs'aɪrɪz] n Buenos Aires nt.
buff [bʌf] adj gelbbraun ♦ n (inf) Fan m.
buffalo ['bʌfələu] (pl ~ or ~es) n (BRIT) Büffel m; (US) Bison m.
buffer ['bʌfə*] n (COMPUT) Puffer m, Pufferspeicher m; (RAIL) Prellbock m; (fig) Polster nt.
buffering ['bʌfərɪŋ] n (COMPUT) Pufferung f.
buffer state n Pufferstaat m.
buffer zone n Pufferzone f.
buffet[1] ['bufeɪ] (BRIT) n Büfett nt, Bahnhofsrestaurant nt; (food) kaltes Buffet nt.
buffet[2] ['bʌfɪt] vt (subj: sea) hin und her werfen; (: wind) schütteln.
buffet car (BRIT) n Speisewagen m.
buffet lunch n Buffet nt.
buffoon [bə'fu:n] n Clown m.

bug [bʌg] n (esp US) Insekt nt; (COMPUT: of program) Programmfehler m; (: of equipment) Fehler m; (fig: germ) Bazillus m; (hidden microphone) Wanze f ♦ vt (inf) nerven; (telephone etc) abhören; (room) verwanzen; **I've got the travel ~** (fig) mich hat die Reiselust gepackt.
bugbear ['bʌgbeə*] n Schreckgespenst nt.
bugger ['bʌgə*] (infl) n Scheißkerl m, Arschloch nt ♦ vb: **~ off!** hau ab!; **~ (it)!** Scheiße!
buggy ['bʌgɪ] n (for baby) Sportwagen m.
bugle ['bju:gl] n Bügelhorn nt.
build [bɪld] (pt, pp **built**) n Körperbau m ♦ vt bauen.
►**build on** vt fus (fig) aufbauen auf +dat.
►**build up** vt aufbauen; (production) steigern; (morale) stärken; (stocks) anlegen; **don't ~ your hopes up too soon** mach dir nicht zu früh Hoffnungen.
builder ['bɪldə*] n Bauunternehmer m.
building ['bɪldɪŋ] n (industry) Bauindustrie f; (construction) Bau m; (structure) Gebäude nt, Bau.
building contractor n Bauunternehmer m.
building industry n Bauindustrie f.
building site n Baustelle f.
building society (BRIT) n Bausparkasse f.
building trade n = building industry.
build-up ['bɪldʌp] n Ansammlung f; (publicity): **to give sb/sth a good ~** jdn/etw ganz groß herausbringen.
built [bɪlt] pt, pp of build ♦ adj: **~-in** eingebaut, Einbau-; (safeguards) eingebaut; **well-~** gut gebaut.
built-up area ['bɪltʌp-] n bebautes Gebiet nt.
bulb [bʌlb] n (Blumen)zwiebel f; (ELEC) (Glüh)birne f.
bulbous ['bʌlbəs] adj knollig.
Bulgaria [bʌl'geərɪə] n Bulgarien nt.
Bulgarian [bʌl'geərɪən] adj bulgarisch ♦ n Bulgare m, Bulgarin f; (LING) Bulgarisch nt.
bulge [bʌldʒ] n Wölbung f; (in birth rate, sales) Zunahme f ♦ vi (pocket) prall gefüllt sein; (cheeks) voll sein; (file) (zum Bersten) voll sein; **to be bulging with** prall gefüllt sein mit.
bulimia [bə'lɪmɪə] n Bulimie f.
bulk [bʌlk] n (of thing) massige Form f; (of person) massige Gestalt f; **in ~** im großen, en gros; **the ~ of** der Großteil +gen.
bulk buying [-'baɪɪŋ] n Mengeneinkauf m, Großeinkauf m.
bulk carrier n Bulkcarrier m.
bulkhead ['bʌlkhɛd] n Schott nt.
bulky ['bʌlkɪ] adj sperrig.
bull [bul] n Stier m; (male elephant or whale) Bulle m; (STOCK EXCHANGE) Haussier m, Haussespekulant m; (REL) Bulle f.
bulldog ['buldɔg] n Bulldogge f.
bulldoze ['buldəuz] vt mit Bulldozern wegräumen; (building) mit Bulldozern

abreißen; **I was ~d into it** (*fig: inf*) ich wurde gezwungen *or* unter Druck gesetzt, es zu tun.
bulldozer ['buldəuzə*] *n* Bulldozer *m*, Planierraupe *f*.
bullet ['bulɪt] *n* Kugel *f*.
bulletin ['bulɪtɪn] *n* (*TV etc*) Kurznachrichten *pl*; (*journal*) Bulletin *nt*.
bulletin board *n* (*COMPUT*) Schwarzes Brett *nt*.
bulletproof ['bulɪtpruːf] *adj* kugelsicher.
bullfight ['bulfaɪt] *n* Stierkampf *m*.
bullfighter ['bulfaɪtə*] *n* Stierkämpfer *m*.
bullfighting ['bulfaɪtɪŋ] *n* Stierkampf *m*.
bullion ['buljən] *n:* **gold/silver** ~ Barrengold *nt*/-silber *nt*.
bullock ['bulək] *n* Ochse *m*.
bullring ['bulrɪŋ] *n* Stierkampfarena *f*.
bull's-eye ['bulzaɪ] *n* (*on a target*): **the** ~ der Scheibenmittelpunkt, das Schwarze.
bullshit ['bulʃɪt] (*inf!*) *n* Scheiß *m*, Quatsch *m* ♦ *vi* Scheiß erzählen; ~**!** Quatsch!
bully ['bulɪ] *n* Tyrann *m* ♦ *vt* tyrannisieren; (*frighten*) einschüchtern.
bullying ['bulɪŋ] *n* Tyrannisieren *nt*.
bum [bʌm] (*inf*) *n* Hintern *m*; (*esp US: good-for-nothing*) Rumtreiber *m*; (*tramp*) Penner *m*.
►**bum around** (*inf*) *vi* herumgammeln.
bumblebee ['bʌmblbiː] *n* Hummel *f*.
bumf [bʌmf] (*inf*) *n* Papierkram *m*.
bump [bʌmp] *n* Zusammenstoß *m*; (*jolt*) Erschütterung *f*; (*swelling*) Beule *f*; (*on road*) Unebenheit *f* ♦ *vt* stoßen; (*car*) eine Delle fahren in +*acc*.
►**bump along** *vi* entlangholpern.
►**bump into** *vt fus* (*obstacle*) stoßen gegen; (*inf: person*) treffen.
bumper ['bʌmpə*] *n* Stoßstange *f* ♦ *adj:* ~ **crop**, ~ **harvest** Rekordernte *f*.
bumper cars *npl* Autoskooter *pl*.
bumper sticker *n* Aufkleber *m*.
bumph [bʌmf] *n* = **bumf**.
bumptious ['bʌmpʃəs] *adj* wichtigtuerisch.
bumpy ['bʌmpɪ] *adj* holperig; **it was a** ~ **flight/ride** während des Fluges/auf der Fahrt wurden wir tüchtig durchgerüttelt.
bun [bʌn] *n* Brötchen *nt*; (*of hair*) Knoten *m*.
bunch [bʌntʃ] *n* Strauß *m*; (*of keys*) Bund *m*; (*of bananas*) Büschel *nt*; (*of people*) Haufen *m*; **bunches** *npl* (*in hair*) Zöpfe *pl*; ~ **of grapes** Weintraube *f*.
bundle ['bʌndl] *n* Bündel *nt* ♦ *vt* (*also:* ~ **up**) bündeln; (*put*): **to** ~ **sth into** etw stopfen *or* packen in +*acc*; **to** ~ **sb into** jdn schaffen in +*acc*.
►**bundle off** *vt* schaffen.
►**bundle out** *vt* herausschaffen.
bun fight (*BRIT: inf*) *n* Festivitäten *pl*; (*tea party*) Teegesellschaft *f*.
bung [bʌŋ] *n* Spund *m*, Spundzapfen *m* ♦ *vt* (*BRIT: inf: also:* ~ **in**) schmeißen; (*also:* ~ **up**)

verstopfen; **my nose is** ~**ed up** meine Nase ist verstopft.
bungalow ['bʌŋgələu] *n* Bungalow *m*.
bungee jumping ['bʌndʒiːˈdʒʌmpɪŋ] *n* Bungee-Springen *nt*.
bungle ['bʌŋgl] *vt* verpfuschen.
bunion ['bʌnjən] *n* entzündeter Ballen *m*.
bunk [bʌŋk] *n* Bett *nt*, Koje *f*; **to do a** ~ (*inf*) abhauen.
►**bunk off** (*inf*) *vi* abhauen.
bunk beds *npl* Etagenbett *nt*.
bunker ['bʌŋkə*] *n* Kohlenbunker *m*; (*MIL, GOLF*) Bunker *m*.
bunny ['bʌnɪ] *n* (*also:* ~ **rabbit**) Hase *m*, Häschen *nt*.
bunny girl (*BRIT*) *n* Häschen *nt*.
bunny hill (*US*) *n* (*SKI*) Anfängerhügel *m*.
bunting ['bʌntɪŋ] *n* (*flags*) Wimpel *pl*, Fähnchen *pl*.
buoy [bɔɪ] *n* Boje *f*.
►**buoy up** *vt* (*fig*) Auftrieb geben +*dat*.
buoyancy ['bɔɪənsɪ] *n* (*of ship, object*) Schwimmfähigkeit *f*.
buoyant ['bɔɪənt] *adj* (*ship, object*) schwimmfähig; (*market*) fest; (*economy*) stabil; (*prices, currency*) fest, stabil; (*person, nature*) heiter.
burden ['bəːdn] *n* Belastung *f*; (*load*) Last *f* ♦ *vt:* **to** ~ **sb with sth** jdn mit etw belasten; **to be a** ~ **to sb** jdm zur Last fallen.
bureau ['bjuərəu] (*pl* ~**x**) *n* (*BRIT: writing desk*) Sekretär *m*; (*US: chest of drawers*) Kommode *f*; (*office*) Büro *nt*.
bureaucracy [bjuəˈrɔkrəsɪ] *n* Bürokratie *f*.
bureaucrat ['bjuərəkræt] *n* Bürokrat(in) *m(f)*.
bureaucratic [bjuərəˈkrætɪk] *adj* bürokratisch.
bureaux ['bjuərəuz] *npl of* **bureau**.
burgeon ['bəːdʒən] *vi* hervorsprießen.
burger ['bəːgə*] (*inf*) *n* Hamburger *m*.
burglar ['bəːglə*] *n* Einbrecher(in) *m(f)*.
burglar alarm *n* Alarmanlage *f*.
burglarize ['bəːgləraɪz] (*US*) *vt* einbrechen in +*acc*.
burglary ['bəːglərɪ] *n* Einbruch *m*.
burgle ['bəːgl] *vt* einbrechen in +*acc*.
Burgundy ['bəːgəndɪ] *n* Burgund *nt*.
burial ['bɛrɪəl] *n* Beerdigung *f*.
burial ground *n* Begräbnisstätte *f*.
burlesque [bəːˈlɛsk] *n* (*parody*) Persiflage *f*; (*US: THEAT*) Burleske *f*.
burly ['bəːlɪ] *adj* kräftig, stämmig.
Burma ['bəːmə] *n* Birma *nt*, Burma *nt*.
Burmese [bəːˈmiːz] *adj* birmanisch, burmesisch ♦ *n inv* Birmane *m*, Burmese *m*, Birmanin *f*, Burmesin *f* ♦ *n* (*LING*) Birmanisch *nt*, Burmesisch *nt*.
burn [bəːn] (*pt, pp* **burned** *or* **burnt**) *vt* verbrennen; (*fuel*) als Brennstoff verwenden; (*food*) anbrennen lassen; (*house etc*) niederbrennen ♦ *vi* brennen; (*food*) anbrennen ♦ *n* Verbrennung *f*; **the cigarette** ~**t a hole in her dress** die Zigarette brannte

ein Loch in ihr Kleid; **I've ~t myself!** ich habe mich verbrannt!

►**burn down** vt abbrennen.

►**burn out** vt: **to ~ o.s. out** (writer etc) sich völlig verausgaben; **the fire ~t itself out** das Feuer brannte aus.

burner ['bə:nə*] n Brenner m.

burning ['bə:nɪŋ] adj brennend; (sand, desert) glühend heiß.

burnish ['bə:nɪʃ] vt polieren.

Burns' Night ist der am 25. Januar begangene Gedenktag für den schottischen Dichter Robert Burns (1759-1796). Wo Schotten leben, sei es in Schottland oder im Ausland, wird dieser Tag mit einem Abendessen gefeiert, bei dem es als Hauptgericht **Haggis** gibt, der mit Dudelsackbegleitung aufgetischt wird. Dazu ißt man Steckrüben- und Kartoffelpüree und trinkt Whisky. Während des Essens werden Burns' Gedichte vorgelesen, seine Lieder gesungen, bestimmte Reden gehalten und Trinksprüche ausgegeben.

---

burnt [bə:nt] pt, pp of **burn**.

burnt sugar (BRIT) n Karamel m.

burp [bə:p] (inf) n Rülpser m ♦ vt (baby) aufstoßen lassen ♦ vi rülpsen.

burrow ['bʌrəʊ] n Bau m ♦ vi graben; (rummage) wühlen.

bursar ['bə:sə*] n Schatzmeister m, Finanzverwalter m.

bursary ['bə:sərɪ] (BRIT) n Stipendium nt.

burst [bə:st] (pt, pp **burst**) vt zum Platzen bringen, platzen lassen ♦ vi platzen ♦ n Salve f; (also: ~ **pipe**) (Rohr)bruch m; **the river has ~ its banks** der Fluß ist über die Ufer getreten; **to ~ into flames** in Flammen aufgehen; **to ~ into tears** in Tränen ausbrechen; **to ~ out laughing** in Lachen ausbrechen; **~ blood vessel** geplatzte Ader f; **to be ~ing with** zum Bersten voll sein mit; (pride) fast platzen vor +dat; **to ~ open** aufspringen; **a ~ of energy** ein Ausbruch m von Energie; **a ~ of enthusiasm** ein Begeisterungsausbruch m; **a ~ of speed** ein Spurt m; **~ of laughter** Lachsalve f; **~ of applause** Beifallssturm m.

►**burst in on** vt fus: **to ~ in on sb** bei jdm hereinplatzen.

►**burst into** vt fus (into room) platzen in +acc.

►**burst out of** vt fus (of room) stürmen or stürzen aus.

bury ['berɪ] vt begraben; (at funeral) beerdigen; **to ~ one's face in one's hands** das Gesicht in den Händen vergraben; **to ~ one's head in the sand** (fig) den Kopf in den Sand stecken; **to ~ the hatchet** (fig) das Kriegsbeil begraben.

bus [bʌs] n (Auto)bus m, (Omni)bus m; (double decker) Doppeldecker m (inf).

bus boy (US) n Bedienungshilfe f.

bush [buʃ] n Busch m, Strauch m; (scrubland) Busch; **to beat about the ~** um den heißen Brei herumreden.

bushed [buʃt] (inf) adj (exhausted) groggy.

bushel ['buʃl] n Scheffel m.

bushfire n Buschfeuer nt.

bushy ['buʃɪ] adj buschig.

busily ['bɪzɪlɪ] adv eifrig; **to be ~ doing sth** eifrig etw tun.

business ['bɪznɪs] n (matter) Angelegenheit f; (trading) Geschäft nt; (firm) Firma f, Betrieb m; (occupation) Beruf m; **to be away on ~** geschäftlich unterwegs sein; **I'm here on ~** ich bin geschäftlich hier; **he's in the insurance/transport ~** er arbeitet in der Versicherungs-/Transportbranche; **to do ~ with sb** Geschäfte pl mit jdm machen; **it's my ~ to ...** es ist meine Aufgabe, zu ...; **it's none of my ~** es geht mich nichts an; **he means ~** er meint es ernst.

business address n Geschäftsadresse f.

business card n (Visiten)karte f.

businesslike ['bɪznɪslaɪk] adj geschäftsmäßig.

businessman ['bɪznɪsmən] (irreg: like **man**) n Geschäftsmann m.

business trip n Geschäftsreise f.

businesswoman ['bɪznɪswʊmən] (irreg: like **woman**) n Geschäftsfrau f.

busker ['bʌskə*] (BRIT) n Straßenmusikant(in) m(f).

bus lane (BRIT) n Busspur f.

bus shelter n Wartehäuschen nt.

bus station n Busbahnhof m.

bus stop n Bushaltestelle f.

bust [bʌst] n Busen m; (measurement) Oberweite f; (sculpture) Büste f ♦ adj (inf) kaputt ♦ vt (inf) verhaften; **to go ~** pleite gehen.

bustle ['bʌsl] n Betrieb m ♦ vi eilig herumlaufen.

bustling ['bʌslɪŋ] adj belebt.

bust-up ['bʌstʌp] (BRIT: inf) n Krach m.

busty ['bʌstɪ] adj (woman) vollbusig.

BUSWE (BRIT) n abbr (= British Union of Social Work Employees) Sozialarbeiter- gewerkschaft.

busy ['bɪzɪ] adj (person) beschäftigt; (shop, street) belebt; (TEL: esp US) besetzt ♦ vt: **to ~ o.s. with** sich beschäftigen mit; **he's a ~ man** er ist ein vielbeschäftigter Mann; **he's ~** er hat (zur Zeit) viel zu tun.

busybody ['bɪzɪbɒdɪ] n: **to be a ~** sich ständig einmischen.

busy signal (US) n (TEL) Besetztzeichen nt.

═══════════════════ KEYWORD

but [bʌt] conj **1** (yet) aber; **not blue ~ red** nicht blau, sondern rot; **he's not very bright, ~ he's hard-working** er ist nicht sehr intelligent, aber er ist fleißig

2 (however): **I'd love to come, ~ I'm busy** ich würde gern kommen, bin aber beschäftigt

3 (*showing disagreement, surprise etc*):
~ **that's far too expensive!** aber das ist viel
zu teuer!; ~ **that's fantastic!** das ist doch
toll!

♦ *prep* (*apart from, except*) außer +*dat*; **nothing**
~ **trouble** nichts als Ärger; **no-one** ~ **him**
can do it keiner außer ihm kann es machen;
~ **for you** wenn Sie nicht gewesen wären;
~ **for your help** ohne Ihre Hilfe; **I'll do**
anything ~ **that** ich mache alles, nur nicht
das; **the last house** ~ **one** das vorletzte
Haus; **the next street** ~ **one** die übernächste
Straße

♦ *adv* (*just, only*) nur; **she's** ~ **a child** sie ist
doch noch ein Kind; **I can** ~ **try** ich kann es
ja versuchen.

butane ['bjuːteɪn] *n* (*also:* ~ **gas**) Butan(gas)
nt.
butch [butʃ] (*inf*) *adj* maskulin.
butcher ['butʃə*] *n* Fleischer *m*, Metzger *m*;
(*pej: murderer*) Schlächter *m* ♦ *vt* schlachten;
(*prisoners etc*) abschlachten.
butcher's (shop) ['butʃəz-] *n* Fleischerei *f*,
Metzgerei *f*.
butler ['bʌtlə*] *n* Butler *m*.
butt [bʌt] *n* großes Faß *nt*, Tonne *f*; (*thick end*)
dickes Ende *nt*; (*of gun*) Kolben *m*; (*of*
cigarette) Kippe *f*; (*BRIT, fig: target*)
Zielscheibe *f*; (*US: inf!*) Arsch *m* ♦ *vt* (*goat*)
mit den Hörnern stoßen; (*person*) mit dem
Kopf stoßen.
►**butt in** *vi* sich einmischen,
dazwischenfunken (*inf*).
butter ['bʌtə*] *n* Butter *f* ♦ *vt* buttern.
buttercup ['bʌtəkʌp] *n* Butterblume *f*.
butter dish *n* Butterdose *f*.
butterfingers ['bʌtəfɪŋgəz] (*inf*) *n* Schussel *m*.
butterfly ['bʌtəflaɪ] *n* Schmetterling *m*;
(*SWIMMING: also:* ~ **stroke**)
Schmetterlingsstil *m*, Butterfly *m*.
buttocks ['bʌtəks] *npl* Gesäß *nt*.
button ['bʌtn] *n* Knopf *m*; (*US: badge*)
Plakette *f* ♦ *vt* (*also:* ~ **up**) zuknöpfen ♦ *vi*
geknöpft werden.
buttonhole ['bʌtnhəul] *n* Knopfloch *nt*;
(*flower*) Blume *f* im Knopfloch ♦ *vt* zu fassen
bekommen, sich *dat* schnappen (*inf*).
buttress ['bʌtrɪs] *n* Strebepfeiler *m*.
buxom ['bʌksəm] *adj* drall.
buy [baɪ] (*pt, pp* **bought**) *vt* kaufen; (*company*)
aufkaufen ♦ *n* Kauf *m*; **that was a good/bad**
~ das war ein guter/schlechter Kauf; **to**
~ **sb sth** jdm etw kaufen; **to** ~ **sth from sb**
etw bei jdm kaufen; (*from individual*) jdm
etw abkaufen; **to** ~ **sb a drink** jdm einen
ausgeben (*inf*).
►**buy back** *vt* zurückkaufen.
►**buy in** (*BRIT*) *vt* einkaufen.
►**buy into** (*BRIT*) *vt fus* sich einkaufen in +*acc*.
►**buy off** *vt* kaufen.
►**buy out** *vt* (*partner*) auszahlen; (*business*)

aufkaufen.
►**buy up** *vt* aufkaufen.
buyer ['baɪə*] *n* Käufer(in) *m(f)*; (*COMM*)
Einkäufer(in) *m(f)*.
buyer's market ['baɪəz-] *n* Käufermarkt *m*.
buyout ['baɪaut] *n* (*of firm: by workers,*
management) Aufkauf *m*.
buzz [bʌz] *vi* summen, brummen; (*saw*)
kreischen ♦ *vt* rufen; (*with buzzer*) (mit dem
Summer) rufen; (*AVIAT: plane, building*)
dicht vorbeifliegen an +*dat* ♦ *n* Summen *nt*,
Brummen *nt*; (*inf*): **to give sb a** ~ jdn
anrufen; **my head is** ~**ing** mir schwirrt der
Kopf.
►**buzz off** (*inf*) *vi* abhauen.
buzzard ['bʌzəd] *n* Bussard *m*.
buzzer ['bʌzə*] *n* Summer *m*.
buzz word (*inf*) *n* Modewort *nt*.

══════════════════════ *KEYWORD*

by [baɪ] *prep* **1** (*referring to cause, agent*) von
+*dat*, durch +*acc*; **killed** ~ **lightning** vom Blitz
or durch einen Blitz getötet; **a painting**
~ **Picasso** ein Bild von Picasso
2 (*referring to method, manner, means*):
~ **bus/car/train** mit dem Bus/Auto/Zug; **to**
pay ~ **cheque** mit *or* per Scheck bezahlen;
~ **saving hard, he was able to ...** indem er
eisern sparte, konnte er ...
3 (*via, through*) über +*acc*; **we came** ~ **Dover**
wir sind über Dover gekommen
4 (*close to*) bei +*dat*, an +*dat*; **the house** ~ **the**
river das Haus am Fluß
5 (*past*) an ... *dat* vorbei; **she rushed** ~ **me** sie
eilte an mir vorbei
6 (*not later than*) bis +*acc*; ~ **4 o'clock** bis 4
Uhr; ~ **this time tomorrow** morgen um
diese Zeit
7 (*amount*): ~ **the kilo/metre** kilo-/
meterweise; **to be paid** ~ **the hour**
stundenweise bezahlt werden
8 (*MATH, measure*): **to divide** ~ **3** durch 3
teilen; **to multiply** ~ **3** mit 3 malnehmen; **it**
missed me ~ **inches** es hat mich um
Zentimeter verfehlt
9 (*according to*): **to play** ~ **the rules** sich an
die Regeln halten; **it's all right** ~ **me** von
mir aus ist es in Ordnung
10: (**all**) ~ **myself/himself** *etc* (ganz) allein
11: ~ **the way** übrigens
♦ *adv* **1** *see* **go, pass** *etc*
2: ~ **and** irgendwann
3: ~ **and large** im großen und ganzen.

bye(-bye) ['baɪ('baɪ)] *excl* (auf) Wiedersehen,
tschüs (*inf*).
bye-law ['baɪlɔː] *n* Verordnung *f*.
by-election ['baɪɪlekʃən] (*BRIT*) *n* Nachwahl *f*.
Byelorussia [bjɛləu'rʌʃə] *n* = **Belorussia**.
Byelorussian [bjɛləu'rʌʃən] *adj, n*
= **Belarussian**.
bygone ['baɪgɔn] *adj* (längst) vergangen ♦ *n*:

let ~s be ~s wir sollten die Vergangenheit ruhen lassen.
by-law ['baɪlɔː] *n* = **bye-law.**
bypass ['baɪpɑːs] *n* Umgehungsstraße *f*; (*MED*) Bypass-Operation *f* ♦ *vt* (*also fig*) umgehen.
by-product ['baɪprɒdʌkt] *n* Nebenprodukt *nt*.
byre ['baɪə'] (*BRIT*) *n* Kuhstall *m*.
bystander ['baɪstændə'] *n* Zuschauer(in) *m(f)*.
byte [baɪt] *n* (*COMPUT*) Byte *nt*.
byway ['baɪweɪ] *n* Seitenweg *m*.
byword ['baɪwɜːd] *n*: **to be a ~ for** der Inbegriff +*gen* sein, gleichbedeutend sein mit.
by-your-leave ['baɪjɔː'liːv] *n*: **without so much as a ~** ohne auch nur (um Erlaubnis) zu fragen.

C, c

C¹, c¹ [siː] *n* (*letter*) C *nt*, c *nt*; (*SCOL*) ≈ Drei *f*, Befriedigend *nt*; ~ **for Charlie** ≈ C wie Cäsar.
C² [siː] *n* (*MUS*) C *nt*, c *nt*.
C³ [siː] *abbr* = **Celsius; centigrade.**
c² *abbr* = **century**; (= *circa*) ca.; (*US etc*: = *cent(s)*) Cent.
CA *n abbr* (*BRIT*) = **chartered accountant** ♦ *abbr* = **Central America**; (*US: POST: = California*).
C/A *abbr* (*COMM*) = **capital account; credit account; current account.**
ca. *abbr* (= *circa*) ca.
CAA *n abbr* (*BRIT*) = **Civil Aviation Authority**; (*US: = Civil Aeronautics Authority*) Zivilluftfahrtbehörde.
CAB (*BRIT*) *n abbr* = **Citizens' Advice Bureau.**
cab [kæb] *n* Taxi *nt*; (*of truck, train etc*) Führerhaus *nt*; (*horse-drawn*) Droschke *f*.
cabaret ['kæbəreɪ] *n* Kabarett *nt*.
cabbage ['kæbɪdʒ] *n* Kohl *m*.
cabbie, cabby ['kæbɪ] *n* Taxifahrer(in) *m(f)*.
cab driver *n* Taxifahrer(in) *m(f)*.
cabin ['kæbɪn] *n* Kabine *f*; (*house*) Hütte *f*.
cabin cruiser *n* Kajütboot *nt*.
cabinet ['kæbɪnɪt] *n* kleiner Schrank *m*; (*also*: **display ~**) Vitrine *f*; (*POL*) Kabinett *nt*.
cabinet-maker ['kæbɪnɪt'meɪkə'] *n* Möbeltischler *m*.
cabinet minister *n* Mitglied *nt* des Kabinetts, Minister(in) *m(f)*.
cable ['keɪbl] *n* Kabel *nt* ♦ *vt* kabeln.
cable car *n* (Draht)seilbahn *f*.
cablegram ['keɪblgræm] *n* (Übersee)telegramm *nt*, Kabel *nt*.
cable railway *n* Seilbahn *f*.

cable television *n* Kabelfernsehen *nt*.
cable TV *n* = **cable television.**
cache [kæʃ] *n* Versteck *nt*, geheimes Lager *nt*; **a ~ of food** ein geheimes Proviantlager.
cackle ['kækl] *vi* (*person: laugh*) meckernd lachen; (*hen*) gackern.
cacti ['kæktaɪ] *npl of* **cactus.**
cactus ['kæktəs] (*pl* **cacti**) *n* Kaktus *m*.
CAD *n abbr* (= *computer-aided design*) CAD *nt*.
caddie ['kædɪ] *n* (*GOLF*) Caddie *m*.
caddy ['kædɪ] *n* = **caddie.**
cadence ['keɪdəns] *n* (*of voice*) Tonfall *m*.
cadet [kə'dɛt] *n* Kadett *m*; **police ~** Polizeianwärter(in) *m(f)*.
cadge [kædʒ] (*inf*) *vt*: **to ~ (from** *or* **off)** schnorren (bei *or* von +*dat*); **to ~ a lift with sb** von jdm mitgenommen werden.
cadger ['kædʒə'] (*BRIT: inf*) *n* Schnorrer(in) *m(f)*.
cadre ['kædrɪ] *n* Kader *m*.
Caesarean [siː'zɛərɪən] *n*: ~ **(section)** Kaiserschnitt *m*.
CAF (*BRIT*) *abbr* (= *cost and freight*) cf.
café ['kæfeɪ] *n* Café *nt*.
cafeteria [kæfɪ'tɪərɪə] *n* Cafeteria *f*.
caffein(e) ['kæfiːn] *n* Koffein *nt*.
cage [keɪdʒ] *n* Käfig *m*; (*of lift*) Fahrkorb *m* ♦ *vt* einsperren.
cagey ['keɪdʒɪ] (*inf*) *adj* vorsichtig; (*evasive*) ausweichend.
cagoule [kə'guːl] *n* Regenjacke *f*.
cahoots [kə'huːts] (*inf*) *n*: **to be in ~ with** unter einer Decke stecken mit.
CAI *n abbr* (= *computer-aided instruction*) CAI *nt*.
Cairo ['kaɪərəu] *n* Kairo *nt*.
cajole [kə'dʒəul] *vt*: **to ~ sb into doing sth** jdn bereden, etw zu tun.
cake [keɪk] *n* Kuchen *m*; (*small*) Gebäckstück *nt*; (*of soap*) Stück *nt*; **it's a piece of ~** (*inf*) das ist ein Kinderspiel *or* ein Klacks; **he wants to have his ~ and eat it (too)** (*fig*) er will das eine, ohne das andere zu lassen.
caked [keɪkt] *adj*: ~ **with** (*mud, blood*) verkrustet mit.
cake shop *n* Konditorei *f*.
Cal. (*US*) *abbr* (*POST*: = *California*).
calamine lotion ['kæləmaɪn-] *n* Galmeilotion *f*.
calamitous [kə'læmɪtəs] *adj* katastrophal.
calamity [kə'læmɪtɪ] *n* Katastrophe *f*.
calcium ['kælsɪəm] *n* Kalzium *nt*.
calculate ['kælkjuleɪt] *vt* (*work out*) berechnen; (*estimate*) abschätzen.
▶**calculate on** *vt fus*: **to ~ on sth** mit etw rechnen; **to ~ on doing sth** damit rechnen, etw zu tun.
calculated ['kælkjuleɪtɪd] *adj* (*insult*) bewußt; (*action*) vorsätzlich; **a ~ risk** ein kalkuliertes Risiko.
calculating ['kælkjuleɪtɪŋ] *adj* (*scheming*) berechnend.

calculation [kælkjuˈleɪʃən] n (*see vt*)
Berechnung f; Abschätzung f; (*sum*)
Rechnung f.
calculator [ˈkælkjuleɪtəˈ] n Rechner m.
calculus [ˈkælkjuləs] n Infinitesimalrechnung
f; **integral/differential** ~ Integral-/
Differentialrechnung f.
calendar [ˈkæləndəˈ] n Kalender m; (*timetable,
schedule*) (Termin)kalender m.
calendar month n Kalendermonat m.
calendar year n Kalenderjahr nt.
calf [kɑːf] (*pl* **calves**) n Kalb nt; (*of elephant, seal
etc*) Junge(s) nt; (*also:* ~**skin**) Kalb(s)leder nt;
(*ANAT*) Wade f.
caliber [ˈkælɪbəˈ] (*US*) n = **calibre**.
calibrate [ˈkælɪbreɪt] vt (*gun etc*) kalibrieren;
(*scale of measuring instrument*) eichen.
calibre, (*US*) **caliber** [ˈkælɪbəˈ] n Kaliber nt;
(*of person*) Format nt.
calico [ˈkælɪkəu] n (*BRIT*) Kattun m, Kaliko m;
(*US*) bedruckter Kattun.
Calif. (*US*) abbr (*POST:* = *California*).
California [kælɪˈfɔːnɪə] n Kalifornien nt.
calipers [ˈkælɪpəz] (*US*) npl = **callipers**.
call [kɔːl] vt (*name, consider*) nennen; (*shout
out, summon*) rufen; (*TEL*) anrufen; (*witness,
flight*) aufrufen; (*meeting*) einberufen;
(*strike*) ausrufen ♦ vi rufen; (*TEL*) anrufen;
(*visit: also:* ~ **in,** ~ **round**) vorbeigehen,
vorbeikommen ♦ n Ruf m; (*TEL*) Anruf m;
(*visit*) Besuch m; (*for a service etc*) Nachfrage
f; (*for flight etc*) Aufruf m; (*fig: lure*) Ruf m,
Verlockung f; **to be** ~**ed** (*named*) heißen;
who is ~**ing?** (*TEL*) wer spricht da bitte?;
London ~**ing** (*RADIO*) hier ist London;
please give me a ~ **at 7** rufen Sie mich bitte
um 7 an; **to make a** ~ ein (Telefon)gespräch
führen; **to pay a** ~ **on sb** jdn besuchen; **to
be on** ~ einsatzbereit sein; (*doctor etc*)
Bereitschaftsdienst haben; **there's not
much** ~ **for these items** es besteht keine
große Nachfrage nach diesen Dingen.
▶**call at** vt fus (*subj: ship*) anlaufen; (*: train*)
halten in +dat.
▶**call back** vi (*return*) wiederkommen; (*TEL*)
zurückrufen ♦ vt (*TEL*) zurückrufen.
▶**call for** vt fus (*demand*) fordern; (*fetch*)
abholen.
▶**call in** vt (*doctor, expert, police*) zu Rate
ziehen; (*books, cars, stock etc*) aus dem
Verkehr ziehen ♦ vi vorbeigehen,
vorbeikommen.
▶**call off** vt absagen.
▶**call on** vt fus besuchen; (*appeal to*)
appellieren an +acc; **to** ~ **on sb to do sth** jdn
bitten or auffordern, etw zu tun.
▶**call out** vi rufen ♦ vt rufen; (*police, troops*)
alarmieren.
▶**call up** vt (*MIL*) einberufen; (*TEL*) anrufen.
Callanetics ® n sing Callanetics f.
call box (*BRIT*) n Telefonzelle f.
caller [ˈkɔːləˈ] n Besucher(in) m(f); (*TEL*)

Anrufer(in) m(f); **hold the line,** ~! (*TEL*) bitte
bleiben Sie am Apparat!
call girl n Callgirl nt.
call-in [ˈkɔːlɪn] (*US*) n (*RADIO, TV*) Phone-in nt.
calling [ˈkɔːlɪŋ] n (*trade*) Beruf m; (*vocation*)
Berufung f.
calling card (*US*) n Visitenkarte f.
callipers, (*US*) **calipers** [ˈkælɪpəz] npl (*MATH*)
Tastzirkel m; (*MED*) Schiene f.
callous [ˈkæləs] adj herzlos.
callousness [ˈkæləsnɪs] n Herzlosigkeit f.
callow [ˈkæləu] adj unreif.
calm [kɑːm] adj ruhig; (*unworried*) gelassen ♦ n
Ruhe f ♦ vt beruhigen; (*fears*) zerstreuen;
(*grief*) lindern.
▶**calm down** vt beruhigen ♦ vi sich
beruhigen.
calmly [ˈkɑːmlɪ] adv (*see adj*) ruhig; gelassen.
calmness [ˈkɑːmnɪs] n (*see adj*) Ruhe f;
Gelassenheit f.
Calor gas ® [ˈkælə-] n Butangas nt.
calorie [ˈkælərɪ] n Kalorie f; **low-**~ **product**
kalorienarmes Produkt nt.
calve [kɑːv] vi kalben.
calves [kɑːvz] npl of **calf**.
CAM n abbr (= *computer-aided manufacture*)
CAM nt.
camber [ˈkæmbəˈ] n Wölbung f.
Cambodia [kæmˈbəudɪə] n Kambodscha nt.
Cambodian [kæmˈbəudɪən] adj
kambodschanisch ♦ n Kambodschaner(in)
m(f).
Cambs (*BRIT*) abbr (*POST:* = *Cambridgeshire*).
camcorder [ˈkæmkɔːdəˈ] n Camcorder m,
Kamera-Recorder m.
came [keɪm] pt of **come**.
camel [ˈkæməl] n Kamel nt.
cameo [ˈkæmɪəu] n Kamee f; (*THEAT, LITER*)
Miniatur f.
camera [ˈkæmərə] n (*CINE, PHOT*) Kamera f;
(*also:* **cine** ~, **movie** ~) Filmkamera f; **35 mm**
~ Kleinbildkamera f; **in** ~ (*LAW*) unter
Ausschluß der Öffentlichkeit.
cameraman [ˈkæmərəmæn] (*irreg: like* **man**) n
Kameramann m.
Cameroon [kæməˈruːn] n Kamerun nt.
Cameroun [kæməˈruːn] n = **Cameroon**.
camomile [ˈkæməumaɪl] n Kamille f.
camouflage [ˈkæməflɑːʒ] n Tarnung f ♦ vt
tarnen.
camp [kæmp] n Lager nt; (*barracks*) Kaserne f
♦ vi zelten ♦ adj (*effeminate*) tuntenhaft (*inf*).
campaign [kæmˈpeɪn] n (*MIL*) Feldzug m; (*POL
etc*) Kampagne f ♦ vi kämpfen; **to** ~ **for/
against** sich einsetzen für/gegen.
campaigner [kæmˈpeɪnəˈ] n: ~ **for**
Befürworter(in) m(f) +gen; ~ **against**
Gegner(in) m(f) +gen.
camp bed (*BRIT*) n Campingliege f.
camper [ˈkæmpəˈ] n (*person*) Camper m;
(*vehicle*) Wohnmobil nt.
camping [ˈkæmpɪŋ] n Camping nt; **to go** ~

zelten gehen, campen.
camp(ing) site n Campingplatz m.
campus ['kæmpəs] n (UNIV)
Universitätsgelände nt, Campus m.
camshaft ['kæmʃɑːft] n Nockenwelle f.
can[1] [kæn] n Büchse f, Dose f; (for oil, water)
Kanister m ♦ vt eindosen, in Büchsen or
Dosen einmachen; **a ~ of beer** eine Dose
Bier; **he had to carry the ~** (BRIT: inf) er
mußte die Sache ausbaden.

═══════════════════ KEYWORD

can[2] (negative **cannot, can't**, conditional and pt
could) aux vb **1** (be able to, know how to)
können; **you ~ do it if you try** du kannst es,
wenn du es nur versuchst; **I can't see you**
ich kann dich nicht sehen; **I ~ swim/drive**
ich kann schwimmen/Auto fahren; **~ you
speak English?** sprechen Sie Englisch?
2 (may) können, dürfen; **~ I use your phone?**
kann or darf ich Ihr Telefon benutzen?;
could I have a word with you? könnte ich
Sie mal sprechen?
3 (expressing disbelief, puzzlement): **it can't be
true!** das darf doch nicht wahr sein!
4 (expressing possibility, suggestion, etc): **he
could be in the library** er könnte in der
Bibliothek sein.

Canada ['kænədə] n Kanada nt.
Canadian [kə'neɪdɪən] adj kanadisch ♦ n
Kanadier(in) m(f).
canal [kə'næl] n (also ANAT) Kanal m.
Canaries [kə'nɛərɪz] npl = **Canary Islands.**
canary [kə'nɛərɪ] n Kanarienvogel m.
Canary Islands [kə'nɛərɪ 'aɪləndz] npl: **the ~**
die Kanarischen Inseln pl.
Canberra ['kænbərə] n Canberra nt.
cancel ['kænsəl] vt absagen; (reservation)
abbestellen; (train, flight) ausfallen lassen;
(contract) annullieren; (order) stornieren;
(cross out) durchstreichen; (stamp)
entwerten; (cheque) ungültig machen.
►**cancel out** vt aufheben; **they ~ each other
out** sie heben sich gegenseitig auf.
cancellation [kænsə'leɪʃən] n Absage f; (of
reservation) Abbestellung f; (of train, flight)
Ausfall m; (TOURISM) Rücktritt m.
cancer ['kænsə] n (also: **C~**: ASTROL) Krebs m;
to be C~ (ein) Krebs sein.
cancerous ['kænsrəs] adj krebsartig.
cancer patient n Krebskranke(r) f(m).
cancer research n Krebsforschung f.
c and f (BRIT) abbr (COMM: = cost and freight)
cf.
candid ['kændɪd] adj offen, ehrlich.
candidacy ['kændɪdəsɪ] n Kandidatur f.
candidate ['kændɪdeɪt] n Kandidat(in) m(f);
(for job) Bewerber(in) m(f).
candidature ['kændɪdətʃə] (BRIT) n
= **candidacy.**
candied ['kændɪd] adj kandiert; **~ apple** (US)

kandierter Apfel m.
candle ['kændl] n Kerze f; (of tallow) Talglicht
nt.
candleholder ['kændlhəuldə] n see
candlestick.
candlelight ['kændllaɪt] n: **by ~** bei
Kerzenlicht.
candlestick ['kændlstɪk] n (also: **candleholder**)
Kerzenhalter m; (bigger, ornate)
Kerzenleuchter m.
candour, (US) candor ['kændə] n Offenheit f.
C & W n abbr = **country and western (music).**
candy ['kændɪ] n (also: **sugar-~**)
Kandis(zucker) m; (US) Bonbon nt or m.
candyfloss ['kændɪflɔs] (BRIT) n Zuckerwatte
f.
candy store (US) n Süßwarenhandlung f.
cane [keɪn] n Rohr nt; (stick) Stock m; (: for
walking) (Spazier)stock m ♦ vt (BRIT: SCOL)
mit dem Stock schlagen.
canine ['keɪnaɪn] adj (species) Hunde-.
canister ['kænɪstə] n Dose f; (pressurized
container) Sprühdose f; (of gas, chemicals etc)
Kanister m.
cannabis ['kænəbɪs] n Haschisch nt; (also:
~ plant) Hanf m, Cannabis m.
canned [kænd] adj Dosen-; (inf: music) aus der
Konserve; (US: inf: worker) entlassen,
rausgeschmissen inf.
cannibal ['kænɪbəl] n Kannibale m, Kannibalin
f.
cannibalism ['kænɪbəlɪzəm] n Kannibalismus
m.
cannon ['kænən] n (pl ~ or ~s) Kanone f.
cannonball ['kænənbɔːl] n Kanonenkugel f.
cannon fodder n Kanonenfutter nt.
cannot ['kænɒt] = **can not.**
canny ['kænɪ] adj schlau.
canoe [kə'nuː] n Kanu nt.
canoeing [kə'nuːɪŋ] n Kanusport m.
canon ['kænən] n Kanon m; (clergyman)
Kanoniker m, Kanonikus m.
canonize ['kænənaɪz] vt kanonisieren,
heiligsprechen.
can-opener ['kænəupnə] n Dosenöffner m,
Büchsenöffner m.
canopy ['kænəpɪ] n (also fig) Baldachin m.
cant [kænt] n scheinheiliges Gerede nt.
can't [kænt] = **can not.**
Cantab. (BRIT) abbr (in degree titles:
= Cantabrigiensis) der Universität
Cambridge.
cantankerous [kæn'tæŋkərəs] adj mürrisch.
canteen [kæn'tiːn] n (in school, workplace)
Kantine f; (: mobile) Feldküche f; (BRIT: of
cutlery) Besteckkasten m.
canter ['kæntə] vi leicht galoppieren, kantern
♦ n leichter Galopp m, Kanter m.
cantilever ['kæntɪliːvə] n Ausleger m.
canvas ['kænvəs] n Leinwand f; (painting)
Gemälde nt; (NAUT) Segeltuch nt; **under ~**
im Zelt.

canvass ['kænvəs] vt (opinions, views) erforschen; (person) für seine Partei zu gewinnen suchen; (place) Wahlwerbung machen in +dat ♦ vi: **to ~ for ...** (POL) um Stimmen für ... werben.

canvasser ['kænvəsə*] n (POL) Wahlhelfer(in) m(f).

canvassing ['kænvəsɪŋ] n (POL) Wahlwerbung f.

canyon ['kænjən] n Cañon m.

CAP n abbr (= Common Agricultural Policy) gemeinsame Agrarpolitik f der EG.

cap [kæp] n Mütze f, Kappe f; (of pen) (Verschluß)kappe f; (of bottle) Verschluß m, Deckel m; (contraceptive: also: **Dutch ~**) Pessar nt; (for toy gun) Zündplättchen nt; (for swimming) Bademütze f, Badekappe f; (SPORT) Ehrenkappe, die Nationalspielern verliehen wird ♦ vt (outdo) überbieten; (SPORT) für die Nationalmannschaft aufstellen; **~ped with ...** mit ... obendrauf; **and to ~ it all, ...** und obendrein ...

capability [keɪpə'bɪlɪtɪ] n Fähigkeit f; (MIL) Potential nt.

capable ['keɪpəbl] adj fähig; **to be ~ of doing sth** etw tun können, fähig sein, etw zu tun; **to be ~ of sth** (interpretation etc) etw zulassen.

capacious [kə'peɪʃəs] adj geräumig.

capacity [kə'pæsɪtɪ] n Fassungsvermögen nt; (of lift etc) Höchstlast f; (capability) Fähigkeit f; (position, role) Eigenschaft f; (of factory) Kapazität f; **filled to ~** randvoll; (stadium etc) bis auf den letzten Platz besetzt; **in his ~ as** ... in seiner Eigenschaft als ...; **this work is beyond my ~** zu dieser Arbeit bin ich nicht fähig; **in an advisory ~** in beratender Funktion; **to work at full ~** voll ausgelastet sein.

cape [keɪp] n Kap nt; (cloak) Cape nt, Umhang m.

Cape of Good Hope n: **the ~** das Kap der guten Hoffnung.

caper ['keɪpə*] n (CULIN: usu pl) Kaper f; (prank) Eskapade f, Kapriole f.

Cape Town n Kapstadt nt.

capita ['kæpɪtə] see **per capita**.

capital ['kæpɪtl] n (also: **~ city**) Hauptstadt f; (money) Kapital nt; (also: **~ letter**) Großbuchstabe m.

capital account n Kapitalverkehrsbilanz f; (of country) Kapitalkonto nt.

capital allowance n (Anlage)abschreibung f.

capital assets npl Kapitalvermögen nt.

capital expenditure n Kapitalaufwendungen pl.

capital gains tax n Kapitalertragssteuer f.

capital goods npl Investitionsgüter pl.

capital-intensive ['kæpɪtlɪn'tɛnsɪv] adj kapitalintensiv.

capitalism ['kæpɪtəlɪzəm] n Kapitalismus m.

capitalist ['kæpɪtəlɪst] adj kapitalistisch ♦ n Kapitalist(in) m(f).

capitalize ['kæpɪtəlaɪz] vt (COMM) kapitalisieren ♦ vi: **to ~ on** Kapital schlagen aus.

capital punishment n Todesstrafe f.

capital transfer tax (BRIT) n Erbschafts- und Schenkungssteuer f.

Capitol ['kæpɪtl] n: **the ~** das Kapitol.

> Capitol ist das Gebäude in Washington auf dem Capitol Hill, in dem der Kongreß der USA zusammentritt. Die Bezeichnung wird in vielen amerikanischen Bundesstaaten auch für das Parlamentsgebäude des jeweiligen Staates verwendet.

capitulate [kə'pɪtjuleɪt] vi kapitulieren.

capitulation [kəpɪtju'leɪʃən] n Kapitulation f.

capricious [kə'prɪʃəs] adj launisch.

Capricorn ['kæprɪkɔːn] n (ASTROL) Steinbock m; **to be ~** (ein) Steinbock sein.

caps [kæps] abbr (= capital letters) Großbuchstaben pl.

capsize [kæp'saɪz] vt zum Kentern bringen ♦ vi kentern.

capstan ['kæpstən] n Poller m.

capsule ['kæpsjuːl] n Kapsel f.

Capt. abbr (MIL) = **captain**.

captain ['kæptɪn] n Kapitän m; (of plane) (Flug)kapitän m; (in army) Hauptmann m ♦ vt (ship) befehligen; (team) anführen.

caption ['kæpʃən] n Bildunterschrift f.

captivate ['kæptɪveɪt] vt fesseln.

captive ['kæptɪv] adj gefangen ♦ n Gefangene(r) f(m).

captivity [kæp'tɪvɪtɪ] n Gefangenschaft f.

captor ['kæptə*] n: **his ~s** diejenigen, die ihn gefangennahmen.

capture ['kæptʃə*] vt (animal) (ein)fangen; (person) gefangennehmen; (town, country, share of market) erobern; (attention) erregen; (COMPUT) erfassen ♦ n (of animal) Einfangen nt; (of person) Gefangennahme f; (of town etc) Eroberung f; (data capture) Erfassung f.

car [kɑː*] n Auto nt, Wagen m; (RAIL) Wagen m; **by ~** mit dem Auto or Wagen.

Caracas [kə'rækəs] n Caracas nt.

carafe [kə'ræf] n Karaffe f.

caramel ['kærəməl] n Karamelle f, Karamelbonbon m or nt; (burnt sugar) Karamel m.

carat ['kærət] n Karat nt; **18 ~ gold** achtzehnkarätiges Gold.

caravan ['kærəvæn] n (BRIT) Wohnwagen m; (in desert) Karawane f.

caravan site (BRIT) n Campingplatz m für Wohnwagen.

caraway seed n Kümmel m.

carbohydrate [kɑːbəu'haɪdreɪt] n Kohle(n)hydrat nt.

carbolic acid [kɑː'bɒlɪk-] n Karbolsäure f.

car bomb n Autobombe f.
carbon ['kɑːbən] n Kohlenstoff m.
carbonated ['kɑːbəneɪtɪd] adj mit
  Kohlensäure (versetzt).
carbon copy n Durchschlag m.
carbon dioxide n Kohlendioxyd nt.
carbon monoxide [mɔ'nɔksaɪd] n
  Kohlenmonoxyd nt.
carbon paper n Kohlepapier nt.
carbon ribbon n Kohlefarbband nt.
car-boot sale n auf einem Parkplatz
  stattfindender Flohmarkt mit dem
  Kofferraum als Auslage.
carburettor, (US) carburetor [kɑːbjuˈrɛtə•] n
  Vergaser m.
carcass ['kɑːkəs] n Kadaver m.
carcinogenic [kɑːsɪnəˈdʒɛnɪk] adj
  krebserregend, karzinogen.
card [kɑːd] n Karte f; (material) (dünne) Pappe
  f, Karton m; (record card, index card etc)
  (Kartei)karte f; (membership card)
  (Mitglieds)ausweis m; (playing card)
  (Spiel)karte f; (visiting card) (Visiten)karte f;
  to play ~s Karten spielen.
cardamom ['kɑːdəməm] n Kardamom m.
cardboard ['kɑːdbɔːd] n Pappe f.
cardboard box n (Papp)karton m.
card-carrying ['kɑːdˈkærɪŋ] adj: **~ member**
  eingetragenes Mitglied nt.
card game n Kartenspiel nt.
cardiac ['kɑːdɪæk] adj (failure, patient) Herz-.
cardigan ['kɑːdɪgən] n Strickjacke f.
cardinal ['kɑːdɪnl] adj (principle, importance)
  Haupt- ♦ n Kardinal m; **~ number**
  Kardinalzahl f; **~ sin** Todsünde f.
card index n Kartei f.
cardphone n Kartentelefon nt.
cardsharp ['kɑːdʃɑːp] n Falschspieler m.
card vote (BRIT) n Abstimmung f durch
  Wahlmänner.
CARE [kɛə•] n abbr (= Cooperative for American
  Relief Everywhere) karitative Organisation.
care [kɛə•] n (attention) Versorgung f; (worry)
  Sorge f; (charge) Obhut f, Fürsorge f ♦ vi: **to
  ~ about** sich kümmern um; **~ of** bei;
  "handle with ~" „Vorsicht, zerbrechlich";
  in sb's ~ in jds dat Obhut; **to take ~**
  aufpassen; **to take ~ to do sth** sich
  bemühen, etw zu tun; **to take ~ of** sich
  kümmern um; **the child has been taken into
  ~** das Kind ist in Pflege genommen worden;
  would you ~ to/for ...? möchten Sie gerne
  ...?; **I wouldn't ~ to do it** ich möchte es nicht
  gern tun; **I don't ~** es ist mir egal or
  gleichgültig; **I couldn't ~ less** es ist mir
  völlig egal or gleichgültig.
▶**care for** vt fus (look after) sich kümmern um;
  (like) mögen.
career [kəˈrɪə•] n Karriere f; (job, profession)
  Beruf m; (life) Laufbahn f ♦ vi (also: **~ along**)
  rasen.
career girl n Karrierefrau f.

careers officer [kəˈrɪəz-] n Berufsberater(in)
  m(f).
career woman n Karrierefrau f.
carefree ['kɛəfriː] adj sorglos.
careful ['kɛəful] adj vorsichtig; (thorough)
  sorgfältig; **(be) ~!** Vorsicht!, paß auf!; **to be
  ~ with one's money** sein Geld gut
  zusammenhalten.
carefully ['kɛəfəlɪ] adv vorsichtig;
  (methodically) sorgfältig.
careless ['kɛəlɪs] adj leichtsinnig; (negligent)
  nachlässig; (remark) gedankenlos.
carelessly ['kɛəlɪslɪ] adv (see adj) leichtsinnig;
  nachlässig; gedankenlos.
carelessness ['kɛəlɪsnɪs] n (see adj)
  Leichtsinn m; Nachlässigkeit f;
  Gedankenlosigkeit f.
caress [kəˈrɛs] n Streicheln nt ♦ vt streicheln.
caretaker ['kɛəteɪkə•] n Hausmeister(in) m(f).
caretaker government (BRIT) n
  geschäftsführende Regierung f.
car ferry n Autofähre f.
cargo ['kɑːgəu] (pl **~es**) n Fracht f, Ladung f.
cargo boat n Frachter m, Frachtschiff nt.
cargo plane n Transportflugzeug nt.
car hire (BRIT) n Autovermietung f.
Caribbean [kærɪˈbiːən] adj karibisch ♦ n: **the
  ~ (Sea)** die Karibik, das Karibische Meer.
caricature ['kærɪkətjuə•] n Karikatur f.
caring ['kɛərɪŋ] adj liebevoll; (society,
  organization) sozial; (behaviour) fürsorglich.
carjacking n Angriff durch Banditen, die
  gewaltsam in PKWs eindringen und den
  Wagen samt Insassen entführen.
carnage ['kɑːnɪdʒ] n (MIL) Blutbad nt,
  Gemetzel nt.
carnal ['kɑːnl] adj fleischlich, sinnlich.
carnation [kɑːˈneɪʃən] n Nelke f.
carnival ['kɑːnɪvl] n Karneval m; (US: funfair)
  Kirmes f.
carnivorous [kɑːˈnɪvərəs] adj fleischfressend.
carol ['kærəl] n: **(Christmas) ~** Weihnachtslied
  nt.
carouse [kəˈrauz] vi zechen.
carousel [kærəˈsɛl] (US) n Karussell nt.
carp [kɑːp] n Karpfen m.
▶**carp at** vt fus herumnörgeln an +dat.
car park (BRIT) n Parkplatz m; (building)
  Parkhaus nt.
carpenter ['kɑːpɪntə•] n Zimmermann m.
carpentry ['kɑːpɪntrɪ] n Zimmerhandwerk nt;
  (school subject, hobby) Tischlern nt.
carpet ['kɑːpɪt] n (also fig) Teppich m ♦ vt (mit
  Teppichen/Teppichboden) auslegen; **fitted
  ~** (BRIT) Teppichboden m.
carpet bombing n Flächenbombardierung f.
carpet slippers npl Pantoffeln pl.
carpet-sweeper ['kɑːpɪtswiːpə•] n
  Teppichkehrer m.
car phone n (TELEC) Autotelefon nt.
carport ['kɑːpɔːt] n Einstellplatz m.
car rental n Autovermietung f.

carriage ['kærɪdʒ] n (RAIL, of typewriter)
Wagen m; (horse-drawn vehicle) Kutsche f; (of
goods) Beförderung f; (transport costs)
Beförderungskosten pl; ~ **forward** Fracht
zahlt Empfänger; ~ **free** frachtfrei; ~ **paid**
frei Haus.

carriage return n (on typewriter)
Wagenrücklauf m; (COMPUT) Return nt.

carriageway ['kærɪdʒweɪ] (BRIT) n Fahrbahn f.

carrier ['kærɪə'] n Spediteur m,
Transportunternehmer m; (MED)
Überträger m.

carrier bag (BRIT) n Tragetasche f, Tragetüte
f.

carrier pigeon n Brieftaube f.

carrion ['kærɪən] n Aas nt.

carrot ['kærət] n Möhre f, Mohrrübe f, Karotte
f; (fig) Köder m.

carry ['kærɪ] vt tragen; (transport)
transportieren; (a motion, bill) annehmen;
(reponsibilities etc) mit sich bringen; (disease,
virus) übertragen ♦ vi (sound) tragen; **to get
carried away** (fig) sich hinreißen lassen; **this
loan carries 10% interest** dieses Darlehen
wird mit 10% verzinst.

▶**carry forward** vt übertragen, vortragen.

▶**carry on** vi weitermachen; (inf: make a fuss)
(ein) Theater machen ♦ vt fortführen; **to
~ on with sth** mit etw weitermachen; **to
~ on singing/eating** weitersingen/-essen.

▶**carry out** vt (orders) ausführen;
(investigation) durchführen; (idea) in die Tat
umsetzen; (threat) wahrmachen.

carrycot ['kærɪkɔt] (BRIT) n Babytragetasche
f.

carry-on ['kærɪ'ɔn] (inf) n Theater nt.

cart [kɑːt] n Wagen m, Karren m; (for
passengers) Wagen m; (handcart)
(Hand)wagen m ♦ vt (inf) mit sich
herumschleppen.

carte blanche ['kɑːt'blɒnʃ] n: **to give sb** ~ jdm
Carte Blanche or (eine) Blankovollmacht
geben.

cartel [kɑː'tɛl] n Kartell nt.

cartilage ['kɑːtɪlɪdʒ] n Knorpel m.

cartographer [kɑː'tɔgrəfə'] n Kartograph(in)
m(f).

cartography [kɑː'tɔgrəfɪ] n Kartographie f.

carton ['kɑːtən] n (Papp)karton m; (of yogurt)
Becher m; (of milk) Tüte f; (of cigarettes)
Stange f.

cartoon [kɑː'tuːn] n (drawing) Karikatur f;
(BRIT: comic strip) Cartoon m; (CINE)
Zeichentrickfilm m.

cartoonist [kɑː'tuːnɪst] n Karikaturist(in) m(f).

cartridge ['kɑːtrɪdʒ] n (for gun, pen) Patrone f;
(music tape, for camera) Kassette f; (of
record-player) Tonabnehmer m.

cartwheel ['kɑːtwiːl] n Rad nt; **to turn a** ~
radschlagen.

carve [kɑːv] vt (meat) (ab)schneiden; (wood)
schnitzen; (stone) meißeln; (initials, design)
einritzen.

▶**carve up** vt (land etc) aufteilen; (meat)
aufschneiden.

carving ['kɑːvɪŋ] n Skulptur f; (in wood etc)
Schnitzerei f.

carving knife n Tranchiermesser nt.

car wash n Autowaschanlage f.

Casablanca [kæsə'blæŋkə] n Casablanca nt.

cascade [kæs'keɪd] n Wasserfall m, Kaskade f;
(of money) Regen m; (of hair) wallende Fülle
f ♦ vi (in Kaskaden) herabfallen; (hair etc)
wallen; (people) strömen.

case [keɪs] n Fall m; (for spectacles etc) Etui nt;
(BRIT: also: **suit**~) Koffer m; (of wine, whisky
etc) Kiste f; (TYP): **lower/upper** ~ groß/klein
geschrieben; **to have a good** ~ gute
Chancen haben, durchzukommen; **there's a
strong** ~ **for reform** es spricht viel für eine
Reform; **in** ~ ... **falls** ...; **in** ~ **of fire** bei
Feuer; **in** ~ **of emergency** im Notfall; **in
~ he comes** falls er kommt; **in any** ~
sowieso; **just in** ~ für alle Fälle.

case-hardened ['keɪshɑːdnd] adj (fig)
abgebrüht (inf).

case history n (MED) Krankengeschichte f.

case study n Fallstudie f.

cash [kæʃ] n (Bar)geld nt ♦ vt (cheque etc)
einlösen; **to pay (in)** ~ bar bezahlen; ~ **on
delivery** per Nachnahme; ~ **with order**
zahlbar bei Bestellung.

▶**cash in** vt einlösen.

▶**cash in on** vt fus Kapital schlagen aus.

cash account n Kassenbuch nt.

cash-and-carry [kæʃən'kærɪ] n Abholmarkt m.

cash-book ['kæʃbuk] n Kassenkonto nt.

cash box n (Geld)kassette f.

cash card (BRIT) n (Geld)automatenkarte f.

cash crop n zum Verkauf bestimmte Ernte f.

cash desk (BRIT) n Kasse f.

cash discount n Skonto m or nt.

cash dispenser (BRIT) n Geldautomat m.

cashew [kæ'ʃuː] n (also: ~ **nut**) Cashewnuß f.

cash flow n Cash-flow m.

cashier [kæ'ʃɪə'] n Kassierer(in) m(f).

cashmere ['kæʃmɪə'] n Kaschmir m.

cash point n Geldautomat m.

cash price n Bar(zahlungs)preis m.

cash register n Registrierkasse f.

cash sale n Barverkauf m.

casing ['keɪsɪŋ] n Gehäuse nt.

casino [kə'siːnəu] n Kasino nt.

cask [kɑːsk] n Faß nt.

casket ['kɑːskɪt] n Schatulle f; (US: coffin) Sarg
m.

Caspian Sea ['kæspɪən-] n: **the** ~ das
Kaspische Meer.

casserole ['kæsərəul] n Auflauf m; (pot,
container) Kasserolle f.

cassette [kæ'sɛt] n Kassette f.

cassette deck n Kassettendeck nt.

cassette player n Kassettenrekorder m.

cassette recorder n Kassettenrekorder m.

cast [kɑːst] (*pt, pp* **cast**) *vt* werfen; (*net, fishing-line*) auswerfen; (*metal, statue*) gießen ♦ *vi* die Angel auswerfen ♦ *n* (*THEAT*) Besetzung *f*; (*mould*) (Guß)form *f*; (*also:* **plaster ~**) Gipsverband *m*; **to ~ sb as Hamlet** (*THEAT*) die Rolle des Hamlet mit jdm besetzen; **to ~ one's vote** seine Stimme abgeben; **to ~ one's eyes over sth** einen Blick auf etw *acc* werfen; **to ~ aspersions on sb/sth** abfällige Bemerkungen über jdn/etw machen; **to ~ doubts on sth** etw in Zweifel ziehen; **to ~ a spell on sb/sth** jdn/etw verzaubern; **to ~ its skin** sich häuten.
▶**cast aside** *vt* fallenlassen.
▶**cast off** *vi* (*NAUT*) losmachen; (*KNITTING*) abketten ♦ *vt* abketten.
▶**cast on** *vi, vt* (*KNITTING*) anschlagen, aufschlagen.
castaway ['kɑːstəweɪ] *n* Schiffbrüchige(r) *f(m)*.
caste [kɑːst] *n* Kaste *f*; (*system*) Kastenwesen *nt*.
caster sugar ['kɑːstə-] (*BRIT*) *n* Raffinade *f*.
casting vote ['kɑːstɪŋ-] (*BRIT*) *n* ausschlaggebende Stimme *f*.
cast iron *n* Gußeisen *nt* ♦ *adj:* **cast-iron** (*fig: will*) eisern; (: *alibi, excuse etc*) hieb- und stichfest.
castle ['kɑːsl] *n* Schloß *nt*; (*manor*) Herrenhaus *nt*; (*fortified*) Burg *f*; (*CHESS*) Turm *m*.
cast off *n* abgelegtes Kleidungsstück *nt*.
castor ['kɑːstə'] *n* Rolle *f*.
castor oil *n* Rizinusöl *nt*.
castrate [kæs'treɪt] *vt* kastrieren.
casual ['kæʒjul] *adj* (*by chance*) zufällig; (*work etc*) Gelegenheits-; (*unconcerned*) lässig, gleichgültig; (*clothes*) leger; **~ wear** Freizeitkleidung *f*.
casual labour *n* Gelegenheitsarbeit *f*.
casually ['kæʒjulɪ] *adv* lässig; (*glance*) beiläufig; (*dress*) leger; (*by chance*) zufällig.
casualty ['kæʒjultɪ] *n* (*of war etc*) Opfer *nt*; (*someone injured*) Verletzte(r) *f(m)*; (*someone killed*) Tote(r) *f(m)*; (*MED*) Unfallstation *f*; **heavy casualties** (*MIL*) schwere Verluste *pl*.
casualty ward (*BRIT*) *n* Unfallstation *f*.
cat [kæt] *n* Katze *f*; (*lion etc*) (Raub)katze *f*.
catacombs ['kætəkuːmz] *npl* Katakomben *pl*.
catalogue, (*US*) **catalog** ['kætəlɔg] *n* Katalog *m* ♦ *vt* katalogisieren.
catalyst ['kætəlɪst] *n* Katalysator *m*.
catalytic converter [kætə'lɪtɪk kən'vɜːtə'] *n* (*AUT*) Katalysator *m*.
catapult ['kætəpʌlt] (*BRIT*) *n* Schleuder *f*; (*MIL*) Katapult *nt or m* ♦ *vi* geschleudert *or* katapultiert werden ♦ *vt* schleudern, katapultieren.
cataract ['kætərækt] *n* (*MED*) grauer Star *m*.
catarrh [kə'tɑː'] *n* Katarrh *m*.
catastrophe [kə'tæstrəfɪ] *n* Katastrophe *f*.
catastrophic [kætə'strɔfɪk] *adj* katastrophal.

catcalls ['kætkɔːlz] *npl* Pfiffe und Buhrufe *pl*.
catch-22 ['kætʃtwentɪ'tuː] *n:* **it's a ~ situation** es ist eine Zwickmühle.
catch [kætʃ] (*pt, pp* **caught**) *vt* fangen; (*take: bus, train etc*) nehmen; (*arrest*) festnehmen; (*surprise*) erwischen, ertappen; (*breath*) holen; (*attention*) erregen; (*hit*) treffen; (*hear*) mitbekommen; (*illness*) sich *dat* zuziehen *or* holen; (*person: also:* **~ up**) einholen ♦ *vi* (*fire*) (anfangen zu) brennen; (*become trapped*) hängenbleiben ♦ *n* Fang *m*; (*trick, hidden problem*) Haken *m*; (*of lock*) Riegel *m*; (*game*) Fangen *nt*; **to ~ sb's attention/eye** jdn auf sich *acc* aufmerksam machen; **to ~ fire** Feuer fangen; **to ~ sight of** erblicken.
▶**catch on** *vi* (*grow popular*) sich durchsetzen; **to ~ on (to sth)** (etw) kapieren.
▶**catch out** (*BRIT*) *vt* (*fig*) hereinlegen.
▶**catch up** *vi* (*fig: with person*) mitkommen; (: *on work*) aufholen ♦ *vt:* **to ~ sb up, to ~ up with sb** jdn einholen.
catching ['kætʃɪŋ] *adj* ansteckend.
catchment area ['kætʃmənt-] (*BRIT*) *n* Einzugsgebiet *nt*.
catch phrase *n* Schlagwort *nt*, Slogan *m*.
catchy ['kætʃɪ] *adj* (*tune*) eingängig.
catechism ['kætɪkɪzəm] *n* Katechismus *m*.
categoric(al) [kætɪ'gɔrɪk(l)] *adj* kategorisch.
categorize ['kætɪgəraɪz] *vt* kategorisieren.
category ['kætɪgərɪ] *n* Kategorie *f*.
cater ['keɪtə'] *vi:* **to ~ (for)** die Speisen und Getränke liefern (für).
▶**cater for** (*BRIT*) *vt fus* (*needs, tastes*) gerecht werden +*dat*; (*readers, consumers*) eingestellt *or* ausgerichtet sein auf +*acc*.
caterer ['keɪtərə'] *n* Lieferant(in) *m(f)* von Speisen und Getränken; (*company*) Lieferfirma *f* für Speisen und Getränke.
catering ['keɪtərɪŋ] *n* Gastronomie *f*.
caterpillar ['kætəpɪlə'] *n* Raupe *f* ♦ *cpd* (*vehicle*) Raupen-.
caterpillar track *n* Raupenkette *f*, Gleiskette *f*.
cat flap *n* Katzentür *f*.
cathedral [kə'θiːdrəl] *n* Kathedrale *f*, Dom *m*.
cathode ['kæθəʊd] *n* Kathode *f*.
cathode-ray tube [kæθəʊd'reɪ-] *n* Kathodenstrahlröhre *f*.
Catholic ['kæθəlɪk] *adj* katholisch ♦ *n* Katholik(in) *m(f)*.
catholic ['kæθəlɪk] *adj* vielseitig.
CAT scanner *n abbr* (*MED:* = *computerized axial tomography scanner*) CAT-Scanner *m*.
Catseye ® ['kæts'aɪ] (*BRIT*) *n* (*AUT*) Katzenauge *nt*.
catsup ['kætsəp] (*US*) *n* Ketchup *m or nt*.
cattle ['kætl] *npl* Vieh *nt*.
catty ['kætɪ] *adj* gehässig.
catwalk ['kætwɔːk] *n* Steg *m*; (*for models*) Laufsteg *m*.
Caucasian [kɔː'keɪzɪən] *adj* kaukasisch ♦ *n*

Kaukasier(in) *m(f)*.
Caucasus ['kɔːkəsəs] *n* Kaukasus *m*.
caucus ['kɔːkəs] *n* (*group*) Gremium *nt*,
Ausschuß *m*; (*US*) Parteiversammlung *f*.

Caucus *bedeutet vor allem in den USA ein
privates Treffen von Parteifunktionären, bei
dem z.B. Kandidaten ausgewählt oder
Grundsatzentscheidungen getroffen werden.
Meist wird ein solches Treffen vor einer
öffentlichen Parteiversammlung abgehalten.
Der Begriff bezieht sich im weiteren Sinne
auch auf den kleinen, aber mächtigen Kreis
von Parteifunktionären, der beim caucus
zusammentrifft.*

---

caught [kɔːt] *pt, pp of* **catch**.
cauliflower ['kɔlıflaʊə°] *n* Blumenkohl *m*.
cause [kɔːz] *n* Ursache *f*; (*reason*) Grund *m*;
(*aim*) Sache *f* ♦ *vt* verursachen; **there is no**
~ **for concern** es besteht kein Grund zur
Sorge; **to** ~ **sth to be done** veranlassen, daß
etw getan wird; **to** ~ **sb to do sth** jdn
veranlassen, etw zu tun.
causeway ['kɔːzweɪ] *n* Damm *m*.
caustic ['kɔːstɪk] *adj* ätzend, kaustisch;
(*remark*) bissig.
cauterize ['kɔːtəraɪz] *vt* kauterisieren.
caution ['kɔːʃən] *n* Vorsicht *f*; (*warning*)
Warnung *f*; (: *LAW*) Verwarnung *f* ♦ *vt*
warnen; (*LAW*) verwarnen.
cautious ['kɔːʃəs] *adj* vorsichtig.
cautiously ['kɔːʃəslı] *adv* vorsichtig.
cautiousness ['kɔːʃəsnıs] *n* Vorsicht *f*.
cavalier [kævə'lıə°] *adj* unbekümmert.
cavalry ['kævəlrı] *n* Kavallerie *f*.
cave [keɪv] *n* Höhle *f* ♦ *vi*: **to go caving** auf
Höhlenexpedition(en) gehen.
▶**cave in** *vi* einstürzen; (*to demands*)
nachgeben.
caveman ['keɪvmæn] (*irreg: like* **man**) *n*
Höhlenmensch *m*.
cavern ['kævən] *n* Höhle *f*.
caviar(e) ['kævıɑː'] *n* Kaviar *m*.
cavity ['kævıtı] *n* Hohlraum *m*; (*in tooth*) Loch
nt.
cavity wall insulation *n* Schaumisolierung *f*.
cavort [kə'vɔːt] *vi* tollen, toben.
cayenne [keɪ'ɛn] *n* (*also:* ~ **pepper**)
Cayennepfeffer *m*.
CB *n abbr* (= *Citizens' Band (Radio)*) CB-Funk *m*.
CBC *n abbr* (= *Canadian Broadcasting
Corporation*) *kanadische
Rundfunkgesellschaft.*
CBE (*BRIT*) *n abbr* (= *Commander of (the Order
of) the British Empire*) *britischer Ordenstitel.*
CBI *n abbr* (= *Confederation of British Industry*)
britischer Unternehmerverband, ≈ BDI *m*.
CBS (*US*) *n abbr* (= *Columbia Broadcasting
System*) *Rundfunkgesellschaft.*
CC (*BRIT*) *abbr* = **county council.**
cc *abbr* (= *cubic centimetre*) ccm; = **carbon**

copy.
CCA (*US*) *n abbr* (= *Circuit Court of Appeals*)
Berufungsgericht *nt*.
CCU (*US*) *n abbr* (= *cardiac or coronary care
unit*) Intensivstation *für* Herzpatienten.
CD *abbr* (*BRIT*: = *Corps Diplomatique*) CD ♦ *n
abbr* (*MIL: BRIT*: = *Civil Defence (Corps)*)
Zivilschutz *m*; (: *US*: = *Civil Defense*)
Zivilschutz *m*; (= *compact disk*) CD *f*;
~ **player** CD-Spieler *m*.
CDC (*US*) *n abbr* (= *Center for Disease Control*)
Seuchenkontrollbehörde.
CD-I *n abbr* (= *Compact Disk Interactive*) CD-I *f*.
Cdr *abbr* (*MIL*) = **commander.**
CD-ROM *n abbr* (= *compact disc read-only
memory*) CD-ROM *f*.
CDT (*US*) *abbr* (= *Central Daylight Time*)
mittelamerikanische Sommerzeit.
cease [siːs] *vt* beenden ♦ *vi* aufhören.
ceasefire ['siːsfaɪə'] *n* Waffenruhe *f*.
ceaseless ['siːslıs] *adj* endlos, unaufhörlich.
CED (*US*) *n abbr* (= *Committee for Economic
Development*) *Komitee für wirtschaftliche
Entwicklung.*
cedar ['siːdə'] *n* Zeder *f*; (*wood*) Zedernholz *nt*.
cede [siːd] *vt* abtreten.
cedilla [sı'dılə] *n* Cedille *f*.
CEEB (*US*) *n abbr* (= *College Entry Examination
Board*) *akademische Zulassungsstelle.*
ceilidh ['keɪlı] (*SCOT*) *n Fest mit Volksmusik,
Gesang und Tanz.*
ceiling ['siːlıŋ] *n* Decke *f*; (*upper limit*)
Obergrenze *f*, Höchstgrenze *f*.
celebrate ['sɛlıbreıt] *vt* feiern; (*mass*)
zelebrieren ♦ *vi* feiern.
celebrated ['sɛlıbreıtıd] *adj* gefeiert.
celebration [sɛlı'breıʃən] *n* Feier *f*.
celebrity [sı'lɛbrıtı] *n* berühmte
Persönlichkeit *f*.
celeriac [sə'lɛrıæk] *n* (Knollen)sellerie *f*.
celery ['sɛlərı] *n* (Stangen)sellerie *f*.
celestial [sı'lɛstıəl] *adj* himmlisch.
celibacy ['sɛlıbəsı] *n* Zölibat *nt or m*.
cell [sɛl] *n* Zelle *f*.
cellar ['sɛlə'] *n* Keller *m*; (*for wine*)
(Wein)keller *m*.
cellist ['tʃɛlıst] *n* Cellist(in) *m(f)*.
cello ['tʃɛləʊ] *n* Cello *nt*.
cellophane ['sɛləfeın] *n* Cellophan *nt*.
cellphone ['sɛlfəʊn] *n* Funktelefon *nt*.
cellular ['sɛljulə'] *adj* (*BIOL*) zellular, Zell-;
(*fabrics*) aus porösem Material.
Celluloid ® ['sɛljulɔıd] *n* Zelluloid *nt*.
cellulose ['sɛljuləus] *n* Zellulose *f*, Zellstoff *m*.
Celsius ['sɛlsıəs] *adj* (*scale*) Celsius-.
Celt [kɛlt] *n* Kelte *m*, Keltin *f*.
Celtic ['kɛltık] *adj* keltisch ♦ *n* (*LING*) Keltisch
nt.
cement [sə'mɛnt] *n* Zement *m*; (*concrete*)
Beton *m*; (*glue*) Klebstoff *m* ♦ *vt*
zementieren; (*stick, glue*) kleben; (*fig*)
festigen.

cement mixer n Betonmischmaschine f.
cemetery ['sɛmɪtrɪ] n Friedhof m.
cenotaph ['sɛnətɑːf] n Ehrenmal nt.
censor ['sɛnsə*] n Zensor(in) m(f) ♦ vt
  zensieren.
censorship ['sɛnsəʃɪp] n Zensur f.
censure ['sɛnʃə*] vt tadeln ♦ n Tadel m.
census ['sɛnsəs] n Volkszählung f.
cent [sɛnt] n (US: coin) Cent m; see also per
  cent.
centenary [sɛn'tiːnərɪ] n hundertster
  Jahrestag m.
centennial [sɛn'tɛnɪəl] (US) n = **centenary**.
center etc ['sɛntə*] (US) = **centre** etc.
centigrade ['sɛntɪɡreɪd] adj (scale) Celsius-.
centilitre, (US) **centiliter** ['sɛntɪliːtə*] n
  Zentiliter m or nt.
centimetre, (US) **centimeter** ['sɛntɪmiːtə*] n
  Zentimeter m or nt.
centipede ['sɛntɪpiːd] n Tausendfüßler m.
central ['sɛntrəl] adj zentral; (committee,
  government) Zentral-; (idea) wesentlich.
Central African Republic n
  Zentralafrikanische Republik f.
Central America n Mittelamerika nt.
central heating n Zentralheizung f.
centralize ['sɛntrəlaɪz] vt zentralisieren.
central processing unit n (COMPUT)
  Zentraleinheit f.
central reservation (BRIT) n Mittelstreifen
  m.
centre, (US) **center** ['sɛntə*] n Mitte f; (health
  centre etc, town centre) Zentrum nt; (of
  attention, interest) Mittelpunkt m; (of action,
  belief etc) Kern m ♦ vt zentrieren; (ball) zur
  Mitte spielen ♦ vi (concentrate): **to ~ on** sich
  konzentrieren auf +acc.
centrefold, (US) **centerfold** ['sɛntəfəʊld] n
  doppelseitiges Bild in der Mitte einer
  Zeitschrift.
centre forward n Mittelstürmer(in) m(f).
centre half n Stopper(in) m(f).
centrepiece, (US) **centerpiece** ['sɛntəpiːs] n
  Tafelaufsatz m; (fig) Kernstück nt.
centre spread (BRIT) n Doppelseite in der
  Mitte einer Zeitschrift.
centre-stage [sɛntə'steɪdʒ] (fig) adv: **to be ~**
  im Mittelpunkt stehen ♦ n **to take centre
  stage** in den Mittelpunkt rücken.
centrifugal [sɛn'trɪfjuɡl] adj (force)
  Zentrifugal-.
centrifuge ['sɛntrɪfjuːʒ] n Zentrifuge f,
  Schleuder f.
century ['sɛntjʊrɪ] n Jahrhundert nt;
  (CRICKET) Hundert f; **in the twentieth ~** im
  zwanzigsten Jahrhundert.
CEO (US) n abbr = **chief executive officer**.
ceramic [sɪ'ræmɪk] adj keramisch; (tiles)
  Keramik-.
ceramics [sɪ'ræmɪks] npl Keramiken pl.
cereal ['siːrɪəl] n Getreide nt; (food)
  Getreideflocken pl (Cornflakes etc).

cerebral ['sɛrɪbrəl] adj (MED) zerebral;
  (intellectual) geistig.
ceremonial [sɛrɪ'məʊnɪəl] n Zeremoniell nt
  ♦ adj zeremoniell.
ceremony ['sɛrɪmənɪ] n Zeremonie f;
  (behaviour) Förmlichkeit f; **to stand on ~**
  förmlich sein.
cert [sɜːt] (BRIT: inf) n: **it's a dead ~** es ist
  todsicher.
certain ['sɜːtən] adj sicher; **a ~ Mr Smith** ein
  gewisser Herr Smith; **~ days/places**
  bestimmte Tage/Orte; **a ~ coldness** eine
  gewisse Kälte; **to make ~ of** sich
  vergewissern +gen; **for ~** ganz sicher, ganz
  genau.
certainly ['sɜːtənlɪ] adv bestimmt; (of course)
  sicherlich; **~!** (aber) sicher!
certainty ['sɜːtəntɪ] n Sicherheit f;
  (inevitability) Gewißheit f.
certificate [sə'tɪfɪkɪt] n Urkunde f; (diploma)
  Zeugnis nt.
certified letter ['sɜːtɪfaɪd-] (US) n
  Einschreibebrief m.
certified mail (US) n Einschreiben nt.
certified public accountant ['sɜːtɪfaɪd-] (US)
  n geprüfter Buchhalter m, geprüfte
  Buchhalterin f.
certify ['sɜːtɪfaɪ] vt bescheinigen; (award a
  diploma to) ein Zeugnis verleihen +dat;
  (declare insane) für unzurechnungsfähig
  erklären ♦ vi: **to ~ to** sich verbürgen für.
cervical ['sɜːvɪkl] adj: **~ cancer**
  Gebärmutterhalskrebs m; **~ smear**
  Abstrich m.
cervix ['sɜːvɪks] n Gebärmutterhals m.
Cesarean [sɪ'zɛərɪən] (US) n = **Caesarean**.
cessation [sə'seɪʃən] n (of hostilities etc)
  Einstellung f, Ende nt.
cesspit ['sɛspɪt] n (sewage tank) Senkgrube f.
CET abbr (= Central European Time) MEZ.
Ceylon [sɪ'lɒn] n Ceylon nt.
cf. abbr (= compare) vgl.
c/f abbr (COMM: = carried forward) Übertr.
CFC n abbr (= chlorofluorocarbon) FCKW m.
CG (US) n abbr = **coastguard**.
cg abbr (= centigram) cg.
CH (BRIT) n abbr (= Companion of Honour)
  britischer Ordenstitel.
ch. abbr (= chapter) Kap.
c.h. (BRIT) abbr (= central heating) ZH.
Chad [tʃæd] n Tschad m.
chafe [tʃeɪf] vt (wund)reiben ♦ vi (fig): **to
  ~ against** sich ärgern über +acc.
chaffinch ['tʃæfɪntʃ] n Buchfink m.
chagrin ['ʃæɡrɪn] n Ärger m.
chain [tʃeɪn] n Kette f ♦ vt (also: ~ **up**: prisoner)
  anketten; (: dog) an die Kette legen.
chain reaction n Kettenreaktion f.
chain-smoke ['tʃeɪnsməʊk] vi eine Zigarette
  nach der anderen rauchen, kettenrauchen.
chain store n Kettenladen m.
chair [tʃɛə*] n Stuhl m; (armchair) Sessel m; (of

university) Lehrstuhl *m*; (*of meeting, committee*) Vorsitz *m* ♦ *vt* den Vorsitz führen bei; **the ~** (*US*) der elektrische Stuhl.

chair lift *n* Sessellift *m*.

chairman ['tʃɔːmən] (*irreg: like* **man**) *n* Vorsitzende(r) *f(m)*; (*BRIT: of company*) Präsident *m*.

chairperson ['tʃɛəpəːsn] *n* Vorsitzende(r) *f(m)*.

chairwoman ['tʃɛəwumən] (*irreg: like* **woman**) *n* Vorsitzende *f*.

chalet ['ʃæleɪ] *n* Chalet *nt*.

chalice ['tʃælɪs] *n* Kelch *m*.

chalk [tʃɔːk] *n* Kalkstein *m*, Kreide *f*; (*for writing*) Kreide *f*.

▶**chalk up** *vt* aufschreiben, notieren; (*fig: success etc*) verbuchen.

challenge ['tʃælɪndʒ] *n* (*of new job*) Anforderungen *pl*; (*of unknown etc*) Reiz *m*; (*to authority etc*) Infragestellung *f*; (*dare*) Herausforderung *f* ♦ *vt* herausfordern; (*authority, right, idea etc*) in Frage stellen; **to ~ sb to do sth** jdn dazu auffordern, etw zu tun; **to ~ sb to a fight/game** jdn zu einem Kampf/Spiel herausfordern.

challenger ['tʃælɪndʒəˊ] *n* Herausforderer *m*, Herausforderin *f*.

challenging ['tʃælɪndʒɪŋ] *adj* (*career, task*) anspruchsvoll; (*tone, look etc*) herausfordernd.

chamber ['tʃeɪmbəˊ] *n* Kammer *f*; (*BRIT: LAW: gen pl: of barristers*) Kanzlei *f*; (: *of judge*) Amtszimmer *nt*; **~ of commerce** Handelskammer *f*.

chambermaid ['tʃeɪmbəmeɪd] *n* Zimmermädchen *nt*.

chamber music *n* Kammermusik *f*.

chamber pot *n* Nachttopf *m*.

chameleon [kə'miːlɪən] *n* Chamäleon *nt*.

chamois ['ʃæmwɑː] *n* Gemse *f*; (*cloth*) Ledertuch *nt*, Fensterleder *nt*.

chamois leather ['ʃæmɪ-] *n* Ledertuch *nt*, Fensterleder *nt*.

champagne [ʃæm'peɪn] *n* Champagner *m*.

champers ['ʃæmpəz] (*inf*) *n* (*champagne*) Schampus *m*.

champion ['tʃæmpɪən] *n* Meister(in) *m(f)*; (*of cause, principle*) Verfechter(in) *m(f)*; (*of person*) Fürsprecher(in) *m(f)* ♦ *vt* eintreten für, sich engagieren für.

championship ['tʃæmpɪənʃɪp] *n* Meisterschaft *f*; (*title*) Titel *m*.

chance [tʃɑːns] *n* (*hope*) Aussicht *f*; (*likelihood, possibility*) Möglichkeit *f*; (*opportunity*) Gelegenheit *f*; (*risk*) Risiko *nt* ♦ *vt* riskieren ♦ *adj* zufällig; **the ~s are that ...** aller Wahrscheinlichkeit nach ..., wahrscheinlich ...; **there is little ~ of his coming** es ist unwahrscheinlich, daß er kommt; **to take a ~** es darauf ankommen lassen; **by ~** durch Zufall, zufällig; **it's the ~ of a lifetime** es ist eine einmalige Chance; **to ~ to do sth** zufällig etw tun; **to ~ it** es riskieren.

▶**chance (up)on** *vt fus* (*person*) zufällig begegnen +*dat*, zufällig treffen; (*thing*) zufällig stoßen auf +*acc*.

chancel ['tʃɑːnsəl] *n* Altarraum *m*.

chancellor ['tʃɑːnsələˊ] *n* Kanzler *m*.

Chancellor of the Exchequer (*BRIT*) *n* Schatzkanzler *m*, Finanzminister *m*.

chancy ['tʃɑːnsɪ] *adj* riskant.

chandelier [ʃændə'lɪəˊ] *n* Kronleuchter *m*.

change [tʃeɪndʒ] *vt* ändern; (*wheel, job, money, baby's nappy*) wechseln; (*bulb*) auswechseln; (*baby*) wickeln ♦ *vi* sich verändern; (*traffic lights*) umspringen ♦ *n* Veränderung *f*; (*difference*) Abwechslung *f*; (*coins*) Kleingeld *nt*; (*money returned*) Wechselgeld *nt*; **to ~ sb into** jdn verwandeln in +*acc*; **to ~ gear** (*AUT*) schalten; **to ~ one's mind** seine Meinung ändern, es sich *dat* anders überlegen; **to ~ hands** den Besitzer wechseln; **to ~ (trains/buses/planes etc)** umsteigen; **to ~ (one's clothes)** sich umziehen; **to ~ into** (*be transformed*) sich verwandeln in +*acc*; **she ~d into an old skirt** sie zog einen alten Rock an; **a ~ of clothes** Kleidung *f* zum Wechseln; **~ of government/climate/job** Regierungs-/Klima-/Berufswechsel *m*; **small ~** Kleingeld *nt*; **to give sb ~ for** *or* **of £10** jdm £10 wechseln; **keep the ~** das stimmt so, der Rest ist für Sie; **for a ~** zur Abwechslung.

changeable ['tʃeɪndʒəbl] *adj* (*weather*) wechselhaft, veränderlich; (*mood*) wechselnd; (*person*) unbeständig.

change machine *n* (Geld)wechselautomat *m*.

changeover ['tʃeɪndʒəuvəˊ] *n* Umstellung *f*.

changing ['tʃeɪndʒɪŋ] *adj* sich verändernd.

changing room (*BRIT*) *n* (Umkleide)kabine *f*; (*SPORT*) Umkleideraum *m*.

channel ['tʃænl] *n* (*TV*) Kanal *m*; (*of river, waterway*) (Fluß)bett *nt*; (*for boats*) Fahrrinne *f*; (*groove*) Rille *f*; (*fig: means*) Weg *m* ♦ *vt* leiten; (*fig*): **to ~ into** lenken auf +*acc*; **through the usual ~s** auf dem üblichen Wege; **green ~** (*CUSTOMS*) „nichts zu verzollen"; **red ~** (*CUSTOMS*) „Waren zu verzollen"; **the (English) C~** der Ärmelkanal; **the C~ Islands** die Kanalinseln *pl*.

Channel Tunnel *n*: **the ~** der Kanaltunnel.

chant [tʃɑːnt] *n* Sprechchor *m*; (*REL*) Gesang *m* ♦ *vt* im (Sprech)chor rufen; (*REL*) singen ♦ *vi* Sprechchöre anstimmen; (*REL*) singen; **the demonstrators ~ed their disapproval** die Demonstranten machten ihrem Unmut in Sprechchören Luft.

chaos ['keɪɔs] *n* Chaos *nt*, Durcheinander *nt*.

chaos theory *n* Chaostheorie *f*.

chaotic [keɪ'ɔtɪk] *adj* chaotisch.

chap [tʃæp] (*BRIT: inf*) *n* Kerl *m*, Typ *m*; **old ~** alter Knabe *or* Junge.

chapel ['tʃæpl] *n* Kapelle *f*; (*BRIT: non-conformist chapel*) Sektenkirche *f*; (: *of union*) *Betriebsgruppe innerhalb der*

*Gewerkschaft der Drucker und
Journalisten.*
chaperone ['ʃæpərəun] n Anstandsdame f ♦ vt
begleiten.
chaplain ['tʃæplɪn] n Pfarrer(in) m(f); (Roman
Catholic) Kaplan m.
chapped [tʃæpt] adj aufgesprungen, rauh.
chapter ['tʃæptə'] n Kapitel nt; **a ~ of
accidents** eine Serie von Unfällen.
char [tʃɑː'] vt verkohlen ♦ vi (BRIT) putzen
gehen ♦ n (BRIT) = **charlady**.
character ['kærɪktə'] n Charakter m;
(personality) Persönlichkeit f; (in novel, film)
Figur f, Gestalt f; (eccentric) Original nt;
(letter: also COMPUT) Zeichen nt; **a person of
good ~** ein guter Mensch.
character code n (COMPUT) Zeichencode m.
characteristic [kærɪktə'rɪstɪk] n Merkmal nt
♦ adj: ~ **(of)** charakteristisch (für), typisch
(für).
characterize ['kærɪktəraɪz] vt kennzeichnen,
charakterisieren; (describe the character of):
to ~ (as) beschreiben (als).
charade [ʃə'rɑːd] n Scharade f.
charcoal ['tʃɑːkəul] n Holzkohle f; (for
drawing) Kohle f, Kohlestift m.
charge [tʃɑːdʒ] n (fee) Gebühr f; (accusation)
Anklage f; (responsibility) Verantwortung f;
(attack) Angriff m ♦ vt (customer) berechnen
+dat; (sum) berechnen; (battery) (auf)laden;
(gun) laden; (enemy) angreifen; (sb with task)
beauftragen ♦ vi angreifen; (usu with: up,
along etc) stürmen; **charges** npl Gebühren pl;
labour ~s Arbeitskosten pl; **to reverse the
~s** (BRIT: TEL) ein R-Gespräch führen; **is
there a ~?** kostet das etwas?; **there's no ~**
es ist umsonst, es kostet nichts; **at no extra
~** ohne Aufpreis; **free of ~** kostenlos, gratis;
to take ~ of (child) sich kümmern um;
(company) übernehmen; **to be in ~ of** die
Verantwortung haben für; (business) leiten;
they ~d us £10 for the meal das Essen
kostete £10; **how much do you ~?** was
verlangen Sie?; **to ~ an expense (up) to sb's
account** eine Ausgabe auf jds Rechnung acc
setzen; **to ~ sb (with)** (LAW) jdn anklagen
(wegen).
charge account n Kunden(kredit)konto nt.
charge card n Kundenkreditkarte f.
chargé d'affaires n Chargé d'affaires m.
charge hand (BRIT) n Vorarbeiter(in) m(f).
charger ['tʃɑːdʒə'] n (also: **battery ~**)
Ladegerät nt; (warhorse) (Schlacht)roß nt.
chariot ['tʃærɪət] n (Streit)wagen m.
charisma [kæ'rɪsmə] n Charisma nt.
charitable ['tʃærɪtəbl] adj (organization)
karitativ, Wohltätigkeits-; (remark)
freundlich.
charity ['tʃærɪtɪ] n (organization) karitative
Organisation f, Wohltätigkeitsverein m;
(kindness, generosity) Menschenfreund-
lichkeit f; (money, gifts) Almosen nt.

charlady ['tʃɑːleɪdɪ] (irreg: like **lady**) (BRIT) n
Putzfrau f, Reinemachefrau f.
charlatan ['ʃɑːlətən] n Scharlatan m.
charm [tʃɑːm] n Charme m; (to bring good luck)
Talisman m; (on bracelet etc) Anhänger m ♦ vt
bezaubern.
charm bracelet n Armband nt mit
Anhängern.
charming ['tʃɑːmɪŋ] adj reizend, charmant;
(place) bezaubernd.
chart [tʃɑːt] n Schaubild nt, Diagramm nt;
(map) Karte f; (weather chart) Wetterkarte f
♦ vt (course) planen; (progress) aufzeichnen;
charts npl (hit parade) Hitliste f.
charter ['tʃɑːtə'] vt chartern ♦ n Charta f; (of
university, company) Gründungsurkunde f;
on ~ gechartert.
chartered accountant ['tʃɑːtəd-] (BRIT) n
Wirtschaftsprüfer(in) m(f).
charter flight n Charterflug m.
charwoman ['tʃɑːwumən] (irreg: like **woman**) n
Putzfrau f, Reinemachefrau f.
chary ['tʃɛərɪ] adj: **to be ~ of doing sth** zögern,
etw zu tun.
chase [tʃeɪs] vt jagen, verfolgen; (also:
~ away) wegjagen, vertreiben; (business,
job etc) hersein hinter +dat (inf) ♦ n
Verfolgungsjagd f.
►**chase down** (US) vt = **chase up**.
►**chase up** (BRIT) vt (person) rankriegen (inf);
(information) ranschaffen (inf).
chasm ['kæzəm] n Kluft f.
chassis ['ʃæsɪ] n Fahrgestell nt.
chaste [tʃeɪst] adj keusch.
chastened ['tʃeɪsnd] adj zur Einsicht
gebracht.
chastening ['tʃeɪsnɪŋ] adj ernüchternd.
chastise [tʃæs'taɪz] vt (scold) schelten.
chastity ['tʃæstɪtɪ] n Keuschheit f.
chat [tʃæt] vi (also: **have a ~**) plaudern, sich
unterhalten ♦ n Plauderei f, Unterhaltung f.
►**chat up** (BRIT: inf) vt anmachen.
chatline ['tʃætlaɪn] n Telefondienst, der
Anrufern die Teilnahme an einer
Gesprächsrunde ermöglicht.
chat show (BRIT) n Talkshow f.
chattel ['tʃætl] n: **goods and ~s** see **good**.
chatter ['tʃætə'] vi schwatzen; (monkey)
schnattern; (teeth) klappern ♦ n (see vi)
Schwatzen nt; Schnattern nt; Klappern nt;
my teeth are ~ing mir klappern die Zähne.
chatterbox ['tʃætəbɒks] (inf) n Quasselstrippe
f.
chattering classes ['tʃætərɪŋ 'klɑːsɪz] npl: **the
~** die intellektuellen Schwätzer pl.
chatty ['tʃætɪ] adj geschwätzig; (letter) im
Plauderton.
chauffeur ['ʃəufə'] n Chauffeur m, Fahrer m.
chauvinism ['ʃəuvɪnɪzəm] n (also: **male ~**)
Chauvinismus m.
chauvinist ['ʃəuvɪnɪst] n Chauvinist m.
chauvinistic [ʃəuvɪ'nɪstɪk] adj chauvinistisch.

ChE *abbr* (= *chemical engineer*) *Titel für Chemotechniker.*

cheap [tʃiːp] *adj* billig; (*reduced*) ermäßigt; (*poor quality*) billig, minderwertig; (*behaviour, joke*) ordinär ♦ *adv*: **to buy/sell sth** ~ etw billig kaufen/verkaufen.

cheapen ['tʃiːpn] *vt* entwürdigen.

cheaper ['tʃiːpə*] *adj* billiger.

cheaply ['tʃiːplɪ] *adv* billig.

cheat [tʃiːt] *vi* mogeln (*inf*), schummeln (*inf*) ♦ *n* Betrüger(in) *m(f)* ♦ *vt*: **to** ~ **sb** (**out of sth**) jdn (um etw) betrügen; **to** ~ **on sb** (*inf*) jdn betrügen.

cheating ['tʃiːtɪŋ] *n* Mogeln *nt* (*inf*), Schummeln *nt* (*inf*).

check [tʃɛk] *vt* überprüfen; (*passport, ticket*) kontrollieren; (*facts*) nachprüfen; (*enemy, disease*) aufhalten; (*impulse*) unterdrücken; (*person*) zurückhalten ♦ *vi* nachprüfen ♦ *n* Kontrolle *f*; (*curb*) Beschränkung *f*; (*US*) = **cheque**; (: *bill*) Rechnung *f*; (*pattern: gen pl*) Karo(muster) *nt* ♦ *adj* kariert; **to** ~ **o.s.** sich beherrschen; **to** ~ **with sb** bei jdm nachfragen; **to keep a** ~ **on sb/sth** jdn/etw kontrollieren.

▸**check in** *vi* (*at hotel*) sich anmelden; (*at airport*) einchecken ♦ *vt* (*luggage*) abfertigen lassen.

▸**check off** *vt* abhaken.

▸**check out** *vi* (*of hotel*) abreisen ♦ *vt* (*luggage*) abfertigen; (*investigate*) überprüfen.

▸**check up** *vi*: **to** ~ **up on sth** etw überprüfen; **to** ~ **up on sb** Nachforschungen über jdn anstellen.

checkered, (*US*) *adj* = **chequered**.

checkers ['tʃɛkəz] (*US*) *npl* Damespiel *nt*.

check guarantee card (*US*) *n* Scheckkarte *f*.

check-in (desk) ['tʃɛkɪn-] *n* (*at airport*) Abfertigung *f*, Abfertigungsschalter *m*.

checking account ['tʃɛkɪŋ-] (*US*) *n* Girokonto *nt*.

check list *n* Prüfliste *f*, Checkliste *f*.

checkmate ['tʃɛkmeɪt] *n* Schachmatt *nt*.

checkout ['tʃɛkaut] *n* Kasse *f*.

checkpoint ['tʃɛkpɔɪnt] *n* Kontrollpunkt *m*.

checkroom ['tʃɛkrum] (*US*) *n* (*left-luggage office*) Gepäckaufbewahrung *f*.

checkup ['tʃɛkʌp] *n* Untersuchung *f*.

cheek [tʃiːk] *n* Backe *f*; (*impudence*) Frechheit *f*; (*nerve*) Unverschämtheit *f*.

cheekbone ['tʃiːkbəun] *n* Backenknochen *m*.

cheeky ['tʃiːkɪ] *adj* frech.

cheep [tʃiːp] *vi* (*bird*) piep(s)en ♦ *n* Piep(s) *m*, Piepser *m*.

cheer [tʃɪə*] *vt* zujubeln +*dat*; (*gladden*) aufmuntern, aufheitern ♦ *vi* jubeln, hurra rufen ♦ *n* (*gen pl*) Hurraruf *m*, Beifallsruf *m*; **cheers** *npl* Hurrageschrei *nt*, Jubel *m*; ~**s!** prost!

▸**cheer on** *vt* anspornen, anfeuern.

▸**cheer up** *vi* vergnügter *or* fröhlicher werden ♦ *vt* aufmuntern, aufheitern.

cheerful ['tʃɪəful] *adj* fröhlich.

cheerfulness ['tʃɪəfulnɪs] *n* Fröhlichkeit *f*.

cheerio [tʃɪərɪ'əu] (*BRIT*) *excl* tschüs (*inf*).

cheerleader ['tʃɪəliːdə*] *n* jd, der bei Sportveranstaltungen etc die Zuschauer zu Beifallsrufen anfeuert.

cheerless ['tʃɪəlɪs] *adj* freudlos, trüb; (*room*) trostlos.

cheese [tʃiːz] *n* Käse *m*.

cheeseboard ['tʃiːzbɔːd] *n* Käsebrett *nt*; (*with cheese on it*) Käseplatte *f*.

cheeseburger ['tʃiːzbəːgə*] *n* Cheeseburger *m*.

cheesecake ['tʃiːzkeɪk] *n* Käsekuchen *m*.

cheetah ['tʃiːtə] *n* Gepard *m*.

chef [ʃɛf] *n* Küchenchef(in) *m(f)*.

chemical ['kɛmɪkl] *adj* chemisch ♦ *n* Chemikalie *f*.

chemical engineering *n* Chemotechnik *f*.

chemist ['kɛmɪst] *n* (*BRIT: pharmacist*) Apotheker(in) *m(f)*; (*scientist*) Chemiker(in) *m(f)*.

chemistry ['kɛmɪstrɪ] *n* Chemie *f*.

chemist's (shop) ['kɛmɪsts-] (*BRIT*) *n* Drogerie *f*; (*also*: **dispensing chemist's**) Apotheke *f*.

chemotherapy [kiːməu'θɛrəpɪ] *n* Chemotherapie *f*.

cheque [tʃɛk] (*BRIT*) *n* Scheck *m*; **to pay by** ~ mit (einem) Scheck bezahlen.

chequebook ['tʃɛkbuk] *n* Scheckbuch *nt*.

cheque card (*BRIT*) *n* Scheckkarte *f*.

chequered, (*US*) **checkered** ['tʃɛkəd] *adj* (*fig*) bewegt.

cherish ['tʃɛrɪʃ] *vt* (*person*) liebevoll sorgen für; (*memory*) in Ehren halten; (*dream*) sich hingeben +*dat*; (*hope*) hegen.

cheroot [ʃə'ruːt] *n* Stumpen *m*.

cherry ['tʃɛrɪ] *n* Kirsche *f*; (*also*: ~ **tree**) Kirschbaum *m*.

chervil ['tʃəːvɪl] *n* Kerbel *m*.

Ches. (*BRIT*) *abbr* (*POST*: = *Cheshire*).

chess [tʃɛs] *n* Schach(spiel) *nt*.

chessboard ['tʃɛsbɔːd] *n* Schachbrett *nt*.

chessman ['tʃɛsmən] (*irreg: like* **man**) *n* Schachfigur *f*.

chess player *n* Schachspieler(in) *m(f)*.

chest [tʃɛst] *n* Brust *f*, Brustkorb *m*; (*box*) Kiste *f*, Truhe *f*; **to get sth off one's** ~ (*inf*) sich *dat* etw von der Seele reden.

chest measurement *n* Brustweite *f*, Brustumfang *m*.

chestnut ['tʃɛsnʌt] *n* Kastanie *f* ♦ *adj* kastanienbraun.

chest of drawers *n* Kommode *f*.

chesty ['tʃɛstɪ] *adj* (*cough*) tief sitzend.

chew [tʃuː] *vt* kauen.

chewing gum ['tʃuːɪŋ-] *n* Kaugummi *m*.

chic [ʃiːk] *adj* schick, elegant.

chick [tʃɪk] *n* Küken *nt*; (*inf*: *girl*) Mieze *f*.

chicken ['tʃɪkɪn] *n* Huhn *nt*; (*meat*) Hähnchen

nt; (*inf: coward*) Feigling *m*.
►**chicken out** (*inf*) *vi:* **to ~ out of doing sth** davor kneifen, etw zu tun.
chicken feed *n* ein paar Pfennige *pl*; (*as salary*) ein Hungerlohn *m*.
chickenpox ['tʃɪkɪnpɒks] *n* Windpocken *pl*.
chickpea ['tʃɪkpiː] *n* Kichererbse *f*.
chicory ['tʃɪkərɪ] *n* (*in coffee*) Zichorie *f*; (*salad vegetable*) Chicorée *f or m*.
chide [tʃaɪd] *vt:* **to ~ sb (for)** jdn schelten (wegen).
chief [tʃiːf] *n* Häuptling *m*; (*of organization, department*) Leiter(in) *m(f)*, Chef(in) *m(f)* ♦ *adj* Haupt-, wichtigste(r, s).
chief constable (*BRIT*) *n* Polizeipräsident *m*, Polizeichef *m*.
chief executive, (*US*) **chief executive officer** *n* Generaldirektor(in) *m(f)*.
chiefly ['tʃiːflɪ] *adv* hauptsächlich.
Chief of Staff *n* Stabschef *m*.
chiffon ['ʃɪfɔn] *n* Chiffon *m*.
chilblain ['tʃɪlbleɪn] *n* Frostbeule *f*.
child [tʃaɪld] (*pl* ~**ren**) *n* Kind *nt*; **do you have any ~ren?** haben Sie Kinder?
child benefit (*BRIT*) *n* Kindergeld *nt*.
childbirth ['tʃaɪldbɜːθ] *n* Geburt *f*, Entbindung *f*.
childhood ['tʃaɪldhud] *n* Kindheit *f*.
childish ['tʃaɪldɪʃ] *adj* kindisch.
childless ['tʃaɪldlɪs] *adj* kinderlos.
childlike ['tʃaɪldlaɪk] *adj* kindlich.
child minder (*BRIT*) *n* Tagesmutter *f*.
child prodigy *n* Wunderkind *nt*.
children ['tʃɪldrən] *npl of* **child**.
children's home ['tʃɪldrənz-] *n* Kinderheim *nt*.
child's play ['tʃaɪldz-] *n:* **it was ~** es war ein Kinderspiel.
Chile ['tʃɪlɪ] *n* Chile *nt*.
Chilean ['tʃɪlɪən] *adj* chilenisch ♦ *n* Chilene *m*, Chilenin *f*.
chill [tʃɪl] *n* Kühle *f*; (*illness*) Erkältung *f* ♦ *adj* kühl; (*fig: reminder*) erschreckend ♦ *vt* kühlen; (*person*) frösteln *or* frieren lassen; **"serve ~ed"** „gekühlt servieren".
chilli, (*US*) **chili** ['tʃɪlɪ] *n* Peperoni *pl*.
chilling ['tʃɪlɪŋ] *adj* (*wind, morning*) eisig; (*fig: effect, prospect etc*) beängstigend.
chill out (*inf*) *vi* sich entspannen, relaxen.
chilly ['tʃɪlɪ] *adj* kühl; (*person, response, look*) kühl, frostig; **to feel ~** frösteln, frieren.
chime [tʃaɪm] *n* Glockenspiel *nt* ♦ *vi* läuten.
chimney ['tʃɪmnɪ] *n* Schornstein *m*.
chimney sweep *n* Schornsteinfeger(in) *m(f)*.
chimpanzee [tʃɪmpæn'ziː] *n* Schimpanse *m*.
chin [tʃɪn] *n* Kinn *nt*.
China ['tʃaɪnə] *n* China *nt*.
china ['tʃaɪnə] *n* Porzellan *nt*.
Chinese [tʃaɪ'niːz] *adj* chinesisch ♦ *n inv* Chinese *m*, Chinesin *f*; (*LING*) Chinesisch *nt*.
chink [tʃɪŋk] *n* (*in door, wall etc*) Ritze *f*, Spalt *m*; (*of bottles etc*) Klirren *nt*.

chintz [tʃɪnts] *n* Chintz *m*.
chinwag ['tʃɪnwæg] (*BRIT: inf*) *n* Schwatz *m*.
chip [tʃɪp] *n* (*gen pl*) Pommes frites *pl*; (*US: also:* **potato ~**) Chip *m*; (*of wood*) Span *m*; (*of glass, stone*) Splitter *m*; (*in glass, cup etc*) abgestoßene Stelle *f*; (*in gambling*) Chip *m*, Spielmarke *f*; (*COMPUT: also:* **microchip**) Chip *m* ♦ *vt* (*cup, plate*) anschlagen; **when the ~s are down** (*fig*) wenn es drauf ankommt.
►**chip in** (*inf*) *vi* (*contribute*) etwas beisteuern; (*interrupt*) sich einschalten.
chipboard ['tʃɪpbɔːd] *n* Spanplatte *f*.
chipmunk ['tʃɪpmʌŋk] *n* Backenhörnchen *nt*.
chippings ['tʃɪpɪŋz] *npl:* **loose ~** (*on road*) Schotter *m*.

Chip shop, auch fish-and-chip shop, ist die traditionelle britische Imbißbude, in der vor allem fritierte Fischfilets und Pommes frites, aber auch andere einfache Mahlzeiten angeboten werden. Früher wurde das Essen zum Mitnehmen in Zeitungspapier verpackt. Manche chip shops haben auch einen Eßraum.

---

chiropodist [kɪ'rɒpədɪst] (*BRIT*) *n* Fußpfleger(in) *m(f)*.
chiropody [kɪ'rɒpədɪ] (*BRIT*) *n* Fußpflege *f*.
chirp [tʃɜːp] *vi* (*bird*) zwitschern; (*crickets*) zirpen.
chirpy ['tʃɜːpɪ] (*inf*) *adj* munter.
chisel ['tʃɪzl] *n* (*for stone*) Meißel *m*; (*for wood*) Beitel *m*.
chit [tʃɪt] *n* Zettel *m*.
chitchat ['tʃɪttʃæt] *n* Plauderei *f*.
chivalrous ['ʃɪvəlrəs] *adj* ritterlich.
chivalry ['ʃɪvəlrɪ] *n* Ritterlichkeit *f*.
chives [tʃaɪvz] *npl* Schnittlauch *m*.
chloride ['klɔːraɪd] *n* Chlorid *nt*.
chlorinate ['klɔrɪneɪt] *vt* chloren.
chlorine ['klɔːriːn] *n* Chlor *nt*.
chock [tʃɒk] *n* Bremskeil *m*, Bremsklotz *m*.
chock-a-block ['tʃɒkə'blɒk] *adj* gerammelt voll.
chock-full [tʃɒk'ful] *adj* = **chock-a-block**.
chocolate ['tʃɒklɪt] *n* Schokolade *f*; (*drink*) Kakao *m*, Schokolade *f*; (*sweet*) Praline *f* ♦ *cpd* Schokoladen-.
choice [tʃɔɪs] *n* Auswahl *f*; (*option*) Möglichkeit *f*; (*preference*) Wahl *f* ♦ *adj* Qualitäts-, erstklassig; **I did it by** *or* **from ~** ich habe es mir so ausgesucht; **a wide ~** eine große Auswahl.
choir ['kwaɪə] *n* Chor *m*.
choirboy ['kwaɪə'bɔɪ] *n* Chorknabe *m*.
choke [tʃəuk] *vi* ersticken; (*with smoke, dust, anger etc*) keine Luft mehr bekommen ♦ *vt* erwürgen, erdrosseln ♦ *n* (*AUT*) Choke *m*, Starterklappe *f*; **to be ~d (with)** verstopft sein (mit).
cholera ['kɒlərə] *n* Cholera *f*.
cholesterol [kə'lestərɒl] *n* Cholesterin *nt*.
choose [tʃuːz] (*pt* **chose,** *pp* **chosen**) *vt*

(aus)wählen; (_profession, friend_) sich _dat_
aussuchen ♦ _vi:_ **to ~ between** wählen
zwischen +_dat_, eine Wahl treffen zwischen
+_dat_; **to ~ from** wählen aus _or_ unter +_dat_,
eine Wahl treffen aus _or_ unter +_dat_; **to ~ to
do sth** beschließen, etw zu tun.
choosy ['tʃuːzɪ] _adj_ wählerisch.
chop [tʃɔp] _vt_ (_wood_) hacken; (_also:_ ~ **up:**
vegetables, fruit, meat) kleinschneiden ♦ _n_
Kotelett _nt_; **chops** (_inf_) _npl_ (_of animal_) Maul
_nt_; (_of person_) Mund _m_; **to get the ~** (_BRIT: inf:
project_) dem Rotstift zum Opfer fallen; (: :
be sacked) rausgeschmissen werden.
▶**chop down** _vt_ (_tree_) fällen.
chopper ['tʃɔpə·] (_inf_) _n_ Hubschrauber _m_.
choppy ['tʃɔpɪ] _adj_ (_sea_) kabbelig, bewegt.
chopsticks ['tʃɔpstɪks] _npl_ Stäbchen _pl_.
choral ['kɔːrəl] _adj_ (_singing_) Chor-; (_society_)
Gesang-.
chord [kɔːd] _n_ Akkord _m_; (_MATH_) Sehne _f_.
chore [tʃɔː·] _n_ Hausarbeit _f_; (_routine task_)
lästige Routinearbeit _f_; **household ~s**
Hausarbeit.
choreographer [kɔrɪ'ɔgrəfə·] _n_
Choreograph(in) _m(f)_.
choreography [kɔrɪ'ɔgrəfɪ] _n_ Choreographie
_f_.
chorister ['kɔrɪstə·] _n_ Chorsänger(in) _m(f)_.
chortle ['tʃɔːtl] _vi_ glucksen.
chorus ['kɔːrəs] _n_ Chor _m_; (_refrain_) Refrain _m_;
(_of complaints_) Flut _f_.
chose [tʃəuz] _pt of_ **choose.**
chosen ['tʃəuzn] _pp of_ **choose.**
chow [tʃau] _n_ Chow-Chow _m_.
chowder ['tʃaudə·] _n_ (sämige) Fischsuppe _f_.
Christ [kraɪst] _n_ Christus _m_.
christen ['krɪsn] _vt_ taufen.
christening ['krɪsnɪŋ] _n_ Taufe _f_.
Christian ['krɪstɪən] _adj_ christlich ♦ _n_
Christ(in) _m(f)_.
Christianity [krɪstɪ'ænɪtɪ] _n_ Christentum _nt_.
Christian name _n_ Vorname _m_.
Christmas ['krɪsməs] _n_ Weihnachten _nt_;
Happy _or_ Merry ~! frohe _or_ fröhliche
Weihnachten!
Christmas card _n_ Weihnachtskarte _f_.
Christmas Day _n_ der erste Weihnachtstag.
Christmas Eve _n_ Heiligabend _m_.
Christmas Island _n_ Weihnachtsinsel _f_.
Christmas tree _n_ Weihnachtsbaum _m_,
Christbaum _m_.
chrome [krəum] _n_ = **chromium.**
chromium ['krəumɪəm] _n_ Chrom _nt_; (_also:_
~ **plating**) Verchromung _f_.
chromosome ['krəuməsəum] _n_ Chromosom
_nt_.
chronic ['krɔnɪk] _adj_ (_also fig_) chronisch;
(_severe_) schlimm.
chronicle ['krɔnɪkl] _n_ Chronik _f_.
chronological [krɔnə'lɔdʒɪkl] _adj_
chronologisch.
chrysanthemum [krɪ'sænθəməm] _n_

Chrysantheme _f_.
chubby ['tʃʌbɪ] _adj_ pummelig; ~ **cheeks**
Pausbacken _pl_.
chuck [tʃʌk] (_inf_) _vt_ werfen, schmeißen; (_BRIT:
also:_ ~ **up,** ~ **in**) (_job_) hinschmeißen;
(: _person_) Schluß machen mit.
▶**chuck out** _vt_ (_person_) rausschmeißen;
(_rubbish etc_) wegschmeißen.
chuckle ['tʃʌkl] _vi_ leise in sich _acc_
hineinlachen.
chuffed [tʃʌft] (_BRIT: inf_) _adj_ vergnügt und
zufrieden; (_flattered_) gebauchpinselt.
chug [tʃʌg] _vi_ (_also:_ ~ **along**) tuckern.
chum [tʃʌm] _n_ Kumpel _m_.
chump [tʃʌmp] (_inf_) _n_ Trottel _m_.
chunk [tʃʌŋk] _n_ großes Stück _nt_.
chunky ['tʃʌŋkɪ] _adj_ (_furniture etc_) klobig;
(_person_) stämmig, untersetzt; (_knitwear_)
dick.
church [tʃəːtʃ] _n_ Kirche _f_; **the C~ of England**
die Anglikanische Kirche.
churchyard ['tʃəːtʃjɑːd] _n_ Friedhof _m_.
churlish ['tʃəːlɪʃ] _adj_ griesgrämig; (_behaviour_)
ungehobelt.
churn [tʃəːn] _n_ Butterfaß _nt_; (_also:_ **milk** ~)
Milchkanne _f_.
▶**churn out** _vt_ am laufenden Band
produzieren.
chute [ʃuːt] _n_ (_also:_ **rubbish** ~) Müllschlucker
_m_; (_for coal, parcels etc_) Rutsche _f_; (_BRIT: slide_)
Rutschbahn _f_, Rutsche _f_.
chutney ['tʃʌtnɪ] _n_ Chutney _nt_.
CIA (_US_) _n abbr_ (= _Central Intelligence Agency_)
CIA _f or m_.
cicada [sɪ'kɑːdə] _n_ Zikade _f_.
CID (_BRIT_) _n abbr_ = **Criminal Investigation
Department.**
cider ['saɪdə·] _n_ Apfelwein _m_.
c.i.f. _abbr_ (_COMM_: = _cost, insurance and freight_)
cif.
cigar [sɪ'gɑː·] _n_ Zigarre _f_.
cigarette [sɪgə'ret] _n_ Zigarette _f_.
cigarette case _n_ Zigarettenetui _nt_.
cigarette end _n_ Zigarettenstummel _m_.
cigarette holder _n_ Zigarettenspitze _f_.
C in C _abbr_ (_MIL_) = **commander in chief.**
cinch [sɪntʃ] (_inf_) _n:_ **it's a ~** das ist ein
Kinderspiel _or_ ein Klacks.
Cinderella [sɪndə'relə] _n_ Aschenputtel _nt_,
Aschenbrödel _nt_.
cinders ['sɪndəz] _npl_ Asche _f_.
cine camera ['sɪnɪ-] (_BRIT_) _n_
(Schmal)filmkamera _f_.
cine film (_BRIT_) _n_ Schmalfilm _m_.
cinema ['sɪnəmə] _n_ Kino _nt_; (_film-making_) Film
_m_.
cine projector (_BRIT_) _n_ Filmprojektor _m_.
cinnamon ['sɪnəmən] _n_ Zimt _m_.
cipher ['saɪfə·] _n_ (_code_) Chiffre _f_; (_fig_)
Niemand _m_; **in ~** chiffriert.
circa ['səːkə] _prep_ zirka, circa.
circle ['səːkl] _n_ Kreis _m_; (_in cinema, theatre_)

Rang *m* ♦ *vi* kreisen ♦ *vt* kreisen um;
(*surround*) umgeben.
circuit ['sɜːkɪt] *n* Runde *f*; (*ELEC*) Stromkreis
m; (*track*) Rennbahn *f*.
circuit board *n* (*COMPUT, ELEC*) Platine *f*,
Leiterplatte *f*.
circuitous [sɜː'kjuɪtəs] *adj* umständlich.
circular ['sɜːkjulə*] *adj* rund; (*route*) Rund- ♦ *n*
(*letter*) Rundschreiben *nt*, Rundbrief *m*; (*as
advertisement*) Wurfsendung *f*; ~ **argument**
Zirkelschluß *m*.
circulate ['sɜːkjuleɪt] *vi* (*traffic*) fließen; (*blood,
report*) zirkulieren; (*news, rumour*)
kursieren, in Umlauf sein; (*person*) die
Runde machen ♦ *vt* herumgehen *or*
zirkulieren lassen.
circulating capital [sɜːkju'leɪtɪŋ-] *n* (*COMM*)
flüssiges Kapital *nt*, Umlaufkapital *nt*.
circulation [sɜːkju'leɪʃən] *n* (*of traffic*) Fluß *m*;
(*of air etc*) Zirkulation *f*; (*of newspaper*)
Auflage *f*; (*MED: of blood*) Kreislauf *m*.
circumcise ['sɜːkəmsaɪz] *vt* beschneiden.
circumference [sə'kʌmfərəns] *n* Umfang *m*;
(*edge*) Rand *m*.
circumflex ['sɜːkəmfleks] *n* (*also:* ~ **accent**)
Zirkumflex *m*.
circumscribe ['sɜːkəmskraɪb] *vt* (*MATH*) einen
Kreis umbeschreiben; (*fig*) eingrenzen.
circumspect ['sɜːkəmspekt] *adj* umsichtig.
circumstances ['sɜːkəmstənsɪz] *npl* Umstände
pl; (*financial condition*) (finanzielle)
Verhältnisse *pl*; **in the** ~ unter diesen
Umständen; **under no** ~ unter (gar) keinen
Umständen, auf keinen Fall.
circumstantial [sɜːkəm'stænʃl] *adj*
ausführlich; ~ **evidence** Inizienbeweis *m*.
circumvent [sɜːkəm'vɛnt] *vt* umgehen.
circus ['sɜːkəs] *n* Zirkus *m*; (*also:* **C~**: *in place
names*) Platz *m*.
cirrhosis [sɪ'rəʊsɪs] *n* (*also:* ~ **of the liver**)
Leberzirrhose *f*.
CIS *n abbr* (= *Commonwealth of Independent
States*) GUS *f*.
cissy ['sɪsɪ] *n, adj see* **sissy**.
cistern ['sɪstən] *n* Zisterne *f*; (*of toilet*)
Spülkasten *m*.
citation [saɪ'teɪʃən] *n* Zitat *nt*; (*US*)
Belobigung *f*; (*LAW*) Vorladung *f* (vor
Gericht).
cite [saɪt] *vt* zitieren; (*example*) anführen;
(*LAW*) vorladen.
citizen ['sɪtɪzn] *n* Staatsbürger(in) *m(f)*; (*of
town*) Bürger(in) *m(f)*.
Citizens' Advice Bureau ['sɪtɪznz-] *n*
≈ Bürgerberatungsstelle *f*.
citizenship ['sɪtɪznʃɪp] *n* Staatsbürgerschaft *f*.
citric acid ['sɪtrɪk-] *n* Zitronensäure *f*.
citrus fruit ['sɪtrəs-] *n* Zitrusfrucht *f*.
city ['sɪtɪ] *n* (Groß)stadt *f*; **the C~** (*FIN*) die
City, das Londoner Banken- und
Börsenviertel.
city centre *n* Stadtzentrum *nt*, Innenstadt *f*.

City Hall *n* Rathaus *nt*; (*US: municipal
government*) Stadtverwaltung *f*.
civic ['sɪvɪk] *adj* (*authorities etc*) Stadt-,
städtisch; (*duties, pride*) Bürger-,
bürgerlich.
civic centre (*BRIT*) *n* Stadtverwaltung *f*.
civil ['sɪvɪl] *adj* (*disturbances, rights*) Bürger-;
(*liberties, law*) bürgerlich; (*polite*) höflich.
Civil Aviation Authority (*BRIT*) *n* Behörde *f*
für Zivilluftfahrt.
civil defence *n* Zivilschutz *m*.
civil disobedience *n* ziviler Ungehorsam *m*.
civil engineer *n* Bauingenieur(in) *m(f)*.
civil engineering *n* Hoch- und Tiefbau *m*.
civilian [sɪ'vɪlɪən] *adj* (*population*) Zivil- ♦ *n*
Zivilist *m*; ~ **casualties** Verluste *pl* unter der
Zivilbevölkerung.
civilization [sɪvɪlaɪ'zeɪʃən] *n* Zivilisation *f*; (*a
society*) Kultur *f*.
civilized ['sɪvɪlaɪzd] *adj* zivilisiert; (*person*)
kultiviert; (*place, experience*) gepflegt.
civil law *n* Zivilrecht *nt*, bürgerliches Recht
nt.
civil liberties *n* (bürgerliche)
Freiheitsrechte *pl*.
civil rights *npl* Bürgerrechte *pl*.
civil servant *n* (Staats)beamter *m*,
(Staats)beamtin *f*.
Civil Service *n* Beamtenschaft *f*.
civil war *n* Bürgerkrieg *m*.
civvies ['sɪvɪz] (*inf*) *npl* Zivilklamotten *pl*.
cl *abbr* (= *centilitre*) cl.
clad [klæd] *adj*: ~ (**in**) gekleidet (in *+acc*).
claim [kleɪm] *vt* (*assert*) behaupten;
(*responsibility*) übernehmen; (*credit*) in
Anspruch nehmen; (*rights, inheritance*)
Anspruch erheben auf *+acc*; (*expenses*) sich
dat zurückerstatten lassen; (*compensation,
damages*) verlangen ♦ *vi* (*for insurance*)
Ansprüche geltend machen ♦ *n* (*assertion*)
Behauptung *f*; (*for pension, wage rise,
compensation*) Forderung *f*; (*right: to
inheritance, land*) Anspruch *m*; (*for expenses*)
Spesenabrechnung *f*; (**insurance**) ~
(Versicherungs)anspruch *m*; **to put in a**
~ **for** beantragen.
claimant ['kleɪmənt] *n* Antragsteller(in) *m(f)*.
claim form *n* Antragsformular *nt*.
clairvoyant [kleə'vɔɪənt] *n* Hellseher(in) *m(f)*.
clam [klæm] *n* Venusmuschel *f*.
►**clam up** (*inf*) *vi* keinen Piep (mehr) sagen.
clamber ['klæmbə*] *vi* klettern.
clammy ['klæmɪ] *adj* feucht.
clamour, (*US*) **clamor** ['klæmə*] *n* Lärm *m*;
(*protest*) Protest *m*, Aufschrei *m* ♦ *vi*: **to** ~ **for**
schreien nach.
clamp [klæmp] *n* Schraubzwinge *f*, Klemme *f*
♦ *vt* (*two things together*) zusammen-
klemmen; (*one thing on another*) klemmen;
(*wheel*) krallen.
►**clamp down on** *vt fus* rigoros vorgehen
gegen.

clampdown ['klæmpdaun] *n:* ~ **(on)** hartes Durchgreifen *nt* (gegen).

clan [klæn] *n* Clan *m.*

clandestine [klæn'dɛstɪn] *adj* geheim, Geheim-.

clang [klæŋ] *vi* klappern; (*bell*) läuten ♦ *n* (*see vi*) Klappern *nt;* Läuten *nt.*

clanger ['klæŋə'] (*BRIT: inf*) *n* Fauxpas *m;* **to drop a** ~ ins Fettnäpfchen treten.

clansman ['klænzmən] *n* (*irreg: like* **man**) Clanmitglied *nt.*

clap [klæp] *vi* (Beifall) klatschen ♦ *vt:* **to** ~ **(one's hands)** (in die Hände) klatschen ♦ *n:* **a** ~ **of thunder** ein Donnerschlag *m.*

clapping ['klæpɪŋ] *n* Beifall *m.*

claptrap ['klæptræp] (*inf*) *n* Geschwafel *nt.*

claret ['klærət] *n* roter Bordeaux(wein) *m.*

clarification [klærɪfɪ'keɪʃən] *n* Klärung *f.*

clarify ['klærɪfaɪ] *vt* klären.

clarinet [klærɪ'nɛt] *n* Klarinette *f.*

clarity ['klærɪtɪ] *n* Klarheit *f.*

clash [klæʃ] *n* (*fight*) Zusammenstoß *m;* (*disagreement*) Streit *m,* Auseinandersetzung *f;* (*of beliefs, ideas, views*) Konflikt *m;* (*of colours, styles, personalities*) Unverträglichkeit *f;* (*of events, dates, appointments*) Überschneidung *f;* (*noise*) Klirren *nt* ♦ *vi* (*fight*) zusammenstoßen; (*disagree*) sich streiten, eine Auseinandersetzung haben; (*beliefs, ideas, views*) aufeinanderprallen; (*colours*) sich beißen; (*styles, personalities*) nicht zusammenpassen; (*two events, dates, appointments*) sich überschneiden; (*make noise*) klirrend aneinanderschlagen.

clasp [klɑːsp] *n* Griff *m;* (*embrace*) Umklammerung *f;* (*of necklace, bag*) Verschluß *m* ♦ *vt* (er)greifen; (*embrace*) umklammern.

class [klɑːs] *n* Klasse *f;* (*lesson*) (Unterrichts)stunde *f* ♦ *adj* (*struggle, distinction*) Klassen- ♦ *vt* einordnen, einstufen.

class-conscious ['klɑːs'kɔnʃəs] *adj* klassenbewußt, standesbewußt.

class-consciousness ['klɑːs'kɔnʃəsnɪs] *n* Klassenbewußtsein *nt,* Standesbewußtsein *nt.*

classic ['klæsɪk] *adj* klassisch ♦ *n* Klassiker *m;* (*race*) *bedeutendes Pferderennen für dreijährige Pferde;* **classics** *npl* (*SCOL*) Altphilologie *f.*

classical ['klæsɪkl] *adj* klassisch.

classification [klæsɪfɪ'keɪʃən] *n* Klassifikation *f;* (*category*) Klasse *f;* (*system*) Einteilung *f.*

classified ['klæsɪfaɪd] *adj* geheim.

classified advertisement *n* Kleinanzeige *f.*

classify ['klæsɪfaɪ] *vt* klassifizieren, (ein)ordnen.

classless ['klɑːslɪs] *adj:* ~ **society** klassenlose Gesellschaft *f.*

classmate ['klɑːsmeɪt] *n* Klassenkamerad(in) *m(f).*

classroom ['klɑːsrum] *n* Klassenzimmer *nt.*

classy ['klɑːsɪ] (*inf*) *adj* nobel, exklusiv; (*person*) todschick.

clatter ['klætə'] *n* Klappern *nt;* (*of hooves*) Trappeln *nt* ♦ *vi* (*see n*) klappern; trappeln.

clause [klɔːz] *n* (*LAW*) Klausel *f;* (*LING*) Satz *m.*

claustrophobia [klɔːstrə'fəubɪə] *n* Klaustrophobie *f,* Platzangst *f.*

claustrophobic [klɔːstrə'fəubɪk] *adj* (*place, situation*) beengend; (*person*): **to be/feel** ~ Platzangst haben/bekommen.

claw [klɔː] *n* Kralle *f;* (*of lobster*) Schere *f,* Zange *f.*

► **claw at** *vt fus* sich krallen an +*acc.*

clay [kleɪ] *n* Ton *m;* (*soil*) Lehm *m.*

clean [kliːn] *adj* sauber; (*fight*) fair; (*record, reputation*) einwandfrei; (*joke, story*) stubenrein, anständig; (*edge, MED: fracture*) glatt ♦ *vt* saubermachen; (*car, hands, face etc*) waschen ♦ *adv:* **he** ~ **forgot** er hat es glatt(weg) vergessen; **to have a** ~ **driving licence** *or* (*US*) **record** keine Strafpunkte haben; **to** ~ **one's teeth** (*BRIT*) sich *dat* die Zähne putzen; **the thief got** ~ **away** der Dieb konnte entkommen; **to come** ~ (*inf*) auspacken.

► **clean off** *vt* abwaschen, abwischen.

► **clean out** *vt* gründlich saubermachen; (*inf: person*) ausnehmen.

► **clean up** *vt* aufräumen; (*child*) saubermachen; (*fig*) für Ordnung sorgen in +*dat* ♦ *vi* aufräumen, saubermachen; (*inf: make profit*) absahnen.

clean-cut ['kliːn'kʌt] *adj* gepflegt; (*situation*) klar.

cleaner ['kliːnə'] *n* Raumpfleger(in) *m(f);* (*woman*) Putzfrau *f;* (*substance*) Reinigungsmittel *nt,* Putzmittel *nt.*

cleaner's ['kliːnəz] *n* (*also:* **dry** ~) Reinigung *f.*

cleaning ['kliːnɪŋ] *n* Putzen *nt.*

cleaning lady *n* Putzfrau *f,* Reinemachefrau *f.*

cleanliness ['klɛnlɪnɪs] *n* Sauberkeit *f,* Reinlichkeit *f.*

cleanly ['kliːnlɪ] *adv* sauber.

cleanse [klɛnz] *vt* (*purify*) läutern; (*face, cut*) reinigen.

cleanser ['klɛnzə'] *n* (*for face*) Reinigungscreme *f,* Reinigungsmilch *f.*

clean-shaven ['kliːn'ʃeɪvn] *adj* glattrasiert.

cleansing department ['klɛnzɪŋ-] (*BRIT*) *n* ~ Stadtreinigung *f.*

clean sweep *n:* **to make a** ~ (*SPORT*) alle Preise einstecken.

clean-up ['kliːnʌp] *n:* **to give sth a** ~ etw gründlich saubermachen.

clear [klɪə'] *adj* klar; (*footprint*) deutlich; (*photograph*) scharf; (*commitment*) eindeutig; (*glass, plastic*) durchsichtig; (*road, way, floor etc*) frei; (*conscience, skin*) rein ♦ *vt* (*room*) ausräumen; (*trees*) abholzen; (*weeds*) *etc*) entfernen; (*slums etc, stock*) räumen; (*LAW*) freisprechen; (*fence, wall*) überspringen; (*cheque*) verrechnen ♦ *vi* (*weather, sky*) aufklaren; (*fog, smoke*) sich auflösen; (*room etc*) sich leeren ♦ *adv:* **to be ~ of the ground** den Boden nicht berühren ♦ *n:* **to be in the ~** (*out of debt*) schuldenfrei sein; (*free of suspicion*) von jedem Verdacht frei sein; (*out of danger*) außer Gefahr sein; **~ profit** Reingewinn *m;* **I have a ~ day tomorrow** (*BRIT*) ich habe morgen nichts vor; **to make o.s. ~** sich klar ausdrücken; **to make it ~ to sb that ...** es jdm (unmißverständlich) klarmachen, daß ...; **to ~ the table** den Tisch abräumen; **to ~ a space (for sth)** (für etw) Platz schaffen; **to ~ one's throat** sich räuspern; **to ~ a profit** einen Gewinn machen; **to keep ~ of sb** jdm aus dem Weg gehen; **to keep ~ of sth** etw meiden; **to keep ~ of trouble** allem Ärger aus dem Weg gehen.

►**clear off** (*inf*) *vi* abhauen, verschwinden.

►**clear up** *vt* aufräumen; (*mystery*) aufklären; (*problem*) lösen ♦ *vi* (*bad weather*) sich aufklären; (*illness*) sich bessern.

clearance ['klɪərəns] *n* (*of slums*) Räumung *f;* (*of trees*) Abholzung *f;* (*permission*) Genehmigung *f;* (*free space*) lichte Höhe *f.*

clearance sale *n* Räumungsverkauf *m.*

clear-cut ['klɪə'kʌt] *adj* klar.

clearing ['klɪərɪŋ] *n* Lichtung *f;* (*BRIT: BANKING*) Clearing *nt.*

clearing bank (*BRIT*) *n* Clearingbank *f.*

clearing house *n* (*COMM*) Clearingstelle *f.*

clearly ['klɪəlɪ] *adv* klar; (*obviously*) eindeutig.

clearway ['klɪəweɪ] (*BRIT*) *n* Straße *f* mit Halteverbot.

cleavage ['kliːvɪdʒ] *n* (*of woman's breasts*) Dekolleté *nt.*

cleaver ['kliːvə'] *n* Hackbeil *nt.*

clef [klef] *n* (Noten)schlüssel *m.*

cleft [kleft] *n* Spalte *f.*

cleft palate *n* (*MED*) Gaumenspalte *f.*

clemency ['klemənsɪ] *n* Milde *f.*

clement ['klemənt] *adj* mild.

clench [klentʃ] *vt* (*fist*) ballen; (*teeth*) zusammenbeißen.

clergy ['klɜːdʒɪ] *n* Klerus *m,* Geistlichkeit *f.*

clergyman ['klɜːdʒɪmən] (*irreg: like* **man**) *n* Geistliche(r) *m.*

clerical ['klerɪkl] *adj* (*job, worker*) Büro-; (*error*) Schreib-; (*REL*) geistlich.

clerk [klɑːk, (*US*) klɜːrk] *n* (*BRIT*) Büroangestellte(r) *f(m);* (*US: sales person*) Verkäufer(in) *m(f).*

Clerk of Court *n* Protokollführer(in) *m(f).*

clever ['klevə'] *adj* klug; (*deft, crafty*) schlau, clever (*inf*); (*device, arrangement*) raffiniert.

cleverly ['klevəlɪ] *adv* geschickt.

clew [kluː] (*US*) *n* = **clue**.

cliché ['kliːʃeɪ] *n* Klischee *nt.*

click [klɪk] *vi* klicken ♦ *vt:* **to ~ one's tongue**

mit der Zunge schnalzen; **to ~ one's heels** die Hacken zusammenschlagen.

client ['klaɪənt] *n* Kunde *m,* Kundin *f;* (*of bank, lawyer*) Klient(in) *m(f);* (*of restaurant*) Gast *m.*

clientele [kliːɑːn'tel] *n* Kundschaft *f.*

cliff [klɪf] *n* Kliff *nt.*

cliffhanger ['klɪfhæŋə'] *n* spannungsgeladene Szene am Ende einer Filmepisode, Cliffhanger *m.*

climactic [klaɪ'mæktɪk] *adj:* **~ point** Höhepunkt *m.*

climate ['klaɪmɪt] *n* Klima *nt.*

climax ['klaɪmæks] *n* (*also: sexual*) Höhepunkt *m.*

climb [klaɪm] *vi* klettern; (*plane, sun, prices, shares*) steigen ♦ *vt* (*stairs, ladder*) hochsteigen, hinaufsteigen; (*tree*) klettern auf +*acc;* (*hill*) steigen auf +*acc* ♦ *n* Aufstieg *m;* (*of prices etc*) Anstieg *m;* **to ~ over a wall/into a car** über eine Mauer/in ein Auto steigen *or* klettern.

►**climb down** (*BRIT*) *vi* (*fig*) nachgeben.

climb-down ['klaɪmdaun] *n* Nachgeben *nt,* Rückzieher *m* (*inf*).

climber ['klaɪmə'] *n* Bergsteiger(in) *m(f);* (*plant*) Kletterpflanze *f.*

climbing ['klaɪmɪŋ] *n* Bergsteigen *nt.*

clinch [klɪntʃ] *vt* (*deal*) perfekt machen; (*argument*) zum Abschluß bringen.

clincher ['klɪntʃə'] *n* ausschlaggebender Faktor *m.*

cling [klɪŋ] (*pt, pp* **clung**) *vi:* **to ~ to** (*mother, support*) sich festklammern an +*dat;* (*idea, belief*) festhalten an +*dat;* (*subj: clothes, dress*) sich anschmiegen +*dat.*

clingfilm ['klɪŋfɪlm] *n* Frischhaltefolie *f.*

clinic ['klɪnɪk] *n* Klinik *f;* (*session*) Sprechstunde *f;* (*: SPORT*) Trainingstunde *f.*

clinical ['klɪnɪkl] *adj* klinisch; (*fig*) nüchtern, kühl; (*: building, room*) steril.

clink [klɪŋk] *vi* klirren.

clip [klɪp] *n* (*also:* **paper ~**) Büroklammer *f;* (*BRIT: also:* **bulldog ~**) Klammer *f;* (*holding wire, hose etc*) Klemme *f;* (*for hair*) Spange *f;* (*TV, CINE*) Ausschnitt *m* ♦ *vt* festklemmen; (*also:* **~ together**) zusammenheften; (*cut*) schneiden.

clippers ['klɪpəz] *npl* (*for gardening*) Schere *f;* (*also:* **nail ~**) Nagelzange *f.*

clipping ['klɪpɪŋ] *n* (*from newspaper*) Ausschnitt *m.*

clique [kliːk] *n* Clique *f,* Gruppe *f.*

clitoris ['klɪtərɪs] *n* Klitoris *f.*

cloak [kləuk] *n* Umhang *m* ♦ *vt* (*fig*) hüllen.

cloakroom ['kləukrum] *n* Garderobe *f;* (*BRIT: WC*) Toilette *f.*

clobber ['klɒbə'] (*inf*) *n* Klamotten *pl* ♦ *vt* (*hit*) hauen, schlagen; (*defeat*) in die Pfanne hauen.

clock [klɒk] *n* Uhr *f;* **round the ~** rund um die Uhr; **30,000 on the ~** (*BRIT: AUT*) ein Tachostand von 30.000; **to work against the**

~ gegen die Uhr arbeiten.

►**clock in** (BRIT) vi (den Arbeitsbeginn) stempeln or stechen.

►**clock off** (BRIT) vi (das Arbeitsende) stempeln or stechen.

►**clock on** (BRIT) vi = **clock in.**

►**clock out** (BRIT) vi = **clock off.**

►**clock up** vt (miles) fahren; (hours) arbeiten.

clockwise ['klɔkwaɪz] adv im Uhrzeigersinn.

clockwork ['klɔkwəːk] n Uhrwerk nt ♦ adj aufziehbar, zum Aufziehen; **like** ~ wie am Schnürchen.

clog [klɔg] n Clog m; (wooden) Holzschuh m ♦ vt verstopfen ♦ vi (also: ~ **up**) verstopfen.

cloister ['klɔɪstə'] n Kreuzgang m.

clone [kləun] n Klon m.

close¹ [kləus] adj (writing, friend, contact) eng; (texture) dicht, fest; (relative) nahe; (examination) genau, gründlich; (watch) streng, scharf; (contest) knapp; (weather) schwül; (room) stickig ♦ adv nahe; ~ **(to)** nahe (+gen); ~ **to** in der Nähe +gen; ~ **by,** ~ **at hand** in der Nähe; **how** ~ **is Edinburgh to Glasgow?** wie weit ist Edinburgh von Glasgow entfernt?; **a** ~ **friend** ein guter or enger Freund; **to have a** ~ **shave** (fig) gerade noch davonkommen; **at** ~ **quarters** aus der Nähe.

close² [kləuz] vt schließen, zumachen; (sale, deal, case) abschließen; (speech) schließen, beenden ♦ vi schließen, zumachen; (door, lid) sich schließen, zugehen; (end) aufhören ♦ n Ende nt, Schluß m; **to bring sth to a** ~ etw beenden.

►**close down** vi (factory) stillgelegt werden; (magazine etc) eingestellt werden.

►**close in** vi (night) hereinbrechen; (fog) sich verdichten; **to** ~ **in on sb/sth** jdm/etw auf den Leib rücken; **the days are closing in** die Tage werden kürzer.

►**close off** vt (area) abriegeln; (road) sperren.

closed [kləuzd] adj geschlossen; (road) gesperrt.

closed-circuit television n Fernseh-überwachungsanlage f.

closed shop n Betrieb m mit Gewerk-schaftszwang.

close-knit ['kləus'nɪt] adj eng zusammen-gewachsen.

closely ['kləuslɪ] adv (examine, watch) genau; (connected) eng; **we are** ~ **related** wir sind nah verwandt; **a** ~ **guarded secret** ein streng gehütetes Geheimnis.

close season ['kləus-] n Schonzeit f; (SPORT) Sommerpause f.

closet ['klɔzɪt] n Wandschrank m.

close-up ['kləusʌp] n Nahaufnahme f.

closing ['kləuzɪŋ] adj (stages) Schluß-; (remarks) abschließend.

closing price n (STOCK EXCHANGE) Schlußkurs m, Schlußnotierung f.

closing time (BRIT) n (in pub) Polizeistunde f,

Sperrstunde f.

closure ['kləuʒə'] n (of factory) Stillegung f; (of magazine) Einstellung f; (of road) Sperrung f; (of border) Schließung f.

clot [klɔt] n (blood clot) (Blut)gerinnsel nt; (inf: idiot) Trottel m ♦ vi gerinnen; (external bleeding) zum Stillstand kommen.

cloth [klɔθ] n (material) Stoff m, Tuch nt; (rag) Lappen m; (BRIT: also: **teacloth**) (Spül)tuch nt; (also: **tablecloth**) Tischtuch nt, Tischdecke f.

clothe [kləuð] vt anziehen, kleiden.

clothes [kləuðz] npl Kleidung f, Kleider pl; **to put one's** ~ **on** sich anziehen; **to take one's** ~ **off** sich ausziehen.

clothes brush n Kleiderbürste f.

clothesline ['kləuðzlaɪn] n Wäscheleine f.

clothes peg, (US) **clothes pin** n Wäscheklammer f.

clothing ['kləuðɪŋ] n = **clothes.**

clotted cream ['klɔtɪd-] (BRIT) n Sahne aus erhitzter Milch.

cloud [klaud] n Wolke f ♦ vt trüben; **every** ~ **has a silver lining** (proverb) auf Regen folgt Sonnenschein; **to** ~ **the issue** es unnötig kompliziert machen; (deliberately) die Angelegenheit verschleiern.

►**cloud over** vi (sky) sich bewölken, sich bedecken; (face, eyes) sich verfinstern.

cloudburst ['klaudbəːst] n Wolkenbruch m.

cloud-cuckoo-land [klaud'kuku:lænd] (BRIT) n Wolkenkuckucksheim nt.

cloudy ['klaudɪ] adj wolkig, bewölkt; (liquid) trüb.

clout [klaut] vt schlagen, hauen ♦ n (fig) Schlagkraft f.

clove [kləuv] n Gewürznelke f; ~ **of garlic** Knoblauchzehe f.

clover ['kləuvə'] n Klee m.

cloverleaf ['kləuvəli:f] n Kleeblatt nt.

clown [klaun] n Clown m ♦ vi (also: ~ **about,** ~ **around**) herumblödeln, herumkaspern.

cloying ['klɔɪɪŋ] adj süßlich.

club [klʌb] n Klub m, Verein m; (weapon) Keule f, Knüppel m; (also: **golf** ~: object) Golfschläger m ♦ vt knüppeln ♦ vi: **to** ~ **together** zusammenlegen; **clubs** npl (CARDS) Kreuz nt.

club car (US) n Speisewagen m.

club class n Club-Klasse f.

clubhouse ['klʌbhaus] n Klubhaus nt.

club soda (US) n (soda water) Sodawasser nt.

cluck [klʌk] vi glucken.

clue [klu:] n Hinweis m, Anhaltspunkt m; (in crossword) Frage f; **I haven't a** ~ ich habe keine Ahnung.

clued-up ['klu:dʌp], (US) **clued in** (inf) adj: **to be** ~ **on sth** über etw acc im Bilde sein.

clueless ['klu:lɪs] adj ahnungslos, unbedarft.

clump [klʌmp] n Gruppe f.

clumsy ['klʌmzɪ] adj ungeschickt; (object) unförmig; (effort, attempt) plump.

clung [klʌŋ] pt, pp of **cling.**

cluster ['klʌstə*] n Gruppe f ♦ vi (people) sich scharen; (houses) sich drängen.

clutch [klʌtʃ] n Griff m; (AUT) Kupplung f ♦ vt (purse, hand) umklammern; (stick) sich festklammern an +dat ♦ vi: **to ~ at** sich klammern an +acc.

clutter ['klʌtə*] vt (also: ~ **up**: room) vollstopfen; (: table) vollstellen ♦ n Kram m (inf).

CM (US) abbr (POST: = North Mariana Islands).

cm abbr (= centimetre) cm.

CNAA (BRIT) n abbr (= Council for National Academic Awards) Zentralstelle zur Vergabe von Qualifikationsnachweisen.

CND n abbr (= Campaign for Nuclear Disarmament) Organisation für atomare Abrüstung.

CO n abbr = **commanding officer**; (BRIT: = Commonwealth Office) Regierungsstelle für Angelegenheiten des Commonwealth ♦ abbr (US: POST: = Colorado).

Co. abbr = **company; county**.

c/o abbr (= care of) bei, c/o.

coach [kəutʃ] n (Reise)bus m; (horse-drawn) Kutsche f; (of train) Wagen m; (SPORT) Trainer m; (SCOL) Nachhilfelehrer(in) m(f) ♦ vt trainieren; (student) Nachhilfeunterricht geben +dat.

coach trip n Busfahrt f.

coagulate [kəu'ægjuleɪt] vi (blood) gerinnen; (paint etc) eindicken ♦ vt (blood) gerinnen lassen; (paint) dick werden lassen.

coal [kəul] n Kohle f.

coalface ['kəulfeɪs] n Streb m.

coalfield ['kəulfiːld] n Kohlenrevier nt.

coalition [kəuə'lɪʃən] n (POL) Koalition f; (of pressure groups etc) Zusammenschluß m.

coalman ['kəulmən] (irreg: like man) n Kohlenhändler m.

coal merchant n = **coalman**.

coal mine n Kohlenbergwerk nt, Zeche f.

coal miner n Bergmann m, Kumpel m (inf).

coal mining n (Kohlen)bergbau m.

coarse [kɔːs] adj (texture) grob; (vulgar) gewöhnlich, derb; (salt, sand etc) grobkörnig.

coast [kəust] n Küste f ♦ vi (im Leerlauf) fahren.

coastal ['kəustl] adj Küsten-.

coaster ['kəustə*] n (NAUT) Küstenfahrzeug nt; (for glass) Untersetzer m.

coastguard ['kəustgɑːd] n (officer) Küstenwächter m; (service) Küstenwacht f.

coastline ['kəustlaɪn] n Küste f.

coat [kəut] n Mantel m; (of animal) Fell nt; (layer) Schicht f; (: of paint) Anstrich m ♦ vt überziehen.

coat hanger n Kleiderbügel m.

coating ['kəutɪŋ] n (of chocolate etc) Überzug m; (of dust etc) Schicht f.

coat of arms n Wappen nt.

coauthor ['kəu'ɔːθə*] n Mitautor(in) m(f),

Mitverfasser(in) m(f).

coax [kəuks] vt (person) überreden.

cob [kɔb] n see **corn**.

cobbler ['kɔblə*] n Schuster m.

cobbles ['kɔblz] npl Kopfsteinpflaster nt.

cobblestones ['kɔblstəunz] npl = **cobbles**.

COBOL ['kəubɔl] n COBOL nt.

cobra ['kəubrə] n Kobra f.

cobweb ['kɔbwɛb] n Spinnennetz nt.

cocaine [kə'keɪn] n Kokain nt.

cock [kɔk] n Hahn m; (male bird) Männchen nt ♦ vt (gun) entsichern; **to ~ one's ears** (fig) die Ohren spitzen.

cock-a-hoop [kɔkə'huːp] adj ganz aus dem Häuschen.

cockerel ['kɔkərl] n junger Hahn m.

cock-eyed ['kɔkaɪd] adj (fig) verrückt, widersinnig.

cockle ['kɔkl] n Herzmuschel f.

cockney ['kɔknɪ] n Cockney m, echter Londoner m; (LING) Cockney nt.

cockpit ['kɔkpɪt] n Cockpit nt.

cockroach ['kɔkrəutʃ] n Küchenschabe f, Kakerlak m.

cocktail ['kɔkteɪl] n Cocktail m; **fruit ~** Obstsalat m; **prawn ~** Krabbencocktail m.

cocktail cabinet n Hausbar f.

cocktail party n Cocktailparty f.

cocktail shaker [-'ʃeɪkə*] n Mixbecher m.

cock-up ['kɔkʌp] (infl) n Schlamassel m.

cocky ['kɔkɪ] adj großspurig.

cocoa ['kəukəu] n Kakao m.

coconut ['kəukənʌt] n Kokosnuß f.

cocoon [kə'kuːn] n Puppe f, Kokon m; (fig) schützende Umgebung f.

COD abbr (BRIT) = **cash on delivery**; (US) = **collect on delivery**.

cod [kɔd] n Kabeljau m.

code [kəud] n (cipher) Chiffre f; (dialling code) Vorwahl f; (post code) Postleitzahl f; **~ of behaviour** Sittenkodex m; **~ of practice** Verfahrensregeln pl.

codeine ['kəudiːn] n Kodein nt.

codger ['kɔdʒə*] (inf) n: **old ~** komischer Kauz m.

codicil ['kɔdɪsɪl] n (LAW) Kodizill nt.

codify ['kəudɪfaɪ] vt kodifizieren.

cod-liver oil ['kɔdlɪvə-] n Lebertran m.

co-driver ['kəu'draɪvə*] n Beifahrer(in) m(f).

co-ed ['kəu'ɛd] (SCOL) adj abbr = **coeducational** ♦ n abbr (US: female pupil/student) Schülerin/ Studentin an einer gemischten Schule/ Universität; (BRIT: school) gemischte Schule f.

coeducational ['kəuɛdju'keɪʃənl] adj (school) Koedukations-, gemischt.

coerce [kəu'əːs] vt zwingen.

coercion [kəu'əːʃən] n Zwang m.

coexistence ['kəuɪg'zɪstəns] n Koexistenz f.

C of C n abbr = **chamber of commerce**.

C of E abbr = **Church of England**.

coffee ['kɔfɪ] n Kaffee m; **black ~** schwarzer

Kaffee _m_; **white** ~ Kaffee mit Milch; ~ **with cream** Kaffee mit Sahne.
coffee bar (_BRIT_) _n_ Café _nt_.
coffee bean _n_ Kaffeebohne _f_.
coffee break _n_ Kaffeepause _f_.
coffee cake (_US_) _n_ Kuchen _m_ zum Kaffee.
coffee cup _n_ Kaffeetasse _f_.
coffeepot ['kɔfɪpɔt] _n_ Kaffeekanne _f_.
coffee table _n_ Couchtisch _m_.
coffin ['kɔfɪn] _n_ Sarg _m_.
C of I _abbr_ (= _Church of Ireland_) anglikanische Kirche Irlands.
C of S _abbr_ (= _Church of Scotland_) presbyterianische Kirche in Schottland.
cog [kɔg] _n_ (_wheel_) Zahnrad _nt_; (_tooth_) Zahn _m_.
cogent ['kəudʒənt] _adj_ stichhaltig, zwingend.
cognac ['kɔnjæk] _n_ Kognak _m_.
cogwheel ['kɔgwiːl] _n_ Zahnrad _nt_.
cohabit [kəu'hæbɪt] _vi_ (_formal_) in eheähnlicher Gemeinschaft leben; **to** ~ **(with sb)** (mit jdm) zusammenleben.
coherent [kəu'hɪərənt] _adj_ (_speech_) zusammenhängend; (_answer, theory_) schlüssig; (_person_) bei klarem Verstand.
cohesion [kəu'hiːʒən] _n_ Geschlossenheit _f_.
cohesive [kə'hiːsɪv] _adj_ geschlossen.
COI (_BRIT_) _n abbr_ (= _Central Office of Information_) regierungsamtliche Informationsstelle.
coil [kɔɪl] _n_ Rolle _f_; (_one loop_) Windung _f_; (_of smoke_) Kringel _m_; (_AUT, ELEC_) Spule _f_; (_contraceptive_) Spirale _f_ ♦ _vt_ aufrollen, aufwickeln.
coin [kɔɪn] _n_ Münze _f_ ♦ _vt_ prägen.
coinage ['kɔɪnɪdʒ] _n_ Münzen _pl_; (_LING_) Prägung _f_.
coin box (_BRIT_) _n_ Münzfernsprecher _m_.
coincide [kəuɪn'saɪd] _vi_ (_events_) zusammenfallen; (_ideas, views_) übereinstimmen.
coincidence [kəu'ɪnsɪdəns] _n_ Zufall _m_.
coin-operated ['kɔɪn'ɔpəreɪtɪd] _adj_ Münz-.
Coke ® [kəuk] _n_ Coca-Cola ® _nt or f_, Coke ® _nt_.
coke [kəuk] _n_ Koks _m_.
Col. _abbr_ = **colonel**.
COLA (_US_) _n abbr_ (= _cost-of-living adjustment_) Anpassung der Löhne und Gehälter an steigende Lebenshaltungskosten.
colander ['kɔləndə'] _n_ Durchschlag _m_.
cold [kəuld] _adj_ kalt; (_unemotional_) kalt, kühl ♦ _n_ Kälte _f_; (_MED_) Erkältung _f_; **it's** ~ es ist kalt; **to be/feel** ~ (_person_) frieren; (_object_) kalt sein; **in** ~ **blood** kaltblütig; **to have** ~ **feet** (_fig_) kalte Füße bekommen; **to give sb the** ~ **shoulder** jdm die kalte Schulter zeigen; **to catch** ~, **to catch a** ~ sich erkälten.
cold-blooded ['kəuld'blʌdɪd] _adj_ kaltblütig.
cold cream _n_ (halbfette) Feuchtigkeitscreme _f_.
coldly ['kəuldlɪ] _adv_ kalt, kühl.
cold-shoulder [kəuld'ʃəuldə'] _vt_ die kalte

Schulter zeigen +_dat_.
cold sore _n_ Bläschenausschlag _m_.
cold sweat _n_: **to come out in a** ~ **(about sth)** (wegen etw) in kalten Schweiß ausbrechen.
cold turkey _n_: **to do** ~ Totalentzug machen.
Cold War _n_: **the** ~ der kalte Krieg.
coleslaw ['kəulslɔː] _n_ Krautsalat _m_.
colic ['kɔlɪk] _n_ Kolik _f_.
colicky ['kɔlɪkɪ] _adj_: **to be** ~ Kolik _f or_ Leibschmerzen _pl_ haben.
collaborate [kə'læbəreɪt] _vi_ zusammenarbeiten; (_with enemy_) kollaborieren.
collaboration [kəlæbə'reɪʃən] _n_ (_see vb_) Zusammenarbeit _f_; Kollaboration _f_.
collaborator [kə'læbəreɪtə'] _n_ (_see vb_) Mitarbeiter(in) _m(f)_; Kollaborateur(in) _m(f)_.
collage [kɔ'lɑːʒ] _n_ Collage _f_.
collagen ['kɔlədʒən] _n_ Kollagen _nt_.
collapse [kə'læps] _vi_ zusammenbrechen; (_building_) einstürzen; (_plans_) scheitern; (_government_) stürzen ♦ _n_ (_see vb_) Zusammenbruch _m_; Einsturz _m_; Scheitern _nt_; Sturz _m_.
collapsible [kə'læpsəbl] _adj_ Klapp-, zusammenklappbar.
collar ['kɔlə'] _n_ Kragen _m_; (_of dog, cat_) Halsband _nt_; (_TECH_) Bund _m_ ♦ _vt_ (_inf_) schnappen.
collarbone ['kɔləbəun] _n_ Schlüsselbein _nt_.
collate [kɔ'leɪt] _vt_ vergleichen.
collateral [kə'lætərl] _n_ (_COMM_) (zusätzliche) Sicherheit _f_.
collateral damage _n_ (_MIL_) Schäden _pl_ in Wohngebieten; (: _casualties_) Opfer _pl_ unter der Zivilbevölkerung.
collation [kə'leɪʃən] _n_ Vergleich _m_; (_CULIN_): **a cold** ~ ein kalter Imbiß _m_.
colleague ['kɔliːg] _n_ Kollege _m_, Kollegin _f_.
collect [kə'lɛkt] _vt_ sammeln; (_mail, BRIT: fetch_) abholen; (_debts_) eintreiben; (_taxes_) einziehen ♦ _vi_ sich ansammeln ♦ _adv_ (_US: TEL_): **to call** ~ ein R-Gespräch führen; **to** ~ **one's thoughts** seine Gedanken ordnen, sich sammeln; ~ **on delivery** (_US: COMM_) per Nachnahme.
collected [kə'lɛktɪd] _adj_: ~ **works** gesammelte Werke _pl_.
collection [kə'lɛkʃən] _n_ Sammlung _f_; (_from place, person, of mail_) Abholung _f_; (_in church_) Kollekte _f_.
collective [kə'lɛktɪv] _adj_ kollektiv, gemeinsam ♦ _n_ Kollektiv _nt_; ~ **farm** landwirtschaftliche Produktionsgenossenschaft _f_.
collective bargaining _n_ Tarifverhandlungen _pl_.
collector [kə'lɛktə'] _n_ Sammler(in) _m(f)_; (_of taxes etc_) Einnehmer(in) _m(f)_; (_of rent, cash_) Kassierer(in) _m(f)_; ~'**s item** _or_ **piece** Sammlerstück _nt_, Liebhaberstück _nt_.
college ['kɔlɪdʒ] _n_ College _nt_; (_of agriculture, technology_) Fachhochschule _f_; **to go to** ~

studieren; ~ **of education** Pädagogische
Hochschule *f.*
collide [kə'laɪd] *vi:* **to** ~ **(with)**
zusammenstoßen (mit); (*fig: clash*) eine
heftige Auseinandersetzung haben (mit).
collie ['kɔlɪ] *n* Collie *m.*
colliery ['kɔlɪərɪ] (*BRIT*) *n* (Kohlen)bergwerk
nt, Zeche *f.*
collision [kə'lɪʒən] *n* Zusammenstoß *m*; **to be
on a** ~ **course** (*also fig*) auf Kollisionskurs
sein.
collision damage waiver *n* (*INSURANCE*)
Verzicht auf Haftungsbeschränkung bei
Unfällen mit Mietwagen.
colloquial [kə'ləukwɪəl] *adj*
umgangssprachlich.
collusion [kə'luːʒən] *n* (geheime) Absprache *f*;
to be in ~ **with** gemeinsame Sache machen
mit.
Colo. (*US*) *abbr* (*POST:* = *Colorado*).
Cologne [kə'ləun] *n* Köln *nt.*
cologne [kə'ləun] *n* (*also:* **eau de** ~)
Kölnischwasser *nt*, Eau de Cologne *nt.*
Colombia [kə'lɔmbɪə] *n* Kolumbien *nt.*
Colombian [kə'lɔmbɪən] *adj* kolumbianisch
♦ *n* Kolumbianer(in) *m(f).*
colon ['kəulən] *n* Doppelpunkt *m*; (*ANAT*)
Dickdarm *m.*
colonel ['kɔːnl] *n* Oberst *m.*
colonial [kə'ləunɪəl] *adj* Kolonial-.
colonize ['kɔlənaɪz] *vt* kolonisieren.
colony ['kɔlənɪ] *n* Kolonie *f.*
color *etc* ['kʌlə*] (*US*) = **colour** *etc.*
Colorado beetle [kɔlə'rɑːdəu-] *n*
Kartoffelkäfer *m.*
colossal [kə'lɔsl] *adj* riesig, kolossal.
colour, (*US*) **color** ['kʌlə*] *n* Farbe *f*; (*skin
colour*) Hautfarbe *f*; (*of spectacle etc*)
Atmosphäre *f* ♦ *vt* bemalen; (*with crayons*)
ausmalen; (*dye*) färben; (*fig*) beeinflussen
♦ *vi* (*blush*) erröten, rot werden ♦ *cpd* Farb-;
colours *npl* (*of party, club etc*) Farben *pl*; **in** ~
(*film*) in Farbe; (*illustrations*) bunt.
►**colour in** *vt* ausmalen.
colour bar *n* Rassenschranke *f.*
colour-blind ['kʌləblaɪnd] *adj* farbenblind.
coloured ['kʌləd] *adj* farbig; (*photo*) Farb-;
(*illustration etc*) bunt.
colour film *n* Farbfilm *m.*
colourful ['kʌləful] *adj* bunt; (*account, story*)
farbig, anschaulich; (*personality*) schillernd.
colouring ['kʌlərɪŋ] *n* Gesichtsfarbe *f*, Teint
m; (*in food*) Farbstoff *m.*
colour scheme *n* Farbzusammenstellung *f.*
colour supplement (*BRIT*) *n* Farbbeilage *f*,
Magazin *nt.*
colour television *n* Farbfernsehen *nt*; (*set*)
Farbfernseher *m.*
colt [kəult] *n* Hengstfohlen *nt.*
column ['kɔləm] *n* Säule *f*; (*of people*) Kolonne
f; (*of print*) Spalte *f*; (*gossip/sports column*)
Kolumne *f*; **the editorial** ~ der Leitartikel.

columnist ['kɔləmnɪst] *n* Kolumnist(in) *m(f).*
coma ['kəumə] *n* Koma *nt*; **to be in a** ~ im
Koma liegen.
comb [kəum] *n* Kamm *m* ♦ *vt* kämmen; (*area*)
durchkämmen.
combat ['kɔmbæt] *n* Kampf *m* ♦ *vt* bekämpfen.
combination [kɔmbɪ'neɪʃən] *n* Kombination *f.*
combination lock *n* Kombinationsschloß *nt.*
combine [*vti* kəm'baɪn, *n* 'kɔmbaɪn] *vt*
verbinden ♦ *vi* sich zusammenschließen;
(*CHEM*) sich verbinden ♦ *n* Konzern *m*;
(*AGR*) = **combine harvester**; ~**d effort**
vereintes Unternehmen.
combine harvester *n* Mähdrescher *m.*
combo ['kɔmbəu] *n* Combo *f.*
combustible [kəm'bʌstɪbl] *adj* brennbar.
combustion [kəm'bʌstʃən] *n* Verbrennung *f.*

═══════════════════════════ *KEYWORD*

come [kʌm] (*pt* **came**, *pp* **come**) *vi* **1** (*movement
towards*) kommen; ~ **with me** kommen Sie
mit mir; **to** ~ **running** angelaufen kommen;
coming! ich komme!
2 (*arrive*) kommen; **they came to a river** sie
kamen an einen Fluß; **to** ~ **home** nach
Hause kommen
3 (*reach*): **to** ~ **to** kommen an +*acc*; **her hair
came to her waist** ihr Haar reichte ihr bis
zur Hüfte; **to** ~ **to a decision** zu einer
Entscheidung kommen
4 (*occur*): **an idea came to me** mir kam eine
Idee
5 (*be, become*) werden; **I've** ~ **to like him**
mittlerweile mag ich ihn; **if it** ~**s to it** wenn
es darauf ankommt
►**come about** *vi* geschehen.
►**come across** *vt fus* (*find: person, thing*)
stoßen auf +*acc* ♦ *vi:* **to** ~ **across well/badly**
(*idea etc*) gut/schlecht ankommen; (*meaning*)
gut/schlecht verstanden werden.
►**come along** *vi* (*arrive*) daherkommen;
(*make progress*) vorankommen; ~ **along!**
komm schon!
►**come apart** *vi* (*break in pieces*)
auseinandergehen.
►**come away** *vi* (*leave*) weggehen; (*become
detached*) abgehen.
►**come back** *vi* (*return*) zurückkommen;: **to**
~ **back into fashion** wieder in Mode
kommen.
►**come by** *vt fus* (*acquire*) kommen zu.
►**come down** *vi* (*price*) sinken, fallen;
(*building: be demolished*) abgerissen werden;
(*tree: during storm*) umstürzen.
►**come forward** *vi* (*volunteer*) sich melden.
►**come from** *vt fus* kommen von, stammen
aus; (*person*) kommen aus.
►**come in** *vi* (*enter*) hereinkommen; (*report,
news*) eintreffen; (*on deal etc*) sich
beteiligen; ~ **in!** herein!
►**come in for** *vt fus* (*criticism etc*) einstecken
müssen.

►**come into** *vt fus* (*inherit: money*) erben; **to ~ into fashion** in Mode kommen; **money doesn't ~ into it** Geld hat nichts damit zu tun.

►**come off** *vi* (*become detached: button, handle*) sich lösen; (*succeed: attempt, plan*) klappen ♦ *vt fus* (*inf*): **~ off it!** mach mal halblang!

►**come on** *vi* (*pupil, work, project*) vorankommen; (*lights etc*) angehen; **~ on!** (*hurry up*) mach schon!; (*giving encouragement*) los!

►**come out** *vi* herauskommen; (*stain*) herausgehen; **to ~ out (on strike)** in den Streik treten.

►**come over** *vt fus*: **I don't know what's ~ over him!** ich weiß nicht, was in ihn gefahren ist.

►**come round** *vi* (*after faint, operation*) wieder zu sich kommen; (*visit*) vorbeikommen; (*agree*) zustimmen.

►**come through** *vi* (*survive*) durchkommen; (*telephone call*) (durch)kommen ♦ *vt fus* (*illness etc*) überstehen.

►**come to** *vi* (*regain consciousness*) wieder zu sich kommen ♦ *vt fus* (*add up to*): **how much does it ~ to?** was macht das zusammen?

►**come under** *vt fus* (*heading*) kommen unter +*acc*; (*criticism, pressure, attack*) geraten unter +*acc*.

►**come up** *vi* (*approach*) herankommen; (*sun*) aufgehen; (*problem*) auftauchen; (*event*) bevorstehen; (*in conversation*) genannt werden; **something's come up** etwas ist dazwischengekommen.

►**come up against** *vt fus* (*resistance, difficulties*) stoßen auf +*acc*.

►**come upon** *vt fus* (*find*) stoßen auf +*acc*.

►**come up to** *vt fus*: **the film didn't come up to our expectations** der Film entsprach nicht unseren Erwartungen; **it's coming up to 10 o'clock** es ist gleich 10 Uhr.

►**come up with** *vt fus* (*idea*) aufwarten mit; (*money*) aufbringen.

comeback ['kʌmbæk] *n* (*of film star etc*) Comeback *nt*; (*reaction, response*) Reaktion *f*.

Comecon ['kɔmɪkɔn] *n abbr* (= *Council for Mutual Economic Assistance*) Comecon *m*.

comedian [kə'miːdɪən] *n* Komiker *m*.

comedienne [kəmiːdɪ'ɛn] *n* Komikerin *f*.

comedown ['kʌmdaun] (*inf*) *n* Enttäuschung *f*; (*professional*) Abstieg *m*.

comedy ['kɔmɪdɪ] *n* Komödie *f*; (*humour*) Witz *m*.

comet ['kɔmɪt] *n* Komet *m*.

comeuppance [kʌm'ʌpəns] *n*: **to get one's ~** die Quittung bekommen.

comfort ['kʌmfət] *n* (*physical*) Behaglichkeit *f*; (*material*) Komfort *m*; (*solace, relief*) Trost *m* ♦ *vt* trösten; **comforts** *npl* (*of home etc*) Komfort *m*, Annehmlichkeiten *pl*.

comfortable ['kʌmfətəbl] *adj* bequem; (*room*) komfortabel; (*walk, climb etc*) geruhsam; (*income*) ausreichend; (*majority*) sicher; **to be ~** (*physically*) sich wohl fühlen; (*financially*) sehr angenehm leben; **the patient is ~** dem Patienten geht es den Umständen entsprechend gut; **I don't feel very ~ about it** mir ist nicht ganz wohl bei der Sache.

comfortably ['kʌmfətəblɪ] *adv* (*sit*) bequem; (*live*) angenehm.

comforter ['kʌmfətəʳ] (*US*) *n* Schnuller *m*.

comfort station (*US*) *n* öffentliche Toilette *f*.

comic ['kɔmɪk] *adj* (*also*: ~**al**) komisch ♦ *n* Komiker(in) *m(f)*; (*BRIT: magazine*) Comicheft *nt*.

comical ['kɔmɪkl] *adj* komisch.

comic strip *n* Comic strip *m*.

coming ['kʌmɪŋ] *n* Ankunft *f*, Kommen *nt* ♦ *adj* kommend; (*next*) nächste(r, s); **in the ~ weeks** in den nächsten Wochen.

coming(s) and going(s) *n(pl)* Kommen und Gehen *nt*.

Comintern ['kɔmɪntəːn] *n* (*POL*) Komintern *f*.

comma ['kɔmə] *n* Komma *nt*.

command [kə'mɑːnd] *n* (*also COMPUT*) Befehl *m*; (*control, charge*) Führung *f*; (*MIL: authority*) Kommando *nt*, Befehlsgewalt *f*; (*mastery*) Beherrschung *f* ♦ *vt* (*troops*) befehligen, kommandieren; (*be able to get*) verfügen über +*acc*; (*deserve: respect, admiration etc*) verdient haben; **to be in ~ of** das Kommando or den (Ober)befehl haben über +*acc*; **to have ~ of** das Kommando haben über +*acc*; **to take ~ of** das Kommando übernehmen +*gen*; **to have at one's ~** verfügen über +*acc*; **to ~ sb to do sth** jdm befehlen, etw zu tun.

commandant ['kɔməndænt] *n* Kommandant *m*.

command economy *n* Kommandowirtschaft *f*.

commandeer [kɔmən'dɪəʳ] *vt* requirieren, beschlagnahmen; (*fig*) sich aneignen.

commander [kə'mɑːndəʳ] *n* Befehlshaber *m*, Kommandant *m*.

commander in chief *n* Oberbefehlshaber *m*.

commanding [kə'mɑːndɪŋ] *adj* (*appearance*) imposant; (*voice, tone*) gebieterisch; (*lead*) entscheidend; (*position*) vorherrschend.

commanding officer *n* befehlshabender Offizier *m*.

commandment [kə'mɑːndmənt] *n* Gebot *nt*.

command module *n* Kommandokapsel *f*.

commando [kə'mɑːndəu] *n* Kommando *nt*, Kommandotrupp *m*; (*soldier*) Angehörige(r) *m* eines Kommando(trupp)s.

commemorate [kə'mɛməreɪt] *vt* gedenken +*gen*.

commemoration [kəmɛmə'reɪʃən] *n* Gedenken *nt*.

commemorative [kə'mɛmərətɪv] *adj* Gedenk-.

commence [kə'mɛns] *vt, vi* beginnen.
commend [kə'mɛnd] *vt* loben; **to ~ sth to sb** jdm etw empfehlen.
commendable [kə'mɛndəbl] *adj* lobenswert.
commendation [kɔmɛn'deɪʃən] *n* Auszeichnung *f*.
commensurate [kə'mɛnʃərɪt] *adj:* **~ with** *or* **to** entsprechend +*dat*.
comment ['kɔmɛnt] *n* Bemerkung *f*; (*on situation etc*) Kommentar *m* ♦ *vi:* **to ~ (on)** sich äußern (über +*acc or* zu); (*on situation etc*) einen Kommentar abgeben (zu); **"no ~"** „kein Kommentar!"; **to ~ that ...** bemerken, daß ...
commentary ['kɔməntərɪ] *n* Kommentar *m*; (*SPORT*) Reportage *f*.
commentator ['kɔmənteɪtə'] *n* Kommentator(in) *m(f)*; (*SPORT*) Reporter(in) *m(f)*.
commerce ['kɔmɜːs] *n* Handel *m*.
commercial [kə'mɜːʃəl] *adj* kommerziell; (*organization*) Wirtschafts- ♦ *n* (*advertisement*) Werbespot *m*.
commercial bank *n* Handelsbank *f*.
commercial break *n* Werbung *f*.
commercial college *n* Fachschule *f* für kaufmännische Berufe.
commercialism [kə'mɜːʃəlɪzəm] *n* Kommerzialisierung *f*.
commercialize [kə'mɜːʃəlaɪz] *vt* kommerzialisieren.
commercialized [kə'mɜːʃəlaɪzd] (*pej*) *adj* kommerzialisiert.
commercial radio *n* kommerzielles Radio *nt*.
commercial television *n* kommerzielles Fernsehen *nt*.
commercial traveller *n* Handels-vertreter(in) *m(f)*.
commercial vehicle *n* Lieferwagen *m*.
commiserate [kə'mɪzəreɪt] *vi:* **to ~ with sb** jdm sein Mitgefühl zeigen.
commission [kə'mɪʃən] *n* (*order for work*) Auftrag *m*; (*COMM*) Provision *f*; (*committee*) Kommission *f*; (*MIL*) Offizierspatent *nt* ♦ *vt* (*work of art*) in Auftrag geben; (*MIL*) (zum Offizier) ernennen; **out of ~** außer Betrieb; (*NAUT*) nicht im Dienst; **I get 10% ~** ich bekomme 10% Provision; **~ of inquiry** Untersuchungsausschuß *m*, Untersuchungskommission *f*; **to ~ sb to do sth** jdn damit beauftragen, etw zu tun; **to ~ sth from sb** jdm etw in Auftrag geben.
commissionaire [kəmɪʃə'nɛə'] (*BRIT*) *n* Portier *m*.
commissioner [kə'mɪʃənə'] *n* Polizeipräsident *m*.
commit [kə'mɪt] *vt* (*crime*) begehen; (*money, resources*) einsetzen; (*to sb's care*) anvertrauen; **to ~ o.s.** sich festlegen; **to ~ o.s. to do sth** sich (dazu) verpflichten, etw zu tun; **to ~ suicide** Selbstmord begehen; **to ~ to writing** zu Papier bringen;

to ~ sb for trial jdn einem Gericht überstellen.
commitment [kə'mɪtmənt] *n* Verpflichtung *f*; (*to ideology, system*) Engagement *nt*.
committed [kə'mɪtɪd] *adj* engagiert.
committee [kə'mɪtɪ] *n* Ausschuß *m*, Komitee *nt*; **to be on a ~** in einem Ausschuß *or* Komitee sein *or* sitzen.
committee meeting *n* Ausschußsitzung *f*.
commodity [kə'mɔdɪtɪ] *n* Ware *f*; (*food*) Nahrungsmittel *nt*.
common ['kɔmən] *adj* (*shared by all*) gemeinsam; (*good*) Gemein-; (*property*) Gemeinschafts-; (*usual, ordinary*) häufig; (*vulgar*) gewöhnlich ♦ *n* Gemeindeland *nt*; **the Commons** (*BRIT: POL*) *npl* das Unterhaus; **in ~ use** allgemein gebräuchlich; **it's ~ knowledge that** es ist allgemein bekannt, daß; **to the ~ good** für das Gemeinwohl; **to have sth in ~ (with sb)** etw (mit jdm) gemein haben.
common cold *n* Schnupfen *m*.
common denominator *n* (*MATH, fig*) gemeinsamer Nenner *m*.
commoner ['kɔmənə'] *n* Bürgerliche(r) *f(m)*.
common ground *n* (*fig*) gemeinsame Basis *f*.
common land *n* Gemeindeland *nt*.
common law *n* Gewohnheitsrecht *nt*.
common-law ['kɔmənlɔ:] *adj:* **she is his ~ wife** sie lebt mit ihm in eheähnlicher Gemeinschaft.
commonly ['kɔmənlɪ] *adv* häufig.
Common Market *n:* **the ~** der Gemeinsame Markt.
commonplace ['kɔmənpleɪs] *adj* alltäglich.
common room *n* Aufenthaltsraum *m*, Tagesraum *m*.
common sense *n* gesunder Menschenverstand *m*.
Commonwealth ['kɔmənwɛlθ] (*BRIT*) *n:* **the ~** das Commonwealth.

Das **Commonwealth**, *offiziell Commonwealth of Nations, ist ein lockerer Zusammenschluß aus souveränen Staaten, die früher unter britischer Regierung standen, und von Großbritannien abhängigen Gebieten. Die Mitgliedsstaaten erkennen den britischen Monarchen als Oberhaupt des Commonwealth an. Bei der Commonwealth Conference, einem Treffen der Staatsoberhäupter der Commonwealthländer, werden Angelegenheiten von gemeinsamem Interesse diskutiert.*

---

commotion [kə'məuʃən] *n* Tumult *m*.
communal ['kɔmju:nl] *adj* gemeinsam, Gemeinschafts-; (*life*) Gemeinschafts-.
commune [*n* 'kɔmju:n, *vi* kə'mju:n] *n* Kommune *f* ♦ *vi:* **to ~ with** Zwiesprache halten mit.
communicate [kə'mju:nɪkeɪt] *vt* mitteilen;

(idea, feeling) vermitteln ♦ *vi:* **to ~ (with)** *(by speech, gesture)* sich verständigen (mit); *(in writing)* in Verbindung *or* Kontakt stehen (mit).

communication [kəmjuːnɪˈkeɪʃən] *n* Kommunikation *f*; *(letter, call)* Mitteilung *f*.

communication cord *(BRIT) n* Notbremse *f*.

communications network [kəmjuːnɪˈkeɪ-ʃənz-] *n* Kommunikationsnetz *nt*.

communications satellite *n* Kommunikationssatellit *m*, Nachrichtensatellit *m*.

communicative [kəˈmjuːnɪkətɪv] *adj* gesprächig, mitteilsam.

communion [kəˈmjuːnɪən] *n (also:* **Holy C~**: *Catholic)* Kommunion *f*; (: *Protestant)* Abendmahl *nt*.

communiqué [kəˈmjuːnɪkeɪ] *n* Kommuniqué *nt*, (amtliche) Verlautbarung *f*.

communism [ˈkɔmjunɪzəm] *n* Kommunismus *m*.

communist [ˈkɔmjunɪst] *adj* kommunistisch ♦ *n* Kommunist(in) *m(f)*.

community [kəˈmjuːnɪtɪ] *n* Gemeinschaft *f*; *(within larger group)* Bevölkerungsgruppe *f*.

community centre *n* Gemeindezentrum *nt*.

community charge *(BRIT) n (formerly)* Gemeindesteuer *f*.

community chest *(US) n* Wohltätigkeitsfonds *m*, Hilfsfonds *m*.

community health centre *n* Gemeinde-Ärztezentrum *nt*.

community home *(BRIT) n* Erziehungsheim *nt*.

community service *n* Sozialdienst *m*.

community spirit *n* Gemeinschaftssinn *m*.

commutation ticket [kɔmjuˈteɪʃən-] *(US) n* Zeitkarte *f*.

commute [kəˈmjuːt] *vi* pendeln ♦ *vt (LAW, MATH)* umwandeln.

commuter [kəˈmjuːtəˈ] *n* Pendler(in) *m(f)*.

compact *[adj* kəmˈpækt, *n* ˈkɔmpækt] *adj* kompakt ♦ *n (also:* **powder ~)** Puderdose *f*.

compact disc *n* Compact Disk *f*, CD *f*.

compact disc player *n* CD-Spieler *m*.

companion [kəmˈpænjən] *n* Begleiter(in) *m(f)*.

companionship [kəmˈpænjənʃɪp] *n* Gesellschaft *f*.

companionway [kəmˈpænjənweɪ] *n (NAUT)* Niedergang *m*.

company [ˈkʌmpənɪ] *n* Firma *f*; *(THEAT)* (Schauspiel)truppe *f*; *(MIL)* Kompanie *f*; *(companionship)* Gesellschaft *f*; **he's good ~** seine Gesellschaft ist angenehm; **to keep sb ~** jdm Gesellschaft leisten; **to part ~ with** sich trennen von; **Smith and C~** Smith & Co.

company car *n* Firmenwagen *m*.

company director *n* Direktor(in) *m(f)*, Firmenchef(in) *m(f)*.

company secretary *(BRIT) n ≈* Prokurist(in) *m(f)*.

comparable [ˈkɔmpərəbl] *adj* vergleichbar.

comparative [kəmˈpærətɪv] *adj* relativ; *(study, literature)* vergleichend; *(LING)* komparativ.

comparatively [kəmˈpærətɪvlɪ] *adv* relativ.

compare [kəmˈpɛəˈ] *vt:* **to ~ (with** *or* **to)** vergleichen (mit) ♦ *vi:* **to ~ (with)** sich vergleichen lassen (mit); **how do the prices ~?** wie lassen sich die Preise vergleichen?; **~d with** *or* **to** im Vergleich zu, verglichen mit.

comparison [kəmˈpærɪsn] *n* Vergleich *m*; **in ~ (with)** im Vergleich (zu).

compartment [kəmˈpɑːtmənt] *n (RAIL)* Abteil *nt*; *(section)* Fach *nt*.

compass [ˈkʌmpəs] *n* Kompaß *m*; *(fig: scope)* Bereich *m*; **compasses** *npl (also:* **pair of ~es)** Zirkel *m*; **within the ~ of** im Rahmen *or* Bereich +gen; **beyond the ~ of** über den Rahmen *or* Bereich +gen hinaus.

compassion [kəmˈpæʃən] *n* Mitgefühl *nt*.

compassionate [kəmˈpæʃənɪt] *adj* mitfühlend; **on ~ grounds** aus familiären Gründen.

compassionate leave *n (esp MIL) Beurlaubung wegen Krankheit oder Trauerfall in der Familie.*

compatibility [kəmpætɪˈbɪlɪtɪ] *n (see adj)* Vereinbarkeit *f*; Zueinanderpassen *nt*; Kompatibilität *f*.

compatible [kəmˈpætɪbl] *adj (ideas etc)* vereinbar; *(people)* zueinander passend; *(COMPUT)* kompatibel.

compel [kəmˈpɛl] *vt* zwingen.

compelling [kəmˈpɛlɪŋ] *adj* zwingend.

compendium [kəmˈpɛndɪəm] *n* Kompendium *nt*.

compensate [ˈkɔmpənseɪt] *vt* entschädigen ♦ *vi:* **to ~ for** *(loss)* ersetzen; *(disappointment, change etc)* (wieder) ausgleichen.

compensation [kɔmpənˈseɪʃən] *n (see vb)* Entschädigung *f*; Ersatz *m*; Ausgleich *m*; *(money)* Schaden(s)ersatz *m*.

compère [ˈkɔmpɛəˈ] *n* Conférencier *m*.

compete [kəmˈpiːt] *vi (in contest, game)* teilnehmen; *(two theories, statements)* unvereinbar sein; **to ~ (with)** *(companies, rivals)* konkurrieren (mit).

competence [ˈkɔmpɪtəns] *n* Fähigkeit *f*.

competent [ˈkɔmpɪtənt] *adj* fähig.

competing [kəmˈpiːtɪŋ] *adj* konkurrierend.

competition [kɔmpɪˈtɪʃən] *n* Konkurrenz *f*; *(contest)* Wettbewerb *m*; **in ~ with** im Wettbewerb mit.

competitive [kəmˈpɛtɪtɪv] *adj (industry, society)* wettbewerbsbetont, wettbewerbsorientiert; *(person)* vom Konkurrenzdenken geprägt; *(price, product)* wettbewerbsfähig, konkurrenzfähig; *(sport)* (Wett)kampf-.

competitive examination *n (for places)* Auswahlprüfung *f*; *(for prizes)* Wettbewerb *m*.

competitor [kəmˈpɛtɪtəˈ] *n* Konkurrent(in)

m(f); (*participant*) Teilnehmer(in) *m(f)*.
compilation [kɔmpɪ'leɪʃən] *n*
Zusammenstellung *f*.
compile [kəm'paɪl] *vt* zusammenstellen;
(*book*) verfassen.
complacency [kəm'pleɪsnsɪ] *n*
Selbstzufriedenheit *f*, Selbstgefälligkeit *f*.
complacent [kəm'pleɪsnt] *adj* selbstzufrieden,
selbstgefällig.
complain [kəm'pleɪn] *vi* (*protest*) sich
beschweren; **to ~ (about)** sich beklagen
(über +*acc*); **to ~ of** (*headache etc*) klagen
über +*acc*.
complaint [kəm'pleɪnt] *n* Klage *f*; (*in shop etc*)
Beschwerde *f*; (*illness*) Beschwerden *pl*.
complement ['kɔmplɪmənt] *n* Ergänzung *f*;
(*esp ship's crew*) Besatzung *f* ♦ *vt* ergänzen;
to have a full ~ of ... (*people*) die volle
Stärke an ... *dat* haben; (*items*) die volle Zahl
an ... *dat* haben.
complementary [kɔmplɪ'mentərɪ] *adj*
komplementär, einander ergänzend.
complete [kəm'pliːt] *adj* (*total: silence*)
vollkommen; (: *change*) völlig; (: *success*)
voll; (*whole*) ganz; (: *set*) vollständig;
(: *edition*) Gesamt-; (*finished*) fertig ♦ *vt*
fertigstellen; (*task*) beenden; (*set, group etc*)
vervollständigen; (*fill in*) ausfüllen; **it's a
~ disaster** es ist eine totale Katastrophe.
completely [kəm'pliːtlɪ] *adv* völlig,
vollkommen.
completion [kəm'pliːʃən] *n* Fertigstellung *f*;
(*of contract*) Abschluß *m*; **to be nearing ~**
kurz vor dem Abschluß sein *or* stehen; **on
~ of the contract** bei Vertragsabschluß.
complex ['kɔmplɛks] *adj* kompliziert ♦ *n*
Komplex *m*.
complexion [kəm'plɛkʃən] *n* Teint *m*,
Gesichtsfarbe *f*; (*of event etc*) Charakter *m*;
(*political, religious*) Anschauung *f*; **to put a
different ~ on sth** etw in einem anderen
Licht erscheinen lassen.
complexity [kəm'plɛksɪtɪ] *n* Kompliziertheit *f*.
compliance [kəm'plaɪəns] *n* Fügsamkeit *f*;
(*agreement*) Einverständnis *nt*; **~ with**
Einverständnis mit, Zustimmung *f* zu; **in
~ with** gemäß +*dat*.
compliant [kəm'plaɪənt] *adj* gefällig,
entgegenkommend.
complicate ['kɔmplɪkeɪt] *vt* komplizieren.
complicated ['kɔmplɪkeɪtɪd] *adj* kompliziert.
complication [kɔmplɪ'keɪʃən] *n* Komplikation
f.
complicity [kəm'plɪsɪtɪ] *n* Mittäterschaft *f*.
compliment [*n* 'kɔmplɪmənt, *vt* 'kɔmplɪment] *n*
Kompliment *nt* ♦ *vt* ein Kompliment/
Komplimente machen; **compliments** *npl*
(*regards*) Grüße *pl*; **to pay sb a ~** jdm ein
Kompliment machen; **to ~ sb (on sth)** jdm
Komplimente (wegen etw) machen; **to ~ sb
on doing sth** jdm Komplimente machen,
daß er/sie etw getan hat.

complimentary [kɔmplɪ'mentərɪ] *adj*
schmeichelhaft; (*ticket, copy of book etc*)
Frei-.
compliments slip *n* Empfehlungszettel *m*.
comply [kəm'plaɪ] *vi*: **to ~ with** (*law*) einhalten
+*acc*; (*ruling*) sich richten nach.
component [kəm'pəunənt] *adj* einzeln ♦ *n*
Bestandteil *m*.
compose [kəm'pəuz] *vt* (*music*) komponieren;
(*poem*) verfassen; (*letter*) abfassen; **to be ~d
of** bestehen aus; **to ~ o.s.** sich sammeln.
composed [kəm'pəuzd] *adj* ruhig, gelassen.
composer [kəm'pəuzə*] *n* Komponist(in) *m(f)*.
composite ['kɔmpəzɪt] *adj* zusammengesetzt;
(*BOT*) Korbblütler-; (*MATH*) teilbar; (*BOT*):
~ plant Korbblütler *m*.
composition [kɔmpə'zɪʃən] *n*
Zusammensetzung *f*; (*essay*) Aufsatz *m*;
(*MUS*) Komposition *f*.
compositor [kəm'pɔzɪtə*] *n*
(Schrift)setzer(in) *m(f)*.
compos mentis ['kɔmpɔs 'mentɪs] *adj*
zurechnungsfähig.
compost ['kɔmpɔst] *n* Kompost *m*; (*also*:
potting ~) Blumenerde *f*.
composure [kəm'pəuʒə*] *n* Fassung *f*,
Beherrschung *f*.
compound [*n, adj* 'kɔmpaund, *vt* kəm'paund] *n*
(*CHEM*) Verbindung *f*; (*enclosure*) umzäuntes
Gebiet *or* Gelände *nt*; (*LING*) Kompositum *nt*
♦ *adj* zusammengesetzt; (*eye*) Facetten- ♦ *vt*
verschlimmern, vergrößern.
compound fracture *n* komplizierter Bruch
m.
compound interest *n* Zinseszins *m*.
comprehend [kɔmprɪ'hend] *vt* begreifen,
verstehen.
comprehension [kɔmprɪ'henʃən] *n*
Verständnis *nt*.
comprehensive [kɔmprɪ'hensɪv] *adj*
umfassend; (*insurance*) Vollkasko- ♦ *n*
= **comprehensive school**.
comprehensive school (*BRIT*) *n*
Gesamtschule *f*.

> **Comprehensive school** *ist in Großbritannien
> eine nicht selektive weiterführende Schule, an
> der alle Kinder aus einem Einzugsgebiet
> gemeinsam unterrichtet werden. An einer
> solchen Gesamtschule können alle
> Schulabschlüsse gemacht werden. Die meisten
> staatlichen Schulen in Großbritannien sind
> comprehensive schools.*

compress [*vt* kəm'pres, *n* 'kɔmpres] *vt*
(*information etc*) verdichten; (*air*)
komprimieren; (*cotton, paper etc*)
zusammenpressen ♦ *n* (*MED*) Kompresse *f*.
compressed air [kəm'prest-] *n* Druckluft *f*,
Preßluft *f*.
compression [kəm'preʃən] *n* (*see vb*)
Verdichtung *f*; Kompression *f*;

Zusammenpressen *nt*.
comprise [kəm'praɪz] *vt (also:* **be ~d of)**
bestehen aus; *(constitute)* bilden,
ausmachen.
compromise ['kɔmprəmaɪz] *n* Kompromiß *m*
♦ *vt (beliefs, principles)* verraten; *(person)*
kompromittieren ♦ *vi* Kompromisse
schließen ♦ *cpd (solution etc)* Kompromiß-.
compulsion [kəm'pʌlʃən] *n* Zwang *m; (force)*
Druck *m*, Zwang *m;* **under ~** unter Druck *or*
Zwang.
compulsive [kəm'pʌlsɪv] *adj* zwanghaft; **it**
makes ~ viewing/reading das muß man
einfach sehen/lesen; **he's a ~ smoker** das
Rauchen ist bei ihm zur Sucht geworden.
compulsory [kəm'pʌlsərɪ] *adj* obligatorisch;
(retirement) Zwangs-.
compulsory purchase *n* Enteignung *f*.
compunction [kəm'pʌŋkʃən] *n* Schuldgefühle
pl, Gewissensbisse *pl;* **to have no ~ about**
doing sth etw tun, ohne sich schuldig zu
fühlen.
computer [kəm'pjuːtə•] *n* Computer *m*,
Rechner *m* ♦ *cpd* Computer-; **the process is**
done by ~ das Verfahren wird per
Computer durchgeführt.
computer game *n* Computerspiel *nt*.
computerization [kəmpjuːtəraɪ'zeɪʃən] *n*
Computerisierung *f*.
computerize [kəm'pjuːtəraɪz] *vt* auf
Computer umstellen; *(information)*
computerisieren.
computer literate *adj:* **to be ~** Computer-
kenntnisse haben.
computer programmer *n* Program-
mierer(in) *m(f)*.
computer programming *n* Programmieren
nt.
computer science *n* Informatik *f*.
computer scientist *n* Informatiker(in) *m(f)*.
computing [kəm'pjuːtɪŋ] *n* Informatik *f;*
(activity) Computerarbeit *f*.
comrade ['kɔmrɪd] *n* Genosse *m*, Genossin *f;*
(friend) Kamerad(in) *m(f)*.
comradeship ['kɔmrɪdʃɪp] *n* Kameradschaft *f*.
comsat ['kɔmsæt] *n abbr* = **communications**
satellite.
con [kɔn] *vt* betrügen; *(cheat)* hereinlegen ♦ *n*
Schwindel *m;* **to ~ sb into doing sth** jdn
durch einen Trick dazu bringen, daß er/sie
etw tut.
concave ['kɔnkeɪv] *adj* konkav.
conceal [kən'siːl] *vt* verbergen; *(information)*
verheimlichen.
concede [kən'siːd] *vt* zugeben ♦ *vi* nachgeben;
(admit defeat) sich geschlagen geben; **to**
~ defeat sich geschlagen geben; **to ~ a**
point to sb jdm in einem Punkt recht
geben.
conceit [kən'siːt] *n* Einbildung *f*.
conceited [kən'siːtɪd] *adj* eingebildet.
conceivable [kən'siːvəbl] *adj* denkbar,

vorstellbar; **it is ~ that ...** es ist denkbar,
daß ...
conceivably [kən'siːvəblɪ] *adv:* **he may ~ be**
right es ist durchaus denkbar, daß er recht
hat.
conceive [kən'siːv] *vt (child)* empfangen;
(plan) kommen auf +*acc; (policy)* konzipieren
♦ *vi* empfangen; **to ~ of sth** sich *dat* etw
vorstellen; **to ~ of doing sth** sich *dat*
vorstellen, etw zu tun.
concentrate ['kɔnsəntreɪt] *vi* sich
konzentrieren ♦ *vt* konzentrieren.
concentration [kɔnsən'treɪʃən] *n*
Konzentration *f*.
concentration camp *n* Konzentrationslager
nt, KZ *nt*.
concentric [kɔn'sentrɪk] *adj* konzentrisch.
concept ['kɔnsept] *n* Vorstellung *f; (principle)*
Begriff *m*.
conception [kən'sepʃən] *n* Vorstellung *f; (of*
child) Empfängnis *f*.
concern [kən'sɜːn] *n* Angelegenheit *f; (anxiety,*
worry) Sorge *f; (COMM)* Konzern *m* ♦ *vt*
Sorgen machen +*dat; (involve)* angehen;
(relate to) betreffen; **to be ~ed (about)** sich
dat Sorgen machen (um); **"to whom it may**
~" *(on certificate)* „Bestätigung"; *(on*
reference) „Zeugnis"; **as far as I am ~ed** was
mich betrifft; **to be ~ed with** sich
interessieren für; **the department ~ed**
(under discussion) die betreffende
Abteilung; *(involved)* die zuständige
Abteilung.
concerning [kən'sɜːnɪŋ] *prep* bezüglich +*gen*,
hinsichtlich +*gen*.
concert ['kɔnsət] *n* Konzert *nt;* **in ~** *(MUS)*
live; *(activities, actions etc)* gemeinsam.
concerted [kən'sɜːtɪd] *adj* gemeinsam.
concert hall *n* Konzerthalle *f*, Konzertsaal *m*.
concertina [kɔnsə'tiːnə] *n* Konzertina *f* ♦ *vi*
sich wie eine Ziehharmonika
zusammenschieben.
concerto [kən'tʃɜːtəʊ] *n* Konzert *nt*.
concession [kən'seʃən] *n* Zugeständnis *nt*,
Konzession *f; (COMM)* Konzession; **tax ~**
Steuervergünstigung *f*.
concessionaire [kənseʃə'neə•] *n* Konzessionär
m.
concessionary [kən'seʃənrɪ] *adj* ermäßigt.
conciliation [kənsɪlɪ'eɪʃən] *n* Schlichtung *f*.
conciliatory [kən'sɪlɪətrɪ] *adj* versöhnlich.
concise [kən'saɪs] *adj* kurzgefaßt, prägnant.
conclave ['kɔnkleɪv] *n* Klausur *f; (REL)*
Konklave *f*.
conclude [kən'kluːd] *vt* beenden, schließen;
(treaty, deal etc) abschließen; *(decide)*
schließen, folgern ♦ *vi* schließen; *(events):* **to**
~ (with) enden (mit); **"That," he ~d, "is why**
we did it." „Darum", schloß er, „haben wir
es getan"; **I ~ that ...** ich komme zu dem
Schluß, daß ...
concluding [kən'kluːdɪŋ] *adj (remarks etc)*

abschließend, Schluß-.
conclusion [kən'klu:ʒən] n (see vb) Ende nt;
Schluß m; Abschluß m; Folgerung f; **to come
to the ~ that** ... zu dem Schluß kommen,
daß ...
conclusive [kən'klu:sɪv] adj (evidence)
schlüssig; (defeat) endgültig.
concoct [kən'kɔkt] vt (excuse etc) sich dat
ausdenken; (meal, sauce) improvisieren.
concoction [kən'kɔkʃən] n Zusammenstellung
f; (drink) Gebräu nt.
concord ['kɔŋkɔːd] n Eintracht f; (treaty)
Vertrag m.
concourse ['kɔŋkɔːs] n (Eingangs)halle f;
(crowd) Menge f.
concrete ['kɔŋkriːt] n Beton m ◆ adj (ceiling,
block) Beton-; (proposal, idea) konkret.
concrete mixer n Betonmischmaschine f.
concur [kən'kəː] vi übereinstimmen; **to
~ with** beipflichten +dat.
concurrently [kən'kʌrntlɪ] adv gleichzeitig.
concussion [kən'kʌʃən] n
Gehirnerschütterung f.
condemn [kən'dɛm] vt verurteilen; (building)
für abbruchreif erklären.
condemnation [kɔndɛm'neɪʃən] n
Verurteilung f.
condensation [kɔndɛn'seɪʃən] n Kondens-
wasser nt.
condense [kən'dɛns] vi kondensieren, sich
niederschlagen ◆ vt zusammenfassen.
condensed milk [kən'dɛnst-] n Kondensmilch
f, Büchsenmilch f.
condescend [kɔndɪ'sɛnd] vi herablassend
sein; **to ~ to do sth** sich dazu herablassen,
etw zu tun.
condescending [kɔndɪ'sɛndɪŋ] adj
herablassend.
condition [kən'dɪʃən] n Zustand m;
(requirement) Bedingung f; (illness) Leiden nt
◆ vt konditionieren; (hair) in Form bringen;
conditions npl (circumstances) Verhältnisse
pl; **in good/poor ~** (person) in guter/
schlechter Verfassung; (thing) in gutem/
schlechtem Zustand; **a heart ~** ein
Herzleiden nt; **weather ~s** die Wetterlage;
on ~ that ... unter der Bedingung, daß ...
conditional [kən'dɪʃənl] adj bedingt; **to be
~ upon** abhängen von.
conditioner [kən'dɪʃənə*] n (for hair)
Pflegespülung f; (for fabrics) Weichspüler m.
condo ['kɔndəu] (US: inf) n abbr
= condominium.
condolences [kən'dəulənsɪz] npl Beileid nt.
condom ['kɔndəm] n Kondom m or nt.
condominium [kɔndə'mɪnɪəm] (US) n Haus nt
mit Eigentumswohnungen; (rooms)
Eigentumswohnung f.
condone [kən'dəun] vt gutheißen.
conducive [kən'djuːsɪv] adj: **~ to** förderlich
+dat.
conduct [n 'kɔndʌkt, vt kən'dʌkt] n Verhalten

nt ◆ vt (investigation etc) durchführen;
(manage) führen; (orchestra, choir etc)
dirigieren; (heat, electricity) leiten; **to ~ o.s.**
sich verhalten.
conducted tour [kən'dʌktɪd-] n Führung f.
conductor [kən'dʌktə*] n (of orchestra)
Dirigent(in) m(f); (on bus) Schaffner m; (US:
on train) Zugführer(in) m(f); (ELEC) Leiter m.
conductress [kən'dʌktrɪs] n (on bus)
Schaffnerin f.
conduit ['kɔndjuɪt] n (TECH) Leitungsrohr nt;
(ELEC) Isolierrohr nt.
cone [kəun] n Kegel m; (on road) Leitkegel m;
(BOT) Zapfen m; (ice cream cornet) (Eis)tüte f.
confectioner [kən'fɛkʃənə*] n (maker)
Süßwarenhersteller(in) m(f); (seller)
Süßwarenhändler(in) m(f); (of cakes)
Konditor(in) m(f).
confectioner's (shop) [kən'fɛkʃənəz-] n
Süßwarenladen m; (cake shop) Konditorei f.
confectionery [kən'fɛkʃənrɪ] n Süßwaren pl,
Süßigkeiten pl; (cakes) Konditorwaren pl.
confederate [kən'fɛdrɪt] adj verbündet ◆ n
(pej) Komplize m, Komplizin f; (US: HIST) **the
C~s** die Konföderierten pl.
confederation [kənfɛdə'reɪʃən] n Bund m;
(POL) Bündnis nt; (COMM) Verband m.
confer [kən'fəː*] vt: **to ~ sth (on sb)** (jdm) etw
verleihen ◆ vi sich beraten; **to ~ with sb
about sth** sich mit jdm über etw acc
beraten, etw mit jdm besprechen.
conference ['kɔnfərəns] n Konferenz f; (more
informal) Besprechung f; **to be in ~** in or bei
einer Konferenz/Besprechung sein.
conference room n Konferenzraum m;
(smaller) Besprechungszimmer nt.
confess [kən'fɛs] vt bekennen; (sin) beichten;
(crime) zugeben, gestehen ◆ vi (admit)
gestehen; **to ~ to sth** (crime) etw gestehen;
(weakness etc) sich zu etw bekennen; **I must
~ that I didn't enjoy it at all** ich muß sagen,
daß es mir überhaupt keinen Spaß gemacht
hat.
confession [kən'fɛʃən] n Geständnis nt; (REL)
Beichte f; **to make a ~** ein Geständnis
ablegen.
confessor [kən'fɛsə*] n Beichtvater m.
confetti [kən'fɛtɪ] n Konfetti nt.
confide [kən'faɪd] vi: **to ~ in** sich anvertrauen
+dat.
confidence ['kɔnfɪdns] n Vertrauen nt; (self-
assurance) Selbstvertrauen nt; (secret)
vertrauliche Mitteilung f, Geheimnis nt; **to
have ~ in sb/sth** Vertrauen zu jdm/etw
haben; **to have (every) ~ that** ... ganz
zuversichtlich sein, daß ...; **motion of no ~**
Mißtrauensantrag m; **to tell sb sth in strict ~**
jdm etw ganz im Vertrauen sagen; **in ~**
vertraulich.
confidence trick n Schwindel m.
confident ['kɔnfɪdənt] adj (selbst)sicher;
(positive) zuversichtlich.

confidential [kɔnfɪ'denʃəl] *adj* vertraulich; (*secretary*) Privat-.
confidentiality [kɔnfɪdenʃɪ'ælɪtɪ] *n* Vertraulichkeit *f*.
configuration [kənfɪgju'reɪʃən] *n* Anordnung *f*; (*COMPUT*) Konfiguration *f*.
confine [kən'faɪn] *vt* (*shut up*) einsperren; **to ~ (to)** beschränken (auf *+acc*); **to ~ o.s. to sth** sich auf etw *acc* beschränken; **to ~ o.s. to doing sth** sich darauf beschränken, etw zu tun.
confined [kən'faɪnd] *adj* begrenzt.
confinement [kən'faɪnmənt] *n* Haft *f*; (*MED*) Entbindung *f*.
confines ['kɔnfaɪnz] *npl* Grenzen *pl*; (*of situation*) Rahmen *m*.
confirm [kən'fɜːm] *vt* bestätigen; **to be ~ed** (*REL*) konfirmiert werden.
confirmation [kɔnfə'meɪʃən] *n* Bestätigung *f*; (*REL*) Konfirmation *f*.
confirmed [kən'fɜːmd] *adj* (*bachelor*) eingefleischt; (*teetotaller*) überzeugt.
confiscate ['kɔnfɪskeɪt] *vt* beschlagnahmen, konfiszieren.
confiscation [kɔnfɪs'keɪʃən] *n* Beschlagnahme *f*, Konfiszierung *f*.
conflagration [kɔnflə'greɪʃən] *n* Feuersbrunst *f*.
conflict ['kɔnflɪkt] *n* Konflikt *m*; (*fighting*) Zusammenstoß *m*, Kampf *m* ♦ *vi*: **to ~ (with)** im Widerspruch stehen (zu).
conflicting [kən'flɪktɪŋ] *adj* widersprüchlich.
conform [kən'fɔːm] *vi* sich anpassen; **to ~ to** entsprechen *+dat*.
conformist [kən'fɔːmɪst] *n* Konformist(in) *m(f)*.
confound [kən'faund] *vt* verwirren; (*amaze*) verblüffen.
confounded [kən'faundɪd] *adj* verdammt, verflixt (*inf*).
confront [kən'frʌnt] *vt* (*problems, task*) sich stellen *+dat*; (*enemy, danger*) gegenübertreten *+dat*.
confrontation [kɔnfrən'teɪʃən] *n* Konfrontation *f*.
confuse [kən'fjuːz] *vt* verwirren; (*mix up*) verwechseln; (*complicate*) durcheinanderbringen.
confused [kən'fjuːzd] *adj* (*person*) verwirrt; (*situation*) verworren, konfus; **to get ~** konfus werden.
confusing [kən'fjuːzɪŋ] *adj* verwirrend.
confusion [kən'fjuːʒən] *n* (*mix-up*) Verwechslung *f*; (*perplexity*) Verwirrung *f*; (*disorder*) Durcheinander *nt*.
congeal [kən'dʒiːl] *vi* (*blood*) gerinnen; (*sauce, oil*) erstarren.
congenial [kən'dʒiːnɪəl] *adj* ansprechend, sympathisch; (*atmosphere, place, work, company*) angenehm.
congenital [kən'dʒenɪtl] *adj* angeboren.
conger eel ['kɔŋgər-] *n* Seeaal *m*.

congested [kən'dʒestɪd] *adj* (*road*) verstopft; (*area*) überfüllt; (*nose*) verstopft; **his lungs are ~** in seiner Lunge hat sich Blut angestaut.
congestion [kən'dʒestʃən] *n* (*MED*) Blutstau *m*; (*of road*) Verstopfung *f*; (*of area*) Überfüllung *f*.
conglomerate [kən'glɒmərɪt] *n* (*COMM*) Konglomerat *nt*.
conglomeration [kənglɒmə'reɪʃən] *n* Ansammlung *f*.
Congo ['kɔŋgəu] *n* (*state*) Kongo *m*.
congratulate [kən'grætjuleɪt] *vt* gratulieren; **to ~ sb (on sth)** jdm (zu etw) gratulieren.
congratulations [kəngrætju'leɪʃənz] *npl* Glückwunsch *m*, Glückwünsche *pl*; **~!** Herzlichen Glückwunsch!; **~ on** Glückwünsche zu.
congregate ['kɔŋgrɪgeɪt] *vi* sich versammeln.
congregation [kɔŋgrɪ'geɪʃən] *n* Gemeinde *f*.
congress ['kɔŋgres] *n* Kongreß *m*; (*US*): **C~** der Kongreß.

Der Congress ist die nationale gesetzgebende Versammlung der USA, die in Washington im Capitol zusammentritt. Der Kongreß besteht aus dem Repräsentantenhaus (435 Abgeordnete, entsprechend den Bevölkerungszahlen auf die einzelnen Bundesstaaten verteilt und jeweils für 2 Jahre gewählt) und dem Senat (100 Senatoren, 2 für jeden Bundesstaat, für 6 Jahre gewählt, wobei ein Drittel alle zwei Jahre neu gewählt wird). Sowohl die Abgeordneten als auch die Senatoren werden in direkter Wahl vom Volk gewählt.

---

congressman ['kɔŋgresmən] (*US*) *n* (*irreg: like man*) Kongreßabgeordnete(r) *m*.
congresswoman ['kɔŋgreswumən] (*US*) (*irreg: like woman*) *n* Kongreßabgeordnete *f*.
conical ['kɔnɪkl] *adj* kegelförmig, konisch.
conifer ['kɔnɪfə*] *n* Nadelbaum *m*.
coniferous [kə'nɪfərəs] *adj* Nadel-.
conjecture [kən'dʒektʃə*] *n* Vermutung *f*, Mutmaßung *f* ♦ *vi* vermuten, mutmaßen.
conjugal ['kɔndʒugl] *adj* ehelich.
conjugate ['kɔndʒugeɪt] *vt* konjugieren.
conjugation [kɔndʒə'geɪʃən] *n* Konjugation *f*.
conjunction [kən'dʒʌŋkʃən] *n* Konjunktion *f*; **in ~ with** zusammen mit, in Verbindung mit.
conjunctivitis [kəndʒʌŋktɪ'vaɪtɪs] *n* Bindehautentzündung *f*.
conjure ['kʌndʒə*] *vi* zaubern ♦ *vt* (*also fig*) hervorzaubern.
►conjure up *vt* (*ghost, spirit*) beschwören; (*memories*) heraufbeschwören.
conjurer ['kʌndʒərə*] *n* Zauberer *m*, Zauberkünstler(in) *m(f)*.
conjuring trick ['kʌndʒərɪŋ-] *n* Zaubertrick *m*, Zauberkunststück *nt*.

conker ['kɔŋkə*] n (BRIT) n (Roß)kastanie f.
conk out [kɔŋk-] (inf) vi den Geist aufgeben.
con man n Schwindler m.
Conn. (US) abbr (POST: = Connecticut).
connect [kə'nɛkt] vt verbinden; (ELEC) anschließen; (TEL: caller) verbinden; (: subscriber) anschließen; (fig: associate) in Zusammenhang bringen ♦ vi: **to ~ with** (train, plane etc) Anschluß haben an +acc; **to ~ sth to sth** etw mit einer Sache verbinden; **to be ~ed with** (associated) in einer Beziehung or in Verbindung stehen zu; (have dealings with) zu tun haben mit; **I am trying to ~ you** (TEL) ich versuche, Sie zu verbinden.
connection [kə'nɛkʃən] n Verbindung f; (ELEC) Kontakt m; (train, plane etc, TEL: subscriber) Anschluß m; (fig: association) Beziehung f, Zusammenhang m; **in ~ with** in Zusammenhang mit; **what is the ~ between them?** welche Verbindung besteht zwischen ihnen?; **business ~s** Geschäftsbeziehungen pl; **to get/miss one's ~** seinen Anschluß erreichen/verpassen.
connexion [kə'nɛkʃən] (BRIT) n = **connection**.
conning tower ['kɔnɪŋ-] n Kommandoturm m.
connive [kə'naɪv] vi: **to ~ at** stillschweigend dulden.
connoisseur [kɔnɪ'sə:*] n Kenner(in) m(f).
connotation [kɔnə'teɪʃən] n Konnotation f.
connubial [kə'nju:bɪəl] adj ehelich.
conquer ['kɔŋkə*] vt erobern; (enemy, fear, feelings) besiegen.
conqueror ['kɔŋkərə*] n Eroberer m.
conquest ['kɔŋkwɛst] n Eroberung f.
cons [kɔnz] npl see **convenience, pro.**
conscience ['kɔnʃəns] n Gewissen nt; **to have a guilty/clear ~** ein schlechtes/gutes Gewissen haben; **in all ~** allen Ernstes.
conscientious [kɔnʃɪ'ɛnʃəs] adj gewissenhaft.
conscientious objector n Wehrdienst- or Kriegsdienstverweigerer m (aus Gewissensgründen).
conscious ['kɔnʃəs] adj bewußt; (awake) bei Bewußtsein; **to become ~ of sth** sich dat einer Sache gen bewußt werden; **to become ~ that** ... sich dat bewußt werden, daß ...
consciousness ['kɔnʃəsnɪs] n Bewußtsein nt; **to lose ~** bewußtlos werden; **to regain ~** wieder zu sich kommen.
conscript ['kɔnskrɪpt] n Wehrpflichtige(r) m.
conscription [kən'skrɪpʃən] n Wehrpflicht f.
consecrate ['kɔnsɪkreɪt] vt weihen.
consecutive [kən'sɛkjutɪv] adj aufeinander-folgend; **on three ~ occasions** dreimal hintereinander.
consensus [kən'sɛnsəs] n Übereinstimmung f; **the ~ (of opinion)** die allgemeine Meinung.
consent [kən'sɛnt] n Zustimmung f ♦ vi: **to ~ to** zustimmen +dat; **age of ~** Ehemündigkeitsalter nt; **by common ~** auf allgemeinen Wunsch.
consenting [kən'sɛntɪŋ] adj: **between ~ adults** ≈ zwischen Erwachsenen.
consequence ['kɔnsɪkwəns] n Folge f; **of ~** bedeutend, wichtig; **it's of little ~** es spielt kaum eine Rolle; **in ~** folglich.
consequently ['kɔnsɪkwəntlɪ] adv folglich.
conservation [kɔnsə'veɪʃən] n Erhaltung f, Schutz m; (of energy) Sparen nt; (also: **nature ~**) Umweltschutz m; (of paintings, books) Erhaltung f, Konservierung f; **energy ~** Energieeinsparung f.
conservationist [kɔnsə'veɪʃnɪst] n Umweltschützer(in) m(f).
conservative [kən'sə:vətɪv] adj konservativ; (cautious) vorsichtig; (BRIT: POL): **C~** konservativ ♦ n (BRIT: POL): **C~** Konservative(r) f(m).
Conservative Party n: **the ~** die Konservative Partei f.
conservatory [kən'sə:vətrɪ] n Wintergarten m; (MUS) Konservatorium nt.
conserve [kən'sə:v] vt erhalten; (supplies, energy) sparen ♦ n Konfitüre f.
consider [kən'sɪdə*] vt (study) sich dat überlegen; (take into account) in Betracht ziehen; **to ~ that** ... der Meinung sein, daß ...; **to ~ sb/sth as** ... jdn/etw für ... halten; **to ~ doing sth** in Erwägung ziehen, etw zu tun; **they ~ themselves to be superior** sie halten sich für etwas Besseres; **she ~ed it a disaster** sie betrachtete es als eine Katastrophe; **~ yourself lucky** Sie können sich glücklich schätzen; **all things ~ed** alles in allem.
considerable [kən'sɪdərəbl] adj beträchtlich.
considerably [kən'sɪdərəblɪ] adv beträchtlich; (bigger, smaller etc) um einiges.
considerate [kən'sɪdərɪt] adj rücksichtsvoll.
consideration [kənsɪdə'reɪʃən] n Überlegung f; (factor) Gesichtspunkt m, Faktor m; (thoughtfulness) Rücksicht f; (reward) Entgelt nt; **out of ~ for** aus Rücksicht auf +acc; **to be under ~** geprüft werden; **my first ~ is my family** ich denke zuerst an meine Familie.
considered [kən'sɪdəd] adj: **~ opinion** ernsthafte Überzeugung.
considering [kən'sɪdərɪŋ] prep in Anbetracht +gen; **~ (that)** wenn man bedenkt(, daß).
consign [kən'saɪn] vt: **to ~ to** (object: to place) verbannen in +acc; (person: to sb's care) anvertrauen +dat; (: to poverty) verurteilen zu; (send) versenden an +acc.
consignment [kən'saɪnmənt] n Sendung f, Lieferung f.
consignment note n Frachtbrief m.
consist [kən'sɪst] vi: **to ~ of** bestehen aus.
consistency [kən'sɪstənsɪ] n (of actions etc) Konsequenz f; (of cream etc) Konsistenz f, Dicke f.
consistent [kən'sɪstənt] adj konsequent;

(*argument, idea*) logisch, folgerichtig; **to be ~ with** entsprechen +*dat*.
consolation [kɔnsəˈleɪʃən] n Trost m.
console [kənˈsəul] vt trösten ♦ n (*panel*) Schalttafel f.
consolidate [kənˈsɔlɪdeɪt] vt festigen.
consols [ˈkɔnsɔlz] (*BRIT*) npl (*STOCK EXCHANGE*) Konsols pl, konsolidierte Staatsanleihen pl.
consommé [kənˈsɔmeɪ] n Kraftbrühe f, Consommé f.
consonant [ˈkɔnsənənt] n Konsonant m, Mitlaut m.
consort [ˈkɔnsɔːt] n Gemahl(in) m(f), Gatte m, Gattin f ♦ vi: **to ~ with sb** mit jdm verkehren; **prince ~** Prinzgemahl m.
consortium [kənˈsɔːtɪəm] n Konsortium nt.
conspicuous [kənˈspɪkjuəs] adj auffallend; **to make o.s. ~** auffallen.
conspiracy [kənˈspɪrəsɪ] n Verschwörung f, Komplott nt.
conspiratorial [kənspɪrəˈtɔːrɪəl] adj verschwörerisch.
conspire [kənˈspaɪə*] vi sich verschwören; (*events*) zusammenkommen.
constable [ˈkʌnstəbl] (*BRIT*) n Polizist m; **chief ~** Polizeipräsident m, Polizeichef m.
constabulary [kənˈstæbjulərɪ] (*BRIT*) n Polizei f.
constant [ˈkɔnstənt] adj dauernd, ständig; (*fixed*) konstant, gleichbleibend.
constantly [ˈkɔnstəntlɪ] adv (an)dauernd, ständig.
constellation [kɔnstəˈleɪʃən] n Sternbild nt.
consternation [kɔnstəˈneɪʃən] n Bestürzung f.
constipated [ˈkɔnstɪpeɪtɪd] adj: **to be ~** Verstopfung haben, verstopft sein.
constipation [kɔnstɪˈpeɪʃən] n Verstopfung f.
constituency [kənˈstɪtjuənsɪ] n (*POL*) Wahlkreis m; (*electors*) Wähler pl (*eines Wahlkreises*).
constituency party n Parteiorganisation in einem Wahlkreis.
constituent [kənˈstɪtjuənt] n (*POL*) Wähler(in) m(f); (*component*) Bestandteil m.
constitute [ˈkɔnstɪtjuːt] vt (*represent*) darstellen; (*make up*) bilden, ausmachen.
constitution [kɔnstɪˈtjuːʃən] n (*POL*) Verfassung f; (*of club etc*) Satzung f; (*health*) Konstitution f, Gesundheit f; (*make-up*) Zusammensetzung f.
constitutional [kɔnstɪˈtjuːʃnl] adj (*government*) verfassungsmäßig; (*reform etc*) Verfassungs-.
constitutional monarchy n konstitutionelle Monarchie f.
constrain [kənˈstreɪn] vt zwingen.
constrained [kənˈstreɪnd] adj gezwungen.
constraint [kənˈstreɪnt] n Beschränkung f, Einschränkung f; (*compulsion*) Zwang m; (*embarrassment*) Befangenheit f.
constrict [kənˈstrɪkt] vt einschnüren; (*blood*

vessel) verengen; (*limit, restrict*) einschränken.
constriction [kənˈstrɪkʃən] n Einschränkung f; (*tightness*) Verengung f; (*squeezing*) Einschnürung f.
construct [kənˈstrʌkt] vt bauen; (*machine*) konstruieren; (*theory, argument*) entwickeln.
construction [kənˈstrʌkʃən] n Bau m; (*structure*) Konstruktion f; (*fig: interpretation*) Deutung f; **under ~** in or im Bau.
construction industry n Bauindustrie f.
constructive [kənˈstrʌktɪv] adj konstruktiv.
construe [kənˈstruː] vt auslegen, deuten.
consul [ˈkɔnsl] n Konsul(in) m(f).
consulate [ˈkɔnsjulɪt] n Konsulat nt.
consult [kənˈsʌlt] vt (*doctor, lawyer*) konsultieren; (*friend*) sich beraten or besprechen mit; (*reference book*) nachschlagen in +*dat*; **to ~ sb (about sth)** jdn (wegen etw) fragen.
consultancy [kənˈsʌltənsɪ] n Beratungsbüro nt; (*MED: job*) Facharztstelle f.
consultant [kənˈsʌltənt] n (*MED*) Facharzt m, Fachärztin f; (*other specialist*) Berater(in) m(f) ♦ cpd: **~ engineer** beratender Ingenieur m; **~ paediatrician** Facharzt/-ärztin m/f für Pädiatrie or Kinderheilkunde; **legal/management ~** Rechts-/Unternehmensberater(in) m(f).
consultation [kɔnsəlˈteɪʃən] n (*MED, LAW*) Konsultation f; (*discussion*) Beratung f, Besprechung f; **in ~ with** in gemeinsamer Beratung mit.
consultative [kənˈsʌltətɪv] adj beratend.
consulting room [kənˈsʌltɪŋ-] (*BRIT*) n Sprechzimmer nt.
consume [kənˈsjuːm] vt (*food, drink*) zu sich nehmen, konsumieren; (*fuel, energy*) verbrauchen; (*time*) in Anspruch nehmen; (*subj: emotion*) verzehren; (: *fire*) vernichten.
consumer [kənˈsjuːmə*] n Verbraucher(in) m(f).
consumer credit n Verbraucherkredit m.
consumer durables npl (langlebige) Gebrauchsgüter pl.
consumer goods npl Konsumgüter pl.
consumerism [kənˈsjuːmərɪzəm] n Verbraucherschutz m.
consumer society n Konsumgesellschaft f.
consumer watchdog n Verbraucherschutzorganisation f.
consummate [ˈkɔnsʌmeɪt] vt (*marriage*) vollziehen; (*ambition etc*) erfüllen.
consumption [kənˈsʌmpʃən] n Verbrauch m; (*of food*) Verzehr m; (*of drinks, buying*) Konsum m; (*MED*) Schwindsucht f; **not fit for human ~** zum Verzehr ungeeignet.
cont. abbr (= *continued*) Forts.
contact [ˈkɔntækt] n Kontakt m; (*touch*) Berührung f; (*person*) Kontaktperson f ♦ vt sich in Verbindung setzen mit; **to be in ~ with sb/sth** mit jdm/etw in Verbindung or

Kontakt stehen; (*touch*) jdn/etw berühren;
business ~s Geschäftsverbindungen *pl*.
contact lenses *npl* Kontaktlinsen *pl*.
contagious [kən'teɪdʒəs] *adj* ansteckend.
contain [kən'teɪn] *vt* enthalten; (*growth,
spread*) in Grenzen halten; (*feeling*)
beherrschen; **to ~ o.s.** an sich *acc* halten.
container [kən'teɪnə*] *n* Behälter *m*; (*for
shipping etc*) Container *m* ♦ *cpd* Container-.
containerize [kən'teɪnəraɪz] *vt* in Container
verpacken; (*port*) auf Container umstellen.
container ship *n* Containerschiff *nt*.
contaminate [kən'tæmɪneɪt] *vt* (*water, food*)
verunreinigen; (*soil etc*) verseuchen.
contamination [kəntæmɪ'neɪʃən] *n* (*see vb*)
Verunreinigung *f*; Verseuchung *f*.
cont'd *abbr* (= *continued*) Forts.
contemplate ['kɔntəmpleɪt] *vt* nachdenken
über +*acc*; (*course of action*) in Erwägung
ziehen; (*person, painting etc*) betrachten.
contemplation [kɔntəm'pleɪʃən] *n*
Betrachtung *f*.
contemporary [kən'tempərərɪ] *adj*
zeitgenössisch; (*present-day*) modern ♦ *n*
Altersgenosse *m*, Altersgenossin *f*; **Samuel
Pepys and his contemporaries** Samuel
Pepys und seine Zeitgenossen.
contempt [kən'tempt] *n* Verachtung *f*; ~ **of
court** (*LAW*) Mißachtung *f* (der Würde) des
Gerichts, Ungebühr *f* vor Gericht; **to have
~ for sb/sth** jdn/etw verachten; **to hold sb
in** ~ jdn verachten.
contemptible [kən'temptəbl] *adj*
verachtenswert.
contemptuous [kən'temptjuəs] *adj*
verächtlich, geringschätzig.
contend [kən'tend] *vt*: **to ~ that** ... behaupten,
daß ...; **to ~ with** fertigwerden mit; **to ~ for**
kämpfen um; **to have to ~ with** es zu tun
haben mit; **he has a lot to ~ with** er hat viel
um die Ohren.
contender [kən'tendə*] *n* (*SPORT*)
Wettkämpfer(in) *m(f)*; (*for title*) Anwärter(in)
m(f); (*POL*) Kandidat(in) *m(f)*.
content [*adj, vt* kən'tent, *n* 'kɔntent] *adj*
zufrieden ♦ *vt* zufriedenstellen ♦ *n* Inhalt *m*;
(*fat content, moisture content etc*) Gehalt *m*;
contents *npl* Inhalt; (**table of**) ~s
Inhaltsverzeichnis *nt*; **to be ~ with**
zufrieden sein mit; **to ~ o.s. with sth** sich
mit etw zufriedengeben *or* begnügen; **to
~ o.s. with doing sth** sich damit
zufriedengeben *or* begnügen, etw zu tun.
contented [kən'tentɪd] *adj* zufrieden.
contentedly [kən'tentɪdlɪ] *adv* zufrieden.
contention [kən'tenʃən] *n* Behauptung *f*;
(*disagreement, argument*) Streit *m*; **bone of** ~
Zankapfel *m*.
contentious [kən'tenʃəs] *adj* strittig,
umstritten.
contentment [kən'tentmənt] *n* Zufriedenheit
f.

contest [*n* 'kɔntest, *vt* kən'test] *n* (*competition*)
Wettkampf *m*; (*for control, power etc*) Kampf
m ♦ *vt* (*election, competition*) teilnehmen an
+*dat*; (*compete for*) kämpfen um; (*statement*)
bestreiten; (*decision*) angreifen; (*LAW*)
anfechten.
contestant [kən'testənt] *n* (*in quiz*)
Kandidat(in) *m(f)*; (*in competition*)
Teilnehmer(in) *m(f)*; (*in fight*) Kämpfer(in)
m(f).
context ['kɔntekst] *n* Zusammenhang *m*,
Kontext *m*; **in** ~ im Zusammenhang; **out of**
~ aus dem Zusammenhang gerissen.
continent ['kɔntɪnənt] *n* Kontinent *m*, Erdteil
m; **the C~** (*BRIT*) (Kontinental)europa *nt*; **on
the C~** in (Kontinental)europa, auf dem
Kontinent.
continental [kɔntɪ'nentl] *adj* kontinental;
(*European*) europäisch ♦ *n* (*BRIT*)
(Festlands)europäer(in) *m(f)*.
continental breakfast *n* kleines Frühstück
nt.
continental quilt (*BRIT*) *n* Steppdecke *f*.
contingency [kən'tɪndʒənsɪ] *n* möglicher Fall
m, Eventualität *f*.
contingency plan *n* Plan *m* für den
Eventualfall.
contingent [kən'tɪndʒənt] *n* Kontingent *nt*
♦ *adj*: **to be ~ upon** abhängen von.
continual [kən'tɪnjuəl] *adj* ständig; (*process*)
ununterbrochen.
continually [kən'tɪnjuəlɪ] *adv* (*see adj*) ständig;
ununterbrochen.
continuation [kəntɪnju'eɪʃən] *n* Fortsetzung *f*;
(*extension*) Weiterführung *f*.
continue [kən'tɪnju:] *vi* andauern;
(*performance, road*) weitergehen; (*person:
talking*) fortfahren ♦ *vt* fortsetzen; **to ~ to do
sth/doing sth** etw weiter tun; **"to be ~d"**
„Fortsetzung folgt"; **"~d on page 10"**
„Fortsetzung auf Seite 10".
continuing education [kən'tɪnjuɪŋ-] *n*
Erwachsenenbildung *f*.
continuity [kɔntɪ'njuːɪtɪ] *n* Kontinuität *f* ♦ *cpd*
(*TV*): ~ **announcer** Ansager(in) *m(f)*; ~ **studio**
Ansagestudio *nt*.
continuous [kən'tɪnjuəs] *adj* ununterbrochen;
(*growth etc*) kontinuierlich; ~ **form** (*LING*)
Verlaufsform *f*; ~ **performance** (*CINE*)
durchgehende Vorstellung *f*.
continuously [kən'tɪnjuəslɪ] *adv* dauernd,
ständig; (*uninterruptedly*) ununterbrochen.
continuous stationery *n* (*COMPUT*)
Endlospapier *nt*.
contort [kən'tɔːt] *vt* (*body*) verrenken,
verdrehen; (*face*) verziehen.
contortion [kən'tɔːʃən] *n* Verrenkung *f*.
contortionist [kən'tɔːʃənɪst] *n*
Schlangenmensch *m*.
contour ['kɔntuə*] *n* (*also*: ~ **line**) Höhenlinie *f*;
(*shape, outline: gen pl*) Kontur *f*, Umriß *m*.
contraband ['kɔntrəbænd] *n* Schmuggelware *f*

♦ *adj* Schmuggel-.
contraception [kɔntrə'sɛpʃən] *n*
Empfängnisverhütung *f*.
contraceptive [kɔntrə'sɛptɪv] *adj*
empfängnisverhütend ♦ *n* Verhütungsmittel
nt.
contract [*n, cpd* 'kɔntrækt, *vb* kɔn'trækt] *n*
Vertrag *m* ♦ *vi* schrumpfen; (*metal, muscle*)
sich zusammenziehen ♦ *vt* (*illness*)
erkranken an +*dat* ♦ *cpd* vertraglich
festgelegt; (*work*) Auftrags-; ~ **of**
employment/service Arbeitsvertrag *m*; **to**
~ **to do sth** (*COMM*) sich vertraglich
verpflichten, etw zu tun.
▶**contract in** (*BRIT*) *vi* beitreten.
▶**contract out** (*BRIT*) *vi* austreten.
contraction [kɔn'trækʃən] *n* Zusammenziehen
nt; (*LING*) Kontraktion *f*; (*MED*) Wehe *f*.
contractor [kɔn'træktə*] *n* Auftragnehmer *m*;
(*building contractor*) Bauunternehmer *m*.
contractual [kɔn'træktʃuəl] *adj* vertraglich.
contradict [kɔntrə'dɪkt] *vt* widersprechen
+*dat*.
contradiction [kɔntrə'dɪkʃən] *n* Widerspruch
m; **to be in** ~ **with** im Widerspruch stehen
zu; **a** ~ **in terms** ein Widerspruch in sich.
contradictory [kɔntrə'dɪktəri] *adj*
widersprüchlich.
contralto [kɔn'træltəu] *n* (*MUS*) Altistin *f*;
(: *voice*) Alt *m*.
contraption [kɔn'træpʃən] (*pej*) *n* (*device*)
Vorrichtung *f*; (*machine*) Gerät *nt*, Apparat
m.
contrary[1] ['kɔntrəri] *adj* entgegengesetzt;
(*ideas, opinions*) gegensätzlich;
(*unfavourable*) widrig ♦ *n* Gegenteil *nt*; ~ **to**
what we thought im Gegensatz zu dem,
was wir dachten; **on the** ~ im Gegenteil;
unless you hear to the ~ sofern Sie nichts
Gegenteiliges hören.
contrary[2] [kɔn'trɛəri] *adj* widerspenstig.
contrast ['kɔntrɑːst] *n* Gegensatz *m*, Kontrast
m ♦ *vt* vergleichen, gegenüberstellen; **in**
~ **to** *or* **with** im Gegensatz zu.
contrasting [kɔn'trɑːstɪŋ] *adj* (*colours*)
kontrastierend; (*attitudes*) gegensätzlich.
contravene [kɔntrə'viːn] *vt* verstoßen gegen.
contravention [kɔntrə'vɛnʃən] *n* Verstoß *m*;
to be in ~ **of sth** gegen etw verstoßen.
contribute [kɔn'trɪbjuːt] *vi* beitragen ♦ *vt*: **to**
~ **£10/an article to** £10/einen Artikel
beisteuern zu; **to** ~ **to** (*charity*) spenden für;
(*newspaper*) schreiben für; (*discussion,*
problem etc) beitragen zu.
contribution [kɔntrɪ'bjuːʃən] *n* Beitrag *m*;
(*donation*) Spende *f*.
contributor [kɔn'trɪbjutə*] *n* (*to appeal*)
Spender(in) *m(f)*; (*to newspaper*)
Mitarbeiter(in) *m(f)*.
contributory [kɔn'trɪbjutəri] *adj*: **a** ~ **cause**
ein Faktor, der mit eine Rolle spielt; **it was**
a ~ **factor in ...** es trug zu ... bei.

contributory pension scheme (*BRIT*) *n*
beitragspflichtige Rentenversicherung *f*.
contrite ['kɔntraɪt] *adj* zerknirscht.
contrivance [kɔn'traɪvəns] *n* (*scheme*) List *f*;
(*device*) Vorrichtung *f*.
contrive [kɔn'traɪv] *vt* (*meeting*) arrangieren
♦ *vi*: **to** ~ **to do sth** es fertigbringen, etw zu
tun.
control [kɔn'trəul] *vt* (*country*) regieren;
(*organization*) leiten; (*machinery, process*)
steuern; (*wages, prices*) kontrollieren;
(*temper*) zügeln; (*disease, fire*) unter
Kontrolle bringen ♦ *n* (*of country*) Kontrolle
f; (*of organization*) Leitung *f*; (*of oneself,*
emotions) Beherrschung *f*; (*SCI: also:*
~ **group**) Kontrollgruppe *f*; **controls** *npl* (*of*
vehicle) Steuerung *f*; (*on radio, television etc*)
Bedienungsfeld *nt*; (*governmental*) Kontrolle
f; **to** ~ **o.s.** sich beherrschen; **to take** ~ **of**
die Kontrolle übernehmen über +*acc*;
(*COMM*) übernehmen; **to be in** ~ **of** unter
Kontrolle haben; (*in charge of*) unter sich *dat*
haben; **out of/under** ~ außer/unter
Kontrolle; **everything is under** ~ ich habe/
wir haben *etc* die Sache im Griff (*inf*); **the**
car went out of ~ der Fahrer verlor die
Kontrolle über den Wagen; **circumstances**
beyond our ~ unvorhersehbare Umstände.
control key *n* (*COMPUT*) Control-Taste *f*.
controller [kɔn'trəulə*] *n* (*RADIO, TV*)
Intendant(in) *m(f)*.
controlling interest [kɔn'trəulɪŋ-] *n*
Mehrheitsanteil *m*.
control panel *n* Schalttafel *f*; (*on television*)
Bedienungsfeld *nt*.
control point *n* Kontrollpunkt *m*,
Kontrollstelle *f*.
control room *n* (*NAUT*) Kommandoraum *m*;
(*MIL*) (Operations)zentrale *f*; (*RADIO, TV*)
Regieraum *m*.
control tower *n* Kontrollturm *m*.
control unit *n* (*COMPUT*) Steuereinheit *f*.
controversial [kɔntrə'vəːʃl] *adj* umstritten,
kontrovers.
controversy ['kɔntrəvəːsi] *n* Streit *m*,
Kontroverse *f*.
conurbation [kɔnə'beɪʃən] *n* Ballungsgebiet
nt, Ballungsraum *m*.
convalesce [kɔnvə'lɛs] *vi* genesen.
convalescence [kɔnvə'lɛsns] *n* Genesungszeit
f.
convalescent [kɔnvə'lɛsnt] *adj* (*leave etc*)
Genesungs-, Kur- ♦ *n* Genesende(r) *f(m)*.
convector [kɔn'vɛktə*] *n* Heizlüfter *m*.
convene [kɔn'viːn] *vt* einberufen ♦ *vi*
zusammentreten.
convener [kɔn'viːnə*] *n* (*organizer*)
Organisator(in) *m(f)*; (*chairperson*)
Vorsitzende(r) *f(m)*.
convenience [kɔn'viːnɪəns] *n* Annehmlichkeit
f; (*suitability*): **the** ~ **of this arrangement/**
location diese günstige Vereinbarung/Lage;

I like the ~ **of having a shower** mir gefällt, wie angenehm es ist, eine Dusche zu haben; **I like the** ~ **of living in the city** mir gefällt, wie praktisch es ist, in der Stadt zu wohnen; **at your** ~ wann es Ihnen paßt; **at your earliest** ~ möglichst bald, baldmöglichst; **with all modern** ~**s** or (*BRIT*) **all mod cons** mit allem modernen Komfort; *see also* **public convenience**.

convenience foods *npl* Fertiggerichte *pl*.

convenient [kən'viːnɪənt] *adj* günstig; (*handy*) praktisch; (*house etc*) günstig gelegen; **if it is** ~ **to you** wenn es Ihnen (so) paßt, wenn es Ihnen keine Umstände macht.

conveniently [kən'viːnɪəntlɪ] *adv* (*happen*) günstigerweise; (*situated*) günstig.

convenor [kən'viːnəʳ] *n* = **convener**.

convent ['kɔnvənt] *n* Kloster *nt*.

convention [kən'vɛnʃən] *n* Konvention *f*; (*conference*) Tagung *f*, Konferenz *f*; (*agreement*) Abkommen *nt*.

conventional [kən'vɛnʃənl] *adj* konventionell.

convent school *n* Klosterschule *f*.

converge [kən'vəːdʒ] *vi* (*roads*) zusammenlaufen ♦ *vi* sich einander annähern; **to** ~ **on sb/a place** (*people*) von überallher zu jdm/an einen Ort strömen.

conversant [kən'vəːsnt] *adj:* **to be** ~ **with** vertraut sein mit.

conversation [kɔnvə'seɪʃən] *n* Gespräch *nt*, Unterhaltung *f*.

conversational [kɔnvə'seɪʃənl] *adj* (*tone, style*) Unterhaltungs-; (*language*) gesprochen; ~ **mode** (*COMPUT*) Dialogbetrieb *m*.

conversationalist [kɔnvə'seɪʃnəlɪst] *n* Unterhalter(in) *m(f)*, Gesprächspartner(in) *m(f)*.

converse [*n* 'kɔnvəːs, *vi* kən'vəːs] *n* Gegenteil *nt* ♦ *vi:* **to** ~ **(with sb) (about sth)** sich (mit jdm) (über etw) unterhalten.

conversely [kɔn'vəːslɪ] *adv* umgekehrt.

conversion [kən'vəːʃən] *n* Umwandlung *f*; (*of weights etc*) Umrechnung *f*; (*REL*) Bekehrung *f*; (*BRIT: of house*) Umbau *m*.

conversion table *n* Umrechnungstabelle *f*.

convert [*vt* kən'vəːt, *n* 'kɔnvəːt] *vt* umwandeln; (*person*) bekehren; (*building*) umbauen; (*vehicle*) umrüsten; (*COMM*) konvertieren; (*RUGBY*) verwandeln ♦ *n* Bekehrte(r) *f(m)*.

convertible [kən'vəːtəbl] *adj* (*currency*) konvertierbar ♦ *n* (*AUT*) Kabriolett *nt*.

convex ['kɔnvɛks] *adj* konvex.

convey [kən'veɪ] *vt* (*information etc*) vermitteln; (*cargo, traveller*) befördern; (*thanks*) übermitteln.

conveyance [kən'veɪəns] *n* Beförderung *f*, Spedition *f*; (*vehicle*) Gefährt *nt*.

conveyancing [kən'veɪənsɪŋ] *n* (Eigentums)übertragung *f*.

conveyor belt *n* Fließband *nt*.

convict [*vt* kən'vɪkt, *n* 'kɔnvɪkt] *vt* verurteilen ♦ *n* Sträfling *m*.

conviction [kən'vɪkʃən] *n* Überzeugung *f*; (*LAW*) Verurteilung *f*.

convince [kən'vɪns] *vt* überzeugen; **to** ~ **sb (of sth)** jdn (von etw) überzeugen; **to** ~ **sb that** ... jdn davon überzeugen, daß ...

convinced [kən'vɪnst] *adj:* ~ **(of)** überzeugt (von); ~ **that** ... überzeugt davon, daß ...

convincing [kən'vɪnsɪŋ] *adj* überzeugend.

convincingly [kən'vɪnsɪŋlɪ] *adv* überzeugend.

convivial [kən'vɪvɪəl] *adj* freundlich; (*event*) gesellig.

convoluted ['kɔnvəluːtɪd] *adj* verwickelt, kompliziert; (*shape*) gewunden.

convoy ['kɔnvɔɪ] *n* Konvoi *m*.

convulse [kən'vʌls] *vt:* **to be** ~**d with laughter/pain** sich vor Lachen schütteln/ Schmerzen krümmen.

convulsion [kən'vʌlʃən] *n* Schüttelkrampf *m*.

coo [kuː] *vi* gurren.

cook [kuk] *vt* kochen, zubereiten ♦ *vi* (*person, food*) kochen; (*fry, roast*) braten; (*pie*) backen ♦ *n* Koch *m*, Köchin *f*.

▶**cook up** (*inf*) *vt* sich *dat* einfallen lassen, zurechtbasteln.

cookbook ['kukbuk] *n* Kochbuch *nt*.

cook-chill ['kuktʃɪl] *adj* durch rasches Kühlen haltbar gemacht.

cooker ['kukəʳ] *n* Herd *m*.

cookery ['kukərɪ] *n* Kochen *nt*, Kochkunst *f*.

cookery book (*BRIT*) *n* = **cookbook**.

cookie ['kukɪ] (*US*) *n* Keks *m or nt*, Plätzchen *nt*.

cooking ['kukɪŋ] *n* Kochen *nt*; (*food*) Essen *nt* ♦ *cpd* Koch-; (*chocolate*) Block-.

cookout ['kukaut] (*US*) *n* ~ Grillparty *f*.

cool [kuːl] *adj* kühl; (*dress, clothes*) leicht, luftig; (*person: calm*) besonnen; (: *unfriendly*) kühl ♦ *vt* kühlen ♦ *vi* abkühlen; **it's** ~ es ist kühl; **to keep sth** ~ *or* **in a** ~ **place** etw kühl aufbewahren; **to keep one's** ~ die Ruhe bewahren.

▶**cool down** *vi* abkühlen; (*fig*) sich beruhigen.

coolant ['kuːlənt] *n* Kühlflüssigkeit *f*.

cool box *n* Kühlbox *f*.

cooler ['kuːləʳ] (*US*) *n* = **cool box**.

cooling ['kuːlɪŋ] *adj* (*drink, shower*) kühlend; (*feeling, emotion*) abkühlend.

cooling tower ['kuːlɪŋ-] *n* Kühlturm *m*.

coolly ['kuːlɪ] *adv* (*calmly*) besonnen, ruhig; (*in unfriendly way*) kühl.

coolness ['kuːlnɪs] *n* (*see adj*) Kühle *f*; Leichtigkeit *f*, Luftigkeit *f*; Besonnenheit *f*.

coop [kuːp] *n* (*for rabbits*) Kaninchenstall *m*; (*for poultry*) Hühnerstall *m* ♦ *vt:* **to** ~ **up** (*fig*) einsperren.

co-op ['kəuɔp] *n abbr* (= *cooperative (society)*) Genossenschaft *f*.

cooperate [kəu'ɔpəreɪt] *vi* zusammenarbeiten; (*assist*) mitmachen, kooperieren; **to** ~ **with sb** mit jdm zusammenarbeiten.

cooperation [kəuɔpə'reɪʃən] *n (see vb)* Zusammenarbeit *f*; Mitarbeit *f*, Kooperation *f*.

cooperative [kəu'ɔpərətɪv] *adj (farm, business)* auf Genossenschaftsbasis; *(person)* kooperativ; (: *helpful*) hilfsbereit ♦ *n* Genossenschaft *f*, Kooperative *f*.

coopt [kəu'ɔpt] *vt:* **to ~ sb onto a committee** jdn in ein Komitee hinzuwählen *or* kooptieren.

coordinate [kəu'ɔ:dɪneɪt] *vt* koordinieren ♦ *n (MATH)* Koordinate *f*; **coordinates** *npl (clothes)* Kleidung *f* zum Kombinieren.

coordination [kəuɔ:dɪ'neɪʃən] *n* Koordinierung *f*, Koordination *f*.

coownership [kəu'əunəʃɪp] *n* Mitbesitz *m*.

cop [kɔp] *(inf) n* Polizist(in) *m(f)*, Bulle *m (pej)*.

cope [kəup] *vi* zurechtkommen; **to ~ with** fertigwerden mit.

Copenhagen ['kəupn'heɪgən] *n* Kopenhagen *nt*.

copier ['kɔpɪə•] *n (also:* **photocopier***)* Kopiergerät *nt*, Kopierer *m*.

copilot ['kəupaɪlət] *n* Kopilot(in) *m(f)*.

copious ['kəupɪəs] *adj* reichlich.

copper ['kɔpə•] *n* Kupfer *nt*; *(BRIT: inf)* Polizist(in) *m(f)*, Bulle *m (pej)*; **coppers** *npl (small change, coins)* Kleingeld *nt*.

coppice ['kɔpɪs] *n* Wäldchen *nt*.

copse [kɔps] *n* = **coppice.**

copulate ['kɔpjuleɪt] *vi* kopulieren.

copy ['kɔpɪ] *n* Kopie *f*; *(of book, record, newspaper)* Exemplar *nt*; *(for printing)* Artikel *m* ♦ *vt (person)* nachahmen; *(idea etc)* nachmachen; *(something written)* abschreiben; **this murder story will make good ~** *(PRESS)* aus diesem Mord kann man etwas machen.

▶**copy out** *vt* abschreiben.

copycat ['kɔpɪkæt] *(pej) n* Nachahmer(in) *m(f)*.

copyright ['kɔpɪraɪt] *n* Copyright *nt*, Urheberrecht *nt*; **~ reserved** urheberrechtlich geschützt.

copy typist *n* Schreibkraft *f (die mit Textvorlagen arbeitet).*

copywriter ['kɔpɪraɪtə•] *n* Werbetexter(in) *m(f)*.

coral ['kɔrəl] *n* Koralle *f*.

coral reef *n* Korallenriff *nt*.

Coral Sea *n:* **the ~** das Korallenmeer.

cord [kɔ:d] *n* Schnur *f*; *(string)* Kordel *f*; *(ELEC)* Kabel *nt*, Schnur *f*; *(fabric)* Kord(samt) *m*; **cords** *npl (trousers)* Kordhosen *pl*.

cordial ['kɔ:dɪəl] *adj* herzlich ♦ *n (BRIT)* Fruchtsaftkonzentrat *nt*.

cordless ['kɔ:dlɪs] *adj* schnurlos.

cordon ['kɔ:dn] *n* Kordon *m*, Absperrkette *f*.

▶**cordon off** *vt (area)* absperren, abriegeln; *(crowd)* mit einer Absperrkette zurückhalten.

corduroy ['kɔ:dərɔɪ] *n* Kord(samt) *m*.

CORE [kɔ:•] *(US) n abbr* (= *Congress of Racial*

Equality) Ausschuß für Rassengleichheit.

core [kɔ:•] *n* Kern *m*; *(of fruit)* Kerngehäuse *nt* ♦ *vt* das Kerngehäuse ausschneiden aus; **rotten to the ~** durch und durch schlecht.

Corfu [kɔ:'fu:] *n* Korfu *nt*.

coriander [kɔrɪ'ændə•] *n* Koriander *m*.

cork [kɔ:k] *n (stopper)* Korken *m*; *(substance)* Kork *m*.

corkage ['kɔ:kɪdʒ] *n* Korkengeld *nt*.

corked [kɔ:kt] *adj:* **the wine is ~** der Wein schmeckt nach Kork.

corkscrew ['kɔ:kskru:] *n* Korkenzieher *m*.

corky ['kɔ:kɪ] *(US) adj* = **corked.**

corm [kɔ:m] *n* Knolle *f*.

cormorant ['kɔ:mərnt] *n* Kormoran *m*.

Corn *(BRIT) abbr (POST:* = *Cornwall).*

corn [kɔ:n] *n (BRIT)* Getreide *nt*, Korn *nt*; *(US)* Mais *m*; *(on foot)* Hühnerauge *nt*; **~ on the cob** Maiskolben *m*.

cornea ['kɔ:nɪə] *n* Hornhaut *f*.

corned beef ['kɔ:nd-] *n* Corned beef *nt*.

corner ['kɔ:nə•] *n* Ecke *f*; *(bend)* Kurve *f* ♦ *vt* in die Enge treiben; *(COMM: market)* monopolisieren ♦ *vi (in car)* die Kurve nehmen; **to cut ~s** *(fig)* das Verfahren abkürzen.

corner flag *n* Eckfahne *f*.

corner kick *n* Eckball *m*.

cornerstone ['kɔ:nəstəun] *n (fig)* Grundstein *m*, Eckstein *m*.

cornet ['kɔ:nɪt] *n (MUS)* Kornett *nt*; *(BRIT: for ice cream)* Eistüte *f*.

cornflakes ['kɔ:nfleɪks] *npl* Corn-flakes *pl*.

cornflour ['kɔ:nflauə•] *(BRIT) n* Stärkemehl *nt*.

cornice ['kɔ:nɪs] *n (Ge)sims nt*.

Cornish ['kɔ:nɪʃ] *adj* kornisch, aus Cornwall.

corn oil *n (Mais)keimöl nt*.

cornstarch ['kɔ:nstɑ:tʃ] *(US) n* = **cornflour.**

cornucopia [kɔ:nju'kəupɪə] *n* Fülle *f*.

Cornwall ['kɔ:nwəl] *n* Cornwall *nt*.

corny ['kɔ:nɪ] *(inf) adj (joke)* blöd.

corollary [kə'rɔlərɪ] *n (logische) Folge f*.

coronary ['kɔrənərɪ] *n (also:* **~ thrombosis***)* Herzinfarkt *m*.

coronation [kɔrə'neɪʃən] *n* Krönung *f*.

coroner ['kɔrənə•] *n* Beamter, der Todesfälle untersucht, die nicht eindeutig eine natürliche Ursache haben.

coronet ['kɔrənɪt] *n* Krone *f*.

Corp. *abbr* = **corporation;** *(MIL)* = **corporal.**

corporal ['kɔ:pərl] *n* Stabsunteroffizier *m*.

corporal punishment *n* Prügelstrafe *f*.

corporate ['kɔ:pərɪt] *adj (organization)* körperschaftlich; *(action, effort, ownership)* gemeinschaftlich; *(finance)* Unternehmens-; *(image, identity)* Firmen-.

corporate hospitality *n Empfänge, Diners etc auf Kosten der aus richtenden Firma.*

corporation [kɔ:pə'reɪʃən] *n (COMM)* Körperschaft *f*; *(of town)* Gemeinde *f*, Stadt *f*.

corporation tax *n* Körperschaftssteuer *f*.

corps [kɔː*] (*pl* ~) *n* Korps *nt*; **the press** ~ die Presse.

corpse [kɔːps] *n* Leiche *f*.

corpuscle ['kɔːpʌsl] *n* Blutkörperchen *nt*.

corral [kə'rɑːl] *n* Korral *m*.

correct [kə'rɛkt] *adj* richtig; (*proper*) korrekt ♦ *vt* korrigieren; (*mistake*) berichtigen, verbessern; **you are** ~ Sie haben recht.

correction [kə'rɛkʃən] *n* (*see vb*) Korrektur *f*; Berichtigung *f*, Verbesserung *f*.

correctly [kə'rɛktlɪ] *adv* (*see adj*) richtig; korrekt.

correlate ['kɔrɪleɪt] *vt* zueinander in Beziehung setzen ♦ *vi:* **to** ~ **with** in einer Beziehung stehen zu.

correlation [kɔrɪ'leɪʃən] *n* Beziehung *f*, Zusammenhang *m*.

correspond [kɔrɪs'pɔnd] *vi:* **to** ~ **(with)** (*write*) korrespondieren (mit); (*be in accordance*) übereinstimmen (mit); **to** ~ **to** (*be equivalent*) entsprechen +*dat*.

correspondence [kɔrɪs'pɔndəns] *n* Korrespondenz *f*, Briefwechsel *m*; (*relationship*) Beziehung *f*.

correspondence column *n* Leserbriefspalte *f*.

correspondence course *n* Fernkurs *m*.

correspondent [kɔrɪs'pɔndənt] *n* Korrespondent(in) *m(f)*.

corresponding [kɔrɪs'pɔndɪŋ] *adj* entsprechend.

corridor ['kɔrɪdɔː*] *n* Korridor *m*; (*in train*) Gang *m*.

corroborate [kə'rɔbəreɪt] *vt* bestätigen.

corrode [kə'rəud] *vt* zerfressen ♦ *vi* korrodieren.

corrosion [kə'rəuʒən] *n* Korrosion *f*.

corrosive [kə'rəuzɪv] *adj* korrosiv.

corrugated ['kɔrəgeɪtɪd] *adj* (*roof*) gewellt; (*cardboard*) Well-.

corrugated iron *n* Wellblech *nt*.

corrupt [kə'rʌpt] *adj* korrupt; (*depraved*) verdorben ♦ *vt* korrumpieren; (*morally*) verderben; ~ **practices** Korruption *f*.

corruption [kə'rʌpʃən] *n* Korruption *f*.

corset ['kɔːsɪt] *n* Korsett *nt*; (*MED*) Stützkorsett *nt*.

Corsica ['kɔːsɪkə] *n* Korsika *nt*.

Corsican ['kɔːsɪkən] *adj* korsisch ♦ *n* Korse *m*, Korsin *f*.

cortège [kɔː'teɪʒ] *n* (*also:* **funeral** ~) Leichenzug *m*.

cortisone ['kɔːtɪzəun] *n* Kortison *nt*.

coruscating ['kɔrəskeɪtɪŋ] *adj* sprühend.

c.o.s. *abbr* (= *cash on shipment*) Barzahlung bei Versand.

cosh [kɔʃ] (*BRIT*) *n* Totschläger *m*.

cosignatory ['kəu'sɪgnətərɪ] *n* Mitunterzeichner(in) *m(f)*.

cosiness ['kəuzɪnɪs] *n* Gemütlichkeit *f*, Behaglichkeit *f*.

cos lettuce ['kɔs-] *n* römischer Salat *m*.

cosmetic [kɔz'mɛtɪk] *n* Kosmetikum *nt* ♦ *adj* kosmetisch; ~ **surgery** (*MED*) kosmetische Chirurgie *f*.

cosmic ['kɔzmɪk] *adj* kosmisch.

cosmonaut ['kɔzmənɔːt] *n* Kosmonaut(in) *m(f)*.

cosmopolitan [kɔzmə'pɔlɪtn] *adj* kosmopolitisch.

cosmos ['kɔzmɔs] *n:* **the** ~ der Kosmos.

cosset ['kɔsɪt] *vt* verwöhnen.

cost [kɔst] (*pt, pp* **cost**) *n* Kosten *pl*; (*fig: loss, damage etc*) Preis *m* ♦ *vt* kosten; (*find out cost of*) (*pt, pp* **costed**) veranschlagen; **costs** *npl* (*COMM, LAW*) Kosten *pl*; **the** ~ **of living** die Lebenshaltungskosten *pl*; **at all** ~**s** um jeden Preis; **how much does it** ~? wieviel *or* was kostet es?; **it** ~**s £5/too much** es kostet £5/ ist zu teuer; **what will it** ~ **to have it repaired?** wieviel kostet die Reparatur?; **to** ~ **sb time/effort** jdn Zeit/Mühe kosten; **it** ~ **him his life/job** es kostete ihn das Leben/ seine Stelle.

cost accountant *n* Kostenbuchhalter(in) *m(f)*.

co-star ['kəustɑː*] *n* einer der Hauptdarsteller *m*, eine der Hauptdarstellerinnen *f*; **she was Sean Connery's** ~ **in** ... sie spielte neben Sean Connery in ...

Costa Rica ['kɔstə'riːkə] *n* Costa Rica *nt*.

cost centre *n* Kostenstelle *f*.

cost control *n* Kostenkontrolle *f*.

cost-effective ['kɔstɪ'fɛktɪv] *adj* rentabel; (*COMM*) kostengünstig.

cost-effectiveness ['kɔstɪ'fɛktɪvnɪs] *n* Rentabilität *f*.

costing ['kɔstɪŋ] *n* Kalkulation *f*.

costly ['kɔstlɪ] *adj* teuer, kostspielig; (*in time, effort*) aufwendig.

cost-of-living ['kɔstəv'lɪvɪŋ] *adj* Lebenshaltungskosten-; (*index*) Lebenshaltungs-.

cost price (*BRIT*) *n* Selbstkostenpreis *m*; **to sell/buy at** ~ zum Selbstkostenpreis verkaufen/kaufen.

costume ['kɔstjuːm] *n* Kostüm *nt*; (*BRIT: also:* **swimming** ~) Badeanzug *m*.

costume jewellery *n* Modeschmuck *m*.

cosy, (*US*) **cozy** ['kəuzɪ] *adj* gemütlich, behaglich; (*bed, scarf, gloves*) warm; (*chat, evening*) gemütlich; **I'm very** ~ **here** ich fühle mich hier sehr wohl, ich finde es hier sehr gemütlich.

cot [kɔt] *n* (*BRIT*) Kinderbett *nt*; (*US: campbed*) Feldbett *nt*.

cot death *n* Krippentod *m*, plötzlicher Kindstod *m*.

Cotswolds ['kɔtswəuldz] *npl:* **the** ~ die Cotswolds *pl*.

cottage ['kɔtɪdʒ] *n* Cottage *nt*, Häuschen *nt*.

cottage cheese *n* Hüttenkäse *m*.

cottage industry *n* Heimindustrie *f*.

cottage pie *n Hackfleisch mit Kartoffelbrei überbacken*.

cotton ['kɔtn] n (*fabric*) Baumwollstoff m; (*plant*) Baumwollstrauch m; (*thread*) (Baumwoll)garn nt ♦ cpd (*dress etc*) Baumwoll-.
►**cotton on** (*inf*) vi: **to ~ on** es kapieren or schnallen; **to ~ on to sth** etw kapieren or schnallen.
cotton candy (*US*) n Zuckerwatte f.
cotton wool (*BRIT*) n Watte f.
couch [kautʃ] n Couch f ♦ vt formulieren.
couchette [ku:'ʃɛt] n Liegewagen(platz) m.
couch potato (*esp US: inf*) n Dauerglotzer(in) m(f).
cough [kɔf] vi husten; (*engine*) stottern ♦ n Husten m.
cough drop n Hustenpastille f.
cough mixture n Hustensaft m.
cough syrup n = **cough mixture**.
could [kud] pt of **can²**.
couldn't ['kudnt] = **could not**.
council ['kaunsl] n Rat m; **city/town ~** Stadtrat m; **C~ of Europe** Europarat m.
council estate (*BRIT*) n Siedlung f mit Sozialwohnungen.
council house (*BRIT*) n Sozialwohnung f.
council housing n sozialer Wohnungsbau m; (*accommodation*) Sozialwohnungen pl.
councillor ['kaunslə*] n Stadtrat m, Stadträtin f.
council tax (*BRIT*) n Gemeindesteuer f.
counsel ['kaunsl] n Rat(schlag) m; (*lawyer*) Rechtsanwalt m, Rechtsanwältin f ♦ vt beraten; **to ~ sth** etw raten or empfehlen; **to ~ sb to do sth** jdm raten or empfehlen, etw zu tun; **~ for the defence** Verteidiger(in) m(f); **~ for the prosecution** Vertreter(in) m(f) der Anklage.
counsellor ['kaunslə*] n Berater(in) m(f); (*US: lawyer*) Rechtsanwalt m, Rechtsanwältin f.
count [kaunt] vt zählen; (*include*) mitrechnen, mitzählen ♦ vi zählen; (*be considered*) betrachtet or angesehen werden ♦ n Zählung f; (*level*) Zahl f; (*nobleman*) Graf m; **to ~ (up) to 10** bis 10 zählen; **not ~ing the children** die Kinder nicht mitgerechnet; **10 ~ing him** 10, wenn man ihn mitrechnet; **to ~ the cost of sth** die Folgen von etw abschätzen; **it ~s for very little** es zählt nicht viel; **~ yourself lucky** Sie können sich glücklich schätzen; **to keep ~ of sth** die Übersicht über etw acc behalten; **blood ~** Blutbild nt; **cholesterol/alcohol ~** Cholesterin-/Alkoholspiegel m.
►**count on** vt fus rechnen mit; (*depend on*) sich verlassen auf +acc; **to ~ on doing sth** die feste Absicht haben, etw zu tun.
►**count up** vt zusammenzählen, zusammenrechnen.
countdown ['kauntdaun] n Countdown m.
countenance ['kauntɪnəns] n Gesicht nt ♦ vt gutheißen.
counter ['kauntə*] n (*in shop*) Ladentisch m;

(*in café*) Theke f; (*in bank, post office*) Schalter m; (*in game*) Spielmarke f; (*TECH*) Zähler m ♦ vt (*oppose: sth said, sth done*) begegnen +dat; (*blow*) kontern ♦ adv: **~ to** gegen +acc; **to buy sth under the ~** (*fig*) etw unter dem Ladentisch bekommen; **to ~ sth with sth** auf etw acc mit etw antworten; **to ~ sth by doing sth** einer Sache damit begegnen, daß man etw tut.
counteract ['kauntər'ækt] vt entgegenwirken +dat; (*effect*) neutralisieren.
counterattack ['kauntərə'tæk] n Gegenangriff m ♦ vi einen Gegenangriff starten.
counterbalance ['kauntə'bæləns] vt Gegengewicht nt.
counterclockwise ['kauntə'klɔkwaɪz] adv gegen den Uhrzeigersinn.
counterespionage ['kauntər'ɛspɪənɑːʒ] n Gegenspionage f, Spionageabwehr f.
counterfeit ['kauntəfɪt] n Fälschung f ♦ vt fälschen ♦ adj (*coin*) Falsch-.
counterfoil ['kauntəfɔɪl] n Kontrollabschnitt m.
counterintelligence ['kauntərɪn'tɛlɪdʒəns] n Gegenspionage f, Spionageabwehr f.
countermand ['kauntəmɑːnd] vt aufheben, widerrufen.
countermeasure ['kauntəmɛʒə*] n Gegenmaßnahme f.
counteroffensive ['kauntərə'fɛnsɪv] n Gegenoffensive f.
counterpane ['kauntəpeɪn] n Tagesdecke f.
counterpart ['kauntəpɑːt] n Gegenüber nt; (*of document etc*) Gegenstück nt, Pendant nt.
counterproductive ['kauntəprə'dʌktɪv] adj widersinnig.
counterproposal ['kauntəprə'pəuzl] n Gegenvorschlag m.
countersign ['kauntəsaɪn] vt gegenzeichnen.
countersink ['kauntəsɪŋk] vt senken.
countess ['kauntɪs] n Gräfin f.
countless ['kauntlɪs] adj unzählig, zahllos.
countrified ['kʌntrɪfaɪd] adj ländlich.
country ['kʌntrɪ] n Land nt; (*native land*) Heimatland nt; **in the ~** auf dem Land; **mountainous ~** gebirgige Landschaft f.
country and western (**music**) n Country- und-Western-Musik f.
country dancing (*BRIT*) n Volkstanz m.
country house n Landhaus nt.
countryman ['kʌntrɪmən] (*irreg: like* **man**) n (*compatriot*) Landsmann m; (*country dweller*) Landmann m.
countryside ['kʌntrɪsaɪd] n Land nt; (*scenery*) Landschaft f, Gegend f.
country-wide ['kʌntrɪ'waɪd] adj, adv landesweit.
county ['kauntɪ] n (*BRIT*) Grafschaft f; (*US*) (Verwaltungs)bezirk m.
county council (*BRIT*) n Gemeinderat m (*einer Grafschaft*).

county town (*BRIT*) *n* Hauptstadt *einer Grafschaft.*

coup [kuː] (*pl* ~**s**) *n* (*also:* ~ **d'état**) Staatsstreich *m*, Coup d'Etat *m*; (*achievement*) Coup *m*.

coupé [kuːˈpeɪ] *n* Coupé *nt*.

couple [ˈkʌpl] *n* Paar *nt*; (*married couple*) Ehepaar *nt* ♦ *vt* verbinden; (*vehicles*) koppeln; **a** ~ **of** (*two*) zwei; (*a few*) ein paar.

couplet [ˈkʌplɪt] *n* Verspaar *nt*.

coupling [ˈkʌplɪŋ] *n* Kupplung *f*.

coupon [ˈkuːpɔn] *n* Gutschein *m*; (*detachable form*) Abschnitt *m*; (*COMM*) Coupon *m*.

courage [ˈkʌrɪdʒ] *n* Mut *m*.

courageous [kəˈreɪdʒəs] *adj* mutig.

courgette [kuəˈʒɛt] (*BRIT*) *n* Zucchino *m*.

courier [ˈkurɪə*] *n* (*messenger*) Kurier(in) *m(f)*; (*for tourists*) Reiseleiter(in) *m(f)*.

course [kɔːs] *n* (*SCOL*) Kurs(us) *m*; (*of ship*) Kurs *m*; (*of life, events, time etc, of river*) Lauf *m*; (*of argument*) Richtung *f*; (*part of meal*) Gang *m*; (*for golf*) Platz *m*; **of** ~ natürlich; **of** ~**!** (*aber*) natürlich!, (*aber*) selbstverständlich!; (**no**) **of** ~ **not!** natürlich nicht!; **in the** ~ **of the next few days** während *or* im Laufe der nächsten paar Tage; **in due** ~ zu gegebener Zeit; ~ (**of action**) Vorgehensweise *f*; **the best** ~ **would be to** ... das beste wäre es, zu ...; **we have no other** ~ **but to** ... es bleibt uns nichts anderes übrig, als zu ...; ~ **of lectures** Vorlesungsreihe *f*; ~ **of treatment** (*MED*) Behandlung *f*; **first/last** ~ erster/letzter Gang, Vor-/Nachspeise *f*.

court [kɔːt] *n* Hof *m*; (*LAW*) Gericht *nt*; (*for tennis, badminton etc*) Platz *m* ♦ *vt* den Hof machen +*dat*; (*favour, popularity*) werben um; (*death, disaster*) herausfordern; **out of** ~ (*LAW*) außergerichtlich; **to take to** ~ (*LAW*) verklagen, vor Gericht bringen.

courteous [ˈkɔːtɪəs] *adj* höflich.

courtesan [kɔːtɪˈzæn] *n* Kurtisane *f*.

courtesy [ˈkɔːtəsɪ] *n* Höflichkeit *f*; (**by**) ~ **of** freundlicherweise zur Verfügung gestellt von.

courtesy coach *n* gebührenfreier Bus *m*.

courtesy light *n* Innenleuchte *f*.

courthouse [ˈkɔːthaus] (*US*) *n* Gerichtsgebäude *nt*.

courtier [ˈkɔːtɪə*] *n* Höfling *m*.

court martial (*pl* **courts martial**) *n* Militärgericht *nt*.

court of appeal (*pl* **courts of appeal**) *n* Berufungsgericht *nt*.

court of inquiry (*pl* **courts of inquiry**) *n* Untersuchungskommission *f*.

courtroom [ˈkɔːtrum] *n* Gerichtssaal *m*.

court shoe *n* Pumps *m*.

courtyard [ˈkɔːtjɑːd] *n* Hof *m*.

cousin [ˈkʌzn] *n* (*male*) Cousin *m*, Vetter *m*; (*female*) Cousine *f*, Kusine *f*; **first** ~ Cousin(e) ersten Grades.

cove [kəuv] *n* (kleine) Bucht *f*.

covenant [ˈkʌvənənt] *n* Schwur *m* ♦ *vt*: **to** ~ **£200 per year to a charity** sich vertraglich verpflichten, £200 im Jahr für wohltätige Zwecke zu spenden.

Coventry [ˈkɔvəntrɪ] *n*: **to send sb to** ~ (*fig*) jdn schneiden (*inf*).

cover [ˈkʌvə*] *vt* bedecken; (*distance*) zurücklegen; (*INSURANCE*) versichern; (*topic*) behandeln; (*include*) erfassen; (*PRESS: report on*) berichten über +*acc* ♦ *n* (*for furniture*) Bezug *m*; (*for typewriter, PC etc*) Hülle *f*; (*of book, magazine*) Umschlag *m*; (*shelter*) Schutz *m*; (*INSURANCE*) Versicherung *f*; (*fig: for illegal activities*) Tarnung *f*; **to be** ~**ed in** *or* **with** bedeckt sein mit; **£10 will** ~ **my expenses** £10 decken meine Unkosten; **to take** ~ (*from rain*) sich unterstellen; ~ **of** geschützt; **under** ~ **of darkness** im Schutz(e) der Dunkelheit; **under separate** ~ getrennt.

▶**cover up** *vt* zudecken; (*fig: facts, feelings*) verheimlichen; (: *mistakes*) vertuschen ♦ *vi* (*fig*): **to** ~ **up for sb** jdn decken.

coverage [ˈkʌvərɪdʒ] *n* Berichterstattung *f*; **television** ~ **of the conference** Fernsehberichte *pl* über die Konferenz; **to give full** ~ **to** ausführlich berichten über +*acc*.

coveralls [ˈkʌvərɔːlz] (*US*) *npl* Overall *m*.

cover charge *n* Kosten *pl* für ein Gedeck.

covering [ˈkʌvərɪŋ] *n* Schicht *f*; (*of snow, dust etc*) Decke *f*.

covering letter, (*US*) **cover letter** *n* Begleitbrief *m*.

cover note *n* (*INSURANCE*) Deckungszusage *f*.

cover price *n* Einzel(exemplar)preis *m*.

covert [ˈkʌvət] *adj* versteckt; (*glance*) verstohlen.

cover-up [ˈkʌvərʌp] *n* Vertuschung *f*, Verschleierung *f*.

covet [ˈkʌvɪt] *vt* begehren.

cow [kau] *n* (*animal, infl: woman*) Kuh *f* ♦ *cpd* Kuh- ♦ *vt* einschüchtern.

coward [ˈkauəd] *n* Feigling *m*.

cowardice [ˈkauədɪs] *n* Feigheit *f*.

cowardly [ˈkauədlɪ] *adj* feige.

cowboy [ˈkaubɔɪ] *n* (*in US*) Cowboy *m*; (*pej: tradesman*) Pfuscher *m*.

cow elephant *n* Elefantenkuh *f*.

cower [ˈkauə*] *vi* sich ducken; (*squatting*) kauern.

cowshed [ˈkauʃɛd] *n* Kuhstall *m*.

cowslip [ˈkauslɪp] *n* Schlüsselblume *f*.

cox [kɔks] *n abbr* = **coxswain**.

coxswain [ˈkɔksn] *n* Steuermann *m*; (*of ship*) Boot(s)führer *m*.

coy [kɔɪ] *adj* verschämt.

coyote [kɔɪˈəutɪ] *n* Kojote *m*.

cozy [ˈkəuzɪ] (*US*) *adj* = **cosy**.

CP *n abbr* (= *Communist Party*) KP *f*.

cp. *abbr* (= *compare*) vgl.

c/p (*BRIT*) *abbr* = **carriage paid.**

CPA (*US*) *n abbr* = **certified public accountant.**

CPI *n abbr* (= *Consumer Price Index*) (Verbraucher)preisindex *m.*

Cpl *abbr* (*MIL*) = **corporal.**

CP/M *n abbr* (= *Control Program for Microprocessors*) CP/M *nt.*

cps *abbr* (*COMPUT, TYP*: = *characters per second*) cps, Zeichen *pl* pro Sekunde.

CPSA (*BRIT*) *n abbr* (= *Civil and Public Services Association*) Gewerkschaft im öffentlichen Dienst.

CPU *n abbr* (*COMPUT*) = **central processing unit.**

cr. *abbr* = **credit; creditor.**

crab [kræb] *n* Krabbe *f*, Krebs *m*; (*meat*) Krabbe *f.*

crab apple *n* Holzapfel *m.*

crack [kræk] *n* (*noise*) Knall *m*; (*of wood breaking*) Knacks *m*; (*gap*) Spalte *f*; (*in bone, dish, glass*) Sprung *m*; (*in wall*) Riß *m*; (*joke*) Witz *m*; (*DRUGS*) Crack *nt* ♦ *vt* (*whip*) knallen mit; (*twig*) knacken mit; (*dish, glass*) einen Sprung machen in +*acc*; (*bone*) anbrechen; (*nut, code*) knacken; (*wall*) rissig machen; (*problem*) lösen; (*joke*) reißen ♦ *adj* erstklassig; **to have a ~ at sth** (*inf*) etw mal probieren; **to ~ jokes** (*inf*) Witze reißen; **to get ~ing** (*inf*) loslegen.

► **crack down on** *vt fus* hart durchgreifen gegen.

► **crack up** *vi* durchdrehen, zusammenbrechen.

crackdown ['krækdaun] *n:* **~ (on)** scharfes Durchgreifen *nt* (gegen).

cracked [krækt] (*inf*) *adj* übergeschnappt.

cracker ['krækə*] *n* (*biscuit*) Kräcker *m*; (*Christmas cracker*) Knallbonbon *nt*; (*firework*) Knallkörper *m*, Kracher *m*; **a ~ of a ...** (*BRIT: inf*) ein(e) tolle(r, s) ...; **he's ~s** (*BRIT: inf*) er ist übergeschnappt.

crackle ['krækl] *vi* (*fire*) knistern, prasseln; (*twig*) knacken.

crackling ['kræklɪŋ] *n* (*of fire*) Knistern *nt*, Prasseln *nt*; (*of twig, on radio, telephone*) Knacken *nt*; (*of pork*) Kruste *f* (*des Schweinebratens*).

crackpot ['krækpɔt] (*inf*) *n* Spinner(in) *m(f)* ♦ *adj* verrückt.

cradle ['kreɪdl] *n* Wiege *f* ♦ *vt* fest in den Armen halten.

craft [krɑːft] *n* (*skill*) Geschicklichkeit *f*; (*art*) Kunsthandwerk *nt*; (*trade*) Handwerk *nt*; (*pl inv: boat*) Boot *nt*; (*pl inv: plane*) Flugzeug *nt.*

craftsman ['krɑːftsmən] (*irreg: like* **man**) *n* Handwerker *m.*

craftsmanship ['krɑːftsmənʃɪp] *n* handwerkliche Ausführung *f.*

crafty ['krɑːftɪ] *adj* schlau, clever.

crag [kræg] *n* Fels *m.*

craggy ['krægɪ] *adj* (*mountain*) zerklüftet;

(*cliff*) felsig; (*face*) kantig.

cram [kræm] *vt* vollstopfen ♦ *vi* pauken (*inf*), büffeln (*inf*); **to ~ with** vollstopfen mit; **to ~ sth into** etw hineinstopfen in +*acc.*

cramming ['kræmɪŋ] *n* (*for exams*) Pauken *nt*, Büffeln *nt.*

cramp [kræmp] *n* Krampf *m* ♦ *vt* hemmen.

cramped [kræmpt] *adj* eng.

crampon ['kræmpən] *n* Steigeisen *nt.*

cranberry ['krænbərɪ] *n* Preiselbeere *f.*

crane [kreɪn] *n* Kran *m*; (*bird*) Kranich *m* ♦ *vt:* **to ~ one's neck** den Hals recken ♦ *vi:* **to ~ forward** den Hals recken.

crania ['kreɪnɪə] *npl of* **cranium.**

cranium ['kreɪnɪəm] (*pl* **crania**) *n* Schädel *m.*

crank [kræŋk] *n* Spinner(in) *m(f)*; (*handle*) Kurbel *f.*

crankshaft ['kræŋkʃɑːft] *n* Kurbelwelle *f.*

cranky ['kræŋkɪ] *adj* verrückt.

cranny ['krænɪ] *n see* **nook.**

crap [kræp] (*inf!*) *n* Scheiße *f* (*!*) ♦ *vi* scheißen (*!*); **to have a ~** scheißen (*!*).

crappy ['kræpɪ] (*inf!*) *adj* beschissen (*!*).

crash [kræʃ] *n* (*noise*) Krachen *nt*; (*of car*) Unfall *m*; (*of plane etc*) Unglück *nt*; (*collision*) Zusammenstoß *m*; (*of stock market, business etc*) Zusammenbruch *m* ♦ *vt* (*car*) einen Unfall haben mit; (*plane etc*) abstürzen mit ♦ *vi* (*plane*) abstürzen; (*car*) einen Unfall haben; (*two cars*) zusammenstoßen; (*market*) zusammenbrechen; (*firm*) Pleite machen; **to ~ into** krachen *or* knallen gegen; **he ~ed the car into a wall** er fuhr mit dem Auto gegen eine Mauer.

crash barrier (*BRIT*) *n* Leitplanke *f.*

crash course *n* Schnellkurs *m*, Intensivkurs *m.*

crash helmet *n* Sturzhelm *m.*

crash-landing ['kræʃlændɪŋ] *n* Bruchlandung *f.*

crass [kræs] *adj* kraß; (*behaviour*) unfein, derb.

crate [kreɪt] *n* (*also inf*) Kiste *f*; (*for bottles*) Kasten *m.*

crater ['kreɪtə*] *n* Krater *m.*

cravat [krə'væt] *n* Halstuch *nt.*

crave [kreɪv] *vt, vi:* **to ~ (for)** sich sehnen nach.

craven ['kreɪvən] *adj* feige.

craving ['kreɪvɪŋ] *n:* **~ (for)** Verlangen *nt* (nach).

crawl [krɔːl] *vi* kriechen; (*child*) krabbeln ♦ *n* (*SWIMMING*) Kraulstil *m*, Kraul(en) *nt*; **to ~ to sb** (*inf*) vor jdm kriechen; **to drive along at a ~** im Schneckentempo *or* Kriechtempo vorankommen.

crawler lane (*BRIT*) *n* (*AUT*) Kriechspur *f.*

crayfish ['kreɪfɪʃ] *n inv* (*freshwater*) Flußkrebs *m*; (*saltwater*) Languste *f.*

crayon ['kreɪən] *n* Buntstift *m.*

craze [kreɪz] *n* Fimmel *m*; **to be all the ~** große Mode sein.

crazed [kreɪzd] *adj* wahnsinnig; (*pottery, glaze*) rissig.

crazy ['kreızı] *adj* wahnsinnig, verrückt;
~ **about sb/sth** (*inf*) verrückt *or* wild auf
jdn/etw; **to go** ~ wahnsinnig *or* verrückt
werden.
crazy paving (*BRIT*) *n* Mosaikpflaster *nt*.
creak [kriːk] *vi* knarren.
cream [kriːm] *n* Sahne *f*, Rahm *m* (*S Ger*);
(*artificial cream, cosmetic*) Creme *f*; (*élite*)
Crème *f*, Elite *f* ♦ *adj* cremefarben; **whipped**
~ Schlagsahne *f*.
►**cream off** *vt* absahnen (*inf*).
cream cake *n* Sahnetorte *f*; (*small*)
Sahnetörtchen *nt*.
cream cheese *n* (Doppelrahm)frischkäse *m*.
creamery ['kriːmərı] *n* (*shop*) Milchgeschäft
nt; (*factory*) Molkerei *f*.
creamy ['kriːmı] *adj* (*colour*) cremefarben;
(*taste*) sahnig.
crease [kriːs] *n* Falte *f*; (*in trousers*) Bügelfalte
f ♦ *vt* zerknittern; (*forehead*) runzeln ♦ *vi*
knittern; (*forehead*) sich runzeln.
crease-resistant ['kriːsrızıstənt] *adj*
knitterfrei.
create [kriː'eɪt] *vt* schaffen; (*interest*)
hervorrufen; (*problems*) verursachen;
(*produce*) herstellen; (*design*) entwerfen,
kreieren; (*impression, fuss*) machen.
creation [kriː'eɪʃən] *n* (*see vb*) Schaffung *f*;
Hervorrufen *nt*; Verursachung *f*;
Herstellung *f*; Entwurf *m*, Kreation *f*; (*REL*)
Schöpfung *f*.
creative [kriː'eɪtɪv] *adj* kreativ, schöpferisch.
creativity [kriːeɪ'tɪvɪtɪ] *n* Kreativität *f*.
creator [kriː'eɪtə*] *n* Schöpfer(in) *m(f)*.
creature ['kriːtʃə*] *n* Geschöpf *nt*; (*living
animal*) Lebewesen *nt*.
creature comforts [- 'kʌmfəts] *npl*
Lebensgenüsse *pl*.
crèche [krɛʃ] *n* (Kinder)krippe *f*; (*all day*)
(Kinder)tagesstätte *f*.
credence ['kriːdns] *n*: **to lend** *or* **give** ~ **to sth**
etw glaubwürdig erscheinen lassen *or*
machen.
credentials [krɪ'dɛnʃlz] *npl* Referenzen *pl*,
Zeugnisse *pl*; (*papers of identity*)
(Ausweis)papiere *pl*.
credibility [krɛdɪ'bɪlɪtɪ] *n* Glaubwürdigkeit *f*.
credible ['krɛdɪbl] *adj* glaubwürdig.
credit ['krɛdɪt] *n* (*loan*) Kredit *m*; (*recognition*)
Anerkennung *f*; (*SCOL*) Schein *m* ♦ *adj*
(*COMM: terms etc*) Kredit- ♦ *vt* (*COMM*)
gutschreiben; (*believe: also:* **give** ~ **to**)
glauben; **credits** *npl* (*CINE, TV: at beginning*)
Vorspann *m*; (: *at end*) Nachspann *m*; **to be in**
~ (*person*) Geld auf dem Konto haben; (*bank
account*) im Haben sein; **on** ~ auf Kredit; **it
is to his** ~ **that ...** es ehrt ihn, daß ...; **to take
the** ~ **for** das Verdienst in Anspruch
nehmen für; **it does him** ~ es spricht für
ihn; **he's a** ~ **to his family** er macht seiner
Familie Ehre; **to** ~ **sb with sth** (*fig*) jdm etw
zuschreiben; **to** ~ **£5 to sb** jdm £5

gutschreiben.
creditable ['krɛdɪtəbl] *adj* lobenswert,
anerkennenswert.
credit account *n* Kreditkonto *nt*.
credit agency (*BRIT*) *n* Kreditauskunftei *f*.
credit balance *n* Kontostand *m*.
credit bureau (*US*) *n* = **credit agency**.
credit card *n* Kreditkarte *f*.
credit control *n* Kreditüberwachung *f*.
credit facilities *npl* (*COMM*)
Kreditmöglichkeiten *pl*.
credit limit *n* Kreditgrenze *f*.
credit note (*BRIT*) *n* Gutschrift *f*.
creditor ['krɛdɪtə*] *n* Gläubiger *m*.
credit transfer *n* Banküberweisung *f*.
creditworthy ['krɛdɪt'wəːðɪ] *adj*
kreditwürdig.
credulity [krɪ'djuːlɪtɪ] *n* Leichtgläubigkeit *f*.
creed [kriːd] *n* Glaubensbekenntnis *nt*.
creek [kriːk] *n* (kleine) Bucht *f*; (*US: stream*)
Bach *m*; **to be up the** ~ (*inf*) in der Tinte
sitzen.
creel [kriːl] *n* (*also:* **lobster** ~) Hummer-
(fang)korb *m*.
creep [kriːp] (*pt, pp* **crept**) *vi* schleichen; (*plant:
horizontally*) kriechen; (: *vertically*) klettern
♦ *n* (*inf*) Kriecher *m*; **to** ~ **up on sb** sich an
jdn heranschleichen; (*time etc*) langsam auf
jdn zukommen; **he's a** ~ er ist ein
widerlicher *or* fieser Typ; **it gives me the** ~**s**
davon kriege ich das kalte Grausen.
creeper ['kriːpə*] *n* Kletterpflanze *f*.
creepers ['kriːpəz] (*US*) *npl* Schuhe mit
weichen Sohlen.
creepy ['kriːpı] *adj* gruselig; (*experience*)
unheimlich, gruselig.
creepy-crawly ['kriːpı'krɔːlı] (*inf*) *n*
Krabbeltier *nt*.
cremate [krɪ'meɪt] *vt* einäschern.
cremation [krɪ'meɪʃən] *n* Einäscherung *f*,
Kremation *f*.
crematoria [krɛmə'tɔːrɪə] *npl of* **crematorium**.
crematorium [krɛmə'tɔːrɪəm] (*pl* **crematoria**)
n Krematorium *nt*.
creosote ['krɪəsəʊt] *n* Kreosot *nt*.
crepe [kreıp] *n* Krepp *m*, Crêpe *m*; (*rubber*)
Krepp(gummi) *m*.
crepe bandage (*BRIT*) *n* elastische Binde *f*.
crepe paper *n* Kreppapier *nt*.
crepe sole *n* Kreppsohle *f*.
crept [krɛpt] *pt, pp of* **creep**.
crescendo [krɪ'ʃɛndəʊ] *n* Höhepunkt *m*; (*MUS*)
Crescendo *nt*.
crescent ['krɛsnt] *n* Halbmond *m*; (*street*)
halbkreisförmig verlaufende Straße.
cress [krɛs] *n* Kresse *f*.
crest [krɛst] *n* (*of hill*) Kamm *m*; (*of bird*)
Haube *f*; (*coat of arms*) Wappen *nt*.
crestfallen ['krɛstfɔːlən] *adj*
niedergeschlagen.
Crete [kriːt] *n* Kreta *nt*.
crevasse [krɪ'væs] *n* Gletscherspalte *f*.

crevice ['krɛvɪs] n Spalte f.
crew [kruː] n Besatzung f; (TV, CINE) Crew f;
(gang) Bande f.
crew cut n Bürstenschnitt m.
crew neck n runder (Hals)ausschnitt m.
crib [krɪb] n Kinderbett nt; (REL) Krippe f ♦ vt
(inf: copy) abschreiben.
cribbage ['krɪbɪdʒ] n Cribbage nt.
crib death (US) n = **cot death**.
crick [krɪk] n Krampf m.
cricket ['krɪkɪt] n Kricket nt; (insect) Grille f.
cricketer ['krɪkɪtə*] n Kricketspieler(in) m(f).
crime [kraɪm] n (no pl: illegal activities)
Verbrechen pl; (illegal action, fig)
Verbrechen nt; **minor ~** kleinere Vergehen
pl.
crime wave n Verbrechenswelle f.
criminal ['krɪmɪnl] n Kriminelle(r) f(m),
Verbrecher(in) m(f) ♦ adj kriminell;
C~ Investigation Department
Kriminalpolizei f.
criminal code n Strafgesetzbuch nt.
crimp [krɪmp] vt kräuseln; (hair) wellen.
crimson ['krɪmzn] adj purpurrot.
cringe [krɪndʒ] vi (in fear) zurückweichen; (in
embarrassment) zusammenzucken.
crinkle ['krɪŋkl] vt (zer)knittern.
cripple ['krɪpl] n Krüppel m ♦ vt zum Krüppel
machen; (ship, plane) aktionsunfähig
machen; (production, exports) lahmlegen,
lähmen; **~d with rheumatism** von Rheuma
praktisch gelähmt.
crippling ['krɪplɪŋ] adj (disease) schwer;
(taxation, debts) erdrückend.
crises ['kraɪsiːz] npl of **crisis**.
crisis ['kraɪsɪs] (pl **crises**) n Krise f.
crisp [krɪsp] adj (vegetables etc) knackig;
(bacon etc) knusprig; (weather) frisch;
(manner, tone, reply) knapp.
crisps [krɪsps] (BRIT) npl Chips pl.
crisscross ['krɪskrɔs] adj (pattern) Kreuz- ♦ vt
kreuz und quer durchziehen.
criteria [kraɪ'tɪərɪə] npl of **criterion**.
criterion [kraɪ'tɪərɪən] (pl **criteria**) n Kriterium
nt.
critic ['krɪtɪk] n Kritiker(in) m(f).
critical ['krɪtɪkl] adj kritisch; **to be ~ of sb/sth**
jdn/etw kritisieren; **he is in a ~ condition**
sein Zustand ist kritisch.
critically ['krɪtɪklɪ] adv kritisch; (ill) schwer.
criticism ['krɪtɪsɪzəm] n Kritik f.
criticize ['krɪtɪsaɪz] vt kritisieren.
critique [krɪ'tiːk] n Kritik f.
croak [krəuk] vi (frog) quaken; (bird, person)
krächzen.
Croat n Kroate m, Kroatin f; (LING) Kroatisch
nt.
Croatia [krəu'eɪʃə] n Kroatien nt.
Croatian [krəu'eɪʃən] adj kroatisch.
crochet ['krəuʃeɪ] n (activity) Häkeln nt; (result)
Häkelei f.
crock [krɔk] n Topf m; (inf: also: **old ~**) (vehicle)

Kiste f; (: person) Wrack nt.
crockery ['krɔkərɪ] n Geschirr nt.
crocodile ['krɔkədaɪl] n Krokodil nt.
crocus ['krəukəs] n Krokus m.
croft [krɔft] (BRIT) n kleines Pachtgut nt.
crofter ['krɔftə*] (BRIT) n Kleinpächter(in)
m(f).
crone [krəun] n alte Hexe f.
crony ['krəunɪ] (inf: pej) n Kumpan(in) m(f).
crook [kruk] n (criminal) Gauner m; (of
shepherd) Hirtenstab m; (of arm) Beuge f.
crooked ['krukɪd] adj krumm; (dishonest)
unehrlich.
crop [krɔp] n (Feld)frucht f; (amount produced)
Ernte f; (riding crop) Reitpeitsche f; (of bird)
Kropf m ♦ vt (hair) stutzen; (subj: animal:
grass) abfressen.
►**crop up** vi aufkommen.
cropper ['krɔpə*] (inf) n: **to come a ~**
hinfallen; (fig: fail) auf die Nase fallen.
crop spraying [-'spreɪɪŋ] n Schädlingsbekämpfung f (durch Besprühen).
croquet ['krəukeɪ] (BRIT) n Krocket nt.
croquette [krə'kɛt] n Krokette f.
cross [krɔs] n Kreuz nt; (BIOL, BOT) Kreuzung f
♦ vt (street) überqueren; (room etc)
durchqueren; (cheque) zur Verrechnung
ausstellen; (arms) verschränken; (legs)
übereinanderschlagen; (animal, plant)
kreuzen; (thwart: person) verärgern; (: plan)
durchkreuzen ♦ adj ärgerlich, böse ♦ vi: **the
boat ~es from ... to ...** das Schiff fährt von
... nach ...; **to ~ o.s.** sich bekreuzigen; **we
have a ~ed line** (BRIT) es ist jemand in der
Leitung; **they've got their lines** or **wires ~ed**
(fig) sie reden aneinander vorbei; **to be/get
~ with sb (about sth)** mit jdm or auf jdn
(wegen etw) böse sein/werden.
►**cross out** vt streichen.
►**cross over** vi hinübergehen.
crossbar ['krɔsbaː*] n (SPORT) Querlatte f; (of
bicycle) Stange f.
crossbow n Armbrust f.
crossbreed ['krɔsbriːd] n Kreuzung f.
cross-Channel ferry ['krɔs'tʃænl-] n
Kanalfähre f.
crosscheck ['krɔstʃɛk] n Gegenprobe f ♦ vt
überprüfen.
cross-country (race) ['krɔs'kʌntrɪ-] n
Querfeldeinrennen nt.
cross-dressing [krɔs'drɛsɪŋ] n (transvestism)
Transvestismus m.
cross-examination ['krɔsɪgzæmɪ'neɪʃən] n
Kreuzverhör nt.
cross-examine ['krɔsɪg'zæmɪn] vt ins
Kreuzverhör nehmen.
cross-eyed ['krɔsaɪd] adj schielend; **to be ~**
schielen.
crossfire ['krɔsfaɪə*] n Kreuzfeuer nt; **to get
caught in the ~** (also fig) ins Kreuzfeuer
geraten.
crossing ['krɔsɪŋ] n Überfahrt f; (also:

pedestrian ~) Fußgängerüberweg *m*.
crossing guard (*US*) *n* ≈ Schülerlotse *m*.
crossing point *n* Übergangsstelle *f*.
cross-purposes ['krɔs'pəːpəsɪz] *npl*: **to be at ~ with sb** jdn mißverstehen; **we're (talking) at ~** wir reden aneinander vorbei.
cross-question ['krɔs'kwɛstʃən] *vt* ins Kreuzverhör nehmen.
cross-reference ['krɔs'rɛfrəns] *n* (Quer)verweis *m*.
crossroads ['krɔsrəudz] *n* Kreuzung *f*.
cross section *n* Querschnitt *m*.
crosswalk ['krɔswɔːk] (*US*) *n* Fußgängerüberweg *m*.
crosswind ['krɔswɪnd] *n* Seitenwind *m*.
crosswise ['krɔswaɪz] *adv* quer.
crossword ['krɔswəːd] *n* (*also*: ~ **puzzle**) Kreuzworträtsel *nt*.
crotch [krɔtʃ] *n* Unterleib *m*; (*of garment*) Schritt *m*.
crotchet ['krɔtʃɪt] *n* Viertelnote *f*.
crotchety ['krɔtʃɪtɪ] *adj* reizbar.
crouch [krautʃ] *vi* kauern.
croup [kruːp] *n* (*MED*) Krupp *m*.
croupier ['kruːpɪə'] *n* Croupier *m*.
crouton ['kruːtɔn] *n* Crouton *m*.
crow [krəu] *n* (*bird*) Krähe *f*; (*of cock*) Krähen *nt* ♦ *vi* krähen; (*fig*) sich brüsten, angeben.
crowbar ['krəubɑː'] *n* Brechstange *f*.
crowd [kraud] *n* (Menschen)menge *f* ♦ *vt* (*room, stadium*) füllen ♦ *vi*: **to ~ round** sich herumdrängen; **~s of people** Menschenmassen *pl*; **the/our ~** (*of friends*) die/unsere Clique *f*; **to ~ sb/sth in** jdn/etw hineinstopfen; **to ~ sb/sth into** jdn pferchen/etw stopfen in +*acc*; **to ~ in** sich hineindrängen.
crowded ['kraudɪd] *adj* überfüllt; (*densely populated*) dicht besiedelt; **~ with** voll von.
crowd scene *n* Massenszene *f*.
crown [kraun] *n* (*also of tooth*) Krone *f*; (*of head*) Wirbel *m*; (*of hill*) Kuppe *f*; (*of hat*) Kopf *m* ♦ *vt* krönen; (*tooth*) überkronen; **the C~** die Krone; **and to ~ it all** ... (*fig*) und zur Krönung des Ganzen ...

Crown Court *ist ein Strafgericht, das in etwa 90 verschiedenen Städten in England und Wales zusammentritt. Schwere Verbrechen wie Mord, Totschlag, Vergewaltigung und Raub werden nur vor dem* crown court *unter Vorsitz eines Richters mit Geschworenen verhandelt.*

---

crowning ['krauniŋ] *adj* krönend.
crown jewels *npl* Kronjuwelen *pl*.
crown prince *n* Kronprinz *m*.
crow's-feet ['krəuzfiːt] *npl* Krähenfüße *pl*.
crow's-nest ['krəuznɛst] *n* Krähennest *nt*, Mastkorb *m*.
crucial ['kruːʃl] *adj* (*decision*) äußerst wichtig; (*vote*) entscheidend; **~ to** äußerst wichtig für.

crucifix ['kruːsɪfɪks] *n* Kruzifix *nt*.
crucifixion [kruːsɪ'fɪkʃən] *n* Kreuzigung *f*.
crucify ['kruːsɪfaɪ] *vt* kreuzigen; (*fig*) in der Luft zerreißen.
crude [kruːd] *adj* (*oil, fibre*) Roh-; (*fig: basic*) primitiv; (: *vulgar*) ordinär ♦ *n* = **crude oil**.
crude oil *n* Rohöl *nt*.
cruel ['kruəl] *adj* grausam.
cruelty ['kruəltɪ] *n* Grausamkeit *f*.
cruet ['kruːɪt] *n* Gewürzständer *m*.
cruise [kruːz] *n* Kreuzfahrt *f* ♦ *vi* (*ship*) kreuzen; (*car*) (mit Dauergeschwindigkeit) fahren; (*aircraft*) (mit Reisegeschwindigkeit) fliegen; (*taxi*) gemächlich fahren.
cruise missile *n* Marschflugkörper *m*.
cruiser ['kruːzə'] *n* Motorboot *nt*; (*warship*) Kreuzer *m*.
cruising speed *n* Reisegeschwindigkeit *f*.
crumb [krʌm] *n* Krümel *m*; (*fig: of information*) Brocken *m*; **a ~ of comfort** ein winziger Trost.
crumble ['krʌmbl] *vt* (*bread*) zerbröckeln; (*biscuit etc*) zerkrümeln ♦ *vi* (*building, earth etc*) zerbröckeln; (*plaster*) abbröckeln; (*fig: opposition*) sich auflösen; (: *belief*) ins Wanken geraten.
crumbly ['krʌmblɪ] *adj* krümelig.
crummy ['krʌmɪ] (*inf*) *adj* mies.
crumpet ['krʌmpɪt] *n* Teekuchen *m* (*zum Toasten*).
crumple ['krʌmpl] *vt* zerknittern.
crunch [krʌntʃ] *vt* (*biscuit, apple etc*) knabbern; (*underfoot*) zertreten ♦ *n*: **the ~** der große Krach; **if it comes to the ~** wenn es wirklich dahin kommt; **when the ~ comes** wenn es hart auf hart geht.
crunchy ['krʌntʃɪ] *adj* knusprig; (*apple etc*) knackig; (*gravel, snow etc*) knirschend.
crusade [kruː'seɪd] *n* Feldzug *m* ♦ *vi*: **to ~ for/against sth** für/gegen etw zu Felde ziehen.
crusader [kruː'seɪdə'] *n* Kreuzritter *m*; (*fig*): **~ (for)** Apostel *m* (+*gen*).
crush [krʌʃ] *n* (*crowd*) Gedränge *nt* ♦ *vt* quetschen; (*grapes*) zerquetschen; (*paper, clothes*) zerknittern; (*garlic, ice*) (zer)stoßen; (*defeat*) niederschlagen; (*devastate*) vernichten; **to have a ~ on sb** (*love*) schwärmen für jdn; **lemon ~** Zitronensaftgetränk *nt*.
crush barrier (*BRIT*) *n* Absperrung *f*.
crushing ['krʌʃɪŋ] *adj* vernichtend.
crust [krʌst] *n* Kruste *f*.
crustacean [krʌs'teɪʃən] *n* Schalentier *nt*, Krustazee *f*.
crusty ['krʌstɪ] *adj* knusprig.
crutch [krʌtʃ] *n* Krücke *f*; (*support*) Stütze *f*; *see also* **crotch**.
crux [krʌks] *n* Kern *m*.
cry [kraɪ] *vi* weinen; (*also*: ~ **out**) aufschreien ♦ *n* Schrei *m*; (*shout*) Ruf *m*; **what are you ~ing about?** warum weinst du?; **to ~ for**

help um Hilfe rufen; **she had a good** ~ sie hat sich (mal richtig) ausgeweint; **it's a far** ~ **from ...** (*fig*) das ist etwas ganz anderes als ...

►**cry off** (*inf*) *vi* absagen.

crying ['kraıŋ] *adj* (*fig: need*) dringend; **it's a** ~ **shame** es ist ein Jammer.

crypt [krıpt] *n* Krypta *f*.

cryptic ['krıptık] *adj* hintergründig, rätselhaft; (*clue*) verschlüsselt.

crystal ['krıstl] *n* Kristall *m*; (*glass*) Kristall(glas) *nt*.

crystal clear *adj* glasklar.

crystallize ['krıstəlaız] *vt* (*opinion, thoughts*) (feste) Form geben +*dat* ♦ *vi* (*sugar etc*) kristallisieren; ~**d fruits** (*BRIT*) kandierte Früchte *pl*.

CSA *n abbr* (= *Child Support Agency*) *Amt zur Regelung von Unterhaltszahlungen für Kinder.*

CSC *n abbr* (= *Civil Service Commission*) *Einstellungsbehörde für den öffentlichen Dienst.*

CSE (*BRIT*) *n abbr* (*formerly: = Certificate of Secondary Education*) *Schulabschlußzeugnis,* ≈ mittlere Reife *f*.

CS gas (*BRIT*) *n* ≈ Tränengas *nt*.

CST (*US*) *abbr* (= *Central Standard Time*) *mittelamerikanische Standardzeit.*

CT (*US*) *abbr* (*POST:* = *Connecticut*).

ct *abbr* = **carat**.

CTC (*BRIT*) *n abbr* = **city technology college**.

CT scanner *n abbr* (*MED:* = *computerized tomography scanner*) CT-Scanner *m*.

cu. *abbr* = **cubic**.

cub [kʌb] *n* Junge(s) *nt*; (*also:* ~ **scout**) Wölfling *m*.

Cuba ['kju:bə] *n* Kuba *nt*.

Cuban ['kju:bən] *adj* kubanisch ♦ *n* Kubaner(in) *m(f)*.

cubbyhole ['kʌbıhəul] *n* (*room*) Kabuff *nt*; (*space*) Eckchen *nt*.

cube [kju:b] *n* Würfel *m*; (*MATH: of number*) dritte Potenz *f* ♦ *vt* (*MATH*) in die dritte Potenz erheben, hoch drei nehmen.

cube root *n* Kubikwurzel *f*.

cubic ['kju:bık] *adj* (*volume*) Kubik-; ~ **metre** *etc* Kubikmeter *m etc*.

cubic capacity *n* Hubraum *m*.

cubicle ['kju:bıkl] *n* Kabine *f*; (*in hospital*) Bettnische *f*.

cuckoo ['kuku:] *n* Kuckuck *m*.

cuckoo clock *n* Kuckucksuhr *f*.

cucumber ['kju:kʌmbə*] *n* Gurke *f*.

cud [kʌd] *n*: **to chew the** ~ (*animal*) wiederkäuen; (*fig: person*) vor sich *acc* hin grübeln.

cuddle ['kʌdl] *vt* in den Arm nehmen, drücken ♦ *vi* schmusen.

cuddly ['kʌdlı] *adj* (*toy*) zum Liebhaben *or* Drücken; (*person*) knuddelig (*inf*).

cudgel ['kʌdʒl] *n* Knüppel *m* ♦ *vt*: **to** ~ **one's**

brains sich *dat* das (Ge)hirn zermartern.

cue [kju:] *n* (*SPORT*) Billardstock *m*, Queue *nt*; (*THEAT: word*) Stichwort *nt*; (: *action*) (Einsatz)zeichen *nt*; (*MUS*) Einsatz *m*.

cuff [kʌf] *n* (*of sleeve*) Manschette *f*; (*US: of trousers*) Aufschlag *m*; (*blow*) Klaps *m* ♦ *vt* einen Klaps geben +*dat*; **off the** ~ aus dem Stegreif.

cuff links *npl* Manschettenknöpfe *pl*.

cu. in. *abbr* (= *cubic inches*) Kubikzoll.

cuisine [kwı'zi:n] *n* Küche *f*.

cul-de-sac ['kʌldəsæk] *n* Sackgasse *f*.

culinary ['kʌlınərı] *adj* (*skill*) Koch-; (*delight*) kulinarisch.

cull [kʌl] *vt* (zusammen)sammeln; (*animals*) ausmerzen ♦ *n Erlegen überschüssiger Tierbestände.*

culminate ['kʌlmıneıt] *vi*: **to** ~ **in** gipfeln in +*dat*.

culmination [kʌlmı'neıʃən] *n* Höhepunkt *m*.

culottes [kju:'lɔts] *npl* Hosenrock *m*.

culpable ['kʌlpəbl] *adj* schuldig.

culprit ['kʌlprıt] *n* Täter(in) *m(f)*.

cult [kʌlt] *n* Kult *m*.

cult figure *n* Kultfigur *f*.

cultivate ['kʌltıveıt] *vt* (*land*) bebauen, landwirtschaftlich nutzen; (*crop*) anbauen; (*feeling*) entwickeln; (*person*) sich *dat* warmhalten (*inf*), die Beziehung pflegen zu.

cultivation [kʌltı'veıʃən] *n* (*of land*) Bebauung *f*, landwirtschaftliche Nutzung *f*; (*of crop*) Anbau *m*.

cultural ['kʌltʃərəl] *adj* kulturell.

culture ['kʌltʃə*] *n* Kultur *f*.

cultured ['kʌltʃəd] *adj* kultiviert; (*pearl*) Zucht-.

cumbersome ['kʌmbəsəm] *adj* (*suitcase etc*) sperrig, unhandlich; (*piece of machinery*) schwer zu handhaben; (*clothing*) hinderlich; (*process*) umständlich.

cumin ['kʌmın] *n* Kreuzkümmel *m*.

cumulative ['kju:mjulətıv] *adj* (*effect, result*) Gesamt-.

cunning ['kʌnıŋ] *n* Gerissenheit *f* ♦ *adj* gerissen; (*device, idea*) schlau.

cunt [kʌnt] (*inf!*) *n* (*vagina*) Fotze *f* (*!*); (*term of abuse*) Arsch *m* (*!*).

cup [kʌp] *n* Tasse *f*; (*as prize*) Pokal *m*; (*of bra*) Körbchen *nt*; **a** ~ **of tea** eine Tasse Tee.

cupboard ['kʌbəd] *n* Schrank *m*.

cup final (*BRIT*) *n* Pokalendspiel *nt*.

cupful ['kʌpful] *n* Tasse *f*.

Cupid ['kju:pıd] *n* Amor *m*; (*figurine*) Amorette *f*.

cupidity [kju:'pıdıtı] *n* Begierde *f*, Gier *f*.

cupola ['kju:pələ] *n* Kuppel *f*.

cuppa ['kʌpə] (*BRIT: inf*) *n* Tasse *f* Tee.

cup tie (*BRIT*) *n* Pokalspiel *nt*.

curable ['kjuərəbl] *adj* heilbar.

curate ['kjuərıt] *n* Vikar *m*.

curator [kjuə'reıtə*] *n* Kustos *m*.

curb [kə:b] *vt* einschränken; (*person*) an die

Kandare nehmen ♦ *n* Einschränkung *f*; (*US: kerb*) Bordstein *m*.

curd cheese *n* Weißkäse *m*.

curdle ['kɜːdl] *vi* gerinnen.

curds [kɜːdz] *npl* ≈ Quark *m*.

cure [kjuə*] *vt* heilen; (*CULIN: salt*) pökeln; (: *smoke*) räuchern; (: *dry*) trocknen; (*problem*) abhelfen +*dat* ♦ *n* (*remedy*) (Heil)mittel *nt*; (*treatment*) Heilverfahren *nt*; (*solution*) Abhilfe *f*; **to be ~d of sth** von etw geheilt sein.

cure-all ['kjuərɔːl] *n* (*also fig*) Allheilmittel *nt*.

curfew ['kɜːfjuː] *n* Ausgangssperre *f*; (*time*) Sperrstunde *f*.

curio ['kjuəriəu] *n* Kuriosität *f*.

curiosity [kjuərɪ'ɒsɪtɪ] *n* (*see adj*) Wißbegier(de) *f*; Neugier *f*; Merkwürdigkeit *f*.

curious ['kjuərɪəs] *adj* (*interested*) wißbegierig; (*nosy*) neugierig; (*strange, unusual*) sonderbar, merkwürdig; **I'm ~ about him** ich bin gespannt auf ihn.

curiously ['kjuərɪəslɪ] *adv* neugierig; (*inquisitively*) wißbegierig; **~ enough, ...** merkwürdigerweise ...

curl [kɜːl] *n* Locke *f*; (*of smoke etc*) Kringel *m* ♦ *vt* (*hair: loosely*) locken; (: *tightly*) kräuseln ♦ *vi* sich locken; sich kräuseln; (*smoke*) sich kringeln.

►**curl up** *vi* sich zusammenrollen.

curler ['kɜːlə*] *n* Lockenwickler *m*; (*SPORT*) Curlingspieler(in) *m(f)*.

curlew ['kɜːluː] *n* Brachvogel *m*.

curling ['kɜːlɪŋ] *n* (*SPORT*) Curling *nt*.

curling tongs, (*US*) **curling irons** *npl* Lockenschere *f*, Brennschere *f*.

curly ['kɜːlɪ] *adj* lockig; (*tightly curled*) kraus.

currant ['kʌrnt] *n* Korinthe *f*; (*blackcurrant, redcurrant*) Johannisbeere *f*.

currency ['kʌrnsɪ] *n* (*system*) Währung *f*; (*money*) Geld *nt*; **foreign ~** Devisen *pl*; **to gain ~** (*fig*) sich verbreiten, um sich greifen.

current ['kʌrnt] *n* Strömung *f*; (*ELEC*) Strom *m*; (*of opinion*) Tendenz *f*, Trend *m* ♦ *adj* gegenwärtig; (*expression*) gebräuchlich; (*idea, custom*) verbreitet; **direct/alternating ~** (*ELEC*) Gleich-/Wechselstrom *m*; **the ~ issue of a magazine** die neueste *or* letzte Nummer einer Zeitschrift; **in ~ use** allgemein gebräuchlich.

current account (*BRIT*) *n* Girokonto *nt*.

current affairs *npl* Tagespolitik *f*.

current assets *npl* (*COMM*) Umlaufvermögen *nt*.

current liabilities *npl* (*COMM*) kurzfristige Verbindlichkeiten *pl*.

currently ['kʌrntlɪ] *adv* zur Zeit.

curricula [kə'rɪkjulə] *npl of* **curriculum**.

curriculum [kə'rɪkjuləm] (*pl* **~s** *or* **curricula**) *n* Lehrplan *m*.

curriculum vitae [-'viːtaɪ] *n* Lebenslauf *m*.

curry ['kʌrɪ] *n* (*dish*) Currygericht *nt* ♦ *vt*: **to ~ favour with** sich einschmeicheln bei.

curry powder *n* Curry *m or nt*, Currypulver *nt*.

curse [kɜːs] *vi* fluchen ♦ *vt* verfluchen ♦ *n* Fluch *m*.

cursor ['kɜːsə*] *n* (*COMPUT*) Cursor *m*.

cursory ['kɜːsərɪ] *adj* flüchtig; (*examination*) oberflächlich.

curt [kɜːt] *adj* knapp, kurz angebunden.

curtail [kɜː'teɪl] *vt* einschränken; (*visit etc*) abkürzen.

curtain ['kɜːtn] *n* Vorhang *m*; (*net*) Gardine *f*; **to draw the ~s** (*together*) die Vorhänge zuziehen; (*apart*) die Vorhänge aufmachen.

curtain call *n* (*THEAT*) Vorhang *m*.

curts(e)y ['kɜːtsɪ] *vi* knicksen ♦ *n* Knicks *m*.

curvature ['kɜːvətʃə*] *n* Krümmung *f*.

curve [kɜːv] *n* Bogen *m*; (*in the road*) Kurve *f* ♦ *vi* einen Bogen machen; (*surface, arch*) sich wölben ♦ *vt* biegen.

curved [kɜːvd] *adj* (*line*) gebogen; (*table legs etc*) geschwungen; (*surface, arch, sides of ship*) gewölbt.

cushion ['kuʃən] *n* Kissen *nt* ♦ *vt* dämpfen; (*seat*) polstern.

cushy ['kuʃɪ] (*inf*) *adj*: **a ~ job** ein gemütlicher *or* ruhiger Job; **to have a ~ time** eine ruhige Kugel schieben.

custard ['kʌstəd] *n* (*for pouring*) Vanillesoße *f*.

custard powder (*BRIT*) *n* Vanillesoßenpulver *nt*.

custodial [kʌs'təudɪəl] *adj*: **~ sentence** Gefängnisstrafe *f*.

custodian [kʌs'təudɪən] *n* Verwalter(in) *m(f)*; (*of museum etc*) Aufseher(in) *m(f)*, Wächter(in) *m(f)*.

custody ['kʌstədɪ] *n* (*of child*) Vormundschaft *f*; (*for offenders*) (polizeilicher) Gewahrsam *m*, Haft *f*; **to take into ~** verhaften; **in the ~ of** unter der Obhut +*gen*; **the mother has ~ of the children** die Kinder sind der Mutter zugesprochen worden.

custom ['kʌstəm] *n* Brauch *m*; (*habit*) (An)gewohnheit *f*; (*LAW*) Gewohnheitsrecht *nt*; (*COMM*) Kundschaft *f*.

customary ['kʌstəmərɪ] *adj* (*conventional*) üblich; (*habitual*) gewohnt; **it is ~ to do it** es ist üblich, es zu tun.

custom-built ['kʌstəm'bɪlt] *adj* spezial- angefertigt.

customer ['kʌstəmə*] *n* Kunde *m*, Kundin *f*; **he's an awkward ~** (*inf*) er ist ein schwieriger Typ.

customer profile *n* Kundenprofil *nt*.

customized ['kʌstəmaɪzd] *adj* individuell aufgemacht.

custom-made ['kʌstəm'meɪd] *adj* (*shirt etc*) maßgefertigt, nach Maß; (*car etc*) spezialangefertigt.

customs ['kʌstəmz] *npl* Zoll *m*; **to go through (the) ~** durch den Zoll gehen.

Customs and Excise (*BRIT*) *n* die Zollbehörde *f*.
customs duty *n* Zoll *m*.
customs officer *n* Zollbeamte(r) *m*, Zollbeamtin *f*.
cut [kʌt] (*pt, pp* **cut**) *vt* schneiden; (*text, programme, spending*) kürzen; (*prices*) senken, herabsetzen; (*supply*) einschränken; (*cloth*) zuschneiden; (*road*) schlagen, hauen; (*inf: lecture, appointment*) schwänzen ♦ *vi* schneiden; (*lines*) sich schneiden ♦ *n* Schnitt *m*; (*in skin*) Schnittwunde *f*; (*in salary, spending etc*) Kürzung *f*; (*of meat*) Stück *nt*; (*of jewel*) Schnitt *m*, Schliff *m*; **to ~ a tooth** zahnen, einen Zahn bekommen; **to ~ one's finger/ hand/knee** sich in den Finger/in die Hand/ am Knie schneiden; **to get one's hair ~** sich *dat* die Haare schneiden lassen; **to ~ sth short** etw vorzeitig abbrechen; **to ~ sb dead** jdn wie Luft behandeln; **cold ~s** (*US*) Aufschnitt *m*; **power ~** Stromausfall *m*.
► **cut back** *vt* (*plants*) zurückschneiden; (*production*) zurückschrauben; (*expenditure*) einschränken.
► **cut down** *vt* (*tree*) fällen; (*consumption*) einschränken; **to ~ sb down to size** (*fig*) jdn auf seinen Platz verweisen.
► **cut down on** *vt fus* einschränken.
► **cut in** *vi* (*AUT*) sich direkt vor ein anderes Auto setzen; **to ~ in (on)** (*conversation*) sich einschalten (in +*acc*).
► **cut off** *vt* abschneiden; (*supply*) sperren; (*TEL*) unterbrechen; **we've been ~ off** (*TEL*) wir sind unterbrochen worden.
► **cut out** *vt* ausschneiden; (*an activity etc*) aufhören mit; (*remove*) herausschneiden.
► **cut up** *vt* kleinschneiden; **it really ~ me up** (*inf*) es hat mich ziemlich mitgenommen; **to feel ~ up about sth** (*inf*) betroffen über etw *acc* sein.
cut and dried *adj* (*also:* **cut-and-dry:** *answer*) eindeutig; (: *solution*) einfach.
cutaway ['kʌtəweɪ] *n* (*coat*) Cut(away) *m*; (*drawing*) Schnittdiagramm *nt*; (*model*) Schnittmodell *nt*; (*CINE, TV*) Schnitt *m*.
cutback ['kʌtbæk] *n* Kürzung *f*.
cute [kju:t] *adj* süß, niedlich; (*clever*) schlau.
cut glass *n* geschliffenes Glas *nt*.
cuticle ['kju:tɪkl] *n* Nagelhaut *f*; **~ remover** Nagelhautentferner *m*.
cutlery ['kʌtlərɪ] *n* Besteck *nt*.
cutlet ['kʌtlɪt] *n* Schnitzel *nt*; (*vegetable cutlet, nut cutlet*) Bratling *m*.
cutoff ['kʌtɔf] *n* (*also:* **~ point**) Trennlinie *f*.
cutoff switch *n* Ausschaltmechanismus *m*.
cutout ['kʌtaut] *n* (*switch*) Unterbrecher *m*; (*shape*) Ausschneidemodell *nt*; (*paper figure*) Ausschneidepuppe *f*.
cut-price ['kʌt'praɪs] *adj* (*goods*) heruntergesetzt; (*offer*) Billig-.
cut-rate ['kʌt'reɪt] (*US*) *adj* = **cut-price**.

cutthroat ['kʌtθrəut] *n* Mörder(in) *m(f)* ♦ *adj* unbarmherzig, mörderisch.
cutting ['kʌtɪŋ] *adj* (*edge, remark*) scharf ♦ *n* (*BRIT: from newspaper*) Ausschnitt *m*; (: *RAIL*) Durchstich *m*; (*from plant*) Ableger *m*.
cutting edge *n* (*fig*) Spitzenstellung *f*; **on the ~ (of)** an der Spitze +*gen*.
cuttlefish ['kʌtlfɪʃ] *n* Tintenfisch *m*.
CV *n abbr* = **curriculum vitae**.
c.w.o. *abbr* (*COMM*) = **cash with order**.
cwt *abbr* = **hundredweight**.
cyanide ['saɪənaɪd] *n* Zyanid *nt*.
cybernetics [saɪbə'netɪks] *n* Kybernetik *f*.
cyclamen ['sɪkləmən] *n* Alpenveilchen *nt*.
cycle ['saɪkl] *n* (*bicycle*) (Fahr)rad *nt*; (*series: of seasons, songs etc*) Zyklus *m*; (: *of events*) Gang *m*; (: *TECH*) Periode *f* ♦ *vi* radfahren.
cycle race *n* Radrennen *nt*.
cycle rack *n* Fahrradständer *m*.
cycling ['saɪklɪŋ] *n* Radfahren *nt*; **to go on a ~ holiday** (*BRIT*) Urlaub mit dem Fahrrad machen.
cyclist ['saɪklɪst] *n* (Fahr)radfahrer(in) *m(f)*.
cyclone ['saɪkləun] *n* Zyklon *m*.
cygnet ['sɪgnɪt] *n* Schwanjunge(s) *nt*.
cylinder ['sɪlɪndə*] *n* Zylinder *m*; (*of gas*) Gasflasche *f*.
cylinder block *n* Zylinderblock *m*.
cylinder head *n* Zylinderkopf *m*.
cylinder-head gasket ['sɪlɪndəhɛd-] *n* Zylinderkopfdichtung *f*.
cymbals ['sɪmblz] *npl* (*MUS*) Becken *nt*.
cynic ['sɪnɪk] *n* Zyniker(in) *m(f)*.
cynical ['sɪnɪkl] *adj* zynisch.
cynicism ['sɪnɪsɪzəm] *n* Zynismus *m*.
CYO (*US*) *n abbr* (= *Catholic Youth Organization*) katholische Jugendorganisation.
cypress ['saɪprɪs] *n* Zypresse *f*.
Cypriot ['sɪprɪət] *adj* zypriotisch, zyprisch ♦ *n* Zypriot(in) *m(f)*.
Cyprus ['saɪprəs] *n* Zypern *nt*.
cyst [sɪst] *n* Zyste *f*.
cystitis [sɪs'taɪtɪs] *n* Blasenentzündung *f*, Zystitis *f*.
CZ (*US*) *n abbr* (= *Canal Zone*) Bereich des Panamakanals.
czar [za:*] *n* = **tsar**.
Czech [tʃɛk] *adj* tschechisch ♦ *n* Tscheche *m*, Tschechin *f*; (*language*) Tschechisch *nt*; **the ~ Republic** die Tschechische Republik *f*.
Czechoslovak [tʃɛkə'sləuvæk] *adj, n* = **Czechoslovak(ian)**.
Czechoslovakia [tʃɛkəslə'vækɪə] *n* (*formerly*) die Tschechoslowakei *f*.
Czechoslovak(ian) [tʃɛkə'sləuvæk, tʃɛkəslə'vækɪən] (*formerly*) *adj* tschechoslowakisch ♦ *n* Tschechoslowake *m*, Tschechoslowakin *f*.

D, d

D¹, d¹ [di:] n (letter) D nt, d nt; ~ **for David,** (US) ~ **for Dog** ≈ D wie Dora.

D² [di:] n (MUS) D nt, d nt.

D³ [di:] (US) abbr (POL) = **democrat; democratic.**

d² (BRIT: formerly) abbr = **penny.**

d. abbr (= died): **Henry Jones, ~ 1754** Henry Jones, gest. 1754.

DA (US) n abbr = **district attorney.**

dab [dæb] vt betupfen; (paint, cream) tupfen ♦ n Tupfer m; **to be a ~ hand at sth** gut in etw dat sein; **to be a ~ hand at doing sth** sich darauf verstehen, etw zu tun.
► **dab at** vt betupfen.

dabble ['dæbl] vi: **to ~ in** sich (nebenbei) beschäftigen mit.

dachshund ['dækshund] n Dackel m.

dad [dæd] (inf) n Papa m, Vati m.

daddy ['dædɪ] (inf) n = **dad.**

daddy-longlegs [dædɪ'lɒŋlɛgz] (inf) n Schnake f.

daffodil ['dæfədɪl] n Osterglocke f, Narzisse f.

daft [dɑːft] (inf) adj doof (inf), blöd (inf); **to be ~ about sb/sth** verrückt nach jdm/etw sein.

dagger ['dægə*] n Dolch m; **to be at ~s drawn with sb** mit jdm auf Kriegsfuß stehen; **to look ~s at sb** jdn mit Blicken durchbohren.

dahlia ['deɪljə] n Dahlie f.

daily ['deɪlɪ] adj täglich; (wages) Tages- ♦ n (paper) Tageszeitung f; (BRIT: also: ~ **help**) Putzfrau f ♦ adv täglich; **twice ~** zweimal täglich or am Tag.

dainty ['deɪntɪ] adj zierlich.

dairy ['deərɪ] n (BRIT: shop) Milchgeschäft nt; (company) Molkerei f; (on farm) Milchkammer f ♦ cpd Milch-; (herd, industry, farming) Milchvieh-.

dairy farm n auf Milchviehhaltung spezialisierter Bauernhof.

dairy products npl Milchprodukte pl, Molkereiprodukte pl.

dairy store (US) n Milchgeschäft nt.

dais ['deɪs] n Podium nt.

daisy ['deɪzɪ] n Gänseblümchen nt.

daisywheel ['deɪzɪwiːl] n Typenrad nt.

daisywheel printer n Typenraddrucker m.

Dakar ['dækə*] n Dakar nt.

dale [deɪl] (BRIT) n Tal nt.

dally ['dælɪ] vi (herum)trödeln; **to ~ with** (plan, idea) spielen mit.

dalmatian [dæl'meɪʃən] n Dalmatiner m.

dam [dæm] n (Stau)damm m; (reservoir) Stausee m ♦ vt stauen.

damage ['dæmɪdʒ] n Schaden m ♦ vt schaden +dat; (spoil, break) beschädigen; **damages** npl (LAW) Schaden(s)ersatz m; ~ **to property** Sachbeschädigung f; **to pay £5,000 in ~s** 5000 Pfund Schaden(s)ersatz (be)zahlen.

damaging ['dæmɪdʒɪŋ] adj: ~ **(to)** schädlich (für).

Damascus [də'mɑːskəs] n Damaskus nt.

dame [deɪm] n Dame f; (US: inf) Weib nt; (THEAT) (komische) Alte f (von einem Mann gespielt).

damn [dæm] vt verfluchen; (condemn) verurteilen ♦ adj (inf: also: ~**ed**) verdammt ♦ n (inf): **I don't give a ~** das ist mir scheißegal (!); ~ **(it)!** verdammt (noch mal)!

damnable ['dæmnəbl] adj gräßlich.

damnation [dæm'neɪʃən] n Verdammnis f ♦ excl (inf) verdammt.

damning ['dæmɪŋ] adj belastend.

damp [dæmp] adj feucht ♦ n Feuchtigkeit f ♦ vt (also: ~**en**) befeuchten, anfeuchten; (enthusiasm etc) dämpfen.

dampcourse ['dæmpkɔːs] n Dämmschicht f.

damper ['dæmpə*] n (MUS) Dämpfer m; (of fire) (Luft)klappe f; **to put a ~ on** (fig) einen Dämpfer aufsetzen +dat.

dampness ['dæmpnɪs] n Feuchtigkeit f.

damson ['dæmzən] n Damaszenerpflaume f.

dance [dɑːns] n Tanz m; (social event) Tanz(abend) m ♦ vi tanzen; **to ~ about** (herum)tänzeln.

dance hall n Tanzsaal m.

dancer ['dɑːnsə*] n Tänzer(in) m(f).

dancing ['dɑːnsɪŋ] n Tanzen nt ♦ cpd (teacher, school, class etc) Tanz-.

D and C n abbr (MED: = dilation and curettage) Ausschabung f.

dandelion ['dændɪlaɪən] n Löwenzahn m.

dandruff ['dændrəf] n Schuppen pl.

dandy ['dændɪ] n Dandy m ♦ adj (US: inf) prima.

Dane [deɪn] n Däne m, Dänin f.

danger ['deɪndʒə*] n Gefahr f; **there is ~ of fire/poisoning** es besteht Feuer-/ Vergiftungsgefahr; **there is a ~ of sth happening** es besteht die Gefahr, daß etw geschieht; "~!" „Achtung!"; **in ~** in Gefahr; **to be in ~ of doing sth** Gefahr laufen, etw zu tun; **out of ~** außer Gefahr.

danger list n: **on the ~** in Lebensgefahr.

dangerous ['deɪndʒrəs] adj gefährlich.

dangerously ['deɪndʒrəslɪ] adv gefährlich; (close) bedenklich; ~ **ill** schwer krank.

danger zone n Gefahrenzone f.

dangle ['dæŋgl] vt baumeln lassen ♦ vi baumeln.

Danish ['deɪnɪʃ] adj dänisch ♦ n (LING) Dänisch nt.

Danish pastry n Plundergebäck nt.

dank [dæŋk] adj (unangenehm) feucht.

Danube ['dænjuːb] n: **the ~** die Donau.

dapper ['dæpə'] *adj* gepflegt.
Dardanelles [daːdə'nɛlz] *npl*: **the** ~ **die** Dardanellen *pl*.
dare [dɛə'] *vt*: **to** ~ **sb to do sth** jdn dazu herausfordern, etw zu tun ♦ *vi*: **to** ~ **(to) do sth** es wagen, etw zu tun; **I** ~**n't tell him** (*BRIT*) ich wage nicht, es ihm zu sagen; **I** ~ **say** ich nehme an.
daredevil ['dɛədɛvl] *n* Draufgänger *m*.
Dar-es-Salaam ['daːrɛssə'laːm] *n* Daressalam *nt*.
daring ['dɛərɪŋ] *adj* kühn, verwegen; (*bold*) gewagt ♦ *n* Kühnheit *f*.
dark [daːk] *adj* dunkel; (*look*) finster ♦ *n*: **in the** ~ im Dunkeln; **to be in the** ~ **about** (*fig*) keine Ahnung haben von; **after** ~ nach Einbruch der Dunkelheit; **it is/is getting** ~ es ist/wird dunkel; ~ **chocolate** Zartbitterschokolade *f*.
Dark Ages *npl*: **the** ~ das finstere Mittelalter.
darken [daːkn] *vt* dunkel machen ♦ *vi* sich verdunkeln.
dark glasses *npl* Sonnenbrille *f*.
dark horse *n* (*fig: in competition*) Unbekannte(r) *f(m)* (mit Außenseiterchancen); (*quiet person*) stilles Wasser *nt*.
darkly ['daːklɪ] *adv* finster.
darkness ['daːknɪs] *n* Dunkelheit *f*, Finsternis *f*.
darkroom ['daːkrum] *n* Dunkelkammer *f*.
darling ['daːlɪŋ] *adj* lieb ♦ *n* Liebling *m*; **to be the** ~ **of** der Liebling +*gen* sein; **she is a** ~ sie ist ein Schatz.
darn [daːn] *vt* stopfen.
dart [daːt] *n* (*in game*) (Wurf)pfeil *m*; (*in sewing*) Abnäher *m* ♦ *vi*: **to** ~ **towards** (*also*: **make a** ~ **towards**) zustürzen auf +*acc*; **to** ~ **away/along** davon-/entlangflitzen.
dartboard ['daːtbɔːd] *n* Dartscheibe *f*.
darts [daːts] *n* Darts *nt*, Pfeilwurfspiel *nt*.
dash [dæʃ] *n* (*sign*) Gedankenstrich *m*; (*rush*) Jagd *f* ♦ *vt* (*throw*) schleudern; (*hopes*) zunichte machen ♦ *vi*: **to** ~ **towards** zustürzen auf +*acc*; **a** ~ **of** ... (*small quantity*) etwas ..., ein Schuß *m* ...; **to make a** ~ **for sth** auf etw *acc* zustürzen; **we'll have to make a** ~ **for it** wir müssen rennen, so schnell wir können.
▶**dash away** *vi* losstürzen.
▶**dash off** *vi* = **dash away.**
dashboard ['dæʃbɔːd] *n* Armaturenbrett *nt*.
dashing ['dæʃɪŋ] *adj* flott.
dastardly ['dæstədlɪ] *adj* niederträchtig.
DAT *n abbr* (= *digital audio tape*) DAT *nt*.
data ['deɪtə] *npl* Daten *pl*.
database ['deɪtəbeɪs] *n* Datenbank *f*.
data capture *n* Datenerfassung *f*.
data processing *n* Datenverarbeitung *f*.
data transmission *n* Datenübertragung *f*.
date [deɪt] *n* Datum *nt*; (*with friend*) Verabredung *f*; (*fruit*) Dattel *f* ♦ *vt* datieren; (*person*) ausgehen mit; **what's the** ~ **today?**

der Wievielte ist heute?; ~ **of birth** Geburtsdatum *nt*; **closing** ~ Einsendeschluß *m*; **to** ~ bis heute; **out of** ~ altmodisch; (*expired*) abgelaufen; **up to** ~ auf dem neuesten Stand; **to bring up to** ~ auf den neuesten Stand bringen; (*person*) über den neuesten Stand der Dinge informieren; **a letter** ~**d 5th July** *or* (*US*) **July 5th** ein vom 5. Juli datierter Brief.
dated ['deɪtɪd] *adj* altmodisch.
dateline ['deɪtlaɪn] *n* (*GEOG*) Datumsgrenze *f*; (*PRESS*) Datumszeile *f*.
date rape *n* Vergewaltigung *f* einer Bekannten (*mit der der Täter eine Verabredung hatte*).
date stamp *n* Datumsstempel *m*.
dative ['deɪtɪv] *n* Dativ *m*.
daub [dɔːb] *vt* schmieren; **to** ~ **with** beschmieren mit.
daughter ['dɔːtə'] *n* Tochter *f*.
daughter-in-law ['dɔːtərɪnlɔː] *n* Schwiegertochter *f*.
daunt [dɔːnt] *vt* entmutigen.
daunting ['dɔːntɪŋ] *adj* entmutigend.
dauntless ['dɔːntlɪs] *adj* unerschrocken, beherzt.
dawdle ['dɔːdl] *vi* trödeln; **to** ~ **over one's work** bei der Arbeit bummeln *or* trödeln.
dawn [dɔːn] *n* Tagesanbruch *m*, Morgengrauen *nt*; (*of period*) Anbruch *m* ♦ *vi* dämmern; (*fig*): **it** ~**ed on him that ...** es dämmerte ihm, daß ...; **from** ~ **to dusk** von morgens bis abends.
dawn chorus (*BRIT*) *n* Morgenkonzert *nt* der Vögel.
day [deɪ] *n* Tag *m*; (*heyday*) Zeit *f*; **the** ~ **before/after** am Tag zuvor/danach; **the** ~ **after tomorrow** übermorgen; **the** ~ **before yesterday** vorgestern; **(on) the following** ~ am Tag danach; **the** ~ **that ...** (am Tag,) als ...; ~ **by** ~ jeden Tag, täglich; **by** ~ tagsüber; **paid by the** ~ tageweise bezahlt; **to work an eight hour** ~ einen Achtstundentag haben; **these** ~**s, in the present** ~ heute, heutzutage.
daybook ['deɪbuk] (*BRIT*) *n* Journal *nt*.
dayboy ['deɪbɔɪ] *n* Externe(r) *m*.
daybreak ['deɪbreɪk] *n* Tagesanbruch *m*.
day-care centre ['deɪkɛə-] *n* (*for children*) (Kinder)tagesstätte *f*; (*for old people*) Altentagesstätte *f*.
daydream ['deɪdriːm] *vi* (mit offenen Augen) träumen ♦ *n* Tagtraum *m*, Träumerei *f*.
daygirl ['deɪgɜːl] *n* Externe *f*.
daylight ['deɪlaɪt] *n* Tageslicht *nt*.
daylight robbery (*inf*) *n* Halsabschneiderei *f*.
daylight-saving time (*US*) *n* Sommerzeit *f*.
day release *n*: **to be on** ~ tageweise (zur Weiterbildung) freigestellt sein.
day return (*BRIT*) *n* Tagesrückfahrkarte *f*.
day shift *n* Tagschicht *f*.
daytime ['deɪtaɪm] *n* Tag *m*; **in the** ~

tagsüber, bei Tage.

day-to-day ['deɪtə'deɪ] adj täglich, Alltags-; **on a ~ basis** tageweise.

day trip n Tagesausflug m.

day-tripper ['deɪ'trɪpə*] n Tagesausflügler(in) m(f).

daze [deɪz] vt benommen machen ♦ n: **in a ~** ganz benommen.

dazed [deɪzd] adj benommen.

dazzle ['dæzl] vt blenden.

dazzling ['dæzlɪŋ] adj (light) blendend; (smile) strahlend; (career, achievements) glänzend.

DC abbr = **direct current**; (US: POST: = District of Columbia).

DCC n abbr (= digital compact cassette) DCC f.

DD n abbr (= Doctor of Divinity) ≈ Dr. theol.

D/D abbr = **direct debit**.

dd. abbr (COMM: = delivered) geliefert.

D-day ['diːdeɪ] n der Tag X.

DDS (US) n abbr (= Doctor of Dental Surgery) ≈ Dr. med. dent.

DDT n abbr (= dichlorodiphenyltrichloroethane) DDT nt.

DE (US) abbr (POST: = Delaware).

DEA (US) n abbr (= Drug Enforcement Administration) amerikanische Drogenbehörde.

deacon ['diːkən] n Diakon m.

dead [dɛd] adj tot; (flowers) verwelkt; (numb) abgestorben, taub; (battery) leer; (place) wie ausgestorben ♦ adv total, völlig; (directly, exactly) genau ♦ npl: **the ~** die Toten pl; **to shoot sb ~** jdn erschießen; **~ silence** Totenstille f; **in the ~ centre (of)** genau in der Mitte +gen; **the line has gone ~** (TEL) die Leitung ist tot; **~ on time** auf die Minute pünktlich; **~ tired** todmüde; **to stop ~** abrupt stehenbleiben.

dead beat (inf) adj (tired) völlig kaputt.

deaden [dɛdn] vt (blow) abschwächen; (pain) mildern; (sound) dämpfen.

dead end n Sackgasse f.

dead-end ['dɛdɛnd] adj: **a ~ job** ein Job m ohne Aufstiegsmöglichkeiten.

dead heat n: **to finish in a ~** unentschieden ausgehen.

dead letter office n Amt nt für unzustellbare Briefe.

deadline ['dɛdlaɪn] n (letzter) Termin m; **to work to a ~** auf einen Termin hinarbeiten.

deadlock ['dɛdlɔk] n Stillstand m; **the meeting ended in ~** die Verhandlung war festgefahren.

dead loss (inf) n: **to be a ~** ein hoffnungsloser Fall sein.

deadly ['dɛdlɪ] adj tödlich ♦ adv: **~ dull** tödlich langweilig.

deadpan ['dɛdpæn] adj (look) unbewegt; (tone) trocken.

Dead Sea n: **the ~** das Tote Meer.

dead season n tote Saison f.

deaf [dɛf] adj taub; (partially) schwerhörig; **to**

turn a ~ ear to sth sich einer Sache dat gegenüber taub stellen.

deaf aid (BRIT) n Hörgerät nt.

deaf-and-dumb ['dɛfən'dʌm] adj taubstumm; **~ alphabet** Taubstummensprache f.

deafen ['dɛfn] vt taub machen.

deafening ['dɛfnɪŋ] adj ohrenbetäubend.

deaf-mute ['dɛfmjuːt] n Taubstumme(r) f(m).

deafness ['dɛfnɪs] n Taubheit f.

deal [diːl] (pt, pp dealt) n Geschäft nt, Handel m ♦ vt (blow) versetzen; (card) geben, austeilen; **to strike a ~ with sb** ein Geschäft mit jdm abschließen; **it's a ~!** (inf) abgemacht!; **he got a fair/bad ~ from them** er ist von ihnen anständig/schlecht behandelt worden; **a good ~ (a lot)** ziemlich viel; **a great ~ (of)** ziemlich viel.

▶**deal in** vt fus handeln mit.

▶**deal with** vt fus (person) sich kümmern um; (problem) sich befassen mit; (successfully) fertigwerden mit; (subject) behandeln.

dealer ['diːlə*] n Händler(in) m(f); (in drugs) Dealer m; (CARDS) Kartengeber(in) m(f).

dealership ['diːləʃɪp] n (Vertrags)händler m.

dealings ['diːlɪŋz] npl Geschäfte pl; (relations) Beziehungen pl.

dealt [dɛlt] pt, pp of **deal**.

dean [diːn] n Dekan m; (US: SCOL: administrator) Schul- oder Collegeverwalter mit Beratungs- und Disziplinarfunktion.

dear [dɪə*] adj lieb; (expensive) teuer ♦ n: **(my) ~** (mein) Liebling m ♦ excl: **~ me!** (ach) du liebe Zeit!; **D~ Sir/Madam** Sehr geehrte Damen und Herren; **D~ Mr/Mrs X** Sehr geehrter Herr/geehrte Frau X; (less formal) Lieber Herr/Liebe Frau X.

dearly ['dɪəlɪ] adv (love) von ganzem Herzen; (pay) teuer.

dear money n (COMM) teures Geld nt.

dearth [dɜːθ] n: **a ~ of** ein Mangel m an +dat.

death [dɛθ] n Tod m; (fatality) Tote(r) f(m), Todesfall m.

deathbed ['dɛθbɛd] n: **to be on one's ~** auf dem Sterbebett liegen.

death certificate n Sterbeurkunde f, Totenschein m.

deathly ['dɛθlɪ] adj (silence) eisig ♦ adv (pale etc) toten-.

death penalty n Todesstrafe f.

death rate n Sterbeziffer f.

death row [-rəʊ] (US) n Todestrakt m.

death sentence n Todesurteil nt.

death squad n Todeskommando nt.

death toll n Zahl f der Todesopfer or Toten.

deathtrap ['dɛθtræp] n Todesfalle f.

deb [dɛb] (inf) n abbr = **debutante**.

debacle [deɪ'bɑːkl] n Debakel nt.

debar [dɪ'bɑː*] vt: **to ~ sb from doing sth** jdn davon ausschließen, etw zu tun; **to ~ sb from a club** jdn aus einem Klub ausschließen.

debase [dɪ'beɪs] vt (value, quality) mindern,

herabsetzen; (*person*) erniedrigen, entwürdigen.

debatable [dɪ'beɪtəbl] *adj* fraglich.

debate [dɪ'beɪt] *n* Debatte *f* ♦ *vt* debattieren über +*acc*; (*course of action*) überlegen ♦ *vi*: **to ~ whether** hin und her überlegen, ob.

debauchery [dɪ'bɔːtʃərɪ] *n* Ausschweifungen *pl*.

debenture [dɪ'bɛntʃə*] *n* Schuldschein *m*.

debilitate [dɪ'bɪlɪteɪt] *vt* schwächen.

debilitating [dɪ'bɪlɪteɪtɪŋ] *adj* schwächend.

debit ['dɛbɪt] *n* Schuldposten *m* ♦ *vt*: **to ~ a sum to sb/sb's account** jdn/jds Konto mit einer Summe belasten; *see also* **direct**.

debit balance *n* Sollsaldo *nt*, Debetsaldo *nt*.

debit note *n* Lastschriftanzeige *f*.

debonair *adj* flott.

debrief [diː'briːf] *vt* befragen.

debriefing [diː'briːfɪŋ] *n* Befragung *f*.

debris ['dɛbriː] *n* Trümmer *pl*, Schutt *m*.

debt [dɛt] *n* Schuld *f*; (*state of owing money*) Schulden *pl*, Verschuldung *f*; **to be in ~** Schulden haben, verschuldet sein; **bad ~** uneinbringliche Forderung *f*.

debt collector *n* Inkassobeauftragte(r) *f(m)*, Schuldeneintreiber(in) *m(f)*.

debtor ['dɛtə*] *n* Schuldner(in) *m(f)*.

debug ['diː'bʌg] *vt* (*COMPUT*) Fehler beseitigen in +*dat*.

debunk [diː'bʌŋk] *vt* (*myths, ideas*) bloßstellen; (*claim*) entlarven; (*person, institution*) vom Sockel stoßen.

debut ['deɪbjuː] *n* Debüt *nt*.

debutante ['dɛbjutænt] *n* Debütantin *f*.

Dec. *abbr* = **December.**

decade ['dɛkeɪd] *n* Jahrzehnt *nt*.

decadence ['dɛkədəns] *n* Dekadenz *f*.

decadent ['dɛkədənt] *adj* dekadent.

decaff ['diːkæf] *n* koffeinfreier Kaffee *m*.

decaffeinated [dɪ'kæfɪneɪtɪd] *adj* koffeinfrei.

decamp [dɪ'kæmp] (*inf*) *vi* verschwinden, sich aus dem Staub machen.

decant [dɪ'kænt] *vt* umfüllen.

decanter [dɪ'kæntə*] *n* Karaffe *f*.

decarbonize [diː'kɑːbənaɪz] *vt* entkohlen.

decathlon [dɪ'kæθlən] *n* Zehnkampf *m*.

decay [dɪ'keɪ] *n* Verfall *m*; (*of tooth*) Fäule *f* ♦ *vi* (*body*) verwesen; (*teeth*) faulen; (*leaves*) verrotten; (*fig: society etc*) verfallen.

decease [dɪ'siːs] *n* (*LAW*): **upon your ~** bei Ihrem Ableben.

deceased [dɪ'siːst] *n*: **the ~** der/die Tote *or* Verstorbene.

deceit [dɪ'siːt] *n* Betrug *m*.

deceitful [dɪ'siːtful] *adj* betrügerisch.

deceive [dɪ'siːv] *vt* täuschen; (*husband, wife etc*) betrügen; **to ~ o.s.** sich *dat* etwas vormachen.

decelerate [diː'sɛləreɪt] *vi* (*car etc*) langsamer werden; (*driver*) die Geschwindigkeit herabsetzen.

December [dɪ'sɛmbə*] *n* Dezember *m*; *see also*

July.

decency ['diːsənsɪ] *n* (*propriety*) Anstand *m*; (*kindness*) Anständigkeit *f*.

decent ['diːsənt] *adj* anständig; **we expect you to do the ~ thing** wir erwarten, daß Sie die Konsequenzen ziehen; **they were very ~ about it** sie haben sich sehr anständig verhalten; **that was very ~ of him** das war sehr anständig von ihm; **are you ~?** (*dressed*) hast du etwas an?

decently ['diːsəntlɪ] *adv* anständig.

decentralization ['diːsɛntrəlaɪ'zeɪʃən] *n* Dezentralisierung *f*.

decentralize [diː'sɛntrəlaɪz] *vt* dezentralisieren.

deception [dɪ'sɛpʃən] *n* Täuschung *f*, Betrug *m*.

deceptive [dɪ'sɛptɪv] *adj* irreführend, täuschend.

decibel ['dɛsɪbɛl] *n* Dezibel *nt*.

decide [dɪ'saɪd] *vt* entscheiden; (*persuade*) veranlassen ♦ *vi* sich entscheiden; **to ~ to do sth/that** beschließen, etw zu tun/daß; **to ~ on sth** sich für etw entscheiden; **to ~ on/against doing sth** sich dafür/dagegen entscheiden, etw zu tun.

decided [dɪ'saɪdɪd] *adj* entschieden; (*character*) entschlossen; (*difference*) deutlich.

decidedly [dɪ'saɪdɪdlɪ] *adv* entschieden; (*emphatically*) entschlossen.

deciding [dɪ'saɪdɪŋ] *adj* entscheidend.

deciduous [dɪ'sɪdjuəs] *adj* (*tree, woods*) Laub-.

decimal ['dɛsɪməl] *adj* (*system, number*) Dezimal- ♦ *n* Dezimalzahl *f*; **to three ~ places** auf drei Dezimalstellen.

decimalize ['dɛsɪməlaɪz] (*BRIT*) *vt* auf das Dezimalsystem umstellen.

decimal point *n* Komma *nt*.

decimate ['dɛsɪmeɪt] *vt* dezimieren.

decipher [dɪ'saɪfə*] *vt* entziffern.

decision [dɪ'sɪʒən] *n* Entscheidung *f*; (*decisiveness*) Bestimmtheit *f*, Entschlossenheit *f*; **to make a ~** eine Entscheidung treffen.

decisive [dɪ'saɪsɪv] *adj* (*action etc*) entscheidend; (*person*) entschlußfreudig; (*manner, reply*) bestimmt, entschlossen.

deck [dɛk] *n* Deck *nt*; (*record deck*) Plattenspieler *m*; (*of cards*) Spiel *nt*; **to go up on ~** an Deck gehen; **below ~** unter Deck; **top ~** (*of bus*) Oberdeck *nt*; **cassette ~** Tape-deck *nt*.

deck chair *n* Liegestuhl *m*.

deck hand *n* Deckshelfer(in) *m(f)*.

declaration [dɛklə'reɪʃən] *n* Erklärung *f*.

declare [dɪ'klɛə*] *vt* erklären; (*result*) bekanntgeben, veröffentlichen; (*income etc*) angeben; (*goods at customs*) verzollen.

declassify [diː'klæsɪfaɪ] *vt* freigeben.

decline [dɪ'klaɪn] *n* Rückgang *m*; (*decay*) Verfall *m* ♦ *vt* ablehnen ♦ *vi* (*strength*) nachlassen; (*business*) zurückgehen; (*old* *person*) abbauen; ~ **in/of** Rückgang *m* +*gen*; ~ **in living standards** Sinken *nt* des Lebensstandards.

declutch ['diː'klʌtʃ] *vi* auskuppeln.

decode ['diː'kəud] *vt* entschlüsseln.

decoder [diː'kəudəᵉ] *n* Decoder *m*.

decompose [diːkəm'pəuz] *vi* (*organic matter*) sich zersetzen; (*corpse*) verwesen.

decomposition [diːkɔmpə'zɪʃən] *n* Zersetzung *f*.

decompression [diːkəm'preʃən] *n* Dekompression *f*, Druckverminderung *f*.

decompression chamber *n* Dekompressionskammer *f*.

decongestant [diːkən'dʒestənt] *n* (*MED*) abschwellendes Mittel *nt*; (: *drops*) Nasentropfen *pl*.

decontaminate [diːkən'tæmɪneɪt] *vt* entgiften.

decontrol [diːkən'trəul] *vt* freigeben.

décor ['deɪkɔːᵉ] *n* Ausstattung *f*, (*THEAT*) Dekor *m or nt*.

decorate ['dekəreɪt] *vt*: **to ~ (with)** verzieren (mit); (*tree, building*) schmücken (mit) ♦ *vt* (*room, house: from bare walls*) anstreichen und tapezieren; (*redecorate*) renovieren.

decoration [dekə'reɪʃən] *n* Verzierung *f*; (*on tree, building*) Schmuck *m*; (*act: see verb*) Verzieren *nt*; Schmücken *nt*; (An)streichen *nt*; Tapezieren *nt*; (*medal*) Auszeichnung *f*.

decorative ['dekərətɪv] *adj* dekorativ.

decorator ['dekəreɪtəᵉ] *n* Maler(in) *m(f)*, Anstreicher(in) *m(f)*.

decorum [dɪ'kɔːrəm] *n* Anstand *m*.

decoy ['diːkɔɪ] *n* Lockvogel *m*; (*object*) Köder *m*; **they used him as a ~ for the enemy** sie benutzten ihn dazu, den Feind anzulocken.

decrease ['diːkriːs] *vt* verringern, reduzieren ♦ *vi* abnehmen, zurückgehen ♦ *n*: ~ **(in)** Abnahme *f* (+*gen*); Rückgang *m* (+*gen*); **to be on the ~** abnehmen, zurückgehen.

decreasing [diː'kriːsɪŋ] *adj* abnehmend, zurückgehend.

decree [dɪ'kriː] *n* (*ADMIN, LAW*) Verfügung *f*; (*POL*) Erlaß *m*; (*REL*) Dekret *nt* ♦ *vt*: **to ~ (that)** verfügen(, daß), verordnen(, daß).

decree absolute *n* endgültiges Scheidungsurteil *nt*.

decree nisi [-'naɪsaɪ] *n* vorläufiges Scheidungsurteil *nt*.

decrepit [dɪ'krepɪt] *adj* (*shack*) baufällig; (*person*) klapprig (*inf*).

decry [dɪ'kraɪ] *vt* schlechtmachen.

dedicate ['dedɪkeɪt] *vt*: **to ~ to** widmen +*dat*.

dedicated ['dedɪkeɪtɪd] *adj* hingebungsvoll, engagiert; (*COMPUT*) dediziert; ~ **word processor** dediziertes Textverarbeitungssystem *nt*.

dedication [dedɪ'keɪʃən] *n* Hingabe *f*; (*in book, on radio*) Widmung *f*.

deduce [dɪ'djuːs] *vt*: **to ~ (that)** schließen(, daß), folgern(, daß).

deduct [dɪ'dʌkt] *vt* abziehen; **to ~ sth (from)** etw abziehen (von); (*esp from wage etc*) etw einbehalten (von).

deduction [dɪ'dʌkʃən] *n* (*act of deducting*) Abzug *m*; (*act of deducing*) Folgerung *f*.

deed [diːd] *n* Tat *f*; (*LAW*) Urkunde *f*; ~ **of covenant** Vertragsurkunde *f*.

deem [diːm] *vt* (*formal*) erachten für, halten für; **to ~ it wise/helpful to do sth** es für klug/hilfreich halten, etw zu tun.

deep [diːp] *adj* tief ♦ *adv*: **the spectators stood 20 ~** die Zuschauer standen in 20 Reihen hintereinander; **to be 4 metres ~** 4 Meter tief sein; **knee-~ in water** bis zu den Knien im Wasser; **he took a ~ breath** er holte tief Luft.

deepen ['diːpn] *vt* vertiefen ♦ *vi* (*crisis*) sich verschärfen; (*mystery*) größer werden.

deepfreeze ['diːp'friːz] *n* Tiefkühltruhe *f*.

deep-fry ['diːp'fraɪ] *vt* fritieren.

deeply ['diːplɪ] *adv* (*breathe*) tief; (*interested*) höchst; (*moved, grateful*) zutiefst.

deep-rooted ['diːp'ruːtɪd] *adj* tief verwurzelt; (*habit*) fest eingefahren.

deep-sea ['diːp'siː] *cpd* Tiefsee-; (*fishing*) Hochsee-.

deep-seated ['diːp'siːtɪd] *adj* tiefsitzend.

deep-set ['diːpset] *adj* tiefliegend.

deer [dɪəᵉ] *n inv* Reh *nt*; (*male*) Hirsch *m*; (**red**) ~ Rotwild *nt*; (**roe**) ~ Reh *nt*; (**fallow**) ~ Damwild *nt*.

deerskin ['dɪəskɪn] *n* Hirschleder *nt*, Rehleder *nt*.

deerstalker ['dɪəstɔːkəᵉ] *n* ≈ Sherlock-Holmes-Mütze *f*.

deface [dɪ'feɪs] *vt* (*with paint etc*) beschmieren; (*slash, tear*) zerstören.

defamation [defə'meɪʃən] *n* Diffamierung *f*, Verleumdung *f*.

defamatory [dɪ'fæmətrɪ] *adj* diffamierend, verleumderisch.

default [dɪ'fɔːlt] *n* (*also*: ~ **value**) Voreinstellung *f* ♦ *vi*: **to ~ on a debt** einer Zahlungsverpflichtung nicht nachkommen; **to win by ~** kampflos gewinnen.

defaulter [dɪ'fɔːltəᵉ] *n* säumiger Zahler *m*, säumige Zahlerin *f*.

default option *n* Voreinstellung *f*.

defeat [dɪ'fiːt] *vt* besiegen, schlagen ♦ *n* (*failure*) Niederlage *f*; (*of enemy*): ~ **(of)** Sieg *m* (über +*acc*).

defeatism [dɪ'fiːtɪzəm] *n* Defätismus *m*.

defeatist [dɪ'fiːtɪst] *adj* defätistisch ♦ *n* Defätist(in) *m(f)*.

defect [*n* 'diːfekt, *vi* dɪ'fekt] *n* Fehler *m* ♦ *vi*: **to ~ to the enemy** zum Feind überlaufen; **physical/mental ~** körperlicher/geistiger Schaden *m or* Defekt *m*; **to ~ to the West** sich in den Westen absetzen.

defective [dɪ'fektɪv] *adj* fehlerhaft.

defector [dɪ'fektəᵉ] *n* Überläufer(in) *m(f)*.

defence, (*US*) **defense** [dɪ'fens] *n*

Verteidigung *f*, (*justification*) Rechtfertigung *f*; in ~ of zur Verteidigung +*gen*; witness for the ~ Zeuge *m*/Zeugin *f* der Verteidigung; the Ministry of D~, (*US*) the Department of Defense das Verteidigungsministerium.

defenceless [dɪ'fɛnslɪs] *adj* schutzlos.

defend [dɪ'fɛnd] *vt* verteidigen.

defendant [dɪ'fɛndənt] *n* Angeklagte(r) *f(m)*; (*in civil case*) Beklagte(r) *f(m)*.

defender [dɪ'fɛndə·] *n* Verteidiger(in) *m(f)*.

defending champion [dɪ'fɛndɪŋ-] *n* (*SPORT*) Titelverteidiger(in) *m(f)*.

defending counsel [dɪ'fɛndɪŋ-] *n* Verteidiger(in) *m(f)*.

defense [dɪ'fɛns] (*US*) *n* = defence.

defensive [dɪ'fɛnsɪv] *adj* defensiv ♦ *n*: on the ~ in der Defensive.

defer [dɪ'fə:·] *vt* verschieben.

deference ['dɛfərəns] *n* Achtung *f*, Respekt *m*; out of *or* in ~ to aus Rücksicht auf +*acc*.

deferential [dɛfə'rɛnʃəl] *adj* ehrerbietig, respektvoll.

defiance [dɪ'faɪəns] *n* Trotz *m*; in ~ of sth einer Sache *dat* zum Trotz, unter Mißachtung einer Sache *gen*.

defiant [dɪ'faɪənt] *adj* trotzig; (*challenging*) herausfordernd.

defiantly [dɪ'faɪəntlɪ] *adv* (*see adj*) trotzig; herausfordernd.

deficiency [dɪ'fɪʃənsɪ] *n* Mangel *m*; (*defect*) Unzulänglichkeit *f*; (*deficit*) Defizit *nt*.

deficiency disease *n* Mangelkrankheit *f*.

deficient [dɪ'fɪʃənt] *adj*: sb/sth is ~ in sth jdm/etw fehlt es an etw *dat*.

deficit ['dɛfɪsɪt] *n* Defizit *nt*.

defile [dɪ'faɪl] *vt* (*memory*) beschmutzen; (*statue etc*) schänden ♦ *n* Hohlweg *m*.

define [dɪ'faɪn] *vt* (*limits, boundaries*) bestimmen, festlegen; (*word*) definieren.

definite ['dɛfɪnɪt] *adj* definitiv; (*date etc*) fest; (*clear, obvious*) klar, eindeutig; (*certain*) bestimmt; he was ~ about it er war sich *dat* sehr sicher.

definite article *n* bestimmter Artikel *m*.

definitely ['dɛfɪnɪtlɪ] *adv* bestimmt; (*decide*) fest, definitiv.

definition [dɛfɪ'nɪʃən] *n* (*of word*) Definition *f*; (*of photograph etc*) Schärfe *f*.

definitive [dɪ'fɪnɪtɪv] *adj* (*account*) definitiv; (*version*) maßgeblich.

deflate [di:'fleɪt] *vt* (*tyre, balloon*) die Luft ablassen aus; (*person*) einen Dämpfer versetzen +*dat*; (*ECON*) deflationieren.

deflation [di:'fleɪʃən] *n* Deflation *f*.

deflationary [di:'fleɪʃənrɪ] *adj* deflationistisch.

deflect [dɪ'flɛkt] *vt* (*attention*) ablenken; (*criticism*) abwehren; (*shot*) abfälschen; (*light*) brechen, beugen.

defog ['di:'fɔg] (*US*) *vt* von Beschlag freimachen.

defogger ['di:'fɔgə·] (*US*) *n* Gebläse *nt*.

deform [dɪ'fɔ:m] *vt* deformieren, verunstalten.

deformed [dɪ'fɔ:md] *adj* deformiert, mißgebildet.

deformity [dɪ'fɔ:mɪtɪ] *n* Deformität *f*, Mißbildung *f*.

defraud [dɪ'frɔ:d] *vt*: to ~ sb (of sth) jdn (um etw) betrügen.

defray [dɪ'freɪ] *vt*: to ~ sb's expenses jds Unkosten tragen *or* übernehmen.

defrost [di:'frɔst] *vt* (*fridge*) abtauen; (*windscreen*) entfrosten; (*food*) auftauen.

defroster [di:'frɔstə·] (*US*) *n* (*AUT*) Gebläse *nt*.

deft [dɛft] *adj* geschickt.

defunct [dɪ'fʌŋkt] *adj* (*industry*) stillgelegt; (*organization*) nicht mehr bestehend.

defuse [di:'fju:z] *vt* entschärfen.

defy [dɪ'faɪ] *vt* sich widersetzen +*dat*; (*challenge*) auffordern; it defies description es spottet jeder Beschreibung.

degenerate [dɪ'dʒɛnəreɪt] *vi* degenerieren ♦ *adj* degenerieren.

degradation [dɛgrə'deɪʃən] *n* Erniedrigung *f*.

degrade [dɪ'greɪd] *vt* erniedrigen; (*reduce the quality of*) degradieren.

degrading [dɪ'greɪdɪŋ] *adj* erniedrigend.

degree [dɪ'gri:] *n* Grad *m*; (*SCOL*) akademischer Grad *m*; 10 ~s below (zero) 10 Grad unter Null; 6 ~s of frost 6 Grad Kälte *or* unter Null; a considerable ~ of risk ein gewisses Risiko; a ~ in maths ein Hochschulabschluß *m* in Mathematik; by ~s nach und nach; to some ~, to a certain ~ einigermaßen, in gewissem Maße.

dehydrated [di:haɪ'dreɪtɪd] *adj* ausgetrocknet, dehydriert; (*milk, eggs*) pulverisiert, Trocken-.

dehydration [di:haɪ'dreɪʃən] *n* Austrocknung *f*, Dehydration *f*.

de-ice ['di:'aɪs] *vt* enteisen.

de-icer ['di:'aɪsə·] *n* Defroster *m*.

deign [deɪn] *vi*: to ~ to do sth sich herablassen, etw zu tun.

deity ['di:ɪtɪ] *n* Gottheit *f*.

dejected [dɪ'dʒɛktɪd] *adj* niedergeschlagen, deprimiert.

dejection [dɪ'dʒɛkʃən] *n* Niedergeschlagenheit *f*, Depression *f*.

Del. (*US*) *abbr* (*POST*: = *Delaware*).

del. *abbr* = delete.

delay [dɪ'leɪ] *vt* (*decision, ceremony*) verschieben, aufschieben; (*person, plane, train*) aufhalten ♦ *vi* zögern ♦ *n* Verzögerung *f*; (*postponement*) Aufschub *m*; to be ~ed (*person*) sich verspäten; (*departure etc*) verspätet sein; (*flight etc*) Verspätung haben; without ~ unverzüglich.

delayed-action [dɪ'leɪd'ækʃən] *adj* (*bomb, mine*) mit Zeitzünder; (*PHOT*): ~ shutter release Selbstauslöser *m*.

delectable [dɪ'lɛktəbl] *adj* (*person*) reizend; (*food*) köstlich.

delegate ['dɛlɪgɪt] *n* Delegierte(r) *f(m)* ♦ *vt*

delegieren; **to ~ sth to sb** jdm mit etw beauftragen; **to ~ sb to do sth** jdn damit beauftragen, etw zu tun.
delegation [dɛlɪˈɡeɪʃən] n Delegation f; (group) Abordnung f, Delegation f.
delete [dɪˈliːt] vt streichen; (COMPUT) löschen.
Delhi [ˈdɛlɪ] n Delhi nt.
deli [ˈdɛlɪ] n Feinkostgeschäft nt.
deliberate [adj dɪˈlɪbərɪt, vi dɪˈlɪbəreɪt] adj absichtlich; (action, insult) bewußt; (slow) bedächtig ♦ vi überlegen.
deliberately [dɪˈlɪbərɪtlɪ] adv absichtlich, bewußt; (slowly) bedächtig.
deliberation [dɪlɪbəˈreɪʃən] n Überlegung f; (usu pl: discussions) Beratungen pl.
delicacy [ˈdɛlɪkəsɪ] n Feinheit f, Zartheit f; (of problem) Delikatheit f; (choice food) Delikatesse f.
delicate [ˈdɛlɪkɪt] adj fein; (colour, health) zart; (approach) feinfühlig; (problem) delikat, heikel.
delicately [ˈdɛlɪkɪtlɪ] adv zart, fein; (act, express) feinfühlig.
delicatessen [dɛlɪkəˈtɛsn] n Feinkostgeschäft nt.
delicious [dɪˈlɪʃəs] adj köstlich; (feeling, person) herrlich.
delight [dɪˈlaɪt] n Freude f ♦ vt erfreuen; **sb takes (a) ~ in sth** etw bereitet jdm große Freude; **sb takes (a) ~ in doing sth** es bereitet jdm große Freude, etw zu tun; **to be the ~ of** die Freude +gen sein; **she was a ~ to interview** es war eine Freude, sie zu interviewen; **the ~s of country life** die Freuden des Landlebens.
delighted [dɪˈlaɪtɪd] adj: **~ (at or with)** erfreut (über +acc), entzückt (über +acc); **to be ~ to do sth** etw gern tun; **I'd be ~** ich würde mich sehr freuen.
delightful [dɪˈlaɪtful] adj reizend, wunderbar.
delimit [diːˈlɪmɪt] vt abgrenzen.
delineate [dɪˈlɪnɪeɪt] vt (fig) beschreiben.
delinquency [dɪˈlɪŋkwənsɪ] n Kriminalität f.
delinquent [dɪˈlɪŋkwənt] adj straffällig ♦ n Delinquent(in) m(f).
delirious [dɪˈlɪrɪəs] adj: **to be ~** (with fever) im Delirium sein; (with excitement) im Taumel sein.
delirium [dɪˈlɪrɪəm] n Delirium nt.
deliver [dɪˈlɪvə*] vt liefern; (letters, papers) zustellen; (hand over) übergeben; (message) überbringen; (speech) halten; (blow) versetzen; (MED: baby) zur Welt bringen; (warning) geben; (ultimatum) stellen; (free): **to ~ (from)** befreien (von); **to ~ the goods** (fig) halten, was man versprochen hat.
deliverance [dɪˈlɪvrəns] n Befreiung f.
delivery [dɪˈlɪvərɪ] n Lieferung f; (of letters, papers) Zustellung f; (of speaker) Vortrag m; (MED) Entbindung f; **to take ~ of sth** etw in Empfang nehmen.

delivery note n Lieferschein m.
delivery van, (US) **delivery truck** n Lieferwagen m.
delouse [ˈdiːˈlaus] vt entlausen.
delta [ˈdɛltə] n Delta nt.
delude [dɪˈluːd] vt täuschen; **to ~ o.s.** sich dat etwas vormachen.
deluge [ˈdɛljuːdʒ] n (of rain) Guß m; (fig: of petitions, requests) Flut f.
delusion [dɪˈluːʒən] n Irrglaube m; **to have ~s of grandeur** größenwahnsinnig sein.
de luxe [dəˈlʌks] adj (hotel, model) Luxus-.
delve [dɛlv] vi: **to ~ into** (subject) sich eingehend befassen mit; (cupboard, handbag) tief greifen in +acc.
Dem. (US) abbr (POL) = **democrat; democratic.**
demagogue [ˈdɛməɡɔɡ] n Demagoge m, Demagogin f.
demand [dɪˈmaːnd] vt verlangen; (rights) fordern; (need) erfordern, verlangen ♦ n Verlangen nt; (claim) Forderung f; (ECON) Nachfrage f; **to ~ sth (from or of sb)** etw (von jdm) verlangen or fordern; **to be in ~** gefragt sein; **on ~** (available) auf Verlangen; (payable) bei Vorlage or Sicht.
demand draft n Sichtwechsel m.
demanding [dɪˈmaːndɪŋ] adj anspruchsvoll; (work, child) anstrengend.
demarcation [diːmaːˈkeɪʃən] n (of area, tasks) Abgrenzung f.
demarcation dispute n Streit m um den Zuständigkeitsbereich.
demean [dɪˈmiːn] vt: **to ~ o.s.** sich erniedrigen.
demeanour, (US) **demeanor** [dɪˈmiːnə*] n Benehmen nt, Auftreten nt.
demented [dɪˈmɛntɪd] adj wahnsinnig.
demilitarized zone [diːˈmɪlɪtəraɪzd-] n entmilitarisierte Zone f.
demise [dɪˈmaɪz] n Ende nt; (death) Tod m.
demist [diːˈmɪst] (BRIT) vt (AUT: windscreen) von Beschlag freimachen.
demister [diːˈmɪstə*] (BRIT) n (AUT) Gebläse nt.
demo [ˈdɛməu] (inf) n abbr = **demonstration.**
demob [diːˈmɔb] (inf) vt = **demobilize.**
demobilize [diːˈməubɪlaɪz] vt aus dem Kriegsdienst entlassen, demobilisieren.
democracy [dɪˈmɔkrəsɪ] n Demokratie f.
democrat [ˈdɛməkræt] n Demokrat(in) m(f).
democratic [dɛməˈkrætɪk] adj demokratisch.
Democratic Party (US) n: **the ~** die Demokratische Partei.
demography [dɪˈmɔɡrəfɪ] n Demographie f.
demolish [dɪˈmɔlɪʃ] vt abreißen, abbrechen; (fig: argument) widerlegen.
demolition [dɛməˈlɪʃən] n Abriß m, Abbruch m; (of argument) Widerlegung f.
demon [ˈdiːmən] n Dämon m ♦ adj teuflisch gut.
demonstrate [ˈdɛmənstreɪt] vt (theory)

demonstrieren; (*skill*) zeigen, beweisen; (*appliance*) vorführen ♦ vi: **to ~ (for/against)** demonstrieren (für/gegen).

demonstration [dɛmən'streɪʃən] n Demonstration f; (*of gadget, machine etc*) Vorführung f; **to hold a ~** eine Demonstration veranstalten or durchführen.

demonstrative [dɪ'mɒnstrətɪv] adj demonstrativ.

demonstrator ['dɛmənstreɪtə*] n Demonstrant(in) m(f); (*sales person*) Vorführer(in) m(f); (*car*) Vorführwagen m; (*computer etc*) Vorführgerät nt.

demoralize [dɪ'mɒrəlaɪz] vt entmutigen.

demote [dɪ'məʊt] vt zurückstufen; (*MIL*) degradieren.

demotion [dɪ'məʊʃən] n Zurückstufung f; (*MIL*) Degradierung f.

demur [dɪ'mə:*] (*form*) vi Einwände pl erheben ♦ n: **without ~** widerspruchslos; **they ~red at the suggestion** sie erhoben Einwände gegen den Vorschlag.

demure [dɪ'mjʊə*] adj zurückhaltend; (*smile*) höflich; (*dress*) schlicht.

demurrage [dɪ'mʌrɪdʒ] n Liegegeld nt.

den [dɛn] n Höhle f; (*of fox*) Bau m; (*room*) Bude f.

denationalization ['di:næʃnəlaɪ'zeɪʃən] n Privatisierung f.

denationalize [di:'næʃnəlaɪz] vt privatisieren.

denatured alcohol [di:'neɪtʃəd-] (*US*) n vergällter Alkohol m.

denial [dɪ'naɪəl] n Leugnen nt; (*of rights*) Verweigerung f.

denier ['dɛnɪə*] n Denier nt.

denigrate ['dɛnɪgreɪt] vt verunglimpfen.

denim ['dɛnɪm] n Jeansstoff m; **denims** npl (Blue) Jeans pl.

denim jacket n Jeansjacke f.

denizen ['dɛnɪzn] n Bewohner(in) m(f); (*person in town*) Einwohner(in) m(f); (*foreigner*) eingebürgerter Ausländer m, eingebürgerte Ausländerin f.

Denmark ['dɛnmɑːk] n Dänemark nt.

denomination [dɪnɒmɪ'neɪʃən] n (*of money*) Nennwert m; (*REL*) Konfession f.

denominator [dɪ'nɒmɪneɪtə*] n Nenner m.

denote [dɪ'nəʊt] vt (*indicate*) hindeuten auf +acc; (*represent*) bezeichnen.

denounce [dɪ'naʊns] vt (*person*) anprangern; (*action*) verurteilen.

dense [dɛns] adj dicht; (*inf: person*) beschränkt.

densely ['dɛnslɪ] adv dicht.

density ['dɛnsɪtɪ] n Dichte f; **single/double- ~ disk** (*COMPUT*) Diskette f mit einfacher/doppelter Dichte.

dent [dɛnt] n Beule f; (*in pride, ego*) Knacks m ♦ vt (*also*: **make a ~ in**) einbeulen; (*pride, ego*) anknacksen.

dental ['dɛntl] adj (*filling, hygiene etc*) Zahn-;

(*treatment*) zahnärztlich.

dental floss [-flɒs] n Zahnseide f.

dental surgeon n Zahnarzt m, Zahnärztin f.

dentifrice ['dɛntɪfrɪs] n Zahnpasta f.

dentist ['dɛntɪst] n Zahnarzt m, Zahnärztin f; (*also*: **~'s (surgery)**) Zahnarzt m, Zahnarztpraxis f.

dentistry ['dɛntɪstrɪ] n Zahnmedizin f.

dentures ['dɛntʃəz] npl Zahnprothese f; (*full*) Gebiß nt.

denuded [di:'nju:dɪd] adj: **~ of** entblößt von.

denunciation [dɪnʌnsɪ'eɪʃən] n (*of person*) Anprangerung f; (*of action*) Verurteilung f.

deny [dɪ'naɪ] vt leugnen; (*involvement*) abstreiten; (*permission, chance*) verweigern; (*country, religion etc*) verleugnen; **he denies having said it** er leugnet or bestreitet, das gesagt zu haben.

deodorant [di:'əʊdərənt] n Deodorant nt.

depart [dɪ'pɑːt] vi (*visitor*) abreisen; (: *on foot*) weggehen; (*bus, train*) abfahren; (*plane*) abfliegen; **to ~ from** (*fig*) abweichen von.

departed [dɪ'pɑːtɪd] adj: **the (dear) ~** der/die (liebe) Verstorbene m/f; **die (lieben) Verstorbenen** pl.

department [dɪ'pɑːtmənt] n Abteilung f; (*SCOL*) Fachbereich m; (*POL*) Ministerium nt; **that's not my ~** (*fig*) dafür bin ich nicht zuständig; **D~ of State** (*US*) Außenministerium nt.

departmental [dɪ:pɑːt'mɛntl] adj (*budget, costs*) der Abteilung; (*level*) Abteilungs-; **~ manager** Abteilungsleiter(in) m(f).

department store n Warenhaus nt.

departure [dɪ'pɑːtʃə*] n (*of visitor*) Abreise f; (*on foot, of employee etc*) Weggang m; (*of bus, train*) Abfahrt f; (*of plane*) Abflug m; (*fig*): **~ from** Abweichen nt von; **a new ~** ein neuer Weg m.

departure lounge n Abflughalle f.

depend [dɪ'pɛnd] vi: **to ~ on** abhängen von; (*rely on, trust*) sich verlassen auf +acc; (*financially*) abhängig sein von, angewiesen sein auf +acc; **it ~s** es kommt darauf an; **~ing on the result ...** je nachdem, wie das Ergebnis ausfällt, ...

dependable [dɪ'pɛndəbl] adj zuverlässig.

dependant [dɪ'pɛndənt] n abhängige(r) (Familien)angehörige(r) f(m).

dependence [dɪ'pɛndəns] n Abhängigkeit f.

dependent [dɪ'pɛndənt] adj: **to be ~ on** (*person*) abhängig sein von, angewiesen sein auf +acc; (*decision*) abhängen von ♦ n = **dependant**.

depict [dɪ'pɪkt] vt (*in picture*) darstellen; (*describe*) beschreiben.

depilatory [dɪ'pɪlətrɪ] n (*also*: **~ cream**) Enthaarungsmittel nt.

depleted [dɪ'pli:tɪd] adj (*reserves*) aufgebraucht; (*stocks*) erschöpft.

deplorable [dɪ'plɔ:rəbl] adj bedauerlich.

deplore [dɪ'plɔ:*] vt verurteilen.

deploy [dɪ'plɔɪ] *vt* einsetzen.
depopulate [diː'pɔpjuleɪt] *vt* entvölkern.
depopulation ['diːpɔpju'leɪʃən] *n*
Entvölkerung *f*.
deport [dɪ'pɔːt] *vt* (*criminal*) deportieren;
(*illegal immigrant*) abschieben.
deportation [diːpɔː'teɪʃən] *n* (*see vb*)
Deportation *f*; Abschiebung *f*.
deportation order *n* Ausweisung *f*.
deportee [diːpɔː'tiː] *n* Deportierte(r) *f(m)*.
deportment [dɪ'pɔːtmənt] *n* Benehmen *nt*.
depose [dɪ'pəuz] *vt* absetzen.
deposit [dɪ'pɔzɪt] *n* (*in account*) Guthaben *nt*;
(*down payment*) Anzahlung *f*; (*for hired goods
etc*) Sicherheit *f*, Kaution *f*; (*on bottle etc*)
Pfand *nt*; (*CHEM*) Ablagerung *f*; (*of ore, oil*)
Lagerstätte *f* ♦ *vt* deponieren; (*subj: river:
sand etc*) ablagern; **to put down a ~ of £50**
eine Anzahlung von £50 machen.
deposit account *n* Sparkonto *nt*.
depositary [dɪ'pɔzɪtərɪ] *n* Treuhänder(in) *m(f)*.
depositor [dɪ'pɔzɪtəʳ] *n* Deponent(in) *m(f)*,
Einzahler(in) *m(f)*.
depository [dɪ'pɔzɪtərɪ] *n* (*person*)
Treuhänder(in) *m(f)*; (*place*) Lager(haus) *nt*.
depot ['depəu] *n* Lager(haus) *nt*; (*for vehicles*)
Depot *nt*; (*US: station*) Bahnhof *m*; (: *bus
station*) Busbahnhof *m*.
depraved [dɪ'preɪvd] *adj* verworfen.
depravity [dɪ'prævɪtɪ] *n* Verworfenheit *f*.
deprecate ['deprɪkeɪt] *vt* mißbilligen.
deprecating ['deprɪkeɪtɪŋ] *adj* (*disapproving*)
mißbilligend; (*apologetic*) entschuldigend.
depreciate [dɪ'priːʃɪeɪt] *vi* an Wert verlieren;
(*currency*) an Kaufkraft verlieren; (*value*)
sinken.
depreciation [dɪpriːʃɪ'eɪʃən] *n* (*see vb*)
Wertminderung *f*; Kaufkraftverlust *m*;
Sinken *nt*.
depress [dɪ'pres] *vt* deprimieren; (*price,
wages*) drücken; (*press down*)
herunterdrücken.
depressant [dɪ'presnt] *n* Beruhigungsmittel
nt.
depressed [dɪ'prest] *adj* deprimiert,
niedergeschlagen; (*price*) gesunken;
(*industry*) geschwächt; (*area*) Notstands-; **to
get ~** deprimiert werden.
depressing [dɪ'presɪŋ] *adj* deprimierend.
depression [dɪ'preʃən] *n* (*PSYCH*)
Depressionen *pl*; (*ECON*) Wirtschaftskrise *f*;
(*MET*) Tief(druckgebiet) *nt*; (*hollow*)
Vertiefung *f*.
deprivation [deprɪ'veɪʃən] *n* Entbehrung *f*,
Not *f*; (*of freedom, rights etc*) Entzug *m*.
deprive [dɪ'praɪv] *vt*: **to ~ sb of sth** (*liberty*)
jdm etw entziehen; (*life*) jdm etw nehmen.
deprived [dɪ'praɪvd] *adj* benachteiligt; (*area*)
notleidend.
dept *abbr* = **department**.
depth [depθ] *n* Tiefe *f*; **in the ~s of** in den
Tiefen +*gen*; **in the ~s of despair** in tiefster

Verzweiflung; **in the ~s of winter** im
tiefsten Winter; **at a ~ of 3 metres** in 3
Meter Tiefe; **to be out of one's ~** (*in water*)
nicht mehr stehen können; (*fig*) überfordert
sein; **to study sth in ~** etw gründlich *or*
eingehend studieren.
depth charge *n* Wasserbombe *f*.
deputation [depju'teɪʃən] *n* Abordnung *f*.
deputize ['depjutaɪz] *vi*: **to ~ for sb** jdn
vertreten.
deputy ['depjutɪ] *cpd* stellvertretend ♦ *n*
(Stell)vertreter(in) *m(f)*; (*POL*)
Abgeordnete(r) *f(m)*; (*US: also:* **~ sheriff**)
Hilfssheriff *m*; **~ head** (*BRIT: SCOL*)
Konrektor(in) *m(f)*.
derail [dɪ'reɪl] *vt*: **to be ~ed** entgleisen.
derailment [dɪ'reɪlmənt] *n* Entgleisung *f*.
deranged [dɪ'reɪndʒd] *adj*: **to be mentally ~**
geistesgestört sein.
derby ['dɜːrbɪ] *n* Derby *nt*; (*US: hat*) Melone *f*.
Derbys (*BRIT*) *abbr* (*POST:* = **Derbyshire**).
deregulate [dɪ'regjuleɪt] *vt* staatliche
Kontrollen aufheben bei.
deregulation [dɪ'regju'leɪʃən] *n* Aufhebung *f*
staatlicher Kontrollen.
derelict ['derɪlɪkt] *adj* verfallen.
deride [dɪ'raɪd] *vt* sich lustig machen über
+*acc*.
derision [dɪ'rɪʒən] *n* Hohn *m*, Spott *m*.
derisive [dɪ'raɪsɪv] *adj* spöttisch.
derisory [dɪ'raɪsərɪ] *adj* spöttisch; (*sum*)
lächerlich.
derivation [derɪ'veɪʃən] *n* Ableitung *f*.
derivative [dɪ'rɪvətɪv] *n* (*LING*) Ableitung *f*;
(*CHEM*) Derivat *nt* ♦ *adj* nachahmend.
derive [dɪ'raɪv] *vt*: **to ~ (from)** gewinnen (aus);
(*benefit*) ziehen (aus) ♦ *vi*: **to ~ from**
(*originate in*) sich herleiten *or* ableiten von;
to ~ pleasure from Freude haben an +*dat*.
dermatitis [dɜːmə'taɪtɪs] *n* Hautentzündung *f*,
Dermatitis *f*.
dermatology [dɜːmə'tɔlədʒɪ] *n* Dermatologie
f.
derogatory [dɪ'rɔgətərɪ] *adj* abfällig.
derrick ['derɪk] *n* (*on ship*) Derrickkran *m*; (*on
well*) Bohrturm *m*.
derv [dɜːv] (*BRIT*) *n* (*AUT*) Diesel(kraftstoff)
m.
desalination [diːsælɪ'neɪʃən] *n* Entsalzung *f*.
descend [dɪ'send] *vt* hinuntergehen,
hinuntersteigen; (*lift, vehicle*)
hinunterfahren; (*road*) hinunterführen ♦ *vi*
hinuntergehen; (*lift*) nach unten fahren; **to
~ from** abstammen von; **to ~ to** sich
erniedrigen zu; **in ~ing order of importance**
nach Wichtigkeit geordnet.
▶**descend on** *vt fus* überfallen; (*subj:
misfortune*) hereinbrechen über +*acc*;
(: *gloom*) befallen; (: *silence*) sich senken auf
+*acc*; **visitors ~ed (up)on us** der Besuch hat
uns überfallen.
descendant [dɪ'sendənt] *n* Nachkomme *m*.

descent [dɪ'sɛnt] n Abstieg m; (origin) Abstammung f.

describe [dɪs'kraɪb] vt beschreiben.

description [dɪs'krɪpʃən] n Beschreibung f; (sort): **of every** ~ aller Art.

descriptive [dɪs'krɪptɪv] adj (writing, painting) deskriptiv.

desecrate ['dɛsɪkreɪt] vt schänden.

desegregate [diː'sɛgrɪgeɪt] vt die Rassentrennung aufheben in +dat.

desert [n 'dɛzət, vb dɪ'zəːt] n Wüste f ♦ vt verlassen ♦ vi desertieren; see also **deserts**.

deserter [dɪ'zəːtə*] n Deserteur m.

desertion [dɪ'zəːʃən] n Desertion f, Fahnenflucht f; (LAW) böswilliges Verlassen nt.

desert island n einsame or verlassene Insel f.

deserts [dɪ'zəːts] npl: **to get one's just** ~ bekommen, was man verdient.

deserve [dɪ'zəːv] vt verdienen.

deservedly [dɪ'zəːvɪdlɪ] adv verdientermaßen.

deserving [dɪ'zəːvɪŋ] adj verdienstvoll.

desiccated ['dɛsɪkeɪtɪd] adj vertrocknet; (coconut) getrocknet.

design [dɪ'zaɪn] n Design nt; (process) Entwurf m, Gestaltung f; (sketch) Entwurf m; (layout, shape) Form f; (pattern) Muster nt; (of car) Konstruktion f; (intention) Plan m, Absicht f ♦ vt entwerfen; **to have** ~**s on** es abgesehen haben auf +acc; **well-**~**ed** mit gutem Design.

designate [vt 'dɛzɪgneɪt, adj 'dɛzɪgnɪt] vt bestimmen, ernennen ♦ adj designiert.

designation [dɛzɪg'neɪʃən] n Bezeichnung f.

designer [dɪ'zaɪnə*] n Designer(in) m(f); (TECH) Konstrukteur(in) m(f); (fashion designer) Modeschöpfer(in) m(f) ♦ adj (clothes etc) Designer-.

desirability [dɪzaɪərə'bɪlɪtɪ] n: **they discussed the** ~ **of the plan** sie besprachen, ob der Plan wünschenswert sei.

desirable [dɪ'zaɪərəbl] adj (proper) wünschenswert; (attractive) reizvoll, attraktiv.

desire [dɪ'zaɪə*] n Wunsch m; (sexual) Verlangen nt, Begehren nt ♦ vt wünschen; (lust after) begehren; **to** ~ **to do sth/that** wünschen, etw zu tun/daß.

desirous [dɪ'zaɪərəs] adj: **to be** ~ **of doing sth** den Wunsch haben, etw zu tun.

desist [dɪ'zɪst] vi: **to** ~ **(from)** absehen (von), Abstand nehmen (von).

desk [dɛsk] n Schreibtisch m; (for pupil) Pult nt; (in hotel) Empfang m; (at airport) Schalter m; (BRIT: in shop, restaurant) Kasse f.

desk job n Bürojob m.

desktop ['dɛsktɒp] n Arbeitsfläche f.

desktop publishing n Desktop-Publishing nt.

desolate ['dɛsəlɪt] adj trostlos.

desolation [dɛsə'leɪʃən] n Trostlosigkeit f.

despair [dɪs'pɛə*] n Verzweiflung f ♦ vi: **to** ~ **of** alle Hoffnung aufgeben auf +acc; **to be in** ~ verzweifelt sein.

despatch [dɪs'pætʃ] n, vt = **dispatch**.

desperate ['dɛspərɪt] adj verzweifelt; (shortage) akut; (criminal) zum Äußersten entschlossen; **to be** ~ **for sth/to do sth** etw dringend brauchen/unbedingt tun wollen.

desperately ['dɛspərɪtlɪ] adv (shout, struggle etc) verzweifelt; (ill) schwer; (unhappy etc) äußerst.

desperation [dɛspə'reɪʃən] n Verzweiflung f; **in (sheer)** ~ aus (reiner) Verzweiflung.

despicable [dɪs'pɪkəbl] adj (action) verabscheuungswürdig; (person) widerwärtig.

despise [dɪs'paɪz] vt verachten.

despite [dɪs'paɪt] prep trotz +gen.

despondent [dɪs'pɒndənt] adj niedergeschlagen, mutlos.

despot ['dɛspɒt] n Despot m.

dessert [dɪ'zəːt] n Nachtisch m, Dessert nt.

dessertspoon [dɪ'zəːtspuːn] n Dessertlöffel m.

destabilize [diː'steɪbɪlaɪz] vt destabilisieren.

destination [dɛstɪ'neɪʃən] n (Reise)ziel nt; (of mail) Bestimmungsort m.

destined ['dɛstɪnd] adj: **to be** ~ **to do sth** dazu bestimmt or ausersehen sein, etw zu tun; **to be** ~ **for** bestimmt or ausersehen sein für.

destiny ['dɛstɪnɪ] n Schicksal nt.

destitute ['dɛstɪtjuːt] adj mittellos.

destroy [dɪs'trɔɪ] vt zerstören; (animal) töten.

destroyer [dɪs'trɔɪə*] n Zerstörer m.

destruction [dɪs'trʌkʃən] n Zerstörung f.

destructive [dɪs'trʌktɪv] adj zerstörerisch; (child, criticism etc) destruktiv.

desultory ['dɛsəltərɪ] adj flüchtig; (conversation) zwanglos.

detach [dɪ'tætʃ] vt (remove) entfernen; (unclip) abnehmen; (unstick) ablösen.

detachable [dɪ'tætʃəbl] adj abnehmbar.

detached [dɪ'tætʃt] adj distanziert; (house) freistehend, Einzel-.

detachment [dɪ'tætʃmənt] n Distanz f; (MIL) Sonderkommando nt.

detail ['diːteɪl] n Einzelheit f; (no pl: in picture, one's work etc) Detail nt; (trifle) unwichtige Einzelheit f ♦ vt (einzeln) aufführen; **in** ~ in Einzelheiten; **to go into** ~**s** auf Einzelheiten eingehen, ins Detail gehen.

detailed ['diːteɪld] adj detailliert, genau.

detain [dɪ'teɪn] vt aufhalten; (in captivity) in Haft halten; (in hospital) festhalten.

detainee [diːteɪ'niː] n Häftling m.

detect [dɪ'tɛkt] vt wahrnehmen; (MED, TECH) feststellen; (MIL) ausfindig machen.

detection [dɪ'tɛkʃən] n Entdeckung f, Feststellung f; **crime** ~ Ermittlungsarbeit f; **to escape** ~ (criminal) nicht gefaßt werden; (mistake) der Aufmerksamkeit dat entgehen.

detective [dɪ'tɛktɪv] n Kriminalbeamte(r) m; **private** ~ Privatdetektiv m.

detective story n Kriminalgeschichte f,
   Detektivgeschichte f.
detector [dɪ'tɛktə*] n Detektor m.
détente [deɪ'taːnt] n Entspannung f, Détente f.
detention [dɪ'tɛnʃən] n (arrest) Festnahme f;
   (captivity) Haft f; (SCOL) Nachsitzen nt.
deter [dɪ'təː*] vt (discourage) abschrecken;
   (dissuade) abhalten.
detergent [dɪ'təːdʒənt] n Reinigungsmittel nt;
   (for clothes) Waschmittel nt; (for dishes)
   Spülmittel nt.
deteriorate [dɪ'tɪərɪəreɪt] vi sich
   verschlechtern.
deterioration [dɪtɪərɪə'reɪʃən] n
   Verschlechterung f.
determination [dɪtəːmɪ'neɪʃən] n
   Entschlossenheit f; (establishment)
   Festsetzung f.
determine [dɪ'təːmɪn] vt (facts) feststellen;
   (limits etc) festlegen; **to ~ that** beschließen,
   daß; **to ~ to do sth** sich entschließen, etw
   zu tun.
determined [dɪ'təːmɪnd] adj entschlossen;
   (quantity) bestimmt; **to be ~ to do sth** (fest)
   entschlossen sein, etw zu tun.
deterrence [dɪ'tɛrəns] n Abschreckung f.
deterrent [dɪ'tɛrənt] n Abschreckungsmittel
   nt; **to act as a ~** als Abschreckung(smittel)
   dienen.
detest [dɪ'tɛst] vt verabscheuen.
detestable [dɪ'tɛstəbl] adj abscheulich,
   widerwärtig.
detonate ['dɛtəneɪt] vi detonieren ♦ vt zur
   Explosion bringen.
detonator ['dɛtəneɪtə*] n Sprengkapsel f.
detour ['diːtuə*] n Umweg m; (US: AUT)
   Umleitung f.
detract [dɪ'trækt] vi: **to ~ from** schmälern;
   (effect) beeinträchtigen.
detractor [dɪ'træktə*] n Kritiker(in) m(f).
detriment ['dɛtrɪmənt] n: **to the ~ of** zum
   Schaden +gen; **without ~ to** ohne Schaden
   für.
detrimental [dɛtrɪ'mɛntl] adj: **to be ~ to**
   schaden +dat.
deuce [djuːs] n (TENNIS) Einstand m.
devaluation [dɪvælju'eɪʃən] n Abwertung f.
devalue ['diː'væljuː] vt abwerten.
devastate ['dɛvəsteɪt] vt verwüsten; (fig:
   shock): **to be ~d by** niedergeschmettert sein
   von.
devastating ['dɛvəsteɪtɪŋ] adj verheerend;
   (announcement, news) niederschmetternd.
devastation [dɛvəs'teɪʃən] n Verwüstung f.
develop [dɪ'vɛləp] vt entwickeln; (business)
   erweitern, ausbauen; (land, resource)
   erschließen; (disease) bekommen ♦ vi sich
   entwickeln; (facts) an den Tag kommen;
   (symptoms) auftreten; **to ~ a taste for sth**
   Geschmack an etw finden; **the machine/car**
   ~ed a fault/engine trouble an dem Gerät/
   dem Wagen trat ein Defekt/ein

Motorschaden auf; **to ~ into** sich
   entwickeln zu, werden.
developer [dɪ'vɛləpə*] n (also: **property ~**)
   Bauunternehmer und Immobilienmakler.
developing country [dɪ'vɛləpɪŋ-] n
   Entwicklungsland nt.
development [dɪ'vɛləpmənt] n Entwicklung f;
   (of land) Erschließung f.
development area n Entwicklungsgebiet nt.
deviant ['diːvɪənt] adj abweichend.
deviate ['diːvɪeɪt] vi: **to ~ (from)** abweichen
   (von).
deviation [diːvɪ'eɪʃən] n Abweichung f.
device [dɪ'vaɪs] n Gerät nt; (ploy, stratagem)
   Trick m; **explosive ~** Sprengkörper m.
devil ['dɛvl] n Teufel m; **go on, be a ~!** nur zu,
   riskier mal was!; **talk of the ~!** wenn man
   vom Teufel spricht!
devilish ['dɛvlɪʃ] adj teuflisch.
devil's advocate ['dɛvlz-] n Advocatus
   Diaboli m.
devious ['diːvɪəs] adj (person) verschlagen;
   (route, path) gewunden.
devise [dɪ'vaɪz] vt sich dat ausdenken;
   (machine) entwerfen.
devoid [dɪ'vɔɪd] adj: **~ of** bar +gen, ohne +acc.
devolution [diːvə'luːʃən] n Dezentralisierung
   f.
devolve [dɪ'vɒlv] vt übertragen ♦ vi: **to**
   ~ (up)on übergehen auf +acc.
devote [dɪ'vəʊt] vt: **to ~ sth/o.s. to** etw/sich
   widmen +dat.
devoted [dɪ'vəʊtɪd] adj treu; (admirer) eifrig;
   to be ~ to sb jdn innig lieben; **the book is**
   ~ to politics das Buch widmet sich ganz der
   Politik dat.
devotee [dɛvəʊ'tiː] n (fan) Liebhaber(in) m(f);
   (REL) Anhänger(in) m(f).
devotion [dɪ'vəʊʃən] n (affection) Ergebenheit
   f; (dedication) Hingabe f; (REL) Andacht f.
devour [dɪ'vaʊə*] vt verschlingen.
devout [dɪ'vaʊt] adj fromm.
dew [djuː] n Tau m.
dexterity [dɛks'tɛrɪtɪ] n Geschicklichkeit f;
   (mental) Gewandtheit f.
dext(e)rous ['dɛkstrəs] adj geschickt.
DFE (BRIT) n abbr (= Department for Education)
   ≈ Bildungsministerium nt.
dg abbr (= decigram) dg.
DH (BRIT) n abbr (= Department of Health)
   ≈ Gesundheitsministerium nt.
Dhaka ['dækə] n Dhaka nt.
DHSS (BRIT) n abbr (formerly: = Department of
   Health and Social Security) Ministerium für
   Gesundheit und Sozialfürsorge.
diabetes [daɪə'biːtiːz] n Zuckerkrankheit f.
diabetic [daɪə'bɛtɪk] adj zuckerkrank;
   (chocolate, jam) Diabetiker- ♦ n
   Diabetiker(in) m(f).
diabolical [daɪə'bɒlɪkl] (inf) adj schrecklich,
   fürchterlich.
diaeresis [daɪ'ɛrɪsɪs] n Diärese f.

diagnose [daɪəg'nəuz] vt diagnostizieren.
diagnoses [-si:z] pl of **diagnosis**.
diagnosis [daɪəg'nəusɪs] (pl **diagnoses**) n
Diagnose f.
diagonal [daɪ'ægənl] adj diagonal ♦ n
Diagonale f.
diagram ['daɪəgræm] n Diagramm nt,
Schaubild nt.
dial ['daɪəl] n Zifferblatt nt; (on radio set)
Einstellskala f; (of phone) Wählscheibe f ♦ vt
wählen; **to ~ a wrong number** sich
verwählen; **can I ~ London direct?** kann ich
nach London durchwählen?
dial. abbr = **dialect.**
dial code (US) n = **dialling code.**
dialect ['daɪəlɛkt] n Dialekt m.
dialling code ['daɪəlɪŋ-], (US) **dial code** n
Vorwahl f.
dialling tone, (US) **dial tone** n Amtszeichen
nt.
dialogue, (US) **dialog** ['daɪəlɒg] n Dialog m;
(conversation) Gespräch nt, Dialog m.
dial tone (US) n = **dialling tone.**
dialysis [daɪ'ælɪsɪs] n Dialyse f.
diameter [daɪ'æmɪtə*] n Durchmesser m.
diametrically [daɪə'mɛtrɪklɪ] adv: **~ opposed
(to)** diametral entgegengesetzt (+dat).
diamond ['daɪəmənd] n Diamant m; (shape)
Raute f; **diamonds** npl (CARDS) Karo nt.
diamond ring n Diamantring m.
diaper ['daɪəpə*] (US) n Windel f.
diaphragm ['daɪəfræm] n Zwerchfell nt;
(contraceptive) Pessar nt.
diarrhoea, (US) **diarrhea** [daɪə'ri:ə] n
Durchfall m.
diary ['daɪərɪ] n (Termin)kalender m; (daily
account) Tagebuch nt; **to keep a ~** Tagebuch
führen.
diatribe ['daɪətraɪb] n Schmährede f; (written)
Schmähschrift f.
dice [daɪs] n inv Würfel m ♦ vt in Würfel
schneiden.
dicey ['daɪsɪ] (inf) adj riskant.
dichotomy [daɪ'kɒtəmɪ] n Dichotomie f, Kluft
f.
dickhead ['dɪkhɛd] (inf) n Knallkopf m.
Dictaphone ® ['dɪktəfəun] n Diktaphon nt,
Diktiergerät nt.
dictate [dɪk'teɪt] vt diktieren ♦ n Diktat nt;
(principle): **the ~s of** die Gebote +gen ♦ vi: **to
~ to** diktieren +dat; **I won't be ~d to** ich
lasse mir keine Vorschriften machen.
dictation [dɪk'teɪʃən] n Diktat nt; **at ~ speed**
im Diktiertempo.
dictator [dɪk'teɪtə*] n Diktator m.
dictatorship [dɪk'teɪtəʃɪp] n Diktatur f.
diction ['dɪkʃən] n Diktion f.
dictionary ['dɪkʃənrɪ] n Wörterbuch nt.
did [dɪd] pt of **do.**
didactic [daɪ'dæktɪk] adj didaktisch.
diddle ['dɪdl] (inf) vt übers Ohr hauen.
didn't ['dɪdnt] = **did not.**

die [daɪ] n (pl: dice) Würfel m; (: dies) Gußform
f ♦ vi sterben; (plant) eingehen; (fig: noise)
aufhören; (: smile) vergehen; (engine)
stehenbleiben; **to ~ of** or **from** sterben an
+dat; **to be dying** im Sterben liegen; **to be
dying for sth** etw unbedingt brauchen; **to be
dying to do sth** darauf brennen, etw zu tun.
►**die away** vi (sound) schwächer werden;
(light) nachlassen.
►**die down** vi (wind) sich legen; (fire)
herunterbrennen; (excitement, noise)
nachlassen.
►**die out** vi aussterben.
die-hard ['daɪhɑ:d] n Ewiggestrige(r) f(m).
diesel ['di:zl] n (vehicle) Diesel m; (also: ~ **oil**)
Diesel(kraftstoff) m.
diesel engine n Dieselmotor m.
diet ['daɪət] n Ernährung f; (MED) Diät f; (when
slimming) Schlankheitskur f ♦ vi (also: **be on
a ~**) eine Schlankheitskur machen; **to live
on a ~ of** sich ernähren von, leben von.
dietician [daɪə'tɪʃən] n Diätassistent(in) m(f).
differ ['dɪfə*] vi (be different): **to ~ (from)** sich
unterscheiden (von); (disagree): **to ~ (about)**
anderer Meinung sein (über +acc); **to agree
to ~** sich dat verschiedene Meinungen
zugestehen.
difference ['dɪfrəns] n Unterschied m;
(disagreement) Differenz f, Auseinandersetzung f; **it makes no ~ to me** das ist mir
egal or einerlei; **to settle one's ~s** die Dif-
ferenzen or Meinungsverschiedenheiten
beilegen.
different ['dɪfrənt] adj (various people, things)
verschieden, unterschiedlich; **to be
~ (from)** anders sein (als).
differential [dɪfə'rɛnʃəl] n (MATH)
Differential nt; (BRIT: in wages)
(Einkommens)unterschied m.
differentiate [dɪfə'rɛnʃɪeɪt] vi: **to ~ (between)**
unterscheiden (zwischen) ♦ vt: **to ~ A from
B** A von B unterscheiden.
differently ['dɪfrəntlɪ] adv anders; (shaped,
designed) verschieden, unterschiedlich.
difficult ['dɪfɪkəlt] adj schwierig; (task,
problem) schwer, schwierig; **~ to
understand** schwer zu verstehen.
difficulty ['dɪfɪkəltɪ] n Schwierigkeit f; **to be
in/get into difficulties** in Schwierigkeiten
sein/geraten.
diffidence ['dɪfɪdəns] n Bescheidenheit f,
Zurückhaltung f.
diffident ['dɪfɪdənt] adj bescheiden,
zurückhaltend.
diffuse [dɪ'fju:s] adj diffus ♦ vt verbreiten.
dig [dɪg] (pt, pp dug) vt graben; (garden)
umgraben ♦ n (prod) Stoß m; (archaeological)
(Aus)grabung f; (remark) Seitenhieb m,
spitze Bemerkung f; **to ~ one's nails into
sth** seine Nägel in etw acc krallen.
►**dig in** vi (fig: inf: eat) reinhauen ♦ vt
(compost) untergraben, eingraben; (knife)

hineinstoßen; (*claw*) festkrallen; **to ~ one's heels in** (*fig*) sich auf die Hinterbeine stellen (*inf*).

▶**dig into** *vt fus* (*savings*) angreifen; (*snow, soil*) ein Loch graben in +*acc*; **to ~ into one's pockets for sth** in seinen Taschen nach etw suchen *or* wühlen.

▶**dig out** *vt* ausgraben.

▶**dig up** *vt* ausgraben.

digest [daɪ'dʒɛst] *vt* verdauen ♦ *n* Digest *m or nt*, Auswahl *f*.

digestible [dɪ'dʒɛstəbl] *adj* verdaulich.

digestion [dɪ'dʒɛstʃən] *n* Verdauung *f*.

digestive [dɪ'dʒɛstɪv] *adj* (*system, upsets*) Verdauungs- ♦ *n* Keks aus Vollkornmehl.

digit ['dɪdʒɪt] *n* (*number*) Ziffer *f*; (*finger*) Finger *m*.

digital ['dɪdʒɪtl] *adj* (*watch, display etc*) Digital-.

digital computer *n* Digitalrechner *m*.

dignified ['dɪɡnɪfaɪd] *adj* würdevoll.

dignitary ['dɪɡnɪtərɪ] *n* Würdenträger(in) *m(f)*.

dignity ['dɪɡnɪtɪ] *n* Würde *f*.

digress [daɪ'ɡrɛs] *vi*: **to ~ (from)** abschweifen (von).

digression [daɪ'ɡrɛʃən] *n* Abschweifung *f*.

digs [dɪɡz] (*BRIT: inf*) *npl* Bude *f*.

dike [daɪk] *n* = **dyke**.

dilapidated [dɪ'læpɪdeɪtɪd] *adj* verfallen.

dilate [daɪ'leɪt] *vi* sich weiten ♦ *vt* weiten.

dilatory ['dɪlətərɪ] *adj* langsam.

dilemma [daɪ'lɛmə] *n* Dilemma *nt*; **to be in a ~** sich in einem Dilemma befinden, in der Klemme sitzen (*inf*).

diligence ['dɪlɪdʒəns] *n* Fleiß *m*.

diligent ['dɪlɪdʒənt] *adj* fleißig; (*research*) sorgfältig, genau.

dill [dɪl] *n* Dill *m*.

dilly-dally ['dɪlɪ'dælɪ] *vi* trödeln.

dilute [daɪ'luːt] *vt* verdünnen; (*belief, principle*) schwächen ♦ *adj* verdünnt.

dim [dɪm] *adj* schwach; (*outline, figure*) undeutlich, verschwommen; (*room*) dämmerig; (*future*) düster; (*prospects*) schlecht; (*inf: person*) schwer von Begriff ♦ *vt* (*light*) dämpfen; (*US: AUT*) abblenden; **to take a ~ view of sth** wenig *or* nicht viel von etw halten.

dime [daɪm] (*US*) *n* Zehncentstück *nt*.

dimension [daɪ'mɛnʃən] *n* (*aspect*) Dimension *f*; (*measurement*) Abmessung *f*, Maß *nt*; (*also pl: scale, size*) Ausmaß *nt*.

-dimensional [dɪ'mɛnʃənl] *adj suff* -dimensional.

diminish [dɪ'mɪnɪʃ] *vi* sich verringern ♦ *vt* verringern.

diminished responsibility *n* verminderte Zurechnungsfähigkeit *f*.

diminutive [dɪ'mɪnjutɪv] *adj* winzig ♦ *n* Verkleinerungsform *f*.

dimly ['dɪmlɪ] *adv* schwach; (*see*) undeutlich, verschwommen.

dimmer ['dɪmə*] *n* (*also:* **~ switch**) Dimmer *m*; (*US: AUT*) Abblendschalter *m*.

dimmers ['dɪməz] (*US*) *npl* (*AUT: dipped headlights*) Abblendlicht *nt*; (*parking lights*) Parklicht *nt*.

dimmer (switch) ['dɪmə-] *n* (*ELEC*) Dimmer *m*; (*US: AUT*) Abblendschalter *m*.

dimple ['dɪmpl] *n* Grübchen *nt*.

dim-witted ['dɪm'wɪtɪd] (*inf*) *adj* dämlich.

din [dɪn] *n* Lärm *m*, Getöse *nt* ♦ *vt* (*inf*): **to ~ sth into sb** jdm etw einbleuen.

dine [daɪn] *vi* speisen.

diner ['daɪnə*] *n* Gast *m*; (*US: restaurant*) Eßlokal *nt*.

dinghy ['dɪŋɡɪ] *n* (*also:* **rubber ~**) Schlauchboot *nt*; (*also:* **sailing ~**) Dingi *nt*.

dingy ['dɪndʒɪ] *adj* schäbig; (*clothes, curtains etc*) schmuddelig.

dining car ['daɪnɪŋ-] (*BRIT*) *n* Speisewagen *m*.

dining room *n* Eßzimmer *nt*; (*in hotel*) Speiseraum *m*.

dinner ['dɪnə*] *n* (*evening meal*) Abendessen *nt*; (*lunch*) Mittagessen *nt*; (*banquet*) (Fest)essen *nt*.

dinner jacket *n* Smokingjackett *nt*.

dinner party *n* Abendgesellschaft *f* (mit Essen).

dinner service *n* Tafelservice *nt*.

dinner time *n* Essenszeit *f*.

dinosaur ['daɪnəsɔː*] *n* Dinosaurier *m*.

dint [dɪnt] *n*: **by ~ of** durch +*acc*.

diocese ['daɪəsɪs] *n* Diözese *f*.

dioxide [daɪ'ɔksaɪd] *n* Dioxyd *nt*.

Dip. (*BRIT*) *abbr* = **diploma**.

dip [dɪp] *n* Senke *f*; (*in sea*) kurzes Bad *nt*; (*CULIN*) Dip *m*; (*for sheep*) Desinfektionslösung *f* ♦ *vt* eintauchen; (*BRIT: AUT*) abblenden ♦ *vi* abfallen.

diphtheria [dɪf'θɪərɪə] *n* Diphtherie *f*.

diphthong ['dɪfθɒŋ] *n* Diphthong *m*.

diploma [dɪ'pləʊmə] *n* Diplom *nt*.

diplomacy [dɪ'pləʊməsɪ] *n* Diplomatie *f*.

diplomat ['dɪpləmæt] *n* Diplomat(in) *m(f)*.

diplomatic [dɪplə'mætɪk] *adj* diplomatisch; **to break off ~ relations (with)** die diplomatischen Beziehungen abbrechen (mit).

diplomatic corps *n* diplomatisches Korps *nt*.

diplomatic immunity *n* Immunität *f*.

dip rod ['dɪprɒd] (*US*) *n* Ölmeßstab *m*.

dipstick ['dɪpstɪk] (*BRIT*) *n* Ölmeßstab *m*.

dip switch (*BRIT*) *n* Abblendschalter *m*.

dire [daɪə*] *adj* (*consequences, effects*) schrecklich.

direct [daɪ'rɛkt] *adj, adv* direkt ♦ *vt* richten; (*company, project, programme etc*) leiten; (*play, film*) Regie führen bei; **to ~ sb to do sth** jdn anweisen, etw zu tun; **can you ~ me to ...?** können Sie mir den Weg nach ... sagen?

direct access *n* (*COMPUT*) Direktzugriff *m*.

direct cost *n* direkte Kosten *pl*.

direct current n Gleichstrom m.
direct debit (*BRIT*) n Einzugsauftrag m;
  (*transaction*) automatische Abbuchung f.
direct dialling n Selbstwahl f.
direct hit n Volltreffer m.
direction [dɪ'rɛkʃən] n Richtung f; (*TV, RADIO*)
  Leitung f; (*CINE*) Regie f; **directions** npl
  (*instructions*) Anweisungen pl; **sense of** ~
  Orientierungssinn m; ~**s for use**
  Gebrauchsanweisung f,
  Gebrauchsanleitung f; **to ask for** ~**s** nach
  dem Weg fragen; **in the** ~ **of** in Richtung.
directional [dɪ'rɛkʃənl] adj (*aerial*) Richt-.
directive [dɪ'rɛktɪv] n Direktive f, Weisung f;
  government ~ Regierungserlaß m.
direct labour n (*COMM*) Produktionsarbeit f;
  (*BRIT*) eigene Arbeitskräfte pl.
directly [dɪ'rɛktlɪ] adv direkt; (*at once*) sofort,
  gleich.
direct mail n Werbebriefe pl.
direct mailshot (*BRIT*) n Direktwerbung f
  per Post.
directness [daɪ'rɛktnɪs] n Direktheit f.
director [dɪ'rɛktə*] n Direktor(in) m(f); (*of
  project, TV, RADIO*) Leiter(in) m(f); (*CINE*)
  Regisseur(in) m(f).
Director of Public Prosecutions (*BRIT*) n
  ≈ Generalstaatsanwalt m,
  Generalstaatsanwältin f.
directory [dɪ'rɛktərɪ] n (*also:* **telephone** ~)
  Telefonbuch nt; (*also:* **street** ~)
  Einwohnerverzeichnis nt; (*COMPUT*)
  Verzeichnis nt; (*COMM*)
  Branchenverzeichnis nt.
directory enquiries, (*US*) **directory
  assistance** n (Fernsprech)auskunft f.
dirt [dɜːt] n Schmutz m; (*earth*) Erde f; **to treat
  sb like** ~ jdn wie (den letzten) Dreck
  behandeln.
dirt-cheap ['dɜːt'tʃiːp] adj spottbillig.
dirt road n unbefestigte Straße f.
dirty ['dɜːtɪ] adj schmutzig; (*story*)
  unanständig ♦ vt beschmutzen.
dirty trick n gemeiner Trick m.
disability [dɪsə'bɪlɪtɪ] n Behinderung f.
disability allowance n Behindertenbeihilfe
  f.
disable [dɪs'eɪbl] vt zum Invaliden machen;
  (*tank, gun*) unbrauchbar machen.
disabled [dɪs'eɪbld] adj behindert ♦ npl: **the** ~
  die Behinderten pl.
disabuse [dɪsə'bjuːz] vt: **to** ~ **sb** (**of**) jdn
  befreien (von).
disadvantage [dɪsəd'vɑːntɪdʒ] n Nachteil m;
  (*detriment*) Schaden m; **to be at a** ~
  benachteiligt or im Nachteil sein.
disadvantaged [dɪsəd'vɑːntɪdʒd] adj
  benachteiligt.
disadvantageous [dɪsædvɑːn'teɪdʒəs] adj
  ungünstig.
disaffected [dɪsə'fɛktɪd] adj entfremdet.
disaffection [dɪsə'fɛkʃən] n Entfremdung f.

disagree [dɪsə'griː] vi nicht übereinstimmen;
  (*to be against, think differently*): **to** ~ (**with**)
  nicht einverstanden sein (mit); **I** ~ **with you**
  ich bin anderer Meinung; **garlic** ~**s with me**
  ich vertrage keinen Knoblauch, Knoblauch
  bekommt mir nicht.
disagreeable [dɪsə'griːəbl] adj unangenehm;
  (*person*) unsympathisch.
disagreement [dɪsə'griːmənt] n Uneinigkeit f;
  (*argument*) Meinungsverschiedenheit f; **to
  have a** ~ **with sb** sich mit jdm nicht einig
  sein.
disallow ['dɪsə'lau] vt (*appeal*) abweisen;
  (*goal*) nicht anerkennen, nicht geben.
disappear [dɪsə'pɪə*] vi verschwinden;
  (*custom etc*) aussterben.
disappearance [dɪsə'pɪərəns] n (*see vi*)
  Verschwinden nt; Aussterben nt.
disappoint [dɪsə'pɔɪnt] vt enttäuschen.
disappointed [dɪsə'pɔɪntɪd] adj enttäuscht.
disappointing [dɪsə'pɔɪntɪŋ] adj
  enttäuschend.
disappointment [dɪsə'pɔɪntmənt] n
  Enttäuschung f.
disapproval [dɪsə'pruːvəl] n Mißbilligung f.
disapprove [dɪsə'pruːv] vi dagegen sein; **to** ~
  ~ **of** mißbilligen +acc.
disapproving [dɪsə'pruːvɪŋ] adj mißbilligend.
disarm [dɪs'ɑːm] vt entwaffnen; (*criticism*) zum
  Verstummen bringen ♦ vi abrüsten.
disarmament [dɪs'ɑːməmənt] n Abrüstung f.
disarming [dɪs'ɑːmɪŋ] adj entwaffnend.
disarray [dɪsə'reɪ] n: **in** ~ (*army, organization*)
  in Auflösung (begriffen); (*hair, clothes*)
  unordentlich; (*thoughts*) durcheinander; **to
  throw into** ~ durcheinanderbringen.
disaster [dɪ'zɑːstə*] n Katastrophe f; (*AVIAT
  etc*) Unglück nt; (*fig: mess*) Fiasko nt.
disaster area n Katastrophengebiet nt; (*fig:
  person*) Katastrophe f; **my office is a** ~ in
  meinem Büro sieht es katastrophal aus.
disastrous [dɪ'zɑːstrəs] adj katastrophal.
disband [dɪs'bænd] vt auflösen ♦ vi sich
  auflösen.
disbelief ['dɪsbə'liːf] n Ungläubigkeit f; **in** ~
  ungläubig.
disbelieve ['dɪsbə'liːv] vt (*person*) nicht
  glauben +dat; (*story*) nicht glauben; **I don't**
  ~ **you** ich bezweifle nicht, was Sie sagen.
disc [dɪsk] n (*ANAT*) Bandscheibe f; (*record*)
  Platte f; (*COMPUT*) = **disk**.
disc. abbr (*COMM*) = **discount**.
discard [dɪs'kɑːd] vt ausrangieren; (*fig: idea,
  plan*) verwerfen.
disc brake n Scheibenbremse f.
discern [dɪ'sɜːn] vt wahrnehmen; (*identify*)
  erkennen.
discernible [dɪ'sɜːnəbl] adj erkennbar; (*object*)
  wahrnehmbar.
discerning [dɪ'sɜːnɪŋ] adj (*judgement*)
  scharfsinnig; (*look*) kritisch; (*listeners etc*)
  anspruchsvoll.

discharge [dɪs'tʃɑːdʒ] vt (duties) nachkommen +dat; (debt) begleichen; (waste) ablassen; (ELEC) entladen; (MED) ausscheiden, absondern; (patient, employee, soldier) entlassen; (defendant) freisprechen ♦ n (of gas) Ausströmen nt; (of liquid) Ausfließen nt; (ELEC) Entladung f; (MED) Ausfluß m; (of patient, employee, soldier) Entlassung f; (of defendant) Freispruch m; to ~ a gun ein Gewehr abfeuern.

discharged bankrupt [dɪs'tʃɑːdʒd-] n (LAW) entlasteter Konkursschuldner m, entlastete Konkursschuldnerin f.

disciple [dɪ'saɪpl] n Jünger m; (fig: follower) Schüler(in) m(f).

disciplinary ['dɪsɪplɪnərɪ] adj (powers etc) Disziplinar-; to take ~ action against sb ein Disziplinarverfahren gegen jdn einleiten.

discipline ['dɪsɪplɪn] n Disziplin f ♦ vt disziplinieren; (punish) bestrafen; to ~ o.s. to do sth sich dazu anhalten or zwingen, etw zu tun.

disc jockey n Diskjockey m.

disclaim [dɪs'kleɪm] vt (knowledge) abstreiten; (responsibility) von sich weisen.

disclaimer [dɪs'kleɪmə*] n Dementi nt; to issue a ~ eine Gegenerklärung abgeben.

disclose [dɪs'kləuz] vt enthüllen, bekanntgeben.

disclosure [dɪs'kləuʒə*] n Enthüllung f.

disco ['dɪskəu] n abbr = discotheque.

discolor etc [dɪs'kʌlə*] (US) = discolour etc.

discolour [dɪs'kʌlə*] vt verfärben ♦ vi sich verfärben.

discolouration [dɪskʌlə'reɪʃən] n Verfärbung f.

discoloured [dɪs'kʌləd] adj verfärbt.

discomfort [dɪs'kʌmfət] n (unease) Unbehagen nt; (physical) Beschwerden pl.

disconcert [dɪskən'səːt] vt beunruhigen, irritieren.

disconcerting [dɪskən'səːtɪŋ] adj beunruhigend, irritierend.

disconnect [dɪskə'nekt] vt abtrennen; (ELEC, RADIO) abstellen; I've been ~ed (TEL) das Gespräch ist unterbrochen worden; (supply, connection) man hat mir das Telefon/den Strom/das Gas etc abgestellt.

disconnected [dɪskə'nektɪd] adj unzusammenhängend.

disconsolate [dɪs'kɔnsəlɪt] adj niedergeschlagen.

discontent [dɪskən'tent] n Unzufriedenheit f.

discontented [dɪskən'tentɪd] adj unzufrieden.

discontinue [dɪskən'tɪnjuː] vt einstellen; "~d" (COMM) „ausgelaufene Serie".

discord ['dɪskɔːd] n Zwietracht f; (MUS) Dissonanz f.

discordant [dɪs'kɔːdənt] adj unharmonisch.

discotheque ['dɪskəutek] n Diskothek f.

discount [n 'dɪskaunt, vt dɪs'kaunt] n Rabatt m ♦ vt nachlassen; (idea, fact) unberücksichtigt lassen; to give sb a ~ on sth jdm auf etw acc Rabatt geben; ~ for cash Skonto nt or m (bei Barzahlung); at a ~ mit Rabatt.

discount house n Diskontbank f; (also: discount store) Diskontgeschäft nt.

discount rate n Diskontsatz m.

discourage [dɪs'kʌrɪdʒ] vt entmutigen; to ~ sb from doing sth jdm davon abraten, etw zu tun.

discouragement [dɪs'kʌrɪdʒmənt] n Mutlosigkeit f; to act as a ~ to sb entmutigend für jdn sein.

discouraging [dɪs'kʌrɪdʒɪŋ] adj entmutigend.

discourteous [dɪs'kəːtɪəs] adj unhöflich.

discover [dɪs'kʌvə*] vt entdecken; (missing person) finden; to ~ that ... herausfinden, daß ...

discovery [dɪs'kʌvərɪ] n Entdeckung f.

discredit [dɪs'kredɪt] vt in Mißkredit bringen ♦ n: to sb's ~ zu jds Schande.

discreet [dɪs'kriːt] adj diskret; (unremarkable) dezent.

discreetly [dɪs'kriːtlɪ] adv diskret; (unremarkably) dezent.

discrepancy [dɪs'krepənsɪ] n Diskrepanz f.

discretion [dɪs'kreʃən] n Diskretion f; at the ~ of im Ermessen +gen; use your own ~ Sie müssen nach eigenem Ermessen handeln.

discretionary [dɪs'kreʃənrɪ] adj: ~ powers Ermessensspielraum m; ~ payments Ermessenszahlungen pl.

discriminate [dɪs'krɪmɪneɪt] vi: to ~ between unterscheiden zwischen +dat; to ~ against diskriminieren +acc.

discriminating [dɪs'krɪmɪneɪtɪŋ] adj anspruchsvoll, kritisch; (tax, duty) Differential-.

discrimination [dɪskrɪmɪ'neɪʃən] n Diskriminierung f; (discernment) Urteilsvermögen nt; racial ~ Rassendiskriminierung f; sexual ~ Diskriminierung aufgrund des Geschlechts.

discus ['dɪskəs] n Diskus m; (event) Diskuswerfen nt.

discuss [dɪs'kʌs] vt besprechen; (debate) diskutieren; (analyse) erörtern, behandeln.

discussion [dɪs'kʌʃən] n Besprechung f; (debate) Diskussion f; under ~ in der Diskussion.

disdain [dɪs'deɪn] n Verachtung f ♦ vt verachten ♦ vi: to ~ to do sth es für unter seiner Würde halten, etw zu tun.

disease [dɪ'ziːz] n Krankheit f.

diseased [dɪ'ziːzd] adj krank; (tree) befallen.

disembark [dɪsɪm'bɑːk] vt ausschiffen ♦ vi (passengers) von Bord gehen.

disembarkation [dɪsɛmbɑː'keɪʃən] n Ausschiffung f.

disembodied ['dɪsɪm'bɔdɪd] adj (voice) geisterhaft; (hand) körperlos.

disembowel ['dɪsɪm'bauəl] vt die Eingeweide

herausnehmen +dat.

disenchanted ['dɪsɪn'tʃɑːntɪd] *adj:* ~ **(with)** enttäuscht (von).

disenfranchise ['dɪsɪn'fræntʃaɪz] *vt* (*POL*) das Wahlrecht entziehen +dat; (*COMM*) die Konzession entziehen +dat.

disengage [dɪsɪn'geɪdʒ] *vt* (*TECH*) ausrasten; **to ~ the clutch** auskuppeln.

disengagement [dɪsɪn'geɪdʒmənt] *n* (*POL*) Disengagement *nt.*

disentangle [dɪsɪn'tæŋgl] *vt* befreien; (*wool, wire*) entwirren.

disfavour, (*US*) **disfavor** [dɪs'feɪvə*] *n* Mißfallen *nt;* **to fall into ~ (with sb)** (bei jdm) in Ungnade fallen.

disfigure [dɪs'fɪgə*] *vt* entstellen; (*object, place*) verunstalten.

disgorge [dɪs'gɔːdʒ] *vt* (*liquid*) ergießen; (*people*) ausspeien.

disgrace [dɪs'greɪs] *n* Schande *f;* (*scandal*) Skandal *m* ♦ *vt* Schande bringen über +acc.

disgraceful [dɪs'greɪsful] *adj* skandalös.

disgruntled [dɪs'grʌntld] *adj* verärgert.

disguise [dɪs'gaɪz] *n* Verkleidung *f* ♦ *vt:* **to ~ (as)** (*person*) verkleiden (als); (*object*) tarnen (als); **in ~** (*person*) verkleidet; **there's no disguising the fact that** ... es kann nicht geleugnet werden, daß ...; **to ~ o.s. as** sich verkleiden als.

disgust [dɪs'gʌst] *n* Abscheu *m* ♦ *vt* anwidern; **she walked off in ~** sie ging voller Empörung weg.

disgusting [dɪs'gʌstɪŋ] *adj* widerlich.

dish [dɪʃ] *n* Schüssel *f;* (*flat*) Schale *f,* (*recipe, food*) Gericht *nt;* (*also:* **satellite ~**) Parabolantenne *f,* Schüssel (*inf*); **to do** *or* **wash the ~es** Geschirr spülen, abwaschen.

▶**dish out** *vt* verteilen; (*food, money*) austeilen; (*advice*) erteilen.

▶**dish up** *vt* (*food*) auftragen, servieren; (*facts, statistics*) auftischen (*inf*).

dishcloth ['dɪʃklɔθ] *n* Spültuch *nt,* Spüllappen *m.*

dishearten [dɪs'hɑːtn] *vt* entmutigen.

dishevelled, (*US*) **disheveled** [dɪ'ʃɛvəld] *adj* unordentlich; (*hair*) zerzaust.

dishonest [dɪs'ɒnɪst] *adj* unehrlich; (*means*) unlauter.

dishonesty [dɪs'ɒnɪstɪ] *n* Unehrlichkeit *f.*

dishonor *etc* [dɪs'ɒnə*] (*US*) = **dishonour** *etc.*

dishonour [dɪs'ɒnə*] *n* Schande *f.*

dishonourable [dɪs'ɒnərəbl] *adj* unehrenhaft.

dish soap (*US*) *n* Spülmittel *nt.*

dishtowel ['dɪʃtauəl] (*US*) *n* Geschirrtuch *nt.*

dishwasher ['dɪʃwɒʃə*] *n* (*machine*) (Geschirr)spülmaschine *f.*

dishy ['dɪʃɪ] (*inf: BRIT*) *adj* attraktiv.

disillusion [dɪsɪ'luːʒən] *vt* desillusionieren ♦ *n* = **disillusionment; to become ~ed (with)** seine Illusionen (über +acc) verlieren.

disillusionment [dɪsɪ'luːʒənmənt] *n* Desillusionierung *f.*

disincentive [dɪsɪn'sɛntɪv] *n* Entmutigung *f;* **it's a ~** es hält die Leute ab; **to be a ~ to sb** jdm keinen Anreiz bieten.

disinclined [dɪsɪn'klaɪnd] *adj:* **to be ~ to do sth** abgeneigt sein, etw zu tun.

disinfect [dɪsɪn'fɛkt] *vt* desinfizieren.

disinfectant [dɪsɪn'fɛktənt] *n* Desinfektionsmittel *nt.*

disinflation [dɪsɪn'fleɪʃən] *n* (*ECON*) Rückgang *m* einer inflationären Entwicklung.

disinformation [dɪsɪnfə'meɪʃən] *n* Desinformation *f.*

disingenuous [dɪsɪn'dʒɛnjuəs] *adj* unaufrichtig.

disinherit [dɪsɪn'hɛrɪt] *vt* enterben.

disintegrate [dɪs'ɪntɪgreɪt] *vi* zerfallen; (*marriage, partnership*) scheitern; (*organization*) sich auflösen.

disinterested [dɪs'ɪntrəstɪd] *adj* (*advice*) unparteiisch, unvoreingenommen; (*help*) uneigennützig.

disjointed [dɪs'dʒɔɪntɪd] *adj* unzusammenhängend.

disk [dɪsk] *n* Diskette *f;* **single-/double-sided ~** einseitige/zweiseitige Diskette.

disk drive *n* Diskettenlaufwerk *nt.*

diskette [dɪs'kɛt] (*US*) *n* = **disk.**

disk operating system *n* Betriebssystem *nt.*

dislike [dɪs'laɪk] *n* Abneigung *f* ♦ *vt* nicht mögen; **to take a ~ to sb/sth** eine Abneigung gegen jdn/etw entwickeln; **I ~ the idea** die Idee gefällt mir nicht; **he ~s it** er kann es nicht leiden, er mag es nicht.

dislocate ['dɪsləkeɪt] *vt* verrenken, ausrenken; **he has ~d his shoulder** er hat sich *dat* den Arm ausgekugelt.

dislodge [dɪs'lɔdʒ] *vt* verschieben.

disloyal [dɪs'lɔɪəl] *adj* illoyal.

dismal ['dɪzml] *adj* trübe, trostlos; (*song, person, mood*) trübsinnig; (*failure*) kläglich.

dismantle [dɪs'mæntl] *vt* (*machine*) demontieren.

dismast [dɪs'mɑːst] *vt* (*NAUT*) entmasten.

dismay [dɪs'meɪ] *n* Bestürzung *f* ♦ *vt* bestürzen; **much to my ~** zu meiner Bestürzung; **in ~** bestürzt.

dismiss [dɪs'mɪs] *vt* entlassen; (*case*) abweisen; (*possibility, idea*) abtun.

dismissal [dɪs'mɪsl] *n* Entlassung *f.*

dismount [dɪs'maunt] *vi* absteigen.

disobedience [dɪsə'biːdɪəns] *n* Ungehorsam *m.*

disobedient [dɪsə'biːdɪənt] *adj* ungehorsam.

disobey [dɪsə'beɪ] *vt* nicht gehorchen +dat; (*order*) nicht befolgen.

disorder [dɪs'ɔːdə*] *n* Unordnung *f;* (*rioting*) Unruhen *pl;* (*MED*) (Funktions)störung *f;* **civil ~** öffentliche Unruhen *pl.*

disorderly [dɪs'ɔːdəlɪ] *adj* unordentlich; (*meeting*) undiszipliniert; (*behaviour*) ungehörig.

disorderly conduct *n* (*LAW*) ungebührliches

Benehmen nt.

disorganize [dɪs'ɔːgənaɪz] vt durcheinanderbringen.

disorganized [dɪs'ɔːgənaɪzd] adj chaotisch.

disorientated [dɪs'ɔːrɪenteɪtɪd] adj desorientiert, verwirrt.

disown [dɪs'əun] vt (action) verleugnen; (child) verstoßen.

disparaging [dɪs'pærɪdʒɪŋ] adj (remarks) abschätzig, geringschätzig; **to be ~ about sb/sth** (person) abschätzig or geringschätzig über jdn/etw urteilen.

disparate ['dɪspərɪt] adj völlig verschieden.

disparity [dɪs'pærɪtɪ] n Unterschied m.

dispassionate [dɪs'pæʃənət] adj nüchtern.

dispatch [dɪs'pætʃ] vt senden, schicken; (deal with) erledigen; (kill) töten ♦ n Senden nt, Schicken nt; (PRESS) Bericht m; (MIL) Depesche f.

dispatch department n Versandabteilung f.

dispatch rider n (MIL) Meldefahrer m.

dispel [dɪs'pɛl] vt (myths) zerstören; (fears) zerstreuen.

dispensary [dɪs'pɛnsərɪ] n Apotheke f; (in chemist's) Raum in einer Apotheke, wo Arzneimittel abgefüllt werden.

dispensation [dɪspən'seɪʃən] n (of treatment) Vergabe f; (special permission) Dispens m; **~ of justice** Rechtsprechung f.

dispense [dɪs'pɛns] vt (medicines) abgeben; (charity) austeilen; (advice) erteilen.

▶**dispense with** vt fus verzichten auf +acc.

dispenser [dɪs'pɛnsə*] n (machine) Automat m.

dispensing chemist [dɪs'pɛnsɪŋ-] (BRIT) n (shop) Apotheke f.

dispersal [dɪs'pəːsl] n (of objects) Verstreuen nt; (of group, crowd) Auflösung f, Zerstreuen nt.

disperse [dɪs'pəːs] vt (objects) verstreuen; (crowd etc) auflösen, zerstreuen; (knowledge, information) verbreiten ♦ vi (crowd) sich auflösen or zerstreuen.

dispirited [dɪs'pɪrɪtɪd] adj entmutigt.

displace [dɪs'pleɪs] vt ablösen.

displaced person [dɪs'pleɪst-] n Verschleppte(r) f(m).

displacement [dɪs'pleɪsmənt] n Ablösung f; (of people) Vertreibung f; (PHYS) Verdrängung f.

display [dɪs'pleɪ] n (in shop) Auslage f; (exhibition) Ausstellung f; (of feeling) Zeigen nt; (pej) Zurschaustellung f; (COMPUT, TECH) Anzeige f ♦ vt zeigen; (ostentatiously) zur Schau stellen; (results, departure times) aushängen; **on ~** ausgestellt.

display advertising n Displaywerbung f.

displease [dɪs'pliːz] vt verstimmen, verärgern.

displeased [dɪs'pliːzd] adj: **I am very ~ with you** ich bin sehr enttäuscht von dir.

displeasure [dɪs'plɛʒə*] n Mißfallen nt.

disposable [dɪs'pəuzəbl] adj (lighter)

Wegwerf-; (bottle) Einweg-; (income) verfügbar.

disposable nappy (BRIT) n Papierwindel f.

disposal [dɪs'pəuzl] n (of goods for sale) Loswerden nt; (of property, belongings: by selling) Verkauf m; (: by giving away) Abgeben nt; (of rubbish) Beseitigung f; **at one's ~** zur Verfügung; **to put sth at sb's ~** jdm etw zur Verfügung stellen.

dispose [dɪs'pəuz]: **~ of** vt fus (body) aus dem Weg schaffen; (unwanted goods) loswerden; (problem, task) erledigen; (stock) verkaufen.

disposed [dɪs'pəuzd] adj: **to be ~ to do sth** (inclined) geneigt sein, etw zu tun; (willing) bereit sein, etw zu tun; **to be well ~ towards sb** jdm wohlwollen.

disposition [dɪspə'zɪʃən] n (nature) Veranlagung f; (inclination) Neigung f.

dispossess ['dɪspə'zɛs] vt enteignen; **to ~ sb of his/her land** jds Land enteignen.

disproportion [dɪsprə'pɔːʃən] n Mißverhältnis nt.

disproportionate [dɪsprə'pɔːʃənət] adj unverhältnismäßig; (amount) unverhältnismäßig hoch/niedrig.

disprove [dɪs'pruːv] vt widerlegen.

dispute [dɪs'pjuːt] n Streit m; (also: **industrial ~**) Auseinandersetzung f zwischen Arbeitgebern und Arbeitnehmern; (POL, MIL) Streitigkeiten pl ♦ vt bestreiten; (ownership etc) anfechten; **to be in or under ~** umstritten sein.

disqualification [dɪskwɔlɪfɪ'keɪʃən] n: **~ (from)** Ausschluß m (von); (SPORT) Disqualifizierung f (von); **~ (from driving)** (BRIT) Führerscheinentzug m.

disqualify [dɪs'kwɔlɪfaɪ] vt disqualifizieren; **to ~ sb for sth** jdn für etw ungeeignet machen; **to ~ sb from doing sth** jdn ungeeignet machen, etw zu tun; **to ~ sb from driving** (BRIT) jdm den Führerschein entziehen.

disquiet [dɪs'kwaɪət] n Unruhe f.

disquieting [dɪs'kwaɪətɪŋ] adj beunruhigend.

disregard [dɪsrɪ'gɑːd] vt nicht beachten, ignorieren ♦ n: **~ (for)** Mißachtung f (+gen); (for danger, money) Geringschätzung f (+gen).

disrepair ['dɪsrɪ'pɛə*] n: **to fall into ~** (machine) vernachlässigt werden; (building) verfallen.

disreputable [dɪs'rɛpjutəbl] adj (person) unehrenhaft; (behaviour) unfein.

disrepute ['dɪsrɪ'pjuːt] n schlechter Ruf m; **to bring/fall into ~** in Verruf bringen/kommen.

disrespectful [dɪsrɪ'spɛktful] adj respektlos.

disrupt [dɪs'rʌpt] vt (plans) durcheinanderbringen; (conversation, proceedings) unterbrechen.

disruption [dɪs'rʌpʃən] n Unterbrechung f; (disturbance) Störung f.

disruptive [dɪs'rʌptɪv] adj störend; (action) Stör-.

dissatisfaction [dɪssætɪs'fækʃən] *n* Unzufriedenheit *f*.

dissatisfied [dɪs'sætɪsfaɪd] *adj:* ~ **(with)** unzufrieden (mit).

dissect [dɪ'sɛkt] *vt* sezieren.

disseminate [dɪ'sɛmɪneɪt] *vt* verbreiten.

dissent [dɪ'sɛnt] *n* abweichende Meinungen *pl*.

dissenter [dɪ'sɛntə*] *n* Abweichler(in) *m(f)*.

dissertation [dɪsə'teɪʃən] *n* (*speech*) Vortrag *m*; (*piece of writing*) Abhandlung *f*; (*for PhD*) Dissertation *f*.

disservice [dɪs'sə:vɪs] *n:* **to do sb a** ~ jdm einen schlechten Dienst erweisen.

dissident ['dɪsɪdnt] *adj* andersdenkend; (*voice*) kritisch ♦ *n* Dissident(in) *m(f)*.

dissimilar [dɪ'sɪmɪlə*] *adj:* ~ **(to)** anders (als).

dissipate ['dɪsɪpeɪt] *vt* (*heat*) neutralisieren; (*clouds*) auflösen; (*money, effort*) verschwenden.

dissipated ['dɪsɪpeɪtɪd] *adj* zügellos, ausschweifend.

dissociate [dɪ'səuʃɪeɪt] *vt* trennen; **to** ~ **o.s. from** sich distanzieren von.

dissolute ['dɪsəlu:t] *adj* zügellos, ausschweifend.

dissolution [dɪsə'lu:ʃən] *n* Auflösung *f*.

dissolve [dɪ'zɔlv] *vt* auflösen ♦ *vi* sich auflösen; **to** ~ **in(to) tears** in Tränen zerfließen.

dissuade [dɪ'sweɪd] *vt:* **to** ~ **sb (from sth)** jdn (von etw) abbringen.

distaff ['dɪstɑ:f] *n:* **the** ~ **side** die mütterliche Seite.

distance ['dɪstns] *n* Entfernung *f*; (*in time*) Abstand *m*; (*reserve*) Abstand, Distanz *f* ♦ *vt:* **to** ~ **o.s. (from)** sich distanzieren (von); **in the** ~ in der Ferne; **what's the** ~ **to London?** wie weit ist es nach London?; **it's within walking** ~ es ist zu Fuß erreichbar; **at a** ~ **of 2 metres** in 2 Meter(n) Entfernung; **keep your** ~! halten Sie Abstand!

distant ['dɪstnt] *adj* (*place*) weit entfernt, fern; (*time*) weit zurückliegend; (*relative*) entfernt; (*manner*) distanziert, kühl.

distaste [dɪs'teɪst] *n* Widerwille *m*.

distasteful [dɪs'teɪstful] *adj* widerlich; **to be** ~ **to sb** jdm zuwider sein.

Dist. Atty. (*US*) *abbr* = **district attorney**.

distemper [dɪs'tɛmpə*] *n* (*paint*) Temperafarbe *f*; (*disease of dogs*) Staupe *f*.

distend [dɪs'tɛnd] *vt* blähen ♦ *vi* sich blähen.

distended [dɪs'tɛndɪd] *adj* aufgebläht.

distil, (*US*) **distill** [dɪs'tɪl] *vt* destillieren; (*fig*) (heraus)destillieren.

distillery [dɪs'tɪlərɪ] *n* Brennerei *f*.

distinct [dɪs'tɪŋkt] *adj* deutlich, klar; (*possibility*) eindeutig; (*different*) verschieden; **as** ~ **from** im Unterschied zu.

distinction [dɪs'tɪŋkʃən] *n* Unterschied *m*; (*honour*) Ehre *f*; (*in exam*) Auszeichnung *f*; **to draw a** ~ **between** einen Unterschied

machen zwischen +*dat*; **a writer of** ~ ein Schriftsteller von Rang.

distinctive [dɪs'tɪŋktɪv] *adj* unverwechselbar.

distinctly [dɪs'tɪŋktlɪ] *adv* deutlich, klar; (*tell*) ausdrücklich; (*unhappy*) ausgeprochen; (*better*) entschieden.

distinguish [dɪs'tɪŋgwɪʃ] *vt* unterscheiden; (*details etc*) erkennen, ausmachen; **to** ~ **(between)** unterscheiden (zwischen +*dat*); **to** ~ **o.s.** sich hervortun.

distinguished [dɪs'tɪŋgwɪʃt] *adj* von hohem Rang; (*career*) hervorragend; (*in appearance*) distinguiert.

distinguishing [dɪs'tɪŋgwɪʃɪŋ] *adj* charakteristisch.

distort [dɪs'tɔ:t] *vt* verzerren; (*argument*) verdrehen.

distortion [dɪs'tɔ:ʃən] *n* (*see vb*) Verzerrung *f*; Verdrehung *f*.

distract [dɪs'trækt] *vt* ablenken.

distracted [dɪs'træktɪd] *adj* unaufmerksam; (*anxious*) besorgt, beunruhigt.

distraction [dɪs'trækʃən] *n* Unaufmerksamkeit *f*; (*confusion*) Verstörtheit *f*; (*sth which distracts*) Ablenkung *f*; (*amusement*) Zerstreuung *f*; **to drive sb to** ~ jdn zur Verzweiflung treiben.

distraught [dɪs'trɔ:t] *adj* verzweifelt.

distress [dɪs'trɛs] *n* Verzweiflung *f* ♦ *vt* Kummer machen +*dat*; **in** ~ (*ship*) in Seenot; (*person*) verzweifelt; ~**ed area** (*BRIT*) Notstandsgebiet *nt*.

distressing [dɪs'trɛsɪŋ] *adj* beunruhigend.

distress signal *n* Notsignal *nt*.

distribute [dɪs'trɪbju:t] *vt* verteilen; (*profits*) aufteilen.

distribution [dɪstrɪ'bju:ʃən] *n* Vertrieb *m*; (*of profits*) Aufteilung *f*.

distribution costs *npl* Vertriebskosten *pl*.

distributor [dɪs'trɪbjutə*] *n* (*COMM*) Vertreiber(in) *m(f)*; (*AUT, TECH*) Verteiler *m*.

district ['dɪstrɪkt] *n* Gebiet *nt*; (*of town*) Stadtteil *m*; (*ADMIN*) (Verwaltungs)bezirk *m*.

district attorney (*US*) *n* Bezirksstaatsanwalt *m*, Bezirksstaatsanwältin *f*.

District Council *heißt der in jedem der britischen* **districts** *(Bezirke) alle vier Jahre neu gewählte Bezirksrat, der für bestimmte Bereiche der Kommunalverwaltung (Gesundheitsschutz, Wohnungsbeschaffung, Baugenehmigungen, Müllabfuhr) zuständig ist. Die district councils werden durch Kommunalabgaben und durch einen Zuschuß von der Regierung finanziert. Ihre Ausgaben werden von einer unabhängigen Prüfungskommission kontrolliert, und bei zu hohen Ausgaben wird der Regierungszuschuß gekürzt.*

district nurse (*BRIT*) *n* Gemeindeschwester *f*.

distrust [dɪs'trʌst] *n* Mißtrauen *nt* ♦ *vt*

mißtrauen +dat.

distrustful [dɪs'trʌstful] adj: ~ **(of)** mißtrauisch (gegenüber +dat).

disturb [dɪs'təːb] vt stören; (upset) beunruhigen; (disorganize) durcheinanderbringen; **sorry to ~ you** entschuldigen Sie bitte die Störung.

disturbance [dɪs'təːbəns] n Störung f; (political etc) Unruhe f; (violent event) Unruhen pl; (by drunks etc) (Ruhe)störung f; **to cause a ~** Unruhe/eine Ruhestörung verursachen; **~ of the peace** Ruhestörung.

disturbed [dɪs'təːbd] adj beunruhigt; (childhood) unglücklich; **mentally/ emotionally ~** geistig/seelisch gestört.

disturbing [dɪs'təːbɪŋ] adj beunruhigend.

disuse [dɪs'juːs] n: **to fall into ~** nicht mehr benutzt werden.

disused [dɪs'juːzd] adj (building) leerstehend; (airfield) stillgelegt.

ditch [dɪtʃ] n Graben m ♦ vt (inf: partner) sitzenlassen; (: plan) sausenlassen; (: car etc) loswerden.

dither ['dɪðə'] (pej) vi zaudern.

ditto ['dɪtəu] adv dito, ebenfalls.

divan [dɪ'væn] n (also: ~ **bed**) Polsterbett nt.

dive [daɪv] n Sprung m; (underwater) Tauchen nt; (of submarine) Untertauchen nt; (pej: place) Spelunke f (inf) ♦ vi springen; (under water) tauchen; (bird) einen Sturzflug machen; (submarine) untertauchen; **to ~ into** (bag, drawer etc) greifen in +acc; (shop, car etc) sich stürzen in +acc.

diver ['daɪvə'] n Taucher(in) m(f); (deep-sea diver) Tiefseetaucher(in) m(f).

diverge [daɪ'vəːdʒ] vi auseinandergehen.

divergent [daɪ'vəːdʒənt] adj unterschiedlich; (views) voneinander abweichend; (interests) auseinandergehend.

diverse [daɪ'vəːs] adj verschiedenartig.

diversification [daɪvəːsɪfɪ'keɪʃən] n Diversifikation f.

diversify [daɪ'vəːsɪfaɪ] vi diversifizieren.

diversion [daɪ'vəːʃən] n (BRIT: AUT) Umleitung f; (distraction) Ablenkung f; (of funds) Umlenkung f.

diversionary [daɪ'vəːʃənrɪ] adj: ~ **tactics** Ablenkungsmanöver pl.

diversity [daɪ'vəːsɪtɪ] n Vielfalt f.

divert [daɪ'vəːt] vt (sb's attention) ablenken; (funds) umlenken; (re-route) umleiten.

divest [daɪ'vest] vt: **to ~ sb of office/his authority** jdn seines Amtes entkleiden/ seiner Macht entheben.

divide [dɪ'vaɪd] vt trennen; (MATH) dividieren, teilen; (share out) verteilen ♦ vi sich teilen; (road) sich gabeln; (people, groups) sich aufteilen ♦ n Kluft f; **to ~** (between or among) aufteilen (unter +dat); **40 ~d by 5** 40 geteilt or dividiert durch 5.

►**divide out** vt: **to ~ out (between or among)** aufteilen (unter +dat).

divided [dɪ'vaɪdɪd] adj geteilt; **to be ~ about or over sth** geteilter Meinung über etw acc sein.

divided highway (US) n ≈ Schnellstraße f.

dividend ['dɪvɪdend] n Dividende f; (fig): **to pay ~s** sich bezahlt machen.

dividend cover n (COMM) Dividendendeckung f.

dividers [dɪ'vaɪdəz] npl (MATH, TECH) Stechzirkel m; (between pages) Register nt.

divine [dɪ'vaɪn] adj göttlich ♦ vt (future) weissagen, prophezeien; (truth) erahnen; (water, metal) aufspüren.

diving ['daɪvɪŋ] n Tauchen nt; (SPORT) Kunstspringen nt.

diving board n Sprungbrett nt.

diving suit n Taucheranzug m.

divinity [dɪ'vɪnɪtɪ] n Göttlichkeit f; (god or goddess) Gottheit f; (SCOL) Theologie f.

divisible [dɪ'vɪzəbl] adj: ~ **(by)** teilbar (durch); **to be ~ into** teilbar sein in +acc.

division [dɪ'vɪʒən] n Teilung f, (MATH) Teilen nt, Division f; (sharing out) Verteilung f; (disagreement) Uneinigkeit f; (BRIT: POL) Abstimmung f durch Hammelsprung; (COMM) Abteilung f, (MIL) Division f; (esp FOOTBALL) Liga f; ~ **of labour** Arbeitsteilung f.

divisive [dɪ'vaɪsɪv] adj: **to be ~** (tactics) auf Spaltung abzielen; (system) zu Feindseligkeit führen.

divorce [dɪ'vɔːs] n Scheidung f ♦ vt sich scheiden lassen von; (dissociate) trennen.

divorced [dɪ'vɔːst] adj geschieden.

divorcee [dɪvɔː'siː] n Geschiedene(r) f(m).

divot ['dɪvət] n vom Golfschläger etc ausgehacktes Rasenstück.

divulge [daɪ'vʌldʒ] vt preisgeben.

DIY (BRIT) n abbr = **do-it-yourself**.

dizziness ['dɪzɪnɪs] n Schwindel m.

dizzy ['dɪzɪ] adj schwind(e)lig; (turn, spell) Schwindel-; (height) schwindelerregend; **I feel ~** mir ist or ich bin schwind(e)lig.

DJ n abbr = **disc jockey**.

d.j. n abbr = **dinner jacket**.

Djakarta [dʒə'kɑːtə] n Jakarta nt.

DJIA (US) n abbr (= Dow-Jones Industrial Average) Dow-Jones-Index m.

dl abbr (= decilitre) dl.

DLit(t) n abbr (= Doctor of Literature, Doctor of Letters) akademischer Grad in Literaturwissenschaft.

DLO n abbr = **dead letter office**.

dm abbr (= decimetre) dm.

DMus n abbr (= Doctor of Music) Doktor der Musikwissenschaft.

DMZ n abbr = **demilitarized zone**.

DNA n abbr (= deoxyribonucleic acid) DNS f.

== KEYWORD

do [du:] (*pt* **did,** *pp* **done**) *aux vb* **1** (*in negative constructions*): **I don't understand** ich verstehe nicht

2 (*to form questions*): **didn't you know?** wußtest du das nicht?; **what ~ you think? was meinst du?**

3 (*for emphasis*): **she does seem rather upset** sie scheint wirklich recht aufgeregt zu sein; **~ sit down/help yourself** bitte nehmen Sie Platz/bedienen Sie sich; **oh ~ shut up!** halte endlich den Mund!

4 (*to avoid repeating vb*): **she swims better than I ~** sie schwimmt besser als ich; **she lives in Glasgow - so ~ I** sie wohnt in Glasgow - ich auch; **who made this mess? - I did** wer hat dieses Durcheinander gemacht? - ich

5 (*in question tags*): **you like him, don't you?** du magst ihn, nicht wahr?; **I don't know him, ~ I?** ich kenne ihn nicht, oder?

♦ *vt* **1** (*carry out, perform*) tun, machen; **what are you ~ing tonight?** was machen Sie heute abend?; **what ~ you ~ (for a living)?** was machen Sie beruflich?; **to ~ one's teeth/nails** sich *dat* die Zähne putzen/die Nägel schneiden

2 (*AUT etc*) fahren; **the car was ~ing 100** das Auto fuhr 100

♦ *vi* **1** (*act, behave*): **~ as I ~** mach es wie ich

2 (*get on, fare*): **he's ~ing well/badly at school** er ist gut/schlecht in der Schule; **the company is ~ing well** der Firma geht es gut; **how ~ you ~?** guten Tag/Morgen/Abend!

3 (*suit, be sufficient*) reichen; **will that ~?** reicht das?; **will this dress ~ for the party?** ist dieses Kleid gut genug für die Party?; **will £10 ~?** reichen £10?; **that'll ~** das reicht; (*in annoyance*) jetzt reicht's aber!; **to make ~ with** auskommen mit

♦ *n* (*inf: party etc*) Party *f*, Fete *f*; **it was quite a ~** es war ganz schön was los

▶**do away with** *vt fus* (*get rid of*) abschaffen.
▶**do for** (*inf*) *vt fus*: **to be done for** erledigt sein.
▶**do in** (*inf*) *vt* (*kill*) umbringen.
▶**do out of** (*inf*) *vt* (*deprive*) bringen um.
▶**do up** *vt fus* (*laces, dress, buttons*) zumachen; (*renovate: room, house*) renovieren.
▶**do with** *vt fus* **1** (*need*) brauchen; **I could ~ with some help/a drink** ich könnte Hilfe/einen Drink gebrauchen.
2 **it has to ~ with money** es hat mit Geld zu tun.
▶**do without** *vt fus* auskommen ohne.

do. *abbr* = **ditto.**
DOA *abbr* (= *dead on arrival*) bei Einlieferung ins Krankenhaus bereits tot.
d.o.b. *abbr* = **date of birth.**

doc [dɔk] (*inf*) *n* Doktor *m*.
docile ['dəusaɪl] *adj* sanft(mütig).
dock [dɔk] *n* Dock *nt*; (*LAW*) Anklagebank *f*; (*BOT*) Ampfer *m* ♦ *vi* anlegen; (*SPACE*) docken ♦ *vt*: **they ~ed a third of his wages** sie kürzten seinen Lohn um ein Drittel; **docks** *npl* (*NAUT*) Hafen *m*.
dock dues [-dju:z] *npl* Hafengebühr *f*.
docker ['dɔkə*] *n* Hafenarbeiter *m*, Docker *m*.
docket ['dɔkɪt] *n* Inhaltserklärung *f*; (*on parcel etc*) Warenbegleitschein *m*, Laufzettel *m*.
dockyard ['dɔkjɑ:d] *n* Werft *f*.
doctor ['dɔktə*] *n* Arzt *m*, Ärztin *f*; (*PhD etc*) Doktor *m* ♦ *vt*: **to ~ a drink** *etc* einem Getränk *etc* etwas beimischen; **~'s office** (*US*) Sprechzimmer *nt*.
doctorate ['dɔktərɪt] *n* Doktorwürde *f*.

> **Doctorate** ist der höchste akademische Grad auf jedem Wissensgebiet und wird nach erfolgreicher Vorlage einer Doktorarbeit verliehen. Die Studienzeit (meist mindestens 3 Jahre) und Länge der Doktorarbeit ist je nach Hochschule verschieden. Am häufigsten wird der Titel PhD (Doctor of Philosophy) auf dem Gebiet der Geisteswissenschaften, Naturwissenschaften und des Ingenieurwesens verliehen, obwohl es auch andere Doktortitel (in Musik, Jura usw.) gibt. Siehe auch **bachelor's degree, master's degree**.

Doctor of Philosophy *n* Doktor *m* der Philosophie.
doctrine ['dɔktrɪn] *n* Doktrin *f*.
docudrama ['dɔkjudrɑːmə] *n* Dokumentarspiel *nt*.
document ['dɔkjumənt] *n* Dokument *nt* ♦ *vt* dokumentieren.
documentary [dɔkju'mɛntərɪ] *adj* dokumentarisch ♦ *n* Dokumentarfilm *m*.
documentation [dɔkjumən'teɪʃən] *n* Dokumentation *f*.
DOD (*US*) *n abbr* (= *Department of Defense*) Verteidigungsministerium *nt*.
doddering ['dɔdərɪŋ] *adj* (*shaky, unsteady*) zittrig.
doddery ['dɔdərɪ] *adj* = **doddering.**
doddle ['dɔdl] (*inf*) *n*: **a ~** ein Kinderspiel *nt*.
Dodecanese (Islands) [dəudɪkə'niːz ('aɪləndz)] *n(pl)*: **the ~** der Dodekanes.
dodge [dɔdʒ] *n* Trick *m* ♦ *vt* ausweichen +*dat*; (*tax*) umgehen ♦ *vi* ausweichen; **to ~ out of the way** zur Seite springen; **to ~ through the traffic** sich durch den Verkehr schlängeln.
dodgems ['dɔdʒəmz] (*BRIT*) *npl* Autoskooter *pl*.
dodgy ['dɔdʒɪ] (*inf*) *adj* (*person*) zweifelhaft; (*plan etc*) gewagt.
DOE *n abbr* (*BRIT*: = *Department of the Environment*) Umweltministerium; (*US*: = *Department of Energy*) Energie-

ministerium.

doe [dəu] n Reh nt, Ricke f; (rabbit) (Kaninchen)weibchen nt.

does [dʌz] vb see **do**.

doesn't ['dʌznt] = **does not**.

dog [dɒg] n Hund m ♦ vt (subj: person) auf den Fersen bleiben +dat; (: bad luck, memory etc) verfolgen; **to go to the ~s** (inf) vor die Hunde gehen.

dog biscuits npl Hundekuchen pl.

dog collar n Hundehalsband nt; (REL) Kragen m des Geistlichen.

dog-eared ['dɒgɪəd] adj mit Eselsohren.

dog food n Hundefutter nt.

dogged ['dɒgɪd] adj beharrlich.

doggy ['dɒgɪ] n Hündchen nt.

doggy bag ['dɒgɪ-] n Tüte für Essensreste, die man nach Hause mitnehmen möchte.

dogma ['dɒgmə] n Dogma nt.

dogmatic [dɒg'mætɪk] adj dogmatisch.

do-gooder [du:'gudə*] (pej) n Weltverbesserer(in) m(f).

dogsbody ['dɒgzbɒdɪ] (BRIT: inf) n Mädchen nt für alles.

doily ['dɔɪlɪ] n Deckchen nt.

doing ['du:ɪŋ] n: **this is your ~** das ist dein Werk.

doings ['du:ɪŋz] npl Treiben nt.

do-it-yourself ['du:ɪtjɔ:'sɛlf] n Heimwerken nt, Do-it-yourself nt.

doldrums ['dɒldrəmz] npl: **to be in the ~** (person) niedergeschlagen sein; (business) in einer Flaute stecken.

dole [dəul] (BRIT) n Arbeitslosenunter-stützung f; **on the ~** arbeitslos.

▶**dole out** vt austeilen, verteilen.

doleful ['dəulful] adj traurig.

doll [dɒl] n (toy, also US: inf: woman) Puppe f.

dollar ['dɒlə*] (US etc) n Dollar m.

dollar area n Dollarblock m.

dolled up (inf) adj aufgedonnert.

dollop ['dɒləp] (inf) n Schlag m.

dolly ['dɒlɪ] (inf) n (doll, woman) Puppe f.

Dolomites ['dɒləmaɪts] npl: **the ~** die Dolomiten pl.

dolphin ['dɒlfɪn] n Delphin m.

domain [də'meɪn] n Bereich m; (empire) Reich nt.

dome [dəum] n Kuppel f.

domestic [də'mɛstɪk] adj (trade) Innen-; (situation) innenpolitisch; (news) Inland-, aus dem Inland; (tasks, appliances) Haushalts-; (animal) Haus-; (duty, happiness) häuslich.

domesticated [də'mɛstɪkeɪtɪd] adj (animal) zahm; (person) häuslich.

domesticity [dəumɛs'tɪsɪtɪ] n häusliches Leben nt.

domestic servant n Hausangestellte(r) f(m).

domicile ['dɒmɪsaɪl] n Wohnsitz m.

dominant ['dɒmɪnənt] adj dominierend; (share) größte(r, s).

dominate ['dɒmɪneɪt] vt dominieren, beherrschen.

domination [dɒmɪ'neɪʃən] n (Vor)herrschaft f.

domineering [dɒmɪ'nɪərɪŋ] adj herrsch-süchtig.

Dominican Republic [də'mɪnɪkən-] n: **the ~** die Dominikanische Republik.

dominion [də'mɪnɪən] n (territory) Herrschaftsgebiet nt; (authority): **to have ~ over** Macht haben über +acc.

domino ['dɒmɪnəu] (pl ~es) n (block) Domino(stein) m.

domino effect n Dominoeffekt m.

dominoes ['dɒmɪnəuz] n (game) Domino(spiel) nt.

don [dɒn] n (BRIT) (Universitäts)dozent m (besonders in Oxford und Cambridge) ♦ vt anziehen.

donate [də'neɪt] vt: **to ~ (to)** (organization, cause) spenden (für).

donation [də'neɪʃən] n (act of donating) Spenden nt; (contribution) Spende f.

done [dʌn] pp of **do**.

donkey ['dɒŋkɪ] n Esel m.

donkey-work ['dɒŋkɪwə:k] (BRIT: inf) n Dreckarbeit f.

donor ['dəunə*] n Spender(in) m(f).

donor card n Organspenderausweis m.

don't [dəunt] = **do not**.

donut ['dəunʌt] (US) n = **doughnut**.

doodle ['du:dl] vi Männchen malen ♦ n Kritzelei f.

doom [du:m] n Unheil nt ♦ vt: **to be ~ed to failure** zum Scheitern verurteilt sein.

doomsday ['du:mzdeɪ] n der Jüngste Tag.

door [dɔ:*] n Tür f; **to go from ~ to ~** von Tür zu Tür gehen.

door bell n Türklingel f.

door handle n Türklinke f; (of car) Türgriff m.

doorman ['dɔ:mən] (irreg: like **man**) n Portier m.

doormat ['dɔ:mæt] n Fußmatte f; (fig) Fußabtreter m.

doorpost ['dɔ:pəust] n Türpfosten m.

doorstep ['dɔ:stɛp] n Eingangsstufe f, Türstufe f; **on the ~** vor der Haustür.

door-to-door ['dɔ:tə'dɔ:*] adj (selling) von Haus zu Haus; **~ salesman** Vertreter m.

doorway ['dɔ:weɪ] n Eingang m.

dope [dəup] n (inf) Stoff m, Drogen pl; (: person) Esel m, Trottel m; (: information) Informationen pl ♦ vt dopen.

dopey ['dəupɪ] (inf) adj (groggy) benebelt; (stupid) blöd, bekloppt.

dormant ['dɔ:mənt] adj (plant) ruhend; (volcano) untätig; (idea, report etc): **to lie ~** schlummern.

dormer ['dɔ:mə*] n (also: ~ **window**) Mansardenfenster nt.

dormice ['dɔ:maɪs] npl of **dormouse**.

dormitory ['dɔ:mɪtrɪ] n Schlafsaal m; (US:

building) Wohnheim *nt*.

dormouse ['dɔːmaus] (*pl* **dormice**) *n* Haselmaus *f*.

Dors (*BRIT*) *abbr* (*POST*: = *Dorset*).

DOS [dɔs] *n abbr* (*COMPUT*: = *disk operating system*) DOS.

dosage ['dəusɪdʒ] *n* Dosis *f*; (*on label*) Dosierung *f*.

dose [dəus] *n* Dosis *f*; (*BRIT*: *bout*) Ration *f* ♦ *vt*: to ~ o.s. Medikamente nehmen; a ~ of flu eine Grippe.

dosser ['dɔsə•] (*BRIT*: *inf*) *n* Penner(in) *m(f)*.

dosshouse ['dɔshaus] (*BRIT*: *inf*) *n* Obdachlosenheim *nt*.

dossier ['dɔsɪeɪ] *n* Dossier *nt*.

DOT (*US*) *n abbr* (= *Department of Transportation*) ≈ Verkehrsministerium *nt*.

dot [dɔt] *n* Punkt *m* ♦ *vt*: ~ted with übersät mit; on the ~ (auf die Minute) pünktlich.

dote [dəut]: ~ on *vt fus* abgöttisch lieben.

dot-matrix printer [dɔt'meɪtrɪks-] *n* Nadeldrucker *m*.

dotted line ['dɔtɪd-] *n* punktierte Linie *f*; to sign on the ~ (*fig*) seine formelle Zustimmung geben.

dotty ['dɔtɪ] (*inf*) *adj* schrullig.

double ['dʌbl] *adj* doppelt; (*chin*) Doppel- ♦ *adv* (*cost*) doppelt soviel ♦ *n* Doppelgänger(in) *m(f)* ♦ *vt* verdoppeln; (*paper, blanket*) (einmal) falten ♦ *vi* sich verdoppeln; ~ five two six (5526) (*BRIT*: *TEL*) fünfundfünfzig sechsundzwanzig; it's spelt with a ~ "l" es wird mit zwei l geschrieben; an egg with a ~ yolk ein Ei mit zwei Dottern; on the ~, (*BRIT*) at the ~ (*quickly*) schnell; (*immediately*) unverzüglich; to ~ as ... (*person*) auch als ... fungieren; (*thing*) auch als ... dienen.

▶**double back** *vi* kehrtmachen, zurückgehen/-fahren.

▶**double up** *vi* sich krümmen; (*share room*) sich ein Zimmer teilen.

double bass *n* Kontrabaß *m*.

double bed *n* Doppelbett *nt*.

double bend (*BRIT*) *n* S-Kurve *f*.

double-blind *adj*: ~ experiment Doppelblindversuch *m*.

double-breasted ['dʌbl'brestɪd] *adj* (*jacket, coat*) zweireihig.

double-check ['dʌbl'tʃek] *vt* noch einmal (über)prüfen ♦ *vi* es noch einmal (über)prüfen.

double-clutch ['dʌbl'klʌtʃ] (*US*) *vi* mit Zwischengas schalten.

double cream (*BRIT*) *n* Sahne *f* mit hohem Fettgehalt, ≈ Schlagsahne *f*.

double-cross [dʌbl'krɔs] *vt* ein Doppelspiel treiben mit.

double-decker [dʌbl'dekə•] *n* Doppeldecker *m*.

double-declutch ['dʌbldiː'klʌtʃ] (*BRIT*) *vi* mit Zwischengas schalten.

double exposure *n* doppelt belichtetes Foto *nt*.

double glazing [-'gleɪzɪŋ] (*BRIT*) *n* Doppelverglasung *f*.

double-page spread ['dʌblpeɪdʒ-] *n* Doppelseite *f*.

double-parking [dʌbl'pɑːkɪŋ] *n* Parken *nt* in der zweiten Reihe.

double room *n* Doppelzimmer *nt*.

doubles ['dʌblz] *n* (*TENNIS*) Doppel *nt*.

double time *n* doppelter Lohn *m*.

double whammy [-'wæmɪ] (*inf*) *n* Doppelschlag *m*.

doubly ['dʌblɪ] *adv* (ganz) besonders.

doubt [daut] *n* Zweifel *m* ♦ *vt* bezweifeln; without (a) ~ ohne Zweifel; to ~ sb jdm nicht glauben; I ~ it (very much) das bezweifle ich (sehr), das möchte ich (stark) bezweifeln; to ~ if *or* whether ... bezweifeln, daß ...; I don't ~ that ... ich bezweifle nicht, daß ...

doubtful ['dautful] *adj* zweifelhaft; to be ~ about sth an etw *dat* zweifeln; to be ~ about doing sth Bedenken haben, ob man etw tun soll; I'm a bit ~ ich bin nicht ganz sicher.

doubtless ['dautlɪs] *adv* ohne Zweifel, sicherlich.

dough [dəu] *n* Teig *m*; (*inf*: *money*) Kohle *f*, Knete *f*.

doughnut, (*US*) **donut** ['dəunʌt] *n* ≈ Berliner (Pfannkuchen) *m*.

dour [duə•] *adj* mürrisch, verdrießlich.

douse [dauz] *vt* Wasser schütten über +*acc*; (*extinguish*) löschen; to ~ with übergießen mit.

dove [dʌv] *n* Taube *f*.

Dover ['dəuvə•] *n* Dover *nt*.

dovetail ['dʌvteɪl] *vi* übereinstimmen ♦ *n* (*also*: ~ joint) Schwalbenschwanzverbindung *f*.

dowager ['dauədʒə•] *n* (adlige) Witwe *f*.

dowdy ['daudɪ] *adj* ohne jeden Schick; (*clothes*) unmodern.

Dow-Jones average ['dau'dʒəunz-] (*US*) *n* Dow-Jones-Index *m*.

down [daun] *n* Daunen *pl* ♦ *adv* hinunter, herunter; (*on the ground*) unten ♦ *prep* hinunter, herunter; (*movement along*) entlang ♦ *vt* (*inf*: *drink*) runterkippen; ~ there/here da/hier unten; the price of meat is ~ die Fleischpreise sind gefallen; I've got it ~ in my diary ich habe es in meinem Kalender notiert; to pay £2 ~ £2 anzahlen; England is two goals ~ England liegt mit zwei Toren zurück; to ~ tools (*BRIT*) die Arbeit niederlegen; ~ with ...! nieder mit ...!

down-and-out ['daunəndaut] *n* Penner(in) *m(f)* (*inf*).

down-at-heel ['daunət'hiːl] *adj* (*appearance, person*) schäbig, heruntergekommen; (*shoes*) abgetreten.

downbeat ['daunbi:t] n (MUS) erster betonter Taktteil m ♦ adj zurückhaltend.

downcast ['daunkɑ:st] adj niedergeschlagen.

downer ['daunə*] (inf) n (drug) Beruhigungsmittel nt; **to be on a ~** deprimiert sein.

downfall ['daunfɔ:l] n Ruin m; (of dictator etc) Sturz m, Fall m.

downgrade ['daungreɪd] vt herunterstufen.

downhearted ['daun'hɑ:tɪd] adj niedergeschlagen, entmutigt.

downhill ['daun'hɪl] adv bergab ♦ n (SKI: also: ~ race) Abfahrtslauf m; **to go ~** (road) bergab führen; (person) hinuntergehen, heruntergehen; (car) hinunterfahren, herunterfahren; (fig) auf dem absteigenden Ast sein.

> **Downing Street** ist die Straße in London, die von Whitehall zum St James Park führt und in der sich der offizielle Wohnsitz des Premierministers (Nr. 10) und des Finanzministers (Nr. 11) befindet. Im weiteren Sinne bezieht sich der Begriff Downing Street auf die britische Regierung.

download ['daunləud] vt laden.

down-market ['daun'mɑ:kɪt] adj (product) für den Massenmarkt.

down payment n Anzahlung f.

downplay ['daunpleɪ] (US) vt herunterspielen.

downpour ['daunpɔ:*] n Wolkenbruch m.

downright ['daunraɪt] adj (liar etc) ausgesprochen; (refusal, lie) glatt.

Downs [daunz] (BRIT) npl: **the ~** die Downs pl, Hügellandschaft in Südengland.

downsize ['daun'saɪz] vi (ECON: company) sich verkleinern.

Down's Syndrome n (MED) Down-Syndrom nt.

downstairs ['daun'stɛəz] adv unten; (downwards) nach unten.

downstream ['daunstri:m] adv flußabwärts, stromabwärts.

downtime ['dauntaɪm] n Ausfallzeit f.

down-to-earth ['dauntu'ə:θ] adj (person) nüchtern; (solution) praktisch.

downtown ['daun'taun] (esp US) adv im Zentrum, in der (Innen)stadt; (go) ins Zentrum, in die (Innen)stadt ♦ adj: ~ **Chicago** das Zentrum von Chicago.

downtrodden ['dauntrɔdn] adj unterdrückt, geknechtet.

down under adv (be) in Australien/ Neuseeland; (go) nach Australien/ Neuseeland.

downward ['daunwəd] adj, adv nach unten; **a ~ trend** ein Abwärtstrend m.

downwards ['daunwədz] adv = **downward**.

dowry ['daurɪ] n Mitgift f.

doz. abbr = **dozen**.

doze [dəuz] vi ein Nickerchen machen.

▶**doze off** vi einschlafen, einnicken.

dozen ['dʌzn] n Dutzend nt; **a ~ books** ein Dutzend Bücher; **80p a ~** 80 Pence das Dutzend; **~s of** Dutzende von.

DPh n abbr (= Doctor of Philosophy) ≈ Dr. phil.

DPhil n abbr (= Doctor of Philosophy) ≈ Dr. phil.

DPP (BRIT) n abbr = **Director of Public Prosecutions**.

DPT n abbr (= diphtheria, pertussis, tetanus) Diphtherie, Keuchhusten und Tetanus.

DPW (US) n abbr (= Department of Public Works) Ministerium für öffentliche Bauprojekte.

Dr abbr = **doctor**; (in street names: = Drive) ≈ Str.

dr abbr (COMM) = **debtor**.

drab [dræb] adj trist.

draft [drɑ:ft] n Entwurf m; (bank draft) Tratte f; (US: call-up) Einberufung f ♦ vt entwerfen; see also **draught**.

draftsman etc ['drɑ:ftsmən] (US) n = **draughtsman** etc.

drag [dræg] vt schleifen, schleppen; (river) absuchen ♦ vi sich hinziehen ♦ n (AVIAT) Luftwiderstand m; (NAUT) Wasserwiderstand m; (inf): **to be a ~** (boring) langweilig sein; (a nuisance) lästig sein; (women's clothing): **in ~** in Frauenkleidung.

▶**drag away** vt: **to ~ away (from)** wegschleppen or wegziehen (von).

▶**drag on** vi sich hinziehen.

dragnet ['drægnɛt] n Schleppnetz nt; (fig) großangelegte Polizeiaktion f.

dragon ['drægn] n Drache m.

dragonfly ['drægənflaɪ] n Libelle f.

dragoon [drə'gu:n] n Dragoner m ♦ vt: **to ~ sb into doing sth** (BRIT) jdn zwingen, etw zu tun.

drain [dreɪn] n Belastung f; (in street) Gully m ♦ vt entwässern; (pond) trockenlegen; (vegetables) abgießen; (glass, cup) leeren ♦ vi ablaufen; **to feel ~ed (of energy/emotion)** sich ausgelaugt fühlen.

drainage ['dreɪnɪdʒ] n Entwässerungssystem nt; (process) Entwässerung f.

draining board ['dreɪnɪŋ-], (US) **drainboard** ['dreɪnbɔ:d] n Ablaufbrett nt.

drainpipe ['dreɪnpaɪp] n Abflußrohr nt.

drake [dreɪk] n Erpel m, Enterich m.

dram [dræm] (SCOT) n (drink) Schluck m.

drama ['drɑ:mə] n Drama nt.

dramatic [drə'mætɪk] adj dramatisch; (theatrical) theatralisch.

dramatically [drə'mætɪklɪ] adv dramatisch; (say, announce, pause) theatralisch.

dramatist ['dræmətɪst] n Dramatiker(in) m(f).

dramatize ['dræmətaɪz] vt dramatisieren; (for TV/cinema) für das Fernsehen/den Film bearbeiten.

drank [dræŋk] pt of **drink**.

drape [dreɪp] vt drapieren.

drapes [dreɪps] (*US*) *npl* Vorhänge *pl*.
drastic ['dræstɪk] *adj* drastisch.
drastically ['dræstɪklɪ] *adv* drastisch.
draught, (*US*) **draft** [drɑːft] *n* (Luft)zug *m*; (*NAUT*) Tiefgang *m*; (*of chimney*) Zug *m*; **on ~ vom Faß.**
draught beer *n* Bier *nt* vom Faß.
draughtboard ['drɑːftbɔːd] (*BRIT*) *n* Damebrett *nt*.
draughts [drɑːfts] (*BRIT*) *n* Damespiel *nt*.
draughtsman, (*US*) **draftsman** ['drɑːftsmən] (*irreg: like* **man**) *n* Zeichner(in) *m(f)*; (*as job*) technischer Zeichner *m*, technische Zeichnerin *f*.
draughtsmanship, (*US*) **draftsmanship** ['drɑːftsmənʃɪp] *n* zeichnerisches Können *nt*; (*art*) Zeichenkunst *f*.
draw [drɔː] (*pt* **drew,** *pp* **drawn**) *vt* zeichnen; (*cart, gun, tooth, conclusion*) ziehen; (*curtain: open*) aufziehen; (: *close*) zuziehen; (*admiration, attention*) erregen; (*money*) abheben; (*wages*) bekommen ♦ *vi* (*SPORT*) unentschieden spielen ♦ *n* (*SPORT*) Unentschieden *nt*; (*lottery*) Lotterie *f*; (: *picking of ticket*) Ziehung *f*; **to ~ a comparison/distinction (between)** einen Vergleich ziehen/Unterschied machen (zwischen +*dat*); **to ~ near** näherkommen; (*event*) nahen; **to ~ to a close** zu Ende gehen.
▶**draw back** *vi*: **to ~ back (from)** zurückweichen (von).
▶**draw in** *vi* (*BRIT: car*) anhalten; (: *train*) einfahren; (*nights*) länger werden.
▶**draw on** *vt* (*resources*) zurückgreifen auf +*acc*; (*imagination*) zu Hilfe nehmen; (*person*) einsetzen.
▶**draw out** *vi* länger werden ♦ *vt* (*money*) abheben.
▶**draw up** *vi* (an)halten ♦ *vt* (*chair etc*) heranziehen; (*document*) aufsetzen.
drawback ['drɔːbæk] *n* Nachteil *m*.
drawbridge ['drɔːbrɪdʒ] *n* Zugbrücke *f*.
drawee [drɔː'iː] *n* Bezogene(r) *f(m)*.
drawer [drɔː*] *n* Schublade *f*.
drawing ['drɔːɪŋ] *n* Zeichnung *f*; (*skill, discipline*) Zeichnen *nt*.
drawing board *n* Reißbrett *nt*; **back to the ~** (*fig*) das muß noch einmal neu überdacht werden.
drawing pin (*BRIT*) *n* Reißzwecke *f*.
drawing room *n* Salon *m*.
drawl [drɔːl] *n* schleppende Sprechweise *f* ♦ *vi* schleppend sprechen.
drawn [drɔːn] *pp of* **draw** ♦ *adj* abgespannt.
drawstring ['drɔːstrɪŋ] *n* Kordel *f* zum Zuziehen.
dread [drɛd] *n* Angst *f*, Furcht *f* ♦ *vt* große Angst haben vor +*dat*.
dreadful ['drɛdful] *adj* schrecklich, furchtbar; **I feel ~!** (*ill*) ich fühle mich schrecklich; (*ashamed*) es ist mir schrecklich peinlich.

dream [driːm] (*pt, pp* **dreamed** *or* **dreamt**) *n* Traum *m* ♦ *vt, vi* träumen; **to have a ~ about sb/sth** von jdm/etw träumen; **sweet ~s!** träume süß!
▶**dream up** *vt* sich *dat* einfallen lassen, sich *dat* ausdenken.
dreamer ['driːmə*] *n* Träumer(in) *m(f)*.
dreamt [drɛmt] *pt, pp of* **dream**.
dream world *n* Traumwelt *f*.
dreamy ['driːmɪ] *adj* verträumt; (*music*) zum Träumen.
dreary ['drɪərɪ] *adj* langweilig; (*weather*) trüb.
dredge [drɛdʒ] *vt* ausbaggern.
▶**dredge up** *vt* ausbaggern; (*fig: unpleasant facts*) ausgraben.
dredger ['drɛdʒə*] *n* (*ship*) Schwimmbagger *m*; (*machine*) Bagger *m*; (*BRIT: also:* **sugar ~**) Zuckerstreuer *m*.
dregs [drɛgz] *npl* Bodensatz *m*; (*of humanity*) Abschaum *m*.
drench [drɛntʃ] *vt* durchnässen; **~ed to the skin** naß bis auf die Haut.
dress [drɛs] *n* Kleid *nt*; (*no pl: clothing*) Kleidung *f* ♦ *vt* anziehen; (*wound*) verbinden ♦ *vi* sich anziehen; **she ~es very well** sie kleidet sich sehr gut; **to ~ a shop window** ein Schaufenster dekorieren; **to get ~ed** sich anziehen.
▶**dress up** *vi* sich feinmachen; (*in fancy dress*) sich verkleiden.
dress circle (*BRIT*) *n* (*THEAT*) erster Rang *m*.
dress designer *n* Modezeichner(in) *m(f)*.
dresser ['drɛsə*] *n* (*BRIT*) Anrichte *f*; (*US*) Kommode *f*; (*also:* **window ~**) Dekorateur(in) *m(f)*.
dressing ['drɛsɪŋ] *n* Verband *m*; (*CULIN*) (Salat)soße *f*.
dressing gown (*BRIT*) *n* Morgenrock *m*.
dressing room *n* Umkleidekabine *f*; (*THEAT*) (Künstler)garderobe *f*.
dressing table *n* Frisierkommode *f*.
dressmaker ['drɛsmeɪkə*] *n* (Damen)schneider(in) *m(f)*.
dressmaking ['drɛsmeɪkɪŋ] *n* Schneidern *nt*.
dress rehearsal *n* Generalprobe *f*.
dressy ['drɛsɪ] (*inf*) *adj* elegant.
drew [druː] *pt of* **draw**.
dribble ['drɪbl] *vi* tropfen; (*baby*) sabbern; (*FOOTBALL*) dribbeln ♦ *vt* (*ball*) dribbeln mit.
dried [draɪd] *adj* (*fruit*) getrocknet, Dörr-; **~ egg** Trockenei *nt*, Eipulver *nt*; **~ milk** Trockenmilch *f*, Milchpulver *nt*.
drier ['draɪə*] *n* = **dryer**.
drift [drɪft] *n* Strömung *f*; (*of snow*) Schneewehe *f*; (*of questions*) Richtung *f* ♦ *vi* treiben; (*sand*) wehen; **to let things ~** die Dinge treiben lassen; **to ~ apart** sich auseinanderleben; **I get** *or* **catch your ~** ich verstehe, worauf Sie hinauswollen.
drifter ['drɪftə*] *n*: **to be a ~** sich treiben lassen.
driftwood ['drɪftwud] *n* Treibholz *nt*.

drill [drɪl] n Bohrer m; (machine)
Bohrmaschine f; (MIL) Drill m ♦ vt bohren;
(troops) drillen ♦ vi: **to ~ (for)** bohren (nach);
to ~ pupils in grammar mit den Schülern
Grammatik pauken.
drilling ['drɪlɪŋ] n Bohrung f.
drilling rig n Bohrturm m; (at sea) Bohrinsel
f.
drily ['draɪlɪ] adv = **dryly.**
drink [drɪŋk] (pt **drank**, pp **drunk**) n Getränk nt;
(alcoholic) Glas nt, Drink m; (sip) Schluck m
♦ vt, vi trinken; **to have a ~** etwas trinken; **a**
~ of water etwas Wasser; **we had ~s before**
lunch vor dem Mittagessen gab es einen
Drink; **would you like something to ~?**
möchten Sie etwas trinken?
►**drink in** vt (fresh air) einatmen, einsaugen;
(story, sight) (begierig) in sich aufnehmen.
drinkable ['drɪŋkəbl] adj trinkbar.
drink-driving ['drɪŋk'draɪvɪŋ] n Trunkenheit f
am Steuer.
drinker ['drɪŋkə*] n Trinker(in) m(f).
drinking ['drɪŋkɪŋ] n Trinken nt.
drinking fountain n Trinkwasserbrunnen m.
drinking water n Trinkwasser nt.
drip [drɪp] n Tropfen nt; (one drip) Tropfen m;
(MED) Tropf m ♦ vi tropfen; (wall) triefnaß
sein.
drip-dry ['drɪp'draɪ] adj bügelfrei.
drip-feed ['drɪpfiːd] vt künstlich ernähren ♦ n:
to be on a ~ künstlich ernährt werden.
dripping ['drɪpɪŋ] n Bratenfett nt ♦ adj
triefend; **I'm ~** ich bin klatschnaß (inf);
~ wet triefnaß.
drive [draɪv] (pt **drove**, pp **driven**) n Fahrt f;
(also: **~way**) Einfahrt f; (: longer) Auffahrt f;
(energy) Schwung m, Elan m; (campaign)
Aktion f; (SPORT) Treibschlag m; (COMPUT:
also: **disk ~**) Laufwerk nt ♦ vt fahren; (TECH)
antreiben ♦ vi fahren; **to go for a ~** ein
bißchen (raus)fahren; **it's 3 hours' ~ from**
London es ist drei Stunden Fahrt von
London (entfernt); **left-/right-hand ~** Links-
/Rechtssteuerung f; **front-/rear-wheel ~**
Vorderrad-/Hinterradantrieb m; **he ~s a**
taxi er ist Taxifahrer; **to ~ sth into sth** (nail,
stake etc) etw in etw schlagen acc; (animal)
treiben; (ball) weit schlagen; (incite,
encourage: also: **~ on**) antreiben; **to ~ sb**
home/to the airport jdn nach Hause/zum
Flughafen fahren; **to ~ sb mad** jdn
verrückt machen; **to ~ sb to (do) sth** jdn
dazu treiben, etw zu tun; **to ~ at 50 km an**
hour mit (einer Geschwindigkeit von) 50
Stundenkilometern fahren; **what are you**
driving at? worauf wollen Sie hinaus?
►**drive off** vt vertreiben.
►**drive out** vt (evil spirit) austreiben; (person)
verdrängen.
drive-by shooting ['draɪvbaɪ-] n
Schußwaffenangriff aus einem
vorbeifahrenden Wagen.

drive-in ['draɪvɪn] (esp US) adj, n: **~ (cinema)**
Autokino nt; **~ (restaurant)** Autorestaurant
nt.
drive-in window (US) n Autoschalter m.
drivel ['drɪvl] (inf) n Blödsinn m.
driven ['drɪvn] pp of **drive.**
driver ['draɪvə*] n Fahrer(in) m(f); (RAIL)
Führer(in) m(f).
driver's license ['draɪvəz-] (US) n
Führerschein m.
driveway ['draɪvweɪ] n Einfahrt f; (longer)
Auffahrt f.
driving ['draɪvɪŋ] n Fahren nt ♦ adj: **~ rain**
strömender Regen m; **~ snow**
Schneetreiben nt.
driving belt n Treibriemen m.
driving force n treibende Kraft f.
driving instructor n Fahrlehrer(in) m(f).
driving lesson n Fahrstunde f.
driving licence (BRIT) n Führerschein m.
driving mirror n Rückspiegel m.
driving school n Fahrschule f.
driving test n Fahrprüfung f.
drizzle ['drɪzl] n Nieselregen m ♦ vi nieseln.
droll [drəul] adj drollig.
dromedary ['drɔmədərɪ] n Dromedar nt.
drone [drəun] n Brummen nt; (male bee)
Drohne f ♦ vi brummen; (bee) summen; (also:
~ on) eintönig sprechen.
drool [druːl] vi sabbern; **to ~ over sth/sb** etw/
jdn sehnsüchtig anstarren.
droop [druːp] vi (flower) den Kopf hängen
lassen; **his shoulders/head ~ed** er ließ die
Schultern/den Kopf herabhängen.
drop [drɔp] n Tropfen m; (lessening) Rückgang
m; (distance) Höhenunterschied m; (in salary)
Verschlechterung f; (also: **parachute ~**)
(Ab)sprung m ♦ vt fallen lassen; (voice, eyes,
price) senken; (set down from car) absetzen;
(omit) weglassen ♦ vi (herunter)fallen;
(wind) sich legen; **drops** npl Tropfen pl; **a 300**
ft ~ ein Höhenunterschied von 300 Fuß; **a**
~ of 10% ein Rückgang um 10%; **cough ~s**
Hustentropfen pl; **to ~ anchor** ankern, vor
Anker gehen; **to ~ sb a line** jdm ein paar
Zeilen schreiben.
►**drop in** (inf) vi: **to ~ in (on sb)** (bei jdm)
vorbeikommen.
►**drop off** vi einschlafen ♦ vt (passenger)
absetzen.
►**drop out** vi (withdraw) ausscheiden;
(student) sein Studium abbrechen.
droplet ['drɔplɪt] n Tröpfchen nt.
dropout ['drɔpaut] n Aussteiger(in) m(f);
(SCOL) Studienabbrecher(in) m(f).
dropper ['drɔpə*] n Pipette f.
droppings ['drɔpɪŋz] npl Kot m.
dross [drɔs] n Schlacke f; (fig) Schund m.
drought [draut] n Dürre f.
drove [drəuv] pt of **drive** ♦ n: **~s of people**
Scharen pl von Menschen.
drown [draun] vt ertränken; (fig: also: **~ out**)

übertönen ♦ _vi_ ertrinken.
drowse [drauz] _vi_ (vor sich _acc_ hin) dösen _or_
dämmern.
drowsy ['drauzı] _adj_ schläfrig.
drudge [drʌdʒ] _n_ Arbeitstier _nt._
drudgery ['drʌdʒərı] _n_ (stumpfsinnige)
Plackerei _f_ (_inf_); **housework is sheer ~**
Hausarbeit ist eine einzige Plackerei.
drug [drʌg] _n_ Medikament _nt_, Arzneimittel _nt_;
(_narcotic_) Droge _f_, Rauschgift _nt_ ♦ _vt_
betäuben; **to be on ~s** drogensüchtig sein;
hard/soft ~s harte/weiche Drogen _pl._
drug addict _n_ Drogensüchtige(r) _f(m)_,
Rauschgiftsüchtige(r) _f(m)._
druggist ['drʌgıst] (_US_) _n_ Drogist(in) _m(f)._
drug peddler _n_ Drogenhändler(in) _m(f)_,
Dealer _m_ (_inf_).
drugstore ['drʌgstɔː'] (_US_) _n_ Drogerie _f._
drum [drʌm] _n_ Trommel _f_; (_for oil, petrol_) Faß
_nt_ ♦ _vi_ trommeln; **drums** _npl_ (_kit_) Schlagzeug
_nt._
▶**drum up** _vt_ (_enthusiasm_) erwecken;
(_support_) auftreiben.
drummer ['drʌmə'] _n_ Trommler(in) _m(f)_; (_in
band, pop group_) Schlagzeuger(in) _m(f)._
drum roll _n_ Trommelwirbel _m._
drumstick ['drʌmstık] _n_ Trommelstock _m_; (_of
chicken_) Keule _f._
drunk [drʌŋk] _pp of_ **drink** ♦ _adj_ betrunken ♦ _n_
(_also:_ **~ard**) Trinker(in) _m(f)_; **to get ~** sich
betrinken; **a ~ driving offence** Trunkenheit
_f_ am Steuer.
drunken ['drʌŋkən] _adj_ betrunken; (_party_)
feucht-fröhlich; **~ driving** Trunkenheit _f_ am
Steuer.
drunkenness ['drʌŋkənnıs] _n_ (_state_)
Betrunkenheit _f_; (_habit_) Trunksucht _f._
dry [draı] _adj_ trocken ♦ _vt, vi_ trocknen; **on
~ land** auf festem Boden; **to ~ one's
hands/hair/eyes** sich _dat_ die Hände
(ab)trocknen/die Haare trocknen/die
Tränen abwischen; **to ~ the dishes** (das
Geschirr) abtrocknen.
▶**dry up** _vi_ austrocknen; (_in speech_) den
Faden verlieren.
dry-clean ['draı'kliːn] _vt_ chemisch reinigen.
dry-cleaner ['draı'kliːnə'] _n_ (_job_) Inhaber(in)
_m(f)_ einer chemischen Reinigung; (_shop: also:_
~'s) chemische Reinigung _f._
dry-cleaning ['draı'kliːnıŋ] _n_ (_process_)
chemische Reinigung _f._
dry dock _n_ Trockendock _nt._
dryer ['draıə'] _n_ Wäschetrockner _m_; (_US: spin-
dryer_) Wäscheschleuder _f._
dry goods _npl_ Kurzwaren _pl._
dry ice _n_ Trockeneis _nt._
dryly ['draılı] _adv_ (_say, remark_) trocken.
dryness ['draınıs] _n_ Trockenheit _f._
dry rot _n_ (Haus)schwamm _m_,
(Holz)schwamm _m._
dry run _n_ (_fig_) Probe _f._
dry ski slope _n_ Trockenskipiste _f._

DSc _n abbr_ (= _Doctor of Science_) ≈ Dr. rer. nat.
DSS (_BRIT_) _n abbr_ (= _Department of Social
Security_) Ministerium _für_ Sozialfürsorge.
DST (_US_) _abbr_ = **daylight-saving time.**
DT _n abbr_ (_COMPUT_) = **data transmission.**
DTI (_BRIT_) _n abbr_ (= _Department of Trade and
Industry_) ≈ Wirtschaftsministerium _nt._
DTP _n abbr_ (= _desktop publishing_) DTP _nt_; _see
also_ **desktop publishing.**
DT's (_inf_) _npl abbr_ (= _delirium tremens_)
Delirium tremens _nt_; **to have the ~** vom
Trinken den Tatterich haben (_inf_).
dual ['djuəl] _adj_ doppelt; (_personality_)
gespalten.
dual carriageway (_BRIT_) _n_ ≈ Schnellstraße _f._
dual nationality _n_ doppelte Staatsangehörigkeit _f._
dual-purpose ['djuəl'pə:pəs] _adj_ zweifach
verwendbar.
dubbed [dʌbd] _adj_ synchronisiert;
(_nicknamed_) getauft.
dubious ['djuːbıəs] _adj_ zweifelhaft; **I'm very
~ about it** ich habe da (doch) starke
Zweifel.
Dublin ['dʌblın] _n_ Dublin _nt._
Dubliner ['dʌblınə'] _n_ Dubliner(in) _m(f)._
duchess ['dʌtʃıs] _n_ Herzogin _f._
duck [dʌk] _n_ Ente _f_ ♦ _vi_ (_also:_ **~ down**) sich
ducken ♦ _vt_ (_blow_) ausweichen +_dat_; (_duty,
responsibility_) aus dem Weg gehen +_dat._
duckling ['dʌklıŋ] _n_ Entenküken _nt_; (_CULIN_)
(junge) Ente _f._
duct [dʌkt] _n_ Rohr _nt_; (_ANAT_) Röhre _f_; **tear ~**
Tränenkanal _m._
dud [dʌd] _n_ Niete _f_ (_inf_); (_note_) Blüte _f_ (_inf_)
♦ _adj:_ **~ cheque** (_BRIT_) ungedeckter Scheck
_m._
due [djuː] _adj_ fällig; (_attention etc_) gebührend;
(_consideration_) reiflich ♦ _n:_ **to give sb his/her
~** jdn gerecht behandeln ♦ _adv:_ **~ north**
direkt nach Norden; **dues** _npl_ Beitrag _m_; (_in
harbour_) Gebühren _pl_; **in ~ course** zu
gegebener Zeit; (_eventually_) im Laufe der
Zeit; **~ to** (_owing to_) wegen +_gen_, aufgrund
+_gen_; **to be ~ to do sth** etw tun sollen; **the
rent is ~ on the 30th** die Miete ist am 30.
fällig; **the train is ~ at 8** der Zug soll (laut
Fahrplan) um 8 ankommen; **she is ~ back
tomorrow** sie müßte morgen zurück sein; **I
am ~ 6 days' leave** mir stehen 6 Tage
Urlaub zu.
due date _n_ Fälligkeitsdatum _nt._
duel ['djuəl] _n_ Duell _nt._
duet [djuː'ɛt] _n_ Duett _nt._
duff [dʌf] (_BRIT: inf_) _adj_ kaputt.
▶**duff up** _vt_ vermöbeln.
duffel bag ['dʌfl-] _n_ Matchbeutel _m._
duffel coat _n_ Dufflecoat _m._
duffer ['dʌfə'] (_inf_) _n_ Versager _m_, Flasche _f._
dug [dʌg] _pt, pp of_ **dig.**
dugout ['dʌgaut] _n_ (_canoe_) Einbaum _m_;
(_shelter_) Unterstand _m._

duke [djuːk] *n* Herzog *m*.
dull [dʌl] *adj* trüb; (*intelligence, wit*) schwerfällig, langsam; (*event*) langweilig; (*sound, pain*) dumpf ♦ *vt* (*pain, grief*) betäuben; (*mind, senses*) abstumpfen.
duly ['djuːlɪ] *adv* (*properly*) gebührend; (*on time*) pünktlich.
dumb [dʌm] *adj* stumm; (*pej: stupid*) dumm, doof (*inf*); **he was struck ~** es verschlug ihm die Sprache.
dumbbell ['dʌmbɛl] *n* Hantel *f*.
dumbfounded [dʌm'faʊndɪd] *adj* verblüfft.
dummy ['dʌmɪ] *n* (Schneider)puppe *f*; (*mock-up*) Attrappe *f*; (*SPORT*) Finte *f*; (*BRIT: for baby*) Schnuller *m* ♦ *adj* (*firm*) fiktiv; **~ bullets** Übungsmunition *f*.
dummy run *n* Probe *f*.
dump [dʌmp] *n* (*also*: **rubbish ~**) Abfallhaufen *m*; (*inf: place*) Müllkippe *f*; (*MIL*) Depot *nt* ♦ *vt* fallen lassen; (*get rid of*) abladen; (*car*) abstellen; (*COMPUT: data*) ausgeben; **to be down in the ~s** (*inf*) deprimiert *or* down sein; **"no ~ing"** „Schuttabladen verboten".
dumpling ['dʌmplɪŋ] *n* Kloß *m*, Knödel *m*.
dumpy ['dʌmpɪ] *adj* pummelig.
dunce [dʌns] *n* Niete *f*.
dune [djuːn] *n* Düne *f*.
dung [dʌŋ] *n* (*AGR*) Dünger *m*, Mist *m*; (*ZOOL*) Dung *m*.
dungarees [dʌŋɡə'riːz] *npl* Latzhose *f*.
dungeon ['dʌndʒən] *n* Kerker *m*, Verlies *nt*.
dunk [dʌŋk] *vt* (ein)tunken.
Dunkirk [dʌn'kɜːk] *n* Dünkirchen *nt*.
duo ['djuːəʊ] *n* Duo *nt*.
duodenal [djuːəʊ'diːnl] *adj* Duodenal-; **~ ulcer** Zwölffingerdarmgeschwür *nt*.
duodenum [djuːəʊ'diːnəm] *n* Zwölffingerdarm *m*.
dupe [djuːp] *n* Betrogene(r) *f(m)* ♦ *vt* betrügen.
duplex ['djuːplɛks] (*US*) *n* Zweifamilienhaus *nt*; (*apartment*) zweistöckige Wohnung *f*.
duplicate [*n, adj* 'djuːplɪkət, *vt* 'djuːplɪkeɪt] *n* (*also*: **~ copy**) Duplikat *nt*, Kopie *f*; (*also*: **~ key**) Zweitschlüssel *m* ♦ *adj* doppelt ♦ *vt* kopieren; (*repeat*) wiederholen; **in ~** in doppelter Ausfertigung.
duplicating machine ['djuːplɪkeɪtɪŋ-] *n* Vervielfältigungsapparat *m*.
duplicator ['djuːplɪkeɪtə'] *n* Vervielfältigungsapparat *m*.
duplicity [djuː'plɪsɪtɪ] *n* Doppelspiel *nt*.
Dur. (*BRIT*) *abbr* (*POST*: = *Durham*).
durability [djʊərə'bɪlɪtɪ] *n* Haltbarkeit *f*.
durable ['djʊərəbl] *adj* haltbar.
duration [djʊə'reɪʃən] *n* Dauer *f*.
duress [djʊə'rɛs] *n*: **under ~** unter Zwang.
Durex ® ['djʊərɛks] (*BRIT*) *n* Gummi *m* (*inf*).
during ['djʊərɪŋ] *prep* während +*gen*.
dusk [dʌsk] *n* (Abend)dämmerung *f*.
dusky ['dʌskɪ] *adj* (*room*) dunkel; (*light*) Dämmer-.
dust [dʌst] *n* Staub *m* ♦ *vt* abstauben; (*cake*

etc): **to ~ with** bestäuben mit.
▶**dust off** *vt* abwischen, wegwischen; (*fig*) hervorkramen.
dustbin ['dʌstbɪn] (*BRIT*) *n* Mülltonne *f*.
dustbin liner (*BRIT*) *n* Müllsack *m*.
duster ['dʌstə'] *n* Staubtuch *nt*.
dust jacket *n* (Schutz)umschlag *m*.
dustman ['dʌstmən] (*BRIT: irreg: like* **man**) *n* Müllmann *m*.
dustpan ['dʌstpæn] *n* Kehrschaufel *f*, Müllschaufel *f*.
dusty ['dʌstɪ] *adj* staubig.
Dutch [dʌtʃ] *adj* holländisch, niederländisch ♦ *n* Holländisch *nt*, Niederländisch *nt* ♦ *adv*: **to go ~** (*inf*) getrennte Kasse machen; **the Dutch** *npl* die Holländer *pl*, die Niederländer *pl*.
Dutch auction *n* Versteigerung mit stufenweise erniedrigtem Ausbietungspreis.
Dutchman ['dʌtʃmən] (*irreg: like* **man**) *n* Holländer *m*, Niederländer *m*.
Dutchwoman ['dʌtʃwʊmən] (*irreg: like* **woman**) *n* Holländerin *f*, Niederländerin *f*.
dutiable ['djuːtɪəbl] *adj* zollpflichtig.
dutiful ['djuːtɪful] *adj* pflichtbewußt; (*son, daughter*) gehorsam.
duty ['djuːtɪ] *n* Pflicht *f*; (*tax*) Zoll *m*; **duties** *npl* (*functions*) Aufgaben *pl*; **to make it one's ~ to do sth** es sich *dat* zur Pflicht machen, etw zu tun; **to pay ~ on sth** Zoll auf etw *acc* zahlen; **on/off ~** im/nicht im Dienst.
duty-free ['djuːtɪ'friː] *adj* zollfrei; **~ shop** Duty-free-Shop *m*.
duty officer *n* Offizier *m* vom Dienst.
duvet ['duːveɪ] (*BRIT*) *n* Federbett *nt*.
DV *abbr* (= *Deo volente*) so Gott will.
DVLA *n abbr* (= *Driver and Vehicle Licensing Authority*) Zulassungsbehörde für Kraftfahrzeuge.
DVLC (*BRIT*) *n abbr* (= *Driver and Vehicle Licensing Centre*) Zulassungsstelle für Kraftfahrzeuge.
DVM (*US*) *n abbr* (= *Doctor of Veterinary Medicine*) ≈ Dr. med. vet.
dwarf [dwɔːf] (*pl* **dwarves**) *n* Zwerg(in) *m(f)* ♦ *vt*: **to be ~ed by sth** neben etw *dat* klein erscheinen.
dwarves [dwɔːvz] *npl of* **dwarf**.
dwell [dwɛl] (*pt, pp* **dwelt**) *vi* wohnen, leben.
▶**dwell on** *vt fus* (in Gedanken) verweilen bei.
dweller ['dwɛlə'] *n* Bewohner(in) *m(f)*; **city ~** Stadtbewohner(in) *m(f)*.
dwelling ['dwɛlɪŋ] *n* Wohnhaus *nt*.
dwelt [dwɛlt] *pt, pp of* **dwell**.
dwindle ['dwɪndl] *vi* abnehmen; (*interest*) schwinden; (*attendance*) zurückgehen.
dwindling ['dwɪndlɪŋ] *adj* (*strength, interest*) schwindend; (*resources, supplies*) versiegend.
dye [daɪ] *n* Farbstoff *m*; (*for hair*) Färbemittel *nt* ♦ *vt* färben.

dyestuffs ['daɪstʌfs] *npl* Farbstoffe *pl*.
dying ['daɪɪŋ] *adj* sterbend; (*moments, words*) letzte(r, s).
dyke [daɪk] *n* (*BRIT: wall*) Deich *m*, Damm *m*; (*channel*) (Entwässerungs)graben *m*; (*causeway*) Fahrdamm *m*.
dynamic [daɪ'næmɪk] *adj* dynamisch.
dynamics [daɪ'næmɪks] *n or npl* Dynamik *f*.
dynamite ['daɪnəmaɪt] *n* Dynamit *nt* ♦ *vt* sprengen.
dynamo ['daɪnəməu] *n* Dynamo *m*; (*AUT*) Lichtmaschine *f*.
dynasty ['dɪnəstɪ] *n* Dynastie *f*.
dysentery ['dɪsntrɪ] *n* (*MED*) Ruhr *f*.
dyslexia [dɪs'lɛksɪə] *n* Legasthenie *f*.
dyslexic [dɪs'lɛksɪk] *adj* legasthenisch ♦ *n* Legastheniker(in) *m(f)*.
dyspepsia [dɪs'pɛpsɪə] *n* Dyspepsie *f*, Verdauungsstörung *f*.
dystrophy ['dɪstrəfɪ] *n* Dystrophie *f*, Ernährungsstörung *f*; **muscular ~** Muskelschwund *m*.

E, e

E¹, e [iː] *n* (*letter*) E *nt*, e *nt*; **~ for Edward**, (*US*) **~ for Easy** E wie Emil.
E² [iː] *n* (*MUS*) E *nt*, e *nt*.
E³ [iː] *abbr* (= *east*) O ♦ *n abbr* (*drug*: = *Ecstasy*) Ecstasy *nt*.
E111 *n abbr* (*also*: **form ~**) E111-Formular *nt*.
E.A. (*US*) *n abbr* (= *educational age*) Bildungsstand *m*.
ea. *abbr* = **each**.
each [iːtʃ] *adj, pron* jede(r, s); **~ other** sich, einander; **they hate ~ other** sie hassen sich *or* einander; **you are jealous of ~ other** ihr seid eifersüchtig aufeinander; **~ day** jeden Tag; **they have 2 books ~** sie haben je 2 Bücher; **they cost £5 ~** sie kosten 5 Pfund das Stück; **~ of us** jede(r, s) von uns.
eager ['iːgə'] *adj* eifrig; **to be ~ to do sth** etw unbedingt tun wollen; **to be ~ for sth** auf etw *acc* erpicht *or* aus (*inf*) sein.
eagerly ['iːgəlɪ] *adv* eifrig; (*awaited*) gespannt, ungeduldig.
eagle ['iːgl] *n* Adler *m*.
ear [ɪə'] *n* Ohr *nt*; (*of corn*) Ähre *f*; **to be up to one's ~s in debt/work** bis über beide Ohren in Schulden/Arbeit stecken; **to be up to one's ~s in paint/baking** mitten im Anstreichen/Backen stecken; **to give sb a thick ~** jdm ein paar hinter die Ohren geben; **we'll play it by ~** (*fig*) wir werden es auf uns zukommen lassen.

earache ['ɪəreɪk] *n* Ohrenschmerzen *pl*.
eardrum ['ɪədrʌm] *n* Trommelfell *nt*.
earful ['ɪəful] (*inf*) *n*: **to give sb an ~** jdm was erzählen; **to get an ~** was zu hören bekommen.
earl [əːl] (*BRIT*) *n* Graf *m*.
earlier ['əːlɪə'] *adj, adv* früher; **I can't come any ~** ich kann nicht früher *or* eher kommen.
early ['əːlɪ] *adv* früh; (*ahead of time*) zu früh ♦ *adj* früh; (*Christians*) Ur-; (*death, departure*) vorzeitig; (*reply*) baldig; **~ in the morning** früh am Morgen; **to have an ~ night** früh ins Bett gehen; **in the ~ hours** in den frühen Morgenstunden; **in the ~** *or* **in the spring/19th century** Anfang des Frühjahrs/des 19. Jahrhunderts; **take the ~ train** nimm den früheren Zug; **you're ~!** Sie sind früh dran!; **she's in her ~ forties** sie ist Anfang Vierzig; **at your earliest convenience** so bald wie möglich.
early retirement *n*: **to take ~** vorzeitig in den Ruhestand gehen.
early warning system *n* Frühwarnsystem *nt*.
earmark ['ɪəmɑːk] *vt*: **to ~ (for)** bestimmen (für), vorsehen (für).
earn [əːn] *vt* verdienen; (*interest*) bringen; **to ~ one's living** seinen Lebensunterhalt verdienen; **this ~ed him much praise, he ~ed much praise for this** das trug ihm viel Lob ein; **he's ~ed his rest/reward** er hat sich seine Pause/Belohnung verdient.
earned income [əːnd-] *n* Arbeitseinkommen *nt*.
earnest ['əːnɪst] *adj* ernsthaft; (*wish, desire*) innig ♦ *n* (*also*: **~ money**) Angeld *nt*; **in ~** (*adv*) richtig; (*adj*): **to be in ~** es ernst meinen; **work on the tunnel soon began in ~** die Tunnelarbeiten begannen bald richtig; **is the Minister in ~ about these proposals?** meint der Minister diese Vorschläge ernst?
earnings ['əːnɪŋz] *npl* Verdienst *m*; (*of company etc*) Ertrag *m*.
ear, nose and throat specialist *n* Hals-Nasen-Ohren-Arzt *m*, Hals-Nasen-Ohren-Ärztin *f*.
earphones ['ɪəfəunz] *npl* Kopfhörer *pl*.
earplugs ['ɪəplʌgz] *npl* Ohropax ® *nt*.
earring ['ɪərɪŋ] *n* Ohrring *m*.
earshot ['ɪəʃɔt] *n*: **within/out of ~** in/außer Hörweite.
earth [əːθ] *n* Erde *f*; (*of fox*) Bau *m* ♦ *vt* (*BRIT: ELEC*) erden.
earthenware ['əːθnwɛə'] *n* Tongeschirr *nt* ♦ *adj* Ton-.
earthly ['əːθlɪ] *adj* irdisch; **~ paradise** Paradies *nt* auf Erden; **there is no ~ reason to think ...** es besteht nicht der geringste Grund für die Annahme ...
earthquake ['əːθkweɪk] *n* Erdbeben *nt*.
earthshattering ['əːθʃætərɪŋ] *adj* (*fig*) weltbewegend.

earth tremor n Erdstoß m.
earthworks ['ə:θwə:ks] npl Erdarbeiten pl.
earthworm ['ə:θwə:m] n Regenwurm m.
earthy ['ə:θɪ] adj (humour) derb.
earwig ['ɪəwɪg] n Ohrwurm m.
ease [i:z] n Leichtigkeit f; (comfort) Behagen nt ♦ vt (problem) vereinfachen; (pain) lindern; (tension) verringern; (loosen) lockern ♦ vi nachlassen; (situation) sich entspannen; **to ~ sth in/out** (push/pull) etw behutsam hineinschieben/herausziehen; **at ~!** (MIL) rührt euch!; **with ~** mit Leichtigkeit; **life of ~** Leben der Muße; **to ~ in the clutch** die Kupplung behutsam kommen lassen.
▶**ease off** vi nachlassen; (slow down) langsamer werden.
▶**ease up** vi = ease off.
easel ['i:zl] n Staffelei f.
easily ['i:zɪlɪ] adv (see adj) leicht; ungezwungen; bequem.
easiness ['i:zɪnɪs] n Leichtigkeit f; (of manner) Ungezwungenheit f.
east [i:st] n Osten m ♦ adj (coast, Asia etc) Ost- ♦ adv ostwärts, nach Osten; **the E~** der Osten.
Easter ['i:stə'] n Ostern nt ♦ adj (holidays etc) Oster-.
Easter egg n Osterei nt.
Easter Island n Osterinsel f.
easterly ['i:stəlɪ] adj östlich; (wind) Ost-.
Easter Monday n Ostermontag m.
eastern ['i:stən] adj östlich; **E~ Europe** Osteuropa nt; **the E~ bloc** (formerly) der Ostblock.
Easter Sunday n Ostersonntag m.
East Germany n (formerly) die DDR f.
eastward(s) ['i:stwəd(z)] adv ostwärts, nach Osten.
easy ['i:zɪ] adj leicht; (relaxed) ungezwungen; (comfortable) bequem ♦ adv: **to take it/things ~** (go slowly) sich dat Zeit lassen; (not worry) es nicht so schwer nehmen; (rest) sich schonen; **payment on ~ terms** Zahlung zu günstigen Bedingungen; **that's easier said than done** das ist leichter gesagt als getan; **I'm ~** (inf) mir ist alles recht.
easy chair n Sessel m.
easy-going ['i:zɪ'gəuɪŋ] adj gelassen.
easy touch (inf) n: **to be an ~** (for money etc) leicht anzuzapfen sein.
eat [i:t] (pt **ate**, pp **eaten**) vt, vi essen; (animal) fressen.
▶**eat away** vt (subj: sea) auswaschen; (: acid) zerfressen.
▶**eat away at** vt fus (metal) anfressen; (savings) angreifen.
▶**eat into** vt fus = eat away at.
▶**eat out** vi essen gehen.
▶**eat up** vt aufessen; **it ~s up electricity** es verbraucht viel Strom.
eatable ['i:təbl] adj genießbar.

eau de Cologne ['əudəkə'ləun] n Kölnisch Wasser nt, Eau de Cologne nt.
eaves [i:vz] npl Dachvorsprung m.
eavesdrop ['i:vzdrɔp] vi lauschen; **to ~ on** belauschen +acc.
ebb [ɛb] n Ebbe f ♦ vi ebben; (fig: also: ~ **away**) dahinschwinden; (: feeling) abebben; **the ~ and flow** (fig) das Auf und Ab; **to be at a low ~** (fig) auf einem Tiefpunkt angelangt sein.
ebb tide n Ebbe f.
ebony ['ɛbənɪ] n Ebenholz nt.
ebullient [ɪ'bʌlɪənt] adj überschäumend, übersprudelnd.
EC n abbr (= European Community) EG f.
eccentric [ɪk'sɛntrɪk] adj exzentrisch ♦ n Exzentriker(in) m(f).
ecclesiastic(al) [ɪkli:zɪ'æstɪk(l)] adj kirchlich.
ECG n abbr (= electrocardiogram) EKG nt.
echo ['ɛkəu] (pl ~**es**) n Echo nt ♦ vt wiederholen ♦ vi widerhallen; (place) hallen.
éclair [eɪ'klɛə'] n Eclair nt.
eclipse [ɪ'klɪps] n Finsternis f ♦ vt in den Schatten stellen.
ECM (US) n abbr (= European Common Market) EG f.
eco- ['i:kəu] pref Öko-, öko-.
ecofriendly adj umweltfreundlich.
ecological [i:kə'lɔdʒɪkəl] adj ökologisch; (damage, disaster) Umwelt-.
ecologist [ɪ'kɔlədʒɪst] n Ökologe m, Ökologin f.
ecology [ɪ'kɔlədʒɪ] n Ökologie f.
economic [i:kə'nɔmɪk] adj (system, policy etc) Wirtschafts-; (profitable) wirtschaftlich.
economical [i:kə'nɔmɪkl] adj wirtschaftlich; (person) sparsam.
economically [i:kə'nɔmɪklɪ] adv wirtschaftlich; (thriftily) sparsam.
economics [i:kə'nɔmɪks] n Wirtschaftswissenschaften pl ♦ npl Wirtschaftlichkeit f; (of situation) wirtschaftliche Seite f.
economist [ɪ'kɔnəmɪst] n Wirtschaftswissenschaftler(in) m(f).
economize [ɪ'kɔnəmaɪz] vi sparen.
economy [ɪ'kɔnəmɪ] n Wirtschaft f; (financial prudence) Sparsamkeit f; **economies of scale** (COMM) Einsparungen pl durch erhöhte Produktion.
economy class n Touristenklasse f.
economy size n Sparpackung f.
ecosystem ['i:kəusɪstəm] n Ökosystem nt.
ecotourism ['i:kəu'tuərɪzm] n Ökotourismus m.
ECSC n abbr (= European Coal and Steel Community) Europäische Gemeinschaft für Kohle und Stahl.
ecstasy ['ɛkstəsɪ] n Ekstase f; (drug) Ecstasy nt; **to go into ecstasies over** in Verzückung geraten über +acc; **in ~** verzückt.
ecstatic [ɛks'tætɪk] adj ekstatisch.

ECT *n abbr* = **electroconvulsive therapy.**

ECU ['eɪkjuː] *n abbr* (= *European Currency Unit*) Ecu *m*.

Ecuador ['ɛkwədɔː'] *n* Ecuador *nt*, Ekuador *nt*.

ecumenical [iːkjuˈmɛnɪkl] *adj* ökumenisch.

eczema ['ɛksɪmə] *n* Ekzem *nt*.

eddy ['ɛdɪ] *n* Strudel *m*.

edge [ɛdʒ] *n* Rand *m*; (*of table, chair*) Kante *f*; (*of lake*) Ufer *nt*; (*of knife etc*) Schneide *f* ♦ *vt* einfassen ♦ *vi:* **to ~ forward** sich nach vorne schieben; **on ~** (*fig*) = **edgy; to have the ~ on** überlegen sein +*dat*; **to ~ away from** sich allmählich entfernen von; **to ~ past** sich vorbeischieben, sich vorbeidrücken.

edgeways ['ɛdʒweɪz] *adv:* **he couldn't get a word in ~** er kam überhaupt nicht zu Wort.

edging ['ɛdʒɪŋ] *n* Einfassung *f*.

edgy ['ɛdʒɪ] *adj* nervös.

edible ['ɛdɪbl] *adj* eßbar, genießbar.

edict ['iːdɪkt] *n* Erlaß *m*.

edifice ['ɛdɪfɪs] *n* Gebäude *nt*.

edifying ['ɛdɪfaɪɪŋ] *adj* erbaulich.

Edinburgh ['ɛdɪnbərə] *n* Edinburg(h) *nt*.

edit ['ɛdɪt] *vt* (*text*) redigieren; (*book*) lektorieren; (*film, broadcast*) schneiden, cutten; (*newspaper, magazine*) herausgeben; (*COMPUT*) editieren.

edition [ɪˈdɪʃən] *n* Ausgabe *f*.

editor ['ɛdɪtə'] *n* Redakteur(in) *m(f)*; (*of newspaper, magazine*) Herausgeber(in) *m(f)*; (*of book*) Lektor(in) *m(f)*; (*CINE, RADIO, TV*) Cutter(in) *m(f)*.

editorial [ɛdɪˈtɔːrɪəl] *adj* redaktionell; (*staff*) Redaktions- ♦ *n* Leitartikel *m*.

EDP *n abbr* (*COMPUT*) (= *electronic data processing*) EDV *f*.

EDT (*US*) *abbr* (= *Eastern Daylight Time*) ostamerikanische Sommerzeit.

educate ['ɛdjukeɪt] *vt* erziehen; **to ~ at ...** zur Schule/Universität gegangen in ...

educated ['ɛdjukeɪtɪd] *adj* gebildet.

educated guess ['ɛdjukeɪtɪd-] *n* wohlbegründete Vermutung *f*.

education [ɛdjuˈkeɪʃən] *n* Erziehung *f*; (*schooling*) Ausbildung *f*; (*knowledge, culture*) Bildung *f*; **primary** *or* (*US*) **elementary ~** Grundschul(aus)bildung *f*; **secondary ~** höhere Schul(aus)bildung *f*.

educational [ɛdjuˈkeɪʃənl] *adj* pädagogisch; (*experience*) lehrreich; (*toy*) pädagogisch wertvoll; **~ technology** Unterrichtstechnologie *f*.

Edwardian [ɛdˈwɔːdɪən] *adj* aus der Zeit Edwards VII.

EE *abbr* = **electrical engineer.**

EEC *n abbr* (= *European Economic Community*) EWG *f*.

EEG *n abbr* (= *electroencephalogram*) EEG *nt*.

eel [iːl] *n* Aal *m*.

EENT (*US*) *n abbr* (*MED:* = *eye, ear, nose and throat*) Augen und Hals-Nasen-Ohren.

EEOC (*US*) *n abbr* (= *Equal Employment Opportunity Commission*) Kommission *für Gleichberechtigung am Arbeitsplatz.*

eerie ['ɪərɪ] *adj* unheimlich.

EET *abbr* (= *Eastern European Time*) OEZ *f*.

efface [ɪˈfeɪs] *vt* auslöschen; **to ~ o.s.** sich im Hintergrund halten.

effect [ɪˈfɛkt] *n* Wirkung *f*, Effekt *m* ♦ *vt* bewirken; (*repairs*) durchführen; **effects** *npl* Effekten *pl*; (*THEAT, CINE etc*) Effekte *pl*; **to take ~** (*law*) in Kraft treten; (*drug*) wirken; **to put into ~** in Kraft setzen; **to have an ~ on sb/sth** eine Wirkung auf jdn/etw haben; **in ~** eigentlich, praktisch; **his letter is to the ~ that ...** sein Brief hat zum Inhalt, daß ...

effective [ɪˈfɛktɪv] *adj* effektiv, wirksam; (*actual*) eigentlich, wirklich; **to become ~** in Kraft treten; **~ date** Zeitpunkt *m* des Inkrafttretens.

effectively [ɪˈfɛktɪvlɪ] *adv* effektiv.

effectiveness [ɪˈfɛktɪvnɪs] *n* Wirksamkeit *f*, Effektivität *f*.

effeminate [ɪˈfɛmɪnɪt] *adj* feminin, effeminiert.

effervescent [ɛfəˈvɛsnt] *adj* sprudelnd.

efficacy ['ɛfɪkəsɪ] *n* Wirksamkeit *f*.

efficiency [ɪˈfɪʃənsɪ] *n* (*see adj*) Fähigkeit *f*, Tüchtigkeit *f*; Rationalität *f*; Leistungsfähigkeit *f*.

efficiency apartment (*US*) *n* Einzimmerwohnung *f*.

efficient [ɪˈfɪʃənt] *adj* fähig, tüchtig; (*organization*) rationell; (*machine*) leistungsfähig.

efficiently [ɪˈfɪʃəntlɪ] *adv* gut, effizient.

effigy ['ɛfɪdʒɪ] *n* Bildnis *nt*.

effluent ['ɛfluənt] *n* Abwasser *nt*.

effort ['ɛfət] *n* Anstrengung *f*; (*attempt*) Versuch *m*; **to make an ~ to do sth** sich bemühen, etw zu tun.

effortless ['ɛfətlɪs] *adj* mühelos; (*style*) flüssig.

effrontery [ɪˈfrʌntərɪ] *n* Unverschämtheit *f*; **to have the ~ to do sth** die Frechheit besitzen, etw zu tun.

effusive [ɪˈfjuːsɪv] *adj* überschwenglich.

EFL *n abbr* (*SCOL:* = *English as a Foreign Language*) Englisch *nt* als Fremdsprache.

EFTA ['ɛftə] *n abbr* (= *European Free Trade Association*) EFTA *f*.

e.g. *adv abbr* (= *exempli gratia*) z.B.

egalitarian [ɪgælɪˈtɛərɪən] *adj* egalitär; (*principles*) Gleichheits- ♦ *n* Verfechter(in) *m(f)* des Egalitarismus.

egg [ɛg] *n* Ei *nt*; **hard-boiled/soft-boiled ~** hart-/weichgekochtes Ei *nt*.

►**egg on** *vt* anstacheln.

egg cup *n* Eierbecher *m*.

eggplant ['ɛgplɑːnt] *n* (*esp US*) Aubergine *f*.

eggshell ['ɛgʃɛl] *n* Eierschale *f* ♦ *adj* eierschalenfarben.

egg timer *n* Eieruhr *f*.

egg white *n* Eiweiß *nt*.

egg yolk n Eigelb nt.
ego ['i:gəu] n (self-esteem) Selbstbewußtsein nt.
egoism ['ɛgəuɪzəm] n Egoismus m.
egoist ['ɛgəuɪst] n Egoist(in) m(f).
egotism ['ɛgəutɪzəm] n Ichbezogenheit f, Egotismus m.
egotist ['ɛgəutɪst] n ichbezogener Mensch m, Egotist(in) m(f).
ego trip (inf) n Egotrip m.
Egypt ['i:dʒɪpt] n Ägypten nt.
Egyptian [ɪ'dʒɪpʃən] adj ägyptisch ♦ n Ägypter(in) m(f).
eiderdown ['aɪdədaun] n Federbett nt, Daunendecke f.
eight [eɪt] num acht.
eighteen [eɪ'ti:n] num achtzehn.
eighteenth [eɪ'ti:nθ] num achtzehnte(r, s).
eighth [eɪtθ] num achte(r, s) ♦ n Achtel nt.
eighty ['eɪtɪ] num achtzig.
Eire ['ɛərə] n (Republik f) Irland nt.
EIS n abbr (= Educational Institute of Scotland) schottische Lehrergewerkschaft.
either ['aɪðə'] adj (one or other) eine(r, s) (von beiden); (both, each) beide pl, jede(r, s) ♦ pron: ~ (of them) eine(r, s) (davon) ♦ adv auch nicht ♦ conj: ~ yes or no entweder ja oder nein; on ~ side (on both sides) auf beiden Seiten; (on one or other side) auf einer der beiden Seiten; I don't like ~ ich mag beide nicht or keinen von beiden; no, I don't ~ nein, ich auch nicht; I haven't seen ~ one or the other ich habe weder den einen noch den anderen gesehen.
ejaculation [ɪdʒækju'leɪʃən] n Ejakulation f, Samenerguß m.
eject [ɪ'dʒɛkt] vt ausstoßen; (tenant, gatecrasher) hinauswerfen ♦ vi den Schleudersitz betätigen.
ejector seat [ɪ'dʒɛktə-] n Schleudersitz m.
eke out vt (make last) strecken.
EKG (US) n abbr = **electrocardiogram**.
el [ɛl] (US: inf) n abbr = **elevated railroad**.
elaborate [adj ɪ'læbərɪt, vb ɪ'læbəreɪt] adj kompliziert; (plan) ausgefeilt ♦ vt näher ausführen; (refine) ausarbeiten ♦ vi mehr ins Detail gehen; to ~ on näher ausführen.
elapse [ɪ'læps] vi vergehen, verstreichen.
elastic [ɪ'læstɪk] n Gummi nt ♦ adj elastisch.
elastic band (BRIT) n Gummiband nt.
elasticity [ɪlæs'tɪsɪtɪ] n Elastizität f.
elated [ɪ'leɪtɪd] adj: to be ~ hocherfreut or in Hochstimmung sein.
elation [ɪ'leɪʃən] n große Freude f, Hochstimmung f.
elbow ['ɛlbəu] n Ellbogen m ♦ vt: to ~ one's way through the crowd sich durch die Menge boxen.
elbow grease (inf) n Muskelkraft f.
elbowroom ['ɛlbəurum] n Ellbogenfreiheit f.
elder ['ɛldə'] adj älter ♦ n (BOT) Holunder m; (older person: gen pl) Ältere(r) f(m).

elderly ['ɛldəlɪ] adj ältere(r, s) ♦ npl: the ~ ältere Leute pl.
elder statesman n erfahrener Staatsmann m.
eldest ['ɛldɪst] adj älteste(r, s) ♦ n Älteste(r) f(m).
elect [ɪ'lɛkt] vt wählen ♦ adj: the president ~ der designierte or künftige Präsident; to ~ to do sth sich dafür entscheiden, etw zu tun.
election [ɪ'lɛkʃən] n Wahl f; to hold an ~ eine Wahl abhalten.
election campaign n Wahlkampf m.
electioneering [ɪlɛkʃə'nɪərɪŋ] n Wahlkampf m.
elector [ɪ'lɛktə'] n Wähler(in) m(f).
electoral [ɪ'lɛktərəl] adj Wähler-.
electoral college n Wahlmännergremium nt.
electorate [ɪ'lɛktərɪt] n Wähler pl, Wählerschaft f.
electric [ɪ'lɛktrɪk] adj elektrisch.
electrical [ɪ'lɛktrɪkl] adj elektrisch; (appliance) Elektro-; (failure) Strom-.
electrical engineer n Elektrotechniker m.
electric blanket n Heizdecke f.
electric chair (US) n elektrischer Stuhl m.
electric cooker n Elektroherd m.
electric current n elektrischer Strom m.
electric fire (BRIT) n elektrisches Heizgerät nt.
electrician [ɪlɛk'trɪʃən] n Elektriker(in) m(f).
electricity [ɪlɛk'trɪsɪtɪ] n Elektrizität f; (supply) (elektrischer) Strom m ♦ cpd Strom-; to switch on/off the ~ den Strom an-/ abschalten.
electricity board (BRIT) n Elektrizitätswerk nt.
electric light n elektrisches Licht nt.
electric shock n elektrischer Schlag m, Stromschlag m.
electrify [ɪ'lɛktrɪfaɪ] vt (fence) unter Strom setzen; (rail network) elektrifizieren; (audience) elektrisieren.
electro... [ɪ'lɛktrəu] pref Elektro-.
electrocardiogram [ɪ'lɛktrə'ka:dɪəgræm] n Elektrokardiogramm nt.
electroconvulsive therapy [ɪ'lɛktrəkən'vʌlsɪv-] n Elektroschocktherapie f.
electrocute [ɪ'lɛktrəkju:t] vt durch einen Stromschlag töten; (US: criminal) auf dem elektrischen Stuhl hinrichten.
electrode [ɪ'lɛktrəud] n Elektrode f.
electroencephalogram [ɪ'lɛktrəu-ɛn'sɛfələgræm] n Elektroenzephalogramm nt.
electrolysis [ɪlɛk'trɒlɪsɪs] n Elektrolyse f.
electromagnetic [ɪ'lɛktrəmæg'nɛtɪk] adj elektromagnetisch.
electron [ɪ'lɛktrɒn] n Elektron nt.
electronic [ɪlɛk'trɒnɪk] adj elektronisch.
electronic data processing n elektronische Datenverarbeitung f.
electronic mail n elektronische Post f.

electronics [ɪlɛk'trɒnɪks] *n* Elektronik *f*.
electron microscope *n*
Elektronenmikroskop *nt*.
electroplated [ɪ'lɛktrə'pleɪtɪd] *adj*
galvanisiert.
electrotherapy [ɪ'lɛktrə'θɛrəpɪ] *n*
Elektrotherapie *f*.
elegance ['ɛlɪgəns] *n* Eleganz *f*.
elegant ['ɛlɪgənt] *adj* elegant.
element ['ɛlɪmənt] *n* Element *nt*; (*of heater, kettle etc*) Heizelement *nt*.
elementary [ɛlɪ'mɛntərɪ] *adj* grundlegend;
~ **school** Grundschule *f*; ~ **education**
Elementarunterricht *m*; ~ **maths/French**
Grundbegriffe *pl* der Mathematik/des
Französischen.

> **Elementary School** *ist in den USA und Kanada
> eine Grundschule, an der ein Kind die ersten
> sechs bis acht Schuljahre verbringt. In den
> USA heißt diese Schule auch* grade school *oder*
> grammar school. *Siehe auch* **high school**.

elephant ['ɛlɪfənt] *n* Elefant *m*.
elevate ['ɛlɪveɪt] *vt* erheben; (*physically*)
heben.
elevated railroad ['ɛlɪveɪtɪd-] (*US*) *n*
Hochbahn *f*.
elevation [ɛlɪ'veɪʃən] *n* Erhebung *f*; (*height*)
Höhe *f* über dem Meeresspiegel; (*ARCHIT*)
Aufriß *m*.
elevator ['ɛlɪveɪtə*] *n* (*US*) Aufzug *m*,
Fahrstuhl *m*; (*in warehouse etc*)
Lastenaufzug *m*.
eleven [ɪ'lɛvn] *num* elf.
elevenses [ɪ'lɛvnzɪz] (*BRIT*) *npl* zweites
Frühstück *nt*.
eleventh [ɪ'lɛvnθ] *num* elfte(r, s); **at the**
~ **hour** (*fig*) in letzter Minute.
elf [ɛlf] (*pl* **elves**) *n* Elf *m*, Elfe *f*; (*mischievous*)
Kobold *m*.
elicit [ɪ'lɪsɪt] *vt*: **to** ~ (**from sb**) (*information*)
(aus jdm) herausbekommen; (*reaction, response*) (von jdm) bekommen.
eligible ['ɛlɪdʒəbl] *adj* (*marriage partner*)
begehrt; **to be** ~ **for sth** für etw in Frage
kommen; **to be** ~ **for a pension**
pensionsberechtigt sein.
eliminate [ɪ'lɪmɪneɪt] *vt* beseitigen; (*candidate etc*) ausschließen; (*team, contestant*) aus dem
Wettbewerb werfen.
elimination [ɪlɪmɪ'neɪʃən] *n* (*see vb*)
Beseitigung *f*; Ausschluß *m*; Ausscheiden *nt*;
by process of ~ durch negative Auslese.
élite [eɪ'liːt] *n* Elite *f*.
élitist [eɪ'liːtɪst] (*pej*) *adj* elitär.
elixir [ɪ'lɪksə*] *n* Elixier *nt*.
Elizabethan [ɪlɪzə'biːθən] *adj* elisabethanisch.
ellipse [ɪ'lɪps] *n* Ellipse *f*.
elliptical [ɪ'lɪptɪkl] *adj* elliptisch.
elm [ɛlm] *n* Ulme *f*.
elocution [ɛlə'kjuːʃən] *n* Sprechtechnik *f*.

elongated ['iːlɒŋgeɪtɪd] *adj* langgestreckt;
(*shadow*) verlängert.
elope [ɪ'ləʊp] *vi* weglaufen.
elopement [ɪ'ləʊpmənt] *n* Weglaufen *nt*.
eloquence ['ɛləkwəns] *n* (*see adj*) Beredtheit *f*,
Wortgewandtheit *f*; Ausdrucksfülle *f*.
eloquent ['ɛləkwənt] *adj* beredt, wort-
gewandt; (*speech, description*)
ausdrucksvoll.
else [ɛls] *adv* andere(r, s); **something** ~ etwas
anderes; **somewhere** ~ woanders,
anderswo; **everywhere** ~ sonst überall;
where ~? wo sonst?; **is there anything** ~ **I
can do?** kann ich sonst noch etwas tun?;
there was little ~ **to do** es gab nicht viel
anderes zu tun; **everyone** ~ alle anderen;
nobody ~ **spoke** niemand anders sagte
etwas, sonst sagte niemand etwas.
elsewhere [ɛls'wɛə*] *adv* woanders,
anderswo; (*go*) woandershin, anderswohin.
ELT *n abbr* (*SCOL*: = *English Language Teaching*)
Englisch als Unterrichtsfach.
elucidate [ɪ'luːsɪdeɪt] *vt* erläutern.
elude [ɪ'luːd] *vt* (*captor*) entkommen +*dat*;
(*capture*) sich entziehen +*dat*; **this fact/idea**
~**d him** diese Tatsache/Idee entging ihm.
elusive [ɪ'luːsɪv] *adj* schwer zu fangen;
(*quality*) unerreichbar; **he's very** ~ er ist
sehr schwer zu erreichen.
elves [ɛlvz] *npl of* **elf**.
emaciated [ɪ'meɪsɪeɪtɪd] *adj* abgezehrt,
ausgezehrt.
E-mail *n abbr* (= *electronic mail*) E-Mail *f*.
emanate ['ɛməneɪt] *vi*: **to** ~ **from** stammen
von; (*sound, light etc*) ausgehen von.
emancipate [ɪ'mænsɪpeɪt] *vt* (*women*)
emanzipieren; (*poor*) befreien; (*slave*)
freilassen.
emancipation [ɪmænsɪ'peɪʃən] *n* (*see vb*)
Emanzipation *f*; Befreiung *f*; Freilassung *f*.
emasculate [ɪ'mæskjuleɪt] *vt* schwächen.
embalm [ɪm'bɑːm] *vt* einbalsamieren.
embankment [ɪm'bæŋkmənt] *n* Böschung *f*;
(*of railway*) Bahndamm *m*; (*of river*) Damm *m*.
embargo [ɪm'bɑːgəʊ] (*pl* ~**es**) *n* Embargo *nt*
♦ *vt* mit einem Embargo belegen; **to put** *or*
impose *or* **place an** ~ **on sth** ein Embargo
über etw *acc* verhängen; **to lift an** ~ ein
Embargo aufheben.
embark [ɪm'bɑːk] *vt* einschiffen ♦ *vi*: **to** ~ (**on**)
sich einschiffen (auf); **to** ~ **on** (*journey*)
beginnen; (*task*) in Angriff nehmen; (*course
of action*) einschlagen.
embarkation [ɛmbɑː'keɪʃən] *n* Einschiffung *f*.
embarkation card *n* Bordkarte *f*.
embarrass [ɪm'bærəs] *vt* in Verlegenheit
bringen.
embarrassed [ɪm'bærəst] *adj* verlegen.
embarrassing [ɪm'bærəsɪŋ] *adj* peinlich.
embarrassment [ɪm'bærəsmənt] *n*
Verlegenheit *f*; (*embarrassing problem*)
Peinlichkeit *f*.

embassy ['ɛmbəsɪ] n Botschaft f; **the Swiss E~** die Schweizer Botschaft.

embedded [ɪm'bɛdɪd] adj eingebettet; (attitude, belief, feeling) verwurzelt.

embellish [ɪm'bɛlɪʃ] vt (account) ausschmücken; **to be ~ed with** geschmückt sein mit.

embers ['ɛmbəz] npl Glut f.

embezzle [ɪm'bɛzl] vt unterschlagen.

embezzlement [ɪm'bɛzlmənt] n Unterschlagung f.

embezzler [ɪm'bɛzlə*] n jd, der eine Unterschlagung begangen hat.

embitter [ɪm'bɪtə*] vt verbittern.

embittered [ɪm'bɪtəd] adj verbittert.

emblem ['ɛmbləm] n Emblem nt; (symbol) Wahrzeichen nt.

embodiment [ɪm'bɔdɪmənt] n Verkörperung f; **to be the ~ of** ... (subj: thing) ... verkörpern; (: person) ... in Person sein.

embody [ɪm'bɔdɪ] vt verkörpern; (include, contain) enthalten.

embolden [ɪm'bəuldn] vt ermutigen.

embolism ['ɛmbəlɪzəm] n Embolie f.

embossed [ɪm'bɔst] adj geprägt; **~ with a logo** mit geprägtem Logo.

embrace [ɪm'breɪs] vt umarmen; (include) umfassen ♦ vi sich umarmen ♦ n Umarmung f.

embroider [ɪm'brɔɪdə*] vt (cloth) besticken; (fig: story) ausschmücken.

embroidery [ɪm'brɔɪdərɪ] n Stickerei f; (activity) Sticken nt.

embroil [ɪm'brɔɪl] vt: **to become ~ed (in sth)** (in etw acc) verwickelt or hineingezogen werden.

embryo ['ɛmbrɪəu] n Embryo m; (fig) Keim m.

emcee [ɛm'siː] n Conférencier m.

emend [ɪ'mɛnd] vt verbessern, korrigieren.

emerald ['ɛmərəld] n Smaragd m.

emerge [ɪ'məːdʒ] vi: **to ~ (from)** auftauchen (aus); (from sleep) erwachen (aus); (from imprisonment) entlassen werden (aus); (from discussion etc) sich herausstellen (bei); (new idea, industry, society) entstehen (aus); **it ~s that** (BRIT) es stellt sich heraus, daß.

emergence [ɪ'məːdʒəns] n Entstehung f.

emergency [ɪ'məːdʒənsɪ] n Notfall m ♦ cpd Not-; (repair) notdürftig; **in an ~** im Notfall; **state of ~** Notstand m.

emergency cord (US) n Notbremse f.

emergency exit n Notausgang m.

emergency landing n Notlandung f.

emergency lane (US) n Seitenstreifen m.

emergency road service (US) n Pannendienst m.

emergency services npl: **the ~** der Notdienst.

emergency stop (BRIT) n Vollbremsung f.

emergent [ɪ'məːdʒənt] adj jung, aufstrebend.

emeritus [ɪ'mɛrɪtəs] adj emeritiert.

emery board ['ɛmərɪ-] n Papiernagelfeile f.

emery paper ['ɛmərɪ-] n Schmirgelpapier nt.

emetic [ɪ'mɛtɪk] n Brechmittel nt.

emigrant ['ɛmɪgrənt] n Auswanderer m, Auswanderin f, Emigrant(in) m(f).

emigrate ['ɛmɪgreɪt] vi auswandern, emigrieren.

emigration [ɛmɪ'greɪʃən] n Auswanderung f, Emigration f.

émigré ['ɛmɪgreɪ] n Emigrant(in) m(f).

eminence ['ɛmɪnəns] n Bedeutung f.

eminent ['ɛmɪnənt] adj bedeutend.

eminently ['ɛmɪnəntlɪ] adv ausgesprochen.

emirate ['ɛmɪrɪt] n Emirat nt.

emission [ɪ'mɪʃən] n Emission f.

emissions [ɪ'mɪʃənz] npl Emissionen pl.

emit [ɪ'mɪt] vt abgeben; (smell) ausströmen; (light, heat) ausstrahlen.

emolument [ɪ'mɔljumənt] n (often pl) Vergütung f; (fee) Honorar nt; (salary) Bezüge pl.

emotion [ɪ'məuʃən] n Gefühl nt.

emotional [ɪ'məuʃənl] adj emotional; (exhaustion) seelisch; (scene) ergreifend; (speech) gefühlsbetont.

emotionally [ɪ'məuʃnəlɪ] adv emotional; (be involved) gefühlsmäßig; (speak) gefühlvoll; **~ disturbed** seelisch gestört.

emotive [ɪ'məutɪv] adj emotional.

empathy ['ɛmpəθɪ] n Einfühlungsvermögen nt; **to feel ~ with sb** sich in jdn einfühlen.

emperor ['ɛmpərə*] n Kaiser m.

emphases ['ɛmfəsiːz] npl of **emphasis**.

emphasis ['ɛmfəsɪs] (pl **emphases**) n Betonung f; (importance) (Schwer)gewicht nt; **to lay** or **place ~ on sth** etw betonen; **the ~ is on reading** das Schwergewicht liegt auf dem Lesen.

emphasize ['ɛmfəsaɪz] vt betonen; (feature) hervorheben; **I must ~ that** ... ich möchte betonen, daß ...

emphatic [ɛm'fætɪk] adj nachdrücklich; (denial) energisch; (person, manner) bestimmt, entschieden.

emphatically [ɛm'fætɪklɪ] adv nachdrücklich; (certainly) eindeutig.

emphysema [ɛmfɪ'siːmə] n Emphysem nt.

empire ['ɛmpaɪə*] n Reich nt.

empirical [ɛm'pɪrɪkl] adj empirisch.

employ [ɪm'plɔɪ] vt beschäftigen; (tool, weapon) verwenden; **he's ~ed in a bank** er ist bei einer Bank angestellt.

employee [ɪmplɔɪ'iː] n Angestellte(r) f(m).

employer [ɪm'plɔɪə*] n Arbeitgeber(in) m(f).

employment [ɪm'plɔɪmənt] n Arbeit f; **to find ~** Arbeit or eine (An)stellung finden; **without ~** stellungslos; **your place of ~** Ihre Arbeitsstätte f.

employment agency n Stellenvermittlung f.

employment exchange (BRIT) n Arbeitsamt nt.

empower [ɪm'pauə*] vt: **to ~ sb to do sth** jdn ermächtigen, etw zu tun.

empress ['ɛmprɪs] n Kaiserin f.

empties ['ɛmptɪz] npl Leergut nt.

emptiness ['ɛmptɪnɪs] n Leere f.

empty ['ɛmptɪ] adj leer; (house, room) leerstehend; (space) frei ♦ vt leeren; (place, house etc) räumen ♦ vi sich leeren; (liquid) abfließen; (river) münden; **on an ~ stomach** auf nüchternen Magen; **to ~ into** (river) münden or sich ergießen in +acc.

empty-handed ['ɛmptɪ'hændɪd] adj mit leeren Händen; **he returned ~** er kehrte unverrichteterdinge zurück.

empty-headed ['ɛmptɪ'hɛdɪd] adj strohdumm.

EMS n abbr (= European Monetary System) EWS nt.

EMT (US) n abbr (= emergency medical technician) ≈ Sanitäter(in) m(f).

EMU n abbr (= economic and monetary union) EWU f.

emu ['iːmjuː] n Emu m.

emulate ['ɛmjuleɪt] vt nacheifern +dat.

emulsion [ɪ'mʌlʃən] n Emulsion f; (also: ~ paint) Emulsionsfarbe f.

enable [ɪ'neɪbl] vt: **to ~ sb to do sth** (permit) es jdm erlauben, etw zu tun; (make possible) es jdm ermöglichen, etw zu tun.

enact [ɪ'nækt] vt (law) erlassen; (play) aufführen; (role) darstellen, spielen.

enamel [ɪ'næməl] n Email nt, Emaille f; (also: ~ paint) Email(le)lack m; (of tooth) Zahnschmelz m.

enamoured [ɪ'næməd] adj: **to be ~ of** (person) verliebt sein in +acc; (pastime, idea, belief) angetan sein von.

encampment [ɪn'kæmpmənt] n Lager nt.

encased [ɪn'keɪst] adj: **~ in** (shell) umgeben von; **to be ~ in** (limb) in Gips liegen or sein.

encash [ɪn'kæʃ] (BRIT) vt einlösen.

enchant [ɪn'tʃɑːnt] vt bezaubern.

enchanted [ɪn'tʃɑːntɪd] adj verzaubert.

enchanting [ɪn'tʃɑːntɪŋ] adj bezaubernd.

encircle [ɪn'sɜːkl] vt umgeben; (person) umringen; (building: police etc) umstellen.

encl. abbr (on letters etc: = enclosed, enclosure) Anl.

enclave ['ɛnkleɪv] n: **an ~ (of)** eine Enklave (+gen).

enclose [ɪn'kləuz] vt umgeben; (land, space) begrenzen; (with fence) einzäunen; (letter etc): **to ~ (with)** beilegen (+dat); **please find ~d** als Anlage übersenden wir Ihnen.

enclosure [ɪn'kləuʒə*] n eingefriedeter Bereich m; (in letter etc) Anlage f.

encoder [ɪn'kəudə*] n Kodierer m.

encompass [ɪn'kʌmpəs] vt umfassen.

encore [ɔŋ'kɔː*] excl Zugabe! ♦ n Zugabe f.

encounter [ɪn'kauntə*] n Begegnung f ♦ vt begegnen +dat; (problem) stoßen auf +acc.

encourage [ɪn'kʌrɪdʒ] vt (activity, attitude) unterstützen; (growth, industry) fördern; **to ~ sb (to do sth)** jdn ermutigen(, etw zu tun).

encouragement [ɪn'kʌrɪdʒmənt] n (see vb)

Unterstützung f; Förderung f; Ermutigung f.

encouraging [ɪn'kʌrɪdʒɪŋ] adj ermutigend.

encroach [ɪn'krəutʃ] vi: **to ~ (up)on** (rights) eingreifen in +acc; (property) eindringen in +acc; (time) in Anspruch nehmen.

encrusted [ɪn'krʌstɪd] adj: **~ with** (gems) besetzt mit; (snow, dirt) verkrustet mit.

encumber [ɪn'kʌmbə*] vt: **to be ~ed with** beladen sein mit; (debts) belastet sein mit.

encyclop(a)edia [ɛnsaɪkləu'piːdɪə] n Lexikon nt, Enzyklopädie f.

end [ɛnd] n Ende nt; (of film, book) Schluß m, Ende nt; (of table) Schmalseite f; (of pointed object) Spitze f; (aim) Zweck m, Ziel nt ♦ vt (also: **bring to an ~, put an ~ to**) beenden ♦ vi enden; **from ~ to ~** von einem Ende zum anderen; **to come to an ~** zu Ende gehen; **to be at an ~** zu Ende sein; **in the ~** schließlich; **on ~** hochkant; **to stand on ~** (hair) zu Berge stehen; **for hours on ~** stundenlang ununterbrochen; **for 5 hours on ~** 5 Stunden ununterbrochen; **at the ~ of the street** am Ende der Straße; **at the ~ of the day** (BRIT, fig) letztlich; **to this ~, with this ~ in view** mit diesem Ziel vor Augen.

▶**end up** vi: **to ~ up in** (place) landen in +dat; **to ~ up in trouble** Ärger bekommen; **to ~ up doing sth** etw schließlich tun.

endanger [ɪn'deɪndʒə*] vt gefährden; **an ~ed species** eine vom Aussterben bedrohte Art.

endear [ɪn'dɪə*] vt: **to ~ o.s. to sb** sich bei jdm beliebt machen.

endearing [ɪn'dɪərɪŋ] adj gewinnend.

endearment [ɪn'dɪəmənt] n: **to whisper ~s** zärtliche Worte flüstern; **term of ~** Kosewort nt, Kosename m.

endeavour, (US) **endeavor** [ɪn'dɛvə*] n Anstrengung f, Bemühung f; (effort) Bestrebung f ♦ vi: **to ~ to do sth** (attempt) sich anstrengen or bemühen, etw zu tun; (strive) bestrebt sein, etw zu tun.

endemic [ɛn'dɛmɪk] adj endemisch, verbreitet.

ending ['ɛndɪŋ] n Ende nt, Schluß m; (LING) Endung f.

endive ['ɛndaɪv] n Endivie f; (chicory) Chicorée f or m.

endless ['ɛndlɪs] adj endlos; (patience, resources, possibilities) unbegrenzt.

endorse [ɪn'dɔːs] vt (cheque) indossieren, auf der Rückseite unterzeichnen; (proposal, plan) billigen; (candidate) unterstützen.

endorsee [ɪndɔː'siː] n Indossat m.

endorsement [ɪn'dɔːsmənt] n Billigung f; (of candidate) Unterstützung f; (BRIT: on driving licence) Strafvermerk m.

endow [ɪn'dau] vt (institution) eine Stiftung machen an +acc; **to be ~ed with** besitzen.

endowment [ɪn'daumənt] n Stiftung f; (quality) Begabung f.

endowment assurance n Versicherung f auf den Erlebensfall, Erlebensversicherung *f*.

endowment mortgage *n* Hypothek *f* mit Lebensversicherung.

end product *n* Endprodukt *nt*; (*fig*) Produkt *nt*.

end result *n* Endergebnis *nt*.

endurable [ɪn'djuərəbl] *adj* erträglich.

endurance [ɪn'djuərəns] *n* Durchhaltevermögen *nt*; (*patience*) Geduld *f*.

endurance test *n* Belastungsprobe *f*.

endure [ɪn'djuə•] *vt* ertragen ♦ *vi* Bestand haben.

enduring [ɪn'djuərɪŋ] *adj* dauerhaft.

end user *n* (*COMPUT*) Endbenutzer *m*.

enema ['enɪmə] *n* Klistier *nt*, Einlauf *m*.

enemy ['enəmɪ] *adj* feindlich; (*strategy*) des Feindes ♦ *n* Feind(in) *m(f)*; **to make an ~ of sb** sich *dat* jdn zum Feind machen.

energetic [enə'dʒetɪk] *adj* aktiv.

energy ['enədʒɪ] *n* Energie *f*; **Department of E~** Energieministerium *nt*.

energy crisis *n* Energiekrise *f*.

energy-saving ['enədʒɪ'seɪvɪŋ] *adj* energiesparend; (*policy*) energiebewußt.

enervating ['enəveɪtɪŋ] *adj* strapazierend.

enforce [ɪn'fɔːs] *vt* (*law, rule, decision*) Geltung verschaffen +*dat*.

enforced [ɪn'fɔːst] *adj* erzwungen.

enfranchise [ɪn'fræntʃaɪz] *vt* das Wahlrecht geben *or* erteilen +*dat*.

engage [ɪn'geɪdʒ] *vt* in Anspruch nehmen; (*employ*) einstellen; (*lawyer*) sich *dat* nehmen; (*MIL*) angreifen ♦ *vi* (*TECH*) einrasten; **to ~ the clutch** einkuppeln; **to ~ sb in conversation** jdn in ein Gespräch verwickeln; **to ~ in** sich beteiligen an +*dat*; **to ~ in commerce** kaufmännisch tätig sein; **to ~ in study** studieren.

engaged [ɪn'geɪdʒd] *adj* verlobt; (*BRIT: busy, in use*) besetzt; **to get ~** sich verloben; **he is ~ in research/a survey** er ist mit Forschungsarbeit/einer Umfrage beschäftigt.

engaged tone (*BRIT*) *n* Besetztzeichen *nt*.

engagement [ɪn'geɪdʒmənt] *n* Verabredung *f*; (*booking*) Engagement *nt*; (*to marry*) Verlobung *f*; (*MIL*) Gefecht *nt*, Kampf *m*; **I have a previous ~** ich habe schon eine Verabredung.

engagement ring *n* Verlobungsring *m*.

engaging [ɪn'geɪdʒɪŋ] *adj* einnehmend.

engender [ɪn'dʒendə•] *vt* erzeugen.

engine ['endʒɪn] *n* Motor *m*; (*RAIL*) Lok(omotive) *f*.

engine driver *n* (*RAIL*) Lok(omotiv)führer(in) *m(f)*.

engineer [endʒɪ'nɪə•] *n* Ingenieur(in) *m(f)*; (*BRIT: for repairs*) Techniker(in) *m(f)*; (*US: RAIL*) Lok(omotiv)führer(in) *m(f)*; (*on ship*) Maschinist(in) *m(f)*; **civil/mechanical ~** Bau-/Maschinenbauingenieur(in) *m(f)*.

engineering [endʒɪ'nɪərɪŋ] *n* Technik *f*;

(*design, construction*) Konstruktion *f* ♦ *cpd*: **~ works** *or* **factory** Maschinenfabrik *f*.

engine failure *n* Maschinenschaden *m*; (*AUT*) Motorschaden *m*.

engine trouble *n* Maschinenschaden *m*; (*AUT*) Motorschaden *m*.

England ['ɪŋglənd] *n* England *nt*.

English ['ɪŋglɪʃ] *adj* englisch ♦ *n* Englisch *nt*; **the English** *npl* die Engländer *pl*; **an ~ speaker** *jd*, der Englisch spricht.

English Channel *n*: **the ~** der Ärmelkanal.

Englishman ['ɪŋglɪʃmən] (*irreg: like* **man**) *n* Engländer *m*.

English-speaking ['ɪŋglɪʃ'spiːkɪŋ] *adj* (*country*) englischsprachig.

Englishwoman ['ɪŋglɪʃwumən] (*irreg: like* **woman**) *n* Engländerin *f*.

engrave [ɪn'greɪv] *vt* gravieren; (*name etc*) eingravieren; (*fig*) einprägen.

engraving [ɪn'greɪvɪŋ] *n* Stich *m*.

engrossed [ɪn'grəust] *adj*: **~ in** vertieft in +*acc*.

engulf [ɪn'gʌlf] *vt* verschlingen; (*subj: panic, fear*) überkommen.

enhance [ɪn'hɑːns] *vt* verbessern; (*enjoyment, beauty*) erhöhen.

enigma [ɪ'nɪgmə] *n* Rätsel *nt*.

enigmatic [enɪg'mætɪk] *adj* rätselhaft.

enjoy [ɪn'dʒɔɪ] *vt* genießen; (*health, fortune*) sich erfreuen +*gen*; (*success*) haben; **to ~ o.s.** sich amüsieren; **I ~ dancing** ich tanze gerne.

enjoyable [ɪn'dʒɔɪəbl] *adj* nett, angenehm.

enjoyment [ɪn'dʒɔɪmənt] *n* Vergnügen *nt*; (*activity*) Freude *f*.

enlarge [ɪn'lɑːdʒ] *vt* vergrößern; (*scope*) erweitern ♦ *vi*: **to ~ on** weiter ausführen.

enlarged [ɪn'lɑːdʒd] *adj* erweitert; (*MED*) vergrößert.

enlargement [ɪn'lɑːdʒmənt] *n* Vergrößerung *f*.

enlighten [ɪn'laɪtn] *vt* aufklären.

enlightened [ɪn'laɪtnd] *adj* aufgeklärt.

enlightening [ɪn'laɪtnɪŋ] *adj* aufschlußreich.

enlightenment [ɪn'laɪtnmənt] *n* (*also HIST: Enlightenment*) Aufklärung *f*.

enlist [ɪn'lɪst] *vt* anwerben; (*support, help*) gewinnen ♦ *vi*: **to ~ in** eintreten in +*acc*; **~ed man** (*US: MIL*) gemeiner Soldat *m*; (*US: in navy*) Matrose *m*.

enliven [ɪn'laɪvn] *vt* beleben.

enmity ['enmɪtɪ] *n* Feindschaft *f*.

ennoble [ɪ'nəubl] *vt* adeln; (*fig: dignify*) erheben.

enormity [ɪ'nɔːmɪtɪ] *n* ungeheure Größe *f*.

enormous [ɪ'nɔːməs] *adj* gewaltig, ungeheuer; (*pleasure, success etc*) riesig.

enormously [ɪ'nɔːməslɪ] *adv* enorm; (*rich*) ungeheuer.

enough [ɪ'nʌf] *adj* genug, genügend ♦ *pron* genug ♦ *adv*: **big ~** groß genug; **he has not worked ~** er hat nicht genug *or* genügend gearbeitet; **have you got ~?** haben Sie

genug?; ~ **to eat** genug zu essen; **will 5 be
~?** reichen 5?; **I've had ~!** jetzt reicht's mir
aber!; **it's hot ~ (as it is)** es ist heiß genug;
he was kind ~ to lend me the money er war
so gut und hat mir das Geld geliehen; **~!** es
reicht!; **that's ~, thanks** danke, das reicht *or*
ist genug; **I've had ~ of him** ich habe genug
von ihm; **funnily/oddly ~** ... komischerweise ...

enquire [ɪn'kwaɪə*] *vt, vi* = inquire.

enrage [ɪn'reɪdʒ] *vt* wütend machen.

enrich [ɪn'rɪtʃ] *vt* bereichern.

enrol, (*US*) **enroll** [ɪn'rəul] *vt* anmelden; (*at
university*) einschreiben, immatrikulieren
♦ *vi* (*see vt*) sich anmelden; sich
einschreiben, sich immatrikulieren.

enrolment, (*US*) **enrollment** [ɪn'rəulmənt] *n*
(*v vb*) Anmeldung *f*; Einschreibung *f*,
Immatrikulation *f*.

en route [ɔn'ruːt] *adv* unterwegs; **~ for** auf
dem Weg nach; **~ from London to Berlin** auf
dem Weg von London nach Berlin.

ensconced [ɪn'skɔnst] *adj*: **she is ~ in** ... sie
hat es sich *dat* in ... *dat* gemütlich gemacht.

ensemble [ɔn'sɔmbl] *n* Ensemble *nt*.

enshrine [ɪn'ʃraɪn] *vt* bewahren; **to be ~d in**
verankert sein in *+dat*.

ensue [ɪn'sjuː] *vi* folgen.

ensuing [ɪn'sjuːɪŋ] *adj* folgend.

ensure [ɪn'ʃuə*] *vt* garantieren; **to ~ that**
sicherstellen, daß.

ENT *n abbr* (*MED*: = *ear, nose and throat*) HNO.

entail [ɪn'teɪl] *vt* mit sich bringen.

entangled [ɪn'tæŋgld] *adj*: **to become ~ (in)**
sich verfangen (in *+dat*).

enter ['entə*] *vt* betreten; (*club*) beitreten *+dat*;
(*army*) gehen zu; (*profession*) ergreifen;
(*race, contest*) sich beteiligen an *+dat*; (*sb for
a competition*) anmelden; (*write down*)
eintragen; (*COMPUT: data*) eingeben ♦ *vi*
(*come in*) hereinkommen; (*go in*)
hineingehen.

►**enter for** *vt fus* anmelden für.

►**enter into** *vt fus* (*discussion, negotiations*)
aufnehmen; (*correspondence*) treten in *+acc*;
(*agreement*) schließen.

►**enter up** *vt* eintragen.

►**enter (up)on** *vt fus* (*career, policy*)
einschlagen.

enteritis [entə'raɪtɪs] *n* Dünndarmentzündung
f.

enterprise ['entəpraɪz] *n* Unternehmen *nt*;
(*initiative*) Initiative *f*; **free ~** freies
Unternehmertum *nt*; **private ~**
Privatunternehmertum *nt*.

enterprising ['entəpraɪzɪŋ] *adj* einfallsreich.

entertain [entə'teɪn] *vt* unterhalten; (*invite*)
einladen; (*idea, plan*) erwägen.

entertainer [entə'teɪnə*] *n* Unterhalter(in)
m(f), Entertainer(in) *m(f)*.

entertaining [entə'teɪnɪŋ] *adj* amüsant ♦ *n*: **to
do a lot of ~** sehr oft Gäste haben.

entertainment [entə'teɪnmənt] *n*
Unterhaltung *f*, (*show*) Darbietung *f*.

entertainment allowance *n*
Aufwandspauschale *f*.

enthral [ɪn'θrɔːl] *vt* begeistern; (*story*) fesseln.

enthralled [ɪn'θrɔːld] *adj* gefesselt; **he was
~ by** *or* **with the book** das Buch fesselte
ihn.

enthralling [ɪn'θrɔːlɪŋ] *adj* fesselnd; (*details*)
spannend.

enthuse [ɪn'θuːz] *vi*: **to ~ about** *or* **over**
schwärmen von.

enthusiasm [ɪn'θuːzɪæzəm] *n* Begeisterung *f*.

enthusiast [ɪn'θuːzɪæst] *n* Enthusiast(in) *m(f)*;
he's a jazz/sports ~ er begeistert sich für
Jazz/Sport.

enthusiastic [ɪnθuːzɪ'æstɪk] *adj* begeistert;
(*response, reception*) enthusiastisch; **to be
~ about** begeistert sein von.

entice [ɪn'taɪs] *vt* locken; (*tempt*) verleiten.

enticing [ɪn'taɪsɪŋ] *adj* verlockend.

entire [ɪn'taɪə*] *adj* ganz.

entirely [ɪn'taɪəlɪ] *adv* völlig.

entirety [ɪn'taɪərətɪ] *n*: **in its ~** in seiner
Gesamtheit.

entitle [ɪn'taɪtl] *vt*: **to ~ sb to sth** jdn zu etw
berechtigen; **to ~ sb to do sth** jdn dazu
berechtigen, etw zu tun.

entitled [ɪn'taɪtld] *adj*: **a book/film** *etc* **~** ... ein
Buch/Film *etc* mit dem Titel ...; **to be ~ to
do sth** das Recht haben, etw zu tun.

entity ['entɪtɪ] *n* Wesen *nt*.

entourage [ɔntu'rɑːʒ] *n* Gefolge *nt*.

entrails ['entreɪlz] *npl* Eingeweide *pl*.

entrance [*n* 'entrns, *vt* ɪn'trɑːns] *n* Eingang *m*;
(*arrival*) Ankunft *f*; (*on stage*) Auftritt *m* ♦ *vt*
bezaubern; **to gain ~ to** (*building etc*) sich
dat Zutritt verschaffen zu; (*university*) die
Zulassung erhalten zu; (*profession etc*)
Zugang erhalten zu.

entrance examination *n* Aufnahmeprüfung
f.

entrance fee *n* Eintrittsgeld *nt*.

entrance ramp (*US*) *n* Auffahrt *f*.

entrancing [ɪn'trɑːnsɪŋ] *adj* bezaubernd.

entrant ['entrnt] *n* Teilnehmer(in) *m(f)*; (*BRIT*:
in exam) Prüfling *m*.

entreat [en'triːt] *vt*: **to ~ sb to do sth** jdn
anflehen, etw zu tun.

entreaty [en'triːtɪ] *n* (flehentliche) Bitte *f*.

entrée ['ɔntreɪ] *n* Hauptgericht *nt*.

entrenched [en'trentʃt] *adj* verankert; (*ideas*)
festgesetzt.

entrepreneur ['ɔntrəprə'nəː*] *n*
Unternehmer(in) *m(f)*.

entrepreneurial ['ɔntrəprə'nəːrɪəl] *adj*
unternehmerisch.

entrust [ɪn'trʌst] *vt*: **to ~ sth to sb** jdm etw
anvertrauen; **to ~ sb with sth** (*task*) jdn mit
etw betrauen; (*secret, valuables*) jdm etw
anvertrauen.

entry ['entrɪ] *n* Eingang *m*; (*in competition*)

Meldung *f*; (*in register, account book, reference book*) Eintrag *m*; (*arrival*) Eintritt *m*; (*to country*) Einreise *f*; **"no ~ "** „Zutritt verboten"; (*AUT*) „Einfahrt verboten"; **single/double** ~ **book-keeping** einfache/ doppelte Buchführung *f*.

entry form *n* Anmeldeformular *nt*.

entry phone (*BRIT*) *n* Türsprechanlage *f*.

entwine [ɪn'twaɪn] *vt* verflechten.

enumerate [ɪ'nju:məreɪt] *vt* aufzählen.

enunciate [ɪ'nʌnsɪeɪt] *vt* artikulieren; (*principle, plan etc*) formulieren.

envelop [ɪn'vɛləp] *vt* einhüllen.

envelope ['ɛnvələup] *n* Umschlag *m*.

enviable ['ɛnvɪəbl] *adj* beneidenswert.

envious ['ɛnvɪəs] *adj* neidisch; **to be ~ of sth/ sb** auf etw/jdn neidisch sein.

environment [ɪn'vaɪərnmənt] *n* Umwelt *f*; **Department of the E~** (*BRIT*) Umweltministerium *nt*.

environmental [ɪnvaɪərn'mɛntl] *adj* (*problems, pollution etc*) Umwelt-; ~ **studies** Umweltkunde *f*.

environmentalist [ɪnvaɪərn'mɛntlɪst] *n* Umweltschützer(in) *m(f)*.

Environmental Protection Agency (*US*) *n* staatliche Umweltbehörde der USA.

environment-friendly *adj* umweltfreundlich.

envisage [ɪn'vɪzɪdʒ] *vt* sich *dat* vorstellen; **I ~ that ...** ich stelle mir vor, daß ...

envision [ɪn'vɪʒən] (*US*) *vt* = **envisage**.

envoy ['ɛnvɔɪ] *n* Gesandte(r) *f(m)*.

envy ['ɛnvɪ] *n* Neid *m* ♦ *vt* beneiden; **to ~ sb sth** jdn um etw beneiden.

enzyme ['ɛnzaɪm] *n* Enzym *nt*.

eon ['i:ən] *n* Äon *m*, Ewigkeit *f*.

EPA (*US*) *n abbr* = **Environmental Protection Agency**.

ephemeral [ɪ'fɛmərl] *adj* kurzlebig.

epic ['ɛpɪk] *n* Epos *nt* ♦ *adj* (*journey*) lang und abenteuerlich.

epicentre, (*US*) **epicenter** ['ɛpɪsɛntə*] *n* Epizentrum *nt*.

epidemic [ɛpɪ'dɛmɪk] *n* Epidemie *f*.

epigram ['ɛpɪgræm] *n* Epigramm *nt*.

epilepsy ['ɛpɪlɛpsɪ] *n* Epilepsie *f*.

epileptic [ɛpɪ'lɛptɪk] *adj* epileptisch ♦ *n* Epileptiker(in) *m(f)*.

epilogue ['ɛpɪlɔg] *n* Epilog *m*, Nachwort *nt*.

Epiphany [ɪ'pɪfənɪ] *n* Dreikönigsfest *nt*.

episcopal [ɪ'pɪskəpl] *adj* bischöflich; **the E~ Church** die Episkopalkirche.

episode ['ɛpɪsəud] *n* Episode *f*; (*TV, RADIO*) Folge *f*.

epistle [ɪ'pɪsl] *n* Epistel *f*; (*REL*) Brief *m*.

epitaph ['ɛpɪtɑ:f] *n* Epitaph *nt*; (*on gravestone etc*) Grab(in)schrift *f*.

epithet ['ɛpɪθɛt] *n* Beiname *m*.

epitome [ɪ'pɪtəmɪ] *n* Inbegriff *m*.

epitomize [ɪ'pɪtəmaɪz] *vt* verkörpern.

epoch ['i:pɔk] *n* Epoche *f*.

epoch-making ['i:pɔkmeɪkɪŋ] *adj* epochal; (*discovery*) epochemachend.

eponymous [ɪ'pɒnɪməs] *adj* namengebend.

equable ['ɛkwəbl] *adj* ausgeglichen; (*reply*) sachlich.

equal ['i:kwl] *adj* gleich ♦ *n* Gleichgestellte(r) *f(m)* ♦ *vt* gleichkommen +*dat*; (*number*) gleich sein +*dat*; **they are roughly ~ in size** sie sind ungefähr gleich groß; **the number of exports should be ~ to imports** Export- und Importzahlen sollten gleich sein; **~ opportunities** Chancengleichheit *f*; **to be ~ to** (*task*) gewachsen sein +*dat*; **two times two ~s four** zwei mal zwei ist (gleich) vier.

equality [i:'kwɔlɪtɪ] *n* Gleichheit *f*; ~ **of opportunity** Chancengleichheit *f*.

equalize ['i:kwəlaɪz] *vt* angleichen ♦ *vi* (*SPORT*) ausgleichen.

equally ['i:kwəlɪ] *adv* gleichmäßig; (*good, bad etc*) gleich; **they are ~ clever** sie sind beide gleich klug.

Equal Opportunities Commission, (*US*) **Equal Employment Opportunity Commission** *n* Ausschuß *m* für Chancengleichheit am Arbeitsplatz.

equal(s) sign *n* Gleichheitszeichen *nt*.

equanimity [ɛkwə'nɪmɪtɪ] *n* Gleichmut *m*, Gelassenheit *f*.

equate [ɪ'kweɪt] *vt*: **to ~ sth with** etw gleichsetzen mit ♦ *vt* (*compare*) auf die gleiche Stufe stellen; **to ~ A to B** A und B auf die gleiche Stufe stellen.

equation [ɪ'kweɪʃən] *n* Gleichung *f*.

equator [ɪ'kweɪtə*] *n* Äquator *m*.

equatorial [ɛkwə'tɔ:rɪəl] *adj* äquatorial.

Equatorial Guinea *n* Äquatorial-Guinea *nt*.

equestrian [ɪ'kwɛstrɪən] *adj* (*sport, dress etc*) Reit-; (*statue*) Reiter- ♦ *n* Reiter(in) *m(f)*.

equilibrium [i:kwɪ'lɪbrɪəm] *n* Gleichgewicht *nt*.

equinox ['i:kwɪnɔks] *n* Tagundnachtgleiche *f*; **the spring/autumn ~** die Frühjahrs-/die Herbst-Tagundnachtgleiche *f*.

equip [ɪ'kwɪp] *vt*: **to ~ (with)** (*person, army*) ausrüsten (mit); (*room, car etc*) ausstatten (mit); **to ~ sb for** jdn vorbereiten auf +*acc*; **to be well ~ped** gut ausgerüstet sein.

equipment [ɪ'kwɪpmənt] *n* Ausrüstung *f*.

equitable ['ɛkwɪtəbl] *adj* gerecht.

equities ['ɛkwɪtɪz] (*BRIT*) *npl* Stammaktien *pl*.

equity ['ɛkwɪtɪ] *n* Gerechtigkeit *f*.

equity capital *n* Eigenkapital *nt*.

equivalent [ɪ'kwɪvələnt] *adj* gleich, gleichwertig ♦ *n* Gegenstück *nt*; **to be ~ to** *or* **the ~ of** entsprechen +*dat*.

equivocal [ɪ'kwɪvəkl] *adj* vieldeutig; (*open to suspicion*) zweifelhaft.

equivocate [ɪ'kwɪvəkeɪt] *vi* ausweichen, ausweichend antworten.

equivocation [ɪkwɪvə'keɪʃən] *n* Ausflucht *f*, ausweichende Antwort *f*.

ER (*BRIT*) *abbr* (= *Elizabeth Regina*) *offizieller*

Namenszug der Königin.
ERA (*US*) *n abbr* (*POL:* = *Equal Rights Amendment*) *Artikel der amerikanischen Verfassung zur Gleichberechtigung;* (*BASEBALL:* = *earned run average*) *durch Eigenleistung erzielte Läufe.*
era ['ɪərə] *n* Ära *f*, Epoche *f*.
eradicate [ɪ'rædɪkeɪt] *vt* ausrotten.
erase [ɪ'reɪz] *vt* (*tape, COMPUT*) löschen; (*writing*) ausradieren; (*thought, feeling*) auslöschen.
eraser [ɪ'reɪzə*] *n* Radiergummi *m*.
erect [ɪ'rɛkt] *adj* aufrecht; (*tail*) hocherhoben; (*ears*) gespitzt ♦ *vt* bauen; (*assemble*) aufstellen.
erection [ɪ'rɛkʃən] *n* Bauen *nt*; (*of statue*) Errichten *nt*; (*of tent, machinery etc*) Aufstellen *nt*; (*PHYSIOL*) Erektion *f*.
ergonomics [ə:gə'nɔmɪks] *n sing* Ergonomie *f*, Ergonomik *f*.
ERISA (*US*) *n abbr* (= *Employee Retirement Income Security Act*) *Gesetz zur Regelung der Rentenversicherung.*
Eritrea *n* Eritrea *nt*.
ERM *n abbr* (= *Exchange Rate Mechanism*) Wechselkursmechanismus *m*.
ermine ['ə:mɪn] *n* (*fur*) Hermelin *m*.
ERNIE, Ernie ['ə:nɪ] (*BRIT*) *n abbr* (= *Electronic Random Number Indicator Equipment*) *Gerät zur Ermittlung von Gewinnummern für Prämiensparer.*
erode [ɪ'rəud] *vt* erodieren, auswaschen; (*metal*) zerfressen; (*confidence, power*) untergraben.
erogenous [ɪ'rɔdʒənəs] *adj* erogen.
erosion [ɪ'rəuʒən] *n* (*see vb*) Erosion *f*, Auswaschen *nt*; Zerfressen *nt*; Untergraben *nt*.
erotic [ɪ'rɔtɪk] *adj* erotisch.
eroticism [ɪ'rɔtɪsɪzəm] *n* Erotik *f*.
err [ə:*] *vi* sich irren; **to ~ on the side of caution/simplicity** (im Zweifelsfall) zur Vorsicht/Vereinfachung neigen.
errand ['ɛrənd] *n* Besorgung *f*; (*to give a message etc*) Botengang *m*; **to run ~s** Besorgungen/Botengänge machen; **~ of mercy** Rettungsaktion *f*.
erratic [ɪ'rætɪk] *adj* unberechenbar; (*attempts*) unkoordiniert; (*noise*) unregelmäßig.
erroneous [ɪ'rəunɪəs] *adj* irrig.
error ['ɛrə*] *n* Fehler *m*; **typing/spelling ~** Tipp-/Rechtschreibfehler *m*; **in ~** irrtümlicherweise; **~s and omissions excepted** Irrtum vorbehalten.
error message *n* Fehlermeldung *f*.
erstwhile ['ə:stwaɪl] *adj* einstig, vormalig.
erudite ['ɛrjudaɪt] *adj* gelehrt.
erupt [ɪ'rʌpt] *vi* ausbrechen.
eruption [ɪ'rʌpʃən] *n* Ausbruch *m*.
ESA *n abbr* (= *European Space Agency*) Europäische Weltraumbehörde *f*.
escalate ['ɛskəleɪt] *vi* eskalieren, sich

ausweiten.
escalation [ɛskə'leɪʃən] *n* Eskalation *f*.
escalator ['ɛskəleɪtə*] *n* Rolltreppe *f*.
escalator clause *n* Gleitklausel *f*.
escapade [ɛskə'peɪd] *n* Eskapade *f*.
escape [ɪs'keɪp] *n* Flucht *f*; (*TECH: of liquid*) Ausfließen *nt*; (*of gas*) Ausströmen *nt*; (*of air, heat*) Entweichen *nt* ♦ *vi* entkommen; (*from prison*) ausbrechen; (*liquid*) ausfließen; (*gas*) ausströmen; (*air, heat*) entweichen ♦ *vt* (*pursuers etc*) entkommen +*dat*; (*punishment etc*) entgehen +*dat*; **his name ~s me** sein Name ist mir entfallen; **to ~ from** flüchten aus; (*prison*) ausbrechen aus; (*person*) entkommen +*dat*; **to ~ to Peru** nach Peru fliehen; **to ~ to safety** sich in Sicherheit bringen; **to ~ notice** unbemerkt bleiben.
escape artist *n* Entfesselungskünstler(in) *m(f)*.
escape clause *n* (*in contract*) Befreiungsklausel *f*.
escapee [ɪskeɪ'pi:] *n* entwichener Häftling *m*.
escape hatch *n* Notluke *f*.
escape key *n* (*COMPUT*) Escape-Taste *f*.
escape route *n* Fluchtweg *m*.
escapism [ɪs'keɪpɪzəm] *n* Wirklichkeitsflucht *f*, Eskapismus *m*.
escapist [ɪs'keɪpɪst] *adj* eskapistisch.
escapologist [ɛskə'pɔlədʒɪst] (*BRIT*) *n* = **escape artist**.
escarpment [ɪs'ka:pmənt] *n* Steilhang *m*.
eschew [ɪs'tʃu:] *vt* meiden.
escort [*n* 'ɛskɔːt, *vt* ɪs'kɔːt] *n* Eskorte *f*; (*companion*) Begleiter(in) *m(f)* ♦ *vt* begleiten; **his ~** seine Begleiterin; **her ~** ihr Begleiter.
escort agency *n* Agentur *f* für Begleiter(innen).
Eskimo ['ɛskɪməu] *n* Eskimo(frau) *m(f)*.
ESL *n abbr* (*SCOL:* = *English as a Second Language*) Englisch *nt* als Zweitsprache.
esophagus [i:'sɔfəgəs] (*US*) *n* = **oesophagus**.
esoteric [ɛsə'tɛrɪk] *adj* esoterisch.
ESP *n abbr* = **extrasensory perception**; (*SCOL:* = *English for Special Purposes*) *Englischunterricht für spezielle Fachbereiche.*
esp. *abbr* = **especially**.
especially [ɪs'pɛʃlɪ] *adv* besonders.
espionage ['ɛspɪəna:ʒ] *n* Spionage *f*.
esplanade [ɛsplə'neɪd] *n* Promenade *f*.
espouse [ɪs'pauz] *vt* eintreten für.
Esquire [ɪs'kwaɪə*] *n* (*abbr* Esq.): **J. Brown, ~** Herrn J. Brown.
essay ['ɛseɪ] *n* Aufsatz *m*; (*LITER*) Essay *m or nt*.
essence ['ɛsns] *n* Wesen *nt*; (*CULIN*) Essenz *f*; **in ~** im wesentlichen; **speed is of the ~** Geschwindigkeit ist von entscheidender Bedeutung.
essential [ɪ'sɛnʃl] *adj* notwendig; (*basic*) wesentlich ♦ *n* (*see adj*) Notwendigste(s) *nt*; Wesentliche(s) *nt*; **it is ~ that** es ist unbedingt *or* absolut erforderlich, daß.

essentially [ɪ'sɛnʃəlɪ] adv im Grunde genommen.

EST (US) abbr (= Eastern Standard Time) ostamerikanische Standardzeit.

est. abbr = established; estimate(d).

establish [ɪs'tæblɪʃ] vt gründen; (facts) feststellen; (proof) erstellen; (relations, contact) aufnehmen; (reputation) sich dat verschaffen.

established [ɪs'tæblɪʃt] adj üblich; (business) eingeführt.

establishment [ɪs'tæblɪʃmənt] n (see vb) Gründung f; Feststellung f; Erstellung f; Aufnahme f; (of reputation) Begründung f; (shop etc) Unternehmen nt; **the E~** das Establishment.

estate [ɪs'teɪt] n Gut nt; (BRIT: also: **housing** ~) Siedlung f; (LAW) Nachlaß m.

estate agency (BRIT) n Maklerbüro nt.

estate agent (BRIT) n Immobilienmakler(in) m(f).

estate car (BRIT) n Kombiwagen m.

esteem [ɪs'tiːm] n: **to hold sb in high** ~ eine hohe Meinung von jdm haben.

esthetic [ɪs'θɛtɪk] (US) adj = aesthetic.

estimate ['ɛstɪmət] n Schätzung f; (assessment) Einschätzung f; (COMM) (Kosten)voranschlag m ♦ vt schätzen ♦ vi (BRIT: COMM): **to** ~ **for** einen Kostenvoranschlag machen für; **to give sb an** ~ **of sth** jdm eine Vorstellung von etw geben; **to** ~ **for** einen Kostenvoranschlag machen für; **at a rough** ~ grob geschätzt, über den Daumen gepeilt (inf); **I** ~ **that** ich schätze, daß.

estimation [ɛstɪ'meɪʃən] n Schätzung f; (opinion) Einschätzung f; **in my** ~ meiner Einschätzung nach.

estimator ['ɛstɪmeɪtə*] n Schätzer(in) m(f).

Estonia [ɛs'təʊnɪə] n Estland nt.

Estonian [ɛs'təʊnɪən] adj estnisch ♦ n Este m, Estin f; (LING) Estnisch nt.

estranged [ɪs'treɪndʒd] adj entfremdet; (from spouse) getrennt; (couple) getrennt lebend.

estrangement [ɪs'treɪndʒmənt] n Entfremdung f; (from spouse) Trennung f.

estrogen ['iːstrəʊdʒən] (US) n = oestrogen.

estuary ['ɛstjʊərɪ] n Mündung f.

ET (BRIT) n abbr (= Employment Training) Ausbildungsmaßnahmen für Arbeitslose.

ETA n abbr (= estimated time of arrival) voraussichtliche Ankunftszeit f.

et al. abbr (= et alii) u.a.

etc. abbr (= et cetera) etc.

etch [ɛtʃ] vt (design, surface: with needle) radieren; (: with acid) ätzen; (: with chisel) meißeln; **it will be** ~**ed on my memory** es wird sich tief in mein Gedächtnis eingraben.

etching ['ɛtʃɪŋ] n Radierung f.

ETD n abbr (= estimated time of departure) voraussichtliche Abflugzeit f.

eternal [ɪ'təːnl] adj ewig.

eternity [ɪ'təːnɪtɪ] n Ewigkeit f.

ether ['iːθə*] n Äther m.

ethereal [ɪ'θɪərɪəl] adj ätherisch.

ethical ['ɛθɪkl] adj ethisch.

ethics ['ɛθɪks] n Ethik f ♦ npl (morality) Moral f.

Ethiopia [iːθɪ'əʊpɪə] n Äthiopien nt.

Ethiopian [iːθɪ'əʊpɪən] adj äthiopisch ♦ n Äthiopier(in) m(f).

ethnic ['ɛθnɪk] adj ethnisch; (music) folkloristisch; (culture etc) urwüchsig.

ethnic cleansing [-'klɛnzɪŋ] n ethnische Säuberung f.

ethnology [ɛθ'nɒlədʒɪ] n Ethnologie f, Völkerkunde f.

ethos ['iːθɒs] n Ethos nt.

etiquette ['ɛtɪkɛt] n Etikette f.

ETV (US) n abbr (= educational television) Fernsehsender, der Bildungs- und Kulturprogramme ausstrahlt.

etymology [ɛtɪ'mɒlədʒɪ] n Etymologie f; (of word) Herkunft f.

EU n abbr (= European Union) EU f.

eucalyptus [juːkə'lɪptəs] n Eukalyptus m.

Eucharist ['juːkərɪst] n: **the** ~ die Eucharistie, das (heilige) Abendmahl.

eulogy ['juːlədʒɪ] n Lobrede f.

euphemism ['juːfəmɪzəm] n Euphemismus m.

euphemistic [juːfə'mɪstɪk] adj euphemistisch, verhüllend.

euphoria [juː'fɔːrɪə] n Euphorie f.

Eurasia [jʊə'reɪʃə] n Eurasien nt.

Eurasian [jʊə'reɪʃən] adj eurasisch ♦ n Eurasier(in) m(f).

Euratom [jʊə'rætəm] n abbr (= European Atomic Energy Community) Euratom f.

Euro- ['jʊərəʊ] pref Euro-.

Eurocheque ['jʊərəʊtʃɛk] n Euroscheck m.

Eurocrat ['jʊərəʊkræt] n Eurokrat(in) m(f).

Eurodollar ['jʊərəʊdɒlə*] n Eurodollar m.

Europe ['jʊərəp] n Europa nt.

European [jʊərə'piːən] adj europäisch ♦ n Europäer(in) m(f).

European Community n: **the** ~ die Europäische Gemeinschaft.

European Court of Justice n: **the** ~ der Europäische Gerichtshof.

European Economic Community n: **the** ~ die Europäische Wirtschaftsgemeinschaft.

Euro-sceptic ['jʊərəʊskɛptɪk] n Euroskeptiker(in) m(f).

euthanasia [juːθə'neɪzɪə] n Euthanasie f.

evacuate [ɪ'vækjueɪt] vt evakuieren; (place) räumen.

evacuation [ɪvækju'eɪʃən] n (see verb) Evakuierung f; Räumung f.

evacuee [ɪvækju'iː] n Evakuierte(r) f(m).

evade [ɪ'veɪd] vt (person, question) ausweichen +dat; (tax) hinterziehen; (duty, responsibility) sich entziehen +dat.

evaluate [ɪ'væljueɪt] vt bewerten; (situation) einschätzen.

evangelical [i:væn'dʒɛlɪkl] *adj* evangelisch.
evangelist [ɪ'vændʒəlɪst] *n* Evangelist(in) *m(f)*.
evangelize [ɪ'vændʒəlaɪz] *vi* evangelisieren.
evaporate [ɪ'væpəreɪt] *vi* verdampfen;
(*feeling, attitude*) dahinschwinden.
evaporated milk [ɪ'væpəreɪtɪd-] *n*
Kondensmilch *f*, Büchsenmilch *f*.
evaporation [ɪvæpə'reɪʃən] *n* Verdampfung *f*.
evasion [ɪ'veɪʒən] *n* Ausweichen *nt*; (*of tax*)
Hinterziehung *f*.
evasive [ɪ'veɪsɪv] *adj* ausweichend; **to take**
~ **action** ein Ausweichmanöver machen.
eve [i:v] *n*: **on the ~ of** am Tag vor +*dat*;
Christmas E~ Heiligabend *m*; **New Year's**
E~ Silvester *m or nt*.
even [i:vn] *adj* (*level*) eben; (*smooth*) glatt;
(*equal*) gleich; (*number*) gerade ♦ *adv* sogar,
selbst; (*introducing a comparison*) sogar noch;
~ **if**, ~ **though** selbst wenn; ~ **more** sogar
noch mehr; **he loves her** ~ **more** er liebt sie
um so mehr; **it's going** ~ **faster now** es fährt
jetzt sogar noch schneller; ~ **so** (aber)
trotzdem; **not** ~ nicht einmal; ~ **he was**
there sogar er war da; **to break** ~ **die**
Kosten decken; **to get** ~ **with sb** es jdm
heimzahlen.
►**even out** *vi* sich ausgleichen ♦ *vt*
ausgleichen.
even-handed [i:vnhændɪd] *adj* gerecht.
evening [i:vnɪŋ] *n* Abend *m*; **in the** ~ abends,
am Abend; **this** ~ heute abend; **tomorrow/**
yesterday ~ morgen/gestern abend.
evening class *n* Abendkurs *m*.
evening dress *n* (*no pl*) Abendkleidung *f*;
(*woman's*) Abendkleid *nt*.
evenly [i:vnlɪ] *adv* gleichmäßig.
evensong [i:vnsɔŋ] *n* Abendandacht *f*.
event [ɪ'vɛnt] *n* Ereignis *nt*; (*SPORT*)
Wettkampf *m*; **in the normal course of** ~**s**
normalerweise; **in the** ~ **of** im Falle +*gen*; **in**
the ~ schließlich; **at all** ~**s** (*BRIT*), **in any** ~
auf jeden Fall.
eventful [ɪ'vɛntful] *adj* ereignisreich.
eventing [ɪ'vɛntɪŋ] *n* (*HORSERIDING*) Military
f.
eventual [ɪ'vɛntʃuəl] *adj* schließlich; (*goal*)
letztlich.
eventuality [ɪvɛntʃu'ælɪtɪ] *n* Eventualität *f*.
eventually [ɪ'vɛntʃuəlɪ] *adv* endlich; (*in time*)
schließlich.
ever [ɛvə'] *adv* immer; (*at any time*) je(mals);
why ~ **not?** warum denn bloß nicht?; **the**
best ~ **seen** der/die/das Allerbeste; **have you**
~ **seen it?** haben Sie es schon einmal
gesehen?; **for** ~ für immer; **hardly** ~ kaum
je(mals); **better than** ~ besser als je zuvor;
~ **since** *adv* seitdem ♦ *conj* seit, seitdem; ~ **so**
pretty unheimlich hübsch (*inf*); **thank you**
~ **so much** ganz herzlichen Dank; **yours** ~
(*BRIT: in letters*) alles Liebe.
Everest [ɛvərɪst] *n* (*also*: **Mount** ~) Mount
Everest *m*.

evergreen [ɛvəgri:n] *n* (*tree/bush*)
immergrüner Baum/Strauch *m*.
everlasting [ɛvə'lɑːstɪŋ] *adj* ewig.

═══════════════════════════ *KEYWORD*

every [ɛvrɪ] *adj* **1** jede(r, s); ~ **one of them**
(*persons*) jede(r) (einzelne) von ihnen;
(*objects*) jedes einzelne Stück; ~ **day** jeden
Tag; ~ **week** jede Woche; ~ **other car** jedes
zweite Auto; ~ **other/third day** alle zwei/
drei Tage; ~ **shop in the town was closed**
alle Geschäfte der Stadt waren
geschlossen; ~ **now and then** ab und zu, hin
und wieder
2 (*all possible*): **I have** ~ **confidence in him**
ich habe volles Vertrauen in ihn; **we wish**
you ~ **success** wir wünschen Ihnen alles
Gute.

everybody [ɛvrɪbɔdɪ] *pron* jeder, alle *pl*;
~ **knows about it** alle wissen es; ~ **else** alle
anderen *pl*.
everyday [ɛvrɪdeɪ] *adj* täglich; (*usual,*
common) alltäglich; (*life, language*) Alltags-.
everyone [ɛvrɪwʌn] *pron* = **everybody**.
everything [ɛvrɪθɪŋ] *pron* alles; **he did**
~ **possible** er hat sein Möglichstes getan.
everywhere [ɛvrɪwɛə'] *adv* überall;
(*wherever*) wo auch *or* immer; ~ **you go you**
meet ... wo man auch *or* wo immer man
hingeht, trifft man ...
evict [ɪ'vɪkt] *vt* zur Räumung zwingen.
eviction [ɪ'vɪkʃən] *n* Ausweisung *f*.
eviction notice *n* Räumungskündigung *f*.
eviction order *n* Räumungsbefehl *m*.
evidence [ɛvɪdns] *n* Beweis *m*; (*of witness*)
Aussage *f*; (*sign, indication*) Zeichen *nt*, Spur
f; **to give** ~ (als Zeuge) aussagen; **to show**
~ **of** zeigen; **in** ~ sichtbar.
evident [ɛvɪdnt] *adj* offensichtlich.
evidently [ɛvɪdntlɪ] *adv* offensichtlich.
evil [i:vl] *adj* böse; (*influence*) schlecht ♦ *n*
Böse(s) *nt*; (*unpleasant situation or activity*)
Übel *nt*.
evocative [ɪ'vɔkətɪv] *adj* evokativ.
evoke [ɪ'vəuk] *vt* hervorrufen; (*memory*)
wecken.
evolution [i:və'lu:ʃən] *n* Evolution *f*;
(*development*) Entwicklung *f*.
evolve [ɪ'vɔlv] *vt* entwickeln ♦ *vi* sich
entwickeln.
ewe [ju:] *n* Mutterschaf *nt*.
ewer [ju:ə'] *n* (Wasser)krug *m*.
ex- [ɛks] *pref* Ex-, frühere(r, s); **the price**
~ **works** der Preis ab Werk.
exacerbate [ɛks'æsəbeɪt] *vt* verschärfen;
(*pain*) verschlimmern.
exact [ɪg'zækt] *adj* genau; (*word*) richtig ♦ *vt*:
to ~ **sth (from)** etw verlangen (von);
(*payment*) etw eintreiben (von).
exacting [ɪg'zæktɪŋ] *adj* anspruchsvoll.
exactly [ɪg'zæktlɪ] *adv* genau; ~**!** (ganz)

genau!; **not** ~ (*hardly*) nicht gerade.
exaggerate [ɪg'zædʒəreɪt] *vt, vi* übertreiben.
exaggerated [ɪg'zædʒəreɪtɪd] *adj* übertrieben.
exaggeration [ɪgzædʒə'reɪʃən] *n*
Übertreibung *f*.
exalt [ɪg'zɔːlt] *vt* preisen.
exalted [ɪg'zɔːltɪd] *adj* hoch; (*elated*) exaltiert.
exam [ɪg'zæm] *n abbr* = **examination**.
examination [ɪgzæmɪ'neɪʃən] *n* (*see vb*)
Untersuchung *f*; Prüfung *f*; Verhör *nt*; **to
take** *or* (*BRIT*) **sit an** ~ eine Prüfung
machen; **the matter is under** ~ die
Angelegenheit wird geprüft *or* untersucht.
examine [ɪg'zæmɪn] *vt* untersuchen; (*accounts,
candidate*) prüfen; (*witness*) verhören.
examiner [ɪg'zæmɪnə*] *n* Prüfer(in) *m(f)*.
example [ɪg'zaːmpl] *n* Beispiel *nt*; **for** ~ zum
Beispiel; **to set a good/bad** ~ ein gutes/
schlechtes Beispiel geben.
exasperate [ɪg'zaːspəreɪt] *vt* (*annoy*)
verärgern; (*frustrate*) zur Verzweiflung
bringen; ~**d by** *or* **with** verärgert/
verzweifelt über +*acc*.
exasperating [ɪg'zaːspəreɪtɪŋ] *adj* ärgerlich;
(*job*) leidig.
exasperation [ɪgzaːspə'reɪʃən] *n* Verzweiflung
f; **in** ~ verzweifelt.
excavate ['ɛkskəveɪt] *vt* ausgraben; (*hole*)
graben ♦ *vi* Ausgrabungen machen.
excavation [ɛkskə'veɪʃən] *n* Ausgrabung *f*.
excavator ['ɛkskəveɪtə*] *n* Bagger *m*.
exceed [ɪk'siːd] *vt* übersteigen; (*hopes*)
übertreffen; (*limit, budget, powers*)
überschreiten.
exceedingly [ɪk'siːdɪŋlɪ] *adv* äußerst.
excel [ɪk'sɛl] *vt* übertreffen ♦ *vi*: **to** ~ (**in** *or* **at**)
sich auszeichnen (in +*dat*); **to** ~ **o.s.** (*BRIT*)
sich selbst übertreffen.
excellence ['ɛksələns] *n* hervorragende
Leistung *f*.
Excellency ['ɛksələnsɪ] *n*: **His** ~ Seine
Exzellenz.
excellent ['ɛksələnt] *adj* ausgezeichnet,
hervorragend.
except [ɪk'sɛpt] *prep* (*also*: ~ **for**) außer +*dat*
♦ *vt*: **to** ~ **sb** (**from**) jdn ausnehmen (bei);
~ **if**, ~ **when** außer wenn; ~ **that** nur daß.
excepting [ɪk'sɛptɪŋ] *prep* außer +*dat*, mit
Ausnahme +*gen*.
exception [ɪk'sɛpʃən] *n* Ausnahme *f*; **to take**
~ **to** Anstoß nehmen an +*dat*; **with the** ~ **of**
mit Ausnahme von.
exceptional [ɪk'sɛpʃənl] *adj* außergewöhnlich.
excerpt ['ɛksəːpt] *n* Auszug *m*.
excess [ɪk'sɛs] *n* Übermaß *nt*; (*INSURANCE*)
Selbstbeteiligung *f*; **excesses** *npl* Exzesse *pl*;
an ~ **of £15, a £15** ~ eine Selbstbeteiligung
von £15; **in** ~ **of** über +*dat*.
excess baggage *n* Übergepäck *nt*.
excess fare (*BRIT*) *n* Nachlösegebühr *f*.
excessive [ɪk'sɛsɪv] *adj* übermäßig.
excess supply *n* Überangebot *nt*.

exchange [ɪks'tʃeɪndʒ] *n* Austausch *m*;
(*conversation*) Wortwechsel *m*; (*also*:
telephone ~) Fernsprechamt *nt* ♦ *vt*: **to**
~ (**for**) tauschen (gegen); (*in shop*)
umtauschen (gegen); **in** ~ **for**; **foreign** ~
Devisenhandel *m*; (*money*) Devisen *pl*.
exchange control *n* Devisenkontrolle *f*.
exchange market *n* Devisenmarkt *m*.
exchange rate *n* Wechselkurs *m*.
Exchequer [ɪks'tʃɛkə*] (*BRIT*) *n*: **the** ~ das
Finanzministerium.
excisable [ɪk'saɪzəbl] *adj* steuerpflichtig.
excise ['ɛksaɪz] *n* Verbrauchssteuer *f* ♦ *vt*
entfernen.
excise duties *npl* Verbrauchssteuern *pl*.
excitable [ɪk'saɪtəbl] *adj* (leicht) erregbar.
excite [ɪk'saɪt] *vt* aufregen; (*arouse*) erregen;
to get ~**d** sich aufregen.
excitement [ɪk'saɪtmənt] *n* Aufregung *f*;
(*exhilaration*) Hochgefühl *nt*.
exciting [ɪk'saɪtɪŋ] *adj* aufregend.
excl. *abbr* = **excluding; exclusive (of)**.
exclaim [ɪks'kleɪm] *vi* aufschreien.
exclamation [ɛksklə'meɪʃən] *n* Ausruf *m*; ~ **of
joy** Freudenschrei *m*.
exclamation mark *n* Ausrufezeichen *nt*.
exclude [ɪks'kluːd] *vt* ausschließen.
excluding [ɪks'kluːdɪŋ] *prep*: ~ **VAT** ohne
Mehrwertsteuer.
exclusion [ɪks'kluːʒən] *n* Ausschluß *m*; **to
concentrate on sth to the** ~ **of everything
else** sich ausschließlich auf etw *dat*
konzentrieren.
exclusion clause *n* Freizeichnungsklausel *f*.
exclusion zone *n* Sperrzone *f*.
exclusive [ɪks'kluːsɪv] *adj* exklusiv; (*story,
interview*) Exklusiv-; (*use*) ausschließlich ♦ *n*
Exklusivbericht *m* ♦ *adv*: **from 1st to 15th
March** ~ vom 1. bis zum 15. März
ausschließlich; ~ **of postage** ohne *or*
exklusive Porto; ~ **of tax** ausschließlich *or*
exklusive Steuern; **to be mutually** ~ sich *or*
einander ausschließen.
exclusively [ɪks'kluːsɪvlɪ] *adv* ausschließlich.
exclusive rights *npl* Exklusivrechte *pl*.
excommunicate [ɛkskə'mjuːnɪkeɪt] *vt*
exkommunizieren.
excrement ['ɛkskrəmənt] *n* Kot *m*,
Exkremente *pl*.
excruciating [ɪks'kruːʃɪeɪtɪŋ] *adj* gräßlich,
fürchterlich; (*noise, embarrassment*)
unerträglich.
excursion [ɪks'kəːʃən] *n* Ausflug *m*.
excursion ticket *n* verbilligte Fahrkarte *f*.
excusable [ɪks'kjuːzəbl] *adj* verzeihlich,
entschuldbar.
excuse [ɪks'kjuːs] *n* Entschuldigung *f* ♦ *vt*
entschuldigen; (*forgive*) verzeihen; **to** ~ **sb
from sth** jdm etw erlassen; **to** ~ **sb from
doing sth** jdn davon befreien, etw zu tun;
~ **me!** entschuldigen Sie!, Entschuldigung!;
if you will ~ **me ...** entschuldigen Sie mich

bitte ...; **to ~ o.s. for sth** sich für *or* wegen
etw entschuldigen; **to ~ o.s. for doing sth**
sich entschuldigen, daß man etw tut; **to
make ~s for sb** jdn entschuldigen; **that's no
~!** das ist keine Ausrede!

ex-directory ['ɛksdɪ'rɛktərɪ] (*BRIT*) *adj*
(*number*) geheim; **she's ~** sie steht nicht im
Telefonbuch.

execrable ['ɛksɪkrəbl] *adj* scheußlich;
(*manners*) abscheulich.

execute ['ɛksɪkjuːt] *vt* ausführen; (*person*)
hinrichten.

execution [ɛksɪ'kjuːʃən] *n* (*see vb*)
Ausführung *f*; Hinrichtung *f*.

executioner [ɛksɪ'kjuːʃnə˟] *n* Scharfrichter *m*.

executive [ɪg'zɛkjutɪv] *n* leitende(r)
Angestellte(r) *f(m)*; (*committee*) Vorstand *m*
♦ *adj* geschäftsführend; (*role*) führend;
(*secretary*) Chef-; (*car, chair*) für gehobene
Ansprüche; (*toys*) Manager-; (*plane*)
≈ Privat-.

executive director *n* leitender Direktor *m*,
leitende Direktorin *f*.

executor [ɪg'zɛkjutə˟] *n* Testaments-
vollstrecker(in) *m(f)*.

exemplary [ɪg'zɛmplərɪ] *adj* vorbildlich,
beispielhaft; (*punishment*) exemplarisch.

exemplify [ɪg'zɛmplɪfaɪ] *vt* verkörpern;
(*illustrate*) veranschaulichen.

exempt [ɪg'zɛmpt] *adj*: **~ from** befreit von ♦ *vt*:
to ~ sb from jdn befreien von.

exemption [ɪg'zɛmpʃən] *n* Befreiung *f*.

exercise ['ɛksəsaɪz] *n* Übung *f*; (*no pl: keep-fit*)
Gymnastik *f*; (: *energetic movement*)
Bewegung *f*, (: *of authority etc*) Ausübung *f*
♦ *vt* (*patience*) üben; (*right*) ausüben; (*dog*)
ausführen; (*mind*) beschäftigen ♦ *vi* (*also*: **to
take ~**) Sport treiben.

exercise book *n* (Schul)heft *nt*.

exert [ɪg'zɜːt] *vt* (*influence*) ausüben;
(*authority*) einsetzen; **to ~ o.s.** sich
anstrengen.

exertion [ɪg'zɜːʃən] *n* Anstrengung *f*.

ex gratia ['ɛks'greɪʃə] *adj*: **~ payment**
freiwillige Zahlung *f*.

exhale [ɛks'heɪl] *vt, vi* ausatmen.

exhaust [ɪg'zɔːst] *n* (*also*: **~ pipe**) Auspuff *m*;
(*fumes*) Auspuffgase *pl* ♦ *vt* erschöpfen;
(*money*) aufbrauchen; (*topic*) erschöpfend
behandeln; **to ~ o.s.** sich verausgaben.

exhausted [ɪg'zɔːstɪd] *adj* erschöpft.

exhausting [ɪg'zɔːstɪŋ] *adj* anstrengend.

exhaustion [ɪg'zɔːstʃən] *n* Erschöpfung *f*;
nervous ~ nervöse Erschöpfung.

exhaustive [ɪg'zɔːstɪv] *adj* erschöpfend.

exhibit [ɪg'zɪbɪt] *n* Ausstellungsstück *nt*;
(*LAW*) Beweisstück *nt* ♦ *vt* zeigen, an den
Tag legen; (*paintings*) ausstellen.

exhibition [ɛksɪ'bɪʃən] *n* Ausstellung *f*; **to
make an ~ of o.s.** sich unmöglich
aufführen; **an ~ of bad manners** schlechte
Manieren *pl*; **an ~ of draughtsmanship**

zeichnerisches Können *nt*.

exhibitionist [ɛksɪ'bɪʃənɪst] *n*
Exhibitionist(in) *m(f)*.

exhibitor [ɪg'zɪbɪtə˟] *n* Aussteller(in) *m(f)*.

exhilarating [ɪg'zɪləreɪtɪŋ] *adj* erregend,
berauschend; (*news*) aufregend.

exhilaration [ɪgzɪlə'reɪʃən] *n* Hochgefühl *nt*.

exhort [ɪg'zɔːt] *vt*: **to ~ sb to do sth** jdn
ermahnen, etw zu tun.

exile ['ɛksaɪl] *n* Exil *nt*; (*person*) Verbannte(r)
f(m) ♦ *vt* verbannen; **in ~** im Exil.

exist [ɪg'zɪst] *vi* existieren.

existence [ɪg'zɪstəns] *n* Existenz *f*; **to be in ~**
existieren.

existentialism [ɛgzɪs'tɛnʃlɪzəm] *n*
Existentialismus *m*.

existing [ɪg'zɪstɪŋ] *adj* bestehend.

exit ['ɛksɪt] *n* Ausgang *m*; (*from motorway*)
Ausfahrt *f*; (*departure*) Abgang *m* ♦ *vi*
(*THEAT*) abgehen; (*COMPUT: from program/
file etc*) das Programm/die Datei *etc*
verlassen; **to ~ from** hinausgehen aus;
(*motorway etc*) abfahren von.

exit poll *n* bei Wählern unmittelbar nach
Verlassen der Wahllokale durchgeführte
Umfrage.

exit ramp (*US*) *n* Ausfahrt *f*.

exit visa *n* Ausreisevisum *nt*.

exodus ['ɛksədəs] *n* Auszug *m*; **the ~ to the
cities** die Abwanderung in die Städte.

ex officio ['ɛksə'fɪʃɪəu] *adj* von Amts wegen
♦ *adv* kraft seines Amtes.

exonerate [ɪg'zɒnəreɪt] *vt*: **to ~ from** entlasten
von.

exorbitant [ɪg'zɔːbɪtnt] *adj* (*prices, rents*)
astronomisch, unverschämt; (*demands*)
maßlos, übertrieben.

exorcize ['ɛksɔːsaɪz] *vt* exorzieren; (*spirit*)
austreiben.

exotic [ɪg'zɒtɪk] *adj* exotisch.

expand [ɪks'pænd] *vt* erweitern; (*staff,
numbers etc*) vergrößern; (*influence*)
ausdehnen ♦ *vi* expandieren; (*population*)
wachsen; (*gas, metal*) sich ausdehnen; **to
~ on** weiter ausführen.

expanse [ɪks'pæns] *n* Weite *f*.

expansion [ɪks'pænʃən] *n* Expansion *f*; (*of
population*) Wachstum *nt*; (*of gas, metal*)
Ausdehnung *f*.

expansionism [ɪks'pænʃənɪzəm] *n*
Expansionspolitik *f*.

expansionist [ɪks'pænʃənɪst] *adj* Expansions-,
expansionistisch.

expatriate [ɛks'pætrɪət] *n* im Ausland
Lebende(r) *f(m)*.

expect [ɪks'pɛkt] *vt* erwarten; (*suppose*)
denken, glauben; (*count on*) rechnen mit
♦ *vi*: **to be ~ing** ein Kind erwarten; **to ~ sb
to do sth** erwarten, daß jd etw tut; **to ~ to
do sth** vorhaben, etw zu tun; **as ~ed** wie
erwartet; **I ~ so** ich glaube schon.

expectancy [ɪks'pɛktənsɪ] *n* Erwartung *f*; **life**

~ Lebenserwartung *f.*

expectant [ɪks'pɛktənt] *adj* erwartungsvoll.

expectantly [ɪks'pɛktəntlɪ] *adv* erwartungsvoll.

expectant mother *n* werdende Mutter *f.*

expectation [ɛkspɛk'teɪʃən] *n* Erwartung *f*; (*hope*) Hoffnung *f*; **in ~ of** in Erwartung +*gen*; **against** *or* **contrary to all ~(s)** wider Erwarten; **to come** *or* **live up to sb's ~s** jds Erwartungen *dat* entsprechen.

expedience [ɪks'piːdɪəns] *n* = **expediency.**

expediency [ɪks'piːdɪənsɪ] *n* Zweckmäßigkeit *f*; **for the sake of** ~ aus Gründen der Zweckmäßigkeit.

expedient [ɪks'piːdɪənt] *adj* zweckmäßig ♦ *n* Hilfsmittel *nt.*

expedite ['ɛkspədaɪt] *vt* beschleunigen.

expedition [ɛkspə'dɪʃən] *n* Expedition *f*; (*for shopping etc*) Tour *f.*

expeditionary force [ɛkspə'dɪʃənrɪ-] *n* Expeditionskorps *nt.*

expeditious [ɛkspə'dɪʃəs] *adj* schnell.

expel [ɪks'pɛl] *vt* (*from school*) verweisen; (*from organization*) ausschließen; (*from place*) vertreiben; (*gas, liquid*) ausstoßen.

expend [ɪks'pɛnd] *vt* ausgeben; (*time, energy*) aufwenden.

expendable [ɪks'pɛndəbl] *adj* entbehrlich.

expenditure [ɪks'pɛndɪtʃə*] *n* Ausgaben *pl*; (*of energy, time*) Aufwand *m.*

expense [ɪks'pɛns] *n* Kosten *pl*; (*expenditure*) Ausgabe *f*; **expenses** *npl* Spesen *pl*; **at the ~ of** auf Kosten +*gen*; **to go to the ~ of buying a new car** (viel) Geld für ein neues Auto anlegen; **at great/little ~** mit hohen/ geringen Kosten.

expense account *n* Spesenkonto *nt.*

expensive [ɪks'pɛnsɪv] *adj* teuer; **to have ~ tastes** einen teuren Geschmack haben.

experience [ɪks'pɪərɪəns] *n* Erfahrung *f*; (*event, activity*) Erlebnis *nt* ♦ *vt* erleben; **by** *or* **from** ~ aus Erfahrung; **to learn by** ~ durch eigene Erfahrung lernen.

experienced [ɪks'pɪərɪənst] *adj* erfahren.

experiment [ɪks'pɛrɪmənt] *n* Experiment *nt*, Versuch *m* ♦ *vi*: **to** ~ **(with/on)** experimentieren (mit/an +*dat*); **to perform** *or* **carry out an** ~ einen Versuch *or* ein Experiment durchführen; **as an** ~ versuchsweise.

experimental [ɪkspɛrɪ'mɛntl] *adj* experimentell; **at the** ~ **stage** im Versuchsstadium.

expert ['ɛkspəːt] *adj* ausgezeichnet, geschickt; (*opinion, help etc*) eines Fachmanns ♦ *n* Fachmann *m*, Fachfrau *f*, Experte *m*, Expertin *f*; **to be** ~ **in** *or* **at doing sth** etw ausgezeichnet können; **an** ~ **on sth/on the subject of sth** ein Experte für etw/auf dem Gebiet einer Sache *gen*; ~ **witness** (*LAW*) sachverständiger Zeuge *m.*

expertise [ɛkspəː'tiːz] *n* Sachkenntnis *f.*

expire [ɪks'paɪə*] *vi* ablaufen.

expiry [ɪks'paɪərɪ] *n* Ablauf *m.*

expiry date *n* Ablauftermin *m*; (*of voucher, special offer etc*) Verfallsdatum *nt.*

explain [ɪks'pleɪn] *vt* erklären.

▶**explain away** *vt* eine Erklärung finden für.

explanation [ɛksplə'neɪʃən] *n* Erklärung *f*; **to find an** ~ **for sth** eine Erklärung für etw finden.

explanatory [ɪks'plænətrɪ] *adj* erklärend.

expletive [ɪks'pliːtɪv] *n* Kraftausdruck *m.*

explicable [ɪks'plɪkəbl] *adj* erklärbar; **for no ~ reason** aus unerfindlichen Gründen.

explicit [ɪks'plɪsɪt] *adj* ausdrücklich; (*sex, violence*) deutlich, unverhüllt; **to be** ~ (*frank*) sich deutlich ausdrücken.

explode [ɪks'pləud] *vi* explodieren; (*population*) sprunghaft ansteigen ♦ *vt* zur Explosion bringen; (*myth, theory*) zu Fall bringen.

exploit ['ɛksplɔɪt] *n* Heldentat *f* ♦ *vt* ausnutzen; (*workers etc*) ausbeuten; (*resources*) nutzen.

exploitation [ɛksplɔɪ'teɪʃən] *n* (*see vb*) Ausnutzung *f*; Ausbeutung *f*; Nutzung *f.*

exploration [ɛksplə'reɪʃən] *n* (*see vb*) Erforschung *f*; Erkundung *f*; Untersuchung *f.*

exploratory [ɪks'plɔrətrɪ] *adj* exploratorisch; (*expedition*) Forschungs-; ~ **operation** (*MED*) Explorationsoperation *f*; ~ **talks** Sondierungsgespräche *pl.*

explore [ɪks'plɔː*] *vt* erforschen; (*with hands etc, idea*) untersuchen.

explorer [ɪks'plɔːrə*] *n* Forschungsreisende(r) *f(m)*; (*of place*) Erforscher(in) *m(f).*

explosion [ɪks'pləuʒən] *n* Explosion *f*; (*outburst*) Ausbruch *m.*

explosive [ɪks'pləusɪv] *adj* explosiv; (*device*) Spreng-; (*temper*) aufbrausend ♦ *n* Sprengstoff *m*; (*device*) Sprengkörper *m.*

exponent [ɪks'pəunənt] *n* Vertreter(in) *m(f)*, Exponent(in) *m(f)*; (*MATH*) Exponent *m.*

exponential [ɛkspəu'nɛnʃl] *adj* exponentiell; (*MATH: function etc*) Exponential-.

export [ɛks'pɔːt] *vt* exportieren, ausführen; (*ideas, values*) verbreiten ♦ *n* Export *m*, Ausfuhr *f*; (*product*) Exportgut *nt* ♦ *cpd* Export-, Ausfuhr-.

exportation [ɛkspɔː'teɪʃən] *n* Export *m*, Ausfuhr *f.*

exporter [ɛks'pɔːtə*] *n* Exporteur *m.*

expose [ɪks'pəuz] *vt* freilegen; (*to heat, radiation*) aussetzen; (*unmask*) entlarven; **to ~ o.s.** sich entblößen.

exposé [ɪk'spəuzeɪ] *n* Enthüllung *f.*

exposed [ɪks'pəuzd] *adj* ungeschützt; (*wire*) bloßliegend; **to be ~ to** (*radiation, heat etc*) ausgesetzt sein +*dat.*

exposition [ɛkspə'zɪʃən] *n* Erläuterung *f*; (*exhibition*) Ausstellung *f.*

exposure [ɪks'pəuʒə*] *n* (*to heat, radiation*)

Aussetzung *f*; (*publicity*) Publicity *f*; (*of person*) Entlarvung *f*; (*PHOT*) Belichtung *f*; (: *shot*) Aufnahme *f*; **to be suffering from ~** an Unterkühlung leiden; **to die from ~** erfrieren.

exposure meter *n* Belichtungsmesser *m*.

expound [ɪks'paund] *vt* darlegen, erläutern.

express [ɪks'prɛs] *adj* ausdrücklich; (*intention*) bestimmt; (*BRIT: letter etc*) Expreß-, Eil- ♦ *n* (*train*) Schnellzug *m*; (*bus*) Schnellbus *m* ♦ *adv* (*send*) per Expreß ♦ *vt* ausdrücken; (*view, emotion*) zum Ausdruck bringen; **to ~ o.s.** sich ausdrücken.

expression [ɪks'prɛʃən] *n* Ausdruck *m*; (*on face*) (Gesichts)ausdruck *m*.

expressionism [ɪks'prɛʃənɪzəm] *n* Expressionismus *m*.

expressive [ɪks'prɛsɪv] *adj* ausdrucksvoll; **~ ability** Ausdrucksfähigkeit *f*.

expressly [ɪks'prɛslɪ] *adv* ausdrücklich; (*intentionally*) absichtlich.

expressway [ɪks'prɛsweɪ] (*US*) *n* Schnellstraße *f*.

expropriate [ɛks'prəuprɪeɪt] *vt* enteignen.

expulsion [ɪks'pʌlʃən] *n* (*SCOL*) Verweisung *f*; (*POL*) Ausweisung *f*; (*of gas, liquid etc*) Ausstoßen *nt*.

expurgate ['ɛkspɔːgeɪt] *vt* zensieren; **the ~d version** die zensierte *or* bereinigte Fassung.

exquisite [ɛks'kwɪzɪt] *adj* exquisit, erlesen; (*keenly felt*) köstlich.

exquisitely [ɛks'kwɪzɪtlɪ] *adv* exquisit; (*carved*) kunstvoll; (*polite, sensitive*) äußerst.

ex-serviceman ['ɛks'səːvɪsmən] (*irreg: like* **man**) *n* ehemaliger Soldat *m*.

ext. *abbr* (*TEL*) = **extension**.

extemporize [ɪks'tɛmpəraɪz] *vi* improvisieren.

extend [ɪks'tɛnd] *vt* verlängern; (*building*) anbauen an +*acc*; (*offer, invitation*) aussprechen; (*arm, hand*) ausstrecken; (*deadline*) verschieben ♦ *vi* sich erstrecken; (*period*) dauern.

extension [ɪks'tɛnʃən] *n* Verlängerung *f*; (*of building*) Anbau *m*; (*of time*) Aufschub *m*; (*of campaign, rights*) Erweiterung *f*; (*TEL*) (Neben)anschluß *m*; **~ 3718** (*TEL*) Apparat 3718.

extension cable *n* Verlängerungskabel *nt*.

extension lead *n* Verlängerungsschnur *f*.

extensive [ɪks'tɛnsɪv] *adj* ausgedehnt; (*effect*) weitreichend; (*damage*) beträchtlich; (*coverage, discussion*) ausführlich; (*inquiries*) umfangreich; (*use*) häufig.

extensively [ɪks'tɛnsɪvlɪ] *adv*: **he's travelled ~** er ist viel gereist.

extent [ɪks'tɛnt] *n* Ausdehnung *f*; (*of problem, damage, loss etc*) Ausmaß *nt*; **to some ~** bis zu einem gewissen Grade; **to a certain ~** in gewissem Maße; **to a large ~** in hohem Maße; **to the ~ of ...** (*debts*) in Höhe von ...; **to go to the ~ of doing sth** so weit gehen,

etw zu tun; **to such an ~ that ...** dermaßen, daß ...; **to what ~?** inwieweit?

extenuating [ɪks'tɛnjueɪtɪŋ] *adj*: **~ circumstances** mildernde Umstände *pl*.

exterior [ɛks'tɪərɪə*] *adj* (*surface, angle, world*) Außen- ♦ *n* Außenseite *f*; (*appearance*) Äußere(s) *nt*.

exterminate [ɪks'təːmɪneɪt] *vt* ausrotten.

extermination [ɪkstəːmɪ'neɪʃən] *n* Ausrottung *f*.

external [ɛks'təːnl] *adj* (*wall etc*) Außen-; (*use*) äußerlich; (*evidence*) unabhängig; (*examiner, auditor*) extern ♦ *n*: **the ~s** die Äußerlichkeiten *pl*; **for ~ use only** nur äußerlich (anzuwenden); **~ affairs** (*POL*) auswärtige Angelegenheiten *pl*.

externally [ɛks'təːnəlɪ] *adv* äußerlich.

extinct [ɪks'tɪŋkt] *adj* ausgestorben; (*volcano*) erloschen.

extinction [ɪks'tɪŋkʃən] *n* Aussterben *nt*.

extinguish [ɪks'tɪŋgwɪʃ] *vt* löschen; (*hope*) zerstören.

extinguisher [ɪks'tɪŋgwɪʃə*] *n* (*also:* **fire ~**) Feuerlöscher *m*.

extol, (*US*) **extoll** [ɪks'təul] *vt* preisen, rühmen.

extort [ɪks'tɔːt] *vt* erpressen; (*confession*) erzwingen.

extortion [ɪks'tɔːʃən] *n* (*see vb*) Erpressung *f*; Erzwingung *f*.

extortionate [ɪks'tɔːʃnɪt] *adj* überhöht; (*price*) Wucher-.

extra ['ɛkstrə] *adj* zusätzlich ♦ *adv* extra ♦ *n* Extra *nt*; (*surcharge*) zusätzliche Kosten *pl*; (*CINE, THEAT*) Statist(in) *m(f)*; **wine will cost ~** Wein wird extra berechnet.

extra... ['ɛkstrə] *pref* außer-, extra-.

extract [*vt* ɪks'trækt, *n* 'ɛkstrækt] *vt* (*tooth*) ziehen; (*mineral*) gewinnen ♦ *n* Auszug *m*; (*malt extract, vanilla extract etc*) Extrakt *m*; **to ~ (from)** (*object*) herausziehen (aus); (*money*) herausholen (aus); (*promise*) abringen +*dat*.

extraction [ɪks'trækʃən] *n* (*see vb*) Ziehen *nt*; Gewinnung *f*; Herausziehen *nt*; Herausholen *nt*; Abringen *nt*; (*DENTISTRY*) Extraktion *f*; (*descent*) Herkunft *f*, Abstammung *f*; **to be of Scottish ~, to be Scottish by ~** schottischer Herkunft *or* Abstammung sein.

extractor fan [ɪks'træktə-] *n* Sauglüfter *m*.

extracurricular ['ɛkstrəkə'rɪkjulə*] *adj* außerhalb des Lehrplans.

extradite ['ɛkstrədaɪt] *vt* ausliefern.

extradition [ɛkstrə'dɪʃən] *n* Auslieferung *f* ♦ *cpd* Auslieferungs-.

extramarital ['ɛkstrə'mærɪtl] *adj* außerehelich.

extramural ['ɛkstrə'mjuərl] *adj* außerhalb der Universität; **~ classes** von der Universität veranstaltete Teilzeitkurse *pl*.

extraneous [ɛks'treɪnɪəs] *adj* unwesentlich.

extraordinary [ɪks'trɔːdnrɪ] adj ungewöhnlich; (special) außerordentlich; **the ~ thing is that** ... das Merkwürdige ist, daß ...

extraordinary general meeting n außerordentliche Hauptversammlung f.

extrapolation [ɛkstræpə'leɪʃən] n Extrapolation f.

extrasensory perception ['ɛkstrə'sɛnsərɪ-] n außersinnliche Wahrnehmung f.

extra time n (FOOTBALL) Verlängerung f.

extravagance [ɪks'trævəgəns] n (no pl) Verschwendungssucht f; (example of spending) Luxus m.

extravagant [ɪks'trævəgənt] adj extravagant; (tastes, gift) teuer; (wasteful) verschwenderisch; (praise) übertrieben; (ideas) ausgefallen.

extreme [ɪks'triːm] adj extrem; (point, edge, poverty) äußerste(r, s) ♦ n Extrem nt; **the ~ right/left** (POL) die äußerste or extreme Rechte/Linke; **~s of temperature** extreme Temperaturen pl.

extremely [ɪks'triːmlɪ] adv äußerst, extrem.

extremist [ɪks'triːmɪst] n Extremist(in) m(f) ♦ adj extremistisch.

extremities [ɪks'trɛmɪtɪz] npl Extremitäten pl.

extremity [ɪks'trɛmɪtɪ] n Rand m; (end) äußerstes Ende nt; (of situation) Ausmaß nt.

extricate ['ɛkstrɪkeɪt] vt: **to ~ sb/sth (from)** jdn/etw befreien (aus).

extrovert ['ɛkstrəvəːt] n extravertierter Mensch m.

exuberance [ɪg'zjuːbərns] n Überschwenglichkeit f.

exuberant [ɪg'zjuːbərnt] adj überschwenglich; (imagination etc) lebhaft.

exude [ɪg'zjuːd] vt ausstrahlen; (liquid) absondern; (smell) ausströmen.

exult [ɪg'zʌlt] vi: **to ~ (in)** jubeln (über +acc).

exultant [ɪg'zʌltənt] adj jubelnd; (shout) Jubel-; **to be ~** jubeln.

exultation [ɛgzʌl'teɪʃən] n Jubel m.

eye [aɪ] n Auge nt; (of needle) Öhr nt ♦ vt betrachten; **to keep an ~ on** aufpassen auf +acc; **as far as the ~ can see** soweit das Auge reicht; **in the public ~** im Blickpunkt der Öffentlichkeit; **to have an ~ for sth** einen Blick für etw haben; **with an ~ to doing sth** (BRIT) mit der Absicht, etw zu tun; **there's more to this than meets the ~** da steckt mehr dahinter(, als man auf den ersten Blick meint).

eyeball ['aɪbɔːl] n Augapfel m.

eyebath ['aɪbɑːθ] (BRIT) n Augenbadewanne f.

eyebrow ['aɪbrau] n Augenbraue f.

eyebrow pencil ['aɪkætʃɪŋ] adj auffallend.

eye-catching ['aɪkætʃɪŋ] adj auffallend.

eyecup ['aɪkʌp] (US) n = **eyebath**.

eye drops npl Augentropfen pl.

eyeful ['aɪful] n: **to get an ~ of sth** (lit) etw ins Auge bekommen; (fig: have a good look) einiges von etw zu sehen bekommen; **she's**

quite an ~ sie hat allerhand zu bieten.

eyeglass ['aɪglɑːs] n Augenglas nt.

eyelash ['aɪlæʃ] n Augenwimper f.

eyelet ['aɪlɪt] n Öse f.

eye level n: **at ~** in Augenhöhe.

eyelevel ['aɪlɛvl] adj in Augenhöhe.

eyelid ['aɪlɪd] n Augenlid nt.

eyeliner ['aɪlaɪnə'] n Eyeliner m.

eye-opener ['aɪəupnə'] n Überraschung f; **to be an ~ to sb** jdm die Augen öffnen.

eye shadow n Lidschatten m.

eyesight ['aɪsaɪt] n Sehvermögen nt.

eyesore ['aɪsɔː'] n Schandfleck m.

eyestrain ['aɪstreɪn] n: **to get ~** seine Augen überanstrengen.

eyetooth ['aɪtuːθ] (pl **eyeteeth**) n Eckzahn m, Augenzahn m; **to give one's eyeteeth for sth** alles für etw geben; **to give one's eyeteeth to do sth** alles darum geben, etw zu tun.

eyewash ['aɪwɔʃ] n Augenwasser nt; (fig) Gewäsch nt.

eyewitness ['aɪwɪtnɪs] n Augenzeuge m, Augenzeugin f.

eyrie ['ɪərɪ] n Horst m.

F, f

F¹, f [ɛf] n (letter) F nt, f nt; **~ for Frederick**, (US) **~ for Fox** ≈ F wie Friedrich.

F² [ɛf] n (MUS) F nt, f nt.

F³ [ɛf] abbr (= Fahrenheit) F.

FA (BRIT) n abbr (= Football Association) englischer Fußball-Dachverband, ≈ DFB m.

FAA (US) n abbr (= Federal Aviation Administration) amerikanische Luftfahrtbehörde.

fable ['feɪbl] n Fabel f.

fabric ['fæbrɪk] n Stoff m; (of society) Gefüge nt; (of building) Bausubstanz f.

fabricate ['fæbrɪkeɪt] vt herstellen; (story) erfinden; (evidence) fälschen.

fabrication [fæbrɪ'keɪʃən] n Herstellung f; (lie) Erfindung f.

fabric ribbon n (for typewriter) Gewebefarbband nt.

fabulous ['fæbjuləs] adj fabelhaft, toll (inf); (extraordinary) sagenhaft; (mythical) legendär.

façade [fə'sɑːd] n Fassade f.

face [feɪs] n Gesicht nt; (expression) Gesichtsausdruck m; (grimace) Grimasse f; (of clock) Zifferblatt nt; (of mountain, cliff) (Steil)wand f; (of building) Fassade f; (side, surface) Seite f ♦ vt (subj: person) gegenübersitzen/-stehen +dat etc; (: building, street *etc*) liegen zu; (: : *north, south etc*) liegen nach; (*unpleasant situation*) sich gegenübersehen +*dat*; (*facts*) ins Auge sehen +*dat*; ~ **down** mit dem Gesicht nach unten; (*card*) mit der Bildseite nach unten; (*object*) mit der Vorderseite nach unten; **to lose/ save** ~ das Gesicht verlieren/wahren; **to make** *or* **pull a** ~ das Gesicht verziehen; **in the** ~ **of** trotz +*gen*; **on the** ~ **of it** so, wie es aussieht; **to come** ~ **to** ~ **with sb** jdn treffen; **to come** ~ **to** ~ **with a problem** einem Problem gegenüberstehen; **to** ~ **each other** einander gegenüberstehen/ -liegen/-sitzen *etc*; **to** ~ **the fact that ...** der Tatsache ins Auge sehen, daß ...; **the man facing me** der Mann mir gegenüber.

▶**face up to** *vt fus* (*obligations, difficulty*) auf sich *acc* nehmen; (*situation, possibility*) sich abfinden mit; (*danger, fact*) ins Auge sehen +*dat*.

face cloth (*BRIT*) *n* Waschlappen *m*.

face cream *n* Gesichtscreme *f*.

faceless ['feɪslɪs] *adj* (*fig*) anonym.

face-lift ['feɪslɪft] *n* Facelifting *nt*; (*of building etc*) Verschönerung *f*.

face powder *n* Gesichtspuder *m*.

face-saving ['feɪsˈeɪvɪŋ] *adj*: **a** ~ **excuse/ tactic** eine Entschuldigung/Taktik, um das Gesicht zu wahren.

facet ['fæsɪt] *n* Seite *f*, Aspekt *m*; (*of gem*) Facette *f*.

facetious [fəˈsiːʃəs] *adj* witzelnd.

face-to-face [feɪstəˈfeɪs] *adj* persönlich; (*confrontation*) direkt.

face value *n* Nennwert *m*; **to take sth at** ~ (*fig*) etw für bare Münze nehmen.

facia ['feɪʃə] *n* = **fascia**.

facial ['feɪʃl] *adj* (*expression, massage etc*) Gesichts- ♦ *n* kosmetische Gesichtsbehandlung *f*.

facile ['fæsaɪl] *adj* oberflächlich; (*comment*) nichtssagend.

facilitate [fəˈsɪlɪteɪt] *vt* erleichtern.

facilities [fəˈsɪlɪtɪz] *npl* Einrichtungen *pl*; **cooking** ~ Kochgelegenheit *f*; **credit** ~ Kreditmöglichkeiten *pl*.

facility [fəˈsɪlɪtɪ] *n* Einrichtung *f*; **to have a** ~ **for** (*skill, aptitude*) eine Begabung haben für.

facing ['feɪsɪŋ] *prep* gegenüber +*dat* ♦ *n* (*SEWING*) Besatz *m*.

facsimile [fækˈsɪmɪlɪ] *n* Faksimile *nt*; (*also:* ~ **machine**) Fernkopierer *m*, (Tele)faxgerät *nt*; (*transmitted document*) Fernkopie *f*, (Tele)fax *nt*.

fact [fækt] *n* Tatsache *f*; (*truth*) Wirklichkeit *f*; **in** ~ eigentlich; (*in reality*) tatsächlich, in Wirklichkeit; **to know for a** ~ **that ...** ganz genau wissen, daß ...; **the** ~ (**of the matter**) **is that ...** die Sache ist die, daß ...; **it's a** ~ **of life that ...** es ist eine Tatsache, daß ...; **to tell sb the** ~**s of life** (*sex*) jdn aufklären.

fact-finding ['fæktfaɪndɪŋ] *adj*: **a** ~ **tour** *or* **mission** eine Informationstour.

faction ['fækʃən] *n* Fraktion *f*.

factional ['fækʃənl] *adj* (*dispute, system*) Fraktions-.

factor ['fæktə*] *n* Faktor *m*; (*COMM*) Kommissionär *m*; (: *agent*) Makler *m*; **safety** ~ Sicherheitsfaktor *m*; **human** ~ menschlicher Faktor.

factory ['fæktərɪ] *n* Fabrik *f*.

factory farming (*BRIT*) *n* industriell betriebene Viehzucht *f*.

factory floor *n*: **the** ~ (*workers*) die Fabrikarbeiter *pl*; **on the** ~ bei *or* unter den Fabrikarbeitern.

factory ship *n* Fabrikschiff *nt*.

factual ['fæktjuəl] *adj* sachlich; (*information*) Sach-.

faculty ['fækəltɪ] *n* Vermögen *nt*, Kraft *f*; (*ability*) Talent *nt*; (*of university*) Fakultät *f*; (*US: teaching staff*) Lehrkörper *m*.

fad [fæd] *n* Fimmel *m*, Tick *m*.

fade [feɪd] *vi* verblassen; (*light*) nachlassen; (*sound*) schwächer werden; (*flower*) verblühen; (*hope*) zerrinnen; (*smile*) verschwinden.

▶**fade in** *vt sep* allmählich einblenden.

▶**fade out** *vt sep* ausblenden.

faeces, (*US*) **feces** ['fiːsiːz] *npl* Kot *m*.

fag [fæg] *n* (*BRIT: inf: cigarette*) Glimmstengel *m*; (: : *chore*) Schinderei *f* (*inf*), Plackerei *f* (*inf*); (*US: inf: homosexual*) Schwule(r) *m*.

fail [feɪl] *vt* (*exam*) nicht bestehen; (*candidate*) durchfallen lassen; (*subj: courage*) verlassen; (: *leader, memory*) im Stich lassen ♦ *vi* (*candidate*) durchfallen; (*attempt*) fehlschlagen; (*brakes*) versagen; (*also:* be ~**ing:** *health*) sich verschlechtern; (: *eyesight, light*) nachlassen; **to** ~ **to do sth** etw nicht tun; (*neglect*) (es) versäumen, etw zu tun; **without** ~ ganz bestimmt.

failing ['feɪlɪŋ] *n* Schwäche *f*, Fehler *m* ♦ *prep* in Ermangelung +*gen*; ~ **that** (oder) sonst, und wenn das nicht möglich ist.

fail-safe ['feɪlseɪf] *adj* (ab)gesichert.

failure ['feɪljə*] *n* Mißerfolg *m*; (*person*) Versager(in) *m(f)*; (*of brakes, heart*) Versagen *nt*; (*of engine, power*) Ausfall *m*; (*of crops*) Mißernte *f*; (*in exam*) Durchfall *m*; **his** ~ **to turn up meant that we had to ...** weil er nicht kam, mußten wir ...; **it was a complete** ~ es war ein totaler Fehlschlag.

faint [feɪnt] *adj* schwach; (*breeze, trace*) leicht ♦ *n* Ohnmacht *f* ♦ *vi* ohnmächtig werden, in Ohnmacht fallen; **she felt** ~ ihr wurde schwach.

faintest ['feɪntɪst] *adj, n*: **I haven't the** ~ (**idea**) ich habe keinen blassen Schimmer.

faint-hearted ['feɪntˈhɑːtɪd] *adj* zaghaft.

faintly ['feɪntlɪ] *adv* schwach.

fair [fɛə*] *adj* gerecht, fair; (*size, number*) ansehnlich; (*chance, guess*) recht gut; (*hair*)

blond; (skin, complexion) hell; (weather)
schön ◆ adv: to play ~ fair spielen ◆ n (also:
trade ~) Messe f; (BRIT: funfair) Jahrmarkt
m, Rummel m; it's not ~! das ist nicht fair!;
a ~ amount of ziemlich viel.
fair copy n Reinschrift f.
fair game n: to be ~ (for) (for attack, criticism)
Freiwild nt sein (für).
fairground ['fɛəgraund] n Rummelplatz m.
fair-haired [fɛə'hɛəd] adj blond.
fairly ['fɛəlɪ] adv gerecht; (quite) ziemlich; I'm
~ sure ich bin (mir) ziemlich sicher.
fairness ['fɛənɪs] n Gerechtigkeit f; in all ~
gerechterweise, fairerweise.
fair play n faires Verhalten nt, Fair play nt.
fairway ['fɛəweɪ] n (GOLF): the ~ das
Fairway.
fairy ['fɛərɪ] n Fee f.
fairy godmother n gute Fee f.
fairy lights (BRIT) npl bunte Lichter pl.
fairy tale n Märchen nt.
faith [feɪθ] n Glaube m; (trust) Vertrauen nt; to
have ~ in sb jdm vertrauen; to have ~ in
sth Vertrauen in etw acc haben.
faithful ['feɪθful] adj (account) genau; ~ (to)
(person) treu +dat.
faithfully ['feɪθəlɪ] adv (see adj) genau; treu.
faith healer n Gesundbeter(in) m(f).
fake [feɪk] n Fälschung f; (person)
Schwindler(in) m(f) ◆ adj gefälscht ◆ vt
fälschen; (illness, emotion) vortäuschen; his
illness is a ~ er simuliert seine Krankheit
nur.
falcon ['fɔːlkən] n Falke m.
Falkland Islands ['fɔːlklənd-] npl: the ~ die
Falkland-Inseln pl.
fall [fɔːl] (pt fell, pp fallen) n Fall m; (of price,
temperature) Sinken nt; (: sudden) Sturz m;
(US: autumn) Herbst m ◆ vi fallen; (night,
darkness) hereinbrechen; (silence) eintreten;
falls npl (waterfall) Wasserfall m; a ~ of snow
ein Schneefall m; a ~ of earth ein Erdrutsch
m; to ~ flat auf die Nase fallen; (plan) ins
Wasser fallen; (joke) nicht ankommen; to
~ in love (with sb/sth) sich (in jdn/etw)
verlieben; to ~ short of sb's expectations
jds Erwartungen nicht erfüllen.
▶**fall apart** vi auseinanderfallen,
kaputtgehen; (inf: emotionally) durchdrehen.
▶**fall back** vi zurückweichen.
▶**fall back on** vi zurückgreifen auf +acc; to
have sth to ~ back on auf etw acc
zurückgreifen können.
▶**fall behind** vi zurückbleiben; (fig: with
payment) in Rückstand geraten.
▶**fall down** vi hinfallen; (building) einstürzen.
▶**fall for** vt fus (trick, story) hereinfallen auf
+acc; (person) sich verlieben in +acc.
▶**fall in** vi einstürzen; (MIL) antreten.
▶**fall in with** vt fus eingehen auf +acc.
▶**fall off** vi herunterfallen; (takings,
attendance) zurückgehen.

▶**fall out** vi (hair, teeth) ausfallen; to ~ out
with sb sich mit jdm zerstreiten.
▶**fall over** vi hinfallen; (object) umfallen ◆ vt:
to ~ over o.s. to do sth sich dat die größte
Mühe geben, etw zu tun.
▶**fall through** vi (plan, project) ins Wasser
fallen.
fallacy ['fæləsɪ] n Irrtum m.
fall-back ['fɔːlbæk] adj: ~ position
Rückzugsbasis f.
fallen ['fɔːlən] pp of fall.
fallible ['fæləbl] adj fehlbar.
falling ['fɔːlɪŋ] adj: ~ market (COMM)
Baissemarkt m.
falling off n Rückgang m.
falling-out ['fɔːlɪŋ'aut] n (break-up) Bruch m.
Fallopian tube [fə'ləupɪən-] n Eileiter m.
fallout ['fɔːlaut] n radioaktiver Niederschlag
m.
fallout shelter n Atombunker m.
fallow ['fæləu] adj brach(liegend).
false [fɔːls] adj falsch; (imprisonment)
widerrechtlich.
false alarm n falscher or blinder Alarm m.
falsehood ['fɔːlshud] n Unwahrheit f.
falsely ['fɔːlslɪ] adv (accuse) zu Unrecht.
false pretences npl: under ~ unter
Vorspiegelung falscher Tatsachen.
false teeth (BRIT) npl Gebiß nt.
falsify ['fɔːlsɪfaɪ] vt fälschen.
falter ['fɔːltə*] vi stocken; (hesitate) zögern.
fame [feɪm] n Ruhm m.
familiar [fə'mɪlɪə*] adj vertraut; (intimate)
vertraulich; to be ~ with vertraut sein mit;
to make o.s. ~ with sich mit etw
vertraut machen; to be on ~ terms with sb
mit jdm auf vertrautem Fuß stehen.
familiarity [fəmɪlɪ'ærɪtɪ] n (see adj)
Vertrautheit f; Vertraulichkeit f.
familiarize [fə'mɪlɪəraɪz] vt: to ~ o.s. with sth
sich mit etw vertraut machen.
family ['fæmɪlɪ] n Familie f; (relations)
Verwandtschaft f.
family business n Familienbetrieb m.
family credit n Beihilfe für
einkommensschwache Familien.
family doctor n Hausarzt m, Hausärztin f.
family life n Familienleben nt.
family man n (home-loving) häuslich
veranlagter Mann m; (with a family)
Familienvater m.
family planning n Familienplanung f;
~ clinic ≈ Familienberatungsstelle f.
family tree n Stammbaum m.
famine ['fæmɪn] n Hungersnot f.
famished ['fæmɪʃt] (inf) adj ausgehungert; I'm
~ ich sterbe vor Hunger.
famous ['feɪməs] adj berühmt.
famously ['feɪməslɪ] adv (get on) prächtig.
fan [fæn] n (person) Fan m; (object: folding)
Fächer m; (: ELEC) Ventilator m ◆ vt fächeln;
(fire) anfachen; (quarrel) schüren.

▶**fan out** *vi* ausschwärmen; (*unfurl*) sich fächerförmig ausbreiten.

fanatic [fəˈnætɪk] *n* Fanatiker(in) *m(f)*; (*enthusiast*) Fan *m*.

fanatical [fəˈnætɪkl] *adj* fanatisch.

fan belt *n* (*AUT*) Keilriemen *m*.

fanciful [ˈfænsɪful] *adj* (*idea*) abstrus, seltsam; (*design, name*) phantasievoll; (*object*) reich verziert.

fan club *n* Fanclub *m*.

fancy [ˈfænsɪ] *n* Laune *f*; (*imagination*) Phantasie *f*; (*fantasy*) Phantasievorstellung *f* ♦ *adj* (*clothes, hat*) toll, schick; (*hotel*) fein, vornehm; (*food*) ausgefallen ♦ *vt* mögen; (*imagine*) sich *dat* einbilden; (*think*) glauben; **to take a ~ to sth** Lust auf etw *acc* bekommen; **when the ~ takes him** wenn ihm gerade danach ist; **it took** *or* **caught my ~** es gefiel mir; **to ~ that ... meinen, daß ...;** **~ that!** (nein) so was!; **he fancies her** (*inf*) sie gefällt ihm.

fancy dress *n* Verkleidung *f*, (Masken)kostüm *nt*.

fancy-dress ball [ˈfænsɪdrɛs-] *n* Maskenball *m*.

fancy goods *npl* Geschenkartikel *pl*.

fanfare [ˈfænfɛəˈ] *n* Fanfare *f*.

fanfold paper [ˈfænfəuld-] *n* Endlospapier *nt*.

fang [fæŋ] *n* (*tooth*) Fang *m*; (: *of snake*) Giftzahn *m*.

fan heater (*BRIT*) *n* Heizlüfter *m*.

fanlight [ˈfænlaɪt] *n* Oberlicht *nt*.

fanny [ˈfænɪ] *n* (*US: inf: bottom*) Po *m*; (*BRIT: infl: genitals*) Möse *f* (*!*).

fantasize [ˈfæntəsaɪz] *vi* phantasieren.

fantastic [fænˈtæstɪk] *adj* phantastisch.

fantasy [ˈfæntəsɪ] *n* Phantasie *f*; (*dream*) Traum *m*.

fanzine [ˈfænziːn] *n* Fanmagazin *nt*.

FAO *n abbr* (= *Food and Agriculture Organization*) FAO *f*.

f.a.q. *abbr* (= *free alongside quay*) frei Kai.

far [fɑːˈ] *adj*: **at the ~ side** auf der anderen Seite ♦ *adv* weit; **at the ~ end** am anderen Ende; **the ~ left/right** die extreme Linke/ Rechte; **~ away, ~ off** weit entfernt *or* weg; **her thoughts were ~ away** sie war mit ihren Gedanken weit weg; **~ from** (*fig*) alles andere als; **by ~** bei weitem; **is it ~ to London?** ist es weit bis nach London?; **it's not ~ from here** es ist nicht weit von hier; **go as ~ as the church** gehen/fahren Sie bis zur Kirche; **as ~ back as the 13th century** schon im 13. Jahrhundert; **as ~ as I know** soweit ich weiß; **as ~ as possible** soweit wie möglich; **how ~?** wie weit?; **how ~ have you got with your work?** wie weit sind Sie mit Ihrer Arbeit (gekommen)?

faraway [ˈfɑːrəweɪ] *adj* weit entfernt; (*look, voice*) abwesend.

farce [fɑːs] *n* Farce *f*.

farcical [ˈfɑːsɪkl] *adj* absurd, grotesk.

fare [fɛəˈ] *n* Fahrpreis *m*; (*money*) Fahrgeld *nt*; (*passenger*) Fahrgast *m*; (*food*) Kost *f* ♦ *vi*: **he ~d well/badly** es ging ihm gut/schlecht; **half/full ~** halber/voller Fahrpreis; **how did you ~?** wie ist es Ihnen ergangen?; **they ~d badly in the recent elections** sie haben bei den letzten Wahlen schlecht abgeschnitten.

Far East *n*: **the ~** der Ferne Osten.

farewell [fɛəˈwel] *excl* lebe/lebt *etc* wohl! ♦ *n* Abschied *m* ♦ *cpd* Abschieds-.

far-fetched [ˈfɑːˈfetʃt] *adj* weit hergeholt.

farm [fɑːm] *n* Bauernhof *m* ♦ *vt* bebauen.

▶**farm out** *vt* (*work etc*) vergeben.

farmer [ˈfɑːməˈ] *n* Bauer *m*, Bäu(e)rin *f*, Landwirt(in) *m(f)*.

farm hand *n* Landarbeiter(in) *m(f)*.

farmhouse [ˈfɑːmhaus] *n* Bauernhaus *nt*.

farming [ˈfɑːmɪŋ] *n* Landwirtschaft *f*; (*of crops*) Ackerbau *m*; (*of animals*) Viehzucht *f*; **sheep ~** Schafzucht *f*, **intensive ~** (*of crops*) Intensivanbau *m*; (*of animals*) Intensivhaltung *f*.

farm labourer *n* = **farm hand**.

farmland [ˈfɑːmlænd] *n* Ackerland *nt*.

farm produce *n* landwirtschaftliche Produkte *pl*.

farm worker *n* = **farm hand**.

farmyard [ˈfɑːmjɑːd] *n* Hof *m*.

Faroe Islands [ˈfɛərəu-] *npl*: **the ~** die Färöer *pl*.

Faroes [ˈfɛərəuz] *npl* = **Faroe Islands**.

far-reaching [ˈfɑːˈriːtʃɪŋ] *adj* weitreichend.

far-sighted [ˈfɑːˈsaɪtɪd] *adj* weitsichtig; (*fig*) weitblickend.

fart [fɑːt] *vi* furzen (*inf!*) ♦ *n* Furz *m* (*inf!*).

farther [ˈfɑːðəˈ] *adv* weiter ♦ *adj* weiter entfernt.

farthest [ˈfɑːðɪst] *superl of* **far**.

FAS, f.a.s. (*BRIT*) *abbr* (= *free alongside ship*) frei Kai.

fascia [ˈfeɪʃə] *n* (*AUT*) Armaturenbrett *nt*.

fascinate [ˈfæsɪneɪt] *vt* faszinieren.

fascinating [ˈfæsɪneɪtɪŋ] *adj* faszinierend.

fascination [fæsɪˈneɪʃən] *n* Faszination *f*.

fascism [ˈfæʃɪzəm] *n* Faschismus *m*.

fascist [ˈfæʃɪst] *adj* faschistisch ♦ *n* Faschist(in) *m(f)*.

fashion [ˈfæʃən] *n* Mode *f*; (*manner*) Art *f* ♦ *vt* formen; **in ~** modern; **out of ~** unmodern; **after a ~** recht und schlecht; **in the Greek ~** im griechischen Stil.

fashionable [ˈfæʃnəbl] *adj* modisch, modern; (*subject*) Mode-; (*club, writer*) in Mode.

fashion designer *n* Modezeichner(in) *m(f)*.

fashion show *n* Modenschau *f*.

fast [fɑːst] *adj* schnell; (*dye, colour*) farbecht ♦ *adv* schnell; (*stuck, held*) fest ♦ *n* Fasten *nt*; (*period of fasting*) Fastenzeit *f* ♦ *vi* fasten; **my watch is (5 minutes) ~** meine Uhr geht (5 Minuten) vor; **to be ~ asleep** tief *or* fest schlafen; **as ~ as I can** so schnell ich kann; **to make a boat ~** (*BRIT*) ein Boot

festmachen.
fasten ['fɑːsn] vt festmachen; (coat, belt etc)
zumachen ♦ vi (see vt) festgemacht werden;
zugemacht werden.
▶**fasten (up)on** vt fus sich dat in den Kopf
setzen.
fastener ['fɑːsnəʳ] n Verschluß m.
fastening ['fɑːsnɪŋ] n = **fastener**.
fast food n Fast food nt, Schnellgerichte pl.
fast-food ['fɑːstfuːd] cpd (industry, chain)
Fast-food-; ~ **restaurant** Schnellimbiß m.
fastidious [fæs'tɪdɪəs] adj penibel.
fast lane n (AUT): **the** ~ die Überholspur.
fat [fæt] adj dick; (person) dick, fett (pej);
(animal) fett; (profit) üppig ♦ n Fett nt; **that's
a ~ lot of use** (inf) das hilft herzlich wenig;
to live off the ~ of the land wie Gott in
Frankreich or wie die Made im Speck
leben.
fatal ['feɪtl] adj tödlich; (mistake)
verhängnisvoll.
fatalistic [feɪtə'lɪstɪk] adj fatalistisch.
fatality [fə'tælɪtɪ] n Todesopfer nt.
fatally ['feɪtəlɪ] adv (see adj) tödlich;
verhängnisvoll.
fate [feɪt] n Schicksal nt; **to meet one's** ~ vom
Schicksal ereilt werden.
fated ['feɪtɪd] adj (person) unglückselig;
(project) zum Scheitern verurteilt; (governed
by fate) vorherbestimmt.
fateful ['feɪtfʊl] adj schicksalhaft.
fat-free ['fæt'friː] adj fettfrei.
father ['fɑːðəʳ] n Vater m.
Father Christmas n der Weihnachtsmann.
fatherhood ['fɑːðəhʊd] n Vaterschaft f.
father-in-law ['fɑːðərənlɔː] n Schwiegervater
m.
fatherland ['fɑːðəlænd] n Vaterland nt.
fatherly ['fɑːðəlɪ] adj väterlich.
fathom ['fæðəm] n (NAUT) Faden m ♦ vt (also:
~ **out**) verstehen.
fatigue [fə'tiːg] n Erschöpfung f; **fatigues** npl
(MIL) Arbeitsanzug m; **metal** ~
Metallermüdung f.
fatness ['fætnɪs] n Dicke f.
fatten ['fætn] vt mästen ♦ vi (person) dick
werden; (animal) fett werden; **chocolate is**
~**ing** Schokolade macht dick.
fatty ['fætɪ] adj fett ♦ n (inf) Dickerchen nt.
fatuous ['fætjʊəs] adj albern, töricht.
faucet ['fɔːsɪt] (US) n (Wasser)hahn m.
fault [fɔːlt] n Fehler m; (blame) Schuld f; (in
machine) Defekt m; (GEOG) Verwerfung f
♦ vt (also: **find** ~ **with**) etwas auszusetzen
haben an +dat; **it's my** ~ es ist meine Schuld;
at ~ im Unrecht; **generous to a** ~
übermäßig großzügig.
faultless ['fɔːltlɪs] adj fehlerlos.
faulty ['fɔːltɪ] adj defekt.
fauna ['fɔːnə] n Fauna f.
faux pas ['fəu'pɑː] n inv Fauxpas m.
favor etc (US) = **favour** etc.

favour, (US) **favor** ['feɪvəʳ] n (approval)
Wohlwollen nt; (help) Gefallen m ♦ vt
bevorzugen; (be favourable for) begünstigen;
to ask a ~ **of sb** jdn um einen Gefallen
bitten; **to do sb a** ~ jdm einen Gefallen tun;
to find ~ **with sb** bei jdm Anklang finden; **in**
~ **of** (biased) zugunsten von; (rejected)
zugunsten +gen; **to be in** ~ **of sth** für etw
sein; **to be in** ~ **of doing sth** dafür sein, etw
zu tun.
favourable ['feɪvrəbl] adj günstig; (reaction)
positiv; (comparison) vorteilhaft.
favourably ['feɪvrəblɪ] adv (react) positiv;
(compare) vorteilhaft.
favourite ['feɪvrɪt] adj Lieblings- ♦ n Liebling
m; (in race) Favorit(in) m(f).
favouritism ['feɪvrɪtɪzəm] n Günstlings-
wirtschaft f.
fawn [fɔːn] n Rehkitz nt ♦ adj (also: ~-coloured)
hellbraun ♦ vi: **to** ~ **(up)on** sich
einschmeicheln bei.
fax [fæks] n Fax nt; (machine) Fax(gerät) nt ♦ vt
faxen.
FBI (US) n abbr (= Federal Bureau of
Investigation) FBI nt.
FCC (US) n abbr (= Federal Communications
Commission) Aufsichtsbehörde im
Medienbereich.
FCO (BRIT) n abbr (= Foreign and
Commonwealth Office) ≈ Auswärtiges Amt
nt.
FD (US) n abbr = **fire department**.
FDA (US) n abbr (= Food and Drug
Administration) Nahrungs- und
Arzneimittelbehörde.
FE n abbr (= further education) Fortbildung f.
fear [fɪəʳ] n Furcht f, Angst f ♦ vt fürchten,
Angst haben vor +dat; (be worried about)
befürchten ♦ vi sich fürchten; ~ **of heights**
Höhenangst f; **for** ~ **of doing sth** aus Angst,
etw zu tun; **to** ~ **for** fürchten um; **to** ~ **that**
... befürchten, daß ....
fearful ['fɪəfʊl] adj (frightening) furchtbar,
schrecklich; (apprehensive) ängstlich; **to be**
~ **of** Angst haben vor +dat.
fearfully ['fɪəfəlɪ] adv ängstlich; (inf: very)
furchtbar, schrecklich.
fearless ['fɪəlɪs] adj furchtlos.
fearsome ['fɪəsəm] adj furchterregend.
feasibility [fiːzə'bɪlɪtɪ] n Durchführbarkeit f.
feasibility study n Durchführbarkeitsstudie
f.
feasible ['fiːzəbl] adj machbar; (proposal, plan)
durchführbar.
feast [fiːst] n Festmahl nt; (REL: also: ~ **day**)
Festtag m, Feiertag m ♦ vi schlemmen; **to**
~ **on** sich gütlich tun an +dat.
feat [fiːt] n Leistung f.
feather ['feðəʳ] n Feder f ♦ cpd Feder-;
(mattress) Federkern- ♦ vt: **to** ~ **one's nest**
(fig) sein Schäfchen ins trockene bringen.
featherweight ['feðəweɪt] n Leichtgewicht nt;

(*BOXING*) Federgewicht *nt*.

feature ['fiːtʃəˡ] *n* Merkmal *nt*; (*PRESS, TV*) Feature *nt* ♦ *vt*: **the film ~s Marlon Brando** Marlon Brando spielt in dem Film mit ♦ *vi*: **to ~ in** vorkommen in +*dat*; (*film*) mitspielen in +*dat*; **features** *npl* (*of face*) (Gesichts)züge *pl*; **it ~d prominently in** es spielte eine große Rolle in +*dat*; **a special ~ on sth/sb** ein Sonderbeitrag *m* über etw/jdn.

feature film *n* Spielfilm *m*.

featureless ['fiːtʃəlɪs] *adj* (*landscape*) eintönig.

Feb. *abbr* (= *February*) Feb.

February ['fɛbruərɪ] *n* Februar *m*; *see also* **July.**

feces ['fiːsiːz] (*US*) *npl* = **faeces.**

feckless ['fɛklɪs] *adj* nutzlos.

Fed (*US*) *abbr* = **federal**; **federation.**

Fed. [fɛd] (*US: inf*) *n abbr* = **Federal Reserve Board.**

fed [fɛd] *pt, pp of* **feed.**

federal ['fɛdərəl] *adj* föderalistisch.

Federal Republic of Germany *n* Bundesrepublik *f* Deutschland.

Federal Reserve Board (*US*) *n Kontroll-organ der US-Zentralbank.*

Federal Trade Commission (*US*) *n Handels-Kontrollbehörde.*

federation [fɛdəˈreɪʃən] *n* Föderation *f*, Bund *m*.

fed up *adj*: **to be ~ with** die Nase voll haben von.

fee [fiː] *n* Gebühr *f*; (*of doctor, lawyer*) Honorar *nt*; **school ~s** Schulgeld *nt*; **entrance ~** Eintrittsgebühr *f*; **membership ~** Mitgliedsbeitrag *m*; **for a small ~** gegen eine geringe Gebühr.

feeble ['fiːbl] *adj* schwach; (*joke*) lahm.

feeble-minded ['fiːblˈmaɪndɪd] *adj* dümmlich.

feed [fiːd] (*pt, pp* **fed**) *n* Mahlzeit *f*; (*of animal*) Fütterung *f*; (*on printer*) Papiervorschub *m* ♦ *vt* füttern; (*family etc*) ernähren; (*machine*) versorgen; **to ~ sth into sth** etw in etw *acc* einfüllen *or* eingeben; (*data, information*) etw in etw *acc* eingeben; **to ~ material into sth** Material in etw *acc* eingeben.

▶**feed back** *vt* zurückleiten.

▶**feed on** *vt fus* sich nähren von.

feedback ['fiːdbæk] *n* Feedback *nt*, Rückmeldung *f*; (*from person*) Reaktion *f*.

feeder ['fiːdəˡ] *n* (*road*) Zubringer *m*; (*railway line, air route*) Zubringerlinie *f*; (*baby's bottle*) Flasche *f*.

feeding bottle ['fiːdɪŋ-] (*BRIT*) *n* Flasche *f*.

feel [fiːl] (*pt, pp* **felt**) *n* (*sensation, touch*) Gefühl *nt*; (*impression*) Atmosphäre *f* ♦ *vt* (*object*) fühlen; (*desire, anger, grief*) empfinden; (*pain*) spüren; (*cold*) leiden unter +*dat*; (*think, believe*): **I ~ that you ought to do it** ich meine *or* ich bin der Meinung, daß Sie es tun sollten; **it has a soft ~** es fühlt sich weich an; **I ~ hungry** ich habe Hunger; **I ~ cold** mir ist kalt; **to ~ lonely/better** sich einsam/besser fühlen; **I don't ~ well** mir

geht es nicht gut; **I ~ sorry for him** er tut mir leid; **it ~s soft** es fühlt sich weich an; **it ~s colder here** es kommt mir hier kälter vor; **it ~s like velvet** es fühlt sich wie Samt an; **to ~ like** (*desire*) Lust haben auf +*acc*; **to ~ like doing sth** Lust haben, etw zu tun; **to get the ~ of sth** ein Gefühl für etw bekommen; **I'm still ~ing my way** ich versuche noch, mich zu orientieren.

▶**feel about** *vi* umhertasten; **to ~ about** *or* **around in one's pocket for** in seiner Tasche herumsuchen nach.

▶**feel around** *vi* = **feel about.**

feeler ['fiːləˡ] *n* Fühler *m*; **to put out a ~** *or* **~s** (*fig*) seine Fühler ausstrecken.

feeling ['fiːlɪŋ] *n* Gefühl *nt*; (*impression*) Eindruck *m*; **~s ran high about it** man ereiferte sich sehr darüber; **what are your ~s about the matter?** was meinen Sie dazu?; **I have a ~ that ...** ich habe das Gefühl, daß ...; **my ~ is that ...** meine Meinung ist, daß ...; **to hurt sb's ~s** jdn verletzen.

fee-paying ['fiːpeɪɪŋ] *adj* (*school*) Privat-; **~ pupils** *Schüler, deren Eltern Schulgeld zahlen.*

feet [fiːt] *npl of* **foot.**

feign [feɪn] *vt* vortäuschen.

feigned [feɪnd] *adj* vorgetäuscht.

feint [feɪnt] *n* fein liniertes Papier *nt*.

felicitous [fɪˈlɪsɪtəs] *adj* glücklich.

feline ['fiːlaɪn] *adj* (*eyes etc*) Katzen-; (*features, grace*) katzenartig.

fell [fɛl] *pt of* **fall** ♦ *vt* fällen; (*opponent*) niederstrecken ♦ *n* (*BRIT: mountain*) Berg *m*; (: *moorland*): **the ~s** das Moor(land) ♦ *adj*: **in one ~ swoop** auf einen Schlag.

fellow ['fɛləu] *n* Mann *m*, Typ *m* (*inf*); (*comrade*) Kamerad *m*; (*of learned society*) Mitglied *nt*; (*of university*) Fellow *m*; **their ~ prisoners/students** ihre Mitgefangenen/Kommilitonen (und Kommilitoninnen); **his ~ workers** seine Kollegen (und Kolleginnen).

fellow citizen *n* Mitbürger(in) *m(f)*.

fellow countryman (*irreg: like* **man**) *n* Landsmann *m*, Landsmännin *f*.

fellow men *npl* Mitmenschen *pl*.

fellowship ['fɛləuʃɪp] *n* Kameradschaft *f*; (*society*) Gemeinschaft *f*; (*SCOL*) Forschungsstipendium *nt*.

fell-walking ['fɛlwɔːkɪŋ] (*BRIT*) *n* Bergwandern *nt*.

felon ['fɛlən] *n* (*LAW*) (Schwer)verbrecher *m*.

felony ['fɛlənɪ] *n* (*LAW*) (schweres) Verbrechen *nt*.

felt [fɛlt] *pt, pp of* **feel** ♦ *n* Filz *m*.

felt-tip pen ['fɛltɪp-] *n* Filzstift *m*.

female ['fiːmeɪl] *n* Weibchen *nt*; (*pej: woman*) Frau *f*, Weib *nt* (*pej*) ♦ *adj* weiblich; (*vote etc*) Frauen-; (*ELEC: connector, plug*) Mutter-, Innen-; **male and ~ students** Studenten und Studentinnen.

female impersonator n Damen-Imitator m.
Femidom ® ['fɛmɪdɔm] n Kondom nt für die Frau, Femidom ® nt.
feminine ['fɛmɪnɪn] adj weiblich, feminin ♦ n Femininum nt.
femininity [fɛmɪ'nɪnɪtɪ] n Weiblichkeit f.
feminism ['fɛmɪnɪzəm] n Feminismus m.
feminist ['fɛmɪnɪst] n Feminist(in) m(f).
fen [fɛn] (BRIT) n: **the F~s** die Niederungen in East Anglia.
fence [fɛns] n Zaun m; (SPORT) Hindernis nt ♦ vt (also: ~ **in**) einzäunen ♦ vi (SPORT) fechten; **to sit on the** ~ (fig) neutral bleiben, nicht Partei ergreifen.
fencing ['fɛnsɪŋ] n (SPORT) Fechten nt.
fend [fɛnd] vi: **to** ~ **for o.s.** für sich (selbst) sorgen, sich allein durchbringen.
▶**fend off** vt abwehren.
fender ['fɛndə*] n Kamingitter nt; (on boat) Fender m; (US: of car) Kotflügel m.
fennel ['fɛnl] n Fenchel m.
ferment [vi fə'mɛnt, n 'fɜːmɛnt] vi gären ♦ n (fig: unrest) Unruhe f.
fermentation [fɜːmɛn'teɪʃən] n Gärung f.
fern [fɜːn] n Farn m.
ferocious [fə'rəuʃəs] adj wild; (behaviour) heftig; (competition) scharf.
ferocity [fə'rɔsɪtɪ] n (see adj) Wildheit f; Heftigkeit f; Schärfe f.
ferret ['fɛrɪt] n Frettchen nt.
▶**ferret about** vi herumstöbern.
▶**ferret around** vi = ferret about.
▶**ferret out** vt aufspüren.
ferry ['fɛrɪ] n (also: ~**boat**) Fähre f ♦ vt transportieren; **to** ~ **sth/sb across** or **over** jdn/etw übersetzen.
ferryman ['fɛrɪmən] (irreg: like man) n Fährmann m.
fertile ['fɜːtaɪl] adj fruchtbar; ~ **period** fruchtbare Tage pl.
fertility [fə'tɪlɪtɪ] n Fruchtbarkeit f.
fertility drug n Fruchtbarkeitsmedikament nt.
fertilization [fɜːtɪlaɪ'zeɪʃən] n (BIOL) Befruchtung f.
fertilize ['fɜːtɪlaɪz] vt düngen; (BIOL) befruchten.
fertilizer ['fɜːtɪlaɪzə*] n Dünger m.
fervent ['fɜːvənt] adj leidenschaftlich; (admirer) glühend.
fervour, (US) **fervor** ['fɜːvə*] n Leidenschaft f.
fester ['fɛstə*] vi (wound) eitern; (insult) nagen; (row) sich verschlimmern.
festival ['fɛstɪvəl] n Fest nt; (ART, MUS) Festival nt, Festspiele pl.
festive ['fɛstɪv] adj festlich; **the** ~ **season** (BRIT: Christmas and New Year) die Festzeit f.
festivities [fɛs'tɪvɪtɪz] npl Feierlichkeiten pl.
festoon [fɛs'tuːn] vt: **to** ~ **with** schmücken mit.
fetch [fɛtʃ] vt holen; (sell for) (ein)bringen; **would you** ~ **me a glass of water please?**

kannst du mir bitte ein Glas Wasser bringen?; **how much did it** ~**?** wieviel hat es eingebracht?
▶**fetch up** (inf) vi landen (inf).
fetching ['fɛtʃɪŋ] adj bezaubernd, reizend.
fête [feɪt] n Fest nt.
fetid ['fɛtɪd] adj übelriechend.
fetish ['fɛtɪʃ] n Fetisch m.
fetter ['fɛtə*] vt fesseln; (horse) anpflocken; (fig) in Fesseln legen.
fetters ['fɛtəz] npl Fesseln pl.
fettle ['fɛtl] (BRIT) n: **in fine** ~ in bester Form.
fetus ['fiːtəs] (US) n = **foetus**.
feud [fjuːd] n Streit m ♦ vi im Streit liegen; **a family** ~ ein Familienstreit m.
feudal ['fjuːdl] adj (society etc) Feudal-.
feudalism ['fjuːdlɪzəm] n Feudalismus m.
fever ['fiːvə*] n Fieber nt; **he has a** ~ er hat Fieber.
feverish ['fiːvərɪʃ] adj fiebrig; (activity, emotion) fieberhaft.
few [fjuː] adj wenige; **a** ~ (adj) ein paar, einige; (pron) einige; **a** ~ **more (days)** noch ein paar (Tage); **they were** ~ sie waren nur wenige; ~ **succeed** nur wenigen gelingt es; **very** ~ **survive** nur sehr wenige überleben; **I know a** ~ ich kenne einige; **a good** ~, **quite a** ~ ziemlich viele; **in the next/past** ~ **days** in den nächsten/letzten paar Tagen; **every** ~ **days/months** alle paar Tage/Monate.
fewer ['fjuːə*] adj weniger; **there are** ~ **buses on Sundays** Sonntags fahren weniger Busse.
fewest ['fjuːɪst] adj die wenigsten.
FFA n abbr (= Future Farmers of America) Verband von Landwirtschaftsstudenten.
FH (BRIT) n abbr = **fire hydrant**.
FHA (US) n abbr (= Federal Housing Administration): ~ **loan** Baudarlehen nt.
fiancé [fɪ'ɑːŋseɪ] n Verlobte(r) m.
fiancée [fɪ'ɑːŋseɪ] n Verlobte f.
fiasco [fɪ'æskəu] n Fiasko nt.
fib [fɪb] n Flunkerei f (inf).
fibre, (US) **fiber** ['faɪbə*] n Faser f; (cloth) (Faser)stoff m; (roughage) Ballaststoffe pl; (ANAT: tissue) Gewebe nt.
fibreboard, (US) **fiberboard** ['faɪbəbɔːd] n Faserplatte f.
fibreglass, (US) **fiberglass** ['faɪbəglɑːs] n Fiberglas nt.
fibrositis [faɪbrə'saɪtɪs] n Bindegewebsentzündung f.
FICA (US) n abbr (= Federal Insurance Contributions Act) Abgabe zur Sozialversicherung.
fickle ['fɪkl] adj unbeständig; (weather) wechselhaft.
fiction ['fɪkʃən] n Erfindung f; (LITER) Erzählliteratur f, Prosaliteratur f.
fictional ['fɪkʃənl] adj erfunden.
fictionalize ['fɪkʃnəlaɪz] vt fiktionalisieren.

fictitious [fɪk'tɪʃəs] *adj* (*false*) falsch; (*invented*) fiktiv, frei erfunden.

fiddle ['fɪdl] *n* Fiedel *f* (*inf*), Geige *f*; (*fraud, swindle*) Schwindelei *f* ♦ *vt* (*BRIT: accounts*) frisieren (*inf*); **tax** ~ Steuermanipulation *f*; **to work a** ~ ein krummes Ding drehen (*inf*).

▶**fiddle with** *vt fus* herumspielen mit.

fiddler ['fɪdlə*] *n* Geiger(in) *m(f)*.

fiddly ['fɪdlɪ] *adj* knifflig (*inf*); (*object*) fummelig.

fidelity [fɪ'dɛlɪtɪ] *n* Treue *f*; (*accuracy*) Genauigkeit *f*.

fidget ['fɪdʒɪt] *vi* zappeln.

fidgety ['fɪdʒɪtɪ] *adj* zappelig.

fiduciary [fɪ'djuːʃɪərɪ] *n* (*LAW*) Treuhänder *m*.

field [fiːld] *n* Feld *nt*; (*SPORT: ground*) Platz *m*; (*subject, area of interest*) Gebiet *nt*; (*COMPUT*) Datenfeld *nt* ♦ *cpd* Feld-; **to lead the** ~ das Feld anführen; ~ **trip** Exkursion *f*.

field day *n:* **to have a** ~ einen herrlichen Tag haben.

field glasses *npl* Feldstecher *m*.

field hospital *n* Feldlazarett *nt*.

field marshal *n* Feldmarschall *m*.

field work *n* Feldforschung *f*; (*ARCHAEOLOGY, GEOG*) Arbeit *f* im Gelände.

fiend [fiːnd] *n* Teufel *m*.

fiendish ['fiːndɪʃ] *adj* teuflisch; (*problem*) verzwickt.

fierce [fɪəs] *adj* wild; (*look*) böse; (*fighting, wind*) heftig; (*loyalty*) leidenschaftlich; (*enemy*) erbittert; (*heat*) glühend.

fiery ['faɪərɪ] *adj* glühend; (*temperament*) feurig, hitzig.

FIFA ['fiːfə] *n abbr* (= *Fédération Internationale de Football Association*) FIFA *f*.

fifteen [fɪf'tiːn] *num* fünfzehn.

fifteenth [fɪf'tiːnθ] *num* fünfzehnte(r, s).

fifth [fɪfθ] *num* fünfte(r, s) ♦ *n* Fünftel *nt*.

fiftieth ['fɪftɪɪθ] *num* fünfzigste(r, s).

fifty ['fɪftɪ] *num* fünfzig.

fifty-fifty ['fɪftɪ'fɪftɪ] *adj, adv* halbe-halbe, fifty-fifty; **to go/share** ~ **with sb** mit jdm halbe-halbe *or* fifty-fifty machen; **we have a** ~ **chance (of success)** unsere Chancen stehen fifty-fifty.

fig [fɪg] *n* Feige *f*.

fight [faɪt] *n* (*pt, pp* **fought**) *n* Kampf *m*; (*quarrel*) Streit *m*; (*punch-up*) Schlägerei *f* ♦ *vt* kämpfen mit *or* gegen; (*prejudice etc*) bekämpfen; (*election*) kandidieren bei; (*emotion*) ankämpfen gegen; (*LAW: case*) durchkämpfen, durchfechten ♦ *vi* kämpfen; (*quarrel*) sich streiten; (*punch-up*) sich schlagen; **to put up a** ~ sich zur Wehr setzen; **to** ~ **one's way through a crowd/the undergrowth** sich *dat* einen Weg durch die Menge/das Unterholz bahnen; **to** ~ **against** bekämpfen; **to** ~ **for one's rights** für seine Rechte kämpfen.

▶**fight back** *vi* zurückschlagen; (*SPORT*) zurückkämpfen; (*after illness*) zu Kräften

kommen ♦ *vt fus* unterdrücken.

▶**fight down** *vt* unterdrücken.

▶**fight off** *vt* abwehren; (*sleep, urge*) ankämpfen gegen.

▶**fight out** *vt:* **to** ~ **it out** es untereinander ausfechten.

fighter ['faɪtə*] *n* Kämpfer(in) *m(f)*; (*plane*) Jagdflugzeug *nt*; (*fig*) Kämpfernatur *f*.

fighter pilot *n* Jagdflieger *m*.

fighting ['faɪtɪŋ] *n* Kämpfe *pl*; (*brawl*) Schlägereien *pl*.

figment ['fɪgmənt] *n:* **a** ~ **of the imagination** ein Hirngespinst *nt*, pure Einbildung *f*.

figurative ['fɪgjurətɪv] *adj* bildlich, übertragen; (*style*) gegenständlich.

figure ['fɪgə*] *n* Figur *f*; (*illustration*) Abbildung *f*; (*number, statistic, cipher*) Zahl *f*; (*person*) Gestalt *f*; (*personality*) Persönlichkeit *f* ♦ *vt* (*esp US*) glauben, schätzen ♦ *vi* eine Rolle spielen; **to put a** ~ **on sth** eine Zahl für etw angeben; **public** ~ Persönlichkeit *f* des öffentlichen Lebens.

▶**figure out** *vt* ausrechnen.

figurehead ['fɪgəhɛd] *n* Galionsfigur *f*.

figure of speech *n* Redensart *f*, Redewendung *f*.

figure skating *n* Eiskunstlaufen *nt*.

Fiji (Islands) ['fiːdʒiː-] *n(pl)* Fidschiinseln *pl*.

filament ['fɪləmənt] *n* Glühfaden *m*; (*BOT*) Staubfaden *m*.

filch [fɪltʃ] (*inf*) *vt* filzen.

file [faɪl] *n* Akte *f*; (*folder*) (Akten)ordner *m*; (*for loose leaf*) (Akten)mappe *f*; (*COMPUT*) Datei *f*; (*row*) Reihe *f*; (*tool*) Feile *f* ♦ *vt* ablegen, abheften; (*claim*) einreichen; (*wood, metal, fingernails*) feilen ♦ *vi:* **to** ~ **in/ out** nacheinander hereinkommen/ hinausgehen; **to** ~ **a suit against sb** eine Klage gegen jdn erheben; **to** ~ **past** in einer Reihe vorbeigehen; **to** ~ **for divorce** die Scheidung einreichen.

filename ['faɪlneɪm] *n* (*COMPUT*) Dateiname *m*.

filibuster ['fɪlɪbʌstə*] (*esp US: POL*) *n* (*also:* ~**er**) Dauerredner(in) *m(f)* ♦ *vi* filibustern, Obstruktion betreiben.

filing ['faɪlɪŋ] *n* Ablegen *nt*, Abheften *nt*.

filing cabinet *n* Aktenschrank *m*.

filing clerk *n* Angestellte(r) *f(m)* in der Registratur.

Filipino [fɪlɪ'piːnəu] *n* Filipino *m*, Filipina *f*; (*LING*) Philippinisch *nt*.

fill [fɪl] *vt* füllen; (*space, area*) ausfüllen; (*tooth*) plombieren; (*need*) erfüllen ♦ *vi* sich füllen ♦ *n:* **to eat one's** ~ sich satt essen; **we've already** ~**ed that vacancy** wir haben diese Stelle schon besetzt.

▶**fill in** *vt* füllen; (*time*) überbrücken; (*form*) ausfüllen ♦ *vi:* **to** ~ **in for sb** für jdn einspringen; **to** ~ **sb in on sth** (*inf*) jdn über etw *acc* ins Bild setzen.

▶**fill out** *vt* ausfüllen.

▶**fill up** vt füllen ♦ vi (AUT) tanken; ~ **it up, please** (AUT) bitte volltanken.
fillet ['fɪlɪt] n Filet nt ♦ vt filetieren.
fillet steak n Filetsteak nt.
filling ['fɪlɪŋ] n Füllung f; (for tooth) Plombe f.
filling station n Tankstelle f.
fillip ['fɪlɪp] n (stimulus) Ansporn m.
filly ['fɪlɪ] n Stutfohlen nt.
film [fɪlm] n Film m; (of powder etc) Schicht f; (for wrapping) Plastikfolie f ♦ vt, vi filmen.
film star n Filmstar m.
film strip n Filmstreifen m.
film studio n Filmstudio nt.
Filofax ® ['faɪleufæks] n Filofax ® nt, Terminplaner m.
filter ['fɪltə*] n Filter m ♦ vt filtern.
▶**filter in** vi durchsickern.
▶**filter through** vi = **filter in.**
filter coffee n Filterkaffee m.
filter lane (BRIT) n Abbiegespur f.
filter tip n Filter m.
filter-tipped ['fɪltə'tɪpt] adj (cigarette) Filter-.
filth [fɪlθ] n Dreck m, Schmutz m.
filthy ['fɪlθɪ] adj dreckig, schmutzig; (language) unflätig.
fin [fɪn] n Flosse f; (TECH) Seitenflosse f.
final ['faɪnl] adj letzte(r, s); (ultimate) letztendlich; (definitive) endgültig ♦ n Finale nt, Endspiel nt; **finals** npl (UNIV) Abschlußprüfung f.
final demand n letzte Zahlungsaufforderung f.
finale [fɪ'nɑːlɪ] n Finale nt; (THEAT) Schlußszene f.
finalist ['faɪnəlɪst] n Endrundenteilnehmer(in) m(f), Finalist(in) m(f).
finality [faɪ'nælɪtɪ] n Endgültigkeit f; **with an air of** ~ mit Bestimmtheit.
finalize ['faɪnəlaɪz] vt endgültig festlegen.
finally ['faɪnəlɪ] adv endlich, schließlich; (lastly) schließlich, zum Schluß; (irrevocably) endgültig.
finance [faɪ'næns] n Geldmittel pl; (money management) Finanzwesen nt ♦ vt finanzieren; **finances** npl (personal) Finanzen pl, Finanzlage f.
financial [faɪ'nænʃəl] adj finanziell; ~ **statement** Bilanz f.
financially [faɪ'nænʃəlɪ] adv finanziell.
financial year n Geschäftsjahr nt.
financier [faɪ'nænsɪə*] n Finanzier m.
find [faɪnd] (pt, pp found) vt finden; (discover) entdecken ♦ n Fund m; **to** ~ **sb guilty** jdn für schuldig befinden; **to** ~ **(some) difficulty in doing sth** (einige) Schwierigkeiten haben, etw zu tun.
▶**find out** vt herausfinden; (person) erwischen ♦ vi: **to** ~ **out about** etwas herausfinden über +acc; (by chance) etwas erfahren über +acc.
findings ['faɪndɪŋz] npl (LAW) Urteil nt; (of report) Ergebnis nt.

fine [faɪn] adj fein; (excellent) gut; (thin) dünn ♦ adv gut; (small) fein ♦ n Geldstrafe f ♦ vt mit einer Geldstrafe belegen; **he's** ~ es geht ihm gut; **the weather is** ~ das Wetter ist schön; **that's cutting it (a bit)** ~ das ist aber (ein bißchen) knapp; **you're doing** ~ das machen Sie gut.
fine arts npl schöne Künste pl.
finely ['faɪnlɪ] adv schön; (chop) klein; (slice) dünn; (adjust) fein.
fine print n: **the** ~ das Kleingedruckte.
finery ['faɪnərɪ] n (of dress) Staat m.
finesse [fɪ'nɛs] n Geschick nt.
fine-tooth comb ['faɪntuː·θ-] n: **to go through sth with a** ~ (fig) etw genau unter die Lupe nehmen.
finger ['fɪŋgə*] n Finger m ♦ vt befühlen; **little** ~ kleiner Finger; **index** ~ Zeigefinger m.
fingernail ['fɪŋgəneɪl] n Fingernagel m.
fingerprint ['fɪŋgəprɪnt] n Fingerabdruck m ♦ vt Fingerabdrücke abnehmen +dat.
fingerstall ['fɪŋgəstɔːl] n Fingerling m.
fingertip ['fɪŋgətɪp] n Fingerspitze f; **to have sth at one's** ~**s** (to hand) etw parat haben; (know well) etw aus dem Effeff kennen (inf).
finicky ['fɪnɪkɪ] adj pingelig.
finish ['fɪnɪʃ] n Schluß m, Ende nt; (SPORT) Finish nt; (polish etc) Verarbeitung f ♦ vt fertig sein mit; (work) erledigen; (book) auslesen; (use up) aufbrauchen ♦ vi enden; (person) fertig sein; **to** ~ **doing sth** mit etw fertig werden; **to** ~ **third** als dritter durchs Ziel gehen; **to have** ~**ed with sth** mit etw fertig sein; **she's** ~**ed with him** sie hat mit ihm Schluß gemacht.
▶**finish off** vt fertigmachen; (kill) den Gnadenstoß geben.
▶**finish up** vt (food) aufessen; (drink) austrinken ♦ vi (end up) landen.
finished ['fɪnɪʃt] adj fertig; (performance) ausgereift; (inf: tired) erledigt.
finishing line ['fɪnɪʃɪŋ-] n Ziellinie f.
finishing school n höhere Mädchenschule f (in der auch Etikette und gesellschaftliches Verhalten gelehrt wird).
finishing touches npl: **the** ~ der letzte Schliff.
finite ['faɪnaɪt] adj begrenzt; (verb) finit.
Finland ['fɪnlənd] n Finnland nt.
Finn [fɪn] n Finne m, Finnin f.
Finnish ['fɪnɪʃ] adj finnisch ♦ n (LING) Finnisch nt.
fiord [fjɔːd] n = **fjord.**
fir [fɜː*] n Tanne f.
fire ['faɪə*] n Feuer nt; (in hearth) (Kamin)feuer nt; (accidental fire) Brand m ♦ vt abschießen; (imagination) beflügeln; (enthusiasm) befeuern; (inf: dismiss) feuern ♦ vi feuern, schießen; **to** ~ **a gun** ein Gewehr abschießen; **to be on** ~ brennen; **to set** ~ **to sth, set sth on** ~ etw anzünden; **insured against** ~ feuerversichert; **electric/gas** ~

Elektro-/Gasofen *m*; **to come/be under ~ (from)** unter Beschuß (von) geraten/ stehen.
fire alarm *n* Feuermelder *m*.
firearm ['faɪrɑːm] *n* Feuerwaffe *f*, Schußwaffe *f*.
fire brigade *n* Feuerwehr *f*.
fire chief *n* Branddirektor *m*.
fire department (*US*) *n* Feuerwehr *f*.
fire door *n* Feuertür *f*.
fire drill *n* Probealarm *m*.
fire engine *n* Feuerwehrauto *nt*.
fire escape *n* Feuertreppe *f*.
fire-extinguisher ['faɪərɪk'stɪŋgwɪʃə'] *n* Feuerlöscher *m*.
fireguard ['faɪəgɑːd] (*BRIT*) *n* (Schutz)gitter *nt* (*vor dem Kamin*).
fire hazard *n*: **that's a ~** das ist feuergefährlich.
fire hydrant *n* Hydrant *m*.
fire insurance *n* Feuerversicherung *f*.
fireman ['faɪəmən] (*irreg: like* **man**) *n* Feuerwehrmann *m*.
fireplace ['faɪəpleɪs] *n* Kamin *m*.
fireplug ['faɪəplʌg] (*US*) *n* = **fire hydrant**.
fire practice *n* = **fire drill**.
fireproof ['faɪəpruːf] *adj* feuerfest.
fire regulations *npl* Brandschutz- bestimmungen *pl*.
fire screen *n* Ofenschirm *m*.
fireside ['faɪəsaɪd] *n*: **by the ~** am Kamin.
fire station *n* Feuerwache *f*.
firewood ['faɪəwud] *n* Brennholz *nt*.
fireworks ['faɪəwɜːks] *npl* Feuerwerkskörper *pl*; (*display*) Feuerwerk *nt*.
firing line ['faɪərɪŋ-] *n* Feuerlinie *f*, Schußlinie *f*; **to be in the ~** (*fig*) in der Schußlinie sein.
firing squad *n* Exekutionskommando *nt*.
firm [fɜːm] *adj* fest; (*mattress*) hart; (*measures*) durchgreifend ♦ *n* Firma *f*; **to be a ~ believer in sth** fest von etw überzeugt sein.
firmly ['fɜːmlɪ] *adv* (*see adj*) fest; hart; (*definitely*) entschlossen.
firmness ['fɜːmnɪs] *n* (*see adj*) Festigkeit *f*; Härte *f*; (*definiteness*) Entschlossenheit *f*.
first [fɜːst] *adj* erste(r, s) ♦ *adv* als erste(r, s); (*before other things*) zuerst; (*when listing reasons etc*) erstens; (*for the first time*) zum ersten Mal ♦ *n* Erste(r, s); (*AUT: also:* **~ gear**) der erste Gang; (*BRIT: SCOL*) ≈ Eins *f*; **the ~ of January** der erste Januar; **at ~** zuerst, zunächst; **~ of all** vor allem; **in the ~ instance** zuerst *or* zunächst einmal; **I'll do it ~ thing (tomorrow)** ich werde es (morgen) als erstes tun; **from the very ~** gleich von Anfang an.
first aid *n* Erste Hilfe *f*.
first-aid kit [fɜːst'eɪd-] *n* Erste-Hilfe- Ausrüstung *f*.
first-class ['fɜːst'klɑːs] *adj* erstklassig; (*carriage, ticket*) Erste(r)-Klasse-; (*post*)

bevorzugt befördert ♦ *adv* (*travel, send*) erster Klasse.
first-hand ['fɜːst'hænd] *adj* aus erster Hand.
first lady (*US*) *n* First Lady *f*; **the ~ of jazz** die Königin des Jazz.
firstly ['fɜːstlɪ] *adv* erstens, zunächst einmal.
first name *n* Vorname *m*.
first night *n* Premiere *f*.
first-rate ['fɜːst'reɪt] *adj* erstklassig.
first-time buyer ['fɜːsttaɪm-] *n* jd, der zum ersten Mal ein Haus/eine Wohnung kauft.
fir tree *n* Tannenbaum *m*.
FIS (*BRIT*) *n abbr* (= *Family Income Supplement*) Beihilfe für einkommensschwache Familien.
fiscal ['fɪskl] *adj* (*year*) Steuer-; (*policies*) Finanz-.
fish [fɪʃ] *n inv* Fisch *m* ♦ *vt* (*area*) fischen in +*dat*; (*river*) angeln in +*dat* ♦ *vi* fischen; (*as sport, hobby*) angeln; **to go ~ing** fischen/ angeln gehen.
▶**fish out** *vt* herausfischen.
fish bone *n* (Fisch)gräte *f*.
fish cake *n* Fischfrikadelle *f*.
fisherman ['fɪʃəmən] (*irreg: like* **man**) *n* Fischer *m*.
fishery ['fɪʃərɪ] *n* Fischereigebiet *nt*.
fish factory (*BRIT*) *n* Fischfabrik *f*.
fish farm *n* Fischzucht(anlage) *f*.
fishfingers [fɪʃ'fɪŋgəz] (*BRIT*) *npl* Fischstäbchen *pl*.
fish-hook ['fɪʃhuk] *n* Angelhaken *m*.
fishing boat ['fɪʃɪŋ-] *n* Fischerboot *nt*.
fishing line *n* Angelschnur *f*.
fishing net *n* Fischnetz *nt*.
fishing rod *n* Angelrute *f*.
fishing tackle *n* Angelgeräte *pl*.
fish market *n* Fischmarkt *m*.
fishmonger ['fɪʃmʌŋgə'] (*esp BRIT*) *n* Fischhändler(in) *m(f)*.
fishmonger's (shop) ['fɪʃmʌŋgəz-] (*esp BRIT*) *n* Fischgeschäft *nt*.
fish slice (*BRIT*) *n* Fischvorlegemesser *nt*.
fish sticks (*US*) *npl* = **fishfingers**.
fishy ['fɪʃɪ] (*inf*) *adj* verdächtig, faul.
fission ['fɪʃən] *n* Spaltung *f*; **atomic** *or* **nuclear ~** Atomspaltung *f*, Kernspaltung *f*.
fissure ['fɪʃə'] *n* Riß *m*, Spalte *f*.
fist [fɪst] *n* Faust *f*.
fist fight *n* Faustkampf *m*.
fit [fɪt] *adj* geeignet; (*healthy*) gesund; (*SPORT*) fit ♦ *vt* passen +*dat*; (*adjust*) anpassen; (*match*) entsprechen +*dat*; (*be suitable for*) passen auf +*acc*; (*put in*) einbauen; (*attach*) anbringen; (*equip*) ausstatten ♦ *vi* passen; (*parts*) zusammenpassen; (*in space, gap*) hineinpassen ♦ *n* (*MED*) Anfall *m*; **to ~ the description** der Beschreibung entsprechen; **~ to** bereit zu; **~ to eat** eßbar; **~ to drink** trinkbar; **to be ~ to keep** es wert sein, aufbewahrt zu werden; **~ for** geeignet für; **~ for work** arbeitsfähig; **to keep ~** sich fit

halten; **do as you think** or **see** ~ tun Sie, was Sie für richtig halten; **a** ~ **of anger** ein Wutanfall *m*; **a** ~ **of pride** eine Anwandlung von Stolz; **to have a** ~ einen Anfall haben; (*inf, fig*) einen Anfall kriegen; **this dress is a good** ~ dieses Kleid sitzt or paßt gut; **by** ~**s and starts** unregelmäßig.

▶**fit in** *vi* (*person*) sich einfügen; (*object*) hineinpassen ♦ *vt* (*fig: appointment*) unterbringen, einschieben; (*visitor*) Zeit finden für; **to** ~ **in with sb's plans** sich mit jds Plänen vereinbaren lassen.

fitful ['fɪtful] *adj* unruhig.

fitment ['fɪtmənt] *n* Einrichtungsgegenstand *m*.

fitness ['fɪtnɪs] *n* Gesundheit *f*; (*SPORT*) Fitneß *f*.

fitted carpet ['fɪtɪd-] *n* Teppichboden *m*.

fitted cupboards *npl* Einbauschränke *pl*.

fitted kitchen (*BRIT*) *n* Einbauküche *f*.

fitter ['fɪtə*] *n* Monteur *m*; (*for machines*) (Maschinen)schlosser *m*.

fitting ['fɪtɪŋ] *adj* passend; (*thanks*) gebührend ♦ *n* (*of dress*) Anprobe *f*; (*of piece of equipment*) Installation *f*; **fittings** *npl* Ausstattung *f*.

fitting room *n* Anprobe(kabine) *f*.

five [faɪv] *num* fünf.

five-day week ['faɪvdeɪ-] *n* Fünftagewoche *f*.

fiver ['faɪvə*] (*inf*) *n* (*BRIT*) Fünfpfundschein *m*; (*US*) Fünfdollarschein *m*.

fix [fɪks] *vt* (*attach*) befestigen; (*arrange*) festsetzen, festlegen; (*mend*) reparieren; (*meal, drink*) machen; (*inf*) manipulieren ♦ *n*: **to be in a** ~ in der Patsche or Klemme sitzen; **to** ~ **sth to/on sth** etw an/auf etw *dat* befestigen; **to** ~ **one's eyes/attention on** seinen Blick/seine Aufmerksamkeit richten auf +*acc*; **the fight was a** ~ (*inf*) der Kampf war eine abgekartete Sache.

▶**fix up** *vt* arrangieren; **to** ~ **sb up with sth** jdm etw besorgen.

fixation [fɪk'seɪʃən] *n* Fixierung *f*.

fixative ['fɪksətɪv] *n* Fixativ *nt*.

fixed [fɪkst] *adj* fest; (*ideas*) fix; (*smile*) starr; ~ **charge** Pauschale *f*; **how are you** ~ **for money?** wie sieht es bei dir mit dem Geld aus?

fixed assets *npl* Anlagevermögen *nt*.

fixture ['fɪkstʃə*] *n* Ausstattungsgegenstand *m*; (*FOOTBALL etc*) Spiel *nt*; (*ATHLETICS etc*) Veranstaltung *f*.

fizz [fɪz] *vi* sprudeln; (*firework*) zischen.

fizzle out ['fɪzl-] *vi* (*plan*) im Sande verlaufen; (*interest*) sich verlieren.

fizzy ['fɪzɪ] *adj* sprudelnd.

fjord [fjɔːd] *n* Fjord *m*.

FL, Fla. (*US*) *abbr* (*POST:* = *Florida*).

flabbergasted ['flæbəgɑːstɪd] *adj* verblüfft.

flabby ['flæbɪ] *adj* schwammig, wabbelig (*inf*).

flag [flæg] *n* Fahne *f*; (*of country*) Flagge *f*; (*for signalling*) Signalflagge *f*; (*also:* ~**stone**)

(Stein)platte *f* ♦ *vi* erlahmen; ~ **of convenience** Billigflagge *f*; **to** ~ **down** anhalten.

flagon ['flægən] *n* Flasche *f*; (*jug*) Krug *m*.

flagpole ['flægpəul] *n* Fahnenstange *f*.

flagrant ['fleɪgrənt] *adj* flagrant; (*injustice*) himmelschreiend.

flagship ['flægʃɪp] *n* Flaggschiff *nt*.

flagstone ['flægstəun] *n* (Stein)platte *f*.

flag stop (*US*) *n* Bedarfshaltestelle *f*.

flair [flɛə*] *n* Talent *nt*; (*style*) Flair *nt*.

flak [flæk] *n* Flakfeuer *nt*; **to get a lot of** ~ (*for sth*) (*inf: criticism*) (wegen etw) unter Beschuß geraten.

flake [fleɪk] *n* Splitter *m*; (*of snow, soap powder*) Flocke *f* ♦ *vi* (*also:* ~ **off**) abblättern, absplittern.

▶**flake out** (*inf*) *vi* aus den Latschen kippen; (*go to sleep*) einschlafen.

flaky ['fleɪkɪ] *adj* brüchig; (*skin*) schuppig.

flaky pastry *n* Blätterteig *m*.

flamboyant [flæm'bɔɪənt] *adj* extravagant.

flame [fleɪm] *n* Flamme *f*; **to burst into** ~**s** in Flammen aufgehen; **an old** ~ (*inf*) eine alte Flamme.

flaming ['fleɪmɪŋ] (*inf!*) *adj* verdammt.

flamingo [flə'mɪŋgəu] *n* Flamingo *m*.

flammable ['flæməbl] *adj* leicht entzündbar.

flan [flæn] *n* Kuchen *m*; ~ **case** Tortenboden *m*.

Flanders ['flɑːndəz] *n* Flandern *nt*.

flange [flændʒ] *n* Flansch *m*.

flank [flæŋk] *n* Flanke *f* ♦ *vt* flankieren.

flannel ['flænl] *n* Flanell *m*; (*BRIT: also:* **face** ~) Waschlappen *m*; (: *inf*) Geschwafel *nt*; **flannels** *npl* (*trousers*) Flanellhose *f*.

flannelette [flænə'lɛt] *n* Baumwollflanell *m*, Biber *m* or *nt*.

flap [flæp] *n* Klappe *f*; (*of envelope*) Lasche *f* ♦ *vt* schlagen mit ♦ *vi* flattern; (*inf: also:* **be in a** ~) in heller Aufregung sein.

flapjack ['flæpdʒæk] *n* (*US: pancake*) Pfannkuchen *m*; (*BRIT: biscuit*) Haferkeks *m*.

flare [flɛə*] *n* Leuchtsignal *nt*; (*in skirt etc*) Weite *f*.

▶**flare up** *vi* auflodern; (*person*) aufbrausen; (*fighting, violence, trouble*) ausbrechen; *see also* **flared**.

flared ['flɛəd] *adj* (*trousers*) mit Schlag; (*skirt*) ausgestellt.

flash [flæʃ] *n* Aufblinken *nt*; (*also:* **news**~) Eilmeldung *f*; (*PHOT*) Blitz *m*, Blitzlicht *nt*; (*US: torch*) Taschenlampe *f* ♦ *vt* aufleuchten lassen; (*news, message*) durchgeben; (*look, smile*) zuwerfen ♦ *vi* aufblinken; (*light on ambulance*) blinken; (*eyes*) blitzen; **in a** ~ im Nu; **quick as a** ~ blitzschnell; ~ **of inspiration** Geistesblitz *m*; **to** ~ **one's headlights** die Lichthupe betätigen; **the thought** ~**ed through his mind** der Gedanke schoß ihm durch den Kopf; **to** ~ **by** or **past** vorbeiflitzen (*inf*).

flashback ['flæʃbæk] *n* Rückblende *f*.
flashbulb ['flæʃbʌlb] *n* Blitzbirne *f*.
flash card *n* Leselernkarte *f*.
flashcube ['flæʃkjuːb] *n* Blitzwürfel *m*.
flasher ['flæʃə*] *n* (*AUT*) Lichthupe *f*; (*infl: man*) Exhibitionist *m*.
flashlight ['flæʃlaɪt] *n* Blitzlicht *nt*.
flash point *n* (*fig*): **to be at ~** auf dem Siedepunkt sein.
flashy ['flæʃɪ] (*pej*) *adj* auffällig, protzig.
flask [flɑːsk] *n* Flakon *m*; (*CHEM*) Glaskolben *m*; (*also:* **vacuum ~**) Thermosflasche ® *f*.
flat [flæt] *adj* flach; (*surface*) eben; (*tyre*) platt; (*battery*) leer; (*beer*) schal; (*refusal, denial*) glatt; (*note, voice*) zu tief; (*rate, fee*) Pauschal- ♦ *n* (*BRIT: apartment*) Wohnung *f*; (*AUT*) (Reifen)panne *f*; (*MUS*) Erniedrigungszeichen *nt*; **to work ~ out** auf Hochtouren arbeiten; **~ rate of pay** Pauschallohn *m*.
flat-footed ['flæt'futɪd] *adj:* **to be ~** Plattfüße *pl* haben.
flatly ['flætlɪ] *adv* (*refuse, deny*) glatt, kategorisch.
flatmate ['flætmeɪt] (*BRIT*) *n* Mitbewohner(in) *m(f)*.
flatness ['flætnɪs] *n* Flachheit *f*.
flat screen *n* Flachbildschirm *m*.
flatten ['flætn] *vt* (*also:* **~ out**) (ein)ebnen; (*paper, fabric etc*) glätten; (*building, city*) dem Erdboden gleichmachen; (*crop*) zu Boden drücken; (*inf: person*) umhauen; **to ~ o.s. against a wall/door** *etc* sich platt gegen *or* an eine Wand/Tür *etc* drücken +*dat*.
flatter ['flætə*] *vt* schmeicheln +*dat*.
flatterer ['flætərə*] *n* Schmeichler(in) *m(f)*.
flattering ['flætərɪŋ] *adj* schmeichelhaft; (*dress etc*) vorteilhaft.
flattery ['flætərɪ] *n* Schmeichelei *f*.
flatulence ['flætjuləns] *n* Blähungen *pl*.
flaunt [flɔːnt] *vt* zur Schau stellen, protzen mit.
flavour, (*US*) **flavor** ['fleɪvə*] *n* Geschmack *m*; (*of ice-cream etc*) Geschmacksrichtung *f* ♦ *vt* Geschmack verleihen +*dat*; **to give** *or* **add ~ to** Geschmack verleihen +*dat*; **music with an African ~** (*fig*) Musik mit einer afrikanischen Note; **strawberry-~ed** mit Erdbeergeschmack.
flavouring ['fleɪvərɪŋ] *n* Aroma *nt*.
flaw [flɔː] *n* Fehler *m*.
flawless ['flɔːlɪs] *adj* (*performance*) fehlerlos; (*complexion*) makellos.
flax [flæks] *n* Flachs *m*.
flaxen ['flæksən] *adj* (*hair*) flachsblond.
flea [fliː] *n* Floh *m*.
flea market *n* Flohmarkt *m*.
fleck [flek] *n* Tupfen *m*, Punkt *m*; (*of dust*) Flöckchen *nt*; (*of mud, paint, colour*) Fleck(en) *m* ♦ *vt* bespritzen; **brown ~ed with white** braun mit weißen Punkten.
fled [fled] *pt, pp of* **flee**.

fledg(e)ling ['fledʒlɪŋ] *n* Jungvogel *m* ♦ *adj* (*inexperienced: actor etc*) Nachwuchs-; (*newly started: business etc*) jung.
flee [fliː] (*pt, pp* **fled**) *vt* fliehen *or* flüchten vor +*dat*; (*country*) fliehen *or* flüchten aus ♦ *vi* fliehen, flüchten.
fleece [fliːs] *n* Schafwolle *f*; (*sheep's coat*) Schaffell *nt*, Vlies *nt* ♦ *vt* (*inf: cheat*) schröpfen.
fleecy ['fliːsɪ] *adj* flauschig; (*cloud*) Schäfchen-.
fleet [fliːt] *n* Flotte *f*; (*of lorries, cars*) Fuhrpark *m*.
fleeting ['fliːtɪŋ] *adj* flüchtig.
Flemish ['flemɪʃ] *adj* flämisch ♦ *n* (*LING*) Flämisch *nt*; **the Flemish** *npl* die Flamen.
flesh [fleʃ] *n* Fleisch *nt*; (*of fruit*) Fruchtfleisch *nt*.
▶**flesh out** *vt* ausgestalten.
flesh wound [-wuːnd] *n* Fleischwunde *f*.
flew [fluː] *pt of* **fly**.
flex [fleks] *n* Kabel *nt* ♦ *vt* beugen; (*muscles*) spielen lassen.
flexibility [fleksɪ'bɪlɪtɪ] *n* (*see adj*) Flexibilität *f*; Biegsamkeit *f*.
flexible ['fleksəbl] *adj* flexibel; (*material*) biegsam.
flexitime ['fleksɪtaɪm] *n* gleitende Arbeitszeit *f*, Gleitzeit *f*.
flick [flɪk] *n* (*of finger*) Schnipsen *nt*; (*of hand*) Wischen *nt*; (*of whip*) Schnalzen *nt*; (*of towel etc*) Schlagen *nt*; (*of switch*) Knipsen *nt* ♦ *vt* schnipsen; (*with hand*) wischen; (*whip*) knallen mit; (*switch*) knipsen; **flicks** (*inf*) *npl* Kino *nt*; **to ~ a towel at sb** mit einem Handtuch nach jdm schlagen.
▶**flick through** *vt fus* durchblättern.
flicker ['flɪkə*] *vi* flackern; (*eyelids*) zucken ♦ *n* Flackern *nt*; (*of pain, fear*) Aufflackern *nt*; (*of smile*) Anflug *m*; (*of eyelid*) Zucken *nt*.
flick knife (*BRIT*) *n* Klappmesser *nt*.
flier ['flaɪə*] *n* Flieger(in) *m(f)*.
flight [flaɪt] *n* Flug *m*; (*escape*) Flucht *f*; (*also:* **~ of steps**) Treppe *f*; **to take ~** die Flucht ergreifen; **to put to ~** in die Flucht schlagen.
flight attendant (*US*) *n* Flugbegleiter(in) *m(f)*.
flight crew *n* Flugbesatzung *f*.
flight deck *n* (*AVIAT*) Cockpit *nt*; (*NAUT*) Flugdeck *nt*.
flight path *n* Flugbahn *f*.
flight recorder *n* Flugschreiber *m*.
flimsy ['flɪmzɪ] *adj* leicht, dünn; (*building*) leicht gebaut; (*excuse*) fadenscheinig; (*evidence*) nicht stichhaltig.
flinch [flɪntʃ] *vi* zusammenzucken; **to ~ from** zurückschrecken vor +*dat*.
fling [flɪŋ] (*pt, pp* **flung**) *vt* schleudern; (*arms*) werfen; (*oneself*) stürzen ♦ *n* (flüchtige) Affäre *f*.
flint [flɪnt] *n* Feuerstein *m*.

flip [flɪp] vt (switch) knipsen; (coin) werfen; (US: pancake) umdrehen ♦ vi: **to ~ for sth** (US) um etw mit einer Münze knobeln.
▶**flip through** vt fus durchblättern; (records etc) durchgehen.
flippant ['flɪpənt] adj leichtfertig.
flipper ['flɪpə*] n Flosse f; (for swimming) (Schwimm)flosse f.
flip side n (of record) B-Seite f.
flirt [fləːt] vi flirten; (with idea) liebäugeln ♦ n: **he/she is a ~** er/sie flirtet gern.
flirtation [fləːˈteɪʃən] n Flirt m.
flit [flɪt] vi flitzen; (expression, smile) huschen.
float [fləut] n Schwimmkork m; (for fishing) Schwimmer m; (lorry) Festwagen m; (money) Wechselgeld nt ♦ vi schwimmen; (swimmer) treiben; (through air) schweben; (currency) floaten ♦ vt (currency) freigeben, floaten lassen; (company) gründen; (idea, plan) in den Raum stellen.
▶**float around** vi im Umlauf sein; (person) herumschweben (inf); (object) herumfliegen (inf).
flock [flɔk] n Herde f; (of birds) Schwarm m ♦ vi: **to ~ to** (place) strömen nach; (event) in Scharen kommen zu.
floe [fləu] n (also: **ice ~**) Eisscholle f.
flog [flɔg] vt auspeitschen; (inf: sell) verscherbeln.
flood [flʌd] n Überschwemmung f; (of letters, imports etc) Flut f ♦ vt überschwemmen; (AUT) absaufen lassen (inf) ♦ vi überschwemmt werden; **to be in ~** Hochwasser führen; **to ~ the market** den Markt überschwemmen; **to ~ into Hungary/the square/the palace** nach Ungarn/auf den Platz/in den Palast strömen.
flooding ['flʌdɪŋ] n Überschwemmung f.
floodlight ['flʌdlaɪt] n Flutlicht nt ♦ vt (mit Flutlicht) beleuchten; (building) anstrahlen.
floodlit ['flʌdlɪt] pt, pp of **floodlight** ♦ adj (mit Flutlicht) beleuchtet; (building) angestrahlt.
flood tide n Flut f.
floodwater ['flʌdwɔːtə*] n Hochwasser nt.
floor [flɔː*] n (Fuß)boden m; (storey) Stock nt; (of sea, valley) Boden m ♦ vt (subj: blow) zu Boden werfen; (: question, remark) die Sprache verschlagen +dat; **on the ~** auf dem Boden; **ground** (BRIT) or **first** (US) **~** Erdgeschoß nt; **first** (BRIT) or **second** (US) **~** erster Stock m; **top ~** oberstes Stockwerk nt; **to have the ~** (speaker: at meeting) das Wort haben.
floorboard ['flɔːbɔːd] n Diele f.
flooring ['flɔːrɪŋ] n (Fuß)boden m; (covering) Fußbodenbelag m.
floor lamp (US) n Stehlampe f.
floor show n Show f, Vorstellung f.
floorwalker ['flɔːwɔːkə*] (esp US) n Ladenaufsicht f.
floozy ['fluːzɪ] (inf) n Flittchen nt.

flop [flɔp] n Reinfall m ♦ vi (play, book) durchfallen; (fall) sich fallenlassen; (scheme) ein Reinfall sein.
floppy ['flɔpɪ] adj schlaff, schlapp ♦ n (also: **~ disk**) Diskette f, Floppy disk f; **~ hat** Schlapphut m.
floppy disk n Diskette f, Floppy disk f.
flora ['flɔːrə] n Flora f.
floral ['flɔːrl] adj geblümt.
Florence ['flɔrəns] n Florenz nt.
Florentine ['flɔrəntaɪn] adj florentinisch.
florid ['flɔrɪd] adj (style) blumig; (complexion) kräftig.
florist ['flɔrɪst] n Blumenhändler(in) m(f).
florist's (shop) ['flɔrɪsts-] n Blumengeschäft nt.
flotation [fləuˈteɪʃən] n (of shares) Auflegung f; (of company) Umwandlung f in eine Aktiengesellschaft.
flotsam ['flɔtsəm] n (also: **~ and jetsam**) Strandgut nt; (floating) Treibgut nt.
flounce [flauns] n Volant m.
▶**flounce out** vi hinausstolzieren.
flounder ['flaundə*] vi sich abstrampeln; (fig: speaker) ins Schwimmen kommen; (economy) in Schwierigkeiten geraten ♦ n Flunder f.
flour ['flauə*] n Mehl nt.
flourish ['flʌrɪʃ] vi gedeihen; (business) blühen, florieren ♦ vt schwenken ♦ n (in writing) Schnörkel m; (bold gesture): **with a ~** mit einer schwungvollen Bewegung.
flourishing ['flʌrɪʃɪŋ] adj gutgehend, florierend.
flout [flaut] vt sich hinwegsetzen über +acc.
flow [fləu] n Fluß m; (of sea) Flut f ♦ vi fließen; (clothes, hair) wallen.
flow chart n Flußdiagramm nt.
flow diagram n = **flow chart**.
flower ['flauə*] n Blume f; (blossom) Blüte f ♦ vi blühen; **to be in ~** blühen.
flowerbed ['flauəbed] n Blumenbeet nt.
flowerpot ['flauəpɔt] n Blumentopf m.
flowery ['flauərɪ] adj blumig; (pattern) Blumen-.
flown [fləun] pp of **fly**.
flu [fluː] n Grippe f.
fluctuate ['flʌktjueɪt] vi schwanken; (opinions, attitudes) sich ändern.
fluctuation [flʌktjuˈeɪʃən] n: **~ (in)** Schwankung f (+gen).
flue [fluː] n Rauchfang m, Rauchabzug m.
fluency ['fluːənsɪ] n Flüssigkeit f; **his ~ in German** sein flüssiges Deutsch.
fluent ['fluːənt] adj flüssig; **he speaks ~ German, he's ~ in German** er spricht fließend Deutsch.
fluently ['fluːəntlɪ] adv flüssig; (speak a language) fließend.
fluff [flʌf] n Fussel m; (fur) Flaum m ♦ vt (inf: do badly) verpatzen; (also: **~ out**) aufplustern.
fluffy ['flʌfɪ] adj flaumig; (jacket etc) weich,

kuschelig; ~ **toy** Kuscheltier nt.
fluid ['fluːɪd] adj fließend; (situation, arrangement) unklar ♦ n Flüssigkeit f.
fluid ounce (BRIT) n flüssige Unze f (= 28 ml).
fluke [fluːk] (inf) n Glücksfall m; **by a ~** durch einen glücklichen Zufall.
flummox ['flʌməks] vt verwirren, durcheinanderbringen.
flung [flʌŋ] pt, pp of **fling**.
flunky ['flʌŋkɪ] n Lakai m.
fluorescent [fluə'rɛsnt] adj fluoreszierend; (paint) Leucht-; (light) Neon-.
fluoride ['fluəraɪd] n Fluorid nt.
fluorine ['fluəriːn] n Fluor nt.
flurry ['flʌrɪ] n (of snow) Gestöber nt; **a ~ of activity/excitement** hektische Aktivität/Aufregung.
flush [flʌʃ] n Röte f; (fig: of beauty etc) Blüte f ♦ vt (durch)spülen, (aus)spülen ♦ vi erröten ♦ adj: ~ **with** auf gleicher Ebene mit; ~ **against** direkt an +dat; **in the first ~ of youth** in der ersten Jugendblüte; **in the first ~ of freedom** im ersten Freiheitstaumel; **hot ~es** (BRIT) Hitzewallungen pl; **to ~ the toilet** spülen, die Wasserspülung betätigen.
▶**flush out** vt aufstöbern.
flushed [flʌʃt] adj rot.
fluster ['flʌstə*] n: **in a ~** nervös; (confused) durcheinander ♦ vt nervös machen; (confuse) durcheinanderbringen.
flustered ['flʌstəd] adj nervös; (confused) durcheinander.
flute [fluːt] n Querflöte f.
fluted ['fluːtɪd] adj gerillt; (column) kanneliert.
flutter ['flʌtə*] n Flattern nt; (of panic, nerves) kurzer Anfall m; (of excitement) Beben nt ♦ vi flattern; (person) tänzeln; **to have a ~** (BRIT: inf: gamble) sein Glück (beim Wetten) versuchen.
flux [flʌks] n: **in a state of ~** im Fluß.
fly [flaɪ] (pt **flew**, pp **flown**) n Fliege f, (on trousers: also: **flies**) (Hosen)schlitz m ♦ vt fliegen; (kite) steigen lassen ♦ vi fliegen; (escape) fliehen; (flag) wehen; **to ~ open** auffliegen; **to ~ off the handle** an die Decke gehen (inf); **pieces of metal went ~ing everywhere** überall flogen Metallteile herum; **she came ~ing into the room** sie kam ins Zimmer gesaust; **her glasses flew off** die Brille flog ihr aus dem Gesicht.
▶**fly away** vi wegfliegen.
▶**fly in** vi einfliegen; **he flew in yesterday** er ist gestern mit dem Flugzeug gekommen.
▶**fly off** vi = fly away.
▶**fly out** vi ausfliegen; **he flew out yesterday** er ist gestern hingeflogen.
fly-fishing ['flaɪfɪʃɪŋ] n Fliegenfischen nt.
flying ['flaɪɪŋ] n Fliegen nt ♦ adj: **a ~ visit** ein Blitzbesuch m; **he doesn't like ~** er fliegt nicht gerne; **with ~ colours** mit fliegenden Fahnen.
flying buttress n Strebebogen m.

flying picket n mobiler Streikposten m.
flying saucer n fliegende Untertasse f.
flying squad n mobiles Einsatzkommando nt.
flying start n: **to get off to a ~** (SPORT) hervorragend wegkommen; (fig) einen glänzenden Start haben.
flyleaf ['flaɪliːf] n Vorsatzblatt nt.
flyover ['flaɪəuvə*] n (BRIT) Überführung f; (US) Luftparade f.
fly-past ['flaɪpɑːst] n Luftparade f.
flysheet ['flaɪʃiːt] n (for tent) Überzelt nt.
flyweight ['flaɪweɪt] n (BOXING) Fliegengewicht nt.
flywheel ['flaɪwiːl] n Schwungrad nt.
FM abbr (BRIT: MIL) = **field marshal**; (RADIO: = frequency modulation) FM, ≈ UKW.
FMB (US) n abbr (= Federal Maritime Board) Dachausschuß der Handelsmarine.
FMCS (US) n abbr (= Federal Mediation and Conciliation Service) Schlichtungsstelle für Arbeitskonflikte.
FO (BRIT) n abbr = **Foreign Office**.
foal [fəul] n Fohlen nt.
foam [fəum] n Schaum m; (also: ~ **rubber**) Schaumgummi m ♦ vi schäumen.
fob [fɔb] vt: **to ~ sb off** jdn abspeisen ♦ n (also: **watch ~**) Uhrkette f.
f.o.b. abbr (COMM: = free on board) frei Schiff.
foc (BRIT) abbr (COMM: = free of charge) gratis.
focal point ['fəukl-] n Mittelpunkt m; (of camera, telescope etc) Brennpunkt m.
focus ['fəukəs] (pl **~es**) n Brennpunkt m; (of storm) Zentrum nt ♦ vt einstellen; (light rays) bündeln ♦ vi: **to ~ (on)** (with camera) klar or scharf einstellen +acc; (person) sich konzentrieren (auf +acc); **in/out of ~** (camera etc) scharf/unscharf eingestellt; (photograph) scharf/unscharf.
fodder ['fɔdə*] n Futter nt.
FoE n abbr (= Friends of the Earth) Umweltschutzorganisation f.
foe [fəu] n Feind(in) m(f).
foetus, (US) **fetus** ['fiːtəs] n Fötus m.
fog [fɔg] n Nebel m.
fogbound ['fɔgbaund] adj (airport) wegen Nebel geschlossen.
foggy ['fɔgɪ] adj neb(e)lig.
fog lamp, (US) **fog light** n (AUT) Nebelscheinwerfer m.
foible ['fɔɪbl] n Eigenheit f.
foil [fɔɪl] vt vereiteln ♦ n Folie f; (complement) Kontrast m; (FENCING) Florett nt; **to act as a ~ to** einen Kontrast darstellen zu.
foist [fɔɪst] vt: **to ~ sth on sb** (goods) jdm etw andrehen; (task) etw an jdn abschieben; (ideas, views) jdm etw aufzwingen.
fold [fəuld] n Falte f; (AGR) Pferch m; (fig) Schoß m ♦ vt (zusammen)falten; (arms) verschränken ♦ vi (business) eingehen (inf).
▶**fold up** vi sich zusammenfalten lassen; (bed, table) sich zusammenklappen lassen; (business) eingehen (inf) ♦ vt

zusammenfalten.
folder ['fəʊldə·] *n* Aktenmappe *f*; (*binder*)
Hefter *m*; (*brochure*) Informationsblatt *nt*.
folding ['fəʊldɪŋ] *adj* (*chair, bed*) Klapp-.
foliage ['fəʊlɪɪdʒ] *n* Laubwerk *nt*.
folk [fəʊk] *npl* Leute *pl* ♦ *cpd* Volks-; **my ~s**
(*parents*) meine alten Herrschaften.
folklore ['fəʊklɔ:·] *n* Folklore *f*.
folk music *n* Volksmusik *f*; (*contemporary*)
Folk *m*.
folk song *n* Volkslied *nt*; (*contemporary*)
Folksong *m*.
follow ['fɒləʊ] *vt* folgen +*dat*; (*with eyes*)
verfolgen; (*advice, instructions*) befolgen ♦ *vi*
folgen; **to ~ in sb's footsteps** in jds
Fußstapfen *acc* treten; **I don't quite ~ you**
ich kann Ihnen nicht ganz folgen; **it ~s that**
daraus folgt, daß; **to ~ suit** (*fig*) jds Beispiel
dat folgen.
▶**follow on** *vi* (*continue*): **to ~ on from**
aufbauen auf +*dat*.
▶**follow out** *vt* (*idea, plan*) zu Ende verfolgen.
▶**follow through** *vt* = **follow out**.
▶**follow up** *vt* nachgehen +*dat*; (*offer*)
aufgreifen; (*case*) weiterverfolgen.
follower ['fɒləʊə·] *n* Anhänger(in) *m(f)*.
following ['fɒləʊɪŋ] *adj* folgend ♦ *n*
Anhängerschaft *f*.
follow-up ['fɒləʊʌp] *n* Weiterführung *f* ♦ *adj*:
~ treatment Nachbehandlung *f*.
folly ['fɒlɪ] *n* Torheit *f*; (*building*) exzentrisches
Bauwerk *nt*.
fond [fɒnd] *adj* liebevoll; (*memory*) lieb;
(*hopes, dreams*) töricht; **to be ~ of** mögen;
she's ~ of swimming sie schwimmt gerne.
fondle ['fɒndl] *vt* streicheln.
fondly ['fɒndlɪ] *adv* liebevoll; (*naïvely*)
törichterweise; **he ~ believed that ...** er war
so naiv zu glauben, daß ...
fondness ['fɒndnɪs] *n* (*for things*) Vorliebe *f*;
(*for people*) Zuneigung *f*; **a special ~ for** eine
besondere Vorliebe für/Zuneigung zu.
font [fɒnt] *n* Taufbecken *nt*; (*TYP*) Schrift *f*.
food [fu:d] *n* Essen *nt*; (*for animals*) Futter *nt*;
(*nourishment*) Nahrung *f*; (*groceries*)
Lebensmittel *pl*.
food chain *n* Nahrungskette *f*.
food mixer *n* Küchenmixer *m*.
food poisoning *n* Lebensmittelvergiftung *f*.
food processor *n* Küchenmaschine *f*.
food stamp *n* Lebensmittelmarke *f*.
foodstuffs ['fu:dstʌfs] *npl* Lebensmittel *pl*.
fool [fu:l] *n* Dummkopf *m*; (*CULIN*)
Sahnespeise aus Obstpüree ♦ *vt*
hereinlegen, täuschen ♦ *vi* herumalbern; **to
make a ~ of sb** jdn lächerlich machen;
(*trick*) jdn hereinlegen; **to make a ~ of o.s.**
sich blamieren; **you can't ~ me** du kannst
mich nicht zum Narren halten.
▶**fool about** (*pej*) *vi* herumtrödeln; (*behave
foolishly*) herumalbern.
▶**fool around** *vi* = **fool about**.

foolhardy ['fu:lhɑ:dɪ] *adj* tollkühn.
foolish ['fu:lɪʃ] *adj* dumm.
foolishly ['fu:lɪʃlɪ] *adv* dumm; **~, I forgot ...**
dummerweise habe ich ... vergessen.
foolishness ['fu:lɪʃnɪs] *n* Dummheit *f*.
foolproof ['fu:lpru:f] *adj* idiotensicher.
foolscap ['fu:lskæp] *n* ≈ Kanzleipapier *nt*.
foot [fʊt] (*pl* **feet**) *n* Fuß *m*; (*of animal*) Pfote *f*
♦ *vt* (*bill*) bezahlen; **on ~** zu Fuß; **to find
one's feet** sich eingewöhnen; **to put one's
~ down** (*AUT*) Gas geben; (*say no*) ein
Machtwort sprechen.
footage ['fʊtɪdʒ] *n* Filmmaterial *nt*.
foot-and-mouth (disease) [fʊtən'maʊθ-] *n*
Maul- und Klauenseuche *f*.
football ['fʊtbɔ:l] *n* Fußball *m*; (*US*) Football
m, amerikanischer Fußball *m*.
footballer ['fʊtbɔ:lə·] (*BRIT*) *n*
Fußballspieler(in) *m(f)*.
football ground *n* Fußballplatz *m*.
football match (*BRIT*) *n* Fußballspiel *nt*.
football player *n* (*BRIT*) Fußballspieler(in)
m(f); (*US*) Football-Spieler(in) *m(f)*.

Football Pools, *umgangssprachlich auch* **the
pools** *genannt, ist das in Großbritannien sehr
beliebte Fußballtoto, das dem auf die
Ergebnisse der samstäglichen Fußballspiele
gewettet wird. Teilnehmer schicken ihren
ausgefüllten Totoschein vor den Spielen an die
Totogesellschaft und vergleichen nach den
Spielen die Ergebnisse mit ihrem Schein. Die
Gewinne können sehr hoch sein und
gelegentlich Millionen von Pfund betragen.*

---

foot brake *n* Fußbremse *f*.
footbridge ['fʊtbrɪdʒ] *n* Fußgängerbrücke *f*.
foothills ['fʊthɪlz] *npl* (Gebirgs)ausläufer *pl*.
foothold ['fʊthəʊld] *n* Halt *m*; **to get a ~** Fuß
fassen.
footing ['fʊtɪŋ] *n* Stellung *f*; (*relationship*)
Verhältnis *nt*; **to lose one's ~** den Halt
verlieren; **on an equal ~** auf gleicher
Basis.
footlights ['fʊtlaɪts] *npl* Rampenlicht *nt*.
footman ['fʊtmən] (*irreg: like* **man**) *n* Lakai *m*.
footnote ['fʊtnəʊt] *n* Fußnote *f*.
footpath ['fʊtpɑ:θ] *n* Fußweg *m*; (*in street*)
Bürgersteig *m*.
footprint ['fʊtprɪnt] *n* Fußabdruck *m*; (*of
animal*) Spur *f*.
footrest ['fʊtrest] *n* Fußstütze *f*.
Footsie ['fʊtsɪ] (*inf*) *n* = **FTSE 100 Index**.
footsie ['fʊtsɪ] (*inf*) *n*: **to play ~ with sb** mit
jdm füßeln.
footsore ['fʊtsɔ:·] *adj*: **to be ~** wunde Füße
haben.
footstep ['fʊtstep] *n* Schritt *m*; (*footprint*)
Fußabdruck *m*; **to follow in sb's ~s** in jds
Fußstapfen *acc* treten.
footwear ['fʊtwɛə·] *n* Schuhe *pl*, Schuhwerk
nt.

=================================== *KEYWORD*

for [fɔː*] *prep* **1** für *+acc*; **is this ~ me?** ist das für mich?; **the train ~ London** der Zug nach London; **it's time ~ lunch** es ist Zeit zum Mittagessen; **what's it ~?** wofür ist das?; **he works ~ the government/a local firm** er arbeitet für die Regierung/eine Firma am Ort; **he's mature ~ his age** er ist reif für sein Alter; **I sold it ~ £20** ich habe es für £20 verkauft; **I'm all ~ it** ich bin ganz dafür; **G ~ George** ≈ G wie Gustav
2 (*because of*): **~ this reason** aus diesem Grund; **~ fear of being criticised** aus Angst, kritisiert zu werden
3 (*referring to distance*): **there are roadworks ~ 5 km** die Straßenbauarbeiten erstrecken sich über 5 km; **we walked ~ miles** wir sind meilenweit gelaufen
4 (*referring to time*): **he was away ~ 2 years** er war 2 Jahre lang weg; **I have known her ~ years** ich kenne sie bereits seit Jahren
5 (*with infinitive clause*): **it is not ~ me to decide** es liegt nicht an mir, das zu entscheiden; **~ this to be possible ...** um dies möglich zu machen, ...
6 (*in spite of*) trotz *+gen or dat*; **~ all his complaints, he is very fond of her** trotz seiner vielen Klagen mag er sie sehr
♦ *conj* (*form: since, as*) denn; **she was very angry, ~ he was late again** sie war sehr böse, denn er kam wieder zu spät.

f.o.r. *abbr* (*COMM: = free on rail*) frei Bahn.
forage ['fɔrɪdʒ] *n* Futter *nt* ♦ *vi* herumstöbern; **to ~** (*for food*) nach Futter suchen.
forage cap *n* Schiffchen *nt*.
foray ['fɔreɪ] *n* (Raub)überfall *m*.
forbad(e) [fə'bæd] *pt of* forbid.
forbearing [fɔː'bɛərɪŋ] *adj* geduldig.
forbid [fə'bɪd] (*pt* forbade, *pp* forbidden) *vt* verbieten; **to ~ sb to do sth** jdm verbieten, etw zu tun.
forbidden [fə'bɪdn] *pp of* forbid ♦ *adj* verboten.
forbidding [fə'bɪdɪŋ] *adj* (*look*) streng; (*prospect*) grauenhaft.
force [fɔːs] *n* Kraft *f*; (*violence*) Gewalt *f*; (*of blow, impact*) Wucht *f*; (*influence*) Macht *f* ♦ *vt* zwingen; (*push*) drücken; (: *person*) drängen; (*lock, door*) aufbrechen; **the Forces** (*BRIT*) *npl* die Streitkräfte *pl*; (*law etc*) geltend; (*people: arrive etc*) zahlreich; **to come into ~** in Kraft treten; **to join ~s** sich zusammentun; **a ~ 5 wind** Windstärke 5; **the sales ~** das Verkaufspersonal; **to ~ o.s./sb to do sth** sich/jdn zwingen, etw zu tun.
▶**force back** *vt* zurückdrängen; (*tears*) unterdrücken.
▶**force down** *vt* (*food*) hinunterwürgen (*inf*).
forced [fɔːst] *adj* gezwungen; **~ labour** Zwangsarbeit *f*; **~ landing** Notlandung *f*.

force-feed ['fɔːsfiːd] *vt* zwangsernähren; (*animal*) stopfen.
forceful ['fɔːsful] *adj* energisch; (*attack*) wirkungsvoll; (*point*) überzeugend.
forceps ['fɔːsɛps] *npl* Zange *f*.
forcible ['fɔːsəbl] *adj* gewaltsam; (*reminder, lesson*) eindringlich.
forcibly ['fɔːsəblɪ] *adv* mit Gewalt; (*express*) eindringlich.
ford [fɔːd] *n* Furt *f* ♦ *vt* durchqueren; (*on foot*) durchwaten.
fore [fɔː*] *n*: **to come to the ~** ins Blickfeld geraten.
forearm ['fɔːrɑːm] *n* Unterarm *m*.
forebear ['fɔːbɛə*] *n* Vorfahr(in) *m(f)*, Ahn(e) *m(f)*.
foreboding [fɔː'bəudɪŋ] *n* Vorahnung *f*.
forecast ['fɔːkɑːst] *n* Prognose *f*; (*of weather*) (Wetter)vorhersage *f* ♦ *vt* (*irreg: like* cast) voraussagen.
foreclose [fɔː'kləuz] *vt* (*LAW: also: ~ on*) kündigen; **to ~ sb** (*on loan/mortgage*) jds Darlehen/Hypothek kündigen.
foreclosure [fɔː'kləuʒə*] *n* Zwangsvollstreckung *f*.
forecourt ['fɔːkɔːt] *n* Vorplatz *m*.
forefathers ['fɔːfɑːðəz] *npl* Vorfahren *pl*.
forefinger ['fɔːfɪŋgə*] *n* Zeigefinger *m*.
forefront ['fɔːfrʌnt] *n*: **in the ~ of** an der Spitze *+gen*.
forego [fɔː'gəu] (*irreg: like* go) *vt* verzichten auf *+acc*.
foregoing ['fɔːgəuɪŋ] *adj* vorhergehend ♦ *n*: **the ~** das Vorhergehende.
foregone ['fɔːgɔn] *pp of* forego ♦ *adj*: **it's a ~ conclusion** es steht von vornherein fest.
foreground ['fɔːgraund] *n* Vordergrund *m*.
forehand ['fɔːhænd] *n* (*TENNIS*) Vorhand *f*.
forehead ['fɔrɪd] *n* Stirn *f*.
foreign ['fɔrɪn] *adj* ausländisch; (*holiday*) im Ausland; (*customs, appearance*) fremdartig; (*trade, policy*) Außen-; (*correspondent*) Auslands-; (*object, matter*) fremd; **goods from ~ countries/a ~ country** Waren aus dem Ausland.
foreign body *n* Fremdkörper *m*.
foreign currency *n* Devisen *pl*.
foreigner ['fɔrɪnə*] *n* Ausländer(in) *m(f)*.
foreign exchange *n* Devisenhandel *m*; (*money*) Devisen *pl*.
foreign exchange market *n* Devisenmarkt *m*.
foreign exchange rate *n* Devisenkurs *m*.
foreign investment *n* Auslandsinvestition *f*.
foreign minister *n* Außenminister(in) *m(f)*.
Foreign Office (*BRIT*) *n* Außenministerium *nt*.
Foreign Secretary (*BRIT*) *n* Außenminister(in) *m(f)*.
foreleg ['fɔːlɛg] *n* Vorderbein *nt*.
foreman ['fɔːmən] (*irreg: like* man) *n* Vorarbeiter *m*; (*of jury*) Obmann *m*.
foremost ['fɔːməust] *adj* führend ♦ *adv*: **first**

and ~ zunächst, vor allem.

forename ['fɔːneɪm] n Vorname m.

forensic [fə'rɛnsɪk] adj (test) forensisch; (medicine) Gerichts-; (expert) Spurensicherungs-.

foreplay ['fɔːpleɪ] n Vorspiel nt.

forerunner ['fɔːrʌnə*] n Vorläufer m.

foresee [fɔː'siː] (irreg: like see) vt vorhersehen.

foreseeable [fɔː'siːəbl] adj vorhersehbar; **in the ~ future** in absehbarer Zeit.

foreseen [fɔː'siːn] pp of **foresee**.

foreshadow [fɔː'ʃædəʊ] vt andeuten.

foreshore ['fɔːʃɔː*] n Strand m.

foreshorten [fɔː'ʃɔːtn] vt perspektivisch verkürzen.

foresight ['fɔːsaɪt] n Voraussicht f, Weitblick m.

foreskin ['fɔːskɪn] n (ANAT) Vorhaut f.

forest ['fɔrɪst] n Wald m.

forestall [fɔː'stɔːl] vt zuvorkommen +dat; (discussion) im Keim ersticken.

forestry ['fɔrɪstrɪ] n Forstwirtschaft f.

foretaste ['fɔːteɪst] n: **a ~ of** ein Vorgeschmack von.

foretell [fɔː'tɛl] (irreg: like tell) vt vorhersagen.

forethought ['fɔːθɔːt] n Vorbedacht m.

foretold [fɔː'təʊld] pt, pp of **foretell**.

forever [fə'rɛvə*] adv für immer; (endlessly) ewig; (consistently) dauernd, ständig; **you're ~ finding difficulties** du findest ständig or dauernd neue Schwierigkeiten.

forewarn [fɔː'wɔːn] vt vorwarnen.

forewent [fɔː'wɛnt] pt of **forego**.

forewoman ['fɔːwʊmən] (irreg: like woman) n Vorarbeiterin f; (of jury) Obmännin f.

foreword ['fɔːwəːd] n Vorwort nt.

forfeit ['fɔːfɪt] n Strafe f, Buße f ♦ vt (right) verwirken; (friendship etc) verlieren; (one's happiness, health) einbüßen.

forgave [fə'geɪv] pt of **forgive**.

forge [fɔːdʒ] n Schmiede f ♦ vt fälschen; (wrought iron) schmieden.

▶**forge ahead** vi große or schnelle Fortschritte machen.

forger ['fɔːdʒə*] n Fälscher(in) m(f).

forgery ['fɔːdʒərɪ] n Fälschung f.

forget [fə'gɛt] (pt forgot, pp forgotten) vt vergessen ♦ vi es vergessen; **to ~ o.s.** sich vergessen.

forgetful [fə'gɛtful] adj vergeßlich; **~ of sth** (of duties etc) nachlässig gegenüber etw.

forgetfulness [fə'gɛtfulnɪs] n Vergeßlichkeit f; (oblivion) Vergessenheit f.

forget-me-not [fə'gɛtmɪnɔt] n Vergißmeinnicht nt.

forgive [fə'gɪv] (pt forgave, pp forgiven) vt verzeihen +dat, vergeben +dat; **to ~ sb for sth** jdm etw verzeihen or vergeben; **to ~ sb for doing sth** jdm verzeihen or vergeben, daß er etw getan hat; **~ me, but ...** entschuldigen Sie, aber ...; **they could be ~n for thinking that ...** es ist verständlich, wenn

sie denken, daß ...

forgiveness [fə'gɪvnɪs] n Verzeihung f.

forgiving [fə'gɪvɪŋ] adj versöhnlich.

forgo [fɔː'gəʊ] (pt forwent, pp forgone) vt = **forego**.

forgot [fə'gɔt] pt of **forget**.

forgotten [fə'gɔtn] pp of **forget**.

fork [fɔːk] n Gabel f; (in road, river, railway) Gabelung f ♦ vi (road) sich gabeln.

▶**fork out** (inf) vt, vi (pay) blechen.

forked [fɔːkt] adj (lightning) zickzackförmig.

fork-lift truck ['fɔːklɪft-] n Gabelstapler m.

forlorn [fə'lɔːn] adj verlassen; (person) einsam und verlassen; (attempt) verzweifelt; (hope) schwach.

form [fɔːm] n Form f; (SCOL) Klasse f; (questionnaire) Formular nt ♦ vt formen, gestalten; (queue, organization, group) bilden; (idea, habit) entwickeln; **in the ~ of** in Form von or +gen; **in the ~ of Peter** in Gestalt von Peter; **to be in good ~** gut in Form sein; **in top ~** in Hochform; **on ~** in Form; **to ~ part of sth** Teil von etw sein.

formal ['fɔːməl] adj offiziell; (person, behaviour) förmlich, formell; (occasion, dinner) feierlich; (clothes) Gesellschafts-; (garden) formell angelegt; (ART, PHILOSOPHY) formal; **~ dress** Gesellschaftskleidung f.

formalities [fɔː'mælɪtɪz] npl Formalitäten pl.

formality [fɔː'mælɪtɪ] n Förmlichkeit f; (procedure) Formalität f.

formalize ['fɔːməlaɪz] vt formell machen.

formally ['fɔːməlɪ] adv (see adj) offiziell; förmlich, formell; feierlich; **to be ~ invited** ausdrücklich eingeladen sein.

format ['fɔːmæt] n Format nt; (form, style) Aufmachung f ♦ vt (COMPUT) formatieren.

formation [fɔː'meɪʃən] n Bildung f; (of theory) Entstehung f; (of business) Gründung f; (pattern: of rocks, clouds) Formation f.

formative ['fɔːmətɪv] adj (influence) prägend; (years) entscheidend.

former ['fɔːmə*] adj früher; **the ~ ... the latter ...** erstere(r, s) ... letztere(r, s); **the ~ president** der ehemalige Präsident; **the ~ East Germany** die ehemalige DDR.

formerly ['fɔːməlɪ] adv früher.

form feed n (on printer) Papiervorschub m.

Formica ® [fɔː'maɪkə] n Resopal ® nt.

formidable ['fɔːmɪdəbl] adj (task) gewaltig, enorm; (opponent) furchterregend.

formula ['fɔːmjulə] (pl ~e or ~s) n Formel f; **F~ One** (AUT) Formel Eins.

formulate ['fɔːmjuleɪt] vt formulieren.

fornicate ['fɔːnɪkeɪt] vi Unzucht treiben.

forsake [fə'seɪk] (pt forsook, pp forsaken) vt im Stich lassen; (belief) aufgeben.

forsook [fə'suk] pt of **forsake**.

fort [fɔːt] n Fort nt; **to hold the ~** die Stellung halten.

forte ['fɔːtɪ] n Stärke f, starke Seite f.

forth [fɔ:θ] *adv* aus; **back and** ~ hin und her; **to go back and** ~ auf und ab gehen; **to bring** ~ hervorbringen; **and so** ~ und so weiter.

forthcoming [fɔ:θ'kʌmɪŋ] *adj (event)* bevorstehend; *(person)* mitteilsam; **to be** ~ *(help)* erfolgen; *(evidence)* geliefert werden.

forthright ['fɔ:θraɪt] *adj* offen.

forthwith ['fɔ:θ'wɪθ] *adv* umgehend.

fortieth ['fɔ:tɪɪθ] *num* vierzigste(r, s).

fortification [fɔ:tɪfɪ'keɪʃən] *n* Befestigung *f*, Festungsanlage *f*.

fortified wine ['fɔ:tɪfaɪd-] *n* weinhaltiges Getränk *nt (Sherry, Portwein etc)*.

fortify ['fɔ:tɪfaɪ] *vt (city)* befestigen; *(person)* bestärken; (: *subj: food, drink)* stärken.

fortitude ['fɔ:tɪtju:d] *n* innere Kraft *or* Stärke *f*.

fortnight ['fɔ:tnaɪt] *(BRIT) n* vierzehn Tage *pl*, zwei Wochen *pl*; **it's a** ~ **since** ... es ist vierzehn Tage *or* zwei Wochen her, daß ...

fortnightly ['fɔ:tnaɪtlɪ] *adj* vierzehntägig, zweiwöchentlich ♦ *adv* alle vierzehn Tage, alle zwei Wochen.

FORTRAN ['fɔ:træn] *n* FORTRAN *nt*.

fortress ['fɔ:trɪs] *n* Festung *f*.

fortuitous [fɔ:'tju:ɪtəs] *adj* zufällig.

fortunate ['fɔ:tʃənɪt] *adj* glücklich; **to be** ~ Glück haben; **he is** ~ **to have** ... er kann sich glücklich schätzen, ... zu haben; **it is** ~ **that** ... es ist ein Glück, daß ...

fortunately ['fɔ:tʃənɪtlɪ] *adv* glücklicherweise, zum Glück.

fortune ['fɔ:tʃən] *n* Glück *nt*; *(wealth)* Vermögen *nt*; **to make a** ~ ein Vermögen machen; **to tell sb's** ~ jdm wahrsagen.

fortune-teller ['fɔ:tʃəntelə*] *n* Wahrsager(in) *m(f)*.

forty ['fɔ:tɪ] *num* vierzig.

forum ['fɔ:rəm] *n* Forum *nt*.

forward ['fɔ:wəd] *adj* vordere(r, s); *(movement)* Vorwärts-; *(not shy)* dreist; *(COMM: buying, price)* Termin- ♦ *adv* nach vorn; *(movement)* vorwärts; *(in time)* voraus ♦ *n (SPORT)* Stürmer *m* ♦ *vt (letter etc)* nachsenden; *(career, plans)* voranbringen; ~ **planning** Vorausplanung *f*; **to move** ~ vorwärtskommen; **"please** ~" „bitte nachsenden".

forwards ['fɔ:wədz] *adv* nach vorn; *(movement)* vorwärts; *(in time)* voraus.

fossil ['fɔsl] *n* Fossil *nt*.

fossil fuel *n* fossiler Brennstoff *m*.

foster ['fɔstə*] *vt (child)* in Pflege nehmen; *(idea, activity)* fördern.

foster child *n* Pflegekind *nt*.

foster mother *n* Pflegemutter *f*.

fought [fɔ:t] *pt, pp of* **fight**.

foul [faul] *adj* abscheulich; *(taste, smell, temper)* übel; *(water)* faulig; *(air)* schlecht; *(language)* unflätig ♦ *n (SPORT)* Foul *nt* ♦ *vt* beschmutzen; *(SPORT)* foulen; *(entangle)* sich verheddern in +*dat*.

foul play *n* unnatürlicher *or* gewaltsamer Tod *m*; ~ **is not suspected** es besteht kein Verdacht auf ein Verbrechen.

found [faund] *pt, pp of* **find** ♦ *vt* gründen.

foundation [faun'deɪʃən] *n* Gründung *f*; *(base: also fig)* Grundlage *f*; *(organization)* Stiftung *f*; *(also:* ~ **cream)** Grundierungscreme *f*; **foundations** *npl (of building)* Fundament *nt*; **the rumours are without** ~ die Gerüchte entbehren jeder Grundlage; **to lay the** ~**s** *(fig)* die Grundlagen schaffen.

foundation stone *n* Grundstein *m*.

founder ['faundə*] *n* Gründer(in) *m(f)* ♦ *vi (ship)* sinken.

founder member *n* Gründungsmitglied *nt*.

founding ['faundɪŋ] *adj*: ~ **fathers** *(esp US)* Väter *pl*.

foundry ['faundrɪ] *n* Gießerei *f*.

fount [faunt] *n* Quelle *f*; *(TYP)* Schrift *f*.

fountain ['fauntɪn] *n* Brunnen *m*.

fountain pen *n* Füllfederhalter *m*, Füller *m*.

four [fɔ:*] *num* vier; **on all** ~**s** auf allen vieren.

four-letter word ['fɔ:letə-] *n* Vulgärausdruck *m*.

four-poster ['fɔ:'pəustə*] *n (also:* ~ **bed)** Himmelbett *nt*.

foursome ['fɔ:səm] *n* Quartett *nt*; **in** *or* **as a** ~ zu viert.

fourteen ['fɔ:'ti:n] *num* vierzehn.

fourteenth ['fɔ:'ti:nθ] *num* vierzehnte(r, s).

fourth [fɔ:θ] *num* vierte(r, s) ♦ *n (AUT: also:* ~ **gear)** der vierte (Gang).

four-wheel drive ['fɔ:wi:l-] *n (AUT)*: **with** ~ mit Vierradantrieb *m*.

fowl [faul] *n* Vogel *m (besonders Huhn, Gans, Ente etc)*.

fox [fɔks] *n* Fuchs *m* ♦ *vt* verblüffen.

foxglove ['fɔksglʌv] *n (BOT)* Fingerhut *m*.

fox-hunting ['fɔkshʌntɪŋ] *n* Fuchsjagd *f*.

foxtrot ['fɔkstrɔt] *n* Foxtrott *m*.

foyer ['fɔɪeɪ] *n* Foyer *nt*.

FPA *(BRIT) n abbr (= Family Planning Association) Organisation für Familienplanung*.

Fr. *abbr (REL)* = **father**; **friar**.

fr. *abbr (= franc)* Fr.

fracas ['fræka:] *n* Aufruhr *m*, Tumult *m*.

fraction ['frækʃən] *n* Bruchteil *m*; *(MATH)* Bruch *m*.

fractionally ['frækʃnəlɪ] *adv* geringfügig.

fractious ['frækʃəs] *adj* verdrießlich.

fracture ['fræktʃə*] *n* Bruch *m* ♦ *vt* brechen.

fragile ['frædʒaɪl] *adj* zerbrechlich; *(economy)* schwach; *(health)* zart; *(person)* angeschlagen.

fragment [*n* 'frægmənt, *vb* fræg'ment] *n* Stück *nt* ♦ *vt* aufsplittern ♦ *vi* sich aufsplittern.

fragmentary ['frægməntərɪ] *adj* fragmentarisch, bruchstückhaft.

fragrance ['freɪgrəns] *n* Duft *m*.

fragrant ['freɪgrənt] *adj* duftend.

frail [freɪl] *adj* schwach, gebrechlich;

(*structure*) zerbrechlich.
frame [freɪm] n Rahmen m; (*of building*) (Grund)gerippe nt; (*of human, animal*) Gestalt f; (*of spectacles: also:* ~**s**) Gestell nt ♦ vt (*picture*) rahmen; (*reply*) formulieren; (*law, theory*) entwerfen; ~ **of mind** Stimmung f, Laune f; **to** ~ **sb** (*inf*) jdm etwas anhängen.
framework ['freɪmwɔːk] n Rahmen m.
France [frɑːns] n Frankreich nt.
franchise ['fræntʃaɪz] n Wahlrecht nt; (*COMM*) Konzession f, Franchise f.
franchisee [fræntʃaɪ'ziː] n Franchisenehmer(in) m(f).
franchiser ['fræntʃaɪzəʳ] n Franchisegeber(in) m(f).
frank [fræŋk] adj offen ♦ vt (*letter*) frankieren.
Frankfurt ['fræŋkfɔːt] n Frankfurt nt.
frankfurter ['fræŋkfɔːtəʳ] n (Frankfurter) Würstchen nt.
franking machine ['fræŋkɪŋ-] n Frankiermaschine f.
frankly ['fræŋklɪ] adv ehrlich gesagt; (*candidly*) offen.
frankness ['fræŋknɪs] n Offenheit f.
frantic ['fræntɪk] adj verzweifelt; (*hectic*) hektisch; (*desperate*) übersteigert.
frantically ['fræntɪklɪ] adv verzweifelt; (*hectically*) hektisch.
fraternal [frə'tɜːnl] adj brüderlich.
fraternity [frə'tɜːnɪtɪ] n Brüderlichkeit f; (*US: UNIV*) Verbindung f; **the legal/medical/ golfing** ~ die Juristen/Mediziner/Golfer pl.
fraternize ['frætənaɪz] vi Umgang haben.
fraud [frɔːd] n Betrug m; (*person*) Betrüger(in) m(f).
fraudulent ['frɔːdjulənt] adj betrügerisch.
fraught [frɔːt] adj (*person*) nervös; **to be** ~ **with danger/problems** voller Gefahren/ Probleme sein.
fray [freɪ] n: **the** ~ der Kampf ♦ vi (*cloth*) ausfransen; (*rope*) sich durchscheuern; **to return to the** ~ sich wieder ins Getümmel stürzen; **tempers were** ~**ed** die Gemüter erhitzten sich; **her nerves were** ~**ed** sie war mit den Nerven am Ende.
FRB (*US*) n abbr = **Federal Reserve Board.**
FRCM (*BRIT*) n abbr (= *Fellow of the Royal College of Music*) Qualifikationsnachweis in Musik.
FRCO (*BRIT*) n abbr (= *Fellow of the Royal College of Organists*) Qualifikationsnachweis für Organisten.
FRCP (*BRIT*) n abbr (= *Fellow of the Royal College of Physicians*) Qualifikationsnachweis für Ärzte.
FRCS (*BRIT*) n abbr (= *Fellow of the Royal College of Surgeons*) Qualifikationsnachweis für Chirurgen.
freak [friːk] n Irre(r) f(m); (*in appearance*) Mißgeburt f; (*event, accident*) außergewöhnlicher Zufall m; (*pej: fanatic*):

health ~ Gesundheitsapostel m.
▶**freak out** (*inf*) vi aussteigen; (*on drugs*) ausflippen.
freakish ['friːkɪʃ] adj verrückt.
freckle ['frɛkl] n Sommersprosse f.
freckled ['frɛkld] adj sommersprossig.
free [friː] adj frei; (*costing nothing*) kostenlos, gratis ♦ vt freilassen; (*jammed object*) lösen; **to give sb a** ~ **hand** jdm freie Hand lassen; ~ **and easy** ungezwungen; **admission** ~ Eintritt frei; ~ (**of charge**), **for** ~ umsonst, gratis.
free agent n: **to be a** ~ sein eigener Herr sein.
freebie ['friːbɪ] (*inf*) n (*promotional gift*) Werbegeschenk nt.
freedom ['friːdəm] n Freiheit f.
freedom fighter n Freiheitskämpfer(in) m(f).
free enterprise n freies Unternehmertum nt.
Freefone ® ['friːfəun] n: **call** ~ **0800** rufen Sie gebührenfrei 0800 an.
free-for-all ['friːfərɔːl] n Gerangel nt; **the fight turned into a** ~ schließlich beteiligten sich alle an der Schlägerei.
free gift n Werbegeschenk nt.
freehold ['friːhəuld] n (*of property*) Besitzrecht nt.
free kick n Freistoß m.
freelance ['friːlɑːns] adj (*journalist etc*) frei(schaffend), freiberuflich tätig.
freelance work n freiberufliche Arbeit f.
freeloader ['friːləudəʳ] (*pej*) n Schmarotzer(in) m(f).
freely ['friːlɪ] adv frei; (*spend*) mit vollen Händen; (*liberally*) großzügig; **drugs are** ~ **available in the city** Drogen sind in der Stadt frei erhältlich.
free-market economy ['friːmɑːkɪt-] n freie Marktwirtschaft f.
Freemason ['friːmeɪsn] n Freimaurer m.
Freemasonry ['friːmeɪsnrɪ] n Freimaurerei f.
Freepost ® ['friːpəust] n ≈ „Gebühr zahlt Empfänger".
free-range ['friː'reɪndʒ] adj (*eggs*) von freilaufenden Hühnern.
free sample n Gratisprobe f.
freesia ['friːzɪə] n Freesie f.
free speech n Redefreiheit f.
freestyle ['friːstaɪl] n Freistil m.
free trade n Freihandel m.
freeway ['friːweɪ] (*US*) n Autobahn f.
freewheel ['friː'wiːl] vi im Freilauf fahren.
free will n freier Wille m; **of one's own** ~ aus freien Stücken.
freeze [friːz] (*pt* **froze**, *pp* **frozen**) vi frieren; (*liquid*) gefrieren; (*pipe*) einfrieren; (*person: stop moving*) erstarren ♦ vt einfrieren; (*water, lake*) gefrieren ♦ n Frost m; (*on arms, wages*) Stopp m.
▶**freeze over** vi (*river*) überfrieren; (*windscreen, windows*) vereisen.
▶**freeze up** vi zufrieren.

freeze-dried ['fri:zdraɪd] adj gefriergetrocknet.

freezer ['fri:zə*] n Tiefkühltruhe f; (upright) Gefrierschrank m; (in fridge: also: ~ compartment) Gefrierfach nt.

freezing ['fri:zɪŋ] adj: ~ (cold) eiskalt ♦ n: 3 degrees below ~ 3 Grad unter Null; I'm ~ mir ist eiskalt.

freezing point n Gefrierpunkt m.

freight [freɪt] n Fracht f; (money charged) Frachtkosten pl; ~ forward Fracht gegen Nachnahme; ~ inward Eingangsfracht f.

freight car (US) n Güterwagen m.

freighter ['freɪtə*] n (NAUT) Frachter m, Frachtschiff nt; (AVIAT) Frachtflugzeug nt.

freight forwarder [-'fɔːwədə*] n Spediteur m.

freight train (US) n Güterzug m.

French [frentʃ] adj französisch ♦ n (LING) Französisch nt; **the French** npl die Franzosen pl.

French bean (BRIT) n grüne Bohne f.

French Canadian adj frankokanadisch ♦ n Frankokanadier(in) m(f).

French dressing n Vinaigrette f.

French fried potatoes npl Pommes frites pl.

French fries [-fraɪz] (US) npl = **French fried potatoes**.

French Guiana [-gaɪ'ænə] n Französisch-Guyana nt.

Frenchman ['frentʃmən] n (irreg: like man) n Franzose m.

French Riviera n: the ~ die französische Riviera.

French stick n Stangenbrot nt.

French window n Verandatür f.

Frenchwoman ['frentʃwumən] (irreg: like woman) n Französin f.

frenetic [frə'netɪk] adj frenetisch, rasend.

frenzied ['frenzɪd] adj rasend.

frenzy ['frenzɪ] n Raserei f; (of joy, excitement) Taumel m; **to drive sb into a ~** jdn zum Rasen bringen; **to be in a ~** in wilder Aufregung sein.

frequency ['fri:kwənsɪ] n Häufigkeit f; (RADIO) Frequenz f.

frequency modulation n Frequenz-modulation f.

frequent [adj 'fri:kwənt, vt frɪ'kwent] adj häufig ♦ vt (pub, restaurant) oft or häufig besuchen.

frequently ['fri:kwəntlɪ] adv oft, häufig.

fresco ['freskəu] n Fresko nt.

fresh [freʃ] adj frisch; (instructions, approach, start) neu; (cheeky) frech; **to make a ~ start** einen neuen Anfang machen.

freshen ['freʃən] vi (wind) auffrischen; (air) frisch werden.

▶**freshen up** vi sich frisch machen.

freshener ['freʃnə*] n: **skin ~** Gesichtswasser nt; **air ~** Raumspray m or nt.

fresher ['freʃə*] (BRIT: inf) n Erstsemester(in) m(f).

freshly ['freʃlɪ] adv frisch.

freshman ['freʃmən] (US: irreg: like man) n = **fresher**.

freshness ['freʃnɪs] n Frische f.

freshwater ['freʃwɔːtə*] adj (fish etc) Süßwasser-.

fret [fret] vi sich dat Sorgen machen.

fretful ['fretful] adj (child) quengelig.

Freudian ['frɔɪdɪən] adj freudianisch, Freudsch; ~ **slip** Freudscher Versprecher m.

FRG n abbr (= Federal Republic of Germany) BRD f.

Fri. abbr (= Friday) Fr.

friar ['fraɪə*] n Mönch m, (Ordens)bruder m.

friction ['frɪkʃən] n Reibung f; (between people) Reibereien pl.

friction feed n (on printer) Friktionsvorschub m.

Friday ['fraɪdɪ] n Freitag m; see also **Tuesday**.

fridge [frɪdʒ] (BRIT) n Kühlschrank m.

fridge-freezer ['frɪdʒ'fri:zə*] n Kühl- und Gefrierkombination f.

fried [fraɪd] pt, pp of **fry** ♦ adj gebraten; ~ **egg** Spiegelei nt; ~ **fish** Bratfisch m.

friend [frend] n Freund(in) m(f); (less intimate) Bekannte(r) f(m); **to make ~s with** sich anfreunden mit.

friendliness ['frendlɪnɪs] n Freundlichkeit f.

friendly ['frendlɪ] adj freundlich; (government) befreundet; (game, match) Freundschafts-♦ n (also: ~ **match**) Freundschaftsspiel nt; **to be ~ with** befreundet sein mit; **to be ~ to** freundlich or nett sein zu.

friendly fire n Beschuß m durch die eigene Seite.

friendly society n Versicherungsverein m auf Gegenseitigkeit.

friendship ['frendʃɪp] n Freundschaft f.

frieze [fri:z] n Fries m.

frigate ['frɪgɪt] n Fregatte f.

fright [fraɪt] n Schreck(en) m; **to take ~** es mit der Angst zu tun bekommen; **she looks a ~** sie sieht verboten or zum Fürchten aus (inf).

frighten ['fraɪtn] vt erschrecken.

▶**frighten away** or **off** vt verscheuchen.

frightened ['fraɪtnd] adj ängstlich; **to be ~ (of)** Angst haben (vor +dat).

frightening ['fraɪtnɪŋ] adj furchterregend.

frightful ['fraɪtful] adj schrecklich, furchtbar.

frightfully ['fraɪtfəlɪ] adv schrecklich, furchtbar; I'm ~ **sorry** es tut mir schrecklich leid.

frigid ['frɪdʒɪd] adj frigide.

frigidity [frɪ'dʒɪdɪtɪ] n Frigidität f.

frill [frɪl] n Rüsche f; **without ~s** (fig) schlicht.

fringe [frɪndʒ] n (BRIT: of hair) Pony m; (decoration) Fransen pl; (edge: also fig) Rand m.

fringe benefits npl zusätzliche Leistungen pl.

fringe theatre n avantgardistisches Theater nt.

Frisbee ® ['frɪzbɪ] n Frisbee ® nt.
frisk [frɪsk] vt durchsuchen, filzen (inf) ♦ vi
umhertollen.
frisky ['frɪskɪ] adj lebendig, ausgelassen.
fritter ['frɪtə*] n Schmalzgebackenes nt no pl
mit Füllung.
►**fritter away** vt vergeuden.
frivolity [frɪ'vɔlɪtɪ] n Frivolität f.
frivolous ['frɪvələs] adj frivol; (activity)
leichtfertig.
frizzy ['frɪzɪ] adj kraus.
fro [frəu] adv: to and ~ hin und her; (walk) auf
und ab.
frock [frɔk] n Kleid nt.
frog [frɔg] n Frosch m; to have a ~ in one's
throat einen Frosch im Hals haben.
frogman ['frɔgmən] (irreg: like man) n
Froschmann m.
frogmarch ['frɔgmɑːtʃ] (BRIT) vt: to ~ sb in/
out jdn herein-/herausschleppen.
frolic ['frɔlɪk] vi umhertollen ♦ n
Ausgelassenheit f; (fun) Spaß m.

══════════════════ KEYWORD

from [frɔm] prep 1 (indicating starting place,
origin) von +dat; where do you come ~?
woher kommen Sie?; ~ London to Glasgow
von London nach Glasgow; a letter/
telephone call ~ my sister ein Brief/Anruf
von meiner Schwester; to drink ~ the bottle
aus der Flasche trinken
2 (indicating time) von (... an); ~ one o'clock
to or until or till now von ein Uhr bis jetzt;
~ January (on) von Januar an, ab Januar
3 (indicating distance) von ... entfernt; the
hotel is 1 km ~ the beach das Hotel ist
1 km vom Strand entfernt
4 (indicating price, number etc): trousers
~ £20 Hosen ab £20; prices range ~ £10 to
£50 die Preise liegen zwischen £10 und £50
5 (indicating difference): he can't tell red
~ green er kann rot und grün nicht
unterscheiden; to be different ~ sb/sth
anders sein als jd/etw
6 (because of, on the basis of): ~ what he says
nach dem, was er sagt; to act ~ conviction
aus Überzeugung handeln; weak ~ hunger
schwach vor Hunger.

frond [frɔnd] n Wedel m.
front [frʌnt] n Vorderseite f; (of dress)
Vorderteil nt; (promenade: also: sea ~)
Strandpromenade f; (MIL, MET) Front f; (fig:
appearances) Fassade f ♦ adj vorderste(r, s);
(wheel, tooth, view) Vorder- ♦ vi: to ~ onto
sth (house) auf etw acc hinausliegen;
(window) auf etw acc hinausgehen; in ~
vorne; in ~ of vor; at the ~ of the coach/
train/car vorne im Bus/Zug/Auto; on the
political ~, little progress has been made an
der politischen Front sind kaum
Fortschritte gemacht worden.

frontage ['frʌntɪdʒ] n Vorderseite f, Front f;
(of shop) Front f.
frontal ['frʌntl] adj (attack etc) Frontal-.
front bench (BRIT) n (POL) vorderste or erste
Reihe f.

> **Front Bench** bezeichnet im britischen
> Unterhaus die vorderste Bank auf der
> Regierungs- und Oppositionsseite zur Rechten
> und Linken des Sprechers. Im weiteren Sinne
> bezieht sich front bench auf die
> Spitzenpolitiker der verschiedenen Parteien,
> die auf dieser Bank sitzen (auch frontbenchers
> genannt), d.h. die Minister auf der einen Seite
> und die Mitglieder des Schattenkabinetts auf
> der anderen.

front desk (US) n Rezeption f.
front door n Haustür f.
frontier ['frʌntɪə*] n Grenze f.
frontispiece ['frʌntɪspiːs] n zweite Titelseite f,
Frontispiz nt.
front page n erste Seite f, Titelseite f.
front room (BRIT) n Wohnzimmer nt.
frontrunner ['frʌntrʌnə*] n Spitzenreiter m.
front-wheel drive ['frʌntwiːl-] n (AUT)
Vorderradantrieb m.
frost [frɔst] n Frost m; (also: hoar~) Rauhreif
m.
frostbite ['frɔstbaɪt] n Erfrierungen pl.
frosted ['frɔstɪd] adj (glass) Milch-; (esp US)
glasiert, mit Zuckerguß überzogen.
frosting ['frɔstɪŋ] (esp US) n Zuckerguß m.
frosty ['frɔstɪ] adj frostig; (look) eisig;
(window) bereift.
froth [frɔθ] n Schaum m.
frothy ['frɔθɪ] adj schäumend.
frown [fraun] n Stirnrunzeln nt ♦ vi die Stirn
runzeln.
►**frown on** vt fus mißbilligen.
froze [frəuz] pt of freeze.
frozen ['frəuzn] pp of freeze ♦ adj tiefgekühlt;
(food) Tiefkühl-; (COMM) eingefroren.
FRS n abbr (BRIT: = Fellow of the Royal Society)
Auszeichnung für Naturwissenschaftler;
(US: = Federal Reserve System)
amerikanische Zentralbank.
frugal ['fruːgl] adj genügsam; (meal) einfach.
fruit [fruːt] n inv Frucht f; (collectively) Obst nt;
(fig: results) Früchte pl.
fruiterer ['fruːtərə*] (esp BRIT) n
Obsthändler(in) m(f).
fruit fly n Fruchtfliege f.
fruitful ['fruːtful] adj fruchtbar.
fruition [fruː'ɪʃən] n: to come to ~ (plan)
Wirklichkeit werden; (efforts) Früchte
tragen; (hope) in Erfüllung gehen.
fruit juice n Fruchtsaft m.
fruitless ['fruːtlɪs] adj fruchtlos, ergebnislos.
fruit machine (BRIT) n Spielautomat m.
fruit salad n Obstsalat m.
fruity ['fruːtɪ] adj (taste, smell etc) Frucht-,

Obst-; (*wine*) fruchtig; (*voice, laugh*) volltönend.

frump [frʌmp] *n:* **to feel a** ~ sich *dat* wie eine Vogelscheuche vorkommen.

frustrate [frʌs'treɪt] *vt* frustrieren; (*attempt*) vereiteln; (*plan*) durchkreuzen.

frustrated [frʌs'treɪtɪd] *adj* frustriert.

frustrating [frʌs'treɪtɪŋ] *adj* frustrierend.

frustration [frʌs'treɪʃən] *n* Frustration *f*; (*of attempt*) Vereitelung *f*; (*of plan*) Zerschlagung *f*.

fry [fraɪ] (*pt, pp* **fried**) *vt* braten; *see also* **small**.

frying pan ['fraɪɪŋ-] *n* Bratpfanne *f*.

FT (*BRIT*) *n abbr* (= *Financial Times*) Wirtschaftszeitung; **the** ~ **index** der Aktienindex der „Financial Times".

ft. *abbr* = **foot; feet.**

FTC (*US*) *n abbr* = **Federal Trade Commission.**

FTSE 100 Index *n Aktienindex der „Financial Times".*

fuchsia ['fju:ʃə] *n* Fuchsie *f*.

fuck [fʌk] (*inf!*) *vt, vi* ficken (*!*); ~ **off!** (*inf!*) verpiß dich! (*!*).

fuddled ['fʌdld] *adj* verwirrt.

fuddy-duddy ['fʌdɪdʌdɪ] (*pej*) *n* Langweiler *m*.

fudge [fʌdʒ] *n* Fondant *m* ♦ *vt* (*issue, problem*) ausweichen +*dat*, aus dem Weg gehen +*dat*.

fuel ['fjuəl] *n* Brennstoff *m*; (*for vehicle*) Kraftstoff *m*; (: *petrol*) Benzin *nt*; (*for aircraft, rocket*) Treibstoff *m* ♦ *vt* (*furnace etc*) betreiben; (*aircraft, ship etc*) antreiben.

fuel oil *n* Gasöl *nt*.

fuel pump *n* (*AUT*) Benzinpumpe *f*.

fuel tank *n* Öltank *m*; (*in vehicle*) (Benzin)tank *m*.

fug [fʌg] (*BRIT: inf*) *n* Mief *m* (*inf*).

fugitive ['fju:dʒɪtɪv] *n* Flüchtling *m*.

fulfil, (*US*) **fulfill** [ful'fɪl] *vt* erfüllen; (*order*) ausführen.

fulfilled [ful'fɪld] *adj* ausgefüllt.

fulfilment, (*US*) **fulfillment** [ful'fɪlmənt] *n* Erfüllung *f*.

full [ful] *adj* voll; (*complete*) vollständig; (*skirt*) weit; (*life*) ausgefüllt ♦ *adv:* **to know** ~ **well that** ... sehr wohl wissen, daß ...; ~ **up** (*hotel etc*) ausgebucht; **I'm** ~ (**up**) ich bin satt; **a** ~ **two hours** volle zwei Stunden; ~ **marks** die beste Note, ≈ eine Eins; (*fig*) höchstes Lob *nt*; **at** ~ **speed** in voller Fahrt; **in** ~ ganz, vollständig; **to pay in** ~ den vollen Betrag bezahlen; **to write one's name** *etc* **in** ~ seinen Namen *etc* ausschreiben.

fullback ['fulbæk] *n* (*RUGBY, FOOTBALL*) Verteidiger *m*.

full-blooded ['ful'blʌdɪd] *adj* (*vigorous*) kräftig; (*virile*) vollblütig.

full board *n* Vollpension *f*.

full-cream ['ful'kri:m] *adj:* ~ **milk** (*BRIT*) Vollmilch *f*.

full employment *n* Vollbeschäftigung *f*.

full grown *adj* ausgewachsen.

full-length ['ful'leŋθ] *adj* (*film*) abendfüllend;

(*coat*) lang; (*portrait*) lebensgroß; (*mirror*) groß; ~ **novel** Roman *m*.

full moon *n* Vollmond *m*.

fullness ['fulnɪs] *n:* **in the** ~ **of time** zu gegebener Zeit.

full-page ['fulpeɪdʒ] *adj* ganzseitig.

full-scale ['fulskeɪl] *adj* (*war*) richtig; (*attack*) Groß-; (*model*) in Originalgröße; (*search*) großangelegt.

full-sized ['ful'saɪzd] *adj* lebensgroß.

full stop *n* Punkt *m*.

full-time ['ful'taɪm] *adj* (*work*) Ganztags-; (*study*) Voll- ♦ *adv* ganztags.

fully ['fulɪ] *adv* völlig; ~ **as big as** mindestens so groß wie.

fully fledged [-'fledʒd] *adj* richtiggehend; (*doctor etc*) voll qualifiziert; (*member*) Voll-; (*bird*) flügge.

fulsome ['fulsəm] (*pej*) *adj* übertrieben.

fumble ['fʌmbl] *vi:* **to** ~ **with** herumfummeln an +*dat* ♦ *vt* (*ball*) nicht sicher fangen.

fume [fju:m] *vi* wütend sein, kochen (*inf*).

fumes [fju:mz] *npl* (*of fire*) Rauch *m*; (*of fuel*) Dämpfe *pl*; (*of car*) Abgase *pl*.

fumigate ['fju:mɪgeɪt] *vt* ausräuchern.

fun [fʌn] *n* Spaß *m*; **he's good** ~ (**to be with**) es macht viel Spaß, mit ihm zusammenzusein; **for** ~ aus *or* zum Spaß; **it's not much** ~ es macht keinen Spaß; **to make** ~ **of, to poke** ~ **at** sich lustig machen über +*acc*.

function ['fʌŋkʃən] *n* Funktion *f*; (*social occasion*) Veranstaltung *f*, Feier *f* ♦ *vi* funktionieren; **to** ~ **as** (*thing*) dienen als; (*person*) fungieren als.

functional ['fʌŋkʃənl] *adj* (*operational*) funktionsfähig; (*practical*) funktionell, zweckmäßig.

function key *n* (*COMPUT*) Funktionstaste *f*.

fund [fʌnd] *n* (*of money*) Fonds *m*; (*source, store*) Schatz *m*, Vorrat *m*; **funds** *npl* (*money*) Mittel *pl*, Gelder *pl*.

fundamental [fʌndə'mentl] *adj* fundamental, grundlegend.

fundamentalism [fʌndə'mentəlɪzəm] *n* Fundamentalismus *m*.

fundamentalist [fʌndə'mentəlɪst] *n* Fundamentalist(in) *m(f)*.

fundamentally [fʌndə'mentəlɪ] *adv* im Grunde; (*radically*) von Grund auf.

fundamentals [fʌndə'mentlz] *npl* Grundbegriffe *pl*.

funding ['fʌndɪŋ] *n* Finanzierung *f*.

fund-raising ['fʌndreɪzɪŋ] *n* Geldbeschaffung *f*.

funeral ['fju:nərəl] *n* Beerdigung *f*.

funeral director *n* Beerdigungsunternehmer(in) *m(f)*.

funeral parlour *n* Leichenhalle *f*.

funeral service *n* Trauergottesdienst *m*.

funereal [fju:'nɪərɪəl] *adj* traurig, trübselig.

funfair ['fʌnfeə*] (*BRIT*) *n* Jahrmarkt *m*.

fungi ['fʌŋgaɪ] *npl of* **fungus.**

fungus ['fʌŋgəs] (*pl* **fungi**) *n* Pilz *m*; (*mould*) Schimmel(pilz) *m*.

funicular [fjuː'nɪkjuləʳ] *n* (*also:* ~ **railway**) Seilbahn *f*.

funky ['fʌŋkɪ] *adj* (*music*) Funk-.

funnel ['fʌnl] *n* Trichter *m*; (*of ship*) Schornstein *m*.

funnily ['fʌnɪlɪ] *adv* komisch; ~ **enough** komischerweise.

funny ['fʌnɪ] *adj* komisch; (*strange*) seltsam, komisch.

funny bone *n* Musikantenknochen *m*.

fun run *n* ~ Volkslauf *m*.

fur [fəːʳ] *n* Fell *nt*, Pelz *m*; (*BRIT: in kettle etc*) Kesselstein *m*.

fur coat *n* Pelzmantel *m*.

furious ['fjuərɪəs] *adj* wütend; (*exchange, argument*) heftig; (*effort*) riesig; (*speed*) rasend; **to be** ~ **with sb** wütend auf jdn sein.

furiously ['fjuərɪəslɪ] *adv* (*see adj*) wütend; (*struggle etc*) heftig; (*run*) schnell.

furl [fəːl] *vt* (*NAUT*) einrollen.

furlong ['fəːlɒŋ] *n* Achtelmeile *f* (= *201,17 m*).

furlough ['fəːləu] *n* (*MIL*) Urlaub *m*.

furnace ['fəːnɪs] *n* (*in foundry*) Schmelzofen *m*; (*in power plant*) Hochofen *m*.

furnish ['fəːnɪʃ] *vt* einrichten; (*room*) möblieren; **to** ~ **sb with sth** jdm etw liefern; ~**ed flat** *or* (*US*) **apartment** möblierte Wohnung *f*.

furnishings ['fəːnɪʃɪŋz] *npl* Einrichtung *f*.

furniture ['fəːnɪtʃəʳ] *n* Möbel *pl*; **piece of** ~ Möbelstück *nt*.

furniture polish *n* Möbelpolitur *f*.

furore [fjuə'rɔːrɪ] *n* (*protests*) Proteste *pl*; (*enthusiasm*) Furore *f or nt*.

furrier ['fʌrɪəʳ] *n* Kürschner(in) *m(f)*.

furrow ['fʌrəu] *n* Furche *f*; (*in skin*) Runzel *f* ♦ *vt* (*brow*) runzeln.

furry ['fəːrɪ] *adj* (*coat, tail*) flauschig; (*animal*) Pelz-; (*toy*) Plüsch-.

further ['fəːðəʳ] *adj* weitere(r, s) ♦ *adv* weiter; (*moreover*) darüber hinaus ♦ *vt* fördern; **until** ~ **notice** bis auf weiteres; **how much** ~ **is it?** wie weit ist es noch?; ~ **to your letter of** ... (*COMM*) bezugnehmend auf Ihr Schreiben vom ...

further education (*BRIT*) *n* Weiterbildung *f*, Fortbildung *f*.

furthermore [fəːðə'mɔːʳ] *adv* außerdem.

furthermost ['fəːðəməust] *adj* äußerste(r, s).

furthest ['fəːðɪst] *superl of* **far**.

furtive ['fəːtɪv] *adj* verstohlen.

furtively ['fəːtɪvlɪ] *adv* verstohlen.

fury ['fjuərɪ] *n* Wut *f*; **to be in a** ~ in Rage sein.

fuse, (*US*) **fuze** [fjuːz] *n* (*ELEC*) Sicherung *f*; (*for bomb etc*) Zündschnur *f* ♦ *vt* (*pieces of metal*) verschmelzen; (*fig*) vereinigen ♦ *vi* (*pieces of metal*) sich verbinden; (*fig*) sich vereinigen; **to** ~ **the lights** (*BRIT*) die Sicherung durchbrennen lassen; **a** ~ **has**

blown eine Sicherung ist durchgebrannt.

fuse box *n* Sicherungskasten *m*.

fuselage ['fjuːzəlɑːʒ] *n* Rumpf *m*.

fuse wire *n* Schmelzdraht *m*.

fusillade [fjuːzɪ'leɪd] *n* Salve *f*.

fusion ['fjuːʒən] *n* Verschmelzung *f*; (*also:* **nuclear** ~) Kernfusion *f*.

fuss [fʌs] *n* Theater *nt* (*inf*) ♦ *vi* sich (unnötig) aufregen ♦ *vt* keine Ruhe lassen +*dat*; **to make a** ~ Krach schlagen (*inf*); **to make a** ~ **of sb** viel Getue um jdn machen (*inf*).

▶**fuss over** *vt fus* bemuttern.

fusspot ['fʌspɒt] *n* Nörgler(in) *m(f)*.

fussy ['fʌsɪ] *adj* kleinlich, pingelig (*inf*); (*clothes, room etc*) verspielt; **I'm not** ~ es ist mir egal.

fusty ['fʌstɪ] *adj* muffig.

futile ['fjuːtaɪl] *adj* vergeblich; (*existence*) sinnlos; (*comment*) zwecklos.

futility [fjuː'tɪlɪtɪ] *n* (*see adj*) Vergeblichkeit *f*; Sinnlosigkeit *f*; Zwecklosigkeit *f*.

futon ['fuːtɒn] *n* Futon *m*.

future ['fjuːtʃəʳ] *adj* zukünftig ♦ *n* Zukunft *f*; (*LING*) Futur *nt*; **futures** *npl* (*COMM*) Termingeschäfte *pl*; **in (the)** ~ in Zukunft; **in the near** ~ in der nahen Zukunft; **in the immediate** ~ sehr bald.

futuristic [fjuːtʃə'rɪstɪk] *adj* futuristisch.

fuze [fjuːz] *n, vt, vi* = **fuse**.

fuzz [fʌz] (*inf*) *n* (*police*): **the** ~ die Bullen *pl*.

fuzzy ['fʌzɪ] *adj* verschwommen; (*hair*) kraus; (*thoughts*) verworren.

fwd. *abbr* = **forward**.

fwy (*US*) *abbr* = **freeway**.

FY *abbr* (= *fiscal year*) Steuerjahr *nt*.

FYI *abbr* (= *for your information*) zu Ihrer Information.

G, g

G¹, g¹ [dʒiː] *n* (*letter*) G *nt*, g *nt*; ~ **for George** ≈ G wie Gustav.

G² [dʒiː] *n* (*MUS*) G *nt*, g *nt*.

G³ [dʒiː] *n abbr* (*BRIT: SCOL*) = **good**; (*US: CINE* = *general (audience)*) Klassifikation für jugendfreie Filme; (*PHYS*): ~-**force** g-Druck *m*.

G7 *n abbr* (*POL:* = *Group of Seven*) G7 *f*.

g² *abbr* (= *gram(me)*) g; (*PHYS*) = **gravity**.

GA (*US*) *n abbr* (*POST:* = *Georgia*).

gab [gæb] (*inf*) *n*: **to have the gift of the** ~ reden können, nicht auf den Mund gefallen sein.

gabble ['gæbl] *vi* brabbeln (*inf*).

gaberdine [gæbə'diːn] *n* Gabardine *m*.

gable ['geɪbl] n Giebel m.
Gabon [gə'bɔn] n Gabun nt.
gad about [gæd-] (inf) vi herumziehen.
gadget ['gædʒɪt] n Gerät nt.
gadgetry ['gædʒɪtrɪ] n Geräte pl.
Gaelic ['geɪlɪk] adj gälisch ♦ n (LING) Gälisch nt.
gaffe [gæf] n Fauxpas m.
gaffer ['gæfə'] (BRIT: inf) n (boss) Chef m; (foreman) Vorarbeiter m; (old man) Alte(r) m.
gag [gæg] n Knebel m; (joke) Gag m ♦ vt knebeln ♦ vi würgen.
gaga ['gɑːgɑː] (inf) adj: to go ~ verkalken.
gage [geɪdʒ] (US) n, vt = **gauge**.
gaiety ['geɪɪtɪ] n Fröhlichkeit f.
gaily ['geɪlɪ] adv fröhlich; ~ coloured farbenfroh, farbenprächtig.
gain [geɪn] n Gewinn m ♦ vt gewinnen ♦ vi (clock, watch) vorgehen; to do sth for ~ etw aus Berechnung tun; (for money) etw des Geldes wegen tun; ~ (in) (increase) Zunahme f (an +dat); (in rights, conditions) Verbesserung f +gen; to ~ ground (an) Boden gewinnen; to ~ speed schneller werden; to ~ weight zunehmen; to ~ 3lbs (in weight) 3 Pfund zunehmen; to ~ (in) confidence sicherer werden;: to ~ from sth von etw profitieren; to ~ in strength stärker werden; to ~ by doing sth davon profitieren, etw zu tun; to ~ on sb jdn einholen.
gainful ['geɪnful] adj: ~ employment Erwerbstätigkeit f.
gainfully ['geɪnfəlɪ] adv: ~ employed erwerbstätig.
gainsay [geɪn'seɪ] (irreg: like say) vt widersprechen +dat; (fact) leugnen.
gait [geɪt] n Gang m; to walk with a slow/ confident ~ mit langsamen Schritten/ selbstbewußt gehen.
gal. abbr = **gallon**.
gala ['gɑːlə] n Galaveranstaltung f; swimming ~ großes Schwimmfest nt.
Galapagos (Islands) [gə'læpəgəs-] npl: (the) ~ die Galapagosinseln pl.
galaxy ['gæləksɪ] n Galaxis f, Sternsystem nt.
gale [geɪl] n Sturm m; ~ force 10 Sturmstärke 10.
gall [gɔːl] n Galle f; (fig: impudence) Frechheit f ♦ vt maßlos ärgern.
gall. abbr = **gallon**.
gallant ['gælənt] adj tapfer; (polite) galant.
gallantry ['gæləntrɪ] n (see adj) Tapferkeit f; Galanterie f.
gall bladder n Gallenblase f.
galleon ['gælɪən] n Galeone f.
gallery ['gælərɪ] n (also: art ~) Galerie f, Museum nt; (private) (Privat)galerie f; (in hall, church) Galerie f; (in theatre) oberster Rang m, Balkon m.
galley ['gælɪ] n Kombüse f; (ship) Galeere f;

(also: ~ proof) Fahne f, Fahnenabzug m.
Gallic ['gælɪk] adj gallisch; (French) französisch.
galling ['gɔːlɪŋ] adj äußerst ärgerlich.
gallon ['gæln] n Gallone f (BRIT = 4,5 l, US = 3,8 l).
gallop ['gæləp] n Galopp m ♦ vi galoppieren; ~ing inflation galoppierende Inflation f.
gallows ['gæləuz] n Galgen m.
gallstone ['gɔːlstəun] n Gallenstein m.
Gallup poll ['gæləp-] n Meinungsumfrage f.
galore [gə'lɔː'] adv in Hülle und Fülle.
galvanize ['gælvənaɪz] vt (fig) mobilisieren; to ~ sb into action jdn plötzlich aktiv werden lassen.
galvanized ['gælvənaɪzd] adj (metal) galvanisiert.
Gambia ['gæmbɪə] n Gambia nt.
gambit ['gæmbɪt] n: (opening) ~ (einleitender) Schachzug m; (in conversation) (einleitende) Bemerkung f.
gamble ['gæmbl] n Risiko nt ♦ vt einsetzen ♦ vi ein Risiko eingehen; (bet) spielen; (on horses etc) wetten; to ~ on the Stock Exchange an der Börse spekulieren; to ~ on sth (horses, race) auf etw acc wetten; (success, outcome etc) sich auf etw acc verlassen.
gambler ['gæmblə'] n Spieler(in) m(f).
gambling ['gæmblɪŋ] n Spielen nt; (on horses etc) Wetten nt.
gambol ['gæmbl] vi herumtollen.
game [geɪm] n Spiel nt; (sport) Sport m; (strategy, scheme) Vorhaben nt; (CULIN, HUNTING) Wild n ♦ adj: to be ~ (for) mitmachen (bei); games npl (SCOL) Sport m; to play a ~ of football/tennis Fußball/(eine Partie) Tennis spielen; big ~ Großwild nt.
game bird n Federwild nt no pl.
gamekeeper ['geɪmkiːpə'] n Wildhüter(in) m(f).
gamely ['geɪmlɪ] adv mutig.
game reserve n Wildschutzreservat nt.
games console ['geɪmz-] n (COMPUT) Gameboy ® m, Konsole f.
game show n (TV) Spielshow f.
gamesmanship ['geɪmzmənʃɪp] n Gerissenheit f beim Spiel.
gaming ['geɪmɪŋ] n (gambling) Spielen nt.
gammon ['gæmən] n Schinken m.
gamut ['gæmət] n Skala f; to run the ~ of die ganze Skala +gen durchlaufen.
gander ['gændə'] n Gänserich m.
gang [gæŋ] n Bande f; (of friends) Haufen m; (of workmen) Kolonne f.
▶**gang up** vi: to ~ up on sb sich gegen jdn zusammentun.
Ganges ['gændʒiːz] n: the ~ der Ganges.
gangland ['gæŋlænd] adj (killer, boss) Unterwelt-.
gangling ['gæŋglɪŋ] adj schlaksig, hochaufgeschossen.
gangly ['gæŋglɪ] adj schlaksig.

gangplank ['gæŋplæŋk] *n* Laufplanke *f*.
gangrene ['gæŋgriːn] *n* (*MED*) Brand *m*.
gangster ['gæŋstə*] *n* Gangster *m*.
gangway ['gæŋweɪ] *n* Laufplanke *f*, Gangway *f*; (*in cinema, bus, plane etc*) Gang *m*.
gantry ['gæntrɪ] *n* (*for crane*) Portal *nt*; (*for railway signal*) Signalbrücke *f*; (*for rocket*) Abschußrampe *f*.
GAO (*US*) *n abbr* (= *General Accounting Office*) Rechnungshof der USA.
gaol [dʒeɪl] (*BRIT*) *n, vt* = **jail**.
gap [gæp] *n* Lücke *f*; (*in time*) Pause *f*; (*difference*): ~ **(between)** Kluft *f* (zwischen +*dat*).
gape [geɪp] *vi* starren, gaffen; (*hole*) gähnen; (*shirt*) offenstehen.
gaping ['geɪpɪŋ] *adj* (*hole*) gähnend; (*shirt*) offen.
garage ['gærɑːʒ] *n* Garage *f*; (*for car repairs*) (Reparatur)werkstatt *f*; (*petrol station*) Tankstelle *f*.
garb [gɑːb] *n* Gewand *nt*, Kluft *f*.
garbage ['gɑːbɪdʒ] *n* (*US: rubbish*) Abfall *m*, Müll *m*; (*inf: nonsense*) Blödsinn *m*, Quatsch *m*; (*fig: film, book*) Schund *m*.
garbage can (*US*) *n* Mülleimer *m*, Abfalleimer *m*.
garbage collector (*US*) *n* Müllmann *m*.
garbage disposal (unit) *n* Müllschlucker *m*.
garbage truck (*US*) *n* Müllwagen *m*.
garbled ['gɑːbld] *adj* (*account*) wirr; (*message*) unverständlich.
garden ['gɑːdn] *n* Garten *m* ♦ *vi* gärtnern; **gardens** *npl* (*public park*) Park *m*; (*private*) Gartenanlagen *pl*; **she was** ~ing sie arbeitete im Garten.
garden centre *n* Gartencenter *nt*.
garden city *n* Gartenstadt *f*.
gardener ['gɑːdnə*] *n* Gärtner(in) *m(f)*.
gardening ['gɑːdnɪŋ] *n* Gartenarbeit *f*.
gargle ['gɑːgl] *vi* gurgeln ♦ *n* Gurgelwasser *nt*.
gargoyle ['gɑːgɔɪl] *n* Wasserspeier *m*.
garish ['gɛərɪʃ] *adj* grell.
garland ['gɑːlənd] *n* Kranz *m*.
garlic ['gɑːlɪk] *n* Knoblauch *m*.
garment ['gɑːmənt] *n* Kleidungsstück *nt*.
garner ['gɑːnə*] *vt* sammeln.
garnish ['gɑːnɪʃ] *vt* garnieren.
garret ['gærɪt] *n* Dachkammer *f*, Mansarde *f*.
garrison ['gærɪsn] *n* Garnison *f*.
garrulous ['gærʊləs] *adj* geschwätzig.
garter ['gɑːtə*] *n* Strumpfband *nt*; (*US: suspender*) Strumpfhalter *m*.
garter belt (*US*) *n* Strumpfgürtel *m*, Hüftgürtel *m*.
gas [gæs] *n* Gas *nt*; (*US: gasoline*) Benzin *nt* ♦ *vt* mit Gas vergiften; (*MIL*) vergasen; **to be given** ~ (*as anaesthetic*) Lachgas bekommen.
gas cooker (*BRIT*) *n* Gasherd *m*.
gas cylinder *n* Gasflasche *f*.
gaseous ['gæsɪəs] *adj* gasförmig.
gas fire (*BRIT*) *n* Gasofen *m*.

gas-fired ['gæsfaɪəd] *adj* (*heater etc*) Gas-.
gash [gæʃ] *n* klaffende Wunde *f*; (*tear*) tiefer Schlitz *m* ♦ *vt* aufschlitzen.
gasket ['gæskɪt] *n* Dichtung *f*.
gas mask *n* Gasmaske *f*.
gas meter *n* Gaszähler *m*.
gasoline ['gæsəliːn] (*US*) *n* Benzin *nt*.
gasp [gɑːsp] *n* tiefer Atemzug *m* ♦ *vi* keuchen; (*in surprise*) nach Luft schnappen; **to give a** ~ **(of shock/horror)** (vor Schreck/Horror) die Luft anhalten; **to be** ~ing **for** sich sehnen nach +*dat*.
▶**gasp out** *vt* hervorstoßen.
gas permeable *adj* (*lenses*) luftdurchlässig.
gas ring *n* Gasbrenner *m*.
gas station (*US*) *n* Tankstelle *f*.
gas stove *n* (*cooker*) Gasherd *m*; (*for camping*) Gaskocher *m*.
gassy ['gæsɪ] *adj* (*drink*) kohlensäurehaltig.
gas tank *n* Benzintank *m*.
gastric ['gæstrɪk] *adj* (*upset, ulcer etc*) Magen-.
gastric flu *n* Darmgrippe *f*.
gastroenteritis ['gæstrəʊentə'raɪtɪs] *n* Magen-Darm-Katarrh *m*.
gastronomy [gæs'trɒnəmɪ] *n* Gastronomie *f*.
gasworks ['gæswɜːks] *n* Gaswerk *nt*.
gate [geɪt] *n* (*of garden*) Pforte *f*; (*of field*) Gatter *nt*; (*of building*) Tor *nt*; (*at airport*) Flugsteig *m*; (*of level crossing*) Schranke *f*; (*of lock*) Tor *nt*.
gateau ['gætəʊ] (*pl* ~**x**) *n* Torte *f*.
gate-crash ['geɪtkræʃ] (*BRIT*) *vt* (*party*) ohne Einladung besuchen; (*concert*) eindringen in +*acc* ♦ *vi* ohne Einladung hingehen; eindringen.
gate-crasher ['geɪtkræʃə*] *n* ungeladener Gast *m*.
gatehouse ['geɪthaʊs] *n* Pförtnerhaus *nt*.
gateway ['geɪtweɪ] *n* (*also fig*) Tor *nt*.
gather ['gæðə*] *vt* sammeln; (*flowers, fruit*) pflücken; (*understand*) schließen; (*SEWING*) kräuseln ♦ *vi* (*assemble*) sich versammeln; (*dust*) sich ansammeln; (*clouds*) sich zusammenziehen; **to** ~ **(from)** schließen (aus); **to** ~ **(that)** annehmen(, daß); **as far as I can** ~ so wie ich es sehe; **to** ~ **speed** schneller werden.
gathering ['gæðərɪŋ] *n* Versammlung *f*.
GATT [gæt] *n abbr* (= *General Agreement on Tariffs and Trade*) GATT *nt*.
gauche [gəʊʃ] *adj* linkisch.
gaudy ['gɔːdɪ] *adj* knallig.
gauge, (*US*) **gage** [geɪdʒ] *n* Meßgerät *nt*, Meßinstrument *nt*; (*RAIL*) Spurweite *f* ♦ *vt* messen; (*fig*) beurteilen; **petrol** ~, **fuel** ~, (*US*) **gas gage** Benzinuhr *f*; **to** ~ **the right moment** den richtigen Moment abwägen.
Gaul [gɔːl] *n* Gallien *nt*; (*person*) Gallier(in) *m(f)*.
gaunt [gɔːnt] *adj* (*haggard*) hager; (*bare, stark*) öde.
gauntlet ['gɔːntlɪt] *n* (Stulpen)handschuh *m*;

(*fig*): **to run the** ~ Spießruten laufen; **to throw down the** ~ den Fehdehandschuh hinwerfen.

gauze [gɔːz] *n* Gaze *f*.

gave [geɪv] *pt of* give.

gavel ['gævl] *n* Hammer *m*.

gawk [gɔːk] (*inf*) *vi* gaffen, glotzen.

gawky ['gɔːkɪ] *adj* schlaksig.

gawp [gɔːp] *vi*: **to** ~ **at** angaffen, anglotzen (*inf*).

gay [geɪ] *adj* (*homosexual*) schwul; (*cheerful*) fröhlich; (*dress*) bunt.

gaze [geɪz] *n* Blick *m* ♦ *vi*: **to** ~ **at sth** etw anstarren.

gazelle [gə'zɛl] *n* Gazelle *f*.

gazette [gə'zɛt] *n* Zeitung *f*; (*official*) Amtsblatt *nt*.

gazetteer [gæzə'tɪə*] *n* alphabetisches Ortsverzeichnis *nt*.

gazump [gə'zʌmp] (*BRIT*) *vt*: **to be** ~**ed** *ein mündlich zugesagtes Haus an einen Höherbietenden verlieren*.

GB *abbr* (= *Great Britain*) GB.

GBH (*BRIT*) *n abbr* (*LAW*) = **grievous bodily harm**.

GC (*BRIT*) *n abbr* (= *George Cross*) *britische Tapferkeitsmedaille*.

GCE (*BRIT*) *n abbr* (= *General Certificate of Education*) *Schulabschlußzeugnis*, ≈ Abitur *nt*.

GCHQ (*BRIT*) *n abbr* (= *Government Communications Headquarters*) *Zentralstelle des britischen Nachrichtendienstes*.

GCSE (*BRIT*) *n abbr* (= *General Certificate of Secondary Education*) *Schulabschlußzeugnis*, ≈ mittlere Reife *f*.

Gdns *abbr* (*in street names*: = *Gardens*) ≈ Str.

GDP *n abbr* = **gross domestic product**.

GDR *n abbr* (*formerly*: = *German Democratic Republic*) DDR *f*.

gear [gɪə*] *n* (*equipment*) Ausrüstung *f*; (*belongings*) Sachen *pl*; (*TECH*) Getriebe *nt*; (*AUT*) Gang *m*; (*on bicycle*) Gangschaltung *f* ♦ *vt* (*fig: adapt*): **to** ~ **sth to** etw ausrichten auf +*acc*; **top** *or* (*US*) **high/low/bottom** ~ hoher/niedriger/erster Gang; **to put a car into** ~ einen Gang einlegen; **to leave the car in** ~ den Gang eingelegt lassen; **to leave out of** ~ im Leerlauf lassen; **our service is** ~**ed to meet the needs of the disabled** unser Betrieb ist auf die Bedürfnisse von Behinderten eingerichtet.

▶**gear up** *vt, vi*: **to** ~ (**o.s.**) **up** (**to**) sich vorbereiten (auf +*acc*) ♦ *vt*: **to** ~ **o.s. up to do sth** sich darauf vorbereiten, etw zu tun.

gearbox ['gɪəbɔks] *n* Getriebe *nt*.

gear lever, (*US*) **gear shift** *n* Schalthebel *m*.

GED (*US*) *n abbr* (*SCOL*: = *general educational development*) *allgemeine Lernentwicklung*.

geese [giːs] *npl of* goose.

geezer ['giːzə*] (*inf*) *n* Kerl *m*, Typ *m*.

Geiger counter ['gaɪgə-] *n* Geigerzähler *m*.

gel [dʒɛl] *n* Gel *nt*.

gelatin(e) ['dʒɛlətiːn] *n* Gelatine *f*.

gelignite ['dʒɛlɪgnaɪt] *n* Plastiksprengstoff *m*.

gem [dʒɛm] *n* Edelstein *m*; **she/the house is a** ~ (*fig*) sie/das Haus ist ein Juwel; **a** ~ **of an idea** eine ausgezeichnete Idee.

Gemini ['dʒɛmɪnaɪ] *n* (*ASTROL*) Zwillinge *pl*; **to be** ~ (ein) Zwilling sein.

gen [dʒɛn] (*BRIT: inf*) *n*: **to give sb the** ~ **on sth** jdn über etw *acc* informieren.

Gen. *abbr* (*MIL*: = *General*) Gen.

gen. *abbr* = **general; generally**.

gender ['dʒɛndə*] *n* Geschlecht *nt*.

gene [dʒiːn] *n* Gen *nt*.

genealogy [dʒiːnɪ'ælədʒɪ] *n* Genealogie *f*, Stammbaumforschung *f*; (*family history*) Stammbaum *m*.

general ['dʒɛnərl] *n* General *m* ♦ *adj* allgemein; (*widespread*) weitverbreitet; (*non-specific*) generell; **in** ~ im allgemeinen; **the** ~ **public** die Öffentlichkeit, die Allgemeinheit; ~ **audit** (*COMM*) Jahresabschlußprüfung *f*.

general anaesthetic *n* Vollnarkose *f*.

general delivery (*US*) *n*: **to send sth** ~ etw postlagernd schicken.

general election *n* Parlamentswahlen *pl*.

generalization ['dʒɛnrəlaɪ'zeɪʃən] *n* Verallgemeinerung *f*.

generalize ['dʒɛnrəlaɪz] *vi* verallgemeinern.

generally ['dʒɛnrəlɪ] *adv* im allgemeinen.

general manager *n* Hauptgeschäftsführer(in) *m(f)*.

general practitioner *n* praktischer Arzt *m*, praktische Ärztin *f*.

general strike *n* Generalstreik *m*.

generate ['dʒɛnəreɪt] *vt* erzeugen; (*jobs*) schaffen; (*profits*) einbringen.

generation [dʒɛnə'reɪʃən] *n* Generation *f*; (*of electricity etc*) Erzeugung *f*.

generator ['dʒɛnəreɪtə*] *n* Generator *m*.

generic [dʒɪ'nɛrɪk] *adj* allgemein; ~ **term** Oberbegriff *m*.

generosity [dʒɛnə'rɔsɪtɪ] *n* Großzügigkeit *f*.

generous ['dʒɛnərəs] *adj* großzügig; (*measure, remuneration*) reichlich.

genesis ['dʒɛnɪsɪs] *n* Entstehung *f*.

genetic [dʒɪ'nɛtɪk] *adj* genetisch.

genetic engineering *n* Gentechnologie *f*.

genetic fingerprinting [-'fɪŋgəprɪntɪŋ] *n* genetische Fingerabdrücke *pl*.

genetics [dʒɪ'nɛtɪks] *n* Genetik *f*.

Geneva [dʒɪ'niːvə] *n* Genf *nt*.

genial ['dʒiːnɪəl] *adj* freundlich; (*climate*) angenehm.

genitals ['dʒɛnɪtlz] *npl* Genitalien *pl*, Geschlechtsteile *pl*.

genitive ['dʒɛnɪtɪv] *n* Genitiv *m*.

genius ['dʒiːnɪəs] *n* Talent *nt*; (*person*) Genie *nt*.

Genoa ['dʒɛnəuə] *n* Genua *nt*.

genocide ['dʒɛnəusaɪd] *n* Völkermord *m*.

Genoese [dʒɛnəu'iːz] *adj* genuesisch ♦ *n inv*

Genuese *m*, Genuesin *f*.
gent [dʒɛnt] (*BRIT: inf*) *n abbr* = **gentleman**.
genteel [dʒɛn'tiːl] *adj* vornehm, fein.
gentle ['dʒɛntl] *adj* sanft; (*movement, breeze*) leicht; **a ~ hint** ein zarter Hinweis.
gentleman ['dʒɛntlmən] (*irreg: like* **man**) *n* Herr *m*; (*referring to social position or good manners*) Gentleman *m*; **~'s agreement** Vereinbarung *f* auf Treu und Glauben.
gentlemanly ['dʒɛntlmənlɪ] *adj* zuvorkommend.
gentleness ['dʒɛntlnɪs] *n* (*see adj*) Sanftheit *f*; Leichtheit *f*; Zartheit *f*.
gently ['dʒɛntlɪ] *adv* (*see adj*) sanft; leicht; zart.
gentry ['dʒɛntrɪ] *n inv*: **the ~** die Gentry, der niedere Adel.
gents [dʒɛnts] *n*: **the ~** die Herrentoilette.
genuine ['dʒɛnjuɪn] *adj* echt; (*person*) natürlich, aufrichtig.
genuinely ['dʒɛnjuɪnlɪ] *adv* wirklich.
geographer [dʒɪ'ɔgrəfə*] *n* Geograph(in) *m(f)*.
geographic(al) [dʒɪə'græfɪk(l)] *adj* geographisch.
geography [dʒɪ'ɔgrəfɪ] *n* Geographie *f*; (*SCOL*) Erdkunde *f*.
geological [dʒɪə'lɔdʒɪkl] *adj* geologisch.
geologist [dʒɪ'ɔlədʒɪst] *n* Geologe *m*, Geologin *f*.
geology [dʒɪ'ɔlədʒɪ] *n* Geologie *f*.
geometric(al) [dʒɪə'mɛtrɪk(l)] *adj* geometrisch.
geometry [dʒɪ'ɔmətrɪ] *n* Geometrie *f*.
Geordie ['dʒɔːdɪ] (*inf*) *n aus dem Gebiet von Newcastle stammende oder dort wohnhafte Person*.
Georgia ['dʒɔːdʒə] *n* (*in Eastern Europe*) Georgien *nt*.
Georgian ['dʒɔːdʒən] *adj* georgisch ♦ *n* Georgier(in) *m(f)*; (*LING*) Georgisch *nt*.
geranium [dʒɪ'reɪnɪəm] *n* Geranie *f*.
geriatric [dʒɛrɪ'ætrɪk] *adj* geriatrisch ♦ *n* Greis(in) *m(f)*.
germ [dʒəːm] *n* Bazillus *m*; (*BIOL, fig*) Keim *m*.
German ['dʒəːmən] *adj* deutsch ♦ *n* Deutsche(r) *f(m)*; (*LING*) Deutsch *nt*.
German Democratic Republic *n* (*formerly*) Deutsche Demokratische Republik *f*.
germane [dʒəː'meɪn] *adj*: **~ (to)** von Belang (für).
German measles (*BRIT*) *n* Röteln *pl*.
German Shepherd (dog) (*esp US*) *n* Schäferhund *m*.
Germany ['dʒəːmənɪ] *n* Deutschland *nt*.
germinate ['dʒəːmɪneɪt] *vi* keimen; (*fig*) aufkeimen.
germination [dʒəːmɪ'neɪʃən] *n* Keimung *f*.
germ warfare *n* biologische Kriegsführung *f*, Bakterienkrieg *m*.
gerrymandering ['dʒɛrɪmændərɪŋ] *n* Wahlkreisschiebungen *pl*.
gestation [dʒɛs'teɪʃən] *n* (*of animals*)

Trächtigkeit *f*; (*of humans*) Schwangerschaft *f*.
gesticulate [dʒɛs'tɪkjuleɪt] *vi* gestikulieren.
gesture ['dʒɛstjə*] *n* Geste *f*; **as a ~ of friendship** als Zeichen der Freundschaft.

═══════════════════════════ *KEYWORD*

get [gɛt] (*pt, pp* **got**, (*US*) *pp* **gotten**) *vi* **1** (*become, be*) werden; **to ~ old/tired/cold** alt/müde/kalt werden; **to ~ dirty** sich schmutzig machen; **to ~ killed** getötet werden; **to ~ married** heiraten
2 (*go*): **to ~ (from ...) to ...** (von ...) nach ... kommen; **how did you ~ here?** wie sind Sie hierhin gekommen?
3 (*begin*): **to ~ to know sb** jdn kennenlernen; **let's ~ going** *or* **started** fangen wir an!
♦ *modal aux vb*: **you've got to do it** du mußt es tun
♦ *vt* **1**: **to ~ sth done** (*do oneself*) etw gemacht bekommen; (*have done*) etw machen lassen; **to ~ one's hair cut** *dat* die Haare schneiden lassen; **to ~ the car going** *or* **to go** das Auto in Gang bringen; **to ~ sb to do sth** etw von jdm machen lassen; (*persuade*) jdn dazu bringen, etw zu tun
2 (*obtain: money, permission, results*) erhalten; (*find: job, flat*) finden; (*fetch: person, doctor, object*) holen; **to ~ sth for sb** jdm etw besorgen; **can I ~ you a drink?** kann ich Ihnen etwas zu trinken anbieten?
3 (*receive, acquire: present, prize*) bekommen; **how much did you ~ for the painting?** wieviel haben Sie für das Bild bekommen?
4 (*catch*) bekommen, kriegen (*inf*); (*hit: target etc*) treffen; **to ~ sb by the arm/throat** jdn am Arm/Hals packen; **the bullet got him in the leg** die Kugel traf ihn ins Bein
5 (*take, move*) bringen; **to ~ sth to sb** jdm etw zukommen lassen
6 (*plane, bus etc: take*) nehmen; (: *catch*) bekommen
7 (*understand: joke etc*) verstehen; **I ~ it** ich verstehe
8 (*have, possess*): **to have got** haben; **how many have you got?** wie viele hast du?
▶**get about** *vi* (*person*) herumkommen; (*news, rumour*) sich verbreiten.
▶**get across** *vt* (*message, meaning*) klarmachen.
▶**get along** *vi* (*be friends*) (miteinander) auskommen; (*depart*) sich auf den Weg machen.
▶**get around** *vt fus* = **get round**.
▶**get at** *vt fus* (*attack, criticize*) angreifen; (*reach*) herankommen an +*acc*; **what are you ~ting at?** worauf willst du hinaus?
▶**get away** *vi* (*leave*) wegkommen; (*on holiday*) verreisen; (*escape*) entkommen.
▶**get away with** *vt fus* (*stolen goods*) entkommen mit; **he'll never ~ away with it!**

damit kommt er nicht durch.
▶**get back** *vi* (*return*) zurückkommen ♦ *vt*
(*regain*) zurückbekommen; ~ **back!** zurück!
▶**get back at** (*inf*) *vt fus:* **to** ~ **back at sb for
sth** jdm etw heimzahlen.
▶**get back to** *vt fus* (*return to*) zurückkehren
zu; (*contact again*) zurückkommen auf +*acc*;
to ~ **back to sleep** wieder einschlafen.
▶**get by** *vi* (*pass*) vorbeikommen; (*manage*)
zurechtkommen; **I can** ~ **by in German** ich
kann mich auf Deutsch verständlich
machen.
▶**get down** *vi* (*from tree, ladder etc*)
heruntersteigen; (*from horse*) absteigen;
(*leave table*) aufstehen; (*bend down*) sich
bücken; (*duck*) sich ducken ♦ *vt* (*depress:
person*) fertigmachen; (*write*) aufschreiben.
▶**get down to** *vt fus:* **to** ~ **down to sth** (*work*)
etw in Angriff nehmen; (*find time*) zu etw
kommen; **to** ~ **down to business** (*fig*) zur
Sache kommen.
▶**get in** *vi* (*be elected: candidate, party*) gewählt
werden; (*arrive*) ankommen ♦ *vt* (*bring in:
harvest*) einbringen; (: *shopping, supplies*)
(herein)holen.
▶**get into** *vt fus* (*conversation, argument, fight*)
geraten in +*acc*; (*vehicle*) einsteigen in +*acc*;
(*clothes*) hineinkommen in +*acc*; **to** ~ **into
bed** ins Bett gehen; **to** ~ **into the habit of
doing sth** sich *dat* angewöhnen, etw zu tun.
▶ **get off** *vi* (*from train etc*) aussteigen; (*escape
punishment*) davonkommen ♦ *vt* (*remove:
clothes*) ausziehen; (: *stain*)
herausbekommen ♦ *vt fus* (*leave: train, bus*)
aussteigen aus; **we** ~ **3 days off at
Christmas** zu Weihnachten bekommen wir 3
Tage frei; **to** ~ **off to a good start** (*fig*) einen
guten Anfang machen.
▶ **get on** *vi* (*be friends*) (miteinander)
auskommen ♦ *vt fus* (*bus, train*) einsteigen in
+*acc*; **how are you** ~**ting on?** wie kommst du
zurecht?; **time is** ~**ting on** es wird langsam
spät.
▶ **get on to** (*BRIT*) *vt fus* (*subject, topic*)
übergehen zu; (*contact: person*) sich in
Verbindung setzen mit.
▶ **get on with** *vt fus* (*person*) auskommen mit;
(*meeting, work etc*) weitermachen mit.
▶ **get out** *vi* (*leave: on foot*) hinausgehen; (*of
vehicle*) aussteigen; (*news etc*)
herauskommen ♦ *vt* (*take out: book etc*)
herausholen; (*remove: stain*)
herausbekommen.
▶ **get out of** *vt fus* (*money: bank etc*) abheben
von; (*avoid: duty etc*) herumkommen um ♦ *vt*
(*extract: confession etc*) herausbekommen
aus; (*derive: pleasure*) haben an +*dat*;
(: *benefit*) haben von.
▶ **get over** *vt fus* (*overcome*) überwinden;
(: *illness*) sich erholen von; (*communicate:
idea etc*) verständlich machen ♦ *vt:* **to** ~ **it
over with** (*finish*) es hinter sich *acc* bringen.

▶ **get round** *vt fus* (*law, rule*) umgehen;
(*person*) herumkriegen.
▶ **get round to** *vt fus:* **to** ~ **round to doing sth**
dazu kommen, etw zu tun.
▶ **get through** *vi* (*TEL*) durchkommen ♦ *vt fus*
(*finish: work*) schaffen; (: *book*) lesen.
▶ **get through to** *vt fus* (*TEL*) durchkommen
zu; (*make o.s. understood*) durchdringen zu.
▶ **get together** *vi* (*people*)
zusammenkommen ♦ *vt* (*people*)
zusammenbringen; (*project, plan etc*)
zusammenstellen.
▶ **get up** *vi* (*rise*) aufstehen ♦ *vt:* **to** ~ **up
enthusiasm for sth** Begeisterung für etw
aufbringen.
▶ **get up to** *vt fus* (*prank etc*) anstellen.

getaway ['gɛtəweɪ] *n:* **to make a/one's** ~ sich
davonmachen.
getaway car *n* Fluchtauto *nt*.
get-together ['gɛttəgɛðə*] *n* Treffen *nt*;
(*party*) Party *f*.
get-up ['gɛtʌp] (*inf*) *n* Aufmachung *f*.
get-well card [gɛt'wɛl-] *n* Karte *f* mit
Genesungswünschen.
geyser ['giːzə*] *n* Geiser *m*; (*BRIT: water heater*)
Durchlauferhitzer *m*.
Ghana ['gɑːnə] *n* Ghana *nt*.
Ghanaian [gɑː'neɪən] *adj* ghanaisch ♦ *n*
Ghanaer(in) *m(f)*.
ghastly ['gɑːstlɪ] *adj* gräßlich; (*complexion*)
totenblaß; **you look** ~! (*ill*) du siehst
gräßlich aus!
gherkin ['gɜːkɪn] *n* Gewürzgurke *f*.
ghetto ['gɛtəʊ] *n* G(h)etto *nt*.
ghetto blaster [-'blɑːstə*] (*inf*) *n*
Ghettoblaster *m*.
ghost [gəʊst] *n* Geist *m*, Gespenst *nt* ♦ *vt* für
jdn (als Ghostwriter) schreiben; **to give up
the** ~ den Geist aufgeben.
ghost town *n* Geisterstadt *f*.
ghostwriter ['gəʊstraɪtə*] *n* Ghostwriter(in)
m(f).
ghoul [guːl] *n* böser Geist *m*.
ghoulish ['guːlɪʃ] *adj* makaber.
GHQ *n abbr* (*MIL:* = *general headquarters*)
Hauptquartier *nt*.
GI (*US: inf*) *n abbr* (= *government issue*) GI *m*.
giant ['dʒaɪənt] *n* (*also fig*) Riese *m* ♦ *adj* riesig,
riesenhaft; ~ (*size*) **packet** Riesenpackung *f*.
giant killer *n* (*fig*) Goliathbezwinger(in) *m(f)*.
gibber ['dʒɪbə*] *vi* brabbeln.
gibberish ['dʒɪbərɪʃ] *n* Quatsch *m*.
gibe [dʒaɪb] *n* spöttische Bemerkung *f* ♦ *vi:* **to**
~ **at** spöttische Bemerkungen machen über
+*acc*.
giblets ['dʒɪblɪts] *npl* Geflügelinnereien *pl*.
Gibraltar [dʒɪ'brɔːltə*] *n* Gibraltar *nt*.
giddiness ['gɪdɪnɪs] *n* Schwindelgefühl *nt*.
giddy ['gɪdɪ] *adj:* **I am/feel** ~ mir ist
schwind(e)lig; (*height*) schwindelerregend;
~ **with excitement** vor Aufregung ganz

ausgelassen.
gift [gɪft] n Geschenk nt; (donation) Spende f;
(COMM: also: **free ~**) (Werbe)geschenk nt;
(ability) Gabe f; **to have a ~ for sth** ein
Talent für etw haben.
gifted ['gɪftɪd] adj begabt.
gift token n Geschenkgutschein m.
gift voucher n = **gift token.**
gig [gɪg] (inf) n Konzert nt.
gigabyte ['dʒɪgəbaɪt] n (COMPUT) Gigabyte nt.
gigantic [dʒaɪˈgæntɪk] adj riesig, riesengroß.
giggle ['gɪgl] vi kichern ♦ n Spaß m; **to do sth
for a ~** etw aus Spaß tun.
GIGO ['gaɪgəʊ] (inf) abbr (COMPUT: = garbage
in, garbage out) GIGO.
gild [gɪld] vt vergolden.
gill [dʒɪl] n Gill nt (BRIT = 15 cl, US = 12 cl).
gills [gɪlz] npl Kiemen pl.
gilt [gɪlt] adj vergoldet ♦ n Vergoldung f;
gilts npl (COMM) mündelsichere
Wertpapiere pl.
gilt-edged ['gɪltɛdʒd] adj (stocks, securities)
mündelsicher.
gimlet ['gɪmlɪt] n Handbohrer m.
gimmick ['gɪmɪk] n Gag m; **sales ~**
Verkaufsmasche f, Verkaufstrick m.
gin [dʒɪn] n Gin m.
ginger ['dʒɪndʒə*] n Ingwer m ♦ adj (hair)
rötlich; (cat) rötlichgelb.
ginger ale n Ginger Ale nt.
ginger beer n Ingwerbier nt.
gingerbread ['dʒɪndʒəbrɛd] n (cake)
Ingwerkuchen m; (biscuit) ≈ Pfefferkuchen
m.
ginger group (BRIT) n Aktionsgruppe f.
gingerly ['dʒɪndʒəlɪ] adv vorsichtig.
gingham ['gɪŋəm] n Gingan m, Gingham m.
ginseng ['dʒɪnsɛŋ] n Ginseng m.
gipsy ['dʒɪpsɪ] n Zigeuner(in) m(f).
gipsy caravan n Zigeunerwagen m.
giraffe [dʒɪˈrɑːf] n Giraffe f.
girder ['gəːdə*] n Träger m.
girdle ['gəːdl] n Hüftgürtel m, Hüfthalter m
♦ vt (fig) umgeben.
girl [gəːl] n Mädchen nt; (young unmarried
woman) (junges) Mädchen nt; (daughter)
Tochter f; **this is my little ~** das ist mein
Töchterchen; **an English ~** eine
Engländerin.
girlfriend ['gəːlfrɛnd] n Freundin f.
Girl Guide n Pfadfinderin f.
girlish ['gəːlɪʃ] adj mädchenhaft.
Girl Scout (US) n Pfadfinderin f.
Giro ['dʒaɪrəʊ] n: **the National ~** (BRIT) der
Postscheckdienst.
giro ['dʒaɪrəʊ] n Giro nt, Giroverkehr m; (post
office giro) Postscheckverkehr m; (BRIT:
welfare cheque) Sozialhilfescheck m.
girth [gəːθ] n Umfang m; (of horse) Sattelgurt
m.
gist [dʒɪst] n Wesentliche(s) nt.

give [gɪv] (pt **gave,** pp **given**) vt **1** (hand over): **to
~ sb sth, ~ sth to sb** jdm etw geben; **I'll
~ you £5 for it** ich gebe dir £5 dafür
2 (used with noun to replace a verb): **to ~ a
sigh/cry/laugh** etc seufzen/schreien/lachen
etc; **to ~ a speech/a lecture** eine Rede/einen
Vortrag halten; **to ~ three cheers** ein
dreifaches Hoch ausbringen
3 (tell, deliver: news, message etc) mitteilen;
(: advice, answer) geben
4 (supply, provide: opportunity, job etc) geben;
(: surprise) bereiten; (bestow: title, honour,
right) geben, verleihen; **that's given me an
idea** dabei kommt mir eine Idee
5 (devote: time, one's life) geben; (: attention)
schenken
6 (organize: party, dinner etc) geben
♦ vi **1** (also: **~ way**: break, collapse) nachgeben
2 (stretch: fabric) sich dehnen.
► **give away** vt (money, opportunity)
verschenken; (secret, information) verraten;
(bride) zum Altar führen; **that immediately
gave him away** dadurch verriet er sich
sofort.
► **give back** vt (money, book etc)
zurückgeben.
► **give in** vi (yield) nachgeben ♦ vt (essay etc)
abgeben.
► **give off** vt (heat, smoke) abgeben.
► **give out** vt (prizes, books, drinks etc)
austeilen ♦ vi (be exhausted: supplies) zu
Ende gehen; (fail) versagen.
► **give up** vt, vi aufgeben; **to ~ up smoking**
das Rauchen aufgeben; **to ~ o.s. up** sich
stellen; (after siege etc) sich ergeben.
► **give way** vi (yield, collapse) nachgeben;
(BRIT: AUT) die Vorfahrt achten.

give-and-take ['gɪvəndˈteɪk] n (gegenseitiges)
Geben und Nehmen nt.
giveaway ['gɪvəweɪ] (inf) n: **her expression
was a ~** ihr Gesichtsausdruck verriet alles;
the exam was a ~! die Prüfung war
geschenkt!; **~ prices** Schleuderpreise pl.
given ['gɪvn] pp of **give** ♦ adj (time, amount)
bestimmt ♦ conj: **~ the circumstances ...**
unter den Umständen ...; **~ that ...**
angesichts der Tatsache, daß ...
glacial ['gleɪsɪəl] adj (landscape etc) Gletscher-;
(fig) eisig.
glacier ['glæsɪə*] n Gletscher m.
glad [glæd] adj froh; **to be ~ about sth** sich
über etw acc freuen; **to be ~ that** sich
freuen, daß; **I was ~ of his help** ich war froh
über seine Hilfe.
gladden ['glædn] vt erfreuen.
glade [gleɪd] n Lichtung f.
gladioli [glædɪˈəʊlaɪ] npl Gladiolen pl.
gladly ['glædlɪ] adv gern(e).
glamorous ['glæmərəs] adj reizvoll; (model

etc) glamourös.
glamour ['glæmə*] n Glanz m, Reiz m.
glance [glɑ:ns] n Blick m ♦ vi: **to ~ at** einen
Blick werfen auf *+acc*.
▶ **glance off** vt *fus* abprallen von.
glancing ['glɑ:nsɪŋ] adj: **to strike sth a ~ blow**
etw streifen.
gland [glænd] n Drüse f.
glandular fever ['glændjulə-] (*BRIT*) n
Drüsenfieber nt.
glare [gleə*] n wütender Blick m; (*of light*)
greller Schein m; (*of publicity*) grelles Licht
nt ♦ vi (*light*) grell scheinen; **to ~ at**
(*wütend*) anstarren.
glaring ['gleərɪŋ] adj eklatant.
glasnost ['glæznɔst] n Glasnost f.
glass [glɑ:s] n Glas nt; **glasses** npl (*spectacles*)
Brille f.
glass-blowing ['glɑ:sbləʊɪŋ] n Glasbläserei f.
glass ceiling n (*fig*) gläserne Decke f.
glass fibre n Glasfaser f.
glasshouse ['glɑ:shaus] n Gewächshaus nt.
glassware ['glɑ:sweə*] n Glaswaren pl.
glassy ['glɑ:sɪ] adj glasig.
Glaswegian [glæs'wi:dʒən] adj Glasgower ♦ n
Glasgower(in) m(f).
glaze [gleɪz] vt (*door, window*) verglasen;
(*pottery*) glasieren ♦ n Glasur f.
glazed [gleɪzd] adj (*eyes*) glasig; (*pottery, tiles*)
glasiert.
glazier ['gleɪzɪə*] n Glaser(in) m(f).
gleam [gli:m] vi (*light*) schimmern; (*polished
surface, eyes*) glänzen ♦ n: **a ~ of hope** ein
Hoffnungsschimmer m.
gleaming ['gli:mɪŋ] adj schimmernd,
glänzend.
glean [gli:n] vt (*information*)
herausbekommen, ausfindig machen.
glee [gli:] n Freude f.
gleeful ['gli:ful] adj fröhlich.
glen [glen] n Tal nt.
glib [glɪb] adj (*person*) glatt; (*promise,
response*) leichthin gemacht.
glibly ['glɪblɪ] adv (*talk*) gewandt; (*answer*)
leichthin.
glide [glaɪd] vi gleiten ♦ n Gleiten nt.
glider ['glaɪdə*] n Segelflugzeug nt.
gliding ['glaɪdɪŋ] n Segelfliegen nt.
glimmer ['glɪmə*] n Schimmer m; (*of interest,
hope*) Funke m ♦ vi schimmern.
glimpse [glɪmps] n Blick m ♦ vt einen Blick
werfen auf *+acc*; **to catch a ~ (of)** einen
flüchtigen Blick erhaschen (von *+dat*).
glint [glɪnt] vi glitzern; (*eyes*) funkeln ♦ n (*see
vb*) Glitzern nt; Funkeln nt.
glisten ['glɪsn] vi glänzen.
glitter ['glɪtə*] vi glitzern; (*eyes*) funkeln ♦ n
(*see vb*) Glitzern nt; Funkeln nt.
glittering ['glɪtərɪŋ] adj glitzernd; (*eyes*)
funkelnd; (*career*) glänzend.
glitz [glɪts] (*inf*) n Glanz m.
gloat [gləʊt] vi: **to ~ (over)** (*own success*) sich

brüsten (mit); (*sb's failure*) sich hämisch
freuen (über *+acc*).
global ['gləʊbl] adj global.
global warming [-'wɔ:mɪŋ] n Erwärmung f
der Erdatmosphäre.
globe [gləʊb] n Erdball m; (*model*) Globus m;
(*shape*) Kugel f.
globetrotter ['gləʊbtrɔtə*] n Globetrotter(in)
m(f), Weltenbummler(in) m(f).
globule ['glɔbju:l] n Tröpfchen nt.
gloom [glu:m] n Düsterkeit f; (*sadness*)
düstere *or* gedrückte Stimmung f.
gloomily ['glu:mɪlɪ] adv düster.
gloomy ['glu:mɪ] adj düster; (*person*)
bedrückt; (*situation*) bedrückend.
glorification [glɔ:rɪfɪ'keɪʃən] n
Verherrlichung f.
glorify ['glɔ:rɪfaɪ] vt verherrlichen.
glorious ['glɔ:rɪəs] adj herrlich; (*victory*)
ruhmreich; (*future*) glanzvoll.
glory ['glɔ:rɪ] n Ruhm m; (*splendour*)
Herrlichkeit f ♦ vi: **to ~ in** sich sonnen in
+dat.
glory hole (*inf*) n Rumpelkammer f.
Glos (*BRIT*) abbr (*POST*: = *Gloucestershire*).
gloss [glɔs] n Glanz m; (*also*: **~ paint**) Lack m,
Lackfarbe f.
▶ **gloss over** vt *fus* vom Tisch wischen.
glossary ['glɔsərɪ] n Glossar n.
glossy ['glɔsɪ] adj glänzend; (*photograph,
magazine*) Hochglanz- ♦ n (*also*: **~ magazine**)
(Hochglanz)magazin nt.
glove [glʌv] n Handschuh m.
glove compartment n Handschuhfach nt.
glow [gləʊ] vi glühen; (*stars, eyes*) leuchten ♦ n
(*see vb*) Glühen nt; Leuchten nt.
glower ['glaʊə*] vi: **to ~ at sb** jdn finster
ansehen.
glowing ['gləʊɪŋ] adj glühend; (*complexion*)
blühend; (*fig: report, description etc*)
begeistert.
glow-worm ['gləʊwə:m] n Glühwürmchen nt.
glucose ['glu:kəus] n Traubenzucker m.
glue [glu:] n Klebstoff m ♦ vt: **to ~ sth onto sth**
etw an etw *acc* kleben; **to ~ sth into place**
etw festkleben.
glue-sniffing ['glu:snɪfɪŋ] n (Klebstoff-)
Schnüffeln nt.
glum [glʌm] adj bedrückt, niedergeschlagen.
glut [glʌt] n: **~ (of)** Überangebot nt (an *+dat*)
♦ vt: **to be ~ted (with)** überschwemmt sein
(mit); **a ~ of pears** eine Birnenschwemme.
glutinous ['glu:tɪnəs] adj klebrig.
glutton ['glʌtn] n Vielfraß m; **a ~ for work** ein
Arbeitstier nt; **a ~ for punishment** ein
Masochist m.
gluttonous ['glʌtənəs] adj gefräßig.
gluttony ['glʌtənɪ] n Völlerei f.
glycerin(e) ['glɪsəri:n] n Glyzerin nt.
gm abbr (= *gram(me)*) g.
GMAT (*US*) n abbr (= *Graduate Management
Admissions Test*) Zulassungsprüfung für

Handelsschulen.

GMB (*BRIT*) *n abbr* (= *General Municipal and Boilermakers (Union)*) *Fabrikarbeitergewerkschaft.*

GMT *abbr* (= *Greenwich Mean Time*) WEZ *f.*

gnarled [nɑːld] *adj* (*tree*) knorrig; (*hand*) knotig.

gnash [næʃ] *vt:* to ~ one's teeth mit den Zähnen knirschen.

gnat [næt] *n* (Stech)mücke *f.*

gnaw [nɔː] *vt* nagen an +*dat* ♦ *vi* (*fig*): to ~ at quälen.

gnome [nəum] *n* Gnom *m*; (*in garden*) Gartenzwerg *m.*

GNP *n abbr* (= *gross national product*) BSP *nt.*

═══════════════════ *KEYWORD*

go [gəu] (*pt* **went**, *pp* **gone**) *vi* **1** gehen; (*travel*) fahren; **a car went by** ein Auto fuhr vorbei **2** (*depart*) gehen; **"I must ~,"** she said „ich muß gehen", sagte sie; **she has gone to Sheffield/Australia** (*permanently*) sie ist nach Sheffield/Australien gegangen **3** (*attend, take part in activity*) gehen; **she went to university in Oxford** sie ist in Oxford zur Universität gegangen; **to ~ for a walk** spazierengehen; **to ~ dancing** tanzen gehen **4** (*work*) funktionieren; **the tape recorder was still ~ing** das Tonband lief noch **5** (*become*): **to ~ pale/mouldy** blaß/schimmelig werden **6** (*be sold*): **to ~ for £100** für £100 weggehen *or* verkauft werden **7** (*be about to, intend to*): **we're ~ing to stop in an hour**, wir hören in einer Stunde auf; **are you ~ing to come?** kommst du?, wirst du kommen? **8** (*time*) vergehen **9** (*event, activity*) ablaufen; **how did it ~?** wie war's? **10** (*be given*): **the job is to ~ to someone else** die Stelle geht an jemand anders **11** (*break etc*) kaputtgehen; **the fuse went** die Sicherung ist durchgebrannt **12** (*be placed*) hingehören; **the milk goes in the fridge** die Milch kommt in den Kühlschrank

♦ *n* **1** (*try*): **to have a ~ at sth** etw versuchen; **I'll have a ~ at mending it** ich will versuchen, es zu reparieren; **to have a ~** es versuchen **2** (*turn*): **whose ~ is it?** wer ist dran *or* an der Reihe? **3** (*move*): **to be on the ~** auf Trab sein.

▶ **go about** *vi* (*also:* ~ **around**: *rumour*) herumgehen ♦ *vt fus:* **how do I ~ about this?** wie soll ich vorgehen?; **to ~ about one's business** seinen eigenen Geschäften nachgehen.

▶ **go after** *vt fus* (*pursue: person*) nachgehen +*dat*; (: *job etc*) sich bemühen um; (: *record*) erreichen wollen.

▶ **go against** *vt fus* (*be unfavourable to*) ungünstig verlaufen für; (*disregard: advice, wishes etc*) handeln gegen.

▶ **go ahead** *vi* (*proceed*) weitergehen; **to ~ ahead with** weitermachen mit.

▶ **go along** *vi* gehen.

▶ **go along with** *vt fus* (*agree with*) zustimmen +*dat*; (*accompany*) mitgehen mit.

▶ **go away** *vi* (*leave*) weggehen.

▶ **go back** *vi* zurückgehen.

▶ **go back on** *vt fus* (*promise*) zurücknehmen.

▶ **go by** *vi* (*years, time*) vergehen ♦ *vt fus* (*rule etc*) sich richten nach.

▶ **go down** *vi* (*descend*) hinuntergehen; (*ship, sun*) untergehen; (*price, level*) sinken ♦ *vt fus* (*stairs, ladder*) hinuntergehen; **went down well** seine Rede kam gut an.

▶ **go for** *vt fus* (*fetch*) holen (gehen); (*like*) mögen; (*attack*) losgehen auf +*acc*; (*apply to*) gelten für.

▶ **go in** *vi* (*enter*) hineingehen.

▶ **go in for** *vt fus* (*competition*) teilnehmen an +*dat*; (*favour*) stehen auf +*acc*.

▶ **go into** *vt fus* (*enter*) hineingehen in +*acc*; (*investigate*) sich befassen mit; (*career*) gehen in +*acc*.

▶ **go off** *vi* (*leave*) weggehen; (*food*) schlecht werden; (*bomb, gun*) losgehen; (*event*) verlaufen; (*lights etc*) ausgehen ♦ *vt fus* (*inf*): **I've gone off it/him** ich mache mir nichts mehr daraus/aus ihm; **the gun went off** das Gewehr ging los; **to ~ off to sleep** einschlafen; **the party went off well** die Party verlief gut.

▶ **go on** *vi* (*continue*) weitergehen; (*happen*) vor sich gehen; (*lights*) angehen ♦ *vt fus* (*be guided by*) sich stützen auf +*acc*; **to ~ on doing sth** mit etw weitermachen; **what's ~ing on here?** was geht hier vor?, was ist hier los?

▶ **go on at** (*inf*) *vt fus* (*nag*) herumnörgeln an +*dat*.

▶ **go on with** *vt fus* weitermachen mit.

▶ **go out** *vt fus* (*leave*) hinausgehen ♦ *vi* (*for entertainment*) ausgehen; (*fire, light*) ausgehen; (*couple*) **they went out for 3 years** sie gingen 3 Jahre lang miteinander.

▶ **go over** *vi* hinübergehen ♦ *vt* (*check*) durchgehen; **to ~ over sth in one's mind** etw überdenken.

▶ **go round** *vi* (*circulate: news, rumour*) umgehen; (*revolve*) sich drehen; (*suffice*) ausreichen; (*visit*): **to ~ round (to sb's)** (bei jdm) vorbeigehen; **there's not enough to ~ round** es reicht nicht (für alle).

▶ **go through** *vt fus* (*place*) gehen durch; (*by car*) fahren durch; (*undergo*) durchmachen; (*search through: files, papers*) durchsuchen; (*describe: list, book, story*) durchgehen; (*perform*) durchgehen.

▶ **go through with** *vt fus* (*plan, crime*) durchziehen; **I couldn't ~ through with it**

ich brachte es nicht fertig.
▶**go under** *vi* (*sink: person*) untergehen; (*fig: business, project*) scheitern.
▶**go up** *vi* (*ascend*) hinaufgehen; (*price, level*) steigen; **to ~ up in flames** in Flammen aufgehen.
▶**go with** *vt fus* (*suit*) passen zu.
▶**go without** *vt fus* (*food, treats*) verzichten auf +*acc*.

goad [gəud] *vt* aufreizen.
▶**goad on** *vt* anstacheln.
go-ahead ['gəuəhɛd] *adj* zielstrebig; (*firm*) fortschrittlich ♦ *n* grünes Licht *nt*; **to give sb the ~** jdm grünes Licht geben.
goal [gəul] *n* Tor *nt*; (*aim*) Ziel *nt*; **to score a ~** ein Tor schießen *or* erzielen.
goal difference *n* Tordifferenz *f*.
goalie ['gəulɪ] (*inf*) *n* Tormann *m*.
goalkeeper ['gəulkiːpə*] *n* Torwart *m*.
goal post *n* Torpfosten *m*.
goat [gəut] *n* Ziege *f*.
gobble ['gɔbl] *vt* (*also: ~ down, ~ up*) verschlingen.
go-between ['gəubɪtwiːn] *n* Vermittler(in) *m(f)*.
Gobi Desert ['gəubɪ-] *n*: **the ~** die Wüste Gobi.
goblet ['gɔblɪt] *n* Pokal *m*.
goblin ['gɔblɪn] *n* Kobold *m*.
go-cart ['gəukaːt] *n* Seifenkiste *f*.
God [gɔd] *n* Gott *m* ♦ *excl* o Gott!
god [gɔd] *n* Gott *m*.
god-awful [gɔd'ɔːfəl] (*inf*) *adj* beschissen (*!*).
godchild ['gɔdtʃaɪld] *n* Patenkind *nt*.
goddamn(ed) ['gɔddæm(d)] (*US: inf*) *adj* gottverdammt.
goddaughter ['gɔddɔːtə*] *n* Patentochter *f*.
goddess ['gɔdɪs] *n* Göttin *f*.
godfather ['gɔdfaːðə*] *n* Pate *m*.
God-fearing ['gɔdfɪərɪŋ] *adj* gottesfürchtig.
godforsaken ['gɔdfəseɪkən] *adj* gottverlassen.
godmother ['gɔdmʌðə*] *n* Patin *f*.
godparent ['gɔdpɛərənt] *n* Pate *m*, Patin *f*.
godsend ['gɔdsɛnd] *n* Geschenk *nt* des Himmels.
godson ['gɔdsʌn] *n* Patensohn *m*.
goes [gəuz] *vb see* go.
gofer ['gəufə*] (*inf*) *n* Mädchen *nt* für alles.
go-getter ['gəugɛtə*] (*inf*) *n* Ellbogentyp (*pej, inf*) *m*.
goggle ['gɔgl] (*inf*) *vi*: **to ~ at** anstarren, anglotzen.
goggles ['gɔglz] *npl* Schutzbrille *f*.
going ['gəuɪŋ] *n*: **it was slow/hard ~** (*fig*) es ging nur langsam/schwer voran ♦ *adj*: **the ~ rate** der gängige Preis; **when the ~ gets tough** wenn es schwierig wird; **a ~ concern** ein gutgehendes Unternehmen.
going-over ['gəuɪŋ'əuvə*] (*inf*) *n* (*check*) Untersuchung *f*; (*beating-up*) Abreibung *f*; **to give sb a good ~** jdm eine tüchtige

Abreibung verpassen.
goings-on ['gəuɪŋz'ɔn] (*inf*) *npl* Vorgänge *pl*, Dinge *pl*.
go-kart ['gəukaːt] *n* = go-cart.
gold [gəuld] *n* Gold *nt*; (*also: ~ medal*) Gold *nt*, Goldmedaille *f* ♦ *adj* golden; (*reserves, jewellery, tooth*) Gold-.
golden ['gəuldən] *adj* (*also fig*) golden.
golden age *n* Blütezeit *f*.
golden handshake (*BRIT*) *n* Abstandssumme *f*.
golden rule *n* goldene Regel *f*.
goldfish ['gəuldfɪʃ] *n* Goldfisch *m*.
gold leaf *n* Blattgold *nt*.
gold medal *n* Goldmedaille *f*.
gold mine *n* (*also fig*) Goldgrube *f*.
gold-plated ['gəuld'pleɪtɪd] *adj* vergoldet.
goldsmith ['gəuldsmɪθ] *n* Goldschmied(in) *m(f)*.
gold standard *n* Goldstandard *m*.
golf [gɔlf] *n* Golf *nt*.
golf ball *n* (*for game*) Golfball *m*; (*on typewriter*) Kugelkopf *m*.
golf club *n* Golfklub *m*; (*stick*) Golfschläger *m*.
golf course *n* Golfplatz *m*.
golfer ['gɔlfə*] *n* Golfspieler(in) *m(f)*, Golfer(in) *m(f)*.
golfing ['gɔlfɪŋ] *n* Golf(spielen) *nt*; **he does a lot of ~** er spielt viel Golf ♦ *cpd* Golf-.
gondola ['gɔndələ] *n* Gondel *f*.
gondolier [gɔndə'lɪə*] *n* Gondoliere *m*.
gone [gɔn] *pp of* go ♦ *adj* weg; (*days*) vorbei.
goner ['gɔnə*] (*inf*) *n*: **to be a ~** hinüber sein.
gong [gɔŋ] *n* Gong *m*.
good [gud] *adj* gut; (*well-behaved*) brav, lieb ♦ *n* (*virtue, morality*) Gute(s) *nt*; (*benefit*) Wohl *nt*; **goods** *npl* (*COMM*) Güter *pl*; **to have a ~ time** sich (gut) amüsieren; **to be ~ at sth** (*swimming, talking etc*) etw gut können; (*science, sports etc*) gut in etw *dat* sein; **to be ~ for sb/sth** gut für jdn/zu etw *dat* sein; **it's ~ for you** das tut dir gut; **it's a ~ thing you were there** gut, daß Sie da waren; **she is ~ with children** sie kann gut mit Kindern umgehen; **she is ~ with her hands** sie ist geschickt; **to feel ~** sich wohlfühlen; **it's ~ to see you** (es ist) schön, Sie zu sehen; **would you be ~ enough to ...?** könnten Sie bitte ...?; **that's very ~ of you** das ist wirklich nett von Ihnen; **a ~ deal (of)** ziemlich viel; **a ~ many** ziemlich viele; **take a ~ look** sieh dir das genau *or* gut an; **a ~ while ago** vor einiger Zeit; **to make ~** (*damage*) wiedergutmachen; (*loss*) ersetzen; **it's no ~ complaining** es ist sinnlos *or* es nützt nichts, sich zu beklagen; **~ morning/afternoon/evening!** guten Morgen/Tag/Abend!; **~ night!** gute Nacht!; **he's up to no ~** er führt nichts Gutes im Schilde; **for the common ~** zum Wohle aller; **is this any ~?** (*will it help you?*) können Sie das

gebrauchen?; (*is it good enough?*) reicht das?; **is the book/film any ~?** was halten Sie von dem Buch/Film?; **for ~** für immer; **~s and chattels** Hab und Gut nt.

goodbye [gud'baɪ] excl auf Wiedersehen!; **to say ~** sich verabschieden.

good-for-nothing ['gudfənʌθɪŋ] adj nichtsnutzig.

Good Friday n Karfreitag m.

good-humoured ['gud'hju:məd] adj gut gelaunt; (*good-natured*) gutmütig; (*remark, joke*) harmlos.

good-looking ['gud'lukɪŋ] adj gutaussehend.

good-natured ['gud'neɪtʃəd] adj gutmütig; (*discussion*) freundlich.

goodness ['gudnɪs] n Güte f; **for ~ sake!** um Himmels willen!; **~ gracious!** ach du liebe or meine Güte!

goods train (*BRIT*) n Güterzug m.

goodwill [gud'wɪl] n Wohlwollen nt; (*COMM*) Goodwill m.

goody ['gudɪ] (*inf*) n Gute(r) m, Held m.

goody-goody ['gudɪgudɪ] (*pej*) n Tugendlamm nt, Musterkind (*inf*) nt.

gooey ['gu:ɪ] (*inf*) adj (*sticky*) klebrig; (*cake*) üppig; (*fig: sentimental*) rührselig.

goose [gu:s] (*pl* **geese**) n Gans f.

gooseberry ['guzbərɪ] n Stachelbeere f; **to play ~** (*BRIT*) das fünfte Rad am Wagen sein.

goose flesh n = **goose pimples**.

goose pimples npl Gänsehaut f.

goose step n Stechschritt m.

GOP (*US: inf*) n abbr (*POL:* = *Grand Old Party*) Republikanische Partei.

gopher ['gəufə*] n (*ZOOL*) Taschenratte f.

gore [gɔ:*] vt aufspießen ♦ n Blut nt.

gorge [gɔ:dʒ] n Schlucht f ♦ vt: **to ~ o.s. (on)** sich vollstopfen (mit).

gorgeous ['gɔ:dʒəs] adj herrlich; (*person*) hinreißend.

gorilla [gə'rɪlə] n Gorilla m.

gormless ['gɔ:mlɪs] (*BRIT: inf*) adj doof.

gorse [gɔ:s] n Stechginster m.

gory ['gɔ:rɪ] adj blutig.

go-slow [gəu'sləu] (*BRIT*) n Bummelstreik m.

gospel ['gɔspl] n Evangelium nt; (*doctrine*) Lehre f.

gossamer ['gɔsəmə*] n Spinnfäden pl; (*light fabric*) hauchdünne Gaze f.

gossip ['gɔsɪp] n (*rumours*) Klatsch m, Tratsch m; (*chat*) Schwatz m; (*person*) Klatschbase f ♦ vi schwatzen; **a piece of ~** eine Neuigkeit.

gossip column n Klatschkolumne f, Klatschspalte f.

got [gɔt] pt, pp of **get**.

Gothic ['gɔθɪk] adj gotisch.

gotten ['gɔtn] (*US*) pp of **get**.

gouge [gaudʒ] vt (*also:* **~ out:** *hole etc*) bohren; (*: initials*) eingravieren; **to ~ sb's eyes out** jdm die Augen ausstechen.

gourd [guəd] n (*container*) Kürbisflasche f.

gourmet ['guəmeɪ] n Feinschmecker(in) m(f), Gourmet m.

gout [gaut] n Gicht f.

govern ['gʌvən] vt (*also LING*) regieren; (*event, conduct*) bestimmen.

governess ['gʌvənɪs] n Gouvernante f.

governing ['gʌvənɪŋ] adj (*POL*) regierend.

governing body n Vorstand m.

government ['gʌvnmənt] n Regierung f ♦ cpd Regierungs-; **local ~** Kommunalverwaltung f, Gemeindeverwaltung f.

governmental [gʌvn'mentl] adj Regierungs-.

government stocks npl Staatspapiere pl, Staatsanleihen pl.

governor ['gʌvənə*] n Gouverneur(in) m(f); (*of bank, hospital, BRIT: of prison*) Direktor(in) m(f); (*of school*) ≈ Mitglied nt des Schulbeirats.

Govt abbr = **government**.

gown [gaun] n (*Abend)kleid nt; (*of teacher, BRIT: of judge*) Robe f.

GP n abbr = **general practitioner**.

GPMU (*BRIT*) n abbr (= *Graphical Paper and Media Union*) Grafiker- und Druckergewerkschaft.

GPO n abbr (*BRIT: formerly:* = *general post office*) Postbehörde f; (*US:* = *Government Printing Office*) regierungsamtliche Druckanstalt.

gr. abbr (*COMM*) = **gross**; (= *gram(me)*) g.

grab [græb] vt packen; (*chance, opportunity*) (beim Schopf) ergreifen ♦ vi: **to ~ at** greifen or grapschen nach +dat; **to ~ some food** schnell etwas essen; **to ~ a few hours sleep** ein paar Stunden schlafen.

grace [greɪs] n Gnade f; (*gracefulness*) Anmut f ♦ vt (*honour*) beehren; (*adorn*) zieren; **5 days' ~** 5 Tage Aufschub; **with (a) good ~** anstandslos; **with (a) bad ~** widerwillig; **his sense of humour is his saving ~** was einen mit ihm versöhnt, ist sein Sinn für Humor; **to say ~** das Tischgebet sprechen.

graceful ['greɪsful] adj anmutig; (*style, shape*) gefällig; (*refusal, behaviour*) charmant.

gracious ['greɪʃəs] adj (*kind, courteous*) liebenswürdig; (*compassionate*) gnädig; (*smile*) freundlich; (*house, mansion etc*) stilvoll; (*living etc*) kultiviert ♦ excl: **(good) ~!** (ach) du meine Güte!, (ach du) lieber Himmel!

gradation [grə'deɪʃən] n Abstufung f.

grade [greɪd] n (*COMM*) (Güte)klasse f; (*in hierarchy*) Rang m; (*SCOL: mark*) Note f; (*US: school class*) Klasse f; (*: gradient: upward*) Neigung f, Steigung f; (*: : downward*) Neigung f, Gefälle nt ♦ vt klassifizieren; (*work, student*) einstufen; **to make the ~** (*fig*) es schaffen.

grade crossing (*US*) n Bahnübergang m.

grade school (*US*) n Grundschule f.

gradient ['greɪdɪənt] n (*upward*) Neigung f, Steigung f; (*downward*) Neigung, Gefälle nt;

(*GEOM*) Gradient *m*.
gradual ['grædjuəl] *adj* allmählich.
gradually ['grædjuəlɪ] *adv* allmählich.
graduate [*n* 'grædjuɪt, *vi* 'grædjueɪt] *n* (*of university*) Hochschulabsolvent(in) *m(f)*; (*US: of high school*) Schulabgänger(in) *m(f)* ♦ *vi* (*from university*) graduieren; (*US*) die (Schul)abschlußprüfung bestehen.
graduated pension ['grædjueɪtɪd-] *n* gestaffelte Rente *f*.
graduation [grædju'eɪʃən] *n* (Ab)schlußfeier *f*.
graffiti [grə'fiːtɪ] *n*, *npl* Graffiti *pl*.
graft [grɑːft] *n* (*AGR*) (Pfropf)reis *nt*; (*MED*) Transplantat *nt*; (*BRIT: inf: hard work*) Schufterei *f*; (*bribery*) Schiebung *f* ♦ *vt*: **to ~ (onto)** (*AGR*) (auf)pfropfen (auf +*acc*); (*MED*) übertragen (auf +*acc*), einpflanzen (in +*acc*); (*fig*) aufpfropfen +*dat*.
grain [greɪn] *n* Korn *nt*; (*no pl: cereals*) Getreide *nt*; (*US: corn*) Getreide *nt*, Korn; (*of wood*) Maserung *f*; **it goes against the ~** (*fig*) es geht einem gegen den Strich.
gram [græm] *n* Gramm *nt*.
grammar ['græmə*] *n* Grammatik *f*, Sprachlehre *f*.
grammar school (*BRIT*) *n* ≈ Gymnasium *nt*.
grammatical [grə'mætɪkl] *adj* grammat(ikal)isch.
gramme [græm] *n* = **gram**.
gramophone ['græməfəun] (*BRIT*) *n* Grammophon *nt*.
granary ['grænərɪ] *n* Kornspeicher *m*; ® (*Granary*): **G~ bread/loaf** Körnerbrot *nt*.
grand [grænd] *adj* großartig; (*inf: wonderful*) phantastisch ♦ *n* (*inf*) ≈ Riese *m* (*1000 Pfund/ Dollar*).
grandchild ['grænt ʃaɪld] (*irreg: like* **child**) *n* Enkelkind *nt*, Enkel(in) *m(f)*.
granddad ['grændæd] (*inf*) *n* Opa *m*.
granddaughter ['grændɔːtə*] *n* Enkelin *f*.
grandeur ['grændjə*] *n* (*of scenery etc*) Erhabenheit *f*; (*of building*) Vornehmheit *f*.
grandfather ['grændfɑːðə*] *n* Großvater *m*.
grandiose ['grændɪəus] (*also pej*) *adj* grandios.
grand jury (*US*) *n* Großes Geschworenengericht *nt*.
grandma ['grænmɑː] (*inf*) *n* Oma *f*.
grandmother ['grænmʌðə*] *n* Großmutter *f*.
grandpa ['grænpɑː] (*inf*) *n* Opa *m*.
grandparents ['grændpɛərənts] *npl* Großeltern *pl*.
grand piano *n* Flügel *m*.
Grand Prix ['grɑ̃ːpriː] *n* (*AUT*) Grand Prix *m*.
grandson ['grænsʌn] *n* Enkel *m*.
grandstand ['grændstænd] *n* Haupttribüne *f*.
grand total *n* Gesamtsumme *f*, Endsumme *f*.
granite ['grænɪt] *n* Granit *m*.
granny ['grænɪ] (*inf*) *n* Oma *f*.
grant [grɑːnt] *vt* (*money*) bewilligen; (*request etc*) gewähren; (*visa*) erteilen; (*admit*) zugeben ♦ *n* Stipendium *nt*; (*subsidy*)

Subvention *f*; **to take sth for ~ed** etw für selbstverständlich halten; **to take sb for ~ed** jdn als selbstverständlich hinnehmen; **to ~ that** zugeben, daß.
granulated sugar ['grænjuleɪtɪd-] *n* (Zucker)raffinade *f*.
granule ['grænjuːl] *n* Körnchen *nt*.
grape [greɪp] *n* (Wein)traube *f*; **a bunch of ~s** eine (ganze) Weintraube.
grapefruit ['greɪpfruːt] (*pl ~ or ~s*) *n* Pampelmuse *f*, Grapefruit *f*.
grapevine ['greɪpvaɪn] *n* Weinstock *m*; **I heard it on the ~** (*fig*) es ist mir zu Ohren gekommen.
graph [grɑːf] *n* (*diagram*) graphische *or* grafische Darstellung *f*, Schaubild *nt*.
graphic ['græfɪk] *adj* plastisch, anschaulich; (*art, design*) graphisch, grafisch; *see also* **graphics**.
graphic designer *n* Graphiker(in) *m(f)*, Grafiker(in) *m(f)*.
graphic equalizer [-iːkwəlaɪzə*] *n* (Graphic) Equalizer *m*.
graphics ['græfɪks] *n* Graphik *f*, Grafik *f* ♦ *npl* (*drawings*) Zeichnungen *pl*, graphische *or* grafische Darstellungen *pl*.
graphite ['græfaɪt] *n* Graphit *m*.
graph paper *n* Millimeterpapier *nt*.
grapple ['græpl] *vi*: **to ~ with sb/sth** mit jdm/ etw kämpfen; **to ~ with a problem** sich mit einem Problem herumschlagen.
grasp [grɑːsp] *vt* (*seize*) ergreifen; (*hold*) festhalten; (*understand*) begreifen ♦ *n* Griff *m*; (*understanding*) Verständnis *nt*; **it slipped from my ~** es entglitt mir; **to have sth within one's ~** etw in greifbarer Nähe haben; **to have a good ~ of sth** (*fig*) etw gut beherrschen.
▶**grasp at** *vt fus* greifen nach; (*fig: opportunity*) ergreifen.
grasping ['grɑːspɪŋ] *adj* habgierig.
grass [grɑːs] *n* Gras *nt*; (*lawn*) Rasen *m*; (*BRIT: inf: informer*) (Polizei)spitzel *m*.
grasshopper ['grɑːshɔpə*] *n* Grashüpfer *m*, Heuschrecke *f*.
grass-roots ['grɑːsruːts] *npl* (*of party etc*) Basis *f* ♦ *adj* (*opinion*) des kleinen Mannes; **at ~ level** an der Basis.
grass snake *n* Ringelnatter *f*.
grassy ['grɑːsɪ] *adj* Gras-, grasig.
grate [greɪt] *n* (Feuer)rost *m* ♦ *vt* reiben; (*carrots etc*) raspeln ♦ *vi*: **to ~ (on)** kratzen (auf +*dat*).
grateful ['greɪtful] *adj* dankbar; (*thanks*) aufrichtig.
gratefully ['greɪtfəlɪ] *adv* dankbar.
grater ['greɪtə*] *n* Reibe *f*.
gratification [grætɪfɪ'keɪʃən] *n* (*pleasure*) Genugtuung *f*; (*satisfaction*) Befriedigung *f*.
gratify ['grætɪfaɪ] *vt* (*please*) erfreuen; (*satisfy*) befriedigen.
gratifying ['grætɪfaɪɪŋ] *adj* (*see vt*) erfreulich;

befriedigend.
grating ['greɪtɪŋ] n Gitter nt ♦ adj (noise)
knirschend; (voice) schrill.
gratitude ['grætɪtjuːd] n Dankbarkeit f.
gratuitous [grəˈtjuːɪtəs] adj unnötig.
gratuity [grəˈtjuːɪtɪ] n Trinkgeld nt.
grave [greɪv] n Grab nt ♦ adj (decision, mistake)
schwer(wiegend); (expression, person) ernst.
grave digger n Totengräber m.
gravel ['grævl] n Kies m.
gravely ['greɪvlɪ] adv (see adj) schwer, ernst;
~ **ill** schwerkrank.
gravestone ['greɪvstəun] n Grabstein m.
graveyard ['greɪvjɑːd] n Friedhof m.
gravitas ['grævɪtæs] n Seriosität f.
gravitate ['grævɪteɪt] vi: **to ~ towards**
angezogen werden von.
gravity ['grævɪtɪ] n Schwerkraft f;
(seriousness) Ernst m, Schwere f.
gravy ['greɪvɪ] n (juice) (Braten)saft m; (sauce)
(Braten)soße f.
gravy boat n Sauciere f, Soßenschüssel f.
gravy train (inf) n: **to ride the ~** leichtes Geld
machen.
gray [greɪ] (US) adj = **grey**.
graze [greɪz] vi grasen, weiden ♦ vt streifen;
(scrape) aufschürfen ♦ n (MED)
Abschürfung f.
grazing ['greɪzɪŋ] n Weideland nt.
grease [griːs] n (lubricant) Schmiere f; (fat)
Fett nt ♦ vt (see n) schmieren; fetten; **to**
~ **the skids** (US, fig) die Maschinerie in
Gang halten.
grease gun n Fettspritze f, Fettpresse f.
greasepaint ['griːspeɪnt] n (Fett)schminke f.
greaseproof paper ['griːspruːf-] (BRIT) n
Pergamentpapier nt.
greasy ['griːsɪ] adj fettig; (food: containing
grease) fett; (tools) schmierig, ölig; (clothes)
speckig; (BRIT: road, surface) glitschig,
schlüpfrig.
great [greɪt] adj groß; (city) bedeutend; (inf:
terrific) prima, toll; **they're ~ friends** sie sind
gute Freunde; **we had a ~ time** wir haben
uns glänzend amüsiert; **it was ~!** es war
toll!; **the ~ thing is that ...** das Wichtigste
ist, daß ...
Great Barrier Reef n: **the ~** das Große
Barriereriff.
Great Britain n Großbritannien nt.
greater ['greɪtə˙] adj see **great**; größer;
bedeutender; **people in G~ Calcutta** die
Leute in Kalkutta und Umgebung;
G~ Manchester Groß-Manchester nt.
great-grandchild [greɪtˈgræntʃaɪld] (irreg: like
child) n Urenkel(in) m(f).
great-grandfather [greɪtˈgrænfɑːðə˙] n
Urgroßvater m.
great-grandmother [greɪtˈgrænmʌðə˙] n
Urgroßmutter f.
Great Lakes npl: **the ~** die Großen Seen pl.
greatly ['greɪtlɪ] adv sehr; (influenced) stark.

greatness ['greɪtnɪs] n Bedeutung f.
Grecian ['griːʃən] adj griechisch.
Greece [griːs] n Griechenland nt.
greed [griːd] n (also: ~iness): ~ **for** Gier f
nach; ~ **for power** Machtgier f; ~ **for money**
Geldgier f.
greedily ['griːdɪlɪ] adv gierig.
greedy ['griːdɪ] adj gierig.
Greek [griːk] adj griechisch ♦ n Grieche m,
Griechin f; (LING) Griechisch nt; **ancient/
modern ~** Alt-/Neugriechisch nt.
green [griːn] adj (also ecological) grün ♦ n (also
GOLF) Grün nt; (stretch of grass) Rasen m,
Grünfläche f; (also: **village ~**) Dorfwiese f,
Anger m; **greens** npl (vegetables)
Grüngemüse nt; (POL): **the G~s** die Grünen
pl; **to have ~ fingers** or (US) **a ~ thumb** (fig)
eine Hand für Pflanzen haben; **to give sb
the ~ light** jdm grünes Licht geben.
green belt n Grüngürtel m.
green card n (AUT) grüne (Versicherungs)karte f; (US) ≈ Aufenthaltserlaubnis
f.
greenery ['griːnərɪ] n Grün nt.
greenfly ['griːnflaɪ] (BRIT) n Blattlaus f.
greengage ['griːngeɪdʒ] n Reineclaude f,
Reneklode f.
greengrocer ['griːngrəusə˙] (BRIT) n Obst- und
Gemüsehändler(in) m(f).
greenhouse ['griːnhaus] n Gewächshaus nt,
Treibhaus nt; ~ **effect** Treibhauseffekt m;
~ **gas** Treibhausgas nt.
greenish ['griːnɪʃ] adj grünlich.
Greenland ['griːnlənd] n Grönland nt.
Greenlander ['griːnləndə˙] n Grönländer(in)
m(f).
green light n grünes Licht nt; **to give sb the
~** jdm grünes Licht or freie Fahrt geben.
Green Party n (POL): **the ~** die Grünen pl.
green pepper n grüne Paprikaschote f.
green pound n grünes Pfund nt.
greet [griːt] vt begrüßen; (news) aufnehmen.
greeting ['griːtɪŋ] n Gruß m; (welcome)
Begrüßung f; **Christmas ~s**
Weihnachtsgrüße pl; **birthday ~s**
Geburtstagsglückwünsche pl; **Season's ~s**
Frohe Weihnachten und ein glückliches
Neues Jahr.
greeting(s) card n Grußkarte f;
(congratulating) Glückwunschkarte f.
gregarious [grəˈgeərɪəs] adj gesellig.
grenade [grəˈneɪd] n (also: **hand ~**)
(Hand)granate f.
grew [gruː] pt of **grow**.
grey, ** (US) **gray [greɪ] adj grau; (dismal) trüb,
grau; **to go ~** grau werden.
grey-haired [greɪˈheəd] adj grauhaarig.
greyhound ['greɪhaund] n Windhund m.
grid [grɪd] n Gitter nt; (ELEC) (Verteiler)netz
nt; (US: AUT: intersection) Kreuzung f.
griddle [grɪdl] n gußeiserne Pfanne zum
Braten und Pfannkuchenbacken.

gridiron ['grɪdaɪən] *n* Bratrost *m*.
gridlock ['grɪdlɔk] *n* (*esp US: on road*) totaler Stau *m*; (*stalemate*) Patt *nt* ♦ *vt*: **to be ~ed** (*roads*) total verstopft sein; (*talks etc*) festgefahren sein.
grief [griːf] *n* Kummer *m*, Trauer *f*; **to come to ~** (*plan*) scheitern; (*person*) zu Schaden kommen; **good ~!** ach du liebe Gute!
grievance ['griːvəns] *n* Beschwerde *f*; (*feeling of resentment*) Groll *m*.
grieve [griːv] *vi* trauern ♦ *vt* Kummer bereiten +*dat*, betrüben; **to ~ for** trauern um.
grievous ['griːvəs] *adj* (*mistake*) schwer; (*situation*) beträchtlich; **~ bodily harm** (*LAW*) schwere Körperverletzung *f*.
grill [grɪl] *n* Grill *m*; (*grilled food: also:* **mixed ~**) Grillgericht *nt*; (*restaurant*) = **grillroom** ♦ *vt* (*BRIT*) grillen; (*inf: question*) in die Zange nehmen, ausquetschen.
grille [grɪl] *n* (*screen*) Gitter *nt*; (*AUT*) Kühlergrill *m*.
grillroom ['grɪlrum] *n* Grillrestaurant *nt*.
grim [grɪm] *adj* trostlos; (*serious, stern*) grimmig.
grimace [grɪ'meɪs] *n* Grimasse *f* ♦ *vi* Grimassen schneiden.
grime [graɪm] *n* Dreck *m*, Schmutz *m*.
grimy ['graɪmɪ] *adj* dreckig, schmutzig.
grin [grɪn] *n* Grinsen *nt* ♦ *vi* grinsen; **to ~ at sb** jdn angrinsen.
grind [graɪnd] (*pt, pp* ground) *vt* zerkleinern; (*coffee, pepper etc*) mahlen; (*US: meat*) hacken, durch den Fleischwolf drehen; (*knife*) schleifen, wetzen; (*gem, lens*) schleifen ♦ *vi* (*car gears*) knirschen ♦ *n* (*work*) Schufterei *f*; **to ~ one's teeth** mit den Zähnen knirschen; **to ~ to a halt** (*vehicle*) quietschend zum Stehen kommen; (*fig: talks, scheme*) sich festfahren; (*work*) stocken; (*production*) zum Erliegen kommen; **the daily ~** (*inf*) der tägliche Trott.
grinder ['graɪndə*] *n* (*for coffee*) Kaffeemühle *f*; (*for waste disposal etc*) Müllzerkleine- rungsanlage *f*.
grindstone ['graɪndstəun] *n*: **to keep one's nose to the ~** hart arbeiten.
grip [grɪp] *n* Griff *m*; (*of tyre, shoe*) Halt *m*; (*holdall*) Reisetasche *f* ♦ *vt* packen; (*audience, attention*) fesseln; **to come to ~s with sth** etw in den Griff bekommen; **to lose one's ~** den Halt verlieren; (*fig*) nachlassen; **to ~ the road** (*car*) gut auf der Straße liegen.
gripe [graɪp] (*inf*) *n* (*complaint*) Meckerei *f* ♦ *vi* meckern; **the ~s** (*MED*) Kolik *f*, Bauchschmerzen *pl*.
gripping ['grɪpɪŋ] *adj* fesselnd, packend.
grisly ['grɪzlɪ] *adj* gräßlich, grausig.
grist [grɪst] *n* (*fig*): **it's all ~ to the mill** das kann man alles verwerten.
gristle ['grɪsl] *n* Knorpel *m*.
grit [grɪt] *n* (*for icy roads: sand*) Sand *m*;

(*crushed stone*) Splitt *m*; (*determination, courage*) Mut *m* ♦ *vt* (*road*) streuen; **grits** *npl* (*US*) Grütze *f*, **I've got a piece of ~ in my eye** ich habe ein Staubkorn im Auge; **to ~ one's teeth** die Zähne zusammenbeißen.
grizzle ['grɪzl] (*BRIT*) *vi* quengeln.
grizzly ['grɪzlɪ] *n* (*also:* **~ bear**) Grislybär *m*, Grizzlybär *m*.
groan [grəun] *n* Stöhnen *nt* ♦ *vi* stöhnen; (*tree, floorboard etc*) ächzen, knarren.
grocer ['grəusə*] *n* Lebensmittelhändler(in) *m(f)*.
groceries ['grəusərɪz] *npl* Lebensmittel *pl*.
grocer's (shop) *n* Lebensmittelgeschäft *nt*.
grog [grɔg] *n* Grog *m*.
groggy ['grɔgɪ] *adj* angeschlagen.
groin [grɔɪn] *n* Leistengegend *f*.
groom [gruːm] *n* Stallbursche *m*; (*also:* **bride~**) Bräutigam *m* ♦ *vt* (*horse*) striegeln; (*fig*): **to ~ sb for** (*job*) jdn aufbauen für; **well-~ed** gepflegt.
groove [gruːv] *n* Rille *f*.
grope [grəup] *vi*: **to ~ for** tasten nach; (*fig: try to think of*) suchen nach.
grosgrain ['grəugreɪn] *n* grob gerippter Stoff *m*.
gross [grəus] *adj* (*neglect*) grob; (*injustice*) kraß; (*behaviour, speech*) grob, derb; (*COMM: income, weight*) Brutto- ♦ *n inv* Gros *nt* ♦ *vt*: **to ~ £500,000** £500 000 brutto einnehmen.
gross domestic product *n* Bruttoinlandsprodukt *nt*.
grossly ['grəuslɪ] *adv* äußerst; (*exaggerated*) grob.
gross national product *n* Bruttosozialprodukt *nt*.
grotesque [grə'tɛsk] *adj* grotesk.
grotto ['grɔtəu] *n* Grotte *f*.
grotty ['grɔtɪ] (*inf*) *adj* mies.
grouch [grautʃ] (*inf*) *vi* schimpfen ♦ *n* (*person*) Miesepeter *m*, Muffel *m*.
ground [graund] *pt, pp of* grind ♦ *n* Boden *m*, Erde *f*; (*land*) Land *nt*; (*SPORT*) Platz *m*, Feld *nt*; (*US: ELEC: also:* **~ wire**) Erde *f*; (*reason: gen pl*) Grund *m* ♦ *vt* (*plane*) aus dem Verkehr ziehen; (*US: ELEC*) erden ♦ *adj* (*coffee etc*) gemahlen ♦ *vi* (*ship*) auflaufen; **grounds** *npl* (*of coffee etc*) Satz *m*; (*gardens etc*) Anlagen *pl*; **below ~** unter der Erde; **to gain/lose ~** Boden gewinnen/verlieren; **common ~** Gemeinsame(s) *nt*; **on the ~s that** mit der Begründung, daß.
ground cloth (*US*) *n* = **groundsheet**.
ground control *n* (*AVIAT, SPACE*) Bodenkontrolle *f*.
ground floor *n* Erdgeschoß *nt*.
grounding ['graundɪŋ] *n* (*in education*) Grundwissen *nt*.
groundless ['graundlɪs] *adj* grundlos, unbegründet.
groundnut ['graundnʌt] *n* Erdnuß *f*.
ground rent (*BRIT*) *n* Erbbauzins *m*.

ground rule n Grundregel f.
groundsheet ['graundʃiːt] (BRIT) n Zeltboden m.
groundskeeper ['graundzkiːpə*] (US) n = **groundsman**.
groundsman ['graundzmən] (irreg: like **man**) n (SPORT) Platzwart m.
ground staff n (AVIAT) Bodenpersonal nt.
ground swell n: **there was a ~ of public opinion against him** die Öffentlichkeit wandte sich gegen ihn.
ground-to-air missile ['graundtə'ɛə*-] n Boden-Luft-Rakete f.
ground-to-ground missile ['graundtə'graund-] n Boden-Boden-Rakete f.
groundwork ['graundwəːk] n Vorarbeit f.
group [gruːp] n Gruppe f; (COMM) Konzern m ♦ vt (also: ~ **together**: in one group) zusammentun; (: in several groups) in Gruppen einteilen ♦ vi (also: ~ **together**) sich zusammentun.
groupie ['gruːpɪ] (inf) n Groupie nt.
group therapy n Gruppentherapie f.
grouse [graus] n inv schottisches Moorhuhn nt ♦ vi (complain) schimpfen.
grove [grəuv] n Hain m, Wäldchen nt.
grovel ['grɔvl] vi (crawl) kriechen; (fig): **to ~ (before)** kriechen (vor +dat).
grow [grəu] (pt **grew**, pp **grown**) vi wachsen; (increase) zunehmen; (become) werden ♦ vt (roses) züchten; (vegetables) anbauen, ziehen; (beard) sich dat wachsen lassen; **to ~ tired of waiting** das Warten leid sein; **to ~ (out of or from)** (develop) entstehen (aus).
▶**grow apart** vi (fig) sich auseinanderentwickeln.
▶**grow away from** vt fus (fig) sich entfremden +dat.
▶**grow on** vt fus: **that painting is ~ing on me** allmählich finde ich Gefallen an dem Bild.
▶**grow out of** vt fus (clothes) herauswachsen aus; (habit) ablegen; **he'll ~ out of it** diese Phase geht auch vorbei.
▶**grow up** vi aufwachsen; (mature) erwachsen werden; (idea, friendship) entstehen.
grower ['grəuə*] n (BOT) Züchter(in) m(f); (AGR) Pflanzer(in) m(f).
growing ['grəuɪŋ] adj wachsend; (number) zunehmend; **~ pains** Wachstumsschmerzen pl; (fig) Kinderkrankheiten pl, Anfangsschwierigkeiten pl.
growl [graul] vi knurren.
grown [grəun] pp of **grow**.
grown-up [grəun'ʌp] n Erwachsene(r) f(m).
growth [grəuθ] n Wachstum nt; (what has grown: of weeds, beard etc) Wuchs m; (of person, character) Entwicklung f; (MED) Gewächs nt, Wucherung f.
growth rate n Wachstumsrate f, Zuwachsrate f.
grub [grʌb] n (larva) Larve f; (inf: food)

Fressalien pl, Futter nt ♦ vi: **to ~ about** or **around (for)** (herum)wühlen (nach).
grubby ['grʌbɪ] adj (dirty) schmuddelig; (fig) schmutzig.
grudge [grʌdʒ] n Groll m ♦ vt: **to ~ sb sth** jdm etw nicht gönnen; **to bear sb a ~** jdm böse sein, einen Groll gegen jdn hegen.
grudging ['grʌdʒɪŋ] adj widerwillig.
grudgingly ['grʌdʒɪŋlɪ] adv widerwillig.
gruelling, (US) grueling ['gruəlɪŋ] adj (encounter) aufreibend; (trip, journey) äußerst strapaziös.
gruesome ['gruːsəm] adj grauenhaft.
gruff [grʌf] adj barsch, schroff.
grumble ['grʌmbl] vi murren, schimpfen.
grumpy ['grʌmpɪ] adj mürrisch, brummig.
grunge [grʌndʒ] (inf) n Grunge nt.
grunt [grʌnt] vi grunzen ♦ n Grunzen nt.
G-string ['dʒiːstrɪŋ] n Minislip m, Tangaslip m.
GSUSA n abbr (= Girl Scouts of the United States of America) amerikanische Pfadfinderinnen.
GT abbr (AUT: = gran turismo) GT.
GU (US) abbr (POST: = Guam).
guarantee [gærən'tiː] n Garantie f ♦ vt garantieren; **he can't ~ (that) he'll come** er kann nicht dafür garantieren, daß er kommt.
guarantor [gærən'tɔː*] n (COMM) Bürge m.
guard [gɑːd] n Wache f; (BOXING, FENCING) Deckung f; (BRIT: RAIL) Schaffner(in) m(f); (on machine) Schutz m, Schutzvorrichtung f; (also: **fire~**) (Schutz)gitter nt ♦ vt (prisoner) bewachen; (protect): **to ~ (against)** (be)schützen (vor +dat); (secret) hüten (vor +dat); **to be on one's ~** auf der Hut sein.
▶**guard against** vt fus (disease) vorbeugen +dat; (damage, accident) verhüten.
guard dog n Wachhund m.
guarded ['gɑːdɪd] adj vorsichtig, zurückhaltend.
guardian ['gɑːdɪən] n Vormund m; (defender) Hüter m.
guardrail ['gɑːdreɪl] n (Schutz)geländer nt.
guard's van (BRIT) n (RAIL) Schaffnerabteil nt, Dienstwagen m.
Guatemala [gwɑːtɪ'mɑːlə] n Guatemala nt.
Guatemalan [gwɑːtɪ'mɑːlən] adj guatemaltekisch, aus Guatemala.
Guernsey ['gəːnzɪ] n Guernsey nt.
guerrilla [gə'rɪlə] n Guerilla m, Guerillakämpfer(in) m(f).
guerrilla warfare n Guerillakrieg m.
guess [gɛs] vt schätzen; (answer) (er)raten; (US: think) schätzen (inf) ♦ vi (see vt) schätzen; raten ♦ n Vermutung f; **I ~ you're right** da haben Sie wohl recht; **to keep sb ~ing** jdn im ungewissen lassen; **to take** or **have a ~** raten; (estimate) schätzen; **my ~ is that ...** ich schätze or vermute, daß ...
guesstimate ['gɛstɪmɪt] (inf) n grobe Schätzung f.

guesswork ['gɛswə:k] n Vermutungen pl; **I got the answer by ~** ich habe die Antwort nur geraten.

guest [gɛst] n Gast m; **be my ~** (inf) nur zu!

guesthouse ['gɛsthaus] n Pension f.

guest room n Gästezimmer nt.

guff [gʌf] (inf) n Quatsch m, Käse m.

guffaw [gʌ'fɔ:] vi schallend lachen ♦ n schallendes Lachen nt.

guidance ['gaɪdəns] n Rat m, Beratung f; **under the ~ of** unter der Leitung von; **vocational ~** Berufsberatung f; **marriage ~** Eheberatung f.

guide [gaɪd] n (person) Führer(in) m(f); (book) Führer m; (BRIT: also: **girl ~**) Pfadfinderin f ♦ vt führen; (direct) lenken; **to be ~d by sb/sth** sich von jdm/etw leiten lassen.

guidebook ['gaɪdbuk] n Führer m.

guided missile n Lenkwaffe f.

guide dog n Blindenhund m.

guidelines ['gaɪdlaɪnz] npl Richtlinien pl.

guild [gɪld] n Verein m.

guildhall ['gɪldhɔ:l] (BRIT) n Gildehaus nt.

guile [gaɪl] n Arglist f.

guileless ['gaɪllɪs] adj arglos.

guillotine ['gɪləti:n] n Guillotine f, Fallbeil nt; (for paper) (Papier)schneidemaschine f.

guilt [gɪlt] n Schuld f; (remorse) Schuldgefühl nt.

guilty ['gɪltɪ] adj schuldig; (expression) schuldbewußt; (secret) dunkel; **to plead ~/ not ~** sich schuldig/nicht schuldig bekennen; **to feel ~ about doing sth** ein schlechtes Gewissen haben, etw zu tun.

Guinea ['gɪnɪ] n: **Republic of ~** Guinea nt.

guinea ['gɪnɪ] (BRIT) n (old) Guinee f.

guinea pig n Meerschweinchen nt; (fig: person) Versuchskaninchen nt.

guise [gaɪz] n: **in** or **under the ~ of** in der Form +gen, in Gestalt +gen.

guitar [gɪ'tɑ:*] n Gitarre f.

guitarist [gɪ'tɑ:rɪst] n Gitarrist(in) m(f).

gulch [gʌltʃ] (US) n Schlucht f.

gulf [gʌlf] n Golf m; (abyss) Abgrund m; (fig: difference) Kluft f; **the (Persian) G~** der (Persische) Golf.

Gulf States npl: **the ~** die Golfstaaten pl.

Gulf Stream n: **the ~** der Golfstrom.

Gulf War n: **the ~** der Golfkrieg.

gull [gʌl] n Möwe f.

gullet ['gʌlɪt] n Speiseröhre f.

gullibility [gʌlɪ'bɪlɪtɪ] n Leichtgläubigkeit f.

gullible ['gʌlɪbl] adj leichtgläubig.

gully ['gʌlɪ] n Schlucht f.

gulp [gʌlp] vi schlucken ♦ vt (also: **~ down**) hinunterschlucken ♦ n: **at one ~** mit einem Schluck.

gum [gʌm] n (ANAT) Zahnfleisch nt; (glue) Klebstoff m; (also: **~drop**) Weingummi nt; (also: **chewing-~**) Kaugummi m ♦ vt: **to ~ (together)** (zusammen)kleben.

▶**gum up** vt: **to ~ up the works** (inf) alles

vermasseln.

gumboots ['gʌmbu:ts] (BRIT) npl Gummistiefel pl.

gumption ['gʌmpʃən] n Grips m (inf).

gumtree ['gʌmtri:] n: **to be up a ~** (fig: inf) aufgeschmissen sein.

gun [gʌn] n (small) Pistole f; (medium-sized) Gewehr nt; (large) Kanone f ♦ vt (also: **~ down**) erschießen; **to stick to one's ~s** (fig) nicht nachgeben, fest bleiben.

gunboat ['gʌnbəut] n Kanonenboot nt.

gun dog n Jagdhund m.

gunfire ['gʌnfaɪə*] n Geschützfeuer nt.

gunge [gʌndʒ] (inf) n Schmiere f.

gung ho ['gʌŋ 'həu] (inf) adj übereifrig.

gunman ['gʌnmən] (irreg: like man) n bewaffneter Verbrecher m.

gunner ['gʌnə*] n Kanonier m, Artillerist m.

gunpoint ['gʌnpɔɪnt] n: **at ~** mit vorgehaltener Pistole; mit vorgehaltenem Gewehr.

gunpowder ['gʌnpaudə*] n Schießpulver nt.

gunrunner ['gʌnrʌnə*] n Waffenschmuggler(in) m(f), Waffenschieber(in) m(f).

gunrunning ['gʌnrʌnɪŋ] n Waffenschmuggel m, Waffenschieberei f.

gunshot ['gʌnʃɔt] n Schuß m.

gunsmith ['gʌnsmɪθ] n Büchsenmacher m.

gurgle ['gə:gl] vi (baby) glucksen; (water) gluckern.

guru ['guru:] n Guru m.

gush [gʌʃ] vi hervorquellen, hervorströmen; (person) schwärmen ♦ n Strahl m.

gushing ['gʌʃɪŋ] adj (fig) überschwenglich.

gusset ['gʌsɪt] n Keil m, Zwickel m.

gust [gʌst] n Windstoß m, Bö(e) f; (of smoke) Wolke f.

gusto ['gʌstəu] n: **with ~** mit Genuß, mit Schwung.

gusty ['gʌstɪ] adj (wind) böig; (day) stürmisch.

gut [gʌt] n (ANAT) Darm m; (for violin, racket) Darmsaiten pl ♦ vt (poultry, fish) ausnehmen; (building) ausräumen; (by fire) ausbrennen; **guts** npl (ANAT) Eingeweide pl; (inf: courage) Mumm m; **to hate sb's ~s** jdn auf den Tod nicht ausstehen können.

gut reaction n rein gefühlsmäßige Reaktion f.

gutsy ['gʌtsɪ] (inf) adj (vivid) rasant; (courageous) mutig.

gutter ['gʌtə*] n (in street) Gosse f, Rinnstein m; (of roof) Dachrinne f.

gutter press n Boulevardpresse f.

guttural ['gʌtərl] adj guttural.

guy [gaɪ] n (inf: man) Typ m, Kerl m; (also: **~rope**) Haltetau nt, Halteseil nt; (for Guy Fawkes' night) (Guy-Fawkes-)Puppe f.

Guy Fawkes' Night, *auch bonfire night genannt, erinnert an den Gunpowder Plot, einen Attentatsversuch auf James I und sein Parlament am 5. November 1605. Einer der*

Verschwörer, Guy Fawkes, wurde auf frischer Tat ertappt, als er das Parlamentsgebäude in die Luft sprengen wollte. Vor der Guy Fawkes' Night basteln Kinder in Großbritannien eine Puppe des Guy Fawkes, mit der sie Geld für Feuerwerkskörper von Passanten erbetteln, und die dann am 5. November auf einem Lagerfeuer mit Feuerwerk verbrannt wird.

Guyana [gaɪ'ænə] n Guyana nt.

guzzle ['gʌzl] vt (food) futtern; (drink) saufen (inf).

gym [dʒɪm] n (also: **gymnasium**) Turnhalle f; (also: **gymnastics**) Gymnastik f, Turnen nt.

gymkhana [dʒɪm'kɑːnə] n Reiterfest nt.

gymnasium [dʒɪm'neɪzɪəm] n Turnhalle f.

gymnast ['dʒɪmnæst] n Turner(in) m(f).

gymnastics [dʒɪm'næstɪks] n Gymnastik f, Turnen nt.

gym shoes npl Turnschuhe pl.

gymslip ['dʒɪmslɪp] (BRIT) n (Schul)trägerrock m.

gynaecologist, (US) gynecologist [gaɪnɪ'kɔlədʒɪst] n Gynäkologe m, Gynäkologin f, Frauenarzt m, Frauenärztin f.

gynaecology, (US) gynecology [gaɪnɪ'kɔlədʒɪ] n Gynäkologie f, Frauenheilkunde f.

gypsy ['dʒɪpsɪ] n = **gipsy**.

gyrate [dʒaɪ'reɪt] vi kreisen, sich drehen.

gyroscope ['dʒaɪərəskəup] n Gyroskop nt.

H, h

H, h [eɪtʃ] n (letter) H, h nt; ~ **for Harry**, (US) ~ **for How** ≈ H wie Heinrich.

habeas corpus ['heɪbɪəs'kɔːpəs] n Habeaskorpusakte f.

haberdashery [hæbə'dæʃərɪ] (BRIT) n Kurzwaren pl.

habit ['hæbɪt] n Gewohnheit f; (esp undesirable) Angewohnheit f; (addiction) Sucht f; (REL) Habit m or nt; **to get out of/into the ~ of doing sth** sich abgewöhnen/ angewöhnen, etw zu tun; **to be in the ~ of doing sth** die (An)gewohnheit haben, etw zu tun.

habitable ['hæbɪtəbl] adj bewohnbar.

habitat ['hæbɪtæt] n Heimat f; (of animals) Lebensraum m, Heimat f.

habitation [hæbɪ'teɪʃən] n Wohnstätte f; **fit for human ~** für Wohnzwecke geeignet, bewohnbar.

habitual [hə'bɪtjuəl] adj (action) gewohnt; (drinker) Gewohnheits-; (liar)

gewohnheitsmäßig.

habitually [hə'bɪtjuəlɪ] adv ständig.

hack [hæk] vt, vi (also COMPUT) hacken ♦ n (pej: writer) Schreiberling m; (horse) Mietpferd nt.

hacker ['hækə*] n (COMPUT) Hacker m.

hackles ['hæklz] npl: **to make sb's ~ rise** (fig) jdn auf die Palme bringen (inf).

hackney cab ['hæknɪ-] n Taxi nt.

hackneyed ['hæknɪd] adj abgedroschen.

hacksaw ['hæksɔː] n Metallsäge f.

had [hæd] pt, pp of **have**.

haddock ['hædək] (pl ~ or ~s) n Schellfisch m.

hadn't ['hædnt] = **had not**.

haematology, (US) hematology ['hiːmə'tɔlədʒɪ] n Hämatologie f.

haemoglobin, (US) hemoglobin ['hiːmə'gləubɪn] n Hämoglobin nt.

haemophilia, (US) hemophilia ['hiːmə'fɪlɪə] n Bluterkrankheit f.

haemorrhage, (US) hemorrhage ['hemərɪdʒ] n Blutung f.

haemorrhoids, (US) hemorrhoids ['hemərɔɪdz] npl Hämorrhoiden pl.

hag [hæg] n alte Hexe f; (witch) Hexe f.

haggard ['hægəd] adj ausgezehrt; (from worry) abgehärmt; (from tiredness) abgespannt.

haggis ['hægɪs] (SCOT) n Gericht aus gehackten Schafsinnereien und Haferschrot, im Schafsmagen gekocht.

haggle ['hægl] vi: **to ~ (over)** feilschen (um).

haggling ['hæglɪŋ] n Feilschen nt.

Hague [heɪg] n: **The ~** Den Haag m.

hail [heɪl] n Hagel m ♦ vt (person) zurufen +dat; (taxi) herbeiwinken, anhalten; (acclaim: person) zujubeln +dat; (: event etc) bejubeln ♦ vi hageln; **he ~s from Scotland** er kommt or stammt aus Schottland.

hailstone ['heɪlstəun] n Hagelkorn nt.

hailstorm ['heɪlstɔːm] n Hagelschauer m.

hair [hɛə*] n (collectively: of person) Haar nt, Haare pl; (: of animal) Fell nt; (single hair) Haar nt; **to do one's ~** sich frisieren; **by a ~'s breadth** um Haaresbreite.

hairbrush ['hɛəbrʌʃ] n Haarbürste f.

haircut ['hɛəkʌt] n Haarschnitt m; (style) Frisur f.

hairdo ['hɛəduː] n Frisur f.

hairdresser ['hɛədresə*] n Friseur m, Friseuse f.

hairdresser's ['hɛədresəz] n Friseursalon m.

hair dryer n Haartrockner m, Fön m.

-haired [hɛəd] suff: **fair-~** blond; **long-~** langhaarig.

hairgrip ['hɛəgrɪp] n Haarklemme f.

hairline ['hɛəlaɪn] n Haaransatz m.

hairline fracture n Haarriß m.

hairnet ['hɛənet] n Haarnetz nt.

hair oil n Haaröl nt.

hairpiece ['hɛəpiːs] n Haarteil nt; (for men) Toupet nt.

hairpin ['hɛəpɪn] n Haarnadel f.

hairpin bend, (US) **hairpin curve** n
Haarnadelkurve f.
hair-raising ['hɛəreɪzɪŋ] adj haarsträubend.
hair remover n Enthaarungscreme f.
hair slide n Haarspange f.
hair spray n Haarspray nt.
hairstyle ['hɛəstaɪl] n Frisur f.
hairy ['hɛərɪ] adj behaart; (inf: situation)
brenzlig, haarig.
Haiti ['heɪtɪ] n Haiti nt.
hake [heɪk] (pl ~ or ~s) n Seehecht m.
halcyon ['hælsɪən] adj glücklich.
hale [heɪl] adj: ~ **and hearty** gesund und
munter.
half [hɑːf] (pl **halves**) n Hälfte f; (of beer etc)
kleines Bier nt etc; (RAIL, bus) Fahrkarte f
zum halben Preis ♦ adj, adv halb; **first/second**
~ (SPORT) erste/zweite Halbzeit f; **two and
a** ~ zweieinhalb; **~-an-hour** eine halbe
Stunde; ~ **a dozen/pound** ein halbes
Dutzend/Pfund; **a week and a** ~ eineinhalb
or anderthalb Wochen; ~ **(of it)** die Hälfte;
~ **(of)** die Hälfte (von or +gen); ~ **the amount
of** die halbe Menge an +dat; **to cut sth in** ~
etw halbieren; ~ **past three** halb vier; **to go
halves (with sb)** (mit jdm) halbe-halbe
machen; **she never does things by halves** sie
macht keine halben Sachen; **he's too clever
by** ~ er ist ein richtiger Schlaumeier;
~ **empty** halbleer; ~ **closed**
halbgeschlossen.
half-baked ['hɑːf'beɪkt] adj blödsinnig (inf).
half board n Halbpension f.
half-breed ['hɑːfbriːd] n = **half-caste**.
half-brother ['hɑːfbrʌðə*] n Halbbruder m.
half-caste ['hɑːfkɑːst] n Mischling m.
half-day [hɑːf'deɪ] n halber freier Tag m.
half-hearted ['hɑːf'hɑːtɪd] adj halbherzig,
lustlos.
half-hour [hɑːf'auə*] n halbe Stunde f.
half-life ['hɑːflaɪf] n (TECH) Halbwertszeit f.
half-mast ['hɑːf'mɑːst]: **at** ~ adv (auf)
halbmast.
halfpenny ['heɪpnɪ] (BRIT) n halber Penny m.
half-price ['hɑːf'praɪs] adj, adv zum halben
Preis.
half-sister ['hɑːfsɪstə*] n Halbschwester f.
half term (BRIT) n kleine Ferien pl (in der Mitte
des Trimesters).
half-timbered [hɑːf'tɪmbəd] adj (house)
Fachwerk-.
half-time [hɑːf'taɪm] n (SPORT) Halbzeit f.
halfway ['hɑːf'weɪ] adv: ~ **to** auf halbem
Wege nach; ~ **through** mitten in +dat; **to
meet sb** ~ (fig) jdm auf halbem Wege
entgegenkommen.
halfway house n (hostel) offene Anstalt f;
(fig) Zwischending nt; (: compromise)
Kompromiß m.
halfwit ['hɑːfwɪt] n Schwachsinnige(r) f(m);
(fig: inf) Schwachkopf m.
half-yearly [hɑːf'jɪəlɪ] adv halbjährlich, jedes

halbe Jahr ♦ adj halbjährlich.
halibut ['hælɪbət] n inv Heilbutt m.
halitosis [hælɪ'təusɪs] n schlechter Atem m,
Mundgeruch m.
hall [hɔːl] n Diele f, (Haus)flur m; (corridor)
Korridor m, Flur m; (mansion) Herrensitz m,
Herrenhaus nt; (for concerts etc) Halle f; **to
live in** ~ (BRIT) im Wohnheim wohnen.
hallmark ['hɔːlmɑːk] n (on gold, silver)
(Feingehalts)stempel m; (of writer, artist etc)
Kennzeichen nt.
hallo [hə'ləu] excl = **hello**.
hall of residence (pl **halls of residence**)
(BRIT) n Studentenwohnheim nt.
hallowed ['hæləud] adj (ground) heilig; (fig:
respected, revered) geheiligt.
Hallowe'en ['hæləu'iːn] n der Tag vor
Allerheiligen.

Hallowe'en ist der 31. Oktober, der Vorabend
von Allerheiligen und nach altem Glauben der
Abend, an dem man Geister und Hexen sehen
kann. In Großbritannien und vor allem in den
USA feiern die Kinder Hallowe'en, indem sie
sich verkleiden und mit selbstgemachten
Laternen aus Kürbissen von Tür zu Tür ziehen.

---

hallucination [həluːsɪ'neɪʃən] n Halluzination
f.
hallucinogenic [həluːsɪnəu'dʒɛnɪk] adj (drug)
halluzinogen ♦ n Halluzinogen nt.
hallway ['hɔːlweɪ] n Diele f, (Haus)flur m.
halo ['heɪləu] n Heiligenschein m; (circle of
light) Hof m.
halt [hɔːlt] vt anhalten; (progress etc) zum
Stillstand bringen ♦ vi anhalten, zum
Stillstand kommen ♦ n: **to come to a** ~ zum
Stillstand kommen; **to call a** ~ **to sth** (fig)
einer Sache dat ein Ende machen.
halter ['hɔːltə*] n Halfter nt.
halter-neck ['hɔːltənɛk] adj (dress) rückenfrei
mit Nackenverschluß.
halve [hɑːv] vt halbieren.
halves [hɑːvz] pl of **half**.
ham [hæm] n Schinken m; (inf: also: **radio** ~)
Funkamateur m; (: actor)
Schmierenkomödiant(in) m(f).
Hamburg ['hæmbəːg] n Hamburg nt.
hamburger ['hæmbəːgə*] n Hamburger m.
ham-fisted ['hæm'fɪstɪd], (US) **ham-handed**
['hæm'hændɪd] adj ungeschickt.
hamlet ['hæmlɪt] n Weiler m, kleines Dorf nt.
hammer ['hæmə*] n Hammer m ♦ vt hämmern;
(fig: criticize) vernichtend kritisieren;
(: defeat) vernichtend schlagen ♦ vi
hämmern; **to** ~ **sth into sb, to** ~ **sth across
to sb** jdm etw einhämmern or einbleuen.
►**hammer out** vt hämmern; (solution,
agreement) ausarbeiten.
hammock ['hæmək] n Hängematte f.
hamper ['hæmpə*] vt behindern ♦ n Korb m.
hamster ['hæmstə*] n Hamster m.

hamstring ['hæmstrɪŋ] n Kniesehne f ♦ vt einengen.

hand [hænd] n Hand f; (of clock) Zeiger m; (handwriting) Hand(schrift) f; (worker) Arbeiter(in) m(f); (of cards) Blatt nt; (measurement: of horse) ≈ 10 cm ♦ vt geben, reichen; **to give** or **lend sb a ~** jdm helfen; **at ~** (place) in der Nähe; (time) unmittelbar bevorstehend; **by ~** von Hand; **in ~** (time) zur Verfügung; (job) anstehend; (situation) unter Kontrolle; **we have the matter in ~** wir haben die Sache im Griff; **on ~** zur Verfügung; **out of ~** adj außer Kontrolle ♦ adv (reject etc) rundweg; **to ~** zur Hand; **on the one ~ ...**, **on the other ~ ...** einerseits ... andererseits ...; **to force sb's ~** jdn zwingen; **to have a free ~** freie Hand haben; **to change ~s** den Besitzer wechseln; **to have in one's ~** (also fig) in der Hand halten; **"~s off!"** „Hände weg!".
▶**hand down** vt (knowledge) weitergeben; (possessions) vererben; (LAW: judgement, sentence) fällen.
▶**hand in** vt abgeben, einreichen.
▶**hand out** vt verteilen; (information) austeilen; (punishment) verhängen.
▶**hand over** vt übergeben.
▶**hand round** vt (BRIT) verteilen; (chocolates etc) herumreichen.

handbag ['hændbæg] n Handtasche f.
hand baggage n Handgepäck nt.
handball ['hændbɔːl] n Handball m.
hand basin n Handwaschbecken nt.
handbook ['hændbʊk] n Handbuch nt.
handbrake ['hændbreɪk] n Handbremse f.
h & c (BRIT) abbr (= hot and cold (water)) h.u.k.
hand cream n Handcreme f.
handcuff ['hændkʌf] vt Handschellen anlegen +dat.
handcuffs ['hændkʌfs] npl Handschellen pl.
handful ['hændfʊl] n Handvoll f.
hand-held ['hænd'held] adj (camera) Hand-.
handicap ['hændɪkæp] n Behinderung f; (disadvantage) Nachteil m; (SPORT) Handicap nt ♦ vt benachteiligen; **mentally/physically ~ped** geistig/körperlich behindert.
handicraft ['hændɪkrɑːft] n Kunsthandwerk nt; (object) Kunsthandwerksarbeit f.
handiwork ['hændɪwɜːk] n Arbeit f; **this looks like his ~** (pej) das sieht nach seiner Arbeit aus.
handkerchief ['hæŋkətʃɪf] n Taschentuch nt.
handle ['hændl] n Griff m; (of door) Klinke f; (of cup) Henkel m; (of broom, brush etc) Stiel m; (for winding) Kurbel f; (CB RADIO: name) Sendezeichen nt ♦ vt anfassen, berühren; (problem etc) sich befassen mit; (: successfully) fertigwerden mit; (people) umgehen mit; **"~ with care"** „Vorsicht - zerbrechlich"; **to fly off the ~** an die Decke gehen; **to get a ~ on a problem** (inf) ein

Problem in den Griff bekommen.
handlebar(s) ['hændlbɑː(z)] n(pl) Lenkstange f.
handling ['hændlɪŋ] n: **~ (of)** (of plant, animal, issue etc) Behandlung f +gen; (of person, tool, machine etc) Umgang m (mit); (ADMIN) Bearbeitung f +gen.
handling charges npl Bearbeitungsgebühr f; (BANKING) Kontoführungsgebühr f.
hand luggage n Handgepäck nt.
hand-out ['hændaut] n (money, food etc) Unterstützung f; (publicity leaflet) Flugblatt nt; (summary) Informationsblatt nt.
hand-picked ['hænd'pɪkt] adj von Hand geerntet; (staff etc) handverlesen.
handrail ['hændreɪl] n Geländer nt.
handset ['hændset] n (TEL) Hörer m.
handshake ['hændʃeɪk] n Händedruck m.
handsome ['hænsəm] adj gutaussehend; (building) schön; (gift) großzügig; (profit, return) ansehnlich.
hands-on ['hændz'ɔn] adj (training) praktisch; (approach etc) aktiv; **~ experience** praktische Erfahrung.
handstand ['hændstænd] n: **to do a ~** einen Handstand machen.
hand-to-mouth ['hændtə'mauθ] adj: **to lead a ~ existence** von der Hand in den Mund leben.
handwriting ['hændraɪtɪŋ] n Handschrift f.
handwritten ['hændrɪtn] adj handgeschrieben.
handy ['hændɪ] adj praktisch; (skilful) geschickt; (close at hand) in der Nähe; **to come in ~** sich als nützlich erweisen.
handyman ['hændɪmæn] (irreg: like **man**) n (at home) Heimwerker m; (in hotel etc) Faktotum nt.
hang [hæŋ] (pt, pp **hung**) vt aufhängen; (criminal) (pt, pp **hanged**) hängen; (head) hängen lassen ♦ vi hängen; (hair, drapery) fallen ♦ n: **to get the ~ of sth** (inf) den richtigen Dreh (bei etw) herauskriegen.
▶**hang about** vi herumlungern.
▶**hang around** vi = hang about.
▶**hang back** vi: **to ~ back (from doing sth)** zögern(, etw zu tun).
▶**hang on** vi warten ♦ vt fus (depend on) abhängen von; **to ~ on to** festhalten; (for protection, support) sich festhalten an +dat; (hope, position) sich klammern an +acc; (ideas) festhalten an +dat; (keep) behalten.
▶**hang out** vt draußen aufhängen ♦ vi heraushängen; (inf: live) wohnen.
▶**hang together** vi (argument) folgerichtig or zusammenhängend sein; (story, explanation) zusammenhängend sein; (statements) zusammenpassen.
▶**hang up** vt aufhängen ♦ vi (TEL): **to ~ up (on sb)** einfach auflegen.
hangar ['hæŋə*] n Hangar m, Flugzeughalle f.
hangdog ['hæŋdɔg] adj zerknirscht.

hanger ['hæŋə'] n Bügel m.
hanger-on [hæŋər'ɔn] n (parasite) Trabant m (inf); **the ~s-~** der Anhang.
hang-glide ['hæŋglaɪd] vi drachenfliegen.
hang-glider ['hæŋglaɪdə'] n (Flug)drachen m.
hang-gliding ['hæŋglaɪdɪŋ] n Drachenfliegen nt.
hanging ['hæŋɪŋ] n (execution) Hinrichtung f durch den Strang; (for wall) Wandbehang m.
hangman ['hæŋmən] (irreg: like **man**) n Henker m.
hangover ['hæŋəuvə'] n Kater m; (from past) Überbleibsel nt.
hang-up ['hæŋʌp] n Komplex m.
hank [hæŋk] n Strang m.
hanker ['hæŋkə'] vi: **to ~ after** sich sehnen nach.
hankering ['hæŋkərɪŋ] n: ~ **(for)** Verlangen nt (nach).
hankie ['hæŋkɪ] n abbr = **handkerchief**.
hanky ['hæŋkɪ] n abbr = **handkerchief**.
Hants [hænts] (BRIT) abbr (POST: = Hampshire).
haphazard [hæp'hæzəd] adj planlos, wahllos.
hapless ['hæplɪs] adj glücklos.
happen ['hæpən] vi geschehen; **to ~ to do sth** zufällig(erweise) etw tun; **as it ~s** zufälligerweise; **what's ~ing?** was ist los?; **she ~ed to be free** sie hatte zufällig(erweise) gerade Zeit; **if anything ~ed to him** wenn ihm etwas zustoßen or passieren sollte.
► **happen (up)on** vt fus zufällig stoßen auf +acc; (person) zufällig treffen.
happening ['hæpnɪŋ] n Ereignis nt, Vorfall m.
happily ['hæpɪlɪ] adv (luckily) glücklicherweise; (cheerfully) fröhlich.
happiness ['hæpɪnɪs] n Glück nt.
happy ['hæpɪ] adj glücklich; (cheerful) fröhlich; **to be ~ (with)** zufrieden sein (mit); **to be ~ to do sth** etw gerne tun; ~ **birthday!** herzlichen Glückwunsch zum Geburtstag!
happy-go-lucky ['hæpɪgəu'lʌkɪ] adj unbekümmert.
happy hour n Zeit, in der Bars, Pubs usw Getränke zu ermäßigten Preisen anbieten.
harangue [hə'ræŋ] vt predigen +dat (inf).
harass ['hærəs] vt schikanieren.
harassed ['hærəst] adj geplagt.
harassment ['hærəsmənt] n Schikanierung f; **sexual ~** sexuelle Belästigung f.
harbour, (US) **harbor** ['hɑːbə'] n Hafen m ♦ vt (hope, fear, grudge etc) hegen; (criminal, fugitive) Unterschlupf gewähren +dat.
harbour dues npl Hafengebühren pl.
harbour master n Hafenmeister m.
hard [hɑːd] adj hart; (question, problem) schwierig; (evidence) gesichert ♦ adv (work) hart, schwer; (think) scharf; (try) sehr; ~ **luck!** Pech!; **no ~ feelings!** ich nehme es dir nicht übel; **to be ~ of hearing** schwerhörig sein; **to be ~ done by**

ungerecht behandelt werden; **I find it ~ to believe that** ... ich kann es kaum glauben, daß ...; **to look ~ at sth** (object) sich +dat etw genau ansehen; (idea) etw gründlich prüfen.
hard-and-fast ['hɑːdən'fɑːst] adj fest.
hardback ['hɑːdbæk] n gebundene Ausgabe f.
hardboard ['hɑːdbɔːd] n Hartfaserplatte f.
hard-boiled egg ['hɑːd'bɔɪld-] n hartgekochtes Ei nt.
hard cash n Bargeld nt.
hard copy n (COMPUT) Ausdruck m.
hard core n harter Kern m.
hard-core ['hɑːd'kɔː'] adj (pornography) hart; (supporters) zum harten Kern gehörend.
hard court n (TENNIS) Hartplatz m.
hard disk n (COMPUT) Festplatte f.
harden ['hɑːdn] vt härten; (attitude, person) verhärten ♦ vi hart werden, sich verhärten.
hardened ['hɑːdnd] adj (criminal) Gewohnheits-; **to be ~ to sth** gegen etw abgehärtet sein.
hardening ['hɑːdnɪŋ] n Verhärtung f.
hard graft n: **by sheer ~** durch harte Arbeit.
hard-headed ['hɑːd'hedɪd] adj nüchtern.
hardhearted ['hɑːd'hɑːtɪd] adj hartherzig.
hard-hitting ['hɑːd'hɪtɪŋ] adj (fig: speech, journalist etc) knallhart.
hard labour n Zwangsarbeit f.
hardliner [hɑːd'laɪnə'] n Vertreter(in) m(f) der harten Linie.
hard-luck story ['hɑːd'lʌk-] n Leidensgeschichte f.
hardly ['hɑːdlɪ] adv kaum; (harshly) hart, streng; **it's ~ the case** (ironic) das ist wohl kaum der Fall; **I can ~ believe it** ich kann es kaum glauben.
hard-nosed [hɑːd'nəuzd] adj abgebrüht.
hard-pressed [hɑːd'prest] adj: **to be ~** unter Druck sein; ~ **for money** in Geldnot.
hard sell n aggressive Verkaufstaktik f.
hardship ['hɑːdʃɪp] n Not f.
hard shoulder (BRIT) n (AUT) Seitenstreifen m.
hard up (inf) adj knapp bei Kasse.
hardware ['hɑːdwɛə'] n Eisenwaren pl; (household goods) Haushaltswaren pl; (COMPUT) Hardware f; (MIL) Waffen pl.
hardware shop n Eisenwarenhandlung f.
hard-wearing [hɑːd'wɛərɪŋ] adj strapazierfähig.
hard-won [hɑːd'wʌn] adj schwer erkämpft.
hard-working [hɑːd'wəːkɪŋ] adj fleißig.
hardy ['hɑːdɪ] adj (animals) zäh; (people) abgehärtet; (plant) winterhart.
hare [hɛə'] n Hase m.
harebrained ['hɛəbreɪnd] adj verrückt.
harelip ['hɛəlɪp] n Hasenscharte f.
harem [hɑː'riːm] n Harem m.
hark back [hɑːk-] vi: **to ~ to** zurückkommen auf +acc.
harm [hɑːm] n Schaden m; (injury) Verletzung f ♦ vt schaden +dat; (person: physically)

verletzen; **to mean no ~** es nicht böse meinen; **out of ~'s way** in Sicherheit; **there's no ~ in trying** es kann nicht schaden, es zu versuchen.

harmful ['hɑːmful] *adj* schädlich.

harmless ['hɑːmlɪs] *adj* harmlos.

harmonic [hɑːˈmɔnɪk] *adj* harmonisch.

harmonica [hɑːˈmɔnɪkə] *n* Harmonika *f*.

harmonics [hɑːˈmɔnɪks] *npl* Harmonik *f*.

harmonious [hɑːˈməunɪəs] *adj* harmonisch.

harmonium [hɑːˈməunɪəm] *n* Harmonium *nt*.

harmonize [ˈhɑːmənaɪz] *vi* (*MUS*) mehrstimmig singen/spielen; (: *one person*) die zweite Stimme singen/spielen; (*colours, ideas*) harmonieren.

harmony [ˈhɑːmənɪ] *n* Einklang *m*; (*MUS*) Harmonie *f*.

harness [ˈhɑːnɪs] *n* (*for horse*) Geschirr *nt*; (*for child*) Laufgurt *m*; (*safety harness*) Sicherheitsgurt *m* ♦ *vt* (*resources, energy etc*) nutzbar machen; (*horse, dog*) anschirren.

harp [hɑːp] *n* Harfe *f* ♦ *vi:* **to ~ on about** (*pej*) herumreiten auf +*dat*.

harpist [ˈhɑːpɪst] *n* Harfenspieler(in) *m(f)*.

harpoon [hɑːˈpuːn] *n* Harpune *f*.

harpsichord [ˈhɑːpsɪkɔːd] *n* Cembalo *nt*.

harried [ˈhærɪd] *adj* bedrängt.

harrow [ˈhærəu] *n* Egge *f*.

harrowing [ˈhærəuɪŋ] *adj* (*film*) erschütternd; (*experience*) grauenhaft.

harry [ˈhærɪ] *vt* bedrängen, zusetzen +*dat*.

harsh [hɑːʃ] *adj* (*sound, light*) grell; (*judge, winter*) streng; (*criticism, life*) hart.

harshly [ˈhɑːʃlɪ] *adv* (*judge*) streng; (*say*) barsch; (*criticize*) hart.

harshness [ˈhɑːʃnɪs] *n* (*see adj*) Grelle *f*; Strenge *f*; Härte *f*.

harvest [ˈhɑːvɪst] *n* Ernte *f* ♦ *vt* ernten.

harvester [ˈhɑːvɪstə*] *n* (*also:* **combine ~**) Mähdrescher *m*.

has [hæz] *vb see* **have**.

has-been [ˈhæzbiːn] (*inf*) *n:* **he's/she's a ~** er/ sie ist eine vergangene *or* vergessene Größe.

hash [hæʃ] *n* (*CULIN*) Haschee *nt*; (*fig*) **to make a ~ of sth** etw verpfuschen (*inf*); ♦ (*inf*) *n abbr* (= *hashish*) Hasch *nt*.

hashish [ˈhæʃɪʃ] *n* Haschisch *nt*.

hasn't [ˈhæznt] = **has not**.

hassle [ˈhæsl] (*inf*) *n* (*bother*) Theater *nt* ♦ *vt* schikanieren.

haste [heɪst] *n* Hast *f*; (*speed*) Eile *f*; **in ~** in Eile; **to make ~ (to do sth)** sich beeilen(, etw zu tun).

hasten [ˈheɪsn] *vt* beschleunigen ♦ *vi:* **to ~ to do sth** sich beeilen, etw zu tun; **I ~ to add** ... ich muß allerdings hinzufügen, ...; **she ~ed back to the house** sie eilte zum Haus zurück.

hastily [ˈheɪstɪlɪ] *adv* (*see adj*) hastig, eilig; vorschnell.

hasty [ˈheɪstɪ] *adj* hastig, eilig; (*rash*) vorschnell.

hat [hæt] *n* Hut *m*; **to keep sth under one's ~** etw für sich behalten.

hatbox [ˈhætbɔks] *n* Hutschachtel *f*.

hatch [hætʃ] *n* (*NAUT: also:* **~way**) Luke *f*; (*also:* **service ~**) Durchreiche *f* ♦ *vi* (*bird*) ausschlüpfen ♦ *vt* ausbrüten; **the eggs ~ed after 10 days** nach 10 Tagen schlüpften die Jungen aus.

hatchback [ˈhætʃbæk] *n* (*AUT: car*) Heckklappenmodell *nt*.

hatchet [ˈhætʃɪt] *n* Beil *nt*; **to bury the ~** das Kriegsbeil begraben.

hatchet job (*inf*) *adj:* **to do a ~ on sb** jdn fertigmachen.

hatchet man (*inf*) *n* (*fig*) Vollstrecker *m*.

hate [heɪt] *vt* hassen ♦ *n* Haß *m*; **I ~ him/milk** ich kann ihn/ Milch nicht ausstehen; **to ~ to do/doing sth** es hassen, etw zu tun; (*weaker*) etw ungern tun; **I ~ to trouble you, but ...** es ist mir sehr unangenehm, daß ich Sie belästigen muß, aber ...

hateful [ˈheɪtful] *adj* abscheulich.

hatred [ˈheɪtrɪd] *n* Haß *m*; (*dislike*) Abneigung *f*.

hat trick *n* Hattrick *m*.

haughty [ˈhɔːtɪ] *adj* überheblich.

haul [hɔːl] *vt* ziehen; (*by lorry*) transportieren; (*NAUT*) den Kurs ändern +*gen* ♦ *n* Beute *f*; (*of fish*) Fang *m*; **he ~ed himself out of the pool** er stemmte sich aus dem Schwimmbecken.

haulage [ˈhɔːlɪdʒ] *n* (*cost*) Transportkosten *pl*; (*business*) Transport *m*.

haulage contractor (*BRIT*) *n* Transportunternehmen *nt*, Spedition *f*; (*person*) Transportunternehmer(in) *m(f)*, Spediteur *m*.

hauler [ˈhɔːlə*] (*US*) *n* Transportunternehmer(in) *m(f)*, Spediteur *m*.

haulier [ˈhɔːlɪə*] (*BRIT*) *n* Transportunternehmer(in) *m(f)*, Spediteur *m*.

haunch [hɔːntʃ] *n* Hüftpartie *f*; (*of meat*) Keule *f*.

haunt [hɔːnt] *vt* (*place*) spuken in +*dat*, umgehen in +*dat*; (*person, also fig*) verfolgen ♦ *n* Lieblingsplatz *m*; (*of crooks etc*) Treffpunkt *m*.

haunted [ˈhɔːntɪd] *adj* (*expression*) gehetzt, gequält; **this building/room is ~** in diesem Gebäude/Zimmer spukt es.

haunting [ˈhɔːntɪŋ] *adj* (*music*) eindringlich; **a ~ sight** ein Anblick, der einen nicht losläßt.

Havana [həˈvænə] *n* Havanna *nt*.

========================= *KEYWORD*

have [hæv] (*pt, pp* **had**) *aux vb* **1** haben; (*with verbs of motion*) sein; **to ~ arrived/gone** angekommen/gegangen sein; **to ~ eaten/ slept** gegessen/geschlafen haben; **he has been promoted** er ist befördert worden; **having eaten** *or* **when he had eaten, he left** nachdem er gegessen hatte, ging er

2 (*in tag questions*): **you've done it, ~n't you?** du hast es gemacht, nicht wahr?; **he hasn't done it, has he?** er hat es nicht gemacht, oder?

3 (*in short answers and questions*): **you've made a mistake - no I ~'t/so I ~** du hast einen Fehler gemacht - nein(, das habe ich nicht)/ja, stimmt; **we ~'t paid - yes we ~!** wir haben nicht bezahlt - doch!; **I've been there before - ~ you?** ich war schon einmal da - wirklich *or* tatsächlich?

♦ *modal aux vb* (*be obliged*): **to ~ (got) to do sth** etw tun müssen; **this has (got) to be a mistake** das muß ein Fehler sein

♦ *vt* **1** (*possess*) haben; **she has (got) blue eyes/dark hair** sie hat blaue Augen/dunkle Haare; **I ~ (got) an idea** ich habe eine Idee **2** (*referring to meals etc*): **to ~ breakfast** frühstücken; **to ~ lunch/dinner** zu Mittag/ Abend essen; **to ~ a drink** etwas trinken; **to ~ a cigarette** eine Zigarette rauchen **3** (*receive, obtain etc*) haben; **may I ~ your address?** kann ich Ihre Adresse haben *or* bekommen?; **to ~ a baby** ein Kind bekommen **4** (*allow*): **I won't ~ this nonsense** dieser Unsinn kommt nicht in Frage!; **we can't ~ that** das kommt nicht in Frage **5: to ~ sth done** etw machen lassen; **to ~ one's hair cut** sich *dat* die Haare schneiden lassen; **to ~ sb do sth** (*order*) jdn etw tun lassen; **he soon had them all laughing/working** bald hatte er alle zum Lachen/Arbeiten gebracht **6** (*experience, suffer*): **to ~ a cold/flu** eine Erkältung/die Grippe haben; **she had her bag stolen** ihr *dat* wurde die Tasche gestohlen **7** (+ *noun: take, hold etc*): **to ~ a swim** schwimmen gehen; **to ~ a walk** spazierengehen; **to ~ a rest** sich ausruhen; **to ~ a meeting** eine Besprechung haben; **to ~ a party** eine Party geben **8** (*inf: dupe*): **you've been had** man hat dich hereingelegt.

▶**have in** (*inf*) *vt:* **to ~ it in for sb** jdn auf dem Kieker haben.

▶**have on** *vt* (*wear*) anhaben; (*BRIT: inf: tease*) auf den Arm nehmen; **I don't ~ any money on me** ich habe kein Geld bei mir; **do you ~ or ~ you anything on tomorrow?** haben Sie morgen etwas vor?

▶**have out** *vt:* **to ~ it out with sb** (*settle a problem etc*) ein Wort mit jdm reden.

haven ['heɪvn] *n* Hafen *m*; (*safe place*) Zufluchtsort *m*.

haven't ['hævnt] = **have not**.

haversack ['hævəsæk] *n* Rucksack *m*.

haves [hævz] (*inf*) *npl:* **the ~ and the have-nots** die Betuchten und die Habenichtse.

havoc ['hævək] *n* Verwüstung *f*; (*confusion*)

Chaos *nt*; **to play ~ with sth** (*disrupt*) etw völlig durcheinanderbringen.

Hawaii [hə'waɪiː] *n* Hawaii *nt*.

Hawaiian [hə'waɪjən] *adj* hawaiisch ♦ *n* Hawaiianer(in) *m(f)*; (*LING*) Hawaiisch *nt*.

hawk [hɔːk] *n* Habicht *m*.

hawker ['hɔːkə*] *n* Hausierer(in) *m(f)*.

hawkish ['hɔːkɪʃ] *adj* (*person, approach*) knallhart.

hawthorn ['hɔːθɔːn] *n* Weißdorn *m*, Rotdorn *m*.

hay [heɪ] *n* Heu *nt*.

hay fever *n* Heuschnupfen *m*.

haystack ['heɪstæk] *n* Heuhaufen *m*; **like looking for a needle in a ~** als ob man eine Stecknadel im Heuhaufen suchte.

haywire ['heɪwaɪə*] (*inf*) *adj:* **to go ~** (*machine*) verrückt spielen; (*plans etc*) über den Haufen geworfen werden.

hazard ['hæzəd] *n* Gefahr *f* ♦ *vt* riskieren; **to be a health/fire ~** eine Gefahr für die Gesundheit/feuergefährlich sein; **to ~ a guess** (es) wagen, eine Vermutung anzustellen.

hazardous ['hæzədəs] *adj* gefährlich.

hazard pay (*US*) *n* Gefahrenzulage *f*.

hazard (warning) lights *npl* (*AUT*) Warnblinkanlage *f*.

haze [heɪz] *n* Dunst *m*.

hazel ['heɪzl] *n* Hasel(nuß)strauch *m*, Haselbusch *m* ♦ *adj* haselnußbraun.

hazelnut ['heɪzlnʌt] *n* Haselnuß *f*.

hazy ['heɪzɪ] *adj* dunstig, diesig; (*idea, memory*) unklar, verschwommen; **I'm rather ~ about the details** an die Einzelheiten kann ich mich nur vage *or* verschwommen erinnern; (*ignorant*) die genauen Einzelheiten sind mir nicht bekannt.

H-bomb ['eɪtʃbɔm] *n* H-Bombe *f*.

HE *abbr* (*REL, DIPLOMACY:* = *His/Her Excellency*) Seine/Ihre Exzellenz; (= *high explosive*) hochexplosiver Sprengstoff *m*.

he [hiː] *pron* er ♦ *pref* männlich; **~ who ...** wer ...

head ['hɛd] *n* Kopf *m*; (*of table*) Kopfende *nt*; (*of queue*) Spitze *f*; (*of company, organization*) Leiter(in) *m(f)*; (*of school*) Schulleiter(in) *m(f)*; (*on coin*) Kopfseite *f*; (*on tape recorder*) Tonkopf *m* ♦ *vt* anführen, an der Spitze stehen von; (*group, company*) leiten; (*FOOTBALL: ball*) köpfen; **~s (or tails)** Kopf (oder Zahl); **~ over heels** Hals über Kopf; (*in love*) bis über beide Ohren; **£10 a** *or* **per ~** 10 Pfund pro Kopf; **at the ~ of the list** oben auf der Liste; **to have a ~ for business** einen guten Geschäftssinn haben; **to have no ~ for heights** nicht schwindelfrei sein; **to come to a ~** sich zuspitzen; **they put their ~s together** sie haben sich zusammengesetzt; **off the top of my** *etc* **~** ohne lange zu überlegen; **on your own ~ be it!** auf Ihre eigene Verantwortung *or* Kappe (*inf*)!; **to bite** *or* **snap sb's** ~ **off** jdn grob anfahren; **he won't bite your** ~ **off** er wird dir schon nicht den Kopf abreißen; **it went to my** ~ es ist mir in den Kopf *or* zu Kopf gestiegen; **to lose/keep one's** ~ den Kopf verlieren/nicht verlieren; **I can't make** ~ **nor tail of this** hieraus werde ich nicht schlau; **he's off his** ~! (*inf*) er ist nicht (ganz) bei Trost!

▶**head for** *vt fus* (*on foot*) zusteuern auf +*acc*; (*by car*) in Richtung ... fahren; (*plane, ship*) Kurs nehmen auf +*acc*; **you are** ~**ing for trouble** du wirst Ärger bekommen.

▶**head off** *vt* abwenden.

headache ['hɛdeɪk] *n* Kopfschmerzen *pl*, Kopfweh *nt*; (*fig*) Problem *nt*; **to have a** ~ Kopfschmerzen *or* Kopfweh haben.

headband ['hɛdbænd] *n* Stirnband *nt*.

headboard ['hɛdbɔːd] *n* Kopfteil *nt*.

head cold *n* Kopfgrippe *f*.

headdress ['hɛddrɛs] (*BRIT*) *n* Kopfschmuck *m*.

headed notepaper ['hɛdɪd-] *n* Schreibpapier *nt* mit Briefkopf.

header ['hɛdə'] (*BRIT: inf*) *n* (*FOOTBALL*) Kopfball *m*.

headfirst ['hɛd'fəːst] *adv* (*lit*) kopfüber; (*fig*) Hals über Kopf.

headgear ['hɛdgɪə'] *n* Kopfbedeckung *f*.

head-hunt ['hɛdhʌnt] *vt* abwerben.

head-hunter ['hɛdhʌntə'] *n* (*COMM*) Kopfjäger(in) *m(f)*.

heading ['hɛdɪŋ] *n* Überschrift *f*.

headlamp ['hɛdlæmp] (*BRIT*) *n* = **headlight**.

headland ['hɛdlənd] *n* Landspitze *f*.

headlight ['hɛdlaɪt] *n* Scheinwerfer *m*.

headline ['hɛdlaɪn] *n* Schlagzeile *f*; (*RADIO, TV*): **(news)** ~**s** Nachrichtenüberblick *m*.

headlong ['hɛdlɔŋ] *adv* kopfüber; (*rush*) Hals über Kopf.

headmaster [hɛd'mɑːstə'] *n* Schulleiter *m*.

headmistress [hɛd'mɪstrɪs] *n* Schulleiterin *f*.

head office *n* Zentrale *f*.

head of state (*pl* **heads of state**) *n* Staatsoberhaupt *nt*.

head-on ['hɛd'ɔn] *adj* (*collision*) frontal; (*confrontation*) direkt.

headphones ['hɛdfəunz] *npl* Kopfhörer *pl*.

headquarters ['hɛdkwɔːtəz] *npl* Zentrale *f*; (*MIL*) Hauptquartier *nt*.

headrest ['hɛdrɛst] *n* (*AUT*) Kopfstütze *f*.

headroom ['hɛdrum] *n* (*in car*) Kopfraum *m*; (*under bridge*) lichte Höhe *f*.

headscarf ['hɛdskɑːf] *n* Kopftuch *nt*.

headset ['hɛdsɛt] *n* = **headphones**.

head start *n* Vorsprung *m*.

headstone ['hɛdstəun] *n* Grabstein *m*.

headstrong ['hɛdstrɔŋ] *adj* eigensinnig.

head waiter *n* Oberkellner *m*.

headway ['hɛdweɪ] *n*: **to make** ~ vorankommen.

headwind ['hɛdwɪnd] *n* Gegenwind *m*.

heady ['hɛdɪ] *adj* (*experience etc*) aufregend; (*drink, atmosphere*) berauschend.

heal [hiːl] *vt*, *vi* heilen.

health [hɛlθ] *n* Gesundheit *f*.

health care *n* Gesundheitsfürsorge *f*.

health centre (*BRIT*) *n* Ärztezentrum *nt*.

health food *n* Reformkost *f*, Naturkost *f*.

health food shop *n* Reformhaus *nt*, Naturkostladen *m*.

health hazard *n* Gefahr *f* für die Gesundheit.

health service (*BRIT*) *n*: **the H~ S~** das Gesundheitswesen.

healthy ['hɛlθɪ] *adj* gesund; (*profit*) ansehnlich.

heap [hiːp] *n* Haufen *m* ♦ *vt*: **to** ~ **(up)** (auf)häufen; ~**s of** (*inf*) jede Menge; **to** ~ **sth with** etw beladen mit; **to** ~ **sth on** etw häufen auf +*acc*; **to** ~ **favours/gifts** *etc* **on sb** jdn mit Gefälligkeiten/Geschenken *etc* überhäufen; **to** ~ **praises on sb** jdn mit Lob überschütten.

hear [hɪə'] (*pt, pp* **heard**) *vt* hören; (*LAW: case*) verhandeln; (: *witness*) vernehmen; **to** ~ **about** hören von; **to** ~ **from sb** von jdm hören; **I've never heard of that book** von dem Buch habe ich noch nie etwas gehört; **I wouldn't** ~ **of it!** davon will ich nichts hören.

▶**hear out** *vt* ausreden lassen.

heard [həːd] *pt, pp of* **hear**.

hearing ['hɪərɪŋ] *n* Gehör *nt*; (*of facts, by committee*) Anhörung *f*; (*of witnesses*) Vernehmung *f*; (*of a case*) Verhandlung *f*; **to give sb a** ~ (*BRIT*) jdn anhören.

hearing aid *n* Hörgerät *nt*.

hearsay ['hɪəseɪ] *n* Gerüchte *pl*; **by** ~ vom Hörensagen.

hearse [həːs] *n* Leichenwagen *m*.

heart [hɑːt] *n* Herz *nt*; (*of problem*) Kern *m*; **hearts** *npl* (*CARDS*) Herz *nt*; **to lose** ~ den Mut verlieren; **to take** ~ Mut fassen; **at** ~ im Grunde; **by** ~ auswendig; **to set one's** ~ **on sth** sein Herz an etw *acc* hängen; **to set one's** ~ **on doing sth** alles daransetzen, etw zu tun; **the** ~ **of the matter** der Kern der Sache.

heartache ['hɑːteɪk] *n* Kummer *m*.

heart attack *n* Herzanfall *m*.

heartbeat ['hɑːtbiːt] *n* Herzschlag *m*.

heartbreak ['hɑːtbreɪk] *n* großer Kummer *m*, Leid *nt*.

heartbreaking ['hɑːtbreɪkɪŋ] *adj* herzzerreißend.

heartbroken ['hɑːtbrəukən] *adj*: **to be** ~ todunglücklich sein.

heartburn ['hɑːtbəːn] *n* Sodbrennen *nt*.

-hearted ['hɑːtɪd] *suff*: **kind-**~ gutherzig.

heartening ['hɑːtnɪŋ] *adj* ermutigend.

heart failure *n* Herzversagen *nt*.

heartfelt ['hɑːtfɛlt] *adj* tief empfunden.

hearth [hɑːθ] *n* ≈ Kamin *m*.

heartily ['hɑːtɪlɪ] *adv* (*see adj*) (laut und)

herzlich; herzhaft; tief; ungeteilt.

heartland ['hɑːtlænd] *n* Herz *nt*; **Britain's industrial** ~ Großbritanniens Industriezentrum.

heartless ['hɑːtlɪs] *adj* herzlos.

heartstrings ['hɑːtstrɪŋz] *npl:* **to tug at sb's** ~ bei jdm auf die Tränendrüsen drücken.

heart-throb ['hɑːtθrɔb] *(inf) n* Schwarm *m*.

heart-to-heart ['hɑːt'tə'hɑːt] *adj, adv* ganz im Vertrauen.

heart transplant *n* Herztransplantation *f*, Herzverpflanzung *f*.

heart-warming ['hɑːtwɔːmɪŋ] *adj* herzerfreuend.

hearty ['hɑːtɪ] *adj (person)* laut und herzlich; *(laugh, appetite)* herzhaft; *(welcome)* herzlich; *(dislike)* tief; *(support)* ungeteilt.

heat [hiːt] *n* Hitze *f*; *(warmth)* Wärme *f*; *(temperature)* Temperatur *f*; *(SPORT: also:* **qualifying** ~*)* Vorrunde *f* ♦ *vt* erhitzen, heiß machen; *(room, house)* heizen; **in** *or (BRIT)* **on** ~ *(ZOOL)* brünstig, läufig.

►**heat up** *vi* sich erwärmen, warm werden ♦ *vt* aufwärmen; *(water, room)* erwärmen.

heated ['hiːtɪd] *adj* geheizt; *(pool)* beheizt; *(argument)* hitzig.

heater ['hiːtə*] *n* (Heiz)ofen *m*; *(in car)* Heizung *f*.

heath [hiːθ] *(BRIT) n* Heide *f*.

heathen ['hiːðn] *n* Heide *m*, Heidin *f*.

heather ['hɛðə*] *n* Heidekraut *nt*, Erika *f*.

heating ['hiːtɪŋ] *n* Heizung *f*.

heat-resistant ['hiːtrɪzɪstənt] *adj* hitzebeständig.

heat-seeking ['hiːtsiːkɪŋ] *adj* wärmesuchend.

heatstroke ['hiːtstrəuk] *n* Hitzschlag *m*.

heat wave *n* Hitzewelle *f*.

heave [hiːv] *vt (pull)* ziehen; *(push)* schieben; *(lift)* (hoch)heben ♦ *vi* sich heben und senken; *(retch)* sich übergeben ♦ *n (see vt)* Zug *m*; Stoß *m*; Heben *nt*; **to** ~ **a sigh** einen Seufzer ausstoßen.

►**heave to** *(pt, pp* **hove)** *vi (NAUT)* beidrehen.

heaven ['hɛvn] *n* Himmel *m*; **thank** ~! Gott sei Dank!; ~ **forbid!** bloß nicht!; **for** ~**'s sake!** um Himmels *or* Gottes willen!

heavenly ['hɛvnlɪ] *adj* himmlisch.

heaven-sent [hɛvn'sɛnt] *adj* ideal.

heavily ['hɛvɪlɪ] *adv* schwer; *(drink, smoke, depend, rely)* stark; *(sleep, sigh)* tief; *(say)* mit schwerer Stimme.

heavy ['hɛvɪ] *adj* schwer; *(clothes)* dick; *(rain, snow, drinker, smoker)* stark; *(build, frame)* kräftig; *(breathing, sleep)* tief; *(schedule, week)* anstrengend; *(weather)* drückend, schwül; **the conversation was** ~ **going** die Unterhaltung war mühsam; **the book was** ~ **going** das Buch las sich schwer.

heavy cream *(US) n* Sahne mit hohem Fettgehalt, ≈ Schlagsahne *f*.

heavy-duty ['hɛvɪ'djuːtɪ] *adj* strapazierfähig.

heavy goods vehicle *n* Lastkraftwagen *m*.

heavy-handed ['hɛvɪ'hændɪd] *adj* schwerfällig, ungeschickt.

heavy industry *n* Schwerindustrie *f*.

heavy metal *n (MUS)* Heavy metal *nt*.

heavyset ['hɛvɪ'sɛt] *(esp US) adj* kräftig gebaut.

heavyweight ['hɛvɪweɪt] *n (SPORT)* Schwergewicht *nt*.

Hebrew ['hiːbruː] *adj* hebräisch ♦ *n (LING)* Hebräisch *nt*.

Hebrides ['hɛbrɪdiːz] *npl:* **the** ~ die Hebriden *pl*.

heck [hɛk] *(inf) interj:* **oh** ~! zum Kuckuck! ♦ *n:* **a** ~ **of a lot** irrsinnig viel.

heckle ['hɛkl] *vt* durch Zwischenrufe stören.

heckler ['hɛklə*] *n* Zwischenrufer(in) *m(f)*, Störer(in) *m(f)*.

hectare ['hɛktɑː*] *(BRIT) n* Hektar *nt or m*.

hectic ['hɛktɪk] *adj* hektisch.

hector ['hɛktə*] *vt* tyrannisieren.

he'd [hiːd] = **he would; he had.**

hedge [hɛdʒ] *n* Hecke *f* ♦ *vi* ausweichen, sich nicht festlegen ♦ *vt:* **to** ~ **one's bets** *(fig)* sich absichern; **as a** ~ **against inflation** als Absicherung *or* Schutz gegen die Inflation.

►**hedge in** *vt (person)* (in seiner Freiheit) einschränken; *(proposals etc)* behindern.

hedgehog ['hɛdʒhɔg] *n* Igel *m*.

hedgerow ['hɛdʒrəu] *n* Hecke *f*.

hedonism ['hiːdənɪzəm] *n* Hedonismus *m*.

heed [hiːd] *vt (also:* **take** ~ **of)** beachten ♦ *n:* **to pay (no)** ~ **to, take (no)** ~ **of** (nicht) beachten.

heedless ['hiːdlɪs] *adj* achtlos; ~ **of sb/sth** ohne auf jdn/etw zu achten.

heel [hiːl] *n* Ferse *f*; *(of shoe)* Absatz *m* ♦ *vt (shoe)* mit einem neuen Absatz versehen; **to bring to** ~ *(dog)* bei Fuß gehen lassen; *(fig: person)* an die Kandare nehmen; **to take to one's** ~**s** *(inf)* sich aus dem Staub machen.

hefty ['hɛftɪ] *adj* kräftig; *(parcel etc)* schwer; *(profit)* ansehnlich.

heifer ['hɛfə*] *n* Färse *f*.

height [haɪt] *n* Höhe *f*; *(of person)* Größe *f*; *(fig: of luxury, good taste etc)* Gipfel *m*; **what** ~ **are you?** wie groß bist du?; **of average** ~ durchschnittlich groß; **to be afraid of** ~**s** nicht schwindelfrei sein; **it's the** ~ **of fashion** das ist die neueste Mode; **at the** ~ **of the tourist season** in der Hauptsaison.

heighten ['haɪtn] *vt* erhöhen.

heinous ['heɪnəs] *adj* abscheulich, verabscheuungswürdig.

heir [ɛə*] *n* Erbe *m*; **the** ~ **to the throne** der Thronfolger.

heir apparent *n* gesetzlicher Erbe *m*.

heiress ['ɛərɛs] *n* Erbin *f*.

heirloom ['ɛəluːm] *n* Erbstück *nt*.

heist [haɪst] *(US: inf) n* Raubüberfall *m*.

held [hɛld] *pt, pp of* **hold.**

helicopter ['hɛlɪkɔptə*] *n* Hubschrauber *m*.

heliport ['hɛlɪpɔːt] *n* Hubschrauberflugplatz

m, Heliport m.

helium ['hi:lɪəm] n Helium nt.

hell [hɛl] n Hölle f; ~! (inf!) verdammt! (inf!); a ~ of a lot (inf) verdammt viel (inf); a ~ of a mess (inf) ein wahnsinniges Chaos (inf); a ~ of a noise (inf) ein Höllenlärm m; a ~ of a nice guy ein wahnsinnig netter Typ.

he'll [hi:l] = **he will; he shall.**

hellbent [hɛl'bɛnt] adj: ~ (on) versessen (auf +acc).

hellish ['hɛlɪʃ] (inf) adj höllisch.

hello [hə'ləʊ] excl hallo; (expressing surprise) nanu, he.

Hell's Angels npl Hell's Angels pl.

helm [hɛlm] n Ruder nt, Steuer nt; at the ~ am Ruder.

helmet ['hɛlmɪt] n Helm m.

helmsman ['hɛlmzmən] (irreg: like **man**) n Steuermann m.

help [hɛlp] n Hilfe f; (charwoman) (Haushalts)hilfe f ♦ vt helfen +dat; with the ~ of (person) mit (der) Hilfe +gen; (tool etc) mit Hilfe +gen; to be of ~ to sb jdm behilflich sein, jdm helfen; can I ~ you? (in shop) womit kann ich Ihnen dienen?; ~ yourself bedienen Sie sich; he can't ~ it er kann nichts dafür; I can't ~ thinking that ... ich kann mir nicht helfen, ich glaube, daß ...

helper ['hɛlpə•] n Helfer(in) m(f).

helpful ['hɛlpful] adj hilfsbereit; (advice, suggestion) nützlich, hilfreich.

helping ['hɛlpɪŋ] n Portion f.

helping hand n: to give or lend sb a ~ jdm behilflich sein.

helpless ['hɛlplɪs] adj hilflos.

helplessly ['hɛlplɪslɪ] adv hilflos.

helpline ['hɛlplaɪn] n (for emergencies) Notruf m; (for information) Informationsdienst m.

Helsinki ['hɛlsɪŋkɪ] n Helsinki nt.

helter-skelter ['hɛltə'skɛltə•] (BRIT) n Rutschbahn f.

hem [hɛm] n Saum m ♦ vt säumen.

▶**hem in** vt einschließen, umgeben; to feel ~med in (fig) sich eingeengt fühlen.

hematology ['hi:mə'tɔlədʒɪ] (US) n = haematology.

hemisphere ['hɛmɪsfɪə•] n Hemisphäre f; (of sphere) Halbkugel f.

hemlock ['hɛmlɔk] n Schierling m.

hemoglobin ['hi:mə'gləʊbɪn] (US) n = haemoglobin.

hemophilia ['hi:mə'fɪlɪə] (US) n = haemophilia.

hemorrhage ['hɛmərɪdʒ] (US) n = haemorrhage.

hemorrhoids ['hɛmərɔɪdz] (US) npl = haemorrhoids.

hemp [hɛmp] n Hanf m.

hen [hɛn] n Henne f, Huhn nt; (female bird) Weibchen nt.

hence [hɛns] adv daher; **2 years** ~ in zwei Jahren.

henceforth [hɛns'fɔ:θ] adv von nun an; (from that time on) von da an.

henchman ['hɛntʃmən] (irreg: like **man**) (pej) n Spießgeselle m.

henna ['hɛnə] n Henna nt.

hen night, hen party (inf) n Damenkränzchen nt.

Als **hen night** bezeichnet man eine feuchtfröhliche Frauenparty, die kurz vor einer Hochzeit von der Braut und ihren Freundinnen meist in einem Gasthaus oder Nachtklub abgehalten wird, und bei der die Freundinnen dafür sorgen, daß vor allem die Braut große Mengen an Alkohol konsumiert. Siehe auch **stag night.**

---

henpecked ['hɛnpɛkt] adj: to be ~ unter dem Pantoffel stehen; ~ husband Pantoffelheld m.

hepatitis [hɛpə'taɪtɪs] n Hepatitis f.

her [hɜ:•] pron sie; (indirect) ihr ♦ adj ihr; I see ~ ich sehe sie; give ~ a book gib ihr ein Buch; after ~ nach ihr; see also **me; my.**

herald ['hɛrəld] n (Vor)bote m ♦ vt ankündigen.

heraldic [hɛ'rældɪk] adj heraldisch, Wappen-.

heraldry ['hɛrəldrɪ] n Wappenkunde f, Heraldik f; (coats of arms) Wappen pl.

herb [hɜ:b] n Kraut nt.

herbaceous [hɜ:'beɪʃəs] adj: ~ border Staudenrabatte f; ~ plant Staude f.

herbal ['hɜ:bl] adj (tea, medicine) Kräuter-.

herbicide ['hɜ:bɪsaɪd] n Unkrautvertilgungsmittel nt, Herbizid nt.

herd [hɜ:d] n Herde f; (of wild animals) Rudel nt ♦ vt treiben; (gather) zusammentreiben; ~ed together zusammengetrieben.

here [hɪə•] adv hier; she left ~ yesterday sie ist gestern von hier abgereist; ~ is/are... hier ist/sind...; ~ you are (giving) (hier,) bitte; ~ we are! (finding sth) da ist es ja!; ~ she is! da ist sie ja!; ~ she comes da kommt sie ja; come ~! komm hierher or hierhin!; ~ and there hier und da; "~'s to ..." „auf ... acc".

hereabouts ['hɪərə'baʊts] adv hier.

hereafter [hɪər'ɑ:ftə•] adv künftig.

hereby [hɪə'baɪ] adv hiermit.

hereditary [hɪ'rɛdɪtrɪ] adj erblich, Erb-.

heredity [hɪ'rɛdɪtɪ] n Vererbung f.

heresy ['hɛrəsɪ] n Ketzerei f.

heretic ['hɛrətɪk] n Ketzer(in) m(f).

heretical [hɪ'rɛtɪkl] adj ketzerisch.

herewith [hɪə'wɪð] adv hiermit.

heritage ['hɛrɪtɪdʒ] n Erbe nt; our national ~ unser nationales Erbe.

hermetically [hɜ:'mɛtɪklɪ] adv: ~ sealed hermetisch verschlossen.

hermit ['hɜ:mɪt] n Einsiedler(in) m(f).

hernia ['hɜ:nɪə] n Bruch m.

hero ['hɪərəʊ] (*pl* ~**es**) *n* Held *m*; (*idol*) Idol *nt*.
heroic [hɪ'rəʊɪk] *adj* heroisch; (*figure, person*) heldenhaft.
heroin ['herəʊɪn] *n* Heroin *nt*.
heroin addict *n* Heroinsüchtige(r) *f(m)*.
heroine ['herəʊɪn] *n* Heldin *f*; (*idol*) Idol *nt*.
heroism ['herəʊɪzəm] *n* Heldentum *nt*.
heron ['herən] *n* Reiher *m*.
hero worship *n* Heldenverehrung *f*.
herring ['herɪŋ] *n* Hering *m*.
hers [hɜːz] *pron* ihre(r, s); **a friend of** ~ ein Freund von ihr; **this is** ~ das gehört ihr; *see also* **mine**.
herself [hə'self] *pron* sich; (*emphatic*) (sie) selbst; *see also* **oneself**.
Herts [hɑːts] (*BRIT*) *abbr* (*POST:* = *Hertfordshire*).
he's [hiːz] = **he is; he has.**
hesitant ['hezɪtənt] *adj* zögernd; **to be** ~ **about doing sth** zögern, etw zu tun.
hesitate ['hezɪteɪt] *vi* zögern; (*be unwilling*) Bedenken haben; **to** ~ **about** Bedenken haben wegen; **don't** ~ **to see a doctor if you are worried** gehen Sie ruhig zum Arzt, wenn Sie sich Sorgen machen.
hesitation [hezɪ'teɪʃən] *n* Zögern *nt*; Bedenken *pl*; **to have no** ~ **in saying sth** etw ohne weiteres sagen können.
hessian ['hesɪən] *n* Sackleinwand *f*, Rupfen *m*.
heterogenous [hetə'rɔdʒɪnəs] *adj* heterogen.
heterosexual ['hetərəʊ'seksjʊəl] *adj* heterosexuell ♦ *n* Heterosexuelle(r) *f(m)*.
het up [het-] (*inf*) *adj:* **to get** ~ **(about)** sich aufregen (über +*acc*).
HEW (*US*) *n abbr* (= *Department of Health, Education and Welfare*) *Ministerium für Gesundheit, Erziehung und Sozialfürsorge.*
hew [hjuː] (*pt, pp* **hewed** *or* **hewn**) *vt* (*stone*) behauen; (*wood*) hacken.
hex [heks] (*US*) *n* Fluch *m* ♦ *vt* verhexen.
hexagon ['heksəgən] *n* Sechseck *nt*.
hexagonal [hek'sægənl] *adj* sechseckig.
hey [heɪ] *excl* he; (*to attract attention*) he du/Sie.
heyday ['heɪdeɪ] *n:* **the** ~ **of** (*person*) die Glanzzeit +*gen*; (*nation, group etc*) die Blütezeit +*gen*.
HF *n abbr* (= *high frequency*) HF.
HGV (*BRIT*) *n abbr* (= *heavy goods vehicle*) LKW *m*.
HI (*US*) *abbr* (*POST:* = *Hawaii*).
hi [haɪ] *excl* hallo.
hiatus [haɪ'eɪtəs] *n* Unterbrechung *f*.
hibernate ['haɪbəneɪt] *vi* Winterschlaf halten *or* machen.
hibernation [haɪbə'neɪʃən] *n* Winterschlaf *m*.
hiccough ['hɪkʌp] *vi* hicksen.
hiccoughs ['hɪkʌps] *npl* Schluckauf *m*; **to have (the)** ~ den Schluckauf haben.
hiccup ['hɪkʌp] *vi* = **hiccough.**
hiccups ['hɪkʌps] *npl* = **hiccoughs.**
hick [hɪk] (*US: inf*) *n* Hinterwäldler *m*.
hid [hɪd] *pt of* **hide.**

hidden ['hɪdn] *pp of* **hide** ♦ *adj* (*advantage, danger*) unsichtbar; (*place*) versteckt; **there are no** ~ **extras** es gibt keine versteckten Extrakosten.
hide [haɪd] (*pt* **hid**, *pp* **hidden**) *n* Haut *f*, Fell *nt*; (*of birdwatcher etc*) Versteck *nt* ♦ *vt* verstecken; (*feeling, information*) verbergen; (*obscure*) verdecken ♦ *vi:* **to** ~ **(from sb)** sich (vor jdm) verstecken; **to** ~ **sth (from sb)** etw (vor jdm) verstecken.
hide-and-seek ['haɪdən'siːk] *n* Versteckspiel *nt*; **to play** ~ Verstecken spielen.
hideaway ['haɪdəweɪ] *n* Zufluchtsort *m*.
hideous ['hɪdɪəs] *adj* scheußlich; (*conditions*) furchtbar.
hideously ['hɪdɪəsli] *adv* furchtbar.
hide-out ['haɪdaʊt] *n* Versteck *nt*.
hiding ['haɪdɪŋ] *n* Tracht *f* Prügel; **to be in** ~ (*concealed*) sich versteckt halten.
hiding place *n* Versteck *nt*.
hierarchy ['haɪərɑːkɪ] *n* Hierarchie *f*.
hieroglyphic [haɪərə'glɪfɪk] *adj* hieroglyphisch.
hieroglyphics [haɪərə'glɪfɪks] *npl* Hieroglyphen *pl*.
hi-fi ['haɪfaɪ] *n abbr* (= *high fidelity*) Hi-Fi *nt* ♦ *adj* (*equipment etc*) Hi-Fi-.
higgledy-piggledy ['hɪgldɪ'pɪgldɪ] *adj* durcheinander.
high [haɪ] *adj* hoch; (*wind*) stark; (*risk*) groß; (*quality*) gut; (*inf: on drugs*) high; (: *on drink*) blau; (*BRIT: food*) schlecht; (: *game*) anbrüchig ♦ *adv* hoch ♦ *n:* **exports have reached a new** ~ der Export hat einen neuen Höchststand erreicht; **to pay a** ~ **price for sth** etw teuer bezahlen; **it's** ~ **time you did it** es ist *or* wird höchste Zeit, daß du es machst; ~ **in the air** hoch oben in der Luft.
highball ['haɪbɔːl] (*US*) *n* Highball *m*.
highboy ['haɪbɔɪ] (*US*) *n* hohe Kommode *f*.
highbrow ['haɪbraʊ] *adj* intellektuell; (*book, discussion etc*) anspruchsvoll.
highchair ['haɪtʃɛə*] *n* Hochstuhl *m*.
high-class ['haɪ'klɑːs] *adj* erstklassig; (*neighbourhood*) vornehm.

High Court ist in *England und Wales* die Kurzform für *High Court of Justice* und bildet zusammen mit dem *Berufungsgericht* den *Obersten Gerichtshof.* In *Schottland* ist es die Kurzform für *High Court of Justiciary*, das höchste Strafgericht in Schottland, das in Edinburgh und anderen Großstädten (immer mit Richter und Geschworenen) zusammentritt und für Verbrechen wie Mord, Vergewaltigung und Hochverrat zuständig ist. Weniger schwere Verbrechen werden vor dem *sheriff court* verhandelt, und leichtere Vergehen vor dem *district court.*

---

higher ['haɪə*] *adj* (*form of study, life etc*) höher

(entwickelt) ♦ *adv* höher.
higher education *n* Hochschulbildung *f.*
highfalutin [haɪfə'luːtɪn] (*inf*) *adj* (*behaviour, ideas*) hochtrabend.
high finance *n* Hochfinanz *f.*
high-flier, high-flyer [haɪ'flaɪə*] *n* Senkrechtstarter(in) *m(f).*
high-flying [haɪ'flaɪɪŋ] *adj* (*person*) erfolgreich; (*lifestyle*) exklusiv.
high-handed [haɪ'hændɪd] *adj* eigenmächtig.
high-heeled [haɪ'hiːld] *adj* hochhackig.
high heels *npl* hochhackige Schuhe *pl.*
high jump *n* Hochsprung *m.*
Highlands ['haɪləndz] *npl:* **the ~** das Hochland.
high-level ['haɪlɛvl] *adj* (*talks etc*) auf höchster Ebene; **~ language** (*COMPUT*) höhere Programmiersprache *f.*
highlight ['haɪlaɪt] *n* (*of event*) Höhepunkt *m*; (*in hair*) Strähnchen *nt* ♦ *vt* (*problem, need*) ein Schlaglicht werfen auf *+acc.*
highlighter ['haɪlaɪtə*] *n* Textmarker *m.*
highly ['haɪlɪ] *adv* hoch-; **to speak ~ of** sich sehr positiv äußern über *+acc;* **to think ~ of** eine hohe Meinung haben von.
highly strung *adj* nervös.
High Mass *n* Hochamt *nt.*
highness ['haɪnɪs] *n:* **Her/His/Your H~** Ihre/Seine/Eure Hoheit *f.*
high-pitched [haɪ'pɪtʃt] *adj* hoch.
high point *n* Höhepunkt *m.*
high-powered ['haɪ'pauəd] *adj* (*engine*) Hochleistungs-; (*job*) Spitzen-; (*businessman*) dynamisch; (*person*) äußerst fähig; (*course*) anspruchsvoll.
high-pressure ['haɪprɛʃə*] *adj* (*area, system*) Hochdruck-; (*inf: sales technique*) aggressiv.
high-rise ['haɪraɪz] *adj* (*apartment, block*) Hochhaus-; **~ building/flats** Hochhaus *nt.*
high school *n* ≈ Oberschule *f.*

High school ist eine weiterführende Schule in den USA. Man unterscheidet zwischen **junior high school** (im Anschluß an die Grundschule, umfaßt das 7., 8. und 9. Schuljahr) und **senior high school** (10., 11. und 12. Schuljahr, mit akademischen und berufsbezogenen Fächern). Weiterführende Schulen in Großbritannien werden manchmal auch als high school bezeichnet. Siehe auch **elementary school**.

---

high season (*BRIT*) *n* Hochsaison *f.*
high spirits *npl* Hochstimmung *f.*
high street (*BRIT*) *n* Hauptstraße *f.*
high strung (*US*) *adj* = **highly strung.**
high tide *n* Flut *f.*
highway ['haɪweɪ] (*US*) *n* Straße *f*; (*between towns, states*) Landstraße *f*; **information ~** Datenautobahn *f.*
Highway Code (*BRIT*) *n* Straßenverkehrsordnung *f.*
highwayman ['haɪweɪmən] (*irreg: like* **man**) *n*

Räuber *m*, Wegelagerer *m.*
hijack ['haɪdʒæk] *vt* entführen ♦ *n* (*also:* **~ing**) Entführung *f.*
hijacker ['haɪdʒækə*] *n* Entführer(in) *m(f).*
hike [haɪk] *vi* wandern ♦ *n* Wanderung *f*; (*inf: in prices etc*) Erhöhung *f* ♦ *vt* (*inf*) erhöhen.
hiker ['haɪkə*] *n* Wanderer *m*, Wanderin *f.*
hiking ['haɪkɪŋ] *n* Wandern *nt.*
hilarious [hɪ'lɛərɪəs] *adj* urkomisch.
hilarity [hɪ'lærɪtɪ] *n* übermütige Ausgelassenheit *f.*
hill [hɪl] *n* Hügel *m*; (*fairly high*) Berg *m*; (*slope*) Hang *m*; (*on road*) Steigung *f.*
hillbilly ['hɪlbɪlɪ] (*US*) *n* Hillbilly *m*; (*pej*) Hinterwäldler(in) *m(f)*, Landpomeranze *f.*
hillock ['hɪlək] *n* Hügel *m*, Anhöhe *f.*
hillside ['hɪlsaɪd] *n* Hang *m.*
hill start *n* (*AUT*) Anfahren *nt* am Berg.
hilltop ['hɪltɔp] *n* Gipfel *m.*
hilly ['hɪlɪ] *adj* hügelig.
hilt [hɪlt] *n* (*of sword, knife*) Heft *nt*; **to the ~** voll und ganz.
him [hɪm] *pron* ihn; (*indirect*) ihm; *see also* **me.**
Himalayas [hɪmə'leɪəz] *npl:* **the ~** der Himalaja.
himself [hɪm'sɛlf] *pron* sich; (*emphatic*) (er) selbst; *see also* **oneself.**
hind [haɪnd] *adj* (*legs*) Hinter- ♦ *n* (*female deer*) Hirschkuh *f.*
hinder ['hɪndə*] *vt* behindern; **to ~ sb from doing sth** jdn daran hindern, etw zu tun.
hindquarters ['haɪnd'kwɔːtəz] *npl* Hinterteil *nt.*
hindrance ['hɪndrəns] *n* Behinderung *f.*
hindsight ['haɪndsaɪt] *n:* **with ~** im nachhinein.
Hindu ['hɪnduː] *adj* hinduistisch, Hindu-.
hinge [hɪndʒ] *n* (*on door*) Angel *f* ♦ *vi:* **to ~ on** anhängen von.
hint [hɪnt] *n* Andeutung *f*; (*advice*) Tip *m*; (*sign, glimmer*) Spur *f* ♦ *vt:* **to ~ that** andeuten, daß ♦ *vi:* **to ~ at** andeuten; **to drop a ~** eine Andeutung machen; **give me a ~** geben Sie mir einen Hinweis; **white with a ~ of pink** weiß mit einem Hauch von Rosa.
hip [hɪp] *n* Hüfte *f.*
hip flask *n* Taschenflasche *f*, Flachmann *m* (*inf*).
hip-hop ['hɪphɔp] *n* Hip-Hop *nt.*
hippie ['hɪpɪ] *n* Hippie *m.*
hippo ['hɪpəu] *n* Nilpferd *nt.*
hip pocket *n* Gesäßtasche *f.*
hippopotamus [hɪpə'pɔtəməs] (*pl* **~es** *or* **hippopotami**) *n* Nilpferd *nt.*
hippy ['hɪpɪ] *n* = **hippie.**
hire ['haɪə*] *vt* (*BRIT*) mieten; (*worker*) einstellen ♦ *n* (*BRIT*) Mieten *nt*; **for ~** (*taxi*) frei; (*boat*) zu vermieten; **on ~** gemietet.
►**hire out** *vt* vermieten.
hire(d) car (*BRIT*) *n* Mietwagen *m*, Leihwagen *m.*
hire-purchase [haɪə'pɜːtʃɪs] (*BRIT*) *n*

Ratenkauf *m*; **to buy sth on** ~ etw auf Raten kaufen.

his [hɪz] *pron* seine(r, s) ♦ *adj* sein; *see also* **my**; **mine**.

hiss [hɪs] *vi* zischen; (*cat*) fauchen ♦ *n* Zischen *nt*; (*of cat*) Fauchen *nt*.

histogram ['hɪstəgræm] *n* Histogramm *nt*.

historian [hɪ'stɔːrɪən] *n* Historiker(in) *m(f)*.

historic [hɪ'stɔrɪk] *adj* historisch.

historical [hɪ'stɔrɪkl] *adj* historisch.

history ['hɪstərɪ] *n* Geschichte *f*; **there's a** ~ **of heart disease in his family** Herzleiden liegen bei ihm in der Familie; **medical** ~ Krankengeschichte *f*.

hit [hɪt] (*pt, pp* **hit**) *vt* schlagen; (*reach, affect*) treffen; (*vehicle: another vehicle*) zusammenstoßen mit; (: *wall, tree*) fahren gegen; (: : *more violently*) prallen gegen; (: *person*) anfahren ♦ *n* Schlag *m*; (*success*) Erfolg *m*; (*song*) Hit *m*; **to** ~ **it off with sb** sich gut mit jdm verstehen; **to** ~ **the headlines** Schlagzeilen machen; **to** ~ **the road** (*inf*) sich auf den Weg *or* die Socken (*inf*) machen; **to** ~ **the roof** (*inf*) an die Decke *or* in die Luft gehen.

►**hit back** *vi:* **to** ~ **back at sb** jdn zurückschlagen; (*fig*) jdm Kontra geben.

►**hit out at** *vt fus* auf jdn losschlagen; (*fig*) jdn scharf angreifen.

►**hit (up)on** *vt fus* stoßen auf +*acc*, finden.

hit-and-miss ['hɪtən'mɪs] *adj* = **hit-or-miss**.

hit-and-run driver ['hɪtən'rʌn-] *n* unfallflüchtiger Fahrer *m*, unfallflüchtige Fahrerin *f*.

hitch [hɪtʃ] *vt* festmachen, anbinden; (*also:* ~ **up**: *trousers, skirt*) hochziehen ♦ *n* Schwierigkeit *f*, Problem *nt*; **to** ~ **a lift** trampen, per Anhalter fahren; **technical** ~ technische Panne *f*.

►**hitch up** *vt* anspannen; *see also* **hitch**.

hitchhike ['hɪtʃhaɪk] *vi* trampen, per Anhalter fahren.

hitchhiker ['hɪtʃhaɪkə*] *n* Tramper(in) *m(f)*, Anhalter(in) *m(f)*.

hi-tech ['haɪ'tɛk] *adj* High-Tech-, hochtechnisiert ♦ *n* High-Tech *nt*, Hochtechnologie *f*.

hitherto [hɪðə'tuː] *adv* bisher, bis jetzt.

'hit list *n* Abschußliste *f*.

hit man (*inf*) *n* Killer *m*.

hit-or-miss ['hɪtə'mɪs] *adj* ungeplant; **to be a** ~ **affair** eine unsichere Sache sein; **it's** ~ **whether** ... es ist nicht zu sagen, ob ...

hit parade *n* Hitparade *f*.

HIV *n abbr* (= *human immunodeficiency virus*) HIV; ~-**negative** HIV-negativ; ~-**positive** HIV-positiv.

hive [haɪv] *n* Bienenkorb *m*; **to be a** ~ **of activity** einem Bienenhaus gleichen.

►**hive off** (*inf*) *vt* ausgliedern, abspalten.

hl *abbr* (= *hectolitre*) hl.

HM *abbr* (= *His/Her Majesty*) S./I.M.

HMG (*BRIT*) *abbr* (= *His/Her Majesty's Government*) die Regierung Seiner/Ihrer Majestät.

HMI (*BRIT*) *n abbr* (*SCOL:* = *His/Her Majesty's Inspector*) *regierungsamtlicher Schulaufsichtsbeauftragter.*

HMO (*US*) *n abbr* (= *health maintenance organization*) Organisation zur Gesundheitsfürsorge.

HMS (*BRIT*) *abbr* (= *His (or Her) Majesty's Ship*) *Namensteil von Schiffen der Kriegsmarine.*

HMSO (*BRIT*) *n abbr* (= *His (or Her) Majesty's Stationery Office*) *regierungsamtliche Druckerei.*

HNC (*BRIT*) *n abbr* (= *Higher National Certificate*) *Berufsschulabschluß.*

HND (*BRIT*) *n abbr* (= *Higher National Diploma*) *Qualifikationsnachweis in technischen Fächern.*

hoard [hɔːd] *n* (*of food*) Vorrat *m*; (*of money, treasure*) Schatz *m* ♦ *vt* (*food*) hamstern; (*money*) horten.

hoarding ['hɔːdɪŋ] (*BRIT*) *n* Plakatwand *f*.

hoarfrost ['hɔːfrɔst] *n* (Rauh)reif *m*.

hoarse [hɔːs] *adj* heiser.

hoax [həʊks] *n* (*false alarm*) blinder Alarm *m*.

hob [hɔb] *n* Kochmulde *f*.

hobble ['hɔbl] *vi* humpeln.

hobby ['hɔbɪ] *n* Hobby *nt*, Steckenpferd *nt*.

hobbyhorse ['hɔbɪhɔːs] *n* (*fig*) Lieblingsthema *nt*.

hobnail boot ['hɔbneɪl-] *n* Nagelschuh *m*.

hobnob ['hɔbnɔb] *vi:* **to** ~ **with** auf du und du stehen mit.

hobo ['həʊbəʊ] (*US*) *n* Penner *m* (*inf*).

hock [hɔk] *n* (*BRIT*) weißer Rheinwein *m*; (*of animal*) Sprunggelenk *nt*; (*US: CULIN*) Gelenkstück *nt*; (*inf*): **to be in** ~ (*person: in debt*) in Schulden stecken; (*object*) verpfändet *or* im Leihhaus sein.

hockey ['hɔkɪ] *n* Hockey *nt*.

hocus-pocus ['həʊkəs'pəʊkəs] *n* Hokuspokus *m*; (*trickery*) faule Tricks *pl*; (*jargon*) Jargon *m*.

hod [hɔd] *n* (*for bricks etc*) Tragemulde *f*.

hodgepodge ['hɔdʒpɔdʒ] (*US*) *n* = **hotchpotch**.

hoe [həʊ] *n* Hacke *f* ♦ *vt* hacken.

hog [hɔg] *n* (Mast)schwein *nt* ♦ *vt* (*road*) für sich beanspruchen; (*telephone etc*) in Beschlag nehmen; **to go the whole** ~ Nägel mit Köpfen machen.

Hogmanay [hɔgmə'neɪ] (*SCOT*) *n* Silvester *nt*.

hogwash ['hɔgwɔʃ] (*inf*) *n* (*nonsense*) Quatsch *m*.

ho hum ['həʊ'hʌm] *interj* na gut.

hoist [hɔɪst] *n* Hebevorrichtung *f* ♦ *vt* hochheben; (*flag, sail*) hissen.

hoity-toity [hɔɪtɪ'tɔɪtɪ] (*inf: pej*) *adj* hochnäsig.

hold [həʊld] (*pt, pp* **held**) *vt* halten; (*contain*) enthalten; (*power, qualification*) haben; (*opinion*) vertreten; (*meeting*) abhalten;

(*conversation*) führen; (*prisoner, hostage*) festhalten ♦ *vi* halten; (*be valid*) gelten; (*weather*) sich halten ♦ *n* (*grasp*) Griff *m*; (*of ship, plane*) Laderaum *m*; **to ~ one's head up** den Kopf hochhalten; **to ~ sb responsible/ liable** *etc* jdn verantwortlich/haftbar *etc* machen; **~ the line!** (*TEL*) bleiben Sie am Apparat!; **~ it!** Moment mal!; **to ~ one's own** sich behaupten; **he ~s the view that ...** er ist der Meinung *or* er vertritt die Ansicht, daß ...; **to ~ firm** *or* **fast** halten; **~ still!, ~ steady!** stillhalten!; **his luck held** das Glück blieb ihm treu; **I don't ~ with ...** ich bin gegen ...; **to catch** *or* **get (a) ~ of** sich festhalten an +*dat*; **to get ~ of** (*fig*) finden, auftreiben; **to get ~ of o.s.** sich in den Griff bekommen; **to have a ~ over** in der Hand haben.

►**hold back** *vt* zurückhalten; (*tears, laughter*) unterdrücken; (*secret*) verbergen; (*information*) geheimhalten.

►**hold down** *vt* niederhalten; (*job*) sich halten in +*dat*.

►**hold forth** *vi*: **to ~ forth (about)** sich ergehen *or* sich auslassen (über +*acc*).

►**hold off** *vt* abwehren ♦ *vi*: **if the rain ~s off** wenn es nicht regnet.

►**hold on** *vi* sich festhalten; (*wait*) warten; **~ on!** (*TEL*) einen Moment bitte!

►**hold on to** *vt fus* sich festhalten an; (*keep*) behalten.

►**hold out** *vt* (*hand*) ausstrecken; (*hope*) haben; (*prospect*) bieten ♦ *vi* nicht nachgeben.

►**hold over** *vt* vertagen.

►**hold up** *vt* hochheben; (*support*) stützen; (*delay*) aufhalten; (*rob*) überfallen.

holdall ['həʊldɔːl] (*BRIT*) *n* Tasche *f*; (*for clothes*) Reisetasche *f*.

holder ['həʊldə*] *n* Halter *m*; (*of ticket, record, office, title etc*) Inhaber(in) *m(f)*.

holding ['həʊldɪŋ] *n* (*share*) Anteil *m*; (*small farm*) Gut *nt* ♦ *adj* (*operation, tactic*) zur Schadensbegrenzung.

holding company *n* Dachgesellschaft *f*, Holdinggesellschaft *f*.

hold-up ['həʊldʌp] *n* bewaffneter Raubüberfall *m*; (*delay*) Verzögerung *f*; (*BRIT: in traffic*) Stockung *f*.

hole [həʊl] *n* Loch *nt*; (*unpleasant town*) Kaff *nt* (*inf*) ♦ *vt* (*ship*) leck schlagen; (*building etc*) durchlöchern; **~ in the heart** Loch im Herz(en); **to pick ~s** (*fig*) (über)kritisch sein; **to pick ~s in sth** (*fig*) an etw *dat* herumkritisieren.

►**hole up** *vi* sich verkriechen.

holiday ['hɒlɪdeɪ] *n* (*BRIT*) Urlaub *m*; (*SCOL*) Ferien *pl*; (*day off*) freier Tag *m*; (*public holiday*) Feiertag *m*; **on ~** im Urlaub, in den Ferien.

holiday camp (*BRIT*) *n* (*also:* **holiday centre**) Feriendorf *nt*.

holiday-maker ['hɒlɪdeɪmeɪkə*] (*BRIT*) *n* Urlauber(in) *m(f)*.

holiday pay *n* Lohn-/Gehaltsfortzahlung während des Urlaubs.

holiday resort *n* Ferienort *m*.

holiday season *n* Urlaubszeit *f*.

holiness ['həʊlɪnɪs] *n* Heiligkeit *f*.

holistic [həʊ'lɪstɪk] *adj* holistisch.

Holland ['hɒlənd] *n* Holland *nt*.

holler ['hɒlə*] (*inf*) *vi* brüllen ♦ *n* Schrei *m*.

hollow ['hɒləʊ] *adj* hohl; (*eyes*) tiefliegend; (*laugh*) unecht; (*sound*) dumpf; (*fig*) leer; (: *victory, opinion*) wertlos ♦ *n* Vertiefung *f* ♦ *vt*: **to ~ out** aushöhlen.

holly ['hɒlɪ] *n* Stechpalme *f*, Ilex *m*; (*leaves*) Stechpalmenzweige *pl*.

hollyhock ['hɒlɪhɒk] *n* Malve *f*.

holocaust ['hɒləkɔːst] *n* Inferno *nt*; (*in Third Reich*) Holocaust *m*.

hologram ['hɒləgræm] *n* Hologramm *nt*.

hols [hɒlz] (*inf*) *npl* Ferien *pl*.

holster ['həʊlstə*] *n* Pistolenhalfter *m or nt*.

holy ['həʊlɪ] *adj* heilig.

Holy Communion *n* Heilige Kommunion *f*.

Holy Father *n* Heiliger Vater *m*.

Holy Ghost *n* Heiliger Geist *m*.

Holy Land *n*: **the ~** das Heilige Land.

holy orders *npl* Priesterweihe *f*.

Holy Spirit *n* Heiliger Geist *m*.

homage ['hɒmɪdʒ] *n* Huldigung *f*; **to pay ~ to** huldigen +*dat*.

home [həʊm] *n* Heim *nt*; (*house, flat*) Zuhause *nt*; (*area, country*) Heimat *f*; (*institution*) Anstalt *f* ♦ *cpd* Heim-; (*ECON, POL*) Innen- ♦ *adv* (*go etc*) nach Hause, heim; **at ~** zu Hause; (*in country*) im Inland; **to be** *or* **feel at ~** (*fig*) sich wohl fühlen; **make yourself at ~** machen Sie es sich *dat* gemütlich *or* bequem; **to make one's ~ somewhere** sich irgendwo niederlassen; **the ~ of free enterprise/jazz** *etc* die Heimat des freien Unternehmertums/Jazz *etc*; **when will you be ~?** wann bist du wieder zu Hause?; **a ~ from ~** ein zweites Zuhause *nt*; **~ and dry** aus dem Schneider; **to drive a nail ~** einen Nagel einschlagen; **to bring sth ~ to sb** jdm etw klarmachen.

►**home in on** *vt fus* (*missiles*) sich ausrichten auf +*acc*.

home address *n* Heimatanschrift *f*.

home-brew [həʊm'bruː] *n* selbstgebrautes Bier *nt*.

homecoming ['həʊmkʌmɪŋ] *n* Heimkehr *f*.

home computer *n* Heimcomputer *m*.

Home Counties (*BRIT*) *npl*: **the ~** die Grafschaften, die an London angrenzen.

home economics *n* Hauswirtschaft(slehre) *f*.

home ground *n* (*SPORT*) eigener Platz *m*; **to be on ~** (*fig*) sich auf vertrautem Terrain bewegen.

home-grown ['həʊmgrəʊn] *adj* (*not foreign*)

einheimisch; *(from garden)* selbstgezogen.
home help n Haushaltshilfe f.
homeland ['həumlænd] n Heimat f,
Heimatland nt.
homeless ['həumlɪs] adj obdachlos; *(refugee)*
heimatlos.
home loan n Hypothek f.
homely ['həumlɪ] adj einfach; *(US: plain)*
unscheinbar.
home-made [həum'meɪd] adj selbstgemacht.
Home Office *(BRIT)* n Innenministerium nt.
homeopath ['həumɪəupæθ] *(US)* n =
homoeopath.
homeopathy [həumɪ'ɔpəθɪ] *(US)* n
= homoeopathy.
home rule n Selbstbestimmung f,
Selbstverwaltung f.
Home Secretary *(BRIT)* n Innenminister(in)
m(f).
homesick ['həumsɪk] adj heimwehkrank; **to
be** ~ Heimweh haben.
homestead ['həumstɛd] n Heimstätte f; *(farm)*
Gehöft nt.
home town n Heimatstadt f.
home truth n bittere Wahrheit f; **to tell sb
some** ~s jdm deutlich die Meinung sagen.
homeward ['həumwəd] adj *(journey)* Heim-
♦ adv = homewards.
homewards ['həumwədz] adv nach Hause,
heim.
homework ['həumwəːk] n Hausaufgaben pl.
homicidal [hɔmɪ'saɪdl] adj gemeingefährlich.
homicide ['hɔmɪsaɪd] *(US)* n Mord m.
homily ['hɔmɪlɪ] n Predigt f.
homing ['həumɪŋ] adj *(device, missile)* mit
Zielsucheinrichtung; ~ **pigeon** Brieftaube f.
homoeopath, *(US)* **homeopath**
['həumɪəupæθ] n Homöopath(in) m(f).
homoeopathy, *(US)* **homeopathy**
[həumɪ'ɔpəθɪ] n Homöopathie f.
homogeneous [hɔməu'dʒiːnɪəs] adj homogen.
homogenize [hə'mɔdʒənaɪz] vt
homogenisieren.
homosexual [hɔməu'sɛksjuəl] adj
homosexuell ♦ n Homosexuelle(r) f(m).
Hon. abbr = **honourable; honorary.**
Honduras [hɔn'djuərəs] n Honduras nt.
hone [həun] n Schleifstein m ♦ vt schleifen;
(fig: groom) erziehen.
honest ['ɔnɪst] adj ehrlich; *(trustworthy)*
redlich; *(sincere)* aufrichtig; **to be quite**
~ **with you** ... um ehrlich zu sein, ...
honestly ['ɔnɪstlɪ] adv *(see adj)* ehrlich;
redlich; aufrichtig.
honesty ['ɔnɪstɪ] n *(see adj)* Ehrlichkeit f;
Redlichkeit f; Aufrichtigkeit f.
honey ['hʌnɪ] n Honig m; *(US: inf)* Schätzchen
nt.
honeycomb ['hʌnɪkəum] n Bienenwabe f;
(pattern) Wabe f ♦ vt: **to** ~ **with** durchlöchern
mit.
honeymoon ['hʌnɪmuːn] n Flitterwochen pl;

(trip) Hochzeitsreise f.
honeysuckle ['hʌnɪsʌkl] n Geißblatt nt.
Hong Kong ['hɔŋ'kɔŋ] n Hongkong nt.
honk [hɔŋk] vi *(AUT)* hupen.
Honolulu [hɔnə'luːluː] n Honolulu nt.
honor etc ['ɔnə*] *(US)* = **honour** etc.
honorary ['ɔnərərɪ] adj ehrenamtlich; *(title,
degree)* Ehren-.
honour, *(US)* **honor** ['ɔnə*] vt ehren;
(commitment, promise) stehen zu ♦ n Ehre f;
(tribute) Auszeichnung f; **in** ~ **of** zu Ehren
von or +gen.
honourable ['ɔnərəbl] adj *(person)* ehrenwert;
(action, defeat) ehrenvoll.
honour-bound ['ɔnə'baund] adj: **to be** ~ **to do
sth** moralisch verpflichtet sein, etw zu tun.
honours degree ['ɔnəz-] n akademischer
Grad mit Prüfung im Spezialfach.

Honours Degree ist ein Universitätsabschluß
mit einer guten Note, also der Note I *(first
class)*, II:1 *(upper second class)*, II:2 *(lower
second class)* oder III *(third class)*. Wer ein
honours degree erhalten hat, darf die
Abkürzung **Hons** nach seinem Namen und Titel
führen, z.B. Mary Smith BA Hons. Heute sind
fast alle Universitätsabschlüsse in
Großbritannien *honours degrees*. Siehe auch
ordinary degree.

---

honours list n Liste verliehener/zu
verleihender Ehrentitel.

Honours List ist eine Liste von Adelstiteln und
Orden, die der britische Monarch zweimal
jährlich *(zu Neujahr und am offiziellen
Geburtstag des Monarchen)* an Bürger in
Großbritannien und im Commonwealth
verleiht. Die Liste wird vom Premierminister
zusammengestellt, aber drei Orden *(der
Hosenbandorden, der Verdienstorden und der
Victoria-Orden)* werden vom Monarchen
persönlich vergeben. Erfolgreiche Geschäfts-
leute, Militärangehörige, Sportler und andere
Prominente, aber auch im sozialen Bereich
besonders aktive Bürger werden auf diese
Weise geehrt.

Hons. abbr *(UNIV)* = **honours degree.**
hood [hud] n *(of coat etc)* Kapuze f; *(of cooker)*
Abzugshaube f; *(AUT: BRIT: folding roof)*
Verdeck nt; *(: US: bonnet)* (Motor)haube f.
hooded ['hudɪd] adj maskiert; *(jacket etc)* mit
Kapuze.
hoodlum ['huːdləm] n Gangster m.
hoodwink ['hudwɪŋk] vt (he)reinlegen.
hoof [huːf] *(pl hooves)* n Huf m.
hook [huk] n Haken m ♦ vt festhaken; *(fish)* an
die Angel bekommen; **by** ~ **or by crook** auf
Biegen und Brechen; **to be** ~ed **on** *(inf: film,
exhibition, etc)* fasziniert sein von; *(: drugs)*
abhängig sein von; *(: person)* stehen auf

+acc.

▶**hook up** vt (RADIO, TV etc) anschließen.
hook and eye (pl **hooks and eyes**) n Haken und Öse pl.
hooligan ['hu:lɪgən] n Rowdy m.
hooliganism ['hu:lɪgənɪzəm] n Rowdytum nt.
hoop [hu:p] n Reifen m; (for croquet: arch) Tor nt.
hooray [hu:'reɪ] excl = **hurrah**.
hoot [hu:t] vi hupen; (siren) heulen; (owl) schreien, rufen; (person) johlen ♦ vt (horn) drücken auf +acc ♦ n (see vi) Hupen nt; Heulen nt; Schreien nt, Rufen nt; Johlen nt; **to ~ with laughter** in johlendes Gelächter ausbrechen.
hooter ['hu:tə*] n (BRIT: AUT) Hupe f; (NAUT, factory) Sirene f.
hoover ® ['hu:və*] (BRIT) n Staubsauger m ♦ vt (carpet) saugen.
hooves [hu:vz] npl of hoof.
hop [hɔp] vi hüpfen ♦ n Hüpfer m; see also **hops**.
hope [həup] vi hoffen ♦ n Hoffnung f ♦ vt: **to ~ that** hoffen, daß; **I ~ so** ich hoffe es, hoffentlich; **I ~ not** ich hoffe nicht, hoffentlich nicht; **to ~ for the best** das Beste hoffen; **to have no ~ of sth/doing sth** keine Hoffnung auf etw +acc haben/darauf haben, etw zu tun; **in the ~ of/that** in der Hoffnung auf/, daß; **to ~ to do sth** hoffen, etw zu tun.
hopeful ['həupful] adj hoffnungsvoll; (situation) vielversprechend; **I'm ~ that she'll manage** ich hoffe, daß sie es schafft.
hopefully ['həupfulɪ] adv hoffnungsvoll; (one hopes) hoffentlich; **~, he'll come back** hoffentlich kommt er wieder.
hopeless ['həuplɪs] adj hoffnungslos; (situation) aussichtslos; (useless): **to be ~ at sth** etw überhaupt nicht können.
hopper ['hɔpə*] n Einfülltrichter m.
hops [hɔps] npl Hopfen m.
horde [hɔ:d] n Horde f.
horizon [hə'raɪzn] n Horizont m.
horizontal [hɔrɪ'zɔntl] adj horizontal.
hormone ['hɔ:məun] n Hormon nt.
hormone replacement therapy n Hormonersatztherapie f.
horn [hɔ:n] n Horn nt; (AUT) Hupe f.
horned [hɔ:nd] adj (animal) mit Hörnern.
hornet ['hɔ:nɪt] n Hornisse f.
horn-rimmed ['hɔ:n'rɪmd] adj (spectacles) Horn-.
horny ['hɔ:nɪ] (inf) adj (aroused) scharf, geil.
horoscope ['hɔrəskəup] n Horoskop nt.
horrendous [hə'rɛndəs] adj abscheulich, entsetzlich.
horrible ['hɔrɪbl] adj fürchterlich, schrecklich; (scream, dream) furchtbar.
horrid ['hɔrɪd] adj entsetzlich, schrecklich.
horrific [hɔ'rɪfɪk] adj entsetzlich, schrecklich.
horrify ['hɔrɪfaɪ] vt entsetzen.

horrifying ['hɔrɪfaɪɪŋ] adj schrecklich, fürchterlich, entsetzlich.
horror ['hɔrə*] n Entsetzen nt, Grauen nt; **~ (of sth)** (abhorrence) Abscheu m (vor etw dat); **the ~s of war** die Schrecken pl des Krieges.
horror film n Horrorfilm m.
horror-stricken ['hɔrəstrɪkn] adj = **horror-struck**.
horror-struck ['hɔrəstrʌk] adj von Entsetzen or Grauen gepackt.
hors d'oeuvre [ɔ:'də:vrə] n Hors d'oeuvre nt, Vorspeise f.
horse [hɔ:s] n Pferd nt.
horseback ['hɔ:sbæk] n: **on ~** adj, adv zu Pferd.
horsebox ['hɔ:sbɔks] n Pferdetransporter m.
horse chestnut n Roßkastanie f.
horse-drawn ['hɔ:sdrɔ:n] adj von Pferden gezogen.
horsefly ['hɔ:sflaɪ] n (Pferde)bremse f.
horseman ['hɔ:smən] (irreg: like **man**) n Reiter m.
horsemanship ['hɔ:smənʃɪp] n Reitkunst f.
horseplay ['hɔ:spleɪ] n Alberei f, Balgerei f.
horsepower ['hɔ:spauə*] n Pferdestärke f.
horse racing n Pferderennen nt.
horseradish ['hɔ:srædɪʃ] n Meerrettich m.
horseshoe ['hɔ:sʃu:] n Hufeisen nt.
horse show n Reitturnier nt.
horse trading n Kuhhandel m.
horse trials npl = **horse show**.
horsewhip ['hɔ:swɪp] n Reitpeitsche f ♦ vt auspeitschen.
horsewoman ['hɔ:swumən] (irreg: like **woman**) n Reiterin f.
horsey ['hɔ:sɪ] adj pferdenärrisch; (appearance) pferdeähnlich.
horticulture ['hɔ:tɪkʌltʃə*] n Gartenbau m.
hose [həuz] n (also: ~ **pipe**) Schlauch m.
▶**hose down** vt abspritzen.
hosiery ['həuzɪərɪ] n Strumpfwaren pl.
hospice ['hɔspɪs] n Pflegeheim nt (für unheilbar Kranke).
hospitable ['hɔspɪtəbl] adj gastfreundlich; (climate) freundlich.
hospital ['hɔspɪtl] n Krankenhaus nt; **in ~**, (US) **in the ~** im Krankenhaus.
hospitality [hɔspɪ'tælɪtɪ] n Gastfreundschaft f.
hospitalize ['hɔspɪtəlaɪz] vt ins Krankenhaus einweisen.
host [həust] n Gastgeber m; (REL) Hostie f ♦ adj Gast- ♦ vt Gastgeber sein bei; **a ~ of** eine Menge.
hostage ['hɔstɪdʒ] n Geisel f; **to be taken/held ~** als Geisel genommen/festgehalten werden.
hostel ['hɔstl] n (Wohn)heim nt; (also: **youth ~**) Jugendherberge f.
hostelling ['hɔstlɪŋ] n: **to go (youth) ~** in Jugendherbergen übernachten.
hostess ['həustɪs] n Gastgeberin f; (BRIT: air hostess) Stewardeß f; (in night-club) Hosteß f.

hostile ['hɔstaıl] *adj* (*conditions*) ungünstig; (*environment*) unwirtlich; (*person*): ~ **(to or towards)** feindselig (gegenüber +*dat*).
hostility [hɔ'stılıtı] *n* Feindseligkeit *f*; **hostilities** *npl* (*fighting*) Feindseligkeiten *pl*.
hot [hɔt] *adj* heiß; (*moderately hot*) warm; (*spicy*) scharf; (*temper*) hitzig; **I am** *or* **feel** ~ mir ist heiß; **to be** ~ **on sth** (*knowledgeable etc*) sich gut mit etw auskennen; (*strict*) sehr auf etw *acc* achten.
▶**hot up** (*BRIT: inf*) *vi* (*situation*) sich verschärfen *or* zuspitzen; (*party*) in Schwung kommen ♦ *vt* (*pace*) steigern; (*engine*) frisieren.
hot air *n* leeres Gerede *nt*.
hot-air balloon [hɔt'ɛə*-] *n* Heißluftballon *m*.
hotbed ['hɔtbɛd] *n* (*fig*) Brutstätte *f*.
hot-blooded [hɔt'blʌdıd] *adj* heißblütig.
hotchpotch ['hɔtʃpɔtʃ] (*BRIT*) *n* Durcheinander *nt*, Mischmasch *m*.
hot dog *n* Hot dog *m or nt*.
hotel [həu'tɛl] *n* Hotel *nt*.
hotelier [həu'tɛlıə*] *n* Hotelier(in) *m(f)*.
hotel industry *n* Hotelgewerbe *nt*.
hotel room *n* Hotelzimmer *nt*.
hot flash (*US*) *n* = **hot flush**.
hot flush *n* (*MED*) Hitzewallung *f*.
hotfoot ['hɔtfut] *adv* eilends.
hothead ['hɔthɛd] *n* Hitzkopf *m*.
hot-headed [hɔt'hɛdıd] *adj* hitzköpfig.
hothouse ['hɔthaus] *n* Treibhaus *nt*.
hot line *n* (*POL*) heißer Draht *m*.
hotly ['hɔtlı] *adv* (*contest*) heiß; (*speak, deny*) heftig.
hotplate ['hɔtpleıt] *n* Kochplatte *f*.
hotpot ['hɔtpɔt] (*BRIT*) *n* Fleischeintopf *m*.
hot potato (*fig: inf*) *n* heißes Eisen *nt*; **to drop sb like a** ~ jdn wie eine heiße Kartoffel fallenlassen.
hot seat *n*: **to be in the** ~ auf dem Schleudersitz sitzen.
hot spot *n* (*fig*) Krisenherd *m*.
hot spring *n* heiße Quelle *f*, Thermalquelle *f*.
hot stuff *n* große Klasse *f*.
hot-tempered ['hɔt'tɛmpəd] *adj* leicht aufbrausend, jähzornig.
hot-water bottle [hɔt'wɔːtə*-] *n* Wärmflasche *f*.
hot-wire (*inf*) *vt* (*car*) kurzschließen.
hound [haund] *vt* hetzen, jagen ♦ *n* Jagdhund *m*; **the** ~**s** die Meute.
hour ['auə*] *n* Stunde *f*; (*time*) Zeit *f*; **at 60 miles an** ~ mit 60 Meilen in der Stunde; **lunch** ~ Mittagspause *f*; **to pay sb by the** ~ jdn stundenweise bezahlen.
hourly ['auəlı] *adj* stündlich; (*rate*) Stunden- ♦ *adv* stündlich, jede Stunde; (*soon*) jederzeit.
house [haus] *n* Haus *nt*; (*household*) Haushalt *m*; (*dynasty*) Geschlecht *nt*, Haus *nt*; (*THEAT: performance*) Vorstellung *f* ♦ *vt* unterbringen; **at my** ~ bei mir (zu Hause);

to my ~ zu mir (nach Hause); **on the** ~ (*fig*) auf Kosten des Hauses; **the H**~ **(of Commons)** (*BRIT*) das Unterhaus; **the H**~ **(of Lords)** (*BRIT*) das Oberhaus; **the H**~ **(of Representatives)** (*US*) das Repräsentantenhaus.
house arrest *n* Hausarrest *m*.
houseboat ['hausbəut] *n* Hausboot *nt*.
housebound ['hausbaund] *adj* ans Haus gefesselt.
housebreaking ['hausbreıkıŋ] *n* Einbruch *m*.
house-broken ['hausbrəukn] (*US*) *adj* = **house-trained**.
housecoat ['hauskəut] *n* Morgenrock *m*.
household ['haushəuld] *n* Haushalt *m*; **to be a** ~ **name** ein Begriff sein.
householder ['haushəuldə*] *n* Hausinhaber(in) *m(f)*; (*of flat*) Wohnungsinhaber(in) *m(f)*.
house-hunting ['haushʌntıŋ] *n*: **to go** ~ nach einem Haus suchen.
housekeeper ['hauski:pə*] *n* Haushälterin *f*.
housekeeping ['hauski:pıŋ] *n* Hauswirtschaft *f*; (*money*) Haushaltsgeld *nt*, Wirtschaftsgeld *nt*.
houseman ['hausmən] (*BRIT: irreg: like* **man**) *n* (*MED*) Assistenzarzt *m*, Assistenzärztin *f*.

Das **House of Commons** *ist das Unterhaus des britischen Parlaments, mit 651 Abgeordneten, die in Wahlkreisen in allgemeiner Wahl gewählt werden. Das Unterhaus hat die Regierungsgewalt inne und tagt etwa 175 Tage im Jahr unter Vorsitz des Sprechers. Als* **House of Lords** *wird das Oberhaus des britischen Parlaments bezeichnet. Die Mitglieder sind nicht gewählt, sondern werden auf Lebenszeit ernannt (life peers), oder sie haben ihren Oberhaussitz geerbt (hereditary peers). Das House of Lords setzt sich aus Kirchenmännern und Adeligen zusammen (Lords Spiritual/Temporal). Es hat im Grunde keine Regierungsgewalt, aber kann vom Unterhaus erlassene Gesetze abändern und ist das oberste Berufungsgericht in Großbritannien (außer Schottland). Das* **House of Representatives** *bildet zusammen mit dem Senat die amerikanische gesetzgebende Versammlung (den Kongreß). Es besteht aus 435 Abgeordneten, die entsprechend den Bevölkerungszahlen auf die einzelnen Bundesstaaten verteilt sind und jeweils für 2 Jahre direkt vom Volk gewählt werden. Es tritt im* Capitol *in* Washington *zusammen. Siehe auch* congress.

house owner *n* Hausbesitzer(in) *m(f)*.
house party *n* mehrtägige Einladung *f*; (*people*) Gesellschaft *f*.
house plant *n* Zimmerpflanze *f*.
house-proud ['hauspraud] *adj* auf Ordnung und Sauberkeit im Haushalt bedacht.

house-to-house ['hausta'haus] *adj* von Haus zu Haus.

house-trained ['haustreind] (*BRIT*) *adj* (*animal*) stubenrein.

house-warming (party) ['hauswɔ:mɪŋ-] *n* Einzugsparty *f*.

housewife ['hauswaɪf] (*irreg: like* **wife**) *n* Hausfrau *f*.

housework ['hauswə:k] *n* Hausarbeit *f*.

housing ['hauzɪŋ] *n* Wohnungen *pl*; (*provision*) Wohnungsbeschaffung *f* ♦ *cpd* Wohnungs-.

housing association *n* Wohnungsbaugesellschaft *f*.

housing benefit *n* ≈ Wohngeld *nt*.

housing conditions *npl* Wohnbedingungen *pl*, Wohnverhältnisse *pl*.

housing development *n* (Wohn)siedlung *f*.

housing estate *n* (Wohn)siedlung *f*.

hovel ['hɔvl] *n* (armselige) Hütte *f*.

hover ['hɔvə*] *vi* schweben; (*person*) herumstehen; **to ~ round sb** jdm nicht von der Seite weichen.

hovercraft ['hɔvəkrɑːft] *n* Hovercraft *nt*, Luftkissenfahrzeug *nt*.

hoverport ['hɔvəpɔːt] *n* Anlegestelle *f* für Hovercrafts.

=========================== KEYWORD

how [hau] *adv* **1** (*in what way*) wie; **~ was the film?** wie war der Film?; **~ is school?** was macht die Schule?; **~ are you?** wie geht es Ihnen?
2 (*to what degree*): **~ much milk?** wieviel Milch?; **~ many people?** wie viele Leute?; **~ long have you been here?** wie lange sind Sie schon hier?; **~ old are you?** wie alt bist du?; **~ lovely/awful!** wie schön/furchtbar!

however [hau'ɛvə*] *conj* jedoch, aber ♦ *adv* wie ... auch; (*in questions*) wie ... bloß *or* nur.

howl [haul] *vi* heulen; (*animal*) jaulen; (*baby, person*) schreien ♦ *n* (*see vb*) Heulen *nt*; Jaulen *nt*; Schreien *nt*.

howler ['haulə*] (*inf*) *n* (*mistake*) Schnitzer *m*.

howling ['haulɪŋ] *adj* (*wind, gale*) heulend.

HP (*BRIT*) *n abbr* = **hire-purchase**.

h.p. *abbr* (*AUT*: = *horsepower*) PS.

HQ *abbr* = **headquarters**.

HR (*US*) *n abbr* (*POL*: = *House of Representatives*) Repräsentantenhaus *nt*.

hr *abbr* (= *hour*) Std.

HRH (*BRIT*) *abbr* (= *His/Her Royal Highness*) Seine/Ihre Königliche Hoheit.

hrs *abbr* (= *hours*) Std.

HS (*US*) *abbr* = **high school**.

HST (*US*) *abbr* (= *Hawaiian Standard Time*) Normalzeit in Hawaii.

hub [hʌb] *n* (Rad)nabe *f*; (*fig: centre*) Mittelpunkt *m*, Zentrum *nt*.

hubbub ['hʌbʌb] *n* Lärm *m*; (*commotion*) Tumult *m*.

hubcap ['hʌbkæp] *n* Radkappe *f*.

HUD (*US*) *n abbr* (= *Department of Housing and Urban Development*) Ministerium *für* Wohnungsbau und Stadtentwicklung.

huddle ['hʌdl] *vi*: **to ~ together** sich zusammendrängen ♦ *n*: **in a ~** dicht zusammengedrängt.

hue [hjuː] *n* Farbton *m*.

hue and cry *n* großes Geschrei *nt*.

huff [hʌf] *n*: **in a ~** beleidigt, eingeschnappt ♦ *vi*: **to ~ and puff** sich aufregen.

huffy ['hʌfɪ] (*inf*) *adj* beleidigt.

hug [hʌg] *vt* umarmen; (*thing*) umklammern ♦ *n* Umarmung *f*; **to give sb a ~** jdn umarmen.

huge [hjuːdʒ] *adj* riesig.

hugely ['hjuːdʒlɪ] *adv* ungeheuer.

hulk [hʌlk] *n* (*wrecked ship*) Wrack *nt*; (*person, building etc*) Klotz *m*.

hulking ['hʌlkɪŋ] *adj*: **~ great** massig.

hull [hʌl] *n* Schiffsrumpf *m*; (*of nuts*) Schale *f*; (*of strawberries etc*) Blättchen *nt* ♦ *vt* (*fruit*) entstielen.

hullaballoo [hʌləbə'luː] (*inf*) *n* Spektakel *m*.

hullo [hə'ləu] *excl* = **hello**.

hum [hʌm] *vt* summen ♦ *vi* summen; (*machine*) brummen ♦ *n* Summen *nt*; (*of traffic*) Brausen *nt*; (*of machines*) Brummen *nt*; (*of voices*) Gemurmel *nt*.

human ['hjuːmən] *adj* menschlich ♦ *n* (*also*: **~ being**) Mensch *m*.

humane [hjuː'meɪn] *adj* human.

humanism ['hjuːmənɪzəm] *n* Humanismus *m*.

humanitarian [hjuːmænɪ'tɛərɪən] *adj* humanitär.

humanity [hjuː'mænɪtɪ] *n* Menschlichkeit *f*; (*mankind*) Menschheit *f*; (*humaneness*) Humanität *f*; **humanities** *npl* (*SCOL*): **the humanities** die Geisteswissenschaften *pl*.

humanly ['hjuːmənlɪ] *adv* menschlich; **if (at all) ~ possible** wenn es irgend möglich ist.

humanoid ['hjuːmənɔɪd] *adj* menschenähnlich ♦ *n* menschenähnliches Wesen *nt*.

human rights *npl* Menschenrechte *pl*.

humble ['hʌmbl] *adj* bescheiden ♦ *vt* demütigen.

humbly ['hʌmblɪ] *adv* bescheiden.

humbug ['hʌmbʌg] *n* Humbug *m*, Mumpitz *m*; (*BRIT: sweet*) Pfefferminzbonbon *m or nt*.

humdrum ['hʌmdrʌm] *adj* eintönig, langweilig.

humid ['hjuːmɪd] *adj* feucht.

humidifier [hjuː'mɪdɪfaɪə*] *n* Luftbefeuchter *m*.

humidity [hjuː'mɪdɪtɪ] *n* Feuchtigkeit *f*.

humiliate [hjuː'mɪlɪeɪt] *vt* demütigen.

humiliating [hjuː'mɪlɪeɪtɪŋ] *adj* demütigend.

humiliation [hjuːmɪlɪ'eɪʃən] *n* Demütigung *f*.

humility [hjuː'mɪlɪtɪ] *n* Bescheidenheit *f*.

humor *etc* (*US*) = **humour** *etc*.

humorist ['hjuːmərɪst] *n* Humorist(in) *m(f)*.

humorous ['hjuːmərəs] *adj* (*remark*) witzig; (*book*) lustig; (*person*) humorvoll.

humour, (*US*) **humor** ['hjuːmə*] *n* Humor *m*;

(*mood*) Stimmung *f* ♦ *vt* seinen Willen lassen +*dat*; **sense of** ~ (Sinn *m* für) Humor; **to be in good/bad** ~ gute/schlechte Laune haben.
humourless ['hju:məlɪs] *adj* humorlos.
hump [hʌmp] *n* Hügel *m*; (*of camel*) Höcker *m*; (*deformity*) Buckel *m*.
humpbacked ['hʌmpbækt] *adj*: ~ **bridge** gewölbte Brücke *f*.
humus ['hju:məs] *n* Humus *m*.
hunch [hʌntʃ] *n* Gefühl *nt*, Ahnung *f*; **I have a** ~ **that** ... ich habe den (leisen) Verdacht, daß ...
hunchback ['hʌntʃbæk] *n* Bucklige(r) *f(m)*.
hunched [hʌntʃt] *adj* gebeugt; (*shoulders*) hochgezogen; (*back*) krumm.
hundred ['hʌndrəd] *num* hundert; **a** *or* **one** ~ **books/people/dollars** (ein)hundert Bücher/Personen/Dollar; ~**s of** Hunderte von; **I'm a** ~ **per cent sure** ich bin absolut sicher.
hundredth ['hʌndrədθ] *num* hundertste(r, s).
hundredweight ['hʌndrɪdweɪt] *n* Gewichtseinheit *f* (*BRIT* = 50,8 kg; *US* = 45,3 kg); ≈ Zentner *m*.
hung [hʌŋ] *pt, pp of* **hang**.
Hungarian [hʌŋ'gɛərɪən] *adj* ungarisch ♦ *n* Ungar(in) *m(f)*; (*LING*) Ungarisch *nt*.
Hungary ['hʌŋgərɪ] *n* Ungarn *nt*.
hunger ['hʌŋgə*] *n* Hunger *m* ♦ *vi*: **to** ~ **for** hungern nach.
hunger strike *n* Hungerstreik *m*.
hung over (*inf*) *adj* verkatert.
hungrily ['hʌŋgrəlɪ] *adv* hungrig.
hungry ['hʌŋgrɪ] *adj* hungrig; **to be** ~ Hunger haben; **to be** ~ **for** hungern nach; (*news*) sehnsüchtig warten auf; **to go** ~ hungern.
hung up (*inf*) *adj*: **to be** ~ **on** (*person*) ein gestörtes Verhältnis haben zu; **to be** ~ **about** nervös sein wegen.
hunk [hʌŋk] *n* großes Stück *nt*; (*inf: man*) (großer, gutaussehender) Mann *m*.
hunt [hʌnt] *vt* jagen; (*criminal, fugitive*) fahnden nach ♦ *vi* (*SPORT*) jagen ♦ *n* (*see vb*) Jagd *f*; Fahndung *f*; (*search*) Suche *f*; **to** ~ **for** (*search*) suchen (nach).
▶**hunt down** *vt* Jagd machen auf +*acc*.
hunter ['hʌntə*] *n* Jäger(in) *m(f)*.
hunting ['hʌntɪŋ] *n* Jagd *f*, Jagen *nt*.
hurdle ['hə:dl] *n* Hürde *f*.
hurl [hə:l] *vt* schleudern; **to** ~ **sth at sb** (*also fig*) jdm etw entgegenschleudern.
hurling ['hə:lɪŋ] *n* (*SPORT*) Hurling *nt*, irische Hockeyart.
hurly-burly ['hə:lɪ'bə:lɪ] *n* Rummel *m*.
hurrah [hu'rɑ:] *n* Hurra *nt* ♦ *excl* hurra.
hurray [hu'reɪ] *n* = **hurrah**.
hurricane ['hʌrɪkən] *n* Orkan *m*.
hurried ['hʌrɪd] *adj* eilig; (*departure*) überstürzt.
hurriedly ['hʌrɪdlɪ] *adv* eilig.
hurry ['hʌrɪ] *n* Eile *f* ♦ *vi* eilen; (*to do sth*) sich beeilen ♦ *vt* (zur Eile) antreiben; (*work*)

beschleunigen; **to be in a** ~ es eilig haben; **to do sth in a** ~ etw schnell tun; **there's no** ~ es eilt nicht; **what's the** ~**?** warum so eilig?; **they hurried to help him** sie eilten ihm zu Hilfe; **to** ~ **home** nach Hause eilen.
▶**hurry along** *vi* sich beeilen.
▶**hurry away** *vi* schnell weggehen, forteilen.
▶**hurry off** *vi* = **hurry away**.
▶**hurry up** *vt* (zur Eile) antreiben ♦ *vi* sich beeilen.
hurt [hə:t] (*pt, pp* **hurt**) *vt* weh tun +*dat*; (*injure, fig*) verletzen ♦ *vi* weh tun ♦ *adj* verletzt; **I've** ~ **my arm** ich habe mir am Arm weh getan; (*injured*) ich habe mir den Arm verletzt; **where does it** ~**?** wo tut es weh?
hurtful ['hə:tful] *adj* verletzend.
hurtle ['hə:tl] *vi*: **to** ~ **past** vorbeisausen; **to** ~ **down** (*fall*) hinunterfallen.
husband ['hʌzbənd] *n* (Ehe)mann *m*.
hush [hʌʃ] *n* Stille *f* ♦ *vt* zum Schweigen bringen; ~**! pst!**
▶**hush up** *vt* vertuschen.
hushed [hʌʃt] *adj* still; (*voice*) gedämpft.
hush-hush [hʌʃ'hʌʃ] (*inf*) *adj* streng geheim.
husk [hʌsk] *n* Schale *f*; (*of wheat*) Spelze *f*; (*of maize*) Hüllblatt *nt*.
husky ['hʌskɪ] *adj* (*voice*) rauh ♦ *n* Schlittenhund *m*.
hustings ['hʌstɪŋz] (*BRIT*) *npl* (*POL*) Wahlkampf *m*.
hustle ['hʌsl] *vt* drängen ♦ *n*: ~ **and bustle** Geschäftigkeit *f*.
hut [hʌt] *n* Hütte *f*.
hutch [hʌtʃ] *n* (Kaninchen)stall *m*.
hyacinth ['haɪəsɪnθ] *n* Hyazinthe *f*.
hybrid ['haɪbrɪd] *n* (*plant, animal*) Kreuzung *f*; (*mixture*) Mischung *f* ♦ *adj* Misch-.
hydrant ['haɪdrənt] *n* (*also:* **fire** ~) Hydrant *m*.
hydraulic [haɪ'drɔ:lɪk] *adj* hydraulisch.
hydraulics [haɪ'drɔ:lɪks] *n* Hydraulik *f*.
hydrochloric acid ['haɪdrəu'klɔrɪk-] *n* Salzsäure *f*.
hydroelectric ['haɪdrəuɪ'lɛktrɪk] *adj* hydroelektrisch.
hydrofoil ['haɪdrəfɔɪl] *n* Tragflächenboot *nt*, Tragflügelboot *nt*.
hydrogen ['haɪdrədʒən] *n* Wasserstoff *m*.
hydrogen bomb *n* Wasserstoffbombe *f*.
hydrophobia ['haɪdrə'fəubɪə] *n* Hydrophobie *f*, Wasserscheu *f*.
hydroplane ['haɪdrəpleɪn] *n* Gleitboot *nt*; (*plane*) Wasserflugzeug *nt* ♦ *vi* (*boat*) abheben.
hyena [haɪ'i:nə] *n* Hyäne *f*.
hygiene ['haɪdʒi:n] *n* Hygiene *f*.
hygienic [haɪ'dʒi:nɪk] *adj* hygienisch.
hymn [hɪm] *n* Kirchenlied *nt*.
hype [haɪp] (*inf*) *n* Rummel *m*.
hyperactive ['haɪpər'æktɪv] *adj* überaktiv.
hyperinflation ['haɪpərɪn'fleɪʃən] *n* galoppierende Inflation *f*.
hypermarket ['haɪpəmɑ:kɪt] (*BRIT*) *n*

Verbrauchermarkt *m.*

hypertension ['haɪpə'tɛnʃən] *n* Hypertonie *f*, Bluthochdruck *m.*

hyphen ['haɪfn] *n* Bindestrich *m*; (*at end of line*) Trennungsstrich *m.*

hyphenated ['haɪfəneɪtɪd] *adj* mit Bindestrich (geschrieben).

hypnosis [hɪp'nəusɪs] *n* Hypnose *f.*

hypnotic [hɪp'nɔtɪk] *adj* hypnotisierend; (*trance*) hypnotisch.

hypnotism ['hɪpnətɪzəm] *n* Hypnotismus *m.*

hypnotist ['hɪpnətɪst] *n* Hypnotiseur *m*, Hypnotiseuse *f.*

hypnotize ['hɪpnətaɪz] *vt* hypnotisieren.

hypoallergenic ['haɪpəuælə'dʒɛnɪk] *adj* für äußerst empfindliche Haut.

hypochondriac [haɪpə'kɔndrɪæk] *n* Hypochonder *m.*

hypocrisy [hɪ'pɔkrɪsɪ] *n* Heuchelei *f.*

hypocrite ['hɪpəkrɪt] *n* Heuchler(in) *m(f).*

hypocritical [hɪpə'krɪtɪkl] *adj* heuchlerisch.

hypodermic [haɪpə'dəːmɪk] *adj* (*injection*) subkutan ♦ *n* (Injektions)spritze *f.*

hypotenuse [haɪ'pɔtɪnjuːz] *n* Hypotenuse *f.*

hypothermia [haɪpə'θəːmɪə] *n* Unterkühlung *f.*

hypothesis [haɪ'pɔθɪsɪs] (*pl* **hypotheses**) *n* Hypothese *f.*

hypothesize [haɪ'pɔθɪsaɪz] *vi* Hypothesen aufstellen ♦ *vt* annehmen.

hypothetic(al) [haɪpəu'θɛtɪk(l)] *adj* hypothetisch.

hysterectomy [hɪstə'rɛktəmɪ] *n* Hysterektomie *f.*

hysteria [hɪ'stɪərɪə] *n* Hysterie *f.*

hysterical [hɪ'stɛrɪkl] *adj* hysterisch; (*situation*) wahnsinnig komisch; **to become** ~ hysterisch werden.

hysterically [hɪ'stɛrɪklɪ] *adv* hysterisch; ~ **funny** wahnsinnig komisch.

hysterics [hɪ'stɛrɪks] *npl*: **to be in** *or* **to have** ~ einen hysterischen Anfall haben; (*laughter*) einen Lachanfall haben.

Hz *abbr* (= *hertz*) Hz.

I, i

I¹, i [aɪ] *n* (*letter*) I *nt*, i *nt*; ~ **for Isaac**, (*US*) ~ **for Item** ≈ I wie Ida.

I² [aɪ] *pron* ich.

I. *abbr* = **island; isle.**

IA (*US*) *abbr* (*POST:* = *Iowa*).

IAEA *n abbr* = **International Atomic Energy Agency.**

ib *abbr* (= *ibidem*) ib(id).

Iberian [aɪ'bɪərɪən] *adj:* **the** ~ **Peninsula** die Iberische Halbinsel.

IBEW (*US*) *n abbr* (= *International Brotherhood of Electrical Workers*) Elektriker- gewerkschaft.

ibid *abbr* (= *ibidem*) ib(id).

i/c (*BRIT*) *abbr* (= *in charge (of)*) *see* **charge.**

ICBM *n abbr* (= *intercontinental ballistic missile*) Interkontinentalrakete *f.*

ICC *n abbr* = **International Chamber of Commerce;** (*US:* = *Interstate Commerce Commission*) Kommission zur Regelung des Warenverkehrs zwischen den US- Bundesstaaten.

ice [aɪs] *n* Eis *nt*; (*on road*) Glatteis *nt* ♦ *vt* (*cake*) mit Zuckerguß überziehen, glasieren ♦ *vi* (*also:* ~ **over,** ~ **up**) vereisen; (*puddle etc*) zufrieren; **to put sth on** ~ (*fig*) etw auf Eis legen.

Ice Age *n* Eiszeit *f.*

ice axe *n* Eispickel *m.*

iceberg ['aɪsbəːg] *n* Eisberg *m*; **the tip of the** ~ (*fig*) die Spitze des Eisbergs.

icebox ['aɪsbɔks] *n* (*US: fridge*) Kühlschrank *m*; (*BRIT: compartment*) Eisfach *nt*; (*insulated box*) Kühltasche *f.*

icebreaker ['aɪsbreɪkə*] *n* Eisbrecher *m.*

ice bucket *n* Eiskühler *m.*

icecap ['aɪskæp] *n* Eisdecke *f*; (*polar*) Eiskappe *f.*

ice-cold ['aɪs'kəuld] *adj* eiskalt.

ice cream *n* Eis *nt.*

ice-cream soda ['aɪskriːm-] *n* Eisbecher mit Sirup und Sodawasser.

ice cube *n* Eiswürfel *m.*

iced [aɪst] *adj* (*cake*) mit Zuckerguß überzogen, glasiert; (*beer etc*) eisgekühlt; (*tea, coffee*) Eis-.

ice hockey *n* Eishockey *nt.*

Iceland ['aɪslənd] *n* Island *nt.*

Icelander ['aɪsləndə*] *n* Isländer(in) *m(f).*

Icelandic [aɪs'lændɪk] *adj* isländisch ♦ *n* (*LING*) Isländisch *nt.*

ice lolly (*BRIT*) *n* Eis *nt* am Stiel.

ice pick *n* Eispickel *m.*

ice rink *n* (Kunst)eisbahn *f*, Schlittschuhbahn *f.*

ice skate *n* Schlittschuh *m.*

ice-skate ['aɪsskeɪt] *vi* Schlittschuh laufen.

ice-skating ['aɪsskeɪtɪŋ] *n* Eislauf *m*, Schlittschuhlaufen *nt.*

icicle ['aɪsɪkl] *n* Eiszapfen *m.*

icing ['aɪsɪŋ] *n* (*CULIN*) Zuckerguß *m*; (*AVIAT etc*) Vereisung *f.*

icing sugar (*BRIT*) *n* Puderzucker *m.*

ICJ *n abbr* = **International Court of Justice.**

icon ['aɪkɔn] *n* Ikone *f*; (*COMPUT*) Ikon *nt.*

ICR (*US*) *n abbr* (= *Institute for Cancer Research*) Krebsforschungsinstitut.

ICRC *n abbr* (= *International Committee of the Red Cross*) IKRK *nt.*

ICU *n abbr* (*MED*) = **intensive care unit.**

icy ['aɪsɪ] *adj* eisig; (*road*) vereist.
ID, Ida. (*US*) *abbr* (*POST:* = *Idaho*).
I'd [aɪd] = **I would; I had.**
ID card *n* = **identity card.**
IDD (*BRIT*) *n abbr* (*TEL:* = *international direct dialling*) *Selbstwählferndienst ins Ausland.*
idea [aɪ'dɪə] *n* Idee *f*; (*opinion*) Ansicht *f*; (*notion*) Vorstellung *f*; (*objective*) Ziel *nt*; **good ~!** gute Idee!; **to have a good ~ that** sich *dat* ziemlich sicher sein, daß; **I haven't the least ~** ich habe nicht die leiseste Ahnung.
ideal [aɪ'dɪəl] *n* Ideal *nt* ♦ *adj* ideal.
idealist [aɪ'dɪəlɪst] *n* Idealist(in) *m(f)*.
ideally [aɪ'dɪəlɪ] *adv* ideal; **~ the book should ...** idealerweise *or* im Idealfall sollte das Buch ...; **she's ~ suited for ...** sie eignet sich hervorragend für ...
identical [aɪ'dɛntɪkl] *adj* identisch; (*twins*) eineiig.
identification [aɪdɛntɪfɪ'keɪʃən] *n* Identifizierung *f*; (**means of**) **~** Ausweispapiere *pl*.
identify [aɪ'dɛntɪfaɪ] *vt* (*recognize*) erkennen; (*distinguish*) identifizieren; **to ~ sb/sth with** jdn/etw identifizieren mit.
Identikit ® [aɪ'dɛntɪkɪt] *n:* **~ (picture)** Phantombild *nt*.
identity [aɪ'dɛntɪtɪ] *n* Identität *f*.
identity card *n* (Personal)ausweis *m*.
identity papers *npl* Ausweispapiere *pl*.
identity parade (*BRIT*) *n* Gegenüberstellung *f*.
ideological [aɪdɪə'lɒdʒɪkl] *adj* ideologisch, weltanschaulich.
ideology [aɪdɪ'ɒlədʒɪ] *n* Ideologie *f*, Weltanschauung *f*.
idiocy ['ɪdɪəsɪ] *n* Idiotie *f*, Dummheit *f*.
idiom ['ɪdɪəm] *n* (*style*) Ausdrucksweise *f*; (*phrase*) Redewendung *f*.
idiomatic [ɪdɪə'mætɪk] *adj* idiomatisch.
idiosyncrasy [ɪdɪəu'sɪŋkrəsɪ] *n* Eigenheit *f*, Eigenart *f*.
idiosyncratic [ɪdɪəusɪŋ'krætɪk] *adj* eigenartig; (*way, method, style*) eigen.
idiot ['ɪdɪət] *n* Idiot(in) *m(f)*, Dummkopf *m*.
idiotic [ɪdɪ'ɒtɪk] *adj* idiotisch, blöd(sinnig).
idle ['aɪdl] *adj* untätig; (*lazy*) faul; (*unemployed*) unbeschäftigt; (*machinery, factory*) stillstehend; (*question*) müßig; (*conversation, pleasure*) leer ♦ *vi* leerlaufen, im Leerlauf sein; **to lie ~** (*machinery*) außer Betrieb sein; (*factory*) die Arbeit eingestellt haben.
▶**idle away** *vt* (*time*) vertrödeln, verbummeln.
idleness ['aɪdlnɪs] *n* Untätigkeit *f*; (*laziness*) Faulheit *f*.
idler ['aɪdlə*] *n* Faulenzer(in) *m(f)*.
idle time *n* (*COMM*) Leerlaufzeit *f*.
idly ['aɪdlɪ] *adv* untätig; (*glance*) abwesend.
idol ['aɪdl] *n* Idol *nt*; (*REL*) Götzenbild *nt*.
idolize ['aɪdəlaɪz] *vt* vergöttern.

idyllic [ɪ'dɪlɪk] *adj* idyllisch.
i.e. *abbr* (= *id est*) d.h.

═══════════════════ *KEYWORD*

if [ɪf] *conj* **1** (*given that, providing that etc*) wenn, falls; **~ anyone comes in** wenn *or* falls jemand hereinkommt; **~ necessary** wenn *or* falls nötig; **~ I were you** wenn ich Sie wäre, an Ihrer Stelle
2 (*whenever*) wenn
3 (*although*): (**even**) **~** auch *or* selbst wenn; **I like it, (even) ~ you don't** mir gefällt es, auch wenn du es nicht magst
4 (*whether*) ob; **ask him ~ he can come** frag ihn, ob er kommen kann
5: **~ so/not** falls ja/nein; **~ only** wenn nur; *see also* **as.**

iffy ['ɪfɪ] (*inf*) *adj* (*uncertain*) unsicher; (*plan, proposal*) fragwürdig; **he was a bit ~ about it** er hat sich sehr vage ausgedrückt.
igloo ['ɪgluː] *n* Iglu *m or nt*.
ignite [ɪg'naɪt] *vt* entzünden ♦ *vi* sich entzünden.
ignition [ɪg'nɪʃən] *n* (*AUT*) Zündung *f*.
ignition key *n* (*AUT*) Zündschlüssel *m*.
ignoble [ɪg'nəubl] *adj* schändlich, unehrenhaft.
ignominious [ɪgnə'mɪnɪəs] *adj* schmachvoll.
ignoramus [ɪgnə'reɪməs] *n* Ignorant(in) *m(f)*.
ignorance ['ɪgnərəns] *n* Unwissenheit *f*, Ignoranz *f*; **to keep sb in ~ of sth** jdn in Unkenntnis über etw *acc* lassen.
ignorant ['ɪgnərənt] *adj* unwissend, ignorant; **to be ~ of** (*subject*) sich nicht auskennen in *+dat*; (*events*) nicht informiert sein über *+acc*.
ignore [ɪg'nɔː*] *vt* ignorieren; (*fact*) außer Acht lassen.
ikon ['aɪkɒn] *n* = **icon.**
IL (*US*) *abbr* (*POST:* = *Illinois*).
ILA (*US*) *n abbr* (= *International Longshoremen's Association*) *Hafenarbeitergewerkschaft.*
I'll [aɪl] = **I will; I shall.**
ill [ɪl] *adj* krank; (*effects*) schädlich ♦ *n* Übel *nt*; (*trouble*) Schlechte(s) *nt* ♦ *adv:* **to speak ~ of sb** Schlechtes über jdn sagen; **to be taken ~** krank werden; **to think ~ of sb** schlecht von jdm denken.
ill-advised [ɪləd'vaɪzd] *adj* unklug; (*person*) schlecht beraten.
ill at ease *adj* unbehaglich.
ill-considered [ɪlkən'sɪdəd] *adj* unüberlegt.
ill-disposed [ɪldɪs'pəuzd] *adj:* **to be ~ toward sb/sth** jdm/etw nicht wohlgesinnt sein.
illegal [ɪ'liːgl] *adj* illegal.
illegally [ɪ'liːgəlɪ] *adv* illegal.
illegible [ɪ'lɛdʒɪbl] *adj* unleserlich.
illegitimate [ɪlɪ'dʒɪtɪmət] *adj* (*child*) unehelich; (*activity, treaty*) unzulässig.
ill-fated [ɪl'feɪtɪd] *adj* unglückselig.
ill-favoured, (*US*) **ill-favored** [ɪl'feɪvəd] *adj* ungestalt (*liter*), häßlich.

ill feeling n Verstimmung f.
ill-gotten ['ɪlgɔtn] adj: ~**gains** unrechtmäßig erworbener Gewinn m.
ill health n schlechter Gesundheitszustand m.
illicit [ɪ'lɪsɪt] adj verboten.
ill-informed [ɪlɪn'fɔːmd] adj (judgement) wenig sachkundig; (person) schlecht informiert or unterrichtet.
illiterate [ɪ'lɪtərət] adj (person) des Lesens und Schreibens unkundig; (letter) voller Fehler.
ill-mannered [ɪl'mænəd] adj unhöflich.
illness ['ɪlnɪs] n Krankheit f.
illogical [ɪ'lɔdʒɪkl] adj unlogisch.
ill-suited [ɪl'suːtɪd] adj nicht zusammenpassend; **he is** ~ **to the job** er ist für die Stelle ungeeignet.
ill-timed [ɪl'taɪmd] adj ungelegen, unpassend.
ill-treat [ɪl'triːt] vt mißhandeln.
ill-treatment [ɪl'triːtmənt] n Mißhandlung f.
illuminate [ɪ'luːmɪneɪt] vt beleuchten.
illuminated sign [ɪ'luːmɪneɪtɪd-] n Leuchtzeichen nt.
illuminating [ɪ'luːmɪneɪtɪŋ] adj aufschlußreich.
illumination [ɪluːmɪ'neɪʃən] n Beleuchtung f; **illuminations** npl (decorative lights) festliche Beleuchtung f, Illumination f.
illusion [ɪ'luːʒən] n Illusion f; (trick) (Zauber)trick m; **to be under the** ~ **that** ... sich dat einbilden, daß ...
illusive [ɪ'luːsɪv] adj = **illusory**.
illusory [ɪ'luːsərɪ] adj illusorisch, trügerisch.
illustrate ['ɪləstreɪt] vt veranschaulichen; (book) illustrieren.
illustration [ɪlə'streɪʃən] n Illustration f; (example) Veranschaulichung f.
illustrator ['ɪləstreɪtə*] n Illustrator(in) m(f).
illustrious [ɪ'lʌstrɪəs] adj (career) glanzvoll; (predecessor) berühmt.
ill will n böses Blut nt.
ILO n abbr = **International Labour Organization**.
ILWU (US) n abbr (= International Longshoremen's and Warehousemen's Union) Hafen- und Lagerarbeitergewerkschaft.
I'm [aɪm] = **I am**.
image ['ɪmɪdʒ] n Bild nt; (public face) Image nt; (reflection) Abbild nt.
imagery ['ɪmɪdʒərɪ] n (in writing) Metaphorik f; (in painting) Symbolik f.
imaginable [ɪ'mædʒɪnəbl] adj vorstellbar, denkbar; **we've tried every** ~ **solution** wir haben jede denkbare Lösung ausprobiert; **she had the prettiest hair** ~ sie hatte das schönste Haar, das man sich vorstellen kann.
imaginary [ɪ'mædʒɪnərɪ] adj erfunden; (being) Phantasie-; (danger) eingebildet.
imagination [ɪmædʒɪ'neɪʃən] n Phantasie f; (illusion) Einbildung f; **it's just your** ~ das bildest du dir nur ein.
imaginative [ɪ'mædʒɪnətɪv] adj phantasievoll;

(solution) einfallsreich.
imagine [ɪ'mædʒɪn] vt sich dat vorstellen; (dream) sich dat träumen lassen; (suppose) vermuten.
imbalance [ɪm'bæləns] n Unausgeglichenheit f.
imbecile ['ɪmbəsiːl] n Schwachkopf m, Idiot m.
imbue [ɪm'bjuː] vt: **to** ~ **sb/sth with** jdn/etw durchdringen mit.
IMF n abbr (= International Monetary Fund) IWF m.
imitate ['ɪmɪteɪt] vt imitieren; (mimic) nachahmen.
imitation [ɪmɪ'teɪʃən] n Imitation f, Nachahmung f.
imitator ['ɪmɪteɪtə*] n Imitator(in) m(f), Nachahmer(in) m(f).
immaculate [ɪ'mækjulət] adj makellos; (appearance, piece of work) tadellos; (REL) unbefleckt.
immaterial [ɪmə'tɪərɪəl] adj unwichtig, unwesentlich.
immature [ɪmə'tjuə*] adj unreif; (organism) noch nicht voll entwickelt.
immaturity [ɪmə'tjuərɪtɪ] n Unreife f.
immeasurable [ɪ'mɛʒrəbl] adj unermeßlich groß.
immediacy [ɪ'miːdɪəsɪ] n Unmittelbarkeit f, Direktheit f; (of needs) Dringlichkeit f.
immediate [ɪ'miːdɪət] adj sofortig; (need) dringend; (neighbourhood, family) nächste(r, s).
immediately [ɪ'miːdɪətlɪ] adv sofort; (directly) unmittelbar; ~ **next to** direkt neben.
immense [ɪ'mɛns] adj riesig, enorm.
immensely [ɪ'mɛnslɪ] adv unheimlich; (grateful, complex etc) äußerst.
immensity [ɪ'mɛnsɪtɪ] n ungeheure Größe f, Unermeßlichkeit f; (of problems etc) gewaltiges Ausmaß nt.
immerse [ɪ'mɜːs] vt eintauchen; **to** ~ **sth in** etw tauchen in +acc; **to be** ~**d in** (fig) vertieft sein in +acc.
immersion heater [ɪ'mɜːʃən-] (BRIT) n elektrischer Heißwasserboiler m.
immigrant ['ɪmɪgrənt] n Einwanderer m, Einwanderin f.
immigration [ɪmɪ'greɪʃən] n Einwanderung f; (at airport etc) Einwanderungsstelle f ♦ cpd Einwanderungs-.
imminent ['ɪmɪnənt] adj bevorstehend.
immobile [ɪ'məubaɪl] adj unbeweglich.
immobilize [ɪ'məubɪlaɪz] vt (person) handlungsunfähig machen; (machine) zum Stillstand bringen.
immoderate [ɪ'mɔdərət] adj unmäßig; (opinion, reaction) extrem; (demand) maßlos.
immodest [ɪ'mɔdɪst] adj unanständig; (boasting) unbescheiden.
immoral [ɪ'mɔrl] adj unmoralisch; (behaviour) unsittlich.
immorality [ɪmə'rælɪtɪ] n (see adj) Unmoral f;

Unsittlichkeit *f.*

immortal [ı'mɔːtl] *adj* unsterblich.

immortality [ımɔː'tælıtı] *n* Unsterblichkeit *f.*

immortalize [ı'mɔːtlaız] *vt* unsterblich machen.

immovable [ı'muːvəbl] *adj* unbeweglich; (*person, opinion*) fest.

immune [ı'mjuːn] *adj:* ~ **(to)** (*disease*) immun (gegen); (*flattery*) unempfänglich (für); (*criticism*) unempfindlich (gegen); (*attack*) sicher (vor +*dat*).

immune system *n* Immunsystem *nt.*

immunity [ı'mjuːnıtı] *n* (*see adj*) Immunität *f;* Unempfänglichkeit *f;* Unempfindlichkeit *f;* Sicherheit *f;* (*of diplomat, from prosecution*) Immunität *f.*

immunization [ımjunaı'zeıʃən] *n* Immunisierung *f.*

immunize ['ımjunaız] *vt:* **to** ~ **(against)** immunisieren (gegen).

imp [ımp] *n* Kobold *m;* (*child*) Racker *m* (*inf*).

impact ['ımpækt] *n* Aufprall *m;* (*of crash*) Wucht *f;* (*of law, measure*) (Aus)wirkung *f.*

impair [ım'pɛə*] *vt* beeinträchtigen.

impaired [ım'pɛəd] *adj* beeinträchtigt; (*hearing*) schlecht; ~ **vision** schlechte Augen *pl.*

impale [ım'peıl] *vt:* **to** ~ **sth (on)** etw aufspießen (auf +*dat*).

impart [ım'paːt] *vt:* **to** ~ **(to)** (*information*) mitteilen +*dat*; (*flavour*) verleihen +*dat.*

impartial [ım'paːʃl] *adj* unparteiisch.

impartiality [ımpaːʃı'ælıtı] *n* Unparteilichkeit *f.*

impassable [ım'paːsəbl] *adj* unpassierbar.

impasse [æm'paːs] *n* Sackgasse *f.*

impassive [ım'pæsıv] *adj* gelassen.

impatience [ım'peıʃəns] *n* Ungeduld *f.*

impatient [ım'peıʃənt] *adj* ungeduldig; **to get** *or* **grow** ~ ungeduldig werden; **to be** ~ **to do sth** es nicht erwarten können, etw zu tun.

impatiently [ım'peıʃəntlı] *adv* ungeduldig.

impeach [ım'piːtʃ] *vt* anklagen; (*public official*) eines Amtsvergehens anklagen.

impeachment [ım'piːtʃmənt] *n* Anklage *f* wegen eines Amtsvergehens, Impeachment *nt.*

impeccable [ım'pɛkəbl] *adj* (*dress*) untadelig; (*manners*) tadellos.

impecunious [ımpı'kjuːnıəs] *adj* mittellos.

impede [ım'piːd] *vt* behindern.

impediment [ım'pɛdımənt] *n* Hindernis *nt;* (*also:* **speech** ~) Sprachfehler *m.*

impel [ım'pɛl] *vt:* **to** ~ **sb to do sth** jdn (dazu) nötigen, etw zu tun.

impending [ım'pɛndıŋ] *adj* bevorstehend; (*catastrophe*) drohend.

impenetrable [ım'pɛnıtrəbl] *adj* undurchdringlich; (*fig*) unergründlich.

imperative [ım'pɛrətıv] *adj* dringend; (*tone*) Befehls- ♦ *n* (*LING*) Imperativ *m,*

Befehlsform *f.*

imperceptible [ımpə'sɛptıbl] *adj* nicht wahrnehmbar, unmerklich.

imperfect [ım'pəːfıkt] *adj* mangelhaft; (*goods*) fehlerhaft ♦ *n* (*LING: also:* ~ **tense**) Imperfekt *nt,* Vergangenheit *f.*

imperfection [ımpəː'fɛkʃən] *n* Fehler *m.*

imperial [ım'pıərıəl] *adj* kaiserlich; (*BRIT: measure*) britisch.

imperialism [ım'pıərıəlızəm] *n* Imperialismus *m.*

imperil [ım'pɛrıl] *vt* gefährden.

imperious [ım'pıərıəs] *adj* herrisch, gebieterisch.

impersonal [ım'pəːsənl] *adj* unpersönlich.

impersonate [ım'pəːsəneıt] *vt* sich ausgeben als; (*THEAT*) imitieren.

impersonation [ımpəːsə'neıʃən] *n* (*THEAT*) Imitation *f;* ~ **of** (*LAW*) Auftreten *nt* als.

impertinent [ım'pəːtınənt] *adj* unverschämt.

imperturbable [ımpə'təːbəbl] *adj* unerschütterlich.

impervious [ım'pəːvıəs] *adj:* ~ **to** (*criticism, pressure*) unberührt von; (*charm, influence*) unempfänglich für.

impetuous [ım'pɛtjuəs] *adj* ungestüm, stürmisch; (*act*) impulsiv.

impetus ['ımpətəs] *n* Schwung *m;* (*fig: driving force*) treibende Kraft *f.*

impinge [ım'pındʒ]: **to** ~ **on** *vt fus* sich auswirken auf +*acc*; (*rights*) einschränken.

impish ['ımpıʃ] *adj* schelmisch.

implacable [ım'plækəbl] *adj* unerbittlich, erbittert.

implant [ım'plaːnt] *vt* (*MED*) einpflanzen; (*fig: idea, principle*) einimpfen.

implausible [ım'plɔːzıbl] *adj* unglaubwürdig.

implement [*n* 'ımplımənt, *vt* 'ımplımɛnt] *n* Gerät *nt,* Werkzeug *nt* ♦ *vt* durchführen.

implicate ['ımplıkeıt] *vt* verwickeln.

implication [ımplı'keıʃən] *n* Auswirkung *f;* (*involvement*) Verwicklung *f;* **by** ~ implizit.

implicit [ım'plısıt] *adj* (*inferred*) implizit, unausgesprochen; (*unquestioning*) absolut.

implicitly [ım'plısıtlı] *adv* (*see adj*) implizit; absolut.

implore [ım'plɔː*] *vt* anflehen.

imply [ım'plaı] *vt* andeuten; (*mean*) bedeuten.

impolite [ımpə'laıt] *adj* unhöflich.

imponderable [ım'pɔndərəbl] *adj* unberechenbar ♦ *n* unberechenbare Größe *f.*

import [*vt* ım'pɔːt, *n* 'ımpɔːt] *vt* importieren, einführen ♦ *n* Import *m,* Einfuhr *f;* (*article*) Importgut *nt* ♦ *cpd* Import-, Einfuhr-.

importance [ım'pɔːtns] *n* (*see adj*) Wichtigkeit *f;* Bedeutung *f;* **to be of little/great** ~ nicht besonders wichtig/sehr wichtig sein.

important [ım'pɔːtnt] *adj* wichtig; (*influential*) bedeutend; **it's not** ~ es ist unwichtig.

importantly [ım'pɔːtntlı] *adv* wichtigtuerisch;

but more ~ ... aber was noch wichtiger ist, ...

importation [ɪmpɔːˈteɪʃən] n Import m, Einfuhr f.

imported [ɪmˈpɔːtɪd] adj importiert, eingeführt.

importer [ɪmˈpɔːtə*] n Importeur m.

impose [ɪmˈpəuz] vt auferlegen; (sanctions) verhängen ♦ vi: **to** ~ **on sb** jdm zur Last fallen.

imposing [ɪmˈpəuzɪŋ] adj eindrucksvoll.

imposition [ɪmpəˈzɪʃən] n (of tax etc) Auferlegung f; **to be an** ~ **on** eine Zumutung sein für.

impossibility [ɪmpɔsəˈbɪlɪtɪ] n Unmöglichkeit f.

impossible [ɪmˈpɔsɪbl] adj unmöglich; **it's** ~ **for me to leave now** ich kann jetzt unmöglich gehen.

impossibly [ɪmˈpɔsɪblɪ] adv unmöglich.

imposter [ɪmˈpɔstə*] n = **impostor**.

impostor [ɪmˈpɔstə*] n Hochstapler(in) m(f).

impotence [ˈɪmpətns] n (see adj) Machtlosigkeit f; Impotenz f.

impotent [ˈɪmpətnt] adj machtlos; (MED) impotent.

impound [ɪmˈpaund] vt beschlagnahmen.

impoverished [ɪmˈpɔvərɪʃt] adj verarmt.

impracticable [ɪmˈpræktɪkəbl] adj (idea) undurchführbar; (solution) unbrauchbar.

impractical [ɪmˈpræktɪkl] adj (plan) undurchführbar; (person) unpraktisch.

imprecise [ɪmprɪˈsaɪs] adj ungenau.

impregnable [ɪmˈprɛgnəbl] adj uneinnehmbar; (fig) unerschütterlich.

impregnate [ˈɪmprɛgneɪt] vt tränken.

impresario [ɪmprɪˈsɑːrɪəu] n (THEAT) Impresario m.

impress [ɪmˈprɛs] vt beeindrucken; (mark) aufdrücken; **to** ~ **sth on sb** jdm etw einschärfen.

impression [ɪmˈprɛʃən] n Eindruck m; (of stamp, seal) Abdruck m; (imitation) Nachahmung f, Imitation f; **to make a good/bad** ~ **on sb** einen guten/schlechten Eindruck auf jdn machen; **to be under the** ~ **that** ... den Eindruck haben, daß ...

impressionable [ɪmˈprɛʃnəbl] adj leicht zu beeindrucken.

impressionist [ɪmˈprɛʃənɪst] n Impressionist(in) m(f); (entertainer) Imitator(in) m(f).

impressive [ɪmˈprɛsɪv] adj beeindruckend.

imprint [ˈɪmprɪnt] n (of hand etc) Abdruck m; (PUBLISHING) Impressum nt.

imprinted [ɪmˈprɪntɪd] adj: **it is** ~ **on my memory/mind** es hat sich mir eingeprägt.

imprison [ɪmˈprɪzn] vt inhaftieren, einsperren.

imprisonment [ɪmˈprɪznmənt] n Gefangenschaft f; **three years'** ~ drei Jahre Gefängnis or Freiheitsstrafe.

improbable [ɪmˈprɔbəbl] adj unwahrscheinlich.

impromptu [ɪmˈprɔmptjuː] adj improvisiert.

improper [ɪmˈprɔpə*] adj ungehörig; (procedure) unrichtig; (dishonest) unlauter.

impropriety [ɪmprəˈpraɪətɪ] n (see adj) Ungehörigkeit f; Unrichtigkeit f; Unlauterkeit f.

improve [ɪmˈpruːv] vt verbessern ♦ vi sich bessern; **the patient is improving** dem Patienten geht es besser.

►**improve (up)on** vt fus verbessern.

improvement [ɪmˈpruːvmənt] n: ~ **(in)** Verbesserung f (+gen); **to make ~s to** Verbesserungen durchführen an +dat.

improvisation [ɪmprəvaɪˈzeɪʃən] n Improvisation f.

improvise [ˈɪmprəvaɪz] vt, vi improvisieren.

imprudence [ɪmˈpruːdns] n Unklugheit f.

imprudent [ɪmˈpruːdnt] adj unklug.

impudent [ˈɪmpjudnt] adj unverschämt.

impugn [ɪmˈpjuːn] vt angreifen; (sincerity, motives, reputation) in Zweifel ziehen.

impulse [ˈɪmpʌls] n Impuls m; (urge) Drang m; **to act on** ~ aus einem Impuls heraus handeln.

impulse buy n Impulsivkauf m.

impulsive [ɪmˈpʌlsɪv] adj impulsiv, spontan; (purchase) Impulsiv-.

impunity [ɪmˈpjuːnɪtɪ] n: **with** ~ ungestraft.

impure [ɪmˈpjuə*] adj unrein; (adulterated) verunreinigt.

impurity [ɪmˈpjuərɪtɪ] n Verunreinigung f.

IN (US) abbr (POST: = Indiana).

═══════════════════════════ KEYWORD

in [ɪn] prep **1** (indicating place, position) in +dat; (with motion) in +acc; ~ **the house/garden** im Haus/Garten; ~ **town** in der Stadt; ~ **the country** auf dem Land; ~ **here** hierin; ~ **there** darin

2 (with place names: of town, region, country) in +dat; ~ **London/Bavaria** in London/Bayern

3 (indicating time) in +dat; ~ **spring/summer/ May** im Frühling/Sommer/Mai; ~ **1994** 1994; ~ **the afternoon** am Nachmittag; **at 4 o'clock** ~ **the afternoon** um 4 Uhr nachmittags; **I did it** ~ **3 hours/days** ich habe es in 3 Stunden/Tagen gemacht; ~ **2 weeks** or **2 weeks' time** in 2 Wochen

4 (indicating manner, circumstances, state) in +dat; ~ **a loud/soft voice** mit lauter/weicher Stimme; ~ **English/German** auf Englisch/ Deutsch; ~ **the sun** in der Sonne; ~ **the rain** im Regen; ~ **good condition** in guter Verfassung

5 (with ratios, numbers): **1** ~ **10** eine(r, s) von 10; **20 pence** ~ **the pound** 20 Pence pro Pfund; **they lined up** ~ **twos** sie stellten sich in Zweierreihen auf

6 (referring to people, works): **the disease is common** ~ **children** die Krankheit ist bei

Kindern verbreitet; ~ **(the works of)**
Dickens bei Dickens; **they have a good**
leader ~ **him** in ihm haben sie einen guten
Führer
7 (*indicating profession etc*) **to be**
~ **teaching/the army** Lehrer(in)/beim
Militär sein
8 (*with present participle*): ~ **saying this, I ...**
wenn ich das sage, ...
♦ *adv:* **to be** ~ (*person: at home, work*) da sein;
(*train, ship, plane*) angekommen sein; (*in
fashion*) in sein; **to ask sb** ~ jdn
hereinbitten; **to run/limp etc** ~
hereinlaufen/-humpeln *etc*
♦ *n:* **the ~s and outs** (*of proposal, situation etc*)
die Einzelheiten *pl*.

in. *abbr* = **inch**.
inability [ɪnə'bɪlɪtɪ] *n* Unfähigkeit *f*.
inaccessible [ɪnək'sɛsɪbl] *adj* unzugänglich.
inaccuracy [ɪn'ækjurəsɪ] *n* (*see adj*)
Ungenauigkeit *f*; Unrichtigkeit *f*; (*mistake*)
Fehler *m*.
inaccurate [ɪn'ækjurət] *adj* ungenau; (*not
correct*) unrichtig.
inaction [ɪn'ækʃən] *n* Untätigkeit *f*.
inactive [ɪn'æktɪv] *adj* untätig.
inactivity [ɪnæk'tɪvɪtɪ] *n* Untätigkeit *f*.
inadequacy [ɪn'ædɪkwəsɪ] *n* Unzulänglichkeit
f.
inadequate [ɪn'ædɪkwət] *adj* unzulänglich.
inadmissible [ɪnəd'mɪsəbl] *adj* unzulässig.
inadvertently [ɪnəd'vɜːtntlɪ] *adv* ungewollt.
inadvisable [ɪnəd'vaɪzəbl] *adj* unratsam; **it is**
~ **to ...** es ist nicht ratsam, zu ...
inane [ɪ'neɪn] *adj* dumm.
inanimate [ɪn'ænɪmət] *adj* unbelebt.
inapplicable [ɪn'æplɪkəbl] *adj* unzutreffend.
inappropriate [ɪnə'prəuprɪət] *adj* unpassend;
(*word, expression*) unangebracht.
inapt [ɪn'æpt] *adj* unpassend.
inarticulate [ɪnɑː'tɪkjulət] *adj* (*speech*)
unverständlich; **he is** ~ er kann sich nur
schlecht ausdrücken.
inasmuch as [ɪnəz'mʌtʃ-] *adv* da, weil; (*in so
far as*) insofern als.
inattention [ɪnə'tɛnʃən] *n* Unaufmerksamkeit
f.
inattentive [ɪnə'tɛntɪv] *adj* unaufmerksam.
inaudible [ɪn'ɔːdɪbl] *adj* unhörbar.
inaugural [ɪ'nɔːgjurəl] *adj* (*speech, meeting*)
Eröffnungs-.
inaugurate [ɪ'nɔːgjureɪt] *vt* einführen;
(*president, official*) (feierlich) in sein/ihr Amt
einführen.
inauguration [ɪnɔːgju'reɪʃən] *n* (*see vb*)
Einführung *f*; (feierliche) Amtseinführung
f.
inauspicious [ɪnɔːs'pɪʃəs] *adj*
unheilverheißend.
in-between [ɪnbɪ'twiːn] *adj* Mittel-,
Zwischen-.

inborn [ɪn'bɔːn] *adj* angeboren.
inbred [ɪn'brɛd] *adj* angeboren; **an** ~ **family**
eine Familie, in der Inzucht herrscht.
inbreeding [ɪn'briːdɪŋ] *n* Inzucht *f*.
in-built ['ɪnbɪlt] *adj* (*quality*) ihm/ihr *etc* eigen;
(*feeling etc*) angeboren.
Inc. *abbr* = **incorporated company**.
Inca ['ɪŋkə] *adj* (*also:* ~**n**) Inka-, inkaisch ♦ *n*
Inka *mf*.
incalculable [ɪn'kælkjuləbl] *adj* (*effect*)
unabsehbar; (*loss*) unermeßlich.
incapable [ɪn'keɪpəbl] *adj* hilflos; **to be** ~ **of**
sth unfähig zu etw sein; **to be** ~ **of doing sth**
unfähig sein, etw zu tun.
incapacitate [ɪnkə'pæsɪteɪt] *vt:* **to** ~ **sb** jdn
unfähig machen.
incapacitated [ɪnkə'pæsɪteɪtɪd] *adj* (*LAW*)
entmündigt.
incapacity [ɪnkə'pæsɪtɪ] *n* Hilflosigkeit *f*;
(*inability*) Unfähigkeit *f*.
incarcerate [ɪn'kɑːsəreɪt] *vt* einkerkern.
incarnate [ɪn'kɑːnɪt] *adj* leibhaftig, in Person;
evil ~ das leibhaftige Böse.
incarnation [ɪnkɑː'neɪʃən] *n* Inbegriff *m*; (*REL*)
Menschwerdung *f*.
incendiary [ɪn'sɛndɪərɪ] *adj* (*bomb*) Brand-;
~ **device** Brandsatz *m*.
incense [*n* 'ɪnsɛns, *vt* ɪn'sɛns] *n* Weihrauch *m*;
(*perfume*) Duft *m* ♦ *vt* wütend machen.
incense burner *n* Weihrauchschwenker *m*.
incentive [ɪn'sɛntɪv] *n* Anreiz *m*.
inception [ɪn'sɛpʃən] *n* Beginn *m*, Anfang *m*.
incessant [ɪn'sɛsnt] *adj* unablässig.
incessantly [ɪn'sɛsntlɪ] *adv* unablässig.
incest ['ɪnsɛst] *n* Inzest *m*.
inch [ɪntʃ] *n* Zoll *m*; **to be within an** ~ **of sth**
kurz vor etw *dat* stehen; **he didn't give an** ~
(*fig*) er gab keinen Fingerbreit nach.
▶**inch forward** *vi* sich millimeterweise *or*
stückchenweise vorwärtsschieben.
incidence ['ɪnsɪdns] *n* Häufigkeit *f*.
incident ['ɪnsɪdnt] *n* Vorfall *m*; (*diplomatic etc*)
Zwischenfall *m*.
incidental [ɪnsɪ'dɛntl] *adj* zusätzlich;
(*unimportant*) nebensächlich; ~ **to**
verbunden mit; ~ **expenses** Nebenkosten *pl*.
incidentally [ɪnsɪ'dɛntəlɪ] *adv* übrigens.
incidental music *n* Begleitmusik *f*.
incident room *n* Einsatzzentrale *f*.
incinerate [ɪn'sɪnəreɪt] *vt* verbrennen.
incinerator [ɪn'sɪnəreɪtə*] *n* (*for waste, refuse*)
(Müll)verbrennungsanlage *f*.
incipient [ɪn'sɪpɪənt] *adj* einsetzend.
incision [ɪn'sɪʒən] *n* Einschnitt *m*.
incisive [ɪn'saɪsɪv] *adj* treffend.
incisor [ɪn'saɪzə*] *n* Schneidezahn *m*.
incite [ɪn'saɪt] *vt* (*rioters*) aufhetzen; (*violence,
hatred*) schüren.
incl. *abbr* = **including; inclusive (of)**.
inclement [ɪn'klɛmənt] *adj* (*weather*) rauh,
unfreundlich.
inclination [ɪnklɪ'neɪʃən] *n* Neigung *f*.

incline [*n* 'ınklaın, *vb* ın'klaın] *n* Abhang *m* ♦ *vt* neigen ♦ *vi* sich neigen; **to be ~d to** neigen zu; **to be well ~d towards sb** jdm geneigt *or* gewogen sein.

include [ın'kluːd] *vt* einbeziehen; (*in price*) einschließen; **the tip is not ~d in the price** Trinkgeld ist im Preis nicht inbegriffen.

including [ın'kluːdıŋ] *prep* einschließlich; **~ service charge** inklusive Bedienung.

inclusion [ın'kluːʒən] *n* (*see vb*) Einbeziehung *f*; Einschluß *m*.

inclusive [ın'kluːsıv] *adj* (*terms*) inklusive; (*price*) Inklusiv-, Pauschal-; **~ of** einschließlich +*gen*.

incognito [ınkɔg'niːtəu] *adv* inkognito.

incoherent [ınkəu'hıərənt] *adj* zusammenhanglos; (*speech*) wirr; (*person*) sich unklar *or* undeutlich ausdrückend.

income ['ınkʌm] *n* Einkommen *nt*; (*from property, investment, pension*) Einkünfte *pl*; **gross/net ~** Brutto-/Nettoeinkommen *nt*; **~ and expenditure account** Gewinn- und Verlustrechnung *f*; **~ bracket** Einkommensklasse *f*.

income support *n* ≈ Sozialhilfe *f*.

income tax *n* Einkommenssteuer *f* ♦ *cpd* Steuer-.

incoming ['ınkʌmıŋ] *adj* (*passenger*) ankommend; (*flight*) landend; (*call, mail*) eingehend; (*government, official*) neu; (*wave*) hereinbrechend; **~ tide** Flut *f*.

incommunicado ['ınkəmjunı'kaːdəu] *adj:* **to hold sb ~** jdn ohne jede Verbindung zur Außenwelt halten.

incomparable [ın'kɔmpərəbl] *adj* unvergleichlich.

incompatible [ınkəm'pætıbl] *adj* unvereinbar.

incompetence [ın'kɔmpıtns] *n* Unfähigkeit *f*.

incompetent [ın'kɔmpıtnt] *adj* unfähig; (*job*) unzulänglich.

incomplete [ınkəm'pliːt] *adj* unfertig; (*partial*) unvollständig.

incomprehensible [ınkɔmprı'hɛnsıbl] *adj* unverständlich.

inconceivable [ınkən'siːvəbl] *adj:* **it is ~ (that ...)** es ist unvorstellbar *or* undenkbar(, daß ...).

inconclusive [ınkən'kluːsıv] *adj* (*experiment, discussion*) ergebnislos; (*evidence, argument*) nicht überzeugend; (*result*) unbestimmt.

incongruous [ın'kɔŋgruəs] *adj* (*strange*) absurd; (*inappropriate*) unpassend.

inconsequential [ınkɔnsı'kwɛnʃl] *adj* unbedeutend, unwichtig.

inconsiderable [ınkən'sıdərəbl] *adj:* **not ~** beachtlich; (*sum*) nicht unerheblich.

inconsiderate [ınkən'sıdərət] *adj* rücksichtslos.

inconsistency [ınkən'sıstənsı] *n* (*see adj*) Widersprüchlichkeit *f*; Inkonsequenz *f*; Unbeständigkeit *f*.

inconsistent [ınkən'sıstnt] *adj* widersprüchlich; (*person*) inkonsequent; (*work*) unbeständig; **to be ~ with** im Widerspruch stehen zu.

inconsolable [ınkən'səuləbl] *adj* untröstlich.

inconspicuous [ınkən'spıkjuəs] *adj* unauffällig; **to make o.s. ~** sich unauffällig benehmen.

incontinence [ın'kɔntınəns] *n* (*MED*) Unfähigkeit *f*, Stuhl und/oder Harn zurückzuhalten, Inkontinenz *f*.

incontinent [ın'kɔntınənt] *adj* (*MED*) unfähig, Stuhl und/oder Harn zurückzuhalten, inkontinent.

inconvenience [ınkən'viːnjəns] *n* Unannehmlichkeit *f*; (*trouble*) Umstände *pl* ♦ *vt* Umstände bereiten +*dat*; **don't ~ yourself** machen Sie sich keine Umstände.

inconvenient [ınkən'viːnjənt] *adj* (*time, place*) ungünstig; (*house*) unbequem, unpraktisch; (*visitor*) ungelegen.

incorporate [ın'kɔːpəreıt] *vt* aufnehmen; (*contain*) enthalten; **safety features have been ~d in the design** in der Konstruktion sind auch Sicherheitsvorkehrungen enthalten.

incorporated company [ın'kɔːpəreıtıd-] (*US*) *n* eingetragene Gesellschaft *f*.

incorrect [ınkə'rɛkt] *adj* falsch.

incorrigible [ın'kɔrıdʒıbl] *adj* unverbesserlich.

incorruptible [ınkə'rʌptıbl] *adj* unbestechlich.

increase [*vb* ın'kriːs, *n* 'ınkriːs] *vi* (*level etc*) zunehmen; (*price*) steigen; (*in size*) sich vergrößern; (*in number, quantity*) sich vermehren ♦ *vt* vergrößern; (*price*) erhöhen ♦ *n:* **~ (in)** Zunahme *f* (+*gen*); (*in wages, spending etc*) Erhöhung *f* (+*gen*); **an ~ of 5%** eine Erhöhung von 5%, eine Zunahme um 5%; **to be on the ~** zunehmen.

increasing [ın'kriːsıŋ] *adj* zunehmend.

increasingly [ın'kriːsıŋlı] *adv* zunehmend.

incredible [ın'krɛdıbl] *adj* unglaublich; (*amazing, wonderful*) unwahrscheinlich (*inf*), sagenhaft (*inf*).

incredulity [ınkrı'djuːlıtı] *n* Ungläubigkeit *f*.

incredulous [ın'krɛdjuləs] *adj* ungläubig.

increment ['ınkrımənt] *n* (*in salary*) Erhöhung *f*, Zulage *f*.

incriminate [ın'krımıneıt] *vt* belasten.

incriminating [ın'krımıneıtıŋ] *adj* belastend.

incrusted [ın'krʌstıd] *adj* = **encrusted**.

incubate ['ınkjubeıt] *vt* ausbrüten ♦ *vi* ausgebrütet werden; (*disease*) zum Ausbruch kommen.

incubation [ınkju'beıʃən] *n* Ausbrüten *nt*; (*of illness*) Inkubation *f*.

incubation period *n* Inkubationszeit *f*.

incubator ['ınkjubeıtə*] *n* (*for babies*) Brutkasten *m*, Inkubator *m*.

inculcate ['ınkʌlkeıt] *vt:* **to ~ sth in(to) sb** jdm etw einprägen.

incumbent [ın'kʌmbənt] *n* Amtsinhaber(in)

m(f) ♦ *adj:* **it is ~ on him to** ... es obliegt ihm
or es ist seine Pflicht, zu ...
incur [ɪn'kɔː'] *vt (expenses, debt)* machen;
(loss) erleiden; *(disapproval, anger)* sich *dat*
zuziehen.
incurable [ɪn'kjuərəbl] *adj* unheilbar.
incursion [ɪn'kɔːʃən] *n (MIL)* Einfall *m*.
Ind. *(US) abbr (POST: = Indiana).*
indebted [ɪn'dɛtɪd] *adj:* **to be ~ to sb** jdm (zu
Dank) verpflichtet sein.
indecency [ɪn'diːsnsɪ] *n* Unanständigkeit *f*,
Anstößigkeit *f*.
indecent [ɪn'diːsnt] *adj* unanständig, anstößig;
(haste) ungebührlich.
indecent assault *(BRIT) n* Sexualverbrechen
nt.
indecent exposure *n* Erregung *f*
öffentlichen Ärgernisses.
indecipherable [ɪndɪ'saɪfərəbl] *adj* unleserlich; *(expression, glance etc)* unergründlich.
indecision [ɪndɪ'sɪʒən] *n* Unentschlossenheit
f.
indecisive [ɪndɪ'saɪsɪv] *adj* unentschlossen.
indeed [ɪn'diːd] *adv* aber sicher; *(in fact)*
tatsächlich, in der Tat; *(furthermore)* sogar;
yes ~! oh ja!, das kann man wohl sagen!
indefatigable [ɪndɪ'fætɪgəbl] *adj* unermüdlich.
indefensible [ɪndɪ'fɛnsɪbl] *adj (conduct)*
unentschuldbar.
indefinable [ɪndɪ'faɪnəbl] *adj* undefinierbar.
indefinite [ɪn'dɛfɪnɪt] *adj* unklar, vage; *(period,
number)* unbestimmt.
indefinite article *n (LING)* unbestimmter
Artikel *m*.
indefinitely [ɪn'dɛfɪnɪtlɪ] *adv (continue)* endlos;
(wait) unbegrenzt (lange); *(postpone)* auf
unbestimmte Zeit.
indelible [ɪn'dɛlɪbl] *adj (mark, stain)* nicht zu
entfernen; **~ pen** Tintenstift *m*; **~ ink**
Wäschetinte *f*.
indelicate [ɪn'dɛlɪkɪt] *adj* taktlos; *(not polite)*
ungehörig.
indemnify [ɪn'dɛmnɪfaɪ] *vt* entschädigen.
indemnity [ɪn'dɛmnɪtɪ] *n (insurance)*
Versicherung *f*; *(compensation)*
Entschädigung *f*.
indent [ɪn'dɛnt] *vt (text)* einrücken, einziehen.
indentation [ɪndɛn'teɪʃən] *n* Einkerbung *f*;
(TYP) Einrückung *f*, Einzug *m*; *(on metal)*
Delle *f*.
indenture [ɪn'dɛntʃə'] *n* Ausbildungsvertrag
m, Lehrvertrag *m*.
independence [ɪndɪ'pɛndns] *n*
Unabhängigkeit *f*.

Independence Day *(der 4. Juli)* ist in den USA
ein gesetzlicher Feiertag zum Gedenken an die
*Unabhängigkeitserklärung am 4. Juli 1776, mit
der die 13 amerikanischen Kolonien ihre
Freiheit und Unabhängigkeit von
Großbritannien erklärten.*

---

independent [ɪndɪ'pɛndnt] *adj* unabhängig.
independently [ɪndɪ'pɛndntlɪ] *adv*
unabhängig.
in-depth ['ɪndɛpθ] *adj* eingehend.
indescribable [ɪndɪs'kraɪbəbl] *adj*
unbeschreiblich.
indestructible [ɪndɪs'trʌktəbl] *adj*
unzerstörbar.
indeterminate [ɪndɪ'tɔːmɪnɪt] *adj* unbestimmt.
index ['ɪndɛks] *(pl ~es) n (in book)* Register *nt*;
(in library etc) Katalog *m*; *(card index)* Kartei
f; *(pl* **indices**: *ratio)* Index *m*; *(: sign)*
(An)zeichen *nt*.
index card *n* Karteikarte *f*.
indexed ['ɪndɛkst] *(US) n* = **index-linked**.
index finger *n* Zeigefinger *m*.
index-linked ['ɪndɛks'lɪŋkt] *adj* der
Inflationsrate *dat* angeglichen.
India ['ɪndɪə] *n* Indien *nt*.
Indian ['ɪndɪən] *adj* indisch; *(American Indian)*
indianisch ♦ *n* Inder(in) *m(f)*; **American ~**
Indianer(in) *m(f)*.
Indian Ocean *n:* **the ~** der Indische Ozean.
Indian Summer *n* Altweibersommer *m*.
India paper *n* Dünndruckpapier *nt*.
India rubber *n* Gummi *m*, Kautschuk *m*.
indicate ['ɪndɪkeɪt] *vt* (an)zeigen; *(point to)*
deuten auf *+acc*; *(mention)* andeuten ♦ *vi*
(BRIT: AUT): **to ~ left/right** links/rechts
blinken.
indication [ɪndɪ'keɪʃən] *n* (An)zeichen *nt*.
indicative [ɪn'dɪkətɪv] *n (LING)* Indikativ *m*,
Wirklichkeitsform *f* ♦ *adj:* **to be ~ of sth** auf
etw *acc* schließen lassen.
indicator ['ɪndɪkeɪtə'] *n (instrument, gauge)*
Anzeiger *m*; *(fig)* (An)zeichen *nt*; *(AUT)*
Richtungsanzeiger *m*, Blinker *m*.
indices ['ɪndɪsiːz] *npl of* **index**.
indict [ɪn'daɪt] *vt* anklagen.
indictable [ɪn'daɪtəbl] *adj (person)*
strafrechtlich verfolgbar; **~ offence**
strafbare Handlung *f*.
indictment [ɪn'daɪtmənt] *n* Anklage *f*; **to be an
~ of sth** *(fig)* ein Armutszeugnis *nt* für etw
sein.
indifference [ɪn'dɪfrəns] *n* Gleichgültig-
keit *f*.
indifferent [ɪn'dɪfrənt] *adj* gleichgültig;
(mediocre) mittelmäßig.
indigenous [ɪn'dɪdʒɪnəs] *adj* einheimisch.
indigestible [ɪndɪ'dʒɛstɪbl] *adj* unverdaulich.
indigestion [ɪndɪ'dʒɛstʃən] *n*
Magenverstimmung *f*.
indignant [ɪn'dɪgnənt] *adj:* **to be ~ at sth/with
sb** entrüstet über etw/jdn sein.
indignation [ɪndɪg'neɪʃən] *n* Entrüstung *f*.
indignity [ɪn'dɪgnɪtɪ] *n* Demütigung *f*.
indigo ['ɪndɪgəu] *n* Indigo *nt or m*.
indirect [ɪndɪ'rɛkt] *adj* indirekt; **~ way** *or*
route Umweg *m*.
indirectly [ɪndɪ'rɛktlɪ] *adv* indirekt.
indiscreet [ɪndɪs'kriːt] *adj* indiskret.

indiscretion [ɪndɪs'krɛʃən] n Indiskretion f.
indiscriminate [ɪndɪs'krɪmɪnət] adj wahllos; (*taste*) unkritisch.
indispensable [ɪndɪs'pɛnsəbl] adj unentbehrlich.
indisposed [ɪndɪs'pəuzd] adj unpäßlich.
indisputable [ɪndɪs'pju:təbl] adj unbestreitbar.
indistinct [ɪndɪs'tɪŋkt] adj undeutlich; (*image*) verschwommen; (*noise*) schwach.
indistinguishable [ɪndɪs'tɪŋgwɪʃəbl] adj: ~ **from** nicht zu unterscheiden von.
individual [ɪndɪ'vɪdjuəl] n Individuum nt, Einzelne(r) f(m) ♦ adj eigen; (*single*) einzeln; (*case, portion*) Einzel-; (*particular*) individuell.
individualist [ɪndɪ'vɪdjuəlɪst] n Individualist(in) m(f).
individuality [ɪndɪvɪdju'ælɪtɪ] n Individualität f.
individually [ɪndɪ'vɪdjuəlɪ] adv einzeln, individuell.
indivisible [ɪndɪ'vɪzɪbl] adj unteilbar.
Indochina [ɪndəu'tʃaɪnə] n Indochina nt.
indoctrinate [ɪn'dɒktrɪneɪt] vt indoktrinieren.
indoctrination [ɪndɒktrɪ'neɪʃən] n Indoktrination f.
indolence ['ɪndələns] n Trägheit f.
indolent ['ɪndələnt] adj träge.
Indonesia [ɪndə'ni:zɪə] n Indonesien nt.
Indonesian [ɪndə'ni:zɪən] adj indonesisch ♦ n Indonesier(in) m(f); (*LING*) Indonesisch nt.
indoor ['ɪndɔ:ˑ] adj (*plant, aerial*) Zimmer-; (*clothes, shoes*) Haus-; (*swimming pool, sport*) Hallen-; (*games*) im Haus.
indoors [ɪn'dɔ:z] adv drinnen; **to go** ~ hineingehen.
indubitable [ɪn'dju:bɪtəbl] adj unzweifelhaft.
indubitably [ɪn'dju:bɪtəblɪ] adv zweifellos.
induce [ɪn'dju:s] vt herbeiführen; (*persuade*) dazu bringen; (*MED: birth*) einleiten; **to** ~ **sb to do sth** jdn dazu bewegen or bringen, etw zu tun.
inducement [ɪn'dju:smənt] n Anreiz m; (*pej: bribe*) Bestechung f.
induct [ɪn'dʌkt] vt (in sein/ihr etc Amt) einführen.
induction [ɪn'dʌkʃən] n (*MED: of birth*) Einleitung f.
induction course (*BRIT*) n Einführungskurs m.
indulge [ɪn'dʌldʒ] vt nachgeben +dat; (*person, child*) verwöhnen ♦ vi: **to** ~ **in** sich hingeben +dat.
indulgence [ɪn'dʌldʒəns] n (*pleasure*) Luxus m; (*leniency*) Nachgiebigkeit f.
indulgent [ɪn'dʌldʒənt] adj nachsichtig.
industrial [ɪn'dʌstrɪəl] adj industriell; (*accident*) Arbeits-; (*city*) Industrie-.
industrial action n Arbeitskampf- maßnahmen pl.
industrial design n Industriedesign nt.

industrial estate (*BRIT*) n Industriegebiet nt.
industrialist [ɪn'dʌstrɪəlɪst] n Industrielle(r) f(m).
industrialize [ɪn'dʌstrɪəlaɪz] vt industrialisieren.
industrial park (*US*) n = **industrial estate**.
industrial relations npl Beziehungen zwischen Arbeitgebern, Arbeitnehmern und Gewerkschaften.
industrial tribunal (*BRIT*) n Arbeitsgericht nt.
industrial unrest (*BRIT*) n Arbeitsunruhen pl.
industrious [ɪn'dʌstrɪəs] adj fleißig.
industry ['ɪndəstrɪ] n Industrie f; (*diligence*) Fleiß m.
inebriated [ɪ'ni:brɪeɪtɪd] adj betrunken.
inedible [ɪn'ɛdɪbl] adj ungenießbar.
ineffective [ɪnɪ'fɛktɪv] adj wirkungslos; (*government*) unfähig.
ineffectual [ɪnɪ'fɛktʃuəl] adj = **ineffective**.
inefficiency [ɪnɪ'fɪʃənsɪ] n (*see adj*) Ineffizienz f; Leistungsunfähigkeit f.
inefficient [ɪnɪ'fɪʃənt] adj ineffizient; (*machine*) leistungsunfähig.
inelegant [ɪn'ɛlɪgənt] adj unelegant.
ineligible [ɪn'ɛlɪdʒɪbl] adj (*candidate*) nicht wählbar; **to be** ~ **for sth** zu etw nicht berechtigt sein.
inept [ɪ'nɛpt] adj (*politician*) unfähig; (*management*) stümperhaft.
ineptitude [ɪ'nɛptɪtju:d] n (*see adj*) Unfähigkeit f; Stümperhaftigkeit f.
inequality [ɪnɪ'kwɒlɪtɪ] n Ungleichheit f.
inequitable [ɪn'ɛkwɪtəbl] adj ungerecht.
inert [ɪ'nə:t] adj unbeweglich; ~ **gas** Edelgas nt.
inertia [ɪ'nə:ʃə] n Trägheit f.
inertia-reel seat belt [ɪ'nə:ʃə'ri:l-] n Automatikgurt m.
inescapable [ɪnɪ'skeɪpəbl] adj unvermeidlich; (*conclusion*) zwangsläufig.
inessential [ɪnɪ'sɛnʃl] adj unwesentlich; (*furniture etc*) entbehrlich.
inessentials [ɪnɪ'sɛnʃlz] npl Nebensächlichkeiten pl.
inestimable [ɪn'ɛstɪməbl] adj unschätzbar.
inevitability [ɪnɛvɪtə'bɪlɪtɪ] n Unvermeid- lichkeit f; **it is an** ~ es ist nicht zu vermeiden.
inevitable [ɪn'ɛvɪtəbl] adj unvermeidlich; (*result*) zwangsläufig.
inevitably [ɪn'ɛvɪtəblɪ] adv zwangsläufig; ~, **he was late** es konnte ja nicht ausbleiben, daß er zu spät kam; **as** ~ **happens** ... wie es immer so ist ...
inexact [ɪnɪg'zækt] adj ungenau.
inexcusable [ɪnɪks'kju:zəbl] adj unentschuldbar, unverzeihlich.
inexhaustible [ɪnɪg'zɔ:stɪbl] adj unerschöpflich.
inexorable [ɪn'ɛksərəbl] adj unaufhaltsam.
inexpensive [ɪnɪk'spɛnsɪv] adj preisgünstig.

inexperience [ɪnɪk'spɪərɪəns] n
Unerfahrenheit f.
inexperienced [ɪnɪk'spɪərɪənst] adj
unerfahren; (swimmer etc) ungeübt; **to be
~ in sth** wenig Erfahrung mit etw haben.
inexplicable [ɪnɪk'splɪkəbl] adj unerklärlich.
inexpressible [ɪnɪk'spresɪbl] adj
unbeschreiblich.
inextricable [ɪnɪk'strɪkəbl] adj unentwirrbar;
(dilemma) unlösbar.
inextricably [ɪnɪk'strɪkəblɪ] adv unentwirrbar;
(linked) untrennbar.
infallibility [ɪnfælə'bɪlɪtɪ] n Unfehlbarkeit f.
infallible [ɪn'fælɪbl] adj unfehlbar.
infamous ['ɪnfəməs] adj niederträchtig.
infamy ['ɪnfəmɪ] n Verrufenheit f.
infancy ['ɪnfənsɪ] n frühe Kindheit f; (of
movement, firm) Anfangsstadium nt.
infant ['ɪnfənt] n Säugling m; (young child)
Kleinkind nt ♦ cpd Säuglings-.
infantile ['ɪnfəntaɪl] adj kindisch, infantil;
(disease) Kinder-.
infantry ['ɪnfəntrɪ] n Infanterie f.
infantryman ['ɪnfəntrɪmən] (irreg: like **man**) n
Infanterist m.
infant school (BRIT) n Grundschule f (für die
ersten beiden Jahrgänge).
infatuated [ɪn'fætjueɪtɪd] adj: ~ **with** vernarrt
in +acc; **to become ~ with** sich vernarren in
+acc.
infatuation [ɪnfætju'eɪʃən] n Vernarrtheit f.
infect [ɪn'fekt] vt anstecken (also fig),
infizieren; (food) verseuchen; **to become
~ed** (wound) sich entzünden.
infection [ɪn'fekʃən] n Infektion f,
Entzündung f; (contagion) Ansteckung f.
infectious [ɪn'fekʃəs] adj ansteckend.
infer [ɪn'fɜː'] vt schließen; (imply) andeuten.
inference ['ɪnfərəns] n (see vb) Schluß m;
Andeutung f.
inferior [ɪn'fɪərɪə'] adj (in rank) untergeordnet,
niedriger; (in quality) minderwertig; (in
quantity, number) geringer ♦ n
Untergebene(r) f(m); **to feel ~ (to sb)** sich
(jdm) unterlegen fühlen.
inferiority [ɪnfɪərɪ'ɔrətɪ] n (see adj)
untergeordnete Stellung f, niedriger Rang
m; Minderwertigkeit f; geringere Zahl f.
inferiority complex n Minderwertig-
keitskomplex m.
infernal [ɪn'fɜːnl] adj höllisch; (temper)
schrecklich.
inferno [ɪn'fɜːnəu] n (blaze) Flammenmeer nt.
infertile [ɪn'fɜːtaɪl] adj unfruchtbar.
infertility [ɪnfɜː'tɪlɪtɪ] n Unfruchtbarkeit f.
infested [ɪn'festɪd] adj: ~ **(with)** verseucht
(mit).
infidelity [ɪnfɪ'delɪtɪ] n Untreue f.
infighting ['ɪnfaɪtɪŋ] n interne Machtkämpfe
pl.
infiltrate ['ɪnfɪltreɪt] vt (organization etc)
infiltrieren, unterwandern; (: to spy)

einschleusen.
infinite ['ɪnfɪnɪt] adj unendlich; (time, money)
unendlich viel.
infinitely ['ɪnfɪnɪtlɪ] adv unendlich viel.
infinitesimal [ɪnfɪnɪ'tesɪməl] adj unendlich
klein, winzig.
infinitive [ɪn'fɪnɪtɪv] n (LING) Infinitiv m,
Grundform f.
infinity [ɪn'fɪnɪtɪ] n Unendlichkeit f; (MATH,
PHOT) Unendliche nt; **an ~ of ...** unendlich
viel(e) ...
infirm [ɪn'fɜːm] adj schwach, gebrechlich.
infirmary [ɪn'fɜːmərɪ] n Krankenhaus nt.
infirmity [ɪn'fɜːmɪtɪ] n Schwäche f,
Gebrechlichkeit f.
inflame [ɪn'fleɪm] vt (person, crowd)
aufbringen.
inflamed [ɪn'fleɪmd] adj entzündet.
inflammable [ɪn'flæməbl] adj feuergefährlich.
inflammation [ɪnflə'meɪʃən] n Entzündung f.
inflammatory [ɪn'flæmətərɪ] adj (speech)
aufrührerisch, Hetz-.
inflatable [ɪn'fleɪtəbl] adj aufblasbar; (dinghy)
Schlauch-.
inflate [ɪn'fleɪt] vt aufpumpen; (balloon)
aufblasen; (price) hochtreiben; (expectation)
steigern; (position, ideas etc) hochspielen.
inflated [ɪn'fleɪtɪd] adj (style) geschwollen;
(value, price) überhöht.
inflation [ɪn'fleɪʃən] n Inflation f.
inflationary [ɪn'fleɪʃənərɪ] adj inflationär;
(spiral) Inflations-.
inflexible [ɪn'fleksɪbl] adj inflexibel; (rule)
starr.
inflict [ɪn'flɪkt] vt: **to ~ sth on sb** (damage,
suffering, wound) jdm etw zufügen;
(punishment) jdm etw auferlegen; (fig:
problems) jdn mit etw belasten.
infliction [ɪn'flɪkʃən] n (see vb) Zufügen nt;
Auferlegung f; Belastung f.
in-flight ['ɪnflaɪt] adj während des Fluges.
inflow ['ɪnfləu] n Zustrom m.
influence ['ɪnfluəns] n Einfluß m ♦ vt
beeinflussen; **under the ~ of alcohol** unter
Alkoholeinfluß.
influential [ɪnflu'enʃl] adj einflußreich.
influenza [ɪnflu'enzə] n (MED) Grippe f.
influx ['ɪnflʌks] n (of refugees) Zustrom m; (of
funds) Zufuhr f.
inform [ɪn'fɔːm] vt: **to ~ sb of sth** jdn von etw
unterrichten, jdn über etw acc informieren
♦ vi: **to ~ on sb** jdn denunzieren.
informal [ɪn'fɔːml] adj ungezwungen; (manner,
clothes) leger; (unofficial) inoffiziell;
(announcement, invitation) informell.
informality [ɪnfɔː'mælɪtɪ] n (see adj)
Ungezwungenheit f; legere Art f;
inoffizieller Charakter m; informeller
Charakter m.
informally [ɪn'fɔːməlɪ] adv (see adj)
ungezwungen; leger; inoffiziell; informell.
informant [ɪn'fɔːmənt] n Informant(in) m(f).

information [ˌɪnfəˈmeɪʃən] n Informationen pl,
Auskunft f; (knowledge) Wissen nt; **to get
~ on** sich informieren über +acc; **a piece of
~** eine Auskunft or Information; **for your ~**
zu Ihrer Information.
information bureau n Auskunftsbüro nt.
information desk n Auskunftsschalter m.
information office n Auskunftsbüro nt.
information processing n Informations-
verarbeitung f.
information retrieval n Informationsabruf
m, Datenabruf m.
information science n Informatik f.
information technology n
Informationstechnik f.
informative [ɪnˈfɔːmətɪv] adj aufschlußreich.
informed [ɪnˈfɔːmd] adj informiert; (guess,
opinion) wohlbegründet; **to be well/better ~**
gut/besser informiert sein.
informer [ɪnˈfɔːmə*] n Informant(in) m(f); (also:
police ~) Polizeispitzel m.
infra dig [ˈɪnfrəˈdɪg] (inf) adj abbr (= infra
dignitatem) unter meiner/seiner etc Würde.
infrared [ɪnfrəˈred] adj infrarot.
infrastructure [ˈɪnfrəstrʌktʃə*] n
Infrastruktur f.
infrequent [ɪnˈfriːkwənt] adj selten.
infringe [ɪnˈfrɪndʒ] vt (law) verstoßen gegen,
übertreten ♦ vi: **to ~ on** (rights) verletzen.
infringement [ɪnˈfrɪndʒmənt] n (see vb)
Verstoß m, Übertretung f, Verletzung f.
infuriate [ɪnˈfjʊərieɪt] vt wütend machen.
infuriating [ɪnˈfjʊərieɪtɪŋ] adj äußerst
ärgerlich.
infuse [ɪnˈfjuːz] vt (tea etc) aufgießen; **to ~ sb
with sth** (fig) jdm etw einflößen.
infusion [ɪnˈfjuːʒən] n (tea etc) Aufguß m.
ingenious [ɪnˈdʒiːnjəs] adj genial.
ingenuity [ɪndʒɪˈnjuːɪtɪ] n Einfallsreichtum m;
(skill) Geschicklichkeit f.
ingenuous [ɪnˈdʒenjuəs] adj offen, aufrichtig;
(innocent) naiv.
ingot [ˈɪŋgət] n Barren m.
ingrained [ɪnˈgreɪnd] adj (habit) fest; (belief)
unerschütterlich.
ingratiate [ɪnˈgreɪʃieɪt] vt: **to ~ o.s. with sb**
sich bei jdm einschmeicheln.
ingratiating [ɪnˈgreɪʃieɪtɪŋ] adj
schmeichlerisch.
ingratitude [ɪnˈgrætɪtjuːd] n Undank m.
ingredient [ɪnˈgriːdiənt] n (of cake etc) Zutat f;
(of situation) Bestandteil m.
ingrowing [ˈɪngrəʊɪŋ] adj: **~ toenail**
eingewachsener Zehennagel m.
inhabit [ɪnˈhæbɪt] vt bewohnen, wohnen in
+dat.
inhabitant [ɪnˈhæbɪtnt] n Einwohner(in) m(f);
(of street, house) Bewohner(in) m(f).
inhale [ɪnˈheɪl] vt einatmen ♦ vi einatmen;
(when smoking) inhalieren.
inhaler [ɪnˈheɪlə*] n Inhalationsapparat m.
inherent [ɪnˈhɪərənt] adj: **~ in** or **to** eigen +dat.

inherently [ɪnˈhɪərəntlɪ] adv von Natur aus.
inherit [ɪnˈherɪt] vt erben.
inheritance [ɪnˈherɪtəns] n Erbe nt.
inhibit [ɪnˈhɪbɪt] vt hemmen.
inhibited [ɪnˈhɪbɪtɪd] adj gehemmt.
inhibiting [ɪnˈhɪbɪtɪŋ] adj hemmend; **~ factor**
Hemmnis nt.
inhibition [ɪnhɪˈbɪʃən] n Hemmung f.
inhospitable [ɪnhɔsˈpɪtəbl] adj ungastlich;
(place, climate) unwirtlich.
in-house [ˈɪnˈhaus] adj, adv hausintern.
inhuman [ɪnˈhjuːmən] adj (behaviour)
unmenschlich; (appearance) nicht
menschlich.
inhumane [ɪnhjuːˈmeɪn] adj inhuman;
(treatment) menschenunwürdig.
inimitable [ɪˈnɪmɪtəbl] adj unnachahmlich.
iniquitous [ɪˈnɪkwɪtəs] adj (unfair) ungerecht.
iniquity [ɪˈnɪkwɪtɪ] n Ungerechtigkeit f;
(wickedness) Ungeheuerlichkeit f.
initial [ɪˈnɪʃl] adj anfänglich; (stage) Anfangs-
♦ n Initiale f, Anfangsbuchstabe m ♦ vt
(document) abzeichnen; **initials** npl Initialen
pl; (as signature) Namenszeichen nt.
initialize [ɪˈnɪʃəlaɪz] vt initialisieren.
initially [ɪˈnɪʃəlɪ] adv zu Anfang; (first) zuerst.
initiate [ɪˈnɪʃieɪt] vt (talks) eröffnen; (process)
einleiten; (new member) feierlich
aufnehmen; **to ~ sb into a secret** jdn in ein
Geheimnis einweihen; **to ~ proceedings
against sb** (LAW) einen Prozeß gegen jdn
anstrengen.
initiation [ɪnɪʃɪˈeɪʃən] n (beginning)
Einführung f; (into secret etc) Einweihung f.
initiative [ɪˈnɪʃətɪv] n Initiative f; **to take the
~** die Initiative ergreifen.
inject [ɪnˈdʒekt] vt (ein)spritzen; (fig: funds)
hineinpumpen; **to ~ sb with sth** jdm etw
spritzen or injizieren; **to ~ money into sth**
(fig) Geld in etw acc pumpen.
injection [ɪnˈdʒekʃən] n Spritze f, Injektion f;
to give/have an ~ eine Spritze or Injektion
geben/bekommen; **an ~ of money/funds**
(fig) eine Finanzspritze.
injudicious [ɪndʒuˈdɪʃəs] adj unklug.
injunction [ɪnˈdʒʌŋkʃən] n (LAW) gerichtliche
Verfügung f.
injure [ˈɪndʒə*] vt verletzen; (reputation)
schaden +dat; **to ~ o.s.** sich verletzen.
injured [ˈɪndʒəd] adj verletzt; (tone) gekränkt;
~ party (LAW) Geschädigte(r) f(m).
injurious [ɪnˈdʒʊəriəs] adj: **to be ~ to** schaden
+dat, schädlich sein +dat.
injury [ˈɪndʒərɪ] n Verletzung f; **to escape
without ~** unverletzt davonkommen.
injury time n (SPORT) Nachspielzeit f; **to play
~** nachspielen.
injustice [ɪnˈdʒʌstɪs] n Ungerechtigkeit f; **you
do me an ~** Sie tun mir unrecht.
ink [ɪŋk] n Tinte f; (in printing) Druckfarbe f.
ink-jet printer [ˈɪŋkdʒet-] n
Tintenstrahldrucker m.

inkling ['ıŋklıŋ] *n* (dunkle) Ahnung *f*; **to have an ~ of** ahnen.

ink pad *n* Stempelkissen *nt*.

inky ['ıŋkı] *adj* tintenschwarz; (*fingers*) tintenbeschmiert.

inlaid ['ınleıd] *adj* eingelegt.

inland ['ınlənd] *adj* (*port, sea, waterway*) Binnen- ♦ *adv* (*travel*) landeinwärts.

Inland Revenue (*BRIT*) *n* ≈ Finanzamt *nt*.

in-laws ['ınlɔːz] *npl* (*parents-in-law*) Schwiegereltern *pl*; (*other relatives*) angeheiratete Verwandte *pl*.

inlet ['ınlet] *n* (schmale) Bucht *f*.

inlet pipe *n* Zuleitung *f*, Zuleitungsrohr *nt*.

inmate ['ınmeıt] *n* Insasse *m*, Insassin *f*.

inmost ['ınməust] *adj* innerst.

inn [ın] *n* Gasthaus *nt*.

innards ['ınədz] (*inf*) *npl* Innereien *pl*.

innate [ı'neıt] *adj* angeboren.

inner ['ınə*] *adj* innere(r, s); (*courtyard*) Innen-.

inner city *n* Innenstadt *f*.

innermost ['ınəməust] *adj* = **inmost**.

inner tube *n* (*of tyre*) Schlauch *m*.

innings ['ınıŋz] *n* (*CRICKET*) Innenrunde *f*; **he's had a good ~** (*fig*) er kann auf ein langes, ausgefülltes Leben zurückblicken.

innocence ['ınəsns] *n* Unschuld *f*.

innocent ['ınəsnt] *adj* unschuldig.

innocuous [ı'nɔkjuəs] *adj* harmlos.

innovation [ınəu'veıʃən] *n* Neuerung *f*.

innuendo [ınju'ɛndəu] (*pl* **~es**) *n* versteckte Andeutung *f*.

innumerable [ı'njuːmrəbl] *adj* unzählig.

inoculate [ı'nɔkjuleıt] *vt*: **to ~ sb against sth** jdn gegen etw impfen; **to ~ sb with sth** jdm etw einimpfen.

inoculation [ınɔkju'leıʃən] *n* Impfung *f*.

inoffensive [ınə'fɛnsıv] *adj* harmlos.

inopportune [ın'ɔpətjuːn] *adj* unangebracht; (*moment*) ungelegen.

inordinate [ı'nɔːdınət] *adj* (*thirst etc*) unmäßig; (*amount, pleasure*) ungeheuer.

inordinately [ı'nɔːdınətlı] *adv* (*proud*) unmäßig; (*long, large etc*) ungeheuer.

inorganic [ınɔː'gænık] *adj* anorganisch.

inpatient ['ınpeıʃənt] *n* stationär behandelter Patient *m*, stationär behandelte Patientin *f*.

input ['ınput] *n* (*of capital, manpower*) Investition *f*; (*of energy*) Zufuhr *f*; (*COMPUT*) Eingabe *f*, Input *m or nt* ♦ *vt* (*COMPUT*) eingeben.

inquest ['ınkwɛst] *n* gerichtliche Untersuchung *f* der Todesursache.

inquire [ın'kwaıə*] *vi*: **to ~ about** sich erkundigen nach, fragen nach ♦ *vt* sich erkundigen nach, fragen nach; **to ~ when/where/whether** fragen *or* sich erkundigen, wann/wo/ob.

▶**inquire after** *vt fus* sich erkundigen nach.

▶**inquire into** *vt fus* untersuchen.

inquiring [ın'kwaıərıŋ] *adj* wissensdurstig.

inquiry [ın'kwaıərı] *n* Untersuchung *f*; (*question*) Anfrage *f*; **to hold an ~ into sth** eine Untersuchung +*gen* durchführen.

inquiry desk (*BRIT*) *n* Auskunft *f*, Auskunftsschalter *m*.

inquiry office (*BRIT*) *n* Auskunft *f*, Auskunftsbüro *nt*.

inquisition [ınkwı'zıʃən] *n* Untersuchung *f*; (*REL*): **the I~** die Inquisition.

inquisitive [ın'kwızıtıv] *adj* neugierig.

inroads ['ınrəudz] *npl*: **to make ~ into** (*savings, supplies*) angreifen.

ins *abbr* (= *inches*) *see* **inch**.

insane [ın'seın] *adj* wahnsinnig; (*MED*) geisteskrank.

insanitary [ın'sænıtərı] *adj* unhygienisch.

insanity [ın'sænıtı] *n* Wahnsinn *m*; (*MED*) Geisteskrankheit *f*.

insatiable [ın'seıʃəbl] *adj* unersättlich.

inscribe [ın'skraıb] *vt* (*on ring*) eingravieren; (*on stone*) einmeißeln; (*on banner*) schreiben; **to ~ a ring/stone/banner with sth** etw in einen Ring eingravieren/in einen Stein einmeißeln/auf ein Spruchband schreiben; **to ~ a book** eine Widmung in ein Buch schreiben.

inscription [ın'skrıpʃən] *n* Inschrift *f*; (*in book*) Widmung *f*.

inscrutable [ın'skruːtəbl] *adj* (*comment*) unergründlich; (*expression*) undurchdringlich.

inseam measurement ['ınsiːm-] (*US*) *n* innere Beinlänge *f*.

insect ['ınsɛkt] *n* Insekt *nt*.

insect bite *n* Insektenstich *m*.

insecticide [ın'sɛktısaıd] *n* Insektizid *nt*, Insektengift *nt*.

insect repellent *n* Insektenbekämpfungsmittel *nt*.

insecure [ınsı'kjuə*] *adj* unsicher.

insecurity [ınsı'kjuərıtı] *n* Unsicherheit *f*.

insemination [ınsɛmı'neıʃən] *n*: **artificial ~** künstliche Besamung *f*.

insensible [ın'sɛnsıbl] *adj* bewußtlos; **~ to** unempfindlich gegen; **~ of** nicht bewußt +*gen*.

insensitive [ın'sɛnsıtıv] *adj* gefühllos.

insensitivity [ınsɛnsı'tıvıtı] *n* Gefühllosigkeit *f*.

inseparable [ın'sɛprəbl] *adj* untrennbar; (*friends*) unzertrennlich.

insert [*vt* ın'səːt, *n* 'ınsəːt] *vt* einfügen; (*into sth*) hineinstecken ♦ *n* (*in newspaper etc*) Beilage *f*; (*in shoe*) Einlage *f*.

insertion [ın'səːʃən] *n* Hineinstecken *nt*; (*of needle*) Einstechen *nt*; (*of comment*) Einfügen *nt*.

in-service ['ın'səːvıs] *adj*: **~ training** (berufsbegleitende) Fortbildung *f*, **~ course** Fortbildungslehrgang *m*.

inshore [ın'ʃɔː*] *adj* (*fishing, waters*) Küsten- ♦ *adv* in Küstennähe; (*move*) auf die Küste zu.

inside ['ɪn'saɪd] n Innere(s) nt, Innenseite f; (of road: BRIT) linke Spur f; (: US, Europe etc) rechte Spur f ♦ adj innere(r, s); (pocket, cabin, light) Innen- ♦ adv (go) nach innen, hinein; (be) drinnen ♦ prep (location) in +dat; (motion) in +acc; ~ **10 minutes** innerhalb von 10 Minuten; **insides** npl (inf) Bauch m; (innards) Eingeweide pl.

inside forward n (SPORT) Halbstürmer m.

inside information n interne Informationen pl.

inside lane n (BRIT) linke Spur f; (US, Europe etc) rechte Spur f.

inside leg measurement (BRIT) n innere Beinlänge f.

inside out adv (know) in- und auswendig; (piece of clothing: be) links or verkehrt herum; (: turn) nach links.

insider [ɪn'saɪdə*] n Insider m, Eingeweihte(r) f(m).

insider dealing n (STOCK EXCHANGE) Insiderhandel m.

insider trading n = **insider dealing**.

inside story n Inside-Story f.

insidious [ɪn'sɪdɪəs] adj heimtückisch.

insight ['ɪnsaɪt] n Verständnis nt; **to gain (an)** ~ **into** einen Einblick gewinnen in +acc.

insignia [ɪn'sɪgnɪə] npl Insignien pl.

insignificant [ɪnsɪg'nɪfɪknt] adj belanglos.

insincere [ɪnsɪn'sɪə*] adj unaufrichtig, falsch.

insincerity [ɪnsɪn'sɛrɪtɪ] n Unaufrichtigkeit f, Falschheit f.

insinuate [ɪn'sɪnjueɪt] vt anspielen auf +acc.

insinuation [ɪnsɪnju'eɪʃən] n Anspielung f.

insipid [ɪn'sɪpɪd] adj fad(e); (colour) langweilig.

insist [ɪn'sɪst] vi bestehen; **to** ~ **on** bestehen auf +dat; **to** ~ **that** darauf bestehen, daß; (claim) behaupten, daß.

insistence [ɪn'sɪstəns] n (determination) Bestehen nt.

insistent [ɪn'sɪstənt] adj (determined) hartnäckig; (continual) andauernd, penetrant (pej).

in so far as adv insofern als.

insole ['ɪnsəul] n Einlegesohle f.

insolence ['ɪnsələns] n Frechheit f, Unverschämtheit f.

insolent ['ɪnsələnt] adj frech, unverschämt.

insoluble [ɪn'sɔljubl] adj unlösbar.

insolvency [ɪn'sɔlvənsɪ] n Zahlungsunfähigkeit f.

insolvent [ɪn'sɔlvənt] adj zahlungsunfähig.

insomnia [ɪn'sɔmnɪə] n Schlaflosigkeit f.

insomniac [ɪn'sɔmnɪæk] n: **to be an** ~ an Schlaflosigkeit leiden.

inspect [ɪn'spɛkt] vt kontrollieren; (examine) prüfen; (troops) inspizieren.

inspection [ɪn'spɛkʃən] n (see vb) Kontrolle f; Prüfung f; Inspektion f.

inspector [ɪn'spɛktə*] n Inspektor(in) m(f); (BRIT: on buses, trains) Kontrolleur(in) m(f);

(: POLICE) Kommissar(in) m(f).

inspiration [ɪnspə'reɪʃən] n Inspiration f; (idea) Eingebung f.

inspire [ɪn'spaɪə*] vt inspirieren; (confidence, hope etc) (er)wecken.

inspired [ɪn'spaɪəd] adj genial; **in an** ~ **moment** in einem Augenblick der Inspiration.

inspiring [ɪn'spaɪərɪŋ] adj inspirierend.

inst. (BRIT) abbr (COMM: = instant): **of the 16th** ~ vom 16. d.M.

instability [ɪnstə'bɪlɪtɪ] n Instabilität f; (of person) Labilität f.

install [ɪn'stɔːl] vt installieren; (telephone) anschließen; (official) einsetzen; **to** ~ **o.s.** sich niederlassen.

installation [ɪnstə'leɪʃən] n Installation f; (of telephone) Anschluß m; (INDUSTRY, MIL: plant) Anlage f.

installment plan (US) n Ratenzahlung f.

installment, (US) installment [ɪn'stɔːlmənt] n Rate f; (of story) Fortsetzung f; (of TV serial etc) (Sende)folge f; **in** ~**s** in Raten.

instance ['ɪnstəns] n Beispiel nt; **for** ~ zum Beispiel; **in that** ~ in diesem Fall; **in many** ~**s** in vielen Fällen; **in the first** ~ zuerst or zunächst (einmal).

instant ['ɪnstənt] n Augenblick m ♦ adj (reaction) unmittelbar; (success) sofortig; ~ **food** Schnellgerichte pl; ~ **coffee** Pulverkaffee m; **the 10th** ~ (COMM, ADMIN) der 10. dieses Monats.

instantaneous [ɪnstən'teɪnɪəs] adj unmittelbar.

instantly ['ɪnstəntlɪ] adv sofort.

instant replay n (TV) Wiederholung f.

instead [ɪn'stɛd] adv statt dessen; ~ **of** statt +gen; ~ **of sb** an jds Stelle dat; ~ **of doing sth** anstatt or anstelle etw zu tun.

instep ['ɪnstɛp] n (of foot) Spann m; (of shoe) Blatt nt.

instigate ['ɪnstɪgeɪt] vt anstiften, anzetteln; (talks etc) initiieren.

instigation [ɪnstɪ'geɪʃən] n (see vb) Anstiftung f, Anzettelung f; Initiierung f; **at sb's** ~ auf jds Betreiben acc.

instil [ɪn'stɪl] vt: **to** ~ **sth into sb** (confidence, fear etc) jdm etw einflößen.

instinct ['ɪnstɪŋkt] n Instinkt m; (reaction, inclination) instinktive Reaktion f.

instinctive [ɪn'stɪŋktɪv] adj instinktiv.

instinctively [ɪn'stɪŋktɪvlɪ] adv instinktiv.

institute ['ɪnstɪtjuːt] n Institut nt; (for teaching) Hochschule f; (professional body) Bund m, Verband m ♦ vt einführen; (inquiry, course of action) einleiten; (proceedings) anstrengen.

institution [ɪnstɪ'tjuːʃən] n Einführung f; (organization) Institution f, Einrichtung f; (hospital, mental home) Anstalt f, Heim nt.

institutional [ɪnstɪ'tjuːʃnl] adj (education) institutionell; (value, quality etc) institutionalisiert; ~ **care** Unterbringung in

einem Heim *or* einer Anstalt; **to be in
~ care** in einem Heim *or* einer Anstalt sein.
instruct [ɪn'strʌkt] *vt*: **to ~ sb in sth** jdn in etw
dat unterrichten; **to ~ sb to do sth** jdn
anweisen, etw zu tun.
instruction [ɪn'strʌkʃən] *n* Unterricht *m*;
instructions *npl (orders)* Anweisungen *pl*; **~s
(for use)** Gebrauchsanweisung *f*,
Gebrauchsanleitung *f*; **~ book/manual/
leaflet** *etc* Bedienungsanleitung *f*.
instructive [ɪn'strʌktɪv] *adj* lehrreich;
(response) aufschlußreich.
instructor [ɪn'strʌktə*] *n* Lehrer(in) *m(f)*.
instrument ['ɪnstrumənt] *n* Instrument *nt*;
(MUS) (Musik)instrument *nt*.
instrumental [ɪnstru'mentl] *adj (MUS: music,
accompaniment)* Instrumental-; **to be ~ in**
eine bedeutende Rolle spielen bei.
instrumentalist [ɪnstru'mentəlɪst] *n*
Instrumentalist(in) *m(f)*.
instrument panel *n* Armaturenbrett *nt*.
insubordination [ɪnsəbɔ:dɪ'neɪʃən] *n*
Gehorsamsverweigerung *f*.
insufferable [ɪn'sʌfrəbl] *adj* unerträglich.
insufficient [ɪnsə'fɪʃənt] *adj* unzureichend.
insufficiently [ɪnsə'fɪʃəntlɪ] *adv* unzureichend.
insular ['ɪnsjulə*] *adj* engstirnig.
insulate ['ɪnsjuleɪt] *vt* isolieren; *(person,
group)* abschirmen.
insulating tape ['ɪnsjuleɪtɪŋ-] *n* Isolierband
nt.
insulation [ɪnsju'leɪʃən] *n (see vb)* Isolierung
f; Abschirmung *f*.
insulator ['ɪnsjuleɪtə*] *n* Isolierstoff *m*.
insulin ['ɪnsjulɪn] *n* Insulin *nt*.
insult [*n* 'ɪnsʌlt, *vt* ɪn'sʌlt] *n* Beleidigung *f* ♦ *vt*
beleidigen.
insulting [ɪn'sʌltɪŋ] *adj* beleidigend.
insuperable [ɪn'sju:prəbl] *adj* unüberwindlich.
insurance [ɪn'ʃuərəns] *n* Versicherung *f*; **fire/
life ~** Brand-/Lebensversicherung *f*; **to take
out ~ (against)** eine Versicherung
abschließen (gegen).
insurance agent *n* Versicherungs-
vertreter(in) *m(f)*.
insurance broker *n* Versicherungs-
makler(in) *m(f)*.
insurance policy *n* Versicherungspolice *f*.
insurance premium *n* Versicherungsprämie
f.
insure [ɪn'ʃuə*] *vt* versichern; **to ~ o.s./sth
against sth** sich/etw gegen etw versichern;
to ~ o.s. *or* **one's life** eine
Lebensversicherung abschließen; **to
~ (o.s.) against sth** *(fig)* sich gegen etw
absichern; **to be ~d for £5,000** für £5000
versichert sein.
insured [ɪn'ʃuəd] *n*: **the ~** der/die Versicherte.
insurer [ɪn'ʃuərə*] *n* Versicherer *m*.
insurgent [ɪn'sɔ:dʒənt] *adj* aufständisch ♦ *n*
Aufständische(r) *f(m)*.
insurmountable [ɪnsə'mauntəbl] *adj*

unüberwindlich.
insurrection [ɪnsə'rekʃən] *n* Aufstand *m*.
intact [ɪn'tækt] *adj* intakt; *(whole)* ganz;
(unharmed) unversehrt.
intake ['ɪnteɪk] *n (of food)* Aufnahme *f*; *(of air)*
Zufuhr *f*; *(BRIT: SCOL)*: **an ~ of 200 a year**
200 neue Schüler pro Jahr.
intangible [ɪn'tændʒɪbl] *adj* unbestimmbar;
(idea) vage; *(benefit)* immateriell.
integer ['ɪntɪdʒə*] *n (MATH)* ganze Zahl *f*.
integral ['ɪntɪgrəl] *adj* wesentlich.
integrate ['ɪntɪgreɪt] *vt* integrieren ♦ *vi* sich
integrieren.
integrated circuit ['ɪntɪgreɪtɪd-] *n (COMPUT)*
integrierter Schaltkreis *m*.
integration [ɪntɪ'greɪʃən] *n* Integration *f*;
racial ~ Rassenintegration *f*.
integrity [ɪn'tegrɪtɪ] *n* Integrität *f*; *(of group)*
Einheit *f*; *(of culture, text)* Unversehrtheit *f*.
intellect ['ɪntəlekt] *n* Intellekt *m*.
intellectual [ɪntə'lektjuəl] *adj* intellektuell,
geistig ♦ *n* Intellektuelle(r) *f(m)*.
intelligence [ɪn'telɪdʒəns] *n* Intelligenz *f*;
(information) Informationen *pl*.
intelligence quotient *n* Intelligenzquotient
m.
intelligence service *n* Nachrichtendienst *m*,
Geheimdienst *m*.
intelligence test *n* Intelligenztest *m*.
intelligent [ɪn'telɪdʒənt] *adj* intelligent;
(decision) klug.
intelligently [ɪn'telɪdʒəntlɪ] *adv* intelligent.
intelligentsia [ɪntelɪ'dʒentsɪə] *n*: **the ~** die
Intelligenz.
intelligible [ɪn'telɪdʒɪbl] *adj* verständlich.
intemperate [ɪn'tempərət] *adj* unmäßig;
(remark) überzogen.
intend [ɪn'tend] *vt*: **to be ~ed for sb** für jdn
gedacht sein; **to ~ to do sth** beabsichtigen,
etw zu tun.
intended [ɪn'tendɪd] *adj (effect, victim)*
beabsichtigt; *(journey)* geplant; *(insult)*
absichtlich.
intense [ɪn'tens] *adj* intensiv; *(anger, joy)*
äußerst groß; *(person)* ernsthaft.
intensely [ɪn'tenslɪ] *adv* äußerst; **I dislike him
~** ich verabscheue ihn.
intensify [ɪn'tensɪfaɪ] *vt* intensivieren,
verstärken.
intensity [ɪn'tensɪtɪ] *n* Intensität *f*; *(of anger)*
Heftigkeit *f*.
intensive [ɪn'tensɪv] *adj* intensiv.
intensive care *n*: **to be in ~** auf der
Intensivstation sein.
intensive care unit *n* Intensivstation *f*.
intent [ɪn'tent] *n* Absicht *f* ♦ *adj (attentive)*
aufmerksam; *(absorbed)*: **~ (on)** versunken
(in +*acc*); **to all ~s and purposes** im Grunde;
to be ~ on doing sth entschlossen sein, etw
zu tun.
intention [ɪn'tenʃən] *n* Absicht *f*.
intentional [ɪn'tenʃənl] *adj* absichtlich.

intentionally [ɪn'tenʃnəlɪ] *adv* absichtlich.
intently [ɪn'tentlɪ] *adv* konzentriert.
inter [ɪn'tə:'] *vt* bestatten.
interact [ɪntər'ækt] *vi* (*people*) interagieren;
(*things*) aufeinander einwirken; (*ideas*) sich
gegenseitig beeinflussen; **to ~ with**
interagieren mit; einwirken auf *+acc*;
beeinflussen.
interaction [ɪntər'ækʃən] *n* (*see vb*)
Interaktion *f*; gegenseitige Einwirkung *f*;
gegenseitige Beeinflussung *f*.
interactive [ɪntər'æktɪv] *adj* (*also COMPUT*)
interaktiv.
intercede [ɪntə'si:d] *vi:* **to ~ (with sb/on
behalf of sb)** sich (bei jdm/für jdn)
einsetzen.
intercept [ɪntə'sept] *vt* abfangen.
interception [ɪntə'sepʃən] *n* Abfangen *nt*.
interchange ['ɪntətʃeɪndʒ] *n* Austausch *m*; (*on
motorway*) (Autobahn)kreuz *nt*.
interchangeable [ɪntə'tʃeɪndʒəbl] *adj*
austauschbar.
intercity [ɪntə'sɪtɪ] *adj:* **~ train** Intercityzug *m*.
intercom ['ɪntəkɔm] *n* (Gegen)sprechanlage *f*.
interconnect [ɪntəkə'nekt] *vi* (*rooms*)
miteinander verbunden sein.
intercontinental ['ɪntəkɔntɪ'nentl] *adj* (*flight,
missile*) Interkontinental-.
intercourse ['ɪntəkɔ:s] *n* (*sexual*)
(Geschlechts)verkehr *m*; (*social, verbal*)
Verkehr *m*.
interdependence [ɪntədɪ'pendəns] *n*
gegenseitige Abhängigkeit *f*.
interdependent [ɪntədɪ'pendənt] *adj*
voneinander abhängig.
interest ['ɪntrɪst] *n* Interesse *nt*; (*COMM: in
company*) Anteil *m*; (*: sum of money*) Zinsen
pl ♦ *vt* interessieren; **compound ~**
Zinseszins *m*; **simple ~** einfache Zinsen;
British ~s in the Middle East britische
Interessen im Nahen Osten; **his main ~ is ...**
er interessiert sich hauptsächlich für ...
interested ['ɪntrɪstɪd] *adj* interessiert; (*party,
body etc*) beteiligt; **to be ~ in sth** sich für
etw interessieren; **to be ~ in doing sth**
daran interessiert sein, etw zu tun.
interest-free ['ɪntrɪst'fri:] *adj, adv* zinslos.
interesting ['ɪntrɪstɪŋ] *adj* interessant.
interest rate *n* Zinssatz *m*.
interface ['ɪntəfeɪs] *n* Verbindung *f*; (*COMPUT*)
Schnittstelle *f*.
interfere [ɪntə'fɪə'] *vi:* **to ~ in** sich einmischen
in *+acc*; **to ~ with** (*object*) sich zu schaffen
machen an *+dat*; (*plans*) durchkreuzen;
(*career, duty, decision*) beeinträchtigen; **don't
~** misch dich nicht ein.
interference [ɪntə'fɪərəns] *n* Einmischung *f*;
(*RADIO, TV*) Störung *f*.
interfering [ɪntə'fɪərɪŋ] *adj* (*person*) sich
ständig einmischend.
interim ['ɪntərɪm] *adj* (*agreement, government
etc*) Übergangs- ♦ *n:* **in the ~** in der

Zwischenzeit.
interim dividend *n* (*COMM*)
Abschlagsdividende *f*.
interior [ɪn'tɪərɪə'] *n* Innere(s) *nt*; (*decor etc*)
Innenausstattung *f* ♦ *adj* Innen-.
interior decorator *n* Innenausstatter(in) *m(f)*.
interior designer *n* Innenarchitekt(in) *m(f)*.
interjection [ɪntə'dʒekʃən] *n* Einwurf *m*;
(*LING*) Interjektion *f*.
interlock [ɪntə'lɔk] *vi* ineinandergreifen.
interloper ['ɪntələupə'] *n* Eindringling *m*.
interlude ['ɪntəlu:d] *n* Unterbrechung *f*, Pause
f; (*THEAT*) Zwischenspiel *nt*.
intermarry [ɪntə'mærɪ] *vi* untereinander
heiraten.
intermediary [ɪntə'mi:dɪərɪ] *n* Vermittler(in)
m(f).
intermediate [ɪntə'mi:dɪət] *adj* (*stage*)
Zwischen-; **an ~ student** ein
fortgeschrittener Anfänger.
interment [ɪn'tə:mənt] *n* Bestattung *f*.
interminable [ɪn'tə:mɪnəbl] *adj* endlos.
intermission [ɪntə'mɪʃən] *n* Pause *f*.
intermittent [ɪntə'mɪtnt] *adj* (*noise*)
periodisch auftretend; (*publication*) in
unregelmäßigen Abständen veröffentlicht.
intermittently [ɪntə'mɪtntlɪ] *adv* (*see adj*)
periodisch; in unregelmäßigen Abständen.
intern [*vt* ɪn'tə:n, *n* 'ɪntə:n] *vt* internieren ♦ *n*
(*US*) Assistenzarzt *m*, Assistenzärztin *f*.
internal [ɪn'tə:nl] *adj* innere(r, s); (*pipes*) im
Haus; (*politics*) Innen-; (*dispute, reform,
memo, structure etc*) intern.
internally [ɪn'tə:nəlɪ] *adv:* **"not to be taken ~"**
„nicht zum Einnehmen".
Internal Revenue Service (*US*) *n*
~ Finanzamt *nt*.
international [ɪntə'næʃnl] *adj* international
♦ *n* (*BRIT: SPORT*) Länderspiel *nt*.
International Atomic Energy Agency *n*
Internationale Atomenergiebehörde.
International Chamber of Commerce *n*
Internationale Handelskammer *f*.
International Court of Justice *n*
Internationaler Gerichtshof *m*.
international date line *n* Datumsgrenze *f*.
International Labour Organization *n*
Internationale Arbeitsorganisation *f*.
internationally [ɪntə'næʃnəlɪ] *adv*
international.
International Monetary Fund *n*
Internationaler Währungsfonds *m*.
international relations *npl*
zwischenstaatliche Beziehungen *pl*.
internecine [ɪntə'ni:saɪn] *adj* mörderisch;
(*war*) Vernichtungs-.
internee [ɪntə:'ni:] *n* Internierte(r) *f(m)*.
internment [ɪn'tə:nmənt] *n* Internierung *f*.
interplay ['ɪntəpleɪ] *n:* **~ (of or between)**
Zusammenspiel *nt* (von).
Interpol ['ɪntəpɔl] *n* Interpol *f*.
interpret [ɪn'tə:prɪt] *vt* auslegen,

interpretieren; (*translate*) dolmetschen ♦ *vi* dolmetschen.

interpretation [ɪntəːprɪ'teɪʃən] *n* (*see vb*) Auslegung *f*, Interpretation *f*; Dolmetschen *nt*.

interpreter [ɪn'təːprɪtə*] *n* Dolmetscher(in) *m(f)*.

interpreting [ɪn'təːprɪtɪŋ] *n* Dolmetschen *nt*.

interrelated [ɪntərɪ'leɪtɪd] *adj* zusammenhängend.

interrogate [ɪn'tɛrəʊgeɪt] *vt* verhören; (*witness*) vernehmen.

interrogation [ɪntɛrəʊ'geɪʃən] *n* (*see vb*) Verhör *nt*; Vernehmung *f*.

interrogative [ɪntə'rɔgətɪv] *adj* (*LING: pronoun*) Interrogativ-, Frage-.

interrogator [ɪn'tɛrəgeɪtə*] *n* (*POLICE*) Vernehmungsbeamte(r) *m*; **the hostage's ~** derjenige, der die Geisel verhörte.

interrupt [ɪntə'rʌpt] *vt*, *vi* unterbrechen.

interruption [ɪntə'rʌpʃən] *n* Unterbrechung *f*.

intersect [ɪntə'sɛkt] *vi* sich kreuzen ♦ *vt* durchziehen; (*MATH*) schneiden.

intersection [ɪntə'sɛkʃən] *n* Kreuzung *f*; (*MATH*) Schnittpunkt *m*.

intersperse [ɪntə'spəːs] *vt*: **to be ~d with** durchsetzt sein mit; **he ~d his lecture with** ... er spickte seine Rede mit ...

intertwine [ɪntə'twaɪn] *vi* sich ineinander verschlingen.

interval ['ɪntəvl] *n* Pause *f*; (*MUS*) Intervall *nt*; **bright ~s** (*in weather*) Aufheiterungen *pl*; **at ~s** in Abständen.

intervene [ɪntə'viːn] *vi* eingreifen; (*event*) dazwischenkommen; (*time*) dazwischenliegen.

intervening [ɪntə'viːnɪŋ] *adj* (*period, years*) dazwischenliegend.

intervention [ɪntə'vɛnʃən] *n* Eingreifen *nt*.

interview ['ɪntəvjuː] *n* (*for job*) Vorstellungsgespräch *nt*; (*for place at college etc*) Auswahlgespräch *nt*; (*RADIO, TV etc*) Interview *nt* ♦ *vt* (*see n*) ein Vorstellungsgespräch/Auswahlgespräch führen mit; interviewen.

interviewee [ɪntəvjuː'iː] *n* (*for job*) Stellenbewerber(in) *m(f)*; (*TV etc*) Interviewgast *m*.

interviewer ['ɪntəvjuə*] *n* Leiter(in) *m(f)* des Vorstellungsgesprächs/Auswahlgesprächs; (*RADIO, TV etc*) Interviewer(in) *m(f)*.

intestate [ɪn'tɛsteɪt] *adv*: **to die ~** ohne Testament sterben.

intestinal [ɪn'tɛstɪnl] *adj* (*infection etc*) Darm-.

intestine [ɪn'tɛstɪn] *n* Darm *m*.

intimacy ['ɪntɪməsɪ] *n* Vertrautheit *f*.

intimate [*adj* 'ɪntɪmət, *vt* 'ɪntɪmeɪt] *adj* eng; (*sexual, also restaurant, dinner, atmosphere*) intim; (*conversation, matter, detail*) vertraulich; (*knowledge*) gründlich ♦ *vt* andeuten; (*make known*) zu verstehen geben.

intimately ['ɪntɪmətlɪ] *adv* (*see adj*) eng; intim; vertraulich; gründlich.

intimation [ɪntɪ'meɪʃən] *n* Andeutung *f*.

intimidate [ɪn'tɪmɪdeɪt] *vt* einschüchtern.

intimidation [ɪntɪmɪ'deɪʃən] *n* Einschüchterung *f*.

═══════════════════════ *KEYWORD*

into ['ɪntu] *prep* **1** (*indicating motion or direction*) in +*acc*; **to go ~ town** in die Stadt gehen; **he worked late ~ the night** er arbeitete bis spät in die Nacht; **the car bumped ~ the wall** der Wagen fuhr gegen die Mauer **2** (*indicating change of condition, result*): **it broke ~ pieces** es zerbrach in Stücke; **she translated ~ English** sie übersetzte ins Englische; **to change pounds ~ dollars** Pfund in Dollar wechseln; **5 ~ 25** 25 durch 5

intolerable [ɪn'tɔlərəbl] *adj* unerträglich.

intolerance [ɪn'tɔlərns] *n* Intoleranz *f*.

intolerant [ɪn'tɔlərnt] *adj*: **~ (of)** intolerant (gegenüber).

intonation [ɪntəʊ'neɪʃən] *n* Intonation *f*.

intoxicated [ɪn'tɔksɪkeɪtɪd] *adj* betrunken; (*fig*) berauscht.

intoxication [ɪntɔksɪ'keɪʃən] *n* (Be)trunkenheit *f*; (*fig*) Rausch *m*.

intractable [ɪn'træktəbl] *adj* hartnäckig; (*child*) widerspenstig; (*temper*) unbeugsam.

intransigence [ɪn'trænsɪdʒəns] *n* Unnachgiebigkeit *f*.

intransigent [ɪn'trænsɪdʒənt] *adj* unnachgiebig.

intransitive [ɪn'trænsɪtɪv] *adj* (*LING*) intransitiv.

intrauterine device ['ɪntrə'juːtəraɪn-] *n* (*MED*) Intrauterinpessar *nt*, Spirale *f* (*inf*).

intravenous [ɪntrə'viːnəs] *adj* intravenös.

in-tray ['ɪntreɪ] *n* Ablage *f* für Eingänge.

intrepid [ɪn'trɛpɪd] *adj* unerschrocken.

intricacy ['ɪntrɪkəsɪ] *n* Kompliziertheit *f*.

intricate ['ɪntrɪkət] *adj* kompliziert.

intrigue [ɪn'triːg] *n* Intrigen *pl* ♦ *vt* faszinieren.

intriguing [ɪn'triːgɪŋ] *adj* faszinierend.

intrinsic [ɪn'trɪnsɪk] *adj* wesentlich.

introduce [ɪntrə'djuːs] *vt* (*sth new*) einführen; (*speaker, TV show etc*) ankündigen; **to ~ sb (to sb)** jdn (jdm) vorstellen; **to ~ sb to** (*pastime, technique*) jdn einführen in +*acc*; **may I ~ ...?** darf ich ... vorstellen?

introduction [ɪntrə'dʌkʃən] *n* Einführung *f*; (*of person*) Vorstellung *f*; (*to book*) Einleitung *f*; **a letter of ~** ein Einführungsschreiben *nt*.

introductory [ɪntrə'dʌktərɪ] *adj* Einführungs-; **~ remarks** einführende Bemerkungen *pl*; **~ offer** Einführungsangebot *nt*.

introspection [ɪntrəʊ'spɛkʃən] *n* Selbstbeobachtung *f*, Introspektion *f*.

introspective [ɪntrəʊ'spɛktɪv] *adj* in sich

gekehrt.
introvert ['ɪntrəuvəːt] n Introvertierte(r) f(m)
♦ adj (also: ~ed) introvertiert.
intrude [ɪn'truːd] vi eindringen; **to ~ on**
stören; (conversation) sich einmischen in
+acc; **am I intruding?** störe ich?
intruder [ɪn'truːdə*] n Eindringling m.
intrusion [ɪn'truːʒən] n Eindringen nt.
intrusive [ɪn'truːsɪv] adj aufdringlich.
intuition [ɪntjuː'ɪʃən] n Intuition f.
intuitive [ɪn'tjuːɪtɪv] adj intuitiv; (feeling)
instinktiv.
inundate ['ɪnʌndeɪt] vt: **to ~ with**
überschwemmen mit.
inure [ɪn'juə*] vt: **to ~ o.s. to** sich gewöhnen
an +acc.
invade [ɪn'veɪd] vt einfallen in +acc; (fig)
heimsuchen.
invader [ɪn'veɪdə*] n Invasor m.
invalid [n 'ɪnvəlɪd, adj ɪn'vælɪd] n Kranke(r)
f(m); (disabled) Invalide m ♦ adj ungültig.
invalidate [ɪn'vælɪdeɪt] vt entkräften; (law,
marriage, election) ungültig machen.
invaluable [ɪn'væljuəbl] adj unschätzbar.
invariable [ɪn'vɛərɪəbl] adj unveränderlich.
invariably [ɪn'vɛərɪəblɪ] adv ständig,
unweigerlich; **she is ~ late** sie kommt
immer zu spät.
invasion [ɪn'veɪʒən] n Invasion f; **an ~ of**
privacy ein Eingriff m in die Privatsphäre.
invective [ɪn'vɛktɪv] n Beschimpfungen pl.
inveigle [ɪn'viːgl] vt: **to ~ sb into sth/doing sth**
jdn zu etw verleiten/dazu verleiten, etw zu
tun.
invent [ɪn'vɛnt] vt erfinden.
invention [ɪn'vɛnʃən] n Erfindung f.
inventive [ɪn'vɛntɪv] adj erfinderisch.
inventiveness [ɪn'vɛntɪvnɪs] n
Einfallsreichtum m.
inventor [ɪn'vɛntə*] n Erfinder(in) m(f).
inventory ['ɪnvəntrɪ] n Inventar nt,
Bestandsverzeichnis nt.
inventory control n (COMM)
Bestandskontrolle f.
inverse [ɪn'vəːs] adj umgekehrt; **in**
~ proportion (to) im umgekehrten
Verhältnis (zu).
invert [ɪn'vəːt] vt umdrehen.
invertebrate [ɪn'vəːtɪbrət] n wirbelloses Tier
nt.
inverted commas [ɪn'vəːtɪd-] (BRIT) npl
Anführungszeichen pl.
invest [ɪn'vɛst] vt investieren ♦ vi: **~ in**
investieren in +acc; (fig) sich dat anschaffen;
to ~ sb with sth jdm etw verleihen.
investigate [ɪn'vɛstɪgeɪt] vt untersuchen.
investigation [ɪnvɛstɪ'geɪʃən] n
Untersuchung f.
investigative [ɪn'vɛstɪgeɪtɪv] adj: **~ journalism**
Enthüllungsjournalismus m.
investigator [ɪn'vɛstɪgeɪtə*] n Ermittler(in)
m(f); **private ~** Privatdetektiv(in) m(f).

investiture [ɪn'vɛstɪtʃə*] n (of chancellor)
Amtseinführung f; (of prince) Investitur f.
investment [ɪn'vɛstmənt] n Investition f.
investment income n Kapitalerträge pl.
investment trust n Investmenttrust m.
investor [ɪn'vɛstə*] n (Kapital)anleger(in) m(f).
inveterate [ɪn'vɛtərət] adj unverbesserlich.
invidious [ɪn'vɪdɪəs] adj (task, job)
unangenehm; (comparison, decision)
ungerecht.
invigilator [ɪn'vɪdʒɪleɪtə*] n Aufsicht f.
invigorating [ɪn'vɪgəreɪtɪŋ] adj belebend;
(experience etc) anregend.
invincible [ɪn'vɪnsɪbl] adj unbesiegbar; (belief,
conviction) unerschütterlich.
inviolate [ɪn'vaɪələt] adj sicher; (truth)
unantastbar.
invisible [ɪn'vɪzɪbl] adj unsichtbar.
invisible mending n Kunststopfen nt.
invitation [ɪnvɪ'teɪʃən] n Einladung f; **by**
~ only nur auf Einladung; **at sb's ~** auf jds
Aufforderung acc (hin).
invite [ɪn'vaɪt] vt einladen; (discussion)
auffordern zu; (criticism) herausfordern; **to**
~ sb to do sth jdn auffordern, etw zu tun;
to ~ sb to dinner jdn zum Abendessen
einladen.
▶**invite out** vt einladen.
inviting [ɪn'vaɪtɪŋ] adj einladend; (desirable)
verlockend.
invoice ['ɪnvɔɪs] n Rechnung f ♦ vt in
Rechnung stellen; **to ~ sb for goods** jdm
für Waren eine Rechnung ausstellen.
invoke [ɪn'vəuk] vt anrufen; (feelings,
memories etc) heraufbeschwören.
involuntary [ɪn'vɔləntrɪ] adj unbeabsichtigt;
(reflex) unwillkürlich.
involve [ɪn'vɔlv] vt (person) beteiligen; (thing)
verbunden sein mit; (concern, affect)
betreffen; **to ~ sb in sth** jdn in etw acc
verwickeln.
involved [ɪn'vɔlvd] adj kompliziert; **the work/**
problems ~ die damit verbundene Arbeit/
verbundenen Schwierigkeiten; **to be ~ in**
beteiligt sein an +dat; (be engrossed)
engagiert sein in +dat; **to become ~ with sb**
Umgang mit jdm haben; (emotionally) mit
jdm eine Beziehung anfangen.
involvement [ɪn'vɔlvmənt] n Engagement nt;
(participation) Beteiligung f.
invulnerable [ɪn'vʌlnərəbl] adj unverwundbar;
(ship, building etc) uneinnehmbar.
inward ['ɪnwəd] adj innerste(r, s); (movement)
nach innen ♦ adv nach innen.
inwardly ['ɪnwədlɪ] adv innerlich.
inwards ['ɪnwədz] adv nach innen.
I/O abbr (COMPUT: = input/output) E/A.
IOC n abbr (= International Olympic Committee)
IOC nt, IOK nt.
iodine ['aɪəudiːn] n Jod nt.
IOM (BRIT) abbr (POST: = Isle of Man).
ion ['aɪən] n Ion nt.

Ionian Sea [aɪˈəunɪən-] *n:* **the** ~ das Ionische Meer.

ionizer [ˈaɪənaɪzə*] *n* Ionisator *m.*

iota [aɪˈəutə] *n* Jota *nt.*

IOU *n abbr* (= *I owe you*) Schuldschein *m.*

IOW (*BRIT*) *abbr* (*POST:* = *Isle of Wight*).

IPA *n abbr* (= *International Phonetic Alphabet*) internationale Lautschrift *f.*

IQ *n abbr* (= *intelligence quotient*) IQ *m.*

IRA *n abbr* (= *Irish Republican Army*) IRA *f;* (*US:* = *individual retirement account*) *privates Rentensparkonto.*

Iran [ɪˈrɑːn] *n* (der) Iran.

Iranian [ɪˈreɪnɪən] *adj* iranisch ♦ *n* Iraner(in) *m(f)*; (*LING*) Iranisch *nt.*

Iraq [ɪˈrɑːk] *n* (der) Irak.

Iraqi [ɪˈrɑːkɪ] *adj* irakisch ♦ *n* Iraker(in) *m(f).*

irascible [ɪˈræsɪbl] *adj* jähzornig.

irate [aɪˈreɪt] *adj* zornig.

Ireland [ˈaɪələnd] *n* Irland *nt;* **the Republic of** ~ die Republik Irland.

iris [ˈaɪrɪs] (*pl* ~**es**) *n* (*ANAT*) Iris *f,* Regenbogenhaut *f;* (*BOT*) Iris, Schwertlilie *f.*

Irish [ˈaɪrɪʃ] *adj* irisch ♦ *npl:* **the** ~ die Iren *pl,* die Irländer *pl.*

Irishman [ˈaɪrɪʃmən] (*irreg: like* **man**) *n* Ire *m,* Irländer *m.*

Irish Sea *n:* **the** ~ die Irische See.

Irishwoman [ˈaɪrɪʃwumən] (*irreg: like* **woman**) *n* Irin *f,* Irländerin *f.*

irk [əːk] *vt* ärgern.

irksome [ˈəːksəm] *adj* lästig.

IRN *n abbr* (= *Independent Radio News*) *Nachrichtendienst des kommerziellen Rundfunks.*

iron [ˈaɪən] *n* Eisen *nt;* (*for clothes*) Bügeleisen *nt* ♦ *cpd* Eisen-; (*will, discipline etc*) eisern ♦ *vt* bügeln.

►**iron out** *vt* (*fig: problems*) aus dem Weg räumen.

Iron Curtain *n* (*POL*): **the** ~ der Eiserne Vorhang.

iron foundry *n* (Eisen)gießerei *f.*

ironic(al) [aɪˈrɒnɪk(l)] *adj* ironisch; (*situation*) paradox, witzig.

ironically [aɪˈrɒnɪklɪ] *adv* ironisch; ~, **the intelligence chief was the last to find out** witzigerweise war der Geheimdienstchef der letzte, der es erfuhr.

ironing [ˈaɪənɪŋ] *n* Bügeln *nt;* (*clothes*) Bügelwäsche *f.*

ironing board *n* Bügelbrett *nt.*

iron lung *n* (*MED*) eiserne Lunge *f.*

ironmonger [ˈaɪənmʌŋgə*] (*BRIT*) *n* Eisen- und Haushaltswarenhändler(in) *m(f).*

ironmonger's (shop) [ˈaɪənmʌŋgəz-] *n* Eisen- und Haushaltswarenhandlung *f.*

iron ore *n* Eisenerz *nt.*

irons [ˈaɪənz] *npl* Hand- und Fußschellen *pl;* **to clap sb in** ~ jdn in Eisen legen.

ironworks [ˈaɪənwəːks] *n* Eisenhütte *f.*

irony [ˈaɪrənɪ] *n* Ironie *f;* **the** ~ **of it is that ...**

das Ironische daran ist, daß ...

irrational [ɪˈræʃənl] *adj* irrational.

irreconcilable [ɪrɛkənˈsaɪləbl] *adj* unvereinbar.

irredeemable [ɪrɪˈdiːməbl] *adj* (*COMM*) nicht einlösbar; (*loan*) unkündbar; (*fault, character*) unverbesserlich.

irrefutable [ɪrɪˈfjuːtəbl] *adj* unwiderlegbar.

irregular [ɪˈregjulə*] *adj* unregelmäßig; (*surface*) uneben; (*behaviour*) ungehörig.

irregularity [ɪregjuˈlærɪtɪ] *n* (*see adj*) Unregelmäßigkeit *f;* Unebenheit *f;* Ungehörigkeit *f.*

irrelevance [ɪˈrɛləvəns] *n* Irrelevanz *f.*

irrelevant [ɪˈrɛləvənt] *adj* unwesentlich, irrelevant.

irreligious [ɪrɪˈlɪdʒəs] *adj* unreligiös.

irreparable [ɪˈrɛprəbl] *adj* nicht wiedergutzumachen.

irreplaceable [ɪrɪˈpleɪsəbl] *adj* unersetzlich.

irrepressible [ɪrɪˈprɛsəbl] *adj* (*good humour*) unerschütterlich; (*enthusiasm etc*) unbändig; (*person*) nicht unterzukriegen.

irreproachable [ɪrɪˈprəutʃəbl] *adj* untadelig.

irresistible [ɪrɪˈzɪstɪbl] *adj* unwiderstehlich.

irresolute [ɪˈrɛzəluːt] *adj* unentschlossen.

irrespective [ɪrɪˈspɛktɪv]: ~ **of** *prep* ungeachtet +*gen.*

irresponsible [ɪrɪˈspɒnsɪbl] *adj* verantwortungslos; (*action*) unverantwortlich.

irretrievable [ɪrɪˈtriːvəbl] *adj* (*object*) nicht mehr wiederzubekommen; (*loss*) unersetzlich; (*damage*) nicht wiedergutzumachen.

irreverent [ɪˈrɛvərnt] *adj* respektlos.

irrevocable [ɪˈrɛvəkəbl] *adj* unwiderruflich.

irrigate [ˈɪrɪgeɪt] *vt* bewässern.

irrigation [ɪrɪˈgeɪʃən] *n* Bewässerung *f.*

irritable [ˈɪrɪtəbl] *adj* reizbar.

irritant [ˈɪrɪtənt] *n* Reizerreger *m;* (*situation etc*) Ärgernis *nt.*

irritate [ˈɪrɪteɪt] *vt* ärgern, irritieren; (*MED*) reizen.

irritating [ˈɪrɪteɪtɪŋ] *adj* ärgerlich, irritierend; **he is** ~ er kann einem auf die Nerven gehen.

irritation [ɪrɪˈteɪʃən] *n* Ärger *m;* (*MED*) Reizung *f;* (*annoying thing*) Ärgernis *nt.*

IRS (*US*) *n abbr* (= *Internal Revenue Service*) *Steuereinzugsbehörde.*

is [ɪz] *vb see* **be.**

ISBN *n abbr* (= *International Standard Book Number*) ISBN *f.*

Islam [ˈɪzlɑːm] *n* der Islam; (*Islamic countries*) die islamischen Länder *pl.*

Islamic [ɪzˈlæmɪk] *adj* islamisch.

island [ˈaɪlənd] *n* Insel *f;* (*also:* **traffic** ~) Verkehrsinsel *f.*

islander [ˈaɪləndə*] *n* Inselbewohner(in) *m(f).*

isle [aɪl] *n* Insel *f.*

isn't [ˈɪznt] = **is not.**

isobar [ˈaɪsəubɑː*] *n* Isobare *f.*

isolate ['aɪsəleɪt] vt isolieren.
isolated ['aɪsəleɪtɪd] adj isoliert; (place)
abgelegen; ~ **incident** Einzelfall m.
isolation [aɪsə'leɪʃən] n Isolierung f.
isolationism [aɪsə'leɪʃənɪzəm] n
Isolationismus m.
isotope ['aɪsəutəup] n Isotop nt.
Israel ['ɪzreɪl] n Israel nt.
Israeli [ɪz'reɪlɪ] adj israelisch ♦ n Israeli mf.
issue ['ɪʃuː] n Frage f; (subject) Thema nt;
(problem) Problem nt; (of book, stamps etc)
Ausgabe f; (offspring) Nachkommenschaft f
♦ vt ausgeben; (statement) herausgeben;
(documents) ausstellen ♦ vi: **to ~ (from)**
dringen (aus); (liquid) austreten (aus); **the
point at ~** der Punkt, um den es geht; **to
avoid the ~** ausweichen; **to confuse** or
obscure the ~ es unnötig kompliziert
machen; **to ~ sth to sb** or ~ **sb with sth** jdm
etw geben; (documents) jdm etw ausstellen;
(gun etc) jdn mit etw ausstatten; **to take
~ with sb (over)** jdm widersprechen (in
+dat); **to make an ~ of sth** etw aufbauschen.
Istanbul [ɪstæn'buːl] n Istanbul nt.
isthmus ['ɪsməs] n Landenge f, Isthmus m.
IT n abbr = **information technology.**

══════════════ KEYWORD

it [ɪt] pron **1** (specific: subject) er/sie/es; (: direct
object) ihn/sie/es; (: indirect object) ihm/ihr/
ihm; **it's on the table** es ist auf dem Tisch; **I
can't find ~** ich kann es nicht finden; **give
~ to me** gib es mir; **about ~** darüber; **from
~** davon; **in ~** darin; **of ~** davon; **what did
you learn from ~?** was hast du daraus
gelernt?; **I'm proud of ~** ich bin stolz darauf
2 (impersonal) es; **it's raining** es regnet; **it's
Friday tomorrow** morgen ist Freitag; **who is
~? - it's me** wer ist da? - ich bin's.

ITA, (BRIT) **i.t.a.** n abbr (= initial teaching
alphabet) Alphabet zum Lesenlernen.
Italian [ɪ'tæljən] adj italienisch ♦ n
Italiener(in) m(f); (LING) Italienisch nt; **the
~s** die Italiener pl.
italics [ɪ'tælɪks] npl Kursivschrift f.
Italy ['ɪtəlɪ] n Italien nt.
ITC (BRIT) n abbr (= Independent Television
Commission) Fernseh-Aufsichtsgremium.
itch [ɪtʃ] n Juckreiz m ♦ vi jucken; **I am ~ing
all over** mich juckt es überall; **to ~ to do sth**
darauf brennen, etw zu tun.
itchy ['ɪtʃɪ] adj juckend; **my back is ~** mein
Rücken juckt.
it'd ['ɪtd] = **it would; it had.**
item ['aɪtəm] n Punkt m; (of collection) Stück nt;
(also: **news ~**) Meldung f; (: in newspaper)
Zeitungsnotiz f; **~s of clothing**
Kleidungsstücke pl.
itemize ['aɪtəmaɪz] vt einzeln aufführen.
itemized bill ['aɪtəmaɪzd-] n Rechnung, auf
der die Posten einzeln aufgeführt sind.

itinerant [ɪ'tɪnərənt] adj (labourer, priest etc)
Wander-; (salesman) reisend.
itinerary [aɪ'tɪnərərɪ] n Reiseroute f.
it'll ['ɪtl] = **it will; it shall.**
ITN (BRIT) n abbr (TV: = Independent Television
News) Nachrichtendienst des
kommerziellen Fernsehens.
its [ɪts] adj sein(e), ihr(e) ♦ pron seine(r, s),
ihre(r, s).
it's [ɪts] = **it is; it has.**
itself [ɪt'sɛlf] pron sich; (emphatic) selbst.
ITV (BRIT) n abbr (TV: = Independent Television)
kommerzieller Fernsehsender.

ITV steht für Independent Television und ist
ein landesweiter privater Fernsehsender in
Großbritannien. Unter der Oberaufsicht einer
unabhängigen Rundfunkbehörde produzieren
Privatfirmen die Programme für die
verschiedenen Sendegebiete. ITV, das seit
1955 Programme ausstrahlt, wird ganz durch
Werbung finanziert und bietet etwa ein Drittel
Informationssendungen (Nachrichten,
Dokumentarfilme, Aktuelles) und ansonsten
Unterhaltung (Sport, Komödien, Drama,
Spielshows, Filme).

IUD n abbr = **intrauterine device.**
I've [aɪv] = **I have.**
ivory ['aɪvərɪ] n Elfenbein nt.
Ivory Coast n Elfenbeinküste f.
ivory tower n (fig) Elfenbeinturm m.
ivy ['aɪvɪ] n Efeu m.
Ivy League (US) n Eliteuniversitäten der
USA.

Als Ivy League bezeichnet man die acht
renommiertesten Universitäten im Nordosten
der Vereinigten Staaten (Brown, Columbia,
Cornell, Dartmouth College, Harvard,
Princeton, University of Pennsylvania, Yale),
die untereinander Sportwettkämpfe austragen.
Der Name bezieht sich auf die
efeubewachsenen Mauern der
Universitätsgebäude.

J, j

J, j [dʒeɪ] n (letter) J nt, j nt; ~ **for Jack,** (US) ~ **for Jig** ≈ J wie Julius.
JA n abbr = **judge advocate; joint account.**
J/A abbr = **joint account.**
jab [dʒæb] vt stoßen; (with finger, needle) stechen ♦ n (inf) Spritze f ♦ vi: **to ~ at** einstechen auf +acc; **to ~ sth into sth** etw in etw acc stoßen/stechen.
jack [dʒæk] n (AUT) Wagenheber m; (BOWLS) Zielkugel f; (CARDS) Bube m.
▶**jack in** (inf) vt aufgeben.
▶**jack up** vt (AUT) aufbocken.
jackal ['dʒækl] n Schakal m.
jackass ['dʒækæs] (inf) n (person) Esel m.
jackdaw ['dʒækdɔː] n Dohle f.
jacket ['dʒækɪt] n Jackett nt; (of book) Schutzumschlag m; **potatoes in their ~s, ~ potatoes** in der Schale gebackene Kartoffeln pl.
jack-in-the-box ['dʒækɪnðəbɔks] n Schachtelteufel m, Kastenteufel m.
jack-knife ['dʒæknaɪf] n Klappmesser nt ♦ vi: **the lorry ~d** der Anhänger (des Lastwagens) hat sich quergestellt.
jack-of-all-trades ['dʒækəvˈɔːltreɪdz] n Alleskönner m.
jack plug n Bananenstecker m.
jackpot ['dʒækpɔt] n Hauptgewinn m; **to hit the ~** (fig) das große Los ziehen.
jacuzzi [dʒəˈkuːzɪ] n Whirlpool m.
jade [dʒeɪd] n Jade m or f.
jaded ['dʒeɪdɪd] adj abgespannt; **to get ~** die Nase voll haben.
JAG n abbr = **Judge Advocate General.**
jagged ['dʒægɪd] adj gezackt.
jaguar ['dʒægjuə*] n Jaguar m.
jail [dʒeɪl] n Gefängnis nt ♦ vt einsperren.
jailbird ['dʒeɪlbəːd] n Knastbruder m (inf).
jailbreak ['dʒeɪlbreɪk] n (Gefängnis)ausbruch m.
jalopy [dʒəˈlɔpɪ] (inf) n alte (Klapper)kiste f or Mühle f.
jam [dʒæm] n Marmelade f, Konfitüre f; (also: **traffic ~**) Stau m; (inf: difficulty) Klemme f ♦ vt blockieren; (mechanism, drawer etc) verklemmen; (RADIO) stören ♦ vi klemmen; (gun) Ladehemmung haben; **I'm in a real ~** (inf) ich stecke wirklich in der Klemme; **to get sb out of a ~** (inf) jdm aus der Klemme helfen; **to ~ sth into sth** etw in etw acc stopfen; **the telephone lines are ~med** die Leitungen sind belegt.

Jamaica [dʒəˈmeɪkə] n Jamaika nt.
Jamaican [dʒəˈmeɪkən] adj jamaikanisch ♦ n Jamaikaner(in) m(f).
jamb [dʒæm] n (of door) (Tür)pfosten m; (of window) (Fenster)pfosten m.
jamboree [dʒæmbəˈriː] n Fest nt.
jam-packed [dʒæmˈpækt] adj: ~ **(with)** vollgestopft (mit).
jam session n (MUS) Jam Session f.
Jan. abbr (= January) Jan.
jangle ['dʒæŋgl] vi klimpern.
janitor ['dʒænɪtə*] n Hausmeister(in) m(f).
January ['dʒænjuərɪ] n Januar m; see also **July.**
Japan [dʒəˈpæn] n Japan nt.
Japanese [dʒæpəˈniːz] adj japanisch ♦ n inv Japaner(in) m(f); (LING) Japanisch nt.
jar [dʒɑː*] n Topf m, Gefäß nt; (glass) Glas nt ♦ vi (sound) gellen; (colours) nicht harmonieren, sich beißen ♦ vt erschüttern; **to ~ on sb** jdm auf die Nerven gehen.
jargon ['dʒɑːgən] n Jargon m.
jarring ['dʒɑːrɪŋ] adj (sound) gellend, schrill; (colour) schreiend.
Jas. abbr (= James).
jasmine ['dʒæzmɪn] n Jasmin m.
jaundice ['dʒɔːndɪs] n Gelbsucht f.
jaundiced ['dʒɔːndɪst] adj (view, attitude) zynisch.
jaunt [dʒɔːnt] n Spritztour f.
jaunty ['dʒɔːntɪ] adj munter; (step) schwungvoll.
Java ['dʒɑːvə] n Java nt.
javelin ['dʒævlɪn] n Speer m.
jaw [dʒɔː] n Kiefer m.
jawbone ['dʒɔːbəun] n Kieferknochen m.
jay [dʒeɪ] n Eichelhäher m.
jaywalker ['dʒeɪwɔːkə*] n unachtsamer Fußgänger m, unachtsame Fußgängerin f.
jazz [dʒæz] n Jazz m.
▶**jazz up** vt aufpeppen (inf).
jazz band n Jazzband f.
JCB ® n Erdräummaschine f.
JCS (US) n abbr (= Joint Chiefs of Staff) Stabschefs pl.
JD (US) n abbr (= Doctor of Laws) ≈ Dr. jur.; (= Justice Department) ≈ Justizministerium nt.
jealous ['dʒɛləs] adj eifersüchtig; (envious) neidisch.
jealously ['dʒɛləslɪ] adv eifersüchtig; (enviously) neidisch; (watchfully) sorgsam.
jealousy ['dʒɛləsɪ] n Eifersucht f; (envy) Neid m.
jeans [dʒiːnz] npl Jeans pl.
jeep [dʒiːp] n Jeep m.
jeer [dʒɪə*] vi höhnische Bemerkungen machen; **to ~ at** verhöhnen.
jeering ['dʒɪərɪŋ] adj höhnisch; (crowd) johlend ♦ n Johlen nt.
jeers ['dʒɪəz] npl Buhrufe pl.
jelly ['dʒɛlɪ] n Götterspeise f; (jam) Gelee m or nt.

jelly baby (*BRIT*) *n* Gummibärchen *nt*.
jellyfish ['dʒɛlɪfɪʃ] *n* Qualle *f*.
jeopardize ['dʒɛpədaɪz] *vt* gefährden.
jeopardy ['dʒɛpədɪ] *n*: **to be in** ~ gefährdet
sein.
jerk [dʒɜːk] *n* Ruck *m*; (*inf: idiot*) Trottel *m* ♦ *vt*
reißen ♦ *vi* (*vehicle*) ruckeln.
jerkin ['dʒɜːkɪn] *n* Wams *nt*.
jerky ['dʒɜːkɪ] *adj* ruckartig.
jerry-built ['dʒɛrɪbɪlt] *adj* schlampig gebaut.
jerry can ['dʒɛrɪ-] *n* großer Blechkanister *m*.
Jersey ['dʒɜːzɪ] *n* Jersey *nt*.
jersey ['dʒɜːzɪ] *n* Pullover *m*; (*fabric*) Jersey *m*.
Jerusalem [dʒə'ruːsləm] *n* Jerusalem *nt*.
jest [dʒɛst] *n* Scherz *m*.
jester ['dʒɛstə*] *n* Narr *m*.
Jesus ['dʒiːzəs] *n* Jesus *m*; ~ **Christ** Jesus
Christus *m*.
jet [dʒɛt] *n* Strahl *m*; (*AVIAT*) Düsenflugzeug *nt*;
(*MINERALOGY, JEWELLERY*) Jett *m or nt*,
Gagat *m*.
jet-black ['dʒɛt'blæk] *adj* pechschwarz.
jet engine *n* Düsentriebwerk *nt*.
jet lag *n* Jet-lag *nt*.
jet-propelled ['dʒɛtprə'pɛld] *adj* Düsen-, mit
Düsenantrieb.
jetsam ['dʒɛtsəm] *n* Strandgut *nt*; (*floating*)
Treibgut *nt*.
jet-setter ['dʒɛtsɛtə*] *n*: **to be a** ~ zum Jet-Set
gehören.
jettison ['dʒɛtɪsn] *vt* abwerfen; (*from ship*)
über Bord werfen.
jetty ['dʒɛtɪ] *n* Landesteg *m*, Pier *m*.
Jew [dʒuː] *n* Jude *m*, Jüdin *f*.
jewel ['dʒuːəl] *n* Edelstein *m*, Juwel *nt* (*also
fig*); (*in watch*) Stein *m*.
jeweller, (*US*) **jeweler** ['dʒuːələ*] *n* Juwelier
m.
jeweller's (shop) *n* Juwelier *m*,
Juweliergeschäft *nt*.
jewellery, (*US*) **jewelry** ['dʒuːəlrɪ] *n* Schmuck
m.
Jewess ['dʒuːɪs] *n* Jüdin *f*.
Jewish ['dʒuːɪʃ] *adj* jüdisch.
JFK (*US*) *n abbr* (= *John Fitzgerald Kennedy
International Airport*) John-F.-Kennedy-
Flughafen *m*.
jib [dʒɪb] *n* (*NAUT*) Klüver *m*; (*of crane*)
Ausleger *m* ♦ *vi* (*horse*) scheuen, bocken; **to**
~ **at doing sth** sich dagegen sträuben, etw
zu tun.
jibe [dʒaɪb] *n* = **gibe**.
jiffy ['dʒɪfɪ] (*inf*) *n*: **in a** ~ sofort.
jig [dʒɪg] *n lebhafter Volkstanz*.
jigsaw ['dʒɪgsɔː] *n* (*also:* ~ **puzzle**)
Puzzle(spiel) *nt*; (*tool*) Stichsäge *f*.
jilt [dʒɪlt] *vt* sitzenlassen.
jingle ['dʒɪŋgl] *n* (*tune*) Jingle *m* ♦ *vi* (*bracelets*)
klimpern; (*bells*) bimmeln.
jingoism ['dʒɪŋgəuɪzəm] *n* Hurrapatriotismus
m.
jinx [dʒɪŋks] (*inf*) *n* Fluch *m*; **there's a** ~ **on it**

es ist verhext.
jitters ['dʒɪtəz] (*inf*) *npl*: **to get the** ~ das große
Zittern bekommen.
jittery ['dʒɪtərɪ] (*inf*) *adj* nervös, rappelig.
jiujitsu [dʒuːˈdʒɪtsuː] *n* Jiu-Jitsu *nt*.
job [dʒɔb] *n* Arbeit *f*; (*post, employment*) Stelle
f, Job *m*; **it's not my** ~ es ist nicht meine
Aufgabe; **a part-time** ~ eine
Teilzeitbeschäftigung; **a full-time** ~ eine
Ganztagsstelle; **he's only doing his** ~ er tut
nur seine Pflicht; **it's a good** ~ **that ...** nur
gut, daß ...; **just the** ~! genau das Richtige!
jobber ['dʒɔbə*] (*BRIT*) *n* Börsenhändler *m*.
jobbing ['dʒɔbɪŋ] (*BRIT*) *adj* Gelegenheits-.
job centre (*BRIT*) *n* Arbeitsamt *nt*.
job creation scheme *n* Arbeitsbeschaffungsmaßnahmen *pl*.
job description *n* Tätigkeitsbeschreibung *f*.
jobless ['dʒɔblɪs] *adj* arbeitslos ♦ *npl*: **the** ~ die
Arbeitslosen *pl*.
job lot *n* (*Waren*)posten *m*.
job satisfaction *n* Zufriedenheit *f* am
Arbeitsplatz.
job security *n* Sicherheit *f* des
Arbeitsplatzes.
job sharing *n* Job-sharing *nt*,
Arbeitsplatzteilung *f*.
job specification *n* Tätigkeitsbeschreibung
f.
Jock [dʒɔk] (*inf*) *n* Schotte *m*.
jockey ['dʒɔkɪ] *n* Jockei *m* ♦ *vi*: **to** ~ **for
position** um eine gute Position rangeln.
jockey box (*US*) *n* (*AUT*) Handschuhfach *nt*.
jocular ['dʒɔkjulə*] *adj* spaßig, witzig.
jog [dʒɔg] *vt* (an)stoßen ♦ *vi* joggen, Dauerlauf
machen; **to** ~ **sb's memory** jds Gedächtnis
dat nachhelfen.
▶**jog along** *vi* entlangzuckeln (*inf*).
jogger ['dʒɔgə*] *n* Jogger(in) *m(f)*.
jogging ['dʒɔgɪŋ] *n* Jogging *nt*, Joggen *nt*.
john [dʒɔn] (*US: inf*) *n* (*toilet*) Klo *nt*.
join [dʒɔɪn] *vt* (*club, party*) beitreten +*dat*;
(*queue*) sich stellen in +*acc*; (*things, places*)
verbinden; (*group of people*) sich
anschließen +*dat* ♦ *vi* (*roads*) sich treffen;
(*rivers*) zusammenfließen ♦ *n*
Verbindungsstelle *f*; **to** ~ **forces (with)** (*fig*)
sich zusammentun (mit); **will you** ~ **us for
dinner?** wollen Sie mit uns zu Abend essen?;
I'll ~ **you later** ich komme später.
▶**join in** *vi* mitmachen ♦ *vt fus* sich beteiligen
an +*dat*.
▶**join up** *vi* sich treffen; (*MIL*) zum Militär
gehen.
joiner ['dʒɔɪnə*] (*BRIT*) *n* Schreiner(in) *m(f)*.
joinery ['dʒɔɪnərɪ] (*BRIT*) *n* Schreinerei *f*.
joint [dʒɔɪnt] *n* (*in woodwork*) Fuge *f*; (*in pipe
etc*) Verbindungsstelle *f*; (*ANAT*) Gelenk *nt*;
(*BRIT: CULIN*) Braten *m*; (*inf: place*) Laden *m*;
(: *of cannabis*) Joint *m* ♦ *adj* gemeinsam;
(*combined*) vereint.
joint account *n* gemeinsames Konto *nt*.

jointly ['dʒɔɪntlɪ] *adv* gemeinsam.
joint ownership *n* Miteigentum *nt*.
joint-stock company ['dʒɔɪnt'stɔk-] *n* Aktiengesellschaft *f*.
joint venture *n* Gemeinschaftsunternehmen *nt*, Joint-venture *nt*.
joist [dʒɔɪst] *n* Balken *m*, Träger *m*.
joke [dʒəuk] *n* Witz *m*; (*also:* **practical** ~) Streich *m* ♦ *vi* Witze machen; **to play a** ~ **on sb** jdm einen Streich spielen.
joker ['dʒəukə*] *n* (*CARDS*) Joker *m*.
joking ['dʒəukɪŋ] *adj* scherzhaft.
jokingly ['dʒəukɪŋlɪ] *adv* scherzhaft, im Spaß.
jollity ['dʒɔlɪtɪ] *n* Fröhlichkeit *f*.
jolly ['dʒɔlɪ] *adj* fröhlich; (*enjoyable*) lustig ♦ *adv* (*BRIT: inf: very*) ganz (schön) ♦ *vt* (*BRIT*): **to** ~ **sb along** jdm aufmunternd zureden; ~ **good!** prima!
jolt [dʒəult] *n* Ruck *m*; (*shock*) Schock *m* ♦ *vt* schütteln; (*subj: bus etc*) durchschütteln; (*emotionally*) aufrütteln.
Jordan ['dʒɔːdən] *n* Jordanien *nt*; (*river*) Jordan *m*.
Jordanian [dʒɔː'deɪnɪən] *adj* jordanisch ♦ *n* Jordanier(in) *m(f)*.
joss stick [dʒɔs-] *n* Räucherstäbchen *nt*.
jostle ['dʒɔsl] *vt* anrempeln ♦ *vi* drängeln.
jot [dʒɔt] *n*: **not one** ~ kein bißchen.
▶**jot down** *vt* notieren.
jotter ['dʒɔtə*] (*BRIT*) *n* Notizbuch *nt*; (*pad*) Notizblock *m*.
journal ['dʒɜːnl] *n* Zeitschrift *f*; (*diary*) Tagebuch *nt*.
journalese [dʒɜːnə'liːz] (*pej*) *n* Pressejargon *m*.
journalism ['dʒɜːnəlɪzəm] *n* Journalismus *m*.
journalist ['dʒɜːnəlɪst] *n* Journalist(in) *m(f)*.
journey ['dʒɜːnɪ] *n* Reise *f* ♦ *vi* reisen; **a 5-hour** ~ eine Fahrt von 5 Stunden; **return** ~ Rückreise *f*; (*both ways*) Hin- und Rückreise *f*.
jovial ['dʒəuvɪəl] *adj* fröhlich; (*atmosphere*) freundlich, herzlich.
jowl [dʒaul] *n* Backe *f*.
joy [dʒɔɪ] *n* Freude *f*.
joyful ['dʒɔɪful] *adj* freudig.
joyride ['dʒɔɪraɪd] *n Spritztour in einem gestohlenen Auto*.
joyrider ['dʒɔɪraɪdə*] *n Autodieb, der den Wagen nur für eine Spritztour benutzt*.
joystick ['dʒɔɪstɪk] *n* (*AVIAT*) Steuerknüppel *m*; (*COMPUT*) Joystick *m*.
JP *n abbr* = **Justice of the Peace**.
Jr *abbr* (*in names:* = *junior*) jun.
JTPA (*US*) *n abbr* (= *Job Training Partnership Act*) *Arbeitsbeschaffungsprogramm für benachteiligte Bevölkerungsteile und Minderheiten*.
jubilant ['dʒuːbɪlnt] *adj* überglücklich.
jubilation [dʒuːbɪ'leɪʃən] *n* Jubel *m*.
jubilee ['dʒuːbɪliː] *n* Jubiläum *nt*; **silver** ~

25jähriges Jubiläum; **golden** ~ 50jähriges Jubiläum.
judge [dʒʌdʒ] *n* Richter(in) *m(f)*; (*in competition*) Preisrichter(in) *m(f)*; (*fig: expert*) Kenner(in) *m(f)* ♦ *vt* (*LAW: person*) die Verhandlung führen über *+acc*; (: *case*) verhandeln; (*competition*) Preisrichter(in) sein bei; (*person etc*) beurteilen; (*consider*) halten für; (*estimate*) einschätzen ♦ *vi*: **judging by** *or* **to** ~ **by his expression** seinem Gesichtsausdruck nach zu urteilen; **she's a good** ~ **of character** sie ist ein guter Menschenkenner; **I'll be the** ~ **of that** das müssen Sie mich schon selbst beurteilen lassen; **as far as I can** ~ soweit ich es beurteilen kann; **I** ~**d it necessary to inform him** ich hielt es für nötig, ihn zu informieren.
judge advocate *n* (*MIL*) Beisitzer(in) *m(f)* bei einem Kriegsgericht.
Judge Advocate General *n* (*MIL*) *Vorsitzender des obersten Militärgerichts*.
judg(e)ment ['dʒʌdʒmənt] *n* Urteil *nt*; (*REL*) Gericht *nt*; (*view, opinion*) Meinung *f*; (*discernment*) Urteilsvermögen *nt*; **in my** ~ meiner Meinung nach; **to pass** ~ (**on**) (*LAW*) das Urteil sprechen (über *+acc*); (*fig*) ein Urteil fällen (über *+acc*).
judicial [dʒuː'dɪʃl] *adj* gerichtlich, Justiz-; (*fig*) kritisch; ~ **review** gerichtliche Überprüfung *f*.
judiciary [dʒuː'dɪʃɪərɪ] *n*: **the** ~ die Gerichtsbehörden *pl*.
judicious [dʒuː'dɪʃəs] *adj* klug.
judo ['dʒuːdəu] *n* Judo *nt*.
jug [dʒʌg] *n* Krug *m*.
jugged hare ['dʒʌgd-] (*BRIT*) *n* ≈ Hasenpfeffer *m*.
juggernaut ['dʒʌgənɔːt] (*BRIT*) *n* Fernlastwagen *m*.
juggle ['dʒʌgl] *vi* jonglieren.
juggler ['dʒʌglə*] *n* Jongleur *m*.
Jugoslav *etc* ['juːgəu'slɑːv] = **Yugoslav** *etc*.
jugular ['dʒʌgjulə*] *adj*: ~ (**vein**) Drosselvene *f*.
juice [dʒuːs] *n* Saft *m*; (*inf: petrol*): **we've run out of** ~ wir haben keinen Sprit mehr.
juicy ['dʒuːsɪ] *adj* saftig.
jukebox ['dʒuːkbɔks] *n* Musikbox *f*.
Jul. *abbr* = **July**.
July [dʒuː'laɪ] *n* Juli *m*; **the first of** ~ der erste Juli; **on the eleventh of** ~ am elften Juli; **in the month of** ~ im (Monat) Juli; **at the beginning/end of** ~ Anfang/Ende Juli; **in the middle of** ~ Mitte Juli; **during** ~ im Juli; **in** ~ **of next year** im Juli nächsten Jahres; **each** *or* **every** ~ jedes Jahr im Juli; ~ **was wet this year** der Juli war dieses Jahr ein nasser Monat.
jumble ['dʒʌmbl] *n* Durcheinander *nt*; (*items for sale*) gebrauchte Sachen *pl* ♦ *vt* (*also:* ~ **up**) durcheinanderbringen.

Jumble sale *ist ein Wohltätigkeitsbasar, meist in einer Aula oder einem Gemeindehaus abgehalten, bei dem alle möglichen Gebrauchtwaren (vor allem Kleidung, Spielzeug, Bücher, Geschirr und Möbel) verkauft werden. Der Erlös fließt entweder einer Wohltätigkeitsorganisation zu oder wird für örtliche Zwecke verwendet, z.B. die Pfadfinder, die Grundschule, Reparatur der Kirche usw.*

jumbo (jet) ['dʒʌmbəu-] *n* Jumbo(-Jet) *m*.
jumbo-size ['dʒʌmbəusaɪz] *adj (packet etc)* Riesen-.
jump [dʒʌmp] *vi* springen; *(with fear, surprise)* zusammenzucken; *(increase)* sprunghaft ansteigen ♦ *vt* springen über +*acc* ♦ *n (see vb)* Sprung *m*; Zusammenzucken *nt*; sprunghafter Anstieg *m*; **to ~ the queue** *(BRIT)* sich vordrängeln.
▶**jump about** *vi* herumspringen.
▶**jump at** *vt fus (idea)* sofort aufgreifen; *(chance)* sofort ergreifen; **he ~ed at the offer** er griff bei dem Angebot sofort zu.
▶**jump down** *vi* herunterspringen.
▶**jump up** *vi* hochspringen; *(from seat)* aufspringen.
jumped-up ['dʒʌmptʌp] *(BRIT: pej) adj* eingebildet.
jumper ['dʒʌmpə'] *n (BRIT)* Pullover *m*; *(US: dress)* Trägerkleid *nt*; *(SPORT)* Springer(in) *m(f)*.
jumper cables *(US) npl* = **jump leads**.
jumping jack *n* Knallfrosch *m*.
jump jet *n* Senkrechtstarter *m*.
jump leads *(BRIT) npl* Starthilfekabel *nt*.
jump-start ['dʒʌmpstɑːt] *vt (AUT: engine)* durch Anschieben des Wagens in Gang bringen.
jump suit *n* Overall *m*.
jumpy ['dʒʌmpɪ] *adj* nervös.
Jun. *abbr* = **June**.
junction ['dʒʌŋkʃən] *(BRIT) n* Kreuzung *f*; *(RAIL)* Gleisanschluß *m*.
juncture ['dʒʌŋktʃə'] *n*: **at this ~** zu diesem Zeitpunkt.
June [dʒuːn] *n* Juni *m*; *see also* **July**.
jungle ['dʒʌŋgl] *n* Urwald *m*, Dschungel *m* *(also fig)*.
junior ['dʒuːnɪə'] *adj* jünger; *(subordinate)* untergeordnet ♦ *n* Jüngere(r) *f(m)*; *(young person)* Junior *m*; **he's ~ to me (by 2 years)**, **he's my ~ (by 2 years)** *(younger)* er ist (2 Jahre) jünger als ich; **he's ~ to me** *(subordinate)* er steht unter mir.
junior executive *n* zweiter Geschäftsführer *m*, zweite Geschäftsführerin *f*.
junior high school *(US) n* ≈ Mittelschule *f*.
junior minister *(BRIT) n* Staatssekretär(in) *m(f)*.
junior partner *n* Juniorpartner(in) *m(f)*.

junior school *(BRIT) n* ≈ Grundschule *f*.
junior sizes *npl (COMM)* Kindergrößen *pl*.
juniper ['dʒuːnɪpə'] *n*: **~ berry** Wacholderbeere *f*.
junk [dʒʌŋk] *n (rubbish)* Gerümpel *nt*; *(cheap goods)* Ramsch *m*; *(ship)* Dschunke *f* ♦ *vt (inf)* ausrangieren.
junk bond *n (FIN)* niedrig eingestuftes Wertpapier mit hohen Ertragschancen bei erhöhtem Risiko.
junket ['dʒʌŋkɪt] *n* Dickmilch *f*; *(inf: pej: free trip)*: **to go on a ~** eine Reise auf Kosten des Steuerzahlers machen.
junk food *n* ungesundes Essen *nt*.
junkie ['dʒʌŋkɪ] *(inf) n* Fixer(in) *m(f)*.
junk mail *n* (Post)wurfsendungen *pl*.
junk room *n* Rumpelkammer *f*.
junk shop *n* Trödelladen *m*.
Junr *abbr (in names:* = *junior)* jun.
junta ['dʒʌntə] *n* Junta *f*.
Jupiter ['dʒuːpɪtə'] *n* Jupiter *m*.
jurisdiction [dʒuərɪs'dɪkʃən] *n* Gerichtsbarkeit *f*; *(ADMIN)* Zuständigkeit *f*, Zuständigkeitsbereich *m*; **it falls** or **comes within/outside my ~** dafür bin ich zuständig/nicht zuständig.
jurisprudence [dʒuərɪs'pruːdəns] *n* Jura *pl*, Rechtswissenschaft *f*.
juror ['dʒuərə'] *n* Schöffe *m*, Schöffin *f*; *(for capital crimes)* Geschworene(r) *f(m)*; *(in competition)* Preisrichter(in) *m(f)*.
jury ['dʒuərɪ] *n*: **the ~** die Schöffen *pl*; *(for capital crimes)* die Geschworenen *pl*; *(for competition)* die Jury, das Preisgericht.
jury box *n* Schöffenbank *f*; Geschworenenbank *f*.
juryman ['dʒuərɪmən] *(irreg: like* **man**) *n* = **juror**.
just [dʒʌst] *adj* gerecht ♦ *adv (exactly)* genau; *(only)* nur; **he's ~ done it/left** er hat es gerade getan/ist gerade gegangen; **~ as I expected** genau wie ich erwartet habe; **~ right** genau richtig; **~ two o'clock** erst zwei Uhr; **we were ~ going** wir wollten gerade gehen; **I was ~ about to phone** ich wollte gerade anrufen; **she's ~ as clever as you** sie ist genauso klug wie du; **it's ~ as well (that ...)** nur gut, daß ...; **~ as he was leaving** gerade als er gehen wollte; **~ before** gerade noch; **~ enough** gerade genug; **~ here** genau hier, genau an dieser Stelle; **he ~ missed** er hat genau danebengetroffen; **it's ~ me** ich bin's nur; **it's ~ a mistake** es ist nur ein Fehler; **~ listen** hör mal; **~ ask someone the way** frage doch einfach jemanden nach dem Weg; **not ~ now** nicht gerade jetzt; **~ a minute!**, **~ one moment!** einen Moment, bitte!
justice ['dʒʌstɪs] *n* Justiz *f*; *(of cause, complaint)* Berechtigung *f*; *(fairness)* Gerechtigkeit *f*; *(US: judge)* Richter(in) *m(f)*; **Lord Chief J~** *(BRIT)* oberster Richter in

Großbritannien; **to do ~ to** (*fig*) gerecht werden +*dat*.

Justice of the Peace *n* Friedensrichter(in) *m(f)*.

justifiable [dʒʌstɪ'faɪəbl] *adj* gerechtfertigt, berechtigt.

justifiably [dʒʌstɪ'faɪəblɪ] *adv* zu Recht, berechtigterweise.

justification [dʒʌstɪfɪ'keɪʃən] *n* Rechtfertigung *f*; (*TYP*) Justierung *f*.

justify ['dʒʌstɪfaɪ] *vt* rechtfertigen; (*text*) justieren; **to be justified in doing sth** etw zu *or* mit Recht tun.

justly ['dʒʌstlɪ] *adv* zu *or* mit Recht; (*deservedly*) gerecht.

jut [dʒʌt] *vi* (*also:* ~ **out**) vorstehen.

jute [dʒuːt] *n* Jute *f*.

juvenile ['dʒuːvənaɪl] *adj* (*crime, offenders*) Jugend-; (*humour, mentality*) kindisch, unreif ♦ *n* Jugendliche(r) *f(m)*.

juvenile delinquency *n* Jugendkriminalität *f*.

juvenile delinquent *n* jugendlicher Straftäter *m*, jugendliche Straftäterin *f*.

juxtapose ['dʒʌkstəpəuz] *vt* nebeneinanderstellen.

juxtaposition ['dʒʌkstəpə'zɪʃən] *n* Nebeneinanderstellung *f*.

K, k

K¹, k [keɪ] *n* (*letter*) K *nt*, k *nt*; ~ **for King** ≈ K wie Kaufmann.

K² [keɪ] *abbr* (= *one thousand*) K; (*COMPUT: = kilobyte*) KB; (*BRIT: in titles*) = **knight**.

kaftan ['kæftæn] *n* Kaftan *m*.

Kalahari Desert [kælə'hɑːrɪ-] *n:* **the ~** die Kalahari.

kale [keɪl] *n* Grünkohl *m*.

kaleidoscope [kə'laɪdəskəup] *n* Kaleidoskop *nt*.

kamikaze ['kæmɪ'kɑːzɪ] *adj* (*mission etc*) Kamikaze-, Selbstmord-.

Kampala [kæm'pɑːlə] *n* Kampala *nt*.

Kampuchea [kæmpu'tʃɪə] *n* Kampuchea *nt*.

Kampuchean [kæmpu'tʃɪən] *adj* kampucheanisch.

kangaroo [kæŋgə'ruː] *n* Känguruh *nt*.

Kans. (*US*) *abbr* (*POST:* = *Kansas*).

kaput [kə'put] (*inf*) *adj:* **to be ~** kaputt sein.

karaoke [kɑːrə'əukɪ] *n* Karaoke *nt*.

karate [kə'rɑːtɪ] *n* Karate *nt*.

Kashmir [kæʃ'mɪə*] *n* Kaschmir *nt*.

kayak ['kaɪæk] *n* Kajak *m or nt*.

Kazakhstan [kæzæk'stɑːn] *n* Kasachstan *nt*.

KC (*BRIT*) *n abbr* (*LAW:* = *King's Counsel*) Kronanwalt *m*.

kd (*US*) *abbr* (*COMM:* = *knocked down*) (in Einzelteile) zerlegt.

kebab [kə'bæb] *n* Kebab *m*.

keel [kiːl] *n* Kiel *m*; **on an even ~** (*fig*) stabil.

▶**keel over** *vi* kentern; (*person*) umkippen.

keen [kiːn] *adj* begeistert, eifrig; (*interest*) groß; (*desire*) heftig; (*eye, intelligence, competition, edge*) scharf; **to be ~ to do or on doing sth** scharf darauf sein, etw zu tun (*inf*); **to be ~ on sth** an etw *dat* sehr interessiert sein; **to be ~ on sb** von jdm sehr angetan sein; **I'm not ~ on going** ich brenne nicht gerade darauf zu gehen.

keenly ['kiːnlɪ] *adv* (*enthusiastically*) begeistert; (*feel*) leidenschaftlich; (*look*) aufmerksam.

keenness ['kiːnnɪs] *n* Begeisterung *f*, Eifer *m*; **his ~ to go is suspicious** daß er so unbedingt gehen will, ist verdächtig.

keep [kiːp] (*pt, pp* **kept**) *vt* behalten; (*preserve, store*) aufbewahren; (*house, shop, accounts, diary*) führen; (*garden etc*) pflegen; (*chickens, bees, fig: promise*) halten; (*family etc*) versorgen, unterhalten; (*detain*) aufhalten; (*prevent*) abhalten ♦ *vi* (*remain*) bleiben; (*food*) sich halten ♦ *n* (*food etc*) Unterhalt *m*; (*of castle*) Bergfried *m*; **to ~ doing sth** etw immer wieder tun; **to ~ sb happy** jdn zufriedenstellen; **to ~ a room tidy** ein Zimmer in Ordnung halten; **to ~ sb waiting** jdn warten lassen; **to ~ an appointment** eine Verabredung einhalten; **to ~ a record of sth** über etw *acc* Buch führen; **to ~ sth to o.s.** etw für sich behalten; **to ~ sth (back) from sb** etw vor jdm geheimhalten; **to ~ sb from doing sth** jdn davon abhalten, etw zu tun; **to ~ sth from happening** etw verhindern; **to ~ time** (*clock*) genau gehen; **enough for his ~** genug für seinen Unterhalt.

▶**keep away** *vt* fernhalten ♦ *vi:* **to ~ away (from)** wegbleiben (von).

▶**keep back** *vt* zurückhalten; (*tears*) unterdrücken; (*money*) einbehalten ♦ *vi* zurückbleiben.

▶**keep down** *vt* (*prices*) niedrig halten; (*spending*) einschränken; (*food*) bei sich behalten ♦ *vi* unten bleiben.

▶**keep in** *vt* im Haus behalten; (*at school*) nachsitzen lassen ♦ *vi* (*inf*): **to ~ in with sb** sich mit jdm gut stellen.

▶**keep off** *vt* fernhalten ♦ *vi* wegbleiben; "~ **off the grass**" „Betreten des Rasens verboten"; ~ **your hands off** Hände weg.

▶**keep on** *vi:* **to ~ on doing sth** (*continue*) etw weiter tun; **to ~ on (about sth)** unaufhörlich (von etw) reden.

▶**keep out** *vt* fernhalten; "~ **out**" „Zutritt verboten".

▶**keep up** *vt* (*payments*) weiterbezahlen; (*standards etc*) aufrechterhalten ♦ *vi:* **to ~ up**

(with) mithalten können (mit).
keeper ['ki:pə*] n Wärter(in) m(f).
keep fit n Fitneßtraining nt.
keeping ['ki:pɪŋ] n (care) Obhut f; **in ~ with** in Übereinstimmung mit; **out of ~ with** nicht im Einklang mit; **I'll leave this in your ~** ich vertraue dies deiner Obhut an.
keeps [ki:ps] n: **for ~** (inf) für immer.
keepsake ['ki:pseɪk] n Andenken nt.
keg [kɛg] n Fäßchen nt; **~ beer** Bier nt vom Faß.
Ken. (US) abbr (POST: = Kentucky).
kennel ['kɛnl] n Hundehütte f.
kennels ['kɛnlz] n Hundeheim nt; **we had to leave our dog in ~ over Christmas** wir mußten unseren Hund über Weihnachten in ein Heim geben.
Kenya ['kɛnjə] n Kenia nt.
Kenyan ['kɛnjən] adj kenianisch ♦ n Kenianer(in) m(f).
kept [kɛpt] pt, pp of **keep**.
kerb [kə:b] n (BRIT) n Bordstein m.
kerb crawler [-'krɔ:lə*] (inf) n Freier m im Autostrich.
kernel ['kə:nl] n Kern m.
kerosene ['kɛrəsi:n] n Kerosin nt.
kestrel ['kɛstrəl] n Turmfalke m.
ketchup ['kɛtʃəp] n Ketchup m or nt.
kettle ['kɛtl] n Kessel m.
kettledrum ['kɛtldrʌm] n (Kessel)pauke f.
key [ki:] n Schlüssel m; (MUS) Tonart f; (of piano, computer, typewriter) Taste f ♦ cpd (issue etc) Schlüssel- ♦ vt (also: ~ **in**) eingeben.
keyboard ['ki:bɔ:d] n Tastatur f.
keyboarder ['ki:bɔ:də*] n Datentypist(in) m(f).
keyed up [ki:d-] adj: **to be (all) ~** (ganz) aufgedreht sein (inf).
keyhole ['ki:həul] n Schlüsselloch nt.
keyhole surgery n Schlüssellochchirurgie f, minimal invasive Chirurgie f.
keynote ['ki:nəut] n Grundton m; (of speech) Leitgedanke m.
keypad ['ki:pæd] n Tastenfeld nt.
key ring n Schlüsselring m.
keystroke ['ki:strəuk] n Anschlag m.
kg abbr (= kilogram) kg.
KGB n abbr (POL: formerly) KGB m.
khaki ['kɑ:kɪ] n K(h)aki nt.
kHz abbr (= kilohertz) kHz.
kibbutz [kɪ'buts] n Kibbuz m.
kick [kɪk] vt treten; (table, ball) treten gegen +acc; (inf: habit) ablegen; (: addiction) wegkommen von ♦ vi (horse) ausschlagen ♦ n Tritt m; (to ball) Schuß m; (of rifle) Rückstoß m; (thrill): **he does it for ~s** er macht es zum Spaß.
►**kick around** (inf) vi (person) rumhängen; (thing) rumliegen.
►**kick off** vi (SPORT) anstoßen.
kickoff ['kɪkɔf] n (SPORT) Anstoß m.
kick start n (AUT: also: ~**er**) Kickstarter m.

kid [kɪd] n (inf: child) Kind nt; (animal) Kitz nt; (leather) Ziegenleder nt, Glacéleder nt ♦ vi (inf) Witze machen; **~ brother** kleiner Bruder m; **~ sister** kleine Schwester f.
kid gloves npl: **to treat sb with ~** (fig) jdn mit Samthandschuhen anfassen.
kidnap ['kɪdnæp] vt entführen, kidnappen.
kidnapper ['kɪdnæpə*] n Entführer(in) m(f), Kidnapper(in) m(f).
kidnapping ['kɪdnæpɪŋ] n Entführung f, Kidnapping nt.
kidney ['kɪdnɪ] n Niere f.
kidney bean n Gartenbohne f.
kidney machine n (MED) künstliche Niere f.
Kilimanjaro [kɪlɪmən'dʒɑ:rəu] n: **Mount ~** der Kilimandscharo.
kill [kɪl] vt töten; (murder) ermorden, umbringen; (plant) eingehen lassen; (proposal) zu Fall bringen; (rumour) ein Ende machen +dat ♦ n Abschuß m; **to ~ time** die Zeit totschlagen; **to ~ o.s. to do sth** (fig) sich fast umbringen, um etw zu tun; **to ~ o.s. (laughing)** (fig) sich totlachen.
►**kill off** vt abtöten; (fig: romance) beenden.
killer ['kɪlə*] n Mörder(in) m(f).
killer instinct n (fig) Tötungsinstinkt m.
killing ['kɪlɪŋ] n Töten nt; (instance) Mord m; **to make a ~** (inf) einen Riesengewinn machen.
killjoy ['kɪldʒɔɪ] n Spielverderber(in) m(f).
kiln [kɪln] n Brennofen m.
kilo ['ki:ləu] n Kilo nt.
kilobyte ['ki:ləubaɪt] n Kilobyte nt.
kilogram(me) ['kɪləugræm] n Kilogramm nt.
kilohertz ['kɪləuhə:ts] n inv Kilohertz nt.
kilometre, (US) **kilometer** ['kɪləmi:tə*] n Kilometer m.
kilowatt ['kɪləuwɔt] n Kilowatt nt.
kilt [kɪlt] n Kilt m, Schottenrock m.
kilter ['kɪltə*] n: **out of ~** nicht in Ordnung.
kimono [kɪ'məunəu] n Kimono m.
kin [kɪn] n see **kith, next**.
kind [kaɪnd] adj freundlich ♦ n Art f; (sort) Sorte f; **would you be ~ enough to ...?**, **would you be so ~ as to ...?** wären Sie (vielleicht) so nett und ...?; **it's very ~ of you (to do ...)** es ist wirklich nett von Ihnen(, ... zu tun); **in ~** (COMM) in Naturalien; **a ~ of** ... eine Art ...; **they are two of a ~** sie sind beide von der gleichen Art; (people) sie sind vom gleichen Schlag.
kindergarten ['kɪndəgɑ:tn] n Kindergarten m.
kind-hearted [kaɪnd'hɑ:tɪd] adj gutherzig.
kindle ['kɪndl] vt anzünden; (emotion) wecken.
kindling ['kɪndlɪŋ] n Anzündholz nt.
kindly ['kaɪndlɪ] adj, adv freundlich, nett; **will you ~ ...** würden Sie bitte ...; **he didn't take it ~** er konnte sich damit nicht anfreunden.
kindness ['kaɪndnɪs] n Freundlichkeit f.
kindred ['kɪndrɪd] adj: **~ spirit** Gleichgesinnte(r) f(m).
kinetic [kɪ'nɛtɪk] adj kinetisch.
king [kɪŋ] n (also fig) König m.

kingdom ['kɪŋdəm] n Königreich nt.
kingfisher ['kɪŋfɪʃə*] n Eisvogel m.
kingpin ['kɪŋpɪn] n (TECH) Bolzen m; (AUT) Achsschenkelbolzen m; (fig) wichtigste Stütze f.
king-size(d) ['kɪŋsaɪz(d)] adj extra groß; (cigarette) King-size-.
kink [kɪŋk] n Knick m; (in hair) Welle f; (fig) Schrulle f.
kinky ['kɪŋkɪ] (pej) adj schrullig; (sexually) abartig.
kinship ['kɪnʃɪp] n Verwandtschaft f.
kinsman ['kɪnzmən] (irreg: like man) n Verwandte(r) m.
kinswoman ['kɪnzwʊmən] (irreg: like woman) n Verwandte f.
kiosk ['kiːɒsk] n Kiosk m; (BRIT) (Telefon)zelle f; (also: **newspaper ~**) (Zeitungs)kiosk m.
kipper ['kɪpə*] n Räucherhering m.
Kirghizia [kəːˈgɪzɪə] n Kirgistan nt.
kiss [kɪs] n Kuß m ♦ vt küssen ♦ vi sich küssen; **to ~ (each other)** sich küssen; **to ~ sb goodbye** jdm einen Abschiedskuß geben.
kissagram ['kɪsəgræm] n durch eine(n) Angestellte(n) einer Agentur persönlich übermittelter Kuß.
kiss of life (BRIT) n: **the ~** Mund-zu-Mund-Beatmung f.
kit [kɪt] n Zeug nt, Sachen pl; (equipment: also MIL) Ausrüstung f; (set of tools) Werkzeug nt; (for assembly) Bausatz m.
►**kit out** (BRIT) vt ausrüsten, ausstatten.
kitbag ['kɪtbæg] n Seesack m.
kitchen ['kɪtʃɪn] n Küche f.
kitchen garden n Küchengarten m.
kitchen sink n Spüle f.
kitchen unit (BRIT) n Küchenschrank m.
kitchenware ['kɪtʃɪnwɛə*] n Küchengeräte pl.
kite [kaɪt] n Drachen m; (ZOOL) Milan m.
kith [kɪθ] n: **~ and kin** Freunde und Verwandte pl.
kitten ['kɪtn] n Kätzchen nt.
kitty ['kɪtɪ] n (gemeinsame) Kasse f.
kiwi (fruit) ['kiːwiː-] n Kiwi(frucht) f.
KKK (US) n abbr (= Ku Klux Klan) Ku-Klux-Klan m.
Kleenex® ['kliːnɛks] n Tempo(taschentuch) ® nt.
kleptomaniac [klɛptəʊˈmeɪnɪæk] n Kleptomane m, Kleptomanin f.
km abbr (= kilometre) km.
km/h abbr (= kilometres per hour) km/h.
knack [næk] n: **to have the ~ of doing sth** es heraushaben, wie man etw macht; **there's a ~ to doing this** da ist ein Trick or Kniff dabei.
knackered ['nækəd] (BRIT: inf) adj kaputt.
knapsack ['næpsæk] n Rucksack m.
knead [niːd] vt kneten.
knee [niː] n Knie nt.
kneecap ['niːkæp] n Kniescheibe f.
kneecapping ['niːkæpɪŋ] n Durchschießen nt

der Kniescheibe.
knee-deep ['niːˈdiːp] adj, adv: **the water was ~** das Wasser ging mir etc bis zum Knie; **~ in mud** knietief or bis zu den Knien im Schlamm.
kneejerk reaction ['niːdʒɜːk-] n (fig) instinktive Reaktion f.
kneel [niːl] (pt, pp **knelt**) vi knien; (also: **~ down**) niederknien.
kneepad ['niːpæd] n Knieschützer m.
knell [nɛl] n Totengeläut(e) nt; (fig) Ende nt.
knelt [nɛlt] pt, pp of **kneel**.
knew [njuː] pt of **know**.
knickers ['nɪkəz] (BRIT) npl Schlüpfer m.
knick-knacks ['nɪknæks] npl Nippsachen pl.
knife [naɪf] (pl **knives**) n Messer nt ♦ vt (injure, attack) einstechen auf +acc; **~, fork and spoon** Messer, Gabel und Löffel.
knife edge n: **to be balanced on a ~** (fig) auf Messers Schneide stehen.
knight [naɪt] n (BRIT) Ritter m; (CHESS) Springer m, Pferd nt.
knighthood ['naɪthʊd] (BRIT) n: **to get a ~** in den Adelsstand erhoben werden.
knit [nɪt] vt stricken ♦ vi stricken; (bones) zusammenwachsen; **to ~ one's brows** die Stirn runzeln.
knitted ['nɪtɪd] adj gestrickt, Strick-.
knitting ['nɪtɪŋ] n Stricken nt; (garment being made) Strickzeug nt.
knitting machine n Strickmaschine f.
knitting needle n Stricknadel f.
knitting pattern n Strickmuster nt.
knitwear ['nɪtwɛə*] n Strickwaren pl.
knives [naɪvz] npl of **knife**.
knob [nɒb] n Griff m; (of stick) Knauf m; (on radio, TV etc) Knopf m; **a ~ of butter** (BRIT) ein Stückchen nt Butter.
knobbly ['nɒblɪ], **knobby** ['nɒbɪ] (US) adj (wood) knorrig; (surface) uneben; **~ knees** Knubbelknie pl (inf).
knock [nɒk] vt schlagen; (bump into) stoßen gegen +acc; (inf: criticize) runtermachen ♦ vi klopfen ♦ n Schlag m; (bump) Stoß m; (on door) Klopfen nt; **to ~ a nail into sth** einen Nagel in etw acc schlagen; **to ~ some sense into sb** jdn zur Vernunft bringen; **to ~ at/on** klopfen an/auf +acc; **he ~ed at the door** er klopfte an, er klopfte an die Tür.
►**knock about** (inf) vt schlagen, verprügeln ♦ vi rumziehen; **~ about with** sich rumtreiben mit.
►**knock around** vt, vi = **knock about**.
►**knock back** (inf) vt (drink) sich dat hinter die Binde kippen.
►**knock down** vt anfahren; (fatally) überfahren; (building etc) abreißen; (price: buyer) herunterhandeln; (: seller) heruntergehen mit.
►**knock off** vi (inf) Feierabend machen ♦ vt (from price) nachlassen; (inf: steal) klauen; **to ~ off £10** £10 nachlassen.

►**knock out** vt bewußtlos schlagen; (subj: drug) bewußtlos werden lassen; (BOXING) k.o. schlagen; (in game, competition) besiegen.
►**knock over** vt umstoßen; (with car) anfahren.
knockdown ['nɔkdaun] adj: ~ **price** Schleuderpreis m.
knocker ['nɔkə*] n Türklopfer m.
knock-for-knock ['nɔkfə'nɔk] (BRIT) adj: ~ **agreement** Vereinbarung, bei der jede Versicherungsgesellschaft den Schaden am von ihr versicherten Fahrzeug übernimmt.
knocking ['nɔkɪŋ] n Klopfen nt.
knock-kneed [nɔk'niːd] adj X-beinig; **to be ~** X-Beine haben.
knockout ['nɔkaut] n (BOXING) K.o.-Schlag m ♦ cpd (competition etc) Ausscheidungs-.
knock-up ['nɔkʌp] n (TENNIS): **to have a ~** ein paar Bälle schlagen.
knot [nɔt] n Knoten m; (in wood) Ast m ♦ vt einen Knoten machen in +acc; (knot together) verknoten; **to tie a ~** einen Knoten machen.
knotty ['nɔtɪ] adj (fig: problem) verwickelt.
know [nəu] (pt **knew**, pp **known**) vt kennen; (facts) wissen; (language) können ♦ vi: **to ~ about** or **of sth/sb** von etw/jdm gehört haben; **to ~ how to swim** schwimmen können; **to get to ~ sth** etw erfahren; (place) etw kennenlernen; **I don't ~ him** ich kenne ihn nicht; **to ~ right from wrong** Gut und Böse unterscheiden können; **as far as I ~** soviel ich weiß; **yes, I ~** ja, ich weiß; **I don't ~** ich weiß (es) nicht.
know-all ['nəuɔːl] (BRIT: pej) n Alleswisser m.
know-how ['nəuhau] n Know-how nt, Sachkenntnis f.
knowing ['nəuɪŋ] adj wissend.
knowingly ['nəuɪŋlɪ] adv (purposely) bewußt; (smile, look) wissend.
know-it-all ['nəuɪtɔːl] (US) n = **know-all**.
knowledge ['nɔlɪdʒ] n Wissen nt, Kenntnis f; (learning, things learnt) Kenntnisse pl; **to have no ~ of** nichts wissen von; **not to my ~** nicht, daß ich wüßte; **without my ~** ohne mein Wissen; **it is common ~ that ...** es ist allgemein bekannt, daß ...; **it has come to my ~ that ...** ich habe erfahren, daß ...; **to have a working ~ of French** Grundkenntnisse in Französisch haben.
knowledgeable ['nɔlɪdʒəbl] adj informiert.
known [nəun] pp of **know** ♦ adj bekannt; (expert) anerkannt.
knuckle ['nʌkl] n (Finger)knöchel m.
►**knuckle down** (inf) vi sich dahinter-klemmen; **to ~ down to work** sich an die Arbeit machen.
►**knuckle under** (inf) vi sich fügen, spuren.
knuckle-duster ['nʌkl'dʌstə*] n Schlagring m.
KO n abbr (= knockout) K.o. m ♦ vt k.o. schlagen.
koala [kəu'ɑːlə] n (also: ~ **bear**) Koala(bär) m.

kook [kuːk] (US: inf) n Spinner m.
Koran [kɔ'rɑːn] n: **the ~** der Koran.
Korea [kə'rɪə] n Korea nt; **North ~** Nordkorea nt; **South ~** Südkorea nt.
Korean [kə'rɪən] adj koreanisch ♦ n Koreaner(in) m(f).
kosher ['kəuʃə*] adj koscher.
kowtow ['kau'tau] vi: **to ~ to sb** vor jdm dienern or einen Kotau machen.
Kremlin ['kremlɪn] n: **the ~** der Kreml.
KS (US) abbr (POST: = Kansas).
Kt (BRIT) abbr (in titles) = **knight**.
Kuala Lumpur ['kwɑːlə'lumpuə*] n Kuala Lumpur nt.
kudos ['kjuːdɔs] n Ansehen nt, Ehre f.
Kurd [kəːd] n Kurde m, Kurdin f.
Kuwait [ku'weɪt] n Kuwait nt.
Kuwaiti [ku'weɪtɪ] adj kuwaitisch ♦ n Kuwaiter(in) m(f).
kW abbr (= kilowatt) kW.
KY (US) abbr (POST: = Kentucky).

L, l

L¹, l¹ [ɛl] n (letter) L nt, l nt; ~ **for Lucy**, (US) ~ **for Love** ≈ L wie Ludwig.
L² [ɛl] abbr (BRIT: AUT: = learner) am Auto angebrachtes Kennzeichen für Fahrschüler; (= lake); (= large) gr.; (= left) l.
l² abbr (= litre) l.
LA (US) n abbr (= Los Angeles) ♦ abbr (POST: = Louisiana).
La. (US) abbr (POST: = Louisiana).
lab [læb] n abbr = **laboratory**.
label ['leɪbl] n Etikett nt; (brand: of record) Label n ♦ vt etikettieren; (fig: person) abstempeln.
labor etc ['leɪbə*] (US) n = **labour** etc.
laboratory [lə'bɔrətərɪ] n Labor nt.

Labor Day ist in den USA und Kanada der Name für den Tag der Arbeit. Er wird dort als gesetzlicher Feiertag am ersten Montag im September begangen.

laborious [lə'bɔːrɪəs] adj mühsam.
labor union (US) n Gewerkschaft f.
labour, (US) **labor** ['leɪbə*] n Arbeit f; (work force) Arbeitskräfte pl; (MED): **to be in ~** in den Wehen liegen ♦ vi: **to ~ (at sth)** sich (mit etw) abmühen ♦ vt: **to ~ a point** auf einem Thema herumreiten; **L~, the L~ Party** (BRIT) die Labour Party; **hard ~** Zwangsarbeit f.
labour camp n Arbeitslager nt.

labour cost n Lohnkosten pl.
labour dispute n Arbeitskampf m.
laboured ['leɪbəd] adj (breathing) schwer; (movement, style) schwerfällig.
labourer ['leɪbərə*] n Arbeiter(in) m(f); **farm ~** Landarbeiter(in) m(f).
labour force n Arbeiterschaft f.
labour intensive adj arbeitsintensiv.
labour market n Arbeitsmarkt m.
labour pains npl Wehen pl.
labour relations npl Beziehungen pl zwischen Arbeitnehmern, Arbeitgebern und Gewerkschaften.
labour-saving ['leɪbəseɪvɪŋ] adj arbeitssparend.
laburnum [lə'bɜːnəm] n (BOT) Goldregen m.
labyrinth ['læbɪrɪnθ] n Labyrinth nt.
lace [leɪs] n (fabric) Spitze f; (of shoe etc) (Schuh)band nt, Schnürsenkel m ♦ vt (also: **~ up**) (zu)schnüren; **to ~ a drink** einen Schuß Alkohol in ein Getränk geben.
lacemaking ['leɪsmeɪkɪŋ] n Klöppelei f.
lacerate ['læsəreɪt] vt zerschneiden.
laceration [læsə'reɪʃən] n Schnittwunde f.
lace-up ['leɪsʌp] adj (shoes etc) Schnür-.
lack [læk] n Mangel m ♦ vt, vi: **sb ~s sth, sb is ~ing in sth** jdm fehlt es an etw dat; **through** or **for ~ of** aus Mangel an +dat; **to be ~ing** fehlen.
lackadaisical [lækə'deɪzɪkl] adj lustlos.
lackey ['lækɪ] (pej) n Lakai m.
lacklustre, (US) lackluster ['læklʌstə*] adj farblos, langweilig.
laconic [lə'kɒnɪk] adj lakonisch.
lacquer ['lækə*] n Lack m; (also: **hair ~**) Haarspray nt.
lacrosse [lə'krɒs] n Lacrosse nt.
lacy ['leɪsɪ] adj Spitzen-; (like lace) spitzenartig.
lad [læd] n Junge m.
ladder ['lædə*] n (also fig) Leiter f; (BRIT: in tights) Laufmasche f ♦ vt (BRIT) Laufmaschen bekommen in +dat ♦ vi (BRIT) Laufmaschen bekommen.
laden ['leɪdn] adj: **~ (with)** beladen (mit); **fully ~** voll beladen.
ladle ['leɪdl] n Schöpflöffel m, (Schöpf)kelle f ♦ vt schöpfen.
▶**ladle out** vt (fig) austeilen.
lady ['leɪdɪ] n (woman) Frau f; (: dignified, graceful etc) Dame f; (BRIT: title) Lady f; **ladies and gentlemen** ... meine Damen und Herren ...; **young ~** junge Dame; **the ladies' (room)** die Damentoilette.
ladybird ['leɪdɪbɜːd], **ladybug** ['leɪdɪbʌg] (US) n Marienkäfer m.
lady-in-waiting ['leɪdɪɪn'weɪtɪŋ] n Hofdame f.
lady-killer ['leɪdɪkɪlə*] n Herzensbrecher m.
ladylike ['leɪdɪlaɪk] adj damenhaft.
ladyship ['leɪdɪʃɪp] n: **your L~** Ihre Ladyschaft.
lag [læg] n (period of time) Zeitabstand m ♦ vi (also: **~ behind**) zurückbleiben; (trade,

investment etc) zurückgehen ♦ vt (pipes etc) isolieren; **old ~** (inf: prisoner) (ehemaliger) Knacki m.
lager ['lɑːgə*] n helles Bier nt.
lager lout (BRIT: inf) n betrunkener Rowdy m.
lagging ['lægɪŋ] n Isoliermaterial nt.
lagoon [lə'guːn] n Lagune f.
Lagos ['leɪgɒs] n Lagos nt.
laid [leɪd] pt, pp of **lay**.
laid-back [leɪd'bæk] (inf) adj locker.
laid up adj: **to be ~ (with)** im Bett liegen (mit).
lain [leɪn] pp of **lie**.
lair [lɛə*] n Lager nt; (cave) Höhle f; (den) Bau m.
laissez faire [lɛseɪ'fɛə*] n Laisser-faire nt.
laity ['leɪətɪ] n or npl Laien pl.
lake [leɪk] n See m.
Lake District (BRIT) n: **the ~** der Lake Distrikt, Seengebiet im NW Englands.
lamb [læm] n Lamm nt; (meat) Lammfleisch nt.
lamb chop n Lammkotelett nt.
lambskin ['læmskɪn] n Lammfell nt.
lamb's wool n Lammwolle f.
lame [leɪm] adj lahm; (argument, answer) schwach.
lame duck n (person) Niete f; (business) unwirtschaftliche Firma f.
lamely ['leɪmlɪ] adv lahm.
lament [lə'mɛnt] n Klage f ♦ vt beklagen.
lamentable ['læməntəbl] adj beklagenswert.
laminated ['læmɪneɪtɪd] adj laminiert; (metal) geschichtet; **~ glass** Verbundglas nt; **~ wood** Sperrholz nt.
lamp [læmp] n Lampe f.
lamplight ['læmplaɪt] n: **by ~** bei Lampenlicht.
lampoon [læm'puːn] n Schmähschrift f ♦ vt verspotten.
lamppost ['læmppəʊst] (BRIT) n Laternenpfahl m.
lampshade ['læmpʃeɪd] n Lampenschirm m.
lance [lɑːns] n Lanze f ♦ vt (MED) aufschneiden.
lance corporal (BRIT) n Obergefreite(r) m.
lancet ['lɑːnsɪt] n (MED) Lanzette f.
Lancs [læŋks] (BRIT) abbr (POST: = Lancashire).
land [lænd] n Land nt; (as property) Grund und Boden m ♦ vi (AVIAT, fig) landen; (from ship) an Land gehen ♦ vt (passengers) absetzen; (goods) an Land bringen; **to own ~** Land besitzen; **to go** or **travel by ~** auf dem Landweg reisen; **to ~ on one's feet** (fig) auf die Füße fallen; **to ~ sb with sth** (inf) jdm etw aufhalsen.
▶**land up** vi: **to ~ up in/at** landen in +dat.
landed gentry ['lændɪd-] n Landadel m.
landfill site ['lændfɪl-] n ≈ Mülldeponie f.
landing ['lændɪŋ] n (of house) Flur m; (outside flat door) Treppenabsatz m; (AVIAT) Landung f.
landing card n Einreisekarte f.

landing craft n inv Landungsboot nt.
landing gear n (AVIAT) Fahrgestell nt.
landing stage n Landesteg m.
landing strip n Landebahn f.
landlady ['lændleɪdɪ] n Vermieterin f; (of pub) Wirtin f.
landlocked ['lændlɔkt] adj von Land eingeschlossen; ~ **country** Binnenstaat m.
landlord ['lændlɔ:d] n Vermieter m; (of pub) Wirt m.
landlubber ['lændlʌbə•] (old) n Landratte f.
landmark ['lændmɑ:k] n Orientierungspunkt m; (famous building) Wahrzeichen nt; (fig) Meilenstein m.
landowner ['lændəʊnə•] n Grundbesitzer(in) m(f).
landscape ['lændskeɪp] n Landschaft f ♦ vt landschaftlich or gärtnerisch gestalten.
landscape architect n Landschaftsarchitekt(in) m(f).
landscape gardener n Landschaftsgärtner(in) m(f).
landscape painting n Landschaftsmalerei f.
landslide ['lændslaɪd] n Erdrutsch m; (fig: electoral) Erdrutschsieg m.
lane [leɪn] n (in country) Weg m; (in town) Gasse f; (of carriageway) Spur f; (of race course, swimming pool) Bahn f; **shipping** ~ Schiffahrtsweg m.
language ['læŋgwɪdʒ] n Sprache f; **bad** ~ Kraftausdrücke pl.
language laboratory n Sprachlabor nt.
languid ['læŋgwɪd] adj träge, matt.
languish ['læŋgwɪʃ] vi schmachten; (project, case) erfolglos bleiben.
lank [læŋk] adj (hair) strähnig.
lanky ['læŋkɪ] adj schlaksig.
lanolin(e) ['lænəlɪn] n Lanolin nt.
lantern ['læntən] n Laterne f.
Laos [laʊs] n Laos nt.
lap [læp] n Schoß m; (in race) Runde f ♦ vt (also: ~ **up**) aufschlecken ♦ vi (water) plätschern.
►**lap up** vt (fig) genießen.
lapdog ['læpdɔg] (pej) n (fig) Schoßhund m.
lapel [lə'pel] n Aufschlag m, Revers nt or m.
Lapland ['læplænd] n Lappland nt.
Lapp [læp] adj lappländisch ♦ n Lappe m, Lappin f; (LING) Lappländisch nt.
lapse [læps] n (bad behaviour) Fehltritt m; (of memory etc) Schwäche f; (of time) Zeitspanne f ♦ vi ablaufen; (law) ungültig werden; **to** ~ **into bad habits** in schlechte Gewohnheiten verfallen.
laptop ['læptɔp] (COMPUT) n Laptop m ♦ cpd Laptop-.
larceny ['lɑ:sənɪ] n Diebstahl m.
larch [lɑ:tʃ] n Lärche f.
lard [lɑ:d] n Schweineschmalz nt.
larder ['lɑ:də•] n Speisekammer f; (cupboard) Speiseschrank m.
large [lɑ:dʒ] adj groß; (person) korpulent; **to make** ~**r** vergrößern; **a** ~ **number of people**

eine große Anzahl von Menschen; **on a** ~ **scale** im großen Rahmen; (extensive) weitreichend; **at** ~ (as a whole) im allgemeinen; (at liberty) auf freiem Fuß; **by and** ~ im großen und ganzen.
large goods vehicle n Lastkraftwagen m.
largely ['lɑ:dʒlɪ] adv (mostly) zum größten Teil; (mainly) hauptsächlich.
large-scale ['lɑ:dʒ'skeɪl] adj im großen Rahmen; (extensive) weitreichend; (map, diagram) in einem großen Maßstab.
largesse [lɑ:'ʒes] n Großzügigkeit f.
lark [lɑ:k] n (bird) Lerche f; (joke) Spaß m, Jux m.
►**lark about** vi herumalbern.
larva ['lɑ:və] (pl ~**e**) n Larve f.
larvae ['lɑ:vi:] npl of **larva**.
laryngitis [lærɪn'dʒaɪtɪs] n Kehlkopfentzündung f.
larynx ['lærɪŋks] n Kehlkopf m.
lasagne [lə'zænjə] n Lasagne pl.
lascivious [lə'sɪvɪəs] adj lüstern.
laser ['leɪzə•] n Laser m.
laser beam n Laserstrahl m.
laser printer n Laserdrucker m.
lash [læʃ] n (also: **eyelash**) Wimper f; (blow with whip) Peitschenhieb m ♦ vt peitschen; (rain, wind) peitschen gegen; (tie): **to** ~ **to** festbinden an +dat; **to** ~ **together** zusammenbinden.
►**lash down** vt festbinden ♦ vi (rain) niederprasseln.
►**lash out** vi um sich schlagen; **to** ~ **out at sb** auf jdn losschlagen; **to** ~ **out at or against sb** (criticize) gegen jdn wettern.
lashing ['læʃɪŋ] n: ~**s of** (BRIT: inf) massenhaft.
lass [læs] (BRIT) n Mädchen nt.
lasso [læ'su:] n Lasso nt ♦ vt mit dem Lasso einfangen.
last [lɑ:st] adj letzte(r, s) ♦ adv (most recently) zuletzt, das letzte Mal; (finally) als letztes ♦ vi (continue) dauern; (: in good condition) sich halten; (money, commodity) reichen; ~ **week** letzte Woche; ~ **night** gestern abend; ~ **but one** vorletzte(r, s); **the** ~ **time** das letzte Mal; **at** ~ endlich; **it** ~**s (for) 2 hours** es dauert 2 Stunden.
last-ditch ['lɑ:st'dɪtʃ] adj (attempt) allerletzte(r, s).
lasting ['lɑ:stɪŋ] adj dauerhaft.
lastly ['lɑ:stlɪ] adv (finally) schließlich; (last of all) zum Schluß.
last-minute ['lɑ:stmɪnɪt] adj in letzter Minute.
latch [lætʃ] n Riegel m; **to be on the** ~ nur eingeklinkt sein.
►**latch on to** vt fus (person) sich anschließen +dat; (idea) abfahren auf +acc (inf).
latchkey ['lætʃki:] n Hausschlüssel m.
latchkey child n Schlüsselkind nt.
late [leɪt] adj spät; (not on time) verspätet ♦ adv spät; (behind time) zu spät; (recently): ~ **of Dechmont** bis vor kurzem in Dechmont

wohnhaft; **the ~ Mr X** (*deceased*) der
verstorbene Herr X; **in ~ May** Ende Mai; **to
be (10 minutes) ~** (10 Minuten) zu spät
kommen; (*train etc*) (10 Minuten)
Verspätung haben; **to work ~** länger
arbeiten; **~ in life** relativ spät (im Leben); **of
~** in letzter Zeit.
latecomer ['leɪtkʌmə'] *n* Nachzügler(in) *m(f)*.
lately ['leɪtlɪ] *adv* in letzter Zeit.
lateness ['leɪtnɪs] *n* (*of person*)
Zuspätkommen *nt*; (*of train, event*)
Verspätung *f*.
latent ['leɪtnt] *adj* (*energy*) ungenutzt; (*skill,
ability*) verborgen.
later ['leɪtə'] *adj, adv* später; **~ on** nachher.
lateral ['lætərl] *adj* seitlich; **~ thinking**
kreatives Denken *nt*.
latest ['leɪtɪst] *adj* neueste(r, s) ♦ *n*: **at the ~**
spätestens.
latex ['leɪtɛks] *n* Latex *m*.
lathe [leɪð] *n* Drehbank *f*.
lather ['lɑːðə'] *n* (Seifen)schaum *m* ♦ *vt*
einschäumen.
Latin ['lætɪn] *n* Latein *nt*; (*person*)
Südländer(in) *m(f)* ♦ *adj* lateinisch;
(*temperament etc*) südländisch.
Latin America *n* Lateinamerika *nt*.
Latin American *adj* lateinamerikanisch ♦ *n*
Lateinamerikaner(in) *m(f)*.
Latino [læ'tiːnəʊ] (*US*) *adj* aus Lateinamerika
stammend ♦ *n* Latino *mf*, in den USA
lebende(r) Lateinamerikaner(in).
latitude ['lætɪtjuːd] *n* (*GEOG*) Breite *f*; (*fig:
freedom*) Freiheit *f*.
latrine [lə'triːn] *n* Latrine *f*.
latter ['lætə'] *adj* (*of two*) letztere(r, s); (*later*)
spätere(r, s); (*second part of period*) zweite(r,
s); (*recent*) letzte(r, s) ♦ *n*: **the ~** der/die/das
letztere, die letzteren.
latter-day ['lætədeɪ] *adj* modern.
latterly ['lætəlɪ] *adv* in letzter Zeit.
lattice ['lætɪs] *n* Gitter *nt*.
lattice window *n* Gitterfenster *nt*.
Latvia ['lætvɪə] *n* Lettland *nt*.
Latvian ['lætvɪən] *adj* lettisch ♦ *n* Lette *m*,
Lettin *f*; (*LING*) Lettisch *nt*.
laudable ['lɔːdəbl] *adj* lobenswert.
laudatory ['lɔːdətrɪ] *adj* (*comments*) lobend;
(*speech*) Lob-.
laugh [lɑːf] *n* Lachen *nt* ♦ *vi* lachen; **(to do sth)
for a ~** (etw) aus Spaß (tun).
►**laugh at** *vt fus* lachen über +*acc*.
►**laugh off** *vt* mit einem Lachen abtun.
laughable ['lɑːfəbl] *adj* lächerlich, lachhaft.
laughing gas ['lɑːfɪŋ-] *n* Lachgas *nt*.
laughing matter *n*: **this is no ~** das ist nicht
zum Lachen.
laughing stock *n*: **to be the ~ of** zum
Gespött +*gen* werden.
laughter ['lɑːftə'] *n* Lachen *nt*, Gelächter *nt*.
launch [lɔːntʃ] *n* (*of rocket, missile*) Abschuß *m*;
(*of satellite*) Start *m*; (*COMM: of product*)

Einführung *f*; (: *with publicity*) Lancierung *f*;
(*motorboat*) Barkasse *f* ♦ *vt* (*ship*) vom Stapel
lassen; (*rocket, missile*) abschießen; (*satellite*)
starten; (*fig: start*) beginnen mit; (*COMM*)
auf den Markt bringen; (: *with publicity*)
lancieren.
►**launch into** *vt fus* (*speech*) vom Stapel
lassen; (*activity*) in Angriff nehmen.
►**launch out** *vi*: **to ~ out (into)** beginnen
(mit).
launching ['lɔːntʃɪŋ] *n* (*of ship*) Stapellauf *m*;
(*of rocket, missile*) Abschuß *m*; (*of satellite*)
Start *m*; (*fig: start*) Beginn *m*; (*COMM: of
product*) Einführung *f*; (: *with publicity*)
Lancierung *f*.
launch(ing) pad *n* Startrampe *f*,
Abschußrampe *f*.
launder ['lɔːndə'] *vt* waschen und bügeln; (*pej:
money*) waschen.
laundrette [lɔːn'drɛt] (*BRIT*) *n* Waschsalon *m*.
Laundromat® ['lɔːndrəmæt] (*US*) *n*
Waschsalon *m*.
laundry ['lɔːndrɪ] *n* Wäsche *f*; (*dirty*)
(schmutzige) Wäsche; (*business*) Wäscherei
f; (*room*) Waschküche *f*; **to do the ~**
(Wäsche) waschen.
laureate ['lɔːrɪət] *adj see* **poet laureate**.
laurel ['lɔrl] *n* (*tree*) Lorbeer(baum) *m*; **to rest
on one's ~s** sich auf seinen Lorbeeren
ausruhen.
Lausanne [ləʊ'zæn] *n* Lausanne *nt*.
lava ['lɑːvə] *n* Lava *f*.
lavatory ['lævətərɪ] *n* Toilette *f*.
lavatory paper *n* Toilettenpapier *nt*.
lavender ['lævəndə'] *n* Lavendel *m*.
lavish ['lævɪʃ] *adj* großzügig; (*meal*) üppig;
(*surroundings*) feudal; (*wasteful*)
verschwenderisch ♦ *vt*: **to ~ sth on sb** jdn
mit etw überhäufen.
lavishly ['lævɪʃlɪ] *adv* (*generously*) großzügig;
(*sumptuously*) aufwendig.
law [lɔː] *n* Recht *nt*; (*a rule: also of nature,
science*) Gesetz *nt*; (*professions connected with
law*) Rechtswesen *nt*; (*SCOL*) Jura *no art*;
against the ~ rechtswidrig; **to study ~** Jura
or Recht(swissenschaft) studieren; **to go to
~** vor Gericht gehen; **to break the ~** gegen
das Gesetz verstoßen.
law-abiding ['lɔːəbaɪdɪŋ] *adj* gesetzestreu.
law and order *n* Ruhe und Ordnung *f*.
lawbreaker ['lɔːbreɪkə'] *n* Rechtsbrecher(in)
m(f).
law court *n* Gerichtshof *m*, Gericht *nt*.
lawful ['lɔːful] *adj* rechtmäßig.
lawfully ['lɔːfəlɪ] *adv* rechtmäßig.
lawless ['lɔːlɪs] *adj* gesetzwidrig.
Law Lord (*BRIT*) *n* Mitglied des Oberhauses
mit besonderem Verantwortungsbereich in
Rechtsfragen.
lawn [lɔːn] *n* Rasen *m*.
lawn mower *n* Rasenmäher *m*.
lawn tennis *n* Rasentennis *nt*.

law school (*US*) *n* juristische Hochschule *f*.
law student *n* Jurastudent(in) *m(f)*.
lawsuit ['lɔːsuːt] *n* Prozeß *m*.
lawyer ['lɔːjəʳ] *n* (Rechts)anwalt *m*,
(Rechts)anwältin *f*.
lax [læks] *adj* lax.
laxative ['læksətɪv] *n* Abführmittel *nt*.
laxity ['læksɪtɪ] *n* Laxheit *f*; **moral ~** lockere *or*
laxe Moral *f*.
lay [leɪ] (*pt, pp* **laid**) *pt of* **lie** ♦ *adj* (*REL: preacher
etc*) Laien- ♦ *vt* legen; (*table*) decken; (*carpet,
cable etc*) verlegen; (*plans*) schmieden; (*trap*)
stellen; **the ~ person** (*not expert*) der Laie;
to ~ facts/proposals before sb jdm
Tatsachen vorlegen/Vorschläge
unterbreiten; **to ~ one's hands on sth** (*fig*)
etw in die Finger bekommen; **to get laid**
(*inf!*) bumsen (*!*).
▶**lay aside** *vt* weglegen, zur Seite legen.
▶**lay by** *vt* beiseite *or* auf die Seite legen.
▶**lay down** *vt* hinlegen; (*rules, laws etc*)
festlegen; **to ~ down the law** Vorschriften
machen; **to ~ down one's life** sein Leben
geben.
▶**lay in** *vt* (*supply*) anlegen.
▶**lay into** *vt fus* losgehen auf +*acc*; (*criticize*)
herunterputzen.
▶**lay off** *vt* (*workers*) entlassen.
▶**lay on** *vt* (*meal*) auftischen; (*entertainment
etc*) sorgen für; (*water, gas*) anschließen;
(*paint*) auftragen.
▶**lay out** *vt* ausbreiten; (*inf: spend*) ausgeben.
▶**lay up** *vt* (*illness*) außer Gefecht setzen; *see
also* **lay by**.
layabout ['leɪəbaut] (*inf: pej*) *n* Faulenzer *m*.
lay-by ['leɪbaɪ] (*BRIT*) *n* Parkbucht *f*.
lay days *npl* Liegezeit *f*.
layer ['leɪəʳ] *n* Schicht *f*.
layette [leɪ'ɛt] *n* Babyausstattung *f*.
layman ['leɪmən] (*irreg: like* **man**) *n* Laie *m*.
lay-off ['leɪɔf] *n* Entlassung *f*.
layout ['leɪaut] *n* (*of garden*) Anlage *f*; (*of
building*) Aufteilung *f*; (*TYP*) Layout *nt*.
laze [leɪz] *vi* (*also:* ~ **about**) (herum)faulenzen.
laziness ['leɪzɪnɪs] *n* Faulheit *f*.
lazy ['leɪzɪ] *adj* faul; (*movement, action*)
langsam, träge.
LB (*CANADA*) *abbr* (= *Labrador*).
lb *abbr* (= *pound (weight)*) britisches Pfund
(*0,45 kg*), ≈ Pfd.
lbw *abbr* (*CRICKET: = leg before wicket*)
Regelverletzung beim Kricket.
LC (*US*) *n abbr* (= *Library of Congress*)
Bibliothek des US-Parlaments.
L/C *abbr* = **letter of credit**.
lc *abbr* (*TYP: = lower case*) *see* **case**.
LCD *n abbr* (= *liquid-crystal display*) LCD *nt*.
Ld (*BRIT*) *abbr* (*in titles*) = **lord**.
LDS *n abbr* (*BRIT: = Licentiate in Dental Surgery*)
≈ Dr. med. dent. ♦ *n abbr* (= *Latter-day Saints*)
Heilige *pl* der Letzten Tage.
LEA (*BRIT*) *n abbr* (= *Local Education Authority*)

örtliche Schulbehörde.
lead¹ [liːd] (*pt, pp* **led**) *n* (*SPORT, fig*) Führung *f*;
(*clue*) Spur *f*; (*in play, film*) Hauptrolle *f*; (*for
dog*) Leine *f*; (*ELEC*) Kabel *nt* ♦ *vt* anführen;
(*guide*) führen; (*organization, BRIT: orchestra*)
leiten ♦ *vi* führen; **to be in the ~** (*SPORT, fig*)
in Führung liegen; **to take the ~** (*SPORT*) in
Führung gehen; **to ~ the way** vorangehen;
to ~ sb astray jdn vom rechten Weg
abführen; (*mislead*) jdn irreführen; **to ~ sb
to believe that** ... jdm den Eindruck
vermitteln, daß ...; **to ~ sb to do sth** jdn
dazu bringen, etw zu tun.
▶**lead away** *vt* wegführen; (*prisoner etc*)
abführen.
▶**lead back** *vt* zurückführen.
▶**lead off** *vi* (*in conversation etc*) den Anfang
machen; (*room, road*) abgehen ♦ *vt fus*
abgehen von.
▶**lead on** *vt* (*tease*) aufziehen.
▶**lead to** *vt fus* führen zu.
▶**lead up to** *vt fus* (*events*) vorangehen +*dat*;
(*in conversation*) hinauswollen auf +*acc*.
lead² [lɛd] *n* Blei *nt*; (*in pencil*) Mine *f*.
leaded ['lɛdɪd] *adj* (*window*) bleiverglast;
(*petrol*) verbleit.
leaden ['lɛdn] *adj* (*sky, sea*) bleiern;
(*movements*) bleischwer.
leader ['liːdəʳ] *n* Führer(in) *m(f)*; (*SPORT*)
Erste(r) *f(m)*; (*in newspaper*) Leitartikel *m*;
the L~ of the House (of Commons/of Lords)
(*BRIT*) der Führer des Unterhauses/des
Oberhauses.
leadership ['liːdəʃɪp] *n* Führung *f*; (*position*)
Vorsitz *m*; (*quality*) Führungsqualitäten *pl*.
lead-free ['lɛdfriː] (*old*) *adj* bleifrei.
leading ['liːdɪŋ] *adj* führend; (*role*) Haupt-;
(*first, front*) vorderste(r, s).
leading lady *n* (*THEAT*) Hauptdarstellerin *f*.
leading light *n* führende Persönlichkeit *f*.
leading man *n* (*THEAT*) Hauptdarsteller *m*.
leading question *n* Suggestivfrage *f*.
lead pencil [lɛd-] *n* Bleistift *m*.
lead poisoning [lɛd-] *n* Bleivergiftung *f*.
lead singer [liːd-] *n* Leadsänger(in) *m(f)*.
lead time [liːd-] *n* (*COMM: for production*)
Produktionszeit *f*; (: *for delivery*) Lieferzeit *f*.
lead-up ['liːdʌp] *n*: **the ~ to sth** die Zeit vor
etw *dat*.
leaf [liːf] (*pl* **leaves**) *n* Blatt *nt*; (*of table*)
Ausziehplatte *f*; **to turn over a new ~** einen
neuen Anfang machen; **to take a ~ out of
sb's book** sich *dat* von jdm eine Scheibe
abschneiden.
▶**leaf through** *vt fus* durchblättern.
leaflet ['liːflɪt] *n* Informationsblatt *nt*.
leafy ['liːfɪ] *adj* (*tree, branch*) belaubt; (*lane,
suburb*) grün.
league [liːg] *n* (*of people, clubs*) Verband *m*; (*of
countries*) Bund *m*; (*FOOTBALL*) Liga *f*; **to be
in ~ with sb** mit jdm gemeinsame Sache
machen.

league table n Tabelle f.

leak [liːk] n Leck nt; (in roof, pipe etc) undichte Stelle f; (piece of information) zugespielte Information f ♦ vi (shoes, roof, pipe) undicht sein; (ship) lecken; (liquid) auslaufen; (gas) ausströmen ♦ vt (information) durchsickern lassen; **to ~ sth to sb** jdm etw zuspielen.

▶**leak out** vi (liquid) auslaufen; (news, information) durchsickern.

leakage ['liːkɪdʒ] n (of liquid) Auslaufen nt; (of gas) Ausströmen nt.

leaky ['liːkɪ] adj (roof, container) undicht.

lean [liːn] (pt, pp **leaned** or **leant**) adj (person) schlank; (meat, fig: time) mager ♦ vt: **to ~ sth on sth** etw an etw acc lehnen; (rest) etw auf etw acc stützen ♦ vi (slope) sich neigen; **to ~ against** sich lehnen gegen; **to ~ on sich** stützen auf +acc; **to ~ forward/back** sich vorbeugen/zurücklehnen; **to ~ towards** tendieren zu.

▶**lean out** vi sich hinauslehnen.

▶**lean over** vi sich vorbeugen.

leaning ['liːnɪŋ] n Hang m, Neigung f.

leant [lɛnt] pt, pp of **lean**.

lean-to ['liːntuː] n Anbau m.

leap [liːp] (pt, pp **leaped** or **leapt**) n Sprung m; (in price, number etc) sprunghafter Anstieg m ♦ vi springen; (price, number etc) sprunghaft (an)steigen.

▶**leap at** vt fus (offer) sich stürzen auf +acc; (opportunity) beim Schopf ergreifen.

▶**leap up** vi aufspringen.

leapfrog ['liːpfrɔg] n Bockspringen nt.

leapt [lɛpt] pt, pp of **leap**.

leap year n Schaltjahr nt.

learn [ləːn] (pt, pp **learned** or **learnt**) vt lernen; (facts) erfahren ♦ vi lernen; **to ~ about** or **of sth** von etw erfahren; **to ~ about sth** (study) etw lernen; **to ~ that ...** (hear, read) erfahren, daß ...; **to ~ to do sth** etw lernen.

learned ['ləːnɪd] adj gelehrt; (book, paper) wissenschaftlich.

learner ['ləːnəʳ] (BRIT) n (also: ~ **driver**) Fahrschüler(in) m(f).

learning ['ləːnɪŋ] n Gelehrsamkeit f.

learnt [ləːnt] pt, pp of **learn**.

lease [liːs] n Pachtvertrag m ♦ vt: **to ~ sth (to sb)** etw (an jdn) verpachten; **on ~ (to)** verpachtet (an +acc); **to ~ sth (from sb)** etw (von jdm) pachten.

▶**lease back** vt rückmieten.

leaseback ['liːsbæk] n Verkauf und Rückmiete pl.

leasehold ['liːshəuld] n Pachtbesitz m ♦ adj gepachtet.

leash [liːʃ] n Leine f.

least [liːst] adv am wenigsten ♦ adj: **the ~** (+ noun) der/die/das wenigste; (: slightest) der/die/das geringste; **the ~ expensive car** das billigste Auto; **at ~** mindestens; (still, rather) wenigstens; **you could at ~ have written** du hättest wenigstens schreiben

können; **not in the ~** nicht im geringsten; **it was the ~ I could do** das war das wenigste, was ich tun konnte.

leather ['lɛðəʳ] n Leder nt.

leather goods npl Lederwaren pl.

leave [liːv] (pt, pp **left**) vt verlassen; (leave behind) zurücklassen; (mark, stain) hinterlassen; (object: accidentally) liegenlassen, stehenlassen; (food) übriglassen; (space, time etc) lassen ♦ vi (go away) (weg)gehen; (bus, train) abfahren ♦ n Urlaub m; **to ~ sth to sb** (money etc) jdm etw hinterlassen; **to ~ sb with sth** (impose) jdm etw aufhalsen; (possession) jdm etw lassen; **they were left with nothing** ihnen blieb nichts; **to be left** übrig sein; **to be left over** (remain) übrig(geblieben) sein; **to ~ for** gehen/fahren nach; **to take one's ~ of sb** sich von jdm verabschieden; **on ~** auf Urlaub.

▶**leave behind** vt zurücklassen; (object: accidentally) liegenlassen, stehenlassen.

▶**leave off** vt (cover, lid) ablassen; (heating, light) auslassen ♦ vi (inf: stop) aufhören.

▶**leave on** vt (light, heating) anlassen.

▶**leave out** vt auslassen.

leave of absence n Beurlaubung f.

leaves [liːvz] npl of **leaf**.

Lebanese [lɛbəˈniːz] adj libanesisch ♦ n inv Libanese m, Libanesin f.

Lebanon ['lɛbənən] n Libanon m.

lecherous ['lɛtʃərəs] (pej) adj lüstern.

lectern ['lɛktəːn] n Rednerpult nt.

lecture ['lɛktʃəʳ] n Vortrag m; (UNIV) Vorlesung f ♦ vi Vorträge/Vorlesungen halten ♦ vt (scold): **to ~ sb on** or **about sth** jdm wegen etw eine Strafpredigt halten; **to give a ~ on** einen Vortrag/eine Vorlesung halten über +acc.

lecture hall n Hörsaal m.

lecturer ['lɛktʃərəʳ] (BRIT) n Dozent(in) m(f); (speaker) Redner(in) m(f).

LED n abbr (ELEC: = light-emitting diode) LED f.

led [lɛd] pt, pp of **lead**[1].

ledge [lɛdʒ] n (of mountain) (Fels)vorsprung m; (of window) Fensterbrett nt; (on wall) Leiste f.

ledger ['lɛdʒəʳ] n (COMM) Hauptbuch nt.

lee [liː] n Windschatten m; (NAUT) Lee f.

leech [liːtʃ] n Blutegel m; (fig: person) Blutsauger m.

leek [liːk] n Porree m, Lauch m.

leer [lɪəʳ] vi: **to ~ at sb** jdm lüsterne Blicke zuwerfen.

leeward ['liːwəd] (NAUT) adj (side etc) Lee- ♦ adv leewärts ♦ n: **to ~** an der Leeseite; (direction) nach der Leeseite.

leeway ['liːweɪ] n (fig): **to have some ~** etwas Spielraum haben; **there's a lot of ~ to make up** ein großer Rückstand muß aufgeholt werden.

left [lɛft] pt, pp of **leave** ♦ adj (remaining) übrig;

(of position) links; (of direction) nach links ♦ n linke Seite f ♦ adv links; nach links; **on the ~, to the ~** links; **the L~** (POL) die Linke.
left-hand drive ['lɛfthænd-] adj mit Linkssteuerung.
left-handed [lɛft'hændɪd] adj linkshändig.
left-hand side ['lɛfthænd-] n linke Seite f.
leftie ['lɛftɪ] (inf) n Linke(r) f(m).
leftist ['lɛftɪst] (POL) n Linke(r) f(m) ♦ adj linke(r, s).
left-luggage (office) [lɛft'lʌɡɪdʒ(-)] (BRIT) n Gepäckaufbewahrung f.
leftovers ['lɛftəuvəz] npl Reste pl.
left-wing ['lɛft'wɪŋ] adj (POL) linke(r, s).
left-winger ['lɛft'wɪŋɡə'] n (POL) Linke(r) f(m).
lefty ['lɛftɪ] n = **leftie**.
leg [lɛɡ] n Bein nt; (CULIN) Keule f; (SPORT) Runde f; (: of relay race) Teilstrecke f; (of journey etc) Etappe f; **to stretch one's ~s** sich dat die Beine vertreten; **to get one's ~ over** (inf) bumsen.
legacy ['lɛɡəsɪ] n Erbschaft f; (fig) Erbe nt.
legal ['liːɡl] adj (requirement) rechtlich, gesetzlich; (system) Rechts-; (allowed by law) legal, rechtlich zulässig; **to take ~ action or proceedings against sb** jdn verklagen.
legal adviser n juristischer Berater m.
legal holiday (US) n gesetzlicher Feiertag m.
legality [lɪ'ɡælɪtɪ] n Legalität f.
legalize ['liːɡəlaɪz] vt legalisieren.
legally ['liːɡəlɪ] adv rechtlich, gesetzlich; (in accordance with the law) rechtmäßig; **~ binding** rechtsverbindlich.
legal tender n gesetzliches Zahlungsmittel nt.
legation [lɪ'ɡeɪʃən] n Gesandtschaft f.
legend ['lɛdʒənd] n Legende f, Sage f; (fig: person) Legende f.
legendary ['lɛdʒəndərɪ] adj legendär; (very famous) berühmt.
-legged ['lɛɡɪd] suff -beinig.
leggings ['lɛɡɪŋz] npl Leggings pl.
leggy ['lɛɡɪ] adj langbeinig.
legibility [lɛdʒɪ'bɪlɪtɪ] n Lesbarkeit f.
legible ['lɛdʒəbl] adj leserlich.
legibly ['lɛdʒəblɪ] adv leserlich.
legion ['liːdʒən] n Legion f ♦ adj zahlreich.
legionnaire [liːdʒə'nɛə'] n Legionär m.
legionnaire's disease n Legionärskrankheit f.
legislate ['lɛdʒɪsleɪt] vi Gesetze/ein Gesetz erlassen.
legislation [lɛdʒɪs'leɪʃən] n Gesetzgebung f; (laws) Gesetze pl.
legislative ['lɛdʒɪslətɪv] adj gesetzgebend; **~ reforms** Gesetzesreformen pl.
legislator ['lɛdʒɪsleɪtə'] n Gesetzgeber m.
legislature ['lɛdʒɪslətʃə'] n Legislative f.
legitimacy [lɪ'dʒɪtɪməsɪ] n (validity) Berechtigung f; (legality) Rechtmäßigkeit f.
legitimate [lɪ'dʒɪtɪmət] adj (reasonable) berechtigt; (excuse) begründet; (legal)

rechtmäßig.
legitimize [lɪ'dʒɪtɪmaɪz] vt legitimieren.
legless ['lɛɡlɪs] (inf) adj (drunk) sternhagelvoll.
legroom ['lɛɡruːm] n Beinfreiheit f.
Leics (BRIT) abbr (POST: = Leicestershire).
leisure ['lɛʒə'] n Freizeit f; **at ~** in Ruhe.
leisure centre n Freizeitzentrum nt.
leisurely ['lɛʒəlɪ] adj geruhsam.
leisure suit n Freizeitanzug m.
lemon ['lɛmən] n Zitrone f; (colour) Zitronengelb nt.
lemonade [lɛmə'neɪd] n Limonade f.
lemon cheese n = **lemon curd**.
lemon curd n zähflüssiger Brotaufstrich mit Zitronengeschmack.
lemon juice n Zitronensaft m.
lemon squeezer n Zitronenpresse f.
lemon tea n Zitronentee m.
lend [lɛnd] (pt, pp lent) vt: **to ~ sth to sb** jdm etw leihen; **to ~ sb a hand (with sth)** jdm (bei etw) helfen; **it ~s itself to ...** es eignet sich für ...
lender ['lɛndə'] n Verleiher(in) m(f).
lending library ['lɛndɪŋ-] n Leihbücherei f.
length [lɛŋθ] n Länge f; (piece) Stück nt; (amount of time) Dauer f; **the ~ of the island** (all along) die ganze Insel entlang; **2 metres in ~** 2 Meter lang; **at ~** (at last) schließlich; (for a long time) lange; **to go to great ~s to do sth** sich dat sehr viel Mühe geben, etw zu tun; **to fall full-~** lang hinfallen; **to lie full-~** in voller Länge daliegen.
lengthen ['lɛŋθn] vt verlängern ♦ vi länger werden.
lengthways ['lɛŋθweɪz] adv der Länge nach.
lengthy ['lɛŋθɪ] adj lang.
leniency ['liːnɪənsɪ] n Nachsicht f.
lenient ['liːnɪənt] adj nachsichtig.
leniently ['liːnɪəntlɪ] adv nachsichtig.
lens [lɛnz] n (of spectacles) Glas nt; (of camera) Objektiv nt; (of telescope) Linse f.
Lent [lɛnt] n Fastenzeit f.
lent [lɛnt] pt, pp of **lend**.
lentil ['lɛntɪl] n Linse f.
Leo ['liːəu] n Löwe m; **to be ~** Löwe sein.
leopard ['lɛpəd] n Leopard m.
leotard ['liːətɑːd] n Gymnastikanzug m.
leper ['lɛpə'] n Leprakranke(r) f(m).
leper colony n Leprasiedlung f.
leprosy ['lɛprəsɪ] n Lepra f.
lesbian ['lɛzbɪən] adj lesbisch ♦ n Lesbierin f.
lesion ['liːʒən] n Verletzung f.
Lesotho [lɪ'suːtuː] n Lesotho nt.
less [lɛs] adj, pron, adv weniger ♦ prep: **~ tax/ 10% discount** abzüglich Steuer/10% Rabatt; **~ than half** weniger als die Hälfte; **~ than ever** weniger denn je; **~ and ~** immer weniger; **the ~ he works ...** je weniger er arbeitet ...; **the Prime Minister, no ~** kein Geringerer als der Premierminister.
lessee [lɛ'siː] n Pächter(in) m(f).
lessen ['lɛsn] vi nachlassen, abnehmen ♦ vt

verringern.
lesser ['lesə'] *adj* geringer; **to a ~ extent** in geringerem Maße.
lesson ['lesn] *n* (*class*) Stunde *f*; (*example, warning*) Lehre *f*; **to teach sb a ~** (*fig*) jdm eine Lektion erteilen.
lessor ['lesɔː'] *n* Verpächter(in) *m(f)*.
lest [lest] *conj* damit ... nicht.
let [let] (*pt, pp* **let**) *vt* (*allow*) lassen; (*BRIT: lease*) vermieten; **to ~ sb do sth** jdn etw tun lassen, jdm erlauben, etw zu tun; **to ~ sb know sth** jdn etw wissen lassen; **~'s go** gehen wir!; **~ him come** lassen Sie ihn kommen; **"to ~"** „zu vermieten".
▶**let down** *vt* (*tyre etc*) die Luft herauslassen aus; (*person*) im Stich lassen; (*dress etc*) länger machen; (*hem*) auslassen; **to ~ one's hair down** (*fig*) aus sich herausgehen.
▶**let go** *vi* loslassen ♦ *vt* (*release*) freilassen; **to ~ go of** loslassen; **to ~ o.s. go** aus sich herausgehen; (*neglect o.s.*) sich gehenlassen.
▶**let in** *vt* hereinlassen; (*water*) durchlassen.
▶**let off** *vt* (*culprit*) laufenlassen; (*firework, bomb*) hochgehen lassen; (*gun*) abfeuern; **to ~ sb off sth** (*excuse*) jdm etw erlassen; **to ~ off steam** (*inf, fig*) sich abreagieren.
▶**let on** *vi* verraten.
▶**let out** *vt* herauslassen; (*sound*) ausstoßen; (*house, room*) vermieten.
▶**let up** *vi* (*cease*) aufhören; (*diminish*) nachlassen.
letdown ['letdaun] *n* Enttäuschung *f*.
lethal ['liːθl] *adj* tödlich.
lethargic [lɛ'θɑːdʒɪk] *adj* träge, lethargisch.
lethargy ['leθədʒɪ] *n* Trägheit *f*, Lethargie *f*.
letter ['letə'] *n* Brief *m*; (*of alphabet*) Buchstabe *m*; **small/capital ~** Klein-/Großbuchstabe *m*.
letter bomb *n* Briefbombe *f*.
letter box (*BRIT*) *n* Briefkasten *m*.
letterhead ['letəhɛd] *n* Briefkopf *m*.
lettering ['letərɪŋ] *n* Beschriftung *f*.
letter of credit *n* Akkreditiv *nt*.
letter opener *n* Brieföffner *m*.
letterpress ['letəpres] *n* Hochdruck *m*.
letter-quality printer ['letəkwɔlɪtɪ-] *n* Schönschreibdrucker *m*.
letters patent *npl* Patent *nt*, Patenturkunde *f*.
lettuce ['letɪs] *n* Kopfsalat *m*.
let-up ['letʌp] *n* Nachlassen *nt*; **there was no ~** es ließ nicht nach.
leukaemia, (*US*) **leukemia** [luːˈkiːmɪə] *n* Leukämie *f*.
level ['levl] *adj* eben ♦ *n* (*on scale, of liquid*) Stand *m*; (*of lake, river*) Wasserstand *m*; (*height*) Höhe *f*; (*fig: standard*) Niveau *nt*; (*also:* **spirit ~**) Wasserwaage *f* ♦ *vt* (*building*) abreißen; (*forest etc*) einebnen ♦ *vi*: **to ~ with sb** (*inf*) ehrlich mit jdm sein ♦ *adv*: **to draw ~ with** einholen; **to be ~ with** auf gleicher Höhe sein mit; **to do one's ~ best** sein

möglichstes tun; **"A" ~s** (*BRIT*) ≈ Abitur *nt*; **"O" ~s** (*BRIT*) ≈ mittlere Reife *f*; **on the ~** (*fig: honest*) ehrlich, reell; **to ~ a gun at sb** ein Gewehr auf jdn richten; **to ~ an accusation at** *or* **against sb** eine Anschuldigung gegen jdn erheben; **to ~ a criticism at** *or* **against sb** Kritik an jdm üben.
▶**level off** *vi* (*prices etc*) sich beruhigen.
▶**level out** *vi* = **level off.**
level crossing (*BRIT*) *n* (beschrankter) Bahnübergang *m*.
level-headed [levl'hedɪd] *adj* (*calm*) ausgeglichen.
levelling ['levlɪŋ] *n* Nivellierung *f*.
level playing field *n* Chancengleichheit *f*; **to compete on a ~** unter gleichen Bedingungen antreten.
lever ['liːvə'] *n* Hebel *m*; (*bar*) Brechstange *f*; (*fig*) Druckmittel *nt* ♦ *vt*: **to ~ up** hochhieven; **to ~ out** heraushieven.
leverage ['liːvərɪdʒ] *n* Hebelkraft *f*; (*fig: influence*) Einfluß *m*.
levity ['levɪtɪ] *n* Leichtfertigkeit *f*.
levy ['levɪ] *n* (*tax*) Steuer *f*; (*charge*) Gebühr *f* ♦ *vt* erheben.
lewd [luːd] *adj* (*look etc*) lüstern; (*remark*) anzüglich.
lexicographer [leksɪˈkɔgrəfə'] *n* Lexikograph(in) *m(f)*.
lexicography [leksɪˈkɔgrəfɪ] *n* Lexikographie *f*.
LGV (*BRIT*) *n abbr* (= *large goods vehicle*) LKW *m*.
LI (*US*) *abbr* (= *Long Island*).
liability [laɪəˈbɪlətɪ] *n* Belastung *f*; (*LAW*) Haftung *f*; **liabilities** *npl* (*COMM*) Verbindlichkeiten *pl*.
liable ['laɪəbl] *adj*: **to be ~ to** (*subject to*) unterliegen +*dat*; (*prone to*) anfällig sein für; **~ for** (*responsible*) haftbar für; **to be ~ to do sth** dazu neigen, etw zu tun.
liaise [liːˈeɪz] *vi*: **to ~ (with)** sich in Verbindung setzen (mit).
liaison [liːˈeɪzɔn] *n* Zusammenarbeit *f*; (*sexual relationship*) Liaison *f*.
liar ['laɪə'] *n* Lügner(in) *m(f)*.
libel ['laɪbl] *n* Verleumdung *f* ♦ *vt* verleumden.
libellous, (*US*) **libelous** ['laɪbləs] *adj* verleumderisch.
liberal ['lɪbərl] *adj* (*POL*) liberal; (*tolerant*) aufgeschlossen; (*generous: offer*) großzügig; (: *amount etc*) reichlich ♦ *n* (*tolerant person*) liberal eingestellter Mensch *m*; (*POL*): **L~** Liberale(r) *f(m)*; **~ with** großzügig mit.
Liberal Democrat *n* Liberaldemokrat(in) *m(f)*.
liberalize ['lɪbərəlaɪz] *vt* liberalisieren.
liberally ['lɪbrəlɪ] *adv* großzügig.
liberal-minded ['lɪbərl'maɪndɪd] *adj* liberal (eingestellt).
liberate ['lɪbəreɪt] *vt* befreien.

liberation [lɪbə'reɪʃən] *n* Befreiung *f*.
liberation theology *n* Befreiungstheologie *f*.
Liberia [laɪ'bɪərɪə] *n* Liberia *nt*.
Liberian [laɪ'bɪərɪən] *adj* liberianisch ♦ *n* Liberianer(in) *m(f)*.
liberty ['lɪbətɪ] *n* Freiheit *f*; **to be at ~** (*criminal*) auf freiem Fuß sein; **to be at ~ to do sth** etw tun dürfen; **to take the ~ of doing sth** sich *dat* erlauben, etw zu tun.
libido [lɪ'biːdəʊ] *n* Libido *f*.
Libra ['liːbrə] *n* Waage *f*; **to be ~** Waage sein.
librarian [laɪ'brɛərɪən] *n* Bibliothekar(in) *m(f)*.
library ['laɪbrərɪ] *n* Bibliothek *f*; (*institution*) Bücherei *f*.
library book *n* Buch *nt* aus der Bücherei.
libretto [lɪ'brɛtəʊ] *n* Libretto *nt*.
Libya ['lɪbɪə] *n* Libyen *nt*.
Libyan ['lɪbɪən] *adj* libysch ♦ *n* Libyer(in) *m(f)*.
lice [laɪs] *npl of* **louse**.
licence, (*US*) **license** ['laɪsns] *n* (*document*) Genehmigung *f*; (*also*: **driving ~**) Führerschein *m*; (*COMM*) Lizenz *f*; (*excessive freedom*) Zügellosigkeit *f*; **to get a TV ~** ≈ Fernsehgebühren bezahlen; **under ~** (*COMM*) in Lizenz.
license ['laɪsns] *n* (*US*) = **licence** ♦ *vt* (*person, organization*) eine Lizenz vergeben an +*acc*; (*activity*) eine Genehmigung erteilen für.
licensed ['laɪsnst] *adj*: **the car is ~** die Kfz-Steuer für das Auto ist bezahlt; **~ hotel/restaurant** Hotel/Restaurant mit Schankerlaubnis.
licensee [laɪsən'siː] *n* (*of bar*) Inhaber(in) *m(f)* einer Schankerlaubnis.
license plate (*US*) *n* Nummernschild *nt*.
licensing hours ['laɪsnsɪŋ] (*BRIT*) *npl* Ausschankzeiten *pl*.
licentious [laɪ'sɛnʃəs] *adj* ausschweifend, zügellos.
lichen ['laɪkən] *n* Flechte *f*.
lick [lɪk] *vt* lecken; (*stamp etc*) lecken an +*dat*; (*inf: defeat*) in die Pfanne hauen ♦ *n* Lecken *nt*; **to ~ one's lips** sich *dat* die Lippen lecken; (*fig*) sich *dat* die Finger lecken; **a ~ of paint** ein Anstrich *m*.
licorice ['lɪkərɪs] (*US*) *n* = **liquorice**.
lid [lɪd] *n* Deckel *m*; (*eyelid*) Lid *nt*; **to take the ~ off sth** (*fig*) etw enthüllen *or* aufdecken.
lido ['laɪdəʊ] (*BRIT*) *n* Freibad *nt*.
lie¹ [laɪ] (*pt, pp* **lied**) *vi* lügen ♦ *n* Lüge *f*; **to tell ~s** lügen.
lie² [laɪ] (*pt* **lay**, *pp* **lain**) *vi* (*lit, fig*) liegen; **to ~ low** (*fig*) untertauchen.
▶**lie about** *vi* herumliegen.
▶**lie around** *vi* = **lie about**.
▶**lie back** *vi* sich zurücklehnen; (*fig: accept the inevitable*) sich fügen.
▶**lie down** *vi* sich hinlegen.
▶**lie up** *vi* (*hide*) untertauchen; (*rest*) im Bett bleiben.
Liechtenstein ['lɪktənstaɪn] *n* Liechtenstein *nt*.

lie detector *n* Lügendetektor *m*.
lie-down ['laɪdaʊn] (*BRIT*) *n*: **to have a ~** ein Schläfchen machen.
lie-in ['laɪɪn] (*BRIT*) *n*: **to have a ~** (sich) ausschlafen.
lieu [luː]: **in ~ of** *prep* an Stelle von, anstatt +*gen*.
Lieut. *abbr* (*MIL:* = *lieutenant*) Lt.
lieutenant [lɛf'tɛnənt, (*US*) luː'tɛnənt] *n* Leutnant *m*.
lieutenant colonel *n* Oberstleutnant *m*.
life [laɪf] (*pl* **lives**) *n* Leben *nt*; (*of machine etc*) Lebensdauer *f*; **true to ~** lebensecht; **painted from ~** aus dem Leben gegriffen; **to be sent to prison for ~** zu einer lebenslänglichen Freiheitsstrafe verurteilt werden; **such is ~** so ist das Leben; **to come to ~** (*fig: person*) munter werden; (: *party etc*) in Schwung kommen.
life annuity *n* Leibrente *f*.
life assurance (*BRIT*) *n* = **life insurance**.
life belt (*BRIT*) *n* Rettungsgürtel *m*.
lifeblood ['laɪfblʌd] *n* (*fig*) Lebensnerv *m*.
lifeboat ['laɪfbəʊt] *n* Rettungsboot *nt*.
life buoy *n* Rettungsring *m*.
life expectancy *n* Lebenserwartung *f*.
lifeguard ['laɪfgɑːd] *n* (*at beach*) Rettungsschwimmer(in) *m(f)*; (*at swimming pool*) Bademeister(in) *m(f)*.
life imprisonment *n* lebenslängliche Freiheitsstrafe *f*.
life insurance *n* Lebensversicherung *f*.
life jacket *n* Schwimmweste *f*.
lifeless ['laɪflɪs] *adj* leblos; (*fig: person, party etc*) langweilig.
lifelike ['laɪflaɪk] *adj* lebensecht; (*painting*) naturgetreu.
lifeline ['laɪflaɪn] *n* (*fig*) Rettungsanker *m*; (*rope*) Rettungsleine *f*.
lifelong ['laɪflɒŋ] *adj* lebenslang.
life preserver (*US*) *n* = **life belt; life jacket**.
lifer ['laɪfə*] (*inf*) *n* Lebenslängliche(r) *f(m)*.
life raft *n* Rettungsfloß *nt*.
life-saver ['laɪfseɪvə*] *n* Lebensretter(in) *m(f)*.
life sciences *npl* Biowissenschaften *pl*.
life sentence *n* lebenslängliche Freiheitsstrafe *f*.
life-size(d) ['laɪfsaɪz(d)] *adj* in Lebensgröße.
life span *n* Lebensdauer *f*; (*of person*) Lebenszeit *f*.
life style ['laɪfstaɪl] *n* Lebensstil *m*.
life-support system ['laɪfsəpɔːt-] *n* (*MED*) Lebenserhaltungssystem *nt*.
lifetime ['laɪftaɪm] *n* Lebenszeit *f*; (*of thing*) Lebensdauer *f*; (*of parliament*) Legislaturperiode *f*; **in my ~** während meines Lebens; **the chance of a ~** eine einmalige Chance.
lift [lɪft] *vt* (*raise*) heben; (*end: ban etc*) aufheben; (*plagiarize*) abschreiben; (*inf: steal*) mitgehen lassen, klauen ♦ *vi* (*fog*) sich auflösen ♦ *n* (*BRIT*) Aufzug *m*, Fahrstuhl *m*;

to take the ~ mit dem Aufzug *or* Fahrstuhl fahren; **to give sb a** ~ (*BRIT*) jdn (im Auto) mitnehmen.
▶**lift off** *vi* abheben.
▶**lift up** *vt* hochheben.
liftoff ['lɪftɔf] *n* Abheben *nt*.
ligament ['lɪgəmənt] *n* (*ANAT*) Band *nt*.
light [laɪt] (*pt, pp* **lit**) *n* Licht *nt* ♦ *vt* (*candle, cigarette, fire*) anzünden; (*room*) beleuchten ♦ *adj* leicht; (*pale, bright*) hell; (*traffic etc*) gering; (*music*) Unterhaltungs- ♦ *adv*: **to travel** ~ mit leichtem Gepäck reisen; **lights** *npl* (*AUT: also*: **traffic** ~**s**) Ampel *f*; **the** ~**s** (*of car*) die Beleuchtung; **have you got a** ~? haben Sie Feuer?; **to turn the** ~ **on/off** das Licht an-/ausmachen; **to come to** ~ ans Tageslicht kommen; **to cast** *or* **shed** *or* **throw** ~ **on** (*fig*) Licht bringen in +*acc*; **in the** ~ **of** angesichts +*gen*; **to make** ~ **of sth** (*fig*) etw auf die leichte Schulter nehmen; ~ **blue/green** *etc* hellblau/-grün *etc*.
▶**light up** *vi* (*face*) sich erhellen ♦ *vt* (*illuminate*) beleuchten, erhellen.
light bulb *n* Glühbirne *f*.
lighten ['laɪtn] *vt* (*make less heavy*) leichter machen ♦ *vi* (*become less dark*) sich aufhellen.
lighter ['laɪtə*] *n* (*also*: **cigarette** ~) Feuerzeug *nt*.
light-fingered [laɪt'fɪŋgəd] (*inf*) *adj* langfingerig.
light-headed [laɪt'hɛdɪd] *adj* (*dizzy*) benommen; (*excited*) ausgelassen.
light-hearted [laɪt'hɑːtɪd] *adj* unbeschwert; (*question, remark etc*) scherzhaft.
lighthouse ['laɪthaus] *n* Leuchtturm *m*.
lighting ['laɪtɪŋ] *n* Beleuchtung *f*.
lighting-up time [laɪtɪŋ'ʌp-] *n* Zeitpunkt, zu dem die Fahrzeugbeleuchtung eingeschaltet werden muß.
lightly ['laɪtlɪ] *adv* leicht; (*not seriously*) leichthin; **to get off** ~ glimpflich davonkommen.
light meter *n* Belichtungsmesser *m*.
lightness ['laɪtnɪs] *n* (*in weight*) Leichtigkeit *f*.
lightning ['laɪtnɪŋ] *n* Blitz *m* ♦ *adj* (*attack etc*) Blitz-; **with** ~ **speed** blitzschnell.
lightning conductor *n* Blitzableiter *m*.
lightning rod (*US*) *n* = **lightning conductor**.
light pen *n* Lichtstift *m*, Lichtgriffel *m*.
lightship ['laɪtʃɪp] *n* Feuerschiff *nt*.
lightweight ['laɪtweɪt] *adj* leicht ♦ *n* (*BOXING*) Leichtgewichtler *m*.
light year *n* Lichtjahr *nt*.
like [laɪk] *vt* mögen ♦ *prep* wie; (*such as*) wie (zum Beispiel) ♦ *n*: **and the** ~ und dergleichen; **I would** ~, **I'd** ~ ich hätte *or* möchte gern; **would you** ~ **a coffee?** möchten Sie einen Kaffee?; **if you** ~ wenn Sie wollen; **to be/look** ~ **sb/sth** jdm/etw ähnlich sein/sehen; **something** ~ **that** so etwas ähnliches; **what does it look/taste/**

sound ~? wie sieht es aus/schmeckt es/hört es sich an?; **what's he/the weather** ~? wie ist er/das Wetter?; **I feel** ~ **a drink** ich möchte gerne etwas trinken; **there's nothing** ~ ... es gibt nichts über +*acc*; **that's just** ~ **him** das sieht ihm ähnlich; **do it** ~ **this** mach es so; **it is nothing** ~ (+*noun*) es ist ganz anders als; (+*adj*) es ist alles andere als; **it is nothing** ~ **as** ... es ist bei weitem nicht so ...; **his** ~**s and dislikes** seine Vorlieben und Abneigungen.
likeable ['laɪkəbl] *adj* sympathisch.
likelihood ['laɪklɪhud] *n* Wahrscheinlichkeit *f*; **there is every** ~ **that** ... es ist sehr wahrscheinlich, daß ...; **in all** ~ aller Wahrscheinlichkeit nach.
likely ['laɪklɪ] *adj* wahrscheinlich; **to be** ~ **to do sth** wahrscheinlich etw tun; **not** ~! (*inf*) wohl kaum!
like-minded [laɪk'maɪndɪd] *adj* gleichgesinnt.
liken ['laɪkən] *vt*: **to** ~ **sth to sth** etw mit etw vergleichen.
likeness ['laɪknɪs] *n* Ähnlichkeit *f*; **that's a good** ~ (*photo, portrait*) das ist ein gutes Bild von ihm/ihr *etc*.
likewise ['laɪkwaɪz] *adv* ebenso; **to do** ~ das gleiche tun.
liking ['laɪkɪŋ] *n*: ~ (**for**) (*person*) Zuneigung *f* (zu); (*thing*) Vorliebe *f* (für); **to be to sb's** ~ nach jds Geschmack sein; **to take a** ~ **to sb** an jdm Gefallen finden.
lilac ['laɪlək] *n* (*BOT*) Flieder *m* ♦ *adj* fliederfarben, (zart)lila.
Lilo ® ['laɪləu] *n* Luftmatratze *f*.
lilt [lɪlt] *n* singender Tonfall *m*.
lilting ['lɪltɪŋ] *adj* singend.
lily ['lɪlɪ] *n* Lilie *f*.
lily of the valley *n* Maiglöckchen *nt*.
Lima ['liːmə] *n* Lima *nt*.
limb [lɪm] *n* Glied *nt*; (*of tree*) Ast *m*; **to be out on a** ~ (*fig*) (ganz) allein (da)stehen.
limber up ['lɪmbə*-] *vi* Lockerungsübungen machen.
limbo ['lɪmbəu] *n*: **to be in** ~ (*fig: plans etc*) in der Schwebe sein; (: *person*) in der Luft hängen (*inf*).
lime [laɪm] *n* (*fruit*) Limone *f*; (*tree*) Linde *f*; (*also*: ~ **juice**) Limonensaft *m*; (*for soil*) Kalk *m*; (*rock*) Kalkstein *m*.
limelight ['laɪmlaɪt] *n*: **to be in the** ~ im Rampenlicht stehen.
limerick ['lɪmərɪk] *n* Limerick *m*.
limestone ['laɪmstəun] *n* Kalkstein *m*.
limit ['lɪmɪt] *n* Grenze *f*; (*restriction*) Beschränkung *f* ♦ *vt* begrenzen, einschränken; **within** ~**s** innerhalb gewisser Grenzen.
limitation [lɪmɪ'teɪʃən] *n* Einschränkung *f*; **limitations** *npl* (*shortcomings*) Grenzen *pl*.
limited ['lɪmɪtɪd] *adj* begrenzt, beschränkt; **to be** ~ **to** beschränkt sein auf +*acc*.
limited edition *n* beschränkte Ausgabe *f*.

limited (liability) company (*BRIT*) *n*
~ Gesellschaft *f* mit beschränkter Haftung.
limitless ['lɪmɪtlɪs] *adj* grenzenlos.
limousine ['lɪməziːn] *n* Limousine *f*.
limp [lɪmp] *adj* schlaff; (*material etc*) weich ♦ *vi*
hinken ♦ *n:* **to have a** ~ hinken.
limpet ['lɪmpɪt] *n* Napfschnecke *f*.
limpid ['lɪmpɪd] *adj* klar.
limply ['lɪmplɪ] *adj* schlaff.
linchpin ['lɪntʃpɪn] *n* (*fig*) wichtigste Stütze *f*.
Lincs [lɪŋks] (*BRIT*) *abbr* (*POST:* = Lincolnshire).
line [laɪn] *n* Linie *f*; (*written, printed*) Zeile *f*;
(*wrinkle*) Falte *f*; (*row: of people*) Schlange *f*;
(*: of things*) Reihe *f*; (*for fishing, washing*)
Leine *f*; (*wire, TEL*) Leitung *f*; (*railway track*)
Gleise *pl*; (*fig: attitude*) Standpunkt *m*;
(*: business*) Branche *f*; (*COMM: of product(s)*)
Art *f* ♦ *vt* (*road*) säumen; (*container*)
auskleiden; (*clothing*) füttern; **hold the**
~ **please!** (*TEL*) bleiben Sie am Apparat!; **to**
cut in ~ (*US*) sich vordrängeln; **in** ~ **in einer**
Reihe; **in** ~ **with** im Einklang mit, in
Übereinstimmung mit; **to be in** ~ **for sth**
mit etw an der Reihe sein; **to bring sth into**
~ **with sth** etw auf die gleiche Linie wie
etw *acc* bringen; **on the right** ~**s** auf dem
richtigen Weg; **to draw the** ~ **at that** da
mache ich nicht mehr mit; **to** ~ **sth with sth**
etw mit etw auskleiden; (*drawers etc*) etw
mit etw auslegen; **to** ~ **the streets** die
Straßen säumen.
► **line up** *vi* sich aufstellen ♦ *vt* (*in a row*)
aufstellen; (*engage*) verpflichten; (*prepare*)
arrangieren; **to have sb** ~**d up** jdn
verpflichtet haben; **to have sth** ~**d up** etw
geplant haben.
linear ['lɪnɪə*] *adj* linear; (*shape, form*) gerade.
lined [laɪnd] *adj* (*face*) faltig; (*paper*) liniert;
(*skirt, jacket*) gefüttert.
line editing *n* (*COMPUT*) zeilenweise
Aufbereitung *f*.
line feed *n* (*COMPUT*) Zeilenvorschub *m*.
lineman ['laɪnmən] (*US: irreg: like* man) *n*
(*FOOTBALL*) Stürmer *m*.
linen ['lɪnɪn] *n* (*cloth*) Leinen *nt*; (*tablecloths,*
sheets etc) Wäsche *f*.
line printer *n* (*COMPUT*) Zeilendrucker *m*.
liner ['laɪnə*] *n* (*ship*) Passagierschiff *nt*; (*also:*
bin ~) Müllbeutel *m*.
linesman ['laɪnzmən] (*irreg: like* man) *n* (*SPORT*)
Linienrichter *m*.
line-up ['laɪnʌp] *n* (*US: queue*) Schlange *f*;
(*SPORT*) Aufstellung *f*; (*at concert etc*)
Künstleraufgebot *nt*; (*identity parade*)
Gegenüberstellung *f*.
linger ['lɪŋɡə*] *vi* (*smell*) sich halten; (*tradition*
etc) fortbestehen; (*person*) sich aufhalten.
lingerie ['lænʒəriː] *n* (*Damen*)unterwäsche *f*.
lingering ['lɪŋɡərɪŋ] *adj* bleibend.
lingo ['lɪŋɡəu] (*pl* ~**es**) (*inf*) *n* Sprache *f*.
linguist ['lɪŋɡwɪst] *n* (*person who speaks several*
languages) Sprachkundige(r) *f(m)*.

linguistic [lɪŋ'ɡwɪstɪk] *adj* sprachlich.
linguistics [lɪŋ'ɡwɪstɪks] *n*
Sprachwissenschaft *f*.
liniment ['lɪnɪmənt] *n* Einreibemittel *nt*.
lining ['laɪnɪŋ] *n* (*cloth*) Futter *nt*; (*ANAT: of*
stomach) Magenschleimhaut *f*; (*TECH*)
Auskleidung *f*; (*of brakes*) (Brems)belag *m*.
link [lɪŋk] *n* Verbindung *f*, Beziehung *f*;
(*communications link*) Verbindung; (*of a*
chain) Glied *nt* ♦ *vt* (*join*) verbinden; **links** *npl*
(*GOLF*) Golfplatz *m*; **rail** ~ Bahnverbindung
f.
► **link up** *vt* verbinden ♦ *vi* verbunden
werden.
linkup ['lɪŋkʌp] *n* Verbindung *f*; (*of spaceships*)
Koppelung *f*.
lino ['laɪnəu] *n* = **linoleum**.
linoleum [lɪ'nəulɪəm] *n* Linoleum *nt*.
linseed oil ['lɪnsiːd-] *n* Leinöl *nt*.
lint [lɪnt] *n* Mull *m*.
lintel ['lɪntl] *n* (*ARCHIT*) Sturz *m*.
lion ['laɪən] *n* Löwe *m*.
lion cub *n* Löwenjunge(s) *nt*.
lioness ['laɪənɪs] *n* Löwin *f*.
lip [lɪp] *n* (*ANAT*) Lippe *f*; (*of cup etc*) Rand *m*;
(*inf: insolence*) Frechheiten *pl*.
liposuction ['lɪpəusʌkʃən] *n* Liposuktion *f*.
lip-read ['lɪpriːd] *vi* von den Lippen ablesen.
lip salve *n* Fettstift *m*.
lip service (*pej*) *n:* **to pay** ~ **to sth** ein
Lippenbekenntnis zu etw ablegen.
lipstick ['lɪpstɪk] *n* Lippenstift *m*.
liquefy ['lɪkwɪfaɪ] *vt* verflüssigen ♦ *vi* sich
verflüssigen.
liqueur [lɪ'kjuə*] *n* Likör *m*.
liquid ['lɪkwɪd] *adj* flüssig ♦ *n* Flüssigkeit *f*.
liquid assets *npl* flüssige Vermögenswerte *pl*.
liquidate ['lɪkwɪdeɪt] *vt* liquidieren.
liquidation [lɪkwɪ'deɪʃən] *n* Liquidation *f*.
liquidation sale (*US*) *n* Verkauf *m* wegen
Geschäftsaufgabe.
liquidator ['lɪkwɪdeɪtə*] *n* Liquidator *m*.
liquid-crystal display ['lɪkwɪd'krɪstl-] *n*
Flüssigkristallanzeige *f*.
liquidity [lɪ'kwɪdɪtɪ] *n* Liquidität *f*.
liquidize ['lɪkwɪdaɪz] *vt* (im Mixer) pürieren.
liquidizer ['lɪkwɪdaɪzə*] *n* Mixer *m*.
liquor ['lɪkə*] *n* Spirituosen *pl*, Alkohol *m*; **hard**
~ harte Drinks *pl*.
liquorice ['lɪkərɪs] (*BRIT*) *n* Lakritze *f*.
liquor store (*US*) *n* Spirituosengeschäft *nt*.
Lisbon ['lɪzbən] *n* Lissabon *nt*.
lisp [lɪsp] *n* Lispeln *nt* ♦ *vi* lispeln.
lissom(e) ['lɪsəm] *adj* geschmeidig.
list [lɪst] *n* Liste *f* ♦ *vt* aufführen; (*COMPUT*)
auflisten; (*write down*) aufschreiben ♦ *vi*
(*ship*) Schlagseite haben.
listed building ['lɪstɪd-] (*BRIT*) *n* unter
Denkmalschutz stehendes Gebäude *nt*.
listed company *n* börsennotierte Firma *f*.
listen ['lɪsn] *vi* hören; **to** ~ **(out) for** horchen
auf +*acc*; **to** ~ **to sb** jdm zuhören; **to** ~ **to sth**

etw hören; ~! hör zu!

listener ['lɪsnə'] n Zuhörer(in) m(f); (*RADIO*) Hörer(in) m(f).

listeria [lɪs'tɪərɪə] n Listeriose f.

listing ['lɪstɪŋ] n Auflistung f; (*entry*) Eintrag m.

listless ['lɪstlɪs] adj lustlos.

listlessly ['lɪstlɪslɪ] adv lustlos.

list price n Listenpreis m.

lit [lɪt] pt, pp of **light**.

litany ['lɪtənɪ] n Litanei f.

liter ['liːtə'] (*US*) n = **litre**.

literacy ['lɪtərəsɪ] n die Fähigkeit, lesen und schreiben zu können.

literacy campaign n Kampagne f gegen das Analphabetentum.

literal ['lɪtərəl] adj wörtlich, eigentlich; (*translation*) (wort)wörtlich.

literally ['lɪtrəlɪ] adv buchstäblich.

literary ['lɪtərərɪ] adj literarisch.

literate ['lɪtərət] adj (*educated*) gebildet; **to be ~** lesen und schreiben können.

literature ['lɪtrɪtʃə'] n Literatur f; (*printed information*) Informationsmaterial nt.

lithe [laɪð] adj gelenkig; (*animal*) geschmeidig.

lithograph ['lɪθəgrɑːf] n Lithographie f.

lithography [lɪ'θɒgrəfɪ] n Lithographie f.

Lithuania [lɪθju'eɪnɪə] n Litauen nt.

Lithuanian [lɪθju'eɪnɪən] adj litauisch ♦ n Litauer(in) m(f); (*LING*) Litauisch nt.

litigation [lɪtɪ'geɪʃən] n Prozeß m.

litmus paper ['lɪtməs-] n Lackmuspapier nt.

litre, (US) liter ['liːtə'] n Liter m or nt.

litter ['lɪtə'] n (*rubbish*) Abfall m; (*young animals*) Wurf m.

litter bin (*BRIT*) n Abfalleimer m.

litterbug ['lɪtəbʌg] n Dreckspatz m.

littered ['lɪtəd] adj: **~ with** (*scattered*) übersät mit.

litter lout n Dreckspatz m.

little ['lɪtl] adj klein; (*short*) kurz ♦ adv wenig; **a ~** ein wenig, ein bißchen; **a ~ bit** ein kleines bißchen; **to have ~ time/money** wenig Zeit/ Geld haben; **~ by ~** nach und nach.

little finger n kleiner Finger m.

little-known ['lɪtl'nəʊn] adj wenig bekannt.

liturgy ['lɪtədʒɪ] n Liturgie f.

live [vi lɪv, adj laɪv] vi leben; (*in house, town*) wohnen ♦ adj lebend; (*TV, RADIO*) live; (*performance, pictures etc*) Live-; (*ELEC*) stromführend; (*bullet, bomb etc*) scharf; **to ~ with sb** mit jdm zusammenleben.

▶**live down** vt hinwegkommen über +acc.

▶**live for** vt leben für.

▶**live in** vi (*student/servant*) im Wohnheim/ Haus wohnen.

▶**live off** vt fus leben von; (*parents etc*) auf Kosten +gen leben.

▶**live on** vt fus leben von.

▶**live out** vi (*BRIT: student/servant*) außerhalb (des Wohnheims/Hauses) wohnen ♦ vt: **to ~ out one's days** or **life** sein Leben

verbringen.

▶**live together** vi zusammenleben.

▶**live up** vt: **to ~ it up** einen draufmachen (*inf*).

▶**live up to** vt fus erfüllen, entsprechen +dat.

live-in ['lɪvɪn] adj (*cook, maid*) im Haus wohnend; **her ~ lover** ihr Freund, der bei ihr wohnt.

livelihood ['laɪvlɪhud] n Lebensunterhalt m.

liveliness ['laɪvlɪnɪs] n (*see adj*) Lebhaftigkeit f; Lebendigkeit f.

lively ['laɪvlɪ] adj lebhaft; (*place, event, book etc*) lebendig.

liven up ['laɪvn-] vt beleben, Leben bringen in +acc; (*person*) aufmuntern ♦ vi (*person*) aufleben; (*discussion, evening etc*) in Schwung kommen.

liver ['lɪvə'] n (*ANAT, CULIN*) Leber f.

liverish ['lɪvərɪʃ] adj: **to be ~** sich unwohl fühlen.

Liverpudlian [lɪvə'pʌdlɪən] adj Liverpooler ♦ n Liverpooler(in) m(f).

livery ['lɪvərɪ] n Livree f.

lives [laɪvz] npl of **life**.

livestock ['laɪvstɒk] n Vieh nt.

live wire (*inf*) n (*person*) Energiebündel nt.

livid ['lɪvɪd] adj (*colour*) bleifarben; (*inf: furious*) fuchsteufelswild.

living ['lɪvɪŋ] adj lebend ♦ n: **to earn** or **make a ~** sich dat seinen Lebensunterhalt verdienen; **within ~ memory** seit Menschengedenken; **the cost of ~** die Lebenshaltungskosten pl.

living conditions npl Wohnverhältnisse pl.

living expenses npl Lebenshaltungskosten pl.

living room n Wohnzimmer nt.

living standards npl Lebensstandard m.

living wage n ausreichender Lohn m.

lizard ['lɪzəd] n Eidechse f.

llama ['lɑːmə] n Lama nt.

LLB n abbr (= *Bachelor of Laws*) akademischer Grad für Juristen.

LLD n abbr (= *Doctor of Laws*) ≈ Dr. jur.

LMT (*US*) abbr (= *Local Mean Time*) Ortszeit.

load [ləud] n Last f; (*of vehicle*) Ladung f; (*weight, ELEC*) Belastung f ♦ vt (also: **~ up**) beladen; (*gun, COMPUT: program, data*) laden; **that's a ~ of rubbish** (*inf*) das ist alles Blödsinn; **~s of, a ~ of** (*fig*) jede Menge; **to ~ a camera** einen Film einlegen.

loaded ['ləudɪd] adj (*inf: rich*) steinreich; (*dice*) präpariert; (*vehicle*): **to be ~ with** beladen sein mit; **a ~ question** eine Fangfrage.

loading bay ['ləudɪŋ-] n Ladeplatz m.

loaf [ləuf] (*pl* **loaves**) n Brot nt, Laib m ♦ vi (also: **~ about, ~ around**) faulenzen; **use your ~!** (*inf*) streng deinen Grips an!

loam [ləum] n Lehmerde f.

loan [ləun] n Darlehen nt ♦ vt: **to ~ sth to sb** jdm etw leihen; **on ~** geliehen.

loan account n Darlehenskonto nt.

loan capital *n* Anleihekapital *nt*.
loan shark (*inf*) *n* Kredithai *m*.
loath [ləuθ] *adj*: **to be ~ to do sth** etw ungern tun.
loathe [ləuð] *vt* verabscheuen.
loathing ['ləuðɪŋ] *n* Abscheu *m*.
loathsome ['ləuðsəm] *adj* abscheulich.
loaves [ləuvz] *npl of* **loaf**.
lob [lɔb] *vt* (*ball*) lobben.
lobby ['lɔbɪ] *n* (*of building*) Eingangshalle *f*; (*POL: pressure group*) Interessenverband *m* ♦ *vt* Einfluß nehmen auf +*acc*.
lobbyist ['lɔbɪɪst] *n* Lobbyist(in) *m(f)*.
lobe [ləub] *n* Ohrläppchen *nt*.
lobster ['lɔbstə*] *n* Hummer *m*.
lobster pot *n* Hummer(fang)korb *m*.
local ['ləukl] *adj* örtlich; (*council*) Stadt-, Gemeinde-; (*paper*) Lokal- ♦ *n* (*pub*) Stammkneipe *f*; **the locals** *npl* (*local inhabitants*) die Einheimischen *pl*.
local anaesthetic *n* örtliche Betäubung *f*.
local authority *n* Gemeindeverwaltung *f*, Stadtverwaltung *f*.
local call *n* Ortsgespräch *nt*.
locale [ləu'kɑːl] *n* Umgebung *f*.
local government *n* Kommunalverwaltung *f*.
locality [ləu'kælɪtɪ] *n* Gegend *f*.
localize ['ləukəlaɪz] *vt* lokalisieren.
locally ['ləukəlɪ] *adv* am Ort.
locate [ləu'keɪt] *vt* (*find*) ausfindig machen; **to be ~d in** sich befinden in +*dat*.
location [ləu'keɪʃən] *n* Ort *m*; (*position*) Lage *f*; (*CINE*) Drehort *m*; **he's on ~ in Mexico** er ist bei Außenaufnahmen in Mexiko; **to be filmed on ~** als Außenaufnahme gedreht werden.
loch [lɔx] (*SCOT*) *n* See *m*.
lock [lɔk] *n* (*of door etc*) Schloß *nt*; (*on canal*) Schleuse *f*; (*also: ~ of hair*) Locke *f* ♦ *vt* (*door etc*) abschließen; (*steering wheel*) sperren; (*COMPUT: keyboard*) verriegeln ♦ *vi* (*door etc*) sich abschließen lassen; (*wheels, mechanism etc*) blockieren; **on full ~** (*AUT*) voll eingeschlagen; **~, stock and barrel** mit allem Drum und Dran; **his jaw ~ed** er hatte Mundsperre.
►**lock away** *vt* wegschließen; (*criminal*) einsperren.
►**lock in** *vt* einschließen.
►**lock out** *vt* aussperren.
►**lock up** *vt* (*criminal etc*) einsperren; (*house*) abschließen ♦ *vi* abschließen.
locker ['lɔkə*] *n* Schließfach *nt*.
locker room *n* Umkleideraum *m*.
locket ['lɔkɪt] *n* Medaillon *nt*.
lockjaw ['lɔkdʒɔː] *n* Wundstarrkrampf *m*.
lockout ['lɔkaut] *n* Aussperrung *f*.
locksmith ['lɔksmɪθ] *n* Schlosser *m*.
lockup ['lɔkʌp] *n* (*US: inf: jail*) Gefängnis *nt*; (*also*: **lock-up garage**) Garage *f*.
locomotive [ləukə'məutɪv] *n* Lokomotive *f*.

locum ['ləukəm] *n* (*MED*) Vertreter(in) *m(f)*.
locust ['ləukəst] *n* Heuschrecke *f*.
lodge [lɔdʒ] *n* Pförtnerhaus *nt*; (*hunting lodge*) Hütte *f*; (*FREEMASONRY*) Loge *f* ♦ *vt* (*complaint, protest etc*) einlegen ♦ *vi* (*bullet*) steckenbleiben; (*person*): **to ~ (with)** zur Untermiete wohnen (bei).
lodger ['lɔdʒə*] *n* Untermieter(in) *m(f)*.
lodging ['lɔdʒɪŋ] *n* Unterkunft *f*.
lodging house *n* Pension *f*.
lodgings ['lɔdʒɪŋz] *npl* möbliertes Zimmer *nt*; (*several rooms*) Wohnung *f*.
loft [lɔft] *n* Boden *m*, Speicher *m*.
lofty ['lɔftɪ] *adj* (*noble*) hoch(fliegend); (*self-important*) hochmütig; (*high*) hoch.
log [lɔg] *n* (*of wood*) Holzblock *m*, Holzklotz *m*; (*written account*) Log *nt* ♦ *n abbr* (*MATH*: = *logarithm*) log ♦ *vt* (ins Logbuch) eintragen.
►**log in** *vi* (*COMPUT*) sich anmelden.
►**log into** *vt fus* (*COMPUT*) sich anmelden bei.
►**log off** *vi* (*COMPUT*) sich abmelden.
►**log on** *vi* (*COMPUT*) = **log in**.
►**log out** *vi* (*COMPUT*) = **log off**.
logarithm ['lɔgərɪðm] *n* Logarithmus *m*.
logbook ['lɔgbuk] *n* (*NAUT*) Logbuch *nt*; (*AVIAT*) Bordbuch *nt*; (*of car*) Kraftfahrzeugbrief *m*; (*of lorry driver*) Fahrtenbuch *nt*; (*of events*) Tagebuch *nt*; (*of movement of goods etc*) Dienstbuch *nt*.
log fire *n* Holzfeuer *nt*.
logger ['lɔgə*] *n* (*lumberjack*) Holzfäller *m*.
loggerheads ['lɔgəhɛdz] *npl*: **to be at ~** Streit haben.
logic ['lɔdʒɪk] *n* Logik *f*.
logical ['lɔdʒɪkl] *adj* logisch.
logically ['lɔdʒɪkəlɪ] *adv* logisch; (*reasonably*) logischerweise.
logistics [lɔ'dʒɪstɪks] *n* Logistik *f*.
log jam *n* (*fig*) Blockierung *f*; **to break the ~** freie Bahn schaffen.
logo ['ləugəu] *n* Logo *nt*.
loin [lɔɪn] *n* Lende *f*.
loincloth ['lɔɪnklɔθ] *n* Lendenschurz *m*.
loiter ['lɔɪtə*] *vi* sich aufhalten.
loll [lɔl] *vi* (*also*: ~ **about**: *person*) herumhängen; (*head*) herunterhängen; (*tongue*) heraushängen.
lollipop ['lɔlɪpɔp] *n* Lutscher *m*.
lollipop lady (*BRIT*) *n* ≈ Schülerlotsin *f*.
lollipop man (*BRIT*) *n* ≈ Schülerlotse *m*.

> **Lollipop Man/Lady** *heißen in Großbritannien die Männer bzw. Frauen, die mit Hilfe eines runden Stoppschildes den Verkehr anhalten, damit Schulkinder die Straße gefahrlos überqueren können. Der Name bezieht sich auf die Form des Schildes, die an einen Lutscher erinnert.*

lollop ['lɔləp] *vi* zockeln.
lolly ['lɔlɪ] (*inf*) *n* (*lollipop*) Lutscher *m*;

(*money*) Mäuse *pl*.
London ['lʌndən] *n* London *nt*.
Londoner ['lʌndənə'] *n* Londoner(in) *m(f)*.
lone [ləun] *adj* einzeln, einsam; (*only*) einzig.
loneliness ['ləunlinis] *n* Einsamkeit *f*.
lonely ['ləunli] *adj* einsam.
lonely hearts *adj*: ~ **ad** Kontaktanzeige *f*; **the**
  ~ **column** die Kontaktanzeigen *pl*.
lone parent *n* Alleinerziehende(r) *f(m)*.
loner ['ləunə'] *n* Einzelgänger(in) *m(f)*.
long [lɒŋ] *adj* lang ♦ *adv* lang(e) ♦ *vi*: **to ~ for**
  sth sich nach etw sehnen; **in the ~ run** auf
  die Dauer; **how ~ is the lesson?** wie lange
  dauert die Stunde?; **6 metres/months ~** 6
  Meter/Monate lang; **so** or **as ~ as** (*on*
  condition that) solange; (*while*) während;
  don't be ~! bleib nicht so lange!; **all night ~**
  die ganze Nacht; **he no ~er comes** er
  kommt nicht mehr; **~ ago** vor langer Zeit;
  ~ before/after vorher/danach; **before**
  ~ bald; **at ~ last** schließlich und endlich;
  the ~ and the short of it is that ... kurz
  gesagt, ...
long-distance [lɒŋ'distəns] *adj* (*travel, phone*
  call) Fern-; (*race*) Langstrecken-.
longevity [lɒn'dʒɛviti] *n* Langlebigkeit *f*.
long-haired ['lɒŋ'hɛəd] *adj* langhaarig;
  (*animal*) Langhaar-.
longhand ['lɒŋhænd] *n* Langschrift *f*.
longing ['lɒŋiŋ] *n* Sehnsucht *f*.
longingly ['lɒŋiŋli] *adv* sehnsüchtig.
longitude ['lɒŋgitjuːd] *n* Länge *f*.
long johns [-dʒɒnz] *npl* lange Unterhose *f*.
long jump *n* Weitsprung *m*.
long-life ['lɒŋlaif] *adj* (*batteries etc*) mit langer
  Lebensdauer; **~ milk** H-Milch *f*.
long-lost ['lɒŋlɒst] *adj* verloren geglaubt.
long-playing record ['lɒŋpleiŋ-] *n*
  Langspielplatte *f*.
long-range ['lɒŋ'reindʒ] *adj* (*plan, forecast*)
  langfristig; (*missile, plane etc*)
  Langstrecken-.
longshoreman ['lɒŋʃɔːmən] (*US*) (*irreg: like*
  man) *n* Hafenarbeiter *m*.
long-sighted ['lɒŋ'saitid] *adj* weitsichtig.
long-standing ['lɒŋ'stændiŋ] *adj* langjährig.
long-suffering [lɒŋ'sʌfəriŋ] *adj* schwer
  geprüft.
long-term ['lɒŋtəːm] *adj* langfristig.
long wave *n* Langwelle *f*.
long-winded [lɒŋ'windid] *adj* umständlich,
  langatmig.
loo [luː] *n* (*BRIT: inf*) Klo *nt*.
loofah ['luːfə] *n* Luffa(schwamm) *m*.
look [luk] *vi* sehen, schauen, gucken (*inf*);
  (*seem, appear*) aussehen ♦ *n* (*glance*) Blick *m*;
  (*appearance*) Aussehen *nt*; (*expression*) Miene
  f; (*FASHION*) Look *m*; **looks** *npl* (*good looks*)
  (gutes) Aussehen; **to ~ (out) onto the sea/**
  south (*building etc*) Blick aufs Meer/nach
  Süden haben; **~ (here)!** (*expressing*
  annoyance) hör (mal) zu!; **~!** (*expressing*

surprise) sieh mal!; **to ~ like sb/sth** wie jd/
  etw aussehen; **it ~s like him** es sieht ihm
  ähnlich; **it ~s about 4 metres long** es
  scheint etwa 4 Meter lang zu sein; **it ~s all**
  right to me es scheint mir in Ordnung zu
  sein; **to ~ ahead** vorausschauen; **to have a**
  ~ at sth sich *dat* etw ansehen; **let me have a**
  ~ laß mich mal sehen; **to have a ~ for sth**
  nach etw suchen.
►**look after** *vt fus* sich kümmern um.
►**look at** *vt fus* ansehen; (*read quickly*)
  durchsehen; (*study, consider*) betrachten.
►**look back** *vi*: **to ~ back (on)** zurückblicken
  (auf +*acc*); **to ~ back at sth/sb** sich nach
  jdm/etw umsehen.
►**look down on** *vt fus* (*fig*) herabsehen auf
  +*acc*.
►**look for** *vt fus* suchen.
►**look forward to** *vt fus* sich freuen auf +*acc*;
  we ~ forward to hearing from you (*in letters*)
  wir hoffen, bald von Ihnen zu hören.
►**look in** *vi*: **to ~ in on sb** bei jdm
  vorbeikommen.
►**look into** *vt fus* (*investigate*) untersuchen.
►**look on** *vi* (*watch*) zusehen.
►**look out** *vi* (*beware*) aufpassen.
►**look out for** *vt fus* Ausschau halten nach.
►**look over** *vt* (*essay etc*) durchsehen; (*house,*
  town etc) sich *dat* ansehen; (*person*) mustern.
►**look round** *vi* sich umsehen.
►**look through** *vt fus* durchsehen.
►**look to** *vt fus* (*rely on*) sich verlassen auf
  +*acc*.
►**look up** *vi* aufsehen; (*situation*) sich bessern
  ♦ *vt* (*word etc*) nachschlagen; **things are ~ing**
  up es geht bergauf.
►**look up to** *vt fus* aufsehen zu.
lookalike ['lukəlaik] *n* Doppelgänger(in) *m(f)*.
look-in ['lukin] *n*: **to get a ~** (*inf*) eine Chance
  haben.
lookout ['lukaut] *n* (*tower etc*) Ausguck *m*;
  (*person*) Wachtposten *m*; **to be on the ~ for**
  sth nach etw Ausschau halten.
loom [luːm] *vi* (*also*: **~ up**: *object, shape*) sich
  abzeichnen; (*event*) näherrücken ♦ *n*
  Webstuhl *m*.
loony ['luːni] (*inf*) *adj* verrückt ♦ *n*
  Verrückte(r) *f(m)*.
loop [luːp] *n* Schlaufe *f*; (*COMPUT*) Schleife *f*
  ♦ *vt*: **to ~ sth around sth** etw um etw
  schlingen.
loophole ['luːphəul] *n* Hintertürchen *nt*; **a ~ in**
  the law eine Lücke im Gesetz.
loose [luːs] *adj* locker, locker; (*clothes etc*) weit;
  (*long hair*) offen; (*not strictly controlled,*
  promiscuous) locker; (*definition*) ungenau;
  (*translation*) frei ♦ *vt* (*animal*) loslassen;
  (*prisoner*) freilassen; (*set off, unleash*)
  entfesseln ♦ *n*: **to be on the ~** frei
  herumlaufen.
loose change *n* Kleingeld *nt*.
loose chippings *npl* Schotter *m*.

loose end n: to be at a ~ or (US) at ~s nichts mit sich dat anzufangen wissen; to tie up ~s die offenstehenden Probleme lösen.

loose-fitting ['luːsfɪtɪŋ] adj weit.

loose-leaf ['luːsliːf] adj Loseblatt-; ~ binder Ringbuch nt.

loose-limbed [luːs'lɪmd] adj gelenkig, beweglich.

loosely ['luːslɪ] adv lose, locker.

loosely-knit ['luːslɪ'nɪt] adj (fig) locker.

loosen ['luːsn] vt lösen, losmachen; (clothing, belt etc) lockern.

loosen up vi (before game) sich auflockern; (relax) auftauen.

loot [luːt] n (inf) Beute f ♦ vt plündern.

looter ['luːtəˀ] n Plünderer m.

looting ['luːtɪŋ] n Plünderung f.

lop off [lɔp-] vt abhacken.

lopsided ['lɔp'saɪdɪd] adj schief.

lord [lɔːd] n (BRIT) Lord m; L~ Smith Lord Smith; the L~ (REL) der Herr; my ~ (to bishop) Exzellenz; (to noble) Mylord; (to judge) Euer Ehren; good L~! ach, du lieber Himmel!; the (House of) L~s (BRIT) das Oberhaus.

lordly ['lɔːdlɪ] adj hochmütig.

lordship ['lɔːdʃɪp] n: your L~ Eure Lordschaft.

lore [lɔːˀ] n Überlieferungen pl.

lorry ['lɔrɪ] (BRIT) n Lastwagen m, Lkw m.

lorry driver (BRIT) n Lastwagenfahrer m.

lose [luːz] (pt, pp lost) vt verlieren; (opportunity) verpassen; (pursuers) abschütteln ♦ vi verlieren; to ~ (time) (clock) nachgehen; to ~ weight abnehmen; to ~ 5 pounds 5 Pfund abnehmen; to ~ sight of sth (also fig) etw aus den Augen verlieren.

loser ['luːzəˀ] n Verlierer(in) m(f); (inf: failure) Versager m; to be a good/bad ~ ein guter/schlechter Verlierer sein.

loss [lɔs] n Verlust m; to make a ~ (of £1,000) (1000 Pfund) Verlust machen; to sell sth at a ~ etw mit Verlust verkaufen; heavy ~es schwere Verluste pl; to cut one's ~es aufgeben, bevor es noch schlimmer wird; to be at a ~ nicht mehr weiterwissen.

loss adjuster n Schadenssachverständige(r) f(m).

loss leader n (COMM) Lockvogelangebot nt.

lost [lɔst] pt, pp of lose ♦ adj (person, animal) vermißt; (object) verloren; to be ~ sich verlaufen/verfahren haben; to get ~ sich verlaufen/verfahren; get ~! (inf) verschwinde!; ~ in thought in Gedanken verloren.

lost and found (US) n = lost property.

lost cause n aussichtslose Sache f.

lost property (BRIT) n Fundsachen pl; (also: ~ office) Fundbüro nt.

lot [lɔt] n (kind) Art f; (group) Gruppe f; (at auctions, destiny) Los nt; to draw ~s losen, Lose ziehen; the ~ alles; a ~ (of) (a large number (of)) viele; (a great deal (of)) viel; ~s of viele; I read a ~ ich lese viel; this happens a ~ das kommt oft vor.

loth [ləʊθ] adj = loath.

lotion ['ləʊʃən] n Lotion f.

lottery ['lɔtərɪ] n Lotterie f.

loud [laud] adj laut; (clothes) schreiend ♦ adv laut; to be ~ in one's support of sb/sth jdn/etw lautstark unterstützen; out ~ (read, laugh etc) laut.

loud-hailer [laud'heɪləˀ] (BRIT) n Megaphon nt.

loudly ['laudlɪ] adv laut.

loudmouthed ['laudmauθt] adj großmäulig.

loudspeaker [laud'spiːkəˀ] n Lautsprecher m.

lounge [laundʒ] n (in house) Wohnzimmer nt; (in hotel) Lounge f; (at airport, station) Wartehalle f; (BRIT: also: ~ bar) Salon m ♦ vi faulenzen.

▶**lounge about** vi herumliegen, herumsitzen, herumstehen.

▶**lounge around** vi = lounge about.

lounge suit (BRIT) n Straßenanzug m.

louse [laus] (pl lice) n Laus f.

▶**louse up** (inf) vt vermasseln.

lousy ['lauzɪ] (inf) adj (bad-quality) lausig, mies; (despicable) fies, gemein; (ill): to feel ~ sich miserabel or elend fühlen.

lout [laut] n Lümmel m, Flegel m.

louvre, (US) **louver** ['luːvəˀ] adj (door, window) Lamellen-.

lovable ['lʌvəbl] adj liebenswert.

love [lʌv] n Liebe f ♦ vt lieben; (thing, activity etc) gern mögen; "~ (from) Anne" (on letter) „mit herzlichen Grüßen, Anne"; to be in ~ with verliebt sein in +acc; to fall in ~ with sich verlieben in +acc; to make ~ sich lieben; ~ at first sight Liebe auf den ersten Blick; to send one's ~ to sb jdn grüßen lassen; "fifteen ~" (TENNIS) „fünfzehn null"; to ~ doing sth etw gern tun; I'd ~ to come ich würde sehr gerne kommen; I ~ chocolate ich esse Schokolade liebend gern.

love affair n Verhältnis nt, Liebschaft f.

love child n uneheliches Kind nt, Kind nt der Liebe.

loved ones ['lʌvdwʌnz] npl enge Freunde und Verwandte pl.

love-hate relationship ['lʌvheɪt-] n Haßliebe f.

love letter n Liebesbrief m.

love life n Liebesleben nt.

lovely ['lʌvlɪ] adj (beautiful) schön; (delightful) herrlich; (person) sehr nett.

lover ['lʌvəˀ] n Geliebte(r) f(m); (person in love) Liebende(r) f(m); ~ of art/music Kunst-/Musikliebhaber(in) m(f); to be ~s ein Liebespaar sein.

lovesick ['lʌvsɪk] adj liebeskrank.

love song n Liebeslied nt.

loving ['lʌvɪŋ] adj liebend; (actions) liebevoll.

low [ləu] *adj* niedrig; (*bow, curtsey*) tief; (*quality*) schlecht; (*sound: deep*) tief; (: *quiet*) leise; (*depressed*) niedergeschlagen, bedrückt ♦ *adv* (*sing*) leise; (*fly*) tief ♦ *n* (*MET*) Tief *nt*; **to be/run** ~ knapp sein/ werden; **sb is running** ~ **on sth** jdm wird etw knapp; **to reach a new** *or* **an all-time** ~ einen neuen Tiefstand erreichen.

low-alcohol ['ləu'ælkəhɔl] *adj* alkoholarm.

lowbrow ['ləubrau] *adj* (geistig) anspruchslos.

low-calorie ['ləu'kælərɪ] *adj* kalorienarm.

low-cut ['ləukʌt] *adj* (*dress*) tief ausgeschnitten.

lowdown ['ləudaun] (*inf*) *n*: **he gave me the** ~ **on it** er hat mich darüber informiert.

lower ['ləuə*] *adj* untere(r, s); (*lip, jaw, arm*) Unter- ♦ *vt* senken.

low-fat ['ləu'fæt] *adj* fettarm.

low-key ['ləu'kiː] *adj* zurückhaltend; (*not obvious*) unaufdringlich.

lowlands ['ləuləndz] *npl* Flachland *nt*.

low-level language ['ləulɛvl-] *n* (*COMPUT*) niedere Programmiersprache *f*.

low-loader ['ləu'ləudə*] *n* Tieflader *m*.

lowly ['ləulɪ] *adj* (*position*) niedrig; (*origin*) bescheiden.

low-lying [ləu'laɪɪŋ] *adj* tiefgelegen.

low-paid [ləu'peɪd] *adj* schlechtbezahlt.

low-rise ['ləuraɪz] *adj* niedrig (gebaut).

low-tech ['ləutɛk] *adj* nicht mit Hi-Tech ausgestattet.

loyal ['lɔɪəl] *adj* treu; (*support*) loyal.

loyalist ['lɔɪəlɪst] *n* Loyalist(in) *m(f)*.

loyalty ['lɔɪəltɪ] *n* (*see adj*) Treue *f*; Loyalität *f*.

lozenge ['lɔzɪndʒ] *n* Pastille *f*; (*shape*) Raute *f*.

LP *n abbr* (= *long player*) LP *f*; *see also* **long-playing record**.

Als **L-Plates** werden in Großbritannien die weißen Schilder mit einem roten 'L' bezeichnet, die vorne und hinten an jedem von einem Fahrschüler geführten Fahrzeug befestigt werden müssen. Fahrschüler müssen einen vorläufigen Führerschein beantragen und dürfen damit unter der Aufsicht eines erfahrenen Autofahrers auf allen Straßen außer Autobahnen fahren.

LPN (*US*) *n abbr* (= *Licensed Practical Nurse*) staatlich anerkannte Krankenschwester *f*, staatlich anerkannter Krankenpfleger *m*.

LRAM (*BRIT*) *n abbr* (= *Licentiate of the Royal Academy of Music*) Qualifikationsnachweis in Musik.

LSAT (*US*) *n abbr* (= *Law School Admission Test*) Zulassungsprüfung für juristische Hochschulen.

LSD *n abbr* (= *lysergic acid diethylamide*) LSD *nt*; (*BRIT: also*: **L.S.D.** = *pounds, shillings and pence*) früheres britisches Währungssystem.

LSE (*BRIT*) *n abbr* (= *London School of Economics*) Londoner Wirtschaftshochschule.

LT *abbr* (*ELEC*: = *low-tension*) Niederspannung *f*; (*cable etc*) Niederspannungs-.

Lt *abbr* (*MIL*: = *lieutenant*) Lt.

Ltd *abbr* (*COMM*: = *limited (liability)*) ≈ GmbH *f*.

lubricant ['luːbrɪkənt] *n* Schmiermittel *nt*.

lubricate ['luːbrɪkeɪt] *vt* schmieren, ölen.

lucid ['luːsɪd] *adj* klar; (*person*) bei klarem Verstand.

lucidity [luːˈsɪdɪtɪ] *n* Klarheit *f*.

luck [lʌk] *n* (*esp good luck*) Glück *nt*; **bad** ~ Unglück *nt*; **good** ~! viel Glück!; **bad** *or* **hard** *or* **tough** ~! so ein Pech!; **hard** *or* **tough** ~! (*showing no sympathy*) Pech gehabt!; **to be in** ~ Glück haben; **to be out of** ~ kein Glück haben.

luckily ['lʌkɪlɪ] *adv* glücklicherweise.

luckless ['lʌklɪs] *adj* glücklos.

lucky ['lʌkɪ] *adj* (*situation, event*) glücklich; (*object*) glücksbringend; (*person*): **to be** ~ Glück haben; **to have a** ~ **escape** noch einmal davonkommen; ~ **charm** Glücksbringer *m*.

lucrative ['luːkrətɪv] *adj* einträglich.

ludicrous ['luːdɪkrəs] *adj* grotesk.

ludo ['luːdəu] *n* Mensch, ärgere dich nicht *nt*.

lug [lʌg] (*inf*) *vt* schleppen.

luggage ['lʌgɪdʒ] *n* Gepäck *nt*.

luggage car (*US*) *n* = **luggage van**.

luggage rack *n* Gepäckträger *m*; (*in train*) Gepäckablage *f*.

luggage van (*BRIT*) *n* (*RAIL*) Gepäckwagen *m*.

lugubrious [luˈguːbrɪəs] *adj* schwermütig.

lukewarm ['luːkwɔːm] *adj* lauwarm; (*fig: person, reaction etc*) lau.

lull [lʌl] *n* Pause *f* ♦ *vt*: **to** ~ **sb to sleep** jdn einlullen *or* einschläfern; **to be** ~**ed into a false sense of security** in trügerische Sicherheit gewiegt werden.

lullaby ['lʌləbaɪ] *n* Schlaflied *nt*.

lumbago [lʌmˈbeɪgəu] *n* Hexenschuß *m*.

lumber ['lʌmbə*] *n* (*wood*) Holz *nt*; (*junk*) Gerümpel *nt* ♦ *vi*: **to** ~ **about/along** herum-/entlangtapsen.

▶**lumber with** *vt*: **to be/get** ~**ed with sth** etw am Hals haben/aufgehalst bekommen.

lumberjack ['lʌmbədʒæk] *n* Holzfäller *m*.

lumber room (*BRIT*) *n* Rumpelkammer *f*.

lumberyard ['lʌmbəjɑːd] (*US*) *n* Holzlager *nt*.

luminous ['luːmɪnəs] *adj* leuchtend, Leucht-.

lump [lʌmp] *n* Klumpen *m*; (*on body*) Beule *f*; (*in breast*) Knoten *m*; (*also*: **sugar** ~) Stück *nt* (Zucker) ♦ *vt*: **to** ~ **together** in einen Topf werfen; **a** ~ **sum** eine Pauschalsumme.

lumpy ['lʌmpɪ] *adj* klumpig.

lunacy ['luːnəsɪ] *n* Wahnsinn *m*.

lunar ['luːnə*] *adj* Mond-.

lunatic ['luːnətɪk] *adj* wahnsinnig ♦ *n* Wahnsinnige(r) *f(m)*, Irre(r) *f(m)*.

lunatic asylum *n* Irrenanstalt *f*.

lunatic fringe *n*: **the** ~ die Extremisten *pl*.

lunch [lʌntʃ] n Mittagessen nt; (time)
Mittagszeit f ♦ vi zu Mittag essen.
lunch break n Mittagspause f.
luncheon ['lʌntʃən] n Mittagessen nt.
luncheon meat n Frühstücksfleisch nt.
luncheon voucher (BRIT) n Essensmarke f.
lunch hour n Mittagspause f.
lunch time n Mittagszeit f.
lung [lʌŋ] n Lunge f.
lunge [lʌndʒ] vi (also: ~ forward) sich nach
vorne stürzen; **to ~ at** sich stürzen auf +acc.
lupin ['luːpɪn] n Lupine f.
lurch [lɜːtʃ] vi ruckeln; (person) taumeln ♦ n
Ruck m; (of person) Taumeln nt; **to leave sb
in the ~** jdn im Stich lassen.
lure [luə*] n Verlockung f ♦ vt locken.
lurid ['luərɪd] adj (story etc) reißerisch; (pej:
brightly coloured) grell, in grellen Farben.
lurk [lɜːk] vi (also fig) lauern.
luscious ['lʌʃəs] adj (attractive) phantastisch;
(food) köstlich, lecker.
lush [lʌʃ] adj (fields) saftig; (gardens) üppig;
(luxurious) luxuriös.
lust [lʌst] (pej) n (sexual) (sinnliche) Begierde
f; (for money, power etc) Gier f.
▶**lust after** vt fus (sexually) begehren; (crave)
gieren nach.
▶**lust for** vt fus = lust after.
lustful ['lʌstful] adj lüstern.
lustre, (US) **luster** ['lʌstə*] n Schimmer m,
Glanz m.
lusty ['lʌstɪ] adj gesund und munter.
lute [luːt] n Laute f.
luvvie, luvvy ['lʌvɪ] (inf) n Schätzchen nt.
Luxembourg ['lʌksəmbɜːg] n Luxemburg nt.
luxuriant [lʌg'zjuərɪənt] adj üppig.
luxuriate [lʌg'zjuərɪeɪt] vi: **to ~ in sth** sich in
etw dat aalen.
luxurious [lʌg'zjuərɪəs] adj luxuriös.
luxury ['lʌkʃərɪ] n Luxus m (no pl) ♦ cpd (hotel,
car etc) Luxus-; **little luxuries** kleine
Genüsse.
LV n abbr = luncheon voucher.
LW abbr (RADIO: = long wave) LW.
Lycra ® ['laɪkrə] n Lycra nt.
lying ['laɪɪŋ] n Lügen nt ♦ adj verlogen.
lynch [lɪntʃ] vt lynchen.
lynx [lɪŋks] n Luchs m.
lyric ['lɪrɪk] adj lyrisch.
lyrical ['lɪrɪkl] adj lyrisch; (fig: praise etc)
schwärmerisch.
lyricism ['lɪrɪsɪzəm] n Lyrik f.
lyrics ['lɪrɪks] npl (of song) Text m.

M, m

M¹, m¹ [ɛm] n (letter) M nt, m nt; **~ for Mary,**
(US) **~ for Mike** ≈ M wie Martha.
M² [ɛm] n abbr (BRIT: = motorway): **the M8**
≈ die A8 ♦ abbr = medium.
m² abbr (= metre) m; = mile; (= million) Mio.
MA n abbr (= Master of Arts) akademischer
Grad für Geisteswissenschaftler; (= military
academy) Militärakademie f ♦ abbr (US:
POST: = Massachusetts).
mac [mæk] (BRIT) n Regenmantel m.
macabre [mə'kɑːbrə] adj makaber.
macaroni [mækə'rəʊnɪ] n Makkaroni pl.
macaroon [mækə'ruːn] n Makrone f.
mace [meɪs] n (weapon) Keule f; (ceremonial)
Amtsstab m; (spice) Muskatblüte f.
Macedonia [mæsɪ'dəʊnɪə] n Makedonien nt.
Macedonian [mæsɪ'dəʊnɪən] adj makedonisch
♦ n Makedonier(in) m(f); (LING)
Makedonisch nt.
machinations [mækɪ'neɪʃənz] npl
Machenschaften pl.
machine [mə'ʃiːn] n Maschine f; (fig: party
machine etc) Apparat m ♦ vt (TECH)
maschinell herstellen or bearbeiten; (dress
etc) mit der Maschine nähen.
machine code n Maschinencode m.
machine gun n Maschinengewehr nt.
machine language n Maschinensprache f.
machine-readable [mə'ʃiːnriːdəbl] adj
maschinenlesbar.
machinery [mə'ʃiːnərɪ] n Maschinen pl; (fig: of
government) Apparat m.
machine shop n Maschinensaal m.
machine tool n Werkzeugmaschine f.
machine washable adj waschmaschinen-
fest.
machinist [mə'ʃiːnɪst] n Maschinist(in) m(f).
macho ['mætʃəʊ] adj Macho-; **a ~ man** ein
Macho m.
mackerel ['mækrl] n inv Makrele f.
mackintosh ['mækɪntɔʃ] (BRIT) n
Regenmantel m.
macro... ['mækrəʊ] pref Makro-, makro-.
macroeconomics ['mækrəʊiːkə'nɒmɪks] npl
Makroökonomie f.
mad [mæd] adj wahnsinnig, verrückt; (angry)
böse, sauer (inf); **to be ~ about** verrückt
sein auf +acc; **to be ~ at sb** böse or sauer auf
jdn sein; **to go ~** (insane) verrückt or
wahnsinnig werden; (angry) böse or sauer
werden.
madam ['mædəm] n gnädige Frau f; **yes, ~**

ja(wohl); **M~ Chairman** Frau Vorsitzende.
madcap ['mædkæp] *adj (idea)* versponnen; *(tricks)* toll.
mad cow disease *n* Rinderwahn *m*.
madden ['mædn] *vt* ärgern, fuchsen *(inf)*.
maddening ['mædnɪŋ] *adj* unerträglich.
made [meɪd] *pt, pp of* **make**.
Madeira [mə'dɪərə] *n* Madeira *nt*; *(wine)* Madeira *m*.
made-to-measure ['meɪdtə'mɛʒə'] *(BRIT) adj* maßgeschneidert.
madhouse ['mædhaus] *n (also fig)* Irrenhaus *nt*.
madly ['mædlɪ] *adv* wie verrückt; ~ **in love** bis über beide Ohren verliebt.
madman ['mædmən] *(irreg: like* **man***) n* Verrückte(r) *m*, Irre(r) *m*.
madness ['mædnɪs] *n* Wahnsinn *m*.
Madrid [mə'drɪd] *n* Madrid *nt*.
Mafia ['mæfɪə] *n* Mafia *f*.
mag [mæg] *(BRIT: inf) n abbr* = **magazine**.
magazine [mægə'ziːn] *n* Zeitschrift *f*; *(RADIO, TV, of firearm)* Magazin *nt*; *(MIL: store)* Depot *nt*.
maggot ['mægət] *n* Made *f*.
magic ['mædʒɪk] *n* Magie *f*; *(conjuring)* Zauberei *f* ♦ *adj* magisch; *(formula)* Zauber-; *(fig: place, moment etc)* zauberhaft.
magical ['mædʒɪkl] *adj* magisch; *(experience, evening)* zauberhaft.
magician [mə'dʒɪʃən] *n (wizard)* Magier *m*; *(conjurer)* Zauberer *m*.
magistrate ['mædʒɪstreɪt] *n* Friedensrichter(in) *m(f)*.
magnanimous [mæg'nænɪməs] *adj* großmütig.
magnate ['mægneɪt] *n* Magnat *m*.
magnesium [mæg'niːzɪəm] *n* Magnesium *nt*.
magnet ['mægnɪt] *n* Magnet *m*.
magnetic [mæg'nɛtɪk] *adj* magnetisch; *(field, compass, pole etc)* Magnet-; *(personality)* anziehend.
magnetic disk *n (COMPUT)* Magnetplatte *f*.
magnetic tape *n* Magnetband *nt*.
magnetism ['mægnɪtɪzəm] *n* Magnetismus *m*; *(of person)* Anziehungskraft *f*.
magnetize ['mægnɪtaɪz] *vt* magnetisieren.
magnification [mægnɪfɪ'keɪʃən] *n* Vergrößerung *f*.
magnificence [mæg'nɪfɪsns] *n* Großartigkeit *f*; *(of robes)* Pracht *f*.
magnificent [mæg'nɪfɪsnt] *adj* großartig; *(robes)* prachtvoll.
magnify ['mægnɪfaɪ] *vt* vergrößern; *(sound)* verstärken; *(fig: exaggerate)* aufbauschen.
magnifying glass ['mægnɪfaɪɪŋ-] *n* Vergrößerungsglas *nt*, Lupe *f*.
magnitude ['mægnɪtjuːd] *n (size)* Ausmaß *nt*, Größe *f*; *(importance)* Bedeutung *f*.
magnolia [mæg'nəʊlɪə] *n* Magnolie *f*.
magpie ['mægpaɪ] *n* Elster *f*.
mahogany [mə'hɔgənɪ] *n* Mahagoni *nt* ♦ *cpd* Mahagoni-.

maid [meɪd] *n* Dienstmädchen *nt*; **old** ~ *(pej)* alte Jungfer.
maiden ['meɪdn] *n (liter)* Mädchen *nt* ♦ *adj* unverheiratet; *(speech, voyage)* Jungfern-.
maiden name *n* Mädchenname *m*.
mail [meɪl] *n* Post *f* ♦ *vt* aufgeben; **by** ~ mit der Post.
mailbox ['meɪlbɔks] *n (US)* Briefkasten *m*; *(COMPUT)* Mailbox *f*, elektronischer Briefkasten *m*.
mailing list ['meɪlɪŋ-] *n* Anschriftenliste *f*.
mailman ['meɪlmæn] *(US: irreg: like* **man***) n* Briefträger *m*, Postbote *m*.
mail order *n (system)* Versand *m* ♦ *cpd*: **mail-order firm** *or* **business** Versandhaus *nt*; **mail-order catalogue** Versandhauskatalog *m*; **by** ~ durch Bestellung per Post.
mailshot ['meɪlʃɔt] *(BRIT) n* Werbebrief *m*.
mail train *n* Postzug *m*.
mail truck *(US) n* Postauto *nt*.
mail van *(BRIT) n (AUT)* Postauto *nt*; *(RAIL)* Postwagen *m*.
maim [meɪm] *vt* verstümmeln.
main [meɪn] *adj* Haupt-, wichtigste(r, s); *(door, entrance, meal)* Haupt- ♦ *n* Hauptleitung *f*; **the mains** *npl (ELEC)* das Stromnetz; *(gas, water)* die Hauptleitung; **in the** ~ im großen und ganzen.
main course *n (CULIN)* Hauptgericht *nt*.
mainframe ['meɪnfreɪm] *n (COMPUT)* Großrechner *m*.
mainland ['meɪnlənd] *n* Festland *nt*.
mainline ['meɪnlaɪn] *adj*: ~ **station** Fernbahnhof *m* ♦ *vt (drugs slang)* spritzen ♦ *vi (drugs slang)* fixen.
main line *n* Hauptstrecke *f*.
mainly ['meɪnlɪ] *adv* hauptsächlich.
main road *n* Hauptstraße *f*.
mainstay ['meɪnsteɪ] *n (foundation)* (wichtigste) Stütze *f*; *(chief constituent)* Hauptbestandteil *m*.
mainstream ['meɪnstriːm] *n* Hauptrichtung *f* ♦ *adj (cinema etc)* populär; *(politics)* der Mitte.
maintain [meɪn'teɪn] *vt (preserve)* aufrechterhalten; *(keep up)* beibehalten; *(provide for)* unterhalten; *(look after: building)* instand halten; *(: equipment)* warten; *(affirm: opinion)* vertreten; *(: innocence)* beteuern; **to** ~ **that ...** behaupten, daß ...
maintenance ['meɪntənəns] *n (of building)* Instandhaltung *f*; *(of equipment)* Wartung *f*; *(preservation)* Aufrechterhaltung *f*; *(LAW: alimony)* Unterhalt *m*.
maintenance contract *n* Wartungsvertrag *m*.
maintenance order *n (LAW)* Unterhaltsurteil *nt*.
maisonette [meɪzə'nɛt] *(BRIT) n* Maisonettewohnung *f*.
maize [meɪz] *n* Mais *m*.
Maj. *abbr (MIL)* = **major**.

majestic [mə'dʒɛstɪk] adj erhaben.
majesty ['mædʒɪstɪ] n (title): **Your M~** Eure
Majestät; (splendour) Erhabenheit f.
major ['meɪdʒə*] n Major m ♦ adj bedeutend;
(MUS) Dur ♦ vi (US): **to ~ in French**
Französisch als Hauptfach belegen; **a
~ operation** eine größere Operation.
Majorca [mə'jɔːkə] n Mallorca nt.
major general n Generalmajor m.
majority [mə'dʒɔrɪtɪ] n Mehrheit f ♦ cpd
(verdict, holding) Mehrheits-.
make [meɪk] (pt, pp **made**) vt machen; (clothes)
nähen; (cake) backen; (speech) halten;
(manufacture) herstellen; (earn) verdienen;
(cause to be): **to ~ sb sad** jdn traurig
machen; (force): **to ~ sb do sth** jdn zwingen,
etw zu tun; (cause) jdn dazu bringen, etw zu
tun; (equal): **2 and 2 ~ 4** 2 und 2 ist or macht
4 ♦ n Marke f, Fabrikat nt; **to ~ a fool of sb**
jdn lächerlich machen; **to ~ a profit/loss**
Gewinn/Verlust machen; **to ~ it** (arrive) es
schaffen; (succeed) Erfolg haben; **what time
do you ~ it?** wie spät hast du?; **to ~ good**
erfolgreich sein; (threat) wahrmachen;
(promise) einlösen; (damage)
wiedergutmachen; (loss) ersetzen; **to ~ do
with** auskommen mit.
▶**make for** vt fus (place) zuhalten auf +acc.
▶**make off** vi sich davonmachen.
▶**make out** vt (decipher) entziffern;
(understand) verstehen; (see) ausmachen;
(write: cheque) ausstellen; (claim, imply)
behaupten; (pretend) so tun, als ob; **to ~ out
a case for sth** für etw argumentieren.
▶**make over** vt: **to ~ over (to)** überschreiben
(+dat).
▶**make up** vt (constitute) bilden; (invent)
erfinden; (prepare: bed) zurechtmachen;
(: parcel) zusammenpacken ♦ vi (after quarrel)
sich versöhnen; (with cosmetics) sich
schminken; **to ~ up one's mind** sich
entscheiden; **to be made up of** bestehen
aus.
▶**make up for** vt fus (loss) ersetzen;
(disappointment etc) ausgleichen.
make-believe ['meɪkbɪliːv] n Phantasie f; **a
world of ~** eine Phantasiewelt; **it's just ~** es
ist nicht wirklich.
maker ['meɪkə*] n Hersteller m; **film ~**
Filmemacher(in) m(f).
makeshift ['meɪkʃɪft] adj behelfsmäßig.
make-up ['meɪkʌp] n Make-up nt, Schminke f.
make-up bag n Kosmetiktasche f.
make-up remover n Make-up-Entferner m.
making ['meɪkɪŋ] n (fig): **in the ~** im
Entstehen; **to have the ~s of** das Zeug
haben zu.
maladjusted [mælə'dʒʌstɪd] adj
verhaltensgestört.
maladroit [mælə'drɔɪt] adj ungeschickt.
malaise [mæ'leɪz] n Unbehagen nt.
malaria [mə'lɛərɪə] n Malaria f.

Malawi [mə'lɑːwɪ] n Malawi nt.
Malay [mə'leɪ] adj malaiisch ♦ n Malaie m,
Malaiin f; (LING) Malaiisch nt.
Malaya [mə'leɪə] n Malaya nt.
Malayan [mə'leɪən] adj, n = **Malay**.
Malaysia [mə'leɪzɪə] n Malaysia nt.
Malaysian [mə'leɪzɪən] adj malaysisch ♦ n
Malaysier(in) m(f).
Maldives ['mɔːldaɪvz] npl Malediven pl.
male [meɪl] n (animal) Männchen nt; (man)
Mann m ♦ adj männlich; (ELEC): ~ **plug**
Stecker m; **because he is ~** weil er ein
Mann/Junge ist; ~ **and female students**
Studenten und Studentinnen; **a ~ child** ein
Junge.
male chauvinist n Chauvinist m.
male nurse n Krankenpfleger m.
malevolence [mə'lɛvələns] n Boshaftigkeit f;
(of action) Böswilligkeit f.
malevolent [mə'lɛvələnt] adj boshaft;
(intention) böswillig.
malfunction [mæl'fʌŋkʃən] n (of computer)
Funktionsstörung f; (of machine) Defekt m
♦ vi (computer) eine Funktionsstörung
haben; (machine) defekt sein.
malice ['mælɪs] n Bosheit f.
malicious [mə'lɪʃəs] adj boshaft; (LAW)
böswillig.
malign [mə'laɪn] vt verleumden ♦ adj
(influence) schlecht; (interpretation)
böswillig.
malignant [mə'lɪgnənt] adj bösartig;
(intention) böswillig.
malingerer [mə'lɪŋgərə*] n Simulant(in) m(f).
mall [mɔːl] n (also: **shopping ~**)
Einkaufszentrum nt.
malleable ['mælɪəbl] adj (lit, fig) formbar.
mallet ['mælɪt] n Holzhammer m.
malnutrition [mælnjuː'trɪʃən] n
Unterernährung f.
malpractice [mæl'præktɪs] n Berufsvergehen
nt.
malt [mɔːlt] n Malz nt; (also: ~ **whisky**) Malt
Whisky m.
Malta ['mɔːltə] n Malta nt.
Maltese [mɔːl'tiːz] adj maltesisch ♦ n inv
Malteser(in) m(f); (LING) Maltesisch nt.
maltreat [mæl'triːt] vt schlecht behandeln;
(violently) mißhandeln.
mammal ['mæml] n Säugetier nt.
mammoth ['mæməθ] n Mammut nt ♦ adj (task)
Mammut-.
man [mæn] (pl **men**) n Mann m; (mankind) der
Mensch, die Menschen pl; (CHESS) Figur f
♦ vt (ship) bemannen; (gun, machine)
bedienen; (post) besetzen; ~ **and wife** Mann
und Frau.
manage ['mænɪdʒ] vi: **to ~ to do sth** es
schaffen, etw zu tun; (get by financially)
zurechtkommen ♦ vt (business, organization)
leiten; (control) zurechtkommen mit; **to
~ without sb/sth** ohne jdn/etw auskommen;

well ~**d** (*business, shop etc*) gut geführt.
manageable ['mænɪdʒəbl] *adj* (*task*) zu
bewältigen; (*number*) überschaubar.
management ['mænɪdʒmənt] *n* Leitung *f*,
Führung *f*; (*persons*) Unternehmensleitung *f*;
"under new ~**"** „unter neuer Leitung".
management accounting *n* Kosten- und
Leistungsrechnung *f*.
management consultant *n* Unternehmens-
berater(in) *m(f)*.
manager ['mænɪdʒə*] *n* (*of business*)
Geschäftsführer(in) *m(f)*; (*of institution etc*)
Direktor(in) *m(f)*; (*of department*) Leiter(in)
m(f); (*of pop star*) Manager(in) *m(f)*; (*SPORT*)
Trainer(in) *m(f)*; **sales** ~ Verkaufsleiter(in)
m(f).
manageress [mænɪdʒə'rɛs] *n* (*of shop,
business*) Geschäftsführerin *f*; (*of office,
department etc*) Leiterin *f*.
managerial [mænɪ'dʒɪərɪəl] *adj* (*role, post*)
leitend; (*decisions*) geschäftlich; ~ **staff/
skills** Führungskräfte *pl*/-qualitäten *pl*.
managing director ['mænɪdʒɪŋ-] *n*
Geschäftsführer(in) *m(f)*.
Mancunian [mæŋ'kju:nɪən] *n* Bewohner(in)
m(f) Manchesters.
mandarin ['mændərɪn] *n* (*also:* ~ **orange**)
Mandarine *f*; (*official: Chinese*) Mandarin *m*;
(: *gen*) Funktionär *m*.
mandate ['mændeɪt] *n* Mandat *nt*; (*task*)
Auftrag *m*.
mandatory ['mændətərɪ] *adj* obligatorisch.
mandolin(e) ['mændəlɪn] *n* Mandoline *f*.
mane [meɪn] *n* Mähne *f*.
maneuver *etc* [mə'nu:və*] (*US*) = **manoeuvre**
etc.
manfully ['mænfəlɪ] *adv* mannhaft, beherzt.
manganese [mæŋgə'ni:z] *n* Mangan *nt*.
mangetout ['mɔnʒ'tu:] (*BRIT*) *n* Zuckererbse
f.
mangle ['mæŋgl] *vt* (übel) zurichten ♦ *n*
Mangel *f*.
mango ['mæŋgəu] (*pl* ~**es**) *n* Mango *f*.
mangrove ['mæŋgrəuv] *n* Mangrove(n)baum
m.
mangy ['meɪndʒɪ] *adj* (*animal*) räudig.
manhandle ['mænhændl] *vt* (*mistreat*) grob
behandeln; (*move by hand*) (von Hand)
befördern.
manhole ['mænhəul] *n* Kanalschacht *m*.
manhood ['mænhud] *n* Mannesalter *nt*.
man-hour ['mænauə*] *n* Arbeitsstunde *f*.
manhunt ['mænhʌnt] *n* Fahndung *f*.
mania ['meɪnɪə] *n* Manie *f*; (*craze*) Sucht *f*;
persecution ~ Verfolgungswahn *m*.
maniac ['meɪnɪæk] *n* Wahnsinnige(r) *f(m)*,
Verrückte(r) *f(m)*; (*fig*) Fanatiker(in) *m(f)*.
manic ['mænɪk] *adj* (*behaviour*) manisch;
(*activity*) rasend.
manic-depressive ['mænɪkdɪ'prɛsɪv] *n*
Manisch-Depressive(r) *f(m)* ♦ *adj* manisch-
depressiv.

manicure ['mænɪkjuə*] *n* Maniküre *f* ♦ *vt*
maniküren.
manicure set *n* Nageletui *nt*, Maniküreetui
nt.
manifest ['mænɪfɛst] *vt* zeigen, bekunden
♦ *adj* offenkundig ♦ *n* Manifest *nt*.
manifestation [mænɪfɛs'teɪʃən] *n* Anzeichen
nt.
manifesto [mænɪ'fɛstəu] *n* Manifest *nt*.
manifold ['mænɪfəuld] *adj* vielfältig ♦ *n*:
exhaust ~ Auspuffkrümmer *m*.
Manila [mə'nɪlə] *n* Manila *nt*.
manila [mə'nɪlə] *adj*: ~ **envelope** brauner
Briefumschlag *m*.
manipulate [mə'nɪpjuleɪt] *vt* manipulieren.
manipulation [mənɪpju'leɪʃən] *n*
Manipulation *f*.
mankind [mæn'kaɪnd] *n* Menschheit *f*.
manliness ['mænlɪnɪs] *n* Männlichkeit *f*.
manly ['mænlɪ] *adj* männlich.
man-made ['mæn'meɪd] *adj* künstlich; (*fibre*)
synthetisch.
manna ['mænə] *n* Manna *nt*.
mannequin ['mænɪkɪn] *n* (*dummy*)
Schaufensterpuppe *f*; (*fashion model*)
Mannequin *nt*.
manner ['mænə*] *n* (*way*) Art *f*, Weise *f*;
(*behaviour*) Art *f*; (*type, sort*): **all** ~ **of things**
die verschiedensten Dinge; **manners** *npl*
(*conduct*) Manieren *pl*, Umgangsformen *pl*;
bad ~**s** schlechte Manieren; **that's bad** ~**s**
das gehört sich nicht.
mannerism ['mænərɪzəm] *n* Eigenheit *f*.
mannerly ['mænəlɪ] *adj* wohlerzogen.
manning ['mænɪŋ] *n* Besatzung *f*.
manoeuvrable, (*US*) **maneuverable**
[mə'nu:vrəbl] *adj* manövrierfähig.
manoeuvre, (*US*) **maneuver** [mə'nu:və*] *vt*
manövrieren; (*situation*) manipulieren ♦ *vi*
manövrieren ♦ *n* (*skilful move*) Manöver *nt*;
manoeuvres *npl* (*MIL*) Manöver *nt*,
Truppenübungen *pl*; **to** ~ **sb into doing sth**
jdn dazu bringen, etw zu tun.
manor ['mænə*] *n* (*also:* ~ **house**) Herrenhaus
nt.
manpower ['mænpauə*] *n* Personal *nt*,
Arbeitskräfte *pl*.
Manpower Services Commission (*BRIT*) *n*
*Behörde für Arbeitsbeschaffung,
Arbeitsvermittlung und Berufsausbildung.*
manservant ['mænsɑ:vənt] (*pl* **menservants**) *n*
Diener *m*.
mansion ['mænʃən] *n* Villa *f*.
manslaughter ['mænslɔ:tə*] *n* Totschlag *m*.
mantelpiece ['mæntlpi:s] *n* Kaminsims *nt* or *m*.
mantle ['mæntl] *n* Decke *f*; (*fig*) Deckmantel
m.
man-to-man ['mæntə'mæn] *adj, adv* von Mann
zu Mann.
manual ['mænjuəl] *adj* manuell, Hand-;
(*controls*) von Hand ♦ *n* Handbuch *nt*.
manufacture [mænju'fæktʃə*] *vt* herstellen

◆ n Herstellung f.
manufactured goods npl Fertigerzeugnisse pl.
manufacturer [mænju'fæktʃərə*] n Hersteller m.
manufacturing [mænju'fæktʃərɪŋ] n Herstellung f.
manure [mə'njuə*] n Dung m.
manuscript ['mænjuskrɪpt] n Manuskript nt; (old document) Handschrift f.
many ['mɛnɪ] adj, pron viele; **a great** ~ eine ganze Reihe; **how** ~? wie viele?; **too** ~ **difficulties** zu viele Schwierigkeiten; **twice as** ~ doppelt so viele; ~ **a time** so manches Mal.
Maori ['maurɪ] adj maorisch ◆ n Maori mf.
map [mæp] n (Land)karte f; (of town) Stadtplan m ◆ vt eine Karte anfertigen von.
▶**map out** vt planen; (plan) entwerfen; (essay) anlegen.
maple ['meɪpl] n (tree, wood) Ahorn m.
Mar. abbr = **March**.
mar [mɑː*] vt (appearance) verunstalten; (day) verderben; (event) stören.
marathon ['mærəθən] n Marathon m ◆ adj: **a** ~ **session** eine Marathonsitzung.
marathon runner n Marathonläufer(in) m(f).
marauder [mə'rɔːdə*] n (robber) Plünderer m; (killer) Mörder m.
marble ['mɑːbl] n Marmor m; (toy) Murmel f.
marbles ['mɑːblz] n (game) Murmeln pl.
March [mɑːtʃ] n März m; see also **July**.
march [mɑːtʃ] vi marschieren; (protesters) ziehen ◆ n Marsch m; (demonstration) Demonstration f; **to** ~ **out of/into** (heraus)marschieren aus +dat/ (herein)marschieren in +acc.
marcher ['mɑːtʃə*] n Demonstrant(in) m(f).
marching orders ['mɑːtʃɪŋ-] npl: **to give sb his/her** ~ (employee) jdn entlassen; (lover) jdm den Laufpaß geben.
march past n Vorbeimarsch m.
mare [mɛə*] n Stute f.
margarine [mɑːdʒə'riːn] n Margarine f.
marge [mɑːdʒ] (BRIT: inf) n abbr = **margarine**.
margin ['mɑːdʒɪn] n Rand m; (of votes) Mehrheit f; (for safety, error etc) Spielraum m; (COMM) Gewinnspanne f.
marginal ['mɑːdʒɪnl] adj geringfügig; (note) Rand-.
marginally ['mɑːdʒɪnəlɪ] adv nur wenig, geringfügig.
marginal (seat) n (POL) mit knapper Mehrheit gewonnener Wahlkreis.
marigold ['mærɪɡəuld] n Ringelblume f.
marijuana [mærɪ'wɑːnə] n Marihuana nt.
marina [mə'riːnə] n Yachthafen m.
marinade [mærɪ'neɪd] n Marinade f ◆ vt = **marinate**.
marinate ['mærɪneɪt] vt marinieren.
marine [mə'riːn] adj (plant, biology) Meeres- ◆ n (BRIT: soldier) Marineinfanterist m; (US:

sailor) Marinesoldat m; ~ **engineer** Schiff(s)bauingenieur m; ~ **engineering** Schiff(s)bau m.
marine insurance n Seeversicherung f.
marital ['mærɪtl] adj ehelich; (problem) Ehe-; ~ **status** Familienstand m.
maritime ['mærɪtaɪm] adj (nation) Seefahrer-; (museum) Seefahrts-; (law) See-.
marjoram ['mɑːdʒərəm] n Majoran m.
mark [mɑːk] n Zeichen nt; (stain) Fleck m; (in snow, mud etc) Spur f; (BRIT: SCOL) Note f; (level, point): **the halfway** ~ die Hälfte f; (currency) Mark f; (BRIT: TECH): **M**~ **2/3** Version f 2/3 ◆ vt (with pen) beschriften; (with shoes etc) schmutzig machen; (with tyres etc) Spuren hinterlassen auf +dat; (damage) beschädigen; (stain) Flecken machen auf +dat; (indicate) markieren; (: price) auszeichnen; (commemorate) begehen; (characterize) kennzeichnen; (BRIT: SCOL) korrigieren (und benoten); (SPORT: player) decken; **punctuation** ~s Satzzeichen pl; **to be quick off the** ~ **(in doing sth)** (fig) blitzschnell reagieren (und etw tun); **to be up to the** ~ den Anforderungen entsprechen; **to** ~ **time** auf der Stelle treten.
▶**mark down** vt (prices, goods) herabsetzen, heruntersetzen.
▶**mark off** vt (tick off) abhaken.
▶**mark out** vt markieren; (person) auszeichnen.
▶**mark up** vt (price) heraufsetzen.
marked [mɑːkt] adj deutlich.
markedly ['mɑːkɪdlɪ] adv deutlich.
marker ['mɑːkə*] n Markierung f; (bookmark) Lesezeichen nt.
market ['mɑːkɪt] n Markt m ◆ vt (sell) vertreiben; (new product) auf den Markt bringen; **to be on the** ~ auf dem Markt sein; **on the open** ~ auf dem freien Markt; **to play the** ~ (STOCK EXCHANGE) an der Börse spekulieren.
marketable ['mɑːkɪtəbl] adj marktfähig.
market analysis n Marktanalyse f.
market day n Markttag m.
market demand n Marktbedarf m.
market economy n Marktwirtschaft f.
market forces npl Marktkräfte pl.
market garden (BRIT) n Gemüseanbaubetrieb m.
marketing ['mɑːkɪtɪŋ] n Marketing nt.
marketing manager n Marketing-manager(in) m(f).
marketplace ['mɑːkɪtpleɪs] n Marktplatz m; (COMM) Markt m.
market price n Marktpreis m.
market research n Marktforschung f.
market value n Marktwert m.
marking ['mɑːkɪŋ] n (on animal) Zeichnung f; (on road) Markierung f.
marksman ['mɑːksmən] (irreg: like **man**) n

Scharfschütze *m*.
marksmanship ['mɑːksmənʃɪp] *n*
Treffsicherheit *f*.
mark-up ['mɑːkʌp] *n* (*COMM: margin*)
Handelsspanne *f*; (: *increase*)
(Preis)aufschlag *m*.
marmalade ['mɑːməleɪd] *n*
Orangenmarmelade *f*.
maroon [mə'ruːn] *vt:* **to be ~ed** festsitzen
♦ *adj* kastanienbraun.
marquee [mɑː'kiː] *n* Festzelt *nt*.
marquess, marquis ['mɑːkwɪs] *n* Marquis *m*.
Marrakech, Marrakesh [mærə'keʃ] *n* Marra-
kesch *nt*.
marriage ['mærɪdʒ] *n* Ehe *f*; (*institution*) die
Ehe; (*wedding*) Hochzeit *f*; **~ of convenience**
Vernunftehe *f*.
marriage bureau *n* Ehevermittlung *f*.
marriage certificate *n* Heiratsurkunde *f*.
marriage guidance, (*US*) **marriage
counseling** *n* Eheberatung *f*.
married ['mærɪd] *adj* verheiratet; (*life*) Ehe-;
(*love*) ehelich; **to get ~** heiraten.
marrow ['mærəu] *n* (*vegetable*) Kürbis *m*;
(*bone marrow*) (Knochen)mark *nt*.
marry ['mærɪ] *vt* heiraten; (*father*)
verheiraten; (*priest*) trauen ♦ *vi* heiraten.
Mars [mɑːz] *n* Mars *m*.
Marseilles [mɑː'seɪlz] *n* Marseilles *nt*.
marsh [mɑːʃ] *n* Sumpf *m*; (*salt marsh*)
Salzsumpf *m*.
marshal ['mɑːʃl] *n* (*MIL: also:* **field ~**)
(Feld)marschall *m*; (*official*) Ordner *m*; (*US:
of police*) Bezirkspolizeichef *m* ♦ *vt*
(*thoughts*) ordnen; (*support*) auftreiben;
(*soldiers*) aufstellen.
marshalling yard ['mɑːʃlɪŋ-] *n* (*RAIL*)
Rangierbahnhof *m*.
marshmallow [mɑːʃ'mæləu] *n* (*BOT*) Eibisch
m; (*sweet*) Marshmallow *m*.
marshy ['mɑːʃɪ] *adj* sumpfig.
marsupial [mɑː'suːpɪəl] *n* Beuteltier *nt*.
martial ['mɑːʃl] *adj* kriegerisch.
martial arts *npl* Kampfsport *m*; **the ~** die
Kampfkunst *sing*.
martial law *n* Kriegsrecht *nt*.
Martian ['mɑːʃən] *n* Marsmensch *m*.
martin ['mɑːtɪn] *n* (*also:* **house ~**) Schwalbe *f*.
martyr ['mɑːtə*] *n* Märtyrer(in) *m(f)* ♦ *vt*
martern.
martyrdom ['mɑːtədəm] *n* Martyrium *nt*.
marvel ['mɑːvl] *n* Wunder *nt* ♦ *vi:* **to ~ (at)**
staunen (über +*acc*).
marvellous, (*US*) **marvelous** ['mɑːvləs] *adj*
wunderbar.
Marxism ['mɑːksɪzəm] *n* Marxismus *m*.
Marxist ['mɑːksɪst] *adj* marxistisch ♦ *n*
Marxist(in) *m(f)*.
marzipan ['mɑːzɪpæn] *n* Marzipan *nt*.
mascara [mæs'kɑːrə] *n* Wimperntusche *f*.
mascot ['mæskət] *n* Maskottchen *nt*.
masculine ['mæskjulɪn] *adj* männlich;

(*atmosphere, woman*) maskulin; (*LING*)
männlich, maskulin.
masculinity [mæskju'lɪnɪtɪ] *n* Männlichkeit *f*.
MASH [mæʃ] (*US*) *n abbr* (= *mobile army
surgical hospital*) mobiles Lazarett *nt*.
mash [mæʃ] *vt* zerstampfen.
mashed potatoes [mæʃt-] *npl*
Kartoffelpüree *nt*, Kartoffelbrei *m*.
mask [mɑːsk] *n* Maske *f* ♦ *vt* (*cover*)
verdecken; (*hide*) verbergen; **surgical ~**
Mundschutz *m*.
masking tape ['mɑːskɪŋ-] *n* Abdeckband *nt*.
masochism ['mæsəukɪzəm] *n* Masochismus *m*.
masochist ['mæsəukɪst] *n* Masochist(in) *m(f)*.
mason ['meɪsn] *n* (*also:* **stone ~**) Steinmetz *m*;
(*also:* **freemason**) Freimaurer *m*.
masonic [mə'sɔnɪk] *adj* (*lodge etc*)
Freimaurer-.
masonry ['meɪsnrɪ] *n* Mauerwerk *nt*.
masquerade [mæskə'reɪd] *vi:* **to ~ as** sich
ausgeben als ♦ *n* Maskerade *f*.
Mass. (*US*) *abbr* (*POST:* = *Massachusetts*).
mass [mæs] *n* Masse *f*; (*of people*) Menge *f*;
(*large amount*) Fülle *f*; (*REL*): **M~** Messe *f*
♦ *cpd* Massen- ♦ *vi* (*troops*) sich massieren;
(*protesters*) sich versammeln; **the masses** *npl*
(*ordinary people*) die Masse, die Massen *pl*;
to go to M~ zur Messe gehen; **~es of** (*inf*)
massenhaft, jede Menge.
massacre ['mæsəkə*] *n* Massaker *nt* ♦ *vt*
massakrieren.
massage ['mæsɑːʒ] *n* Massage *f* ♦ *vt*
massieren.
masseur [mæ'sə:*] *n* Masseur *m*.
masseuse [mæ'sə:z] *n* Masseurin *f*.
massive ['mæsɪv] *adj* (*furniture, person*)
wuchtig; (*support*) massiv; (*changes,
increase*) enorm.
mass market *n* Massenmarkt *m*.
mass media *npl* Massenmedien *pl*.
mass meeting *n* Massenveranstaltung *f*; (*of
everyone concerned*) Vollversammlung *f*;
(*POL*) Massenkundgebung *f*.
mass-produce ['mæsprə'djuːs] *vt* in
Massenproduktion herstellen.
mass-production ['mæsprə'dʌkʃən] *n*
Massenproduktion *f*.
mast [mɑːst] *n* (*NAUT*) Mast *m*; (*RADIO etc*)
Sendeturm *m*.
mastectomy [mæs'tektəmɪ] *n*
Brustamputation *f*.
master ['mɑːstə*] *n* Herr *m*; (*teacher*) Lehrer
m; (*title*): **M~ X** (der junge) Herr X; (*ART,
MUS, of craft etc*) Meister *m* ♦ *cpd:* **~ baker/
plumber** *etc* Bäcker-/Klempnermeister *etc m*
♦ *vt* meistern; (*feeling*) unter Kontrolle
bringen; (*skill, language*) beherrschen.
master disk *n* (*COMPUT*) Stammdiskette *f*.
masterful ['mɑːstəful] *adj* gebieterisch;
(*skilful*) meisterhaft.
master key *n* Hauptschlüssel *m*.
masterly ['mɑːstəlɪ] *adj* meisterhaft.

mastermind ['mɑːstəmaɪnd] n (führender) Kopf m ♦ vt planen und ausführen.
Master of Arts n Magister m der philosophischen Fakultät.
Master of Ceremonies n Zeremonienmeister m; (for variety show etc) Conférencier m.
Master of Science n Magister m der naturwissenschaftlichen Fakultät.
masterpiece ['mɑːstəpiːs] n Meisterwerk nt.
master plan n kluger Plan m.

Master's Degree ist ein höherer akademischer Grad, den man in der Regel nach dem **bachelor's degree** erwerben kann. Je nach Universität erhält man ein master's degree nach einem entsprechenden Studium und/oder einer Dissertation. Die am häufigsten verliehenen Grade sind **MA** (Master of Arts) und **MSc** (Master of Science), die beide Studium und Dissertation erfordern, während für **MLitt** (Master of Letters) und **MPhil** (Master of Philosophy) meist nur eine Dissertation nötig ist. Siehe auch **bachelor's degree**, **doctorate**.

---

masterstroke ['mɑːstəstrəuk] n Meisterstück nt.
mastery ['mɑːstərɪ] n (of language etc) Beherrschung f; (skill) (meisterhaftes) Können nt.
mastiff ['mæstɪf] n Dogge f.
masturbate ['mæstəbeɪt] vi masturbieren, onanieren.
masturbation [mæstə'beɪʃən] n Masturbation f, Onanie f.
mat [mæt] n Matte f; (also: **doormat**) Fußmatte f; (also: **table** ~) Untersetzer m; (: of cloth) Deckchen nt ♦ adj = **matt**.
match [mætʃ] n Wettkampf m; (team game) Spiel nt; (TENNIS) Match nt; (for lighting fire etc) Streichholz nt; (equivalent): **to be a good/perfect** ~ gut/perfekt zusammenpassen ♦ vt (go well with) passen zu; (equal) gleichkommen +dat; (correspond to) entsprechen +dat; (suit) sich anpassen +dat; (also: ~ **up**: pair) passend zusammenbringen ♦ vi zusammenpassen; **to be a good** ~ gut zusammenpassen; **to be no** ~ **for** sich nicht messen können mit; **with shoes to** ~ mit (dazu) passenden Schuhen.
▶**match up** vi zusammenpassen.
matchbox ['mætʃbɔks] n Streichholzschachtel f.
matching ['mætʃɪŋ] adj (dazu) passend.
matchless ['mætʃlɪs] adj unvergleichlich.
mate [meɪt] n (inf: friend) Freund(in) m(f), Kumpel m; (animal) Männchen nt, Weibchen nt; (assistant) Gehilfe m, Gehilfin f; (in merchant navy) Maat m ♦ vi (animals) sich paaren.
material [mə'tɪərɪəl] n Material nt; (cloth)

Stoff m ♦ adj (possessions, existence) materiell; (relevant) wesentlich; **materials** npl (equipment) Material nt.
materialistic [mətɪərɪə'lɪstɪk] adj materialistisch.
materialize [mə'tɪərɪəlaɪz] vi (event) zustande kommen; (plan) verwirklicht werden; (hope) sich verwirklichen; (problem) auftreten; (crisis, difficulty) eintreten.
maternal [mə'təːnl] adj mütterlich, Mutter-.
maternity [mə'təːnɪtɪ] n Mutterschaft f ♦ cpd (ward etc) Entbindungs-; (care) für werdende und junge Mütter.
maternity benefit n Mutterschaftsgeld nt.
maternity dress n Umstandskleid nt.
maternity hospital n Entbindungsheim nt.
maternity leave n Mutterschaftsurlaub m.
matey ['meɪtɪ] (BRIT: inf) adj kumpelhaft.
math [mæθ] (US) n abbr = **maths**.
mathematical [mæθə'mætɪkl] adj mathematisch.
mathematician [mæθəmə'tɪʃən] n Mathematiker(in) m(f).
mathematics [mæθə'mætɪks] n Mathematik f.
maths [mæθs], (US) **math** [mæθ] n abbr Mathe f.
matinée ['mætɪneɪ] n Nachmittagsvorstellung f.
mating ['meɪtɪŋ] n Paarung f.
mating call n Lockruf m.
mating season n Paarungszeit f.
matriarchal [meɪtrɪ'ɑːkl] adj matriarchalisch.
matrices ['meɪtrɪsiːz] npl of **matrix**.
matriculation [mətrɪkju'leɪʃən] n Immatrikulation f.
matrimonial [mætrɪ'məunɪəl] adj Ehe-.
matrimony ['mætrɪmənɪ] n Ehe f.
matrix ['meɪtrɪks] (pl **matrices**) n (MATH) Matrix f; (framework) Gefüge nt.
matron ['meɪtrən] n (in hospital) Oberschwester f; (in school) Schwester f.
matronly ['meɪtrənlɪ] adj matronenhaft.
matt [mæt] adj matt; (paint) Matt-.
matted ['mætɪd] adj verfilzt.
matter ['mætə*] n (event, situation) Sache f, Angelegenheit f; (PHYS) Materie f; (substance, material) Stoff m; (MED: pus) Eiter m ♦ vi (be important) wichtig sein; **matters** npl (affairs) Angelegenheiten pl, Dinge pl; (situation) Lage f; **what's the** ~? was ist los?; **no** ~ **what** egal, was (passiert); **that's another** ~ das ist etwas anderes; **as a** ~ **of course** selbstverständlich; **as a** ~ **of fact** eigentlich; **it's a** ~ **of habit** es ist eine Gewohnheitssache; **vegetable** ~ pflanzliche Stoffe pl; **printed** ~ Drucksachen pl; **reading** ~ (BRIT) Lesestoff m; **it doesn't** ~ es macht nichts.
matter-of-fact ['mætərəv'fækt] adj sachlich.
matting ['mætɪŋ] n Matten pl; **rush** ~ Binsenmatten pl.
mattress ['mætrɪs] n Matratze f.

mature [mə'tjuə*] *adj* reif; (*wine*) ausgereift
♦ *vi* reifen; (*COMM*) fällig werden.
mature student *n* älterer Student *m*, ältere
Studentin *f*.
maturity [mə'tjuərɪtɪ] *n* Reife *f*; **to have
reached** ~ (*person*) erwachsen sein; (*animal*)
ausgewachsen sein.
maudlin ['mɔ:dlɪn] *adj* gefühlsselig.
maul [mɔ:l] *vt* (anfallen und) übel zurichten.
Mauritania [mɔ:rɪ'teɪnɪə] *n* Mauritanien *nt*.
Mauritius [mə'rɪʃəs] *n* Mauritius *nt*.
mausoleum [mɔ:sə'lɪəm] *n* Mausoleum *nt*.
mauve [məuv] *adj* mauve.
maverick ['mævrɪk] *n* (*dissenter*)
Abtrünnige(r) *m*; (*independent thinker*)
Querdenker *m*.
mawkish ['mɔ:kɪʃ] *adj* rührselig.
max. *abbr* = **maximum**.
maxim ['mæksɪm] *n* Maxime *f*.
maxima ['mæksɪmə] *npl of* **maximum**.
maximize ['mæksɪmaɪz] *vt* maximieren.
maximum ['mæksɪməm] (*pl* **maxima** *or* ~**s**) *adj*
(*amount, speed etc*) Höchst-; (*efficiency*)
maximal ♦ *n* Maximum *nt*.
May [meɪ] *n* Mai *m*; *see also* **July**.
may [meɪ] (*conditional* **might**) *vi* (*be possible*)
können; (*have permission*) dürfen; **he**
~ **come** vielleicht kommt er; ~ **I smoke?**
darf ich rauchen?; ~ **God bless you!** (*wish*)
Gott segne dich!; ~ **I sit here?** kann ich
mich hier hinsetzen?; **he might be there** er
könnte da sein; **you might like to try**
vielleicht möchten Sie es mal versuchen;
you ~ **as well go** Sie können ruhig gehen.
maybe ['meɪbi:] *adv* vielleicht; ~ **he'll** ... es
kann sein, daß er ...; ~ **not** vielleicht nicht.
Mayday ['meɪdeɪ] *n* Maydaysignal *nt*, ≈ SOS-
Ruf *m*.
May Day *n* der 1. Mai.
mayhem ['meɪhem] *n* Chaos *nt*.
mayonnaise [meɪə'neɪz] *n* Mayonnaise *f*.
mayor [mɛə*] *n* Bürgermeister *m*.
mayoress ['mɛərɛs] *n* Bürgermeisterin *f*;
(*partner*) Frau *f* des Bürgermeisters.
maypole ['meɪpəul] *n* Maibaum *m*.
maze [meɪz] *n* Irrgarten *m*; (*fig*) Wirrwarr *m*.
MB *abbr* (*COMPUT*: = *megabyte*) MB;
(*CANADA*: = *Manitoba*).
MBA *n abbr* (= *Master of Business
Administration*) akademischer Grad in
Betriebswirtschaft.
MBE (*BRIT*) *n abbr* (= *Member of (the Order of)
the British Empire*) britischer Ordenstitel.
MC *n abbr* = **Master of Ceremonies**.
MCAT (*US*) *n abbr* (= *Medical College
Admissions Test*) Zulassungsprüfung für
medizinische Fachschulen.
MCP (*BRIT*: *inf*) *n abbr* (= *male chauvinist pig*)
Chauvinistenschwein *nt*.
MD *n abbr* (= *Doctor of Medicine*) ≈ Dr. med.;
(*COMM*) = **managing director** ♦ *abbr* (*US*:
POST: = *Maryland*).

MDT (*US*) *abbr* (= *Mountain Daylight Time*)
amerikanische Sommerzeitzone.
ME *n abbr* (*US*) = **medical examiner**; (*MED*:
= *myalgic encephalomyelitis*) *krankhafter
Energiemangel (oft nach Virus-
erkrankungen)* ♦ *abbr* (*US*: *POST*: = *Maine*).

════════════════════ *KEYWORD*

me [mi:] *pron* **1** (*direct*) mich; **can you hear** ~?
können Sie mich hören?; **it's** ~ ich bin's
2 (*indirect*) mir; **he gave** ~ **the money, he
gave the money to** ~ er gab mir das Geld
3 (*after prep*): **it's for** ~ es ist für mich; **with**
~ mit mir; **give them to** ~ gib sie mir;
without ~ ohne mich.

meadow ['mɛdəu] *n* Wiese *f*.
meagre, (*US*) **meager** ['mi:gə*] *adj* (*amount*)
kläglich; (*meal*) dürftig.
meal [mi:l] *n* Mahlzeit *f*; (*food*) Essen *nt*; (*flour*)
Schrotmehl *nt*; **to go out for a** ~ essen
gehen; **to make a** ~ **of sth** (*fig*) etw auf sehr
umständliche Art machen.
meals on wheels *n sing* Essen *nt* auf Rädern.
mealtime ['mi:ltaɪm] *n* Essenszeit *f*.
mealy-mouthed ['mi:lɪmauðd] *adj*
unaufrichtig; (*politician*) schönfärberisch.
mean [mi:n] (*pt, pp* **meant**) *adj* (*with money*)
geizig; (*unkind*) gemein; (*US*: *inf*: *animal*)
bösartig; (*shabby*) schäbig; (*average*)
Durchschnitts-, mittlere(r, s) ♦ *vt* (*signify*)
bedeuten; (*refer to*) meinen; (*intend*)
beabsichtigen ♦ *n* (*average*) Durchschnitt *m*;
means *npl* (*way*) Möglichkeit *f*; (*money*)
Mittel *pl*; **by** ~**s of** durch; **by all** ~**s!** aber
natürlich *or* selbstverständlich!; **do you**
~ **it?** meinst du das ernst?; **what do you** ~?
was willst du damit sagen?; **to be meant for
sb/sth** für jdn/etw bestimmt sein; **to** ~ **to
do sth** etw tun wollen.
meander [mɪ'ændə*] *vi* (*river*) sich schlängeln;
(*person: walking*) schlendern; (: *talking*)
abschweifen.
meaning ['mi:nɪŋ] *n* Sinn *m*; (*of word, gesture*)
Bedeutung *f*.
meaningful ['mi:nɪŋful] *adj* sinnvoll; (*glance,
remark*) vielsagend, bedeutsam;
(*relationship*) tiefergehend.
meaningless ['mi:nɪŋlɪs] *adj* sinnlos; (*word,
song*) bedeutungslos.
meanness ['mi:nnɪs] *n* (*with money*) Geiz *m*;
(*unkindness*) Gemeinheit *f*; (*shabbiness*)
Schäbigkeit *f*.
means test [mi:nz-] *n* Überprüfung *f* der
Einkommens- und Vermögensverhältnisse.
means-tested ['mi:nztestɪd] *adj* von den
Einkommens- und Vermögensverhältnissen
abhängig.
meant [ment] *pt, pp of* **mean**.
meantime ['mi:ntaɪm] *adv* (*also*: **in the** ~)
inzwischen.
meanwhile ['mi:nwaɪl] *adv* = **meantime**.

measles ['miːzlz] n Masern pl.
measly ['miːzlɪ] (inf) adj mick(e)rig.
measurable ['mɛʒərəbl] adj meßbar.
measure ['mɛʒəˈ] vt, vi messen ♦ n (amount)
Menge f; (ruler) Meßstab m; (of achievement)
Maßstab m; (action) Maßnahme f; **a litre ~**
ein Meßbecher m, der einen Liter faßt; **a/
some ~ of** ein gewisses Maß an +dat; **to take
~s to do sth** Maßnahmen ergreifen, um etw
zu tun.
▶**measure up** vi: **to ~ up to** herankommen
an +acc.
measured ['mɛʒəd] adj (tone) bedächtig;
(step) gemessen.
measurement ['mɛʒəmənt] n (measure) Maß
nt; (act) Messung f; **chest/hip ~** Brust-/
Hüftumfang m.
measurements ['mɛʒəmənts] npl Maße pl; **to
take sb's ~** bei jdm Maß nehmen.
meat [miːt] n Fleisch nt; **cold ~s** (BRIT)
Aufschnitt m; **crab ~** Krabbenfleisch nt.
meatball ['miːtbɔːl] n Fleischkloß m.
meat pie n Fleischpastete f.
meaty ['miːtɪ] adj (meal, dish) mit viel Fleisch;
(fig: satisfying: book etc) gehaltvoll; (: brawny:
person) kräftig (gebaut).
Mecca ['mɛkə] n (GEOG, fig) Mekka nt.
mechanic [mɪˈkænɪk] n Mechaniker(in) m(f).
mechanical [mɪˈkænɪkl] adj mechanisch.
mechanical engineering n Maschinenbau
m.
mechanics [mɪˈkænɪks] n (PHYS) Mechanik f
♦ npl (of reading etc) Technik f; (of
government etc) Mechanismus m.
mechanism ['mɛkənɪzəm] n Mechanismus m.
mechanization [mɛkənaɪˈzeɪʃən] n
Mechanisierung f.
mechanize ['mɛkənaɪz] vt, vi mechanisieren.
MEd n abbr (= Master of Education)
akademischer Grad für Lehrer.
medal ['mɛdl] n Medaille f; (decoration) Orden
m.
medallion [mɪˈdælɪən] n Medaillon nt.
medallist, (US) medalist ['mɛdlɪst] n
Medaillengewinner(in) m(f).
meddle ['mɛdl] vi: **to ~ (in)** sich einmischen
(in +acc); **to ~ with sb** sich mit jdm
einlassen; **to ~ with sth** (tamper) sich dat an
etw dat zu schaffen machen.
meddlesome ['mɛdlsəm], **meddling** ['mɛdlɪŋ]
adj sich ständig einmischend.
media ['miːdɪə] npl Medien pl.
media circus n Medienrummel m.
mediaeval [mɛdɪˈiːvl] adj = **medieval**.
median ['miːdɪən] (US) n (also: ~ **strip**)
Mittelstreifen m.
mediate ['miːdɪeɪt] vi vermitteln.
mediation [miːdɪˈeɪʃən] n Vermittlung f.
mediator ['miːdɪeɪtəˈ] n Vermittler(in) m(f).
Medicaid ['mɛdɪkeɪd] (US) n staatliche
Krankenversicherung und Gesundheitsfürsorge für Einkommensschwache.

medical ['mɛdɪkl] adj (care) medizinisch;
(treatment) ärztlich ♦ n (ärztliche)
Untersuchung f.
medical certificate n (confirming health)
ärztliches Gesundheitszeugnis nt;
(confirming illness) ärztliches Attest nt.
medical examiner (US) n
≈ Gerichtsmediziner(in) m(f); (performing
autopsy) Leichenbeschauer m.
medical student n Medizinstudent(in) m(f).
Medicare ['mɛdɪkeəˈ] (US) n staatliche
Krankenversicherung und
Gesundheitsfürsorge für ältere Bürger.
medicated ['mɛdɪkeɪtɪd] adj medizinisch.
medication [mɛdɪˈkeɪʃən] n Medikamente pl.
medicinal [mɛˈdɪsɪnl] adj (substance) Heil-;
(qualities) heilend; (purposes) medizinisch.
medicine ['mɛdsɪn] n Medizin f; (drug) Arznei
f.
medicine ball n Medizinball m.
medicine chest n Hausapotheke f.
medicine man n Medizinmann m.
medieval [mɛdɪˈiːvl] adj mittelalterlich.
mediocre [miːdɪˈəukəˈ] adj mittelmäßig.
mediocrity [miːdɪˈɔkrɪtɪ] n Mittelmäßigkeit f.
meditate ['mɛdɪteɪt] vi nachdenken; (REL)
meditieren.
meditation [mɛdɪˈteɪʃən] n Nachdenken nt;
(REL) Meditation f.
Mediterranean [mɛdɪtəˈreɪnɪən] adj (country,
climate etc) Mittelmeer-; **the ~ (Sea)** das
Mittelmeer.
medium ['miːdɪəm] (pl **media** or **~s**) adj
mittlere(r, s) ♦ n (means) Mittel nt;
(substance, material) Medium nt; (pl **~s**)
(person) Medium nt; **of ~ height** mittelgroß;
to strike a happy ~ den goldenen Mittelweg
finden.
medium-dry ['miːdɪəm'draɪ] adj (wine, sherry)
halbtrocken.
medium-sized ['miːdɪəm'saɪzd] adj
mittelgroß.
medium wave n (RADIO) Mittelwelle f.
medley ['mɛdlɪ] n Gemisch nt; (MUS) Medley
nt.
meek [miːk] adj sanft(mütig), duldsam.
meet [miːt] (pt, pp **met**) vt (encounter) treffen;
(by arrangement) sich treffen mit; (for the
first time) kennenlernen; (go and fetch)
abholen; (opponent) treffen auf +acc;
(condition, standard) erfüllen; (need,
expenses) decken; (problem) stoßen auf +acc;
(challenge) begegnen +dat; (bill) begleichen;
(join: lines) sich schneiden mit; (: road etc)
treffen auf +acc ♦ vi (encounter) sich
begegnen; (by arrangement) sich treffen; (for
the first time) sich kennenlernen; (for talks
etc) zusammenkommen; (committee) tagen;
(join: lines) sich schneiden; (: roads etc)
aufeinandertreffen ♦ n (BRIT: HUNTING)
Jagd f; (US: SPORT) Sportfest nt; **pleased to
~ you!** (sehr) angenehm!

▶**meet up** *vi:* **to** ~ **up with sb** sich mit jdm treffen.
▶**meet with** *vt fus* (*difficulty, success*) haben.
meeting ['mi:tɪŋ] *n* (*assembly, people assembling*) Versammlung *f*; (*COMM, of committee etc*) Sitzung *f*; (*also:* **business** ~) Besprechung *f*; (*encounter*) Begegnung *f*; (*: arranged*) Treffen *nt*; (*POL*) Gespräch *nt*; (*SPORT*) Veranstaltung *f*; **she's at** *or* **in a** ~ (*COMM*) sie ist bei einer Besprechung; **to call a** ~ eine Sitzung/Versammlung einberufen.
meeting-place ['mi:tɪŋpleɪs] *n* Treffpunkt *m*.
megabyte ['mɛgəbaɪt] *n* Megabyte *nt*.
megalomaniac [mɛgələ'meɪnɪæk] *n* Größenwahnsinnige(r) *f(m)*.
megaphone ['mɛgəfəʊn] *n* Megaphon *nt*.
megawatt ['mɛgəwɔt] *n* Megawatt *nt*.
melancholy ['mɛlənkəlɪ] *n* Melancholie *f*, Schwermut *f* ♦ *adj* melancholisch, schwermütig.
mellow ['mɛləʊ] *adj* (*sound*) voll, weich; (*light, colour, stone*) warm; (*weathered*) verwittert; (*person*) gesetzt; (*wine*) ausgereift ♦ *vi* (*person*) gesetzter werden.
melodious [mɪ'ləʊdɪəs] *adj* melodisch.
melodrama ['mɛləʊdrɑːmə] *n* Melodrama *nt*.
melodramatic [mɛlədrə'mætɪk] *adj* melodramatisch.
melody ['mɛlədɪ] *n* Melodie *f*.
melon ['mɛlən] *n* Melone *f*.
melt [mɛlt] *vi* (*lit, fig*) schmelzen ♦ *vt* schmelzen; (*butter*) zerlassen.
▶**melt down** *vt* einschmelzen.
meltdown ['mɛltdaʊn] *n* (*in nuclear reactor*) Kernschmelze *f*.
melting point ['mɛltɪŋ-] *n* Schmelzpunkt *m*.
melting pot *n* (*lit, fig*) Schmelztiegel *m*; **to be in the** ~ in der Schwebe sein.
member ['mɛmbə*] *n* Mitglied *nt*; (*ANAT*) Glied *nt* ♦ *cpd:* ~ **country** Mitgliedsland *nt*; ~ **state** Mitgliedsstaat *m*; **M**~ **of Parliament** (*BRIT*) Abgeordnete(r) *f(m)* (des Unterhauses); **M**~ **of the European Parliament** (*BRIT*) Abgeordnete(r) *f(m)* des Europaparlaments.
membership ['mɛmbəʃɪp] *n* Mitgliedschaft *f*; (*members*) Mitglieder *pl*; (*number of members*) Mitgliederzahl *f*.
membership card *n* Mitgliedsausweis *m*.
membrane ['mɛmbreɪn] *n* Membran(e) *f*.
memento [mə'mɛntəʊ] *n* Andenken *nt*.
memo ['mɛməʊ] *n* Memo *nt*, Mitteilung *f*.
memoir ['mɛmwɑː*] *n* Kurzbiographie *f*.
memoirs ['mɛmwɑːz] *npl* Memoiren *pl*.
memo pad *n* Notizblock *m*.
memorable ['mɛmərəbl] *adj* denkwürdig; (*unforgettable*) unvergeßlich.
memorandum [mɛmə'rændəm] (*pl* **memoranda**) *n* Mitteilung *f*.
memorial [mɪ'mɔːrɪəl] *n* Denkmal *nt* ♦ *adj* (*service, prize*) Gedenk-.

Memorial Day (*US*) *n* ≈ Volkstrauertag *m*.

> **Memorial Day** ist in den USA ein gesetzlicher Feiertag am letzten Montag im Mai zum Gedenken der in allen Kriegen gefallenen amerikanischen Soldaten. Siehe auch **Remembrance Sunday**.

memorize ['mɛməraɪz] *vt* sich *dat* einprägen.
memory ['mɛmərɪ] *n* Gedächtnis *nt*; (*sth remembered*) Erinnerung *f*; (*COMPUT*) Speicher *m*; **in** ~ **of** zur Erinnerung an +*acc*; **to have a good/bad** ~ ein gutes/schlechtes Gedächtnis haben; **loss of** ~ Gedächtnisschwund *m*.
men [mɛn] *npl of* **man**.
menace ['mɛnɪs] *n* Bedrohung *f*; (*nuisance*) (Land)plage *f* ♦ *vt* bedrohen; **a public** ~ eine Gefahr für die Öffentlichkeit.
menacing ['mɛnɪsɪŋ] *adj* drohend.
menagerie [mɪ'nædʒərɪ] *n* Menagerie *f*.
mend [mɛnd] *vt* reparieren; (*darn*) flicken ♦ *n:* **to be on the** ~ auf dem Wege der Besserung sein; **to** ~ **one's ways** sich bessern.
mending ['mɛndɪŋ] *n* Reparaturen *pl*; (*clothes*) Flickarbeiten *pl*.
menial ['miːnɪəl] (*often pej*) *adj* niedrig, untergeordnet.
meningitis [mɛnɪn'dʒaɪtɪs] *n* Hirnhautentzündung *f*.
menopause ['mɛnəʊpɔːz] *n:* **the** ~ die Wechseljahre *pl*.
menservants ['mɛnsəːvənts] *npl of* **manservant**.
men's room (*US*) *n* Herrentoilette *f*.
menstrual ['mɛnstruəl] *adj* (*BIOL: cycle etc*) Menstruations-; ~ **period** Monatsblutung *f*.
menstruate ['mɛnstrueɪt] *vi* die Menstruation haben.
menstruation [mɛnstru'eɪʃən] *n* Menstruation *f*.
menswear ['mɛnzwɛə*] *n* Herren(be)kleidung *f*.
mental ['mɛntl] *adj* geistig; (*illness*) Geistes-; ~ **arithmetic** Kopfrechnen *nt*.
mental hospital *n* psychiatrische Klinik *f*.
mentality [mɛn'tælɪtɪ] *n* Mentalität *f*.
mentally ['mɛntlɪ] *adv:* **to be** ~ **handicapped** geistig behindert sein.
menthol ['mɛnθɒl] *n* Menthol *nt*.
mention ['mɛnʃən] *n* Erwähnung *f* ♦ *vt* erwähnen; **don't** ~ **it!** (bitte,) gern geschehen!; **not to** ~ ... von ... ganz zu schweigen.
mentor ['mɛntɔː*] *n* Mentor *m*.
menu ['mɛnjuː] *n* Menü *nt*; (*printed*) Speisekarte *f*.
menu-driven ['mɛnjuːdrɪvn] *adj* (*COMPUT*) menügesteuert.
MEP (*BRIT*) *n abbr* (= *Member of the European Parliament*) Abgeordnete(r) *f(m)* des

Europaparlaments.

mercantile ['mɜːkəntaɪl] adj (class, society) handeltreibend; (law) Handels-.

mercenary ['mɜːsɪnərɪ] adj (person) geldgierig ♦ n Söldner m.

merchandise ['mɜːtʃəndaɪz] n Ware f.

merchandiser ['mɜːtʃəndaɪzə'] n Verkaufsförderungsexperte m.

merchant ['mɜːtʃənt] n Kaufmann m; **timber/ wine** ~ Holz-/Weinhändler m.

merchant bank (BRIT) n Handelsbank f.

merchantman ['mɜːtʃəntmən] (irreg: like **man**) n Handelsschiff nt.

merchant navy, (US) **merchant marine** n Handelsmarine f.

merciful ['mɜːsɪful] adj gnädig; **a** ~ **release** eine Erlösung.

mercifully ['mɜːsɪflɪ] adv glücklicherweise.

merciless ['mɜːsɪlɪs] adj erbarmungslos.

mercurial [mɜː'kjuərɪəl] adj (unpredictable) sprunghaft, wechselhaft; (lively) quecksilbrig.

mercury ['mɜːkjurɪ] n Quecksilber nt.

mercy ['mɜːsɪ] n Gnade f; **to have** ~ **on sb** Erbarmen mit jdm haben; **at the** ~ **of** ausgeliefert +dat.

mercy killing n Euthanasie f.

mere [mɪə'] adj bloß; **his** ~ **presence irritates her** schon or allein seine Anwesenheit ärgert sie; **she is a** ~ **child** sie ist noch ein Kind; **it's a** ~ **trifle** es ist eine Lappalie; **by** ~ **chance** rein durch Zufall.

merely ['mɪəlɪ] adv lediglich, bloß.

merge [mɜːdʒ] vt (combine) vereinen; (COMPUT: files) mischen ♦ vi (COMM) fusionieren; (colours, sounds, shapes) ineinander übergehen; (roads) zusammenlaufen.

merger ['mɜːdʒə'] n (COMM) Fusion f.

meridian [mə'rɪdɪən] n Meridian m.

meringue [mə'ræŋ] n Baiser nt.

merit ['mɛrɪt] n (worth, value) Wert m; (advantage) Vorzug m; (achievement) Verdienst nt ♦ vt verdienen.

meritocracy [mɛrɪ'tɔkrəsɪ] n Leistungsgesellschaft f.

mermaid ['mɜːmeɪd] n Seejungfrau f, Meerjungfrau f.

merrily ['mɛrɪlɪ] adv vergnügt.

merriment ['mɛrɪmənt] n Heiterkeit f.

merry ['mɛrɪ] adj vergnügt; (music) fröhlich; **M**~ **Christmas!** Fröhliche or Frohe Weihnachten!

merry-go-round ['mɛrɪgəʊraʊnd] n Karussell nt.

mesh [mɛʃ] n Geflecht nt; **wire** ~ Maschendraht m.

mesmerize ['mɛzməraɪz] vt (fig) faszinieren.

mess [mɛs] n Durcheinander nt; (dirt) Dreck m; (MIL) Kasino nt; **to be in a** ~ (untidy) unordentlich sein; (in difficulty) in Schwierigkeiten stecken; **to be a** ~ (fig: life)

verkorkst sein; **to get o.s. in a** ~ in Schwierigkeiten geraten.

▶**mess about** (inf) vi (fool around) herumalbern.

▶**mess about with** (inf) vt fus (play around with) herumfummeln an +dat.

▶**mess around** (inf) vi = **mess about**.

▶**mess around with** (inf) vt fus = **mess about with**.

▶**mess up** vt durcheinanderbringen; (dirty) verdrecken.

message ['mɛsɪdʒ] n Mitteilung f, Nachricht f; (meaning) Aussage f; **to get the** ~ (inf, fig) kapieren.

message switching [-'swɪtʃɪŋ] n (COMPUT) Speichervermittlung f.

messenger ['mɛsɪndʒə'] n Bote m.

Messiah [mɪ'saɪə] n Messias m.

Messrs ['mɛsəz] abbr (on letters: = messieurs) An (die Herren).

messy ['mɛsɪ] adj (dirty) dreckig; (untidy) unordentlich.

Met [mɛt] (US) n abbr (= Metropolitan Opera) Met f.

met [mɛt] pt, pp of **meet**.

met. adj abbr (= meteorological): **the M**~ **Office** das Wetteramt.

metabolism [mɛ'tæbəlɪzəm] n Stoffwechsel m.

metal ['mɛtl] n Metall nt.

metal fatigue n Metallermüdung f.

metalled ['mɛtld] adj (road) asphaltiert.

metallic [mɪ'tælɪk] adj metallisch; (made of metal) aus Metall.

metallurgy [mɛ'tælədʒɪ] n Metallurgie f.

metalwork ['mɛtlwɜːk] n Metallarbeit f.

metamorphosis [mɛtə'mɔːfəsɪs] (pl **metamorphoses**) n Verwandlung f.

metaphor ['mɛtəfə'] n Metapher f.

metaphorical [mɛtə'fɔrɪkl] adj metaphorisch.

metaphysics [mɛtə'fɪzɪks] n Metaphysik f.

meteor ['miːtɪə'] n Meteor m.

meteoric [miːtɪ'ɔrɪk] adj (fig) kometenhaft.

meteorite ['miːtɪəraɪt] n Meteorit m.

meteorological [miːtɪərə'lɒdʒɪkl] adj (conditions, office etc) Wetter-.

meteorology [miːtɪə'rɒlədʒɪ] n Wetterkunde f, Meteorologie f.

mete out [miːt-] vt austeilen; **to** ~ **justice** Recht sprechen.

meter ['miːtə'] n Zähler m; (water meter) Wasseruhr f; (parking meter) Parkuhr f; (US: unit) = **metre**.

methane ['miːθeɪn] n Methan nt.

method ['mɛθəd] n Methode f; ~ **of payment** Zahlungsweise f.

methodical [mɪ'θɔdɪkl] adj methodisch.

Methodist ['mɛθədɪst] n Methodist(in) m(f).

methodology [mɛθə'dɔlədʒɪ] n Methodik f.

meths [mɛθs] (BRIT) n = **methylated spirit**.

methylated spirit ['mɛθɪleɪtɪd-] (BRIT) n (Brenn)spiritus m.

meticulous [mɪ'tɪkjuləs] *adj* sorgfältig; *(detail)* genau.

metre, *(US)* **meter** ['miːtə*] *n* Meter *m or nt*.

metric ['mɛtrɪk] *adj* metrisch; **to go** ~ auf das metrische Maßsystem umstellen.

metrical ['mɛtrɪkl] *adj* metrisch.

metrication [mɛtrɪ'keɪʃən] *n* Umstellung *f* auf das metrische Maßsystem.

metric system *n* metrisches Maßsystem *nt*.

metric ton *n* Metertonne *f*.

metronome ['mɛtrənəum] *n* Metronom *nt*.

metropolis [mɪ'trɔpəlɪs] *n* Metropole *f*.

metropolitan [mɛtrə'pɔlɪtn] *adj* großstädtisch.

Metropolitan Police *(BRIT) n:* **the** ~ **die** Londoner Polizei.

mettle ['mɛtl] *n:* **to be on one's** ~ auf dem Posten sein.

mew [mjuː] *vi* miauen.

mews [mjuːz] *(BRIT) n* Gasse *f* mit ehemaligen Kutscherhäuschen.

Mexican ['mɛksɪkən] *adj* mexikanisch ♦ *n* Mexikaner(in) *m(f)*.

Mexico ['mɛksɪkəu] *n* Mexiko *nt*.

Mexico City *n* Mexico City *f*.

mezzanine ['mɛtsəniːn] *n* Mezzanin *nt*.

MFA *(US) n abbr (= Master of Fine Arts)* akademischer Grad in Kunst.

mfr *abbr* = **manufacture; manufacturer**.

mg *abbr (= milligram(me))* mg.

Mgr *abbr (= Monseigneur, Monsignor)* Mgr.; *(COMM)* = **manager**.

MHR *(US, AUSTRALIA) n abbr (= Member of the House of Representatives)* Abgeordnete(r) *f(m)* des Repräsentantenhauses.

MHz *abbr (= megahertz)* MHz.

MI *(US) abbr (POST: = Michigan)*.

MI5 *(BRIT) n abbr (= Military Intelligence 5)* britischer Spionageabwehrdienst.

MI6 *(BRIT) n abbr (= Military Intelligence 6)* britischer Geheimdienst.

MIA *abbr (MIL: = missing in action)* vermißt.

miaow [miː'au] *vi* miauen.

mice [maɪs] *npl of* **mouse**.

Mich. *(US) abbr (POST: = Michigan)*.

micro... ['maɪkrəu] *pref* mikro-, Mikro-.

microbe ['maɪkrəub] *n* Mikrobe *f*.

microbiology [maɪkrəubaɪ'ɔlədʒɪ] *n* Mikrobiologie *f*.

microchip ['maɪkrəutʃɪp] *n* Mikrochip *m*.

micro(computer) ['maɪkrəu(kəm'pjuːtə*)] *n* Mikrocomputer *m*.

microcosm ['maɪkrəukɔzəm] *n* Mikrokosmos *m*.

microeconomics ['maɪkrəuiːkə'nɔmɪks] *n* Mikroökonomie *f*.

microelectronics ['maɪkrəuɪlɛk'trɔnɪks] *n* Mikroelektronik *f*.

microfiche ['maɪkrəufiːʃ] *n* Mikrofiche *m or nt*.

microfilm ['maɪkrəufɪlm] *n* Mikrofilm *m*.

microlight ['maɪkrəulaɪt] *n* Ultraleichtflugzeug *nt*.

micrometer [maɪ'krɔmɪtə*] *n* Meßschraube *f*.

microphone ['maɪkrəfəun] *n* Mikrofon *nt*, Mikrophon *nt*.

microprocessor ['maɪkrəu'prəusɛsə*] *n* Mikroprozessor *m*.

microscope ['maɪkrəskəup] *n* Mikroskop *nt*; **under the** ~ unter dem Mikroskop.

microscopic [maɪkrə'skɔpɪk] *adj* mikroskopisch; *(creature)* mikroskopisch klein.

microwave ['maɪkrəuweɪv] *n* Mikrowelle *f*; *(also:* ~ **oven)** Mikrowellenherd *m*.

mid- [mɪd] *adj:* **in** ~**-May** Mitte Mai; **in** ~**-afternoon** *(mitten)* am Nachmittag; **in** ~**-air** *(mitten)* in der Luft; **he's in his** ~**-thirties** er ist Mitte dreißig.

midday [mɪd'deɪ] *n* Mittag *m*.

middle ['mɪdl] *n* Mitte *f* ♦ *adj* mittlere(r, s); **in the** ~ **of the night** mitten in der Nacht; **I'm in the** ~ **of reading it** ich bin mittendrin; **a** ~ **course** ein Mittelweg *m*.

middle age *n* mittleres Lebensalter *nt*.

middle-aged [mɪdl'eɪdʒd] *adj* mittleren Alters.

Middle Ages *npl* Mittelalter *nt*.

middle-class [mɪdl'klɑːs] *adj* mittelständisch.

middle class(es) *n(pl)* Mittelstand *m*.

Middle East *n* Naher Osten *m*.

middleman ['mɪdlmæn] *(irreg: like* **man)** *n* Zwischenhändler *m*.

middle management *n* mittleres Management *nt*.

middle name *n* zweiter Vorname *m*.

middle-of-the-road ['mɪdləvðə'rəud] *adj* gemäßigt; *(politician)* der Mitte; *(MUS)* leicht.

middleweight ['mɪdlweɪt] *n* *(BOXING)* Mittelgewicht *nt*.

middling ['mɪdlɪŋ] *adj* mittelmäßig.

Middx *(BRIT) abbr (POST: = Middlesex)*.

midge [mɪdʒ] *n* Mücke *f*.

midget ['mɪdʒɪt] *n* Liliputaner(in) *m(f)*.

midi system ['mɪdɪ-] *n* Midi-System *nt*.

Midlands ['mɪdləndz] *(BRIT) npl:* **the** ~ Mittelengland *nt*.

midnight ['mɪdnaɪt] *n* Mitternacht *f* ♦ *cpd* Mitternachts-; **at** ~ um Mitternacht.

midriff ['mɪdrɪf] *n* Taille *f*.

midst [mɪdst] *n:* **in the** ~ **of** mitten in +*dat*; **to be in the** ~ **of doing sth** mitten dabei sein, etw zu tun.

midsummer [mɪd'sʌmə*] *n* Hochsommer *m*; **M~('s) Day** Sommersonnenwende *f*.

midway [mɪd'weɪ] *adj:* **we have reached the** ~ **point** wir haben die Hälfte hinter uns *dat* ♦ *adv* auf halbem Weg; ~ **between** *(in space)* auf halbem Weg zwischen; ~ **through** *(in time)* mitten in +*dat*.

midweek [mɪd'wiːk] *adv* mitten in der Woche ♦ *adj* Mitte der Woche.

midwife ['mɪdwaɪf] *(pl* **midwives)** *n* Hebamme *f*.

midwifery ['mɪdwɪfərɪ] n Geburtshilfe f.
midwinter [mɪd'wɪntə*] n: **in** ~ im tiefsten Winter.
miffed [mɪft] (inf) adj: **to be** ~ eingeschnappt sein.
might [maɪt] vb see **may** ♦ n Macht f; **with all one's** ~ mit aller Kraft.
mighty ['maɪtɪ] adj mächtig.
migraine ['miːgreɪn] n Migräne f.
migrant ['maɪgrənt] adj (bird) Zug-; (worker) Wander- ♦ n (bird) Zugvogel m; (worker) Wanderarbeiter(in) m(f).
migrate [maɪ'greɪt] vi (bird) ziehen; (person) abwandern.
migration [maɪ'greɪʃən] n Wanderung f; (to cities) Abwanderung f; (of birds) (Vogel)zug m.
mike [maɪk] n abbr = **microphone**.
Milan [mɪ'læn] n Mailand nt.
mild [maɪld] adj mild; (gentle) sanft; (slight: infection etc) leicht; (: interest) gering.
mildew ['mɪldjuː] n Schimmel m.
mildly ['maɪldlɪ] adv (say) sanft; (slight) leicht; **to put it** ~ gelinde gesagt.
mildness ['maɪldnɪs] n Milde f; (gentleness) Sanftheit f; (of infection etc) Leichtigkeit f.
mile [maɪl] n Meile f; **to do 30** ~**s per gallon** ≈ 9 Liter auf 100 km verbrauchen.
mileage ['maɪlɪdʒ] n Meilenzahl f; (fig) Nutzen m; **to get a lot of** ~ **out of sth** etw gründlich ausnutzen; **there is a lot of** ~ **in the idea** aus der Idee läßt sich viel machen.
mileage allowance n ≈ Kilometergeld nt.
mileometer [maɪ'lɔmɪtə*] n ≈ Kilometerzähler m.
milestone ['maɪlstəʊn] n (lit, fig) Meilenstein m.
milieu ['miːljəː] n Milieu n.
militant ['mɪlɪtnt] adj militant ♦ n Militante(r) f(m).
militarism ['mɪlɪtərɪzəm] n Militarismus m.
militaristic [mɪlɪtə'rɪstɪk] adj militaristisch.
military ['mɪlɪtərɪ] adj (history, leader etc) Militär- ♦ n: **the** ~ das Militär.
military police n Militärpolizei f.
military service n Militärdienst m.
militate ['mɪlɪteɪt] vi: **to** ~ **against** negative Auswirkungen haben auf +acc.
militia [mɪ'lɪʃə] n Miliz f.
milk [mɪlk] n Milch f ♦ vt (lit, fig) melken.
milk chocolate n Vollmilchschokolade f.
milk float (BRIT) n Milchwagen m.
milking ['mɪlkɪŋ] n Melken nt.
milkman ['mɪlkmən] (irreg: like **man**) n Milchmann m.
milk shake n Milchmixgetränk nt.
milk tooth n Milchzahn m.
milk truck (US) n = **milk float**.
milky ['mɪlkɪ] adj milchig; (drink) mit viel Milch; ~ **coffee** Milchkaffee m.
Milky Way n Milchstraße f.
mill [mɪl] n Mühle f; (factory) Fabrik f; (woollen mill) Spinnerei f ♦ vt mahlen ♦ vi (also: ~ **about**) umherlaufen.
millennium [mɪ'lɛnɪəm] (pl ~**s** or **millennia**) n Jahrtausend nt.
miller ['mɪlə*] n Müller m.
millet ['mɪlɪt] n Hirse f.
milli... ['mɪlɪ] pref Milli-.
milligram(me) ['mɪlɪgræm] n Milligramm nt.
millilitre, (US) **milliliter** ['mɪlɪliːtə*] n Milliliter m or nt.
millimetre, (US) **millimeter** ['mɪlɪmiːtə*] n Millimeter m or nt.
millinery ['mɪlɪnərɪ] n Hüte pl.
million ['mɪljən] n Million f; **a** ~ **times** (fig) tausendmal, x-mal.
millionaire [mɪljə'nɛə*] n Millionär m.
millipede ['mɪlɪpiːd] n Tausendfüßler m.
millstone ['mɪlstəʊn] n (fig): **it's a** ~ **round his neck** es ist für ihn ein Klotz am Bein.
millwheel ['mɪlwiːl] n Mühlrad nt.
milometer [maɪ'lɔmɪtə*] n = **mileometer**.
mime [maɪm] n Pantomime f; (actor) Pantomime m ♦ vt pantomimisch darstellen.
mimic ['mɪmɪk] n Imitator m ♦ vt (for amusement) parodieren; (animal, person) imitieren, nachahmen.
mimicry ['mɪmɪkrɪ] n Nachahmung f.
Min. (BRIT) abbr (POL) = **ministry**.
min. abbr (= minute) Min.; = **minimum**.
minaret [mɪnə'rɛt] n Minarett nt.
mince [mɪns] vt (meat) durch den Fleischwolf drehen ♦ vi (in walking) trippeln ♦ n (BRIT: meat) Hackfleisch nt; **he does not** ~ **(his) words** er nimmt kein Blatt vor den Mund.
mincemeat ['mɪnsmiːt] n süße Gebäckfüllung aus Dörrobst und Sirup; (US: meat) Hackfleisch nt; **to make** ~ **of sb** (inf) Hackfleisch aus jdm machen.
mince pie n mit Mincemeat gefülltes Gebäck.
mincer ['mɪnsə*] n Fleischwolf m.
mincing ['mɪnsɪŋ] adj (walk) trippelnd; (voice) geziert.
mind [maɪnd] n Geist m, Verstand m; (thoughts) Gedanken pl; (memory) Gedächtnis nt ♦ vt aufpassen auf +acc; (office etc) nach dem Rechten sehen in +dat; (object to) etwas haben gegen; **to my** ~ meiner Meinung nach; **to be out of one's** ~ verrückt sein; **it is on my** ~ es beschäftigt mich; **to keep** or **bear sth in** ~ etw nicht vergessen, an etw denken; **to make up one's** ~ sich entscheiden; **to change one's** ~ es sich dat anders überlegen; **to be in two** ~**s about sth** sich dat über etw acc nicht im klaren sein; **to have it in** ~ **to do sth** die Absicht haben, etw zu tun; **to have sb/sth in** ~ jdn/etw denken; **it slipped my** ~ ich habe es vergessen; **to bring** or **call sth to** ~ etw in Erinnerung rufen; **I can't get it out of my** ~ es geht mir nicht aus dem Kopf; **his** ~ **was on other things** er war mit den

Gedanken woanders; "~ **the step**"
„Vorsicht Stufe"; **do you** ~ **if ...?** macht es
Ihnen etwas aus, wenn ...?; **I don't** ~ es ist
mir egal; ~ **you,** ... allerdings ...; **never** ~! (*it
makes no odds*) ist doch egal!; (*don't worry*)
macht nichts!

mind-boggling ['maɪndbɒglɪŋ] (*inf*) *adj*
atemberaubend.

-minded ['maɪndɪd] *adj:* **fair-**~ gerecht; **an
industrially-**~ **nation** ein auf Industrie
ausgerichtetes Land.

minder ['maɪndə*] *n* Betreuer(in) *m(f)*; (*inf:
bodyguard*) Aufpasser(in) *m(f)*.

mindful ['maɪndful] *adj:* ~ **of** unter
Berücksichtigung +*gen*.

mindless ['maɪndlɪs] *adj* (*violence*) sinnlos;
(*work*) geistlos.

mine¹ [maɪn] *n* (*coal mine, gold mine*)
Bergwerk *nt*; (*bomb*) Mine *f* ♦ *vt* (*coal*)
abbauen; (*beach etc*) verminen; (*ship*) eine
Mine befestigen an +*dat*.

mine² [maɪn] *pron* meine(r, s); **that book is** ~
das Buch ist mein(e)s, das Buch gehört
mir; **this is** ~ das ist meins; **a friend of** ~ ein
Freund/eine Freundin von mir.

mine detector *n* Minensuchgerät *nt*.

minefield ['maɪnfiːld] *n* Minenfeld *nt*; (*fig*)
brisante Situation *f*.

miner ['maɪnə*] *n* Bergmann *m*, Bergarbeiter
m.

mineral ['mɪnərəl] *adj* (*deposit, resources*)
Mineral- ♦ *n* Mineral *nt*; **minerals** *npl* (*BRIT:
soft drinks*) Erfrischungsgetränke *pl*.

mineralogy [mɪnə'rælədʒɪ] *n* Mineralogie *f*.

mineral water *n* Mineralwasser *nt*.

minesweeper ['maɪnswiːpə*] *n*
Minensuchboot *nt*.

mingle ['mɪŋgl] *vi:* **to** ~ **(with)** sich
vermischen (mit); **to** ~ **with** (*people*)
Umgang haben mit; (*at party etc*) sich
unterhalten mit; **you should** ~ **a bit** du
solltest dich unter die Leute mischen.

mingy ['mɪndʒɪ] (*inf*) *adj* knick(e)rig; (*amount*)
mick(e)rig.

mini... ['mɪnɪ] *pref* Mini-.

miniature ['mɪnətʃə*] *adj* winzig; (*version etc*)
Miniatur- ♦ *n* Miniatur *f*; **in** ~ im kleinen, im
Kleinformat.

minibus ['mɪnɪbʌs] *n* Kleinbus *m*.

minicab ['mɪnɪkæb] *n* Kleintaxi *nt*.

minicomputer ['mɪnɪkəm'pjuːtə*] *n*
Minicomputer *m*.

minim ['mɪnɪm] *n* (*MUS*) halbe Note *f*.

minima ['mɪnɪmə] *npl of* **minimum**.

minimal ['mɪnɪml] *adj* minimal.

minimalist ['mɪnɪməlɪst] *adj* minimalistisch.

minimize ['mɪnɪmaɪz] *vt* auf ein Minimum
reduzieren; (*play down*) herunterspielen.

minimum ['mɪnɪməm] (*pl* **minima**) *n* Minimum
nt ♦ *adj* (*income, speed*) Mindest-; **to reduce
to a** ~ auf ein Mindestmaß reduzieren;
~ **wage** Mindestlohn *m*.

minimum lending rate *n* Diskontsatz *m*.

mining ['maɪnɪŋ] *n* Bergbau *m* ♦ *cpd* Bergbau-.

minion ['mɪnjən] (*pej*) *n* Untergebene(r) *f(m)*.

miniseries ['mɪnɪsɪəriːz] *n* Miniserie *f*.

miniskirt ['mɪnɪskəːt] *n* Minirock *m*.

minister ['mɪnɪstə*] *n* (*BRIT: POL*) Minister(in)
m(f); (*REL*) Pfarrer *m* ♦ *vi:* **to** ~ **to** sich
kümmern um; (*needs*) befriedigen.

ministerial [mɪnɪs'tɪərɪəl] (*BRIT*) *adj* (*POL*)
ministeriell.

ministry ['mɪnɪstrɪ] *n* (*BRIT: POL*) Ministerium
nt; **to join the** ~ (*REL*) Geistliche(r) werden.

Ministry of Defence (*BRIT*) *n*
Verteidigungsministerium *nt*.

mink [mɪŋk] (*pl* ~**s** *or* ~) *n* Nerz *m*.

mink coat *n* Nerzmantel *m*.

Minn. (*US*) *abbr* (*POST*: = Minnesota).

minnow ['mɪnəu] *n* Elritze *f*.

minor ['maɪnə*] *adj* kleinere(r, s); (*poet*)
unbedeutend; (*planet*) klein; (*MUS*) Moll ♦ *n*
Minderjährige(r) *f(m)*.

Minorca [mɪ'nɔːkə] *n* Menorca *nt*.

minority [maɪ'nɒrɪtɪ] *n* Minderheit *f*; **to be in a**
~ in der Minderheit sein.

minster ['mɪnstə*] *n* Münster *nt*.

minstrel ['mɪnstrəl] *n* Spielmann *m*.

mint [mɪnt] *n* Minze *f*; (*sweet*)
Pfefferminz(bonbon) *nt*; (*place*): **the M**~ die
Münzanstalt ♦ *vt* (*coins*) prägen; **in**
~ **condition** neuwertig.

mint sauce *n* Minzsoße *f*.

minuet [mɪnju'et] *n* Menuett *nt*.

minus ['maɪnəs] *n* (*also:* ~ **sign**) Minuszeichen
nt ♦ *prep* minus, weniger; ~ **24ºC** 24 Grad
unter Null.

minuscule ['mɪnəskjuːl] *adj* winzig.

minute¹ [maɪ'njuːt] *adj* winzig; (*search*)
peinlich genau; (*detail*) kleinste(r, s); **in**
~ **detail** in allen Einzelheiten.

minute² ['mɪnɪt] *n* Minute *f*; (*fig*) Augenblick
m, Moment *m*; **minutes** *npl* (*of meeting*)
Protokoll *nt*; **it is 5** ~**s past 3** es ist 5
Minuten nach 3; **wait a** ~! einen Augenblick
or Moment!; **up-to-the-**~ (*news*)
hochaktuell; (*technology*) allerneueste(r, s);
at the last ~ in letzter Minute.

minute book *n* Protokollbuch *nt*.

minute hand *n* Minutenzeiger *m*.

minutely [maɪ'njuːtlɪ] *adv* (*in detail*)
genauestens; (*by a small amount*) ganz
geringfügig.

minutiae [mɪ'njuːʃiː] *npl* Einzelheiten *pl*.

miracle ['mɪrəkl] *n* (*REL, fig*) Wunder *nt*.

miraculous [mɪ'rækjuləs] *adj* wunderbar;
(*powers, effect, cure*) Wunder-; (*success,
change*) unglaublich; **to have a** ~ **escape** wie
durch ein Wunder entkommen.

mirage ['mɪrɑːʒ] *n* Fata Morgana *f*; (*fig*)
Trugbild *nt*.

mire ['maɪə*] *n* Morast *m*.

mirror ['mɪrə*] *n* Spiegel *m* ♦ *vt* (*lit, fig*)
widerspiegeln.

mirror image n Spiegelbild nt.
mirth [mə:θ] n Heiterkeit f.
misadventure [mɪsəd'vɛntʃə˙] n Mißgeschick nt; **death by** ~ (BRIT) Tod m durch Unfall.
misanthropist [mɪ'zænθrəpɪst] n Misanthrop m, Menschenfeind m.
misapply [mɪsə'plaɪ] vt (term) falsch verwenden; (rule) falsch anwenden.
misapprehension ['mɪsæprɪ'hɛnʃən] n Mißverständnis nt; **you are under a** ~ Sie befinden sich im Irrtum.
misappropriate [mɪsə'prəuprɪeɪt] vt veruntreuen.
misappropriation ['mɪsəprəuprɪ'eɪʃən] n Veruntreuung f.
misbehave [mɪsbɪ'heɪv] vi sich schlecht benehmen.
misbehaviour, (US) **misbehavior** [mɪsbɪ'heɪvjə˙] n schlechtes Benehmen nt.
misc. abbr = **miscellaneous.**
miscalculate [mɪs'kælkjuleɪt] vt falsch berechnen; (misjudge) falsch einschätzen.
miscalculation ['mɪskælkju'leɪʃən] n Rechenfehler m; (misjudgement) Fehleinschätzung f.
miscarriage ['mɪskærɪdʒ] n (MED) Fehlgeburt f; ~ **of justice** (LAW) Justizirrtum m.
miscarry [mɪs'kærɪ] vi (MED) eine Fehlgeburt haben; (fail: plans) fehlschlagen.
miscellaneous [mɪsɪ'leɪnɪəs] adj verschieden; (subjects, items) divers; ~ **expenses** sonstige Unkosten pl.
mischance [mɪs'tʃɑːns] n unglücklicher Zufall m.
mischief ['mɪstʃɪf] n (bad behaviour) Unfug m; (playfulness) Verschmitztheit f; (harm) Schaden m; (pranks) Streiche pl; **to get into** ~ etwas anstellen; **to do sb a** ~ jdm etwas antun.
mischievous ['mɪstʃɪvəs] adj (naughty) ungezogen; (playful) verschmitzt.
misconception ['mɪskən'sɛpʃən] n fälschliche Annahme f.
misconduct [mɪs'kɒndʌkt] n Fehlverhalten nt; **professional** ~ Berufsvergehen nt.
misconstrue [mɪskən'struː] vt mißverstehen.
miscount [mɪs'kaunt] vt falsch zählen ♦ vi sich verzählen.
misdemeanour, (US) **misdemeanor** [mɪsdɪ'miːnə˙] n Vergehen nt.
misdirect [mɪsdɪ'rɛkt] vt (person) in die falsche Richtung schicken; (talent) vergeuden.
miser ['maɪzə˙] n Geizhals m.
miserable ['mɪzərəbl] adj (unhappy) unglücklich; (wretched) erbärmlich, elend; (unpleasant: weather) trostlos; (: person) gemein; (contemptible: offer, donation) armselig; (: failure) kläglich; **to feel** ~ sich elend fühlen.
miserably ['mɪzərəblɪ] adv (fail) kläglich; (live) elend; (smile, speak) unglücklich; (small)

jämmerlich.
miserly ['maɪzəlɪ] adj geizig; (amount) armselig.
misery ['mɪzərɪ] n (unhappiness) Kummer m; (wretchedness) Elend nt; (inf: person) Miesepeter m.
misfire [mɪs'faɪə˙] vi (plan) fehlschlagen; (car engine) fehlzünden.
misfit ['mɪsfɪt] n Außenseiter(in) m(f).
misfortune [mɪs'fɔːtʃən] n Pech nt, Unglück nt.
misgiving [mɪs'gɪvɪŋ] n Bedenken pl; **to have** ~**s about sth** bei etw nicht wohl fühlen.
misguided [mɪs'gaɪdɪd] adj töricht; (opinion, view) irrig; (misplaced) unangebracht.
mishandle [mɪs'hændl] vt falsch handhaben.
mishap [mɪs'hæp] n Mißgeschick nt.
mishear [mɪs'hɪə˙] (irreg: like **hear**) vt falsch hören ♦ vi sich verhören.
misheard [mɪs'hɜːd] pt, pp of **mishear.**
mishmash ['mɪʃmæʃ] (inf) n Mischmasch m.
misinform [mɪsɪn'fɔːm] vt falsch informieren.
misinterpret [mɪsɪn'tɜːprɪt] vt (gesture, situation) falsch auslegen; (comment) falsch auffassen.
misinterpretation ['mɪsɪntɜːprɪ'teɪʃən] n falsche Auslegung f.
misjudge [mɪs'dʒʌdʒ] vt falsch einschätzen.
mislay [mɪs'leɪ] (irreg: like **lay**) vt verlegen.
mislead [mɪs'liːd] (irreg: like **lead**) vt irreführen.
misleading [mɪs'liːdɪŋ] adj irreführend.
misled [mɪs'lɛd] pt, pp of **mislead.**
mismanage [mɪs'mænɪdʒ] vt (business) herunterwirtschaften; (institution) schlecht führen.
mismanagement [mɪs'mænɪdʒmənt] n Mißwirtschaft f.
misnomer [mɪs'nəumə˙] n unzutreffende Bezeichnung f.
misogynist [mɪ'sɒdʒɪnɪst] n Frauenfeind m.
misplaced [mɪs'pleɪst] adj (misguided) unangebracht; (wrongly positioned) an der falschen Stelle.
misprint ['mɪsprɪnt] n Druckfehler m.
mispronounce [mɪsprə'nauns] vt falsch aussprechen.
misquote ['mɪs'kwəut] vt falsch zitieren.
misread [mɪs'riːd] (irreg: like **read**) vt falsch lesen; (misinterpret) falsch verstehen.
misrepresent [mɪsrɛprɪ'zɛnt] vt falsch darstellen; **he was** ~**ed** seine Worte wurden verfälscht wiedergegeben.
Miss [mɪs] n Fräulein nt; **Dear** ~ **Smith** Liebe Frau Smith.
miss [mɪs] vt (train etc, chance, opportunity) verpassen; (target) verfehlen; (notice loss of, regret absence of) vermissen; (class, meeting) fehlen bei ♦ vi danebentreffen; (missile, object) danebengehen ♦ n Fehltreffer m; **you can't** ~ **it** du kannst es nicht verfehlen; **the bus just** ~**ed the wall** der Bus wäre um ein Haar gegen die Mauer gefahren; **you're**

~ing the point das geht an der Sache
vorbei.

►**miss out** (*BRIT*) *vt* auslassen.

►**miss out on** *vt fus* (*party*) verpassen; (*fun*)
zu kurz kommen bei.

missal ['mɪsl] *n* Meßbuch *nt*.

misshapen [mɪs'ʃeɪpən] *adj* mißgebildet.

missile ['mɪsaɪl] *n* (*MIL*) Rakete *f*; (*object
thrown*) (Wurf)geschoß *nt*.

missile base *n* Raketenbasis *f*.

missile launcher [-'lɔːntʃə•] *n* Startrampe *f*.

missing ['mɪsɪŋ] *adj* (*lost: person*) vermißt;
(: *object*) verschwunden; (*absent, removed*)
fehlend; **to be ~** fehlen; **to go ~**
verschwinden; **~ person** Vermißte(r) *f(m)*.

mission ['mɪʃən] *n* (*task*) Mission *f*, Auftrag *m*;
(*representatives*) Gesandtschaft *f*; (*MIL*)
Einsatz *m*; (*REL*) Mission *f*; **on a ~ to ...** (*to
place/people*) im Einsatz in +*dat*/bei ...

missionary ['mɪʃənrɪ] *n* Missionar(in) *m(f)*.

missive ['mɪsɪv] (*form*) *n* Schreiben *nt*.

misspell ['mɪs'spɛl] (*irreg: like* **spell**) *vt* falsch
schreiben.

misspent ['mɪs'spɛnt] *adj* (*youth*) vergeudet.

mist [mɪst] *n* Nebel *m*; (*light*) Dunst *m* ♦ *vi* (*also:
~ over: eyes*) sich verschleiern; (*BRIT: also:
~ over, ~ up*) (*windows*) beschlagen.

mistake [mɪs'teɪk] (*irreg: like* **take**) *n* Fehler *m*
♦ *vt* sich irren in +*dat*; (*intentions*) falsch
verstehen; **by ~** aus Versehen; **to make a ~**
(*in writing, calculation*) sich vertun; **to make a
~ (about sb/sth)** sich (in jdm/etw) irren; **to
~ A for B** A mit B verwechseln.

mistaken [mɪs'teɪkən] *pp of* **mistake** ♦ *adj*
falsch; **to be ~** sich irren.

mistaken identity *n* Verwechslung *f*.

mistakenly [mɪs'teɪkənlɪ] *adv*
irrtümlicherweise.

mister ['mɪstə•] (*inf*) *n* (*sir*) *not translated; see*
Mr.

mistletoe ['mɪsltəu] *n* Mistel *f*.

mistook [mɪs'tuk] *pt of* **mistake**.

mistranslation [mɪstræns'leɪʃən] *n* falsche
Übersetzung *f*.

mistreat [mɪs'triːt] *vt* schlecht behandeln.

mistress ['mɪstrɪs] *n* (*lover*) Geliebte *f*; (*of
house, servant, situation*) Herrin *f*; (*BRIT:
teacher*) Lehrerin *f*.

mistrust [mɪs'trʌst] *vt* mißtrauen +*dat* ♦ *n*:
~ (of) Mißtrauen *nt* (gegenüber).

mistrustful [mɪs'trʌstful] *adj*: **~ (of)**
mißtrauisch (gegenüber).

misty ['mɪstɪ] *adj* (*day etc*) neblig; (*glasses,
windows*) beschlagen.

misty-eyed ['mɪstɪ'aɪd] *adj* mit
verschleiertem Blick.

misunderstand [mɪsʌndə'stænd] (*irreg: like*
understand) *vt* mißverstehen, falsch
verstehen ♦ *vi* es falsch verstehen.

misunderstanding ['mɪsʌndə'stændɪŋ] *n*
Mißverständnis *nt*; (*disagreement*)
Meinungsverschiedenheit *f*.

misunderstood [mɪsʌndə'stud] *pt, pp of*
misunderstand.

misuse [*n* mɪs'juːs, *vt* mɪs'juːz] *n* Mißbrauch *m*
♦ *vt* mißbrauchen; (*word*) falsch
gebrauchen.

MIT (*US*) *n abbr* (= *Massachusetts Institute of
Technology*) *private technische
Fachhochschule.*

mite [maɪt] *n* (*small quantity*) bißchen *nt*; (*BRIT:
small child*) Würmchen *nt*.

miter ['maɪtə•] (*US*) *n* = **mitre**.

mitigate ['mɪtɪgeɪt] *vt* mildern; **mitigating
circumstances** mildernde Umstände *pl*.

mitigation [mɪtɪ'geɪʃən] *n* Milderung *f*.

mitre, (*US*) miter ['maɪtə•] *n* (*of bishop*) Mitra
f; (*CARPENTRY*) Gehrung *f*.

mitt(en) ['mɪt(n)] *n* Fausthandschuh *m*.

mix [mɪks] *vt* mischen; (*drink*) mixen; (*sauce,
cake*) zubereiten; (*ingredients*) verrühren
♦ *vi*: **to ~ (with)** verkehren (mit) ♦ *n*
Mischung *f*; **to ~ sth with sth** etw mit etw
vermischen; **to ~ business with pleasure**
das Angenehme mit dem Nützlichen
verbinden; **cake ~** Backmischung *f*.

►**mix in** *vt* (*eggs etc*) unterrühren.

►**mix up** *vt* (*people*) verwechseln; (*things*)
durcheinanderbringen; **to be ~ed up in sth**
in etw *acc* verwickelt sein.

mixed [mɪkst] *adj* gemischt; **~ marriage**
Mischehe *f*.

mixed-ability ['mɪkstə'bɪlɪtɪ] *adj* (*group etc*)
mit unterschiedlicher Fähigkeiten.

mixed bag *n* (*of things, problems*)
Sammelsurium *nt*; (*of people*) gemischter
Haufen *m*.

mixed blessing *n*: **it's a ~** das ist ein
zweischneidiges Schwert.

mixed doubles *npl* gemischtes Doppel *nt*.

mixed economy *n* gemischte
Wirtschaftsform *f*.

mixed grill (*BRIT*) *n* Grillteller *m*.

mixed-up [mɪkst'ʌp] *adj* durcheinander.

mixer ['mɪksə•] *n* (*for food*) Mixer *m*; (*drink*)
Tonic etc zum Auffüllen von alkoholischen
Mixgetränken; **to be a good ~** (*sociable
person*) kontaktfreudig sein.

mixer tap *n* Mischbatterie *f*.

mixture ['mɪkstʃə•] *n* Mischung *f*; (*CULIN*)
Gemisch *nt*; (: *for cake*) Teig *m*; (*MED*)
Mixtur *f*.

mix-up ['mɪksʌp] *n* Durcheinander *nt*.

MK (*BRIT*) *abbr* (*TECH*) = **mark**.

mk *abbr* (*FIN*) = **mark**.

mkt *abbr* = **market**.

MLitt *n abbr* (= *Master of Literature, Master of
Letters*) *akademischer Grad in
Literaturwissenschaft.*

MLR (*BRIT*) *n abbr* = **minimum lending rate**.

mm *abbr* (= *millimetre*) mm.

MN *abbr* (*BRIT*) = **merchant navy**; (*US: POST:
= Minnesota*).

MO *n abbr* (= *medical officer*) Sanitätsoffizier

m; (US: inf) = **modus operandi** ♦ abbr (US: POST: = Missouri).

m.o. abbr = **money order**.

moan [məun] n Stöhnen nt ♦ vi stöhnen; (inf: complain): **to ~ (about)** meckern (über +acc).

moaner ['məunə'] (inf) n Miesmacher(in) m(f).

moat [məut] n Wassergraben m.

mob [mɔb] n Mob m; (organized) Bande f ♦ vt herfallen über +acc.

mobile ['məubaıl] adj beweglich; (workforce, society) mobil ♦ n (decoration) Mobile nt; **applicants must be ~** Bewerber müssen motorisiert sein.

mobile home n Wohnwagen m.

mobile phone n Funktelefon nt.

mobility [məu'bılıtı] n Beweglichkeit f; (of workforce etc) Mobilität f.

mobility allowance n Beihilfe für Gehbehinderte.

mobilize ['məubılaız] vt mobilisieren; (MIL) mobil machen ♦ vi (MIL) mobil machen.

moccasin ['mɔkəsın] n Mokassin m.

mock [mɔk] vt sich lustig machen über +acc ♦ adj (fake: Elizabethan etc) Pseudo-; (exam) Probe-; (battle) Schein-.

mockery ['mɔkərı] n Spott m; **to make a ~ of sb** jdn zum Gespött machen; **to make a ~ of sth** etw zur Farce machen.

mocking ['mɔkıŋ] adj spöttisch.

mockingbird ['mɔkıŋbə:d] n Spottdrossel f.

mock-up ['mɔkʌp] n Modell nt.

MOD (BRIT) n abbr = **Ministry of Defence**.

mod cons ['mɔd'kɔnz] (BRIT) npl abbr (= modern conveniences) Komfort m.

mode [məud] n Form f; (COMPUT, TECH) Betriebsart f; **~ of life** Lebensweise f; **~ of transport** Transportmittel nt.

model ['mɔdl] n Modell nt; (fashion model) Mannequin nt; (example) Muster nt ♦ adj (excellent) vorbildlich; (small scale: railway etc) Modell- ♦ vt (clothes) vorführen; (with clay etc) modellieren, formen ♦ vi (for designer, photographer etc) als Modell arbeiten; **to ~ o.s. on sb** sich dat jdn zum Vorbild nehmen.

modeller, (US) **modeler** ['mɔdlə'] n Modellbauer m.

model railway n Modelleisenbahn f.

modem ['məudɛm] n Modem nt.

moderate [adj 'mɔdərət, vb 'mɔdəreıt] adj gemäßigt; (amount) nicht allzu groß; (change) leicht ♦ n Gemäßigte(r) f(m) ♦ vi (storm, wind etc) nachlassen ♦ vt (tone, demands) mäßigen.

moderately ['mɔdərətlı] adv mäßig; (expensive, difficult) nicht allzu; (pleased, happy) einigermaßen; **~ priced** nicht allzu teuer.

moderation [mɔdə'reıʃən] n Mäßigung f; **in ~** in or mit Maßen.

moderator ['mɔdəreıtə'] n (ECCL) Synodalpräsident m.

modern ['mɔdən] adj modern; **~ languages** moderne Fremdsprachen pl.

modernization [mɔdənaı'zeıʃən] n Modernisierung f.

modernize ['mɔdənaız] vt modernisieren.

modest ['mɔdıst] adj bescheiden; (chaste) schamhaft.

modestly ['mɔdıstlı] adv bescheiden; (behave) schamhaft; (to a moderate extent) mäßig.

modesty ['mɔdıstı] n Bescheidenheit f; (chastity) Schamgefühl nt.

modicum ['mɔdıkəm] n: **a ~ of** ein wenig or bißchen.

modification [mɔdıfı'keıʃən] n Änderung f; (to policy etc) Modifizierung f; **to make ~s to** (Ver)änderungen vornehmen an +dat, modifizieren.

modify ['mɔdıfaı] vt (ver)ändern; (policy etc) modifizieren.

modish ['məudıʃ] adj (fashionable) modisch.

Mods [mɔdz] (BRIT) n abbr (SCOL: = (Honour) Moderations) akademische Prüfung an der Universität Oxford.

modular ['mɔdjulə'] adj (unit, furniture) aus Bauelementen (zusammengesetzt); (COMPUT) modular.

modulate ['mɔdjuleıt] vt modulieren; (process, activity) umwandeln.

modulation [mɔdju'leıʃən] n Modulation f; (modification) Veränderung f.

module ['mɔdju:l] n (Bau)element nt; (SPACE) Raumkapsel f; (SCOL) Kurs m.

modus operandi ['məudəsɔpə'rændi:] n Modus operandi m.

Mogadishu [mɔgə'dıʃu:] n Mogadischu nt.

mogul ['məugl] n (fig) Mogul m.

MOH (BRIT) n abbr (= Medical Officer of Health) Amtsarzt m, Amtsärztin f.

mohair ['məuhɛə'] n Mohair m.

Mohammed [mə'hæmɛd] n Mohammed m.

moist [mɔıst] adj feucht.

moisten ['mɔısn] vt anfeuchten.

moisture ['mɔıstʃə'] n Feuchtigkeit f.

moisturize ['mɔıstʃəraız] vt (skin) mit einer Feuchtigkeitscreme behandeln.

moisturizer ['mɔıstʃəraızə'] n Feuchtigkeitscreme f.

molar ['məulə'] n Backenzahn m.

molasses [mə'læsız] n Melasse f.

mold etc [məuld] (US) n, vt = **mould** etc.

Moldavia [mɔl'deıvıə] n Moldawien nt.

Moldavian [mɔl'deıvıən] adj moldawisch.

Moldova [mɔl'dəuvə] n Moldawien nt.

Moldovan adj moldawisch.

mole [məul] n (on skin) Leberfleck m; (ZOOL) Maulwurf m; (fig: spy) Spion(in) m(f).

molecular [məu'lekjulə'] adj molekular; (biology) Molekular-.

molecule ['mɔlıkju:l] n Molekül nt.

molehill ['məulhıl] n Maulwurfshaufen m.

molest [mə'lest] vt (assault sexually) sich vergehen an +dat; (harass) belästigen.

mollusc ['mɔləsk] *n* Weichtier *nt*.
mollycoddle ['mɔlıkɔdl] *vt* verhätscheln.
Molotov cocktail ['mɔlətɔf-] *n*
Molotowcocktail *m*.
molt [məult] (*US*) *vi* = **moult**.
molten ['məultən] *adj* geschmolzen, flüssig.
mom [mɔm] (*US*) *n* = **mum**.
moment ['məumənt] *n* Moment *m*, Augenblick
m; (*importance*) Bedeutung *f*; **for a** ~ (für)
einen Moment *or* Augenblick; **at that** ~ in
diesem Moment *or* Augenblick; **at the** ~
momentan; **for the** ~ vorläufig; **in a** ~
gleich; **"one** ~ **please"** (*TEL*) „bleiben Sie
am Apparat".
momentarily ['məuməntrılı] *adv* für einen
Augenblick *or* Moment; (*US: very soon*)
jeden Augenblick *or* Moment.
momentary ['məuməntərı] *adj* (*brief*) kurz.
momentous [məu'mɛntəs] *adj* (*occasion*)
bedeutsam; (*decision*) von großer
Tragweite.
momentum [məu'mɛntəm] *n* (*PHYS*) Impuls
m; (*fig: of movement*) Schwung *m*; (: *of events,
change*) Dynamik *f*; **to gather** ~ schneller
werden; (*fig*) richtig in Gang kommen.
mommy ['mɔmı] (*US*) *n* = **mummy**.
Mon. *abbr* (= *Monday*) Mo.
Monaco ['mɔnəkəu] *n* Monaco *nt*.
monarch ['mɔnək] *n* Monarch(in) *m(f)*.
monarchist ['mɔnəkıst] *n* Monarchist(in) *m(f)*.
monarchy ['mɔnəkı] *n* Monarchie *f*; **the M**~
(*royal family*) die königliche Familie.
monastery ['mɔnəstərı] *n* Kloster *nt*.
monastic [mə'næstık] *adj* Kloster-,
klösterlich; (*fig*) mönchisch, klösterlich
einfach.
Monday ['mʌndı] *n* Montag *m*; *see also*
Tuesday.
Monegasque [mɔnə'gæsk] *adj* monegassisch
♦ *n* Monegasse *m*, Monegassin *f*.
monetarist ['mʌnıtərıst] *n* Monetarist(in) *m(f)*
♦ *adj* monetaristisch.
monetary ['mʌnıtərı] *adj* (*system, union*)
Währungs-.
money ['mʌnı] *n* Geld *nt*; **to make** ~ (*person*)
Geld verdienen; (*business*) etwas
einbringen; **danger** ~ (*BRIT*)
Gefahrenzulage *f*; **I've got no** ~ **left** ich habe
kein Geld mehr.
moneyed ['mʌnıd] (*form*) *adj* begütert.
moneylender ['mʌnılɛndə'] *n*
Geldverleiher(in) *m(f)*.
moneymaker ['mʌnımeıkə'] *n* (*person*)
Finanzgenie *nt*; (*idea*) einträgliche Sache *f*;
(*product*) Verkaufserfolg *m*.
moneymaking ['mʌnımeıkıŋ] *adj* einträglich.
money market *n* Geldmarkt *m*.
money order *n* Zahlungsanweisung *f*.
money-spinner ['mʌnıspınə'] (*inf*) *n*
Verkaufsschlager *m*; (*person, business*)
Goldgrube *f*.
money supply *n* Geldvolumen *nt*.

Mongol ['mɔŋgəl] *n* Mongole *m*, Mongolin *f*;
(*LING*) Mongolisch *nt*.
mongol ['mɔŋgəl] (*offensive*) *n* Mongoloide(r)
f(m).
Mongolia [mɔŋ'gəulıə] *n* Mongolien *nt*.
Mongolian [mɔŋ'gəulıən] *adj* mongolisch ♦ *n*
Mongole *m*, Mongolin *f*; (*LING*) Mongolisch
nt.
mongoose ['mɔŋguːs] *n* Mungo *m*.
mongrel ['mʌŋgrəl] *n* Promenadenmischung *f*.
monitor ['mɔnıtə'] *n* Monitor *m* ♦ *vt*
überwachen; (*broadcasts*) mithören.
monk [mʌŋk] *n* Mönch *m*.
monkey ['mʌŋkı] *n* Affe *m*.
monkey business (*inf*) *n* faule Sachen *pl*.
monkey nut (*BRIT*) *n* Erdnuß *f*.
monkey tricks *npl* = **monkey business.**
monkey wrench *n* verstellbarer
Schraubenschlüssel *m*.
mono ['mɔnəu] *adj* (*recording etc*) Mono-.
monochrome ['mɔnəkrəum] *adj* (*photograph,
television*) Schwarzweiß-; (*COMPUT: screen*)
Monochrom-.
monogamous [mɔ'nɔgəməs] *adj* monogam.
monogamy [mɔ'nɔgəmı] *n* Monogamie *f*.
monogram ['mɔnəgræm] *n* Monogramm *nt*.
monolith ['mɔnəlıθ] *n* Monolith *m*.
monolithic [mɔnə'lıθık] *adj* monolithisch.
monologue ['mɔnəlɔg] *n* Monolog *m*.
monoplane ['mɔnəpleın] *n* Eindecker *m*.
monopolize [mə'nɔpəlaız] *vt* beherrschen;
(*person*) mit Beschlag belegen;
(*conversation*) an sich *acc* reißen.
monopoly [mə'nɔpəlı] *n* Monopol *nt*; **to have a**
~ **on** *or* **of sth** (*fig: domination*) etw für sich
gepachtet haben; **Monopolies and Mergers
Commission** (*BRIT*) ≈ Kartellamt *nt*.
monorail ['mɔnəureıl] *n* Einschienenbahn *f*.
monosodium glutamate
[mɔnə'səudıəm'gluːtəmeıt] *n* Glutamat *nt*.
monosyllabic [mɔnəsı'læbık] *adj* einsilbig.
monosyllable ['mɔnəsıləbl] *n* einsilbiges
Wort *nt*.
monotone ['mɔnətəun] *n*: **in a** ~ monoton.
monotonous [mə'nɔtənəs] *adj* monoton,
eintönig.
monotony [mə'nɔtənı] *n* Monotonie *f*,
Eintönigkeit *f*.
monsoon [mɔn'suːn] *n* Monsun *m*.
monster ['mɔnstə'] *n* Ungetüm *nt*, Monstrum
nt; (*imaginary creature*) Ungeheuer *nt*,
Monster *nt*; (*person*) Unmensch *m*.
monstrosity [mɔn'strɔsıtı] *n* Ungetüm *nt*,
Monstrum *nt*.
monstrous ['mɔnstrəs] *adj* (*huge*) riesig;
(*ugly*) abscheulich; (*atrocious*)
ungeheuerlich.
Mont. (*US*) *abbr* (*POST*: = *Montana*).
montage [mɔn'tɑːʒ] *n* Montage *f*.
Mont Blanc [mɔ̃blɑ̃] *n* Montblanc *m*.
month [mʌnθ] *n* Monat *m*; **every** ~ jeden
Monat; **300 dollars a** ~ 300 Dollar im Monat.

monthly ['mʌnθlɪ] *adj* monatlich; (*ticket, magazine*) Monats- ♦ *adv* monatlich; **twice ~** zweimal im Monat.

Montreal [mɒntrɪ'ɔːl] *n* Montreal *nt*.

monument ['mɒnjumənt] *n* Denkmal *nt*.

monumental [mɒnju'mentl] *adj* (*building, statue*) gewaltig, monumental; (*book, piece of work*) unsterblich; (*storm, row*) ungeheuer.

moo [muː] *vi* muhen.

mood [muːd] *n* Stimmung *f*; (*of person*) Laune *f*, Stimmung *f*; **to be in a good/bad ~** gut/ schlecht gelaunt sein; **to be in the ~ for** aufgelegt sein zu.

moodily ['muːdɪlɪ] *adv* launisch; (*sullenly*) schlecht gelaunt.

moody ['muːdɪ] *adj* launisch; (*sullen*) schlecht gelaunt.

moon [muːn] *n* Mond *m*.

moonlight ['muːnlaɪt] *n* Mondschein *m* ♦ *vi* (*inf*) schwarzarbeiten.

moonlighting ['muːnlaɪtɪŋ] (*inf*) *n* Schwarzarbeit *f*.

moonlit ['muːnlɪt] *adj* (*night*) mondhell.

moonshot ['muːnʃɒt] *n* Mondflug *m*.

moor [muə'] *n* (Hoch)moor *nt*, Heide *f* ♦ *vt* vertäuen ♦ *vi* anlegen.

mooring ['muərɪŋ] *n* Anlegeplatz *m*; **moorings** *npl* (*chains*) Verankerung *f*.

Moorish ['muərɪʃ] *adj* maurisch.

moorland ['muələnd] *n* Moorlandschaft *f*, Heidelandschaft *f*.

moose [muːs] *n inv* Elch *m*.

moot [muːt] *vt*: **to be ~ed** vorgeschlagen werden ♦ *adj*: **it's a ~ point** das ist fraglich.

mop [mɒp] *n* (*for floor*) Mop *m*; (*for dishes*) Spülbürste *f*; (*of hair*) Mähne *f* ♦ *vt* (*floor*) wischen; (*face*) abwischen; (*eyes*) sich *dat* wischen; **to ~ the sweat from one's brow** sich *dat* den Schweiß von der Stirn wischen.

▶**mop up** *vt* aufwischen.

mope [məup] *vi* Trübsal blasen.

▶**mope about** *vi* mit einer Jammermiene herumlaufen.

▶**mope around** *vi* = mope about.

moped ['məupɛd] *n* Moped *nt*.

moquette [mɒ'kɛt] *n* Mokett *m*.

MOR *adj abbr* (*MUS*) = **middle-of-the-road**.

moral ['mɒrl] *adj* moralisch; (*welfare, values*) sittlich; (*behaviour*) moralisch einwandfrei ♦ *n* Moral *f*; **morals** *npl* (*principles, values*) Moralvorstellungen *pl*; **~ support** moralische Unterstützung *f*.

morale [mɒ'rɑːl] *n* Moral *f*.

morality [mə'rælɪtɪ] *n* Sittlichkeit *f*; (*system of morals*) Moral *f*, Ethik *f*; (*correctness*) moralische Richtigkeit *f*.

moralize ['mɒrəlaɪz] *vi* moralisieren; **to ~ about** sich moralisch entrüsten über +*acc*.

morally ['mɒrəlɪ] *adv* moralisch; (*live, behave*) moralisch einwandfrei.

moral victory *n* moralischer Sieg *m*.

morass [mə'ræs] *n* Morast *m*, Sumpf *m* (*also*

fig).

moratorium [mɒrə'tɔːrɪəm] *n* Stopp *m*, Moratorium *nt*.

morbid ['mɔːbɪd] *adj* (*imagination*) krankhaft; (*interest*) unnatürlich; (*comments, behaviour*) makaber.

═══════════════════ *KEYWORD*

more [mɔː'] *adj* **1** (*greater in number etc*) mehr; **~ people/work/letters than we expected** mehr Leute/Arbeit/Briefe, als wir erwarteten; **I have ~ wine/money than you** ich habe mehr Wein/Geld als du
2 (*additional*): **do you want (some) ~ tea?** möchten Sie noch mehr Tee?; **is there any ~ wine?** ist noch Wein da?; **I have no ~ money, I don't have any ~ money** ich habe kein Geld mehr
♦ *pron* **1** (*greater amount*) mehr; **~ than 10** mehr als 10; **it cost ~ than we expected** es kostete mehr, als wir erwarteten
2 (*further or additional amount*): **is there any ~?** gibt es noch mehr?; **there's no ~** es ist nichts mehr da; **many/much ~** viel mehr
♦ *adv* mehr; **~ dangerous/difficult/easily etc (than)** gefährlicher/schwerer/leichter *etc* (als); **~ and ~** mehr und mehr, immer mehr; **~ and ~ excited/expensive** immer aufgeregter/teurer; **~ or less** mehr oder weniger; **~ than ever** mehr denn je, mehr als jemals zuvor; **~ beautiful than ever** schöner denn je; **no ~, not any ~** nicht mehr.

moreover [mɔː'rəuvə'] *adv* außerdem, zudem.

morgue [mɔːg] *n* Leichenschauhaus *nt*.

MORI ['mɔːrɪ] (*BRIT*) *n abbr* (= *Market and Opinion Research Institute*) Markt- und Meinungsforschungsinstitut.

moribund ['mɔrɪbʌnd] *adj* dem Untergang geweiht.

Mormon ['mɔːmən] *n* Mormone *m*, Mormonin *f*.

morning ['mɔːnɪŋ] *n* Morgen *m*; (*as opposed to afternoon*) Vormittag *m* ♦ *cpd* Morgen-; **in the ~** morgens; vormittags; (*tomorrow*) morgen früh; **7 o'clock in the ~** 7 Uhr morgens; **this ~** heute morgen.

morning-after pill ['mɔːnɪŋ'ɑːftə-] *n* Pille *f* danach.

morning sickness *n* (Schwangerschafts)übelkeit *f*.

Moroccan [mə'rɒkən] *adj* marokkanisch ♦ *n* Marokkaner(in) *m(f)*.

Morocco [mə'rɒkəu] *n* Marokko *nt*.

moron ['mɔːrɒn] (*inf*) *n* Schwachkopf *m*.

moronic [mə'rɒnɪk] (*inf*) *adj* schwachsinnig.

morose [mə'rəus] *adj* mißmutig.

morphine ['mɔːfiːn] *n* Morphium *nt*.

morris dancing ['mɒrɪs-] *n* Moriskentanz *m*, *alter englischer Volkstanz*.

Morse [mɔːs] *n* (*also:* **~ code**) Morsealphabet

nt.

morsel ['mɔːsl] *n* Stückchen *nt*.

mortal ['mɔːtl] *adj* sterblich; (*wound, combat*) tödlich; (*danger*) Todes-; (*sin, enemy*) Tod- ♦ *n* (*human being*) Sterbliche(r) *f(m)*.

mortality [mɔː'tælɪtɪ] *n* Sterblichkeit *f*; (*number of deaths*) Todesfälle *pl*.

mortality rate *n* Sterblichkeitsziffer *f*.

mortar ['mɔːtə•] *n* (*MIL*) Minenwerfer *m*; (*CONSTR*) Mörtel *m*; (*CULIN*) Mörser *m*.

mortgage ['mɔːgɪdʒ] *n* Hypothek *f* ♦ *vt* mit einer Hypothek belasten; **to take out a ~** eine Hypothek aufnehmen.

mortgage company (*US*) *n* Hypotheken-bank *f*.

mortgagee [mɔːgə'dʒiː] *n* Hypotheken-gläubiger *m*.

mortgagor ['mɔːgədʒə•] *n* Hypotheken-schuldner *m*.

mortician [mɔː'tɪʃən] (*US*) *n* Bestattungs-unternehmer *m*.

mortified ['mɔːtɪfaɪd] *adj*: **he was ~** er empfand das als beschämend; (*embarrassed*) es war ihm schrecklich peinlich.

mortify ['mɔːtɪfaɪ] *vt* beschämen.

mortise lock ['mɔːtɪs-] *n* Einsteckschloß *nt*.

mortuary ['mɔːtjuərɪ] *n* Leichenhalle *f*.

mosaic [məu'zeɪɪk] *n* Mosaik *nt*.

Moscow ['mɒskəu] *n* Moskau *nt*.

Moslem ['mɒzləm] *adj, n* = **Muslim**.

mosque [mɒsk] *n* Moschee *f*.

mosquito [mɒs'kiːtəu] (*pl* ~**es**) *n* Stechmücke *f*; (*in tropics*) Moskito *m*.

mosquito net *n* Moskitonetz *nt*.

moss [mɒs] *n* Moos *nt*.

mossy ['mɒsɪ] *adj* bemoost.

============================= *KEYWORD*

most [məust] *adj* **1** (*almost all: people, things etc*) meiste(r, s); ~ **people** die meisten Leute
2 (*largest, greatest: interest, money etc*) meiste(r, s); **who has (the) ~ money?** wer hat das meiste Geld?
♦ *pron* (*greatest quantity, number*) der/die/das meiste; ~ **of it** das meiste (davon); ~ **of them** die meisten von ihnen; ~ **of the time/ work** die meiste Zeit/Arbeit; ~ **of the time he's very helpful** er ist meistens sehr hilfsbereit; **to make the ~ of sth** das Beste aus etw machen; **at the (very) ~** (aller)höchstens
♦ *adv* (+ *vb: spend, eat, work etc*) am meisten; (+ *adj*): **the ~ intelligent/expensive** *etc* der/ die/das intelligenteste/teuerste *etc*; (+ *adv: carefully, easily etc*) äußerst; (*very: polite, interesting etc*) höchst; **a ~ interesting book** ein höchst interessantes Buch.

mostly ['məustlɪ] *adv* (*chiefly*) hauptsächlich; (*usually*) meistens.

MOT (*BRIT*) *n abbr* (= *Ministry of Transport*):

~ **(test)** ≈ TÜV *m*; **the car failed its ~** das Auto ist nicht durch den TÜV gekommen.

motel [məu'tel] *n* Motel *nt*.

moth [mɒθ] *n* Nachtfalter *m*; (*clothes moth*) Motte *f*.

mothball ['mɒθbɔːl] *n* Mottenkugel *f*.

moth-eaten ['mɒθiːtn] (*pej*) *adj* mottenzerfressen.

mother ['mʌðə•] *n* Mutter *f* ♦ *adj* (*country*) Heimat-; (*company*) Mutter- ♦ *vt* großziehen; (*pamper, protect*) bemuttern.

motherboard ['mʌðəbɔːd] *n* (*COMPUT*) Hauptplatine *f*.

motherhood ['mʌðəhud] *n* Mutterschaft *f*.

mother-in-law ['mʌðərɪnlɔː] *n* Schwiegermutter *f*.

motherly ['mʌðəlɪ] *adj* mütterlich.

mother-of-pearl ['mʌðərəv'pɜːl] *n* Perlmutt *nt*.

mother's help *n* Haushaltshilfe *f*.

mother-to-be ['mʌðətə'biː] *n* werdende Mutter *f*.

mother tongue *n* Muttersprache *f*.

mothproof ['mɒθpruːf] *adj* mottenfest.

motif [məu'tiːf] *n* Motiv *nt*.

motion ['məuʃən] *n* Bewegung *f*; (*proposal*) Antrag *m*; (*BRIT: also:* **bowel ~**) Stuhlgang *m* ♦ *vt, vi*: **to ~ (to) sb to do sth** jdm ein Zeichen geben, daß er/sie etw tun solle; **to be in ~** (*vehicle*) fahren; **to set in ~** in Gang bringen; **to go through the ~s (of doing sth)** (*fig*) etw der Form halber tun; (*pretend*) so tun, als ob (man etw täte).

motionless ['məuʃənlɪs] *adj* reg(ungs)los.

motion picture *n* Film *m*.

motivate ['məutɪveɪt] *vt* motivieren.

motivated ['məutɪveɪtɪd] *adj* motiviert; ~ **by** getrieben von.

motivation [məutɪ'veɪʃən] *n* Motivation *f*.

motive ['məutɪv] *n* Motiv *nt*, Beweggrund *m* ♦ *adj* (*power, force*) Antriebs-; **from the best (of) ~s** mit den besten Absichten.

motley ['mɒtlɪ] *adj* bunt(gemischt).

motor ['məutə•] *n* Motor *m*; (*BRIT: inf: car*) Auto *nt* ♦ *cpd* (*industry, trade*) Auto(mobil)-.

motorbike ['məutəbaɪk] *n* Motorrad *nt*.

motorboat ['məutəbəut] *n* Motorboot *nt*.

motorcade ['məutəkeɪd] *n* Fahrzeugkolonne *f*.

motorcar ['məutəkɑː] (*BRIT*) *n* (Personenkraft)wagen *m*.

motorcoach ['məutəkəutʃ] (*BRIT*) *n* Reisebus *m*.

motorcycle ['məutəsaɪkl] *n* Motorrad *nt*.

motorcycle racing *n* Motorradrennen *nt*.

motorcyclist ['məutəsaɪklɪst] *n* Motorradfahrer(in) *m(f)*.

motoring ['məutərɪŋ] (*BRIT*) *n* Autofahren *nt* ♦ *cpd* Auto-; (*offence, accident*) Verkehrs-.

motorist ['məutərɪst] *n* Autofahrer(in) *m(f)*.

motorized ['məutəraɪzd] *adj* motorisiert.

motor oil *n* Motorenöl *nt*.

motor racing (*BRIT*) *n* Autorennen *nt*.

motor scooter n Motorroller m.
motor vehicle n Kraftfahrzeug nt.
motorway ['məutəweɪ] (BRIT) n Autobahn f.
mottled ['mɔtld] adj gesprenkelt.
motto ['mɔtəu] (pl ~es) n Motto nt.
mould, (US) mold [məuld] n (cast) Form f;
(: for metal) Gußform f; (mildew) Schimmel m
♦ vt (lit, fig) formen.
moulder ['məuldə*] vi (decay) vermodern.
moulding ['məuldɪŋ] n (ARCHIT) Zierleiste f.
mouldy ['məuldɪ] adj schimmelig; (smell)
moderig.
moult, (US) molt [məult] vi (animal) sich
haaren; (bird) sich mausern.
mound [maund] n (of earth) Hügel m; (heap)
Haufen m.
mount [maunt] n (in proper names):
M~ Carmel der Berg Karmel; (horse) Pferd
nt; (for picture) Passepartout nt ♦ vt (horse)
besteigen; (exhibition etc) vorbereiten;
(jewel) (ein)fassen; (picture) mit einem
Passepartout versehen; (staircase)
hochgehen; (stamp) aufkleben; (attack,
campaign) organisieren ♦ vi (increase)
steigen; (: problems) sich häufen; (on horse)
aufsitzen.
►**mount up** vi (costs, savings) sich
summieren, sich zusammenläppern (inf).
mountain ['mauntɪn] n Berg m ♦ cpd (road,
stream) Gebirgs-; **to make a ~ out of a
molehill** aus einer Mücke einen Elefanten
machen.
mountain bike n Mountain-Bike nt.
mountaineer [mauntɪ'nɪə*] n Bergsteiger(in)
m(f).
mountaineering [mauntɪ'nɪərɪŋ] n
Bergsteigen nt; **to go ~** bergsteigen gehen.
mountainous ['mauntɪnəs] adj gebirgig.
mountain range n Gebirgskette f.
mountain rescue team n Bergwacht f.
mountainside ['mauntɪnsaɪd] n (Berg)hang m.
mounted ['mauntɪd] adj (police, soldiers)
beritten.
Mount Everest n Mount Everest m.
mourn [mɔ:n] vt betrauern ♦ vi: **to ~ (for)**
trauern (um).
mourner ['mɔ:nə*] n Trauernde(r) f(m).
mournful ['mɔ:nful] adj traurig.
mourning ['mɔ:nɪŋ] n Trauer f; **to be in ~**
trauern; (wear special clothes) Trauer tragen.
mouse [maus] (pl mice) n (ZOOL, COMPUT)
Maus f; (fig: person) schüchternes Mäuschen
nt.
mousetrap ['maustræp] n Mausefalle f.
moussaka [mu'sɑ:kə] n Moussaka f.
mousse [mu:s] n (CULIN) Mousse f; (cosmetic)
Schaumfestiger m.
moustache, (US) mustache [məs'tɑ:ʃ] n
Schnurrbart m.
mousy ['mausɪ] adj (hair) mausgrau.
mouth [mauθ] (pl ~s) n Mund m; (of cave, hole,
bottle) Öffnung f; (of river) Mündung f.

mouthful ['mauθful] n (of food) Bissen m; (of
drink) Schluck m.
mouth organ n Mundharmonika f.
mouthpiece ['mauθpi:s] n Mundstück nt;
(spokesman) Sprachrohr nt.
mouth-to-mouth ['mauθtə'mauθ] adj:
~ **resuscitation** Mund-zu-Mund-Beatmung f.
mouthwash ['mauθwɔʃ] n Mundwasser nt.
mouth-watering ['mauθwɔ:tərɪŋ] adj
appetitlich.
movable ['mu:vəbl] adj beweglich; ~ **feast**
beweglicher Feiertag m.
move [mu:v] n (movement) Bewegung f; (in
game) Zug m; (change: of house) Umzug m;
(: of job) Stellenwechsel m ♦ vt bewegen;
(furniture) (ver)rücken; (car) umstellen; (in
game) ziehen mit; (emotionally) bewegen,
ergreifen; (POL: resolution etc) beantragen
♦ vi sich bewegen; (traffic) vorankommen; (in
game) ziehen; (also: ~ **house**) umziehen;
(develop) sich entwickeln; **it's my ~** ich bin
am Zug; **to get a ~ on** sich beeilen; **to ~ sb
to do sth** jdn (dazu) veranlassen, etw zu
tun; **to ~ towards** sich nähern +dat.
►**move about** vi sich (hin- und her)bewegen;
(travel) unterwegs sein; (from place to place)
umherziehen; (change residence) umziehen;
(change job) die Stelle wechseln; **I can hear
him moving about** ich höre ihn
herumlaufen.
►**move along** vi weitergehen.
►**move around** vi = move about.
►**move away** vi (from town, area) wegziehen.
►**move back** vi (return) zurückkommen.
►**move forward** vi (advance) vorrücken.
►**move in** vi (to house) einziehen; (police,
soldiers) anrücken.
►**move off** vi (car) abfahren.
►**move on** vi (leave) weitergehen; (travel)
weiterfahren ♦ vt (onlookers) zum
Weitergehen auffordern.
►**move out** vi (of house) ausziehen.
►**move over** vi (to make room) (zur Seite)
rücken.
►**move up** vi (employee) befördert werden;
(pupil) versetzt werden; (deputy) aufrücken.
moveable ['mu:vəbl] adj = movable.
movement ['mu:vmənt] n (action, group)
Bewegung f; (freedom to move)
Bewegungsfreiheit f; (transportation)
Beförderung f; (shift) Trend m; (MUS) Satz
m; (MED: also: bowel ~) Stuhlgang m.
mover ['mu:və*] n (of proposal)
Antragsteller(in) m(f).
movie ['mu:vɪ] n Film m; **to go to the ~s** ins
Kino gehen.
movie camera n Filmkamera f.
moviegoer ['mu:vɪgəuə*] (US) n
Kinogänger(in) m(f).
moving ['mu:vɪŋ] adj beweglich; (emotional)
ergreifend; (instigating): **the ~ spirit/force**
die treibende Kraft.

mow [məu] (_pt_ **mowed,** _pp_ **mowed** _or_ **mown**) _vt_ mähen.

▶**mow down** _vt_ (_kill_) niedermähen.

mower ['məuə'] _n_ (_also:_ **lawnmower**) Rasenmäher _m._

Mozambique [məuzəm'bi:k] _n_ Mosambik _nt._

MP _n abbr_ (= _Member of Parliament_) ≈ MdB; = **military police**; (_CANADA:_ = _Mounted Police_) berittene Polizei _f._

mpg _n abbr_ (= _miles per gallon_) _see_ **mile.**

mph _abbr_ (= _miles per hour_) Meilen pro Stunde.

MPhil _n abbr_ (= _Master of Philosophy_) ≈ M.A.

MPS (_BRIT_) _n abbr_ (= _Member of the Pharmaceutical Society_) _Qualifikationsnachweis für Pharmazeuten._

Mr, (_US_) **Mr.** ['mɪstə'] _n:_ ~ **Smith** Herr Smith.

MRC (_BRIT_) _n abbr_ (= _Medical Research Council_) _medizinischer Forschungsausschuß._

MRCP (_BRIT_) _n abbr_ (= _Member of the Royal College of Physicians_) _höchster akademischer Grad in Medizin._

MRCS (_BRIT_) _n abbr_ (= _Member of the Royal College of Surgeons_) _höchster akademischer Grad für Chirurgen._

MRCVS (_BRIT_) _n abbr_ (= _Member of the Royal College of Veterinary Surgeons_) _höchster akademischer Grad für Tiermediziner._

Mrs, (_US_) **Mrs.** ['mɪsɪz] _n:_ ~ **Smith** Frau Smith.

MS _n abbr_ (= _multiple sclerosis_) MS _f_; (_US:_ = _Master of Science_) _akademischer Grad in Naturwissenschaften_ ♦ _abbr_ (_US: POST:_ = _Mississippi_).

MS. (_pl_ **MSS.**) _n abbr_ (= _manuscript_) Ms.

Ms, (_US_) **Ms.** [mɪz] _n_ (= _Miss or Mrs_): ~ **Smith** Frau Smith.

MSA (_US_) _n abbr_ (= _Master of Science in Agriculture_) _akademischer Grad in Agronomie._

MSc _n abbr_ (= _Master of Science_) _akademischer Grad in Naturwissenschaften._

MSG _n abbr_ = **monosodium glutamate.**

MSS. _n abbr_ (= _manuscripts_) Mss.

MST (_US_) _abbr_ (= _Mountain Standard Time_) _amerikanische Standardzeitzone._

MSW (_US_) _n abbr_ (= _Master of Social Work_) _akademischer Grad in Sozialwissenschaft._

MT _n abbr_ (_COMPUT, LING:_ = _machine translation_) maschinelle Übersetzung _f_ ♦ _abbr_ (_US: POST:_ = _Montana_).

Mt _abbr_ (_GEOG_) = **mount.**

MTV (_esp US_) _n abbr_ (= _music television_) MTV _nt._

================= _KEYWORD_

much [mʌtʃ] _adj_ (_time, money, effort_) viel; **how** ~ **money/time do you need?** wieviel Geld/ Zeit brauchen Sie?; **he's done so** ~ **work for us** er hat so viel für uns gearbeitet; **as** ~ **as** soviel wie; **I have as** ~ **money/intelligence**

as you ich besitze genauso viel Geld/ Intelligenz wie du
♦ _pron_ viel; **how** ~ **is it?** was kostet es?
♦ _adv_ **1** (_greatly, a great deal_) sehr; **thank you very** ~ vielen Dank, danke sehr; **I read as** ~ **as I can** ich lese soviel wie ich kann
2 (_by far_) viel; **I'm** ~ **better now** mir geht es jetzt viel besser
3 (_almost_) fast; **how are you feeling?** - ~ **the same** wie fühlst du dich? - fast genauso; **the two books are** ~ **the same** die zwei Bücher sind sich sehr ähnlich.

muck [mʌk] _n_ (_dirt_) Dreck _m._

▶**muck about** (_inf_) _vi_ (_fool about_) herumalbern ♦ _vt:_ **to** ~ **sb about** mit jdm beliebig umspringen.

▶**muck around** _vi_ = **muck about.**

▶**muck in** (_BRIT: inf_) _vi_ mit anpacken.

▶**muck out** _vt_ (_stable_) ausmisten.

▶**muck up** (_inf_) _vt_ (_exam etc_) verpfuschen.

muckraking ['mʌkreɪkɪŋ] (_fig: inf_) _n_ Sensationsmache _f_ ♦ _adj_ sensationslüstern.

mucky ['mʌkɪ] _adj_ (_dirty_) dreckig; (_field_) matschig.

mucus ['mju:kəs] _n_ Schleim _m._

mud [mʌd] _n_ Schlamm _m._

muddle ['mʌdl] _n_ (_mess_) Durcheinander _nt_; (_confusion_) Verwirrung _f_ ♦ _vt_ (_person_) verwirren; (_also:_ ~ **up**) durcheinanderbringen; **to be in a** ~ völlig durcheinander sein; **to get in a** ~ (_person_) konfus werden; (_things_) durcheinandergeraten.

▶**muddle along** _vi_ vor sich _acc_ hinwursteln.

▶**muddle through** _vi_ (_get by_) sich durchschlagen.

muddle-headed [mʌdl'hedɪd] _adj_ zerstreut.

muddy ['mʌdɪ] _adj_ (_floor_) schmutzig; (_field_) schlammig.

mud flats _npl_ Watt(enmeer) _nt._

mudguard ['mʌdgɑ:d] (_BRIT_) _n_ Schutzblech _nt_; (_on old car_) Kotflügel _m._

mudpack ['mʌdpæk] _n_ Schlammpackung _f._

mud-slinging ['mʌdslɪŋɪŋ] _n_ (_fig_) Schlechtmacherei _f._

muesli ['mju:zlɪ] _n_ Müsli _nt._

muffin ['mʌfɪn] _n_ (_BRIT_) weiches, flaches Milchbrötchen, meist warm gegessen; (_US_) kleiner runder Rührkuchen.

muffle ['mʌfl] _vt_ (_sound_) dämpfen; (_against cold_) einmummeln.

muffled ['mʌfld] _adj_ (_see vt_) gedämpft; eingemummelt.

muffler ['mʌflə'] _n_ (_US: AUT_) Auspufftopf _m_; (_scarf_) dicker Schal _m._

mufti ['mʌftɪ] _n:_ **in** ~ in Zivil.

mug [mʌg] _n_ (_cup_) Becher _m_; (_for beer_) Krug _m_; (_inf: face_) Visage _f_; (: _fool_) Trottel _m_ ♦ _vt_ (auf der Straße) überfallen; **it's a** ~**'s game** (_BRIT_) das ist doch Schwachsinn.

▶**mug up** (_BRIT: inf_) _vt_ (_also:_ ~ **up on**) pauken.

mugger ['mʌgə'] _n_ Straßenräuber _m._

mugging ['mʌgɪŋ] n Straßenraub m.
muggins ['mʌgɪnz] (BRIT: inf) n Dummkopf m; **... and ~ does all the work** ... und ich bin mal wieder der/die Dumme und mache die ganze Arbeit.
muggy ['mʌgɪ] adj (weather, day) schwül.
mug shot (inf) n (of criminal) Verbrecherfoto nt; (for passport) Paßbild nt.
mulatto [mju:'lætəu] (pl ~es) n Mulatte m, Mulattin f.
mulberry ['mʌlbrɪ] n (fruit) Maulbeere f; (tree) Maulbeerbaum m.
mule [mju:l] n Maultier nt.
mulled [mʌld] adj: ~ **wine** Glühwein m.
mullioned ['mʌlɪənd] adj (windows) längs unterteilt.
mull over [mʌl-] vt sich dat durch den Kopf gehen lassen.
multi... ['mʌltɪ] pref multi-, Multi-.
multi-access ['mʌltɪ'æksɛs] adj (COMPUT: system etc) Mehrplatz-.
multicoloured, (US) **multicolored** ['mʌltɪkʌləd] adj mehrfarbig.
multifarious [mʌltɪ'fɛərɪəs] adj vielfältig.
multilateral [mʌltɪ'lætərl] adj multilateral.
multi-level ['mʌltɪlevl] (US) adj = **multistorey**.
multimillionaire [mʌltɪmɪljə'nɛə*] n Multimillionär m.
multinational [mʌltɪ'næʃənl] adj multinational ♦ n multinationaler Konzern m, Multi m (inf).
multiple ['mʌltɪpl] adj (injuries) mehrfach; (interests, causes) vielfältig ♦ n Vielfache(s) nt; ~ **collision** Massenkarambolage f.
multiple-choice ['mʌltɪpltʃɔɪs] adj (question etc) Multiple-Choice-.
multiple sclerosis n multiple Sklerose f.
multiplex ['mʌltɪplɛks] n: ~ **transmitter** Multiplex-Sender m; ~ **cinema** Kinocenter nt.
multiplication [mʌltɪplɪ'keɪʃən] n Multiplikation f; (increase) Vervielfachung f.
multiplication table n Multiplikations-tabelle f.
multiplicity [mʌltɪ'plɪsɪtɪ] n: **a ~ of** eine Vielzahl von.
multiply ['mʌltɪplaɪ] vt multiplizieren ♦ vi (increase: problems) stark zunehmen; (: number) sich vervielfachen; (breed) sich vermehren.
multiracial [mʌltɪ'reɪʃl] adj gemischtrassig; (school) ohne Rassentrennung; ~ **policy** Politik f der Rassenintegration.
multistorey [mʌltɪ'stɔːrɪ] (BRIT) adj (building, car park) mehrstöckig.
multitude ['mʌltɪtjuːd] n Menge f; **a ~ of** eine Vielzahl von, eine Menge.
mum [mʌm] (BRIT: inf) n Mutti f, Mama f ♦ adj: **to keep ~** den Mund halten; ~**'s the word** nichts verraten!
mumble ['mʌmbl] vt, vi (indistinctly) nuscheln; (quietly) murmeln.
mumbo jumbo ['mʌmbəu-] n (nonsense)

Geschwafel nt.
mummify ['mʌmɪfaɪ] vt mumifizieren.
mummy ['mʌmɪ] n (BRIT: mother) Mami f; (embalmed body) Mumie f.
mumps [mʌmps] n Mumps m or f.
munch [mʌntʃ] vt, vi mampfen.
mundane [mʌn'deɪn] adj (life) banal; (task) stumpfsinnig.
Munich ['mjuːnɪk] n München nt.
municipal [mju:'nɪsɪpl] adj städtisch, Stadt-; (elections, administration) Kommunal-.
municipality [mju:nɪsɪ'pælɪtɪ] n Gemeinde f, Stadt f.
munitions [mju:'nɪʃənz] npl Munition f.
mural ['mjuərl] n Wandgemälde nt.
murder ['mɔːdə*] n Mord m ♦ vt ermorden; (spoil: piece of music, language) verhunzen; **to commit ~** einen Mord begehen.
murderer ['mɔːdərə*] n Mörder m.
murderess ['mɔːdərɪs] n Mörderin f.
murderous ['mɔːdərəs] adj blutrünstig; (attack) Mord-; (fig: look, attack) vernichtend; (: pace, heat) mörderisch.
murk [mɔːk] n Düsternis f.
murky ['mɔːkɪ] adj düster; (water) trübe.
murmur ['mɔːmə*] n (of voices) Murmeln nt; (of wind, waves) Rauschen nt ♦ vt, vi murmeln; **heart ~** Herzgeräusche pl.
MusB(ac) n abbr (= Bachelor of Music) akademischer Grad in Musikwissenschaft.
muscle ['mʌsl] n Muskel m; (fig: strength) Macht f.
►**muscle in** vi: **to ~ in (on sth)** (bei etw) mitmischen.
muscular ['mʌskjulə*] adj (pain, dystrophy) Muskel-; (person, build) muskulös.
muscular dystrophy n Muskeldystrophie f.
MusD(oc) n abbr (= Doctor of Music) Doktorat in Musikwissenschaft.
muse [mju:z] vi nachgrübeln ♦ n Muse f.
museum [mju:'zɪəm] n Museum nt.
mush [mʌʃ] n Brei m; (pej) Schmalz m.
mushroom ['mʌʃrum] n (edible) (eßbarer) Pilz m; (poisonous) Giftpilz m; (button mushroom) Champignon m ♦ vi (fig: buildings etc) aus dem Boden schießen; (: town, organization) explosionsartig wachsen.
mushroom cloud n Atompilz m.
mushy ['mʌʃɪ] adj matschig; (consistency) breiig; (inf: sentimental) rührselig; ~ **peas** Erbsenbrei m.
music ['mju:zɪk] n Musik f; (written music, score) Noten pl.
musical ['mju:zɪkl] adj musikalisch; (sound, tune) melodisch ♦ n Musical nt.
music(al) box n Spieldose f.
musical chairs n die Reise f nach Jerusalem.
musical instrument n Musikinstrument nt.
music centre n Musik-Center nt.
music hall n Varieté nt.
musician [mju:'zɪʃən] n Musiker(in) m(f).
music stand n Notenständer m.

musk [mʌsk] n Moschus m.
musket ['mʌskɪt] n Muskete f.
muskrat ['mʌskræt] n Bisamratte f.
musk rose n Moschusrose f.
Muslim ['mʌzlɪm] adj moslemisch ♦ n Moslem m, Moslime f.
muslin ['mʌzlɪn] n Musselin m.
musquash ['mʌskwɔʃ] n Bisamratte f; (fur) Bisam m.
mussel ['mʌsl] n (Mies)muschel f.
must [mʌst] aux vb müssen; (in negative) dürfen ♦ n Muß nt; **I ~ do it** ich muß es tun; **you ~ not do that** das darfst du nicht tun; **he ~ be there by now** jetzt müßte er schon dort sein; **you ~ come and see me soon** Sie müssen mich bald besuchen; **why ~ he behave so badly?** warum muß er sich so schlecht benehmen?; **I ~ have made a mistake** ich muß mich geirrt haben; **the film is a ~** den Film muß man unbedingt gesehen haben.
mustache ['mʌstæʃ] (US) n = moustache.
mustard ['mʌstəd] n Senf m.
mustard gas n (MIL) Senfgas nt.
muster ['mʌstə*] vt (support) zusammenbekommen; (also: ~ up: energy, strength, courage) aufbringen; (troops, members) antreten lassen ♦ n: **to pass ~** den Anforderungen genügen.
mustiness ['mʌstɪnɪs] n Muffigkeit f.
mustn't ['mʌsnt] = must not.
musty ['mʌstɪ] adj muffig; (building) moderig.
mutant ['mju:tənt] n Mutante f.
mutate [mju:'teɪt] vi (BIOL) mutieren.
mutation [mju:'teɪʃən] n (BIOL) Mutation f; (alteration) Veränderung f.
mute [mju:t] adj stumm.
muted ['mju:tɪd] adj (colour) gedeckt; (reaction, criticism) verhalten; (sound, trumpet, MUS) gedämpft.
mutilate ['mju:tɪleɪt] vt verstümmeln.
mutilation [mju:tɪ'leɪʃən] n Verstümmelung f.
mutinous ['mju:tɪnəs] adj meuterisch; (attitude) rebellisch.
mutiny ['mju:tɪnɪ] n Meuterei f ♦ vi meutern.
mutter ['mʌtə*] vt, vi murmeln.
mutton ['mʌtn] n Hammelfleisch nt.
mutual ['mju:tʃuəl] adj (feeling, attraction) gegenseitig; (benefit) beiderseitig; (interest, friend) gemeinsam; **the feeling was ~** das beruhte auf Gegenseitigkeit.
mutually ['mju:tʃuəlɪ] adv (beneficial, satisfactory) für beide Seiten; (accepted) von beiden Seiten; **to be ~ exclusive** einander ausschließen; **~ incompatible** nicht miteinander vereinbar.
Muzak ® ['mju:zæk] n Berieselungsmusik f (inf).
muzzle ['mʌzl] n (of dog) Maul nt; (of gun) Mündung f; (guard: for dog) Maulkorb m ♦ vt (dog) einen Maulkorb anlegen +dat; (fig: press, person) mundtot machen.

MV abbr (= motor vessel) MS.
MVP (US) n abbr (SPORT: = most valuable player) wertvollster Spieler m, wertvollste Spielerin f.
MW abbr (RADIO: = medium wave) MW.

═══════════════════════════ KEYWORD

my [maɪ] adj mein(e); **this is ~ brother/sister/ house** das ist mein Bruder/meine Schwester/mein Haus; **I've washed ~ hair/ cut ~ finger** ich habe mir die Haare gewaschen/mir or mich in den Finger geschnitten; **is this ~ pen or yours?** ist das mein Stift oder deiner?

Myanmar ['maɪænmɑː] n Myanmar nt.
myopic [maɪ'ɔpɪk] adj (MED, fig) kurzsichtig.
myriad ['mɪrɪəd] n Unzahl f.
myrrh [mə:*] n Myrrhe f.
myself [maɪ'self] pron (acc) mich; (dat) mir; (emphatic) selbst; see also oneself.
mysterious [mɪs'tɪərɪəs] adj geheimnisvoll, mysteriös.
mysteriously [mɪs'tɪərɪəslɪ] adv auf mysteriöse Weise; (smile) geheimnisvoll.
mystery ['mɪstərɪ] n (puzzle) Rätsel nt; (strangeness) Rätselhaftigkeit f ♦ cpd (guest, voice) mysteriös; **~ story** n Kriminalgeschichte f.
mystic ['mɪstɪk] n Mystiker(in) m(f).
mystic(al) ['mɪstɪk(l)] adj mystisch.
mystify ['mɪstɪfaɪ] vt vor ein Rätsel stellen.
mystique [mɪs'ti:k] n geheimnisvoller Nimbus m.
myth [mɪθ] n Mythos m; (fallacy) Märchen nt.
mythical ['mɪθɪkl] adj mythisch; (jobs, opportunities etc) fiktiv.
mythological [mɪθə'lɔdʒɪkl] adj mythologisch.
mythology [mɪ'θɔlədʒɪ] n Mythologie f.

═══════════════ *N, n*

N¹, n [ɛn] n (letter) N nt, n nt; **~ for Nellie**, (US) **~ for Nan** ≈ N wie Nordpol.
N² [ɛn] abbr (= north) N.
NA (US) n abbr (= Narcotics Anonymous) Hilfsorganisation für Drogensüchtige; (= National Academy) Dachverband verschiedener Forschungsunternehmen.
n/a abbr (= not applicable) entf.; (COMM etc: = no account) kein Konto.
NAACP (US) n abbr (= National Association for the Advancement of Colored People) Vereinigung zur Förderung Farbiger.
NAAFI ['næfɪ] (BRIT) n abbr (= Navy, Army and

Air Force Institutes) *Laden für britische Armeeangehörige.*

NACU (*US*) *n abbr* (= *National Association of Colleges and Universities*) *Fachhochschul- und Universitätsverband.*

nadir ['neɪdɪə*] *n* (*fig*) Tiefstpunkt *m*; (*ASTRON*) Nadir *m.*

NAFTA *n abbr* (= *North Atlantic Free Trade Agreement*) *amerikanische Freihandelszone.*

nag [næg] *vt* herumnörgeln an +*dat* ♦ *vi* nörgeln ♦ *n* (*pej: horse*) Gaul *m*; (: *person*) Nörgler(in) *m(f)*; **to ~ at sb** jdn plagen, jdm keine Ruhe lassen.

nagging ['nægɪŋ] *adj* (*doubt, suspicion*) quälend; (*pain*) dumpf.

nail [neɪl] *n* Nagel *m* ♦ *vt* (*inf: thief etc*) drankriegen; (: *fraud*) aufdecken; **to ~ sth to sth** etw an etw *acc* nageln; **to ~ sb down (to sth)** jdn (auf etw *acc*) festnageln.

nailbrush ['neɪlbrʌʃ] *n* Nagelbürste *f.*

nailfile ['neɪlfaɪl] *n* Nagelfeile *f.*

nail polish *n* Nagellack *m.*

nail polish remover *n* Nagellackentferner *m.*

nail scissors *npl* Nagelschere *f.*

nail varnish (*BRIT*) *n* = **nail polish.**

Nairobi [naɪ'rəʊbɪ] *n* Nairobi *nt.*

naive [naɪ'iːv] *adj* naiv.

naïveté [naːiːv'teɪ] *n* = **naivety.**

naivety [naɪ'iːvtɪ] *n* Naivität *f.*

naked ['neɪkɪd] *adj* nackt; (*flame, light*) offen; **with the ~ eye** mit bloßem Auge; **to the ~ eye** für das bloße Auge.

nakedness ['neɪkɪdnɪs] *n* Nacktheit *f.*

NAM (*US*) *n abbr* (= *National Association of Manufacturers*) *nationaler Verband der verarbeitenden Industrie.*

name [neɪm] *n* Name *m* ♦ *vt* nennen; (*ship*) taufen; (*identify*) (beim Namen) nennen; (*date etc*) bestimmen, festlegen; **what's your ~?** wie heißen Sie?; **my ~ is Peter** ich heiße Peter; **by ~** mit Namen; **in the ~ of** im Namen +*gen*; **to give one's ~ and address** Namen und Adresse angeben; **to make a ~ for o.s.** sich *dat* einen Namen machen; **to give sb a bad ~** jdn in Verruf bringen; **to call sb ~s** jdn beschimpfen; **to be ~d after sb/sth** nach jdm/etw benannt werden.

name-dropping ['neɪmdrɒpɪŋ] *n* Angeberei *f* mit berühmten Namen.

nameless ['neɪmlɪs] *adj* namenlos; **who/which shall remain ~** der/die/das ungenannt bleiben soll.

namely ['neɪmlɪ] *adv* nämlich.

nameplate ['neɪmpleɪt] *n* Namensschild *nt.*

namesake ['neɪmseɪk] *n* Namensvetter(in) *m(f).*

nan bread [naːn-] *n* Nan-Brot *nt*, *fladenförmiges Weißbrot als Beilage zu indischen Gerichten.*

nanny ['nænɪ] *n* Kindermädchen *nt.*

nanny-goat ['nænɪɡəʊt] *n* Geiß *f.*

nap [næp] *n* Schläfchen *nt*; (*of fabric*) Strich *m* ♦ *vi:* **to be caught ~ping** (*fig*) überrumpelt werden; **to have a ~** ein Schläfchen *or* ein Nickerchen (*inf*) machen.

NAPA (*US*) *n abbr* (= *National Association of Performing Artists*) *Künstlergewerkschaft.*

napalm ['neɪpɑːm] *n* Napalm *nt.*

nape [neɪp] *n:* **the ~ of the neck** der Nacken.

napkin ['næpkɪn] *n* (*also:* **table ~**) Serviette *f.*

Naples ['neɪplz] *n* Neapel *nt.*

Napoleonic [nəpəʊlɪ'ɒnɪk] *adj* Napoleonisch.

nappy ['næpɪ] (*BRIT*) *n* Windel *f.*

nappy liner (*BRIT*) *n* Windeleinlage *f.*

nappy rash *n* Wundsein *nt.*

narcissistic [nɑːsɪ'sɪstɪk] *adj* narzißtisch.

narcissus [nɑː'sɪsəs] (*pl* **narcissi**) *n* Narzisse *f.*

narcotic [nɑː'kɒtɪk] *adj* narkotisch ♦ *n* Narkotikum *nt*; **narcotics** *npl* (*drugs*) Drogen *pl*; **~ drug** Rauschgift *nt.*

nark [nɑːk] (*BRIT: inf*) *vt:* **to be ~ed at sth** sauer über etw *acc* sein.

narrate [nə'reɪt] *vt* erzählen; (*film, programme*) kommentieren.

narration [nə'reɪʃən] *n* Kommentar *m.*

narrative ['nærətɪv] *n* Erzählung *f*; (*of journey etc*) Schilderung *f.*

narrator [nə'reɪtə*] *n* Erzähler(in) *m(f)*; (*in film etc*) Kommentator(in) *m(f).*

narrow ['nærəʊ] *adj* eng; (*ledge etc*) schmal; (*majority, advantage, victory, defeat*) knapp; (*ideas, view*) engstirnig ♦ *vi* sich verengen; (*gap, difference*) sich verringern ♦ *vt* (*gap, difference*) verringern; (*eyes*) zusammenkneifen; **to have a ~ escape** mit knapper Not davonkommen; **to ~ sth down (to sth)** etw (auf etw *acc*) beschränken.

narrow gauge ['nærəʊɡeɪdʒ] *adj* (*RAIL*) Schmalspur-.

narrowly ['nærəʊlɪ] *adv* knapp; (*escape*) mit knapper Not.

narrow-minded [nærəʊ'maɪndɪd] *adj* engstirnig.

NAS (*US*) *n abbr* (= *National Academy of Sciences*) *Akademie der Wissenschaften.*

NASA ['næsə] (*US*) *n abbr* (= *National Aeronautics and Space Administration*) NASA *f.*

nasal ['neɪzl] *adj* Nasen-; (*voice*) näselnd.

Nassau ['næsɔː] *n* Nassau *nt.*

nastily ['nɑːstɪlɪ] *adv* gemein; (*say*) gehässig.

nastiness ['nɑːstɪnɪs] *n* Gemeinheit *f*; (*of remark*) Gehässigkeit *f*; (*of smell, taste etc*) Ekelhaftigkeit *f.*

nasturtium [nəs'təːʃəm] *n* Kapuziner- kresse *f.*

nasty ['nɑːstɪ] *adj* (*remark*) gehässig; (*person*) gemein; (*taste, smell*) ekelhaft; (*wound, disease, accident, shock*) schlimm; (*problem, question*) schwierig; (*weather, temper*) abscheulich; **to turn ~** unangenehm werden; **it's a ~ business** es ist schrecklich; **he's got a ~ temper** mit ihm ist nicht gut

Kirschen essen.

NAS/UWT *(BRIT)* *n abbr* (= *National Association of Schoolmasters/Union of Women Teachers) Lehrergewerkschaft.*

nation ['neɪʃən] *n* Nation *f*; *(people)* Volk *nt*.

national ['næʃənl] *adj (character, flag)* National-; *(interests)* Staats-; *(newspaper)* überregional ♦ *n* Staatsbürger(in) *m(f)*; **foreign** ~ Ausländer(in) *m(f)*.

national anthem *n* Nationalhymne *f*.

National Curriculum *n zentraler Lehrplan für Schulen in England und Wales.*

national debt *n* Staatsverschuldung *f*.

national dress *n* Nationaltracht *f*.

National Guard *(US)* *n* Nationalgarde *f*.

National Health Service *(BRIT)* *n* Staatlicher Gesundheitsdienst *m*.

National Insurance *(BRIT)* *n* Sozialversicherung *f*.

nationalism ['næʃnəlɪzəm] *n* Nationalismus *m*.

nationalist ['næʃnəlɪst] *adj* nationalistisch ♦ *n* Nationalist(in) *m(f)*.

nationality [næʃə'nælɪtɪ] *n* Staatsangehörigkeit *f*, Nationalität *f*.

nationalization [næʃnəlaɪ'zeɪʃən] *n* Verstaatlichung *f*.

nationalize ['næʃnəlaɪz] *vt* verstaatlichen.

National Lottery *n* ≈ Lotto *nt*.

nationally ['næʃnəlɪ] *adv* landesweit.

national park *n* Nationalpark *m*.

national press *n* überregionale Presse *f*.

National Security Council *(US)* *n* Nationaler Sicherheitsrat *m*.

national service *n* Wehrdienst *m*.

National Trust *(BRIT)* *n Organisation zum Schutz historischer Bauten und Denkmäler sowie zum Landschaftsschutz.*

Der **National Trust** *ist ein 1895 gegründeter Natur- und Denkmalschutzverband in Großbritannien, der Gebäude und Gelände von besonderem historischem oder ästhetischem Interesse erhält und der Öffentlichkeit zugänglich macht. Viele Gebäude im Besitz des National Trust sind (z.T. gegen ein Eintrittsgeld) zu besichtigen.*

---

nationwide ['neɪʃənwaɪd] *adj, adv* landesweit.

native ['neɪtɪv] *n* Einheimische(r) *f(m)* ♦ *adj* einheimisch; *(country)* Heimat-; *(language)* Mutter-; *(innate)* angeboren; **a** ~ **of Germany, a** ~ **German** ein gebürtiger Deutscher, eine gebürtige Deutsche; ~ **to** beheimatet in *+dat*.

Native American *adj* indianisch, der Ureinwohner Amerikas ♦ *n* Ureinwohner(in) *m(f)* Amerikas.

native speaker *n* Muttersprachler(in) *m(f)*.

Nativity [nə'tɪvɪtɪ] *n*: **the** ~ Christi Geburt *f*.

nativity play *n* Krippenspiel *nt*.

NATO ['neɪtəʊ] *n abbr* (= *North Atlantic Treaty Organization)* NATO *f*.

natter ['nætə*] *(BRIT)* *vi* quatschen *(inf)* ♦ *n*: **to have a** ~ einen Schwatz halten.

natural ['nætʃrəl] *adj* natürlich; *(disaster)* Natur-; *(innate)* angeboren; *(born)* geboren; *(MUS)* ohne Vorzeichen; **to die of** ~ **causes** eines natürlichen Todes sterben; ~ **foods** Naturkost *f*; **she played F** ~ **not F sharp** sie spielte f statt fis.

natural childbirth *n* natürliche Geburt *f*.

natural gas *n* Erdgas *nt*.

natural history *n* Naturkunde *f*; **the** ~ **of England** die Naturgeschichte Englands.

naturalist ['nætʃrəlɪst] *n* Naturforscher(in) *m(f)*.

naturalize ['nætʃrəlaɪz] *vt*: **to become** ~**d** eingebürgert werden.

naturally ['nætʃrəlɪ] *adv* natürlich; *(happen)* auf natürlichem Wege; *(die)* eines natürlichen Todes; *(occur: cheerful, talented, blonde)* von Natur aus.

naturalness ['nætʃrəlnɪs] *n* Natürlichkeit *f*.

natural resources *npl* Naturschätze *pl*.

natural selection *n* natürliche Auslese *f*.

natural wastage *n* natürliche Personalreduzierung *f*.

nature ['neɪtʃə*] *n (also: Nature)* Natur *f*; *(kind, sort)* Art *f*; *(character)* Wesen *nt*; **by** ~ von Natur aus; **by its (very)** ~ naturgemäß; **documents of a confidential** ~ Unterlagen vertraulicher Art.

-natured ['neɪtʃəd] *suff*: **good-**~ gutmütig; **ill-**~ bösartig.

nature reserve *(BRIT)* *n* Naturschutzgebiet *nt*.

nature trail *n* Naturlehrpfad *m*.

naturist ['neɪtʃərɪst] *n* Anhänger(in) *m(f)* der Freikörperkultur.

naught [nɔːt] *n* = nought.

naughtiness ['nɔːtɪnɪs] *n (see adj)* Unartigkeit *f*, Ungezogenheit *f*; Unanständigkeit *f*.

naughty ['nɔːtɪ] *adj (child)* unartig, ungezogen; *(story, film, words)* unanständig.

nausea ['nɔːsɪə] *n* Übelkeit *f*.

nauseate ['nɔːsɪeɪt] *vt* Übelkeit verursachen *+dat*; *(fig)* anwidern.

nauseating ['nɔːsɪeɪtɪŋ] *adj* ekelerregend; *(fig)* widerlich.

nauseous ['nɔːsɪəs] *adj* ekelhaft; **I feel** ~ mir ist übel.

nautical ['nɔːtɪkl] *adj (chart)* See-; *(uniform)* Seemanns-.

nautical mile *n* Seemeile *f*.

naval ['neɪvl] *adj* Marine-; *(battle, forces)* See-.

naval officer *n* Marineoffizier *m*.

nave [neɪv] *n* Hauptschiff *nt*, Mittelschiff *nt*.

navel ['neɪvl] *n* Nabel *m*.

navigable ['nævɪgəbl] *adj* schiffbar.

navigate ['nævɪgeɪt] *vt (river)* befahren; *(path)* begehen ♦ *vi* navigieren; *(AUT)* den Fahrer dirigieren.

navigation [nævɪ'geɪʃən] *n* Navigation *f*.

navigator ['nævɪgeɪtə*] *n (NAUT)* Steuermann

m; (*AVIAT*) Navigator(in) *m(f);* (*AUT*)
Beifahrer(in) *m(f).*
navvy ['nævɪ] (*BRIT*) *n* Straßenarbeiter *m.*
navy ['neɪvɪ] *n* (Kriegs)marine *f;* (*ships*)
(Kriegs)flotte *f;* **Department of the N~** (*US*)
Marineministerium *nt.*
navy(-blue) ['neɪvɪ('blu:)] *adj* marineblau.
Nazareth ['næzərɪθ] *n* Nazareth *nt.*
Nazi ['nɑːtsɪ] *n* Nazi *m.*
NB *abbr* (= *nota bene*) NB; (*CANADA:* = *New
Brunswick*).
NBA (*US*) *n abbr* (= *National Basketball
Association*) Basketball-Dachverband;
(= *National Boxing Association*) Boxsport-
Dachverband.
NBC (*US*) *n abbr* (= *National Broadcasting
Company*) Fernsehsender.
NBS (*US*) *n abbr* (= *National Bureau of
Standards*) amerikanischer
Normenausschuß.
NC *abbr* (*COMM etc:* = *no charge*) frei; (*US:
POST:* = *North Carolina*).
NCC *n abbr* (*BRIT:* = *Nature Conservancy
Council*) Naturschutzverband; (*US:
* = *National Council of Churches*)
Zusammenschluß protestantischer und
orthodoxer Kirchen.
NCCL (*BRIT*) *n abbr* (= *National Council for Civil
Liberties*) Organisation zum Schutz von
Freiheitsrechten.
NCO *n abbr* (*MIL:* = *noncommissioned officer*)
Uffz.
ND (*US*) *abbr* (*POST:* = *North Dakota*).
N.Dak. (*US*) *abbr* (*POST:* = *North Dakota*).
NE *abbr* = **north-east;** (*US: POST:* = *New
England; Nebraska*).
NEA (*US*) *n abbr* (= *National Education
Association*) Verband für das
Erziehungswesen.
neap [niːp] *n* (*also:* **~ tide**) Nippflut *f.*
Neapolitan [nɪə'pɔlɪtən] *adj* neapolitanisch ♦ *n*
Neapolitaner(in) *m(f).*
near [nɪə·] *adj* nahe ♦ *adv* nahe; (*almost*) fast,
beinahe ♦ *prep* (*also:* **~ to:** *in space*) nahe an
+*dat;* (: *in time*) um *acc* ... herum; (: *in situation,
in intimacy*) nahe +*dat* ♦ *vt* sich nähern +*dat;*
(*state, situation*) kurz vor +*dat* stehen;
Christmas is ~ bald ist Weihnachten;
£25,000 or ~est offer (*BRIT*) £25.000 oder das
nächstbeste Angebot; **in the ~ future** in
naher Zukunft, bald; **in ~ darkness** fast im
Dunkeln; **a ~ tragedy** beinahe eine
Tragödie; **~ here/there** hier/dort in der
Nähe; **to be ~ (to) doing sth** nahe daran
sein, etw zu tun; **the building is ~ing
completion** der Bau steht kurz vor dem
Abschluß.
nearby [nɪə'baɪ] *adj* nahegelegen ♦ *adv* in der
Nähe.
Near East *n:* **the ~** der Nahe Osten.
nearer ['nɪərə·] *adj, adv comp of* **near.**
nearest [nɪərəst] *adj, adv superl of* **near.**

nearly ['nɪəlɪ] *adv* fast; **I ~ fell** ich wäre
beinahe gefallen; **it's not ~ big enough** es
ist bei weitem nicht groß genug; **she was
~ crying** sie war den Tränen nahe.
near miss *n* Beinahezusammenstoß *m;* **that
was a ~** (*shot*) das war knapp daneben.
nearness ['nɪənɪs] *n* Nähe *f.*
nearside ['nɪəsaɪd] (*AUT*) *adj* (*when driving on
left*) linksseitig; (*when driving on right*)
rechtsseitig ♦ *n:* **the ~** (*when driving on left*)
die linke Seite; (*when driving on right*) die
rechte Seite.
near-sighted [nɪə'saɪtɪd] *adj* kurzsichtig.
neat [niːt] *adj* ordentlich; (*handwriting*) sauber;
(*plan, solution*) elegant; (*description*)
prägnant; (*spirits*) pur; **I drink it ~** ich trinke
es pur.
neatly ['niːtlɪ] *adv* ordentlich; (*conveniently*)
sauber.
neatness ['niːtnɪs] *n* Ordentlichkeit *f;* (*of
solution, plan*) Sauberkeit *f.*
Nebr. (*US*) *abbr* (*POST:* = *Nebraska*).
nebulous ['nɛbjuləs] *adj* vage, unklar.
necessarily ['nɛsɪsrɪlɪ] *adv* notwendigerweise;
not ~ nicht unbedingt.
necessary ['nɛsɪsrɪ] *adj* notwendig, nötig;
(*inevitable*) unausweichlich; **if ~** wenn nötig,
nötigenfalls; **it is ~ to** ... man muß ...
necessitate [nɪ'sɛsɪteɪt] *vt* erforderlich
machen.
necessity [nɪ'sɛsɪtɪ] *n* Notwendigkeit *f;* **of ~**
notgedrungen; **out of ~** aus Not; **the
necessities (of life)** das Notwendigste (zum
Leben).
neck [nɛk] *n* Hals *m;* (*of shirt, dress, jumper*)
Ausschnitt *m* ♦ *vi* (*inf*) knutschen; **~ and ~**
Kopf an Kopf; **to stick one's ~ out** (*inf*)
seinen Kopf riskieren.
necklace ['nɛklɪs] *n* (Hals)kette *f.*
neckline ['nɛklaɪn] *n* Ausschnitt *m.*
necktie ['nɛktaɪ] (*esp US*) *n* Krawatte *f.*
nectar ['nɛktə·] *n* Nektar *m.*
nectarine ['nɛktərɪn] *n* Nektarine *f.*
NEDC (*BRIT*) *n abbr* (= *National Economic
Development Council*) Rat für
Wirtschaftsentwicklung.
Neddy ['nɛdɪ] (*BRIT: inf*) *n abbr* = **NEDC.**
née [neɪ] *prep:* **~ Scott** geborene Scott.
need [niːd] *n* Bedarf *m;* (*necessity*)
Notwendigkeit *f;* (*requirement*) Bedürfnis *nt;*
(*poverty*) Not *f* ♦ *vt* brauchen; (*could do with*)
nötig haben; **in ~** bedürftig; **to be in ~ of
sth** etw nötig haben; **£10 will meet my
immediate ~s** mit £ 10 komme ich erst
einmal aus; **(there's) no ~** (das ist) nicht
nötig; **there's no ~ to get so worked up
about it** du brauchst dich darüber nicht so
aufzuregen; **he had no ~ to work** er hatte es
nicht nötig zu arbeiten; **I ~ to do it** ich muß
es tun; **you don't ~ to go, you ~n't go** du
brauchst nicht zu gehen; **a signature is ~ed**
das bedarf einer Unterschrift *gen.*

needle ['niːdl] *n* Nadel *f* ♦ *vt* (*fig: inf: goad*) ärgern, piesacken.

needless ['niːdlɪs] *adj* unnötig; ~ **to say** natürlich.

needlessly ['niːdlɪslɪ] *adv* unnötig.

needlework ['niːdlwəːk] *n* Handarbeit *f*.

needn't ['niːdnt] = need not.

needy ['niːdɪ] *adj* bedürftig ♦ *npl:* **the** ~ **die** Bedürftigen *pl.*

negation [nɪ'geɪʃən] *n* Verweigerung *f*.

negative ['nɛgətɪv] *adj* negativ; (*answer*) abschlägig ♦ *n* (*PHOT*) Negativ *nt*; (*LING*) Verneinungswort *nt*, Negation *f*; **to answer in the** ~ eine verneinende Antwort geben.

negative equity *n Differenz zwischen gefallenem Wert und hypothekarischer Belastung eines Wohnungseigentums.*

neglect [nɪ'glɛkt] *vt* vernachlässigen; (*writer, artist*) unterschätzen ♦ *n* Vernachlässigung *f*.

neglected [nɪ'glɛktɪd] *adj* vernachlässigt; (*writer, artist*) unterschätzt.

neglectful [nɪ'glɛktful] *adj* nachlässig; (*father*) pflichtvergessen; **to be** ~ **of sth** etw vernachlässigen.

negligee ['nɛglɪʒeɪ] *n* Negligé *nt.*

negligence ['nɛglɪdʒəns] *n* Nachlässigkeit *f*; (*LAW*) Fahrlässigkeit *f*.

negligent ['nɛglɪdʒənt] *adj* nachlässig; (*LAW*) fahrlässig; (*casual*) lässig.

negligently ['nɛglɪdʒəntlɪ] *adv* (*see adj*) nachlässig; fahrlässig; lässig.

negligible ['nɛglɪdʒɪbl] *adj* geringfügig.

negotiable [nɪ'gəuʃɪəbl] *adj* verhandlungs-fähig; (*path, river*) passierbar; **not** ~ (*on cheque etc*) nicht übertragbar.

negotiate [nɪ'gəuʃɪeɪt] *vi* verhandeln ♦ *vt* aushandeln; (*obstacle, hill*) überwinden; (*bend*) nehmen; **to** ~ **with sb** (**for sth**) mit jdm (über etw *acc*) verhandeln.

negotiating table [nɪ'gəuʃɪeɪtɪŋ-] *n* Verhandlungstisch *m*.

negotiation [nɪgəuʃɪ'eɪʃən] *n* Verhandlung *f*; **the matter is still under** ~ über die Sache wird noch verhandelt.

negotiator [nɪ'gəuʃɪeɪtə*] *n* Unterhändler(in) *m(f).*

Negress ['niːgrɪs] *n* Negerin *f*.

Negro ['niːgrəu] (*pl* ~**es**) *adj* (*boy, slave*) Neger- ♦ *n* Neger *m.*

neigh [neɪ] *vi* wiehern.

neighbour, (*US*) **neighbor** ['neɪbə*] *n* Nachbar(in) *m(f).*

neighbourhood ['neɪbəhud] *n* (*place*) Gegend *f*; (*people*) Nachbarschaft *f*; **in the** ~ **of** ... in der Nähe von ...; (*sum of money*) so um die ...

neighbourhood watch *n Vereinigung von Bürgern, die Straßenwachen etc zur Unterstützung der Polizei bei der Verbrechensbekämpfung organisiert.*

neighbouring ['neɪbərɪŋ] *adj* benachbart, Nachbar-.

neighbourly ['neɪbəlɪ] *adj* nachbarlich.

neither ['naɪðə*] *conj:* **I didn't move and** ~ **did John** ich bewegte mich nicht, und John auch nicht ♦ *pron* keine(r, s) (von beiden) ♦ *adv:* ~ ... **nor** ... weder ... noch ...; ~ **story is true** keine der beiden Geschichten stimmt; ~ **is true** beides stimmt nicht; ~ **do I/have I** ich auch nicht.

neo... ['niːəu] *pref* neo-, Neo-.

neolithic [niə'lɪθɪk] *adv* jungsteinzeitlich, neolithisch.

neologism [nɪ'ɔlədʒɪzəm] *n* (Wort)neubildung *f*, Neologismus *m*.

neon ['niːɔn] *n* Neon *nt*.

neon light *n* Neonlampe *f*.

neon sign *n* Neonreklame *f*.

Nepal [nɪ'pɔːl] *n* Nepal *nt*.

nephew ['nɛvjuː] *n* Neffe *m*.

nepotism ['nɛpətɪzəm] *n* Vetternwirtschaft *f*.

nerd [nəːd] (*inf*) *n* Schwachkopf *m*.

nerve [nəːv] *n* (*ANAT*) Nerv *m*; (*courage*) Mut *m*; (*impudence*) Frechheit *f*; **nerves** *npl* (*anxiety*) Nervosität *f*; (*emotional strength*) Nerven *pl*; **he gets on my** ~**s** er geht mir auf die Nerven; **to lose one's** ~ die Nerven verlieren.

nerve-centre, (*US*) **nerve-center** ['nəːvsɛntə*] *n* (*fig*) Schaltzentrale *f*.

nerve gas *n* Nervengas *nt*.

nerve-racking ['nəːvrækɪŋ] *adj* nervenaufreibend.

nervous ['nəːvəs] *adj* Nerven-, nervlich; (*anxious*) nervös; **to be** ~ **of/about** Angst haben vor +*dat*.

nervous breakdown *n* Nerven-zusammenbruch *m*.

nervously ['nəːvəslɪ] *adv* nervös.

nervousness ['nəːvəsnɪs] *n* Nervosität *f*.

nervous system *n* Nervensystem *nt*.

nervous wreck (*inf*) *n* Nervenbündel *nt*; **to be a** ~ mit den Nerven völlig am Ende sein.

nervy ['nəːvɪ] (*inf*) *adj* (*BRIT: tense*) nervös; (*US: cheeky*) dreist.

nest [nɛst] *n* Nest *nt* ♦ *vi* nisten; **a** ~ **of tables** ein Satz Tische *or* von Tischen.

nest egg *n* Notgroschen *m*.

nestle ['nɛsl] *vi* sich kuscheln; (*house*) eingebettet sein.

nestling ['nɛstlɪŋ] *n* Nestling *m*.

net [nɛt] *n* Netz *nt*; (*fabric*) Tüll *m* ♦ *adj* (*COMM*) Netto-; (*final: result, effect*) End- ♦ *vt* (mit einem Netz) fangen; (*profit*) einbringen; (*deal, sale, fortune*) an Land ziehen; ~ **of tax** steuerfrei; **he earns £10,000** ~ **per year** er verdient £ 10.000 netto im Jahr; **it weighs 250g** ~ es wiegt 250 g netto.

netball ['nɛtbɔːl] *n* Netzball *m*.

net curtains *npl* Gardinen *pl*, Stores *pl*.

Netherlands ['nɛðələndz] *npl:* **the** ~ **die** Niederlande *pl*.

nett [nɛt] *adj* = net.

netting ['nɛtɪŋ] *n* (*for fence etc*) Maschendraht *m*; (*fabric*) Netzgewebe *nt*, Tüll *m*.

nettle ['nɛtl] n Nessel f; **to grasp the ~** (fig) in den sauren Apfel beißen.

network ['nɛtwəːk] n Netz nt; (TV, RADIO) Sendenetz nt ♦ vt (RADIO, TV) im ganzen Netzbereich ausstrahlen; (computers) in einem Netzwerk zusammenschließen.

neuralgia [njuə'rældʒə] n Neuralgie f, Nervenschmerzen pl.

neurological [njuərə'lɔdʒɪkl] adj neurologisch.

neurotic [njuə'rɔtɪk] adj neurotisch ♦ n Neurotiker(in) m(f).

neuter ['njuːtə*] adj (LING) sächlich ♦ vt kastrieren; (female) sterilisieren.

neutral ['njuːtrəl] adj neutral ♦ n (AUT) Leerlauf m.

neutrality [njuː'trælɪtɪ] n Neutralität f.

neutralize ['njuːtrəlaɪz] vt neutralisieren, aufheben.

neutron ['njuːtrɔn] n Neutron nt.

neutron bomb n Neutronenbombe f.

Nev. (US) abbr (POST: = Nevada).

never ['nɛvə*] adv nie; (not) nicht; **~ in my life** noch nie; **~ again** nie wieder; **well I ~!** nein, so was!; see also **mind**.

never-ending [nɛvər'ɛndɪŋ] adj endlos.

nevertheless [nɛvəðə'lɛs] adv trotzdem, dennoch.

new [njuː] adj neu; (mother) jung; **as good as ~** so gut wie neu; **to be ~ to sb** jdm neu sein.

New Age n New Age nt.

newborn ['njuːbɔːn] adj neugeboren.

newcomer ['njuːkʌmə*] n Neuankömmling m; (in job) Neuling m.

new-fangled ['njuː'fæŋgld] (pej) adj neumodisch.

new-found ['njuːfaund] adj neuentdeckt; (confidence) neugeschöpft.

Newfoundland ['njuːfənlənd] n Neufundland nt.

New Guinea n Neuguinea nt.

newly ['njuːlɪ] adv neu.

newly-weds ['njuːlɪwɛdz] npl Neuvermählte pl, Frischvermählte pl.

new moon n Neumond m.

newness ['njuːnɪs] n Neuheit f; (of cheese, bread etc) Frische f.

New Orleans [-'ɔːliːənz] n New Orleans nt.

news [njuːz] n Nachricht f; **a piece of ~** eine Neuigkeit; **the ~** (RADIO, TV) die Nachrichten pl; **good/bad ~** gute/schlechte Nachrichten.

news agency n Nachrichtenagentur f.

newsagent ['njuːzeɪdʒənt] (BRIT) n Zeitungshändler(in) m(f).

news bulletin n Bulletin nt.

newscaster ['njuːzkaːstə*] n Nachrichten- sprecher(in) m(f).

newsdealer ['njuːzdiːlə*] (US) n = newsagent.

newsflash ['njuːzflæʃ] n Kurzmeldung f.

newsletter ['njuːzlɛtə*] n Rundschreiben nt, Mitteilungsblatt nt.

newspaper ['njuːzpeɪpə*] n Zeitung f; **daily/ weekly ~** Tages-/Wochenzeitung f.

newsprint ['njuːzprɪnt] n Zeitungspapier nt.

newsreader ['njuːzriːdə*] n = newscaster.

newsreel ['njuːzriːl] n Wochenschau f.

newsroom ['njuːzruːm] n Nachrichten- redaktion f; (RADIO, TV) Nachrichtenstudio nt.

newsstand ['njuːzstænd] n Zeitungsstand m.

newsworthy ['njuːzwəːðɪ] adj: **to be ~** Neuigkeitswert haben.

newt [njuːt] n Wassermolch m.

new town (BRIT) n neue, teilweise mit Regierungsgeldern errichtete städtische Siedlung.

New Year n neues Jahr nt; (New Year's Day) Neujahr nt; **Happy ~!** (ein) glückliches or frohes neues Jahr!

New Year's Day n Neujahr nt, Neujahrstag m.

New Year's Eve n Silvester nt.

New York [-'jɔːk] n New York nt; (also: **~ State**) der Staat New York.

New Zealand [-'ziːlənd] n Neuseeland nt ♦ adj neuseeländisch.

New Zealander [-'ziːləndə*] n Neuseeländer(in) m(f).

next [nɛkst] adj nächste(r, s); (room) Neben- ♦ adv dann; (do, happen) als nächstes; (afterwards) danach; **the ~ day** am nächsten or folgenden Tag; **~ time** das nächste Mal; **~ year** nächstes Jahr; **~ please!** der nächste bitte!; **who's ~?** wer ist der nächste?; **"turn to the ~ page"** „bitte umblättern"; **the week after ~** übernächste Woche; **the ~ on the right/left** der/die/das nächste rechts/ links; **the ~ thing I knew** das nächste, woran ich mich erinnern konnte; **~ to** neben +dat; **~ to nothing** so gut wie nichts; **when do we meet ~?** wann treffen wir uns wieder or das nächste Mal?; **the ~ best** der/ die/das nächstbeste.

next door adv nebenan ♦ adj: **next-door** nebenan; **the house ~** das Nebenhaus; **to go ~** nach nebenan gehen; **my next-door neighbour** mein direkter Nachbar.

next-of-kin ['nɛkstəv'kɪn] n nächster Verwandter m, nächste Verwandte f.

NF n abbr (BRIT: POL: = National Front) rechtsradikale Partei ♦ abbr (CANADA: = Newfoundland).

NFL (US) n abbr (= National Football League) Fußball-Nationalliga.

NG (US) abbr = National Guard.

NGO n abbr (= nongovernmental organization) nichtstaatliche Organisation.

NH (US) abbr (POST: = New Hampshire).

NHL (US) n abbr (= National Hockey League) Hockey-Nationalliga.

NHS (BRIT) n abbr = National Health Service.

NI abbr = Northern Ireland; (BRIT) = National Insurance.

Niagara Falls [naɪ'ægərə-] *npl* Niagarafälle *pl*.
nib [nɪb] *n* Feder *f*.
nibble ['nɪbl] *vt* knabbern; (*bite*) knabbern an +*dat* ♦ *vi:* **to** ~ **at** knabbern an +*dat*.
Nicaragua [nɪkə'rægjuə] *n* Nicaragua *nt*.
Nicaraguan [nɪkə'rægjuən] *adj* nicaraguanisch ♦ *n* Nicaraguaner(in) *m(f)*.
Nice [niːs] *n* Nizza *nt*.
nice [naɪs] *adj* nett; (*holiday, weather, picture etc*) schön; (*taste*) gut; (*person, clothes etc*) hübsch.
nicely ['naɪslɪ] *adv* (*attractively*) hübsch; (*politely*) nett; (*satisfactorily*) gut; **that will do** ~ das reicht (vollauf).
niceties ['naɪsɪtɪz] *npl:* **the** ~ die Feinheiten *pl*.
niche [niːʃ] *n* Nische *f*; (*job, position*) Plätzchen *nt*.
nick [nɪk] *n* Kratzer *m*; (*in metal, wood etc*) Kerbe *f* ♦ *vt* (*BRIT: inf: steal*) klauen; (: : *arrest*) einsperren, einlochen; (*cut*): **to** ~ **o.s.** sich schneiden; **in good** ~ (*BRIT: inf*) gut in Schuß; **in the** ~ (*BRIT: inf: in prison*) im Knast; **in the** ~ **of time** gerade noch rechtzeitig.
nickel ['nɪkl] *n* Nickel *nt*; (*US*) Fünfcentstück *nt*.
nickname ['nɪkneɪm] *n* Spitzname *m* ♦ *vt* betiteln, taufen (*inf*).
Nicosia [nɪkə'siːə] *n* Nikosia *nt*.
nicotine ['nɪkətiːn] *n* Nikotin *nt*.
nicotine patch *n* Nikotinpflaster *nt*.
niece [niːs] *n* Nichte *f*.
nifty ['nɪftɪ] (*inf*) *adj* flott; (*gadget, tool*) schlau.
Niger ['naɪdʒə*] *n* Niger *m*.
Nigeria [naɪ'dʒɪərɪə] *n* Nigeria *nt*.
Nigerian [naɪ'dʒɪərɪən] *adj* nigerianisch ♦ *n* Nigerianer(in) *m(f)*.
niggardly ['nɪgədlɪ] *adj* knauserig; (*allowance, amount*) armselig.
nigger [nɪgə*] (*inf*) *n* Nigger *m* (*inf!*).
niggle ['nɪgl] *vt* plagen, zu schaffen machen +*dat* ♦ *vi* herumkritisieren.
niggling ['nɪglɪŋ] *adj* quälend; (*pain, ache*) bohrend.
night [naɪt] *n* Nacht *f*; (*evening*) Abend *m*; **the** ~ **before last** vorletzte Nacht, vorgestern abend; **at** ~, **by** ~ nachts, abends; **nine o'clock at** ~ = neun Uhr abends; **in the** ~, **during the** ~ in der Nacht; ~ **and day** Tag und Nacht.
nightcap ['naɪtkæp] *n* Schlaftrunk *m*.
nightclub ['naɪtklʌb] *n* Nachtlokal *nt*.
nightdress ['naɪtdrɛs] *n* Nachthemd *nt*.
nightfall ['naɪtfɔːl] *n* Einbruch *m* der Dunkelheit.
nightgown ['naɪtgaun] *n* = **nightdress**.
nightie ['naɪtɪ] *n* = **nightdress**.
nightingale ['naɪtɪŋgeɪl] *n* Nachtigall *f*.
nightlife ['naɪtlaɪf] *n* Nachtleben *nt*.
nightly ['naɪtlɪ] *adj* (all)nächtlich, Nacht-; (*every evening*) (all)abendlich, Abend- ♦ *adv* jede Nacht; (*every evening*) jeden Abend.

nightmare ['naɪtmɛə*] *n* Alptraum *m*.
night porter *n* Nachtportier *m*.
night safe *n* Nachtsafe *m*.
night school *n* Abendschule *f*.
nightshade ['naɪtʃeɪd] *n:* **deadly** ~ Tollkirsche *f*.
night shift *n* Nachtschicht *f*.
night-time ['naɪttaɪm] *n* Nacht *f*.
night watchman *n* Nachtwächter *m*.
nihilism ['naɪɪlɪzəm] *n* Nihilismus *m*.
nil [nɪl] *n* Nichts *nt*; (*BRIT: SPORT*) Null *f*.
Nile [naɪl] *n:* **the** ~ der Nil.
nimble ['nɪmbl] *adj* flink; (*mind*) beweglich.
nine [naɪn] *num* neun.
nineteen ['naɪn'tiːn] *num* neunzehn.
nineteenth [naɪn'tiːnθ] *num* neunzehnte(r, s).
ninety ['naɪntɪ] *num* neunzig.
ninth [naɪnθ] *num* neunte(r, s) ♦ *n* Neuntel *nt*.
nip [nɪp] *vt* zwicken ♦ *n* Biß *m*; (*drink*) Schlückchen *nt* ♦ *vi* (*BRIT: inf*): **to** ~ **out/ down/up** kurz raus-/runter-/raufgehen; **to** ~ **into a shop** (*BRIT: inf*) kurz in einen Laden gehen.
nipple ['nɪpl] *n* (*ANAT*) Brustwarze *f*.
nippy ['nɪpɪ] (*BRIT*) *adj* (*quick: person*) flott; (: *car*) spritzig; (*cold*) frisch.
nit [nɪt] *n* Nisse *f*; (*inf: idiot*) Dummkopf *m*.
nitpicking ['nɪtpɪkɪŋ] (*inf*) *n* Kleinigkeitskrämerei *f*.
nitrogen ['naɪtrədʒən] *n* Stickstoff *m*.
nitroglycerin(e) ['naɪtrəu'glɪsəriːn] *n* Nitroglyzerin *nt*.
nitty-gritty ['nɪtɪ'grɪtɪ] (*inf*) *n:* **to get down to the** ~ zur Sache kommen.
nitwit ['nɪtwɪt] (*inf*) *n* Dummkopf *m*.
NJ (*US*) *abbr* (*POST:* = *New Jersey*).
NLF *n abbr* (= *National Liberation Front*) vietnamesische Befreiungsbewegung während des Vietnamkrieges.
NLQ *abbr* (*COMPUT, TYP:* = *near letter quality*) NLQ.
NLRB (*US*) *n abbr* (= *National Labor Relations Board*) Ausschuß zur Regelung der Beziehungen zwischen Arbeitgebern und Arbeitnehmern.
NM, N.Mex. (*US*) *abbr* (*POST:* = *New Mexico*)

═══════════════════════ KEYWORD

no [nəu] (*pl* **noes**) *adv* (*opposite of "yes"*) nein; ~ **thank you** nein danke
♦ *adj* (*not any*) kein(e); **I have** ~ **money/ time/books** ich habe kein Geld/keine Zeit/ keine Bücher; "~ **entry**" „kein Zutritt"; "~ **smoking**" „Rauchen verboten"
♦ *n* Nein *nt*; **there were 20 noes and one abstention** es gab 20 Neinstimmen und eine Enthaltung; **I won't take** ~ **for an answer** ich bestehe darauf.

═══════════════════════

no. *abbr* (= *number*) Nr.
nobble ['nɔbl] (*BRIT: inf*) *vt* (*bribe*) (sich *dat*) kaufen; (*grab*) sich *dat* schnappen; (*RACING:*

horse, dog) lahmlegen.
Nobel Prize [nəu'bɛl-] *n* Nobelpreis *m*.
nobility [nəu'bɪlɪtɪ] *n* Adel *m*; *(quality)* Edelmut *m*.
noble ['nəubl] *adj* edel, nobel; *(aristocratic)* ad(e)lig; *(impressive)* prächtig.
nobleman ['nəublmən] *(irreg: like* **man***) n* Ad(e)lige(r) *f(m)*.
nobly ['nəublɪ] *adv* edel.
nobody ['nəubədɪ] *pron* niemand, keiner ♦ *n:* **he's a ~** er ist ein Niemand *m*.
no-claims bonus [nəu'kleɪmz-] *n* Schadenfreiheitsrabatt *m*.
nocturnal [nɔk'tə:nl] *adj* nächtlich; *(animal)* Nacht-.
nod [nɔd] *vi* nicken; *(fig: flowers etc)* wippen ♦ *vt:* **to ~ one's head** mit dem Kopf nicken ♦ *n* Nicken *nt;* **they ~ded their agreement** sie nickten zustimmend.
▶**nod off** *vi* einnicken.
no-fly zone [nəu'flaɪ-] *n* Sperrzone *f* für den Flugverkehr.
noise [nɔɪz] *n* Geräusch *nt;* *(din)* Lärm *m*.
noiseless ['nɔɪzlɪs] *adj* geräuschlos.
noisily ['nɔɪzɪlɪ] *adv* laut.
noisy ['nɔɪzɪ] *adj* laut.
nomad ['nəumæd] *n* Nomade *m*, Nomadin *f*.
nomadic [nəu'mædɪk] *adj* Nomaden-, nomadisch.
no-man's-land ['nəumænzlænd] *n* Niemandsland *nt*.
nominal ['nɔmɪnl] *adj* nominell.
nominate ['nɔmɪneɪt] *vt* nominieren; *(appoint)* ernennen.
nomination [nɔmɪ'neɪʃən] *n* Nominierung *f;* *(appointment)* Ernennung *f*.
nominee [nɔmɪ'ni:] *n* Kandidat(in) *m(f)*.
non- [nɔn] *pref* nicht-, Nicht-.
non-alcoholic [nɔnælkə'hɔlɪk] *adj* alkoholfrei.
non-aligned [nɔnə'laɪnd] *adj* blockfrei.
non-breakable [nɔn'breɪkəbl] *adj* unzerbrechlich.
nonce word ['nɔns-] *n* Ad-hoc-Bildung *f*.
nonchalant ['nɔnʃələnt] *adj* lässig, nonchalant.
noncommissioned officer [nɔnkə'mɪʃənd-] *n* Unteroffizier *m*.
non-committal [nɔnkə'mɪtl] *adj* zurückhaltend; *(answer)* unverbindlich.
nonconformist [nɔnkən'fɔ:mɪst] *n* Nonkonformist(in) *m(f)* ♦ *adj* nonkonformistisch.
non-cooperation ['nɔnkəuɔpə'reɪʃən] *n* unkooperative Haltung *f*.
nondescript ['nɔndɪskrɪpt] *adj* unauffällig; *(colour)* unbestimmbar.
none [nʌn] *pron (not one)* kein(e, er, es); *(not any)* nichts; **~ of us** keiner von uns; **I've ~ left** *(not any)* ich habe nichts übrig; *(not one)* ich habe kein(e, en, es) übrig; **~ at all** *(not any)* überhaupt nicht; *(not one)* überhaupt kein(e, er, es); **I was ~ the wiser**

ich war auch nicht klüger; **she would have ~ of it** sie wollte nichts davon hören; **it was ~ other than X** es war kein anderer als X.
nonentity [nɔ'nentɪtɪ] *n (person)* Nichts *nt*, unbedeutende Figur *f*.
non-essential [nɔnɪ'senʃl] *adj* unnötig ♦ *n:* **~s** nicht (lebens)notwendige Dinge *pl*.
nonetheless ['nʌnðə'lɛs] *adv* nichtsdestoweniger, trotzdem.
nonevent [nɔnɪ'vɛnt] *n* Reinfall *m*.
non-existent [nɔnɪg'zɪstənt] *adj* nicht vorhanden.
non-fiction [nɔn'fɪkʃən] *n* Sachbücher *pl* ♦ *adj (book)* Sach-; *(prize)* Sachbuch-.
non-flammable [nɔn'flæməbl] *adj* nicht entzündbar.
non-intervention ['nɔnɪntə'vɛnʃən] *n* Nichteinmischung *f*, Nichteingreifen *nt*.
no-no ['nəunəu] *n:* **it's a ~** *(inf)* das kommt nicht in Frage.
non obst. *abbr (= non obstante)* dennoch.
no-nonsense [nəu'nɔnsəns] *adj (approach, look)* nüchtern.
non-payment [nɔn'peɪmənt] *n* Nichtzahlung *f*, Zahlungsverweigerung *f*.
nonplussed [nɔn'plʌst] *adj* verdutzt, verblüfft.
non-profit making ['nɔn'prɔfɪt-] *adj (organization)* gemeinnützig.
nonreturnable [nɔnrə'tə:nəbl] *adj:* **~ bottle** Einwegflasche *f*.
nonsense ['nɔnsəns] *n* Unsinn *m;* **~!** Unsinn!, Quatsch!; **it is ~ to say that ...** es ist dummes Gerede, zu sagen, daß ...; **to make (a) ~ of sth** etw ad absurdum führen.
nonsensical [nɔn'sɛnsɪkl] *adj (idea, action etc)* unsinnig.
non-shrink [nɔn'ʃrɪŋk] *(BRIT) adj* nicht einlaufend.
non-smoker ['nɔn'sməukə*] *n* Nichtraucher(in) *m(f)*.
nonstarter [nɔn'stɑ:tə*] *n (fig):* **it's a ~** *(idea etc)* es hat keine Erfolgschance.
non-stick ['nɔn'stɪk] *adj* kunststoffbeschichtet, Teflon- ®.
non-stop ['nɔn'stɔp] *adj* ununterbrochen; *(flight)* Nonstop- ♦ *adv* ununterbrochen; *(fly)* nonstop.
non-taxable [nɔn'tæksəbl] *adj* nichtsteuerpflichtig.
non-U [nɔn'ju:] *(BRIT: inf) adj abbr (= non-upper class)* nicht vornehm.
non-white [nɔn'waɪt] *adj* farbig ♦ *n* Farbige(r) *f(m)*.
noodles ['nu:dlz] *npl* Nudeln *pl*.
nook [nuk] *n:* **every ~ and cranny** jeder Winkel.
noon [nu:n] *n* Mittag *m*.
no-one ['nəuwʌn] *pron* = **nobody**.
noose [nu:s] *n* Schlinge *f*.
nor [nɔ:*] *conj, adv* = **neither**.
Norf *(BRIT) abbr (POST:* = *Norfolk)*.

norm [nɔ:m] n Norm f.
normal ['nɔ:ml] adj normal ♦ n: **to return to** ~ sich wieder normalisieren.
normality [nɔ:'mælɪtɪ] n Normalität f.
normally ['nɔ:məlɪ] adv normalerweise; (act, behave) normal.
Normandy ['nɔ:məndɪ] n Normandie f.
north [nɔ:θ] n Norden m ♦ adj nördlich, Nord- ♦ adv nach Norden; ~ **of** nördlich von.
North Africa n Nordafrika nt.
North African adj nordafrikanisch ♦ n Nordafrikaner(in) m(f).
North America n Nordamerika nt.
North American adj nordamerikanisch ♦ n Nordamerikaner(in) m(f).
Northants [nɔ:'θænts] (BRIT) abbr (POST: = Northamptonshire).
northbound ['nɔ:θbaʊnd] adj in Richtung Norden; (carriageway) nach Norden (führend).
Northd (BRIT) abbr (POST: = Northumberland).
north-east [nɔ:θ'i:st] n Nordosten m ♦ adj nordöstlich, Nordost- ♦ adv nach Nordosten; ~ **of** nordöstlich von.
northerly ['nɔ:ðəlɪ] adj nördlich.
northern ['nɔ:ðən] adj nördlich, Nord-.
Northern Ireland n Nordirland nt.
North Korea n Nordkorea nt.
North Pole n: **the** ~ der Nordpol.
North Sea n: **the** ~ die Nordsee f.
North Sea oil n Nordseeöl nt.
northward(s) ['nɔ:θwəd(z)] adv nach Norden, nordwärts.
north-west [nɔ:θ'wɛst] n Nordwesten m ♦ adj nordwestlich, Nordwest- ♦ adv nach Nordwesten; ~ **of** nordwestlich von.
Norway ['nɔ:weɪ] n Norwegen nt.
Norwegian [nɔ:'wi:dʒən] adj norwegisch ♦ n Norweger(in) m(f); (LING) Norwegisch nt.
nos. abbr (= numbers) Nrn.
nose [nəʊz] n Nase f; (of car) Schnauze f ♦ vi (also: ~ **one's way**) sich schieben; **to follow one's** ~ immer der Nase nach gehen; **to get up one's** ~ (inf) auf die Nerven gehen +dat; **to have a (good)** ~ **for sth** eine (gute) Nase für etw haben; **to keep one's** ~ **clean** (inf) eine saubere Weste behalten; **to look down one's** ~ **at sb/sth** (inf) auf jdn/etw herabsehen; **to pay through the** ~ **(for sth)** (inf) (für etw) viel blechen; **to rub sb's** ~ **in sth** (inf) jdm etw unter die Nase reiben; **to turn one's** ~ **up at sth** (inf) die Nase über etw acc rümpfen; **under sb's** ~ vor jds Augen.
▶**nose about** vi herumschnüffeln.
▶**nose around** vi = nose about.
nosebleed ['nəʊzbli:d] n Nasenbluten nt.
nose-dive ['nəʊzdaɪv] n (of plane) Sturzflug m ♦ vi (plane) im Sturzflug herabgehen.
nose drops npl Nasentropfen pl.
nosey ['nəʊzɪ] (inf) adj = nosy.
nostalgia [nɔs'tældʒɪə] n Nostalgie f.

nostalgic [nɔs'tældʒɪk] adj nostalgisch.
nostril ['nɔstrɪl] n Nasenloch nt; (of animal) Nüster f.
nosy ['nəʊzɪ] (inf) adj neugierig.

═══════════════════════════ *KEYWORD*

not [nɔt] adv nicht; **he is** ~ or **isn't here** er ist nicht hier; **you must** ~ or **you mustn't do that** das darfst du nicht tun; **it's too late, isn't it?** es ist zu spät, nicht wahr?; ~ **that I don't like him** nicht, daß ich ihn nicht mag; ~ **yet** noch nicht; ~ **now** nicht jetzt; see also **all, only.**

notable ['nəʊtəbl] adj bemerkenswert.
notably ['nəʊtəblɪ] adv hauptsächlich; (markedly) bemerkenswert.
notary ['nəʊtərɪ] n (also: ~ **public**) Notar(in) m(f).
notation [nəʊ'teɪʃən] n Notation f; (MUS) Notenschrift f.
notch [nɔtʃ] n Kerbe f; (in blade, saw) Scharte f; (fig) Klasse f.
▶**notch up** vt erzielen; (victory) erringen.
note [nəʊt] n Notiz f; (of lecturer) Manuskript nt; (of student etc) Aufzeichnung f; (in book etc) Anmerkung f; (letter) paar Zeilen pl; (banknote) Note f, Schein m; (MUS: sound) Ton m; (: symbol) Note f; (tone) Ton m, Klang m ♦ vt beachten; (point out) anmerken; (also: ~ **down**) notieren; **of** ~ bedeutend; **to make a** ~ **of sth** dat etw notieren; **to take** ~**s** Notizen machen, mitschreiben; **to take** ~ **of sth** etw zur Kenntnis nehmen.
notebook ['nəʊtbʊk] n Notizbuch nt; (for shorthand) Stenoblock m.
notecase ['nəʊtkeɪs] (BRIT) n Brieftasche f.
noted ['nəʊtɪd] adj bekannt.
notepad ['nəʊtpæd] n Notizblock m.
notepaper ['nəʊtpeɪpə*] n Briefpapier nt.
noteworthy ['nəʊtwə:ðɪ] adj beachtenswert.
nothing ['nʌθɪŋ] n nichts; ~ **new/worse** etc nichts Neues/Schlimmeres etc; ~ **much** nicht viel; ~ **else** sonst nichts; **for** ~ umsonst; ~ **at all** überhaupt nichts.
notice ['nəʊtɪs] n Bekanntmachung f; (sign) Schild nt; (warning) Ankündigung f; (dismissal) Kündigung f; (BRIT: review) Kritik f, Rezension f ♦ vt bemerken; **to bring sth to sb's** ~ jdn auf etw acc aufmerksam machen; **to take no** ~ **of** ignorieren, nicht beachten; **to escape sb's** ~ jdm entgehen; **it has come to my** ~ **that ...** es ist mir zu Ohren gekommen, daß ...; **to give sb** ~ **of sth** jdm von etw Bescheid geben; **without** ~ ohne Ankündigung; **advance** ~ Vorankündigung f; **at short/a moment's** ~ kurzfristig/innerhalb kürzester Zeit; **until further** ~ bis auf weiteres; **to hand in one's** ~ kündigen; **to be given one's** ~ gekündigt werden +dat.
noticeable ['nəʊtɪsəbl] adj deutlich.
noticeboard ['nəʊtɪsbɔ:d] (BRIT) n

Anschlagbrett nt.
notification [nəʊtɪfɪ'keɪʃən] n
Benachrichtigung f.
notify ['nəʊtɪfaɪ] vt: **to ~ sb (of sth)** jdn (von
etw) benachrichtigen.
notion ['nəʊʃən] n Vorstellung f; **notions** (US)
npl (haberdashery) Kurzwaren pl.
notoriety [nəʊtə'raɪətɪ] n traurige
Berühmtheit f.
notorious [nəʊ'tɔːrɪəs] adj berüchtigt.
notoriously [nəʊ'tɔːrɪəslɪ] adv notorisch.
Notts [nɒts] (BRIT) abbr (POST:
= Nottinghamshire).
notwithstanding [nɒtwɪθ'stændɪŋ] adv
trotzdem ♦ prep trotz +dat.
nougat ['nuːgɑː] n Nougat m.
nought [nɔːt] n Null f.
noun [naʊn] n Hauptwort nt, Substantiv nt.
nourish ['nʌrɪʃ] vt nähren.
nourishing ['nʌrɪʃɪŋ] adj nahrhaft.
nourishment ['nʌrɪʃmənt] n Nahrung f.
Nov. abbr (= November) Nov.
Nova Scotia ['nəʊvə'skəʊʃə] n Neuschottland
nt.
novel ['nɒvl] n Roman m ♦ adj neu(artig).
novelist ['nɒvəlɪst] n Romanschriftsteller(in)
m(f).
novelty ['nɒvəltɪ] n Neuheit f; (object)
Kleinigkeit f.
November [nəʊ'vɛmbə*] n November m; see
also **July.**
novice ['nɒvɪs] n Neuling m, Anfänger(in) m(f);
(REL) Novize m, Novizin f.
NOW [naʊ] (US) n abbr (= National Organization
for Women) Frauenvereinigung.
now [naʊ] adv jetzt; (these days) heute ♦ conj:
~ (that) jetzt, wo; **right ~** gleich, sofort; **by
~** inzwischen, mittlerweile; **that's the
fashion just ~** das ist gerade modern; **I saw
her just ~** ich habe sie gerade gesehen;
(every) ~ and then, (every) ~ and again ab
und zu, gelegentlich; **from ~ on** von nun an;
in 3 days from ~ (heute) in 3 Tagen;
between ~ and Monday bis Montag; **that's
all for ~** das ist erst einmal alles; **any day ~**
jederzeit; **~ then** also.
nowadays ['naʊədeɪz] adv heute.
nowhere ['nəʊwɛə*] adv (be) nirgends,
nirgendwo; (go) nirgendwohin; **~ else**
nirgendwo anders.
no-win situation [nəʊ'wɪn-] n aussichtslose
Lage f.
noxious ['nɒkʃəs] adj (gas, fumes) schädlich;
(smell) übel.
nozzle ['nɒzl] n Düse f.
NP n abbr (LAW) = **notary public.**
NS (CANADA) abbr (= Nova Scotia).
NSC (US) n abbr = **National Security Council.**
NSF (US) n abbr (= National Science Foundation)
Organisation zur Förderung der
Wissenschaft.
NSPCC (BRIT) n abbr (= National Society for the

Prevention of Cruelty to Children)
Kinderschutzbund m.
NSW (AUSTRALIA) abbr (POST: = New South
Wales).
NT n abbr (BIBLE: = New Testament) NT.
nth [ɛnθ] (inf) adj: **to the ~ degree** in der
n-ten Potenz.
nuance ['njuːɑːns] n Nuance f.
nubile ['njuːbaɪl] adj gut entwickelt.
nuclear ['njuːklɪə*] adj (bomb, industry etc)
Atom-; **~ physics** Kernphysik f; **~ war**
Atomkrieg m.
nuclear disarmament n nukleare or
atomare Abrüstung f.
nuclear family n Kleinfamilie f, Kernfamilie
f.
nuclear-free zone ['njuːklɪə'friː-] n
atomwaffenfreie Zone f.
nuclei ['njuːklɪaɪ] npl of **nucleus.**
nucleus ['njuːklɪəs] (pl **nuclei**) n Kern m.
NUCPS (BRIT) n abbr (= National Union of Civil
and Public Servants) Gewerkschaft für
Beschäftigte im öffentlichen Dienst.
nude [njuːd] adj nackt ♦ n (ART) Akt m; **in the
~** nackt.
nudge [nʌdʒ] vt anstoßen.
nudist ['njuːdɪst] n Nudist(in) m(f).
nudist colony n FKK-Kolonie f.
nudity ['njuːdɪtɪ] n Nacktheit f.
nugget ['nʌgɪt] n (of gold) Klumpen m; (fig: of
information) Brocken m.
nuisance ['njuːsns] n: **to be a ~** lästig sein;
(situation) ärgerlich sein; **he's a ~** er geht
einem auf die Nerven; **what a ~!** wie
ärgerlich/lästig!
NUJ (BRIT) n abbr (= National Union of
Journalists) Journalistengewerkschaft.
null [nʌl] adj: **~ and void** null und nichtig.
nullify ['nʌlɪfaɪ] vt zunichte machen; (claim,
law) für null und nichtig erklären.
NUM (BRIT) n abbr (= National Union of
Mineworkers) Bergarbeitergewerkschaft.
numb [nʌm] adj taub, gefühllos; (fig: with fear
etc) wie betäubt ♦ vt taub or gefühllos
machen; (pain, fig: mind) betäuben.
number ['nʌmbə*] n Zahl f; (quantity) (An)zahl
f; (of house, bank account, bus etc) Nummer f
♦ vt (pages etc) numerieren; (amount to)
zählen; **a ~ of** einige; **any ~ of** beliebig
viele; (reasons) alle möglichen; **wrong ~**
(TEL) falsch verbunden; **to be ~ed among**
zählen zu.
number plate (BRIT) n (AUT)
Nummernschild nt.
Number Ten (BRIT) n (POL: = 10 Downing
Street) Nummer zehn f (Downing Street).
numbness ['nʌmnɪs] n Taubheit f, Starre f;
(fig) Benommenheit f, Betäubung f.
numbskull ['nʌmskʌl] n = **numskull.**
numeral ['njuːmərəl] n Ziffer f.
numerate ['njuːmərɪt] (BRIT) adj: **to be ~**
rechnen können.

numerical [nju:'mɛrɪkl] *adj* numerisch.
numerous ['nju:mərəs] *adj* zahlreich.
numskull ['nʌmskʌl] (*inf*) *n* Holzkopf *m*.
nun [nʌn] *n* Nonne *f*.
nunnery ['nʌnərɪ] *n* (Nonnen)kloster *nt*.
nuptial ['nʌpʃəl] *adj* (*feast, celebration*)
  Hochzeits-; ~ **bliss** Eheglück *nt*.
nurse [nɜːs] *n* Krankenschwester *f*; (*also:*
  ~**maid**) Kindermädchen *nt* ♦ *vt* pflegen;
  (*cold, toothache etc*) auskurieren; (*baby*)
  stillen; (*fig: desire, grudge*) hegen.
nursery ['nɜːsərɪ] *n* Kindergarten *m*; (*room*)
  Kinderzimmer *nt*; (*for plants*) Gärtnerei *f*.
nursery rhyme *n* Kinderreim *m*.
nursery school *n* Kindergarten *m*.
nursery slope (*BRIT*) *n* (*SKI*) Anfängerhügel
  m.
nursing ['nɜːsɪŋ] *n* Krankenpflege *f*; (*care*)
  Pflege *f*.
nursing home *n* Pflegeheim *nt*.
nursing mother *n* stillende Mutter *f*.
nurture ['nɜːtʃə'] *vt* hegen und pflegen; (*fig:*
  ideas, creativity) fördern.
NUS (*BRIT*) *n abbr* (= *National Union of*
  Students) Studentengewerkschaft.
NUT (*BRIT*) *n abbr* (= *National Union of*
  Teachers) Lehrergewerkschaft.
nut [nʌt] *n* (*TECH*) (Schrauben)mutter *f*; (*BOT*)
  Nuß *f*; (*inf: lunatic*) Spinner(in) *m(f)*.
nutcase ['nʌtkeɪs] (*inf*) *n* Spinner(in) *m(f)*.
nutcrackers ['nʌtkrækəz] *npl* Nußknacker *m*.
nutmeg ['nʌtmɛg] *n* Muskat *m*, Muskatnuß *f*.
nutrient ['nju:trɪənt] *n* Nährstoff *m*.
nutrition [nju:'trɪʃən] *n* Ernährung *f*;
  (*nourishment*) Nahrung *f*.
nutritionist [nju:'trɪʃənɪst] *n*
  Ernährungswissenschaftler(in) *m(f)*.
nutritious [nju:'trɪʃəs] *adj* nahrhaft.
nuts [nʌts] (*inf*) *adj* verrückt; **he's** ~ er spinnt.
nutshell ['nʌtʃɛl] *n* Nußschale *f*; **in a** ~ (*fig*)
  kurz gesagt.
nutty ['nʌtɪ] *adj* (*flavour*) Nuß-; (*inf: idea etc*)
  bekloppt.
nuzzle ['nʌzl] *vi*: **to** ~ **up to** sich drücken *or*
  schmiegen an +*acc*.
NV (*US*) *abbr* (*POST:* = *Nevada*).
NW *abbr* = **north-west**.
NWT (*CANADA*) *abbr* (= *Northwest Territories*).
NY (*US*) *abbr* (*POST:* = *New York*).
NYC (*US*) *abbr* (*POST:* = *New York City*).
nylon ['naɪlɔn] *n* Nylon *nt* ♦ *adj* Nylon-; **nylons**
  npl (*stockings*) Nylonstrümpfe *pl*.
nymph [nɪmf] *n* Nymphe *f*.
nymphomaniac ['nɪmfəu'meɪnɪæk] *n*
  Nymphomanin *f*.
NYSE (*US*) *n abbr* (= *New York Stock Exchange*)
  New Yorker Börse.
NZ *abbr* = **New Zealand**.

O, o

O, o [əu] *n* (*letter*) O *nt*, o *nt*; (*US: SCOL:*
  outstanding) ≈ Eins *f*; (*TEL etc*) Null *f*; ~ **for**
  Olive, (*US*) ~ **for Oboe** ≈ O wie Otto.
oaf [əuf] *n* Trottel *m*.
oak [əuk] *n* (*tree, wood*) Eiche *f* ♦ *adj* (*furniture,*
  door) Eichen-.
O & M *n abbr* (= *organization and method*)
  Organisation und Arbeitsweise *pl*.
OAP (*BRIT*) *n abbr* = **old age pensioner**.
oar [ɔː'] *n* Ruder *nt*; **to put** *or* **shove one's** ~ **in**
  (*inf, fig*) mitmischen, sich einmischen.
oarsman ['ɔːzmən] (*irreg: like* **man**) *n* Ruderer
  m.
oarswoman ['ɔːzwumən] (*irreg: like* **woman**) *n*
  Ruderin *f*.
OAS *n abbr* (= *Organization of American States*)
  OAS *f*.
oasis [əu'eɪsɪs] (*pl* **oases**) *n* (*lit, fig*) Oase *f*.
oath [əuθ] *n* (*promise*) Eid *m*, Schwur *m*; (*swear*
  word) Fluch *m*; **on** (*BRIT*) *or* **under** ~ unter
  Eid; **to take the** ~ (*LAW*) vereidigt werden.
oatmeal ['əutmiːl] *n* Haferschrot *m*; (*colour*)
  Hellbeige *nt*.
oats [əuts] *npl* Hafer *m*; **he's getting his** ~
  (*BRIT: inf, fig*) er kommt im Bett auf seine
  Kosten.
OAU *n abbr* (= *Organization of African Unity*)
  OAU *f*.
obdurate ['ɔbdjurɪt] *adj* unnachgiebig.
OBE (*BRIT*) *n abbr* (= *Officer of (the order of) the*
  British Empire) britischer Ordenstitel.
obedience [ə'biːdɪəns] *n* Gehorsam *m*; **in** ~ **to**
  gemäß +*dat*.
obedient [ə'biːdɪənt] *adj* gehorsam; **to be** ~ **to**
  sb jdm gehorchen.
obelisk ['ɔbɪlɪsk] *n* Obelisk *m*.
obese [əu'biːs] *adj* fettleibig.
obesity [əu'biːsɪtɪ] *n* Fettleibigkeit *f*.
obey [ə'beɪ] *vt* (*person*) gehorchen +*dat*, folgen
  +*dat*; (*orders, law*) befolgen ♦ *vi* gehorchen.
obituary [ə'bɪtjuərɪ] *n* Nachruf *m*.
object [*n* 'ɔbdʒɪkt, *vi* əb'dʒɛkt] *n* (*also LING*)
  Objekt *nt*; (*purpose*) Ziel *nt*, Zweck *m* ♦ *vi*
  dagegen sein; **to be an** ~ **of ridicule** (*person*)
  sich lächerlich machen; (*thing*) lächerlich
  wirken; **money is no** ~ Geld spielt keine
  Rolle; **he** ~**ed that** ... er wandte ein, daß ...; **I**
  ~**!** ich protestiere!; **do you** ~ **to my**
  smoking? haben Sie etwas dagegen, wenn
  ich rauche?
objection [əb'dʒɛkʃən] *n* (*argument*) Einwand
  m; **I have no** ~ **to** ... ich habe nichts

dagegen, daß ...; **if you have no** ~ wenn Sie nichts dagegen haben; **to raise** or **voice an** ~ einen Einwand erheben or vorbringen.
objectionable [əb'dʒɛkʃənəbl] adj (language, conduct) anstößig; (person) unausstehlich.
objective [əb'dʒɛktɪv] adj objektiv ♦ n Ziel nt.
objectively [əb'dʒɛktɪvlɪ] adv objektiv.
objectivity [ɔbdʒɪk'tɪvɪtɪ] n Objektivität f.
object lesson n: **an** ~ **in** ein Paradebeispiel nt für.
objector [əb'dʒɛktə'] n Gegner(in) m(f).
obligation [ɔblɪ'geɪʃən] n Pflicht f; **to be under an** ~ **to do sth** verpflichtet sein, etw zu tun; **to be under an** ~ **to sb** jdm verpflichtet sein; **"no** ~ **to buy"** (COMM) „kein Kaufzwang".
obligatory [ə'blɪɡətərɪ] adj obligatorisch.
oblige [ə'blaɪdʒ] vt (compel) zwingen; (do a favour for) einen Gefallen tun +dat; **I felt** ~**d to invite him in** ich fühlte mich verpflichtet, ihn hereinzubitten; **to be** ~**d to sb for sth** (grateful) jdm für etw dankbar sein; **anything to** ~! (inf) stets zu Diensten!
obliging [ə'blaɪdʒɪŋ] adj entgegenkommend.
oblique [ə'bliːk] adj (line, angle) schief; (reference, compliment) indirekt, versteckt ♦ n (BRIT: also: ~ **stroke**) Schrägstrich m.
obliterate [ə'blɪtəreɪt] vt (village etc) vernichten; (fig: memory, error) auslöschen.
oblivion [ə'blɪvɪən] n (unconsciousness) Bewußtlosigkeit f; (being forgotten) Vergessenheit f; **to sink into** ~ (event etc) in Vergessenheit geraten.
oblivious [ə'blɪvɪəs] adj: **he was** ~ **of** or **to it** er war sich dessen nicht bewußt.
oblong ['ɔblɔŋ] adj rechteckig ♦ n Rechteck nt.
obnoxious [əb'nɔkʃəs] adj widerwärtig, widerlich.
o.b.o. (US) abbr (in classified ads: = or best offer) bzw. Höchstgebot.
oboe ['əubəu] n Oboe f.
obscene [əb'siːn] adj obszön; (fig: wealth) unanständig; (income etc) unverschämt.
obscenity [əb'sɛnɪtɪ] n Obszönität f.
obscure [əb'skjuə'] adj (little known) unbekannt, obskur; (difficult to understand) unklar ♦ vt (obstruct, conceal) verdecken.
obscurity [əb'skjuərɪtɪ] n (of person, book) Unbekanntheit f; (of remark etc) Unklarheit f.
obsequious [əb'siːkwɪəs] adj unterwürfig.
observable [əb'zə:vəbl] adj wahrnehmbar; (noticeable) erkennbar.
observance [əb'zə:vns] n (of law etc) Befolgung f; **religious** ~**s** religiöse Feste pl.
observant [əb'zə:vənt] adj aufmerksam.
observation [ɔbzə'veɪʃən] n (remark) Bemerkung f; (act of observing, MED) Beobachtung f; **she's in hospital under** ~ sie ist zur Beobachtung im Krankenhaus.
observation post n Beobachtungsposten m.
observatory [əb'zə:vətrɪ] n Observatorium nt.
observe [əb'zə:v] vt (watch) beobachten;

(notice, comment) bemerken; (abide by: rule etc) einhalten.
observer [əb'zə:və'] n Beobachter(in) m(f).
obsess [əb'sɛs] vt verfolgen; **to be** ~**ed by** or **with sb/sth** von jdm/etw besessen sein.
obsession [əb'sɛʃən] n Besessenheit f.
obsessive [əb'sɛsɪv] adj (person) zwanghaft; (interest, hatred, tidiness) krankhaft; **to be** ~ **about cleaning/tidying up** einen Putz-/Ordnungsfimmel haben (inf).
obsolescence [ɔbsə'lɛsns] n Veralten nt; **built-in** or **planned** ~ (COMM) geplanter Verschleiß m.
obsolete ['ɔbsəliːt] adj veraltet.
obstacle ['ɔbstəkl] n (lit, fig) Hindernis nt.
obstacle race n Hindernisrennen nt.
obstetrician [ɔbstə'trɪʃən] n Geburtshelfer(in) m(f).
obstetrics [ɔb'stɛtrɪks] n Geburtshilfe f.
obstinacy ['ɔbstɪnəsɪ] n (of person) Starrsinn m.
obstinate ['ɔbstɪnɪt] adj (person) starrsinnig, stur; (refusal, cough etc) hartnäckig.
obstruct [əb'strʌkt] vt (road, path) blockieren; (traffic, fig) behindern.
obstruction [əb'strʌkʃən] n (object) Hindernis nt; (of plan, law) Behinderung f.
obstructive [əb'strʌktɪv] adj hinderlich, obstruktiv (esp POL); **she's being** ~ sie macht Schwierigkeiten.
obtain [əb'teɪn] vt erhalten, bekommen ♦ vi (form: exist, be the case) gelten.
obtainable [əb'teɪnəbl] adj erhältlich.
obtrusive [əb'truːsɪv] adj aufdringlich; (conspicuous) auffällig.
obtuse [əb'tjuːs] adj (person, remark) einfältig; (MATH) stumpf.
obverse ['ɔbvə:s] n (of situation, argument) Kehrseite f.
obviate ['ɔbvɪeɪt] vt (need, problem etc) vorbeugen +dat.
obvious ['ɔbvɪəs] adj offensichtlich; (lie) klar; (predictable) naheliegend.
obviously ['ɔbvɪəslɪ] adv (clearly) offensichtlich; (of course) natürlich; ~! selbstverständlich!; ~ **not** offensichtlich nicht; **he was** ~ **not drunk** er war natürlich nicht betrunken; **he was not** ~ **drunk** offenbar war er nicht betrunken.
OCAS n abbr (= Organization of Central American States) mittelamerikanischer Staatenbund.
occasion [ə'keɪʒən] n Gelegenheit f; (celebration etc) Ereignis nt ♦ vt (form: cause) verursachen; **on** ~ (sometimes) gelegentlich; **on that** ~ bei der Gelegenheit; **to rise to the** ~ sich der Lage gewachsen zeigen.
occasional [ə'keɪʒənl] adj gelegentlich; **he likes the** ~ **cigar** er raucht gelegentlich gern eine Zigarre.
occasionally [ə'keɪʒənəlɪ] adv gelegentlich;

very ~ sehr selten.

occasional table *n* Beistelltisch *m*.

occult [ɔ'kʌlt] *n*: **the** ~ der Okkultismus ♦ *adj* okkult.

occupancy ['ɔkjupənsɪ] *n* (*of room etc*) Bewohnen *nt*.

occupant ['ɔkjupənt] *n* (*of house etc*) Bewohner(in) *m(f)*; (*temporary: of car*) Insasse *m*, Insassin *f*; **the** ~ **of this table/ office** derjenige, der an diesem Tisch sitzt/ in diesem Büro arbeitet.

occupation [ɔkju'peɪʃən] *n* (*job*) Beruf *m*; (*pastime*) Beschäftigung *f*; (*of building, country etc*) Besetzung *f*.

occupational guidance [ɔku'peɪʃənl-] (*BRIT*) *n* Berufsberatung *f*.

occupational hazard *n* Berufsrisiko *nt*.

occupational pension scheme *n* betriebliche Altersversorgung *f*.

occupational therapy *n* Beschäftigungs-therapie *f*.

occupier ['ɔkjupaɪə*] *n* Bewohner(in) *m(f)*.

occupy ['ɔkjupaɪ] *vt* (*house, office*) bewohnen; (*place etc*) belegen; (*building, country etc*) besetzen; (*time, attention*) beanspruchen; (*position, space*) einnehmen; **to** ~ **o.s. (in** *or* **with sth)** sich (mit etw) beschäftigen; **to** ~ **o.s. in** *or* **with doing sth** sich damit beschäftigen, etw zu tun; **to be occupied in** *or* **with sth** mit etw beschäftigt sein; **to be occupied in** *or* **with doing sth** damit beschäftigt sein, etw zu tun.

occur [ə'kɔː*] *vi* (*take place*) geschehen, sich ereignen; (*exist*) vorkommen; **to** ~ **to sb** jdm einfallen.

occurrence [ə'kʌrəns] *n* (*event*) Ereignis *nt*; (*incidence*) Auftreten *nt*.

ocean ['əuʃən] *n* Ozean *m*, Meer *nt*; ~**s of** (*inf*) jede Menge.

ocean bed *n* Meeresgrund *m*.

ocean-going ['əuʃəngəuɪŋ] *adj* (*ship, vessel*) Hochsee-.

Oceania [əuʃɪ'eɪnɪə] *n* Ozeanien *nt*.

ocean liner *n* Ozeandampfer *m*.

ochre, (*US*) **ocher** ['əukə*] *adj* ockerfar-ben.

o'clock [ə'klɔk] *adv*: **it is 5** ~ es ist 5 Uhr.

OCR *n abbr* (*COMPUT*) = **optical character reader; optical character recogniton.**

Oct. *abbr* (= *October*) Okt.

octagonal [ɔk'tægənl] *adj* achteckig.

octane ['ɔkteɪn] *n* Oktan *nt*; **high-**~ **petrol** *or* (*US*) **gas** Benzin *nt* mit hoher Oktan-zahl.

octave ['ɔktɪv] *n* Oktave *f*.

October [ɔk'təubə*] *n* Oktober *m*; *see also* July.

octogenarian ['ɔktəudʒɪ'nɛərɪən] *n* Achtzigjährige(r) *f(m)*.

octopus ['ɔktəpəs] *n* Tintenfisch *m*.

odd [ɔd] *adj* (*person*) sonderbar, komisch; (*behaviour, shape*) seltsam; (*number*)

ungerade; (*sock, shoe etc*) einzeln; (*occasional*) gelegentlich; **60-**~ etwa 60; **at** ~ **times** ab und zu; **to be the** ~ **one out** der Außenseiter/die Außenseiterin sein; **add meat or the** ~ **vegetable to the soup** fügen Sie der Suppe Fleisch oder auch etwas Gemüse bei.

oddball ['ɔdbɔːl] (*inf*) *n* komischer Kauz *m*.

oddity ['ɔdɪtɪ] *n* (*person*) Sonderling *m*; (*thing*) Merkwürdigkeit *f*.

odd-job man [ɔd'dʒɔb-] *n* Mädchen *nt* für alles.

odd jobs *npl* Gelegenheitsarbeiten *pl*.

oddly ['ɔdlɪ] *adv* (*behave, dress*) seltsam; *see also* **enough.**

oddments ['ɔdmənts] *npl* (*COMM*) Restposten *m*.

odds [ɔdz] *npl* (*in betting*) Gewinnquote *f*; (*fig*) Chancen *pl*; **the** ~ **are in favour of/against his coming** es sieht so aus, als ob er kommt/nicht kommt; **to succeed against all the** ~ allen Erwartungen zum Trotz erfolgreich sein; **it makes no** ~ es spielt keine Rolle; **to be at** ~ **(with)** (*in disagreement*) uneinig sein (mit); (*at variance*) sich nicht vertragen (mit).

odds and ends *npl* Kleinigkeiten *pl*.

odds-on [ɔdz'ɔn] *adj*: **the** ~ **favourite** der klare Favorit ♦ *adv*: **it's** ~ **that she'll win** es ist so gut wie sicher, daß sie gewinnt.

ode [əud] *n* Ode *f*.

odious ['əudɪəs] *adj* widerwärtig.

odometer [ɔ'dɔmɪtə*] (*US*) *n* Tacho(meter) *m*.

odor *etc* (*US*) = **odour** *etc*.

odour, (*US*) **odor** ['əudə*] *n* Geruch *m*.

odourless ['əudəlɪs] *adj* geruchlos.

OECD *n abbr* (= *Organization for Economic Cooperation and Development*) OECD *f*.

oesophagus, (*US*) **esophagus** [iː'sɔfəgəs] *n* Speiseröhre *f*.

oestrogen, (*US*) **estrogen** ['iːstrəudʒən] *n* Östrogen *nt*.

========================= *KEYWORD*

of [ɔv] *prep* **1** von; **the history** ~ **Germany** die Geschichte Deutschlands; **a friend** ~ **ours** ein Freund von uns; **a boy** ~ **ten** ein Junge von zehn Jahren, ein zehnjähriger Junge; **that was kind** ~ **you** das war nett von Ihnen; **the city** ~ **New York** die Stadt New York

2 (*expressing quantity, amount, dates etc*): **a kilo** ~ **flour** ein Kilo Mehl; **how much** ~ **this do you need?** wieviel brauchen Sie davon?; **3** ~ **them** (*people*) 3 von ihnen; (*objects*) 3 davon; **a cup** ~ **tea** eine Tasse Tee; **a vase** ~ **flowers** eine Vase mit Blumen; **the 5th** ~ **July** der 5. Juli

3 (*from, out of*) aus; **a bracelet** ~ **solid gold** ein Armband aus massivem Gold; **made** ~ **wood** aus Holz (gemacht).

===================== KEYWORD

off [ɔf] *adv* **1** (*referring to distance, time*): **it's a long way** ~ es ist sehr weit weg; **the game is 3 days** ~ es sind noch 3 Tage bis zum Spiel
2 (*departure*): **to go** ~ **to Paris/Italy** nach Paris/Italien fahren; **I must be** ~ ich muß gehen
3 (*removal*): **to take** ~ **one's coat/clothes** seinen Mantel/sich ausziehen; **the button came** ~ der Knopf ging ab; **10 %** ~ (*COMM*) 10% Nachlaß
4: to be ~ (*on holiday*) im Urlaub sein; (*due to sickness*) krank sein; **I'm** ~ **on Fridays** freitags habe ich frei; **he was** ~ **on Friday** Freitag war er nicht da; **to have a day** ~ (*from work*) einen Tag frei haben; **to be** ~ **sick** wegen Krankheit fehlen
♦ *adj* **1** (*not turned on: machine, light, engine etc*) aus; (: *water, gas*) abgedreht; (: *tap*) zu
2: to be ~ (*meeting, match*) ausfallen; (*agreement*) nicht mehr gelten
3 (*BRIT: not fresh: milk, cheese, meat etc*) verdorben, schlecht
4: on the ~ **chance that** ... für den Fall, daß ...; **to have an** ~ **day** (*not as good as usual*) nicht in Form sein; **to be badly** ~ sich schlecht stehen
♦ *prep* **1** (*indicating motion, removal etc*) von +*dat*; **to fall** ~ **a cliff** von einer Klippe fallen; **to take a picture** ~ **the wall** ein Bild von der Wand nehmen
2 (*distant from*): **5 km** ~ **the main road** 5 km von der Hauptstraße entfernt; **an island** ~ **the coast** eine Insel vor der Küste
3: I'm ~ **meat/beer** (*no longer eat/drink it*) ich esse kein Fleisch/trinke kein Bier mehr; (*no longer like it*) ich kann kein Fleisch/Bier *etc* mehr sehen

offal ['ɔfl] *n* (*CULIN*) Innereien *pl*.
off-beat ['ɔfbiːt] *adj* (*clothes, ideas*) ausgefallen.
off-centre, (*US*) **off-center** [ɔf'sɛntə*] *adj* nicht genau in der Mitte, links/rechts von der Mitte ♦ *adv* asymmetrisch.
off-colour ['ɔf'kʌlə*] (*BRIT*) *adj* (*ill*) unpäßlich; **to feel** ~ sich unwohl fühlen.
offence, (*US*) **offense** [ə'fɛns] *n* (*crime*) Vergehen *nt*; (*insult*) Beleidigung *f*, Kränkung *f*; **to commit an** ~ eine Straftat begehen; **to take** ~ **(at)** Anstoß nehmen (an +*dat*); **to give** ~ **(to)** Anstoß erregen (bei); "**no** ~" „nichts für ungut".
offend [ə'fɛnd] *vt* (*upset*) kränken; **to** ~ **against** (*law, rule*) verstoßen gegen.
offender [ə'fɛndə*] *n* Straftäter(in) *m(f)*.
offending [ə'fɛndɪŋ] *adj* (*item etc*) Anstoß erregend.
offense [ə'fɛns] (*US*) *n* = **offence**.
offensive [ə'fɛnsɪv] *adj* (*remark, behaviour*)

verletzend; (*smell etc*) übel; (*weapon*) Angriffs- ♦ *n* (*MIL*) Offensive *f*.
offer ['ɔfə*] *n* Angebot *nt* ♦ *vt* anbieten; (*money, opportunity, service*) bieten; (*reward*) aussetzen; **to make an** ~ **for sth** ein Angebot für etw machen; **on** ~ (*COMM: available*) erhältlich; (: *cheaper*) im Angebot; **to** ~ **sth to sb** jdm etw anbieten; **to** ~ **to do sth** anbieten, etw zu tun.
offering ['ɔfərɪŋ] *n* Darbietung *f*; (*REL*) Opfergabe *f*.
off-hand [ɔf'hænd] *adj* (*casual*) lässig; (*impolite*) kurz angebunden ♦ *adv* auf Anhieb; **I can't tell you** ~ das kann ich Ihnen auf Anhieb nicht sagen.
office ['ɔfɪs] *n* Büro *nt*; (*position*) Amt *nt*; **doctor's** ~ (*US*) Praxis *f*; **to take** ~ das Amt antreten; **in** ~ (*minister etc*) im Amt; **through his good** ~**s** durch seine guten Dienste; **O**~ **of Fair Trading** (*BRIT*) Behörde *f* gegen unlauteren Wettbewerb.
office block, (*US*) **office building** *n* Bürogebäude *nt*.
office boy *n* Bürogehilfe *m*.
office holder *n* Amtsinhaber(in) *m(f)*.
office hours *npl* (*COMM*) Bürostunden *pl*; (*US: MED*) Sprechstunde *f*.
office manager *n* Büroleiter(in) *m(f)*.
officer ['ɔfɪsə*] *n* (*MIL etc*) Offizier *m*; (*also:* **police** ~) Polizeibeamte(r) *m*, Polizeibeamtin *f*; (*of organization*) Funktionär *m*.
office work *n* Büroarbeit *f*.
office worker *n* Büroangestellte(r) *f(m)*.
official [ə'fɪʃl] *adj* offiziell ♦ *n* (*in government*) Beamte(r) *m*, Beamtin *f*; (*in trade union etc*) Funktionär *m*.
officialdom [ə'fɪʃldəm] (*pej*) *n* Bürokratie *f*.
officially [ə'fɪʃəlɪ] *adv* offiziell.
official receiver *n* (*COMM*) Konkursverwalter *m*.
officiate [ə'fɪʃɪeɪt] *vi* amtieren; **to** ~ **at a marriage** eine Trauung vornehmen.
officious [ə'fɪʃəs] *adj* übereifrig.
offing ['ɔfɪŋ] *n:* **in the** ~ in Sicht.
off-key [ɔf'kiː] *adj* (*MUS: sing, play*) falsch; (*instrument*) verstimmt.
off-licence ['ɔflaɪsns] (*BRIT*) *n* ≈ Wein- und Spirituosenhandlung *f*.

> **Off-licence** ist ein Geschäft (oder eine Theke in einer Gaststätte), wo man alkoholische Getränke kaufen kann, die aber anderswo konsumiert werden müssen. In solchen Geschäften, die oft von landesweiten Ketten betrieben werden, kann man auch andere Getränke, Süßigkeiten, Zigaretten und Knabbereien kaufen.

off-limits [ɔf'lɪmɪts] *adj* verboten.
off-line [ɔf'laɪn] (*COMPUT*) *adj* Off-line- ♦ *adv* off line; (*switched off*) abgetrennt.

off-load ['ɔfləud] *vt* abladen.

off-peak ['ɔf'pi:k] *adj* (*heating*) Nachtspeicher-; (*electricity*) Nacht-; (*train*) außerhalb der Stoßzeit; ~ **ticket** Fahrkarte *f* zur Fahrt außerhalb der Stoßzeit.

off-putting ['ɔfputɪŋ] (*BRIT*) *adj* (*remark, behaviour*) abstoßend.

off-season ['ɔf'si:zn] *adj, adv* außerhalb der Saison.

offset ['ɔfsɛt] (*irreg: like* **set**) *vt* (*counteract*) ausgleichen.

offshoot ['ɔfʃu:t] *n* (*BOT, fig*) Ableger *m*.

offshore [ɔf'ʃɔ:ʳ] *adj* (*breeze*) ablandig; (*oil rig, fishing*) küstennah.

offside ['ɔf'saɪd] *adj* (*SPORT*) im Abseits; (*AUT: when driving on left*) rechtsseitig; (: *when driving on right*) linksseitig ♦ *n:* **the** ~ (*AUT: when driving on left*) die rechte Seite; (: *when driving on right*) die linke Seite.

offspring ['ɔfsprɪŋ] *n inv* Nachwuchs *m*.

offstage [ɔf'steɪdʒ] *adv* hinter den Kulissen.

off-the-cuff [ɔfðə'kʌf] *adj* (*remark*) aus dem Stegreif.

off-the-job ['ɔfðə'dʒɔb] *adj:* ~ **training** außerbetriebliche Weiterbildung *f*.

off-the-peg ['ɔfðə'pɛg], (*US*) **off-the-rack** ['ɔfðə'ræk] *adv* von der Stange.

off-the-record ['ɔfðə'rɛkɔ:d] *adj* (*conversation, briefing*) inoffiziell; **that's strictly** ~ das ist ganz im Vertrauen.

off-white ['ɔfwaɪt] *adj* gebrochen weiß.

Ofgas ['ɔfgæs] *n Überwachungsgremium zum Verbraucherschutz nach Privatisierung der Gasindustrie*.

Oftel ['ɔftɛl] *n Überwachungsgremium zum Verbraucherschutz nach Privatisierung der Telekommunikationsindustrie*.

often ['ɔfn] *adv* oft; **how** ~? wie oft?; **more** ~ **than not** meistens; **as** ~ **as not** ziemlich oft; **every so** ~ ab und zu.

Ofwat ['ɔfwɔt] *n Überwachungsgremium zum Verbraucherschutz nach Privatisierung der Wasserindustrie*.

ogle ['əugl] *vt* schielen nach, begaffen (*pej*).

ogre ['əugəʳ] *n* (*monster*) Menschenfresser *m*.

OH (*US*) *abbr* (*POST: =* Ohio).

oh [əu] *excl* oh.

ohm [əum] *n* Ohm *nt*.

OHMS (*BRIT*) *abbr* (*= On His/Her Majesty's Service*) *Aufdruck auf amtlichen Postsendungen*.

oil [ɔɪl] *n* Öl *nt*; (*petroleum*) (Erd)öl *nt* ♦ *vt* ölen.

oilcan ['ɔɪlkæn] *n* Ölkanne *f*.

oil change *n* Ölwechsel *m*.

oilcloth ['ɔɪlklɔθ] *n* Wachstuch *nt*.

oilfield ['ɔɪlfi:ld] *n* Ölfeld *nt*.

oil filter *n* Ölfilter *m*.

oil-fired ['ɔɪlfaɪəd] *adj* (*boiler, central heating*) Öl-.

oil gauge *n* Ölstandsmesser *m*.

oil painting *n* Ölgemälde *nt*.

oil refinery *n* Ölraffinerie *f*.

oil rig *n* Ölförderturm *m*; (*at sea*) Bohrinsel *f*.

oilskins ['ɔɪlskɪnz] *npl* Ölzeug *nt*.

oil slick *n* Ölteppich *m*.

oil tanker *n* (*ship*) (Öl)tanker *m*; (*truck*) Tankwagen *m*.

oil well *n* Ölquelle *f*.

oily ['ɔɪlɪ] *adj* (*substance*) ölig; (*rag*) öldurchtränkt; (*food*) fettig.

ointment ['ɔɪntmənt] *n* Salbe *f*.

OK (*US*) *abbr* (*POST: =* Oklahoma).

O.K. ['əu'keɪ] (*inf*) *excl* okay; (*granted*) gut ♦ *adj* (*average*) einigermaßen; (*acceptable*) in Ordnung ♦ *vt* genehmigen ♦ *n:* **to give sb/sth the** ~ jdm/etw seine Zustimmung geben; **is it** ~? ist es in Ordnung?; **are you** ~? bist du in Ordnung?; **are you** ~ **for money?** hast du (noch) genug Geld?; **it's** ~ **with** *or* **by me** mir ist es recht.

okay ['əu'keɪ] *excl* = **O.K.**

Okla. (*US*) *abbr* (*POST: =* Oklahoma).

old [əuld] *adj* alt; **how** ~ **are you?** wie alt bist du?; **he's 10 years** ~ er ist 10 Jahre alt; ~**er brother** ältere(r) Bruder; **any** ~ **thing will do for him** ihm ist alles recht.

old age *n* Alter *nt*.

old age pension *n* Rente *f*.

old age pensioner (*BRIT*) *n* Rentner(in) *m(f)*.

old-fashioned ['əuld'fæʃnd] *adj* altmodisch.

old hand *n* alter Hase *m*.

old hat *adj:* **to be** ~ ein alter Hut sein.

old maid *n* alte Jungfer *f*.

old people's home *n* Altersheim *nt*.

old-style ['əuldstaɪl] *adj* im alten Stil.

old-time dancing ['əuldtaɪm-] *n* Tänze *pl* im alten Stil.

old-timer [əuld'taɪməʳ] (*esp US*) *n* Veteran *m*.

old wives' tale *n* Ammenmärchen *nt*.

oleander [əuli'ændəʳ] *n* Oleander *m*.

O level (*BRIT*) *n* (*formerly*) ≈ Abschluß *m* der Sekundarstufe 1, mittlere Reife *f*.

olive ['ɔlɪv] *n* Olive *f*; (*tree*) Olivenbaum *m* ♦ *adj* (*also:* ~-**green**) olivgrün; **to offer an** ~ **branch to sb** (*fig*) jdm ein Friedensangebot machen.

olive oil *n* Olivenöl *nt*.

Olympic [əu'lɪmpɪk] *adj* olympisch.

Olympic Games *npl:* **the** ~ (*also:* **the Olympics**) die Olympischen Spiele *pl*.

OM (*BRIT*) *n abbr* (*= Order of Merit*) *britischer Verdienstorden*.

Oman [əu'mɑ:n] *n* Oman *m*.

OMB (*US*) *n abbr* (*= Office of Management and Budget*) *Regierungsbehörde für Verwaltung und Etat*.

ombudsman ['ɔmbudzmən] *n* Ombudsmann *m*.

omelette, (*US*) **omelet** ['ɔmlɪt] *n* Omelett *nt*; **ham/cheese omelet(te)** Schinken-/ Käseomelett *nt*.

omen ['əumən] *n* Omen *nt*.

ominous ['ɔmɪnəs] *adj* (*silence, warning*) ominös; (*clouds, smoke*) bedrohlich.

omission [əuˈmɪʃən] n (*thing omitted*) Auslassung f; (*act of omitting*) Auslassen nt.
omit [əuˈmɪt] vt (*deliberately*) unterlassen; (*by mistake*) auslassen ♦ vi: **to ~ to do sth** es unterlassen, etw zu tun.
omnivorous [ɔmˈnɪvrəs] adj: **to be ~** Allesfresser sein.
ON (*CANADA*) abbr (= *Ontario*).

━━━━━━━━━━━━━━━━━━━━━ *KEYWORD*

on [ɔn] prep **1** (*indicating position*) auf +dat; (*with vb of motion*) auf +acc; **it's ~ the table** es ist auf dem Tisch; **she put the book ~ the table** sie legte das Buch auf den Tisch; **~ the left** links; **~ the right** rechts; **the house is ~ the main road** das Haus liegt an der Hauptstraße
2 (*indicating means, method, condition etc*) **~ foot** (go, be) zu Fuß; **to be ~ the train/ plane** im Zug/Flugzeug sein; **to go ~ the train/plane** mit dem Zug/Flugzeug reisen; **(to be wanted) ~ the telephone** am Telefon (verlangt werden); **~ the radio/television** im Radio/Fernsehen; **to be ~ drugs** Drogen nehmen; **to be ~ holiday** im Urlaub sein; **I'm here ~ business** ich bin geschäftlich hier
3 (*referring to time*): **~ Friday** am Freitag; **~ Fridays** freitags; **~ June 20th** am 20. Juni; **~ Friday, June 20th** am Freitag, dem 20. Juni; **a week ~ Friday** Freitag in einer Woche; **~ (his) arrival he went straight to his hotel** bei seiner Ankunft ging er direkt in sein Hotel; **~ seeing this he ...** als er das sah, ... er ...
4 (*about, concerning*) über +acc; **a book ~ physics** ein Buch über Physik
♦ adv **1** (*referring to dress*): **to have one's coat ~** seinen Mantel anhaben; **what's she got ~?** was hat sie an?
2 (*referring to covering*) **screw the lid ~ tightly** dreh den Deckel fest zu
3 (*further, continuously*): **to walk/drive/read ~** weitergehen/-fahren/-lesen
♦ adj **1** (*functioning, in operation: machine, radio, TV, light*) an; (: *tap*) auf; (: *handbrake*) angezogen; **there's a good film ~ at the cinema** im Kino läuft ein guter Film
2: **that's not ~!** (*inf: of behaviour*) das ist nicht drin!

━━━━━━━━━━━━━━━━━━━━━

ONC (*BRIT*) n abbr (= *Ordinary National Certificate*) höherer Schulabschluß.
once [wʌns] adv (*on one occasion*) einmal; (*formerly*) früher; (*a long time ago*) früher einmal ♦ conj (*as soon as*) sobald; **at ~** (*immediately*) sofort; (*simultaneously*) gleichzeitig; **~ a week** einmal pro Woche; **~ more** or **again** noch einmal; **~ and for all** ein für allemal; **~ upon a time** es war einmal; **~ in a while** ab und zu; **all at ~** (*suddenly*) plötzlich; **for ~** ausnahmsweise (einmal); **~ or twice** ein paarmal; **~ he had**

left sobald er gegangen war; **~ it was done** nachdem es getan war.
oncoming [ˈɔnkʌmɪŋ] adj (*traffic etc*) entgegenkommend.
OND (*BRIT*) n abbr (= *Ordinary National Diploma*) technisches Diplom.

━━━━━━━━━━━━━━━━━━━━━ *KEYWORD*

one [wʌn] num ein(e); (*counting*) eins; **~ hundred and fifty** (ein)hundert(und)-fünfzig; **~ day there was a sudden knock at the door** eines Tages klopfte es plötzlich an der Tür; **~ by ~** einzeln
♦ adj **1** (*sole*) einzige(r, s); **the ~ book which ...** das einzige Buch, das ...
2 (*same*): **they came in the ~ car** sie kamen in demselben Wagen; **they all belong to the ~ family** sie alle gehören zu ein und derselben Familie
♦ pron **1**: **this ~** diese(r, s); **that ~** der/die/das (da); **which ~?** welcher/welche/welches?; **he is ~ of us** er ist einer von uns; **I've already got ~/a red ~** ich habe schon eins/ein rotes
2: **another ~** einander; **do you two ever see ~ another?** seht ihr zwei euch jemals?
3 (*impersonal*) man; **~ never knows** man weiß nie; **to cut ~'s finger** sich dat in den Finger schneiden.

━━━━━━━━━━━━━━━━━━━━━

one-day excursion [ˈwʌndeɪ-] (*US*) n (*day return*) Tagesrückfahrkarte f.
one-man [ˈwʌnˈmæn] adj (*business, show*) Einmann-.
one-man band n Einmannkapelle f.
one-off [wʌnˈɔf] (*BRIT: inf*) n einmaliges Ereignis nt.
one-parent family [ˈwʌnpɛərənt-] n Familie f mit nur einem Elternteil.
one-piece [ˈwʌnpiːs] adj: **~ swimsuit** einteiliger Badeanzug m.
onerous [ˈɔnərəs] adj (*duty etc*) schwer.

━━━━━━━━━━━━━━━━━━━━━ *KEYWORD*

oneself [wʌnˈsɛlf] pron (*reflexive: after prep*) sich; (*emphatic*) selbst; **to hurt ~** sich dat weh tun; **to keep sth for ~** etw für sich behalten; **to talk to ~** Selbstgespräche führen.

━━━━━━━━━━━━━━━━━━━━━

one-shot [ˈwʌnʃɔt] (*US*) n = **one-off**.
one-sided [wʌnˈsaɪdɪd] adj einseitig.
one-time [ˈwʌntaɪm] adj ehemalig.
one-to-one [ˈwʌntəwʌn] adj (*relationship, tuition*) Einzel-.
one-upmanship [wʌnˈʌpmənʃɪp] n: **the art of ~** die Kunst, anderen um einen Schritt voraus zu sein.
one-way [ˈwʌnweɪ] adj (*street, traffic*) Einbahn-; (*ticket*) Einzel-.
ongoing [ˈɔngəuɪŋ] adj (*project*) laufend; (*situation etc*) andauernd.
onion [ˈʌnjən] n Zwiebel f.

on-line ['ɔnlaɪn] (*COMPUT*) *adj* (*printer, database*) On-line-; (*switched on*) gekoppelt ♦ *adv* on line.
onlooker ['ɔnlukə*] *n* Zuschauer(in) *m(f)*.
only ['əunlɪ] *adv* nur ♦ *adj* einzige(r, s) ♦ *conj* nur, bloß; **I ~ took one** ich nahm nur eins; **I saw her ~ yesterday** ich habe sie erst gestern gesehen; **I'd be ~ too pleased to help** ich würde allzu gern helfen; **not ~ ... but (also) ...** nicht nur ... sondern auch ...; **an ~ child** ein Einzelkind *nt*; **I would come, ~ I'm too busy** ich würde kommen, wenn ich nicht so viel zu tun hätte.
ono (*BRIT*) *abbr* (*in classified ads*: = or near(est) offer) *see* **near.**
onset ['ɔnsɛt] *n* Beginn *m*.
onshore ['ɔnʃɔː*] *adj* (*wind*) auflandig, See-.
onslaught ['ɔnslɔːt] *n* Attacke *f*.
on-the-job ['ɔnðə'dʒɔb] *adj*: **~ training** Ausbildung *f* am Arbeitsplatz.
onto ['ɔntu] *prep* = **on to.**
onus ['əunəs] *n* Last *f*, Pflicht *f*; **the ~ is on him to prove it** er trägt die Beweislast.
onward(s) ['ɔnwəd(z)] *adv* weiter; **from that time ~** von der Zeit an ♦ *adj* fortschreitend.
onyx ['ɔnɪks] *n* Onyx *m*.
ooze [uːz] *vi* (*mud, water etc*) triefen.
opacity [əu'pæsɪtɪ] *n* (*of substance*) Undurchsichtigkeit *f*.
opal ['əupl] *n* Opal *m*.
opaque [əu'peɪk] *adj* (*substance*) undurchsichtig, trüb.
OPEC ['əupɛk] *n abbr* (= *Organization of Petroleum-Exporting Countries*) OPEC *f*.
open ['əupn] *adj* offen; (*packet, shop, museum*) geöffnet; (*view*) frei; (*meeting, debate*) öffentlich; (*ticket, return*) unbeschränkt; (*vacancy*) verfügbar ♦ *vt* öffnen, aufmachen; (*book, paper etc*) aufschlagen; (*account*) eröffnen; (*blocked road*) freimachen ♦ *vi* (*door, eyes, mouth*) sich öffnen; (*shop, bank etc*) aufmachen; (*commence*) beginnen; (*film, play*) Premiere haben; (*flower*) aufgehen; **in the ~ (air)** im Freien; **the ~ sea** das offene Meer; **to have an ~ mind on sth** etw *dat* aufgeschlossen gegenüberstehen; **to be ~ to** (*ideas etc*) offen sein für; **to be ~ to criticism** der Kritik *dat* ausgesetzt sein; **to be ~ to the public** für die Öffentlichkeit zugänglich sein; **to ~ one's mouth** (*speak*) den Mund aufmachen.
▶**open on to** *vt fus* (*room, door*) führen auf +*acc*.
▶**open up** *vi* (*unlock*) aufmachen; (*confide*) sich äußern.
open-air [əupn'ɛə*] *adj* im Freien; **~ concert** Open-air-Konzert *nt*; **~ swimming pool** Freibad *nt*.
open-and-shut ['əupənən'ʃʌt] *adj*: **~ case** klarer Fall *m*.
open day *n* Tag *m* der offenen Tür.
open-ended [əupn'ɛndɪd] *adj* (*question etc*) mit

offenem Ausgang; (*contract*) unbefristet.
opener ['əupnə*] *n* (*also*: **tin ~, can ~**) Dosenöffner *m*.
open-heart [əupən'hɑːt] *adj*: **~ surgery** Eingriff *m* am offenen Herzen.
opening ['əupnɪŋ] *adj* (*commencing: stages, scene*) erste(r, s); (*remarks, ceremony etc*) Eröffnungs- ♦ *n* (*gap, hole*) Öffnung *f*; (*of play etc*) Anfang *m*; (*of new building etc*) Eröffnung *f*; (*opportunity*) Gelegenheit *f*.
opening hours *npl* Öffnungszeiten *pl*.
opening night *n* (*THEAT*) Eröffnungsabend *m*.
open learning *n* Weiterbildungssystem auf Teilzeitbasis.
openly ['əupnlɪ] *adv* offen.
open-minded [əupn'maɪndɪd] *adj* aufgeschlossen.
open-necked ['əupnnɛkt] *adj* (*shirt*) mit offenem Kragen.
openness ['əupnnɪs] *n* (*frankness*) Offenheit *f*.
open-plan ['əupn'plæn] *adj* (*office*) Großraum-.
open prison *n* offenes Gefängnis *nt*.
open sandwich *n* belegtes Brot *nt*.
open shop *n* Unternehmen ohne Gewerkschaftszwang.
Open University (*BRIT*) *n* ≈ Fernuniversität *f*.

> **Open University** *ist eine 1969 in Großbritannien gegründete Fernuniversität für Spätstudierende. Der Unterricht findet durch Fernseh- und Radiosendungen statt, schriftliche Arbeiten werden mit der Post verschickt, und der Besuch von Sommerkursen ist Pflicht. Die Studenten müssen eine bestimmte Anzahl von Unterrichtseinheiten in einem bestimmten Zeitraum absolvieren und für die Verleihung eines akademischen Grades eine Mindestzahl von Scheinen machen.*

open verdict *n* (*LAW*) Todesfeststellung ohne Angabe der Todesursache.
opera ['ɔpərə] *n* Oper *f*.
opera glasses *npl* Opernglas *nt*.
opera house *n* Opernhaus *nt*.
opera singer *n* Opernsänger(in) *m(f)*.
operate ['ɔpəreɪt] *vt* (*machine etc*) bedienen ♦ *vi* (*machine etc*) funktionieren; (*company*) arbeiten; (*laws, forces*) wirken; (*MED*) operieren; **to ~ on sb** jdn operieren.
operatic [ɔpə'rætɪk] *adj* (*singer etc*) Opern-.
operating room ['ɔpəreɪtɪŋ-] (*US*) *n* Operationssaal *m*.
operating system *n* (*COMPUT*) Betriebssystem *nt*.
operating table *n* (*MED*) Operationstisch *m*.
operating theatre *n* (*MED*) Operationssaal *m*.
operation [ɔpə'reɪʃən] *n* (*activity*) Unternehmung *f*; (*of machine etc*) Betrieb *m*; (*MIL, MED*) Operation *f*; (*COMM*) Geschäft *nt*;

to be in ~ (law, scheme) in Kraft sein; **to have an** ~ (MED) operiert werden; **to perform an** ~ (MED) eine Operation vornehmen.
operational [ɔpə'reɪʃənl] adj (machine etc) einsatzfähig.
operative ['ɔpərətɪv] adj (measure, system) wirksam; (law) gültig ♦ n (in factory) Maschinenarbeiter(in) m(f); **the** ~ **word** das entscheidende Wort.
operator ['ɔpəreɪtə*] n (TEL) Vermittlung f; (of machine) Bediener(in) m(f).
operetta [ɔpə'rɛtə] n Operette f.
ophthalmic [ɔf'θælmɪk] adj (department) Augen-.
ophthalmic optician n Augenoptiker(in) m(f).
ophthalmologist [ɔfθæl'mɔlədʒɪst] n Augenarzt m, Augenärztin f.
opinion [ə'pɪnjən] n Meinung f; **in my** ~ meiner Meinung nach; **to have a good/high** ~ **of sb/o.s.** eine gute/hohe Meinung von jdm/sich haben; **to be of the** ~ **that** ... der Ansicht or Meinung sein, daß ...; **to get a second** ~ (MED etc) ein zweites Gutachten einholen.
opinionated [ə'pɪnjəneɪtɪd] (pej) adj rechthaberisch.
opinion poll n Meinungsumfrage f.
opium ['əupɪəm] n Opium nt.
opponent [ə'pəunənt] n Gegner(in) m(f).
opportune ['ɔpətjuːn] adj (moment) günstig.
opportunism [ɔpə'tjuːnɪsəm] (pej) n Opportunismus m.
opportunist [ɔpə'tjuːnɪst] (pej) n Opportunist(in) m(f).
opportunity [ɔpə'tjuːnɪtɪ] n Gelegenheit f, Möglichkeit f; (prospects) Chance f; **to take the** ~ **of doing sth** die Gelegenheit ergreifen, etw zu tun.
oppose [ə'pəuz] vt (opinion, plan) ablehnen; **to be** ~**d to sth** gegen etw sein; **as** ~**d to** im Gegensatz zu.
opposing [ə'pəuzɪŋ] adj (side, team) gegnerisch; (ideas, tendencies) entgegengesetzt.
opposite ['ɔpəzɪt] adj (house, door) gegenüberliegend; (end, direction) entgegengesetzt; (point of view, effect) gegenteilig ♦ adv gegenüber ♦ prep (in front of) gegenüber; (next to: on list, form etc) neben ♦ n: **the** ~ das Gegenteil; **the** ~ **sex** das andere Geschlecht; **"see** ~ **page"** „siehe gegenüber".
opposite number n (person) Gegenspieler(in) m(f).
opposition [ɔpə'zɪʃən] n (resistance) Widerstand m; (SPORT) Gegner pl; **the O**~ (POL) die Opposition.
oppress [ə'prɛs] vt unterdrücken.
oppressed [ə'prɛst] adj unterdrückt.
oppression [ə'prɛʃən] n Unterdrückung f.

oppressive [ə'prɛsɪv] adj (weather, heat) bedrückend; (political regime) repressiv.
opprobrium [ə'prəubrɪəm] n (form) Schande f, Schmach f.
opt [ɔpt] vi: **to** ~ **for** sich entscheiden für; **to** ~ **to do sth** sich entscheiden, etw zu tun.
▶**opt out (of)** vi (not participate) sich nicht beteiligen (an +dat); (of insurance scheme etc) kündigen; **to** ~ **out (of local authority control)** (POL: hospital, school) aus der Kontrolle der Gemeindeverwaltung austreten.
optical ['ɔptɪkl] adj optisch.
optical character reader n optischer Klarschriftleser m.
optical character recognition n optische Zeichenerkennung f.
optical illusion n optische Täuschung f.
optician [ɔp'tɪʃən] n Optiker(in) m(f).
optics ['ɔptɪks] n Optik f.
optimism ['ɔptɪmɪzəm] n Optimismus m.
optimist ['ɔptɪmɪst] n Optimist(in) m(f).
optimistic [ɔptɪ'mɪstɪk] adj optimistisch.
optimum ['ɔptɪməm] adj optimal.
option ['ɔpʃən] n (choice) Möglichkeit f; (SCOL) Wahlfach nt; (COMM) Option f; **to keep one's** ~**s open** sich dat alle Möglichkeiten offenhalten; **to have no** ~ keine (andere) Wahl haben.
optional ['ɔpʃənl] adj freiwillig; ~ **extras** (COMM) Extras pl.
opulence ['ɔpjuləns] n Reichtum m.
opulent ['ɔpjulənt] adj (very wealthy) reich, wohlhabend.
OR (US) abbr (POST: = Oregon).
or [ɔː*] conj oder; **he hasn't seen** ~ **heard anything** er hat weder etwas gesehen noch gehört; ~ **else** (otherwise) sonst; **fifty** ~ **sixty people** fünfzig bis sechzig Leute.
oracle ['ɔrəkl] n Orakel nt.
oral ['ɔːrəl] adj (test, report) mündlich; (MED: vaccine, contraceptive) zum Einnehmen ♦ n (exam) mündliche Prüfung f.
orange ['ɔrɪndʒ] n Orange f, Apfelsine f ♦ adj (colour) orange.
orangeade [ɔrɪndʒ'eɪd] n Orangenlimonade f.
oration [ɔː'reɪʃən] n Ansprache f.
orator ['ɔrətə*] n Redner(in) m(f).
oratorio [ɔrə'tɔːrɪəu] n (MUS) Oratorium nt.
orb [ɔːb] n Kugel f.
orbit ['ɔːbɪt] n (of planet etc) Umlaufbahn f ♦ vt umkreisen.
orbital motorway ['ɔːbɪtəl-] n Ringautobahn f.
orchard ['ɔːtʃəd] n Obstgarten m; **apple** ~ Obstgarten mit Apfelbäumen.
orchestra ['ɔːkɪstrə] n Orchester nt; (US: stalls) Parkett nt.
orchestral [ɔː'kɛstrəl] adj (piece, musicians) Orchester-.
orchestrate ['ɔːkɪstreɪt] vt orchestrieren.
orchid ['ɔːkɪd] n Orchidee f.

ordain [ɔːˈdeɪn] *vt (REL)* ordinieren; *(decree)* verfügen.

ordeal [ɔːˈdiːl] *n* Qual *f*.

order [ˈɔːdə*] *n (command)* Befehl *m*; *(COMM, in restaurant)* Bestellung *f*; *(sequence)* Reihenfolge *f*; *(discipline, organization)* Ordnung *f*; *(REL)* Orden *m* ♦ *vt (command)* befehlen; *(COMM, in restaurant)* bestellen; *(also:* put in ~) ordnen; in ~ *(permitted)* in Ordnung; in (working) ~ betriebsfähig; in ~ to do sth um etw zu tun; in ~ of size nach Größe (geordnet); on ~ *(COMM)* bestellt; out of ~ *(not working)* außer Betrieb; *(in the wrong sequence)* durcheinander; *(motion, proposal)* nicht zulässig; to place an ~ for sth with sb eine Bestellung für etw bei jdm aufgeben; made to ~ *(COMM)* auf Bestellung (gemacht); to be under ~s to do sth die Anweisung haben, etw zu tun; to take ~s Befehle entgegennehmen; a point of ~ *(in debate etc)* eine Verfahrensfrage; "pay to the ~ of ..." „zahlbar an *+dat* ..."; of *or* in the ~ of in der Größenordnung von; to ~ sb to do sth jdn anweisen, etw zu tun.
▶**order around** *vt (also:* order about) herumkommandieren.

order book *n (COMM)* Auftragsbuch *nt*.

order form *n* Bestellschein *m*.

orderly [ˈɔːdəlɪ] *n (MIL)* Offiziersbursche *m*; *(MED)* Pfleger(in) *m(f)* ♦ *adj (manner)* ordentlich; *(sequence, system)* geordnet.

order number *n (COMM)* Bestellnummer *f*.

ordinal [ˈɔːdɪnl] *adj:* ~ number Ordinalzahl *f*.

ordinarily [ˈɔːdnrɪlɪ] *adv* normalerweise.

ordinary [ˈɔːdnrɪ] *adj (everyday)* gewöhnlich, normal; *(pej: mediocre)* mittelmäßig; out of the ~ außergewöhnlich.

Ordinary degree *ist ein Universitätsabschluß, der an Studenten vergeben wird, die entweder die für ein* honours degree *nötige Note nicht erreicht haben, aber trotzdem nicht durchgefallen sind, oder die sich nur für ein ordinary degree eingeschrieben haben, wobei das Studium meist kürzer ist.*

---

ordinary seaman *(BRIT) n* Leichtmatrose *m*.

ordinary shares *npl* Stammaktien *pl*.

ordination [ɔːdɪˈneɪʃən] *n (REL)* Ordination *f*.

ordnance [ˈɔːdnəns] *n (unit)* Technische Truppe *f* ♦ *adj (factory, supplies)* Munitions-.

Ordnance Survey *(BRIT) n* Landesvermessung *f*.

ore [ɔː*] *n* Erz *nt*.

Ore. *(US) abbr (POST:* = *Oregon)*.

organ [ˈɔːgən] *n (ANAT)* Organ *nt*; *(MUS)* Orgel *f*.

organic [ɔːˈgænɪk] *adj* organisch.

organism [ˈɔːgənɪzəm] *n* Organismus *m*.

organist [ˈɔːgənɪst] *n* Organist(in) *m(f)*.

organization [ɔːgənaɪˈzeɪʃən] *n* Organisation *f*.

organization chart *n* Organisationsplan *m*.

organize [ˈɔːgənaɪz] *vt* organisieren; to get ~d sich fertigmachen.

organized crime *n* organisiertes Verbrechen *nt*.

organized labour *n* organisierte Arbeiterschaft *f*.

organizer [ˈɔːgənaɪzə*] *n (of conference etc)* Organisator *m*, Veranstalter *m*.

orgasm [ˈɔːgæzəm] *n* Orgasmus *m*.

orgy [ˈɔːdʒɪ] *n* Orgie *f*; an ~ of destruction eine Zerstörungsorgie.

Orient [ˈɔːrɪənt] *n:* the ~ der Orient.

orient [ˈɔːrɪənt] *vt:* to ~ o.s. (to) sich orientieren (in *+dat*); to be ~ed towards ausgerichtet sein auf *+acc*.

oriental [ɔːrɪˈɛntl] *adj* orientalisch.

orientate [ˈɔːrɪənteɪt] *vt:* to ~ o.s. sich orientieren; *(fig)* sich zurechtfinden; to be ~d towards ausgerichtet sein auf *+acc*.

orifice [ˈɔrɪfɪs] *n (ANAT)* Öffnung *f*.

origin [ˈɔrɪdʒɪn] *n* Ursprung *m*; *(of person)* Herkunft *f*; country of ~ Herkunftsland *nt*.

original [əˈrɪdʒɪnl] *adj (first)* ursprünglich; *(genuine)* original; *(imaginative)* originell ♦ *n* Original *nt*.

originality [ərɪdʒɪˈnælɪtɪ] *n* Originalität *f*.

originally [əˈrɪdʒɪnəlɪ] *adv (at first)* ursprünglich.

originate [əˈrɪdʒɪneɪt] *vi:* to ~ in *(idea, custom etc)* entstanden sein in *+dat*; to ~ with *or* from stammen von.

originator [əˈrɪdʒɪneɪtə*] *n (of idea, custom)* Urheber(in) *m(f)*.

Orkneys [ˈɔːknɪz] *npl:* the ~ *(also:* the Orkney Islands) die Orkneyinseln *pl*.

ornament [ˈɔːnəmənt] *n (object)* Ziergegenstand *m*; *(decoration)* Verzierungen *pl*.

ornamental [ɔːnəˈmɛntl] *adj (garden, pond)* Zier-.

ornamentation [ɔːnəmɛnˈteɪʃən] *n* Verzierungen *pl*.

ornate [ɔːˈneɪt] *adj (necklace, design)* kunstvoll.

ornithologist [ɔːnɪˈθɔlədʒɪst] *n* Ornithologe *m*, Ornithologin *f*.

ornithology [ɔːnɪˈθɔlədʒɪ] *n* Ornithologie *f*, Vogelkunde *f*.

orphan [ˈɔːfn] *n* Waise *f*, Waisenkind *nt* ♦ *vt:* to be ~ed zur Waise werden.

orphanage [ˈɔːfənɪdʒ] *n* Waisenhaus *nt*.

orthodox [ˈɔːθədɔks] *adj* orthodox; ~ medicine die konventionelle Medizin.

orthodoxy [ˈɔːθədɔksɪ] *n* Orthodoxie *f*.

orthopaedic, *(US)* **orthopedic** [ɔːθəˈpiːdɪk] *adj* orthopädisch.

OS *abbr (BRIT)* = **Ordnance Survey;** *(NAUT)* = **ordinary seaman;** *(DRESS)* = **outsize.**

O/S *abbr (COMM:* = *out of stock)* nicht auf Lager.

Oscar [ˈɔskə*] *n* Oscar *m*.

oscillate ['ɔsɪleɪt] *vi (ELEC, PHYS)* schwingen, oszillieren; *(fig)* schwanken.

OSHA *(US) n abbr (= Occupational Safety and Health Administration) Regierungsstelle für Arbeitsschutzvorschriften.*

Oslo ['ɔzləu] *n* Oslo *nt*.

OST *n abbr (= Office of Science and Technology) Ministerium für Wissenschaft und Technologie.*

ostensible [ɔs'tɛnsɪbl] *adj* vorgeblich, angeblich.

ostensibly [ɔs'tɛnsɪblɪ] *adv* angeblich.

ostentation [ɔstɛn'teɪʃən] *n* Pomp *m*, Protz *m*.

ostentatious [ɔstɛn'teɪʃəs] *adj (building, car etc)* pompös; *(person)* protzig.

osteopath ['ɔstɪəpæθ] *n* Osteopath(in) *m(f)*.

ostracize ['ɔstrəsaɪz] *vt* ächten.

ostrich ['ɔstrɪtʃ] *n* Strauß *m*.

OT *abbr (BIBLE: = Old Testament)* AT.

OTB *(US) n abbr (= offtrack betting) Wetten außerhalb des Rennbahngeländes.*

OTE *abbr (COMM: = on-target earnings)* Einkommensziel *nt*.

other ['ʌðə'] *adj* andere(r, s) ♦ *pron*: **the ~ (one)** der/die/das andere; **~s** andere *pl*; **the ~s** die anderen *pl*; **~ than** *(apart from)* außer; **the ~ day** *(recently)* neulich; **some actor or ~** irgendein Schauspieler; **somebody or ~** irgend jemand; **the car was none ~ than Robert's** das Auto gehörte keinem anderen als Robert.

otherwise ['ʌðəwaɪz] *adv (differently)* anders; *(apart from that, if not)* sonst, ansonsten; **an ~ good piece of work** eine im übrigen gute Arbeit.

OTT *(inf) abbr (= over the top) see* **top**.

otter ['ɔtə'] *n* Otter *m*.

OU *(BRIT) n abbr =* **Open University**.

ouch [autʃ] *excl* autsch.

ought [ɔːt] *(pt* **ought)** *aux vb*: **I ~ to do it** ich sollte es tun; **this ~ to have been corrected** das hätte korrigiert werden müssen; **he ~ to win** *(he probably will win)* er dürfte wohl gewinnen; **you ~ to go and see it** das solltest du dir ansehen.

ounce [auns] *n* Unze *f*; *(fig: small amount)* bißchen *nt*.

our ['auə'] *adj* unsere(r, s); *see also* **my**.

ours [auəz] *pron* unsere(r, s); *see also* **mine**[1].

ourselves [auə'sɛlvz] *pron pl* uns (selbst); *(emphatic)* selbst; **we did it (all) by ~** wir haben alles selbst gemacht; *see also* **oneself**.

oust [aust] *vt (forcibly remove)* verdrängen.

====== *KEYWORD* ======

out[1] [aut] *adv* **1** *(not in)* draußen; **~ in the rain/snow** draußen im Regen/Schnee; **~ here** hier; **~ there** dort; **to go/come etc ~** hinausgehen/-kommen *etc*; **to speak ~ loud** laut sprechen

2 *(not at home, absent)* nicht da

3 *(indicating distance):* **the boat was 10 km ~**

das Schiff war 10 km weit draußen; **3 days ~ from Plymouth** 3 Tage nach dem Auslaufen von Plymouth

4 *(SPORT)* aus; **the ball is ~/has gone ~** der Ball ist aus

♦ *adj* **1**: **to be ~** *(person: unconscious)* bewußtlos sein; *(: out of game)* ausgeschieden sein; *(out of fashion: style, singer)* out sein

2 *(have appeared: flowers)* da; *(: news, secret)* heraus

3 *(extinguished, finished: fire, light, gas)* aus; **before the week was ~** ehe die Woche zu Ende war

4: to be ~ to do sth *(intend)* etw tun wollen

5 *(wrong):* **to be ~ in one's calculations** sich in seinen Berechnungen irren.

out[2] [aut] *vt (inf: expose as homosexual)* outen.

outage ['autɪdʒ] *(esp US) n (power failure)* Stromausfall *m*.

out-and-out ['autəndaut] *adj (liar, thief etc)* ausgemacht.

outback ['autbæk] *n (in Australia):* **the ~** das Hinterland.

outbid [aut'bɪd] *vt* überbieten.

outboard ['autbɔːd] *n (also:* **~ motor)** Außenbordmotor *m*.

outbound ['autbaund] *adj (ship)* auslaufend.

outbreak ['autbreɪk] *n (of war, disease etc)* Ausbruch *m*.

outbuilding ['autbɪldɪŋ] *n* Nebengebäude *nt*.

outburst ['autbəːst] *n (of anger etc)* Gefühlsausbruch *m*.

outcast ['autkɑːst] *n* Ausgestoßene(r) *f(m)*.

outclass [aut'klɑːs] *vt* deklassieren.

outcome ['autkʌm] *n* Ergebnis *nt*, Resultat *nt*.

outcrop ['autkrɔp] *n (of rock)* Block *m*.

outcry ['autkraɪ] *n* Aufschrei *m*.

outdated [aut'deɪtɪd] *adj (custom, idea)* veraltet.

outdo [aut'duː] *(irreg: like* **do)** *vt* übertreffen.

outdoor [aut'dɔː'] *adj (activities)* im Freien; *(clothes)* für draußen; **~ swimming pool** Freibad *nt*; **she's an ~ person** sie liebt die freie Natur.

outdoors [aut'dɔːz] *adv (play, sleep)* draußen, im Freien.

outer ['autə'] *adj* äußere(r, s); **~ suburbs** (äußere) Vorstädte *pl*; **the ~ office** das Vorzimmer.

outer space *n* der Weltraum.

outfit ['autfɪt] *n (clothes)* Kleidung *f*; *(inf: team)* Verein *m*.

outfitter's ['autfɪtəz] *(BRIT) n (shop)* Herrenausstatter *m*.

outgoing ['autgəuɪŋ] *adj (extrovert)* kontaktfreudig; *(retiring: president etc)* scheidend; *(mail etc)* ausgehend.

outgoings ['autgəuɪŋz] *(BRIT) npl* Ausgaben *pl*.

outgrow [aut'grəu] *(irreg: like* **grow)** *vt (clothes)* herauswachsen aus; *(habits etc)* ablegen.

outhouse ['authaus] *n* Nebengebäude *nt*.
outing ['autɪŋ] *n* Ausflug *m*.
outlandish [aut'lændɪʃ] *adj* eigenartig, seltsam.
outlast [aut'lɑːst] *vt* überleben.
outlaw ['autlɔː] *n* Geächtete(r) *f(m)* ♦ *vt* verbieten.
outlay ['autleɪ] *n* Auslagen *pl*.
outlet ['autlɛt] *n* (*hole, pipe*) Abfluß *m*; (*US: ELEC*) Steckdose *f*; (*COMM: also:* **retail ~**) Verkaufsstelle *f*; (*fig: for grief, anger etc*) Ventil *nt*.
outline ['autlaɪn] *n* (*shape*) Umriß *m*; (*brief explanation*) Abriß *m*; (*rough sketch*) Skizze *f* ♦ *vt* (*fig: theory, plan etc*) umreißen, skizzieren.
outlive [aut'lɪv] *vt* (*survive*) überleben.
outlook ['autluk] *n* (*attitude*) Einstellung *f*; (*prospects*) Aussichten *pl*; (*for weather*) Vorhersage *f*.
outlying ['autlaɪɪŋ] *adj* (*area, town etc*) entlegen.
outmanoeuvre, (*US*) **outmaneuver** [autmə'nuːvə] *vt* ausmanövrieren.
outmoded [aut'məudɪd] *adj* veraltet.
outnumber [aut'nʌmbə] *vt* zahlenmäßig überlegen sein *+dat*; **to be ~ed (by) 5 to 1** im Verhältnis 5 zu 1 in der Minderheit sein

═══════════════════════ *KEYWORD*

out of *prep* **1** (*outside, beyond: position*) nicht in *+dat*; (*: motion*) aus *+dat*; **to look ~ the window** aus dem Fenster blicken; **to be ~ danger** außer Gefahr sein
2 (*cause, origin*) aus *+dat*; **~ curiosity/fear/ greed** aus Neugier/Angst/Habgier; **to drink sth ~ a cup** etw aus einer Tasse trinken
3 (*from among*) von *+dat*; **one ~ every three smokers** einer von drei Rauchern
4 (*without*): **to be ~ sugar/milk/petrol** *etc* keinen Zucker/keine Milch/kein Benzin *etc* mehr haben.

out of bounds *adj*: **to be ~** verboten sein.
out-of-court [autəv'kɔːt] *adj* (*settlement*) außergerichtlich; *see also* **court**.
out-of-date [autəv'deɪt] *adj* (*passport, ticket etc*) abgelaufen; (*clothes, idea*) veraltet.
out-of-doors [autəv'dɔːz] *adv* (*play, stay etc*) im Freien.
out-of-the-way ['autəvðə'weɪ] *adj* (*place*) entlegen; (*pub, restaurant etc*) kaum bekannt.
out-of-work ['autəvwəːk] *adj* arbeitslos.
outpatient ['autpeɪʃənt] *n* ambulanter Patient *m*, ambulante Patientin *f*.
outpost ['autpəust] *n* (*MIL, COMM*) Vorposten *m*.
outpouring ['autpɔːrɪŋ] *n* (*of emotion etc*) Erguß *m*.
output ['autput] *n* (*production: of factory, writer etc*) Produktion *f*; (*COMPUT*) Output *m*, Ausgabe *f* ♦ *vt* (*COMPUT*) ausgeben.

outrage ['autreɪdʒ] *n* (*scandal*) Skandal *m*; (*atrocity*) Verbrechen *nt*, Ausschreitung *f*; (*anger*) Empörung *f* ♦ *vt* (*shock, anger*) empören.
outrageous [aut'reɪdʒəs] *adj* (*remark etc*) empörend; (*clothes*) unmöglich; (*scandalous*) skandalös.
outrider ['autraɪdə] *n* (*on motorcycle*) Kradbegleiter *m*.
outright [aut'raɪt] *adv* (*kill*) auf der Stelle; (*win*) überlegen; (*buy*) auf einen Schlag; (*ask, refuse*) ohne Umschweife ♦ *adj* (*winner, victory*) unbestritten; (*refusal, hostility*) total.
outrun [aut'rʌn] (*irreg: like* **run**) *vt* schneller laufen als.
outset ['autsɛt] *n* Anfang *m*, Beginn *m*; **from the ~** von Anfang an; **at the ~** am Anfang.
outshine [aut'ʃaɪn] (*irreg: like* **shine**) *vt* (*fig*) in den Schatten stellen.
outside [aut'saɪd] *n* (*of building etc*) Außenseite *f* ♦ *adj* (*wall, lavatory*) Außen- ♦ *adv* (*be, wait*) draußen; (*go*) nach draußen ♦ *prep* außerhalb *+gen*; (*door etc*) vor *+dat*; **at the ~** (*at the most*) höchstens; (*at the latest*) spätestens; **an ~ chance** eine geringe Chance.
outside broadcast *n* außerhalb des Studios produzierte Sendung *f*.
outside lane *n* Überholspur *f*.
outside line *n* (*TEL*) Amtsanschluß *m*.
outsider [aut'saɪdə] *n* (*stranger*) Außenstehende(r) *f(m)*; (*odd one out, in race etc*) Außenseiter(in) *m(f)*.
outsize ['autsaɪz] *adj* (*clothes*) übergroß.
outskirts ['autskəːts] *npl* (*of town*) Stadtrand *m*.
outsmart [aut'smɑːt] *vt* austricksen (*inf*).
outspoken [aut'spəukən] *adj* offen.
outspread [aut'sprɛd] *adj* (*wings, arms etc*) ausgebreitet.
outstanding [aut'stændɪŋ] *adj* (*exceptional*) hervorragend; (*remaining*) ausstehend; **your account is still ~** Ihr Konto weist noch Außenstände auf.
outstay [aut'steɪ] *vt*: **to ~ one's welcome** länger bleiben als erwünscht.
outstretched [aut'strɛtʃt] *adj* ausgestreckt.
outstrip [aut'strɪp] *vt* (*competitors, supply*): **to ~ (in)** übertreffen (an *+dat*).
out tray *n* Ablage *f* für Ausgänge.
outvote [aut'vəut] *vt* überstimmen.
outward ['autwəd] *adj* (*sign, appearances*) äußere(r, s); **~ journey** Hinreise *f*.
outwardly ['autwədlɪ] *adv* (*on the surface*) äußerlich.
outward(s) ['autwəd(z)] *adv* (*move, face*) nach außen.
outweigh [aut'weɪ] *vt* schwerer wiegen als.
outwit [aut'wɪt] *vt* überlisten.
ova ['əuvə] *npl of* **ovum**.
oval ['əuvl] *adj* oval ♦ *n* Oval *nt*.

Oval Office, *ein großer ovaler Raum im Weißen Haus, ist das private Büro des amerikanischen Präsidenten. Im weiteren Sinne bezieht sich dieser Begriff oft auf die Präsidentschaft selbst.*

ovarian [əu'vɛəriən] *adj* (*ANAT*) des Eierstocks/der Eierstöcke; **~ cyst** Zyste *f* im Eierstock.
ovary ['əuvərɪ] *n* (*ANAT, MED*) Eierstock *m*.
ovation [əu'veɪʃən] *n* Ovation *f*.
oven ['ʌvn] *n* (*CULIN*) Backofen *m*.
ovenproof ['ʌvnpru:f] *adj* (*dish etc*) feuerfest.
oven-ready ['ʌvnrɛdɪ] *adj* backfertig.
ovenware ['ʌvnwɛə*] *n* feuerfestes Geschirr *nt*.

=========================== KEYWORD

over ['əuvə*] *adv* **1** (*across: walk, jump, fly etc*) hinüber; **~ here** hier; **~ there** dort (drüben); **to ask sb ~** (*to one's house*) jdn zu sich einladen
2 (*indicating movement*): **to fall ~** (*person*) hinfallen; (*object*) umfallen; **to knock sth ~** etw umstoßen; **to turn ~** (*in bed*) sich umdrehen; **to bend ~** sich bücken
3 (*finished*): **to be ~** (*game, life, relationship etc*) vorbei sein, zu Ende sein
4 (*excessively: clever, rich, fat etc*) übermäßig
5 (*remaining: money, food etc*) übrig; **is there any cake (left) ~?** ist noch Kuchen übrig?
6: all ~ (*everywhere*) überall
7 (*repeatedly*): **~ and ~ (again)** immer (und immer) wieder; **five times ~** fünfmal
♦ *prep* **1** (*on top of, above*) über +*dat*; (*with vb of motion*) über +*acc*; **to spread a sheet ~ sth** ein Laken über etw *acc* breiten
2 (*on the other side of*): **the pub ~ the road** die Kneipe gegenüber; **he jumped ~ the wall** er sprang über die Mauer
3 (*more than*) über +*acc*; **~ 200 people** über 200 Leute; **~ and above my normal duties** über meine normalen Pflichten hinaus; **~ and above that** darüber hinaus
4 (*during*) während; **let's discuss it ~ dinner** wir sollten es beim Abendessen besprechen.

over... ['əuvə*] *pref* über-.
overact [əuvər'ækt] *vi* übertreiben.
overall ['əuvərɔ:l] *adj* (*length, cost etc*) Gesamt-; (*impression, view*) allgemein ♦ *adv* (*measure, cost*) insgesamt; (*generally*) im allgemeinen ♦ *n* (*BRIT*) Kittel *m*; **overalls** *npl* Overall *m*.
overall majority *n* absolute Mehrheit *f*.
overanxious [əuvər'æŋkʃəs] *adj* überängstlich.
overawe [əuvər'ɔ:] *vt*: **to be ~d (by)** überwältigt sein (von).
overbalance [əuvə'bæləns] *vi* das

Gleichgewicht verlieren.
overbearing [əuvə'bɛərɪŋ] *adj* (*person, manner*) aufdringlich.
overboard ['əuvəbɔ:d] *adv* (*NAUT*) über Bord; **to go ~** (*fig*) es übertreiben, zu weit gehen.
overbook [əuvə'buk] *vt* überbuchen.
overcame [əuvə'keɪm] *pt of* **overcome**.
overcapitalize [əuvə'kæpɪtəlaɪz] *vt* überkapitalisieren.
overcast ['əuvəkɑ:st] *adj* (*day, sky*) bedeckt.
overcharge [əuvə'tʃɑ:dʒ] *vt* zuviel berechnen +*dat*.
overcoat ['əuvəkəut] *n* Mantel *m*.
overcome [əuvə'kʌm] (*irreg: like* **come**) *vt* (*problem, fear*) überwinden ♦ *adj* überwältigt; **she was ~ with grief** der Schmerz übermannte sie.
overconfident [əuvə'kɔnfɪdənt] *adj* zu selbstsicher.
overcrowded [əuvə'kraudɪd] *adj* überfüllt.
overcrowding [əuvə'kraudɪŋ] *n* Überfüllung *f*.
overdo [əuvə'du:] (*irreg: like* **do**) *vt* übertreiben; **to ~ it** es übertreiben.
overdose ['əuvədəus] *n* Überdosis *f*.
overdraft ['əuvədrɑ:ft] *n* Kontoüberziehung *f*; **to have an ~** sein Konto überziehen.
overdrawn [əuvə'drɔ:n] *adj* (*account*) überzogen; **I am ~** ich habe mein Konto überzogen.
overdrive ['əuvədraɪv] *n* (*AUT*) Schongang *m*.
overdue [əuvə'dju:] *adj* überfällig; **that change was long ~** diese Änderung war schon lange fällig.
overemphasis [əuvər'emfəsɪs] *n*: **~ on** Überbetonung +*gen*.
overestimate [əuvər'estɪmeɪt] *vt* überschätzen.
overexcited [əuvərɪk'saɪtɪd] *adj* ganz aufgeregt.
overexertion [əuvərɪg'zə:ʃən] *n* Überanstrengung *f*.
overexpose [əuvərɪk'spəuz] *vt* (*PHOT*) überbelichten.
overflow [əuvə'fləu] *vi* (*river*) über die Ufer treten; (*bath, jar etc*) überlaufen ♦ *n* (*also:* **~ pipe**) Überlaufrohr *nt*.
overgenerous [əuvə'dʒenərəs] *adj* allzu großzügig.
overgrown [əuvə'grəun] *adj* (*garden*) verwildert; **he's just an ~ schoolboy** er ist nur ein großes Kind.
overhang ['əuvə'hæŋ] (*irreg: like* **hang**) *vt* herausragen über +*acc* ♦ *vi* überhängen ♦ *n* Überhang *m*.
overhaul [əuvə'hɔ:l] *vt* (*equipment, car etc*) überholen ♦ *n* Überholung *f*.
overhead [əuvə'hɛd] *adv* (*above*) oben; (*in the sky*) in der Luft ♦ *adj* (*lighting*) Decken-; (*cables, wires*) Überland- ♦ *n* (*US*) = **overheads; overheads** *npl* allgemeine Unkosten *pl*.
overhear [əuvə'hɪə*] (*irreg: like* **hear**) *vt*

(zufällig) mit anhören.

overheat [əuvə'hiːt] vi (engine) heißlaufen.

overjoyed [əuvə'dʒɔɪd] adj überglücklich; **to be ~ (at)** überglücklich sein (über +acc).

overkill ['əuvəkɪl] n (fig): **it would be ~** das wäre zuviel des Guten.

overland ['əuvəlænd] adj (journey) Überland- ♦ adv (travel) über Land.

overlap [əuvə'læp] vi (figures, ideas etc) sich überschneiden.

overleaf [əuvə'liːf] adv umseitig, auf der Rückseite.

overload [əuvə'ləud] vt (vehicle) überladen; (ELEC) überbelasten; (fig: with work etc) überlasten.

overlook [əuvə'luk] vt (have view over) überblicken; (fail to notice) übersehen; (excuse, forgive) hinwegsehen über +acc.

overlord ['əuvəlɔːd] n oberster Herr m.

overmanning [əuvə'mænɪŋ] n Überbesetzung f.

overnight [əuvə'naɪt] adv über Nacht ♦ adj (bag, clothes) Reise-; (accommodation, stop) für die Nacht; **to travel ~** nachts reisen; **he'll be away ~** (tonight) er kommt erst morgen zurück; **to stay ~** über Nacht bleiben; **~ stay** Übernachtung f.

overpass ['əuvəpɑːs] (esp US) n Überführung f.

overpay [əuvə'peɪ] vt: **to ~ sb by £50** jdm £ 50 zuviel bezahlen.

overplay [əuvə'pleɪ] vt (overact) übertrieben darstellen; **to ~ one's hand** den Bogen überspannen.

overpower [əuvə'pauə*] vt überwältigen.

overpowering [əuvə'pauərɪŋ] adj (heat) unerträglich; (stench) durchdringend; (feeling, desire) überwältigend.

overproduction ['əuvəprə'dʌkʃən] n Überproduktion f.

overrate [əuvə'reɪt] vt überschätzen.

overreach [əuvə'riːtʃ] vt: **to ~ o.s.** sich übernehmen.

overreact [əuvəriː'ækt] vi übertrieben reagieren.

override [əuvə'raɪd] (irreg: like ride) vt (order etc) sich hinwegsetzen über +acc.

overriding [əuvə'raɪdɪŋ] adj vorrangig.

overrule [əuvə'ruːl] vt (claim, person) zurückweisen; (decision) aufheben.

overrun [əuvə'rʌn] (irreg: like run) vt (country, continent) einfallen in +acc ♦ vi (meeting etc) zu lange dauern; **the town is ~ with tourists** die Stadt ist von Touristen überlaufen.

overseas [əuvə'siːz] adv (live, work) im Ausland; (travel) ins Ausland ♦ adj (market, trade) Übersee-; (student, visitor) aus dem Ausland.

oversee [əuvə'siː] vt (supervise) beaufsichtigen, überwachen.

overseer ['əuvəsɪə*] n Aufseher(in) m(f).

overshadow [əuvə'ʃædəu] vt (place, building

etc) überschatten; (fig) in den Schatten stellen.

overshoot [əuvə'ʃuːt] (irreg: like shoot) vt (target, runway) hinausschießen über +acc.

oversight ['əuvəsaɪt] n Versehen nt; **due to an ~** aus Versehen.

oversimplify [əuvə'sɪmplɪfaɪ] vt zu stark vereinfachen.

oversleep [əuvə'sliːp] (irreg: like sleep) vi verschlafen.

overspend [əuvə'spend] (irreg: like spend) vi zuviel ausgeben; **we have overspent by 5,000 dollars** wir haben 5000 Dollar zuviel ausgegeben.

overspill ['əuvəspɪl] n (excess population) Bevölkerungsüberschuß m.

overstaffed [əuvə'stɑːft] adj: **to be ~** überbesetzt sein.

overstate [əuvə'steɪt] vt (exaggerate) zu sehr betonen.

overstatement [əuvə'steɪtmənt] n Übertreibung f.

overstay [əuvə'steɪ] vt see **outstay**.

overstep [əuvə'step] vt: **to ~ the mark** zu weit gehen.

overstock [əuvə'stɔk] vt zu große Bestände anlegen in +dat.

overstretched [əuvə'stretʃt] adj (person, resources) überfordert.

overstrike ['əuvəstraɪk] (irreg: like strike) n (on printer) Mehrfachdruck m ♦ vt mehrfach-drucken.

oversubscribed [əuvəsəb'skraɪbd] adj (COMM etc) überzeichnet.

overt [əu'vəːt] adj offen.

overtake [əuvə'teɪk] (irreg: like take) vt (AUT) überholen; (event, change) hereinbrechen über +acc; (emotion) befallen ♦ vi (AUT) überholen.

overtaking [əuvə'teɪkɪŋ] n (AUT) Überholen nt.

overtax [əuvə'tæks] vt (ECON) zu hoch besteuern; (strength, patience) überfordern; **to ~ o.s.** sich übernehmen.

overthrow [əuvə'θrəu] (irreg: like throw) vt (government etc) stürzen.

overtime ['əuvətaɪm] n Überstunden pl; **to do or work ~** Überstunden machen.

overtime ban n Überstundenverbot nt.

overtone ['əuvətəun] n (fig: also: ~s): **~s of** Untertöne pl von.

overture ['əuvətʃuə*] n (MUS) Ouvertüre f; (fig) Annäherungsversuch m.

overturn [əuvə'təːn] vt (car, chair) umkippen; (fig: decision) aufheben; (: government) stürzen ♦ vi (train etc) umkippen; (car) sich überschlagen; (boat) kentern.

overview ['əuvəvjuː] n Überblick m.

overweight [əuvə'weɪt] adj (person) übergewichtig.

overwhelm [əuvə'welm] vt überwältigen.

overwhelming [əuvə'welmɪŋ] adj

überwältigend; **one's ~ impression is of
heat/noise** man bemerkt vor allem die
Hitze/den Lärm.
overwhelmingly [əuvə'wɛlmɪŋlɪ] adv (vote,
reject) mit überwältigender Mehrheit;
(appreciative, generous etc) über alle Maßen;
(opposed etc) überwiegend.
overwork [əuvə'wəːk] n Überarbeitung f ♦ vt
(person) (mit Arbeit) überlasten; (cliché etc)
überstrapazieren ♦ vi sich überarbeiten.
overwrite [əuvə'raɪt] vt (COMPUT)
überschreiben.
overwrought [əuvə'rɔːt] adj (person)
überreizt.
ovulate ['ɔvjuleɪt] vi ovulieren.
ovulation [ɔvju'leɪʃən] n Eisprung m,
Ovulation f.
ovum ['əuvəm] (pl **ova**) n Eizelle f.
owe [əu] vt: **to ~ sb sth, to ~ sth to sb** (lit, fig)
jdm etw schulden; (life, talent, good looks etc)
jdm etw verdanken.
owing to ['əuɪŋ-] prep (because of) wegen +gen,
aufgrund +gen.
owl [aul] n Eule f.
own [əun] vt (possess) besitzen ♦ vi (BRIT:
form): **to ~ up to sth** etw zugeben ♦ adj
eigen; **a room of my ~** mein eigenes
Zimmer; **to get one's ~ back** (take revenge)
sich rächen; **on one's ~** allein; **to come into
one's ~** sich entfalten.
►**own up** vi gestehen, es zugeben.
own brand n (COMM) Hausmarke f.
owner ['əunə*] n Besitzer(in) m(f),
Eigentümer(in) m(f).
owner-occupier ['əunər'ɔkjupaɪə*] n (ADMIN,
LAW) Bewohner(in) m(f) im eigenen Haus.
ownership ['əunəʃɪp] n Besitz m; **under new
~** (shop etc) unter neuer Leitung.
own goal n (also fig) Eigentor nt.
ox [ɔks] (pl **~en**) n Ochse m.

> **Oxbridge**, eine Mischung aus Ox(ford) und
> (Cam)bridge, bezieht sich auf die uralten
> Universitäten von Oxford und Cambridge.
> Dieser Begriff ist oft wertend und bringt das
> Prestige und die Privilegien zum Ausdruck, die
> traditionellerweise mit diesen Universitäten in
> Verbindung gebracht werden.

OXFAM (BRIT) n abbr (= Oxford Committee for
Famine Relief) karitative Vereinigung zur
Hungerhilfe.
oxide ['ɔksaɪd] n Oxyd nt.
oxidize ['ɔksɪdaɪz] vi oxydieren.
Oxon. ['ɔksn] (BRIT) abbr (POST:
= Oxfordshire); (in degree titles: = Oxoniensis)
der Universität Oxford.
oxtail ['ɔksteɪl] n: **~ soup**
Ochsenschwanzsuppe f.
oxyacetylene ['ɔksɪə'setɪliːn] adj (flame)
Azetylensauerstoff-; **~ burner**
Schweißbrenner m; **~ welding**

Autogenschweißen nt.
oxygen ['ɔksɪdʒən] n Sauerstoff m.
oxygen mask n Sauerstoffmaske f.
oxygen tent n Sauerstoffzelt nt.
oyster ['ɔɪstə*] n Auster f.
oz abbr = **ounce**.
ozone ['əuzəun] n Ozon nt.
ozone hole n Ozonloch nt.
ozone layer n: **the ~** die Ozonschicht.

P, p

P, p¹ [piː] n (letter) P nt, p nt; **~ for Peter** ≈ P
wie Paula.
P. abbr = **president; prince**.
p² (BRIT) abbr = **penny; pence**.
p. abbr (= page) S.
PA n abbr = **personal assistant; public-address
system** ♦ abbr (US: POST: = Pennsylvania).
pa [paː] (inf) n Papa m.
p.a. abbr (= per annum) p.a.
PAC (US) n abbr (= political action committee)
politisches Aktionskomitee.
pace [peɪs] n (step) Schritt m; (speed) Tempo
nt ♦ vi: **to ~ up and down** auf und ab gehen;
to keep ~ with Schritt halten mit; **to set the
~** das Tempo angeben; **to put sb through
his/her ~s** (fig) jdn auf Herz und Nieren
prüfen.
pacemaker ['peɪsmeɪkə*] n (MED)
(Herz)schrittmacher m; (SPORT: also:
pacesetter) Schrittmacher m.
pacesetter ['peɪssetə*] n (SPORT)
= **pacemaker**.
Pacific [pə'sɪfɪk] n (GEOG): **the ~ (Ocean)** der
Pazifik, der Pazifische Ozean.
pacific [pə'sɪfɪk] adj (intentions etc) friedlich.
pacifier ['pæsɪfaɪə*] (US) n (dummy) Schnuller
m.
pacifist ['pæsɪfɪst] n Pazifist(in) m(f).
pacify ['pæsɪfaɪ] vt (person, fears) beruhigen.
pack [pæk] n (packet) Packung f; (US: of
cigarettes) Schachtel f; (of people)
Meute f; (back pack) Rucksack m; (of cards)
(Karten)spiel nt ♦ vt (clothes etc) einpacken;
(suitcase etc, COMPUT) packen; (press down)
pressen ♦ vi packen; **to ~ one's bags** (fig)
die Koffer packen; **to ~ into** (cram: people,
objects) hineinstopfen in +acc; **to send sb
~ing** (inf) jdn kurz abfertigen.
►**pack in** (BRIT: inf) vt (job) hinschmeißen;
~ it in! hör auf!
►**pack off** vt schicken.
►**pack up** vi (BRIT: inf: machine) den Geist
aufgeben; (: : person) Feierabend machen

♦ *vt (belongings)* zusammenpacken.
package ['pækɪdʒ] *n (parcel, COMPUT)* Paket *nt*; *(also:* ~ **deal)** Pauschalangebot *nt* ♦ *vt* verpacken.
package holiday *(BRIT)*, **package tour** *(US)* *n* Pauschalreise *f*.
packaging ['pækɪdʒɪŋ] *n* Verpackung *f*.
packed [pækt] *adj (crowded)* randvoll.
packed lunch *(BRIT)* *n* Lunchpaket *nt*.
packer ['pækə*] *n* Packer(in) *m(f)*.
packet ['pækɪt] *n* Packung *f*; *(of cigarettes)* Schachtel *m*; **to make a** ~ *(BRIT: inf)* einen Haufen Geld verdienen.
packet switching *n (COMPUT)* Paketvermittlung *f*.
pack ice ['pækaɪs] *n* Packeis *nt*.
packing ['pækɪŋ] *n (act)* Packen *nt*; *(material)* Verpackung *f*.
packing case *n* Kiste *f*.
pact [pækt] *n* Pakt *m*.
pad [pæd] *n (paper)* Block *m*; *(to prevent damage)* Polster *nt*; *(inf: home)* Bude *f* ♦ *vt (upholstery etc)* polstern ♦ *vi*: **to** ~ **about/in** herum-/hereintrotten.
padded cell ['pædɪd-] *n* Gummizelle *f*.
padding ['pædɪŋ] *n (material)* Polsterung *f*; *(fig)* Füllwerk *nt*.
paddle ['pædl] *n (oar)* Paddel *nt*; *(US: for table tennis)* Schläger *m* ♦ *vt* paddeln ♦ *vi (at seaside)* planschen.
paddle steamer *n* Raddampfer *m*.
paddling pool ['pædlɪŋ-] *(BRIT)* *n* Planschbecken *nt*.
paddock ['pædək] *n (small field)* Koppel *f*; *(at race course)* Sattelplatz *m*.
paddy field ['pædɪ-] *n* Reisfeld *nt*.
padlock ['pædlɔk] *n* Vorhängeschloß *nt* ♦ *vt* (mit einem Vorhängeschloß) verschließen.
padre ['paːdrɪ] *n (REL)* Feldgeistliche(r) *m*.
paediatrician [piːdɪə'trɪʃən] *n* Kinderarzt *m*, Kinderärztin *f*.
paediatrics, *(US)* **pediatrics** [piːdɪ'ætrɪks] *n* Kinderheilkunde *f*, Pädiatrie *f*.
paedophile ['piːdəufaɪl] *n* Pädophile(r) *f(m)* ♦ *adj* pädophil.
paedophilia [piːdəu'fɪlɪə] *n* Pädophilie *f*.
pagan ['peɪgən] *adj* heidnisch ♦ *n* Heide *m*, Heidin *f*.
page [peɪdʒ] *n (of book etc)* Seite *f*; *(also:* ~**boy:** *in hotel)* Page *m* ♦ *vt (in hotel etc)* ausrufen lassen.
pageant ['pædʒənt] *n (historical procession)* Festzug *m*; *(show)* Historienspiel *nt*.
pageantry ['pædʒəntrɪ] *n* Prunk *m*.
pageboy ['peɪdʒbɔɪ] *n see* **page**.
pager ['peɪdʒə*] *n* Funkrufempfänger *m*, Piepser *m (inf)*.
paginate ['pædʒɪneɪt] *vt* paginieren.
pagination [pædʒɪ'neɪʃən] *n* Paginierung *f*.
pagoda [pə'gəudə] *n* Pagode *f*.
paid [peɪd] *pt, pp of* **pay** ♦ *adj* bezahlt; **to put** ~ **to** *(BRIT)* zunichte machen.

paid-in ['peɪdɪn] *(US) adj* = **paid-up**.
paid-up ['peɪdʌp], *(US)* **paid-in** ['peɪdɪn] *adj (member)* zahlend; *(COMM: shares)* eingezahlt; ~ **capital** eingezahltes Kapital *nt*.
pail [peɪl] *n* Eimer *m*.
pain [peɪn] *n* Schmerz *m*; *(also:* ~ **in the neck:** *inf: nuisance)* Plage *f*; **to have a** ~ **in the chest/arm** Schmerzen in der Brust/im Arm haben; **to be in** ~ Schmerzen haben; **to take** ~**s to do sth** *(make an effort)* sich *dat* Mühe geben, etw zu tun; **on** ~ **of death** bei Todesstrafe; **he is/it is a right** ~ **(in the neck)** *(inf)* er/das geht einem auf den Wecker.
pained [peɪnd] *adj (expression)* gequält.
painful ['peɪnful] *adj (back, injury etc)* schmerzhaft; *(sight, decision etc)* schmerzlich; *(laborious)* mühsam; *(embarrassing)* peinlich.
painfully ['peɪnfəlɪ] *adv (fig: extremely)* furchtbar.
painkiller ['peɪnkɪlə*] *n* schmerzstillendes Mittel *nt*.
painless ['peɪnlɪs] *adj* schmerzlos.
painstaking ['peɪnzteɪkɪŋ] *adj (work, person)* gewissenhaft.
paint [peɪnt] *n* Farbe *f* ♦ *vt (door, house etc)* anstreichen; *(person, picture)* malen; *(fig)* zeichnen; **a tin of** ~ eine Dose Farbe; **to** ~ **the door blue** die Tür blau streichen; **to** ~ **in oils** in Öl malen.
paintbox ['peɪntbɔks] *n* Farbkasten *m*, Malkasten *m*.
paintbrush ['peɪntbrʌʃ] *n* Pinsel *m*.
painter ['peɪntə*] *n (artist)* Maler(in) *m(f)*; *(decorator)* Anstreicher(in) *m(f)*.
painting ['peɪntɪŋ] *n (activity: of artist)* Malerei *f*; *(: of decorator)* Anstreichen *nt*; *(picture)* Bild *nt*, Gemälde *nt*.
paint stripper *n* Abbeizmittel *nt*.
paintwork ['peɪntwəːk] *n (of wall etc)* Anstrich *m*; *(of car)* Lack *m*.
pair [pɛə*] *n* Paar *nt*; **a** ~ **of scissors** eine Schere; **a** ~ **of trousers** eine Hose.
▶**pair off** *vi*: **to** ~ **off with sb** sich jdm anschließen.
pajamas [pə'dʒaːməz] *(US) npl* Schlafanzug *m*, Pyjama *m*.
Pakistan [paːkɪ'staːn] *n* Pakistan *nt*.
Pakistani [paːkɪ'staːnɪ] *adj* pakistanisch ♦ *n* Pakistani *m*, Pakistaner(in) *m(f)*.
PAL *n abbr (TV:* = *phase alternation line)* PAL *nt*.
pal [pæl] *(inf) n (friend)* Kumpel *m*, Freund(in) *m(f)*.
palace ['pæləs] *n* Palast *m*.
palaeontology [pælɪɔn'tɔlədʒɪ] *n* Paläontologie *f*.
palatable ['pælɪtəbl] *adj (food, drink)* genießbar; *(fig: idea, fact etc)* angenehm.
palate ['pælɪt] *n (ANAT)* Gaumen *m*; *(sense of taste)* Geschmackssinn *m*.

palatial [pə'leɪʃəl] adj (residence etc)
prunkvoll.
palaver [pə'lɑːvə•] (inf) n (fuss) Theater nt.
pale [peɪl] adj blaß; (light) fahl ♦ vi erblassen
♦ n: **beyond the** ~ (unacceptable: behaviour)
indiskutabel; **to grow** or **turn** ~ erblassen,
blaß werden; ~ **blue** zartblau; **to** ~ **into
insignificance (beside)** zur Bedeutungs-
losigkeit herabsinken (gegenüber +dat).
paleness ['peɪlnɪs] n Blässe f.
Palestine ['pælɪstaɪn] n Palästina nt.
Palestinian [pælɪs'tɪnɪən] adj palästinensisch
♦ n Palästinenser(in) m(f).
palette ['pælɪt] n Palette f.
palings ['peɪlɪŋz] npl (fence) Lattenzaun m.
palisade [pælɪ'seɪd] n Palisade f.
pall [pɔːl] n (cloud of smoke) (Rauch)wolke f
♦ vi an Reiz verlieren.
pallet ['pælɪt] n (for goods) Palette f.
palliative ['pælɪətɪv] n (MED)
Linderungsmittel nt; (fig) Beschönigung f.
pallid ['pælɪd] adj bleich.
pallor ['pælə•] n Bleichheit f.
pally ['pælɪ] (inf) adj: **they're very** ~ sie sind
dicke Freunde.
palm [pɑːm] n (also: ~ **tree**) Palme f; (of hand)
Handteller m ♦ vt: **to** ~ **sth off on sb** (inf)
jdm etw andrehen.
palmistry ['pɑːmɪstrɪ] n Handlesekunst f.
Palm Sunday n Palmsonntag m.
palpable ['pælpəbl] adj (obvious)
offensichtlich.
palpitations [pælpɪ'teɪʃənz] npl (MED)
Herzklopfen nt.
paltry ['pɔːltrɪ] adj (amount, wage) armselig.
pamper ['pæmpə•] vt verwöhnen.
pamphlet ['pæmflət] n Broschüre f; (political)
Flugschrift f.
pan [pæn] n (also: **saucepan**) Topf m; (also:
frying ~) Pfanne f ♦ vi (CINE, TV) schwenken
♦ vt (inf: book, film) verreißen; **to** ~ **for gold**
Gold waschen.
panacea [pænə'sɪə] n Allheilmittel nt.
panache [pə'næʃ] n Elan m, Schwung m.
Panama ['pænəmɑː] n Panama nt.
panama [pænə'mɑː] n (also: ~ **hat**) Panamahut
m.
Panama Canal n: **the** ~ der Panamakanal.
Panamanian [pænə'meɪnɪən] adj panamaisch
♦ n Panamaer(in) m(f).
pancake ['pænkeɪk] n Pfannkuchen m.
Pancake Day (BRIT) n Fastnachtsdienstag m.
pancake roll n gefüllte Pfannkuchenrolle.
pancreas ['pæŋkrɪəs] n Bauchspeicheldrüse f.
panda ['pændə] n Panda m.
panda car (BRIT) n Streifenwagen m.
pandemonium [pændɪ'məʊnɪəm] n Chaos nt.
pander ['pændə•] vi: **to** ~ **to** (person, desire etc)
sich richten nach, entgegenkommen +dat.
p & h (US) abbr (= postage and handling) Porto
und Bearbeitungsgebühr.
P & L abbr (= profit and loss) Gewinn und

Verlust; see also **profit**.
p & p (BRIT) abbr (= postage and packing)
Porto und Verpackung.
pane [peɪn] n (of glass) Scheibe f.
panel ['pænl] n (wood, metal, glass etc) Platte f,
Tafel f; (group of experts etc)
Diskussionsrunde f; ~ **of judges** Jury f.
panel game (BRIT) n Ratespiel nt.
panelling, (US) **paneling** ['pænəlɪŋ] n
Täfelung f.
panellist, (US) **panelist** ['pænəlɪst] n
Diskussionsteilnehmer(in) m(f).
pang [pæŋ] n: **to have** or **feel a** ~ **of regret**
Reue empfinden; **hunger** ~s quälender
Hunger m; ~s **of conscience** Gewissensbisse
pl.
panhandler ['pænhændlə•] (US: inf) n
Bettler(in) m(f).
panic ['pænɪk] n Panik f ♦ vi in Panik geraten.
panic buying [-baɪɪŋ] n Panikkäufe pl.
panicky ['pænɪkɪ] adj (person) überängstlich;
(feeling) Angst-; (reaction) Kurzschluß-.
panic-stricken ['pænɪkstrɪkən] adj (person,
face) von Panik erfaßt.
pannier ['pænɪə•] n (on bicycle) Satteltasche f;
(on animal) (Trage)korb m.
panorama [pænə'rɑːmə] n (view) Panorama nt.
panoramic [pænə'ræmɪk] adj (view)
Panorama-.
pansy ['pænzɪ] n (BOT) Stiefmütterchen nt;
(inf: pej: sissy) Tunte f.
pant [pænt] vi (person) keuchen; (animal)
hecheln.
pantechnicon [pæn'teknɪkən] (BRIT) n
Möbelwagen m.
panther ['pænθə•] n Panther m.
panties ['pæntɪz] npl Höschen nt.
panto ['pæntəʊ] n see **pantomime**.

> Pantomime oder umgangssprachlich **panto** ist
> in Großbritannien ein zur Weihnachtszeit
> aufgeführtes Märchenspiel mit possenhaften
> Elementen, Musik, Standardrollen (ein als
> Frau verkleideter Mann, ein Junge, ein
> Bösewicht) und aktuellen Witzen.
> Publikumsbeteiligung wird gern gesehen (z.B.
> warnen die Kinder den Helden mit dem Ruf
> 'He's behind you' vor einer drohenden Gefahr),
> und viele der Witze sprechen vor allem
> Erwachsene an, so daß pantomimes
> Unterhaltung für die ganze Familie bieten.

pantry ['pæntrɪ] n (cupboard) Vorratsschrank
m; (room) Speisekammer f.
pants [pænts] npl (BRIT: woman's) Höschen nt;
(: man's) Unterhose f; (US: trousers) Hose f.
panty hose (US) npl Strumpfhose f.
papacy ['peɪpəsɪ] n Papsttum nt; **during the**
~ **of Paul VI** während der Amtszeit von
Papst Paul VI.
papal ['peɪpəl] adj päpstlich.
paparazzi [pæpə'rætsiː] npl Pressefotografen

_pl_, Paparazzi _pl_.

paper ['peɪpə*] _n_ Papier _nt_; (_also:_ **newspaper**) Zeitung _f_; (_exam_) Arbeit _f_; (_academic essay_) Referat _nt_; (_document_) Dokument _nt_, Papier; (_wallpaper_) Tapete _f_ ♦ _adj_ (_made from paper: hat, plane etc_) Papier-, aus Papier ♦ _vt_ (_room_) tapezieren; **papers** _npl_ (_also:_ **identity** ~**s**) Papiere _pl_; **a piece of** ~ (_odd bit_) ein Stück Papier, ein Zettel; (_sheet_) ein Blatt Papier; **to put sth down on** ~ etw schriftlich festhalten.

paper advance _n_ (_on printer_) Papiervorschub _m_.

paperback ['peɪpəbæk] _n_ Taschenbuch _nt_, Paperback _nt_ ♦ _adj_: ~ **edition** Taschenbuchausgabe _f_.

paper bag _n_ Tüte _f_.

paperboy ['peɪpəbɔɪ] _n_ Zeitungsjunge _m_.

paperclip ['peɪpəklɪp] _n_ Büroklammer _f_.

paper hankie _n_ Tempotaschentuch ® _nt_.

paper mill _n_ Papierfabrik _f_.

paper money _n_ Papiergeld _nt_.

paper shop _n_ Zeitungsladen _m_.

paperweight ['peɪpəweɪt] _n_ Briefbeschwerer _m_.

paperwork ['peɪpəwɜːk] _n_ Schreibarbeit _f_.

papier-mâché [pæpjeɪ'mæʃeɪ] _n_ Papiermaché _nt_.

paprika ['pæprɪkə] _n_ Paprika _m_.

Pap Smear, Pap Test _n_ (_MED_) Abstrich _m_.

par [pɑː*] _n_ (_GOLF_) Par _nt_; **to be on a** ~ **with** sich messen können mit; **at** ~ (_COMM_) zum Nennwert; **above/below** ~ (_COMM_) über/ unter dem Nennwert; **above** _or_ **over** ~ (_GOLF_) über dem Par; **below** _or_ **under** ~ (_GOLF_) unter dem Par; **to feel below** _or_ **under** ~ sich nicht auf der Höhe fühlen; **to be** ~ **for the course** (_fig_) zu erwarten sein.

parable ['pærəbl] _n_ Gleichnis _nt_.

parabola [pə'ræbələ] _n_ (_MATH_) Parabel _f_.

parachute ['pærəʃuːt] _n_ Fallschirm _m_.

parachute jump _n_ Fallschirmabsprung _m_.

parachutist ['pærəʃuːtɪst] _n_ Fallschirm-springer(in) _m(f)_.

parade [pə'reɪd] _n_ (_procession_) Parade _f_; (_ceremony_) Zeremonie _f_ ♦ _vt_ (_people_) aufmarschieren lassen; (_wealth, knowledge etc_) zur Schau stellen ♦ _vi_ (_MIL_) aufmarschieren; **fashion** ~ Modenschau _f_.

parade ground _n_ Truppenübungsplatz _m_, Exerzierplatz _m_.

paradise ['pærədaɪs] _n_ (_also fig_) Paradies _nt_.

paradox ['pærədɒks] _n_ Paradox _nt_.

paradoxical [pærə'dɒksɪkl] _adj_ (_situation_) paradox.

paradoxically [pærə'dɒksɪklɪ] _adv_ paradoxerweise.

paraffin ['pærəfɪn] (_BRIT_) _n_ (_also:_ ~ **oil**) Petroleum _nt_; **liquid** ~ Paraffinöl _nt_.

paraffin heater (_BRIT_) _n_ Petroleumofen _m_.

paraffin lamp (_BRIT_) _n_ Petroleumlampe _f_.

paragon ['pærəgən] _n_: **a** ~ **of** (_honesty, virtue etc_) ein Muster _nt_ an +_dat_.

paragraph ['pærəgrɑːf] _n_ Absatz _m_, Paragraph _m_; **to begin a new** ~ einen neuen Absatz beginnen.

parallel ['pærəlɛl] _adj_ (_also COMPUT_) parallel; (_fig: similar_) vergleichbar ♦ _n_ Parallele _f_; (_GEOG_) Breitenkreis _m_; **to run** ~ (**with** _or_ **to**) (_lit, fig_) parallel verlaufen (zu); **to draw** ~**s between/with** Parallelen ziehen zwischen/ mit; **in** ~ (_ELEC_) parallel.

paralyse ['pærəlaɪz] (_BRIT_) _vt_ (_also fig_) lähmen.

paralysis [pə'rælɪsɪs] (_pl_ **paralyses**) _n_ Lähmung _f_.

paralytic [pærə'lɪtɪk] _adj_ paralytisch, Lähmungs-; (_BRIT: inf: drunk_) sternhagelvoll.

paralyze ['pærəlaɪz] (_US_) _vt_ = **paralyse**.

paramedic [pærə'mɛdɪk] _n_ Sanitäter(in) _m(f)_; (_in hospital_) medizinisch-technischer Assistent _m_, medizinisch-technische Assistentin _f_.

parameter [pə'ræmɪtə*] _n_ (_MATH_) Parameter _m_; (_fig: factor_) Faktor _m_; (: _limit_) Rahmen _m_.

paramilitary [pærə'mɪlɪtərɪ] _adj_ paramilitärisch.

paramount ['pærəmaunt] _adj_ vorherrschend; **of** ~ **importance** von höchster _or_ größter Wichtigkeit.

paranoia [pærə'nɔɪə] _n_ Paranoia _f_.

paranoid ['pærənɔɪd] _adj_ paranoid.

paranormal [pærə'nɔːml] _adj_ übersinnlich, paranormal ♦ _n_: **the** ~ das Übersinnliche.

parapet ['pærəpɪt] _n_ Brüstung _f_.

paraphernalia [pærəfə'neɪlɪə] _n_ Utensilien _pl_.

paraphrase ['pærəfreɪz] _vt_ umschreiben.

paraplegic [pærə'pliːdʒɪk] _n_ Paraplegiker(in) _m(f)_, doppelseitig Gelähmte(r) _f(m)_.

parapsychology [pærəsaɪ'kɔlədʒɪ] _n_ Parapsychologie _f_.

parasite ['pærəsaɪt] _n_ (_also fig_) Parasit _m_.

parasol ['pærəsɒl] _n_ Sonnenschirm _m_.

paratrooper ['pærətruːpə*] _n_ Fallschirmjäger _m_.

parcel ['pɑːsl] _n_ Paket _nt_ ♦ _vt_ (_also:_ ~ **up**) verpacken.

▶**parcel out** _vt_ aufteilen.

parcel bomb (_BRIT_) _n_ Paketbombe _f_.

parcel post _n_ Paketpost _f_.

parch [pɑːtʃ] _vt_ ausdörren, austrocknen.

parched [pɑːtʃt] _adj_ ausgetrocknet; **I'm** ~ (_inf: thirsty_) ich bin am Verdursten.

parchment ['pɑːtʃmənt] _n_ Pergament _nt_.

pardon ['pɑːdn] _n_ (_LAW_) Begnadigung _f_ ♦ _vt_ (_forgive_) verzeihen +_dat_, vergeben +_dat_; (_LAW_) begnadigen; ~ **me!, I beg your** ~! (_I'm sorry!_) verzeihen Sie bitte!; (**I beg your**) ~**?**, (_US_) ~ **me?** (_what did you say?_) bitte?

pare [peə*] _vt_ (_BRIT: nails_) schneiden; (_fruit etc_) schälen; (_fig: costs etc_) reduzieren.

parent ['peərənt] _n_ (_mother_) Mutter _f_; (_father_) Vater _m_; **parents** _npl_ (_mother and father_) Eltern _pl_.

parentage ['peərəntɪdʒ] _n_ Herkunft _f_; **of**

unknown ~ unbekannter Herkunft.
parental [pə'rɛntl] adj (love, control etc)
elterlich.
parent company n Mutterunternehmen nt.
parentheses [pə'rɛnθɪsi:z] npl of **parenthesis**.
parenthesis [pə'rɛnθɪsɪs] (pl **parentheses**) n
Klammer f; **in** ~ in Klammern.
parenthood ['pɛərənthud] n Elternschaft f.
parenting ['pɛərəntɪŋ] n elterliche Pflege f.
Paris ['pærɪs] n Paris nt.
parish ['pærɪʃ] n Gemeinde f.
parish council (BRIT) n Gemeinderat m.
parishioner [pə'rɪʃənə*] n Gemeindemitglied
nt.
Parisian [pə'rɪzɪən] adj Pariser inv,
paris(er)isch ♦ n Pariser(in) m(f).
parity ['pærɪtɪ] n (equality) Gleichstellung f.
park [pɑ:k] n Park m ♦ vt, vi (AUT) parken.
parka ['pɑ:kə] n Parka m.
parking ['pɑ:kɪŋ] n Parken nt; **"no** ~**"**
„Parken verboten".
parking lights npl Parklicht nt.
parking lot (US) n Parkplatz m.
parking meter n Parkuhr f.
parking offence (BRIT) n Parkvergehen nt.
parking place n Parkplatz m.
parking ticket n Strafzettel m.
parking violation (US) n = **parking offence**.
Parkinson's (disease) ['pɑ:kɪnsənz-] n
Parkinsonsche Krankheit f.
parkway ['pɑ:kweɪ] (US) n Allee f.
parlance ['pɑ:ləns] n: **in common/modern** ~
im allgemeinen/modernen Sprachgebrauch.
parliament ['pɑ:ləmənt] n Parlament nt.

Parliament ist die höchste gesetzgebende
Versammlung in Großbritannien und tritt im
Parlamentsgebäude in London zusammen. Die
Legislaturperiode beträgt normalerweise 5
Jahre, von einer Wahl zur nächsten. Das
Parlament besteht aus zwei Kammern, dem
Oberhaus (siehe **House of Lords**) und dem
Unterhaus (siehe **House of Commons**).

---

parliamentary [pɑ:lə'mɛntərɪ] adj
parlamentarisch.
parlour, (US) **parlor** ['pɑ:lə*] n Salon m.
parlous ['pɑ:ləs] adj (state) prekär.
Parmesan [pɑ:mɪ'zæn] n (also: ~ **cheese**)
Parmesan(käse) m.
parochial [pə'rəukɪəl] (pej) adj (person,
attitude) engstirnig.
parody ['pærədɪ] n Parodie f ♦ vt parodieren.
parole [pə'rəul] n (LAW) Bewährung f; **on** ~
auf Bewährung.
paroxysm ['pærəksɪzəm] n (also MED) Anfall
m.
parquet ['pɑ:keɪ] n (also: ~ **floor(ing)**)
Parkettboden m.
parrot ['pærət] n Papagei m.
parrot-fashion ['pærətfæʃən] adv (say, learn)
mechanisch; (repeat) wie ein Papagei.

parry ['pærɪ] vt (blow, argument) parieren,
abwehren.
parsimonious [pɑ:sɪ'məunɪəs] adj geizig.
parsley ['pɑ:slɪ] n Petersilie f.
parsnip ['pɑ:snɪp] n Pastinake f.
parson ['pɑ:sn] n Pfarrer m.
part [pɑ:t] n Teil m; (TECH) Teil nt; (THEAT,
CINE etc: role) Rolle f; (US: in hair) Scheitel m;
(MUS) Stimme f ♦ adv = **partly** ♦ vt (separate)
trennen; (hair) scheiteln ♦ vi (roads, fig:
people) sich trennen; (crowd) sich teilen; **to
take** ~ **in** teilnehmen an +dat; **to take sth in
good** ~ etw nicht übelnehmen; **to take sb's**
~ (support) sich auf jds Seite acc stellen; **on
his** ~ seinerseits; **for my** ~ für meinen Teil;
for the most ~ (generally) zumeist; **for the
better** or **best** ~ **of the day** die meiste Zeit
des Tages; **to be** ~ **and parcel of**
dazugehören zu; ~ **of speech** (LING) Wortart
f.
▶**part with** vt fus sich trennen von.
partake [pɑ:'teɪk] (irreg: like **take**) vi (form): **to**
~ **of sth** etw zu sich nehmen.
part exchange (BRIT) n: **to give/take sth in** ~
etw in Zahlung geben/nehmen.
partial ['pɑ:ʃl] adj (victory, solution) Teil-;
(support) teilweise; (biassed) parteiisch; **to
be** ~ **to** (person, drink etc) eine Vorliebe
haben für.
partially ['pɑ:ʃəlɪ] adv (to some extent)
teilweise, zum Teil.
participant [pɑ:'tɪsɪpənt] n Teilnehmer(in)
m(f).
participate [pɑ:'tɪsɪpeɪt] vi sich beteiligen; **to**
~ **in** teilnehmen an +dat.
participation [pɑ:tɪsɪ'peɪʃən] n Teilnahme f.
participle ['pɑ:tɪsɪpl] n Partizip nt.
particle ['pɑ:tɪkl] n Teilchen nt, Partikel f.
particular [pə'tɪkjulə*] adj (distinct: person,
time, place etc) bestimmt, speziell; (special)
speziell, besondere(r, s) ♦ n: **in** ~ im
besonderen, besonders; **particulars** npl
Einzelheiten pl; (name, address etc)
Personalien pl; **to be very** ~ **about sth**
(fussy) in bezug auf etw acc sehr eigen sein.
particularly [pə'tɪkjulǝlɪ] adv besonders.
parting ['pɑ:tɪŋ] n (action) Teilung f; (farewell)
Abschied m; (BRIT: in hair) Scheitel m ♦ adj
(words, gift etc) Abschieds-; **his** ~ **shot was**
... (fig) seine Bemerkung zum Abschied war
...
partisan [pɑ:tɪ'zæn] adj (politics, views)
voreingenommen ♦ n (supporter)
Anhänger(in) m(f); (fighter) Partisan m.
partition [pɑ:'tɪʃən] n (wall, screen)
Trennwand f; (of country) Teilung f ♦ vt
(room, office) aufteilen; (country) teilen.
partly ['pɑ:tlɪ] adv teilweise, zum Teil.
partner ['pɑ:tnə*] n Partner(in) m(f); (COMM)
Partner(in), Teilhaber(in) m(f) ♦ vt (at dance,
cards etc) als Partner(in) haben.
partnership ['pɑ:tnəʃɪp] n (POL etc)

Partnerschaft *f*; (*COMM*) Teilhaberschaft *f*;
to go into ~ **(with sb)**, **form a** ~ **(with sb)**
(mit jdm) eine Partnerschaft eingehen.
part payment *n* Anzahlung *f*.
partridge ['pɑːtrɪdʒ] *n* Rebhuhn *nt*.
part-time ['pɑːt'taɪm] *adj* (*work, staff*) Teilzeit-,
Halbtags- ♦ *adv*: **to work** ~ Teilzeit arbeiten;
to study ~ Teilzeitstudent(in) *m(f)* sein.
part-timer [pɑːt'taɪməˈ] *n* (*also*: **part-time
worker**) Teilzeitbeschäftigte(r) *f(m)*.
party ['pɑːtɪ] *n* (*POL, LAW*) Partei *f*;
(*celebration, social event*) Party *f*, Fete *f*;
(*group of people*) Gruppe *f*, Gesellschaft *f*
♦ *cpd* (*POL*) Partei-; **dinner** ~
Abendgesellschaft *f*; **to give** *or* **throw a** ~
eine Party geben, eine Fete machen; **we're
having a** ~ **next Saturday** bei uns ist
nächsten Samstag eine Party; **our son's
birthday** ~ die Geburtstagsfeier unseres
Sohnes; **to be a** ~ **to a crime** an einem
Verbrechen beteiligt sein.
party dress *n* Partykleid *nt*.
party line *n* (*TEL*) Gemeinschaftsanschluß *m*;
(*POL*) Parteilinie *f*.
party piece (*inf*) *n*: **to do one's** ~ auf einer
Party etwas zum besten geben.
party political *adj* parteipolitisch.
party political broadcast *n* parteipolitische
Sendung *f*.
par value *n* (*COMM: of share, bond*) Nennwert
m.
pass [pɑːs] *vt* (*spend: time*) verbringen; (*hand
over*) reichen, geben; (*go past*)
vorbeikommen an +*dat*; (: *in car*)
vorbeifahren an +*dat*; (*overtake*) überholen;
(*fig: exceed*) übersteigen; (*exam*) bestehen;
(*law, proposal*) genehmigen ♦ *vi* (*go past*)
vorbeigehen; (: *in car*) vorbeifahren; (*in
exam*) bestehen ♦ *n* (*permit*) Ausweis *m*; (*in
mountains, SPORT*) Paß *m*; **to** ~ **sth through
sth** etw durch etw führen; **to** ~ **the ball to**
den Ball zuspielen +*dat*; **could you** ~ **the
vegetables round?** könnten Sie das Gemüse
herumreichen?; **to get a** ~ **in** ... (*SCOL*) die
Prüfung in ... bestehen; **things have come to
a pretty** ~ **when** ... (*BRIT: inf*) so weit ist es
schon gekommen, daß ...; **to make a** ~ **at sb**
(*inf*) jdn anmachen.
▶**pass away** *vi* (*die*) dahinscheiden.
▶**pass by** *vi* (*go past*) vorbeigehen; (: *in car*)
vorbeifahren ♦ *vt* (*ignore*) vorbeigehen an
+*dat*.
▶**pass down** *vt* (*customs, inheritance*)
weitergeben.
▶**pass for** *vt*: **she could** ~ **for 25** sie könnte
für 25 durchgehen.
▶**pass on** *vi* (*die*) verscheiden ♦ *vt*: **to** ~ **on
(to)** weitergeben (an +*acc*).
▶**pass out** *vi* (*faint*) ohnmächtig werden;
(*BRIT: MIL*) die Ausbildung beenden.
▶**pass over** *vt* (*ignore*) übergehen ♦ *vi* (*die*)
entschlafen.

▶**pass up** *vt* (*opportunity*) sich *dat* entgehen
lassen.
passable ['pɑːsəbl] *adj* (*road*) passierbar;
(*acceptable*) passabel.
passage ['pæsɪdʒ] *n* Gang *m*; (*in book*) Passage
f; (*way through crowd etc, ANAT*) Weg *m*; (*act
of passing: of train etc*) Durchfahrt *f*; (*journey:
on boat*) Überfahrt *f*.
passageway ['pæsɪdʒweɪ] *n* Gang *m*.
passenger ['pæsɪndʒəˈ] *n* (*in boat, plane*)
Passagier *m*; (*in car*) Fahrgast *m*.
passer-by [pɑːsə'baɪ] (*pl* ~**s**-~) *n* Passant(in)
m(f).
passing ['pɑːsɪŋ] *adj* (*moment, thought etc*)
flüchtig; **in** ~ (*incidentally*) beiläufig,
nebenbei; **to mention sth in** ~ etw beiläufig
or nebenbei erwähnen.
passing place *n* (*AUT*) Ausweichstelle *f*.
passion ['pæʃən] *n* Leidenschaft *f*; **to have a**
~ **for sth** eine Leidenschaft für etw haben.
passionate ['pæʃənɪt] *adj* leidenschaftlich.
passion fruit *n* Passionsfrucht *f*, Maracuja *f*.
Passion play *n* Passionsspiel *nt*.
passive ['pæsɪv] *adj* passiv; (*LING*) Passiv- ♦ *n*
(*LING*) Passiv *nt*.
passive smoking *n* passives Rauchen,
Passivrauchen *nt*.
passkey ['pɑːskiː] *n* Hauptschlüssel *m*.
Passover ['pɑːsəuvəˈ] *n* Passah(fest) *nt*.
passport ['pɑːspɔːt] *n* Paß *m*; (*fig: to success
etc*) Schlüssel *m*.
passport control *n* Paßkontrolle *f*.
password ['pɑːswɜːd] *n* Kennwort *nt*;
(*COMPUT*) Paßwort *nt*.
past [pɑːst] *prep* (*in front of*) vorbei an +*dat*;
(*beyond*) hinter +*dat*; (*later than*) nach ♦ *adj*
(*government etc*) früher, ehemalig; (*week,
month etc*) vergangen ♦ *n* Vergangenheit *f*
♦ *adv*: **to run** ~ vorbeilaufen; **he's** ~ **40** er ist
über 40; **it's** ~ **midnight** es ist nach
Mitternacht; **ten/quarter** ~ **eight** zehn/
viertel nach acht; **he ran** ~ **me** er lief an
mir vorbei; **I'm** ~ **caring** es kümmert mich
nicht mehr; **to be** ~ **it** (*BRIT: inf: person*) es
nicht mehr bringen; **for the** ~ **few/3 days**
während der letzten Tage/3 Tage; **in the** ~
(*also LING*) in der Vergangenheit.
pasta ['pæstə] *n* Nudeln *pl*.
paste [peɪst] *n* (*wet mixture*) Teig *m*; (*glue*)
Kleister *m*; (*jewellery*) Straß *m*; (*fish, tomato
etc paste*) Paste *f* ♦ *vt* (*stick*) kleben.
pastel ['pæstl] *adj* (*colour*) Pastell-.
pasteurized ['pæstʃəraɪzd] *adj* pasteurisiert.
pastille ['pæstɪl] *n* Pastille *f*.
pastime ['pɑːstaɪm] *n* Zeitvertreib *m*, Hobby
nt.
past master (*BRIT*) *n*: **to be a** ~ **at sth** ein
Experte in etw *dat* sein.
pastor ['pɑːstəˈ] *n* Pastor(in) *m(f)*.
pastoral ['pɑːstərl] *adj* (*REL: duties etc*) als
Pastor.
pastry ['peɪstrɪ] *n* (*dough*) Teig *m*; (*cake*)

Gebäckstück nt.
pasture ['pɑːstʃər] n Weide f.
pasty [n 'pæstɪ, adj 'peɪstɪ] n (pie) Pastete f
♦ adj (complexion) bläßlich.
pat [pæt] vt (with hand) tätscheln ♦ adj (answer,
remark) glatt ♦ n: **to give sb/o.s. a ~ on the
back** (fig) jdm/sich auf die Schulter klopfen;
he knows it off ~, (US) **he has it down ~** er
kennt das in- und auswendig.
patch [pætʃ] n (piece of material) Flicken m;
(also: **eye ~**) Augenklappe f; (damp, bald etc)
Fleck m; (of land) Stück nt; (: for growing
vegetables etc) Beet nt ♦ vt (clothes) flicken;
(to go through) a bad ~ eine schwierige
Zeit (durchmachen).
▶**patch up** vt (clothes etc) flicken; (quarrel)
beilegen.
patchwork ['pætʃwəːk] n (SEWING)
Patchwork nt.
patchy ['pætʃɪ] adj (colour) ungleichmäßig;
(information, knowledge etc) lückenhaft.
pate [peɪt] n: **a bald ~** eine Glatze.
pâté ['pæteɪ] n Pastete f.
patent ['peɪtnt] n Patent nt ♦ vt patentieren
lassen ♦ adj (obvious) offensichtlich.
patent leather n Lackleder nt.
patently ['peɪtntlɪ] adv (obvious, wrong)
vollkommen.
patent medicine n patentrechtlich
geschütztes Arzneimittel nt.
Patent Office n Patentamt nt.
paternal [pə'təːnl] adj väterlich; **my
~ grandmother** meine Großmutter
väterlicherseits.
paternalistic [pətəːnə'lɪstɪk] adj
patriarchalisch.
paternity [pə'təːnɪtɪ] n Vaterschaft f.
paternity leave n Vaterschaftsurlaub m.
paternity suit n Vaterschaftsprozeß m.
path [pɑːθ] n (also fig) Weg m; (trail, track) Pfad
m; (trajectory: of bullet, aircraft, planet) Bahn f.
pathetic [pə'θɛtɪk] adj (pitiful)
mitleiderregend; (very bad) erbärmlich.
pathological [pæθə'lɒdʒɪkl] adj (liar, hatred)
krankhaft; (MED) pathologisch.
pathologist [pə'θɒlədʒɪst] n Pathologe m,
Pathologin f.
pathology [pə'θɒlədʒɪ] n Pathologie f.
pathos ['peɪθɒs] n Pathos nt.
pathway ['pɑːθweɪ] n Pfad m, Weg m; (fig)
Weg.
patience ['peɪʃns] n Geduld f; (BRIT: CARDS)
Patience f; **to lose (one's) ~** die Geduld
verlieren.
patient ['peɪʃnt] n Patient(in) m(f) ♦ adj
geduldig; **to be ~ with sb** Geduld mit jdm
haben.
patiently ['peɪʃntlɪ] adv geduldig.
patio ['pætɪəʊ] n Terrasse f.
patriot ['peɪtrɪət] n Patriot(in) m(f).
patriotic [pætrɪ'ɒtɪk] adj patriotisch.
patriotism ['pætrɪətɪzəm] n Patriotismus m.

patrol [pə'trəʊl] n (MIL) Patrouille f; (POLICE)
Streife f ♦ vt (MIL, POLICE: city, streets etc)
patrouillieren; **to be on ~** (MIL) auf
Patrouille sein; (POLICE) auf Streife sein.
patrol boat n Patrouillenboot nt.
patrol car n Streifenwagen m.
patrolman [pə'trəʊlmən] (US: irreg: like man) n
(POLICE) (Streifen)polizist m.
patron ['peɪtrən] n (customer) Kunde m,
Kundin f; (benefactor) Förderer m; **~ of the
arts** Kunstmäzen m.
patronage ['pætrənɪdʒ] n (of artist, charity etc)
Förderung f.
patronize ['pætrənaɪz] vt (pej: look down on)
von oben herab behandeln; (artist etc)
fördern; (shop, club) besuchen.
patronizing ['pætrənaɪzɪŋ] adj herablassend.
patron saint n Schutzheilige(r) f(m).
patter ['pætər] n (of feet) Trappeln nt; (of rain)
Prasseln nt; (sales talk etc) Sprüche pl ♦ vi
(footsteps) trappeln; (rain) prasseln.
pattern ['pætən] n Muster nt; (SEWING)
Schnittmuster nt; **behaviour ~s**
Verhaltensmuster pl.
patterned ['pætənd] adj gemustert; **~ with
flowers** mit Blumenmuster.
paucity ['pɔːsɪtɪ] n: **a ~ of** ein Mangel m an
+dat.
paunch [pɔːntʃ] n Bauch m, Wanst m.
pauper ['pɔːpər] n Arme(r) f(m); **~'s grave**
Armengrab m.
pause [pɔːz] n Pause f ♦ vi eine Pause machen;
(hesitate) innehalten; **to ~ for breath** eine
Verschnaufpause einlegen.
pave [peɪv] vt (street, yard etc) pflastern; **to
~ the way for** (fig) den Weg bereiten or
bahnen für.
pavement ['peɪvmənt] n (BRIT) Bürgersteig
m; (US: roadway) Straße f.
pavilion [pə'vɪlɪən] n (SPORT) Klubhaus nt.
paving ['peɪvɪŋ] n (material) Straßenbelag m.
paving stone n Pflasterstein m.
paw [pɔː] n (of cat, dog etc) Pfote f; (of lion,
bear etc) Tatze f, Pranke f ♦ vt (pej: touch)
betatschen; **to ~ the ground** (animal)
scharren.
pawn [pɔːn] n (CHESS) Bauer m; (fig)
Schachfigur f ♦ vt versetzen.
pawnbroker ['pɔːnbrəʊkər] n Pfandleiher m.
pawnshop ['pɔːnʃɒp] n Pfandhaus nt.
pay [peɪ] (pt, pp paid) n (wage) Lohn m; (salary)
Gehalt nt ♦ vt (sum of money, wage) zahlen;
(bill, person) bezahlen ♦ vi (be profitable) sich
bezahlt machen; (fig) sich lohnen; **how
much did you ~ for it?** wieviel hast du dafür
bezahlt?; **I paid 10 pounds for that book** ich
habe 10 Pfund für das Buch bezahlt, das
Buch hat mich 10 Pfund gekostet; **to
~ one's way** seinen Beitrag leisten; **to
~ dividends** (fig) sich bezahlt machen; **to
~ the price/penalty for sth** (fig) den Preis/
die Strafe für etw zahlen; **to ~ sb a**

compliment jdm ein Kompliment machen; **to ~ attention (to)** achtgeben (auf +acc); **to ~ sb a visit** jdn besuchen; **to ~ one's respects to sb** jdm seine Aufwartung machen.

►**pay back** *vt* zurückzahlen; **I'll ~ you back next week** ich gebe dir das Geld nächste Woche zurück.

►**pay for** *vt fus* (*also fig*) (be)zahlen für.

►**pay in** *vt* einzahlen.

►**pay off** *vt* (*debt*) abbezahlen; (*person*) auszahlen; (*creditor*) befriedigen; (*mortgage*) tilgen ♦ *vi* sich auszahlen; **to ~ sth off in instalments** etw in Raten (ab)zahlen.

►**pay out** *vt* (*money*) ausgeben; (*rope*) ablaufen lassen.

►**pay up** *vi* zahlen.

payable ['peɪəbl] *adj* zahlbar; **to make a cheque ~ to sb** einen Scheck auf jdn ausstellen.

pay award *n* Lohn-/Gehaltserhöhung *f*.

payday ['peɪdeɪ] *n* Zahltag *m*.

PAYE (*BRIT*) *n abbr* (= *pay as you earn*) *Lohnsteuerabzugsverfahren*.

payee [peɪˈiː] *n* Zahlungsempfänger *m*.

pay envelope (*US*) *n* = **pay packet**.

paying guest ['peɪɪŋ-] *n* zahlender Gast *m*.

payload ['peɪləud] *n* Nutzlast *f*.

payment ['peɪmənt] *n* (*act*) Zahlung *f*, Bezahlung *f*; (*of bill*) Begleichung *f*; (*sum of money*) Zahlung *f*; **advance ~** (*part sum*) Anzahlung *f*; (*total sum*) Vorauszahlung *f*; **deferred ~**, **~ by instalments** Ratenzahlung *f*; **monthly ~** (*sum of money*) Monatsrate *f*; **on ~ of** gegen Zahlung von.

pay packet (*BRIT*) *n* Lohntüte *f*.

payphone ['peɪfəun] *n* Münztelefon *nt*; (*card phone*) Kartentelefon *nt*.

payroll ['peɪrəul] *n* Lohnliste *f*; **to be on a firm's ~** bei einer Firma beschäftigt sein.

pay slip (*BRIT*) *n* (*see* **pay**) Lohnstreifen *m*; Gehaltsstreifen *m*.

pay station (*US*) *n* = **payphone**.

PBS (*US*) *n abbr* (= *Public Broadcasting Service*) *öffentliche Rundfunkanstalt*.

PC *n abbr* (= *personal computer*) PC *m*; (*BRIT*) = **police constable** ♦ *adj abbr* = **politically correct** ♦ *abbr* (*BRIT*) = **Privy Councillor**.

pc *abbr* = **per cent; postcard**.

p/c *abbr* = **petty cash**.

PCB *n abbr* (*ELEC, COMPUT*) = **printed circuit board**; (= *polychlorinated biphenyl*) PCB *nt*.

pcm *abbr* (= *per calendar month*) pro Monat.

PD (*US*) *n abbr* = **police department**.

pd *abbr* (= *paid*) bez.

pdq (*inf*) *adv abbr* (= *pretty damn quick*) verdammt schnell.

PDSA (*BRIT*) *n abbr* (= *People's Dispensary for Sick Animals*) *kostenloses Behandlungszentrum für Haustiere*.

PDT (*US*) *abbr* (= *Pacific Daylight Time*) *pazifische Sommerzeit*.

PE *n abbr* (*SCOL*) = **physical education** ♦ *abbr* (*CANADA*: = *Prince Edward Island*).

pea [piː] *n* Erbse *f*.

peace [piːs] *n* Frieden *m*; **to be at ~ with sb/ sth** mit jdm/etw in Frieden leben; **to keep the ~** (*policeman*) die öffentliche Ordnung aufrechterhalten; (*citizen*) den Frieden wahren.

peaceable ['piːsəbl] *adj* friedlich.

peaceful ['piːsful] *adj* friedlich.

peacekeeper ['piːskiːpə*] *n* Friedenswächter(in) *m(f)*.

peacekeeping force ['piːskiːpɪŋ-] *n* Friedenstruppen *pl*.

peace offering *n* Friedensangebot *nt*.

peach [piːtʃ] *n* Pfirsich *m*.

peacock ['piːkɔk] *n* Pfau *m*.

peak [piːk] *n* (*of mountain*) Spitze *f*, Gipfel *m*; (*of cap*) Schirm *m*; (*fig*) Höhepunkt *m*.

peak hours *npl* Stoßzeit *f*.

peak period *n* Spitzenzeit *f*, Stoßzeit *f*.

peak rate *n* Höchstrate *f*.

peaky ['piːkɪ] (*BRIT: inf*) *adj* blaß.

peal [piːl] *n* (*of bells*) Läuten *nt*; **~s of laughter** schallendes Gelächter *nt*.

peanut ['piːnʌt] *n* Erdnuß *f*.

peanut butter *n* Erdnußbutter *f*.

pear [pɛə*] *n* Birne *f*.

pearl [pəːl] *n* Perle *f*.

peasant ['pɛznt] *n* Bauer *m*.

peat [piːt] *n* Torf *m*.

pebble ['pɛbl] *n* Kieselstein *m*.

peck [pɛk] *vt* (*bird*) picken; (*also:* **~ at**) picken an +*dat* ♦ *n* (*of bird*) Schnabelhieb *m*; (*kiss*) Küßchen *nt*.

pecking order ['pɛkɪŋ-] *n* (*fig*) Hackordnung *f*.

peckish ['pɛkɪʃ] (*BRIT: inf*) *adj* (*hungry*) leicht hungrig; **I'm feeling ~** ich könnte was zu essen gebrauchen.

peculiar [pɪˈkjuːlɪə*] *adj* (*strange*) seltsam; **~ to** (*exclusive to*) charakteristisch für.

peculiarity [pɪkjuːlɪˈærɪtɪ] *n* (*strange habit*) Eigenart *f*; (*distinctive feature*) Besonderheit *f*, Eigentümlichkeit *f*.

peculiarly [pɪˈkjuːlɪəlɪ] *adv* (*oddly*) seltsam; (*distinctively*) unverkennbar.

pecuniary [pɪˈkjuːnɪərɪ] *adj* finanziell.

pedal ['pɛdl] *n* Pedal *nt* ♦ *vi* in die Pedale treten.

pedal bin (*BRIT*) *n* Treteimer *m*.

pedant ['pɛdənt] *n* Pedant(in) *m(f)*.

pedantic [pɪˈdæntɪk] *adj* pedantisch.

peddle ['pɛdl] *vt* (*goods*) feilbieten, verkaufen; (*drugs*) handeln mit; (*gossip*) verbreiten.

peddler ['pɛdlə*] *n* (*also:* **drug ~**) Pusher(in) *m(f)*.

pedestal ['pɛdəstl] *n* Sockel *m*.

pedestrian [pɪˈdɛstrɪən] *n* Fußgänger(in) *m(f)* ♦ *adj* Fußgänger-; (*fig*) langweilig.

pedestrian crossing (*BRIT*) *n*

Fußgängerüberweg *m*.
pedestrian precinct (*BRIT*) *n* Fußgängerzone
f.
pediatrics [pi:dɪ'ætrɪks] (*US*) *n* = **paediatrics**.
pedigree ['pedɪgri:] *n* (*of animal*) Stammbaum
m; (*fig: background*) Vorgeschichte *f* ♦ *cpd*
(*dog*) Rasse-, reinrassig.
pee [pi:] (*inf*) *vi* pinkeln.
peek [pi:k] *vi*: **to** ~ **at/over/into** *etc* gucken
nach/über +*acc*/in +*acc* *etc* ♦ *n*: **to have** *or* **take
a** ~ (**at**) einen (kurzen) Blick werfen (auf
+*acc*).
peel [pi:l] *n* Schale *f* ♦ *vt* schälen ♦ *vi* (*paint*)
abblättern; (*wallpaper*) sich lösen; (*skin, back
etc*) sich schälen.
▶**peel back** *vt* abziehen.
peeler ['pi:lə*] *n* (*potato peeler etc*)
Schälmesser *nt*.
peelings ['pi:lɪŋz] *npl* Schalen *pl*.
peep [pi:p] *n* (*look*) kurzer Blick *m*; (*sound*)
Pieps *m* ♦ *vi* (*look*) gucken; **to have** *or* **take a**
~ (**at**) einen kurzen Blick werfen (auf +*acc*).
▶**peep out** *vi* (*be visible*) hervorgucken.
peephole ['pi:phəul] *n* Guckloch *nt*.
peer [pɪə*] *n* (*noble*) Peer *m*; (*equal*)
Gleichrangige(r) *f(m)*; (*contemporary*)
Gleichaltrige(r) *f(m)* ♦ *vi*: **to** ~ **at** starren auf
+*acc*.
peerage ['pɪərɪdʒ] *n* (*title*) Adelswürde *f*;
(*position*) Adelsstand *m*; **the** ~ (*all the peers*)
der Adel.
peerless ['pɪəlɪs] *adj* unvergleichlich.
peeved [pi:vd] *adj* verärgert, sauer (*inf*).
peevish ['pi:vɪʃ] *adj* (*bad-tempered*) mürrisch.
peg [peg] *n* (*hook, knob*) Haken *m*; (*BRIT: also:
clothes* ~) Wäscheklammer *f*; (*also: tent* ~)
Zeltpflock *m*, Hering *m* ♦ *vt* (*washing*)
festklammern; (*prices*) festsetzen; **off the** ~
von der Stange.
pejorative [pɪ'dʒɔrətɪv] *adj* abwertend.
Pekin [pi:'kɪn] *n* = **Peking**.
Pekinese [pi:kɪ'ni:z] *n* = **Pekingese**.
Peking [pi:'kɪŋ] *n* Peking *nt*.
Pekingese [pi:kɪ'ni:z] *n* (*dog*) Pekinese *m*.
pelican ['pelɪkən] *n* Pelikan *m*.
pelican crossing (*BRIT*) *n* (*AUT*)
Fußgängerüberweg *m* mit Ampel.
pellet ['pelɪt] *n* (*of paper etc*) Kügelchen *nt*; (*of
mud etc*) Klümpchen *nt*; (*for shotgun*)
Schrotkugel *f*.
pell-mell ['pel'mel] *adv* in heillosem
Durcheinander.
pelmet ['pelmɪt] *n* (*wooden*) Blende *f*; (*fabric*)
Querbehang *m*.
pelt [pelt] *vi* (*rain: also:* ~ **down**)
niederprasseln; (*inf: run*) rasen ♦ *n* (*animal
skin*) Pelz *m*, Fell *nt* ♦ *vt*: **to** ~ **sb with sth** jdn
mit etw bewerfen.
pelvis ['pelvɪs] *n* Becken *nt*.
pen [pen] *n* (*also:* **fountain** ~) Füller *m*; (*also:*
ballpoint ~) Kugelschreiber *m*; (*also:* **felt-tip**
~) Filzstift *m*; (*enclosure: for sheep, pigs etc*)

Pferch *m*; (*US: inf: prison*) Knast *m*; **to put**
~ **to paper** zur Feder greifen.
penal ['pi:nl] *adj* (*LAW: colony, institution*)
Straf-; (: *system, reform*) Strafrechts-;
~ **code** Strafgesetzbuch *nt*.
penalize ['pi:nəlaɪz] *vt* (*punish*) bestrafen; (*fig*)
benachteiligen.
penal servitude [-'sə:vɪtju:d] *n* Zwangsarbeit
f.
penalty ['penltɪ] *n* Strafe *f*; (*SPORT*) Strafstoß
m; (: *FOOTBALL*) Elfmeter *m*.
penalty area (*BRIT*) *n* (*SPORT*) Strafraum *m*.
penalty clause *n* Strafklausel *f*.
penalty kick *n* (*RUGBY*) Strafstoß *m*;
(*FOOTBALL*) Elfmeter *m*.
penalty shoot-out [-'ʃu:taut] *n* (*FOOTBALL*)
Elfmeterschießen *nt*.
penance ['penəns] *n* (*REL*): **to do** ~ **for one's
sins** für seine Sünden Buße tun.
pence [pens] *npl of* **penny**.
penchant ['pã:ʃã:ŋ] *n* Vorliebe *f*, Schwäche *f*;
to have a ~ **for** eine Schwäche haben für.
pencil ['pensl] *n* Bleistift *m* ♦ *vt*: **to** ~ **sb/sth in**
jdn/etw vormerken.
pencil case *n* Federmäppchen *nt*.
pencil sharpener *n* Bleistiftspitzer *m*.
pendant ['pendnt] *n* Anhänger *m*.
pending ['pendɪŋ] *adj* anstehend ♦ *prep*: ~ **his
return** bis zu seiner Rückkehr; ~ **a decision**
bis eine Entscheidung getroffen ist.
pendulum ['pendjuləm] *n* Pendel *nt*.
penetrate ['penɪtreɪt] *vt* (*person: territory etc*)
durchdringen; (*light, water, sound*)
eindringen in +*acc*.
penetrating ['penɪtreɪtɪŋ] *adj* (*sound, gaze*)
durchdringend; (*mind, observation*) scharf.
penetration [penɪ'treɪʃən] *n* Durchdringen *nt*.
pen friend (*BRIT*) *n* Brieffreund(in) *m(f)*.
penguin ['peŋgwɪn] *n* Pinguin *m*.
penicillin [penɪ'sɪlɪn] *n* Penizillin *nt*.
peninsula [pə'nɪnsjulə] *n* Halbinsel *f*.
penis ['pi:nɪs] *n* Penis *m*.
penitence ['penɪtns] *n* Reue *f*.
penitent ['penɪtnt] *adj* reuig.
penitentiary [penɪ'tenʃərɪ] (*US*) *n* Gefängnis
nt.
penknife ['pennaɪf] *n* Taschenmesser *nt*.
Penn. (*US*) *abbr* (*POST:* = *Pennsylvania*).
pen name *n* Pseudonym *nt*.
pennant ['penənt] *n* (*NAUT*) Wimpel *m*.
penniless ['penɪlɪs] *adj* mittellos.
Pennines ['penaɪnz] *npl*: **the** ~ die Pennines *pl*.
penny ['penɪ] *n* (*pl* **pennies** *or* (*BRIT*) **pence**) *n*
Penny *m*; (*US*) Cent *m*; **it was worth every** ~
es war jeden Pfennig wert; **it won't cost
you a** ~ es kostet dich keinen Pfennig.
pen pal *n* Brieffreund(in) *m(f)*.
penpusher ['penpuʃə*] *n* Schreiberling *m*.
pension ['penʃən] *n* Rente *f*.
▶**pension off** *vt* (*vorzeitig*) pensionieren.
pensionable ['penʃnəbl] *adj* (*age*) Pensions-;
(*job*) mit Pensionsberechtigung.

pensioner ['pɛnʃənə*] (*BRIT*) n Rentner(in) m(f).
pension scheme n Rentenversicherung f.
pensive ['pɛnsɪv] adj nachdenklich.
pentagon ['pɛntəgən] (*US*) n: **the P~** das Pentagon.

Pentagon *heißt das fünfeckige Gebäude in Arlington, Virginia, in dem das amerikanische Verteidigungsministerium untergebracht ist. Im weiteren Sinne bezieht sich dieses Wort auf die amerikanische Militärführung.*

Pentecost ['pɛntɪkɔst] n (*in Judaism*) Erntefest nt; (*in Christianity*) Pfingsten nt.
penthouse ['pɛnthaus] n Penthouse nt.
pent-up ['pɛntʌp] adj (*feelings*) aufgestaut.
penultimate [pɛ'nʌltɪmət] adj vorletzte(r, s).
penury ['pɛnjurɪ] n Armut f, Not f.
people ['piːpl] npl (*persons*) Leute pl; (*inhabitants*) Bevölkerung f ♦ n (*nation, race*) Volk nt; **old ~** alte Menschen or Leute; **young ~** junge Leute; **the room was full of ~** das Zimmer war voller Leute or Menschen; **several ~ came** mehrere (Leute) kamen; **~ say that ...** man sagt, daß ...; **the ~** (*POL*) das Volk; **a man of the ~** ein Mann des Volkes.
PEP n abbr (= *personal equity plan*) steuerbegünstigte Kapitalinvestition.
pep [pɛp] (*inf*) n Schwung m, Pep m.
▶**pep up** vt (*person*) aufmöbeln; (*food*) pikanter machen.
pepper ['pɛpə*] n (*spice*) Pfeffer m; (*vegetable*) Paprika m ♦ vt: **to ~ with** (*fig*) übersäen mit; **two ~s** zwei Paprikaschoten.
peppercorn ['pɛpəkɔːn] n Pfefferkorn nt.
pepper mill n Pfeffermühle f.
peppermint ['pɛpəmɪnt] n (*sweet*) Pfefferminz nt; (*plant*) Pfefferminze f.
pepperoni [pɛpə'rəunɪ] n ≈ Pfeffersalami f.
pepper pot n Pfefferstreuer m.
pep talk (*inf*) n aufmunternde Worte pl.
per [pɜː*] prep (*for each*) pro; **~ day/person/ kilo** pro Tag/Person/Kilo; **~ annum** pro Jahr; **as ~ your instructions** gemäß Ihren Anweisungen.
per capita [-'kæpɪtə] adj (*income*) Pro-Kopf- ♦ adv pro Kopf.
perceive [pə'siːv] vt (*see*) wahrnehmen; (*view, understand*) verstehen.
per cent n Prozent nt; **a 20 ~ discount** 20 Prozent Rabatt.
percentage [pə'sɛntɪdʒ] n Prozentsatz m; **on a ~ basis** auf Prozentbasis.
percentage point n Prozent nt.
perceptible [pə'sɛptɪbl] adj (*difference, change*) wahrnehmbar, merklich.
perception [pə'sɛpʃən] n (*insight*) Einsicht f; (*opinion, understanding*) Erkenntnis f; (*faculty*) Wahrnehmung f.
perceptive [pə'sɛptɪv] adj (*person*)

aufmerksam; (*analysis etc*) erkenntnisreich.
perch [pɜːtʃ] n (*for bird*) Stange f; (*fish*) Flußbarsch m ♦ vi: **to ~ (on)** (*bird*) sitzen (auf +dat); (*person*) hocken (auf +dat).
percolate ['pɜːkəleɪt] vt (*coffee*) (mit einer Kaffeemaschine) zubereiten ♦ vi (*coffee*) durchlaufen; **to ~ through/into** (*idea, light etc*) durchsickern durch/in +acc.
percolator ['pɜːkəleɪtə*] n (*also*: **coffee ~**) Kaffeemaschine f.
percussion [pə'kʌʃən] n (*MUS*) Schlagzeug nt.
peremptory [pə'rɛmptərɪ] (*pej*) adj (*person*) herrisch; (*order*) kategorisch.
perennial [pə'rɛnɪəl] adj (*plant*) mehrjährig; (*fig: problem, feature etc*) immer wiederkehrend ♦ n (*BOT*) mehrjährige Pflanze f.
perfect [adj, n 'pɜːfɪkt, vt pə'fɛkt] adj perfekt; (*nonsense, idiot etc*) ausgemacht ♦ vt (*technique*) perfektionieren ♦ n: **the ~** (*also*: **the ~ tense**) das Perfekt; **he's a ~ stranger to me** er ist mir vollkommen fremd.
perfection [pə'fɛkʃən] n Perfektion f, Vollkommenheit f.
perfectionist [pə'fɛkʃənɪst] n Perfektionist(in) m(f).
perfectly ['pɜːfɪktlɪ] adv vollkommen; (*faultlessly*) perfekt; **I'm ~ happy with the situation** ich bin mit der Lage vollkommen zufrieden; **you know ~ well that ...** Sie wissen ganz genau, daß ...
perforate ['pɜːfəreɪt] vt perforieren.
perforated ulcer ['pɜːfəreɪtəd-] n durchgebrochenes Geschwür nt.
perforation [pɜːfə'reɪʃən] n (*small hole*) Loch nt; (*line of holes*) Perforation f.
perform [pə'fɔːm] vt (*operation, ceremony etc*) durchführen; (*task*) erfüllen; (*piece of music, play etc*) aufführen ♦ vi auftreten; **to ~ well/badly** eine gute/schlechte Leistung zeigen.
performance [pə'fɔːməns] n Leistung f; (*of play, show*) Vorstellung f; **the team put up a good ~** die Mannschaft zeigte eine gute Leistung.
performer [pə'fɔːmə*] n Künstler(in) m(f).
performing [pə'fɔːmɪŋ] adj (*animal*) dressiert.
performing arts npl: **the ~** die darstellenden Künste pl.
perfume ['pɜːfjuːm] n Parfüm nt; (*fragrance*) Duft m ♦ vt parfümieren.
perfunctory [pə'fʌŋktərɪ] adj flüchtig.
perhaps [pə'hæps] adv vielleicht; **~ he'll come** er kommt vielleicht; **~ not** vielleicht nicht.
peril ['pɛrɪl] n Gefahr f.
perilous ['pɛrɪləs] adj gefährlich.
perilously ['pɛrɪləslɪ] adv: **they came ~ close to being caught** sie wären um ein Haar gefangen worden.
perimeter [pə'rɪmɪtə*] n Umfang m.
perimeter fence n Umzäunung f.
period ['pɪərɪəd] n (*length of time*) Zeitraum m,

Periode *f*; (*era*) Zeitalter *nt*; (*SCOL*) Stunde *f*; (*esp US: full stop*) Punkt *m*; (*MED: also:* **menstrual** ~) Periode ♦ *adj* (*costume etc*) zeitgenössisch; **for a** ~ **of 3 weeks** für eine Dauer *or* einen Zeitraum von 3 Wochen; **the holiday** ~ (*BRIT*) die Urlaubszeit; **I won't do it. P~.** ich mache das nicht, und damit basta!

periodic [pɪərɪ'ɔdɪk] *adj* periodisch.

periodical [pɪərɪ'ɔdɪkl] *n* Zeitschrift *f* ♦ *adj* periodisch.

periodically [pɪərɪ'ɔdɪklɪ] *adv* periodisch.

period pains (*BRIT*) *npl* Menstruationsschmerzen *pl*.

peripatetic [pɛrɪpə'tɛtɪk] *adj* (*BRIT: teacher*) an mehreren Schulen tätig; ~ **life** Wanderleben *nt*.

peripheral [pə'rɪfərəl] *adj* (*feature, issue*) Rand-, nebensächlich; (*vision*) peripher ♦ *n* (*COMPUT*) Peripheriegerät *nt*.

periphery [pə'rɪfərɪ] *n* Peripherie *f*.

periscope ['pɛrɪskəup] *n* Periskop *nt*.

perish ['pɛrɪʃ] *vi* (*die*) umkommen; (*rubber, leather etc*) verschleißen.

perishable ['pɛrɪʃəbl] *adj* (*food*) leicht verderblich.

perishables ['pɛrɪʃəblz] *npl* leicht verderbliche Waren *pl*.

perishing ['pɛrɪʃɪŋ] (*BRIT: inf*) *adj*: **it's** ~ (**cold**) es ist eisig kalt.

peritonitis [pɛrɪtə'naɪtɪs] *n* Bauchfellentzündung *f*.

perjure ['pɜːdʒə*] *vt*: **to** ~ **o.s.** einen Meineid leisten.

perjury ['pɜːdʒərɪ] *n* (*in court*) Meineid *m*; (*breach of oath*) Eidesverletzung *f*.

perks [pɜːks] (*inf*) *npl* (*extras*) Vergünstigungen *pl*.

perk up *vi* (*cheer up*) munter werden.

perky ['pɜːkɪ] *adj* (*cheerful*) munter.

perm [pɜːm] *n* Dauerwelle *f* ♦ *vt*: **to have one's hair** ~**ed** sich *dat* eine Dauerwelle machen lassen.

permanence ['pɜːmənəns] *n* Dauerhaftigkeit *f*.

permanent ['pɜːmənənt] *adj* dauerhaft; (*job, position*) fest; ~ **address** ständiger Wohnsitz *m*; **I'm not** ~ **here** ich bin hier nicht fest angestellt.

permanently ['pɜːmənəntlɪ] *adv* (*damage*) dauerhaft; (*stay, live*) ständig; (*locked, open, frozen etc*) dauernd.

permeable ['pɜːmɪəbl] *adj* durchlässig.

permeate ['pɜːmɪeɪt] *vt* durchdringen ♦ *vi*: **to** ~ **through** dringen durch.

permissible [pə'mɪsɪbl] *adj* zulässig.

permission [pə'mɪʃən] *n* Erlaubnis *f*, Genehmigung *f*; **to give sb** ~ **to do sth** jdm die Erlaubnis geben, etw zu tun.

permissive [pə'mɪsɪv] *adj* (*society, age*) permissiv.

permit [*n* 'pɜːmɪt, *vt* pə'mɪt] *n* Genehmigung *f* ♦ *vt* (*allow*) erlauben; (*make possible*) gestatten; **fishing** ~ Angelschein *m*; **to** ~ **sb to do sth** jdm erlauben, etw zu tun; **weather** ~**ting** wenn das Wetter es zuläßt.

permutation [pə:mju'teɪʃən] *n* Permutation *f*; (*fig*) Variation *f*.

pernicious [pə:'nɪʃəs] *adj* (*lie, nonsense*) bösartig; (*effect*) schädlich.

pernickety [pə'nɪkɪtɪ] (*inf*) *adj* pingelig.

perpendicular [pə:pən'dɪkjulə*] *adj* senkrecht ♦ *n*: **the** ~ die Senkrechte; ~ **to** senkrecht zu.

perpetrate ['pɜːpɪtreɪt] *vt* (*crime*) begehen.

perpetual [pə'pɛtjuəl] *adj* ständig, dauernd.

perpetuate [pə'pɛtjueɪt] *vt* (*custom, belief etc*) bewahren; (*situation*) aufrechterhalten.

perpetuity [pə:pɪ'tjuːɪtɪ] *n*: **in** ~ auf ewig.

perplex [pə'plɛks] *vt* verblüffen.

perplexing [pə:'plɛksɪŋ] *adj* verblüffend.

perquisites ['pɜːkwɪzɪts] (*form*) *npl* Vergünstigungen *pl*.

per se [-seɪ] *adv* an sich.

persecute ['pɜːsɪkjuːt] *vt* verfolgen.

persecution [pə:sɪ'kjuːʃən] *n* Verfolgung *f*.

perseverance [pə:sɪ'vɪərns] *n* Beharrlichkeit *f*, Ausdauer *f*.

persevere [pə:sɪ'vɪə*] *vi* durchhalten, beharren.

Persia ['pɜːʃə] *n* Persien *nt*.

Persian ['pɜːʃən] *adj* persisch ♦ *n* (*LING*) Persisch *nt*; **the** ~ **Gulf** der (Persische) Golf.

Persian cat *n* Perserkatze *f*.

persist [pə'sɪst] *vi*: **to** ~ (**with** *or* **in**) beharren (auf +*dat*), festhalten (an +*dat*); **to** ~ **in doing sth** darauf beharren, etw zu tun.

persistence [pə'sɪstəns] *n* (*determination*) Beharrlichkeit *f*.

persistent [pə'sɪstənt] *adj* (*person, noise*) beharrlich; (*smell, cough etc*) hartnäckig; (*lateness, rain*) andauernd; ~ **offender** Wiederholungstäter(in) *m(f)*.

persnickety [pə'snɪkɪtɪ] (*US: inf*) *adj* = **pernickety**.

person ['pɜːsn] *n* Person *f*, Mensch *m*; **in** ~ persönlich; **on** *or* **about one's** ~ bei sich; ~ **to** ~ **call** (*TEL*) Gespräch *nt* mit Voranmeldung.

personable ['pɜːsnəbl] *adj* von angenehmer Erscheinung.

personal ['pɜːsnl] *adj* persönlich; (*life*) Privat-; **nothing** ~! nehmen Sie es nicht persönlich!

personal allowance *n* (*TAX*) persönlicher Steuerfreibetrag *m*.

personal assistant *n* persönlicher Referent *m*, persönliche Referentin *f*.

personal column *n* private Kleinanzeigen *pl*.

personal computer *n* Personalcomputer *m*.

personal details *npl* Personalien *pl*.

personal hygiene *n* Körperhygiene *f*.

personal identification number *n* (*BANKING*) Geheimnummer *f*, PIN-Nummer *f*.

personality [pɜːsə'nælɪtɪ] n (*character, person*) Persönlichkeit *f*.
personal loan n Personaldarlehen *nt*.
personally ['pɜːsnəlɪ] adv persönlich; **to take sth ~** etw persönlich nehmen.
personal organizer n Terminplaner *m*.
personal stereo n Walkman ® *m*.
personify [pɜː'sɒnɪfaɪ] vt personifizieren; (*embody*) verkörpern.
personnel [pɜːsə'nɛl] n Personal *nt*.
personnel department n Personalabteilung *f*.
personnel manager n Personalleiter(in) *m(f)*.
perspective [pə'spɛktɪv] n (*also fig*) Perspektive *f*; **to get sth into ~** (*fig*) etw in Relation zu anderen Dingen sehen.
Perspex ® ['pɜːspɛks] n Acrylglas *nt*.
perspicacity [pɜːspɪ'kæsɪtɪ] n Scharfsinn *m*.
perspiration [pɜːspɪ'reɪʃən] n Transpiration *f*.
perspire [pə'spaɪə'] vi transpirieren.
persuade [pə'sweɪd] vt: **to ~ sb to do sth** jdn dazu überreden, etw zu tun; **to ~ sb that** jdn davon überzeugen, daß; **to be ~d of sth** von etw überzeugt sein.
persuasion [pə'sweɪʒən] n (*act*) Überredung *f*; (*creed*) Überzeugung *f*.
persuasive [pə'sweɪsɪv] adj (*person, argument*) überzeugend.
pert [pɜːt] adj (*person*) frech; (*nose, buttocks*) keck; (*hat*) keß.
pertaining [pɜː'teɪnɪŋ]: **~ to** prep betreffend +*acc*.
pertinent ['pɜːtɪnənt] adj relevant.
perturb [pə'tɜːb] vt beunruhigen.
Peru [pə'ruː] n Peru *nt*.
perusal [pə'ruːzl] n Durchsicht *f*.
peruse [pə'ruːz] vt durchsehen.
Peruvian [pə'ruːvjən] adj peruanisch ♦ n Peruaner(in) *m(f)*.
pervade [pə'veɪd] vt (*smell, feeling*) erfüllen.
pervasive [pə'veɪzɪv] adj (*smell*) durchdringend; (*influence*) weitreichend; (*mood, atmosphere*) allumfassend.
perverse [pə'vɜːs] adj (*person*) borniert; (*behaviour*) widernatürlich, pervers.
perversion [pə'vɜːʃən] n (*sexual*) Perversion *f*; (*of truth, justice*) Verzerrung *f*, Pervertierung *f*.
perversity [pə'vɜːsɪtɪ] n Widernatürlichkeit *f*.
pervert [n 'pɜːvɜːt, vt pə'vɜːt] n (*sexual deviant*) perverser Mensch *m* ♦ vt (*person, mind*) verderben; (*distort: truth, custom*) verfälschen.
pessimism ['pɛsɪmɪzəm] n Pessimismus *m*.
pessimist ['pɛsɪmɪst] n Pessimist(in) *m(f)*.
pessimistic [pɛsɪ'mɪstɪk] adj pessimistisch.
pest [pɛst] n (*insect*) Schädling *m*; (*fig: nuisance*) Plage *f*.
pest control n Schädlingsbekämpfung *f*.
pester ['pɛstə'] vt belästigen.
pesticide ['pɛstɪsaɪd] n Schädlingsbekämp-

fungsmittel *nt*, Pestizid *nt*.
pestilence ['pɛstɪləns] n Pest *f*.
pestle ['pɛsl] n Stößel *m*.
pet [pɛt] n (*animal*) Haustier *nt* ♦ adj (*theory etc*) Lieblings- ♦ vt (*stroke*) streicheln ♦ vi (*inf: sexually*) herumknutschen; **teacher's ~** (*favourite*) Lehrers Liebling *m*; **a ~ rabbit/ snake** *etc* ein Kaninchen/eine Schlange *etc* (als Haustier); **that's my ~ hate** das hasse ich besonders.
petal ['pɛtl] n Blütenblatt *nt*.
peter out ['piːtə-] vi (*road etc*) allmählich aufhören, zu Ende gehen; (*conversation, meeting*) sich totlaufen.
petite [pə'tiːt] adj (*woman*) zierlich.
petition [pə'tɪʃən] n (*signed document*) Petition *f*; (*LAW*) Klage *f* ♦ vt ersuchen ♦ vi: **to ~ for divorce** die Scheidung einreichen.
pet name (*BRIT*) n Kosename *m*.
petrified ['pɛtrɪfaɪd] adj (*fig: terrified*) starr vor Angst.
petrify ['pɛtrɪfaɪ] vt (*fig: terrify*) vor Angst erstarren lassen.
petrochemical [pɛtrə'kɛmɪkl] adj petrochemisch.
petrodollars ['pɛtrəudɒləz] npl Petrodollar *pl*.
petrol ['pɛtrəl] (*BRIT*) n Benzin *nt*; **two-star ~** Normalbenzin *nt*; **four-star ~** Super(benzin) *nt*; **unleaded ~** bleifreies *or* unverbleites Benzin.
petrol bomb n Benzinbombe *f*.
petrol can (*BRIT*) n Benzinkanister *m*.
petrol engine (*BRIT*) n Benzinmotor *m*.
petroleum [pə'trəuliəm] n Petroleum *nt*.
petroleum jelly n Vaseline *f*.
petrol pump (*BRIT*) n (*in garage*) Zapfsäule *f*; (*in engine*) Benzinpumpe *f*.
petrol station (*BRIT*) n Tankstelle *f*.
petrol tank (*BRIT*) n Benzintank *m*.
petticoat ['pɛtɪkəut] n (*underskirt: full-length*) Unterkleid *nt*; (*: waist*) Unterrock *m*.
pettifogging ['pɛtɪfɒgɪŋ] adj kleinlich.
pettiness ['pɛtɪnɪs] n Kleinlichkeit *f*.
petty ['pɛtɪ] adj (*trivial*) unbedeutend; (*small-minded*) kleinlich; (*crime*) geringfügig; (*official*) untergeordnet; (*excuse*) billig; (*remark*) spitz.
petty cash n (*in office*) Portokasse *f*.
petty officer n Maat *m*.
petulant ['pɛtjulənt] adj (*person, expression*) gereizt.
pew [pjuː] n (*in church*) Kirchenbank *f*.
pewter ['pjuːtə'] n Zinn *nt*.
Pfc (*US*) abbr (*MIL: = private first class*) ≈ Obergefreite(r) *m*.
PG n abbr (*CINE: = parental guidance*) *Klassifikation für Filme, die Kinder nur in Begleitung Erwachsener sehen dürfen.*
PGA n abbr (= *Professional Golfers' Association*) *Golf-Profiverband.*
PH (*US*) n abbr (*MIL: = Purple Heart*) *Verwundetenauszeichnung.*

pH n abbr (= potential of hydrogen) pH.
PHA (US) n abbr (= Public Housing Administration) Regierungsbehörde für sozialen Wohnungsbau.
phallic ['fælɪk] adj phallisch; (symbol) Phallus-.
phantom ['fæntəm] n Phantom nt ♦ adj (fig) Phantom-.
Pharaoh ['fɛərəu] n Pharao m.
pharmaceutical [fɑːmə'sjuːtɪkl] adj pharmazeutisch.
pharmaceuticals [fɑːmə'sjuːtɪklz] npl Arzneimittel pl, Pharmaka pl.
pharmacist ['fɑːməsɪst] n Apotheker(in) m(f).
pharmacy ['fɑːməsɪ] n (shop) Apotheke f; (science) Pharmazie f.
phase [feɪz] n Phase f ♦ vt: **to ~ sth in/out** etw stufenweise einführen/abschaffen.
PhD n abbr (= Doctor of Philosophy) ≈ Dr. phil.
pheasant ['fɛznt] n Fasan m.
phenomena [fə'nɒmɪnə] npl of phenomenon.
phenomenal [fə'nɒmɪnl] adj phänomenal.
phenomenon [fə'nɒmɪnən] (pl phenomena) n Phänomen nt.
phew [fjuː] excl puh!
phial ['faɪəl] n Fläschchen nt.
philanderer [fɪ'lændərə*] n Schwerenöter m.
philanthropic [fɪlən'θrɒpɪk] adj philanthropisch.
philanthropist [fɪ'lænθrəpɪst] n Philanthrop(in) m(f).
philatelist [fɪ'lætəlɪst] n Philatelist(in) m(f).
philately [fɪ'lætəlɪ] n Philatelie f.
Philippines ['fɪlɪpiːnz] npl: **the ~** die Philippinen pl.
Philistine ['fɪlɪstaɪn] n (boor) Banause m.
philosopher [fɪ'lɒsəfə*] n Philosoph(in) m(f).
philosophical [fɪlə'sɒfɪkl] adj philosophisch; (fig: calm, resigned) gelassen.
philosophize [fɪ'lɒsəfaɪz] vi philosophieren.
philosophy [fɪ'lɒsəfɪ] n Philosophie f.
phlegm [flɛm] n (MED) Schleim m.
phlegmatic [flɛg'mætɪk] adj phlegmatisch.
phobia ['fəubjə] n Phobie f.
phone [fəun] n Telefon nt ♦ vt anrufen ♦ vi anrufen, telefonieren; **to be on the ~** (possess a phone) Telefon haben; (be calling) telefonieren.
▶**phone back** vt, vi zurückrufen.
▶**phone up** vt, vi anrufen.
phone book n Telefonbuch nt.
phone booth n Telefonzelle f.
phone box (BRIT) n Telefonzelle f.
phone call n Anruf m.
phonecard ['fəunkɑːd] n Telefonkarte f.
phone-in ['fəunɪn] (BRIT) n (RADIO, TV) Radio-/Fernsehsendung mit Hörer-/Zuschauerbeteiligung per Telefon, Phone-in nt ♦ adj mit Hörer-/Zuschaueranrufen.
phone tapping [-tæpɪŋ] n Abhören nt von Telefonleitungen.
phonetics [fə'nɛtɪks] n Phonetik f.

phoney ['fəunɪ] adj (address) falsch; (accent) unecht; (person) unaufrichtig.
phonograph ['fəunəgrɑːf] (US) n Grammophon nt.
phony ['fəunɪ] adj = phoney.
phosphate ['fɒsfeɪt] n Phosphat nt.
phosphorus ['fɒsfərəs] n Phosphor m.
photo ['fəutəu] n Foto nt.
photo... ['fəutəu] pref Foto-.
photocopier ['fəutəukɒpɪə*] n Fotokopierer m.
photocopy ['fəutəukɒpɪ] n Fotokopie f ♦ vt fotokopieren.
photoelectric [fəutəuɪ'lɛktrɪk] adj (effect) photoelektrisch; (cell) Photo-.
photo finish n Fotofinish nt.
Photofit ® ['fəutəufɪt] n (also: ~ **picture**) Phantombild nt.
photogenic [fəutəu'dʒɛnɪk] adj fotogen.
photograph ['fəutəgræf] n Fotografie f ♦ vt fotografieren; **to take a ~ of sb** jdn fotografieren.
photographer [fə'tɒgrəfə*] n Fotograf(in) m(f).
photographic [fəutə'græfɪk] adj (equipment etc) fotografisch, Foto-.
photography [fə'tɒgrəfɪ] n Fotografie f.
photo opportunity n Fototermin m; (accidental) Fotogelegenheit f.
photostat ['fəutəustæt] n Fotokopie f.
photosynthesis [fəutəu'sɪnθəsɪs] n Photosynthese f.
phrase [freɪz] n Satz m; (LING) Redewendung f; (MUS) Phrase f ♦ vt ausdrücken; (letter) formulieren.
phrase book n Sprachführer m.
physical ['fɪzɪkl] adj (bodily) körperlich; (geography, properties) physikalisch; (law, explanation) natürlich; **~ examination** ärztliche Untersuchung f; **the ~ sciences** die Naturwissenschaften.
physical education n Sportunterricht m.
physically ['fɪzɪklɪ] adv (fit, attractive) körperlich.
physician [fɪ'zɪʃən] n Arzt m, Ärztin f.
physicist ['fɪzɪsɪst] n Physiker(in) m(f).
physics ['fɪzɪks] n Physik f.
physiological ['fɪzɪə'lɒdʒɪkl] adj physiologisch.
physiology [fɪzɪ'ɒlədʒɪ] n Physiologie f.
physiotherapist [fɪzɪəu'θɛrəpɪst] n Physiotherapeut(in) m(f).
physiotherapy [fɪzɪəu'θɛrəpɪ] n Physiotherapie f.
physique [fɪ'ziːk] n Körperbau m.
pianist ['piːənɪst] n Pianist(in) m(f).
piano [pɪ'ænəu] n Klavier nt, Piano nt.
piano accordion (BRIT) n Akkordeon nt.
piccolo ['pɪkələu] n Pikkoloflöte f.
pick [pɪk] n (also: ~axe) Spitzhacke f ♦ vt (select) aussuchen; (gather: fruit, mushrooms) sammeln; (: flowers) pflücken; (remove, take out) herausnehmen; (lock) knacken; (scab,

spot) kratzen an +*dat*; **take your** ~ (*choose*) Sie haben die Wahl; **the** ~ **of** (*best*) das Beste +*gen*; **to** ~ **one's nose** in der Nase bohren; **to** ~ **one's teeth** in den Zähnen stochern; **to** ~ **sb's brains** jdn als Informationsquelle nutzen; **to** ~ **sb's pocket** jdn bestehlen; **to** ~ **a quarrel (with sb)** einen Streit (mit jdm) anfangen.

▶**pick at** *vt fus* (*food*) herumstochern in +*dat*.

▶**pick off** *vt* (*shoot*) abschießen.

▶**pick on** *vt fus* (*criticize*) herumhacken auf +*dat*.

▶**pick out** *vt* (*distinguish*) ausmachen; (*select*) aussuchen.

▶**pick up** *vi* (*health*) sich verbessern; (*economy*) sich erholen ♦ *vt* (*from floor etc*) aufheben; (*arrest*) festnehmen; (*collect: person, parcel etc*) abholen; (*hitchhiker*) mitnehmen; (*for sexual encounter*) aufreißen; (*learn: skill etc*) mitbekommen; (*RADIO*) empfangen; **to** ~ **up where one left off** da weitermachen, wo man aufgehört hat; **to** ~ **up speed** schneller werden; **to** ~ **o.s. up** (*after falling etc*) sich aufrappeln.

pickaxe, (*US*) **pickax** ['pɪkæks] *n* Spitzhacke *f*.

picket ['pɪkɪt] *n* (*in strike*) Streikposten *m* ♦ *vt* (*factory etc*) Streikposten aufstellen vor +*dat*.

picketing ['pɪkɪtɪŋ] *n* Aufstellen *nt* von Streikposten.

picket line *n* Streikpostenkette *f*.

pickings ['pɪkɪŋz] *npl*: **there are rich** ~ **to be had here** hier ist die Ausbeute gut.

pickle ['pɪkl] *n* (*also*: ~**s**: *as condiment*) Pickles *pl* ♦ *vt* einlegen; **to be in a** ~ in der Klemme sitzen; **to get in a** ~ in eine Klemme geraten.

pick-me-up ['pɪkmiːʌp] *n* Muntermacher *m*.

pickpocket ['pɪkpɔkɪt] *n* Taschendieb(in) *m(f)*.

pick-up ['pɪkʌp] *n* (*also*: ~ **truck**) offener Kleintransporter *m*; (*BRIT: on record player*) Tonabnehmer *m*.

picnic ['pɪknɪk] *n* Picknick *nt* ♦ *vi* picknicken.

picnicker ['pɪknɪkə*] *n* Picknicker(in) *m(f)*.

pictorial [pɪk'tɔːrɪəl] *adj* (*record, coverage etc*) bildlich.

picture ['pɪktʃə*] *n* (*also TV, fig*) Bild *nt*; (*film*) Film *m* ♦ *vt* (*imagine*) sich vorstellen; **the** ~**s** (*BRIT: inf: the cinema*) das Kino; **to take a** ~ **of sb** ein Bild von jdm machen; **to put sb in the** ~ jdn ins Bild setzen.

picture book *n* Bilderbuch *nt*.

picturesque [pɪktʃə'rɛsk] *adj* malerisch.

picture window *n* Aussichtsfenster *nt*.

piddling ['pɪdlɪŋ] (*inf*) *adj* lächerlich.

pidgin ['pɪdʒɪn] *adj*: ~ **English** Pidgin-Englisch *nt*.

pie [paɪ] *n* (*vegetable, meat*) Pastete *f*; (*fruit*) Torte *f*.

piebald ['paɪbɔːld] *adj* (*horse*) scheckig.

piece [piːs] *n* Stück *nt*; (*DRAUGHTS etc*) Stein *m*; (*CHESS*) Figur *f*; **in** ~**s** (*broken*) kaputt; (*taken apart*) auseinandergenommen, in

Einzelteilen; **a** ~ **of clothing/furniture/music** ein Kleidungs-/Möbel-/Musikstück *nt*; **a** ~ **of machinery** eine Maschine; **a** ~ **of research** eine Forschungsarbeit; **a** ~ **of advice** ein Rat *m*; **to take sth to** ~**s** etw auseinandernehmen; **in one** ~ (*object*) unbeschädigt; (*person*) wohlbehalten; **a 10p** ~ (*BRIT*) ein 10-Pence-Stück *nt*; ~ **by** ~ Stück für Stück; **a six-**~ **band** eine sechsköpfige Band; **let her say her** ~ laß sie ausreden.

▶**piece together** *vt* zusammenfügen.

piecemeal ['piːsmiːl] *adv* stückweise, Stück für Stück.

piecework ['piːswəːk] *n* Akkordarbeit *f*.

pie chart *n* Tortendiagramm *nt*.

pier [pɪə*] *n* Pier *m*.

pierce [pɪəs] *vt* durchstechen; **to have one's ears** ~**d** sich *dat* die Ohrläppchen durchstechen lassen.

piercing ['pɪəsɪŋ] *adj* (*fig: cry, eyes, stare*) durchdringend; (*wind*) schneidend.

piety ['paɪətɪ] *n* Frömmigkeit *f*.

piffling ['pɪflɪŋ] (*inf*) *adj* lächerlich.

pig [pɪg] *n* (*also pej*) Schwein *nt*; (*greedy person*) Vielfraß *m*.

pigeon ['pɪdʒən] *n* Taube *f*.

pigeonhole ['pɪdʒənhəul] *n* (*for letters etc*) Fach *nt*; (*fig*) Schublade *f* ♦ *vt* (*fig: person*) in eine Schublade stecken.

pigeon-toed ['pɪdʒəntəud] *adj* mit einwärts gerichteten Zehen.

piggy bank ['pɪgɪ-] *n* Sparschwein *nt*.

pig-headed ['pɪg'hɛdɪd] (*pej*) *adj* dickköpfig.

piglet ['pɪglɪt] *n* Schweinchen *nt*, Ferkel *nt*.

pigment ['pɪgmənt] *n* Pigment *nt*.

pigmentation [pɪgmən'teɪʃən] *n* Pigmentierung *f*, Färbung *f*.

pigmy ['pɪgmɪ] *n* = **pygmy**.

pigskin ['pɪgskɪn] *n* Schweinsleder *nt*.

pigsty ['pɪgstaɪ] *n* (*also fig*) Schweinestall *m*.

pigtail ['pɪgteɪl] *n* Zopf *m*.

pike [paɪk] *n* (*fish*) Hecht *m*; (*spear*) Spieß *m*.

pilchard ['pɪltʃəd] *n* Sardine *f*.

pile [paɪl] *n* (*heap*) Haufen *m*; (*stack*) Stapel *m*; (*of carpet, velvet*) Flor *m*; (*pillar*) Pfahl *m* ♦ *vt* (*also*: ~ **up**) (auf)stapeln; **in a** ~ in einem Haufen; **to** ~ **into/out of** (*vehicle*) sich drängen in +*acc*/aus.

▶**pile on** *vt*: **to** ~ **it on** (*inf*) zu dick auftragen.

▶**pile up** *vi* (*papers, problems, work*) sich stapeln.

piles [paɪlz] *npl* (*MED*) Hämorrhoiden *pl*.

pile-up ['paɪlʌp] *n* (*AUT*) Massenkarambolage *f*.

pilfer ['pɪlfə*] *vt, vi* stehlen.

pilfering ['pɪlfərɪŋ] *n* Diebstahl *m*.

pilgrim ['pɪlgrɪm] *n* Pilger(in) *m(f)*.

pilgrimage ['pɪlgrɪmɪdʒ] *n* Pilgerfahrt *f*, Wallfahrt *f*.

pill [pɪl] *n* Tablette *f*, Pille *f*; **the** ~ (*contraceptive*) die Pille; **to be on the** ~ die

Pille nehmen.

pillage ['pɪlɪdʒ] *n* Plünderung *f* ♦ *vt* plündern.

pillar ['pɪlə'] *n* Säule *f*; **a ~ of society** (*fig*) eine Säule *or* Stütze der Gesellschaft.

pillar box (*BRIT*) *n* Briefkasten *m*.

pillion ['pɪljən] *n*: **to ride ~** (*on motorcycle*) auf dem Soziussitz mitfahren; (*on horse*) hinten auf dem Pferd mitreiten.

pillory ['pɪlərɪ] *vt* (*criticize*) anprangern ♦ *n* Pranger *m*.

pillow ['pɪləu] *n* (Kopf)kissen *nt*.

pillowcase ['pɪləukeɪs] *n* (Kopf)kissenbezug *m*.

pillowslip ['pɪləuslɪp] *n* = **pillowcase**.

pilot ['paɪlət] *n* (*AVIAT*) Pilot(in) *m(f)*; (*NAUT*) Lotse *m* ♦ *adj* (*scheme, study etc*) Pilot- ♦ *vt* (*aircraft*) steuern; (*fig: new law, scheme*) sich zum Fürsprecher machen +*gen*.

pilot boat *n* Lotsenboot *nt*.

pilot light *n* (*on cooker, boiler*) Zündflamme *f*.

pimento [pɪ'mɛntəu] *n* (*spice*) Piment *nt*.

pimp [pɪmp] *n* Zuhälter *m*.

pimple ['pɪmpl] *n* Pickel *m*.

pimply ['pɪmplɪ] *adj* pick(e)lig.

PIN *n abbr* (= *personal identification number*) PIN; **~ number** PIN-Nummer *f*.

pin [pɪn] *n* (*metal: for clothes, papers*) Stecknadel *f*; (*TECH*) Stift *m*; (*BRIT: also:* **drawing ~**) Heftzwecke *f*; (*in grenade*) Sicherungsstift *m*; (*BRIT: ELEC*) Pol *m* ♦ *vt* (*fasten with pin*) feststecken; **~s and needles** (*in arms, legs etc*) Kribbeln *nt*; **to ~ sb against/to sth** jdn gegen/an etw *acc* pressen; **to ~ sth on sb** (*fig*) jdm etw anhängen.

▶**pin down** *vt* (*fig: person*) festnageln; **there's something strange here but I can't quite ~ it down** hier stimmt etwas nicht, aber ich weiß nicht genau was.

pinafore ['pɪnəfɔː'] (*BRIT*) *n* (*also:* **~ dress**) Trägerkleid *nt*.

pinball ['pɪnbɔːl] *n* (*game*) Flippern *nt*; (*machine*) Flipper *m*.

pincers ['pɪnsəz] *npl* (*tool*) Kneifzange *f*; (*of crab, lobster etc*) Schere *f*.

pinch [pɪntʃ] *n* (*of salt etc*) Prise *f* ♦ *vt* (*with finger and thumb*) zwicken, kneifen; (*inf: steal*) klauen ♦ *vi* (*shoe*) drücken; **at a ~** zur Not; **to feel the ~** (*fig*) die schlechte Lage zu spüren bekommen.

pinched [pɪntʃt] *adj* (*face*) erschöpft; **~ with cold** verfroren.

pincushion ['pɪnkuʃən] *n* Nadelkissen *nt*.

pine [paɪn] *n* (*also:* **~ tree**) Kiefer *f*; (*wood*) Kiefernholz *nt* ♦ *vi*: **to ~ for** sich sehnen nach.

▶**pine away** *vi* sich (vor Kummer) verzehren.

pineapple ['paɪnæpl] *n* Ananas *f*.

pine cone *n* Kiefernzapfen *m*.

pine needles *npl* Kiefernnadeln *pl*.

ping [pɪŋ] *n* (*noise*) Klingeln *nt*.

Ping-Pong ® ['pɪŋpɔŋ] *n* Pingpong *nt*.

pink [pɪŋk] *adj* rosa *inv* ♦ *n* (*colour*) Rosa *nt*; (*BOT*) Gartennelke *f*.

pinking shears *npl* Zickzackschere *f*.

pin money (*BRIT: inf*) *n* Nadelgeld *nt*.

pinnacle ['pɪnəkl] *n* (*of building, mountain*) Spitze *f*; (*fig*) Gipfel *m*.

pinpoint ['pɪnpɔɪnt] *vt* (*identify*) genau festlegen, identifizieren; (*position of sth*) genau aufzeigen.

pinstripe ['pɪnstraɪp] *adj*: **~ suit** Nadelstreifenanzug *m*.

pint [paɪnt] *n* (*BRIT:* = *568 cc*) (britisches) Pint *nt*; (*US:* = *473 cc*) (amerikanisches) Pint; **a ~** (*BRIT: inf: of beer*) ≈ eine Halbe.

pin-up ['pɪnʌp] *n* (*picture*) Pin-up-Foto *nt*.

pioneer [paɪə'nɪə'] *n* (*lit, fig*) Pionier *m* ♦ *vt* (*invention etc*) Pionierarbeit leisten für.

pious ['paɪəs] *adj* fromm.

pip [pɪp] *n* (*of apple, orange*) Kern *m* ♦ *vt*: **to be ~ped at the post** (*BRIT, fig*) um Haaresbreite geschlagen werden; **the pips** *npl* (*BRIT: RADIO*) das Zeitzeichen.

pipe [paɪp] *n* (*for water, gas*) Rohr *nt*; (*for smoking*) Pfeife *f*; (*MUS*) Flöte *f* ♦ *vt* (*water, gas, oil*) (durch Rohre) leiten; **pipes** *npl* (*also:* **bagpipes**) Dudelsack *m*.

▶**pipe down** (*inf*) *vi* (*be quiet*) ruhig sein.

pipe cleaner *n* Pfeifenreiniger *m*.

piped music [paɪpt-] *n* Berieselungsmusik *f*.

pipe dream *n* Hirngespinst *nt*.

pipeline ['paɪplaɪn] *n* Pipeline *f*; **it's in the ~** (*fig*) es ist in Vorbereitung.

piper ['paɪpə'] *n* (*bagpipe player*) Dudelsackspieler(in) *m(f)*.

pipe tobacco *n* Pfeifentabak *m*.

piping ['paɪpɪŋ] *adv*: **~ hot** kochendheiß.

piquant ['piːkənt] *adj* (*also fig*) pikant.

pique ['piːk] *n*: **in a fit of ~** eingeschnappt, pikiert.

piracy ['paɪərəsɪ] *n* Piraterie *f*, Seeräuberei *f*; (*COMM*): **to commit ~** ein Plagiat begehen.

pirate ['paɪərət] *n* Pirat *m*, Seeräuber *m* ♦ *vt* (*COMM: video tape, cassette etc*) illegal herstellen.

pirate radio station (*BRIT*) *n* Piratensender *m*.

pirouette [pɪru'et] *n* Pirouette *f* ♦ *vi* Pirouetten drehen.

Pisces ['paɪsiːz] *n* Fische *pl*; **to be ~** Fische *or* (ein) Fisch sein.

piss [pɪs] (*infl*) *vi* pissen ♦ *n* Pisse *f*; **~ off!** verpiß dich!; **to be ~ed off (with sb/sth)** (von jdm/etw) die Schnauze voll haben; **it's ~ing down** (*BRIT: raining*) es schifft; **to take the ~ out of sb** (*BRIT*) jdn verarschen.

pissed [pɪst] (*infl*) *adj* (*drunk*) besoffen.

pistol ['pɪstl] *n* Pistole *f*.

piston ['pɪstən] *n* Kolben *m*.

pit [pɪt] *n* Grube *f*; (*in surface of road*) Schlagloch *nt*; (*coal mine*) Zeche *f*; (*also:* **orchestra ~**) Orchestergraben *m* ♦ *vt*: **to ~ one's wits against sb** seinen Verstand an

jdm messen; **the pits** *npl* (*AUT*) die Box; **to
~ o.s. against sth** den Kampf gegen etw
aufnehmen; **to ~ sb against sb** jdn gegen
jdn antreten lassen; **the ~ of one's stomach**
die Magengrube.

pitapat ['pɪtə'pæt] (*BRIT*) *adv:* **to go ~** (*heart*)
pochen, klopfen; (*rain*) prasseln.

pitch [pɪtʃ] *n* (*BRIT: SPORT: field*) Spielfeld *nt*;
(*MUS*) Tonhöhe *f*; (*fig: level, degree*) Grad *m*;
(*tar*) Pech *nt*; (*also:* **sales ~**) Verkaufsmasche
f; (*NAUT*) Stampfen *nt* ♦ *vt* (*throw*) werfen,
schleudern; (*set: price, message*) ansetzen
♦ *vi* (*fall forwards*) hinschlagen; (*NAUT*)
stampfen; **to ~ a tent** ein Zelt aufschlagen;
to be ~ed forward vornüber geworfen
werden.

pitch-black ['pɪtʃ'blæk] *adj* pechschwarz.

pitched battle [pɪtʃt-] *n* offene Schlacht *f*.

pitcher ['pɪtʃə*] *n* (*jug*) Krug *m*; (*US:
BASEBALL*) Werfer *m*.

pitchfork ['pɪtʃfɔːk] *n* Heugabel *f*.

piteous ['pɪtɪəs] *adj* kläglich, erbärmlich.

pitfall ['pɪtfɔːl] *n* Falle *f*.

pith [pɪθ] *n* (*of orange etc*) weiße Haut *f*; (*of
plant*) Mark *nt*; (*fig*) Kern *m*.

pithead ['pɪthɛd] *n* Schachtanlagen *pl* über
Tage.

pithy ['pɪθɪ] *adj* (*comment etc*) prägnant.

pitiable ['pɪtɪəbl] *adj* mitleiderregend.

pitiful ['pɪtɪful] *adj* (*sight etc*) mitleiderregend;
(*excuse, attempt*) jämmerlich, kläglich.

pitifully ['pɪtɪfəlɪ] *adv* (*thin, frail*) jämmerlich;
(*inadequate, ill-equipped*) fürchterlich.

pitiless ['pɪtɪlɪs] *adj* mitleidlos.

pittance ['pɪtns] *n* Hungerlohn *m*.

pitted ['pɪtɪd] *adj:* **~ with** übersät mit; **~ with
rust** voller Rost.

pity ['pɪtɪ] *n* Mitleid *nt* ♦ *vt* bemitleiden,
bedauern; **what a ~!** wie schade!; **it is a
~ that you can't come** schade, daß du nicht
kommen kannst; **to take ~ on sb** Mitleid
mit jdm haben.

pitying ['pɪtɪɪŋ] *adj* mitleidig.

pivot ['pɪvət] *n* (*TECH*) Drehpunkt *m*; (*fig*)
Dreh- und Angelpunkt *m* ♦ *vi* sich drehen.

▶**pivot on** (*depend on*) abhängen von.

pixel ['pɪksl] *n* (*COMPUT*) Pixel *nt*.

pixie ['pɪksɪ] *n* Elf *m*, Elfe *f*.

pizza ['piːtsə] *n* Pizza *f*.

placard ['plækɑːd] *n* Plakat *nt*, Aushang *m*; (*in
march etc*) Transparent *nt*.

placate [plə'keɪt] *vt* beschwichtigen,
besänftigen.

placatory [plə'keɪtərɪ] *adj* beschwichtigend,
besänftigend.

place [pleɪs] *n* Platz *m*; (*position*) Stelle *f*, Ort
m; (*seat: on committee etc*) Sitz *m*; (*home*)
Wohnung *f*; (*in street names*) ≈ Straße *f* ♦ *vt*
(*put: object*) stellen, legen; (*identify: person*)
unterbringen; **~ of birth** Geburtsort *m*; **to
take ~** (*happen*) geschehen, passieren; **at/to
his ~** (*home*) bei/zu ihm; **from ~ to ~** von

Ort zu Ort; **all over the ~** überall; **in ~s**
stellenweise; **in sb's/sth's ~** anstelle von
jdm/etw; **to take sb's/sth's ~** an die Stelle
von jdm/etw treten, jdn/etw ersetzen; **out of
~** (*inappropriate*) unangebracht; **I feel out of
~ here** ich fühle mich hier fehl am Platze;
in the first ~ (*first of all*) erstens; **to change
~s with sb** mit jdm den Platz tauschen; **to
put sb in his ~** (*fig*) jdn in seine Schranken
weisen; **he's going ~s** er bringt es noch mal
weit; **it's not my ~ to do it** es ist nicht an
mir, das zu tun; **to be ~d** (*in race, exam*)
plaziert sein; **to be ~d third** den dritten
Platz belegen; **to ~ an order with sb (for sth)**
eine Bestellung bei jdm (für etw) aufgeben;
how are you ~d next week? wie sieht es bei
Ihnen nächste Woche aus?

placebo [plə'siːbəu] *n* Placebo *nt*; (*fig*)
Beruhigungsmittel *nt*.

place mat *n* Set *nt or m*.

placement ['pleɪsmənt] *n* Plazierung *f*.

place name *n* Ortsname *m*.

placenta [plə'sɛntə] *n* Plazenta *f*.

place setting *n* Gedeck *nt*.

placid ['plæsɪd] *adj* (*person*) ruhig, gelassen;
(*place, river etc*) friedvoll.

plagiarism ['pleɪdʒərɪzəm] *n* Plagiat *nt*.

plagiarist ['pleɪdʒərɪst] *n* Plagiator(in) *m(f)*.

plagiarize ['pleɪdʒəraɪz] *vt* (*idea, work*)
kopieren, plagiieren.

plague [pleɪg] *n* (*MED*) Seuche *f*; (*fig: of locusts
etc*) Plage *f* ♦ *vt* (*fig: problems etc*) plagen; **to
~ sb with questions** jdn mit Fragen quälen.

plaice [pleɪs] *n inv* Scholle *f*.

plaid [plæd] *n* Plaid *nt*.

plain [pleɪn] *adj* (*unpatterned*) einfarbig;
(*simple*) einfach, schlicht; (*clear, easily
understood*) klar; (*not beautiful*) unattraktiv;
(*frank*) offen ♦ *adv* (*wrong, stupid etc*) einfach
♦ *n* (*area of land*) Ebene *f*, (*KNITTING*) rechte
Masche *f*; **to make sth ~ to sb** jdm etw
klarmachen.

plain chocolate *n* Bitterschokolade *f*.

plain-clothes ['pleɪnkləuðz] *adj* (*police officer*)
in Zivil.

plainly ['pleɪnlɪ] *adv* (*obviously*) eindeutig;
(*clearly*) deutlich, klar.

plainness ['pleɪnnɪs] *n* (*of person*)
Reizlosigkeit *f*.

plain speaking *n* Offenheit *f*; **a bit of ~** ein
paar offene Worte.

plain-spoken ['pleɪn'spəukən] *adj* offen.

plaintiff ['pleɪntɪf] *n* Kläger(in) *m(f)*.

plaintive ['pleɪntɪv] *adj* (*cry, voice*) klagend;
(*song*) schwermütig; (*look*) traurig.

plait [plæt] *n* (*of hair*) Zopf *m*; (*of rope, leather*)
Geflecht *nt* ♦ *vt* flechten.

plan [plæn] *n* Plan *m* ♦ *vt* planen; (*building,
schedule*) entwerfen ♦ *vi* planen; **to ~ to do
sth** planen *or* vorhaben, etw zu tun; **how
long do you ~ to stay?** wie lange haben Sie
vor, zu bleiben?; **to ~ for *or* on** (*expect*) sich

einstellen auf +acc; **to ~ on doing sth**
vorhaben, etw zu tun.

plane [pleɪn] n (AVIAT) Flugzeug nt; (MATH)
Ebene f; (fig: level) Niveau nt; (tool) Hobel m;
(also: ~ **tree**) Platane f ♦ vt (wood) hobeln ♦ vi
(NAUT, AUT) gleiten.

planet ['plænɪt] n Planet m.

planetarium [plænɪ'tɛərɪəm] n Planetarium nt.

plank [plæŋk] n (of wood) Brett nt; (fig: of
policy etc) Schwerpunkt m.

plankton ['plæŋktən] n Plankton nt.

planned economy ['plænd-] n Planwirtschaft
f.

planner ['plænə•] n Planer(in) m(f).

planning ['plænɪŋ] n Planung f.

planning permission (BRIT) n
Baugenehmigung f.

plant [plɑːnt] n (BOT) Pflanze f; (machinery)
Maschinen pl; (factory) Anlage f ♦ vt (seed,
plant, crops) pflanzen; (field, garden)
bepflanzen; (microphone, bomb etc)
anbringen; (incriminating evidence)
schleusen; (fig: object) stellen; (: kiss)
drücken.

plantation [plæn'teɪʃən] n Plantage f; (wood)
Anpflanzung f.

plant pot (BRIT) n Blumentopf m.

plaque [plæk] n (on building etc) Tafel f,
Plakette f; (on teeth) Zahnbelag m.

plasma ['plæzmə] n Plasma nt.

plaster ['plɑːstə•] n (for walls) Putz m; (also:
~ **of Paris**) Gips m; (BRIT: also: sticking ~)
Pflaster nt ♦ vt (wall, ceiling) verputzen; **in ~**
(BRIT) in Gips; **to ~ with** (cover) bepflastern
mit.

plasterboard ['plɑːstəbɔːd] n Gipskarton m.

plaster cast n (MED) Gipsverband m; (model,
statue) Gipsform f.

plastered ['plɑːstəd] (inf) adj (drunk)
sturzbesoffen.

plasterer ['plɑːstərə•] n Gipser m.

plastic ['plæstɪk] n Plastik nt ♦ adj (bucket, cup
etc) Plastik-; (flexible) formbar; **the ~ arts**
die bildende Kunst.

plastic bag n Plastiktüte f.

plastic bullet n Plastikgeschoß nt.

plastic explosive n Plastiksprengstoff m.

Plasticine ® ['plæstɪsiːn] n Plastilin nt.

plastic surgery n plastische Chirurgie f.

plate [pleɪt] n Teller m; (metal cover) Platte f;
(TYP) Druckplatte f; (in book: picture) Tafel f; (dental plate)
Gaumenplatte f; (on door) Schild nt; (gold/
silver plate) vergoldeter/versilberter Artikel
m; **that necklace is just ~** die Halskette ist
nur vergoldet/versilbert.

plateau ['plætəu] (pl ~**s** or ~**x**) n (GEOG)
Plateau nt, Hochebene f; (fig) stabiler
Zustand m.

plateful ['pleɪtful] n Teller m.

plate glass n Tafelglas nt.

platen ['plætən] n (on typewriter, printer)
(Schreib)walze f.

plate rack n Geschirrständer m.

platform ['plætfɔːm] n (stage) Podium nt; (for
landing, loading on etc, BRIT: of bus) Plattform
f; (RAIL) Bahnsteig m; (POL) Programm nt;
the train leaves from ~ 7 der Zug fährt von
Gleis 7 ab.

platform ticket (BRIT) n (RAIL)
Bahnsteigkarte f.

platinum ['plætɪnəm] n Platin nt.

platitude ['plætɪtjuːd] n Platitüde f,
Gemeinplatz m.

platonic [plə'tɔnɪk] adj (relationship)
platonisch.

platoon [plə'tuːn] n Zug m.

platter ['plætə•] n Platte f.

plaudits ['plɔːdɪts] npl Ovationen pl.

plausible ['plɔːzɪbl] adj (theory, excuse)
plausibel; (liar etc) glaubwürdig.

play [pleɪ] n (THEAT) (Theater)stück nt; (TV)
Fernsehspiel nt; (RADIO) Hörspiel nt;
(activity) Spiel nt ♦ vt spielen; (team,
opponent) spielen gegen ♦ vi spielen; **to
bring into ~** ins Spiel bringen; **a ~ on words**
ein Wortspiel nt; **to ~ a trick on sb** jdn
hereinlegen; **to ~ a part** or **role in sth** (fig)
eine Rolle bei etw spielen; **to ~ for time**
(fig) auf Zeit spielen, Zeit gewinnen wollen;
to ~ safe auf Nummer Sicher gehen; **to
~ into sb's hands** jdm in die Hände spielen.
► **play about with** vt fus = play around with.
► **play along with** vt fus (person) sich richten
nach; (plan, idea) eingehen auf +acc.
► **play around with** vt fus (fiddle with)
herumspielen mit.
► **play at** vt fus (do casually) spielen mit; **to
~ at being sb/sth** jdn/etw spielen.
► **play back** vt (recording) abspielen.
► **play down** vt herunterspielen.
► **play on** vt fus (sb's feelings etc) ausnutzen; **to
~ on sb's mind** jdm im Kopf herumgehen.
► **play up** vi (machine, knee etc)
Schwierigkeiten machen; (children) frech
werden.

play-act ['pleɪækt] vi Theater spielen.

playboy ['pleɪbɔɪ] n Playboy m.

player ['pleɪə•] n (SPORT, MUS) Spieler(in)
m(f); (THEAT) Schauspieler(in) m(f).

playful ['pleɪful] adj (person, gesture)
spielerisch; (animal) verspielt.

playgoer ['pleɪɡəuə•] n Theaterbesucher(in)
m(f).

playground ['pleɪɡraund] n (in park) Spielplatz
m; (in school) Schulhof m.

playgroup ['pleɪɡruːp] n Spielgruppe f.

playing card ['pleɪɪŋ-] n Spielkarte f.

playing field n Sportplatz m.

playmaker ['pleɪmeɪkə•] n (SPORT)
Spielmacher(in) m(f).

playmate ['pleɪmeɪt] n Spielkamerad(in) m(f).

play-off ['pleɪɔf] n Entscheidungsspiel nt.

playpen ['pleɪpɛn] n Laufstall m.

playroom ['pleɪruːm] n Spielzimmer nt.
playschool ['pleɪskuːl] n = **playgroup**.
plaything ['pleɪθɪŋ] n (also fig) Spielzeug nt.
playtime ['pleɪtaɪm] n (kleine) Pause f.
playwright ['pleɪraɪt] n Dramatiker(in) m(f).
plc (BRIT) n abbr (= public limited company)
≈ AG f.
plea [pliː] n (request) Bitte f; (LAW): **to enter a
~ of guilty/not guilty** sich schuldig/
unschuldig erklären; (excuse) Vorwand m.
plea bargaining n Verhandlungen zwischen
Anklage und Verteidigung mit dem Ziel,
bestimmte Anklagepunkte fallenzulassen,
wenn der Angeklagte sich in anderen
Punkten schuldig bekennt.
plead [pliːd] vi (LAW) vor Gericht eine
Schuld-/Unschuldserklärung abgeben ♦ vt
(LAW): **to ~ sb's case** jdn vertreten; (give as
excuse: ignorance, ill health etc) vorgeben,
sich berufen auf +acc; **to ~ with sb** (beg) jdn
inständig bitten; **to ~ for sth** um etw
nachsuchen; **to ~ guilty/not guilty** sich
schuldig/nicht schuldig bekennen.
pleasant ['plɛznt] adj angenehm; (smile)
freundlich.
pleasantly ['plɛzntlɪ] adv (surprised)
angenehm; (say, behave) freundlich.
pleasantries ['plɛzntrɪz] npl Höflichkeiten pl,
Nettigkeiten pl.
please [pliːz] excl bitte ♦ vt (satisfy)
zufriedenstellen ♦ vi (give pleasure) gefällig
sein; **~ Miss/Sir!** (to attract teacher's
attention) ≈ Frau/Herr X!; **yes, ~** ja, bitte;
my bill, ~ die Rechnung, bitte; **~ don't cry!**
bitte wein doch nicht!; **~ yourself!** (inf) wie
du willst!; **do as you ~** machen Sie, was Sie
für richtig halten.
pleased [pliːzd] adj (happy) erfreut; (satisfied)
zufrieden; **~ to meet you** freut mich(, Sie
kennenzulernen); **~ with** zufrieden mit; **we
are ~ to inform you that …** wir freuen uns,
Ihnen mitzuteilen, daß …
pleasing ['pliːzɪŋ] adj (remark, picture etc)
erfreulich; (person) sympathisch.
pleasurable ['plɛʒərəbl] adj angenehm.
pleasure ['plɛʒə'] n (happiness, satisfaction)
Freude f; (fun, enjoyable experience)
Vergnügen nt; **it's a ~**, **my ~** gern
geschehen; **with ~** gern, mit Vergnügen; **is
this trip for business or ~?** ist diese Reise
geschäftlich oder zum Vergnügen?
pleasure boat n Vergnügungsschiff nt.
pleasure cruise n Vergnügungsfahrt f.
pleat [pliːt] n Falte f.
pleb [plɛb] (inf: pej) n Prolet m.
plebiscite ['plɛbɪsɪt] n Volksentscheid m,
Plebiszit nt.
plectrum ['plɛktrəm] n Plektron nt, Plektrum
nt.
pledge [plɛdʒ] n (promise) Versprechen nt ♦ vt
(promise) versprechen; **to ~ sb to secrecy**
jdn zum Schweigen verpflichten.

plenary ['pliːnərɪ] adj (powers) unbeschränkt;
~ session Plenarsitzung f; **~ meeting**
Vollversammlung f.
plentiful ['plɛntɪful] adj reichlich.
plenty ['plɛntɪ] n (lots) eine Menge; (sufficient)
reichlich; **~ of** eine Menge; **we've got ~ of
time to get there** wir haben jede Menge
Zeit, dorthin zu kommen.
plethora ['plɛθərə] n: **a ~ of** eine Fülle von,
eine Unmenge an +dat.
pleurisy ['pluərɪsɪ] n Rippenfellentzündung f.
Plexiglas® ['plɛksɪglɑːs] (US) n Plexiglas®
nt.
pliable ['plaɪəbl] adj (material) biegsam; (fig:
person) leicht beeinflußbar.
pliant ['plaɪənt] adj = **pliable**.
pliers ['plaɪəz] npl Zange f.
plight [plaɪt] n (of person, country) Not f.
plimsolls ['plɪmsəlz] (BRIT) npl Turnschuhe pl.
plinth [plɪnθ] n Sockel m.
PLO n abbr (= Palestine Liberation Organization)
PLO f.
plod [plɔd] vi (walk) trotten; (fig) sich
abplagen.
plodder ['plɔdə'] (pej) n (slow worker) zäher
Arbeiter m, zähe Arbeiterin f.
plonk [plɔŋk] (inf) n (BRIT: wine) (billiger)
Wein m ♦ vt: **to ~ sth down** etw hinknallen.
plot [plɔt] n (secret plan) Komplott nt,
Verschwörung f; (of story, play, film)
Handlung f ♦ vt (sb's downfall etc) planen; (on
chart, graph) markieren ♦ vi (conspire) sich
verschwören; **a ~ of land** ein Grundstück; **a
vegetable ~** (BRIT) ein Gemüsebeet nt.
plotter ['plɔtə'] n (instrument, also COMPUT)
Plotter m.
plough, (US) **plow** [plau] n Pflug m ♦ vt
pflügen; **to ~ money into sth** (project etc)
Geld in etw acc stecken.
▶**plough back** vt (COMM) reinvestieren.
▶**plough into** vt fus (crowd) rasen in +acc.
ploughman, (US) **plowman** ['plaumən] (irreg:
like **man**) n Pflüger m.
ploughman's lunch ['plaumənz-] (BRIT) n
Imbiß aus Brot, Käse und Pickles.
plow etc (US) = **plough** etc.
ploy [plɔɪ] n Trick m.
pluck [plʌk] vt (fruit, flower, leaf) pflücken;
(musical instrument, eyebrows) zupfen; (bird)
rupfen ♦ n (courage) Mut m; **to ~ up courage**
allen Mut zusammennehmen.
plucky ['plʌkɪ] (inf) adj (person) tapfer.
plug [plʌg] n (ELEC) Stecker m; (stopper)
Stöpsel m; (AUT: also: **spark(ing) ~**)
Zündkerze f ♦ vt (hole) zustopfen; (inf:
advertise) Reklame machen für; **to give sb/
sth a ~** für jdn/etw Reklame machen.
▶**plug in** vt (ELEC) einstöpseln, anschließen
♦ vi angeschlossen werden.
plughole ['plʌghəul] (BRIT) n Abfluß m.
plum [plʌm] n (fruit) Pflaume f ♦ adj (inf): **a
~ job** ein Traumjob m.

plumage ['pluːmɪdʒ] n Gefieder nt.
plumb [plʌm] vt: **to ~ the depths of despair/
humiliation** die tiefste Verzweiflung/
Erniedrigung erleben.
▶**plumb in** vt (washing machine, shower etc)
anschließen, installieren.
plumber ['plʌmə*] n Installateur m, Klempner
m.
plumbing ['plʌmɪŋ] n (piping) Installationen
pl, Rohrleitungen pl; (trade) Klempnerei f;
(work) Installationsarbeiten pl.
plumb line n Lot nt, Senkblei nt.
plume [pluːm] n (of bird) Feder f; (on helmet,
horse's head) Federbusch m; ~ **of smoke**
Rauchfahne f.
plummet ['plʌmɪt] vi (bird, aircraft)
(hinunter)stürzen; (price, rate) rapide
absacken.
plump [plʌmp] adj (person) füllig, mollig.
▶**plump for** (inf) vt fus sich entscheiden für.
▶**plump up** vt (cushion) aufschütteln.
plunder ['plʌndə*] n (activity) Plünderung f;
(stolen things) Beute f ♦ vt (city, tomb)
plündern.
plunge [plʌndʒ] n (of bird, person) Sprung m;
(fig: of prices, rates etc) Sturz m ♦ vt (hand,
knife) stoßen ♦ vi (thing) stürzen; (bird,
person) sich stürzen; (fig: prices, rates etc)
abfallen, stürzen; **to take the ~** (fig) den
Sprung wagen; **the room was ~d into
darkness** das Zimmer war in Dunkelheit
getaucht.
plunger ['plʌndʒə*] n (for sink) Sauger m.
plunging ['plʌndʒɪŋ] adj: ~ **neckline** tiefer
Ausschnitt m.
pluperfect [pluː'pəːfɪkt] n: **the ~** das
Plusquamperfekt.
plural ['pluərl] adj Plural- ♦ n Plural m,
Mehrzahl f.
plus [plʌs] n (also: ~ **sign**) Pluszeichen nt
♦ prep, adj plus; **it's a ~** (fig) es ist ein Vorteil
or ein Pluspunkt; **ten/twenty ~** (more than)
über zehn/zwanzig; **B ~** (SCOL) ≈ Zwei plus.
plus fours npl Überfallhose f.
plush [plʌʃ] adj (car, hotel etc) feudal ♦ n
(fabric) Plüsch m.
plutonium [pluː'təunɪəm] n Plutonium nt.
ply [plaɪ] vt (a trade) ausüben, nachgehen +dat;
(tool) gebrauchen, anwenden ♦ vi (ship)
verkehren ♦ n (of wool, rope) Stärke f; (also:
~**wood**) Sperrholz nt; **to ~ sb with drink** jdn
ausgiebig bewirten; **to ~ sb with questions**
jdm viele Fragen stellen; **two-/three-
~ wool** zwei-/dreifädige Wolle.
plywood ['plaɪwud] n Sperrholz nt.
PM (BRIT) abbr = **Prime Minister.**
p.m. adv abbr (= post meridiem) nachmittags;
(later) abends.
PMT abbr = **premenstrual tension.**
pneumatic [njuː'mætɪk] adj pneumatisch.
pneumatic drill n Preßluftbohrer m.
pneumonia [njuː'məunɪə] n

Lungenentzündung f.
PO n abbr = **Post Office**; (MIL) = **petty officer.**
p.o. abbr = **postal order.**
POA (BRIT) n abbr (= Prison Officers'
Association) Gewerkschaft der
Gefängnisbeamten.
poach [pəutʃ] vt (steal: fish, animals, birds)
illegal erbeuten, wildern; (CULIN: egg)
pochieren; (: fish) dünsten ♦ vi (steal)
wildern.
poached [pəutʃt] adj: ~ **eggs** verlorene Eier.
poacher ['pəutʃə*] n Wilderer m.
PO Box n abbr (= Post Office Box) Postf.
pocket ['pɔkɪt] n Tasche f; (fig: small area)
vereinzelter Bereich m ♦ vt (put in one's
pocket, steal) einstecken; **to be out of ~**
(BRIT) Verlust machen; ~ **of resistance**
Widerstandsnest nt.
pocketbook ['pɔkɪtbuk] n (notebook)
Notizbuch nt; (US: wallet) Brieftasche f;
(: handbag) Handtasche f.
pocket calculator n Taschenrechner m.
pocketknife ['pɔkɪtnaɪf] n Taschenmesser nt.
pocket money n Taschengeld nt.
pocket-sized ['pɔkɪtsaɪzd] adj im
Taschenformat.
pockmarked ['pɔkmɑːkt] adj (face)
pockennarbig.
pod [pɔd] n Hülse f.
podgy ['pɔdʒɪ] (inf) adj rundlich, pummelig.
podiatrist [pɔ'diːətrɪst] (US) n
Fußspezialist(in) m(f).
podiatry [pɔ'diːətrɪ] (US) n Fußpflege f.
podium ['pəudɪəm] n Podium nt.
POE n abbr (= port of embarkation)
Ausgangshafen m; (= port of entry)
Eingangshafen m.
poem ['pəuɪm] n Gedicht nt.
poet ['pəuɪt] n Dichter(in) m(f).
poetic [pəu'etɪk] adj poetisch, dichterisch;
(fig) malerisch.
poetic justice n ausgleichende
Gerechtigkeit f.
poetic licence n dichterische Freiheit f.
poet laureate n Hofdichter m.

Poet laureate ist in Großbritannien ein Dichter,
der ein Gehalt als Hofdichter bezieht und kraft
seines Amtes ein lebenslanges Mitglied des
britischen Königshofes ist. Der Poet Laureate
schrieb traditionellerweise ausführliche
Gedichte zu Staatsanlässen; ein Brauch, der
heute kaum noch befolgt wird. Der erste Poet
Laureate 1616 war Ben Jonson.

---

poetry ['pəuɪtrɪ] n (poems) Gedichte pl;
(writing) Poesie f.
poignant ['pɔɪnjənt] adj ergreifend; (situation)
herzzerreißend.
point [pɔɪnt] n Punkt m; (of needle, knife etc)
Spitze f; (purpose) Sinn m, Zweck m;
(significant part) Entscheidende(s) nt;

(*moment*) Zeitpunkt *m*; (*ELEC: also:* **power** ~) Steckdose *f*; (*also:* **decimal** ~) ≈ Komma *nt* ♦ *vt* (*show, mark*) deuten auf +*acc* ♦ *vi* (*with finger, stick etc*) zeigen, deuten; **points** *npl* (*AUT*) (Unterbrecher)kontakte *pl*; (*RAIL*) Weichen *pl*; **two** ~ **five** (= 2.5) zwei Komma fünf; **good/bad** ~**s** (*of person*) gute/ schlechte Seiten *or* Eigenschaften; **the train stops at Carlisle and all** ~**s south** der Zug hält in Carlisle und allen Orten weiter südlich; **to be on the** ~ **of doing sth** im Begriff sein, etw zu tun; **to make a** ~ **of doing sth** besonders darauf achten, etw zu tun; (*make a habit of*) Wert darauf legen, etw zu tun; **to get/miss the** ~ verstehen/nicht verstehen, worum es geht; **to come** *or* **get to the** ~ zur Sache kommen; **to make one's** ~ seinen Standpunkt klarmachen; **that's the whole** ~! darum geht es ja gerade!; **what's the** ~? was soll's?; **to be beside the** ~ unwichtig *or* irrelevant sein; **there's no** ~ **talking to you** es ist sinnlos, mit dir zu reden; **you've got a** ~ **there!** da könnten Sie recht haben!; **in** ~ **of fact** in Wirklichkeit; ~ **of sale** (*COMM*) Verkaufsstelle *f*; **to** ~ **sth at sb** (*gun etc*) etw auf jdn richten; (*finger*) mit etw auf jdn *acc* zeigen; **to** ~ **at** zeigen auf +*acc*; **to** ~ **to** zeigen auf +*acc*; (*fig*) hinweisen auf +*acc*.

▶**point out** *vt* hinweisen auf +*acc*.

▶**point to** *vt fus* hindeuten auf +*acc*.

point-blank ['pɔɪnt'blæŋk] *adv* (*say, ask*) direkt; (*refuse*) glatt; (*also:* **at** ~ **range**) aus unmittelbarer Entfernung.

point duty (*BRIT*) *n:* **to be on** ~ Verkehrsdienst haben.

pointed ['pɔɪntɪd] *adj* spitz; (*fig: remark*) spitz, scharf.

pointedly ['pɔɪntɪdlɪ] *adv* (*ask, reply etc*) spitz, scharf.

pointer ['pɔɪntə*] *n* (*on chart, machine*) Zeiger *m*; (*fig: piece of information or advice*) Hinweis *m*; (*stick*) Zeigestock *m*; (*dog*) Pointer *m*.

pointing ['pɔɪntɪŋ] *n* (*CONSTR*) Ausfugung *f*.

pointless ['pɔɪntlɪs] *adj* sinnlos, zwecklos.

point of view *n* Ansicht *f*, Standpunkt *m*; **from a practical** ~ von einem praktischen Standpunkt aus.

poise [pɔɪz] *n* (*composure*) Selbstsicherheit *f*; (*balance*) Haltung *f* ♦ *vt:* **to be** ~**d for sth** (*fig*) bereit zu etw sein.

poison ['pɔɪzn] *n* Gift *nt* ♦ *vt* vergiften.

poisoning ['pɔɪznɪŋ] *n* Vergiftung *f*.

poisonous ['pɔɪznəs] *adj* (*animal, plant*) Gift-; (*fumes, chemicals etc*) giftig; (*fig: rumours etc*) zersetzend.

poison-pen letter [pɔɪzn'pɛn] *n* anonymer Brief *m* (*mit Indiskretionen*).

poke [pəuk] *vt* (*with finger, stick etc*) stoßen; (*fire*) schüren ♦ *n* (*jab*) Stoß *m*, Schubs *m* (*inf*); **to** ~ **sth in(to)** (*put*) etw stecken in +*acc*; **to** ~ **one's head out of the window** seinen

Kopf aus dem Fenster strecken; **to** ~ **fun at sb** sich über jdn lustig machen.

▶**poke about** *vi* (*search*) herumstochern.

▶**poke out** *vi* (*stick out*) vorstehen.

poker ['pəukə*] *n* (*metal bar*) Schürhaken *m*; (*CARDS*) Poker *nt*.

poker-faced ['pəukə'feɪst] *adj* mit unbewegter Miene, mit Pokergesicht.

poky ['pəukɪ] (*pej*) *adj* (*room, house*) winzig.

Poland ['pəulənd] *n* Polen *nt*.

polar ['pəulə*] *adj* (*icecap*) polar; (*region*) Polar-.

polar bear *n* Eisbär *m*.

polarize ['pəuləraɪz] *vt* polarisieren.

Pole [pəul] *n* Pole *m*, Polin *f*.

pole [pəul] *n* (*post, stick*) Stange *f*; (*flag pole, telegraph pole etc*) Mast *m*; (*GEOG, ELEC*) Pol *m*; **to be** ~**s apart** (*fig*) durch Welten (voneinander) getrennt sein.

poleaxe, (*US*) **poleax** ['pəulæks] *vt* (*fig*) umhauen.

pole bean (*US*) *n* (*runner bean*) Stangenbohne *f*.

polecat ['pəulkæt] *n* Iltis *m*.

Pol. Econ. ['pɔlɪkɔn] *n abbr* (= *political economy*) Volkswirtschaft *f*.

polemic [pɔ'lɛmɪk] *n* Polemik *f*.

Pole Star *n* Polarstern *m*.

pole vault ['pəulvɔːlt] *n* Stabhochsprung *m*.

police [pə'liːs] *npl* (*organization*) Polizei *f*; (*members*) Polizisten *pl*, Polizeikräfte *pl* ♦ *vt* (*street, area, town*) kontrollieren; **a large number of** ~ **were hurt** viele Polizeikräfte wurden verletzt.

police car *n* Polizeiauto *nt*.

police constable (*BRIT*) *n* Polizist(in) *m(f)*, Polizeibeamte(r) *m*, Polizeibeamtin *f*.

police department (*US*) *n* Polizei *f*.

police force *n* Polizei *f*.

policeman [pə'liːsmən] (*irreg: like* **man**) *n* Polizist *m*.

police officer *n* = **police constable**.

police record *n:* **to have a** ~ vorbestraft sein.

police state *n* (*POL*) Polizeistaat *m*.

police station *n* Polizeiwache *f*.

policewoman [pə'liːswumən] (*irreg: like* **woman**) *n* Polizistin *f*.

policy ['pɔlɪsɪ] *n* (*POL, ECON*) Politik *f*; (*also:* **insurance** ~) (Versicherungs)police *f*; (*of newspaper*) Grundsatz *m*; **to take out a** ~ (*INSURANCE*) eine Versicherung abschließen.

policyholder ['pɔlɪsɪ'həuldə*] *n* (*INSURANCE*) Versicherungsnehmer(in) *m(f)*.

policy making *n* Strategieplanung *f*.

polio ['pəulɪəu] *n* Kinderlähmung *f*, Polio *f*.

Polish ['pəulɪʃ] *adj* polnisch ♦ *n* (*LING*) Polnisch *nt*.

polish ['pɔlɪʃ] *n* (*for shoes*) Creme *f*; (*for furniture*) Politur *f*; (*for floors*) Bohnerwachs *nt*; (*shine: on shoes, floor etc*) Glanz *m*; (*fig: refinement*) Schliff *m* ♦ *vt* (*shoes*) putzen;

(*floor, furniture etc*) polieren.
▶**polish off** vt (*work*) erledigen; (*food*) verputzen.
polished ['pɒlɪʃt] adj (*fig: person*) mit Schliff; (: *style*) geschliffen.
polite [pə'laɪt] adj höflich; (*company, society*) fein; **it's not ~ to do that** es gehört sich nicht, das zu tun.
politely [pə'laɪtlɪ] adv höflich.
politeness [pə'laɪtnɪs] n Höflichkeit f.
politic ['pɒlɪtɪk] adj klug, vernünftig.
political [pə'lɪtɪkl] adj politisch.
political asylum n politisches Asyl nt.
politically [pə'lɪtɪklɪ] adv politisch; **~ correct** politisch korrekt.
politician [pɒlɪ'tɪʃən] n Politiker(in) m(f).
politics ['pɒlɪtɪks] n Politik f ♦ npl (*beliefs, opinions*) politische Ansichten pl.
polka ['pɒlkə] n Polka f.
poll [pəul] n (*also:* **opinion ~**) (Meinungs)-umfrage f; (*election*) Wahl f ♦ vt (*in opinion poll*) befragen; (*number of votes*) erhalten; **to go to the ~s** (*voters*) zur Wahl gehen; (*government*) sich den Wählern stellen.
pollen ['pɒlən] n Pollen m, Blütenstaub m.
pollen count n Pollenkonzentration f.
pollinate ['pɒlɪneɪt] vt bestäuben.
polling booth ['pəulɪŋ-] n (*BRIT*) n Wahlkabine f.
polling day (*BRIT*) n Wahltag m.
polling station (*BRIT*) n Wahllokal nt.
pollster ['pəulstə*] n Meinungsforscher(in) m(f).
poll tax n Kopfsteuer f.
pollutant [pə'lu:tənt] n Schadstoff m.
pollute [pə'lu:t] vt verschmutzen.
pollution [pə'lu:ʃən] n (*process*) Verschmutzung f; (*substances*) Schmutz m.
polo ['pəuləu] n Polo nt.
polo neck n (*jumper*) Rollkragenpullover m.
polo-necked ['pəuləunɛkt] adj (*jumper, sweater*) Rollkragen-.
poltergeist ['pɔːltəgaɪst] n Poltergeist m.
poly ['pɒlɪ] (*BRIT*) n abbr = **polytechnic**.
poly bag (*inf*) n Plastiktüte f.
polyester [pɒlɪ'ɛstə*] n Polyester m.
polygamy [pə'lɪgəmɪ] n Polygamie f.
polygraph ['pɒlɪgrɑːf] (*US*) n (*lie detector*) Lügendetektor m.
Polynesia [pɒlɪ'niːzɪə] n Polynesien nt.
Polynesian [pɒlɪ'niːzɪən] adj polynesisch ♦ n Polynesier(in) m(f).
polyp ['pɒlɪp] n Polyp m.
polystyrene [pɒlɪ'staɪriːn] n ≈ Styropor ® nt.
polytechnic [pɒlɪ'tɛknɪk] n technische Hochschule f.
polythene ['pɒlɪθiːn] n Polyäthylen nt.
polythene bag n Plastiktüte f.
polyurethane [pɒlɪ'juərɪθeɪn] n Polyurethan nt.
pomegranate ['pɒmɪgrænɪt] n Granatapfel m.
pommel ['pɒml] n (*on saddle*) Sattelknopf m

♦ vt (*US*) = **pummel**.
pomp [pɒmp] n Pomp m, Prunk m.
pompom ['pɒmpɒm] n Troddel f.
pompous ['pɒmpəs] (*pej*) adj (*person*) aufgeblasen; (*piece of writing*) geschwollen.
pond [pɒnd] n Teich m.
ponder ['pɒndə*] vt nachdenken über +acc ♦ vi nachdenken.
ponderous ['pɒndərəs] adj (*style, language*) schwerfällig.
pong [pɒŋ] (*BRIT: inf*) n Gestank m ♦ vi stinken.
pontiff ['pɒntɪf] n Papst m.
pontificate [pɒn'tɪfɪkeɪt] vi dozieren.
pontoon [pɒn'tuːn] n (*floating platform*) Ponton m; (*CARDS*) Siebzehnundvier nt.
pony ['pəunɪ] n Pony nt.
ponytail ['pəunɪteɪl] n Pferdeschwanz m; **to have one's hair in a ~** einen Pferdeschwanz tragen.
pony trekking (*BRIT*) n Ponytrecken nt.
poodle ['puːdl] n Pudel m.
pooh-pooh [puː'puː] vt verächtlich abtun.
pool [puːl] n (*pond*) Teich m; (*also: swimming ~*) Schwimmbad nt; (*of blood*) Lache f; (*SPORT*) Poolbillard nt; (*of cash, workers*) Bestand m; (*CARDS: kitty*) Kasse f; (*COMM: consortium*) Interessengemeinschaft f ♦ vt (*money*) zusammenlegen; (*knowledge, resources*) vereinigen; **pools** npl (*football pools*) ≈ Fußballtoto nt; **a ~ of sunlight/shade** eine sonnige/schattige Stelle; **car ~** Fahrgemeinschaft f; **typing ~**, (*US*) **secretary ~** Schreibzentrale f; **to do the (football) ~s** ≈ im Fußballtoto spielen.
poor [puə*] adj arm; (*bad*) schlecht ♦ npl: **the ~** die Armen pl; **~ in** (*resources etc*) arm an +dat; **~ Bob** der arme Bob.
poorly ['puəlɪ] adj elend, krank ♦ adv (*badly: designed, paid, furnished*) schlecht.
pop [pɒp] n (*MUS*) Pop m; (*fizzy drink*) Limonade f; (*US: inf: father*) Papa m; (*sound*) Knall m ♦ vi (*balloon*) platzen; (*cork*) knallen ♦ vt: **to ~ sth into/onto sth** etw schnell in etw acc stecken/auf etw acc legen; **his eyes ~ped out of his head** (*inf*) ihm fielen fast die Augen aus dem Kopf; **she ~ped her head out of the window** sie streckte den Kopf aus dem Fenster.
▶**pop in** vi vorbeikommen.
▶**pop out** vi kurz weggehen.
▶**pop up** vi auftauchen.
popcorn ['pɒpkɔːn] n Popcorn nt.
pope [pəup] n Papst m.
poplar ['pɒplə*] n Pappel f.
poplin ['pɒplɪn] n Popeline f.
popper ['pɒpə*] (*BRIT: inf*) n (*for fastening*) Druckknopf m.
poppy ['pɒpɪ] n Mohn m.
poppycock ['pɒpɪkɒk] (*inf*) n Humbug m, dummes Zeug nt.
Popsicle ® ['pɒpsɪkl] (*US*) n Eis nt am Stiel.

pop star n Popstar m.
populace ['pɔpjuləs] n: **the ~** die
Bevölkerung, das Volk.
popular ['pɔpjulə*] adj (*well-liked, fashionable*)
beliebt, populär; (*general, non-specialist*)
allgemein; (*idea*) weitverbreitet; (*POL:
movement*) Volks-; (: *cause*) des Volkes; **to
be ~ with** beliebt sein bei; **the ~ press** die
Boulevardpresse.
popularity [pɔpju'lærɪtɪ] n Beliebtheit f,
Popularität f.
popularize ['pɔpjuləraɪz] vt (*sport, music,
fashion*) populär machen; (*science, ideas*)
popularisieren.
popularly ['pɔpjuləlɪ] adv (*commonly*)
allgemein.
population [pɔpju'leɪʃən] n Bevölkerung f; (*of
a species*) Zahl f, Population f; **a prison ~ of
44,000** (eine Zahl von) 44.000
Gefängnisinsassen; **the civilian ~** die
Zivilbevölkerung.
population explosion n Bevölkerungs-
explosion f.
populous ['pɔpjuləs] adj dicht besiedelt.
porcelain ['pɔ:slɪn] n Porzellan nt.
porch [pɔ:tʃ] n (*entrance*) Vorbau m; (*US*)
Veranda f.
porcupine ['pɔ:kjupaɪn] n Stachelschwein nt.
pore [pɔ:*] n Pore f ♦ vi: **to ~ over** (*book etc*)
gründlich studieren.
pork [pɔ:k] n Schweinefleisch nt.
pork chop n Schweinekotelett nt.
porn [pɔ:n] (*inf*) n Porno m; **~ channel/
magazine/shop** Pornokanal m/-magazin
nt/-laden m.
pornographic [pɔ:nə'græfɪk] adj
pornographisch.
pornography [pɔ:'nɔgrəfɪ] n Pornographie f.
porous ['pɔ:rəs] adj porös.
porpoise ['pɔ:pəs] n Tümmler m.
porridge ['pɔrɪdʒ] n Haferbrei m, Porridge nt.
port [pɔ:t] n (*harbour*) Hafen m; (*NAUT: left
side*) Backbord nt; (*wine*) Portwein m;
(*COMPUT*) Port m ♦ adj (*NAUT*) Backbord-; **to
~** (*NAUT*) an Backbord; **~ of call** (*NAUT*)
Anlaufhafen nt.
portable ['pɔ:təbl] adj (*television, typewriter etc*)
tragbar, portabel.
portal ['pɔ:tl] n Portal nt.
portcullis [pɔ:t'kʌlɪs] n Fallgitter nt.
portend [pɔ:'tend] vt hindeuten auf +acc.
portent ['pɔ:tent] n Vorzeichen nt.
porter ['pɔ:tə*] n (*for luggage*) Gepäckträger
m; (*doorkeeper*) Pförtner m; (*US: RAIL*)
Schlafwagenschaffner(in) m(f).
portfolio [pɔ:t'fəulɪəu] n (*case*) Aktenmappe f;
(*POL*) Geschäftsbereich m; (*FIN*)
Portefeuille nt; (*of artist*) Kollektion f.
porthole ['pɔ:thəul] n Bullauge nt.
portico ['pɔ:tɪkəu] n Säulenhalle f.
portion ['pɔ:ʃən] n (*part*) Teil m; (*helping of
food*) Portion f.

portly ['pɔ:tlɪ] adj beleibt, korpulent.
portrait ['pɔ:treɪt] n Porträt nt.
portray [pɔ:'treɪ] vt darstellen.
portrayal [pɔ:'treɪəl] n Darstellung f.
Portugal ['pɔ:tjugl] n Portugal nt.
Portuguese [pɔ:tju'gi:z] adj portugiesisch ♦ n
inv (*person*) Portugiese m, Portugiesin f;
(*LING*) Portugiesisch nt.
Portuguese man-of-war [-mænəv'wɔ:*] n
(*ZOOL*) Röhrenqualle f, Portugiesische
Galeere f.
pose [pəuz] n Pose f ♦ vt (*question, problem*)
aufwerfen; (*danger*) mit sich bringen ♦ vi: **to
~ as** (*pretend*) sich ausgeben als; **to strike a
~** sich in Positur werfen; **to ~ for** (*painting
etc*) Modell sitzen für, posieren für.
poser ['pəuzə*] n (*problem, puzzle*) harte Nuß f
(*inf*); (*person*) = **poseur.**
poseur [pəu'zɜ:*] (*pej*) n Angeber(in) m(f).
posh [pɔʃ] (*inf*) adj vornehm; **to talk ~**
vornehm daherreden.
position [pə'zɪʃən] n (*place: of thing, person*)
Position f, Lage f; (*of person's body*) Stellung
f; (*job*) Stelle f; (*in race etc*) Platz m; (*attitude*)
Haltung f, Standpunkt m; (*situation*) Lage
♦ vt (*person, thing*) stellen; **to be in a ~ to do
sth** in der Lage sein, etw zu tun.
positive ['pɔzɪtɪv] adj positiv; (*certain*) sicher;
(*decisive: action, policy*) konstruktiv.
positively ['pɔzɪtɪvlɪ] adv (*emphatic: rude,
stupid etc*) eindeutig; (*encouragingly, also
ELEC*) positiv; **the body has been
~ identified** die Leiche ist eindeutig
identifiziert worden.
posse ['pɔsɪ] (*US*) n (Polizei)truppe f.
possess [pə'zes] vt besitzen; (*subj: feeling,
belief*) Besitz ergreifen von; **like a man ~ed**
wie besessen; **whatever ~ed you to do it?**
was ist in dich gefahren, das zu tun?
possession [pə'zeʃən] n Besitz m; **possessions**
npl (*belongings*) Besitz m; **to take ~ of** Besitz
ergreifen von.
possessive [pə'zesɪv] adj (*nature etc*)
besitzergreifend; (*LING: pronoun*)
Possessiv-; (: *adjective*) besitzanzeigend; **to
be ~ about sb/sth** Besitzansprüche an jdn/
etw acc stellen.
possessiveness [pə'zesɪvnɪs] n
besitzergreifende Art f.
possessor [pə'zesə*] n Besitzer(in) m(f).
possibility [pɔsɪ'bɪlɪtɪ] n Möglichkeit f.
possible ['pɔsɪbl] adj möglich; **it's ~** (*may be
true*) es ist möglich, es kann sein; **it's ~ to
do it** es ist machbar *or* zu machen; **as far as
~** so weit wie möglich; **if ~** falls *or* wenn
möglich; **as soon as ~** so bald wie möglich.
possibly ['pɔsɪblɪ] adv (*perhaps*)
möglicherweise, vielleicht; (*conceivably*)
überhaupt; **if you ~ can** falls überhaupt
möglich; **what could they ~ want?** was um
alles in der Welt wollen sie?; **I cannot
~ come** ich kann auf keinen Fall kommen.

post [pəust] *n* (*BRIT*) Post *f*; (*pole, goal post*)
Pfosten *m*; (*job*) Stelle *f*; (*MIL*) Posten *m*; (*also:*
trading ~) Handelsniederlassung *f* ♦ *vt*
(*BRIT: letter*) aufgeben; (*MIL*) aufstellen; **by**
~ (*BRIT*) per Post; **by return of ~** (*BRIT*)
postwendend, umgehend; **to keep sb ~ed**
(*informed*) jdn auf dem laufenden halten; **to**
~ sb to (*town, country*) jdn versetzen nach;
(*embassy, office*) jdn versetzen zu; (*MIL*) jdn
abkommandieren nach.

▶**post up** *vt* anschlagen.

post... [pəust] *pref* Post-, post-; **~-1990** nach
1990.

postage ['pəustɪdʒ] *n* Porto *nt*.

postage stamp *n* Briefmarke *f*.

postal ['pəustl] *adj* (*charges, service*) Post-.

postal order (*BRIT*) *n* Postanweisung *f*.

postbag ['pəustbæg] (*BRIT*) *n* Postsack *m*;
(*letters*) Posteingang *m*.

postbox ['pəustbɔks] *n* Briefkasten *m*.

postcard ['pəustkɑːd] *n* Postkarte *f*.

postcode ['pəustkəud] (*BRIT*) *n* Postleitzahl *f*.

postdate ['pəust'deɪt] *vt* (*cheque*) vordatieren.

poster ['pəustə*] *n* Poster *nt*, Plakat *nt*.

poste restante [pəust'rɛstãːnt] (*BRIT*) *n* Stelle
f für postlagernde Sendungen ♦ *adv*
postlagernd.

posterior [pɔs'tɪərɪə*] (*hum*) *n*
Allerwerteste(r) *m*.

posterity [pɔs'tɛrɪtɪ] *n* die Nachwelt.

poster paint *n* Plakatfarbe *f*.

post exchange (*US*) *n* (*MIL*) *Laden für US-
Militärpersonal*.

post-free [pəust'friː] (*BRIT*) *adj, adv* portofrei.

postgraduate ['pəust'grædjuət] *n*
Graduierte(r) *f(m)* (*im Weiterstudium*).

posthumous ['pɔstjuməs] *adj* posthum.

posthumously ['pɔstjuməslɪ] *adv* posthum.

posting ['pəustɪŋ] *n* (*job*) Stelle *f*.

postman ['pəustmən] (*irreg: like* **man**) *n*
Briefträger *m*, Postbote *m*.

postmark ['pəustmɑːk] *n* Poststempel *m*.

postmaster ['pəustmɑːstə*] *n* Postmeister *m*.

Postmaster General *n* ≈ Postminister(in)
m(f).

postmistress ['pəustmɪstrɪs] *n* Postmeisterin
f.

postmortem [pəust'mɔːtəm] *n* (*MED*)
Obduktion *f*; (*fig*) nachträgliche Erörterung
f.

postnatal ['pəust'neɪtl] *adj* nach der Geburt,
postnatal.

post office *n* (*building*) Post *f*, Postamt *nt*; **the**
Post Office (*organization*) die Post.

Post Office Box *n* Postfach *nt*.

post-paid ['pəust'peɪd] *adj, adv* = **post-free**.

postpone [pəus'pəun] *vt* verschieben.

postponement [pəus'pəunmənt] *n* Aufschub
m.

postscript ['pəustskrɪpt] *n* (*to letter*)
Nachschrift *f*, PS *nt*.

postulate ['pɔstjuleɪt] *vt* ausgehen von,

postulieren.

posture ['pɔstʃə*] *n* (*also fig*) Haltung *f* ♦ *vi*
(*pej*) posieren.

postwar [pəust'wɔː*] *adj* Nachkriegs-.

posy ['pəuzɪ] *n* Blumensträußchen *nt*.

pot [pɔt] *n* Topf *m*; (*teapot, coffee pot, potful*)
Kanne *f*; (*inf: marijuana*) Pot *nt* ♦ *vt* (*plant*)
eintopfen; **to go to ~** (*inf*) auf den Hund
kommen; **~s of** (*BRIT: inf*) jede Menge.

potash ['pɔtæʃ] *n* Pottasche *f*.

potassium [pə'tæsɪəm] *n* Kalium *nt*.

potato [pə'teɪtəu] (*pl* **~es**) *n* Kartoffel *f*.

potato chips (*US*) *npl* = **potato crisps**.

potato crisps *npl* Kartoffelchips *pl*.

potato flour *n* Kartoffelmehl *nt*.

potato peeler *n* Kartoffelschäler *m*.

potbellied ['pɔtbɛlɪd] *adj* (*from overeating*)
dickbäuchig; (*from malnutrition*)
blähbäuchig.

potency ['pəutnsɪ] *n* (*sexual*) Potenz *f*; (*of drink,*
drug) Stärke *f*.

potent ['pəutnt] *adj* (*powerful*) stark; (*sexually*)
potent.

potentate ['pəutnteɪt] *n* Machthaber *m*,
Potentat *m*.

potential [pə'tɛnʃl] *adj* potentiell ♦ *n* Potential
nt; **to have ~** (*person, machine*) Fähigkeiten
or Potential haben; (*idea, plan*) ausbaufähig
sein.

potentially [pə'tɛnʃəlɪ] *adv* potentiell; **it's**
~ dangerous es könnte gefährlich sein.

pothole ['pɔthəul] *n* (*in road*) Schlagloch *nt*;
(*cave*) Höhle *f*.

potholing ['pɔthəulɪŋ] (*BRIT*) *n*: **to go ~**
Höhlenforschung betreiben.

potion ['pəuʃən] *n* Elixier *nt*.

potluck [pɔt'lʌk] *n*: **to take ~** sich
überraschen lassen.

potpourri [pəu'purɪ] *n* (*dried petals*)
Duftsträußchen *nt*; (*fig*) Sammelsurium *nt*.

pot roast *n* Schmorbraten *m*.

pot shot *n*: **to take a ~ at** aufs Geratewohl
schießen auf +*acc*.

potted ['pɔtɪd] *adj* (*food*) eingemacht; (*plant*)
Topf-; (*abbreviated: history etc*) Kurz-,
kurzgefaßt.

potter ['pɔtə*] *n* Töpfer(in) *m(f)* ♦ *vi*: **to**
~ around, ~ about (*BRIT*) herumhantieren;
to ~ around the house im Haus
herumwerkeln.

potter's wheel *n* Töpferscheibe *f*.

pottery ['pɔtərɪ] *n* (*pots, dishes etc*) Keramik *f*,
Töpferwaren *pl*; (*work, hobby*) Töpfern *nt*;
(*factory, workshop*) Töpferei *f*; **a piece of ~**
ein Töpferstück *nt*.

potty ['pɔtɪ] *adj* (*inf: mad*) verrückt ♦ *n* (*for*
child) Töpfchen *nt*.

potty-training ['pɔtɪtreɪnɪŋ] *n* Entwöhnung *f*
vom Windeltragen.

pouch [pautʃ] *n* Beutel *m* (*also ZOOL*).

pouf(fe) [puːf] *n* (*stool*) gepolsterter Hocker
m.

poultice ['pəultɪs] n Umschlag m.
poultry ['pəultrɪ] n Geflügel nt.
poultry farm n Geflügelfarm f.
poultry farmer n Geflügelzüchter(in) m(f).
pounce [pauns] vi: **to ~ on** (also fig) sich stürzen auf +acc.
pound [paund] n (unit of money) Pfund nt; (unit of weight) (britisches) Pfund (= 453,6g); (for dogs) Zwinger m; (for cars) Abholstelle f (für abgeschleppte Fahrzeuge) ♦ vt (beat: table, wall etc) herumhämmern auf +dat; (crush: grain, spice etc) zerstoßen; (bombard) beschießen ♦ vi (heart) klopfen, pochen; (head) dröhnen; **half a ~ of butter** ein halbes Pfund Butter; **a five-~ note** ein Fünfpfundschein m.
pounding ['paundɪŋ] n: **to take a ~** (fig) schwer angegriffen werden; (team) eine Schlappe einstecken müssen.
pound sterling n Pfund nt Sterling.
pour [pɔː] vt (tea, wine etc) gießen; (cereal etc) schütten ♦ vi strömen; **to ~ sb a glass of wine/a cup of tea** jdm ein Glas Wein/eine Tasse Tee einschenken; **to ~ with rain** in Strömen gießen.
►**pour away** vt wegschütten.
►**pour in** vi (people) hereinströmen; (letters etc) massenweise eintreffen.
►**pour out** vi (people) herausströmen ♦ vt (tea, wine etc) eingießen; (fig: thoughts, feelings, etc) freien Lauf lassen +dat.
pouring ['pɔːrɪŋ] adj: **~ rain** strömender Regen m.
pout [paut] vi einen Schmollmund ziehen.
poverty ['pɔvətɪ] n Armut f.
poverty line n Armutsgrenze f.
poverty-stricken ['pɔvətɪstrɪkn] adj verarmt, notleidend.
poverty trap (BRIT) n gleichbleibend schlechte wirtschaftliche Situation aufgrund des Wegfalls von Sozialleistungen bei verbessertem Einkommen, Armutsfalle f.
POW n abbr = **prisoner of war**.
powder ['paudə] n Pulver nt ♦ vt: **to ~ one's face** sich dat das Gesicht pudern; **to ~ one's nose** (euph) kurz mal verschwinden.
powder compact n Puderdose f.
powdered milk ['paudəd-] n Milchpulver nt.
powder keg n (also fig) Pulverfaß nt.
powder puff n Puderquaste f.
powder room n (euph) n Damentoilette f.
power ['pauə] n (control, legal right) Macht f; (ability) Fähigkeit f; (of muscles, ideas, words) Kraft f; (of explosion, engine) Gewalt f; (electricity) Strom m; **2 to the ~ (of) 3** (MATH) 2 hoch 3; **to do everything in one's ~ to help** alles in seiner Macht Stehende tun, um zu helfen; **a world ~** eine Weltmacht; **the ~s that be** (authority) diejenigen, die das Sagen haben; **~ of attorney** Vollmacht f; **to be in ~** (POL etc) an der Macht sein.
powerboat ['pauəbəut] n schnelles Motorboot

nt, Rennboot nt.
power cut n Stromausfall m.
powered ['pauəd] adj: **~ by** angetrieben von; **nuclear-~ submarine** atomgetriebenes U-Boot.
power failure n Stromausfall m.
powerful ['pauəful] adj (person, organization) mächtig; (body, voice, blow etc) kräftig; (engine) stark; (unpleasant: smell) streng; (emotion) überwältigend; (argument, evidence) massiv.
powerhouse ['pauəhaus] n: **he is a ~ of ideas** er hat ständig neue Ideen.
powerless ['pauəlɪs] adj machtlos; **to be ~ to do sth** nicht die Macht haben, etw zu tun.
power line n Stromkabel nt.
power point (BRIT) n Steckdose f.
power station n Kraftwerk nt.
power steering n (AUT) Servolenkung f.
powwow ['pauwau] n Besprechung f.
pp abbr (= per procurationem) ppa.
pp. abbr (= pages) S.
PPE (BRIT) n abbr (UNIV: = philosophy, politics and economics) Studiengang bestehend aus Philosophie, Politologie und Volkswirtschaft.
PPS n abbr (= post postscriptum) PPS; (BRIT: = parliamentary private secretary) Privatsekretär eines Ministers.
PQ (CANADA) abbr (= Province of Quebec).
PR n abbr = **public relations**; (POL) = **proportional representation** ♦ abbr (US: POST: = Puerto Rico).
Pr. abbr = **prince**.
practicability [præktɪkə'bɪlɪtɪ] n Durchführbarkeit f.
practicable ['præktɪkəbl] adj (scheme, idea) durchführbar.
practical ['præktɪkl] adj praktisch; (person: good with hands) praktisch veranlagt; (ideas, methods) praktikabel.
practicality [præktɪ'kælɪtɪ] n (of person) praktische Veranlagung f; **practicalities** npl (of situation etc) praktische Einzelheiten pl.
practical joke n Streich m.
practically ['præktɪklɪ] adv praktisch.
practice ['præktɪs] n (also MED, LAW) Praxis f; (custom) Brauch m; (exercise) Übung f ♦ vt, vi (US) = **practise**; **in ~** in der Praxis; **out of ~** aus der Übung; **2 hours' piano ~** 2 Stunden Klavierübungen; **it's common or standard ~** es ist allgemein üblich; **to put sth into ~** etw in die Praxis umsetzen; **target ~** Zielschießen nt.
practice match n Übungsspiel nt.
practise, (US) **practice** ['præktɪs] vt (train at) üben; (carry out: custom) pflegen; (: activity etc) ausüben; (profession) praktizieren ♦ vi (train) üben; (lawyer, doctor etc) praktizieren.
practised ['præktɪst] (BRIT) adj (person, liar) geübt; (performance) gekonnt; **with a ~ eye** mit geschultem Auge.

practising ['præktɪsɪŋ] *adj* praktizierend.
practitioner [præk'tɪʃənə*] *n:* **medical ~** praktischer Arzt *m,* praktische Ärztin *f;* **legal ~** Rechtsanwalt *m,* Rechtsanwältin *f.*
pragmatic [præg'mætɪk] *adj* pragmatisch.
pragmatism ['prægmətɪzəm] *n* Pragmatismus *m.*
Prague [prɑːg] *n* Prag *nt.*
prairie ['preərɪ] *n* (Gras)steppe *f;* **the ~s** (*US*) die Prärien.
praise [preɪz] *n* Lob *nt* ♦ *vt* loben; (*REL*) loben, preisen.
praiseworthy ['preɪzwəːðɪ] *adj* lobenswert.
pram [præm] (*BRIT*) *n* Kinderwagen *m.*
prance [prɑːns] *vi* (*horse*) tänzeln; **to ~ about/in/out** (*person*) herum-/hinein-/hinausstolzieren.
prank [præŋk] *n* Streich *m.*
prat [præt] (*BRIT: inf*) *n* (*idiot*) Trottel *m.*
prattle ['prætl] *vi:* **to ~ on (about)** pausenlos plappern (über +*acc*).
prawn [prɔːn] *n* (*CULIN, ZOOL*) Garnele *f,* Krabbe *f;* **~ cocktail** Krabbencocktail *m.*
pray [preɪ] *vi* beten; **to ~ for sb/sth** (*REL, fig*) für jdn/um etw beten.
prayer [preə*] *n* Gebet *nt;* **to say one's ~s** beten.
prayer book *n* Gebetbuch *nt.*
pre... [priː] *pref* Prä-, prä-; **~-1970** vor 1970.
preach [priːtʃ] *vi* (*REL*) predigen; (*pej: moralize*) Predigten halten ♦ *vt* (*sermon*) direkt halten; (*fig: advocate*) predigen, verkünden; **to ~ at sb** (*fig*) jdm Moralpredigten halten; **to ~ to the converted** (*fig*) offene Türen einrennen.
preacher ['priːtʃə*] *n* Prediger(in) *m(f).*
preamble [priː'æmbl] *n* Vorbemerkung *f.*
prearranged [priːə'reɪndʒd] *adj* (vorher) vereinbart.
precarious [prɪ'keərɪəs] *adj* prekär.
precaution [prɪ'kɔːʃən] *n* Vorsichtsmaßnahme *f;* **to take ~s** Vorsichtsmaßnahmen treffen.
precautionary [prɪ'kɔːʃənrɪ] *adj* (*measure*) vorbeugend, Vorsichts-.
precede [prɪ'siːd] *vt* (*event*) vorausgehen +*dat;* (*person*) vorangehen +*dat;* (*words, sentences*) vorangestellt sein +*dat.*
precedence ['presɪdəns] *n* (*priority*) Vorrang *m;* **to take ~ over** Vorrang haben vor +*dat.*
precedent ['presɪdənt] *n* (*LAW*) Präzedenzfall *m;* **without ~** noch nie dagewesen; **to establish** *or* **set a ~** einen Präzedenzfall schaffen.
preceding [prɪ'siːdɪŋ] *adj* vorhergehend.
precept ['priːsept] *n* Grundsatz *m,* Regel *f.*
precinct ['priːsɪŋkt] *n* (*US: part of city*) Bezirk *m;* **precincts** *npl* (*of cathedral, palace*) Gelände *nt;* **shopping ~** (*BRIT*) Einkaufsviertel *nt;* (*under cover*) Einkaufscenter *nt.*
precious ['preʃəs] *adj* wertvoll, kostbar; (*pej: person, writing*) geziert; (*ironic: damned*)

heißgeliebt, wundervoll ♦ *adv* (*inf*): **~ little/ few** herzlich wenig/wenige.
precious stone *n* Edelstein *m.*
precipice ['presɪpɪs] *n* (*also fig*) Abgrund *m.*
precipitate [*vt* prɪ'sɪpɪteɪt, *adj* prɪ'sɪpɪtɪt] *vt* (*event*) heraufbeschwören ♦ *adj* (*hasty*) überstürzt, übereilt.
precipitation [prɪsɪpɪ'teɪʃən] *n* (*rain*) Niederschlag *m.*
precipitous [prɪ'sɪpɪtəs] *adj* (*steep*) steil; (*hasty*) übereilt.
précis ['preɪsiː] *n inv* Zusammenfassung *f.*
precise [prɪ'saɪs] *adj* genau, präzise; **at 4 o'clock to be ~** um 4 Uhr, um genau zu sein.
precisely [prɪ'saɪslɪ] *adv* genau, exakt; (*emphatic*) ganz genau; **~!** genau!
precision [prɪ'sɪʒən] *n* Genauigkeit *f,* Präzision *f.*
preclude [prɪ'kluːd] *vt* ausschließen; **to ~ sb from doing sth** jdn daran hindern, etw zu tun.
precocious [prɪ'kəʊʃəs] *adj* (*child, behaviour*) frühreif.
preconceived [priːkən'siːvd] *adj* (*idea*) vorgefaßt.
preconception ['priːkən'sepʃən] *n* vorgefaßte Meinung *f.*
precondition ['priːkən'dɪʃən] *n* Vorbedingung *f.*
precursor [priː'kəːsə*] *n* Vorläufer *m.*
predate ['priː'deɪt] *vt* (*precede*) vorausgehen +*dat.*
predator ['predətə*] *n* (*ZOOL*) Raubtier *nt;* (*fig*) Eindringling *m.*
predatory ['predətərɪ] *adj* (*animal*) Raub-; (*person, organization*) auf Beute lauernd.
predecessor ['priːdɪsesə*] *n* Vorgänger(in) *m(f).*
predestination [priːdestɪ'neɪʃən] *n* Vorherbestimmung *f.*
predetermine [priːdɪ'təːmɪn] *vt* vorherbestimmen.
predicament [prɪ'dɪkəmənt] *n* Notlage *f,* Dilemma *nt;* **to be in a ~** in einer Notlage *or* einem Dilemma stecken.
predicate ['predɪkɪt] *n* (*LING*) Prädikat *nt.*
predict [prɪ'dɪkt] *vt* vorhersagen.
predictable [prɪ'dɪktəbl] *adj* vorhersagbar.
predictably [prɪ'dɪktəblɪ] *adv* (*behave, react*) wie vorherzusehen; **~ she didn't come** wie vorherzusehen war, kam sie nicht.
prediction [prɪ'dɪkʃən] *n* Voraussage *f.*
predispose ['priːdɪs'pəʊz] *vt:* **to ~ sb to sth** jdn zu etw veranlassen; **to be ~d to do sth** geneigt sein, etw zu tun.
predominance [prɪ'dɒmɪnəns] *n* Vorherrschaft *f.*
predominant [prɪ'dɒmɪnənt] *adj* vorherrschend; **to become ~** vorherrschend werden.
predominantly [prɪ'dɒmɪnəntlɪ] *adv* überwiegend.

predominate [prɪ'dɔmɪneɪt] _vi_ (_in number, size_) vorherrschen; (_in strength, influence_) überwiegen.

pre-eminent [pri:'emɪnənt] _adj_ herausragend.

pre-empt [pri:'emt] _vt_ zuvorkommen +_dat_.

pre-emptive [pri:'emtɪv] _adj_: ~-~ **strike** Präventivschlag _m_.

preen [pri:n] _vt_: **to** ~ **itself** (_bird_) sich putzen; **to** ~ **o.s.** sich herausputzen.

prefab ['pri:fæb] _n_ Fertighaus _nt_.

prefabricated [pri:'fæbrɪkeɪtɪd] _adj_ vorgefertigt.

preface ['prefəs] _n_ Vorwort _nt_ ♦ _vt_: **to** ~ **with/ by** (_speech, action_) einleiten mit/durch.

prefect ['pri:fekt] (_BRIT_) _n_ (_in school_) Aufsichtsschüler(in) _m(f)_.

prefer [prɪ'fɜː'] _vt_ (_like better_) vorziehen; **to** ~ **charges** (_LAW_) Anklage erheben; **to** ~ **doing** _or_ **to do sth** (es) vorziehen, etw zu tun; **I** ~ **tea to coffee** ich mag lieber Tee als Kaffee.

preferable ['prefrəbl] _adj_: **to be** ~ (**to**) vorzuziehen sein (+_dat_).

preferably ['prefrəblɪ] _adv_ vorzugsweise, am besten.

preference ['prefrəns] _n_: **to have a** ~ **for** (_liking_) eine Vorliebe haben für; **I drink beer in** ~ **to wine** ich trinke lieber Bier als Wein; **to give** ~ **to** (_priority_) vorziehen, Vorrang einräumen +_dat_.

preference shares (_BRIT_) _npl_ (_COMM_) Vorzugsaktien _pl_.

preferential [prefə'renʃəl] _adj_: ~ **treatment** bevorzugte Behandlung _f_; **to give sb** ~ **treatment** jdn bevorzugt behandeln.

preferred stock [prɪ'fɜd-] (_US_) _npl_ = **preference shares.**

prefix ['pri:fɪks] _n_ (_LING_) Präfix _nt_.

pregnancy ['pregnənsɪ] _n_ (_of woman_) Schwangerschaft _f_; (_of female animal_) Trächtigkeit _f_.

pregnancy test _n_ Schwangerschaftstest _m_.

pregnant ['pregnənt] _adj_ (_woman_) schwanger; (_female animal_) trächtig; (_fig: pause, remark_) bedeutungsschwer; **3 months** ~ im vierten Monat (schwanger).

prehistoric ['pri:hɪs'tɔrɪk] _adj_ prähistorisch, vorgeschichtlich.

prehistory [pri:'hɪstərɪ] _n_ Vorgeschichte _f_.

prejudge [pri:'dʒʌdʒ] _vt_ vorschnell beurteilen.

prejudice ['predʒudɪs] _n_ (_bias against_) Vorurteil _nt_; (_bias in favour_) Voreingenommenheit _f_ ♦ _vt_ beeinträchtigen; **without** ~ (_form_) unbeschadet +_gen_, ohne Beeinträchtigung +_gen_; **to** ~ **sb in favour of/ against sth** jdn für/gegen etw einnehmen.

prejudiced ['predʒudɪst] _adj_ (_person, view_) voreingenommen.

prelate ['prelət] _n_ Prälat _m_.

preliminaries [prɪ'lɪmɪnərɪz] _npl_ Vorbereitungen _pl_; (_of competition_) Vorrunde _f_.

preliminary [prɪ'lɪmɪnərɪ] _adj_ (_step, arrangements_) vorbereitend; (_remarks_) einleitend.

prelude ['prelju:d] _n_ (_MUS_) Präludium _nt_; (: _as introduction_) Vorspiel _nt_; **a** ~ **to** (_fig_) ein Vorspiel _or_ ein Auftakt zu.

premarital ['pri:'mærɪtl] _adj_ vorehelich.

premature ['prematʃuə'] _adj_ (_earlier than expected_) vorzeitig; (_too early_) verfrüht; **you are being a little** ~ Sie sind etwas voreilig; ~ **baby** Frühgeburt _f_.

premeditated [pri:'medɪteɪtɪd] _adj_ vorsätzlich.

premeditation [pri:medɪ'teɪʃən] _n_ Vorsatz _m_.

premenstrual tension [pri:'menstruəl-] _n_ prämenstruelles Syndrom _nt_.

premier ['premɪə'] _adj_ (_best_) beste(r, s), bedeutendste(r, s) ♦ _n_ (_POL_) Premierminister(in) _m(f)_.

premiere ['premɪeə'] _n_ Premiere _f_.

premise ['premɪs] _n_ (_of argument_) Voraussetzung _f_; **premises** _npl_ (_of business etc_) Räumlichkeiten _pl_; **on the** ~**s** im Hause.

premium ['pri:mɪəm] _n_ (_COMM, INSURANCE_) Prämie _f_; **to be at a** ~ (_expensive_) zum Höchstpreis gehandelt werden; (_hard to get_) Mangelware sein.

premium bond (_BRIT_) _n_ Prämienanleihe _f_.

Premium Bonds, _eigentlich_ **Premium Savings Bonds,** _sind Lotterieaktien, die seit 1956 vom britischen Finanzministerium ausgegeben werden und keine Zinsen bringen, sondern statt dessen an einer monatlichen Auslosung teilnehmen. Die Gewinnummern für die verschiedenen Geldpreise werden in Blackpool von einem Computer namens_ **ERNIE** (Electronic Random Number Indicator Equipment) _ermittelt._

---

premium gasoline (_US_) _n_ Super(benzin) _nt_.

premonition [premə'nɪʃən] _n_ Vorahnung _f_.

preoccupation [pri:ɔkju'peɪʃən] _n_: ~ **with** (vorrangige) Beschäftigung mit.

preoccupied [pri:'ɔkjupaɪd] _adj_ (_thoughtful_) gedankenverloren; (_with work, family_) beschäftigt.

prep [prep] (_SCOL_) _adj abbr_ (= _preparatory_) _see_ **preparatory school** ♦ _n abbr_ (= _preparation_) Hausaufgaben _pl_.

prepaid [pri:'peɪd] _adj_ (_paid in advance_) im voraus bezahlt; (_envelope_) frankiert.

preparation [prepə'reɪʃən] _n_ Vorbereitung _f_; (_food, medicine, cosmetic_) Zubereitung _f_; **preparations** _npl_ Vorbereitungen _pl_; **in** ~ **for sth** als Vorbereitung für etw.

preparatory [prɪ'pærətərɪ] _adj_ vorbereitend; ~ **to sth/to doing sth** als Vorbereitung für etw/, um etw zu tun.

prepare [prɪ'peə'] _vt_ vorbereiten; (_food, meal_) zubereiten ♦ _vi_: **to** ~ **for** sich vorbereiten auf +*acc*.

prepared [prɪ'pɛəd] *adj:* **to be ~ to do sth**
(*willing*) bereit sein, etw zu tun; **to be ~ for**
sth (*ready*) auf etw *acc* vorbereitet sein.

preponderance [prɪ'pɔndərns] *n* Übergewicht
nt.

preposition [prɛpə'zɪʃən] *n* Präposition *f*.

prepossessing [priːpə'zɛsɪŋ] *adj* von
angenehmer Erscheinung.

preposterous [prɪ'pɔstərəs] *adj* grotesk,
widersinnig.

prep school *n* = **preparatory school.**

Prep(aratory) school *ist in Großbritannien eine
meist private Schule für Kinder im Alter von 7
bis 13 Jahren, die auf eine weiterführende
Privatschule vorbereiten soll.*

---

prerecorded ['priːrɪ'kɔːdɪd] *adj* (*broadcast*)
aufgezeichnet; (*cassette, video*) bespielt.

prerequisite [priː'rɛkwɪzɪt] *n* Vorbedingung *f*,
Grundvoraussetzung *f*.

prerogative [prɪ'rɔgətɪv] *n* Vorrecht *nt*,
Privileg *nt*.

Presbyterian [prɛzbɪ'tɪərɪən] *adj*
presbyterianisch ♦ *n* Presbyterianer(in)
m(f).

presbytery ['prɛzbɪtərɪ] *n* Pfarrhaus *nt*.

preschool ['priː'skuːl] *adj* (*age, child, education*)
Vorschul-.

prescribe [prɪ'skraɪb] *vt* (*MED*) verschreiben;
(*demand*) anordnen, vorschreiben.

prescribed *adj* (*duties, period*)
vorgeschrieben.

prescription [prɪ'skrɪpʃən] *n* (*MED: slip of
paper*) Rezept *nt*; (: *medicine*) Medikament *nt*;
to make up *or* (*US*) **fill a ~** ein Medikament
zubereiten; **"only available on ~"**
„rezeptpflichtig".

prescription charges (*BRIT*) *npl*
Rezeptgebühr *f*.

prescriptive [prɪ'skrɪptɪv] *adj* normativ.

presence ['prɛzns] *n* Gegenwart *f*,
Anwesenheit *f*; (*fig: personality*)
Ausstrahlung *f*; (*spirit, invisible influence*)
Erscheinung *f*; **in sb's ~** in jds *dat*
Gegenwart *or* Beisein; **~ of mind**
Geistesgegenwart *f*.

present [*adj, n* 'prɛznt, *vt* prɪ'zɛnt] *adj* (*current*)
gegenwärtig, derzeitig; (*in attendance*)
anwesend ♦ *n* (*gift*) Geschenk *nt*; (*LING: also:*
~ tense) Präsens *nt*, Gegenwart *f* ♦ *vt* (*give:
prize etc*) überreichen; (*plan, report*)
vorlegen; (*cause, provide, portray*) darstellen;
(*information, view*) darlegen; (*RADIO, TV*)
leiten; **to be ~ at** anwesend *or* zugegen sein
bei; **those ~** die Anwesenden; **to give sb a ~**
jdm ein Geschenk geben; **the ~** (*actuality*)
die Gegenwart; **at ~** gegenwärtig, im
Augenblick; **to ~ sth to sb, ~ sb with sth**
jdm etw übergeben *or* überreichen; **to ~ sb
(to)** (*formally: introduce*) jdn vorstellen +*dat*;

to ~ itself (*opportunity*) sich bieten.

presentable [prɪ'zɛntəbl] *adj* (*person*)
präsentabel, ansehnlich.

presentation [prɛzn'teɪʃən] *n* (*of prize*)
Überreichung *f*; (*of plan, report etc*) Vorlage
f; (*appearance*) Erscheinungsbild *nt*; (*talk*)
Vortrag *m*; **on ~ of** (*voucher etc*) gegen
Vorlage +*gen*.

present-day ['prɛzntdeɪ] *adj* heutig,
gegenwärtig.

presenter [prɪ'zɛntə*] *n* (*on radio, TV*)
Moderator(in) *m(f)*.

presently ['prɛzntlɪ] *adv* (*soon after*) gleich
darauf; (*soon*) bald, in Kürze; (*currently*)
derzeit, gegenwärtig.

present participle *n* Partizip *nt* Präsens.

preservation [prɛzə'veɪʃən] *n* (*of peace,
standards etc*) Erhaltung *f*; (*of furniture,
building*) Konservierung *f*.

preservative [prɪ'zɔːvətɪv] *n*
Konservierungsmittel *nt*.

preserve [prɪ'zɔːv] *vt* erhalten; (*peace*)
wahren; (*wood*) schützen; (*food*)
konservieren ♦ *n* (*often pl: jam, chutney etc*)
Eingemachte(s) *nt*; (*for game, fish*) Revier *nt*;
a male ~ (*fig*) eine männliche Domäne; **a
working class ~** (*fig*) eine Domäne der
Arbeiterklasse.

preshrunk ['priː'ʃrʌŋk] *adj* (*jeans etc*)
vorgewaschen.

preside [prɪ'zaɪd] *vi:* **to ~ over** (*meeting etc*)
vorsitzen +*dat*, den Vorsitz haben bei.

presidency ['prɛzɪdənsɪ] *n* (*POL*)
Präsidentschaft *f*; (*US: of company*) Vorsitz
m.

president ['prɛzɪdənt] *n* (*POL*) Präsident(in)
m(f); (*of organization*) Vorsitzende(r) *f(m)*.

presidential [prɛzɪ'dɛnʃl] *adj* (*election,
campaign etc*) Präsidentschafts-; (*adviser,
representative etc*) des Präsidenten.

press [prɛs] *n* (*printing press*) Presse *f*; (*of
switch, bell*) Druck *m*; (*for wine*) Kelter *f* ♦ *vt*
drücken, pressen; (*button, sb's hand etc*)
drücken; (*iron: clothes*) bügeln; (*put pressure
on: person*) drängen; (*pursue: idea, claim*)
vertreten ♦ *vi* (*squeeze*) drücken, pressen;
the P~ (*newspapers, journalists*) die Presse;
to go to ~ (*newspaper*) in Druck gehen; **to
be in ~** (*at the printer's*) im Druck sein; **to be
in the ~** (*in the newspapers*) in der Zeitung
stehen; **at the ~ of a button** auf
Knopfdruck; **to ~ sth (up)on sb** (*force*) jdm
etw aufdrängen; **we are ~ed for time/
money** wir sind in Geldnot/Zeitnot; **to ~ sb
for an answer** auf jds *acc* Antwort drängen;
to ~ sb to do *or* **into doing sth** jdn drängen,
etw zu tun; **to ~ charges (against sb)** (*LAW*)
Klage (gegen jdn) erheben; **to ~ for**
(*changes etc*) drängen auf +*acc*.

▶**press ahead** *vi* weitermachen; **to ~ ahead
with sth** etw durchziehen.

▶**press on** *vi* weitermachen.

press agency n Presseagentur f.
press clipping n Zeitungsausschnitt m.
press conference n Pressekonferenz f.
press cutting n = **press clipping**.
press-gang ['prɛsgæŋ] vt: **to ~ sb into doing sth** jdn bedrängen, etw zu tun.
pressing ['prɛsɪŋ] adj (urgent) dringend.
press officer n Pressesprecher(in) m(f).
press release n Pressemitteilung f.
press stud (BRIT) n Druckknopf m.
press-up ['prɛsʌp] (BRIT) n Liegestütz m.
pressure ['prɛʃə°] n (also fig) Druck m ♦ vt: **to ~ sb to do sth** jdn dazu drängen, etw zu tun; **to put ~ on sb (to do sth)** Druck auf jdn ausüben(, etw zu tun); **high/low ~** (TECH, MET) Hoch-/Tiefdruck m.
pressure cooker n Schnellkochtopf m.
pressure gauge n Druckmesser m, Manometer nt.
pressure group n Interessenverband m, Pressure-group f.
pressurize ['prɛʃəraɪz] vt: **to ~ sb (to do sth or into doing sth)** jdn unter Druck setzen(, etw zu tun).
pressurized ['prɛʃəraɪzd] adj (cabin, container etc) Druck-.
Prestel ® ['prɛstɛl] n ~ Bildschirmtext m, Btx nt.
prestige [prɛsˈtiːʒ] n Prestige nt.
prestigious [prɛsˈtɪdʒəs] adj (institution, appointment) mit hohem Prestigewert.
presumably [prɪˈzjuːməblɪ] adv vermutlich; **~ he did it** vermutlich or wahrscheinlich hat er es getan.
presume [prɪˈzjuːm] vt: **to ~ (that)** (assume) annehmen(, daß); **to ~ to do sth** (dare) sich anmaßen, etw zu tun; **I ~ so** das nehme ich an.
presumption [prɪˈzʌmpʃən] n (supposition) Annahme f; (audacity) Anmaßung f.
presumptuous [prɪˈzʌmpʃəs] adj anmaßend.
presuppose [priːsəˈpəuz] vt voraussetzen.
presupposition [priːsʌpəˈzɪʃən] n Voraussetzung f.
pretax [priːˈtæks] adj (profit) vor (Abzug der) Steuern.
pretence, (US) **pretense** [prɪˈtɛns] n (false appearance) Vortäuschung f; **under false ~s** unter Vorspiegelung falscher Tatsachen; **she is devoid of all ~** sie ist völlig natürlich; **to make a ~ of doing sth** vortäuschen, etw zu tun.
pretend [prɪˈtɛnd] vt (feign) vorgeben ♦ vi (feign) sich verstellen, so tun, als ob; **I don't ~ to understand it** (claim) ich erhebe nicht den Anspruch, es zu verstehen.
pretense [prɪˈtɛns] (US) n = **pretence**.
pretentious [prɪˈtɛnʃəs] adj anmaßend.
preterite ['prɛtərɪt] n Imperfekt nt, Präteritum nt.
pretext ['priːtɛkst] n Vorwand m; **on or under the ~ of doing sth** unter dem Vorwand, etw

zu tun.
pretty ['prɪtɪ] adj hübsch, nett ♦ adv: **~ clever** ganz schön schlau; **~ good** ganz gut.
prevail [prɪˈveɪl] vi (be current) vorherrschen; (triumph) siegen; **to ~ (up)on sb to do sth** (persuade) jdn dazu bewegen or überreden, etw zu tun.
prevailing [prɪˈveɪlɪŋ] adj (wind, fashion etc) vorherrschend.
prevalent ['prɛvələnt] adj (belief, custom) vorherrschend.
prevaricate [prɪˈværɪkeɪt] vi (by saying sth) Ausflüchte machen; (by doing sth) Ausweichmanöver machen.
prevarication [prɪværɪˈkeɪʃən] n (see vi) Ausflucht f; Ausweichmanöver nt.
prevent [prɪˈvɛnt] vt verhindern; **to ~ sb from doing sth** jdn daran hindern, etw zu tun; **to ~ sth from happening** verhindern, daß etw geschieht.
preventable [prɪˈvɛntəbl] adj verhütbar, vermeidbar.
preventative [prɪˈvɛntətɪv] adj = **preventive**.
prevention [prɪˈvɛnʃən] n Verhütung f.
preventive [prɪˈvɛntɪv] adj (measures, medicine) vorbeugend.
preview ['priːvjuː] n (of film) Vorpremiere f; (of exhibition) Vernissage f.
previous ['priːvɪəs] adj (earlier) früher; (preceding) vorhergehend; **~ to** vor +dat.
previously ['priːvɪəslɪ] adv (before) zuvor; (formerly) früher.
prewar [priːˈwɔː] adj (period) Vorkriegs-.
prey [preɪ] n Beute f; **to fall ~ to** (fig) zum Opfer fallen +dat.
▶**prey on** vt fus (animal) Jagd machen auf +acc; **it was ~ing on his mind** es ließ ihn nicht los.
price [praɪs] n (also fig) Preis m ♦ vt (goods) auszeichnen; **what is the ~ of ...?** was kostet ...?; **to go up or rise in ~** im Preis steigen, teurer werden; **to put a ~ on sth** (also fig) einen Preis für etw festsetzen; **what ~ his promises now?** wie steht es jetzt mit seinen Versprechungen?; **he regained his freedom, but at a ~** er hat seine Freiheit wieder, aber zu welchem Preis!; **to be ~d at £30** £30 kosten; **to ~ o.s. out of the market** durch zu hohe Preise konkurrenzunfähig werden.
price control n Preiskontrolle f.
price-cutting ['praɪskʌtɪŋ] n Preissenkungen pl.
priceless ['praɪslɪs] adj (diamond, painting) von unschätzbarem Wert; (inf: amusing) unbezahlbar, köstlich.
price list n Preisliste f.
price range n Preisklasse f; **it's within my ~** ich kann es mir nicht leisten.
price tag n Preisschild nt; (fig) Preis m.
price war n Preiskrieg m.
pricey ['praɪsɪ] (inf) adj kostspielig.
prick [prɪk] n (sting) Stich m; (infl: penis)

Schwanz m; (: idiot) Arsch m ♦ vt stechen;
(sausage, balloon) einstechen; **to ~ up one's
ears** die Ohren spitzen.
prickle ['prɪkl] n (of plant) Dorn m, Stachel m;
(sensation) Prickeln nt.
prickly ['prɪklɪ] adj (plant) stachelig; (fabric)
kratzig.
prickly heat n Hitzebläschen pl.
prickly pear n Feigenkaktus m.
pride [praɪd] n Stolz m; (pej: arrogance)
Hochmut m ♦ vt: **to ~ o.s.** on sich rühmen
+gen; **to take (a) ~ in** stolz sein auf +acc; **to
take a ~ in doing sth** etw mit Stolz tun; **to
have** or **take ~ of place** (BRIT) die Krönung
sein.
priest [priːst] n Priester m.
priestess ['priːstɪs] n Priesterin f.
priesthood ['priːsthud] n Priestertum nt.
prig [prɪg] n: **he's a ~** er hält sich für ein
Tugendlamm.
prim [prɪm] (pej) adj (person) etepetete.
primacy ['praɪməsɪ] n (supremacy) Vorrang m;
(position) Vorrangstellung f.
prima-facie ['praɪmə'feɪʃɪ] adj: **to have a
~ case** (LAW) eine gute Beweisgrundlage
haben.
primal ['praɪməl] adj ursprünglich; **~ scream**
Urschrei m.
primarily ['praɪmərɪlɪ] adv in erster Linie,
hauptsächlich.
primary ['praɪmərɪ] adj (principal) Haupt-,
hauptsächlich; (education, teacher)
Grundschul- ♦ n (US: election) Vorwahl f.

Als **primary** wird im amerikanischen
Präsidentschaftswahlkampf eine Vorwahl
bezeichnet, die mitentscheidet, welche
Präsidentschaftskandidaten die beiden großen
Parteien aufstellen. Vorwahlen werden nach
komplizierten Regeln von Februar (New
Hampshire) bis Juni in etwa 35 Staaten
abgehalten. Der von den Kandidaten in den
primaries erzielte Stimmenanteil bestimmt,
wie viele Abgeordnete bei der endgültigen
Auswahl der demokratischen bzw.
republikanischen Kandidaten bei den
nationalen Parteitagen im Juli/August für sie
stimmen.

---

primary colour n Primärfarbe f.
primary school (BRIT) n Grundschule f.

Primary school ist in Großbritannien eine
Grundschule für Kinder im Alter von 5 bis 11
Jahren. Oft wird sie aufgeteilt in **infant school**
(5 bis 7 Jahre) und **junior school** (7 bis 11
Jahre). Siehe auch **secondary school**.

---

primate ['praɪmɪt] n (ZOOL) Primat m; (REL)
Primas m.
prime [praɪm] adj (most important) oberste(r,
s); (best quality) erstklassig ♦ n (of person's

life) die besten Jahre pl ♦ vt (wood)
grundieren; (fig: person) informieren; (gun)
schußbereit machen; (pump) auffüllen;
~ example erstklassiges Beispiel; **in the
~ of life** im besten Alter.
Prime Minister n Premierminister(in) m(f).
primer ['praɪmə*] n (paint) Grundierung f;
(book) Einführung f.
prime time n (RADIO, TV) Hauptsendezeit f.
primeval [praɪ'miːvl] adj (beast) urzeitlich;
(fig: feelings) instinktiv; **~ forest** Urwald m.
primitive ['prɪmɪtɪv] adj (tribe, tool, conditions
etc) primitiv; (life form, machine etc)
frühzeitlich; (man) der Urzeit.
primrose ['prɪmrəuz] n Primel f, gelbe
Schlüsselblume f.
primula ['prɪmjulə] n Primel f.
Primus (stove) ® (BRIT) n Primuskocher m.
prince [prɪns] n Prinz m.
Prince Charming (hum) n Märchenprinz m.
princess [prɪn'sɛs] n Prinzessin f.
principal ['prɪnsɪpl] adj (most important)
Haupt-, wichtigste(r, s) ♦ n (of school,
college) Rektor(in) m(f); (THEAT)
Hauptdarsteller(in) m(f); (FIN)
Kapitalsumme f.
principality [prɪnsɪ'pælɪtɪ] n Fürstentum nt.
principally ['prɪnsɪplɪ] adv vornehmlich.
principle ['prɪnsɪpl] n Prinzip nt; **in ~** im
Prinzip, prinzipiell; **on ~** aus Prinzip.
print [prɪnt] n (type, ART) Druck m; (PHOT)
Abzug m; (fabric) bedruckter Stoff m ♦ vt
(produce) drucken; (publish)
veröffentlichen; (cloth, pattern) bedrucken;
(write in capitals) in Druckschrift schreiben;
prints npl (fingerprints etc) Abdrücke pl; **out
of ~** vergriffen; **in ~** erhältlich; **the fine** or
small ~ das Kleingedruckte.
▶**print out** vt (COMPUT) ausdrucken.
printed circuit ['prɪntɪd-] n gedruckte
Schaltung f.
printed circuit board n Leiterplatte f.
printed matter n Drucksache f.
printer ['prɪntə*] n (person) Drucker(in) m(f);
(firm) Druckerei f; (machine) Drucker m.
printhead ['prɪnthɛd] n Druckkopf m.
printing ['prɪntɪŋ] n (activity) Drucken nt.
printing press n Druckerpresse f.
print-out ['prɪntaut] (COMPUT) n Ausdruck m.
print run n Auflage f.
printwheel ['prɪntwiːl] n (COMPUT) Typenrad
nt.
prior ['praɪə*] adj (previous: knowledge, warning)
vorherig; (: engagement) früher; (more
important: claim, duty) vorrangig ♦ n (REL)
Prior m; **without ~ notice** ohne vorherige
Ankündigung; **to have a ~ claim on sth** ein
Vorrecht auf etw acc haben; **~ to** vor +dat.
priority [praɪ'ɒrɪtɪ] n vorrangige
Angelegenheit f; **priorities** npl Prioritäten pl;
to take or **have ~ (over sth)** Vorrang (vor
etw dat) haben; **to give ~ to sb/sth** jdm/etw

Vorrang einräumen.
priory ['praɪərɪ] *n* Kloster *nt*.
prise [praɪz] (*BRIT*) *vt*: **to ~ open** aufbrechen.
prism ['prɪzəm] *n* Prisma *nt*.
prison ['prɪzn] *n* Gefängnis *nt* ♦ *cpd* (*officer, food, cell etc*) Gefängnis-.
prison camp *n* Gefangenenlager *nt*.
prisoner ['prɪznə*] *n* Gefangene(r) *f(m)*; **the ~ at the bar** (*LAW*) der/die Angeklagte; **to take sb ~** jdn gefangennehmen.
prisoner of war *n* Kriegsgefangene(r) *f(m)*.
prissy ['prɪsɪ] (*pej*) *adj* zimperlich.
pristine ['prɪstiːn] *adj* makellos; **in ~ condition** in makellosem Zustand.
privacy ['prɪvəsɪ] *n* Privatsphäre *f*.
private ['praɪvɪt] *adj* privat; (*life*) Privat-; (*thoughts, plans etc*) persönlich; (*place*) abgelegen; (*secretive: person*) verschlossen ♦ *n* (*MIL*) Gefreite(r) *m*; "~" (*on envelope*) „vertraulich"; (*on door*) „privat"; **in ~** privat; **in (his) ~ life** in seinem Privatleben; **to be in ~ practice** (*MED*) Privatpatienten haben; **~ hearing** (*LAW*) nichtöffentliche Verhandlung.
private enterprise *n* Privatunternehmen *nt*.
private eye *n* Privatdetektiv *m*.
private limited company (*BRIT*) *n* (*COMM*) ≈ Aktiengesellschaft *f*.
privately ['praɪvɪtlɪ] *adv* privat; (*secretly*) insgeheim; **a ~ owned company** eine Firma im Privatbesitz.
private parts *npl* (*ANAT*) Geschlechtsteile *pl*.
private property *n* Privatbesitz *m*.
private school *n* (*fee-paying*) Privatschule *f*.
privation [praɪˈveɪʃən] *n* Not *f*.
privatize ['praɪvɪtaɪz] *vt* privatisieren.
privet ['prɪvɪt] *n* Liguster *m*.
privilege ['prɪvɪlɪdʒ] *n* (*advantage*) Privileg *nt*; (*honour*) Ehre *f*.
privileged ['prɪvɪlɪdʒd] *adj* privilegiert; **to be ~ to do sth** das Privileg *or* die Ehre haben, etw zu tun.
privy ['prɪvɪ] *adj*: **to be ~ to** eingeweiht sein in +*acc*.

> **Privy Council** *ist eine Gruppe von königlichen Beratern, die ihren Ursprung im normannischen England hat. Heute hat dieser Rat eine rein formale Funktion. Kabinettsmitglieder und andere bedeutende politische, kirchliche oder juristische Persönlichkeiten sind automatisch Mitglieder.*

Privy Councillor (*BRIT*) *n* Geheimer Rat *m*.
prize [praɪz] *n* Preis *m* ♦ *adj* (*prize-winning*) preisgekrönt; (*classic: example*) erstklassig ♦ *vt* schätzen; **~ idiot** (*inf*) Vollidiot *m*.
prizefighter ['praɪzfaɪtə*] *n* Preisboxer *m*.
prizegiving ['praɪzgɪvɪŋ] *n* Preisverleihung *f*.
prize money *n* Geldpreis *m*.
prizewinner ['praɪzwɪnə*] *n* Preisträger(in) *m(f)*.

prizewinning ['praɪzwɪnɪŋ] *adj* preisgekrönt.
PRO *n abbr* = **public relations officer**.
pro [prəʊ] *n* (*SPORT*) Profi *m* ♦ *prep* (*in favour of*) pro +*acc*, für +*acc*; **the ~s and cons** das Für und Wider.
pro- [prəʊ] *pref* (*in favour of*) Pro-, pro-; **~-disarmament campaign** Kampagne *f* für Abrüstung.
proactive [prəʊˈæktɪv] *adj* proaktiv.
probability [prɒbəˈbɪlɪtɪ] *n* Wahrscheinlichkeit *f*; **in all ~** aller Wahrscheinlichkeit nach.
probable ['prɒbəbl] *adj* wahrscheinlich; **it seems ~ that ...** es ist wahrscheinlich, daß ...
probably ['prɒbəblɪ] *adv* wahrscheinlich.
probate ['prəʊbɪt] *n* gerichtliche Testamentsbestätigung *f*.
probation [prəˈbeɪʃən] *n*: **on ~** (*lawbreaker*) auf Bewährung; (*employee*) auf Probe.
probationary [prəˈbeɪʃənrɪ] *adj* (*period*) Probe-.
probationer [prəˈbeɪʃənə*] *n* (*nurse: female*) Lernschwester *f*; (: *male*) Lernpfleger *m*.
probation officer *n* Bewährungshelfer(in) *m(f)*.
probe [prəʊb] *n* (*MED, SPACE*) Sonde *f*; (*enquiry*) Untersuchung *f* ♦ *vt* (*investigate*) untersuchen; (*poke*) bohren in +*dat*.
probity ['prəʊbɪtɪ] *n* Rechtschaffenheit *f*.
problem ['prɒbləm] *n* Problem *nt*; **to have ~s with the car** Probleme *or* Schwierigkeiten mit dem Auto haben; **what's the ~?** wo fehlt's?; **I had no ~ finding her** ich habe sie ohne Schwierigkeiten gefunden; **no ~!** kein Problem!
problematic(al) [prɒbləˈmætɪk(l)] *adj* problematisch.
problem-solving ['prɒbləmsɒlvɪŋ] *adj* (*skills, ability*) zur Problemlösung ♦ *n* Problemlösung *f*.
procedural [prəˈsiːdjʊrəl] *adj* (*agreement, problem*) verfahrensmäßig.
procedure [prəˈsiːdʒə*] *n* Verfahren *nt*.
proceed [prəˈsiːd] *vi* (*carry on*) fortfahren; (*person: go*) sich bewegen; **to ~ to do sth** etw tun; **to ~ with** fortfahren mit; **I am not sure how to ~** ich bin nicht sicher über die weitere Vorgehensweise; **to ~ against sb** (*LAW*) gegen jdn gerichtlich vorgehen.
proceedings [prəˈsiːdɪŋz] *npl* (*organized events*) Vorgänge *pl*; (*LAW*) Verfahren *nt*; (*records*) Protokoll *nt*.
proceeds ['prəʊsiːdz] *npl* Erlös *m*.
process ['prəʊsɛs] *n* (*series of actions*) Verfahren *nt*; (*BIOL, CHEM*) Prozeß *m* ♦ *vt* (*raw materials, food, COMPUT: data*) verarbeiten; (*application*) bearbeiten; (*PHOT*) entwickeln; **in the ~** dabei; **to be in the ~ of doing sth** (gerade) dabei sein, etw zu tun.
processed cheese ['prəʊsɛst-], (*US*) **process cheese** *n* Schmelzkäse *m*.

processing ['prəusesıŋ] n (PHOT) Entwickeln nt.

procession [prə'sɛʃən] n Umzug m, Prozession f; **wedding/funeral** ~ Hochzeits-/Trauerzug m.

proclaim [prə'kleɪm] vt verkünden, proklamieren.

proclamation [prɔklə'meɪʃən] n Proklamation f.

proclivity [prə'klɪvɪtɪ] (form) n Vorliebe f.

procrastinate [prəu'kræstɪneɪt] vi zögern, zaudern.

procrastination [prəukræstɪ'neɪʃən] n Zögern nt, Zaudern nt.

procreation [prəukrɪ'eɪʃən] n Fortpflanzung f.

procurator fiscal ['prɔkjureɪtə-] n (pl **procurators fiscal**) (SCOT) ≈ Staatsanwalt m, Staatsanwältin f.

procure [prə'kjuə*] vt (obtain) beschaffen.

procurement [prə'kjuəmənt] n (COMM) Beschaffung f.

prod [prɔd] vt (push: with finger, stick etc) stoßen, stupsen (inf); (fig: urge) anspornen ♦ n (with finger, stick etc) Stoß m, Stups m (inf); (fig: reminder) mahnender Hinweis m.

prodigal ['prɔdɪgl] adj: ~ **son** verlorener Sohn m.

prodigious [prə'dɪdʒəs] adj (cost, memory) ungeheuer.

prodigy ['prɔdɪdʒɪ] n (person) Naturtalent nt; **child** ~ Wunderkind nt.

produce [n 'prɔdjuːs, vt prə'djuːs] n (AGR) (Boden)produkte pl ♦ vt (result etc) hervorbringen; (goods, commodity) produzieren, herstellen; (BIOL, CHEM) erzeugen; (fig: evidence etc) liefern; (: passport etc) vorlegen; (play, film, programme) produzieren.

producer [prə'djuːsə*] n (person) Produzent(in) m(f); (country, company) Produzent m, Hersteller m.

product ['prɔdʌkt] n Produkt nt.

production [prə'dʌkʃən] n Produktion f; (THEAT) Inszenierung f; **to go into** ~ (goods) in Produktion gehen; **on** ~ **of** gegen Vorlage +gen.

production agreement (US) n Produktivitätsabkommen nt.

production line n Fließband nt, Fertigungsstraße f.

production manager n Produktionsleiter(in) m(f).

productive [prə'dʌktɪv] adj produktiv.

productivity [prɔdʌk'tɪvɪtɪ] n Produktivität f.

productivity agreement (BRIT) n Produktivitätsabkommen nt.

productivity bonus n Leistungszulage f.

Prof. n abbr (= professor) Prof.

profane [prə'feɪn] adj (language etc) profan; (secular) weltlich.

profess [prə'fɛs] vt (claim) vorgeben; (express: feeling, opinion) zeigen, bekunden; **I do not**

~ **to be an expert** ich behaupte nicht, ein Experte zu sein.

professed [prə'fɛst] adj (self-declared) erklärt.

profession [prə'fɛʃən] n Beruf m; (people) Berufsstand m; **the** ~**s** die gehobenen Berufe.

professional [prə'fɛʃənl] adj (organization, musician etc) Berufs-; (misconduct, advice) beruflich; (skilful) professionell ♦ n (doctor, lawyer, teacher etc) Fachmann m, Fachfrau f; (SPORT) Profi m; (skilled person) Experte m, Expertin f; **to seek** ~ **advice** fachmännischen Rat einholen.

professionalism [prə'fɛʃnəlɪzəm] n fachliches Können nt.

professionally [prə'fɛʃnəlɪ] adv beruflich; (for a living) berufsmäßig; **I only know him** ~ ich kenne ihn nur beruflich.

professor [prə'fɛsə*] n (BRIT) Professor(in) m(f); (US, CANADA) Dozent(in) m(f).

professorship [prə'fɛsəʃɪp] n Professur f.

proffer ['prɔfə*] vt (advice, drink, one's hand) anbieten; (apologies) aussprechen; (plate etc) hinhalten.

proficiency [prə'fɪʃənsɪ] n Können nt, Fertigkeiten pl.

proficient [prə'fɪʃənt] adj fähig; **to be** ~ **at** or **in** gut sein in +dat.

profile ['prəufaɪl] n (of person's face) Profil nt; (fig: biography) Porträt nt; **to keep a low** ~ (fig) sich zurückhalten; **to have a high** ~ (fig) eine große Rolle spielen.

profit ['prɔfɪt] n (COMM) Gewinn m, Profit m ♦ vi: **to** ~ **by** or **from** (fig) profitieren von; ~ **and loss account** Gewinn-und-Verlust-Rechnung; **to make a** ~ einen Gewinn machen; **to sell (sth) at a** ~ (etw) mit Gewinn verkaufen.

profitability [prɔfɪtə'bɪlɪtɪ] n Rentabilität f.

profitable ['prɔfɪtəbl] adj (business, deal) rentabel, einträglich; (fig: useful) nützlich.

profit centre n Bilanzabteilung f.

profiteering [prɔfɪ'tɪərɪŋ] (pej) n Profitmacherei f.

profit-making ['prɔfɪtmeɪkɪŋ] adj (organization) gewinnorientiert.

profit margin n Gewinnspanne f.

profit-sharing ['prɔfɪtʃɛərɪŋ] n Gewinnbeteiligung f.

profits tax (BRIT) n Ertragssteuer f.

profligate ['prɔflɪgɪt] adj (person, spending) verschwenderisch; (waste) sinnlos; ~ **with** (extravagant) verschwenderisch mit.

pro forma ['prəu'fɔːmə] adj: ~ **invoice** Pro-forma-Rechnung f.

profound [prə'faund] adj (shock) schwer, tief; (effect, differences) weitreichend; (idea, book) tiefschürfend.

profuse [prə'fjuːs] adj (apologies) überschwenglich.

profusely [prə'fjuːslɪ] adv (apologise, thank) vielmals; (sweat, bleed) stark.

profusion [prə'fju:ʒən] *n* Überfülle *f*.
progeny ['prɒdʒɪnɪ] *n* Nachkommenschaft *f*.
prognoses [prɒg'nəusi:z] *npl of* **prognosis**.
prognosis [prɒg'nəusis] (*pl* **prognoses**) *n* (*MED, fig*) Prognose *f*.
program ['prəugræm] (*COMPUT*) *n* Programm *nt* ♦ *vt* programmieren.
programme, (*US*) **program** ['prəugræm] *n* Programm *nt* ♦ *vt* (*machine, system*) programmieren.
programmer ['prəugræmə*] *n* Programmierer(in) *m(f)*.
programming, (*US*) **programing** ['prəugræmɪŋ] *n* Programmierung *f*.
programming language *n* Programmiersprache *f*.
progress [*n* 'prəugres, *vi* prə'gres] *n* Fortschritt *m*; (*improvement*) Fortschritte *pl* ♦ *vi* (*advance*) vorankommen; (*become higher in rank*) aufsteigen; (*continue*) sich fortsetzen; **in** ~ (*meeting, battle, match*) im Gange; **to make** ~ Fortschritte machen.
progression [prə'greʃən] *n* (*development*) Fortschritt *m*, Entwicklung *f*; (*series*) Folge *f*.
progressive [prə'gresiv] *adj* (*enlightened*) progressiv, fortschrittlich; (*gradual*) fortschreitend.
progressively [prə'gresivlɪ] *adv* (*gradually*) zunehmend.
progress report *n* (*MED*) Fortschrittsbericht *m*; (*ADMIN*) Tätigkeitsbericht *m*.
prohibit [prə'hɪbɪt] *vt* (*ban*) verbieten; **to** ~ **sb from doing sth** jdm verbieten *or* untersagen, etw zu tun; **"smoking ~ed"** „Rauchen verboten".
prohibition [prəuɪ'bɪʃən] *n* Verbot *nt*; **P**~ (*US*) Prohibition *f*.
prohibitive [prə'hɪbɪtɪv] *adj* (*cost etc*) untragbar.
project [*n* 'prɒdʒekt, *vt, vi* prə'dʒekt] *n* (*plan, scheme*) Projekt *nt*; (*SCOL*) Referat *nt* ♦ *vt* (*plan*) planen; (*estimate*) schätzen, voraussagen; (*light, film, picture*) projizieren ♦ *vi* (*stick out*) hervorragen.
projectile [prə'dʒektaɪl] *n* Projektil *nt*, Geschoß *nt*.
projection [prə'dʒekʃən] *n* (*estimate*) Schätzung *f*, Voraussage *f*; (*overhang*) Vorsprung *m*; (*CINE*) Projektion *f*.
projectionist [prə'dʒekʃənɪst] *n* Filmvorführer(in) *m(f)*.
projection room *n* Vorführraum *m*.
projector [prə'dʒektə*] *n* Projektor *m*.
proletarian [prəulɪ'teərɪən] *adj* proletarisch.
proletariat [prəulɪ'teərɪət] *n*: **the** ~ das Proletariat.
proliferate [prə'lɪfəreɪt] *vi* sich vermehren.
proliferation [prəlɪfə'reɪʃən] *n* Vermehrung *f*, Verbreitung *f*.
prolific [prə'lɪfɪk] *adj* (*artist, writer*) produktiv.
prologue, (*US*) **prolog** ['prəulɒg] *n* (*of play,*

book) Prolog *m*.
prolong [prə'lɒŋ] *vt* verlängern.
prom [prɒm] *n abbr* = **promenade**; (*MUS*) = **promenade concert**; (*US: college ball*) Studentenball *m*.

Prom (*promenade concert*) ist in Großbritannien ein Konzert, bei dem ein Teil der Zuhörer steht (*ursprünglich spazierenging*). Die seit 1895 alljährlich stattfindenden Proms (seit 1941 immer in der Londoner *Royal Albert Hall*) zählen zu den bedeutendsten Musikereignissen in England. Der letzte Abend der Proms steht ganz im Zeichen des Patriotismus und gipfelt im Singen des Liedes '*Land of Hope and Glory*'. In den USA und Kanada steht das Wort für **promenade**, ein Ball an einer **High School** oder einem **College**.

---

promenade [prɒmə'nɑ:d] *n* Promenade *f*.
promenade concert (*BRIT*) *n* Promenadenkonzert *nt*.
promenade deck *n* Promenadendeck *nt*.
prominence ['prɒmɪnəns] *n* (*importance*) Bedeutung *f*; **to rise to** ~ bekannt werden.
prominent ['prɒmɪnənt] *adj* (*person*) prominent; (*thing*) bedeutend; (*very noticeable*) herausragend; **he is** ~ **in the field of science** er ist eine führende Persönlichkeit im naturwissenschaftlichen Bereich.
prominently ['prɒmɪnəntlɪ] *adv* (*display, set*) deutlich sichtbar; **he figured** ~ **in the case** er spielte in dem Fall eine bedeutende Rolle.
promiscuity [prɒmɪs'kju:ɪtɪ] *n* Promiskuität *f*.
promiscuous [prə'mɪskjuəs] *adj* promisk.
promise ['prɒmɪs] *n* (*vow*) Versprechen *nt*; (*potential, hope*) Hoffnung *f* ♦ *vi* versprechen ♦ *vt*: **to** ~ **sb sth,** ~ **sth to sb** jdm etw versprechen; **to make/break/keep a** ~ ein Versprechen geben/brechen/halten; **a young man of** ~ ein vielversprechender junger Mann; **she shows** ~ sie gibt zu Hoffnungen Anlaß; **it** ~**s to be lively** es verspricht lebhaft zu werden; **to** ~ (**sb**) **to do sth** (jdm) versprechen, etw zu tun.
promising ['prɒmɪsɪŋ] *adj* vielversprechend.
promissory note ['prɒmɪsərɪ-] *n* Schuldschein *m*.
promontory ['prɒməntrɪ] *n* Felsvorsprung *m*.
promote [prə'məut] *vt* (*employee*) befördern; (*advertise*) werben für; (*encourage: peace etc*) fördern; **the team was** ~**d to the first division** (*BRIT: FOOTBALL*) die Mannschaft stieg in die erste Division auf.
promoter [prə'məutə*] *n* (*of concert, event*) Veranstalter(in) *m(f)*; (*of cause, idea*) Förderer *m*, Förderin *f*.
promotion [prə'məuʃən] *n* (*at work*) Beförderung *f*; (*of product, event*) Werbung *f*;

(*of idea*) Förderung *f*; (*publicity campaign*) Werbekampagne *f*.

prompt [prɔmpt] *adj* prompt, sofortig ♦ *adv* (*exactly*) pünktlich ♦ *n* (*COMPUT*) Prompt *m* ♦ *vt* (*cause*) veranlassen; (*when talking*) auf die Sprünge helfen +*dat*; (*THEAT*) soufflieren +*dat*; **they're very** ~ (*punctual*) sie sind sehr pünktlich; **he was** ~ **to accept** er nahm unverzüglich an; **at 8 o'clock** ~ (um) Punkt 8 Uhr; **to** ~ **sb to do sth** jdn dazu veranlassen, etw zu tun.

prompter ['prɔmptə•] *n* (*THEAT*) Souffleur *m*, Souffleuse *f*.

promptly ['prɔmptlɪ] *adv* (*immediately*) sofort; (*exactly*) pünktlich.

promptness ['prɔmptnɪs] *n* Promptheit *f*.

promulgate ['prɔmǝlgeɪt] *vt* (*policy*) bekanntmachen, verkünden; (*idea*) verbreiten.

prone [prǝun] *adj* (*face down*) in Bauchlage; **to be** ~ **to sth** zu etw neigen; **she is** ~ **to burst into tears if …** sie neigt dazu, in Tränen auszubrechen, wenn …

prong [prɔŋ] *n* (*of fork*) Zinke *f*.

pronoun ['prǝunaun] *n* Pronomen *nt*, Fürwort *nt*.

pronounce [prǝ'nauns] *vt* (*word*) aussprechen; (*give verdict, opinion*) erklären ♦ *vi*: **to** ~ **(up)on** sich äußern zu; **they** ~**d him dead/unfit to drive** sie erklärten ihn für tot/ fahruntüchtig.

pronounced [prǝ'naunst] *adj* (*noticeable*) ausgeprägt, deutlich.

pronouncement [prǝ'naunsmǝnt] *n* Erklärung *f*.

pronto ['prɔntǝu] (*inf*) *adv* fix.

pronunciation [prǝnʌnsɪ'eɪʃǝn] *n* Aussprache *f*.

proof [pru:f] *n* (*evidence*) Beweis *m*; (*TYP*) (Korrektur)fahne *f* ♦ *adj*: ~ **against** sicher vor +*dat*; **to be 70 %** ~ (*alcohol*) ≈ einen Alkoholgehalt von 40% haben.

proofreader ['pru:fri:dǝ•] *n* Korrektor(in) *m(f)*.

Prop. *abbr* (*COMM*: = *proprietor*) Inh.

prop [prɔp] *n* (*support, also fig*) Stütze *f* ♦ *vt* (*lean*): **to** ~ **sth against sth** etw an etw *acc* lehnen.

▶**prop up** *vt sep* (*thing*) (ab)stützen; (*fig: government, industry*) unterstützen.

propaganda [prɔpǝ'gændǝ] *n* Propaganda *f*.

propagate ['prɔpǝgeɪt] *vt* (*plants*) züchten; (*ideas etc*) propagieren ♦ *vi* (*plants, animals*) sich fortpflanzen.

propagation [prɔpǝ'geɪʃǝn] *n* (*of ideas etc*) Propagierung *f*; (*of plants, animals*) Fortpflanzung *f*.

propel [prǝ'pɛl] *vt* (*vehicle, machine*) antreiben; (*person*) schubsen; (*fig: person*) treiben.

propeller [prǝ'pɛlǝ•] *n* Propeller *m*.

propelling pencil [prǝ'pɛlɪŋ-] (*BRIT*) *n* Drehbleistift *m*.

propensity [prǝ'pɛnsɪtɪ] *n*: **a** ~ **for** *or* **to sth** ein

Hang *m or* eine Neigung zu etw; **to have a** ~ **to do sth** dazu neigen, etw zu tun.

proper ['prɔpǝ•] *adj* (*genuine, correct*) richtig; (*socially acceptable*) schicklich; (*inf: real*) echt; **the town/city** ~ die Stadt selbst; **to go through the** ~ **channels** den Dienstweg einhalten.

properly ['prɔpǝlɪ] *adv* (*eat, work*) richtig; (*behave*) anständig.

proper noun *n* Eigenname *m*.

property ['prɔpǝtɪ] *n* (*possessions*) Eigentum *nt*; (*building and its land*) Grundstück *nt*; (*quality*) Eigenschaft *f*; **it's their** ~ es gehört ihnen.

property developer *n* ≈ Grundstücks-makler(in) *m(f)*.

property market *n* Immobilienmarkt *m*.

property owner *n* Grundbesitzer(in) *m(f)*.

property tax *n* Vermögenssteuer *f*.

prophecy ['prɔfɪsɪ] *n* Prophezeiung *f*.

prophesy ['prɔfɪsaɪ] *vt* prophezeien ♦ *vi* Prophezeiungen machen.

prophet ['prɔfɪt] *n* Prophet *m*; ~ **of doom** Unheilsprophet(in) *m(f)*.

prophetic [prǝ'fɛtɪk] *adj* prophetisch.

proportion [prǝ'pɔ:ʃǝn] *n* (*part*) Teil *m*; (*number of people, things*) Anteil *m*; (*ratio*) Verhältnis *nt*; **in** ~ **to** im Verhältnis zu; **to be out of all** ~ **to sth** in keinem Verhältnis zu etw stehen; **to get sth in/out of** ~ etw im richtigen/falschen Verhältnis sehen; **a sense of** ~ (*fig*) ein Sinn für das Wesentliche.

proportional [prǝ'pɔ:ʃǝnl] *adj*: ~ **to** proportional zu.

proportional representation *n* Verhältniswahlrecht *nt*.

proportionate [prǝ'pɔ:ʃǝnɪt] *adj* = **proportional**.

proposal [prǝ'pǝuzl] *n* (*plan*) Vorschlag *m*; ~ **(of marriage)** Heiratsantrag *m*.

propose [prǝ'pǝuz] *vt* (*plan, idea*) vorschlagen; (*motion*) einbringen; (*toast*) ausbringen ♦ *vi* (*offer marriage*) einen Heiratsantrag machen; **to** ~ **to do sth** *or* **doing sth** (*intend*) die Absicht haben, etw zu tun.

proposer [prǝ'pǝuzǝ•] *n* (*of motion etc*) Antragsteller(in) *m(f)*.

proposition [prɔpǝ'zɪʃǝn] *n* (*statement*) These *f*; (*offer*) Angebot *nt*; **to make sb a** ~ jdm ein Angebot machen.

propound [prǝ'paund] *vt* (*idea etc*) darlegen.

proprietary [prǝ'praɪǝtǝrɪ] *adj* (*brand, medicine*) Marken-; (*tone, manner*) besitzergreifend.

proprietor [prǝ'praɪǝtǝ•] *n* (*of hotel, shop etc*) Inhaber(in) *m(f)*; (*of newspaper*) Besitzer(in) *m(f)*.

propriety [prǝ'praɪǝtɪ] *n* (*seemliness*) Schicklichkeit *f*.

props [prɔps] *npl* (*THEAT*) Requisiten *pl*.

propulsion [prǝ'pʌlʃǝn] *n* Antrieb *m*.

pro rata [prəuˈrɑːtə] *adj, adv* anteilmäßig; **on a**
~ basis anteilmäßig.
prosaic [prəuˈzeɪɪk] *adj* prosaisch, nüchtern.
Pros. Atty. (*US*) *abbr* = **prosecuting attorney**.
proscribe [prəˈskraɪb] (*form*) *vt* verbieten,
untersagen.
prose [prəuz] *n* (*not poetry*) Prosa *f*; (*BRIT:*
SCOL: translation) Übersetzung *f* in die
Fremdsprache.
prosecute [ˈprɒsɪkjuːt] *vt* (*LAW: person*)
strafrechtlich verfolgen; (: *case*) die
Anklage vertreten in +*dat*.
prosecuting attorney [ˈprɒsɪkjuːtɪŋ-] (*US*) *n*
Staatsanwalt *m*, Staatsanwältin *f*.
prosecution [prɒsɪˈkjuːʃən] *n* (*LAW: action*)
strafrechtliche Verfolgung *f*; (: *accusing*
side) Anklage(vertretung) *f*.
prosecutor [ˈprɒsɪkjuːtə*] *n*
Anklagevertreter(in) *m(f)*; (*also:* **public ~**)
Staatsanwalt *m*, Staatsanwältin *f*.
prospect [*n* ˈprɒspɛkt, *vi* prəˈspɛkt] *n* Aussicht
f ♦ *vi:* **to ~ (for)** suchen (nach); **prospects** *npl*
(*for work etc*) Aussichten *pl*, Chancen *pl*; **we**
are faced with the ~ of higher
unemployment wir müssen mit der
Möglichkeit rechnen, daß die
Arbeitslosigkeit steigt.
prospecting [ˈprɒspɛktɪŋ] *n* (*for gold, oil etc*)
Suche *f*.
prospective [prəˈspɛktɪv] *adj* (*son-in-law*)
zukünftig; (*customer, candidate*)
voraussichtlich.
prospectus [prəˈspɛktəs] *n* (*of college,*
company) Prospekt *m*.
prosper [ˈprɒspə*] *vi* (*person*) Erfolg haben;
(*business, city etc*) gedeihen, florieren.
prosperity [prɒˈspɛrɪtɪ] *n* Wohlstand *m*.
prosperous [ˈprɒspərəs] *adj* (*person*)
wohlhabend; (*business, city etc*) blühend.
prostate [ˈprɒsteɪt] *n* (*also:* **~ gland**) Prostata *f*.
prostitute [ˈprɒstɪtjuːt] *n* (*female*)
Prostituierte *f*; (*male*) männliche(r)
Prostituierte(r) *m*, Strichjunge *m* (*inf*) ♦ *vt:* **to**
~ o.s. (*fig*) sich prostituieren, sich unter
Wert verkaufen.
prostitution [prɒstɪˈtjuːʃən] *n* Prostitution *f*.
prostrate [ˈprɒstreɪt] *adj* (*face down*)
ausgestreckt (liegend); (*fig*)
niedergeschmettert ♦ *vt:* **to ~ o.s. before**
sich zu Boden werfen vor +*dat*.
protagonist [prəˈtægənɪst] *n* (*of idea,*
movement) Verfechter(in) *m(f)*; (*THEAT,*
LITER) Protagonist(in) *m(f)*.
protect [prəˈtɛkt] *vt* schützen.
protection [prəˈtɛkʃən] *n* Schutz *m*; **police ~**
Polizeischutz *m*.
protectionism [prəˈtɛkʃənɪzəm] *n*
Protektionismus *m*.
protection racket *n* Organisation *f* zur
Erpressung von Schutzgeld.
protective [prəˈtɛktɪv] *adj* (*clothing, layer etc*)
Schutz-; (*person*) fürsorglich; **~ custody**

Schutzhaft *f*.
protector [prəˈtɛktə*] *n* (*person*)
Beschützer(in) *m(f)*; (*device*) Schutz *m*.
protégé(e) [ˈprəutɪʒeɪ] *n* Schützling *m*.
protein [ˈprəutiːn] *n* Protein *nt*, Eiweiß *nt*.
pro tem [prəuˈtɛm] *adv abbr* (= *pro tempore*)
vorläufig.
protest [*n* ˈprəutɛst, *vi, vt* prəˈtɛst] *n* Protest *m*
♦ *vi:* **to ~ about** *or* **against** *or* **at sth** gegen
etw protestieren ♦ *vt:* **to ~ (that)** (*insist*)
beteuern(, daß).
Protestant [ˈprɒtɪstənt] *adj* protestantisch ♦ *n*
Protestant(in) *m(f)*.
protester [prəˈtɛstə*] *n* (*in demonstration*)
Demonstrant(in) *m(f)*.
protest march *n* Protestmarsch *m*.
protestor [prəˈtɛstə*] *n* = **protester**.
protocol [ˈprəutəkɒl] *n* Protokoll *nt*.
prototype [ˈprəutətaɪp] *n* Prototyp *m*.
protracted [prəˈtræktɪd] *adj* (*meeting etc*)
langwierig, sich hinziehend; (*absence*)
länger.
protractor [prəˈtræktə*] *n* (*GEOM*)
Winkelmesser *m*.
protrude [prəˈtruːd] *vi* (*rock, ledge, teeth*)
vorstehen.
protuberance [prəˈtjuːbərəns] *n* Auswuchs *m*.
proud [praud] *adj* stolz; (*arrogant*) hochmütig;
~ of sb/sth stolz auf jdn/etw; **to be ~ to do**
sth stolz (darauf) sein, etw zu tun; **to do**
sb/o.s. ~ (*inf*) jdn/sich verwöhnen.
proudly [ˈpraudlɪ] *adv* stolz.
prove [pruːv] *vt* beweisen ♦ *vi:* **to ~ (to be)**
correct sich als richtig herausstellen *or*
erweisen; **to ~ (o.s./itself) (to be) useful** sich
als nützlich erweisen; **he was ~d right in**
the end er hat schließlich recht behalten.
proverb [ˈprɒvɜːb] *n* Sprichwort *nt*.
proverbial [prəˈvɜːbɪəl] *adj* sprichwörtlich.
provide [prəˈvaɪd] *vt* (*food, money, shelter etc*)
zur Verfügung stellen; (*answer, example etc*)
liefern; **to ~ sb with sth** jdm etw zur
Verfügung stellen.
▶**provide for** *vt fus* (*person*) sorgen für; (*future*
event) vorsorgen für.
provided [prəˈvaɪdɪd] *conj:* **~ (that)**
vorausgesetzt(, daß).
Providence [ˈprɒvɪdəns] *n* die Vorsehung.
providing [prəˈvaɪdɪŋ] *conj:* **~ (that)**
vorausgesetzt(, daß).
province [ˈprɒvɪns] *n* (*of country*) Provinz *f*;
(*responsibility etc*) Bereich *m*, Gebiet *nt*;
provinces *npl:* **the ~s** *außerhalb der*
Hauptstadt liegende Landesteile, Provinz *f*.
provincial [prəˈvɪnʃəl] *adj* (*town, newspaper*
etc) Provinz-; (*pej: parochial*) provinziell.
provision [prəˈvɪʒən] *n* (*supplying*)
Bereitstellung *f*; (*preparation*) Vorsorge *f*,
Vorkehrungen *pl*; (*stipulation, clause*)
Bestimmung *f*; **provisions** *npl* (*food*) Proviant
m; **to make ~ for** vorsorgen für; (*for people*)
sorgen für; **there's no ~ for this in the**

contract dies ist im Vertrag nicht vorgesehen.

provisional [prə'vɪʒənl] adj vorläufig, provisorisch ♦ n: **P~** (IRISH: POL) Mitglied der provisorischen irisch-republikanischen Armee.

provisional licence (BRIT) n (AUT) vorläufige Fahrerlaubnis f.

provisionally [prə'vɪʒnəlɪ] adv vorläufig.

proviso [prə'vaɪzəu] n Vorbehalt m; **with the ~ that** ... unter dem Vorbehalt, daß ...

Provo ['prɔvəu] (IRISH: inf) n abbr (POL) = **Provisional**.

provocation [prɔvə'keɪʃən] n Provokation f, Herausforderung f; **to be under ~** provoziert werden.

provocative [prə'vɔkətɪv] adj provozierend, herausfordernd; (sexually stimulating) aufreizend.

provoke [prə'vəuk] vt (person) provozieren, herausfordern; (fight) herbeiführen; (reaction etc) hervorrufen; **to ~ sb to do** or **into doing sth** jdn dazu provozieren, etw zu tun.

provost ['prɔvəst] n (BRIT: of university) Dekan m; (SCOT) Bürgermeister(in) m(f).

prow [prau] n (of boat) Bug m.

prowess ['prauɪs] n Können nt, Fähigkeiten pl; **his ~ as a footballer** sein fußballerisches Können.

prowl [praul] vi (also: ~ **about**, ~ **around**) schleichen ♦ n: **on the ~** (animal, fig: person) auf Streifzug.

prowler ['praulə*] n Herumtreiber m.

proximity [prɔk'sɪmɪtɪ] n Nähe f.

proxy ['prɔksɪ] n: **by ~** durch einen Stellvertreter.

prude [pru:d] n: **to be a ~** prüde sein.

prudence ['pru:dns] n Klugheit f, Umsicht f.

prudent ['pru:dnt] adj (sensible) klug.

prudish ['pru:dɪʃ] adj prüde.

prune [pru:n] n Backpflaume f ♦ vt (plant) stutzen, beschneiden.

pry [praɪ] vi: **to ~ (into)** seine Nase hineinstecken (in +acc), herumschnüffeln (in +dat).

PS abbr (= postscript) PS.

psalm [sɑ:m] n Psalm m.

PSAT (US) n abbr (= Preliminary Scholastic Aptitude Test) Schuleignungstest.

PSBR (BRIT) n abbr (ECON: = public sector borrowing requirement) staatlicher Kreditbedarf m.

pseud [sju:d] (BRIT: inf: pej) n Angeber(in) m(f).

pseudo- ['sju:dəu] pref Pseudo-.

pseudonym ['sju:dənɪm] n Pseudonym nt.

PST (US) abbr (= Pacific Standard Time) pazifische Standardzeit.

PSV (BRIT) n abbr = **public-service vehicle**.

psyche ['saɪkɪ] n Psyche f.

psychedelic [saɪkə'dɛlɪk] adj (drug) psychedelisch; (clothes, colours) in psychedelischen Farben.

psychiatric [saɪkɪ'ætrɪk] adj psychiatrisch.

psychiatrist [saɪ'kaɪətrɪst] n Psychiater(in) m(f).

psychiatry [saɪ'kaɪətrɪ] n Psychiatrie f.

psychic ['saɪkɪk] adj (person) übersinnlich begabt; (damage, disorder) psychisch ♦ n Mensch m mit übersinnlichen Fähigkeiten.

psycho ['saɪkəu] (US: inf) n Verrückte(r) f(m).

psychoanalyse [saɪkəu'ænəlaɪz] vt psychoanalytisch behandeln, psychoanalysieren.

psychoanalysis [saɪkəuə'nælɪsɪs] n Psychoanalyse f.

psychoanalyst [saɪkəu'ænəlɪst] n Psychoanalytiker(in) m(f).

psychological [saɪkə'lɔdʒɪkl] adj psychologisch.

psychologist [saɪ'kɔlədʒɪst] n Psychologe m, Psychologin f.

psychology [saɪ'kɔlədʒɪ] n (science) Psychologie f; (character) Psyche f.

psychopath ['saɪkəupæθ] n Psychopath(in) m(f).

psychoses [saɪ'kəusi:z] npl of **psychosis**.

psychosis [saɪ'kəusɪs] (pl **psychoses**) n Psychose f.

psychosomatic ['saɪkəusə'mætɪk] adj psychosomatisch.

psychotherapy [saɪkəu'θɛrəpɪ] n Psychotherapie f.

psychotic [saɪ'kɔtɪk] adj psychotisch.

PT (BRIT) n abbr (SCOL: = physical training) Turnen nt.

Pt abbr (in place names: = Point) Pt.

pt abbr = **pint; point**.

PTA n abbr (= Parent-Teacher Association) Lehrer- und Elternverband.

Pte (BRIT) abbr (MIL) = **private**.

PTO abbr (= please turn over) b.w.

PTV (US) n abbr (= pay television) Pay-TV nt; (= public television) öffentliches Fernsehen nt.

pub [pʌb] n = **public house**.

Pub ist ein Gasthaus mit einer Lizenz zum Ausschank von alkoholischen Getränken. Ein Pub besteht meist aus verschiedenen gemütlichen (**lounge, snug**) oder einfacheren Räumen (**public bar**), in der oft auch Spiele wie Darts, Domino und Poolbillard zur Verfügung stehen. In Pubs werden vor allem Mittags oft auch Mahlzeiten angeboten. Pubs sind normalerweise von 11 bis 23 Uhr geöffnet, aber manchmal nachmittags geschlossen.

pub-crawl ['pʌbkrɔ:l] (inf) n: **to go on a ~** eine Kneipentour machen.

puberty ['pju:bətɪ] n Pubertät f.

pubic ['pju:bɪk] adj (hair) Scham-; ~ **bone** Schambein nt.

public ['pʌblɪk] adj öffentlich ♦ n: **the ~** (in

general) die Öffentlichkeit; (*particular set of people)* das Publikum; **to be ~ knowledge** allgemein bekannt sein; **to make sth ~ etw** bekanntmachen; **to go ~** (*COMM*) in eine Aktiengesellschaft umgewandelt werden; **in ~** in aller Öffentlichkeit; **the general ~** die Allgemeinheit.

public-address system [pʌblɪkə'drɛs-] *n* Lautsprecheranlage *f*.

publican ['pʌblɪkən] *n* Gastwirt(in) *m(f)*.

publication [pʌblɪ'keɪʃən] *n* Veröffentlichung *f*.

public company *n* Aktiengesellschaft *f*.

public convenience (*BRIT*) *n* öffentliche Toilette *f*.

public holiday *n* gesetzlicher Feiertag *m*.

public house (*BRIT*) *n* Gaststätte *f*.

publicity [pʌb'lɪsɪtɪ] *n* (*information*) Werbung *f*; (*attention*) Publicity *f*.

publicize ['pʌblɪsaɪz] *vt* (*fact*) bekanntmachen; (*event*) Publicity machen für.

public limited company *n* ≈ Aktien-gesellschaft *f*.

publicly ['pʌblɪklɪ] *adv* öffentlich; **to be ~ owned** (*COMM*) in Staatsbesitz sein.

public opinion *n* die öffentliche Meinung.

public ownership *n:* **to be taken into ~** verstaatlicht werden.

Public Prosecutor *n* Staatsanwalt *m*, Staatsanwältin *f*.

public relations *n* Public Relations *pl*, Öffentlichkeitsarbeit *f*.

public relations officer *n* Beauftragte(r) *f(m)* für Öffentlichkeitsarbeit.

public school *n* (*BRIT*) Privatschule *f*; (*US*) staatliche Schule *f*.

Public school *bezeichnet vor allem in England eine weiterführende Privatschule, meist eine Internatsschule mit hohem Prestige, an die oft auch eine* **preparatory school** *angeschlossen ist. Public schools werden von einem Schulbeirat verwaltet und durch Stiftungen und Schulgelder, die an den bekanntesten Schulen wie Eton, Harrow und Westminster sehr hoch sein können, finanziert. Die meisten Schüler einer Public school gehen zur Universität, oft nach Oxford oder Cambridge. Viele Industrielle, Abgeordnete und hohe Beamte haben eine Public school besucht. In Schottland und den USA bedeutet Public school eine öffentliche, vom Steuerzahler finanzierte Schule.*

---

public sector *n:* **the ~** der öffentliche Sektor.

public-service vehicle [pʌblɪk'sɜːvɪs-] (*BRIT*) *n* öffentliches Verkehrsmittel *nt*.

public-spirited [pʌblɪk'spɪrɪtɪd] *adj* gemeinsinnig.

public transport *n* öffentliche Verkehrsmittel *pl*.

public utility *n* öffentlicher

Versorgungsbetrieb *m*.

public works *npl* öffentliche Bauprojekte *pl*.

publish ['pʌblɪʃ] *vt* veröffentlichen.

publisher ['pʌblɪʃə*] *n* (*person*) Verleger(in) *m(f)*; (*company*) Verlag *m*.

publishing ['pʌblɪʃɪŋ] *n* (*profession*) das Verlagswesen.

publishing company *n* Verlag *m*, Verlagshaus *nt*.

puce [pjuːs] *adj* (*face*) hochrot.

puck [pʌk] *n* (*ICE HOCKEY*) Puck *m*.

pucker ['pʌkə*] *vi* (*lips, face*) sich verziehen; (*fabric etc*) Falten werfen ♦ *vt* (*lips, face*) verziehen; (*fabric etc*) Falten machen in +*acc*.

pudding ['pudɪŋ] *n* (*cooked sweet food*) Süßspeise *f*; (*BRIT: dessert*) Nachtisch *m*; **rice ~** Milchreis *m*; **black ~,** (*US*) **blood ~** ≈ Blutwurst *f*.

puddle ['pʌdl] *n* (*of rain*) Pfütze *f*; (*of blood*) Lache *f*.

puerile ['pjuəraɪl] *adj* kindisch.

Puerto Rico ['pwɜːtəu'riːkəu] *n* Puerto Rico *nt*.

puff [pʌf] *n* (*of cigarette, pipe*) Zug *m*; (*gasp*) Schnaufer *m*; (*of air*) Stoß *m*; (*of smoke*) Wolke *f* ♦ *vt* (*also:* **~ on, ~ at:** *cigarette, pipe*) ziehen an +*dat* ♦ *vi* (*gasp*) keuchen, schnaufen.

►**puff out** *vt* (*one's chest*) herausdrücken; (*one's cheeks*) aufblasen.

puffed [pʌft] (*inf*) *adj* außer Puste.

puffin ['pʌfɪn] *n* Papageientaucher *m*.

puff pastry, (*US*) **puff paste** *n* Blätterteig *m*.

puffy ['pʌfɪ] *adj* (*eye*) geschwollen; (*face*) aufgedunsen.

pugnacious [pʌg'neɪʃəs] *adj* (*person*) streitsüchtig.

pull [pul] *vt* (*rope, handle etc*) ziehen an +*dat*; (*cart etc*) ziehen; (*close: curtain*) zuziehen; (: *blind*) herunterlassen; (*inf: attract: people*) anlocken; (: *sexual partner*) aufreißen; (*pint of beer*) zapfen ♦ *vi* ziehen ♦ *n* (*also fig: attraction*) Anziehungskraft *f*; **to ~ the trigger** abdrücken; **to ~ a face** ein Gesicht schneiden; **to ~ a muscle** sich *dat* einen Muskel zerren; **not to ~ one's** *or* **any punches** (*fig*) sich *dat* keine Zurückhaltung auferlegen; **to ~ to pieces** (*fig*) zerreißen; **to ~ one's weight** (*fig*) sich ins Zeug legen; **to ~ o.s. together** sich zusammenreißen; **to ~ sb's leg** (*fig*) jdn auf den Arm nehmen; **to ~ strings (for sb)** seine Beziehungen (für jdn) spielen lassen; **to give sth a ~** an etw *dat* ziehen.

►**pull apart** *vt* (*separate*) trennen.

►**pull away** *vi* (*AUT*) losfahren.

►**pull back** *vi* (*retreat*) sich zurückziehen; (*fig*) einen Rückzieher machen (*inf*).

►**pull down** *vt* (*building*) abreißen.

►**pull in** *vi* (*AUT: at kerb*) anhalten; (*RAIL*) einfahren ♦ *vt* (*inf: money*) einsacken; (*crowds, people*) anlocken; (*police: suspect*) sich *dat* schnappen (*inf*).

▶**pull off** vt (clothes etc) ausziehen; (fig: difficult thing) schaffen, bringen (inf).

▶**pull out** vi (AUT: from kerb) losfahren; (: when overtaking) ausscheren; (RAIL) ausfahren; (withdraw) sich zurückziehen ♦ vt (extract) herausziehen.

▶**pull over** vi (AUT) an den Straßenrand fahren.

▶**pull through** vi (MED) durchkommen.

▶**pull up** vi (AUT, RAIL: stop) anhalten ♦ vt (raise) hochziehen; (uproot) herausreißen; (chair) heranrücken.

pullback ['pulbæk] n (retreat) Rückzug m.

pulley ['pulɪ] n Flaschenzug m.

pull-out ['pulaut] n (in magazine) Beilage f (zum Heraustrennen).

pullover ['puləuvə'] n Pullover m.

pulp [pʌlp] n (of fruit) Fruchtfleisch nt; (for paper) (Papier)brei m; (LITER: pej) Schund m ♦ adj (pej: magazine, novel) Schund-; **to reduce sth to a ~** etw zu Brei machen.

pulpit ['pulpɪt] n Kanzel f.

pulsate [pʌl'seɪt] vi (heart) klopfen; (music) pulsieren.

pulse [pʌls] n (ANAT) Puls m; (rhythm) Rhythmus m; **pulses** npl (BOT) Hülsenfrüchte pl; (TECH) Impuls m; vi pulsieren; **to take** or **feel sb's ~** jdm den Puls fühlen; **to have one's finger on the ~ (of sth)** (fig) den Finger am Puls (einer Sache gen) haben.

pulverize ['pʌlvəraɪz] vt pulverisieren; (fig: destroy) vernichten.

puma ['pju:mə] n Puma m.

pumice ['pʌmɪs] n (also: ~ stone) Bimsstein m.

pummel ['pʌml] vt mit Faustschlägen bearbeiten.

pump [pʌmp] n Pumpe f; (petrol pump) Zapfsäule f; (shoe) Turnschuh m ♦ vt pumpen; **to ~ sb for information** jdn aushorchen; **she had her stomach ~ed** ihr wurde der Magen ausgepumpt.

▶**pump up** vt (inflate) aufpumpen.

pumpkin ['pʌmpkɪn] n Kürbis m.

pun [pʌn] n Wortspiel nt.

punch [pʌntʃ] n (blow) Schlag m; (fig: force) Schlagkraft f; (tool) Locher m; (drink) Bowle f, Punsch m ♦ vt (hit) schlagen; (make a hole in) lochen; **to ~ a hole in sth** ein Loch in etw acc stanzen.

▶**punch in** (US) vi (bei Arbeitsbeginn) stempeln.

▶**punch out** (US) vi (bei Arbeitsende) stempeln.

Punch and Judy show n ≈ Kasper(le)theater nt.

punch card, (US) punched card [pʌntʃt-] n Lochkarte f.

punch-drunk ['pʌntʃdrʌŋk] (BRIT) adj (boxer) angeschlagen.

punch line n Pointe f.

punch-up ['pʌntʃʌp] (BRIT: inf) n Schlägerei f.

punctual ['pʌŋktjuəl] adj pünktlich.

punctuality [pʌŋktju'ælɪtɪ] n Pünktlichkeit f.

punctually ['pʌŋktjuəlɪ] adv pünktlich; **it will start ~ at 6** es beginnt um Punkt 6 or pünktlich um 6.

punctuation [pʌŋktju'eɪʃən] n Zeichensetzung f.

punctuation mark n Satzzeichen nt.

puncture ['pʌŋktʃə'] n (AUT) Reifenpanne f ♦ vt durchbohren; **I have a ~** ich habe eine Reifenpanne.

pundit ['pʌndɪt] n Experte m, Expertin f.

pungent ['pʌndʒənt] adj (smell, taste) scharf; (fig: speech, article etc) spitz, scharf.

punish ['pʌnɪʃ] vt bestrafen; **to ~ sb for sth** jdn für etw bestrafen; **to ~ sb for doing sth** jdn dafür bestrafen, daß er etw getan hat.

punishable ['pʌnɪʃəbl] adj strafbar.

punishing ['pʌnɪʃɪŋ] adj (fig: exercise, ordeal) hart.

punishment ['pʌnɪʃmənt] n (act) Bestrafung f; (way of punishing) Strafe f; **to take a lot of ~** (fig: car, person etc) viel abbekommen.

punitive ['pju:nɪtɪv] adj (action) Straf-, zur Strafe; (measure) (extrem) hart.

punk [pʌŋk] n (also: ~ rocker) Punker(in) m(f); (also: ~ rock) Punk m; (US: inf: hoodlum) Gangster m.

punnet ['pʌnɪt] n (of raspberries etc) Körbchen nt.

punt¹ [pʌnt] n (boat) Stechkahn m ♦ vi mit dem Stechkahn fahren.

punt² [pʌnt] (IRISH) n (currency) irisches Pfund nt.

punter ['pʌntə'] (BRIT) n (gambler) Wetter(in) m(f); **the ~s** (inf: customers) die Leute; **the average ~** (inf) Otto Normalverbraucher m.

puny ['pju:nɪ] adj (person, arms etc) schwächlich; (efforts) kläglich, kümmerlich.

pup [pʌp] n (young dog) Welpe m, junger Hund m; **seal ~** Welpenjunge(s) nt.

pupil ['pju:pl] n (SCOL) Schüler(in) m(f); (of eye) Pupille f.

puppet ['pʌpɪt] n (with strings, Handpuppe f; fig: person) Marionette f.

puppet government n Marionettenregierung f.

puppy ['pʌpɪ] n (young dog) Welpe m, junger Hund m.

purchase ['pə:tʃɪs] n Kauf m; (grip) Halt m ♦ vt kaufen; **to get** or **gain (a) ~ on** (grip) Halt finden an +dat.

purchase order n Bestellung f.

purchase price n Kaufpreis m.

purchaser ['pə:tʃɪsə'] n Käufer(in) m(f).

purchase tax n Kaufsteuer f.

purchasing power ['pə:tʃɪsɪŋ-] n Kaufkraft f.

pure [pjuə'] adj rein; **a ~ wool jumper** ein Pullover aus reiner Wolle; **it's laziness ~ and simple** es ist nichts als reine Faulheit.

purebred ['pjuəbrɛd] adj reinrassig.

puree ['pjʊəreɪ] *n* Püree *nt*.

purely ['pjʊəlɪ] *adv* rein.

purgatory ['pɜːgətərɪ] *n* (*REL*) das Fegefeuer; (*fig*) die Hölle.

purge [pɜːdʒ] *n* (*POL*) Säuberung *f* ♦ *vt* (*POL: organization*) säubern; (: *extremists etc*) entfernen; (*fig: thoughts, mind etc*) befreien.

purification [pjʊərɪfɪ'keɪʃən] *n* Reinigung *f*.

purify ['pjʊərɪfaɪ] *vt* reinigen.

purist ['pjʊərɪst] *n* Purist(in) *m(f)*.

puritan ['pjʊərɪtən] *n* Puritaner(in) *m(f)*.

puritanical [pjʊərɪ'tænɪkl] *adj* puritanisch.

purity ['pjʊərɪtɪ] *n* Reinheit *f*.

purl [pɜːl] (*KNITTING*) *n* linke Masche *f* ♦ *vt* links stricken.

purloin [pɜː'lɔɪn] (*form*) *vt* entwenden.

purple ['pɜːpl] *adj* violett.

purport [pɜː'pɔːt] *vi*: **to ~ to be/do sth** vorgeben, etw zu sein/tun.

purpose ['pɜːpəs] *n* (*reason*) Zweck *m*; (*aim*) Ziel *nt*, Absicht *f*; **on ~** absichtlich; **for illustrative ~s** zu Illustrationszwecken; **for all practical ~s** praktisch (gesehen); **for the ~s of this meeting** zum Zweck dieses Treffens; **to little ~** mit wenig Erfolg; **to no ~** ohne Erfolg; **a sense of ~** ein Zielbewußtsein *nt*.

purpose-built ['pɜːpəs'bɪlt] (*BRIT*) *adj* speziell angefertigt, Spezial-.

purposeful ['pɜːpəsful] *adj* entschlossen.

purposely ['pɜːpəslɪ] *adv* absichtlich, bewußt.

purr [pɜː] *vi* (*cat*) schnurren.

purse [pɜːs] *n* (*BRIT: for money*) Geldbörse *f*, Portemonnaie *nt*; (*US: handbag*) Handtasche *f* ♦ *vt* (*lips*) kräuseln.

purser ['pɜːsə] *n* (*NAUT*) Zahlmeister *m*.

purse-snatcher ['pɜːssnætʃə] (*US*) *n* Handtaschendieb *m*.

pursue [pə'sjuː] *vt* (*person, vehicle, plan, aim*) verfolgen; (*fig: interest etc*) nachgehen +*dat*.

pursuer [pə'sjuːə] *n* Verfolger(in) *m(f)*.

pursuit [pə'sjuːt] *n* (*chase*) Verfolgung *f*; (*pastime*) Beschäftigung *f*; (*fig*): **~ of** (*of happiness etc*) Streben *nt* nach; **in ~ of** (*person, car etc*) auf der Jagd nach; (*fig: happiness etc*) im Streben nach.

purveyor [pə'veɪə] (*form*) *n* (*of goods etc*) Lieferant *m*.

pus [pʌs] *n* Eiter *m*.

push [pʊʃ] *n* Stoß *m*, Schub *m* ♦ *vt* (*press*) drücken; (*shove*) schieben; (*fig: put pressure on: person*) bedrängen; (: *promote: product*) werben für; (*inf: sell: drugs*) pushen ♦ *vi* (*press*) drücken; (*shove*) schieben; **at the ~ of a button** auf Knopfdruck; **at a ~** (*BRIT: inf*) notfalls; **to ~ a door open/shut** eine Tür auf-/zudrücken; **"~"** (*on door*) „drücken"; (*on bell*) „klingeln"; **to be ~ed for time/money** (*inf*) in Zeitnot/Geldnot sein; **she is ~ing fifty** (*inf*) sie geht auf die Fünfzig zu; **to ~ for** (*demand*) drängen auf +*acc*.

▶**push around** *vt* (*bully*) herumschubsen.

▶**push aside** *vt* beiseite schieben.

▶**push in** *vi* sich dazwischendrängeln.

▶**push off** (*inf*) *vi* abhauen.

▶**push on** *vi* (*continue*) weitermachen.

▶**push over** *vt* umstoßen.

▶**push through** *vt* (*measure etc*) durchdrücken.

▶**push up** *vt* (*total, prices*) hochtreiben.

push-bike ['pʊʃbaɪk] (*BRIT*) *n* Fahrrad *nt*.

push-button ['pʊʃbʌtn] *adj* (*machine, calculator*) Drucktasten-.

pushchair ['pʊʃtʃɛə] (*BRIT*) *n* Sportwagen *m*.

pusher ['pʊʃə] *n* (*drug dealer*) Pusher *m*.

pushover ['pʊʃəʊvə] (*inf*) *n*: **it's a ~** das ist ein Kinderspiel.

push-up ['pʊʃʌp] (*US*) *n* Liegestütz *m*.

pushy ['pʊʃɪ] (*pej*) *adj* aufdringlich.

puss [pʊs] (*inf*) *n* Mieze *f*.

pussy(cat) ['pʊsɪ(kæt)] (*inf*) *n* Mieze(katze) *f*.

put [pʊt] (*pt, pp* **put**) *vt* (*thing*) tun; (: *upright*) stellen; (: *flat*) legen; (*person: in room, institution etc*) stecken; (: *in state, situation*) versetzen; (*express: idea etc*) ausdrücken; (*present: case, view*) vorbringen; (*ask: question*) stellen; (*classify*) einschätzen; (*write, type*) schreiben; **to ~ sb in a good/ bad mood** jdn gut/schlecht stimmen; **to ~ sb to bed** jdn ins Bett bringen; **to ~ sb to a lot of trouble** jdm viele Umstände machen; **how shall I ~ it?** wie soll ich es sagen *or* ausdrücken?; **to ~ a lot of time into sth** viel Zeit auf etw *acc* verwenden; **to ~ money on a horse** Geld auf ein Pferd setzen; **the cost is now ~ at 2 million pounds** die Kosten werden jetzt auf 2 Millionen Pfund geschätzt; **I ~ it to you that ...** (*BRIT*) ich behaupte, daß ...; **to stay ~** (an Ort und Stelle) bleiben.

▶**put about** *vi* (*NAUT*) den Kurs ändern ♦ *vt* (*rumour*) verbreiten.

▶**put across** *vt* (*ideas etc*) verständlich machen.

▶**put around** *vt* = **put about**.

▶**put aside** *vt* (*work*) zur Seite legen; (*idea, problem*) unbeachtet lassen; (*sum of money*) zurücklegen.

▶**put away** *vt* (*store*) wegräumen; (*inf: consume*) verdrücken; (*save: money*) zurücklegen; (*imprison*) einsperren.

▶**put back** *vt* (*replace*) zurücktun; (: *upright*) zurückstellen; (: *flat*) zurücklegen; (*postpone*) verschieben; (*delay*) zurückwerfen.

▶**put by** *vt* (*money, supplies etc*) zurücklegen.

▶**put down** *vt* (*upright*) hinstellen; (*flat*) hinlegen; (*cup, glass*) absetzen; (*in writing*) aufschreiben; (*riot, rebellion*) niederschlagen; (*humiliate*) demütigen; (*kill*) töten.

▶**put down to** *vt* (*attribute*) zurückführen auf +*acc*.

▶**put forward** *vt* (*ideas etc*) vorbringen;

(*watch, clock*) vorstellen; (*date, meeting*) vorverlegen.

▶**put in** *vt* (*application, complaint*) einreichen; (*time, effort*) investieren; (*gas, electricity etc*) installieren ♦ *vi* (*NAUT*) einlaufen.

▶**put in for** *vt fus* (*promotion*) sich bewerben um; (*leave*) beantragen.

▶**put off** *vt* (*delay*) verschieben; (*distract*) ablenken; **to ~ sb off sth** (*discourage*) jdn von etw abbringen.

▶**put on** *vt* (*clothes, brake*) anziehen; (*glasses, kettle*) aufsetzen; (*make-up, ointment etc*) auftragen; (*light, TV*) anmachen; (*play etc*) aufführen; (*record, tape, video*) auflegen; (*dinner etc*) aufsetzen; (*assume: look, behaviour etc*) annehmen; (*inf: tease*) auf den Arm nehmen; (*extra bus, train etc*) einsetzen; **to ~ on airs** sich zieren; **to ~ on weight** zunehmen.

▶**put on to** *vt* (*tell about*) vermitteln.

▶**put out** *vt* (*fire, light*) ausmachen; (*take out: rubbish*) herausbringen; (*: cat etc*) vor die Tür setzen; (*one's hand*) ausstrecken; (*story, announcement*) verbreiten; (*BRIT: dislocate: shoulder etc*) verrenken; (*inf: inconvenience*) Umstände machen +*dat* ♦ *vi* (*NAUT*): **to ~ out to sea** in See stechen; **to ~ out from Plymouth** von Plymouth auslaufen.

▶**put through** *vt* (*TEL: person*) verbinden; (*: call*) durchstellen; (*plan, agreement*) durchbringen; **~ me through to Ms Blair** verbinden Sie mich mit Frau Blair.

▶**put together** *vt* (*furniture etc*) zusammenbauen; (*plan, campaign*) ausarbeiten; **more than the rest of them ~ together** mehr als alle anderen zusammen.

▶**put up** *vt* (*fence, building*) errichten; (*tent*) aufstellen; (*umbrella*) aufspannen; (*hood*) hochschlagen; (*poster, sign etc*) anbringen; (*price, cost*) erhöhen; (*accommodate*) unterbringen; **to ~ up resistance** Widerstand leisten; **to ~ up a fight** sich zur Wehr setzen; **to ~ sb up to sth** jdn zu etw anstiften; **to ~ sb up to doing sth** jdn dazu anstiften, etw zu tun; **to ~ sth up for sale** etw zum Verkauf anbieten.

▶**put upon** *vt fus*: **to be ~ upon** (*imposed on*) ausgenutzt werden.

▶**put up with** *vt fus* sich abfinden mit.

putative ['pju:tətɪv] *adj* mutmaßlich.

putrid ['pju:trɪd] *adj* (*mess, meat*) faul.

putt [pʌt] *n* Putt *m*.

putter ['pʌtə*] *n* (*GOLF*) Putter *m* ♦ *vi* (*US*) = **potter**.

putting green ['pʌtɪŋ-] *n* kleiner Golfplatz *m* zum Putten.

putty ['pʌtɪ] *n* Kitt *m*.

put-up ['pʊtʌp] *adj*: **a ~ job** ein abgekartetes Spiel *nt*.

puzzle ['pʌzl] *n* (*game, toy*) Geschicklichkeitsspiel *nt*; (*mystery*) Rätsel *nt* ♦ *vt*

verwirren ♦ *vi*: **to ~ over sth** sich *dat* über etw *acc* den Kopf zerbrechen; **to be ~d as to why ...** vor einem Rätsel stehen, warum ...

puzzling ['pʌzlɪŋ] *adj* verwirrend; (*mysterious*) rätselhaft.

PVC *n abbr* (= *polyvinyl chloride*) PVC *nt*.

Pvt. (*US*) *abbr* (*MIL*) = **private**.

PW (*US*) *n abbr* = **prisoner of war**.

p.w. *abbr* (= *per week*) pro Woche.

PX (*US*) *n abbr* (*MIL*) = **post exchange**.

pygmy ['pɪgmɪ] *n* Pygmäe *m*.

pyjamas, (*US*) **pajamas** [pə'dʒɑːməz] *npl* Pyjama *m*, Schlafanzug *m*; **a pair of ~** ein Schlafanzug.

pylon ['paɪlən] *n* Mast *m*.

pyramid ['pɪrəmɪd] *n* Pyramide *f*.

Pyrenean [pɪrə'niːən] *adj* pyrenäisch.

Pyrenees [pɪrə'niːz] *npl*: **the ~** die Pyrenäen *pl*.

Pyrex ® ['paɪreks] *n* ~ Jenaer Glas ® *nt* ♦ *adj* (*dish, bowl*) aus Jenaer Glas ®.

python ['paɪθən] *n* Pythonschlange *f*.

Q, q

Q, q [kjuː] *n* (*letter*) Q *nt*, q *nt*; **~ for Queen** ≈ Q wie Quelle.

Qatar [kæ'tɑː*] *n* Katar *nt*.

QC (*BRIT*) *n abbr* (*LAW*: = *Queen's Counsel*) Kronanwalt *m*.

> **QC** (*kurz für Queen's Counsel, bzw. KC für King's Counsel*) ist in Großbritannien ein hochgestellter **barrister**, *der auf Empfehlung des Lordkanzlers ernannt wird und zum Zeichen seines Amtes einen seidenen Umhang trägt und daher auch als* **silk** *bezeichnet wird. Ein QC muß vor Gericht in Begleitung eines rangniedrigeren Anwaltes erscheinen.*

QED *abbr* (= *quod erat demonstrandum*) q.e.d.

QM *n abbr* (*MIL*) = **quartermaster**.

q.t. (*inf*) *n abbr* (= *quiet*): **on the ~** heimlich.

qty *abbr* = **quantity**.

quack [kwæk] *n* (*of duck*) Schnattern *nt*, Quaken *nt*; (*inf: pej: doctor*) Quacksalber *m* ♦ *vi* schnattern, quaken.

quad [kwɔd] *abbr* = **quadrangle**; (= *quadruplet*) Vierling *m*.

quadrangle ['kwɔdræŋgl] *n* (*courtyard*) Innenhof *m*.

quadrilateral [kwɔdrɪ'lætərəl] *n* Viereck *nt*.

quadruped ['kwɔdruped] *n* Vierfüßer *m*.

quadruple [kwɔ'druːpl] *vt* vervierfachen ♦ *vi* sich vervierfachen.

quadruplets [kwɔ'druːplɪts] *npl* Vierlinge *pl*.

quagmire ['kwægmaɪə'] *n (also fig)* Sumpf *m*.

quail [kweɪl] *n* Wachtel *f* ♦ *vi:* **he ~ed at the thought/before her anger** ihm schauderte bei dem Gedanken/vor ihrem Zorn.

quaint [kweɪnt] *adj (house, village)* malerisch; *(ideas, customs)* urig, kurios.

quake [kweɪk] *vi* beben, zittern ♦ *n* = **earthquake**.

Quaker ['kweɪkə'] *n* Quäker(in) *m(f)*.

qualification [kwɔlɪfɪ'keɪʃən] *n (often pl: degree etc)* Qualifikation *f*; *(attribute)* Voraussetzung *f*; *(reservation)* Vorbehalt *m*; **what are your ~s?** welche Qualifikationen haben Sie?

qualified ['kwɔlɪfaɪd] *adj (trained: doctor etc)* qualifiziert, ausgebildet; *(limited: agreement, praise)* bedingt; **to be/feel ~ to do sth** *(fit, competent)* qualifiziert sein/sich qualifiziert fühlen, etw zu tun; **it was a ~ success** es war kein voller Erfolg; **he's not ~ for the job** ihm fehlen die Qualifikationen für die Stelle.

qualify ['kwɔlɪfaɪ] *vt (entitle)* qualifizieren; *(modify: statement)* einschränken ♦ *vi (pass examination)* sich qualifizieren; **to ~ for** *(be eligible)* die Berechtigung erlangen für; *(in competition)* sich qualifizieren für; **to ~ as an engineer** die Ausbildung zum Ingenieur abschließen.

qualifying ['kwɔlɪfaɪɪŋ] *adj:* **~ exam** Auswahlprüfung *f*; **~ round** Qualifikationsrunde *f*.

qualitative ['kwɔlɪtətɪv] *adj* qualitativ.

quality ['kwɔlɪtɪ] *n* Qualität *f*; *(characteristic)* Eigenschaft *f* ♦ *cpd* Qualitäts-; **of good/poor ~** von guter/schlechter Qualität; **~ of life** Lebensqualität *f*.

quality control *n* Qualitätskontrolle *f*.

quality papers *(BRIT) npl:* **the ~** die seriösen Zeitungen *pl*.

> **Quality press** *bezeichnet auf die seriösen Tages- und Wochenzeitungen, im Gegensatz zu den Massenblättern. Diese Zeitungen sind fast alle großformatig und wenden sich an den anspruchsvolleren Leser, der voll informiert sein möchte und bereit ist, für die Zeitungslektüre viel Zeit aufzuwenden. Siehe auch* **tabloid press**.

qualm [kwɑːm] *n* Bedenken *pl*; **to have ~s about sth** Bedenken wegen etw haben.

quandary ['kwɔndrɪ] *n:* **to be in a ~** in einem Dilemma sein.

quango ['kwæŋgəu] *(BRIT) n abbr (= quasi-autonomous nongovernmental organization)* ≈ (regierungsunabhängige) Kommission *f*.

quantifiable ['kwɔntɪfaɪəbl] *adj* quantifizierbar.

quantitative ['kwɔntɪtətɪv] *adj* quantitativ.

quantity ['kwɔntɪtɪ] *n (amount)* Menge *f*; **in large/small quantities** in großen/kleinen Mengen; **in ~** *(in bulk)* in großen Mengen; **an unknown ~** *(fig)* eine unbekannte Größe.

quantity surveyor *n* Baukosten-kalkulator(in) *m(f)*.

quantum leap ['kwɔntəm-] *n (PHYS)* Quantensprung *m*; *(fig)* Riesenschritt *m*.

quarantine ['kwɔrntiːn] *n* Quarantäne *f*; **in ~** in Quarantäne.

quark [kwɑːk] *n (cheese)* Quark *m*; *(PHYS)* Quark *nt*.

quarrel ['kwɔrl] *n (argument)* Streit *m* ♦ *vi* sich streiten; **to have a ~ with sb** sich mit jdm streiten; **I've no ~ with him** ich habe nichts gegen ihn; **I can't ~ with that** dagegen kann ich nichts einwenden.

quarrelsome ['kwɔrəlsəm] *adj* streitsüchtig.

quarry ['kwɔrɪ] *n (for stone)* Steinbruch *m*; *(prey)* Beute *f* ♦ *vt (marble etc)* brechen;

quart [kwɔːt] *n* Quart *nt*.

quarter ['kwɔːtə'] *n* Viertel *nt*; *(US: coin)* 25-Cent-Stück *nt*; *(of year)* Quartal *nt*; *(district)* Viertel *nt* ♦ *vt (divide)* vierteln; *(MIL: lodge)* einquartieren; **quarters** *npl (MIL)* Quartier *nt*; *(also: living ~s)* Unterkünfte *pl*; **a ~ of an hour** eine Viertelstunde; **it's a ~ to three,** *(US)* **it's a ~ of three** es ist Viertel vor drei; **it's a ~ past three,** *(US)* **it's a ~ after three** es ist Viertel nach drei; **from all ~s** aus allen Richtungen; **at close ~s** aus unmittelbarer Nähe.

quarterback ['kwɔːtəbæk] *n (AMERICAN FOOTBALL)* Quarterback *m*.

quarterdeck ['kwɔːtədek] *n (NAUT)* Quarterdeck *nt*.

quarterfinal ['kwɔːtə'faɪnl] *n* Viertelfinale *nt*.

quarterly ['kwɔːtəlɪ] *adj, adv* vierteljährlich ♦ *n* Vierteljahresschrift *f*.

quartermaster ['kwɔːtəmɑːstə'] *n (MIL)* Quartiermeister *m*.

quartet [kwɔː'tet] *n (MUS)* Quartett *nt*.

quarto ['kwɔːtəu] *n (size of paper)* Quartformat *nt*; *(book)* im Quartformat.

quartz [kwɔːts] *n* Quarz *m* ♦ *cpd (watch, clock)* Quarz-.

quash [kwɔʃ] *vt (verdict)* aufheben.

quasi- ['kweɪzaɪ] *pref* quasi-.

quaver ['kweɪvə'] *n (BRIT: MUS)* Achtelnote *f* ♦ *vi (voice)* beben, zittern.

quay [kiː] *n* Kai *m*.

quayside ['kiːsaɪd] *n* Kai *m*.

queasiness ['kwiːzɪnɪs] *n* Übelkeit *f*.

queasy ['kwiːzɪ] *adj (nauseous)* übel; **I feel ~** mir ist übel *or* schlecht.

Quebec [kwɪ'bek] *n* Quebec *nt*.

queen [kwiːn] *n (also ZOOL)* Königin *f*; *(CARDS, CHESS)* Dame *f*.

queen mother *n* Königinmutter *f*.

Queen's speech *(BRIT) n* ≈ Regierungserklärung *f*.

Queen's Speech (bzw King's Speech) ist eine vom britischen Monarchen bei der feierlichen alljährlichen Parlamentseröffnung im Oberhaus vor dem versammelten Ober- und Unterhaus verlesene Rede. Sie wird vom Premierminister in Zusammenarbeit mit dem Kabinett verfaßt und enthält die Regierungsverklärung.

queer [kwɪə*] adj (odd) sonderbar, seltsam ♦ n (infl: pej: male homosexual) Schwule(r) m; **I feel ~** (BRIT: unwell) mir ist ganz komisch.

quell [kwɛl] vt (riot) niederschlagen; (fears) überwinden.

quench [kwɛntʃ] vt: **to ~ one's thirst** seinen Durst stillen.

querulous ['kwɛrʊləs] adj nörglerisch.

query ['kwɪərɪ] n Anfrage f ♦ vt (check) nachfragen bezüglich +gen; (express doubt about) bezweifeln.

quest [kwɛst] n Suche f.

question ['kwɛstʃən] n Frage f ♦ vt (interrogate) befragen; (doubt) bezweifeln; **to ask sb a ~, put a ~ to sb** jdm eine Frage stellen; **to bring** or **call sth into ~** etw in Frage stellen; **the ~ is ...** die Frage ist ...; **there's no ~ of him playing for England** es ist ausgeschlossen, daß er für England spielt; **the person/night in ~** die fragliche Person/Nacht; **to be beyond ~** außer Frage stehen; **to be out of the ~** nicht in Frage kommen.

questionable ['kwɛstʃənəbl] adj fraglich.

questioner ['kwɛstʃənə*] n Fragesteller(in) m(f).

questioning ['kwɛstʃənɪŋ] adj (look) fragend; (mind) forschend ♦ n (POLICE) Vernehmung f.

question mark n Fragezeichen nt.

questionnaire [kwɛstʃə'nɛə*] n Fragebogen m.

queue [kjuː] (BRIT) n Schlange f ♦ vi (also: ~ up) Schlange stehen.

quibble ['kwɪbl] vi: **to ~ about** or **over** sich streiten über +acc; **to ~ with** herumnörgeln an +dat ♦ n Krittelei f.

quiche [kiːʃ] n Quiche f.

quick [kwɪk] adj schnell; (mind, wit) wach; (look, visit) flüchtig ♦ adv schnell ♦ n: **to cut sb to the ~** (fig) jdn tief verletzen; **be ~!** mach schnell!; **to be ~ to act** schnell handeln; **she was ~ to see that ...** sie begriff schnell, daß ...; **she has a ~ temper** sie wird leicht hitzig.

quicken ['kwɪkən] vt beschleunigen ♦ vi schneller werden, sich beschleunigen.

quick-fire ['kwɪkfaɪə*] adj (questions) wie aus der Maschinenpistole.

quick fix n Sofortlösung f.

quicklime ['kwɪklaɪm] n ungelöschter Kalk m.

quickly ['kwɪklɪ] adv schnell.

quickness ['kwɪknɪs] n Schnelligkeit f; ~ **of mind** Scharfsinn m.

quicksand ['kwɪksænd] n Treibsand m.

quickstep ['kwɪkstɛp] n Quickstep m.

quick-tempered [kwɪk'tɛmpəd] adj hitzig, leicht erregbar.

quick-witted [kwɪk'wɪtɪd] adj schlagfertig.

quid [kwɪd] (BRIT: inf) n inv Pfund nt.

quid pro quo ['kwɪdprəʊ'kwəʊ] n Gegenleistung f.

quiet ['kwaɪət] adj leise; (place) ruhig, still; (silent, reserved) still; (business, day) ruhig; (without fuss etc: wedding) in kleinem Rahmen ♦ n (peacefulness) Stille f, Ruhe f; (silence) Ruhe f ♦ vt, vi (US) = **quieten; keep** or **be ~!** sei still!; **I'll have a ~ word with him** ich werde mal unter vier Augen mit ihm reden; **on the ~** (in secret) heimlich.

quieten ['kwaɪətn] (BRIT: also: ~ **down**) vi ruhiger werden ♦ vt (person, animal) beruhigen.

quietly ['kwaɪətlɪ] adv leise; (silently) still; (calmly) ruhig; ~ **confident** insgeheim sicher.

quietness ['kwaɪətnɪs] n (peacefulness) Ruhe f; (silence) Stille f.

quill [kwɪl] n (pen) Feder f; (of porcupine) Stachel m.

quilt [kwɪlt] n Decke f; (also: **continental** ~) Federbett nt.

quin [kwɪn] (BRIT) n abbr (= quintuplet) Fünfling m.

quince [kwɪns] n Quitte f.

quinine [kwɪ'niːn] n Chinin nt.

quintet [kwɪn'tɛt] n (MUS) Quintett nt.

quintuplets [kwɪn'tjuːplɪts] npl Fünflinge pl.

quip [kwɪp] n witzige or geistreiche Bemerkung f ♦ vt witzeln.

quire ['kwaɪə*] n (of paper) 24 Bogen Papier.

quirk [kwəːk] n Marotte f; **a ~ of fate** eine Laune des Schicksals.

quit [kwɪt] (pt, pp **quit** or **quitted**) vt (smoking) aufgeben; (job) kündigen; (premises) verlassen ♦ vi (give up) aufgeben; (resign) kündigen; **to ~ doing sth** aufhören, etw zu tun; ~ **stalling!** (US: inf) weichen Sie nicht ständig aus!; **notice to ~** (BRIT) Kündigung f.

quite [kwaɪt] adv (rather) ziemlich; (entirely) ganz; **not ~ nicht ganz; I ~ like it** ich mag es ganz gern; **I ~ understand** ich verstehe; **I don't ~ remember** ich erinnere mich nicht genau; **not ~ as many as the last time** nicht ganz so viele wie das letzte Mal; **that meal was ~ something!** das Essen konnte sich sehen lassen!; **it was ~ a sight** das war vielleicht ein Anblick; ~ **a few of them** eine ganze Reihe von Ihnen; ~ **(so)!** ganz recht!

quits [kwɪts] adj: **we're ~** wir sind quitt; **let's call it ~** lassen wir's dabei.

quiver ['kwɪvə*] vi zittern.

quiz [kwɪz] n (game) Quiz nt ♦ vt (question)

befragen.
quizzical ['kwɪzɪkl] *adj (look, smile)* wissend.
quoits [kwɔɪts] *npl (game)* Wurfspiel *mit Ringen*.
quorum ['kwɔːrəm] *n* Quorum *nt*.
quota ['kwəʊtə] *n (allowance)* Quote *f*.
quotation [kwəʊ'teɪʃən] *n (from book etc)* Zitat *nt; (estimate)* Preisangabe *f; (COMM)* Kostenvoranschlag *m*.
quotation marks *npl* Anführungszeichen *pl*.
quote [kwəʊt] *n (from book etc)* Zitat *nt; (estimate)* Kostenvoranschlag *m ♦ vt* zitieren; *(fact, example)* anführen; *(price)* nennen; **quotes** *npl (quotation marks)* Anführungszeichen *pl;* **in ~s** in Anführungszeichen; **the figure ~d for the repairs** die für die Reparatur genannte Summe; **~ ... unquote** Zitat Anfang ... Zitat Ende.
quotient ['kwəʊʃənt] *n* Quotient *m*.
qv *abbr (= quod vide)* s.d.
qwerty keyboard ['kwɜːtɪ-] *n* Qwerty-Tastatur *f*.

R, r

R¹, r [ɑː] *n (letter)* R *nt,* r *nt;* **~ for Robert,** *(US)* **~ for Roger** ≈ R wie Richard.
R² [ɑː] *abbr (= Réaumur (scale))* R; *(US: CINE: = restricted)* Klassifikation *für nicht jugendfreie Filme*.
R. *abbr (= right)* r.; **= river;** *(US: POL)* **= republican;** *(BRIT: = Rex)* König; *(= Regina)* Königin.
RA *abbr (MIL)* **= rear admiral ♦** *n abbr (BRIT: = Royal Academy)* Gesellschaft *zur Förderung der Künste; (= Royal Academician)* Mitglied *der Royal Academy*.
RAAF *n abbr (MIL: = Royal Australian Air Force)* australische Luftwaffe *f*.
Rabat [rə'bɑːt] *n* Rabat *nt*.
rabbi ['ræbaɪ] *n* Rabbi *m*.
rabbit ['ræbɪt] *n* Kaninchen *nt ♦ vi (BRIT: inf: also:* **to ~ on)** quatschen, schwafeln.
rabbit hole *n* Kaninchenbau *m*.
rabbit hutch *n* Kaninchenstall *m*.
rabble ['ræbl] *(pej)* *n* Pöbel *m*.
rabid ['ræbɪd] *adj (animal)* tollwütig; *(fig: fanatical)* fanatisch.
rabies ['reɪbiːz] *n* Tollwut *f*.
RAC *(BRIT)* *n abbr (= Royal Automobile Club)* Autofahrerorganisation, ≈ ADAC *m*.
raccoon [rə'kuːn] *n* Waschbär *m*.
race [reɪs] *n (species)* Rasse *f; (competition)* Rennen *nt; (for power, control)* Wettlauf *m*

♦ *vt (horse, pigeon)* an Wettbewerben teilnehmen lassen; *(car etc)* ins Rennen schicken; *(person)* um die Wette laufen mit **♦** *vi (compete)* antreten; *(hurry)* rennen; *(pulse, heart)* rasen; *(engine)* durchdrehen; **the human ~** die Menschheit; **a ~ against time** ein Wettlauf mit der Zeit; **he ~d across the road** er raste über die Straße; **to ~ in/out** hinein-/hinausstürzen.
race car *(US)* *n* **= racing car.**
race car driver *(US)* *n* **= racing driver.**
racecourse ['reɪskɔːs] *n* Rennbahn *f*.
racehorse ['reɪshɔːs] *n* Rennpferd *nt*.
race meeting *n* Rennveranstaltung *f*.
race relations *npl* Beziehungen *pl* zwischen den Rassen.
racetrack ['reɪstræk] *n* Rennbahn *f; (US)* **= racecourse.**
racial ['reɪʃl] *adj* Rassen-.
racialism ['reɪʃlɪzəm] *n* Rassismus *m*.
racialist ['reɪʃlɪst] *adj* rassistisch **♦** *n (pej)* Rassist(in) *m(f)*.
racing ['reɪsɪŋ] *n (horse racing)* Pferderennen *nt; (motor racing)* Rennsport *m*.
racing car *(BRIT)* *n* Rennwagen *m*.
racing driver *(BRIT)* *n* Rennfahrer(in) *m(f)*.
racism ['reɪsɪzəm] *n* Rassismus *m*.
racist ['reɪsɪst] *adj* rassistisch **♦** *n (pej)* Rassist(in) *m(f)*.
rack [ræk] *n (also:* **luggage ~)** Gepäckablage *f; (also:* **roof ~)** Dachgepäckträger *m; (for dresses etc)* Ständer *m; (for dishes)* Gestell *nt* **♦** *vt:* **~ed by** *(pain etc)* gemartert von; **magazine/toast ~** Zeitungs-/Toastständer *m;* **to ~ one's brains** sich *dat* den Kopf zerbrechen; **to go to ~ and ruin** *(building)* zerfallen; *(business, country)* herunterkommen.
racket ['rækɪt] *n (for tennis etc)* Schläger *m; (noise)* Krach *m,* Radau *m; (swindle)* Schwindel *m*.
racketeer [rækɪ'tɪə] *(esp US)* *n* Gangster *m*.
racoon [rə'kuːn] *n* **= raccoon.**
racquet ['rækɪt] *n (for tennis etc)* Schläger *m*.
racy ['reɪsɪ] *adj (book, story)* rasant.
RADA [rɑːdə] *(BRIT)* *n abbr (= Royal Academy of Dramatic Art)* Schauspielschule *f*.
radar ['reɪdɑː] *n* Radar *m or nt* **♦** *cpd* Radar-.
radar trap *n* Radarfalle *f*.
radial ['reɪdɪəl] *adj (roads)* strahlenförmig verlaufend; *(pattern)* strahlenförmig **♦** *n (also:* **~ tyre)** Gürtelreifen *m*.
radiance ['reɪdɪəns] *n* Glanz *m*.
radiant ['reɪdɪənt] *adj* strahlend; *(PHYS: heat)* Strahlungs-.
radiate ['reɪdɪeɪt] *vt (lit, fig)* ausstrahlen **♦** *vi (lines, roads)* strahlenförmig verlaufen.
radiation [reɪdɪ'eɪʃən] *n (radioactivity)* radioaktive Strahlung *f; (from sun etc)* Strahlung *f*.
radiation sickness *n* Strahlenkrankheit *f*.
radiator ['reɪdɪeɪtə] *n (heater)* Heizkörper *m;*

(*AUT*) Kühler m.
radiator cap n (*AUT*) Kühlerdeckel m.
radiator grill n (*AUT*) Kühlergrill m.
radical ['rædɪkl] adj radikal ♦ n (*person*)
Radikale(r) f(m).
radii ['reɪdɪaɪ] npl of **radius**.
radio ['reɪdɪəu] n (*broadcasting*) Radio nt,
Rundfunk m; (*device: for receiving broadcasts*)
Radio nt; (: *for transmitting and receiving*)
Funkgerät nt ♦ vi: **to ~ to sb** mit jdm per
Funk sprechen ♦ vt (*person*) per Funk
verständigen; (*message, position*) per Funk
durchgeben; **on the ~** im Radio.
radio... ['reɪdɪəu] pref Radio..., radio...
radioactive ['reɪdɪəu'æktɪv] adj radioaktiv.
radioactivity ['reɪdɪəuæk'tɪvɪtɪ] n
Radioaktivität f.
radio announcer n Rundfunksprecher(in)
m(f).
radio-controlled ['reɪdɪəukən'trəuld] adj
ferngesteuert.
radiographer [reɪdɪ'ɔgrəfə*] n Röntgenologe
m, Röntgenologin f.
radiography [reɪdɪ'ɔgrəfɪ] n Röntgenographie
f.
radiologist [reɪdɪ'ɔlədʒɪst] n Radiologe m,
Radiologin f.
radiology [reɪdɪ'ɔlədʒɪ] n Radiologie f.
radio station n Radiosender m.
radio taxi n Funktaxi nt.
radiotelephone ['reɪdɪəu'tɛlɪfəun] n
Funksprechgerät nt.
radio telescope n Radioteleskop nt.
radiotherapist ['reɪdɪəu'θɛrəpɪst] n
Strahlentherapeut(in) m(f).
radiotherapy ['reɪdɪəu'θɛrəpɪ] n
Strahlentherapie f.
radish ['rædɪʃ] n Radieschen nt; (*long white
variety*) Rettich m.
radium ['reɪdɪəm] n Radium nt.
radius ['reɪdɪəs] (pl **radii**) n Radius m; (*area*)
Umkreis m; **within a ~ of 50 miles** in einem
Umkreis von 50 Meilen.
RAF (*BRIT*) n abbr = **Royal Air Force**.
raffia ['ræfɪə] n Bast m.
raffish ['ræfɪʃ] adj (*person*) verwegen; (*place*)
verkommen.
raffle ['ræfl] n Verlosung f, Tombola f ♦ vt
(*prize*) verlosen; **~ ticket** Los nt.
raft [rɑ:ft] n Floß nt; (*also*: **life ~**) Rettungsfloß
nt.
rafter ['rɑ:ftə*] n Dachsparren m.
rag [ræg] n (*piece of cloth*) Lappen m; (*torn
cloth*) Fetzen m; (*pej: newspaper*) Käseblatt
nt; (*BRIT: UNIV*) studentische
Wohltätigkeitsveranstaltung ♦ vt (*BRIT:
tease*) aufziehen; **rags** npl (*torn clothes*)
Lumpen pl; **in ~s** (*person*) zerlumpt; **his was
a ~s-to-riches story** er brachte es vom
Tellerwäscher zum Millionär.
rag-and-bone man [rægən'bəun-] (*BRIT*) n
Lumpensammler m.

ragbag ['rægbæg] n (*assortment*)
Sammelsurium nt.

Rag Day/Week heißt der Tag bzw. die Woche,
wenn Studenten Geld für wohltätige Zwecke
sammeln. Diverse gesponserte Aktionen wie
Volksläufe, Straßentheater und Kneipentouren
werden zur Unterhaltung der Studenten und
der Bevölkerung organisiert.
Studentenzeitschriften mit schlüpfrigen Witzen
werden auf der Straße verkauft, und fast alle
Universitäten und Colleges halten einen Ball
ab. Der Erlös aller Veranstaltungen fließt
Wohltätigkeitsorganisationen zu.

rag doll n Stoffpuppe f.
rage [reɪdʒ] n (*fury*) Wut f, Zorn m ♦ vi toben,
wüten; **it's all the ~** (*fashionable*) es ist der
letzte Schrei; **to fly into a ~** einen Wutanfall
bekommen.
ragged ['rægɪd] adj (*jagged*) zackig; (*clothes,
person*) zerlumpt; (*beard*) ausgefranst.
raging ['reɪdʒɪŋ] adj (*sea, storm, torrent*)
tobend, tosend; (*fever*) heftig; (*thirst*)
brennend; (*toothache*) rasend.
rag trade (*inf*) n: **the ~** die Modebranche f.
raid [reɪd] n (*MIL*) Angriff m, Überfall m; (*by
police*) Razzia f; (*by criminal: forcefully*)
Überfall m; (: *secretly*) Einbruch m ♦ vt (*MIL*)
angreifen, überfallen; (*police*) stürmen;
(*criminal: forcefully*) überfallen; (: *secretly*)
einbrechen in +acc.
rail [reɪl] n Geländer nt; (*on deck of ship*) Reling
f; **rails** npl (*for train*) Schienen pl; **by ~** mit der
Bahn.
railcard ['reɪlkɑ:d] (*BRIT*) n (*for young people*)
≈ Juniorenpaß m; (*for pensioners*)
≈ Seniorenpaß m.
railing(s) ['reɪlɪŋ(z)] n(pl) (*fence*) Zaun m.
railroad ['reɪlrəud] (*US*) n = **railway**.
railway ['reɪlweɪ] (*BRIT*) n Eisenbahn f; (*track*)
Gleis nt; (*company*) Bahn f.
railway engine (*BRIT*) n Lokomotive f.
railway line (*BRIT*) n Bahnlinie f; (*track*) Gleis
nt.
railwayman ['reɪlweɪmən] (*irreg: like* **man**)
(*BRIT*) n Eisenbahner m.
railway station (*BRIT*) n Bahnhof m.
rain [reɪn] n Regen m ♦ vi regnen; **in the ~** im
Regen; **as right as ~** voll auf der Höhe; **it's
~ing** es regnet; **it's ~ing cats and dogs** es
regnet in Strömen.
rainbow ['reɪnbəu] n Regenbogen m.
rain check (*US*) n: **to take a ~ on sth** sich dat
etw noch einmal überlegen.
raincoat ['reɪnkəut] n Regenmantel m.
raindrop ['reɪndrɔp] n Regentropfen m.
rainfall ['reɪnfɔ:l] n Niederschlag m.
rainforest ['reɪnfɔrɪst] n Regenwald m.
rainproof ['reɪnpru:f] adj wasserfest.
rainstorm ['reɪnstɔ:m] n schwere Regenfälle
pl.

rainwater ['reɪnwɔːtə'] n Regenwasser nt.
rainy ['reɪnɪ] adj (day) regnerisch, verregnet; (area) regenreich; ~ **season** Regenzeit f; **to save sth for a ~ day** etw für schlechte Zeiten aufheben.
raise [reɪz] n (pay rise) Gehaltserhöhung f ♦ vt (lift: hand) hochheben; (: window) hochziehen; (siege) beenden; (embargo) aufheben; (increase) erhöhen; (improve) verbessern; (question etc) zur Sprache bringen; (doubts etc) vorbringen; (child, cattle) aufziehen; (crop) anbauen; (army) aufstellen; (funds) aufbringen; (loan) aufnehmen; **to ~ a glass to sb/sth** das Glas auf jdn/etw erheben; **to ~ one's voice** die Stimme erheben; **to ~ sb's hopes** jdm Hoffnungen machen; **to ~ a laugh/smile** Gelächter/ein Lächeln hervorrufen; **this ~s the question...** das wirft die Frage auf...
raisin ['reɪzn] n Rosine f.
Raj [rɑːdʒ] n: **the ~** britische Regierung in Indien vor 1947.
rajah ['rɑːdʒə] n Radscha m.
rake [reɪk] n Harke f; (old: person) Schwerenöter m ♦ vt harken; (light, gun: area) bestreichen; **he's raking it in** (inf) er scheffelt das Geld nur so.
rake-off ['reɪkɔf] (inf) n Anteil m.
rally ['rælɪ] n (POL etc) Kundgebung f; (AUT) Rallye f; (TENNIS etc) Ballwechsel m ♦ vt (support) sammeln ♦ vi (sick person, Stock Exchange) sich erholen.
▶**rally round** vi sich zusammentun ♦ vt fus zu Hilfe kommen +dat.
rallying point ['rælɪɪŋ-] n Sammelstelle f.
RAM [ræm] n abbr (COMPUT: = random access memory) RAM.
ram [ræm] n Widder m ♦ vt rammen.
ramble ['ræmbl] n Wanderung f ♦ vi wandern; (also: ~ **on:** talk) schwafeln.
rambler ['ræmblə'] n Wanderer m, Wanderin f; (BOT) Kletterrose f.
rambling ['ræmblɪŋ] adj (speech, letter) weitschweifig; (house) weitläufig; (BOT) rankend, Kletter-.
rambunctious [ræm'bʌŋkʃəs] (US) adj = **rumbustious.**
RAMC (BRIT) n abbr (= Royal Army Medical Corps) Verband zur Versorgung der Armee mit Stabsärzten und Sanitätern.
ramifications [ræmɪfɪ'keɪʃənz] npl Auswirkungen pl.
ramp [ræmp] n Rampe f; (in garage) Hebebühne f; **on ~** (US: AUT) Auffahrt f; **off ~** (US: AUT) Ausfahrt f.
rampage [ræm'peɪdʒ] n: **to be/go on the ~** randalieren ♦ vi: **they went rampaging through the town** sie zogen randalierend durch die Stadt.
rampant ['ræmpənt] adj: **to be ~** (crime, disease etc) wild wuchern.
rampart ['ræmpɑːt] n Schutzwall m.

ram raiding [-reɪdɪŋ] n Einbruchdiebstahl, wobei die Diebe mit einem Wagen in die Schaufensterfront eines Ladens eindringen.
ramshackle ['ræmʃækl] adj (house) baufällig; (cart) klapprig; (table) altersschwach.
RAN n abbr (= Royal Australian Navy) australische Marine f.
ran [ræn] pt of **run.**
ranch [rɑːntʃ] n Ranch f.
rancher ['rɑːntʃə'] n Rancher(in) m(f); (worker) Farmhelfer(in) m(f).
rancid ['rænsɪd] adj ranzig.
rancour, (US) **rancor** ['ræŋkə'] n Verbitterung f.
R & B n abbr (= rhythm and blues) R & B.
R & D n abbr = **research and development.**
random ['rændəm] adj (arrangement) willkürlich; (selection) zufällig; (COMPUT) wahlfrei; (MATH) Zufalls- ♦ n: **at ~** aufs Geratewohl.
random access n (COMPUT) wahlfreier Zugriff m.
random access memory n (COMPUT) Schreib-Lese-Speicher m.
R & R (US) n abbr (MIL: = rest and recreation) Urlaub m.
randy ['rændɪ] (BRIT: inf) adj geil, scharf.
rang [ræŋ] pt of **ring.**
range [reɪndʒ] n (of mountains) Kette f; (of missile) Reichweite f; (of voice) Umfang m; (series) Reihe f; (of products) Auswahl f; (MIL: also: **rifle ~**) Schießstand m; (also: **kitchen ~**) Herd m ♦ vt (place in a line) anordnen ♦ vi: **to ~ over** (extend) sich erstrecken über +acc; **price ~** Preisspanne f; **do you have anything else in this price ~?** haben Sie noch etwas anderes in dieser Preisklasse?; **within (firing) ~** in Schußweite; **at close ~** aus unmittelbarer Entfernung; **~d left/right** (text) links-/rechtsbündig; **to ~ from ... to ...** sich zwischen ... und ... bewegen.
ranger ['reɪndʒə'] n Förster(in) m(f).
Rangoon [ræŋ'guːn] n Rangun nt.
rank [ræŋk] n (row) Reihe f; (MIL) Rang m; (social class) Schicht f; (BRIT: also: **taxi ~**) Taxistand m ♦ vi: **to ~ as/among** zählen zu ♦ vt: **he is ~ed third in the world** er steht weltweit an dritter Stelle ♦ adj (stinking) stinkend; (sheer: hypocrisy etc) rein; **the ~s** npl (MIL) die Mannschaften pl; **the ~ and file** (ordinary members) die Basis f; **to close ~s** (fig, MIL) die Reihen schließen.
rankle ['ræŋkl] vi (insult) nachwirken; **to ~ with sb** jdn wurmen.
rank outsider n totaler Außenseiter m, totale Außenseiterin f.
ransack ['rænsæk] vt (search) durchwühlen; (plunder) plündern.
ransom ['rænsəm] n (money) Lösegeld nt; **to hold sb to ~** (hostage) jdn als Geisel halten; (fig) jdn erpressen.
rant [rænt] vi schimpfen, wettern; **to ~ and**

rave herumwettern.
ranting ['ræntɪŋ] n Geschimpfe nt.
rap [ræp] vi klopfen ♦ vt: **to ~ sb's knuckles** jdm auf die Finger klopfen ♦ n (at door) Klopfen nt; (also: ~ **music**) Rap m.
rape [reɪp] n Vergewaltigung f; (BOT) Raps m ♦ vt vergewaltigen.
rape(seed) oil ['reɪp(siːd)-] n Rapsöl nt.
rapid ['ræpɪd] adj schnell; (growth, change) schnell, rapide.
rapidity [rə'pɪdɪtɪ] n Schnelligkeit f.
rapidly ['ræpɪdlɪ] adv schnell; (grow, change) schnell, rapide.
rapids ['ræpɪdz] npl Stromschnellen pl.
rapist ['reɪpɪst] n Vergewaltiger m.
rapport [ræ'pɔː] n enges Verhältnis nt.
rapprochement [ræ'prɔʃmɑ̃ːŋ] n Annäherung f.
rapt [ræpt] adj (attention) gespannt; **to be ~ in thought** in Gedanken versunken sein.
rapture ['ræptʃə] n Entzücken nt; **to go into ~s over** ins Schwärmen geraten über +acc.
rapturous ['ræptʃərəs] adj (applause, welcome) stürmisch.
rare [rɛə] adj selten; (steak) nur angebraten, englisch (gebraten); **it is ~ to find that ...** es kommt nur selten vor, daß ...
rarebit ['rɛəbɪt] n see **Welsh rarebit**.
rarefied ['rɛərɪfaɪd] adj (air, atmosphere) dünn; (fig) exklusiv.
rarely ['rɛəlɪ] adv selten.
raring ['rɛərɪŋ] adj: ~ **to go** (inf) in den Startlöchern.
rarity ['rɛərɪtɪ] n Seltenheit f.
rascal ['rɑːskl] n (child) Frechdachs m; (rogue) Schurke m.
rash [ræʃ] adj (person) unbesonnen; (promise, act) übereilt ♦ n (MED) Ausschlag m; (of events etc) Flut f; **to come out in a ~** einen Ausschlag bekommen.
rasher ['ræʃə] n (of bacon) Scheibe f.
rashly ['ræʃlɪ] adv (promise etc) voreilig.
rasp [rɑːsp] n (tool) Raspel f; (sound) Kratzen nt ♦ vt, vi krächzen.
raspberry ['rɑːzbərɪ] n Himbeere f; ~ **bush** Himbeerstrauch m; **to blow a ~** (inf) verächtlich schnauben.
rasping ['rɑːspɪŋ] adj: **a ~ noise** ein kratzendes Geräusch.
Rastafarian n Rastafarier m.
rat [ræt] n Ratte f.
ratable ['reɪtəbl] adj = **rateable**.
ratchet ['rætʃɪt] n Sperrklinke f; ~ **wheel** Sperrad nt.
rate [reɪt] n (speed: of change etc) Tempo nt; (of inflation, unemployment etc) Rate f; (of interest, taxation) Satz m; (price) Preis m ♦ vt einschätzen; **rates** npl (BRIT: property tax) Kommunalabgaben pl; **at a ~ of 60 kph** mit einem Tempo von 60 km/h; ~ **of growth** (ECON) Wachstumsrate f; ~ **of return** (FIN) Rendite f; **pulse ~** Pulszahl f; **at this/that ~**

wenn es so weitergeht; at any ~ auf jeden Fall; **to ~ sb/sth as** jdn/etw einschätzen als; **to ~ sb/sth among** jdn/etw zählen zu; **to ~ sb/sth highly** jdn/etw hoch einschätzen.
rateable ['reɪtəbl] adj: ~ **value** (BRIT) steuerbarer Wert m.
ratepayer ['reɪtpeɪə] (BRIT) n Steuerzahler(in) m(f).
rather ['rɑːðə] adv (somewhat) etwas; (very) ziemlich; ~ **a lot** ziemlich or recht viel; **I would ~ go** ich würde lieber gehen; ~ **than** (instead of) anstelle von; **or ~** (more accurately) oder vielmehr; **I'd ~ not say** das möchte ich lieber nicht sagen; **I ~ think he won't come** ich glaube eher, daß er nicht kommt.
ratification [rætɪfɪ'keɪʃən] n Ratifikation f.
ratify ['rætɪfaɪ] vt (treaty etc) ratifizieren.
rating ['reɪtɪŋ] n (score) Rate f; (assessment) Beurteilung f; (NAUT: BRIT: sailor) Matrose m; **ratings** npl (RADIO, TV) Einschaltquote f.
ratio ['reɪʃɪəu] n Verhältnis nt; **a ~ of 5 to 1** ein Verhältnis von 5 zu 1.
ration ['ræʃən] n Ration f ♦ vt rationieren; **rations** npl (MIL) Rationen pl.
rational ['ræʃənl] adj rational, vernünftig.
rationale [ræʃə'nɑːl] n Grundlage f.
rationalization [ræʃənəlaɪ'zeɪʃən] n (justification) Rechtfertigung f; (of company, system) Rationalisierung f.
rationalize ['ræʃnəlaɪz] vt (see n) rechtfertigen, rationalisieren.
rationally ['ræʃnəlɪ] adv vernünftig, rational.
rationing ['ræʃnɪŋ] n Rationierung f.
ratpack (BRIT: inf) n (reporters) Pressemeute f.
rat poison n Rattengift nt.
rat race n: **the ~** der ständige or tägliche Konkurrenzkampf m.
rattan [ræ'tæn] n Rattan nt, Peddigrohr nt.
rattle ['rætl] n (of door, window, snake) Klappern nt; (of train, car etc) Rattern nt; (of chain) Rasseln nt; (toy) Rassel f ♦ vi (chains) rasseln; (windows) klappern; (bottles) klirren ♦ vt (shake noisily) rütteln an +dat; (fig: unsettle) nervös machen; **to ~ along** (car, bus) dahinrattern.
rattlesnake ['rætlsneɪk] n Klapperschlange f.
ratty ['rætɪ] (inf) adj gereizt.
raucous ['rɔːkəs] adj (voice etc) rauh.
raucously ['rɔːkəslɪ] adv rauh.
raunchy ['rɔːntʃɪ] adj (voice, song) lüstern, geil.
ravage ['rævɪdʒ] vt verwüsten.
ravages ['rævɪdʒɪz] npl (of war) Verwüstungen pl; (of weather) zerstörende Auswirkungen pl; (of time) Spuren pl.
rave [reɪv] vi (in anger) toben ♦ adj (inf: review) glänzend; (scene, culture) Rave- ♦ n (BRIT: inf: party) Rave m, Fete f.
▶**rave about** schwärmen von.
raven ['reɪvən] n Rabe m.
ravenous ['rævənəs] adj (person)

ausgehungert; (*appetite*) unersättlich.
ravine [rə'viːn] *n* Schlucht *f*.
raving ['reɪvɪŋ] *adj:* **a ~ lunatic** ein total
verrückter Typ.
ravings ['reɪvɪŋz] *npl* Phantastereien *pl*.
ravioli [rævɪ'əʊlɪ] *n* Ravioli *pl*.
ravishing ['rævɪʃɪŋ] *adj* hinreißend.
raw [rɔː] *adj* roh; (*sore*) wund; (*inexperienced*)
unerfahren; (*weather, day*) rauh; **to get a
~ deal** ungerecht behandelt werden.
Rawalpindi [rɔːl'pɪndɪ] *n* Rawalpindi *nt*.
raw material *n* Rohmaterial *nt*.
ray [reɪ] *n* Strahl *m*; **~ of hope**
Hoffnungsschimmer *m*.
rayon ['reɪɔn] *n* Reyon *nt*.
raze [reɪz] *vt* (*also:* **to ~ to the ground**) dem
Erdboden gleichmachen.
razor ['reɪzə*] *n* Rasierapparat *m*; (*open ~*)
Rasiermesser *nt*.
razor blade *n* Rasierklinge *f*.
razzle ['ræzl] (*BRIT: inf*) *n:* **to be/go on the ~**
einen draufmachen.
razzmatazz ['ræzmə'tæz] (*inf*) *n* Trubel *m*.
RC *abbr* (= *Roman Catholic*) r.-k.
RCAF *n abbr* (= *Royal Canadian Air Force*)
kanadische Luftwaffe *f*.
RCMP *n abbr* (= *Royal Canadian Mounted Police*)
kanadische berittene Polizei.
RCN *n abbr* (= *Royal Canadian Navy*)
kanadische Marine.
RD (*US*) *abbr* (*POST:* = *rural delivery*)
Landpostzustellung *f*.
Rd *abbr* (= *road*) Str.
RDC (*BRIT*) *n abbr* = **rural district council**.
RE (*BRIT*) *n abbr* (*SCOL*) = **religious education**;
(*MIL:* = *Royal Engineers*) *Königliches
Pionierkorps*.
re [riː] *prep* (*with regard to*) bezüglich +*gen*.
reach [riːtʃ] *n* (*range*) Reichweite *f* ♦ *vt*
erreichen; (*conclusion, decision*) kommen zu;
(*be able to touch*) kommen an +*acc* ♦ *vi* (*stretch
out one's arm*) langen; **reaches** *npl* (*of river*)
Gebiete *pl*; **within/out of ~** in/außer
Reichweite; **within easy ~ of the
supermarket/station** ganz in der Nähe des
Supermarkts/Bahnhofs; **beyond the ~ of
sb/sth** außerhalb der Reichweite von jdm/
etw; **"keep out of the ~ of children"** „von
Kindern fernhalten"; **can I ~ you at your
hotel?** kann ich Sie in Ihrem Hotel
erreichen?
▶**reach out** *vt* (*hand*) ausstrecken ♦ *vi* die
Hand ausstrecken; **to ~ out for sth** nach
etw greifen.
react [riː'ækt] *vi:* **to ~ (to)** (*also MED*)
reagieren (auf +*acc*); (*CHEM*): **to ~ (with)**
reagieren (mit); **to ~ (against)** (*rebel*) sich
wehren (gegen).
reaction [riː'ækʃən] *n* Reaktion *f*; **reactions** *npl*
(*reflexes*) Reaktionen *pl*; **a ~ against sth**
Widerstand gegen etw.
reactionary [riː'ækʃənrɪ] *adj* reaktionär ♦ *n*

Reaktionär(in) *m(f)*.
reactor [riː'æktə*] *n* (*also:* **nuclear ~**)
Kernreaktor *m*.
read [riːd] (*pt, pp* **read** [rɛd]) *vi* lesen; (*piece of
writing etc*) sich lesen ♦ *vt* lesen; (*meter,
thermometer etc*) ablesen; (*understand: mood,
thoughts*) sich versetzen in +*acc*; (*meter,
thermometer etc: measurement*) anzeigen;
(*study*) studieren; **to ~ sb's lips** jdm von den
Lippen ablesen; **to ~ sb's mind** jds
Gedanken lesen; **to ~ between the lines**
zwischen den Zeilen lesen; **to take sth as ~**
(*self-evident*) etw für selbstverständlich
halten; **you can take it as ~ that** ... Sie
können davon ausgehen, daß ...; **do you
~ me?** (*TEL*) verstehen Sie mich?; **to ~ sth
into sb's remarks** etw in jds Bemerkungen
hineininterpretieren.
▶**read out** *vt* vorlesen.
▶**read over** *vt* durchlesen.
▶**read through** *vt* durchlesen.
▶**read up on** *vt fus* sich informieren über
+*acc*.
readable ['riːdəbl] *adj* (*legible*) lesbar; (*book,
author etc*) lesenswert.
reader ['riːdə*] *n* (*person*) Leser(in) *m(f)*; (*book*)
Lesebuch *nt*; (*BRIT: at university*)
≈ Dozent(in) *m(f)*; **to be an avid/slow ~**
eifrig/langsam lesen.
readership ['riːdəʃɪp] *n* (*of newspaper etc*)
Leserschaft *f*.
readily ['rɛdɪlɪ] *adv* (*without hesitation*)
bereitwillig; (*easily*) ohne weiteres.
readiness ['rɛdɪnɪs] *n* Bereitschaft *f*; **in ~ for**
bereit für.
reading ['riːdɪŋ] *n* Lesen *nt*; (*understanding*)
Verständnis *nt*; (*from bible, of poetry etc*)
Lesung *f*; (*on meter, thermometer etc*)
Anzeige *f*.
reading lamp *n* Leselampe *f*.
reading matter *n* Lesestoff *m*.
reading room *n* Lesesaal *m*.
readjust [riːə'dʒʌst] *vt* (*position, knob,
instrument etc*) neu einstellen ♦ *vi:* **to ~ (to)**
sich anpassen (an +*acc*).
readjustment [riːə'dʒʌstmənt] *n* (*fig*)
Neuorientierung *f*.
ready ['rɛdɪ] *adj* (*prepared*) bereit, fertig;
(*willing*) bereit; (*easy*) leicht; (*available*)
fertig ♦ *n:* **at the ~** (*MIL*) einsatzbereit; (*fig*)
griffbereit; **~ for use** gebrauchsfertig; **to
be ~ to do sth** bereit sein, etw zu tun; **to get
~** sich fertigmachen; **to get sth ~** etw
bereitmachen.
ready cash *n* Bargeld *nt*.
ready-cooked ['rɛdɪkʊkt] *adj* vorgekocht.
ready-made ['rɛdɪmeɪd] *adj* (*clothes*) von der
Stange, Konfektions-; **~ meal** Fertiggericht
nt.
ready-mix ['rɛdɪmɪks] *n* (*for cakes etc*)
Backmischung *f*; (*concrete*) Fertigbeton *m*.
ready money *n* = **ready cash**.

ready reckoner [-'rɛkənə•] (*BRIT*) n
Rechentabelle f.
ready-to-wear ['rɛdɪtə'wɛə•] adj (*clothes*) von
der Stange, Konfektions-.
reaffirm [ri:ə'fə:m] vt bestätigen.
reagent [ri:'eɪdʒənt] n: **chemical** ~ Reagens nt.
real [rɪəl] adj (*reason, result etc*) wirklich;
(*leather, gold etc*) echt; (*life, feeling*) wahr; (*for
emphasis*) echt ♦ adv (*US: inf: very*) echt; **in
~ life** im wahren or wirklichen Leben; **in
~ terms** effektiv.
real ale n Real Ale nt.
real estate n Immobilien pl ♦ cpd (*US: agent,
business etc*) Immobilien-.
realign vt neu ausrichten.
realism ['rɪəlɪzəm] n (*also ART*) Realismus m.
realist ['rɪəlɪst] n Realist(in) m(f).
realistic [rɪə'lɪstɪk] adj realistisch.
reality [ri:'ælɪtɪ] n Wirklichkeit f, Realität f; **in
~ in** Wirklichkeit.
realization [rɪəlaɪ'zeɪʃən] n (*understanding*)
Erkenntnis f; (*fulfilment*) Verwirklichung f,
Realisierung f; (*FIN: of asset*) Realisation f.
realize ['rɪəlaɪz] vt (*understand*) verstehen;
(*fulfil*) verwirklichen, realisieren; (*FIN:
amount, profit*) realisieren; **I ~ that** ... es ist
mir klar, daß ...
really ['rɪəlɪ] adv wirklich; **what ~ happened**
was wirklich geschah; **~?** wirklich?; **~!**
(*indicating annoyance*) also wirklich!
realm [rɛlm] n (*fig: field*) Bereich m; (*kingdom*)
Reich nt.
real-time ['ri:ltaɪm] adj (*COMPUT: processing
etc*) Echtzeit-.
realtor ['rɪəltɔ:•] (*US*) n Immobilienmakler(in)
m(f).
ream [ri:m] n (*of paper*) Ries nt; **reams** (*inf, fig*)
Bände pl.
reap [ri:p] vt (*crop*) einbringen, ernten; (*fig:
benefits*) ernten; (: *rewards*) bekommen.
reaper ['ri:pə•] n (*machine*) Mähdrescher m.
reappear [ri:ə'pɪə•] vi wiederauftauchen.
reappearance [ri:ə'pɪərəns] n Wiederauftauchen nt.
reapply [ri:ə'plaɪ] vi: **to ~ for** sich erneut
bewerben um.
reappoint [ri:ə'pɔɪnt] vt (*to job*)
wiedereinstellen.
reappraisal [ri:ə'preɪzl] n (*of idea etc*)
Neubeurteilung f.
rear [rɪə•] adj hintere(r, s); (*wheel etc*) Hinter-
♦ n Rückseite f; (*buttocks*) Hinterteil nt ♦ vt
(*family, animals*) aufziehen ♦ vi (*also*: ~ **up**:
horse*) sich aufbäumen.
rear admiral n Konteradmiral m.
rear-engined ['rɪər'ɛndʒɪnd] adj mit
Heckmotor.
rearguard ['rɪəgɑ:d] n (*MIL*) Nachhut f; **to
fight a ~ action** (*fig*) sich erbittert wehren.
rearm [ri:'ɑ:m] vi (*country*) wiederaufrüsten
♦ vt wiederbewaffnen.
rearmament [ri:'ɑ:məmənt] n

Wiederaufrüstung f.
rearrange [ri:ə'reɪndʒ] vt (*furniture*) umstellen;
(*meeting*) den Termin ändern +gen.
rear-view mirror ['rɪəvju:-] n Rückspiegel m.
reason ['ri:zn] n (*cause*) Grund m; (*rationality*)
Verstand m; (*common sense*) Vernunft f ♦ vi:
to ~ with sb vernünftig mit jdm reden; **the
~ for/why** der Grund für/, warum; **we have
~ to believe that** ... wir haben Grund zu der
Annahme, daß ...; **it stands to ~ that** ... es ist
zu erwarten, daß ...; **she claims with good
~ that** ... sie behauptet mit gutem Grund or
mit Recht, daß ...; **all the more ~ why** ... ein
Grund mehr, warum ...; **yes, but within ~**
ja, solange es sich im Rahmen hält.
reasonable ['ri:znəbl] adj vernünftig; (*number,
amount*) angemessen; (*not bad*) ganz
ordentlich; **be ~!** sei doch vernünftig!
reasonably ['ri:znəblɪ] adv (*fairly*) ziemlich;
(*sensibly*) vernünftig; **one could ~ assume
that** ... man könnte durchaus annehmen,
daß ...
reasoned ['ri:znd] adj (*argument*) durchdacht.
reasoning ['ri:znɪŋ] n Argumentation f.
reassemble [ri:ə'sɛmbl] vt (*machine*) wieder
zusammensetzen ♦ vi sich wieder
versammeln.
reassert [ri:ə'sə:t] vt: **to ~ oneself/one's
authority** seine Autorität wieder geltend
machen.
reassurance [ri:ə'ʃuərəns] n (*comfort*)
Beruhigung f; (*guarantee*) Bestätigung f.
reassure [ri:ə'ʃuə•] vt beruhigen.
reassuring [ri:ə'ʃuərɪŋ] adj beruhigend.
reawakening [ri:ə'weɪknɪŋ] n
Wiedererwachen nt.
rebate ['ri:beɪt] n (*on tax etc*) Rückerstattung
f; (*discount*) Ermäßigung f.
rebel ['rɛbl] n Rebell(in) m(f) ♦ vi rebellieren.
rebellion [rɪ'bɛljən] n Rebellion f.
rebellious [rɪ'bɛljəs] adj rebellisch.
rebirth [ri:'bə:θ] n Wiedergeburt f.
rebound [rɪ'baund] vi (*ball*) zurückprallen ♦ n:
on the ~ (*fig*) als Tröstung.
rebuff [rɪ'bʌf] n Abfuhr f ♦ vt zurückweisen.
rebuild [ri:'bɪld] (*irreg: like* **build**) vt
wiederaufbauen; (*confidence*)
wiederherstellen.
rebuke [rɪ'bju:k] vt zurechtweisen, tadeln ♦ n
Zurechtweisung f, Tadel m.
rebut [rɪ'bʌt] (*form*) vt widerlegen.
rebuttal [rɪ'bʌtl] (*form*) n Widerlegung f.
recalcitrant [rɪ'kælsɪtrənt] adj aufsässig.
recall [rɪ'kɔ:l] vt (*remember*) sich erinnern an
+acc; (*ambassador*) abberufen; (*product*)
zurückrufen ♦ n (*of memories*) Erinnerung f;
(*of ambassador*) Abberufung f; (*of product*)
Rückruf m; **beyond ~** unwiederbringlich.
recant [rɪ'kænt] vi widerrufen.
recap ['ri:kæp] vt, vi zusammenfassen ♦ n
Zusammenfassung f.
recapitulate [ri:kə'pɪtjuleɪt] vt, vi = **recap**.

recapture [riː'kæptʃəˈ] *vt* (*town*)
wiedereinnehmen; (*prisoner*)
wiederergreifen; (*atmosphere etc*)
heraufbeschwören.

rec'd *abbr* (*COMM*: = *received*) erh.

recede [rɪ'siːd] *vi* (*tide*) zurückgehen; (*lights etc*) verschwinden; (*memory, hope*)
schwinden; **his hair is beginning to** ~ er
bekommt eine Stirnglatze.

receding [rɪ'siːdɪŋ] *adj* (*hairline*)
zurückweichend; (*chin*) fliehend.

receipt [rɪ'siːt] *n* (*document*) Quittung *f*; (*act of receiving*) Erhalt *m*; **receipts** *npl* (*COMM*)
Einnahmen *pl*; **on** ~ **of** bei Erhalt *+gen*; **to be in** ~ **of sth** etw erhalten.

receivable [rɪ'siːvəbl] *adj* (*COMM*) zulässig;
(*owing*) ausstehend.

receive [rɪ'siːv] *vt* erhalten, bekommen;
(*injury*) erleiden; (*treatment*) erhalten;
(*visitor, guest*) empfangen; **to be on the receiving end of sth** der/die Leidtragende
von etw sein; **"~d with thanks"** (*COMM*)
„dankend erhalten".

> **Received Pronunciation** *oder* **RP** *ist die
> hochsprachliche Standardaussprache des
> britischen Englisch, die bis vor kurzem in der
> Ober- und Mittelschicht vorherrschte und auch
> heute noch großes Ansehen unter höheren
> Beamten genießt.*

receiver [rɪ'siːvəˈ] *n* (*TEL*) Hörer *m*; (*RADIO, TV*) Empfänger *m*; (*of stolen goods*)
Hehler(in) *m(f)*; (*COMM*) Empfänger(in) *m(f)*.

receivership [rɪ'siːvəʃɪp] *n*: **to go into** ~ in
Konkurs gehen.

recent ['riːsnt] *adj* (*event*) kürzlich; (*times*)
letzte(r, s); **in** ~ **years** in den letzten Jahren.

recently ['riːsntlɪ] *adv* (*not long ago*) kürzlich;
(*lately*) in letzter Zeit; **as** ~ **as** erst; **until** ~
bis vor kurzem.

receptacle [rɪ'sɛptɪkl] *n* Behälter *m*.

reception [rɪ'sɛpʃən] *n* (*in hotel, office etc*)
Rezeption *f*; (*party, RADIO, TV*) Empfang *m*;
(*welcome*) Aufnahme *f*.

reception centre (*BRIT*) *n* Aufnahmelager *nt*.

reception desk *n* Rezeption *f*.

receptionist [rɪ'sɛpʃənɪst] *n* (*in hotel*)
Empfangschef *m*, Empfangsdame *f*; (*in doctor's surgery*) Sprechstundenhilfe *f*.

receptive [rɪ'sɛptɪv] *adj* aufnahmebereit.

recess [rɪ'sɛs] *n* (*in room*) Nische *f*; (*secret place*) Winkel *m*; (*POL etc: holiday*) Ferien *pl*;
(*US: LAW: short break*) Pause *f*; (*esp US: SCOL*)
Pause *f*.

recession [rɪ'sɛʃən] *n* (*ECON*) Rezession *f*.

recharge [riː'tʃɑːdʒ] *vt* (*battery*) aufladen.

rechargeable [riː'tʃɑːdʒəbl] *adj* (*battery*)
aufladbar.

recipe ['rɛsɪpɪ] *n* Rezept *nt*; **a** ~ **for success** ein
Erfolgsrezept *nt*; **to be a** ~ **for disaster** in
die Katastrophe führen.

recipient [rɪ'sɪpɪənt] *n* Empfänger(in) *m(f)*.

reciprocal [rɪ'sɪprəkl] *adj* gegenseitig.

reciprocate [rɪ'sɪprəkeɪt] *vt* (*invitation, feeling*)
erwidern ♦ *vi* sich revanchieren.

recital [rɪ'saɪtl] *n* (*concert*) Konzert *nt*.

recitation [rɛsɪ'teɪʃən] *n* (*of poem etc*) Vortrag
m.

recite [rɪ'saɪt] *vt* (*poem*) vortragen; (*complaints etc*) aufzählen.

reckless ['rɛkləs] *adj* (*driving, driver*)
rücksichtslos; (*spending*) leichtsinnig.

recklessly ['rɛkləslɪ] *adv* (*drive*) rücksichtslos;
(*spend, gamble*) leichtsinnig.

reckon ['rɛkən] *vt* (*consider*) halten für;
(*calculate*) berechnen ♦ *vi*: **he is somebody to be** ~**ed with** mit ihm muß man rechnen; **I** ~ **that** ... (*think*) ich schätze, daß ...; **to** ~ **without sb/sth** nicht mit jdm/etw
rechnen.

▶**reckon on** *vt fus* rechnen mit.

reckoning ['rɛknɪŋ] *n* (*calculation*)
Berechnung *f*; **the day of** ~ der Tag der
Abrechnung.

reclaim [rɪ'kleɪm] *vt* (*luggage*) abholen; (*tax etc*) zurückfordern; (*land*) gewinnen; (*waste materials*) zur Wiederverwertung sammeln.

reclamation [rɛklə'meɪʃən] *n* (*of land*)
Gewinnung *f*.

recline [rɪ'klaɪn] *vi* (*sit or lie back*)
zurückgelehnt sitzen.

reclining [rɪ'klaɪnɪŋ] *adj* (*seat*) Liege-.

recluse [rɪ'kluːs] *n* Einsiedler(in) *m(f)*.

recognition [rɛkəg'nɪʃən] *n* (*of person, place*)
Erkennen *nt*; (*of problem, fact*) Erkenntnis *f*;
(*of achievement*) Anerkennung *f*; **in** ~ **of** in
Anerkennung *+gen*; **to gain** ~ Anerkennung
finden; **she had changed beyond** ~ sie war
nicht wiederzuerkennen.

recognizable ['rɛkəgnaɪzəbl] *adj* erkennbar.

recognize ['rɛkəgnaɪz] *vt* (*person, place, voice*)
wiedererkennen; (*sign, problem*) erkennen;
(*qualifications, government, achievement*)
anerkennen; **to** ~ **sb by/as** jdn erkennen an
+dat/als.

recoil [rɪ'kɔɪl] *vi* (*person*): **to** ~ **from**
zurückweichen vor *+dat*; (*fig*)
zurückschrecken vor *+dat* ♦ *n* (*of gun*)
Rückstoß *m*.

recollect [rɛkə'lɛkt] *vt* (*remember*) sich
erinnern an *+acc*.

recollection [rɛkə'lɛkʃən] *n* Erinnerung *f*; **to the best of my** ~ soweit ich mich erinnern
or entsinnen kann.

recommend [rɛkə'mɛnd] *vt* empfehlen; **she has a lot to** ~ **her** es spricht sehr viel für
sie.

recommendation [rɛkəmɛn'deɪʃən] *n*
Empfehlung *f*; **on the** ~ **of** auf Empfehlung
+gen.

recommended retail price (*BRIT*) *n* (*COMM*)
unverbindlicher Richtpreis *m*.

recompense ['rɛkəmpɛns] *n* (*reward*)

Belohnung *f*; (*compensation*) Entschädigung
f.

reconcilable ['rɛkənsaɪləbl] *adj* (*ideas*)
(miteinander) vereinbar.

reconcile ['rɛkənsaɪl] *vt* (*people*) versöhnen;
(*facts, beliefs*) (miteinander) vereinbaren, in
Einklang bringen; **to ~ o.s. to sth** sich mit
etw abfinden.

reconciliation [rɛkənsɪlɪ'eɪʃən] *n* (*of people*)
Versöhnung *f*; (*of facts, beliefs*)
Vereinbarung *f*.

recondite [rɪ'kɔndaɪt] *adj* obskur.

recondition [riːkən'dɪʃən] *vt* (*machine*)
überholen.

reconditioned [riːkən'dɪʃənd] *adj* (*engine, TV*)
generalüberholt.

reconnaissance [rɪ'kɔnɪsns] *n* (*MIL*)
Aufklärung *f*.

reconnoitre, (*US*) **reconnoiter** [rɛkə'nɔɪtə*]
vt (*MIL*) erkunden.

reconsider [riːkən'sɪdə*] *vt* (noch einmal)
überdenken ♦ *vi* es sich *dat* noch einmal
überlegen.

reconstitute [riː'kɔnstɪtjuːt] *vt* (*organization*)
neu bilden; (*food*) wiederherstellen.

reconstruct [riːkən'strʌkt] *vt* (*building*)
wiederaufbauen; (*policy, system*) neu
organisieren; (*event, crime*) rekonstruieren.

reconstruction [riːkən'strʌkʃən] *n*
Wiederaufbau *m*; (*of crime*) Rekonstruktion
f.

reconvene [riːkən'viːn] *vi* (*meet again*) wieder
zusammenkommen ♦ *vt* (*meeting etc*) wieder
einberufen.

record ['rɛkɔːd] *n* (*written account*)
Aufzeichnung *f*; (*of meeting*) Protokoll *nt*; (*of
decision*) Beleg *m*; (*COMPUT*) Datensatz *m*;
(*file*) Akte *f*; (*MUS: disc*) Schallplatte *f*;
(*history*) Vorgeschichte *f*; (*also:* **criminal ~**)
Vorstrafen *pl*; (*SPORT*) Rekord *m* ♦ *vt*
aufzeichnen; (*song etc*) aufnehmen;
(*temperature, speed etc*) registrieren ♦ *adj*
(*sales, profits*) Rekord-; **~ of attendance**
Anwesenheitsliste *f*; **public ~s** Urkunden *pl*
des Nationalarchivs; **to keep a ~ of sth** etw
schriftlich festhalten; **to have a good/poor
~** gute/schlechte Leistungen vorzuweisen
haben; **to have a (criminal) ~** vorbestraft
sein; **to set** *or* **put the ~ straight** (*fig*)
Klarheit schaffen; **he is on ~ as saying that
...** er hat nachweislich gesagt, daß ...; **off the
~** (*remark*) inoffiziell ♦ *adv* (*speak*) im
Vertrauen; **in ~ time** in Rekordzeit.

recorded delivery [rɪ'kɔːdɪd-] (*BRIT*) *n* (*POST*)
Einschreiben *nt*; **to send sth (by) ~** etw per
Einschreiben senden.

recorder [rɪ'kɔːdə*] *n* (*MUS*) Blockflöte *f*;
(*LAW*) *nebenamtlich als Richter tätiger
Rechtsanwalt*.

record holder *n* (*SPORT*) Rekordinhaber(in)
m(f).

recording [rɪ'kɔːdɪŋ] *n* Aufnahme *f*.

recording studio *n* Aufnahmestudio *nt*.

record library *n* Schallplattenverleih *m*.

record player *n* Plattenspieler *m*.

recount [rɪ'kaunt] *vt* (*story etc*) erzählen.

re-count ['riːkaunt] *n* (*of votes*) Nachzählung *f*
♦ *vt* (*votes*) nachzählen.

recoup [rɪ'kuːp] *vt*: **to ~ one's losses** seine
Verluste ausgleichen.

recourse [rɪ'kɔːs] *n*: **to have ~ to sth** Zuflucht
zu etw nehmen.

recover [rɪ'kʌvə*] *vt* (*get back*)
zurückbekommen; (*stolen goods*)
sicherstellen; (*wreck, body*) bergen; (*financial
loss*) ausgleichen ♦ *vi* sich erholen.

re-cover [riː'kʌvə*] *vt* (*chair etc*) neu beziehen.

recovery [rɪ'kʌvərɪ] *n* (*from illness etc*)
Erholung *f*; (*in economy*) Aufschwung *m*; (*of
lost items*) Wiederfinden *nt*; (*of stolen goods*)
Sicherstellung *f*; (*of wreck, body*) Bergung *f*;
(*of financial loss*) Ausgleich *m*.

re-create [riːkrɪ'eɪt] *vt* (*atmosphere, situation*)
wiederherstellen.

recreation [rɛkrɪ'eɪʃən] *n* (*leisure*) Erholung *f*,
Entspannung *f*.

recreational [rɛkrɪ'eɪʃənl] *adj* (*facilities etc*)
Freizeit-.

recreational drug *n* Freizeitdroge *f*.

recreational vehicle (*US*) *n* Caravan *m*.

recrimination [rɪkrɪmɪ'neɪʃən] *n* gegenseitige
Anschuldigungen *pl*.

recruit [rɪ'kruːt] *n* (*MIL*) Rekrut *m*; (*in
company*) neuer Mitarbeiter *m*, neue
Mitarbeiterin *f* ♦ *vt* (*MIL*) rekrutieren; (*staff,
new members*) anwerben.

recruiting office [rɪ'kruːtɪŋ-] *n* (*MIL*)
Rekrutierungsbüro *nt*.

recruitment [rɪ'kruːtmənt] *n* (*of staff*)
Anwerbung *f*.

rectangle ['rɛktæŋgl] *n* Rechteck *nt*.

rectangular [rɛk'tæŋgjulə*] *adj* (*shape*)
rechteckig.

rectify ['rɛktɪfaɪ] *vt* (*mistake etc*) korrigieren.

rector ['rɛktə*] *n* (*REL*) Pfarrer(in) *m(f)*.

rectory ['rɛktərɪ] *n* Pfarrhaus *nt*.

rectum ['rɛktəm] *n* Rektum *nt*, Mastdarm *m*.

recuperate [rɪ'kjuːpəreɪt] *vi* (*recover*) sich
erholen.

recur [rɪ'kəː*] *vi* (*error, event*) sich
wiederholen; (*pain etc*) wiederholt
auftreten.

recurrence [rɪ'kərns] *n* (*see vi*) Wiederholung
f; wiederholtes Auftreten *nt*.

recurrent [rɪ'kərnt] *adj* (*see vi*) sich
wiederholend; wiederholt auftretend.

recurring [rɪ'kərɪŋ] *adj* (*problem, dream*) sich
wiederholend; (*MATH*): **six point five four ~**
sechs komma fünf Periode vier.

recycle [riː'saɪkl] *vt* (*waste, paper etc*) recyceln,
wiederverwerten.

red [rɛd] *n* Rot *nt*; (*pej: POL*) Rote(r) *f(m)* ♦ *adj*
rot; **to be in the ~** (*business etc*) in den roten
Zahlen sein.

red alert *n*: **to be on** ~ in höchster Alarmbereitschaft sein.
red-blooded ['rɛd'blʌdɪd] *adj* heißblütig.

> Als **redbrick university** *werden die jüngeren britischen Universitäten bezeichnet, die im späten 19. und Anfang des 20. Jh. in Städten wie Manchester, Liverpool und Bristol gegründet wurden. Der Name steht im Gegensatz zu Oxford und Cambridge und bezieht sich auf die roten Backsteinmauern der Universitätsgebäude.*

red carpet treatment *n*: **to give sb the** ~ den roten Teppich für jdn ausrollen.
Red Cross *n* Rotes Kreuz *nt*.
redcurrant ['rɛdkʌrənt] *n* rote Johannisbeere *f*.
redden ['rɛdn] *vt* röten ♦ *vi* (*blush*) erröten.
reddish ['rɛdɪʃ] *adj* rötlich.
redecorate [riː'dɛkəreɪt] *vt, vi* renovieren.
redecoration [riːdɛkə'reɪʃən] *n* Renovierung *f*.
redeem [rɪ'diːm] *vt* (*situation etc*) retten; (*voucher, sth in pawn*) einlösen; (*loan*) abzahlen; (*REL*) erlösen; **to** ~ **oneself for sth** etw wiedergutmachen.
redeemable [rɪ'diːməbl] *adj* (*voucher etc*) einlösbar.
redeeming [rɪ'diːmɪŋ] *adj* (*feature, quality*) versöhnend.
redefine [riːdɪ'faɪn] *vt* neu definieren.
redemption [rɪ'dɛmʃən] *n* (*REL*) Erlösung *f*; **past** *or* **beyond** ~ nicht mehr zu retten.
redeploy [riːdɪ'plɔɪ] *vt* (*resources, staff*) umverteilen; (*MIL*) verlegen.
redeployment [riːdɪ'plɔɪmənt] *n* (*see vt*) Umverteilung *f*; Verlegung *f*.
redevelop [riːdɪ'vɛləp] *vt* (*area*) sanieren.
redevelopment [riːdɪ'vɛləpmənt] *n* Sanierung *f*.
red-handed [rɛd'hændɪd] *adj*: **to be caught** ~ auf frischer Tat ertappt werden.
redhead ['rɛdhɛd] *n* Rotschopf *m*.
red herring *n* (*fig*) falsche Spur *f*.
red-hot [rɛd'hɒt] *adj* (*metal*) rotglühend.
redirect [riːdaɪ'rɛkt] *vt* (*mail*) nachsenden; (*traffic*) umleiten.
rediscover [riːdɪs'kʌvə*] *vt* wiederentdecken.
redistribute [riːdɪs'trɪbjuːt] *vt* umverteilen.
red-letter day ['rɛdlɛtə-] *n* besonderer Tag *m*.
red light *n* (*AUT*): **to go through a** ~ eine Ampel bei Rot überfahren.
red-light district ['rɛdlaɪt-] *n* Rotlichtviertel *nt*.
red meat *n* Rind- und Lammfleisch.
redness ['rɛdnɪs] *n* Röte *f*.
redo [riː'duː] (*irreg: like* do) *vt* noch einmal machen.
redolent ['rɛdələnt] *adj*: **to be** ~ **of sth** nach etw riechen; (*fig*) an etw erinnern.
redouble [riː'dʌbl] *vt*: **to** ~ **one's efforts** seine Anstrengungen verdoppeln.

redraft [riː'drɑːft] *vt* (*agreement*) neu abfassen.
redraw [riː'drɔː] *vt* neu zeichnen.
redress [rɪ'drɛs] *n* (*compensation*) Wiedergutmachung *f* ♦ *vt* wiedergutmachen; **to** ~ **the balance** das Gleichgewicht wiederherstellen.
Red Sea *n*: **the** ~ das Rote Meer.
redskin ['rɛdskɪn] (*old: offensive*) *n* Rothaut *f*.
red tape *n* (*fig*) Bürokratie *f*.
reduce [rɪ'djuːs] *vt* (*spending, numbers, risk etc*) vermindern, reduzieren; **to** ~ **sth by/to 5%** etw um/auf 5% *acc* reduzieren; **to** ~ **sb to tears/silence** jdn zum Weinen/Schweigen bringen; **to** ~ **sb to begging/stealing** jdn zur Bettelei/zum Diebstahl zwingen; **"~ speed now"** (*AUT*) „langsam fahren".
reduced [rɪ'djuːst] *adj* (*goods, ticket etc*) ermäßigt; **"greatly** ~ **prices"** „Preise stark reduziert".
reduction [rɪ'dʌkʃən] *n* (*in price etc*) Ermäßigung, Reduzierung *f*, (*in numbers*) Verminderung *f*.
redundancy [rɪ'dʌndənsɪ] (*BRIT*) *n* (*dismissal*) Entlassung *f*; (*unemployment*) Arbeitslosigkeit *f*; **compulsory** ~ Entlassung *f*, **voluntary** ~ freiwilliger Verzicht *m* auf den Arbeitsplatz.
redundancy payment (*BRIT*) *n* Abfindung *f*.
redundant [rɪ'dʌndnt] *adj* (*BRIT: worker*) arbeitslos; (*word, object*) überflüssig; **to be made** ~ (*worker*) den Arbeitsplatz verlieren.
reed [riːd] *n* (*BOT*) Schilf *nt*; (*MUS: of clarinet etc*) Rohrblatt *nt*.
re-educate [riː'ɛdjukeɪt] *vt* umerziehen.
reedy ['riːdɪ] *adj* (*voice*) Fistel-.
reef [riːf] *n* (*at sea*) Riff *nt*.
reek [riːk] *vi*: **to** ~ (**of**) (*lit, fig*) stinken (nach).
reel [riːl] *n* (*of thread etc, on fishing-rod*) Rolle *f*; (*CINE: scene*) Szene *f*; (*of film, tape*) Spule *f*; (*dance*) Reel *m* ♦ *vi* (*sway*) taumeln; **my head is** ~**ing** mir dreht sich der Kopf.
►**reel in** *vt* (*fish, line*) einholen.
►**reel off** *vt* (*say*) herunterrasseln.
re-election [riːɪ'lɛkʃən] *n* Wiederwahl *f*.
re-enter [riː'ɛntə*] *vt* (*country*) wiedereinreisen in +*acc*; (*SPACE*) wiedereintreten in +*acc*.
re-entry [riː'ɛntrɪ] *n* Wiedereinreise *f*; (*SPACE*) Wiedereintritt *m*.
re-examine [riːɪg'zæmɪn] *vt* (*proposal etc*) nochmals prüfen; (*witness*) nochmals vernehmen.
re-export ['riːɪks'pɔːt] *vt* wiederausführen ♦ *n* Wiederausfuhr *f*; (*commodity*) wiederausgeführte Ware *f*.
ref [rɛf] *n* (*inf*) *n abbr* (*SPORT*) = **referee**.
ref. *abbr* (*COMM*: = with reference to*) betr.; **your** ~ Ihr Zeichen;.
refectory [rɪ'fɛktərɪ] *n* (*in university*) Mensa *f*.
refer [rɪ'fə:*] *vt*: **to** ~ **sb to** (*book etc*) jdn verweisen auf +*acc*; (*doctor, hospital*) jdn

überweisen zu; **to ~ sth to** (*task, problem*) etw übergeben an +*acc*; **he ~red me to the manager** er verwies mich an den Geschäftsführer.

▶**refer to** *vt fus* (*mention*) erwähnen; (*relate to*) sich beziehen auf +*acc*; (*consult*) hinzuziehen.

referee [rɛfə'ri:] *n* (*SPORT*) Schiedsrichter(in) *m(f)*; (*BRIT: for job application*) Referenz *f* ♦ *vt* als Schiedsrichter(in) leiten.

reference ['rɛfrəns] *n* (*mention*) Hinweis *m*; (*in book, article*) Quellenangabe *f*; (*for job application, person*) Referenz *f*; **with ~ to** mit Bezug auf +*acc*; **"please quote this ~"** (*COMM*) „bitte dieses Zeichen angeben".

reference book *n* Nachschlagewerk *nt*.
reference library *n* Präsenzbibliothek *f*.
reference number *n* Aktenzeichen *nt*.
referenda [rɛfə'rɛndə] *npl of* **referendum**.
referendum [rɛfə'rɛndəm] (*pl* **referenda**) *n* Referendum *nt*, Volksentscheid *m*.

referral [rɪ'fə:rəl] *n* (*of matter, problem*) Weiterleitung *f*; (*to doctor, specialist*) Überweisung *f*.

refill [ri:'fɪl] *vt* nachfüllen ♦ *n* (*for pen etc*) Nachfüllmine *f*; (*drink*) Nachfüllung *f*.

refine [rɪ'faɪn] *vt* (*sugar, oil*) raffinieren; (*theory, idea*) verfeinern.

refined [rɪ'faɪnd] *adj* (*person*) kultiviert; (*taste*) fein, vornehm; (*sugar, oil*) raffiniert.

refinement [rɪ'faɪnmənt] *n* (*of person*) Kultiviertheit *f*; (*of system, ideas*) Verfeinerung *f*.

refinery [rɪ'faɪnərɪ] *n* (*for oil etc*) Raffinerie *f*.

refit [ri:'fɪt] (*NAUT*) *n* Überholung *f* ♦ *vt* (*ship*) überholen.

reflate [ri:'fleɪt] *vt* (*economy*) ankurbeln.
reflation [ri:'fleɪʃən] *n* (*ECON*) Reflation *f*.
reflationary [ri:'fleɪʃənrɪ] *adj* (*ECON*) reflationär.

reflect [rɪ'flɛkt] *vt* reflektieren; (*fig*) widerspiegeln ♦ *vi* (*think*) nachdenken.

▶**reflect on** *vt fus* (*discredit*) ein schlechtes Licht werfen auf +*acc*.

reflection [rɪ'flɛkʃən] *n* (*image*) Spiegelbild *nt*; (*of light, heat*) Reflexion *f*; (*fig*) Widerspiegelung *f*; (: *thought*) Gedanke *m*; **on ~** nach genauerer Überlegung; **this is a ~ on ...** (*criticism*) das sagt einiges über ...

reflector [rɪ'flɛktə*] *n* (*AUT etc*) Rückstrahler *m*; (*for light, heat*) Reflektor *m*.

reflex ['ri:flɛks] *adj* Reflex-; **reflexes** *npl* (*PHYSIOL, PSYCH*) Reflexe *pl*.

reflexive [rɪ'flɛksɪv] *adj* (*LING*) reflexiv.

reform [rɪ'fɔ:m] *n* Reform *f* ♦ *vt* reformieren ♦ *vi* (*criminal etc*) sich bessern.

reformat [ri:'fɔ:mæt] *vt* (*COMPUT*) neu formatieren.

Reformation [rɛfə'meɪʃən] *n*: **the ~** die Reformation.

reformatory [rɪ'fɔ:mətərɪ] (*US*) *n* Besserungsanstalt *f*.

reformed [rɪ'fɔ:md] *adj* (*character, alcoholic*) gewandelt.

refrain [rɪ'freɪn] *vi*: **to ~ from doing sth** etw unterlassen ♦ *n* (*of song*) Refrain *m*.

refresh [rɪ'frɛʃ] *vt* erfrischen; **to ~ one's memory** sein Gedächtnis auffrischen.

refresher course [rɪ'frɛʃə-] *n* Auffrischungskurs *m*.

refreshing [rɪ'frɛʃɪŋ] *adj* erfrischend; (*sleep*) wohltuend; (*idea etc*) angenehm.

refreshment [rɪ'frɛʃmənt] *n* Erfrischung *f*.

refreshments [rɪ'frɛʃmənts] *npl* (*food and drink*) Erfrischungen *pl*.

refrigeration [rɪfrɪdʒə'reɪʃən] *n* Kühlung *f*.

refrigerator [rɪ'frɪdʒəreɪtə*] *n* Kühlschrank *m*.

refuel [ri:'fjuəl] *vt, vi* auftanken.

refuelling [ri:'fjuəlɪŋ] *n* Auftanken *nt*.

refuge ['rɛfju:dʒ] *n* Zuflucht *f*; **to seek/take ~ in** Zuflucht suchen/nehmen in +*dat*.

refugee [rɛfju'dʒi:] *n* Flüchtling *m*; **a political ~** ein politischer Flüchtling.

refugee camp *n* Flüchtlingslager *nt*.

refund ['ri:fʌnd] *n* Rückerstattung *f* ♦ *vt* (*money*) zurückerstatten.

refurbish [ri:'fə:bɪʃ] *vt* (*shop etc*) renovieren.

refurbishment [ri:fə:bɪʃmənt] *n* (*of shop etc*) Renovierung *f*.

refurnish [ri:'fə:nɪʃ] *vt* neu möblieren.

refusal [rɪ'fju:zəl] *n* Ablehnung *f*; **a ~ to do sth** eine Weigerung, etw zu tun; **to give sb first ~ on sth** jdm etw zuerst anbieten.

refuse¹ [rɪ'fju:z] *vt* (*request, offer etc*) ablehnen; (*gift*) zurückweisen; (*permission*) verweigern ♦ *vi* ablehnen; (*horse*) verweigern; **to ~ to do sth** sich weigern, etw zu tun.

refuse² ['rɛfju:s] *n* (*rubbish*) Abfall *m*, Müll *m*.

refuse collection *n* Müllabfuhr *f*.

refuse disposal *n* Müllbeseitigung *f*.

refusenik [rɪ'fju:znɪk] *n* (*inf*) Verweigerer(in) *m(f)*; (*in former USSR*) sowjetischer Jude, dem die Emigration nach Israel verweigert wurde.

refute [rɪ'fju:t] *vt* (*argument*) widerlegen.

regain [rɪ'geɪn] *vt* wiedererlangen.

regal ['ri:gl] *adj* königlich.

regale [rɪ'geɪl] *vt*: **to ~ sb with sth** jdn mit etw verwöhnen.

regalia [rɪ'geɪlɪə] *n* (*costume*) Amtstracht *f*.

regard [rɪ'gɑ:d] *n* (*esteem*) Achtung *f* ♦ *vt* (*consider*) ansehen, betrachten; (*view*) betrachten; **to give one's ~s to sb** jdm Grüße bestellen; **"with kindest ~s"** „mit freundlichen Grüßen"; **as ~s, with ~ to** bezüglich +*gen*.

regarding [rɪ'gɑ:dɪŋ] *prep* bezüglich +*gen*.

regardless [rɪ'gɑ:dlɪs] *adv* trotzdem ♦ *adj*: **~ of** ohne Rücksicht auf +*acc*.

regatta [rɪ'gætə] *n* Regatta *f*.

regency ['ri:dʒənsɪ] *n* Regentschaft *f* ♦ *adj*: **R~** (*furniture etc*) Regency-.

regenerate [rɪ'dʒɛnəreɪt] *vt* (*inner cities, arts*)

erneuern; (*person, feelings*) beleben ♦ *vi*
(*BIOL*) sich regenerieren.
regent ['riːdʒənt] *n* Regent(in) *m(f)*.
reggae ['rɛgeɪ] *n* Reggae *m*.
regime [reɪ'ʒiːm] *n* (*government*) Regime *nt*;
(*diet etc*) Kur *f*.
regiment ['rɛdʒɪmənt] *n* (*MIL*) Regiment *nt* ♦ *vt*
reglementieren.
regimental [rɛdʒɪ'mɛntl] *adj* Regiments-.
regimentation [rɛdʒɪmɛn'teɪʃən] *n*
Reglementierung *f*.
region ['riːdʒən] *n* (*of land*) Gebiet *nt*; (*of body*)
Bereich *m*; (*administrative division of country*)
Region *f*; **in the ~ of** (*approximately*) im
Bereich von.
regional ['riːdʒənl] *adj* regional.
regional development *n* regionale
Entwicklung *f*.
register ['rɛdʒɪstə*] *n* (*list, MUS*) Register *nt*;
(*also*: **electoral ~**) Wählerverzeichnis *nt*;
(*SCOL*) Klassenbuch *nt* ♦ *vt* registrieren;
(*car*) anmelden; (*letter*) als Einschreiben
senden; (*amount, measurement*) verzeichnen
♦ *vi* (*person*) sich anmelden; (: *at doctor's*)
sich (als Patient) eintragen; (*amount etc*)
registriert werden; (*make impression*)
(einen) Eindruck machen; **to ~ a protest**
Protest anmelden.
registered ['rɛdʒɪstəd] *adj* (*letter, parcel*)
eingeschrieben; (*drug addict, childminder etc*)
(offiziell) eingetragen.
registered company *n* eingetragene
Gesellschaft *f*.
registered nurse (*US*) *n* staatlich geprüfte
Krankenschwester *f*, staatlich geprüfter
Krankenpfleger *m*.
registered trademark *n* eingetragenes
Warenzeichen *nt*.
register office *n* = **registry office**.
registrar ['rɛdʒɪstrɑː*] *n* (*in registry office*)
Standesbeamte(r) *m*, Standesbeamtin *f*; (*in
college etc*) Kanzler *m*; (*BRIT: in hospital*)
Krankenhausarzt *m*, Krankenhausärztin *f*.
registration [rɛdʒɪs'treɪʃən] *n* Registrierung *f*;
(*of students, unemployed etc*) Anmeldung *f*.
registration number (*BRIT*) *n* (*AUT*)
polizeiliches Kennzeichen *nt*.
registry ['rɛdʒɪstrɪ] *n* Registratur *f*.
registry office (*BRIT*) *n* Standesamt *nt*; **to get
married in a ~** standesamtlich heiraten.
regret [rɪ'grɛt] *n* Bedauern *nt* ♦ *vt* bedauern;
with ~ mit Bedauern; **to have no ~s** nichts
bereuen; **we ~ to inform you that …** wir
müssen Ihnen leider mitteilen, daß …
regretfully [rɪ'grɛtfəlɪ] *adv* mit Bedauern.
regrettable [rɪ'grɛtəbl] *adj* bedauerlich.
regrettably [rɪ'grɛtəblɪ] *adv*
bedauerlicherweise; **~, he said …**
bedauerlicherweise sagte er …
Regt *abbr* (*MIL*: = *regiment*) Rgt.
regular ['rɛgjulə*] *adj* (*also LING*) regelmäßig;
(*usual: time, doctor*) üblich; (: *customer*)

Stamm-; (*soldier*) Berufs-; (*COMM: size*)
normal ♦ *n* (*client*) Stammkunde *m*,
Stammkundin *f*.
regularity [rɛgju'lærɪtɪ] *n* Regelmäßigkeit *f*.
regularly ['rɛgjuləlɪ] *adv* regelmäßig; (*breathe,
beat: evenly*) gleichmäßig.
regulate ['rɛgjuleɪt] *vt* regulieren.
regulation [rɛgju'leɪʃən] *n* Regulierung *f*;
(*rule*) Vorschrift *f*.
regulatory [rɛgju'leɪtrɪ] *adj* (*system*)
Regulierungs-; (*body, agency*)
Überwachungs-.
rehabilitate [riːə'bɪlɪteɪt] *vt* (*criminal, drug
addict*) (in die Gesellschaft)
wiedereingliedern; (*invalid*) rehabilitieren.
rehabilitation ['riːəbɪlɪ'teɪʃən] *n* (*see vt*)
Wiedereingliederung *f* (in die
Gesellschaft); Rehabilitation *f*.
rehash [riː'hæʃ] (*inf*) *vt* (*idea etc*) aufwärmen.
rehearsal [rɪ'hɜːsəl] *n* (*THEAT*) Probe *f*; **dress
~** Generalprobe *f*.
rehearse [rɪ'hɜːs] *vt* (*play, speech etc*) proben.
rehouse [riː'hauz] *vt* neu unterbringen.
reign [reɪn] *n* (*lit, fig*) Herrschaft *f* ♦ *vi* (*lit, fig*)
herrschen.
reigning ['reɪnɪŋ] *adj* regierend; (*champion*)
amtierend.
reimburse [riːɪm'bɜːs] *vt* die Kosten erstatten
+*dat.*
rein [reɪn] *n* Zügel *m*; **to give sb free ~** (*fig*)
jdm freie Hand lassen; **to keep a tight ~ on
sth** (*fig*) bei etw die Zügel kurz halten.
reincarnation [riːɪnkɑː'neɪʃən] *n* (*belief*) die
Wiedergeburt *f*; (*person*) Reinkarnation *f*.
reindeer ['reɪndɪə*] *n inv* Ren(tier) *nt*.
reinforce [riːɪn'fɔːs] *vt* (*strengthen*)
verstärken; (*support: idea etc*) stützen;
(: *prejudice*) stärken.
reinforced concrete *n* Stahlbeton *m*.
reinforcement [riːɪn'fɔːsmənt] *n*
(*strengthening*) Verstärkung *f*; (*of attitude etc*)
Stärkung *f*; **reinforcements** *npl* (*MIL*)
Verstärkung *f*.
reinstate [riːɪn'steɪt] *vt* (*employee*)
wiedereinstellen; (*tax, law*)
wiedereinführen; (*text*) wiedereinfügen.
reinstatement [riːɪn'steɪtmənt] *n* (*of
employee*) Wiedereinstellung *f*.
reissue [riː'ɪʃjuː] *vt* neu herausgeben.
reiterate [riː'ɪtəreɪt] *vt* wiederholen.
reject ['riːdʒɛkt] *n* (*COMM*) Ausschuß *m no pl*
♦ *vt* ablehnen; (*admirer*) abweisen; (*goods*)
zurückweisen; (*machine: coin*) nicht
annehmen; (*MED: heart, kidney*) abstoßen.
rejection [rɪ'dʒɛkʃən] *n* Ablehnung *f*; (*of
admirer*) Abweisung *f*; (*MED*) Abstoßung *f*.
rejoice [rɪ'dʒɔɪs] *vi*: **to ~ at** *or* **over** jubeln über
+*acc.*
rejoinder [rɪ'dʒɔɪndə*] *n* Erwiderung *f*.
rejuvenate [rɪ'dʒuːvəneɪt] *vt* (*person*)
verjüngen; (*organization etc*) beleben.
rekindle [riː'kɪndl] *vt* (*interest, emotion etc*)

wiedererwecken.

relapse [rɪ'læps] n (MED) Rückfall m ♦ vi: **to ~ into** zurückfallen in +acc.

relate [rɪ'leɪt] vt (tell) berichten; (connect) in Verbindung bringen ♦ vi: **to ~ to** (empathize with: person, subject) eine Beziehung finden zu; (connect with) zusammenhängen mit.

related [rɪ'leɪtɪd] adj: **to be ~** (miteinander) verwandt sein; (issues etc) zusammenhängen.

relating to [rɪ'leɪtɪŋ-] prep bezüglich +gen, mit Bezug auf +acc.

relation [rɪ'leɪʃən] n (member of family) Verwandte(r) f(m); (connection) Beziehung f; **relations** npl (contact) Beziehungen pl; **diplomatic/international ~s** diplomatische/ internationale Beziehungen; **in ~ to** im Verhältnis zu; **to bear no ~ to** in keinem Verhältnis stehen zu.

relationship [rɪ'leɪʃənʃɪp] n Beziehung f; (between countries) Beziehungen pl; (affair) Verhältnis nt; **they have a good ~** sie haben ein gutes Verhältnis zueinander.

relative ['rɛlətɪv] n Verwandte(r) f(m) ♦ adj relativ; **all her ~s** ihre ganze Verwandtschaft; **~ to** im Vergleich zu; **it's all ~** es ist alles relativ.

relatively ['rɛlətɪvlɪ] adv relativ.

relative pronoun n Relativpronomen nt.

relax [rɪ'læks] vi (person, muscle) sich entspannen; (calm down) sich beruhigen ♦ vt (one's grip) lockern; (mind, person) entspannen; (control etc) lockern.

relaxation [riːlæk'seɪʃən] n Entspannung f; (of control etc) Lockern nt.

relaxed [rɪ'lækst] adj (person, atmosphere) entspannt; (discussion) locker.

relaxing [rɪ'læksɪŋ] adj entspannend.

relay ['riːleɪ] n (race) Staffel f, Staffellauf m ♦ vt (message etc) übermitteln; (broadcast) übertragen.

release [rɪ'liːs] n (from prison) Entlassung f; (from obligation, situation) Befreiung f; (of documents, funds etc) Freigabe f; (of gas etc) Freisetzung f; (of film, book, record) Herausgabe f; (record, film) Veröffentlichung f; (TECH: device) Auslöser m ♦ vt (from prison) entlassen; (person: from obligation, from wreckage) befreien; (gas etc) freisetzen; (TECH, AUT: catch, brake etc) lösen; (record, film) herausbringen; (news, figures) bekanntgeben; **on general ~** (film) überall in den Kinos; see also **press release**.

relegate ['rɛləgeɪt] vt (downgrade) herunterstufen; (BRIT: SPORT): **to be ~d** absteigen.

relent [rɪ'lɛnt] vi (give in) nachgeben.

relentless [rɪ'lɛntlɪs] adj (heat, noise) erbarmungslos; (enemy etc) unerbittlich.

relevance ['rɛləvəns] n Relevanz f, Bedeutung f; **the ~ of religion to society** die Relevanz or Bedeutung der Religion für die

Gesellschaft.

relevant ['rɛləvənt] adj relevant; (chapter, area) entsprechend; **~ to** relevant für.

reliability [rɪlaɪə'bɪlɪtɪ] n Zuverlässigkeit f.

reliable [rɪ'laɪəbl] adj zuverlässig.

reliably [rɪ'laɪəblɪ] adv: **to be ~ informed that ...** zuverlässige Informationen darüber haben, daß ...

reliance [rɪ'laɪəns] n: **~ (on)** (person) Angewiesenheit f (auf +acc); (drugs, financial support) Abhängigkeit f (von).

reliant [rɪ'laɪənt] adj: **to be ~ on sth/sb** auf etw/jdn angewiesen sein.

relic ['rɛlɪk] n (REL) Reliquie f; (of the past) Relikt nt.

relief [rɪ'liːf] n (from pain etc) Erleichterung f; (aid) Hilfe f; (ART, GEOG) Relief nt ♦ cpd (bus) Entlastungs-; (driver) zur Ablösung; **light ~** leichte Abwechslung f.

relief map n Reliefkarte f.

relief road (BRIT) n Entlastungsstraße f.

relieve [rɪ'liːv] vt (pain) lindern; (fear, worry) mildern; (take over from) ablösen; **to ~ sb of sth** (load) jdm etw abnehmen; (duties, post) jdn einer Sache gen entheben; **to ~ o.s.** (euphemism) sich erleichtern.

relieved [rɪ'liːvd] adj erleichtert; **I'm ~ to hear it** es erleichtert mich, das zu hören.

religion [rɪ'lɪdʒən] n Religion f.

religious [rɪ'lɪdʒəs] adj religiös.

religious education n Religionsunterricht m.

religiously [rɪ'lɪdʒəslɪ] adv (regularly, thoroughly) gewissenhaft.

relinquish [rɪ'lɪŋkwɪʃ] vt (control etc) aufgeben; (claim) verzichten auf +acc.

relish ['rɛlɪʃ] n (CULIN) würzige Soße f, Relish nt; (enjoyment) Genuß m ♦ vt (enjoy) genießen; **to ~ doing sth** etw mit Genuß tun.

relive [riː'lɪv] vt noch einmal durchleben.

reload [riː'ləʊd] vt (gun) neu laden.

relocate [riːləʊ'keɪt] vt verlegen ♦ vi den Standort wechseln; **to ~ in** seinen Standort verlegen nach.

reluctance [rɪ'lʌktəns] n Widerwille m.

reluctant [rɪ'lʌktənt] adj unwillig, widerwillig; **I'm ~ to do that** es widerstrebt mir, das zu tun.

reluctantly [rɪ'lʌktəntlɪ] adv widerwillig, nur ungern.

rely on [rɪ'laɪ-] vt fus (be dependent on) abhängen von; (trust) sich verlassen auf +acc.

remain [rɪ'meɪn] vi bleiben; (survive) übrigbleiben; **to ~ silent** weiterhin schweigen; **to ~ in control** die Kontrolle behalten; **much ~s to be done** es noch viel zu tun; **the fact ~s that ...** Tatsache ist und bleibt, daß ...; **it ~s to be seen whether ...** es bleibt abzuwarten, ob ...

remainder [rɪ'meɪndə*] n Rest m ♦ vt (COMM)

zu ermäßigtem Preis anbieten.

remaining [rɪ'meɪnɪŋ] *adj* übrig.

remains [rɪ'meɪnz] *npl* (*of meal*) Überreste *pl*; (*of building etc*) Ruinen *pl*; (*of body*) sterbliche Überreste *pl*.

remand [rɪ'mɑ:nd] *n*: **to be on** ~ in Untersuchungshaft sein ♦ *vt*: **to be ~ed in custody** in Untersuchungshaft bleiben müssen.

remand home (*formerly: BRIT*) *n* Untersuchungsgefängnis *nt* für Jugendliche.

remark [rɪ'mɑ:k] *n* Bemerkung *f* ♦ *vt* bemerken ♦ *vi*: **to** ~ **on sth** Bemerkungen über etw *acc* machen; **to** ~ **that** die Bemerkung machen, daß.

remarkable [rɪ'mɑ:kəbl] *adj* bemerkenswert.

remarry [ri:'mærɪ] *vi* wieder heiraten.

remedial [rɪ'mi:dɪəl] *adj* (*tuition, classes*) Förder-; ~ **exercise** Heilgymnastik *f*.

remedy ['rɛmədɪ] *n* (*lit, fig*) (Heil)mittel *nt* ♦ *vt* (*mistake, situation*) abhelfen +*dat*.

remember [rɪ'mɛmbə*] *vt* (*call back to mind*) sich erinnern an +*acc*; (*bear in mind*) denken an +*acc*; ~ **me to him** (*send greetings*) grüße ihn von mir; **I** ~ **seeing it, I** ~ **having seen it** ich erinnere mich (daran), es gesehen zu haben; **she ~ed to do it** sie hat daran gedacht, es zu tun.

remembrance [rɪ'mɛmbrəns] *n* Erinnerung *f*; **in** ~ **of sb/sth** im Gedenken an +*acc*.

Remembrance Sunday (*BRIT*) *n* ≈ Volkstrauertag *m*.

> Remembrance Sunday oder Remembrance Day ist der britische Gedenktag für die Gefallenen der beiden Weltkriege und andere Konflikte. Er fällt auf einen Sonntag vor oder nach dem 11. November (am 11. November 1918 endete der erste Weltkrieg) und wird mit einer Schweigeminute, Kranzniederlegungen an Kriegerdenkmälern und dem Tragen von Anstecknadeln in Form einer Mohnblume begangen.

remind [rɪ'maɪnd] *vt*: **to** ~ **sb to do sth** jdn daran erinnern, etw zu tun; **to** ~ **sb of sth** jdn an etw *acc* erinnern; **to** ~ **sb that ...** jdn daran erinnern, daß ...; **she ~s me of her mother** sie erinnert mich an ihre Mutter; **that ~s me!** dabei fällt mir etwas ein!

reminder [rɪ'maɪndə*] *n* (*of person, place etc*) Erinnerung *f*; (*letter*) Mahnung *f*.

reminisce [rɛmɪ'nɪs] *vi*: **to** ~ (**about**) sich in Erinnerungen ergehen (über +*acc*).

reminiscences [rɛmɪ'nɪsnsɪz] *npl* Erinnerungen *pl*.

reminiscent [rɛmɪ'nɪsnt] *adj*: **to be** ~ **of sth** an etw *acc* erinnern.

remiss [rɪ'mɪs] *adj* nachlässig; **it was** ~ **of him** es war nachlässig von ihm.

remission [rɪ'mɪʃən] *n* (*of sentence*) Straferlaß *m*; (*MED*) Remission *f*; (*REL*) Erlaß *m*.

remit [rɪ'mɪt] *vt* (*money*) überweisen ♦ *n* (*of official etc*) Aufgabenbereich *m*.

remittance [rɪ'mɪtns] *n* Überweisung *f*.

remnant ['rɛmnənt] *n* Überrest *m*; (*COMM: of cloth*) Rest *m*.

remonstrate ['rɛmənstreɪt] *vi*: **to** ~ (**with sb about sth**) sich beschweren (bei jdm wegen etw).

remorse [rɪ'mɔ:s] *n* Reue *f*.

remorseful [rɪ'mɔ:sful] *adj* reumütig.

remorseless [rɪ'mɔ:slɪs] *adj* (*noise, pain*) unbarmherzig.

remote [rɪ'məut] *adj* (*distant: place, time*) weit entfernt; (*aloof*) distanziert; (*slight: chance etc*) entfernt; **there is a** ~ **possibility that ...** es besteht eventuell die Möglichkeit, daß ...

remote control *n* Fernsteuerung *f*; (*TV etc*) Fernbedienung *f*.

remote-controlled [rɪ'məutkən'trəuld] *adj* ferngesteuert.

remotely [rɪ'məutlɪ] *adv* (*slightly*) entfernt.

remoteness [rɪ'məutnɪs] *n* (*of place*) Entlegenheit *f*; (*of person*) Distanziertheit *f*.

remould ['ri:məuld] (*BRIT*) *n* (*AUT*) runderneuerter Reifen *m*.

removable [rɪ'mu:vəbl] *adj* (*detachable*) abnehmbar.

removal [rɪ'mu:vəl] *n* (*of object etc*) Entfernung *f*; (*of threat etc*) Beseitigung *f*; (*BRIT: from house*) Umzug *m*; (*dismissal*) Entlassung *f*; (*MED: of kidney etc*) Entfernung *f*.

removal man (*BRIT*) *n* Möbelpacker *m*.

removal van (*BRIT*) *n* Möbelwagen *m*.

remove [rɪ'mu:v] *vt* entfernen; (*clothing*) ausziehen; (*bandage etc*) abnehmen; (*employee*) entlassen; (*name: from list*) streichen; (*doubt, threat, obstacle*) beseitigen; **my first cousin once ~d** mein Vetter ersten Grades.

remover [rɪ'mu:və*] *n* (*for paint, varnish*) Entferner *m*; **stain** ~ Fleckentferner *m*; **make-up** ~ Make-up-Entferner *m*.

remunerate [rɪ'mju:nəreɪt] *vt* vergüten.

remuneration [rɪmju:nə'reɪʃən] *n* Vergütung *f*.

Renaissance [rɪ'neɪsɑ:s] *n*: **the** ~ die Renaissance.

renal ['ri:nl] *adj* (*MED*) Nieren-.

renal failure *n* Nierenversagen *nt*.

rename [ri:'neɪm] *vt* umbenennen.

rend [rɛnd] (*pt, pp* **rent**) *vt* (*air, silence*) zerreißen.

render ['rɛndə*] *vt* (*give: assistance, aid*) leisten; (*cause to become: unconscious, harmless, useless*) machen; (*submit*) vorlegen.

rendering ['rɛndərɪŋ] (*BRIT*) *n* = **rendition**.

rendezvous ['rɔndɪvu:] *n* (*meeting*) Rendezvous *nt*; (*place*) Treffpunkt *m* ♦ *vi* (*people*) sich treffen; (*spacecraft*) ein Rendezvousmanöver durchführen; **to ~ with sb** sich mit jdm treffen.

rendition [rɛn'dɪʃən] *n* (*of song etc*) Vortrag *m*.

renegade ['rɛnɪgeɪd] *n* Renegat(in) *m(f)*, Überläufer(in) *m(f)*.

renew [rɪ'njuː] *vt* erneuern; (*attack, negotiations*) wiederaufnehmen; (*loan, contract etc*) verlängern; (*relationship etc*) wiederaufleben lassen.

renewables *npl* erneuerbare Energien *pl*.

renewal [rɪ'njuːəl] *n* Erneuerung *f*; (*of conflict*) Wiederaufnahme *f*; (*of contract etc*) Verlängerung *f*.

renounce [rɪ'nauns] *vt* verzichten auf +*acc*; (*belief*) aufgeben.

renovate ['rɛnəveɪt] *vt* (*building*) restaurieren; (*machine*) überholen.

renovation [rɛnə'veɪʃən] *n* (*see vb*) Restaurierung *f*; Überholung *f*.

renown [rɪ'naun] *n* Ruf *m*.

renowned [rɪ'naund] *adj* berühmt.

rent [rɛnt] *pt, pp of* **rend** ♦ *n* (*for house*) Miete *f* ♦ *vt* mieten; (*also*: ~ **out**) vermieten.

rental ['rɛntl] *n* (*for television, car*) Mietgebühr *f*.

rent boy (*inf*) *n* Strichjunge *m*.

rent strike *n* Mietstreik *m*.

renunciation [rɪnʌnsɪ'eɪʃən] *n* Verzicht *m*; (*of belief*) Aufgabe *f*; (*self-denial*) Selbstverleugnung *f*.

reopen [riː'əupən] *vt* (*shop etc*) wiedereröffnen; (*negotiations, legal case etc*) wiederaufnehmen.

reopening [riː'əupnɪŋ] *n* (*see vt*) Wiedereröffnung *f*; Wiederaufnahme *f*.

reorder [riː'ɔːdə*] *vt* (*rearrange*) umordnen.

reorganization ['riːɔːgənaɪ'zeɪʃən] *n* Umorganisation *f*.

reorganize [riː'ɔːgənaɪz] *vt* umorganisieren.

Rep. (*US*) *abbr* (*POL*) = **representative; republican**.

rep [rɛp] *n abbr* (*COMM*) = **representative**; (*THEAT*) = **repertory**.

repair [rɪ'pɛə*] *n* Reparatur *f* ♦ *vt* reparieren; (*clothes, road*) ausbessern; **in good/bad** ~ in gutem/schlechtem Zustand; **beyond** ~ nicht mehr zu reparieren; **to be under** ~ (*road*) ausgebessert werden.

repair kit *n* (*for bicycle*) Flickzeug *nt*.

repair man *n* Handwerker *m*.

repair shop *n* Reparaturwerkstatt *f*.

repartee [rɛpɑː'tiː] *n* (*exchange*) Schlagabtausch *m*; (*reply*) schlagfertige Bemerkung *f*.

repast [rɪ'pɑːst] (*form*) *n* Mahl *nt*.

repatriate [riː'pætrɪeɪt] *vt* repatriieren.

repay [riː'peɪ] (*irreg: like* **pay**) *vt* zurückzahlen; (*sb's efforts, attention*) belohnen; (*favour*) erwidern; **I'll ~ you next week** ich zahle es dir nächste Woche zurück.

repayment [riː'peɪmənt] *n* Rückzahlung *f*.

repeal [rɪ'piːl] *n* (*of law*) Aufhebung *f* ♦ *vt* (*law*) aufheben.

repeat [rɪ'piːt] *n* (*RADIO, TV*) Wiederholung *f* ♦ *vt, vi* wiederholen ♦ *cpd* (*performance*) Wiederholungs-; (*order*) Nach-; **to ~ o.s./itself** sich wiederholen; **to ~ an order for sth** etw nachbestellen.

repeatedly [rɪ'piːtɪdlɪ] *adv* wiederholt.

repel [rɪ'pɛl] *vt* (*drive away*) zurückschlagen; (*disgust*) abstoßen.

repellent [rɪ'pɛlənt] *adj* abstoßend ♦ *n*: **insect** ~ Insekten(schutz)mittel *nt*.

repent [rɪ'pɛnt] *vi*: **to ~ of sth** etw bereuen.

repentance [rɪ'pɛntəns] *n* Reue *f*.

repercussions [riːpə'kʌʃənz] *npl* Auswirkungen *pl*.

repertoire ['rɛpətwɑː*] *n* (*MUS, THEAT*) Repertoire *nt*; (*fig*) Spektrum *nt*.

repertory ['rɛpətərɪ] *n* (*also*: ~ **theatre**) Repertoiretheater *nt*.

repertory company *n* Repertoire-Ensemble *nt*.

repetition [rɛpɪ'tɪʃən] *n* (*repeat*) Wiederholung *f*.

repetitious [rɛpɪ'tɪʃəs] *adj* (*speech etc*) voller Wiederholungen.

repetitive [rɪ'pɛtɪtɪv] *adj* eintönig, monoton.

replace [rɪ'pleɪs] *vt* (*put back: upright*) zurückstellen; (: *flat*) zurücklegen; (*take the place of*) ersetzen; **to ~ X with Y** X durch Y ersetzen; **"~ the receiver"** (*TEL*) „Hörer auflegen".

replacement [rɪ'pleɪsmənt] *n* Ersatz *m*.

replacement part *n* Ersatzteil *nt*.

replay ['riːpleɪ] *n* (*of match*) Wiederholungsspiel *nt* ♦ *vt* (*match*) wiederholen; (*track, song: on tape*) nochmals abspielen.

replenish [rɪ'plɛnɪʃ] *vt* (*glass, stock etc*) auffüllen.

replete [rɪ'pliːt] *adj* (*after meal*) gesättigt; ~ **with** reichlich ausgestattet mit.

replica ['rɛplɪkə] *n* (*of object*) Nachbildung *f*.

reply [rɪ'plaɪ] *n* Antwort *f* ♦ *vi*: **to ~ (to sb/sth)** (jdm/auf etw *acc*) antworten; **in ~ to** als Antwort auf +*acc*; **there's no ~** (*TEL*) es meldet sich niemand.

reply coupon *n* Antwortschein *m*.

report [rɪ'pɔːt] *n* Bericht *m*; (*BRIT: also:* **school** ~) Zeugnis *nt*; (*of gun*) Knall *m* ♦ *vt* berichten; (*casualties, damage, theft etc*) melden; (*person: to police*) anzeigen ♦ *vi* (*make a report*) Bericht erstatten; **to ~ to sb** (*present o.s. to*) sich bei jdm melden; (*be responsible to*) jdm unterstellt sein; **to ~ on sth** über etw *acc* Bericht erstatten; **to ~ sick** sich krank melden; **it is ~ed that** es wird berichtet *or* gemeldet, daß ...

report card (*US, SCOT*) *n* Zeugnis *nt*.

reportedly [rɪ'pɔːtɪdlɪ] *adv*: **she is ~ living in Spain** sie lebt angeblich in Spanien.

reported speech *n* (*LING*) indirekte Rede *f*.

reporter [rɪ'pɔːtə*] n Reporter(in) m(f).
repose [rɪ'pəuz] n: **in ~** in Ruhestellung.
repository [rɪ'pɔzɪtərɪ] n (person: of knowledge) Quelle f; (place: of collection etc) Lager nt.
repossess ['riːpə'zɛs] vt (wieder) in Besitz nehmen.
repossession order [riːpə'zɛʃən-] n Beschlagnahmungsverfügung f.
reprehensible [rɛprɪ'hɛnsɪbl] adj verwerflich.
represent [rɛprɪ'zɛnt] vt (person, nation) vertreten; (show: view, opinion) darstellen; (symbolize: idea) symbolisieren, verkörpern; **to ~ sth as** (describe) etw darstellen als.
representation [rɛprɪzɛn'teɪʃən] n (state of being represented) Vertretung f; (picture etc) Darstellung f; **representations** npl (protest) Proteste pl.
representative [rɛprɪ'zɛntətɪv] n (also COMM) Vertreter(in) m(f); (US: POL) Abgeordnete(r) f(m) des Repräsentantenhauses ♦ adj repräsentativ; **~ of** repräsentativ für.
repress [rɪ'prɛs] vt unterdrücken.
repression [rɪ'prɛʃən] n Unterdrückung f.
repressive [rɪ'prɛsɪv] adj repressiv.
reprieve [rɪ'priːv] n (cancellation) Begnadigung f; (postponement) Strafaufschub m; (fig) Gnadenfrist f ♦ vt: **he was ~d** (see n) er wurde begnadigt; ihm wurde Strafaufschub gewährt.
reprimand ['rɛprɪmɑːnd] n Tadel m ♦ vt tadeln.
reprint ['riːprɪnt] n Nachdruck m ♦ vt nachdrucken.
reprisal [rɪ'praɪzl] n Vergeltung f; **reprisals** npl Repressalien pl; (in war) Vergeltungsaktionen pl; **to take ~s** zu Repressalien greifen; (in war) Vergeltungsaktionen durchführen.
reproach [rɪ'prəutʃ] n (rebuke) Vorwurf m ♦ vt: **to ~ sb for sth** jdm etw zum Vorwurf machen; **beyond ~** über jeden Vorwurf erhaben; **to ~ sb with sth** jdm etw vorwerfen.
reproachful [rɪ'prəutʃful] adj vorwurfsvoll.
reproduce [riːprə'djuːs] vt reproduzieren ♦ vi (BIOL) sich vermehren.
reproduction [riːprə'dʌkʃən] n Reproduktion f; (BIOL) Fortpflanzung f.
reproductive [riːprə'dʌktɪv] adj (system, organs) Fortpflanzungs-.
reproof [rɪ'pruːf] n (rebuke) Tadel m; **with ~** tadelnd.
reprove [rɪ'pruːv] vt tadeln; **to ~ sb for sth** jdn wegen etw tadeln.
reproving [rɪ'pruːvɪŋ] adj tadelnd.
reptile ['rɛptaɪl] n Reptil nt.
Repub. (US) abbr (POL) = **republican**.
republic [rɪ'pʌblɪk] n Republik f.
republican [rɪ'pʌblɪkən] adj republikanisch ♦ n Republikaner(in) m(f); **the R~s** (US: POL) die Republikaner.
repudiate [rɪ'pjuːdɪeɪt] vt (accusation) zurückweisen; (violence) ablehnen; (old: friend, wife etc) verstoßen.
repugnance [rɪ'pʌɡnəns] n Abscheu m.
repugnant [rɪ'pʌɡnənt] adj abstoßend.
repulse [rɪ'pʌls] vt (attack etc) zurückschlagen; (sight, picture etc) abstoßen.
repulsion [rɪ'pʌlʃən] n Abscheu m.
repulsive [rɪ'pʌlsɪv] adj widerwärtig, abstoßend.
reputable ['rɛpjutəbl] adj (make, company etc) angesehen.
reputation [rɛpju'teɪʃən] n Ruf m; **to have a ~ for** einen Ruf haben für; **he has a ~ for being awkward** er gilt als schwierig.
repute [rɪ'pjuːt] n: **of ~** angesehen; **to be held in high ~** in hohem Ansehen stehen.
reputed [rɪ'pjuːtɪd] adj angeblich; **he is ~ to be rich** er ist angeblich reich.
reputedly [rɪ'pjuːtɪdlɪ] adv angeblich.
request [rɪ'kwɛst] n (polite) Bitte f; (formal) Ersuchen nt; (RADIO) Musikwunsch m ♦ vt (politely) bitten um; (formally) ersuchen; **at the ~ of** auf Wunsch von; **"you are ~ed not to smoke"** „bitte nicht rauchen".
request stop (BRIT) n Bedarfshaltestelle f.
requiem ['rɛkwɪəm] n (REL: also: ~ **mass**) Totenmesse f; (MUS) Requiem nt.
require [rɪ'kwaɪə*] vt (need) benötigen; (: situation) erfordern; (demand) verlangen; **to ~ sb to do sth** von jdm verlangen, etw zu tun; **if ~d** falls nötig; **what qualifications are ~d?** welche Qualifikationen werden verlangt?; **~d by law** gesetzlich vorgeschrieben.
required [rɪ'kwaɪəd] adj erforderlich.
requirement [rɪ'kwaɪəmənt] n (need) Bedarf m; (condition) Anforderung f; **to meet sb's ~s** jds Anforderungen erfüllen.
requisite [rɪ'kwɪzɪt] adj erforderlich; **requisites** npl: **toilet/travel ~s** Toiletten-/Reiseartikel pl.
requisition [rɛkwɪ'zɪʃən] n: ~ **(for)** (demand) Anforderung f (von) ♦ vt (MIL) beschlagnahmen.
reroute [riː'ruːt] vt (train etc) umleiten.
resale [riː'seɪl] n Weiterverkauf m; **"not for ~"** „nicht zum Weiterverkauf bestimmt".
resale price maintenance n Preisbindung f.
rescind [rɪ'sɪnd] vt (law, order) aufheben; (decision) rückgängig machen; (agreement) widerrufen.
rescue ['rɛskjuː] n Rettung f ♦ vt retten; **to come to sb's ~** jdm zu Hilfe kommen.
rescue party n Rettungsmannschaft f.
rescuer ['rɛskjuə*] n Retter(in) m(f).
research [rɪ'səːtʃ] n Forschung f ♦ vt erforschen ♦ vi: **to ~ into sth** etw erforschen; **to do ~** Forschung betreiben; **a piece of ~** eine Forschungsarbeit; ~ **and development** Forschung und Entwicklung.
researcher [rɪ'səːtʃə*] n Forscher(in) m(f).
research work n Forschungsarbeit f.

research worker n = researcher.

resell [riː'sɛl] (irreg: like sell) vt
weiterverkaufen.

resemblance [rɪ'zɛmbləns] n Ähnlichkeit f; **to
bear a strong ~** to starke Ähnlichkeit haben
mit; **it bears no ~ to ...** es hat keine
Ähnlichkeit mit ...

resemble [rɪ'zɛmbl] vt ähneln +dat, gleichen
+dat.

resent [rɪ'zɛnt] vt (attitude, treatment)
mißbilligen; (person) ablehnen.

resentful [rɪ'zɛntful] adj (person) gekränkt;
(attitude) mißbilligend.

resentment [rɪ'zɛntmənt] n Verbitterung f.

reservation [rɛzə'veɪʃən] n (booking)
Reservierung f; (doubt) Vorbehalt m; (land)
Reservat nt; **to make a ~** (in hotel etc) eine
Reservierung vornehmen; **with ~(s)**
(doubts) unter Vorbehalt.

reservation desk n Reservierungsschalter
m.

reserve [rɪ'zəːv] n Reserve f, Vorrat m; (fig: of
talent etc) Reserve f; (SPORT)
Reservespieler(in) m(f); (also: **nature ~**)
Naturschutzgebiet nt; (restraint)
Zurückhaltung f ♦ vt reservieren; (table,
ticket) reservieren lassen; **reserves** npl (MIL)
Reserve f; **in ~** in Reserve.

reserve currency n Reservewährung f.

reserved [rɪ'zəːvd] adj (restrained)
zurückhaltend; (seat) reserviert.

reserve price (BRIT) n Mindestpreis m.

reserve team (BRIT) n Reservemannschaft f.

reservist [rɪ'zəːvɪst] n (MIL) Reservist m.

reservoir [ˈrɛzəvwɑːˀ] n (lit, fig) Reservoir nt.

reset [riː'sɛt] (irreg: like set) vt (watch) neu
stellen; (broken bone) wieder einrichten;
(COMPUT) zurückstellen.

reshape [riː'ʃeɪp] vt (policy, view)
umgestalten.

reshuffle [riː'ʃʌfl] n: **cabinet ~**
Kabinettsumbildung f.

reside [rɪ'zaɪd] vi (live: person) seinen/ihren
Wohnsitz haben.

▶**reside in** vt fus (exist) liegen in +dat.

residence [ˈrɛzɪdəns] n (form: home) Wohnsitz
m; (length of stay) Aufenthalt m; **to take up ~**
sich niederlassen; **in ~** (queen etc)
anwesend; **writer/artist in ~** Schriftsteller/
Künstler, der in einer Ausbildungsstätte bei
freier Unterkunft lehrt und arbeitet.

residence permit (BRIT) n
Aufenthaltserlaubnis f.

resident [ˈrɛzɪdənt] n (of country, town)
Einwohner(in) m(f); (in hotel) Gast m ♦ adj (in
country, town) wohnhaft; (population)
ansässig; (doctor) hauseigen; (landlord) im
Hause wohnend.

residential [rɛzɪ'dɛnʃəl] adj (area) Wohn-;
(course) mit Wohnung am Ort; (staff) im
Hause wohnend.

residue [ˈrɛzɪdjuː] n (CHEM) Rückstand m;
(fig) Überrest m.

resign [rɪ'zaɪn] vt (one's post) zurücktreten
von ♦ vi (from post) zurücktreten; **to ~ o.s.
to** (situation etc) sich abfinden mit.

resignation [rɛzɪg'neɪʃən] n (from post)
Rücktritt m; (state of mind) Resignation f; **to
tender one's ~** seine Kündigung einreichen.

resigned [rɪ'zaɪnd] adj: **to be ~ to sth** sich mit
etw abgefunden haben.

resilience [rɪ'zɪlɪəns] n (of material)
Widerstandsfähigkeit f; (of person)
Unverwüstlichkeit f.

resilient [rɪ'zɪlɪənt] adj (see n)
widerstandsfähig; unverwüstlich.

resin [ˈrɛzɪn] n Harz nt.

resist [rɪ'zɪst] vt (change, demand) sich
widersetzen +dat; (attack etc) Widerstand
leisten +dat; (urge etc) widerstehen +dat; **I
couldn't ~ (doing) it** ich konnte nicht
widerstehen(, es zu tun).

resistance [rɪ'zɪstəns] n (also ELEC)
Widerstand m; (to illness) Widerstandsfähigkeit f.

resistant [rɪ'zɪstənt] adj: **~ (to)** (to change etc)
widerstandsfähig (gegenüber); (to
antibiotics etc) resistent (gegen).

resolute [ˈrɛzəluːt] adj (person) entschlossen,
resolut; (refusal) entschieden.

resolution [rɛzə'luːʃən] n (decision) Beschluß
m; (determination) Entschlossenheit f; (of
problem) Lösung f; **to make a ~** einen
Entschluß fassen.

resolve [rɪ'zɔlv] n (determination)
Entschlossenheit f ♦ vt (problem) lösen;
(difficulty) beseitigen ♦ vi: **to ~ to do sth**
beschließen, etw zu tun.

resolved [rɪ'zɔlvd] adj (determined)
entschlossen.

resonance [ˈrɛzənəns] n Resonanz f.

resonant [ˈrɛzənənt] adj (sound, voice)
volltönend; (place) widerhallend.

resort [rɪ'zɔːt] n (town) Urlaubsort m;
(recourse) Zuflucht f ♦ vi: **to ~ to** Zuflucht
nehmen zu; **seaside ~** Seebad nt; **winter
sports ~** Wintersportort m; **as a last ~** als
letzter Ausweg; **in the last ~**
schlimmstenfalls.

resound [rɪ'zaund] vi: **to ~ (with)** widerhallen
(von).

resounding [rɪ'zaundɪŋ] adj (noise)
widerhallend; (voice) schallend; (fig: success)
durchschlagend; (: victory) überlegen.

resource [rɪ'sɔːs] n (raw material) Bodenschatz
m; **resources** npl (coal, oil etc) Energiequellen
pl; (money) Mittel pl, Ressourcen pl; **natural
~s** Naturschätze pl.

resourceful [rɪ'sɔːsful] adj einfallsreich.

resourcefulness [rɪ'sɔːsfulnɪs] n
Einfallsreichtum m.

respect [rɪs'pɛkt] n (consideration, esteem)
Respekt m ♦ vt respektieren; **respects** npl
(greetings) Grüße pl; **to have ~ for sb/sth**

Respekt vor jdm/etw haben; **to show sb/sth ~** Respekt vor jdm/etw zeigen; **out of ~ for** aus Rücksicht auf *+acc*; **with ~ to, in ~ of** in bezug auf *+acc*; **in this ~** in dieser Hinsicht; **in some/many ~s** in gewisser/vielfacher Hinsicht; **with (all due) ~** bei allem Respekt.

respectability [rɪspɛktə'bɪlɪtɪ] *n* Anständigkeit *f*.

respectable [rɪs'pɛktəbl] *adj* anständig; (*amount, income*) ansehnlich; (*standard, mark etc*) ordentlich.

respected [rɪs'pɛktɪd] *adj* angesehen.

respectful [rɪs'pɛktful] *adj* respektvoll.

respectfully [rɪs'pɛktfəlɪ] *adv* (*behave*) respektvoll.

respective [rɪs'pɛktɪv] *adj* jeweilig.

respectively [rɪs'pɛktɪvlɪ] *adv* beziehungsweise; **Germany and Britain were 3rd and 4th ~** Deutschland und Großbritannien belegten den 3. beziehungsweise 4. Platz.

respiration [rɛspɪ'reɪʃən] *n see* **artificial**.

respirator ['rɛspɪreɪtə*] *n* Respirator *m*, Beatmungsgerät *nt*.

respiratory ['rɛspərətərɪ] *adj* (*system, failure*) Atmungs-.

respite ['rɛspaɪt] *n* (*rest*) Ruhepause *f*.

resplendent [rɪs'plɛndənt] *adj* (*clothes*) prächtig.

respond [rɪs'pɒnd] *vi* (*answer*) antworten; (*react*) reagieren.

respondent [rɪs'pɒndənt] *n* (*LAW*) Beklagte(r) *f(m)*.

response [rɪs'pɒns] *n* (*to question*) Antwort *f*; (*to event etc*) Reaktion *f*; **in ~ to** als Antwort/Reaktion auf *+acc*.

responsibility [rɪspɒnsɪ'bɪlɪtɪ] *n* Verantwortung *f*; **to take ~ for sth/sb** die Verantwortung für etw/jdn übernehmen.

responsible [rɪs'pɒnsɪbl] *adj* verantwortlich; (*reliable, important*) verantwortungsvoll; **to be ~ for sth** für etw verantwortlich sein; **to be ~ for doing sth** dafür verantwortlich sein, etw zu tun; **to be ~ to sb** jdm gegenüber verantwortlich sein.

responsibly [rɪs'pɒnsɪblɪ] *adv* verantwortungsvoll.

responsive [rɪs'pɒnsɪv] *adj* (*person*) ansprechbar.

rest [rɛst] *n* (*relaxation*) Ruhe *f*; (*pause*) Ruhepause *f*; (*remainder*) Rest *m*; (*support*) Stütze *f*; (*MUS*) Pause *f* ♦ *vi* (*relax*) sich ausruhen ♦ *vt* (*eyes, legs etc*) ausruhen; **the ~ of them** die übrigen; **to put** *or* **set sb's mind at ~** jdn beruhigen; **to come to ~** (*object*) zum Stillstand kommen; **to lay sb to ~** jdn zur letzten Ruhe betten; **to ~ on sth** (*lit, fig*) sich auf etw *acc* stützen; **to let the matter ~** die Sache auf sich beruhen lassen; **~ assured that ...** seien Sie versichert, daß ...; **I won't ~ until ...** ich werde nicht ruhen,

bis .:.; **may he/she ~ in peace** möge er/sie in Frieden ruhen; **to ~ sth on/against sth** (*lean*) etw an etw *acc*/gegen etw lehnen; **to ~ one's eyes** *or* **gaze on sth** den Blick auf etw heften; **I ~ my case** mehr brauche ich dazu wohl nicht zu sagen.

restart [riː'stɑːt] *vt* (*engine*) wieder anlassen; (*work*) wiederaufnehmen.

restaurant ['rɛstərɒŋ] *n* Restaurant *nt*.

restaurant car (*BRIT*) *n* (*RAIL*) Speisewagen *m*.

rest cure *n* Erholung *f*.

restful ['rɛstful] *adj* (*music*) ruhig; (*lighting*) beruhigend; (*atmosphere*) friedlich.

rest home *n* Pflegeheim *nt*.

restitution [rɛstɪ'tjuːʃən] *n*: **to make ~ to sb of sth** jdm etw zurückerstatten; (*as compensation*) jdn für etw entschädigen.

restive ['rɛstɪv] *adj* (*person, crew*) unruhig; (*horse*) störrisch.

restless ['rɛstlɪs] *adj* rastlos; (*audience*) unruhig; **to get ~** unruhig werden.

restlessly ['rɛstlɪslɪ] *adv* (*walk around*) rastlos; (*turn over*) unruhig.

restock [riː'stɒk] *vt* (*shop, freezer*) wieder auffüllen; (*lake, river: with fish*) wieder besetzen.

restoration [rɛstə'reɪʃən] *n* (*of painting etc*) Restauration *f*; (*of law and order, health, sight etc*) Wiederherstellung *f*; (*of land, rights*) Rückgabe *f*; (*HIST*): **the R~** die Restauration.

restorative [rɪ'stɒrətɪv] *adj* (*power, treatment*) stärkend ♦ *n* (*old: drink*) Stärkungsmittel *nt*.

restore [rɪ'stɔː*] *vt* (*painting etc*) restaurieren; (*law and order, health, faith etc*) wiederherstellen; (*property*) zurückgeben; **to ~ sth to** (*to former state*) etw zurückverwandeln in *+acc*; **to ~ sb to power** jdn wieder an die Macht bringen.

restorer [rɪ'stɔːrə*] *n* (*ART etc*) Restaurator(in) *m(f)*.

restrain [rɪs'treɪn] *vt* (*person*) zurückhalten; (*feeling*) unterdrücken; (*growth, inflation*) dämpfen; **to ~ sb from doing sth** jdn davon abhalten, etw zu tun; **to ~ o.s. from doing sth** sich beherrschen, etw nicht zu tun.

restrained [rɪs'treɪnd] *adj* (*person*) beherrscht; (*style etc*) zurückhaltend.

restraint [rɪs'treɪnt] *n* (*restriction*) Einschränkung *f*; (*moderation*) Zurückhaltung *f*; **wage ~** Zurückhaltung *f* bei Lohnforderungen.

restrict [rɪs'trɪkt] *vt* beschränken.

restricted area (*BRIT*) *n* (*AUT*) Bereich *m* mit Geschwindigkeitsbeschränkung.

restriction [rɪs'trɪkʃən] *n* Beschränkung *f*.

restrictive [rɪs'trɪktɪv] *adj* (*law, measure*) restriktiv; (*clothing*) beengend.

restrictive practices (*BRIT*) *npl* (*INDUSTRY*) wettbewerbshemmende Geschäftspraktiken *pl*.

rest room (*US*) *n* Toilette *f*.

restructure [riː'strʌktʃəʳ] vt umstrukturieren.
result [rɪ'zʌlt] n Resultat nt; (of match, election, exam etc) Ergebnis nt ♦ vi: **to ~ in** führen zu; **as a ~ of the accident** als Folge des Unfalls; **he missed the train as a ~ of sleeping in** er verpaßte den Zug, weil er verschlafen hatte; **to ~ from** resultieren or sich ergeben aus; **as a ~ it is too expensive** folglich ist es zu teuer.
resultant [rɪ'zʌltənt] adj resultierend, sich ergebend.
resume [rɪ'zjuːm] vt (work, journey) wiederaufnehmen; (seat) wieder einnehmen ♦ vi (start again) von neuem beginnen.
résumé ['reɪsjuːmeɪ] n Zusammenfassung f; (US: curriculum vitae) Lebenslauf m.
resumption [rɪ'zʌmpʃən] n (of work etc) Wiederaufnahme f.
resurgence [rɪ'səːdʒəns] n Wiederaufleben nt.
resurrection [rɛzə'rɛkʃən] n (of hopes, fears) Wiederaufleben nt; (of custom etc) Wiederbelebung f; (REL): **the R~** die Auferstehung f.
resuscitate [rɪ'sʌsɪteɪt] vt (MED, fig) wiederbeleben.
resuscitation [rɪsʌsɪ'teɪʃən] n Wiederbelebung f.
retail ['riːteɪl] adj (trade, department) Verkaufs-; (shop, goods) Einzelhandels- ♦ adv im Einzelhandel ♦ vt (sell) (im Einzelhandel) verkaufen ♦ vi: **to ~ at** (im Einzelhandel) kosten; **this product retail~s at £25** dieses Produkt kostet im Laden £25.
retailer ['riːteɪləʳ] n Einzelhändler(in) m(f).
retail outlet n Einzelhandelsverkaufsstelle f.
retail price n Einzelhandelspreis m.
retail price index n Einzelhandelspreisindex m.
retain [rɪ'teɪn] vt (keep) behalten; (: heat, moisture) zurückhalten.
retainer [rɪ'teɪnəʳ] n (fee) Vorauszahlung f.
retaliate [rɪ'tælɪeɪt] vi Vergeltung üben.
retaliation [rɪtælɪ'eɪʃən] n Vergeltung f; **in ~ for** als Vergeltung für.
retaliatory [rɪ'tælɪətərɪ] adj (move, attack) Vergeltungs-.
retarded [rɪ'tɑːdɪd] adj zurückgeblieben; **mentally ~** geistig zurückgeblieben.
retch [rɛtʃ] vi würgen.
retention [rɪ'tɛnʃən] n (of tradition etc) Beibehaltung f; (of land, memories) Behalten nt; (of heat, fluid etc) Zurückhalten nt.
retentive [rɪ'tɛntɪv] adj (memory) merkfähig.
rethink ['riː'θɪŋk] vt noch einmal überdenken.
reticence ['rɛtɪsns] n Zurückhaltung f.
reticent ['rɛtɪsnt] adj zurückhaltend.
retina ['rɛtɪnə] n Netzhaut f.
retinue ['rɛtɪnjuː] n Gefolge nt.
retire [rɪ'taɪəʳ] vi (give up work) in den Ruhestand treten; (withdraw, go to bed) sich zurückziehen.
retired [rɪ'taɪəd] adj (person) im Ruhestand.

retirement [rɪ'taɪəmənt] n (state) Ruhestand m; (act) Pensionierung f.
retirement age n Rentenalter nt.
retiring [rɪ'taɪərɪŋ] adj (leaving) ausscheidend; (shy) zurückhaltend.
retort [rɪ'tɔːt] vi erwidern ♦ n (reply) Erwiderung f.
retrace [riː'treɪs] vt: **to ~ one's steps** (lit, fig) seine Schritte zurückverfolgen.
retract [rɪ'trækt] vt (promise) zurücknehmen; (confession) zurückziehen; (claws, undercarriage) einziehen.
retractable [rɪ'træktəbl] adj (undercarriage, aerial) einziehbar.
retrain [riː'treɪn] vt umschulen ♦ vi umgeschult werden.
retraining [riː'treɪnɪŋ] n Umschulung f.
retread ['riːtrɛd] n (tyre) runderneuerter Reifen m.
retreat [rɪ'triːt] n (place) Zufluchtsort m; (withdrawal: also MIL) Rückzug m ♦ vi sich zurückziehen; **to beat a hasty ~** schleunigst den Rückzug antreten.
retrial [riː'traɪəl] n erneute Verhandlung f.
retribution [rɛtrɪ'bjuːʃən] n Strafe f.
retrieval [rɪ'triːvəl] n (of object) Zurückholen nt; (COMPUT) Abruf m.
retrieve [rɪ'triːv] vt (object) zurückholen; (situation) retten; (error) wiedergutmachen; (dog) apportieren; (COMPUT) abrufen.
retriever [rɪ'triːvəʳ] n (dog) Apportierhund m.
retroactive [rɛtrəu'æktɪv] adj rückwirkend.
retrograde ['rɛtrəgreɪd] adj (step) Rück-.
retrospect ['rɛtrəspɛkt] n: **in ~** rückblickend, im Rückblick.
retrospective [rɛtrə'spɛktɪv] adj (opinion etc) im Nachhinein; (law, tax) rückwirkend ♦ n (ART) Retrospektive f.
return [rɪ'təːn] n (going or coming back) Rückkehr f; (of sth stolen etc) Rückgabe f; (also: ~ **ticket**: BRIT) Rückfahrkarte f; (FIN: from investment etc) Ertrag m; (of merchandise) Rücksendung f; (official report) Erklärung f ♦ cpd (journey) Rück- ♦ vi (person etc: come or go back) zurückkehren; (feelings, symptoms etc) wiederkehren ♦ vt (favour, greetings etc) erwidern; (sth stolen etc) zurückgeben; (LAW: verdict) fällen; (POL: candidate) wählen; (ball) zurückspielen; **returns** npl (COMM) Gewinne pl; **in ~ (for)** als Gegenleistung (für); **by ~ of post** postwendend; **many happy ~s (of the day)!** herzlichen Glückwunsch zum Geburtstag!; **~ match** Rückspiel nt.
▶**return to** vt fus (regain: consciousness, power) wiedererlangen.
returnable [rɪ'təːnəbl] adj (bottle etc) Mehrweg-.
returner n jd, der nach längerer Abwesenheit wieder in die Arbeitswelt zurückkehrt.
returning officer [rɪ'təːnɪŋ-] (BRIT) n Wahlleiter(in) m(f).

return key n (*COMPUT*) Return-Taste f.
reunion [riːˈjuːnɪən] n Treffen nt; (*after long separation*) Wiedervereinigung f.
reunite [riːjuːˈnaɪt] vt wiedervereinigen.
Rev. abbr (*REL*) = **Reverend.**
rev [rɛv] n abbr (*AUT*: = *revolution per minute*) Umdrehung f pro Minute, U/min. ♦ vt (*also:* ~ **up**: *engine*) aufheulen lassen.
revaluation [riːvæljuˈeɪʃən] n (*of property*) Neuschätzung f; (*of currency*) Aufwertung f; (*of attitudes*) Neubewertung f.
revamp [riːˈvæmp] vt (*company, system*) auf Vordermann bringen.
rev counter (*BRIT*) n (*AUT*) Drehzahlmesser m.
Revd. abbr (*REL*) = **Reverend.**
reveal [rɪˈviːl] vt (*make known*) enthüllen; (*make visible*) zum Vorschein bringen.
revealing [rɪˈviːlɪŋ] adj (*comment, action*) aufschlußreich; (*dress*) tief ausgeschnitten.
reveille [rɪˈvælɪə] n (*MIL*) Wecksignal nt.
revel [ˈrɛvl] vi: **to ~ in sth** in etw schwelgen; **to ~ in doing sth** es genießen, etw zu tun.
revelation [rɛvəˈleɪʃən] n (*disclosure*) Enthüllung f.
reveller [ˈrɛvlə] n Zecher(in) m(f).
revelry [ˈrɛvlrɪ] n Gelage nt.
revenge [rɪˈvɛndʒ] n (*for insult etc*) Rache f ♦ vt rächen; **to get one's ~ (for sth)** seine Rache (für etw) bekommen; **to ~ o.s.** or **take one's ~ (on sb)** sich (an jdm) rächen.
revengeful [rɪˈvɛndʒful] adj rachsüchtig.
revenue [ˈrɛvənjuː] n (*of person, company*) Einnahmen pl; (*of government*) Staatseinkünfte pl.
reverberate [rɪˈvɜːbəreɪt] vi (*sound etc*) widerhallen; (*fig: shock etc*) Nachwirkungen haben.
reverberation [rɪvɜːbəˈreɪʃən] n (*of sound*) Widerhall m; (*fig: of event etc*) Nachwirkungen pl.
revere [rɪˈvɪə] vt verehren.
reverence [ˈrɛvərəns] n Ehrfurcht f.
Reverend [ˈrɛvərənd] adj (*in titles*) Pfarrer; **the ~ John Smith** Pfarrer John Smith.
reverent [ˈrɛvərənt] adj ehrfürchtig.
reverie [ˈrɛvərɪ] n Träumerei f.
reversal [rɪˈvɜːsl] n (*of policy, trend*) Umkehr f; **a ~ of roles** ein Rollentausch m.
reverse [rɪˈvɜːs] n (*opposite*) Gegenteil nt; (*back: of cloth*) linke Seite f, (: *of coin, paper*) Rückseite f; (*AUT: also:* ~ **gear**) Rückwärtsgang m; (*setback*) Rückschlag m ♦ adj (*side*) Rück-; (*process*) umgekehrt ♦ vt (*position, trend etc*) umkehren; (*LAW: verdict*) revidieren; (*roles*) vertauschen; (*car*) zurücksetzen ♦ vi (*BRIT: AUT*) zurücksetzen; **in ~** umgekehrt; **to go into ~** den Rückwärtsgang einlegen; **in ~ order** in umgekehrter Reihenfolge; **to ~ direction** sich um 180 Grad drehen.
reverse-charge call [rɪˈvɜːstʃɑːdʒ-] (*BRIT*) n

R-Gespräch nt.
reverse video n (*COMPUT*) invertierte Darstellung f.
reversible [rɪˈvɜːsəbl] adj (*garment*) auf beiden Seiten tragbar; (*decision, operation*) umkehrbar.
reversing lights [rɪˈvɜːsɪŋ-] (*BRIT*) npl Rückfahrscheinwerfer m.
reversion [rɪˈvɜːʃən] n: ~ **to** Rückfall in +acc; (*ZOOL*) Rückentwicklung f.
revert [rɪˈvɜːt] vi: **to ~ to** (*former state*) zurückkehren zu, zurückfallen in +acc; (*LAW: money, property*) zurückfallen an +acc.
review [rɪˈvjuː] n (*magazine*) Zeitschrift f; (*MIL*) Inspektion f; (*of book, film etc*) Kritik f, Besprechung f, Rezension f; (*of policy etc*) Überprüfung f ♦ vt (*MIL: troops*) inspizieren; (*book, film etc*) besprechen, rezensieren; (*policy etc*) überprüfen; **to be/come under ~** überprüft werden.
reviewer [rɪˈvjuːə] n Kritiker(in) m(f), Rezensent(in) m(f).
revile [rɪˈvaɪl] vt schmähen.
revise [rɪˈvaɪz] vt (*manuscript*) überarbeiten, revidieren; (*opinion etc*) ändern; (*price, procedure*) revidieren ♦ vi (*study*) wiederholen; ~**d edition** überarbeitete Ausgabe.
revision [rɪˈvɪʒən] n (*of manuscript, law etc*) Überarbeitung f, Revision f; (*for exam*) Wiederholung f.
revitalize [riːˈvaɪtəlaɪz] vt neu beleben.
revival [rɪˈvaɪvəl] n (*recovery*) Aufschwung m; (*of interest, faith*) Wiederaufleben nt; (*THEAT*) Wiederaufnahme f.
revive [rɪˈvaɪv] vt (*person*) wiederbeleben; (*economy etc*) Auftrieb geben +dat; (*custom*) wiederaufleben lassen; (*hope, interest etc*) neu beleben; (*play*) wiederaufnehmen ♦ vi (*person*) wieder zu sich kommen; (*activity, economy etc*) wieder aufblühen; (*hope, interest etc*) wiedererweckt werden.
revoke [rɪˈvəuk] vt (*law etc*) aufheben; (*title, licence*) entziehen +dat; (*promise, decision*) widerrufen.
revolt [rɪˈvəult] n Revolte f, Aufstand m ♦ vi rebellieren ♦ vt abstoßen; **to ~ against sb/ sth** gegen jdn/etw rebellieren.
revolting [rɪˈvəultɪŋ] adj (*disgusting*) abscheulich, ekelhaft.
revolution [rɛvəˈluːʃən] n (*POL etc*) Revolution f; (*rotation*) Umdrehung f.
revolutionary [rɛvəˈluːʃənrɪ] adj revolutionär; (*leader, army*) Revolutions- ♦ n Revolutionär(in) m(f).
revolutionize [rɛvəˈluːʃənaɪz] vt revolutionieren.
revolve [rɪˈvɒlv] vi sich drehen; **to ~ (a)round** sich drehen um.
revolver [rɪˈvɒlvə] n Revolver m.
revolving [rɪˈvɒlvɪŋ] adj (*chair*) Dreh-; (*sprinkler etc*) drehbar.

revolving door n Drehtür f.
revue [rɪ'vjuː] n (THEAT) Revue f.
revulsion [rɪ'vʌlʃən] n (disgust) Abscheu m, Ekel m.
reward [rɪ'wɔːd] n Belohnung f; (satisfaction) Befriedigung f ♦ vt belohnen.
rewarding [rɪ'wɔːdɪŋ] adj lohnend; **financially** ~ einträglich.
rewind [riː'waɪnd] (irreg: like wind) vt (tape etc) zurückspulen.
rewire [riː'waɪə'] vt neu verkabeln.
reword [riː'wɔːd] vt (message, note) umformulieren.
rework [riː'wɔːk] vt (use again: theme etc) wieder verarbeiten; (revise) neu fassen.
rewrite [riː'raɪt] (irreg: like write) vt neu schreiben.
Reykjavik ['reɪkjəviːk] n Reykjavik nt.
RFD (US) abbr (POST: = rural free delivery) freie Landpostzustellung.
RGN (BRIT) n abbr (= Registered General Nurse) staatlich geprüfte Krankenschwester f, staatlich geprüfter Krankenpfleger m.
Rh abbr (MED: = rhesus) Rh.
rhapsody ['ræpsədɪ] n (MUS) Rhapsodie f.
rhesus negative adj Rhesus negativ.
rhesus positive adj Rhesus positiv.
rhetoric ['retərɪk] n Rhetorik f.
rhetorical [rɪ'tɒrɪkl] adj rhetorisch.
rheumatic [ruː'mætɪk] adj rheumatisch.
rheumatism ['ruːmətɪzəm] n Rheuma nt, Rheumatismus m.
rheumatoid arthritis ['ruːmətɔɪd-] n Gelenkrheumatismus m.
Rhine [raɪn] n: **the** ~ der Rhein.
rhinestone ['raɪnstəun] n Rheinkiesel m.
rhinoceros [raɪ'nɒsərəs] n Rhinozeros nt.
Rhodes [rəudz] n Rhodos nt.
Rhodesia [rəu'diːʒə] (formerly) n (GEOG) Rhodesien nt.
rhododendron [rəudə'dendrən] n Rhododendron m or nt.
Rhone [rəun] n: **the** ~ die Rhone.
rhubarb ['ruːbɑːb] n Rhabarber m.
rhyme [raɪm] n Reim m; (verse) Verse pl ♦ vi: **to** ~ **(with)** sich reimen (mit); **without** ~ **or reason** ohne Sinn und Verstand.
rhythm ['rɪðm] n Rhythmus m.
rhythmic(al) ['rɪðmɪk(l)] adj rhythmisch.
rhythmically ['rɪðmɪklɪ] adv (move, beat) rhythmisch, im Rhythmus.
rhythm method n Knaus-Ogino-Methode f.
RI n abbr (BRIT: SCOL: = religious instruction) Religionsunterricht m ♦ abbr (US: POST: = Rhode Island).
rib [rɪb] n Rippe f ♦ vt (mock) aufziehen.
ribald ['rɪbəld] adj (laughter, joke) rüde; (person) anzüglich.
ribbed [rɪbd] adj (socks, sweater) gerippt.
ribbon ['rɪbən] n (for hair, decoration) Band nt; (of typewriter) Farbband nt; **in** ~**s** (torn) in Fetzen.

rice [raɪs] n Reis m.
ricefield ['raɪsfiːld] n Reisfeld nt.
rice pudding n Milchreis m.
rich [rɪtʃ] adj reich; (soil) fruchtbar; (food) schwer; (diet) reichhaltig; (colour) satt; (voice) volltönend; (tapestries, silks) prächtig ♦ npl: **the** ~ die Reichen; ~ **in** reich an +dat.
riches ['rɪtʃɪz] npl Reichtum m.
richly ['rɪtʃlɪ] adv (decorated, carved) reich; (reward, benefit) reichlich; ~ **deserved/ earned** wohlverdient.
richness ['rɪtʃnɪs] n (wealth) Reichtum m; (of life, culture, food) Reichhaltigkeit f; (of soil) Fruchtbarkeit f; (of costumes, furnishings) Pracht f.
rickets ['rɪkɪts] n Rachitis f.
rickety ['rɪkɪtɪ] adj (chair etc) wackelig.
rickshaw ['rɪkʃɔː] n Rikscha f.
ricochet ['rɪkəʃeɪ] vi abprallen ♦ n Abpraller m.
rid [rɪd] (pt, pp rid) vt: **to** ~ **sb/sth of** jdn/etw befreien von; **to get** ~ **of** loswerden; (inhibitions, illusions etc) sich befreien von.
riddance ['rɪdns] n: **good** ~! gut, daß wir den/ die/das los sind!
ridden ['rɪdn] pp of **ride**.
riddle ['rɪdl] n Rätsel nt ♦ vt: **to be** ~**d with** (guilt, doubts) geplagt sein von; (holes, corruption) durchsetzt sein von.
ride [raɪd] (pt **rode**, pp **ridden**) n (in car, on bicycle) Fahrt f; (on horse) Ritt m; (path) Reitweg m ♦ vi (on horse) reiten; (on bicycle, bus etc) fahren ♦ vt (see vi) reiten; fahren; **car** ~ Autofahrt f; **to go for a** ~ eine Fahrt/ einen Ausritt machen; **to take sb for a** ~ (fig) jdn hereinlegen; **we rode all day/all the way** wir sind den ganzen Tag/den ganzen Weg geritten/gefahren; **to** ~ **at anchor** (NAUT) vor Anker liegen; **can you** ~ **a bike?** kannst du Fahrrad fahren?
▶**ride out** vt: **to** ~ **out the storm** (fig) den Sturm überstehen.
rider ['raɪdə'] n (on horse) Reiter(in) m(f); (on bicycle etc) Fahrer(in) m(f); (in document etc) Zusatz m.
ridge [rɪdʒ] n (of hill) Grat m; (of roof) First m; (in sand etc) Rippelmarke f.
ridicule ['rɪdɪkjuːl] n Spott m ♦ vt (person) verspotten; (proposal, system etc) lächerlich machen; **she was the object of** ~ alle machten sich über sie lustig.
ridiculous [rɪ'dɪkjuləs] adj lächerlich.
riding ['raɪdɪŋ] n Reiten nt.
riding school n Reitschule f.
rife [raɪf] adj: **to be** ~ (corruption, disease etc) grassieren; **to be** ~ **with** (rumours etc) durchsetzt sein von.
riffraff ['rɪfræf] n Gesindel nt.
rifle ['raɪfl] n (gun) Gewehr nt ♦ vt (wallet etc) plündern.
▶**rifle through** vt fus (papers etc) durchwühlen.

rifle range n Schießstand m.

rift [rɪft] n Spalt m; (fig) Kluft f.

rig [rɪg] n (also: **oil ~**: at sea) Bohrinsel f; (: on land) Bohrturm m ♦ vt (election, game etc) manipulieren.

▶**rig out** (BRIT) vt: to ~ sb out as/in jdn ausstaffieren als/in +dat.

▶**rig up** vt (device) montieren.

rigging ['rɪgɪŋ] n (NAUT) Takelage f.

right [raɪt] adj (correct) richtig; (not left) rechte(r, s) ♦ n Recht nt ♦ adv (correctly, properly) richtig; (directly, exactly) genau; (not on the left) rechts ♦ vt (ship, car etc) aufrichten; (fault, situation) berichtigen ♦ excl okay; **the ~ time** (exact) die genaue Zeit; (most suitable) die richtige Zeit; **to be ~** (person) recht haben; (answer, fact) richtig sein; (clock) genau gehen; (reading etc) korrekt sein; **to get sth ~** etw richtig machen; **let's get it ~ this time!** diesmal machen wir es richtig!; **you did the ~ thing** du hast das Richtige getan; **to put sth ~** (mistake etc) etw berichtigen; **on/to the ~** rechts; **the R~** (POL) die Rechte; **by ~s** richtig genommen; **to be in the ~** im Recht sein; **you're within your ~s (to do that)** es ist dein gutes Recht(, das zu tun); **he is a well-known author in his own ~** er ist selbst auch ein bekannter Autor; **film ~s** Filmrechte pl; **~ now** im Moment; **~ before/after the party** gleich vor/nach der Party; **~ against the wall** unmittelbar an der Wand; **~ ahead** geradeaus; **~ away** (immediately) sofort; **~ in the middle** genau in der Mitte; **he went ~ to the end of the road** er ging bis ganz ans Ende der Straße.

right angle n rechter Winkel m.

righteous ['raɪtʃəs] adj (person) rechtschaffen; (indignation) gerecht.

righteousness ['raɪtʃəsnɪs] n Rechtschaffenheit f.

rightful ['raɪtful] adj rechtmäßig.

rightfully ['raɪtfəlɪ] adv von Rechts wegen.

right-hand drive adj (vehicle) mit Rechtssteuerung.

right-handed [raɪt'hændɪd] adj rechtshändig.

right-hand man n rechte Hand f.

right-hand side n rechte Seite f.

rightly ['raɪtlɪ] adv (with reason) zu Recht; **if I remember ~** (BRIT) wenn ich mich recht entsinne.

right-minded [raɪt'maɪndɪd] adj vernünftig.

right of way n (on path etc) Durchgangsrecht f, (AUT) Vorfahrt f.

rights issue n (STOCK EXCHANGE) Bezugsrechtsemission f.

right wing n (POL, SPORT) rechter Flügel m.

right-wing [raɪt'wɪŋ] adj (POL) rechtsgerichtet.

right-winger [raɪt'wɪŋə*] n (POL) Rechte(r) f(m); (SPORT) Rechtsaußen m.

rigid ['rɪdʒɪd] adj (structure, views) starr; (principle, control etc) streng.

rigidity [rɪ'dʒɪdɪtɪ] n (of structure etc) Starrheit f; (of attitude, views etc) Strenge f.

rigidly ['rɪdʒɪdlɪ] adv (hold, fix etc) starr; (control, interpret) streng.

rigmarole ['rɪgmərəʊl] n (procedure) Gedöns nt (inf).

rigor ['rɪgə*] (US) n = **rigour**.

rigor mortis ['rɪgə'mɔ:tɪs] n Totenstarre f.

rigorous ['rɪgərəs] adj (control etc) streng; (training) gründlich.

rigorously ['rɪgərəslɪ] adv (test, assess etc) streng.

rigour, (US) **rigor** ['rɪgə*] n (of argument, law) Strenge f; (of research) Gründlichkeit f; **the ~s of life/winter** die Härten des Lebens/des Winters.

rig-out ['rɪgaut] (BRIT: inf) n (clothes) Aufzug m.

rile [raɪl] vt ärgern.

rim [rɪm] n (of glass, spectacles) Rand m; (of wheel) Felge f, Radkranz m.

rimless ['rɪmlɪs] adj (spectacles) randlos.

rimmed [rɪmd] adj: ~ **with** umrandet von; **gold-~ spectacles** Brille f mit Goldfassung or Goldrand.

rind [raɪnd] n (of bacon) Schwarte f; (of lemon, melon) Schale f; (of cheese) Rinde f.

ring [rɪŋ] (pt **rang**, pp **rung**) n Ring m; (of people, objects) Kreis m; (of circus) Manege f; (bullring) Arena f; (sound of telephone) Klingeln nt; (sound of bell) Läuten nt; (on cooker) Kochstelle m ♦ vi (TEL: person) anrufen; (telephone, doorbell) klingeln; (bell) läuten; (also: ~ **out**) ertönen ♦ vt (BRIT: TEL) anrufen; (bell etc) läuten; (encircle) einen Kreis machen um; **to give sb a ~** (BRIT: TEL) jdn anrufen; **that has a ~ of truth about it** das könnte stimmen; **to run ~s round sb** (inf, fig) jdn in die Tasche stecken; **to ~ true/false** wahr/falsch klingen; **my ears are ~ing** mir klingen die Ohren; **to ~ the doorbell** klingeln; **the name doesn't ~ a bell (with me)** der Name sagt mir nichts.

▶**ring back** (BRIT) vt, vi (TEL) zurückrufen.

▶**ring off** (BRIT) vi (TEL) (den Hörer) auflegen.

▶**ring up** (BRIT) vt (TEL) anrufen.

ring binder n Ringbuch nt.

ring finger n Ringfinger m.

ringing ['rɪŋɪŋ] n (of telephone) Klingeln nt; (of bell) Läuten nt; (in ears) Klingen nt.

ringing tone (BRIT) n (TEL) Rufzeichen nt.

ringleader ['rɪŋliːdə*] n Rädelsführer(in) m(f).

ringlets ['rɪŋlɪts] npl Ringellocken pl; **in ~** in Ringellocken.

ring road (BRIT) n Ringstraße f.

rink [rɪŋk] n (also: **ice ~**) Eisbahn f; (also: **roller skating ~**) Rollschuhbahn f.

rinse [rɪns] n Spülen nt; (of hands) Abspülen nt; (hair dye) Tönung f ♦ vt spülen; (hands) abspülen; (also: ~ **out**: clothes) auswaschen;

(: *mouth*) ausspülen; **to give sth a ~** etw spülen; (*dishes*) etw abspülen.

Rio (de Janeiro) ['riːəu(dədʒəˈnɪərəu)] *n* Rio (de Janeiro) *nt.*

riot ['raɪət] *n* (*disturbance*) Aufruhr *m* ♦ *vi* randalieren; **a ~ of colours** ein Farbenmeer *nt*; **to run ~** randalieren.

rioter ['raɪətə*] *n* Randalierer *m.*

riot gear *n* Schutzausrüstung *f.*

riotous ['raɪətəs] *adj* (*crowd*) randalierend; (*nights, party*) ausschweifend; (*welcome etc*) tumultartig.

riotously ['raɪətəslɪ] *adv:* ~ **funny** *or* **comic** urkomisch.

riot police *n* Bereitschaftspolizei *f*; **hundreds of** ~ Hunderte von Bereitschaftspolizisten.

RIP *abbr* (= *rest in peace*) R.I.P.

rip [rɪp] *n* (*tear*) Riß *m* ♦ *vt* zerreißen ♦ *vi* reißen.

▶**rip off** *vt* (*clothes*) herunterreißen; (*inf: swindle*) übers Ohr hauen.

▶**rip up** *vt* zerreißen.

ripcord ['rɪpkɔːd] *n* Reißleine *f.*

ripe [raɪp] *adj* reif; **to be ~ for sth** (*fig*) reif für etw sein; **he lived to a ~ old age** er erreichte ein stolzes Alter.

ripen ['raɪpn] *vt* reifen lassen ♦ *vi* reifen.

ripeness ['raɪpnɪs] *n* Reife *f.*

rip-off ['rɪpɔf] (*inf*) *n:* **it's a ~!** das ist Wucher!

riposte [rɪˈpɔst] *n* scharfe Entgegnung *f.*

ripple ['rɪpl] *n* (*wave*) kleine Welle *f*; (*of laughter, applause*) Welle *f* ♦ *vi* (*water*) sich kräuseln; (*muscles*) spielen ♦ *vt* (*surface*) kräuseln.

rise [raɪz] (*pt* **rose**, *pp* **risen**) *n* (*incline*) Steigung *f*; (*BRIT: salary increase*) Gehaltserhöhung *f*; (*in prices, temperature etc*) Anstieg *m*; (*fig: to fame etc*) Aufstieg *m* ♦ *vi* (*prices, water*) steigen; (*sun, moon*) aufgehen; (*wind*) aufkommen; (*from bed, chair*) aufstehen; (*sound, voice*) ansteigen; (*also:* ~ **up:** *tower, rebel*) sich erheben; (*in rank*) aufsteigen; **to give ~ to** Anlaß geben zu; **to ~ to power** an die Macht kommen.

risen ['rɪzn] *pp of* **rise.**

rising ['raɪzɪŋ] *adj* (*increasing*) steigend; (*up-and-coming*) aufstrebend.

rising damp *n* aufsteigende Feuchtigkeit *f.*

rising star *n* (*fig: person*) Aufsteiger(in) *m(f).*

risk [rɪsk] *n* (*danger, chance*) Gefahr *f*; (*deliberate*) Risiko *nt* ♦ *vt* riskieren; **to take a ~** ein Risiko eingehen; **to run the ~ of sth** etw zu fürchten haben; **to run the ~ of doing sth** Gefahr laufen, etw zu tun; **at ~** in Gefahr; **at one's own ~** auf eigene Gefahr; **at the ~ of sounding rude** ... auf die Gefahr hin, unhöflich zu klingen, ...; **it's a fire/ health ~** es ist ein Feuer-/ Gesundheitsrisiko; **I'll ~ it** ich riskiere es.

risk capital *n* Risikokapital *nt.*

risky ['rɪskɪ] *adj* riskant.

risqué ['riːskeɪ] *adj* (*joke*) gewagt.

rissole ['rɪsəul] *n* (*of meat, fish etc*) Frikadelle *f.*

rite [raɪt] *n* Ritus *m*; **last ~s** (*REL*) Letzte Ölung *f.*

ritual ['rɪtjuəl] *adj* (*law, murder*) Ritual-; (*dance*) rituell ♦ *n* Ritual *nt.*

rival ['raɪvl] *n* Rivale *m*, Rivalin *f* ♦ *adj* (*firm, newspaper etc*) Konkurrenz-; (*teams, groups etc*) rivalisierend ♦ *vt* (*match*) sich messen können mit; **to ~ sth/sb in sth** sich mit etw/ jdm in bezug auf etw messen können.

rivalry ['raɪvlrɪ] *n* Rivalität *f.*

river ['rɪvə*] *n* Fluß *m*; (*fig: of blood etc*) Strom *m* ♦ *cpd* (*port, traffic*) Fluß-; **up/down ~** flußaufwärts/-abwärts.

river bank *n* Flußufer *nt.*

river bed *n* Flußbett *nt.*

riverside ['rɪvəsaɪd] *n* = **river bank.**

rivet ['rɪvɪt] *n* Niete *f* ♦ *vt* (*fig: attention*) fesseln; (: *eyes*) heften.

riveting ['rɪvɪtɪŋ] *adj* (*fig*) fesselnd.

Riviera [rɪvɪˈɛərə] *n:* **the (French)** ~ die (französische) Riviera; **the Italian** ~ die italienische Riviera.

Riyadh [rɪˈjɑːd] *n* Riad *nt.*

RMT *n abbr* (= *National Union of Rail, Maritime and Transport Workers*) Gewerkschaft der Eisenbahner, Seeleute und Transportarbeiter.

RN *n abbr* (*BRIT*) = **Royal Navy;** (*US*) = **registered nurse.**

RNA *n abbr* (= *ribonucleic acid*) RNS *f.*

RNLI (*BRIT*) *n abbr* (= *Royal National Lifeboat Institution*) *durch Spenden finanzierter Seenot-Rettungsdienst,* ≈ DLRG *f.*

RNZAF *n abbr* (= *Royal New Zealand Air Force*) neuseeländische Luftwaffe *f.*

RNZN *n abbr* (= *Royal New Zealand Navy*) neuseeländische Marine *f.*

road [rəud] *n* Straße *f*; (*fig*) Weg *m* ♦ *cpd* (*accident, sense*) Verkehrs-; **main** ~ Hauptstraße *f*; **it takes four hours by** ~ man braucht vier Stunden mit dem Auto; **let's hit the** ~ machen wir uns auf den Weg!; **to be on the** ~ (*salesman etc*) unterwegs sein; (*pop group etc*) auf Tournee sein; **on the** ~ **to success** auf dem Weg zum Erfolg; **major/minor** ~ Haupt-/Nebenstraße *f.*

roadblock ['rəudblɔk] *n* Straßensperre *f.*

road haulage *n* Spedition *f.*

roadhog ['rəudhɔg] *n* Verkehrsrowdy *m.*

road map *n* Straßenkarte *f.*

road safety *n* Verkehrssicherheit *f.*

roadside ['rəudsaɪd] *n* Straßenrand *m* ♦ *cpd* (*building, sign etc*) am Straßenrand; **by the** ~ am Straßenrand.

road sign *n* Verkehrszeichen *nt.*

roadsweeper ['rəudswiːpə*] (*BRIT*) *n* (*person*) Straßenkehrer(in) *m(f)*; (*vehicle*) Straßenkehrmaschine *f.*

road user *n* Verkehrsteilnehmer(in) *m(f).*

roadway ['rəudweɪ] *n* Fahrbahn *f.*

road works *npl* Straßenbauarbeiten *pl.*

roadworthy ['rəudwə:ðɪ] *adj* verkehrstüchtig.
roam [rəum] *vi* wandern, streifen ♦ *vt* (*streets, countryside*) durchstreifen.
roar [rɔː*] *n* (*of animal, crowd*) Brüllen *nt*; (*of vehicle*) Getöse *nt*; (*of storm*) Heulen *nt* ♦ *vi* (*animal, person*) brüllen; (*engine, wind etc*) heulen; ~**s of laughter** brüllendes Gelächter; **to ~ with laughter** vor Lachen brüllen.
roaring ['rɔːrɪŋ] *adj*: **a ~ fire** ein prasselndes Feuer; **a ~ success** ein Bombenerfolg *m*; **to do a ~ trade (in sth)** ein Riesengeschäft (mit etw) machen.
roast [rəust] *n* Braten *m* ♦ *vt* (*meat, potatoes*) braten; (*coffee*) rösten.
roast beef *n* Roastbeef *nt*.
roasting ['rəustɪŋ] (*inf*) *adj* (*hot*) knallheiß ♦ *n* (*criticism*) Verriß *m*; (*telling-off*) Standpauke *f*; **to give sb a ~** (*criticize*) jdn verreißen; (*scold*) jdm eine Standpauke halten.
rob [rɔb] *vt* (*person*) bestehlen; (*house, bank*) ausrauben; **to ~ sb of sth** jdm etw rauben; (*fig: deprive*) jdm etw vorenthalten.
robber ['rɔbə*] *n* Räuber(in) *m(f)*.
robbery ['rɔbərɪ] *n* Raub *m*.
robe [rəub] *n* (*for ceremony etc*) Gewand *nt*; (*also:* **bath ~**) Bademantel *m*; (*US*) Morgenrock *m* ♦ *vt*: **to be ~d in** (*form*) (festlich) in etw *acc* gekleidet sein.
robin ['rɔbɪn] *n* Rotkehlchen *nt*.
robot ['rəubɔt] *n* Roboter *m*.
robotics [rə'bɔtɪks] *n* Robotik *f*.
robust [rəu'bʌst] *adj* robust; (*appetite*) gesund.
rock [rɔk] *n* (*substance*) Stein *m*; (*boulder*) Felsen *m*; (*US: small stone*) Stein *m*; (*BRIT: sweet*) ≈ Zuckerstange *f*; (*MUS: also:* ~ **music**) Rock *m*, Rockmusik *f* ♦ *vt* (*swing gently: cradle*) schaukeln; (: *child*) wiegen; (*shake: also fig*) erschüttern ♦ *vi* (*object*) schwanken; (*person*) schaukeln; **on the ~s** (*drink*) mit Eis; (*ship*) (auf Felsen) aufgelaufen; (*marriage etc*) gescheitert; **to ~ the boat** (*fig*) Unruhe stiften.
rock and roll *n* Rock and Roll *m*.
rock-bottom ['rɔk'bɔtəm] *adj* (*prices*) Tiefst- ♦ *n*: **to reach** *or* **touch** *or* **hit ~** (*person, prices*) den Tiefpunkt erreichen.
rock cake *n* ≈ Rosinenbrötchen *nt*.
rock climber *n* Felsenkletterer(in) *m(f)*.
rock climbing *n* Felsenklettern *nt*.
rockery ['rɔkərɪ] *n* Steingarten *m*.
rocket ['rɔkɪt] *n* Rakete *f* ♦ *vi* (*prices*) in die Höhe schießen.
rocket launcher *n* Raketenwerfer *m*.
rock face *n* Felswand *f*.
rock fall *n* Steinschlag *m*.
rocking chair ['rɔkɪŋ-] *n* Schaukelstuhl *m*.
rocking horse *n* Schaukelpferd *nt*.
rocky ['rɔkɪ] *adj* (*path, ground*) felsig; (*fig: business, marriage*) wackelig.
Rocky Mountains *npl*: **the ~** die Rocky Mountains *pl*.

rod [rɔd] *n* (*also TECH*) Stange *f*; (*also:* **fishing ~**) Angelrute *f*.
rode [rəud] *pt of* **ride**.
rodent ['rəudnt] *n* Nagetier *nt*.
rodeo ['rəudɪəu] (*US*) *n* Rodeo *nt*.
roe [rəu] *n* (*CULIN*): **hard ~** Rogen *m*; **soft ~** Milch *f*.
roe deer *n inv* Reh *nt*.
rogue [rəug] *n* Gauner *m*.
roguish ['rəugɪʃ] *adj* schelmisch.
role [rəul] *n* Rolle *f*.
role model *n* Rollenmodell *nt*.
role play *n* Rollenspiel *nt*.
roll [rəul] *n* (*of paper*) Rolle *f*; (*of cloth*) Ballen *m*; (*of banknotes*) Bündel *nt*; (*also:* **bread ~**) Brötchen *nt*; (*register, list*) Verzeichnis *nt*; (*of drums etc*) Wirbel *m* ♦ *vt* rollen; (*also:* ~ **up:** *string*) aufrollen; (: *sleeves*) aufkrempeln; (*cigarette*) drehen; (*also:* ~ **out:** *pastry*) ausrollen; (*flatten: lawn, road*) walzen ♦ *vi* rollen; (*drum*) wirbeln; (*thunder*) grollen; (*ship*) schlingern; (*tears, sweat*) fließen; (*camera, printing press*) laufen; **cheese/ham ~** Käse-/Schinkenbrötchen *nt*; **he's ~ing in it** (*inf: rich*) er schwimmt im Geld.
►**roll about** *vi* sich wälzen.
►**roll around** *vi* = **roll about**.
►**roll in** *vi* (*money, invitations*) hereinströmen.
►**roll over** *vi* sich umdrehen.
►**roll up** *vi* (*inf: arrive*) aufkreuzen ♦ *vt* (*carpet, umbrella etc*) aufrollen; **to ~ o.s. up into a ball** sich zusammenrollen.
roll call *n* namentlicher Aufruf *m*.
rolled gold [rəuld-] *n* Dubleegold *nt*.
roller ['rəulə*] *n* Rolle *f*; (*for lawn, road*) Walze *f*; (*for hair*) Lockenwickler *m*.
roller blind *n* Rollo *nt*.
roller coaster *n* Achterbahn *f*.
roller skates *npl* Rollschuhe *pl*.
rollicking ['rɔlɪkɪŋ] *adj* toll, Mords-; **to have a ~ time** sich ganz toll amüsieren.
rolling ['rəulɪŋ] *adj* (*hills*) wellig.
rolling mill *n* Walzwerk *nt*.
rolling pin *n* Nudelholz *nt*.
rolling stock *n* (*RAIL*) Fahrzeuge *pl*.
roll-on-roll-off ['rəulɔn'rəulɔf] (*BRIT*) *adj* (*ferry*) Roll-on-roll-off-.
roly-poly ['rəulɪ'pəulɪ] (*BRIT*) *n* ≈ Strudel *m*.
ROM [rɔm] *n abbr* (*COMPUT*: = *read only memory*) ROM.
Roman ['rəumən] *adj* römisch ♦ *n* (*person*) Römer(in) *m(f)*.
Roman Catholic *adj* römisch-katholisch ♦ *n* Katholik(in) *m(f)*.
romance [rə'mæns] *n* (*love affair*) Romanze *f*; (*romanticism*) Romantik *f*; (*novel*) phantastische Erzählung *f*.
Romanesque [rəumə'nesk] *adj* romanisch.
Romania [rəu'meɪnɪə] *n* Rumänien *nt*.
Romanian [rəu'meɪnɪən] *adj* rumänisch ♦ *n* (*person*) Rumäne *m*, Rumänin *f*; (*LING*) Rumänisch *nt*.

Roman numeral n römische Ziffer f.

romantic [rə'mæntɪk] adj romantisch.

romanticism [rə'mæntɪsɪzəm] n (also ART, LITER) Romantik f.

Romany ['rɔmənɪ] adj Roma- ♦ n (person) Roma mf; (LING) Romani nt.

Rome [rəum] n Rom nt.

romp [rɔmp] n Klamauk m ♦ vi (also: ~ about) herumtollen; **to ~ home** (horse) spielend gewinnen.

rompers ['rɔmpəz] npl (clothing) einteiliger Spielanzug für Babys.

rondo ['rɔndəu] n (MUS) Rondo nt.

roof [ru:f] (pl ~s) n Dach nt ♦ vt (house etc) überdachen; **the ~ of the mouth** der Gaumen.

roof garden n Dachgarten m.

roofing ['ru:fɪŋ] n Deckung f; ~ **felt** Dachpappe f.

roof rack n Dachgepäckträger m.

rook [ruk] n (bird) Saatkrähe f; (CHESS) Turm m.

rookie ['rukɪ] (inf) n (esp MIL) Grünschnabel m.

room [ru:m] n (in house, hotel) Zimmer nt; (space) Raum m, Platz m; (scope: for change etc) Raum m ♦ vi: **to ~ with sb** (esp US) ein Zimmer mit jdm teilen; **rooms** npl (lodging) Zimmer pl; "~s **to let**", (US) "~s **for rent**" „Zimmer zu vermieten"; **single/double ~** Einzel-/Doppelzimmer nt; **is there ~ for this?** ist dafür Platz vorhanden?; **to make ~ for sb** für jdn Platz machen; **there is ~ for improvement** es gibt Möglichkeiten zur Verbesserung.

rooming house ['ru:mɪŋ-] (US) n Mietshaus nt.

roommate ['ru:mmeɪt] n Zimmergenosse m, Zimmergenossin f.

room service n Zimmerservice m.

room temperature n Zimmertemperatur f.

roomy ['ru:mɪ] adj (building, car) geräumig.

roost [ru:st] vi (birds) sich niederlassen.

rooster ['ru:stə*] (esp US) n Hahn m.

root [ru:t] n (also MATH) Wurzel f ♦ vi (plant) Wurzeln schlagen ♦ vt: **to be ~ed in** verwurzelt sein in +dat; **roots** npl (family origins) Wurzeln pl; **to take ~** (plant, idea) Wurzeln schlagen; **the ~ cause of the problem** die Wurzel des Problems.

▶**root about** vi (search) herumwühlen.

▶**root for** vt fus (support) anfeuern.

▶**root out** vt ausrotten.

root beer (US) n kohlensäurehaltiges Getränk aus Wurzel- und Kräuterextrakten.

rope [rəup] n Seil nt; (NAUT) Tau nt ♦ vt (tie) festbinden; (also: ~ **together**) zusammenbinden; **to know the ~s** (fig) sich auskennen.

▶**rope in** vt (fig: person) einspannen.

▶**rope off** vt (area) mit einem Seil absperren.

rope ladder n Strickleiter f.

rop(e)y (inf) adj (ill, poor quality) miserabel.

rosary ['rəuzərɪ] n Rosenkranz m.

rose [rəuz] pt of **rise** ♦ n (flower) Rose f; (also: ~**bush**) Rosenstrauch m; (on watering can) Brause f ♦ adj rosarot.

rosé ['rəuzeɪ] n (wine) Rosé m.

rosebed ['rəuzbɛd] n Rosenbeet nt.

rosebud ['rəuzbʌd] n Rosenknospe f.

rosebush ['rəuzbuʃ] n Rosenstrauch m.

rosemary ['rəuzmərɪ] n Rosmarin m.

rosette [rəu'zɛt] n Rosette f.

ROSPA ['rɔspə] (BRIT) n abbr (= Royal Society for the Prevention of Accidents) Verband, der Maßnahmen zur Unfallverhütung propagiert.

roster ['rɔstə*] n: **duty ~** Dienstplan m.

rostrum ['rɔstrəm] n Rednerpult nt.

rosy ['rəuzɪ] adj (colour) rosarot; (face, situation) rosig; **a ~ future** eine rosige Zukunft.

rot [rɔt] n (decay) Fäulnis f; (fig: rubbish) Quatsch m ♦ vt verfaulen lassen ♦ vi (teeth, wood, fruit etc) verfaulen; **to stop the ~** (BRIT, fig) den Verfall stoppen; **dry ~** Holzschwamm m; **wet ~** Naßfäule f.

rota ['rəutə] n Dienstplan m; **on a ~ basis** reihum nach Plan.

rotary ['rəutərɪ] adj (cutter) rotierend; (motion) Dreh-.

rotate [rəu'teɪt] vt (spin) drehen, rotieren lassen; (crops) im Wechsel anbauen; (jobs) turnusmäßig wechseln ♦ vi (revolve) rotieren, sich drehen.

rotating [rəu'teɪtɪŋ] adj (revolving) rotierend; (drum, mirror) Dreh-.

rotation [rəu'teɪʃən] n (of planet, drum etc) Rotation f, Drehung f; (of crops) Wechsel m; (of jobs) turnusmäßiger Wechsel m; **in ~** der Reihe nach.

rote [rəut] n: **by ~** auswendig.

rotor ['rəutə*] n (also: ~ **blade**) Rotor m.

rotten ['rɔtn] adj (decayed) faul, verfault; (inf: person, situation) gemein; (: film, weather, driver etc) mies; **to feel ~** sich elend fühlen.

rotund [rəu'tʌnd] adj (person) rundlich.

rouble, (US) **ruble** ['ru:bl] n Rubel m.

rouge [ru:ʒ] n Rouge nt.

rough [rʌf] adj rauh; (terrain, road) uneben; (person, plan, drawing, guess) grob; (life, conditions, journey) hart; (sea, crossing) stürmisch ♦ n (GOLF): **in the ~** im Rough ♦ vt: **to ~ it** primitiv or ohne Komfort leben; **the sea is ~ today** die See ist heute stürmisch; **to have a ~ time** eine harte Zeit durchmachen; **can you give me a ~ idea of the cost?** können Sie mir eine ungefähre Vorstellung von den Kosten geben?; **to feel ~** (BRIT) sich elend fühlen; **to sleep ~** (BRIT) im Freien übernachten; **to play ~** (fig) auf die grobe Tour kommen.

▶**rough out** vt (drawing, idea etc) skizzieren.

roughage ['rʌfɪdʒ] n Ballaststoffe pl.

rough-and-ready ['rʌfən'rɛdɪ] *adj*
provisorisch.
rough-and-tumble ['rʌfən'tʌmbl] *n (fighting)*
Balgerei *f*; *(fig)* Schlachtfeld *nt*.
roughcast ['rʌfkɑːst] *n* Rauhputz *m*.
rough copy *n* Entwurf *m*.
rough draft *n =* **rough copy**.
rough justice *n* Justizwillkür *f*.
roughly ['rʌflɪ] *adv* grob; *(approximately)*
ungefähr; ~ **speaking** grob gesagt.
roughness ['rʌfnɪs] *n* Rauheit *f*; *(of manner)*
Grobheit *f*.
roughshod ['rʌfʃɒd] *adv:* **to ride ~ over** sich
rücksichtslos hinwegsetzen über +*acc*.
roulette [ruː'lɛt] *n* Roulette *nt*.
Roumania *etc* [ruː'meɪnɪə] *n =* **Romania** *etc*.
round [raund] *adj* rund ♦ *n* Runde *f*; *(of*
ammunition) Ladung *f* ♦ *vt (corner)* biegen
um; *(cape)* umrunden ♦ *prep* um ♦ *adv:* **all ~**
rundherum; **in ~ figures** rund gerechnet;
the daily ~ *(fig)* der tägliche Trott; **a ~ of**
applause Beifall *m*; **a ~ of drinks)** eine
Runde; **a ~ of sandwiches** ein Butterbrot; **a**
~ of toast *(BRIT)* eine Scheibe Toast; **it's just**
~ the corner *(fig)* es steht vor der Tür; **to go**
~ the back hinten herum gehen; **to go ~ (an**
obstacle) (um ein Hindernis) herumgehen;
~ the clock rund um die Uhr; **~ his neck/**
the table um seinen Hals/den Tisch; **to sail**
~ the world die Welt umsegeln; **to walk**
~ the room/park im Zimmer/Park
herumgehen; **~ about 300** *(approximately)*
ungefähr 300; **the long way ~** auf
Umwegen; **all (the) year ~** das ganze Jahr
über; **the wrong way ~** falsch herum; **to ask**
sb ~ jdn zu sich einladen; **I'll be ~ at 6**
o'clock ich komme um 6 Uhr; **to go ~**
(rotate) sich drehen; **to go ~ to sb's (house)**
jdn (zu Hause) besuchen; **enough to go ~**
genug für alle.
▶**round off** *vt* abrunden.
▶**round up** *vt (cattle etc)* zusammentreiben;
(people) versammeln; *(figure)* aufrunden.
roundabout ['raundəbaut] *(BRIT) n (AUT)*
Kreisverkehr *m*; *(at fair)* Karussell *nt* ♦ *adj:*
by a ~ route auf Umwegen; **in a ~ way** auf
Umwegen.
rounded ['raundɪd] *adj (hill, figure etc)*
rundlich.
rounders ['raundəz] *n ≈* Schlagball *m*.
roundly ['raundlɪ] *adv (fig: criticize etc)*
nachdrücklich.
round robin *(esp US) n (SPORT)* Wettkampf *m*,
bei dem jeder gegen jeden spielt.
round-shouldered ['raund'ʃəuldəd] *adj* mit
runden Schultern.
round trip *n* Rundreise *f*.
roundup ['raundʌp] *n (of news etc)*
Zusammenfassung *f*; *(of animals)*
Zusammentreiben *nt*; *(of criminals)*
Aufgreifen *nt*; **a ~ of the latest news** ein
Nachrichtenüberblick *m*.

rouse [rauz] *vt (wake up)* aufwecken; *(stir up)*
reizen.
rousing ['rauzɪŋ] *adj (speech)* mitreißend;
(welcome) stürmisch.
rout [raut] *(MIL) n* totale Niederlage *f* ♦ *vt*
(defeat) vernichtend schlagen.
route [ruːt] *n* Strecke *f*; *(of bus, train, shipping)*
Linie *f*; *(of procession, fig)* Weg *m*; **"all ~s"**
(AUT) „alle Richtungen"; **the best ~ to**
London der beste Weg nach London.
route map *(BRIT) n* Streckenkarte *f*.
routine [ruː'tiːn] *adj (work, check etc)* Routine-
♦ *n (habits)* Routine *f*; *(drudgery)* Stumpfsinn
m; *(THEAT)* Nummer *f*; **~ procedure**
Routinesache *f*.
rove [rəuv] *vt (area, streets)* ziehen durch.
roving reporter ['rəuvɪŋ] *n* Reporter(in) *m(f)*
im Außendienst.
row¹ [rəu] *n (line)* Reihe *f* ♦ *vi (in boat)* rudern
♦ *vt (boat)* rudern; **three times in a ~**
dreimal hintereinander.
row² [rau] *n (din)* Krach *m*, Lärm *m*; *(dispute)*
Streit *m* ♦ *vi (argue)* sich streiten; **to have a**
~ sich streiten.
rowboat ['rəubaut] *(US) n =* **rowing boat**.
rowdiness ['raudɪnɪs] *n* Rowdytum *nt*.
rowdy ['raudɪ] *adj (person)* rüpelhaft; *(party*
etc) lärmend.
rowdyism ['raudɪɪzəm] *n =* **rowdiness**.
rowing ['rəuɪŋ] *n (sport)* Rudern *nt*.
rowing boat *(BRIT) n* Ruderboot *nt*.
rowlock ['rɒlək] *(BRIT) n* Dolle *f*.
royal ['rɔɪəl] *adj* königlich; **the ~ family** die
königliche Familie.

Die **Royal Academy** *oder* **Royal Academy of**
Arts, *eine Akademie zur Förderung der*
Malerei, Bildhauerei und Architektur, wurde
1768 unter der Schirmherrschaft von George II
gegründet und befindet sich seit 1869 in
Burlington House, Piccadilly, London. Jeden
Sommer findet dort eine Ausstellung mit
Werken zeitgenössischer Künstler statt. Die
Royal Academy unterhält auch Schulen, an
denen Malerei, Bildhauerei und Architektur
unterrichtet wird.

Royal Air Force *(BRIT) n:* **the ~** die
Königliche Luftwaffe.
royal blue *adj* königsblau.
royalist ['rɔɪəlɪst] *n* Royalist(in) *m(f)* ♦ *adj*
royalistisch.
Royal Navy *(BRIT) n:* **the ~** die Königliche
Marine.
royalty ['rɔɪəltɪ] *n (royal persons)* die
königliche Familie; **royalties** *npl (to author)*
Tantiemen *pl*; *(to inventor)* Honorar *nt*.
RP *(BRIT) n abbr (= received pronunciation)*
Standardaussprache des Englischen; see also
receive.
rpm *abbr (= revolutions per minute)* U/min.
RR *(US) abbr =* **railroad**.

RRP (*BRIT*) *n abbr* = **recommended retail price.**
RSA (*BRIT*) *n abbr* (= *Royal Society of Arts*) *akademischer Verband zur Vergabe von Diplomen*; (= *Royal Scottish Academy*) *Kunstakademie.*
RSI *n abbr* (*MED:* = *repetitive strain injury*) RSI *nt*, *Schmerzempfindung durch ständige Wiederholung bestimmter Bewegungen.*
RSPB (*BRIT*) *n abbr* (= *Royal Society for the Protection of Birds*) *Vogelschutzorganisation.*
RSPCA (*BRIT*) *n abbr* (= *Royal Society for the Prevention of Cruelty to Animals*) *Tierschutzverein m.*
RSVP *abbr* (= *répondez s'il vous plaît*) u.A.w.g.
RTA *n abbr* (= *road traffic accident*) *Verkehrsunfall m.*
Rt Hon. (*BRIT*) *abbr* (= *Right Honourable*) *Titel für Abgeordnete des Unterhauses.*
Rt Rev. *abbr* (*REL:* = *Right Reverend*) *Titel für Bischöfe.*
rub [rʌb] *vt* reiben ♦ *n:* **to give sth a ~** (*polish*) etw polieren; **he ~bed his hands together** er rieb sich *dat* die Hände; **to ~ sb up** *or* (*US*) **~ sb the wrong way** bei jdm anecken.
▶**rub down** *vt* (*body, horse*) abreiben.
▶**rub in** *vt* (*ointment*) einreiben; **don't ~ it in!** (*fig*) reite nicht so darauf herum!
▶**rub off** *vi* (*paint*) abfärben.
▶**rub off on** *vt fus* abfärben auf +*acc.*
▶**rub out** *vt* (*with eraser*) ausradieren.
rubber ['rʌbə*] *n* (*also inf: condom*) Gummi *nt or m*; (*BRIT: eraser*) Radiergummi *m.*
rubber band *n* Gummiband *nt.*
rubber bullet *n* Gummigeschoß *nt.*
rubber plant *n* Gummibaum *m.*
rubber ring *n* (*for swimming*) Schwimmreifen *m.*
rubber stamp *n* Stempel *m.*
rubber-stamp [rʌbə'stæmp] *vt* (*fig: decision*) genehmigen.
rubbery ['rʌbərɪ] *adj* (*material*) gummiartig; (*meat, food*) wie Gummi.
rubbish ['rʌbɪʃ] (*BRIT*) *n* (*waste*) Abfall *m*; (*fig: junk*) Schrott *m*; (: *pej: nonsense*) Quatsch *m* ♦ *vt* (*inf*) heruntermachen; ~! Quatsch!
rubbish bin (*BRIT*) *n* Abfalleimer *m.*
rubbish dump (*BRIT*) *n* Müllabladeplatz *m.*
rubbishy ['rʌbɪʃɪ] (*BRIT: inf*) *adj* miserabel, mies.
rubble ['rʌbl] *n* (*debris*) Trümmer *pl*; (*CONSTR*) Schutt *m.*
ruble ['ruːbl] (*US*) *n* = **rouble.**
ruby ['ruːbɪ] *n* (*gem*) Rubin *m* ♦ *adj* (*red*) rubinrot.
RUC (*BRIT*) *n abbr* (= *Royal Ulster Constabulary*) *nordirische Polizeibehörde.*
rucksack ['rʌksæk] *n* Rucksack *m.*
ructions ['rʌkʃənz] (*inf*) *npl* Krach *m*, Ärger *m.*
rudder ['rʌdə*] *n* (*of ship, plane*) Ruder *nt.*
ruddy ['rʌdɪ] *adj* (*complexion etc*) rötlich; (*inf: damned*) verdammt.
rude [ruːd] *adj* (*impolite*) unhöflich; (*naughty*)

unanständig; (*unexpected: shock etc*) böse; (*crude: table, shelter etc*) primitiv; **to be ~ to sb** unhöflich zu jdm sein; **a ~ awakening** ein böses Erwachen.
rudely ['ruːdlɪ] *adv* (*interrupt*) unhöflich; (*say, push*) grob.
rudeness ['ruːdnɪs] *n* (*impoliteness*) Unhöflichkeit *f.*
rudimentary [ruːdɪ'mɛntərɪ] *adj* (*equipment*) primitiv; (*knowledge*) Grund-.
rudiments ['ruːdɪmənts] *npl* Grundlagen *pl.*
rue [ruː] *vt* bereuen.
rueful ['ruːful] *adj* (*expression, person*) reuevoll.
ruff [rʌf] *n* (*collar*) Halskrause *f.*
ruffian ['rʌfɪən] *n* Rüpel *m.*
ruffle ['rʌfl] *vt* (*hair, feathers*) zerzausen; (*water*) kräuseln; (*fig: person*) aus der Fassung bringen.
rug [rʌg] *n* (*on floor*) Läufer *m*; (*BRIT: blanket*) Decke *f.*
rugby ['rʌgbɪ] *n* (*also: ~ football*) Rugby *nt.*
rugged ['rʌgɪd] *adj* (*landscape*) rauh; (*man*) robust; (*features, face*) markig; (*determination, independence*) wild.
rugger ['rʌgə*] (*BRIT: inf*) *n* Rugby *nt.*
ruin ['ruːɪn] *n* (*destruction, downfall*) Ruin *m*; (*remains*) Ruine *f* ♦ *vt* ruinieren; (*building*) zerstören; (*clothes, carpet etc*) verderben;
ruins *npl* (*of castle*) Ruinen *pl*; (*of building*) Trümmer *pl*; **in ~s** (*lit, fig*) in Trümmern.
ruination [ruːɪ'neɪʃən] *n* (*of building etc*) Zerstörung *f*; (*of person, life*) Ruinierung *f.*
ruinous ['ruːɪnəs] *adj* (*expense, interest*) ruinös.
rule [ruːl] *n* (*norm*) Regel *f*; (*regulation*) Vorschrift *f*; (*government*) Herrschaft *f*; (*also: ruler*) Lineal *nt* ♦ *vt* (*country, people*) herrschen über +*acc* ♦ *vi* (*monarch etc*) herrschen; **it's against the ~s** das ist nicht gestattet; **as a ~ of thumb** als Faustregel; **under British ~** unter britischer Herrschaft; **as a ~** in der Regel; **to ~ in favour of/against/on sth** (*LAW*) für/gegen/ über etw *acc* entscheiden; **to ~ that ...** (*umpire, judge etc*) entscheiden, daß ...
▶**rule out** *vt* (*possibility etc*) ausschließen; **murder cannot be ~d out** Mord ist nicht auszuschließen.
ruled [ruːld] *adj* (*paper*) liniert.
ruler ['ruːlə*] *n* (*sovereign*) Herrscher(in) *m(f)*; (*for measuring*) Lineal *nt.*
ruling ['ruːlɪŋ] *adj* (*party*) Regierungs-; (*body*) maßgebend ♦ *n* (*LAW*) Entscheidung *f*; **the ~ class** die herrschende Klasse.
rum [rʌm] *n* Rum *m* ♦ *adj* (*BRIT: inf: peculiar*) komisch.
Rumania *etc n* = **Romania** *etc.*
rumble ['rʌmbl] *n* (*of thunder*) Grollen *nt*; (*of traffic*) Rumpeln *nt*; (*of guns*) Donnern *nt*; (*of voices*) Gemurmel *nt* ♦ *vi* (*stomach*) knurren; (*thunder*) grollen; (*traffic*) rumpeln; (*guns*) donnern.

rumbustious [rʌm'bʌstʃəs] *adj* (*person*)
ungebärdig.

ruminate ['ruːmɪneɪt] *vi* (*person*) grübeln;
(*cow, sheep etc*) wiederkäuen.

rummage ['rʌmɪdʒ] *vi* herumstöbern.

rummage sale (*US*) *n* Trödelmarkt *m*.

rumour, (*US*) **rumor** ['ruːmə*] *n* Gerücht *nt*
♦ *vt*: **it is** ~**ed that** ... man sagt, daß ...

rump [rʌmp] *n* (*of animal*) Hinterteil *nt*; (*of
group etc*) Rumpf *m*.

rumple ['rʌmpl] *vt* (*clothes etc*) zerknittern;
(*hair*) zerzausen.

rump steak *n* Rumpsteak *nt*.

rumpus ['rʌmpəs] *n* Krach *m*; **to kick up a** ~
Krach schlagen.

run [rʌn] (*pt* **ran**, *pp* **run**) *n* (*as exercise, sport*)
Lauf *m*; (*in car, train etc*) Fahrt *f*; (*series*) Serie
f; (*SKI*) Abfahrt *f*; (*CRICKET, BASEBALL*) Run
m; (*THEAT*) Spielzeit *f*; (*in tights etc*)
Laufmasche *f* ♦ *vt* (*race, distance*) laufen,
rennen; (*operate: business*) leiten; (*: hotel,
shop*) führen; (*: competition, course*)
durchführen; (*COMPUT: program*) laufen
lassen; (*hand, fingers*) streichen mit; (*water,
bath*) einlaufen lassen; (*PRESS: feature,
article*) bringen ♦ *vi* laufen, rennen; (*flee*)
weglaufen; (*bus, train*) fahren; (*river, tears*)
fließen; (*colours*) auslaufen; (*jumper*) färben;
(*in election*) antreten; (*road, railway etc*)
verlaufen; **to go for a** ~ (*as exercise*) einen
Dauerlauf machen; **to break into a** ~ zu
laufen *or* rennen beginnen; **a** ~ **of good/bad
luck** eine Glücks-/Pechsträhne; **to have the**
~ **of sb's house** jds Haus zur freien
Verfügung haben; **there was a** ~ **on** ...
(*meat, tickets*) es gab einen Ansturm auf
+*acc*; **in the long** ~ langfristig; **in the short** ~
kurzfristig; **to make a** ~ **for it** die Beine in
die Hand nehmen; **on the** ~ (*fugitive*) auf
der Flucht; **I'll** ~ **you to the station** ich fahre
dich zum Bahnhof; **to** ~ **the risk of doing sth**
Gefahr laufen, etw zu tun; **she ran her
finger down the list** sie ging die Liste mit
dem Finger durch; **it's very cheap to** ~ (*car,
machine*) es ist sehr billig im Verbrauch; **to**
~ **a bath** das Badewasser einlaufen lassen; **to
be** ~ **off one's feet** (*BRIT*) ständig auf
Trab sein; **the baby's nose was** ~**ning** dem
Baby lief die Nase; **the train** ~**s between
Gatwick and Victoria** der Zug verkehrt
zwischen Gatwick und Victoria; **the bus** ~**s
every 20 minutes** der Bus fährt alle 20
Minuten; **to** ~ **on petrol/off batteries** mit
Benzin/auf Batterie laufen; **to** ~ **for
president** für das Amt des Präsidenten
kandidieren; **to** ~ **dry** (*well etc*)
austrocknen; **tempers were** ~**ning high** alle
waren sehr erregt; **unemployment is** ~**ning
at 20 per cent** die Arbeitslosigkeit beträgt
20 Prozent; **blonde hair** ~**s in the family**
blonde Haare liegen in der Familie.

▶**run across** *vt fus* (*find*) stoßen auf +*acc*.

▶**run after** *vt fus* nachlaufen +*dat*.

▶**run away** *vi* weglaufen.

▶**run down** *vt* (*production*) verringern;
(*factory*) allmählich stillegen; (*AUT: person*)
überfahren; (*criticize*) schlechtmachen ♦ *vi*
(*battery*) leer werden.

▶**run in** (*BRIT*) *vt* (*car*) einfahren.

▶**run into** *vt fus* (*meet: person*) begegnen +*dat*;
(*: trouble etc*) bekommen; (*collide with*)
laufen/fahren gegen; **to** ~ **into debt** in
Schulden geraten; **their losses ran into
millions** ihre Schulden gingen in die
Millionen.

▶**run off** *vt* (*liquid*) ablassen; (*copies*) machen
♦ *vi* weglaufen.

▶**run out** *vi* (*time, passport*) ablaufen; (*money*)
ausgehen; (*luck*) zu Ende gehen.

▶**run out of** *vt fus*: **we're** ~**ning out of
money/petrol** uns geht das Geld/das Benzin
aus; **we're** ~**ning out of time** wir haben
keine Zeit mehr.

▶**run over** *vt* (*AUT*) überfahren ♦ *vt fus*
(*repeat*) durchgehen ♦ *vi* (*bath, water*)
überlaufen.

▶**run through** *vt fus* (*instructions, lines*)
durchgehen.

▶**run up** *vt* (*debt*) anhäufen.

▶**run up against** *vt fus* (*difficulties*) stoßen auf
+*acc*.

runabout ['rʌnəbaut] *n* (*AUT*) Flitzer *m*.

run-around ['rʌnəraund] (*inf*) *n*: **to give sb the**
~ jdn an der Nase herumführen.

runaway ['rʌnəweɪ] *adj* (*horse*) ausgerissen;
(*truck, train*) außer Kontrolle geraten; (*child,
slave*) entlaufen; (*fig: inflation*) unkontrollierbar; (*: success*) überwältigend.

rundown ['rʌndaun] *n* (*of industry etc*)
allmähliche Stillegung *f* ♦ *adj*: **to be run-
down** (*person*) total erschöpft sein; (*building,
area*) heruntergekommen.

rung [rʌŋ] *pp of* **ring** ♦ *n* (*also fig*) Sprosse *f*.

run-in ['rʌnɪn] (*inf*) *n* Auseinandersetzung *f*.

runner ['rʌnə*] *n* Läufer(in) *m(f)*; (*horse*)
Rennpferd *nt*; (*on sledge, drawer etc*) Kufe *f*.

runner bean (*BRIT*) *n* Stangenbohne *f*.

runner-up [rʌnər'ʌp] *n* Zweitplazierte(r) *f(m)*.

running ['rʌnɪŋ] *n* (*sport*) Laufen *nt*; (*of
business etc*) Leitung *f*; (*of machine etc*)
Betrieb *m* ♦ *adj* (*water, stream*) laufend; **to be
in/out of the** ~ **for sth** bei etw im Rennen
liegen/aus dem Rennen sein; **to make the** ~
(*in race, fig*) das Rennen machen; **6 days** ~ 6
Tage hintereinander; **to have a** ~ **battle
with sb** ständig im Streit mit jdm liegen; **to
give a** ~ **commentary on sth** etw
fortlaufend kommentieren; **a** ~ **sore** eine
nässende Wunde.

running costs *npl* (*of car, machine*)
Unterhaltskosten *pl*.

running head *n* (*TYP, COMPUT*)
Kolumnentitel *m*.

running mate (*US*) *n* (*POL*)

Vizepräsidentschaftskandidat m.
runny ['rʌnɪ] adj (egg, butter) dünnflüssig;
(nose, eyes) triefend.
run-off ['rʌnɔf] n (in contest, election)
Entscheidungsrunde f; (extra race)
Entscheidungsrennen nt.
run-of-the-mill ['rʌnəvðə'mɪl] adj gewöhnlich.
runt [rʌnt] n (animal) kleinstes und
schwächstes Tier eines Wurfs; (pej: person)
Zwerg m.
run-through ['rʌnθruː] n (rehearsal) Probe f.
run-up ['rʌnʌp] n: **the ~ to** (election etc) die
Zeit vor +dat.
runway ['rʌnweɪ] n (AVIAT) Start- und
Landebahn f.
rupee [ruː'piː] n Rupie f.
rupture ['rʌptʃə] n (MED) Bruch m; (conflict)
Spaltung f ♦ vt: **to ~ o.s.** (MED) sich dat einen
Bruch zuziehen.
rural ['ruərl] adj ländlich; (crime) auf dem
Lande.
rural district council (BRIT) n
Landbezirksverwaltung f.
ruse [ruːz] n List f.
rush [rʌʃ] n (hurry) Eile f, Hetze f; (COMM:
sudden demand) starke Nachfrage f; (of
water, air) Stoß m; (of feeling) Woge f ♦ vt
(lunch, job etc) sich beeilen bei; (person,
supplies etc) schnellstens bringen ♦ vi
(person) sich beeilen; (air, water) strömen;
rushes npl (BOT) Schilf nt; (for chair, basket
etc) Binsen pl; **is there any ~ for this?** eilt
das?; **we've had a ~ of orders** wir hatten
einen Zustrom von Bestellungen; **I'm in a
~ (to do sth)** ich habe es eilig (, etw zu tun);
gold ~ Goldrausch m; **don't ~ me!** drängen
Sie mich nicht!; **to ~ sth off** (send) etw
schnellstens abschicken; **to ~ sb into doing
sth** jdn dazu drängen, etw zu tun.
►**rush through** vt (order, application)
schnellstens erledigen.
rush hour n Hauptverkehrszeit f, Rush-hour
f.
rush job n Eilauftrag m.
rush matting n Binsenmatte f.
rusk [rʌsk] n Zwieback m.
Russia ['rʌʃə] n Rußland nt.
Russian ['rʌʃən] adj russisch ♦ n (person)
Russe m, Russin f; (LING) Russisch nt.
rust [rʌst] n Rost m ♦ vi rosten.
rustic ['rʌstɪk] adj (style, furniture) rustikal ♦ n
(pej: person) Bauer m.
rustle ['rʌsl] vi (paper, leaves) rascheln ♦ vt
(paper) rascheln mit; (US: cattle) stehlen.
rustproof ['rʌstpruːf] adj nichtrostend.
rustproofing ['rʌstpruːfɪŋ] n Rostschutz m.
rusty ['rʌstɪ] adj (car) rostig; (fig: skill etc)
eingerostet.
rut [rʌt] n (in path etc) Furche f; (ZOOL: season)
Brunft f, Brunst f; **to be in a ~** (fig) im Trott
stecken.
rutabaga [ruːtə'beɪgə] (US) n Steckrübe f.

ruthless ['ruːθlɪs] adj rücksichtslos.
ruthlessness ['ruːθlɪsnɪs] n
Rücksichtslosigkeit f.
RV abbr (BIBLE: = revised version) englische
Bibelübersetzung von 1885 ♦ n abbr (US)
= recreational vehicle.
Rwanda [ru'ændə] n Ruanda nt.
Rwandan [ru'ændən] adj ruandisch.
rye [raɪ] n (cereal) Roggen m.
rye bread n Roggenbrot nt.

S, s

S¹, s [ɛs] n (letter) S nt, s nt; (US: SCOL:
satisfactory) ≈ 3; **~ for sugar** ≈ S wie
Samuel.
S² [ɛs] abbr (= saint) St.; (= small) kl.;
(= south) S.
SA abbr = **South Africa, South America**;
(= South Australia) Südaustralien nt.
Sabbath ['sæbəθ] n (Jewish) Sabbat m;
(Christian) Sonntag m.
sabbatical [sə'bætɪkl] n (also: **~ year**)
Forschungsjahr nt.
sabotage ['sæbətɑːʒ] n Sabotage f ♦ vt einen
Sabotageakt verüben auf +acc; (plan,
meeting) sabotieren.
sabre ['seɪbə] n Säbel m.
sabre-rattling ['seɪbərætlɪŋ] n Säbelrasseln nt.
saccharin(e) ['sækərɪn] n Saccharin nt ♦ adj
(fig) zuckersüß.
sachet ['sæʃeɪ] n (of shampoo) Beutel m; (of
sugar etc) Tütchen nt.
sack [sæk] n Sack m ♦ vt (dismiss) entlassen;
(plunder) plündern; **to get the ~** rausfliegen
(inf); **to give sb the ~** jdn rausschmeißen
(inf).
sackful ['sækful] n: **a ~ of** ein Sack.
sacking ['sækɪŋ] n (dismissal) Entlassung f;
(material) Sackleinen nt.
sacrament ['sækrəmənt] n Sakrament nt.
sacred ['seɪkrɪd] adj heilig; (music, history)
geistlich; (memory) geheiligt; (building)
sakral.
sacred cow n (lit, fig) heilige Kuh f.
sacrifice ['sækrɪfaɪs] n Opfer nt ♦ vt opfern; **to
make ~s (for sb)** (für jdn) Opfer bringen.
sacrilege ['sækrɪlɪdʒ] n Sakrileg nt; **that would
be ~** das wäre ein Sakrileg.
sacrosanct ['sækrəusæŋkt] adj (lit, fig)
sakrosankt.
sad [sæd] adj traurig; **he was ~ to see her go**
er war traurig (darüber), daß sie wegging.
sadden ['sædn] vt betrüben.
saddle ['sædl] n Sattel m ♦ vt (horse) satteln; **to**

be ~d with sb/sth (inf) jdn/etw am Hals
haben.
saddlebag ['sædlbæg] n Satteltasche f.
sadism ['seɪdɪzəm] n Sadismus m.
sadist ['seɪdɪst] n Sadist(in) m(f).
sadistic [sə'dɪstɪk] adj sadistisch.
sadly ['sædlɪ] adv traurig, betrübt;
(unfortunately) leider, bedauerlicherweise;
(seriously) schwer; **he is ~ lacking in humour**
ihm fehlt leider jeglicher Humor.
sadness ['sædnɪs] n Traurigkeit f.
sadomasochism [seɪdəʊ'mæsəkɪzəm] n
Sadomasochismus m.
s.a.e. (BRIT) abbr (= stamped addressed
envelope) see **stamp.**
safari [sə'fɑːrɪ] n Safari f; **to go on ~** auf
Safari gehen.
safari park n Safaripark m.
safe [seɪf] adj sicher; (out of danger) in
Sicherheit ♦ n Safe m or nt, Tresor m; **~ from**
sicher vor +dat; **~ and sound** gesund und
wohlbehalten; **(just) to be on the ~ side**
(nur) um sicherzugehen; **to play ~** auf
Nummer Sicher gehen (inf); **it is ~ to say**
that ... man kann wohl sagen, daß ...;
~ journey! gute Fahrt or Reise!
safe bet n: **it's a ~ that ...** es ist sicher,
daß ...
safe-breaker ['seɪfbreɪkə*] (BRIT) n
Safeknacker m (inf).
safe-conduct [seɪf'kɒndʌkt] n freies or
sicheres Geleit nt.
safe-cracker ['seɪfkrækə*] n = **safe-breaker.**
safe-deposit ['seɪfdɪpɒzɪt] n (vault)
Tresorraum m; (also: **~ box**) Banksafe m.
safeguard ['seɪfgɑːd] n Schutz m ♦ vt
schützen; (interests) wahren; (future)
sichern; **as a ~ against** zum Schutz gegen.
safe haven n Zufluchtsort m.
safe house n geheimer Unterschlupf m.
safekeeping ['seɪf'kiːpɪŋ] n sichere
Aufbewahrung f.
safely ['seɪflɪ] adv sicher; (assume, say) wohl,
ruhig; (arrive) wohlbehalten; **I can ~ say ...**
ich kann wohl sagen ...
safe passage n sichere Durchreise f.
safe sex n geschützter Sex m.
safety ['seɪftɪ] n Sicherheit f; **~ first!**
Sicherheit geht vor!
safety belt n Sicherheitsgurt m.
safety catch n (on gun) Sicherung f; (on
window, door) Sperre f.
safety net n Sprungnetz nt, Sicherheitsnetz
nt; (fig) Sicherheitsvorkehrung f.
safety pin n Sicherheitsnadel f.
safety valve n Sicherheitsventil nt.
saffron ['sæfrən] n Safran m.
sag [sæg] vi durchhängen; (breasts) hängen;
(fig: spirits, demand) sinken.
saga ['sɑːgə] n Saga f; (fig) Geschichte f.
sage [seɪdʒ] n (herb) Salbei m; (wise man)
Weise(r) m.

Sagittarius [sædʒɪ'tɛərɪəs] n Schütze m; **to be
~ Schütze sein.**
sago ['seɪgəʊ] n Sago m.
Sahara [sə'hɑːrə] n: **the ~ (Desert)** die (Wüste)
Sahara.
Sahel [sæ'hɛl] n Sahel m, Sahelzone f.
said [sɛd] pt, pp of **say.**
Saigon [saɪ'gɒn] n Saigon nt.
sail [seɪl] n Segel m ♦ vt segeln ♦ vi fahren;
(SPORT) segeln; (begin voyage: ship)
auslaufen; (: passenger) abfahren; (fig: ball
etc) fliegen, segeln; **to go for a ~** segeln
gehen; **to set ~** losfahren, abfahren.
▶**sail through** vt fus (fig: exam etc) spielend
schaffen.
sailboat ['seɪlbəʊt] (US) n = **sailing boat.**
sailing ['seɪlɪŋ] n (SPORT) Segeln nt; (voyage)
Überfahrt f; **to go ~** segeln gehen.
sailing boat n Segelboot nt.
sailing ship n Segelschiff nt.
sailor ['seɪlə*] n Seemann m, Matrose m.
saint [seɪnt] n (lit, fig) Heilige(r) f(m).
saintly ['seɪntlɪ] adj heiligmäßig; (expression)
fromm.
sake [seɪk] n: **for the ~ of sb/sth, for sb's/sth's
~** um jds/einer Sache gen willen; (out of
consideration for) jdm/etw zuliebe; **he enjoys
talking for talking's ~** er redet gerne, nur
damit etwas gesagt wird; **for the ~ of
argument** rein theoretisch; **art for art's ~**
Kunst um der Kunst willen; **for heaven's ~!**
um Gottes willen!
salad ['sæləd] n Salat m; **tomato ~**
Tomatensalat m; **green ~** grüner Salat m.
salad bowl n Salatschüssel f.
salad cream (BRIT) n ≈ Mayonnaise f.
salad dressing n Salatsoße f.
salami [sə'lɑːmɪ] n Salami f.
salaried ['sælərɪd] adj: **~ staff**
Gehaltsempfänger pl.
salary ['sælərɪ] n Gehalt nt.
salary scale n Gehaltsskala f.
sale [seɪl] n Verkauf m; (at reduced prices)
Ausverkauf m; (auction) Auktion f; **sales** npl
(total amount sold) Absatz m ♦ cpd (campaign)
Verkaufs-; (conference) Vertreter-; (figures)
Absatz-; **"for ~"** „zu verkaufen"; **on ~** im
Handel; **on ~ or return** auf
Kommissionsbasis; **closing-down** or (US)
liquidation ~ Räumungsverkauf m.
sale and lease back n (COMM) Verkauf m
mit Rückmiete.
saleroom ['seɪlruːm] n Auktionsraum m.
sales assistant, (US) **sales clerk** [seɪlz-] n
Verkäufer(in) m(f).
sales force n Vertreterstab m.
salesman ['seɪlzmən] (irreg: like **man**) n
Verkäufer m; (representative) Vertreter m.
sales manager n Verkaufsleiter m.
salesmanship ['seɪlzmənʃɪp] n
Verkaufstechnik f.
sales tax (US) n Verkaufssteuer f.

saleswoman ['seɪlzwumən] (*irreg: like* **woman**) *n* Verkäuferin *f*; (*representative*) Vertreterin *f*.

salient ['seɪlɪənt] *adj* (*features*) hervorstechend; (*points*) Haupt-.

saline ['seɪlaɪn] *adj* (*solution etc*) Salz-.

saliva [sə'laɪvə] *n* Speichel *m*.

sallow ['sæləu] *adj* (*complexion*) fahl.

sally forth ['sælɪ-] (*old*) *vi* sich aufmachen.

sally out *vi* = **sally forth**.

salmon ['sæmən] *n inv* Lachs *m*.

salmon trout *n* Lachsforelle *f*.

salon ['sælɔn] *n* Salon *m*.

saloon [sə'luːn] *n* (*US: bar*) Saloon *m*; (*BRIT: AUT*) Limousine *f*; (*ship's lounge*) Salon *m*.

SALT [sɔːlt] *n abbr* (= *Strategic Arms Limitation Talks/Treaty*) SALT.

salt [sɔːlt] *n* Salz *nt* ♦ *vt* (*preserve*) einsalzen; (*put salt on*) salzen; (*road*) mit Salz streuen ♦ *cpd* Salz-; (*pork, beef*) gepökelt; **the ~ of the earth** (*fig*) das Salz der Erde; **to take sth with a pinch** *or* **grain of ~** (*fig*) etw nicht ganz so erst nehmen.

salt cellar *n* Salzstreuer *m*.

salt-free ['sɔːlt'friː] *adj* salzlos.

salt mine *n* Salzbergwerk *nt*.

saltwater ['sɔːlt'wɔːtə*] *adj* (*fish, plant*) Meeres-.

salty ['sɔːltɪ] *adj* salzig.

salubrious [sə'luːbrɪəs] *adj* (*district etc*) fein; (*air, living conditions*) gesund.

salutary ['sæljutərɪ] *adj* heilsam.

salute [sə'luːt] *n* (*MIL, greeting*) Gruß *m*; (*MIL: with guns*) Salut *m* ♦ *vt* (*MIL*) grüßen, salutieren vor +*dat*; (*fig*) begrüßen.

salvage ['sælvɪdʒ] *n* Bergung *f*; (*things saved*) Bergungsgut *nt* ♦ *vt* bergen; (*fig*) retten.

salvage vessel *n* Bergungsschiff *nt*.

salvation [sæl'veɪʃən] *n* (*REL*) Heil *nt*; (*economic etc*) Rettung *f*.

Salvation Army *n* Heilsarmee *f*.

salver ['sælvə*] *n* Tablett *nt*.

salvo ['sælvəu] (*pl* **~es**) *n* Salve *f*.

Samaritan [sə'mærɪtən] *n*: **the ~s** ≈ die Telefonseelsorge.

same [seɪm] *adj* (*similar*) gleiche(r, s); (*identical*) selbe(r, s) ♦ *pron*: **the ~** (*similar*) der/die/das gleiche; (*identical*) derselbe/dieselbe/dasselbe; **the ~ book as** das gleiche Buch wie; **they are the ~ age** sie sind gleichaltrig; **they are exactly the ~** sie sind genau gleich; **on the ~ day** am gleichen *or* selben Tag; **at the ~ time** (*simultaneously*) gleichzeitig, zur gleichen Zeit; (*yet*) doch; **they're one and the ~** (*person*) das ist doch ein und derselbe/dieselbe; (*thing*) das ist doch dasselbe; **~ again** (*in bar etc*) das gleiche noch mal; **all** *or* **just the ~** trotzdem; **to do the ~ (as sb)** das gleiche (wie jd) tun; **the ~ to you!** (*danke*) gleichfalls!; **~ here!** ich/wir *etc* auch!; **thanks all the ~** trotzdem vielen Dank; **it's all the ~ to me** es ist mir egal.

sample ['sɑːmpl] *n* Probe *f*; (*of merchandise*) Probe *f*, Muster *nt* ♦ *vt* probieren; **to take a ~** eine Stichprobe machen; **free ~** kostenlose Probe.

sanatorium [sænə'tɔːrɪəm] (*pl* **sanatoria**) *n* Sanatorium *nt*.

sanctify ['sæŋktɪfaɪ] *vt* heiligen.

sanctimonious [sæŋktɪ'məunɪəs] *adj* scheinheilig.

sanction ['sæŋkʃən] *n* Zustimmung *f* ♦ *vt* sanktionieren; **sanctions** *npl* (*POL*) Sanktionen *pl*; **to impose economic ~s on** *or* **against** Wirtschaftssanktionen verhängen gegen.

sanctity ['sæŋktɪtɪ] *n* (*holiness*) Heiligkeit *f*; (*inviolability*) Unantastbarkeit *f*.

sanctuary ['sæŋktjuərɪ] *n* (*for birds/animals*) Schutzgebiet *nt*; (*place of refuge*) Zuflucht *f*; (*REL: in church*) Altarraum *m*.

sand [sænd] *n* Sand *m* ♦ *vt* (*also:* **~ down**) abschmirgeln; *see also* **sands**.

sandal ['sændl] *n* Sandale *f*.

sandbag ['sændbæg] *n* Sandsack *m*.

sandblast ['sændblɑːst] *vt* sandstrahlen.

sandbox ['sændbɔks] (*US*) *n* Sandkasten *m*.

sandcastle ['sændkɑːsl] *n* Sandburg *f*.

sand dune *n* Sanddüne *f*.

sander ['sændə*] *n* (*tool*) Schleifmaschine *f*.

S & M (*US*) *n abbr* (= *sadomasochism*) S/M.

sandpaper ['sændpeɪpə*] *n* Schmirgelpapier *nt*.

sandpit ['sændpɪt] *n* Sandkasten *m*.

sands [sændz] *npl* (*beach*) Sandstrand *m*.

sandstone ['sændstəun] *n* Sandstein *m*.

sandstorm ['sændstɔːm] *n* Sandsturm *m*.

sandwich ['sændwɪtʃ] *n* Sandwich *nt* ♦ *vt*: **~ed between** eingequetscht zwischen; **cheese/ham ~** Käse-/Schinkenbrot *nt*.

sandwich board *n* Reklametafel *f*.

sandwich course (*BRIT*) *n* Ausbildungsgang, bei dem sich Theorie und Praxis abwechseln.

sandwich man *n* Sandwichmann *m*, Plakatträger *m*.

sandy ['sændɪ] *adj* sandig; (*beach*) Sand-; (*hair*) rotblond.

sane [seɪn] *adj* geistig gesund; (*sensible*) vernünftig.

sang [sæŋ] *pt of* **sing**.

sanguine ['sæŋgwɪn] *adj* zuversichtlich.

sanitarium [sænɪ'tɛərɪəm] (*US*) (*pl* **sanitaria**) *n* = **sanatorium**.

sanitary ['sænɪtərɪ] *adj* hygienisch; (*facilities*) sanitär; (*inspector*) Gesundheits-.

sanitary towel, (*US*) **sanitary napkin** *n* Damenbinde *f*.

sanitation [sænɪ'teɪʃən] *n* Hygiene *f*; (*toilets etc*) sanitäre Anlagen *pl*; (*drainage*) Kanalisation *f*.

sanitation department (*US*) *n* Stadtreinigung *f*.

sanity ['sænɪtɪ] n geistige Gesundheit f; (*common sense*) Vernunft f.

sank [sæŋk] pt of **sink**.

San Marino ['sænmə'riːnəu] n San Marino nt.

Santa Claus [sæntə'klɔːz] n ≈ der Weihnachtsmann.

Santiago [sæntɪ'ɑːgəu] n (*also:* ~ **de Chile**) Santiago (de Chile) nt.

sap [sæp] n Saft m ♦ vt (*strength*) zehren an +dat; (*confidence*) untergraben.

sapling ['sæplɪŋ] n junger Baum m.

sapper ['sæpə'] n (MIL) Pionier m.

sapphire ['sæfaɪə'] n Saphir m.

sarcasm ['sɑːkæzm] n Sarkasmus m.

sarcastic [sɑː'kæstɪk] adj sarkastisch.

sarcophagus [sɑː'kɔfəgəs] (pl **sarcophagi**) n Sarkophag m.

sardine [sɑː'diːn] n Sardine f.

Sardinia [sɑː'dɪnɪə] n Sardinien nt.

Sardinian [sɑː'dɪnɪən] adj sardinisch, sardisch ♦ n (*person*) Sardinier(in) m(f); (LING) Sardinisch nt.

sardonic [sɑː'dɔnɪk] adj (*smile*) süffisant.

sari ['sɑːrɪ] n Sari m.

sartorial [sɑː'tɔːrɪəl] adj: **his ~ elegance** seine elegante Art, sich zu kleiden.

SAS (BRIT) n abbr (MIL: = Special Air Service) Spezialeinheit der britischen Armee.

SASE (US) n abbr (= self-addressed stamped envelope) frankierter Rückumschlag m.

sash [sæʃ] n Schärpe f; (*of window*) Fensterrahmen m.

sash window n Schiebefenster nt.

SAT (US) n abbr (= Scholastic Aptitude Test) Hochschul-Aufnahmeprüfung.

Sat. abbr (= Saturday) Sa.

sat [sæt] pt, pp of **sit**.

Satan ['seɪtn] n Satan m.

satanic [sə'tænɪk] adj satanisch.

satanism ['seɪtnɪzəm] n Satanismus m.

satchel ['sætʃl] n (*child's*) Schultasche f.

sated ['seɪtɪd] adj gesättigt; **to be ~ with sth** (fig) von etw übersättigt sein.

satellite ['sætəlaɪt] n Satellit m; (*also:* ~ **state**) Satellitenstaat m.

satellite dish n Satellitenantenne f, Parabolantenne f.

satellite television n Satellitenfernsehen nt.

satiate ['seɪʃɪeɪt] vt (*food*) sättigen; (fig: *pleasure etc*) übersättigen.

satin ['sætɪn] n Satin m ♦ adj (*dress etc*) Satin-; **with a ~ finish** mit Seidenglanz.

satire ['sætaɪə'] n Satire f.

satirical [sə'tɪrɪkl] adj satirisch.

satirist ['sætɪrɪst] n Satiriker(in) m(f).

satirize ['sætɪraɪz] vt satirisch darstellen.

satisfaction [sætɪs'fækʃən] n Befriedigung f; **to get ~ from sb** (*refund, apology etc*) Genugtuung von jdm erhalten; **has it been done to your ~?** sind Sie damit zufrieden?

satisfactorily [sætɪs'fæktərɪlɪ] adv zufriedenstellend.

satisfactory [sætɪs'fæktərɪ] adj zufriedenstellend.

satisfied ['sætɪsfaɪd] adj zufrieden.

satisfy ['sætɪsfaɪ] vt zufriedenstellen; (*needs, demand*) befriedigen; (*requirements, conditions*) erfüllen; **to ~ sb/o.s. that ...** jdn/ sich davon überzeugen, daß ...

satisfying ['sætɪsfaɪɪŋ] adj befriedigend; (*meal*) sättigend.

satsuma [sæt'suːmə] n Satsuma f.

saturate ['sætʃəreɪt] vt: **to ~ (with)** durchnässen (mit); (CHEM, fig: *market*) sättigen; (fig: *area etc*) überschwemmen.

saturated fat ['sætʃəreɪtɪd-] n gesättigtes Fett nt.

saturation [sætʃə'reɪʃən] n (CHEM, fig) Sättigung f; ~ **advertising** flächendeckende Werbung f; ~ **bombing** Flächenbombardierung f.

Saturday ['sætədɪ] n Samstag m; *see also* **Tuesday**.

sauce [sɔːs] n Soße f, Sauce f.

saucepan ['sɔːspən] n Kochtopf m.

saucer ['sɔːsə'] n Untertasse f.

saucy ['sɔːsɪ] adj frech.

Saudi ['saudi-] adj (*also:* ~ **Arabian**) saudisch, saudiarabisch.

Saudi Arabia ['saudi-] n Saudi-Arabien nt.

sauna ['sɔːnə] n Sauna f.

saunter ['sɔːntə'] vi schlendern.

sausage ['sɔsɪdʒ] n Wurst f.

sausage roll n Wurst f im Schlafrock.

sauté ['səuteɪ] vt kurz anbraten ♦ adj: ~**ed potatoes** Bratkartoffeln pl.

savage ['sævɪdʒ] adj (*attack etc*) brutal; (*dog*) gefährlich; (*criticism*) schonungslos ♦ n (*old: pej*) Wilde(r) f(m) ♦ vt (*maul*) zerfleischen; (fig: *criticize*) verreißen.

savagely ['sævɪdʒlɪ] adv (*attack etc*) brutal; (*criticize*) schonungslos.

savagery ['sævɪdʒrɪ] n (*of attack*) Brutalität f.

save [seɪv] vt (*rescue*) retten; (*money, time*) sparen; (*food etc*) aufheben; (*work, trouble*) (er)sparen; (*keep: receipts etc*) aufbewahren; (: *seat etc*) freihalten; (COMPUT: *file*) abspeichern; (SPORT: *shot, ball*) halten ♦ vi (*also:* ~ **up**) sparen ♦ n (SPORT) (Ball)abwehr f ♦ prep (*form*) außer +dat; **it will ~ me an hour** dadurch spare ich eine Stunde; **to ~ face** das Gesicht wahren; **God ~ the Queen!** Gott schütze die Königin!

saving ['seɪvɪŋ] n (*on price etc*) Ersparnis f ♦ adj: **the ~ grace of sth** das einzig Gute an etw dat; **savings** npl (*money*) Ersparnisse pl; **to make ~s** sparen.

savings account n Sparkonto nt.

savings bank n Sparkasse f.

saviour, (US) **savior** ['seɪvjə'] n Retter(in) m(f); (REL) Erlöser m.

savoir-faire ['sævwɑːfɛə'] n Gewandtheit f.

savour, (US) **savor** ['seɪvə'] vt genießen ♦ n (*of food*) Geschmack m.

savoury, (*US*) **savory** ['seɪvərɪ] *adj* pikant.
savvy ['sævɪ] (*inf*) *n* Grips *m*; **he hasn't got much** ~ er hat keine Ahnung.
saw [sɔː] (*pt* sawed, *pp* sawed *or* sawn) *vt* sägen ♦ *n* Säge *f* ♦ *pt of* see; **to** ~ **sth up** etw zersägen.
sawdust ['sɔːdʌst] *n* Sägemehl *nt*.
sawmill ['sɔːmɪl] *n* Sägewerk *nt*.
sawn [sɔːn] *pp of* saw.
sawn-off ['sɔːnɒf], (*US*) **sawed-off** ['sɔːdɒf] *adj:* ~ **shotgun** Gewehr *nt* mit abgesägtem Lauf.
saxophone ['sæksəfəun] *n* Saxophon *nt*.
say [seɪ] (*pt, pp* said) *vt* sagen ♦ *n:* **to have one's** ~ seine Meinung äußern; **could you** ~ **that again?** können Sie das wiederholen?; **my watch** ~s **3 o'clock** auf meiner Uhr ist es 3 Uhr; **it** ~s **on the sign "No Smoking"** auf dem Schild steht „Rauchen verboten"; **shall we** ~ **Tuesday?** sagen wir Dienstag?; **come for dinner at,** ~, **8 o'clock** kommt um, sagen wir mal, 8 Uhr, zum Essen; **that doesn't** ~ **much for him** das spricht nicht gerade für ihn; **when all is said and done** letzten Endes; **there is something/a lot to be said for it** es spricht einiges/vieles dafür; **you can** ~ **that again!** das kann man wohl sagen!; **that is to** ~ das heißt; **that goes without** ~**ing** das versteht sich von selbst; **to** ~ **nothing of ...** von ... ganz zu schweigen; ~ **(that)** ... angenommen, (daß) ...; **to have a** *or* **some** ~ **in sth** ein Mitspracherecht bei etw haben.
saying ['seɪɪŋ] *n* Redensart *f*.
say-so ['seɪsəu] *n* Zustimmung *f*; **to do sth on sb's** ~ etw auf jds Anweisung *acc* hin tun.
SBA (*US*) *n abbr* (= *Small Business Administration*) *Regierungsstelle zur Unterstützung kleiner und mittelständischer Betriebe.*
SC (*US*) *n abbr* = **Supreme Court** ♦ *abbr* (*POST:* = *South Carolina*).
s/c *abbr* = **self-contained.**
scab [skæb] *n* (*on wound*) Schorf *m*; (*pej*) Streikbrecher(in) *m(f)*.
scabby ['skæbɪ] (*pej*) *adj* (*hands, skin*) schorfig.
scaffold ['skæfəld] *n* (*for execution*) Schafott *nt*.
scaffolding ['skæfəldɪŋ] *n* Gerüst *nt*.
scald [skɔːld] *n* Verbrühung *f* ♦ *vt* (*burn*) verbrühen.
scalding ['skɔːldɪŋ] *adj* (*also:* ~ **hot**) siedend heiß.
scale [skeɪl] *n* Skala *f*; (*of fish*) Schuppe *f*; (*MUS*) Tonleiter *f*; (*size, extent*) Ausmaß *nt*, Umfang *m*; (*of map, model*) Maßstab *m* ♦ *vt* (*cliff, tree*) erklettern; (*pair of*) **scales** *npl* (*for weighing*) Waage *f*; **pay** ~ Lohnskala *f*; **to draw sth to** ~ etw maßstabgetreu zeichnen; **a small-**~ **model** ein Modell in verkleinertem Maßstab; **on a large** ~ im großen Rahmen; ~ **of charges** Gebührenordnung *f*.
▶**scale down** *vt* verkleinern; (*fig*)

verringern.
scaled-down [skeɪld'daun] *adj* verkleinert; (*project, forecast*) eingeschränkt.
scale drawing *n* maßstabgetreue Zeichnung *f*.
scallion ['skæljən] *n* Frühlingszwiebel *f*; (*US: shallot*) Schalotte *f*; (: *leek*) Lauch *m*.
scallop ['skɒləp] *n* (*ZOOL*) Kammuschel *f*; (*SEWING*) Bogenkante *f*.
scalp [skælp] *n* Kopfhaut *f* ♦ *vt* skalpieren.
scalpel ['skælpl] *n* Skalpell *nt*.
scalper ['skælpə*] (*US: inf*) *n* (*ticket tout*) (Karten)schwarzhändler(in) *m(f)*.
scam [skæm] (*inf*) *n* Betrug *m*.
scamp [skæmp] (*inf*) *n* Frechdachs *m*.
scamper ['skæmpə*] *vi:* **to** ~ **away** *or* **off** verschwinden.
scampi ['skæmpɪ] (*BRIT*) *npl* Scampi *pl*.
scan [skæn] *vt* (*horizon*) absuchen; (*newspaper etc*) überfliegen; (*TV, RADAR*) abtasten ♦ *vi* (*poetry*) das richtige Versmaß haben ♦ *n* (*MED*) Scan *m*.
scandal ['skændl] *n* Skandal *m*; (*gossip*) Skandalgeschichten *pl*.
scandalize ['skændəlaɪz] *vt* schockieren.
scandalous ['skændələs] *adj* skandalös.
Scandinavia [skændɪ'neɪvɪə] *n* Skandinavien *nt*.
Scandinavian [skændɪ'neɪvɪən] *adj* skandinavisch ♦ *n* Skandinavier(in) *m(f)*.
scanner ['skænə*] *n* (*MED*) Scanner *m*; (*RADAR*) Richtantenne *f*.
scant [skænt] *adj* wenig.
scantily ['skæntɪlɪ] *adv:* ~ **clad** *or* **dressed** spärlich bekleidet.
scanty ['skæntɪ] *adj* (*information*) dürftig; (*meal*) kärglich; (*bikini*) knapp.
scapegoat ['skeɪpgəut] *n* Sündenbock *m*.
scar [skɑː] *n* Narbe *f*; (*fig*) Wunde *f* ♦ *vt* eine Narbe hinterlassen auf +*dat*; (*fig*) zeichnen.
scarce [skɛəs] *adj* knapp; **to make o.s.** ~ (*inf*) verschwinden.
scarcely ['skɛəslɪ] *adv* kaum; (*certainly not*) wohl kaum; ~ **anybody** kaum jemand; **I can** ~ **believe it** ich kann es kaum glauben.
scarcity ['skɛəsɪtɪ] *n* Knappheit *f*; ~ **value** Seltenheitswert *m*.
scare [skɛə*] *n* (*fright*) Schreck(en) *m*; (*public fear*) Panik *f* ♦ *vt* (*frighten*) erschrecken; (*worry*) Angst machen +*dat*; **to give sb a** ~ jdm einen Schrecken einjagen; **bomb** ~ Bombendrohung *f*.
▶**scare away** *vt* (*animal*) verscheuchen; (*investor, buyer*) abschrecken.
▶**scare off** *vt* = **scare away.**
scarecrow ['skɛəkrəu] *n* Vogelscheuche *f*.
scared ['skɛəd] *adj:* **to be** ~ Angst haben; **to be** ~ **stiff** fürchterliche Angst haben.
scaremonger ['skɛəmʌŋgə*] *n* Panikmacher *m*.
scarf [skɑːf] (*pl* ~**s** *or* **scarves**) *n* Schal *m*; (*headscarf*) Kopftuch *nt*.

scarlet ['skɑ:lɪt] *adj* (scharlach)rot.
scarlet fever *n* Scharlach *m*.
scarper ['skɑ:pə*] (*BRIT: inf*) *vi* abhauen.
scarred [skɑ:d] *adj* narbig; (*fig*) gezeichnet.
scarves [skɑ:vz] *npl of* **scarf**.
scary ['skɛərɪ] (*inf*) *adj* unheimlich; (*film*) gruselig.
scathing ['skeɪðɪŋ] *adj* (*comments*) bissig; (*attack*) scharf; **to be ~ about sth** bissige Bemerkungen über etw *acc* machen.
scatter ['skætə*] *vt* verstreuen; (*flock of birds*) aufscheuchen; (*crowd*) zerstreuen ♦ *vi* (*crowd*) sich zerstreuen.
scatterbrained ['skætəbreɪnd] (*inf*) *adj* schusselig.
scattered ['skætəd] *n* verstreut; **~ showers** vereinzelte Regenschauer *pl*.
scatty ['skætɪ] (*BRIT: inf*) *adj* schusselig.
scavenge ['skævəndʒ] *vi*: **to ~ for sth** nach etw suchen.
scavenger ['skævəndʒə*] *n* (*person*) Aasgeier *m* (*inf*); (*animal, bird*) Aasfresser *m*.
SCE *n abbr* (= *Scottish Certificate of Education*) *Schulabschlußzeugnis in Schottland.*
scenario [sɪ'nɑ:rɪəu] *n* (*THEAT, CINE*) Szenarium *nt*; (*fig*) Szenario *nt*.
scene [si:n] *n* (*lit, fig*) Szene *f*; (*of crime*) Schauplatz *m*; (*of accident*) Ort *m*; (*sight*) Anblick *m*; **behind the ~s** (*fig*) hinter den Kulissen; **to make a ~** (*inf: fuss*) eine Szene machen; **to appear on the ~** (*fig*) auftauchen, auf der Bildfläche erscheinen; **the political ~** die politische Landschaft.
scenery ['si:nərɪ] *n* (*THEAT*) Bühnenbild *nt*; (*landscape*) Landschaft *f*.
scenic ['si:nɪk] *adj* malerisch, landschaftlich schön.
scent [sɛnt] *n* (*fragrance*) Duft *m*; (*track*) Fährte *f*; (*fig*) Spur *f*; (*liquid perfume*) Parfüm *nt*; **to put** *or* **throw sb off the ~** (*fig*) jdn von der Spur abbringen.
sceptic, (*US*) **skeptic** ['skɛptɪk] *n* Skeptiker(in) *m(f)*.
sceptical, (*US*) **skeptical** ['skɛptɪkl] *adj* skeptisch.
scepticism, (*US*) **skepticism** ['skɛptɪsɪzəm] *n* Skepsis *f*.
sceptre, (*US*) **scepter** ['sɛptə*] *n* Zepter *nt*.
schedule ['ʃɛdju:l, (*US*) 'skɛdju:l] *n* (*of trains, buses*) Fahrplan *m*; (*of events*) Programm *nt*; (*of prices, details etc*) Liste *f* ♦ *vt* planen; (*visit, meeting etc*) ansetzen; **on ~** wie geplant, pünktlich; **we are working to a very tight ~** wir arbeiten nach einem sehr knappen Zeitplan; **everything went according to ~** alles ist planmäßig verlaufen; **to be ahead of/behind ~** dem Zeitplan voraus sein/im Rückstand sein; **he was ~d to leave yesterday** laut Zeitplan hätte er gestern abfahren sollen.
scheduled ['ʃɛdju:ld, (*US*) 'skɛdju:ld] *adj* (*date, time*) vorgesehen; (*visit, event*) geplant;

(*train, bus, stop*) planmäßig.
scheduled flight *n* Linienflug *m*.
schematic [skɪ'mætɪk] *adj* schematisch.
scheme [ski:m] *n* (*personal plan*) Plan *m*; (*plot*) raffinierter Plan *m*, Komplott *nt*; (*formal plan*) Programm *nt* ♦ *vi* Pläne schmieden, intrigieren; **colour ~** Farbzusammenstellung *f*; **pension ~** Rentenversicherung *f*.
scheming ['ski:mɪŋ] *adj* intrigierend ♦ *n* Machenschaften *pl*.
schism ['skɪzəm] *n* Spaltung *f*.
schizophrenia [skɪtsə'fri:nɪə] *n* Schizophrenie *f*.
schizophrenic [skɪtsə'frɛnɪk] *adj* schizophren ♦ *n* Schizophrene(r) *f(m)*.
scholar ['skɔlə*] *n* Gelehrte(r) *f(m)*; (*pupil*) Student(in) *m(f)*, Schüler(in) *m(f)*; (*scholarship holder*) Stipendiat(in) *m(f)*.
scholarly ['skɔləlɪ] *adj* gelehrt; (*text, approach*) wissenschaftlich.
scholarship ['skɔləʃɪp] *n* Gelehrsamkeit *f*; (*grant*) Stipendium *nt*.
school [sku:l] *n* Schule *f*; (*US: inf: university*) Universität *f*; (*of whales, porpoises etc*) Schule *f*, Schwarm *m* ♦ *cpd* Schul-.
school age *n* Schulalter *nt*.
schoolbook ['sku:lbuk] *n* Schulbuch *nt*.
schoolboy ['sku:lbɔɪ] *n* Schuljunge *m*, Schüler *m*.
schoolchildren ['sku:ltʃɪldrən] *npl* Schulkinder *pl*, Schüler *pl*.
schooldays ['sku:ldeɪz] *npl* Schulzeit *f*.
schooled [sku:ld] *adj* geschult; **to be ~ in sth** über etw *acc* gut Bescheid wissen.
schoolgirl ['sku:lɡə:l] *n* Schulmädchen *nt*, Schülerin *f*.
schooling ['sku:lɪŋ] *n* Schulbildung *f*.
school-leaver [sku:l'li:və*] (*BRIT*) *n* Schulabgänger(in) *m(f)*.
schoolmaster ['sku:lmɑ:stə*] *n* Lehrer *m*.
schoolmistress ['sku:lmɪstrɪs] *n* Lehrerin *f*.
school report (*BRIT*) *n* Zeugnis *nt*.
schoolroom ['sku:lru:m] *n* Klassenzimmer *nt*.
schoolteacher ['sku:lti:tʃə*] *n* Lehrer(in) *m(f)*.
schoolyard ['sku:ljɑ:d] *n* Schulhof *m*.
schooner ['sku:nə*] *n* (*ship*) Schoner *m*; (*BRIT: for sherry*) großes Sherryglas *nt*; (*US etc: for beer*) großes Bierglas *nt*.
sciatica [saɪ'ætɪkə] *n* Ischias *m or nt*.
science ['saɪəns] *n* Naturwissenschaft *f*; (*branch of knowledge*) Wissenschaft *f*; **the ~s** Naturwissenschaften *pl*.
science fiction *n* Science-fiction *f*.
scientific [saɪən'tɪfɪk] *adj* wissenschaftlich.
scientist ['saɪəntɪst] *n* Wissenschaftler(in) *m(f)*.
sci-fi ['saɪfaɪ] (*inf*) *n abbr* (= *science fiction*) SF.
Scillies ['sɪlɪz] *npl* = **Scilly Isles**.
Scilly Isles ['sɪlɪ'aɪlz] *npl*: **the ~** die Scilly-Inseln *pl*.
scintillating ['sɪntɪleɪtɪŋ] *adj* (*fig: conversation*)

faszinierend; (*wit*) sprühend.
scissors ['sɪzəz] *npl* Schere *f*; **a pair of** ~ eine Schere.
sclerosis [sklɪ'rəusɪs] *n* Sklerose *f*.
scoff [skɔf] *vt* (*BRIT: inf: eat*) futtern, verputzen ♦ *vi*: **to** ~ (**at**) (*mock*) spotten (über +*acc*), sich lustig machen (über +*acc*).
scold [skəuld] *vt* ausschimpfen.
scolding ['skəuldɪŋ] *n* Schelte *f*; **to get a** ~ ausgeschimpft werden.
scone [skɔn] *n* brötchenartiges Teegebäck.
scoop [sku:p] *n* (*for flour etc*) Schaufel *f*; (*for ice cream etc*) Portionierer *m*; (*amount*) Kugel *f*; (*PRESS*) Knüller *m*.
▶**scoop out** *vt* aushöhlen.
▶**scoop up** *vt* aufschaufeln; (*liquid*) aufschöpfen.
scooter ['sku:tə*] *n* (*also*: **motor** ~) Motorroller *m*; (*toy*) (Tret)roller *m*.
scope [skəup] *n* (*opportunity*) Möglichkeiten *pl*; (*range*) Ausmaß *nt*, Umfang *m*; (*freedom*) Freiheit *f*; **within the** ~ **of** im Rahmen +*gen*; **there is plenty of** ~ **for improvement** (*BRIT*) es könnte noch viel verbessert werden.
scorch [skɔːtʃ] *vt* versengen; (*earth, grass*) verbrennen.
scorched earth policy *n* (*MIL*) Politik *f* der verbrannten Erde.
scorcher ['skɔːtʃə*] (*inf*) *n* heißer Tag *m*.
scorching ['skɔːtʃɪŋ] *adj* (*day, weather*) brütend heiß.
score [skɔː*] *n* (*number of points*) (Punkte)stand *m*; (*of game*) Spielstand *m*; (*MUS*) Partitur *f*; (*twenty*) zwanzig ♦ *vt* (*goal*) schießen; (*point, success*) erzielen; (*mark*) einkerben; (*cut*) einritzen ♦ *vi* (*in game*) einen Punkt/Punkte erzielen; (*FOOTBALL etc*) ein Tor schießen; (*keep score*) (Punkte) zählen; **to settle an old** ~ **with sb** (*fig*) eine alte Rechnung mit jdm begleichen; **what's the** ~? (*SPORT*) wie steht's?; ~**s of** Hunderte von; **on that** ~ in dieser Hinsicht; **to** ~ **well** gut abschneiden; **to** ~ **6 out of 10** 6 von 10 Punkten erzielen; **to** ~ (**a point**) **over sb** (*fig*) jdn ausstechen.
▶**score out** *vt* ausstreichen.
scoreboard ['skɔːbɔːd] *n* Anzeigetafel *f*.
scorecard ['skɔːkɑːd] *n* (*SPORT*) Spielprotokoll *nt*.
score line *n* (*SPORT*) Spielstand *m*; (: *final score*) Endergebnis *nt*.
scorer ['skɔːrə*] *n* (*FOOTBALL etc*) Torschütze *m*, Torschützin *f*; (*person keeping score*) Anschreiber(in) *m(f)*.
scorn [skɔːn] *n* Verachtung *f* ♦ *vt* verachten; (*reject*) verschmähen.
scornful ['skɔːnful] *adj* verächtlich, höhnisch.
Scorpio ['skɔːpɪəu] *n* Skorpion *m*; **to be** ~ Skorpion sein.
scorpion ['skɔːpɪən] *n* Skorpion *m*.
Scot [skɔt] *n* Schotte *m*, Schottin *f*.
Scotch [skɔtʃ] *n* Scotch *m*.

scotch [skɔtʃ] *vt* (*rumour*) aus der Welt schaffen; (*plan, idea*) unterbinden.
Scotch tape ® *n* ≈ Tesafilm ® *m*.
scot-free ['skɔt'friː] *adv*: **to get off** ~ ungeschoren davonkommen.
Scotland ['skɔtlənd] *n* Schottland *nt*.
Scots [skɔts] *adj* schottisch.
Scotsman ['skɔtsmən] (*irreg: like* **man**) *n* Schotte *m*.
Scotswoman ['skɔtswumən] (*irreg: like* **woman**) *n* Schottin *f*.
Scottish ['skɔtɪʃ] *adj* schottisch.
Scottish National Party *n* Partei, die für die Unabhängigkeit Schottlands eintritt.
scoundrel ['skaundrl] *n* Schurke *m*.
scour ['skauə*] *vt* (*search*) absuchen; (*clean*) scheuern.
scourer ['skauərə*] *n* Topfkratzer *m*.
scourge [skəːdʒ] *n* (*lit, fig*) Geißel *f*.
scout [skaut] *n* (*MIL*) Kundschafter *m*, Späher *m*; (*also*: **boy** ~) Pfadfinder *m*; **girl** ~ (*US*) Pfadfinderin *f*.
▶**scout around** *vi* sich umsehen.
scowl [skaul] *vi* ein böses Gesicht machen ♦ *n* böses Gesicht *nt*; **to** ~ **at sb** jdn böse ansehen.
scrabble ['skræbl] *vi* (*also*: ~ **around**) herumtasten ♦ *n*: **S**~ ® Scrabble ® *nt*; **to** ~ **at sth** nach etw krallen; **to** ~ **about** *or* **around for sth** nach etw herumsuchen.
scraggy ['skrægɪ] *adj* (*animal*) mager; (*body, neck etc*) dürr.
scram [skræm] (*inf*) *vi* abhauen, verschwinden.
scramble ['skræmbl] *n* (*climb*) Kletterpartie *f*; (*rush*) Hetze *f*; (*struggle*) Gerangel *nt* ♦ *vi*: **to** ~ **up/over** klettern auf/über +*acc*; **to** ~ **for** sich drängeln um; **to go scrambling** (*SPORT*) Querfeldeinrennen fahren.
scrambled eggs ['skræmbld-] *n* Rührei *nt*.
scrap [skræp] *n* (*bit*) Stückchen *nt*; (*fig: of truth, evidence*) Spur *f*; (*fight*) Balgerei *f*; (*also*: ~ **metal**) Altmetall *nt*, Schrott *m* ♦ *vt* (*machines etc*) verschrotten; (*fig: plans etc*) fallenlassen ♦ *vi* (*fight*) sich balgen; **scraps** *npl* (*leftovers*) Reste *pl*; **to sell sth for** ~ etw als Schrott *or* zum Verschrotten verkaufen.
scrapbook ['skræpbuk] *n* Sammelalbum *nt*.
scrap dealer *n* Schrotthändler(in) *m(f)*.
scrape [skreɪp] *vt* abkratzen; (*hand etc*) abschürfen; (*car*) verschrammen ♦ *n*: **to get into a** ~ (*difficult situation*) in Schwulitäten *pl* kommen (*inf*).
▶**scrape through** *vt* (*exam etc*) durchrutschen durch (*inf*).
▶**scrape together** *vt* (*money*) zusammenkratzen.
scraper ['skreɪpə*] *n* Kratzer *m*.
scrap heap *n*: **to be on the** ~ (*fig*) zum alten Eisen gehören.
scrap merchant (*BRIT*) *n* Schrotthändler(in) *m(f)*.

scrap metal n Altmetall nt, Schrott m.
scrap paper n Schmierpapier nt.
scrappy ['skræpɪ] adj zusammengestoppelt (inf).
scrap yard n Schrottplatz m.
scratch [skrætʃ] n Kratzer m ♦ vt kratzen; (one's nose etc) sich kratzen an +dat; (paint, car, record) verkratzen; (COMPUT) löschen ♦ vi sich kratzen ♦ cpd (team, side) zusammengewürfelt; **to start from ~** ganz von vorne anfangen; **to be up to ~** den Anforderungen entsprechen; **to ~ the surface** (fig) an der Oberfläche bleiben.
scratch pad (US) n Notizblock m.
scrawl [skrɔːl] n Gekritzel nt; (handwriting) Klaue f (inf) ♦ vt hinkritzeln.
scrawny ['skrɔːnɪ] adj dürr.
scream [skriːm] n Schrei m ♦ vi schreien; **to be a ~** (inf) zum Schreien sein; **to ~ at sb (to do sth)** jdn anschreien(, etw zu tun).
scree [skriː] n Geröll nt.
screech [skriːtʃ] vi kreischen; (tyres, brakes) quietschen ♦ n Kreischen nt; (of tyres, brakes) Quietschen nt.
screen [skriːn] n (CINE) Leinwand f; (TV, COMPUT) Bildschirm m; (movable barrier) Wandschirm m; (fig: cover) Tarnung f; (also: **windscreen**) Windschutzscheibe f ♦ vt (protect) abschirmen; (from the wind etc) schützen; (conceal) verdecken; (film) zeigen, vorführen; (programme) senden; (candidates etc) überprüfen; (for illness): **to ~ sb for sth** jdn auf etw acc (hin) untersuchen.
screen editing n (COMPUT) Bildschirm-aufbereitung f.
screening ['skriːnɪŋ] n (MED) Untersuchung f; (of film) Vorführung f; (TV) Sendung f; (for security) Überprüfung f.
screen memory n (COMPUT) Bildschirmspeicher m.
screenplay ['skriːnpleɪ] n Drehbuch nt.
screen test n Probeaufnahmen pl.
screw [skruː] n Schraube f ♦ vt schrauben; (inf!) bumsen (!); **to ~ sth in** etw einschrauben; **to ~ sth to the wall** etw an der Wand festschrauben; **to have one's head ~ed on** (fig) ein vernünftiger Mensch sein.
▶**screw up** vt (paper etc) zusammenknüllen; (inf: ruin) vermasseln; **to ~ up one's eyes** die Augen zusammenkneifen.
screwdriver ['skruːdraɪvə*] n Schrauben-zieher m.
screwed-up ['skruːd'ʌp] (inf) adj: **to be/get ~ about sth** sich wegen etw ganz verrückt machen.
screwy ['skruːɪ] (inf) adj verrückt.
scribble ['skrɪbl] n Gekritzel nt ♦ vt, vi kritzeln; **to ~ sth down** etw hinkritzeln.
scribe [skraɪb] n Schreiber m.
script [skrɪpt] n (CINE) Drehbuch nt; (of speech, play etc) Text m; (alphabet) Schrift f;

(in exam) schriftliche Arbeit f.
scripted ['skrɪptɪd] adj (speech etc) vorbereitet.
scripture(s) ['skrɪptʃə(z)] n(pl) (heilige) Schrift f; **the S~(s)** (the Bible) die Heilige Schrift f.
scriptwriter ['skrɪptraɪtə*] n (RADIO, TV) Autor(in) m(f); (CINE) Drehbuchautor(in) m(f).
scroll [skrəul] n Schriftrolle f ♦ vt (COMPUT) scrollen.
scrotum ['skrəutəm] n Hodensack m.
scrounge [skraundʒ] (inf) vt: **to ~ sth off sb** etw bei jdm schnorren ♦ vi schnorren ♦ n: **on the ~** am Schnorren.
scrounger ['skraundʒə*] (inf) n Schnorrer(in) m(f).
scrub [skrʌb] n Gestrüpp nt ♦ vt (floor etc) schrubben; (inf: idea, plan) fallenlassen.
scrubbing brush ['skrʌbɪŋ-] n Scheuerbürste f.
scruff [skrʌf] n: **by the ~ of the neck** am Genick.
scruffy ['skrʌfɪ] adj gammelig, verwahrlost.
scrum(mage) ['skrʌm(ɪdʒ)] n (RUGBY) Gedränge nt.
scruple ['skruːpl] n (gen pl) Skrupel m, Bedenken nt; **to have no ~s about doing sth** keine Skrupel or Bedenken haben, etw zu tun.
scrupulous ['skruːpjuləs] adj gewissenhaft; (honesty) unbedingt.
scrupulously ['skruːpjuləslɪ] adv gewissenhaft; (honest, fair) äußerst; (clean) peinlich.
scrutinize ['skruːtɪnaɪz] vt prüfend ansehen; (data, records etc) genau prüfen or untersuchen.
scrutiny ['skruːtɪnɪ] n genaue Untersuchung f; **under the ~ of sb** unter jds prüfendem Blick.
scuba ['skuːbə] n (Schwimm)tauchgerät nt.
scuba diving n Sporttauchen nt.
scuff [skʌf] vt (shoes, floor) abwetzen.
scuffle ['skʌfl] n Handgemenge nt.
scull [skʌl] n Skull nt.
scullery ['skʌlərɪ] n (old) Spülküche f.
sculptor ['skʌlptə*] n Bildhauer(in) m(f).
sculpture ['skʌlptʃə*] n (art) Bildhauerei f; (object) Skulptur f.
scum [skʌm] n (on liquid) Schmutzschicht f; (pej) Abschaum m.
scupper ['skʌpə*] (BRIT: inf) vt (plan, idea) zerschlagen.
scurrilous ['skʌrɪləs] adj verleumderisch.
scurry ['skʌrɪ] vi huschen.
▶**scurry off** vi forthasten.
scurvy ['skəːvɪ] n Skorbut m.
scuttle ['skʌtl] n (also: **coal ~**) Kohleneimer m ♦ vt (ship) versenken ♦ vi: **to ~ away** or **off** verschwinden.
scythe [saɪð] n Sense f.

SD, S.Dak. (*US*) *abbr* (*POST:* = *South Dakota*).
SDI (*US*) *n abbr* (*MIL:* = *Strategic Defense Initiative*) SDI *f*.
SDLP (*BRIT*) *n abbr* (*POL:* = *Social Democratic and Labour Party*) *sozialdemokratische Partei in Nordirland*.
SDP (*BRIT*) *n abbr* (*POL: formerly:* = *Social Democratic Party*) *sozialdemokratische Partei*.
SE *abbr* (= *south-east*) SO.
sea [siː] *n* Meer *nt*, See *f*; (*fig*) Meer *nt* ♦ *cpd* See-; **by** ~ (*travel*) mit dem Schiff; **beside** *or* **by the** ~ (*holiday*) am Meer, an der See; (*village*) am Meer; **on the** ~ (*boat*) auf See; **at** ~ auf See; **to be all at** ~ (*fig*) nicht durchblicken (*inf*); **out to** ~ aufs Meer (hinaus); **to look out to** ~ aufs Meer hinausblicken; **heavy/rough** ~(**s**) schwere/rauhe See *f*.
sea anemone *n* Seeanemone *f*.
sea bed *n* Meeresboden *m*.
seaboard [ˈsiːbɔːd] *n* Küste *f*.
seafarer [ˈsiːfɛərə] *n* Seefahrer *m*.
seafaring [ˈsiːfɛərɪŋ] *adj* (*life, nation*) Seefahrer-.
seafood [ˈsiːfuːd] *n* Meeresfrüchte *pl*.
seafront [ˈsiːfrʌnt] *n* Strandpromenade *f*.
seagoing [ˈsiːɡəʊɪŋ] *adj* hochseetüchtig.
seagull [ˈsiːɡʌl] *n* Möwe *f*.
seal [siːl] *n* (*animal*) Seehund *m*; (*official stamp*) Siegel *nt*; (*in machine etc*) Dichtung *f*; (*on bottle etc*) Verschluß *m* ♦ *vt* (*envelope*) zukleben; (*crack, opening*) abdichten; (*with seal*) versiegeln; (*agreement, sb's fate*) besiegeln; **to give sth one's** ~ **of approval** einer Sache *dat* seine offizielle Zustimmung geben.
▶**seal off** *vt* (*place*) abriegeln.
sea level *n* Meeresspiegel *m*; **2,000 ft above/below** ~ 2000 Fuß über/unter dem Meeresspiegel.
sealing wax [ˈsiːlɪŋ-] *n* Siegelwachs *nt*.
sea lion *n* Seelöwe *m*.
sealskin [ˈsiːlskɪn] *n* Seehundfell *nt*.
seam [siːm] *n* Naht *f*; (*lit, fig: where edges join*) Übergang *m*; (*of coal etc*) Flöz *nt*; **the hall was bursting at the** ~**s** der Saal platzte aus allen Nähten.
seaman [ˈsiːmən] (*irreg: like* **man**) *n* Seemann *m*.
seamanship [ˈsiːmənʃɪp] *n* Seemannschaft *f*.
seamless [ˈsiːmlɪs] *adj* (*lit, fig*) nahtlos.
seamy [ˈsiːmɪ] *adj* zwielichtig; **the** ~ **side of life** die Schattenseite des Lebens.
séance [ˈseɪɒns] *n* spiritistische Sitzung *f*.
seaplane [ˈsiːpleɪn] *n* Wasserflugzeug *nt*.
seaport [ˈsiːpɔːt] *n* Seehafen *m*.
search [sɜːtʃ] *n* Suche *f*; (*inspection*) Durchsuchung *f*; (*COMPUT*) Suchlauf *m* ♦ *vt* durchsuchen; (*mind, memory*) durchforschen ♦ *vi*: **to** ~ **for** suchen nach; "~ **and replace**" (*COMPUT*) „suchen und ersetzen"; **in** ~ **of** auf der Suche nach.

▶**search through** *vt fus* durchsuchen.
searcher [ˈsɜːtʃə] *n* Suchende(r) *f(m)*.
searching [ˈsɜːtʃɪŋ] *adj* (*question*) bohrend; (*look*) prüfend; (*examination*) eingehend.
searchlight [ˈsɜːtʃlaɪt] *n* Suchscheinwerfer *m*.
search party *n* Suchtrupp *m*; **to send out a** ~ einen Suchtrupp ausschicken.
search warrant *n* Durchsuchungsbefehl *m*.
searing [ˈsɪərɪŋ] *adj* (*heat*) glühend; (*pain*) scharf.
seashore [ˈsiːʃɔː] *n* Strand *m*; **on the** ~ am Strand.
seasick [ˈsiːsɪk] *adj* seekrank.
seasickness [ˈsiːsɪknɪs] *n* Seekrankheit *f*.
seaside [ˈsiːsaɪd] *n* Meer *nt*, See *f*; **to go to the** ~ ans Meer *or* an die See fahren; **at the** ~ am Meer, an der See.
seaside resort *n* Badeort *m*.
season [ˈsiːzn] *n* Jahreszeit *f*; (*AGR*) Zeit *f*; (*SPORT, of films etc*) Saison *f*; (*THEAT*) Spielzeit *f* ♦ *vt* (*food*) würzen; **strawberries are in** ~/**out of** ~ für Erdbeeren ist jetzt die richtige Zeit/nicht die richtige Zeit; **the busy** ~ die Hochsaison *f*; **the open** ~ (*HUNTING*) die Jagdzeit *f*.
seasonal [ˈsiːznl] *adj* (*work*) Saison-.
seasoned [ˈsiːznd] *adj* (*fig: traveller*) erfahren; (*wood*) abgelagert; **she's a** ~ **campaigner** sie ist eine alte Kämpferin.
seasoning [ˈsiːznɪŋ] *n* Gewürz *nt*.
season ticket *n* (*RAIL*) Zeitkarte *f*; (*SPORT*) Dauerkarte *f*; (*THEAT*) Abonnement *nt*.
seat [siːt] *n* (*chair, of government, POL*) Sitz *m*; (*place*) Platz *m*; (*buttocks*) Gesäß *nt*; (*of trousers*) Hosenboden *m*; (*of learning*) Stätte *f* ♦ *vt* setzen; (*have room for*) Sitzplätze bieten für; **are there any** ~**s left?** sind noch Plätze frei?; **to take one's** ~ sich setzen; **please be** ~**ed** bitte nehmen Sie Platz; **to be** ~**ed** sitzen.
seat belt *n* Sicherheitsgurt *m*.
seating arrangements [ˈsiːtɪŋ-] *npl* Sitzordnung *f*.
seating capacity *n* Sitzplätze *pl*.
SEATO [ˈsiːtəʊ] *n abbr* (= *Southeast Asia Treaty Organization*) SEATO *f*.
sea urchin *n* Seeigel *m*.
sea water *n* Meerwasser *nt*.
seaweed [ˈsiːwiːd] *n* Seetang *m*.
seaworthy [ˈsiːwəːðɪ] *adj* seetüchtig.
SEC (*US*) *n abbr* (= *Securities and Exchange Commission*) *amerikanische Börsenaufsichtsbehörde*.
sec. *abbr* (= *second*) Sek.
secateurs [sɛkəˈtəːz] *npl* Gartenschere *f*.
secede [sɪˈsiːd] *vi* (*POL*): **to** ~ (**from**) sich abspalten (von).
secluded [sɪˈkluːdɪd] *adj* (*place*) abgelegen; (*life*) zurückgezogen.
seclusion [sɪˈkluːʒən] *n* Abgeschiedenheit *f*; **in** ~ zurückgezogen.
second¹ [sɪˈkɒnd] (*BRIT*) *vt* (*employee*)

abordnen.

second² ['sɛkənd] *adj* zweite(r, s) ♦ *adv* (*come, be placed*) zweite(r, s); (*when listing*) zweitens ♦ *n* (*time*) Sekunde *f*; (*AUT: also:* ~ **gear**) der zweite Gang; (*COMM: imperfect*) zweite Wahl *f* ♦ *vt* (*motion*) unterstützen; **upper/lower** ~ (*BRIT: UNIV*) ≈ Zwei plus/minus; **Charles the S**~ Karl der Zweite; **just a** ~! einen Augenblick!; ~ **floor** (*BRIT*) zweiter Stock *m*; (*US*) erster Stock *m*; **to ask for a** ~ **opinion** ein zweites Gutachten einholen.

secondary ['sɛkəndərı] *adj* weniger wichtig.

secondary education *n* höhere Schulbildung *f*.

secondary picketing *n Aufstellung von Streikposten bei nur indirekt beteiligten Firmen.*

secondary school *n* höhere Schule *f*.

Secondary school *ist in Großbritannien eine weiterführende Schule für Kinder von 11 bis 18 Jahren. Manche Schüler gehen schon mit 16 Jahren, wenn die allgemeine Schulpflicht endet, von der Schule ab. Die meisten secondary schools sind heute Gesamtschulen, obwohl es auch noch selektive Schulen gibt. Siehe auch* **comprehensive school, primary school**.

---

second-best [sɛkənd'bɛst] *adj* zweitbeste(r, s) ♦ *n:* **as a** ~ als Ausweichlösung; **don't settle for** ~ gib dich nur mit dem Besten zufrieden.

second-class ['sɛkənd'klɑːs] *adj* zweitklassig; (*citizen*) zweiter Klasse; (*RAIL, POST*) Zweite-Klasse- ♦ *adv* (*RAIL, POST*) zweiter Klasse; **to send sth** ~ etw zweiter Klasse schicken; **to travel** ~ zweiter Klasse reisen.

second cousin *n* Cousin *m*/Cousine *f* zweiten Grades.

seconder ['sɛkəndə*] *n* Befürworter(in) *m(f)*.

second-guess ['sɛkənd'gɛs] *vt* vorhersagen; **to** ~ **sb** vorhersagen, was jd machen wird.

secondhand ['sɛkənd'hænd] *adj* gebraucht; (*clothing*) getragen ♦ *adv* (*buy*) gebraucht; **to hear sth** ~ etw aus zweiter Hand haben; ~ **car** Gebrauchtwagen *m*.

second hand *n* (*on clock*) Sekundenzeiger *m*.

second-in-command ['sɛkəndınkə'mɑːnd] *n* (*MIL*) stellvertretender Kommandeur *m*; (*ADMIN*) stellvertretender Leiter *m*.

secondly ['sɛkəndlı] *adv* zweitens.

secondment [sı'kɔndmənt] (*BRIT*) *n* Abordnung *f*; **to be on** ~ abgeordnet sein.

second-rate ['sɛkənd'reıt] *adj* zweitklassig.

second thoughts *npl:* **on** ~ *or* (*US*) **thought** wenn ich es mir (recht) überlege; **to have** ~ (**about doing sth**) es sich dat anders überlegen (und etw doch nicht tun).

Second World War *n:* **the** ~ der Zweite Weltkrieg.

secrecy ['siːkrəsı] *n* Geheimhaltung *f*; (*of person*) Verschwiegenheit *f*; **in** ~ heimlich.

secret ['siːkrıt] *adj* geheim; (*admirer*) heimlich ♦ *n* Geheimnis *nt*; **in** ~ heimlich; ~ **passage** Geheimgang *m*; **to keep sth** ~ **from sb** etw vor jdm geheimhalten; **can you keep a** ~? kannst du schweigen?; **to make no** ~ **of sth** kein Geheimnis *or* keinen Hehl aus etw machen.

secret agent *n* Geheimagent(in) *m(f)*.

secretarial [sɛkrı'tɛərıəl] *adj* (*work*) Büro-; (*course*) Sekretärinnen-; (*staff*) Sekretariats-.

secretariat [sɛkrı'tɛərıət] *n* (*POL, ADMIN*) Sekretariat *nt*.

secretary ['sɛkrətərı] *n* (*COMM*) Sekretär(in) *m(f)*; (*of club*) Schriftführer(in) *m(f)*; **S**~ **of State (for)** (*BRIT: POL*) Minister(in) *m(f)* (für); **S**~ **of State** (*US: POL*) Außenminister(in) *m(f)*.

secretary-general ['sɛkrətərı'dʒɛnərl] (*pl* **secretaries-general**) *n* Generalsekretär(in) *m(f)*.

secrete [sı'kriːt] *vt* (*ANAT, BIOL, MED*) absondern; (*hide*) verbergen.

secretion [sı'kriːʃən] *n* (*substance*) Sekret *nt*.

secretive ['siːkrətıv] *adj* verschlossen; (*pej*) geheimnistuerisch.

secretly ['siːkrıtlı] *adv* heimlich; (*hope*) insgeheim.

secret police *n* Geheimpolizei *f*.

secret service *n* Geheimdienst *m*.

sect [sɛkt] *n* Sekte *f*.

sectarian [sɛk'tɛərıən] *adj* (*killing etc*) konfessionell motiviert; ~ **violence** gewalttätige Konfessionsstreitigkeiten *pl*.

section ['sɛkʃən] *n* (*part*) Teil *m*; (*department*) Abteilung *f*; (*of document*) Absatz *m*; (*cross-section*) Schnitt *m* ♦ *vt* (*divide*) teilen; **the business/sport** ~ (*PRESS*) der Wirtschafts-/Sportteil.

sectional ['sɛkʃənl] *adj:* ~ **drawing** Darstellung *f* im Schnitt.

sector ['sɛktə*] *n* Sektor *m*.

secular ['sɛkjulə*] *adj* weltlich.

secure [sı'kjuə*] *adj* sicher; (*firmly fixed*) fest ♦ *vt* (*fix*) festmachen; (*votes etc*) erhalten; (*contract etc*) (sich *dat*) sichern; (*COMM: loan*) (ab)sichern; **to make sth** ~ etw sichern; **to** ~ **sth for sb** jdm etw sichern.

secured creditor [sı'kjuəd-] *n* (*COMM*) abgesicherter Gläubiger *m*.

securely [sı'kjuəlı] *adv* (*firmly*) fest; (*safely*) sicher.

security [sı'kjuərıtı] *n* Sicherheit *f*; (*freedom from anxiety*) Geborgenheit *f*; **securities** *npl* (*STOCK EXCHANGE*) Effekten *pl*, Wertpapiere *pl*; **to increase/tighten** ~ die Sicherheitsvorkehrungen verschärfen; ~ **of tenure** Kündigungsschutz *m*.

Security Council *n* Sicherheitsrat *m*.

security forces *npl* Sicherheitskräfte *pl*.

security guard n Sicherheitsbeamte(r) m; (*transporting money*) Wachmann m.
security risk n Sicherheitsrisiko nt.
secy. *abbr* = **secretary**.
sedan [sə'dæn] (*US*) n (*AUT*) Limousine f.
sedate [sı'deıt] *adj* (*person*) ruhig, gesetzt; (*life*) geruhsam; (*pace*) gemächlich ♦ *vt* (*MED*) Beruhigungsmittel geben +dat.
sedation [sı'deıʃən] n (*MED*) Beruhigungsmittel pl; **to be under** ~ unter dem Einfluß von Beruhigungsmitteln stehen.
sedative ['sɛdıtıv] n (*MED*) Beruhigungsmittel nt.
sedentary ['sɛdntrı] *adj* (*occupation, work*) sitzend.
sediment ['sɛdımənt] n (*in bottle*) (Boden)satz m; (*in lake etc*) Ablagerung f.
sedimentary [sɛdı'mɛntərı] *adj* (*GEOG*) sedimentär; ~ **rock** Sedimentgestein nt.
sedition [sı'dıʃən] n Aufwiegelung f.
seduce [sı'djuːs] *vt* verführen; **to** ~ **sb into doing sth** jdn dazu verleiten, etw zu tun.
seduction [sı'dʌkʃən] n (*attraction*) Verlockung f; (*act of seducing*) Verführung f.
seductive [sı'dʌktıv] *adj* verführerisch; (*fig: offer*) verlockend.
see [siː] (*pt* **saw**, *pp* **seen**) *vt* sehen; (*look at*) sich *dat* ansehen; (*understand*) verstehen; (*ein*)sehen; (*doctor etc*) aufsuchen ♦ *vi* sehen ♦ n (*REL*) Bistum nt; **to** ~ **that** (*ensure*) dafür sorgen, daß; **to** ~ **sb to the door** jdn zur Tür bringen; **there was nobody to be** ~**n** es war niemand zu sehen; **to go and** ~ **sb** jdn besuchen (gehen); **to** ~ **a doctor** zum Arzt gehen; ~ **you!** tschüs! (*inf*); ~ **you soon!** bis bald!; **let me** ~ (*show me*) laß mich mal sehen; (*let me think*) laß mich mal überlegen; **I** ~ ich verstehe, aha; (*annoyed*) ach so; **you** ~ weißt du, siehst du; ~ **for yourself** überzeug dich doch selbst; **I don't know what she** ~**s in him** ich weiß nicht, was sie an ihm findet; **as far as I can** ~ so wie ich das sehe.
▶**see about** *vt fus* sich kümmern um +acc.
▶**see off** *vt* verabschieden.
▶**see through** *vt fus* durchschauen ♦ *vt:* **to** ~ **sb through sth** jdm in etw *dat* beistehen; **to** ~ **sth through to the end** etw zu Ende bringen; **this should** ~ **you through** das müßte dir reichen.
▶**see to** *vt fus* sich kümmern um +acc.
seed [siːd] n Samen m; (*of fruit*) Kern m; (*fig: usu pl*) Keim m; (*TENNIS*) gesetzter Spieler m, gesetzte Spielerin f; **to go to** ~ (*plant*) Samen bilden; (*lettuce etc*) schießen; (*fig: person*) herunterkommen.
seedless ['siːdlıs] *adj* kernlos.
seedling ['siːdlıŋ] n (*BOT*) Sämling m.
seedy ['siːdı] *adj* (*person, place*) zwielichtig, zweifelhaft.
seeing ['siːıŋ] *conj:* ~ **as** *or* **that** da.
seek [siːk] (*pt, pp* **sought**) *vt* suchen; **to** ~ **advice from sb** jdn um Rat fragen; **to** ~ **help from sb** jdn um Hilfe bitten.
▶**seek out** *vt* ausfindig machen.
seem [siːm] *vi* scheinen; **there** ~**s to be a mistake** da scheint ein Fehler zu sein; **it** ~**s (that)** es scheint(, daß); **it** ~**s to me that** ... mir scheint, daß ...; **what** ~**s to be the trouble?** worum geht es denn?; (*doctor*) was fehlt Ihnen denn?
seemingly ['siːmıŋlı] *adv* anscheinend.
seemly ['siːmlı] *adj* schicklich.
seen [siːn] *pp of* **see**.
seep [siːp] *vi* sickern.
seersucker ['sıəsʌkə*] n Krepp m, Seersucker m.
seesaw ['siːsɔː] n Wippe f.
seethe [siːð] *vi:* **to** ~ **with** (*place*) wimmeln von; **to** ~ **with anger** vor Wut kochen.
see-through ['siːθruː] *adj* durchsichtig.
segment ['sɛgmənt] n Teil m; (*of orange*) Stück nt.
segregate ['sɛgrıgeıt] *vt* trennen, absondern.
segregation [sɛgrı'geıʃən] n Trennung f.
Seine [seın] n: **the** ~ die Seine f.
seismic shock n Erdstoß m.
seize [siːz] *vt* packen, ergreifen; (*fig: opportunity*) ergreifen; (*power, control*) an sich *acc* reißen; (*territory, airfield*) besetzen; (*hostage*) nehmen; (*LAW*) beschlagnahmen.
▶**seize up** *vi* (*engine*) sich festfressen.
▶**seize (up)on** *vt fus* sich stürzen auf +acc.
seizure ['siːʒə*] n (*MED*) Anfall m; (*of power*) Ergreifung f; (*LAW*) Beschlagnahmung f.
seldom ['sɛldəm] *adv* selten.
select [sı'lɛkt] *adj* exklusiv ♦ *vt* (aus)wählen; (*SPORT*) aufstellen; **a** ~ **few** wenige Auserwählte.
selection [sı'lɛkʃən] n (*being chosen*) Wahl f; (*range*) Auswahl f.
selection committee n Auswahlkomitee nt.
selective [sı'lɛktıv] *adj* wählerisch; (*not general*) selektiv.
selector [sı'lɛktə*] n (*SPORT*) Mannschaftsaufsteller(in) m(f); (*TECH*) Wählschalter m; (: *button*) Taste f.
self [sɛlf] (*pl* **selves**) n Selbst nt, Ich nt; **she was her normal** ~ **again** sie war wieder ganz die alte.
self... [sɛlf] *pref* selbst-, Selbst-.
self-addressed ['sɛlfə'drɛst] *adj:* ~ **envelope** addressierter Rückumschlag m.
self-adhesive [sɛlfəd'hiːzıv] *adj* selbstklebend.
self-appointed [sɛlfə'pɔıntıd] *adj* selbsternannt.
self-assertive [sɛlfə'səːtıv] *adj* selbstbewußt.
self-assurance [sɛlfə'ʃuərəns] n Selbstsicherheit f.
self-assured [sɛlfə'ʃuəd] *adj* selbstsicher.
self-catering [sɛlf'keıtərıŋ] (*BRIT*) *adj* (*holiday, flat*) für Selbstversorger.
self-centred, (*US*) **self-centered** [sɛlf'sɛntəd]

adj egozentrisch, ichbezogen.

self-cleaning [sɛlf'kliːnɪŋ] *adj* selbstreinigend.

self-confessed [sɛlfkən'fɛst] *adj* erklärt.

self-confidence [sɛlf'kɔnfɪdns] *n* Selbstbewußtsein *nt*, Selbstvertrauen *nt*.

self-confident [sɛlf'kɔnfɪdənt] *adj* selbstbewußt, selbstsicher.

self-conscious [sɛlf'kɔnʃəs] *adj* befangen, gehemmt.

self-contained [sɛlfkən'teɪnd] (*BRIT*) *adj* (*flat*) abgeschlossen; (*person*) selbständig.

self-control [sɛlfkən'trəʊl] *n* Selbstbeherrschung *f*.

self-defeating [sɛlfdɪ'fiːtɪŋ] *adj* unsinnig.

self-defence, (*US*) **self-defense** [sɛlfdɪ'fɛns] *n* Selbstverteidigung *f*; (*LAW*) Notwehr *f*; **in ~** zu seiner/ihrer *etc* Verteidigung; (*LAW*) in Notwehr.

self-discipline [sɛlf'dɪsɪplɪn] *n* Selbstdisziplin *f*.

self-employed [sɛlfɪm'plɔɪd] *adj* selbständig.

self-esteem [sɛlfɪs'tiːm] *n* Selbstachtung *f*.

self-evident [sɛlf'ɛvɪdnt] *adj* offensichtlich.

self-explanatory [sɛlfɪks'plænətrɪ] *adj* unmittelbar verständlich.

self-financing [sɛlffaɪ'nænsɪŋ] *adj* selbstfinanzierend.

self-governing [sɛlf'gʌvənɪŋ] *adj* selbstverwaltet.

self-help ['sɛlf'hɛlp] *n* Selbsthilfe *f*.

self-importance [sɛlfɪm'pɔːtns] *n* Aufgeblasenheit *f*.

self-indulgent [sɛlfɪn'dʌldʒənt] *adj* genießerisch; **to be ~** sich verwöhnen.

self-inflicted [sɛlfɪn'flɪktɪd] *adj* selbst zugefügt.

self-interest [sɛlf'ɪntrɪst] *n* Eigennutz *m*.

selfish ['sɛlfɪʃ] *adj* egoistisch, selbstsüchtig.

selfishly ['sɛlfɪʃlɪ] *adv* egoistisch, selbstsüchtig.

selfishness ['sɛlfɪʃnɪs] *n* Egoismus *m*, Selbstsucht *f*.

selfless ['sɛlflɪs] *adj* selbstlos.

selflessly ['sɛlflɪslɪ] *adv* selbstlos.

selflessness ['sɛlflɪsnɪs] *n* Selbstlosigkeit *f*.

self-made ['sɛlfmeɪd] *adj:* **~ man** Selfmademan *m*.

self-pity [sɛlf'pɪtɪ] *n* Selbstmitleid *nt*.

self-portrait [sɛlf'pɔːtreɪt] *n* Selbstporträt *nt*, Selbstbildnis *nt*.

self-possessed [sɛlfpə'zɛst] *adj* selbstbeherrscht.

self-preservation ['sɛlfprɛzə'veɪʃən] *n* Selbsterhaltung *f*.

self-raising ['sɛlf'reɪzɪŋ], (*US*) **self-rising** ['sɛlf'raɪzɪŋ] *adj:* **~ flour** *Mehl mit bereits beigemischtem Backpulver.*

self-reliant [sɛlfrɪ'laɪənt] *adj* selbständig.

self-respect [sɛlfrɪs'pɛkt] *n* Selbstachtung *f*.

self-respecting [sɛlfrɪs'pɛktɪŋ] *adj* mit Selbstachtung; (*genuine*) der/die/das etwas auf sich hält.

self-righteous [sɛlf'raɪtʃəs] *adj* selbstgerecht.

self-rising [sɛlf'raɪzɪŋ] (*US*) *adj* = **self-raising**.

self-sacrifice [sɛlf'sækrɪfaɪs] *n* Selbstaufopferung *f*.

self-same ['sɛlfseɪm] *adj:* **the ~** genau derselbe/dieselbe/dasselbe.

self-satisfied [sɛlf'sætɪsfaɪd] *adj* selbstzufrieden.

self-sealing [sɛlf'siːlɪŋ] *adj* selbstklebend.

self-service [sɛlf'səːvɪs] *adj* (*shop, restaurant etc*) Selbstbedienungs-.

self-styled ['sɛlfstaɪld] *adj* selbsternannt.

self-sufficient [sɛlfsə'fɪʃənt] *adj* (*country*) autark; (*person*) selbständig, unabhängig; **to be ~ in coal** seinen Kohlebedarf selbst decken können.

self-supporting [sɛlfsə'pɔːtɪŋ] *adj* (*business*) sich selbst tragend.

self-taught [sɛlf'tɔːt] *adj:* **to be ~** Autodidakt sein; **he is a ~ pianist** er hat sich das Klavierspielen selbst beigebracht.

self-test ['sɛlftɛst] *n* (*COMPUT*) Selbsttest *m*.

sell [sɛl] (*pt, pp* **sold**) *vt* verkaufen; (*shop: goods*) führen, haben (*inf*); (*fig: idea*) schmackhaft machen +*dat*, verkaufen (*inf*) ♦ *vi* sich verkaufen (lassen); **to ~ at or for 10 pounds** für 10 Pfund verkauft werden; **to ~ sb sth** jdm etw verkaufen; **to ~ o.s.** sich verkaufen.

▶**sell off** *vt* verkaufen.

▶**sell out** *vi:* **we/the tickets are sold out** wir/die Karten sind ausverkauft; **we have sold out of ...** wir haben kein ... mehr, ... ist ausverkauft.

▶**sell up** *vi* sein Haus/seine Firma *etc* verkaufen.

sell-by date ['sɛlbaɪ-] *n ≈* Haltbarkeitsdatum *nt*.

seller ['sɛlə*] *n* Verkäufer(in) *m(f)*; **~'s market** Verkäufermarkt *m*.

selling price ['sɛlɪŋ-] *n* Verkaufspreis *m*.

sellotape ® ['sɛləʊteɪp] (*BRIT*) *n* Klebeband *nt*, ≈ Tesafilm ® *m*.

sellout ['sɛlaʊt] *n* (*inf: betrayal*) Verrat *m*; **the match was a ~** das Spiel war ausverkauft.

selves [sɛlvz] *pl of* **self**.

semantic [sɪ'mæntɪk] *adj* semantisch.

semantics [sɪ'mæntɪks] *n* (*LING*) Semantik *f*.

semaphore ['sɛməfɔː*] *n* Flaggenalphabet *nt*.

semblance ['sɛmblns] *n* Anschein *m*.

semen ['siːmən] *n* Samenflüssigkeit *f*, Sperma *nt*.

semester [sɪ'mɛstə*] (*esp US*) *n* Semester *nt*.

semi ['sɛmɪ] *n* = **semidetached (house)**.

semi... ['sɛmɪ] *pref* halb-, Halb-.

semibreve ['sɛmɪbriːv] (*BRIT*) *n* (*MUS*) ganze Note *f*.

semicircle ['sɛmɪsəːkl] *n* Halbkreis *m*.

semicircular ['sɛmɪ'səːkjʊlə*] *adj* halbkreisförmig.

semicolon [sɛmɪ'kəʊlən] *n* Strichpunkt *m*, Semikolon *nt*.

semiconductor [semɪkən'dʌktə*] n Halbleiter m.

semiconscious [semɪ'kɔnʃəs] adj halb bewußtlos.

semidetached (house) (BRIT) n Doppelhaushälfte f.

semifinal [semɪ'faɪnl] n Halbfinale nt.

seminar ['semɪnɑː*] n Seminar nt.

seminary ['semɪnərɪ] n (REL) Priesterseminar nt.

semi-precious stone n Halbedelstein m.

semiquaver ['semɪkweɪvə*] (BRIT) n (MUS) Sechzehntelnote f.

semiskilled [semɪ'skɪld] adj (work) Anlern-; (worker) angelernt.

semi-skimmed [semɪ'skɪmd] adj (milk) teilentrahmt, Halbfett-.

semitone ['semɪtəʊn] n (MUS) Halbton m.

semolina [semə'liːnə] n Grieß m.

SEN (BRIT) n abbr (formerly: = State Enrolled Nurse) staatlich anerkannte Krankenschwester f, staatlich anerkannter Krankenpfleger m.

Sen., sen. abbr (US) = senator; (in names: = senior) sen.

senate ['senɪt] n Senat m.

Senate ist das Oberhaus des amerikanischen Kongresses (das Unterhaus ist das **House of Representatives**). Der Senat besteht aus 100 Senatoren, 2 für jeden Bundesstaat, die für 6 Jahre gewählt werden, wobei ein Drittel alle zwei Jahre neu gewählt wird. Die Senatoren werden in direkter Wahl vom Volk gewählt. Siehe auch **congress**.

---

senator ['senɪtə*] n Senator(in) m(f).

send [send] (pt, pp sent) vt schicken; (transmit) senden; **to ~ sth by post** or (US) **mail** etw mit der Post schicken; **to ~ sb for sth** (for check-up etc) jdn zu etw schicken; **to ~ word that** ... Nachricht geben, daß ...; **she ~s (you) her love** sie läßt dich grüßen; **to ~ sb to Coventry** (BRIT) jdn schneiden (inf); **to ~ sb to sleep** jdn einschläfern; **to ~ sth flying** etw umwerfen.

▶**send away** vt wegschicken.

▶**send away for** vt fus (per Post) anfordern.

▶**send back** vt zurückschicken.

▶**send for** vt fus (per Post) anfordern; (doctor, police) rufen.

▶**send in** vt einsenden, einschicken.

▶**send off** vt abschicken; (BRIT: player) vom Platz weisen.

▶**send on** vt (BRIT: letter) nachsenden; (luggage etc) vorausschicken.

▶**send out** vt verschicken; (light, heat) abgeben; (signal) aussenden.

▶**send round** vt schicken; (circulate) zirkulieren lassen.

▶**send up** vt (astronaut) hochschießen; (price, blood pressure) hochtreiben; (BRIT: parody)

verulken (inf).

sender ['sendə*] n Absender(in) m(f).

sending-off ['sendɪŋɔf] n (SPORT) Platzverweis m.

send-off ['sendɔf] n: **a good ~** eine große Verabschiedung.

send-up ['sendʌp] n Verulkung f (inf).

Senegal [senɪ'gɔːl] n Senegal nt.

Senegalese [senɪgə'liːz] adj senegalesisch ♦ n inv Senegalese m, Senegalesin f.

senile ['siːnaɪl] adj senil.

senility [sɪ'nɪlɪtɪ] n Senilität f.

senior ['siːnɪə*] adj (staff, manager) leitend; (officer) höher; (post, position) leitend ♦ n (SCOL): **the ~s** die Oberstufenschüler pl; **to be ~ to sb** jdm übergeordnet sein; **she is 15 years his ~** sie ist 15 Jahre älter als er; **P. Jones ~** P. Jones senior.

senior citizen n Senior(in) m(f).

senior high school (US) n Oberstufe f.

seniority [siːnɪ'ɔrɪtɪ] n (in service) (längere) Betriebszugehörigkeit f; (in rank) (höhere) Position f.

sensation [sen'seɪʃən] n (feeling) Gefühl nt; (great success) Sensation f; **to cause a ~** großes Aufsehen erregen.

sensational [sen'seɪʃənl] adj (wonderful) wunderbar; (result) sensationell; (headlines etc) reißerisch.

sense [sens] n Sinn m; (feeling) Gefühl nt; (good sense) Verstand m, gesunder Menschenverstand m; (meaning) Bedeutung f, Sinn m ♦ vt spüren; **~ of smell** Geruchssinn m; **it makes ~** (can be understood) es ergibt einen Sinn; (is sensible) es ist vernünftig or sinnvoll; **there's no ~ in that** das hat keinen Sinn; **there is no ~ in doing that** es hat keinen Sinn, das zu tun; **to come to one's ~s** Vernunft annehmen; **to take leave of one's ~s** den Verstand verlieren.

senseless ['senslɪs] adj (pointless) sinnlos; (unconscious) besinnungslos, bewußtlos.

sense of humour n Sinn m für Humor.

sensibility [sensɪ'bɪlɪtɪ] n Empfindsamkeit f; (sensitivity) Empfindlichkeit f; **to offend sb's sensibilities** jds Zartgefühl verletzen.

sensible ['sensɪbl] adj vernünftig; (shoes, clothes) praktisch.

sensitive ['sensɪtɪv] adj empfindlich; (understanding) einfühlsam; (touchy: person) sensibel; (: issue) heikel; **to be ~ to sth** in bezug auf etw acc empfindlich sein; **he is very ~ about it/to criticism** er reagiert sehr empfindlich darauf/auf Kritik.

sensitivity [sensɪ'tɪvɪtɪ] n Empfindlichkeit f; (understanding) Einfühlungsvermögen nt; (of issue etc) heikle Natur f; **an issue of great ~** ein sehr heikles Thema.

sensual ['sensjʊəl] adj sinnlich; (person, life) sinnenfroh.

sensuous ['sensjʊəs] adj sinnlich.

sent [sɛnt] *pt, pp of* **send.**

sentence ['sɛntns] *n* (*LING*) Satz *m*; (*LAW: judgement*) Urteil *nt*; (: *punishment*) Strafe *f* ♦ *vt:* **to ~ sb to death/to 5 years in prison** jdn zum Tode/zu 5 Jahren Haft verurteilen; **to pass ~ on sb** das Urteil über jdn verkünden; (*fig*) jdn verurteilen; **to serve a life ~** eine lebenslängliche Freiheitsstrafe verbüßen.

sentiment ['sɛntɪmənt] *n* Sentimentalität *f*; (*also pl: opinion*) Ansicht *f*.

sentimental [sɛntɪ'mɛntl] *adj* sentimental.

sentimentality [sɛntɪmɛn'tælɪtɪ] *n* Sentimentalität *f*.

sentry ['sɛntrɪ] *n* Wachtposten *m*.

sentry duty *n:* **to be on ~** auf Wache sein.

Seoul [səʊl] *n* Seoul *nt*.

separable ['sɛprəbl] *adj:* **to be ~ from** trennbar sein von.

separate ['sɛprɪt] *adj* getrennt; (*occasions*) verschieden; (*rooms*) separat ♦ *vt* trennen ♦ *vi* sich trennen; **~ from** getrennt von; **to go ~ ways** getrennte Wege gehen; **under ~ cover** (*COMM*) mit getrennter Post; **to ~ into** aufteilen in +*acc*; *see also* **separates.**

separately ['sɛprɪtlɪ] *adv* getrennt.

separates ['sɛprɪts] *npl* (*clothes*) kombinierbare Einzelteile *pl*.

separation [sɛpə'reɪʃən] *n* Trennung *f*.

sepia ['si:pjə] *adj* sepiafarben.

Sept. *abbr* (= *September*) Sept.

September [sɛp'tɛmbə*] *n* September *m; see also* **July.**

septic ['sɛptɪk] *adj* vereitert, septisch; **to go ~** eitern.

septicaemia, (*US*) **septicemia** [sɛptɪ'si:mɪə] *n* Blutvergiftung *f*.

septic tank *n* Faulbehälter *m*.

sequel ['si:kwl] *n* (*follow-up*) Nachspiel *nt*; (*of film, story*) Fortsetzung *f*.

sequence ['si:kwəns] *n* Folge *f*; (*dance/film sequence*) Sequenz *f*; **in ~** der Reihe nach.

sequential [sɪ'kwɛnʃəl] *adj* aufeinanderfolgend; **~ access** (*COMPUT*) sequentieller Zugriff *m*.

sequestrate [sɪ'kwɛstreɪt] *vt* (*LAW, COMM*) sequestrieren, beschlagnahmen.

sequin ['si:kwɪn] *n* Paillette *f*.

Serbia ['sə:bɪə] *n* Serbien *nt*.

Serbian ['sə:bɪən] *adj* serbisch ♦ *n* Serbier(in) *m(f)*; (*LING*) Serbisch *nt*.

Serbo-Croat ['sə:bəʊ'krəʊæt] *n* (*LING*) Serbokroatisch *nt*.

serenade [sɛrə'neɪd] *n* Serenade *f* ♦ *vt* ein Ständchen *nt* bringen +*dat*.

serene [sɪ'ri:n] *adj* (*landscape etc*) friedlich; (*expression*) heiter; (*person*) gelassen.

serenity [sə'rɛnɪtɪ] *n* (*of landscape*) Friedlichkeit *f*; (*of expression*) Gelassenheit *f*.

sergeant ['sɑ:dʒənt] *n* (*MIL etc*) Feldwebel *m*; (*POLICE*) Polizeimeister *m*.

sergeant-major ['sɑ:dʒənt'meɪdʒə*] *n* Oberfeldwebel *m*.

serial ['sɪərɪəl] *n* (*TV*) Serie *f*; (*RADIO*) Sendereihe *f*; (*in magazine*) Fortsetzungsroman *m* ♦ *adj* (*COMPUT*) seriell.

serialize ['sɪərɪəlaɪz] *vt* in Fortsetzungen veröffentlichen; (*TV, RADIO*) in Fortsetzungen senden.

serial killer *n* Serienmörder(in) *m(f)*.

serial number *n* Seriennummer *f*.

series ['sɪərɪz] *n inv* (*group*) Serie *f*, Reihe *f*; (*of books*) Reihe *f*; (*TV*) Serie *f*.

serious ['sɪərɪəs] *adj* ernst; (*important*) wichtig; (: *illness*) schwer; (: *condition*) bedenklich; **are you ~ (about it)?** meinst du das ernst?

seriously ['sɪərɪəslɪ] *adv* ernst; (*talk, interested*) ernsthaft; (*ill, hurt, damaged*) schwer; (*not jokingly*) im Ernst; **to take sb/sth ~** jdn/etw ernst nehmen; **do you ~ believe that ...** glauben Sie ernsthaft *or* im Ernst, daß ...

seriousness ['sɪərɪəsnɪs] *n* Ernst *m*, Ernsthaftigkeit *f*; (*of problem*) Bedenklichkeit *f*.

sermon ['sə:mən] *n* Predigt *f*; (*fig*) Moralpredigt *f*.

serrated [sɪ'reɪtɪd] *adj* gezackt; **~ knife** Sägemesser *nt*.

serum ['sɪərəm] *n* Serum *nt*.

servant ['sə:vənt] *n* (*lit, fig*) Diener(in) *m(f)*; (*domestic*) Hausangestellte(r) *f(m)*.

serve [sə:v] *vt* dienen +*dat*; (*in shop, with food/ drink*) bedienen; (*food, meal*) servieren; (*purpose*) haben; (*apprenticeship*) durchmachen; (*prison term*) verbüßen ♦ *vi* (*at table*) auftragen, servieren; (*TENNIS*) aufschlagen; (*soldier*) dienen; (*be useful*): **to ~ as/for** dienen als ♦ *n* (*TENNIS*) Aufschlag *m*; **are you being ~d?** werden Sie schon bedient?; **to ~ its purpose** seinen Zweck erfüllen; **to ~ sb's purpose** jds Zwecken dienen; **it ~s him right** das geschieht ihm recht; **to ~ on a committee** einem Ausschuß angehören; **to ~ on a jury** Geschworene(r) *f(m)* sein; **it's my turn to ~** (*TENNIS*) ich habe Aufschlag; **it ~s to show/explain ...** das zeigt/erklärt ...

▶**serve out** *vt* (*food*) auftragen, servieren.

▶**serve up** *vt* = **serve out.**

service ['sə:vɪs] *n* Dienst *m*; (*commercial*) Dienstleistung *f*; (*in hotel, restaurant*) Bedienung *f*, Service *m*; (*also:* **train ~**) Bahnverbindung *f*; (: *generally*) Zugverkehr *m*; (*REL*) Gottesdienst *m*; (*AUT*) Inspektion *f*; (*TENNIS*) Aufschlag *m*; (*plates etc*) Service *nt* ♦ *vt* (*car, machine*) warten; **the Services** *npl* (*army, navy etc*) die Streitkräfte *pl*; **military/ national ~** Militärdienst *m*; **to be of ~ to sb** jdm nützen; **to do sb a ~** jdm einen Dienst erweisen; **to put one's car in for a ~** sein Auto zur Inspektion geben; **dinner ~** Eßservice *nt*.

serviceable ['sə:vɪsəbl] *adj* zweckmäßig.
service area *n* (*on motorway*) Raststätte *f.*
service charge (*BRIT*) *n* Bedienungsgeld *nt.*
service industry *n* Dienstleistungsbranche *f.*
serviceman ['sə:vɪsmən] (*irreg: like* **man**) *n*
  Militärangehörige(r) *m.*
service station *n* Tankstelle *f.*
serviette [sə:vɪ'ɛt] (*BRIT*) *n* Serviette *f.*
servile ['sə:vaɪl] *adj* unterwürfig.
session ['sɛʃən] *n* Sitzung *f*; (*US, SCOT: SCOL*)
  Studienjahr *nt*; (: : *term*) Semester *nt*;
  recording ~ Aufnahme *f*; **to be in** ~ tagen.
session musician *n* Session-Musiker(in) *m(f).*
set [sɛt] (*pt, pp* **set**) *n* (*of saucepans, books, keys
  etc*) Satz *m*; (*group*) Reihe *f*; (*of cutlery*)
  Garnitur *f*; (*also:* **radio** ~) Radio(gerät) *nt*;
  (*also:* **TV** ~) Fernsehgerät *nt*; (*TENNIS*) Satz
  m; (*group of people*) Kreis *m*; (*MATH*) Menge
  f; (*THEAT: stage*) Bühne *f*; (: *scenery*)
  Bühnenbild *nt*; (*CINE*) Drehort *m*;
  (*HAIRDRESSING*) (Ein)legen *nt* ♦ *adj* (*fixed*)
  fest; (*ready*) fertig, bereit ♦ *vt* (*table*)
  decken; (*place*) auflegen; (*time, price, rules
  etc*) festsetzen; (*record*) aufstellen; (*alarm,
  watch, task*) stellen; (*exam*)
  zusammenstellen; (*TYP*) setzen ♦ *vi* (*sun*)
  untergehen; (*jam, jelly, concrete*) fest
  werden; (*bone*) zusammenwachsen; **a** ~ **of
  false teeth** ein Gebiß; **a** ~ **of dining-room
  furniture** eine Eßzimmergarnitur; **a chess** ~
  ein Schachspiel; **to be** ~ **on doing sth** etw
  unbedingt tun wollen; **to be all** ~ **to do sth**
  bereit sein, etw zu tun; **he's** ~ **in his ways** er
  ist in seinen Gewohnheiten festgefahren; **a**
  ~ **phrase** eine feste Redewendung; **a novel**
  ~ **in Rome** ein Roman, der in Rom spielt; **to**
  ~ **to music** vertonen; **to** ~ **on fire**
  anstecken; **to** ~ **free** freilassen; **to** ~ **sail**
  losfahren.
►**set about** *vt fus* (*task*) anpacken; **to** ~ **about
  doing sth** sich daranmachen, etw zu tun.
►**set aside** *vt* (*money etc*) beiseite legen;
  (*time*) einplanen.
►**set back** *vt:* **to** ~ **sb back 5 pounds** jdn 5
  Pfund kosten; **to** ~ **sb back (by)** (*in time*) jdn
  zurückwerfen (um); **a house** ~ **back from
  the road** ein Haus, das etwas von der
  Straße abliegt.
►**set in** *vi* (*bad weather*) einsetzen; (*infection*)
  sich einstellen; **the rain has** ~ **in for the day**
  es hat sich für heute eingeregnet.
►**set off** *vi* (*depart*) aufbrechen ♦ *vt* (*bomb*)
  losgehen lassen; (*alarm, chain of events*)
  auslösen; (*show up well*) hervorheben.
►**set out** *vi* (*depart*) aufbrechen ♦ *vt* (*goods
  etc*) ausbreiten; (*chairs etc*) aufstellen;
  (*arguments*) darlegen; **to** ~ **out to do sth**
  sich *dat* vornehmen, etw zu tun; **to** ~ **out
  from home** zu Hause aufbrechen.
►**set up** *vt* (*organization*) gründen;
  (*monument*) errichten; **to** ~ **up shop** ein
  Geschäft eröffnen; (*fig*) sich selbständig

machen.
setback ['sɛtbæk] *n* Rückschlag *m.*
set menu *n* Menü *nt.*
set square *n* Zeichendreieck *nt.*
settee [sɛ'ti:] *n* Sofa *nt.*
setting ['sɛtɪŋ] *n* (*background*) Rahmen *m*;
  (*position*) Einstellung *f*; (*of jewel*) Fassung *f.*
setting lotion *n* (Haar)festiger *m.*
settle ['sɛtl] *vt* (*matter*) regeln; (*argument*)
  beilegen; (*accounts*) begleichen; (*affairs,
  business*) in Ordnung bringen; (*colonize:
  land*) besiedeln ♦ *vi* (*also:* ~ **down**) sich
  niederlassen; (*sand, dust etc*) sich legen;
  (*sediment*) sich setzen; (*calm down*) sich
  beruhigen; **to** ~ **one's stomach** den Magen
  beruhigen; **that's** ~**d then!** das ist also
  abgemacht!; **to** ~ **down to work** sich an die
  Arbeit setzen; **to** ~ **down to watch TV** es
  sich *dat* vor dem Fernseher gemütlich
  machen.
►**settle for** *vt fus* sich zufriedengeben mit.
►**settle in** *vi* sich einleben; (*in job etc*) sich
  eingewöhnen.
►**settle on** *vt fus* sich entscheiden für.
►**settle up** *vi:* **to** ~ **up with sb** mit jdm
  abrechnen.
settlement ['sɛtlmənt] *n* (*payment*)
  Begleichung *f*; (*LAW*) Vergleich *m*;
  (*agreement*) Übereinkunft *f*; (*of conflict*)
  Beilegung *f*; (*village etc*) Siedlung *f*,
  Niederlassung *f*; (*colonization*) Besiedelung
  f; **in** ~ **of our account** (*COMM*) zum
  Ausgleich unseres Kontos.
settler ['sɛtlə*] *n* Siedler(in) *m(f).*
setup, set-up ['sɛtʌp] *n* (*organization*)
  Organisation *f*; (*system*) System *nt.*
seven ['sɛvn] *num* sieben.
seventeen [sɛvn'ti:n] *num* siebzehn.
seventh ['sɛvnθ] *num* siebte(r, s).
seventy ['sɛvntɪ] *num* siebzig.
sever ['sɛvə*] *vt* durchtrennen; (*fig: relations*)
  abbrechen; (: *ties*) lösen.
several ['sɛvərl] *adj* einige, mehrere ♦ *pron*
  einige; ~ **of us** einige von uns; ~ **times**
  einige Male, mehrmals.
severance ['sɛvərəns] *n* (*of relations*) Abbruch
  m.
severance pay *n* Abfindung *f.*
severe [sɪ'vɪə*] *adj* (*damage, shortage*) schwer;
  (*pain*) stark; (*person, expression, dress, winter*)
  streng; (*punishment*) hart; (*climate*) rauh.
severely [sɪ'vɪəlɪ] *adv* (*damage*) stark; (*punish*)
  hart; (*wounded, ill*) schwer.
severity [sɪ'vɛrɪtɪ] *n* (*gravity: of punishment*)
  Härte *f*; (: *of manner, voice, winter*) Strenge *f*;
  (: *of weather*) Rauheit *f*, (*austerity*) Strenge *f.*
sew [səu] (*pt* **sewed**, *pp* **sewn**) *vt, vi* nähen.
►**sew up** *vt* (*zusammen*)nähen; **it is all** ~**n up**
  (*fig*) es ist unter Dach und Fach.
sewage ['su:ɪdʒ] *n* Abwasser *nt.*
sewage works *n* Kläranlage *f.*
sewer ['su:ə*] *n* Abwasserkanal *m.*

sewing ['səʊɪŋ] *n* Nähen *nt*; (*items*) Näharbeit *f*.
sewing machine *n* Nähmaschine *f*.
sewn [səʊn] *pp of* sew.
sex [sɛks] *n* (*gender*) Geschlecht *nt*; (*lovemaking*) Sex *m*; **to have ~ with sb** (Geschlechts)verkehr mit jdm haben.
sex act *n* Geschlechtsakt *m*.
sex appeal *n* Sex-Appeal *m*.
sex education *n* Sexualerziehung *f*.
sexism ['sɛksɪzəm] *n* Sexismus *m*.
sexist ['sɛksɪst] *adj* sexistisch.
sex life *n* Sexualleben *nt*.
sex object *n* Sexualobjekt *nt*.
sextet [sɛks'tɛt] *n* Sextett *nt*.
sexual ['sɛksjʊəl] *adj* sexuell; (*reproduction*) geschlechtlich; (*equality*) der Geschlechter.
sexual assault *n* Vergewaltigung *f*.
sexual harassment *n* sexuelle Belästigung *f*.
sexual intercourse *n* Geschlechtsverkehr *m*.
sexually ['sɛksjʊəlɪ] *adv* sexuell; (*segregate*) nach Geschlechtern; (*discriminate*) auf Grund des Geschlechts; (*reproduce*) geschlechtlich.
sexual orientation *n* sexuelle Orientierung *f*.
sexy ['sɛksɪ] *adj* sexy; (*pictures, underwear*) sexy, aufreizend.
Seychelles [seɪ'ʃɛl(z)] *npl*: **the ~** die Seychellen *pl*.
SF *n abbr* (= *science fiction*) SF.
SG (*US*) *n abbr* (*MIL, MED*) = **Surgeon General**.
Sgt *abbr* (*POLICE, MIL*) = **sergeant**.
shabbiness ['ʃæbɪnɪs] *n* Schäbigkeit *f*.
shabby ['ʃæbɪ] *adj* schäbig.
shack [ʃæk] *n* Hütte *f*.
▶**shack up** (*inf*) *vi*: **to ~ up (with sb)** (mit jdm) zusammenziehen.
shackles ['ʃæklz] *npl* Ketten *pl*; (*fig*) Fesseln *pl*.
shade [ʃeɪd] *n* Schatten *m*; (*for lamp*) (Lampen)schirm *m*; (*of colour*) (Farb)ton *m*; (*US: also:* **window ~**) Jalousie *f*, Rollo *nt* ♦ *vt* beschatten; (*eyes*) abschirmen; **shades** *npl* (*inf: sunglasses*) Sonnenbrille *f*; **in the ~** im Schatten; **a ~ of blue** ein Blauton; **a ~ (more/too large)** (*small quantity*) etwas *or* eine Spur (mehr/zu groß).
shadow ['ʃædəʊ] *n* Schatten *m* ♦ *vt* (*follow*) beschatten; **without** *or* **beyond a ~ of a doubt** ohne den geringsten Zweifel.
shadow cabinet (*BRIT*) *n* Schattenkabinett *nt*.
shadowy ['ʃædəʊɪ] *adj* schattig; (*figure, shape*) schattenhaft.
shady ['ʃeɪdɪ] *adj* schattig; (*fig: dishonest*) zwielichtig; **~ deals** dunkle Geschäfte.
shaft [ʃɑːft] *n* (*of arrow, spear*) Schaft *m*; (*AUT, TECH*) Welle *f*; (*of mine, lift*) Schacht *m*; (*of light*) Strahl *m*; **ventilation ~** Luftschacht *m*.
shaggy ['ʃægɪ] *adj* zottelig; (*dog, sheep*) struppig.
shake [ʃeɪk] (*pt* **shook**, *pp* **shaken**) *vt* schütteln;

(*weaken, upset, surprise*) erschüttern; (*weaken: resolve*) ins Wanken bringen ♦ *vi* zittern, beben; (*building, table*) wackeln; (*earth*) beben ♦ *n* Schütteln *nt*; **to ~ one's head** den Kopf schütteln; **to ~ hands with sb** jdm die Hand schütteln; **to ~ one's fist (at sb)** (jdm) mit der Faust drohen; **give it a good ~** schütteln Sie es gut durch; **a ~ of the head** ein Kopfschütteln.
▶**shake off** *vt* (*lit, fig*) abschütteln.
▶**shake up** *vt* schütteln; (*fig: upset*) erschüttern.
shake-out ['ʃeɪkaʊt] *n* Freisetzung *f* von Arbeitskräften.
shake-up ['ʃeɪkʌp] *n* (radikale) Veränderung *f*.
shakily ['ʃeɪkɪlɪ] *adv* (*reply*) mit zittriger Stimme; (*walk, stand*) unsicher, wackelig.
shaky ['ʃeɪkɪ] *adj* (*hand, voice*) zittrig; (*memory*) schwach; (*knowledge, prospects, future, start*) unsicher.
shale [ʃeɪl] *n* Schiefer *m*.
shall [ʃæl] *aux vb*: **I ~ go** ich werde gehen; **~ I open the door?** soll ich die Tür öffnen?; **I'll go, ~ I?** soll ich gehen?
shallot [ʃə'lɒt] (*BRIT*) *n* Schalotte *f*.
shallow ['ʃæləʊ] *adj* flach; (*fig*) oberflächlich; **the shallows** *npl* die Untiefen *pl*.
sham [ʃæm] *n* Heuchelei *f*; (*person*) Heuchler(in) *m(f)*; (*object*) Attrappe *f* ♦ *adj* unecht; (*fight*) Schein- ♦ *vt* vortäuschen.
shambles ['ʃæmblz] *n* heilloses Durcheinander *nt*; **the economy is (in) a complete ~** die Wirtschaft befindet sich in einem totalen Chaos.
shambolic [ʃæm'bɒlɪk] (*inf*) *adj* chaotisch.
shame [ʃeɪm] *n* Scham *f*; (*disgrace*) Schande *f* ♦ *vt* beschämen; **it is a ~ that ...** es ist eine Schande, daß ...; **what a ~!** wie schade!; **to bring ~ on** Schande bringen über +*acc*; **to put sb/sth to ~** jdn/etw in den Schatten stellen.
shamefaced ['ʃeɪmfeɪst] *adj* betreten.
shameful ['ʃeɪmfʊl] *adj* schändlich.
shameless ['ʃeɪmlɪs] *adj* schamlos.
shampoo [ʃæm'puː] *n* Shampoo(n) *nt* ♦ *vt* waschen.
shampoo and set *n* Waschen und Legen *nt*.
shamrock ['ʃæmrɒk] *n* (*plant*) Klee *m*; (*leaf*) Kleeblatt *nt*.
shandy ['ʃændɪ] *n* Bier *nt* mit Limonade, Radler *m*.
shan't [ʃɑːnt] = **shall not**.
shanty town ['ʃæntɪ-] *n* Elendsviertel *nt*.
SHAPE [ʃeɪp] *n abbr* (*MIL:* = *Supreme Headquarters Allied Powers, Europe*) *Hauptquartier der alliierten Streitkräfte in Europa während des 2. Weltkriegs*.
shape [ʃeɪp] *n* Form *f* ♦ *vt* gestalten; (*form*) formen; (*sb's ideas*) prägen; (*sb's life*) bestimmen; **to take ~** Gestalt annehmen; **in the ~ of a heart** in Herzform; **I can't bear**

gardening in any ~ or form ich kann
Gartenarbeit absolut nicht ausstehen; **to
get (o.s.) into** ~ in Form kommen.
▶**shape up** *vi* sich entwickeln.
-shaped [ʃeɪpt] *suff:* **heart-**~ herzförmig.
shapeless [ˈʃeɪplɪs] *adj* formlos.
shapely [ˈʃeɪplɪ] *adj* (*woman*) wohl-
proportioniert; (*legs*) wohlgeformt.
share [ʃɛəˈ] *n* (*part*) Anteil *m*; (*contribution*)
Teil *m*; (*COMM*) Aktie *f* ◆ *vt* teilen; (*room,
bed, taxi*) sich *dat* teilen; (*have in common*)
gemeinsam haben; **to** ~ **in** (*joy, sorrow*)
teilen; (*profits*) beteiligt sein an +*dat*; (*work*)
sich beteiligen an +*dat*.
▶**share out** *vt* aufteilen.
share capital *n* Aktienkapital *nt*.
share certificate *n* Aktienurkunde *f*.
shareholder [ˈʃɛəhəʊldəˈ] *n* Aktionär(in) *m(f)*.
share index *n* Aktienindex *m*; **the 100 Share
Index** *Aktienindex der Financial Times*.
share issue *n* Aktienemission *f*.
shark [ʃɑːk] *n* Hai(fisch) *m*.
sharp [ʃɑːp] *adj* scharf; (*point, nose, chin*)
spitz; (*pain*) heftig; (*cold*) schneidend; (*MUS*)
zu hoch; (*increase*) stark; (*person: quick-
witted*) clever; (: *dishonest*) gerissen ◆ *n*
(*MUS*) Kreuz *nt* ◆ *adv*: **at 2 o'clock** ~ um
Punkt 2 Uhr; **turn** ~ **left** biegen Sie scharf
nach links ab; **to be** ~ **with sb** schroff mit
jdm sein; ~ **practices** (*COMM*) unsaubere
Geschäfte *pl*; **C** ~ (*MUS*) Cis *nt*; **look** ~! (ein
bißchen) dalli! (*inf*).
sharpen [ˈʃɑːpn] *vt* schleifen, schärfen;
(*pencil, stick etc*) (an)spitzen; (*fig: appetite*)
anregen.
sharpener [ˈʃɑːpnəˈ] *n* (*also:* **pencil** ~)
(Bleistift)spitzer *m*; (*also:* **knife** ~)
Schleifgerät *nt*.
sharp-eyed [ʃɑːpˈaɪd] *adj* scharfsichtig.
sharpish [ˈʃɑːpɪʃ] (*inf*) *adj* (*instantly*) auf der
Stelle.
sharply [ˈʃɑːplɪ] *adv* scharf; (*stop*) plötzlich;
(*retort*) schroff.
sharp-tempered [ʃɑːpˈtɛmpəd] *adj* jähzornig.
sharp-witted [ʃɑːpˈwɪtɪd] *adj* scharfsinnig.
shatter [ˈʃætəˈ] *vt* zertrümmern; (*fig: hopes,
dreams*) zunichte machen; (: *confidence*)
zerstören ◆ *vi* zerbrechen, zerspringen.
shattered [ˈʃætəd] *adj* erschüttert; (*inf:
exhausted*) fertig, kaputt.
shattering [ˈʃætərɪŋ] *adj* erschütternd,
niederschmetternd; (*exhausting*) äußerst
anstrengend.
shatterproof [ˈʃætəpruːf] *adj* splitterfest,
splitterfrei.
shave [ʃeɪv] *vt* rasieren ◆ *vi* sich rasieren ◆ *n*:
to have a ~ sich rasieren.
shaven [ˈʃeɪvn] *adj* (*head*) kahlgeschoren.
shaver [ˈʃeɪvəˈ] *n* (*also:* **electric** ~)
Rasierapparat *m*.
shaving [ˈʃeɪvɪŋ] *n* Rasieren *nt*; **shavings** *npl*
(*of wood etc*) Späne *pl*.

shaving brush *n* Rasierpinsel *m*.
shaving cream *n* Rasiercreme *f*.
shaving foam *n* Rasierschaum *m*.
shaving point *n* Steckdose *f* für
Rasierapparate.
shaving soap *n* Rasierseife *f*.
shawl [ʃɔːl] *n* (Woll)tuch *nt*.
she [ʃiː] *pron* sie ◆ *pref* weiblich; ~-**bear** Bärin
f; **there** ~ **is** da ist sie.
sheaf [ʃiːf] (*pl* **sheaves**) *n* (*of corn*) Garbe *f*; (*of
papers*) Bündel *nt*.
shear [ʃɪəˈ] (*pt* **sheared**, *pp* **shorn**) *vt* scheren.
▶**shear off** *vi* abbrechen.
shears [ˈʃɪəz] *npl* (*for hedge*) Heckenschere *f*.
sheath [ʃiːθ] *n* (*of knife*) Scheide *f*;
(*contraceptive*) Kondom *nt*.
sheathe [ʃiːð] *vt* ummanteln; (*sword*) in die
Scheide stecken.
sheath knife *n* Fahrtenmesser *nt*.
sheaves [ʃiːvz] *npl of* **sheaf**.
shed [ʃɛd] (*pt, pp* **shed**) *n* Schuppen *m*;
(*INDUSTRY, RAIL*) Halle *f* ◆ *vt* (*tears, blood*)
vergießen; (*load*) verlieren; (*workers*)
entlassen; **to** ~ **its skin** sich häuten; **to**
~ **light on** (*problem*) erhellen.
she'd [ʃiːd] = **she had**; **she would**.
sheen [ʃiːn] *n* Glanz *m*.
sheep [ʃiːp] *n inv* Schaf *nt*.
sheepdog [ˈʃiːpdɒg] *n* Hütehund *m*.
sheep farmer *n* Schaffarmer *m*.
sheepish [ˈʃiːpɪʃ] *adj* verlegen.
sheepskin [ˈʃiːpskɪn] *n* Schaffell *nt* ◆ *cpd*
Schaffell-.
sheer [ʃɪəˈ] *adj* (*utter*) rein; (*steep*) steil;
(*almost transparent*) (hauch)dünn ◆ *adv*
(*straight up*) senkrecht; **by** ~ **chance** rein
zufällig.
sheet [ʃiːt] *n* (*on bed*) (Bett)laken *nt*; (*of paper*)
Blatt *nt*; (*of glass, metal*) Platte *f*; (*of ice*)
Fläche *f*.
sheet feed *n* (*on printer*) Papiereinzug *m*.
sheet lightning *n* Wetterleuchten *nt*.
sheet metal *n* Walzblech *nt*.
sheet music *n* Notenblätter *pl*.
sheik(h) [ʃeɪk] *n* Scheich *m*.
shelf [ʃɛlf] (*pl* **shelves**) *n* Brett *nt*, Bord *nt*; **set
of shelves** Regal *nt*.
shelf life *n* Lagerfähigkeit *f*.
shell [ʃɛl] *n* (*on beach*) Muschel *f*; (*of egg, nut
etc*) Schale *f*; (*explosive*) Granate *f*; (*of
building*) Mauern *pl* ◆ *vt* (*peas*) enthülsen;
(*MIL: fire on*) (mit Granaten) beschießen.
▶**shell out** (*inf*) *vt*: **to** ~ **out (for)** blechen
(für).
she'll [ʃiːl] = **she will**; **she shall**.
shellfish [ˈʃɛlfɪʃ] *n inv* Schalentier *nt*; (*scallop
etc*) Muschel *f*; (*as food*) Meeresfrüchte *pl*.
shelter [ˈʃɛltəˈ] *n* (*building*) Unterstand *m*;
(*refuge*) Schutz *m*; (*also:* **bus** ~)
Wartehäuschen *nt*; (*also:* **night** ~)
Obdachlosenasyl *nt* ◆ *vt* (*protect*) schützen;
(*homeless, refugees*) aufnehmen; (*wanted*

man) Unterschlupf gewähren +dat ♦ vi sich
unterstellen; (*from storm*) Schutz suchen; **to
take ~ (from)** (*from danger*) sich in
Sicherheit bringen (vor +dat); (*from storm
etc*) Schutz suchen (vor +dat).

sheltered ['ʃɛltəd] *adj* (*life*) behütet; (*spot*)
geschützt; **~ housing** (*for old people*)
Altenwohnungen *pl*; (*for handicapped people*)
Behindertenwohnungen *pl*.

shelve [ʃɛlv] *vt* (*fig: plan*) ad acta legen.

shelves [ʃɛlvz] *npl of* **shelf**.

shelving ['ʃɛlvɪŋ] *n* Regale *pl*.

shepherd ['ʃɛpəd] *n* Schäfer *m* ♦ *vt* (*guide*)
führen.

shepherdess ['ʃɛpədɪs] *n* Schäferin *f*.

shepherd's pie (*BRIT*) *n* Auflauf aus
Hackfleisch und Kartoffelbrei.

sherbet ['ʃəːbət] *n* (*BRIT: powder*) Brausepulver *nt*; (*US: water ice*) Fruchteis *nt*.

sheriff ['ʃɛrɪf] (*US*) *n* Sheriff *m*.

sherry ['ʃɛrɪ] *n* Sherry *m*.

she's [ʃiːz] = **she is; she has.**

Shetland ['ʃɛtlənd] *n* (*also:* **the ~ Islands**) die
Shetlandinseln *pl*.

Shetland pony *n* Shetlandpony *nt*.

shield [ʃiːld] *n* (*MIL*) Schild *m*; (*trophy*)
Trophäe *f*; (*fig: protection*) Schutz *m* ♦ *vt*: **to
~ (from)** schützen (vor +dat).

shift [ʃɪft] *n* (*change*) Änderung *f*; (*work-period,
workers*) Schicht *f* ♦ *vt* (*move*) bewegen;
(*furniture*) (ver)rücken; (*stain*)
herausbekommen ♦ *vi* (*move*) sich bewegen;
(*wind*) drehen; **a ~ in demand** (*COMM*) eine
Nachfrageverschiebung.

shift key *n* Umschalttaste *f*.

shiftless ['ʃɪftlɪs] *adj* träge.

shift work *n* Schichtarbeit *f*; **to do ~** Schicht
arbeiten.

shifty ['ʃɪftɪ] *adj* verschlagen.

Shiite ['ʃiːaɪt] *adj* schiitisch ♦ *n* Schiit(in) *m(f)*.

shilling ['ʃɪlɪŋ] (*BRIT: old*) *n* Shilling *m*.

shilly-shally ['ʃɪlɪʃælɪ] *vi* unschlüssig sein.

shimmer ['ʃɪmə] *vi* schimmern.

shimmering ['ʃɪmərɪŋ] *adj* schimmernd.

shin [ʃɪn] *n* Schienbein *nt* ♦ *vi*: **to ~ up a tree**
einen Baum hinaufklettern.

shindig ['ʃɪndɪɡ] (*inf*) *n* Remmidemmi *nt*.

shine [ʃaɪn] (*pt, pp* **shone**) *n* Glanz *m* ♦ *vi* (*sun,
light*) scheinen; (*eyes*) leuchten; (*hair, fig:
person*) glänzen ♦ *vt* (*polish: pt, pp* **shined**)
polieren; **to ~ a torch on sth** etw mit einer
Taschenlampe anleuchten.

shingle ['ʃɪŋɡl] *n* (*on beach*) Kiesel(steine) *pl*;
(*on roof*) Schindel *f*.

shingles ['ʃɪŋɡlz] *npl* (*MED*) Gürtelrose *f*.

shining ['ʃaɪnɪŋ] *adj* glänzend; (*example*)
leuchtend.

shiny ['ʃaɪnɪ] *adj* glänzend.

ship [ʃɪp] *n* Schiff *nt* ♦ *vt* verschiffen; (*send*)
versenden; (*water*) übernehmen; **on board ~**
an Bord.

shipbuilder ['ʃɪpbɪldə] *n* Schiffbauer *m*.

shipbuilding ['ʃɪpbɪldɪŋ] *n* Schiffbau *m*.

ship canal *n* Seekanal *m*.

ship chandler [-'tʃɑːndlə] *n* Schiffsausrüster
m.

shipment ['ʃɪpmənt] *n* (*of goods*) Versand *m*;
(*amount*) Sendung *f*.

shipowner ['ʃɪpəʊnə] *n* Schiffseigner *m*; (*of
many ships*) Reeder *m*.

shipper ['ʃɪpə] *n* (*person*) Spediteur *m*;
(*company*) Spedition *f*.

shipping ['ʃɪpɪŋ] *n* (*transport*) Versand *m*;
(*ships*) Schiffe *pl*.

shipping agent *n* Reeder *m*.

shipping company *n* Schiffahrtslinie *f*,
Reederei *f*.

shipping lane *n* Schiffahrtsstraße *f*.

shipping line *n* = **shipping company**.

shipshape ['ʃɪpʃeɪp] *adj* tipptopp (*inf*).

shipwreck ['ʃɪprɛk] *n* Schiffbruch *m*; (*ship*)
Wrack *nt* ♦ *vt*: **to be ~ed** schiffbrüchig sein.

shipyard ['ʃɪpjɑːd] *n* Werft *f*.

shire ['ʃaɪə] (*BRIT*) *n* Grafschaft *f*.

shirk [ʃəːk] *vt* sich drücken vor +dat.

shirt [ʃəːt] *n* (*Ober*)hemd *nt*; (*woman's*)
(Hemd)bluse *f*; **in (one's) ~ sleeves** in
Hemdsärmeln.

shirty ['ʃəːtɪ] (*BRIT: inf*) *adj* sauer (*inf*).

shit [ʃɪt] (*inf!*) *excl* Scheiße! (*!*)

shiver ['ʃɪvə] *n* Schauer *m* ♦ *vi* zittern; **to
~ with cold** vor Kälte zittern.

shoal [ʃəʊl] *n* (*of fish*) Schwarm *m*; (*also:* **~s,**
fig) Scharen *pl*.

shock [ʃɔk] *n* Schock *m*; (*impact*)
Erschütterung *f*; (*also:* **electric ~**) Schlag *m*
♦ *vt* (*upset*) erschüttern; (*offend*)
schockieren; **to be suffering from ~** (*MED*)
einen Schock haben; **to be in ~** unter
Schock stehen; **it gave us a ~** es hat uns
erschreckt; **it came as a ~ to hear that ...**
wir hörten mit Bestürzung, daß ...

shock absorber *n* (*AUT*) Stoßdämpfer *m*.

shocker ['ʃɔkə] (*inf*) *n* (*film etc*) Schocker *m*,
Reißer *m*; **that's a real ~** (*event etc*) das haut
einen echt um.

shocking ['ʃɔkɪŋ] *adj* schrecklich,
fürchterlich; (*outrageous*) schockierend.

shockproof ['ʃɔkpruːf] *adj* stoßfest.

shock therapy *n* Schocktherapie *f*.

shock treatment *n* = **shock therapy**.

shock wave *n* (*lit*) Druckwelle *f*; (*fig*)
Schockwelle *f*.

shod [ʃɔd] *pt, pp of* **shoe**.

shoddy ['ʃɔdɪ] *adj* minderwertig.

shoe [ʃuː] (*pt, pp* **shod**) *n* Schuh *m*; (*for horse*)
Hufeisen *nt*; (*also:* **brake ~**) Bremsbacke *f*
♦ *vt* (*horse*) beschlagen.

shoebrush ['ʃuːbrʌʃ] *n* Schuhbürste *f*.

shoehorn ['ʃuːhɔːn] *n* Schuhanzieher *m*.

shoelace ['ʃuːleɪs] *n* Schnürsenkel *m*.

shoemaker ['ʃuːmeɪkə] *n* Schuhmacher *m*,
Schuster *m*.

shoe polish *n* Schuhcreme *f*.

shoe shop n Schuhgeschäft nt.
shoestring ['ʃuːstrɪŋ] n (fig): **on a ~** mit ganz wenig Geld.
shoetree ['ʃuːtriː] n Schuhspanner m.
shone [ʃɒn] pt, pp of **shine**.
shoo [ʃuː] excl (to dog etc) pfui ♦ vt (also: **~ away, ~ off,** etc) verscheuchen; (somewhere) scheuchen.
shook [ʃuk] pt of **shake**.
shoot [ʃuːt] (pt, pp **shot**) n (on branch) Trieb m; (seedling) Sämling m; (SPORT) Jagd f ♦ vt (gun) abfeuern; (arrow, goal) schießen; (kill, execute) erschießen; (wound) anschießen; (BRIT: game birds) schießen; (film) drehen ♦ vi: **to ~ (at)** schießen (auf +acc); **to ~ past** (sb/sth) (an jdm/etw) vorbeischießen.
►**shoot down** vt abschießen.
►**shoot in** vi hereingeschossen kommen.
►**shoot out (of)** vi herausgeschossen kommen (aus +dat).
►**shoot up** vi (fig: increase) in die Höhe schnellen.
shooting ['ʃuːtɪŋ] n Schießen nt, Schüsse pl; (attack) Schießerei f; (murder) Erschießung f; (CINE) Drehen nt; (HUNTING) Jagen nt.
shooting range n Schießplatz m.
shooting star n Sternschnuppe f.
shop [ʃɒp] n Geschäft nt, Laden m; (workshop) Werkstatt f ♦ vi (also: **go ~ping**) einkaufen (gehen); **repair ~** Reparaturwerkstatt f; **to talk ~** (fig) über die Arbeit reden.
►**shop around** vi Preise vergleichen; (fig) sich umsehen.
shopaholic ['ʃɒpə'hɒlɪk] (inf) n: **to be a ~** einen Einkaufsfimmel haben.
shop assistant (BRIT) n Verkäufer(in) m(f).
shop floor (BRIT) n (workers) Arbeiter pl; **on the ~** bei or unter den Arbeitern.
shopkeeper ['ʃɒpkiːpə*] n Geschäfts- inhaber(in) m(f), Ladenbesitzer(in) m(f).
shoplifter ['ʃɒplɪftə*] n Ladendieb(in) m(f).
shoplifting ['ʃɒplɪftɪŋ] n Ladendiebstahl m.
shopper ['ʃɒpə*] n Käufer(in) m(f).
shopping ['ʃɒpɪŋ] n (goods) Einkäufe pl.
shopping bag n Einkaufstasche f.
shopping centre, (US) **shopping center** n Einkaufszentrum nt.
shopping mall n Shopping-Center nt.
shop-soiled ['ʃɒpsɔɪld] adj angeschmutzt.
shop steward (BRIT) n gewerkschaftlicher Vertrauensmann m.
shop window n Schaufenster nt.
shore [ʃɔː*] n Ufer nt; (beach) Strand m ♦ vt: **to ~ (up)** abstützen; **on ~** an Land.
shore leave n (NAUT) Landurlaub m.
shorn [ʃɔːn] pp of **shear**; **to be ~ of** (power etc) entkleidet sein +gen.
short [ʃɔːt] adj kurz; (person) klein; (curt) schroff, kurz angebunden (inf); (scarce) knapp ♦ n (also: **~ film**) Kurzfilm m; **to be ~ of ...** zuwenig ... haben; **I'm 3 ~** ich habe 3 zu wenig, mir fehlen 3; **in ~** kurz gesagt; **to**

be in ~ supply knapp sein; **it is ~ for ...** es ist die Kurzform von ...; **a ~ time ago** vor kurzem; **in the ~ term** auf kurze Sicht; **~ of doing sth** außer etw zu tun; **to cut ~** abbrechen; **everything ~ of ...** alles außer ... +dat; **to fall ~ of sth** etw nicht erreichen; (expectations) etw nicht erfüllen; **to run ~ of** ... nicht mehr viel ... haben; **to stop ~** plötzlich innehalten; **to stop ~ of** haltmachen vor +dat; see also **shorts**.
shortage ['ʃɔːtɪdʒ] n: **a ~ of** ein Mangel m an +dat.
shortbread ['ʃɔːtbrɛd] n Mürbegebäck nt.
short-change [ʃɔːt'tʃeɪndʒ] vt: **to ~ sb** jdm zuwenig Wechselgeld geben.
short circuit n Kurzschluß m.
shortcoming ['ʃɔːtkʌmɪŋ] n Fehler m, Mangel m.
shortcrust pastry (BRIT) n Mürbeteig m.
short cut n Abkürzung f; (fig) Schnellverfahren nt.
shorten ['ʃɔːtn] vt verkürzen.
shortening ['ʃɔːtnɪŋ] n (Back)fett nt.
shortfall ['ʃɔːtfɔːl] n Defizit nt.
shorthand ['ʃɔːthænd] n Kurzschrift f, Stenographie f; (fig) Kurzform f; **to take sth down in ~** etw stenographieren.
shorthand notebook (BRIT) n Stenoblock m.
shorthand typist (BRIT) n Stenotypist(in) m(f).
short list (BRIT) n Auswahlliste f; **to be on the ~** in der engeren Wahl sein.
short-list ['ʃɔːtlɪst] (BRIT) vt in die engere Wahl ziehen; **to be ~ed** in die engere Wahl kommen.
short-lived ['ʃɔːt'lɪvd] adj kurzlebig; **to be ~** nicht von Dauer sein.
shortly ['ʃɔːtlɪ] adv bald.
shorts [ʃɔːts] npl: **(a pair of) ~** Shorts pl.
short-sighted [ʃɔːt'saɪtɪd] (BRIT) adj (lit, fig) kurzsichtig.
short-sightedness [ʃɔːt'saɪtɪdnɪs] n Kurzsichtigkeit f.
short-staffed [ʃɔːt'stɑːft] adj: **to be ~** zuwenig Personal haben.
short story n Kurzgeschichte f.
short-tempered [ʃɔːt'tɛmpəd] adj gereizt.
short-term ['ʃɔːttɜːm] adj kurzfristig.
short time n: **to work ~, to be on ~** kurzarbeiten, Kurzarbeit haben.
short-wave ['ʃɔːtweɪv] (RADIO) adj auf Kurzwelle ♦ n Kurzwelle f.
shot [ʃɒt] pt, pp of **shoot** ♦ n Schuß m; (shotgun pellets) Schrot m; (injection) Spritze f; (PHOT) Aufnahme f; **to fire a ~ at sb/sth** einen Schuß auf jdn/etw abgeben; **to have a ~ at (doing) sth** etw mal versuchen; **to get ~ of sb/sth** (inf) jdn/etw loswerden; **a big ~** (inf) ein hohes Tier; **a good/poor ~** (person) ein guter/schlechter Schütze; **like a ~** sofort.
shotgun ['ʃɒtgʌn] n Schrotflinte f.
should [ʃud] aux vb: **I ~ go now** ich sollte jetzt

gehen; **he ~ be there now** er müßte eigentlich schon da sein; **I ~ go if I were you** an deiner Stelle würde ich gehen; **I ~ like to** ich möchte gerne, ich würde gerne; **~ he phone ...** falls er anruft ...

shoulder ['ʃəuldə*] n Schulter f ♦ vt (fig) auf sich acc nehmen; **to rub ~s with sb** (fig) mit jdm in Berührung kommen; **to give sb the cold ~** (fig) jdm die kalte Schulter zeigen.

shoulder bag n Umhängetasche f.

shoulder blade n Schulterblatt nt.

shoulder strap n (on clothing) Träger m; (on bag) Schulterriemen m.

shouldn't ['ʃudnt] = should not.

shout [ʃaut] n Schrei m, Ruf m ♦ vt schreien, rufen ♦ vi (also: ~ out) aufschreien; **to give sb a ~** jdn rufen.

▶**shout down** vt niederbrüllen.

shouting ['ʃautɪŋ] n Geschrei nt.

shouting match (inf) n: **to have a ~** sich gegenseitig anschreien.

shove [ʃʌv] vt schieben; (with one push) stoßen, schubsen (inf) ♦ n: **to give sb a ~** jdn stoßen or schubsen (inf); **to give sth a ~** etw verrücken; (door) gegen etw stoßen; **to ~ sth in sth** (inf: put) etw in etw acc stecken; **he ~d me out of the way** er stieß mich zur Seite.

▶**shove off** (inf) vi abschieben.

shovel ['ʃʌvl] n Schaufel f; (mechanical) Bagger m ♦ vt schaufeln.

show [ʃəu] (pt showed, pp shown) n (exhibition) Ausstellung f, Schau f; (THEAT) Aufführung f; (TV) Show f; (CINE) Vorstellung f ♦ vt zeigen; (exhibit) ausstellen ♦ vi: **it ~s** man sieht es; (is evident) man merkt es; **to ask for a ~ of hands** um Handzeichen bitten; **without any ~ of emotion** ohne jede Gefühlsregung; **it's just for ~** es ist nur zur Schau; **on ~** ausgestellt, zu sehen; **who's running the ~ here?** (inf) wer ist hier verantwortlich?; **to ~ sb to his seat/the door** jdn an seinen Platz/zur Tür bringen; **to ~ a profit/loss** Gewinn/Verlust aufweisen; **it just goes to ~ that ...** da sieht man's mal wieder, daß ...

▶**show in** vt hereinführen.

▶**show off** (pej) vi angeben ♦ vt vorführen.

▶**show out** vt hinausbegleiten.

▶**show up** vi (stand out) sich abheben; (inf: turn up) auftauchen ♦ vt (uncover) deutlich erkennen lassen; (shame) blamieren.

show biz n = show business.

show business n Showgeschäft nt.

showcase ['ʃəukeɪs] n Schaukasten m; (fig) Werbung f.

showdown ['ʃəudaun] n Kraftprobe f.

shower ['ʃauə*] n (of rain) Schauer m; (of stones etc) Hagel m; (for bathing in) Dusche f; (US: party) Party, bei der jeder ein Geschenk für den Ehrengast mitbringt ♦ vi duschen ♦ vt: **to ~ sb with** (gifts etc) jdn

überschütten mit; (missiles, abuse etc) auf jdn niederhageln lassen; **to have or take a ~** duschen; **a ~ of sparks** ein Funkenregen.

showercap ['ʃauəkæp] n Duschhaube f.

showerproof ['ʃauəpru:f] adj regenfest.

showery ['ʃauərɪ] adj regnerisch.

showground ['ʃəugraund] n Ausstellungsgelände nt.

showing ['ʃəuɪŋ] n (of film) Vorführung f.

show jumping n Springreiten nt.

showman ['ʃəumən] (irreg: like man) n (at fair) Schausteller m; (at circus) Artist m; (fig) Schauspieler m.

showmanship ['ʃəumənʃɪp] n Talent nt für effektvolle Darbietung.

shown [ʃəun] pp of show.

show-off ['ʃəuɔf] (inf) n Angeber(in) m(f).

showpiece ['ʃəupi:s] n (of exhibition etc) Schaustück nt; (best example) Paradestück nt; (prime example) Musterbeispiel nt.

showroom ['ʃəurum] n Ausstellungsraum m.

show trial n Schauprozeß m.

showy ['ʃəuɪ] adj auffallend.

shrank [ʃræŋk] pt of shrink.

shrapnel ['ʃræpnl] n Schrapnell nt.

shred [ʃred] n (gen pl) Fetzen m; (fig): **not a ~ of truth** kein Fünkchen Wahrheit; **not a ~ of evidence** keine Spur eines Beweises ♦ vt zerfetzen; (CULIN) raspeln.

shredder ['ʃredə*] n (vegetable shredder) Raspel f; (document shredder) Reißwolf m; (garden shredder) Häcksler m.

shrew [ʃru:] n (ZOOL) Spitzmaus f; (pej: woman) Xanthippe f.

shrewd [ʃru:d] adj klug.

shrewdness ['ʃru:dnɪs] n Klugheit f.

shriek [ʃri:k] n schriller Schrei m ♦ vi schreien; **to ~ with laughter** vor Lachen quietschen.

shrift [ʃrɪft] n: **to give sb short ~** jdn kurz abfertigen.

shrill [ʃrɪl] adj schrill.

shrimp [ʃrɪmp] n Garnele f.

shrine [ʃraɪn] n Schrein m; (fig) Gedenkstätte f.

shrink [ʃrɪŋk] (pt shrank, pp shrunk) vi (cloth) einlaufen; (profits, audiences) schrumpfen; (forests) schwinden; (also: ~ away) zurückweichen ♦ vt (cloth) einlaufen lassen ♦ n (inf: pej) Klapsdoktor m; **to ~ from sth** vor etw dat zurückschrecken; **to ~ from doing sth** davor zurückschrecken, etw zu tun.

shrinkage ['ʃrɪŋkɪdʒ] n (of clothes) Einlaufen nt.

shrink-wrap ['ʃrɪŋkræp] vt einschweißen.

shrivel ['ʃrɪvl] (also: ~ up) vt austrocknen ♦ vi austrocknen, verschrumpeln.

shroud [ʃraud] n Leichentuch nt ♦ vt: **~ed in mystery** von einem Geheimnis umgeben.

Shrove Tuesday ['ʃrəuv-] n Fastnachtsdienstag m.

shrub [ʃrʌb] n Strauch m, Busch m.
shrubbery ['ʃrʌbərɪ] n Gebüsch nt.
shrug [ʃrʌg] n: ~ **(of the shoulders)**
Achselzucken nt ♦ vi, vt: **to ~ (one's
shoulders)** mit den Achseln zucken.
►**shrug off** vt (criticism) auf die leichte
Schulter nehmen; (illness) abschütteln.
shrunk [ʃrʌŋk] pp of **shrink.**
shrunken ['ʃrʌŋkn] adj (ein)geschrumpft.
shudder ['ʃʌdə'] n Schauder m ♦ vi schaudern;
I ~ to think of it (fig) mir graut, wenn ich
nur daran denke.
shuffle ['ʃʌfl] vt (cards) mischen ♦ vi
schlurfen; **to ~ (one's feet)** mit den Füßen
scharren.
shun [ʃʌn] vt meiden; (publicity) scheuen.
shunt [ʃʌnt] vt rangieren.
shunting yard ['ʃʌntɪŋ-] n Rangierbahnhof m.
shush [ʃuʃ] excl pst!, sch!
shut [ʃʌt] (pt, pp shut) vt schließen, zumachen
(inf) ♦ vi sich schließen, zugehen; (shop)
schließen, zumachen (inf).
►**shut down** vt (factory etc) schließen;
(machine) abschalten ♦ vi schließen,
zumachen (inf).
►**shut off** vt (gas, electricity) abstellen; (oil
supplies etc) abschneiden.
►**shut out** vt (person) aussperren; (cold,
noise) nicht hereinlassen; (view)
versperren; (memory, thought) verdrängen.
►**shut up** vi (inf: keep quiet) den Mund halten
♦ vt (silence) zum Schweigen bringen.
shutdown ['ʃʌtdaun] n Schließung f.
shutter ['ʃʌtə'] n Fensterladen m; (PHOT)
Verschluß m.
shuttle ['ʃʌtl] n (plane) Pendelflugzeug nt;
(train) Pendelzug m; (space shuttle)
Raumtransporter m; (also: ~ service)
Pendelverkehr m; (for weaving) Schiffchen
nt ♦ vi: **to ~ to and fro** pendeln; **to
~ between** pendeln zwischen ♦ vt
(passengers) transportieren.
shuttlecock ['ʃʌtlkɔk] n Federball m.
shuttle diplomacy n Reisediplomatie f.
shy [ʃaɪ] adj schüchtern; (animal) scheu ♦ vi: **to
~ away from doing sth** (fig) davor
zurückschrecken, etw zu tun; **to fight ~ of**
aus dem Weg gehen +dat; **to be ~ of doing
sth** Hemmungen haben, etw zu tun.
shyly ['ʃaɪlɪ] adv schüchtern, scheu.
shyness ['ʃaɪnɪs] n Schüchternheit f, Scheu f.
Siam [saɪ'æm] n Siam nt.
Siamese [saɪə'miːz] adj: ~ **cat** Siamkatze f;
~ **twins** siamesische Zwillinge pl.
Siberia [saɪ'bɪərɪə] n Sibirien nt.
sibling ['sɪblɪŋ] n Geschwister nt.
Sicilian [sɪ'sɪlɪən] adj sizilianisch ♦ n
Sizilianer(in) m(f).
Sicily ['sɪsɪlɪ] n Sizilien nt.
sick [sɪk] adj krank; (humour, joke) makaber;
to be ~ (vomit) brechen, sich übergeben; **I
feel ~** mir ist schlecht; **to fall ~** krank

werden; **to be (off)** ~ wegen Krankheit
fehlen; **a ~ person** ein Kranker, eine
Kranke; **to be ~ of** (fig) satt haben +acc.
sickbag ['sɪkbæg] n Spucktüte f.
sickbay ['sɪkbeɪ] n Krankenrevier nt.
sickbed ['sɪkbɛd] n Krankenbett nt.
sick building syndrome n Kopfschmerzen,
Allergien etc, die in modernen,
vollklimatisierten Bürogebäuden
entstehen.
sicken ['sɪkn] vt (disgust) anwidern ♦ vi: **to be
~ing for a cold/flu** eine Erkältung/Grippe
bekommen.
sickening ['sɪknɪŋ] adj (fig) widerlich,
ekelhaft.
sickle ['sɪkl] n Sichel f.
sick leave n: **to be on ~** krank geschrieben
sein.
sickle-cell anaemia n Sichelzellenanämie f.
sick list n: **to be on the ~** auf der
Krankenliste stehen.
sickly ['sɪklɪ] adj kränklich; (causing nausea)
widerlich, ekelhaft.
sickness ['sɪknɪs] n Krankheit f; (vomiting)
Erbrechen nt.
sickness benefit n Krankengeld nt.
sick note n Krankmeldung f.
sick pay n Lohnfortzahlung f im
Krankheitsfall; (paid by insurance)
Krankengeld nt.
sickroom ['sɪkruːm] n Krankenzimmer nt.
side [saɪd] n Seite f; (team) Mannschaft f; (in
conflict etc) Partei f, Seite f; (of hill) Hang m
♦ adj (door, entrance) Seiten-, Neben- ♦ vi: **to
~ with sb** jds Partei ergreifen; **by the ~ of**
neben +dat; ~ **by** ~ Seite an Seite; **the right/
wrong ~** (of cloth) die rechte/linke Seite;
they are on our ~ sie stehen auf unserer
Seite; **she never left my ~** sie wich mir
nicht von der Seite; **to put sth to one ~** etw
beiseite legen; **from ~ to ~** von einer Seite
zur anderen; **to take ~s (with)** Partei
ergreifen (für); **a ~ of beef** ein halbes Rind;
a ~ of bacon eine Speckseite.
sideboard ['saɪdbɔːd] n Sideboard nt;
sideboards (BRIT) npl = **sideburns.**
sideburns ['saɪdbəːnz] npl Koteletten pl.
sidecar ['saɪdkɑː'] n Beiwagen m.
side dish n Beilage f.
side drum n kleine Trommel f.
side effect n (MED, fig) Nebenwirkung f.
sidekick ['saɪdkɪk] (inf) n Handlanger m.
sidelight ['saɪdlaɪt] n (AUT)
Begrenzungsleuchte f.
sideline ['saɪdlaɪn] n (SPORT) Seitenlinie f; (fig:
job) Nebenerwerb m; **to stand on the ~s**
(fig) unbeteiligter Zuschauer sein; **to wait
on the ~s** (fig) in den Kulissen warten.
sidelong ['saɪdlɔŋ] adj (glance) Seiten-;
(: surreptitious) verstohlen; **to give sb a
~ glance** jdn kurz aus den Augenwinkeln
ansehen.

side plate *n* kleiner Teller *m*.

side road *n* Nebenstraße *f*.

side-saddle ['saɪdsædl] *adv* (*ride*) im Damensitz.

sideshow ['saɪdʃəu] *n* Nebenattraktion *f*.

sidestep ['saɪdstɛp] *vt* (*problem*) umgehen; (*question*) ausweichen +*dat* ♦ *vi* (*BOXING etc*) seitwärts ausweichen.

side street *n* Seitenstraße *f*.

sidetrack ['saɪdtræk] *vt* (*fig*) ablenken.

sidewalk ['saɪdwɔːk] (*US*) *n* Bürgersteig *m*.

sideways ['saɪdweɪz] *adv* seitwärts; (*lean, look*) zur Seite.

siding ['saɪdɪŋ] *n* Abstellgleis *nt*.

sidle ['saɪdl] *vi:* **to ~ up (to)** sich heranschleichen (an +*acc*).

SIDS *n abbr* (*MED: = sudden infant death syndrome*) plötzlicher Kindstod *m*.

siege [siːdʒ] *n* Belagerung *f*; **to be under ~** belagert sein; **to lay ~ to** belagern.

siege economy *n* Belagerungswirtschaft *f*.

siege mentality *n* Belagerungsmentalität *f*.

Sierra Leone [sɪˈɛrəlɪˈəun] *n* Sierra Leone *f*.

siesta [sɪˈɛstə] *n* Siesta *f*.

sieve [sɪv] *n* Sieb *nt* ♦ *vt* sieben.

sift [sɪft] *vt* sieben; (*also:* **~ through**) durchgehen.

sigh [saɪ] *n* Seufzer *m* ♦ *vi* seufzen; **to breathe a ~ of relief** erleichtert aufseufzen.

sight [saɪt] *n* (*faculty*) Sehvermögen *nt*, Augenlicht *nt*; (*spectacle*) Anblick *m*; (*on gun*) Visier *nt* ♦ *vt* sichten; **in ~** in Sicht; **on ~** (*shoot*) sofort; **out of ~** außer Sicht; **at ~** (*COMM*) bei Sicht; **at first ~** auf den ersten Blick; **I know her by ~** ich kenne sie vom Sehen; **to catch ~ of sb/sth** jdn/etw sehen; **to lose ~ of sth** (*fig*) etw aus den Augen verlieren; **to set one's ~s on sth** ein Auge auf etw werfen.

sighted ['saɪtɪd] *adj* sehend; **partially ~** sehbehindert.

sightseeing ['saɪtsiːɪŋ] *n* Besichtigungen *pl*; **to go ~** auf Besichtigungstour gehen.

sightseer ['saɪtsiːə*] *n* Tourist(in) *m(f)*.

sign [saɪn] *n* Zeichen *nt*; (*notice*) Schild *nt*; (*evidence*) Anzeichen *nt*; (*also:* **road ~**) Verkehrsschild *nt* ♦ *vt* unterschreiben; (*player*) verpflichten; **a ~ of the times** ein Zeichen unserer Zeit; **it's a good/bad ~** es ist ein gutes/schlechtes Zeichen; **plus/minus ~** Plus-/Minuszeichen *nt*; **there's no ~ of her changing her mind** nichts deutet darauf hin, daß sie es sich anders überlegen wird; **he was showing ~s of improvement** er ließ Anzeichen einer Verbesserung erkennen; **to ~ one's name** unterschreiben; **to ~ sth over to sb** jdm etw überschreiben.

▶**sign away** *vt* (*rights etc*) verzichten auf +*acc*.

▶**sign in** *vi* sich eintragen.

▶**sign off** *vi* (*RADIO, TV*) sich verabschieden; (*in letter*) Schluß machen.

▶**sign on** *vi* (*MIL*) sich verpflichten; (*BRIT: as unemployed*) sich arbeitslos melden; (*for course*) sich einschreiben ♦ *vt* (*MIL*) verpflichten; (*employee*) anstellen.

▶**sign out** *vi* (*from hotel etc*) sich (aus dem Hotelgästebuch *etc*) austragen.

▶**sign up** *vi* (*MIL*) sich verpflichten; (*for course*) sich einschreiben ♦ *vt* (*player, recruit*) verpflichten.

signal ['sɪgnl] *n* Zeichen *nt*; (*RAIL*) Signal *nt* ♦ *vi* (*AUT*) Zeichen/ein Zeichen geben ♦ *vt* ein Zeichen geben +*dat*; **to ~ a right/left turn** (*AUT*) rechts/links blinken.

signal box *n* Stellwerk *nt*.

signalman ['sɪgnlmən] (*irreg: like* **man**) *n* Stellwerkswärter *m*.

signatory ['sɪgnətərɪ] *n* Unterzeichner *m*; (*state*) Signatarstaat *m*.

signature ['sɪgnətʃə*] *n* Unterschrift *f*; (*ZOOL, BIOL*) Kennzeichen *nt*.

signature tune *n* Erkennungsmelodie *f*.

signet ring ['sɪgnət-] *n* Siegelring *m*.

significance [sɪgˈnɪfɪkəns] *n* Bedeutung *f*; **that is of no ~** das ist belanglos *or* bedeutungslos.

significant [sɪgˈnɪfɪkənt] *adj* bedeutend, wichtig; (*look, smile*) vielsagend, bedeutsam; **it is ~ that ...** es ist bezeichnend, daß ...

significantly [sɪgˈnɪfɪkəntlɪ] *adv* bedeutend; (*smile*) vielsagend, bedeutsam.

signify ['sɪgnɪfaɪ] *vt* bedeuten; (*person*) zu erkennen geben.

sign language *n* Zeichensprache *f*.

signpost ['saɪnpəust] *n* (*lit, fig*) Wegweiser *m*.

Sikh [siːk] *n* Sikh *mf* ♦ *adj* (*province etc*) Sikh-.

silage ['saɪlɪdʒ] *n* Silage *f*, Silofutter *nt*.

silence ['saɪləns] *n* Stille *f*; (*of person*) Schweigen *nt* ♦ *vt* zum Schweigen bringen; **in ~** still; (*not talking*) schweigend.

silencer ['saɪlənsə*] *n* (*on gun*) Schalldämpfer *m*; (*BRIT: AUT*) Auspufftopf *m*.

silent ['saɪlənt] *adj* still; (*machine*) ruhig; **~ film** Stummfilm *m*; **to remain ~** still bleiben; (*about sth*) sich nicht äußern.

silently ['saɪləntlɪ] *adv* lautlos; (*not talking*) schweigend.

silent partner *n* stiller Teilhaber *m*.

silhouette [sɪluːˈɛt] *n* Silhouette *f*, Umriß *m* ♦ *vt:* **to be ~d against sth** sich als Silhouette gegen etw abheben.

silicon ['sɪlɪkən] *n* Silizium *nt*.

silicon chip *n* Silikonchip *m*.

silicone ['sɪlɪkəun] *n* Silikon *nt*.

Silicon Valley *n* Silicon Valley *nt*.

silk [sɪlk] *n* Seide *f* ♦ *adj* (*dress etc*) Seiden-.

silky ['sɪlkɪ] *adj* seidig.

sill [sɪl] *n* (*also:* **window ~**) (Fenster)sims *m or nt*; (*of door*) Schwelle *f*; (*AUT*) Türleiste *f*.

silly ['sɪlɪ] *adj* (*person*) dumm; **to do something ~** etwas Dummes tun.

silo ['saɪləu] *n* Silo *nt*; (*for missile*) Raketensilo nt.

silt [sɪlt] n Schlamm m, Schlick m.
▶**silt up** vi verschlammen ♦ vt
verschlämmen.
silver ['sɪlvə*] n Silber nt; (coins) Silbergeld nt
♦ adj silbern.
silver foil (BRIT) n Alufolie f.
silver paper (BRIT) n Silberpapier nt.
silver-plated [sɪlvə'pleɪtɪd] adj versilbert.
silversmith ['sɪlvəsmɪθ] n Silberschmied(in)
m(f).
silverware ['sɪlvəwɛə*] n Silber nt.
silver wedding (anniversary) n
Silberhochzeit f.
silvery ['sɪlvrɪ] adj silbern; (sound) silberhell.
similar ['sɪmɪlə*] adj: ~ (to) ähnlich (wie or
+dat).
similarity [sɪmɪ'lærɪtɪ] n Ähnlichkeit f.
similarly ['sɪmɪləlɪ] adv ähnlich; (likewise)
genauso.
simile ['sɪmɪlɪ] n (LING) Vergleich m.
simmer ['sɪmə*] vi auf kleiner Flamme
kochen.
▶**simmer down** (inf) vi (fig) sich abregen.
simper ['sɪmpə*] vi geziert lächeln.
simpering ['sɪmprɪŋ] adj geziert.
simple ['sɪmpl] adj einfach; (dress) einfach,
schlicht; (foolish) einfältig; **the ~ truth is
that** ... es ist einfach so, daß ...
simple interest n Kapitalzinsen pl.
simple-minded [sɪmpl'maɪndɪd] (pej) adj
einfältig.
simpleton ['sɪmpltən] (pej) n Einfaltspinsel m.
simplicity [sɪm'plɪsɪtɪ] n Einfachheit f; (of
dress) Schlichtheit f.
simplification [sɪmplɪfɪ'keɪʃən] n
Vereinfachung f.
simplify ['sɪmplɪfaɪ] vt vereinfachen.
simply ['sɪmplɪ] adv (just, merely) nur, bloß; (in
a simple way) einfach.
simulate ['sɪmjuleɪt] vt vortäuschen, spielen;
(illness) simulieren.
simulated ['sɪmjuleɪtɪd] adj (hair, fur) imitiert;
(TECH) simuliert.
simulation [sɪmju'leɪʃən] n Vortäuschung f;
(simulated object) Imitation f; (TECH)
Simulation f.
simultaneous [sɪməl'teɪnɪəs] adj gleichzeitig;
(translation, interpreting) Simultan-.
simultaneously [sɪməl'teɪnɪəslɪ] adv
gleichzeitig.
sin [sɪn] n Sünde f ♦ vi sündigen.
Sinai ['saɪneɪaɪ] n Sinai m.
since [sɪns] adv inzwischen, seitdem ♦ prep seit
♦ conj (time) seit(dem); (because) da; ~ **then,
ever** ~ seitdem.
sincere [sɪn'sɪə*] adj aufrichtig, offen;
(apology, belief) aufrichtig.
sincerely [sɪn'sɪəlɪ] adv aufrichtig, offen;
yours ~ (in letter) mit freundlichen Grüßen.
sincerity [sɪn'sɛrɪtɪ] n Aufrichtigkeit f.
sine [saɪn] n Sinus m.

sine qua non [sɪnɪkwɑː'nɔn] n unerläßliche
Voraussetzung f.
sinew ['sɪnjuː] n Sehne f.
sinful ['sɪnful] adj sündig, sündhaft.
sing [sɪŋ] (pt **sang**, pp **sung**) vt, vi singen.
Singapore [sɪŋgə'pɔː*] n Singapur nt.
singe [sɪndʒ] vt versengen; (lightly) ansengen.
singer ['sɪŋə*] n Sänger(in) m(f).
Singhalese [sɪŋə'liːz] adj = **Sinhalese**.
singing ['sɪŋɪŋ] n Singen nt, Gesang m; **a ~ in
the ears** ein Dröhnen in den Ohren.
single ['sɪŋgl] adj (solitary) einzige(r, s);
(individual) einzeln; (unmarried) ledig,
unverheiratet; (not double) einfach ♦ n
(BRIT: also: ~ **ticket**) Einzelfahrschein m;
(record) Single f; **not a ~ one was left** es war
kein einziges mehr übrig; **every** ~ **day**
jeden Tag; ~ **spacing** einfacher
Zeilenabstand m.
▶**single out** vt auswählen; **to** ~ **out for praise**
lobend erwähnen.
single bed n Einzelbett nt.
single-breasted ['sɪŋglbrestɪd] adj einreihig.
Single European Market n: **the** ~ der
Europäische Binnenmarkt.
single file n: **in** ~ im Gänsemarsch.
single-handed [sɪŋgl'hændɪd] adv ganz allein.
single-minded [sɪŋgl'maɪndɪd] adj zielstrebig.
single parent n Alleinerziehende(r) f(m).
single room n Einzelzimmer nt.
singles ['sɪŋglz] npl (TENNIS) Einzel nt.
singles bar n Singles-Bar f.
single-sex school n reine Jungen-/
Mädchenschule f; **education in** ~s nach
Geschlechtern getrennte Schulerziehung.
singly ['sɪŋglɪ] adv einzeln.
singsong ['sɪŋsɔŋ] adj (tone) singend ♦ n: **to
have a** ~ zusammen singen.
singular ['sɪŋgjulə*] adj (odd) eigenartig;
(outstanding) einzigartig; (LING: form etc)
Singular- ♦ n (LING) Singular m, Einzahl f; **in
the** ~ im Singular.
singularly ['sɪŋgjuləlɪ] adv außerordentlich.
Sinhalese [sɪnhə'liːz] adj singhalesisch.
sinister ['sɪnɪstə*] adj unheimlich.
sink [sɪŋk] (pt **sank**, pp **sunk**) n Spülbecken nt
♦ vt (ship) versenken; (well) bohren;
(foundations) absenken ♦ vi (ship) sinken,
untergehen; (ground) sich senken; (person)
sinken; **to** ~ **one's teeth/claws into sth** die
Zähne/seine Klauen in etw acc schlagen; **his
heart/spirits sank at the thought** bei dem
Gedanken verließ ihn der Mut; **he sank into
the mud/a chair** er sank in den Schlamm
ein/in einen Sessel.
▶**sink back** vi (zurück)sinken.
▶**sink down** vi (nieder)sinken.
▶**sink in** vi (fig) verstanden werden; **it's only
just sunk in** ich begreife es erst jetzt.
sinking ['sɪŋkɪŋ] n (of ship) Untergang m;
(: deliberate) Versenkung f ♦ adj: ~ **feeling**
flaues Gefühl nt (im Magen).

sinking fund n Tilgungsfonds m.
sink unit n Spüle f.
sinner ['sɪnə'] n Sünder(in) m(f).
Sinn Féin [ʃɪn'feɪn] n republikanisch-nationalistische irische Partei.
Sino- ['saɪnəu] pref chinesisch-.
sinuous ['sɪnjuəs] adj (snake) gewunden; (dance) geschmeidig.
sinus ['saɪnəs] n (Nasen)nebenhöhle f.
sip [sɪp] n Schlückchen nt ♦ vt nippen an +dat.
siphon ['saɪfən] n Heber m; (also: **soda** ~) Siphon m.
▶**siphon off** vt absaugen; (petrol) abzapfen.
SIPS n abbr (= side impact protection system) Seitenaufprallschutz m.
sir [sə'] n mein Herr, Herr X; **S~ John Smith** Sir John Smith; **yes,** ~ ja(, Herr X); **Dear S~ (or Madam)** (in letter) Sehr geehrte (Damen und) Herren!
siren ['saɪərn] n Sirene f.
sirloin ['sə:lɔɪn] n (also: ~ **steak**) Filetsteak nt.
sirocco [sɪ'rɒkəu] n Schirokko m.
sisal ['saɪsəl] n Sisal m.
sissy ['sɪsɪ] (inf: pej) n Waschlappen m ♦ adj weichlich.
sister ['sɪstə'] n Schwester f; (nun) (Ordens)schwester f; (BRIT: nurse) Oberschwester f ♦ cpd: ~ **organization** Schwesterorganisation f; ~ **ship** Schwesterschiff nt.
sister-in-law ['sɪstərɪnlɔ:] n Schwägerin f.
sit [sɪt] (pt, pp **sat**) vi (sit down) sich setzen; (be sitting) sitzen; (assembly) tagen; (for painter) Modell sitzen ♦ vt (exam) machen; **to** ~ **on a committee** in einem Ausschuß sitzen; **to** ~ **tight** abwarten.
▶**sit about** vi herumsitzen.
▶**sit around** vi = **sit about**.
▶**sit back** vi sich zurücklehnen.
▶**sit down** vi sich (hin)setzen; **to be** ~**ting down** sitzen.
▶**sit in on** vt fus dabeisein bei.
▶**sit up** vi sich aufsetzen; (straight) sich gerade hinsetzen; (not go to bed) aufbleiben.
sitcom ['sɪtkɒm] n abbr (TV) = **situation comedy**.
sit-down ['sɪtdaun] adj: **a** ~ **strike** ein Sitzstreik m; **a** ~ **meal** eine richtige Mahlzeit.
site [saɪt] n (place) Platz m; (of crime) Ort m; (also: **building** ~) Baustelle f ♦ vt (factory) legen; (missiles) stationieren.
sit-in ['sɪtɪn] n Sit-in nt.
siting ['saɪtɪŋ] n (location) Lage f.
sitter ['sɪtə'] n (for painter) Modell nt; (also: **baby-**~) Babysitter m.
sitting ['sɪtɪŋ] n Sitzung f; **we have two** ~**s for lunch** bei uns wird das Mittagessen in zwei Schüben serviert; **at a single** ~ auf einmal.
sitting member n (POL) (derzeitiger) Abgeordnete(r) m, (derzeitige) Abgeordnete f.

sitting room n Wohnzimmer nt.
sitting tenant (BRIT) n (derzeitiger) Mieter m.
situate ['sɪtjueɪt] vt legen.
situated ['sɪtjueɪtɪd] adj gelegen; **to be** ~ liegen.
situation [sɪtju'eɪʃən] n Situation f, Lage f; (job) Stelle f; (location) Lage f; "~**s vacant**" (BRIT) „Stellenangebote".
situation comedy n (TV) Situationskomödie f.
six [sɪks] num sechs.
six-pack ['sɪkspæk] n Sechserpack m.
sixteen [sɪks'ti:n] num sechzehn.
sixth [sɪksθ] num sechste(r, s); **the upper/lower** ~ (BRIT: SCOL) ≈ die Ober-/Unterprima.
sixty ['sɪkstɪ] num sechzig.
size [saɪz] n Größe f; (extent) Ausmaß nt; **I take** ~ **14** ich habe Größe 14; **the small/large** ~ (of soap powder etc) die kleine/große Packung; **it's the** ~ **of** ... es ist so groß wie ...; **cut to** ~ auf die richtige Größe zurechtschnitten.
▶**size up** vt einschätzen.
sizeable ['saɪzəbl] adj ziemlich groß; (income etc) ansehnlich.
sizzle ['sɪzl] vi brutzeln.
SK (CANADA) abbr (= Saskatchewan).
skate [skeɪt] n (ice skate) Schlittschuh m; (roller skate) Rollschuh m; (fish: pl inv) Rochen m ♦ vi Schlittschuh laufen.
▶**skate around** vt fus (problem, issue) einfach übergehen.
▶**skate over** vt fus = **skate around**.
skateboard ['skeɪtbɔ:d] n Skateboard nt.
skater ['skeɪtə'] n Schlittschuhläufer(in) m(f).
skating ['skeɪtɪŋ] n Eislauf m.
skating rink n Eisbahn f.
skeleton ['skelɪtn] n Skelett nt ♦ attrib (plan, outline) skizzenhaft.
skeleton key n Dietrich m, Nachschlüssel m.
skeleton staff n Minimalbesetzung f.
skeptic etc ['skeptɪk] (US) = **sceptic** etc.
sketch [sketʃ] n Skizze f; (THEAT, TV) Sketch m ♦ vt skizzieren; (also: ~ **out**: ideas) umreißen.
sketchbook ['sketʃbuk] n Skizzenbuch m.
sketchpad ['sketʃpæd] n Skizzenblock m.
sketchy ['sketʃɪ] adj (coverage) oberflächlich; (notes etc) bruchstückhaft.
skew [skju:] adj schief.
skewed [skju:d] adj (distorted) verzerrt.
skewer ['skju:ə'] n Spieß m.
ski [ski:] n Ski m, Schi m ♦ vi Ski laufen or fahren.
ski boot n Skistiefel m.
skid [skɪd] n (AUT) Schleudern nt ♦ vi rutschen; (AUT) schleudern; **to go into a** ~ ins Schleudern geraten or kommen.
skid marks npl Reifenspuren pl; (from braking) Bremsspuren pl.
skier ['ski:ə'] n Skiläufer(in) m(f),

Skifahrer(in) *m(f)*.
skiing ['ski:ɪŋ] *n* Skilaufen *nt*, Skifahren *nt*; **to go** ~ Skilaufen *or* Skifahren gehen.
ski instructor *n* Skilehrer(in) *m(f)*.
ski jump *n* (*event*) Skispringen *nt*; (*ramp*) Sprungschanze *f*.
skilful, (*US*) **skillful** ['skɪlful] *adj* geschickt.
skilfully *adv* geschickt.
ski lift *n* Skilift *m*.
skill [skɪl] *n* (*ability*) Können *nt*; (*dexterity*) Geschicklichkeit *f*; **skills** (*acquired abilities*) Fähigkeiten *pl*; **computer/language** ~**s** Computer-/Sprachkenntnisse *pl*; **to learn a new** ~ etwas Neues lernen.
skilled [skɪld] *adj* (*skilful*) geschickt; (*trained*) ausgebildet; (*work*) qualifiziert.
skillet ['skɪlɪt] *n* Bratpfanne *f*.
skillful *etc* ['skɪlful] (*US*) = **skilful** *etc*.
skim [skɪm] *vt* (*also*: ~ **off**: *cream, fat*) abschöpfen; (*glide over*) gleiten über +*acc* ♦ *vi*: **to** ~ **through** (*book etc*) überfliegen.
skimmed milk [skɪmd-] *n* Magermilch *f*.
skimp [skɪmp] (*also*: ~ **on**) *vt* (*work etc*) nachlässig machen; (*cloth etc*) sparen an +*dat*.
skimpy ['skɪmpɪ] *adj* (*meagre*) dürftig; (*too small*) knapp.
skin [skɪn] *n* Haut *f*; (*fur*) Fell *nt*; (*of fruit*) Schale *f* ♦ *vt* (*animal*) häuten; **wet** *or* **soaked to the** ~ naß bis auf die Haut.
skin cancer *n* Hautkrebs *m*.
skin-deep ['skɪn'di:p] *adj* oberflächlich.
skin diver *n* Sporttaucher(in) *m(f)*.
skin diving *n* Sporttauchen *nt*.
skinflint ['skɪnflɪnt] *n* Geizkragen *m*.
skin graft *n* Hautverpflanzung *f*.
skinhead ['skɪnhɛd] *n* Skinhead *m*.
skinny ['skɪnɪ] *adj* dünn.
skin test *n* Hauttest *m*.
skintight ['skɪntaɪt] *adj* hauteng.
skip [skɪp] *n* Sprung *m*, Hüpfer *m*; (*BRIT: container*) (Müll)container *m* ♦ *vi* springen, hüpfen; (*with rope*) seilspringen ♦ *vt* überspringen; (*miss: lunch, lecture*) ausfallen lassen; **to** ~ **school** (*esp US*) die Schule schwänzen.
ski pants *npl* Skihose *f*.
ski pole *n* Skistock *m*.
skipper ['skɪpə*] *n* (*NAUT*) Kapitän *m*; (*inf: SPORT*) Mannschaftskapitän *m* ♦ *vt*: **to** ~ **a boat/team** Kapitän eines Schiffes/einer Mannschaft sein.
skipping rope ['skɪpɪŋ-] (*BRIT*) *n* Sprungseil *nt*.
ski resort *n* Wintersportort *m*.
skirmish ['skə:mɪʃ] *n* (*MIL*) Geplänkel *nt*; (*political etc*) Zusammenstoß *m*.
skirt [skə:t] *n* Rock *m* ♦ *vt* (*fig*) umgehen.
skirting board ['skə:tɪŋ-] (*BRIT*) *n* Fußleiste *f*.
ski run *n* Skipiste *f*.
ski slope *n* Skipiste *f*.
ski suit *n* Skianzug *m*.

skit [skɪt] *n* Parodie *f*.
ski tow *n* Schlepplift *m*.
skittle ['skɪtl] *n* Kegel *m*.
skittles ['skɪtlz] *n* (*game*) Kegeln *nt*.
skive [skaɪv] (*BRIT: inf*) *vi* blaumachen; (*from school*) schwänzen.
skulk [skʌlk] *vi* sich herumdrücken.
skull [skʌl] *n* Schädel *m*.
skullcap ['skʌlkæp] *n* Scheitelkäppchen *nt*.
skunk [skʌŋk] *n* Skunk *m*, Stinktier *nt*; (*fur*) Skunk *m*.
sky [skaɪ] *n* Himmel *m*; **to praise sb to the skies** jdn in den Himmel heben.
sky-blue [skaɪ'blu:] *adj* himmelblau.
skydiving ['skaɪdaɪvɪŋ] *n* Fallschirmspringen *nt*.
sky-high ['skaɪ'haɪ] *adj* (*prices, confidence*) himmelhoch ♦ *adv*: **to blow a bridge** ~ eine Brücke in die Luft sprengen.
skylark ['skaɪlɑ:k] *n* Feldlerche *f*.
skylight ['skaɪlaɪt] *n* Dachfenster *nt*.
skyline ['skaɪlaɪn] *n* (*horizon*) Horizont *m*; (*of city*) Skyline *f*, Silhouette *f*.
skyscraper ['skaɪskreɪpə*] *n* Wolkenkratzer *m*.
slab [slæb] *n* (*stone*) Platte *f*; (*of wood*) Tafel *f*; (*of cake, cheese*) großes Stück *nt*.
slack [slæk] *adj* (*loose*) locker; (*rope*) durchhängend; (*skin*) schlaff; (*careless*) nachlässig; (*COMM: market*) flau; (: *demand*) schwach; (*period*) ruhig ♦ *n* (*in rope etc*) durchhängendes Teil *nt*; **slacks** *npl* (*trousers*) Hose *f*; **business is** ~ das Geschäft geht schlecht.
slacken ['slækn] *vi* (*also*: ~ **off**: *speed, rain*) nachlassen; (: *pace*) langsamer werden; (: *demand*) zurückgehen ♦ *vt* (*grip*) lockern; (*speed*) verringern; (*pace*) verlangsamen.
slag heap [slæg-] *n* Schlackenhalde *f*.
slag off (*BRIT: inf*) *vt* (*criticize*) (he)runtermachen.
slain [sleɪn] *pp of* **slay**.
slake [sleɪk] *vt* (*thirst*) stillen.
slalom ['slɑ:ləm] *n* Slalom *m*.
slam [slæm] *vt* (*door*) zuschlagen, zuknallen (*inf*); (*throw*) knallen (*inf*); (*criticize*) verreißen ♦ *vi* (*door*) zuschlagen, zuknallen (*inf*); **to** ~ **on the brakes** (*AUT*) auf die Bremse steigen (*inf*).
slammer ['slæmə*] (*inf*) *n* (*prison*) Knast *m*.
slander ['slɑ:ndə*] *n* (*LAW*) Verleumdung *f*; (*insult*) Beleidigung *f* ♦ *vt* verleumden.
slanderous ['slɑ:ndrəs] *adj* verleumderisch.
slang [slæŋ] *n* Slang *m*; (*jargon*) Jargon *m*.
slanging match ['slæŋɪŋ-] *n* gegenseitige Beschimpfungen *pl*.
slant [slɑ:nt] *n* Neigung *f*, Schräge *f*; (*fig: approach*) Perspektive *f* ♦ *vi* (*floor*) sich neigen; (*ceiling*) schräg sein.
slanted ['slɑ:ntɪd] *adj* (*roof*) schräg; (*eyes*) schräggestellt.
slanting ['slɑ:ntɪŋ] *adj* = **slanted**.
slap [slæp] *n* Schlag *m*, Klaps *m* ♦ *vt* schlagen

♦ *adv* (*inf: directly*) direkt; **to ~ sth on sth** etw auf etw *acc* klatschen; **it fell ~(-bang) in the middle** es fiel genau in die Mitte.

slapdash ['slæpdæʃ] *adj* nachlässig, schludrig (*inf*).

slapstick ['slæpstɪk] *n* Klamauk *m*.

slap-up ['slæpʌp] *adj*: **a ~ meal** (*BRIT*) ein Essen mit allem Drum und Dran.

slash [slæʃ] *vt* aufschlitzen; (*fig: prices*) radikal senken; **to ~ one's wrists** sich *dat* die Pulsadern aufschneiden.

slat [slæt] *n* Leiste *f*, Latte *f*.

slate [sleɪt] *n* Schiefer *m*; (*piece*) Schieferplatte *f* ♦ *vt* (*criticize*) verreißen.

slaughter ['slɔːtə*] *n* (*of animals*) Schlachten *nt*; (*of people*) Gemetzel *nt* ♦ *vt* (*animals*) schlachten; (*people*) abschlachten.

slaughterhouse ['slɔːtəhaus] *n* Schlachthof *m*.

Slav [slɑːv] *adj* slawisch ♦ *n* Slawe *m*, Slawin *f*.

slave [sleɪv] *n* Sklave *m*, Sklavin *f* ♦ *vi* (*also*: **~ away**) sich abplagen, schuften (*inf*); **to ~ (away) at sth** sich mit etw herumschlagen.

slave-driver ['sleɪvdraɪvə*] *n* Sklaventreiber(in) *m(f)*.

slave labour *n* Sklavenarbeit *f*; **it's just ~** (*fig*) es ist die reinste Sklavenarbeit.

slaver ['slævə*] *vi* (*dribble*) geifern.

slavery ['sleɪvərɪ] *n* Sklaverei *f*.

Slavic ['slævɪk] *adj* slawisch.

slavish ['sleɪvɪʃ] *adj* sklavisch.

slavishly ['sleɪvɪʃlɪ] *adv* sklavisch.

Slavonic [slə'vɒnɪk] *adj* slawisch.

slay [sleɪ] (*pt* **slew**, *pp* **slain**) *vt* (*liter*) erschlagen.

SLD (*BRIT*) *n abbr* (*POL*: = *Social and Liberal Democratic Party*) sozialliberale Partei.

sleazy ['sliːzɪ] *adj* schäbig.

sledge [sledʒ] *n* Schlitten *m*.

sledgehammer ['sledʒhæmə*] *n* Vorschlaghammer *m*.

sleek [sliːk] *adj* glatt, glänzend; (*car, boat etc*) schnittig.

sleep [sliːp] (*pt, pp* **slept**) *n* Schlaf *m* ♦ *vi* schlafen ♦ *vt*: **we can ~ 4** bei uns können 4 Leute schlafen; **to go to ~** einschlafen; **to have a good night's ~** sich richtig ausschlafen; **to put to ~** (*euph: kill*) einschläfern; **to ~ lightly** einen leichten Schlaf haben; **to ~ with sb** (*euph: have sex*) mit jdm schlafen.

▶**sleep around** *vi* mit jedem/jeder schlafen.

▶**sleep in** *vi* (*oversleep*) verschlafen; (*rise late*) lange schlafen.

sleeper ['sliːpə*] *n* (*train*) Schlafwagenzug *m*; (*berth*) Platz *m* im Schlafwagen; (*BRIT: on track*) Schwelle *f*; (*person*) Schläfer(in) *m(f)*.

sleepily ['sliːpɪlɪ] *adv* müde, schläfrig.

sleeping accommodation *n* (*beds etc*) Schlafgelegenheiten *pl*.

sleeping arrangements *npl* Bettenverteilung *f*.

sleeping bag *n* Schlafsack *m*.

sleeping car *n* Schlafwagen *m*.

sleeping partner (*BRIT*) = **silent partner**.

sleeping pill *n* Schlaftablette *f*.

sleeping sickness *n* Schlafkrankheit *f*.

sleepless ['sliːplɪs] *adj* (*night*) schlaflos.

sleeplessness ['sliːplɪsnɪs] *n* Schlaflosigkeit *f*.

sleepwalk ['sliːpwɔːk] *vi* schlafwandeln.

sleepwalker ['sliːpwɔːkə*] *n* Schlafwandler(in) *m(f)*.

sleepy ['sliːpɪ] *adj* müde, schläfrig; (*fig: village etc*) verschlafen; **to be** *or* **feel ~** müde sein.

sleet [sliːt] *n* Schneeregen *m*.

sleeve [sliːv] *n* Ärmel *m*; (*of record*) Hülle *f*; **to have sth up one's ~** (*fig*) etw in petto haben.

sleeveless ['sliːvlɪs] *adj* (*garment*) ärmellos.

sleigh [sleɪ] *n* (Pferde)schlitten *m*.

sleight [slaɪt] *n*: **~ of hand** Fingerfertigkeit *f*.

slender ['slendə*] *adj* schlank, schmal; (*small*) knapp.

slept [slept] *pt, pp of* **sleep**.

sleuth [sluːθ] *n* Detektiv *m*.

slew [sluː] *vi* (*BRIT: also*: **~ round**) herumschwenken; **the bus ~ed across the road** der Bus rutschte über die Straße ♦ *pt of* **slay**.

slice [slaɪs] *n* Scheibe *f*; (*utensil*) Wender *m* ♦ *vt* (in Scheiben) schneiden; **~d bread** aufgeschnittenes Brot *nt*; **the best thing since ~d bread** der/die/das Allerbeste.

slick [slɪk] *adj* professionell; (*pej*) glatt ♦ *n* (*also*: **oil ~**) Ölteppich *m*.

slid [slɪd] *pt, pp of* **slide**.

slide [slaɪd] (*pt, pp* **slid**) *n* (*on ice etc*) Rutschen *nt*; (*fig: to ruin etc*) Abgleiten *nt*; (*in playground*) Rutschbahn *f*; (*PHOT*) Dia *nt*; (*BRIT: also*: **hair ~**) Spange *f*; (*microscope slide*) Objektträger *m*; (*in prices*) Preisrutsch *m* ♦ *vt* schieben ♦ *vi* (*slip*) rutschen; (*glide*) gleiten; **to let things ~** (*fig*) die Dinge schleifen lassen.

slide projector *n* Diaprojektor *m*.

slide rule *n* Rechenschieber *m*.

sliding ['slaɪdɪŋ] *adj* (*door, window etc*) Schiebe-.

sliding roof *n* (*AUT*) Schiebedach *nt*.

sliding scale *n* gleitende Skala *f*.

slight [slaɪt] *adj* zierlich; (*small*) gering; (*error, accent, pain etc*) leicht; (*trivial*) leicht ♦ *n*: **a ~ (on sb/sth)** ein Affront *m* (gegen jdn/etw); **the ~est noise** der geringste Lärm; **the ~est problem** das kleinste Problem; **I haven't the ~est idea** ich habe nicht die geringste Ahnung; **not in the ~est** nicht im geringsten.

slightly ['slaɪtlɪ] *adv* etwas, ein bißchen; **~ built** zierlich.

slim [slɪm] *adj* schlank; (*chance*) gering ♦ *vi* eine Schlankheitskur machen, abnehmen.

slime [slaɪm] *n* Schleim *m*.

slimming ['slɪmɪŋ] *n* Abnehmen *nt*.

slimy ['slaɪmɪ] *adj* (*lit, fig*) schleimig.

sling [slɪŋ] (*pt, pp* **slung**) *n* Schlinge *f*; (*for baby*) Tragetuch *nt*; (*weapon*) Schleuder *f* ♦ *vt* schleudern; **to have one's arm in a ~** den Arm in der Schlinge tragen.

slingshot ['slɪŋʃɔt] *n* Steinschleuder *f*.

slink [slɪŋk] (*pt, pp* **slunk**) *vi*: **to ~ away** *or* **off** sich davonschleichen.

slinky ['slɪŋkɪ] *adj* (*dress*) enganliegend.

slip [slɪp] *n* (*fall*) Ausrutschen *nt*; (*mistake*) Fehler *m*, Schnitzer *m*; (*underskirt*) Unterrock *m*; (*also:* **~ of paper**) Zettel *m* ♦ *vt* (*slide*) stecken ♦ *vi* ausrutschen; (*decline*) fallen; **he had a nasty ~** er ist ausgerutscht und böse gefallen; **to give sb the ~** jdm entwischen; **a ~ of the tongue** ein Versprecher *m*; **to ~ into/out of sth, to ~ sth on/off** in etw *acc*/aus etw schlüpfen; **to let a chance ~ by** eine Gelegenheit ungenutzt lassen; **it ~ped from her hand** es rutschte ihr aus der Hand.

▶**slip away** *vi* sich davonschleichen.

▶**slip in** *vt* stecken in +*acc*.

▶**slip out** *vi* kurz weggehen.

▶**slip up** *vi* sich vertun (*inf*).

slip-on ['slɪpɔn] *adj* zum Überziehen; **~ shoes** Slipper *pl*.

slipped disc [slɪpt-] *n* Bandscheibenschaden *m*.

slipper ['slɪpə*] *n* Pantoffel *m*, Hausschuh *m*.

slippery ['slɪpərɪ] *adj* (*lit, fig*) glatt; (*fish etc*) schlüpfrig.

slippy ['slɪpɪ] *adj* (*slippery*) glatt.

slip road (*BRIT*) *n* (*to motorway etc*) Auffahrt *f*; (*from motorway etc*) Ausfahrt *f*.

slipshod ['slɪpʃɔd] *adj* schludrig (*inf*).

slipstream ['slɪpstriːm] *n* (*TECH*) Sog *m*; (*AUT*) Windschatten *m*.

slip-up ['slɪpʌp] *n* Fehler *m*, Schnitzer *m*.

slipway ['slɪpweɪ] *n* (*NAUT*) Ablaufbahn *f*.

slit [slɪt] (*pt, pp* **slit**) *n* Schlitz *m*; (*tear*) Riß *m* ♦ *vt* aufschlitzen; **to ~ sb's throat** jdm die Kehle aufschlitzen.

slither ['slɪðə*] *vi* rutschen; (*snake etc*) gleiten.

sliver ['slɪvə*] *n* (*of glass, wood*) Splitter *m*; (*of cheese etc*) Scheibchen *nt*.

slob [slɔb] (*inf*) *n* Drecksau *f* (*!*).

slog [slɔg] (*BRIT*) *vi* (*work hard*) schuften ♦ *n*: **it was a hard ~** es war eine ganz schöne Schufterei; **to ~ away at sth** sich mit etw abrackern.

slogan ['sləʊgən] *n* Slogan *m*.

slop [slɔp] *vi* schwappen ♦ *vt* verschütten.

▶**slop out** *vi* (*in prison etc*) den Toiletteneimer ausleeren.

slope [sləʊp] *n* Hügel *m*; (*side of mountain*) Hang *m*; (*ski slope*) Piste *f*; (*slant*) Neigung *f* ♦ *vi*: **to ~ down** abfallen; **to ~ up** ansteigen.

sloping ['sləʊpɪŋ] *adj* (*upwards*) ansteigend; (*downwards*) abfallend; (*roof, handwriting*) schräg.

sloppy ['slɔpɪ] *adj* (*work*) nachlässig; (*appearance*) schlampig; (*sentimental*) rührselig.

slops [slɔps] *npl* Abfallbrühe *f*.

slosh [slɔʃ] (*inf*) *vi*: **to ~ around** *or* **about** (*person*) herumplanschen; (*liquid*) herumschwappen.

sloshed [slɔʃt] (*inf*) *adj* (*drunk*) blau.

slot [slɔt] *n* Schlitz *m*; (*fig: in timetable*) Termin *m*; (*: RADIO, TV*) Sendezeit *f* ♦ *vt*: **to ~ sth in** etw hineinstecken ♦ *vi*: **to ~ into** sich einfügen lassen in +*acc*.

sloth [sləʊθ] *n* (*laziness*) Trägheit *f*, Faulheit *f*; (*ZOOL*) Faultier *nt*.

slot machine *n* (*BRIT*) Münzautomat *m*; (*for gambling*) Spielautomat *m*.

slot meter (*BRIT*) *n* Münzzähler *m*.

slouch [slautʃ] *vi* eine krumme Haltung haben; (*when walking*) krumm gehen ♦ *n*: **he's no ~** er hat etwas los (*inf*); **she was ~ed in a chair** sie hing auf einem Stuhl.

Slovak ['sləʊvæk] *adj* slowakisch ♦ *n* Slowake *m*, Slowakin *f*; (*LING*) Slowakisch *nt*; **the ~ Republic** die Slowakische Republik.

Slovakia [sləʊˈvækɪə] *n* die Slowakei.

Slovakian [sləʊˈvækɪən] *adj, n* = **Slovak**.

Slovene ['sləʊviːn] *n* Slowene *m*, Slowenin *f*; (*LING*) Slowenisch *nt* ♦ *adj* slowenisch.

Slovenia [sləʊˈviːnɪə] *n* Slowenien *nt*.

Slovenian [sləʊˈviːnɪən] *adj, n* = **Slovene**.

slovenly ['slʌvənlɪ] *adj* schlampig; (*careless*) nachlässig, schludrig (*inf*).

slow [sləʊ] *adj* langsam; (*not clever*) langsam, begriffsstutzig ♦ *adv* langsam ♦ *vt* (*also:* **~ down, ~ up**) verlangsamen; (*business*) verschlechtern ♦ *vi* (*also:* **~ down, ~ up**) sich verlangsamen; (*business*) schlechter gehen; **to be ~** (*watch, clock*) nachgehen; **"~"** „langsam fahren"; **at a ~ speed** langsam; **to be ~ to act** sich *dat* Zeit lassen; **to be ~ to decide** lange brauchen, um sich zu entscheiden; **my watch is 20 minutes ~** meine Uhr geht 20 Minuten nach; **business is ~** das Geschäft geht schlecht; **to go ~** (*driver*) langsam fahren; (*BRIT: in industrial dispute*) einen Bummelstreik machen.

slow-acting [sləʊˈæktɪŋ] *adj* mit Langzeitwirkung.

slowly ['sləʊlɪ] *adv* langsam.

slow motion *n*: **in ~** in Zeitlupe.

slow-moving [sləʊˈmuːvɪŋ] *adj* langsam; (*traffic*) kriechend.

slowness ['sləʊnɪs] *n* Langsamkeit *f*.

sludge [slʌdʒ] *n* Schlamm *m*.

slue [sluː] (*US*) *vi* = **slew**.

slug [slʌg] *n* Nacktschnecke *f*; (*US: inf: bullet*) Kugel *f*.

sluggish ['slʌgɪʃ] *adj* träge; (*engine*) lahm; (*COMM*) flau.

sluice [sluːs] *n* Schleuse *f*; (*channel*) (Wasch)rinne *f* ♦ *vt*: **to ~ down** *or* **out** abspritzen.

slum [slʌm] *n* Slum *m*, Elendsviertel *nt*.

slumber ['slʌmbə*] *n* Schlaf *m*.

slump [slʌmp] *n* Rezession *f* ◆ *vi* fallen; ~ **in sales** Absatzflaute *f*; ~ **in prices** Preissturz *m*; **he was ~ed over the wheel** er war über dem Steuer zusammengesackt.

slung [slʌŋ] *pt, pp of* **sling**.

slunk [slʌŋk] *pt, pp of* **slink**.

slur [slɜ:ʳ] *n* (*fig*): ~ **(on)** Beleidigung *f* (für) ◆ *vt* (*words*) undeutlich aussprechen; **to cast a ~ on** verunglimpfen.

slurp [slɜ:p] (*inf*) *vt, vi* schlürfen.

slurred [slɜ:d] *adj* (*speech, voice*) undeutlich.

slush [slʌʃ] *n* (*melted snow*) Schneematsch *m*.

slush fund *n* Schmiergelder *pl*, Schmiergeldfonds *m*.

slushy ['slʌʃɪ] *adj* matschig; (*BRIT, fig*) schmalzig.

slut [slʌt] (*pej*) *n* Schlampe *f*.

sly [slaɪ] *adj* (*smile, expression*) wissend; (*remark*) vielsagend; (*person*) schlau, gerissen; **on the ~** heimlich.

S/M *n abbr* (= *sadomasochism*) S/M.

smack [smæk] *n* Klaps *m*; (*on face*) Ohrfeige *f* ◆ *vt* (*hit*) schlagen; (: *child*) einen Klaps geben +*dat*; (: *on face*) ohrfeigen ◆ *vi*: **to ~ of** riechen nach ◆ *adv*: **it fell ~ in the middle** (*inf*) es fiel genau in die Mitte; **to ~ one's lips** schmatzen.

smacker ['smækəʳ] (*inf*) *n* (*kiss*) Schmatzer *m*.

small [smɔ:l] *adj* klein ◆ *n*: **the ~ of the back** das Kreuz; **to get** *or* **grow ~er** (*thing*) kleiner werden; (*numbers*) zurückgehen; **to make ~er** (*amount, income*) kürzen; (*object, garment*) kleiner machen; **a ~ shopkeeper** der Inhaber eines kleinen Geschäfts; **a ~ business** ein Kleinunternehmen *nt*.

small ads (*BRIT*) *npl* Kleinanzeigen *pl*.

small arms *n* Handfeuerwaffen *pl*.

small business *n* Kleinunternehmen *nt*.

small change *n* Kleingeld *nt*.

small fry *npl* (*unimportant people*) kleine Fische *pl*.

smallholder ['smɔ:lhəuldəʳ] (*BRIT*) *n* Kleinbauer *m*.

smallholding ['smɔ:lhəuldɪŋ] (*BRIT*) *n* kleiner Landbesitz *m*.

small hours *npl*: **in the ~** in den frühen Morgenstunden.

smallish ['smɔ:lɪʃ] *adj* ziemlich klein.

small-minded [smɔ:l'maɪndɪd] *adj* engstirnig.

smallpox ['smɔ:lpɔks] *n* Pocken *pl*.

small print *n*: **the ~** das Kleingedruckte.

small-scale ['smɔ:lskeɪl] *adj* (*map, model*) in verkleinertem Maßstab; (*business, farming*) kleinangelegt.

small talk *n* (oberflächliche) Konversation *f*.

small-time ['smɔ:ltaɪm] *adj* (*farmer etc*) klein; **a ~ thief** ein kleiner Ganove.

small-town ['smɔ:ltaun] *adj* kleinstädtisch.

smarmy ['smɑ:mɪ] (*BRIT: pej*) *adj* schmierig.

smart [smɑ:t] *adj* (*neat*) ordentlich, gepflegt; (*fashionable*) schick, elegant; (*clever*) intelligent, clever (*inf*); (*quick*) schnell ◆ *vi*

(*sting*) brennen; (*suffer*) leiden; **the ~ set** die Schickeria (*inf*); **and look ~ (about it)!** und zwar ein bißchen plötzlich! (*inf*).

smart card *n* Chipkarte *f*.

smarten up ['smɑ:tn-] *vi* sich feinmachen ◆ *vt* verschönern.

smash [smæʃ] *n* (*also*: ~**-up**) Unfall *m*; (*sound*) Krachen *nt*; (*song, play, film*) Superhit *m*; (*TENNIS*) Schmetterball *m* ◆ *vt* (*break*) zerbrechen; (*car etc*) kaputtfahren; (*hopes*) zerschlagen; (*SPORT: record*) haushoch schlagen ◆ *vi* (*break*) zerbrechen; (*against wall, into sth etc*) krachen.

▶**smash up** *vt* (*car*) kaputtfahren; (*room*) kurz und klein schlagen (*inf*).

smash hit *n* Superhit *m*.

smashing ['smæʃɪŋ] (*inf*) *adj* super, toll.

smattering ['smætərɪŋ] *n*: **a ~ of Greek** *etc* ein paar Brocken Griechisch *etc*.

smear [smɪəʳ] *n* (*trace*) verschmierter Fleck *m*; (*insult*) Verleumdung *f*; (*MED*) Abstrich *m* ◆ *vt* (*spread*) verschmieren; (*make dirty*) beschmieren; **his hands were ~ed with oil/ink** seine Hände waren mit Öl/Tinte beschmiert.

smear campaign *n* Verleumdungskampagne *f*.

smear test *n* Abstrich *m*.

smell [smel] (*pt, pp* **smelt** *or* **smelled**) *n* Geruch *m*; (*sense*) Geruchssinn *m* ◆ *vt* riechen ◆ *vi* riechen; (*pej*) stinken; (*pleasantly*) duften; **to ~ of** riechen nach.

smelly ['smelɪ] (*pej*) *adj* stinkend.

smelt [smelt] *pt, pp of* **smell** ◆ *vt* schmelzen.

smile [smaɪl] *n* Lächeln *nt* ◆ *vi* lächeln.

smiling ['smaɪlɪŋ] *adj* lächelnd.

smirk [smɜ:k] (*pej*) *n* Grinsen *nt*.

smithy ['smɪðɪ] *n* Schmiede *f*.

smitten ['smɪtn] *adj*: ~ **with** vernarrt in +*acc*.

smock [smɔk] *n* Kittel *m*; (*US: overall*) Overall *m*.

smog [smɔg] *n* Smog *m*.

smoke [sməuk] *n* Rauch *m* ◆ *vi, vt* rauchen; **to have a ~** eine rauchen; **to go up in ~** in Rauch (und Flammen) aufgehen; (*fig*) sich in Rauch auflösen; **do you ~?** rauchen Sie?

smoked [sməukt] *adj* geräuchert, Räucher-; ~ **glass** Rauchglas *nt*.

smokeless fuel ['sməuklɪs-] *n* rauchlose Kohle *f*.

smokeless zone (*BRIT*) *n* rauchfreie Zone *f*.

smoker ['sməukəʳ] *n* Raucher(in) *m(f)*; (*RAIL*) Raucherabteil *nt*.

smoke screen *n* Rauchvorhang *m*; (*fig*) Deckmantel *m*.

smoke shop (*US*) *n* Tabakladen *m*.

smoking ['sməukɪŋ] *n* Rauchen *nt*; "**no ~**" „Rauchen verboten".

smoking compartment, (*US*) **smoking car** *n* Raucherabteil *nt*.

smoking room *n* Raucherzimmer *nt*.

smoky ['sməukɪ] *adj* verraucht; (*taste*)

rauchig.
smolder ['sməuldə'] (US) vi = **smoulder.**
smoochy ['smu:tʃɪ] adj (music, tape) zum
Schmusen.
smooth [smu:ð] adj (lit, fig: pej) glatt; (flavour,
whisky) weich; (movement) geschmeidig;
(flight) ruhig.
▶**smooth out** vt glätten; (fig: difficulties) aus
dem Weg räumen.
▶**smooth over** vt: to ~ **things over** (fig) die
Sache bereinigen.
smoothly ['smu:ðlɪ] adv reibungslos, glatt;
everything went ~ alles ging glatt über die
Bühne.
smoothness ['smu:ðnɪs] n Glätte f; (of flight)
Ruhe f.
smother ['smʌðə'] vt (fire, person) ersticken;
(repress) unterdrücken.
smoulder, (US) **smolder** ['sməuldə'] vi (lit,
fig) glimmen, schwelen.
smudge [smʌdʒ] n Schmutzfleck m ♦ vt
verwischen.
smug [smʌg] (pej) adj selbstgefällig.
smuggle ['smʌgl] vt schmuggeln; to ~ **in/out**
einschmuggeln/herausschmuggeln.
smuggler ['smʌglə'] n Schmuggler(in) m(f).
smuggling ['smʌglɪŋ] n Schmuggel m.
smut [smʌt] n (grain of soot) Rußflocke f; (in
conversation etc) Schmutz m.
smutty ['smʌtɪ] adj (fig: joke, book) schmutzig.
snack [snæk] n Kleinigkeit f (zu essen); to
have a ~ eine Kleinigkeit essen.
snack bar n Imbißstube f.
snag [snæg] n Haken m, Schwierigkeit f.
snail [sneɪl] n Schnecke f.
snake [sneɪk] n Schlange f.
snap [snæp] n Knacken nt; (photograph)
Schnappschuß m; (card game)
≈ Schnippschnapp nt ♦ adj (decision)
plötzlich, spontan ♦ vt (break) (zer)brechen
♦ vi (break) (zer)brechen; (rope, thread etc)
reißen; **a cold** ~ ein Kälteeinbruch m; **his
patience** ~**ped** ihm riß der Geduldsfaden;
his temper ~**ped** er verlor die
Beherrschung; to ~ **one's fingers** mit den
Fingern schnipsen or schnalzen; to
~ **open/shut** auf-/zuschnappen.
▶**snap at** vt fus (dog) schnappen nach; (fig:
person) anschnauzen (inf).
▶**snap off** vt (break) abbrechen.
▶**snap up** vt (bargains) wegschnappen.
snap fastener n Druckknopf m.
snappy ['snæpɪ] (inf) adj (answer) kurz und
treffend; (slogan) zündend; **make it** ~ ein
bißchen dalli!; **he is a** ~ **dresser** er zieht
sich flott an.
snapshot ['snæpʃɔt] n Schnappschuß m.
snare [snɛə'] n Falle f ♦ vt (lit, fig) fangen.
snarl [snɑ:l] vi knurren ♦ vt: **to get** ~**ed up**
(plans) durcheinanderkommen; (traffic)
stocken.
snarl-up ['snɑ:lʌp] n Verkehrschaos nt.

snatch [snætʃ] n (of conversation) Fetzen m; (of
song) **paar Takte** pl ♦ vt (grab) greifen;
(steal) stehlen, klauen (inf); (child)
entführen; (fig: opportunity) ergreifen;
(: look) werfen ♦ vi: **don't** ~! nicht
grapschen!; to ~ **a sandwich** schnell ein
Butterbrot essen; to ~ **some sleep** etwas
Schlaf ergattern.
▶**snatch up** vt schnappen.
snazzy ['snæzɪ] (inf) adj flott.
sneak [sni:k] (pt (US) also **snuck**) vi: to ~ **in/out**
sich einschleichen/sich hinausschleichen
♦ vt: to ~ **a look at sth** heimlich auf etw acc
schielen ♦ n (inf: pej) Petze f.
▶**sneak up** vi: to ~ **up on sb** sich an jdn
heranschleichen.
sneakers ['sni:kəz] npl Freizeitschuhe pl.
sneaking ['sni:kɪŋ] adj: **to have a** ~ **feeling/
suspicion that** ... das ungute Gefühl/den
leisen Verdacht haben, daß ...
sneaky ['sni:kɪ] (pej) adj raffiniert.
sneer [snɪə'] vi (smile nastily) spöttisch
lächeln; (mock): **to** ~ **at** verspotten ♦ n
(smile) spöttisches Lächeln nt; (remark)
spöttische Bemerkung f.
sneeze [sni:z] n Niesen nt ♦ vi niesen.
▶**sneeze at** vt fus: **it's not to be** ~**d at** es ist
nicht zu verachten.
snicker ['snɪkə'] vi see **snigger.**
snide [snaɪd] (pej) adj abfällig.
sniff [snɪf] n Schniefen nt; (smell) Schnüffeln
nt ♦ vi schniefen ♦ vt riechen, schnuppern an
+dat; (glue) schnüffeln.
sniffer dog ['snɪfə-] n Spürhund m.
snigger ['snɪgə'] vi kichern.
snip [snɪp] n Schnitt m; (BRIT: inf: bargain)
Schnäppchen nt ♦ vt schnippeln; to ~ **sth
off/through sth** etw abschnippeln/
durchschnippeln.
sniper ['snaɪpə'] n Heckenschütze m.
snippet ['snɪpɪt] n (of information) Bruchstück
nt; (of conversation) Fetzen m.
snivelling, (US) **sniveling** ['snɪvlɪŋ] adj
heulend.
snob [snɔb] n Snob m.
snobbery ['snɔbərɪ] n Snobismus m.
snobbish ['snɔbɪʃ] adj snobistisch, versnobt
(inf).
snog [snɔg] (BRIT: inf) n Knutscherei f; **to have
a** ~ **with sb** mit jdm (rum)knutschen ♦ vi
(rum)knutschen.
snooker ['snu:kə'] n Snooker nt ♦ vt (BRIT: inf):
to be ~**ed** festsitzen.
snoop [snu:p] vi: **to** ~ **about**
herumschnüffeln; **to** ~ **on sb** jdm
nachschnüffeln.
snooper ['snu:pə'] n Schnüffler(in) m(f).
snooty ['snu:tɪ] adj hochnäsig.
snooze [snu:z] n Schläfchen nt ♦ vi ein
Schläfchen machen.
snore [snɔ:'] n Schnarchen nt ♦ vi schnarchen.
snoring ['snɔ:rɪŋ] n Schnarchen nt.

snorkel ['snɔ:kl] *n* Schnorchel *m*.

snort [snɔ:t] *n* Schnauben *nt* ♦ *vi* (*animal*) schnauben; (*person*) prusten ♦ *vt* (*inf: cocaine*) schnüffeln.

snotty ['snɔtɪ] (*inf*) *adj* (*handkerchief, nose*) Rotz-; (*pej: snobbish*) hochnäsig.

snout [snaut] *n* Schnauze *f*.

snow [snəu] *n* Schnee *m* ♦ *vi* schneien ♦ *vt*: **to be ~ed under with work** mit Arbeit reichlich eingedeckt sein; **it's ~ing** es schneit.

snowball ['snəubɔ:l] *n* Schneeball *m* ♦ *vi* (*fig: problem*) eskalieren; (: *campaign*) ins Rollen kommen.

snowbound ['snəubaund] *adj* eingeschneit.

snow-capped ['snəukæpt] *adj* schneebedeckt.

snowdrift ['snəudrɪft] *n* Schneewehe *f*.

snowdrop ['snəudrɔp] *n* Schneeglöckchen *nt*.

snowfall ['snəufɔ:l] *n* Schneefall *m*.

snowflake ['snəufleɪk] *n* Schneeflocke *f*.

snowline ['snəulaɪn] *n* Schneegrenze *f*.

snowman ['snəumæn] (*irreg: like* **man**) *n* Schneemann *m*.

snowplough, (*US*) **snowplow** ['snəuplau] *n* Schneepflug *m*.

snowshoe ['snəuʃu:] *n* Schneeschuh *m*.

snowstorm ['snəustɔ:m] *n* Schneesturm *m*.

snowy ['snəuɪ] *adj* schneeweiß; (*covered with snow*) verschneit.

SNP (*BRIT*) *n abbr* (*POL*) = **Scottish National Party**.

snub [snʌb] *vt* (*person*) vor den Kopf stoßen ♦ *n* Abfuhr *f*.

snub-nosed [snʌb'nəuzd] *adj* stupsnasig.

snuff [snʌf] *n* Schnupftabak *m* ♦ *vt* (*also: ~ out: candle*) auslöschen.

snuff movie *n* Pornofilm, in dem jemand tatsächlich stirbt.

snug [snʌg] *adj* behaglich, gemütlich; (*well-fitting*) gutsitzend; **it's a ~ fit** es paßt genau.

snuggle ['snʌgl] *vi*: **to ~ up to sb** sich an jdn kuscheln; **to ~ down in bed** sich ins Bett kuscheln.

snugly ['snʌglɪ] *adv* behaglich; **it fits ~** (*object in pocket etc*) es paßt genau hinein; (*garment*) es paßt wie angegossen.

SO *n abbr* (*BANKING*) = **standing order**.

═══════════════ *KEYWORD* ═══════════════

so [səu] *adv* **1** (*thus, likewise*) so; **~ saying he walked away** mit diesen Worten ging er weg; **if ~** falls ja; **I didn't do it - you did ~!** ich hab es nicht getan - hast du wohl!; **~ do I, ~ am I** *etc* ich auch; **it's 5 o'clock - ~ it is!** es ist 5 Uhr - tatsächlich!; **I hope/think ~** ich hoffe/glaube ja; **~ far** bis jetzt

2 (*in comparisons etc: to such a degree*) so; **~ big/quickly (that)** so groß/schnell(, daß); **I'm ~ glad to see you** ich bin ja so froh, dich zu sehen

3: **~ much** so viel; **I've got ~ much work** ich habe so viel Arbeit; **I love you ~ much** ich

liebe dich so sehr; **~ many** so viele

4 (*phrases*): **10 or ~** 10 oder so; **~ long!** (*inf: goodbye*) tschüs!

♦ *conj* **1** (*expressing purpose*): **~ as to do sth** um etw zu tun; **~ (that)** damit

2 (*expressing result*) also; **~ I was right after all** ich hatte also doch recht; **~ you see, I could have gone** wie Sie sehen, hätte ich gehen können; **~ (what)?** na und?

soak [səuk] *vt* (*drench*) durchnässen; (*steep*) einweichen ♦ *vi* einweichen; **to be ~ed through** völlig durchnäßt sein.

►**soak in** *vi* einziehen.

►**soak up** *vt* aufsaugen.

soaking ['səukɪŋ] *adj* (*also: ~ wet*) patschnaß.

so-and-so ['səuənsəu] *n* (*somebody*) Soundso *no art*; **Mr/Mrs ~** Herr/Frau Soundso; **the little ~!** (*pej*) das Biest!

soap [səup] *n* Seife *f*; (*TV: also: ~ opera*) Fernsehserie *f*, Seifenoper *f* (*inf*).

soapbox ['səupbɔks] *n* (*lit*) Seifenkiste *f*; (*fig: platform*) Apfelsinenkiste *f*.

soapflakes ['səupfleɪks] *npl* Seifenflocken *pl*.

soap opera *n* (*TV*) Fernsehserie *f*, Seifenoper *f* (*inf*).

soap powder *n* Seifenpulver *nt*.

soapsuds ['səupsʌdz] *npl* Seifenschaum *m*.

soapy ['səupɪ] *adj* seifig; **~ water** Seifenwasser *nt*.

soar [sɔ:*] *vi* aufsteigen; (*price, temperature*) hochschnellen; (*building etc*) aufragen.

soaring ['sɔ:rɪŋ] *adj* (*prices*) in die Höhe schnellend; (*inflation*) unaufhaltsam.

sob [sɔb] *n* Schluchzer *m* ♦ *vi* schluchzen.

s.o.b. (*US: inf!*) *n abbr* (= *son of a bitch*) Scheißkerl *m*.

sober ['səubə*] *adj* nüchtern; (*serious*) ernst; (*colour*) gedeckt; (*style*) schlicht.

►**sober up** *vt* nüchtern machen ♦ *vi* nüchtern werden.

sobriety [sə'braɪətɪ] *n* Nüchternheit *f*; (*seriousness*) Ernst *m*.

sobriquet ['səubrɪkeɪ] *n* Spitzname *m*.

sob story *n* rührselige Geschichte *f*.

Soc. *abbr* (= *society*) Ges.

so-called ['səu'kɔ:ld] *adj* sogenannt.

soccer ['sɔkə*] *n* Fußball *m*.

soccer pitch *n* Fußballplatz *m*.

soccer player *n* Fußballspieler(in) *m(f)*.

sociable ['səuʃəbl] *adj* gesellig.

social ['səuʃl] *adj* sozial; (*history*) Sozial-; (*structure*) Gesellschafts-; (*event, contact*) gesellschaftlich; (*person*) gesellig; (*animal*) gesellig lebend ♦ *n* (*party*) geselliger Abend *m*; **~ life** gesellschaftliches Leben *nt*; **to have no ~ life** nicht mit anderen Leuten zusammenkommen.

social class *n* Gesellschaftsklasse *f*.

social climber (*pej*) *n* Emporkömmling *m*, sozialer Aufsteiger *m*.

social club *n* Klub *m* für geselliges

Beisammensein.

Social Democrat n Sozialdemokrat(in) m(f).

social insurance (US) n Sozialversicherung f.

socialism ['səuʃəlɪzəm] n Sozialismus m.

socialist ['səuʃəlɪst] adj sozialistisch ♦ n Sozialist(in) m(f).

socialite ['səuʃəlaɪt] n Angehörige(r) f(m) der Schickeria.

socialize ['səuʃəlaɪz] vi unter die Leute kommen; **to ~ with** (meet socially) gesellschaftlich verkehren mit; (chat to) sich unterhalten mit.

socially ['səuʃəlɪ] adv (visit) privat; (acceptable) in Gesellschaft.

social science n Sozialwissenschaft f.

social security (BRIT) n Sozialhilfe f; **Department of Social Security** Ministerium nt für Soziales.

social services npl soziale Einrichtungen pl.

social welfare n soziales Wohl nt.

social work n Sozialarbeit f.

social worker n Sozialarbeiter(in) m(f).

society [sə'saɪətɪ] n Gesellschaft f; (people, their lifestyle) die Gesellschaft; (club) Verein m; (also: **high ~**) High-Society f ♦ cpd (party, lady) Gesellschafts-.

socioeconomic ['səusɪəuiːkə'nɒmɪk] adj sozioökonomisch.

sociological [səusɪə'lɒdʒɪkl] adj soziologisch.

sociologist [səusɪ'ɒlədʒɪst] n Soziologe m, Soziologin f.

sociology [səusɪ'ɒlədʒɪ] n Soziologie f.

sock [sɒk] n Socke f ♦ vt (inf: hit) hauen; **to pull one's ~s up** (fig) sich am Riemen reißen.

socket ['sɒkɪt] n (of eye) Augenhöhle f; (of joint) Gelenkpfanne f; (BRIT: ELEC: wall socket) Steckdose f; (: : for light bulb) Fassung f.

sod [sɒd] n (earth) Sode f; (BRIT: inf!) Sau f (!); **the poor ~** das arme Schwein.

▶**sod off** (BRIT: inf!) vi: **sod off!** verpiß dich!

soda ['səudə] n Soda nt; (also: **~ water**) Soda(wasser) nt; (US: also: **~ pop**) Brause f.

sodden ['sɒdn] adj durchnäßt.

sodium ['səudɪəm] n Natrium nt.

sodium chloride n Natriumchlorid nt, Kochsalz nt.

sofa ['səufə] n Sofa nt.

Sofia ['səufɪə] n Sofia nt.

soft [sɒft] adj weich; (not rough) zart; (voice, music, light, colour) gedämpft; (lenient) nachsichtig; **~ in the head** (inf) nicht ganz richtig im Kopf.

soft-boiled ['sɒftbɔɪld] adj (egg) weich(gekocht).

soft drink n alkoholfreies Getränk nt.

soft drugs npl weiche Drogen pl.

soften ['sɒfn] vt weich machen; (effect, blow) mildern ♦ vi weich werden; (voice, expression) sanfter werden.

softener ['sɒfnə*] n (water softener)

Enthärtungsmittel nt; (fabric softener) Weichspüler m.

soft fruit (BRIT) n Beerenobst nt.

soft furnishings npl Raumtextilien pl.

soft-hearted [sɒft'hɑːtɪd] adj weichherzig.

softly ['sɒftlɪ] adv (gently) sanft; (quietly) leise.

softness ['sɒftnɪs] n Weichheit f; (gentleness) Sanftheit f.

soft option n Weg m des geringsten Widerstandes.

soft sell n weiche Verkaufstaktik f.

soft spot n: **to have a ~ for sb** eine Schwäche für jdn haben.

soft target n leicht verwundbares Ziel nt.

soft toy n Stofftier nt.

software ['sɒftwɛə*] n (COMPUT) Software f.

software package n (COMPUT) Softwarepaket nt.

soft water n weiches Wasser nt.

soggy ['sɒgɪ] adj (ground) durchweicht; (sandwiches etc) matschig.

soil [sɔɪl] n Erde f, Boden m ♦ vt beschmutzen.

soiled [sɔɪld] adj schmutzig.

sojourn ['sɒdʒəːn] (form) n Aufenthalt m.

solace ['sɒlɪs] n Trost m.

solar ['səulə*] adj (eclipse, power station etc) Sonnen-.

solarium [sə'lɛərɪəm] (pl **solaria**) n Solarium nt.

solar panel n Sonnenkollektor m.

solar plexus [-'plɛksəs] n (ANAT) Solarplexus m, Magengrube f.

solar power n Sonnenenergie f.

solar system n Sonnensystem nt.

solar wind n Sonnenwind m.

sold [səuld] pt, pp of **sell**.

solder ['səuldə*] vt löten ♦ n Lötmittel nt.

soldier ['səuldʒə*] n Soldat m ♦ vi: **to ~ on** unermüdlich weitermachen; **toy ~** Spielzeugsoldat m.

sold out adj ausverkauft.

sole [səul] n Sohle f; (fish: pl inv) Seezunge f ♦ adj einzig, Allein-; (exclusive) alleinig; **the ~ reason** der einzige Grund.

solely ['səullɪ] adv nur, ausschließlich; **I will hold you ~ responsible** ich mache Sie allein dafür verantwortlich.

solemn ['sɒləm] adj feierlich; (person) ernst.

sole trader n (COMM) Einzelunternehmer m.

solicit [sə'lɪsɪt] vt (request) erbitten, bitten um ♦ vi (prostitute) Kunden anwerben.

solicitor [sə'lɪsɪtə*] (BRIT) n Rechtsanwalt m, Rechtsanwältin f.

solid ['sɒlɪd] adj (not hollow, pure) massiv; (not liquid) fest; (reliable) zuverlässig; (strong: structure) stabil; (: foundations) solide; (substantial: advice) gut; (: experience) solide; (unbroken) ununterbrochen ♦ n (solid object) Festkörper m; **solids** npl (food) feste Nahrung f; **to be on ~ ground** (fig) sich auf festem Boden befinden; **I read for 2 hours ~** ich habe 2 Stunden ununterbrochen gelesen.

solidarity [sɔlɪ'dærɪtɪ] n Solidarität f.
solid fuel n fester Brennstoff m.
solidify [sə'lɪdɪfaɪ] vi fest werden ♦ vt fest
werden lassen.
solidity [sə'lɪdɪtɪ] n (of structure) Stabilität f;
(of foundations) Solidität f.
solidly ['sɔlɪdlɪ] adv (built) solide; (in favour)
geschlossen, einmütig; a ~ respectable
family eine durch und durch respektable
Familie.
solid-state ['sɔlɪdsteɪt] adj (ELEC: equipment)
Halbleiter-.
soliloquy [sə'lɪləkwɪ] n Monolog m.
solitaire [sɔlɪ'tɛə*] n (gem) Solitär m; (game)
Patience f.
solitary ['sɔlɪtərɪ] adj einsam; (single) einzeln.
solitary confinement n Einzelhaft f.
solitude ['sɔlɪtjuːd] n Einsamkeit f; to live in ~
einsam leben.
solo ['səʊləʊ] n Solo nt ♦ adv (fly) allein; (play,
perform) solo; ~ flight Alleinflug m.
soloist ['səʊləʊɪst] n Solist(in) m(f).
Solomon Islands ['sɔləmən-] npl: the ~ die
Salomoninseln pl.
solstice ['sɔlstɪs] n Sonnenwende f.
soluble ['sɔljʊbl] adj löslich.
solution [sə'luːʃən] n (answer, liquid) Lösung f;
(to crossword) Auflösung f.
solve [sɔlv] vt lösen; (mystery) enträtseln.
solvency ['sɔlvənsɪ] n (COMM)
Zahlungsfähigkeit f.
solvent ['sɔlvənt] adj (COMM) zahlungsfähig
♦ n (CHEM) Lösungsmittel nt.
solvent abuse n Lösungsmittelmißbrauch m.
Som. (BRIT) abbr (POST: = Somerset).
Somali [sə'mɑːlɪ] adj somalisch ♦ n
Somalier(in) m(f).
Somalia [sə'mɑːlɪə] n Somalia nt.
Somaliland n (formerly) Somaliland nt.
sombre, (US) **somber** ['sɔmbə*] adj (dark)
dunkel, düster; (serious) finster.

========================== KEYWORD

some [sʌm] adj 1 (a certain amount or number
of) einige; ~ tea/water/money etwas Tee/
Wasser/Geld; ~ biscuits ein paar Plätzchen;
~ children came einige Kinder kamen; he
asked me ~ questions er stellte mir ein
paar Fragen
2 (certain: in contrasts) manche(r, s);
~ people say that ... manche Leute sagen,
daß ...; ~ films were excellent einige or
manche Filme waren ausgezeichnet
3 (unspecified) irgendein(e); ~ woman was
asking for you eine Frau hat nach Ihnen
gefragt; ~ day eines Tages; ~ day next
week irgendwann nächste Woche; that's
~ house! das ist vielleicht ein Haus!
♦ pron 1 (a certain number) einige; I've got ~
(books etc) ich habe welche
2 (a certain amount) etwas; I've got ~ (money,
milk) ich habe welche(s); I've read ~ of the

book ich habe das Buch teilweise gelesen
♦ adv: ~ 10 people etwa 10 Leute.

somebody ['sʌmbədɪ] pron = someone.
someday ['sʌmdeɪ] adv irgendwann.
somehow ['sʌmhaʊ] adv irgendwie.
someone ['sʌmwʌn] pron (irgend) jemand;
there's ~ coming es kommt jemand; I saw
~ in the garden ich habe jemanden im
Garten gesehen.
someplace ['sʌmpleɪs] (US) adv = somewhere.
somersault ['sʌməsɔːlt] n Salto m ♦ vi einen
Salto machen; (vehicle) sich überschlagen.
something ['sʌmθɪŋ] pron etwas; ~ nice etwas
Schönes; there's ~ wrong da stimmt etwas
nicht; would you like ~ to eat/drink?
möchten Sie etwas zu essen/trinken?
sometime ['sʌmtaɪm] adv irgendwann; ~ last
month irgendwann letzten Monat; I'll finish
it ~ ich werde es irgendwann
fertigmachen.
sometimes ['sʌmtaɪmz] adv manchmal.
somewhat ['sʌmwɔt] adv etwas, ein wenig;
~ to my surprise ziemlich zu meiner
Überraschung.
somewhere ['sʌmwɛə*] adv (be) irgendwo;
(go) irgendwohin; ~ (or other) in Scotland
irgendwo in Schottland; ~ else (be)
woanders; (go) woandershin.
son [sʌn] n Sohn m.
sonar ['səʊnɑː*] n Sonar(gerät) nt, Echolot nt.
sonata [sə'nɑːtə] n Sonate f.
song [sɔŋ] n Lied nt; (of bird) Gesang m.
songbook ['sɔŋbʊk] n Liederbuch nt.
songwriter ['sɔŋraɪtə*] n Liedermacher m.
sonic ['sɔnɪk] adj (speed) Schall-; ~ boom
Überschallknall m.
son-in-law ['sʌnɪnlɔː] n Schwiegersohn m.
sonnet ['sɔnɪt] n Sonett nt.
sonny ['sʌnɪ] (inf) n Junge m.
soon [suːn] adv bald; (a short time after) bald,
schnell; (early) früh; ~ afterwards kurz or
bald danach; quite ~ ziemlich bald; how
~ can you finish it? bis wann haben Sie es
fertig?; how ~ can you come back? wann
können Sie frühestens wiederkommen?;
see you ~! bis bald!; see also as.
sooner ['suːnə*] adv (time) früher, eher;
(preference) lieber; I would ~ do that das
würde ich lieber tun; ~ or later früher oder
später; the ~ the better je eher, desto
besser; no ~ said than done gesagt, getan;
no ~ had we left than ... wir waren gerade
gegangen, da ...
soot [sʊt] n Ruß m.
soothe [suːð] vt beruhigen; (pain) lindern.
soothing ['suːðɪŋ] adj beruhigend; (ointment
etc) schmerzlindernd; (drink) wohltuend;
(bath) entspannend.
SOP n abbr (= standard operating procedure)
normale Vorgehensweise f.
sop [sɔp] n: that's only a ~ das soll nur zur

Beschwichtigung dienen.

sophisticated [sə'fɪstɪkeɪtɪd] adj (woman, lifestyle) kultiviert; (audience) anspruchsvoll; (machinery) hochentwickelt; (arguments) differenziert.

sophistication [səfɪstɪ'keɪʃən] n (of person) Kultiviertheit f; (of machine) hoher Entwicklungsstand m; (of argument etc) Differenziertheit f.

sophomore ['sɔfəmɔː*] (US) n Student(in) im 2. Studienjahr.

soporific [sɔpə'rɪfɪk] adj einschläfernd ♦ n Schlafmittel nt.

sopping ['sɔpɪŋ] adj: ~ (wet) völlig durchnäßt.

soppy ['sɔpɪ] (pej) adj (person) sentimental; (film) schmalzig.

soprano [sə'prɑːnəu] n Sopranist(in) m(f).

sorbet ['sɔːbeɪ] n Sorbet nt or m, Fruchteis nt.

sorcerer ['sɔːsərə*] n Hexenmeister m.

sordid ['sɔːdɪd] adj (dirty) verkommen; (wretched) elend.

sore [sɔː*] adj wund; (esp US: offended) verärgert, sauer (inf) ♦ n wunde Stelle f; to have a ~ throat Halsschmerzen haben; it's a ~ point (fig) es ist ein wunder Punkt.

sorely ['sɔːlɪ] adv: I am ~ tempted (to) ich bin sehr in Versuchung(, zu).

soreness ['sɔːnɪs] n (pain) Schmerz m.

sorrel ['sɔrəl] n (BOT) (großer) Sauerampfer m.

sorrow ['sɔrəu] n Trauer f; **sorrows** npl (troubles) Sorgen und Nöte pl.

sorrowful ['sɔrəuful] adj traurig.

sorry ['sɔrɪ] adj traurig; (excuse) faul; (sight) jämmerlich; ~! Entschuldigung!, Verzeihung!; ~? wie bitte?; I feel ~ for him er tut mir leid; I'm ~ to hear that ... es tut mir leid, daß ...; I'm ~ about ... es tut mir leid wegen ...

sort [sɔːt] n Sorte f; (make: of car etc) Marke f ♦ vt (also: ~ **out**) sortieren; (: problems) ins reine bringen; (COMPUT) sortieren; **all ~s of reasons** alle möglichen Gründe; **what ~ do you want?** welche Sorte möchten Sie?; **what ~ of car?** was für ein Auto?; **I'll do nothing of the ~!** das kommt überhaupt nicht in Frage!; **it's ~ of awkward** (inf) es ist irgendwie schwierig; **to ~ sth out** etw in Ordnung bringen.

sort code n Bankleitzahl f.

sortie ['sɔːtɪ] n (MIL) Ausfall m; (fig) Ausflug m.

sorting office ['sɔːtɪŋ-] n Postverteilstelle f.

SOS n abbr (= save our souls) SOS nt.

so-so ['səusəu] adv, adj so lala.

soufflé ['suːfleɪ] n Soufflé nt.

sought [sɔːt] pt, pp of **seek**.

sought-after ['sɔːtɑːftə*] adj begehrt, gesucht; **a much ~ item** ein vielbegehrtes Stück.

soul [səul] n Seele f; (MUS) Soul m; **the poor ~ had nowhere to sleep** der Ärmste hatte

keine Unterkunft; **I didn't see a ~** ich habe keine Menschenseele gesehen.

soul-destroying ['səuldɪstrɔɪɪŋ] adj geisttötend.

soulful ['səulful] adj (eyes) seelenvoll; (music) gefühlvoll.

soulless ['səullɪs] adj (place) seelenlos; (job) eintönig.

soul mate n Seelenfreund(in) m(f).

soul-searching ['səulsɜːtʃɪŋ] n: **after much ~** nach reiflicher Überlegung.

sound [saund] adj (healthy) gesund; (safe, secure) sicher; (not damaged) einwandfrei; (reliable) solide; (thorough) gründlich; (sensible, valid) vernünftig ♦ adv: **to be ~ asleep** tief und fest schlafen ♦ n Geräusch nt; (MUS) Klang m; (on TV etc) Ton m; (GEOG) Meerenge f, Sund m ♦ vt: **to ~ the alarm** Alarm schlagen ♦ vi (alarm, horn) ertönen; (fig: seem) sich anhören, klingen; **to be of ~ mind** bei klarem Verstand sein; **I don't like the ~ of it** das klingt gar nicht gut; **to ~ one's horn** (AUT) hupen; **to ~ like** sich anhören wie; **that ~s like them arriving** das hört sich so an, als ob sie ankommen; **it ~s as if ...** es klingt or es hört sich so an, als ob ...

▶**sound off** (inf) vi: **to ~ off (about)** sich auslassen (über +acc).

▶**sound out** vt (person) aushorchen; (opinion) herausbekommen.

sound barrier n Schallmauer f.

sound bite n prägnantes Zitat nt.

sound effects npl Toneffekte pl.

sound engineer n Toningenieur(in) m(f).

sounding ['saundɪŋ] n (NAUT) Loten nt, Peilung f.

sounding board n (MUS) Resonanzboden m; (fig): **to use sb as a ~ for one's ideas** seine Ideen an jdm testen.

soundly ['saundlɪ] adv (sleep) tief und fest; (beat) tüchtig.

soundproof ['saundpruːf] adj schalldicht ♦ vt schalldicht machen.

sound system n Verstärkersystem nt.

soundtrack ['saundtræk] n Filmmusik f.

sound wave n Schallwelle f.

soup [suːp] n Suppe f; **to be in the ~** (fig) in der Tinte sitzen.

soup course n Vorsuppe f.

soup kitchen n Suppenküche f.

soup plate n Suppenteller m.

soupspoon ['suːpspuːn] n Suppenlöffel m.

sour ['sauə*] adj sauer; (fig: bad-tempered) säuerlich; **to go** or **turn ~** (milk, wine) sauer werden; (fig: relationship) sich trüben; **it's ~ grapes** (fig) die Trauben hängen zu hoch.

source [sɔːs] n Quelle f; (fig: of problem, anxiety) Ursache f; **I have it from a reliable ~ that ...** ich habe es aus sicherer Quelle, daß ...

south [sauθ] n Süden m ♦ adj südlich, Süd-

◆ *adv* nach Süden; **(to the)** ~ **of** im Süden *or* südlich von; **to travel** ~ nach Süden fahren; **the S~ of France** Südfrankreich *nt.*

South Africa *n* Südafrika *nt.*

South African *adj* südafrikanisch ◆ *n* Südafrikaner(in) *m(f).*

South America *n* Südamerika *nt.*

South American *adj* südamerikanisch ◆ *n* Südamerikaner(in) *m(f).*

southbound ['sauθbaund] *adj* in Richtung Süden; *(carriageway)* Richtung Süden.

south-east [sauθ'i:st] *n* Südosten *m.*

South-East Asia *n* Südostasien *nt.*

southerly ['sʌðəlɪ] *adj* südlich; *(wind)* aus südlicher Richtung.

southern ['sʌðən] *adj* südlich, Süd-; **the ~ hemisphere** die südliche Halbkugel *or* Hemisphäre.

South Korea *n* Südkorea *nt.*

South Pole *n* Südpol *m.*

South Sea Islands *npl* Südseeinseln *pl.*

South Seas *npl* Südsee *f.*

southward(s) ['sauθwəd(z)] *adv* nach Süden, in Richtung Süden.

south-west [sauθ'wɛst] *n* Südwesten *m.*

souvenir [su:və'nɪə*] *n* Andenken *nt,* Souvenir *nt.*

sovereign ['sɔvrɪn] *n* Herrscher(in) *m(f).*

sovereignty ['sɔvrɪntɪ] *n* Oberhoheit *f,* Souveränität *f.*

soviet ['səuvɪət] *(formerly) adj* sowjetisch ◆ *n* Sowjetbürger(in) *m(f);* **the S~ Union** die Sowjetunion *f.*

sow¹ [sau] *n* Sau *f.*

sow² [səu] *(pt* **sowed,** *pp* **sown)** *vt (lit, fig)* säen.

soya ['sɔɪə], *(US)* **soy** [sɔɪ] *n:* ~ **bean** Sojabohne *f;* ~ **sauce** Sojasoße *f.*

sozzled ['sɔzld] *(BRIT: inf) adj* besoffen.

spa [spɑ:] *n (town)* Heilbad *nt; (US: also:* **health** ~) Fitneßzentrum *nt.*

space [speɪs] *n* Platz *m,* Raum *m; (gap)* Lücke *f; (beyond Earth)* der Weltraum; *(interval, period)* Zeitraum *m* ◆ *cpd* Raum- ◆ *vt (also:* ~ **out)** verteilen; **to clear a** ~ **for sth** für etw Platz schaffen; **in a confined** ~ auf engem Raum; **in a short** ~ **of time** in kurzer Zeit; **(with)in the** ~ **of an hour** innerhalb einer Stunde.

space bar *n (on keyboard)* Leertaste *f.*

spacecraft ['speɪskrɑ:ft] *n* Raumfahrzeug *nt.*

spaceman ['speɪsmæn] *(irreg: like* **man)** *n* Raumfahrer *m.*

spaceship ['speɪsʃɪp] *n* Raumschiff *nt.*

space shuttle *n* Raumtransporter *m.*

spacesuit ['speɪssu:t] *n* Raumanzug *m.*

spacewoman ['speɪswumən] *(irreg: like* **woman)** *n* Raumfahrerin *f.*

spacing ['speɪsɪŋ] *n* Abstand *m;* **single/double** ~ einfacher/doppelter Zeilenabstand.

spacious ['speɪʃəs] *adj* geräumig.

spade [speɪd] *n* Spaten *m; (child's)* Schaufel *f;*

spades *npl (CARDS)* Pik *nt.*

spadework ['speɪdwə:k] *n (fig)* Vorarbeit *f.*

spaghetti [spə'gɛtɪ] *n* Spaghetti *pl.*

Spain [speɪn] *n* Spanien *nt.*

span [spæn] *n (of bird, plane, arch)* Spannweite *f; (in time)* Zeitspanne *f* ◆ *vt* überspannen; *(fig: time)* sich erstrecken über *+acc.*

Spaniard ['spænjəd] *n* Spanier(in) *m(f).*

spaniel ['spænjəl] *n* Spaniel *m.*

Spanish ['spænɪʃ] *adj* spanisch ◆ *n (LING)* Spanisch *nt;* **the Spanish** *npl* die Spanier *pl;* ~ **omelette** Omelett mit Paprikaschoten, Zwiebeln, Tomaten etc.

spank [spæŋk] *vt:* **to** ~ **sb's bottom** jdm den Hintern versohlen *(inf).*

spanner ['spænə*] *(BRIT) n* Schraubenschlüssel *m.*

spar [spɑ:*] *n (NAUT)* Sparren *m* ◆ *vi (BOXING)* ein Sparring *nt* machen.

spare [spɛə*] *adj (free)* frei; *(extra: part, fuse etc)* Ersatz- ◆ *n* = **spare part** ◆ *vt (save: trouble etc)* (er)sparen; *(make available)* erübrigen; *(afford to give)* übrig haben; *(refrain from hurting)* verschonen; **these 2 are going** ~ diese beiden sind noch übrig; **to** ~ *(surplus)* übrig; **to** ~ **no expense** keine Kosten scheuen, an nichts sparen; **can you** ~ **the time?** haben Sie Zeit?; **I've a few minutes to** ~ ich habe ein paar Minuten Zeit; **there is no time to** ~ es ist keine Zeit; ~ **me the details** verschone mich mit den Einzelheiten.

spare part *n* Ersatzteil *nt.*

spare room *n* Gästezimmer *nt.*

spare time *n* Freizeit *f.*

spare tyre *n* Reservereifen *m.*

spare wheel *n* Reserverad *nt.*

sparing ['spɛərɪŋ] *adj:* **to be** ~ **with** sparsam umgehen mit.

sparingly ['spɛərɪŋlɪ] *adv* sparsam.

spark [spɑ:k] *n (lit, fig)* Funke *m.*

spark(ing) plug ['spɑ:k(ɪŋ)-] *n* Zündkerze *f.*

sparkle ['spɑ:kl] *n* Funkeln *nt,* Glitzern *nt* ◆ *vi* funkeln, glitzern.

sparkler ['spɑ:klə*] *n (firework)* Wunderkerze *f.*

sparkling ['spɑ:klɪŋ] *adj (water)* mit Kohlensäure; *(conversation)* vor Geist sprühend; *(performance)* glänzend; ~ **wine** Schaumwein *m.*

sparring partner ['spɑ:rɪŋ-] *n (also fig)* Sparringspartner *m.*

sparrow ['spærəu] *n* Spatz *m.*

sparse [spɑ:s] *adj* spärlich; *(population)* dünn.

spartan ['spɑ:tən] *adj (fig)* spartanisch.

spasm ['spæzəm] *n (MED)* Krampf *m; (fig: of anger etc)* Anfall *m.*

spasmodic [spæz'mɔdɪk] *adj (fig)* sporadisch.

spastic ['spæstɪk] *(old) n* Spastiker(in) *m(f)* ◆ *adj* spastisch.

spat [spæt] *pt, pp of* **spit** ◆ *n (US: quarrel)* Krach *m.*

spate [speɪt] n (fig): **a ~ of** eine Flut von; **to be in full ~** (river) Hochwasser führen.

spatial ['speɪʃl] adj räumlich.

spatter ['spætə*] vt (liquid) verspritzen; (surface) bespritzen ♦ vi spritzen.

spatula ['spætjulə] n (CULIN) Spachtel m; (MED) Spatel m.

spawn [spɔːn] vi laichen ♦ vt hervorbringen, erzeugen ♦ n Laich m.

SPCA (US) n abbr (= Society for the Prevention of Cruelty to Animals) Tierschutzverein m.

SPCC (US) n abbr (= Society for the Prevention of Cruelty to Children) Kinderschutzbund m.

speak [spiːk] (pt **spoke**, pp **spoken**) vt (say) sagen; (language) sprechen ♦ vi sprechen, reden; (make a speech) sprechen; **to ~ one's mind** seine Meinung sagen; **to ~ to sb/of** or **about sth** mit jdm/über etw acc sprechen or reden; **~ up!** sprich lauter!; **to ~ at a conference** bei einer Tagung einen Vortrag halten; **to ~ in a debate** in einer Debatte sprechen; **he has no money to ~ of** er hat so gut wie kein Geld; **so to ~** so zusagen.

▸**speak for** vt fus: **to ~ for sb** (on behalf of) in jds Namen dat or für jdn sprechen; **that picture is already spoken for** (in shop) das Bild ist schon verkauft or vergeben; **~ for yourself!** das meinst auch nur du!

speaker ['spiːkə*] n (in public) Redner(in) m(f); (also: **loudspeaker**) Lautsprecher m; (POL): **the S~** (BRIT, US) der Sprecher, die Sprecherin; **are you a Welsh ~?** sprechen Sie Walisisch?

speaking ['spiːkɪŋ] adj sprechend; **Italian-~ people** Italienischsprechende pl; **to be on ~ terms** miteinander reden or sprechen; **~ clock** telefonische Zeitansage.

spear [spɪə*] n Speer m ♦ vt aufspießen.

spearhead ['spɪəhed] vt (MIL, fig) anführen.

spearmint ['spɪəmɪnt] n grüne Minze f.

spec [spek] (inf): **on ~** auf Verdacht, auf gut Glück; **to buy/go on ~** auf gut Glück kaufen/hingehen.

spec. n abbr (TECH) = **specification**.

special ['speʃl] adj besondere(r, s); (service, performance, adviser, permission, school) Sonder- ♦ n (train) Sonderzug m; **take ~ care** paß besonders gut auf; **nothing ~** nichts Besonderes; **today's ~** (at restaurant) Tagesgericht nt.

special agent n Agent(in) m(f).

special correspondent n Sonderberichterstatter(in) m(f).

special delivery n (POST): **by ~** durch Eilzustellung.

special effects npl Spezialeffekte pl.

specialist ['speʃəlɪst] n Spezialist(in) m(f); (MED) Facharzt m, Fachärztin f; **heart ~** Facharzt m/Fachärztin f für Herzkrankheiten.

speciality [speʃɪ'ælɪtɪ] n Spezialität f; (study) Spezialgebiet nt.

specialize ['speʃəlaɪz] vi: **to ~ (in)** sich spezialisieren (auf +acc).

specially ['speʃlɪ] adv besonders, extra.

special offer n Sonderangebot nt.

specialty ['speʃəltɪ] (esp US) = **speciality**.

species ['spiːʃiːz] n inv Art f.

specific [spə'sɪfɪk] adj (fixed) bestimmt; (exact) genau; **to be ~ to** eigentümlich sein für.

specifically [spə'sɪfɪklɪ] adv (specially) speziell; (exactly) genau; **more ~** und zwar.

specification [spesɪfɪ'keɪʃən] n genaue Angabe f; (requirement) Bedingung f; **specifications** npl (TECH) technische Daten pl.

specify ['spesɪfaɪ] vt angeben; **unless otherwise specified** wenn nicht anders angegeben.

specimen ['spesɪmən] n Exemplar nt; (MED) Probe f.

specimen copy n Belegexemplar nt, Probeexemplar nt.

specimen signature n Unterschriftsprobe f.

speck [spek] n Fleckchen nt; (of dust) Körnchen nt.

speckled ['spekld] adj gesprenkelt.

specs [speks] (inf) npl Brille f.

spectacle ['spektəkl] n (scene) Schauspiel nt; (sight) Anblick m; (grand event) Spektakel nt; **spectacles** npl (glasses) Brille f.

spectacle case (BRIT) n Brillenetui nt.

spectacular [spek'tækjulə*] adj sensationell; (success) spektakulär ♦ n (THEAT etc) Show f.

spectator [spek'teɪtə*] n Zuschauer(in) m(f); **~ sport** Publikumssport m.

spectra ['spektrə] npl of **spectrum**.

spectre, (US) **specter** ['spektə*] n Gespenst nt; (fig) (Schreck)gespenst nt.

spectrum ['spektrəm] (pl **spectra**) n (lit, fig) Spektrum nt.

speculate ['spekjuleɪt] vi (FIN) spekulieren; **to ~ about** spekulieren or Vermutungen anstellen über +acc.

speculation [spekju'leɪʃən] n Spekulation f.

speculative ['spekjulətɪv] adj spekulativ.

speculator ['spekjuleɪtə*] n Spekulant(in) m(f).

sped [sped] pt, pp of **speed**.

speech [spiːtʃ] n Sprache f; (manner of speaking) Sprechweise f; (enunciation) (Aus)sprache f; (formal talk: THEAT) Rede f.

speech day (BRIT) n (SCOL) Schulfeier f.

speech impediment n Sprachfehler m.

speechless ['spiːtʃlɪs] adj sprachlos.

speech therapist n Logopäde m, Logopädin f, Sprachtherapeut(in) m(f).

speech therapy n Logopädie f, Sprachtherapie f.

speed [spiːd] n Geschwindigkeit f, Schnelligkeit f ♦ vi (exceed speed limit) zu schnell fahren; **to ~ along** dahinsausen; **to ~ by** (car etc) vorbeischießen; (years) verfliegen; **at ~** (BRIT) mit hoher Geschwindigkeit; **at full** or **top ~** mit

Höchstgeschwindigkeit; **at a ~ of 70km/h** mit (einer Geschwindigkeit *or* einem Tempo von) 70 km/h; **shorthand/typing ~s** Silben/Anschläge pro Minute; **a five-~ gearbox** ein Fünfganggetriebe *nt*.
▸**speed up** (*pt, pp* **speeded up**) *vi* beschleunigen; (*fig*) sich beschleunigen ♦ *vt* beschleunigen.
speedboat ['spiːdbəut] *n* Rennboot *nt*.
speedily ['spiːdɪlɪ] *adv* schnell.
speeding ['spiːdɪŋ] *n* Geschwindigkeitsüberschreitung *f*.
speed limit *n* Tempolimit *nt*, Geschwindigkeitsbegrenzung *f*.
speedometer [spɪˈdɒmɪtə'] *n* Tachometer *m*.
speed trap *n* Radarfalle *f*.
speedway ['spiːdweɪ] *n* (*also:* ~ **racing**) Speedwayrennen *nt*.
speedy ['spiːdɪ] *adj* schnell; (*reply, settlement*) prompt.
speleologist [spɛlɪˈɒlədʒɪst] *n* Höhlenkundler(in) *m(f)*.
spell [spɛl] (*pt, pp* **spelt** (*BRIT*) *or* **spelled**) *n* (*also:* **magic ~**) Zauber *m*; (*incantation*) Zauberspruch *m*; (*period of time*) Zeit *f*, Weile *f* ♦ *vt* schreiben; (*also:* ~ **out:** *aloud*) buchstabieren; (*signify*) bedeuten; **to cast a ~ on sb** jdn verzaubern; **cold ~** Kältewelle *f*; **how do you ~ your name?** wie schreibt sich Ihr Name?; **can you ~ it for me?** können Sie das bitte buchstabieren?; **he can't ~** er kann keine Rechtschreibung.
spellbound ['spɛlbaund] *adj* gebannt.
spelling ['spɛlɪŋ] *n* Schreibweise *f*; (*ability*) Rechtschreibung *f*; ~ **mistake** Rechtschreibfehler *m*.
spelt [spɛlt] *pt, pp of* **spell**.
spend [spɛnd] (*pt, pp* **spent**) *vt* (*money*) ausgeben; (*time, life*) verbringen; **to ~ time/money/effort on sth** Zeit/Geld/Mühe für etw aufbringen.
spending ['spɛndɪŋ] *n* Ausgaben *pl*; **government ~** öffentliche Ausgaben *pl*.
spending money *n* Taschengeld *nt*.
spending power *n* Kaufkraft *f*.
spendthrift ['spɛndθrɪft] *n* Verschwender(in) *m(f)*.
spent [spɛnt] *pt, pp of* **spend** ♦ *adj* (*patience*) erschöpft; (*cartridge, bullets*) verbraucht; (*match*) abgebrannt.
sperm [spəːm] *n* Samenzelle *f*, Spermium *nt*.
sperm bank *n* Samenbank *f*.
sperm whale *n* Pottwal *m*.
spew [spjuː] *vt* (*also:* ~ **up**) erbrechen; (*fig*) ausspucken.
sphere [sfɪə'] *n* Kugel *f*; (*area*) Gebiet *nt*, Bereich *m*.
spherical ['sfɛrɪkl] *adj* kugelförmig.
sphinx [sfɪŋks] *n* Sphinx *f*.
spice [spaɪs] *n* Gewürz *nt* ♦ *vt* würzen.
spick-and-span ['spɪkən'spæn] *adj* blitzsauber.

spicy ['spaɪsɪ] *adj* stark gewürzt.
spider ['spaɪdə'] *n* Spinne *f*; ~**'s web** Spinnengewebe *nt*, Spinnennetz *nt*.
spidery ['spaɪdərɪ] *adj* (*handwriting*) krakelig.
spiel [spiːl] (*inf*) *n* Sermon *m*.
spike [spaɪk] *n* (*point*) Spitze *f*; (*BOT*) Ähre *f*; (*ELEC*) Spannungsspitze *f*; **spikes** *npl* (*SPORT*) Spikes *pl*.
spike heel (*US*) *n* Pfennigabsatz *m*.
spiky ['spaɪkɪ] *adj* stachelig; (*branch*) dornig.
spill [spɪl] (*pt, pp* **spilt** *or* **spilled**) *vt* verschütten ♦ *vi* verschüttet werden; **to ~ the beans** (*inf, fig*) alles ausplaudern.
▸**spill out** *vi* (*people*) herausströmen.
▸**spill over** *vi* überlaufen; (*fig: spread*) sich ausbreiten; **to ~ over into** sich auswirken auf +*acc*.
spillage ['spɪlɪdʒ] *n* (*act*) Verschütten *nt*; (*quantity*) verschüttete Menge *f*.
spin [spɪn] (*pt* **spun, span**, *pp* **spun**) *n* (*trip*) Spritztour *f*; (*revolution*) Drehung *f*; (*AVIAT*) Trudeln *nt*; (*on ball*) Drall *m* ♦ *vt* (*wool etc*) spinnen; (*ball, coin*) (hoch)werfen; (*wheel*) drehen; (*BRIT: also:* ~-**dry**) schleudern ♦ *vi* (*make thread*) spinnen; (*person*) sich drehen; (*car etc*) schleudern; **to ~ a yarn** Seemannsgarn spinnen; **to ~ a coin** (*BRIT*) eine Münze werfen; **my head is ~ning** mir dreht sich alles.
▸**spin out** *vt* (*talk*) ausspinnen; (*job, holiday*) in die Länge ziehen; (*money*) strecken.
spina bifida ['spaɪnə'bɪfɪdə] *n* offene Wirbelsäule *f*, Spina bifida *f*.
spinach ['spɪnɪtʃ] *n* Spinat *m*.
spinal ['spaɪnl] *adj* (*injury etc*) Rückgrat-.
spinal column *n* Wirbelsäule *f*.
spinal cord *n* Rückenmark *nt*.
spindly ['spɪndlɪ] *adj* spindeldürr.
spin doctor *n* PR-Fachmann *m*, PR-Fachfrau *f*.
spin-dry ['spɪn'draɪ] *vt* schleudern.
spin-dryer [spɪn'draɪə'] (*BRIT*) *n* (Wäsche)schleuder *f*.
spine [spaɪn] *n* (*ANAT*) Rückgrat *nt*; (*thorn*) Stachel *m*.
spine-chilling ['spaɪntʃɪlɪŋ] *adj* schaurig, gruselig.
spineless ['spaɪnlɪs] *adj* (*fig*) rückgratlos.
spinner ['spɪnə'] *n* (*of thread*) Spinner(in) *m(f)*.
spinning ['spɪnɪŋ] *n* (*art*) Spinnen *nt*.
spinning top *n* Kreisel *m*.
spinning wheel *n* Spinnrad *nt*.
spin-off ['spɪnɒf] *n* (*fig*) Nebenprodukt *nt*.
spinster ['spɪnstə'] *n* unverheiratete Frau; (*pej*) alte Jungfer *f*.
spiral ['spaɪərl] *n* Spirale *f* ♦ *vi* (*fig: prices etc*) in die Höhe klettern; **the inflationary ~** die Inflationsspirale.
spiral staircase *n* Wendeltreppe *f*.
spire ['spaɪə'] *n* Turmspitze *f*.
spirit ['spɪrɪt] *n* Geist *m*; (*soul*) Seele *f*; (*energy*) Elan *m*, Schwung *m*; (*courage*) Mut *m*; (*sense*)

Geist *m*, Sinn *m*; (*frame of mind*) Stimmung *f*; **spirits** *npl* (*drink*) Spirituosen *pl*; **in good ~s** guter Laune; **community ~** Gemeinschaftssinn *m*.

spirited ['spɪrɪtɪd] *adj* (*resistance, defence*) mutig; (*performance*) lebendig.

spirit level *n* Wasserwaage *f*.

spiritual ['spɪrɪtjuəl] *adj* geistig, seelisch; (*religious*) geistlich ♦ *n* (*also:* **Negro ~**) Spiritual *nt*.

spiritualism ['spɪrɪtjuəlɪzəm] *n* Spiritismus *m*.

spit [spɪt] (*pt, pp* **spat**) *n* (*for roasting*) Spieß *m*; (*saliva*) Spucke *f* ♦ *vi* spucken; (*fire*) Funken sprühen; (*cooking*) spritzen; (*inf: rain*) tröpfeln.

spite [spaɪt] *n* Boshaftigkeit *f* ♦ *vt* ärgern; **in ~ of** trotz *+gen*.

spiteful ['spaɪtful] *adj* boshaft, gemein.

spitroast ['spɪtrəust] *n* Spießbraten *m*.

spitting ['spɪtɪŋ] *n*: "**~ prohibited**" „Spucken verboten" ♦ *adj*: **to be the ~ image of sb** jdm wie aus dem Gesicht geschnitten sein.

spittle ['spɪtl] *n* Speichel *m*, Spucke *f*.

spiv [spɪv] (*BRIT: inf: pej*) *n* schmieriger Typ *m*.

splash [splæʃ] *n* (*sound*) Platschen *nt*; (*of colour*) Tupfer *m* ♦ *excl* platsch! ♦ *vt* bespritzen ♦ *vi* (*also: ~ **about***) herumplanschen; (*water, rain*) spritzen; **to ~ paint on the floor** den Fußboden mit Farbe bespritzen.

splashdown ['splæʃdaun] *n* (*SPACE*) Wasserung *f*.

splayfooted ['spleɪfutɪd] *adj* mit nach außen gestellten Füßen.

spleen [spliːn] *n* Milz *f*.

splendid ['splendɪd] *adj* hervorragend, ausgezeichnet; (*impressive*) prächtig.

splendour, (*US*) **splendor** ['splendə*] *n* Pracht *f*; **splendours** *npl* Pracht *f*.

splice [splaɪs] *vt* spleißen, kleben.

splint [splɪnt] *n* Schiene *f*.

splinter ['splɪntə*] *n* Splitter *m* ♦ *vi* (zer)splittern.

splinter group *n* Splittergruppe *f*.

split [splɪt] (*pt, pp* **split**) *n* (*tear*) Riß *m*; (*fig: division*) Aufteilung *f*; (*: difference*) Kluft *f*; (*POL*) Spaltung *f* ♦ *vt* (*divide*) aufteilen; (*party*) spalten; (*share equally*) teilen ♦ *vi* (*divide*) sich aufteilen; (*tear*) reißen; **to do the ~s** (einen) Spagat machen; **let's ~ the difference** teilen wir uns die Differenz.

▶**split up** *vi* sich trennen; (*meeting*) sich auflösen.

split-level ['splɪtlevl] *adj* mit versetzten Geschossen.

split peas *npl* getrocknete (halbe) Erbsen *pl*.

split personality *n* gespaltene Persönlichkeit *f*.

split second *n* Bruchteil *m* einer Sekunde.

splitting ['splɪtɪŋ] *adj*: **a ~ headache** rasende Kopfschmerzen *pl*.

splutter ['splʌtə*] *vi* (*engine etc*) stottern;

(*person*) prusten.

spoil [spɔɪl] (*pt, pp* **spoilt** *or* **spoiled**) *vt* verderben; (*child*) verwöhnen; (*ballot paper, vote*) ungültig machen ♦ *vi*: **to be ~ing for a fight** Streit suchen.

spoils [spɔɪlz] *npl* Beute *f*; (*fig*) Gewinn *m*.

spoilsport ['spɔɪlspɔːt] (*pej*) *n* Spielverderber *m*.

spoilt [spɔɪlt] *pt, pp of* **spoil** ♦ *adj* (*child*) verwöhnt; (*ballot paper*) ungültig.

spoke [spəuk] *pt of* **speak** ♦ *n* Speiche *f*.

spoken ['spəukn] *pp of* **speak**.

spokesman ['spəuksmən] (*irreg: like* **man**) *n* Sprecher *m*.

spokesperson ['spəukspɜːsn] *n* Sprecher(in) *m(f)*.

spokeswoman ['spəukswumən] (*irreg: like* **woman**) *n* Sprecherin *f*.

sponge [spʌndʒ] *n* Schwamm *m*; (*also: ~* **cake**) Biskuit(kuchen) *m* ♦ *vt* mit einem Schwamm waschen ♦ *vi*: **to ~ off** *or* **on sb** jdm auf der Tasche liegen.

sponge bag (*BRIT*) *n* Waschbeutel *m*, Kulturbeutel *m*.

sponger ['spʌndʒə*] (*pej*) *n* Schmarotzer *m*.

spongy ['spʌndʒɪ] *adj* schwammig.

sponsor ['spɔnsə*] *n* Sponsor(in) *m(f)*, Geldgeber(in) *m(f)*; (*BRIT: for charitable event*) Sponsor(in) *m(f)*; (*for application, bill etc*) Befürworter(in) *m(f)* ♦ *vt* sponsern, finanziell unterstützen; (*fund-raiser*) sponsern; (*applicant*) unterstützen; (*proposal, bill etc*) befürworten; **I ~ed him at 3p a mile** (*in fund-raising race*) ich habe mich verpflichtet, ihm 3 Pence pro Meile zu geben.

sponsorship ['spɔnsəʃɪp] *n* finanzielle Unterstützung *f*.

spontaneity [spɔntə'neɪɪtɪ] *n* Spontaneität *f*.

spontaneous [spɔn'teɪnɪəs] *adj* spontan; **~ combustion** Selbstentzündung *f*.

spoof [spuːf] *n* (*parody*) Parodie *f*; (*hoax*) Ulk *m*.

spooky ['spuːkɪ] (*inf*) *adj* gruselig.

spool [spuːl] *n* Spule *f*.

spoon [spuːn] *n* Löffel *m*.

spoon-feed ['spuːnfiːd] *vt* (mit dem Löffel) füttern; (*fig*) gängeln.

spoonful ['spuːnful] *n* Löffel *m*.

sporadic [spə'rædɪk] *adj* sporadisch, vereinzelt.

sport [spɔːt] *n* Sport *m*; (*type*) Sportart *f*; (*also:* **good ~**: *person*) feiner Kerl *m* ♦ *vt* (*wear*) tragen; **indoor ~s** Hallensport *m*; **outdoor ~s** Sport *m* im Freien.

sporting ['spɔːtɪŋ] *adj* (*event etc*) Sport-; (*generous*) großzügig; **to give sb a ~ chance** jdm eine faire Chance geben.

sport jacket (*US*) *n* = **sports jacket**.

sports car *n* Sportwagen *m*.

sports centre *n* Sportzentrum *nt*.

sports ground *n* Sportplatz *m*.

sports jacket (_BRIT_) n Sakko m.
sportsman ['spɔːtsmən] (_irreg: like_ **man**) n
Sportler m.
sportsmanship ['spɔːtsmənʃɪp] n
Sportlichkeit f.
sports page n Sportseite f.
sportswear ['spɔːtswɛə*] n Sportkleidung f.
sportswoman ['spɔːtswumən] (_irreg: like_
woman) n Sportlerin f.
sporty ['spɔːtɪ] adj sportlich.
spot [spɔt] n (_mark_) Fleck m; (_dot_) Punkt m;
(_on skin_) Pickel m; (_place_) Stelle f, Platz m;
(_RADIO, TV_) Nummer f, Auftritt m; (_also:_
~ **advertisement**) Werbespot m; (_small
amount_): **a** ~ **of** ein bißchen ♦ vt entdecken;
on the ~ (_in that place_) an Ort und Stelle;
(_immediately_) auf der Stelle; **to be in a** ~ in
der Klemme sitzen; **to put sb on the** ~ jdn
in Verlegenheit bringen; **to come out in** ~**s**
Pickel bekommen.
spot check n Stichprobe f.
spotless ['spɔtlɪs] adj makellos sauber.
spotlight ['spɔtlaɪt] n Scheinwerfer m; (_in
room_) Strahler m.
spot-on [spɔt'ɔn] (_BRIT: inf_) adj genau richtig.
spot price n Kassapreis m.
spotted ['spɔtɪd] adj gepunktet.
spotty ['spɔtɪ] adj pickelig.
spouse [spaus] n (_male_) Gatte m; (_female_)
Gattin f.
spout [spaut] n (_of jug, teapot_) Tülle f; (_of pipe_)
Ausfluß m; (_of liquid_) Strahl m ♦ vi spritzen;
(_flames_) sprühen.
sprain [spreɪn] n Verstauchung f ♦ vt: **to**
~ **one's ankle/wrist** sich dat den Knöchel/
das Handgelenk verstauchen.
sprang [spræŋ] pt of **spring**.
sprawl [sprɔːl] vi (_person_) sich ausstrecken;
(_place_) wild wuchern ♦ n: **urban** ~
wildwuchernde Ausbreitung des
Stadtgebietes; **to send sb** ~**ing** jdn zu
Boden werfen.
spray [spreɪ] n (_small drops_) Sprühnebel m;
(_sea spray_) Gischt m or f; (_container_)
Sprühdose f; (_garden spray_) Sprühgerät nt;
(_of flowers_) Strauß m ♦ vt sprühen, spritzen;
(_crops_) spritzen ♦ cpd (_deodorant_) Sprüh-;
~ **can** Sprühdose f.
spread [sprɛd] (_pt, pp_ **spread**) n (_range_)
Spektrum nt; (_selection_) Auswahl f;
(_distribution_) Verteilung f; (_for bread_)
(Brot)aufstrich m; (_inf: food_) Festessen nt;
(_PRESS, TYP: two pages_) Doppelseite f ♦ vt
ausbreiten; (_butter_) streichen; (_workload,
wealth, repayments etc_) verteilen; (_scatter_)
verstreuen; (_rumour, disease_) verbreiten ♦ vi
(_disease, news_) sich verbreiten; (_also:_ ~ **out:**
stain) sich ausbreiten; **to get a middle-age** ~
in den mittleren Jahren Speck ansetzen.
▶**spread out** vi (_move apart_) sich verteilen.
spread-eagled ['sprɛdiːɡld] adj mit
ausgestreckten Armen und Beinen; **to be or**

lie ~ mit ausgestreckten Armen und
Beinen daliegen.
spreadsheet ['sprɛdʃiːt] n (_COMPUT_)
Tabellenkalkulation f.
spree [spriː] n: **to go on a** ~ (_drinking_) eine
Zechtour machen; (_spending_) groß
einkaufen gehen.
sprig [sprɪɡ] n Zweig m.
sprightly ['spraɪtlɪ] adj rüstig.
spring [sprɪŋ] (_pt_ **sprang**, _pp_ **sprung**) n (_coiled
metal_) Sprungfeder f; (_season_) Frühling m,
Frühjahr nt; (_of water_) Quelle f ♦ vi (_leap_)
springen ♦ vt: **to** ~ **a leak** (_pipe etc_) undicht
werden; **in** ~ im Frühling or Frühjahr; **to
walk with a** ~ **in one's step** mit federnden
Schritten gehen; **to** ~ **from** (_result_)
herrühren von; **to** ~ **into action** aktiv
werden; **he sprang the news on me** er hat
mich mit der Nachricht überrascht.
▶**spring up** vi (_building, plant_) aus dem Boden
schießen.
springboard ['sprɪŋbɔːd] n (_SPORT, fig_)
Sprungbrett nt.
spring-clean(ing) [sprɪŋ'kliːn(ɪŋ)] n
Frühjahrsputz m.
spring onion (_BRIT_) n Frühlingszwiebel f.
spring roll n Frühlingsrolle f.
springtime ['sprɪŋtaɪm] n Frühling m.
springy ['sprɪŋɪ] adj federnd; (_mattress_) weich
gefedert.
sprinkle ['sprɪŋkl] vt (_liquid_) sprenkeln; (_salt,
sugar_) streuen; **to** ~ **water on,** ~ **with water**
mit Wasser besprengen; **to** ~ **sugar etc on,**
~ **with sugar etc** mit Zucker etc bestreuen.
sprinkler ['sprɪŋklə*] n (_for lawn_) Rasen-
sprenger m; (_to put out fire_) Sprinkler m.
sprinkling ['sprɪŋklɪŋ] n: **a** ~ **of** (_water_) ein
paar Tropfen; (_salt, sugar_) eine Prise; (_fig_)
ein paar.
sprint [sprɪnt] n Sprint m ♦ vi rennen; (_SPORT_)
sprinten; **the 200 metres** ~ der 200-Meter-
Lauf.
sprinter ['sprɪntə*] n Sprinter(in) m(f).
sprite [spraɪt] n Kobold m.
spritzer ['sprɪtsə*] n Schorle f.
sprocket ['sprɔkɪt] n Kettenzahnrad nt.
sprout [spraut] vi (_vegetable_) sprießen;
keimen.
sprouts [sprauts] npl (_also:_ **Brussels** ~)
Rosenkohl m.
spruce [spruːs] n inv Fichte f ♦ adj gepflegt,
adrett.
▶**spruce up** vt auf Vordermann bringen (_inf_);
to ~ **o.s. up** sein Äußeres pflegen.
sprung [sprʌŋ] pp of **spring**.
spry [spraɪ] adj rüstig.
SPUC n abbr (= _Society for the Protection of the
Unborn Child_) Gesellschaft f zum Schutz des
ungeborenen Lebens.
spud [spʌd] (_inf_) n Kartoffel f.
spun [spʌn] pt, pp of **spin**.
spur [spɜː*] n Sporn m; (_fig_) Ansporn m ♦ vt

(*also:* ~ **on**, *fig*) anspornen; **on the ~ of the moment** ganz spontan.

spurious ['spjuərıəs] *adj* falsch.

spurn [spə:n] *vt* verschmähen.

spurt [spə:t] *n* (*of blood etc*) Strahl *m*; (*of energy*) Anwandlung *f* ♦ *vi* (*blood*) (heraus)spritzen; **to put on a ~** (*lit, fig*) einen Spurt einlegen.

sputter ['spʌtə*] *vi* = **splutter**.

spy [spaı] *n* Spion(in) *m(f)* ♦ *vi:* **to ~ on** nachspionieren +*dat* ♦ *vt* sehen ♦ *cpd* (*film, story*) Spionage-.

spying ['spaııŋ] *n* Spionage *f*.

Sq. *abbr* (*in address:* = *square*) ≈ Pl.

sq. *abbr* = **square**.

squabble ['skwɔbl] *vi* (sich) zanken ♦ *n* Streit *m*.

squad [skwɔd] *n* (*MIL*) Trupp *m*; (*POLICE*) Kommando *nt*; (: *drug/fraud squad*) Dezernat *nt*; (*SPORT*) Mannschaft *f*; **flying ~** (*POLICE*) Überfallkommando *nt*.

squad car (*BRIT*) *n* (*POLICE*) Streifenwagen *m*.

squaddie ['skwɔdı] (*BRIT*) *n* (*private soldier*) Gefreite(r) *m*.

squadron ['skwɔdrn] *n* (*MIL*) Schwadron *f*; (*AVIAT*) Staffel *f*; (*NAUT*) Geschwader *nt*.

squalid ['skwɔlıd] *adj* verkommen; (*conditions*) elend; (*sordid*) erbärmlich.

squall [skwɔ:l] *n* Bö(e) *f*.

squalor ['skwɔlə*] *n* Elend *nt*.

squander ['skwɔndə*] *vt* verschwenden; (*chances*) vertun.

square [skwɛə*] *n* Quadrat *nt*; (*in town*) Platz *m*; (*US: block of houses*) Block *m*; (*also:* **set ~**) Zeichendreieck *nt*; (*inf: person*) Spießer *m* ♦ *adj* quadratisch; (*inf: ideas, person*) spießig ♦ *vt* (*arrange*) ausrichten; (*MATH*) quadrieren; (*reconcile*) in Einklang bringen ♦ *vi* (*accord*) übereinstimmen; **we're back to ~ one** jetzt sind wir wieder da, wo wir angefangen haben; **all ~** (*SPORT*) unentschieden; (*fig*) quitt; **a ~ meal** eine ordentliche Mahlzeit; **2 metres ~** 2 Meter im Quadrat; **2 ~ metres** 2 Quadratmeter; **I'll ~ it with him** (*inf*) ich mache das mit ihm ab; **can you ~ it with your conscience?** können Sie das mit Ihrem Gewissen vereinbaren?

▶**square up** (*BRIT*) *vi* abrechnen.

square bracket *n* eckige Klammer *f*.

squarely ['skwɛəlı] *adv* (*directly*) direkt, genau; (*firmly*) fest; (*honestly*) ehrlich; (*fairly*) gerecht, fair.

square root *n* Quadratwurzel *f*.

squash [skwɔʃ] *n* (*BRIT*): **lemon/orange ~** Zitronen-/Orangensaftgetränk *nt*; (*US: marrow etc*) Kürbis *m*; (*SPORT*) Squash *nt* ♦ *vt* zerquetschen.

squat [skwɔt] *adj* gedrungen ♦ *vi* (*also:* ~ **down**) hocken (sich hin)hocken; (*on property*): **to ~ (in a house)** ein Haus besetzen.

squatter ['skwɔtə*] *n* Hausbesetzer(in) *m(f)*.

squawk [skwɔ:k] *vi* kreischen.

squeak [skwi:k] *vi* quietschen; (*mouse etc*) piepsen ♦ *n* Quietschen *nt*; (*of mouse etc*) Piepsen *nt*.

squeaky-clean [skwi:kı'kli:n] (*inf*) *adj* blitzsauber.

squeal [skwi:l] *vi* quietschen.

squeamish ['skwi:mıʃ] *adj* empfindlich.

squeeze [skwi:z] *n* Drücken *nt*; (*ECON*) Beschränkung *f*; (*also:* **credit ~**) Kreditbeschränkung *f* ♦ *vt* drücken; (*lemon etc*) auspressen ♦ *vi:* **to ~ past sth** sich an etw *dat* vorbeidrücken; **to ~ under sth** sich unter etw *dat* durchzwängen; **to give sth a ~** etw drücken; **a ~ of lemon** ein Spritzer Zitronensaft.

▶**squeeze out** *vt* (*juice etc*) (her)auspressen; (*fig: exclude*) hinausdrängen.

squelch [skwɛltʃ] *vi* (*mud etc*) quatschen.

squib [skwıb] *n* Knallfrosch *m*.

squid [skwıd] *n* Tintenfisch *m*.

squiggle ['skwıgl] *n* Schnörkel *m*.

squint [skwınt] *vi* (*in the sunlight*) blinzeln ♦ *n* (*MED*) Schielen *nt*; **he has a ~** er schielt.

squire ['skwaıə*] (*BRIT*) *n* Gutsherr *m*; (*inf*) Chef *m*.

squirm [skwə:m] *vi* (*lit, fig*) sich winden.

squirrel ['skwırəl] *n* Eichhörnchen *nt*.

squirt [skwə:t] *vi, vt* spritzen.

Sr *abbr* (*in names:* = *senior*) sen.; (*REL*) = **sister**.

SRC (*BRIT*) *n abbr* (= *Students' Representative Council*) *studentische Vertretung*.

Sri Lanka [srı'læŋkə] *n* Sri Lanka *nt*.

SRN (*BRIT*) *n abbr* (*formerly:* = *State Registered Nurse*) staatlich geprüfte Krankenschwester *f*, staatlich geprüfter Krankenpfleger *m*.

SRO (*US*) *abbr* (= *standing room only*) nur Stehplätze.

SS *abbr* = **steamship**.

SSA (*US*) *n abbr* (= *Social Security Administration*) Sozialversicherungsbehörde *f*.

SST (*US*) *n abbr* (= *supersonic transport*) Überschallverkehr *m*.

ST (*US*) *abbr* = **standard time**.

St *abbr* (= *saint*) St.; (= *street*) Str.

stab [stæb] *n* Stich *m*, Stoß *m*; (*inf: try*): **to have a ~ at sth** etw probieren ♦ *vt* (*person*) niederstechen; (*body*) einstechen auf +*acc*; **a ~ of pain** ein stechender Schmerz; **to ~ sb to death** jdn erstechen.

stabbing ['stæbıŋ] *n* Messerstecherei *f* ♦ *adj* (*pain*) stechend.

stability [stə'bılıtı] *n* Stabilität *f*.

stabilization [steɪbəlaɪ'zeɪʃən] *n* Stabilisierung *f*.

stabilize ['steɪbəlaɪz] *vt* stabilisieren ♦ *vi* sich stabilisieren.

stabilizer ['steɪbəlaɪzə*] *n* (*AVIAT*) Stabilisierungsfläche *f*; (*NAUT, food additive*) Stabilisator *m*.

stable ['steɪbl] *adj* stabil; (*marriage*) dauerhaft

◆ *n* Stall *m*; **riding** ~**s** Reitstall *m*.

staccato [stə'kɑːtəu] *adv* (*MUS*) stakkato ◆ *adj* abgehackt.

stack [stæk] *n* Stapel *m*; (*of books etc*) Stoß *m* ◆ *vt* (*also*: ~ **up**) aufstapeln; ~**s of time** (*BRIT: inf*) jede Menge Zeit; **to** ~ **with** vollstapeln mit.

stadia ['steɪdɪə] *npl of* **stadium**.

stadium ['steɪdɪəm] (*pl* **stadia** *or* ~**s**) *n* Stadion *nt*.

staff [stɑːf] *n* (*workforce, servants*) Personal *nt*; (*BRIT: also*: **teaching** ~) (Lehrer)kollegium *nt*; (*stick: MIL*) Stab *m* ◆ *vt* (mit Personal) besetzen; **one of his** ~ einer seiner Mitarbeiter; **a member of** ~ ein(e) Mitarbeiter(in) *m(f)*; (*SCOL*) ein(e) Lehrer(in) *m(f)*.

staffroom ['stɑːfruːm] *n* (*SCOL*) Lehrerzimmer *nt*.

Staffs (*BRIT*) *abbr* (*POST*: = Staffordshire).

stag [stæg] *n* Hirsch *m*; (*BRIT: STOCK EXCHANGE*) Spekulant *m* (*der junge Aktien aufkauft*); ~ **market** (*BRIT: STOCK EXCHANGE*) Spekulantenmarkt *m*.

stage [steɪdʒ] *n* Bühne *f*; (*platform*) Podium *nt*; (*point, period*) Stadium *nt* ◆ *vt* (*play*) aufführen; (*demonstration*) organisieren; (*perform: recovery etc*) schaffen; **the** ~ das Theater, die Bühne; **in** ~**s** etappenweise; **to go through a difficult** ~ eine schwierige Phase durchmachen; **in the early/final** ~**s** im Anfangs-/Endstadium.

stagecoach ['steɪdʒkəutʃ] *n* Postkutsche *f*.

stage door *n* Bühneneingang *m*.

stage fright *n* Lampenfieber *nt*.

stagehand ['steɪdʒhænd] *n* Bühnenarbeiter(in) *m(f)*.

stage-manage ['steɪdʒmænɪdʒ] *vt* (*fig*) inszenieren.

stage manager *n* Inspizient(in) *m(f)*.

stagger ['stægə'] *vi* schwanken, taumeln ◆ *vt* (*amaze*) die Sprache verschlagen +*dat*; (*hours, holidays*) staffeln.

staggering ['stægərɪŋ] *adj* (*amazing*) atemberaubend.

staging post ['steɪdʒɪŋ-] *n* Zwischenstation *f*.

stagnant ['stægnənt] *adj* (*water*) stehend; (*economy etc*) stagnierend.

stagnate [stæg'neɪt] *vi* (*economy etc*) stagnieren; (*person*) verdummen.

stagnation [stæg'neɪʃən] *n* Stagnation *f*.

stag night, stag party *n* Herrenabend *m*.

> Als **stag night** bezeichnet man eine feuchtfröhliche Männerparty, die kurz vor einer Hochzeit vom Bräutigam und seinen Freunden meist in einem Gasthaus oder Nachtklub abgehalten wird. Diese Feiern sind oft sehr ausgelassen und können manchmal auch zu weit gehen (wenn die betrunkenen Bräutigam ein Streich gespielt wird). Siehe auch **hen night**.

staid [steɪd] *adj* gesetzt.

stain [steɪn] *n* Fleck *m*; (*colouring*) Beize *f* ◆ *vt* beflecken; (*wood*) beizen.

stained glass window [steɪnd-] *n* buntes Glasfenster *nt*.

stainless steel ['steɪnlɪs-] *n* (rostfreier) Edelstahl *m*.

stain remover *n* Fleckentferner *m*.

stair [stɛə'] *n* (*step*) Stufe *f*; **stairs** *npl* (*flight of steps*) Treppe *f*; **on the** ~**s** auf der Treppe.

staircase ['stɛəkeɪs] *n* Treppe *f*.

stairway ['stɛəweɪ] *n* = **staircase**.

stairwell ['stɛəwɛl] *n* Treppenhaus *nt*.

stake [steɪk] *n* (*post*) Pfahl *m*, Pfosten *m*; (*COMM*) Anteil *m*; (*BETTING: gen pl*) Einsatz *m* ◆ *vt* (*money*) setzen; (*also*: ~ **out**: *area*) abstecken; **to be at** ~ auf dem Spiel stehen; **to have a** ~ **in sth** einen Anteil an etw *dat* haben; **to** ~ **a claim (to sth)** sich *dat* ein Anrecht (auf etw *acc*) sichern; **to** ~ **one's life on sth** seinen Kopf auf etw *acc* wetten; **to** ~ **one's reputation on sth** sich für etw verbürgen.

stakeout ['steɪkaut] *n* (*surveillance*) Überwachung *f*.

stalactite ['stæləktaɪt] *n* Stalaktit *m*.

stalagmite ['stæləgmaɪt] *n* Stalagmit *m*.

stale [steɪl] *adj* (*bread*) altbacken; (*food*) alt; (*smell*) muffig; (*air*) verbraucht; (*beer*) schal.

stalemate ['steɪlmeɪt] *n* (*CHESS*) Patt *nt*; (*fig*) Sackgasse *f*.

stalk [stɔːk] *n* Stiel *m* ◆ *vt* sich heranpirschen an +*acc* ◆ *vi*: **to** ~ **out/off** hinaus-/davonstolzieren.

stall [stɔːl] *n* (*BRIT: in market etc*) Stand *m*; (*in stable*) Box *f* ◆ *vt* (*engine, car*) abwürgen; (*fig: person*) hinhalten; (: *decision etc*) hinauszögern ◆ *vi* (*engine*) absterben; (*car*) stehenbleiben; (*fig: person*) ausweichen; **stalls** *npl* (*BRIT: in cinema, theatre*) Parkett *nt*; **a seat in the** ~**s** ein Platz im Parkett; **a clothes/flower** ~ ein Kleidungs-/Blumenstand; **to** ~ **for time** versuchen, Zeit zu gewinnen.

stallholder ['stɔːlhəuldə'] (*BRIT*) *n* Standbesitzer(in) *m(f)*.

stallion ['stæljən] *n* Hengst *m*.

stalwart ['stɔːlwət] *adj* treu.

stamen ['steɪmɛn] *n* Staubgefäß *nt*.

stamina ['stæmɪnə] *n* Ausdauer *f*.

stammer ['stæmə'] *n* Stottern *nt* ◆ *vi* stottern; **to have a** ~ stottern.

stamp [stæmp] *n* (*lit, fig*) Stempel *m*; (*postage stamp*) Briefmarke *f* ◆ *vi* stampfen; (*also*: ~ **one's foot**) (mit dem Fuß) aufstampfen ◆ *vt* stempeln; (*with postage stamp*) frankieren; ~**ed addressed envelope** frankierter Rückumschlag.

▶**stamp out** *vt* (*fire*) austreten; (*fig: crime*) ausrotten; (: *opposition*) unterdrücken.

stamp album *n* Briefmarkenalbum *nt*.

stamp collecting n Briefmarkensammeln nt.
stamp duty (BRIT) n (Stempel)gebühr f.
stampede [stæm'pi:d] n (of animals) wilde Flucht f; (fig) Massenandrang m.
stamp machine n Briefmarkenautomat m.
stance [stæns] n Haltung f; (fig) Einstellung f.
stand [stænd] (pt, pp **stood**) n (COMM) Stand m; (SPORT) Tribüne f; (piece of furniture) Ständer m ♦ vi stehen; (rise) aufstehen; (remain) bestehenbleiben; (in election etc) kandidieren ♦ vt stellen; (tolerate, withstand) ertragen; **to make a ~ against sth** Widerstand gegen etw leisten; **to take a ~ on sth** einen Standpunkt zu etw vertreten; **to take the ~** (US: LAW) in den Zeugenstand treten; **to ~ at** (value, score etc) betragen; (level) liegen bei; **to ~ for parliament** (BRIT) in den Parlamentswahlen kandidieren; **to ~ to gain/lose sth** etw gewinnen/verlieren können; **it ~s to reason** es ist einleuchtend; **as things ~** nach Lage der Dinge; **to ~ sb a drink/meal** jdm einen Drink/ein Essen spendieren; **I can't ~ him** ich kann ihn nicht leiden or ausstehen; **we don't ~ a chance** wir haben keine Chance; **to ~ trial** vor Gericht stehen.
►**stand by** vi (be ready) sich bereithalten; (fail to help) (unbeteiligt) danebenstehen ♦ vt fus (opinion, decision) stehen zu; (person) halten zu.
►**stand down** vi zurücktreten.
►**stand for** vt fus (signify) bedeuten; (represent) stehen für; (tolerate) sich dat gefallen lassen.
►**stand in for** vt fus vertreten.
►**stand out** vi hervorstechen.
►**stand up** vi aufstehen.
►**stand up for** vt fus eintreten für.
►**stand up to** vt fus standhalten +dat; (person) sich behaupten gegenüber +dat.
stand-alone ['stændələun] adj (COMPUT) selbständig.
standard ['stændəd] n (level) Niveau nt; (norm) Norm f; (criterion) Maßstab m; (flag) Standarte f ♦ adj (size, model, value etc) Standard-; (normal) normal; **standards** npl (morals) (sittliche) Maßstäbe pl; **to be** or **to come up to ~** den Anforderungen genügen; **to apply a double ~** mit zweierlei Maß messen.
standardization [stændədaɪ'zeɪʃən] n Vereinheitlichung f.
standardize ['stændədaɪz] vt vereinheitlichen.
standard lamp (BRIT) n Stehlampe f.
standard of living n Lebensstandard m.
standard time n Normalzeit f.
stand-by, standby ['stændbaɪ] n Reserve f; (also: **standby ticket**) Standby-Ticket nt ♦ adj (generator) Reserve-, Ersatz-; **to be on ~** (doctor) Bereitschaftsdienst haben; (crew, firemen etc) in Bereitschaft sein, einsatzbereit sein.

stand-by ticket n Standby-Ticket nt.
stand-in ['stændin] n Ersatz m.
standing ['stændiŋ] adj (permanent) ständig; (army) stehend ♦ n (status) Rang m, Stellung f; **a ~ ovation** stürmischer Beifall; **of many years' ~** von langjähriger Dauer; **a relationship of 6 months' ~** eine seit 6 Monaten bestehende Beziehung; **a man of some ~** ein angesehener Mann.
standing committee n ständiger Ausschuß m.
standing joke n Standardwitz m.
standing order (BRIT) n (at bank) Dauerauftrag m.
standing room n Stehplätze pl.
standoff n (situation) ausweglose or verfahrene Situation f.
stand-offish [stænd'ɔfiʃ] adj distanziert.
standpat ['stændpæt] (US) adj konservativ.
standpipe ['stændpaɪp] n Steigrohr nt.
standpoint ['stændpɔɪnt] n Standpunkt m.
standstill ['stændstɪl] n: **to be at a ~** stillstehen; (fig: negotiations) in eine Sackgasse geraten sein; **to come to a ~** (traffic) zum Stillstand kommen.
stank [stæŋk] pt of **stink**.
stanza ['stænzə] n Strophe f.
staple ['steɪpl] n (for papers) Heftklammer f; (chief product) Hauptartikel m ♦ adj (food, diet) Grund-, Haupt- ♦ vt heften.
stapler ['steɪplə*] n Hefter m.
star [sta:*] n Stern m; (celebrity) Star m ♦ vt (THEAT, CINE) in der Hauptrolle zeigen ♦ vi: **to ~ in** die Hauptrolle haben in; **the stars** npl (horoscope) das Horoskop; **4-~ hotel** 4-Sterne-Hotel nt; **2-~ petrol** (BRIT) Normal(benzin) nt; **4-~ petrol** (BRIT) Super(benzin) nt.
star attraction n Hauptattraktion f.
starboard ['sta:bɔ:d] adj (side) Steuerbord-; **to ~** (nach) Steuerbord.
starch [sta:tʃ] n Stärke f.
starched [sta:tʃt] adj gestärkt.
starchy ['sta:tʃɪ] adj (food) stärkehaltig; (pej: person) steif.
stardom ['sta:dəm] n Berühmtheit f.
stare [stɛə*] n starrer Blick m ♦ vi: **to ~ at** anstarren.
starfish ['sta:fɪʃ] n Seestern m.
stark [sta:k] adj (bleak) kahl; (simplicity) schlicht; (colour) eintönig; (reality, poverty) nackt ♦ adv: **~ naked** splitternackt.
starkers ['sta:kəz] (inf) adj splitter(faser)nackt.
starlet ['sta:lɪt] n (Film)sternchen nt, Starlet nt.
starlight ['sta:laɪt] n Sternenlicht nt.
starling ['sta:lɪŋ] n Star m.
starlit ['sta:lɪt] adj sternklar.
starry ['sta:rɪ] adj sternklar; **~ sky** Sternenhimmel m.
starry-eyed [sta:rɪ'aɪd] adj (innocent) arglos,

blauäugig; (*from wonder*) verzückt.
Stars and Stripes *n sing* Sternenbanner *nt*.
star sign *n* Sternzeichen *nt*.
star-studded ['stɑːstʌdɪd] *adj:* **a ~ cast** eine
Starbesetzung *f*.
START *n abbr* (*MIL:* = *Strategic Arms Reduction
Talks*) START.
start [stɑːt] *n* Beginn *m*, Anfang *m*; (*departure*)
Aufbruch *m*; (*advantage*) Vorsprung *m* ♦ *vt*
anfangen mit; (*panic*) auslösen; (*fire*)
anzünden; (*found*) gründen; (: *restaurant etc*)
eröffnen; (*engine*) anlassen; (*car*) starten
♦ *vi* anfangen; (*with fright*) zusammenfahren;
(*engine etc*) anspringen; **at the ~** am
Anfang, zu Beginn; **for a ~** erstens; **to make
an early ~** frühzeitig aufbrechen; **to give a
~** zusammenfahren; **to wake up with a ~**
aus dem Schlaf hochschrecken; **to ~ doing**
or **to do sth** anfangen, etw zu tun; **to ~ (off)
with ...** (*firstly*) erstens; (*at the beginning*)
zunächst.
►**start off** *vi* (*begin*) anfangen; (*begin moving*)
losgehen/-fahren.
►**start out** *vi* (*leave*) sich aufmachen.
►**start over** (*US*) *vi* noch einmal von vorn
anfangen.
►**start up** *vt* (*business*) gründen; (*restaurant
etc*) eröffnen; (*car*) starten; (*engine*)
anlassen.
starter ['stɑːtə'] *n* (*AUT*) Anlasser *m*; (*SPORT:
official, runner, horse*) Starter *m*; (*BRIT: CULIN*)
Vorspeise *f*; **for ~s** (*inf*) für den Anfang.
starting point ['stɑːtɪŋ-] *n* (*lit, fig*)
Ausgangspunkt *m*.
starting price *n* (*at auction*)
Ausgangsangebot *nt*.
startle ['stɑːtl] *vt* erschrecken.
startling ['stɑːtlɪŋ] *adj* (*news etc*)
überraschend.
star turn (*BRIT*) *n* Sensation *f*,
Hauptattraktion *f*.
starvation [stɑːˈveɪʃən] *n* Hunger *m*; **to die
of/from ~** verhungern.
starve [stɑːv] *vi* hungern; (*to death*)
verhungern ♦ *vt* hungern lassen; (*fig:
deprive*): **to ~ sb of sth** jdm etw
vorenthalten; **I'm starving** ich sterbe vor
Hunger.
Star Wars *n* Krieg *m* der Sterne.
stash [stæʃ] *vi* (*also:* **~ away**) beiseite
schaffen ♦ *n* (*secret store*) geheimes Lager
nt.
state [steɪt] *n* (*condition*) Zustand *m*; (*POL*)
Staat *m* ♦ *vt* (*say*) feststellen; (*declare*)
erklären; **the States** *npl* (*GEOG*) die
(Vereinigten) Staaten *pl*; **to be in a ~**
aufgeregt sein; (*on edge*) nervös sein; (*in a
mess*) in einem schrecklichen Zustand sein;
to get into a ~ durchdrehen (*inf*); **in ~**
feierlich; **to lie in ~** (feierlich) aufgebahrt
sein; **~ of emergency** Notstand *m*; **~ of mind**
Verfassung *f*.

state control *n* staatliche Kontrolle *f*.
stated ['steɪtɪd] *adj* erklärt.
State Department (*US*) *n*
Außenministerium *nt*.
state education (*BRIT*) *n* staatliche
Erziehung *f*; (*system*) staatliches
Bildungswesen *nt*.
stateless ['steɪtlɪs] *adj* staatenlos.
stately ['steɪtlɪ] *adj* würdevoll; (*walk*)
gemessen; **~ home** Schloß *nt*.
statement ['steɪtmənt] *n* (*thing said*)
Feststellung *f*; (*declaration*) Erklärung *f*;
(*FIN*) (Konto)auszug *m*; **official ~** (amtliche)
Erklärung *f*; **bank ~** Kontoauszug *m*.
state of the art *n:* **the ~** der neueste Stand
der Technik ♦ *adj:* **state-of-the-art** auf dem
neuesten Stand der Technik; (*technology*)
Spitzen-.
state-owned ['steɪtəund] *adj* staatseigen.
state school *n* öffentliche Schule *f*.
state secret *n* Staatsgeheimnis *nt*.
statesman ['steɪtsmən] (*irreg: like* **man**) *n*
Staatsmann *m*.
statesmanship ['steɪtsmənʃɪp] *n* Staatskunst
f.
static ['stætɪk] *n* (*RADIO, TV*) atmosphärische
Störungen *pl* ♦ *adj* (*not moving*) konstant.
static electricity *n* Reibungselektrizität *f*.
station ['steɪʃən] *n* (*RAIL*) Bahnhof *m*; (*also:*
bus ~) Busbahnhof *m*; (*also:* **police ~**)
(Polizei)wache *f*; (*RADIO*) Sender *m* ♦ *vt*
(*guards etc*) postieren; (*soldiers etc*)
stationieren; **action ~s** (*MIL*) Stellung *f*;
above one's ~ über seinem Stand.
stationary ['steɪʃnərɪ] *adj* (*vehicle*) haltend; **to
be ~** stehen.
stationer ['steɪʃnə'] *n* Schreibwaren-
händler(in) *m(f)*.
stationer's (shop) *n* Schreibwarenhandlung
f.
stationery ['steɪʃnərɪ] *n* Schreibwaren *pl*;
(*writing paper*) Briefpapier *nt*.
stationmaster ['steɪʃənmɑːstə'] *n*
Bahnhofsvorsteher *m*.
station wagon (*US*) *n* Kombi(wagen) *m*.
statistic [stəˈtɪstɪk] *n* Statistik *f*.
statistical [stəˈtɪstɪkl] *adj* statistisch.
statistics [stəˈtɪstɪks] *n* (*science*) Statistik *f*.
statue ['stætjuː] *n* Statue *f*.
statuesque [stætjuˈɛsk] *adj* stattlich.
statuette [stætjuˈɛt] *n* Statuette *f*.
stature ['stætʃə'] *n* Wuchs *m*, Statur *f*; (*fig:
reputation*) Format *nt*.
status ['steɪtəs] *n* Status *m*; (*position*) Stellung
f; **the ~ quo** der Status quo.
status line *n* (*COMPUT*) Statuszeile *f*.
status symbol *n* Statussymbol *nt*.
statute ['stætjuːt] *n* Gesetz *nt*; **statutes** *npl* (*of
club etc*) Satzung *f*.
statute book *n:* **to be on the ~** geltendes
Recht sein.
statutory ['stætjutrɪ] *adj* gesetzlich;

~ **declaration** eidesstattliche Erklärung *f*.
staunch [stɔːntʃ] *adj* treu ♦ *vt* (*flow*) stauen; (*blood*) stillen.
stave [steɪv] *n* (*MUS*) Notensystem *nt*.
▶**stave off** *vt* (*attack*) abwehren; (*threat*) abwenden.
stay [steɪ] *n* Aufenthalt *m* ♦ *vi* bleiben; (*with sb, as guest*) wohnen; (*in hotel*) übernachten; ~ **of execution** (*LAW*) Aussetzung *f*; **to ~ put** bleiben; **to ~ with friends** bei Freunden untergebracht sein; **to ~ the night** übernachten.
▶**stay behind** *vi* zurückbleiben.
▶**stay in** *vi* (*at home*) zu Hause bleiben.
▶**stay on** *vi* bleiben.
▶**stay out** *vi* (*of house*) wegbleiben; (*remain on strike*) weiterstreiken.
▶**stay up** *vi* (*at night*) aufbleiben.
staying power ['steɪɪŋ-] *n* Stehvermögen *nt*, Durchhaltevermögen *nt*.
STD *n abbr* (*BRIT: TEL:* = *subscriber trunk dialling*) Selbstwählferndienst *m*; (*MED:* = *sexually transmitted disease*) durch Geschlechtsverkehr übertragene Krankheit *f*.
stead [stɛd] *n:* **in sb's ~** an jds Stelle; **to stand sb in good ~** jdm zugute *or* zustatten kommen.
steadfast ['stɛdfɑːst] *adj* standhaft.
steadily ['stɛdɪlɪ] *adv* (*regularly*) regelmäßig; (*constantly*) stetig; (*fixedly*) fest, unverwandt.
steady ['stɛdɪ] *adj* (*job, boyfriend, girlfriend, look*) fest; (*income*) regelmäßig; (*speed*) gleichmäßig; (*rise*) stetig; (*person, character*) zuverlässig, solide; (*voice, hand etc*) ruhig ♦ *vt* (*stabilize*) ruhig halten; (*nerves*) beruhigen; **to ~ o.s. on sth** sich auf etw *acc* stützen; **to ~ o.s. against sth** sich an etw *dat* abstützen.
steak [steɪk] *n* Steak *nt*; (*fish*) Filet *nt*.
steakhouse ['steɪkhaʊs] *n* Steakrestaurant *nt*.
steal [stiːl] (*pt* **stole**, *pp* **stolen**) *vt* stehlen ♦ *vi* stehlen; (*move secretly*) sich stehlen, schleichen.
▶**steal away** *vi* sich davonschleichen.
stealth [stɛlθ] *n:* **by ~** heimlich.
stealthy ['stɛlθɪ] *adj* heimlich, verstohlen.
steam [stiːm] *n* Dampf *m* ♦ *vt* (*CULIN*) dämpfen, dünsten ♦ *vi* dampfen; **covered with ~** (*window etc*) beschlagen; **under one's own ~** (*fig*) allein, ohne Hilfe; **to run out of ~** (*fig*) den Schwung verlieren; **to let off ~** (*inf, fig*) Dampf ablassen.
▶**steam up** *vi* (*window*) beschlagen; **to get ~ed up about sth** (*inf, fig*) sich über etw *acc* aufregen.
steam engine *n* (*RAIL*) Dampflok(omotive) *f*.
steamer ['stiːmə'] *n* Dampfer *m*; (*CULIN*) Dämpfer *m*.
steam iron *n* Dampfbügeleisen *nt*.
steamroller ['stiːmrəʊlə'] *n* Dampfwalze *f*.

steamship ['stiːmʃɪp] *n* = **steamer**.
steamy ['stiːmɪ] *adj* (*room*) dampfig; (*window*) beschlagen; (*book, film*) heiß.
steed [stiːd] (*liter*) *n* Roß *nt*.
steel [stiːl] *n* Stahl *m* ♦ *adj* (*girder, wool etc*) Stahl-.
steel band *n* (*MUS*) Steelband *f*.
steel industry *n* Stahlindustrie *f*.
steel mill *n* Stahlwalzwerk *nt*.
steelworks ['stiːlwɜːks] *n* Stahlwerk *nt*.
steely ['stiːlɪ] *adj* (*determination*) eisern; (*eyes, gaze*) hart, stählern.
steep [stiːp] *adj* steil; (*increase, rise*) stark; (*price, fees*) gepfeffert ♦ *vt* einweichen; **to be ~ed in history** geschichtsträchtig sein.
steeple ['stiːpl] *n* Kirchturm *m*.
steeplechase ['stiːpltʃeɪs] *n* (*for horses*) Hindernisrennen *nt*; (*for runners*) Hindernislauf *m*.
steeplejack ['stiːpldʒæk] *n* Turmarbeiter *m*.
steeply ['stiːplɪ] *adv* steil.
steer [stɪə'] *vt* steuern; (*car etc*) lenken; (*person*) lotsen ♦ *vi* steuern; (*in car etc*) lenken; **to ~ for** zusteuern auf +*acc*; **to ~ clear of sb** (*fig*) jdm aus dem Weg gehen; **to ~ clear of sth** (*fig*) etw meiden.
steering ['stɪərɪŋ] *n* (*AUT*) Lenkung *f*.
steering column *n* (*AUT*) Lenksäule *f*.
steering committee *n* Lenkungsausschuß *m*.
steering wheel *n* (*AUT*) Lenkrad *nt*, Steuer *nt*.
stellar ['stɛlə'] *adj* stellar.
stem [stɛm] *n* Stiel *m*; (*of pipe*) Hals *m* ♦ *vt* aufhalten; (*flow*) eindämmen; (*bleeding*) zum Stillstand bringen.
▶**stem from** *vt fus* zurückgehen auf +*acc*.
stench [stɛntʃ] (*pej*) *n* Gestank *m*.
stencil ['stɛnsl] *n* Schablone *f* ♦ *vt* mit Schablone zeichnen.
stenographer [stɛ'nɒɡrəfə'] (*US*) *n* Stenograph(in) *m(f)*.
stenography [stɛ'nɒɡrəfɪ] (*US*) *n* Stenographie *f*.
step [stɛp] *n* (*lit, fig*) Schritt *m*; (*of stairs*) Stufe *f* ♦ *vi:* **to ~ forward/back** vor-/zurücktreten; **steps** *npl* (*BRIT*) = **stepladder**; ~ **by** ~ (*fig*) Schritt für Schritt; **in/out of ~ (with)** im/nicht im Tritt (mit); (*fig*) im/nicht im Gleichklang (mit).
▶**step down** *vi* (*fig: resign*) zurücktreten.
▶**step in** *vi* (*fig*) eingreifen.
▶**step off** *vt fus* aussteigen aus +*dat*.
▶**step on** *vt fus* treten auf +*acc*.
▶**step over** *vt fus* steigen über +*acc*.
▶**step up** *vt* (*efforts*) steigern; (*pace etc*) beschleunigen.
stepbrother ['stɛpbrʌðə'] *n* Stiefbruder *m*.
stepchild ['stɛptʃaɪld] *n* Stiefkind *nt*.
stepdaughter ['stɛpdɔːtə'] *n* Stieftochter *f*.
stepfather ['stɛpfɑːðə'] *n* Stiefvater *m*.
stepladder ['stɛplædə'] (*BRIT*) *n* Trittleiter *f*.

stepmother ['stɛpmʌðə*] n Stiefmutter f.
stepping stone ['stɛpɪŋ-] n Trittstein m; (fig) Sprungbrett nt.
stepsister ['stɛpsɪstə*] n Stiefschwester f.
stepson ['stɛpsʌn] n Stiefsohn m.
stereo ['stɛrɪəu] n (system) Stereoanlage f ♦ adj (sound etc) Stereo-; **in** ~ in Stereo.
stereotype ['stɪərɪətaɪp] n Klischee nt, Klischeevorstellung f ♦ vt in ein Klischee zwängen; ~**d** stereotyp.
sterile ['stɛraɪl] adj steril, keimfrei; (barren) unfruchtbar; (fig: debate) fruchtlos.
sterility [stɛ'rɪlɪtɪ] n Unfruchtbarkeit f.
sterilization [stɛrɪlaɪ'zeɪʃən] n Sterilisation f, Sterilisierung f.
sterilize ['stɛrɪlaɪz] vt sterilisieren.
sterling ['stə:lɪŋ] adj (silver) Sterling-; (fig) gediegen ♦ n (ECON) das Pfund Sterling, das englische Pfund; **one pound** ~ ein Pfund Sterling.
sterling area n (ECON) Sterlingländer pl.
stern [stə:n] adj streng ♦ n Heck nt.
sternum ['stə:nəm] n Brustbein nt.
steroid ['stɪərɔɪd] n Steroid nt.
stethoscope ['stɛθəskəup] n Stethoskop nt.
stevedore ['sti:vədɔ:*] n Stauer m, Schauermann m.
stew [stju:] n Eintopf m ♦ vt schmoren; (fruit, vegetables) dünsten ♦ vi schmoren; ~**ed tea** bitterer Tee m; ~**ed fruit** (Obst)kompott nt.
steward ['stju:əd] n Steward m; (at public event) Ordner(in) m(f); (also: **shop** ~) gewerkschaftliche Vertrauensperson f.
stewardess ['stju:ədɛs] n Stewardeß f.
stewardship ['stju:ədʃɪp] n Verwaltung f.
stewing steak, (US) **stew meat** ['stju:ɪŋ-] n (Rinder)schmorfleisch nt.
St. Ex. abbr = **stock exchange.**
stg abbr = **sterling.**
stick [stɪk] (pt, pp **stuck**) n Zweig m; (of dynamite) Stange f; (of chalk etc) Stück nt; (as weapon) Stock m; (also: **walking** ~) (Spazier)stock m ♦ vt (with glue etc) kleben; (inf: put) tun, stecken; (: tolerate) aushalten; (thrust) stoßen ♦ vi: **to** ~ (**to**) kleben (an +dat); (remain) (hängen)bleiben; (door etc) klemmen; (lift) steckenbleiben; **to get hold of the wrong end of the** ~ (BRIT, fig) es falsch verstehen; **to** ~ **in sb's mind** jdm im Gedächtnis (haften)bleiben.
►**stick around** (inf) vi hier-/dableiben.
►**stick out** vi (ears etc) abstehen ♦ vt: **to** ~ **it out** (inf) durchhalten.
►**stick to** vt fus (one's word, promise) halten; (agreement, rules) sich halten an +acc; (the truth, facts) bleiben bei.
►**stick up** vi hochstehen.
►**stick up for** vt fus eintreten für.
sticker ['stɪkə*] n Aufkleber m.
sticking plaster ['stɪkɪŋ-] n Heftpflaster nt.
sticking point n Hindernis nt; (in discussion etc) strittiger Punkt m.

stickleback ['stɪklbæk] n Stichling m.
stickler ['stɪklə*] n: **to be a** ~ **for sth** es mit etw peinlich genau nehmen.
stick shift (US) n Schaltknüppel m; (car) Wagen m mit Handschaltung.
stick-up ['stɪkʌp] (inf) n Überfall m.
sticky ['stɪkɪ] adj klebrig; (label, tape) Klebe-; (weather, day) schwül.
stiff [stɪf] adj steif; (hard, firm) hart; (paste, egg-white) fest; (door, zip etc) schwer gehend; (competition) hart; (sentence) schwer; (drink) stark ♦ adv (bored, worried, scared) zu Tode; **to be** or **feel** ~ steif sein; **to have a** ~ **neck** einen steifen Hals haben; **to keep a** ~ **upper lip** (BRIT, fig) die Haltung bewahren.
stiffen ['stɪfn] vi steif werden; (body) erstarren.
stiffness ['stɪfnɪs] n Steifheit f.
stifle ['staɪfl] vt unterdrücken; (heat) erdrücken.
stifling ['staɪflɪŋ] adj (heat) drückend.
stigma ['stɪgmə] n Stigma nt; (BOT) Narbe f, Stigma nt; **stigmata** pl (MED) Wundmal nt.
stile [staɪl] n Zaunübertritt m.
stiletto [stɪ'lɛtəu] (BRIT) n (also: ~ **heel**) Bleistiftabsatz m.
still [stɪl] adj (motionless) bewegungslos; (tranquil) ruhig; (air, water) still; (BRIT: drink) ohne Kohlensäure ♦ adv (immer) noch; (yet, even) noch; (nonetheless) trotzdem ♦ n (CINE) Standfoto nt; **to stand** ~ stillstehen; **keep** ~! halte still!; **he** ~ **hasn't arrived** er ist immer noch nicht angekommen.
stillborn ['stɪlbɔ:n] adj totgeboren.
still life n Stilleben nt.
stilt [stɪlt] n (pile) Pfahl m; (for walking on) Stelze f.
stilted ['stɪltɪd] adj gestelzt.
stimulant ['stɪmjulənt] n Anregungsmittel nt.
stimulate ['stɪmjuleɪt] vt anregen, stimulieren; (demand) ankurbeln.
stimulating ['stɪmjuleɪtɪŋ] adj anregend, stimulierend.
stimulation [stɪmju'leɪʃən] n Anregung f, Stimulation f.
stimuli ['stɪmjulaɪ] npl of **stimulus.**
stimulus ['stɪmjuləs] (pl **stimuli**) n (incentive) Anreiz m; (BIOL) Reiz m; (PSYCH) Stimulus m.
sting [stɪŋ] (pt, pp **stung**) n Stich m; (pain) Stechen nt; (organ: of insect) Stachel m; (inf: confidence trick) Ding nt ♦ vt stechen; (fig) treffen, verletzen ♦ vi stechen; (eyes, ointment, plant etc) brennen; **my eyes are** ~**ing** mir brennen die Augen.
stingy ['stɪndʒɪ] (pej) adj geizig, knauserig.
stink [stɪŋk] (pt **stank,** pp **stunk**) n Gestank m ♦ vi stinken.
stinker ['stɪŋkə*] (inf) n (problem) harter Brocken m; (person) Ekel nt.
stinking ['stɪŋkɪŋ] (inf) adj (fig) beschissen (!);

a ~ **cold** eine scheußliche Erkältung; ~ **rich** stinkreich.

stint [stɪnt] n (*period*) Zeit f; (*batch of work*) Pensum nt; (*share*) Teil m ♦ vi: **to** ~ **on** sparen mit.

stipend ['staɪpend] n Gehalt nt.

stipendiary [staɪ'pendɪərɪ] adj: ~ **magistrate** bezahlter Friedensrichter m.

stipulate ['stɪpjuleɪt] vt festsetzen; (*condition*) stellen.

stipulation [stɪpju'leɪʃən] n Bedingung f, Auflage f.

stir [stɜː*] n (*fig*) Aufsehen nt ♦ vt umrühren; (*fig: emotions*) aufwühlen; (: *person*) bewegen ♦ vi sich bewegen; **to give sth a** ~ etw umrühren; **to cause a** ~ Aufsehen erregen.

►**stir up** vt: **to** ~ **up trouble** Unruhe stiften; **to** ~ **things up** stänkern.

stir-fry ['stɜː'fraɪ] vt unter Rühren kurz anbraten ♦ n Pfannengericht nt (*das unter Rühren kurz angebraten wurde*).

stirring ['stɜːrɪŋ] adj bewegend.

stirrup ['stɪrəp] n Steigbügel m.

stitch [stɪtʃ] n (*SEWING*) Stich m; (*KNITTING*) Masche f; (*MED*) Faden m; (*pain*) Seitenstiche pl ♦ vt nähen; **he had to have** ~**es** er mußte genäht werden.

stoat [stəut] n Wiesel nt.

stock [stɔk] n Vorrat m; (*COMM*) Bestand m; (*AGR*) Vieh nt; (*CULIN*) Brühe f; (*descent, origin*) Abstammung f, Herkunft f; (*FIN*) Wertpapiere pl; (*RAIL: also: rolling* ~) rollendes Material nt ♦ adj (*reply, excuse etc*) Standard- ♦ vt (*in shop*) führen; **in/out of** ~ vorrätig/nicht vorrätig; ~**s and shares** (Aktien und) Wertpapiere pl; **government** ~ Staatsanleihe f; **to take** ~ **of** (*fig*) Bilanz ziehen über +acc; **well-**~**ed** (*shop*) mit gutem Sortiment.

►**stock up** vi: **to** ~ **up (with)** sich eindecken (mit).

stockade [stɔ'keɪd] n Palisade f.

stockbroker ['stɔkbrəukə*] n Börsenmakler m.

stock control n Bestandsüberwachung f.

stock cube (*BRIT*) n Brühwürfel m.

stock exchange n Börse f.

stockholder ['stɔkhəuldə*] (*esp US*) n Aktionär(in) m(f).

Stockholm ['stɔkhəum] n Stockholm nt.

stocking ['stɔkɪŋ] n Strumpf m.

stock-in-trade ['stɔkɪn'treɪd] n (*fig*): **it's his** ~ es gehört zu seinem festen Repertoire.

stockist ['stɔkɪst] (*BRIT*) n Händler m.

stock market (*BRIT*) n Börse f.

stock phrase n Standardsatz m.

stockpile ['stɔkpaɪl] n Vorrat m; (*of weapons*) Lager nt ♦ vt horten.

stockroom ['stɔkruːm] n Lager nt, Lagerraum m.

stocktaking ['stɔkteɪkɪŋ] (*BRIT*) n Inventur f.

stocky ['stɔkɪ] adj stämmig.

stodgy ['stɔdʒɪ] adj (*food*) pampig (*inf*), schwer.

stoic ['stəuɪk] n Stoiker(in) m(f).

stoic(al) ['stəuɪk(l)] adj stoisch.

stoke [stəuk] vt (*fire*) schüren; (*furnace, boiler*) heizen.

stoker ['stəukə*] n Heizer m.

stole [stəul] pt of **steal** ♦ n Stola f.

stolen ['stəuln] pp of **steal**.

stolid ['stɔlɪd] adj phlegmatisch, stur (*inf*).

stomach ['stʌmək] n Magen m; (*belly*) Bauch m ♦ vt (*fig*) vertragen.

stomach ache n Magenschmerzen pl.

stomach pump n Magenpumpe f.

stomach ulcer n Magengeschwür nt.

stomp [stɔmp] vi stapfen.

stone [stəun] n Stein m; (*BRIT: weight*) Gewichtseinheit (= 6,35 kg) ♦ adj (*wall, jar etc*) Stein-, steinern ♦ vt (*person*) mit Steinen bewerfen; (*fruit*) entkernen, entsteinen; **within a** ~**'s throw of the station** nur einen Katzensprung vom Bahnhof entfernt.

Stone Age n Steinzeit f.

stone-cold ['stəun'kəuld] adj eiskalt.

stoned [stəund] (*inf*) adj (*on drugs*) stoned; (*drunk*) total zu.

stone-deaf ['stəun'def] adj stocktaub.

stonemason ['stəunmeɪsn] n Steinmetz m.

stonewall [stəun'wɔːl] vi mauern; (*in answering questions*) ausweichen.

stonework ['stəunwɜːk] n Mauerwerk nt.

stony ['stəunɪ] adj steinig; (*fig: silence etc*) steinern.

stood [stud] pt, pp of **stand**.

stooge [stuːdʒ] n (*inf*) Handlanger(in) m(f); (*THEAT*) Stichwortgeber(in) m(f).

stool [stuːl] n Hocker m.

stoop [stuːp] vi (*also:* ~ **down**) sich bücken; (*walk*) gebeugt gehen; **to** ~ **to sth** (*fig*) sich zu etw herablassen; **to** ~ **to doing sth** sich dazu herablassen, etw zu tun.

stop [stɔp] n Halt m; (*short stay*) Aufenthalt m; (*in punctuation: also: full* ~) Punkt m; (*bus stop etc*) Haltestelle f ♦ vt stoppen; (*car etc*) anhalten; (*block*) sperren; (*prevent*) verhindern ♦ vi (*car etc*) anhalten; (*train*) halten; (*pedestrian, watch, clock*) stehenbleiben; (*end*) aufhören; **to come to a** ~ anhalten; **to put a** ~ **to** einen Riegel vorschieben +dat; **to** ~ **doing sth** aufhören, etw zu tun; **to** ~ **sb (from) doing sth** jdn davon abhalten, etw zu tun; ~ **it!** laß das!, hör auf!

►**stop by** vi kurz vorbeikommen.

►**stop off** vi kurz haltmachen, Zwischenstation machen.

►**stop up** vt (*hole*) zustopfen.

stopcock ['stɔpkɔk] n Absperrhahn m.

stopgap ['stɔpgæp] n (*person*) Lückenbüßer m; (*thing*) Notbehelf m; ~ **measure** Überbrückungsmaßnahme f.

stop-go [stɔp'gəu] adj (*economic cycle etc*) mit

ständigem Auf und Ab.

stoplights ['stɔplaɪts] _npl_ (_AUT_) Bremslichter _pl._

stopover ['stɔpəʊvə*] _n_ Zwischenaufenthalt _m_; (_AVIAT_) Zwischenlandung _f_.

stoppage ['stɔpɪdʒ] _n_ (_strike_) Streik _m_; (_blockage_) Unterbrechung _f_; (_of pay, cheque_) Sperrung _f_; (_deduction_) Abzug _m_.

stopper ['stɔpə*] _n_ Stöpsel _m_.

stop press _n_ letzte Meldungen _pl._

stopwatch ['stɔpwɔtʃ] _n_ Stoppuhr _f_.

storage ['stɔːrɪdʒ] _n_ Lagerung _f_; (_also:_ ~ _space_) Stauraum _m_; (_COMPUT_) Speicherung _f_.

storage capacity _n_ (_COMPUT_) Speicherkapazität _f_.

storage heater (_BRIT_) _n_ (Nacht)speicherofen _m_.

store [stɔː*] _n_ Vorrat _m_; (_depot_) Lager _nt_; (_BRIT: large shop_) Geschäft _nt_, Kaufhaus _nt_; (_US: shop_) Laden _m_; (_fig_): **a ~ of** eine Fülle an +_dat_ ♦ _vt_ lagern; (_information etc, COMPUT_) speichern; (_food, medicines etc_) aufbewahren; (_in filing system_) ablegen; **stores** _npl_ (_provisions_) Vorräte _pl_; **in ~** eingelagert; **who knows what's in ~ for us?** wer weiß, was uns bevorsteht?; **to set great/little ~ by sth** viel/wenig von etw halten.

▶**store up** _vt_ einen Vorrat anlegen von; (_memories_) im Gedächtnis bewahren.

storehouse ['stɔːhaʊs] _n_ (_US: COMM_) Lager(haus) _nt_; (_fig_) Fundgrube _f_.

storekeeper ['stɔːkiːpə*] (_US_) _n_ Ladenbesitzer(in) _m(f)_.

storeroom ['stɔːruːm] _n_ Lagerraum _m_.

storey, **(_US_) **story ['stɔːrɪ] _n_ Stock _m_, Stockwerk _nt_.

stork [stɔːk] _n_ Storch _m_.

storm [stɔːm] _n_ (_lit, fig_) Sturm _m_; (_bad weather_) Unwetter _nt_; (_also:_ **electrical ~**) Gewitter _nt_ ♦ _vi_ (_fig_) toben ♦ _vt_ (_attack_) stürmen.

storm cloud _n_ Gewitterwolke _f_.

storm door _n_ äußere Windfangtür _f_.

stormy ['stɔːmɪ] _adj_ (_lit, fig_) stürmisch.

story ['stɔːrɪ] _n_ Geschichte _f_; (_PRESS_) Artikel _m_; (_lie_) Märchen _nt_; (_US_) = **storey**.

storybook ['stɔːrɪbʊk] _n_ Geschichtenbuch _nt_.

storyteller ['stɔːrɪtelə*] _n_ Geschichtenerzähler(in) _m(f)_.

stout [staʊt] _adj_ (_strong_) stark; (_fat_) untersetzt; (_resolute_) energisch ♦ _n_ Starkbier _nt_.

stove [stəʊv] _n_ Herd _m_; (_small_) Kocher _m_; (_for heating_) (Heiz)ofen _m_; **gas ~** Gasherd _m_.

stow [stəʊ] _vt_ (_also:_ ~ **away**) verstauen.

stowaway ['stəʊəweɪ] _n_ blinder Passagier _m_.

straddle ['strædl] _vt_ (_sitting_) rittlings sitzen auf +_dat_; (_standing_) breitbeinig stehen über +_dat_; (_jumping_) grätschen über +_acc_; (_fig_) überspannen.

strafe [strɑːf] _vt_ beschießen.

straggle ['strægl] _vi_ (_houses etc_) verstreut liegen; (_people etc_) zurückbleiben.

straggler ['stræglə*] _n_ Nachzügler _m_.

straggly ['stræglɪ] _adj_ (_hair_) unordentlich.

straight [streɪt] _adj_ gerade; (_hair_) glatt; (_honest_) offen, direkt; (_simple_) einfach; (: _fight_) direkt; (_THEAT_) ernst; (_inf: heterosexual_) hetero; (_whisky etc_) pur ♦ _adv_ (_in time_) sofort; (_in direction_) direkt; (_drink_) pur ♦ _n_ (_SPORT_) Gerade _f_; **to put** _or_ **get sth ~** (_make clear_) etw klären; (_make tidy_) etw in Ordnung bringen; **let's get this ~** das wollen wir mal klarstellen; **10 ~ wins** 10 Siege hintereinander; **to win in ~ sets** (_TENNIS_) ohne Satzverlust gewinnen; **to go ~ home** direkt nach Hause gehen; **~ out** rundheraus; **~ away, ~ off** sofort, gleich.

straighten ['streɪtn] _vt_ (_skirt, sheet etc_) geradeziehen.

▶**straighten out** _vt_ (_fig_) klären.

straight-faced [streɪt'feɪst] _adj_: **to be/remain ~** ernst bleiben ♦ _adv_ ohne zu lachen.

straightforward [streɪt'fɔːwəd] _adj_ (_simple_) einfach; (_honest_) offen.

straight sets _npl_ (_TENNIS_): **to win in ~** ohne Satzverlust gewinnen.

strain [streɪn] _n_ Belastung _f_; (_MED: also:_ **back ~**) überanstrengter Rücken _m_; (: _tension_) Überlastung _f_; (_of virus_) Art _f_; (_breed_) Sorte _f_ ♦ _vt_ (_back etc_) überanstrengen; (_resources_) belasten; (_CULIN_) abgießen ♦ _vi_: **to ~ to do sth** sich anstrengen, etw zu tun; **strains** _npl_ (_MUS_) Klänge _pl_; **he's been under a lot of ~** er hat unter viel Streß gestanden.

strained [streɪnd] _adj_ (_back_) überanstrengt; (_muscle_) gezerrt; (_forced_) gezwungen; (_relations_) gespannt.

strainer ['streɪnə*] _n_ Sieb _nt_.

strait [streɪt] _n_ Meerenge _f_, Straße _f_; **straits** _npl_ (_fig_): **to be in dire ~s** in großen Nöten sein.

straitjacket ['streɪtdʒækɪt] _n_ Zwangsjacke _f_.

strait-laced [streɪt'leɪst] _adj_ prüde, puritanisch.

strand [strænd] _n_ (_lit, fig_) Faden _m_; (_of wire_) Litze _f_; (_of hair_) Strähne _f_.

stranded ['strændɪd] _adj_: **to be ~** (_traveller_) festsitzen; (_ship, sea creature_) gestrandet.

strange [streɪndʒ] _adj_ fremd; (_odd_) seltsam, merkwürdig.

strangely ['streɪndʒlɪ] _adv_ seltsam, merkwürdig; _see also_ **enough**.

stranger ['streɪndʒə*] _n_ Fremde(r) _f(m)_; **I'm a ~ here** ich bin hier fremd.

strangle ['stræŋgl] _vt_ erwürgen, erdrosseln; (_fig: economy etc_) ersticken.

stranglehold ['stræŋglhəʊld] _n_ (_fig_) absolute Machtposition _f_.

strangulation [stræŋgju'leɪʃən] _n_ Erwürgen _nt_, Erdrosseln _nt_.

strap [stræp] _n_ Riemen _m_; (_of dress etc_) Träger _m_ ♦ _vt_ (_also:_ ~ **in**) anschnallen; (_also:_ ~ **on**) umschnallen.

straphanging ['stræphæŋɪŋ] n Pendeln nt (als stehender Fahrgast).

strapless ['stræplɪs] adj trägerlos, schulterfrei.

strapped [stræpt] (inf) adj: ~ **(for cash)** pleite.

strapping ['stræpɪŋ] adj stramm.

Strasbourg ['stræzbɔːg] n Straßburg nt.

strata ['strɑːtə] npl of **stratum**.

stratagem ['strætɪdʒəm] n List f.

strategic [strə'tiːdʒɪk] adj strategisch; (error) taktisch.

strategist ['strætɪdʒɪst] n Stratege m, Strategin f.

strategy ['strætɪdʒɪ] n Strategie f.

stratosphere ['strætəsfɪə'] n Stratosphäre f.

stratum ['strɑːtəm] (pl **strata**) n Schicht f.

straw [strɔː] n Stroh nt; (drinking straw) Strohhalm m; **that's the last ~!** das ist der Gipfel!

strawberry ['strɔːbərɪ] n Erdbeere f.

stray [streɪ] adj (animal) streunend; (bullet) verirrt; (scattered) einzeln, vereinzelt ♦ vi (children) sich verirren; (animals) streunen; (thoughts) abschweifen.

streak [striːk] n Streifen m; (in hair) Strähne f; (fig: of madness etc) Zug m ♦ vt streifen ♦ vi: **to ~ past** vorbeiflitzen; **a winning/losing ~** eine Glücks-/Pechsträhne.

streaker ['striːkə'] (inf) n Blitzer(in) m(f).

streaky ['striːkɪ] adj (bacon) durchwachsen.

stream [striːm] n (small river) Bach m; (current) Strömung f; (of people, vehicles) Strom m; (of questions, insults etc) Flut f, Schwall m; (of smoke) Schwaden m; (SCOL) Leistungsgruppe f ♦ vt (SCOL) in Leistungsgruppen einteilen ♦ vi strömen; **against the ~** gegen den Strom; **to come on ~** (new power plant etc) in Betrieb genommen werden.

streamer ['striːmə'] n Luftschlange f.

stream feed n automatischer Papiereinzug m.

streamline ['striːmlaɪn] vt Stromlinienform geben +dat; (fig) rationalisieren.

streamlined ['striːmlaɪnd] adj stromlinienförmig; (AVIAT, AUT) windschlüpfrig; (fig) rationalisiert.

street [striːt] n Straße f; **the back ~s** die Seitensträßchen pl; **to be on the ~s** (homeless) obdachlos sein; (as prostitute) auf den Strich gehen.

streetcar ['striːtkɑː'] (US) n Straßenbahn f.

street cred [-krɛd] (inf) n Glaubwürdigkeit f.

street lamp n Straßenlaterne f.

street lighting n Straßenbeleuchtung f.

street map n Stadtplan m.

street market n Straßenmarkt m.

street plan n Stadtplan m.

streetwise ['striːtwaɪz] (inf) adj: **to be ~** wissen, wo's langgeht.

strength [strɛŋθ] n (lit, fig) Stärke f; (physical) Kraft f, Stärke f; (of girder etc) Stabilität f; (of knot etc) Festigkeit f; (of chemical solution) Konzentration f; (of wine) Schwere f; **on the ~ of** auf Grund +gen; **at full ~** vollzählig; **to be below ~** nicht die volle Stärke haben.

strengthen ['strɛŋθn] vt (lit, fig) verstärken; (muscle) kräftigen; (economy, currency, relationship) festigen.

strenuous ['strɛnjuəs] adj anstrengend; (determined) unermüdlich.

strenuously ['strɛnjuəslɪ] adv energisch; **she ~ denied the rumour** sie leugnete das Gerücht hartnäckig.

stress [strɛs] n Druck m; (mental) Belastung f, Streß m; (LING) Betonung f; (emphasis) Akzent m, Gewicht nt ♦ vt betonen; **to lay great ~ on sth** großen Wert auf etw acc legen; **to be under ~** großen Belastungen ausgesetzt sein, unter Streß stehen.

stressful ['strɛsful] adj anstrengend, stressig; (situation) angespannt.

stretch [strɛtʃ] n (of sand, water etc) Stück nt; (of time) Zeit f ♦ vi (person, animal) sich strecken; (land, area) sich erstrecken ♦ vt (pull) spannen; (fig: job, task) fordern; **at a ~** an einem Stück, ohne Unterbrechung; **by no ~ of the imagination** beim besten Willen nicht; **to ~ to** or **as far as the frontier** (extend) sich bis zur Grenze erstrecken; **to ~ one's legs** sich dat die Beine vertreten.

▶**stretch out** vi sich ausstrecken ♦ vt ausstrecken.

▶**stretch to** vt fus (be enough) reichen für.

stretcher ['strɛtʃə'] n (Trag)bahre f.

stretcher-bearer ['strɛtʃəbɛərə'] n Krankenträger m.

stretch marks npl Dehnungsstreifen pl; (through pregnancy) Schwangerschaftsstreifen pl.

strewn [struːn] adj: ~ **with** übersät mit.

stricken ['strɪkən] adj (person) leidend; (city, industry etc) notleidend; ~ **with** (disease) geschlagen mit; (fear etc) erfüllt von.

strict [strɪkt] adj streng; (precise) genau; **in the ~est confidence** streng vertraulich; **in the ~ sense of the word** streng genommen.

strictly ['strɪktlɪ] adv streng; (exactly) genau; (solely) ausschließlich; ~ **confidential** streng vertraulich; ~ **speaking** genau genommen; **not ~ true** nicht ganz richtig; ~ **between ourselves** ganz unter uns.

strictness ['strɪktnɪs] n Strenge f.

stridden ['strɪdn] pp of **stride**.

stride [straɪd] (pt **strode**, pp **stridden**) n Schritt m ♦ vi schreiten; **to take sth in one's ~** (fig) mit etw spielend fertig werden.

strident ['straɪdnt] adj schrill, durchdringend; (demands) lautstark.

strife [straɪf] n Streit m, Zwietracht f.

strike [straɪk] (pt, pp **struck**) n Streik m, Ausstand m; (MIL) Angriff m ♦ vt (hit) schlagen; (fig: idea, thought) in den Sinn kommmen +dat; (oil etc) finden, stoßen auf

+*acc*; (*bargain, deal*) aushandeln; (*coin, medal*) prägen ♦ *vi* streiken; (*illness, killer*) zuschlagen; (*disaster*) hereinbrechen; (*clock*) schlagen; **on** ~ streikend; **to be on** ~ streiken; **to** ~ **a balance** einen Mittelweg finden; **to be struck by lightning** vom Blitz getroffen werden; **to** ~ **a match** ein Streichholz anzünden.
►**strike back** *vi* (*MIL*) zurückschlagen; (*fig*) sich wehren.
►**strike down** *vt* niederschlagen.
►**strike off** *vt* (*from list*) (aus)streichen; (*doctor etc*) die Zulassung entziehen +*dat*.
►**strike out** *vi* losziehen, sich aufmachen ♦ *vt* (*word, sentence*) (aus)streichen.
►**strike up** *vt* (*MUS*) anstimmen; (*conversation*) anknüpfen; (*friendship*) schließen.
strikebreaker ['straɪkbreɪkə*] *n* Streikbrecher *m*.
strike pay *n* Streikgeld *nt*.
striker ['straɪkə*] *n* Streikende(r) *f(m)*; (*SPORT*) Stürmer *m*.
striking ['straɪkɪŋ] *adj* auffallend; (*attractive*) attraktiv.
strimmer ['strɪmə*] *n* Rasentrimmer *m*.
string [strɪŋ] (*pt, pp* **strung**) *n* Schnur *f*; (*of islands*) Kette *f*; (*of people, cars*) Schlange *f*; (*series*) Serie *f*; (*COMPUT*) Zeichenfolge *f*; (*MUS*) Saite *f* ♦ *vt*: **to** ~ **together** aneinanderreihen; **the strings** *npl* (*MUS*) die Streichinstrumente *pl*; **to pull** ~**s** (*fig*) Beziehungen spielen lassen; **with no** ~**s attached** (*fig*) ohne Bedingungen; **to** ~ **sth out** etw verteilen.
string bean *n* grüne Bohne *f*.
stringed instrument *n* Saiteninstrument *nt*.
stringent ['strɪndʒənt] *adj* streng; (*measures*) drastisch.
string quartet *n* Streichquartett *nt*.
strip [strɪp] *n* Streifen *m*; (*of metal*) Band *nt*; (*SPORT*) Trikot *nt*, Dreß *m* ♦ *vt* (*undress*) ausziehen; (*paint*) abbeizen; (*also:* ~ **down**: *machine etc*) auseinandernehmen ♦ *vi* (*undress*) sich ausziehen.
strip cartoon *n* Comic(strip) *m*.
stripe [straɪp] *n* Streifen *m*; **stripes** *npl* (*MIL, POLICE*) (Ärmel)streifen *pl*.
striped [straɪpt] *adj* gestreift.
strip lighting (*BRIT*) *n* Neonlicht *nt*.
stripper ['strɪpə*] *n* Stripper(in) *m(f)*, Stripteasetänzer(in) *m(f)*.
strip-search ['strɪpsɛːtʃ] *n* Leibesvisitation *f* (*bei der man sich ausziehen muß*) ♦ *vt*: **to be** ~**ed** sich ausziehen müssen und durchsucht werden.
striptease ['strɪptiːz] *n* Striptease *m or nt*.
strive [straɪv] (*pt* **strove**, *pp* **striven**) *vi*: **to** ~ **for sth** nach etw streben; **to** ~ **to do sth** danach streben, etw zu tun.
striven ['strɪvn] *pp of* **strive**.
strobe [strəʊb] *n* (*also:* ~ **lights**)

Stroboskoplicht *nt*.
strode [strəʊd] *pt of* **stride**.
stroke [strəʊk] *n* Schlag *m*, Hieb *m*; (*SWIMMING: style*) Stil *m*; (*MED*) Schlaganfall *m*; (*of clock*) Schlag *m*; (*of paintbrush*) Strich *m* ♦ *vt* (*caress*) streicheln; **at a** ~ mit einem Schlag; **on the** ~ **of 5** Punkt 5 (Uhr); **a** ~ **of luck** ein Glücksfall *m*; **a 2-**~ **engine** ein Zweitaktmotor *m*.
stroll [strəʊl] *n* Spaziergang *m* ♦ *vi* spazieren; **to go for a** ~, **have** *or* **take a** ~ einen Spaziergang machen.
stroller ['strəʊlə*] (*US*) *n* (*pushchair*) Sportwagen *m*.
strong [strɔŋ] *adj* stark; (*person, arms, grip*) stark, kräftig; (*healthy*) kräftig; (*object, material*) solide, stabil; (*letter*) geharnischt; (*measure*) drastisch; (*language*) derb; (*nerves*) gut; (*taste, smell*) streng ♦ *adv*: **to be going** ~ (*company*) sehr erfolgreich sein; (*person*) gut in Schuß sein; **I have no** ~ **feelings about it** es ist mir ziemlich egal; **they are 50** ~ sie sind insgesamt 50.
strong-arm ['strɔŋɑːm] *adj* brutal.
strongbox ['strɔŋbɒks] *n* (Geld)kassette *f*.
stronghold ['strɔŋhəʊld] *n* Festung *f*; (*fig*) Hochburg *f*.
strongly ['strɔŋlɪ] *adv* (*solidly*) stabil; (*forcefully*) entschieden; (*deeply*) fest; **to feel** ~ **that** ... fest davon überzeugt sein, daß ...; **I feel** ~ **about it** mir liegt sehr viel daran; (*negatively*) ich bin sehr dagegen.
strongman ['strɔŋmæn] (*irreg: like* **man**) *n* (*lit, fig*) starker Mann *m*.
strongroom ['strɔŋruːm] *n* Tresorraum *m*.
stroppy ['strɔpɪ] (*BRIT: inf*) *adj* pampig; (*obstinate*) stur.
strove [strəʊv] *pt of* **strive**.
struck [strʌk] *pt, pp of* **strike**.
structural ['strʌktʃərəl] *adj* strukturell; (*damage*) baulich; (*defect*) Konstruktions-.
structurally ['strʌktʃərəlɪ] *adv*: ~ **sound** mit guter Bausubstanz.
structure ['strʌktʃə*] *n* Struktur *f*, Aufbau *m*; (*building*) Gebäude *nt*.
struggle ['strʌgl] *n* Kampf *m*; (*difficulty*) Anstrengung *f* ♦ *vi* (*try hard*) sich abmühen; (*fight*) kämpfen; (*in self-defence*) sich wehren; **to have a** ~ **to do sth** Mühe haben, etw zu tun; **to be a** ~ **for sb** jdm große Schwierigkeiten bereiten.
strum [strʌm] *vt* (*guitar*) klimpern auf +*dat*.
strung [strʌŋ] *pt, pp of* **string**.
strut [strʌt] *n* Strebe *f*, Stütze *f* ♦ *vi* stolzieren.
strychnine ['strɪkniːn] *n* Strychnin *nt*.
stub [stʌb] *n* (*of cheque, ticket etc*) Abschnitt *m*; (*of cigarette*) Kippe *f* ♦ *vt*: **to** ~ **one's toe** sich dat den Zeh stoßen.
►**stub out** *vt* (*cigarette*) ausdrücken.
stubble ['stʌbl] *n* Stoppeln *pl*.
stubborn ['stʌbən] *adj* hartnäckig; (*child*) störrisch.

stubby ['stʌbɪ] *adj* kurz und dick.

stucco ['stʌkəu] *n* Stuck *m*.

stuck [stʌk] *pt, pp of* **stick** ♦ *adj:* **to be ~** (*jammed*) klemmen; (*unable to answer*) nicht klarkommen; **to get ~** steckenbleiben; (*fig*) nicht weiterkommen.

stuck-up [stʌk'ʌp] (*inf*) *adj* hochnäsig.

stud [stʌd] *n* (*on clothing etc*) Niete *f*; (*on collar*) Kragenknopf *m*; (*earring*) Ohrstecker *m*; (*on boot*) Stollen *m*; (*also:* **~ farm**) Gestüt *nt*; (*also:* **~ horse**) Zuchthengst *m* ♦ *vt* (*fig*): **~ded with** übersät mit; (*with jewels*) dicht besetzt mit.

student ['stjuːdənt] *n* Student(in) *m(f)*; (*at school*) Schüler(in) *m(f)* ♦ *cpd* Studenten-; **law/medical ~** Jura-/Medizinstudent(in) *m(f)*; **~ nurse** Krankenpflegeschüler(in) *m(f)*; **~ teacher** Referendar(in) *m(f)*.

student driver (*US*) *n* Fahrschüler(in) *m(f)*.

students' union ['stjuːdənts-] (*BRIT*) *n* Studentenvereinigung *f*, ≈ AStA *m*; (*building*) Gebäude *nt* der Studentenvereinigung.

studied ['stʌdɪd] *adj* (*expression*) einstudiert; (*attitude*) berechnet.

studio ['stjuːdɪəu] *n* Studio *nt*; (*sculptor's etc*) Atelier *nt*.

studio flat, (*US*) **studio apartment** *n* Einzimmerwohnung *f*.

studious ['stjuːdɪəs] *adj* lernbegierig.

studiously ['stjuːdɪəslɪ] *adv* (*carefully*) sorgsam.

study ['stʌdɪ] *n* Studium *nt*, Lernen *nt*; (*room*) Arbeitszimmer *nt* ♦ *vt* studieren; (*face*) prüfend ansehen; (*evidence*) prüfen ♦ *vi* studieren, lernen; **studies** *npl* (*studying*) Studien *pl*; **to make a ~ of sth** etw untersuchen; (*academic*) etw studieren; **to ~ for an exam** sich auf eine Prüfung vorbereiten.

stuff [stʌf] *n* Zeug *nt* ♦ *vt* ausstopfen; (*CULIN*) füllen; (*inf: push*) stopfen; **my nose is ~ed up** ich habe eine verstopfte Nase; **get ~ed!** (*inf!*) du kannst mich mal!

stuffed toy [stʌft-] *n* Stofftier *nt*.

stuffing ['stʌfɪŋ] *n* Füllung *f*; (*in sofa etc*) Polstermaterial *nt*.

stuffy ['stʌfɪ] *adj* (*room*) stickig; (*person, ideas*) spießig.

stumble ['stʌmbl] *vi* stolpern; **to ~ across** *or* **on** (*fig*) (zufällig) stoßen auf *+acc*.

stumbling block ['stʌmblɪŋ-] *n* Hürde *f*, Hindernis *nt*.

stump [stʌmp] *n* Stumpf *m* ♦ *vt:* **to be ~ed** überfragt sein.

stun [stʌn] *vt* betäuben; (*news*) fassungslos machen.

stung [stʌŋ] *pt, pp of* **sting**.

stunk [stʌŋk] *pp of* **stink**.

stunning ['stʌnɪŋ] *adj* (*news, event*) sensationell; (*girl, dress*) hinreißend.

stunt [stʌnt] *n* (*in film*) Stunt *m*; (*publicity stunt*) (Werbe)gag *m*.

stunted ['stʌntɪd] *adj* verkümmert.

stuntman ['stʌntmæn] (*irreg: like* **man**) *n* Stuntman *m*.

stupefaction [stjuːpɪ'fækʃən] *n* Verblüffung *f*.

stupefy ['stjuːpɪfaɪ] *vt* benommen machen; (*fig*) verblüffen.

stupendous [stjuː'pɛndəs] *adj* enorm.

stupid ['stjuːpɪd] *adj* dumm.

stupidity [stjuː'pɪdɪtɪ] *n* Dummheit *f*.

stupidly ['stjuːpɪdlɪ] *adv* dumm.

stupor ['stjuːpə*] *n* Benommenheit *f*; **in a ~** benommen.

sturdily ['stəːdɪlɪ] *adv:* **~ built** (*person*) kräftig gebaut; (*thing*) stabil gebaut.

sturdy ['stəːdɪ] *adj* (*person*) kräftig; (*thing*) stabil.

sturgeon ['stəːdʒən] *n* Stör *m*.

stutter ['stʌtə*] *n* Stottern *nt* ♦ *vi* stottern; **to have a ~** stottern.

Stuttgart ['stʊtɡɑːt] *n* Stuttgart *nt*.

sty [staɪ] *n* Schweinestall *m*.

stye [staɪ] *n* Gerstenkorn *nt*.

style [staɪl] *n* Stil *m*; (*design*) Modell *nt*; **in the latest ~** nach der neuesten Mode; **hair ~** Frisur *f*.

styli ['staɪlaɪ] *npl of* **stylus**.

stylish ['staɪlɪʃ] *adj* elegant.

stylist ['staɪlɪst] *n* (*hair stylist*) Friseur *m*, Friseuse *f*; (*literary stylist*) Stilist(in) *m(f)*.

stylized ['staɪlaɪzd] *adj* stilisiert.

stylus ['staɪləs] (*pl* **styli** *or* **~es**) *n* Nadel *f*.

Styrofoam ® ['staɪrəfəum] *n* ≈ Styropor *nt* ®.

suave [swɑːv] *adj* zuvorkommend.

sub [sʌb] *n abbr* (*NAUT*) = **submarine**; (*ADMIN*) = **subscription**; (*BRIT: PRESS*) = **subeditor**.

sub... [sʌb] *pref* Unter-, unter-.

subcommittee ['sʌbkəmɪtɪ] *n* Unterausschuß *m*.

subconscious [sʌb'kɒnʃəs] *adj* unterbewußt.

subcontinent [sʌb'kɒntɪnənt] *n:* **the (Indian) ~** der (indische) Subkontinent.

subcontract [*vt* 'sʌbkən'trækt, *n* 'sʌb'kɒntrækt] *vt* (vertraglich) weitervergeben ♦ *n* Nebenvertrag *m*.

subcontractor ['sʌbkən'træktə*] *n* Subunternehmer *m*.

subdivide [sʌbdɪ'vaɪd] *vt* unterteilen.

subdivision ['sʌbdɪvɪʒən] *n* Unterteilung *f*.

subdue [səb'djuː] *vt* unterwerfen; (*emotions*) dämpfen.

subdued [səb'djuːd] *adj* (*light*) gedämpft; (*person*) bedrückt.

subeditor [sʌb'ɛdɪtə*] (*BRIT*) *n* Redakteur(in) *m(f)*.

subject [*n* 'sʌbdʒɪkt, *vt* səb'dʒɛkt] *n* (*matter*) Thema *nt*; (*SCOL*) Fach *nt*; (*of country*) Staatsbürger(in) *m(f)*; (*GRAM*) Subjekt *nt* ♦ *vt:* **to ~ sb to sth** jdn einer Sache *dat* unterziehen; (*expose*) jdn einer Sache *dat* aussetzen; **to change the ~** das Thema wechseln; **to be ~ to** (*law, tax*) unterworfen sein *+dat*; (*heart attacks etc*) anfällig sein für;

~ **to confirmation in writing** vorausgesetzt, es wird schriftlich bestätigt.
subjection [səb'dʒɛkʃən] n Unterwerfung f.
subjective [səb'dʒɛktɪv] adj subjektiv.
subject matter n Stoff m; (content) Inhalt m.
sub judice [sʌb'dju:dɪsɪ] adj (LAW): **to be** ~ verhandelt werden.
subjugate ['sʌbdʒugeɪt] vt unterwerfen.
subjunctive [səb'dʒʌŋktɪv] n Konjunktiv m; **in the** ~ im Konjunktiv.
sublet [sʌb'lɛt] vt untervermieten.
sublime [sə'blaɪm] adj erhaben, vollendet; **that's going from the** ~ **to the ridiculous** das ist ein Abstieg ins Profane.
subliminal [sʌb'lɪmɪnl] adj unterschwellig.
submachine gun ['sʌbmə'ʃi:n-] n Maschinenpistole f.
submarine [sʌbmə'ri:n] n Unterseeboot nt, U-Boot nt.
submerge [səb'mə:dʒ] vt untertauchen; (flood) überschwemmen ♦ vi tauchen; ~**d** unter Wasser.
submersion [səb'mə:ʃən] n Untertauchen nt; (of submarine) Tauchen nt; (by flood) Überschwemmung f.
submission [səb'mɪʃən] n (subjection) Unterwerfung f; (of plan, application etc) Einreichung f; (proposal) Vorlage f.
submissive [səb'mɪsɪv] adj gehorsam; (gesture) demütig.
submit [səb'mɪt] vt (proposal) vorlegen; (application etc) einreichen ♦ vi: **to** ~ **to sth** sich einer Sache dat unterwerfen.
subnormal [sʌb'nɔ:ml] adj (below average) unterdurchschnittlich; (old: child etc) minderbegabt; **educationally** ~ lernbehindert.
subordinate [sə'bɔ:dɪnət] n Untergebene(r) f(m); (LING): ~ **clause** Nebensatz m ♦ adj untergeordnet; **to be** ~ **to sb** jdm untergeordnet sein.
subpoena [səb'pi:nə] n (LAW) Vorladung f ♦ vt vorladen.
subroutine [sʌbru:'ti:n] n (COMPUT) Unterprogramm nt.
subscribe [səb'skraɪb] vi spenden; **to** ~ **to** (opinion, theory) sich anschließen +dat; (fund, charity) regelmäßig spenden an +acc; (magazine etc) abonnieren.
subscriber [səb'skraɪbə*] n (to magazine) Abonnent(in) m(f); (TEL) Teilnehmer(in) m(f).
subscript ['sʌbskrɪpt] n tiefgestelltes Zeichen nt.
subscription [səb'skrɪpʃən] n (to magazine etc) Abonnement nt; (membership dues) (Mitglieds)beitrag m; **to take out a** ~ **to** (magazine etc) abonnieren.
subsequent ['sʌbsɪkwənt] adj später, nachfolgend; (further) weiter; ~ **to** im Anschluß an +acc.
subsequently ['sʌbsɪkwəntlɪ] adv später.
subservient [səb'sə:vɪənt] adj unterwürfig;

('less important) untergeordnet; **to be** ~ **to** untergeordnet sein +dat.
subside [səb'saɪd] vi (feeling, pain) nachlassen; (flood) sinken; (earth) sich senken.
subsidence [səb'saɪdns] n Senkung f.
subsidiarity [səbsɪdɪ'ærɪtɪ] n Subsidiarität f.
subsidiary [səb'sɪdɪərɪ] adj (question, role, BRIT: SCOL: subject) Neben- ♦ n (also: ~ **company**) Tochtergesellschaft f.
subsidize ['sʌbsɪdaɪz] vt subventionieren.
subsidy ['sʌbsɪdɪ] n Subvention f.
subsist [səb'sɪst] vi: **to** ~ **on sth** sich von etw ernähren.
subsistence [səb'sɪstəns] n Existenz f; **enough for** ~ genug zum (Über)leben.
subsistence allowance n Unterhaltszuschuß m.
subsistence level n Existenzminimum nt.
substance ['sʌbstəns] n Substanz f, Stoff m; (fig: essence) Kern m; **a man of** ~ ein vermögender Mann; **to lack** ~ (book) keine Substanz haben; (argument) keine Durchschlagskraft haben.
substance abuse n Mißbrauch von Alkohol, Drogen, Arzneimitteln etc.
substandard [sʌb'stændəd] adj minderwertig; (housing) unzulänglich.
substantial [səb'stænʃl] adj (solid) solide; (considerable) beträchtlich, größere(r, s); (meal) kräftig.
substantially [səb'stænʃəlɪ] adv erheblich; (in essence) im wesentlichen.
substantiate [səb'stænʃɪeɪt] vt erhärten, untermauern.
substitute ['sʌbstɪtju:t] n Ersatz m ♦ vt: **to** ~ **A for B** B durch A ersetzen.
substitute teacher (US) n Vertretung f.
substitution [sʌbstɪ'tju:ʃən] n Ersetzen nt; (FOOTBALL) Auswechseln nt.
subterfuge ['sʌbtəfju:dʒ] n Tricks pl; (trickery) Täuschung f.
subterranean [sʌbtə'reɪnɪən] adj unterirdisch.
subtitle ['sʌbtaɪtl] n Untertitel m.
subtle ['sʌtl] adj fein; (indirect) raffiniert.
subtlety ['sʌtltɪ] n Feinheit f; (art of being subtle) Finesse f.
subtly ['sʌtlɪ] adv (change, vary) leicht; (different) auf subtile Weise; (persuade) raffiniert.
subtotal [sʌb'təʊtl] n Zwischensumme f.
subtract [səb'trækt] vt abziehen, subtrahieren.
subtraction [səb'trækʃən] n Abziehen nt, Subtraktion f.
subtropical [sʌb'trɒpɪkl] adj subtropisch.
suburb ['sʌbə:b] n Vorort m.
suburban [sə'bə:bən] adj (train etc) Vorort-; (lifestyle etc) spießig, kleinbürgerlich.
suburbia [sə'bə:bɪə] n die Vororte pl.
subvention [səb'vɛnʃən] n Subvention f.
subversion [səb'və:ʃən] n Subversion f.
subversive [səb'və:sɪv] adj subversiv.

subway ['sʌbweɪ] n (US) Untergrundbahn f, U-Bahn f; (BRIT: underpass) Unterführung f.
sub-zero [sʌb'zɪərəu] adj: ~ **temperatures** Temperaturen unter Null.
succeed [sək'siːd] vi (plan etc) gelingen, erfolgreich sein; (person) erfolgreich sein, Erfolg haben ♦ vt (in job) Nachfolger werden +gen; (in order) folgen +dat; **sb ~s in doing sth** es gelingt jdm, etw zu tun.
succeeding [sək'siːdɪŋ] adj folgend; ~ **generations** spätere or nachfolgende Generationen pl.
success [sək'sɛs] n Erfolg m; **without** ~ ohne Erfolg, erfolglos.
successful [sək'sɛsful] adj erfolgreich; **to be** ~ erfolgreich sein, Erfolg haben; **sb is ~ in doing sth** es gelingt jdm, etw zu tun.
successfully [sək'sɛsfəlɪ] adv erfolgreich, mit Erfolg.
succession [sək'sɛʃən] n Folge f, Serie f; (to throne etc) Nachfolge f; **3 years in** ~ 3 Jahre nacheinander or hintereinander.
successive [sək'sɛsɪv] adj aufeinanderfolgend; **on 3** ~ **days** 3 Tage nacheinander or hintereinander.
successor [sək'sɛsə*] n Nachfolger(in) m(f).
succinct [sək'sɪŋkt] adj knapp, prägnant.
succulent ['sʌkjulənt] adj saftig ♦ n Fettpflanze f, Sukkulente f.
succumb [sə'kʌm] vi: **to** ~ **to** (temptation) erliegen +dat; (illness: become affected by) bekommen; (: die of) erliegen +dat.
such [sʌtʃ] adj (of that kind): ~ **a book** so ein Buch; (so much): ~ **courage** so viel Mut; (emphasizing similarity): **or some** ~ **place/ name** etc oder so ähnlich ♦ adv so; ~ **books** solche Bücher; ~ **a lot of** so viel; **she made** ~ **a noise that** ... sie machte so einen Lärm, daß ...; ~ **books as I have** was ich an Büchern habe; **I said no** ~ **thing** das habe ich nie gesagt; ~ **a long trip** so eine lange Reise; ~ **as** wie (zum Beispiel); **as** ~ **an** sich.
such-and-such ['sʌtʃənsʌtʃ] adj die und die, der und der, das und das.
suchlike ['sʌtʃlaɪk] (inf) pron: **and** ~ und dergleichen.
suck [sʌk] vt (sweet etc) lutschen; (ice-lolly) lutschen an +dat; (baby) saugen an +dat; (pump, machine) saugen.
sucker ['sʌkə*] n (ZOOL) Saugnapf m; (TECH) Saugfuß m; (BOT) unterirdischer Ausläufer m; (inf) Dummkopf m.
suckle ['sʌkl] vt (baby) stillen; (animal) säugen.
sucrose ['suːkrəuz] n (pflanzlicher) Zucker m.
suction ['sʌkʃən] n Saugwirkung f.
suction pump n Saugpumpe f.
Sudan [su'dɑːn] n der Sudan.
Sudanese [suːdə'niːz] adj sudanesisch ♦ n Sudanese m, Sudanesin f.
sudden ['sʌdn] adj plötzlich; **all of a** ~ ganz

plötzlich.
sudden death n (also: **sudden-death play-off**) Stichkampf m.
suddenly ['sʌdnlɪ] adv plötzlich.
suds [sʌdz] npl Seifenschaum m.
sue [suː] vt verklagen ♦ vi klagen, vor Gericht gehen; **to** ~ **sb for damages** jdn auf Schadenersatz verklagen; **to** ~ **for divorce** die Scheidung einreichen.
suede [sweɪd] n Wildleder nt ♦ cpd Wildleder-.
suet ['suɪt] n Nierenfett nt.
Suez ['suːɪz] n: **the** ~ **Canal** der Suezkanal.
Suff. (BRIT) abbr (POST: = Suffolk).
suffer ['sʌfə*] vt erleiden; (rudeness etc) ertragen ♦ vi leiden; **to** ~ **from** leiden an +dat; **to** ~ **the effects of sth** an den Folgen von etw leiden.
sufferance ['sʌfərns] n: **he was only there on** ~ er wurde dort nur geduldet.
sufferer ['sʌfərə*] n Leidende(r) f(m).
suffering ['sʌfərɪŋ] n Leid nt.
suffice [sə'faɪs] vi genügen.
sufficient [sə'fɪʃənt] adj ausreichend; ~ **money** genug Geld.
sufficiently [sə'fɪʃəntlɪ] adv genug, ausreichend; ~ **powerful/enthusiastic** mächtig/begeistert genug.
suffix ['sʌfɪks] n Suffix nt, Nachsilbe f.
suffocate ['sʌfəkeɪt] vi (lit, fig) ersticken.
suffocation [sʌfə'keɪʃən] n Ersticken nt.
suffrage ['sʌfrɪdʒ] n Wahlrecht nt.
suffragette [sʌfrə'dʒɛt] n Suffragette f.
suffused [sə'fjuːzd] adj: ~ **with** erfüllt von; ~ **with light** lichtdurchflutet.
sugar ['ʃugə*] n Zucker m ♦ vt zuckern.
sugar beet n Zuckerrübe f.
sugar bowl n Zuckerdose f.
sugar cane n Zuckerrohr nt.
sugar-coated ['ʃugə'kəutɪd] adj mit Zucker überzogen.
sugar lump n Zuckerstück nt.
sugar refinery n Zuckerraffinerie f.
sugary ['ʃugərɪ] adj süß; (fig: smile, phrase) süßlich.
suggest [sə'dʒɛst] vt vorschlagen; (indicate) andeuten, hindeuten auf +acc; **what do you** ~ **I do?** was schlagen Sie vor?
suggestion [sə'dʒɛstʃən] n Vorschlag m; (indication) Anflug m; (trace) Spur f.
suggestive [sə'dʒɛstɪv] (pej) adj anzüglich.
suicidal [suɪ'saɪdl] adj selbstmörderisch; (person) selbstmordgefährdet; **to be** or **feel** ~ Selbstmordgedanken haben.
suicide ['suɪsaɪd] n (lit, fig) Selbstmord m; (person) Selbstmörder(in) m(f); see also **commit**.
suicide attempt, suicide bid n Selbstmordversuch m.
suit [suːt] n (man's) Anzug m; (woman's) Kostüm nt; (LAW) Prozeß m, Verfahren nt; (CARDS) Farbe f ♦ vt passen +dat; (colour, clothes) stehen +dat; **to bring a** ~ **against sb**

(*LAW*) gegen jdn Klage erheben *or* einen Prozeß anstrengen; **to follow** ~ (*fig*) das Gleiche tun; **to** ~ **sth to** etw anpassen an +*acc*; **to be** ~**ed to do sth** sich dafür eignen, etw zu tun; ~ **yourself!** wie du willst!; **well** ~**ed** (*couple*) gut zusammenpassend.

suitability [suːtəˈbɪlɪtɪ] *n* Eignung *f*.

suitable [ˈsuːtəbl] *adj* (*convenient*) passend; (*appropriate*) geeignet; **would tomorrow be** ~? würde Ihnen morgen passen?; **Monday isn't** ~ Montag paßt nicht; **we found somebody** ~ wir haben jemand Passenden gefunden.

suitably [ˈsuːtəblɪ] *adv* passend; (*impressed*) gebührend.

suitcase [ˈsuːtkeɪs] *n* Koffer *m*.

suite [swiːt] *n* (*of rooms*) Suite *f*, Zimmerflucht *f*; (*MUS*) Suite *f*; **bedroom/dining room** ~ Schlafzimmer-/Eßzimmereinrichtung *f*; **a three-piece** ~ eine dreiteilige Polstergarnitur.

suitor [ˈsuːtə*] *n* Kläger(in) *m(f)*.

sulfate [ˈsʌlfeɪt] (*US*) *n* = **sulphate**.

sulfur [ˈsʌlfə*] (*US*) *n* = **sulphur**.

sulfuric [sʌlˈfjuərɪk] (*US*) *adj* = **sulphuric**.

sulk [sʌlk] *vi* schmollen.

sulky [ˈsʌlkɪ] *adj* schmollend.

sullen [ˈsʌlən] *adj* mürrisch, verdrossen.

sulphate, (*US*) **sulfate** [ˈsʌlfeɪt] *n* Sulfat *nt*, schwefelsaures Salz *nt*.

sulphur, (*US*) **sulfur** [ˈsʌlfə*] *n* Schwefel *m*.

sulphur dioxide *n* Schwefeldioxid *nt*.

sulphuric, (*US*) **sulfuric** [sʌlˈfjuərɪk] *adj*: ~ **acid** Schwefelsäure *f*.

sultan [ˈsʌltən] *n* Sultan *m*.

sultana [sʌlˈtɑːnə] *n* Sultanine *f*.

sultry [ˈsʌltrɪ] *adj* schwül.

sum [sʌm] *n* (*calculation*) Rechenaufgabe *f*; (*amount*) Summe *f*, Betrag *m*.

▶**sum up** *vt* zusammenfassen; (*evaluate rapidly*) einschätzen ♦ *vi* zusammenfassen.

Sumatra [suˈmɑːtrə] *n* Sumatra *nt*.

summarize [ˈsʌməraɪz] *vt* zusammenfassen.

summary [ˈsʌmərɪ] *n* Zusammenfassung *f* ♦ *adj* (*justice, executions*) im Schnellverfahren.

summer [ˈsʌmə*] *n* Sommer *m* ♦ *cpd* Sommer-; **in** ~ im Sommer.

summer camp (*US*) *n* Ferienlager *nt*.

summer holidays *npl* Sommerferien *pl*.

summerhouse [ˈsʌməhaus] *n* (*in garden*) Gartenhaus *nt*, Gartenlaube *f*.

summertime [ˈsʌmətaɪm] *n* Sommer *m*, Sommerszeit *f*.

summer time *n* Sommerzeit *f*.

summery [ˈsʌmərɪ] *adj* sommerlich.

summing-up [sʌmɪŋˈʌp] *n* (*LAW*) Resümee *nt*.

summit [ˈsʌmɪt] *n* Gipfel *m*; (*also:* ~ **conference/meeting**) Gipfelkonferenz *f* /-treffen *nt*.

summon [ˈsʌmən] *vt* rufen, kommen lassen; (*help*) holen; (*meeting*) einberufen; (*LAW: witness*) vorladen.

▶**summon up** *vt* aufbringen.

summons [ˈsʌmənz] *n* (*LAW*) Vorladung *f*; (*fig*) Aufruf *m* ♦ *vt* (*LAW*) vorladen; **to serve a** ~ **on sb** jdn vor Gericht laden.

sumo (wrestling) [ˈsuːməu] *n* Sumo(-Ringen) *nt*.

sump [sʌmp] (*BRIT*) *n* Ölwanne *f*.

sumptuous [ˈsʌmptjuəs] *adj* (*meal*) üppig; (*costume*) aufwendig.

Sun. *abbr* (= *Sunday*) So.

sun [sʌn] *n* Sonne *f*; **to catch the** ~ einen Sonnenbrand bekommen; **everything under the** ~ alles Mögliche.

sunbathe [ˈsʌnbeɪð] *vi* sich sonnen.

sunbeam [ˈsʌnbiːm] *n* Sonnenstrahl *m*.

sunbed [ˈsʌnbed] *n* (*with sun lamp*) Sonnenbank *f*.

sunburn [ˈsʌnbəːn] *n* Sonnenbrand *m*.

sunburned [ˈsʌnbəːnd] *adj* = **sunburnt**.

sunburnt [ˈsʌnbəːnt] *adj* sonnenverbrannt, sonnengebräunt; **to be** ~ (*painfully*) einen Sonnenbrand haben.

sun-cream [ˈsʌnkriːm] *n* Sonnencreme *f*.

sundae [ˈsʌndeɪ] *n* Eisbecher *m*.

Sunday [ˈsʌndɪ] *n* Sonntag *m*; *see also* **Tuesday**.

Sunday paper *n* Sonntagszeitung *f*.

Die **Sunday papers** *umfassen sowohl Massenblätter als auch seriöse Zeitungen. The Observer ist die älteste überregionale Sonntagszeitung der Welt. Die Sonntagszeitungen sind alle sehr umfangreich mit vielen Farb- und Sonderbeilagen. Zu den meisten Tageszeitungen gibt es parallele Sonntagsblätter, die aber separate Redaktionen haben.*

Sunday school *n* Sonntagsschule *f*.

sundial [ˈsʌndaɪəl] *n* Sonnenuhr *f*.

sundown [ˈsʌndaun] (*esp US*) *n* Sonnenuntergang *m*.

sundries [ˈsʌndrɪz] *npl* Verschiedenes *nt*.

sundry [ˈsʌndrɪ] *adj* verschiedene; **all and** ~ jedermann.

sunflower [ˈsʌnflauə*] *n* Sonnenblume *f*.

sunflower oil *n* Sonnenblumenöl *nt*.

sung [sʌŋ] *pp of* **sing**.

sunglasses [ˈsʌnglɑːsɪz] *npl* Sonnenbrille *f*.

sunk [sʌŋk] *pp of* **sink**.

sunken [ˈsʌŋkn] *adj* versunken; (*eyes*) tiefliegend; (*cheeks*) eingefallen; (*bath*) eingelassen.

sunlamp [ˈsʌnlæmp] *n* Höhensonne *f*.

sunlight [ˈsʌnlaɪt] *n* Sonnenlicht *nt*.

sunlit [ˈsʌnlɪt] *adj* sonnig, sonnenbeschienen.

sunny [ˈsʌnɪ] *adj* sonnig; (*fig*) heiter.

sunrise [ˈsʌnraɪz] *n* Sonnenaufgang *m*.

sun roof *n* (*AUT*) Schiebedach *nt*; (*on building*) Sonnenterrasse *f*.

sun screen *n* Sonnenschutzmittel *nt*.

sunset [ˈsʌnset] *n* Sonnenuntergang *m*.

sunshade ['sʌnʃeɪd] n Sonnenschirm m.
sunshine ['sʌnʃaɪn] n Sonnenschein m.
sunspot ['sʌnspɒt] n Sonnenfleck m.
sunstroke ['sʌnstrəuk] n Sonnenstich m.
suntan ['sʌntæn] n (Sonnen)bräune f; **to get a**
~ braun werden.
suntan lotion n Sonnenmilch f.
suntanned ['sʌntænd] adj braun(gebrannt).
suntan oil n Sonnenöl m.
suntrap ['sʌntræp] n sonniges Eckchen nt.
super ['suːpə⁎] (inf) adj phantastisch, toll.
superannuation [suːpərænjuˈeɪʃən] n Beitrag
m zur Rentenversicherung.
superb [suːˈpəːb] adj ausgezeichnet,
großartig; (meal) vorzüglich.
Super Bowl n Super Bowl m, American-
Football-Turnier zwischen den
Spitzenreitern der Nationalligen.
supercilious [suːpəˈsɪlɪəs] adj herablassend.
superconductor [suːpəkənˈdʌktə⁎] n (PHYS)
Superleiter m.
superficial [suːpəˈfɪʃəl] adj oberflächlich.
superficially [suːpəˈfɪʃəlɪ] adv oberflächlich;
(from a superficial point of view) oberflächlich
gesehen.
superfluous [suːˈpəːfluəs] adj überflüssig.
superglue ['suːpəgluː] n Sekundenkleber m.
superhighway (US) n ≈ Autobahn f;
information ~ Datenautobahn f.
superhuman [suːpəˈhjuːmən] adj
übermenschlich.
superimpose ['suːpərɪmˈpəuz] vt (two things)
übereinanderlegen; **to** ~ **on** legen auf +acc;
to ~ **with** überlagern mit.
superintend [suːpərɪnˈtɛnd] vt beaufsichtigen,
überwachen.
superintendent [suːpərɪnˈtɛndənt] n
Aufseher(in) m(f); (POLICE) Kommissar(in)
m(f).
superior [suˈpɪərɪə⁎] adj besser, überlegen
+dat; (more senior) höhergestellt; (smug)
überheblich; (: smile) überlegen ♦ n
Vorgesetzte(r) f(m); **Mother S~** (REL) Mutter
Oberin.
superiority [supɪərɪˈɒrɪtɪ] n Überlegenheit f.
superlative [suˈpəːlətɪv] n Superlativ m ♦ adj
überragend.
superman ['suːpəmæn] (irreg: like **man**) n
Übermensch m.
supermarket ['suːpəmɑːkɪt] n Supermarkt m.
supermodel ['suːpəmɒdl] n Supermodell nt.
supernatural [suːpəˈnætʃərəl] adj
übernatürlich ♦ n: **the** ~ das
Übernatürliche.
supernova [suːpəˈnəuvə] n Supernova f.
superpower ['suːpəpauə⁎] n Supermacht f.
superscript ['suːpəskrɪpt] n hochgestelltes
Zeichen nt.
supersede [suːpəˈsiːd] vt ablösen, ersetzen.
supersonic ['suːpəˈsɒnɪk] adj (aircraft etc)
Überschall-.
superstar ['suːpəstɑː⁎] n Superstar m.

superstition [suːpəˈstɪʃən] n Aberglaube m.
superstitious [suːpəˈstɪʃəs] adj abergläubisch.
superstore ['suːpəstɔː⁎] (BRIT) n Großmarkt
m.
supertanker ['suːpətæŋkə⁎] n Supertanker m.
supertax ['suːpətæks] n Höchststeuer f.
supervise ['suːpəvaɪz] vt beaufsichtigen.
supervision [suːpəˈvɪʒən] n Beaufsichtigung f;
under medical ~ unter ärztlicher Aufsicht.
supervisor ['suːpəvaɪzə⁎] n Aufseher(in) m(f);
(of students) Tutor(in) m(f).
supervisory ['suːpəvaɪzərɪ] adj
beaufsichtigend, Aufsichts-.
supine ['suːpaɪn] adj: **to be** ~ auf dem Rücken
liegen ♦ adv auf dem Rücken.
supper ['sʌpə⁎] n Abendessen nt; **to have** ~ zu
Abend essen.
supplant [səˈplɑːnt] vt ablösen, ersetzen.
supple ['sʌpl] adj geschmeidig; (person)
gelenkig.
supplement ['sʌplɪmənt] n Zusatz m; (of book)
Ergänzungsband m; (of newspaper etc)
Beilage f ♦ vt ergänzen.
supplementary [sʌplɪˈmɛntərɪ] adj zusätzlich,
ergänzend.
supplementary benefit (BRIT: old) n
≈ Sozialhilfe f.
supplier [səˈplaɪə⁎] n Lieferant(in) m(f).
supply [səˈplaɪ] vt liefern; (provide) sorgen
für; (a need) befriedigen ♦ n Vorrat m;
(supplying) Lieferung f; **supplies** npl (food)
Vorräte pl; (MIL) Nachschub m; **to** ~ **sth to
sb** jdm etw liefern; **to** ~ **sth with sth** etw
mit etw versorgen; **it comes supplied with
an adaptor** es wird mit einem Adapter
geliefert; **office supplies** Bürobedarf m; **to
be in short** ~ knapp sein; **the electricity/
water/gas** ~ die Strom-/Wasser-/
Gasversorgung f; ~ **and demand** Angebot nt
und Nachfrage.
supply teacher (BRIT) n Vertretung f.
support [səˈpɔːt] n Unterstützung f; (TECH)
Stütze f ♦ vt unterstützen, eintreten für;
(financially: family etc) unterhalten; (: party
etc) finanziell unterstützen; (TECH)
(ab)stützen; (theory etc) untermauern; **they
stopped work in** ~ **of** ... sie sind in den
Streik getreten, um für ... einzutreten; **to**
~ **o.s.** (financially) finanziell unabhängig
sein; **to** ~ **Arsenal** Arsenal-Fan sein.
supporter [səˈpɔːtə⁎] n (POL etc) Anhänger(in)
m(f); (SPORT) Fan m.
supporting [səˈpɔːtɪŋ] adj: ~ **role** Nebenrolle f;
~ **actor** Schauspieler m in einer Nebenrolle;
~ **film** Vorfilm m.
supportive [səˈpɔːtɪv] n hilfreich; **to be** ~ **of
sb/sth** jdn/etw unterstützen.
suppose [səˈpəuz] vt annehmen, glauben;
(imagine) sich dat vorstellen; **to be** ~**d to do
sth** etw tun sollen; **it was worse than she'd**
~**d** es war schlimmer, als sie es sich
vorgestellt hatte; **I don't** ~ **she'll come** ich

glaube kaum, daß sie kommt; **he's about sixty, I ~** er muß wohl so um die Sechzig sein; **he's ~d to be an expert** er ist angeblich ein Experte; **I ~ so/not** ich glaube schon/nicht.

supposedly [sə'pəʊzɪdlɪ] *adv* angeblich.

supposing [sə'pəʊzɪŋ] *conj* angenommen.

supposition [sʌpə'zɪʃən] *n* Annahme *f*.

suppository [sə'pɒzɪtrɪ] *n* Zäpfchen *nt*.

suppress [sə'prɛs] *vt* unterdrücken; (*publication*) verbieten.

suppression [sə'prɛʃən] *n* Unterdrückung *f*.

suppressor [sə'prɛsə'] *n* (*ELEC etc*) Entstörungselement *nt*.

supremacy [su'prɛməsɪ] *n* Vormachtstellung *f*.

supreme [su'priːm] *adj* Ober-, oberste(r, s); (*effort*) äußerste(r, s); (*achievement*) höchste(r, s).

Supreme Court (*US*) *n* Oberster Gerichtshof *m*.

supremo [su'priːməʊ] (*BRIT: inf*) *n* Boß *m*.

Supt *abbr* (*POLICE*) = **superintendent.**

surcharge ['səːtʃɑːdʒ] *n* Zuschlag *m*.

sure [ʃʊə'] *adj* sicher; (*reliable*) zuverlässig, sicher ♦ *adv* (*inf: esp US*): **that ~ is pretty, that's ~ pretty** das ist aber schön; **to make ~ of sth** sich einer Sache *gen* vergewissern; **to make ~ that** sich vergewissern, daß; **I'm ~ of it** ich bin mir da sicher; **I'm not ~ how/why/when** ich bin mir nicht sicher *or* ich weiß nicht genau, wie/warum/wann; **to be ~ of o.s.** selbstsicher sein; **~!** klar!; **~ enough** tatsächlich.

sure-fire ['ʃʊəfaɪə'] (*inf*) *adj* todsicher.

sure-footed [ʃʊə'fʊtɪd] *adj* trittsicher.

surely ['ʃʊəlɪ] *adv* sicherlich, bestimmt; **~ you don't mean that!** das meinen Sie doch bestimmt *or* sicher nicht (so)!

surety ['ʃʊərətɪ] *n* Bürgschaft *f*, Sicherheit *f*; **to go** *or* **stand ~ for sb** für jdn bürgen.

surf [səːf] *n* Brandung *f*.

surface ['səːfɪs] *n* Oberfläche *f* ♦ *vt* (*road*) mit einem Belag versehen ♦ *vi* (*lit, fig*) auftauchen; (*feeling*) hochkommen; (*rise from bed*) hochkommen; **on the ~** (*fig*) oberflächlich betrachtet.

surface area *n* Fläche *f*.

surface mail *n* Post *f* auf dem Land-/Seeweg.

surface-to-surface ['səːfɪstə'səːfɪs] *adj* (*missile*) Boden-Boden-.

surfboard ['səːfbɔːd] *n* Surfbrett *nt*.

surfeit ['səːfɪt] *n*: **a ~ of** ein Übermaß an +*dat*.

surfer ['səːfə'] *n* Surfer(in) *m(f)*.

surfing ['səːfɪŋ] *n* Surfen *nt*; **to go ~** Surfen gehen.

surge [səːdʒ] *n* Anstieg *m*; (*fig: of emotion*) Woge *f*; (*ELEC*) Spannungsstoß *m* ♦ *vi* (*water*) branden; (*people*) sich drängen; (*vehicles*) sich wälzen; (*emotion*) aufwallen; (*ELEC: power*) ansteigen; **to ~ forward** nach vorne drängen.

surgeon ['səːdʒən] *n* Chirurg(in) *m(f)*.

Surgeon General (*US*) *n* (*MED*) ≈ Gesundheitsminister(in) *m(f)*; (*MIL*) Sanitätsinspekteur(in) *m(f)*.

surgery ['səːdʒərɪ] *n* Chirurgie *f*; (*BRIT: room*) Sprechzimmer *nt*; (: *building*) Praxis *f*; (*also:* **~ hours**: *of doctor, MP etc*) Sprechstunde *f*; **to have ~** operiert werden; **to need ~** operiert werden müssen.

surgical ['səːdʒɪkl] *adj* chirurgisch; (*treatment*) operativ.

surgical spirit (*BRIT*) *n* Wundbenzin *nt*.

surly ['səːlɪ] *adj* verdrießlich, mürrisch.

surmise [səː'maɪz] *vt* vermuten, mutmaßen.

surmount [səː'maʊnt] *vt* (*fig*) überwinden.

surname ['səːneɪm] *n* Nachname *m*.

surpass [səː'pɑːs] *vt* übertreffen.

surplus ['səːpləs] *n* Überschuß *m* ♦ *adj* überschüssig; **it is ~ to our requirements** das benötigen wir nicht.

surprise [sə'praɪz] *n* Überraschung *f* ♦ *vt* überraschen; (*astonish*) erstaunen; (*army*) überrumpeln; (*thief*) ertappen; **to take sb by ~** jdn überraschen.

surprising [sə'praɪzɪŋ] *adj* überraschend; (*situation*) erstaunlich; **it is ~ how/that** es ist erstaunlich, wie/daß.

surprisingly [sə'praɪzɪŋlɪ] *adv* überraschend, erstaunlich; (*somewhat*) **~, he agreed** erstaunlicherweise war er damit einverstanden.

surrealism [sə'rɪəlɪzəm] *n* Surrealismus *m*.

surrealist [sə'rɪəlɪst] *adj* surrealistisch.

surrender [sə'rɛndə'] *n* Kapitulation *f* ♦ *vi* sich ergeben ♦ *vt* aufgeben.

surrender value *n* Rückkaufswert *m*.

surreptitious [sʌrəp'tɪʃəs] *adj* heimlich, verstohlen.

surrogate ['sʌrəgɪt] *n* Ersatz *m* ♦ *adj* (*parents*) Ersatz-.

surrogate mother *n* Leihmutter *f*.

surround [sə'raʊnd] *vt* umgeben; (*MIL, POLICE etc*) umstellen.

surrounding [sə'raʊndɪŋ] *adj* umliegend; **the ~ area** die Umgebung.

surroundings [sə'raʊndɪŋz] *npl* Umgebung *f*.

surtax ['səːtæks] *n* Steuerzuschlag *m*.

surveillance [səː'veɪləns] *n* Überwachung *f*; **to be under ~** überwacht werden.

survey ['səːveɪ] *n* (*of land*) Vermessung *f*; (*of house*) Begutachtung *f*; (*investigation*) Untersuchung *f*; (*report*) Gutachten *nt*; (*comprehensive view*) Überblick *m* ♦ *vt* (*land*) vermessen; (*house*) inspizieren; (*look at*) betrachten.

surveying [sə'veɪɪŋ] *n* (*of land*) Vermessung *f*.

surveyor [sə'veɪə'] *n* (*of land*) Landvermesser(in) *m(f)*; (*of house*) Baugutachter(in) *m(f)*.

survival [sə'vaɪvl] *n* Überleben *nt*; (*relic*) Überbleibsel *nt*; **~ course/kit** Überlebenstraining *nt*/-ausrüstung *f*; **~ bag**

Expeditionsschlafsack *m*.
survive [sə'vaɪv] *vi* überleben; (*custom etc*)
weiterbestehen ♦ *vt* überleben.
survivor [sə'vaɪvə*] *n* Überlebende(r) *f(m)*.
susceptible [sə'sɛptəbl] *adj*: ~ **(to)** anfällig
(für); (*influenced by*) empfänglich (für).
suspect ['sʌspɛkt] *adj* verdächtig ♦ *n*
Verdächtige(r) *f(m)* ♦ *vt*: to ~ **sb of** jdn
verdächtigen *+gen*; (*think*) vermuten; (*doubt*)
bezweifeln.
suspected [səs'pɛktɪd] *adj* (*terrorist etc*)
mutmaßlich; **he is a ~ member of this
organization** er steht im Verdacht, Mitglied
dieser Organisation zu sein.
suspend [səs'pɛnd] *vt* (*hang*) (auf)hängen;
(*delay, stop*) einstellen; (*from employment*)
suspendieren; **to be ~ed (from)** (*hang*)
hängen (an *+dat*).
suspended animation [səs'pɛndɪd-] *n*
vorübergehender Stillstand aller
Körperfunktionen.
suspended sentence *n* (*LAW*) zur
Bewährung ausgesetzte Strafe *f*.
suspender belt [səs'pɛndə*-] *n*
Strumpfhaltergürtel *m*.
suspenders [səs'pɛndəz] *npl* (*BRIT*)
Strumpfhalter *pl*; (*US*) Hosenträger *pl*.
suspense [səs'pɛns] *n* Spannung *f*;
(*uncertainty*) Ungewißheit *f*; **to keep sb in ~**
jdn auf die Folter spannen.
suspension [səs'pɛnʃən] *n* (*from job*)
Suspendierung *f*; (*from team*) Sperrung *f*;
(*AUT*) Federung *f*; (*of driving licence*)
zeitweiliger Entzug *m*; (*of payment*)
zeitweilige Einstellung *f*.
suspension bridge *n* Hängebrücke *f*.
suspicion [səs'pɪʃən] *n* Verdacht *m*; (*distrust*)
Mißtrauen *nt*; (*trace*) Spur *f*; **to be under ~**
unter Verdacht stehen; **arrested on ~ of
murder** wegen Mordverdachts
festgenommen.
suspicious [səs'pɪʃəs] *adj* (*suspecting*)
mißtrauisch; (*causing suspicion*) verdächtig;
to be ~ of or **about sb/sth** jdn/etw mit
Mißtrauen betrachten.
suss out [sʌs-] - (*BRIT: inf*) *vt* (*discover*)
rauskriegen; (*understand*) durchschauen.
sustain [səs'teɪn] *vt* (*continue*)
aufrechterhalten; (*food, drink*) bei Kräften
halten; (*suffer: injury*) erleiden.
sustainable [səs'teɪnəbl] *adj*: **to be ~**
aufrechtzuerhalten sein; ~ **growth** stetiges
Wachstum *nt*.
sustained [səs'teɪnd] *adj* (*effort*) ausdauernd;
(*attack*) anhaltend.
sustenance ['sʌstɪnəns] *n* Nahrung *f*.
suture ['suːtʃə*] *n* Naht *f*.
SW *abbr* (= *south-west*) SW; (*RADIO*: = *short-
wave*) KW.
swab [swɔb] *n* (*MED*) Tupfer *m* ♦ *vt* (*NAUT*:
also: ~ **down**) wischen.
swagger ['swægə*] *vi* stolzieren.

swallow ['swɔləu] *n* (*bird*) Schwalbe *f*; (*of food,
drink etc*) Schluck *m* ♦ *vt*
(herunter)schlucken; (*fig: story, insult, one's
pride*) schlucken; **to ~ one's words** (*speak
indistinctly*) seine Worte verschlucken;
(*retract*) alles zurücknehmen.
▸**swallow up** *vt* verschlingen.
swam [swæm] *pt of* **swim**.
swamp [swɔmp] *n* Sumpf *m* ♦ *vt* (*lit, fig*)
überschwemmen.
swampy ['swɔmpɪ] *adj* sumpfig.
swan [swɔn] *n* Schwan *m*.
swank [swæŋk] (*inf*) *vi* angeben.
swan song *n* (*fig*) Schwanengesang *m*.
swap [swɔp] *n* Tausch *m* ♦ *vt*: **to ~ (for)**
(ein)tauschen (gegen).
SWAPO ['swɑːpəu] *n abbr* (= *South-West Africa
People's Organization*) SWAPO *f*.
swarm [swɔːm] *n* Schwarm *m*; (*of people*)
Schar *f* ♦ *vi* (*bees, people*) schwärmen; **to be
~ing with** wimmeln von.
swarthy ['swɔːðɪ] *adj* (*person, face*)
dunkelhäutig; (*complexion*) dunkel.
swashbuckling ['swɔʃbʌklɪŋ] *adj*
draufgängerisch; (*hero*) verwegen.
swastika ['swɔstɪkə] *n* Hakenkreuz *nt*.
SWAT (*US*) *n abbr* (= *Special Weapons and
Tactics*): ~ **team** ≈ schnelle Eingreiftruppe
f.
swat [swɔt] *vt* totschlagen ♦ *n* (*BRIT: also*: **fly**
~) Fliegenklatsche *f*.
swathe [sweɪð] *vt*: **to ~ in** wickeln in *+acc*.
swatter ['swɔtə*] *n* (*also*: **fly** ~)
Fliegenklatsche *f*.
sway [sweɪ] *vi* schwanken ♦ *vt* (*influence*)
beeinflussen ♦ *n*: **to hold ~** herrschen; **to
hold ~ over sb** jdn beherrschen *or* in seiner
Macht haben.
Swaziland ['swɑːzɪlænd] *n* Swasiland *nt*.
swear [swɛə*] (*pt* **swore**, *pp* **sworn**) *vi* (*curse*)
fluchen ♦ *vt* (*promise*) schwören; **to ~ an
oath** einen Eid ablegen.
▸**swear in** *vt* vereidigen.
swearword ['swɛəwɔːd] *n* Fluch *m*,
Kraftausdruck *m*.
sweat [swɛt] *n* Schweiß *m* ♦ *vi* schwitzen; **to
be in a ~** schwitzen.
sweatband ['swɛtbænd] *n* Schweißband *nt*.
sweater ['swɛtə*] *n* Pullover *m*.
sweatshirt ['swɛtʃəːt] *n* Sweatshirt *nt*.
sweatshop ['swɛtʃɔp] (*pej*) *n*
Ausbeuterbetrieb *m*.
sweaty ['swɛtɪ] *adj* verschwitzt; (*hands*)
schweißig.
Swede [swiːd] *n* Schwede *m*, Schwedin *f*.
swede [swiːd] (*BRIT*) *n* Steckrübe *f*.
Sweden ['swiːdn] *n* Schweden *nt*.
Swedish ['swiːdɪʃ] *adj* schwedisch ♦ *n*
Schwedisch *nt*.
sweep [swiːp] (*pt, pp* **swept**) *n*: **to give sth a ~**
etw fegen *or* kehren; (*curve*) Bogen *m*;
(*range*) Bereich *m*; (*also*: **chimney ~**)

Kaminkehrer m, Schornsteinfeger m ♦ vt fegen, kehren; (current) reißen ♦ vi (through air) gleiten; (wind) fegen.
►**sweep away** vt hinwegfegen.
►**sweep past** vi vorbeirauschen.
►**sweep up** vi zusammenfegen, zusammenkehren.
sweeper ['swiːpə*] n (FOOTBALL) Ausputzer m.
sweeping ['swiːpɪŋ] adj (gesture) weit ausholend; (changes, reforms) weitreichend; (statement) verallgemeinernd.
sweepstake ['swiːpsteɪk] n Pferdewette, bei der der Preis aus der Summe der Einsätze besteht.
sweet [swiːt] n (candy) Bonbon nt or m; (BRIT: CULIN) Nachtisch m ♦ adj süß; (air, water) frisch; (kind) lieb ♦ adv: to smell/taste ~ süß duften/schmecken; ~ and sour süß-sauer.
sweetbread ['swiːtbred] n Bries nt.
sweetcorn ['swiːtkɔːn] n Mais m.
sweeten ['swiːtn] vt süßen; (temper) bessern; (person) gnädig stimmen.
sweetener ['swiːtnə*] n Süßstoff m; (fig) Anreiz m.
sweetheart ['swiːthaːt] n Freund(in) m(f); (in speech, writing) Schatz m, Liebling m.
sweetness ['swiːtnɪs] n Süße f; (kindness) Liebenswürdigkeit f.
sweet pea n (Garten)wicke f.
sweet potato n Süßkartoffel f, Batate f.
sweet shop (BRIT) n Süßwarengeschäft nt.
sweet tooth n: to have a ~ gern Süßes essen.
swell [swel] (pt swelled, pp swollen or swelled) n Seegang m ♦ adj (US: inf) toll, prima ♦ vi (increase) anwachsen; (sound) anschwellen; (feeling) stärker werden; (also: ~ up) anschwellen.
swelling ['swelɪŋ] n Schwellung f.
sweltering ['sweltərɪŋ] adj (heat) glühend; (weather, day) glühend heiß.
swept [swept] pt, pp of **sweep**.
swerve [swɜːv] vi (animal) ausbrechen; (driver, vehicle) ausschwenken; to ~ off the road ausschwenken und von der Straße abkommen.
swift [swift] n Mauersegler m ♦ adj schnell.
swiftly ['swiftlɪ] adv schnell.
swiftness ['swiftnɪs] n Schnelligkeit f.
swig [swig] (inf) n Schluck m ♦ vt herunterkippen.
swill [swil] vt (also: ~ out) ausspülen; (also: ~ down) abspülen ♦ n (for pigs) Schweinefutter nt.
swim [swim] (pt swam, pp swum) vi schwimmen; (before one's eyes) verschwimmen ♦ vt (the Channel etc) durchschwimmen; (a length) schwimmen ♦ n: to go for a ~ schwimmen gehen; to go ~ming schwimmen gehen; my head is ~ming mir dreht sich der Kopf.

swimmer ['swimə*] n Schwimmer(in) m(f).
swimming ['swimɪŋ] n Schwimmen nt.
swimming baths (BRIT) npl Schwimmbad nt.
swimming cap n Badekappe f, Bademütze f.
swimming costume (BRIT) n Badeanzug m.
swimmingly ['swimɪŋlɪ] (inf) adv glänzend.
swimming pool n Schwimmbad nt.
swimming trunks npl Badehose f.
swimsuit ['swimsuːt] n Badeanzug m.
swindle ['swindl] n Schwindel m, Betrug m ♦ vt: to ~ sb (out of sth) jdn (um etw) betrügen or beschwindeln.
swindler ['swindlə*] n Schwindler(in) m(f).
swine [swain] (inf!) n Schwein nt.
swing [swiŋ] (pt, pp swung) n (in playground) Schaukel f; (movement) Schwung m; (change) Umschwung m; (MUS) Swing m ♦ vt (arms, legs) schwingen (mit); (also: ~ round) herumschwenken ♦ vi schwingen; (also: ~ round) sich umdrehen; (vehicle) herumschwenken; a ~ to the left (POL) ein Linksruck m; to get into the ~ of things richtig reinkommen; to be in full ~ (party etc) in vollem Gang sein.
swing bridge n Drehbrücke f.
swing door, (US) **swinging door** n Pendeltür f.
swingeing ['swindʒɪŋ] (BRIT) adj (blow) hart; (attack) scharf; (cuts, increases) extrem.
swinging ['swiŋɪŋ] adj (music) schwungvoll; (movement) schaukelnd.
swipe [swaip] vt (also: ~ at) schlagen nach; (inf: steal) klauen ♦ n Schlag m.
swirl [swɜːl] vi wirbeln ♦ n Wirbeln nt.
swish [swiʃ] vi rauschen; (tail) schlagen ♦ n Rauschen nt; (of tail) Schlagen nt ♦ adj (inf) schick.
Swiss [swis] adj schweizerisch, Schweizer ♦ n inv Schweizer(in) m(f).
Swiss French adj französischschweizerisch.
Swiss German adj deutschschweizerisch.
Swiss roll n Biskuitrolle f.
switch [switʃ] n Schalter m; (change) Änderung f ♦ vt (change) ändern; (exchange) tauschen, wechseln; to ~ (round or over) vertauschen.
►**switch off** vt abschalten; (light) ausschalten ♦ vi (fig) abschalten.
►**switch on** vt einschalten; (radio) anstellen; (engine) anlassen.
switchback ['switʃbæk] (BRIT) n (road) auf und ab führende Straße f; (roller-coaster) Achterbahn f.
switchblade ['switʃbleid] n Schnappmesser nt.
switchboard ['switʃbɔːd] n Vermittlung f, Zentrale f.
switchboard operator n Telefonist(in) m(f).
Switzerland ['switsələnd] n die Schweiz f.
swivel ['swivl] vi (also: ~ round) sich (herum)drehen.
swollen ['swəulən] pp of **swell** ♦ adj

geschwollen; (*lake etc*) angeschwollen.
swoon [swuːn] *vi* beinahe ohnmächtig
werden ♦ *n* Ohnmacht *f*.
swoop [swuːp] *n* (*by police etc*) Razzia *f*; (*of
bird etc*) Sturzflug *m* ♦ *vi* (*also*: ~ **down**: *bird*)
herabstoßen; (*plane*) einen Sturzflug
machen.
swop [swɔp] = **swap**.
sword [sɔːd] *n* Schwert *nt*.
swordfish ['sɔːdfɪʃ] *n* Schwertfisch *m*.
swore [swɔː*] *pt of* **swear**.
sworn [swɔːn] *pp of* **swear** ♦ *adj* (*statement*)
eidlich; (*evidence*) unter Eid; (*enemy*)
geschworen.
swot [swɔt] *vi* pauken ♦ *n* (*pej*) Streber(in)
m(f).
►**swot up** *vt*: **to** ~ **up** (**on**) pauken (+*acc*).
swum [swʌm] *pp of* **swim**.
swung [swʌŋ] *pt*, *pp of* **swing**.
sycamore ['sɪkəmɔː*] *n* Bergahorn *m*.
sycophant ['sɪkəfænt] *n* Kriecher *m*,
Speichellecker *m*.
sycophantic [sɪkə'fæntɪk] *adj* kriecherisch.
Sydney ['sɪdnɪ] *n* Sydney *nt*.
syllable ['sɪləbl] *n* Silbe *f*.
syllabus ['sɪləbəs] *n* Lehrplan *m*; **on the** ~ im
Lehrplan.
symbol ['sɪmbl] *n* Symbol *nt*.
symbolic(al) [sɪm'bɔlɪk(l)] *adj* symbolisch; **to
be** ~ **of sth** etw symbolisieren, ein Symbol
für etw sein.
symbolism ['sɪmbəlɪzəm] *n* Symbolismus *m*.
symbolize ['sɪmbəlaɪz] *vt* symbolisieren.
symmetrical [sɪ'mɛtrɪkl] *adj* symmetrisch.
symmetry ['sɪmɪtrɪ] *n* Symmetrie *f*.
sympathetic [sɪmpə'θɛtɪk] *adj* (*understanding*)
verständnisvoll; (*showing pity*) mitfühlend;
(*likeable*) sympathisch; (*supportive*)
wohlwollend; **to be** ~ **to a cause** (*well-
disposed*) einer Sache wohlwollend
gegenüberstehen.
sympathetically [sɪmpə'θɛtɪklɪ] *adv* (*showing
understanding*) verständnisvoll; (*showing
support*) wohlwollend.
sympathize ['sɪmpəθaɪz] *vi*: **to** ~ **with** (*person*)
Mitleid haben mit; (*feelings*) Verständnis
haben für; (*cause*) sympathisieren mit.
sympathizer ['sɪmpəθaɪzə*] *n* (*POL*)
Sympathisant(in) *m(f)*.
sympathy ['sɪmpəθɪ] *n* Mitgefühl *nt*;
sympathies *npl* (*support, tendencies*)
Sympathien *pl*; **with our deepest** ~ mit
aufrichtigem *or* herzlichem Beileid; **to
come out in** ~ (*workers*) in einen
Sympathiestreik treten.
symphonic [sɪm'fɔnɪk] *adj* sinfonisch.
symphony ['sɪmfənɪ] *n* Sinfonie *f*.
symphony orchestra *n* Sinfonieorchester
nt.
symposia [sɪm'pəuzɪə] *npl of* **symposium**.
symposium [sɪm'pəuzɪəm] (*pl* ~**s** *or*
symposia) *n* Symposium *nt*.

symptom ['sɪmptəm] *n* (*MED, fig*) Symptom *nt*,
Anzeichen *nt*.
symptomatic [sɪmptə'mætɪk] *adj*: ~ **of**
symptomatisch für.
synagogue ['sɪnəgɔg] *n* Synagoge *f*.
sync [sɪŋk] *n abbr* (= *synchronization*): **in** ~
synchron; **out of** ~ nicht synchron.
synchromesh [sɪŋkrəu'mɛʃ] *n*
Synchrongetriebe *nt*.
synchronize ['sɪŋkrənaɪz] *vt* (*watches*)
gleichstellen; (*movements*) aufeinander
abstimmen; (*sound*) synchronisieren ♦ *vi*: **to**
~ **with** (*sound*) synchron sein mit.
synchronized swimming ['sɪŋkrənaɪzd-] *n*
Synchronschwimmen *nt*.
syncopated ['sɪŋkəpeɪtɪd] *adj* synkopiert.
syndicate ['sɪndɪkɪt] *n* Interessengemeinschaft *f*; (*of businesses*) Verband *m*;
(*of newspapers*) Pressezentrale *f*.
syndrome ['sɪndrəum] *n* Syndrom *nt*; (*fig*)
Phänomen *nt*.
synonym ['sɪnənɪm] *n* Synonym *nt*.
synonymous [sɪ'nɔnɪməs] *adj* (*fig*): ~ (**with**)
gleichbedeutend (mit).
synopses [sɪ'nɔpsiːz] *npl of* **synopsis**.
synopsis [sɪ'nɔpsɪs] (*pl* **synopses**) *n* Abriß *m*,
Zusammenfassung *f*.
syntactic [sɪn'tæktɪk] *adj* syntaktisch.
syntax ['sɪntæks] *n* Syntax *f*.
syntax error *n* (*COMPUT*) Syntaxfehler *m*.
syntheses ['sɪnθəsiːz] *npl of* **synthesis**.
synthesis ['sɪnθəsɪs] (*pl* **syntheses**) *n* Synthese
f.
synthesizer ['sɪnθəsaɪzə*] *n* Synthesizer *m*.
synthetic [sɪn'θɛtɪk] *adj* synthetisch; (*speech*)
künstlich; **synthetics** *npl* (*man-made fabrics*)
Synthetik *f*.
syphilis ['sɪfɪlɪs] *n* Syphilis *f*.
syphon ['saɪfən] = **siphon**.
Syria ['sɪrɪə] *n* Syrien *nt*.
Syrian ['sɪrɪən] *adj* syrisch ♦ *n* Syrer(in) *m(f)*.
syringe [sɪ'rɪndʒ] *n* Spritze *f*.
syrup ['sɪrəp] *n* Sirup *m*; (*also*: **golden** ~)
(gelber) Sirup *m*.
syrupy ['sɪrəpɪ] *adj* sirupartig; (*pej, fig*:
sentimental) schmalzig.
system ['sɪstəm] *n* System *nt*; (*body*) Körper
m; (*ANAT*) Apparat *m*, System *nt*; **it was a
shock to his** ~ er hatte schwer damit zu
schaffen.
systematic [sɪstə'mætɪk] *adj* systematisch.
system disk *n* (*COMPUT*) Systemdiskette *f*.
systems analyst ['sɪstəmz-] *n*
Systemanalytiker(in) *m(f)*.

T, t

T, t [tiː] n (*letter*) T nt, t nt; ~ **for Tommy** ≈ T wie Theodor.
TA (*BRIT*) n abbr = **Territorial Army.**
ta [taː] (*BRIT: inf*) interj danke.
tab [tæb] n abbr = **tabulator** ♦ n (*on drinks can*) Ring m; (*on garment*) Etikett nt; **to keep ~s on sb/sth** (*fig*) jdn/etw im Auge behalten.
tabby ['tæbɪ] n (*also:* ~ **cat**) getigerte Katze f.
tabernacle ['tæbənækl] n Tabernakel nt.
table ['teɪbl] n Tisch m; (*MATH, CHEM etc*) Tabelle f ♦ vt (*BRIT: PARL: motion etc*) einbringen; **to lay** or **set the** ~ den Tisch decken; **to clear the** ~ den Tisch abräumen; **league** ~ (*BRIT: SPORT*) Tabelle f.
tablecloth ['teɪblklɔθ] n Tischdecke f.
table d'hôte [taːbl'dəut] adj (*menu, meal*) Tagesmenü nt.
table lamp n Tischlampe f.
tablemat ['teɪblmæt] n (*of cloth*) Set nt or m; (*for hot dish*) Untersatz m.
table of contents n Inhaltsverzeichnis nt.
table salt n Tafelsalz nt.
tablespoon ['teɪblspuːn] n Eßlöffel m; (*also:* ~**ful**) Eßlöffel(voll) m.
tablet ['tæblɪt] n (*MED*) Tablette f; (*HIST: for writing*) Tafel f; (*plaque*) Plakette f; ~ **of soap** (*BRIT*) Stück nt Seife.
table tennis n Tischtennis nt.
table wine n Tafelwein m.
tabloid ['tæblɔɪd] n (*newspaper*) Boulevardzeitung f; **the ~s** die Boulevardpresse.

Der Ausdruck **tabloid press** *bezieht sich auf kleinformatige Zeitungen (ca 30 × 40cm); die sind in Großbritannien fast ausschließlich Massenblätter. Im Gegensatz zur* **quality press** *verwenden diese Massenblätter viele Fotos und einen knappen, oft reißerischen Stil. Sie kommen den Lesern entgegen, die mehr Wert auf Unterhaltung legen.*

---

taboo [tə'buː] n Tabu nt ♦ adj tabu; **a** ~ **subject/word** ein Tabuthema/Tabuwort.
tabulate ['tæbjuleɪt] vt tabellarisieren.
tabulator ['tæbjuleɪtə*] n (*on typewriter*) Tabulator m.
tachograph ['tækəgrɑːf] n Fahrtenschreiber m.
tachometer [tæ'kɒmɪtə*] n Tachometer m.
tacit ['tæsɪt] adj stillschweigend.
taciturn ['tæsɪtɜːn] adj schweigsam.
tack [tæk] n (*nail*) Stift m ♦ vt (*nail*) anheften;

(*stitch*) heften ♦ vi (*NAUT*) kreuzen; **to change** ~ (*fig*) den Kurs ändern; **to** ~ **sth on to (the end of) sth** etw (hinten) an etw acc anheften.
tackle ['tækl] n (*for fishing*) Ausrüstung f; (*for lifting*) Flaschenzug m; (*FOOTBALL, RUGBY*) Angriff m ♦ vt (*deal with: difficulty*) in Angriff nehmen; (*challenge: person*) zur Rede stellen; (*physically, also SPORT*) angreifen.
tacky ['tækɪ] adj (*sticky*) klebrig; (*pej: cheap-looking*) schäbig.
tact [tækt] n Takt m.
tactful ['tæktful] adj taktvoll; **to be** ~ taktvoll sein.
tactfully ['tæktfəlɪ] adv taktvoll.
tactical ['tæktɪkl] adj taktisch; ~ **error** taktischer Fehler; ~ **voting** taktische Stimmabgabe.
tactician [tæk'tɪʃən] n Taktiker(in) m(f).
tactics ['tæktɪks] npl Taktik f.
tactless ['tæktlɪs] adj taktlos.
tactlessly ['tæktlɪslɪ] adv taktlos.
tadpole ['tædpəul] n Kaulquappe f.
taffy ['tæfɪ] (*US*) n (*toffee*) Toffee nt, Sahnebonbon nt.
tag [tæg] n (*label*) Anhänger m; **price/name** ~ Preis-/Namensschild nt.
▶**tag along** vi sich anschließen.
Tahiti [taː'hiːtɪ] n Tahiti nt.
tail [teɪl] n (*of animal*) Schwanz m; (*of plane*) Heck nt; (*of shirt, coat*) Schoß m ♦ vt (*follow*) folgen +dat; **tails** npl (*formal suit*) Frack m; **to turn** ~ die Flucht ergreifen; *see also* **head.**
▶**tail off** vi (*in size etc*) abnehmen; (*voice*) schwächer werden.
tailback ['teɪlbæk] (*BRIT*) n (*AUT*) Stau m.
tail coat n = **tails.**
tail end n Ende nt.
tailgate ['teɪlgeɪt] n (*AUT*) Heckklappe f.
taillight ['teɪllaɪt] n (*AUT*) Rücklicht nt.
tailor ['teɪlə*] n Schneider(in) m(f) ♦ vt: **to** ~ **sth (to)** etw abstimmen (auf +acc); ~'**s shop** Schneiderei f.
tailoring ['teɪlərɪŋ] n (*craft*) Schneiderei f; (*cut*) Verarbeitung f.
tailor-made ['teɪlə'meɪd] adj (*also fig*) maßgeschneidert.
tailwind ['teɪlwɪnd] n Rückenwind m.
taint [teɪnt] vt (*meat, food*) verderben; (*fig: reputation etc*) beschmutzen.
tainted ['teɪntɪd] adj (*food, water, air*) verdorben; (*fig: profits, reputation etc*): ~ **with** behaftet mit.
Taiwan [taɪ'waːn] n Taiwan nt.
Tajikistan [taːdʒɪkɪ'staːn] n Tadschikistan nt.
take [teɪk] (*pt* **took,** *pp* **taken**) vt nehmen; (*photo, notes*) machen; (*decision*) fällen; (*require: courage, time*) erfordern; (*tolerate: pain etc*) ertragen; (*hold: passengers etc*) fassen; (*accompany: person*) begleiten; (*carry, bring*) mitnehmen; (*exam, test*) machen; (*conduct: meeting*) leiten; (: *class*)

unterrichten ♦ vi (have effect: drug) wirken;
(: dye) angenommen werden ♦ n (CINE)
Aufnahme f; to ~ sth from (drawer etc) etw
nehmen aus +dat; I ~ it (that) ich nehme an(,
daß); I took him for a doctor (mistake) ich
hielt ihn für einen Arzt; to ~ sb's hand jds
Hand nehmen; to ~ sb for a walk mit jdm
spazierengehen; to be ~n ill krank werden;
to ~ it upon o.s. to do sth es auf sich
nehmen, etw zu tun; ~ the first (street) on
the left nehmen Sie die erste Straße links;
to ~ Russian at university Russisch
studieren; it won't ~ long es dauert nicht
lange; I was quite ~n with her/it (attracted
to) ich war von ihr/davon recht angetan.
►**take after** vt fus (resemble) ähneln +dat,
ähnlich sein +dat.
►**take apart** vt auseinandernehmen.
►**take away** vt wegnehmen; (carry off)
wegbringen; (MATH) abziehen ♦ vi: to
~ away from (detract from) schmälern,
beeinträchtigen.
►**take back** vt (return) zurückbringen; (one's
words) zurücknehmen.
►**take down** vt (write down) aufschreiben;
(dismantle) abreißen.
►**take in** vt (deceive: person) hereinlegen,
täuschen; (understand) begreifen; (include)
einschließen; (lodger) aufnehmen; (orphan,
stray dog) zu sich nehmen; (dress, waistband)
enger machen.
►**take off** vi (AVIAT) starten; (go away) sich
absetzen ♦ vt (clothes) ausziehen; (glasses)
abnehmen; (make-up) entfernen; (time) frei
nehmen; (imitate: person) nachmachen.
►**take on** vt (work, responsibility)
übernehmen; (employee) einstellen;
(compete against) antreten gegen.
►**take out** vt (invite) ausgehen mit; (remove:
tooth) herausnehmen; (licence) erwerben; to
~ sth out of sth (drawer, pocket etc) etw aus
etw nehmen; don't ~ it out on me! laß es
nicht an mir aus!
►**take over** vt (business) übernehmen;
(country) Besitz ergreifen von ♦ vi (replace):
to ~ over from sb jdn ablösen.
►**take to** vt fus (person, thing) mögen; (activity)
Gefallen finden an +dat; (form habit of): to
~ to doing sth sich dat angewöhnen, etw zu
tun.
►**take up** vt (hobby, sport) anfangen mit; (job)
antreten; (idea etc) annehmen; (time, space)
beanspruchen; (continue: task, story)
fortfahren mit; (shorten: hem, garment)
kürzer machen ♦ vi (befriend): to ~ up with
sb sich mit jdm anfreunden; to ~ sb up on
an offer/a suggestion auf jds Angebot/
Vorschlag eingehen.
takeaway ['teɪkəweɪ] (BRIT) n (shop,
restaurant) ≈ Schnellimbiß m; (food) Imbiß m
(zum Mitnehmen).
take-home pay ['teɪkhəum-] n Nettolohn m.

taken ['teɪkən] pp of take.
takeoff ['teɪkɔf] n (AVIAT) Start m.
takeout ['teɪkaut] (US) n = takeaway.
takeover ['teɪkəuvə*] n (COMM) Übernahme f;
(of country) Inbesitznahme f.
takeover bid n Übernahmeangebot nt.
takings ['teɪkɪŋz] npl Einnahmen pl.
talc [tælk] n (also: talcum powder)
Talkumpuder nt.
tale [teɪl] n Geschichte f; to tell ~s (to sb)
(child) (jdm) Geschichten erzählen.
talent ['tælnt] n Talent nt.
talented ['tæləntɪd] adj talentiert, begabt.
talent scout n Talentsucher(in) m(f).
talisman ['tælɪzmən] n Talisman m.
talk [tɔːk] n (speech) Vortrag m; (conversation,
discussion) Gespräch nt; (gossip) Gerede nt
♦ vi (speak) sprechen; (chat) reden; (gossip)
klatschen; **talks** npl (POL etc) Gespräche pl;
to give a ~ einen Vortrag halten; **to ~ about**
(discuss) sprechen or reden über; **~ing of
films, have you seen ...?** da wir gerade von
Filmen sprechen: hast du ... gesehen?; **to
~ sb into doing sth** jdn zu etw überreden;
to ~ sb out of doing sth jdm etw ausreden.
►**talk over** vt (problem etc) besprechen,
bereden.
talkative ['tɔːkətɪv] adj gesprächig.
talker ['tɔːkə*] n: **to be a good/entertaining/
fast** etc ~ gut/amüsant/schnell etc reden
können.
talking point ['tɔːkɪŋ-] n Gesprächsthema nt.
talking-to ['tɔːkɪŋtu] n: **to give sb a (good) ~**
jdm eine (ordentliche) Standpauke halten
(inf).
talk show n Talkshow f.
tall [tɔːl] adj (person) groß; (glass, bookcase,
tree, building) hoch; (ladder) lang; **to be 6 feet
~** (person) ≈ 1,80m groß sein; **how ~ are
you?** wie groß bist du?
tallboy ['tɔːlbɔɪ] (BRIT) n Kommode f.
tallness ['tɔːlnɪs] n (of person) Größe f; (of tree,
building etc) Höhe f.
tall story n unglaubliche Geschichte f.
tally ['tælɪ] n (of marks, amounts etc) aktueller
Stand m ♦ vi: **to ~ (with)** (figures, stories etc)
übereinstimmen mit; **to keep a ~ of sth**
über etw acc Buch führen.
talon ['tælən] n Kralle f.
tambourine [tæmbə'riːn] n Tamburin nt.
tame [teɪm] adj (animal, bird) zahm; (fig: story,
party, performance) lustlos, lahm (inf).
Tamil ['tæmɪl] adj tamilisch ♦ n Tamile m,
Tamilin f; (LING) Tamil nt.
tamper ['tæmpə*] vi: **to ~ with sth** an etw dat
herumpfuschen (inf).
tampon ['tæmpɔn] n Tampon m.
tan [tæn] n (also: suntan) (Sonnen)bräune f ♦ vi
(person, skin) braun werden ♦ vt (hide)
gerben; (skin) bräunen ♦ adj (colour)
hellbraun; **to get a ~** braun werden.
tandem ['tændəm] n Tandem nt; (together): in

~ (*fig*) zusammen.
tandoori [tæn'duərɪ] *n*: ~ **oven** Tandoori-Ofen *m*; ~ **chicken** *im Tandoori-Ofen gebratenes Huhn*.
tang [tæŋ] *n* (*smell*) Geruch *m*; (*taste*) Geschmack *m*.
tangent ['tændʒənt] *n* (*MATH*) Tangente *f*; **to go off at a** ~ (*fig*) vom Thema abschweifen.
tangerine [tændʒə'riːn] *n* (*fruit*) Mandarine *f*; (*colour*) Orangerot *nt*.
tangible ['tændʒəbl] *adj* greifbar; ~ **assets** (*COMM*) Sachanlagevermögen *nt*.
Tangier [tæn'dʒɪə*] *n* Tanger *nt*.
tangle ['tæŋgl] *n* (*of branches, wire etc*) Gewirr *nt*; **to be in a** ~ verheddert sein; (*fig*) durcheinander sein; **to get in a** ~ sich verheddern; (*fig*) durcheinandergeraten.
tango ['tæŋgəu] *n* Tango *m*.
tank [tæŋk] *n* Tank *m*; (*for photographic processing*) Wanne *f*; (*also*: **fish** ~) Aquarium *nt*; (*MIL*) Panzer *m*.
tankard ['tæŋkəd] *n* Bierkrug *m*.
tanker ['tæŋkə*] *n* (*ship*) Tanker *m*; (*truck*) Tankwagen *m*.
tanned [tænd] *adj* (*person*) braungebrannt; (*hide*) gegerbt.
tannin ['tænɪn] *n* Tannin *nt*.
tanning ['tænɪŋ] *n* (*of leather*) Gerben *nt*.
Tannoy® ['tænɔɪ] (*BRIT*) *n* Lautsprechersystem *nt*; **over the** ~ über Lautsprecher.
tantalizing ['tæntəlaɪzɪŋ] *adj* (*smell*) verführerisch; (*possibility*) verlockend.
tantamount ['tæntəmaunt] *adj*: ~ **to** gleichbedeutend mit.
tantrum ['tæntrəm] *n* Wutanfall *m*; **to throw a** ~ einen Wutanfall bekommen.
Tanzania [tænzə'nɪə] *n* Tansania *nt*.
Tanzanian [tænzə'nɪən] *adj* tansanisch ♦ *n* (*person*) Tansanier(in) *m(f)*.
tap [tæp] *n* (*on sink, gas tap*) Hahn *m*; (*gentle blow*) leichter Schlag *m*, Klaps *m* ♦ *vt* (*hit gently*) klopfen; (*exploit: resources, energy*) nutzen; (*telephone*) abhören, anzapfen; **on** ~ (*fig: resources, information*) zur Verfügung; (*beer*) vom Faß.
tap-dancing ['tæpdɑːnsɪŋ] *n* Steptanz *m*.
tape [teɪp] *n* (*also*: **magnetic** ~) Tonband *nt*; (*cassette*) Kassette *f*; (*also*: **sticky** ~) Klebeband *nt*; (*for tying*) Band *nt* ♦ *vt* (*record, conversation*) aufnehmen, aufzeichnen; (*stick with tape*) mit Klebeband befestigen; **on** ~ (*song etc*) auf Band.
tape deck *n* Tapedeck *nt*.
tape measure *n* Bandmaß *nt*.
taper ['teɪpə*] *n* (*candle*) lange, dünne Kerze ♦ *vi* sich verjüngen.
tape recorder *n* Tonband(gerät) *nt*.
tape recording *n* Tonbandaufnahme *f*.
tapered ['teɪpəd] *adj* (*skirt, jacket*) nach unten enger werdend.
tapering ['teɪpərɪŋ] *adj* spitz zulaufend.
tapestry ['tæpɪstrɪ] *n* (*on wall*) Wandteppich

m; (*fig*) Kaleidoskop *nt*.
tapeworm ['teɪpwəːm] *n* Bandwurm *m*.
tapioca [tæpɪ'əukə] *n* Tapioka *f*.
tappet ['tæpɪt] *n* (*AUT*) Stößel *m*.
tar [tɑː] *n* Teer *m*; **low/middle** ~ **cigarettes** Zigaretten mit niedrigem/mittlerem Teergehalt.
tarantula [tə'ræntjulə] *n* Tarantel *f*.
tardy ['tɑːdɪ] *adj* (*reply, letter*) verspätet; (*progress*) langsam.
target ['tɑːgɪt] *n* Ziel *nt*; (*fig: of joke, criticism etc*) Zielscheibe *f*; **to be on** ~ (*project, work*) nach Plan verlaufen.
target practice *n* Zielschießen *nt*.
tariff ['tærɪf] *n* (*tax on goods*) Zoll *m*; (*BRIT: in hotels etc*) Preisliste *f*.
tariff barrier *n* Zollschranke *f*.
tarmac® ['tɑːmæk] *n* (*BRIT: on road*) Asphalt *m*; (*AVIAT*): **on the** ~ auf dem Rollfeld ♦ *vt* (*BRIT: road etc*) asphaltieren.
tarn [tɑːn] *n* Bergsee *m*.
tarnish ['tɑːnɪʃ] *vt* (*silver, brass etc*) stumpf werden lassen; (*fig: reputation etc*) beflecken, in Mitleidenschaft ziehen.
tarot ['tærəu] *n* Tarot *nt or m*.
tarpaulin [tɑː'pɔːlɪn] *n* Plane *f*.
tarragon ['tærəgən] *n* Estragon *m*.
tart [tɑːt] *n* (*CULIN*) Torte *f*; (: *small*) Törtchen *nt*; (*BRIT: inf: prostitute*) Nutte *f* ♦ *adj* (*apple, grapefruit etc*) säuerlich.
►**tart up** (*BRIT: inf*) *vt* (*room, building*) aufmotzen; **to** ~ **o.s. up** sich feinmachen; (*pej*) sich auftakeln.
tartan ['tɑːtn] *n* Tartan *m*, Schottenstoff *m* ♦ *adj* (*scarf etc*) mit Schottenmuster.
tartar ['tɑːtə*] *n* (*on teeth*) Zahnstein *m*; (*pej: person*) Tyrann(in) *m(f)*.
tartar(e) sauce ['tɑːtə-] *n* Remouladensoße *f*.
task [tɑːsk] *n* Aufgabe *f*; **to take sb to** ~ jdn ins Gebet nehmen.
task force *n* (*MIL*) Sonderkommando *nt*; (*POLICE*) Spezialeinheit *f*.
taskmaster ['tɑːskmɑːstə*] *n*: **a hard** ~ ein strenger Lehrmeister.
Tasmania [tæz'meɪnɪə] *n* Tasmanien *nt*.
tassel ['tæsl] *n* Quaste *f*.
taste [teɪst] *n* Geschmack *m*; (*sample*) Kostprobe *f*; (*fig: of suffering, freedom etc*) Vorgeschmack *m* ♦ *vt* (*get flavour of*) schmecken; (*test*) probieren, versuchen ♦ *vi*: **to** ~ **of/like sth** nach/wie etw schmecken; **sense of** ~ Geschmackssinn *m*; **to have a** ~ **of sth** (*sample*) etw probieren; **to acquire a** ~ **for sth** (*liking*) Geschmack an etw *dat* finden; **to be in good/bad** ~ (*joke etc*) geschmackvoll/geschmacklos sein; **you can** ~ **the garlic (in it)** (*detect*) man schmeckt den Knoblauch durch; **what does it** ~ **like?** wie schmeckt es?
taste buds *npl* Geschmacksknospen *pl*.
tasteful ['teɪstful] *adj* geschmackvoll.
tastefully ['teɪstfəlɪ] *adv* geschmackvoll.

tasteless ['teɪstlɪs] *adj* geschmacklos.
tasty ['teɪstɪ] *adj* schmackhaft.
tattered ['tætəd] *adj* (*clothes, paper etc*) zerrissen; (*fig: hopes etc*) angeschlagen.
tatters ['tætəz] *npl:* **to be in ~** (*clothes*) in Fetzen sein.
tattoo [tə'tuː] *n* (*on skin*) Tätowierung *f*; (*spectacle*) Zapfenstreich *m* ♦ *vt:* **to ~ sth on sth** etw auf etw *acc* tätowieren.
tatty ['tætɪ] (*BRIT: inf*) *adj* schäbig.
taught [tɔːt] *pt, pp of* **teach.**
taunt [tɔːnt] *n* höhnische Bemerkung *f* ♦ *vt* (*person*) verhöhnen.
Taurus ['tɔːrəs] *n* Stier *m*; **to be ~** (ein) Stier sein.
taut [tɔːt] *adj* (*skin, thread etc*) straff.
tavern ['tævən] *n* Taverne *f*.
tawdry ['tɔːdrɪ] *adj* (*jewellery, clothes etc*) billig.
tawny ['tɔːnɪ] *adj* gelbbraun.
tawny owl *n* Waldkauz *m*.
tax [tæks] *n* Steuer *f* ♦ *vt* (*earnings, goods etc*) besteuern; (*fig: memory, knowledge*) strapazieren; (: *patience etc*) auf die Probe stellen; **before/after ~** vor/nach Abzug der Steuern; **free of ~** steuerfrei.
taxable ['tæksəbl] *adj* steuerpflichtig; (*income*) steuerbar.
tax allowance *n* Steuerfreibetrag *m*.
taxation [tæk'seɪʃən] *n* (*system*) Besteuerung *f*; (*money paid*) Steuern *pl*.
tax avoidance *n* Steuerumgehung *f*.
tax collector *n* Steuerbeamte(r) *m*, Steuerbeamtin *f*.
tax disc (*BRIT*) *n* (*AUT*) Steuerplakette *f*.
tax evasion *n* Steuerhinterziehung *f*.
tax exemption *n* Steuerbefreiung *f*.
tax exile (*person*) *n* Steuerflüchtling *m*.
tax-free ['tæksfriː] *adj* steuerfrei.
tax haven *n* Steuerparadies *nt*.
taxi ['tæksɪ] *n* Taxi *nt* ♦ *vi* (*AVIAT: plane*) rollen.
taxidermist ['tæksɪdəːmɪst] *n* Taxidermist(in) *m(f)*, Tierpräparator(in) *m(f)*.
taxi driver *n* Taxifahrer(in) *m(f)*.
tax inspector (*BRIT*) *n* Steuerinspektor(in) *m(f)*.
taxi rank (*BRIT*) *n* Taxistand *m*.
taxi stand *n* = **taxi rank.**
taxpayer ['tækspeɪə'] *n* Steuerzahler(in) *m(f)*.
tax rebate *n* Steuerrückvergütung *f*.
tax relief *n* Steuernachlaß *m*.
tax return *n* Steuererklärung *f*.
tax shelter *n* (*COMM*) System zur Verhinderung von Steuerbelastung.
tax year *n* Steuerjahr *nt*.
TB *n abbr* (= *tuberculosis*) Tb *f*, Tbc *f*.
TD (*US*) *n abbr* = **Treasury Department;** (*FOOTBALL*) = **touchdown.**
tea [tiː] *n* (*drink*) Tee *m*; (*BRIT: evening meal*) Abendessen *nt*; **afternoon ~** (*BRIT*) Nachmittagstee *m*.
tea bag *n* Teebeutel *m*.

tea break (*BRIT*) *n* Teepause *f*.
teacake ['tiːkeɪk] (*BRIT*) *n* Rosinenbrötchen *nt*.
teach [tiːtʃ] (*pt, pp* **taught**) *vt:* **to ~ sb sth, ~ sth to sb** (*instruct*) jdm etw beibringen; (*in school*) jdn in etw *dat* unterrichten ♦ *vi* unterrichten; **it taught him a lesson** (*fig*) er hat seine Lektion gelernt.
teacher ['tiːtʃə'] *n* Lehrer(in) *m(f)*; **German ~** Deutschlehrer(in) *m(f)*.
teacher training college *n* (*for primary schools*) ≈ pädagogische Hochschule *f*; (*for secondary schools*) ≈ Studienseminar *nt*.
teaching ['tiːtʃɪŋ] *n* (*work of teacher*) Unterricht *m*.
teaching aids *npl* Lehrmittel *pl*.
teaching hospital (*BRIT*) *n* Ausbildungskrankenhaus *nt*.
teaching staff (*BRIT*) *n* Lehrerkollegium *nt*.
tea cosy *n* Teewärmer *m*.
teacup ['tiːkʌp] *n* Teetasse *f*.
teak [tiːk] *n* Teak *nt*.
tea leaves *npl* Teeblätter *pl*.
team [tiːm] *n* (*of experts etc*) Team *nt*; (*SPORT*) Mannschaft *f*, Team *nt*; (*of horses, oxen*) Gespann *nt*.
▶**team up** *vi:* **to ~ up (with)** sich zusammentun (mit).
team game *n* Mannschaftsspiel *nt*.
team spirit *n* Teamgeist *m*.
teamwork ['tiːmwəːk] *n* Teamwork *nt*, Teamarbeit *f*.
tea party *n* Teegesellschaft *f*.
teapot ['tiːpɔt] *n* Teekanne *f*.
tear¹ [tɛə'] (*pt* **tore**, *pp* **torn**) *n* (*hole*) Riß *m* ♦ *vt* (*rip*) zerreißen ♦ *vi* (*become torn*) reißen; **to ~ sth to pieces** *or* **bits** *or* **shreds** (*lit, fig*) etw in Stücke reißen; **to ~ sb to pieces** jdn fertigmachen.
▶**tear along** *vi* (*rush: driver, car*) entlanggrasen.
▶**tear apart** *vt* (*book, clothes, people*) auseinanderreißen; (*upset: person*) hin- und herreißen.
▶**tear away** *vt:* **to ~ o.s. away (from sth)** (*fig*) sich (von etw) losreißen.
▶**tear out** *vt* (*sheet of paper etc*) herausreißen.
▶**tear up** *vt* (*sheet of paper etc*) zerreißen.
tear² [tɪə'] *n* (*in eye*) Träne *f*; **in ~s** in Tränen; **to burst into ~s** in Tränen ausbrechen.
tearaway ['tɛərəweɪ] (*BRIT: inf*) *n* Rabauke *m*.
teardrop ['tɪədrɔp] *n* Träne *f*.
tearful ['tɪəful] *adj* (*person*) weinend; (*face*) tränenüberströmt.
tear gas *n* Tränengas *nt*.
tearing ['tɛərɪŋ] *adj:* **to be in a ~ hurry** es unheimlich eilig haben.
tearoom ['tiːruːm] *n* = **teashop.**
tease [tiːz] *vt* necken; (*unkindly*) aufziehen ♦ *n:* **she's a real ~** sie zieht einen ständig auf.
tea set *n* Teeservice *nt*.
teashop ['tiːʃɔp] (*BRIT*) *n* Teestube *f*.
Teasmade ® ['tiːzmeɪd] *n* Teemaschine *f* (*mit Zeiteinstellung*).

teaspoon ['tiːspuːn] n Teelöffel m; (also: ~ful: measure) Teelöffel(voll) m.
tea strainer n Teesieb nt.
teat [tiːt] n (on bottle) Sauger m.
teatime ['tiːtaɪm] n Teestunde f.
tea towel (BRIT) n Geschirrtuch nt.
tea urn n Teespender m.
tech [tɛk] (inf) n abbr = **technical college; technology.**
technical ['tɛknɪkl] adj technisch; (terms, language) Fach-.
technical college (BRIT) n Technische Fachschule f.
technicality [tɛknɪ'kælɪtɪ] n (point of law) Formalität f; (detail) technische Einzelheit f; **on a (legal)** ~ aufgrund einer (juristischen) Formalität.
technically ['tɛknɪklɪ] adv (strictly speaking) genau genommen; (regarding technique) technisch (gesehen).
technician [tɛk'nɪʃən] n Techniker(in) m(f).
technique [tɛk'niːk] n Technik f.
techno ['tɛknəu] n (MUS) Techno nt.
technocrat ['tɛknəkræt] n Technokrat(in) m(f).
technological [tɛknə'lɔdʒɪkl] adj technologisch.
technologist [tɛk'nɔlədʒɪst] n Technologe m, Technologin f.
technology [tɛk'nɔlədʒɪ] n Technologie f.
technology college n Oberstufenkolleg mit technischem Schwerpunkt.
teddy (bear) ['tɛdɪ(-)] n Teddy(bär) m.
tedious ['tiːdɪəs] adj langweilig.
tedium ['tiːdɪəm] n Langeweile f.
tee [tiː] n (GOLF) Tee nt.
▸**tee off** vi (vom Tee) abschlagen.
teem [tiːm] vi: **to** ~ **with** (tourists etc) wimmeln von; **it is** ~**ing down** es gießt in Strömen.
teenage ['tiːneɪdʒ] adj (fashions etc) Jugend-; (children) im Teenageralter.
teenager ['tiːneɪdʒə*] n Teenager m, Jugendliche(r) f(m).
teens [tiːnz] npl: **to be in one's** ~ im Teenageralter sein.
tee shirt n = **T-shirt.**
teeter ['tiːtə*] vi (also fig) schwanken, taumeln.
teeth [tiːθ] npl of **tooth.**
teethe [tiːð] vi Zähne bekommen, zahnen.
teething ring ['tiːðɪŋ-] n Beißring m.
teething troubles npl (fig) Kinderkrankheiten pl.
teetotal ['tiː'təutl] adj (person) abstinent.
teetotaller, (US) **teetotaler** ['tiː'təutlə*] n Abstinenzler(in) m(f), Antialkoholiker(in) m(f).
TEFL ['tɛfl] n abbr (= Teaching of English as a Foreign Language) Unterricht in Englisch als Fremdsprache.
Teflon ® ['tɛflɔn] n Teflon ® nt.
Teheran [tɛə'raːn] n Teheran nt.

tel. abbr (= telephone) Tel.
Tel Aviv ['tɛlə'viːv] n Tel Aviv nt.
telecast ['tɛlɪkaːst] n Fernsehsendung f.
telecommunications ['tɛlɪkəmjuːnɪ'keɪʃənz] n Nachrichtentechnik f.
telegram ['tɛlɪgræm] n Telegramm nt.
telegraph ['tɛlɪgraːf] n (system) Telegraf m.
telegraphic [tɛlɪ'græfɪk] adj (equipment) telegrafisch.
telegraph pole n Telegrafenmast m.
telegraph wire n Telegrafenleitung f.
telepathic [tɛlɪ'pæθɪk] adj telepathisch.
telepathy [tə'lɛpəθɪ] n Telepathie f.
telephone ['tɛlɪfəun] n Telefon nt ♦ vt (person) anrufen ♦ vi anrufen, telefonieren; **to be on the** ~ (talking) telefonieren; (possessing phone) ein Telefon haben.
telephone box, (US) **telephone booth** n Telefonzelle f.
telephone call n Anruf m.
telephone directory n Telefonbuch nt.
telephone exchange n Telefonzentrale f.
telephone number n Telefonnummer f.
telephone operator n Telefonist(in) m(f).
telephone tapping n Abhören nt von Telefonleitungen.
telephonist [tə'lɛfənɪst] (BRIT) n Telefonist(in) m(f).
telephoto ['tɛlɪ'fəutəu] adj: ~ **lens** Teleobjektiv nt.
teleprinter ['tɛlɪprɪntə*] n Fernschreiber m.
Teleprompter ® ['tɛlɪprɔmptə*] (US) n Teleprompter m.
telesales ['tɛlɪseɪlz] n Verkauf m per Telefon.
telescope ['tɛlɪskəup] n Teleskop nt ♦ vi (fig: bus, lorry) sich ineinanderschieben ♦ vt (make shorter) zusammenschieben.
telescopic [tɛlɪ'skɔpɪk] adj (legs, aerial) ausziehbar; ~ **lens** Fernrohrlinse f.
Teletext ® ['tɛlɪtɛkst] n Videotext m.
telethon ['tɛlɪθɔn] n Spendenaktion für wohltätige Zwecke in Form einer vielstündigen Fernsehsendung.
televise ['tɛlɪvaɪz] vt (im Fernsehen) übertragen.
television ['tɛlɪvɪʒən] n Fernsehen nt; (set) Fernseher m, Fernsehapparat m; **to be on** ~ im Fernsehen sein.
television licence (BRIT) n Fernsehgenehmigung f.
television programme n Fernsehprogramm nt.
television set n Fernseher m, Fernsehapparat m.
telex ['tɛlɛks] n (system, machine, message) Telex nt ♦ vt (message) telexen; (person) ein Telex schicken +dat ♦ vi telexen.
tell [tɛl] (pt, pp told) vt (say) sagen; (relate: story) erzählen; (distinguish): **to** ~ **sth from** etw unterscheiden von; (be sure) wissen ♦ vi (have an effect) sich auswirken; **to** ~ **sb to do sth** jdm sagen, etw zu tun; **to** ~ **sb of or**

about sth jdm von etw erzählen; **to be able to ~ the time** (*know how to*) die Uhr kennen; **can you ~ me the time?** können Sie mir sagen, wie spät es ist?; **(I) ~ you what, let's go to the cinema** weißt du was? Laß uns ins Kino gehen!; **I can't ~ them apart** ich kann sie nicht unterscheiden.

▶**tell off** *vt:* **to ~ sb off** jdn ausschimpfen.

▶**tell on** *vt fus* (*inform against*) verpetzen.

teller ['tɛlə*] *n* (*in bank*) Kassierer(in) *m(f)*.

telling ['tɛlɪŋ] *adj* (*remark etc*) verräterisch.

telltale ['tɛlteɪl] *adj* verräterisch ♦ *n* (*pej*) Petzer *m*, Petze *f*.

telly ['tɛlɪ] (*BRIT: inf*) *n abbr* = **television**.

temerity [tə'mɛrɪtɪ] *n* Unverschämtheit *f*.

temp [tɛmp] (*BRIT: inf*) *n abbr* (= *temporary office worker*) Zeitarbeitskraft *f* ♦ *vi* als Zeitarbeitskraft arbeiten.

temper ['tɛmpə*] *n* (*nature*) Naturell *nt*; (*mood*) Laune *f* ♦ *vt* (*moderate*) mildern; **a (fit of) ~** ein Wutanfall; **to be in a ~** gereizt sein; **to lose one's ~** die Beherrschung verlieren.

temperament ['tɛmprəmənt] *n* Temperament *nt*.

temperamental [tɛmprə'mɛntl] *adj* (*person, car*) launisch.

temperate ['tɛmprət] *adj* gemäßigt.

temperature ['tɛmprətʃə*] *n* Temperatur *f*; **to have** *or* **run a ~** Fieber haben; **to take sb's ~** bei jdm Fieber messen.

temperature chart *n* (*MED*) Fiebertabelle *f*.

tempered ['tɛmpəd] *adj* (*steel*) gehärtet.

tempest ['tɛmpɪst] *n* Sturm *m*.

tempestuous [tɛm'pɛstjuəs] *adj* (*also fig*) stürmisch; (*person*) leidenschaftlich.

tempi ['tɛmpiː] *npl of* **tempo**.

template ['tɛmplɪt] *n* Schablone *f*.

temple ['tɛmpl] *n* (*building*) Tempel *m*; (*ANAT*) Schläfe *f*.

tempo ['tɛmpəu] (*pl ~s or* **tempi**) *n* (*MUS, fig*) Tempo *nt*.

temporal ['tɛmpərl] *adj* (*non-religious*) weltlich; (*relating to time*) zeitlich.

temporarily ['tɛmpərərɪlɪ] *adv* vorübergehend; (*unavailable, alone etc*) zeitweilig.

temporary ['tɛmpərərɪ] *adj* (*arrangement*) provisorisch; (*worker, job*) Aushilfs-; **~ secretary** Sekretärin zur Aushilfe; **~ teacher** Aushilfslehrer(in) *m(f)*.

temporize ['tɛmpəraɪz] *vi* ausweichen.

tempt [tɛmpt] *vt* in Versuchung führen; **to ~ sb into doing sth** jdn dazu verleiten, etw zu tun; **to be ~ed to do sth** versucht sein, etw zu tun.

temptation [tɛmp'teɪʃən] *n* Versuchung *f*.

tempting ['tɛmptɪŋ] *adj* (*offer*) verlockend; (*food*) verführerisch.

ten [tɛn] *num* zehn ♦ *n:* **~s of thousands** Zehntausende *pl*.

tenable ['tɛnəbl] *adj* (*argument, position*) haltbar.

tenacious [tə'neɪʃəs] *adj* zäh, hartnäckig.

tenacity [tə'næsɪtɪ] *n* Zähigkeit *f*, Hartnäckigkeit *f*.

tenancy ['tɛnənsɪ] *n* (*of room*) Mietverhältnis *nt*; (*of land*) Pachtverhältnis *nt*.

tenant ['tɛnənt] *n* (*of room*) Mieter(in) *m(f)*; (*of land*) Pächter(in) *m(f)*.

tend [tɛnd] *vt* (*crops, sick person*) sich kümmern um ♦ *vi:* **to ~ to do sth** dazu neigen *or* tendieren, etw zu tun.

tendency ['tɛndənsɪ] *n* (*of person*) Neigung *f*; (*of thing*) Tendenz *f*.

tender ['tɛndə*] *adj* (*person, care*) zärtlich; (*heart*) gut; (*sore*) empfindlich; (*meat, age*) zart ♦ *n* (*COMM*) Angebot *nt*; (*money*): **legal ~** gesetzliches Zahlungsmittel *nt* ♦ *vt* (*offer*) vorlegen; (*resignation*) einreichen; (*apology*) anbieten; **to put in a ~ (for)** ein Angebot vorlegen (für); **to put work out to ~** (*BRIT*) Arbeiten ausschreiben.

tenderize ['tɛndəraɪz] *vt* (*meat*) zart machen.

tenderly ['tɛndəlɪ] *adv* zärtlich, liebevoll.

tenderness ['tɛndənɪs] *n* (*affection*) Zärtlichkeit *f*; (*of meat*) Zartheit *f*.

tendon ['tɛndən] *n* Sehne *f*.

tendril ['tɛndrɪl] *n* (*BOT*) Ranke *f*; (*of hair etc*) Strähne *f*.

tenement ['tɛnəmənt] *n* Mietshaus *nt*.

Tenerife [tɛnə'riːf] *n* Teneriffa *nt*.

tenet ['tɛnət] *n* Prinzip *nt*.

Tenn. (*US*) *abbr* (*POST:* = *Tennessee*).

tenner ['tɛnə*] (*BRIT: inf*) *n* Zehner *m*.

tennis ['tɛnɪs] *n* Tennis *nt*.

tennis ball *n* Tennisball *m*.

tennis club *n* Tennisclub *m*.

tennis court *n* Tennisplatz *m*.

tennis elbow *n* (*MED*) Tennisell(en)bogen *m*.

tennis match *n* Tennismatch *nt*.

tennis player *n* Tennisspieler(in) *m(f)*.

tennis racket *n* Tennisschläger *m*.

tennis shoes *npl* Tennisschuhe *pl*.

tenor ['tɛnə*] *n* (*MUS*) Tenor *m*; (*of speech etc*) wesentlicher Gehalt *m*.

tenpin bowling ['tɛnpɪn-] (*BRIT*) *n* Bowling *nt*.

tense [tɛns] *adj* (*person, muscle*) angespannt; (*smile*) verkrampft; (*period, situation*) gespannt ♦ *n* (*LING*) Zeit *f*, Tempus *nt* ♦ *vt* (*muscles*) anspannen.

tenseness ['tɛnsnɪs] *n* Gespanntheit *f*.

tension ['tɛnʃən] *n* (*nervousness*) Angespanntheit *f*; (*between ropes etc*) Spannung *f*.

tent [tɛnt] *n* Zelt *nt*.

tentacle ['tɛntəkl] *n* (*ZOOL*) Fangarm *m*; (*fig*) Klaue *f*.

tentative ['tɛntətɪv] *adj* (*person, smile*) zögernd; (*step*) unsicher; (*conclusion, plans*) vorläufig.

tentatively ['tɛntətɪvlɪ] *adv* (*suggest*) versuchsweise; (*wave etc*) zögernd.

tenterhooks ['tɛntəhuks] *npl:* **to be on ~** wie auf glühenden Kohlen sitzen.

tenth [tɛnθ] *num* zehnte(r, s) ♦ *n* Zehntel *nt*.
tent peg *n* Hering *m*.
tent pole *n* Zeltstange *f*.
tenuous ['tɛnjuəs] *adj* (*hold, links etc*)
  schwach.
tenure ['tɛnjuəʳ] *n* (*of land etc*) Nutzungsrecht
  nt; (*of office*) Amtszeit *f*; (*UNIV*): **to have ~**
  eine Dauerstellung haben.
tepid ['tɛpɪd] *adj* (*also fig*) lauwarm.
Ter. *abbr* (*in street names*: = *terrace*) ≈ Str.
term [təːm] *n* (*word*) Ausdruck *m*; (*period in
  power etc*) Amtszeit *f*; (*SCOL: three per year*)
  Trimester *nt* ♦ *vt* (*call*) nennen; **terms** *npl*
  (*also COMM*) Bedingungen *pl*; **in economic/
  political ~s** wirtschaftlich/politisch
  gesehen; **in ~s of business** was das
  Geschäft angeht *or* betrifft; **~ of
  imprisonment** Gefängnisstrafe *f*; **"easy ~s"**
  (*COMM*) „günstige Bedingungen"; **in the
  short/long ~** auf kurze/lange Sicht; **to be on
  good ~s with sb** sich mit jdm gut
  verstehen; **to come to ~s with** (*problem*)
  sich abfinden mit.
terminal ['təːmɪnl] *adj* (*disease, patient*)
  unheilbar ♦ *n* (*AVIAT, COMM, COMPUT*)
  Terminal *nt*; (*ELEC*) Anschluß *m*; (*BRIT: also:
  bus ~) Endstation *f*.
terminate ['təːmɪneɪt] *vt* beenden ♦ *vi*: **to ~ in**
  enden in +*dat*.
termination [təːmɪ'neɪʃən] *n* Beendigung *f*;
  (*expiry: of contract*) Ablauf *m*; (*MED: of
  pregnancy*) Abbruch *m*.
termini ['təːmɪnaɪ] *npl of* **terminus**.
terminology [təːmɪ'nɔlədʒɪ] *n* Terminologie *f*.
terminus ['təːmɪnəs] (*pl* **termini**) *n* (*for buses,
  trains*) Endstation *f*.
termite ['təːmaɪt] *n* Termite *f*.
term paper (*US*) *n* (*UNIV*) ≈ Semesterarbeit
  f.
Terr. *abbr* (*in street names*: = *terrace*) ≈ Str.
terrace ['tɛrəs] *n* (*BRIT: row of houses*)
  Häuserreihe *f*; (*AGR, patio*) Terrasse *f*; **the
  terraces** *npl* (*BRIT: SPORT*) die Ränge *pl*.
terraced ['tɛrəst] *adj* (*house*) Reihen-; (*garden*)
  terrassenförmig angelegt.
terracotta ['tɛrə'kɔtə] *n* (*clay*) Terrakotta *f*;
  (*colour*) Braunrot *nt* ♦ *adj* (*pot, roof etc*)
  Terrakotta-.
terrain [tɛ'reɪn] *n* Gelände *nt*, Terrain *nt*.
terrible ['tɛrɪbl] *adj* schrecklich, furchtbar.
terribly ['tɛrɪblɪ] *adv* (*very*) furchtbar; (*very
  badly*) entsetzlich.
terrier ['tɛrɪəʳ] *n* Terrier *m*.
terrific [tə'rɪfɪk] *adj* (*very great: thunderstorm,
  speed*) unheimlich; (*time, party*) sagenhaft.
terrify ['tɛrɪfaɪ] *vt* erschrecken; **to be terrified**
  schreckliche Angst haben.
terrifying ['tɛrɪfaɪɪŋ] *adj* entsetzlich,
  grauenvoll.
territorial [tɛrɪ'tɔːrɪəl] *adj* (*boundaries, dispute*)
  territorial, Gebiets-; (*waters*) Hoheits- ♦ *n*
  (*MIL*) Soldat *m* der Territorialarmee.

Territorial Army (*BRIT*) *n* (*MIL*): **the ~** die
  Territorialarmee.
territorial waters *npl* Hoheitsgewässer *pl*.
territory ['tɛrɪtərɪ] *n* (*also fig*) Gebiet *nt*.
terror ['tɛrəʳ] *n* (*great fear*) panische Angst *f*.
terrorism ['tɛrərɪzəm] *n* Terrorismus *m*.
terrorist ['tɛrərɪst] *n* Terrorist(in) *m(f)*.
terrorize ['tɛrəraɪz] *vt* terrorisieren.
terse [təːs] *adj* knapp.
tertiary ['təːʃərɪ] *adj* tertiär; **~ education**
  (*BRIT*) Universitätsausbildung *f*.
Terylene® ['tɛrɪliːn] *n* Terylen® *nt* ♦ *adj*
  Terylen-.
TESL ['tɛsl] *n abbr* (= *Teaching of English as a
  Second Language*) Unterricht in Englisch als
  Zweitsprache.
TESSA ['tɛsə] (*BRIT*) *n abbr* (= *Tax Exempt
  Special Savings Account*) steuerfreies
  Sparsystem mit begrenzter Einlagehöhe.
test [tɛst] *n* Test *m*; (*of courage etc*) Probe *f*;
  (*SCOL*) Prüfung *f*; (*also:* **driving ~**)
  Fahrprüfung *f* ♦ *vt* testen; (*check, SCOL*)
  prüfen; **to put sth to the ~** etw auf die
  Probe stellen; **to ~ sth for sth** etw auf etw
  acc prüfen.
testament ['tɛstəmənt] *n* Zeugnis *nt*; **the Old/
  New T~** das Alte/Neue Testament; **last will
  and ~** Testament *nt*.
test ban *n* (*also:* **nuclear ~**) Teststopp *m*.
test card *n* (*TV*) Testbild *nt*.
test case *n* (*LAW*) Musterfall *m*; (*fig*)
  Musterbeispiel *nt*.
testes ['tɛstiːz] *npl* Testikel *pl*, Hoden *pl*.
test flight *n* Testflug *m*.
testicle ['tɛstɪkl] *n* Hoden *m*.
testify ['tɛstɪfaɪ] *vi* (*LAW*) aussagen; **to ~ to
  sth** (*LAW, fig*) etw bezeugen.
testimonial [tɛstɪ'məunɪəl] *n* (*BRIT: reference*)
  Referenz *f*; (*SPORT: also:* **~ match**)
  Benefizspiel, dessen Erlös einem
  verdienten Spieler zugute kommt.
testimony ['tɛstɪmənɪ] *n* (*statement*) Aussage
  f; (*clear proof*): **to be (a) ~ to** ein Zeugnis
  sein für.
testing ['tɛstɪŋ] *adj* schwierig.
test match *n* (*CRICKET, RUGBY*) Test Match
  nt, Länderspiel *nt*.
testosterone [tɛs'tɔstərəun] *n* Testosteron *nt*.
test paper *n* (*SCOL*) Klassenarbeit *f*.
test pilot *n* Testpilot(in) *m(f)*.
test tube *n* Reagenzglas *nt*.
test-tube baby ['tɛsttjuːb-] *n* Retortenbaby
  nt.
testy ['tɛstɪ] *adj* gereizt.
tetanus ['tɛtənəs] *n* Tetanus *m*,
  Wundstarrkrampf *m*.
tetchy ['tɛtʃɪ] *adj* gereizt.
tether ['tɛðəʳ] *vt* (*animal*) festbinden ♦ *n*: **to be
  at the end of one's ~** völlig am Ende sein.
Tex. (*US*) *abbr* (*POST*: = *Texas*).
text [tɛkst] *n* Text *m*.
textbook ['tɛkstbuk] *n* Lehrbuch *nt*.

textiles ['tɛkstaɪlz] *npl* Textilien *pl.*

textual ['tɛkstjuəl] *adj (analysis etc)* Text-.

texture ['tɛkstʃə'] *n* Beschaffenheit *f*, Struktur *f.*

TGWU *(BRIT) n abbr (= Transport and General Workers' Union)* Transportarbeitergewerkschaft.

Thai [taɪ] *adj* thailändisch ♦ *n* Thailänder(in) *m(f).*

Thailand ['taɪlænd] *n* Thailand *nt.*

thalidomide ® [θə'lɪdəmaɪd] *n* Contergan ® *nt.*

Thames [tɛmz] *n:* **the ~** die Themse.

than [ðæn] *conj (in comparisons)* als; **more ~ 10** mehr als 10; **she is older ~ you think** sie ist älter als Sie denken; **more ~ once** mehr als einmal.

thank [θæŋk] *vt* danken +*dat;* **~ you** danke; **~ you very much** vielen Dank; **~ God!** Gott sei Dank!

thankful ['θæŋkful] *adj:* **~ (for/that)** dankbar (für/, daß).

thankfully ['θæŋkfəlɪ] *adv* dankbar; **~ there were few victims** zum Glück gab es nur wenige Opfer.

thankless ['θæŋklɪs] *adj* undankbar.

thanks [θæŋks] *npl* Dank *m* ♦ *excl (also:* **many ~, ~ a lot)** danke, vielen Dank; **~ to** dank +*gen.*

Thanksgiving (Day) ['θæŋksgɪvɪŋ(-)] *(US) n* Thanksgiving Day *m.*

> Thanksgiving (Day) ist ein Feiertag in den USA, der auf den vierten Donnerstag im November fällt. Er soll daran erinnern, wie die Pilgerväter die gute Ernte im Jahre 1621 feierten. In Kanada gibt es einen ähnlichen Erntedanktag (der aber nichts mit den Pilgervätern zu tun hat) am zweiten Montag im Oktober.

─────────── *KEYWORD*

that [ðæt] *(pl* **those)** *adj (demonstrative)* der/die/das; **~ man** der Mann; **~ woman** die Frau; **~ book** das Buch; **~ one** der/die/das da; **I want this one, not ~ one** ich will dieses (hier), nicht das (da)

♦ *pron* **1** *(demonstrative)* das; **who's/what's ~?** wer/was ist das?; **is ~ you?** bist du das?; **will you eat all ~?** ißt du das alles?; **that's what he said** das hat er gesagt; **what happened after ~?** was geschah danach?; **~ is (to say)** das heißt; **and that's that!** und damit Schluß!

2 *(relative: subject)* der/die/das; (: : *pl)* die; (: *direct object)* den/die/das; (: : *pl)* die; (: *indirect object)* dem/der/dem; (: : *pl)* denen; **the man ~ I saw** der Mann, den ich gesehen habe; **all ~ I have** alles, was ich habe; **the people ~ I spoke to** die Leute, mit denen ich geredet habe

3 *(relative: of time)* **the day ~ he came** der Tag, an dem er kam; **the winter ~ he came to see us** der Winter, in dem er uns besuchte

♦ *conj* daß; **he thought ~ I was ill** er dachte, daß ich krank sei, er dachte, ich sei krank

♦ *adv (demonstrative)* so; **I can't work ~ much** ich kann nicht so viel arbeiten; **~ high** so hoch.

───────────

thatched [θætʃt] *adj (roof, cottage)* strohgedeckt.

Thatcherism ['θætʃərɪzəm] *n* Thatcherismus *m.*

Thatcherite ['θætʃəraɪt] *adj* thatcheristisch ♦ *n* Thatcher-Anhänger(in) *m(f).*

thaw [θɔː] *n* Tauwetter *nt* ♦ *vi (ice)* tauen; *(food)* auftauen ♦ *vt (also:* **~ out)** auftauen; **it's ~ing** es taut.

─────────── *KEYWORD*

the [ðiː, ðə] *def art* **1** *(before masculine noun)* der; *(before feminine noun)* die; *(before neuter noun)* das; *(before plural noun)* die; **to play ~ piano/violin** Klavier/Geige spielen; **I'm going to ~ butcher's/the cinema** ich gehe zum Metzger/ins Kino

2 *(+ adj to form noun):* **~ rich and ~ poor** die Reichen und die Armen; **to attempt ~ impossible** das Unmögliche versuchen

3 *(in titles):* **Elizabeth ~ First** Elisabeth die Erste; **Peter ~ Great** Peter der Große

4 *(in comparisons):* **~ more he works ~ more he earns** je mehr er arbeitet, desto mehr verdient er; **~ sooner ~ better** je eher, desto besser.

───────────

theatre, *(US)* **theater** ['θɪətə'] *n* Theater *nt;* *(also:* **lecture ~)** Hörsaal *m;* *(also:* **operating ~)** Operationsaal *m.*

theatre-goer ['θɪətəgəuə'] *n* Theaterbesucher(in) *m(f).*

theatrical [θɪ'ætrɪkl] *adj (event, production)* Theater-; *(gestures etc)* theatralisch.

theft [θɛft] *n* Diebstahl *m.*

their [ðɛə'] *adj* ihr.

theirs [ðɛəz] *pron* ihre(r, s); **it is ~** es gehört ihnen; **a friend of ~** ein Freund/eine Freundin von ihnen; *see also* **my, mine[1].**

them [ðɛm] *pron (direct)* sie; *(indirect)* ihnen; **I see ~** ich sehe sie; **give ~ the book** gib ihnen das Buch; **give me a few of ~** geben Sie mir ein paar davon; **with ~** mit ihnen; **without ~** ohne sie; *see also* **me.**

theme [θiːm] *n (also MUS)* Thema *nt.*

theme park *n* Themenpark *m.*

theme song *n* Titelmusik *f.*

theme tune *n* Titelmelodie *f.*

themselves [ðəm'sɛlvz] *pl pron (reflexive, after prep)* sich; *(emphatic, alone)* selbst; **between ~** unter sich.

then [ðɛn] *adv (at that time)* damals; *(next,*

later) dann ♦ *conj (therefore)* also ♦ *adj:* **the ~ president** der damalige Präsident; **by ~** *(past)* bis dahin; *(future)* bis dann; **from ~ on** von da an; **before ~** davor; **until ~** bis dann; **and ~ what?** und was dann?; **what do you want me to do ~?** was soll ich dann machen?; **... but ~ (again) he's the boss ...** aber er ist ja der Chef.

theologian [θɪə'ləudʒən] *n* Theologe *m*, Theologin *f*.

theological [θɪə'lɒdʒɪkl] *adj* theologisch.

theology [θɪ'ɒlədʒɪ] *n* Theologie *f*.

theorem ['θɪərəm] *n* Lehrsatz *m*.

theoretical [θɪə'rɛtɪkl] *adj* theoretisch.

theorize ['θɪəraɪz] *vi* theoretisieren.

theory ['θɪərɪ] *n* Theorie *f*; **in ~** theoretisch.

therapeutic [θɛrə'pjuːtɪk] *adj* therapeutisch.

therapist ['θɛrəpɪst] *n* Therapeut(in) *m(f)*.

therapy ['θɛrəpɪ] *n* Therapie *f*.

═══════════════════ *KEYWORD*

there [ðɛəʳ] *adv* **1**: **~ is/are** da ist/sind; *(there exist(s))* es gibt; **~ are 3 of them** es gibt 3 davon; **~ has been an accident** da war ein Unfall; **~ will be a meeting tomorrow** morgen findet ein Treffen statt **2** *(referring to place)* da, dort; **down/over ~** da unten/drüben; **put it in/on ~** leg es dort hinein/hinauf; **I want that book ~** ich möchte das Buch da; **~ he is!** da ist er ja! **3**: **~, ~** *(esp to child)* ist ja gut.

thereabouts ['ðɛərə'bauts] *adv:* **or ~** *(place)* oder dortherum; *(amount, time)* oder so.

thereafter [ðɛər'ɑːftəʳ] *adv* danach.

thereby ['ðɛəbaɪ] *adv* dadurch.

therefore ['ðɛəfɔːʳ] *adv* daher, deshalb.

there's ['ðɛəz] = **there is; there has.**

thereupon [ðɛərə'pɒn] *adv (at that point)* darauf(hin).

thermal ['θəːml] *adj (springs)* Thermal-; *(underwear, paper, printer)* Thermo-.

thermodynamics ['θəːmədaɪ'næmɪks] *n* Thermodynamik *f*.

thermometer [θə'mɒmɪtəʳ] *n* Thermometer *nt*.

thermonuclear ['θəːməu'njuːklɪəʳ] *adj* thermonuklear.

Thermos ® ['θəːməs] *n (also:* **~ flask)** Thermosflasche ® *f*.

thermostat ['θəːməustæt] *n* Thermostat *m*.

thesaurus [θɪ'sɔːrəs] *n* Synonymwörterbuch *nt*.

these [ðiːz] *pl adj, pl pron* diese.

theses ['θiːsiːz] *npl of* **thesis.**

thesis ['θiːsɪs] *(pl* **theses)** *n* These *f*; *(for doctorate etc)* Dissertation *f*, Doktorarbeit *f*.

they [ðeɪ] *pl pron* sie; **~ say that ...** *(it is said that)* man sagt, daß ...

they'd [ðeɪd] = **they had; they would.**

they'll [ðeɪl] = **they shall; they will.**

they're [ðɛəʳ] = **they are.**

they've [ðeɪv] = **they have.**

thick [θɪk] *adj* dick; *(sauce etc)* dickflüssig; *(fog, forest, hair etc)* dicht; *(inf: stupid)* blöd ♦ *n:* **in the ~ of the battle** mitten im Gefecht; **it's 20 cm ~** es ist 20 cm dick.

thicken ['θɪkn] *vi (fog etc)* sich verdichten ♦ *vt (sauce etc)* eindicken; **the plot ~s** die Sache wird immer verwickelter.

thicket ['θɪkɪt] *n* Dickicht *nt*.

thickly ['θɪklɪ] *adv (spread, cut)* dick; **~ populated** dicht bevölkert.

thickness ['θɪknɪs] *n (of rope, wire)* Dicke *f*; *(layer)* Lage *f*.

thickset [θɪk'sɛt] *adj (person, body)* gedrungen.

thick-skinned [θɪk'skɪnd] *adj (also fig)* dickhäutig.

thief [θiːf] *(pl* **thieves)** *n* Dieb(in) *m(f)*.

thieves [θiːvz] *npl of* **thief.**

thieving ['θiːvɪŋ] *n* Stehlen *nt*.

thigh [θaɪ] *n* Oberschenkel *m*.

thighbone ['θaɪbəun] *n* Oberschenkelknochen *m*.

thimble ['θɪmbl] *n* Fingerhut *m*.

thin [θɪn] *adj* dünn; *(fog)* leicht; *(hair, crowd)* spärlich ♦ *vt:* **to ~ (down)** *(sauce, paint)* verdünnen ♦ *vi (fog, crowd)* sich lichten; **his hair is ~ning** sein Haar lichtet sich.

thing [θɪŋ] *n* Ding *nt*; *(matter)* Sache *f*; *(inf):* **to have a ~ about sth** *(be fascinated by)* wie besessen sein von etw; *(hate)* etw nicht ausstehen können; **things** *npl (belongings)* Sachen *pl*; **to do sth first ~ (every morning/ tomorrow morning)** etw (morgens/morgen früh) als erstes tun; **I look awful first ~ in the morning** ich sehe frühmorgens immer furchtbar aus; **to do sth last ~ (at night)** etw als letztes (am Abend) tun; **the ~ is ...** die Sache ist die: ...; **for one ~** zunächst mal; **don't worry about a ~** du brauchst dir überhaupt keine Sorgen zu machen; **you'll do no such ~!** das läßt du schön bleiben!; **poor ~** armes Ding; **the best ~ would be to ...** das Beste wäre, zu ...; **how are ~s?** wie geht's?

think [θɪŋk] *(pt, pp* **thought)** *vi (reflect)* nachdenken; *(reason)* denken ♦ *vt (be of the opinion)* denken; *(believe)* glauben; **to ~ of** denken an +*acc*; *(recall)* sich erinnern an +*acc*; **what did you ~ of them?** was hielten Sie von ihnen?; **to ~ about sth/sb** *(ponder)* über etw/jdn nachdenken; **I'll ~ about it** ich werde es mir überlegen; **to ~ of doing sth** daran denken, etw zu tun; **to ~ highly of sb** viel von jdm halten; **to ~ aloud** laut nachdenken; **~ again!** denk noch mal nach!; **I ~ so/not** ich glaube ja/nein.

▶**think over** *vt (offer, suggestion)* überdenken; **I'd like to ~ things over** ich möchte mir die Sache noch einmal überlegen.

▶**think through** *vt* durchdenken.

▶**think up** *vt* sich *dat* ausdenken.

thinking ['θɪŋkɪŋ] n Denken nt; **to my (way of)** ~ meiner Meinung or Ansicht nach.
think-tank ['θɪŋktæŋk] n Expertengremium nt.
thinly ['θɪnlɪ] adv dünn; (disguised, veiled) kaum.
thinness ['θɪnnɪs] n Dünne f.
third [θəːd] num dritte(r, s) ♦ n (fraction) Drittel nt; (AUT: also: ~ **gear**) dritter Gang m; (BRIT: SCOL: degree) ≈ Ausreichend nt; **a** ~ **of** ein Drittel +gen.
third-degree burns ['θəːddɪgriː-] npl Verbrennungen pl dritten Grades.
thirdly ['θəːdlɪ] adv drittens.
third party insurance (BRIT) n ≈ Haftpflichtversicherung f.
third-rate ['θəːd'reɪt] (pej) adj drittklassig.
Third World n: **the** ~ die Dritte Welt ♦ adj der Dritten Welt.
thirst [θəːst] n Durst m.
thirsty ['θəːstɪ] adj durstig; **to be** ~ Durst haben; **gardening is** ~ **work** Gartenarbeit macht durstig.
thirteen [θəː'tiːn] num dreizehn.
thirteenth ['θəː'tiːnθ] num dreizehnte(r, s).
thirtieth ['θəːtɪɪθ] num dreißigste(r, s).
thirty ['θəːtɪ] num dreißig.

========================= *KEYWORD*

this [ðɪs] (pl **these**) adj (demonstrative) diese(r, s); ~ **man** dieser Mann; ~ **woman** diese Frau; ~ **book** dieses Buch; ~ **one** diese(r, s) (hier)
♦ pron (demonstrative) dies, das; **who/what is** ~? wer/was ist das?; ~ **is where I live** hier wohne ich; ~ **is what he said** das hat er gesagt; ~ **is Mr Brown** (in introductions, photo) das ist Herr Brown; (on telephone) hier ist Herr Brown
♦ adv (demonstrative): ~ **high/long** etc so hoch/lang etc.

thistle ['θɪsl] n Distel f.
thong [θɒŋ] n Riemen m.
thorn [θɔːn] n Dorn m.
thorny ['θɔːnɪ] adj dornig; (fig: problem) heikel.
thorough ['θʌrə] adj gründlich.
thoroughbred ['θʌrəbred] n (horse) Vollblüter m.
thoroughfare ['θʌrəfɛə*] n (road) Durchgangsstraße f; **"no** ~**"** (BRIT) „Durchfahrt verboten".
thoroughgoing ['θʌrəgəʊɪŋ] adj (changes, reform) grundlegend; (investigation) gründlich.
thoroughly ['θʌrəlɪ] adv gründlich; (very) äußerst; **I** ~ **agree** ich stimme vollkommen zu.
thoroughness ['θʌrənɪs] n Gründlichkeit f.
those [ðəʊz] pl adj, pl pron die (da); ~ **(of you) who ...** diejenigen (von Ihnen), die ...

though [ðəʊ] conj obwohl ♦ adv aber; **even** ~ obwohl; **it's not easy,** ~ es ist aber nicht einfach.
thought [θɔːt] pt, pp of **think** ♦ n Gedanke m; **thoughts** npl (opinion) Gedanken pl; **after much** ~ nach langer Überlegung; **I've just had a** ~ mir ist gerade etwas eingefallen; **to give sth some** ~ sich dat Gedanken über etw acc machen.
thoughtful ['θɔːtful] adj (deep in thought) nachdenklich; (considerate) aufmerksam.
thoughtfully ['θɔːtfəlɪ] adv (look etc) nachdenklich; (behave etc) rücksichtsvoll; (provide) rücksichtsvollerweise.
thoughtless ['θɔːtlɪs] adj gedankenlos.
thoughtlessly ['θɔːtlɪslɪ] adv gedankenlos.
thoughtlessness ['θɔːtlɪsnɪs] n Gedankenlosigkeit f.
thought-out [θɔːt'aut] adj durchdacht.
thought-provoking ['θɔːtprəvəukɪŋ] adj: **to be** ~ Denkanstöße geben.
thousand ['θauzənd] num (ein)tausend; **two** ~ zweitausend; ~**s of** Tausende von.
thousandth ['θauzəntθ] num tausendste(r, s).
thrash [θræʃ] vt (beat) verprügeln; (defeat) (vernichtend) schlagen.
► **thrash about** vi um sich schlagen.
► **thrash around** vi = thrash about.
► **thrash out** vt (problem) ausdiskutieren.
thrashing ['θræʃɪŋ] n: **to give sb a** ~ jdn verprügeln.
thread [θred] n (yarn) Faden m; (of screw) Gewinde nt ♦ vt (needle) einfädeln; **to** ~ **one's way between** sich hindurchschlängeln zwischen.
threadbare ['θredbɛə*] adj (clothes) abgetragen; (carpet) abgelaufen.
threat [θret] n Drohung f; (fig): ~ **(to)** Gefahr f (für); **to be under** ~ **of** (closure etc) bedroht sein von.
threaten ['θretn] vi bedrohen ♦ vt: **to** ~ **sb with sth** jdm mit etw drohen; **to** ~ **to do sth** (damit) drohen, etw zu tun.
threatening ['θretnɪŋ] adj drohend, bedrohlich.
three [θriː] num drei.
three-dimensional [θriːdɪ'menʃənl] adj dreidimensional.
threefold ['θriːfəuld] adv: **to increase** ~ dreifach or um das Dreifache ansteigen.
three-piece suit ['θriːpiːs-] n dreiteiliger Anzug m.
three-piece suite n dreiteilige Polstergarnitur f.
three-ply [θriː'plaɪ] adj (wool) dreifädig; (wood) dreilagig.
three-quarters [θriː'kwɔːtəz] npl Dreiviertel nt; ~ **full** dreiviertel voll.
three-wheeler ['θriː'wiːlə*] n (car) Dreiradwagen m.
thresh [θreʃ] vt dreschen.
threshing machine ['θreʃɪŋ-] n

Dreschmaschine f.

threshold ['θrɛʃhəʊld] n Schwelle f; **to be on the ~ of sth** (*fig*) an der Schwelle zu etw sein *or* stehen.

threshold agreement n (*ECON*) Tarifvereinbarung über der Inflationsrate angeglichene Lohnerhöhungen.

threw [θruː] pt of **throw**.

thrift [θrɪft] n Sparsamkeit f.

thrifty ['θrɪftɪ] adj sparsam.

thrill [θrɪl] n (*excitement*) Aufregung f; (*shudder*) Erregung f ♦ vi zittern ♦ vt (*person, audience*) erregen; **to be ~ed** (*with gift etc*) sich riesig freuen.

thriller ['θrɪlə'] n Thriller m.

thrilling ['θrɪlɪŋ] adj (*ride, performance etc*) erregend; (*news*) aufregend.

thrive [θraɪv] (*pt* **thrived** *or* **throve**, *pp* **thrived**) vi gedeihen; **to ~ on sth** von etw leben.

thriving ['θraɪvɪŋ] adj (*business, community*) blühend, florierend.

throat [θrəʊt] n Kehle f; **to have a sore ~** Halsschmerzen haben.

throb [θrɒb] n (*of heart*) Klopfen nt; (*pain*) Pochen nt; (*of engine*) Dröhnen nt ♦ vi (*heart*) klopfen; (*pain*) pochen; (*machine*) dröhnen; **my head is ~bing** ich habe rasende Kopfschmerzen.

throes [θrəʊz] npl: **in the ~ of** (*war, moving house etc*) mitten in +dat; **death ~** Todeskampf m.

thrombosis [θrɒm'bəʊsɪs] n Thrombose f.

throne [θrəʊn] n Thron m; **on the ~** auf dem Thron.

throng ['θrɒŋ] n Masse f ♦ vt (*streets etc*) sich drängen in +dat ♦ vi: **to ~ to** strömen zu; **a ~ of people** eine Menschenmenge; **to be ~ed with** wimmeln von.

throttle ['θrɒtl] n (*in car*) Gaspedal nt; (*on motorcycle*) Gashebel m ♦ vt (*strangle*) erdrosseln.

through [θruː] prep durch; (*time*) während; (*owing to*) infolge +gen ♦ adj (*ticket, train*) durchgehend ♦ adv durch; **(from) Monday ~ Friday** (*US*) von Montag bis Freitag; **to be ~** (*TEL*) verbunden sein; **to be ~ with sb/sth** mit jdm/etw fertig sein; **we're ~!** es ist aus zwischen uns!; **"no ~ road** *or* (*US*) **traffic"** „keine Durchfahrt"; **to let sb ~** jdn durchlassen; **to put sb ~ to sb** (*TEL*) jdn mit jdm verbinden.

throughout [θruː'aʊt] adv (*everywhere*) überall; (*the whole time*) die ganze Zeit über ♦ prep (*place*) überall in +dat; (*time*): **~ the morning/afternoon** während des ganzen Morgens/Nachmittags; **~ her life** ihr ganzes Leben lang.

throughput ['θruːpʊt] n (*also COMPUT*) Durchsatz m.

throve [θrəʊv] pt of **thrive**.

throw [θrəʊ] (*pt* **threw**, *pp* **thrown**) n Wurf m ♦ vt werfen; (*rider*) abwerfen; (*fig: confuse*) aus der Fassung bringen; (*pottery*) töpfern; **to ~ a party** eine Party geben; **to ~ open** (*doors, windows*) aufreißen; (*debate*) öffnen.

▸**throw about** vt (*money*) herumwerfen mit.

▸**throw around** vt = **throw about**.

▸**throw away** vt wegwerfen; (*waste*) verschwenden.

▸**throw off** vt (*get rid of: burden*) abwerfen.

▸**throw out** vt (*rubbish*) wegwerfen; (*idea*) verwerfen; (*person*) hinauswerfen.

▸**throw together** vt (*meal*) hinhauen; (*clothes*) zusammenpacken.

▸**throw up** vi (*vomit*) sich übergeben.

throwaway ['θrəʊəweɪ] adj (*cutlery etc*) Einweg-; (*line, remark*) beiläufig.

throwback ['θrəʊbæk] n: **it's a ~ to** (*reminder*) es erinnert an +acc.

throw-in ['θrəʊɪn] n (*FOOTBALL*) Einwurf m.

thrown [θrəʊn] pp of **throw**.

thru [θruː] (*US*) prep, adj, adv = **through**.

thrush [θrʌʃ] n (*bird*) Drossel f; (*MED: esp in children*) Soor m; (: *BRIT: in women*) vaginale Pilzerkrankung f.

thrust [θrʌst] (*pt, pp* **thrust**) n (*TECH*) Schubkraft f; (*push*) Stoß m; (*fig: impetus*) Stoßkraft f ♦ vt stoßen.

thud [θʌd] n dumpfes Geräusch nt.

thug [θʌg] n Schlägertyp m.

thumb [θʌm] n Daumen m ♦ vt: **to ~ a lift** per Anhalter fahren; **to give sb/sth the ~s up** (*approve*) jdm/etw dat grünes Licht geben; **to give sb/sth the ~s down** (*disapprove*) jdn/ etw ablehnen.

▸**thumb through** vt fus (*book*) durchblättern.

thumb index n Daumenregister nt.

thumbnail ['θʌmneɪl] n Daumennagel m.

thumbnail sketch n kurze Darstellung f.

thumbtack ['θʌmtæk] (*US*) n Heftzwecke f.

thump [θʌmp] n (*blow*) Schlag m; (*sound*) dumpfer Schlag m ♦ vt schlagen auf +acc ♦ vi (*heart etc*) heftig pochen.

thumping ['θʌmpɪŋ] adj (*majority, victory etc*) Riesen-; (*headache, cold*) fürchterlich.

thunder ['θʌndə'] n Donner m ♦ vi donnern; (*shout angrily*) brüllen; **to ~ past** (*train etc*) vorbeidonnern.

thunderbolt ['θʌndəbəʊlt] n Blitzschlag m.

thunderclap ['θʌndəklæp] n Donnerschlag m.

thunderous ['θʌndrəs] adj donnernd.

thunderstorm ['θʌndəstɔːm] n Gewitter nt.

thunderstruck ['θʌndəstrʌk] adj: **to be ~** (*shocked*) wie von Donner gerührt sein.

thundery ['θʌndərɪ] adj (*weather*) gewitterig.

Thur(s). abbr (= *Thursday*) Do.

Thursday ['θɜːzdɪ] n Donnerstag m; see also **Tuesday**.

thus [ðʌs] adv (*in this way*) so; (*consequently*) somit.

thwart [θwɔːt] vt (*person*) einen Strich durch die Rechnung machen +dat; (*plans*) vereiteln.

thyme [taɪm] n Thymian m.

thyroid ['θaɪrɔɪd] n (also: ~ **gland**) Schilddrüse f.

tiara [tɪ'ɑːrə] n Diadem nt.

Tiber ['taɪbə*] n: **the** ~ der Tiber.

Tibet [tɪ'bɛt] n Tibet nt.

Tibetan [tɪ'bɛtən] adj tibetanisch ♦ n (person) Tibetaner(in) m(f); (LING) Tibetisch nt.

tibia ['tɪbɪə] n Schienbein nt.

tic [tɪk] n nervöse Zuckung f, Tic m.

tick [tɪk] n (sound) Ticken nt; (mark) Häkchen nt; (ZOOL) Zecke f; (BRIT: inf: moment) Augenblick m; (: credit): **to buy sth on** ~ etw auf Pump kaufen ♦ vi (clock, watch) ticken ♦ vt (item on list) abhaken; **to put a** ~ **against sth** etw abhaken; **what makes him** ~? was ist er für ein Mensch?

►**tick off** vt (item on list) abhaken; (person) rüffeln.

►**tick over** vi (engine) im Leerlauf sein; (fig: business etc) sich über Wasser halten.

ticker tape ['tɪkəteɪp] n Lochstreifen m; (US: in celebrations) ≈ Luftschlangen pl.

ticket ['tɪkɪt] n (for public transport) Fahrkarte f; (for theatre etc) Eintrittskarte f; (in shop: on goods) Preisschild nt; (: from cash register) Kassenbon m; (for raffle) Los nt; (for library) Ausweis m; (also: **parking** ~: fine) Strafzettel m; (US: POL) Wahlliste f; **to get a (parking)** ~ (AUT) einen Strafzettel bekommen.

ticket agency n (THEAT) Vorverkaufsstelle f.

ticket collector n (RAIL: at station) Fahrkartenkontrolleur(in) m(f); (on train) Schaffner(in) m(f).

ticket holder n Karteninhaber(in) m(f).

ticket inspector n Fahrkartenkontrolleur(in) m(f).

ticket office n (RAIL) Fahrkartenschalter m; (THEAT) Theaterkasse f.

tickle ['tɪkl] vt kitzeln; (fig: amuse) amüsieren ♦ vi kitzeln; **it** ~**s!** das kitzelt!

ticklish ['tɪklɪʃ] adj (person, situation) kitzlig.

tidal ['taɪdl] adj (force) Gezeiten-, der Gezeiten; (river) Tide-.

tidal wave n Flutwelle f.

tidbit ['tɪdbɪt] (US) n = **titbit**.

tiddlywinks ['tɪdlɪwɪŋks] n Flohhüpfen nt.

tide [taɪd] n (in sea) Gezeiten pl; (fig: of events, opinion etc) Trend m; **high** ~ Flut f; **low** ~ Ebbe f; **the** ~ **is in/out** es ist Flut/Ebbe; **the** ~ **is coming in** die Flut kommt.

►**tide over** vt über die Runden helfen +dat.

tidily ['taɪdɪlɪ] adv ordentlich.

tidiness ['taɪdɪnɪs] n Ordentlichkeit f.

tidy ['taɪdɪ] adj (room, desk) ordentlich, aufgeräumt; (person) ordnungsliebend; (sum, income) ordentlich ♦ vt (also: ~ **up**) aufräumen.

tie [taɪ] n (BRIT: also: **necktie**) Krawatte f; (string etc) Band nt; (fig: link) Verbindung f; (SPORT: match) Spiel nt; (in competition: draw) Unentschieden nt ♦ vt (parcel) verschnüren; (shoelaces) zubinden; (ribbon) binden ♦ vi

(SPORT etc): **to** ~ **with sb for first place** sich mit jdm den ersten Platz teilen; "**black** ~" „Abendanzug"; "**white** ~" „Frackzwang"; **family** ~**s** familiäre Bindungen; **to** ~ **sth in a bow** etw zu einer Schleife binden; **to** ~ **a knot in sth** einen Knoten in etw acc machen.

►**tie down** vt (fig: restrict) binden; (: : to date, price etc) festlegen.

►**tie in** vi: **to** ~ **in with** zusammenpassen mit.

►**tie on** vt (BRIT) anbinden.

►**tie up** vt (parcel) verschnüren; (dog) anbinden; (boat) festmachen; (person) fesseln; (arrangements) unter Dach und Fach bringen; **to be** ~**d up** (busy) zu tun haben, beschäftigt sein.

tie-break(er) ['taɪbreɪk(ə*)] n (TENNIS) Tie-break m; (in quiz) Entscheidungsfrage f.

tie-on ['taɪɔn] (BRIT) adj (label) Anhänge-.

tiepin ['taɪpɪn] (BRIT) n Krawattennadel f.

tier [tɪə*] n (of stadium etc) Rang m; (of cake) Lage f.

tie-tack ['taɪtæk] (US) n = **tiepin**.

tiff [tɪf] n Krach m.

tiger ['taɪgə*] n Tiger m.

tight [taɪt] adj (screw, knot, grip) fest; (shoes, clothes, bend) eng; (security) streng; (budget, money) knapp; (schedule) gedrängt; (inf: drunk) voll; (: stingy) knickerig ♦ adv fest; **to be packed** ~ (suitcase) prallvoll sein; (room) gerammelt voll sein; **everybody hold** ~! alle festhalten!

tighten ['taɪtn] vt (rope, strap) straffen; (screw, bolt) anziehen; (grip) festigen; (security) verschärfen ♦ vi (grip) sich festigen; (rope etc) sich spannen.

tightfisted [taɪt'fɪstɪd] adj knickerig (inf).

tight-lipped ['taɪt'lɪpt] adj (fig: silence) eisern; **to be** ~ **about sth** über etw acc schweigen.

tightly ['taɪtlɪ] adv fest.

tightrope ['taɪtrəup] n Seil nt; **to be on** or **walking a** ~ (fig) einen Balanceakt vollführen.

tightrope walker n Seiltänzer(in) m(f).

tights [taɪts] (BRIT) npl Strumpfhose f.

tigress ['taɪgrɪs] n Tigerin f.

tilde ['tɪldə] n Tilde f.

tile [taɪl] n (on roof) Ziegel m; (on floor) Fliese f; (on wall) Kachel f ♦ vt (floor) mit Fliesen auslegen; (bathroom) kacheln.

tiled [taɪld] adj (floor) mit Fliesen ausgelegt; (wall) gekachelt.

till [tɪl] n (in shop etc) Kasse f ♦ vt (land) bestellen ♦ prep, conj = **until**.

tiller ['tɪlə*] n (NAUT) Ruderpinne f.

tilt [tɪlt] vt neigen ♦ vi sich neigen ♦ n (slope) Neigung f; **to wear one's hat at a** ~ den Hut schief aufhaben; **(at) full** ~ mit Volldampf.

timber ['tɪmbə*] n (material) Holz nt; (trees) Nutzholz nt.

time [taɪm] n Zeit f; (occasion) Gelegenheit f, Mal nt; (MUS) Takt m ♦ vt (measure time of) die Zeit messen bei; (runner) stoppen; (fix

moment for: visit etc) den Zeitpunkt festlegen
für; **a long** ~ eine lange Zeit; **for the**
~ **being** vorläufig; **4 at a** ~ 4 auf einmal;
from ~ **to** ~ von Zeit zu Zeit; ~ **after** ~,
~ **and again** immer (und immer) wieder; **at**
~**s** manchmal, zuweilen; **in** ~ (*soon enough*)
rechtzeitig; (*eventually*) mit der Zeit; (*MUS*)
im Takt; **in a week's** ~ in einer Woche; **in no**
~ im Handumdrehen; **any** ~ jederzeit; **on** ~
rechtzeitig; **to be 30 minutes behind/ahead**
of ~ 30 Minuten zurück/voraus sein; **by the**
~ **he arrived** als er ankam; **5** ~**s 5** 5 mal 5;
what ~ **is it?** wie spät ist es?; **to have a good**
~ sich amüsieren; **we/they** *etc* **had a hard** ~
wir/sie *etc* **hatten es schwer;** ~**'s up!** die
Zeit ist um!; **I've no** ~ **for it** (*fig*) dafür habe
ich nichts übrig; **he'll do it in his own (good)**
~ (*without being hurried*) er macht es, ohne
sich hetzen zu lassen; **he'll do it in** *or* (*US*)
on his own ~ (*out of working hours*) er macht
es in seiner Freizeit; **to be behind the** ~**s**
rückständig sein; **to** ~ **sth well/badly** den
richtigen/falschen Zeitpunkt für etw
wählen; **the bomb was** ~**d to go off 5**
minutes later die Bombe war so eingestellt,
daß sie 5 Minuten später explodieren sollte.
time-and-motion study ['taɪmənd'məʊʃən-] *n*
Arbeitsstudie *f*.
time bomb *n* (*also fig*) Zeitbombe *f*.
time card *n* Stechkarte *f*.
time clock *n* (*in factory etc*) Stechuhr *f*.
time-consuming ['taɪmkənsjuːmɪŋ] *adj*
zeitraubend.
time difference *n* Zeitunterschied *m*.
time frame *n* zeitlicher Rahmen *m*.
time-honoured, (*US*) **time-honored**
['taɪmɔnəd] *adj* althergebracht.
timekeeper ['taɪmkiːpə'] *n*: **she's a good** ~ sie
erfüllt ihr Zeitsoll.
time-lag ['taɪmlæg] *n* Verzögerung *f*.
timeless ['taɪmlɪs] *adj* zeitlos.
time limit *n* zeitliche Grenze *f*.
timely ['taɪmlɪ] *adj* (*arrival*) rechtzeitig;
(*reminder*) zur rechten Zeit.
time off *n*: **to take** ~ sich *dat* frei nehmen.
timer ['taɪmə'] *n* (*time switch*) Schaltuhr *f*; (*on*
cooker) Zeitmesser *m*; (*on video*) Timer *m*.
time-saving ['taɪmseɪvɪŋ] *adj* zeitsparend.
timescale ['taɪmskeɪl] (*BRIT*) *n* Zeitspanne *f*.
time-share ['taɪmʃɛə'] *n* Ferienwohnung *f* auf
Timesharing-Basis.
time-sharing ['taɪmʃɛərɪŋ] *n* (*of property,*
COMPUT) Timesharing *nt*.
time sheet *n* = **time card.**
time signal *n* (*RADIO*) Zeitzeichen *nt*.
time switch *n* Zeitschalter *m*.
timetable ['taɪmteɪbl] *n* (*RAIL etc*) Fahrplan *m*;
(*SCOL*) Stundenplan *m*; (*programme of*
events) Programm *nt*.
time zone *n* Zeitzone *f*.
timid ['tɪmɪd] *adj* (*person*) schüchtern; (*animal*)
scheu.

timidity [tɪ'mɪdɪtɪ] *n* (*shyness*) Schüchternheit
f.
timing ['taɪmɪŋ] *n* (*SPORT*) Timing *nt*; **the** ~ **of**
his resignation der Zeitpunkt seines
Rücktritts.
timing device *n* (*on bomb*) Zeitzünder *m*.
timpani ['tɪmpənɪ] *npl* Kesselpauken *pl*.
tin [tɪn] *n* (*metal*) Blech *nt*; (*container*) Dose *f*;
(: *for baking*) Form *f*; (: *BRIT: can*) Büchse *f*,
Dose *f*; **two** ~**s of paint** zwei Dosen Farbe.
tinfoil ['tɪnfɔɪl] *n* Alufolie *f*.
tinge [tɪndʒ] *n* (*of colour*) Färbung *f*, (*fig: of*
emotion etc) Anflug *m*, Anstrich *m* ♦ *vt*: ~**d**
with blue/red leicht blau/rot gefärbt; **to be**
~**d with sth** (*fig: emotion etc*) einen Anstrich
von etw haben.
tingle ['tɪŋgl] *vi* prickeln; (*from cold*) kribbeln;
I was tingling with excitement ich zitterte
vor Aufregung.
tinker ['tɪŋkə'] *n* (*gipsy*) Kesselflicker *m*.
►**tinker with** *vt fus* herumbasteln an +*dat*.
tinkle ['tɪŋkl] *vi* klingeln ♦ *n* (*inf*): **to give sb a**
~ (*TEL*) bei jdm anklingeln.
tin mine *n* Zinnbergwerk *nt*.
tinned [tɪnd] (*BRIT*) *adj* (*food, peas*) Dosen-, in
Dosen.
tinnitus ['tɪnɪtəs] *n* Tinnitus *m*, Ohrensummen
nt.
tinny ['tɪnɪ] (*pej*) *adj* (*sound*) blechern; (*car etc*)
Schrott-.
tin-opener ['tɪnəupnə'] (*BRIT*) *n* Dosenöffner
m.
tinsel ['tɪnsl] *n* Rauschgoldgirlanden *pl*.
tint [tɪnt] *n* (*colour*) Ton *m*; (*for hair*) Tönung *f*
♦ *vt* (*hair*) tönen.
tinted ['tɪntɪd] *adj* getönt.
tiny ['taɪnɪ] *adj* winzig.
tip [tɪp] *n* (*end*) Spitze *f*; (*gratuity*) Trinkgeld *nt*;
(*BRIT: for rubbish*) Müllkippe *f*; (: *for coal*)
Halde *f*; (*advice*) Tip *m*, Hinweis *m* ♦ *vt*
(*waiter*) ein Trinkgeld geben +*dat*; (*tilt*)
kippen; (*also:* ~ **over:** *overturn*) umkippen;
(*also:* ~ **out:** *empty*) leeren; (*predict: winner*
etc) tippen *or* setzen auf +*acc*; **he** ~**ped out**
the contents of the box er kippte den Inhalt
der Kiste aus.
►**tip off** *vt* einen Tip *or* Hinweis geben +*dat*.
tip-off ['tɪpɔf] *n* Hinweis *m*.
tipped ['tɪpt] *adj* (*BRIT: cigarette*) Filter-; **steel-**
~ mit Stahlspitze.
Tipp-Ex ® ['tɪpɛks] *n* Tipp-Ex ® *nt*.
tipple ['tɪpl] (*BRIT*) *vi* picheln ♦ *n*: **to have a** ~
einen trinken.
tipster ['tɪpstə'] *n* jd, der bei Pferderennen,
Börsengeschäften etc Tips gegen
Bezahlung weitergibt.
tipsy ['tɪpsɪ] (*inf*) *adj* beschwipst.
tiptoe ['tɪptəu] *n*: **on** ~ auf Zehenspitzen.
tip-top ['tɪp'tɔp] *adj*: **in** ~ **condition** tipptopp.
tirade [taɪ'reɪd] *n* Tirade *f*.
tire ['taɪə'] *n* (*US*) = **tyre** ♦ *vt* müde machen,
ermüden ♦ *vi* (*become tired*) müde werden;

to ~ of sth genug von etw haben.
►**tire out** *vt* erschöpfen.
tired ['taɪəd] *adj* müde; **to be/look ~** müde
sein/aussehen; **to feel ~** sich müde fühlen;
to be ~ of sth etw satt haben; **to be ~ of
doing sth** es satt haben, etw zu tun.
tiredness ['taɪədnɪs] *n* Müdigkeit *f*.
tireless ['taɪəlɪs] *adj* unermüdlich.
tiresome ['taɪəsəm] *adj* lästig.
tiring ['taɪərɪŋ] *adj* ermüdend, anstrengend.
tissue ['tɪʃuː] *n* (*ANAT, BIOL*) Gewebe *nt*;
(*paper handkerchief*) Papiertaschentuch *nt*.
tissue paper *n* Seidenpapier *nt*.
tit [tɪt] *n* (*bird*) Meise *f*; (*inf: breast*) Titte *f*;
~ for tat wie du mir, so ich dir.
titanium [tɪ'teɪnɪəm] *n* Titan *nt*.
titbit, (*US*) **tidbit** ['tɪtbɪt] *n* (*food, news*)
Leckerbissen *m*.
titillate ['tɪtɪleɪt] *vt* erregen, reizen.
titivate ['tɪtɪveɪt] *vt* feinmachen.
title ['taɪtl] *n* Titel *m*; (*LAW*): **~ to** Anspruch
auf +*acc*.
title deed *n* Eigentumsurkunde *f*.
title page *n* Titelseite *f*.
title role *n* Titelrolle *f*.
title track *n* Titelstück *nt*.
titter ['tɪtə*] *vi* kichern.
tittle-tattle ['tɪtltætl] (*inf*) *n* Klatsch *m*,
Gerede *nt*.
tizzy ['tɪzɪ]: **to be in a ~** aufgeregt sein; **to
get in a ~** sich aufregen.
T-junction ['tiː'dʒʌŋkʃən] *n* T-Kreuzung *f*.
TM *abbr* (= *trademark*) Wz; = **transcendental
meditation**.
TN (*US*) *abbr* (*POST:* = *Tennessee*).
TNT *n abbr* (= *trinitrotoluene*) TNT *nt*.

───────────────── *KEYWORD*

to [tuː] *prep* **1** (*direction*) nach +*dat*, zu +*dat*; **to
go ~ France/London/school/the station**
nach Frankreich/nach London/zur Schule/
zum Bahnhof gehen; **~ the left/right** nach
links/rechts; **I have never been ~ Germany**
ich war noch nie in Deutschland
2 (*as far as*) bis; **to count ~ 10** bis 10 zählen
3 (*with expressions of time*) vor +*dat*; **a quarter
~ 5** (*BRIT*) Viertel vor 5
4 (*for, of*): **the key ~ the front door** der
Schlüssel für die Haustür; **a letter ~ his
wife** ein Brief an seine Frau
5 (*expressing indirect object*): **to give sth ~ sb**
jdm etw geben; **to talk ~ sb** mit jdm
sprechen; **I sold it ~ a friend** ich habe es an
einen Freund verkauft; **you've done
something ~ your hair** du hast etwas mit
deinem Haar gemacht
6 (*in relation to*) zu; **A is ~ B as C is ~ D** A
verhält sich zu B wie C zu D; **3 goals ~ 2** 3
zu 2 Tore; **40 miles ~ the gallon** 40 Meilen
pro Gallone
7 (*purpose, result*) zu; **to sentence sb to death**
jdn zum Tode verurteilen; **~ my surprise** zu
meiner Überraschung
♦ *with vb* **1** (*simple infinitive*): **~ go** gehen;
~ eat essen
2 (*following another vb*): **to want ~ do sth**
etw tun wollen; **to try/start ~ do sth**
versuchen/anfangen, etw zu tun
3 (*with vb omitted*): **I don't want ~** ich will
nicht; **you ought ~** du solltest es tun
4 (*purpose, result*) (um ...) zu; **I did it ~ help
you** ich habe es getan, um dir zu helfen
5 (*equivalent to relative clause*) zu; **he has a lot
~ lose** er hat viel zu verlieren; **the main
thing is ~ try** die Hauptsache ist, es zu
versuchen
6 (*after adjective etc*): **ready ~ use**
gebrauchsfertig; **too old/young ~ ...** zu alt/
jung, um zu ...; **it's too heavy ~ lift** es ist zu
schwer zu heben
♦ *adv*: **to push/pull the door ~** die Tür
zudrücken/zuziehen; **~ and fro** hin und her.

toad [təud] *n* Kröte *f*.
toadstool ['təudstuːl] *n* Giftpilz *m*.
toady ['təudɪ] (*pej*) *vi*: **to ~ to sb** vor jdm
kriechen.
toast [təust] *n* (*CULIN, drink*) Toast *m* ♦ *vt*
(*bread etc*) toasten; (*drink to*) einen Toast *or*
Trinkspruch ausbringen auf +*acc*; **a piece** *or*
slice of ~ eine Scheibe Toast.
toaster ['təustə*] *n* Toaster *m*.
toastmaster ['təustmɑːstə*] *n*
Zeremonienmeister *m*.
toast rack *n* Toastständer *m*.
tobacco [tə'bækəu] *n* Tabak *m*; **pipe ~**
Pfeifentabak *m*.
tobacconist [tə'bækənɪst] *n* Tabakhändler(in)
m(f).
tobacconist's (shop) [tə'bækənɪsts-] *n*
Tabakwarenladen *m*.
Tobago [tə'beɪgəu] *n see* **Trinidad**.
toboggan [tə'bɔgən] *n* Schlitten *m*.
today [tə'deɪ] *adv, n* heute; **what day is it ~?**
welcher Tag ist heute?; **what date is it ~?**
der wievielte ist heute?; **~ is the 4th of
March** heute ist der 4. März; **a week ago ~**
heute vor einer Woche; **~'s paper** die
Zeitung von heute.
toddle ['tɔdl] (*inf*) *vi*: **to ~ in/off/along**
herein-/davon-/entlangwatscheln.
toddler ['tɔdlə*] *n* Kleinkind *nt*.
to-do [tə'duː] *n* Aufregung *f*, Theater *nt*.
toe [təu] *n* Zehe *f*, Zeh *m*; (*of shoe, sock*) Spitze
f; **to ~ the line** (*fig*) auf Linie bleiben; **big/
little ~** großer/kleiner Zeh.
toehold ['təuhəuld] *n* (*in climbing*) Halt *m* für
die Fußspitzen; (*fig*): **to get/gain a ~ (in)**
einen Einstieg bekommen/sich *dat* einen
Einstieg verschaffen (in +*dat*).
toenail ['təuneɪl] *n* Zehennagel *m*.
toffee ['tɔfɪ] *n* Toffee *m*.
toffee apple (*BRIT*) *n* ≈ kandierter Apfel *m*.
tofu ['təufuː] *n* Tofu *m*.

toga ['təugə] n Toga f.

together [tə'gɛðə*] adv zusammen; (at the same time) gleichzeitig; ~ **with** gemeinsam mit.

togetherness [tə'gɛðənɪs] n Beisammensein nt.

toggle switch ['tɔgl-] n (COMPUT) Toggle-Schalter m.

Togo ['təugəu] n Togo nt.

togs [tɔgz] (inf) npl Klamotten pl.

toil [tɔɪl] n Mühe f ♦ vi sich abmühen.

toilet ['tɔɪlət] n Toilette f ♦ cpd (kit, accessories etc) Toiletten-; **to go to the** ~ auf die Toilette gehen.

toilet bag (BRIT) n Kulturbeutel m.

toilet bowl n Toilettenbecken nt.

toilet paper n Toilettenpapier nt.

toiletries ['tɔɪlətrɪz] npl Toilettenartikel pl.

toilet roll n Rolle f Toilettenpapier.

toilet soap n Toilettenseife f.

toilet water n Toilettenwasser nt.

to-ing and fro-ing ['tu:ɪŋən'frəuɪŋ] (BRIT) n Hin und Her nt.

token ['təukən] n (sign, souvenir) Zeichen nt; (substitute coin) Wertmarke f ♦ adj (strike, payment etc) symbolisch; **by the same** ~ (fig) in gleicher Weise; **book/record/gift** ~ (BRIT) Bücher-/Platten-/Geschenkgutschein m.

tokenism ['təukənɪzəm] n: **to be (pure)** ~ (nur) eine Alibifunktion haben.

Tokyo ['təukjəu] n Tokio nt.

told [təuld] pt, pp of **tell**.

tolerable ['tɔlərəbl] adj (bearable) erträglich; (fairly good) passabel.

tolerably ['tɔlərəblɪ] adv: ~ **good** ganz annehmbar or passabel.

tolerance ['tɔlərns] n Toleranz f.

tolerant ['tɔlərnt] adj tolerant; **to be** ~ **of sth** tolerant gegenüber etw sein.

tolerate ['tɔləreɪt] vt (pain, noise) erdulden, ertragen; (injustice) tolerieren.

toleration [tɔlə'reɪʃən] n (of person, pain etc) Duldung f; (REL, POL) Toleranz f.

toll [təul] n (of casualties, deaths) (Gesamt)zahl f; (tax, charge) Gebühr f ♦ vi (bell) läuten; **the work took its** ~ **on us** die Arbeit blieb nicht ohne Auswirkungen auf uns.

tollbridge ['təulbrɪdʒ] n gebührenpflichtige Brücke f, Mautbrücke f.

toll call (US) n Ferngespräch nt.

toll-free ['təulfri:] (US) n gebührenfrei.

toll road n gebührenpflichtige Straße f, Mautstraße f.

tomato [tə'mɑːtəu] (pl ~es) n Tomate f.

tomato purée n Tomatenmark nt.

tomb [tu:m] n Grab nt.

tombola [tɔm'bəulə] n Tombola f.

tomboy ['tɔmbɔɪ] n Wildfang m.

tombstone ['tu:mstəun] n Grabstein m.

tomcat ['tɔmkæt] n Kater m.

tome [təum] n (form) n Band m.

tomorrow [tə'mɔrəu] adv morgen ♦ n morgen; (future) Zukunft f; **the day after** ~ übermorgen; **a week** ~ morgen in einer Woche; ~ **morning** morgen früh.

ton [tʌn] n (BRIT) (britische) Tonne f; (US: also: **short** ~) (US-)Tonne f (ca. 907 kg); (metric ton) (metrische) Tonne f; ~s **of** (inf) Unmengen von.

tonal ['təunl] adj (MUS) klanglich, tonal.

tone [təun] n Ton m ♦ vi (also: ~ **in:** colours) (farblich) passen.

►**tone down** vt (also fig) abschwächen.

►**tone up** vt (muscles) kräftigen.

tone-deaf [təun'dɛf] adj ohne Gefühl für Tonhöhen.

toner ['təunə*] n (for photocopier) Toner m.

Tonga [tɔŋə] n Tonga nt.

tongs [tɔŋz] npl Zange f; (also: **curling** ~) Lockenstab m.

tongue [tʌŋ] n Zunge f; (form: language) Sprache f; ~-**in-cheek** (speak, say) ironisch.

tongue-tied ['tʌŋtaɪd] adj (fig) sprachlos.

tongue-twister ['tʌŋtwɪstə*] n Zungenbrecher m.

tonic ['tɔnɪk] n (MED) Tonikum nt; (fig) Wohltat f; (also: ~ **water**) Tonic nt; (MUS) Tonika f, Grundton m.

tonight [tə'naɪt] adv (this evening) heute abend; (this night) heute nacht ♦ n (this evening) der heutige Abend; (this night) die kommende Nacht; **(I'll) see you** ~! bis heute abend!

tonnage ['tʌnɪdʒ] n Tonnage f.

tonne [tʌn] (BRIT) n (metric ton) Tonne f.

tonsil ['tɔnsl] n Mandel f; **to have one's** ~s **out** sich dat die Mandeln herausnehmen lassen.

tonsillitis [tɔnsɪ'laɪtɪs] n Mandelentzündung f.

too [tu:] adv (excessively) zu; (also) auch; **it's** ~ **sweet** es ist zu süß; **I went** ~ ich bin auch mitgegangen; ~ **much** (adj) zuviel; (adv) zu sehr; ~ **many** zu viele; ~ **bad!** das ist eben Pech!

took [tuk] pt of **take**.

tool [tu:l] n (also fig) Werkzeug nt.

tool box n Werkzeugkasten m.

tool kit n Werkzeugsatz m.

toot [tu:t] n (of horn) Hupton m; (of whistle) Pfeifton m ♦ vi (with car-horn) hupen.

tooth [tu:θ] (pl **teeth**) n (also TECH) Zahn m; **to have a** ~ **out** or (US) **pulled** sich dat einen Zahn ziehen lassen; **to brush one's teeth** sich dat die Zähne putzen; **by the skin of one's teeth** (fig) mit knapper Not.

toothache ['tu:θeɪk] n Zahnschmerzen pl; **to have** ~ Zahnschmerzen haben.

toothbrush ['tu:θbrʌʃ] n Zahnbürste f.

toothpaste ['tu:θpeɪst] n Zahnpasta f.

toothpick ['tu:θpɪk] n Zahnstocher m.

tooth powder n Zahnpulver nt.

top [tɔp] n (of mountain, tree, ladder) Spitze f; (of cupboard, table, box) Oberseite f; (of street) Ende nt; (lid) Verschluß m; (AUT: also: ~ **gear**) höchster Gang m; (also: **spinning** ~:

toy) Kreisel *m*; (*blouse etc*) Oberteil *nt*; (*of pyjamas*) Jacke *f* ♦ *adj* höchste(r, s); (*highest in rank*) oberste(r, s); (: *golfer etc*) Top- ♦ *vt* (*poll, vote, list*) anführen; (*estimate etc*) übersteigen; **at the ~ of the stairs/page** oben auf der Treppe/Seite; **at the ~ of the street** am Ende der Straße; **on ~ of** (*above*) auf +*dat*; (*in addition to*) zusätzlich zu; **from ~ to bottom** von oben bis unten; **from ~ to toe** (*BRIT*) von Kopf bis Fuß; **at the ~ of the list** oben auf der Liste; **at the ~ of his voice** so laut er konnte; **over the ~** (*inf: behaviour etc*) übertrieben; **to go over the ~** (*inf*) übertrieben; **at ~ speed** bei Höchstgeschwindigkeit.

►**top up** , (*US*) **top off** *vt* (*drink*) nachfüllen; (*salary*) aufbessern.

topaz ['təupæz] *n* Topas *m*.

top-class ['tɔp'klɑːs] *adj* erstklassig; (*hotel, player etc*) Spitzen-.

topcoat ['tɔpkəut] *n* (*overcoat*) Mantel *m*; (*of paint*) Deckanstrich *m*.

top floor *n* oberster Stock *m*.

top hat *n* Zylinder *m*.

top-heavy [tɔp'hɛvɪ] *adj* (*also fig*) kopflastig.

topic ['tɔpɪk] *n* Thema *nt*.

topical ['tɔpɪkl] *adj* (*issue etc*) aktuell.

topless ['tɔplɪs] *adj* (*waitress*) Oben-ohne-; (*bather*) barbusig ♦ *adv* oben ohne.

top-level ['tɔplɛvl] *adj* auf höchster Ebene.

topmost ['tɔpməust] *adj* oberste(r, s).

top-notch ['tɔp'nɔtʃ] *adj* erstklassig.

topography [tə'pɔgrəfɪ] *n* Topographie *f*.

topping ['tɔpɪŋ] *n* (*CULIN*) Überzug *m*.

topple ['tɔpl] *vt* (*government etc*) stürzen ♦ *vi* (*person*) stürzen; (*object*) fallen.

top-ranking ['tɔpræŋkɪŋ] *adj* (*official*) hochgestellt.

top-secret ['tɔp'siːkrɪt] *adj* streng geheim.

top-security ['tɔpsə'kjuərɪtɪ] (*BRIT*) *adj* (*prison, wing*) Hochsicherheits-.

topsy-turvy ['tɔpsɪ'təːvɪ] *adj* auf den Kopf gestellt ♦ *adv* durcheinander; (*fall, land*) verkehrt herum.

top-up ['tɔpʌp] *n*: **would you like a ~?** darf ich Ihnen nachschenken?

top-up loan *n* Ergänzungsdarlehen *nt*.

torch [tɔːtʃ] *n* Fackel *f*; (*BRIT: electric*) Taschenlampe *f*.

tore [tɔː*] *pt of* tear.

torment [*n* tɔːmɛnt, *vt* tɔː'mɛnt] *n* Qual *f* ♦ *vt* quälen; (*annoy*) ärgern.

torn [tɔːn] *pp of* tear¹ ♦ *adj*: **~ between** (*fig*) hin- und hergerissen zwischen.

tornado [tɔː'neɪdəu] (*pl ~es*) *n* (*storm*) Tornado *m*.

torpedo [tɔː'piːdəu] (*pl ~es*) *n* Torpedo *m*.

torpedo boat *n* Torpedoboot *nt*.

torpor ['tɔːpə*] *n* Trägheit *f*.

torrent ['tɔrnt] *n* (*flood*) Strom *m*; (*fig*) Flut *f*.

torrential [tɔ'rɛnʃl] *adj* (*rain*) wolkenbruchartig.

torrid ['tɔrɪd] *adj* (*weather, love affair*) heiß.

torso ['tɔːsəu] *n* Torso *m*.

tortoise ['tɔːtəs] *n* Schildkröte *f*.

tortoiseshell ['tɔːtəʃɛl] *adj* (*jewellery, ornaments*) aus Schildpatt; (*cat*) braun-gelb-schwarz.

tortuous ['tɔːtjuəs] *adj* (*path*) gewunden; (*argument, mind*) umständlich.

torture ['tɔːtʃə*] *n* Folter *f*; (*fig*) Qual *f* ♦ *vt* foltern; (*fig: torment*) quälen; **it was ~** (*fig*) es war eine Qual.

torturer ['tɔːtʃərə*] *n* Folterer *m*.

Tory ['tɔːrɪ] (*BRIT: POL*) *adj* konservativ ♦ *n* Tory *m*, Konservative(r) *f(m)*.

toss [tɔs] *vt* (*throw*) werfen; (*one's head*) zurückwerfen; (*salad*) anmachen; (*pancake*) wenden ♦ *n*: **with a ~ of her head** mit einer Kopfbewegung; **to ~ a coin** eine Münze werfen; **to win/lose the ~** die Entscheidung per Münzwurf gewinnen/verlieren; **to ~ up for sth** etw per Münzwurf entscheiden; **to ~ and turn** (*in bed*) sich hin und her wälzen.

tot [tɔt] *n* (*BRIT: drink*) Schluck *m*; (*child*) Knirps *m*.

►**tot up** (*BRIT*) *vt* (*figures*) zusammenzählen.

total ['təutl] *adj* (*number etc*) gesamt; (*failure, wreck etc*) völlig, total ♦ *n* Gesamtzahl *f* ♦ *vt* (*add up*) zusammenzählen; (*add up to*) sich belaufen auf; **in ~** insgesamt.

totalitarian [təutælɪ'tɛərɪən] *adj* totalitär.

totality [təu'tælɪtɪ] *n* Gesamtheit *f*.

totally ['təutəlɪ] *adv* völlig.

totem pole ['təutəm-] *n* Totempfahl *m*.

totter ['tɔtə*] *vi* (*person*) wanken, taumeln; (*fig: government*) im Wanken sein.

touch [tʌtʃ] *n* (*sense of touch*) Gefühl *nt*; (*contact*) Berührung *f*; (*skill: of pianist etc*) Hand *f* ♦ *vt* berühren; (*tamper with*) anrühren; (*emotionally*) rühren ♦ *vi* (*make contact*) sich berühren; **the personal ~** die persönliche Note; **to put the finishing ~es to sth** letzte Hand an etw *acc* legen; **a ~ of** (*fig: frost etc*) etwas, ein Hauch von; **in ~ with** (*person, group*) in Verbindung mit; **to get in ~ with sb** mit jdm in Verbindung treten; **I'll be in ~** ich melde mich; **to lose ~** (*friends*) den Kontakt verlieren; **to be out of ~ with sb** keine Verbindung mehr zu jdm haben; **to be out of ~ with events** nicht auf dem laufenden sein; **~ wood!** hoffen wir das Beste!

►**touch on** *vt fus* (*topic*) berühren.

►**touch up** *vt* (*car etc*) ausbessern.

touch-and-go ['tʌtʃən'gəu] *adj* (*situation*) auf der Kippe; **it was ~ whether we'd succeed** es war völlig offen, ob wir Erfolg haben würden.

touchdown ['tʌtʃdaun] *n* (*of rocket, plane*) Landung *f*; (*US: FOOTBALL*) Touchdown *m*.

touched [tʌtʃt] *adj* (*moved*) gerührt; (*inf: mad*) plemplem.

touching ['tʌtʃɪŋ] *adj* rührend.

touchline ['tʌtʃlaɪn] n (SPORT) Seitenlinie f.

touch-sensitive ['tʌtʃ'sensɪtɪv] adj berührungsempfindlich; (switch) Kontakt-.

touch-type ['tʌtʃtaɪp] vi blindschreiben.

touchy ['tʌtʃɪ] adj (person, subject) empfindlich.

tough [tʌf] adj (strong, firm, difficult) hart; (resistant) widerstandsfähig; (meat, animal, person) zäh; (rough) rauh; ~ **luck!** Pech!

toughen ['tʌfn] vt (sb's character) hart machen; (glass etc) härten.

toughness ['tʌfnɪs] n Härte f.

toupee ['tuːpeɪ] n Toupet nt.

tour ['tuə*] n (journey) Reise f, Tour f; (of factory, museum etc) Rundgang m; (: also: **guided** ~) Führung f; (by pop group etc) Tournee f ♦ vt (country, factory etc: on foot) ziehen durch; (: in car) fahren durch; **to go on a** ~ **of a museum/castle** an einer Museums-/Schloßführung teilnehmen; **to go on a** ~ **of the Highlands** die Highlands bereisen; **to go/be on** ~ (pop group, theatre company etc) auf Tournee gehen/sein.

touring ['tuərɪŋ] n Umherreisen nt.

tourism ['tuərɪzm] n Tourismus m.

tourist ['tuərɪst] n Tourist(in) m(f) ♦ cpd (attractions, season) Touristen-; **the** ~ **trade** die Tourismusbranche.

tourist class n Touristenklasse f.

tourist information centre (BRIT) n Touristen-Informationszentrum nt.

tourist office n Verkehrsamt nt.

tournament ['tuənəmənt] n Turnier nt.

tourniquet ['tuənɪkeɪ] n Aderpresse f.

tour operator (BRIT) n Reiseveranstalter m.

tousled ['tauzld] adj (hair) zerzaust.

tout [taut] vi: **to** ~ **for business** die Reklametrommel schlagen; **to** ~ **for custom** auf Kundenfang gehen ♦ n (also: **ticket** ~) Schwarzhändler, der Eintrittskarten zu überhöhten Preisen verkauft.

tow [təu] vt (vehicle) abschleppen; (caravan, trailer) ziehen ♦ n: **to give sb a** ~ (AUT) jdn abschleppen; **"on** or (US) **in** ~" „Fahrzeug wird abgeschleppt".

▶ **tow away** vt (vehicle) abschleppen.

toward(s) [tə'wɔːd(z)] prep (direction) zu; (attitude) gegenüber +dat; (purpose) für; (in time) gegen; ~ **noon/the end of the year** gegen Mittag/Ende des Jahres; **to feel friendly** ~ **sb** jdm freundlich gesinnt sein.

towel ['tauəl] n Handtuch nt; **to throw in the** ~ (fig) das Handtuch werfen.

towelling ['tauəlɪŋ] n Frottee nt or m.

towel rail, (US) **towel rack** n Handtuchstange f.

tower ['tauə*] n Turm m ♦ vi aufragen; **to** ~ **above** or **over sb/sth** über jdm/etw aufragen.

tower block (BRIT) n Hochhaus nt.

towering ['tauərɪŋ] adj hoch aufragend.

towline ['təulaɪn] n Abschleppseil nt.

town [taun] n Stadt f; **to go (in)to** ~ in die Stadt gehen; **to go to** ~ **on sth** (fig) sich bei etw ins Zeug legen; **in** ~ in der Stadt; **to be out of** ~ (person) nicht in der Stadt sein.

town centre n Stadtzentrum nt.

town clerk n Stadtdirektor(in) m(f).

town council n Stadtrat m.

town crier [-'kraɪə*] n Ausrufer m.

town hall n Rathaus nt.

town house n (städtisches) Wohnhaus nt; (US: in a complex) Reihenhaus nt.

townie ['taunɪ] (inf) n (town-dweller) Städter(in) m(f).

town plan n Stadtplan m.

town planner n Stadtplaner(in) m(f).

town planning n Stadtplanung f.

township ['taunʃɪp] n Stadt(gemeinde) f; (formerly: in South Africa) Township f.

townspeople ['taunzpiːpl] npl Stadtbewohner pl.

towpath ['təupɑːθ] n Leinpfad m.

towrope ['təurəup] n Abschleppseil nt.

tow truck (US) n Abschleppwagen m.

toxic ['tɔksɪk] adj giftig, toxisch.

toxin ['tɔksɪn] n Gift nt, Giftstoff m.

toy [tɔɪ] n Spielzeug nt.

▶ **toy with** vt fus (object, idea) spielen mit.

toyshop ['tɔɪʃɔp] n Spielzeugladen m.

trace [treɪs] n (sign, small amount) Spur f ♦ vt (draw) nachzeichnen; (follow) verfolgen; (locate) aufspüren; **without** ~ (disappear) spurlos; **there was no** ~ **of it** es war spurlos verschwunden.

trace element n Spurenelement nt.

tracer ['treɪsə*] n (MIL: also: ~ **bullet**) Leuchtspurgeschoß nt; (MED) Indikator m.

trachea [trə'kiːə] n Luftröhre f.

tracing paper ['treɪsɪŋ-] n Pauspapier nt.

track [træk] n Weg m; (of comet, SPORT) Bahn f; (of suspect, animal) Spur f; (RAIL) Gleis nt; (on tape, record) Stück nt, Track m ♦ vt (follow) verfolgen; **to keep** ~ **of sb/sth** (fig) jdn/etw im Auge behalten; **to be on the right** ~ (fig) auf der richtigen Spur sein.

▶ **track down** vt aufspüren.

tracker dog ['trækə-] (BRIT) n Spürhund m.

track events npl Laufwettbewerbe f.

tracking station ['trækɪŋ-] n Bodenstation f.

track meet (US) n (SPORT) Leichtathletikwettkampf m.

track record n: **to have a good** ~ (fig) gute Leistungen vorzuweisen haben.

tracksuit ['træksuːt] n Trainingsanzug m.

tract [trækt] n (GEOG) Gebiet nt; (pamphlet) Traktat m or nt; **respiratory** ~ Atemwege pl.

traction ['trækʃən] n (power) Zugkraft f; (AUT: grip) Bodenhaftung f; (MED): **in** ~ im Streckverband.

traction engine n Zugmaschine f.

tractor ['træktə*] n Traktor m.

trade [treɪd] n (activity) Handel m; (skill, job) Handwerk nt ♦ vi (do business) handeln ♦ vt:

to ~ sth (for sth) etw (gegen etw)
eintauschen; **foreign** ~ Außenhandel *m*;
Department of T~ and Industry (*BRIT*)
≈ Wirtschaftsministerium *nt*; **to** ~ **with**
Handel treiben mit; **to** ~ **in** (*merchandise*)
handeln in +*dat*.

▶**trade in** *vt* in Zahlung geben.

trade barrier *n* Handelsschranke *f*.

trade deficit *n* Handelsdefizit *nt*.

Trade Descriptions Act (*BRIT*) *n Gesetz über korrekte Warenbeschreibungen*.

trade discount *n* Händlerrabatt *m*.

trade fair *n* Handelsmesse *f*.

trade figures *npl* Handelsziffern *pl*.

trade-in ['treɪdɪn] *n*: **to take sth as a** ~ etw in Zahlung nehmen.

trade-in value *n* Gebrauchtwert *m*.

trademark ['treɪdmɑːk] *n* Warenzeichen *nt*.

trade mission *n* Handelsmission *f*.

trade name *n* Handelsname *m*.

trade-off ['treɪdɔf] *n* Handel *m*; **there's bound to be a** ~ **between speed and quality** es gibt entweder Einbußen bei der Schnelligkeit oder bei der Qualität.

trader ['treɪdə*] *n* Händler(in) *m(f)*.

trade secret *n* (*also fig*) Betriebsgeheimnis *nt*.

tradesman ['treɪdzmən] (*irreg: like* **man**) *n* (*shopkeeper*) Händler *m*.

trade union *n* Gewerkschaft *f*.

trade unionist [-'juːnjənɪst] *n* Gewerkschaftler(in) *m(f)*.

trade wind *n* Passat *m*.

trading ['treɪdɪŋ] *n* Handel *m*.

trading estate (*BRIT*) *n* Industriegelände *nt*.

trading stamp *n* Rabattmarke *f*.

tradition [trə'dɪʃən] *n* Tradition *f*.

traditional [trə'dɪʃənl] *adj* traditionell.

traditionally [trə'dɪʃnəlɪ] *adv* traditionell.

traffic ['træfɪk] *n* Verkehr *m*; (*in drugs etc*) Handel *m* ♦ *vi*: **to** ~ **in** handeln mit.

traffic calming *n* Verkehrsberuhigung *f*.

traffic circle (*US*) *n* Kreisverkehr *m*.

traffic island *n* Verkehrsinsel *f*.

traffic jam *n* Verkehrsstauung *f*, Stau *m*.

trafficker ['træfɪkə*] *n* Händler(in) *m(f)*.

traffic lights *npl* Ampel *f*.

traffic offence (*BRIT*) *n* Verkehrsdelikt *nt*.

traffic sign *n* Verkehrszeichen *nt*.

traffic violation (*US*) *n* = **traffic offence**.

traffic warden *n Verkehrspolizist für Parkvergehen*; (*woman*) ≈ Politesse *f*.

tragedy ['trædʒədɪ] *n* Tragödie *f*.

tragic ['trædʒɪk] *adj* tragisch.

tragically ['trædʒɪkəlɪ] *adv* tragisch.

trail [treɪl] *n* (*path*) Weg *m*; (*track*) Spur *f*; (*of smoke, dust*) Wolke *f* ♦ *vt* (*drag*) schleifen; (*follow*) folgen +*dat* ♦ *vi* (*hang loosely*) schleifen; (*in game, contest*) zurückliegen; **to be on sb's** ~ jdm auf der Spur sein.

▶**trail away** *vi* (*sound, voice*) sich verlieren.

▶**trail behind** *vi* hinterhertrotten.

▶**trail off** *vi* = **trail away**.

trailer ['treɪlə*] *n* (*AUT*) Anhänger *m*; (*US: caravan*) Caravan *m*, Wohnwagen *m*; (*CINE, TV*) Trailer *m*.

trailer truck (*US*) *n* Sattelschlepper *m*.

train [treɪn] *n* (*RAIL*) Zug *m*; (*of dress*) Schleppe *f* ♦ *vt* (*apprentice etc*) ausbilden; (*dog*) abrichten; (*athlete*) trainieren; (*mind*) schulen; (*plant*) ziehen; (*point: camera, gun etc*): **to** ~ **on** richten auf +*acc* ♦ *vi* (*learn a skill*) ausgebildet werden; (*SPORT*) trainieren; ~ **of thought** Gedankengang *m*; **to go by** ~ mit dem Zug fahren; ~ **of events** Ereignisfolge *f*; **to** ~ **sb to do sth** jdn dazu ausbilden, etw zu tun.

train attendant (*US*) *n* Schlafwagenschaffner *m*.

trained [treɪnd] *adj* (*worker*) gelernt; (*teacher*) ausgebildet; (*animal*) dressiert; (*eye*) geschult.

trainee [treɪ'niː] *n* Auszubildende(r) *f(m)*.

trainer ['treɪnə*] *n* (*SPORT: coach*) Trainer(in) *m(f)*; (: *shoe*) Trainingsschuh *m*; (*of animals*) Dresseur(in) *m(f)*.

training ['treɪnɪŋ] *n* (*for occupation*) Ausbildung *f*; (*SPORT*) Training *nt*; **in** ~ (*SPORT*) im Training.

training college *n* (*for teachers*) ≈ Pädagogische Hochschule *f*.

training course *n* Ausbildungskurs *m*.

traipse [treɪps] *vi*: **to** ~ **in/out** hinein-/herauslatschen.

trait [treɪt] *n* Zug *m*, Eigenschaft *f*.

traitor ['treɪtə*] *n* Verräter(in) *m(f)*.

trajectory [trə'dʒɛktərɪ] *n* Flugbahn *f*.

tram [træm] (*BRIT*) *n* (*also*: ~**car**) Straßenbahn *f*.

tramline ['træmlaɪn] *n* Straßenbahnschiene *f*.

tramp [træmp] *n* Landstreicher *m*; (*pej: woman*) Flittchen *nt* ♦ *vi* stapfen ♦ *vt* (*walk through: town, streets*) latschen durch.

trample ['træmpl] *vt*: **to** ~ (**underfoot**) niedertrampeln ♦ *vi* (*also fig*): **to** ~ **on** herumtrampeln auf +*dat*.

trampoline ['træmpəliːn] *n* Trampolin *nt*.

trance [trɑːns] *n* Trance *f*; **to go into a** ~ in Trance verfallen.

tranquil ['træŋkwɪl] *adj* ruhig, friedlich.

tranquillity, (*US*) **tranquility** [træŋ'kwɪlɪtɪ] *n* Ruhe *f*.

tranquillizer, (*US*) **tranquilizer** ['træŋkwɪlaɪzə*] *n* Beruhigungsmittel *nt*.

transact [træn'zækt] *vt* (*business*) abwickeln.

transaction [træn'zækʃən] *n* Geschäft *nt*; **cash** ~ Bargeldtransaktion *f*.

transatlantic ['trænzət'læntɪk] *adj* transatlantisch; (*phone-call*) über den Atlantik.

transcend [træn'sɛnd] *vt* überschreiten.

transcendental [trænsɛn'dɛntl] *adj*: ~ **meditation** transzendentale Meditation *f*.

transcribe [træn'skraɪb] *vt* transkribieren.

transcript ['trænskrɪpt] n Niederschrift f, Transkription f.

transcription [træn'skrɪpʃən] n Transkription f.

transept ['trænsept] n Querschiff nt.

transfer ['trænsfə'] n (of employees) Versetzung f; (of money) Überweisung f; (of power) Übertragung f; (SPORT) Transfer m; (picture, design) Abziehbild nt ♦ vt (employees) versetzen; (money) überweisen; (power, ownership) übertragen; **by bank ~** per Banküberweisung; **to ~ the charges** (BRIT: TEL) ein R-Gespräch führen.

transferable [træns'fə:rəbl] adj übertragbar; "not ~" „nicht übertragbar".

transfix [træns'fɪks] vt aufspießen; **~ed with fear** (fig) starr vor Angst.

transform [træns'fɔ:m] vt umwandeln.

transformation [trænsfə'meɪʃən] n Umwandlung f.

transformer [træns'fɔ:mə'] n (ELEC) Transformator m.

transfusion [træns'fju:ʒən] n (also: blood ~) Bluttransfusion f.

transgress [træns'gres] vt (go beyond) überschreiten; (violate: rules, law) verletzen.

transient ['trænzɪənt] adj vorübergehend.

transistor [træn'zɪstə'] n (ELEC) Transistor m; (also: ~ radio) Transistorradio nt.

transit ['trænzɪt] n: **in ~** unterwegs.

transit camp n Durchgangslager nt.

transition [træn'zɪʃən] n Übergang m.

transitional [træn'zɪʃənl] adj (period, stage) Übergangs-.

transitive ['trænzɪtɪv] adj (verb) transitiv.

transit lounge n Transithalle f.

transitory ['trænzɪtərɪ] adj (emotion, arrangement etc) vorübergehend.

transit visa n Transitvisum nt.

translate [trænz'leɪt] vt übersetzen; **to ~ (from/into)** übersetzen (aus/in +acc).

translation [trænz'leɪʃən] n Übersetzung f; **in ~** als Übersetzung.

translator [trænz'leɪtə'] n Übersetzer(in) m(f).

translucent [trænz'lu:snt] adj (object) lichtdurchlässig.

transmission [trænz'mɪʃən] n (also TV) Übertragung f; (of information) Übermittlung f; (AUT) Getriebe nt.

transmit [trænz'mɪt] vt (also TV) übertragen; (message, signal) übermitteln.

transmitter [trænz'mɪtə'] n (TV, RADIO) Sender m.

transparency [træns'pɛərnsɪ] n (of glass etc) Durchsichtigkeit f; (BRIT: PHOT) Dia nt.

transparent [træns'pærnt] adj durchsichtig; (fig: obvious) offensichtlich.

transpire [træns'paɪə'] vi (turn out) bekannt werden; (happen) passieren; **it finally ~d that ...** schließlich sickerte durch, daß ...

transplant [vt træns'plɑ:nt, n 'trɑ:nsplɑ:nt] vt (organ, seedlings) verpflanzen ♦ n (MED)

Transplantation f; **to have a heart ~** sich einer Herztransplantation unterziehen.

transport ['trænspɔ:t] n Transport m, Beförderung f ♦ vt transportieren; **do you have your own ~?** haben Sie ein Auto?; **public ~** öffentliche Verkehrsmittel pl; **Department of T~** (BRIT) Verkehrsministerium nt.

transportation ['trænspɔ:'teɪʃən] n Transport m, Beförderung f; (means of transport) Beförderungsmittel nt; **Department of T~** (US) Verkehrsministerium nt.

transport café (BRIT) n Fernfahrerlokal nt.

transpose [træns'pəuz] vt versetzen.

transsexual [trænz'seksuəl] adj transsexuell ♦ n Transsexuelle(r) f(m).

transverse ['trænzvə:s] adj (beam etc) Quer-.

transvestite [trænz'vestaɪt] n Transvestit m.

trap [træp] n (also fig) Falle f; (carriage) zweirädriger Pferdewagen m ♦ vt (animal) (mit einer Falle) fangen; (person: trick) in die Falle locken; (: confine) gefangen halten; (immobilize) festsetzen; (capture: energy) stauen; **to set** or **lay a ~ (for sb)** (jdm) eine Falle stellen; **to shut one's ~** (inf) die Klappe halten; **to ~ one's finger in the door** sich dat den Finger in der Tür einklemmen.

trap door n Falltür f.

trapeze [trə'pi:z] n Trapez nt.

trapper ['træpə'] n Fallensteller m, Trapper m.

trappings ['træpɪŋz] npl äußere Zeichen pl; (of power) Insignien pl.

trash [træʃ] n (rubbish) Abfall m, Müll m; (pej: nonsense) Schund m, Mist m.

trash can (US) n Mülleimer m.

trashy ['træʃɪ] adj (goods) minderwertig, wertlos; (novel etc) Schund-.

trauma ['trɔ:mə] n Trauma nt.

traumatic [trɔ:'mætɪk] adj traumatisch.

traumatize ['trɔ:mətaɪz] vt traumatisieren.

travel ['trævl] n (travelling) Reisen nt ♦ vi reisen; (short distance) fahren; (move: car, aeroplane) sich bewegen; (sound etc) sich fortpflanzen; (news) sich verbreiten ♦ vt (distance) zurücklegen; **travels** npl (journeys) Reisen pl; **this wine doesn't ~ well** dieser Wein verträgt den Transport nicht.

travel agency n Reisebüro nt.

travel agent n Reisebürokaufmann m, Reisebürokauffrau f.

travel brochure n Reiseprospekt m.

traveling etc (US) = **travelling** etc.

traveller, (US) **traveler** ['trævlə'] n Reisende(r) f(m); (COMM) Vertreter(in) m(f).

traveller's cheque, (US) **traveler's check** n Reisescheck m.

travelling, (US) **traveling** ['trævlɪŋ] n Reisen nt ♦ cpd (circus, exhibition) Wander-; (bag, clock) Reise-; **~ expenses** Reisespesen pl.

travelling salesman n Vertreter m.

travelogue ['trævəlɔg] n Reisebericht m.

travel sickness n Reisekrankheit f.

traverse ['trævəs] *vt* durchqueren.
travesty ['trævəstɪ] *n* Travestie *f*.
trawler ['trɔːlə*] *n* Fischdampfer *m*.
tray [treɪ] *n* (*for carrying*) Tablett *nt*; (*also:* **in-**
~**/out-**~: *on desk*) Ablage *f* für Eingänge/
Ausgänge.
treacherous ['trɛtʃərəs] *adj* (*person, look*)
verräterisch; (*ground, tide*) tückisch; **road**
conditions are ~ die Straßen sind in
gefährlichem Zustand.
treachery ['trɛtʃərɪ] *n* Verrat *m*.
treacle ['triːkl] *n* Sirup *m*.
tread [trɛd] (*pt* **trod**, *pp* **trodden**) *n* (*of tyre*)
Profil *nt*; (*footstep*) Schritt *m*; (*of stair*) Stufe *f*
♦ *vi* gehen.
►**tread on** *vt fus* treten auf +*acc*.
treadle ['trɛdl] *n* Pedal *nt*.
treas. *abbr* = **treasurer**.
treason ['triːzn] *n* Verrat *m*.
treasure ['trɛʒə*] *n* (*also fig*) Schatz *m* ♦ *vt*
schätzen; **treasures** *npl* (*art treasures etc*)
Schätze *pl*, Kostbarkeiten *pl*.
treasure hunt *n* Schatzsuche *f*.
treasurer ['trɛʒərə*] *n* Schatzmeister(in) *m(f)*.
treasury ['trɛʒərɪ] *n*: **the T**~, (*US*) **the**
T~ **Department** das Finanzministerium.
treasury bill *n* kurzfristiger Schatzwechsel
m.
treat [triːt] *n* (*present*) (besonderes)
Vergnügen *nt* ♦ *vt* (*also MED, TECH*)
behandeln; **it came as a** ~ es war eine
besondere Freude; **to** ~ **sth as a joke** etw
als Witz ansehen; **to** ~ **sb to sth** jdm etw
spendieren.
treatment ['triːtmənt] *n* Behandlung *f*; **to have**
~ **for sth** wegen etw in Behandlung sein.
treaty ['triːtɪ] *n* Vertrag *m*.
treble ['trɛbl] *adj* (*triple*) dreifach; (*MUS: voice,*
part) (Knaben)sopran-; (*instrument*) Diskant-
♦ *n* (*singer*) (Knaben)sopran *m*; (*on hi-fi, radio*
etc) Höhen *pl* ♦ *vt* verdreifachen ♦ *vi* sich
verdreifachen; **to be** ~ **the amount/size of**
sth dreimal soviel/so groß wie etw sein.
treble clef *n* Violinschlüssel *m*.
tree [triː] *n* Baum *m*.
tree-lined ['triːlaɪnd] *adj* baumbestanden.
treetop ['triːtɔp] *n* Baumkrone *f*.
tree trunk *n* Baumstamm *m*.
trek [trɛk] *n* Treck *m*; (*tiring walk*) Marsch *m*
♦ *vi* trecken.
trellis ['trɛlɪs] *n* Gitter *nt*.
tremble ['trɛmbl] *vi* (*voice, body, trees*) zittern;
(*ground*) beben.
trembling ['trɛmblɪŋ] *n* (*of ground*) Beben *nt*,
Erschütterung *f*; (*of trees*) Zittern *nt* ♦ *adj*
(*hand, voice etc*) zitternd.
tremendous [trɪ'mɛndəs] *adj* (*amount, success*
etc) gewaltig, enorm; (*holiday, view etc*)
phantastisch.
tremendously [trɪ'mɛndəslɪ] *adv* (*difficult,*
exciting) ungeheuer; **he enjoyed it** ~ es hat
ihm ausgezeichnet gefallen.

tremor ['trɛmə*] *n* Zittern *nt*; (*also:* **earth** ~)
Beben *nt*, Erschütterung *f*.
trench [trɛntʃ] *n* Graben *m*.
trench coat *n* Trenchcoat *m*.
trench warfare *n* Stellungskrieg *m*.
trend [trɛnd] *n* Tendenz *f*; (*fashion*) Trend *m*; **a**
~ **towards/away from sth** eine Tendenz zu/
weg von etw; **to set a/the** ~
richtungsweisend sein.
trendy ['trɛndɪ] *adj* modisch.
trepidation [trɛpɪ'deɪʃən] *n* (*apprehension*)
Beklommenheit *f*; **in** ~ beklommen.
trespass ['trɛspəs] *vi*: **to** ~ **on** (*private property*)
unbefugt betreten; **"no** ~**ing"** „Betreten
verboten".
trespasser ['trɛspəsə*] *n* Unbefugte(r) *f(m)*;
"~**s will be prosecuted"** „widerrechtliches
Betreten wird strafrechtlich verfolgt".
tress [trɛs] *n* (*of hair*) Locke *f*.
trestle ['trɛsl] *n* Bock *m*.
trestle table *n* Klapptisch *m*.
trial ['traɪəl] *n* (*LAW*) Prozeß *m*; (*test: of*
machine, drug etc) Versuch *m*; (*worry*) Plage *f*;
trials *npl* (*unpleasant experiences*)
Schwierigkeiten *pl*; ~ **by jury**
Schwurgerichtsverfahren *nt*; **to be sent for**
~ vor Gericht gestellt werden; **to be/go on**
~ (*LAW*) angeklagt sein/werden; **by** ~ **and**
error durch Ausprobieren.
trial balance *n* Probebilanz *f*.
trial basis *n*: **on a** ~ probeweise.
trial period *n* Probezeit *f*.
trial run *n* Versuch *m*.
triangle ['traɪæŋgl] *n* Dreieck *nt*; (*US: set*
square) (Zeichen)dreieck *nt*; (*MUS*) Triangel
f.
triangular [traɪ'æŋgjulə*] *adj* dreieckig.
triathlon [traɪ'æθlən] *n* Triathlon *nt*.
tribal ['traɪbl] *adj* (*warrior, warfare, dance*)
Stammes-.
tribe [traɪb] *n* Stamm *m*.
tribesman ['traɪbzmən] (*irreg: like* **man**) *n*
Stammesangehörige(r) *m*.
tribulations [trɪbju'leɪʃənz] *npl* Kümmernisse
pl.
tribunal [traɪ'bjuːnl] *n* Gericht *nt*.
tributary ['trɪbjutərɪ] *n* (*of river*) Nebenfluß *m*.
tribute ['trɪbjuːt] *n* Tribut *m*; **to pay** ~ **to**
Tribut zollen +*dat*.
trice [traɪs] *n*: **in a** ~ im Handumdrehen.
trick [trɪk] *n* Trick *m*; (*CARDS*) Stich *m* ♦ *vt*
hereinlegen; **to play a** ~ **on sb** jdm einen
Streich spielen; **it's a** ~ **of the light** das
Licht täuscht; **that should do the** ~ das
müßte hinhauen; **to** ~ **sb into doing sth** jdn
(mit einem Trick) dazu bringen, etw zu tun;
to ~ **sb out of sth** jdn um etw prellen.
trickery ['trɪkərɪ] *n* Tricks *pl*, Betrügerei *f*.
trickle ['trɪkl] *n* (*of water etc*) Rinnsal *nt* ♦ *vi*
(*water, rain etc*) rinnen; (*people*) sich
langsam bewegen.
trick photography *n* Trickfotografie *f*.

trick question *n* Fangfrage *f*.
trickster ['trɪkstə'] *n* Betrüger(in) *m(f)*.
tricky ['trɪkɪ] *adj* (*job, problem*) schwierig.
tricycle ['traɪsɪkl] *n* Dreirad *nt*.
trifle ['traɪfl] *n* (*detail*) Kleinigkeit *f*; (*CULIN*)
   Trifle *nt* ♦ *adv*: **a ~ long** ein bißchen lang ♦ *vi*:
   to ~ with sb/sth jdn/etw nicht ernst
   nehmen; **he is not (someone) to be ~d with**
   mit ihm ist nicht zu spaßen.
trifling ['traɪflɪŋ] *adj* (*detail*) unbedeutend.
trigger ['trɪgə'] *n* Abzug *m*.
▶**trigger off** *vt fus* auslösen.
trigonometry [trɪgə'nɒmətrɪ] *n*
   Trigonometrie *f*.
trilby ['trɪlbɪ] (*BRIT*) *n* (*also:* **~ hat**) Filzhut *m*.
trill [trɪl] *n* (*MUS*) Triller *m*; (*of birds*) Trillern
   nt.
trilogy ['trɪlədʒɪ] *n* Trilogie *f*.
trim [trɪm] *adj* (*house, garden*) gepflegt; (*figure,
   person*) schlank ♦ *n* (*haircut etc*): **to have a ~**
   sich *dat* die Haare nachschneiden lassen;
   (*on clothes, car*) Besatz *m* ♦ *vt* (*hair, beard*)
   nachschneiden; (*decorate*): **to ~ (with)**
   besetzen (mit); (*NAUT: a sail*) trimmen mit;
   to keep o.s. in (good) ~ (gut) in Form
   bleiben.
trimmings ['trɪmɪŋz] *npl* (*CULIN*): **with all the
   ~** mit allem Drum und Dran; (*cuttings: of
   pastry etc*) Reste *pl*.
Trinidad and Tobago ['trɪnɪdæd-] *n* Trinidad
   und Tobago *nt*.
trinity ['trɪnɪtɪ] *n* (*REL*) Dreieinigkeit *f*.
trinket ['trɪŋkɪt] *n* (*ornament*) Schmuckgegen-
   stand *m*; (*piece of jewellery*) Schmuckstück
   nt.
trio ['triːəu] *n* Trio *nt*.
trip [trɪp] *n* (*journey*) Reise *f*; (*outing*) Ausflug
   m ♦ *vi* (*stumble*) stolpern; (*go lightly*)
   trippeln; **on a ~** auf Reisen.
▶**trip over** *vt fus* stolpern über +*acc*.
▶**trip up** *vi* stolpern ♦ *vt* (*person*) zu Fall
   bringen.
tripartite [traɪ'pɑːtaɪt] *adj* (*agreement, talks*)
   dreiseitig.
tripe [traɪp] *n* (*CULIN*) Kaldaunen *pl*; (*pej:
   rubbish*) Stuß *m*.
triple ['trɪpl] *adj* dreifach ♦ *adv*: **~ the
   distance/the speed** dreimal so weit/schnell;
   ~ the amount dreimal soviel.
triple jump *n* Dreisprung *m*.
triplets ['trɪplɪts] *npl* Drillinge *pl*.
triplicate ['trɪplɪkət] *n*: **in ~** in dreifacher
   Ausfertigung.
tripod ['traɪpɒd] *n* (*PHOT*) Stativ *nt*.
Tripoli ['trɪpəlɪ] *n* Tripolis *nt*.
tripper ['trɪpə'] (*BRIT*) *n* Ausflügler(in) *m(f)*.
tripwire ['trɪpwaɪə'] *n* Stolperdraht *m*.
trite [traɪt] (*pej*) *adj* (*comment, idea etc*) banal.
triumph ['traɪʌmf] *n* Triumph *m* ♦ *vi*: **to
   ~ (over)** triumphieren (über +*acc*).
triumphal [traɪ'ʌmfl] *adj* (*return*) triumphal.
triumphant [traɪ'ʌmfənt] *adj* triumphal;

(*victorious*) siegreich.
triumphantly [traɪ'ʌmfəntlɪ] *adv*
   triumphierend.
trivia ['trɪvɪə] (*pej*) *npl* Trivialitäten *pl*.
trivial ['trɪvɪəl] *adj* trivial.
triviality [trɪvɪ'ælɪtɪ] *n* Trivialität *f*.
trivialize ['trɪvɪəlaɪz] *vt* trivialisieren.
trod [trɒd] *pt of* **tread**.
trodden [trɒdn] *pp of* **tread**.
trolley ['trɒlɪ] *n* (*for luggage*) Kofferkuli *m*; (*for
   shopping*) Einkaufswagen *m*; (*table on
   wheels*) Teewagen *m*; (*also:* **~ bus**)
   Oberleitungsomnibus *m*, Obus *m*.
trollop ['trɒləp] (*pej*) *n* (*woman*) Schlampe *f*.
trombone [trɒm'bəun] *n* Posaune *f*.
troop [truːp] *n* (*of people, monkeys etc*) Gruppe
   f ♦ *vi*: **to ~ in/out** hinein-/hinausströmen;
   troops *npl* (*MIL*) Truppen *pl*.
troop carrier *n* Truppentransporter *m*;
   (*NAUT: also:* **troopship**) Truppentransport-
   schiff *nt*.
trooper ['truːpə'] *n* (*MIL*) Kavallerist *m*; (*US:
   policeman*) Polizist *m*.
trooping the colour ['truːpɪŋ-] (*BRIT*) *n*
   (*ceremony*) Fahnenparade *f*.
troopship ['truːpʃɪp] *n* Truppentransport-
   schiff *nt*.
trophy ['trəufɪ] *n* Trophäe *f*.
tropic ['trɒpɪk] *n* Wendekreis *m*; **the tropics** *npl*
   die Tropen *pl*; **T~ of Cancer/Capricorn**
   Wendekreis des Krebses/Steinbocks.
tropical ['trɒpɪkl] *adj* tropisch.
trot [trɒt] *n* (*fast pace*) Trott *m*; (*of horse*) Trab
   m ♦ *vi* (*horse*) traben; (*person*) trotten; **on the
   ~** (*BRIT, fig*) hintereinander.
▶**trot out** *vt* (*facts, excuse etc*) vorbringen.
trouble ['trʌbl] *n* Schwierigkeiten *pl*; (*bother,
   effort*) Umstände *pl*; (*unrest*) Unruhen *pl* ♦ *vt*
   (*worry*) beunruhigen; (*disturb: person*)
   belästigen ♦ *vi*: **to ~ to do sth** sich *dat* die
   Mühe machen, etw zu tun; **troubles** *npl*
   (*personal*) Probleme *pl*; (*POL etc*) Unruhen *pl*;
   to be in ~ in Schwierigkeiten sein; **to have
   ~ doing sth** Schwierigkeiten *or* Probleme
   haben, etw zu tun; **to go to the ~ of doing
   sth** sich *dat* die Mühe machen, etw zu tun;
   it's no ~! das macht mir nichts aus!; **the
   ~ is ...** das Problem ist ...; **what's the ~?** wo
   fehlt's?; **stomach** *etc* **~** Probleme mit dem
   Magen *etc*; **please don't ~ yourself** bitte
   bemühen Sie sich nicht.
troubled [trʌbld] *adj* (*person*) besorgt;
   (*country, life, era*) von Problemen
   geschüttelt.
trouble-free ['trʌblfriː] *adj* problemlos.
troublemaker ['trʌblmeɪkə'] *n*
   Unruhestifter(in) *m(f)*.
troubleshooter ['trʌblʃuːtə'] *n* Vermittler(in)
   m(f).
troublesome ['trʌblsəm] *adj* (*child*) schwierig;
   (*cough etc*) lästig.
trouble spot *n* (*MIL*) Unruheherd *m*.

troubling ['trʌblɪŋ] adj (question etc)
beunruhigend.

trough [trɔf] n (also: **drinking** ~)
Wassertrog m; (also: **feeding** ~) Futtertrog
m; (channel) Rinne f; (low point) Tief nt; **a** ~
of low pressure ein Tiefdruckkeil m.

trounce [trauns] vt (defeat) vernichtend
schlagen.

troupe [truːp] n Truppe f.

trouser press ['trauzə-] n Hosenpresse f.

trousers ['trauzəz] npl Hose f; **short** ~ kurze
Hose; **a pair of** ~ eine Hose.

trouser suit (BRIT) n Hosenanzug m.

trousseau ['truːsəu] n (pl ~x or ~s) Aussteuer
f.

trout [traut] n inv Forelle f.

trowel ['trauəl] n (garden tool) Pflanzkelle f;
(builder's tool) (Maurer)kelle f.

truant ['truənt] (BRIT) n: **to play** ~ die Schule
schwänzen.

truce [truːs] n Waffenstillstand m.

truck [trʌk] n (lorry) Lastwagen m; (RAIL)
Güterwagen m; (for luggage) Gepäckwagen
m; **to have no** ~ **with sb** nichts mit jdm zu
tun haben.

truck driver n Lkw-Fahrer(in) m(f).

trucker ['trʌkə*] (US) n Lkw-Fahrer(in) m(f).

truck farm (US) n Gemüsefarm f.

trucking ['trʌkɪŋ] (US) n Transport m.

trucking company (US) n Spedition f.

truculent ['trʌkjulənt] adj aufsässig.

trudge [trʌdʒ] vi (also: ~ **along**) sich
dahinschleppen.

true [truː] adj wahr; (accurate) genau; (genuine)
echt; (faithful: friend) treu; (wall, beam)
gerade; (circle) rund; **to come** ~ wahr
werden; ~ **to life** lebensecht.

truffle ['trʌfl] n (fungus, sweet) Trüffel f.

truly ['truːlɪ] adv wahrhaft, wirklich;
(truthfully) wirklich; **yours** ~ (in letter) mit
freundlichen Grüßen.

trump [trʌmp] n (also: ~ **card**, also fig) Trumpf
m; **to turn up** ~s (fig) sich als Retter in der
Not erweisen.

trumped-up adj: **a** ~ **charge** eine erfundene
Anschuldigung.

trumpet ['trʌmpɪt] n Trompete f.

truncated [trʌŋ'keɪtɪd] adj (message, object)
verstümmelt.

truncheon ['trʌntʃən] (BRIT) n
Gummiknüppel m.

trundle ['trʌndl] vt (trolley etc) rollen ♦ vi: **to**
~ **along** (person) dahinschlendern; (vehicle)
dahinrollen.

trunk [trʌŋk] n (of tree) Stamm m; (of person)
Rumpf m; (of elephant) Rüssel m; (case)
Schrankkoffer m; (US: AUT) Kofferraum m;
trunks npl (also: **swimming** ~s) Badehose f.

trunk call (BRIT) n Ferngespräch nt.

trunk road (BRIT) n Fernstraße f.

truss [trʌs] n (MED) Bruchband nt.

▶**truss (up)** vt (CULIN) dressieren; (person)

fesseln.

trust [trʌst] n Vertrauen nt; (COMM: for charity
etc) Stiftung f ♦ vt vertrauen +dat; **to take sth
on** ~ (advice etc) etw einfach glauben; **to be
in** ~ (LAW) treuhänderisch verwaltet
werden; **to** ~ **(that)** (hope) hoffen(, daß).

trust company n Trust m.

trusted ['trʌstɪd] adj (friend, servant) treu.

trustee [trʌs'tiː] n (LAW) Treuhänder(in) m(f);
(of school etc) Aufsichtsratsmitglied nt.

trustful ['trʌstful] adj vertrauensvoll.

trust fund n Treuhandvermögen nt.

trusting ['trʌstɪŋ] adj vertrauensvoll.

trustworthy ['trʌstwɜːðɪ] adj (person)
vertrauenswürdig.

trusty ['trʌstɪ] adj getreu.

truth [truːθ] n (pl ~s) n: **the** ~ die Wahrheit f.

truthful ['truːθful] adj (person) ehrlich; (answer
etc) wahrheitsgemäß.

truthfully ['truːθfəlɪ] adv (answer)
wahrheitsgemäß.

truthfulness ['truːθfəlnɪs] n Ehrlichkeit f.

try [traɪ] n (also RUGBY) Versuch m ♦ vt
(attempt) versuchen; (test) probieren; (LAW)
vor Gericht stellen; (strain: patience) auf die
Probe stellen ♦ vi es versuchen; **to have a** ~
es versuchen, einen Versuch machen; **to**
~ **to do sth** versuchen, etw zu tun; **to**
~ **one's (very) best** or **hardest** sein Bestes
versuchen or tun.

▶**try on** vt (clothes) anprobieren; **she's** ~**ing it
on** (fig) sie probiert, wie weit sie gehen
kann.

▶**try out** vt ausprobieren.

trying ['traɪɪŋ] adj (person) schwierig;
(experience) schwer.

tsar [zɑː*] n Zar m.

T-shirt ['tiːʃəːt] n T-Shirt nt.

T-square ['tiːskwɛə*] n (TECH) Reißschiene f.

TT adj abbr (BRIT: inf) = **teetotal** ♦ abbr (US:
POST: = **Trust Territories**) der US-
Verwaltungshoheit unterstellte Gebiete.

tub [tʌb] n (container) Kübel m; (bath) Wanne f.

tuba ['tjuːbə] n Tuba f.

tubby ['tʌbɪ] adj rundlich.

tube [tjuːb] n (pipe) Rohr nt; (container) Tube f;
(BRIT: underground) U-Bahn f; (US: inf): **the** ~
(television) die Röhre.

tubeless ['tjuːblɪs] adj (tyre) schlauchlos.

tuber ['tjuːbə*] n (BOT) Knolle f.

tuberculosis [tjubɜːkju'ləusɪs] n Tuberkulose
f.

tube station (BRIT) n U-Bahn-Station f.

tubing ['tjuːbɪŋ] n Schlauch m; **a piece of** ~
ein Schlauch.

tubular ['tjuːbjulə*] adj röhrenförmig.

TUC (BRIT) n abbr (= **Trades Union Congress**)
britischer Gewerkschafts-Dachverband.

tuck [tʌk] vt (put) stecken ♦ n (SEWING) Biese
f.

▶**tuck away** vt (money) wegstecken; **to be**
~**ed away** (building) versteckt liegen.

►**tuck in** vt (*clothing*) feststecken; (*child*) zudecken ♦ vi (*eat*) zulangen.
►**tuck up** vt (*invalid, child*) zudecken.
tuck shop n Süßwarenladen m.
Tue(s). abbr (= *Tuesday*) Di.
Tuesday ['tjuːzdɪ] n Dienstag m; **it is ~ 23rd March** heute ist Dienstag, der 23. März; **on ~** am Dienstag; **on ~s** dienstags; **every ~** jeden Dienstag; **every other ~** jeden zweiten Dienstag; **last/next ~** letzten/ nächsten Dienstag; **the following ~** am Dienstag darauf; **~'s newspaper** die Zeitung von Dienstag; **a week/fortnight on ~** Dienstag in einer Woche/in vierzehn Tagen; **the ~ before last** der vorletzte Dienstag; **the ~ after next** der übernächste Dienstag; **~ morning/lunchtime/afternoon/ evening** Dienstag morgen/mittag/ nachmittag/abend; **~ night** (*overnight*) Dienstag nacht.
tuft [tʌft] n Büschel nt.
tug [tʌg] n (*ship*) Schlepper m ♦ vt zerren.
tug of love n Tauziehen nt (*um das Sorgerecht für Kinder*).
tug-of-war [tʌgəv'wɔːʳ] n (*also fig*) Tauziehen nt.
tuition [tjuː'ɪʃən] n (*BRIT*) Unterricht m; (*US: school fees*) Schulgeld nt.
tulip ['tjuːlɪp] n Tulpe f.
tumble ['tʌmbl] n (*fall*) Sturz m ♦ vi (*fall*) stürzen.
►**tumble to** (*inf*) vt fus kapieren.
tumbledown ['tʌmbldaun] adj (*building*) baufällig.
tumble dryer (*BRIT*) n Wäschetrockner m.
tumbler ['tʌmbləʳ] n (*glass*) Trinkglas nt.
tummy ['tʌmɪ] (*inf*) n Bauch m.
tumour, (*US*) **tumor** ['tjuːməʳ] n (*MED*) Tumor m, Geschwulst f.
tumult ['tjuːmʌlt] n Tumult m.
tumultuous [tjuː'mʌltjuəs] adj (*welcome, applause etc*) stürmisch.
tuna ['tjuːnə] n inv (*also:* **~ fish**) Thunfisch m.
tune [tjuːn] n (*melody*) Melodie f ♦ vt (*MUS*) stimmen; (*RADIO, TV, AUT*) einstellen; **to be in/out of ~** (*instrument*) richtig gestimmt/ verstimmt sein; (*singer*) richtig/falsch singen; **to be in/out of ~ with** (*fig*) in Einklang/nicht in Einklang stehen mit; **she was robbed to the ~ of 10,000 pounds** sie wurde um einen Betrag in Höhe von 10.000 Pfund beraubt.
►**tune in** vi (*RADIO, TV*) einschalten; **to ~ in to BBC1** BBC1 einschalten.
►**tune up** vi (*MUS*) (das Instrument/die Instrumente) stimmen.
tuneful ['tjuːnful] adj melodisch.
tuner ['tjuːnəʳ] n: **piano ~** Klavierstimmer(in) m(f); (*radio set*) Tuner m.
tuner amplifier n Steuergerät nt.
tungsten ['tʌŋstən] n Wolfram nt.
tunic ['tjuːnɪk] n Hemdbluse f.

tuning fork ['tjuːnɪŋ-] n Stimmgabel f.
Tunis ['tjuːnɪs] n Tunis nt.
Tunisia [tjuː'nɪzɪə] n Tunesien nt.
Tunisian [tjuː'nɪzɪən] adj tunesisch ♦ n (*person*) Tunesier(in) m(f).
tunnel ['tʌnl] n Tunnel m; (*in mine*) Stollen m ♦ vi einen Tunnel bauen.
tunnel vision n (*MED*) Gesichtsfeld- einengung f; (*fig*) Engstirnigkeit f.
tunny ['tʌnɪ] n Thunfisch m.
turban ['təːbən] n Turban m.
turbid ['təːbɪd] adj (*water*) trüb; (*air*) schmutzig.
turbine ['təːbaɪn] n Turbine f.
turbo ['təːbəu] n Turbo m; **~ engine** Turbomotor m.
turbojet [təːbəu'dʒɛt] n Düsenflugzeug nt.
turboprop [təːbəu'prɔp] n (*engine*) Turbo- Prop-Turbine f.
turbot ['təːbət] n inv Steinbutt m.
turbulence ['təːbjuləns] n (*AVIAT*) Turbulenz f.
turbulent ['təːbjulənt] adj (*water, seas*) stürmisch; (*fig: career, period*) turbulent.
tureen [tə'riːn] n Terrine f.
turf [təːf] n (*grass*) Rasen m; (*clod*) Sode f ♦ vt (*area*) mit Grassoden bedecken; **the T~** (*horse-racing*) der Pferderennsport.
►**turf out** (*inf*) vt (*person*) rausschmeißen.
turf accountant (*BRIT*) n Buchmacher m.
turgid ['təːdʒɪd] adj geschwollen.
Turin ['tjuə'rɪn] n Turin nt.
Turk [təːk] n Türke m, Türkin f.
Turkey ['təːkɪ] n die Türkei f.
turkey ['təːkɪ] n (*bird*) Truthahn m, Truthenne f; (*meat*) Puter m.
Turkish ['təːkɪʃ] adj türkisch ♦ n (*LING*) Türkisch nt.
Turkish bath n türkisches Bad nt.
Turkish delight n geleeartige Süßigkeit, mit Puderzucker oder Schokolade überzogen.
turmeric ['təːmərɪk] n Kurkuma f.
turmoil ['təːmɔɪl] n Aufruhr m; **in ~** in Aufruhr.
turn [təːn] n (*change*) Wende f; (*in road*) Kurve f; (*rotation*) Drehung f; (*performance*) Nummer f; (*inf: MED*) Anfall m ♦ vt (*handle, key*) drehen; (*collar, steak*) wenden; (*page*) umblättern; (*shape: wood*) drechseln; (: *metal*) drehen ♦ vi (*object*) sich drehen; (*person*) sich umdrehen; (*change direction*) abbiegen; (*milk*) sauer werden; **to do sb a good ~** jdm einen guten Dienst erweisen; **a ~ of events** eine Wendung der Dinge; **it gave me quite a ~** (*inf*) das hat mir einen schönen Schrecken eingejagt; **"no left ~"** (*AUT*) „Linksabbiegen verboten"; **it's your ~** du bist dran; **in ~** der Reihe nach; **to take ~s (at)** sich abwechseln (bei); **at the ~ of the century/year** zur Jahrhundertwende/ Jahreswende; **to take a ~ for the worse** (*events*) sich zum Schlechten wenden; **his**

health *or* he has taken a ~ for the worse sein Befinden hat sich verschlechtert; **to ~ nasty/forty/grey** unangenehm/vierzig/grau werden.

▶**turn against** *vt fus* sich wenden gegen.

▶**turn around** *vi* sich umdrehen; (*in car*) wenden.

▶**turn away** *vi* sich abwenden ♦ *vt* (*applicants*) abweisen; (*business*) zurückweisen.

▶**turn back** *vi* umkehren ♦ *vt* (*person, vehicle*) zurückweisen.

▶**turn down** *vt* (*request*) ablehnen; (*heating*) kleiner stellen; (*radio etc*) leiser stellen; (*bedclothes*) aufschlagen.

▶**turn in** *vi* (*inf: go to bed*) sich hinhauen ♦ *vt* (*to police*) anzeigen; **to ~ o.s. in** sich stellen.

▶**turn into** *vt fus* (*change*) sich verwandeln in +*acc* ♦ *vt* machen zu.

▶**turn off** *vi* (*from road*) abbiegen ♦ *vt* (*light, radio etc*) ausmachen; (*tap*) zudrehen; (*engine*) abstellen.

▶**turn on** *vt* (*light, radio etc*) anmachen; (*tap*) aufdrehen; (*engine*) anstellen.

▶**turn out** *vt* (*light*) ausmachen; (*gas*) abstellen ♦ *vi* (*appear, attend*) erscheinen; **to ~ out to be** (*prove to be*) sich erweisen als; **to ~ out well/badly** (*situation*) gut/schlecht enden.

▶**turn over** *vi* (*person*) sich umdrehen ♦ *vt* (*object*) umdrehen, wenden; (*page*) umblättern; **to ~ sth over to** (*to sb*) etw übertragen +*dat*; (*to sth*) etw verlagern zu.

▶**turn round** *vi* sich umdrehen; (*vehicle*) wenden.

▶**turn up** *vi* (*person*) erscheinen; (*lost object*) wieder auftauchen ♦ *vt* (*collar*) hochklappen; (*heater*) höher stellen; (*radio etc*) lauter stellen.

turnabout ['tə:nəbaut] *n* (*fig*) Kehrtwendung *f*.

turnaround ['tə:nəraund] *n* = **turnabout**.

turncoat ['tə:nkəut] *n* Überläufer(in) *m(f)*.

turned-up ['tə:ndʌp] *adj:* ~ **nose** Stupsnase *f*.

turning ['tə:nıŋ] *n* (*in road*) Abzweigung *f*; **the first ~ on the right** die erste Straße rechts.

turning circle (*BRIT*) *n* (*AUT*) Wendekreis *m*.

turning point *n* (*fig*) Wendepunkt *m*.

turning radius (*US*) *n* = **turning circle**.

turnip ['tə:nıp] *n* Rübe *f*.

turnout ['tə:naut] *n* (*of voters etc*) Beteiligung *f*.

turnover ['tə:nəuvə•] *n* (*COMM: amount of money*) Umsatz *m*; (: *of staff*) Fluktuation *f*; (*CULIN*): **apple ~** Apfeltasche *f*; **there is a rapid ~ in staff** der Personalbestand wechselt ständig.

turnpike ['tə:npaık] (*US*) *n* gebührenpflichtige Autobahn *f*.

turnstile ['tə:nstaıl] *n* Drehkreuz *nt*.

turntable ['tə:nteıbl] *n* (*on record player*) Plattenteller *m*.

turn-up ['tə:nʌp] (*BRIT*) *n* (*on trousers*) Aufschlag *m*; **that's a ~ for the books!** (*inf*) das ist eine echte Überraschung!

turpentine ['tə:pəntaın] *n* (*also:* **turps**) Terpentin *nt*.

turquoise ['tə:kwɔız] *n* (*stone*) Türkis *m* ♦ *adj* (*colour*) türkis.

turret ['tʌrıt] *n* Turm *m*.

turtle ['tə:tl] *n* Schildkröte *f*.

turtleneck (sweater) ['tə:tlnɛk(-)] *n* Pullover *m* mit rundem Kragen.

Tuscan ['tʌskən] *adj* toskanisch ♦ *n* (*person*) Toskaner(in) *m(f)*.

Tuscany ['tʌskənı] *n* die Toskana.

tusk [tʌsk] *n* (*of elephant*) Stoßzahn *m*.

tussle ['tʌsl] *n* Gerangel *nt*.

tutor ['tju:tə•] *n* Tutor(in) *m(f)*; (*private tutor*) Privatlehrer(in) *m(f)*.

tutorial [tju:'tɔ:rıəl] *n* Kolloquium *nt*.

tuxedo [tʌk'si:dəu] (*US*) *n* Smoking *m*.

TV [ti:'vi:] *n abbr* (= *television*) TV *nt*.

TV dinner *n* Fertiggericht *nt*.

twaddle ['twɔdl] (*inf*) *n* dummes Zeug *nt*.

twang [twæŋ] *n* (*of instrument*) singender Ton *m*; (*of voice*) näselnder Ton *m* ♦ *vi* einen singenden Ton von sich geben ♦ *vt* (*guitar*) zupfen.

tweak [twi:k] *vt* kneifen.

tweed [twi:d] *n* Tweed *m* ♦ *adj* (*jacket, skirt*) Tweed-.

tweezers ['twi:zəz] *npl* Pinzette *f*.

twelfth [twɛlfθ] *num* zwölfte(r, s) ♦ *n* Zwölftel *nt*.

Twelfth Night *n* ≈ Dreikönige *nt*.

twelve [twɛlv] *num* zwölf; **at ~ (o'clock)** (*midday*) um zwölf Uhr (mittags); (*midnight*) um zwölf Uhr nachts.

twentieth ['twɛntııθ] *num* zwanzigste(r, s).

twenty ['twɛntı] *num* zwanzig.

twerp [twə:p] (*inf*) *n* Schwachkopf *m*.

twice [twaıs] *adv* zweimal; **~ as much** zweimal soviel; **~ a week** zweimal die Woche; **she is ~ your age** sie ist doppelt so alt wie du.

twiddle ['twıdl] *vt* drehen an +*dat* ♦ *vi:* **to ~ (with)** herumdrehen (an +*dat*); **to ~ one's thumbs** (*fig*) Däumchen drehen.

twig [twıg] *n* Zweig *m* ♦ *vi, vt* (*BRIT: inf: realize*) kapieren.

twilight ['twaılaıt] *n* Dämmerung *f*; **in the ~** in der Dämmerung.

twill [twıl] *n* (*cloth*) Köper *m*.

twin [twın] *adj* (*sister, brother*) Zwillings-; (*towers*) Doppel- ♦ *n* Zwilling *m*; (*room in hotel etc*) Zweibettzimmer *nt* ♦ *vt* (*towns etc*): **to be ~ned with ... ...** als Partnerstadt haben.

twin-bedded room ['twın'bɛdıd-] *n* Zweibettzimmer *nt*.

twin beds *npl* zwei (gleiche) Einzelbetten *pl*.

twin-carburettor ['twınkɑ:bju'rɛtə•] *adj* Doppelvergaser-.

twine [twaɪn] n Bindfaden m ♦ vi sich winden.
twin-engined [twɪn'ɛndʒɪnd] adj zweimotorig.
twinge [twɪndʒ] n (of pain) Stechen nt; a ~ of conscience Gewissensbisse pl; a ~ of fear/guilt ein Angst-/Schuldgefühl nt.
twinkle ['twɪŋkl] vi funkeln ♦ n Funkeln nt.
twin town n Partnerstadt f.
twirl [twəːl] vt herumwirbeln ♦ vi wirbeln ♦ n Wirbel m.
twist [twɪst] n (action) Drehung f; (in road) Kurve; (in coil, flex) Biegung f; (in story) Wendung f ♦ vt (turn) drehen; (injure: ankle etc) verrenken; (twine) wickeln; (fig: meaning etc) verdrehen ♦ vi (road, river) sich winden; ~ my arm! (inf) überreden Sie mich einfach!
twisted ['twɪstɪd] adj (wire, rope) gedreht; (ankle) verrenkt; (fig: logic, mind) verdreht.
twit [twɪt] (inf) n Trottel m.
twitch [twɪtʃ] n (jerky movement) Zucken nt ♦ vi zucken.
two [tuː] num zwei; ~ by ~, in ~s zu zweit; to put ~ and ~ together (fig) zwei und zwei zusammenzählen.
two-bit [tuːˈbɪt] (inf) adj (worthless) mies.
two-door [tuːˈdɔː] adj zweitürig.
two-faced [tuːˈfeɪst] (pej) adj scheinheilig.
twofold ['tuːfəʊld] adv: to increase ~ um das Doppelte ansteigen ♦ adj (increase) um das Doppelte; (aim, value etc) zweifach.
two-piece (suit) ['tuːpiːs-] n Zweiteiler m.
two-piece (swimsuit) n zweiteiliger Badeanzug m.
two-ply ['tuːplaɪ] adj (wool) zweifädig; (tissues) zweilagig.
two-seater ['tuːˈsiːtə] n (car) Zweisitzer m.
twosome ['tuːsəm] n (people) Paar nt.
two-stroke ['tuːstrəʊk] n (also: ~ engine) Zweitakter m ♦ adj (engine) Zweitakt-.
two-tone ['tuːtəʊn] adj (in colour) zweifarbig.
two-way ['tuːweɪ] adj: ~ traffic Verkehr m in beiden Richtungen; ~ radio Funksprechgerät nt.
TX (US) abbr (POST: = Texas).
tycoon [taɪˈkuːn] n Magnat m.
type [taɪp] n (category, model, example) Typ m; (TYP) Schrift f ♦ vt (letter etc) tippen, mit der Maschine schreiben; a ~ of eine Art von; what ~ do you want? welche Sorte möchten Sie?; in bold/italic ~ in Fett-/Kursivdruck.
typecast ['taɪpkɑːst] (irreg: like cast) vt (actor) (auf eine Rolle) festlegen.
typeface ['taɪpfeɪs] n Schrift f, Schriftbild nt.
typescript ['taɪpskrɪpt] n (maschinen-geschriebenes) Manuskript nt.
typeset ['taɪpset] (irreg: like set) vt setzen.
typesetter ['taɪpsetə] n Setzer(in) m(f).
typewriter ['taɪpraɪtə] n Schreibmaschine f.
typewritten ['taɪprɪtn] adj maschine(n)-geschrieben.
typhoid ['taɪfɔɪd] n Typhus m.

typhoon [taɪˈfuːn] n Taifun m.
typhus ['taɪfəs] n Fleckfieber nt.
typical ['tɪpɪkl] adj typisch; ~ (of) typisch (für); that's ~! das ist typisch!
typify ['tɪpɪfaɪ] vt typisch sein für.
typing ['taɪpɪŋ] n Maschine(n)schreiben nt.
typing error n Tippfehler m.
typing pool n Schreibzentrale f.
typist ['taɪpɪst] n Schreibkraft f.
typo ['taɪpəʊ] (inf) n abbr (= typographical error) Druckfehler m.
typography [tɪˈpɒɡrəfɪ] n Typographie f.
tyranny ['tɪrənɪ] n Tyrannei f.
tyrant ['taɪərnt] n Tyrann(in) m(f).
tyre, (US) **tire** ['taɪə] n Reifen m.
tyre pressure n Reifendruck m.
Tyrol [tɪˈrəʊl] n Tirol nt.
Tyrolean [tɪrəˈliːən] adj Tiroler ♦ n (person) Tiroler(in) m(f).
Tyrolese [tɪrəˈliːz] = **Tyrolean.**
Tyrrhenian Sea [tɪˈriːnɪən-] n: the ~ das Tyrrhenische Meer.
tzar [zɑː] n = **tsar.**

U, u

U¹, u [juː] n (letter) U nt, u nt; ~ for Uncle ≈ U wie Ulrich.
U² [juː] (BRIT) n abbr (CINE: = universal) Klassifikation für jugendfreie Filme.
UAW (US) n abbr (= United Automobile Workers) Automobilarbeitergewerkschaft.
UB40 (BRIT) n abbr (= unemployment benefit form 40) Arbeitslosenausweis m.
U-bend ['juːbend] n (in pipe) U-Krümmung f.
ubiquitous [juːˈbɪkwɪtəs] adj allgegenwärtig.
UCCA ['ʌkə] (BRIT) n abbr (= Universities Central Council on Admissions) akademische Zulassungsstelle, ≈ ZVS f.
UDA (BRIT) n abbr (= Ulster Defence Association) paramilitärische protestantische Organisation in Nordirland.
UDC (BRIT) n abbr (= Urban District Council) Stadtverwaltung f.
udder ['ʌdə] n Euter nt.
UDI (BRIT) n abbr (POL: = unilateral declaration of independence) einseitige Unabhängig-keitserklärung f.
UDR (BRIT) n abbr (= Ulster Defence Regiment) Regiment aus Teilzeitsoldaten zur Unterstützung der britischen Armee und Polizei in Nordirland.
UEFA [juːˈeɪfə] n abbr (= Union of European Football Associations) UEFA f.
UFO ['juːfəʊ] n abbr (= unidentified flying object)

Ufo nt.

Uganda [juːˈgændə] n Uganda nt.

Ugandan [juːˈgændən] adj ugandisch ♦ n Ugander(in) m(f).

UGC (BRIT) n abbr (= University Grants Committee) Ausschuß zur Verteilung von Geldern an Universitäten.

ugh [əːh] excl igitt.

ugliness [ˈʌglɪnɪs] n Häßlichkeit f.

ugly [ˈʌglɪ] adj häßlich; (nasty) schlimm.

UHF abbr (= ultrahigh frequency) UHF.

UHT abbr (= ultra heat treated): ~ **milk** H-Milch f.

UK n abbr = United Kingdom.

Ukraine [juːˈkreɪn] n Ukraine f.

Ukrainian [juːˈkreɪnɪən] adj ukrainisch ♦ n Ukrainer(in) m(f); (LING) Ukrainisch nt.

ulcer [ˈʌlsə*] n (stomach ulcer etc) Geschwür nt; (also: mouth ~) Abszeß m im Mund.

Ulster [ˈʌlstə*] n Ulster nt.

ulterior [ʌlˈtɪərɪə*] adj: ~ **motive** Hintergedanke m.

ultimata [ʌltɪˈmeɪtə] npl of **ultimatum**.

ultimate [ˈʌltɪmət] adj (final) letztendlich; (greatest) größte(r, s); (: deterrent) äußerste(r, s); (: authority) höchste(r, s) ♦ n: **the** ~ **in luxury** das Äußerste or Höchste an Luxus.

ultimately [ˈʌltɪmətlɪ] adv (in the end) schließlich, letzten Endes; (basically) im Grunde (genommen).

ultimatum [ʌltɪˈmeɪtəm] (pl ~s or ultimata) n Ultimatum nt.

ultrasonic [ʌltrəˈsɒnɪk] adj (sound) Ultraschall-.

ultrasound [ˈʌltrəsaund] n Ultraschall m.

ultraviolet [ˈʌltrəˈvaɪəlɪt] adj ultraviolett.

umbilical cord [ʌmˈbɪlɪkl-] n Nabelschnur f.

umbrage [ˈʌmbrɪdʒ] n: **to take** ~ **at** Anstoß nehmen an +dat.

umbrella [ʌmˈbrelə] n (for rain) (Regen)schirm m; (for sun) Sonnenschirm m; (fig): **under the** ~ **of** unter der Leitung von.

umlaut [ˈumlaut] n Umlaut m; (mark) Umlautzeichen nt.

umpire [ˈʌmpaɪə*] n Schiedsrichter(in) m(f) ♦ vt (game) als Schiedsrichter leiten.

umpteen [ʌmpˈtiːn] adj zig.

umpteenth [ʌmpˈtiːnθ] adj: **for the** ~ **time** zum x-ten Mal.

UMWA n abbr (= United Mineworkers of America) amerikanische Bergarbeitergewerkschaft.

UN n abbr (= United Nations) UNO f.

unabashed [ʌnəˈbæʃt] adj: **to be/seem** ~ unbeeindruckt sein/scheinen.

unabated [ʌnəˈbeɪtɪd] adj unvermindert ♦ adv: **to continue** ~ nicht nachlassen.

unable [ʌnˈeɪbl] adj: **to be** ~ **to do sth** etw nicht tun können.

unabridged [ʌnəˈbrɪdʒd] adj ungekürzt.

unacceptable [ʌnəkˈsɛptəbl] adj unannehmbar, nicht akzeptabel.

unaccompanied [ʌnəˈkʌmpənɪd] adj (child, song) ohne Begleitung; (luggage) unbegleitet.

unaccountably [ʌnəˈkauntəblɪ] adv unerklärlich.

unaccounted [ʌnəˈkauntɪd] adj: **to be** ~ **for** (passengers, money etc) (noch) fehlen.

unaccustomed [ʌnəˈkʌstəmd] adj: **to be** ~ **to** nicht gewöhnt sein an +acc.

unacquainted [ʌnəˈkweɪntɪd] adj: **to be** ~ **with** nicht vertraut sein mit.

unadulterated [ʌnəˈdʌltəreɪtɪd] adj rein.

unaffected [ʌnəˈfɛktɪd] adj (person, behaviour) natürlich, ungekünstelt; **to be** ~ **by sth** von etw nicht berührt werden.

unafraid [ʌnəˈfreɪd] adj: **to be** ~ keine Angst haben.

unaided [ʌnˈeɪdɪd] adv ohne fremde Hilfe.

unanimity [juːnəˈnɪmɪtɪ] n Einstimmigkeit f.

unanimous [juːˈnænɪməs] adj einstimmig.

unanimously [juːˈnænɪməslɪ] adv einstimmig.

unanswered [ʌnˈɑːnsəd] adj unbeantwortet.

unappetizing [ʌnˈæpɪtaɪzɪŋ] adj (food) unappetitlich.

unappreciative [ʌnəˈpriːʃɪətɪv] adj (person) undankbar; (audience) verständnislos.

unarmed [ʌnˈɑːmd] adj unbewaffnet; ~ **combat** Nahkampf m ohne Waffen.

unashamed [ʌnəˈʃeɪmd] adj (pleasure, greed etc) unverhohlen.

unassisted [ʌnəˈsɪstɪd] adv ohne fremde Hilfe.

unassuming [ʌnəˈsjuːmɪŋ] adj bescheiden.

unattached [ʌnəˈtætʃt] adj (single: person) ungebunden; (unconnected) ohne Verbindung.

unattended [ʌnəˈtɛndɪd] adj (car, luggage, child) unbeaufsichtigt.

unattractive [ʌnəˈtræktɪv] adj unattraktiv.

unauthorized [ʌnˈɔːθəraɪzd] adj (visit, use) unbefugt; (version) nicht unautorisiert.

unavailable [ʌnəˈveɪləbl] adj (article, room) nicht verfügbar; (person) nicht zu erreichen; ~ **for comment** nicht zu sprechen.

unavoidable [ʌnəˈvɔɪdəbl] adj unvermeidlich.

unavoidably [ʌnəˈvɔɪdəblɪ] adv (delayed etc) auf unvermeidliche Weise.

unaware [ʌnəˈwɛə*] adj: **he was** ~ **of it** er war sich dat dessen nicht bewußt.

unawares [ʌnəˈwɛəz] adv (catch, take) unerwartet.

unbalanced [ʌnˈbælənst] adj (report) unausgewogen; (mentally) ~ geistig gestört.

unbearable [ʌnˈbɛərəbl] adj unerträglich.

unbeatable [ʌnˈbiːtəbl] adj unschlagbar.

unbeaten [ʌnˈbiːtn] adj ungeschlagen.

unbecoming [ʌnbɪˈkʌmɪŋ] adj (language, behaviour) unpassend; (garment) unvorteilhaft.

unbeknown(st) [ʌnbɪˈnəun(st)] adv: ~ **to me/**

Peter ohne mein/Peters Wissen.

unbelief [ʌnbɪ'liːf] n Ungläubigkeit f.

unbelievable [ʌnbɪ'liːvəbl] adj unglaublich.

unbelievably [ʌnbɪ'liːvəblɪ] adv unglaublich.

unbend [ʌn'bend] (irreg: like bend) vi (relax) aus sich herausgehen ♦ vt (wire etc) geradebiegen.

unbending [ʌn'bendɪŋ] adj (person, attitude) unnachgiebig.

unbias(s)ed [ʌn'baɪəst] adj unvoreingenommen.

unblemished [ʌn'blemɪʃt] adj (also fig) makellos.

unblock [ʌn'blɒk] vt (pipe) frei machen.

unborn [ʌn'bɔːn] adj ungeboren.

unbounded [ʌn'baundɪd] adj grenzenlos.

unbreakable [ʌn'breɪkəbl] adj (object) unzerbrechlich.

unbridled [ʌn'braɪdld] adj ungezügelt.

unbroken [ʌn'brəukən] adj (seal) unversehrt; (silence) ununterbrochen; (record, series) ungebrochen.

unbuckle [ʌn'bʌkl] vt aufschnallen.

unburden [ʌn'bɜːdn] vt: to ~ o.s. (to sb) (jdm) sein Herz ausschütten.

unbusinesslike [ʌn'bɪznɪslaɪk] adj ungeschäftsmäßig.

unbutton [ʌn'bʌtn] vt aufknöpfen.

uncalled-for [ʌn'kɔːldfɔːʳ] adj (remark etc) unnötig.

uncanny [ʌn'kænɪ] adj unheimlich.

unceasing [ʌn'siːsɪŋ] adj (search, flow etc) unaufhörlich; (loyalty) unermüdlich.

unceremonious [ʌnserɪ'məunɪəs] adj (abrupt, rude) brüsk, barsch.

uncertain [ʌn'sɜːtn] adj (person) unsicher; (future, outcome) ungewiß; to be ~ about sth unsicher über etw acc sein; in no ~ terms unzweideutig.

uncertainty [ʌn'sɜːtntɪ] n Ungewißheit f; uncertainties npl (doubts) Unsicherheiten pl.

unchallenged [ʌn'tʃælɪndʒd] adj unbestritten ♦ adv (walk, enter) ungehindert; to go ~ unangefochten bleiben.

unchanged [ʌn'tʃeɪndʒd] adj unverändert.

uncharitable [ʌn'tʃærɪtəbl] adj (remark, behaviour etc) unfreundlich.

uncharted [ʌn'tʃɑːtɪd] adj (land, sea) unverzeichnet.

unchecked [ʌn'tʃekt] adv (grow, continue) ungehindert.

uncivil [ʌn'sɪvɪl] adj (person) grob.

uncivilized [ʌn'sɪvɪlaɪzd] adj unzivilisiert.

uncle ['ʌŋkl] n Onkel m.

unclear [ʌn'klɪəʳ] adj unklar; I'm still ~ about what I'm supposed to do mir ist immer noch nicht klar, was ich tun soll.

uncoil [ʌn'kɔɪl] vt (rope, wire) abwickeln ♦ vi (snake) sich strecken.

uncomfortable [ʌn'kʌmfətəbl] adj (person, chair) unbequem; (room) ungemütlich; (nervous) unbehaglich; (unpleasant: situation, fact) unerfreulich.

uncomfortably [ʌn'kʌmfətəblɪ] adv (sit) unbequem; (smile) unbehaglich.

uncommitted [ʌnkə'mɪtɪd] adj nicht engagiert; ~ to nicht festgelegt auf +acc.

uncommon [ʌn'kɒmən] adj ungewöhnlich.

uncommunicative [ʌnkə'mjuːnɪkətɪv] adj (person) schweigsam.

uncomplicated [ʌn'kɒmplɪkeɪtɪd] adj unkompliziert.

uncompromising [ʌn'kɒmprəmaɪzɪŋ] adj (person, belief) kompromißlos.

unconcerned [ʌnkən'sɜːnd] adj (person) unbekümmert; to be ~ about sth sich nicht um etw kümmern.

unconditional [ʌnkən'dɪʃənl] adj bedingungslos; (acceptance) vorbehaltlos.

uncongenial [ʌnkən'dʒiːnɪəl] adj (surroundings) unangenehm.

unconnected [ʌnkə'nɛktɪd] adj (unrelated) ohne Verbindung; to be ~ with sth nicht mit etw in Beziehung stehen.

unconscious [ʌn'kɒnʃəs] adj (in faint) bewußtlos; (unaware): ~ of nicht bewußt +gen ♦ n: the ~ das Unbewußte; to knock sb ~ jdn bewußtlos schlagen.

unconsciously [ʌn'kɒnʃəslɪ] adv unbewußt.

unconsciousness [ʌn'kɒnʃəsnɪs] n Bewußtlosigkeit f.

unconstitutional ['ʌnkɒnstɪ'tjuːʃənl] adj verfassungswidrig.

uncontested [ʌnkən'tɛstɪd] adj (POL: seat, election) ohne Gegenkandidat; (divorce) ohne Einwände der Gegenseite.

uncontrollable [ʌnkən'trəuləbl] adj unkontrollierbar; (laughter) unbändig.

uncontrolled [ʌnkən'trəuld] adj (behaviour) ungezähmt; (price rises etc) ungehindert.

unconventional [ʌnkən'vɛnʃənl] adj unkonventionell.

unconvinced [ʌnkən'vɪnst] adj: to be/remain ~ nicht überzeugt sein/bleiben.

unconvincing [ʌnkən'vɪnsɪŋ] adj nicht überzeugend.

uncork [ʌn'kɔːk] vt (bottle) entkorken.

uncorroborated [ʌnkə'rɒbəreɪtɪd] adj (evidence) unbestätigt.

uncouth [ʌn'kuːθ] adj (person, behaviour) ungehobelt.

uncover [ʌn'kʌvəʳ] vt aufdecken.

unctuous ['ʌŋktjuəs] (form) adj (person, behaviour) salbungsvoll.

undamaged [ʌn'dæmɪdʒd] adj unbeschädigt.

undaunted [ʌn'dɔːntɪd] adj (person) unverzagt; ~, she struggled on sie kämpfte unverzagt weiter.

undecided [ʌndɪ'saɪdɪd] adj (person) unentschlossen; (question) unentschieden.

undelivered [ʌndɪ'lɪvəd] adj (goods) nicht geliefert; (letters) nicht zugestellt; if ~ return to sender (on envelope) falls unzustellbar, zurück an Absender.

undeniable [ʌndɪˈnaɪəbl] *adj* unbestreitbar.
undeniably [ʌndɪˈnaɪəblɪ] *adv* (*true*)
zweifellos; (*handsome*) unbestreitbar.
under [ˈʌndə*] *prep* (*position*) unter +dat;
(*motion*) unter +acc; (*according to: law etc*)
nach, gemäß +dat ♦ *adv* (*go, fly etc*) darunter;
to come from ~ **sth** unter etw *dat*
hervorkommen; ~ **there** darunter; **in** ~ **2**
hours in weniger als 2 Stunden;
~ **anaesthetic** unter Narkose; **to be**
~ **discussion** diskutiert werden; ~ **repair** in
Reparatur; ~ **the circumstances** unter den
Umständen. .
under... [ˈʌndə*] *pref* Unter-, unter-.
underage [ʌndərˈeɪdʒ] *adj* (*person*)
minderjährig; ~ **drinking** Alkoholgenuß
durch Minderjährige.
underarm [ˈʌndərɑːm] *adv* (*bowl, throw*) von
unten ♦ *adj* (*throw, shot*) von unten;
(*deodorant*) Achselhöhlen-.
undercapitalized [ˈʌndəˈkæpɪtəlaɪzd] *adj*
unterkapitalisiert.
undercarriage [ˈʌndəkærɪdʒ] *n* (*AVIAT*)
Fahrgestell *nt*.
undercharge [ʌndəˈtʃɑːdʒ] *vt* zu wenig
berechnen +dat.
underclass [ˈʌndəklɑːs] *n* Unterklasse *f*.
underclothes [ˈʌndəkləuðz] *npl* Unterwäsche
f.
undercoat [ˈʌndəkəut] *n* (*paint*) Grundierung
f.
undercover [ʌndəˈkʌvə*] *adj* (*duty, agent*)
Geheim- ♦ *adv* (*work*) insgeheim.
undercurrent [ˈʌndəkʌrnt] *n* (*also fig*)
Unterströmung *f*.
undercut [ʌndəˈkʌt] (*irreg: like* cut) *vt* (*person,
prices*) unterbieten.
underdeveloped [ˈʌndədɪˈveləpt] *adj*
unterentwickelt.
underdog [ˈʌndədɒg] *n:* **the** ~ der/die
Benachteiligte.
underdone [ʌndəˈdʌn] *adj* (*food*) nicht gar;
(: *meat*) nicht durchgebraten.
underemployment [ˈʌndərɪmˈplɔɪmənt] *n*
Unterbeschäftigung *f*.
underestimate [ˈʌndərˈestɪmeɪt] *vt*
unterschätzen.
underexposed [ˈʌndərɪksˈpəuzd] *adj* (*PHOT*)
unterbelichtet.
underfed [ʌndəˈfed] *adj* unterernährt.
underfoot [ʌndəˈfut] *adv:* **to crush sth** ~ etw
am Boden zerdrücken; **to trample sth** ~ auf
etw *dat* herumtrampeln.
underfunded [ˈʌndəˈfʌndɪd] *adj*
unterfinanziert.
undergo [ʌndəˈgəu] (*irreg: like* go) *vt* (*change*)
durchmachen; (*test, operation*) sich
unterziehen; **the car is** ~**ing repairs** das
Auto wird gerade repariert.
undergraduate [ʌndəˈgrædjuɪt] *n* Student(in)
m(f) ♦ *cpd:* ~ **courses** Kurse *pl* für
nichtgraduierte Studenten.

underground [ˈʌndəgraund] *adj* unterirdisch;
(*POL: newspaper, activities*) Untergrund- ♦ *adv*
(*work*) unterirdisch; (: *miners*) unter Tage;
(*POL*): **to go** ~ untertauchen ♦ *n:* **the** ~
(*BRIT*) die U-Bahn; (*POL*) die
Untergrundbewegung; ~ **car park**
Tiefgarage *f*.
undergrowth [ˈʌndəgrəuθ] *n* Unterholz *nt*.
underhand(ed) [ʌndəˈhænd(ɪd)] *adj* (*fig:
behaviour, person*) hinterhältig.
underinsured [ʌndərɪnˈʃuəd] *adj*
unterversichert.
underlay [ˈʌndəˈleɪ] *n* Unterlage *f*.
underlie [ʌndəˈlaɪ] (*irreg: like* lie) *vt* (*fig: be basis
of*) zugrunde liegen +dat; **the underlying
cause** der eigentliche Grund.
underline [ʌndəˈlaɪn] *vt* unterstreichen; (*fig:
emphasize*) betonen.
underling [ˈʌndəlɪŋ] (*pej*) *n* Befehls-
empfänger(in) *m(f)*.
undermanning [ʌndəˈmænɪŋ] *n*
Personalmangel *m*.
undermentioned [ʌndəˈmenʃənd] *adj*
untengenannt.
undermine [ʌndəˈmaɪn] *vt* unterminieren,
unterhöhlen.
underneath [ʌndəˈniːθ] *adv* darunter ♦ *prep*
(*position*) unter +dat; (*motion*) unter +acc.
undernourished [ʌndəˈnʌrɪʃt] *adj*
unterernährt.
underpaid [ʌndəˈpeɪd] *adj* unterbezahlt.
underpants [ˈʌndəpænts] *npl* Unterhose *f*.
underpass [ˈʌndəpɑːs] (*BRIT*) *n* Unterführung
f.
underpin [ʌndəˈpɪn] *vt* (*argument*)
untermauern.
underplay [ʌndəˈpleɪ] (*BRIT*) *vt*
herunterspielen.
underpopulated [ʌndəˈpɒpjuleɪtɪd] *adj*
unterbevölkert.
underprice [ʌndəˈpraɪs] *vt* (*goods*) zu billig
anbieten.
underprivileged [ʌndəˈprɪvɪlɪdʒd] *adj*
unterprivilegiert.
underrate [ʌndəˈreɪt] *vt* unterschätzen.
underscore [ʌndəˈskɔː*] *vt* unterstreichen.
underseal [ʌndəˈsiːl] (*BRIT*) *vt* (*car*) mit
Unterbodenschutz versehen ♦ *n* (*of car*)
Unterbodenschutz *m*.
undersecretary [ʌndəˈsekrətərɪ] *n* (*POL*)
Staatssekretär(in) *m(f)*.
undersell [ʌndəˈsel] (*irreg: like* sell) *vt*
(*competitors*) unterbieten.
undershirt [ˈʌndəʃɜːt] (*US*) *n* Unterhemd *nt*.
undershorts [ˈʌndəʃɔːts] (*US*) *npl* Unterhose *f*.
underside [ˈʌndəsaɪd] *n* Unterseite *f*.
undersigned [ˈʌndəˈsaɪnd] *adj* unterzeichnet
♦ *n:* **the** ~ der/die Unterzeichnete; **we the**
~ **agree that ...** wir, die Unterzeichneten,
kommen überein, daß ...
underskirt [ˈʌndəskɜːt] (*BRIT*) *n* Unterrock *m*.
understaffed [ʌndəˈstɑːft] *adj* unterbesetzt.

understand [ʌndə'stænd] (*irreg: like* **stand**) *vt, vi*
verstehen; **I ~ (that) you have ...** (*believe*)
soweit ich weiß, haben Sie ...; **to make o.s.**
understood sich verständlich machen.

understandable [ʌndə'stændəbl] *adj*
verständlich.

understanding [ʌndə'stændɪŋ] *adj*
verständnisvoll ♦ *n* Verständnis *nt*; **to come**
to an ~ with sb mit jdm übereinkommen;
on the ~ that ... unter der Voraussetzung,
daß ...

understate [ʌndə'steɪt] *vt* herunterspielen.

understatement ['ʌndəsteɪtmənt] *n*
Understatement *nt*, Untertreibung *f*; **that's**
an ~! das ist untertrieben!

understood [ʌndə'stud] *pt, pp of* **understand**
♦ *adj* (*agreed*) abgemacht; (*implied*)
impliziert.

understudy ['ʌndəstʌdɪ] *n* zweite Besetzung *f*.

undertake [ʌndə'teɪk] (*irreg: like* **take**) *vt* (*task*)
übernehmen ♦ *vi:* **to ~ to do sth** es
übernehmen, etw zu tun.

undertaker ['ʌndəteɪkə*] *n* (Leichen)bestatter
m.

undertaking ['ʌndəteɪkɪŋ] *n* (*job*)
Unternehmen *nt*; (*promise*) Zusicherung *f*.

undertone ['ʌndətəun] *n* (*of criticism etc*)
Unterton *m*; **in an ~** mit gedämpfter
Stimme.

undervalue [ʌndə'vælju:] *vt* (*person, work etc*)
unterbewerten.

underwater ['ʌndə'wɔːtə*] *adv* (*swim etc*)
unter Wasser ♦ *adj* (*exploration, camera etc*)
Unterwasser-.

underwear ['ʌndəwɛə*] *n* Unterwäsche *f*.

underweight [ʌndə'weɪt] *adj:* **to be ~**
Untergewicht haben.

underworld ['ʌndəwə:ld] *n* Unterwelt *f*.

underwrite [ʌndə'raɪt] *vt* (*FIN*) garantieren;
(*INSURANCE*) versichern.

underwriter ['ʌndəraɪtə*] *n* (*INSURANCE*)
Versicherer(in) *m(f)*.

undeserved [ʌndɪ'zə:vd] *adj* unverdient.

undesirable [ʌndɪ'zaɪərəbl] *adj* unerwünscht.

undeveloped [ʌndɪ'vɛləpt] *adj* (*land*)
unentwickelt; (*resources*) ungenutzt.

undies ['ʌndɪz] (*inf*) *npl* Unterwäsche *f*.

undiluted ['ʌndaɪ'lu:tɪd] *adj* (*substance*)
unverdünnt; (*emotion*) unverfälscht.

undiplomatic ['ʌndɪplə'mætɪk] *adj*
undiplomatisch.

undischarged ['ʌndɪs'tʃɑːdʒd] *adj:* **~ bankrupt**
nicht entlasteter Konkursschuldner *m*,
nicht entlastete Konkursschuldnerin *f*.

undisciplined [ʌn'dɪsɪplɪnd] *adj*
undiszipliniert.

undiscovered ['ʌndɪs'kʌvəd] *adj* unentdeckt.

undisguised ['ʌndɪs'gaɪzd] *adj* (*dislike,*
amusement etc) unverhohlen.

undisputed ['ʌndɪs'pju:tɪd] *adj* unbestritten.

undistinguished ['ʌndɪs'tɪŋgwɪʃt] *adj* (*career,*
person) mittelmäßig; (*appearance*)
durchschnittlich.

undisturbed [ʌndɪs'tə:bd] *adj* ungestört; **to**
leave sth ~ etw unberührt lassen.

undivided [ʌndɪ'vaɪdɪd] *adj:* **you have my**
~ attention Sie haben meine ungeteilte
Aufmerksamkeit.

undo [ʌn'du:] (*irreg: like* **do**) *vt* (*unfasten*)
aufmachen; (*spoil*) zunichte machen.

undoing [ʌn'du:ɪŋ] *n* Verderben *nt*.

undone [ʌn'dʌn] *pp of* **undo** ♦ *adj:* **to come ~**
(*shoelaces etc*) aufgehen.

undoubted [ʌn'dautɪd] *adj* unzweifelhaft.

undoubtedly [ʌn'dautɪdlɪ] *adv* zweifellos.

undress [ʌn'drɛs] *vi* sich ausziehen ♦ *vt*
ausziehen.

undrinkable [ʌn'drɪŋkəbl] *adj* (*unpalatable*)
ungenießbar; (*poisonous*) nicht trinkbar.

undue [ʌn'dju:] *adj* (*excessive*) übertrieben.

undulating ['ʌndjuleɪtɪŋ] *adj* (*movement*)
Wellen-; (*hills*) sanft.

unduly [ʌn'dju:lɪ] *adv* (*excessively*) übermäßig.

undying [ʌn'daɪɪŋ] *adj* (*love, loyalty etc*) ewig.

unearned [ʌn'ə:nd] *adj* (*praise*) unverdient;
~ income Kapitaleinkommen *nt*.

unearth [ʌn'ə:θ] *vt* (*skeleton etc*) ausgraben;
(*fig: secrets etc*) ausfindig machen.

unearthly [ʌn'ə:θlɪ] *adj* (*eerie*) unheimlich; **at**
some ~ hour zu nachtschlafender Zeit.

unease [ʌn'i:z] *n* Unbehagen *nt*.

uneasy [ʌn'i:zɪ] *adj* (*person*) unruhig; (*feeling*)
unbehaglich; (*peace, truce*) unsicher; **to feel**
~ about doing sth ein ungutes Gefühl dabei
haben, etw zu tun.

uneconomic ['ʌni:kə'nɒmɪk] *adj*
unwirtschaftlich.

uneconomical ['ʌni:kə'nɒmɪkl] *adj*
unwirtschaftlich.

uneducated [ʌn'ɛdjukeɪtɪd] *adj* ungebildet.

unemployed [ʌnɪm'plɔɪd] *adj* arbeitslos ♦ *npl:*
the ~ die Arbeitslosen *pl*.

unemployment [ʌnɪm'plɔɪmənt] *n*
Arbeitslosigkeit *f*.

unemployment benefit (*BRIT*) *n*
Arbeitslosenunterstützung *f*.

unemployment compensation (*US*) *n*
= **unemployment benefit**.

unending [ʌn'ɛndɪŋ] *adj* endlos.

unenviable [ʌn'ɛnvɪəbl] *adj* (*task, conditions*
etc) wenig beneidenswert.

unequal [ʌn'i:kwəl] *adj* ungleich; **to feel ~ to**
sich nicht gewachsen fühlen +*dat*.

unequalled, (*US*) **unequaled** [ʌn'i:kwəld] *adj*
unübertroffen.

unequivocal [ʌnɪ'kwɪvəkl] *adj* (*answer*)
unzweideutig; **to be ~ about sth** eine klare
Haltung zu etw haben.

unerring [ʌn'ə:rɪŋ] *adj* unfehlbar.

UNESCO [ju:'nɛskəu] *n abbr* (= *United Nations*
Educational, Scientific and Cultural
Organization) UNESCO *f*.

unethical [ʌn'ɛθɪkl] *adj* (*methods*) unlauter;
(*doctor's behaviour*) unethisch.

uneven [ʌn'iːvn] *adj* (*teeth, road etc*) uneben; (*performance*) ungleichmäßig.

uneventful [ʌnɪ'ventful] *adj* ereignislos.

unexceptional [ʌnɪk'sepʃənl] *adj* durchschnittlich.

unexciting [ʌnɪk'saɪtɪŋ] *adj* (*film, news*) wenig aufregend.

unexpected [ʌnɪks'pektɪd] *adj* unerwartet.

unexpectedly [ʌnɪks'pektɪdlɪ] *adv* unerwartet.

unexplained [ʌnɪks'pleɪnd] *adj* (*mystery, failure*) ungeklärt.

unexploded [ʌnɪks'pləʊdɪd] *adj* nicht explodiert.

unfailing [ʌn'feɪlɪŋ] *adj* (*support, energy*) unerschöpflich.

unfair [ʌn'feə*] *adj* unfair, ungerecht; (*advantage*) ungerechtfertigt; ~ **to** unfair *or* ungerecht zu.

unfair dismissal *n* ungerechtfertigte Entlassung *f*.

unfairly [ʌn'feəlɪ] *adv* (*treat*) unfair, ungerecht; (*dismiss*) ungerechtfertigt.

unfaithful [ʌn'feɪθful] *adj* (*lover, spouse*) untreu.

unfamiliar [ʌnfə'mɪlɪə*] *adj* ungewohnt; (*person*) fremd; **to be** ~ **with sth** mit etw nicht vertraut sein.

unfashionable [ʌn'fæʃnəbl] *adj* (*clothes, ideas*) unmodern; (*place*) unbeliebt.

unfasten [ʌn'fɑːsn] *vt* (*seat belt, strap*) lösen.

unfathomable [ʌn'fæðəməbl] *adj* unergründlich.

unfavourable, (US) unfavorable [ʌn'feɪvrəbl] *adj* (*circumstances, weather*) ungünstig; (*opinion, report*) negativ.

unfavourably, (US) unfavorably [ʌn'feɪvrəblɪ] *adv*: **to compare** ~ **(with sth)** im Vergleich (mit etw) ungünstig sein; **to compare** ~ **(with sb)** im Vergleich (mit jdm) schlechter abschneiden; **to look** ~ **on** (*suggestion etc*) ablehnend gegenüberstehen +*dat*.

unfeeling [ʌn'fiːlɪŋ] *adj* gefühllos.

unfinished [ʌn'fɪnɪʃt] *adj* unvollendet.

unfit [ʌn'fɪt] *adj* (*physically*) nicht fit; (*incompetent*) unfähig; ~ **for work** arbeitsunfähig; ~ **for human consumption** zum Verzehr ungeeignet.

unflagging [ʌn'flægɪŋ] *adj* (*attention, energy*) unermüdlich.

unflappable [ʌn'flæpəbl] *adj* unerschütterlich.

unflattering [ʌn'flætərɪŋ] *adj* (*dress, hairstyle*) unvorteilhaft; (*remark*) wenig schmeichelhaft.

unflinching [ʌn'flɪntʃɪŋ] *adj* unerschrocken.

unfold [ʌn'fəʊld] *vt* (*sheets, map*) auseinanderfalten ♦ *vi* (*situation, story*) sich entfalten.

unforeseeable [ʌnfɔː'siːəbl] *adj* unvorhersehbar.

unforeseen ['ʌnfɔː'siːn] *adj* unvorhergesehen.

unforgettable [ʌnfə'getəbl] *adj* unvergeßlich.

unforgivable [ʌnfə'gɪvəbl] *adj* unverzeihlich.

unformatted [ʌn'fɔːmætɪd] *adj* (*disk, text*) unformatiert.

unfortunate [ʌn'fɔːtʃənət] *adj* (*unlucky*) unglücklich; (*regrettable*) bedauerlich; **it is** ~ **that** ... es ist bedauerlich, daß ...

unfortunately [ʌn'fɔːtʃənətlɪ] *adv* leider.

unfounded [ʌn'faʊndɪd] *adj* (*allegations, fears*) unbegründet.

unfriendly [ʌn'frendlɪ] *adj* unfreundlich.

unfulfilled [ʌnful'fɪld] *adj* (*ambition, prophecy*) unerfüllt; (*person*) unausgefüllt.

unfurl [ʌn'fɜːl] *vt* (*flag etc*) entrollen.

unfurnished [ʌn'fɜːnɪʃt] *adj* unmöbliert.

ungainly [ʌn'geɪnlɪ] *adj* (*person*) unbeholfen.

ungodly [ʌn'gɒdlɪ] *adj* (*annoying*) heillos; **at some** ~ **hour** zu nachtschlafender Zeit.

ungrateful [ʌn'greɪtful] *adj* undankbar.

unguarded [ʌn'gɑːdɪd] *adj*: **in an** ~ **moment** in einem unbedachten Augenblick.

unhappily [ʌn'hæpɪlɪ] *adv* (*miserably*) unglücklich; (*unfortunately*) leider.

unhappiness [ʌn'hæpɪnɪs] *n* Traurigkeit *f*.

unhappy [ʌn'hæpɪ] *adj* unglücklich; ~ **about/with** (*dissatisfied*) unzufrieden über +*acc*/mit.

unharmed [ʌn'hɑːmd] *adj* (*person, animal*) unversehrt.

UNHCR *n abbr* (= *United Nations High Commission for Refugees*) Flüchtlingskommission der Vereinten Nationen.

unhealthy [ʌn'helθɪ] *adj* (*person*) nicht gesund; (*place*) ungesund; (*fig: interest*) krankhaft.

unheard-of [ʌn'hɜːdɒv] *adj* (*unknown*) unbekannt; (*outrageous*) unerhört.

unhelpful [ʌn'helpful] *adj* (*person*) nicht hilfreich; (*advice*) nutzlos.

unhesitating [ʌn'hezɪteɪtɪŋ] *adj* (*loyalty*) bereitwillig; (*reply, offer*) prompt.

unholy [ʌn'həʊlɪ] (*inf*) *adj* (*fig: alliance*) übel; (: *mess*) heillos; (: *row*) furchtbar.

unhook [ʌn'hʊk] *vt* (*unfasten*) losmachen.

unhurt [ʌn'hɜːt] *adj* unverletzt.

unhygienic ['ʌnhaɪ'dʒiːnɪk] *adj* unhygienisch.

UNICEF ['juːnɪsef] *n abbr* (= *United Nations International Children's Emergency Fund*) UNICEF *f*.

unicorn ['juːnɪkɔːn] *n* Einhorn *nt*.

unidentified [ʌnaɪ'dentɪfaɪd] *adj* (*unknown*) unbekannt; (*unnamed*) ungenannt; *see also* UFO.

unification [juːnɪfɪ'keɪʃən] *n* Vereinigung *f*.

uniform ['juːnɪfɔːm] *n* Uniform *f* ♦ *adj* (*length, width etc*) einheitlich.

uniformity [juːnɪ'fɔːmɪtɪ] *n* Einheitlichkeit *f*.

unify ['juːnɪfaɪ] *vt* vereinigen.

unilateral [juːnɪ'lætərəl] *adj* einseitig.

unimaginable [ʌnɪ'mædʒɪnəbl] *adj* unvorstellbar.

unimaginative [ʌnɪ'mædʒɪnətɪv] *adj* phantasielos.

unimpaired [ʌnɪm'pɛəd] *adj* unbeeinträchtigt.
unimportant [ʌnɪm'pɔːtənt] *adj* unwichtig.
unimpressed [ʌnɪm'prɛst] *adj* unbeeindruckt.
uninhabited [ʌnɪn'hæbɪtɪd] *adj* unbewohnt.
uninhibited [ʌnɪn'hɪbɪtɪd] *adj* (*person*) ohne
Hemmungen; (*behaviour*) hemmungslos.
uninjured [ʌn'ɪndʒəd] *adj* unverletzt.
uninspiring [ʌnɪn'spaɪərɪŋ] *adj* wenig
aufregend; (*person*) trocken, nüchtern.
unintelligent [ʌnɪn'tɛlɪdʒənt] *adj*
unintelligent.
unintentional [ʌnɪn'tɛnʃənəl] *adj*
unbeabsichtigt.
unintentionally [ʌnɪn'tɛnʃnəlɪ] *adv*
unabsichtlich.
uninvited [ʌnɪn'vaɪtɪd] *adj* (*guest*) ungeladen.
uninviting [ʌnɪn'vaɪtɪŋ] *adj* (*food*)
unappetitlich; (*place*) wenig einladend.
union ['juːnjən] *n* (*unification*) Vereinigung *f*;
(*also*: **trade** ~) Gewerkschaft *f* ♦ *cpd*
(*activities, leader etc*) Gewerkschafts-; **the
U~** (*US*) die Vereinigten Staaten.
unionize ['juːnjənaɪz] *vt* (*employees*)
gewerkschaftlich organisieren.
Union Jack *n* Union Jack *m*.
union shop *n* gewerkschaftspflichtiger
Betrieb *m*.
unique [juː'niːk] *adj* (*object etc*) einmalig;
(*ability, skill*) einzigartig; **to be ~ to**
charakteristisch sein für.
unisex ['juːnɪsɛks] *adj* (*clothes*) Unisex-;
(*hairdresser*) für Damen und Herren.
UNISON ['juːnɪsn] *n Gewerkschaft der
Angestellten im öffentlichen Dienst.*
unison ['juːnɪsn] *n:* **in ~** (*say, sing*)
einstimmig; (*act*) in Übereinstimmung.
unit ['juːnɪt] *n* Einheit *f*; **production ~**
Produktionsabteilung *f*; **kitchen ~** Küchen-
Einbauelement *nt*.
unitary ['juːnɪtrɪ] *adj* (*state, system etc*)
einheitlich.
unit cost *n* (*COMM*) Stückkosten *pl*.
unite [juː'naɪt] *vt* vereinigen ♦ *vi* sich
zusammenschließen.
united [juː'naɪtɪd] *adj* (*agreed*) einig; (*country,
party*) vereinigt.
United Arab Emirates *npl:* **the ~** die
Vereinigten Arabischen Emirate *pl*.
United Kingdom *n:* **the ~** das Vereinigte
Königreich.
United Nations *npl:* **the ~** die Vereinten
Nationen *pl*.
United States (of America) *n:* **the ~** die
Vereinigten Staaten *pl* (von Amerika).
unit price *n* (*COMM*) Einzelpreis *m*.
unit trust (*BRIT*) *n* (*COMM*) Investmenttrust
m.
unity ['juːnɪtɪ] *n* Einheit *f*.
Univ. *abbr* = **university.**
universal [juːnɪ'vɜːsl] *adj* allgemein.
universe ['juːnɪvɜːs] *n* Universum *nt*.
university [juːnɪ'vɜːsɪtɪ] *n* Universität *f* ♦ *cpd*

(*student, professor*) Universitäts-; (*education,
year*) akademisch.
university degree *n* Universitätsabschluß *m*.
unjust [ʌn'dʒʌst] *adj* ungerecht; (*society*)
unfair.
unjustifiable ['ʌndʒʌstɪ'faɪəbl] *adj* nicht zu
rechtfertigen.
unjustified [ʌn'dʒʌstɪfaɪd] *adj* (*belief, action*)
ungerechtfertigt; (*text*) nicht bündig.
unkempt [ʌn'kɛmpt] *adj* ungepflegt.
unkind [ʌn'kaɪnd] *adj* (*person, comment etc*)
unfreundlich.
unkindly [ʌn'kaɪndlɪ] *adv* unfreundlich.
unknown [ʌn'nəʊn] *adj* unbekannt; **~ to me,
...** ohne daß ich es wußte, ...; **~ quantity** (*fig*)
unbekannte Größe.
unladen [ʌn'leɪdn] *adj* (*ship*) ohne Ladung;
(*weight*) Leer-.
unlawful [ʌn'lɔːful] *adj* gesetzwidrig.
unleaded ['ʌn'lɛdɪd] *adj* (*petrol*) bleifrei,
unverbleit; **I use ~** ich fahre bleifrei.
unleash [ʌn'liːʃ] *vt* (*fig: feeling, forces etc*)
entfesseln.
unleavened [ʌn'lɛvnd] *adj* (*bread*) ungesäuert.
unless [ʌn'lɛs] *conj* es sei denn; **~ he comes**
wenn er nicht kommt; **~ otherwise stated**
wenn nicht anders angegeben; **~ I am
mistaken** wenn ich mich nicht irre; **there
will be a strike ~ ...** es wird zum Streik
kommen, es sei denn, ...
unlicensed [ʌn'laɪsnst] (*BRIT*) *adj* (*restaurant*)
ohne Schankkonzession.
unlike [ʌn'laɪk] *adj* (*not alike*) unähnlich ♦ *prep*
(*different from*) verschieden von; **~ me, she
is very tidy** im Gegensatz zu mir ist sie sehr
ordentlich.
unlikelihood [ʌn'laɪklɪhud] *adj*
Unwahrscheinlichkeit *f*.
unlikely [ʌn'laɪklɪ] *adj* unwahrscheinlich;
(*combination etc*) merkwürdig; **in the
~ event of/that ...** im unwahrscheinlichen
Fall +*gen*/daß ....
unlimited [ʌn'lɪmɪtɪd] *adj* unbeschränkt.
unlisted ['ʌn'lɪstɪd] *adj* (*STOCK EXCHANGE*)
nicht notiert; (*US: TEL*): **to be ~** nicht im
Telefonbuch stehen.
unlit [ʌn'lɪt] *adj* (*room etc*) unbeleuchtet.
unload [ʌn'ləud] *vt* (*box etc*) ausladen; (*car etc*)
entladen.
unlock [ʌn'lɔk] *vt* aufschließen.
unlucky [ʌn'lʌkɪ] *adj* (*object*)
unglückbringend; (*number*) Unglücks-; **to
be ~** (*person*) Pech haben.
unmanageable [ʌn'mænɪdʒəbl] *adj* (*tool,
vehicle*) kaum zu handhaben; (*person, hair*)
widerspenstig; (*situation*) unkontrollierbar.
unmanned [ʌn'mænd] *adj* (*station, spacecraft
etc*) unbemannt.
unmarked [ʌn'mɑːkt] *adj* (*unstained*)
fleckenlos; (*unscarred*) nicht gezeichnet;
(*unblemished*) makellos; **~ police car** nicht
gekennzeichneter Streifenwagen *m*.

unmarried [ʌn'mærɪd] *adj* unverheiratet.
unmarried mother *n* ledige Mutter *f*.
unmask [ʌn'mɑːsk] *vt* (*reveal*) enthüllen.
unmatched [ʌn'mætʃt] *adj* unübertroffen.
unmentionable [ʌn'menʃnəbl] *adj* (*topic, word*) Tabu-; **to be ~** tabu sein.
unmerciful [ʌn'mɔːsɪful] *adj* erbarmungslos.
unmistak(e)able [ʌnmɪs'teɪkəbl] *adj* unverkennbar.
unmistak(e)ably [ʌnmɪs'teɪkəblɪ] *adv* unverkennbar.
unmitigated [ʌn'mɪtɪgeɪtɪd] *adj* (*disaster etc*) total.
unnamed [ʌn'neɪmd] *adj* (*nameless*) namenlos; (*anonymous*) ungenannt.
unnatural [ʌn'nætʃrəl] *adj* unnatürlich; (*against nature: habit*) widernatürlich.
unnecessarily [ʌn'nesəsərɪlɪ] *adv* (*worry etc*) unnötigerweise; (*severe etc*) übertrieben.
unnecessary [ʌn'nesəsərɪ] *adj* unnötig.
unnerve [ʌn'nɔːv] *vt* entnerven.
unnoticed [ʌn'nəʊtɪst] *adj:* **to go** *or* **pass ~** unbemerkt bleiben.
UNO ['juːnəʊ] *n abbr* (= *United Nations Organization*) UNO *f*.
unobservant [ʌnəb'zɔːvnt] *adj* unaufmerksam.
unobtainable [ʌnəb'teɪnəbl] *adj* (*item*) nicht erhältlich; **this number is ~** (*TEL*) kein Anschluß unter dieser Nummer.
unobtrusive [ʌnəb'truːsɪv] *adj* unauffällig.
unoccupied [ʌn'ɔkjupaɪd] *adj* (*seat*) frei; (*house*) leer(stehend).
unofficial [ʌnə'fɪʃl] *adj* inoffiziell.
unopened [ʌn'əʊpənd] *adj* ungeöffnet.
unopposed [ʌnə'pəʊzd] *adj:* **to be ~** (*suggestion*) nicht auf Widerstand treffen; (*motion, bill*) ohne Gegenstimmen angenommen werden.
unorthodox [ʌn'ɔːθədɔks] *adj* (*also REL*) unorthodox.
unpack [ʌn'pæk] *vt, vi* auspacken.
unpaid [ʌn'peɪd] *adj* unbezahlt.
unpalatable [ʌn'pælətəbl] *adj* (*meal*) ungenießbar; (*truth*) bitter.
unparalleled [ʌn'pærəleld] *adj* beispiellos.
unpatriotic ['ʌnpætrɪ'ɔtɪk] *adj* unpatriotisch.
unplanned [ʌn'plænd] *adj* ungeplant.
unpleasant [ʌn'pleznt] *adj* unangenehm; (*person, manner*) unfreundlich.
unplug [ʌn'plʌg] *vt* (*iron, record player etc*) den Stecker herausziehen +*gen*.
unpolluted [ʌnpə'luːtɪd] *adj* unverschmutzt.
unpopular [ʌn'pɔpjʊləʳ] *adj* unpopulär; **to make o.s. ~ (with)** sich unbeliebt machen (bei).
unprecedented [ʌn'presɪdentɪd] *adj* noch nie dagewesen; (*decision*) einmalig.
unpredictable [ʌnprɪ'dɪktəbl] *adj* (*person, weather*) unberechenbar; (*reaction*) unvorhersehbar.
unprejudiced [ʌn'predʒudɪst] *adj*

unvoreingenommen.
unprepared [ʌnprɪ'peəd] *adj* unvorbereitet.
unprepossessing ['ʌnpriːpə'zesɪŋ] *adj* (*person, place*) unattraktiv.
unpretentious [ʌnprɪ'tenʃəs] *adj* (*building, person*) schlicht.
unprincipled [ʌn'prɪnsɪpld] *adj* (*person*) charakterlos.
unproductive [ʌnprə'dʌktɪv] *adj* (*land*) unfruchtbar, ertragsarm; (*discussion*) unproduktiv.
unprofessional [ʌnprə'feʃənl] *adj* unprofessionell.
unprofitable [ʌn'prɔfɪtəbl] *adj* nicht profitabel, unrentabel.
UNPROFOR *n abbr* (= *United Nations Protection Force*) UNPROFOR *f*; **~ troops** UNPROFOR-Truppen, UNO-Schutztruppen.
unprotected ['ʌnprə'tektɪd] *adj* ungeschützt.
unprovoked [ʌnprə'vəʊkt] *adj* (*attack*) grundlos.
unpunished [ʌn'pʌnɪʃt] *adj:* **to go ~** straflos bleiben.
unqualified [ʌn'kwɔlɪfaɪd] *adj* unqualifiziert; (*disaster, success*) vollkommen.
unquestionably [ʌn'kwestʃənəblɪ] *adv* fraglos.
unquestioning [ʌn'kwestʃənɪŋ] *adj* bedingungslos.
unravel [ʌn'rævl] *vt* (*also fig*) entwirren.
unreal [ʌn'rɪəl] *adj* (*artificial*) unecht; (*peculiar*) unwirklich.
unrealistic ['ʌnrɪə'lɪstɪk] *adj* unrealistisch.
unreasonable [ʌn'riːznəbl] *adj* (*person, attitude*) unvernünftig; (*demand, length of time*) unzumutbar.
unrecognizable [ʌn'rekəgnaɪzəbl] *adj* nicht zu erkennen.
unrecognized [ʌn'rekəgnaɪzd] *adj* (*talent etc*) unerkannt; (*POL: regime*) nicht anerkannt.
unreconstructed ['ʌnriːkən'strʌktɪd] (*esp US*) *adj* (*unwilling to accept change*) unverbesserlich.
unrecorded [ʌnrə'kɔːdɪd] *adj* (*piece of music etc*) nicht aufgenommen; (*incident, statement*) nicht schriftlich festgehalten.
unrefined [ʌnrə'faɪnd] *adj* (*sugar, petroleum*) nicht raffiniert.
unrehearsed [ʌnrɪ'hɔːst] *adj* (*THEAT etc*) nicht geprobt; (*spontaneous*) spontan.
unrelated [ʌnrɪ'leɪtɪd] *adj* (*incidents*) ohne Beziehung; (*people*) nicht verwandt.
unrelenting [ʌnrɪ'lentɪŋ] *adj* (*person, behaviour etc*) unnachgiebig.
unreliable [ʌnrɪ'laɪəbl] *adj* unzuverlässig.
unrelieved [ʌnrɪ'liːvd] *adj* ungemindert.
unremitting [ʌnrɪ'mɪtɪŋ] *adj* (*efforts, attempts*) unermüdlich.
unrepeatable [ʌnrɪ'piːtəbl] *adj* (*offer*) einmalig; (*comment*) nicht wiederholbar.
unrepentant [ʌnrɪ'pentənt] *adj:* **to be ~ about**

sth etw nicht bereuen; **he's an ~ Marxist** er bereut es nicht, nach wie vor Marxist zu sein.

unrepresentative ['ʌnrɛprɪ'zɛntətɪv] *adj:* **~ (of)** nicht repräsentativ (für).

unrepresented ['ʌnrɛprɪ'zɛntɪd] *adj* nicht vertreten.

unreserved [ʌnrɪ'zə:vd] *adj* (*seat*) unreserviert; (*approval etc*) uneingeschränkt, vorbehaltlos.

unreservedly [ʌnrɪ'zə:vɪdlɪ] *adv* ohne Vorbehalt.

unresponsive [ʌnrɪs'pɒnsɪv] *adj* unempfänglich.

unrest [ʌn'rɛst] *n* Unruhen *pl*.

unrestricted [ʌnrɪ'strɪktɪd] *adj* unbeschränkt; **to have ~ access to** ungehinderten Zugang haben zu.

unrewarded [ʌnrɪ'wɔ:dɪd] *adj* unbelohnt.

unripe [ʌn'raɪp] *adj* unreif.

unrivalled, (*US*) **unrivaled** [ʌn'raɪvəld] *adj* unübertroffen.

unroll [ʌn'rəul] *vt* entrollen ♦ *vi* sich entrollen.

unruffled [ʌn'rʌfld] *adj* unbewegt; (*hair*) unzerzaust.

unruly [ʌn'ru:lɪ] *adj* (*child, behaviour*) ungebärdig; (*hair*) widerspenstig.

unsafe [ʌn'seɪf] *adj* unsicher; (*machine, bridge, car etc*) gefährlich; **~ to eat/drink** ungenießbar.

unsaid [ʌn'sɛd] *adj:* **to leave sth ~** etw ungesagt lassen.

unsaleable, (*US*) **unsalable** [ʌn'seɪləbl] *adj* unverkäuflich.

unsatisfactory ['ʌnsætɪs'fæktərɪ] *adj* unbefriedigend.

unsatisfied [ʌn'sætɪsfaɪd] *adj* unzufrieden.

unsavoury, (*US*) **unsavory** [ʌn'seɪvərɪ] *adj* (*fig: person, place*) widerwärtig.

unscathed [ʌn'skeɪðd] *adj* unversehrt.

unscientific ['ʌnsaɪən'tɪfɪk] *adj* unwissenschaftlich.

unscrew [ʌn'skru:] *vt* losschrauben.

unscrupulous [ʌn'skru:pjuləs] *adj* skrupellos.

unseat [ʌn'si:t] *vt* (*rider*) abwerfen; (*from office*) aus dem Amt drängen.

unsecured ['ʌnsɪ'kjuəd] *adj:* **~ creditor** nicht gesicherter Gläubiger *m*; **~ loan** Blankokredit *m*.

unseeded [ʌn'si:dɪd] *adj* (*player*) nicht gesetzt.

unseemly [ʌn'si:mlɪ] *adj* unschicklich.

unseen [ʌn'si:n] *adj* (*person, danger*) unsichtbar.

unselfish [ʌn'sɛlfɪʃ] *adj* selbstlos.

unsettled [ʌn'sɛtld] *adj* (*person*) unruhig; (*future*) unsicher; (*question*) ungeklärt; (*weather*) unbeständig.

unsettling [ʌn'sɛtlɪŋ] *adj* beunruhigend.

unshak(e)able [ʌn'ʃeɪkəbl] *adj* unerschütterlich.

unshaven [ʌn'ʃeɪvn] *adj* unrasiert.

unsightly [ʌn'saɪtlɪ] *adj* unansehnlich.

unskilled [ʌn'skɪld] *adj* (*work, worker*) ungelernt.

unsociable [ʌn'səuʃəbl] *adj* ungesellig.

unsocial [ʌn'səuʃl] *adj:* **to work ~ hours** außerhalb der normalen Arbeitszeit arbeiten.

unsold [ʌn'səuld] *adj* unverkauft.

unsolicited [ʌnsə'lɪsɪtɪd] *adj* unerbeten.

unsophisticated [ʌnsə'fɪstɪkeɪtɪd] *adj* (*person*) anspruchslos; (*method, device*) simpel.

unsound [ʌn'saund] *adj* (*floor, foundations*) unsicher; (*policy, advice*) unklug; **of ~ mind** unzurechnungsfähig.

unspeakable [ʌn'spi:kəbl] *adj* (*indescribable*) unsagbar; (*awful*) abscheulich.

unspoken [ʌn'spəukn] *adj* (*word*) unausgesprochen; (*agreement etc*) stillschweigend.

unstable [ʌn'steɪbl] *adj* (*piece of furniture*) nicht stabil; (*government*) instabil; (*person: mentally*) labil.

unsteady [ʌn'stɛdɪ] *adj* (*step, voice, legs*) unsicher; (*ladder*) wack(e)lig.

unstinting [ʌn'stɪntɪŋ] *adj* (*support*) vorbehaltlos; (*generosity*) unbegrenzt.

unstuck [ʌn'stʌk] *adj:* **to come ~** (*label etc*) sich lösen; (*fig: plan, idea etc*) versagen.

unsubstantiated ['ʌnsəb'stænʃɪeɪtɪd] *adj* (*rumour*) unbestätigt; (*accusation*) unbegründet.

unsuccessful [ʌnsək'sɛsful] *adj* erfolglos; (*marriage*) gescheitert; **to be ~** keinen Erfolg haben.

unsuccessfully [ʌnsək'sɛsfəlɪ] *adv* ohne Erfolg, vergeblich.

unsuitable [ʌn'su:təbl] *adj* (*time*) unpassend; (*clothes, person*) ungeeignet.

unsuited [ʌn'su:tɪd] *adj:* **to be ~ for** *or* **to sth** für etw ungeeignet sein.

unsung ['ʌnsʌŋ] *adj:* **an ~ hero** ein unbesungener Held.

unsure [ʌn'ʃuə*] *adj* unsicher; **to be ~ of o.s.** unsicher sein.

unsuspecting [ʌnsəs'pɛktɪŋ] *adj* ahnungslos.

unsweetened [ʌn'swi:tnd] *adj* ungesüßt.

unswerving [ʌn'swə:vɪŋ] *adj* unerschütterlich.

unsympathetic ['ʌnsɪmpə'θɛtɪk] *adj* (*showing little understanding*) abweisend; (*unlikeable*) unsympathisch; **to be ~ to(wards) sth** einer Sache *dat* ablehnend gegenüberstehen.

untangle [ʌn'tæŋgl] *vt* entwirren.

untapped [ʌn'tæpt] *adj* (*resources*) ungenutzt.

untaxed [ʌn'tækst] *adj* (*goods, income*) steuerfrei.

unthinkable [ʌn'θɪŋkəbl] *adj* undenkbar.

unthinking [ʌn'θɪŋkɪŋ] *adj* (*uncritical*) bedenkenlos; (*thoughtless*) gedankenlos.

untidy [ʌn'taɪdɪ] *adj* unordentlich.

untie [ʌn'taɪ] *vt* (*knot, parcel*) aufschnüren; (*prisoner, dog*) losbinden.

until [ən'tɪl] *prep* bis +*acc*; (*after negative*) vor

+*dat* ♦ *conj* bis; (*after negative*) bevor; ~ **now**
bis jetzt; ~ **then** bis dann; **from morning**
~ **night** von morgens bis abends; ~ **he**
comes bis er kommt.
untimely [ʌn'taɪmlɪ] *adj* (*moment*) unpassend;
(*arrival*) ungelegen; (*death*) vorzeitig.
untold [ʌn'təuld] *adj* (*joy, suffering, wealth*)
unermeßlich; **the** ~ **story** die Hintergründe.
untouched [ʌn'tʌtʃt] *adj* unberührt;
(*undamaged*) unversehrt; ~ **by** (*unaffected*)
unberührt von.
untoward [ʌntə'wɔːd] *adj* (*events, effects etc*)
ungünstig.
untrained ['ʌn'treɪnd] *adj* unausgebildet; (*eye,*
hands) ungeschult.
untrammelled [ʌn'træmld] *adj* (*person*)
ungebunden; (*behaviour*) unbeschränkt.
untranslatable [ʌntrænz'leɪtəbl] *adj*
unübersetzbar.
untried [ʌn'traɪd] *adj* (*policy, remedy*)
unerprobt; (*prisoner*) noch nicht vor Gericht
gestellt.
untrue [ʌn'truː] *adj* unwahr.
untrustworthy [ʌn'trʌstwəːðɪ] *adj*
unzuverlässig.
unusable [ʌn'juːzəbl] *adj* (*object*)
unbrauchbar; (*room*) nicht benutzbar.
unused¹ [ʌn'juːzd] *adj* (*new*) unbenutzt.
unused² [ʌn'juːst] *adj:* **to be** ~ **to sth** an etw
acc nicht gewöhnt sein; **to be** ~ **to doing sth**
nicht daran gewöhnt sein, etw zu tun.
unusual [ʌn'juːʒuəl] *adj* ungewöhnlich;
(*exceptional*) außergewöhnlich.
unusually [ʌn'juːʒuəlɪ] *adv* (*large, high etc*)
ungewöhnlich.
unveil [ʌn'veɪl] *vt* (*also fig*) enthüllen.
unwanted [ʌn'wɒntɪd] *adj* unerwünscht.
unwarranted [ʌn'wɒrəntɪd] *adj*
ungerechtfertigt.
unwary [ʌn'wɛərɪ] *adj* unachtsam.
unwavering [ʌn'weɪvərɪŋ] *adj* (*faith, support*)
unerschütterlich; (*gaze*) fest.
unwelcome [ʌn'wɛlkəm] *adj* (*guest*)
unwillkommen; (*news*) unerfreulich; **to feel**
~ sich nicht willkommen fühlen.
unwell [ʌn'wɛl] *adj:* **to be** ~, **to feel** ~ sich
nicht wohl fühlen.
unwieldy [ʌn'wiːldɪ] *adj* (*object*) unhandlich;
(*system*) schwerfällig.
unwilling [ʌn'wɪlɪŋ] *adj:* **to be** ~ **to do sth** etw
nicht tun wollen.
unwillingly [ʌn'wɪlɪŋlɪ] *adv* widerwillig.
unwind [ʌn'waɪnd] (*irreg: like* **wind**) *vt*
abwickeln ♦ *vi* sich abwickeln; (*relax*) sich
entspannen.
unwise [ʌn'waɪz] *adj* unklug.
unwitting [ʌn'wɪtɪŋ] *adj* (*accomplice*)
unwissentlich; (*victim*) ahnungslos.
unworkable [ʌn'wəːkəbl] *adj* (*plan*)
undurchführbar.
unworthy [ʌn'wəːðɪ] *adj* unwürdig; **to be** ~ **of**
sth einer Sache *gen* nicht wert *or* würdig

sein; **to be** ~ **to do sth** es nicht wert sein,
etw zu tun; **that remark is** ~ **of you** diese
Bemerkung ist unter deiner Würde.
unwrap [ʌn'ræp] *vt* auspacken.
unwritten [ʌn'rɪtn] *adj* (*law*) ungeschrieben;
(*agreement*) stillschweigend.
unzip [ʌn'zɪp] *vt* aufmachen.

═══════════════════════════ *KEYWORD*

up [ʌp] *prep:* **to be** ~ **sth** (oben) auf etw *dat*
sein; **to go** ~ **sth** (auf) etw *acc* hinaufgehen;
go ~ **that road and turn left** gehen Sie die
Straße hinauf und biegen Sie links ab
♦ *adv* **1** (*upwards, higher*) oben; **put it a bit**
higher ~ stelle es etwas höher; ~ **there** dort
oben; ~ **above** hoch oben
2: to be ~ (*out of bed*) auf sein; (*prices, level*)
gestiegen sein; (*building, tent*) stehen; **time's**
~ die Zeit ist um *or* vorbei
3: ~ **to** (*as far as*) bis; ~ **to now** bis jetzt
4: to be ~ **to** (*depending on*) abhängen von;
it's ~ **to you** das hängt von dir ab; **it's not**
~ **to me to decide** es liegt nicht bei mir, das
zu entscheiden
5: to be ~ **to** (*equal to*) gewachsen sein +*dat*;
he's not ~ **to it** (*job, task etc*) er ist dem
nicht gewachsen; **his work is not** ~ **to the**
required standard seine Arbeit entspricht
nicht dem gewünschten Niveau
6: to be ~ **to** (*inf: be doing*) vorhaben; **what**
is he ~ **to?** (*showing disapproval, suspicion*)
was führt er im Schilde?
♦ *n:* ~**s and downs** (*in life, career*) Höhen und
Tiefen *pl* ♦ *vi* (*inf*): **she** ~**ped and left** sie
sprang auf und rannte davon
♦ *vt* (*inf: price*) heraufsetzen.

up-and-coming [ʌpənd'kʌmɪŋ] *adj* (*actor,*
company etc) kommend.
upbeat ['ʌpbiːt] *n* (*MUS*) Auftakt *m*; (*in*
economy etc) Aufschwung *m* ♦ *adj* (*optimistic*)
optimistisch.
upbraid [ʌp'breɪd] *vt* tadeln.
upbringing ['ʌpbrɪŋɪŋ] *n* Erziehung *f*.
upcoming ['ʌpkʌmɪŋ] (*esp US*) *adj* kommend.
update [ʌp'deɪt] *vt* aktualisieren.
upend [ʌp'end] *vt* auf den Kopf stellen.
upfront [ʌp'frʌnt] *adj* (*person*) offen ♦ *adv:*
20% ~ 20% (als) Vorschuß, 20% im voraus.
upgrade [ʌp'greɪd] *vt* (*house*)
Verbesserungen durchführen in +*dat*; (*job*)
verbessern; (*employee*) befördern;
(*COMPUT*) nachrüsten.
upheaval [ʌp'hiːvl] *n* Unruhe *f*.
uphill ['ʌp'hɪl] *adj* bergaufwärts (führend);
(*fig: task*) mühsam ♦ *adv* (*push, move*)
bergaufwärts; (*go*) bergauf.
uphold [ʌp'həuld] (*irreg: like* **hold**) *vt* (*law,*
principle) wahren; (*decision*) unterstützen.
upholstery [ʌp'həulstərɪ] *n* Polsterung *f*.
upkeep ['ʌpkiːp] *n* (*maintenance*)
Instandhaltung *f*.

up-market [ʌp'mɑːkɪt] *adj* anspruchsvoll.
upon [ə'pɒn] *prep* (*position*) auf +*dat*; (*motion*) auf +*acc*.
upper ['ʌpə'] *adj* obere(r, s) ♦ *n* (*of shoe*) Oberleder *nt*.
upper class *n*: the ~ die Oberschicht.
upper-class ['ʌpə'klɑːs] *adj* vornehm.
uppercut ['ʌpəkʌt] *n* Uppercut *m*.
upper hand *n*: to have the ~ die Oberhand haben.
Upper House *n* (*POL*) Oberhaus *nt*.
uppermost ['ʌpəməust] *adj* oberste(r, s); **what was ~ in my mind** woran ich in erster Linie dachte.
Upper Volta [-'vɒltə] *n* Obervolta *nt*.
upright ['ʌpraɪt] *adj* (*vertical*) vertikal; (*fig: honest*) rechtschaffen ♦ *adv* (*sit, stand*) aufrecht ♦ *n* (*CONSTR*) Pfosten *m*.
uprising ['ʌpraɪzɪŋ] *n* Aufstand *m*.
uproar ['ʌprɔː'] *n* Aufruhr *m*.
uproarious [ʌp'rɔːriəs] *adj* (*laughter*) brüllend; (*joke*) brüllend komisch; (*mirth*) überwältigend.
uproot [ʌp'ruːt] *vt* (*tree*) entwurzeln; (*fig: people*) aus der gewohnten Umgebung reißen; (: *in war etc*) entwurzeln.
upset [*vt, adj* ʌp'sɛt, *n* 'ʌpsɛt] (*irreg: like* **set**) *vt* (*knock over*) umstoßen; (*person: offend, make unhappy*) verletzen; (*routine, plan*) durcheinanderbringen ♦ *adj* (*unhappy*) aufgebracht; (*stomach*) verstimmt ♦ *n*: **to have/get a stomach ~** (*BRIT*) eine Magenverstimmung haben/bekommen; **to get ~** sich aufregen.
upset price ['ʌpsɛt-] (*US, SCOT*) *n* Mindestpreis *m*.
upsetting [ʌp'sɛtɪŋ] *adj* (*distressing*) erschütternd.
upshot ['ʌpʃɒt] *n* Ergebnis *nt*; **the ~ of it all was that ...** es lief schließlich darauf hinaus, daß ...
upside down ['ʌpsaɪd-] *adv* verkehrt herum; **to turn a room ~** (*fig*) ein Zimmer auf den Kopf stellen.
upstage [ʌp'steɪdʒ] *adv* (*THEAT*) im Bühnenhintergrund ♦ *vt*: **to ~ sb** (*fig*) jdn ausstechen; jdm die Schau stehlen (*inf*).
upstairs [ʌp'stɛəz] *adv* (*be*) oben; (*go*) nach oben ♦ *adj* (*room*) obere(r, s); (*window*) im oberen Stock ♦ *n* oberes Stockwerk *nt*; **there's no ~** das Haus hat kein Obergeschoß.
upstart ['ʌpstɑːt] (*pej*) *n* Emporkömmling *m*.
upstream [ʌp'striːm] *adv, adj* flußaufwärts.
upsurge ['ʌpsəːdʒ] *n* (*of enthusiasm etc*) Schwall *m*.
uptake ['ʌpteɪk] *n*: **to be quick on the ~** schnell kapieren; **to be slow on the ~** schwer von Begriff sein.
uptight [ʌp'taɪt] (*inf*) *adj* nervös.
up-to-date ['ʌptə'deɪt] *adj* (*modern*) modern; (*person*) up to date.

upturn ['ʌptəːn] *n* (*in economy*) Aufschwung *m*.
upturned ['ʌptəːnd] *adj*: **~ nose** Stupsnase *f*.
upward ['ʌpwəd] *adj* (*movement*) Aufwärts-; (*glance*) nach oben gerichtet.
upwardly mobile ['ʌpwədlɪ-] *adj*: **to be ~** ein Aufsteigertyp *m* sein.
upwards ['ʌpwədz] *adv* (*move*) aufwärts; (*glance*) nach oben; **upward(s) of** (*more than*) über +*acc*.
URA (*US*) *n abbr* (= *Urban Renewal Administration*) Stadtsanierungsbehörde.
Ural Mountains ['juərəl-] *n*: **the ~** (*also*: **the Urals**) der Ural.
uranium [juə'reɪnɪəm] *n* Uran *nt*.
Uranus [juə'reɪnəs] *n* Uranus *m*.
urban ['əːbən] *adj* städtisch; (*unemployment*) in den Städten.
urbane [ə'beɪn] *adj* weltgewandt.
urbanization ['əːbənaɪ'zeɪʃən] *n* Urbanisierung *f*, Verstädterung *f*.
urchin ['əːtʃɪn] (*pej*) *n* Gassenkind *nt*.
Urdu ['uəduː] *n* Urdu *nt*.
urge [əːdʒ] *n* (*need, desire*) Verlangen *nt* ♦ *vt*: **to ~ sb to do sth** jdn eindringlich bitten, etw zu tun; **to ~ caution** zur Vorsicht mahnen.
►urge on *vt* antreiben.
urgency ['əːdʒənsɪ] *n* Dringlichkeit *f*.
urgent ['əːdʒənt] *adj* dringend; (*voice*) eindringend.
urgently ['əːdʒəntlɪ] *adv* dringend.
urinal ['juərɪnl] *n* (*building*) Pissoir *nt*; (*vessel*) Urinal *nt*.
urinate ['juərɪneɪt] *vi* urinieren.
urine ['juərɪn] *n* Urin *m*.
urn [əːn] *n* Urne *f*; (*also*: **tea ~**) Teekessel *m*.
Uruguay ['juərəgwaɪ] *n* Uruguay *nt*.
Uruguayan [juərə'gwaɪən] *adj* uruguayisch ♦ *n* (*person*) Uruguayer(in) *m(f)*.
US *n abbr* (= *United States*) USA *pl*.
us [ʌs] *pl pron* uns; (*emphatic*) wir; *see also* **me**.
USA *n abbr* (= *United States of America*) USA *f*; (*MIL*: = *United States Army*) US-Armee *f*.
usable ['juːzəbl] *adj* brauchbar.
USAF *n abbr* (= *United States Air Force*) US-Luftwaffe *f*.
usage ['juːzɪdʒ] *n* (*LING*) (Sprach)gebrauch *m*.
USCG *n abbr* (= *United States Coast Guard*) Küstenwache der USA.
USDA *n abbr* (= *United States Department of Agriculture*) US-Landwirtschafts-ministerium.
USDAW ['ʌzdɔː] (*BRIT*) *n abbr* (= *Union of Shop, Distributive and Allied Workers*) Einzelhandelsgewerkschaft.
USDI *n abbr* (= *United States Department of the Interior*) US-Innenministerium.
use [*n* juːs, *vt* juːz] *n* (*using*) Gebrauch *m*, Verwendung *f*; (*usefulness, purpose*) Nutzen *m* ♦ *vt* benutzen, gebrauchen; (*phrase*) verwenden; **in ~** in Gebrauch; **out of ~**

außer Gebrauch; **to be of** ~ nützlich *or* von Nutzen sein; **to make** ~ **of sth** Gebrauch von etw machen; **it's no** ~ es hat keinen Zweck; **to have the** ~ **of sth** über etw *acc* verfügen können; **what's this** ~**d for?** wofür wird das gebraucht?; **to be** ~**d to sth** etw gewohnt sein; **to get** ~**d to sth** sich an etw *acc* gewöhnen; **she** ~**d to do it** sie hat es früher gemacht.

►**use up** *vt* (*food, leftovers*) aufbrauchen; (*money*) verbrauchen.

used [juːzd] *adj* gebraucht; (*car*) Gebraucht-.

useful ['juːsful] *adj* nützlich; **to come in** ~ sich als nützlich erweisen.

usefulness ['juːsfəlnɪs] *n* Nützlichkeit *f.*

useless ['juːslɪs] *adj* nutzlos; (*person: hopeless*) hoffnungslos.

user ['juːzə*] *n* Benutzer(in) *m(f)*; (*of petrol, gas etc*) Verbraucher(in) *m(f)*.

user-friendly ['juːzə'frɛndlɪ] *adj* benutzerfreundlich.

usher ['ʌʃə*] *n* (*at wedding*) Platzanweiser *m* ♦ *vt:* **to** ~ **sb in** jdn hineinführen.

usherette [ʌʃə'rɛt] *n* Platzanweiserin *f.*

USIA *n abbr* (= *United States Information Agency*) US-Informations- und Kulturinstitut.

USM *n abbr* (= *United States Mint*) US-Münzanstalt; (= *United States Mail*) US-Postbehörde.

USN *n abbr* (= *United States Navy*) US-Marine *f.*

USPHS *n abbr* (= *United States Public Health Service*) US-Gesundheitsbehörde.

USPO *n abbr* (= *United States Post Office*) US-Postbehörde.

USS *abbr* (= *United States Ship*) Namensteil von Schiffen der Kriegsmarine.

USSR *n abbr* (*formerly:* = *Union of Soviet Socialist Republics*) UdSSR *f.*

usu. *abbr* = **usually.**

usual ['juːʒuəl] *adj* üblich, gewöhnlich; **as** ~ wie gewöhnlich.

usually ['juːʒuəlɪ] *adv* gewöhnlich.

usurer ['juːʒərə*] *n* Wucherer *m.*

usurp [juː'zəːp] *vt* (*title, position*) an sich *acc* reißen.

usury ['juːʒurɪ] *n* Wucher *m.*

UT (*US*) *abbr* (*POST:* = *Utah*).

utensil [juː'tɛnsl] *n* Gerät *nt*; **kitchen** ~**s** Küchengeräte *pl.*

uterus ['juːtərəs] *n* Gebärmutter *f*, Uterus *m.*

utilitarian [juːtɪlɪ'tɛərɪən] *adj* (*building, object*) praktisch; (*PHILOSOPHY*) utilitaristisch.

utility [juː'tɪlɪtɪ] *n* (*usefulness*) Nützlichkeit *f*; (*public utility*) Versorgungsbetrieb *m.*

utility room *n* ≈ Hauswirtschaftsraum *m.*

utilization [juːtɪlaɪ'zeɪʃən] *n* Verwendung *f.*

utilize ['juːtɪlaɪz] *vt* verwenden.

utmost ['ʌtməust] *adj* äußerste(r, s) ♦ *n:* **to do one's** ~ sein möglichstes tun; **of the** ~ **importance** von äußerster Wichtigkeit.

utter ['ʌtə*] *adj* (*amazement*) äußerste(r, s); (*rubbish, fool*) total ♦ *vt* (*sounds, words*) äußern.

utterance ['ʌtərəns] *n* Äußerung *f.*

utterly ['ʌtəlɪ] *adv* (*totally*) vollkommen.

U-turn ['juː'təːn] *n* (*also fig*) Kehrtwendung *f.*

Uzbekistan [ʌzbɛkɪ'staːn] *n* Usbekistan *nt.*

V, v

V¹, v [viː] *n* (*letter*) V *nt*, v *nt*; ~ **for Victor** ≈ V wie Viktor.

V² *abbr* (= *volt*) V.

v. *abbr* = **verse;** (= *versus*) vs.; (= *vide*) s.

VA (*US*) *abbr* (*POST:* = *Virginia*).

vac [væk] (*BRIT: inf*) *n abbr* = **vacation.**

vacancy ['veɪkənsɪ] *n* (*BRIT: job*) freie Stelle *f*; (*room in hotel etc*) freies Zimmer *nt*; **"no vacancies"** „belegt"; **have you any vacancies?** (*hotel*) haben Sie Zimmer frei?; (*office*) haben Sie freie Stellen?

vacant ['veɪkənt] *adj* (*room, seat, job*) frei; (*look*) leer.

vacant lot (*US*) *n* unbebautes Grundstück *nt.*

vacate [və'keɪt] *vt* (*house*) räumen; (*one's seat*) frei machen; (*job*) aufgeben.

vacation [və'keɪʃən] (*esp US*) *n* (*holiday*) Urlaub *m*; (*SCOL*) Ferien *pl*; **to take a** ~ Urlaub machen; **on** ~ im Urlaub.

vacation course *n* Ferienkurs *m.*

vaccinate ['væksɪneɪt] *vt:* **to** ~ **sb (against sth)** jdn (gegen etw) impfen.

vaccination [væksɪ'neɪʃən] *n* Impfung *f.*

vaccine ['væksiːn] *n* Impfstoff *m.*

vacuum ['vækjum] *n* (*empty space*) Vakuum *nt.*

vacuum cleaner *n* Staubsauger *m.*

vacuum flask (*BRIT*) *n* Thermosflasche ® *f.*

vacuum-packed ['vækjum'pækt] *adj* vakuumverpackt.

vagabond ['vægəbɔnd] *n* Vagabund *m.*

vagary ['veɪgərɪ] *n:* **the vagaries of** die Launen +*gen.*

vagina [və'dʒaɪnə] *n* Scheide *f*, Vagina *f.*

vagrancy ['veɪgrənsɪ] *n* Landstreicherei *f*; (*in towns, cities*) Stadtstreicherei *f.*

vagrant ['veɪgrənt] *n* Landstreicher(in) *m(f)*; (*in town, city*) Stadtstreicher(in) *m(f)*.

vague [veɪg] *adj* (*memory*) vage; (*outline*) undeutlich; (*look, idea, instructions*) unbestimmt; (*person: not precise*) unsicher; (: *evasive*) unbestimmt; **to look** ~ (*absent-minded*) zerstreut aussehen; **I haven't the** ~**st idea** ich habe nicht die leiseste Ahnung.

vaguely ['veɪglɪ] *adv* (*unclearly*) vage,

unbestimmt; (*slightly*) in etwa.
vagueness ['veignis] *n* Unbestimmtheit *f*.
vain [vein] *adj* (*person*) eitel; (*attempt, action*)
vergeblich; **in** ~ vergebens; **to die in** ~
umsonst sterben.
vainly ['veinli] *adv* vergebens.
valance ['væləns] *n* (*of bed*) Volant *m*.
valedictorian [vælidik'tɔːriən] (*US*) *n* (*SCOL*)
Abschiedsredner(in) *bei der*
Schulentlassungsfeier.
valedictory [væli'diktəri] *adj* (*speech*)
Abschieds-; (*remarks*) zum Abschied.
valentine ['væləntain] *n* (*also:* ~ **card**)
Valentinsgruß *m*; (*person*) Freund/Freundin,
*dem/der man am Valentinstag einen Gruß
schickt*.
valet ['vælit] *n* Kammerdiener *m*.
valet parking *n* Einparken *nt* (*durch
Hotelangestellte etc*).
valet service *n* Reinigungsdienst *m*.
valiant ['væliənt] *adj* (*effort*) tapfer.
valid ['vælid] *adj* (*ticket, document*) gültig;
(*argument, reason*) stichhaltig.
validate ['vælideit] *vt* (*contract, document*) für
gültig erklären; (*argument, claim*)
bestätigen.
validity [və'liditi] *n* (*soundness*) Gültigkeit *f*.
valise [və'liːz] *n* kleiner Koffer *m*.
valley ['væli] *n* Tal *nt*.
valour, (*US*) **valor** ['vælə*] *n* Tapferkeit *f*.
valuable ['væljuəbl] *adj* wertvoll; (*time*)
kostbar.
valuables ['væljuəblz] *npl* Wertsachen *pl*.
valuation [vælju'eiʃən] *n* (*of house etc*)
Schätzung *f*; (*judgement of quality*)
Einschätzung *f*.
value ['væljuː] *n* Wert *m*; (*usefulness*) Nutzen *m*
♦ *vt* schätzen; **values** *npl* (*principles, beliefs*)
Werte *pl*; **you get good** ~ **(for money) in that
shop** in dem Laden bekommt man etwas
für sein Geld; **to lose (in)** ~ an Wert
verlieren; **to gain (in)** ~ im Wert steigen; **to
be of great** ~ **(to sb)** (*fig*) von großem Wert
(für jdn) sein.
value-added tax [vælju:'ædid-] (*BRIT*) *n*
Mehrwertsteuer *f*.
valued ['væljuːd] *adj* (*customer, advice*)
geschätzt.
valuer ['væljuə*] *n* Schätzer(in) *m(f)*.
valve [vælv] *n* Ventil *nt*; (*MED*) Klappe *f*.
vampire ['væmpaiə*] *n* Vampir *m*.
van [væn] *n* (*AUT*) Lieferwagen *m*; (*BRIT: RAIL*)
Waggon *m*.
V and A (*BRIT*) *n abbr* (= *Victoria and Albert
Museum*) *Londoner Museum*.
vandal ['vændl] *n* Rowdy *m*.
vandalism ['vændəlizəm] *n* Vandalismus *m*.
vandalize ['vændəlaiz] *vt* mutwillig zerstören.
vanguard ['vængaːd] *n* (*fig*): **in the** ~ **of** an der
Spitze +*gen*.
vanilla [və'nilə] *n* Vanille *f*.
vanilla ice cream *n* Vanilleeis *nt*.

vanish ['væniʃ] *vi* verschwinden.
vanity ['væniti] *n* (*of person*) Eitelkeit *f*.
vanity case *n* Kosmetikkoffer *m*.
vantage point ['vaːntidʒ-] *n* Aussichtspunkt
m; (*fig*): **from our** ~ aus unserer Sicht.
vaporize ['veipəraiz] *vt* verdampfen ♦ *vi*
verdunsten.
vapour, (*US*) **vapor** ['veipə*] *n* (*gas, steam*)
Dampf *m*; (*mist*) Dunst *m*.
vapour trail *n* (*AVIAT*) Kondensstreifen *m*.
variable ['vɛəriəbl] *adj* (*likely to change: mood,
quality, weather*) veränderlich, wechselhaft;
(*able to be changed: temperature, height,
speed*) variabel ♦ *n* veränderlicher Faktor
m; (*MATH*) Variable *f*.
variance ['vɛəriəns] *n*: **to be at** ~ **(with)** nicht
übereinstimmen (mit).
variant ['vɛəriənt] *n* Variante *f*.
variation [vɛəri'eiʃən] *n* (*change*)
Veränderung *f*; (*different form: of plot, theme
etc*) Variation *f*.
varicose ['værikəus] *adj*: ~ **veins**
Krampfadern *pl*.
varied ['vɛərid] *adj* (*diverse*) unterschiedlich;
(*full of changes*) abwechslungsreich.
variety [və'raiəti] *n* (*diversity*) Vielfalt *f*;
(*varied collection*) Auswahl *f*; (*type*) Sorte *f*; **a
wide** ~ **of ...** eine Vielfalt an +*acc* ...; **for a
** ~ **of reasons** aus verschiedenen Gründen.
variety show *n* Varietévorführung *f*.
various ['vɛəriəs] *adj* (*reasons, people*)
verschiedene; **at** ~ **times** (*different*) zu
verschiedenen Zeiten; (*several*) mehrmals,
mehrfach.
varnish ['vaːniʃ] *n* Lack *m* ♦ *vt* (*wood, one's
nails*) lackieren.
vary ['vɛəri] *vt* verändern ♦ *vi* (*be different*)
variieren; **to** ~ **with** (*weather, season etc*)
sich ändern mit.
varying ['vɛəriiŋ] *adj* unterschiedlich.
vase [vaːz] *n* Vase *f*.
vasectomy [væ'sɛktəmi] *n* Vasektomie *f*.
Vaseline ® ['væsiliːn] *n* Vaseline *f*.
vast [vaːst] *adj* (*knowledge*) enorm; (*expense,
area*) riesig.
vastly ['vaːstli] *adv* (*superior, improved*)
erheblich.
vastness ['vaːstnis] *n* ungeheure Größe *f*.
VAT [væt] (*BRIT*) *n abbr* (= *value-added tax*)
MWSt *f*.
vat [væt] *n* Faß *nt*.
Vatican ['vætikən] *n*: **the** ~ der Vatikan.
vatman ['vætmæn] (*inf: irreg: like* **man**) *n*
~ Fiskus *m* (*bezüglich Einbehaltung der
Mehrwertsteuer*).
vaudeville ['vəudəvil] *n* Varieté *nt*.
vault [vɔːlt] *n* (*of roof*) Gewölbe *nt*; (*tomb*)
Gruft *f*; (*in bank*) Tresorraum *m*; (*jump*)
Sprung *m* ♦ *vt* (*also:* ~ **over**) überspringen.
vaunted ['vɔːntid] *adj*: **much-**~ vielgepriesen.
VC *n abbr* = **vice-chairman**; (*BRIT:* = *Victoria
Cross*) Viktoriakreuz *nt*, höchste britische

Tapferkeitsauszeichnung.

VCR *n abbr* = **video cassette recorder.**

VD *n abbr* = **venereal disease.**

VDU *n abbr* (*COMPUT*) = **visual display unit.**

veal [viːl] *n* Kalbfleisch *nt*.

veer [vɪə*] *vi* (*wind*) sich drehen; (*vehicle*) ausscheren.

veg (*BRIT: inf*) *n abbr* = **vegetable(s).**

vegan ['viːgən] *n* Veganer(in) *m(f)* ♦ *adj* radikal vegetarisch.

vegeburger ['vɛdʒɪbəːgə*] *n* vegetarischer Hamburger *m*.

vegetable ['vɛdʒtəbl] *n* (*plant*) Gemüse *nt*; (*plant life*) Pflanzen *pl* ♦ *cpd* (*oil etc*) Pflanzen-; (*garden, plot*) Gemüse-.

vegetarian [vɛdʒɪ'tɛərɪən] *n* Vegetarier(in) *m(f)* ♦ *adj* vegetarisch.

vegetate ['vɛdʒɪteɪt] *vi* (*fig: person*) dahinvegetieren.

vegetation [vɛdʒɪ'teɪʃən] *n* (*plants*) Vegetation *f*.

vegetative ['vɛdʒɪtətɪv] *adj* vegetativ.

veggieburger ['vɛdʒɪbəːgə*] *n* = **vegeburger.**

vehemence ['viːɪməns] *n* Vehemenz *f*, Heftigkeit *f*.

vehement ['viːɪmənt] *adj* heftig.

vehicle ['viːɪkl] *n* (*machine*) Fahrzeug *nt*; (*fig: means*) Mittel *nt*.

vehicular [vɪ'hɪkjulə*] *adj:* **"no ~ traffic"** „kein Fahrzeugverkehr".

veil [veɪl] *n* Schleier *m* ♦ *vt* (*also fig*) verschleiern; **under a ~ of secrecy** unter einem Schleier von Geheimnissen.

veiled [veɪld] *adj* (*also fig: threat*) verschleiert.

vein [veɪn] *n* Ader *f*; (*fig: mood, style*) Stimmung *f*.

Velcro ® ['vɛlkrəu] *n* (*also:* **~ fastener** *or* **fastening**) Klettverschluß *m*.

vellum ['vɛləm] *n* (*writing paper*) Pergament *nt*.

velocity [vɪ'lɔsɪtɪ] *n* Geschwindigkeit *f*.

velours *n* Velours *m*.

velvet ['vɛlvɪt] *n* Samt *m* ♦ *adj* (*skirt, jacket*) Samt-.

vendetta [vɛn'dɛtə] *n* Vendetta *f*; (*between families*) Blutrache *f*.

vending machine ['vɛndɪŋ-] *n* Automat *m*.

vendor ['vɛndə*] *n* Verkäufer(in) *m(f)*; **street ~** Straßenhändler(in) *m(f)*.

veneer [və'nɪə*] *n* (*on furniture*) Furnier *nt*; (*fig*) Anstrich *m*.

venerable ['vɛnərəbl] *adj* ehrwürdig; (*REL*) hochwürdig.

venereal [vɪ'nɪərɪəl] *adj:* **~ disease** Geschlechtskrankheit *f*.

Venetian [vɪ'niːʃən] *adj* (*GEOG*) venezianisch ♦ *n* (*person*) Venezianer(in) *m(f)*.

Venetian blind *n* Jalousie *f*.

Venezuela [vɛnɛ'zweɪlə] *n* Venezuela *nt*.

Venezuelan [vɛnɛ'zweɪlən] *adj* venezolanisch ♦ *n* (*person*) Venezolaner(in) *m(f)*.

vengeance ['vɛndʒəns] *n* Rache *f*; **with a ~** (*fig: fiercely*) gewaltig; **he broke the rules with a ~** er verstieß die Regeln - und nicht zu knapp.

vengeful ['vɛndʒful] *adj* rachsüchtig.

Venice ['vɛnɪs] *n* Venedig *nt*.

venison ['vɛnɪsn] *n* Rehfleisch *nt*.

venom ['vɛnəm] *n* (*poison*) Gift *nt*; (*bitterness, anger*) Gehässigkeit *f*.

venomous ['vɛnəməs] *adj* (*snake, insect*) giftig; (*look*) gehässig.

vent [vɛnt] *n* (*also:* **air ~**) Abzug *m*; (*in jacket*) Schlitz *m* ♦ *vt* (*fig: feelings*) abreagieren.

ventilate ['vɛntɪleɪt] *vt* (*building*) belüften; (*room*) lüften.

ventilation [vɛntɪ'leɪʃən] *n* Belüftung *f*.

ventilation shaft *n* Luftschacht *m*.

ventilator ['vɛntɪleɪtə*] *n* (*TECH*) Ventilator *m*; (*MED*) Beatmungsgerät *nt*.

ventriloquist [vɛn'trɪləkwɪst] *n* Bauchredner(in) *m(f)*.

venture ['vɛntʃə*] *n* Unternehmung *f* ♦ *vt* (*opinion*) zu äußern wagen ♦ *vi* (*dare to go*) sich wagen; **a business ~** ein geschäftliches Unternehmen; **to ~ to do sth** es wagen, etw zu tun.

venture capital *n* Risikokapital *nt*.

venue ['vɛnjuː] *n* (*for meeting*) Treffpunkt *m*; (*for big events*) Austragungsort *m*.

Venus ['viːnəs] *n* Venus *f*.

veracity [və'ræsɪtɪ] *n* (*of person*) Aufrichtigkeit *f*; (*of evidence etc*) Richtigkeit *f*.

veranda(h) [və'rændə] *n* Veranda *f*.

verb [vəːb] *n* Verb *nt*.

verbal ['vəːbl] *adj* verbal; (*skills*) sprachlich; (*translation*) wörtlich.

verbally ['vəːbəlɪ] *adv* (*communicate etc*) mündlich, verbal.

verbatim [vəː'beɪtɪm] *adj* wörtlich ♦ *adv* Wort für Wort.

verbose [vəː'bəus] *adj* (*person*) wortreich; (*writing*) weitschweifig.

verdict ['vəːdɪkt] *n* (*LAW, fig*) Urteil *nt*; **~ of guilty/not guilty** Schuld-/Freispruch *m*.

verge [vəːdʒ] (*BRIT*) *n* (*of road*) Rand *m*, Bankett *nt*; **"soft ~s"** (*BRIT: AUT*) „Seitenstreifen nicht befahrbar"; **to be on the ~ of doing sth** im Begriff sein, etw zu tun.

▶**verge on** *vt fus* grenzen an +*acc*.

verger ['vəːdʒə*] *n* (*REL*) Küster *m*.

verification [vɛrɪfɪ'keɪʃən] *n* (*see vt*) Bestätigung *f*; Überprüfung *f*.

verify ['vɛrɪfaɪ] *vt* (*confirm*) bestätigen; (*check*) überprüfen.

veritable ['vɛrɪtəbl] *adj* (*real*) wahr.

vermin ['vəːmɪn] *npl* Ungeziefer *nt*.

vermouth ['vəːməθ] *n* Wermut *m*.

vernacular [və'nækjulə*] *n* (*of country*) Landessprache *f*; (*of region*) Dialekt *m*.

versatile ['vəːsətaɪl] *adj* vielseitig.

versatility [vəːsə'tɪlɪtɪ] *n* Vielseitigkeit *f*.

verse [vɔːs] n (poetry) Poesie f; (stanza) Strophe f; (in bible) Vers m; **in ~** in Versform.
versed [vɔːst] adj: **(well-)~ in** (gut) bewandert in +dat.
version ['vɔːʃən] n Version f.
versus ['vɔːsəs] prep gegen.
vertebra ['vɔːtɪbrə] (pl ~e) n Rückenwirbel m.
vertebrae ['vɔːtɪbriː] npl of **vertebra**.
vertebrate ['vɔːtɪbrɪt] n Wirbeltier nt.
vertical ['vɔːtɪkl] adj vertikal, senkrecht ♦ n Vertikale f.
vertically ['vɔːtɪklɪ] adv vertikal.
vertigo ['vɔːtɪgəu] n Schwindelgefühle pl; **to suffer from ~** leicht schwindlig werden.
verve [vɔːv] n Schwung m.
very ['vɛrɪ] adv sehr ♦ adj: **the ~ book which ...** genau das Buch, das ...; **the ~ last** der/die/ das allerletzte; **at the ~ least** allerwenigstens; **~ well/little** sehr gut/ wenig; **~ much** sehr viel; (like, hope) sehr; **the ~ thought (of it) alarms me** der bloße Gedanke (daran) beunruhigt mich; **at the ~ end** ganz am Ende.
vespers ['vɛspəz] npl (REL) Vesper f.
vessel ['vɛsl] n Gefäß nt; (NAUT) Schiff nt; see **blood**.
vest [vɛst] n (BRIT: underwear) Unterhemd nt; (US: waistcoat) Weste f ♦ vt: **to ~ sb with sth, ~ sth in sb** jdm etw verleihen.
vested interest ['vɛstɪd-] n (COMM) finanzielles Interesse nt; **to have a ~ in doing sth** ein besonderes Interesse daran haben, etw zu tun.
vestibule ['vɛstɪbjuːl] n Vorhalle f.
vestige ['vɛstɪdʒ] n Spur f.
vestment ['vɛstmənt] n (REL) Ornat nt.
vestry ['vɛstrɪ] n Sakristei f.
Vesuvius [vɪ'suːvɪəs] n Vesuv m.
vet [vɛt] (BRIT) n abbr = **veterinary surgeon** ♦ vt (examine) überprüfen.
veteran ['vɛtərn] n Veteran(in) m(f) ♦ adj: **she's a ~ campaigner for ...** sie ist eine altgediente Kämpferin für ...
veteran car n Oldtimer m (vor 1919 gebaut).
veterinarian [vɛtrɪ'nɛərɪən] (US) n = **veterinary surgeon**.
veterinary ['vɛtrɪnərɪ] adj (practice, medicine) Veterinär-; (care, training) tierärztlich.
veterinary surgeon (BRIT) n Tierarzt m, Tierärztin f.
veto ['viːtəu] (pl ~es) n Veto nt ♦ vt ein Veto einlegen gegen; **to put a ~ on sth** gegen etw ein Veto einlegen.
vetting ['vɛtɪŋ] n Überprüfung f.
vex [vɛks] vt (irritate, upset) ärgern.
vexed [vɛkst] adj (upset) verärgert; (question) umstritten.
VFD (US) n abbr (= volunteer fire department) ≈ freiwillige Feuerwehr f.
VG (BRIT) n abbr (SCOL etc: = very good) ≈ Sehr Gut nt.

VHF abbr (RADIO: = very high frequency) VHF.
VI (US) abbr (POST: = Virgin Islands).
via ['vaɪə] prep über +acc.
viability [vaɪə'bɪlɪtɪ] n (see adj) Durchführbarkeit f, Rentabilität f.
viable ['vaɪəbl] adj (project) durchführbar; (company) rentabel.
viaduct ['vaɪədʌkt] n Viadukt m.
vial ['vaɪəl] n Fläschchen nt.
vibes [vaɪbz] npl (MUS) see **vibraphone**; (inf: vibrations): **I get good/bad ~ from it/him** das/er/macht mich an/nicht an.
vibrant ['vaɪbrnt] adj (lively) dynamisch; (bright) lebendig; (full of emotion: voice) volltönend.
vibraphone ['vaɪbrəfəun] n Vibraphon nt.
vibrate [vaɪ'breɪt] vi (house) zittern, beben; (machine, sound etc) vibrieren.
vibration [vaɪ'breɪʃən] n (act of vibrating) Vibrieren nt; (instance) Vibration f.
vibrator [vaɪ'breɪtə*] n Vibrator m.
vicar ['vɪkə*] n Pfarrer m.
vicarage ['vɪkərɪdʒ] n Pfarrhaus nt.
vicarious [vɪ'kɛərɪəs] adj (pleasure, experience) indirekt.
vice [vaɪs] n (moral fault) Laster nt; (TECH) Schraubstock m.
vice- [vaɪs] pref Vize-.
vice-chairman [vaɪs'tʃɛəmən] n stellvertretender Vorsitzender m.
vice chancellor (BRIT) n (of university) ≈ Rektor m.
vice president n Vizepräsident(in) m(f).
viceroy ['vaɪsrɔɪ] n Vizekönig m.
vice squad n (POLICE) Sittendezernat nt.
vice versa ['vaɪsɪ'vɔːsə] adv umgekehrt.
vicinity [vɪ'sɪnɪtɪ] n: **in the ~ (of)** in der Nähe or Umgebung (+gen).
vicious ['vɪʃəs] adj (attack, blow) brutal; (words, look) gemein; (horse, dog) bösartig.
vicious circle n Teufelskreis m.
viciousness ['vɪʃəsnɪs] n Bösartigkeit f, Gemeinheit f.
vicissitudes [vɪ'sɪsɪtjuːdz] npl Wechselfälle pl.
victim ['vɪktɪm] n Opfer nt; **to be the ~ of an attack** einem Angriff zum Opfer fallen.
victimization ['vɪktɪmaɪ'zeɪʃən] n Schikanierung f.
victimize ['vɪktɪmaɪz] vt schikanieren.
victor ['vɪktə*] n Sieger(in) m(f).
Victorian [vɪk'tɔːrɪən] adj viktorianisch.
victorious [vɪk'tɔːrɪəs] adj (team) siegreich; (shout) triumphierend.
victory ['vɪktərɪ] n Sieg m; **to win a ~ over sb** einen Sieg über jdn erringen.
video ['vɪdɪəu] n (film, cassette, recorder) Video nt ♦ cpd Video-.
video camera n Videokamera f.
video cassette n Videokassette f.
video cassette recorder n Videorekorder m.
videodisc, videodisk ['vɪdɪəudɪsk] n Bildplatte f.

video game n Videospiel nt, Telespiel nt.
video nasty n *Video mit übertriebenen Gewaltszenen und/oder pornographischem Inhalt.*
videophone ['vɪdɪəʊfəʊn] n Bildtelefon nt.
video recorder n Videorekorder m.
video recording n Videoaufnahme f.
video tape n Videoband nt.
vie [vaɪ] vi: to ~ with sb/for sth mit jdm/um etw wetteifern.
Vienna [vɪ'ɛnə] n Wien nt.
Viennese [vɪə'niːz] adj Wiener.
Vietnam ['vjɛt'næm] n Vietnam nt.
Viet Nam ['vjɛt'næm] n = **Vietnam**.
Vietnamese [vjɛtnə'miːz] adj vietnamesisch ♦ n inv (person) Vietnamese m, Vietnamesin f; (LING) Vietnamesisch nt.
view [vjuː] n (from window etc) Aussicht f; (sight) Blick m; (outlook) Sicht f; (opinion) Ansicht f ♦ vt betrachten; (house) besichtigen; **to be on ~** (in museum etc) ausgestellt sein; **in full ~ of** vor den Augen +gen; **to take the ~ that** ... der Ansicht sein, daß ...; **in ~ of the weather/the fact that** in Anbetracht des Wetters/der Tatsache, daß ...; **in my ~** meiner Ansicht nach; **an overall ~ of the situation** ein allgemeiner Überblick über die Lage; **with a ~ to doing sth** mit der Absicht, etw zu tun.
viewdata ® ['vjuːdeɪtə] (BRIT) n Bildschirmtext m.
viewer ['vjuːə*] n (person) Zuschauer(in) m(f); (viewfinder) Sucher m.
viewfinder ['vjuːfaɪndə*] n Sucher m.
viewpoint ['vjuːpɔɪnt] n (attitude) Standpunkt m; (place) Aussichtspunkt m.
vigil ['vɪdʒɪl] n Wache f; **to keep ~** Wache halten.
vigilance ['vɪdʒɪləns] n Wachsamkeit f.
vigilance committee (US) n Bürgerwehr f.
vigilant ['vɪdʒɪlənt] adj wachsam.
vigilante [vɪdʒɪ'læntɪ] n *Mitglied einer Selbstschutzorganisation oder Bürgerwehr* ♦ adj (group, patrol) Bürgerwehr-, Selbstschutz-.
vigorous ['vɪgərəs] adj (action, campaign) energisch, dynamisch; (plant) kräftig.
vigour, (US) **vigor** ['vɪgə*] n (of person, campaign) Energie f, Dynamik f.
vile [vaɪl] adj abscheulich.
vilify ['vɪlɪfaɪ] vt diffamieren.
villa ['vɪlə] n Villa f.
village ['vɪlɪdʒ] n Dorf nt.
villager ['vɪlɪdʒə*] n Dorfbewohner(in) m(f).
villain ['vɪlən] n (scoundrel) Schurke m; (in novel etc) Bösewicht m; (BRIT: criminal) Verbrecher(in) m(f).
VIN (US) n abbr (= vehicle identification number) amtliches Kennzeichen nt.
vinaigrette [vɪneɪ'grɛt] n Vinaigrette f.
vindicate ['vɪndɪkeɪt] vt (person) rehabilitieren; (action) rechtfertigen.

vindication [vɪndɪ'keɪʃən] n Rechtfertigung f.
vindictive [vɪn'dɪktɪv] adj (person) nachtragend; (action) aus Rache.
vine [vaɪn] n (BOT: producing grapes) Weinrebe f; (: in jungle) Rebengewächs nt.
vinegar ['vɪnɪgə*] n Essig m.
vine grower n Weinbauer m.
vine-growing ['vaɪngrəʊɪŋ] adj (region) Weinbau- ♦ n Weinbau m.
vineyard ['vɪnjɑːd] n Weinberg m.
vintage ['vɪntɪdʒ] n (of wine) Jahrgang m ♦ cpd (classic) klassisch; **the 1980 ~** (of wine) der Jahrgang 1980.
vintage car n Oldtimer m (zwischen 1919 und 1930 gebaut).
vintage wine n erlesener Wein m.
vinyl ['vaɪnl] n Vinyl nt; (records) Schallplatten pl.
viola [vɪ'əʊlə] n Bratsche f.
violate ['vaɪəleɪt] vt (agreement) verletzen; (peace) stören; (graveyard) schänden.
violation [vaɪə'leɪʃən] n (of agreement etc) Verletzung f; **in ~ of** (rule, law) unter Verletzung +gen.
violence ['vaɪələns] n Gewalt f; (strength) Heftigkeit f.
violent ['vaɪələnt] adj (behaviour) gewalttätig; (death) gewaltsam; (explosion, criticism, emotion) heftig; **a ~ dislike of sb/sth** eine heftige Abneigung gegen jdn/etw.
violently ['vaɪələntlɪ] adv heftig; (ill) schwer; (angry) äußerst.
violet ['vaɪələt] adj violett ♦ n (colour) Violett nt; (plant) Veilchen nt.
violin [vaɪə'lɪn] n Geige f, Violine f.
violinist [vaɪə'lɪnɪst] n Violinist(in) m(f), Geiger(in) m(f).
VIP n abbr (= very important person) VIP m.
viper ['vaɪpə*] n Viper f.
viral ['vaɪərəl] adj (disease, infection) Virus-.
virgin ['vɜːdʒɪn] n Jungfrau f ♦ adj (snow, forest etc) unberührt; **she is a ~** sie ist Jungfrau; **the Blessed V~** die Heilige Jungfrau.
virgin birth n unbefleckte Empfängnis f; (BIOL) Jungfernzeugung f.
virginity [vɜː'dʒɪnɪtɪ] n (of person) Jungfräulichkeit f.
Virgo ['vɜːgəʊ] n (sign) Jungfrau f; **to be ~** Jungfrau sein.
virile ['vɪraɪl] adj (person) männlich.
virility [vɪ'rɪlɪtɪ] n (masculine qualities) Männlichkeit f.
virtual ['vɜːtjʊəl] adj (COMPUT, PHYS) virtuell; **it's a ~ impossibility** es ist so gut wie unmöglich; **to be the ~ leader** eigentlich or praktisch der Führer sein.
virtually ['vɜːtjʊəlɪ] adv praktisch, nahezu; **it is ~ impossible** es ist so gut wie unmöglich.
virtual reality n virtuelle Realität f.
virtue ['vɜːtjuː] n Tugend f; (advantage) Vorzug m; **by ~ of** aufgrund +gen.
virtuosi [vɜːtjʊ'əʊzɪ] npl of **virtuoso**.

virtuosity [vəːtjuˈɒsɪtɪ] *n* Virtuosität *f*.
virtuoso [vəːtjuˈəuzəu] (*pl* ~**s** *or* **virtuosi**) *n*
Virtuose *m*.
virtuous [ˈvəːtjuəs] *adj* tugendhaft.
virulence [ˈvɪruləns] *n* (*of disease*)
Bösartigkeit *f*; (*hatred*) Feindseligkeit *f*.
virulent [ˈvɪrulənt] *adj* (*disease*) bösartig;
(*actions, feelings*) feindselig.
virus [ˈvaɪərəs] *n* (*MED, COMPUT*) Virus *m or nt*.
visa [ˈviːzə] *n* Visum *nt*.
vis-à-vis [viːzəˈviː] *prep* gegenüber.
viscose [ˈvɪskəus] *n* (*also CHEM*) Viskose *f*.
viscount [ˈvaɪkaunt] *n* Viscount *m*.
viscous [ˈvɪskəs] *adj* zähflüssig.
vise [vaɪs] (*US*) *n* (*TECH*) = **vice**.
visibility [vɪzɪˈbɪlɪtɪ] *n* (*range of vision*)
Sicht(weite) *f*.
visible [ˈvɪzəbl] *adj* sichtbar; ~ **exports/
imports** sichtbare Ausfuhren/Einfuhren.
visibly [ˈvɪzəblɪ] *adv* sichtlich.
vision [ˈvɪʒən] *n* (*sight*) Sicht *f*; (*foresight*)
Weitblick *m*; (*in dream*) Vision *f*.
visionary [ˈvɪʒənrɪ] *adj* (*with foresight*)
vorausblickend.
visit [ˈvɪzɪt] *n* Besuch *m* ♦ *vt* besuchen; **a
private/official** ~ ein privater/offizieller
Besuch.
visiting [ˈvɪzɪtɪŋ] *adj* (*speaker, team*) Gast-.
visiting card *n* Visitenkarte *f*.
visiting hours *npl* Besuchszeiten *pl*.
visiting professor *n* Gastprofessor(in) *m(f)*.
visitor [ˈvɪzɪtə*] *n* Besucher(in) *m(f)*.
visitors' book [ˈvɪzɪtəz-] *n* Gästebuch *nt*.
visor [ˈvaɪzə*] *n* (*of helmet etc*) Visier *nt*.
VISTA [ˈvɪstə] (*US*) *n abbr* (= *Volunteers in
Service to America*) staatliches
Förderprogramm für strukturschwache
Gebiete.
vista [ˈvɪstə] *n* Aussicht *f*.
visual [ˈvɪzjuəl] *adj* (*image etc*) visuell; **the**
~ **arts** die darstellenden Künste.
visual aid *n* Anschauungsmaterial *nt*.
visual display unit *n* (Daten)sichtgerät *nt*.
visualize [ˈvɪzjuəlaɪz] *vt* sich *dat* vorstellen.
visually [ˈvɪzjuəlɪ] *adv* visuell; ~ **appealing**
optisch ansprechend; ~ **handicapped**
sehbehindert.
vital [ˈvaɪtl] *adj* (*essential*) unerläßlich; (*organ*)
lebenswichtig; (*full of life*) vital; **of**
~ **importance (to sb/sth)** von größter
Wichtigkeit (für jdn/etw).
vitality [vaɪˈtælɪtɪ] *n* (*liveliness*) Vitalität *f*.
vitally [ˈvaɪtəlɪ] *adv*: ~ **important** äußerst
wichtig.
vital statistics *npl* (*fig: of woman*)
Körpermaße *pl*; (*of population*)
Bevölkerungsstatistik *f*.
vitamin [ˈvɪtəmɪn] *n* Vitamin *nt* ♦ *cpd* (*pill,
deficiencies*) Vitamin-.
vitiate [ˈvɪʃɪeɪt] *vt* (*spoil*) verunreinigen.
vitreous [ˈvɪtrɪəs] *adj*: ~ **china** Porzellanemail
nt; ~ **enamel** Glasemail *nt*.

vitriolic [vɪtrɪˈɒlɪk] *adj* (*fig: language, behaviour*)
haßerfüllt.
viva [ˈvaɪvə] *n* (*SCOL: also:* ~ **voce** [-ˈvəutʃɪ])
mündliche Prüfung *f*.
vivacious [vɪˈveɪʃəs] *adj* lebhaft.
vivacity [vɪˈvæsɪtɪ] *n* Lebendigkeit *f*.
vivid [ˈvɪvɪd] *adj* (*description*) lebendig;
(*memory, imagination*) lebhaft; (*colour*)
leuchtend; (*light*) hell.
vividly [ˈvɪvɪdlɪ] *adv* (*describe*) lebendig;
(*remember*) lebhaft.
vivisection [vɪvɪˈsekʃən] *n* Vivisektion *f*.
vixen [ˈvɪksn] *n* (*ZOOL*) Füchsin *f*; (*pej: woman*)
Drachen *m*.
viz [vɪz] *abbr* (= *videlicet*) nämlich.
VLF *abbr* (*RADIO*: = *very low frequency*) VLF.
V-neck [ˈviːnɛk] *n* (*also*: ~ **jumper** *or* **pullover**)
Pullover *m* mit V-Ausschnitt.
VOA *n abbr* (= *Voice of America*) Stimme *f*
Amerikas.
vocabulary [vəuˈkæbjulərɪ] *n* (*words known*)
Vokabular *nt*, Wortschatz *m*.
vocal [ˈvəukl] *adj* (*of the voice*) stimmlich;
(*articulate*) lautstark.
vocal cords *npl* Stimmbänder *pl*.
vocalist [ˈvəukəlɪst] *n* Sänger(in) *m(f)*.
vocals [ˈvəuklz] *npl* (*MUS*) Gesang *m*, Vocals
pl.
vocation [vəuˈkeɪʃən] *n* (*calling*) Berufung *f*;
(*profession*) Beruf *m*.
vocational [vəuˈkeɪʃənl] *adj* (*training, guidance
etc*) Berufs-.
vociferous [vəˈsɪfərəs] *adj* (*protesters,
demands*) lautstark.
vodka [ˈvɒdkə] *n* Wodka *m*.
vogue [vəug] *n* (*fashion*) Mode *f*; (*popularity*)
Popularität *f*; **in** ~ in Mode.
voice [vɔɪs] *n* (*also fig*) Stimme *f* ♦ *vt* (*opinion*)
zum Ausdruck bringen; **in a loud/soft** ~ mit
lauter/leiser Stimme; **to give** ~ **to** Ausdruck
verleihen +*dat*.
voice-over [ˈvɔɪsəuvə*] *n* (Film)kommentar *m*.
void [vɔɪd] *n* (*hole*) Loch *nt*; (*fig: emptiness*)
Leere *f* ♦ *adj* (*invalid*) ungültig; ~ **of** (*empty*)
ohne.
voile [vɔɪl] *n* Voile *m*.
vol. *abbr* (= *volume*) Bd.
volatile [ˈvɒlətaɪl] *adj* (*person*) impulsiv;
(*situation*) unsicher; (*liquid etc*) flüchtig.
volcanic [vɒlˈkænɪk] *adj* (*rock, eruption*)
vulkanisch, Vulkan-.
volcano [vɒlˈkeɪnəu] (*pl* ~**es**) *n* Vulkan *m*.
volition [vəˈlɪʃən] *n*: **of one's own** ~ aus
freiem Willen.
volley [ˈvɒlɪ] *n* (*of gunfire*) Salve *f*; (*of stones,
questions*) Hagel *m*; (*TENNIS etc*) Volley *m*.
volleyball [ˈvɒlɪbɔːl] *n* Volleyball *m*.
volt [vəult] *n* Volt *nt*.
voltage [ˈvəultɪdʒ] *n* Spannung *f*; **high/low** ~
Hoch-/Niederspannung *f*.
volte-face [ˈvɒltˈfɑːs] *n* Kehrtwendung *f*.
voluble [ˈvɒljubl] *adj* (*person*) redselig;

(*speech*) wortreich.

volume ['vɔljuːm] n (*space*) Volumen nt; (*amount*) Umfang m, Ausmaß nt; (*book*) Band m; (*sound level*) Lautstärke f; ~ **one/two** (*of book*) Band eins/zwei; **his expression spoke ~s** sein Gesichtsausdruck sprach Bände.

volume control n (*RADIO, TV*) Lautstärkeregler m.

volume discount n (*COMM*) Mengenrabatt m.

voluminous [və'luːmɪnəs] adj (*clothes*) sehr weit; (*correspondence, notes*) umfangreich.

voluntarily ['vɔləntrɪlɪ] adv freiwillig.

voluntary ['vɔləntərɪ] adj freiwillig.

voluntary liquidation n freiwillige Liquidation f.

volunteer [vɔlən'tɪə'] n Freiwillige(r) f(m) ♦ vt (*information*) vorbringen ♦ vi (*for army etc*) sich freiwillig melden; **to ~ to do sth** sich anbieten, etw zu tun.

voluptuous [və'lʌptjuəs] adj sinnlich, wollüstig.

vomit ['vɔmɪt] n Erbrochene(s) nt ♦ vt erbrechen ♦ vi sich übergeben.

voracious [və'reɪʃəs] adj (*person*) gefräßig; ~ **appetite** Riesenappetit m.

vote [vəut] n Stimme f; (*votes cast*) Stimmen pl; (*right to vote*) Wahlrecht nt; (*ballot*) Abstimmung f ♦ vt (*elect*): **to be ~d chairman etc** zum Vorsitzenden etc gewählt werden; (*propose*): **to ~ that** vorschlagen, daß ♦ vi (*in election etc*) wählen; **to put sth to the ~, (take a) ~ on sth** über etw acc abstimmen; ~ **of censure** Tadelsantrag m; **to pass a ~ of confidence/no confidence** ein Vertrauens-/ Mißtrauensvotum annehmen; **to ~ to do sth** dafür stimmen, etw zu tun; **to ~ yes/no** mit Ja/Nein stimmen; **to ~ Labour/Green etc** Labour/die Grünen etc wählen; **to ~ for** or **in favour of sth/against sth** für/gegen etw stimmen.

vote of thanks n Danksagung f.

voter ['vəutə'] n Wähler(in) m(f).

voting ['vəutɪŋ] n Wahl f.

voting paper (*BRIT*) n Stimmzettel m.

voting right n Stimmrecht nt.

vouch [vautʃ]: ~ **for** vt fus bürgen für.

voucher ['vautʃə'] n Gutschein m; (*receipt*) Beleg m; **gift** ~ Geschenkgutschein m; **luncheon** ~ Essensmarke f; **travel** ~ Reisegutschein m.

vow [vau] n Versprechen nt ♦ vt: **to ~ to do sth/that** geloben, etw zu tun/daß; **to take** or **make a ~ to do sth** geloben, etw zu tun.

vowel ['vauəl] n Vokal m.

voyage ['vɔɪɪdʒ] n Reise f.

voyeur [vwɑː'jəː'] n Voyeur(in) m(f).

voyeurism [vwɑː'jəːrɪzəm] n Voyeurismus m.

VP n abbr = **vice president**.

vs abbr (= *versus*) vs.

V-sign ['viːsaɪn] (*BRIT*) n: **to give sb the** ~ ≈ jdm den Vogel zeigen.

VSO (*BRIT*) n abbr (= *Voluntary Service Overseas*) britischer Entwicklungsdienst.

VT (*US*) abbr (*POST*: = *Vermont*).

vulgar ['vʌlgə'] adj (*remarks, gestures*) vulgär; (*decor, ostentation*) geschmacklos.

vulgarity [vʌl'gærɪtɪ] n (*see adj*) Vulgarität f; Geschmacklosigkeit f.

vulnerability [vʌlnərə'bɪlɪtɪ] n Verletzlichkeit f.

vulnerable ['vʌlnərəbl] adj (*person, position*) verletzlich.

vulture ['vʌltʃə'] n (*also fig*) Geier m.

vulva ['vʌlvə] n Vulva f.

W, w

W¹, w ['dʌbljuː] n (*letter*) W nt, w nt; ~ **for William** ≈ W wie Wilhelm.

W² ['dʌbljuː] abbr (*ELEC*: = *watt*) W; (= *west*) W.

WA abbr (*US: POST*: = *Washington*); (*AUSTRALIA*: = *Western Australia*).

wad [wɔd] n (*of cotton wool*) Bausch m; (*of paper, banknotes*) Bündel nt.

wadding ['wɔdɪŋ] n Füllmaterial nt.

waddle ['wɔdl] vi watscheln.

wade [weɪd] vi: **to ~ across** (*a river, stream*) waten durch; **to ~ through** (*fig: a book*) sich durchkämpfen durch.

wafer ['weɪfə'] n (*biscuit*) Waffel f.

wafer-thin ['weɪfə'θɪn] adj hauchdünn.

waffle ['wɔfl] n (*CULIN*) Waffel f; (*inf: empty talk*) Geschwafel nt ♦ vi (*in speech etc*) schwafeln.

waffle iron n Waffeleisen nt.

waft [wɔft] vt, vi wehen.

wag [wæg] vt (*tail*) wedeln mit; (*finger*) drohen mit ♦ vi (*tail*) wedeln; **the dog ~ged its tail** der Hund wedelte mit dem Schwanz.

wage [weɪdʒ] n (*also*: ~**s**) Lohn m ♦ vt: **to ~ war** Krieg führen; **a day's ~s** ein Tageslohn.

wage claim n Lohnforderung f.

wage differential n Lohnunterschied m.

wage earner [-əːnə'] n Lohnempfänger(in) m(f).

wage freeze n Lohnstopp m.

wage packet n Lohntüte f.

wager ['weɪdʒə'] n Wette f ♦ vt wetten.

waggle ['wægl] vt (*ears etc*) wackeln mit ♦ vi wackeln.

wag(g)on ['wægən] n (*horse-drawn*) Fuhrwerk nt; (*BRIT: RAIL*) Waggon m.

wail [weɪl] n (*of person*) Jammern nt; (*of siren*) Heulen nt ♦ vi (*person*) jammern; (*siren*) heulen.

waist [weɪst] n (*ANAT, of clothing*) Taille f.
waistcoat ['weɪskəut] (*BRIT*) n Weste f.
waistline ['weɪstlaɪn] n Taille f.
wait [weɪt] n Wartezeit f ♦ vi warten; **to lie in ~ for sb** jdm auflauern; **to keep sb ~ing** jdn warten lassen; **I can't ~ to ...** (*fig*) ich kann es kaum erwarten, zu ...; **to ~ for sb/sth** auf jdn/etw warten; **~ a minute!** Moment mal!; **"repairs while you ~"** „Reparaturen sofort".
►**wait behind** vi zurückbleiben.
►**wait on** vt fus (*serve*) bedienen.
►**wait up** vi aufbleiben; **don't ~ up for me** warte nicht auf mich.
waiter ['weɪtə'] n Kellner m.
waiting ['weɪtɪŋ] n: **"no ~"** (*BRIT: AUT*) „Halten verboten".
waiting list n Warteliste f.
waiting room n (*in surgery*) Wartezimmer nt; (*in railway station*) Wartesaal m.
waitress ['weɪtrɪs] n Kellnerin f.
waive [weɪv] vt (*rule*) verzichten auf +acc.
waiver ['weɪvə'] n Verzicht m.
wake [weɪk] (*pt* **woke, waked,** *pp* **woken, waked**) vt (*also:* **~ up**) wecken ♦ vi (*also:* **~ up**) aufwachen ♦ n (*for dead person*) Totenwache f; (*NAUT*) Kielwasser nt; **to ~ up to** (*fig*) sich dat bewußt werden +gen; **in the ~ of** (*fig*) unmittelbar nach, im Gefolge +gen; **to follow in sb's ~** (*fig*) hinter jdm herziehen.
waken ['weɪkn] vt = **wake.**
Wales [weɪlz] n Wales nt; **the Prince of ~** der Prinz von Wales.
walk [wɔːk] n (*hike*) Wanderung f; (*shorter*) Spaziergang m; (*gait*) Gang m; (*path*) Weg m; (*in park, along coast etc*) (Spazier)weg m ♦ vi gehen; (*instead of driving*) zu Fuß gehen; (*for pleasure, exercise*) spazierengehen ♦ vt (*distance*) gehen, laufen; (*dog*) ausführen; **it's 10 minutes' ~ from here** es ist 10 Minuten zu Fuß von hier; **to go for a ~** spazierengehen; **to slow to a ~** im Schrittempo weitergehen; **people from all ~s of life** Leute aus allen Gesellschaftsschichten; **to ~ in one's sleep** schlafwandeln; **I'd rather ~ than take the bus** ich gehe lieber zu Fuß, als mit dem Bus zu fahren; **I'll ~ you home** ich bringe dich nach Hause.
►**walk out** vi (*audience*) den Saal verlassen; (*workers*) in Streik treten.
►**walk out on** (*inf*) vt fus (*family etc*) verlassen.
walkabout ['wɔːkəbaut] n: **the Queen/president went on a ~** die Königin/der Präsident mischte sich unters Volk *or* nahm ein Bad in der Menge.
walker ['wɔːkə'] n (*person*) Spaziergänger(in) m(f).
walkie-talkie ['wɔːkɪ'tɔːkɪ] n Walkie-talkie nt.
walking ['wɔːkɪŋ] n Wandern nt; **it's within**

~ distance es ist zu Fuß erreichbar.
walking holiday n Wanderurlaub m.
walking shoes npl Wanderschuhe pl.
walking stick n Spazierstock m.
Walkman ® ['wɔːkmən] n Walkman ® m.
walk-on ['wɔːkɔn] adj (*THEAT*): **~ part** Statistenrolle f.
walkout ['wɔːkaut] n (*of workers*) Streik m.
walkover ['wɔːkəuvə'] (*inf*) n (*competition, exam etc*) Kinderspiel nt.
walkway ['wɔːkweɪ] n Fußweg m.
wall [wɔːl] n Wand f; (*exterior, city wall etc*) Mauer f; **to go to the ~** (*fig: firm etc*) kaputtgehen.
►**wall in** vt (*enclose*) ummauern.
wall cupboard n Wandschrank m.
walled [wɔːld] adj von Mauern umgeben.
wallet ['wɔlɪt] n Brieftasche f.
wallflower ['wɔːlflauə'] n (*BOT*) Goldlack m; **to be a ~** (*fig*) ein Mauerblümchen sein.
wall hanging n Wandbehang m.
wallop ['wɔləp] (*BRIT: inf*) vt verprügeln.
wallow ['wɔləu] vi (*in mud, water*) sich wälzen; (*in guilt, grief*) schwelgen.
wallpaper ['wɔːlpeɪpə'] n Tapete f ♦ vt tapezieren.
wall-to-wall ['wɔːltə'wɔːl] adj: **~ carpeting** Teppichboden m.
wally ['wɔlɪ] (*inf*) n Trottel m.
walnut ['wɔːlnʌt] n (*nut*) Walnuß f; (*tree*) Walnußbaum m; (*wood*) Nußbaumholz nt.
walrus ['wɔːlrəs] (*pl* **~** *or* **~es**) n Walroß nt.
waltz [wɔːlts] n Walzer m ♦ vi Walzer tanzen.
wan [wɔn] adj bleich; (*smile*) matt.
wand [wɔnd] n (*also:* **magic ~**) Zauberstab m.
wander ['wɔndə'] vi (*person*) herumlaufen; (*mind, thoughts*) wandern ♦ vt (*the streets, the hills etc*) durchstreifen.
wanderer ['wɔndərə'] n Wandervogel m.
wandering ['wɔndrɪŋ] adj (*tribe*) umherziehend; (*minstrel, actor*) fahrend.
wane [weɪn] vi (*moon*) abnehmen; (*influence etc*) schwinden.
wangle ['wæŋgl] (*BRIT: inf*) vt sich dat verschaffen.
wanker ['wæŋkə'] (*inf!*) n Wichser m.
wannabe(e) ['wɔnəbiː] (*inf*) n Möchtegern m; **James Bond ~** Möchtegern-James-Bond m.
want [wɔnt] vt (*wish for*) wollen; (*need*) brauchen ♦ n (*lack*): **for ~ of** aus Mangel an +dat; **wants** npl (*needs*) Bedürfnisse pl; **to ~ to do sth** etw tun wollen; **to ~ sb to do sth** wollen, daß jd etw tut; **to ~ in/out** herein-/hinauswollen; **you're ~ed on the phone** Sie werden am Telefon verlangt; **he is ~ed by the police** er wird von der Polizei gesucht; **a ~ of foresight** ein Mangel an Voraussicht.
want ads (*US*) npl Kaufgesuche pl.
wanted ['wɔntɪd] adj (*criminal etc*) gesucht; **"cook ~"** „Koch/Köchin gesucht".
wanting ['wɔntɪŋ] adj: **to be found ~** sich als

unzulänglich erweisen.

wanton ['wɒntn] *adj* (*violence*) mutwillig; (*promiscuous: woman*) schamlos.

war [wɔːʳ] *n* Krieg *m*; **to go to ~** (*start*) einen Krieg anfangen; **to be at ~** (**with**) sich im Kriegszustand befinden (mit); **to make ~** (**on**) Krieg führen (gegen); **a ~ on drugs/ crime** ein Feldzug gegen Drogen/das Verbrechen.

warble ['wɔːbl] *n* Trällern *nt* ♦ *vi* trällern.

war cry *n* Kriegsruf *m*; (*fig: slogan*) Schlachtruf *m*.

ward [wɔːd] *n* (*in hospital*) Station *f*; (*POL*) Wahlbezirk *m*; (*LAW: also:* **~ of court**) Mündel *nt* unter Amtsvormundschaft.

▶**ward off** *vt* (*attack, enemy, illness*) abwehren.

warden ['wɔːdn] *n* (*of park etc*) Aufseher(in) *m(f)*; (*of jail*) Wärter(in) *m(f)*; (*BRIT: of youth hostel*) Herbergsvater *m*, Herbergsmutter *f*; (: *in university*) Wohnheimleiter(in) *m(f)*; (*:also:* **traffic ~**) Verkehrspolizist(in) *m(f)*.

warder ['wɔːdəʳ] (*BRIT*) *n* Gefängnis- wärter(in) *m(f)*.

wardrobe ['wɔːdrəub] *n* (*for clothes*) Kleiderschrank *m*; (*collection of clothes*) Garderobe *f*; (*CINE, THEAT*) Kostüme *pl*.

warehouse ['wɛəhaus] *n* Lager *nt*.

wares [wɛəz] *npl* Waren *pl*.

warfare ['wɔːfɛəʳ] *n* Krieg *m*.

war game *n* Kriegsspiel *nt*.

warhead ['wɔːhed] *n* Sprengkopf *m*.

warily ['wɛərɪlɪ] *adv* vorsichtig.

Warks (*BRIT*) *abbr* (*POST: = Warwickshire*).

warlike ['wɔːlaɪk] *adj* kriegerisch.

warm [wɔːm] *adj* warm; (*thanks, applause, welcome, person*) herzlich; **it's ~** es ist warm; **I'm ~** mir ist warm; **to keep sth ~** etw warm halten; **with my ~est thanks/ congratulations** mit meinem herzlichsten Dank/meinen herzlichsten Glückwünschen.

▶**warm up** *vi* warm werden; (*athlete*) sich aufwärmen ♦ *vt* aufwärmen.

warm-blooded ['wɔːm'blʌdɪd] *adj* warmblütig.

war memorial *n* Kriegerdenkmal *nt*.

warm-hearted [wɔːm'hɑːtɪd] *adj* warmherzig.

warmly ['wɔːmlɪ] *adv* (*applaud, welcome*) herzlich; (*dress*) warm.

warmonger ['wɔːmʌŋɡəʳ] (*pej*) *n* Kriegshetzer *m*.

warmongering ['wɔːmʌŋɡrɪŋ] (*pej*) *n* Kriegshetze *f*.

warmth [wɔːmθ] *n* Wärme *f*; (*friendliness*) Herzlichkeit *f*.

warm-up ['wɔːmʌp] *n* Aufwärmen *nt*; **~ exercise** Aufwärmübung *f*.

warn [wɔːn] *vt:* **to ~ sb that ...** jdn warnen, daß ...; **to ~ sb of sth** jdn vor etw *dat* warnen; **to ~ sb not to do sth** *or* **against doing sth** jdn davor warnen, etw zu tun.

warning ['wɔːnɪŋ] *n* Warnung *f*; **without (any) ~** (*suddenly*) unerwartet; (*without notifying*)

ohne Vorwarnung; **gale ~** Sturmwarnung *f*.

warning light *n* Warnlicht *nt*.

warning triangle *n* (*AUT*) Warndreieck *nt*.

warp [wɔːp] *vi* (*wood etc*) sich verziehen ♦ *vt* (*fig: character*) entstellen ♦ *n* (*TEXTILES*) Kette *f*.

warpath ['wɔːpɑːθ] *n:* **to be on the ~** auf dem Kriegspfad sein.

warped [wɔːpt] *adj* (*wood*) verzogen; (*fig: character, sense of humour etc*) abartig.

warrant ['wɔrnt] *n* (*LAW: for arrest*) Haftbefehl *m*; (*:also:* **search ~**) Durchsuchungsbefehl *m* ♦ *vt* (*justify, merit*) rechtfertigen.

warrant officer *n* (*MIL*) Dienstgrad zwischen Offizier und Unteroffizier.

warranty ['wɔrntɪ] *n* Garantie *f*; **under ~** (*COMM*) unter Garantie.

warren ['wɔrən] *n* (*of rabbits*) Bau *m*; (*fig: of passages, streets*) Labyrinth *nt*.

warring ['wɔːrɪŋ] *adj* (*nations*) kriegführend; (*interests*) gegensätzlich; (*factions*) verfeindet.

warrior ['wɔrɪəʳ] *n* Krieger *m*.

Warsaw ['wɔːsɔː] *n* Warschau *nt*.

warship ['wɔːʃɪp] *n* Kriegsschiff *nt*.

wart [wɔːt] *n* Warze *f*.

wartime ['wɔːtaɪm] *n:* **in ~** im Krieg.

wary ['wɛərɪ] *adj* (*person*) vorsichtig; **to be ~ about** *or* **of doing sth** Bedenken haben, etw zu tun.

was [wɒz] *pt of* be.

wash [wɒʃ] *vt* waschen; (*dishes*) spülen, abwaschen; (*remove grease, paint etc*) ausspülen ♦ *vi* (*person*) sich waschen ♦ *n* (*clothes etc*) Wäsche *f*; (*washing programme*) Waschgang *m*; (*of ship*) Kielwasser *nt*; **he was ~ed overboard** er wurde über Bord gespült; **to ~ over/against sth** (*sea etc*) über/gegen etw *acc* spülen; **to have a ~** sich waschen; **to give sth a ~** etw waschen.

▶**wash away** *vt* wegspülen.

▶**wash down** *vt* (*wall, car*) abwaschen; (*food: with wine etc*) hinunterspülen.

▶**wash off** *vi* sich herauswaschen ♦ *vt* abwaschen.

▶**wash out** *vt* (*stain*) herauswaschen.

▶**wash up** *vi* (*BRIT: wash dishes*) spülen, abwaschen; (*US: have a wash*) sich waschen.

Wash. (*US*) *abbr* (*POST: = Washington*).

washable ['wɒʃəbl] *adj* (*fabric*) waschbar; (*wallpaper*) abwaschbar.

washbasin ['wɒʃbeɪsn], (*US*) **washbowl** ['wɒʃbəul] *n* Waschbecken *nt*.

washcloth ['wɒʃklɒθ] (*US*) *n* Waschlappen *m*.

washer ['wɒʃəʳ] *n* (*on tap etc*) Dichtungsring *m*.

washing ['wɒʃɪŋ] *n* Wäsche *f*.

washing line (*BRIT*) *n* Wäscheleine *f*.

washing machine *n* Waschmaschine *f*.

washing powder (*BRIT*) *n* Waschpulver *nt*.

Washington ['wɒʃɪŋtən] *n* Washington *nt*.

washing-up [wɔʃɪŋˈʌp] n Abwasch m; **to do the ~** spülen, abwaschen.
washing-up liquid (BRIT) n (Geschirr)spülmittel nt.
wash-out ['wɔʃaut] (inf) n (failed event) Reinfall m.
washroom ['wɔʃrum] (US) n Waschraum m.
wasn't ['wɔznt] = **was not**.
WASP, Wasp [wɔsp] (US: inf) n abbr (= White Anglo-Saxon Protestant) weißer angelsächsischer Protestant m.
wasp [wɔsp] n Wespe f.
waspish ['wɔspɪʃ] adj giftig.
wastage ['weɪstɪdʒ] n Verlust m; **natural ~** natürliche Personalreduzierung.
waste [weɪst] n Verschwendung f; (rubbish) Abfall m ♦ adj (material) Abfall-; (left over: paper etc) ungenutzt ♦ vt verschwenden; (opportunity) vertun; **wastes** npl (area of land) Wildnis f; **it's a ~ of money** das ist Geldverschwendung; **to go to ~** umkommen; **to lay ~** (area, town) verwüsten.
▶**waste away** vi verkümmern.
wastebasket ['weɪstbɑːskɪt] (US) n = **wastepaper basket**.
waste disposal unit (BRIT) n Müllschlucker m.
wasteful ['weɪstful] adj (person) verschwenderisch; (process) aufwendig.
waste ground (BRIT) n unbebautes Grundstück nt.
wasteland ['weɪstlənd] n Ödland nt; (in town) ödes Gebiet nt; (fig) Einöde f.
wastepaper basket ['weɪstpeɪpə-] (BRIT) n Papierkorb m.
waste pipe n Abflußrohr nt.
waste products npl Abfallprodukte pl.
waster ['weɪstə*] n Verschwender(in) m(f); (good-for-nothing) Taugenichts m.
watch [wɔtʃ] n (also: **wristwatch**) (Armband)uhr f; (surveillance) Bewachung f; (MIL, NAUT: group of guards) Wachmannschaft f; (NAUT: spell of duty) Wache f ♦ vt (look at) betrachten; (: match, programme) sich dat ansehen; (spy on, guard) beobachten; (be careful of) aufpassen auf +acc ♦ vi (look) zusehen; **to be on ~** Wache halten; **to keep a close ~ on sb/sth** jdn/etw genau im Auge behalten; **to ~ TV** fernsehen; **~ what you're doing!** paß auf!; **~ how you drive!** fahr vorsichtig!
▶**watch out** vi aufpassen; **~ out!** Vorsicht!
watchband ['wɔtʃbænd] (US) n = **watchstrap**.
watchdog ['wɔtʃdɔg] n (dog) Wachhund m; (fig) Aufpasser(in) m(f).
watchful ['wɔtʃful] adj wachsam.
watchmaker ['wɔtʃmeɪkə*] n Uhrmacher(in) m(f).
watchman ['wɔtʃmən] (irreg: like **man**) n see **night watchman**.
watch stem (US) n (winder) Krone f,

Aufziehrädchen nt.
watchstrap ['wɔtʃstræp] n Uhrarmband nt.
watchword ['wɔtʃwəːd] n Parole f.
water ['wɔːtə*] n Wasser nt ♦ vt (plant) gießen; (garden) bewässern ♦ vi (eyes) tränen; **a drink of ~** ein Schluck Wasser; **in British ~s** in britischen (Hoheits)gewässern; **to pass ~** (urinate) Wasser lassen; **my mouth is ~ing** mir läuft das Wasser im Mund zusammen; **to make sb's mouth ~** jdm den Mund wäßrig machen.
▶**water down** vt (also fig) verwässern.
water biscuit n Kräcker m.
water cannon n Wasserwerfer m.
water closet (BRIT: old) n Wasserklosett nt.
watercolour, (US) **watercolor** ['wɔːtəkʌlə*] n (picture) Aquarell nt; **watercolours** npl (paints) Wasserfarben pl.
water-cooled ['wɔːtəkuːld] adj wassergekühlt.
watercress ['wɔːtəkrɛs] n Brunnenkresse f.
waterfall ['wɔːtəfɔːl] n Wasserfall m.
waterfront ['wɔːtəfrʌnt] n (at seaside) Ufer nt; (at docks) Hafengegend f.
water heater n Heißwassergerät nt.
water hole n Wasserloch nt.
water ice n Fruchteis nt (auf Wasserbasis).
watering can ['wɔːtərɪŋ-] n Gießkanne f.
water level n Wasserstand m; (of flood) Pegelstand m.
water lily n Seerose f.
water line n Wasserlinie f.
waterlogged ['wɔːtəlɔgd] adj (ground) unter Wasser.
water main n Hauptwasserleitung f.
watermark ['wɔːtəmɑːk] n (on paper) Wasserzeichen nt.
watermelon ['wɔːtəmɛlən] n Wassermelone f.
waterproof ['wɔːtəpruːf] adj (trousers, jacket etc) wasserdicht.
water-repellent ['wɔːtərɪˈpɛlnt] adj wasserabstoßend.
watershed ['wɔːtəʃɛd] n (GEOG) Wasserscheide f; (fig) Wendepunkt m.
water-skiing ['wɔːtəskiːɪŋ] n Wasserski nt.
water softener n Wasserenthärter m.
water tank n Wassertank m.
watertight ['wɔːtətaɪt] adj wasserdicht; (fig: excuse, case, agreement etc) hieb- und stichfest.
water vapour n Wasserdampf m.
waterway ['wɔːtəweɪ] n Wasserstraße f.
waterworks ['wɔːtəwəːks] n Wasserwerk nt; (inf, fig: bladder) Blase f.
watery ['wɔːtəri] adj (coffee, soup etc) wäßrig; (eyes) tränend.
watt [wɔt] n Watt nt.
wattage ['wɔtɪdʒ] n Wattleistung f.
wattle ['wɔtl] n Flechtwerk nt.
wattle and daub n Lehmgeflecht nt.
wave [weɪv] n (also fig) Welle f; (of hand) Winken nt ♦ vi (signal) winken; (branches)

sich hin- und herbewegen; (*grass*) wogen; (*flag*) wehen ♦ *vt* (*hand, flag etc*) winken mit; (*gun, stick*) schwenken; (*hair*) wellen; **short/ medium/long** ~ (*RADIO*) Kurz-/Mittel-/ Langwelle *f*; **the new** ~ (*CINE, MUS*) die Neue Welle *f*; **he** ~**d us over to his table** er winkte uns zu seinem Tisch hinüber; **to** ~ **goodbye to sb** jdm zum Abschied winken.

►**wave aside** *vt* (*fig: suggestion etc*) zurückweisen.

waveband ['weɪvbænd] *n* (*RADIO*) Wellenbereich *m*.

wavelength ['weɪvleŋθ] *n* (*RADIO*) Wellenlänge *f*; **on the same** ~ (*fig*) auf derselben Wellenlänge.

waver ['weɪvə*] *vi* (*voice*) schwanken; (*eyes*) zucken; (*love, person*) wanken.

wavy ['weɪvɪ] *adj* (*line*) wellenförmig; (*hair*) wellig.

wax [wæks] *n* Wachs *nt*; (*for sealing*) Siegellack *m*; (*in ear*) Ohrenschmalz *nt* ♦ *vt* (*floor*) bohnern; (*car, skis*) wachsen ♦ *vi* (*moon*) zunehmen.

waxed [wækst] *adj* (*jacket*) gewachst.

waxen [wæksn] *adj* (*face*) wachsbleich.

waxworks ['wækswɔːks] *npl* (*models*) Wachsfiguren *pl* ♦ *n* (*place*) Wachsfigurenkabinett *nt*.

way [weɪ] *n* Weg *m*; (*distance*) Strecke *f*; (*direction*) Richtung *f*; (*manner*) Art *f*; (*method*) Art und Weise *f*; (*habit*) Gewohnheit *f*; **which** ~ **to ...?** wo geht es zu ...?; **this** ~, **please** hier entlang, bitte; **on the** ~ (*en route*) auf dem Weg, unterwegs; **to be on one's** ~ auf dem Weg sein; **to fight one's** ~ **through a crowd** sich *acc* durch die Menge kämpfen; **to lie one's** ~ **out of sth** sich aus etw herauslügen; **to keep out of sb's** ~ jdm aus dem Weg gehen; **it's a long** ~ **away** es ist weit entfernt; (*event*) das ist noch lange hin; **the village is rather out of the** ~ das Dorf ist recht abgelegen; **to go out of one's** ~ **to do sth** sich sehr bemühen, etw zu tun; **to be in the** ~ im Weg sein; **to lose one's** ~ sich verirren; **under** ~ (*project etc*) im Gang; **the** ~ **back** der Rückweg; **to make** ~ (**for sb/sth**) (für jdn/etw) Platz machen; **to get one's own** ~ seinen Willen bekommen; **put it the right** ~ **up** (*BRIT*) stell es richtig herum hin; **to be the wrong** ~ **round** verkehrt herum sein; **he's in a bad** ~ ihm geht es schlecht; **in a** ~ in gewisser Weise; **in some** ~**s** in mancher Hinsicht; **no** ~**!** (*inf*) kommt nicht in Frage!; **by the** ~ ... übrigens ...; "~ **in**" (*BRIT*) „Eingang"; "~ **out**" (*BRIT*) „Ausgang"; "**give** ~" (*BRIT: AUT*) „Vorfahrt beachten"; ~ **of life** Lebensstil *m*.

waybill ['weɪbɪl] *n* Frachtbrief *m*.

waylay [weɪ'leɪ] (*irreg: like* lay) *vt* auflauern +*dat*; **to get waylaid** (*fig*) abgefangen

werden.

wayside ['weɪsaɪd] *adj* am Straßenrand ♦ *n* Straßenrand *m*; **to fall by the** ~ (*fig*) auf der Strecke bleiben.

way station (*US*) *n* (*RAIL*) kleiner Bahnhof *m*; (*fig*) Zwischenstation *f*.

wayward ['weɪwəd] *adj* (*behaviour*) eigenwillig; (*child*) eigensinnig.

WC (*BRIT*) *n abbr* (= *water closet*) WC *nt*.

WCC *n abbr* (= *World Council of Churches*) Weltkirchenrat *m*.

we [wiː] *pl pron* wir; **here** ~ **are** (*arriving*) da sind wir; (*finding sth*) na bitte.

weak [wiːk] *adj* schwach; (*tea, coffee*) dünn; **to grow** ~(**er**) schwächer werden.

weaken ['wiːkn] *vi* (*resolve, person*) schwächer werden; (*influence, power*) nachlassen ♦ *vt* schwächen.

weak-kneed ['wiːk'niːd] *adj* (*fig*) schwächlich.

weakling ['wiːklɪŋ] *n* Schwächling *m*.

weakly ['wiːklɪ] *adv* schwach.

weakness ['wiːknɪs] *n* Schwäche *f*; **to have a** ~ **for** eine Schwäche haben für.

wealth [wɛlθ] *n* Reichtum *m*; (*of details, knowledge etc*) Fülle *f*.

wealth tax *n* Vermögenssteuer *f*.

wealthy ['wɛlθɪ] *adj* wohlhabend, reich.

wean [wiːn] *vt* (*also fig*) entwöhnen.

weapon ['wɛpən] *n* Waffe *f*.

wear [wɛə*] (*pt* wore, *pp* worn) *vt* (*clothes, shoes, beard*) tragen; (*put on*) anziehen ♦ *vi* (*last*) halten; (*become old: carpet, jeans*) sich abnutzen ♦ *n* (*damage*) Verschleiß *m*; (*use*): **I got a lot of/very little** ~ **out of the coat** der Mantel hat lange/nicht sehr lange gehalten; **baby**~ Babykleidung *f*; **sports**~ Sportkleidung *f*; **town/evening** ~ Kleidung für die Stadt/den Abend; **to** ~ **a hole in sth** (*coat etc*) etw durchwetzen.

►**wear away** *vt* verschleißen ♦ *vi* (*inscription etc*) verwittern.

►**wear down** *vt* (*heels*) abnutzen; (*person, strength*) zermürben.

►**wear off** *vi* (*pain etc*) nachlassen.

►**wear on** *vi* sich hinziehen.

►**wear out** *vt* (*shoes, clothing*) verschleißen; (*person, strength*) erschöpfen.

wearable ['wɛərəbl] *adj* tragbar.

wear and tear [-tɛə*] *n* Verschleiß *m*.

wearer ['wɛərə*] *n* Träger(in) *m(f)*.

wearily ['wɪərɪlɪ] *adv* (*say, sit*) lustlos, müde.

weariness ['wɪərɪnɪs] *n* (*tiredness*) Müdigkeit *f*.

wearisome ['wɪərɪsəm] *adj* (*boring*) langweilig; (*tiring*) ermüdend.

weary ['wɪərɪ] *adj* (*tired*) müde; (*dispirited*) lustlos ♦ *vi*: **to** ~ **of sb/sth** jds/etw *gen* überdrüssig werden.

weasel ['wiːzl] *n* Wiesel *nt*.

weather ['wɛðə*] *n* Wetter *nt* ♦ *vt* (*storm, crisis*) überstehen; (*rock, wood*) verwittern; **what's the** ~ **like?** wie ist das Wetter?; **under the** ~

(fig: ill) angeschlagen.
weather-beaten ['wɛðəbiːtn] *adj (face)* vom Wetter gegerbt; *(building, stone)* verwittert.
weathercock ['wɛðəkɔk] *n* Wetterhahn *m*.
weather forecast *n* Wettervorhersage *f*.
weatherman ['wɛðəmæn] *(irreg: like* **man***) n* Mann *m* vom Wetteramt, Wetterfrosch *m (hum inf)*.
weatherproof ['wɛðəpruːf] *adj* wetterfest.
weather report *n* Wetterbericht *m*.
weather vane [-veɪn] *n* = **weathercock**.
weave [wiːv] *(pt* **wove**, *pp* **woven***) vt (cloth)* weben; *(basket)* flechten ♦ *vi (fig: pt, pp* **weaved**: *move in and out)* sich schlängeln.
weaver ['wiːvə'] *n* Weber(in) *m(f)*.
weaving ['wiːvɪŋ] *n* Weberei *f*.
web [wɛb] *n (also fig)* Netz *nt; (on duck's foot)* Schwimmhaut *f*.
webbed ['wɛbd] *adj (foot)* Schwimm-.
webbing ['wɛbɪŋ] *n (on chair)* Gewebe *nt*.
wed [wɛd] *(pt, pp* **wedded***) vt, vi* heiraten ♦ *n:* **the newly-~s** die Jungvermählten *pl*.
Wed. *abbr (=* **Wednesday***)* Mi.
we'd [wiːd] **= we had; we would**.
wedded ['wɛdɪd] *pt, pp of* **wed** ♦ *adj:* **to be ~ to sth** *(idea etc)* mit etw eng verbunden sein.
wedding [wɛdɪŋ] *n* Hochzeit *f;* **silver/golden ~** silberne/goldene Hochzeit.
wedding day *n* Hochzeitstag *m*.
wedding dress *n* Hochzeitskleid *nt*.
wedding present *n* Hochzeitsgeschenk *nt*.
wedding ring *n* Trauring *m*.
wedge [wɛdʒ] *n* Keil *m; (of cake)* Stück *nt* ♦ *vt (fasten)* festklemmen; *(pack tightly)* einkeilen.
wedge-heeled shoes ['wɛdʒhiːld-] *npl* Schuhe *pl* mit Keilabsätzen.
wedlock ['wɛdlɔk] *n* Ehe *f*.
Wednesday ['wɛdnzdɪ] *n* Mittwoch *m; see also* **Tuesday**.
wee [wiː] *(SCOT) adj* klein.
weed [wiːd] *n (BOT)* Unkraut *nt; (pej: person)* Schwächling *m* ♦ *vt (garden)* jäten.
►**weed out** *vt (fig)* aussondern.
weedkiller ['wiːdkɪlə'] *n* Unkrautvertilger *m*.
weedy ['wiːdɪ] *adj (person)* schwächlich.
week [wiːk] *n* Woche *f;* **once/twice a ~** einmal/zweimal die Woche; **in two ~s' time** in zwei Wochen; **a ~ today/on Friday** heute/Freitag in einer Woche.
weekday ['wiːkdeɪ] *n* Wochentag *m; (COMM: Monday to Saturday)* Werktag *m;* **on ~s** an Wochentagen/Werktagen.
weekend [wiːk'ɛnd] *n* Wochenende *nt;* **this/next/last ~** an diesem/am nächsten/am letzten Wochenende; **what are you doing at the ~?** was machen Sie am Wochenende?; **open at ~s** an Wochenenden geöffnet.
weekly ['wiːklɪ] *adv* wöchentlich ♦ *adj (newspaper)* Wochen- ♦ *n (newspaper)* Wochenzeitung *f; (magazine)* Wochenzeitschrift *f*.

weep [wiːp] *(pt, pp* **wept***) vi (person)* weinen; *(wound)* nässen.
weeping willow ['wiːpɪŋ-] *n (tree)* Trauerweide *f*.
weepy ['wiːpɪ] *adj (person)* weinerlich; *(film)* rührselig ♦ *n (film etc)* Schmachtfetzen *m*.
weft [wɛft] *n* Schußfaden *m*.
weigh [weɪ] *vt* wiegen; *(fig: evidence, risks)* abwägen ♦ *vi* wiegen; **to ~ anchor** den Anker lichten.
►**weigh down** *vt* niederdrücken.
►**weigh out** *vt (goods)* auswiegen.
►**weigh up** *vt (person, offer, risk)* abschätzen.
weighbridge ['weɪbrɪdʒ] *n* Brückenwaage *f*.
weighing machine ['weɪɪŋ-] *n* Waage *f*.
weight [weɪt] *n* Gewicht *nt* ♦ *vt (fig):* **to be ~ed in favour of sb/sth** jdn/etw begünstigen; **to be sold by ~** nach Gewicht verkauft werden; **to lose ~** abnehmen; **to put on ~** zunehmen; **~s and measures** Maße und Gewichte.
weighting ['weɪtɪŋ] *n (allowance)* Zulage *f*.
weightlessness ['weɪtlɪsnɪs] *n* Schwerelosigkeit *f*.
weightlifter ['weɪtlɪftə'] *n* Gewichtheber *m*.
weight limit *n* Gewichtsbeschränkung *f*.
weight training *n* Krafttraining *nt*.
weighty ['weɪtɪ] *adj* schwer; *(fig: important)* gewichtig.
weir [wɪə'] *n (in river)* Wehr *nt*.
weird [wɪəd] *adj (object, situation, effect)* komisch; *(person)* seltsam.
weirdo ['wɪədəu] *(inf) n* verrückter Typ *m*.
welcome ['wɛlkəm] *adj* willkommen ♦ *n* Willkommen *nt* ♦ *vt* begrüßen, willkommen heißen; **~ to London!** willkommen in London!; **to make sb ~** jdn freundlich aufnehmen; **you're ~ to try** du kannst es gern versuchen; **thank you - you're ~!** danke - nichts zu danken!
welcoming ['wɛlkəmɪŋ] *adj (smile, room)* einladend; *(person)* freundlich.
weld [wɛld] *n* Schweißnaht *f* ♦ *vt* schweißen.
welder ['wɛldə'] *n (person)* Schweißer(in) *m(f)*.
welding ['wɛldɪŋ] *n* Schweißen *nt*.
welfare ['wɛlfɛə'] *n (well-being)* Wohl *nt; (social aid)* Sozialhilfe *f*.
welfare state *n* Wohlfahrtsstaat *m*.
welfare work *n* Fürsorgearbeit *f*.
well [wɛl] *n (for water)* Brunnen *m; (oil well)* Quelle *f* ♦ *adv* gut; *(for emphasis with adj)* durchaus ♦ *adj:* **to be ~** *(person)* gesund sein ♦ *excl* nun!, na!; **as ~** *(in addition)* ebenfalls; **you might as ~ tell me** sag es mir ruhig; **he did as ~ as he could** er machte es so gut er konnte; **pretty as ~ as rich** sowohl hübsch als auch reich; **~ done!** gut gemacht!; **to do ~** *(person)* gut vorankommen; *(business)* gut gehen; **~ before dawn** lange vor Tagesanbruch; **~ over 40** weit über 40; **I don't feel ~** ich fühle mich nicht gut *or* wohl; **get ~ soon!** gute Besserung!; **~, as I**

was saying ... also, wie ich bereits sagte, ...
▶**well up** vi (tears, emotions) aufsteigen.
we'll [wi:l] = we will; we shall.
well-behaved ['wɛlbɪ'heɪvd] adj wohlerzogen.
well-being ['wɛl'bi:ɪŋ] n Wohl(ergehen) nt.
well-bred ['wɛl'brɛd] adj (person) gut erzogen.
well-built ['wɛl'bɪlt] adj gut gebaut.
well-chosen ['wɛl'tʃəʊzn] adj gut gewählt.
well-deserved ['wɛldɪ'zɜːvd] adj wohlverdient.
well-developed ['wɛldɪ'vɛləpt] adj gut entwickelt.
well-disposed ['wɛl'dɪspəʊzd] adj: ~ to(wards) freundlich gesonnen +dat.
well-dressed ['wɛl'drɛst] adj gut gekleidet.
well-earned ['wɛl'ɜːnd] adj (rest) wohlverdient.
well-groomed ['wɛl'gruːmd] adj gepflegt.
well-heeled ['wɛl'hiːld] (inf) adj betucht.
well-informed ['wɛlɪn'fɔːmd] adj gut informiert.
Wellington ['wɛlɪŋtən] n (GEOG) Wellington nt.
wellingtons ['wɛlɪŋtənz] npl (also: **wellington boots**) Gummistiefel pl.
well-kept ['wɛl'kɛpt] adj (house, grounds) gepflegt; (secret) gut gehütet.
well-known ['wɛl'nəʊn] adj wohlbekannt.
well-mannered ['wɛl'mænəd] adj wohlerzogen.
well-meaning ['wɛl'miːnɪŋ] adj (person) wohlmeinend; (offer etc) gutgemeint.
well-nigh ['wɛl'naɪ] adv: ~ **impossible** geradezu unmöglich.
well-off ['wɛl'ɒf] adj (rich) begütert.
well-read ['wɛl'rɛd] adj belesen.
well-spoken ['wɛl'spəʊkn] adj: **to be** ~ sich gut or gewandt ausdrücken.
well-stocked ['wɛl'stɒkt] adj gut bestückt.
well-timed ['wɛl'taɪmd] adj gut abgepaßt.
well-to-do ['wɛltə'duː] adj wohlhabend.
well-wisher ['wɛlwɪʃəʳ] n (friend, admirer) wohlmeinender Mensch m; **scores of** ~**s had gathered** eine große Gefolgschaft hatte sich versammelt; **letters from** ~**s** Briefe von Leuten, die es gut meinen.
well-woman clinic ['wɛlwʊmən-] n ≈ Frauensprechstunde f.
Welsh [wɛlʃ] adj walisisch ♦ n (LING) Walisisch nt; **the Welsh** npl die Waliser pl.
Welshman ['wɛlʃmən] (irreg: like **man**) n Waliser m.
Welsh rarebit n überbackenes Käsebrot nt.
Welshwoman ['wɛlʃwʊmən] (irreg: like **woman**) n Waliserin f.
welter ['wɛltəʳ] n: **a** ~ **of** eine Flut von.
went [wɛnt] pt of **go**.
wept [wɛpt] pt, pp of **weep**.
were [wɜːʳ] pt of **be**.
we're [wɪəʳ] = we are.
weren't [wɜːnt] = were not.
werewolf ['wɪəwʊlf] (pl **werewolves**) n

Werwolf m.
werewolves ['wɪəwʊlvz] npl of **werewolf**.
west [wɛst] n Westen m ♦ adj (wind, side, coast) West-, westlich ♦ adv (to or towards the west) westwärts; **the W~** (POL) der Westen.
westbound ['wɛstbaʊnd] adj (traffic, carriageway) in Richtung Westen.
West Country (BRIT) n: **the** ~ Südwestengland nt.
westerly ['wɛstəlɪ] adj westlich.
western ['wɛstən] adj westlich ♦ n (CINE) Western m.
westerner ['wɛstənəʳ] n Abendländer(in) m(f).
westernized ['wɛstənaɪzd] adj (society etc) verwestlicht.
West German adj westdeutsch ♦ n (person) Westdeutsche(r) f(m).
West Germany n (formerly) Bundesrepublik f Deutschland.
West Indian adj westindisch ♦ n (person) Westinder(in) m(f).
West Indies [-'ɪndɪz] npl: **the** ~ Westindien nt.
Westminster ['wɛstmɪnstəʳ] n Westminster nt; (parliament) das britische Parlament.
westward(s) ['wɛstwəd(z)] adv westwärts.
wet [wɛt] adj naß ♦ n (BRIT: POL) Gemäßigte(r) f(m), Waschlappen m (pej); **to get** ~ naß werden; "~ **paint**" „frisch gestrichen"; **to be a** ~ **blanket** (fig: pej: person) ein(e) Spielverderber(in) m(f) sein; **to** ~ **one's pants/o.s.** sich dat in die Hosen machen.
wetness ['wɛtnɪs] n Nässe f; (of climate) Feuchtigkeit f.
wet suit n Taucheranzug m.
we've [wiːv] = we have.
whack [wæk] vt schlagen.
whacked [wækt] (BRIT: inf) adj (exhausted) erschlagen.
whale [weɪl] n Wal m.
whaler ['weɪləʳ] n Walfänger m.
whaling ['weɪlɪŋ] n Walfang m.
wharf [wɔːf] (pl **wharves**) n Kai m.
wharves [wɔːvz] npl of **wharf**.

―――――――――――――― KEYWORD

what [wɒt] adj **1** (in direct/indirect questions) welche(r, s); ~ **colour/shape is it?** welche Farbe/Form hat es?; **for** ~ **reason?** aus welchem Grund?
2 (in exclamations) was für ein(e); ~ **a mess!** was für ein Durcheinander!; ~ **a fool I am!** was bin ich doch (für) ein Idiot! ♦ pron (interrogative, relative) was; ~ **are you doing?** was machst du?; ~ **are you talking about?** wovon redest du?; ~ **is it called?** wie heißt das?; ~ **about me?** und ich?; ~ **about a cup of tea?** wie wär's mit einer Tasse Tee?; ~ **about going to the cinema?** sollen wir ins Kino gehen?; **I saw** ~ **you did/what was on the table** ich habe gesehen, was du getan hast/was auf dem Tisch war; **tell me**

~ **you're thinking about** sag mir, woran du denkst
♦ *excl (disbelieving)* was, wie; ~, **no coffee!** was *or* wie, kein Kaffee?

whatever [wɒt'ɛvə*] *adj:* ~ **book** welches Buch auch immer ♦ *pron:* **do** ~ **is necessary/you want** tun Sie, was nötig ist/was immer Sie wollen; ~ **happens** was auch passiert; **no reason** ~ *or* **whatsoever** überhaupt kein Grund; **nothing** ~ *or* **whatsoever** überhaupt nichts.

whatsoever [wɒtsəu'ɛvə*] *adj* = **whatever**.

wheat [wi:t] *n* Weizen *m*.

wheatgerm ['wi:tdʒɜ:m] *n* Weizenkeim *m*.

wheatmeal ['wi:tmi:l] *n* Weizenmehl *nt*.

wheedle ['wi:dl] *vt:* **to** ~ **sb into doing sth** jdn beschwatzen, etw zu tun; **to** ~ **sth out of sb** jdm etw abluchsen.

wheel [wi:l] *n* Rad *nt*; *(also:* **steering** ~) Lenkrad *nt*; *(NAUT)* Steuer *nt* ♦ *vt (pram etc)* schieben ♦ *vi (birds)* kreisen; *(also:* ~ **round:** *person)* sich herumdrehen.

wheelbarrow ['wi:lbærəu] *n* Schubkarre *f*.

wheelbase ['wi:lbeis] *n* Radstand *m*.

wheelchair ['wi:ltʃɛə*] *n* Rollstuhl *m*.

wheel clamp *n* Parkkralle *f*.

wheeler-dealer ['wi:lə'di:lə*] *(pej) n* Geschäftemacher(in) *m(f)*.

wheelie-bin ['wi:lɪbɪn] *n* Mülltonne *f* auf Rädern.

wheeling ['wi:lɪŋ] *n:* ~ **and dealing** *(pej)* Geschäftemacherei *f*.

wheeze [wi:z] *vi (person)* keuchen ♦ *n (idea, joke etc)* Scherz *m*.

wheezy ['wi:zɪ] *adj (person)* mit pfeifendem Atem; *(cough)* keuchend; *(breath)* pfeifend; *(laugh)* asthmatisch.

═══════════════════════ *KEYWORD*

when [wɛn] *adv* wann
♦ *conj* **1** *(at, during, after the time that)* wenn; **she was reading** ~ **I came in** als ich hereinkam, las sie gerade; **be careful** ~ **you cross the road** sei vorsichtig, wenn du die Straße überquerst
2 *(on, at which)* als; **on the day** ~ **I met him** am Tag, als ich ihn traf
3 *(whereas)* wo ... doch, obwohl; **why did you buy that** ~ **you can't afford it?** warum hast du das gekauft, obwohl du es dir nicht leisten kannst?

whenever [wɛn'ɛvə*] *adv, conj (any time that)* wann immer; *(every time that)* (jedesmal,) wenn; **I go** ~ **I can** ich gehe, wann immer ich kann.

where [wɛə*] *adv, conj* wo; **this is** ~ ... hier ...; ~ **possible** soweit möglich; ~ **are you from?** woher kommen Sie?

whereabouts [wɛərə'bauts] *adv* wo ♦ *n:* **nobody knows his** ~ keiner weiß, wo er ist.

whereas [wɛər'æz] *conj* während.

whereby [wɛə'baɪ] *(form) adv* wonach.

whereupon [wɛərə'pɒn] *conj* worauf.

wherever [wɛər'ɛvə*] *conj (position)* wo (auch) immer; *(motion)* wohin (auch) immer ♦ *adv (surprise)* wo (um alles in der Welt); **sit** ~ **you like** nehmen Sie Platz, wo immer Sie wollen.

wherewithal ['wɛəwɪðɔ:l] *n:* **the** ~ **(to do sth)** *(money)* das nötige Kleingeld(, um etw zu tun).

whet [wɛt] *vt (appetite)* anregen; *(tool)* schleifen.

whether ['wɛðə*] *conj* ob; **I don't know** ~ **to accept or not** ich weiß nicht, ob ich annehmen soll oder nicht; ~ **you go or not** ob du gehst oder nicht; **it's doubtful** ~ ... es ist zweifelhaft, ob ...

whey ['weɪ] *n* Molke *f*.

═══════════════════════ *KEYWORD*

which [wɪtʃ] *adj* **1** *(interrogative: direct, indirect)* welche(r, s); ~ **picture?** welches Bild?; ~ **books?** welche Bücher?; ~ **one?** welche(r,s)?
2: in ~ **case** in diesem Fall; **by** ~ **time** zu dieser Zeit
♦ *pron* **1** *(interrogative)* welche(r, s); ~ **of you are coming?** wer von Ihnen kommt?; **I don't mind** ~ mir ist gleich, welche(r,s)
2 *(relative)* der/die/das; **the apple** ~ **you ate/which is on the table** der Apfel, den du gegessen hast/der auf dem Tisch liegt; **the chair on** ~ **you are sitting** der Stuhl, auf dem Sie sitzen; **the book of** ~ **you spoke** das Buch, wovon *or* von dem Sie sprachen; **he said he saw her,** ~ **is true** er sagte, er habe sie gesehen, was auch stimmt; **after** ~ wonach.

whichever [wɪtʃ'ɛvə*] *adj:* **take** ~ **book you want** nehmen Sie irgendein *or* ein beliebiges Buch; ~ **book you take** welches Buch Sie auch nehmen.

whiff [wɪf] *n (of perfume)* Hauch *m*; *(of petrol, smoke)* Geruch *m*; **to catch a** ~ **of sth** den Geruch von etw wahrnehmen.

while [waɪl] *n* Weile *f* ♦ *conj* während; **for a** ~ eine Weile (lang); **in a** ~ gleich; **all the** ~ die ganze Zeit (über); **I'll/we'll** *etc* **make it worth your** ~ es wird sich für Sie lohnen.

▶**while away** *vt (time)* sich *dat* vertreiben.

whilst [waɪlst] *conj* = **while**.

whim [wɪm] *n* Laune *f*.

whimper ['wɪmpə*] *n (cry, moan)* Wimmern *nt* ♦ *vi* wimmern.

whimsical ['wɪmzɪkəl] *adj* wunderlich, seltsam; *(story)* kurios.

whine [waɪn] *n (of pain)* Jammern *nt*; *(of engine, siren)* Heulen *nt* ♦ *vi (person)* jammern; *(dog)* jaulen; *(engine, siren)* heulen.

whip [wɪp] n Peitsche f; (POL)
≈ Fraktionsführer m ♦ vt (person, animal)
peitschen; (cream, eggs) schlagen; (move
quickly): **to ~ sth out/off** etw blitzschnell
hervorholen/wegbringen.

> Der Ausdruck **whip** bezieht sich in der Politik
> auf einen Abgeordneten, der für die Einhaltung
> der Parteidisziplin zuständig ist, besonders für
> die Anwesenheit und das Wahlverhalten der
> Abgeordneten im Unterhaus. Die whips
> fordern die Abgeordneten ihrer Partei
> schriftlich zur Anwesenheit auf und deuten die
> Wichtigkeit der Abstimmungen durch ein-,
> zwei-, oder dreimaliges Unterstreichen an,
> wobei dreimaliges Unterstreichen (3-line whip)
> strengsten Fraktionszwang bedeutet.

▶**whip up** vt (cream) schlagen; (inf: meal)
hinzaubern; (arouse: support) anheizen;
(: people) mitreißen.

whiplash ['wɪplæʃ] n Peitschenhieb m; (MED:
also: ~ **injury**) Schleudertrauma nt.

whipped cream [wɪpt-] n Schlagsahne f.

whipping boy ['wɪpɪŋ-] n (fig) Prügelknabe
m.

whip-round ['wɪpraʊnd] (BRIT: inf) n
(Geld)sammlung f.

whirl [wə:l] vt (arms, sword etc) herumwirbeln
♦ vi wirbeln ♦ n (of activity, pleasure) Wirbel
m; **to be in a ~** (mind, person) völlig verwirrt
sein.

whirlpool ['wə:lpu:l] n (lit) Strudel m.

whirlwind ['wə:lwɪnd] n (lit) Wirbelwind m.

whirr [wə:ʳ] vi (motor etc) surren.

whisk [wɪsk] n (CULIN) Schneebesen m ♦ vt
(cream, eggs) schlagen; **to ~ sb away** or **off**
jdn in Windeseile wegbringen.

whiskers ['wɪskəz] npl (of animal) Barthaare
pl; (of man) Backenbart m.

whisky, (US, Ireland) **whiskey** ['wɪskɪ] n
Whisky m.

whisper ['wɪspəʳ] n Flüstern nt; (fig: of wind)
Wispern nt ♦ vt, vi flüstern; **to ~ sth to sb**
jdm etw zuflüstern.

whispering ['wɪspərɪŋ] n Geflüster nt.

whist [wɪst] (BRIT) n Whist nt.

whistle ['wɪsl] n (sound) Pfiff m; (object)
Pfeife f ♦ vi pfeifen ♦ vt **to ~ a tune** eine
Melodie pfeifen.

whistle-stop ['wɪslstɒp] adj: **to make a ~ tour
of** (fig) eine Rundreise machen durch; (POL)
eine Wahlkampfreise machen durch.

Whit [wɪt] n = **Whitsun**.

white [waɪt] adj weiß ♦ n (colour) Weiß nt;
(person) Weiße(r) f(m); (of egg, eye) Weiße(s)
nt; **to turn** or **go ~** (person: with fear) weiß or
bleich werden; (: with age) weiße Haare
bekommen; (hair) weiß werden; **the ~s**
(washing) die Weißwäsche f; **tennis/cricket
~s** weiße Tennis-/Krickettrikots.

whitebait ['waɪtbeɪt] n eßbare Jungfische

(Heringe, Sprotten etc).

white coffee (BRIT) n Kaffee m mit Milch.

white-collar worker ['waɪtkɒlə-] n
Schreibtischarbeiter(in) m(f).

white elephant n (fig: venture)
Fehlinvestition f.

white goods npl (appliances) große
Haushaltsgeräte pl; (linen etc) Weißwaren pl.

white-hot [waɪt'hɒt] adj (metal) weißglühend.

> **White House,** eine weiß gestrichene Villa in
> Washington, ist der offizielle Wohnsitz des
> amerikanischen Präsidenten. Im weiteren
> Sinne bezieht sich dieser Begriff auf die
> Exekutive der amerikanischen Regierung.

white lie n Notlüge f.

whiteness ['waɪtnɪs] n Weiß nt.

white noise n weißes Rauschen nt.

whiteout ['waɪtaut] n starkes
Schneegestöber nt.

white paper n (POL) Weißbuch nt.

whitewash ['waɪtwɔʃ] n (paint) Tünche f; (inf:
SPORT) totale Niederlage f ♦ vt (building)
tünchen; (fig: incident, reputation)
reinwaschen.

white water n: **white-water rafting**
Wildwasserflößen nt.

whiting ['waɪtɪŋ] n inv (fish) Weißling m.

Whit Monday n Pfingstmontag m.

Whitsun ['wɪtsn] n Pfingsten nt.

whittle ['wɪtl] vt: **to ~ away** or **down** (costs
etc) verringern.

whizz [wɪz] vi: **to ~ past** or **by** vorbeisausen.

whizz kid (inf) n Senkrechtstarter(in) m(f).

WHO n abbr (= World Health Organization)
Weltgesundheitsorganisation f, WHO f.

━━━━━━━━━━━━━━━━━━ KEYWORD

who [hu:] pron **1** (interrogative) wer; (: acc)
wen; (: dat) wem; ~ **is it?, who's there?** wer
ist da?; ~ **did you give it to?** wem hast du es
gegeben?

2 (relative) der/die/das; **the man/woman
~ spoke to me** der Mann, der/die Frau, die
mit mir gesprochen hat.

whodunit, whodunnit [hu:'dʌnɪt] (inf) n
Krimi m.

whoever [hu:'evəʳ] pron: ~ **finds it** wer (auch
immer) es findet; **ask** ~ **you like** fragen Sie,
wen Sie wollen; ~ **he marries** ganz gleich or
egal, wen er heiratet; ~ **told you that?** wer
um alles in der Welt hat dir das erzählt?

whole [həʊl] adj (entire) ganz; (not broken) heil
♦ n Ganze(s) nt; **the ~ lot (of it)** alles; **the
~ lot (of them)** alle; **the ~ (of the) time** die
ganze Zeit; ~ **villages were destroyed** ganze
Dörfer wurden zerstört; **the ~ of** der/die/
das ganze; **the ~ of Glasgow/Europe** ganz
Glasgow/Europa; **the ~ of the town** die
ganze Stadt; **on the ~** im ganzen (gesehen).

wholefood(s) ['həulfu:d(z)] n(pl) Vollwertkost f.

wholefood shop n ≈ Reformhaus nt.

wholehearted [həul'hɑːtɪd] adj (agreement etc) rückhaltlos.

wholeheartedly [həul'hɑːtɪdlɪ] adv (agree etc) rückhaltlos.

wholemeal ['həulmiːl] (BRIT) adj (bread, flour) Vollkorn-.

whole note (US) n ganze Note f.

wholesale ['həulseɪl] n (business) Großhandel m ♦ adj (price) Großhandels-; (destruction etc) umfassend ♦ adv (buy, sell) im Großhandel.

wholesaler ['həulseɪlə*] n Großhändler m.

wholesome ['həulsəm] adj (food) gesund; (effect) zuträglich; (attitude) positiv.

wholewheat ['həulwiːt] adj = **wholemeal**.

wholly ['həulɪ] adv ganz und gar.

================= *KEYWORD*

whom [huːm] pron **1** (interrogative: acc) wen; (: dat) wem; ~ **did you see?** wen hast du gesehen?; **to ~ did you give it?** wem hast du es gegeben?
2 (relative: acc) den/die/das; (: dat) dem/der/dem; **the man ~ I saw/to ~ I spoke** der Mann, den ich gesehen habe/mit dem ich gesprochen habe.

whooping cough ['huːpɪŋ-] n Keuchhusten m.

whoosh [wuʃ] vi: **to ~ along/past/down** entlang-/vorbei-/hinuntersausen ♦ n Sausen nt; **the skiers ~ed past, skiers came by with a ~** die Skifahrer sausten vorbei.

whopper ['wɒpə*] (inf) n (lie) faustdicke Lüge f; (large thing) Mordsding nt.

whopping ['wɒpɪŋ] (inf) adj Riesen-, riesig.

whore [hɔː*] (inf: pej) n Hure f.

================= *KEYWORD*

whose [huːz] adj **1** (possessive: interrogative) wessen; ~ **book is this?**, ~ **is this book?** wessen Buch ist das?, wem gehört das Buch?; **I don't know ~ it is** ich weiß nicht, wem es gehört
2 (possessive: relative) dessen/deren/dessen; **the man ~ son you rescued** der Mann, dessen Sohn du gerettet hast; **the woman ~ car was stolen** die Frau, deren Auto gestohlen worden war
♦ pron ~ **is this?** wem gehört das?; **I know ~ it is** ich weiß, wem es gehört.

Who's Who ['huːz'huː] n (book) Who's Who nt.

================= *KEYWORD*

why [waɪ] adv warum; ~ **not?** warum nicht?
♦ conj warum; **I wonder ~ he said that** ich frage mich, warum er das gesagt hat; **that's not ~ I'm here** ich bin nicht deswegen hier; **the reason ~** der Grund, warum or weshalb

♦ excl (expressing surprise, shock) na so was; (expressing annoyance) ach; ~, **yes (of course)** aber ja doch; ~, **it's you!** na so was, du bist's!

WI n abbr (BRIT: = Women's Institute) britischer Frauenverband ♦ abbr = **West Indies**; (US: POST: = Wisconsin).

wick [wɪk] n Docht m; **he gets on my ~** (BRIT: inf) er geht mir auf den Geist.

wicked ['wɪkɪd] adj (crime, person) böse; (smile, wit) frech; (inf: prices) unverschämt; (: weather) schrecklich.

wicker ['wɪkə*] adj (chair etc) Korb-; (basket) Weiden-.

wickerwork ['wɪkəwɜːk] adj (chair etc) Korb-; (basket) Weiden- ♦ n (objects) Korbwaren pl.

wicket ['wɪkɪt] n (CRICKET: stumps) Tor nt, Wicket nt; (: grass area) Spielbahn f.

wicket-keeper ['wɪkɪtkiːpə*] n Torwächter m.

wide [waɪd] adj breit; (area) weit; (publicity) umfassend ♦ adv: **to open sth ~** etw weit öffnen; **it is 3 metres ~** es ist 3 Meter breit; **to go ~** vorbeigehen.

wide-angle lens ['waɪdæŋgl-] n Weitwinkelobjektiv nt.

wide-awake [waɪdə'weɪk] adj hellwach.

wide-eyed [waɪd'aɪd] adj mit großen Augen; (fig) unschuldig, naiv.

widely ['waɪdlɪ] adv (differ, vary) erheblich; (travel) ausgiebig, viel; (spaced) weit; (believed, known) allgemein; **to be ~ read** (reader) sehr belesen sein.

widen ['waɪdn] vt (road, river) verbreitern; (one's experience) erweitern ♦ vi sich verbreitern.

wideness ['waɪdnɪs] n (of road, river, gap) Breite f.

wide open adj (window, eyes, mouth) weit geöffnet.

wide-ranging [waɪd'reɪndʒɪŋ] adj (effects) weitreichend; (interview, survey) umfassend.

widespread ['waɪdsprɛd] adj weitverbreitet.

widow ['wɪdəu] n Witwe f.

widowed ['wɪdəud] adj verwitwet.

widower ['wɪdəuə*] n Witwer m.

width [wɪdθ] n Breite f; (in swimming pool) (Quer)bahn f; **it's 7 metres in ~** es ist 7 Meter breit.

widthways ['wɪdθweɪz] adv der Breite nach.

wield [wiːld] vt (sword) schwingen; (power) ausüben.

wife [waɪf] (pl **wives**) n Frau f.

wig [wɪg] n Perücke f.

wigging ['wɪgɪŋ] (BRIT: inf) n Standpauke f.

wiggle ['wɪgl] vt wackeln mit.

wiggly ['wɪglɪ] adj: ~ **line** Schlangenlinie f.

wigwam ['wɪgwæm] n Wigwam m.

wild [waɪld] adj wild; (weather) rauh, stürmisch; (person, behaviour) ungestüm; (idea) weithergeholt; (applause) stürmisch
♦ n: **the ~** (natural surroundings) die freie

Natur f; **the wilds** npl die Wildnis; **I'm not ~ about it** ich bin nicht versessen or scharf darauf.

wild card n (COMPUT) Wildcard f, Ersatzzeichen nt.

wildcat ['waɪldkæt] n Wildkatze f.

wildcat strike n wilder Streik m.

wilderness ['wɪldənɪs] n Wildnis f.

wildfire ['waɪldfaɪə*] n: **to spread like ~** sich wie ein Lauffeuer ausbreiten.

wild-goose chase [waɪld'guːs-] n aussichtslose Suche f.

wildlife ['waɪldlaɪf] n (animals) die Tierwelt f.

wildly ['waɪldlɪ] adv wild; (very: romantic) wild-; (: inefficient) furchtbar.

wiles [waɪlz] npl List f.

wilful, (US) **willful** ['wɪlful] adj (obstinate) eigensinnig; (deliberate) vorsätzlich.

===================== KEYWORD

will [wɪl] (vt: pt, pp **willed**) aux vb **1** (forming future tense): I **~ finish it tomorrow** ich werde es morgen fertigmachen, ich mache es morgen fertig; **~ you do it?** - yes I **~**/no I won't machst du es? - ja/nein
2 (in conjectures, predictions): **that ~ be the postman** das ist bestimmt der Briefträger
3 (in commands, requests, offers): **~ you sit down** (politely) bitte nehmen Sie Platz; (angrily) nun setz dich doch; **~ you be quiet!** seid jetzt still!; **~ you help me?** hilfst du mir?; **~ you have a cup of tea?** möchten Sie eine Tasse Tee?; **I won't put up with it!** das lasse ich mir nicht gefallen! ♦ vt: **to ~ sb to do sth** jdn durch Willenskraft dazu bewegen, etw zu tun; **he ~ed himself to go on** er zwang sich dazu, weiterzumachen ♦ n (volition) Wille m; (testament) Testament nt; **he did it against his ~** er tat es gegen seinen Willen.

willful ['wɪlful] (US) adj = **wilful**.

willing ['wɪlɪŋ] adj (having no objection) gewillt; (enthusiastic) bereitwillig; **he's ~ to do it** er ist bereit, es zu tun; **to show ~** guten Willen zeigen.

willingly ['wɪlɪŋlɪ] adv bereitwillig.

willingness ['wɪlɪŋnɪs] n (readiness) Bereitschaft f; (enthusiasm) Bereitwilligkeit f.

will-o'-the-wisp ['wɪləðə'wɪsp] n Irrlicht nt; (fig) Trugbild nt.

willow ['wɪləu] n (tree) Weide f; (wood) Weidenholz nt.

willpower ['wɪlpauə*] n Willenskraft f.

willy-nilly ['wɪlɪ'nɪlɪ] adv (willingly or not) wohl oder übel.

wilt [wɪlt] vi (plant) welken.

Wilts [wɪlts] (BRIT) abbr (POST: = Wiltshire).

wily ['waɪlɪ] adj listig, raffiniert.

wimp [wɪmp] (inf: pej) n Waschlappen m.

wimpish ['wɪmpɪʃ] (inf) adj weichlich.

win [wɪn] (pt, pp **won**) n Sieg m ♦ vt gewinnen ♦ vi siegen, gewinnen.
▶**win over** vt (persuade) gewinnen.
▶**win round** (BRIT) vt = **win over**.

wince [wɪns] vi zusammenzucken.

winch [wɪntʃ] n Winde f.

Winchester disk ['wɪntʃɪstə-] n Winchesterplatte f.

wind¹ [wɪnd] n (air) Wind m; (MED) Blähungen pl; (breath) Atem m ♦ vt (take breath away from) den Atem nehmen +dat; **the winds** npl (MUS) die Bläser pl; **into or against the ~** gegen den Wind; **to get ~ of sth** (fig) von etw Wind bekommen; **to break ~** Darmwind entweichen lassen.

wind² [waɪnd] (pt, pp **wound**) vt (thread, rope, bandage) wickeln; (clock, toy) aufziehen ♦ vi (road, river) sich winden.
▶**wind down** vt (car window) herunterdrehen; (fig: production) zurückschrauben.
▶**wind up** vt (clock, toy) aufziehen; (debate) abschließen.

windbreak ['wɪndbreɪk] n Windschutz m.

windbreaker ['wɪndbreɪkə*] (US) n = **windcheater**.

windcheater ['wɪndtʃiːtə*] n Windjacke f.

winder ['waɪndə*] (BRIT) n (on watch) Krone f, Aufziehrädchen nt.

windfall ['wɪndfɔːl] n (money) unverhoffter Glücksfall m; (apple) Fallobst nt.

winding ['waɪndɪŋ] adj gewunden.

wind instrument ['wɪnd-] n Blasinstrument nt.

windmill ['wɪndmɪl] n Windmühle f.

window ['wɪndəu] n (also COMPUT) Fenster nt; (in shop) Schaufenster nt.

window box n Blumenkasten m.

window cleaner n Fensterputzer(in) m(f).

window dresser n Schaufensterdekorateur(in) m(f).

window envelope n Fensterumschlag m.

window frame n Fensterrahmen m.

window ledge n Fenstersims m.

window pane n Fensterscheibe f.

window-shopping ['wɪndəuʃɔpɪŋ] n Schaufensterbummel m; **to go ~** einen Schaufensterbummel machen.

windowsill ['wɪndəusɪl] n Fensterbank f.

windpipe ['wɪndpaɪp] n Luftröhre f.

wind power ['wɪnd-] n Windkraft f, Windenergie f.

windscreen ['wɪndskriːn] n Windschutzscheibe f.

windscreen washer n Scheibenwaschanlage f.

windscreen wiper [-waɪpə*] n Scheibenwischer m.

windshield ['wɪndʃiːld] (US) n = **windscreen**.

windsurfing ['wɪndsəːfɪŋ] n Windsurfen nt.

windswept ['wɪndswept] adj (place) vom Wind gepeitscht; (person) vom Wind zerzaust.

wind tunnel ['wɪnd-] *n* Windkanal *m*.
windy ['wɪndɪ] *adj* windig; **it's ~ es** ist windig.
wine [waɪn] *n* Wein *m* ♦ *vt:* **to ~ and dine sb** jdm zu einem guten Essen ausführen.
wine bar *n* Weinlokal *nt*.
wine cellar *n* Weinkeller *m*.
wine glass *n* Weinglas *nt*.
wine list *n* Weinkarte *f*.
wine merchant *n* Weinhändler(in) *m(f)*.
wine tasting [-teɪstɪŋ] *n* Weinprobe *f*.
wine waiter *n* Weinkellner *m*.
wing [wɪŋ] *n* (*of bird, insect, plane*) Flügel *m*; (*of building*) Trakt *m*; (*of car*) Kotflügel *m*; **the wings** *npl* (*THEAT*) die Kulissen *pl*.
winger ['wɪŋə*] *n* (*SPORT*) Flügelspieler(in) *m(f)*.
wing mirror (*BRIT*) *n* Seitenspiegel *m*.
wing nut *n* Flügelmutter *f*.
wingspan ['wɪŋspæn] *n* Flügelspannweite *f*.
wingspread ['wɪŋsprɛd] *n* = **wingspan**.
wink [wɪŋk] *n* (*of eye*) Zwinkern *m* ♦ *vi* (*with eye*) zwinkern; (*light etc*) blinken.
winkle [wɪŋkl] *n* Strandschnecke *f*.
winner ['wɪnə*] *n* (*of race, competition*) Sieger(in) *m(f)*; (*of prize*) Gewinner(in) *m(f)*.
winning ['wɪnɪŋ] *adj* (*team, entry*) siegreich; (*shot, goal*) entscheidend; (*smile*) einnehmend; *see also* **winnings**.
winning post *n* (*lit*) Zielpfosten *m*; (*fig*) Ziel *nt*.
winnings ['wɪnɪŋz] *npl* Gewinn *m*.
winsome ['wɪnsəm] *adj* (*expression*) gewinnend; (*person*) reizend.
winter ['wɪntə*] *n* Winter *m* ♦ *vi* (*birds*) überwintern; **in ~** im Winter.
winter sports *npl* Wintersport *m*.
wintry ['wɪntrɪ] *adj* (*weather, day*) winterlich, Winter-.
wipe [waɪp] *vt* wischen; (*dry*) abtrocknen; (*clean*) abwischen; (*erase: tape*) löschen; **to ~ one's nose** sich *dat* die Nase putzen ♦ *n:* **to give sth a ~** etw abwischen.
▶**wipe off** *vt* abwischen.
▶**wipe out** *vt* (*destroy: city etc*) auslöschen.
▶**wipe up** *vt* (*mess*) aufwischen.
wire ['waɪə*] *n* Draht *m*; (*US: telegram*) Telegramm *nt* ♦ *vt* (*US*): **to ~ sb** jdm telegrafieren; (*also:* ~ **up**: *electrical fitting*) anschließen.
wire brush *n* Drahtbürste *f*.
wire cutters *npl* Drahtschere *f*.
wireless ['waɪəlɪs] (*BRIT: old*) *n* Funk *m*; (*set*) Rundfunkgerät *nt*.
wire netting *n* Maschendraht *m*.
wire service (*US*) *n* Nachrichtenagentur *f*.
wire-tapping ['waɪə'tæpɪŋ] *n* Anzapfen *nt* von Leitungen.
wiring ['waɪərɪŋ] *n* elektrische Leitungen *pl*.
wiry ['waɪərɪ] *adj* (*person*) drahtig; (*hair*) borstig.
Wis. (*US*) *abbr* (*POST:* = *Wisconsin*).
wisdom ['wɪzdəm] *n* (*of person*) Weisheit *f*; (*of*

action, remark) Klugheit *f*.
wisdom tooth *n* Weisheitszahn *m*.
wise *adj* (*person*) weise; (*action, remark*) klug; **I'm none the ~r** ich bin genauso klug wie vorher.
▶**wise up** (*inf*) *vi:* **to ~ up to sth** hinter etw *acc* kommen.
...wise [waɪz] *suff:* **timewise/moneywise** *etc* zeitmäßig/geldmäßig *etc*.
wisecrack ['waɪzkræk] *n* Witzelei *f*.
wisely ['waɪzlɪ] *adv* klug, weise.
wish [wɪʃ] *n* Wunsch *m* ♦ *vt* wünschen; **best ~es** (*for birthday etc*) herzliche Grüße, alle guten Wünsche; **with best ~es** (*in letter*) mit den besten Wünschen *or* Grüßen; **give her my best ~es** grüßen Sie sie herzlich von mir; **to make a ~** sich *dat* etw wünschen; **to ~ sb goodbye** jdm auf Wiedersehen sagen; **he ~ed me well** er wünschte mir alles Gute; **to ~ to do sth** etw tun wollen; **to ~ sth on sb** jdm etw wünschen; **to ~ for sth** sich *dat* etw wünschen.
wishbone ['wɪʃbəun] *n* Gabelbein *nt*.
wishful ['wɪʃful] *adj:* **it's ~ thinking** das ist reines Wunschdenken.
wishy-washy ['wɪʃɪ'wɒʃɪ] (*inf*) *adj* (*colour*) verwaschen; (*person*) farblos; (*ideas*) nichtssagend.
wisp [wɪsp] *n* (*of grass*) Büschel *nt*; (*of hair*) Strähne *f*; (*of smoke*) Fahne *f*.
wistful ['wɪstful] *adj* wehmütig.
wit [wɪt] *n* (*wittiness*) geistreiche Art *f*; (*person*) geistreicher Mensch *m*; (*presence of mind*) Verstand *m*; **wits** *npl* (*intelligence*) Verstand *m*; **to be at one's ~s' end** mit seinem Latein am Ende sein; **to have one's ~s about one** einen klaren Kopf haben; **to ~** (*namely*) und zwar.
witch [wɪtʃ] *n* Hexe *f*.
witchcraft ['wɪtʃkrɑːft] *n* Hexerei *f*.
witch doctor *n* Medizinmann *m*.
witch-hunt ['wɪtʃhʌnt] *n* (*fig*) Hexenjagd *f*.

═══════════════════════ *KEYWORD*

with [wɪð] *prep* **1** (*accompanying, in the company of*) mit; **we stayed ~ friends** wir wohnten bei Freunden; **I'll be ~ you in a minute** einen Augenblick, ich bin sofort da; **I'm ~ you** (*I understand*) ich verstehe; **to be ~ it** (*inf: up-to-date*) auf dem laufenden sein; (: *alert*) da sein
2 (*descriptive, indicating manner*) mit; **the man ~ the grey hat/blue eyes** der Mann mit dem grauen Hut/den blauen Augen; ~ **tears in her eyes** mit Tränen in den Augen; **red ~ anger** rot vor Wut.

withdraw [wɪθ'drɔː] (*irreg: like* **draw**) *vt* (*object, offer*) zurückziehen; (*remark*) zurücknehmen ♦ *vi* (*troops*) abziehen; (*person*) sich zurückziehen; **to ~ money** (*from bank*) Geld abheben; **to ~ into o.s.** sich in sich *acc* selbst zurückziehen.

withdrawal [wɪθ'drɔːəl] n (of offer, remark) Zurücknahme f; (of troops) Abzug m; (of participation) Ausstieg m; (of services) Streichung f; (of money) Abhebung f.

withdrawal symptoms npl Entzugserscheinungen pl.

withdrawn [wɪθ'drɔːn] pp of **withdraw** ♦ adj (person) verschlossen.

wither ['wɪðə•] vi (plant) verwelken.

withered ['wɪðəd] adj (plant) verwelkt; (limb) verkümmert.

withhold [wɪθ'həuld] (irreg: like **hold**) vt vorenthalten.

within [wɪð'ɪn] prep (place) innerhalb +gen; (time, distance) innerhalb von ♦ adv innen; ~ **reach** in Reichweite; ~ **sight (of)** in Sichtweite (+gen); ~ **the week** vor Ende der Woche; ~ **a mile of** weniger als eine Meile entfernt von; ~ **an hour** innerhalb einer Stunde; ~ **the law** im Rahmen des Gesetzes.

without [wɪð'aut] prep ohne; ~ **a coat** ohne Mantel; ~ **speaking** ohne zu sprechen; **it goes** ~ **saying** das versteht sich von selbst; ~ **anyone knowing** ohne daß jemand davon wußte.

withstand [wɪθ'stænd] (irreg: like **stand**) vt widerstehen +dat.

witness ['wɪtnɪs] n Zeuge m, Zeugin f ♦ vt (event) sehen, Zeuge/Zeugin sein +gen; (fig) miterleben; **to bear** ~ **to sth** Zeugnis für etw ablegen; ~ **for the prosecution/defence** Zeuge/Zeugin der Anklage/Verteidigung; **to** ~ **to sth** etw bezeugen; **to** ~ **having seen sth** bezeugen, etw gesehen zu haben.

witness box n Zeugenstand m.

witness stand (US) n = **witness box**.

witticism ['wɪtɪsɪzəm] n geistreiche Bemerkung f.

witty ['wɪtɪ] adj geistreich.

wives [waɪvz] npl of **wife**.

wizard ['wɪzəd] n Zauberer m.

wizened ['wɪznd] adj (person) verhutzelt; (fruit, vegetable) verschrumpelt.

wk abbr = **week**.

Wm. abbr (= William).

WO n abbr (MIL) = **warrant officer**.

wobble ['wɔbl] vi wackeln; (legs) zittern.

wobbly ['wɔblɪ] adj (hand, voice) zitt(e)rig; (table, chair) wack(e)lig; **to feel** ~ sich wack(e)lig fühlen.

woe [wəu] n (sorrow) Jammer m; (misfortune) Kummer m.

woeful ['wəuful] adj traurig.

wok [wɔk] n Wok m.

woke [wəuk] pt of **wake**.

woken ['wəukn] pp of **wake**.

wolf [wulf] (pl **wolves**) n Wolf m.

wolves [wulvz] npl of **wolf**.

woman ['wumən] (pl **women**) n Frau f; ~ **friend** Freundin f; ~ **teacher** Lehrerin f; **young** ~ junge Frau; **women's page**

Frauenseite f.

woman doctor n Ärztin f.

womanize ['wumənaɪz] (pej) vi hinter Frauen her sein.

womanly ['wumənlɪ] adj (virtues etc) weiblich.

womb [wuːm] n Mutterleib m; (MED) Gebärmutter f.

women ['wɪmɪn] npl of **woman**.

women's lib ['wɪmɪnz-] (inf) n Frauenbefreiung f.

Women's (Liberation) Movement n Frauenbewegung f.

won [wʌn] pt, pp of **win**.

wonder ['wʌndə•] n (miracle) Wunder nt; (awe) Verwunderung f ♦ vi: **to** ~ **whether/why** etc sich fragen, ob/warum etc; **it's no** ~ **(that)** es ist kein Wunder(, daß); **to** ~ **at** (marvel at) staunen über +acc; **to** ~ **about** sich dat Gedanken machen über +acc; **I** ~ **if you could help me** könnten Sie mir vielleicht helfen.

wonderful ['wʌndəful] adj wunderbar.

wonderfully ['wʌndəfəlɪ] adv wunderbar.

wonky ['wɔŋkɪ] (BRIT: inf) adj wack(e)lig.

wont [wəunt] n: **as is his** ~ wie er zu tun pflegt.

won't [wəunt] = **will not**.

woo [wuː] vt (woman, audience) umwerben.

wood [wud] n (timber) Holz nt; (forest) Wald m ♦ cpd Holz-.

woodcarving ['wudkɑːvɪŋ] n (act, object) Holzschnitzerei f.

wooded ['wudɪd] adj bewaldet.

wooden ['wudn] adj (also fig) hölzern.

woodland ['wudlənd] n Waldland nt.

woodpecker ['wudpɛkə•] n Specht m.

wood pigeon n Ringeltaube f.

woodwind ['wudwɪnd] adj (instrument) Holzblasinstrument nt; **the** ~ die Holzbläser pl.

woodwork ['wudwəːk] n (skill) Holzarbeiten pl.

woodworm ['wudwəːm] n Holzwurm m.

woof [wuf] n (of dog) Wau nt ♦ vi kläffen; ~, ~! wau, wau!

wool [wul] n Wolle f; **to pull the** ~ **over sb's eyes** (fig) jdn hinters Licht führen.

woollen, (US) **woolen** ['wulən] adj (hat) Woll-, wollen.

woollens ['wulənz] npl Wollsachen pl.

woolly, (US) **wooly** ['wulɪ] adj (socks, hat etc) Woll-; (fig: ideas) schwammig; (person) verworren ♦ n (pullover) Wollpullover m.

woozy ['wuːzɪ] (inf) adj duselig.

Worcs (BRIT) abbr (POST: = Worcestershire).

word [wəːd] n Wort nt; (news) Nachricht f ♦ vt (letter, message) formulieren; ~ **for** ~ Wort für Wort, (wort)wörtlich; **what's the** ~ **for "pen" in German?** was heißt „pen" auf deutsch?; **to put sth into** ~**s** etw in Worte fassen; **in other** ~**s** mit anderen Worten; **to break/keep one's** ~ sein Wort brechen/

halten; **to have ~s with sb** eine
Auseinandersetzung mit jdm haben; **to
have a ~ with sb** mit jdm sprechen; **I'll take
your ~ for it** ich verlasse mich auf Sie; **to
send ~ of sth** verlauten lassen; **to leave
~ (with sb/for sb) that** ... (bei jdm/für jdn)
die Nachricht hinterlassen, daß ...; **by ~ of
mouth** durch mündliche Überlieferung.
wording ['wəːdɪŋ] *n* (*of message, contract etc*)
Wortlaut *m*, Formulierung *f*.
word-perfect ['wəːd'pəːfɪkt] *adj*: **to be ~** den
Text perfekt beherrschen.
word processing *n* Textverarbeitung *f*.
word processor [-prəusesəˀ] *n*
Textverarbeitungssystem *nt*.
wordwrap ['wəːdræp] *n* (*COMPUT*)
(automatischer) Zeilenumbruch *m*.
wordy ['wəːdɪ] *adj* (*book*) langatmig; (*person*)
wortreich.
wore [wɔːˀ] *pt of* **wear**.
work [wəːk] *n* Arbeit *f*; (*ART, LITER*) Werk *nt*
♦ *vi* arbeiten; (*mechanism*) funktionieren; (*be
successful: medicine etc*) wirken ♦ *vt* (*clay,
wood, land*) bearbeiten; (*mine*) arbeiten in;
(*machine*) bedienen; (*create: effect, miracle*)
bewirken; **to go to ~** zur Arbeit gehen; **to
set to ~**, **to start ~** sich an die Arbeit
machen; **to be at ~ (on sth)** (an etw *dat*)
arbeiten; **to be out of ~** arbeitslos sein; **to
be in ~** eine Stelle haben; **to ~ hard** hart
arbeiten; **to ~ loose** (*part, knot*) sich lösen;
to ~ on the assumption that ... von der
Annahme ausgehen, daß ...
▶**work on** *vt fus* (*task*) arbeiten an +*dat*;
(*person: influence*) bearbeiten; **he's ~ing on
his car** er arbeitet an seinem Auto.
▶**work out** *vi* (*plans etc*) klappen; (*SPORT*)
trainieren ♦ *vt* (*problem*) lösen; (*plan*)
ausarbeiten; **it ~s out at 100 pounds** es
ergibt 100 Pfund.
▶**work up** *vt*: **to get ~ed up** sich aufregen.
workable ['wəːkəbl] *adj* (*system*)
durchführbar; (*solution*) brauchbar.
workaholic [wəːkə'hɔlɪk] *n* Arbeitstier *nt*.
workbench ['wəːkbentʃ] *n* Werkbank *f*.
worker ['wəːkəˀ] *n* Arbeiter(in) *m(f)*; **office ~**
Büroarbeiter(in) *m(f)*.
workforce ['wəːkfɔːs] *n* Arbeiterschaft *f*.
work-in ['wəːkɪn] (*BRIT*) *n* Fabrikbesetzung *f*.
working ['wəːkɪŋ] *adj* (*day, conditions*)
Arbeits-; (*population*) arbeitend; (*mother*)
berufstätig; **a ~ knowledge of English**
(*adequate*) Grundkenntnisse in Englisch.
working capital *n* Betriebskapital *nt*.
working class *n* Arbeiterklasse *f*.
working-class ['wəːkɪŋ'klɑːs] *adj* (*family,
town*) Arbeiter-.
working man *n* Arbeiter *m*.
working order *n*: **in ~** in betriebsfähigem
Zustand.
working party (*BRIT*) *n* Ausschuß *m*.
working relationship *n* Arbeitsbeziehung *f*.

working week *n* Arbeitswoche *f*.
work-in-progress ['wəːkɪn'prəugres] *n*
laufende Arbeiten *pl*.
workload ['wəːkləud] *n* Arbeitsbelastung *f*.
workman ['wəːkmən] (*irreg: like* **man**) *n*
Arbeiter *m*.
workmanship ['wəːkmənʃɪp] *n*
Arbeitsqualität *f*.
workmate ['wəːkmeɪt] *n* Arbeitskollege *m*,
Arbeitskollegin *f*.
workout ['wəːkaut] *n* Fitneßtraining *nt*.
work permit *n* Arbeitserlaubnis *f*.
works [wəːks] (*BRIT*) *n* (*factory*) Fabrik *f*, Werk
nt ♦ *npl* (*of clock*) Uhrwerk *nt*; (*of machine*)
Getriebe *nt*.
work sheet *n* Arbeitsblatt *nt*.
workshop ['wəːkʃɔp] *n* (*building*) Werkstatt *f*;
(*practical session*) Workshop *nt*.
work station *n* Arbeitsplatz *m*; (*COMPUT*)
Workstation *f*.
work-study ['wəːkstʌdɪ] *n* Arbeitsstudie *f*.
worktop ['wəːktɔp] *n* Arbeitsfläche *f*.
work-to-rule ['wəːktə'ruːl] (*BRIT*) *n* Dienst *m*
nach Vorschrift.
world [wəːld] *n* Welt *f* ♦ *cpd* (*champion, power,
war*) Welt-; **all over the ~** auf der ganzen
Welt; **to think the ~ of sb** große Stücke auf
jdn halten; **what in the ~ is he doing?** was
um alles in der Welt macht er?; **to do sb a
or the ~ of good** jdm unwahrscheinlich gut
tun; **W~ War One/Two** der Erste/Zweite
Weltkrieg; **out of this ~** phantastisch.
World Cup *n*: **the ~** (*FOOTBALL*) die
Fußballweltmeisterschaft *f*.
world-famous [wəːld'feɪməs] *adj*
weltberühmt.
worldly ['wəːldlɪ] *adj* weltlich; (*knowledgeable*)
weltgewandt.
world music *n* World Music *f*, Richtung der
Popmusik, die musikalische Stilelemente
der Dritten Welt verwendet.
World Series (*US*) *n* Endrunde der
Baseball-Weltmeisterschaft zwischen den
Tabellenführern der Spitzenligen.
worldwide ['wəːld'waɪd] *adj, adv* weltweit.
worm [wəːm] *n* Wurm *m*.
▶**worm out** *vt*: **to ~ sth out of sb** jdm etw
entlocken.
worn [wɔːn] *pp of* **wear** ♦ *adj* (*carpet*)
abgenutzt; (*shoe*) abgetragen.
worn-out ['wɔːnaut] *adj* (*object*) abgenutzt;
(*person*) erschöpft.
worried ['wʌrɪd] *adj* besorgt; **to be ~ about
sth** sich wegen etw Sorgen machen.
worrier ['wʌrɪəˀ] *n*: **to be a ~** sich ständig
Sorgen machen.
worrisome ['wʌrɪsəm] *adj* besorgniserregend.
worry ['wʌrɪ] *n* Sorge *f* ♦ *vt* beunruhigen ♦ *vi*
sich *dat* Sorgen machen; **to ~ about or over
sth/sb** sich um etw/jdn Sorgen machen.
worrying ['wʌrɪɪŋ] *adj* beunruhigend.
worse [wəːs] *adj* schlechter, schlimmer ♦ *adv*

schlechter ♦ n Schlechtere(s) nt,
Schlimmere(s) nt; **to get** ~ (*situation etc*)
sich verschlechtern or verschlimmern; **he
is none the** ~ **for it** er hat keinen Schaden
dabei erlitten; **so much the** ~ **for you!** um so
schlimmer für dich!; **a change for the** ~
eine Wendung zum Schlechten.

worsen ['wɜːsn] vt verschlimmern ♦ vi sich
verschlechtern.

worse off adj (*also fig*) schlechter dran; **he is
now** ~ **than before** er ist jetzt schlechter
dran als zuvor.

worship ['wɜːʃɪp] n (*act*) Verehrung f ♦ vt
(*god*) anbeten; (*person, thing*) verehren; **Your
W**~ (*BRIT: to mayor*) verehrter Herr
Bürgermeister; (: *to judge*) Euer Ehren.

worshipper ['wɜːʃɪpə'] n (*in church etc*)
Kirchgänger(in) m(f); (*fig*) Anbeter(in) m(f),
Verehrer(in) m(f).

worst [wɜːst] adj schlechteste(r, s),
schlimmste(r, s) ♦ adv am schlimmsten ♦ n
Schlimmste(s) nt; **at** ~ schlimmstenfalls; **if
the** ~ **comes to the** ~ wenn alle Stricke
reißen.

worst-case scenario ['wɜːstkeɪs-] n
Schlimmstfallszenario nt.

worsted ['wustɪd] n Kammgarn nt.

worth [wɜːθ] n Wert m ♦ adj: **to be** ~ wert
sein; **£2** ~ **of apples** Äpfel für £ 2; **how
much is it** ~? was or wieviel ist es wert?; **it's**
~ **it** (*effort, time*) es lohnt sich; **it's** ~ **every
penny** es ist sein Geld wert.

worthless ['wɜːθlɪs] adj wertlos.

worthwhile ['wɜːθ'waɪl] adj lohnend.

worthy ['wɜːðɪ] adj (*person*) würdig; (*motive*)
ehrenwert; ~ **of** wert +gen.

=============== *KEYWORD* ===============

would [wud] aux vb **1** (*conditional tense*): **if you
asked him he** ~ **do it** wenn du ihn fragtest,
würde er es tun; **if you had asked him he**
~ **have done it** wenn du ihn gefragt hättest,
hätte er es getan
2 (*in offers, invitations, requests*): ~ **you like a
biscuit?** möchten Sie ein Plätzchen?; ~ **you
ask him to come in?** würden Sie ihn bitten,
hereinzukommen?
3 (*in indirect speech*): **I said I** ~ **do it** ich
sagte, ich würde es tun
4 (*emphatic*): **it WOULD have to snow today!**
ausgerechnet heute mußte es schneien!
5 (*insistence*): **she** ~**n't behave** sie wollte
sich partout nicht benehmen
6 (*conjecture*): **it** ~ **have been midnight** es
mochte etwa Mitternacht gewesen sein; **it**
~ **seem so** so scheint es wohl
7 (*indicating habit*): **he** ~ **go there on
Mondays** er ging montags immer dorthin;
he ~ **spend every day on the beach** er
verbrachte jeden Tag am Strand.

would-be ['wudbiː] adj (*singer, writer*)

Möchtegern-.

wouldn't ['wudnt] = **would not**.

wound¹ [waund] pt, pp of **wind²**.

wound² [wuːnd] n Wunde f ♦ vt verwunden;
~**ed in the leg** am Bein verletzt.

wove [wəuv] pt of **weave**.

woven ['wəuvn] pp of **weave**.

WP n abbr = **word processing; word processor**
♦ abbr (*BRIT: inf: = weather permitting*) bei
günstiger Witterung.

WPC (*BRIT*) n abbr (= **woman police constable**)
Polizistin f.

wpm abbr (= **words per minute**) Worte pro
Minute (*beim Maschinenschreiben*).

WRAC (*BRIT*) n abbr (= **Women's Royal Army
Corps**) Frauenkorps der Armee.

WRAF (*BRIT*) n abbr (= **Women's Royal Air
Force**) Frauenkorps der Luftwaffe.

wrangle ['ræŋgl] n Gerangel nt ♦ vi: **to** ~ **with
sb over sth** sich mit jdm um etw zanken.

wrap [ræp] n (*shawl*) Umhang m; (*cape*) Cape
nt ♦ vt einwickeln; (*also:* ~ **up:** *pack*)
einpacken; (*wind: tape etc*) wickeln; **under**
~**s** (*fig: plan*) geheim.

wrapper ['ræpə'] n (*on chocolate*) Papier nt;
(*BRIT: of book*) Umschlag m.

wrapping paper ['ræpɪŋ-] n (*brown*)
Packpapier nt; (*fancy*) Geschenkpapier nt.

wrath [rɔθ] n Zorn m.

wreak [riːk] vt: **to** ~ **havoc (on)** verheerenden
Schaden anrichten (bei); **to** ~ **vengeance** or
revenge on sb Rache an jdm üben.

wreath [riːθ] (pl ~**s**) n Kranz m.

wreck [rɛk] n Wrack nt; (*vehicle*)
Schrotthaufen m ♦ vt kaputtmachen; (*car*) zu
Schrott fahren; (*chances*) zerstören.

wreckage ['rɛkɪdʒ] n (*of car, plane, building*)
Trümmer pl; (*of ship*) Wrackteile pl.

wrecker ['rɛkə'] n (*US*) (*breakdown van*)
Abschleppwagen m.

Wren (*BRIT*) n abbr weibliches Mitglied der
britischen Marine.

wren [rɛn] n (*ZOOL*) Zaunkönig m.

wrench [rɛntʃ] n (*TECH*) Schraubenschlüssel
m; (*tug*) Ruck m; (*fig*) schmerzhaftes
Erlebnis nt ♦ vt (*pull*) reißen; (*injure: arm,
back*) verrenken; **to** ~ **sth from sb** jdm etw
entreißen.

wrest [rɛst] vt: **to** ~ **sth from sb** jdm etw
abringen.

wrestle ['rɛsl] vi: **to** ~ (**with sb**) (mit jdm)
ringen; **to** ~ **with a problem** mit einem
Problem kämpfen.

wrestler ['rɛslə'] n Ringer(in) m(f).

wrestling ['rɛslɪŋ] n Ringen nt; (*also:* **all-in** ~)
Freistilringen nt.

wrestling match n Ringkampf m.

wretch [rɛtʃ] n: **poor** ~ (*man*) armer
Schlucker m; (*woman*) armes Ding nt; **little**
~! (*often humorous*) kleiner Schlingel!

wretched ['rɛtʃɪd] adj (*poor*) erbärmlich;
(*unhappy*) unglücklich; (*inf: damned*) elend.

wriggle ['rɪgl] vi (also: ~ **about**: person)
zappeln; (fish) sich winden; (snake etc) sich
schlängeln ♦ n Zappeln nt.

wring [rɪŋ] (pt, pp **wrung**) vt (wet clothes)
auswringen; (hands) wringen; (neck)
umdrehen; **to ~ sth out of sth/sb** (fig) etw/
jdm etw abringen.

wringer ['rɪŋə*] n Mangel f.

wringing ['rɪŋɪŋ] adj (also: ~ **wet**) tropfnaß.

wrinkle ['rɪŋkl] n Falte f ♦ vt (nose, forehead
etc) runzeln ♦ vi (skin, paint etc) sich runzeln.

wrinkled ['rɪŋkld] adj (fabric, paper)
zerknittert; (surface) gekräuselt; (skin)
runzlig.

wrinkly ['rɪŋklɪ] adj = **wrinkled**.

wrist [rɪst] n Handgelenk nt.

wristband ['rɪstbænd] (BRIT) n (of shirt)
Manschette f; (of watch) Armband nt.

wristwatch ['rɪstwɔtʃ] n Armbanduhr f.

writ [rɪt] n (LAW) (gerichtliche) Verfügung f;
to issue a ~ against sb, serve a ~ on sb eine
Verfügung gegen jdn erlassen.

write [raɪt] (pt **wrote**, pp **written**) vt schreiben;
(cheque) ausstellen ♦ vi schreiben; **to ~ to
sb** jdm schreiben.

▶**write away** vi: **to ~ away for sth** etw
anfordern.

▶**write down** vt aufschreiben.

▶**write off** vt (debt, project) abschreiben;
(wreck: car etc) zu Schrott fahren ♦ vi = **write
away**.

▶**write out** vt (put in writing) schreiben;
(cheque, receipt etc) ausstellen.

▶**write up** vt (report etc) schreiben.

write-off ['raɪtɔf] n (AUT) Totalschaden m.

write-protected ['raɪtprə'tɛktɪd] adj
(COMPUT) schreibgeschützt.

writer ['raɪtə*] n (author) Schriftsteller(in)
m(f); (of report, document etc) Verfasser(in)
m(f).

write-up ['raɪtʌp] n (review) Kritik f.

writhe [raɪð] vi sich krümmen.

writing ['raɪtɪŋ] n Schrift f; (of author)
Arbeiten pl; (activity) Schreiben nt; **in ~**
schriftlich; **in my own ~** in meiner eigenen
Handschrift.

writing case n Schreibmappe f.

writing desk n Schreibtisch m.

writing paper n Schreibpapier nt.

written ['rɪtn] pp of **write**.

WRNS (BRIT) n abbr (= Women's Royal Naval
Service) Frauenkorps der Marine.

wrong [rɔŋ] adj falsch; (morally bad) unrecht;
(unfair) ungerecht ♦ adv falsch ♦ n (injustice)
Unrecht nt; (evil): **right and ~** Gut und Böse
♦ vt (treat unfairly) Unrecht tun +dat; **to be ~**
(answer) falsch sein; (in doing, saying sth)
unrecht haben; **you are ~ to do it** es ist ein
Fehler von dir, das zu tun; **it's ~ to steal,
stealing is ~** Stehlen ist unrecht; **you are
~ about that, you've got it ~** da hast du
unrecht; **what's ~?** wo fehlt's?; **there's**

nothing ~ es ist alles in Ordnung; **to go ~**
(person) einen Fehler machen; (plan)
schiefgehen; (machine) versagen; **to be in
the ~** im Unrecht sein.

wrongdoer ['rɔŋduə*] n Übeltäter(in) m(f).

wrong-foot [rɔŋ'fut] vt: **to ~ sb** (SPORT) jdn
auf dem falschen Fuß erwischen; (fig) jdn
im falschen Moment erwischen.

wrongful ['rɔŋful] adj unrechtmäßig.

wrongly ['rɔŋlɪ] adv falsch; (unjustly) zu
Unrecht.

wrong number n (TEL): **you've got the ~** Sie
sind falsch verbunden.

wrong side n: **the ~** (of material) die linke
Seite.

wrote [rəut] pt of **write**.

wrought [rɔːt] adj: ~ **iron** Schmiedeeisen nt.

wrung [rʌŋ] pt, pp of **wring**.

WRVS (BRIT) n abbr (= Women's Royal
Voluntary Service) karitativer
Frauenverband.

wry [raɪ] adj (smile, humour) trocken.

wt. abbr = **weight**.

WV (US) abbr (POST: = West Virginia).

W.Va. (US) abbr (POST: = West Virginia).

WY, Wyo. (US) abbr (POST: = Wyoming).

WYSIWYG ['wɪzɪwɪg] abbr (COMPUT: = what
you see is what you get) WYSIWYG nt.

X, x

X, x [ɛks] n (letter) X nt, x nt; (BRIT: CINE:
formerly) Klassifikation für nicht jugendfreie
Filme; ~ **for Xmas** ≈ X wie Xanthippe.

Xerox® ['zɪərɔks] n (also: ~ **machine**)
Xerokopierer m; (photocopy) Xerokopie f
♦ vt xerokopieren.

XL abbr (= extra large) XL.

Xmas ['ɛksməs] n abbr = **Christmas**.

X-rated ['ɛks'reɪtɪd] (US) adj (film) nicht
jugendfrei.

X-ray [ɛks'reɪ] n Röntgenstrahl m; (photo)
Röntgenbild nt ♦ vt röntgen; **to have an ~**
sich röntgen lassen.

xylophone ['zaɪləfəun] n Xylophon nt.

Y, y

Y, y [waɪ] n (letter) Y nt, y nt; ~ **for Yellow**, (US) ~ **for Yoke** ≈ Y wie Ypsilon.
yacht [jɔt] n Jacht f.
yachting ['jɔtɪŋ] n Segeln nt.
yachtsman ['jɔtsmən] (irreg: like man) n Segler m.
yam [jæm] n Yamswurzel f.
Yank [jæŋk] (pej) n Ami m.
yank [jæŋk] vt reißen ♦ n Ruck m; **to give sth a** ~ mit einem Ruck an etw dat ziehen.
Yankee ['jæŋkɪ] (pej) n = **Yank**.
yap [jæp] vi (dog) kläffen.
yard [jɑːd] n (of house etc) Hof m; (US: garden) Garten m; (measure) Yard nt (= 0,91 m); **builder's** ~ Bauhof m.
yardstick ['jɑːdstɪk] n (fig) Maßstab m.
yarn [jɑːn] n (thread) Garn nt; (tale) Geschichte f.
yawn [jɔːn] n Gähnen nt ♦ vi gähnen.
yawning ['jɔːnɪŋ] adj (gap) gähnend.
yd abbr = **yard**.
yeah [jɛə] (inf) adv ja.
year [jɪə] n Jahr nt; (referring to wine) Jahrgang m; **every** ~ jedes Jahr; **this** ~ dieses Jahr; **a** or **per** ~ pro Jahr; ~ **in**, ~ **out** jahrein, jahraus; **to be 8** ~**s old** 8 Jahre alt sein; **an eight-**~**-old child** ein achtjähriges Kind.
yearbook ['jɪəbuk] n Jahrbuch nt.
yearling ['jɪəlɪŋ] n (horse) Jährling m.
yearly ['jɪəlɪ] adj, adv (once a year) jährlich; **twice** ~ zweimal jährlich or im Jahr.
yearn [jɔːn] vi: **to** ~ **for sth** sich nach etwas sehnen; **to** ~ **to do sth** sich danach sehnen, etw zu tun.
yearning ['jɔːnɪŋ] n: **to have a** ~ **for sth** ein Verlangen nach etw haben; **to have a** ~ **to do sth** ein Verlangen danach haben, etw zu tun.
yeast [jiːst] n Hefe f.
yell [jɛl] n Schrei m ♦ vi schreien.
yellow ['jɛləu] adj gelb ♦ n Gelb nt.
yellow fever n Gelbfieber nt.
yellowish ['jɛləuɪʃ] adj gelblich.
Yellow Pages ® npl: **the** ~ die Gelben Seiten pl, das Branchenverzeichnis.
Yellow Sea n: **the** ~ das Gelbe Meer.
yelp [jɛlp] n Jaulen nt ♦ vi jaulen.
Yemen ['jɛmən] n: **(the)** ~ (der) Jemen.
Yemeni ['jɛmənɪ] adj jemenitisch ♦ n Jemenit(in) m(f).
yen [jɛn] n (currency) Yen m; (craving): **to have**

a ~ **for** Lust auf etw haben; **to have a** ~ **to do sth** Lust darauf haben, etw zu tun.
yeoman ['jəumən] (irreg: like man) n: **Y**~ **of the Guard** (königlicher) Leibgardist m.
yes [jɛs] adv ja; (in reply to negative) doch ♦ n Ja nt; **to say** ~ ja sagen; **to answer** ~ mit ja antworten.
yes-man ['jɛsmæn] (irreg: like man) (pej) n Jasager m.
yesterday ['jɛstədɪ] adv gestern ♦ n Gestern nt; ~ **morning/evening** gestern morgen/abend; ~**'s paper** die Zeitung von gestern; **the day before** ~ vorgestern; **all day** ~ gestern den ganzen Tag (lang).
yet [jɛt] adv noch ♦ conj jedoch; **it is not finished** ~ es ist noch nicht fertig; **must you go just** ~? mußt du schon gehen?; **the best** ~ der/die/das bisher beste; **as** ~ bisher; **it'll be a few days** ~ es wird noch ein paar Tage dauern; **not for a few days** ~ nicht in den nächsten paar Tagen; ~ **again** wiederum.
yew [juː] n (tree) Eibe f; (wood) Eibenholz nt.
Y-fronts ® ['waɪfrʌnts] npl (Herren-)Slip m (mit Y-förmiger Vorderseite).
YHA (BRIT) n abbr (= Youth Hostels Association) britischer Jugendherbergsverband.
Yiddish ['jɪdɪʃ] n Jiddisch nt.
yield [jiːld] n (AGR) Ertrag m; (COMM) Gewinn m ♦ vt (surrender: control etc) abtreten; (produce: results, profit) hervorbringen ♦ vi (surrender, give way) nachgeben; (US: AUT) die Vorfahrt achten; **a** ~ **of 5%** ein Ertrag or Gewinn von 5%.
YMCA n abbr (organization: = Young Men's Christian Association) CVJM m.
yob(bo) ['jɔb(əu)] (BRIT: inf: pej) n Rowdy m.
yodel ['jəudl] vi jodeln.
yoga ['jəugə] n Yoga m or nt.
yog(h)ourt ['jəugət] n Joghurt m or nt.
yog(h)urt ['jəugət] n = **yog(h)ourt**.
yoke [jəuk] n (also fig) Joch nt ♦ vt (also: ~ **together**: oxen) einspannen.
yolk [jəuk] n (of egg) Dotter m, Eigelb nt.
yonder ['jɔndə] adv: **(over)** ~ dort drüben ♦ adj: **from** ~ **house** von dem Haus dort drüben.
yonks [jɔŋks] (inf) n: **for** ~ seit einer Ewigkeit.
Yorks [jɔːks] (BRIT) abbr (POST: = Yorkshire).

════════ KEYWORD

you [juː] pron **1** (subject: familiar: singular) du; (: : plural) ihr; (: polite) Sie; ~ **Germans enjoy your food** ihr Deutschen eßt gern gut **2** (object: direct: familiar: singular) dich; (: : : plural) euch; (: : polite) Sie; (: indirect: familiar: singular) dir; (: : : plural) euch; (: : polite) Ihnen; **I know** ~ ich kenne dich/euch/Sie; **I gave it to** ~ ich habe es dir/euch/Ihnen gegeben; **if I were** ~ **I would ...** an deiner/eurer/Ihrer Stelle würde ich ... **3** (after prep, in comparisons): **it's for** ~ es ist

für dich/euch/Sie; **she's younger than** ~ sie
ist jünger als du/ihr/Sie
4 (*impersonal: one*) man; ~ **never know** man
weiß nie.

you'd [ju:d] = **you had; you would.**

you'll [ju:l] = **you will; you shall.**

young [jʌŋ] *adj* jung; **the young** *npl* (*of animal*)
die Jungen *pl*; (*people*) die jungen Leute *pl*; **a**
~ **man** ein junger Mann; **a** ~ **lady** eine
junge Dame.

younger [jʌŋgə*] *adj* jünger; **the** ~ **generation**
die jüngere Generation.

youngish ['jʌŋɪʃ] *adj* recht jung.

youngster ['jʌŋstə*] *n* Kind *nt*.

your [jɔ:*] *adj* (*familiar: sing*) dein/deine/dein;
(: *pl*) euer/eure/euer; (*polite*) Ihr/Ihre/Ihr;
(*one's*) sein; **you mustn't eat with** ~ **fingers**
man darf nicht mit den Fingern essen; *see
also* **my.**

you're [juə*] = **you are.**

yours [jɔ:z] *pron* (*familiar: sing*) deiner/deine/
dein(e)s; (: *pl*) eurer/eure/eures; (*polite*)
Ihrer/Ihre/Ihres; **a friend of** ~ ein Freund
von dir/Ihnen; **is it** ~**?** gehört es dir/Ihnen?;
~ **sincerely/faithfully** mit freundlichen
Grüßen; *see also* **mine**[1].

yourself [jɔ:'sɛlf] *pron* (*reflexive: familiar: sing:
acc*) dich; (: : : *dat*) dir; (: : *pl*) euch; (: *polite*)
sich; (*emphatic*) selbst; **you** ~ **told me** das
haben Sie mir selbst gesagt.

yourselves [jɔ:'sɛlvz] *pl pron* (*reflexive: familiar*)
euch; (: *polite*) sich; (*emphatic*) selbst; *see also*
oneself.

youth [ju:θ] *n* Jugend *f*; (*young man: pl youths*)
Jugendliche(r) *m*; **in my** ~ in meiner
Jugend.

youth club *n* Jugendklub *m*.

youthful ['ju:θful] *adj* jugendlich.

youthfulness ['ju:θfəlnɪs] *n* Jugendlichkeit *f*.

youth hostel *n* Jugendherberge *f*.

youth movement *n* Jugendbewegung *f*.

you've [ju:v] = **you have.**

yowl [jaul] *n* (*of animal*) Jaulen *nt*; (*of person*)
Heulen *nt*.

yr *abbr* (= *year*) J.

YT (*CANADA*) *abbr* (= *Yukon Territory*).

Yugoslav ['ju:gəuslɑ:v] (*formerly*) *adj*
jugoslawisch ♦ *n* Jugoslawe *m*, Jugoslawin *f*.

Yugoslavia ['ju:gəu'slɑ:vɪə] (*formerly*) *n*
Jugoslawien *nt*.

Yugoslavian ['ju:gəu'slɑ:vɪən] (*formerly*) *adj*
jugoslawisch.

Yule log [ju:l-] *n* Biskuitrolle mit Überzug,
die zu Weihnachten gegessen wird.

yuppie ['jʌpɪ] (*inf*) *n* Yuppie *m* ♦ *adj*
yuppiehaft; (*job, car*) Yuppie-.

YWCA *n abbr* (*organization*): = *Young Women's
Christian Association*) CVJF *m*.

Z, z

Z, z [zɛd, (*US*) zi:] *n* (*letter*) Z *nt*, z *nt*; ~ **for
Zebra** ≈ Z wie Zacharias.

Zaire [zɑ:'i:ə*] *n* Zaire *nt*.

Zambia ['zæmbɪə] *n* Sambia *nt*.

Zambian ['zæmbɪən] *adj* sambisch ♦ *n*
Sambier(in) *m(f)*.

zany ['zeɪnɪ] *adj* verrückt.

zap [zæp] *vt* (*COMPUT: delete*) löschen.

zeal [zi:l] *n* Eifer *m*.

zealot ['zɛlət] *n* Fanatiker(in) *m(f)*.

zealous ['zɛləs] *adj* eifrig.

zebra ['zi:brə] *n* Zebra *nt*.

zebra crossing (*BRIT*) *n* Zebrastreifen *m*.

zenith ['zɛnɪθ] *n* (*also fig*) Zenit *m*.

zero ['zɪərəu] *n* (*number*) Null *f* ♦ *vi:* **to** ~ **in on
sth** (*target*) etw einkreisen; **5 degrees below**
~ 5 Grad unter Null.

zero hour *n* die Stunde X.

zero option *n* (*esp POL*) Nullösung *f*.

zero-rated ['zi:rəureɪtɪd] (*BRIT*) *adj* (*TAX*)
mehrwertsteuerfrei.

zest [zɛst] *n* (*for life*) Begeisterung *f*; (*of
orange*) Orangenschale *f*.

zigzag ['zɪgzæg] *n* Zickzack *m* ♦ *vi* sich im
Zickzack bewegen.

Zimbabwe [zɪm'bɑ:bwɪ] *n* Zimbabwe *nt*.

Zimbabwean [zɪm'bɑ:bwɪən] *adj*
zimbabwisch.

zimmer ® ['zɪmə*] *n* (*also:* ~ **frame**)
Laufgestell *nt*.

zinc [zɪŋk] *n* Zink *nt*.

Zionism ['zaɪənɪzəm] *n* Zionismus *m*.

Zionist ['zaɪənɪst] *adj* zionistisch ♦ *n*
Zionist(in) *m(f)*.

zip [zɪp] *n* (*also:* ~ **fastener**) Reißverschluß *m*
♦ *vt* (*also:* ~ **up:** *dress etc*) den Reißverschluß
zumachen an +*dat*.

zip code (*US*) *n* Postleitzahl *f*.

zipper ['zɪpə*] (*US*) *n* = **zip.**

zither ['zɪðə*] *n* Zither *f*.

zodiac ['zəudɪæk] *n* Tierkreis *m*.

zombie ['zɔmbɪ] *n* (*fig*) Schwachkopf *m*.

zone [zəun] *n* (*also MIL*) Zone *f*, Gebiet *nt*; (*in
town*) Bezirk *m*.

zonked [zɔŋkt] (*inf*) *adj* (*tired*) total geschafft;
(*high on drugs*) high; (*drunk*) voll.

zoo [zu:] *n* Zoo *m*.

zoological [zuə'lɔdʒɪkl] *adj* zoologisch.

zoologist [zu'ɔlədʒɪst] *n* Zoologe *m*, Zoologin *f*.

zoology [zu:'ɔlədʒɪ] *n* Zoologie *f*.

zoom [zu:m] *vi:* **to** ~ **past** vorbeisausen; **to·
~ in (on sth/sb)** (*PHOT, CINE*) (etw/jdn)

näher heranholen.
zoom lens *n* Zoomobjektiv *nt*.
zucchini [zuːˈkiːnɪ] (*US*) *n(pl)* Zucchini *pl*.

Zulu [ˈzuːluː] *adj* (*tribe, culture*) Zulu- ♦ *n*
(*person*) Zulu *m/f*; (*LING*) Zulu *nt*.
Zürich [ˈzjuərɪk] *n* Zürich *nt*.